Climate Change: A Reader

Climate Change: A Reader

William H. Rodgers Jr.
STIMSON BULLITT PROFESSOR OF LAW
UNIVERSITY OF WASHINGTON SCHOOL OF LAW

Michael Robinson-Dorn
CLINICAL PROFESSOR OF LAW
UNIVERSITY OF CALIFORNIA-IRVINE SCHOOL OF LAW

Jennifer K. Barcelos

Anna T. Moritz

CAROLINA ACADEMIC PRESS
Durham, North Carolina

Library of Congress Cataloging-in-Publication Data

Climate change : a reader / William H. Rodgers, Jr. ... [et al.].
    p. cm.
ISBN 978-1-59460-482-9 (alk. paper)
1. Climatic changes--Law and legislation--United States. I. Rodgers, William H.,
1939- II. Title.

KF3783.C578 2010
344.7304'6342--dc22

                        2010022597

Carolina Academic Press
700 Kent Street
Durham, North Carolina 27701
Telephone (919) 489-7486
Fax (919) 493-5668
www.cap-press.com

This book is dedicated to Janet Rodgers.

Summary Table of Contents

Preface

We must begin with a note of appreciation for the patience and cooperation displayed by the extraordinary authors we have brought together in this volume. The idea looked good on paper when we proposed assembling a number of bright lights and leading thinkers on the overarching contemporary topic of climate change. Law was involved, but much more, and two years in incubation was far too long. For many disciplines, perhaps most, two years is an eternity, which means we were able to assemble only a sample of opinion circa 2008–2010. Nonetheless, we are proud of the assemblage, despite its vulnerabilities to the ravages of time, which allows us to rest assured on the confident assumption that big topics require constant and loving attention.

The great writer, Bill McKibben, lays claim to the first book on global warming for a general audience. It was called THE END OF NATURE and was published in 1989. As he spoke of a river close to his home in the Adirondack Mountains, McKibben reminisced:[1]

> Merely knowing that we'd begun to alter the climate meant that the water flowing in that creek had a different, lesser meaning. Instead of a world where rain had an independent and mysterious existence, the rain had become a subset of human activity ... The rain bore a brand; it was a steer not a deer.

In his latest book, EARTH: MAKING A LIFE ON A TOUGH NEW PLANET, McKibben discusses how the threat of global warming has become reality in a frightfully short time:[2]

> none of that planning works if it suddenly rains harder and faster than it has ever rained before, and that's exactly what's now happening. It's raining harder and evaporating faster; seas are rising and ice is melting, melting far more quickly than we once expected. The first point of this book is simple: global warming is no longer a philosophical threat, *no longer a threat at all*. It's our reality. We've changed the planet, changed it in large and fundamental ways. And these changes are far, far more evident in the toughest parts of the globe, where climate change is already wrecking thousands of lives daily.

"In fact," McKibben writes, "if you've got a spare month some time, google *global warming and grandchildren*."[3] If you do, you will find there Jim Hansen's letter to his grandchildren.[4] This book is our letter to the law students and law teachers and to our grandchildren. We all wonder how governance and law will thrive in this brave new world.

William H. Rodgers, Jr.	Jeni K. Barcelos
Michael Robinson-Dorn	Anna T. Moritz

---

1. BILL McKIBBEN, EARTH: MAKING A LIFE ON A TOUGH NEW PLANET, *Preface* at xi–xii (Times Books, Henry Holt & Co. 2010) [hereinafter 2010 EARTH].
2. *Id*. at xiii (emphasis in original).
3. Id. at 11 (emphasis in original).
4. JAMES HANSEN, STORMS OF MY GRANDCHILDREN: THE TRUTH ABOUT THE COMING CLIMATE CATASTROPHE AND OUR LAST CHANCE TO SAVE HUMANITY (Bloomsbury USA 2009).

Acknowledgments

A reader, by its nature, gathers the works of others into one place. Standard academic citations and credit for contributions has been provided throughout the text. In addition, we acknowledge with appreciation the following authors, publishers and journals who have graciously granted permission to reprint excerpts from their publications or who wrote specifically for this publication.

Adler, Robert W., University of Utah. *Rethinking Water Law in a Changing Climate*. Copyright 2011 by Robert W. Adler. All rights reserved. Used with permission of the author.

Antolini, Denise, University of Hawaii at Manoa. *Drowning Hawai'i: Island Resiliency and Climate Change*. Copyright 2011 by Denise Antolini. All rights reserved. Used with permission of the author.

Arctic Climate Impact Assessment, IMPACTS OF A WARMING ARCTIC (Cambridge Un. Press 2004). Copyright © 2004 Arctic Climate Impact Assessment. Reprinted with the permission of Cambridge University Press.

Baxter, William F., PEOPLE OR PENGUINS: THE CASE FOR OPTIMAL POLLUTION (1974 Columbia Un. Press, N.Y., London). Copyright 1974 Columbia University Press. Used by permission from Columbia University Press.

Boersma, P. Dee, University of Washington. *Penguins as Marine Sentinels*. Copyright 2008 by Dee P. Boersma. All rights reserved. Reprinted with permission of the author. Reprinted from 58(7) BIOSCIENCE 597 (2008).

Bosselman, Fred, Chicago-Kent College of Law. *Overcoming the Loneliness of the Long-Distance Runner: Nuclear Power for 2020*. Copyright 2011 by Fred Bosselman. All rights reserved. Used with permission of the author.

Brenner, David M., Riddell Williams P.S. *Insurance for Potential Climate Change Liability*. Copyright 2011 by David M. Brenner. All rights reserved. Used with permission of the author.

Burns, Dr. William C.G., Santa Clara University School of Law. *Sites for Sore Eyes: The World Heritage Convention and the Specter of Climate Change*. Copyright 2011 by William C.G. Burns. All rights reserved. Used with permission of the author.

Caldicott, Helen, NUCLEAR POWER IS NOT THE ANSWER. Copyright © 2006 by Helen Caldicott. Reprinted with permission The New Press.

Calvin, William H., *Turning Around by 2020, in* GLOBAL FEVER: HOW TO TREAT CLIMATE CHANGE (Un. Chicago Press 2008). By permission University of Chicago Press.

Capriccioso, Rob, *Tribes urged to prepare for possible federal carbon incentives*, INDIAN COUNTRY TODAY, April 10, 2008. Used by permission of INDIAN COUNTRY TODAY.

Carbon Mitigation Initiative (figure and excerpt of stabilization wedges), Princeton University. Reprinted with permission of the Carbon Mitigation Initiative.

Center for Progressive Reform, PROTECTING PUBLIC HEALTH AND ENVIRONMENT BY THE STROKE OF A PRESIDENTIAL PEN: SEVEN EXECUTIVE ORDERS FOR THE PRESIDENT'S FIRST 100 DAYS (2008). Reprinted by permission of the Center for Progressive Reform.

Coleman, Felicia C. and Petes, Laura E., Florida State University, Costal & Marine laboratory. *Life History Trade-offs in Marine Organisms: Consequences of Climate Change.* Copyright 2011 by Felicia C. Coleman and Laura E. Petes. All rights reserved. Used with permission of the author.

Connolly, Kim Diana, State University of NY, Buffalo, School of Law. *Climate Change in Wetland Ecosystems: Meeting the Needs and Welfare of the People and the Planet.* Copyright 2011 by Kim Diana Connolly. All rights reserved. Used with permission of the author.

Craig, Robin Kundis, The Florida State University College of Law. *The Atmosphere, the Oceans, Climate, and Ecosystem Services.* Copyright 2011 by Robin Kundis Craig. All rights reserved. Used with permission of the author.

Dittmer, Kyle, Columbia River Inter-Tribal Fish Commission, Part-time Lecturer at Portland Community College. *Climate Change on Columbia Basin Tribal Lands.* Copyright 2011 by Kyle Dittmer. All rights reserved. Used with permission of the author.

Doremus, Holly, University of California, Berkeley & University of California, Davis. *Lots of Science, Not Much Law; Why Knowledge Has Not (Yet) Been Power over Greenhouse Gas Emissions.* Copyright 2011 by Holly Doremus. All rights reserved. Used with permission of the author.

Doughton, Sandi, *Acidified seawater showing up along coast ahead of schedule,* THE SEATTLE TIMES, May 23, 2008. (Copyright 2008, Seattle Times Company. Used with permission).

Duncan, Myrl L., Washburn University School of Law. *Global Warming and Non-Point Source Pollution in the Great Plains: What's Good for Agriculture Is Also Good for Planet Earth.* Copyright 2011 by Myrl Duncna. All rights reserved. Used with permission of the author.

Farber, Daniel A., *Climate Change, Federalism, and the Constitution,* UC Berkeley Public Law Research Paper No. 1081664 (January 9, 2008). Used with permission.

Feller, Joseph M., Arizona State University. *Climate Change and Livestock Grazing on Western Rangelands.* Copyright 2011 by Joseph M. Feller. All rights reserved. Used with permission of the author.

Ferrey, Steven, Suffolk University Law School in Boston. *The Legal Dilemmas of the Kyoto Protocol for Carbon Control.* Copyright 2011 by Steven Ferrey. All rights reserved. Used with permission of the author.

Flatt, Victor B., University of North Carolina Chapel Hill School of Law. *Evolving Trends in Federal Climate Change Legislation.* Copyright 2007 by Victor B. Flatt and NORTHWESTERN UNIVERSITY LAW REVIEW COLLOQUY. Victor B. Flatt, *The Legislative Temperature for Climate Change,* 102 NW. U. L. REV. COLLOQUY 123 (2007). Condensed and reprinted version used with permission of the author and NORTHWESTERN UNIVERSITY LAW REVIEW COLLOQUY.

Freyfogle, Eric T., University of Illinois. *Making Room for Nature's Refugees.* Copyright 2011 by Eric T. Freyfogle. All rights reserved. Used with permission of the author.

Friedman, Thomas L., HOT, FLAT AND CROWDED. Copyright © 2008 by Thomas Friedman. Reprinted by permission of Farrar, Straus & Giroux, LLC.

Galbraith, James, *How Conservatives Abandoned the Free Market and Why Liberals Should Too,* from THE PREDATOR STATE. Reprinted with the permission of Free Press, a Division of Simon & Schuster, Inc. Copyright © 2008. All rights reserved.

Gardiner, Stephen M., University of Washington. *A Perfect Moral Storm: Climate Change, Intergenerational Ethics and the Problem of Corruption.* Copyright 2011 by Stephen M. Gardiner.

All rights reserved. Used with permission of the author. This paper was originally written for presentation to an interdisciplinary workshop on Values in Nature at Princeton University, the proceedings of which appeared in ENVIRONMENTAL VALUES.

Gelbspan, Ross, THE HEAT IS ON: THE CLIMATE CRISIS, THE COVER-UP, THE PRESCRIPTION. Copyright © 1998 by Ross Gelbspan. Reprinted by permission of BASIC BOOKS, a member of Perseus Books Group.

Gerrard, Michael B., Columbia Law School. *The National Environmental Policy Act and Its Progeny.* Copyright 2011 by Michael B. Gerrard. All rights reserved. Used with permission of the author.

Glicksman, Robert L., University of Kansas. *Facing Unprecedented Stewardship Challenges: Climate Change and Federal Land Management.* Copyright 2011 by Robert L. Glicksman. All rights reserved. Used with permission of the author.

Goodell, Jeff, BIG COAL: THE DIRTY SECRET BEHIND AMERICA'S ENERGY FUTURE. Copyright © 2006 by Jeff Goodell. Reprinted by permission of Houghton Mifflin Harcourt Publishing Company. All rights reserved.

Gordon, Ruth, *Climate Change and the Poorest Nations: Further Reflections on global Inequality*, 78 U. COLO. L. REV. 1559 (2007). Reprinted with the permission of the University of Colorado Law Review.

Guruswamy, Lakshman D., University of Colorado at Boulder. *Energy Justice.* Copyright 2011 by Lakshman D. Guruswamy. All rights reserved. Used with permission of the author.

Hayes, Denis, President/CEO of Bullitt Foundation. *Renewable Energy and the Reagan Revolution: An Unstoppable Force Derailed by an Immovable Object.* Copyright 2011 by Denis Hayes. All rights reserved. Used with permission of the author.

Hykes Steere, Victoria, LLM from University of Washington. *An Iñupiaq Reflection on "Ice".* Copyright 2011 by Victoria Hykes Steere. All rights reserved. Used with permission of the author.

Inslee, Jay and Bracken Hendricks, APOLLO'S FIRE. Copyright © 2008. Reproduced by permission of Island Press, Washington, D.C.

Keiter, Robert B., University of Utah. *Climate Change and Wildfire Policy.* Copyright 2011 by Robert B. Keiter. All rights reserved. Used with permission of the author.

Kolbert, Elizabeth, FIELD NOTES FROM A CATASTROPHE: MAN, NATURE AND CLIMATE CHANGE (Bloomsbury 2007). Copyright 2007. Permission to reprint granted by Bloomsbury USA.

Kravchenko, Svitlana, University of Oregon. *Right to Carbon or Right to Life: Human Rights Approaches to Climate Change.* Copyright 2011 by Svitlana Kravchenko. All rights reserved. Used with permission of the author.

Kunzig, Robert, *Scraping Bottom*, NATIONAL GEOGRAPHIC, March 2009. Copyright 2009. Reprinted by permission, Kunzig, Robert J./National Geographic Stock.

Latin, Howard, Rutgers University School of Law. *Framing Global Climate Change.* Copyright 2011 by Howard Latin. All rights reserved. Used with permission of the author.

Liotta, P.H. & Shearer, Allan W., GAIA'S REVENGE: CLIMATE CHANGE AND HUMANITY'S LOSS (Praeger Publishers 2007). Copyright © 2007 by P.H. Liotta and Allan W. Shearer. Reproduced with permission of Greenwood Publishing Group, Inc. Westport, CT.

Lomborg, Bjorn, *A Better Way Than Cap and Trade*, WASHINGTON POST, A19 (June 26, 2008) Copyright © 2008 by Bjorn Lomborg. Reprinted by permission of Bjorn Lomborg.

Lovelock, James, REVENGE OF THE GAIA. Copyright © 2006 by James Lovelock. Reprinted by permission of the author and BASIC BOOKS, a member of the Perseus Books Group.

Lynas, Mark, Six Degrees: Our Future on a Hotter Planet. Reprinted by permission of HarperCollins Publishers Ltd. © Mark Lynas 2008.

Macartan, Humphreys; Sachs, Jeffrey D. & Stiglitz, Joseph E., Introduction: *What is the Problem with Natural Resource Wealth?, in* Escaping the Resource Curse (2007 Columbia Un. Press, NY 2007).

McCall, William, BPA, tribes reach $900 million deal to help Columbia River salmon, Associated Press *in* The Seattle Times, April 7, 2008, Copyright © 2008. Used with Permission of the YGS Group/AP.

McGinley, Patrick Charles, West Virginia University . *Climate Change and Coal: Exploring the Dark Side.* Copyright 2011 by Patrick Charles McGinley. All rights reserved. Used with permission of the author.

Miles, Edward L., University of Washington. *Principles for Designing International Environmental Agreements: Avoiding the Law of the "Least Ambitious Program".* Copyright 2011 by Edward L. Miles. All rights reserved. Used with permission of the author.

Monbiot, George, Heat: How To Stop The Planet From Burning (South End Press 2007). Copyright © George Monbiot 2007. Reprinted by permission of Penguin (UK), Antony Harwood Ltd.

Moritz, Anna T., University of Washington, J.D. *Scientific Consensus on Climate Change.* Copyright 2011 by Anna T. Moritz. All rights reserved. Used with permission of the author.

Nash, J., El Nino. Copyright © 2002 by J. Nash. By permission of GRAND CENTRAL PUBLISHING.

Ngugi, Joel M., University of Washington. *The "Curse" of Ecological Interdependence: Africa, Climate Change and Social Justice.* Copyright 2011 by Joel M. Ngugi. All rights reserved. Used with permission of the author.

Norton, David W., Arctic Rim Research, *Coastal Sea Ice Watch: Private Confessions of a Convert to Indigenous Knowledge, in* The Earth is Faster Now: Indigenous Observations of Arctic Environmental Change (Arctic Studies Center, Smithsonian Institution 2002). Copyright 2002.

Osofsky, Hari M., *Climate Change Legislation in Context,* 102 Nw. U. L. Rev. Colloquy (2007). Reprinted by special permission of Northwestern University School of Law, *Northwestern University Law Review.*

Parenteau, Patrick, Vermont Law School. *Go Back, It's a Trap! The Perils of Geological Sequestration of CO2.* Copyright 2011 by Patrick Parenteau. All rights reserved. Used with permission of the author.

Pawa, Matt, *Global Warming: The Ultimate Public Nuisance* in Creative Common Law Strategies (Clifford L. Rechtschaffen & Denise E. Antolini, Eds., Environmental Law Institute 2007). Copyright© 2007 Environmental Law Institute®, Washington, DC. Reprinted with permission from ELI®.

Pearce, Fred, With Speed and Violence. Copyright © 2007 by Fred Pearce. Reprinted by permission of Beacon Press, Boston.

Pentland, William, *Alaska's Waters Quietly Reopen to Drilling.* Reprinted by Permission of Forbes.com, © 2009 Forbes LLC.

Peterson, David L. and McKenzie, Don, U.S. Forest Service, Pacific NW Station. *Understanding and Adapting to New Stress Complexes in Forest Ecosystems.* Copyright 2011 by David L. Peterson and Don McKenzie. All rights reserved. Used with permission of the authors.

REN21. 2008. *Renewables 2007 Global Status Report* (Paris: REN21 Secretariat and Washington, DC: Worldwatch Institute). Copyright 2008 By Deutsche Gesellschaft für Technische Zusammenarbeit (GTZ) GmbH.

Richardson, Anthony and Poloczanska, Elvira, *Under-Resourced, Under Threat*, 320 SCIENCE 1294 (2008). Reprinted with permission from AAAS.

Rieser, Alison, University of Hawaii at Manoa. *Whales, Whaling and the Warming Oceans.* Copyright 2008 by Alison Rieser. All rights reserved. Reprinted with permission of the author and the BOSTON COLLEGE ENVIRONMENTAL AFFAIRS LAW REVIEW. An earlier version of this chapter was presented at a symposium on the great whales of the North Atlantic at Boston College Law School on October 16, 2008, sponsored by the MIT Sea Grant Program and the BOSTON COLLEGE ENVIRONMENTAL AFFAIRS LAW REVIEW and published in the Review's volume 36, number 2.

Roach, J. Ashley, Office of the Legal Adviser, U.S. Department of State. *Arctic Sovereignty: Cold Facts, Hot Issues.* Reprinted by permission of the author.

Roberts, Paul, THE END OF OIL: ON THE EDGE OF A PERILOUS NEW WORLD. Copyright © 2004 by Paul Roberts. Reprinted by permission of Houghton Mifflin Harcourt Publishing Company. All rights reserved.

Rodgers, William H., Jr., ENVIRONMENTAL LAW IN INDIAN COUNTRY (Thomson/West 2005). Reprinted with permission of Thomson Reuters.

Roger Rosenblatt, Gregg Grunenfelder, J. Elizabeth Jackson, Catherine Karr, Rich Fenske, State of WA — Human Health Preparation & Adaptation Work Group December 2007, UW Dept. of Environmental and Health Services. *Climate Change and Human Health: The Likely Impact on the Human Community in the United States.* Copyright 2011 by Human Health Preparation & Adaptation Work Group. All rights reserved. Adapted from a report prepared for the State of Washington by the Human Health Preparation and Adaptation Work Group (Dec. 2007). Used with permission of the authors.

Romm, Joseph, HELL AND HIGH WATER: GLOBAL WARMING — THE SOLUTION AND THE POLITICS — AND WHAT WE SHOULD DO. Copyright © 2007 by Joseph Romm. Reprinted by permission of HarperCollins Publishers.

Roston, Eric, THE CARBON AGE: HOW LIFE'S CORE ELEMENT HAS BECOME CIVILIZATION'S GREATEST THREAT. Copyright © 2008. Permission to reprint granted by Walker & Co.

Rowland, Melanie J., National Oceanic and Atmospheric Administration. *Conserving Biodiversity in a No-Analog World: Is the Endangered Species Act Obsolete?.* Copyright 2011 by Melanie J. Rowland. All rights reserved. Used with permission of the author.

Ruddiman, William F.; PLOWS, PLAGUES AND PETROLEUM. Copyright © 2005 by Princeton University Press. Reprinted by permission of Princeton University Press.

Shearman, David & Smith, Joseph Wayne, THE CLIMATE CHANGE CHALLENGE AND THE FAILURE OF DEMOCRACY (Praeger Publishers). Copyright © 2007 by David Shearman and Joseph Wayne Smith. Reproduced with permission of Greenwood Publishing Group, Inc., Westport, CT.

Smith, Jeffrey A., Cravath, Swaine & Moore LLP. *Current Forms of Climate Change Disclosure: Moving Towards a Brave New World.* Copyright 2011 by Jeffrey A. Smith. All rights reserved. Used with permission of the author.

Smith, Jeffrey, Mariani, Michael, Morreale, Matthew, Hamilton, Anne, Cravath, Swaine & Moore LLP. *Corporate Responses to Climate Change.* Copyright 2011. Used with permission of the authors.

Speth, James Gustave, Bridge at the End of the World: Capitalism, the Environment, and Crossing from Crisis to Sustainability. Copyright © 2008 by James Gustave Speth. Yale University Press. Reprinted by permission of the author and Yale University Press.

Sterman, John, *Risk Communication on Climate: Mental Models and Mass Balance*, 322 Science 532 (2008). Reprinted with permission from AAAS.

Stern, Nicolas, *The Stern Report*, © Crown copyright 2006.

Stokstad, Erik, *A Second Chance for Rainforest Biodiversity*, 320 Science 1436–37 (2008). Reprinted with permission from AAAS.

Strauss, Andrew, Widener University School of Law. *Expanding the Jurisdiction of the International Court of Justice as a Means of Addressing Climate Change: Lessons from the Global Trade Regime*. Copyright 2011 by Andrew Strauss. All rights reserved. Used with permission of the author.

The CNA Corporation, National Security and the Threat of Climate Change (2007) (excerpts from the Executive Summary, http://securityandclimate.cna.org/report/). Copyright 2007 by CNA Corporation. Used with permission of CNA Corporation.

Thomas, Chris D. *Recent Evolutionary Effects of Climate Change*, *in* Climate Change and Biodiversity (T.E. Lovejoy & Lee Hannah, eds. Yale Un. Press 2005).

Tomain, Joseph P., University of Cincinnati College of Law. *Rethinking Energy Law*. Copyright 2011 by Joseph P. Tomain. All rights reserved. Used with permission of the author.

Tsosie, Rebecca, *Indigenous People and Environmental Justice: The Impact of Climate Change*, 78 U. Colo. L. Rev. 162 5(2007). Reprinted with permission of the University of Colorado Law Review and Rebecca Tsosie.

Union of Concerned Scientists, *Smoke, Mirrors & Hot Air: How Exxon Mobil Uses Big Tobacco's Tactics to Manufacture Uncertainty on Climate Science*. Copyright © 2007 Union of Concerned Scientists. Reprinted by permission.

Union of Concerned Scientists, *Tobacco's Tactics to Manufacture Uncertainty on Climate Science*. Copyright © 2007 Union of Concerned Scientists. Reprinted by permission.

Union of Concerned Scientists, *Voices of Federal Climate Scientists: Global Warming Solutions Depend on Unimpeded Science*. Copyright © 2006 Union of Concerned Scientists. Reprinted by permission.

Verchick, Robert R.M., Loyola University New Orleans. *Adaptive Justice*. Copyright 2008 by Robert R. M. Verchick and MIT Press. Reprinted with permission from the author and MIT Press. Draws from an earlier essay, *Adaptation, Economics and Justice*, *in* Climate Change and the Neoliberal Model (David Driesen, ed., MIT Press 2008).

Ward, Peter D., University of Washington. *Mass Extinctions in Deep Time as Clues to Potential Future Catastrophes: The Most Dangerous Threat from Global Warming*. Copyright 2011 by Peter D. Ward. All rights reserved. Used with permission of the author.

Weaver, Jacqueline Lang, University of Houston Law Center. *The Future of the Petroleum Industry in a World of Global*. Copyright 2011 by Jacqueline Lang Weaver. All rights reserved. Used with permission of the author.

Weiss, Edith Brown, Conference on Developing Policies for Responding to Climactic Change, Villach, Austria, 28 Sept.—2 Oct. 1987), *in* In Fairness to Future Generations: International Law, Common Patrimony, and Intergenerational Equity (Transnational Publishers, Inc. 1989). Reprinted by permission Koninklijke. Permission to reprint also granted by Vermont Journal of Environmental Law.

Wood, Mary Christina, University of Oregon School of Law. *Atmospheric Trust Litigation.* Copyright 2009 by Mary Christina Wood and Cambridge University Press. Used with permission of the author and Cambridge University Press. Part of this paper is based on material published in Mary Christina Wood, *Atmospheric Trust Litigation, in* ADJUDICATING CLIMATE CHANGE: SUB-NATIONAL, NATIONAL, AND SUPRA-NATIONAL APPROACHES (William C.G. Burns & Hari M. Godowsky, eds., Cambridge Un. Press 2009).

World Energy Council, DECIDING THE FUTURE: ENERGY POLICY SCENARIOS TO 2050 (2007). Reprinted with permission.

Worldwatch Institute, AMERICAN ENERGY: THE RENEWABLE PATH TO ENERGY SECURITY (2006). Reprinted by permission of Worldwatch Institute.

Zang, Dongsheng, University of Washington. *Poisoned Air: The Negotiating State and the Changing Climate in China.* Copyright 2011 by Dongsheng Zang. All rights reserved. Used with permission of the author.

Zerbe, Richard O. and Garland, Nancy, University of Washington. *The Economics of Climate Change.* Copyright 2011 by Richard O. Zerbe and Nancy Garland. All rights reserved. Used with permission of the authors.

Chapter One
Setting the Scientific Stage

Chapter One

Setting the Scientific Stage

I. The Deep History of the Earth

GEORGE MONBIOT, HEAT: HOW TO STOP THE PLANET FROM BURNING 3 (South End Press 2007) [hereinafter 2007 MONBIOT]:

> To doubt, today, that manmade climate change is happening, you must abandon science and revert to some other means of understanding the world, alchemy, perhaps, or magic.

JAMES LOVELOCK, THE REVENGE OF GAIA: EARTH'S CLIMATE CRISIS & THE FATE OF HUMANITY xiv (Perseus Books Group 2006) [hereinafter 2006 LOVELOCK]:

> we are in a fool's climate, accidentally kept cool by smoke, and before this century is over, billions of us will die and the few breeding pairs of people that survive will be in the arctic region where the climate remains tolerable.
>
> The great party of the twentieth century is coming to an end, and unless we now start preparing our survival kit we will soon be just another species eking out an existence in the few remaining habitable regions.... Not only will wildlife and whole ecosystems go extinct but the planet will lose a precious resource: human civilization.

2006 LOVELOCK at 150:

> Economists and politicians have to square the utter necessity of a rapid and controlled shutdown of emissions from fossil fuel burning with the human needs of civilization.

2006 LOVELOCK at 147–48:

> I am not a pessimist.... Even now, when the bell has started tolling to mark our ending, we still talk of sustainable development as if these feeble offerings would be accepted by Gaia as an appropriate and affordable sacrifice.

WILLIAM H. CALVIN, GLOBAL FEVER: HOW TO TREAT CLIMATE CHANGE 4 (U. Chicago Press 2008) [hereinafter 2008 CALVIN]:

> The climate scientists now say we need to stop the growth in worldwide carbon emissions before 2020, even for a compromise goal that will melt much of Greenland, flood major coastal cities, and make a third of all species extinct. (Some compromise). Delay will take us into the territory of half of all species, failing crops, famines, mass migrations, and genocidal wars.

2008 CALVIN at 8:

> We have already stumbled into the high-risk zone. I'd say that we are facing a medium likelihood of widespread catastrophe, rather like flying on a plane with a 30 percent chance of losing a wing before landing.

2008 CALVIN at 13:

> our present climate change isn't a simple one-dimensional problem that can be framed as mere warming, what with floods and droughts becoming much more frequent, deserts expanding, and the like.
>
> Then there are varied causes such as the CO_2 accumulating, the sun brightening, the ozone thinning, the methane soaring, the Gulf Stream slowing, the lower atmosphere thickening, and El Niño possibly settling in for good. All of that tipping, slipping, and flipping. Where do they fit into the big picture?

2008 CALVIN at 52:

> An 80 percent chance of having to live in a vastly disrupted United States is so close to a sure thing that Americans ought to insist that their government treat it that way as a precaution.

Climate scientist Stephen H. Schneider, 2007. Quoted in 2008 CALVIN at 85:

> We're altering the environment far faster than we can possibly predict the consequences.

2008 Calvin at 190:

> What will happen if the earth's fever climbs even more? The simplest way of judging is to consult past history for analogous situations. For example, were the earth to warm up several degrees more, is there data from a past warming to suggest what could happen?

PETER D. WARD, Professor of Biology, Earth and Space Sciences, University of Washington, Astrobiologist, NASA, UNDER A GREEN SKY: GLOBAL WARMING, THE MASS EXTINCTIONS OF THE PAST AND WHAT THEY CAN TELL US ABOUT OUR FUTURE xiii–iv (Smithsonian Books, Harper Collins 2007):

> In this book I will marshal the history of discovery, beginning in the 1970s, that has led an increasing number of scientists across a broad swath of fields to conclude that the past might be our best key to predicting the future. As strewn across this barren, nearly lifeless hillside in the nontouristy middle of Nevada, if there is even the slightest chance that the carbon dioxide in Earth's atmosphere of 200 million years ago caused this mass extinction, as well as numerous other times before and since that ancient calamity, then it is time for we practitioners who study the deep past to begin screaming like the sane madman played by Peter Finch in the classic 1976 film *Network*, who brought forth his pain with the cry: "I'm as mad as hell, and I'm not going to take this anymore."
>
> In our case, this cry must be: "I am scared as hell, and I am not going to be silent anymore!"
>
> This book is my scream, for here in Nevada, on that day when heat was its usual quotidian force of death, we sat on the remains of a greenhouse extinction, and it was not pretty, this graveyard, the evidence clutched in these dirty rocks utterly demolishing any possibility of hyperbole. Is it happening again? Most of us think so, but there are still so few of us who visit the deep past and compare it to the present and future. Thus this book, words tumbling out powered by rage and sorrow but mostly fear, not for us but for our children—and theirs.

This is the question addressed by paleontologist PETER D. WARD, in UNDER A GREEN SKY: GLOBAL WARMING, THE MASS EXTINCTIONS OF THE PAST AND WHAT THEY CAN TELL US ABOUT OUR FUTURE (Smithsonian Books, Harper-Collins 2007) [hereinafter 2007 WARD].

Mass Extinctions in Deep Time as Clues to Potential Future Catastrophes: The Most Dangerous Threat from Global Warming

Peter D. Ward, Department of Biology, Department of Earth and Space Science, University of Washington; and the NASA Astrobiology Institute

Introduction

The fossil record tells us that the biota of our planet has undergone numerous and catastrophic die-offs. But how many of these mass extinctions could take place in the present or future, and how many may have been somehow related to environmental conditions, such as characteristic planetary temperatures of atmospheric gas content (such as different CO_2 and/or O_2)? In this brief review I will look at some of these events to better constrain what kind of future catastrophes could be in store for our planet.

To understand how we can use the past to predict the future, we first must look at some scientific history. Geology as a science came into being at the end of the Eighteenth Century, and its formation was in no small way stimulated by the need to tell time—the time that specific rock formations were formed. The earliest geologists were confronted with this seemingly intractable problem: how could the ages of various rocks visible on the surface of the Earth be deduced? In some rare cases the superpositional contact of rock bodies made clear which was younger and which older, but in general there was little understanding about the age of the Earth and its rocky surface. Because such understanding was of paramount economic, rather than simply scientific interest, learning how to find the relative ages of various rock bodies became one of the most studied scientific problems of its time.

The first solution to this problem became apparent early in the Nineteenth Century, when it was observed that many sedimentary rock bodies contained the remains of fossilized organisms, and that the succession of fossils was similar. Because these successions could be observed in even far distant lands, the succession of fossils could be used to arrive at the relative age of sedimentary rock units. This process led to the formation of what we now call the Geological Time Scale, and even as our understanding of rock ages blossomed with the invention of radiometric time dating during the Twentieth Century, the use of fossils as indicators of relative time remains a useful and widely employed means of understanding the age of rocks. This method has worked, however, for one simple reason: most fossils range only limited distances through strata (where higher strata are younger). For instance, a particular kind of trilobite might be found at the base of a thick limestone bed, but disappears only several beds above. Its appearance marks its formation through new species formation, its disappearance its extinction. And not only did most fossil taxa show rather short periods of existence on Earth as deduced by their vertical, or time ranges in sedimentary rock, but it was early recognized that wholesale disappearance of fossil faunas, to be replaced by an almost entirely new suite of species, was commonplace in the stratigraphic record. No wonder, then, that the earliest geologists were almost all adherents of the Principal of Catastrophism: that our Earth has experienced a succession of ancient calamities that were lethal to large numbers of species living on Earth in the past. The past catastrophes were useful, however—they could be used to define the beginnings and ends of the largest scale units of the Geological Time Scale (the Eras, and some Periods), and are also clues to past perturbations to Earth's habitability. They are called mass extinctions. An illustration of the geological time scale is shown in Figure 1.

Mass extinctions, then, were brief intervals of time when significant proportions of a planet's biota were killed off. They were killed by one or some combination of too much heat or cold, not enough food or nutrients, too little (or too much) water, oxygen or carbon dioxide, excess radiation, incorrect acidity in the environment, or environmental toxins. On Earth there have been about 15 such episodes during the last 500 Myr (Million years), five of which eliminated more than half of all species then inhabiting our planet.

They also did more than threaten biota. They also played a large part in the formation of evolutionary novelty. These events significantly affected the evolutionary history of Earth's biota: for example, if the dinosaurs had not been suddenly killed off following a comet collision with the Earth 65 Ma (Million years ago), the so called "Age of Mammals" (called this because mammals became the most important and numerous of large terrestrial vertebrate animals) would certainly have played out differently, since it has to be assumed that some dinosaurs surely would have competed with mammals, and may have been more successful as both carnivores and herbivores within certain ecosystems. The fact that the wholesale evolution of mammalian diversity

Geologic Time Scale				
Time Millions of Years	Eon	Era	Period	Epoch
-0-	Phanerozoic	Cenozoic	Quarternary	Holocene
				Pleistocene
-1.5-			Tertiary	Pliocene
				Miocene
				Oligocene
				Paleocene
-65-		Mesozoic	Cretaceous	
-145-			Jurassic	
-199-			Triassic	
-251-		Paleozoic	Permian	
-299-			Mississippian	
			Pennsylvanian	
-359-			Devonian	
-416-			Silurian	
-443-			Ordovician	
-542-			Cambrian	
		Eon		
-2500-	Precambrian	Proterozoic		
-4100-		Archean		
-4500-		Hadean		

Figure 1 For: Out of Thin Air

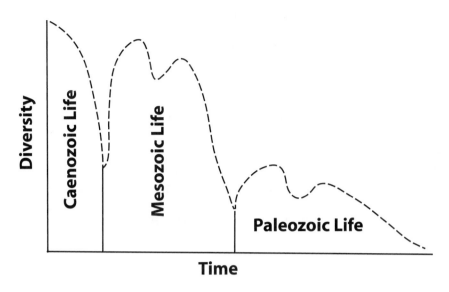

Figure 2. Mass Extinction

took place only after the dinosaurs were swept from the scene was surely not coincidence. Mass extinctions are thus both instigators as well as foils to evolution and innovation.

A Brief History

The two largest mass extinctions, recognized even as early as the mid-19th century, were so profound that they were used in the 1840s by John Phillips, an English naturalist, to subdivide the stratigraphic record—and the history of life it contains—into three large blocks of time: the *Paleozoic Era*, or time of "old life," extending from the first appearance of skeletonized life 530 Ma until it was ended by the mass extinction of 250 Ma; the *Mesozoic Era*, or time of "middle life," beginning immediately after the Paleozoic extinction and ending 65 Ma; and the *Cenozoic Era*, or time of "new life," extending from the last great mass extinction to the present day. (Figure 2).

But while all who studied the Earth agreed on these categories, there was little agreement about how long these mass extinctions took to kill off things. By the Twentieth Century, most geologists had come to view the mass extinctions as gradual, long term events, and a Uniformitarianism view extended until nearly the end of the 20th century.[1] In 1980, however, the field was revolutionized when a multidisciplinary group of scientists from Berkeley, headed by the father/son team of Luis and Walter Alvarez, published what are now known as the Alvarez Hypotheses,[2] namely that (1) the Earth was struck 65 Ma by an Earth-crossing object of some sort (asteroid or comet), and (2) the environmental effects stemming from that impact brought about a mass extinction among the late Cretaceous fauna (animals) sufficient to end the *Mesozoic Era*. Thus, by the end of the Twentieth Century, two very different kinds of causes were postulated for these disasters: one, caused by some combination of climate change coincident with large-scale volcanic activity in the form of flood basalts, accompanying rise or fall of oceanic sealevel, was thought to have been long-term in its power, causing an extinction event that took a million years or more to unfold. The other, asteroid impact, was seen as occurring far more

---

1. References in V.E. Courtillot & P.R. Renne, *On the Ages of Flood Basalt Events*, 335 C. R. Geosci. 113 (2003).

2. L.W. Alvarez *et al.*, *Extraterrestrial Cause for the Cretaceous-Tertiary Extinction—Experimental Results and Theoretical Interpretation*, 208 Science 1095 (1980).

rapidly. But even by the end of the Twentieth Century it was unclear which of these was the dominant mechanism. Let us briefly look at what we now think transpired in the past, first examining the events that took place, and then looking at possible causes of the events.

The Past Catastrophes

Paleontologists have discovered 15 mass extinction events occurring since the "Cambrian Explosion" of 537 million years ago.[3] A summary of these can be found in Figure 3.

There may have been yet other mass extinction events of earlier times that are largely unknown to us because they occurred when organisms rarely made skeletal hard parts, and thus rarely became fossils. Perhaps the long period of Earth history prior to the advent of skeletons was also punctuated by enormous global catastrophes decimating the biota of our planet—mass extinctions without record—or at least without a record that has yet been deciphered. One of the still raging controversies among those who study these past catastrophes concerns microbes.

Name	Time (MA)	Cause	Recovery Fauna	Recovery Time	% Kill
Vendian Extinctions	560–538?	Unknown	Animal phyla	Unknown	100%?
Late Cambrian Extinctions		Anoxia?			40% marine genera
Ordovician Mass Extinction (Big Five)		Anoxia, global cooling			55% marine genera
Devonian Mass Extinction (Big Five)		Anoxia			40% marine genera
Permian Mass Extinction (Big Five)		Anoxia/ global heating, impact?			60% marine genera
Triassic/Jurassic mass extinction (Big Five)		Anoxia/ global heating, impact?			45% marine genera
Toarcian Event (Jurassic)		Anoxia			20% marine genera
Tithonian Event (Late Jurassic)		Anoxia			20% marine genera
Cenomanian-Turonian event (Cretaceous)		Anoxia			20% marine genera
Cretaceous –Paleogene (K/P) Mass Extinction (Big Five)		Impact			45% marine genera
Paleocene Event		Global heating			10% marine genera
Eocene –Oligocene Event		Impact?			15% marine genera
End Pleistocene— Recent Event		Global cooling, Human activity			?

Figure 3. Mass Extinction Events

---

3. A. Hallam & P.B. Wignall, Mass Extinctions and Their Aftermath (Oxford Un. Press 1997).

Do bacteria (and viruses) survive these events relatively unscathed, or do they too succumb to the processes that so obviously kill animal species so readily?

Of the fifteen mass extinctions officially classified as such from the last 500 Myr, six have been especially catastrophic as measured either by the number of families, genera, or species going extinct, or by their effect on subsequent biotic evolution. To this list we should probably add three more that may have occurred prior to 500 Ma, as well as one that might be happening in our time, a *current* biodiversity crisis caused by the effects of a runaway human population. Although the final extinction total for the current mass extinction cannot yet be tallied, it may be representative of what happens whenever an intelligent species arises on a planet.

Our understanding of the various events is in inverse proportion to their age: the older they are, the less we know because of the increasingly corrupted fossil and geological record. The most recent of the larger, ancient events, the Cretaceous/Tertiary mass extinction 65 Ma, is by far the most studied and best understood. In order of appearance, the oldest first, let's look briefly at these events. The more minor ones, such as several in the Mesozoic Era, will be left out so as to concentrate on the most catastrophic.

The oldest of the mass extinctions probably occurred early in Earth History, during the time of the so-called Early Bombardment (4.0–3.8 billion years ago), when the flotsam and jetsam left over from the formation of the Solar System some 4.6 billion years ago found its way to all of the planets. The Earth and Moon were no exception, and one has only to look at our pocked moon to realize how intense this early bombardment phase really was, for almost all of the craters now visible happened during this event. The Earth was even more cratered, but few are left due to the intense nature of weathering on our atmosphere- and ocean-covered planet. The period of early heavy bombardment is thought to have sterilized the surface of the Earth at least several times — assuming that life had evolved at all by this time. This is at best a potential event — if life was indeed present, it may have suffered one or more mass extinctions. The next two events are also intuited, rather than based on evidence from fossils. About 2.5 billion years ago, an intensely poisonous gas (at least to most life of the time) began to accumulate for the first time in the atmosphere: oxygen. This rise of oxygen certainly caused the extinction of many, perhaps most anaerobic bacterial species then on Earth. (But not complete extinction: there were certainly many anaerobic environments, then as now, in the sea and in fresh water.) Soon after the evolution of a new kind of microbe adapted to oxygen caused a major change in global temperatures, which plunged the planet into another mass extinction. The evolution of photosynthetic microbes caused carbon dioxide levels, and therefore greenhouse gas levels, to plummet, and the Earth virtually froze over. There is little or no fossil record of this event, which may have coincided with the first "Snowball Earth" event when geological evidence indicates that even the tropics were frozen. Although either the rise of oxygen, or the Snowball Earth, potentially could have caused a mass extinction, at the present time there is no evidence for this from the fossil record.

The next potential extinction is thought to have occurred about 750 million years ago, and if it occurred, would have been caused by yet another Snowball Earth event. There is almost no information known about this event, which may have included three or four separate extinctions coinciding with repeated glaciations. There appears to have been wholesale extinction among *stromatolites* and planktonic organisms called *acritarchs*. The lack of fossilized animals from this time period obscures these events. The next, however, left a record that we can interpret.

The Cambrian Period of 545–500 million years ago is famous as the time of the so-called "Cambrian Extinction," when most animal groups now on Earth first appeared in the fossil record. Two mass extinctions book-end the Cambrian. The Cambrian Explosion was preceded by the first of all mass extinctions visible among animals, which caused the disappearance of the so-called *Ediacaran* fauna. These were odd assemblages of jellyfish-like and sea-anemone-like animals that can be found in strata immediately below the base of the Cambrian from many parts of the world. They appear to be the first diverse assemblage of animals, perhaps early fore-runners of today's animals such as the *Cnidaria* (jellyfishes, corals, hydras) and various worms, or perhaps an assemblage of phyla now completely extinct. They disappeared in sudden and dramatic fashion immediately prior to the Cambrian period, but the cause of their disappearance remains a mystery. It may have been caused by competition with the newly evolving and more modern groups of animals typifying the Cambrian, or through sudden environmental change. A second wave of extinctions occurred about 60 Myr after the Ediacaran crisis. This second crisis was protracted over several millions of years, and gravely affected the first reef-forming organisms (*archeocyathids*), as well as many groups of trilobites and early mollusks. Again, there is little direct evidence of what brought about these extinctions, other than that they seem to be linked to changes in worldwide sea level and to the formation of deep anoxic bottom water.

Following the Cambrian events, mass extinctions seemingly became more lethal in terms of the percentage of species killed off.[4] This certainly suggests that the number of individuals dying out would have been phenomenal. During the *Paleozoic Era* of 540 to 250 million years ago, there were three more major mass extinctions. In the Ordovician Period (> 400 Ma) and in the Devonian Period (~ 370 Ma), major events decimated the marine faunas of the time. Because our record of land life is poor for both of these intervals, there is still much to learn about the severity of these events on land. In the sea, however, it is clear that the majority of species went extinct, and that more than 20% of marine families were eliminated. Yet as catastrophic as these events were, they were just a warm-up, compared to what happened at the end of the *Paleozoic* (and the reason that there was an end of the *Paleozoic*, and a start of the next era, the *Mesozoic*). This event is known as the Permian Extinction, and colloquially referred to either as the "Great Dying" or the "Mother of all Mass Extinctions."

Based on how many species died out, the Permian Extinction was easily the most catastrophic of all the events.[5] It is clear that the vast majority of animal and plant life on the Earth was extinguished. Yet even though long recognized as being the most catastrophic mass extinction, its cause has been problematic. Several different and independent causes may even have contributed to the event. The most widely reported is that this event, like the mass extinction at the end of the Cretaceous, was caused by asteroids' impact on the Earth. But most new evidence seems to be contrary to this explanation. One possible major cause was an increase in atmospheric CO_2 arising from (1) a short-term release of carbon dioxide from sediments formerly sequestered on the ocean floor, (2) gas emitted during unusually severe volcanic eruptions, and 3) a changeover to a world-wide anoxic ocean that allowed the blooming of H_2S emitting microbes, producing a significant release of poisonous hydrogen sulfide into the atmosphere.[6] The presence of even as little as 200ppm H_2S in the atmosphere would have caused upper atmospheric ozone layer disruption or even complete disappearance, as well as directly poisoning of vertebrate animals and plants.

Such a sudden release of huge volumes of carbon dioxide would cause a direct killing of marine organisms by carbon dioxide poisoning, as well as a direct killing of terrestrial life due to a sudden and intense global heating from a greatly increased greenhouse effect and the poisonous H_2S. A heat spike of perhaps 5–10°C, 10,000 to 100,000 years in duration, was certainly in-

---

4. Hallam & Wignall, *supra* note 3.

5. Hallam & Wignall, *supra* note 3.

6. L.R. Kump *et al.*, *Massive Release of Hydrogen Sulfide to the Surface Ocean and Atmosphere During Intervals of Oceanic Anoxia*, 33 Geology 397 (2005).

volved[7] while a new work using molecular biomarkers[8] certainly supports this new hypothesis that H_2S was a factor. It appears that there may have been a significant land plant die-off at the end of the Permian, perhaps also brought about through the combination of gases and temperature in a newly changed atmosphere. The presence of identifiable cell wall material from microbes that were obligate anaerobes that could photosynthesize as well as use H_2S metabolically indicates that deep anoxia made its way up into the photic zone, a process involving a rise of the chemocline.[9]

The world after the Permian event was a very empty place biologically. Recovery was slow, taking at least 5 million years,[10] and because so much was wiped out in the Permian event, the new species arising in this empty world were mainly of stocks different from those prior to the event. These new species had about 50 million years of peace before they too were overtaken by yet another massive die-off, known as the Triassic mass extinction. Like its immediate predecessor, asteroid impact has been implicated, but also like the Permian event, it now seems far more likely that the Triassic mass extinction event was caused by planetary changes to the atmosphere, not by rocks falling onto our planet from space.

The other notable mass extinctions following the Permian extinction included the Triassic/Jurassic mass extinction event, a smaller event in the early Jurassic, one in the mid Cretaceous, and a very significant event at the end of the *Paleocene*, some 10 million years after the dinosaur killing KT event. All of these are now associated with the same scenario as the Permian event: sudden global warming from flood basalt releasing CO_2 into the atmosphere; anoxia of the oceans; blooming of anoxic photosynthesizing H_2S producing microbes in response to saturation of the upper ocean with H_2S; followed by a flux of this H_2S out of the oceans into the atmosphere, causing a land plant extinction.

Causes

The brief listing of events given above suggests that most of the mass extinctions seem to have been caused by the forces generated by the planet itself. Some still remain mysterious as to their cause, however, and at this time there are other potential catastrophic events that might have affected the Earth. Let us look at some of these.

In one way or another, all mass extinctions appear to have been immediately caused by changes in the "global atmosphere inventory." The specific killing agents arise through changes in the makeup and behavior of the atmosphere, or through factors such as temperature and circulation patterns that are dictated by properties of the atmosphere. Those in turn can be caused by many things: asteroid or comet impact, loss of carbon dioxide or other gases into the oceans and atmosphere during flood basalt extrusion (when great volumes of lava flow out onto the Earth's surface), loss of gases caused by liberation of organic-rich oceanic sediments during sea level change, or changes in ocean circulation patterns.

The geological record on this planet suggests, however, that more than a single cause is usually associated with any given mass extinction. Sometimes these multiple events occur at the same time; sometimes they are separated by hundreds of thousands of years. Perhaps one perturbation stresses the planet, making it more susceptible to the next perturbation.

---

7. Courtillot & Renne, *supra* note 1.

8. K. Grice *et al.*, *Photic Zone Euxinia During the Permian-Triassic Superanoxic Event*, 307 Science 706 (2005).

9. Kump *et al.*, *supra* note 6.

10. J.L. Payne *et al.*, *Large Perturbations of the Carbon Cycle During Recovery from the End-Permian Extinction*, 305 Science 506 (2004).

One such perturbation, difficult to detect, would have been changes in the amount of energy coming from the sun, or periods of intense solar flares and storms of greater magnitude than anything humans have observed in the very short time that scientific observation of the sun has taken place at all. We do know that the sun has been increasing in its energy output over time, and since the formation of the Earth that energy amount hitting the Earth has increased by a third. If that energy were greater still, over short intervals of time, the Earth might experience the fate of Venus—something called a Runaway Greenhouse event that would cause the loss of our oceans. This will be the ultimate fate of the oceans, but that is thought to be still at least two billion years in the future. But that could change if our Sun turns out to be less stable than we now think.

What about the opposite—not a hot greenhouse, but a deep freeze? As we saw above, this has already happened several times. Could it happen again, or if not on a planetary scale, could we be heading for a new interval of glaciation, similar to the times and temperatures of maximum ice covers of the Ice Ages of the last 2.5 million years? The input of massive volumes of human-made greenhouse gases such as carbon dioxide makes this unlikely in the near term. But if civilization stumbles, or runs out of coal or oil, this is a distinct possibility. A new glacial interval would even be more catastrophic (especially to agriculture) than even the globally tropical times that we seem to be heading toward because of human tweaking of the atmosphere.

Humans are not the only producers of greenhouse gases. There is increasing evidence that the occurrences of *flood basalts* [lava flows] in the Earth's past were coincident with mass extinctions. At the end of the Permian, for instance, the so-called Siberian Traps were extruded; while at the end of the Triassic, the largest known flood basalt on earth, the Central Atlantic Magmatic Province, was extruded. These events involve the short-term extrusion of large volumes of basalt onto the surface of the Earth, as well as out-gassing of large volumes of carbon dioxide, a greenhouse gas, and sulfur dioxide, a poisonous gas. At the present time, however, it is not known how extrusion of large amounts of lava onto the surface of the Earth translates into a killing mechanism on land or in the sea. One idea is that short-term global heating is caused by huge amounts of greenhouse gases, including methane (previously bound in clathrates), being liberated at these times. Modeling of temperatures at the end of the Permian confirms a short-term heat spike. It would be naïve to think that such Magmatic episodes have come to an end simply because humans don't want them to happen, and if such a gigantic geological event were to occur, no amount of human engineering could stop it. A graph showing past mass extinctions and atmospheric CO_2 levels appears in Figure 4.

Dangers from Space

One potential, future catastrophe would be impact of a large asteroid or comet on the Earth. Even a small asteroid strike would surely perturb agricultural production by throwing up great volumes of dust into the atmosphere to the point of creating global famine. While most of the Earth-crossing asteroids in our solar system have been found and are being tracked, there are many bodies of less than 1 km diameter that are too small to detect until too late. Any impact hit in the ocean would also cause tsunamis.

What are the odds? Every century the Earth is struck by something large enough (< 50 m in diameter—Tunguska-sized events, which do not strike the surface but airburst above the surface) to perturb climate, and thousand-year events (0.5 m to 100 m diameter) could conceivably wipe out appreciable numbers of humans because of famine resulting from climate change after the impact, as well as potential tsunamis.

There are other potential dangers that are extraterrestrial. The two most dangerous are surely supernova and gamma ray bursts.

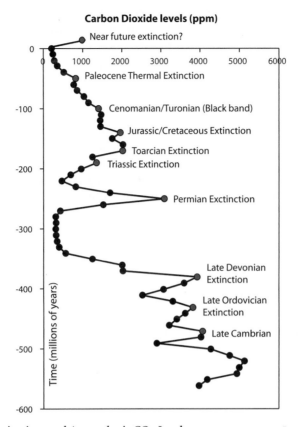

Figure 4. Past Mass Extinctions and Atmospheric CO$_2$ Levels

A supernova is a star that explodes, violently, at the end of its lifetime. Two University of Chicago astronomers[11] calculated that a star going supernova within 30 light years of our Sun would release fluxes of energetic electromagnetic radiation and charged particles (cosmic rays) sufficient to destroy the Earth's ozone layer in 300 years or less. Removal of the ozone layer would then prove calamitous to the biosphere as it would expose both marine and land organisms to potentially lethal solar ultraviolet radiation, as is shown by researchers studying the effect of ultraviolet radiation on current phytoplankton populations under the current "hole" in the ozone that fluctuates in size over Antarctica. These studies suggest that photosynthesizing organisms such as phytoplankton and reef communities would be particularly affected. Based on the average number of stars near the Sun and the rates of supernova explosions (only very rare stars, those with masses at least 8 times that of the Sun, go supernova), they concluded that supernova explosions within 30 light years of the Earth, and therefore presumably dangerous, occur on average every 200–300 million years. Thus, a supernova might have caused several of the still mysterious mass extinctions of the past.

Another potential hazard is *gamma ray bursts*, one type of which lasts a second or less, peaks at ~200 keV energy, and is thought to arise from the merging of two neutron stars into a black hole (most observed bursts originate in very distant galaxies), or is related somehow to supernova explosions. Such a burst of gamma rays hitting the Earth could have many deleterious ef-

11. J. Ellis & D.N. Schramm, *Could a Nearby Supernova Explosion Have Caused a Mass Extinction*, 92 Proc. Natl. Acad. Sci. USA 235 (1995).

fects, such as (a) delivering enough ionizing energy to Earth's surface (after the original gamma rays are transformed into ultraviolet spectral lines) to cause significant genetic damage to organisms, despite the relatively thick atmosphere of Earth, (b) stripping the ozone layer and thus allowing solar ultraviolet radiation to damage life, (c) changing atmospheric chemistry that could lead to, for example, great changes in surface temperature or biogeochemical cycles, or (d) producing harmful radioactive species on Earth.

A critical issue is the frequency of these postulated events in any galaxy. A recent and detailed analysis in 2002 indicated that the Milky Way should have one gamma ray burst every two million years on average, and it may be that a gamma ray burst happening *anywhere* in our Galaxy may well seriously affect Earth's life with a "photon jolt" (as well as any other life in the Galaxy, no matter where located). Long-term biological effects, however, are very uncertain regarding what levels of radiation are necessary to cause significant mutations and other evolutionary effects, and how these vary between different species.

What We Should Worry About

Based on a reading of the past, we humans should care very much about both asteroid impact, as well as global warming. These seem to be the two main causes of past catastrophes. A rapid change in sea level that will occur if the Greenland, or even parts of the Antarctic ice sheets melt, would be particular devastating to agriculture and human habitation. Loss of the Greenland Ice cap would cause sea level rise between 3 and 6m, whereas the loss of all continental ice sheets would cause an 80m rise.

The deep history of the earth has spoken to us many times. Earth scientists are doing their best to interpret the occasions. We hope they are listening out there.

―――――――――

Notes

1. WILLIAM JAMES BURROUGHS, CLIMATE CHANGE IN PREHISTORY: THE END OF THE REIGN OF CHAOS 19 (Cambridge Un. Press 2008 ed.):

> What is now clear is that during the last ice age, and the period that followed it, the climate was much more chaotic than it has been in recent millennia. Generally, the climate was much more variable. Sudden changes occurred from time to time. Collapse of parts of the ice sheets, or release of meltwater lakes that built up behind the ice led to cataclysmic changes. Armadas of icebergs or floods of icy freshwater swept out into the North Atlantic altering the circulation of the ocean at a stroke and with it the climate of the neighboring continents.

2. On the techniques of the climate researchers, see ELIZABETH KOLBERT, FIELD NOTES FROM A CATASTROPHE: MAN, NATURE, AND CLIMATE CHANGE 50–51 (Bloomsbury USA 2006) [hereinafter 2006 KOLBERT]:

> In the Greenland ice, there is nuclear fallout from early atomic tests, volcanic ash from Krakatau, lead pollution from ancient Roman smelters, and dust blown in from Mongolia on ice age winds. Every layer also contains tiny bubbles of trapped air, each of them a sample of a past atmosphere.
>
> …. Over the last decade, three Greenland cores have been drilled to a depth of nearly two miles, and these cores have prompted a wholesale rethinking of how the

climate operates. Where once the system was thought to change, as it were, only glacially, now it is known to be capable of sudden and unpredictable reversals. One such reversal, called the Younger Dryas, ... took place roughly 12,800 years ago.... In Greenland, average annual temperatures shot up nearly twenty degrees in a single decade.

3. P.H. Liotta & Allan W. Shearer, Gaia's Revenge: Climate Change and Humanity's Loss 62 (Praeger 2007) [hereinafter 2007 P.H. Liotta and Allan W. Shearer]:

Regarding the science of climate change, the implications are astonishing. We do not suffer from insufficient information; we suffer from too much scientifically conclusive data. We cannot reduce our uncertainty in order to resolve the definitive debate on climate change and human impact; we can only increase our uncertainty with the insecurity of our increased knowledge.

Ultimately, we are no closer to addressing how best to solve these challenges, even as they collide with environmental, human, and national issues. As subsequent chapters argue, climate change will be the driving force and critical uncertainty that will alter everything.

4. Wallace S. Broecker & Robert Kunzig, Fixing Climate: What Past Climate Changes Reveal About the Current Threat — and How to Counter It xvi (Hill & Wang eds., Farrar, Straus & Giroux 2008):

the message from the study of past climates is that the time for stopping the increase for atmospheric CO_2 is now.... When you have explored the Ice Age for as long as Broecker has and especially the wild swings that happened within the Ice Age, you don't think natural climate variability is benign.

5. 2008 Calvin at 89:

In the climate system, tipping points may be invisible until encountered. That's why studying ancient climate is so important. It shows us many of the past episodes of tip, slip, and flip.

6. Tyler Volk, CO_2 Rising: The World's Greatest Environmental Challenge 158 (MIT Press 2008):

Before about 1850, CO_2 levels were stable at about 280 parts per million in the atmosphere for thousands of years.

Id. at 156:

The rate of increase is increasing—no surprise given that energy use will rise, though more slowly than the 3 percent exponential growth rate of the gross world product. Earth will continue to have an atmosphere with a CO_2 level higher than any shown by ice-core measurements stretching back more than half a million years.

7. David Archer, The Long Thaw: How Humans Are Changing the Next 100,000 Years of Earth's Climate 1 (Princeton Un. Press 2009):

Global warming could be one of humankind's longest lasting legacies. The climatic impacts of releasing fossil fuel CO_2 to the atmosphere will last longer than Stonehenge. Longer than time capsules, longer than nuclear waste, far longer than the age of human civilization so far. Each ton of coal that we burn leaves CO_2 gas in the atmosphere. The CO_2 coming from a quarter of that ton will still be affecting the climate one thousand years from now, at the start of the next millennium. And that is only the beginning.

II. The Progression of Climate Science

Scientific Consensus on Climate Change

Anna Moritz, J.D. Class of 2009, University of Washington School of Law; Ph.D in Neuroscience and in Applied Physiology (2003), University of Colorado at Boulder. Postdoctoral fellowships: University of Colorado Health Sciences Center and the Department of Physiology and Biophysics at the University of Washington Medical School with a research emphasis on input integration and information processing in single neurons, as explored through computer modeling and cellular recordings. Anna switched careers upon witnessing the utter lack of responsiveness to the impending climate catastrophe.

Despite the attempt to make climate change appear controversial in the popular media, there is an overwhelming scientific consensus that human activity that releases greenhouse gases is causing a change in the Earth's climate.[1] An excellent source of information is the Intergovernmental Panel on Climate Change (IPCC).[2]

The literature on climate change is extensive, and selecting a "representative" sample of the many superb studies is difficult. Nonetheless, the studies below exemplify a few of the important moments in the progression of our understanding of climate change.

Svante Arrhenius, *On the Influence of Carbonic Acid in the Air upon the Temperature of the Ground*, 41 PHILOS. MAG. J. SCI. 237 (1896).

> Svante Arrhenius was the first person to calculate—by hand—the effects of increased atmospheric carbon dioxide on global temperatures. His calculations were amazingly accurate and have been little improved upon in today's age of supercomputers. Climate sensitivity is defined as the temperature increase in response to a doubling in carbon dioxide concentration. Arrhenius estimated climate sensitivity to be 5–6° C; the most recent IPCC estimate of climate sensitivity is 2.0–4.5° C, with greater sensitivity possible.[3]

Charles D. Keeling *et al.*, *The Concentration and Isotopic Abundances of Carbon Dioxide in the Atmosphere*, 12 TELLUS 200 (1960).

> Charles Keeling began observing atmospheric carbon dioxide concentrations in 1957. He noticed that the measurement was the same at every location; the data reflected both seasonal variability and a long-term increase due to fossil-fuel consumption. The resulting plot, the "Keeling curve", of atmospheric carbon dioxide concentration versus time has become an icon of anthropogenic climate forcing. This work continues today at Scripps Institution of Oceanography. For an early discussion of the impact of fossil-fuel burning, see C. D. Keeling, *Is Carbon Dioxide from Fossil Fuel Changing Man's Environment?* 114 PROCEEDINGS OF THE AMERICAN PHILOSOPHICAL SOCIETY 10 (1970). (See Figure 5.)

Dansgaard W., *et al.*, *One Thousand Centuries of Climatic Record from Camp Century on the Greenland Ice Sheet*, 166 SCIENCE 377 (1969).

> The analysis of gases and isotopes trapped in air bubbles within ice cores provides a means for analyzing and re-constructing climate from hundreds of thousands of years ago. This allows for predictions of future climate change in the presence of increased at-

---

1. *See, e.g.,* Naomi Oreskes, *The Scientific Consensus on Climate Change*, 306 SCIENCE 1686 (2004).

2. http://www.ipcc.ch/.

3.*Summary for Policymakers, in* CLIMATE CHANGE 2007: THE PHYSICAL SCIENCE BASIS. CONTRIBUTION OF WORKING GROUP I TO THE FOURTH ASSESSMENT REPORT OF THE INTERGOVERNMENTAL PANEL ON CLIMATE CHANGE (S.D. Solomon *et al.* eds., Cambridge Un. Press 2007).

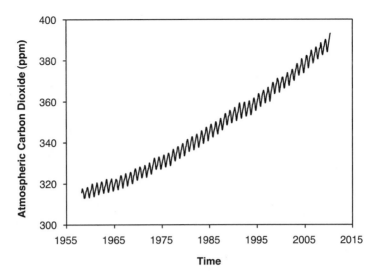

Figure 5. Continuous carbon dioxide measurements at the Mauna Loa Observatory, which began with Keeling's original work and continues today. Atmospheric carbon dioxide concentration is shown on the ordinate and time is shown on the abscissa. Data source: C. D. Keeling, S. C. Piper, R. B. Bacastow, M. Wahlen, T. P. Whorf, M. Heimann, and H. A. Meijer, *Exchanges of atmospheric CO_2 and $13CO_2$ with the terrestrial biosphere and oceans from 1978 to 2000*, I. Global aspects, SIO Reference Series, No. 01-06 (Scripps Institution of Oceanography, San Diego 2001).

mospheric carbon dioxide. Since Dansgaard's early studies, numerous cores have been extracted and analyzed. The longest record to date, extracted in Antarctica, extends to 800,000 years before present. (See Figure 6.)

John Mercer, *West Antarctic Ice Sheet and CO_2 Greenhouse Effect: Threat of Disaster*, 217 Nature 321 (1978).

John Mercer suggested as early as the 1970's that one of the disastrous and underestimated effects of global warming would be loss of the West Antarctic Ice Sheet and a resultant 5 m rise in sea level. Antarctic Ice Shelves have been continually receding; the Larsen B Ice Shelf made news when an area of approximately 3250 km^2 rapidly collapsed on January 31, 2002.[4] The most recent loss is the Wilkins Ice Shelf on the Antarctic Peninsula, which has experienced the greatest warming anywhere on Earth at a rate of 0.9° F/decade.[5] The Wilkins Shelf collapse has scientists surprised because its disintegration is occurring during the coldest time of the year.

James Hansen recently published an excellent discussion of scientific hesitance to be "alarmist" in which he alludes to the difficulty John Mercer faced getting funding after publishing this paper.[6] In the same article Hansen also shows that, in fact, predictions that take into account the current rapidity of ice sheet loss indicate that sea level may rise by as much as 5 m within this century.

W.-C. Wang, Y.L. Yung, A.A. Lacis, T. Mo & J.E. Hansen, *Greenhouse Effects Due to Man-made Perturbation of Trace Gases*, 194 Science 685 (1976).

This study was among the first to quantify the effects of various greenhouse gases on global warming. The importance of non-carbon dioxide greenhouse gases is receiving

---

4. http://nsidc.org/iceshelves/larsenb2002
5. http://nsidc.org/news/press/20080325_Wilkins.html
6. James E. Hansen, *Scientific Reticence and Sea Level Rise*, 2 Environ. Res. Lett. 024002 (2007).

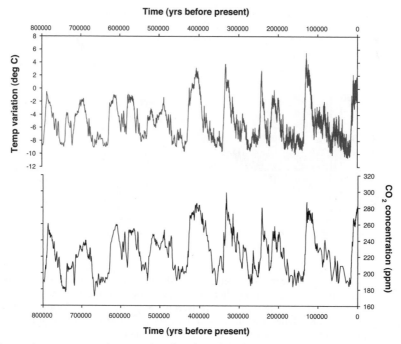

Figure 6. Changes in temperature (top trace) and carbon dioxide concentrations (bottom trace) over the last 800,000 years. Temperature changes are measured relative to the average over the last 1000 years. Time is measured in years before present (BP). Temperature data source: J. Jouzel *et al.*, *Orbital and Millennial Antarctic Climate Variability over the Past 800,000 Years*, 317 SCIENCE 793 (2007). Carbon dioxide data source: D. Luthi *et al. High-resolution carbon dioxide concentration record 650,000–800,000 years before present*, 453 NATURE 379 (2008).

attention. The figure below is taken from a recent paper by Hansen and colleagues that examines the effect of non-carbon dioxide greenhouse gases and focuses on the enhanced sensitivity of the Arctic. (See Figure 7.)

Michael E. Mann *et al.*, *Global-scale Temperature Patterns and Climate Forcing Over the Past Six Centuries*, 392 NATURE 779 (1998).

These authors were the first to publish the "hockey stick" plot of global temperatures, which showed a dramatic increase in the 20th century. Because the authors combined temperature "proxies" such as tree rings and ice cores, the results were much discussed and in some cases criticized. Since this article was published, other reports have largely substantiated the results, including a ten-year follow up by the same researchers.[7] For a particularly comprehensive analysis, see Osborn and Briffa, *The Spatial Extent of 20th-Century Warmth in the Context of the Past 1200 Years*, 311 SCIENCE 841 (2006). Dr. James Hansen recently published data on his website for most of 2007 indicating that the first 11 months of 2007 were the second hottest on record behind 2005.[8] He notes that this is particularly impressive given that we were in a cool phase in the El Niño cycle. The IPCC also has included an analysis of long-term temperatures in its assessment reports. (See Figure 8.)

P. Falkowski *et al.*, *The Global Carbon Cycle: A Test of Our Knowledge of Earth as a System*, 290 SCIENCE 291 (2000).

---

7. M.E. Mann *et al.*, *Proxy-based Reconstructions of Hemispheric and Global Surface Temperature Variations over the Past Two Millennia*, 105 PROC. NATL. ACAD. SCI. 13525 (2008).

8. http://www.columbia.edu/~jeh1.

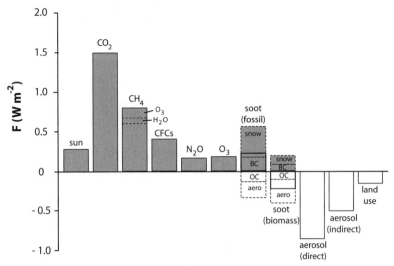

Figure 7. Summary of climate forcings between 1750 and 2000. The warming effect of the sum of all non-carbon dioxide gases is equivalent to the effect of carbon dioxide. Abbreviations: CO_2, carbon dioxide; CH_4, methane; O_3, ozone; H_2O, water vapor; CFCs, chlorofluorocarbons; N_2O, nitrous oxide; BC, black carbon; OC, organic carbon; aero, aerosol. Although technically not a greenhouse gas, black carbon, or soot, also exerts a powerful warming effect, especially through reductions in albedo at the Arctic. Both "direct" and "indirect" forcings are summarized on the plot. Data source: J. Hansen *et al.*, *Efficacy of climate forcings*, 110 J. GEOPHYS. RES. D18104 (2005).

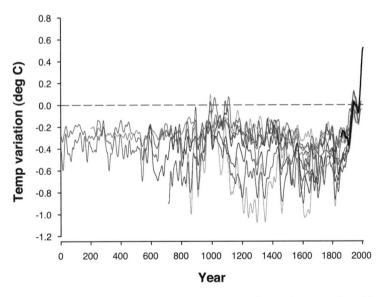

Figure 8. This graph shows temperature changes in the northern hemisphere as reflected in various proxies. Variation is measured relative to the average temperature between 1961 and 1990. This figure includes data for more recent years than the original Mann publication, but the same trend is evident. These plots of temperature are called "hockey sticks" due to the fact that they look like a hockey stick on its side. For data references, see E. Jensen *et al.*, *Paleoclimate*, in CLIMATE CHANGE 2007: THE PHYSICAL SCIENCE BASIS. CONTRIBUTION OF WORKING GROUP I TO THE FOURTH ASSESSMENT REPORT OF THE INTERGOVERNMENTAL PANEL ON CLIMATE CHANGE Figure 6.10 (S. Soloman *et al.* eds., Cambridge Un. Press 2007). Data compiled and made available by Tim Osborn and Keith Briffa at the Climate Reconstruction Unit, School of Environmental Sciences, University of East Anglia, Norwich, UK.

Carbon is stored and released through a variety of mechanisms. The cumulative balance of these sources and sinks dictates atmospheric carbon dioxide levels and thus greenhouse effects. The authors in this paper review the various aspects of the system.

Richard Alley *et al.*, *Abrupt Climate Change*, 299 Science 2005 (2003).

Richard Alley is a well-known glaciologist. In this review article he and his colleagues explain that contrary to popular impression, climate can change dramatically and on a very short time scale. These "tipping points" are now well-accepted as one of the greatest dangers of increased atmospheric greenhouse gases.

C. Thomas *et al.*, *Extinction Risk from Climate Change*, 427 Nature 145 (2004).

One of the significant effects of global warming is loss of biodiversity. This study estimated that up to 37% of species will be committed to extinction by 2050. An example is the plight of polar bears today. The United States Geological Survey recently released a report indicating that 2/3 of the world's polar bears will be gone by 2050.[9]

F. Chapin *et al.*, *Role of Land-Surface Changes in Arctic Summer Warming*, 310 Science 5748 (2005).

"Albedo" refers to the reflectivity of a surface. In climate science, it is a measure of how much radiation the Earth absorbs, or reflects, which in turn drives changes in temperature. Snow is a very effective reflector. For this reason, the Arctic is a particularly important location, as discussed in this study.

Since this paper was published, Arctic sea ice has receded dramatically. The extent of sea ice melt in the summer of 2007 crushed all previous records and far exceeded the extent of sea ice melt predicted by any climate models.[10] This massive sea ice loss was nearly repeated in the summer of 2008, despite much cooler conditions than in the summer of 2007.[11] Perhaps more troubling is that while sea ice extent in 2008 did not reach the 2007 record, the sea ice volume in 2008 was likely the lowest ever recorded which has severe implications for future ice loss.[12] (See Figure 9.)

T.R. Christensen *et al.*, *Thawing Sub-Arctic Permafrost: Effects on Vegetation and Methane Emissions*, 31 Geophysical Research Letters L04501 (2004).

Large amounts of methane are stored in sub-Arctic permafrost. The massive amounts of methane released as a result of thawing could become a new and uncontrolled source of greenhouse gases. A recent study has further explored the impact of Arctic sea ice loss on permafrost melt.[13] Another hazard of permafrost loss is the destabilization of methane clathrates. Methane clathrates are ice lattices that store massive amounts of methane under the sea floor. They are stabilized by both very cold temperatures and high pressure. Clathrates under melting permafrost may be released in large boluses, which has the potential to cause extremely rapid climate change, as reported recently by Kennedy *et al.*[14]

---

9. http://www.usgs.gov/newsroom/special/polar%5Fbears.

10. Julienne Stroeve *et al.*, *Arctic Sea Ice Decline: Faster than Forecast*, 34 Geophys. Res. Lett. L09501 (2007); J. Stroeve *et al.*, *Arctic Sea Ice Extent Plummets in 2007*, 89 Eos 13 (2008).

11. September 16, 2008 report, *available at* http://nsidc.org/arcticseaicenews/.

12. October 2, 2008 report, *available at* http://nsidc.org/arcticseaicenews/.

13. David M. Lawrence *et al.*, *Accelerated Arctic Warming and Permafrost Degradation During Rapid Sea Ice Loss*, 35 Geophys. Res. Letters L11506 (2008).

14. M. Kennedy *et al.*, *Snowball Earth Termination by Destabilization of Equatorial Permafrost Methane Clathrate*, 453 Nature 642 (2008). *See also, supra* at 5, Peter D. Ward, *Mass Extinctions in Deep Time as Clues to Potential Future Catastrophes: The Most Dangerous Threat From Global Warming*.

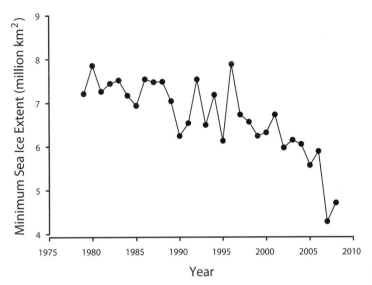

Figure 9. Trends in minimal sea ice extent from 1979 to 2008. Note that sea ice extent decreased precipitously in the summer of 2007 far exceeding normal variability or predicted loss. The extent of September Arctic sea ice is shown on the ordinate and year of observation is shown on the abscissa. Data source: National Snow and Ice Data Center, http://nsidc.org.

J.C. Orr *et al.*, *Anthropogenic Ocean Acidification over the Twenty-First Century and Its Impact on Calcifying Organisms*, 437 NATURE 681 (2005).

Atmospheric carbon dioxide from human activity is absorbed in large quantities by the oceans. Relatively recently, researchers began to realize that this was decreasing oceanic carbonate concentrations and consequently pH. Calcifying organisms from plankton to coral to shellfish require carbonate to build their shells. The loss of these species would destroy the entire ocean food web and ecosystem. For a broader review of ocean acidification, see the 2005 report from the Royal Society.[15]

Unlike atmospheric changes, which can be difficult to predict with certainty, the decrease in ocean pH, or "ocean acidification," is extremely predictable. In a widely-cited study, several top scientists predicted that anthropogenic carbon dioxide may cause changes in ocean pH over the next century that are larger than any in the last 300 million years.[16] Although ocean pH has been decreasing since the Industrial Revolution, the continual decline in pH is apparent even in observations over the 20 years between 1985 and 2005. (See Figure 10.)

Mark Z. Jacobson, *Strong Radiative Heating Due to the Mixing State of Black Carbon in Atmospheric Aerosols*, 409 NATURE 695 (2001).

Black carbon refers to the black portion of soot, which is produced during incomplete combustion. Although it is not technically a greenhouse gas, black carbon is a very strong heating agent, and probably second only to carbon dioxide in its impact on global warming. Black carbon is highly effective at absorbing solar radiation and heating the surrounding atmosphere. Furthermore, when it lands on snow or ice, black carbon reduces the reflectivity, or albedo, of the white surface and accelerates melting. Fi-

---

15. *Available at* http://www.royalsoc.ac.uk/document.asp?id=3249.
16. K. Caldeira & M.E. Wickett, *Anthropogenic Carbon and Ocean pH*, 425 NATURE 365 (2003).

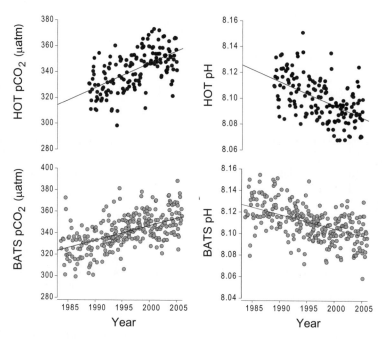

Figure 10. Ocean acidification observed at two locations: [top] Hawaii Ocean Time-series (HOT) and [bottom] Bermuda-Atlantic Time-series Study (BATS). The left panel shows measured partial pressure of carbon dioxide and the right panel shows corresponding changes in ocean pH at each location. HOT data source: J.E. Dore *et al.*, *Climate-driven changes to the atmospheric CO2 sink in the subtropical North Pacific Ocean*, 424 NATURE 754 (2003). BATS data source: N.R. Bates, *Interannual variability of the oceanic CO2 sink in the subtropical gyre of the North Atlantic Ocean over the last two decades*, 112 JOURNAL OF GEOPHYSICAL RESEARCH (OCEANS) C09013 (2007); N. R. Bates and A.J. Peters, *The contribution of atmospheric acid deposition to ocean acidification in the subtropical North Atlantic Ocean*, 107 MARINE CHEMISTRY 547 (2007).

nally, black carbon can interrupt hydrological cycles due to its impacts on cloud formation. Relative to carbon dioxide, black carbon has a much higher "global warming potential." That is, one kilogram of black carbon is estimated to have the same heating effect as approximately 500 kg of carbon dioxide over 100 years; the global warming potential of black carbon is much greater over shorter time scales.

In contrast to carbon dioxide, black carbon remains in the atmosphere for only about one week. Nonetheless, in that time it can travel long distances. Due to its short atmospheric lifetime, black carbon reductions can have an immediate mitigating effect on global warming, in contrast to carbon dioxide which remains in the atmosphere over 100 years. Thus, black carbon reductions could be used to "buy time" for more long-term climate solutions. In addition, the sources of black carbon are more limited than sources of carbon dioxide, which makes reduction strategies easier to implement. In developed countries, the main source of black carbon is diesel-fuel burning, whereas in developing countries, residential cooking and heating stoves as well as small coal plants are the main sources. For a recent review of the state of the science, see V. Ramanathan & G. Carmichael, *Global and Regional Climate Changes Due to Black Carbon*, 1 NATURE GEOSCIENCE 221 (2008).

Notes

1. Paul C.W. Davies, *The Fight Against Global Warming is Lost*, in What Is Your Dangerous Idea? Today's Leading Thinkers on the Unthinkable 43 (John Brockman ed., Harper-Collins 2007):

> Some countries, including the United States and Australia, have been in denial about global warming. They cast doubt on the science that sets alarm bells ringing. Other countries, such as the United Kingdom, are in a panic and want to make drastic cuts in greenhouse emissions. Both stances are irrelevant because the fight is a hopeless one. In spite of the recent hike in the price of oil, the stuff is still cheap enough to burn. Human nature being what it is, people will go on burning it until it starts running out and simple economics puts the brakes on. Meanwhile the carbon dioxide levels in the atmosphere will just go on rising....

2. Gary Braasch, Earth Under Fire: How Global Warming is Changing the World 213–14 (Un. of California Press 2007) ("Epilogue Mission: Possible") [hereinafter 2007 Earth Under Fire]:

> Let me state the goal clearly: No policy should be promulgated, no program initiated, no alliance sealed, no purchase made, no machine designed or built, no land use permitted, no law passed, no politician elected unless the action is a step forward to reduction and reversal of the effect of greenhouse gases.

3. Bill McKibben, "Afterward," *in* 2007 Earth Under Fire at 215:

> Gary Braasch's book shows how such signs and portents are piling up in every corner of the planet—ice melting, seas rising, mosquitoes breeding. The speed of that deterioration of the planet's stability is, as Emmanuel says, faster and broader than we would have expected at the start. But we made another mistake, too: we overestimated the speed with which the world's political systems would react to this greatest of all challenges. Fifteen years after the alarms were sounded, we have very little to show for our efforts—only the modest Kyoto treaty, unsigned by the biggest polluter, and due to expire before long with no coherent plan for an extension or replacement. Perhaps this should come as no great surprise; after all, dealing with global warming means weaning the world from fossil fuel, a substance that underwrites its daily operation. Perhaps, as one academic suggested years ago, this is "the public policy problem from hell," one that simply won't be solved in time.
>
> And yet, and yet. There are so many tantalizing signs of the things that could be done.

4. On the career of Taro Takahasi, who has undertaken the monitoring of the "breath of the ocean," see Wallace S. Broecker & Robert Kunzig, Fixing Climate: What Past Climate Changes Reveal About the Current Threat—And How to Counter It 81, 83 (Hill & Wang 2008) ("Where the Carbon Goes"):

> By extracting large quantities of fossil carbon from the land, and pumping it into the atmosphere, we are increasing the pressure of CO_2 there. Indirectly but inevitably, we are pressing CO_2 into the ocean. But how much of it and how fast? The accumulation of fossil carbon in the ocean cannot be measured as readily as Keeling measured the buildup in the atmosphere, because the ocean started out with fifty times more carbon. The change caused by fossil fuel burning is thus relatively small and hard to detect—nothing like the 20 percent increase in the atmosphere that Keeling documented over his career.

5. *Predicting future climate change.* Discussions of climate change are often divided into the changes that have already occurred and those that are expected to occur in the future. Often the

future effects are considered more important because (1) they will likely be much greater in magnitude than current effects and (2) some of these changes may be prevented.

But how do we know what will happen in the future? There are two common methods of prediction, which are not mutually exclusive. First, future effects of greenhouse gas emissions can be predicted based on paleoclimate data, such as the changes in temperature that accompanied different atmospheric carbon dioxide levels in deep history. These predictions are based on measuring changes in various isotopes in "proxies" such as ice cores. The longest ice-core record has traced changes up to 800,000 years before present.[1] The advantage of paleoclimate data is that we know the observed changes actually occurred and thus are relatively reliable. On the other hand, predictions based on paleoclimate data are limited to the pattern of changes, *e.g.* rate of change in greenhouse gases, that occurred in the past.

Thus, climate scientists sometimes turn to a second method of climate prediction: climate models. A climate model is an intricate set of mathematical equations which is iteratively solved in three-dimensional space for each interval in time. Like weather models, climate models must represent the dynamics and physics of components of the atmosphere and their interactions.[2] These models are called general circulation models (GCMs). Due to the significant interactions between the oceans and the atmosphere, the physical processes must be represented for both the atmosphere and the oceans.

Once the basic physics have been represented, climate scientists must adapt the model to represent the effect of changes in atmospheric greenhouse gas concentrations. This includes not only the basic impact of the "greenhouse effect" but also numerous feedbacks, including changes in albedo, the carbon cycle, cloud processes, and oceanic carbon uptake, to name a few. Each of these relationships can be approximated with a mathematical equation. Throughout this book there will be numerous examples of the effects of increased greenhouse gas concentrations. Virtually all of these have been incorporated in a climate model at some point.

After developing mathematical approximations, supercomputers are used iteratively to solve the equations. First the atmosphere is divided into a three-dimensional grid. The computer then solves all of the equations for a single "cube" in space, feeds the result to neighboring "cubes," and repeats the process for each point in space. This is repeated over intervals in time to extrapolate from present day to future changes in temperature.

The benefit of using a climate model is that different hypothetical changes in greenhouse gas concentrations can be tested by changing the assumptions used in the model. On the other hand, it can be difficult to measure the accuracy of the predictions.

As Dr. Stephen Schneider comments in Laboratory Earth:[3]

> Can models be validated? This is a fundamental philosophical question. Strictly speaking, the logical answer is no, since ... much of what humans are doing to force climate changes is unprecedented, and there is no precise empirical way to validate a model for conditions where there is no exactly comparable test. But there is much that

---

1. D. Lüthi *et al.*, *High-resolution Carbon Dioxide Concentration Record 650,000–800,000 Years Before Present*, 453 Nature 379 (2008).

2. For a description of these basic physics equations, see John Houghton, Global Warming: The Complete Briefing 80 (Cambridge Un. Press, 2004).

3. Stephen Schneider, Laboratory Earth: The Planetary Gamble We Can't Afford to Lose 76 (HarperCollins, 1997).

can be done in practice to test model subcomponents and evaluate overall model performance.

The validation that Dr. Schneider refers to involves running the model using inputs from the recorded past and checking that the results match observed changes. If the match is good, the expectation is that future changes will also be relatively accurate. The problem that arises is that the equations used to describe the fundamental relationships reflect correlations between observations, which may or may not be causally related. That is, they provide good circumstantial evidence, but nothing more. Thus, there may be another causal component of which climate scientists are unaware, or the relative importance of different factors may not be what is assumed by the model equations.

Despite the uncertainty in some details, climate models have become highly detailed and every month more data becomes available to validate the models and their underlying assumptions. One way to increase confidence is to compare the outputs of a number of models, each of which may use different assumptions.[4] Often the big-picture results agree well, which increases the chances that the predictions are accurate.

6. *All is not equal in the world of warming.* While climate change is referred to as a "global" phenomenon, as shown throughout this Reader, the effects vary in different regions. One of the regional differences relates to the complex effect of aerosol particles. Robert Charlson of the University of Washington pioneered research on the effect of one type of aerosol particles—sulfates. Beginning in 1974 he demonstrated these particles may have a cooling effect.[5] Importantly, he showed in 1994 that this effect is localized and non-uniform because industrial processes release sulfates and sulfates do not become "well mixed" in the same sense that other greenhouse gases do.[6] The implication of non-uniform cooling is that regions that experience the greatest warming due to increased greenhouse gases may not be regions that experience the greatest cooling from aerosol particles. Further complicating matters is the fact that some aerosol particles, such as black carbon or soot, exert a warming effect.[7] Despite the potential cooling effect of sulfates, it should be remembered that the cooling effect is much smaller than the heating effect of greenhouse gases.[8] Furthermore, Dr. Charlson has stated unequivocally that geoengineering proposals to intentionally release sulfate particles into the atmosphere should *not* be pursued.[9]

---

4. *See, e.g.,* G.A. Meehl *et al., Global Climate Projections, in* CLIMATE CHANGE 2007: THE PHYSICAL SCIENCE BASIS. CONTRIBUTION OF WORKING GROUP I TO THE FOURTH ASSESSMENT REPORT OF THE INTERGOVERNMENTAL PANEL ON CLIMATE CHANGE 747 (S. Solomon *et al.* eds., Cambridge Un. Press 2007) (comparing the output of all major climate models and suggesting the range of changes that is "very likely" to occur in the future).

5. Bert Bolin, Georg Witt and Robert J. Charlson, *Stockholm Tropospheric Aerosol Seminar: Measurement of Global to Regional Scale Pollution by Airborne Particles,* 55 AMERICAN METEOROLOGICAL SOCIETY BULLETIN 228 (1974).

6. Robert J. Charlson & Tom M.L. Wigley, *Sulfate Aerosol and Climate Change,* 270 SCIENTIFIC AMERICAN 46 (1994).

7. *See, e.g.,* V. Ramanathan & Gregory Carmichael, *Global and Regional Climate Changes Due to Black Carbon,* 1 NATURE GEOSCIENCE 221 (2008).

8. *See* Richard B. Alley *et al., Summary for Policymakers, in* CLIMATE CHANGE 2007: THE PHYSICAL SCIENCE BASIS. CONTRIBUTION OF WORKING GROUP I TO THE FOURTH ASSESSMENT REPORT OF THE INTERGOVERNMENTAL PANEL ON CLIMATE CHANGE 4, Figure SPM.2 (S. Soloman *et al.* eds, Cambridge Un. Press 2007).

9. Robert J. Charlson, *Patchy Cooling in a Warmer World,* Presentation to the Global Warming and Justice Seminar at the University of Washington School of Law (Jan. 21, 2009) (this presentation with minor differences was also given to the King of Sweden when Dr. Charlson accepted the position as King Carl XVI Gustav Professor of Environmental Science, 1999–2000 at Stockholm University).

III. Where We Are Now

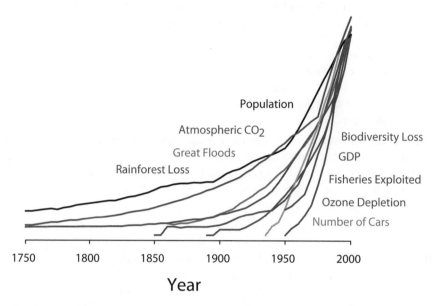

Figure 11. Trends in the state of the Earth. Modified from W. Steffen *et al.*, Global Change and the Earth System: A Planet Under Pressure (Birkhäuser 2005), as used in J.G. Speth, The Bridge at the Edge of the World xx–xxi (Yale Un. Press 2008). The purpose of this representation of the data is to compare the similarity in trends for each variable. See cited sources for data values.

A. An Urgent Present

James E. Hansen, *The Greenhouse Effect: Impacts on Global Temperature and Regional Heat Waves*, Testimony before the U.S. Senate Committee on Energy and Natural Resources (June 23, 1988).

A turning point in public awareness of global warming occurred in the summer of 1988, when Dr. James Hansen testified before a U.S. Senate committee on global warming. He made three main points: (1) the earth is warmer in 1988 than at any time in the history of instrumental measurements; (2) global warming is now sufficiently large that we can ascribe with a high degree of confidence a cause and effect relationship to the greenhouse effect; and (3) in our computer climate simulations the greenhouse effect now is already large enough to begin to affect the probability of occurrence of extreme events such as summer heat waves. The following day, the front page headline of the New York Times was "Global Warming Has Begun." In addition 32 climate-related bills were introduced in Congress. None of them passed.

On the twentieth anniversary of his testimony, Dr. Hansen[10] gave a presentation titled "Global Warming Twenty Years Later: Tipping Points Near." The following is an excerpt from the full presentation:[11]

---

10. Dr. James E. Hansen, a physicist by training, directs the NASA Goddard Institute for Space Studies, a laboratory of the Goddard Space Flight Center and a unit of the Columbia University Earth Institute, but he speaks as a private citizen today at the National Press Club and at a Briefing to the House Select Committee on Energy Independence & Global Warming.

11. June 23, 2008 posting: http://columbia.edu/~jeh1/.

My presentation today is exactly 20 years after my 23 June 1988 testimony to Congress, which alerted the public that global warming was underway. There are striking similarities between then and now, but one big difference.

Again a wide gap has developed between what is understood about global warming by the relevant scientific community and what is known by policymakers and the public. Now, as then, frank assessment of scientific data yields conclusions that are shocking to the body politic. Now, as then, I can assert that these conclusions have a certainty exceeding 99 percent.

The difference is that now we have used up all slack in the schedule for actions needed to defuse the global warming time bomb. The next President and Congress must define a course next year in which the United States exerts leadership commensurate with our responsibility for the present dangerous situation.

Otherwise it will become impractical to constrain atmospheric carbon dioxide, the greenhouse gas produced in burning fossil fuels, to a level that prevents the climate system from passing tipping points that lead to disastrous climate changes that spiral dynamically out of humanity's control.

Changes needed to preserve creation, the planet on which civilization developed, are clear. But the changes have been blocked by special interests, focused on short-term profits, who hold sway in Washington and other capitals.

I argue that a path yielding energy independence and a healthier environment is, barely, still possible. It requires a transformative change of direction in Washington in the next year.

On 23 June 1988 I testified to a hearing, chaired by Senator Tim Wirth of Colorado, that the Earth had entered a long-term warming trend and that human-made greenhouse gases almost surely were responsible. I noted that global warming enhanced both extremes of the water cycle, meaning stronger droughts and forest fires, on the one hand, but also heavier rains and floods.

My testimony two decades ago was greeted with skepticism. But while skepticism is the lifeblood of science, it can confuse the public. As scientists examine a topic from all perspectives, it may appear that nothing is known with confidence. But from such broad open-minded study of all data, valid conclusions can be drawn.

My conclusions in 1988 were built on a wide range of inputs from basic physics, planetary studies, observations of on-going changes, and climate models. The evidence was strong enough that I could say it was time to "stop waffling". I was sure that time would bring the scientific community to a similar consensus, as it has.

....

What is at stake? Warming so far, about two degrees Fahrenheit over land areas, seems almost innocuous, being less than day-to-day weather fluctuations. But more warming is already "in-the-pipeline", delayed only by the great inertia of the world ocean. And climate is nearing dangerous tipping points. Elements of a "perfect storm," a global cataclysm, are assembled.

Climate can reach points such that amplifying feedbacks spur large rapid changes. Arctic sea ice is a current example. Global warming initiated sea ice melt, exposing darker ocean that absorbs more sunlight, melting more ice. As a result, without any additional greenhouse gases, the Arctic soon will be ice-free in the summer.

More ominous tipping points loom. West Antarctic and Greenland ice sheets are vulnerable to even small additional warming. These two-mile-thick behemoths respond slowly at first, but if disintegration gets well underway it will become unstoppable. Debate among scientists is only about how much sea level would rise by a given date. In my opinion, if emissions follow a business-as-usual scenario, sea level rise of at least two meters is likely this century. Hundreds of millions of people would become refugees. No stable shoreline would be reestablished in any time frame that humanity can conceive.

Animal and plant species are already stressed by climate change. Polar and alpine species will be pushed off the planet, if warming continues. Other species attempt to migrate, but as some are extinguished their interdependencies can cause ecosystem collapse. Mass extinctions, of more than half the species on the planet, have occurred several times when the Earth warmed as much as expected if greenhouse gases continue to increase. Biodiversity recovered, but it required hundreds of thousands of years.

The disturbing conclusion, documented in a paper[12] I have written with several of the world's leading climate experts, is that the safe level of atmospheric carbon dioxide is no more than 350 ppm (parts per million) and it may be less. Carbon dioxide amount is already 385 ppm and rising about 2 ppm per year. Stunning corollary: the oft-stated goal to keep global warming less than two degrees Celsius (3.6 degrees Fahrenheit) is a recipe for global disaster, not salvation.

These conclusions are based on paleoclimate data showing how the Earth responded to past levels of greenhouse gases and on observations showing how the world is responding to today's carbon dioxide amount. The consequences of continued increase of greenhouse gases extend far beyond extermination of species and future sea level rise.

Arid subtropical climate zones are expanding poleward. Already an average expansion of about 250 miles has occurred, affecting the southern United States, the Mediterranean region, Australia and southern Africa. Forest fires and drying-up of lakes will increase further unless carbon dioxide growth is halted and reversed.

Mountain glaciers are the source of fresh water for hundreds of millions of people. These glaciers are receding world-wide, in the Himalayas, Andes and Rocky Mountains. They will disappear, leaving their rivers as trickles in late summer and fall, unless the growth of carbon dioxide is reversed.

Coral reefs, the rainforest of the ocean, are home for one-third of the species in the sea. Coral reefs are under stress for several reasons, including warming of the ocean, but especially because of ocean acidification, a direct effect of added carbon dioxide. Ocean life dependent on carbonate shells and skeletons is threatened by dissolution as the ocean becomes more acidic.

Such phenomena, including the instability of Arctic sea ice and the great ice sheets at today's carbon dioxide amount, show that we have already gone too far. We must draw down atmospheric carbon dioxide to preserve the planet we know. A level of no more than 350 ppm is still feasible, with the help of reforestation and improved agricultural practices, but just barely—time is running out.

....

If politicians remain at loggerheads, citizens must lead. We must demand a moratorium on new coal-fired power plants. We must block fossil fuel interests who aim to squeeze every last drop of oil from public lands, off-shore, and wilderness areas. Those last drops are no solution. They yield continued exorbitant profits for a short-sighted self-serving industry, but no alleviation of our addiction or long-term energy source.

---

12. James E. Hansen *et al.*, *Target atmospheric CO$_2$: where should humanity aim?*, *available at* http://arxiv.org/abs/0804.1126 and http://arxiv.org/abs/0804.1135.

Moving from fossil fuels to clean energy is challenging, yet transformative in ways that will be welcomed. Cheap, subsidized fossil fuels engendered bad habits. We import food from halfway around the world, for example, even with healthier products available from nearby fields. Local produce would be competitive if not for fossil fuel subsidies and the fact that climate change damages and costs, due to fossil fuels, are also borne by the public.

A price on emissions that cause harm is essential. Yes, a carbon tax. Carbon tax with 100 percent dividend[13] is needed to wean us off fossil fuel addiction. Tax and dividend allows the marketplace, not politicians, to make investment decisions.

Carbon tax on coal, oil and gas is simple, applied at the first point of sale or port of entry. The entire tax must be returned to the public, an equal amount to each adult, a half-share for children. This dividend can be deposited monthly in an individual's bank account.

Carbon tax with 100 percent dividend is non-regressive. On the contrary, you can bet that low and middle income people will find ways to limit their carbon tax and come out ahead. Profligate energy users will have to pay for their excesses.

Demand for low-carbon high-efficiency products will spur innovation, making our products more competitive on international markets. Carbon emissions will plummet as energy efficiency and renewable energies grow rapidly. Black soot, mercury and other fossil fuel emissions will decline. A brighter, cleaner future, with energy independence, is possible.

....

B. Joint Science Academies' Statement: Global Response to Climate Change (2005)

Climate change is real

There will always be uncertainty in understanding a system as complex as the world's climate. However there is now strong evidence that significant global warming is occurring.[1] The evidence comes from direct measurements of rising surface air temperatures and subsurface ocean temperatures and from phenomena such as increases in average global sea levels, retreating glaciers, and changes to many physical and biological systems. It is likely that most of the warming in recent decades can be attributed to human activities (IPCC 2001).[2] This warming has already led to changes in the Earth's climate.

The existence of greenhouse gases in the atmosphere is vital to life on Earth—in their absence average temperatures would be about 30 centigrade degrees lower than they are today. But human activities are now causing atmospheric concentrations of greenhouse gases—including carbon dioxide, methane, tropospheric ozone, and nitrous oxide—to rise well above pre-industrial levels. Carbon dioxide levels have increased from 280 ppm in 1750 to over 375 ppm today—higher

---

13. The proposed "tax and 100% dividend" is based largely on the cap and dividend approach described by Peter Barnes in Who Owns the Sky: Our Common Assets and the Future of Capitalism (Island Press 2001); http://www.ppionline.org/ppi_ci.cfm?knlgAreaID=116&subsecID=149&contentID=3867.

1. This statement concentrates on climate change associated with global warming. We use the UNFCCC definition of climate change, which is "a change of climate which is attributed directly or indirectly to human activity that alters the composition of the global atmosphere and which is in addition to natural climate variability observed over comparable time periods."

2. IPCC (2001). Third Assessment Report. We recognise the international scientific consensus of the Intergovernmental Panel on Climate Change (IPCC).

than any previous levels that can be reliably measured (*i.e.* in the last 420,000 years). Increasing greenhouse gases are causing temperatures to rise; the Earth's surface warmed by approximately 0.6 centigrade degrees over the twentieth century. The Intergovernmental Panel on Climate Change (IPCC) projected that the average global surface temperatures will continue to increase to between 1.4 centigrade degrees and 5.8 centigrade degrees above 1990 levels, by 2100.

Reduce the causes of climate change

The scientific understanding of climate change is now sufficiently clear to justify nations taking prompt action. It is vital that all nations identify cost-effective steps that they can take now, to contribute to substantial and long-term reduction in net global greenhouse gas emissions.

Action taken now to reduce significantly the build-up of greenhouse gases in the atmosphere will lessen the magnitude and rate of climate change. As the United Nations Framework Convention on Climate Change (UNFCCC) recognises, a lack of full scientific certainty about some aspects of climate change is not a reason for delaying an immediate response that will, at a reasonable cost, prevent dangerous anthropogenic interference with the climate system.

As nations and economies develop over the next 25 years, world primary energy demand is estimated to increase by almost 60%. Fossil fuels, which are responsible for the majority of carbon dioxide emissions produced by human activities, provide valuable resources for many nations and are projected to provide 85% of this demand (IEA 2004).[3] Minimising the amount of this carbon dioxide reaching the atmosphere presents a huge challenge. There are many potentially cost-effective technological options that could contribute to stabilising greenhouse gas concentrations. These are at various stages of research and development. However barriers to their broad deployment still need to be overcome.

Carbon dioxide can remain in the atmosphere for many decades. Even with possible lowered emission rates we will be experiencing the impacts of climate change throughout the 21st century and beyond. Failure to implement significant reductions in net greenhouse gas emissions now, will make the job much harder in the future.

Prepare for the consequences of climate change

Major parts of the climate system respond slowly to changes in greenhouse gas concentrations. Even if greenhouse gas emissions were stabilised instantly at today's levels, the climate would still continue to change as it adapts to the increased emission of recent decades. Further changes in climate are therefore unavoidable. Nations must prepare for them.

The projected changes in climate will have both beneficial and adverse effects at the regional level, for example on water resources, agriculture, natural ecosystems and human health. The larger and faster the changes in climate, the more likely it is that adverse effects will dominate. Increasing temperatures are likely to increase the frequency and severity of weather events such as heat waves and heavy rainfall. Increasing temperatures could lead to large-scale effects such as melting of large ice sheets (with major impacts on low-lying regions throughout the world). The IPCC estimates that the combined effects of ice melting and sea water expansion from ocean warming are projected to cause the global mean sea-level to rise by between 0.1 and 0.9 metres between 1990 and 2100. In Bangladesh alone, a 0.5 metre sea-level rise would place about 6 million people at risk from flooding.

---

3. IEA (2004). WORLD ENERGY OUTLOOK 4. Although long-term projections of future world energy demand and supply are highly uncertain, the World Energy Outlook produced by the International Energy Agency (IEA) is a useful source of information about possible future energy scenarios.

Developing nations that lack the infrastructure or resources to respond to the impacts of climate change will be particularly affected. It is clear that many of the world's poorest people are likely to suffer the most from climate change. Long-term global efforts to create a more healthy, prosperous and sustainable world may be severely hindered by changes in the climate.

The task of devising and implementing strategies to adapt to the consequences of climate change will require worldwide collaborative inputs from a wide range of experts, including physical and natural scientists, engineers, social scientists, medical scientists, those in the humanities, business leaders and economists.

Conclusion

We urge all nations, in the line with the UNFCCC principles,[4] to take prompt action to reduce the causes of climate change, adapt to its impacts and ensure that the issue is included in all relevant national and international strategies. As national science academies, we commit to working with governments to help develop and implement the national and international response to the challenge of climate change.

G8 nations have been responsible for much of the past greenhouse gas emissions. As parties to the UNFCCC, G8 nations are committed to showing leadership in addressing climate change and assisting developing nations to meet the challenges of adaptation and mitigation. We call on world leaders, including those meeting at the Gleneagles G8 Summit in July 2005, to:

- Acknowledge that the threat of climate change is clear and increasing.
- Launch an international study[5] to explore scientifically informed targets for atmospheric greenhouse gas concentrations, and their associated emissions scenarios, that will enable nations to avoid impacts deemed unacceptable.
- Identify cost-effective steps that can be taken now to contribute to substantial and long-term reduction in net global greenhouse gas emissions.
- Recognise that delayed action will increase the risk of adverse environmental effects and will likely incur a greater cost.
- Work with developing nations to build a scientific and technological capacity best suited to their circumstances, enabling them to develop innovative solutions to mitigate and adapt to the adverse effects of climate change, while explicitly recognising their legitimate development rights.
- Show leadership in developing and deploying clean energy technologies and approaches to energy efficiency, and share this knowledge with all other nations.
- Mobilise the science and technology community to enhance research and development efforts, which can better inform climate change decisions.

Academia Brasillera de Ciéncias Brazil	Royal Society of Canada Canada	Chinese Academy of Sciences China
Académie des Sciences France	Deutsche Akademi der Naturforscher Leopolidina, Germany	Indian National Science Academy India
Academia Nazionale del Lincei Italy	Science Council of Japan Japan	Russian Academy of Sciences Russia
Royal Society United Kingdom	National Academy of Sciences United States of America	

---

4. With special emphasis on the first principle of the UNFCCC, which states: "The Parties should protect the climate system for the benefit of present and future generations of humankind, on the basis of equity and in accordance with their common but differentiated responsibilities and respective capabilities. Accordingly, the developed country Parties should take the lead in combating climate change and the adverse effects thereof."

5. Recognising and building on the IPCC's ongoing work on emission scenarios.

C. Intergovernmental Panel on Climate Change

For a superb, candid and explicit account of the Intergovernmental Panel on Climate Change (IPCC), which was formed in 1988 and gradually developed into the key United Nations body offering scientific advice on this topic to governments of the world, see Bert Bolin, A History of the Science and Politics of Climate Change: The Role of the Intergovernmental Panel on Climate Change (Cambridge Un. Press 2007) [hereinafter 2007 Bolin]. The text begins with this summary:

> Written by its first Chairman, this book is a unique overview of the history of the IPCC. It describes and evaluates the intricate interplay between key factors in the science and politics of climate change, the strategy that has been followed, and the regretfully slow pace in getting to grips with the uncertainties that have prevented earlier action being taken. The book also highlights the emerging conflict between establishing a sustainable global energy system and preventing a serious change in global climate. This text provides researchers and policy makers with an insight into the history of the politics of climate change.

Spencer Weart, New Scientist, April 14, 2007, p. 202, quoted in 2008 Calvin at 198:

> The Intergovernmental Panel on Climate Change ... was created by conservatives [in the early 1990s] to forestall "alarmist" declarations from self-appointed committees of scientists. Governments committed the IPCC to repeated rounds of study and debate, forbidding any announcement except by unanimous consensus. It seemed a sure formula for paralysis.
>
> However, the power of democratic methods, combined with rational argument, overcame all obstacles. The IPCC has evolved into a robust transnational institution that provides authoritative conclusions of grave significance.

Howard Latin to David Hunter, August 25, 2008, ENVLAWPROFESSORS list serve:

> Dear David:
>
> If I could persuade the IPCC to evaluate whether the sun is likely to rise in the East tomorrow, they would say it is "very likely" because this is their highest expression of reasonable scientific certainty.

2008 Calvin at 111:

> Surface runoff and thermal expansion of the oceans is what, for the most part, is used to estimate sea-level rise in the 2007 report of the Intergovernmental Panel on Climate Change (IPCC), the major international body that evaluates the science for policymakers.
>
> But this is seriously incomplete. It is merely the part of the problem which can be computed....

2008 Calvin at 128–29:

> Let's start with the minimal sea-level rise for the twenty-first century, which is about 0.5 m (20 inches). The inundation is about two-thirds of that we'd get from a 1.0 m rise, given the way elevations rise near U.S. shorelines. And since most glaciologists I know think that the IPCC figure is an underestimate, I briefly mention what a 1m rise will do.
>
> About the first meter of sea-level rise will submerge the Maldives. Mali, the country's capital, is already a walled city. The country lost 10 percent of its land in the 2004 Indian Ocean tsunami....
>
> ....

It's the first meter (3.3 ft) that will destroy Miami and most coastal areas in Florida. Furthermore, the damage will occur in episodes such as storm surges, long before average sea level rises 1 m.

. . . .

2008 CALVIN at 142–43:

In the 2007 IPCC projection for the twenty-first century, the annual rise in sea level is calculated from the thermal expansion of the warming oceans, to which is added a small amount from the summer melt of the surface layer of the ice sheets. For later this century, the estimate came out to about 0.3 m, just half again as much as the twentieth-century sea-level rise.

. . . .

The Physical Sciences (WG 1) IPCC reports have a tendency to feature only what a giant spreadsheet can calculate. They downplay aspects for which no firm numbers can be attached because mechanisms are not yet understood.

Many climate scientists would say that the IPCC reports are too conservative, that they underestimate the trouble ahead for the policymakers who rely on the reports. As an example, they point to the model in the 2001 IPCC report which underestimated sea-level rise after 1990. And only the models' high-end predictions for temperature can match the actual data.

I suspect that the 2007 IPCC sea-level estimate of 0.3 m in this century is completely inadequate as guidance for policymakers. (A last-minute compromise was appended to the IPCC report that allowed that another 0.4 m could come from a faster melt of Greenland.) But 0.7 m doesn't add up to the 3 m this century that many climate scientists are worried about, just because of what's happened before.

. . . .

2008 CALVIN at 198:

So for the physical science part of the 2007 IPCC report, thousands of scientific findings were reviewed, 600 climate scientists were involved in writing the report, then it went out to peer reviewers, then to additional national reviewers like me—so thousands of reviewers (making a total of 30,000 comments) were involved before it ever landed in the laps of hundreds of government representatives gathered in Paris—who proceeded to tone down some well-established scientific conclusions. Fortunately, someone will always compare the draft report with the finished one to show the changes, put up the comparison on the web, and the countries that pushed the changes then become publicly identified with trying to rewrite the scientists.

To call something "alarmist" that survives such a winnowing process is to risk one's own credibility. It is more likely that the IPCC reports understate the case, that the alarm has been somewhat muffled by the cumbersome process.

As mentioned earlier, the sea-level rise for the twenty-first century in the IPCC report is mostly thermal expansion because they were uncertain how much to add for accelerated iceberg production. The models used for the 2001 IPCC report predicted CO_2 rise correctly but were on the low side for both temperature and sea-level rise.

Remember also that the IPCC estimates leave out anything that can't be assigned a reliable number—and so they leave out quite a lot, including history. A big part of IPCC's problem is its strict adherence to the use of physical models. By IPCC standards, "if it's not in the model, it's speculation," says Stefan Rahmstorf, one of the leading modelers. By ignoring factors that can't yet be modeled, he says, IPCC came up with deceptively reassuring numbers.

The other omission is the whole class of sudden episodes of damage, as when the Amazon burns in a prolonged El Niño.

The culture of science (in contrast to medicine) downplays the possibility of things going badly wrong. Mumbled British understatement is a style not confined to UK scientists. Jim Hansen calls it "scientific reticence."

––––––––––

Quoted in MARVIN MINSKY, THE EMOTION MACHINE: COMMONSENSE THINKING, ARTIFICIAL INTELLIGENCE, AND THE FUTURE OF THE HUMAN MIND 210 (Simon & Schuster 2006):

Never interrupt your enemy when he is making a mistake.

Napoleon Bonaparte.

Strategic behavior is everywhere in law. Here is Dr. Edward Miles predicting that strategic moves of one sort or another affect the very design of international agreements. One would expect similar "gaming" to be directed at the IPCC, whose influence has grown and expanded over time.

––––––––––

Principles for Designing International Environmental Agreements: Avoiding the Law of the "Least Ambitious Program"

Edward L. Miles. Bloedel Professor of Marine Studies and Public Affairs, School of Marine Affairs and the Evans School of Public Affairs, Co-Director of the Center for Science in the Earth System, Joint Institute for the Study of Atmosphere and Ocean, University of Washington, Seattle, WA. 98195; Tel: 206-685-1837 & 206-616-5348, Fax: 206-543-1417 & 206-616-5776, edmiles@u. washington.edu.

Designing a Regime to Control Global Climate Change, the Ultimate Collective Action Problem

Why is global climate change the ultimate collective action problem with clear and persistent application of the "Law of the Least Ambitious Program?" Since the dawn of the nineteenth century fossil fuels have constituted the engine driving economic development for almost all countries.[1] The aggregate burden of these emissions reached a concentration level of 380 parts per million by volume (ppmv) in Winter 2005.[2] The significance of this magnitude and the rate of change, up to 2000, was clearly stated by the IPCC, Working Group I in the THIRD ASSESSMENT:[3] "The atmospheric concentration of carbon dioxide … has increased by 31% since 1750. The present concentration has not been exceeded during the past 420,000 years and likely not during the past 20 million years. The current rate of increase is unprecedented during at least the past 20,000 years."

Continued growth of fossil fuel emissions from anthropogenic sources has resulted in an increase of the global mean atmospheric temperature by 0.6 ± 0.2°C since the late nineteenth cen-

––––––––––

1. Tim Dyson, *On development, demography, and climate change: The end of the world as we know it?* Paper prepared for Session 952 of the XXVth Conference of the International Union for the Scientific Study of Population, Tours, 18–23 July (2005).

2. THE KEELING CURVE, Mauna Loa, HI. NOAA Climate Monitoring and Diagnostic Laboratory (2006).

3. INTERGOVERNMENTAL PANEL ON CLIMATE CHANGE (IPCC), CLIMATE CHANGE 2001: THE SCIENTIFIC BASIS (J.T. Houghton *et al.* eds., Cambridge Un. Press 2001).

tury and future increases threaten destabilizing changes in the planetary climate system with significant and variable impacts at regional levels.[4] These conditions create the ultimate collective action problem because there are very large differences between private and social costs and the distribution of benefits and costs is highly skewed. Considerable uncertainty exists in projecting future trends and their effects, so that all policy measures will be indeterminate in their ultimate impacts. Indeterminacy, when linked to issues of costs, changing lifestyles, and distributive inequities, creates large obstacles to significant short run policy action. Moreover, the traditional application of benefit-cost analysis by business firms tends to discount the future heavily beyond two decades. But governments and corporate executives are not the only significant decision makers in this issue area because the question of what is at stake reaches into every single household in every country. As summarized by White,[5] the global climate change problem represents a classic dilemma of policy formulation " ... involving possibly severe but unknown levels of risk of undesirable consequences, great uncertainty about causes, costs, and consequences, and consequences [that] will be visited on future generations unevenly."

The dynamic of the "Law of the Least Ambitious Program" could be observed clearly when governments in Europe and the United States began to take the problem seriously after 1985. This year was a crucial date because it was the first of two meetings of an incipient epistemic community of university-based scientists, government scientists and NGO experts meeting first in Villach, Austria and in 1987 in Bellagio, Italy, which framed the problem posed by increasing concentrations of CO_2 in the planetary atmosphere.[6] Both 1985 and 1987 are important for the serendipity that fatefully linked the climate change problem to the ozone hole problem which had emerged as a priority problem on the official international agenda, leading to the negotiation of the Vienna Convention in 1985 and the Montreal Protocol in 1987. As a result, the approach adopted for the ozone hole problem became the template for the global warming problem without any deep analysis as to the appropriateness of such a link. The push to action gained strength in 1988 and 1989 as a result of the intense heat waves and drought of those two summers.[7] In 1988 the first non-governmental /governmental conference was convened by the Prime Ministers of Canada and Norway who emerged briefly as the first high level political entrepreneurs on the subject,[8] but in 1988 the Bush 1 Administration in the U.S. found that developments leading to regulation were moving too quickly and sought to slow things down by pushing for creation of IPCC to be the mechanism for developing periodic consensus scientific evaluations of the state of the problem.[9] Thus 1988 became the point at which the official problem definition phase began among the advanced industrial countries, with an emphasis on scientific/environmental assessment followed by economic evaluation as a prelude to action.

By 1989 clear signs of problems to come were evident in three dimensions. Within the Bush 1 Administration, the issue was seen to involve very serious consequences for the U.S. economy and the willingness of the U.S. public to accept strong regulation. Consequently, the White House Domestic Policy Council assumed the coordinating role for development of U.S. policy. This shift signaled a decline of the role of EPA relative to the Departments of Energy, Interior, and Commerce, as well as the Office of Management and Budget and the President's Council of Economic Advisors. The Group of 77 was not yet a significant player in this push to regulation as

---

4. *Ibid.*

5. R.M. White, *Greenhouse Policy and Climate Uncertainty*. 70 Bulletin of the American Meteorological Association 1123–1127 (1989).

6. Daniel M. Bodansky, *The United Nations Framework Convention on Climate Change: A Commentary*, 18 Yale J. Int'l L. 451, 460–461 (1993).

7. *Ibid.*

8. *Id.* at 462.

9. *See id.* at 464.

a group and severe differences were evident within the OECD group concerning quantitative limits on emissions targets and timetables. The European Community, Canada, and Norway were combined in a strong coalition for regulatory action, but they were opposed by the U.S. and Japan within the OECD and the USSR outside. The latter three had severe reservations concerning issues of competitive disadvantage as a result of regulation.[10]

Also in 1989 critical developments occurred in the U.K. which heavily shaped the design of the regime embodied in the Framework Convention for Climate Change (FCCC) of 1992. Prime Minister Thatcher convened a one-day cabinet level briefing on the problem involving UK and some U.S. scientists and emerged convinced of the seriousness of the problem. She then used the occasion of the Noordwijk (The Netherlands) Ministerial Conference of the European Community to seize leadership of the EC on the issue, calling strongly for global regulation by treaty. The Noordwijk Declaration of the EC, issued on November 7, 1989, contained two proposals which show the rationale underlying the design of the regime created by the FCCC, a rationale that came primarily from the UK:

> For the long term safeguarding of our planet and maintaining the ecological balance, joint effort and action should aim at limiting or reducing emissions and increasing sinks for greenhouse gases to a level consistent with the natural capacity of the planet. Such a level should be reached within a time frame sufficient to allow ecosystems to adapt naturally to climate change, to ensure that food production is not threatened and permit economic development in a sustainable and environmentally sound manner. Stabilizing the atmospheric concentrations of green house gases is an imperative goal.

It was thought also that the IPCC should study the possibility of the concept of CO_2 co-equivalence, i.e., *a single parameter for radioactive forcing; and to look into the prospect of quantitative emissions targets to limit or reduce emissions.*

This Declaration was followed the next day, November 8, 1989, by a Thatcher address to the 44th session of the UN General Assembly, which made the following points *inter alia* (United Kingdom Mission to the United Nations, 8 November 1989):

- The problem is vast. "Whole areas of our planet could be subject to drought and starvation if the pattern of rains and monsoons were to change as a result of the destruction of forests and the accumulation of greenhouse gases."
- Before we act we need the best possible scientific assessment. The UK has assumed the task of coordinating such an assessment within the IPCC. [This became the First IPCC Assessment, 1990].[11]
- "But as well as the science, we need to get the economics right. That means first we must have continued economic growth in order to generate the wealth required to pay for the protection of the environment. But it must be growth which does not plunder the planet today and leave our children to deal with the consequences tomorrow."
- We do not need new institutions; better to strengthen the ones we have, in particular the WMO [World Meteorological Organization] and UNEP [United Nations Environmental Program].
- "The most pressing task which faces us at the international level is to negotiate a framework convention on climate change.... Fortunately we have a model in the action already taken to protect the ozone layer. The Vienna Convention in 1985 and the Montreal Proto-

---

10. *Id.* at 467.
11. Intergovernmental Panel on Climate Change (IPCC), Climate Change: The IPCC Scientific Assessment (J. T. Houghton, G. J. Jenkins, and J. J. Ephraums eds., Cambridge Un. Press 1990).

col in 1987 established landmarks in international law. They aimed to prevent rather than just cure a global environmental problem."

- The life of the IPCC should be prolonged to provide authoritative scientific bases for negotiation of a series of protocols.
- "I believe we should aim to have a Convention on global climate change ready by the time the World Conference on Environment and Development meets in 1992." Prime Minister Thatcher also met with President George H. Bush while she was in the U.S. in an attempt to persuade him to join with the E.C. in this effort. She did not succeed.

On the basis of the detailed analysis provided by Bodansky,[12] combined with press coverage of the FCCC negotiations, one can construe that the process of negotiation was simultaneously conducted on three levels: within the North, North vs. South, and within the South. Within the North, the most difficult issues revolved around competitive disadvantage, the pace of regulation and the impacts of taxation on economies, especially the energy and transportation sectors. In the U.S. fears about domestic public reactions were also a factor. Within the South, increasing conflict led to the collapse of the Group of 77 in 1991, particularly over the issue of emission control commitments. Some argued for a united front against strong action on the grounds that the onus lay with Annex I parties (the OECD). Their view was that the people who had created the problem shouldn't now be able to stop economic development within the South and they saw this principle as part of national sovereignty. But completely opposed to this view were those countries who saw themselves most at risk. These were gathered together in the Association of Small Island States (AOSIS), a coalition of those states especially vulnerable to sea level rise. In between these two factions were the members of OPEC led by Saudi Arabia and including China whose representatives argued that their continued economic development required use of their coal resources.

The U.S. remained alone with industry, a Democratically-controlled Congress, and the Bush I Administration all strongly opposed to binding targets and timetables.

The outcome of the negotiations resulted in a regime with basic institutions, differentiation of parties on the basis of their relative energy efficiency, weak obligations, and relatively strong scientific assessment capacity and reporting and review obligations.[13] Bodansky[14] summed it all up with the following comment:

> Like politics generally, building a climate change regime is the art of the possible. Rather than impose strong substantive obligations, which some states might not have accepted, the FCCC promotes consensus-building and cooperation. Because it requires relatively little, most states have been willing to become parties. But once adopted, it may create a dynamic that eventually produces more substantive commitments.

This expectation has not been fulfilled and the Kyoto Protocol, completed in December 1997, was rejected by the U.S. and Australia, with Russia sitting on the fence, waiting to be courted.

The results of the final meeting on December 10, 1997 are as follows:[15]

- Overall AIC [All In-Country] reduction in emissions from 1990 base year at 5%; but differentiation on the basis of relative energy efficiency toward target years 2008–2012:

---

12. Bodansky, *supra* note 6, at 477–478.

13. *See id.* at 555–558.

14. Daniel M. Bodansky, *The Emerging Climate Change Regime*, 20 ANNU. REV. ENERGY ENVIRON. 425, 432 (1995).

15. Framework Convention on Climate Change, Conference of the Parties, Third Session, Kyoto Protocol to the United Nations Convention on Climate Change, Doc. # FCCC/CP/1997/L.7/Add.1 (December 10, 1997). *Available at* http://unfccc.int/documentation/documents/items/ (last visited March 28, 2009).

Canada 6%; EU 8%, but "Bubble" (joint) solution permitted; Japan 6%; US 7%; Iceland 110%; Norway 101%; Russia 100% ["Hot air" as result of collapse of Soviet economy].

- Demonstrable progress by 2005.
- Focus on net changes in GHG emissions from sources and removal from sinks via land use changes, afforestation, reforestation, and deforestation since 1990.
- "Basket" of GHG = CO_2, CH_4, HFCs, PFC, & SF_6. Total radioactive forcing a weighted sum.
- Emissions trading and joint implementation permitted.
- Reporting, independent review, and verification included.
- Penalties not prescribed. [Enforcement issue pending].
- Obligations not extended to developing countries.

The rejection by the U.S. put in jeopardy the entry into force of the Protocol and played into the hands of Japan and Russia since both could, and did, extract additional concessions for securing their signatures and ratification. The Japanese demand was to remove the issue of penalties for non-compliance; the Russian demand was for support from the EU for Russian entry into the WTO as a side payment. Both demands were successful at the Marrakesh session, which followed Kyoto a year later. But what did Kyoto really amount to? Let us first consider the scientific and technical implications. Professor Bert Bolin, then serving as overall Chairman of the IPCC, wrote a commentary for SCIENCE, which appeared on 16 January, 1998. Professor Bolin made five points. First, within the "basket" of six greenhouse gases, which the U.S. had insisted on, the increase of CO_2 alone would account for 70% of the total increase of radioactive forcing. Not many measures were available for decreasing methane (CH_4) and nitrous oxides (NO_X) and the other components of the "basket" contributed only a few percentage points to radiative forcing. Secondly, even with full compliance with the Protocol, by 2010 advanced industrial countries would still be contributing four times the CO_2 emissions of developing countries. Thirdly, even with full compliance with the Protocol, accumulated emissions of CO_2 from 1990 to 2010 would amount to 140GtC, which would imply an increase in the atmospheric concentration by about 29ppmv to a total of 382ppmv. [This is actually an underestimate because in winter 2005 the Keeling Curve registered a reading of 380.] Bolin's fourth point was that if the Protocol were to achieve stabilization of emissions at a concentration level double the pre-industrial ambient concentration of 282ppmv, parties would have to achieve a 30% cut in aggregate emissions by 2050 and an additional 30% cut by 2100. Professor Bolin's fifth and final judgment was: "The Kyoto Conference did not achieve much with respect to limiting the buildup of greenhouse gases in the atmosphere."[16] It should also be said that even with so modest an initial target, only the UK and Germany were on the way in 2006 to meeting their 2010 targets and the 2006 meeting of the Conference of Parties in Kenya ended without any significant measures to break out of the gridlock in which the parties found themselves.

Is there then any evidence of design errors in both the FCCC and the Kyoto Protocol? The answer to this question is in the affirmative. Relative to Kyoto, Victor[17] has argued that the main impediment to effective international policy relative to the global warming problem is the lack of a viable architecture for international cooperation. Targets and timetables constitute fundamental flaws in the regulatory system for controlling emissions. The latter vary with economic growth and technological change but the rigidity of targets and timetables in the Protocol makes them unresponsive to changing economic conditions. Furthermore, emissions trading is in-

---

16. Bert Bolin, *The Kyoto Negotiations on Climate Change: A Science Perspective*, 279 SCIENCE 330, 331 (1998).

17. David G. Victor, THE COLLAPSE OF THE KYOTO PROTOCOL (Princeton Un. Press 2001).

tended to compensate firms, reduce costs of compliance and provide flexibility; allocation permits would be worth hundreds of billions of U.S. dollars. Integrity of such a system requires compulsory membership of all the major players, but the Protocol cannot provide such a guaranty. Victor[18] concludes that the Montreal Protocol was simply the wrong template to apply because global warming is a fundamentally different type of problem.

On the other hand, one finds an alternative view about the fit between the Montreal Protocol and the global warming problem from Parson,[19] at least in one respect. Parson argues that the Montreal Protocol was successful but not because the problem was uniquely benign. There had been policy deadlock for a period of ten years. A powerful contributor to the Montreal Protocol, which Kyoto would have done well to have incorporated in its own design, was the 1988 organization of the Technology Assessment Panel, which became later the Technology and Economics Assessment Panel (TEAP). This organization operated differently from other panels. It was dominated by representatives of the firms, using their knowledge of technology and what the firms could and would adopt to solve the problem. In fact, in this collective entity, the problem-solving capacity of the Panel was greater than even that of the largest firm. Interestingly, the representatives provided the expertise required without becoming swallowed up in inter-firm rivalries. Firms could get help meeting controls in a highly feasible way and Parson states explicitly that he considers a lack of such a capability in both the FCCC and the Kyoto Protocol a serious design flaw. Parson[20] goes further to argue that " ... the most important elements of the 1987 [Montreal] Protocol were its provisions for adapting controls in response to new information and new capabilities, the requirement for periodic review of controls, the independent expert assessment panels, and the linkages between these. Such provisions will be essential if concrete measures are to be taken on any issue under significant uncertainty about whether they are correct in their stringency, form, timing, or breadth—that is, under any attempt to take precautionary action."[21] This subtle difference between the arguments of Victor and Parson is very important. They both agree that Kyoto lacked the flexibility and responsiveness to changing conditions that is to be found in the Montreal Protocol, but Parson would say that the designers of Kyoto learned the wrong lessons from the Montreal Protocol, not that the latter was the wrong template to apply. The critical point here is how uncertainty is to be accommodated in the regulatory design and on this point I will argue that the FCCC has failed in a crucial respect and that failure, combined with the gridlock in the Kyoto approach, argues for starting over because we now know that the stakes are very high indeed.

Article 2 of the FCCC stipulates (emphasis added):

> The ultimate objective of this Convention ... is to achieve ... *stabilization of greenhouse gas concentrations in the atmosphere at a level that would prevent dangerous anthropogenic interference with the climate system.* Such a level should be achieved within a time-frame sufficient to allow ecosystems to adapt naturally to climate change, to ensure that food production is not threatened, and to enable economic development to proceed in a sustainable manner.

This central formulation in the FCCC design assumes that the process of climate change is essentially linear and that there will be time enough to respond in such a way that allows parties to the Convention to enable ecosystems to adjust naturally, to ensure that food production is not

---

18. *Ibid.*

19. Edward A. Parson, *Breaking the policy deadlock on climate change: a new role for technology assessment,* ISSUES IN SCIENCE AND TECHNOLOGY. Summer 2002; PARSON, EDWARD A., PROTECTING THE OZONE LAYER (Oxford Un. Press 2003).

20. EDWARD A PARSON, PROTECTING THE OZONE LAYER 377 (Oxford Un. Press 2003).

21. *Id.* at 270–71.

threatened, and to enable economic development to proceed in a sustainable manner. We now know that all these assumptions are fictitious. While it was not written into the Convention, the parties settled informally on a doubling of the pre-industrial ambient concentration of CO_2 (560ppmv) as the standard; the impacts were presumed to be manageable; and the effect on world GNP was then calculated to be on the order of 1%. We now know that the standard is inappropriate and the other two assumptions are also fictitious.

We also know that "stabilization" may not be the most appropriate standard; that a world of 560ppmv represents a world of considerable environmental destruction; that no single measure of "dangerous interference with the climate system" exists; and that the prior assumptions about time to significant impacts is false because we are now faced with a flood of surprises emerging in a world of 380ppmv. These surprises come from internal feedbacks, nonlinearities, and thresholds in the earth's climate system, many of which are still unknown.[22] So at a time of great uncertainty the design is locked in to a fundamental standard on the basis of fictitious assumptions which are cast in a form of considerable rigidity.

What do we now know about the magnitudes and rates of change of global climate change, how they translate into impacts, and what they tell us about nonlinearities and thresholds in the earth's climate system?

The evidence available can be summarized as follows:

- At 380ppmv there has been a considerable increase in surface & sub-surface heat in the ocean in the amount of 14.5×10^{22} Joules.[23]
- The ocean has taken up 48% of all carbon emitted by humans since 1850 with significant decreases in ocean pH. [24–25]
- Both factors combine to dislocate marine ecosystems at almost all trophic levels and combine again with overfishing to deliver a triple whammy of multiple stresses.
- Recent indications are that both the oceanic and terrestrial[26] carbon sinks are slowing down their rate of uptake. Under what conditions will large sinks become large sources over what timescales? And corals are at great risk even below a global average temperature increase of 1°C.
- If uptake of carbon slows, then projections of maximum temperature increases by 2100 as per IPCC have been significantly understated.
- With respect to glacier disintegration, Hansen[27] poses and explores the question whether anthropogenic global warming can cause ice-sheet melting measured in meters on a timescale of centuries. The dynamics seem to be more than plausible, *i.e.*, increased heat

22. José A. Rial *et al.*, *Nonlinearities, Feedbacks and Critical Thresholds Within the Earth's Climate System*, 65 CLIMATE CHANGE 11 (2004).

23. Sydney Levitus, John I Autonov, Cathy Stephens, *Warming of the World Ocean*, 287 SCIENCE 2225 (2000); S. Levitus, J. Antonov, and T. Boyer, *Warming of the World Ocean 2000–2005*, 32 GEOPHYSICAL RESEARCH LETTERS 1029 (2005).

24. C.L. Sabine *et al.*, *The Oceanic Sink for Anthropogenic CO_2*, 305 SCIENCE 367 (2004); R.A. Feely, *et al.*, *Impact of Anthropogenic CO_2 on the $CaCO_3$ System in the Oceans*, 305 SCIENCE 362 (2004).

25. R.A. Feely, L.D. Talley, G. C. Johnson, C.L. Sabine, and R. Wanninkhof, *Repeat Hydrography Cruises Reveal Chemical Changes in the North Atlantic*, 86 EOS. TRANS. AGU 399, 404–05 (2005); J.A. Kleypas *et al.*, *Impacts of Acidification on Coral Reefs and other Marine Calcifiers: A Guide for Future Research*, Contribution No. 2897 from NOAA/Pacific Marine Environmental Laboratory (2006).

26. R.A. Feely, L.D. Talley, G. C. Johnson, C.L. Sabine, and R. Wanninkhof, *Repeat Hydrography Cruises Reveal Chemical Changes in the North Atlantic*, 86 EOS. TRANS. AGU 399, 404–05 (2005); P. Friedlingstein *et al.*, *Climate-carbon cycle feedback analysis, results from the C^4MIP model intercomparison*, 19 JOURNAL OF CLIMATE 3337 (2006).

27. J.E. Hansen, *A slippery slope: How much global warming constitutes "dangerous anthropogenic interference"?* An editorial essay, 68 CLIMATIC CHANGE 269 (2005).

in the mixed layer increases summer melt on the ice sheet which leads to increased ice stream surges and massive iceberg discharges. In this case the troubling nonlinearity is the observed positive feedback between increased sub-surface heat in the world ocean and sub-surface ice in the Antarctic and the Arctic such that the summer melt rate is significantly higher than expected.

- With respect to increases in hurricane intensity (not frequency), suggestive recent work has been done by Emmanuel[28] which appears to establish a positive correlation with tropical sea surface temperatures (SSTs). There is not yet a consensus on this point, but similar findings have been made by a team using a different approach.[29] A general consensus has emerged from 2007.
- Impacts of both of the above combined mean greater hazards for growing global coastal populations and higher destructive potential. [>30 mega-cities (>8 million people), most in Asia, projected by the UN by 2050].

Additional items have been adduced in a list constructed by Pittock:[30]

- Recent estimates of climate sensitivity based on modeling, with some including recent and/or paleoclimatic data, suggest climate sensitivity lies in a range of 2°–6°C, not 1.5°–4.5°C as per IPCC (2001).[31] This finding implies a higher probability of warming by 2100 in excess of the IPCC mean of 3.0°C.
- Global dimming is decreasing as a function of more effective controls on sulphur emissions. Global dimming delays ocean warming and is most evident in the Northern Hemisphere. Reductions are likely to have asymmetric cross-equatorial effects on both the Australian Monsoon and Atlantic circulation.
- Permafrost melting is widespread and rapid.
- Biomass feedbacks are now evident—some soils and vegetation are now acting as sources of carbon, not sinks.
- Atmospheric circulation changes are occurring in mid-high latitudes in Northern & Southern Hemisphere.
- There is a slowing down of the North Atlantic overturning meridional circulation [global thermohaline circulation which transports heat from the equator to high latitudes in the Northern Hemisphere].

On the basis of these findings, we can answer some questions which have been posed by others about the formulation in Article 2 of the FCCC. For instance, Janetos[32] asked: Different thresholds for different systems? Different thresholds for the same system in different places? Different ways of valuing by different actors?

On the basis of abundant evidence of wide spatial and temporal variability of impacts on a regional and sub-regional basis, there would have to be different thresholds for different systems. Also in the same vein, there would have to be different thresholds for the same systems in different places because there is evidence of changes in precipitation and temperature with respect to elevation, local winds, and the like. Again, widespread spatial and temporal variability is evident and there are substantial differences in valuing impacts and consequences by different actors. Similar

28. Kerry Emmanuel, *Increasing Destructiveness of Tropical Cyclones Over the Past 30 Years*, 436 NATURE 686 (2005).

29. P.J. Webster., *Changes in Tropical Cyclone Number, Duration, and Intensity in a Warming Environment*, 309 SCIENCE 1844 (2005).

30. A. Barrie Pittock, *Are Scientists Underestimating Climate Change?*, 87 EOS 340 (2006).

31. INTERGOVERNMENTAL PANEL ON CLIMATE CHANGE (IPCC), CLIMATE CHANGE 2001: THE SCIENTIFIC BASIS 881 (J.T. Houghton *et al.* eds., Cambridge Un. Press 2001).

32. Anthony C. Janetos, *Targets, Thresholds, and Communication: Presentation to the Board of Trustees*, H. John Heinz III Center for Science, Economics, and the Environment, Washington, D.C. (2004).

replies are possible to two additional questions posed by scientists participating in the workshop on climate change convened in Exeter by the UK Government in February 2005. The two questions are dangerous for whom and dangerous by when? These questions lead logically to two overall questions posed at the UK workshop: Can a global target represent dangers at the local level? How much climate change is too much? The last question was posed by Prime Minister Tony Blair.

So can a global target represent dangers at local levels? Given the observed regional spatial and temporal variability of impacts, the answer is only if the maximum permitted level is 300ppmv, which implies that the over-riding objective is reversal, not stabilization. This, of course, takes us back to the valuing question because the real choice in any global standard has to do with what trade-offs are acceptable to decision-makers between the costs of shifting out of fossil fuels and the scale of environmental destruction implied by threshold changes. In every case, climate change is not the only factor at work. This is always a question of coping with multiple stresses and the synergies which occur as a result of their interaction. Given the uncertainties, the point made by Parson[33] about the need for building into the regime design rules for adapting controls to new information and new capabilities is of particular relevance. Another point of considerable relevance in the light of what we now know about nonlinearities in the earth's climate system and the stark fact that on this issue the scientific community does not know what it does not know, both Rial et al.[34] and Pittock[35] make sensible suggestions about the approach to policy in the face of risks posed by climate change at all spatial scales from local to global. Rial et al. recommend moving away from prediction as the primary policy approach to integrated assessment of vulnerability. Risk assessment and disaster prevention then become the alternative to prediction, both of which should be done quantitatively to derive insight into the relative importance of climate vis-à-vis other environmental influences. Pittock argues that the balance of evidence is swinging towards a higher probability of extreme outcomes at lower levels of greenhouse gas concentrations than the IPCC has recognized. He recommends a focus on low probability/high consequence outcomes in which the objective is not prediction of the most likely outcomes but seeking to avoid unacceptable outcomes. Learning to understand nonlinearities and thresholds and to use that knowledge as best we can becomes one of the central criteria for regime design.

Then what evidence is there of a willingness to start over in seeking approaches to regime design for the global warming problem? The author's informal conversations with European officials after the 2006 meeting of the Conference of the Parties to the Kyoto Protocol revealed increasing disenchantment with the existing process as leading nowhere and a willingness to consider less than global attempts towards smaller groups of like-minded states.[36] This trend is akin to Peter Sand's recommendation about "fast tracks" and clubs within clubs. The author also found similar thinking in informal discussions with senior industry and government officials from OECD countries in September 2006. Their argument is that they should not try to renegotiate both the FCCC and the Kyoto Protocol in the same manner as before, because it would take too long and developing countries are unlikely to accept binding targets at levels that would satisfy advanced industrial countries. There is strong informal agreement to seek energy security as soon as possible through increasing efficiency, moving up from 1% to 2% growth in energy efficiency per year. They accept that rejecting the global approach means accepting individual and/or group approaches among the like-minded. They are aware that in the next thirty years

---

33. EDWARD A. PARSON, PROTECTING THE OZONE LAYER 377 (Oxford Un. Press 2003).

34. José A. Rial et al., *Nonlinearities, Feedbacks and Critical Thresholds Within the Earth's Climate System*, 65 CLIMATIC CHANGE 11 (2004).

35. Pittock, *supra* note 30.

36. Andrew C. Revkin, *Fighting Global Warming: New broad treaties in doubt*, INTERNATIONAL HERALD TRIBUNE, December 5, 2005.

globally, nuclear power and renewable resources are likely to provide only about 10% of world energy needs; therefore coal is the real option for the near term and this fact constitutes a huge problem. But moving beyond conventional resources in the right way is THE major challenge.

When pressed on approaches to decentralized regime design, these officials say coordinated policy agreements should begin in the OECD group, with or without formal legal arrangements at the initial stage. However, they concede that such a decentralized approach would require formal agreements on a monitoring and reporting system to create transparency. A decentralized approach also would require coordinated agreement on carbon taxes and approaches to carbon sequestration, particularly from coal-fired plants. Such a large shift in policy, they admit, would require U.S. leadership, which they think is becoming increasingly possible. They note that there is a significant bottom-up shift in policy views at city, state, and industry levels in view of the rate and magnitude of observed climate change impacts and they are also aware of a split in the fundamentalist coalition in the U.S. on this issue. They view that as politically significant. They also assume that as more significantly adverse climate change impacts are experienced, the stronger will be public support for the policies that will be required. There is also a coalition within this group that is pushing for industry to stake out bold positions, to accept risks, and to move out of R&D into demonstration projects at a large scale. However, others want to know what is the appropriate regulatory environment and whether the governments are going to leave it to industry to take all the risks. They warn that having the capital to take risks is needed to get the market to work. The interesting point underlying all this non-traditional thinking is still an attempt to stabilize emissions at 550ppmv by 2050. They are aware that the nonlinearities in the climate system will mean that a considerable amount of environmental destruction will occur, but they think this is the best we can do and that it will be a struggle to achieve this outcome.

Conclusions

International treaty-making on climate change is a maelstrom of multiple parties, high uncertainties, defectors, and hold-out advantage-seekers. It gave us poor design in the FCCC and in the Kyoto Protocol. Poor design gave us poor performance. "Stabilization" was a casual early concept that has proved long-lived. Casual bargaining assumptions had to be proved wrong by hard-won scientific advance. A happy "learn-as-we-go" burden was placed upon the IPCC though few anticipated at the time the significance of this institution and the stresses that would be placed upon it.

Still, we have learned much about institutional design.

It is worth noting that the available literature is rich in information, which includes case studies and comparative evaluation, much of it guided by theoretical insights gained from collective action theory and game theory. The literature shows signs of maturation and cumulative development and the collective output is highly applicable to and useful for real world attempts at institutional design. I am surprised, however, by how much of the design enterprise, when one looks at the corpus of the work over time, is actually transportable. In the category of "high transportability" I would include the following design elements:

1. The need for flexibility and responsiveness in the control structure, especially when uncertainty is high and given the necessity of creating a mechanism that does iterative assessments of the state of the problem and the impacts of regime performance in a context of high transparency.
2. There must be deliberative mechanisms which constitute pathways for learning and for linking that learning to policy formulation and revision.
3. Transparency also means that NGOs may independently evaluate governmental performance.

4. One should be very careful in the beginning to find the correct architecture of collaboration for the problem.

5. Adopt a management approach to enforcement, especially in the early years to facilitate widespread participation, but do not shy away from strong enforcement where it seems to be necessary.

6. There is a need in the beginning for both epistemic communities and political entrepreneurs but, over time, these may or may not play major roles consistently. However, the importance of the administrative communities at national and international levels grows with time.

7. It is important to understand in a problem whether the critical interface with decision-makers is technology or science. If one accepts that technological fixes exist to environmental problems and that experts can be left alone to find solutions based on market acceptability, then the role of science is to demonstrate that there is an environmental imperative and that technology has the solution. Since economic models are not very good at anticipating technological innovation, the only real test is market acceptability. TEAP was successful because only those executives who made those kinds of decisions could participate. Companies that did not have the technological options were deliberately excluded from participation. Therefore, who is excluded is a very important question since it has impacts both on the framing of the issue and the urgency with which it is pursued.....

Beyond these elements, I think the structure of the problem, combined with political, economic, and social realities, constrains design options to a considerable extent. This is another way of saying that context is very important and that the two most important design elements to understand fully are the problem structure in the human-environment system and the particular context.

Notes

1. In 1989 the World Meteorological Organization (WMO) and the United Nations Environment Program (UNEP) formed the Intergovernmental Panel on Climate Change (IPCC). 2006 LOVELOCK at 50:

Climate forecasts in 1988 quickly fell behind reality. (See Figure 12.)

2. See OLIVER TICKELL, KYOTO 2: HOW TO MANAGE THE GLOBAL GREENHOUSE 1 (Zed Books 2008) (footnotes omitted) [hereinafter 2008 Tickell]:

Economist Nicholas Stern famously described climate change as "the greatest market failure the world has seen." But there is an exception: the attempts of the world's governments to redress that market failure, beginning with the Climate Convention's Kyoto Protocol. Far from overcoming the market failure identified by Stern, the Kyoto Protocol has created a whole new spectrum of market failures—like Hans Christian Andersens' demonic distorting mirror when it was smashed to smithereens.

First among the Protocol's failures is that its key objective—to reduce greenhouse gas emissions—is unmet, as reported by Michael Raupach in 2007. Indeed, the rate of increase in global CO_2 emissions from burning fossil fuels and from industry has accelerated, from 1.1 percent per year for 1990–99 to more than 3 percent per year for

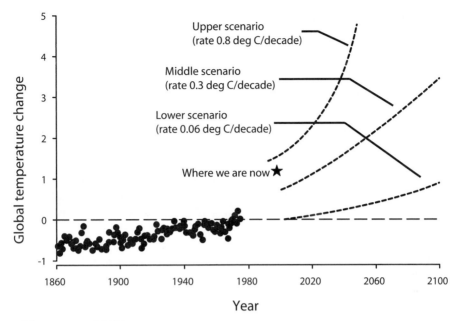

Figure 12. The Revenge of GAIA.

2000–04. The emissions growth rate since 2000, as Raupach writes, "was greater than for the most fossil-fuel intensive of the Intergovernmental Panel on Climate Change emissions scenarios developed in the late 1990s."

3. 2007 KOLBERT at 10–12:

The National Academy of Sciences undertook its first major study of global warming in 1979. [This Ad Hoc Study Group on Carbon Dioxide and Climate] was led by the distinguished meteorologist Jule Charney, of MIT, who, in the 1940s, had been the first meteorologist to demonstrate that numerical weather forecasting was feasible. [It said:] "If carbon dioxide continues to increase, the study group finds no reason to doubt that climate changes will result and no reason to believe that these changes will be negligible." ... Since the Charney report, the National Academy of Sciences alone has produced nearly two hundred more studies on the subject.... During this same period, worldwide carbon-dioxide emissions have continued to increase, from five billion to seven billion metric tons a year, and the earth's temperature ... has steadily risen.

4. *See* THOMAS L. FRIEDMAN, HOT, FLAT AND CROWDED: WHY WE NEED A GREEN REVOLUTION—AND HOW IT CAN RENEW AMERICA 113 (Farrar, Straus & Giroux 2008) [hereinafter 2008 Friedman]:

"The most important conclusions about global climatic disruption—that it's real, that it's accelerating, that it's already doing significant harm, that human activities are responsible for most of it, that tipping points into really catastrophic disruption likely lurk along the 'business as usual' trajectory, and that there is much that could be done to reduce the danger at affordable cost if only we would get started—have not been concocted by the Sierra Club or the enemies of capitalism," noted John Holdren. "They are based on an immense edifice of painstaking studies published in the world's leading peer-reviewed scientific journals. They have been vetted and documented in excruciating detail by the largest, longest, costliest, most international, most interdisciplinary, and most thorough formal review of a scientific topic ever conducted."

5. For the treatise on the topic, see Fred Pearce, With Speed and Violence: Why Scientists Fear Tipping Points in Climate Change (Beacon Press 2007). *Compare id.* at 17:

> By ignoring these outliers (quoting a scientist), IPCC has failed for ten years to investigate the possible effects of more extreme climate change.

with id. at 40:

> Over three days in March 2002, there occurred one of the most dramatic alterations to the map of Antartica since the end of the last ice age.... A shelf of floating ice larger than Luxembourg and some 650 feet thick, which had been attached to the peninsula for thousands of years, shattered like a huge pane of glass. It broke into hundreds of pieces, each of them a huge iceberg that floated away into the South Atlantic.

and id. at 66 (on a Hadley Centre prediction):

> The Amazon rainforest will be dead before the end of the century. Not partly dead, or sick, but dead and gone.

and id. at 67 (on the 1997 wildfires of Borneo):

> The fires got out of control, and the result was one of the greatest forest fires in human history. The smoke spread for thousands of miles. Unsighted planes crashed from the skies, and ships collided at sea; in neighboring Malaysia and distant Thailand, hospitals filled with victims of lung diseases, and schools were closed. The fires became a global news story. The cost of the fires in lost business alone was put at tens of billions of dollars.

Ross Gelbspan, The Heat Is On: The Climate Crisis/The Cover-Up/The Prescription 78–81 (Perseus Books 1998) [hereinafter 1998 Gelbspan Heat Is On]:

In late May 1996, at a symposium in the Rayburn House Office Building, two of the leading IPCC scientists—Dr. Benjamin Santer and Dr. Tom M.L. Wigley—explained the findings contained in the new IPCC report, providing yet more evidence of human-induced global warming. Santer is a climate modeler at the Lawrence Livermore National Laboratory, while Wigley is a senior scientist at the National Center for Atmospheric Research.

The targeting of Santer was no coincidence. Barely a month later, Santer, Wigley, and eleven other researchers would detail their new findings in an article in Nature. The New York Times would call their findings "the most important ... in a decade." An accompanying editorial in Nature would conclude that "the results of Santer *et al.*—using the available data and state-of-the-art climate models—provide the clearest evidence yet that humans may have affected the global climate." The Rayburn building session gave an advance look at the findings, as they were presented in the IPCC report.

In the Rayburn building, addressing a standing-room crowd, Santer used climate modeling to confirm that global warming cannot be attributed to the natural variability of the weather. He demonstrated that the measurable patterns of uneven warming coincide with patterns that would result from the atmospheric buildup of carbon dioxide accompanied by the distribution of airborne sulfates. The structure of that pattern is different from warming that is due to natural weather variations. In a follow-up presentation Wigley demonstrated how scientists have determined that the warming is due primarily to the release of carbon dioxide by human activities.

The session was attended by a number of industry representatives, including William O'-Keefe, chairman of the Global Climate Coalition and an official of the American Petroleum Institute; Donald Pearlman, a Washington attorney who represents an undisclosed number of coal and oil producers and who quarterbacks the delegations of OPEC nations at international climate talks; and S. Fred Singer.

When the scientists had concluded their presentations, Pearlman and O'Keefe accused Santer of secretly altering the IPCC report of the previous year. They charged him with single-handedly suppressing expressions of dissent from other IPCC scientists. They derided Santer for eliminating references to scientific uncertainties.

These startling public accusations before a packed audience left Santer and Wigley visibly shaken. When Santer replied that one section of the 1995 IPCC report in question had been moved to another place simply for the sake of clarity, Pearlman scoffed. When Wigley pointed out that the chapter had been written by forty scientists and peer-reviewed by sixty others, Pearlman dismissed him out of hand.

Shortly thereafter, the coal and oil lobbies placed stories in The Washington Times and the trade paper, Energy Daily. They accused Santer of making "unauthorized" and "politically motivated" changes in the IPCC report. These stories, provided to the newspapers by the Global Climate Coalition, used incomplete and grossly misleading excerpts of the IPCC document that had been taken out of context. Playing on the recent "ethnic cleansing" atrocities in Bosnia, the public relations specialists of the GCC accused Santer of "scientific cleansing." The Energy Daily story, quoting extensively from a GCC handout, concluded: "Unless the management of the IPCC promptly undertakes to republish the printed versions of the underlying ... report ... the IPCC's credibility will have been lost."

Subsequently, in an op-ed piece in The Wall Street Journal, Frederick Seitz, director of the Marshall Institute, castigated Santer for allegedly excising references to scientific uncertainty. Wrote Seitz, "I have never witnessed a more disturbing corruption of the peer-review process than the events that led to this IPCC report." (Several months later, Seitz conceded the reports of his own Marshall Institute, which consistently deny any threat to the global climate, were not based on science but merely "represent opinion.") The story—with all its damning but unsubstantiated allegations—was picked up by the New York Times.

Predictably, the next issue of Pat Michael's coal-funded World Climate Report accused Santer of raising "very serious questions about whether the IPCC has compromised, or even lost, its scientific integrity." The journal referred to the Global Climate Coalition as "a concerned group," never referencing the oil, coal, and automotive interests it represents.

Following this wave of disinformation, Santer wrote a letter that he sent to each of the authors of the 1995 IPCC report: "I am taking the unusual step of writing to you directly in order to keep you apprised of some very serious allegations that have been made recently by the Global Climate Coalition (GCC).... These allegations impugn my own scientific integrity, the integrity of the other Lead Authors of Chapter 8, and the integrity of the IPCC itself. I am troubled that this controversy has surfaced. I had hoped that any controversy regarding the 1995 IPCC Report would focus on the science itself, and not on the scientists. I guess I was being naive."

In an interview, Santer expressed his personal dismay at the unfair accusations. "All I want to do is to be done with this and get back to my science. But the last couple of weeks—both for me and my family—have been the most difficult of my entire professional career."

In their reply to Energy Daily, Santer and Wigley, as well as two other IPCC scientists (Dr. Tim Barnett of the Scripps Institution of Oceanography, and Dr. Ebby Anyamba) of NASA's

Goddard Space Flight Center), cited the "incorrect" nature of the material that had been provided to the paper by the GCC. The article's author, they added, "should at the very least have contacted one of the [IPCC authors] … in order to obtain a more balanced view of how and why revisions were made to this chapter." A separate response to THE WALL STREET JOURNAL was signed by forty-two IPCC scientists.

Another letter to the JOURNAL was signed by IPCC chairman Bert Bolin and by Sir John Houghton and Luiz Gylvan Meira Filho, co-chairs of the IPCC's working group on science. Santer's handling of the chapter in question, they wrote, adhered meticulously to proper IPCC procedure and violated no scientific ethics. "No one could have been more thorough and honest" than Santer, they added, in incorporating the final changes into the text.

Shortly thereafter, William O'Keefe continued the attack he had helped launch in the Rayburn building. He publicly called for "an independent review" to determine whether Santer had substantially altered the IPCC documents. The attack prompted Santer to write his fellow IPCC scientists, "In effect, the Global Climate Coalition would like to put the IPCC—and my own scientific integrity—on trial."

Enter Dana Rohrabacher [former surfer, journalist turned Republican congressman from Orange County, California, chair, Subcommittee on Energy & Environment, House of Representatives]. When the coal and oil lobbies found themselves unable to discredit Santer, they enlisted the help of the "hear-no-science" congressman. In July 1996, responding to the lobbyists' urgings, Rohrabacher wrote to Secretary of Energy Hazel O'Leary, urging her to withdraw Energy Department funding from the laboratory that employs Benjamin Santer.

1998 GELBSPAN HEAT IS ON at 118–24:

Throughout the ongoing Climate Convention negotiations, the OPEC nations and their industry counterparts have consistently warned the large developing giants—China, India, Brazil, and Mexico, for instance—that the "climate scare" is based on flawed science and is basically a plot by the wealthy countries to keep them relatively poor. Consequently, they have urged those countries to accept nothing but the loosest future restrictions. At the same time, the OPEC nations and the fossil fuel industry representatives have put the United Nations on notice that they will accept no restrictions that do not fall equally heavily on the developing giants. Anything less, they argue, would be fundamentally unfair to fossil fuel producers, whose income depends on sales of oil and coal.

It is a strategy designed to guarantee the failure of the talks.

Clearly any attempt to impose the same restrictions on the poor countries—whose per-capita consumption of coal and oil has been comparatively tiny—as would fall on the rich countries—who have built their dominant industrial wealth on a base of fossil fuels—amounts to nothing less than "environmental colonialism," according to Sunita Narain, an Indian researcher and coauthor of GLOBAL WARMING IN AN UNEQUAL WORLD.

But that approach is what the fossil fuel lobbyists are pitching. Saudi Arabia and Kuwait, in league with representatives of the U.S. oil and coal industry, have successfully used these tactics to keep the negotiators from moving forward.

At a preliminary negotiating session in New York in February 1995, China and India, both of which have vast coal resources, argued that unless the United States leads the way by significantly cutting its own emissions, their obligation to develop their own economies outweighs their obligation to [preserve] the global environment. The range of initial positions, according to observers, left some room for negotiation. But that hope was scotched by the OPEC bloc, which steadfastly opposed even the vaguest of goals. The delegations from Saudi Arabia and Kuwait were especially intransigent, according to observers, who express particular irritation with the role of Donald Pearlman, a former official in the Reagan and Bush administrations.

Pearlman, who is a partner in the Washington law and lobbying firm of Patton, Boggs and Blow, has basically functioned behind the scenes as the parliamentary quarterback for the OPEC delegations, directing their efforts to hamstring the negotiations. On several occasions Pearlman was seen passing handwritten notes to Saudi and Kuwaiti delegates, advising them to oppose specific treaty language and providing them with alternative wording more favorable to their interests. Several observers witnessed OPEC delegates carrying Pearlman's notes into negotiating sessions and consulting them during the deliberations.

In the end, the OPEC delegations prevailed in that February 1995 meeting. Supported by the United States, Japan, Australia, Canada, and New Zealand, the meeting rejected calls to limit emissions, declaring such action premature. The following month, a subsequent negotiating round ended with an agreement to negotiate a vehicle for reducing emissions to be adopted in Japan in 1997.

Under the Foreign Agents' Registration Act, Pearlman is registered as a representative of Abu Dhabi, Oman, Quatar, the United Arab Emirates, and other oil-producing countries. But in a telephone interview he emphatically denied that he has ever formally represented any foreign government in connection with international climate deliberations. He did not deny counseling OPEC delegates.

Several years ago Pearlman founded a nonprofit organization called the Climate Council. According to its IRS charter, its purpose is to represent U.S.-based energy companies "whose business could be adversely affected by laws relating to potential global climate change." Pearlman secured official Non-governmental Organization (NGO) status for his Climate Council, which gives him access to briefings from the official U.S. delegation—a situation that enrages his critics in the environmental community, who have dubbed him King of the Carbon Club. Environmentalists charge that Pearlman's official nonprofit status, together with his ties to the Saudis, Kuwaitis, and other OPEC nations, allow him to be privy to information from both camps in the negotiations. Jennifer Morgan, coordinator of the U.S. Climate Action NetWork, an affiliation of U.S.-based environmental NGOs, says that given Pearlman's relationship with OPEC delegations, he should not be permitted to "enjoy official nonpartisan, nongovernmental status." Pearlman dismisses that criticism, insisting he has never received any compensation from any foreign government for any work related to climate issues.

Like the skeptic scientists and their ideological supporters, Pearlman has also criticized the work of the IPCC. In an interview, he bemoaned the politicization of the IPCC process, saying it was being contaminated by the political agendas of its member nations. "The IPCC has been heavily politicized from the beginning," he said. "It is as true of highly technical scientific issues as it is of economic ones. One can count on the fingers of one hand the times when any nation has taken a position before the IPCC ... that would not further its policy preferences."

At the negotiating session in March 1996, the level of discord was as high as ever. As the delegates began to consider several agenda items, they were interrupted by delegates from Saudi Arabia, Kuwait, and China, who claimed they had not had time to read the IPCC report—although they had received them three months earlier, at a meeting in Berlin. But even if they had received the reports only the day before, that excuse would still lack any credibility. According to a newsletter of the environmental NGO community: "This blatant, transparent attempt to undermine the key conclusions of the [report] was even more unbelievable because these same countries negotiated every line, word by word, in the final months leading to the [report's] approval ... last December."

The March 1996 negotiating sessions considered the question of international energy efficiency standards for appliances—a fairly minimal but nonetheless useful step toward emissions reductions. Initially, most of the delegates were agreeable to implementing the relatively innocuous efficiency standards. But following discussions with oil and coal industry representatives, a number of delegates from developing countries rejected the standards, on the ground that they constituted a nontariff trade barrier and hence violated the General Agreement on Tariffs and Trade guidelines. All these delegates used the exact same wording, in which they had been coached by the lobbyists. Not even the adoption of minimal efficiency standards could slip by the guardians of the oil and coal interests.

At that same negotiating session one island-nation delegate suggested that, rather than have 150 governments negotiate regulations for the auto industry, representatives of the leading auto manufacturers might meet and discuss ways in which they could cooperate in setting global standards and developing less-polluting vehicles.

The industry response was disheartening. "Business representatives present at this meeting greeted the suggestion with loud, dismissive and cynical laughter," according to an account in ECO, the environmental NGO newsletter. The account concluded: "Most ... of the business NGOs now straining the capacity of the observers' gallery come to Geneva to slow the Convention's advancement. Their most memorable contribution to last week's workshop ... for example, was to ask, with naive cynicism, whether it might not be more cost-effective to build one meter sea walls around the globe than to invest in mitigating climate change."

As for the OPEC delegations, ECO noted that "Saudi Arabia is still trying to argue that producers of polluting fossil fuels have a right to a special representation ... in the Convention process. But as far as its core work goes, little interest has been shown, and many [OPEC delegations] have arrived without evidence of prior preparation."

The sustained campaign of diplomatic sabotage continues with the relentless obstructions that are raised when IPCC scientists try to get their message out.

Dr. Kevin Trenberth was the head of an IPCC scientific group that, in late 1995, wrote a policymakers' summary of the IPCC scientific draft report. Trenberth, the lead author of the summary, said it was in fairly good shape going into a negotiating session in Madrid near the end of November 1995. But he noted with great frustration in a letter after the session that "there were deliberate attempts to obfuscate and undermine the documents by the OPEC nations, principally Saudi Arabia and Kuwait.... Even with an overwhelming 93 to 2 vote in favor of particular wording, proceedings were delayed time and time again seeking alternative language that would satisfy everyone. Sidebar meetings were held by groups of 10 or so which were supposed to resolve wording of particular sections. But neither the Saudis nor Kuwait would participate in these and instead offered continual amendments...."

"In the final throes of trying to get a document of some sort, the Saudis continued with every ploy including saying there was no quorum," despite the lack of any quorum requirement. "Part of the strategy seemed to be to avoid having a document at all," Trenberth surmised, so frustrated by the blatant obstructionism that he considered taking his name off the document.

Taking their cues from Donald Pearlman, the Saudi and Kuwaiti delegates objected to virtually every word of the summary. Noted Trenberth: "All of the [resulting] wording was that of the Saudis in spite of overwhelming support for alternatives. Every word was approved separately. The result was no macro perspective of the whole document or even sections. It was, at best, disappointing."

The obstructionism was epitomized by the fight over the heading of a section on sulfate aerosols. After intense negotiations, the section was finally titled "Anthropogenic Aerosols Tend to Produce Negative Radiative Forcings," which, Trenberth said, "is true but says nothing. Most people favored my suggested wording, which was 'Anthropogenic Aerosols Tend to Mask Global Warming.'" But that title was rejected by the OPEC delegates. "All this does not augur well for the future of the IPCC. I believe it cannot continue unless substantial changes in rules of procedure are made," Trenberth added.

In a subsequent letter to another IPCC official, Trenberth asked: "The question ... [is] how to deal with small groups whose real intent is to subvert the process? Whether or not this was really the purpose of the Saudis and Iran, this question remains an important one and I believe that procedures should be put in place that are understood by all participants as to how these things should be dealt with in future."

As the time neared for the December 1997 Kyoto Conference, oil and coal interests fought ferociously against any meaningful emissions reductions. Like their U.S. counterparts, the OPEC delegates continued to insist that the state of the science is too ambiguous to take substantial action. In November 1995, after the Saudis and Kuwaitis worked so hard to thwart IPCC scientists in Madrid, Merylyn McKensey Hedger, an officer for the Worldwide Fund for Nature, told a writer for NATURE magazine that "the situation is too serious for countries such as Saudi Arabia and Kuwait to continue ... to subvert the IPCC process." But that complaint was rejected out of hand by Mohammed Al-Sabban, head of the Saudi delegation. "Saudi Arabia's oil income amounts to 96 percent of our total exports," he said, adding: "Until there is clearer evidence of human involvement in climate change, we will not agree to what amounts to a tax on oil."

In Geneva in the summer of 1996, eleven oil- and coal-producing nations continued to attack the findings of the scientists, voting to reject the IPCC's scientific report on growing climatic instability. Kuwait, Saudi Arabia, Syria, Iran, China, Nigeria, and five other oil-producing states declined to approve the IPCC text without substantial modification to its language.

In response, Bert Bolin, then chair of the IPCC, declared: "This is the work of two thousand scientists, reviewed, revised and reviewed again. There is no compromise in any direction. Do not trust any individual scientists, not even me; look at the work of all these, a balanced view." Referring to this and other recent attacks on the IPCC, Bolin said, "We reject accusations and allegations made against us. We have completely and carefully done our work. It is the best science on climate the world has to offer. I stake my reputation and honor that it is so."

Unfortunately, Bolin's honor means little to the fossil fuel industries, whose lobbies will do whatever they can to undermine any process—scientific, diplomatic, or regulatory—that could lead to enforced limits on coal and oil burning.

At the Geneva meeting U.S. undersecretary of state Timothy Wirth heralded a new, more aggressive U.S. policy when he announced for the first time that the United States would support a binding international agreement to limit emissions. "Saying that we want to have a target that is binding is a clear indication that the United States is very serious about taking steps and leading the rest of the world," Wirth said. "We will be getting more and more specific as the next year and a half rolls through.... We are not interested in grand rhetorical goals that are impossible to realize. We want the negotiations to focus on outcomes that are real and achievable."

Wirth called his announcement "a big deal"—and on the scale of diplomacy, perhaps it was. But if, after four years of talks, a call for mandatory but unspecified emissions targets is a "big deal," then progress is being measured according to standards of diplomacy, not those of the biosphere.

Notes

1. George Monbiot, Heat: How to Stop the Planet From Burning 39 (South End Press 2007) (footnotes omitted):

> On February 2001, seventeen days after George W. Bush was sworn in, A.G. (Randy) Randol, ExxonMobil's senior environmental advisor, sent a fax to John Howard, an environmental official at the White House. It began by discussing the role of Robert Watson, the head of the Intergovernmental Panel on Climate Change. It suggested he had a "personal agenda" and asked, "Can Watson now be replaced at the request of the U.S.?" It went on to ask that the United States be represented at the panel's discussions by a Dr. Harlan Watson. Both requests were met. One Watson was sacked, the other was appointed, and he continues to wreak havoc at international climate meetings.

2. *Compare* 2007 Bolin at 73:

> These intentional misinterpretations of the IPCC report were annoying, and almost all scientists that I have met considered [Fred] Singer's activities during the early 1990s, and actually ever since, to be a systematic attempt to discredit the IPCC's efforts by making incorrect or misleading statements both verbally and in the popular press. On the other hand, some of the articles in the [Singer 1992 book] raised legitimate questions and accordingly were considered in later IPCC assessments.

with id. at 85:

> To focus on a revision of the IPCC rules of procedure was then an obvious first step, and in fact, [Donald] Pearlman did have some influence on the modifications of the IPCC rules of procedure for a few years. Controversies between stakeholders, particularly in the energy industry, and the IPCC were still in their early phase in 1992, but would increase and indeed become troublesome during the coming years.

and id. at 189:

> This [2004] declaration by the Russian Academy is indeed a most amazing document, a mixture of poor scientific arguments and national politics. It is surprising that this kind of document was presented by the leading scientific institution of the country.

3. Eli Kintisch, *Projections of Climate Change Go From Bad to Worse, Scientists Report*, 323 Science 1546 (March 20, 2009) ("The worst-case IPCC projections, or even worse, are being realized," says oceanographer, Katherine Richardson, University of Copenhagen, who co-chairs a meeting of 2,000 scientists; the "ice sheets" are shrinking, says Eric Rignot of University of California, Irvine, which puts us on a trajectory of one-meter sea level rise by 2100).

4. Institute for Governance & Sustainable Development, Abrupt Climate Changes Approaching Faster Than Previously Predicted, Jan. 10, 2009 (Durwood Zaelke, President):

> The Paleoclimate records derived from archives such as tree rings, ice cores, corals, and sediments show that past climate changes have included both steady, linear changes as well as abrupt, non-linear changes, where small increases in global warming produced large and irreversible impacts once temperature tipping points were passed. Climate scientists now warn that anthropogenic emissions are pushing the planet's climate system toward such temperature tipping points sooner than previously expected and that impacts could be catastrophic.
>
> Among potential impacts of passing climate tipping points are the disappearance of Arctic summer sea ice, major reduction of area and volume of Himalayan-Tibetan glaciers, deglaciation of Greenland Ice Sheet, dieback of Amazonian and boreal

forests, shutdown of the Atlantic Thermohaline Circulation, and collapse of West Antarctic Ice Sheet.[1] The catastrophic impacts from these events would include many meters of sea level rise, water shortages, megadroughts, and famine and could lead to political instability and resource wars.[2] Other impacts include release of methane and other greenhouse gases (GHGs) from permafrost and ocean hydrates, which could set off runaway feedbacks, something not yet included in climate models. (In December 2008, the International Siberian Shelf Study reported highest ever methane measurements in East Siberian Arctic Shelf, indicating underwater permafrost is already thawing.)[3]

In a recent study in the *Proceedings of the National Academy of Sciences*, V. Ramanathan and Y. Feng from the Scripps Institution of Oceanography, University of California, San Diego, calculate that GHG emissions as of 2005 have committed the planet to warming of "2.4°C (1.4°–4.3°) above the preindustrial surface temperatures,"[4] which is within the range of predicted tipping points. (See Figure 13.)

The present observed temperature increase of 0.76°C[5] is misleading for policy. Warming of at least another 1°C is presently being masked by "atmospheric brown clouds" containing cooling particulates released with GHG emissions and other pollution.[6] As we continue to reduce the pollution creating these clouds for health reasons we are unmasking the 1°C or greater temperature increase that is already committed from current emissions.[7] An additional 0.6°C warming is temporarily delayed by ocean thermal inertia.[8] Of the 2.4°C committed warming, more than 50% is expected within 50 years, as heat stored in oceans is returned to the atmosphere, and as short-lived anthropogenic aerosols that are masking warming continue to be reduced to protect health and local environment resources.[9]

---

1. Timothy Lenton, Hermann Held, Elmar Kriegler, Jim Hall, Wolfgang Lucht, Stefan Rahmstorf & Hans Joachim Schellnhuber, *Tipping elements in the Earth's climate system*, 105 Proc. of the Nat'l Acad. of Sci. 1786, 1786 (2008); *see also* World Wildlife Fund, Climate Change: Faster, Stronger, Sooner (2008) ("It is currently forecast that [Arctic] summer sea ice could completely disappear somewhere between 2013 and 2040 — a state not seen on planet Earth for more than a million years."). *See also* Clark, P.U., A.J. Weaver (coordinating lead authors), E. Brook, E.R. Cook, T.L. Delworth & K. Steffen (chapter lead authors), *2008: Abrupt Climate Change, A report by the U.S. Climate Change Science Program and the Subcommittee on Global Change Research*, U.S. Geological Survey, Reston, VA, 459 pp. (The mass balance loss of the Greenland Ice Sheet doubled from the mid-1990s to the most recent observations in 2006, while the mass balance loss of Antarctica increased ... more than 60% from the mid-1990s to the mid 2000s.)

2. Lenton *et al.*, *supra* note 1, at 1788; Peter Schwartz & Doug Randall, *An Abrupt Climate Change Scenario and Its Implications for United States National Security*, 18–19 (2003), http://handle.dtic.mil/100.2/ADA469325.

3. Rich Monastersky, *Arctic warming spurs record melting*, Nature News, doi:10.1038/news.2008.1314. (The East Siberian Arctic Shelf runs more than 900 miles into the Arctic Ocean.)

4. V. Ramanathan & Y. Feng, *On avoiding dangerous anthropogenic interference with the climate system: Formidable challenges ahead*, 105 Proc. of the Nat'l Acad. of Sci. 14245, 14245 (2008).

5. *Id.* at 14247. *See also* James Hansen, Makiko Sato, Reto Ruedy, Ken Lo, David W. Lea & Martin Medina-Elizade, *Global temperature change*, 103 Proc. of the Nat'l Acad. of Sci. 14288, 14288 (2006) ("Global warming is now 0.6°C in the past three decades and 0.8°C in the past century.").

6. Ramanathan & Feng, *supra* note 4, at 14246–47.

7. *Id.* at 14245–46. *See also* V. Ramanathan *et al.*, United Nations Environment Programme, Atmospheric Brown Clouds: Regional Assessment Report with Focus on Asia 11–12 (2008), *available at* http://www.unep.org/pdf/ABCSummaryFinal.pdf ("[A]ir pollution regulations can have large amplifying effects on global warming. For example, using climate sensitivity recommended in IPCC-AR4, elimination of aerosols in [atmospheric brown clouds] ... could ... push the climate system over the 2°C threshold value for the so-called dangerous climate change.").

8. James Hansen, Makiko Sato, Pushker Kharecha, David Beerling, Valeris Masson-Delmotte, Mark Pagani, Maureen Raymo, Dana L. Royer & James C. Zachos, *Target Atmospheric CO_2: Where Should Humanity Aim?* 2 Open Atmospheric Science Journal 217, 221 (2008) [hereinafter *Target Atmospheric CO_2*].

9. Ramanathan & Feng, *supra* note 4, at 14247.

Impacts from committed warming could include "widespread loss of biodiversity, widespread deglaciation of the Greenland Ice Sheet, and a major reduction of area and volume of Hindu-Kush-Himalaya-Tibetan (HKHT) glaciers, which provide the headwaters for most major river systems of Asia,"[10] including the Yellow, Yangtze, Ganges, Mekong, Indus, and Brahmaputra.[11]

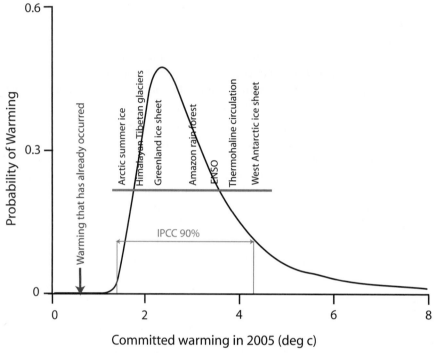

Figure 13. Probability of reaching tipping points. The graph shows the probability that the Earth will warm by the amounts shown on the x-axis and the associated tipping points that will be reached at each level of warming. Re-drawn from: Ramanathan & Y. Feng, *On avoiding dangerous anthropogenic interference with the climate system: Formidable challenges ahead*, 105 Proc. of the Nat'l Acad. of Sci. 14245, 14245 (2008).

---

10. *Id.* at 14245.

11. Lester R. Brown, Plan B 3.0: Mobilizing to Save Civilization 54 (2008) ("Nowhere is the melting of glaciers of more concern than in Asia, where 1.3 billion people depend for their water supply on rivers originating in the Himalayan Mountains and the adjacent Tibet-Qinghai Plateau. India's Gangotri Glacier, which supplies 70 percent of the water to the Ganges, is not only melting, it is doing so at an accelerated rate. If this melting continues to accelerate, the Gangotri's life expectancy will be measured in decades and the Ganges will become a seasonal river, flowing only during the rainy season. For the 407 million Indians and Bangladeshis who live in the Ganges basin, this could be a life-threatening loss of water. In China, which is even more dependent than India on river water for irrigation, the situation is particularly challenging. Chinese government data show the glaciers on the Tibet-Qinghai Plateau that feed both the Yellow and Yangtze Rivers are melting at 7 percent a year. The Yellow River, whose basin is home to 147 million people, could experience a large dry-season flow reduction. The Yangtze River, by far the larger of the two, is threatened by the disappearance of glaciers as well. The basin's 369 million people rely heavily on rice from fields irrigated with Yangtze River water. Yao Tandong, a leading Chinese glaciologist, predicts that two thirds of China's glaciers could be gone by 2060. 'The fullscale glacier shrinkage in the plateau region,' Yao says, 'will eventually lead to an ecological catastrophe.' Other Asian rivers that originate in this rooftop of the world include the Indus, with 178 million people in its basin in India and Pakistan; the Brahmaputra, which flows through Bangladesh; and the Mekong, which waters Cambodia, Laos, Thailand, and Viet Nam.").

At high latitudes, temperatures are rising faster than the global average. The Arctic, Greenland, and the Tibetan Plateau are at particular risk.[12] Between 1965 and 2005, Arctic temperatures increased at least twice as fast as the global average.[13] Melting Arctic sea ice is producing a positive feedback by reducing albedo, or reflectivity, leading to more absorption of heat by exposed Arctic waters.[14] Further darkening is caused when black carbon, or soot, is deposited on snow and ice.[15] The Greenland Ice Sheet is warming even faster than the Arctic at 2.2 times the global average.[16]

The Tibetan Plateau—the planet's largest store of ice after the Arctic and Antarctic—is warming about three times the global average, with temperature increases of 0.3°C or more per decade measured for the past half-century.[17] The majority of Tibetan glaciers are retreating, and across much of the plateau the retreat is accelerating.[18] Himalayan glacier retreat is well documented through remote sensing techniques and aerial photographs.[19] This is now confirmed by ice core samples from Naimona'nyi Glacier in the Himalayas (Tibet).[20]

Since the 1950s, warming in excess of 1°C on the Tibetan side of the Himalayas has contributed to retreat of more than 80% of the glaciers, and the degradation of 10% of its permafrost in the past ten years.[21] The surface area of the Tibetan Plateau is projected

---

12. Lenton *et al.*, *supra* note 1, at 1788 ("Transient warming is generally greater toward the poles and greater on the land than in the ocean."); *see also* Jane Qiu, *The Third Pole*, 454 NATURE 393 (2008).

13. P. LEMKE *et al.*, INTERGOVERNMENTAL PANEL ON CLIMATE CHANGE [IPCC], *Observations: Changes in Snow, Ice and Frozen Ground*, CLIMATE CHANGE 2007: THE PHYSICAL SCIENCE BASIS 339 (S. Solomon *et al.* eds., Cambridge Un. Press 2007) ("Recent decreases in ice mass are correlated with rising surface air temperatures. This is especially true for the region north of 65°N, where temperatures have increased by about twice the global average from 1965 to 2005."). *See also* Rich Monastersky, *Arctic warming spurs record melting*, NATURE NEWS, *available at* http://www.nature.com/news/2008/081217/full/news.2008.1314.html (Recent observations reported 16 December at the meeting of the American Geophysical Union in San Francisco, California, showed record melting in northern Greenland and record release of methane from formerly frozen deposits off the Siberian coast.).

14. Lenton *et al.*, *supra* note 1, at 1788.

15. V. Ramanathan & G. Carmichael, *Global and regional climate changes due to black carbon*, 1 NATURE GEOSCIENCE 221, 224 (2008) at 221. *See also* M.G. Flanner, C.S. Zender, J.T. Randerson & P.J. Rasch, *Present-day climate forcing and response from black carbon in snow*, 112 J. GEOPHYS. RES. D11202 (2007) (noting that "the 'efficacy' of BC/snow forcing is more than three times greater than forcing by CO_2").

16. Petr Chylek & Ulrike Lohmann, *Ratio of the Greenland to global temperature change: Comparison of observations and climate modeling results*, 32GEOPHYS. RES. LETT. L14705 (2005).

17. Qiu, *supra* note 13, at 393. *See also* R.V. CRUZ *et al.*, IPCC, *Asia*, *in* CLIMATE CHANGE 2007: IMPACTS, ADAPTATION AND VULNERABILITY 475 (M.L. Parry *et al.* eds., 2007) (There have been measurements of "0.16 and 0.32°C per decade increase in annual and winter temperatures, respectively").

18. T. Yao, T., J. Pu, A. Lu, Y. Wang & W. Yu, *Recent glacial retreat and its impact on the hydrological processes on the Tibetan Plateau, China, and surrounding regions*, 39 ARCT. ANTARCT. ALP. RES. 642–650 (2007).

19. Y. Ding, S. Liu, J. Li & D. Shangguan, *The retreat of glaciers in response to recent climate warming in western China*, 43 ANN. GLACIOL. 97–105 (2006).

20. N.M. Kehrwald *et al.*, *Mass loss on Himalayan glacier endangers water resources*, GEOPHYS. RES. LETT.,L22503 (2008) ("Naimona'nyi is the highest glacier (6050 masl) documented to be losing mass annually.... Estimates of the impact of Himalayan glacier retreat on water resources have not accounted for mass loss through high elevation thinning such as is currently occurring on the Naimona'nyi ice field. If Naimona'nyi is characteristic of other glaciers in the region, alpine glacier meltwater surpluses are likely to shrink much faster than currently predicted with substantial consequences for approximately half a billion people.").

21. Ramanathan & Carmichael, *supra* note 15; *see also* Qiu, *supra* note 12, at 393 ("The Tibetan plateau gets a lot less attention than the Arctic or Antarctic, but after them it is Earth's largest store of ice. And the store is melting fast. In the past half-century, 82% of the plateau's glaciers have retreated. In the past decade, 10% of its permafrost has degraded. As the changes continue, or even accelerate, their effects will resonate far beyond the isolated plateau, changing the water supply for billions of people and altering the atmospheric cir-

to shrink to 100,000 km^2 by 2030 from 500,000 km^2 in 1995.[22] Under current trends, two-thirds of the glaciers will disappear by 2060, threatening water supply for a billion people, including their critical dry-season irrigation.[23] These and other geographic regions where water supply is dominated by melting snow or ice are predicted to suffer severe consequences as a result of recent warming.[24] Deposition of black carbon is a major driver of glacial retreat in the Hindu-Kush-Himalayan-Tibetan region.[25]

In the Himalayas alone there are approximately 15,000 glaciers (of 46,377 glaciers catalogued by the Chinese Glacier Inventory in western China), storing an estimated 12,000 km^3 of freshwater.[26] The Himalayas glaciers seasonally release meltwater into tributaries of the Indus, Ganges, and Brahmaputra Rivers with glacial melt contributing up to 45% of the total river flow.[27] Approximately 500 million people depend upon water from these three rivers for agriculture and other purposes.[28]

Scientists estimate that temperature tipping points for abrupt climate changes could be passed this century, or even in the next decade.[29] Under a "business-as-usual" scenario, where atmospheric CO_2 concentrations are increasing about 2 ppm per year, the question is not whether abrupt climate change will occur, but rather how soon.[30] Dr. James Hansen, Director of NASA's Goddard Institute for Space Studies, agrees with Ramanathan and Feng that we have already passed the threshold for "dangerous anthropogenic interference" with the natural climate system. Hansen calculates that CO_2 concentrations must be reduced from their current 385 ppm to 350 ppm maximum if we want to preserve planetary conditions similar to those where civilization developed and humanity is adapted.[31] Current projections are that CO_2 concentrations will approach 441 ppm with a corresponding committed warming of 3.1°C by 2030 in the absence of strong countervailing mitigation.[32] By the end of the century, business-as-usual emis-

---

culation over half the planet.... The melting seasons on the plateau now begin earlier and last longer.... If current trends hold, two thirds of the plateau glaciers could be gone by 2050."). In the Tibetan Plateau Steppe, where the headwaters of the Yangtze, Mekong, and Indus are located, there is concern both for short-term flood and long-term reductions in water supplies. *See, e.g., id.* at 395 ("The risk of floods, though, is but a short-term danger far exceeded by long-term issues with water supplies atop the [Tibetan plateau].").

22. Cruz *et al., supra* note 17.

23. Brown, *supra* note 11, at 54. ("Yao Tandong, a leading Chinese glaciologist, predicts that two thirds of China's glaciers could be gone by 2060. 'The fullscale glacier shrinkage in the plateau region,' Yao says, 'will eventually lead to an ecological catastrophe.'").

24. T.P. Barnett, J. C. Adam & D. P. Lettenmaier, *Potential impacts of a warming climate on water availability in snow-dominated regions,* 438 Nature 303–309 (2005); *see also,* Kehrwald *et al., supra* note 20.

25. Ramanathan *et al., supra* note 7, at 6 ("The present report adds that soot in [atmospheric brown clouds] is another major cause of the retreat of [Hindu-Kush-Himalayan-Tibetan] glaciers and snow packs. The warming of the elevated atmospheric layers due to greenhouse warming is amplified by the solar heating by soot at elevated levels and an increase in solar absorption by snow and ice contaminated by the deposition of soot."); *see also id.* at 25 ("Decreased reflection of solar radiation by snow and ice due to black carbon deposition is emerging as another major contributor to the melting of snow packs and glaciers."); *see also* Ramanathan & Carmichael, *supra* note 15, at 224.

26. Ding *et al., supra* note 19; *see also* Cruz *et al., supra* note 17.

27. World Resources Institute (2003), *Watersheds of the World* [CD-ROM], World Resour. Inst., New York.

28. Cruz *et al., supra* note 17.

29. Lenton *et al., supra* note 1, at 1786; Committee on Abrupt Climate Change & National Research Council, Abrupt Climate Change: Inevitable Surprises 107–08 (2003).

30. *Target Atmospheric CO_2, supra* note 8, at 218; *see also* James Hansen, *Climate Catastrophe,* New Scientist, at 32 (July 28, 2007).

31. *Target Atmospheric CO_2, supra* note 8, at 217.

32. Ramanathan & Feng, *supra* note 4, at 14247–49.

sions could cause atmospheric concentrations of CO_2 and other long-lived GHGs to double, leading to an eventual global temperature increase of up to 6°C.[33]

Despite the certainty that abrupt climate changes have occurred in the past and could be triggered again in the near future, current climate policy does not account for abrupt climate change.[34] In particular, abrupt climate change is not incorporated into the projections of the Intergovernmental Panel on Climate Change (IPCC), which is regarded as the most authoritative, if often conservative, source of information on climate issues.[35] While the focus must continue on mid- and long-term mitigation strategies to reduce CO_2 emissions, we also must begin fast-action mitigation strategies that can produce immediate climate mitigation and delay the onset of tipping points.

In his commentary to the Ramanathan and Feng study, Professor Hans Joachim Schellnhuber from the Potsdam Institute for Climate Impact Research concludes that "we are still left with a fair chance to hold the 2°C line, yet the race between climate dynamics and climate policy will be a close one. The odds … may be improved by aerosol management … (taking the warming components such as black carbon out first), and even techniques for extracting atmospheric CO_2 (like bio-sequestration).… However, the quintessential challenges remain, namely bending down the global [climate emis-

---

33. INTERNATIONAL ENERGY AGENCY [IEA], WORLD ENERGY OUTLOOK 45–46 (2008) ("The projected rise in emissions of greenhouse gases in the Reference Scenario puts us on a course of doubling the concentration of those gases in the atmosphere by the end of this century, entailing an eventual global average temperature increase of up to 6°C. The Reference Scenario trends point to continuing growth in emissions of CO_2 and other greenhouse gases. Global energy-related CO_2 emissions rise from 28 Gt in 2006 to 41 Gt in 2030—an increase of 45%. The 2030 projection is only 1 Gt lower than that projected in last year's *Outlook*, even though we assume much higher prices and slightly lower world GDP growth. World greenhouse-gas emissions, including non-energy CO_2 and all other gases, are projected to grow from 44 Gt CO_2-equivalent in 2005 to 60 Gt CO_2-eq in 2030, an increase of 35% over 2005."); *see id.* at 401 ("The total CO_2-equivalent concentration of all long-lived greenhouse gases, taking into account land-use change, is currently around 455 ppm. This is around 60% higher than the level in pre-industrial times.") (footnote omitted).

34. Peter Read & Jonathan Lermit, *Bio-Energy with Carbon Storage (BECS): a Sequential Decision Approach to the threat of Abrupt Climate Change*, 30 ENERGY 2654, 2654 (2005) ("Abrupt Climate Change is an issue that 'haunts the climate change problem' (IPCC, 2001) but has been neglected by policy makers up to now, maybe for want of practicable measures for effective response, save for risky geo-engineering."); *see also* Lenton *et al., supra* note 1, at 1792 ("Society may be lulled into a false sense of security by smooth projections of global change. Our synthesis of present knowledge suggests that a variety of tipping elements could reach their critical point within this century under anthropogenic climate change."). In September 2008, the U.S. Department of Energy announced a new research effort on abrupt climate change called IMPACTS—Investigation of the Magnitudes and Probabilities of Abrupt Climate Transitions. Headed by William Collins of Berkeley Lab's Earth Sciences Division, the program will include six national laboratories. *See IMPACTS: On the Threshold of Abrupt Climate Changes*, Lawrence Berkeley National Laboratory, News Center (2008), at http://newscenter. lbl.gov/feature-stories/2008/09/17/impacts-on-the-threshold-of-abrupt-climate-changes/ (Climate change "has occurred with frightening rapidity in the past and … is highly likely in the future, with wide-ranging economic and social effects." The initial research focus will be on "the Four Horsemen of the Apocalypse": instability among marine ice sheets, particularly the West Antarctic ice sheet, which could cause four to six meters of sea level rise, and submerge small island states and low-lying coastal areas, including port facilities worldwide; positive feedback mechanisms in subarctic forests and arctic ecosystems, leading to rapid methane release or large-scale changes in the surface energy balance, "which could occur over only 20–30 years, [and] may amplify currently predicted warming two to three times, in the Arctic and possibly globally"; destabilization of methane hydrates (vast deposits of methane gas caged in water ice), particularly in the Arctic Ocean; and feedback between biosphere and atmosphere that could lead to megadroughts in North America.).

35. *See, e.g.*, James Hansen, *Scientific reticence and sea level rise*, ENVIRON. RES. 2, 5 (2007).

sions] … in the 2015–2020 window … and phasing out carbon dioxide emissions completely by 2100. This requires an industrial revolution for sustainability starting now."[36]

A suite of fast-action mitigation strategies are urgently needed to avoid passing tipping points for abrupt climate changes. Black carbon may be the second largest contributor to climate warming, and because its atmospheric lifetime is days to weeks, reducing it may offer the fastest mitigation.[37] Other fast-action climate mitigation strategies include reducing other short-lived forcers such as methane and tropospheric ozone precursors,[38] as well as accelerating efforts under the Montreal Protocol on Substances that Deplete the Ozone Layer to reduce ozone-depleting substances (ODSs), most of which are powerful climate gases.[39] (In November 2008, the 193 Parties to the Montreal Protocol unanimously agreed for the second year in a row to strengthen their treaty to provide additional protection for the climate system, as well as for the ozone layer; they also agreed to launch formal discussions for moving HFCs into the Montreal Protocol, where those with high global warming potential could be phased-out.)[40]

---

36. Hans Joachim Schellnhuber, *Global Warming: Stop worrying, start panicking?*, 105 Proc. of the Nat'l Acad. of Sci. 14239, 14239–40 (2008).

37. Ramanathan & Carmichael, *supra* note 15, at 222 ("The BC forcing of 0.9 W m^{-2} (with a range of 0.4 to 1.2 W m^{-2}) … is as much as 55% of the CO_2 forcing and is larger than the forcing due to the other GHGs such as CH_4, CFCs, N_2O or tropospheric ozone."); *see also* Mark Jacobson, *Control of Fossil-Fuel Particulate Black Carbon and Organic Matter, Possibly the Most Effective Method of Slowing Global Warming*, 107 J. Geophys. Res. D19 (2002); and Qiu, *supra* note 12, at 396 ("Reducing emissions of greenhouse gases and black carbon should be the top priority," according to Xu Baiqing of the Institute of Tibetan Plateau Research.).

38. *Role of Black Carbon on Global and Regional Climate Change: Hearing on the role of black carbon as a factor in climate change Before H. Comm. on Oversight and Gov't Reform*, 110th Cong. 4 (2007) (testimony of V. Ramanathan).

39. *See* Guus J. M. Velders, Stephen O. Andersen, John S. Daniel, David W. Fahey & Mack McFarland, *The importance of the Montreal Protocol in protecting climate*, 104 Proc. Nat'l. Acad. Sci. 4814, 4814–19 (2007), *available at* http://www.pnas.org/cgi/content/abstract/104/12/4814 (From 1990 to 2010, the Montreal Protocol will have reduced climate emissions by a net of 135 billion tonnes of CO_2-eq., delaying climate forcing by up to 12 years. This is ~ 13% of the forcing due to accumulated anthropogenic emissions of CO_2 and several times the reductions sought under the first phase of Kyoto Protocol.). In 2007, the Montreal Protocol was further strengthened to accelerate the phase-out of HCFCs; that adjustment has the potential to produce mitigation up to 16 billion tones of CO_2-eq. *See* U.S. EPA 2008 Climate Award Winners, Team Award Winners, http://www.epa.gov/cppd/awards/2008winners.html ("The U.S. EPA estimates that, through 2040, the HCFC agreement could reduce emissions by up to 16 billion metric tonnes of carbon dioxide-equivalent. This is equal to the greenhouse gas emissions from the electricity use of more than 70 million U.S. households over the next 30 years."); Technology and Economic Assessment Panel [TEAP], United Nations Environment Programme, Response to Decision XVIII/12, Report of the Task Force on HCFC Issues (with Particular Focus on the Impact of the Clean Development Mechanism) and Emissions Reductions Benefits Arising from Earlier HCFC Phase-Out and Other Practical Measures 8 (2007) [hereinafter "TEAP Response"], *available at* http://ozone.unep.org/teap/Reports/TEAP_Reports/TEAP-TaskForce-HCFC-Aug2007.pdf.

40. At the 20th Meeting of the Parties to the Montreal Protocol, the Parties agreed to begin collecting and destroying unwanted ODSs in existing stockpiles and discarded products and equipment. *See* The Eighth Meeting of the Conference of the Parties to the Vienna Convention and the Twentieth Meeting of the Parties to the Montreal Protocol, Doha, Qatar, Nov. 16–20, 2008, *Advance Report*, at Decision XX/7 (Nov. 27, 2008) [hereinafter *Advance Report*], *available at* http://ozone.unep.org/Meeting_Documents/mop/20mop/MOP-20-9E.pdf. Without immediate action to prevent emissions of ODSs from banks, these sources will release 6 billion tonnes or more of CO_2–eq. into the atmosphere before 2015 and a further 15 billion tonnes of CO_2–eq. thereafter, and will otherwise cancel the hoped for gains of the current climate treaty. *See* TEAP Response, *supra* note 29, at 12, 27; *see also* IPCC & TEAP, *Technical Summary, in* Special Report on Safeguarding the Ozone Layer and the Global Climate System: Issues Related to Hydrofluorocarbons and Perfluorocarbons [Special Report] 9 (2005), *available at* http://arch.rivm.nl/env/int/ipcc/pages_media/SROC-final/SpecialReportSROC.html.

The Parties also decided to start discussions on moving hydrofluorocarbons, or HFCs, from the climate treaty to the stricter Montreal Protocol, where HFCs with high global warming potential could be phased-out.

Other fast-action mitigation efforts include bio-sequestration in forests and soils. Biochar, for example, removes carbon from the carbon cycle by drawing down atmospheric concentrations of CO_2 in a carbon-negative process and provides near permanent carbon storage while also improving soil productivity and reducing the need for fossil fuel-based fertilizer.[41] Improving energy efficiency[42] and expanding renewables, especially wind, also can produce fast mitigation,[43] as can improving albedo in urban areas,[44] and in deserts.[45] Most of these fast-action strategies have strong co-benefits,

----

See Advance Report, supra, at Decision XX/8. HFCs have global warming potentials hundreds to thousands of times that of CO_2 and are one of the six GHGs included in the Kyoto Protocol; they are used primarily as a replacement for ODSs phased-out under the Montreal Protocol. *See* IPCC & TEAP, *Summary for Policy Makers, in* SPECIAL REPORT, *supra,* at 3. The Parties also provided USD $490 million over three years to assist developing countries to meet their commitments, including the commitment last year to accelerate the phase-out of HCFC, which has the potential to prevent up to 16 billion tonnes of CO_2-eq. emissions if the Parties ensure climate friendly alternatives are used, and not high GWP HFCs. *See id.; see also* TEAP RESPONSE, *supra* note 40.

41. Johannes Lehmann, John Gaunt & Marco Rondon, *Bio-char Sequestration In Terrestrial Ecosystems – A Review,* 11 MITIGATION AND ADAPTATION STRATEGIES FOR GLOBAL CHANGE 403, 404 (2006). *See also,* International Biochar Initiative, *How Much Carbon Can Biochar Systems Offset—and When?, available at* http://www.biochar-international.org/images/final_carbon.pdf (Biochar could provide 3.671 Gt CO_2/yr in climate mitigation by 2040, or cumulative mitigation of more than 145 Gt CO_2 by 2040 when avoided fossil fuel CO_2 is added from co-production of bio-energy.).

42. Group of Eight Summit, Heiligendamm, Ger., June 6–8, 2007, *Growth and Responsibility in the World Economy: Summit Declaration,* ¶46 (June 7, 2007) ("Improving energy efficiency worldwide is the fastest, the most sustainable and the cheapest way to reduce greenhouse gas emissions and enhance energy security.").

43. The IPCC predicts that renewable energy sources, which have "a positive effect on energy security, employment and on air quality," will be able to provide 30–35% of the world's electricity by 2030. IPCC, *Summary for Policymakers, in* CLIMATE CHANGE 2007: MITIGATION 13 (B. Metz *et al.* eds., 2007). The IPCC reports that "wind is the fastest growing energy supply sector." IPCC, IPCC SCOPING MEETING ON RENEWABLE ENERGY SOURCES 4 (Olav Hohmeyer & Tom Trittin eds., 2008); *see also* Greenpeace & Global Wind Energy Council, GLOBAL WIND ENERGY OUTLOOK 2006, at 38 (2006) ("Under the Advanced wind energy growth projection, coupled with ambitious energy saving, wind power could be supplying 29.1% of the world's electricity by 2030 and 34.2% by 2050."). In its most recent report, the International Energy Agency concludes that "[p]reventing catastrophic and irreversible damage to the global climate ultimately requires a major decarbonisation of the world energy sources.... The energy sector will have to play the central role in curbing emissions—through major improvements in efficiency and rapid switching to renewable and other low-carbon technologies...." *See* IEA, *supra* note 34, at 37–38.

44. *See* Hashem Akbari, Surabi Menon & Arthur Rosenfeld, *Global Cooling: Increasing Worldwide Urban Albedos to Offset CO_2,* CLIMATIC CHANGE (forthcoming 2008). (If 100 large urban areas switched their roofs and pavement to highly reflective materials, the authors calculate this would "induce a negative radiative forcing of 4.4×10^{-2} Wm^{-2} equivalent to offsetting 44 Gt of emitted CO_2. A 44 Gt of emitted CO_2 offset resulting from changing the albedo of roofs and paved surfaces is worth about $1100 billion. Assuming a plausible growth rate of 1.5% in the world's CO_2-equivalent emission rate, we estimate that the 44 Gt CO_2-equivalent offset potential for cool roofs and cool pavements would counteract the effect of the growth in CO_2-equivalent emission rates for 11 years."); *see also* Hashem Akbari, Leader, Heat Island Group, Presentation at the Fifth Annual California Climate Change Conference: Global Cooling: Increasing World-wide Urban Albedos to Offset CO_2 (Sept. 9, 2008), *available at* http://www.climatechange.ca.gov/events/2008_ conference/ presentations/2008-09-09/Hashem_Akbari.pdf. In California, which sets strict energy budgets for new construction, residential and some non-residential buildings can receive energy credits toward their energy budgets for installing "cool roofs." Cool roofs can lower roof temperatures up to 100 degrees Fahrenheit, reducing energy use for air conditioning and associated urban heat islands and smog. CAL. CODE REGS. tit. 24 §118 (2007). Cool roof and reflective pavement are two of California's early action measures implementing California Assembly Bill Number 32, the Global Warming Solutions Act. *See* AIR RESOURCES BOARD, CALIFORNIA ENVIRONMENTAL PROTECTION AGENCY, EXPANDED LIST OF EARLY ACTION MEASURES TO REDUCE GREENHOUSE GAS EMISSIONS IN CALIFORNIA RECOMMENDED FOR BOARD CONSIDERATION, at C-14 (2007).

45. Takayuki Toyama & Alan Stainer, *Cosmic Heat Emission concept to "stop" global warming,* 9 INTERNATIONAL J. GLOBAL ENVIRON. ISSUES 151–153 (2009) (In light of the urgent need to cool the planet, researchers in Japan and UK propose "what is believed to be the cheapest and immediately effective concept: To lay the

such as public health benefits from black carbon reductions, earlier recovery of the ozone layer from faster ODS phase-outs and from collecting and destroying ODSs in discarded products and equipment, soil enhancement and reduced fertilizer and water use from biochar, and increased energy security and green jobs from efficiency and renewables. These co-benefits provide further incentives to act now to forestall temperature tipping points visible on the horizon.

Many countries may have some existing legal authority to begin addressing some of these strategies. Where this is the case, improving compliance can help promote near-term climate mitigation.[46] The International Network for Environmental Compliance & Enforcement recently issued *Climate Compliance Alerts* on black carbon[47] and illegally harvested timber.[48]

For further information, contact Durwood Zaelke, President (dzaelke@igsd.org), or Dennis Clare, Law Fellow (dclare@igsd.org), IGSD.

D. Science and the Supreme Court

The undisputed champion of environmental science in the U.S. today is the National Academy of Sciences,[1] which functions through its operating arm, the National Research Council. Incorporated by Act of Congress in 1863 and charged with investigating and reporting on subjects "whenever called upon by any department of the Government,"[2] the Academy today is the preeminent government advisor on questions of science, technology, and the environment. The Academy is organized into a loose network of boards, commissions, offices and councils. It is strongly staffed with scientific expertise and occupies an impressive building on Constitution Avenue in Washington, D.C. The Academy's work is carried out through hundreds of advisory committees of volunteers from segments of the scientific community.[3] Typically, the scope of work and questions to be answered by a particular study are defined by contract negotiations between the sponsoring agency and the relevant arm of the Academy.

Heat Reflecting Sheet (HRS) on Earth's surface which would, at the same time, prevent desertification.... The preparation for such a feasibility study, presented to the Chinese authorities, has already started.").

46. *See* Eighth International Conference on Environmental Compliance and Enforcement, Cape Town, S. Afr., Apr. 5–11, 2008, *Cape Town Statement*, for an affirmation of the benefits of environmental compliance and enforcement.

47. Int'l Network for Environmental Compliance and Enforcement [INECE], *Jump-Starting Climate Protection: INECE Targets Compliance with Laws Controlling Black Carbon* (June 12, 2008), *available at* http://inece.org/climate/INECEClimateComplianceAlert_BlackCarbon.pdf.

48. INECE, *Recent Amendments to U.S. Lacey Act Should Help Protect Forests Worldwide*, *available at* http://www.inece.org/climate/ClimateComplianceAlert_LaceyAct.pdf.

1. A leading if dated text on the work of the Academy is PHILIP BOFFEY, THE BRAIN BANK OF AMERICA: AN INQUIRY INTO THE POLITICS OF SCIENCE (McGraw-Hill 1975) [hereinafter cited as 1975 BRAIN BANK]. Leading journalistic discussions are D.S. Greenberg's three-part series in 156 SCIENCE 222, 360, 498 (1967); Claude E. Barfield's two-part series in 3 NATIONAL J. 101, 220 (1970); and John Walsh's two-part series in 160 SCIENCE 242, 353 (1971). *See also* B.L.R. SMITH, THE ADVISERS: SCIENTISTS IN THE POLICY PROCESS (Brookings Institute 1992) (an excellent study of science advisors other than those within the Academy). This description is elaborated upon and extended in W.H. RODGERS, JR., ENVIRONMENTAL LAW IN INDIAN COUNTRY § 1:13 at 339 (Thomson/West 2005).

2. Act of Mar. 3, 1863, ch. 111, § 3, 12 Stat. 806, 36 U.S.C.A. § 253.

3. 1975 BRAIN BANK at 11–12.

It was established in litigation that the Academy is not an "agency" and its committees are not "advisory committees" for purposes of the Freedom of Information Act and the Advisory Committee Act.[4] In 1997, this status was fixed by legislation.[5]

The Academy undertook its first major study of global warming in 1979, with a panel led by distinguished meteorologist, Jule Charney of MIT.[6] It has completed nearly two hundred additional studies since that time.[7] Here is a sample of the work of the Academy:[8]

Table 4.1

Select climate change reports from the National Academy of Sciences[9]

Understanding Climate Change Feedbacks (2003)
Board on Atmospheric Sciences and Climate (BASC)
Panel on Climate Change Feedbacks, Climate Research Committee, National Research Council

Abrupt Climate Change: Inevitable Surprises (2002)
Ocean Studies Board (OSB), Polar Research Board (PRB)
Committee on Abrupt Climate Change, National Research Council

Climate Change Science: An Analysis of Some Key Questions (2001)
Commission on Geosciences, Environment and Resources (CGER)
Committee on the Science of Climate Change, National Research Council

From Climate to Weather: Impacts on Society and Economy — Summary of a Forum, June 28, 2002, Washington, D.C. (2003)
Natural Disasters Roundtable (NDR)
A Summary to the Natural Disasters Roundtable, The National Academies

Improving the Effectiveness of U.S. Climate Modeling (2001)
Commission on Geosciences, Environment and Resources (CGER)
Committee on Climate, Ecosystems, Infectious Diseases, and Human Health, Board on Atmospheric Sciences and Climate, National Research Council.

The Science of Regional and Global Change: Putting Knowledge to Work (2001)
Policy Division (PD)
Committee on Global Change Research, National Research Council

Global Environmental Change: Research Pathways for the Next Decade (1999)
Policy Division (PD)
Committee on Global Change Research, National Research Council

Making Climate Forecasts Matter (1999)
Paul C. Stern and William E. Easterling, eds.: Panel on Human Dimensions of Seasonal-to-Interannual Climate Variability
Committee on the Human Dimensions of Global Change, National Research Council

Capacity of U.S. Climate Modeling to Support Climate Change Assessment Activities (1998)
Commission on Geosciences, Environment and Resources (CGER)

---

4. Lombardo v. Handler, 397 F. Supp. 792 (D.D.C. 1975) *affirmed per curiam* 546 F.2d 1043 (D.C. Cir. 1976, *cert. denied* 431 U.S. 932, 97 S.Ct. 2639, 53 L.Ed.2d 248 (1977) (Professor Rodgers was an attorney in the proceeding). *Court Lets Justice Mull Academy Case,* 277 Science 755 (Aug. 8, 1997) (Justice Department trying to make up its mind on question of supporting Academy in its campaign to resist FACA).

5. Pub. L. 105–153, 111 Stat. 2689 (Dec. 17, 1997), amending 5 U.S.C.A. App. 2.

6. Report of an Ad Hoc Study Group on Carbon Dioxide and Climate: A Scientific Assessment of the National Academy of Sciences (1979, Nat'l Academy of Sciences, Wash. D.C.) (The Charney Report).

7. *See* Elizabeth Kolbert, Field Notes From a Catastrophe: Man, Nature, and Climate Change 10–13 (Bloomsbury 2006).

8. Ann Rappaport & Sarah Hammond Creighton, Degrees that Matter: Climate Change and the University 58–59 (MIT Press 2007).

9. *Available from* http://books.nap.edu/collections/global_warming/index.html.

Climate Research Committee, National Research Council
Policy Implications of Greenhouse Warming: Mitigation, Adaptation, and the Science Base (1992)
National Academy of Sciences, National Academy of Engineering, Institute of Medicine (SEM)
Panel on Policy Implications of Greenhouse Warming, National Academy of Sciences, National Academy of Engineering, Institute of Medicine

---

In 2004, a group of states, local governments, and private organizations petitioned the U.S. Environmental Protection Agency (EPA) to take action to regulate four greenhouse gases, including carbon dioxide. Under Subsection 202(a)(1) of the Clean Air Act, 42 U.S.C. §7521(a)(1), the Administrator of the agency is empowered to prescribe "standards" applicable to the "emission of any air pollutant" from any class of new motor vehicles, "which may reasonably be anticipated to endanger public health or welfare." A panel of the U.S. Court of Appeals for the District of Columbia upheld EPA's discretion to deny the petition, citing a 2001 National Research Council (NRC) study for the proposition that a "causal linkage" between greenhouse gas emissions and global warming "cannot be unequivocally established." *Commonwealth of Massachusetts v. EPA*, 415 F.3d 50, 67 (D.C. Cir. 2005). Hearing the case *en banc*, seven of nine judges of the court adhered to this view. *Commonwealth of Massachusetts v. EPA*, 433 F.3d 66 (D.C. Cir. 2005) (*en banc*).

On *certiorari* to the Supreme Court, the issue of the state of the science would loom large.

The questions of what courts hear about science and what they choose to hear has never been more important. Proposals have ranged from the establishment of science courts to the recognition of the National Academy of Sciences as a kind of "Solicitor General for Science" with authority to comment to the Supreme Court on cases with a high scientific component. We always have hoped that judges selected for their political loyalties and chosen for their conspicuous ideologies will find "independence" when they "ascend" to the judiciary.

Consider this indictment of the fate of science in one of the global warming legal dramas of the times:

Brief of [Seventeen] *Amici Curiae* Climate Scientists, Supreme Court of the United States, *Commonwealth of Massachusetts v. U.S. EPA*, by John C. Dernbach, Kirsten H. Engel, Robert B. McKinstry, Jr., Stephani Tai, Counsel for *Amici Curiae* Climate Scientists, Aug. 31, 2006 (footnotes as in original):

Argument

I. The Science of Climate Change Indicates that It Is Virtually Certain that Greenhouse Gas Emissions from Human Activities Cause Global Climate Changes, Endangering Human Health and Welfare.

Neither EPA nor the court of appeals correctly applied the science of climate change to the petition for rulemaking. In its report in 2001, CLIMATE CHANGE SCIENCE, a panel of NAS/NRC unambiguously stated that it is virtually certain[7] that greenhouse gas emissions

---

7. In our discussion of climate change science, we use the terminology introduced by INTERGOVERNMENTAL PANEL ON CLIMATE CHANGE THIRD ASSESSMENT REPORT. Intergovernmental Panel on Climate Change ["IPCC"], *Technical Summary of the Working Group I Report of the Intergovernmental Panel on Climate Change* 28 n.4 (2001) ("In this Technical Summary and in the Summary for Policymakers, the following words have been used where appropriate to indicate judgmental estimates of confidence: virtually certain (greater than 99% chance that a result is true); very likely (90–99% chance); likely (66–90% chance); medium likelihood (33–66% chance); unlikely (10–33% chance); very unlikely (1–10% chance); exceptionally unlikely (less than 1% chance). The reader is referred to individual chapters for more details.").

from human activities cause global climate changes. These emissions increase the risk of adverse effects on health and welfare. To aid this Court in understanding the foregoing conclusion, we first clarify what scientific knowledge informs us about anthropogenic climate change.

1. The basic physics underlying the greenhouse effect is firmly established. Two principles in particular are as certain as any phenomena in planetary sciences. First, particular atmospheric gases ("greenhouse gases") absorb radiation that otherwise would be lost to space, and re-radiate it back to the ground. A planet with those gases in its atmosphere is thus warmer at the surface than it would be without them. Second, greater atmospheric concentrations of greenhouse gases, all other things being equal, cause higher temperatures at the surface. The Earth is habitable for its current life forms in part because natural levels of greenhouse gases in the atmosphere warm the surface.

2. Over the last two centuries, it is virtually certain that human activities have increased amounts of important greenhouse gases (primarily CO_2, CH_4, N_2O, and fluorocarbons)[8] in the atmosphere to levels not seen in all of prior human experience, and likely not seen for 3 million years.

3. It is likely or very likely[9] that human-induced increases in these greenhouse gases are already causing global climate to warm. Human activities likely caused most of the approximately 0.6 °C (1.1 °F) rise over the 20th century. J.A. 151, CLIMATE CHANGE SCIENCE at 1. The mean ocean temperature has risen by 0.05 °C (0.09 °F), global average sea level has risen by 0.1 to 0.2 meters (1/3 to 2/3 feet) over the 20th century, and snow cover and Arctic ice have decreased by about 10% and 10–15%, respectively, since the late 1960s (when data first became available for this measurement). *Id.* at 16. A variety of other climate factors are changing consistent with warming induced by greenhouse gases. By contrast, we know of no measures of climate on the global scale that indicate cooling.

4. It is virtually certain that what has been observed so far is only the beginning, and that continued greenhouse gas emissions along current trajectories will cause additional warming of the earth system as a whole. The average time for removal from the atmosphere of added carbon dioxide is measured in centuries. It is very likely that such perturbation would cause the rate of surface warming and sea level rise in the 21st century to be substantially larger and faster than that experienced in the 20th century, without precedent in the past 10,000 years.

5. The first sentences of CLIMATE CHANGE SCIENCE state:

> Greenhouse gases are accumulating in Earth's atmosphere as a result of human activities, causing surface air temperatures and subsurface ocean temperatures to rise. Temperatures are, in fact, rising. The changes observed over the last several decades are likely mostly due to human activities, but we cannot rule out that some significant part of these changes is also a reflection of natural variability. Human-induced warming and associated sea level rises are expected to continue through the 21st century. Secondary effects are suggested by computer model simulations and basic physical reasoning. These include increases in rainfall rates and increased susceptibility of semi-arid regions to drought. The impacts of these changes will be critically dependent on the magnitude of the warming and the rate with which it occurs.

---

8. Water vapor is a greenhouse gas and is an important amplifier of climate change because its atmospheric concentrations tend to increase when the atmosphere and surface waters warm up. Anthropogenic emissions of water vapor to the atmosphere by automobiles and other combustion sources do not significantly affect global atmospheric concentrations of water vapor relative to the natural evaporation and condensation processes, and thus they do not "cause, or contribute," to pollution implicated in anthropogenic climate change. 42 U.S.C. 7521(a)(1).

9. *See* note 7, *supra.*

J.A. 151, Climate Change Science at 1.

6. Although the general link between increased greenhouse gases in the atmosphere and increased warming of the earth system is virtually certain, the complexity of the climate system means that predictions of specific details that follow from this general link are subject to varying degrees of certainty. Among the more certain predictions are the following:

a. It is likely, based on both models and on data from the ice ages over the last 400,000 years, that if atmospheric carbon dioxide doubled from pre-industrial times, and rose no further, the long-term rise of global average surface temperature (the "climate sensitivity") would be between 1.5 and 4.5 °C (2.7–8.1 °F). J.A. 166, Climate Change Science at 7.

b. In the absence of emissions reductions, however, carbon dioxide concentrations in the atmosphere are very likely to increase to much more than twice pre-industrial values, and the consequent rise in global average temperature during the 21st century, projected to be 1.4 to 5.8 °C (2.5 to 10.4 °F), will likely continue to higher values beyond the year 2100. IPCC, *Technical Summary*, at 69.

c. This amount of warming in 6.a and 6.b is very likely to drive melting of arctic ice sheets and further increases in global average sea level by 2100, with continued sea-level rise in the decades and centuries following 2100.

d. The anticipated sea level rise, especially when combined with likely increases in hurricane intensities, would exacerbate storm surges and have direct, negative impacts on health and welfare in the United States, and globally. These negative impacts would be concentrated in low-lying coastal regions, such as Cape Cod, Massachusetts, the Gulf coast, and southern Florida.

e. Rising temperatures are also likely to lead to increases in extreme weather events (especially heat waves, and associated heat-related deaths) and altered patterns of rainfall (*e.g.*, droughts and floods) that will disrupt natural and agricultural ecosystems, and increase the risk of extinction of animal and plant species.

f. Ocean acidity is very likely to increase by several tenths of a pH unit due to continued uptake of carbon dioxide, and this acidification is likely to cause substantial stress to key marine organisms, and hence to whole marine ecosystems, particularly in cold water regions. Although this is an impact of increasing levels of greenhouse gases, it is not an atmospheric climate change and therefore was not addressed in Climate Change Science.

g. Ground level ozone ("smog") levels (and associated risks to human health) are very likely to increase with temperature, especially in the Northeastern United States, where many areas currently experience ozone levels that exceed EPA Clean Air Act standards on hot summer days.

7. The possibilities of the climate changes above have been carefully and extensively assessed, and there is a broad scientific consensus that these changes are likely or very likely. This consensus is clearly expressed in Climate Change Science. It is harder to determine how long it may take for these changes to occur, and what the precise magnitude of the impacts may be. The climate system has a great deal of inertia (especially in the ice sheets and oceans), and thus the effects of greenhouse gases already in the atmosphere are delayed. Emissions of GHGs commit the climate to future warming long after release to the atmosphere.

8. Apart from the likely, very likely, and virtually certain gradual climate changes outlined in points 1–7, there is also an as yet unquantifiable probability that continued greenhouse gas emissions will trigger abrupt climate change surprises that could very rapidly impose large impacts on ecosystems and human welfare and health. The NAS/NRC issued a detailed report (*Abrupt Climate Change*) on this matter in 2002, showing that abrupt climate changes (*e.g.*, large regional cooling or warming, widespread droughts, shifts in hurricane frequency or flood regimes that occur in only a decade or so) are possible because they have happened in the past, at the dawn of

human history and before. We do not understand these switches very well, but there is a finite but unknown risk that continued emission of greenhouse gases will trigger a climate change surprise.

9. The science of climate change (including the uncertainties) implies that delay in reducing greenhouse gas emissions will very likely increase the risks to human societies. Early steps to reduce greenhouse gas emissions to levels below current trajectories will certainly reduce the magnitude of climate change that would otherwise be caused. Because of inertia in the climate system, it will be many decades before effects of emission reductions are realized.

10. Delaying reductions in greenhouse gas emissions heightens the risk to human welfare because climate inertia commits us to large-scale, long term (centuries) climate change consequences before the exact nature of those consequences can be known. The heightened risk of delaying emissions reductions is clearly expressed in CLIMATE CHANGE SCIENCE. J.A. 151–152, CLIMATE CHANGE SCIENCE at 1.

11. Stratospheric ozone depletion and the Antarctic "ozone hole" illustrate how both surprise and inertia may increase the risks from unmitigated global environmental change. Models predicted that the emission of chlorofluorocarbons (CFCs) and other chlorinated halocarbons by human activities would gradually deplete stratospheric ozone. No model predicted the stratospheric ozone hole in advance of its discovery in the mid-1980s. The reality of ozone depletion turned out to be worse than even the worst-case modeled scenario because none of the models anticipated the novel chemistry of ozone depletion via polar stratospheric clouds above the south (and north) poles. The CFC phase-out of the 1990s should allow the ozone hole to recover, but it will take about 75 years, a time lag reflecting the long lifetimes of CFCs (inertia preventing recovery). It is noteworthy that early regulation by the United States (beginning in the 1970s, before the ozone hole was discovered) certainly reduced the risks and damages that unfolded in the case of stratospheric ozone depletion.

12. Developments since the NAS/NRC reports of 2001 and 2002 have only reinforced the finding that recent climate changes are "likely mostly due to human activities."[10] J.A. 151, CLIMATE CHANGE SCIENCE at 1.

a. The five warmest years since pre-industrial times were 1998, 2002, 2003, 2004, and 2005 (2005 is the warmest overall), and the reduction of ice cover in the Arctic has accelerated.[11]

b. A recent NAS/NRC report confirmed temperature trends discussed in CLIMATE CHANGE SCIENCE, concluding that the global mean surface temperature during the last few decades of the 20th century was higher than any comparable period in the past four centuries, and, likely so, in the past 1000 years. *Reconstructions* at 2, Report in Brief; *id.* at 3.

c. The question of the apparent discrepancy between late 20th century temperature rise at the surface, versus satellite-derived temperatures above the surface, regarded as a puzzle in CLI-

---

10. See, *e.g.*, JOINT SCIENCE ACADEMIES' STATEMENT: GLOBAL RESPONSE TO CLIMATE CHANGE, *available at* http:// www.nationalacademies.org/onpi/06072005.pdf (June 2005) (signed by the presidents of the national scientific academies in Brazil, Canada, China, France, Germany, India, Italy, Japan, Russia, United Kingdom, and the United States). The STATEMENT begins:

Climate change is real. There will always be uncertainty in understanding a system as complex as the world's climate. However there is now strong evidence that significant global warming is occurring. The evidence comes from direct measurements of rising surface air temperatures and subsurface ocean temperatures and from phenomena such as increases in average global sea levels, retreating glaciers, and changes to many physical and biological systems. It is likely that most of the warming in recent decades can be attributed to human activities (PCC 2001). This warming has already led to changes in the Earth's climate.

Id. (emphasis added).

11. James Hansen, Makiko Sato, Reto Ruedy, Ken Lo, David W. Lea & Martin Medina-Elizade, *Global temperature change*, 103 PROC. OF THE NAT'L ACAD. OF SCI. 14288, 14288 (2006); J.C. Comiso, *Arctic Warming Signals from Satellite Observations*, 61–3 WEATHER 70–76 (2006).

MATE CHANGE SCIENCE, has been resolved. A recent comprehensive scientific reevaluation, which corrected errors in the initial satellite estimates, concluded that "all available data sets show that both the surface and the troposphere have warmed." U.S. Climate Change Science Program, TEMPERATURE TRENDS IN THE LOWER ATMOSPHERE: STEPS FOR UNDERSTANDING AND RECONCILING DIFFERENCES 1 (Apr. 2006).

II. EPA and the Court of Appeals Mischaracterized the Science of Climate Change, Making It Appear More Uncertain Than It Actually Is.

EPA relied on the NAS/NRC 2001 report, CLIMATE CHANGE SCIENCE, as the authoritative source of scientific information in its decision to deny the petition for rulemaking. The court of appeals cited no other source than CLIMATE CHANGE SCIENCE for its conclusion regarding scientific uncertainty. But EPA and the court of appeals mischaracterized the scientific analysis in CLIMATE CHANGE SCIENCE and arrived at conclusions sharply at variance with the scientific judgments in the report.

To understand the magnitude of their mischaracterization of CLIMATE CHANGE SCIENCE, one must first examine the nature of scientific uncertainty. Scientific knowledge is developed incrementally, using experiment and observation to test and refine hypotheses. A large part of the work of science is directed towards understanding and quantifying uncertainties. The *goal is to place bounds on future outcomes.* An hypothesis is deemed "virtually certain" if the predicted outcome is expected to occur for 99% or more of repeated trials, "very likely" for 90–99%, and "likely" for 66–90%.[12] Absolute certainty is impossible *in principle* in climate science, as in all fields of science.[13] Moreover, there is only a single "trial" with respect to earth's climate, so strict statistical measures of likelihood cannot be applied. These characteristics of scientific knowledge must be expertly considered, and certainties and uncertainties carefully balanced, when applying the protective approach required for decisions to regulate under the Clean Air Act. However, in its denial of the petition for rulemaking, EPA presented an inexpert and unbalanced discussion, and reached conclusions not supported by the scientific evidence it was purporting to use.

A. EPA's Decision

EPA's decision misrepresented the findings in CLIMATE CHANGE SCIENCE, which EPA cited as the only source of evidence in its discussion of scientific uncertainty. See Pet. App. 82, 68 Fed. Reg. 52,922, 52,930 (Sept. 8, 2003) ("We rely in this decision on NRC's objective and independent assessment of the relevant science."); *see also id.* (adding that nothing received during the public comment period "causes us to question the validity of the NRC's conclusions"). CLIMATE CHANGE SCIENCE encompasses both the more certain and the less certain elements of the science, and uncertainties are described explicitly, as is the norm in scientific reports. Thus, it is possible to quote selectively from the report to make the scientific conclusions appear either more or less certain than they actually are.

EPA admitted to three important observations about the global climate: (1) that "concentrations of GHGs are increasing in the atmosphere as a result of human activities," *id.* (citing J.A. 170–180, CLIMATE CHANGE SCIENCE at 9–12), (2) that a "diverse array of evidence points to a warming of global surface air temperatures," *id.* (quoting J.A. 190, CLIMATE CHANGE SCIENCE at 16), and (3) that "the magnitude of the observed warming is large in comparison to natural variability," Pet. App. A83, 68 Fed. Reg. at 52,930 (quoting J.A. 193, CLIMATE CHANGE SCIENCE at 17).

---

12. *See* note 7, *supra.*

13. *See* Erica Beecher-Monas, *The Heuristics of Intellectual Due Process: A Primer for Triers of Science,* 75 N.Y.U.L. REV. 1563, 1581 (2000) ("Scientists understand that fluctuations, instability, multiple choices, and limited predictability are inherent at all levels of observation.") (internal quotation marks omitted).

However, EPA omitted the essential scientific conclusion that constitutes the core of *Climate Change Science:* that these separate observations are causally linked. This is a fundamental omission. It is as if a summary of Newton's Principia—which advanced the theory of gravitation as the common explanation for how apples fall to earth and planets move in the heavens—repeated Newton's description of the motions of apples and planets, but never got around to mentioning gravity. Isaac Newton, Principia Mathematica Philosophiae Naturalis (W.A. Kaminski trans., World Scientific 1987) (1729).

EPA in particular omitted mention of the following two pivotal conclusions. First, the NAS report unambiguously links already observed climate warming, and related impacts, damages, and risks, to human emissions of greenhouse gases. "*The changes observed over the last several decades are likely mostly due to human activities*, but we cannot rule out that some significant part of these changes is also a reflection of natural variability." J.A. 151, Climate Change Science at 1(emphasis added). The key conclusion, in the first part of this sentence, is never cited by EPA. Second, after listing a number of impacts and damages that are likely to occur in response to human-caused climate change, Climate Change Science states, "Hence national policy decisions made now, and in the longer-term future will influence the extent of any damage suffered by vulnerable human populations and ecosystems later in this century." J.A. 152, Climate Change Science at 1. Remarkably, EPA ignored this scientific judgment, which clearly indicated the panel's concern that dangerous human-caused climate change is likely[14] already underway with larger effects committed for the future, particularly if action should not be taken to limit emissions.

EPA focused instead on a statement in the 2001 report that a "causal linkage between the buildup of greenhouse gases in the atmosphere and the observed climate changes during the 20th century cannot be unequivocally established." J.A. 193, Climate Change Science at 17 (cited in Pet. App. A83, 68 Fed. Reg. at 52,930). But EPA was petitioned to initiate rulemaking under Section 202(a)(1) of the Clean Air Act, which requires regulation of motor vehicle pollutants that "may reasonably be *anticipated* to endanger public health or welfare." 42 U.S.C. 7521(a)(1) (emphasis added). It is not required that the link between observed warming and increased greenhouse gas concentrations be "unequivocally established" in order to ascertain whether greenhouse gas emissions "may reasonably be anticipated to harm" human health and welfare under Section 202(a)(1). As noted above, if "unequivocal" means "absolutely certain," this is impossible for climate science, just as absolute certainty is impossible to show for the link between smoking and cancer, or for the links to impacts of many other pollutants that are already regulated under the "reasonably be anticipated to endanger" framework.

EPA also ignored the two-sidedness of scientific uncertainty. Outcomes may turn out better than our best current prediction, but it is just as possible that environmental and health damages will be more severe than best predictions, as happened in the examples of stratospheric ozone depletion (discussed *supra*) and of lead toxicity from automobile emissions (discussed *infra*). Thus, it is wrong to infer that, because a prediction of an undesirable outcome is uncertain, the associated risks are not worth regulating.

EPA's use of selective quotations and its unbalanced treatment of uncertainty allowed it to draw conclusions that are opposed to the actual scientific conclusions of Climate Change Science. EPA stated: "Substantial scientific uncertainties limit our ability to assess each of these factors [that contribute to climate change] and to separate out those changes resulting from natural

---

14. *See* note 7, *supra*.

variability from those that are directly the result of increases in anthropogenic GHGs." Pet. App. A84, 86 Fed. Reg. at 52,930. EPA's conclusion, drawn from this statement, was: "Until more is understood about the causes, extent, and significance of climate change and the potential options for addressing it, EPA believes that it is inappropriate to regulate GHG emissions from motor vehicles." Pet. App. A86, 86 Fed. Reg. at 52,931.

EPA's conclusion implies that there is no significant risk in waiting for future studies. This conclusion directly conflicts with the plain language of Climate Change Science, the authority that EPA claimed to use. The uncertainties are important, but so are the certainties and near-certainties, and the risks of delaying reductions in GHG emissions. In environmental science generally, and climate science in particular, critical decisions must be made in a timely fashion to protect the health and welfare of the population, without absolute certainty or multiple trials, and without the false luxury of waiting for the damage to be observed.

The need for timely decisions in the presence of uncertainty was recognized explicitly by Congress in crafting the Clean Air Act § 202(a)(1). Climate Change Science assessed the science holistically and concluded that human-caused climate change had most likely already occurred and that serious future damage was highly probable.

By failing to properly balance scientific knowledge and uncertainties, and to acknowledge the links between GHGs, climate change, and damage to human health and welfare discussed in Climate Change Science, EPA fundamentally distorted the meaning of the report. There is simply no sign in EPA's decision of the strong base of scientific knowledge described in Climate Change Science. The core conclusions of Climate Change Science (omitted in EPA's discussion) dovetail with the requirements of the Clean Air Act § 202(a)(1). EPA's denial of petition to regulate was based on distortion and misrepresentation of the scientific findings of Climate Change Science.

B. Court of Appeals Decision

The court of appeals assumed that EPA has the statutory authority to regulate greenhouse gas emissions from motor vehicles, but decided that EPA had properly exercised its discretion in refusing to regulate these emissions. In upholding EPA's decision, the court of appeals relied on several factors, including scientific uncertainty. Pet App. 12, *Massachusetts*, 415 F.3d at 57. The court of appeals, relying on EPA's misrepresentation of Climate Change Science, also mischaracterizes the findings of the NAS/NRC panel by emphasizing uncertainties in climate change science while failing even to mention the existence of fundamental areas of certainty or consensus. The court then used scientific uncertainty (which it had mischaracterized) as a basis for upholding EPA's decision. Pet. App. 13, *id.* at 58.

Judge Randolph's opinion for the court cites Climate Change Science six times, with these citations selected in a way that omits important scientific context. For example, the opinion states, "The National Research Council [NAS/NRC] concluded that 'a causal linkage' between greenhouse gas emissions and global warming 'cannot be unequivocally established,'" excluding the intervening words "between the buildup of greenhouse gases in the atmosphere and the observed climate changes in the 20th century." Pet. App. 12, *id.* at 57. Without the intervening words, the reader is given the false impression that the quote applies to a completely different issue, the *general* link between greenhouse gas concentrations and global warming. In fact, as we (including those of us who were members of the 2001 NAS/NRC panel) emphasize above, this link is virtually certain, even though uncertainties attach to the exact magnitude and timing of human-induced climate warming.

III. EPA Did Not Apply the Standard of Scientific Evidence Set Forth in the Clean Air Act.

. . . .

On *certiorari*, the Supreme Court ruled[1] in a 5:4 opinion by Mr. Justice Stevens that the State of Massachusetts has standing to seek relief under the Clean Air Act to protect its territory from rising seas in the same sense that the State of Georgia could bring a lawsuit to defend against incoming SO_2 from a copper smelter.[2] On the particular question of redressability, it was enough that the prospect of a legal victory could alleviate the injury if not fully prevent it.

On the merits, the court holds that greenhouse gas emissions (such as CO_2) are "pollutants" under the Clean Air Act and that the EPA has a duty to regulate "emissions" from new motor vehicles upon a finding of "endangerment."[3] Thus far, according to the majority, EPA "has offered no reasoned explanation for its refusal to decide whether greenhouse gases cause or contribute to climate change."[4]

Chief Justice Roberts, joined by Scalia, Thomas, and Alito, JJs, dissents, insisting that the legal challenges are "nonjusticiable."[5] He takes umbrage at the invocation of *Tennessee Copper* to develop a nontraditional role of standing.[6] And he shows how what he describes as "traditional standing" (dating perhaps to the *Lujan* decision in 1992)[7] creates a set of interlocking traps for would-be plaintiffs:[8]

> Petitioners' reliance on Massachusetts's loss of coastal land as their injury in fact for standing purposes creates insurmountable problems for them with respect to causation and redressability....
>
> ....
>
> Redressability is even more problematic. To the tenuous link between petitioners' alleged injury and the indeterminate fractional domestic emissions at issue here, add the fact that petitioners cannot meaningfully predict what will come of the 80 percent of global greenhouse gas emissions that originate outside the United States ... [T]he domestic emissions at issue here may become an increasingly marginal portion of global emissions, and any decreases produced by petitioners' desired standards are likely to be overwhelmed many times over by emissions increases elsewhere in the world.
>
> ....
>
> Petitioners' difficulty in demonstrating causation and redressability is not surprising given the evident mismatch between the source of their alleged injury—catastrophic global warming—and the narrow subject matter of the Clean Air Act provision at issue in this suit. This mismatch suggests that petitioners' true goal for this litigation may be more symbolic than anything else.

---

1. Massachusetts v. E.P.A., 549 U.S. 497, 127 S.Ct. 1438, 167 L.Ed.2d 248 (2007).

2. 549 U.S. at 520 & n.17 (discussing the famous environmental case of Georgia v. Tennessee Copper Co., 206 U.S. 230 (1907)).

3. *See* 549 U.S. at 527–49, discussing Subsection 302(g), 42 U.S.C.A § 7602(g) (defining "air pollutant") and Subsection 202(a)(1), *id.* § 7521(a)(1) (directing Administrator to regulate the "emission" of "any air pollutant" from any class of "new motor vehicles" upon a determination that it may "cause, or contribute to, air pollution which may reasonably be anticipated to endanger public health or welfare").

4. 549 U.S. at 534.

5. 549 U.S. at 535 (1).

6. 549 U.S. at 537 (3) ("The Court has to go back a full century in an attempt to justify its novel standing rule, but even there it comes up short").

7. Lujan v. Defenders of Wildlife, 504 U.S. 555 (1992).

8. 549 U.S. at 542–43, 545, 546–47.

The dissent concludes with a denunciation of the old *SCRAP* standing case.[9] Its choice of language would apply more fittingly to the repudiations of *SCRAP* the high court has given us in the last thirty years:[10]

> Over time, *SCRAP* became emblematic not of the looseness of Article III standing requirements, but of how utterly manipulable they are if not taken seriously as a matter of judicial self-restraint. *SCRAP* made standing seem a lawyer's game, rather than a fundamental limitation ensuring that courts function as courts and not intrude on the politically accountable branches. Today's decision is *SCRAP* for a new generation.

Mr. Justice Scalia (joined by Chief Justice Roberts and Thomas and Alito, JJs), writes a separate dissent, giving wondrous and strange instruction on the meaning of "air pollutant," "air pollution,"[11] and the adequacy of EPA's reasons for wanting no part of these petitions.

Notes

1. Q. How many law review articles have cited the Supreme Court's decision in *Massachusetts v. EPA*, 549 U.S. 497, 127 S. Ct. 1438 (2007)?

A. 234 or 333.

Search for William H. Rodgers, Jr., Oct. 12, 2008, by Melia Cossette, Intern Reference Librarian, Marian Gould Gallagher Law Library, University of Washington School of Law (databases: Shepard's On Lexis or Westlaw Secondary Sources and Law Reviews).

2. *See* Robert V. Percival, Massachusetts v. EPA: *Escaping the Common Law's Growing Shadow*, 2007 Sup. Ct. Rev. 111, 159–60 (2008):

> Like the litigation in *Georgia v. Tennessee Copper* a century ago, *Massachusetts v. EPA* should spawn renewed efforts to confront a widely acknowledged environmental problem that no court could possibly hope to solve by itself. In the face of what many believe to be the most widespread and serious environmental problem humans face, the Court has taken a modest step to enter the vacuum left by executive inaction. Like its decision a century ago in *Tennessee Copper*, the Court's *Massachusetts v. EPA* decision is a victory for states seeking federal help to begin the long process of combating a problem that extends beyond their jurisdiction. With its decision in *Massachusetts v. EPA* the Court returns in part to the role it played in the early twentieth century by forcing action, at the behest of a state, when no other federal institution was responding to a serious environmental problem.

3. Bradford Mank, *Should States Have Greater Standing Rights Than Ordinary Citizens?* Massachusetts v. EPA's *New Standing Test for States*, 49 Wm. & Mary L. Rev. 1701, 1780 (2008) (footnote omitted):

------

9. United States v. Students Challenging Regulatory Agency Procedures (SCRAP), 412 U.S. 669 (1973), with background in a book by Neil Thomas Proto, To a High Court: The Tumult and Choices that Led to United States of America v. SCRAP (Hamilton Books 2006).

10. 549 U.S. at 548 (footnote omitted).

11. 549 U.S. at 560:

EPA's conception of "air pollution"—focusing on impurities in the "ambient air" "at ground level or near the surface of the earth"—is perfectly consistent with the natural meaning of that term.

The relaxed standing rule for states in *Massachusetts* will make it easier for states and state attorneys general (AGs) to file suit in federal courts.

4. Andrew Long, *Standing & Consensus: Globalism in* Massachusetts v. EPA, 23 J. ENVTL. LAW & LIT. 73, 74 (2008):

> Despite the considerable scholarly attention given to the case in the months since it was decided, three potentially crucial points have received relatively little attention: (1) the integration of an environmentalist world view into standing analysis (by permitting a challenge to one input in an interconnected global system); (2) near embrace of scientific consensus on climate change that runs contrary to professed agency uncertainty; and (3) recognition of EPA's significant, but incomplete role in resolving a global environmental problem.

5. The response to the ruling in *Massachusetts v. EPA* has been remarkable and prolific. Obviously, the U.S. government is capable of directional change. Juliet Eilperin, *EPA Presses Obama to Regulate Warming Under Clean Air Act*, WASH. POST, March 24, 2009, p.1, col. 1.

E. The Law-Science Interface

DAVID SHEARMAN & JOSEPH WAYNE SMITH, THE CLIMATE CHANGE CHALLENGE AND THE FAILURE OF DEMOCRACY at xiii–xv (Praeger 2007) (Preface) (Politics and the Environment series) (footnote omitted):

Preface

This book documents the near certainty of climate change, its serious consequences, and the failure of democratic societies to respond adequately. A new planet is about to be created, one that is inhospitable, producing less food and water and without the necessary ecological services to support the world's population. In February of 2007, the first part of the 4th "Report of the Intergovernmental Panel on Climate Change" was published. A consensus of 2,300 climate scientists, many of them American, reported more severe changes than in the previous report in 2001 and stressed an urgency to act.

We have known about these impending problems for several decades. Each year the certainty of the science has increased, yet we have failed to act appropriately to the threat. We have analyzed the reasons for this indolence. This understanding will lead you to ask yourself if Western civilization can survive in its present state of prosperity, health, and well-being, or will it soon suffer the fate of all previous civilizations — to become a mere page in history?

We will demand from you the reader, far more than your comprehension of the consequences of climate change and the workings of democracy. You will need to examine the limits of your introspection and the motivation bestowed upon you by biology and culture. The questions to be asked are difficult. You have a commitment to your children, but are you committed to the well-being of future generations and those you may never see, such as your great-grandchildren? If so are you prepared to change your lifestyle now? Are you prepared to see society and its governance change if this is a necessary solution?

It is salutary to think where this issue sits in your priority list. Examine how much of your time each day is spent considering matters of importance to you. If we exclude time spent in work and sleep, what proportion of your thinking time is devoted to your career, reputation, colleagues, finances, car, future possessions, prowess, and—not least—sex, desire, and food? Of course you love your partner and children, but how much time does your brain spend on them? If your gender is female, chances are that your priorities have a different emphasis with much more time thinking of relationships and family. We may make ourselves comfortable by saying the future of humanity is a concern to us, but estimate truthfully to yourself how many seconds per day you think about it. How much time compared to your indulgencies of entertainment, television, and the delights and addictions of consumerism?

Human nature being as it is, we do not consider that these world issues threaten us until they impinge directly upon us. The crushing drought in Australia has coincided with a surge of interest in climate change. Hurricane Katrina had a similar though smaller impact on climate change discussion in the United States, but has the issue permeated the people or press of New York or the citizens of Delhi or Toronto? Has it superseded the Grammies or Oscars in public interest? The increase in wild fires in California, British Colombia, Australia, and Iberia has concentrated the minds of inhabitants because the threat is recurrent and has increased visibly. However when it happens to someone else, even though we have played a part in its genesis, it scarcely impinges on our thoughts, unlike those poor souls already subject to the inundation of a South Sea island due to rising sea levels, or the melting of the Inuit land and loss of their livelihood.

In simple terms we have a conflict of interest between our personal needs and desires and the recognition of what we must do personally to alleviate this threat. We are like many patients informed of a diagnosis of cancer. We understand the diagnosis but engage in denial. In the same way death is dismissed when it crosses our minds. Admittedly, denial has been overcome in some countries with the development of alternative fuels, but even those nations with good intent have failed to stem the rising flow of greenhouse emissions.

If conflict of interest presents a problem to all of us, this conflict is an even greater problem to those in government. This conflict explains why government rhetoric is followed by catatonia. Not only does the politician have to contend with the personal conflicts of interest that we all experience, but he or she has a career conflict over reelection, the consuming motive of most. Reelection depends upon economic growth and a booming economy, the root cause of climate change and the rapid depletion of resources available to us. The fundamental political dilemma is illustrated by the view of British Prime Minister Blair, expressed at the Economic Forum in Davos in February 2005 to the effect that if we were to put forward a solution to climate change, something that would involve drastic cuts in economic growth or standards of living, it would not matter how justified it was, it would simply not be agreed to. In other words, democracy itself has a big problem. This negative response is seen to be much more vigorous when we consider the words and actions of U.S. President George Bush or Australian Prime Minister John Howard. Nothing can be done that will harm industry or jobs. Comprehension does not extend to the possibility that there may be fewer future jobs unless action is taken. In this book we provide an analysis of this situation.

This political attitude also explains the obsession with technological development. It offers a fix without having to make difficult and unpopular decisions. Climate change, like all other problems that humanity has encountered, will be solved by technology—pump the carbon dioxide underground and launch space ships with mirrors to reflect sunlight. This solution fits the paradigm of development and progress and more importantly absolves us from any sacrifice of our profligacy. But it won't work this time because there are so many interlocking problems that cannot respond to a technological fix. These problems depend upon population expansion and consumption of natural resources.

Perhaps the most important conflict of interest occurs within the corporate empires, the boiler rooms of our productive society. You will learn from our analysis that profits and responsibility to shareholders rank above all other responsibilities whatever the public face of corporate responsibility. To date, evidence suggests that the gulf cannot be bridged.

Ultimately we are enclosed in an autonomous market economy; no one can flourish outside it and the consequences of its never-ending growth are obvious to all who are prepared to think about it. This intricate form of human organization has become like the ant hill, where the brain ruling the paradigm is the collective neural tissue of all ants, working in concert and eating the world. Fortunately there are predators for ants. The autonomous human brain is "the market."

....

---

1. Science in the Bureaucracy: Suppress, Manipulate, Modify and "Spin"

Ross Gelbspan, Boiling Point: How Politicians, Big Oil and Coal, Journalists, and Activists Have Fueled the Climate Crisis—And What We Can Do to Avert Disaster xvii (Basic Books 2004):

> It is an excruciating experience to watch the planet fall apart piece by piece in the face of persistent and pathological denial.

Mark Bowen, Censoring Science: Inside the Political Attack on Dr. James Hansen and the Truth of Global Warming 239 (Dutton 2008) [hereinafter 2008 Bowen Censoring Science]:

> The tobacco experience does not bode well for a solution to global warming. The industry succeeded in postponing meaningful action on smoking for more than three decades, at the cost of hundreds of thousands of lives per year.

Brown and Williamson tobacco company, quoted in Union of Concerned Scientists, Smoke, Mirrors & Hot Air: How Exxon Mobil Uses Big Tobacco's Tactics to Manufacture Uncertainty on Climate Science (Jan. 2007):

> Doubt is our product, since it is the best means of competing with the "body of fact" that exists in the minds of the general public. It is also the means of establishing a controversy.

David Michaels, Doubt Is Their Product: How Industry's Assault on Science Threatens Your Health xii (Oxford Un. Press 2008) (footnote omitted):

> To give credit where credit is due, the sound science/junk science dichotomy has worked wonders as a public relations gimmick and has gained widespread acceptance in the current debate over the use of scientific evidence in public policy.

a. NASA (National Aeronautics & Space Administration)

George Monbiot, Heat: How to Stop the Planet From Burning, *Forward* to the U.S. Edition iv (South End Press 2007):

> After the war, almost everyone becomes a member of the Resistance.

> Under the [G.W.] Bush administration, the science of climate change has been treated much as the Catholic Church, during Galileo's lifetime, handled the science of planetary motion.

> In February 2007, two senior White House officials published an open letter seeking to correct inaccurate stories in the press "that the President's concern about climate

change is new." "In fact," they reported, "climate change has been a top priority since the President's first year in office." To prove it, they had found 37 words Bush said about the subject in 2001; 45 words in 2002; and 32 words in January 2007. At that point he had even managed to say "climate change." This demonstrated, they claimed, that he has shown "continued leadership on the issue."

2008 Bowen Censoring Science at 297, quoting Michael Griffin, head of NASA (May 2007) and leader of the organization that does more climate-related research than any other entity on earth. Mr. Griffin says he is not sure global warming is a problem "we must wrestle with." This quotation appears in full in the Holly Doremus article at page 97.

See further NASA climate blame, New Scientist, June 7, 2008, p. 7:

> Managers of the press office at NASA's HQ systematically downplayed news on climate research between 2004 and 2006, according to the space agency's watchdog. News on climate science was "marginalized or mischaracterized," according to the Office of the Inspector General, and NASA climate scientists were prevented from speaking freely. The managers in question no longer work at the agency.

b. NOAA (National Oceanic & Atmospheric Administration)

House Comm. on Oversight & Governmental Reform, *Political Interference With Climate Change Science Under the Bush Administration* (Dec. 2007) (Rep. Henry A Waxman):

- White House Censored Climate Change Scientists
  - At NOAA, media requests relating to climate change were routed through the Council on Environmental Quality (formerly environmental champion, more recently environmental underminer).
  - *Id.* at ii: "The White House played a major role in crafting the August 2003 EPA legal opinion disavowing authority to regulate greenhouse gases. CEQ Chairman James Connaugton personally edited the draft legal opinion."
  - *Id.* at 6: "CEQ was the ultimate decision-maker on whether an interview request would be granted."
  - *Id.* at 7: "After Hurricane Katrina, there was a concerted effort by the White House and Department of Commerce to direct media inquiries to scientists who did not think climate change was related to increased hurricane intensity."
  - *Id.* at 9: "selectively providing media access to government scientists who would deny [the existence of a link between global warming and hurricane intensity]."

c. CEQ (Council on Environmental Quality)

2008 Bowen Censoring Science at 111–12:

> On June 19, 2003, Andy Revkin and his colleague Katharine Seelye at The New York Times reported that none other than the Council on Environmental Quality had done some serious editing to a section on global warming in the Environmental Protection Agency's first-ever report on the state of the environment, which had been requested two years earlier by [administrator Christie Whitman] … In the end, the staff at EPA refused to agree to the edits, and the entire section on global warming was dropped from the state of the environment report.…

Richard Cowan, *Senator says White House in climate change cover up*, Reuters, *available at* http://uk.reuters.com/article/latestCrisis/idUKN0831209020080708 (last visited 7/30/2008):

"This cover-up is being directed from the White House and the office of the president," said Sen. Barbara Boxer, the California Democrat who chairs the Senate Environment and Public Works Committee.

At issue is a preliminary finding by the EPA last December that "greenhouse gases may reasonably be anticipated to endanger public welfare, according to Jason Burnett, the agency's former associate deputy administrator who appeared at a news conference with Boxer."

GEORGE MONBIOT, HEAT: HOW TO STOP THE PLANET FROM BURNING 39 (South End Press 2007) (footnotes omitted):

The NEW YORK TIMES later discovered that Phil Cooney, who is a lawyer with no scientific training, had been imported into the White House from the American Petroleum Institute, to control the presentation of climate science. He edited scientific reports, striking out evidence that glaciers were retreating and inserting phrases suggesting that there was serious scientific doubt about global warming. When the revelations were published he resigned and took up a post at Exxon.

Andrew C. Revkin, *Cheney's Office Said to Edit Draft Testimony*, NEW YORK TIMES, July 9, 2008, *available at* http://www.nytimes.com/2008/07/09/washington/09enviro.html?ref=environment (last visited 7/30/2008):

Mr. Burnett said that the offices of Mr. Cheney and the White House [CEQ] "were seeking deletions" of sections of draft testimony describing health risks from warming. The testimony was prepared by Dr. Julie L. Gerberding, the head of the Centers for Disease Control and Prevention, for a hearing last October before Ms. Boxer's Committee.

The full text of the [Jason K.] Burnett Correspondence with Senator Barbara Boxer is as follows:

JASON KESTREL BURNETT

July 6, 2008

The Honorable Barbara Boxer
Chairman, Committee on Environment and Public Works United States Senate
Washington, DC 20510-6175

Dear Senator Boxer:

In order to answer your questions from your letter dated July 1st, 2008 I will provide some background. In my role as Associate Deputy Administrator of the Environmental Protection Agency (EPA), I led and coordinated energy and climate change actions across various EPA offices. The most significant such action was the effort to respond to the *Massachusetts v. EPA* Supreme Court decision. Having found that greenhouse gases are air pollutants under the Clean Air Act, the Supreme Court's decision required that the Administrator of EPA determine whether greenhouse gases "may reasonably be anticipated to endanger public health or welfare" and, if so, to issue greenhouse gas regulations. The basic logic of the statute is straightforward; if the public is endangered, the government must act.

After months of work by EPA professional scientists and lawyers, a number of senior meetings at the White House, and a robust decision-making process, the Administrator asked staff to draft a provisional finding that greenhouse gases may reasonably be anticipated to endanger public welfare.

1.   Your first question concerns the events of December 2007 related to that endangerment finding. In early December EPA was preparing the finding for formal Office of Management and Budget (OMB) review. All of us were very deliberate in our actions knowing the profound consequences ... such a finding caused. I took extra steps to ensure that there was a common understanding within the government regarding this finding. For example, on December 1st, 2007 I read key sections of the provisional endangerment finding to OMB staff to ensure that it correctly reflected the conclusions that had been reached in prior meetings. On the morning of December 5th I discussed the finding with the Administrator of the Office of Information and Regulatory Affairs of the OMB. I got agreement that the finding was ready for formal OMB review provided that EPA make certain modifications.

            We made the requested modifications, I checked with others in senior EPA management, and I sent an email containing the finding. Shortly after I sent the email, EPA received a phone call from the White House asking for us not to send the finding. When we explained that the document had been sent, I was asked to send a follow-up note saying that the email had been sent in error. I explained that I could not do this because it was not true.

            I was then asked to retract the previous email on the grounds that the Energy Bill then working its way through Congress could make such a finding moot. I declined to do so. I and others at EPA explained that if Congress did amend the Clean Air Act to render the Supreme Court decision moot then and only then would the EPA be relieved of the obligation to move forward with an endangerment finding.

2a.   You ask whether I am "aware of any efforts by White House or other officials to encourage or require the redaction of statements by CDC [Centers for Disease Control and Prevention] that global warming endangers human health or the environment." The Council on Environmental Quality (CEQ) and the Office of the Vice President (OVP) were seeking deletions to the CDC testimony. CEQ requested that I work with CDC to remove from the testimony any discussion of the human health consequences of climate change.

2b.   You ask whether "such redactions were sought in order to avoid support for a finding of public endangerment that could trigger regulatory action under the Clean Air Act." During the fall of 2007 there was extensive debate about how the Administrator should make the endangerment finding. CEQ contacted me to argue that I could best keep options open for the Administrator if I would convince CDC to delete particular sections of their testimony. As I have said in other forums, I saw it as a key part of my job to keep options open for the Administrator even if I did not personally agree with those options. However, I only worked to keep options open that were consistent with relevant scientific information.

2c.   You ask "who sought such changes in CDC's testimony" and any role I or White House officials may have played. As stated above, CEQ and OVP were seeking changes and CEQ asked if I would work with CDC to make the desired deletions. I read the testimony, checked with EPA scientists, and came to the conclusion that the draft testimony was fundamentally accurate as written. I therefore declined to make the requested deletions or to suggest to CDC that they do so.

3.   You ask for a description of "any efforts by White House officials to alter any other testimony regarding the threats posed by global warming in hearings before this Committee." In preparation for the January 24th, 2008 hearing before this Committee regarding the Administrator's denial of California's request for a vehicle emission waiver, EPA staff had drafted written testimony that quoted the Administrator's December 19th, 2007 let-

ter to Governor Schwarzenegger. That letter had stated "greenhouse gas emissions harm the environment in California and elsewhere regardless of where the emissions occur." While EPA staff, myself included, did not support the denial, we thought including such language in the testimony would help clarify that the denial was consistent with the Administrator's belief that climate change is a problem.

In the course of interagency review of EPA's draft testimony we received a suggestion to avoid the phrase "greenhouse gas emissions harm the environment." EPA made it clear that we intended to keep the original language since it was accurate and informative.

An official in the OVP called to tell me that his office wanted the language changed. I declined to accept the suggestion, providing again the defense that the testimony was accurate as written. I said if the OVP wanted the language changed then someone more senior would need to talk with the Administrator. In the end this part of the Administrator's testimony remained as EPA had written it.

I have recently resigned from my position at EPA having reached the conclusion that no more productive work responding to the Supreme Court could be accomplished under this Administration. Please feel free to contact me at [redacted].

Sincerely,
Jason K. Burnett

---

d. EPA (Environmental Protection Agency)

Tarck Maassarani, Government Accountability Project, Redacting the Science of Climate Change: An Investigative and Synthesis Report 58 (March 2007) [hereinafter 2007 GAP Report]:

Q. Who gobbled up EPA's June 2003 first-ever Draft Report on the Environment?

OMB (Office of Management and Budget) "suggested removing a discussion of climate change from the report's executive summary."

Office of Science and Technology Policy "asked to strike a discussion of human health and ecological effects of climate change."

CEQ urged EPA to "delete climate change or use previously agreed upon material."

DOE (Department of Energy) "contended that atmospheric concentrations of carbon should be dismissed as poor indicators of climate change."

Brief of [Seventeen] *Amici Curiae* Climate Scientists, Supreme Court of the United States, *Commonwealth of Massachusetts v. U.S. EPA*, Aug. 31, 2006 (at 2–3):

As practicing scientists who study the earth's climate system, we and many in our profession have long understood that continued human-caused emission of greenhouse gases—primarily carbon dioxide (CO_2), but also methane (CH_4), nitrous oxide (N_2O), and fluorocarbons—would eventually warm the earth's surface. Most were skeptical that we would see strong signs of human-induced climate change in our lifetimes. But by the beginning of this decade, we observed that global temperatures are rising, plant and animal ranges are shifting, glaciers are in retreat globally, and arctic sea ice is retreating. Sea levels are rising and the oceans are becoming more acidic. To the extent that these changes result from human alteration of the atmosphere, we know that they are just the first small increment of climate change yet to come if human societies do not curb emissions of greenhouse gases.

The evidence of these changes, though attended by the uncertainty or caveats that appropriately accompany scientific knowledge, is nonetheless so compelling that it has crystallized a remarkable consensus within the scientific community: climate warming is happening, and human activities are very likely a significant causal factor. The nature of this consensus may be obscured in a public debate that sometimes equates consensus with unanimity or complete certainty. We are profoundly troubled by the misunderstanding or misrepresentation of the current state of knowledge of climate change evident in the United States Environmental Protection Agency's ("EPA's") denial of the petition for rulemaking to regulate emissions of greenhouse gases from mobile sources, Pet. App. A59–A93, Control of Emissions From New Highway Vehicles and Engines, 68 Fed. Reg. 52,922, (Sept. 8, 2003), and the subsequent court of appeals review of that action, Pet App. 1–58, *Massachusetts v. EPA,* 415 F.3d 50 (D.C. Cir. 2005).

EPA and the appeals court stated that they considered the NAS/NRC report CLIMATE CHANGE SCIENCE to be the scientific authority for the decision to deny the petition to regulate. We feel an obligation to inform this Court that they misunderstood or misrepresented the science contained in this report, to correct the public record as to what CLIMATE CHANGE SCIENCE and subsequent NAS reports say about climate change, and to offer our professional insight on using scientific evidence to judge whether a particular standard for regulatory action is met in the matter of climate change.

See AL GORE, AN INCONVENIENT TRUTH: THE PLANETARY EMERGENCE OF GLOBAL WARMING AND WHAT WE CAN DO ABOUT IT (2006, Rodale, N.Y., N.Y.), discussing the work of Mr. Phillip Cooney who did some editorial work for the George W. Bush Administration on the subject of global warming. This found its way into the New York Times in 2005:

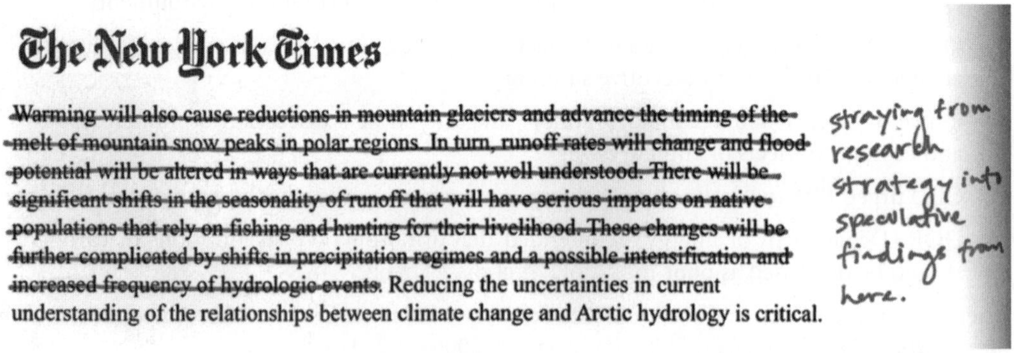

The New York Times

~~Warming will also cause reductions in mountain glaciers and advance the timing of the melt of mountain snow peaks in polar regions. In turn, runoff rates will change and flood potential will be altered in ways that are currently not well understood. There will be significant shifts in the seasonality of runoff that will have serious impacts on native populations that rely on fishing and hunting for their livelihood. These changes will be further complicated by shifts in precipitation regimes and a possible intensification and increased frequency of hydrologic events.~~ Reducing the uncertainties in current understanding of the relationships between climate change and Arctic hydrology is critical.

(handwritten margin note: straying from research strategy into speculative findings from here.)

Q. What is red-lined [crossed out above] by Mr. Cooney in the above NEW YORK TIMES Article?

Warming will also cause reductions in mountain glaciers and advance the timing of the melt of mountain snow peaks in polar regions. In turn, runoff rates will change and flood potential will be altered in ways that are currently not understood. There will be significant shifts in the seasonality of runoff that will have serious impacts on native populations that rely on fishing and hunting for their livelihood. These changes will be further complicated by shifts in precipitation regimes and a possible intensification and increased frequency of hydrologic events.

Q. What is left?

Reducing the uncertainties in current understanding of the relationships between climate change and Arctic hydrology is critical.

e. The 2004 Arctic Climate Impact Assessment

ARCTIC CLIMATE IMPACT ASSESSMENT, IMPACTS OF A WARMING ARCTIC 94 (Cambridge Un. Press 2004):

> As Indigenous Peoples perceive it, the Arctic is becoming an environment at risk in the sense that sea ice is less stable, unusual weather patterns are occurring, vegetation cover is changing, and particular animals are no longer found in traditional hunting areas during specific seasons. Local landscapes, seascapes, and icescapes are becoming unfamiliar, making people feel like strangers in their own land.

CHRIS MOONEY, THE REPUBLICAN WAR ON SCIENCE 82 (Perseus Books 2005):

> Whenever a major new development occurs in climate science, these groups [Exxon-backed entities and other "think tanks"] kick into high dudgeon, nitpicking and debunking state-of-the-art science in online commentaries, reports, press releases, and newspaper op-ed pieces. As a case in point, consider the late 2004 release of the ARCTIC CLIMATE IMPACT ASSESSMENT, which showed that human-fueled global warming has already had alarming impacts on the Arctic region, such as the melting of glaciers and sea ice. The Marshall Institute promptly challenged the report's science; and then [Sen. James Inhofe, Oklahoma, Chairman, Comm. on Environment and Public Works following the 2002 Congressional elections, staunch opponent of the Climate Stewardship Act, author of a 12,000-word Senate floor speech, entitled "The Science of Climate Change" ("the greatest hoax ever perpetrated on the American people")], in issuing his own challenge, cited the Marshall Institute.

TAREK MAASSARANI, REDACTING THE SCIENCE OF CLIMATE CHANGE: AN INVESTIGATIVE AND SYNTHESIS REPORT 60 n. 273 (Government Accountability Project, March 2007), *quoting* Rick Piltz, Memorandum on "Censorship and Secrecy" (June 2005):

> Why has the [Climate Change Science Program] failed to transmit copies of the report that were purchased for distribution to Members of Congress and others? They are still gathering dust in a storeroom, sitting in unopened boxes. What roles have CEQ, the State Department, and the CCSP Director played in what appears to be an administration decision to distance itself from the ARCTIC CLIMATE IMPACT ASSESSMENT, which identifies a range of observed and projected adverse impacts of climate change on Arctic ecosystems and communities, with implications for global climate change and potential global consequences, including accelerated sea level rise? The AICA Chair testifies and gives briefings, but it is on his own. The U.S. government has been sitting out the follow-through process, without acknowledging the findings, briefing Congress, or even delivering the report.

Suzanne Goldenberg & Damian Carrington, *Revealed: the secret evidence of global warming Bush tried to hide,* GUARDIAN—THE OBSERVER, July 26, 2009, *available at* http://www.guardian.co.uk/environment/2009/jul/26/climate-change-obama-administration (last visited August 11, 2009):

> Graphic images that reveal the devastating impact of global warming in the Arctic have been released by the US military. The photographs, taken by spy satellites over the

past decade, confirm that in recent years vast areas in high latitudes have lost their ice cover in summer months.

The pictures, kept secret by Washington during the presidency of George W Bush, were declassified by the White House last week. President Barack Obama is currently trying to galvanise Congress and the American public to take action to halt catastrophic climate change caused by rising levels of carbon dioxide in the atmosphere.

One particularly striking set of images—selected from the 1,000 photographs released—includes views of the Alaskan port of Barrow. One, taken in July 2006, shows sea ice still nestling close to the shore. A second image shows that by the following July the coastal waters were entirely ice-free.

The photographs demonstrate starkly how global warming is changing the Arctic. More than a million square kilometres of sea ice—a record loss—were missing in the summer of 2007 compared with the previous year.

Nor has this loss shown any sign of recovery. Ice cover for 2008 was almost as bad as for 2007, and this year levels look equally sparse.

f. John Grant on Lysenkoism

JOHN GRANT, CORRUPTED SCIENCE: FRAUD, IDEOLOGY AND POLITICS IN SCIENCE 270–75 (Sterling Pub. 2007) (on Lysenkoism in Russia; a case study in extreme politicization of science); Trofim D. Lysenko was a peasant amateur agronomist who climbed the political ladder to lead the Moscow Institute of Genetics under Stalin; a committed Marxist, he believed that plants would do what you wanted them to do if you put them in the right environment):

- Tactics: "His response was that of blusterers anywhere: When a claim is challenged, rather than weigh the merits of the challenge, retaliate by making the claim ever more extravagant."
- Preferred newspaper interviews to publication;
- Hired his own lawyer who helped him formulate a theory of gibberish;
- Created his own journal and used self-publishing as his best mouthpiece;
- Ruthlessly pursued all scientific enemies;
- Used political appointees to strengthen his hold on scientific enterprises;
- Mocked and repudiated Darwinism since competition in the wild "violated Marxist principles of cooperation";
- Killed ten million people "as a consequence of the collectivization of Soviet agriculture and the imposition of Lysenkoist agricultural practices";
- Authorities admired him because his ideas were "Idealogically sound" … ;"if reality stubbornly refused to conform to Marxist science, then it must be reality that was at fault."

g. Union of Concerned Scientists: Big Tobacco Uncertainty Tactics

UNION OF CONCERNED SCIENTISTS, SMOKE, MIRRORS & HOT AIR: HOW EXXON MOBIL USES BIG TOBACCO'S TACTICS TO MANUFACTURE UNCERTAINTY ON CLIMATE SCIENCE (Jan. 2007):

- Manufactured Uncertainty ("Doubt Creation") (quotations are paraphrases, not direct quotes);
- A Strategy of Information Laundering through Front Groups ("Letting Big Oil Speak Through the Temperate Voices of the Fully Disguised");
- Promotion of the Marginalized and Repudiated in the Global Warming Debate ("Giving Extravagant Voice to the Exceedingly Foolish");

- Shift Focus Away from Meaningful Action to Indeterminate Pursuit ("Chasing the Rabbit of 'Sound Science' to the Ends of the Earth");
- "Sticks-in-the-Spokes" Political Strategies.

h. Drawing the Lines

When does "normal" spin (putting the best face on events), "acceptable review," "understand-able" partisanship, "usual" politics, and "vigorous" advocacy cross the line to become political corruption, the dissemination of "material false statements" (18 U.S.C. § 1001) or unethical behavior in violation of judicial and professional canons?

Bothersome Law

Schoeffler and Louisiana Crawfish Producers Ass'n-West v. Kempthorne, 493 F. Supp. 2d 805, 807

(W.D. La. 2007) (Tucker L. Melancon, J.) (granting plaintiffs' motion for summary judgment on claim alleging that Secretary failed to perform a nondiscretionary duty to designate critical habitat for the Louisiana Black Bear) (emphasis in original):

> If this Court were to accept the position espoused by the United States Department of Interior in this proceeding ... there would be no law. The crux of the Secretary's position is: *we did not do our job; we did not follow the law; but ... too bad, plaintiffs did not file suit in time ... this despite our misrepresentations to plaintiffs and to the public to the contrary.*

493 F. Supp. 2d at 807 (emphasis in original):

> There can be no law, much less "the rule of law," if the administrative agencies that have been entrusted to implement the law as enacted by Congress can fail to fulfill their statutory duty without consequence.

---

2. The Use of *Daubert* Motions

All law students are familiar with the so-called "gatekeeping" functions of courts with regard to the admissibility of expert scientific testimony under *Daubert v. Merrell Dow Pharmaceuticals, Inc.*, 509 U.S. 579, 113 S.Ct. 2786, 125 L.Ed.2d 469 (1993). Consider, however, what "legally admissible science" might look like after being run through a ruthlessly selective machine that scorched-earth environmental practice has become in the U.S. courts. The focus here is on "tipping points" that are of acute contemporary interest in the science of climate change.

2008 CALVIN at 37:

> My book is more about the principles of acceleration—which probably won't change—that underlie tip, slip and flip.

2008 CALVIN at 89, 118:

> That's why study of ancient climate is so important. It shows us many of the past episodes of tip, slip and flip.
>
> Were the West Antarctic Ice Sheet to melt or collapse, sea level would increase by 6 m/20 feet.
>
> Were Greenland's ice to melt or collapse, it too would add 6 m/20 feet. If all melted including the rest of Antarctica, sea level rise would be about 70 m, the height of a 20-story building.

Collapse, not melt, is the operative concept. The sea level is rising, mostly from thermal expansion but increasing from ice additions. How fast that happens is, I suspect, largely a function of ice sliding sideways, not melt rate itself.

Glaciologist Richard Alley, *quoted in* 2008 CALVIN at 12:

We used to think that it would take 10,000 years for melting at the surface to penetrate down to the bottom of the ice sheet. But if you make a lake on the surface and a crack opens and the water goes down the crack, it doesn't take 10,000 years, it takes ten seconds. That huge lag time is completely eliminated.

RICHARD B. ALLEY, THE TWO-MILE TIME MACHINE: ICE CORES, ABRUPT CLIMATE CHANGE, AND OUR FUTURE 32 (Princeton Un. Press. 2000):

If all of the ice on Earth today were to melt, global sea level would rise about 200 feet vertically—not "Waterworld," but certainly a disaster, with the coast of Florida moving somewhere up into Georgia. Fortunately, we do not expect such a disaster over at least the next few centuries.

Figure 14. An appropriate photo here would be one of surface melt on the Greenland Ice Sheets. Surface melt can descend into a moulin. A moulin is a vertical shaft worn through the glacier by surface water, which carries the water to the base of the ice sheet. It is a roaring vertical river and it accelerates processes associated with melting. Essays on ice are today much in vogue. See Myron Arms, Riddle of the Ice: A Scientific Adventure Into the Arctic (Doubleday 1998). Henry Pollack has written that "there is a very real possibility that in only a few decades the Arctic Ocean may be ice-free in the summer, for the first time in fifty-five million years." A World Without Ice 209 (Penguin Books 2009) [hereinafter 2009 Pollock]. Pollack continues (id. at 209) (footnote omitted): "Climate scientist Ian Howat of Ohio State University remarked that the loss of Arctic Sea ice might be the largest change in Earth's surface that humans have ever observed." For a well-known photo of a moulin descending into the Greenland ice sheet see http://www.global-greenhouse-warming.com/moulin.html (last visited 7/8/2010).

Green Mountain Chrysler Plymouth Dodge Jeep v. Crombie, 508 F. Supp. 2d 295 (D. Vt. 2007) (Sessions, Chief Judge).

This case upholds Vermont regulations that would establish greenhouse gas emission standards for new autos. Plaintiffs include the Alliance of Automobile Manufacturers and General Motors Corporation. Attorneys for the auto industry make a *Daubert* motion to strike the testimony of Jim Hansen, preeminent climate scientist of the times, director of the Goddard Inst. for Space Studies, singled out for censorship. The motion sought to exclude testimony on these topics:

- *id.* at 312: "[H]is testimony regarding the impact of the regulation, and more specifically his 'tipping point' theory, including his testimony regarding ice sheet disintegration. They apparently do not seek to exclude his testimony regarding species extinction and regional effects of global warming, except insofar as these effects are presented as consequences of the Earth passing a 'tipping point.'"
- *id.* at 313–14: "[Hansen's] 'tipping point' theory posits that at a certain point the changes associated with global warming will become dramatically more rapid and out of control. The 'tipping point' is the point at which very little, if any, additional forcing is needed for substantial changes to occur";
- *id.* at 314 (footnote omitted): "Hansen testified that sea level rise is likely to take place in nonlinear fashion because of multiple positive feedbacks."
- *id.* at 317: Instead of this disturbing information about "tipping points" and "nonlinear" sea level rise, the industry offered decision makers a more satisfying informational diet—

Dr. John Christy, who "testified that Hansen's hypothesis regarding rapid sea level rise is unsupported by the scientific evidence."

This *Daubert* motion was denied. The argument that Hansen's opinions "arise out of pure speculation" (*id.* at 316) is rejected.

Notes

1. On the application of the *Daubert* test to climate models, see Matthew W. Swinehart, *Remedying* Daubert's *Inadequacy in Evaluating the Admissibility of Scientific Models Used in Environmental Tort Litigation*, 86 TEX. L. REV. 1281 (2008).

2. For an excellent summary, see Daniel A. Farber, *Modeling Climate Change and Its Impacts: Law, Policy, and Science*, 86 TEX. L. REV. 1655 (2008). For a thoughtful challenge to modeling as "understatement," see JAMES LOVELOCK, THE VANISHING FACE OF GAIA: A FINAL WARNING ch. 2 (Basic Books 2009).

3. See Thomas O. McGarity, *Our Science is Sound Science and Their Science is Junk Science: Science-Based Strategies for Avoiding Accountability and Responsibility for Risk-Producing Products and Activities*, 52 U. KAN. L. REV. 897, 925 (2004):

> In early 2003, the Competitive Enterprise Institute, a think tank that has historically opposed national and international efforts to abate greenhouse gases filed an [Information Quality Act] challenge in three agencies demanding that they "withdraw" the National Assessment on Climate Change (NACC), an interagency report on the role that greenhouse gases play in global warming. Although the Report had received extensive peer review and public vetting, CEI nevertheless launched a classic corpuscular attack on various aspects of the Report that were not, in CEI's view, based on "sound science." After the White House Office of Science and Technology Policy (OTSP) denied CEI's petition, CEI sued President Bush and the Director of OSTP seeking a judicial ruling on the merits of its IQA challenge. The case subsequently settled when the federal government agreed to place a disclaimer on the NACC advising that it had not been prepared in accordance with the requirements of the IQA.

The Information Quality Act, Pub. L. No. 106–554, 114 Stat. 2763 (2000), was an obscure rider, pushed by a tobacco industry lobbyist, to allow—under OMB guidance—the "correction of information" in agency studies. Thomas O. McGarity, 52 U. KAN. L. REV. at 913 (quoting IQA).

---

3. Legal Retaliation Against a Strategy of "Fictionalization" of Global Warming Science

Native Village of Kivalina and City of Kivalina v. Exxon Mobil Corp. et al., Complaint Filed Feb. 26, 2008 (N.D. Cal).

This lawsuit raises common law claims against U.S. coal and oil companies for releases of greenhouse gases that have led to the flooding—and anticipated abandonment—of a Native Alaska village. The complaint includes a "conspiracy" count that reads in part as follows:

41. Exxon Mobil has taken the lead in the industry efforts to disseminate false information about global warming....

....

189.   There has been a long campaign by power, coal, and oil companies to mislead the public about the science of global warming....

....

190.   The industries have ... formed and used front groups, fake citizens organizations, and bogus scientific bodies, such as the Global Climate Coalition ("GCC"), the Greening Earth Society, the George C. Marshall Institute, and the Cooler Heads Coalition. The most active company in such efforts has been defendant Exxon Mobil.

192–93. One of the earliest and most prominent front groups has been The Advancement of Sound Science Coalition (TASSC).... TASSC has funded a web site, JunkScience.com, which was founded by a public relations consultant working at TASSC.... Exxon Mobil has funded TASSC. The Orwellian use of the terms 'junk science' and 'sound science' were adopted by the power, coal and oil industries—including some of the Conspiracy Defendants—to subvert the global warming debate.

197–204. The Global Climate Coalition [founded in 1989] met at a variety of locations, including the offices of Exxon. [Among its works, it] distributed a video to hundreds of journalists claiming that increased levels of carbon dioxide will increase crop production and help feed the hungry people of the world.

....

213.   On April 10, 1996, the George C. Marshall Institute, as part of the Conspiracy Defendants' disinformation campaign, issued a report falsely claiming that peer-reviewed studies indicated temperature increases were consistent with 'natural climate change.'

214.   Since Exxon Mobil began to support its efforts, the Marshall Institute has served as a clearinghouse for global warming contrarians, conducting round-table events and producing frequent publications. The Marshall Institute has been touting its new book, SHATTERED CONSENSUS: THE TRUE STATE OF GLOBAL WARMING, edited by long-time contrarian Patrick Michaels. Michaels has, over the past several years, been affiliated with at least ten organizations funded by Exxon Mobil.

....

231.   Relying on tactics developed by the tobacco industry to discredit health risks associated with tobacco use, Exxon Mobil has channeled $16 million over the 1998 to 2005 period to 42 organizations that promote disinformation on global warming.

....

234.   Rather than meet its social and legal responsibilities, Exxon Mobil engaged in a multi-faceted attack on global warming which included exploiting science, denying the consensus on global warming, running misleading advertising denying the existence of global warming or its causes, and funding organizations who attacked global warming on these bases and/or the factors causing global warming.

235.   Exxon Mobil has funded and continues to fund groups like the George Marshall Institute, the Frazier Institute, and Free Enterprise to prop up discred-

ited studies and to disseminate misleading information to downplay the severity of global climate change.

....

246.   Exxon Mobil marshaled its considerable resources [to undermine the 2004 Arctic Climate Impact Assessment] that combined the work of some 300 scientists and was four years in the making.

....

———

This lawsuit seeks $400 million to facilitate relocation of the Village of Kivalina. It is guided by experienced counsel, including Steve Berman of Seattle who represented several plaintiff states in the tobacco litigation. Its progress will be closely monitored. And, of course, the scientific and political background against which it proceeds is in constant flux. *See* Andrew C. Revkin, *Climate skeptics meet to roast global warming; New York event draws 600, from former astronaut to MIT professor*, NEW YORK TIMES, March 8, 2009 (Marc Morano, spokesman on environmental issues for Sen. James Inhofe: "The only place where this alleged climate catastrophe is happening is in the virtual world of computer models, not in the real world"; "But large corporations such as Exxon-Mobil, which in the past financed the Heartland Institute and other groups that challenged the climate consensus, have reduced support." Alan Jeffers, spokesman for ExxonMobil: the company has ended support "to several public policy research groups whose position on climate change could divert attention from the important discussion about how the world will secure the energy required for economic growth in an environmentally responsible manner."). (This case is dismissed in Native village of Kivalina v. Exxon Mobile Corporation, 663 F. Supp. 863 (M.D. Cal. 2009.)

———

Lots of Science, Not Much Law; Why Knowledge Has Not (Yet) Been Power over Greenhouse Gas Emissions

Holly Doremus. Professor of Law, University of California, Berkeley, and University of California, Davis. Tel: (510) 643-5699 and (530) 752-2879; hdoremus@law.berkeley .edu and hddoremus@ucdavis.edu.

I.   *Introduction*

For nearly forty years, environmental lawyers and environmentalists more generally in the United States have had a love-hate relationship with science. On the one hand, they have seen science as a powerful political force, providing the justification for legislation that significantly constrains individual choices, which in the absence of scientific justification might seem inconsistent with the foundations of liberal democracy.[1] On the other hand, they have feared that excessive emphasis on science could deprive the movement of its passion, encourage foolish technological optimism, and pose barriers to precautionary regulation.[2] Whether it is bane, boon, or a bit of both, scientific knowledge has always been seen as difficult to integrate with law.

———

1. Dan Tarlock has made the case for the importance of science in legitimizing environmental regulation. A. Dan Tarlock, *Environmental Law: Ethics or Science?*, 7 DUKE ENVTL. L. & POL'Y F. 193 (1996). Fred Smith is among those who have criticized the "environmental gospel" as a significant challenge to "the classical liberal vision." Fred L. Smith, *The Progressive Environmental Gospels Versus Classical Liberalism*, 56 CASE WESTERN L. REV. 621 (2006).

2. The latest (or at least the highest-profile recent) critique of the environmental movement's focus on science is found in TED NORDHAUS & MICHAEL SHELLENBERGER, BREAK THROUGH: FROM THE DEATH OF ENVI-

Global warming policy (or the lack thereof) illustrates the current state of this complicated relationship. Scientific understanding appears to have advanced much faster than policy. The basic physics of the greenhouse effect have been understood for well over 100 years. In the early 1800s, Jean Baptiste Fourier figured out that radiation of heat from the planet's surface kept the earth from heating up to the temperature of the sun. In fact, Fourier's calculations, based on the level of infrared radiation from the earth, suggested that the planet's temperature should be well below freezing. He speculated, without a whole lot of evidence to back it up, that the atmosphere must trap some of the radiated heat.[3] In 1862, John Tyndall provided the first solid evidence to support this theory, publishing the results of experiments showing that water vapor, carbon dioxide, and certain other gases found in the atmosphere at low levels absorb infrared radiation, trapping its heat in the atmosphere.[4] Before 1900, Svente Arrhenius had drawn the connection between the greenhouse effect and human activity. Arrhenius noticed that changing carbon dioxide levels could produce temperature changes that would be magnified by water vapor, because warmer air holds more water, thereby causing more warming, and colder air holds less, bringing about additional cooling. Given the amount of carbon dioxide being spewed into the air by the machines of the industrial revolution, Arrhenius calculated that atmospheric CO_2 levels could eventually double, bringing Sweden a balmy distant future.[5] In 1938, Guy Callendar gave concrete form to Arrheius's theoretical calculations. Callendar, an amateur scientist, explained to Britain's Royal Meteorological Society that his review of published measurements of atmospheric CO_2 showed a small increase since the early nineteenth century; he argued that increase was attributable to the burning of fossil fuels, and was responsible for the observed slight warming over the same time period.[6] In 1958, Charles Keeling worked out the instrumentation to accurately measure atmospheric CO_2 levels, and within two years was able to demonstrate that those levels were rising in Antarctica.[7] Within a few more years, Keeling's now-famous graph of CO_2 concentrations on Mauna Loa provided clear visual evidence that atmospheric greenhouse gas levels were rapidly increasing.[8]

As the data accumulated, atmospheric scientists gradually became policy advocates. Beginning in the 1960s, respected scientists, inside and outside government, began to argue that global climate change presents a serious threat to people and the environment. Yet as of the middle of 2008 the United States had taken essentially no action to combat or adjust to global climate change. Internationally, there is a treaty calling for reductions in greenhouse gas emissions,

---

RONMENTALISM TO THE POLITICS OF POSSIBILITY (Houghton Mifflin Co. 2007). Although Nordhaus and Shellenberger claim to be proposing an entirely new vision of environmentalism, critiques of overreliance on science are not new. *See, e.g.,* Wendy E. Wagner, *The Science Charade in Toxic Risk Regulation,* 95 COLUM. L. REV. 1613 (1995); Donald T. Hornstein, *Reclaiming Environmental Law: A Normative Critique of Comparative Risk Analysis,* 92 COLUM. L. REV. 962 (1992); Eric T. Freyfogle & Julianne Lutz Newton, *Putting Science in its Place,* 16 CONSERVATION BIOLOGY 863 (2002).

3. TIM FLANNERY, THE WEATHER MAKERS: HOW MAN IS CHANGING THE CLIMATE AND WHAT IT MEANS FOR LIFE ON EARTH 38–39 (Atlantic Monthly Press 2005) [hereinafter FLANNERY]; SPENCER R. WEART, THE DISCOVERY OF GLOBAL WARMING 2–3 (Harvard Un. Press 2003) [hereinafter WEART]. Fourier gave rise to our present terminology when he compared the heat-trapping effect of the earth's atmosphere to that of a box covered with glass, leading others to begin talking of the "greenhouse effect" and eventually of "greenhouse gases."

4. John Tyndall, *Further Researches on the Absorption and Radiation of Heat by Gaseous Matter* (1862), cited in WEART, *supra* note 3, at 3–4.

5. FLANNERY, *supra* note 3, at 40; WEART, *supra* note 3, at 5–7.

6. FLANNERY, *supra* note 3, at 40–41; WEART, *supra* note 3, at 2, 18–19.

7. WEART, *supra* note 3, at 36.

8. *See* WEART, *supra* note 3, at 18 (describing the Keeling curve as "the central icon of the greenhouse effect"). By 1966, Keeling's graph had made an impression on then-college student Al Gore. *Id.* at 142.

but the level of cuts it contemplates is widely agreed to be insufficient, and its adherents are having difficulty achieving even that level.

What has gone wrong? It is easy to see the failure to address global warming earlier or more enthusiastically as a simple case of politics trumping science. That surely has been part of the problem, especially during the Bush II administration. But the disjunction between information and response predates 2001, and is more complicated than the "science versus politics" story suggests.

There are a number of other reasons why policymakers have been slow to respond to the information scientists have been feeding them. The global warming problem could fairly be described as a perfect storm for science-policy interaction. First, although the general outlines of global warming have been understood for some time, the kinds of detailed information needed to inform policy choices has been much slower to develop. Second, global warming itself has a significant time lag, so that we have made decisions that committed the world to increasingly large temperature increases before we understood the consequences. Third, there has been a systematic campaign to drown out scientific warnings of climate change and its consequences. Fourth, we in the United States have not been anxious to confront the reality of global warming, in part because we have not seen ourselves as particularly vulnerable to its impacts, and in part because it has seemed beyond our power to change it.

The story of the interaction of science and policy in the global warming context suggests some general lessons for science-dependent policy decisions. Science alone never determines policy decisions. It is a mistake for environmental advocates on the one hand to assume that the policy they want will (or even should) automatically follow when they present their scientific evidence to policymakers. It is equally a mistake, of course, for the defenders of the status quo to insist on absolute scientific certainty as a condition of any policy change. What action is appropriate or politically acceptable will depend not only on the facts and the confidence with which they are known, but also on public beliefs, attitudes, and available policy responses. Although science is never determinative, it is often crucially important to the decision. Policymakers and the public which oversees their work need to understand the nuances of scientific uncertainty better than they currently do. That is a tall order, given the challenges of communication. Scientists and journalists both could do more to raise awareness of the nature and significance of uncertainties, and policymakers could do more to create and support politically independent trustworthy sources of information about policy-relevant science.

II. Limits of the Science

One reason that scientific information about global warming has not yet triggered national legislation in the United States, or a strong international treaty, is that it is not unequivocal. Like the science of most environmental problems, that of global warming remains difficult and incomplete. The general outlines of the problem—that anthropogenic greenhouse gas emissions are changing the world's climate—are now supported by a remarkably powerful scientific consensus. But that consensus is a relatively recent development, and it still does not provide the details policymakers crave.

A. What Do We Know and When Did We Know It?

The story told above of the progress of knowledge of climate change makes it sound as if knowledge advanced smoothly, uncontested, while only policy stood still. But of course the truth is more complicated. Understanding of anthropogenic climate change came in fits and starts, and understanding of its implications developed even more gradually.

Today, there is strong consensus on the reality and seriousness of human-caused climate change. That consensus is embodied in the most recent report of the U.N.-sponsored Intergovernmental Panel on Climate Change (IPCC).[9] Tim Flannery calls the IPCC reports the "lowest common denominator" of global warming science because they must gain the agreement not only of hundreds of scientists but also of the panel's member governments.[10] Yet as the science has become stronger, that cautious body has issued a series of progressively more detailed and confident consensus reports. By its fourth assessment report, issued in late 2007, the lowest common denominator on global warming was pretty high. The IPCC proclaimed that: the planet is unequivocally warming;[11] most of that change is very likely (defined to mean the probability exceeds 90%) due to increases in anthropogenic greenhouse gas emissions rather than natural factors;[12] and unless controls are imposed on emissions, global average temperatures will likely increase anywhere from 1 to more than 6 degrees centigrade by the end of the twenty-first century.[13] Consensus within the scientific community came somewhat faster than at the IPCC, which was deliberately designed to be conservative. A study in the prestigious journal *Science* reported that literally none of the more than 900 papers on climate change published in refereed journals between 1993 and 2003 argued against the basic conclusion that people are significantly altering the climate.[14] Even the highest levels of the U.S. federal government's executive branch, which until recently had fiercely resisted acknowledging the reality of global warming, now are willing to say that the phenomenon is real, and very likely due to anthropogenic greenhouse gas emissions.[15]

But that level of confidence did not arrive quickly. Although the basic physics of the greenhouse effect are simple, the earth's climate is not. Nor was it intensively studied until recently. When Arrhenius made his calculations and Callendar his observations, both were more concerned about the possibility of a new ice age than about runaway heat. While their work did suggest that human actions could affect global climate, that did not frighten them. At the time, greenhouse gases were accumulating slowly enough that any noticeable impacts seemed centuries if not millennia in the future.[16] A bit of warming sounded like a good thing, promising to

---

9. The IPCC was set up in 1988 by the World Meteorological Organization and the United Nations Environment Programme. Hundreds of scientists contribute to and review its reports, but in the end those reports must be approved by the IPCC's member governments. Intergovernmental Panel on Climate Change, About IPCC, http://www.ipcc.ch/about/index.htm. Spencer Weart describes the IPCC as a "unique hybrid" of science and politics. WEART, *supra* note 3, at 158.

10. FLANNERY, *supra* note 3, at 246. Others agree that the IPCC reports err on the side of caution. Richard A. Kerr, *Scientists Tell Policymakers We're All Warming the World*, 315 SCIENCE 754, 757 (2007). Kerr describes the procedures for preparing IPCC reports in detail: "Forty governments nominated the 150 lead authors and 450 authors of [the 2007 IPCC report on the physical science] … Authors had their draft chapters reviewed by all comers. More than 600 volunteered, submitting 30,000 comments. Authors responded to every comment, and reviewers certified each response. With their final draft of the science in hand, authors gathered in Paris, France with 300 representatives of 113 nations for 4 days to hash out the wording of a scientist-written Summary for Policymakers." *Id.* at 754. *See also* INTERGOVERNMENTAL PANEL ON CLIMATE CHANGE, 16 YEARS OF SCIENTIFIC ASSESSMENT IN SUPPORT OF THE CLIMATE CONVENTION 4 (Dec. 2004), *available at* http://www. ipcc.ch/pdf/10th-anniversary/anniversary-brochure.pdf.

11. IPCC, CLIMATE CHANGE 2007: SYNTHESIS REPORT, SUMMARY FOR POLICYMAKERS 2 (Nov. 2007), *available at* http://www.ipcc.ch/ipccreports/ar4-syr.htm.

12. *Id.* at 5.

13. *Id.* at 7–8.

14. Naomi Oreskes, *The Scientific Consensus on Climate Change*, 306 SCIENCE 1686 (2004).

15. NATIONAL SCIENCE AND TECHNOLOGY COUNCIL, COMMITTEE ON ENVIRONMENT AND NATURAL RESOURCES, SCIENTIFIC EFFECT OF GLOBAL CHANGE ON THE UNITED STATES 2 (May 2008), *available at* http://www.ostp.gov/galleries/NSTC%20Reports/Scientific%20Assessment%20FULL%20Report.pdf [hereinafter 2008 NATIONAL SCIENCE AND TECHNOLOGY COUNCIL]. The National Science and Technology Council is chaired by the President, and includes all cabinet-level officials with significant science portfolios. Exec. Order 12881, 58 Fed. Reg. 62491 (Nov. 23, 1993).

16. Through the 1950s, atmospheric scientists assumed that industrial emissions would continue at a constant rate, failing to note that they had been rising exponentially since the onset of the industrial revolution. *See, e.g.*, WEART, *supra* note 3, at 29 (noting that Roger Revelle made that assumption in 1957).

increase crop yields and human comfort in chilly northern Europe and Scandinavia.[17] It was hardly a pressing scientific issue. By 1966, a National Research Council panel had agreed that greenhouse gases were building up in the atmosphere, but concluded that there was no immediate cause for concern, only a need for more research.[18]

In the late 1960s, spurred in part by that report and Keeling's Mauna Loa data, climate research did become a higher priority. Still, progress was slow. Understanding the effects of greenhouse gas emissions on climate required models of the planet's weather systems, which necessarily remained crude until computing power increased. It also required more detailed knowledge of past and present conditions, which was hard to come by. It was not until 1980, for example, that reliable methods were developed for measuring CO_2 levels in ice cores, allowing scientists to accumulate key data in support of the greenhouse effect.[19] The importance of greenhouse gases other than CO_2 was recognized about the same time.[20] Even when the right questions were being asked and the methods to ask them were available, they were tough to answer. The signal of anthropogenic climate change is difficult to pick up, because it is superimposed on a highly variable natural system.

Well into the 1970s, scientists disagreed about whether anthropogenic effects threatened to warm or to cool the planet.[21] Not surprisingly, there was no unified push from the scientific community for policy measures to address whatever the threat might be. In 1977 the National Research Council, while warning of the possibility of climate shocks, declined to call for a policy response.[22] Finally in 1983 EPA issued the first federal report characterizing global warming as a real and near-term threat, but that report came hard on the heels of yet another National Research Council report downplaying concerns.[23]

It was not until the late 1980s and early 1990s that a broad scientific consensus began to coalesce, and the millennium arrived before that consensus solidified. Surveys of climate scientists at that point revealed that, although they agreed that substantial uncertainties remained, two-thirds of them felt that the evidence was sufficient to justify policy responses.[24] Still, the science was hardly bullet-proof.

The models, and the data that supported them, had a variety of shortcomings. It took time to improve them; because climate modeling is so complex, the work is slow and resource-intensive.[25] Key difficulties with the models were not resolved until the late 1990s.[26] At that point the evidence began to cascade, not just from models but also from the increasingly apparent and measurable changes on the ground. A series of ecological studies revealed that climate change was already affecting the range, migration patterns, flowering time, and other traits in a variety

---

17. WEART, *supra* note 3, at 7, 19. *See also* FLANNERY, *supra* note 3, at 237 (suggesting that global warming failed to gain policy traction early because it sounds comforting rather than frightening).

18. NATIONAL RESEARCH COUNCIL, WEATHER AND CLIMATE MODIFICATION: PROBLEMS AND PROSPECTS (1966). The National Research Council is the policy arm of the independent National Academies (which comprise the National Academy of Sciences, National Academy of Engineering, and Institute of Medicine). In response to requests from government agencies or Congress, the National Research Council empanels expert committees to answer questions about the science underlying policy programs or decisions.

19. WEART, *supra* note 3, at 130.

20. *Id.* at 128.

21. *Id.* at 94.

22. National Research Council, Energy and Climate (1977).

23. WEART, *supra* note 3, at 146.

24. *Id.* at 164.

25. Daniel A. Farber, *Climate Models: A User's Guide*, UC Berkeley Public Law Research Paper No. 1030607 at 8 (Nov. 16, 2007), *available at* http://ssrn.com/abstract=1030607.

26. WEART, *supra* note 3, at 177.

of species.[27] By 2003, a study drawing on published scientific papers covering nearly 2000 species concluded that more than 60% of those species were breeding, nesting, flowering, or migrating earlier,[28] and 80% of those whose ranges had shifted had moved toward the poles or to higher altitudes.[29] At that point, the American Geophysical Union decided that the evidence was clear enough to justify the conclusion that global warming was both real and human-caused.[30] Finally, based on its review of published studies, even the conservative IPCC concluded in 2007 that "[t]he vast majority of studies of terrestrial biological systems reveal notable impacts of global warming over the last three to five decades, which are consistent across plant and animal taxa: earlier spring and summer phenology and longer growing seasons in mid- and higher latitudes, production range expansions at higher elevations and latitudes, some evidence for population declines at lower elevational or latitudinal limits to species ranges, and vulnerability of species with restricted ranges, leading to local extinctions."[31] Such studies dovetailed nicely with the observations of ordinary Americans, a majority of whom now believe that they see the effects of global warming in their own lives.[32] By the summer of 2008, observations of Arctic sea ice suggested that the computer models of global warming were still wrong, but not in a comforting way—sea ice loss is decades ahead of the predictions of the models.[33]

27. *See, e.g.,* Lesley Hughes, *Biological Consequences of Global Warming: Is the Signature Already Apparent?*, 15 Trends in Ecology and Evolution 56 (2000); Terry L. Root, *et al., Fingerprints of Global Warming on Wild Animals and Plants,* 421 Nature 57 (2003); Niclas Jonzen *et al., Rapid Advance of Spring Arrival Dates in Long-Distance Migratory Birds,* 312 Science 1959 (2006); 2008 National Science and Technology Council, *supra* note 15, at 9 ("In an analysis of 866 peer-reviewed papers exploring the ecological consequences of climate change worldwide, nearly 60% of the 1,598 species studied exhibited shifts in their distributions and/or timing of their annual cycles that correspond to recent large-scale climate change patterns.").

28. Camille Parmesan and Gary Yohe, *A Globally Coherent Fingerprint of Climate Change Impacts Across Natural Systems,* 421 Nature 37, 38 (2003).

29. *Id.* at 39.

30. Elizabeth Kolbert, Field Notes from a Catastrophe: Man, Nature, and Climate Change 12 (Bloomsbury USA 2006).

31. Cynthia Rosenzweig *et al., Assessment of Observed Changes and Responses in Natural and Managed Systems, in* Climate Change 2007: Impacts, Adaptation and Vulnerability. Contribution of Working Group II to the Fourth Assessment Report of the Intergovernmental Panel on Climate Change 79, 104 (M L. Parry *et al.* eds., Cambridge Un. Press 2007). Marine and freshwater systems were also found to be changing in response to climate change. *Id.* at 94. Overall, the group found that 94% of observed changes in species distribution and phenology were consistent with a warming world. *Id.* at 116.

32. Stanford professor Jon Krosnick, who has done a series of surveys of American attitudes toward global warming since 1998, found that the intensity of concern about global warming spiked in 2006, together with a spike in the proportion of respondents saying that temperatures have risen and the weather has become more unstable where they live and globally. *Intensity Spikes in Concern on Warming; Many See a Change in Weather Patterns,* ABC News/Time/Stanford Poll: Global Warming, Mar. 14, 2006, *available at* http://woods. stanford.edu/docs/surveys/GW_Woods_ABC_Release_on_2006_GW_poll.pdf. Krosnick had previously found that respondent's belief in the existence of global warming was significantly influenced by their personal experience with the weather. Jon A. Krosnick *et al., The Origins and Consequences of Democratic Citizens' Policy Agendas: A Study of Popular Concern About Global Warming,* 77 Climatic Change 7, 21 (2006).

33. *See Sea Ice Outlook, Monthly Reports,* May 2008 Outlook Report, http://www.arcus.org/search/seaice outlook/downloads/monthly-reports/june-reports/sio_full_report_may.pdf (experts predicted the extent of sea ice for summer 2008 would be less than the record minimum of 2007); National Snow and Ice Data Center, Arctic Sea Ice News and Analysis (reporting that as of June 3, 2008, the extent of arctic sea ice approached the record low levels of 2007); Seth Borenstein, *This Summer May See First Ice-Free North Pole,* June 27, 2008, http://ap.google.com/article/ALeqM5hU5i54pX9VdxAcD6Mo3VfWZDWfyQD91ILU4G1. By July, the projections were somewhat less pessimistic for 2008, although the longterm trend toward reduced summer ice remained. *See* Study of Environmental Arctic Change, Sea Ice Outlook: Monthly Reports, June Report, July 16, 2008, http://www.arcus.org/search/seaiceoutlook/report_june.php. For more on the lingering shortcomings of climate models, see Farber, *supra* note 25, at 9–11.

B. *The Importance of Scale*

The basic fact of global warming is now well established. Various climate models show with high confidence that the planet is warming, and project that it will continue to do so due to anthropogenic greenhouse gas emissions. That's important information for policymakers, but it isn't necessarily sufficient to motivate action.

The climate models that provide the confidence now expressed by the IPCC and others are global models. But no one makes global decisions about how to respond to the threat of climate change. Decisions are made at national and sub-national levels. Although their resolution is improving, global climate models are still limited in their ability to predict small-scale climate changes, or changes over short time scales.[34] That matters, because the extent of warming is expected to vary with location, as are effects on precipitation. That means that many localized economic, health, and environmental impacts remain highly uncertain. While humans along with other species can be expected to suffer in various ways worldwide as the planet warms, it is still unclear exactly how climate will respond in many places, including much of the United States. An additional layer of uncertainty surrounds the consequences of any particular level of warming. As explained in more detail below, it is easy for decisionmakers who are not faced with clear evidence of portending disasters to put off taking painful actions.

Some of the most frightening global climate predictions also remain very difficult to evaluate. Should the earth cross a climatic threshold, it could shift rapidly to a new and very different climatic state. That could happen if the North Atlantic warm ocean current slows or the Greenland or West Antarctic ice sheets melt. Although there is a great deal of concern that those events might occur, the evidence for them remains thin and equivocal, and views in the scientific community are still rapidly evolving.[35] Of course, uncertainty works both ways—scientists concerned about catastrophic change cannot prove it will happen or set a definite threshold, but neither can others be certain it won't happen or know what temperatures the world need not exceed. It might seem that the threat of catastrophic climate change, even shrouded in a high degree of uncertainty, should be a great motivator of action, but as explained below it turns out that people are pretty good at ignoring that kind of thing.

C. *The Tortoise and the Hare: Scientific Progress and Policy Commitments*

To further complicate the scientific picture, there is a significant lag between greenhouse gas emissions and climatic responses. Carbon dioxide, in particular, can persist in the atmosphere for up to two hundred years.[36] That means that emissions from the early days of the industrial revolution may still be affecting our climate today. It has taken much longer for scientific understanding to advance than for greenhouse gas levels to build up. The warning of an expert panel in the late 1970s turns out to have been completely accurate—by the time the signal of anthropogenic climate change became clearly discernible, the world was already committed to substantial climate change.[37] By the same token, some environmental changes were noticed, but not tied to anthropogenic climate change until well after they occurred. The golden toad, for example, was last

---

34. *See* 2008 National Science and Technology Council, *supra* note 15, at 3 ("attribution of the drivers of long-term temperature changes on time scales of less than 50 years and at regional scales (*e.g.*, county, state, or multiple states, as opposed to continental), with limited exceptions, has not yet been established.").

35. *See, e.g., id.* at 7.8. For a detailed description of the possibilities and consequences of crossing climatic tipping points, see generally Fred Pearce, With Speed and Violence: Why Scientists Fear Tipping Points in Climate Change (Beacon Press 2007).

36. Intergovernmental Panel on Climate Change, Climate Change 2001: The Scientific Basis 38 (2001).

37. National Research Council, Carbon Dioxide and Climate: A Scientific Assessment 2 (1979).

seen in the Costa Rican cloud forest in the 1980s. It was not until 1999, however, that ecologists understood that drying of the forest as a consequence of global warming accounted for the toad's disappearance.[38]

That understanding persistently lags environmental effects and commitment to environmental effects complicates efforts to make climate change policy on a scientific basis. The only way to avoid serious problems under those conditions is to act decisively *before* there is clear evidence that decisive action is necessary or will be sufficient. That is politically challenging under the best of conditions, because it plays into the status quo bias that characterizes most human institutions. It is particularly challenging if the proponents of policy initiatives rely heavily on science to justify their proposals, as advocates for greenhouse gas regulation have done. Uncertainty plays directly into the rhetoric of "sound science," used by opponents of change to argue that truly "scientific" decisionmaking requires near-certain proof of responsibility and efficacy before drastic policy changes are implemented.[39] Such proof can never be provided in time if environmental impacts and commitments are progressing more rapidly than scientific knowledge.

III. Human Nature and the Climate Change Problem

For all its shortcomings, as explained above the scientific evidence for human-caused global warming is now quite strong. Yet the United States as a nation has yet to respond, and the world has responded only sluggishly and ineffectively. Although states, local governments, and other nations are beginning to take halting steps, nowhere is the response as vigorous as leading scientists say it needs to be to prevent dramatic climate alterations. The reasons for that policy gap are complex and varied. To put it simply, global warming is the perfect storm of a policy problem, one that is hard to get people to care about as well as difficult to solve.

A. The Tragedy of the Atmospheric Commons

The problem of managing collectively-held resources was first articulated by Scott Gordon in 1954.[40] It has become known as the "tragedy of the commons" after the title of Garrett Hardin's famous 1968 essay.[41] In a nutshell, the idea is that when multiple entities have unfettered access to a resource they will not use it sustainably. The rational thing for each to do is to grab as much as possible as quickly as possible. Since no one can force others to restrain themselves, individual self-restraint does not make sense. The resource will disappear anyway, so those who do not join the rush will give up the benefit of their share to no purpose.

Under some circumstances, common resources can be managed effectively through legal restraints, informal social norms, or disaggregating the commons into individually-assigned property rights.[42] But any solution to the commons problem requires that an entity capable of enforc-

---

38. FLANNERY, *supra* note 3, ch. 12.

39. For descriptions of the "sound science" movement and its rhetorical success, see Holly Doremus, *Science Plays Defense: Natural Resource Management in the Bush Administration*, 32 ECOLOGY L.Q. 249, 261–65 (2005); Thomas O. McGarity, *Our Science is Sound Science and Their Science is Junk Science: Science-Based Strategies for Avoiding Accountability and Responsibility for Risk-Producing Products and Activities*, 52 U. KAN. L. REV. 897 (2004).

40. H. Scott ;2204;2204Gordon, *The Economic Theory of a Common-Property Resource: The Fishery*, 62 J. POL. ECON. 124 (1954).

41. Garrett Hardin, *The Tragedy of the Commons*, 162 SCIENCE 1243 (1968).

42. *See, e.g.,* Barton H. Thompson, Jr., *Tragically Difficult: The Obstacles to Governing the Commons*, 30 ENVTL. L. 241, 243–44 (2000) [hereinafter 2000 Thompson]; ELINOR OSTROM, GOVERNING THE COMMONS: THE EVOLUTION OF INSTITUTIONS FOR COLLECTIVE ACTION 58–102 (Cambridge Un. Press 1990).

ing regulations or defining rights, that is a government or cohesive social group, have effective control over access to the resource. That is emphatically not the case for the global atmosphere, the resource whose overuse as a waste sink for greenhouse gases is causing the climate change. Many individual governments control pollution sources within their boundaries, but they have so far proven incapable of joining together to form an effective management coalition. The Kyoto Protocol, the closest thing to an international governance regime for greenhouse gas emissions, does not include the United States, until recently the world's single largest emitting country, and does not impose any limits on emissions from developing countries, including China, which recently overtook the U.S. to become the emissions leader, and India. A more comprehensive agreement is difficult to come by, in part because the most significant players deeply distrust each other's motives, and emissions are difficult to verify, which makes any limitations correspondingly difficult to enforce.

Furthermore, because different nations have contributed to the climate change problem to different extents, and the costs and benefits of limiting global warming will not be evenly shared, there is room for many different views about how emission reductions should be equitably allocated. Not surprisingly, under these sorts of circumstances people (and nations) tend to view as fair allocations that work to their benefit.[43] That dynamic has been one of the major barriers to a more comprehensive climate change treaty, and also to U.S. participation in the Kyoto Protocol. Many environmentalists in the United States blame George W. Bush for the nation's failure to embrace some responsibility to reduce its emissions, but domestic opposition to the Kyoto agreement precedes the Bush administration. The Clinton administration (even with Al Gore, today the country's best known campaigner against global warming, in the Vice Presidential seat) refused to request Senate ratification of the treaty absent restraints on developing nations,[44] which were not forthcoming. Whatever that administration's own views on the matter, Kyoto would have been doomed in the Congress; in 1997, the Senate voted unanimously in favor of a resolution opposing any international climate change agreement that would harm the U.S. economy or exempt developing nations.[45]

Meanwhile, the absence of a comprehensive treaty provides a rationale for inaction on the U.S. domestic front. Perhaps most prominently, the EPA under George W. Bush has refused to invoke its authorities under the Clean Air Act to address greenhouse gas emissions on the grounds that any emission reductions in the United States would likely be countered by increasing emissions in China and India.[46] Scientific information, no matter how strong or frightening, cannot by itself motivate individual action to address a commons problem. Distasteful as it is, it may be economically rational for the United States not to adopt domestic greenhouse gas controls if decision makers are convinced that domestic action will not prevent the harms of global warming. The theory might be that if our children must deal with a warmer globe no matter

---

43. 2000 Thompson, *supra* note 42, at 260–62.

44. Henry D. Jacoby *et al.*, *Kyoto's Unfinished Business*, FOREIGN AFFAIRS, July/Aug. 1998, at 54; 2000 Thompson, *supra* note 42, at 255.

45. S. Res. 98, 105th Cong. (1997).

46. In responding to a petition by environmental groups and states seeking regulation of greenhouse gas emissions from motor vehicles, for example, EPA asserted that "Unilateral EPA regulation of motor vehicle GHG emissions could also weaken U.S. efforts to persuade key developing countries to reduce the GHG intensity of their economies. Considering the large populations and growing economies of some developing countries, increases in their GHG emissions could quickly overwhelm the effects of GHG reduction measures in developed countries. Any potential benefit of EPA regulation could be lost to the extent other nations decided to let their emissions significantly increase in view of U.S. emission reductions." EPA, Control of Emissions from New Highway Vehicles and Engines, 68 Fed. Reg. 52922, 52931 (Sept. 8, 2003). EPA's rationale for refusing to regulate greenhouse gas emissions from cars was invalidated by the Supreme Court in Massachusetts v. EPA, 549 U.S. 497, 127 S. Ct. 1438 (2007), but EPA has yet to commit to regulation.

what we do today, then our best gift to them might be as much wealth as we can accumulate in the short run, maximizing their options for adaptation.

B. "If Something's Hard to Do, It's Not Worth Doing"[47]

Even without the collective action problem, it would not be easy to motivate governments to take on the challenge of addressing climate change. First, human nature inclines people to ignore the problem as long as they can. Second, even when they recognize a problem, people are not inclined to act unless they see a reasonable path forward. Climate change is a challenge on both fronts because it takes us beyond the known. The level of emission reduction apparently needed to avoid potentially catastrophic temperature increases is staggering: cuts of 50% to 80% from 1990 levels by 2050,[48] in the face of demographic and economic changes that are pushing toward rapid increases in emissions.[49] Furthermore, those emissions are the product of combustion, which has for decades been the primary engine of global economies. There are no obvious substitutes waiting in the wings, as there were for most of the chlorofluorocarbons phased out by the Montreal Protocol,[50] and there is no obvious technological fix, as there was for the acid-rain producing sulfur dioxide emissions tackled by the Clean Air Act's best known tradeable permit provision.[51]

Limiting global warming is a difficult challenge by any measure. It may be that, in the end, a lower-carbon economy is better for some economies, but the transition to that economy will inevitably be disruptive. In addition, because of the collective action nature of the problem, because we don't currently have or know of technologies that can fully replace our reliance on fossil fuels, and because our delay in tackling the problem means that we are already committed to substantial warming, there is no guarantee of success. As Homer Simpson well knows, if you are doomed to failure anyway, you might as well make life easier by not even trying to accomplish

---

47. Homer Simpson offered this gem of advice to his son Bart who was (briefly) struggling to learn to play the guitar. Homer told him to put the guitar in the closet and go watch television instead. THE SIMPSONS: A COMPLETE GUIDE TO OUR FAVORITE FAMILY 87 (Ray Richmond & Antonio Coffman eds., Harper Paperbacks 1997). Another of Homer's pearls of wisdoms could be equally applicable here. As he once said to his wife Marge, "Trying is the first step towards failure." THE SIMPSONS AND PHILOSOPHY: THE D'OH! OF HOMER 14 (William Irwin, Mark T. Conard & Aeon J. Skoble eds., Open Court 2001).

48. On the advice of their science academies, the G-8 nations *Joint Science Academies Statement: Climate Change Adaptation and the G-8 Nations* (the world's largest economies) recently agreed to a 50% reduction goal in that time period. Sheryl Gay Stolberg, *G-8 Leaders Pledge to Cut Emissions in Half by 2050*, N.Y. TIMES, July 9, 2008 (noting the nations' commitment); *Joint Science Academies Statement: Climate Change Adaptation and the Transition to a Low Carbon Society*, June 2008, *available at* http://royalsociety.org/downloaddoc.asp?id=5450 (statement from G-8 nations' science academies). Other scientists contend that emissions must be rapidly reduced by at least 80% from 1990 levels to avoid disastrous climate change. Martin Parry *et al.*, *Squaring Up to Reality*, 2 NATURE REPORTS: CLIMATE CHANGE 68 (2008).

49. Between 1990 and 2004, while the Kyoto Protocol, with its detailed schedule of emission reductions from a 1990 baseline, was being negotiated and adopted, global greenhouse gas emission levels rose by 24%. INTERGOVERNMENTAL PANEL ON CLIMATE CHANGE, CONTRIBUTION OF WORKING GROUP III TO THE FOURTH ASSESSMENT REPORT, SUMMARY FOR POLICYMAKERS 3–4 (Cambridge Un. Press 2007), *available at* http://www.ipcc.ch/pdf/assessment-report/ar4/wg3/ar4-wg3-spm.pdf.

50. Cass Sunstein notes that EPA had banned most uses of CFCs in aerosol propellants well before the Montreal Protocol with no objection from consumers. Cass Sunstein, *Of Montreal and Kyoto: A Tale of Two Protocols*, 31 HARV. ENVTL. L. REV. 1, 11 (2007) [hereinafter 2007 Sunstein]. By the time the Protocol was agreed to, American companies had developed substitutes for CFCs, giving them a competitive advantage in a world where those compounds would be phased out. *Id.* at 12–15.

51. Holly Doremus and Michael Hanemann, *Of Babies and Bathwater: Why the Clean Air Act's Cooperative Federalism Framework Is Useful for Addressing Global Warming*, 50 ARIZ. L. REV. 799 (Fall 2008).

difficult things. That mind set is further encouraged by the fact that the worst harm from climate change is still decades in the future (and correspondingly that the ameliorative effects of emission reductions now will redound primarily to the benefit of our children and grandchildren rather than ourselves) and, for those of us in the United States, at considerable geographic remove.[52]

To make matters worse, so far people in the U.S. have not been shown what steps they can personally take to make a difference. Even people who are convinced that they bear some personal responsibility for a serious problem frequently will be frozen if they do not feel competent to address the problem and do not see how to develop the needed competence.[53] A sense of futility, which in the global warming context might quite rationally come from the perception that others are not going to restrain their emissions, from the belief that there is no effective substitute for fossil-fuel-derived energy, or from the knowledge that a significant amount of warming is already inevitable, dampens enthusiasm for action.

Some polls suggest that precisely that dynamic may be operating to inhibit a robust response to global warming. One recent survey found a strong correlation between personal efficacy, a variable which combined both the acceptance of responsibility for global warming and the belief that one could do something about it, and concern about climate change; respondents who scored high on the personal efficacy scale also had high levels of concern.[54] Surprisingly, greater (self-reported) knowledge about the problem correlated with reduced personal efficacy and concern.[55] Another research group has challenged that last conclusion. Jon Krosnick and his colleagues at Stanford find that the effect of added information is sensitive to political ideology, presumably because people with different political identities look to different sources of information. Democrats, they conclude, become more concerned as they gain additional information, while Republicans become less concerned.[56] In either case, however, the underlying point remains that attitudes toward global warming are significantly influenced not only by information about the scientific facts, but also by information and beliefs about responsibility and efficacy.

---

52. Poor and low-lying countries will suffer the worst effects of global warming. *See, e.g.,* NICHOLAS STERN, THE ECONOMICS OF CLIMATE CHANGE: THE STERN REVIEW 37 (Cambridge Un. Press 2007); UNITED NATIONS FRAMEWORK CONVENTION ON CLIMATE CHANGE, CLIMATE CHANGE: IMPACTS, VULNERABILITIES AND ADAPTATION IN DEVELOPING COUNTRIES (2007); Daniel A. Farber, *Basic Compensation for Victims of Climate Change*, 38 ENVTL. L. REP. 10521, 10524 (2008). By some estimates, agriculture in the United States could even benefit; at a minimum the United States does not face the extreme costs that some other nations do. *See* 2007 Sunstein, *supra* note 50, at 33–34 (estimating that implementation of the Kyoto Protocol would impose substantial costs on the United States while providing only minimal benefits). Others sharply disagree. NRDC recently issued a report concluding that climate change will cost $1.9 trillion annually (in today's dollars) by 2100. FRANK ACKERMAN & ELIZABETH A. STANTON, THE COST OF CLIMATE CHANGE: WHAT WE'LL PAY IF GLOBAL WARMING GOES UNCHECKED (May 2008), *available at* http://www.nrdc.org/globalwarming/cost/contents.asp.

53. Birgitta Gatersleben *et al.*, *Measurement and Determinants of Environmentally Significant Consumer Behavior*, 34 ENV'T & BEHAVIOR 335 (2002); Raymond DeYoung, *Some Psychological Aspects of Reduced Consumption Behavior: The Role of Intrinsic Satisfaction and Competence Motivation*, 28 ENV'T & BEHAVIOR 358, 399 (1996). *See also* Ann E. Carlson, *Recycling Norms*, 89 CAL. L. REV. 1231, 1236 (2001); Albert C. Lin, *Evangelizing Climate Change* 23–24 (draft July 29, 2008), unpublished manuscript *available at* http://papers.ssrn.com/sol3/papers.cfm?abstract_id=1186261 [hereinafter 2008 Lin].

54. Paul M. Kellstedt, Sammy Zahran & Arnold Vedlitz, *Personal Efficacy, the Information Environment, and Attitudes Toward Global Warming and Climate Change in the United States*, 28 RISK ANALYSIS 113, 121 (2008).

55. *Id.* at 122.

56. Peter Aldhous, *Knowledgeable Republicans "Less Concerned" Over Climate*, NEW SCIENTIST, May 23, 2008, at 24.

C. Self-Deception and Spin

1. The Psychology of Delusion

As Buzz Thompson has pointed out, scientific uncertainty accentuates the general human tendency to ignore or underplay the importance of problems that seem tough to solve. As he puts it: "Unfortunately, when there is scientific uncertainty, people faced with a tough solution to a commons dilemma engage in tremendous wishful thinking."[57] To the extent that the scientific evidence relevant to any policy choice is equivocal, people tend to read it as supporting their interests or their pre-existing views about the "better" policy choices.[58] They also tend to be optimistic about the ability of technology to solve looming problems before they cause serious harm, about the likelihood that they will escape harm, and about the chances that the government will bail them out if they do not.[59] Global climate change contains generous helpings of all the ingredients needed to promote self-deception. Human nature makes it almost certain that the political community will undervalue the harms global warming will produce, and overvalue the costs that solving it will impose.[60]

2. Adding Spin to the Mix

Absent conscious efforts to escape its trap, people readily fall into it the trap of self-delusion about tough problems without even realizing it. That story is familiar, and it has certainly operated in the context of global warming. But the story of climate change inaction is more complicated, because not only has the psychology of delusion not been countered, it has been abetted, both deliberately and inadvertently.

Deliberate spin came from two sources. The first was the fossil fuel industry, which faces potentially enormous financial losses if greenhouse gas emissions are regulated. The second was the administration of George W. Bush, which despite making some noises in the 2000 election campaign about regulating greenhouse gas emissions,[61] came into office with strong ties to fossil fuel interests and a corresponding commitment to inaction on the global warming front. Both worked hard to present the climate change science as highly uncertain, particularly with respect to the extent to which anthropogenic emissions are driving global warming. They were joined by a loose alliance of bloggers and right-wing pundits.

Exxon-Mobil was apparently the most active industry player. It funded a variety of climate change deniers, issued reports downplaying the work of the IPCC as unscientific, and asserted in various documents that it is difficult to determine the extent to which human actions are causing recent climatic changes. The Union of Concerned Scientists has detailed how Exxon funded front organizations to create the illusion of a substantial community of scientific doubters.[62] One major recipient of Exxon's largesse was the conservative think-tank

---

57. 2008 Thompson, *supra* note 42, at 258.

58. *See, e.g.,* Daniel Sarewitz, *How Science Makes Environmental Controversies Worse,* 7 ENVTL. SCI. & POL'Y 385, 390–92 (2004) [hereinafter 2004 Sarewitz]; Naomi Oreskes, *Science and Public Policy: What's Proof Got to Do With It?,* 7 ENVTL. SCI. & POL'Y 369, 375 (2004); 2008 Thompson, *supra* note 42, at 258–59; Jeffrey J. Rachlinski, *The Psychology of Global Climate Change,* 2000 U. ILL. L. REV. 299, 304–306 (2000) [hereinafter 2000 Rachlinski].

59. 2008 Thompson, *supra* note 42, at 258–59, 263–65.

60. On the psychology of climate change, in addition to 2008 Thompson, *see also* 2000 Rachlinski, *supra* note 58; 2008 Lin, *supra* note 53, at 21–23.

61. Editorial, *Mr. ;25726;25726Bush Reverses Course,* N.Y. TIMES, March 15, 2001, at A24.

62. UNION OF CONCERNED SCIENTISTS, SMOKE, MIRRORS & HOT AIR: HOW EXXON MOBIL USES BIG TOBACCO'S TACTICS TO MANUFACTURE UNCERTAINTY ON CLIMATE SCIENCE (Jan. 2007), *available at* http://www.ucsusa.org/news/press_release/ExxonMobil-GlobalWarming-tobacco.html.

American Enterprise Institute, which offered payments of $10,000 each to scientists and economists for papers critical of the 2007 IPCC report.[63] The Competitive Enterprise Institute, a lobbying organization which has received funding from Exxon and the automobile industry, produced a series of ads deriding the idea that carbon dioxide should be treated as a harmful pollutant.[64] Eventually, England's premier scientific academy, the Royal Society, criticized Exxon for promoting a misleading view of climate science through these sorts of activities, leading other climate skeptics to accuse the Royal Society of trying to stifle debate.[65] A lawsuit filed in early 2008 charges that Exxon, with the help of other oil, coal, and electric power interests, engaged in a deliberate campaign "to mislead the public about the science of global warming."[66]

Inside the government, the George W. Bush White House vigorously used its control over government scientists and the channels of agency communication to reinforce the idea that global warming science is highly uncertain, and to block messages that might have encouraged calls to act against greenhouse gas emissions. Political appointees edited agency reports on global warming to emphasize uncertainty.[67] The media contacts of government climate experts like James Hansen at NASA were screened, and attempts were made to restrict his public statements about global warming, even when he clearly explained that he was speaking only for himself and not as a representative of NASA.[68] The White House insisted on reviewing and clearing testimony presented to Congress by agency scientists including Julie Gelberding, Director of the Centers for Disease Control and Prevention, who was not permitted to describe climate change as a serious public health concern.[69] In addition to emphasizing uncertainty, the administration also sowed doubt about whether global warming would be such a bad thing, or whether controlling it should be seen as a human responsibility. Most prominently, in May 2007 NASA administrator Michael Griffin explained his views to National Public Radio in the following terms:

> I have no doubt that ... a trend of global warming exists. I am not sure that it is fair to say that it is a problem we must wrestle with. To assume that it is a problem is to assume that the state of Earth's climate today is the optimal climate, the best climate that we could have or ever have had and that we need to take steps to make sure that it doesn't change. First of all, I don't think it's within the power of human beings to assure that the climate does not change, as millions of years of history have shown. And second of all, I guess I would ask which human beings—where and when—are to be accorded the privilege of deciding that this particular climate that we have right here today, right now is the best climate for all other human beings. I think that's a rather arrogant position for people to take.[70]

---

63. Ian Sample, *Scientists Offered Cash to Dispute Climate Study*, The Guardian (UK), Feb. 2, 2007.

64. The tag line was "Carbon dioxide: they call it pollution, we call it life." Fred Pearce, *State of Denial*, New Scientist, Nov. 4, 2006 [hereinafter 2006 Pearce].

65. Eliot Marshal, *Royal Society Takes a Shot at Exxon-Mobil*, 313 Science 1871 (2006).

66. Native Village of Kivalina v. ExxonMobil Corp., Complaint for Damages 47–62, Civ. No. N.D. Cal., Feb. 6, 2008, *available at* http://turtletalk.files.wordpress.com/2008/02/kivalina-complaint.pdf.

67. Holly Doremus, *Scientific and Political Integrity in Environmental Policy*, 86 Texas L. Rev. 1601, 1612 (2008) [hereinafter 2008 Doremus]; Tarek Maassarani, Gov't Accountability Project, Redacting the Science of Climate Change: An Investigative and Synthesis Report 47 (2007) *available at* http://www.whistleblower.org/doc/2007/Final%203.28%20Redacting%20Climate%20Science%20Report.pdf; Allegations of Political Interference with Government Climate Change Science: Hearing Before the H. Comm. on Oversight and Government Reform, 110th Cong. 116 (2007) (statement of Rick Pilz, formerly senior associate, U.S. Climate Change Science Program).

68. 2008 Doremus, *supra* note 67, at 1609.

69. Juliet Eilperin, *Sen. Boxer Seeks Answers on Redacted Testimony*, Wash. Post, Oct. 25, 2007, at A2.

70. National Public Radio, *NASA Chief Questions Urgency of Global Warming*, May 31, 2007, http://www.npr.org/templates/story/story.php?storyId=10571499.

Global warming science became a partisan issue in the Congress as well. Senator James Inhofe, chair of the Senate Committee on Environment and Public Works until the Democrats gained the Senate majority in 2007, was particularly aggressive. He convened a series of hearings intended to show that global warming was a hoax perpetrated against the American people by radical environmentalists. The star witness at one hearing was novelist Michael Crichton, whose fictional tale "State of Fear" tells of an environmental group struggling to get the world's attention about global warming in order to improve their fund-raising fortunes.[71] In a move many climate scientists interpreted as intimidation, Inhofe also sought information on funding sources from the employers of U.S. scientists involved in the IPCC process.[72] In the House, Rep. Joe Barton (R-TX) pressured Michael Mann, author of the famous "hockey stick" temperature graph that has been widely cited as strong evidence of anthropogenic global warming. Barton demanded that Mann, and his colleagues produce volumes of information, including unpublished data and responses to detailed questions about their funding sources and methodology,[73] commissioned a report evaluating Mann's work, and held a hearing to criticize Mann.[74] The key conclusions of Mann's work, though, were subsequently endorsed by the National Academy of Sciences and have been replicated by other researchers.[75]

Industry and certain politicians were deliberately spinning, trying to persuade the public that the science of global warming was too uncertain to justify policy intervention. They received an inadvertent boost from the media, which until recently reported the global warming story primarily as one of scientific conflict, even after the scientific community had reached a strong consensus. Proving either that chutzpah knows no bounds or that people have a truly remarkable ability to filter evidence so that it reinforces their own views, Senator Inhofe held a final hearing as chair of the Senate Committee on Environment and Public Works in December 2006 to accuse the media of squelching the voices of climate change skeptics.[76] The reality seems quite different. Several studies have found that media coverage of global warming has tended to focus on uncertainty,[77] to exaggerate the extent and importance of scientific disagreement in the name of balance,[78] and to link indications of uncertainty with claims that policy decisions should be put off.[79]

Recently, the media seem to have become more conscious of the extent to which a search for "balance" focused primarily on including comments from global warming skeptics can distort

---

71. Crichton's may be the first thriller to be stuffed full of footnotes in an attempt to prove a scientific theory (in this case that human burning of fossil fuels is causing global warming) wrong.

72. 2006 Pearce, *supra* note 64.

73. John M. Budd, *Information, Analysis and Ideology: A Case Study of Science and the Public Interest*, 58 J. Am. Soc. Information Sci. & Tech. 2366, 2367 (2007) [hereinafter 2007 Budd]; Wendy Wagner & Rena Steinzor, *Saving Science from Politicians*, Baltimore Sun, Sept. 5, 2006, at A11; 2006 Pearce, *supra* note 64.

74. 2007 Budd, *supra* note 73, at 2368–69.

75. 2006 Pearce, *supra* note 64; Editorial, *Cooling the Hot Air*, St. Louis Post-Dispatch, June 28, 2006; National Research Council, Surface Temperature Reconstructions for the Last 2000 Years (2006).

76. In his opening statement at the hearing, Inhofe claimed that "Much of the mainstream media has subverted its role as an objective source of information on climate change into the role of an advocate." U.S. Senate, Committee on Environment and Public Works, Hearing on Climate Change and the Media, Dec. 6, 2006, Statement of Senator James Inhofe, *available at* http://epw.senate.gov/hearing_statements.cfm?id=266624.

77. Liisa Antilla, *Climate of Scepticism: U.S. Newspaper Coverage of the Science of Climate Change*, 15 Global Envtl. Change 338 (2005).

78. *See, e.g.*, Jules Boykoff and Maxwell Boykoff, *Balance as Bias: Global Warming and the US Prestige Press*, 14 Global Envtl. Change 125 (2004) (finding that more than half of the articles on global warming published in the New York Times, Washington Post, Wall Street Journal and Los Angeles Times between 1988 and 2002 treated as roughly equal the views that climate change is entirely natural and that it is largely human-caused). *See also* Weart, *supra* note 3, at 105 (noting that journalists tended to "present every scientific question as if it were a head-on battle between two equal and diametrically opposite sides").

79. Stephen C. Zehr, *Public Representations of Scientific Uncertainty about Global Climate Change*, 9 Public Understanding of Science 85 (2000).

the story, and have begun to present the scientific consensus that warming is both real and human-caused more clearly. But even without giving undue air time to climate change skeptics, the media can still sow confusion by covering every new story as a major development, without carefully parsing what is known with confidence and what remains unclear. Andrew Revkin of the NEW YORK TIMES, arguably the premier American journalist covering climate change, recently wrote that such coverage can distract and confuse the public, as major breakthroughs are announced one day only to be apparently discredited the next.[80]

The disinformation campaign seems to have been successful, at least to a point. A 2006 survey found that 64% of American adults (wrongly) believe there is a lot of disagreement among scientists about whether global warming is occurring.[81] That level is essentially unchanged from 1997,[82] despite the progressive strengthening of the scientific consensus over that time. Just 30% believe that people are primarily responsible for global warming.[83] But spin can only do so much. It cannot change the way people experience the world. More than half now believe that temperatures are rising and extreme weather events becoming more common, both locally and globally.[84] And although only 38% currently believe it is a serious current threat, 80% see it as a serious future problem if nothing is done.[85]

IV. Lessons for Scientifically-Informed Policy

The global warming problem is distinctive in its importance and its difficulty. It is the defining environmental issue of our time, perhaps the defining policy issue, period. But in many respects it is much like the many other environmental challenges we have been dealing with for more than a generation. If we can understand why abundant scientific information seems to co-exist comfortably with policy inaction on climate change, we may be able to make progress not only on climate change but on those other issues as well.

Three key lessons emerge from this case study of climate change science and policy. First, it is naïve, and potentially counterproductive, to assume that science alone will save the world. While scientific information is often an essential factor, whether and to what extent it motivates changes in government policy or individual behavior depends on the context. Advocates for change need to pay close attention to that context. Second, the status quo is especially resistant to change where the need for change is equivocal, the harm in the future, and the alternatives apparently difficult. That means that uncertainty works in favor of the status quo. Knowing that, and knowing that uncertainty is the hallmark of environmental conflict,[86] environmental advocates and environmental scientists should work to improve the ways that scientific uncertainty are communicated to the public and policymakers. Third, because spinning the facts is so tempting and so easy for scientifically complex problems like global warming, it would be useful to have a trusted neutral source of scientific information. That may simply not be possible in the current partisan climate. Ideally, though, it is a role that would be filled by a politically-independent government agency. Those who seek scientifically educated policymaking, whatever their values, should support the creation and funding of such an agency.

---

80. Andrew Revkin, *Climate Experts Tussle Over Details; Public Gets Whiplash*, N.Y. TIMES, July 29, 2008.

81. ABC News/Time/Stanford Poll, Press Release, *Intensity Spikes in Concern on Warming, Many See a Change in Weather Patterns*, Mar. 14, 2006, at 2.

82. *Id.*

83. *Id.*

84. *Id.* at 1.

85. *Id.* at 3.

86. Holly Doremus, *Constitutive Law and Environmental Policy*, 22 STAN. ENVTL. L.J. 295, 319–21 (2003) [hereinafter 2003 Doremus]; Richard J. Lazarus, *Restoring What's Environmental About Environmental Law in the Supreme Court*, 47 UCLA L. REV. 703, 747 (2000).

Science is never the entire story. Environmentalists and environmental scientists sometimes seem to assume that if only the public understood the facts, the policy they favor would follow automatically. When they present their version of the facts and nothing happens, they conclude that the policy process is not adequately attuned to scientific information. The climate change story shows that while there often are difficulties in communicating scientific information to the public and policymakers, that is not by any means always the reason for inaction. People who are fully and accurately informed of all the information about climate change might nonetheless oppose action, rationally because their calculation of the individual costs and benefits shows that they cannot solve the problem at a cost justified by their benefits, or irrationally because the problem seems distant or hard to address.

To the extent the problem is one of lack of motivation or capacity, rather than lack of information, piling on information or accusing people of being deaf to the science will not help and may even alienate the target audience. Environmental advocates, and environmental scientists who get involved in policy debates, need to be attuned to value differences and value opacity. They need to be ready to explain, patiently and without their exasperation showing too clearly, why people should care about the changes global warming will bring, why they should believe that they bear some individual responsibility for global warming, and what exactly they can do about it.

That last may be the most important at this point. Advocates for greenhouse gas emission limits must be prepared to confront the tough questions of what it will take to reduce emissions enough to prevent drastic climate change. Energy efficiency ought to be an easy sell, because it is almost always an economic benefit to the actor, but it must seem feasible. Simply telling people to drive less or use less electricity is not likely to help; showing them that mass transit is available or how they can reduce wasted electricity use by "vampire" appliances should be more effective.

Committed leadership, which has been sorely lacking at the national level, might go a long way toward increasing motivation to act. A charismatic leader willing to take responsibility for the problem could help the public understand its importance, see the justification for some level of sacrifice or disruption, model steps forward, and show the benefits to be gained from those steps over time. The American political system seems structurally incapable of producing such leaders at this point; the unwillingness or inability of Al Gore, who is clearly personally committed to the cause of preventing global warming, to step forward strongly when he was vice president is a depressing case in point. One reason states and local governments are doing more than the national government, however, is that leaders have stepped forward at those levels. If climate change leadership turns out to be good for the political careers of people like governors Arnold Schwarzenegger (R-CA) and Kathleen Sibelius (D-KS), we might hope to see such leadership on the national level.

The nuances of science matter, but are difficult to communicate. While information is rarely if ever sufficient to motivate action, it is frequently necessary to that purpose. Before they will demand political action, especially at significant cost to their own interests, people must believe that global warming matters in ways that they care about. In a polarized world, that message may be difficult to get across where there is significant scientific uncertainty.

Scientists are accustomed to thinking that the "truth" about the world they study will eventually win out in the marketplace of ideas, but that is not necessarily the case in the rough-and-tumble public marketplace. Very few members of the public have the time or training needed to get their information directly from the scientific literature. The information they get is necessarily mediated in one way or another, and in many cases they will not have much ability to evaluate it themselves.

The nature and relevance of uncertainty in scientific information seem particularly prone to miscommunication. Uncertainty is easily exaggerated. Nearly every scientific study, for example, can be criticized. Professor Tom McGarity has vividly described the ways that uncertainty is magnified in the tort system by seriatim attacks on individual studies. If each individual study can be knocked out as flawed, nothing remains to support a judgment in favor of an injured plaintiff, even if a reasonable scientist working in the field would view the collective weight of the studies as supporting liability.[87] Anti-regulatory interests and the Bush administration have made some efforts to import the same strategy into administrative proceedings.[88]

The importance of uncertainty is also easily overstated. Sometimes uncertainty matters to the policy decision, and sometime it does not. How likely it is that the Greenland ice sheet will melt, and how quickly, are highly relevant to decisions about emission limits and adaptation, because they are closely linked to the extent and rate of sea level rise. Exactly how warm the earth was in 800 A.D. may be far less relevant, unless it tells us something important about the reliability of one or more climate models. But if the difference between important and unimportant uncertainty is not openly discussed in the public debate, it can easily be lost. In fact, opponents of environmental policy decisions often attack the science behind those decisions, frequently blunderbuss-style. If they can blow holes in any part of the supporting science, they may think, they can bring down the decision. One recent study suggests that theory does not work where the agency responsible for interpreting the science is also the relevant audience,[89] but it might be more effective where the relevant audience is the inexpert general public.

Scientists must take the first steps toward a more nuanced treatment of uncertainty. Many environmental scientists, both within agencies and outside them, have tended in the past to downplay the uncertainty in their understanding of controversial policy issues.[90] They quite reasonably fear that any uncertainty may be exploited to prevent or delay action. But their opponents have already learned how to identify and exploit uncertainty; pretending that it does not exist is no longer an option. Instead, scientist-advocates should focus on more accurately describing uncertainty, its relevance to decisions, and its amenability to reduction. They should offer that explanation to journalists, who may be better qualified to translate it for the general public. Admittedly, scientists and journalists both may be skeptical about the ability of the American public, as a group notoriously scientifically illiterate, to follow a nuanced discussion of uncertainty. But the public is not so much illiterate about science as it is about the role of science in society.[91] The discussion I propose should prove both accessible and educational; it requires no specialized knowledge of the details of climate physics or ecology to understand the potential sources of uncertainty and the ways that uncertainty can vary in importance.

Trusted neutral sources of information are desperately needed. Although I have just proposed that scientists with an interest in policy and science journalists can spark an important societal conversation, even I am skeptical that, at this point in the game, anyone would listen. Environmental science in general, and climate change science in particular, have become not just politicized but polarized. Believing in climate change or not has come to be associated with membership in particular tribes—environmentalists or economists to put it in crude shorthand. Those who adopt the "wrong" view are drummed out of the tribe.[92] Members of such polarized fac-

---

87. Thomas O. McGarity, *On the Prospect of "Daubertizing" Judicial Review of Risk Assessment*, 66 Law & Contemp. Probs. 155 (2003).

88. *Id.*; *see also* Holly Doremus, *Data Gaps in Natural Resource Management: Sniffing for Leaks Along the Information Pipeline*, 83 Ind. L.J. 407, 440–42 (2008).

89. David S. Caudill & Donald E. Curley, *Strategic Idealizations of Science to Oppose Environmental Regulation: A Case Study of Five TMDL Controversies*, manuscript on file with the author.

90. 2003 Doremus, *supra* note 86, at 296.

91. Henry Bauer, Scientific Literacy and the Myth of the Scientific Method (Un. of Illinois Press 1992).

92. Douglas Kysar and James Salzman, *Environmental Tribalism*, 87 Minn. L. Rev. 1099 (2003) [hereinafter 2003 Kysar & Salzman]; 2004 Sarewitz, *supra* note 58.

tions accept information only from fellow members, and as they listen only to others who agree with them become ever more set and extreme in their views.[93]

Once polarization has set in, the cycle is difficult to break. Members of one tribe will discount, or even reject entirely, information that comes from the other. That dynamic plays right into the strengths of campaigns to exaggerate uncertainty—those inclined to oppose regulation will be primed to hear such claims as persuasive and important. A strong consensus among the relevant scientific community will not change minds if the entire scientific community (or large chunks of it) are identified as members of the "environmentalist" tribe.

We are well down the road of climate change information polarization. Only a source of information trusted by both sides has a chance to take us off that path. Organized skepticism campaigns and the reaction to them have bred distrust of scientists in general, and of global warming science in particular, among the public.[94]

Getting out of the polarization box will require a more readily trusted source of information. That is a role that, in the abstract, at least, the government ought to be best qualified to fill. But it cannot be filled by the Presidentially-controlled executive branch, which has played a key role in the polarization process. Even a change in administration will not increase the level of trust in administration sources; it likely will only change the identity of the tribes who agree and disagree with the information. Congress should consider creating a politically independent climate science agency, perhaps one modeled on the academic-science-oriented U.S. Geological Survey, but insulated from direct control by a politically-appointed Cabinet member. At the very least, Congress should provide added civil service protection for career government scientists.[95] Because the executive is not the only governmental branch prone to elide the distinctions between science and politics, Congress should also protect this independent agency from its annual cycle of budget politics by providing a dedicated revenue stream independent of annual appropriations.

V. Conclusion

There are many reasons for pessimism about the ability of scientific knowledge to catalyze timely policy responses to global warming. The science itself is complex and poorly matched in scale or time with the policy problem. People are prone to stick their heads in the sand when possible, ignoring important problems that are difficult to tackle. Scientific uncertainty promotes that reaction by making it easier to rationalize inattention.

Still, there is reason for optimism. As Scott Saleska and Kirsten Engel remind us, "facts are stubborn things."[96] As the world warms, the problem becomes harder to ignore. Indeed, the domestic politics of global warming has shifted substantially over the last few years. Many states and cities have established emission reduction goals and taken the first steps toward meeting those goals, driven by a combination of increased public awareness of warming[97] and dramatic

---

93. 2003 Kysar & Salzman, *supra* note 92, at 1121–22.

94. In the 2006 poll, a plurality (41%) of respondents said they only moderately trusted the things scientists say about the environment. Just as many trusted scientists completely as trusted them not at all, supporting the tribal polarization hypothesis. ABC News/Time/Stanford University Poll, *supra* note 81, at 10.

95. 2008 Doremus, *supra* note 67, at 1647.

96. Scott Saleska and Kirsten Engel, *"Facts are Stubborn Things": An Empirical Reality Check in the Theoretical Debate Over the Race to the Bottom in State Environmental Standard-Setting*, 8 CORNELL J. L. & PUB. POL'Y 55 (1998). The quote is from John Adams, who wrote: "Facts are stubborn things; and whatever may be our wishes, our inclinations, or the dictates of our passion, they cannot alter the state of facts and evidence." John Adams, *Argument and Report, in* 3 LEGAL PAPERS OF JOHN ADAMS 98, 269 (L. Kinvin Wroth & Hiller B. Zobel eds., Belknap Press of Harvard Un. Press 1965).

97. *See supra* note 81.

reports about its current and future consequences.[98] The question is whether we can escape the twin traps of scientific uncertainty and flawed human nature in time to prevent a climate catastrophe.

Notes

1. John D. Sterman, *Risk Communication and Climate: Mental Models and Mass Balance*, 322 SCIENCE 532 (Oct. 24, 2008) (reference omitted):

> [A] 2007 survey found a majority of U.S. respondents (54%) advocated a "wait-and-see" or "go slow" approach to emissions reductions. Larger majorities favored wait-and-see or go slow in Russia, China, and India. For most people, uncertainty about the risks of climate change means costly actions to reduce emissions should be deferred; if climate change begins to harm the economy, mitigation policies can then be implemented. However, long delays in the climate's response to anthropogenic forcing means such reasoning is erroneous.

> Wait-and-see works well in simple systems with short lags. We can wait until the teakettle whistles before removing it from the flame because there is little lag between the boil, the whistle, and our response. Similarly, wait-and-see would be a prudent response to climate change if there were short delays in the response of the climate system to intervention. However, there are substantial delays in every link of a long causal chain stretching from the implementation of emissions abatement policies to emissions reductions to changes in atmospheric GHG concentrations to surface warming to changes in ice sheets, sea level, agricultural productivity, extinction rates, and other impacts. Mitigating the risks therefore requires emissions reductions long before additional harm is evident. Wait-and-see policies implicitly presume the climate is roughly a first-order linear system with a short time constant, rather than a complex dynamical system with long delays, multiple positive feedbacks, and nonlinearities that may cause abrupt, costly, and irreversible regime changes.

2. John D. Sterman, *Risk Communication and Climate: Mental Models and Mass Balance*, 322 SCIENCE 532, 533 (Oct. 24, 2008) (reference omitted):

> Obviously, few people are trained in climatology or nonlinear dynamics, and public understanding of these topics is poor. But there is a deeper problem: poor understanding of stocks and flows—the concept of accumulation. Accumulation is pervasive in everyday experience: Our bathtubs accumulate the inflow of water through the drain, our bank accounts accumulate deposits less withdrawals, and we all struggle to control our weight by managing the inflows and outflows of calories through diet and exercise. Yet, despite their ubiquity, research shows that people have difficulty relating the flows into and out of a stock to the level of the stock, even in simple, familiar contexts such as bank accounts and bathtubs. Instead, people often assess system dynamics using a pat-

---

98. *See, e.g.,* CALIFORNIA DEP'T OF WATER RESOURCES, PROGRESS ON INCORPORATING CLIMATE CHANGE INTO PLANNING AND MANAGEMENT OF CALIFORNIA'S WATER RESOURCES, TECHNICAL MEMORANDUM REPORT 2–19 (2006), *available at* http:// www.climatechange.water.ca.gov/docs/DWRClimateChangeJuly06.pdf; NATIONAL SCIENCE AND TECHNOLOGY COUNCIL, *supra* note 15; U.S. CLIMATE CHANGE SCIENCE PROGRAM, Synthesis and Assessment Product 3.3, WEATHER AND CLIMATE EXTREMES IN A CHANGING CLIMATE, REGIONS OF FOCUS: NORTH AMERICA, HAWAII, CARIBBEAN, AND U.S. PACIFIC ISLANDS (June 2008).

tern-matching heuristic, assuming that the output of a system should "look like"—be positively correlated with—its inputs.

....

Poor understanding of accumulation leads to serious errors in reasoning about climate change, [even among students at MIT].

... 84% drew patterns that violated the principles of accumulation. If emissions followed the path in the typical example shown, atmospheric CO_2 would continue to rise. Nearly two-thirds of the participants asserted that atmospheric GHGs can stabilize even though emissions continuously exceed removal—analogous to arguing a bathtub continuously filled faster than it drains will never overflow. Most believe that stopping the growth of emissions stops the growth of GHG concentrations. The erroneous belief that stabilizing emissions would quickly stabilize the climate supports wait-and-see policies but violates basic laws of physics.

3. Andrew C. Revkin, *The Greenhouse Effect and The Bathtub Effect*, THE NEW YORK TIMES, Jan. 28, 2009, *available at* http:dotearth.blogs.nytimes.com/2009/01/28/the-greenhouse-effect-and-the-bathtub-effect:

We tend to think that the output of a process should be correlated with—look like—its input. If greenhouse gas emissions are growing, we think, the climate will warm, and if we cut emissions we imagine that the climate will cool. In systems with significant accumulations, however, such correlational reasoning does not hold. Rather it's more like filling a bathtub. The amount of carbon dioxide in the atmosphere is like the level of water in a bathtub. The level grows as long as you pour more water in through the faucet than drains out. Right now, we pour about twice as much CO_2 into the atmospheric tub than is removed on net by natural processes.

... Further, ... the net removal of CO_2 from the atmosphere is likely to fall as the stocks that absorb all that carbon, particularly the oceans, fill up. There are other key "bathtubs"—accumulations—that contribute to the irreversibility of climate change....

... Because the drains out of the various bathtubs involved in the climate—atmospheric concentrations, the heat balance of the surface and oceans, ice sheet accumulations, and thermal expansion of the oceans are small and slow, the emissions we generate in the next few decades will lead to changes that, on any time scale we can contemplate, are irreversible.

....

4. *See* JAMES LOVELOCK, THE VANISHING FACE OF GAIA: A FINAL WARNING 7 (Basic Books 2009) [hereinafter 2009 LOVELOCK]:

Just think, as I write this in 2008, more than 1000 of the world's best climate scientists have worked for seventeen years to forecast future climates and have failed to predict the climate of today. I have little confidence in the smooth, rising curve of temperature that modelers predict for the next ninety years. The Earth's history and simple climate models based on the notion of a live and responsive Earth suggest that sudden change and surprise are more likely.

5. 2009 LOVELOCK at 31:

It is time to wake up and realize that Gaia is no cozy mother that nurtures humans and can be propitiated by gestures such as carbon trading or sustainable development. Gaia, even though we are part of her, will always dictate the terms of peace.

Chapter Two

The Justice of Transformative Change and the Spread of Global Fever

Chapter Two

The Justice of Transformative Change and the Spread of Global Fever

Atiq Rahman, Bangladesh Centre for Advanced Studies, 1995, *quoted in* J. TIMMONS ROBERTS & BRADLEY C. PARKS, A CLIMATE OF INJUSTICE: GLOBAL INEQUALITY, NORTH-SOUTH POLITICS, AND CLIMATE POLICY 2 (MIT Press 2007) [hereinafter 2007 ROBERTS & PARKS], *citing* TOM ATHANASIOU & PAUL BAER, DEAD HEAT: GLOBAL JUSTICE AND CLIMATE CHANGE 23 (Seven Stories Press 2002):

> If climate change makes our country uninhabitable, we will march with our wet feet into your living rooms.

2007 ROBERTS & PARKS 4–5:

> Scientists and environmentalists in the world's wealthier nations are mystified as to why this life-threatening issue has elicited such an anemic policy response, but many of them miss the point: Responses to climate change are wound up with other social and economic issues facing nations and are fundamentally about inequality and injustice.

CHRISTIAN AID, THE HUMAN FACE OF CLIMATE CHANGE: A CHRISTIAN AID REPORT 4 (2007), *available at* http://www.christianaid.org.uk/Images/CC_Impacts_Adaptation_final.pdf (last visited June 8, 2009):

> Climate change and poverty are mixing in the lives of the world's poorest people, to deadly effect. More frequent drought and more severe seasonal flooding are testing the limits of community resilience, pushing already precarious lives closer to the edge.

2007 ELIZABETH KOLBERT, FIELD NOTES FROM A CATASTROPHE: MAN, NATURE AND CLIMATE CHANGE 20 (Bloomsbury 2007) [hereinafter 2007 KOLBERT]:

> In most parts of Alaska, the permafrost has warmed by three degrees [F] since the early 1980s. In some parts of the state, it has warmed by nearly six degrees.

OLIVER TICKELL, KYOTO 2: HOW TO MANAGE THE GLOBAL GREENHOUSE 21 (Zed Books 2008) [hereinafter 2008 TICKELL]:

> Arctic heating will also warm the tundra regions of the Canadian, Siberian and Alaskan Arctic, with the risk of emitting billions of tonnes of methane—a greenhouse gas some thirty times more powerful than carbon dioxide—presently locked up in the permafrost.... Indeed, this process may already be under way in western Siberia, which has warmed by 3°C over the last forty years, as reported by Fred Pearce in NEW SCIENTIST....

2008 THOMAS L. FRIEDMAN, HOT, FLAT AND CROWDED: WHY WE NEED A GREEN REVOLUTION— AND HOW IT CAN RENEW AMERICA 109 (Farrar, Strauss & Giroux 2008) [hereinafter 2008 FRIEDMAN]:

Based on current science, the IPCC concluded that if the total human influence on the atmosphere reaches the equivalent of 550 ppm of CO_2, which is exactly where we're heading, by mid-century that will probably lead in time (there is a time lag, because it takes a while to heat up the oceans) to an approximately 3-degree-Celsius rise in global average temperature. If, through mitigation efforts, we manage to cap the changes in the atmosphere to the equivalent of 450 ppm of CO_2, that would probably result in an approximately 2-degree-Celsius rise in global average temperature.

2007 KOLBERT at 18:

[Sign just past the treeline at Colfoot on the Dalton Highway, built for Alaskan oil]: An evergreen was marked with a plaque that read "Farthest North Spruce Tree on the Alaska Pipeline: Do Not Cut." Predictably, someone had taken a knife to it.

I. When, Where, and How:
A Simple Matter of Six Degrees

British Journalist and National Geographic explorer, Mark Lynas, hit upon the notion of assembling the vast and rapidly accumulating knowledge about climate change into a degree-by-degree guide to our planet's future. Lynas relies upon a one to six degree centigrade rise in the planet's temperature by the end of this century, the same figures cited by the IPCC.

MARK LYNAS, SIX DEGREES: OUR FUTURE ON A HOTTER PLANET 15 (National Geographic 2008) [hereinafter 2008 LYNAS]:

Scientists have now made hundreds of projections—mostly based on complex computer models—of how future global warming will affect everything from corn crops in Tanzania to snowfall in the Alps.

2008 LYNAS at 16:

My first chapter included all the global-warming impacts I could find associated with a one degree rise in temperature, my second chapter covered two degrees, my third chapter covered three degrees ... and on up the scale to six degrees—the worst-case scenario.

Would small changes in global average temperatures really make discernible differences?

2008 LYNAS at 17–18:

Consider this: Eighteen thousand years ago, during the deepest freeze of the last ice age, global temperatures were about six degrees cooler than today. In that frigid climate, ice sheets stretched across North America from sea to shining sea. As glacial grooves in the rocks in Central Park attest, New York was buried under a thick slab of ice, more than a mile deep as it stretched into the heart of the continent. Northern New Jersey was buried, as was all the Great Lakes area, and almost the entirety of Canada. Farther south, the agricultural heartland of states like Missouri and Iowa would have been freezing tundra, blasted by dust-laden winds sweeping down from the ice cap, and underlain by layers of solid permafrost. During the Ice Age, humans were displaced far to the south, where places that are now subtropical, like Florida and California, maintained a temperate climate.

A. One Degree

2008 LYNAS at 57:

But as the oceans have warmed due to the human-enhanced greenhouse effect, bleaching episodes have hit the world's coral reefs with increasing—and devastating—regularity. The first mass-bleaching event occurred on the Great Barrier Reef in 1998. Since then things have got steadily worse. In 2002 another mass-bleaching event occurred—this time 60 to 95 percent of all the reefs surveyed across the marine park were bleached to some extent. A small number of reefs, particularly those close to shore where the waters were hottest, suffered almost total wipeout.

2008 LYNAS at 58:

By the 2020s, [Ove Hoegh-Guldberg] discovered, with less than a degree of global warming, the seas will have heated up so much that the 1998 Barrier Reef mass-bleaching event would be a "normal" year. Given that it takes 30 years or so for a seriously bleached reef to recover, annual bleaching events will devastate the ecosystem.... Other coral reef ecosystems—from the Caribbean to Thailand—would be similarly transformed. With the end of the coral reefs, one of the world's great treasure troves of biodiversity would be destroyed forever.

2008 LYNAS at 60:

[V]ery few of the world's reefs are in any state to take on the challenges of climate change. Direct human interference—from sewage, overfishing, and agricultural runoff—has already reduced coral reefs across the globe to shadows of their former pristine selves. In total 70 percent of the world's reefs are now either dead or dying. This is a disaster of an almost unimaginable scale for global biodiversity: Second only to rain forests in terms of the vibrancy and diversity of life they nurture, coral reefs worldwide shelter and feed a third of all life in the oceans, including 4,000 types of fish.

B. Two Degrees

2008 LYNAS at 88:

Greenland will tip into irreversible melt once global temperatures rise past a mere 1.2° C.

2008 LYNAS at 94:

Sea levels are currently rising at 3.3 millimeters per year—much faster than the 2.2 millimeters projected by the IPCC's 2001 report. If, as Hansen suggests is likely, melt rates as rapid as those at the end of the last ice age begin to happen this century, the whole Greenland ice sheet could disappear within 140 years. The geography of the world's coastlines would then look radically different. Miami would disappear entirely, as would most of Manhattan. Central London would be flooded. Bangkok, Bombay, and Shanghai would also lose most of their area. In all, half of humanity would have to move to higher ground, leaving landscapes and buildings and monuments that have been central to civilization for over a thousand years to be gradually consumed by the sea.

2008 LYNAS at 76–77:

Humans have already managed to reduce the alkalinity of the seas by 0.1 pH units. As Professor Ken Caldeira of the Carnegie Institution's Global Ecology Department says; "The current rate of carbon dioxide input is nearly 50 times higher than normal. In less than 100 years, the pH of the oceans could drop by as much as half a unit from its natural 8.2 to about 7.7." This drop may not sound like much, but this half point on the pH scale represents a fivefold increase in acidity. And because the oceans circulate only very slowly, even if atmospheric carbon dioxide levels are eventually stabilized— perhaps because humanity wakes up to this warming effect—these changes in ocean chemistry will persist for thousands of years.

This fast-moving area of scientific research was the subject of a major report by the Royal Society in June 2005, which identified some of the main concerns that are increasingly keeping marine biologists awake at night. First and foremost is the possibility that even with relatively low future emissions during this century (equating to two degrees or less of temperature warming), large areas of the Southern Ocean and part of the Pacific will become effectively toxic to organisms with calcium carbonate shells after about 2050. With higher emissions, most of the entire global ocean will become eventually too acidic to support calcereous marine life.

The most important life-forms to be affected are those that form the bedrock of the oceanic food chain: plankton. Although individually tiny (only a few thousandths of a millimeter across), photosynthesizing plankton like coccolithophores are perhaps the most important plant resource on Earth. They compose at least half the biosphere's entire primary production—that's equivalent to all the land plants put together—often forming blooms so extensive that they stain the ocean surface green and can easily be photographed from space. The places where phytoplankton thrive are the breadbaskets of the global oceans: All higher species from mackerel to humpback whales ultimately depend on them. Yet coccolithophores have a calcium carbonate structure, and this makes them especially vulnerable to ocean acidification. When scientists simulated the oceans of the future by pumping artificially high levels of dissolved CO_2 into sections of a Norwegian fjord, they watched in dismay as coccolithophore structures first corroded and then began to disintegrate altogether.

While Lynas provides futuristic narrative to present climate predictions, the daily newspapers are revealing concrete climate impacts unfolding before our eyes.

Sandi Doughton, *Acidified seawater showing up along coast ahead of schedule*, THE SEATTLE TIMES, May 23, 2008:

Climate models predicted it wouldn't happen until the end of the century.

So a team led by Seattle researchers was stunned to discover that vast swaths of acidified seawater already are showing up along the Pacific Coast as greenhouse-gas emissions upset the oceans' chemical balance.

"What we found ... was truly astonishing," said oceanographer Richard Feely, of the National Oceanic and Atmospheric Administration's (NOAA) Pacific Marine Environmental Laboratory in Seattle. "This means ocean acidification may be seriously impacting marine life on the continental shelf right now."

All along the coast, the scientists found regions where the water was acidic enough to dissolve the shells and skeletons of clams, corals and many of the tiny creatures at the base of the marine food chain. Acidified water also can kill fish eggs and a wide range of marine larvae.

"Entire marine ecosystems are likely to be affected," said co-author Debby Ianson, an oceanographer at Fisheries and Oceans Canada.

Though it hasn't received as much attention as global warming, ocean acidification is a flip side of the same phenomenon. The increase in atmospheric carbon dioxide from power plants, factories and cars that is raising temperatures worldwide also is to blame for the increasing acidity of the world's oceans.

Normally, seawater is slightly alkaline. When carbon dioxide from the atmosphere dissolves into the water, it forms carbonic acid—the weak acid that helps give soda pop its tang. The process also robs the water of carbonate, a key ingredient in the formation of calcium carbonate shells.

Since the Industrial Revolution, when humans began pumping massive amounts of carbon dioxide into the atmosphere, Feely estimates the oceans have absorbed 525 billion tons of the man-made greenhouse gas—about one-third of the total released during that period.

By keeping some of the carbon dioxide out of the atmosphere, the oceans have blunted the temperature rise due to global warming. But they've suffered for that service, with a more than 30-percent increase in acidity.

The acidified water does not pose a direct threat to people. "We're not talking battery acid here," said co-author Burke Hales, an oceanographer at Oregon State University.

On the pH scale, which measures acidity, strongly alkaline materials such as oven cleaner measure about 13. Hydrochloric acid has a pH of 1. Seawater usually measures around 8.1. The most acidic water the scientists found off the Pacific Coast measured 7.6 on the pH scale. The numerical difference may seem slight, but it represents a threefold increase in acidity, Hales said.

Until now, researchers believed the most acidified water was confined to the deep oceans. Cold water, which holds more carbon dioxide, sinks. Deep waters also are naturally high in carbon dioxide, which is a byproduct of the decay of plankton.

Feely and his NOAA colleague Christopher Sabine previously have shown that zones of acidified water are growing and moving closer to the surface as the oceans absorb more man-made carbon dioxide.

During surveys on the Pacific Coast last year, a team including Feely and Sabine discovered the natural upwelling that occurs along the West Coast each spring and early summer is pulling the acidified water onto the continental shelf.

"I think this is a red flag for us, because it's right at our doorstep on the West Coast," said Victoria Fabry, a biological oceanographer at California State University, San Marcos, who was not involved with the study. "It's telling us that we really need more monitoring to figure out what's going on."

Climate scientist Ken Caldeira, of the Carnegie Institution at Stanford University, said the finding underscores the limitations of computer models.

"This is another example where what's happening in the natural world seems to be happening much faster than what our climate models predict," he said.

And there's worse to come, the scientists warn.

A network of currents shuffles ocean water around the globe. The acidified water upwelling along the coast today was last exposed to the atmosphere about 50 years ago, when carbon-dioxide levels were much lower than they are now. That means the water that will rise from the depths over the coming decades will have absorbed more carbon dioxide and will be even more acidic.

"We've got 50 years worth of water that's already left the station and is on its way to us," Hales said. "Each one of those years is going to be a little bit more corrosive than the one before."

———————

2008 Lynas at 113:

> Most readers will by now have concluded that two degrees of global warming is likely to be survivable, barring any unpleasant surprises, for the majority of humanity. I agree. The same cannot be said, unfortunately, for a large swath of natural biodiversity—the plants and animals that share this planet with us. With ecosystems already fragmented and marginalized due to incessant human population growth and economic activity, climate change looks set to reap a grim toll on what remains of nature.

2008 Lynas at 116–17:

> In a study published in Nature in 2004, the ecologist Chris Thomas and more than a dozen other experts revealed that according to their models, over a third of all species would be "committed to extinction" by the time global temperatures reached two degrees in 2050. "Well over a million species could be threatened with extinction as a result of climate change," Thomas told the press.

C. Three Degrees

2008 Lynas at 124:

> In their hot, dusty, and largely flat land, the Botswana live for the day when rumbling clouds gather, the heavens open, and fat raindrops splatter onto the sunbaked earth. When Botswana (formerly Bechuanaland) became independent from Britain in 1966, its first president, the still revered Sir Seretse Khama, punched the air and shouted: "Let there be rain!" Rarely can there have been a clearer articulation of national will.
>
> ....
>
> But sadly for Botswana, the long-range forecast shows very little rain. By the time global warming reaches three degrees, drought will have already become perennial in both this country and much of the rest of southern Africa.

2008 Lynas at 138, 139, 142:

> [One obscure paper appearing in Nature in November 2000 should have set off] panic on the streets, people shouting from rooftops, statements to Congress, and 24-hour news coverage. There were none of these things. The paper, modestly entitled "Acceleration of Global Warming Due to Carbon Cycle Feedbacks in a Coupled Climate Model," and written by a team from Britain's Hadley Centre, was largely ignored.
>
> Why should the paper, published in Nature, have rung worldwide alarm bells? First, it showed that global warming could begin to generate its own momentum if a previously unforeseen positive feedback ... came into effect. This, the "carbon cycle feedback" referred to in the paper's title, would potentially leave human beings as powerless bystanders in a devastating runaway global-warming scenario. Second, the Hadley paper revealed that the main furnace of this positive feedback would burn not in the industrial capitals of the world, but in the remote heart of South America, beginning with the near-total collapse of the Amazonian rainforest.
>
> According to the newly updated model, a three-degree rise in global temperatures—something that could happen as early as 2050—effectively reverses the carbon cycle. Instead of absorbing CO_2, vegetation and soils start releasing it in massive quantities, as soil bacteria work faster to break down organic matter in a hotter environment, and plant growth goes into reverse....

> Even if all [ongoing] destruction stopped tomorrow, the Hadley Centre's model suggests that the Amazon rain forest would still be doomed unless global warming levels off at two degrees....

2008 LYNAS at 151–52:

> The three-degree world will see water sluicing off Greenland in phenomenal quantities, converging into immense glacial rivers as the ice edge retreats into the center of the giant island.

2008 LYNAS at 156:

> Drought, unfortunately, is central to the forecasts for [Central America] in the three-degree world. Although precipitation in the deep tropics is projected to increase, the subtropics get drier, and Central America is right in the middle of one of these drying zones.

2008 LYNAS at 163, 164:

> The Last Drops of the Colorado
>
> ....
>
> Although the Colorado dams, which can hold four years' worth of river flow, act as a buffer to changing river levels, long-term drought is still a critical threat. One detailed modeling study of how the Colorado system might behave in a future climate found that for between a quarter and half the time during the second half of the 21st Century, the system would essentially fail.

2008 LYNAS at 176–77 (emphasis added):

> A fascinating—if depressing—study, identifying exactly which areas are going to be the worst hit by "disappearing climates," was published in April 2007, authored by a team led by John Williams, an assistant professor at the University of Wisconsin's Geography Department. It lists the Columbian and Peruvian Andes, Central America, the African Rift Mountains, the Zambian and Angolan Highlands, Cape Province of South Africa, southeast Australia, portions of the Himalaya, the Indonesian and Philippine island archipelagos, and regions around the Arctic. *In total somewhere between 10 and 50 percent of the globe's surface will see its usual climate vanish altogether. Animals and plants that are adapted to these doomed climates will have nowhere to go; no place anywhere on the Earth's surface will still provide a suitable climatic habitat. Most depressing of all is the close association between those areas whose climates are projected to vanish altogether and global biodiversity hot spots. In other words, the places that experience the worst wipeout will be exactly those where today life flourishes in its most glorious abundance and diversity.*

D. Four Degrees

2008 LYNAS at 186:

> in the four-degree world, with global sea levels half a meter or more above current levels, Alexandria's long lifespan will be drawing to a close.

2008 LYNAS at 191–92:

> A global warming of four degrees would be more than enough to allow the melt line to creep across both the Ross and the Ronne ice shelves, fatally damaging their integrity as meltwater pries open gaps in the ice. If either breaks up, just like the Larsen and Wordie ice shelves already have farther north, then nothing will stand in the way of total collapse for the entire West Antarctic sheet and rapid inundation for the world's coastlines.

2008 LYNAS at 192:

> So will it ever happen? Again, geological evidence could be the key. When the Earth was last four degrees warmer, there was no ice at either pole. Global warming of this magnitude would eventually leave the whole planet without ice for the first time in nearly 40 million years.

2008 LYNAS at 194–95:

> One study conducted by the United Kingdom and Chinese governments suggests that by the latter third of the 21st century, if global temperatures are more than three degrees higher than now, China's agricultural production will crash.

2008 LYNAS at 196:

> it is difficult to avoid the conclusion that mass starvation will be a permanent danger for much of the human race in the four-degree world—and possibly, as suggested previously, much earlier. With major global breadbaskets dusty and abandoned, rising demand will be chasing rapidly diminishing supply.

2008 LYNAS at 199:

> hot subtropical climate zones now located in North Africa will spread north into the heart of Europe.

2008 LYNAS at 212:

> This is the ominous conclusion of the four-degree world: That just as with the projected Amazon collapse and carbon cycle feedback of the three-degree world, stabilizing global temperatures at four degrees above current levels may not be possible because of carbon releases from Arctic permafrost. In this scenario, if we reach three degrees, that increase could lead inexorably to four degrees, which in turn could lead inexorably to five.

E. Five Degrees

2008 LYNAS at 215:

> With five degrees of global warming, an entirely new planet is coming into being—one largely unrecognizable from the Earth we know today. The remaining ice sheets are eventually eliminated from both poles. Rain forests have already burned up and disappeared. Rising sea levels have inundated coastal cities and are beginning to penetrate far inland into continental interiors. Humans are herded into shrinking "zones of habitability" by the twin crises of drought and flood. Inland areas see temperatures ten or more degrees higher than now.

2008 LYNAS at 236:

> A drastic reduction in human populations is unambiguously the most likely outcome of a rise in global temperatures toward five degrees—what James Lovelock unhappily terms "the cull."

F. Six Degrees

2008 LYNAS at 261–62, 263:

> So the lesson of the end-Permian [251 mya] is this: The planet can rapidly turn very unfriendly indeed once it is pushed far enough out of kilter. Today, vast volumes of

methane hydrates are again lodged on subsea continental shelves, biding their time for the trigger of rising ocean temperatures. Just how far they can be safely pushed, no one can tell.

Nor is there any reason to rule out ocean stratification and hydrogen sulfide poisoning as another possible disaster scenario. The gradual shutting down of the Gulf Stream could be just one cog in this much larger machine; as the oceans stop circulating, warmer waters would penetrate into the depths, carrying less dissolved oxygen and gradually eliminating aerobic life. Stagnant oceans would be largely invisible to us land dwellers. Indeed, much of the Black Sea today is anoxic, but cold oxygen-rich surface waters keep a lid on the poisonous liquid beneath.

....

Could humanity itself ever go extinct? I think it unlikely....

II. Justice in a Warmer World

A. Generally

The vast literature on climate change is filled with language that law students would recognize as expressions of justice and opinions of injustice. Here is a small sample from a single author, George Monbiot, whose website — www.monbiot.com — is listed by Yahoo as the most popular columnist's site on Earth, outside the United States. The quotations are borrowed from GEORGE MONBIOT, HEAT: HOW TO STOP THE PLANET FROM BURNING 6, 21, 43, 46, 50, 59, 60, 68, 142, 154–55, 214 (South End Press 2007) (footnotes omitted) [hereinafter 2007 MONBIOT]:

> [The World Health Organization] estimates that 150,000 people a year are now dying as a result of climate change, as diseases spread faster at higher temperatures. All this is happening with just 0.6° of warming.

> [T]he richest people, who can buy their way out of trouble, will be harmed last. The blame ... is inversely proportionally to the impacts.

> The lady in the Rolls-Royce car is more damaging to morale than a fleet of Goering's bombing planes [quoting George Orwell, 1940].

> [The European Union's Emissions Trading Scheme], which has been running since the beginning of 2005, began by handing out carbon dioxide emissions permits, free of charge, to big European companies. By and large, those who produced the most carbon emissions were given the most permits: the polluter was paid. This handout was so generous that, in May 2006, the British government's consultants calculated that power firms would be making a windfall profit from the scheme of around [one billion pounds], while doing nothing to reduce their emissions.

> ....

> [The financial costs of Hurricane Katrina], which may have been exacerbated by climate change, amount to some $75 billion, and we can use that number to help derive a price for carbon pollution. But does it capture the suffering of the people whose homes were destroyed? Does it capture the partial destruction, in New Orleans, of one of the quirkiest and most creative communities on earth? Does it, most importantly, capture the value of the lives of those who drowned?

....

Argue with the executives of any industry which is failing to cut its carbon emissions, and they will say the same thing: it doesn't matter because they can pay other people to do it for them.

....

[T]he supersonic jet ... is possibly the most environmentally damaging technology ever developed.

....

There are some good builders in this country, but the government has sided with the bad ones.

....

the automobile ... can't be blamed for anything. Its conscience is ... clear.... It only fulfills its destiny: it is destined to wipe out the world [quoting Ilya Ehrenburg, 1929].

....

The speed and acceleration of our cars is a form of profligacy at which all future generations will goggle.

....

[The internet] creates a false impression of action.... But by itself, as I know to my cost, writing, reading, debate and dissent change nothing. They are of value only if they inspire action.

———————

For starters, then, Mr. Monbiot advises us to watch for genocide and murder of the innocent, discrimination based on wealth, divergence of fault and consequence, unequal sacrifices, rewards for culpability, unethical valuations, shirking of duties, amoral corporate behavior, governmental favoritism, industrial indifference, profligacy, waste, and greed, and free-riding passivity. These estimates supply plenty of room for legal innovation.

J. Timmons Roberts & Bradley C. Parks, A Climate of Injustice: Global Inequality, North-South Politics, and Climate Policy 1–2 (MIT Press 2007) [hereinafter 2007 Roberts & Parks]:

> Imagine you carefully save money your entire life to buy a beautiful piece of land in the country to farm. The land and equipment cost more than you expect, and you quickly become dependent on a narrow margin of profit to sustain yourself and your family. Soon after you move in, however, someone buys the property bordering your land and immediately opens a landfill, accepting trash and hazardous wastes from the entire region. A mountain of trash rapidly grows; the landfill stinks, the noise of the trucks and bulldozers is deafening, and the waste leaks into your groundwater. Since the land is in an unzoned, unincorporated township, you have no recourse to stop the dumping through zoning limits, and the landowner is best friends with the major political and economic players in the county, state, and even the federal government. The value of your property plummets, and you cannot afford to move. The owner of the dump lives elsewhere and grows rich on its income; you suffer all the costs of his operation and gain none of the benefits.
>
> You seek to make an agreement with the neighbor, asking for some limits on his behavior. He negotiates with you for years, but never agrees to any substantial changes in his dumping. Instead, he says it would be unfair to have to do so unless you also agreed

to stop dumping your farm waste, which would prevent you from being able to farm effectively. You turn to your other neighbors, seeking partners who will force the dump owner to clean up or close. Some agree, but these are only the poorest and least powerful of your neighbors—the others are friends of the dump owner, or own businesses that they fear might be hurt by the restrictions you seek.

The dump owner suggests that the impacts of his dumping require more study and promises enormous research projects by scientists of his choosing. Repeatedly and with great fanfare he promises to lend you money on good terms to build a wall as a visual screen, to clean your drinking water, and to help you deal with other effects. Desperate for any progress, you accept his offers, but his promises are quickly forgotten, and the improvements are never completed. He asks you again to sign an agreement that in a few years would make it impossible for you to increase production on your farm to the point where your family could live decently. You and the other less powerful neighbors resist the agreement.

With only slight changes in the details, this is the story of global warming and all the years of discussion and action since the issue was identified in the late 1980s.

———————

Notes

1. "[The Bush administration continues to oppose Kyoto because it is 'an *unfair* and *ineffective* means of addressing global climate change concerns' and *would cause serious harm to the U.S. economy*." Office of the Press Secretary, U.S. President, 2001, quoted in 2007 ROBERTS & PARKS at 4 (emphasis added).

2. Climate optimism, New Scientist, April 4, 2009, p. 4, quoting Todd Stern, chief U.S. climate negotiator, Obama administration:

> We do not doubt the science, we do not doubt the urgency, and we do not doubt the enormity of the challenge before us.... The facts on the ground are outstripping the worst-case scenarios. The cost of inaction—or inadequate actions—are unacceptable.

3. Why might we wish to blame the present stalemate on the Rio Earth Summit in 1992?

> The most controversial issue at Rio was global climate change. Under intense pressure to do something, 187 nations eventually signed the United Nations Framework Convention on Climate Change (UNFCCC) [as of May 24, 2004]. However, the treaty avoided tough details. It called on nations to "protect the climate system ... on the basis of equity and in accordance with their *common but differentiated responsibilities and respective capabilities*," but consensus on these "first principles" masked profound disagreement on the issue of actual obligations. Developing countries interpreted the "common but differentiated" language with great precision: industrialized nations would need to take the lead by cutting their own emissions and transferring large sums of environmental assistance to the South. However, developed countries saw more room for selective interpretation.

2007 ROBERTS & PARKS at 3 (footnotes omitted but *citing* Kevin A. Baumert & Nancy Kete, Introduction, *An Architecture for Climate Protection, in* BUILDING ON THE KYOTO PROTOCOL: OPTIONS FOR PROTECTING THE CLIMATE 8 (Kevin A. Baumert ed., World Resources Institute 2002)).

4. *Thinking About Climate Justice*. 2007 ROBERTS & PARKS 6–7 (footnote omitted):

> .... Our account of the North-South stalemate on climate policy relies on the integration of three types of arguments: general theories about the behavior of states, in-

termediate explanations about international environmental politics and North-South politics, and issue-specific insights concerning the "problem structure" of climate change.

In the first group are issues of trust, worldviews, causal beliefs, and principled beliefs—issues we believe are largely attributable to the position of countries in the global division of labor. Inequality, we argue, dampens utility-enhancing cooperative efforts by reinforcing structuralist worldviews and causal beliefs, creating incentives for zero-sum and negative-sum behavior, polarizing preferences, generating divergent and unstable expectations about future behavior, eroding trust and civic norms among different social groups, destabilizing policy coalitions, and making it difficult to coalesce around a socially shared understanding of what is "fair."

At the intermediate level are explanations of the ongoing development crisis and those arising in environmental debates over the definition of sustainable development, foreign assistance for the environment, and global versus local environmental concerns. Climate negotiations do not take place in a vacuum. They are taking place at a time when concerns about Northern callousness and opportunism in matters of international political economy are rising, levels of generalized trust are declining, and calls for fair processes and fair outcomes are being marginalized. The North-South impasse on climate policy is, in other words, linked to larger systemic problems that hinder cooperation between rich and poor nations more generally. Compounding this problem, for more than thirty years the environmental issues of most concern to developing countries have been brushed aside and replaced with First World issues. However, global commons issues, such as ozone depletion, habitat loss, and climate change, are much less pressing to most poor nations than providing safe drinking water, slowing soil erosion, treating sewage, slowing the spread of deserts, and reducing lung- and eye-burning pollution. This wedge between Northern and Southern interests has put rich donor countries in the difficult business of "persuad[ing] recipient countries ... to take the environmental actions of [lowest] priority to them."

Finally, we rely upon a series of explanations that are specific to the "problem structure" of climate change. Part of the reason cooperation on climate change is so difficult to achieve is intrinsic to the problem itself: the number of parties needed to resolve the problem, the complexity of the problem, the time sensitivity of the solution, the quantity and quality of information, the high levels of uncertainty surrounding the issue, the stability and intensity of actor preferences, the "observability" of climate-related behavior, and the asymmetry of externalities. We argue that to understand why countries are willing or unwilling to cooperate and make sacrifices for the protection of what may be their way of life, we must first identify which nations are most responsible for global climate change, which nations will most suffer the effects of climate change most profoundly, and which nations will most likely bear the largest costs of cleaning up the mess. This "triple inequality" of responsibility, vulnerability, and mitigation, which is also intrinsic to the problem, offers a powerful and parsimonious explanation for the negotiation positions adopted by rich and poor nations.

Citing Barbara Connolly, *Increments for the Earth: The Politics of Environmental Aid, in* Institutions for Environmental Aid 327, 300 (Robert O. Keohane & Marc A. Levy eds., MIT Press 1996).

———

A Perfect Moral Storm: Climate Change, Intergenerational Ethics and the Problem of Corruption[1]

Stephen M. Gardiner. Stephen Gardiner is an Associate Professor of Philosophy at the University of Washington, Seattle. His main areas of interest are ethical theory, political philosophy and environmental ethics. He also teaches topics in applied ethics, philosophy of economics and ancient Greek philosophy. His current research includes projects in the areas of global political philosophy, ethics and global environmental policy (especially global climate change), Aristotelian virtue ethics, and egalitarianism and market systems. In May 2007, he organized the interdisciplinary conference Ethics and Climate Change at the University of Washington. Steve joined the University of Washington in July 2004, having previously been on the faculty at the University of Utah and the University of Canterbury in Christchurch, New Zealand. He received his Ph.D. from Cornell University in 1999. He also has a M.A. in Philosophy from the University of Colorado at Boulder, and a B.A. in Philosophy, Politics and Economics from the University of Oxford. He can be reached at smgard@u.washington.edu.

I. Intergenerational Equity

"There's a quiet clamor for hypocrisy and deception; and pragmatic politicians respond with … schemes that seem to promise something for nothing. Please, spare us the truth."[2]

The most authoritative scientific report on climate change begins by saying:

> Natural, technical, and social sciences can provide essential information and evidence needed for decisions on what constitutes "dangerous anthropogenic interference with the climate system." At the same time, *such decisions are value judgments …* [3]

There are good grounds for this statement. Climate change is a complex problem raising issues across and between a large number of disciplines, including the physical and life sciences, political science, economics, and psychology, to name just a few. But without wishing for a moment to marginalize the contributions of these disciplines, ethics does seem to play a fundamental role.

Why so? At the most general level, the reason is that we cannot get very far in discussing why climate change is a problem without invoking ethical considerations. If we do not think that our own actions are open to moral assessment, or that various interests (our own, those of our kin and country, those of distant people, future people, animals and nature) matter, then it is hard to see why climate change (or much else) poses a problem. But once we see this, then we appear to need some account of moral responsibility, morally important interests, and what to do about both. And this puts us squarely in the domain of ethics.

At a more practical level, ethical questions are fundamental to the main policy decisions that must be made, such as where to set a global ceiling for greenhouse gas emissions, and how to

1. This paper was originally written for presentation to an interdisciplinary workshop on *Values in Nature* at Princeton University, the proceedings of which appeared in *Environmental Values*. I thank the Center for Human Values at Princeton and the University of Washington for research support in the form of a Laurance S. Rockefeller fellowship. I also thank audiences at Iowa State University, Lewis and Clark College, the University of Washington, the Western Political Science Association, and the Pacific Division of the American Philosophical Association. For comments, I am particularly grateful to Chrisoula Andreou, Kristen Hessler, Jay Odenbaugh, John Meyer, Darrel Moellendorf, Peter Singer, Harlan Wilson, Clark Wolf, and two anonymous reviewers. I am especially endebted to Dale Jamieson.

2. Robert J. Samuelson, *Lots of Gain And No Pain!*, NEWSWEEK, February 21, 2005, at 41. Samuelson was talking about another intergenerational issue—social security—but his claims ring true here as well.

3. INTERGOVERNMENTAL PANEL ON CLIMATE CHANGE (IPCC), CLIMATE CHANGE 2001: SYNTHESIS REPORT 2 (2001, Cambridge University Press) (emphasis added), *available at* www.ipcc.ch.

distribute the emissions allowed by such a ceiling. For example, where the global ceiling is set depends on how the interests of the current generation are weighed against those of future generations; and how emissions are distributed under the global cap depends in part on various beliefs about the appropriate role of energy consumption in people's lives, the importance of historical responsibility for the problem, and the current needs and future aspirations of particular societies.

The relevance of ethics to substantive climate policy thus seems clear. But this is not the topic that I wish to take up here.[4] Instead, I want to discuss a further, and to some extent more basic, way in which ethical reflection sheds light on our present predicament. This has nothing much to do with the substance of a defensible climate regime; instead, it concerns the process of making climate policy.

My thesis is this. The peculiar features of the climate change problem pose substantial obstacles to our ability to make the hard choices necessary to address it. Climate change is a perfect moral storm. One consequence of this is that, even if the difficult ethical questions could be answered, we might still find it difficult to act. For the storm makes us extremely vulnerable to moral corruption.[5]

Let us say that a perfect storm is an event constituted by an unusual convergence of independently harmful factors where this convergence is likely to result in substantial, and possibly catastrophic, negative outcomes. The term "the perfect storm" seems to have become prominent in popular culture through Sebastian Junger's book of that name, and the associated Hollywood film.[6] Junger's tale is based on the true story of the *Andrea Gail*, a fishing vessel caught at sea during a convergence of three particularly bad storms.[7] The sense of the analogy is then that climate change appears to be a perfect moral storm because it involves the convergence of a number of factors that threaten our ability to behave ethically.

As climate change is a complex phenomenon, I cannot hope to identify all of the ways in which its features cause problems for ethical behavior. Instead, I will identify three especially salient problems—analogous to the three storms that hit the *Andrea Gail*—that converge in the climate change case. These three "storms" arise in the global, intergenerational and theoretical dimensions, and I will argue that their interaction helps to exacerbate and obscure a lurking problem of moral corruption that may be of greater practical importance than any of them.

A.   The Global Storm

The first two storms arise out of three important characteristics of the climate change problem. I label these characteristics:

- Dispersion of Causes and Effects
- Fragmentation of Agency
- Institutional Inadequacy

---

4. For more on such issues, see Stephen M. Gardiner, *Ethics and Global Climate Change*, 114 ETHICS 555 (2004).

5. One might wonder why, despite the widespread agreement that climate change involves important ethical questions, there is relatively little overt discussion of them. The answer to this question is no doubt complex. But my thesis may constitute part of that answer.

6. SEBASTIAN JUNGER, A PERFECT STORM: A TRUE STORY OF MEN AGAINST THE SEA (Harper 1999).

7. This definition is my own. The term "perfect storm" is in wide usage. However, it is difficult to find definitions of it. An online dictionary of slang offers the following: "When three events, usually beyond one's control, converge and create a large inconvenience for an individual. Each event represents one of the storms that collided on the *Andrea Gail* in the book/movie titled the perfect storm." Urbandictionary.com, 3/25/05.

Since these characteristics manifest themselves in two especially salient dimensions—the spatial and the temporal—it is useful to distinguish two distinct but mutually reinforcing components of the climate change problem. I shall call the first "the Global Storm." This corresponds to the dominant understanding of the climate change problem; and it emerges from a predominantly spatial interpretation of the three characteristics.

Let us begin with the Dispersion of Causes and Effects. Climate change is a truly global phenomenon. Emissions of greenhouse gases from any geographical location on the Earth's surface travel to the upper atmosphere and then play a role in affecting climate globally. Hence, the impact of any particular emission of greenhouse gases is not realized solely at its source, either individual or geographical; rather impacts are dispersed to other actors and regions of the Earth. Such spatial dispersion has been widely discussed.

The second characteristic is the Fragmentation of Agency. Climate change is not caused by a single agent, but by a vast number of individuals and institutions not unified by a comprehensive structure of agency. This is important because it poses a challenge to humanity's ability to respond.

In the spatial dimension, this feature is usually understood as arising out of the shape of the current international system, as constituted by states. Then the problem is that, given that there is not only no world government but also no less centralized system of global governance (or at least no effective one), it is very difficult to coordinate an effective response to global climate change.[8]

This general argument is generally given more bite through the invocation of a certain familiar theoretical model.[9] For the international situation is usually understood in game theoretic terms as a Prisoner's Dilemma, or what Garrett Hardin calls a "Tragedy of the Commons."[10] For the sake of ease of exposition, let us describe the Prisoner's Dilemma scenario in terms of a paradigm case, that of overpollution.[11] Suppose that a number of distinct agents are trying to decide whether or not to engage in a polluting activity, and that their situation is characterized by the following two claims:

---

8. An anonymous reviewer objects that this is a "very American take on the matter," since "the rest of the world" (a) "is less sure that there is an utter absence of effective global governance," (b) "might argue that were it not for recent U.S. resistance a centralized system of governance might be said to at least be in the early stages of evolution," and (c) accepts "Kyoto as a reasonable first step toward global governance on climate change." Much might be said about this, but here I can make only three quick points. First, suppose that (a)–(c) are all true. Even so, their truth does not seem sufficient to undermine the global storm; the claims are just too weak. Second, if there is a system of effective governance, then the current weakness of the international response to climate change becomes more, rather than less, surprising, and this bolsters one of my main claims in this paper, which is that other factors need to be taken into account. Third, elsewhere I have criticized Kyoto as too weak (Gardiner, *The Global Warming Tragedy and the Dangerous Illusion of the Kyoto Protocol*, 18 ETHICS AND INTERNATIONAL AFFAIRS 23 (2004)). Others have criticized me for being too pessimistic here, invoking the "first step" defense (*e.g.*, Elizabeth DeSombre, *Global Warming: More Common than Tragic*, 18 ETHICS AND INTERNATIONAL AFFAIRS 41 (2004). My response is to say that it is the critics who are the pessimists: they believe that Kyoto was the best that humanity could achieve at the time; I am more optimistic about our capabilities.

9. The appropriateness of this model even to the spatial dimension requires some further specific, but usually undefended, background assumptions about the precise nature of the dispersion of effects and fragmentation of agency. But I shall pass over that issue here.

10. Garret Hardin, *Tragedy of the Common*, 162 SCIENCE 1243 (1968). I discuss this in more detail in previous work, especially Stephen M. Gardiner, *The Real Tragedy of the Commons*, 30 PHILOSOPHY AND PUBLIC AFFAIRS 416 (2001).

11. Nothing depends on the case being of this form. For a fuller characterization, see Stephen M. Gardiner, *The Real Tragedy of the Commons*, 30 PHILOSOPHY AND PUBLIC AFFAIRS 416 (2001).

(PD1) It is *collectively rational* to cooperate and restrict overall pollution: each agent prefers the outcome produced by everyone restricting their individual pollution over the outcome produced by no one doing so.

(PD2) It is *individually rational* not to restrict one's own pollution: when each agent has the power to decide whether or not she will restrict her pollution, each (rationally) prefers not to do so, whatever the others do.

Agents in such a situation find themselves in a paradoxical position. On the one hand, given (PD1), they understand that it would be better for everyone if every agent cooperated; but, on the other hand, given (PD2), they also know that they should all choose to defect. This is paradoxical because it implies that if individual agents act rationally in terms of their own interests, then they collectively undermine those interests.[12]

A Tragedy of the Commons is essentially a Prisoner's Dilemma involving a common resource. This has become the standard analytical model for understanding regional and global environmental problems in general, and climate change is no exception. Typically, the reasoning goes as follows. Imagine climate change as an international problem and conceive of the relevant parties as individual countries, who represent the interests of their countries in perpetuity. Then, (PD1) and (PD2) appear to hold. On the one hand, no one wants serious climate change. Hence, each country prefers the outcome produced by everyone restricting their individual emissions over the outcome produced by no one doing so, and so it is collectively rational to cooperate and restrict global emissions. But, on the other hand, each country prefers to free ride on the actions of others. Hence, when each country has the power to decide whether or not she will restrict her emissions, each prefers not to do so, whatever the others do.

From this perspective, it appears that climate change is a normal tragedy of the commons. Still, there is a sense in which this turns out to be encouraging news; for, in the real world, commons problems are often resolvable under certain circumstances, and climate change seems to fill these desiderata.[13] In particular, it is widely said that parties facing a commons problem can resolve it if they benefit from a wider context of interaction; and this appears to be the case with climate change, since countries interact with each other on a number of broader issues, such as trade and security.

---

12. Some will complain that such game theoretical analyses are misguided in general, and in any case irrelevant to the *ethics* of international affairs, since they focus on self-interested motivation. Though a full discussion is not possible here, a couple of quick responses may be helpful. First, I believe that often the best way to make progress in solving a given ethical problem is to get clear on what the problem actually is. Game theoretic analyses are sometimes helpful here (*cf.* their popularity in the actual literature on environmental issues in general, and climate change in particular). Second, my analysis need not assume that actual human individuals, states or generations are exclusively self-interested, nor that their interests are exclusively economic. (In fact, I would reject such claims.) Instead, it can proceed on a much more limited set of assumptions. Suppose, for example, that the following were the case: first, the actual, unreflective *consumption behavior* of most agents is dominated by their *perceived self-interest*; second, this is often seen in rather narrow terms; and third, it is such behavior which drives much of the energy use in the industrialized countries, and so much of the problem of climate change. If such claims are reasonable, then modeling the dynamics of the global warming problem in terms of a simplifying assumption of self-interest is not seriously misleading. For the role of that assumption is simply to suggest (a) that, *if nothing is done to prevent it*, unreflective consumption behavior will dominate individual, state and generational behavior, (b) that this is likely to lead to tragedy, and so (c) that some kind of regulation of normal consumption patterns (whether individual, governmental, market-based, or of some other form) is necessary in order to avoid a moral disaster.

13. This implies that, in the real world, commons problems do not strictly-speaking satisfy all the conditions of the prisoner's dilemma paradigm. For relevant discussion, see Lee Shepski, *Prisoner's Dilemma: the Hard Problem*, paper presented at the Pacific Division of the American Philosophical Association, March 2006, and ELINOR OSTROM, GOVERNING THE COMMONS (Cambridge Un. Press 1990).

This brings us to the third characteristic of the climate change problem, institutional inadequacy. There is wide agreement that the appropriate means for resolving commons problems under the favorable conditions just mentioned is for the parties to agree to change the existing incentive structure through the introduction of a system of enforceable sanctions. (Hardin calls this "mutual coercion, mutually agreed upon.") This transforms the decision situation by foreclosing the option of free riding, so that the collectively rational action also becomes individually rational. Theoretically, then, matters seem simple; but in practice things are different. For the need for enforceable sanctions poses a challenge at the global level because of the limits of our current, largely national, institutions, and the lack of an effective system of global governance. In essence, addressing climate change appears to require global regulation of greenhouse gas emissions, where this includes establishing a reliable enforcement mechanism; but the current global system—or lack of it—makes this difficult, if not impossible.

The implication of this familiar analysis, then, is that the main thing that is needed to solve the global warming problem is an effective system of global governance (at least for this issue). And there is a sense in which this is still good news. For, in principle at least, it should be possible to motivate countries to establish such a regime, since they ought to recognize that it is in their best interests to eliminate the possibility of free riding and so make genuine cooperation the rational strategy at the individual as well as collective level.

Unfortunately, however, this is not the end of the story. For there are other features of the climate change case that make the necessary global agreement more difficult, and so exacerbate the basic Global Storm.[14] Prominent amongst these is scientific uncertainty about the precise magnitude and distribution of effects, particularly at the national level.[15] One reason for this is that the lack of trustworthy data about the costs and benefits of climate change at the national level casts doubt on the truth of (PD1). Perhaps, some nations wonder, we might be better off with climate change than without it. More importantly, some countries might wonder whether they will at least be relatively better off than other countries, and so might get away with paying less to avoid the associated costs.[16] Such factors complicate the game theoretic situation, and so make agreement more difficult.

In other contexts, the problem of scientific uncertainty might not be so serious. But a second characteristic of the climate change problem exacerbates matters in this setting. The source of climate change is located deep in the infrastructure of current human civilizations; hence, attempts to combat it may have substantial ramifications for human social life. Climate change is

---

14. There is one fortunate convergence. Several writers have emphasized that the major ethical arguments all point in the same direction: that the developed countries should bear most of the costs of the transition—including those accruing to developing countries—at least in the early stages of mitigation and adaptation. *See*, for example, Peter Singer, *One Atmosphere*, in Peter Singer, One World: The Ethics of Globalization ch. 2 (Yale Un. Press 2002), *and* Henry Shue, *Global Environment and International Inequality*, 75 International Affairs 531 (1999).

15. Rado Dimitrov argues that we must distinguish between different kinds of uncertainty when we investigate the effects of scientific uncertainty on international regime building, and that it is uncertainties about national impacts that undermines regime formation. *See* Rado Dimitory, *Knowledge, Power and Interests in Environmental Regime Formation*, 47 International Studies Quarterly 123 (2003).

16. This consideration appears to play a role in U.S. deliberation about climate change, where it is often asserted that the U.S. faces lower marginal costs from climate change than other countries. *See*, for example, Robert O. Mendelsohn, Global Warming and the American Economy (Edgar Elgar Publishing 2001); W.A. Nitze, *A Failure of Presidential Leadership*. *in* Irving Mintzer and J. Amber Leonard, Negotiating Climate Change: The Inside Story of the Rio Convention 189–90 (Cambridge Un. Press 1994); *and, by contrast*, National Assessment Synthesis Team, Climate Change Impacts on the United States: The Potential Consequences of Climate Variability and Change (Cambridge Un. Press 2000), *available at* www.usgcrp.gov/usgcrp/nacc/default.htm.

caused by human emissions of greenhouse gases, primarily carbon dioxide. Such emissions are brought about by the burning of fossil fuels for energy. But it is this energy that supports existing economies. Hence, given that halting climate change will require deep cuts in projected global emissions over time, we can expect that such action will have profound effects on the basic economic organization of the developed countries and on the aspirations of the developing countries.

This has several salient implications. First, it suggests that those with vested interests in the continuation of the current system—*e.g.*, many of those with substantial political and economic power—will resist such action. Second, unless ready substitutes are found, real mitigation can be expected to have profound impacts on how humans live and how human societies evolve. Hence, action on climate change is likely to raise serious, and perhaps uncomfortable, questions about who we are and what we want to be. Third, this suggests a *status quo* bias in the face of uncertainty. Contemplating change is often uncomfortable; contemplating basic change may be unnerving, even distressing. Since the social ramifications of action appear to be large, perspicuous and concrete, but those of inaction appear uncertain, elusive and indeterminate, it is easy to see why uncertainty might exacerbate social inertia.[17]

The third feature of the climate change problem that exacerbates the basic Global Storm is that of skewed vulnerabilities. The climate change problem interacts in some unfortunate ways with the present global power structure. For one thing, the responsibility for historical and current emissions lies predominantly with the richer, more powerful nations, and the poor nations are badly situated to hold them accountable. For another, the limited evidence on regional impacts suggests that it is the poorer nations that are most vulnerable to the worst impacts of climate change.[18] Finally, action on climate change creates a moral risk for the developed nations. It embodies a recognition that there are international norms of ethics and responsibility, and reinforces the idea that international cooperation on issues involving such norms is both possible and necessary. Hence, it may encourage attention to other moral defects of the current global system, such as global poverty, human rights violations, and so on.[19]

II. The Intergenerational Storm

We can now return to the three characteristics of the climate change problem identified earlier:

- Dispersion of Causes and Effects

---

17. Much more might be said here. I discuss some of the psychological aspects of political inertia and the role they play independently of scientific uncertainty in S. Gardiner, *Saved by Disaster? Abrupt Climate Change, Political Inertia, and the Possibility of an Intergenerational Arms Race*, 40 JOURNAL OF SOCIAL PHILOSOPHY 140 (2009).

18. This is so both because a greater proportion of their economies are in climate-sensitive sectors, and because—being poor—they are worse placed to deal with those impacts. *See* Intergovernmental Panel on Climate Change (IPCC), CLIMATE CHANGE 2001: SYNTHESIS REPORT 8, 16 (Cambridge Un. Press 2001), *available at* www.ipcc.ch.

19. Of course, it does not help that the climate change problem arises in an unfortunate geopolitical setting. Current international relations occur against a backdrop of distraction, mistrust and severe inequalities of power. The dominant global actor and lone superpower, the United States, refuses to address climate change, and is in any case distracted by the threat of global terrorism. Moreover, the international community, including many of America's historical allies, distrust its motives, its actions and especially its uses of moral rhetoric; so there is global discord. This unfortunate state of affairs is especially problematic in relation to the developing nations, whose cooperation must be secured if the climate change problem is to be addressed. One issue is the credibility of the developed nations' commitment to solving the climate change problem. (*See* the next section.) Another is the North's focus on mitigation to the exclusion of adaptation issues. A third concern is the South's fear of an "abate and switch" strategy on the part of the North. (Note that considered in isolation, these factors do not seem sufficient to explain political inertia. After all, the climate change problem originally became prominent during the 1990s, a decade with a much more promising geopolitical environment.)

- Fragmentation of Agency
- Institutional Inadequacy

The Global Storm emerges from a spatial reading of these characteristics; but I would argue that another, even more serious problem arises when we see them from a temporal perspective. I shall call this "the Intergenerational Storm."

Consider first the Dispersion of Causes and Effects. Human-induced climate change is a severely lagged phenomenon. This is partly because some of the basic mechanisms set in motion by the greenhouse effect—such as sea level rise—take a very long time to be fully realized. But it is also because by far the most important greenhouse gas emitted by human beings is carbon dioxide, and once emitted molecules of carbon dioxide can spend a surprisingly long time in the upper atmosphere.[20]

Let us dwell for a moment on this second factor. The IPCC says that the average time spent by a molecule of carbon dioxide in the upper atmosphere is in the region of 5–200 years. This estimate is long enough to create a serious lagging effect; nevertheless, it obscures the fact that a significant percentage of carbon dioxide molecules remain in the atmosphere for much longer periods of time, on the order of thousands and tens of thousands of years. For instance, in a recent paper, David Archer says:

> The carbon cycle of the biosphere will take a long time to completely neutralize and sequester anthropogenic CO_2. We show a wide range of model forecasts of this effect. For the best-guess cases … we expect that 17–33% of the fossil fuel carbon will still reside in the atmosphere 1kyr from now, decreasing to 10–15% at 10kyr, and 7% at 100 kyr. The mean lifetime of fossil fuel CO_2 is about 30–35 kyr.[21]

"This is a fact," he says, which has not yet "reached general public awareness."[22] Hence, he suggests that "a better shorthand for public discussion [than the IPCC estimate] might be that CO_2 sticks around for hundreds of years, plus 25% that sticks around forever."[23]

The fact that carbon dioxide is a long-lived greenhouse gas has at least three important implications. The first is that climate change is a *resilient* phenomenon. Given that currently it does not seem practical to remove large quantities of carbon dioxide from the upper atmosphere, or to moderate its climatic effects, the upward trend in atmospheric concentration is not easily reversible. Hence, a goal of stabilizing and then reducing carbon dioxide concentrations requires advance planning. Second, climate change impacts are *seriously backloaded*. The climate change that the earth is currently experiencing is primarily the result of emissions from some time in the past, rather than current emissions. As an illustration, it is widely accepted that by 2000 we had already committed ourselves to a rise of at least 0.5 and perhaps more than 1 degree Celsius over the then-observed rise of 0.6°C.[24] Third, backloading implies that the full, cumulative effects of

---

20. For more on both claims, *see* Intergovernmental Panel on Climate Change (IPCC), Climate Change 2001: Synthesis Report 16-7 (Cambridge Un. Press 2001), *available at* www.ipcc.ch/.

21. David Archer, *Fate of Fossil Fuel CO_2 in Geologic Time*, 110 Journal of Geophysical Research 5 (2005). "Kyr" means "thousand years".

22. David Archer, *How Long Will Global Warming Last?* 15 March 2005. *Available at:* http://www. realclimate.org/index.php/archives/2005/03/how-long-will-global-warming-last/#more-134.

23. *Id.*; a similar remark occurs in David Archer, *Fate of Fossil Fuel CO_2 in Geologic Time*, 110 Journal of Geophysical Research 5 (2005).

24. T.M.L. Wigley, *The Climate Change Commitment*. 307 Science 1766 (2005); Gerald Meehl, Warren M. Washington, William D. Collins, Julie M. Arblaster, Aixue Hu, Lawrence E. Buja, Warren G. Strand, and Haiyan Teng, *How Much More Global Warming and Sea Level Rise?* 307 Science 1769 (2005); *and* Richard T. Wetherald, Ronald J. Stouffer, and Keith W. Dixon, *Committed Warming and Its Implications for Climate Change*, 28 No. 8 Geophysical Research Letters 1535, April 15, 2001.

our current emissions will not be realized for some time in the future. So, climate change is a *substantially deferred* phenomenon.

Temporal dispersion creates a number of problems. First, as is widely noted, the resilience of climate change implies that delays in action have serious repercussions for our ability to manage the problem. Second, backloading implies that climate change poses serious epistemic difficulties, especially for normal political actors. For one thing, backloading makes it hard to grasp the connection between causes and effects, and this may undermine the motivation to act;[25] for another, it implies that by the time we realize that things are bad, we will already be committed to much more change, so it undermines the ability to respond. Third, the deferral effect calls into question the ability of standard institutions to deal with the problem. For one thing, democratic political institutions have relatively short time horizons—the next election cycle, a politician's political career—and it is doubtful whether such institutions have the wherewithal to deal with substantially deferred impacts. Even more seriously, substantial deferral is likely to undermine the will to act. This is because there is an incentive problem: the bad effects of current emissions are likely to fall, or fall disproportionately, on future generations, whereas the benefits of emissions accrue largely to the present.[26]

These last two points already raise the specter of institutional inadequacy. But to appreciate this problem fully, we must first say something about the temporal fragmentation of agency. There is some reason to think that the temporal fragmentation of agency might be worse than the spatial fragmentation even considered in isolation. For there is a sense in which temporal fragmentation is more intractable than spatial fragmentation: in principle, spatially fragmented agents may actually become unified and so able really to act as a single agent; but temporally fragmented agents cannot actually become unified, and so may at best only act *as if* they were a single agent.

Interesting as such questions are, they need not detain us here. For temporal fragmentation in the context of the kind of temporal dispersion that characterizes climate change is clearly much worse than the associated spatial fragmentation. For the presence of backloading and deferral together brings on a new collective action problem that adds to the tragedy of the commons caused by the Global Storm, and thereby makes matters much worse.

The problem emerges when one relaxes the assumption that countries can be relied upon adequately to represent the interests of both their present and future citizens. Suppose that this is not true. Suppose instead that countries are biased towards the interests of the current generation. Then, since the benefits of carbon dioxide emission are felt primarily by the present generation, in the form of cheap energy, whereas the costs—in the form of the risk of severe and perhaps catastrophic climate change—are substantially deferred to future generations, climate change might provide an instance of a severe intergenerational collective action problem. Moreover, this problem will be iterated. Each new generation will face the same incentive structure as soon as it gains the power to decide whether or not to act.[27]

The nature of the intergenerational problem is easiest to see if we compare it to the traditional Prisoner's Dilemma. Suppose we consider a pure version of the intergenerational problem,

---

25. This is exacerbated by the fact that the climate is an inherently chaotic system in any case, and that there is no control against which its performance might be compared.

26. The possibility of nonlinear effects, such as in abrupt climate change, complicates this point, but I do not think it undermines it. *See* S. Gardiner, *Saved by Disaster? Abrupt Climate Change, Political Inertia, and the Possibility of an Intergenerational Arms Race*, 40 JOURNAL OF SOCIAL PHILOSOPHY 140 (June 5, 2009), Special Issue on Global Environmental Issues, Edited by Tim Hayward and Carol Gould.

27. Elsewhere, I have argued that it is this background fact that most readily explains the weakness of the Kyoto deal. *See* Gardiner, Stephen, *The Global Warming Tragedy and the Dangerous Illusion of the Kyoto Protocol*, 18 Ethics and International Affairs 23 (2004).

where the generations do not overlap.[28] (Call this the "Pure Intergenerational Problem" (PIP).) In that case, the problem can be (roughly) characterized as follows:[29]

(PIP1) It is *collectively rational* for most generations to cooperate: (almost) every generation prefers the outcome produced by everyone restricting pollution over the outcome produced by everyone overpolluting.

(PIP2) It is *individually rational* for all generations not to cooperate: when each generation has the power to decide whether or not it will overpollute, each generation (rationally) prefers to overpollute, whatever the others do.

Now, the PIP is worse than the Prisoner's Dilemma in two main respects. The first respect is that its two constituent claims are worse. On the one hand, (PIP1) is worse than (PD1) because the first generation is not included. This means not only that one generation is not motivated to accept the collectively rational outcome, but also that the problem becomes iterated. Since subsequent generations have no reason to comply if their predecessors do not, noncompliance by the first generation has a domino effect that undermines the collective project. On the other hand, (PIP2) is worse than (PD2) because the reason for it is deeper. Both of these claims hold because the parties lack access to mechanisms (such as enforceable sanctions) that would make defection irrational. But whereas in normal Prisoner's Dilemma-type cases, this obstacle is largely practical, and can be resolved by creating appropriate institutions, in the PIP it arises because the parties do not coexist, and so seem unable to influence each other's behavior through the creation of appropriate coercive institutions.

This problem of interaction produces the second respect in which the PIP is worse than the Prisoner's Dilemma. This is that the PIP is more difficult to resolve, because the standard solutions to the Prisoner's Dilemma are unavailable: one cannot appeal to a wider context of mutually-beneficial interaction, nor to the usual notions of reciprocity.

The upshot of all this is that in the case of climate change, the intergenerational analysis will be less optimistic about solutions than the tragedy of the commons analysis. For it implies that current populations may not be motivated to establish a fully adequate global regime, since, given the temporal dispersion of effects—and especially backloading and deferral—such a regime is probably not in *their* interests. This is a large moral problem, especially since in my view the intergenerational problem dominates the tragedy of the commons aspect in climate change.

The PIP is bad enough considered in isolation. But in the context of climate change it is also subject to morally relevant multiplier effects. First, climate change is not a static phenomenon. In failing to act appropriately, the current generation does not simply pass an existing problem along to future people, rather it adds to it, making the problem worse. For one thing, it increases the costs of coping with climate change: failing to act now increases the magnitude of future climate change and so its effects. For another, it increases mitigation costs: failing to act now makes it more difficult to change because it allows additional investment in fossil fuel-based infrastructure in developed and especially less developed countries. Hence, inaction raises transition costs, making future change harder than change now. Moreover, and perhaps most importantly, the current generation does not add to the problem in a linear way. Rather, it rapidly accelerates the problem, since global emissions are increasing at a substantial rate: for example, total carbon dioxide emissions have increased more than four-fold in the last fifty years. (See Figure 1.)

---

28. Generational overlap complicates the picture in some ways, but I do not think that it resolves the basic problem. *See* Stephen Gardiner, *The Pure Intergenerational Problem*, 86 MONIST 481 (2003).

29. These matters are discussed in more detail in Gardiner 2003 (*id.*), from which the following description is drawn.

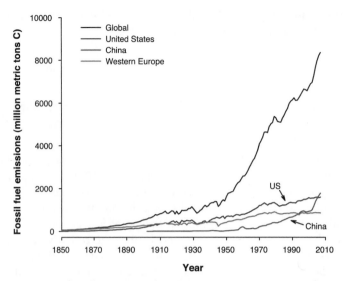

Figure 1. Country/Region Fossil Fuel CO_2 Annual Emissions. Data source: T.A. Boden, G. Marland, and R.J. Andres, Carbon Dioxide Information Analysis Center, Environmental Sciences Division, Oak Ridge National Laboratory.

Moreover, the current growth rate is around 2% per year.[30] Though 2% may not seem like much, the effects of compounding make it significant, even in the near term: "continued growth of CO_2 emissions at 2% per year would yield a 22% increase of emission rate in 10 years and a 35% increase in 15 years."[31]

Second, insufficient action may make some generations suffer unnecessarily. Suppose that, at this point in time, climate change seriously affects the prospects of generations A, B and C. Suppose, then, that if generation A refuses to act, the effect will continue for longer, harming generations D and E. This may make generation A's inaction worse in a significant respect. In addition to failing to aid generations B and C (and probably also increasing the magnitude of harm inflicted on them), generation A now harms generations D and E, who otherwise would be spared. On some views, this might count as especially egregious, since it might be said that it violates a fundamental moral principle of "Do No Harm."[32]

Third, generation A's inaction may create situations where *tragic choices* must be made. One way in which a generation may act badly is if it puts in place a set of future circumstances that make it morally required for its successors (and perhaps even itself) to make other generations suffer either unnecessarily, or at least more than would otherwise be the case. For example, suppose that generation A could and should act now in order to limit climate change such that generation D would be kept below some crucial climate threshold, but delay would mean that they would pass that threshold.[33] If passing the threshold imposes severe costs on generation D, then their situation may be so dire that they are forced to take action that will harm generation F— such as emitting even more greenhouse gases—that they would otherwise not need to consider.

30. James Hansen and Makiko Sato, *Greenhouse Gas Growth Rates*, 46 Proceedings of the National Academy of Sciences 101, 16109 (2004); James Hansen, *Can We Still Avoid Dangerous Human-made Climate Change*? Talk presented at the New School University, February 2006; Graph from Hansen 2006.

31. *Id.* at 9.

32. I owe this suggestion to Henry Shue.

33. *See* Brian C. O'Neill and Michael Oppenheimer, *Dangerous Climate Impacts and the Kyoto Protocol*, 296 Science 1971 (2002).

What I have in mind is this. Under some circumstances actions that harm innocent others may be morally permissible on grounds of self-defense, and such circumstances may arise in the climate change case.[34] Hence, the claim is that, if there is a self-defense exception on the prohibition on harming innocent others, one way in which generation A might behave badly is by creating a situation such that generation D is forced to call on the self-defense exception and so inflict extra suffering on generation F.[35] Moreover, like the basic PIP, this problem can become iterated: perhaps generation F must call on the self-defense exception too, and so inflict harm on generation H, and so on.

III. The Theoretical Storm

The final storm I want to mention is constituted by our current theoretical ineptitude. We are extremely ill-equipped to deal with many problems characteristic of the long-term future. Even our best theories face basic and often severe difficulties addressing basic issues such as scientific uncertainty, intergenerational equity, contingent persons, nonhuman animals and nature. But climate change involves all of these matters and more.[36]

Now I do not want to discuss any of these difficulties in any detail here. Instead, I want to gesture at how, when they converge with each other and with the Global and Intergenerational Storms, they encourage a new and distinct problem for ethical action on climate change, the problem of moral corruption.

IV. Moral Corruption

Corruption of the kind I have in mind can be facilitated in a number of ways. Consider the following examples of possible strategies:

- Distraction
- Complacency
- Unreasonable Doubt
- Selective Attention
- Delusion
- Pandering
- False Witness
- Hypocrisy

Now, the mere listing of these strategies is probably enough to make the main point here; and I suspect that close observers of the political debate about climate change will recognize many of these mechanisms as being in play. Still, I would like to pause for a moment to draw particular attention to selective attention.

The problem is this. Since climate change involves a complex convergence of problems, it is easy to engage in *manipulative or self-deceptive* behavior by applying one's attention selectively to only some of the considerations that make the situation difficult. At the level of practical politics, such strategies are all too familiar. For example, many political actors emphasize considerations that appear to make inaction excusable, or even desirable (such as uncertainty or simple eco-

---

34. Martino Traxler, *Fair Chore Division for Climate Change*, 28 Social Theory and Practice 101, 107 (2002).

35. Henry Shue considers a related case in a recent paper. Henry Shue, *Responsibility of Future Generations and the Technological Transition, in* Perspectives on Climate Change: Science, Economics, Politics, Ethics 265–284, 275–276 (Walter Sinnott-Armstrong and Richard Howarth eds., Elsevier 2005).

36. For some discussion of the problems faced by cost benefit analysis in particular, see John Broome, Counting the Cost of Global Warming Isle of Harris (White Horse Press 1992); Clive L. Spash, Greenhouse Economics: Value and Ethics (Routledge 2002); Stephen Gardiner, *Ethics and Global Climate Change*, 114 Ethics: 555 (2004); Stephen Gardiner, *Protecting Future Generations, in* Handbook of Intergenerational Justice (Jörg Tremmel ed., Edgar Elgar Publishing 2006).

nomic calculations with high discount rates) and action more difficult and contentious (such the basic lifestyles issue) at the expense of those that seem to impose a clearer and more immediate burden (such as scientific consensus and the Pure Intergenerational Problem).

But selective attention strategies may also manifest themselves more generally. And this prompts a very unpleasant thought: perhaps there is a problem of corruption in the theoretical, as well as the practical, debate. For example, it is possible that the prominence of the Global Storm model is not independent of the existence of the Intergenerational Storm, but rather is encouraged by it. After all, the current generation may find it highly advantageous to focus on the Global Storm. For one thing, such a focus tends to draw attention toward various issues of global politics and scientific uncertainty that seem to problematize action, and away from issues of intergenerational ethics, which tend to demand it. Thus, an emphasis on the Global Storm at the expense of the other problems may *facilitate* a strategy of procrastination and delay. For another, since it assumes that the relevant actors are nation-states who represent the interests of their citizens in perpetuity, the Global Storm analysis has the effect of assuming away the intergenerational aspect of the climate change problem.[37] Thus, an undue emphasis on it may obscure much of what is at stake in making climate policy, and in a way that may benefit present people.[38]

In conclusion, the presence of the problem of moral corruption reveals another sense in which climate change may be a perfect moral storm. This is that its complexity may turn out to be *perfectly convenient* for us, the current generation, and indeed for each successor generation as it comes to occupy our position. For one thing, it provides each generation with the cover under which it can seem to be taking the issue seriously—by negotiating weak and largely substanceless global accords, for example, and then heralding them as great achievements[39]—when really it is simply exploiting its temporal position. For another, all of this can occur without the exploitative generation actually having to acknowledge that this is what it is doing. By avoiding overtly selfish behavior, an earlier generation can take advantage of the future without the unpleasantness of admitting it—either to others, or, perhaps more importantly, to itself.

B. Perspectives of Law

1. International Law

a. Intergenerational Equity

[Reprinted from the Vermont Journal of Environmental Law, Winter, 2007–08, 9 Vt. J. Envtl. L. 615] (The Vermont Journal of Environmental Law reprinted this article, which

---

37. In particular, it conceives of the problem as one that self-interested motivation alone should be able to solve, and where failure will result in self-inflicted harm. But the intergenerational analysis makes clear that these claims are not true: current actions will largely harm (innocent) future people, and this suggests that motivations that are not generation-relative must be called upon to protect them.

38. In particular, once one identifies the Intergenerational Storm, it becomes clear that any given generation confronts two versions of the tragedy of the commons. The first version assumes that nations represent the interests of their citizens in perpetuity, and so is genuinely cross-generational; but the second assumes that nations predominantly represent the interests of their current citizens, and so is merely intragenerational. The problem is then that the collectively rational solutions to these two commons problems may be—and very likely are—different. (For example, in the case of climate change, it is probable that the intragenerational problem calls for much less mitigation of greenhouse gas emissions than the cross-generational problem.) So, we cannot take the fact that a particular generation is motivated to and engages in resolving one (the intragenerational tragedy) as evidence that they are interested in solving the other (the cross-generational version). *See* Stephen Gardiner, *The Global Warming Tragedy and the Dangerous Illusion of the Kyoto Protocol*, 18 Ethics and International Affairs 23 (2004).

39. *Id.*

was originally published as Appendix D in Edith Brown Weiss, In Fairness to Future Generations: International Law, Common Patrimony, and Intergenerational Equity 345–51 (Transnational Publishers, Inc. 1989).

Climate Change, Intergenerational Equity, and International Law

Edith Brown Weiss. Francis Cabell Brown Professor of International Law, Georgetown University School of Law, A.B., Stanford University; J.D., Harvard Law School; Ph.D., University of California (Berkeley); LL.D.(Hon.), Chicago-Kent College of Law, Illinois Institute of Technology.

Introduction

Climate change is an inherently intergenerational problem with extremely serious implications for equity between ourselves and future generations and among communities in the present and the future. More than twenty years ago I wrote an article entitled *Climate Change, Intergenerational Equity and International Law.* The basic issues and the analysis remain the same, though a number of international agreements relevant to climate change have been concluded since then.

At the time the Article was drafted, there was still considerable scientific uncertainty as to whether global warming was occurring, when it would occur, and with what effects within geographic regions. In an effort to address these uncertainties, the United Nations Environment Programme, the World Meteorological Organization, and the International Council of Scientific Unions jointly held the First World Climate Conference in 1979. Other international meetings focused on climate and carbon dioxide followed, culminating in a meeting of experts in 1985 in Villach, Austria, where an international consensus was achieved for the first time on the importance of the problem. The Article reprinted here was prepared as a Background Paper for the Villach Conference (Villach Article).

Three years later, in 1988, thirty-five countries founded the Intergovernmental Panel on Climate Change (IPCC), which produced its First Assessment of climate change and its effects in 1991. The IPCC is the most far-reaching international effort to ensure that authoritative scientific assessments are placed before the international community. In 2007, the IPCC produced its Fourth, and most recent, Assessment. The IPCC concluded that "[w]arming of the climate system is unequivocal, as is now evident from observations of increases in global average air and ocean temperatures, widespread melting of snow and ice, and rising global average sea level."[1] It further concluded that "[m]ost of the observed increase in globally-averaged temperatures since the mid-20th century is very likely due to the observed increase in anthropogenic GHG [Green House Gas] concentrations."[2]

The impacts from warming are predicted to be long-term, widespread, and severe. Even if a few countries may experience more favorable local climate in the near term, they are likely to suffer in the long term because of potentially devastating consequences elsewhere that will affect their own economic and social conditions. Developing countries will very likely suffer the worst effects from climate change because they have the least resilience and capacity to adapt.

No longer can we ignore the fact that climate change is an intergenerational problem and that the well-being of future generations depends upon actions that we take today. The Villach Article was included as an appendix to the 1989 book *In Fairness to Future Generations.* This book de-

---

1. U.N. Env't Programme and World Meteorological Org., Intergovernmental Panel on Climate Change [IPCC], IPCC Fourth Assessment Report, Climate Change 2007: The Physical Science Basis (Summary for Policymakers) 5 (Susan Solomon *et al.* eds., Cambrige Un. Press 2007), *available at* http://ipcc-wg1.ucar.edu/wg1/ Report/AR4WG1_Print_SPM.pdf (contribution of Working Group I).

2. *Id.* at 10 (citation omitted).

fines a theory of intergenerational equity, proposes principles of intergenerational equity, and sets forth both rights and obligations of future generations for the robustness and integrity of the Earth and its natural resources and for cultural resources.

The basic concept is that all generations are partners caring for and using the Earth. Every generation needs to pass the Earth and our natural and cultural resources on in at least as good condition as we received them. This leads to three principles of intergenerational equity: options, quality, and access. The first, comparable options, means conserving the diversity of the natural resource base so that future generations can use it to satisfy their own values. The second principle, comparable quality, means ensuring the quality of the environment on balance is comparable between generations. The third one, comparable access, means non-discriminatory access among generations to the Earth and its resources.

These principles satisfy the basic criteria of balance, flexibility, cultural acceptability, and clarity. One criterion is to balance the needs of future generations with those of the present, neither licensing the present generation to consume without attention to the interests of future generations or requiring it to sacrifice unreasonably to meet indeterminate future needs. Since we cannot predict the values of future generations, we also have to provide them with the options and quality to satisfy their own values and needs. In addition, the principles need to be generally acceptable to the many different cultures in the world, and finally they have to be reasonably clear so that they can be implemented and applied.

Despite subsequent relevant legal developments, the intergenerational issues raised in the Villach Article remain. In 1985, States concluded a framework agreement to protect the ozone layer, The Vienna Convention for the Protection of the Ozone Layer, and two years later the Montreal Protocol on Substances that Deplete the Ozone Layer. Some of the chemicals controlled in this Protocol also are greenhouse gases, and the Protocol has made a useful contribution to limiting these greenhouse gas emissions.

In 1992, after eighteen months of negotiation, countries finalized the United Nations Framework Convention on Climate Change and opened it for signature at the Rio Conference on Environment and Development. Notably, the Convention does not contain explicit targets and timetables for stabilizing atmospheric concentrations of greenhouse gases. However, it does obligate States party to provide national inventories of sources and sinks of greenhouse gases, regular national reports on policies, and measures that limit emissions of greenhouse gases and enhance the sinks for them. As of April 1, 2008, 192 countries are parties to the Convention.

At the first meeting of the Conference of the Parties to the UNFCC, countries agreed to a mandate to negotiate a new binding instrument to apply to the period beyond the year 2000 and to consider quantified targets and timetables for controlling greenhouse gas emissions. The Kyoto Protocol to the Convention was concluded in 1997, although it entered into force only in 2005. As of January 15, 2008, 178 countries are parties to the Protocol, but not the United States. The Kyoto Protocol has had only limited effect. States are now looking to negotiate new arrangements to govern the post-Kyoto commitment period, which ends in 2012.

Recently, systems for trading in greenhouse gas emissions as a means to control emissions have emerged in Europe and North America. These include the European Union Emissions Trading Scheme (EU ETS), the voluntary U.S.-based Chicago Climate Exchange (CCX), the Chicago Climate Futures Exchange (CCFE), and a new Montreal Climate Exchange (MCeX). The last is a joint venture of the Montreal Exchange (MX) and the Chicago Climate Exchange, which is expected to be launched at the end of May 2008.

The Villach Article refers to international environmental agreements in other areas. In the past twenty years, there have been significant developments in agreements to control pollution and protect ecosystems in regional seas, in the marine environment, in the atmosphere, and in fresh water. Indeed as of 2000, there were well over 1000 international legal instruments that were either partially or fully concerned with protection of the environment. Many more have been added since then. But despite these developments, we do not yet have international agreements that address climate change effectively, and they do not yet address the intergenerational dimensions of climate change.

The Villach Article proposes a global strategy for climate change, which respects principles of intergenerational equity and a declaration as an initial step. Since then, UNESCO adopted in 1997 a Declaration on the Responsibilities of the Present Generations Toward Future Generations, which focuses on our obligations to future generations (but not their rights). At the end of March 2008, the Human Rights Council adopted a resolution on Human Rights and Climate Change, which requests the Office of the United Nations High Commissioner for Human Rights to conduct "a detailed analytical study of the relationship between climate change and human rights" for submission prior to the Council's tenth session.[3]

Climate change is expected to have the most harmful impacts on impoverished regions and communities, in part because they are most vulnerable to changes in climate and because they have the least capacity to adapt. Intergenerational equity and intragenerational equity are linked in this context. In the present generation, one cannot expect people to fulfill obligations to future generations if they are not able to satisfy their basic needs. As future generations become living generations, they inherit the intergenerational obligations to conserve options, quality, and access in relationship to other members of the present generation.

As reports have indicated, climate change is likely to produce profound effects on the way we live, now and in the future. The article written for the Villach Conference twenty years ago identifies some of the pressing issues in ensuring intergenerational equity. We can choose to leave an impoverished legacy to future generations and to increase the inequalities among peoples today, or we can try to address the poverty issues today and to leave the Earth at least in no worse condition than we received it for future generations. If we have only obligations to future generations, we may act from a sense of noblesse oblige toward them. If, on the other hand, future generations have rights, people living today must consider their interests, examined from their perspective, in the actions we take today.

My congratulations to the VERMONT JOURNAL OF ENVIRONMENTAL LAW and the VERMONT LAW REVIEW for organizing this symposium on climate change and intergenerational equity and for contributing to an understanding of the issues.

Edith Brown Weiss, April 2008

Appendix D

Climate Change, Intergenerational Equity and International Law *

* We are reprinting Dr. Brown Weiss's Villach Article as it was originally published as Appendix D *in* IN FAIRNESS TO FUTURE GENERATIONS: INTERNATIONAL LAW, COMMON PATRIMONY, AND INTERGENERATIONAL EQUITY 345–51 (Hotei Publishing 1989). The footnotes below have been modified to conform to THE BLUEBOOK: A UNIFORM SYSTEM OF CITATION (Columbia Law Review Ass'n *et al.* eds., 18th ed. 2005).

---

3. Laura MacInnis, *U.N. Human Rights Body Turns to Climate Change*, REUTERS, Mar. 28, 2008, http://www.reuters.com/article/environmentNews/idUSL2778449820080328. *See generally* U.N. Human Rights Council, *Promotion and Protection of All Human Rights, Civil, Political, Economic, Social and Cultural Rights, Including the Right to Development*, U.N. Doc. A/HRC/7/L.21/Rev.1 (Mar. 26, 2008) (recognizing climate change as a threat to peoples and communities).

by Dr. Edith Brown Weiss

Background Paper, Conference on Developing Policies for Responding to Future Climatic Change, Villach, Austria, 28 Sept.–2 Oct. 1987)

Global climate change induced partly by human activities raises serious issues of justice between the present generation and future generations, and between communities within future generations. In using the planet's resources for our own benefit, we may pass many of the costs to future generations in the form of climate change and the need to adapt to such change.

Traditionally people have attributed climate to God, other deities, or the vagaries of nature. At least until recently they have not attributed it to human activities. As a corollary they have not considered that they had any obligation to compensate others for harsh climate conditions. But this assumption may falter. It may now be possible at the planetary level to hold one generation responsible for triggering global climate changes for future generations. While it may still be impossible to pinpoint particular countries as responsible for specific climate changes, it is increasingly possible to identify the global cumulative effects of our activities on future climate. We can also identify certain kinds of activities, such as fossil fuel consumption, as contributing significantly to an increase in temperature.

We have certain obligations to future generations which must guide the strategies that we adopt to address issues of global climate change. Unless we recognize this, we will benefit ourselves at the expense of the welfare of future generations. We will also proceed on the unwritten assumption that we must do everything we can to preserve the status quo in climate and prevent change. But change may not necessarily be more harmful to future generations if we can take steps to ensure that the rate of change is slow, that direct damage from change is minimized, and that future generations receive the tools and resources with which to adapt to climate change.

As a first step in addressing our obligation to future generations, we need to identify potential problems of intergenerational equity, develop normative principles to guide us in addressing these problems, and translate these into specific policies and enforceable agreements.

I. *Problems of Intergenerational Equity*

Problems of equity arise both between the present generation (defined as people living today) and future generations, and between different communities within future generations. Some problems relate to the condition of the natural environment future generations will receive; others to the resources they will inherit for adapting to a changed natural environment.

A.   *Changes in the Natural Environment*

Global climate change directly affects the natural environment, although the precise effects and distribution of these effects remains uncertain. If projected temperature increases occur, coastal areas will flood, precipitation patterns will shift, and weather fluctuations may become more frequent and extreme. Depending upon the rate of change, this may lead to degradation in the quality of the climate in major parts of the earth and decreased diversity in the natural resource base.

Degradation in the quality of the environment for future generations may arise at the global level and at regional and local levels. Many present centers of population may have climates that are regarded as less desirable than today. These will have significant societal impacts, such as population migrations and economic dislocations which can be costly for future generations. At the national level, coastlines may flood, causing members of future generations to abandon properties, to clean up polluted areas, and even to relocate urban areas. If coastlines flood in the future, the present generation will have reaped the benefits of coastal development and cheap waste disposal and inflicted potentially large costs on members of future generations.

Harsher climate conditions may also lead to depletion of the diversity of the natural resource base through the loss of existing species of flora and fauna unable to withstand the changes in temperature and precipitation or extreme fluctuations in weather. Advances in agriculture have led to the widespread adoption of crop strains which, while more productive, are also more vulnerable to climatic change. Many wild cultivars, useful in adapting to climate change, are being eliminated.

The depletion of the diversity of the natural resource base raises serious problems of equity for future generations because it narrows the range of options available to them in addressing their own problems and satisfying their needs.

Climate change will also raise significant equity concerns between communities within future generations because the changes will likely produce more favorable climates in a few parts of the world and less favorable in many others. Arguably those who will be better off should then help those who are worse off to share the burden. But those with relatively good climates today have been markedly reluctant to assist those with poorer climates, and such assistance as has been rendered, has not been viewed as compensatory for unfavorable climate conditions.

B.   Access to Resources for Adapting to Global Change

The effects of global climate change upon the welfare of future generations depends upon the rate of climate change. The faster the rate, the heavier the costs are likely to be for future generations. While climate has always changed, the rate of change is unprecedented. While some of the changes in climate may objectively produce better conditions for human habitation in certain areas, all peoples will suffer unless they are able to adapt quickly and effectively to the changed conditions.

We may classify countries according to their level of economic development today and the climate conditions that are projected within the next century. The level of economic development can be used as a guide to a country's ability to adapt to changed climate conditions. The higher the level of economic development, the more likely it is that the country will have resources with which to adapt to global climate change.

The matrix outlined here yields, for simplicity, four basic groups: developed countries expecting possibly better climate conditions (such as Canada), developed countries expecting worse climate conditions (such as the United States and countries in Europe), developing countries expecting better climate conditions, and developing countries expecting worse climate conditions. Of these groups, those countries that are now poor and will suffer worse climate conditions in the future suffer the greatest burden from climate change, for they have the least capacity to adapt to climate change.

In terms of intergenerational equity, the matrix reveals that we can expect not only problems of equity between generations but serious problems of equity between members of any given future generation. In some instances, such as for those poor countries whose climate worsens, the burdens will exacerbate existing inequities in the international community. In other instances, such for those developing countries potentially receiving better climate conditions, the climatic inequities may be alleviated, but other inequities will not be unless the resources and skills for adapting to changed climate conditions are available and can be effectively utilized. Otherwise, climate change will strengthen the economic divisions which already exist between countries, since some countries will have a greater capacity to adapt than will others.

II. The Theory of Intergenerational Equity

Before developing strategies for managing global climate change, it is important to define our obligations to future generations. For this, we adopt the perspective of a generation which is

placed somewhere on the spectrum of time, but does not know in advance where.[4] Such a generation would want to receive the planet in at least as good condition as every other generation receives it and to be able to use it for its own benefit. This requires that each generation pass on the
planet in no worse condition than received and have equitable access to its resources. From this
we can formulate principles of intergenerational equity. As proposed in detail elsewhere, these
principles would call for conservation of options (defined as conserving the diversity of the natural and cultural resources base), conservation of quality (defined as leaving the planet no worse
off than received), and conservation of access (defined as equitable access to the use and benefits
of the legacy).[5]

In the context of global climate change, implementation of these principles of intergenerational equity calls for measures to prevent rapid changes in climate, measures to prevent or mitigate damage from climate change, and measures to assist countries in adapting to climate
change.

A strategy to prevent rapid climate change has been discussed by others. It includes such
components as controlling the use of fuels rich in carbon, preventing deforestation and the misuse of soils, controlling the release of fluorochlorocarbons and other elements which destroy the
ozone layer, and monitoring nitrogen fertilizer use. To fulfill our obligation to future generations, we need to evaluate these strategies against the normative goals of ensuring that our descendants have access to a planet with diversity and quality comparable to prior generations.

Strategies to minimize damage from anticipated climate change include many actions which
we ought to take now for the welfare of our own and future generations, but which become
more urgent in the face of global climate change. These include gathering and conserving
germplasm for additional crops that are now neglected, and conserving the knowledge of traditional peoples of the utility of certain plants and animals, of ecosystems, and of practices
adapted to harsh climate conditions. Many strategies to mitigate damage are appropriately implemented at the national and local levels. These include coastal zone management, particularly
the siting of hazardous waste disposal facilities and nuclear power plants.

Strategies for adapting to climate change will involve research directed at anticipating
changes, monitoring to detect changes, conservation of knowledge about how societies have
adapted to climate changes in the past, development and maintenance of gene banks to assist in
agricultural adaptations, planning for alternative water supplies, changes in land use, incentives
to encourage or discourage population migrations as appropriate, and other measures. Some of
these measures must be designed to assist communities during the transition stage to a new climate; others should have a longer-range focus.

Unless the present generation is willing to undertake such measures, it is reaping the benefits
of its activities but passing the very substantial costs to future generations to bear.

III. The Role of International Law

In order to implement a strategy for managing global climate change, it will be necessary to
develop enforceable norms of behavior as the international, national, and local level.

International law, which dates to the early 17th century and the rise of the sovereign nation-
states, has been spatially oriented. To the extent that it considers the temporal dimension, it focuses mainly on the relationship of the present to the past. Problems of global climate change,

---

4. *See* J. RAWLS, A THEORY OF JUSTICE (Belknap Press 1971).

5. *See* E. BROWN WEISS, IN FAIRNESS TO FUTURE GENERATIONS: INTERNATIONAL LAW, COMMON PATRI-
MONY, AND INTERGENERATIONAL EQUITY (Hotei Publishing 1989). *See also* E. Brown Weiss, *The Planetary
Trust: Conservation and Intergenerational Equity*, 11 ECOLOGY L. Q. 295 (1984).

which focus on the relationship of the present to the future, demand that it turn to the future. As set forth elsewhere, it would be useful to have a Declaration of the Planetary Rights and Obligations to Future Generations which would set forth principles of intergenerational equity to guide specific normative and policy developments in areas such as global climate change.[6] As an initial step, such a Declaration could be drafted for the specific context of global climate change.

In developing a strategy for global climate change, there are already certain existing agreements which can be drawn upon to address specific aspects of the problem. Most of these agreements are intended to control pollution. They include the Vienna Convention for the Protection of the Ozone Layer, the Montreal Protocol on Substances that Deplete the Ozone Layer, the Economic Commission of Europe (ECE) Convention on Long-Range Transboundary Air Pollution, the Protocol to reduce sulphur emissions by 30 percent, the draft Protocol on controlling nitrogen oxides, and the European Economic Community (EEC) directives and regulations on specific pollutants.[7]

Many countries have national legislation controlling the emission of air pollutants to various degrees, which could be extended to controlling emissions of chlorofluorocarbons, nitrous oxides, and perhaps carbon dioxide. Some countries have legislation mandating standards of energy efficiency (which cuts down on fuel or gasoline consumption) or providing incentives to use certain fuels rather than others. Such national legislation could be used to lower carbon dioxide emissions.

There are few international agreements to date which can be viewed as minimizing the direct effects of global climate change, such as coastal flooding and water contamination. International agreements controlling marine pollution offer useful precedents. These include the London Ocean Dumping Convention, the Law of the Sea Convention, the many regional seas conventions, and the recent convention controlling the disposal of wastes in the South Pacific.[8] At the national level, some countries have enacted coastal zone management legislation, which could be useful in developing responses to projected coastal damage from global climate change.[9] In the United States, state and local land use regulations play a critical role.

There are no international agreements to date directed to adapting to climate change. Those agreements providing for the monitoring and exchange of climate data are, of course, relevant to any adaptation strategy. Once there is agreement on what adaptation requires, however, international agreements to facilitate this policy will be needed.

IV. Scientific Uncertainty and International Law

Planning for global climate change inherently involves large scientific uncertainties. As our understanding of how the climate system works, of how human activities affect the system, and of the impacts of global climate change upon the natural and cultural environment in-

6. *See supra* note 2; E Brown Weiss, *Intergenerational Justice and International Law*, unpublished manuscript, presented to the Conference on Human Rights, Oxford University, May 1987.

7. *Vienna Convention for the Protection of the Ozone Layer*, March 22, 1985, 26 I.L.M. 1516 (1987); *Montreal Protocol on Substances That Deplete the Ozone Layer*, Sept. 1987, [Reference File] Int'l Env't Rep. (BNA) 21:3151; *Convention on Long-Range Transboundary Air Pollution*, Nov. 13, 1979, 18 I.L.M. 1440 (1979), T.I.A.S. No. 10541; *Protocol on the Reduction of Sulphur Emissions or Their Transboundary Fluxes by At Least 30 Percent*, July 6, 1985, [Reference File] Int'l Env't Rep. (BNA) 21:3021; *Protocol on the Control of Emissions of Nitrogen Oxides* (revised draft), 17 Envtl. Pol'y & L. 259 (1987); EEC *Directive on Air Quality Standards for Nitrogen Dioxide*, March 7, 1985, 28 O.J.Eur.Comm. 1 (1985).

8. Convention on the Prevention of Marine Pollution by Dumping of Wastes and Other Matter [London Ocean Dumping Convention], Dec. 29, 1972, T.I.A.S. No. 8165; *U.N. Convention of the Law of the Sea*, Dec. 10, 1982, 21 I.L.M. 1261 (1982); *Convention for the Protection of the Natural Resources and Environment of the South Pacific Region*, Nov. 25, 1986, 26 I.L.M. 38 (1987).

9. *See* U.S. Coastal Zone Management Act of 1972, 1985 ed. & 1987 pocket. 16 U.S.C.A. 1451–64; Environmental Protection of Coastal Zone Management in Asia & Pacific (I. Kato *et. al.* eds. 1986).

creases, it must be incorporated into our laws and institutions. In international law, this means drafting agreements in such a way that they can respond to changes in scientific knowledge.

There are several devices already in use in various international agreements for doing so, albeit they may not be adequate. One of the most common is the use of protocols and annexes to implement agreements and to regulate additional activities as scientific understanding advances. The Montreal Protocol on chlorofluorocarbons to the Vienna Convention on Protecting the Ozone Layer, the Protocol on sulphur emission and the draft Protocol on nitrogen oxides to the Convention on Long-Range Transboundary Air Pollution, the annexes to the Great Lakes Water Quality Agreement, the annex to the Convention on the Conservation of Antarctic Seals, and the protocols to many of the regional seas conventions, illustrate these.[10]

International agreements have also used appendices or lists of regulated items effectively. In some instances the appendices set forth scientific criteria for placing items on the list. These agreements include the Great Lakes Water Quality Agreement between Canada and the United States, which lists hazardous and potentially hazardous pollutants in appendices, the London Ocean Dumping Convention, the Rhine Convention Against Pollution by Chlorides, the Convention on the Conservation of Migratory Species of Wild Animals, and the Convention on International Trade in Endangered Species of Wild Fauna and Flora.[11]

One of the most promising approaches is the use of scientific advisory boards which are established as part of the Conventions. These boards are usually authorized to advise on issues relevant to implementing the conventions. For example, the Migratory Species Scientific Council, attached to the Convention on the Conservation of Migratory Species of Wild Animals, is to provide scientific advice to the parties, recommend and evaluate relevant research, recommend migratory species for inclusion in the agreement, and suggest conservation measures.[12] Similarly, the Great Lakes Water Quality Agreement establishes a Science Advisory Board to assist the Water Quality Board and members of the International Joint Commission, and ultimately the parties in implementing the Agreement.[13] The Montreal Protocol on Substances That Deplete the Ozone Layer, the Convention on the Conservation of Antarctic Marine Living Resources, the Convention for the Conservation of Antarctic Seals, and the recent Convention on Antarctic Mineral Resources also provide for scientific advisory councils.[14] In the context of global climate change, serious consideration should be given to include scientific advisory units in international agreements addressed to aspects of climate change.

---

10. Montreal Protocol, *supra* note 7; Protocol on the Reduction of Sulphur Emissions, *supra* note 7; Protocol on the Control of Nitrogen Oxides, *supra* note 7; Great Lakes Water Quality Agreement, Nov. 22, 1978, T.I.A.S. No. 9257 and Protocol Amending the 1978 Agreement, signed Nov. 18, 1987; Convention on the Conservation of Antarctic Seals, June 1, 1972, T.I.A.S. No. 8826, and as an example of protocols to regional sea conventions, *Protocol Concerning Cooperation in Combating Pollution of the Mediterranean Sea by Oil and Other Harmful Substances in Cases of Emergency*, Feb. 16, 1967, 15 I.L.M. 306 (1976).

11. Great Lakes Water Quality Agreement, *supra* note 10; London Ocean Dumping Convention, *supra* note 8; *Rhine Convention Against Pollution by Chlorides*, Dec. 3, 1976, 16 I.L.M. 265 (1976); *Convention on the Conservation of Migratory Species of Wild Animals*, June 23, 1979 19 I.L.M. 11 (1976); Convention on International Trade in Endangered Species of Wild Fauna and Flora, March 3, 1979, T.I.A.S. No. 8249.

12. Art. VIII, Convention on Conservation of Migratory Species of Wild Animals, *supra* note 11.

13. Art. VIII, Great Lakes Water Quality Agreement, *supra* note 10.

14. Migratory Species Convention, *supra* note 11; Great Lakes Water Quality Agreement, *supra* note 10; Montreal Protocol, *supra* note 7; the Conservation of Antarctic Marine Living Resources, May 20, 1980, T.I.A.S. No. 10240; Convention for the Conservation of Antarctic Seals, June 1, 1972, *supra* note 10; *Convention on the Regulation of Antarctic Mineral Resource Activities*, June 2, 1988, 27 I.L.M. 859 (1988).

V. Conclusions

We must recognize that global climate change caused in part by human activities raises serious problems of justice between our generation and future generations, and among communities within these future generations. To fulfill our responsibility to future generations we must respect principles of intergenerational equity. We need a Global Strategy for Climate Change, which reflects principles of intergenerational equity. The strategy should include measures to slow the rate of change, to minimize direct damage from change, and to transfer the resources and tools necessary to adapt to climate change. Elements of such a strategy must be translated into enforceable norms at the international, national, and local levels. As an initial step, we should consider a Declaration of Planetary Rights and Obligations addressed to issues of global change. Only by addressing issues of intergenerational equity now can we ensure that we are passing a planetary legacy to future generations which is no worse than we received it.

International Human Rights Law and Climate Change

According to the Office of the United Nations High Commissioner for Human Rights:[15]

> As a global environmental hazard, climate change affects the enjoyment of human rights as a whole and therefore, it is at the core of the indivisible, interdependent and interrelated nature of each and all human rights as initially emphasized by the Universal Declaration of Human Rights.

Indeed, marginalized groups, whether in industrialized or developing countries and across all cultures and boundaries, are particularly vulnerable to the dire consequences of climate change. For example, small-scale farmers, women in rural areas, those not having adequate access to safe-drinking water, healthcare and social security, refugees, internally displaced, and the poor who are already living at the margins of survival would suffer disproportionately the consequences of global warming.

Indigenous peoples, and residents of small island states and Least Developed Countries, are also among those who will be the first to suffer from climate change. Emerging evidence suggests that the livelihoods and cultural identities of indigenous peoples across all regions, such as the Inuit from North America, the Sami people from the Nordic countries and the Russian Peninsula of Kola, the Massai Tribe from Africa, and indigenous populations in Latin America, Central Asia and the Pacific Rim, are threatened by the detrimental impacts of Climate change partly because their means of subsistence are highly dependent on nature.

The most vulnerable will suffer earliest and the most from climate change. Climate change therefore should be addressed in a way that is fair and just, cognizant of the needs and risks faced by the vulnerable groups, and adherent to the principles of non-discrimination and equality. Any sustainable solution to climate change must take into account its human impact and the needs of all communities in all countries in a holistic manner.

b. International Human Rights Law

Right to Carbon or Right to Life: Human Rights Approaches to Climate Change

Svitlana Kravchenko. Phd, LL.D, Professor and LL.M. Program Director, School of Law, University of Oregon, Eugene, OR 97403-1221; Tel: 541-346-0532; Fax: 541-346-1564; slana@uoregon.edu; J.D.,

---

15. UN Commission for Human Rights http://www.ohchr.org/EN/NewsEvents/Pages/Climate.aspx.

Lviv National University, Ukraine; Ph.D., All-Union Institute of Soviet Legislation, Moscow, U.S.S.R.; LL.D., National Law Academy, Ukraine.

> We, the human species, are confronting a planetary emergency.... But there is hopeful news as well: we have the ability to solve this crisis and avoid the worst—though not all—of its consequences, if we act boldly, decisively and quickly.

Al Gore[1]

> [T]hat which is common to the greatest number has the least care bestowed upon it. Everyone thinks chiefly of his own, hardly at all of the common interest; and only when he is himself concerned as an individual.... [E]verybody is more inclined to neglect the duty which he expects another to fulfill....

Aristotle, Politics[2]

Human rights form a central part of the thought system of many people in the world, including those in the United States. The enforcement of "rights" in the legal system does not, by itself, change government policy, but the embedding of rights in our thought systems can. I want to ask whether the concept of human rights has a role to play in changing minds—and more importantly, hearts—in our political system. The reason that I focus on hearts is that changes there are more permanent; and where the heart goes, the head tends to follow.

If we come to see human-caused global climate change as violating fundamental human rights—as something as unacceptable as other gross violations of human rights—perhaps we can make the breakthrough in our politics that is essential. Perhaps we can rescue ourselves from the planetary emergency that Al Gore, in the quote above, sees so clearly. Perhaps we can overcome the limitations of human nature that Aristotle saw so clearly more than two millennia ago. Perhaps that which is "common to the greatest number"—the precious planet that sustains our lives—may come to have not the least care, but our *loving* care, bestowed upon it.

Dr. James Hansen of the NASA Goddard Institute for Space Studies has said that a global tipping point could be reached by 2016.[3] According to Hansen:

> If global emissions of carbon dioxide continue to rise at the rate of the past decade, ... there will be disastrous effects, including increasingly rapid sea level rise, increased frequency of droughts and floods, and increased stress on wildlife and plants due to rapidly shifting climate zones.[4]

The U.N. Intergovernmental Panel on Climate Change (IPCC), in its 2007 Fourth Assessment Report, concluded that "[w]arming of the climate system is unequivocal, as is now evident from observations of increases in global average air and ocean temperatures, widespread melting of snow and ice, and rising global average sea level."[5] The Report also found "*high agreement* and *much evidence* that with current climate change mitigation policies and related sustainable development practices, global GHG emissions will continue to grow over the next few decades."[6] The

---

1. Al Gore, Former Vice President of the United States, 2007 Nobel Peace Laureate, Nobel Lecture (Dec. 10, 2007), http://nobelprize.org/nobel_prizes/peace/laureates/2007/gore-lecture_en.html.

2. 1 The Politics of Aristotle, ¶ 1261b30-40, p. 30 (Benjamin Jowett trans., Oxford: Clarendon Press 1885).

3. *Earth Climate Approaches Dangerous Tipping Point*, Env't News Service, June 1, 2007, http://www.ens-newswire.com/ens/jun2007/2007-06-01-01.asp.

4. *Id.*

5. U.N. Intergovernmental Panel on Climate Change [IPCC], Climate Change 2007: Synthesis Report 72 (Cambridge Un. Press 2007) [hereinafter IPCC Synthesis Report], *available at* http://www.ipcc.ch/pdf/assessment-report/ar4/syr/ar4_syr.pdf. The Synthesis Report is the fourth element of the IPCC Fourth Assessment Report. *Id.*

6. *Id.* at 44.

Report specifically points out important risks if governments fail to respond, such as species extinction, increases in droughts, heat waves, floods, increased vulnerability of indigenous communities and the poor and elderly, and loss of coastal area and associated impacts.[7]

Even still, the outlook is not completely negative. The Report indicates that there is "substantial economic potential for the mitigation of global GHG emissions over the coming decades that could offset the projected growth of global emissions or reduce emissions below current levels."[8] However, to prevent a catastrophe, we will need to act without delay and adopt a multifaceted approach.[9]

The Conference of the Parties to the U.N. Framework Convention on Climate Change (UN-FCCC) met in Bali, Indonesia, in December 2007 to launch comprehensive and inclusive negotiations for a new multilateral framework.[10] It was intended to create commitments beyond the year 2012,[11] the end of the first commitment period under the Kyoto Protocol.[12] The Bali Action Plan was agreed to, and consensus was achieved, only on the last day of negotiations.[13] Under pressure from the United States, the Plan set no worldwide goals.[14] The targets sought by some such as the European Union were omitted and a footnote in the preamble merely drew attention to the IPCC Fourth Assessment Report.[15] These omissions kept the United States at the negotiating table, but at a meeting in Hawaii in January 2008, the United States again refused to agree to any particular targets.[16] A new treaty—the Copenhagen Protocol—is supposed to be negotiated now, to be completed at the next meeting of the Conference of the Parties in December 2009 in Copenhagen, Denmark.

While diplomats and politicians are slowly starting to negotiate a new post-Kyoto treaty, lawyers in the United States and around the world are wondering how to speed up government action. Some believe that litigation has little role to play.[17] Others are wondering whether both litigation and political advocacy centered on human rights can make a difference. If new agreements are reached in Copenhagen, a further question will arise—whether commitments will be kept. The limitations of compliance mechanisms under international environmental law suggest that we should look to claims of human rights violations for potential enforcement, or at least shaming.

I.   *The Limitations of International Environmental Law Mechanisms*

The normal application and enforcement of international law occurs in diplomatic actions, in the self-restraint of governments, and sometimes in the compliance mechanisms that are set up to monitor whether countries are carrying out their obligations. In dealing with climate change, it is not clear, however, that these methods will be successful.

---

7. *Id.* at 64–65.

8. *Id.* at 58.

9. *Id.* at 64, 17–18, 23 ("Responding to climate change involves an iterative risk management process that includes both adaptation and mitigation, and takes into account climate change damages, co-benefits, sustainability, equity, and attitudes to risk.") (citation omitted).

10. Thomas Fuller & Andrew C. Revkin, *Climate Plan Looks Beyond Bush's Tenure*, N.Y. Times, Dec. 16, 2007, http://www.nytimes.com/2007/12/16/world/16climate.html.

11. *Id.*

12. Kyoto Protocol to the United Nations Framework Convention on Climate Change, Dec. 10, 1997, 37 I.L.M. 22 (1998) [hereinafter Kyoto Protocol], *available at* http://unfccc.int/resource/docs/ convkp/kpeng.pdf.

13. Fuller & Revkin, *supra* note 10.

14. *Id.*

15. *Id.*

16. *Europeans Test US Commitment to Climate Change*, Spiegel, Jan. 30, 2008, http://www.spiegel.de/international/world/0,1518,532077,00.html.

17. *See* Shi-Ling Hsu, *A Realistic Evaluation of Climate Change Litigation Through the Lens of a Hypothetical Lawsuit*, 79 U. Colo. L. Rev. (forthcoming July 2008), *available at* http://ssrn.com/abstract=1014870 (arguing that litigation is unlikely to make a significant difference in climate change).

A.   The United Nations Framework Convention on Climate Change

The UNFCCC plays an important role as a framework for international actions, political decisions, diplomatic negotiations, and coordinated scientific research.[18] It also provides technological and financial assistance for mitigation, adaptation, information exchange, and capacity-building.[19] As a framework convention, the UNFCCC does not contain concrete obligations; however, article 2 of the Convention consists of some arguable legal obligations:

> [T]o achieve in accordance with the relevant provisions of the Convention, stabilization of greenhouse gas concentrations in the atmosphere at a level that would prevent dangerous anthropogenic interference with the climate system. Such a level should be achieved within a time-frame sufficient to allow ecosystems to adapt naturally to climate change, to ensure that food production is not threatened and to enable economic development to proceed in a sustainable manner.[20]

Roda Verheyen has argued that article 2 must be interpreted in accordance with the principles in articles 31 and 32 of the Vienna Convention of the Law of Treaties,[21] giving it at least some persuasive force. Considering that, according to the IPCC Fourth Assessment Report, we have not been able to prevent "dangerous anthropogenic interference with the climate system," that ecosystems do not have sufficient time to adapt to climate change,[22] and that food production is threatened already, the Parties might be seen as already in violation of the UNFCCC. Similarly, it appears that some Parties to the Kyoto Protocol will also fail to meet their obligations, insignificant as those obligations appear to be in light of the size of the problem.

Despite apparent violations of the UNFCCC, the likelihood of effective enforcement action that would to lead to compliance seems slight. Generally, compliance mechanisms of multilateral environmental agreements (MEAs) are weak.[23] Their main goal is to assist and facilitate compliance, not to enforce or punish. They do not have "teeth." They lack serious sanctions, except for a few such as the Basel Convention,[24] the Montreal Protocol,[25] and the Convention on International Trade in Endangered Species (CITES),[26] which use trade sanctions as measures for non-compliance. MEAs even avoid using the term "sanctions." Instead, they use terms such as "measures"[27] or mention the "consequences" of noncompliance.[28]

---

18. U.N. Framework Convention on Climate Change, Essential Background, http://unfccc.int/essential_background/items/2877.php (last visited Apr. 20, 2008).

19. *Id.*

20. United Nations Framework Convention on Climate Change, art. 2, May 9, 1992, 1771 U.N.T.S. 107 [hereinafter UNFCCC], *available at* http://unfccc.int/resource/docs/convkp/conveng.pdf.

21. Roda Verheyen, *The Climate Change Regime After Montreal*, 7 Y.B. OF EUR. ENVT'L L. 237–38 (2007). *See generally* Vienna Convention on the Law of Treaties, *opened for signature* May 23, 1969, 1155 U.N.T.S. 331 (entered into force Jan. 27, 1980).

22. *See, e.g.*, IPCC SYNTHESIS REPORT, *supra* note 5, at 64.

23. Svitlana Kravchenko, *The Aarhus Convention and Innovations in Compliance with Multilateral Environmental Agreements*, 18 COLO. J. OF INT'L ENVTL. L. & POL'Y 1, 15–17 (2007) (explaining some of the shortcomings of MEAs).

24. Basel Convention on the Control of Transboundary Movements of Hazardous Wastes and Their Disposal art. 9, Mar. 22, 1989, 28 I.L.M. 657, *available at* http://www.basel.int/text/con-e-rev.doc.

25. Montreal Protocol on Substances That Deplete the Ozone Layer art. IV, Sept. 16, 1987, 1522 U.N.T.S. 28 [hereinafter Montreal Protocol].

26. Convention of International Trade in Endangered Species of Wild Fauna and Flora art. VIII, *opened for signature* Mar. 3, 1973, 993 U.N.T.S. 243 (entered into force July 1, 1975) [hereinafter CITES].

27. *See, e.g.*, Montreal Protocol, *supra* note 25, art. II; CITES, *supra* note 26, art. VIII (both using the term "measures" instead of "sanctions" to describe the trade sanctions).

28. *See, e.g.*, Kyoto Protocol, *supra* note 12.

The UNFCCC has a Subsidiary Body for Implementation (SBI) that is "established to assist the Conference of the Parties in the assessment and review of the effective implementation of the Convention."[29] Among other duties, it must "assess the overall aggregated effect of the steps taken by the Parties in the light of the latest scientific assessments concerning climate change."[30] The SBI advises the COP on administrative and financial matters, examines information in the national communications and emissions inventories submitted by Parties, and reviews "financial assistance given to non-Annex I Parties";[31] however, this body does not have any enforcement power.

The Convention also has a settlement procedure for a dispute between any two or more Parties concerning the interpretation or application of the Convention, "through negotiation or any other peaceful means of their own choice."[32] In addition, Parties can accept compulsory submission of their dispute to the International Court of Justice (ICJ) or arbitration using procedures adopted by the Conference of the Parties.[33] These provisions appear never to have been used.

B. The Kyoto Protocol

The Kyoto Protocol shares objectives with the UNFCCC. However, in comparison with the Convention, which encourages Parties to stabilize greenhouse gas (GHG) emissions and does not have mandatory obligations, the Protocol has legally binding obligations for developed countries to reduce GHG emissions below a level specified for each of them in Annex B to the Protocol.[34] These reductions would achieve an overall reduction of 5% below the baseline level of 1990 by the year 2012.[35]

The Kyoto Protocol Compliance Mechanism, in contrast to the mechanism under the UNFCCC, is one of the most comprehensive and rigorous amongst all MEAs, although it is just starting to operate. The Kyoto Implementation Committee consists of two branches—a facilitative branch and an enforcement branch.[36] The "facilitative" approach is claimed to have several benefits, including:

> building confidence in the treaty regime; ensuring that all Parties have the institutional, technical, and financial capacity to fulfill their obligations; reinforcing the Parties' sense of collective action and obligation; demonstrating that obligations are reasonable and attainable; and encouraging greater participation in the regime while lowering resistance to the adoption of additional binding commitments.[37]

The facilitative branch started its operation in May 2006 with a case brought to it by South Africa, on behalf of the Group of 77 and China, entitled "Compliance with Article 3.1 of the Kyoto Protocol."[38] The case was brought against Canada and fourteen other countries, alleg-

---

29. UNFCCC, *supra* note 20, art. 10, ¶ 1.

30. *Id.* art. 10, ¶ (2)(a).

31. U.N. Framework Convention on Climate Change, Convention Bodies, http://unfccc.int/essential_background/convention/convention_bodies/items/2629.php (last visited Apr. 20, 2008).

32. UNFCCC, *supra* note 20, art. 14, ¶ 1.

33. *Id.* ¶ 2.

34. Kyoto Protocol, *supra* note 12, Annex B.

35. U.N. Framework Convention on Climate Change, Kyoto Protocol, http://unfccc.int/ kyoto_protocol/items/2830.php (last visited Apr. 20, 2008).

36. Conference of the Parties Serving as the Meeting of the Parties to the Kyoto Protocol, 1st Sess., Montreal, Can., Nov. 28–Dec. 10, 2005, *Decision 27/CMP.1, Procedures and Mechanisms Relating to Compliance Under the Kyoto Protocol*, 92, 94–96, U.N. Doc. FCCC/KP/CMP/2005/8/Add.3 (Mar. 30, 2006).

37. Donald M. Goldberg *et al.*, Ctr. for Int'l Envtl. Law & Euronatura, Building a Compliance Regime Under the Kyoto Protocol 2 (1998), *available at* http://www.ciel.org/Publications/ buildingacomplianceregimeunderKP.pdf.

38. *Report to the Compliance Committee on the Deliberations in the Facilitative Branch Relating to the Submission Entitled "Compliance with Article 3.1 of the Kyoto Protocol,"* 3, U.N. Doc. CC/FB/3/2006/2 (Sept. 6, 2006), *available at* http://unfccc.int/files/kyoto_mechanisms/compliance/ application/pdf/cc-fb-3-2006-2.pdf.

ing that the countries had failed to submit various kinds of information required by the procedures under the Protocol.[39] The facilitative branch found itself paralyzed, however, and could not take action.[40] A report by the facilitative branch to the Compliance Committee stated:

> The branch made a number of attempts to arrive at a consensus. When all efforts to reach agreement on a decision by consensus had been exhausted, a vote was taken electronically on 21 June 2006, resulting in the failure to adopt either a decision to proceed or a decision not to proceed by a majority of three-fourths of the members present and voting, as required.... [41]

The facilitative branch had prepared two draft decisions—one to proceed and one not to proceed. The draft decision to proceed would have stated that the Parties had failed their information obligations and the branch should take "necessary actions to provide advice, facilitation and promotion to each Party concerned;"[42] however, this proposal failed by a vote of 4–4, with two abstentions.[43]

On the decision *not* to proceed, the branch had proposed a finding that:

> a) The communication was not submitted by a Party on its own behalf through a representative duly authorized for this purpose.
>
> The procedures and mechanisms do not provide for the possibility of groups of Parties making submissions by proxy ...
>
> b) The submission does not clearly and individually name the Parties with respect to which it purports to raise a question of implementation.
>
> c) The submission is not supported by information corroborating the question of implementation it purports to raise, nor does it substantiate that this question relates to any of the specific commitments under the Kyoto Protocol identified in either of paragraphs 5 or 6 of section VII.[44]

This proposal failed by a vote of 5–5.[45] The inability of the facilitative branch to reach a decision by the required three-fourths vote, on even these relatively minor matters concerning information submissions, does not make the Committee's work on the more difficult matters it may confront in the future look promising.

C.   The International Court of Justice

There is no international environmental court. Even if one were created, international tribunals have only moral authority and lack the power to force states to comply. Are principles of international environmental law robust enough for a case before the ICJ?

There have been only two environmental cases in the ICJ's jurisprudence to date: the Gabcikovo-Nagymaros case[46] and the Nuclear Testing Case.[47] Some have argued that a small island

---

39. *Id.*

40. *Id.* at 4.

41. *Id.* at 3.

42. *Id.*

43. *Id.* at 4.

44. *Id.*

45. *Id.* at 5.

46. Gabčíkovo-Nagymaros Project (Hung. v. Slovk.), 1997 I.C.J. 7 (Sept. 25), *available at* http://www.icj-cij.org/docket/files/92/7375.pdf.

47. Nuclear Tests (N.Z. v. Fr.), 1995 I.C.J. 288, 342 (Sept. 22), *available at* http://www.icj-cij.org/ docket/files/97/7187.pdf.

state that is likely to be inundated by rising seas could press a claim before the ICJ.[48] Professor Rebecca Elizabeth Jacobs has argued that a suit by the South Pacific island nation of Tuvalu would face several problems:

> Tuvalu must show not only that the United States and Australia are unlawfully caus-
> ing the island damage, but also that it has a right to future damages that have yet to
> occur. Tuvalu might succeed by arguing principles of intergenerational rights and the
> precautionary principle.[49]

The general status of the precautionary principle in international law is not yet settled. In petitioning to the ICJ for damages in the 1995 Nuclear Test Case, New Zealand alleged "by virtue of the adoption into environmental law of the 'Precautionary Principle,' the burden of proof fell on a state [France] wishing to engage in potentially damaging environmental conduct to show in advance that its activities would not cause contamination."[50] The ICJ dismissed New Zealand's claims without ruling on this issue.[51] Justice Weeramantry, however, in his dissent from the court order opinion argued that the precautionary principle is "gaining increasing support as part of the international law of the environment."[52]

In the field of climate change, the status of the principle is stronger. The precautionary principle is embedded within article 3 of the UNFCCC, and provides as follows:

> The Parties should take precautionary measures to anticipate, prevent or minimize
> the causes of climate change and mitigate its adverse effects. Where there are threats of
> serious or irreversible damage, lack of full scientific certainty should not be used as a
> reason for postponing such measures, taking into account that policies and measures to
> deal with climate change should be cost-effective so as to ensure global benefits at the
> lowest possible cost.[53]

The ICJ's Advisory Opinion on the Legality of the Threat or Use of Nuclear Weapons recognized another principle that would be relevant to a climate change lawsuit: it confirmed that the existence of the general obligation of states to ensure that activities within their jurisdiction and control respect the environment of other states or of areas beyond national control is now part of the corpus of international law relating to the environment.[54] This principle of international environmental law was also expressed in the Stockholm Declaration[55] and the Rio Declaration.[56]

Although Tuvalu has yet to bring a case before the ICJ, it continues to claim a right to compensation for damages caused by climate change. Recently the nation changed its approach from international litigation to making a broad request for compensation based on the polluter pays

---

48. Rebeca Elizabeth Jacobs, Abstract, *Treading Deep Waters: Substantive Law Issues in Tuvalu's Threat to Sue the Unitecd States in the International Court of Justice*, 14 Pac. Rim L. & Pol'y 103 (2003).

49. *Id.*

50. Nuclear Tests, 1995 I.C.J. at 298.

51. *Id.* at 307.

52. *Id.* at 342 (Weeramantry, J., dissenting).

53. UNFCCC, *supra* note 20, art. 3, ¶ 3.

54. Legality of the Threat or Use of Nuclear Weapons, Advisory Opinion, 1996 I.C.J. 226, ¶ 29, at 241–42 (July 8), *available at* http://www.icj-cij.org/docket/files/95/7495.pdf.

55. *Declaration of the United Nations Conference on the Human Environment* princ. 21, June 16, 1972, 11 I.L.M. 1420 ("States have, in accordance with the Charter of the United Nations and the principles of international law, the sovereign right to exploit their own resources … and the responsibility to ensure that activities within their jurisdiction or control do not cause damage to the environment of other States or of areas beyond the limits of their national jurisdiction.").

56. U.N. Conference on Environment and Development, Rio de Janiero, Brazil, June 3–14, 1992, *Rio Declaration on Environment and Development*, princ. 2, U.N. Doc. A/CONF.151/26 (Vol. I) (Aug. 12, 1992), *available at* http://www.un.org/documents/ga/conf151/aconf15126-1annex1.htm [hereinafter Rio Declaration].

principle.[57] The Deputy Prime Minister of Tuvalu, the Honorable Tavau Teii, said in a speech to the U.N. High Level Meeting on Climate Change, held at the U.N. headquarters in New York in September 2007, that major greenhouse polluters should pay Tuvalu for the impacts of climate change:

> Rather than relying on aid money we believe that the major greenhouse polluters should pay for the impacts they are causing. According to recent reports, funding to assist countries adapt to the impacts of climate change will cost in the region of US$ 80 billion per year. This cannot be met by aid budgets; it must be new funding based on the polluter pays principle.[58]

Considering Tuvalu, a nation faced with being wiped off the map by climate change, has not pressed forward with a case before the ICJ, it is hard to foresee the ICJ as a likely forum for addressing climate change. Instead, the argument is likely to have more force in strictly political fora.

II. Human Rights and Global Warming

At least four combinations of forums and claims might be used for litigation regarding climate change: international courts or compliance bodies, international human rights bodies, national courts applying international law, and national courts considering human rights claims under domestic law. If international courts or compliance bodies under MEAs offer little hope, what about the means and mechanisms that have been set up to protect human rights, both internationally and nationally?

The Inuit people claimed, in a 2005 petition to the Inter-American Commission on Human Rights, that global warming has an impact on their rights to life, health, culture, and subsistence. While the term "right to life" means something different to most Americans, in other countries it is often associated with the right to a healthy environment. It has been held to require environmentally protective actions in cases decided by regional human rights bodies such as the African Commission of Human Rights and the Inter-American Commission on Human Rights. Other substantive environmental human rights claims have been upheld on other grounds, such as a right to private and family life in the European Court of Human Rights. Finally, the Supreme Courts of India and the Philippines, the Supreme Court of Montana, and trial courts in places like Nigeria (dealing with gas flaring and climate change) have applied substantive environmental human rights claims to resolve cases.

A.   Recognition of Linkages Between Human Rights and the Environment

Linkages between human rights and the environment have been discussed and established during the last fifteen years by several scholars.[59] In 1994, the U.N. Special Rapporteur Fatma Zohra Ksentini prepared a final report titled "Human Rights and the Environment" in which she formulated strong and comprehensive linkages between human rights and the environment and provided environmental dimension of fundamental human rights—to life, health, and culture.[60]

---

57. Press Release, Afelee Pita, Ambassador, Permanent Mission of Tuvalu to the United Nations, Tuvalu Calls for Climate Change Polluters to Pay, Sept. 29, 2007, http://www.tuvaluislands.com/un/
2007/un_2007-09-29.html.

58. *Id.*

59. *See, e.g.*, HUMAN RIGHTS APPROACHES TO ENVIRONMENTAL PROTECTION (Alan E. Boyle & Michael R. Anderson eds., Oxford Un. Press 1996); DINAH SHELTON, *Environmental Rights, in* PEOPLE RIGHTS 187–88 (Philip Alston ed., Oxford Un. Press 2001) (discussing the interconnectedness of human and environmental rights laws); LINKING HUMAN RIGHTS AND ENVIRONMENT (Romina Picolotti & Jorge Daniel Taillant eds., Un. of Arizona Press 2003) (discussing the relationships between human rights and the environment).

60. Comm. on Human Rights, Sub-Comm. on Prevention of Discrimination & Prot. of Minorities, Special Rapporteur, *Human Rights and the Environment, Final Report*, U.N. Doc. E/CN.4/Sub.2/1994/9 (July 6, 1994) (prepared by Mrs. Fatma Zohra Ksentini) [hereinafter *Final Report*].

In 2002, under the organization of the U.N. High Commissioner on Human Rights and the Executive Director of the U.N. Environmental Programme, a group of experts convened for an Expert Seminar on Human Rights and the Environment.[61] The expert participants, which included the present author, reached broad agreement on the growing interconnectedness between the fields of human rights and environmental protection. In their Conclusions the experts noted:

> [L]inkage of human rights and environmental concerns, approaches and techniques is reflected in developments relating to procedural and substantive rights, in the activities of international organizations, and in the drafting and application of national constitutions.... [I]n the last decade a substantial body of case law and decisions has recognized the violation of a fundamental human right as the cause, or result, of environmental degradation. A significant number of decisions at the national and international levels have identified environmental harm to individuals or communities, especially indigenous peoples, arising as a result of violations of the rights to health, to life, to self-determination, to food and water, and to housing.[62]

These linkages were further discussed at the World Summit on Sustainable Development in 2002, being included in the Johannesburg Plan of Implementation.[63] More recently, the interconnectedness of environmental and human rights has been discussed in relation to the issue of global climate change.[64] However, evaluating the connections is not only the domain of academics. The U.N. Human Rights Council in a resolution of March 26, 2008, entitled "Human Rights and Climate Change," emphasized that "climate change poses an immediate and far-reaching threat to people and communities around the world and has implications for the full enjoyment of human rights."[65] The Council decided to undertake "a detailed analytical study of the relationship between climate change and human rights ... and thereafter to make available the study ... to the Conference of Parties to the United Nations Framework Convention on Climate Change for its consideration."[66]

B. International Human Rights Forums

Attempts to enforce MEAs such as the UNFCCC or Kyoto Protocol face several limitations. One limitation is that individuals have no standing to file complaints. State challenges against other states for non-compliance with MEAs are rather rare because states care about their diplomatic relations with other countries. A second limitation is that the members of most compliance mechanisms are not truly independent and instead appear as representatives of their gov-

---

61. Expert Seminar on Human Rights and the Environment, Meeting of Experts' Conclusions (2002), *available at* http://www.unhchr.ch/environment/conclusions.html.

62. *Id.*

63. World Summit on Sustainable Development, Aug. 26–Sept. 4, 2002, *Johannesburg Plan of Implementation*, ¶¶ 164, 169, U.N. Doc. A/CONF.199/20 (2002), *available at* http://www.un.org/esa/sustdev/documents/WSSD_POI_PD/English/WSSD_PlanImpl.pdf.

64. *See, e.g.*, Randall S. Abate, *Climate Change, the United States, and the Impact of Arctic Melting: A Case Study in the Need for Enforceable International Environmental Rights*, 26A STAN. ENVTL. L.J. 3 (2007) (considering the bases of international human rights, the impact of climate change on the Inuit, and the bases for recovery for climate change in human rights lawsuits); Timo Koivurova, *International Legal Avenues to Address the Plight of Victims of Climate Change: Problems and Prospects*, 22 J. ENVTL. L. & LITIG. 267, 285, 295–98 (2007) (discussing the challenges to climate change damage recovery, within the context of the "Inuit Circumpolar Council's (ICC) human rights petition against the United States," as a human rights issue).

65. Office of the High Commissioner for Human Rights, U.N. Human Rights Council, 7th Sess., U.N. Doc. A/HRC/7/L.21/Rev.1 (Mar. 26, 2008), *available at* http://ap.ohchr.org/documents/E/HRC/resolutions/A_HRC_7_L_21_Rev_1.doc.

66. *Id.*

ernments. For example, the UNFCCC SBI is available only to governments complaining about other governments, and its members, although made up of experts on matters related to climate change, represent their home governments.[67]

Human rights bodies, on the other hand, are available for complaints from non-state actors—citizens and non-government organizations (NGOs)—and the bodies themselves usually consist of independent experts. Human rights bodies are well established in the form of U.N. Charter organs, such as the U.N. Human Rights Commission and the U.N. Human Rights Council, and in the form of U.N. human rights treaty organs, which include the Human Rights Committee under the International Covenant on Civil and Political Rights (ICCPR),[68] the Committee on Economic, Social and Cultural Rights established under the Covenant of Economic, Social and Cultural Rights, the Committee on the Rights of the Child established under the Convention on the Rights of the Child, and similar bodies under other human rights treaties.

The U.N. Human Rights Committee is not a judicial body, but it does have authority to hear individual complaints. It has considered various complaints by indigenous peoples for alleged harm to their environment under article 27 of the ICCPR.[69] Some of them were successful. Special Rapporteur Fatma Zohra Ksentini has suggested that the U.N. Human Rights Committee

> could expand its general comment on the right to life in order to include environmental concerns or formulate a general comment defining the links existing between civil and political rights and the environment. Moreover, it should be able, through dealing with complaints, to establish case law that will accommodate environmental concerns.[70]

This U.N. body might be used to raise concerns about violations of human rights caused by climate change.

Previously the Prime Minister of Tuvalu requested environmental refugee status for its citizens from both Australia and New Zealand.[71] While New Zealand responded to the plea by allowing seventy-five Tuvaluans to relocate annually to their country, Australia has refused to make any such offer.[72] At a rate of seventy-five Tuvaluan relocations a year, the island would hypothetically not become uninhabited until 140 years have passed—ninety years after scientists predict it will be under water.[73]

Almost all human rights treaties recognize the "right to life."[74] According to article 6 of the ICCPR, "Every human being has the inherent right to life. This right shall be protected by law.

---

67. UNFCCC, *supra* note 20, art. 10.

68. International Covenant on Civil and Political Rights, Dec. 16, 1966, 999 U.N.T.S. 171 [hereinafter ICCPR].

69. *See, e.g.*, Bernard Ominayak & Lubicon Lake Band v. Canada, ICCPR H.R. Comm. Commc'n No. 167/1984, U.N. Doc. CCPR/C/38/D/167/1984 (1990); Länsman v. Finland, IPCC H.R. Comm., Commc'n No. 511/1992, U.N. Doc. CCPR/C/52/D/511/1992, 6 (1994) (action by reindeer herders under article 27 of the ICCPR, alleging that a government approved stone quarry would adversely affect their environment, herding activities, and culture (denied)).

70. *Final Report*, *supra* note 60, ¶ 259(e).

71. *Australia Unfazed at Tuvalu over Anger on Climate Change*, Tuvalu News, Aug. 30, 2002, *available at* http://www.tuvaluislands.com/news/archived/2002/2002-08-30a.htm.

72. *Pacific Island Villagers Become Climate Change Refugees*, Env't News Service, Dec. 6, 2005, http://www.ens-newswire.com/ens/dec2005/2005-12-06-02.asp.

73. *See* Anwen Roberts, *What Will Become of Tuvalu's Climate Refugees*, Spiegel, Sept. 14, 2007, http://www.spiegel.de/international/world/0,1518,505819,00.html (stating that Tuvalu is expected to be underwater within fifty years).

74. *See, e.g.*, ICCPR, *supra* note 68, art. 6 ("Every human being has an inherent right to life."); Additional Protocol to the American Convention on Human Rights in the Area of Economic, Social and Cultural Rights art. 11, Nov. 17, 1988, O.A.S.T.S. No. 69 [hereinafter Protocol of San Salvador], *available at* http://www.oas.org/juridico/english/Treaties/a-52.html ("Everyone shall have right to live in a healthy environment."); Con-

No one shall be arbitrarily deprived of his life."[75] Conceivably, inhabitants of Tuvalu could present a claim to the Human Rights Committee that their right to life is being violated. In addition, under article 12 of the ICCPR, the people of Tuvalu might claim a violation of the right to liberty of movement and the freedom to choose their residence.[76]

The issue of environmental refugees displaced by climate change is not limited to Tuvalu, of course.[77] Bangladesh, already one of the poorest nations in the world, also has many citizens near sea level who are vulnerable to rising seas and stronger storms. Other nations with substantial populations at risk include Viet Nam, China, Egypt, the Philippines, Indonesia, the Maldives, and the Marshall Islands.[78] The likelihood of displacement due to flooding from sea-level rise is global and massive. According to the FOURTH ASSESSMENT REPORT of the IPCC, more than 100 million people will be displaced each year by flooding even when the sea level has risen only by forty centimeters.[79]

However, the U.N. Human Rights Committee can only consider individual complaints against governments that have ratified the Optional Protocol to the ICCPR, thereby accepting the Committee's jurisdiction over such complaints.[80] Although the United States has ratified the ICCPR,[81] it has neither signed nor ratified the U.N. Optional Protocol.[82] Two other main polluters—China and India—ratified the ICCPR in 2005 and 1979, respectively, but have also not ratified the Optional Protocol.[83] Therefore, none of these present and future main emitters of GHG can be challenged by individuals for human rights violations in the Human Rights Committee. Most European nations, on the other hand, have accepted jurisdiction of the Committee to hear complaints and their actions could therefore be examined by the Committee.[84]

C.   International Human Rights Courts and Other Bodies

A better opportunity to challenge human rights violations related to climate change may lie in the regional human rights systems, namely, the European Court of Human Rights, the Inter-American Commission and Court of Human Rights, and the African Commission and Court of

---

vention on Access to Information, Public Participation in Decision-Making and Access to Justice in Environmental Matters art. 1, June 25, 1998, 38 I.L.M. 517 (1999) [hereinafter Aarhus Convention], *available at* http://www.unece.org/env/pp/documents/cep43e.pdf (endorsing "the right of every person ... to live in an environment adequate to his or her health and well-being....").

75. ICCPR, *supra* note 68, art. 6.

76. *Id.* art. 12.

77. Climate Institute, Climate Change and Sea Level Rise, http://www.climate.org/topics/sea-level/index.shtml (last visited Apr. 20, 2008).

78. *Id.* Some developing countries are especially vulnerable to sea level rise due to their low-lying nature and limited financial resources to respond. Among the most vulnerable are countries with large populations in deltaic coastal regions such as Bangladesh, Viet Nam, China and Egypt. Two populous island nations, the Philippines and Indonesia, have millions who face displacement from their homes from sea level rise. Several small island state nations including the Maldives in the Indian Ocean and the Marshall Islands and Tuvalu in the Pacific could face extinction within this century if rates of sea level rise accelerate. *Id.*

79. INTERGOVERNMENTAL PANEL ON CLIMATE CHANGE FOURTH ASSESSMENT REPORT, CLIMATE CHANGE 2007: IMPACTS, ADAPTATION AND VULNERABILITY 334 fig.6.8 (2007), *available at* http://www.ipcc-wg2.org/index.html.

80. *Id.*

81. U.N. High Comm'r for Human Rights, *Status of Ratifications of the Principal International Human Rights Treaties* 11 (July 14, 2006), *available at* http://www2.ohchr.org/english/bodies/docs/ status.pdf [hereinafter *Status of Ratifications*].

82. *Id.* The U.S. Senate also imposed numerous conditions at the time of advice and consent to ratification of the ICCPR, including a declaration that it is not self-executing. U.S. Ratification of International Covenant on Civil and Political Rights, 58 Fed. Reg. 45,934 (Aug. 31, 1993); 138 CONG. REC. S4781-01, *S4783 (daily ed. Apr 2, 1992), *available at* http://www1.umn.edu/humanrts/ usdocs/civilres.html.

83. *Status of Ratifications, supra* note 81, at 3, 6.

84. *See generally id.* (evidencing ratification of the ICCPR by European countries).

Human and Peoples' Rights. As we will discuss below, human rights treaties have provisions that explicitly or implicitly recognize environmental rights. In recent years, the regional bodies enforcing these rights have moved to the position that degradation of the environment can violate human rights. In addition to explicit or implicit recognition of the right to a healthy environment in some human rights treaties, some courts interpret fundamental human rights—such as the rights to life, to health, to culture, and to subsistence, as well as the right to respect for private and family life—in ways that help protect the environment from pollution or degradation.

1.   European Court of Human Rights

In Europe, the Aarhus Convention recognizes the "right of every person of present and future generations to live in an environment adequate to his or her health and well-being," and requires each Party to guarantee the procedural "rights of access to information, public participation in decision-making and access to justice in environmental matters."[85] Of equal importance, the European Convention on the Protection of Human Rights and Fundamental Freedoms (popularly known as the European Convention on Human Rights) has provisions concerning the right to life (article 2) and right to private and family life (article 8).[86]

Article 2 reads in part: "Everyone's right to life shall be protected by law. No one shall be deprived of his life intentionally save in the execution of a sentence of a court following his conviction of a crime for which this penalty is provided by law."[87]

Article 8 reads in part: "Everyone has the right to respect for his private and family life, his home and his correspondence."[88]

Article 8 has been used in several environmental cases such as *Lopez Ostra v. Spain,*[89] *Guerra v. Italy,*[90] *Fadeyeva v. Russia,*[91] and *Taskin v. Turkey,*[92] while article 2 has been used in one environmental case, *Oneryildiz v. Turkey.*[93]

In *Lopez Ostra v. Spain,* the first and landmark environmental case of the European Court of Human Rights, applicant Gregoria Lopez Ostra of Spain alleged a violation of her right to privacy and family security under article 8 of the European Convention.[94] The applicant based her claim on the siting of a leather processing waste treatment plant near her home, which released fumes, smells, and contamination and "immediately caused health problems and [a] nuisance."[95] Mrs. Lopez Ostra argued that the government had a positive duty to secure her rights under article 8.[96] The Court, while not finding an outright affirmative duty to prevent the pollution, did find the government failed "in striking a fair balance between the interest of the town's economic well-being—that of having a waste-treatment plant—and the applicant's effective enjoyment of her right to respect for her home and her private and family life."[97] Thus,

---

85. Aarhus Convention, *supra* note 74, art.1.

86. Convention for the Protection of Human Rights and Fundamental Freedoms, Nov. 4, 1950, 213 U.N.T.S. 222, *available at* http://www.echr.coe.int/NR/rdonlyres/D5CC24A7-DC13-4318-B457-5C9014916 D7A/0/English

Anglais.pdf [hereinafter European Convention].

87. *Id.* art. 2.

88. *Id.* art. 8.

89. López-Ostra v. Spain, 20 Eur. Ct. H.R. 277 (1995).

90. Guerra v. Italy, 26 Eur. Ct. H.R. 357 (1998).

91. Fadeyeva v. Russia, 45 Eur. Ct. H.R. 10 (2005).

92. Taskin v. Turkey, 2004-III Eur. Ct. H.R. 621 (2004).

93. Öneryildiz v. Turkey (Grand Chamber), 41 Eur. Ct. H. R. 20 (2004).

94. Lopez-Ostra v. Spain, 20 Eur. Ct. H.R. ¶¶ 6, 44.

95. *Id.* ¶ 8.

96. *Id.* ¶ 51.

97. *Id.* ¶ 56.

finding a breach of article 8, the Court ordered the government to pay four million pesetas as compensation.[98]

Similarly, in *Fadeyeva v. Russia,* applicant Nadezhda Mikhaylovna Fadeyeva of Russia alleged a violation under article 8 of the European Convention for the government's "failure to protect her private life and home."[99] The applicant lived about 450 meters from Russia's largest iron smelter and alleged "the extent of environmental [air] pollution at her place of residence was and remains seriously detrimental to her health and wellbeing."[100] The court observed that "over a significant period of time the concentration of various toxic elements in the air near the applicant's house seriously exceeded the [maximum permissible limits]."[101] The court ruled that the government, by not offering any effective solution to help the applicants move from the affected area, "failed to strike a fair balance between the interests of the community and the applicant's effective enjoyment of her right to respect for her home and her private life."[102] Thus finding a breach of article 8, the court ordered the government to pay six thousand euros for non-pecuniary damages.[103]

In *Taskin v. Turkey,* the Turkish government had persisted in authorizing a mining process using sodium cyanide after numerous national court decisions ruling that the authorizations were illegal.[104] The European Court of Human Rights ruled that the mining for gold using sodium cyanide violated the right to respect for private and family life in breach of article 8.[105] The court also concluded that the government's refusal to abide by its own courts' decisions deprived the citizens of "their right to effective judicial protection in the determination of their civil rights."[106] The particular civil right at issue was the national right, under article 56 of the Turkish Constitution, "to live in a healthy [and] balanced environment."[107]

In *Guerra v. Italy* the court discussed both article 2 and article 8.[108] In that case, forty applicants lived in the town of Manfredonia, approximately one kilometer from a "high risk" chemical factory that produced fertilizers and other highly toxic chemicals.[109] Accidents due to malfunctions had occurred in the past. During the most serious accident, "one hundred and fifty people were admitted to the hospital with acute arsenic poisoning."[110]

The court held unanimously that it was unnecessary to consider the case under article 2 of the Convention because it ruled that article 8 had been violated.[111] However, Judge Walsh, in his concurring opinion, said that article 2 was violated as well because it "also guarantees the protection of the bodily integrity of the applicants."[112] Judge Jambrek in his concurring opinion also made "some observations on the possible applicability of article 2 in this case."[113] The protection of health and physical integrity was, in his view, related to the "right to life."[114] He continued:

---

98. *Id.* ¶ 65.

99. Fadeyeva v. Russia, 45 Eur. Ct. H.R. 10, ¶ 64 (2005).

100. *Id.* ¶¶ 10–11, 71.

101. *Id.* ¶¶ 11, 87.

102. *Id.* ¶¶ 133–34.

103. *Id.* ¶¶ 134, 138.

104. Taskin v. Turkey, 2004-III Eur. Ct. H.R. 621, ¶¶ 11–89 (2004).

105. *Id.* ¶ 126.

106. *Id.* ¶ 127.

107. *Id.* ¶¶ 132, 90.

108. Guerra v. Italy, 26 Eur. Ct. H.R. 26, ¶¶ 56–62 (1998).

109. *Id.* ¶ 13 (stating that the factory "was classified as 'high risk' according to the criteria set out in Presidential Decree").

110. *Id.* ¶ 15.

111. *Id.* ¶¶ 62, 75.

112. *Id.* (Walsh, J., concurring).

113. *Id.* (Jambrek, J., concurring).

114. *Id.*

> [P]erson(s) concerned face a real risk of being subjected to circumstances which endanger their health and physical integrity, and thereby put at serious risk their right to life, protected by law.... It may therefore be time for the Court's case-law on Article 2 (the right to life) to start evolving, to develop the respective implied rights, articulate situations of real and serious risk to life, or different aspects of the right to life. Article 2 also appears relevant and applicable to the facts of the instant case, in that 150 people were taken to hospital with severe arsenic poisoning. Through the release of harmful substances into the atmosphere, the activity carried on at the factory thus constituted a "major-accident hazard dangerous to the environment."[115]

In 2002 the European Court of Human Rights for the first time decided to apply article 2 in *Oneryildiz v. Turkey,* an environmental case clearly involving loss of life.[116] The applicant complained that the accident on April 28, 1993, in which nine members of his family died, had occurred as a result of the negligence of the relevant authorities.[117] An expert committee's report indicated that "the waste-collection site in question breached the Environment Act and the Regulation on Solid-Waste Control and consequently pose[d] a health hazard to humans and animals."[118] The report observed that no measures had been taken to prevent a possible explosion of methane gas from the dump, and that such an explosion subsequently occurred.[119] The explosion buried ten homes, including that of the applicant.[120] The court held that as a consequence there had been a violation of article 2.[121]

A dramatic explosion and landslide, along with the widespread knowledge that methane can explode, led the court to the conclusion that the right to life in article 2 had been violated. But what are the prospects for bringing such a claim in Europe concerning loss of life from human-induced climate change? It is increasingly accepted that warm ocean waters fuel hurricanes and that climate change will cause hurricanes and tropical storms to become more intense—lasting longer, unleashing stronger winds, and causing more damage to coastal ecosystems and communities.[122] This will result in dramatic and adverse impacts on life and property, both of which are central concerns of human rights regimes. Hurricane Katrina caused a loss of 1300 lives and $ 80 billion in economic damage.[123] Although hurricanes are not a problem in Europe, heat waves are. For example, heat waves killed more than 52,000 people in 2003 in Europe.[124] "As the mercury climbs, more frequent and more severe heat waves are in store. Accordingly, the World Meteorological Organization estimates that the number of heat-related fatalities could double in less than 20 years."[125]

If sufficient evidence could be accumulated to support a case linking heat wave deaths and GHG emissions, who could be the defendants in a complaint to the European Court of Human Rights? One possibility might be states that are members of the Council of Europe but have not introduced mandatory and significant reduction programs for GHG emissions. The Russian

---

115. *Id.*

116. Öneryildiz v. Turkey (*Grand Chamber*), 41 Eur. Ct. H.R. 20, ¶ 18 (2004).

117. *Id.* ¶ 63.

118. *Id.* ¶ 15.

119. *Id.* ¶ 23.

120. *Id.* ¶ 18.

121. *Id.* ¶ 118.

122. IPCC Synthesis Report, *supra* note 5, at 46.

123. Nat'l Oceanic & Atmospheric Admin. [NOAA], Noteworthy Records of the 2005 Atlantic Hurricane Season, http://www.noaanews.noaa.gov/stories2005/s2540b.htm (last visited Apr. 20, 2008).

124. Janet Larsen, *Setting the Record Straight: More than 52,000 Europeans Died from Heat in Summer 2003,* Earth Pol'y Inst., July 28, 2007, http://www.earth-policy.org/Updates/2006/ Update56.htm.

125. *Id.*

Federation is a party to the European Convention on Human Rights and its Optional Protocol.[126] The European Court of Human Rights has found Russia in violation of article 8 in the past.[127] The Russian Federation ratified the Kyoto Protocol in 2004, and therefore has obligations to reduce GHG emissions below its 1990 levels.

2. Inter-American Commission and Court of Human Rights

The Inter-American Commission and Court of Human Rights are known as strong bodies for the protection of indigenous peoples' rights. Legal instruments include the American Convention on Human Rights[128] and the Additional Protocol to the Convention (the Protocol of San Salvador), which recognizes that "[e]veryone shall have the right to live in a healthy environment."[129] Although the Protocol of San Salvador has been ratified by only six countries, the American Convention has been ratified by twenty-five countries (not including the United States and Canada).[130] The court enforces the Convention, but the commission is willing to make findings in cases of alleged violation of a third document, the American Declaration of the Rights and Duties of Man, even in matters involving the United States and Canada.

The court recognized the land and property rights of indigenous people in the groundbreaking *Awas Tingni* case.[131] The court ruled that the State of Nicaragua violated the right to the use and enjoyment of property by granting a logging concession on traditional lands of the Mayagna (Sumo) Awas Tingni Community.[132] By "evolutionary interpretation" of the right to the use and enjoyment of property, the court held:

> [A]rticle 21 of the Convention protects the right to property in a sense which includes, among others, the rights of members of the indigenous communities within the framework of communal property ... Based on this understanding, the Court considers that the members of the Awas Tingni Community have the right that the State ... carry out the delimitation, demarcation, and titling of the territory belonging to the Community.[133]

The Inter-American Commission on Human Rights has recognized the relationship between human rights and the environmental impacts of development activities. Can it be a tool also for combating climate change? In 2005, for the first time, the commission received a petition requesting relief for a violation of human rights resulting from global warming, allegedly caused by "acts and omissions of the United States."[134] The Inuit peoples of Alaska and Canada argued

---

126. Council of Europe, Parties and Signatories to the European Convention on Human Rights and Additional Protocols, http://conventions.coe.int/Treaty/Commun/ListeTableauCourt.asp? MA=3&CM=16&CL= ENG (last visited Apr. 20, 2008).

127. Fadeyeva v. Russia, 45 Eur. Ct. H.R. 10, ¶ 134 (2005); Ledyayeva v. Russia, Eur. Ct. H.R. Application. Nos. 53157/99, 53247/99, 53695/00, 56850/00, (2008), *available at* http://www.asil.org/ pdfs/ilibledyayeva 061122.pdf.

128. American Convention on Human Rights, Nov. 22, 1969, O.A.S.T.S. No. 36, 1144 U.N.T.S. 123, *available at* http://www.cidh.org/Basicos/English/Basic3.American%20Convention.htm [hereinafter American Convention].

129. Protocol of San Salvador, *supra* note 74, art. 11.

130. Inter-American Commission on Human Rights, *What is the IACHR?*, http://www.cidh.org/ Basicos/English/Basic4.Amer.Conv.Ratif.htm (last visited Apr. 26, 2008).

131. Mayagna (Sumo) Awas Tingni Cmty. v. Nicaragua, 2001 Inter-Am. Ct. H.R. (ser. C) No. 79 (Aug. 31, 2001).

132. *Id.* ¶ 153.

133. *Id.* ¶¶ 148, 153.

134. Petition to the Inter American Commission on Human Rights Seeking Relief from Violations Resulting from Global Warming Caused by Acts and Omissions of the United States at 1 (Dec. 7, 2005), *available at* http://www.earthjustice.org/library/legal_docs/petition-to-the-inter-american-commission-on-human-rights-on-behalf-of-the-inuit-circumpolar-conference.pdf [hereinafter Inuit Petition].

that the adverse impact on wildlife from climate change—changes in the location number and health of plant and animal species—violates their fundamental human rights to life, property, culture, and means of subsistence.[135]

Some species are starting to move to different locations, exacerbating the Inuit's travel problems; other species cannot make their annual migrations because the ice on which they normally travel is gone.[136] Reduction of sea ice drastically shrinks the habitat for polar bears and seals, pushing them toward extinction.[137] The petition argued that this has impaired the Inuits' right to subsist by altering their food sources.[138] Furthermore, "[g]lobal warming violates these rights by melting the ice, snow and permafrost, changing the weather, and radically altering every aspect of the arctic environment on which Inuit lives and culture depend."[139]

The petition focused on the United States of America because it is one of the largest emitters of GHGs and has, up to this point, refused to join the international effort to reduce emissions under the Kyoto Protocol.[140] The petition asked the commission to declare the United States in violation of rights affirmed in the 1948 American Declaration of the Rights and Duties of Man and other instruments of international law.[141]

In November 2006, however, the petitioners received a letter from the commission, stating that it "will not be able to process your petition at present … the information provided does not enable us to determine whether the alleged facts would tend to characterize a violation of rights protected by the American Declaration."[142]

Although it rejected the petition, the commission subsequently held a hearing on March 1, 2007, at the request of petitioners, in which it discussed the connection between human rights and global warming.[143] The former chair of the Inuit Circumpolar Council, 2007 Nobel Peace Prize nominee Sheila Watt-Cloutier, testified to the effects of climate change on the global environment, health, and rights of indigenous peoples.[144] Her testimony went beyond the Arctic to include a broader region—the Caribbean, Central America, Venezuela, and Uruguay.[145] Even without a positive outcome, the petition has become a precedent for using the Inter-American Commission to raise questions of violations of human rights caused by global warming. As Donald M. Goldberg and Martin Wagner, lawyers for the petitioners, have written:

> [A] report by the Commission examining the connection between global warming and human rights could have a powerful impact on worldwide efforts to address global warming. It would demonstrate that the issue is not merely an abstract problem for the

135. *Id.* at 5–6.
136. *Id.* at 3.
137. *Id.* at 4.
138. *Id.* at 3.
139. Press Release, EarthJustice, *Inuit Human Rights Petition Filed over Climate Change* (Dec. 7, 2005), *available at* http://www.earthjustice.org/news/press/005/inuit-human-rights-petition-filed-over-climate-change.html.
140. Inuit Petition, *supra* note 134, at 6.
141. *Id.* at 5.
142. *Letter of the Inter-American Commission on Human Rights to Mr.Crowley, Ref.:Sheila Watt-Cloutier et al.*, Petition N P1413-05, United States, Nov. 16, 2006 (on file with author).
143. Press Release, EarthJustice, *Inter-American Commission on Human Rights to Hold Hearing on Global Warming* (Feb. 6, 2007), *available at* http://www.earthjustice.org/news/press/007/ inter-american-commission-on-human-rights-Hearing-on-Global-Warming.html.
144. Press Release, Earth Justice, *Nobel Prize Nominee Testifies About Global Warming* (Mar. 1, 2007), *available at* http://www.earthjustice.org/news/press/007/nobel-prize-nominee-testifies-about-global-warming.html.
145. *Id.*

future, but is instead a problem of immediate concern to all people everywhere. Recognition by the Commission of a link between global warming and human rights may establish a legal basis for holding responsible countries that have profited from inadequate greenhouse gas regulation and could provide a strong incentive to all countries to participate in effective international response efforts.[146]

At the very least, the filing of the Inuits' petition and the Inter-American Commission on Human Rights' decision to address the question of how climate change affects human rights has advanced the notion that climate change is an issue involving human rights, not just public policy.

3.   African Commission of Human and Peoples' Rights

Article 24 of the African Charter on Human and Peoples' Rights (African Charter) says that "[a]ll peoples shall have the right to a general satisfactory environment favorable to their development."[147] The African Commission on Human Rights enforced the right to health and the right to a satisfactory environment in the case *Social and Economic Rights Action Center v. Nigeria*.[148] The Action Center asserted:

> [The] Nigerian government violated the right to health and the right to clean environment as recognized under Articles 16 and 24 of the African Charter by failing to fulfill the minimum duties required by these rights. This, the Complainants allege, the government has done by:
>
>> Directly participating in the contamination of air, water and soil and thereby harming the health of the Ogoni population,
>>
>> Failing to protect the Ogoni population from the harm caused by the NNPC Shell Consortium but instead using its security forces to facilitate the damage.[149]

The commission's ruling stated:

> [D]espite its obligation to protect persons against interferences in the enjoyment of their rights, the Government of Nigeria facilitated the destruction of the Ogoniland. Contrary to its Charter obligations and despite such internationally established principles, the Nigerian Government has given the green light to private actors, and the oil Companies in particular, to devastatingly affect the well-being of the Ogonis. By any measure of standards, its practice falls short of the minimum conduct expected of governments, and therefore, is in violation of Article 21 of the African Charter.[150]

The commission found Nigeria in violation of articles 2, 4, 14, 16, 18(1), 21 and 24 of the African Charter and appealed to the government of the Federal Republic of Nigeria "to ensure protection of the environment, health and livelihood of the people of Ogoniland."[151] The commission asked Nigeria to ensure "adequate compensation to victims of the human rights violations, including relief and resettlement assistance to victims of government sponsored raids, and

---

146. Donald M. Goldberg & Martin Wagner, *Petitioning for Adverse Impacts of Global Warming in the Inter-American Human Rights System*, *in* CLIMATE CHANGE—FIVE YEARS AFTER KYOTO 191, 195 (Science Publishers 2002), *available at* http://www.ciel.org/Publications/Petitioning_GlobalWarming_ IAHR.pdf.

147. African [Banjul] Charter on Human and Peoples' Rights art. 24, June 27, 1981, 21 I.L.M. 58 (1982), *available at* http://www.achpr.org/english/_info/charter_en.html.

148. Soc. & Econ. Rights Action Ctr. v. Nigeria, No. 155/96 (Afr. Comm'n H. & Peoples' R., May 27, 2002), *available at* http://www.escr-net.org/usr_doc/serac.pdf.

149. *Id.* at 9–10 (bullet points omitted).

150. *Id.* at 12.

151. *Id.* at 15.

[to undertake] a comprehensive cleanup of lands and rivers damaged by oil operations."[152] This case could be useful precedent in climate change litigation in situations where a government violates human rights by not fulfilling its duty to protect the environment, health, and livelihood of people from the negative consequences of climate change, and has to resettle and compensate victims.

D.   National Courts Safeguarding Human Rights

U.S. domestic courts have been unwilling to hold that environmental rights have gained sufficient status under international law to be enforceable in tort. In *Flores v. Southern Peru Copper Corp.*, the plaintiffs alleged a violation of the rights to life and health as violation of customary international law, actionable under the Alien Tort Claims Act (ATCA).[153] The court rejected the argument, holding:

> [T]he asserted "right to life" and "right to health" are insufficiently definite to constitute rules of customary international law.... [I]n order to state a claim under the ATCA, we have required that a plaintiff must allege a violation of a "clear and unambiguous" rule of customary international law.... Far from being "clear and unambiguous," the statements relied on by plaintiffs to define the rights to life and health are vague and amorphous.[154]

The plaintiffs referred to a "right to life" enshrined in the Universal Declaration of Human Rights, the International Covenant on Economic, Social, and Cultural Rights, and the Rio Declaration on Environment and Development; however, the court found these principles "boundless and indeterminate," expressing "virtuous goals" but only "at a level of abstraction" and not establishing the existence of a customary international law "right to life" or "right to health."[155]

On the other hand, in 2005 the Federal High Court of Nigeria (Benin Judicial Division) found that multinational oil companies, by flaring gas during exploration and production activities, violated the "fundamental rights to life (including healthy environment) and dignity of human person guaranteed by Sections 33(1) and 34(1) of the Constitution of [the] Federal Republic of Nigeria, 1999 and reinforced by Arts 4, 16 and 24 of the African Charter on Human and Peoples Rights."[156] The court ordered the respondents to take immediate steps to stop further flaring of gas in the community.[157]

A right to a healthy environment in various formulations is recognized by the constitutions of 118 nations around the world.[158] The Supreme Court of the Philippines used the right to a "balanced and healthful ecology" in the Constitution of the Philippines to overturn and block government action in *Oposa v. Factoran.*[159] The plaintiffs brought the case on behalf of minor children and generations yet unborn to "prevent the misappropriation or impairment" of Philippine rainforests and "arrest the unabated hemorrhage of the country's vital life-support systems and continued rape of Mother Earth."[160] They alleged, "At the pre-

---

152. *Id.*

153. Flores v. S. Peru Copper Corp., 414 F.3d 233, 254 (2nd Cir. 2003).

154. *Id.* (citations omitted).

155. *Id.* at 255.

156. Gbemre v. Shell Petroleum Dev. Co. Nigeria Ltd., No. FHC/B/CS/53/05, at 30 (F.H.C. Nov. 14, 2005) (Nigeria), *available at* http://www.climatelaw.org/cases/case-documents/nigeria/ni-shell-nov05-judgment.pdf.

157. *Id.* at 31.

158. EARTHJUSTICE, ENVTL. RIGHTS REPORT 2007: HUMAN RIGHTS AND THE ENVIRONMENT app. (2007), *available at* http://www.earthjustice.org/library/references/2007-environmental-rights-report.pdf.

159. Oposa v. Factoran, G.R. No. 101083, 224 S.C.R.A. 792 (S.C., July 30, 1993) (Phil.), *available at* http://www.elaw.org/node/1343.

160. *Id.*

sent rate of deforestation, *i.e.* about 200,000 hectares per annum or 25 hectares per hour ...,
the Philippines will be bereft of forest resources after the end of this ensuing decade, if not
earlier."[161]

The plaintiffs asked the court to order the defendant to: (1) "[c]ancel all existing timber license agreements in the country"; and (2) "[c]ease and desist from receiving, accepting, processing, renewing or approving new timber license agreements."[162] The court granted the petition,
stating that "[t]he right to a balanced and healthful ecology carries with it the correlative duty to
refrain from impairing the environment."[163]

The right to life enshrined in the Constitution of India has been interpreted broadly by courts
to include a right to a healthy environment. The Supreme Court of India in *Subhash Kumar v.
State of Bihar* took a strong position on what is encompassed within the right to life:

> Right to live is a fundamental right under Art. 21 of the Constitution and it includes
> the right of enjoyment of pollution free water and air for full enjoyment of life. If any-
> thing endangers or impairs that quality of life in derogation of laws, a citizen has right
> to have recourse to Art. 32 of the Constitution for removing the pollution of water or
> air which may be detrimental to the quality of life. A petition under Art. 32 for the pre-
> vention of pollution is maintainable at the instance of affected persons or even by a
> group of social workers or journalists.[164]

In Hungary, the Constitutional Court overturned national legislation privatizing forests on the
basis of a constitutional right to a "healthy environment."[165] Courts in Bangladesh,[166] Nepal,[167] and
Pakistan[168] have made constitutional rulings about violations of citizens' environmental rights. The
Constitutional Chamber of Costa Rica's Supreme Court of Justice closed a municipal waste site due
to violations of constitutional environmental rights.[169] The Constitutional Tribunal of Peru has ordered officials to set up health monitoring and ordered the Ministry of Mines and private companies to participate in health protection because of violations of health and environmental rights.[170]

The right to a healthy environment has been recognized in the constitutions of several states
of the United States, including in the Montana Constitution.[171] The Supreme Court of Montana
in *Montana Environmental Information Center v. Department of Environmental Quality* enforced

---

161. *Id.* ¶ 12.

162. *Id.* ¶ 20.

163. *Id.*

164. Subhash Kumar v. State of Bihar, (1991) 1 S.C.R. 5, 13 (India), *available at* http://www.elaw.org/
node/2751.

165. Alkotmánybíróság [Constitutional Court], No. 28/1994 (V.20), ABH. (1994) (Hung.); *see also*
Stephen Stec, *Rights and Duties Towards a Healthy Environment, in* Reg'l Envtl. Ctr. for Cent. & E. Europe,
Handbook on Access to Justice Under the Aarhus Convention 73, 74 (Stephen Stec ed., 2003), *avail-
able at* http://www.elaw.org/node/2423 (describing the "protected forest" case).

166. Farooque v. Gov't of Bangladesh, 17 B.L.D. (AD) 1, 1997, 1 B.L.C. (AD) 189 (1996) (Bangl.) (Flood
Action Plan Case), *available at* http://www.elaw.org/node/1300.

167. Prakash Mani Sharma for Pro Public v. His Majesty Government Cabinet Secretariat and others, WP
2991/1995 (1997) (Nepal), *available at* http://www.elaw.org/node/1391 (holding that the court may give orders to give effect to directive principles in constitution, including those concerning the environment).

168. Shehla Zia v. W.A.P.D.A. Human Rights Case No. 15-K of 1992, P.L.D. 1994 Supreme Court 693
(Pak.), *available at* http://www.elaw.org/node/1342 (finding that electromagnetic radiation from power station violated constitutional rights).

169. Carlos Roberto Mejía Chacón v. Santa Ana, No. 3705-93, July 30, 1993 (Sala Constitucional de la
Corte Suprema de Justicia) (Costa Rica), *available at* http://www.elaw.org/node/1312.

170. Pablo Miguel Fabián Martínez y Otros, Exp. N. 2002–2006-PC/TC, Sentencia de la Sala Segunda del
Tribunal Constitucional) (May 12, 2006), *available at*http://www.elaw.org/node/1754.

171. Mont. Const. art. II, § 3 ("[Inalienable rights] include the right to a clean and healthful environment ...").

this right when the State tried to lessen protections for water in the state.[172] The Court held that the State's action violated "the constitutional right to a clean and healthy environment and to be free from unreasonable degradation of that environment."[173]

That the highest courts of some nations and U.S. states have been willing to apply constitutional provisions to stop government actions harmful to the environment is barely known among lawyers or academics in the United States. These cases are sure to strike some as adventurous, but they are becoming numerous. Is it too much to believe that such jurisprudence could be enlisted in the fight against global warming?

III.   Procedural Rights and Global Warming

Procedural rights—the right to know, the right to participate in decision-making, and the right to have access to justice in environmental matters—were formulated in principle 10 of the Rio Declaration.[174] They can be a powerful tool for combating climate change through litigation. Public access to information on climate change and its effects is necessary to assess the actions or inactions of governments and the emissions of polluting industries. Provisions to enhance public participation also open the door to citizens for lobbying governments for the adoption of needed regulations and measures to combat climate change. Access to justice for citizens and nongovernmental organizations ensures that if governments or industries fail to comply with measures that are adopted, the violations can be brought to the attention of the courts.

Procedural rights are included in the U.N. Framework Convention on Climate Change. Article 6 requires Parties to "[p]romote and facilitate at the national and, as appropriate, subregional and regional levels … [p]ublic access to information on climate change and its effects; [and p]ublic participation in addressing climate change and its effects and developing adequate responses."[175]

The Kyoto Protocol similarly requires Parties to facilitate "public access to information on climate change" and to seek and utilize information from NGOs.[176] In addition, procedural human rights can be found in various other international and national instruments, as discussed next.

A.   Access to Information

Access to information is coming to be recognized as a basic human right. For instance, in 1996 the Parliamentary Assembly of the Council of Europe (PACE),[177] with the passage of the Resolution of 1087,[178] took an important step in the recognition of the right to information as a human right. Resolution 1087 on the Consequences of the Chernobyl Disaster stated that "the

---

172. Mont. Envtl. Info. Ctr. v. Dep't of Envtl. Quality, 988 P.2d 1236, 1249 (Mont. 1999).

173. *Id.* at 1249.

174. Rio Declaration, *supra* note 56.

175. UNFCCC, *supra* note 20, art. 6(a).

176. Kyoto Protocol, *supra* note 12, arts. 10(e), 13(4)(i).

177. Council of Europe Parliamentary Assembly, PACE Historical Overview, http://assembly.coe.int/Main.asp?Link=/AboutUs/APCE_history.htm (last visited Apr. 20, 2008). The Parliamentary Assembly of the Council of Europe (PACE) was formed in 1949. It consists of 318 representatives (636 with alternates) sent by the national parliaments of the forty-seven states that are members of the Council of Europe, a pan-European institution whose members stretch from Russia to Portugal. Council of Europe Parliamentary Assembly, Assembly Procedure, http://assembly.coe.int/Main.asp?Link=/AboutUs/APCE_structures.htm (last visited Apr. 20, 2008). The Assembly elects the judges of the European Court of Human Rights, among other duties. Council of Europe Parliamentary Assembly, PACE Assembly Structure, http://assembly.coe.int/Main.asp?Link =/About Us/APCE_ Procedure.htm (last visited Apr. 20, 2008).

178. Eur. Parl. Ass., *Resolution 1087 on the Consequences of the Chernobyl Disaster*, 16th Sitting (Apr. 26, 1996), *available at* http://assembly.coe.int/main.asp?Link=/documents/adoptedtext/ ta96/eres1087.htm; *see also* Comm. on the Env't, Reg'l Planning and Local Auths., *The Consequences of the Chernobyl Disaster*, Doc. No. 7538 (1996), *available at* http://assembly.coe.int/Documents/ WorkingDocs/doc96/EDOC7538.htm.

Assembly believes that public access to clear and full information on this subject—and many others for that matter—must be viewed as a basic human right."[179]

In *Oneryildiz v. Turkey,* the Grand Chamber of the European Court of Human Rights said broadly that where dangerous activities are concerned, "public access to clear and full information is viewed as a basic human right" in Europe.[180] For this proposition, it cited Resolution 1087 and said that the resolution "makes clear that this right must not be taken to be limited to the risks associated with the use of nuclear energy in the civil sector."[181] The Grand Chamber went further, noting that such a human right to information had previously been found by the Court to be part of the right of private and family life under article 8 of the European Convention on Human Rights where pollution was concerned, citing the decision in *Guerra v. Italy.*[182] The Grand Chamber said that this same right to information "may also, in principle, be relied on for the protection of the right to life, particularly as this interpretation is supported by current developments in European standards," referring back to its discussion of Resolution 1087.[183] The Grand Chamber said that "particular emphasis should be placed on the public's right to information" as a way for governments to "take all appropriate steps to safeguard life for the purposes of Article 2."[184] It must be asked whether European courts would be willing to take this right concerning access to information on pollution risks and apply it to information relevant to the pollution causing global warming.[185]

The view that the right to information in environmental matters is a basic human right has been stated even more strongly by the Inter-American Court of Human Rights. The American Convention on Human Rights was cited in *Claude Reyes v. Chile,* a recent decision.[186] The American Convention's direct provision on the human right to information, article 13, states that "[e]veryone has the right to freedom of thought and expression. This right includes freedom to seek, receive, and impart information and ideas of all kinds."[187] This language largely tracks article 10 of the European Convention on Human Rights (regarding freedom of expression) although the American Convention adds the word "seek."[188]

The American Convention's article 13 could be seen as simply an anti-censorship provision, just as the European Court found in *Guerra.*[189] In fact, the American Convention made that link even more directly in section 2 of article 13, which states "[t]he exercise of the right provided ...

---

179. *Id.* ¶ 4.

180. Öneryildiz v. Turkey (Grand Chamber), 41 Eur. Ct. H.R. 20 ¶ 62 (2004).

181. *Id.*

182. *Id.* ¶ 90. This was a rather dramatic, or clever, or just deceptive use of *Guerra*, for in that case Resolution 1087 had been offered to the court as a basis for holding that article 10 recognized a right to obtain information from the government (or at least a duty of government to provide information), and the court had refused to do so. Now, some years later, the Court in *Öneryildiz* chose to refer to another part of the *Guerra* decision in which information had been mentioned as part of article 8—and now the Court used that and Resolution 1087 to assert that the right to information is a "basic human right."

183. *Id.*

184. *Id.* ¶¶ 89–90.

185. In addition to these convention-based or general human rights claims, many countries in Europe also recognize rights to information through legislation. In the case of members of the European Union, these rights are part of the European Union's Directive on Access to Information. European Parliament and Council Directive 2003/4, 2003 O.J. (L 41) 26, *available at* http://eur-lex.europa.eu/LexUriServ/LexUriServ.do?uri= OJ:L:2003:04 1:0026:0032:EN:PDF.

186. Marcel Claude Reyes v. Chile, 2006 Inter-Am. Ct. H.R. (ser. C) No. 151, ¶ 1, *available at* http://www. corteidh.or.cr/docs/casos/articulos/ seriec_151_ing.pdf.

187. American Convention, *supra* note 128, art. 13(1).

188. *Compare id* ("freedom to seek, receive, and impart information"), *with* European Convention, *supra* note 86 ("freedom ... to receive and impart information and ideas without interference by public authority and regardless of frontiers.").

189. American Convention, *supra* note 128, art. 13(1); *Guerra*, 26 Eur. Ct. H.R. ¶ 53.

shall not be subject to prior censorship."[190] But the Inter-American Court took a much broader view in the *Claude Reyes* case, saying that by denying information requests by Mr. Reyes the Chilean government had violated article 13.[191] The Inter-American Commission, in presenting the case to the court, had asserted:

> The disclosure of State-held information should play a very important role in a democratic society, because it enables civil society to control the actions of the Government to which it has entrusted the protection of its interests. "Article 13 of the Convention should be understood as a positive obligation on the part of the State to provide access to the information it holds."[192]

The court found it necessary to "determine whether the failure to hand over part of the information requested from the Foreign Investment Committee in 1998 constituted a violation of the right to freedom of thought and expression of Marcel Claude Reyes, and, consequently, a violation of Article 13 of the American Convention."[193]

The court ruled that, indeed, this was a violation. This kind of ruling indicates that, at least in the Americas, the right to gather information on emissions causing global warming is a basic human right that cannot be limited by restrictive national policies.

Returning to Europe, the Aarhus Convention on Access to Information, Public Participation in Decision-Making, and Access to Justice in Environmental Matters recognizes not only the right of the public to receive information upon request (article 4), but also the duty of the government to collect and disseminate information (article 5).[194] This Convention has been ratified by thirty-nine countries of Europe as well as the European Community. U.N. Secretary-General Kofi Annan has characterized its importance: "Although regional in scope, the significance of the Aarhus Convention is global. It is by far the most impressive elaboration of principle 10 of the Rio Declaration, which stresses the need for citizens' participation in environmental issues and for access to information on the environment held by public authorities."[195]

The Aarhus Convention Compliance Committee enforces these provisions, provides guidance through authoritative interpretations of the Convention in its jurisprudence, and facilitates improvement of laws and practices on national levels.[196] It has done so on the question of access to information in cases involving Kazakhstan and Ukraine.[197]

National legislation and some national constitutions also recognize the right to information.[198] The right to information has been enforced in matters involving climate change in at

---

190. *Compare* American Convention, *supra* note 128, art. 13(2), *with* European Convention, *supra* note 86 (stating that the exercise of the freedom of expression "may be subject to such formalities, conditions, restrictions or penalties as are prescribed by law and are necessary in a democratic society").

191. Marcel Claude Reyes v. Chile, 2006 Inter-Am C. H.R. (ser. C) No. 151, ¶ 148, *available at* http://www.corteidh.or.cr/docs/casos/articulos/seriec_151_ing.pdf.

192. *Id.* ¶ 58.

193. *Id.* ¶ 65.

194. Aarhus Convention, *supra* note 74, arts. 4, 5.

195. Kofi A. Annan, U.N. Secretary-General, *Foreword to* U.N. Econ. Comm'n for Eur., The Aarhus Convention: An Implementation Guide, at v (2000), *available at* http://www.unece.org/ env/pp/acig.pdf.

196. *See* Kravchenko, *supra* note 23, at 34 (summarizing ways that the Aarhus Convention's compliance mechanisms have been effective).

197. *Id.* at 35–39.

198. Const. of Ukraine art. 34, *available at* http://www.rada.gov.ua/const/conengl.htm ("Everyone has the right to freely collect, store, use and disseminate information...."); S. Afr. Const. ch. 2, § 32 (1), *available at* http://www.concourt.gov.za/site/theconstitution/english.pdf ("Everyone has the right of access to—(a) any information held by the state; and (b) any information that is held by another person and that is required for the exercise or protection of any rights.").

least one national court. In Germany, the Berlin Administrative Court in 2006 ordered the release of information about the extent to which Euler Hermes AG, an export credit agency, provides political and economic risk insurance to projects that produce GHGs.[199] The procedural human right to information may well have an important future in disputes where access to information related to climate change is denied to the public.

B.   Public Participation

The U.N. Framework Convention on Climate Change requires public participation in addressing climate change and its effects and developing adequate responses.[200] This provision of the Convention can be used in various ways, including to demand participation in the environmental assessment of certain projects and activities that emit GHGs contributing to climate change. Case law involving environmental impact assessment and climate change is evolving in various national courts. For example, in November 2006, in the case *Gray v. Minister for Planning* in New South Wales (NSW), the Land and Environment Court made a decision that an EIA for a large coal mine known as the Anvil Hill Project *must* address global warming.[201] Judge Nicola Pain decided:

> [T]here is a sufficiently proximate link between the mining of a very substantial reserve of thermal coal in NSW, the only purpose of which is for use as fuel in power stations, and the emission of GHG which contribute to climate change/global warming, which is impacting now and likely to continue to do so on the Australian and consequently NSW environment, to require assessment of that GHG contribution of the coal when burnt in an environmental assessment under Pt 3A.[202]

One of the main arguments of the plaintiff was that members of the public must be properly informed in order to determine if they wish to make submissions.[203] The NSW court found that defendant's failure to take into account the precautionary principle and intergenerational equity were unlawful: "[T]he requirement for prior environmental impact assessment and approval enables the present generation to meet its obligation of intergenerational equity by ensuring the health, diversity, and productivity of the environment is maintained and enhanced for the benefit of future generations."[204] Soon thereafter, the Land and Resources Tribunal of Queensland took the opposite position in *Re Xstrata Coal Queensland Pty Ltd.*, ruling that that an EIA for a coal mine need not assess greenhouse gas emissions.[205]

In the United States, Friends of the Earth, Greenpeace, and four cities sued the Export-Import Bank (Ex-Im) and the Overseas Private Investment Corporation (OPIC).[206] Plaintiffs alleged that the defendants failed to evaluate the effects of their "financial support ... [of] fossil fuel projects that emit greenhouse gases" on global climate change.[207] The parties argued that the defendants were "required to conduct an environmental review under NEPA."[208] The court ruled

---

199. Bund für Umwelt und Naturschutz Deutschland v. Federal Republic of Germany, VerwG 10 A 215.04 (Verwaltungsgericht Berlin, 10th Chamber) (Jan. 10, 2006), *available at* http://www.climatelaw.org/cases/case-documents/germany/de-export-jan06.pdf; *unofficial translation available at* http://www.climatelaw.org/cases/case-documents/germany/de-export-jan06-eng.doc.

200. UNFCCC, *supra* note 20, art. 6(a)(iii).

201. *Id.* ¶¶ 96–100.

202. *Id.* ¶ 100.

203. *Id.* ¶¶ 14–15.

204. *Id.* ¶ 116.

205. *Re Xstrata Coal Queensland Pty Ltd.*, [2007] Q.L.R.T. 33 (Feb. 15, 2007), *available at* http://www.lrt.qld.gov.au/LRT/PDF/Xstrata_a33.pdf.

206. Friends of the Earth v. Mosbacher, 488 F. Supp. 2d 889, 891 n.1 (N.D. Cal. 2007).

207. *Id.* at 892.

208. *Id.*

that Ex-Im and OPIC are not completely exempt from NEPA requirements, but did not yet make a decision about whether Ex-Im or OPIC have enough authority over the specific projects in issue that their funding must be subject to EIA requirements.[209] This lingering issue was left to be decided in a future trial. The door is clearly open in the United States to require NEPA review and its concomitant public participation in at least some projects affecting GHG emissions, even in other countries. Even more recently, the U.S. Court of Appeals for the Ninth Circuit has ruled in a case involving potential emissions in the United States that "[t]he impact of greenhouse gas emissions on climate change is precisely the kind of cumulative impacts analysis that NEPA requires agencies to conduct."[210]

Public participation is an important environmental right. To the extent that EIA processes are initiated for projects that may affect the climate, the public will have an opportunity to participate in assessment of the impact of those projects, require public hearings, and raise comments. The resultant public outcry may halt a project. To the extent that institutions ignore requirements for public participation in decisions that may affect the climate, court actions challenging the decisions as illegal may give environmental procedural rights an important role in overturning them.

Conclusion

The accelerating pace of climate change puts the lives of current and future generations in danger. Human rights instruments can bring new arguments to the international and national debates. Attempts to use international human rights bodies, regional human rights courts, or national courts to combat climate change have met mixed success so far. However, they do start to reframe the debate, which might be their greatest contribution.

Notes

1. Q. How many law review articles have cited or referenced the so-called Inuit Petition to the Inter-American Commission on Human Rights (filed in Dec. 2005)?

   A. 27

Search for Prof. William H. Rodgers, Jr., Oct. 12, 2008, by Cheryl Nyberg, Marian Gould Gallagher Law Library, University of Washington, School of Law (LexisNexis file of U.S. Law Reviews and Journals).

2. Masego Madzwamuse, *A way of life is feeling the heat*, BBC NEWS, June 17, 2008, *available at* http://news.bbc.co.uk/2/hi/science/nature/7456973.stm (last visited Oct. 22, 2008):

International development policies are undermining the long term survival of some of the globe's poorest communities, argues Masego Madzwamuse. In this week's Green Room, she says the skills and knowledge needed to survive in the world's harsh drylands are being sacrificed in the name of progress.

The world's poorest of the poor live in the toughest areas of the planet—the drylands.

These areas all have key factors in common: water is scarce, and rainfall is unpredictable—or it rains only during a very short period every year.

---

209. *Id.* at 889.
210. Ctr. for Biological Diversity v. Nat'l Highway Traffic Safety, 508 F.3d 508, 550 (9th Cir. 2007), *opinion vacated and withdrawn*, 438 F.3d 1172 (9th Cir. 2008) (court declines to order preparation of an EIS but the decision remains a strong application of NEPA in the context of climate change).

Drylands cover more than 40% of the Earth's surface and are home to more than two billion people.

These areas are also home to a disproportionate number of people without secure access to food.

Why are 43% of the world's cultivated lands found in dry areas? And why have decades of development not led to significant improvements?

Rather than improving, it would appear that the situation is getting worse, with more frequent droughts, such as those in Ethiopia and Northern Kenya.

Another important issue that strikes me about drylands is that these areas have been completely neglected despite being the world's home of the poor.

While one international agreement—the United Nations Convention to Combat Desertification (UNCCD)—has been dedicated solely to the drylands of this world, little attention has been paid by the media, development or conservation organisations, or the international donor community.

The only time attention is paid is when droughts (a regular climatic phenomenon in such lands) are allowed to proceed to famine, which in this day and age can only be the result of political failure.

Humanitarian and food relief follow the TV headlines, creating more dependencies rather than developing viable and sustainable economies.

Dry heat

It is expected that these areas will be hardest hit by climate change in the future.

The influential Stern Review noted that a 3C (5.4F) increase in global temperature was likely to result in an extra 150–550m people becoming exposed to the risk of hunger.

The review also said that climate change was likely to result in up to four billion people suffering water shortages.

The world's drylands are likely to bear the brunt of this gloomy prognosis.

In my opinion, the world will only successfully fight poverty and achieve the Millennium Development Goals (MDGs) if we pay more attention to these unique ecosystems and learn from the mistakes of the past.

This means moving away from a colonially biased view of drylands.

It is unfortunately still common to equate drylands with deserts and wastelands, as these areas might not look at first sight very productive, especially during a period of drought.

So, what are the ingredients for success in developing the poorest regions of this world?

First of all, development interventions need to be adapted to the realities of drylands.

Crop production, whether rain-fed or irrigated, will always be a limited opportunity. Yet the major effort in "development" is a green revolution for the desert.

Has half a century of development not taught us the reality for cultivation in the drylands?

Livestock is much more suitable to arid environments and more likely to support rural livelihoods in arid regions.

For instance, Turkana pastoralists of Kenya know that livestock is their mainstay, even though they have some of the fastest maturing varieties of sorghum in the world.

Secondly, we should work with the knowledge and institutional systems of the people who have lived there for centuries.

We need to understand why they have complex common property systems for land and resource management that may span and cover very large territories, and guarantee that a variety of stakeholders can use these scarce resources and survive.

It is important to also understand why they place more emphasis on livestock than crops. Livestock is a better converter of biomass in such harsh lands.

We must not sweep aside this knowledge and experience. Instead, we should build on those systems and support them with so-called "modern and scientific knowledge" to improve productivity and create market opportunities.

Yet we ignore their complex risk management and resilience enhancement strategies.

One classical example has been the numerous efforts to use inappropriate policies to settle nomadic people and restrict their movements.

Nomadic livestock herding has been a key sustainable survival strategy in the more arid areas. Once grass and water become scarce, these communities move with their animals to the next area.

Thus, they are able to use resources sustainably without leaving themselves exposed to the effects of droughts.

While livestock farming in drylands contributes significantly to national economies, most subsidies go to unsustainable ranching projects rather than the small livestock holders.

National treasures

Pastoralism is one of the few land use systems that can be compatible with wildlife conservation.

Yet where are many of the world's national parks? More than 70% of Kenya's are in drylands, which includes a number of important dry season grazing areas for pastoralists.

Dryland peoples depend on the surrounding environment, and they should be able to benefit from conservation through community conserved areas and tourism, rather than having their best lands taken away from them in the name of conservation.

Thirdly, nature's contribution to the survival of the poor needs to be recognised as an important asset.

It is nature that provides food, fodder for livestock, construction material for shelter, medicinal plants, emergency food and climate regulation (shade is highly valued in 40C).

Opportunities for sustainable development exist.

Sudan is the world's largest producer of gum arabic, a principal ingredient of colas and chewing gum, which stems from a 2,000-year agroforestry tradition.

And the arid lands of the Horn of Africa produce the highest quality frankincense and myrrh in the world.

In one district in Botswana that has an average annual rainfall of just 200mm, dryland ecosystem services contributed $190,000 (... 95,000) to the national income. Almost 50% of this came from wild plants such as the medicinal devil's claw.

Instead of building on this natural capital, development and government interventions tend to replace and disregard them.

Even worse, they are not reflected in the national GDP figures. As a consequence, most policy frameworks provide incentives for their exploitation rather than their sustainable use.

We cannot continue to let the world's poor dryland dwellers down.

Panaceas, history tells us, don't work. Instead, we need to invest in the innovative and sustainable use of natural assets.

Masego Madzwamuse is the IUCN's regional programme development officer and focal person for southern African drylands

The Green Room is a series of opinion pieces on environmental topics running weekly on the BBC News website

---

Do you agree with Masego Madzwamuse? Is the international community overlooking the needs of people living in the world's drylands? Are current policies jeopardizing centuries of skills and knowledge needed to survive in some of the planet's harshest environments? Or can modern science and technology deliver a sustainable future for all? What information would we need to have to answer these questions?

---

c. Elaborations of Law

i. Duties to Compensate

Daniel A. Farber, *The Case for Climate Compensation: Justice for Climate Change Victims in a Complex World*, Utah L. Rev. 377, 412–23 (2008), *responding in part to* Eric A. Posner and Cass R. Sunstein, *Climate Change Justice*, 96 Geo. L.J. 1565 (2008):

> The issue of climate justice is admittedly a complex one. Commentators have raised important questions about culpability, causation of harm, and collective responsibility. It seems fairly clear, however, that Americans—not just our ancestors but ourselves—are responsible for a disproportionate amount of greenhouse gases and that we have benefited, at least in the short run, from uncontrolled greenhouse emissions that have enabled our energy-intensive lifestyle and corporate profits; that these gases are causing harm, particularly to the poorest and most vulnerable segments of the global population; and that we have failed to take reasonable measures to limit our emissions. I have argued that these facts form an adequate basis to hold ourselves morally accountable for some share of the harm caused by climate change. In particular, we should support the creation of a system for compensating climate change victims for the costs of adaptation, to the extent that our excessive past emissions and those of other developed countries have created the need for adaptation. It is no excuse that such a system would be expensive or imperfect. Even more clearly, I believe, we have a moral obligation to limit future emissions, not merely in our own benefit (which is likely) but also because of a moral duty to refrain from causing unreasonable harm to others. (As do others, including developing countries, though what conduct is unreasonable may not be the same for every country.) Contrary to the views of commentators such as Posner and Sunstein, climate justice is an imperative, not a quixotic quest for a delusive quarry.
>
> Considerations of justice might, in an ideal world, be a sufficient basis for action. In reality, concerns about future social welfare are likely to dominate among policy analysts, while politicians will be influenced by political advantage and national self-interest—hopefully leavened by substantive concerns about welfare and justice. To raise claims of justice is not to be naive about their prospects in the political rough and tumble. But the least we can do is to try.

Eric A. Posner and Cass R. Sunstein, *Climate Change Justice*, 96 Geo. L. J. 1565, 1570 (2008):

> To the extent that the United States is a net loser, the world should act so as to induce it to participate in an accord [under an international climate change agreement] that

would promote the welfare of the world's citizens, taken as a whole. With side-payments to the United States, of the kind that have elsewhere induced reluctant nations to join environmental treaties, an international agreement could be designed so as to make everyone better off and no one worse off. Who could oppose ... [such] an agreement?

Eric A. Posner and Cass R. Sunstein, *Climate Change Justice* (Univ. of Chi. Law Sch. Law and Econ. Olin Working Paper No. 354, August 2007), available at http://ssrn.com/abstract_id= 1008958:

> The current stock of greenhouse gases in the atmosphere is due to the behavior of people living in the past. Much of it is due to the behavior of people who are dead. The basic problem for corrective justice is that dead wrongdoers cannot be punished or held responsible for their behavior, or forced to compensate those they have harmed. Holding Americans today responsible for the activities of their ancestors is not fair or reasonable on corrective justice grounds, at least not unless contemporary Americans can be said to have benefited from the actions of their ancestors (an issue to which we shall return).

ii. Forms of Compensation

Daniel A. Farber, *Basic Compensation for Victims of Climate Change*, 155 U. Pa. L. Rev. 1605, 1607-07 (2007):

> certain kinds of injuries could be the subject of a workable compensation system. These injuries—involving changes in basic geographic characteristics such as sea level or permafrost—are readily identifiable, do not raise the complicated causation issues that plague other potential forms of damages, and can be measured (at least roughly) in a fairly straightforward way.

Id. at 1613:

> [Identifies "geographic damages"]—diminished coastlines, available water, glaciers, and tundra as a good candidate for the "core of potential damages."

Id. at 1616:

> [Explores a variety of] analogous compensation schemes, including those for terrorists, toxic torts, damages to natural resources, slavery and racial discrimination, natural disasters, and environmental damages caused by war.

Id. at 1616, discussing the 9/11 Fund:

> Clearly, the threat of tort liability pervaded the construction of 9/11 compensation, and the potential for tort liability also will likely prompt climate change compensation in other forms.

Id. at 1621, *quoting Puerto Rico v. SS Zoe Coloctroni*, 628 F.2d 652, 675–76 (1st Cir. 1980):

> [T]he appropriate primary standard for determining damages in a case such as this is the cost reasonably to be incurred by the sovereign or its designated agency to restore or rehabilitate the environment in the affected area to [its] pre-existing condition, or as close thereto as is feasible without grossly disproportionate expenditures.

Id. at 1644, interpreting the 1992 Framework Convention as amounting to:

> a requirement of in-kind contribution to adaptation measures. Thus, at least in principle, the United States and other signatories to the framework agreement already seem to have agreed to compensation at the international level.

Id. at 1655:

> As a preferred measure of damages, I suggest the cost of remedial measures such as monitoring, protecting, restoring, or providing substitutes for existing resources.

iii. Duty to Provide Accurate Information

Does the U.S. government have a duty to refrain from giving its own citizens false information about risks they face? Not in *Benzman v. Whitman*, 523 F.3d 119 (2d Cir. 2008) (Jon D. Newman, C.J.), which was a class action suit by people in lower Manhattan and Brooklyn who claimed that government officials misled them by stating that air quality in the period after the destruction of the World Trade Center towers was safe enough to permit return to homes, schools, and offices. The court affirmed a dismissal of a *Bivens* count against former EPA Administrator, Christine Whitman, charging that her false statements of assurance violated plaintiffs' Fifth Amendment substantive due process right "to be free from government-created health risks." *Id.* at 123. This claim is insufficient because (*id.* at 128): "Whitman did face a choice between competing considerations, although not the stark choice between telling a deliberate falsehood about health risks and issuing an accurate warning about them.... The realistic choice for Whitman was either to accept the White House guidance [to downplay the risks] and reassure the public or disregard the CEQ's views in communicating with the public. A choice of that sort implicates precisely the competing governmental considerations that *Lombardi* recognized would preclude a valid claim of denial of substantive due process in the absence of an allegation that the Government official acted with intent to harm." Thus approved is the "good soldier" defense. Allegations that Whitman's statements were "knowingly false" are insufficient here to plead deliberate injury. Allegations that EPA failed to follow the Nat'l Contingency Plan in matters of monitoring and testing are insufficiently "ministerial" under *SUWA* to support an APA violation (there is no "discrete agency action that [EPA] is required to take"). A CERCLA citizen-suit count is thus dismissed under the authority of *Bennett v. Spear* for failure to identify a "not discretionary" action.

iv. Distributive Justice

Tom Athanasiou & Paul Baer, Dead Heat: Global Justice and Global Warming 71–72 (Seven Stories Press 2002):

> Which presents us, finally, with a crucial moral and political question: Why, now that the atmosphere's ability to absorb carbon is manifestly and critically scarce, should people in some countries continue to enjoy more of it, and thus more wealth, than others?
>
> The answer, of course, is that there are not and cannot be any such reasons, save perhaps for raw power. And this, perhaps more than anything else, provides our rationale. For whatever one's position on "the commodification of nature" or the perils of tradable pollution permits, this remains: The "right" to dump greenhouse gases into the atmosphere has significant economic value, and the economic advantages of this right cannot be ignored.
>
> The issue here is distributive justice. But understand that in a world beset by ecological crisis, distributive justice must mean more than it did in the past. It must include not only the fair distribution of wealth, resources, and opportunities, but the fair distribution of "impacts" as well. Because the elemental truth is that as the storms become more violent and the droughts more fierce, some of us will be hurt far, far more, and far earlier, than others. The rich will be able to hide, but the poor will not, and neither will the plants and the beasts. And because the "ecosystems people"—indigenous peo-

ples, farmers, fishermen—who rely directly on nature for their livelihoods are the most threatened of all, the real priority is finding a politics that makes a low concentration cap possible; it's at least as crucial as finding a fair distribution of emissions rights.

v. Justice as Mitigation

Maxine Burkett, *Just Solutions to Climate Change: A Climate Justice Proposal for a Domestic Clean Development Mechanism*, 56 BUFF. L. REV. 169, 170–73 (2008):

The weighty and unequal toll that climate change is wreaking on the global poor is no less devastating for the poor, black and brown of the United States. The federal response to the climate crisis—which has been both belated and insubstantial—has failed to take seriously the potentially devastating impacts of climate change and climate change policies on poor and of-color communities. This inaction does not reflect the sentiment of significant American institutions and communities who are now demanding immediate change in our domestic climate policy. Congress, by all indications, is pressing for a mechanism that will cap allowable greenhouse gas emissions while permitting the trade of emissions credits between entities. This market-based response to the climate crisis will have inherent disadvantages for poor and of-color communities. In order to protect these communities, this Article, consistent with a climate justice framework, argues for supplementing the emerging cap-and-trade system with a domestic clean development mechanism.

The fundamental purpose of an emergent climate justice movement is to address the issues and concerns that arise from the intersection of climate change with race, poverty, and preexisting environmental risks. To date, issues of climate justice, as a parallel environmental justice concern, have been widely overlooked in policy circles and underappreciated in the legal academic arena as well. This Article seeks to center climate justice in the legal discourse. It also advocates for a domestic climate justice policy-mechanism, which is a critical contribution in making the nation's first comprehensive climate policy a *just* one.

In the lengthy and discordant international negotiations on creating sound climate policies, the disproportionate burdens borne by the global poor inspired repeated calls for distributive and procedural justice. As a result, the Kyoto Protocol did not adopt a cap-and-trade regime without addressing distributive concerns. In particular, the Protocol codified a Clean Development Mechanism (CDM) to specifically address uneven development positions across countries. The mechanism provides credits to be used in international carbon trading in exchange for investment in green and renewable energy projects in developing countries. The exclusive purpose of the mechanism is to assist least developed countries in achieving sustainable development through "green" projects, while providing sellable emissions reduction credits from CDM projects undertaken in these countries.

The domestic clean development mechanism this Article proposes would likewise introduce an infrastructure that provides incentives for economically depressed and of-color communities to become venues for emissions abatement. The mechanism would also include, and partially finance, an adaptation fund. Generally, "adaptation" aims to "realize gains from opportunities or to reduce the damages that result from climate change."[1] "Mitigation," alternatively, describes actions that will slow or constrain cli-

---

1. Neil A. Leary, *A Welfare Theoretic Analysis of Climate Change Inequities, in* FAIRNESS IN ADAPTATION TO CLIMATE CHANGE 155, 155 (W. Neil Adger *et al.* eds., MIT Press 2006). "Unlike mitigation, adaptation is a response to rather than a slowing of global warming." Stephen H. Schneider & Janica Lane, *Dangers and Thresholds in Climate Change and the Implications for Justice, in* FAIRNESS IN ADAPTATION TO CLIMATE CHANGE, *supra*, at 23, 45. The Intergovernmental Panel on Climate Change identifies two types of adaptation, au-

mate change.[2] The fund, similar to the one established by Kyoto and hinted at in currently proposed domestic climate bills, would provide monies for adaptation to those who lack the basic resources to support green development projects, but who are nonetheless expected to bear the most significant burdens.

Given the current domestic legal and political exigencies, the United States will likely adopt a cap-and-trade system, for which a clean development mechanism is a critical supplement. In the coming year, therefore, those crafting climate rules in Congress and beyond will have an unparalleled opportunity to implement policy that accounts for climate justice concerns. This critical window introduces a particular urgency for communities at risk of disproportionate harm to participate meaningfully in the policy set to emerge. This is especially true if that legislated approach threatens to exacerbate harm to poor communities and communities of color, which a pure cap-and-trade program might well do. Instead, a domestic clean development mechanism, as an indispensable component of market-based climate policy, would provide two significant benefits. First, poor and of-color communities would gain entry into the cap-and-trade market that would otherwise exclude them, allowing such communities to create offsetting projects consistent with the emerging policy consensus. Second, the United States as a nation could begin to rectify its overwhelming contribution to the climate crisis, while still meeting its responsibility to those who suffer particularly severe effects of climate change.

To be sure, advocating a domestic CDM is controversial to some. The Kyoto CDM has been the subject of much criticism; however, the global project is floundering for reasons that we need not replicate at a national level. Kyoto's failures, as I will show, are due to weaknesses in implementation of the program, not in the mechanism's foundational concept. In this Article, I do acknowledge these current weaknesses of Kyoto's CDM and point out the disadvantages of market-based remedies, which in the context of U.S. domestic policy, have demonstrated that a least-cost response to emissions abatement efforts can exacerbate certain communities' pollution burden. I maintain, however, that the CDM's innovative framework—once corrected—is currently the most viable option for meeting domestic climate justice goals.

....

vi. Procedural Justice and "Hot Spots"

Alice Kaswan, *Environmental Justice and Domestic Climate Change*, 38 Env. L. Rptr. (Environmental Law Institute) 10287, 10289, 10290, 10291, 10299 (May 2008) (footnotes omitted and renumbered):

The environmental justice movement presents a number of types of claims for justice. Activists seek distributive justice: for example, they oppose facility sitings or permitting actions that would create or increase existing pollution disparities. They also seek participatory justice: they seek an influential role in the decisions that could impact their communities. Environmental justice advocates perceive environmental issues in context: in seeking "social justice," environmental burdens are significant not

---

tonomous (non-policy-driven reactive response) and planned (passive and anticipatory). *See id.* at 45.

In this Article, I use "mitigation" and "aggressive mitigation" to describe the implementation of actions that would reduce seventy percent of greenhouse gas emissions as soon as possible, as urged by climate scientists and environmentalists.

2. Leary, *supra*, note 1, at 155.

only in environmental terms, but are considered a product of broader social, economic, and political forces. The movement's environmental policy goals are therefore designed to achieve not only environmental benefits, but community empowerment as well.

In the climate change context, environmental justice groups are beginning to articulate overarching principles. Domestically, the Environmental Justice and Climate Change Initiative developed a list of 10 climate justice principles.[1] Recognizing the particular vulnerability of the poor and people of color, a number of the principles focus on the potential consequences of climate change and the critical importance of reducing GHG emissions. Several other principles focus on the implications of climate change policies, including a call for adaptation assistance for poor communities, as well as compensation for workers and others impacted by the potential economic costs of climate change policies. The environmental justice movement's participatory goals are reflected in the call for community participation. The principles express caution about the emergence of international and national carbon markets. California environmental justice groups have been even more critical of market-based approaches.

. . . .

At the state level,[2] California is a national leader in incorporating environmental justice. AB 32,[3] adopted in 2006, recognizes the importance of developing climate change policies that take a wide variety of factors into consideration, including environmental justice. The California Air Resources Board (CARB), the primary agency responsible for implementing AB 32, is to develop approaches to meet the state's emissions reduction goals in a manner that minimizes costs and maximizes benefits for California's economy, improves and modernizes California's energy infrastructure and maintains electric system reliability, maximizes additional environmental and economic co-benefits for California, and complements the state's efforts to improve air quality.[4]

Procedurally, the law instructs CARB to develop its policies in consultation with many relevant stakeholders, including "the environmental justice community, industry

---

1. *See* Environmental Justice & Climate Change Initiative, *10 Principles for Just Climate Change Policies in the United States*, http:// www.ejcc.org/ejcc10short_usa.pdf (last visited Mar. 27, 2008) (listing 10 principles); Ansje Miller & Cody Sisco, Ten Actions of Climate Justice Policies (2002), *available at* http:// www.ejrc. cau.edu/summit2/SummIIClimateJustice%20.pdf (explaining the 10 principles). The Environmental Justice and Climate Change Initiative is an effort by 28 domestic organizations, including environmental justice organizations, religious organizations, Native American organizations, and other nonprofits to advocate for climate change action. *Id.*

2. EPA and the Pew Center on Global Climate Change websites provide comprehensive information on state climate change policies. *See* U.S. EPA, *State and Regional Climate Action Table*, http:// www. epa.gov/climatechange/wycd/stateandlocalgov/state_actions list.html (EPA website listing state climate change policies); Pew Ctr. on Global Climate Change, *What's Being Done … in the States*, http://www.pew climate.org/what_s_being_done/in_the_states.

3. Cal. Health & Safety Code §§ 38500–99, *available at* http:// www.climatechange.ca.gov/ documents/ab_ 32_bill_20060927_chaptered.pdf. AB 32 requires the state to reduce to its 1990 levels of emissions by 2020. *Id.* § 38550. That goal is expected to lead to a 25% reduction below 2006 levels. *See* Media Release, California Climate Action Team, State Takes Early Action to Reduce Greenhouse Gases (Mar. 12, 2007), *available at* http://www.calepa.ca. gov/PressRoom/Releases/2007/PR4-031207.pdf.

4. Cal. Health & Safety Code § 38501(h). AB 32 also states that in developing implementing regulations, CARB should "[c]onsider overall societal benefits, including reductions in other air pollutants, diversification of energy sources, and other benefits to the economy, environment, and public health." *Id.* § 38562(b)(6). To the extent a market-based system is adopted, the statute specifies that CARB should "[m]aximize additional environmental and economic benefits for California…." *Id.* § 38570(b)(3).

sectors, business groups, academic institutions, [and] environmental organizations."[5] The law also mandated the creation of an Environmental Justice Advisory Committee and required that it be "comprised of representatives from communities in the state with the most significant exposure to air pollution, including, but not limited to, communities with minority populations or low-income populations...."[6] To develop its scoping plan for regulations, AB 32 also requires CARB to hold public workshops "in regions of the state that have the most significant exposure to air pollutants, including, but not limited to, communities with minority populations [and] communities with low-income populations...."[7]

Substantively, several AB 32 provisions require CARB to consider impacts on low-income minority populations and to ensure that climate change policies do not undermine the achievement of other environmental goals.[8] These provisions are described in more detail below, where I detail AB 32's requirements for integrating environmental justice into a market system as a prelude to exploring actual mechanisms for doing so.

AB 32 also provides a model for how climate change regulation could provide economic benefits to disadvantaged communities, fueled by investments in new technology and its implementation. The relevant provision is discussed below, where I discuss the economic opportunities presented by climate change regulation.[9] At least on paper, California is thus a national leader in recognizing the interrelationships between climate change policy and broader economic and environmental issues.

. . . .

Market proponents and critics have talked past one another on the hot spot issue. Environmental justice advocates routinely critique market-based systems due to the risk of hot spots: the risk that, instead of reducing their emissions, one or more facilities could buy allowances that increase emissions above the existing status quo. In general, environmental justice advocates fear that the hot spots from trading could arise or be perpetuated in the poor communities of color which contain the nation's older, more polluting, facilities. Some market proponents dismiss the hot spot concern because CO_2 does not have adverse local effects. Environmental justice advocates then point to the risks presented by GHG co-pollutants and argue that if facilities can initiate or increase production by purchasing carbon allowances, then co-pollutant emissions are likely to increase. Market proponents respond that carbon trading would not lead to an increase in co-pollutants because existing co-pollutant permits would constrain them.

As explained below, I conclude that a cap-and-trade program would not, in most instances, directly cause co-pollutant hot spots. Nonetheless, because the existing regulatory system does not fully constrain hot spots, a GHG trading system would do less to control the existing risk than a regulatory approach that required all facilities to reduce GHGs. Even if the hot spot risk is generally caused by the existing regula-

---

5. *Id.* § 38501(f).

6. *Id.* § 38591(a).

7. *Id.* § 38561(g).

8. *Id.* § 38562(b)(2) (prohibiting disproportionate impacts on low-income communities); *id.* § 38570(b)(1) (requiring that CARB consider whether market-based systems will lead to direct, indirect, and cumulative impacts, especially on heavily polluted communities); *id.* § 38562(4) (stating that the law should complement the state's efforts to meet clean air goals); *id.* § 38570(b)(2) (stating that CARB should ensure that market-based systems do not increase co-pollutants).

9. *Id.* § 38565.

tory system, not a GHG cap-and-trade system, a GHG-control program that can provide the co-benefit of reducing the existing hot spot risk is superior to one that does not.

....

vii. Adequacy of Compensation and the Role of Retribution

In *Exxon Shipping v. Baker*, ____ U.S. ____, 128 S.Ct. 2605, 171 L.Ed.2d 570 (June 25, 2008), the U.S. Supreme Court rushed past several issues of "justice" that will be drawn upon in future global warming cases. Is it fair for a giant corporation to avoid "derivative" responsibility for misdeeds of its employees? When does an "eccentric" and "unpredictable" punitive damage award offend some background sense of fairness? Will knowledge of consequence or endeavors to "redefine" the science figure in any compensation? When is compensation "adequate" and may victims claim a share of available "retribution"?

The opinion for the court in *Exxon Shipping v. Baker* (by Souter, J.) strongly hints that it would be unfair to hold a shipowner liable for punitive damages without corporate "acquiescence" in the actions causing harm. It holds that it would be unfair to the shipowner to allow an assessment of punitives to exceed allowable compensatory damages. Thus what was once a $5 billion punitive damage award would be reduced tenfold and the shares of 32,000 fishermen who waited for twenty years would be reduced accordingly. The high court holds that Exxon Shipping was fully and adequately punished for the 1989 *Exxon Valdez* oil spill.

The court actually is divided 4:4 on the question of whether the corporation would be liable for the misdeeds of Captain Joseph Hazelwood. (Justice Alito took no part in the consideration of the case.) But this vote will become 5:4 against if Justice Alito votes as expected at first opportunity. Requiring "acquiescence" by giant corporations in the drunken driving (and any number of other foibles and missteps) by the captains of giant vessels[1] gives "deniability" to the corporation and will fuel strategies to let the buck stop far downstream. The Exxon disaster itself shows exactly what you get when there is expected to be no "derivative" liability for an oil spill. Paper rules from above. Poor oversight. Little change in behavior. Deny later that the captain was drunk,[2] even while the company fires him for being drunk.[3] Make a scapegoat of the captain. He will suffer all sanctions while those whose liability could only be "derivative" are praised, honored, and promoted.[4]

As for the punitives (set by the jury at $5 billion in 1994), Mr. Justice Souter dug deeply for a vision of justice (presumed to be buried within each and every one of us) and discovered sentiments against "unpredictability" and "this feature of happenstance" that "is in tension with the function of the awards as punitive, just because of the implication of unfairness that an eccentri-

---

1. *See* Paul Edelman, *Amici Curiae* Brief of Ship Masters and Expert Mariners Captains Mitchell Stoller, Joseph Ahlstrom, Roger Johnson, John Scott Merrill, and Tom Trosvig In Support of Respondents 26 (Jan. 29, 2008) ("In addition to piloting these enormous ships, captains may manage as many as several hundred crew members. In order to run all of the operations on these ships, captains must maintain contact with the shore. As a result, captains of today are much like plant managers of a land-based operation"; *see id.* at 8: "more than half of all cargo transported by sea today is harmful to the environment").

2. *See* Walter Dellinger, Brief for Petitioners 9 n.3 (Dec. 17, 2007) (the question of whether Hazelwood was "impaired by alcohol" is "hotly disputed").

3. *See* David W. Oesting, Brief for Respondents 9 n.8 (Jan. 22, 2008) ("Even Exxon's Chairman conceded shortly after the spill that Hazelwood was 'drunk'... and Exxon fired him for that reason").

4. Exxon Shipping Co. v. Baker, Transcript of Oral Argument, Feb. 27, 2008, p. 76 (Jeffrey L. Fisher, Esq., for Respondents) [hereinafter Feb. 27, 2008 Oral Argument]: ("In the wake of the spill,... Exxon fired one person—Captain Hazelwood. They reassigned the third mate. Everybody else up—further up the chain of command that allowed this to happen received bonuses and raises.")

cally high punitive verdict carries in a system whose commonly held notion of law rests on a sense of fairness in dealing with one another."[5] Empirical support for this vision of "unpredictability" and "outlier" and "eccentric" jury behavior on punitives appears in empirical research. Some of this is blessed and cited by the court, with the curious disclaimer: "Because this research was funded in part by Exxon, we decline to rely on it."[6] There are many other published works not paid for by Exxon and not relied on by the court either.[7]

To correct this wildly unpredictable behavior by juries, Justice Souter took the court on a "quantitative" path, declaring:[8]

> given the need to protect against the possibility (and the disruptive cost to the legal system) of awards that are unpredictable and unnecessary, either for deterrence or for measured retribution, we consider that a 1:1 ratio [of punitives to compensatory damages], which is above the median award, is a fair upper limit in such maritime cases.

Consider whether the unpredictability and caprice declared to exist in the jury system can be surpassed by the imagination (and ample self-deceptions) of a sample of Supreme Court justices. For example—

• *Inadequacy of Compensation*

The Supreme Court announced that this Exxon case "does not support an argument that maritime compensatory awards need supplementing."[9] But of course the attractiveness (and simplemindedness) of insisting upon a "quantitative" ratio between punitive and compensatory damages is that the "punishment" should not greatly exceed the damage inflicted. "Compensatory" in this equation must stand for "damages done" not "the small fraction of damage for which we were made to pay." Perhaps Justice Souter's "unpredictability" beacon could be recalibrated if the compensatory function represented more than a tiny fraction of costs imposed.

How much has Exxon "underpaid" for the economic and environmental damage done in Prince William Sound? We would start with a figure of about $10 billion, more or less.[10] Massive environmental damage was not compensated for in the Exxon case. The court heard something about this in the briefs[11] but not a single advocate before the Supreme Court thought it useful to

---

5. Exxon Shipping Co. v. Baker, 128 S.Ct. at 2627. As of mid-October 2008, not a penny of the punitive damages awarded to class members has been paid.

6. Exxon Shipping Co. v. Baker, 128 S.Ct. at 2126, citing, among other authorities, Schlade, Sunstein & Kahneman, Deliberating About Dollars: The Severity Shift, 100 Colum. L. Rev. 1139 (2000). Obviously, the court relies upon this research while "declining" to rely upon it.

7. Riki Ott, Sound Truth and Corporate Myths: The Legacy of the *Exxon Valdez* Oil Spill (Dragonfly Sisters Press 2005) (by a member of the plaintiff class); Kellie Kvasnikoff, *Exxon Valdez*: 18 Years and Counting (Lulu.com 2007) (another member of the plaintiff class) [hereinafter cited as 2007 Kvasnikoff]; Rodgers, *et al.*, The Exxon Valdez *Reopener: Natural Resource Damage Settlements and Roads Not Taken*, 22 Alask. L. Rev. 135 (2005) [hereinafter cited as 2005 *Exxon Valdez* Reopener].

8. Exxon Shipping Co. v. Baker, 128 S.Ct. at 2633.

9. Exxon Shipping Co. v. Baker, 128 S.Ct. at 2633 n.27.

10. Compare 2005 *Exxon Valdez* Reopener at 148–49 (original contingent valuation studies put damage done to the Sound at 3–14 billion dollars) with Feb. 27, 2008 Oral Argument at 33 (Walter Dellinger, on behalf of Petitioners) ("when you start with payments that have reached $3.4 billion in terms of compensation, fines, remediation, restitution, that clearly obviates the need for deterrence"). There could be another trial on the additional damage inflicted by the "payments" for which Exxon gets full credit. See Riki Ott, Not One Drop: Betrayal and Courage in the Wake of the *Exxon Valdez* Oil Spill (Chelsea Green Pub 2008) [hereinafter cited as 2008 Ott]; David S. Case, Brief of *Amici Curiae* National Congress of American Indians and many other native groups, Jan. 29, 2008 (assertion that class members were "fully compensated" is remarkably "shallow" and "callous").

11. *See* Amy J. Wildermuth, Brief for the Pacific Coast Federation of Fishermen's Associations and the Institute for Fisheries Resources As *Amici Curiae* In Support of Respondents, Jan. 29, 2008, pp. 5–10 (on the

inform the court that the authorities are in the process of trying to collect from Exxon an additional $92 million in reopener monies for ongoing environmental damage.[12] This important environmental case is missing its environmental part.

- *"Unnecessary for Deterrence or for Measured Retribution"*[13]

Justice Souter and the court no doubt chose its fatuous 1:1 ratio because it is not easy for a jury or a court to determine whether a corporate entity has been adequately deterred and appropriately sanctioned. It may well be that Exxon has learned its "drunken captain" lesson. There is little evidence that the corporation will be capsized by a wave of remorse over its broader oil-spill avoidance duties on topics such as vessels with double-bottoms and clean-up plans.[14] Lessons are yet to be learned on other topics such as participation in the corruptions of government or the payment of royalties the company honorably owes.[15]

Exxon Shipping Co. v. Baker declares the company "adequately deterred" though there can be no character test on the matter.

Exxon Shipping Co. v. Baker also declares the company "adequately punished." There is little evidence of that. In the early 1990s criminal proceedings were staged. Exxon pled guilty to three misdemeanors and agreed to pay a $150 million fine. But $125 million of this fine vanished and was "remitted" ("to forgive or pardon") and returned to the corporation.

Another $100 million was declared "restitution" and went to the federal and state governments—but free of the legal restraints of the natural resource damage process.[16]

- *"No Earmarks of Exceptional Blame"*[17]

---

persistence of oil and collapse of the herring); *Exxon Valdez* Oil Spill Trustee Council, Lingering Oil, http://www.evostc.state.ak.us/Habitat/lingering.cfm (visited October 20, 2008).

12. The U.S. and Alaska have made demands for $92 million of the $100 million under the Reopener clause. These funds have not been paid and will necessitate further litigation.

13. Exxon Shipping Co. v. Baker, 128 S.Ct. at 2633.

14. *Compare* 2008 Ott at 23–25 with William M. Walker, Brief of *Amicus Curiae* Prince William Sound Regional Citizens' Advisory Council and Cook Inlet Regional Citizens' Advisory Council in Support of Respondents, Jan. 28, 2008, p. 28 (after twenty years' experience, the RCACs assert that "despite the many safeguards in place today against another oil spill, the elements of human error—indeed recklessness—and the corporate profit-seeking imperative remain substantially the same"; urges continuation of the "threat of punitive damages").

15. *See, e.g.,* ESCAPING THE RESOURCE CURSE, 24–25 (Mascartan Humphreys, Jeffrey D. Sachs & Joseph E. Stiglitz, eds., Columbia Un. Press 2007) (ch. 2, Joseph E. Stiglitz, *What is the Role of the State?* (footnotes omitted) ("In the 1980s I worked on a case involving cheating by the major oil companies in Alaska. This oil-rich state had a mineral lease requiring the oil companies to pay 12.5 percent of the gross receipts, less the cost of transporting the oil out from the far-flung site at Prudhoe Bay on the Arctic Circle. By overestimating their costs by just a few pennies per gallon (and multiplying those pennies by hundreds of millions of gallons) the oil companies would increase their profits enormously. They could not resist the temptation"; "In the end, there was no doubt that the cheating had occurred—and on a massive scale. There followed a series of settlements involving a who's who of global oil companies—including what are now BP, ExxonMobil, and ConocoPhillips—for an amount in excess of 6 billion dollars"); Robert McClure, *Federal Agency bungles oil-gas contracts,* SEATTLE POST-INTELLIGENCER, Sept. 19, 2008, p. 1, col. 2 ("Uncollected royalties by minerals service could hit $14 billion, GAO says"); U.S. Dep't of Interior, Office of Inspector General, "OIG Investigations of MMS Employees," Sept. 9, 2008 (sex, drugs, and "Royalties in Kind"); H. Josef Hebert, *Oil Brokers sex scandal may affect drilling debate,* ASSOCIATED PRESS, Sept. 11, 2008, available at http://ap.google.com/article/ALeqM5jzUY8O1E6qfQWasH6Fewcq6YfYmwD934FHVG0 (visited 10/20/2008).

16. 2005 *Exxon Valdez* Reopener at 149–52.

17. Exxon Shipping Co. v. Baker, 128 S.Ct. at 2633; *see id.* at 2631 ("worse than negligent but less than malicious"); 2631 n. 22 (no "specific purpose to cause harm at the expense of an established duty"); 2631 (not a case of "malicious behavior and dangerous activity carried on for the purpose of increasing a tortfeasor's gain"); *id.* at 2637: "[only a case of] reckless action, profitless to the tortfeasor, resulting in substantial recovery for substantial injury"; *id.* at 2633: "without behavior driven primarily by desire for gain"; "without the modest economic harm or odds of detection that have opened the door to higher awards").

Justice Souter repeatedly downplays Exxon's role in the oil spill disaster with terminology that minimizes culpability. Thousands of fishing people who came to know this corporation far better than they had wanted to get no chance to talk back. One of them, Kellie Kvasnikoff,[18] is given a chance in these pages. He says: "The gloating predictions of Exxon's chief strategist have turned out to be true, and the case has stretched into the 21st century. After 18 years justice has turned out to be misspelled, it is JUST-US. Those with the deep pockets ... can manufacture legal arguments, use the law, buy science, keep Supreme Court Justices and Presidents in their hip pockets and play them like puppets when it is to their benefit."

viii. More on Punitive Damages

What is the scope of the offender's behavior put in issue by a punitive damages claim and award? *Exxon Shipping* and the U.S. Supreme Court say it is limited to the precise behavior (*i.e.*, drunken driving) that yielded the spill. What are the fishing peoples' views on this corporate character inquiry? 2007 KVASNIKOFF, *supra* (eradication of food supply, crushing of elders' spirits, dysfunctional cleanup program, flawed contingency plans, copious motion and litigation extravagance designed to discourage adversaries, misuse of "limited fund" theory to prevent "opt-outs" from the class, extravagant claims of privilege for 12, 000 documents, a secret deal between Exxon and the Seattle Seven fishing companies to undercut the punitives award, numerous fines and penalties on environmental matters, destruction of indigenous peoples' rainforest with the Chad-Cameroon pipeline project, participation in climate-change coverup, recognition as the "sixth-worst" polluter in the U.S., cozy relationships with the brutal Indonesian military, a "History of Pollution and Theft," numerous hazardous waste violations, withdrawal of oil and gas from Texas lands without permission, defrauding Alabama on royalties due from natural gas wells in state waters); 2008 OTT, *supra* (false promises of double-bottom tankers and state-of-the-art vessel traffic control, reduced minimum crew sizes, nonexistence contingency plans, dysfunctional ballast water treatment plant, failure to build the promised sludge incinerator, coverup of sickness among oil cleanup workers, more "charade" than "cleanup," politicization of science, incessant public relations, tanker operators laundering hazardous wastes at Valdez—a "Ballast Watergate," Wackenhut spies, distortion of truth, the pledge of the Exxon chairman to "use every legal means available to overturn this unjust verdict," the Seattle Seven and the "fraud on the Court," Exxon's legal efforts to bring the *Exxon Valdez* back to Prince William Sound, arrested at the Exxon shareholder meeting, seventeen years after the spill nine of twenty-four species originally injured are listed as "recovered," profit by stalling, "Some Corporate Defense Strategies in Adversarial Legislation," Native creation of a "Shame Pole" dedicated to Exxon Mobil).

ix. Intergenerational Equity Revisited

Oliver A. Houck, *Light From the Trees: The Stories of Minors Oposa and the Russian Forest Cases*, 19 GEO. INT'L. ENVTL. L. REV. 321, 324–25 (2007), *commenting on Minors Oposa v. Factoran*, 224 S.C.R.A. 792 (S.C., July 30, 1993), reprinted in 33 I.L.M. 173 (1994) (footnotes omitted):

> Yet the one thing above all else for which Antonio Oposa will be remembered, around the world, is a lawsuit which he brought on behalf of his children, the children of friends, and children yet unborn, to save the rapidly vanishing forests of the Philippines. The case is known as Minors Oposa.

---

18. 2007 KVASNIKOFF at 30; *id.* at 165: "If there are grounds for the death penalty to be inflicted upon an individual, then there should be grounds for a corporate death penalty."

Id. at 333–35 (footnotes omitted):

The threshold question was whom to sue. The most obvious targets were the logging companies, which, after all, were the ones cutting down the trees. The difficulty was that the companies held signed and sealed government permits allowing them to log for decades into the future. They had at their disposal, further, stables of the country's best lawyers ready to bog down the claims in piles of paperwork, supported by hot-and-cold running legislators and politicians on tap as well. The Philippines ranked high among the politically-corrupt countries of the world, and its judiciary was also suspect. All it took was a few, quiet phone calls, and the case could simply disappear. As a legal and practical matter, then, the only feasible defendant was the Department of Environment and Natural Resources, friend or otherwise in the affair.

To the Philippine Ecological Network, the facts behind Minors Oposa were overwhelming. The Department of Environment and Natural Resources and its predecessors had ninety-two long-term TLAs [Timber Logging Allowances] outstanding for over 10 million acres of virgin timber and was considering yet more. That was already five times the amount of original forest left in the entire country. Hillsides were sliding into ravines, soil runoff was smothering the coral reefs, and entire species were disappearing. Clearly, this was wrong. The challenge was to prove that it was also illegal and that the real parties in interest, the proper parties to blow the whistle, harkening back to the idea Oposa had returned with from Norway, were the children and the future of the country, children yet unborn. This was Oposa's vision from the start. What he saw wrong here was an attack on posterity. He also saw a way to frame the case that fused— for the media, the public, and the courts—the wrong with the illegal.

There remained, however, the matter of who, among the living, would dare to bring the suit, in their own names, against the government. Oposa recruited a few friends and family members to join him, with their children, but none had the appetite to go first ("one can imagine how skeptical and afraid they were, why the heck would we sue Government?"). Their fears were understandable. One logging company—out of the 92 concessions at issue—"could simply hire someone to have me shot and killed." They insisted that, because the suit was his idea, Oposa's children would go first. His oldest was three and one-half years old, his youngest nine months old. Hence the caption, Minors Oposa.

The suit was filed on behalf of Oposa and his children, other children and their parents, unnamed children of the future, the parents of the named children, and the Philippine Ecological Network against Secretary Factoran who, whatever his sympathies, was represented by state attorneys sworn to defend government actions. Originally styled as a "taxpayers' action" on behalf of all Filipinos, and with a rhetorical extravagance that few American lawyers would dare ("the unabated hemorrhage of the country's vital life-support systems and continued rape of Mother Earth"), the complaint alleged violations of the environmental protection provisions of the Constitution and the sustainable use mandate of the Executive Order establishing the Department of Environment and Natural Resources. It sought nothing less than the cancellation of all existing TLAs and an injunction against processing new ones. Oposa wanted the whole enchilada.

Id. at 335–38 (footnotes omitted):

[*Minors Oposa* was dismissed by the trial court]. Oposa appealed to the Supreme Court, at which point the Solicitor General questioned, for the first time, the right of Oposa to represent entities as diffuse as all Filipinos, to say nothing of children yet unborn. Unwilling to abandon his theory, Oposa came across writings by an American scholar who spoke in terms of "intergenerational equity," and the term captured his same vision. He had never heard the phrase, but it was precisely what he had been thinking and what he was convinced the Constitution meant. He had no law on his side for this point (nor, in truth, any law contrary—the proposition was new), but he had the credibility of a U.S. publication, and from then on it would be up to the facts, the argument, and the judges. The Philippine Supreme Court then did an astonishing thing. It ruled for Oposa on every argument.

[The scholarship that drives this tale is the work of Edith Brown Weiss, *Our Rights and Future Obligations to Future Generations for the Environment*, 84 AM. J. INT'L L. 198 (1998); Edith Brown Weiss, *Intergenerational Equity in International Law*, 81 AM. SOC'Y INT'L L. PROC. 126 (1987); Edith Brown Weiss, *The Planetary Trust: Conservation and Intergenerational Equity*, 11 ECOLOGY L.Q. 495 (1984).]

The opinion was written by Justice Hilario G. Davide, Jr., the Court's most newly-appointed member, joined by ten other justices of the Court. Three members took no part. Only one member wrote separately, to concur. These numbers are all the more astonishing for what Justice Davide had to say. His opinion reads in part like poetry. In other parts it reads like Oposa had written it himself. Turning first to the issue of the unborn children, Davide found that Oposa had the right to represent his generation's interest in environmental quality, as well as that of succeeding generations. The right flowed naturally, in the Court's mind, from the Constitution's chosen language, "the rhythm and harmony of nature." Nature implied "the created world in its entirety." The maintenance of its "rhythm and harmony" included "indispensably" the "judicious disposition, utilization, management, renewal and conservation" of the country's resources, so that they would be "equitably accessible to the present as well as future generations." Each generation, therefore, held a "responsibility to the next" to preserve nature. That obligation was the basis for its standing to sue, for its own sake and for those to come.

So far so good, but at this point Oposa *et al.* were only past the courthouse door. The next step of the opinion was equally breathtaking. Section 16 of the Constitution, Justice Davide declared, not only accorded the procedural right to litigate but also granted the substantive right to protection as well. The principles of environmental protection it embraced were so fundamental that they had been law all along, in the way of natural law, even had the Constitution said nothing about them. Indeed, these principles were so fundamental (they were "assumed to exist from the inception of mankind") that they could even trump enumerated provisions of the Bill of Rights. Finishing with a flourish, he wrote that, were such rights not implied, "the day would not be too far when all else would be lost not only for the present generation, but also for those to come—generations which stand to inherit nothing but parched earth incapable of sustaining life."

This having been said, the Court was not about to let the impairment of contracts provision stand in the way. In the first instance, it found the TLAs not to be contracts at all in the legal sense, but rather licenses that were capable of being withdrawn for the public welfare. Even if the TLAs were regarded as contracts, the Court continued, the case did not involve a law or an executive order canceling the TLAs (clearly, though, this is what the plaintiffs were seeking), and even if it had, cancellation would be justifiable under these circumstances as a valid exercise of the police power.

Having rolled this far, the Court turned last to the leave-it-to-the-politicians, separation of powers argument, finding ample precedent to support judicial review of government actions. The case did not put "policy formation" by the executive at issue. What was involved, rather, was the enforcement of a right expressed in law. Even if this right did implicate politics, the Constitution had expanded judicial power to "determine whether or not there has been a grave abuse of discretion amounting to lack or excess of jurisdiction" by any branch of government. Your decision to make, Department of Environment and Natural Resources, but our decision to review.

Of the eleven justices sitting, this was the opinion of ten. It would be hard to imagine ten of eleven votes in favor of any of the four conclusions just described, from any court of appeals in the United States, much less the Supreme Court, at any time in history. The opinion was a bombshell. Not just one bomb, but several. Where in the world, one might ask, did it come from? From no single source, doubtless, but one may reasonably postulate several contributors. The judges in this case, like their country, were coming off decades of quasi-dictatorial rule, the antithesis of law, and were asserting their new role. At the same time, during the late 1980s, the Philippines was catching the first heady wave of environmental enthusiasm that had swept the United States two decades before. Front and center was environmental mismanagement writ large, the open scandal of forest management. New ink was barely dry on the far-reaching and aspirational declarations of its Constitution. The politicians may not have been totally ready for the message, but the courts—in many countries both the most educated and the "least political" branch of government—were less shackled to the past and more free to change course. Justice Davide, who, one has the sense, grew into environmental literacy with the experience of this case, went on to lecture to international audiences on the role of an independent judiciary in environmental protection and the need for a corollary offense in legal and public education. Pure Antonio Oposa.

At the end of the day, however, one senses that what won this case was the overwhelming, remorseless, and no-escape mountain of facts. The Court's detailed recitation of Oposa's allegations—a parade of horribles—shows that it understood them and was impressed. The Philippines had taken its greatest natural treasure and turned it into a liability, impoverishing everyone. There seemed no other way to stop the train. At times, hard cases make great law.

x. Sources

Additionally, *see* Ann E. Carlson, *Heat Waves, Global Warming and Mitigation*, 26 UCLA J. ENVTL. L. & POL'Y 169 (2008); Daniel A. Farber, *Apportioning Climate Change Costs*, 25 UCLA J. ENVTL. L. & POL. 21 (2007/2008); Alice Kaswan, *Reconciling Justice and Efficiency: Integrating Environmental Justice Into Cap-and-Trade Programs for Controlling Greenhouse Gases* (May 19, 2008) (in draft); Sarah C. Aminzadeh, *A Moral Imperative: The Human Rights Implications of Climate Change*, 30 HASTINGS INT'L & COMPAR. L. REV. 231 (2007); Audrey Koecher, *Corporate Accountability for Environmental Human Rights Abuse in Developing Nations: Making the Case for Punitive Damages Under the Alien Tort Claims Act*, 17 J. TRANSNAT'L L. & POL'Y 151 (2007); James Goodwin & Armin Rosencranz, *Holding Oil Companies Liable for Human Rights Violations in a Post-Sosa World*, 42 NEW ENGL. L. REV. 701 (2008); Inho Kim, *"Milking" Oil Tankers: The Paradoxical Effect of the Oil Pollution Act of 1990*, 47 NAT. RES. J. 849, 850 (2007) (the "shipping sector has not entirely withdrawn from U.S. waters, but rather changed its operation patterns to take advantage of cost-efficient older single-hull vessels in these waters"). *See also* OLIVER HOUCK, TAKING BACK EDEN: EIGHT ENVIRONMENTAL CASES THAT CHANGED THE WORLD (Island Press 2009).

III. Transformation of the Arctic: The "Barometer" of Indigenous Peoples

Global warming will hit many populations and it will strike indigenous peoples especially hard. For an excellent introduction to this topic, see INDIGENOUS PEOPLES, THE ENVIRONMENT AND LAW: AN ANTHOLOGY (Lawrence Watters ed., Carolina Academic Press 2004) [hereinafter 2004 WATTERS].

For a splendid summary by an experienced scholar of Indian law, *see* Rebecca Tsosie, *Indigenous People and Environmental Justice: The Impact of Climate Change*, 78 U. COLO. L. REV. 1625, 1635 (2007) [hereinafter 2007 Tsosie on *Indigenous Environmental Justice*]:

> The impacts of climate change on indigenous peoples are particularly visible in the Pacific Islands and in the Arctic due to the great interdependence of the people with their local environments and the centrality of traditional life ways to basic survival in these regions. Although these environments are radically different from one another, there are many harms common to the affected indigenous communities in both regions, in part because both environments are extremely susceptible to climate change and in part because of the close, synergistic relationship between the people and the local environment.
>
> ....

2007 Tsosie on *Indigenous Environmental Justice* at 1674–75:

> This article has argued for a right to environmental self-determination for indigenous peoples, which would allow them to maintain their unique cultural and political status as the peoples of traditional lands since before the establishment of current national boundaries. In the context of climate change policy, recognition of a right to self-determination would impose affirmative obligations on nation-states to engage in a mitigation strategy in order to avoid catastrophic harm to indigenous peoples.
>
> This human-rights claim is different from the first generation of indigenous environmental justice claims, which focused on sovereignty and the need to exercise tribal regulatory jurisdiction over reservation lands. In the United States, the political sovereignty of federally recognized Indian nations may enhance their claim for a right to participate in the development of a national policy on climate change. However, the recognition of tribal "sovereignty" is not sufficient to protect indigenous peoples within their traditional environments. Similarly, the claim of environmental self-determination is quite different from tort-based models of human rights litigation, which attempt to hold nation-states and corporations liable for environmental harm. Such claims are limited by the requirements of injury, causation, and damages, and they primarily deal with redress for quantifiable past harm but do little to prevent the prospective harms likely to be caused by the environmental policies, or lack thereof, of nation states.

A. Baseline 2002: Traditional Ecological Knowledge

David W. Norton, Arctic Rim Research, *Coastal Sea Ice Watch: Private Confessions of a Convert to Indigenous Knowledge*, in THE EARTH IS FASTER NOW: INDIGENOUS OBSERVATIONS OF ARCTIC ENVIRONMENTAL CHANGE 127, 130 (Arctic Studies Center, Smithsonian Institution 2002) [hereinafter 2002 NORTON]:

Our research project took shape in early 1999, when colleagues in Barrow, Alaska, were especially concerned with public safety for the hundreds of people who would occupy landfast ice during the annual spring subsistence hunt for the bowhead whale (*Balaena mysticetus*) in April–June of each year. In mid-May of 1997, a large slab of nearshore ice bearing dozens of subsistence whalers had broken loose from landfast ice near Barrow and floated north into the Beaufort Sea. By braving hazardous fog for a night and a day, North Slope Borough Search and Rescue helicopter pilots plucked all 154 marooned crewmembers from twelve camps on the drifting ice....

[Makes note of two "articles of commitment" that inform the National Science Foundation's Office of Polar Programs' initiative on "humans in the Arctic System (HARC)": climate change is happening and indigenous knowledge is useful. Consider the Sept. 2000 Fifty-First Arctic Science Conference conducted by the Arctic Science Division of the AAAS (*id.* at 130). The proceedings volume of that annual conference consisted of abstracts for 129 oral and poster presentations, of which forty (31%) dealt with climate change and forty-seven (36.4%) involved [Traditional Ecological Knowledge or TEK]].

2002 NORTON at 133:

It is hard now to imagine choosing a subject [nearshore sea ice] that so deeply captivates both indigenous subsistence whalers and sealers, and the arctic research community.

Quoting Billy Blair Patkotak, in 2002 NORTON at 142–43:

The rules for interpreting ice [and other variables in the Wainwright nearshore environment] changed after 1975–76. Before that I could tell younger whalers what they were seeing and what to expect. After the rules changed, I tried; but I was often wrong. Pretty soon younger whalers stopped listening to me. I tell you, that made me very sad.

2002 NORTON at 145 [this remark coincides with oceanographers' detections of a Bering Sea ecological regime shift dating from 1976]:

Whalers observe and think about nearshore ice by thinking in two dimensions besides the ones that nonwhalers primarily use.... Satellite imagery in all forms affords users essentially a two-dimensional view.... On a fine scale, whalers' two-dimensional assessment of nearshore ice still tends to outperform satellite imagery....

....

In addition to this two-dimensional analysis, subsistence hunters appraise an expanse of nearshore ice by visualizing its third (vertical) dimension.... [This includes] changes in the atmosphere above the ice, the ice itself, the behavior of the water column on which the ice floats, and the bottom topography of the sea floor. Local naturalists' expertise thus keeps track of a whole array of variables.

[The whaler's "fourth dimension" is to invest the ice with "historical perspective"—*i.e.*, a seasonal "system memory."]

2002 NORTON at 151:

The poll asked respondents [experts of sea ice analysis within agencies of the federal government] to choose the alternative that would make them feel safer out on nearshore sea ice: (a) web connections to satellite imagery and Weather Service ice forecasts, or (b) an Iñupiaq companion traditionally knowledgeable of local ice conditions. Preference for an Iñupiaq guide was unanimous.

2002 NORTON at 152–53:

> With respect to understanding nearshore sea ice, fraternizing with scientists shows no
> sign of displacing traditional knowledge. Nor do scientists' technological shortcuts of
> satellite imagery, tide gauge data, and measurements of under-ice currents seem as
> likely to corrupt traditional knowledge as to encourage it. The health of traditional
> knowledge depends upon continuity or continued receptivity by coming generations
> who must master TEK and pass it on.

B. Baseline 2004: The Old Arctic

Remarkably, events are moving so quickly in the Arctic that a few years have brought radical
changes. This description of "Arctic Environmental Problems" by Jennifer McIver, entitled *The
Arctic*, appears in 2004 WATTERS ch. 8, at 159–61:

> Six factors converge to make the Arctic one of the world's most environmentally vul-
> nerable regions. First, low temperatures drastically slow decomposition of natural and
> synthetic substances and pollutants. Metal objects take centuries to corrode and vanish,
> spilled or leaked oil takes years to degrade, and organic pollutants dumped into water
> resources may travel a thousand kilometers before complete dissipation, compared to a
> few hundred kilometers in more temperate zones.
>
> Second, regeneration of Arctic flora is slow and drawn out due to cold air tempera-
> tures, cold soils and only a few months of sunlight each year. The growing period is lim-
> ited to a short, intense window of opportunity during the short summer months. When
> Arctic tundra or vegetation is disturbed, it can take centuries to regrow. Implications
> for the rest of the Arctic food chain are profound ...
>
> Third, climatic conditions in high latitudes do not allow much diversity of animal
> life, but do allow increases in numbers and concentrations of the species present. For
> example, the George River caribou herd in northern Quebec number between 600,000
> and 900,000. The Bering Sea Pollock fishery is the largest single species in the world.
> These huge numbers of animals remain relatively concentrated in their distribution be-
> cause of their need for protection from predators and the availability of food supply. In
> the case of marine mammals in the winter, only a very limited area of the Arctic Ocean
> is free of ice, so animals are highly concentrated around these few good sources of air
> and nutrients. Such high concentrations of mammals in some areas of the Arctic enor-
> mously heightens vulnerability to detrimental activities.
>
> Fourth, marine areas are of much greater significance in the Arctic than elsewhere
> around the globe, both as habitat and feeding ground. Birds and land mammals, including
> humans, live on the coastal edge to be safe from predators and close to food from the sea.
>
> Fifth, the Arctic climate is highly susceptible to global warming trends due to low
> precipitation, a relatively stagnant low air mass over the region and the ice's high reflec-
> tivity of radiation. During the Arctic winter, warming could be three to four times
> greater than global averages. Regional warming could have numerous effects. Certain
> changes are already registering: "warmer air and ground temperatures, reduced water
> levels in lakes and rivers, less sea ice, more forest fires and insect infestations, increased
> coastal erosion and more snow in winter." Some of these changes can have surprising
> results. For example, warmer air and ground conditions lead to a thaw in the per-
> mafrost ... Finally, severe weather and ice conditions can make environmental clean-up
> extremely difficult, if not impossible in some circumstances.

Some of the most pressing Arctic environmental issues originate far away in the economies of more temperate countries. Heavy metal pollutants in the world's oceans are transported north by ocean currents coming from the equator and "there is very little mechanism to move them south again." Contaminants such as DDT, PCB, radionuclides, carbon dioxide, soot, sulphur dioxide, CFCs, pesticides and heavy metals enter the food chain at the bottom from the air and water and take decades to reach measurable levels further up the chain. Alarmingly, these kinds of chemicals have been discovered both in the bodies of polar bears and the breast milk of indigenous mothers. The 1987 incident at the Chernobyl power plant has had chronic effects on the livelihood and safety of the Sami population ... Largely dependent on gourmet reindeer meat exports, the Sami economy suffered a serious blow from the enforced slaughter of 100,000 animals after the incident. The effects of that incident persist.

Heavy metals and sulphur originating mostly in the South also accumulate low over the Arctic region, forming the "Arctic Haze." The brown haze is visible air pollution made up of suspended particulate matter that scatters solar radiation. It has been visible since the 1950s and is considered an early warning system of emission levels of long-range pollutants. The biggest threat signaled by the presence of the Arctic Haze is climate change. Scientists do not agree as to what effects a warming trend would have on the Arctic. Some project that it could dramatically increase snowfall, triggering an ice age. Others predict a reduction in areas of Arctic tundra and encroachment of forests northward. Food supplies would change together with migration patterns of mammals. All of these effects would have dramatic impact on indigenous-subsistence based societies. What scientists do agree upon is that dramatic climatic change will cause massive climatic imbalance in not only the Arctic but the rest of the globe as well.

The delicate balance of the Arctic ecosystem leads to another arena in which environmental management is crucial, that of habitat protection. Since the *Exxon Valdez* accident in 1989, there is no longer any need to hypothesize about the kind of devastation oil-tanker spills can cause in the Northern environment. Oil and gas activities carry with them other effects, however, which are less often highlighted. First, the pipelines built to transport oil and gas southward not only scar the tundra from their construction, but also affect the migratory habits of critical caribou herds. One author notes that pipelines in both Russia and the United States are in some cases extensively corroded, creating the possibility of major damage from a pipeline spill. More recently, scientists have discovered that noise caused by offshore oil and gas activities may have a very significant impact on the behavior and safety of certain marine species. Finally, dredging of the ocean floor for oil platform construction and earthmoving on land for road and causeway construction disturb spawning grounds and disrupt migration patterns.

Another example of a threat to wildlife habitat is the massive BHP diamond mine proposed for an area in the Canadian Arctic. Not only would the proposed mine open in a region used for centuries by the Dene tribe for hunting and trapping, but the development would be constructed in the headwaters of the Coppermine River, putting the fishing grounds of the Nunavut Inuit at risk. We know that, between 1965 and 1981, sixteen nuclear reactors were dumped from old Soviet naval vessels into the Kara Sea north of the Russian Arctic coast. In addition, liquid nuclear waste was disposed of in the same area as recently as 1992. Many believe that the threat of radioactive contamination may be the most critical environmental hazard for the Arctic today. Finally, a great deal has been heard about over-harvesting of Arctic wildlife resources.

Notes

1. On "the largest single species in the world" referenced by Jennifer McIver, *see Fast-Food Fish Under Threat*, NEW SCIENTIST, Nov. 29, 2008, p. 6:

> Last week, a panel from the U.S. National Marine Fisheries Service recommended an 18 percent reduction in next year's catch in the eastern Bering Sea, the main Pollock region for U.S. boats, bringing the total down to 815,000 tonnes. This is the latest in a series of cuts which have seen the quota drop from almost 1,500,000 tonnes in 2005.

2. On the long-range transport of pollutants referenced by Jennifer McIver, see MARLA CONE, SILENT SNOW: THE SLOW POISONING OF THE ARCTIC 41 (Grove Press 2005) ("It was a pack of seal blubber like this that started Arctic scientists on their journey of toxic discovery.").

3. On the caribou referenced by Jennifer McIver, see Robert Roy Britt, Reindeer & Caribou Populations Plung, Yahoo! News, LiveScience.com (June 11, 2009), available at http://www.live-science.com/environment/090611-reindeer-populations-plunge.html (last visited August 17, 2009) (findings of study by Mark Boyce and Liv Vors, University of Alberta, reported in the Global Change Biology Journal):

> Reindeer and caribou numbers worldwide have plunged nearly 60 percent in the last three decades due to climate change and habitat disturbance, a new study finds.

C. 2004 Arctic Climate Impact Assessment

Lester R. Brown, President, World Resources Institute, flyer distributed with book, entitled "Plan B 3.0 Mobilizing to Save Civilization," Summer 2008:

> Experts were "stunned" this past summer [2007] by the loss of Arctic Sea ice. An area almost twice the size of Britain disappeared in a single week.

MARK LYNAS, SIX DEGREES: OUR FUTURE ON A HOTTER PLANET 98 (National Geographic 2008):

> The culprit is the "Arctic amplifier" of global warming, which means that a temperature rise of two degrees globally would lead to anything from 3.2° C to 6.6° C warming in the Arctic by 2050.

ARCTIC CLIMATE IMPACT ASSESSMENT, IMPACTS OF A WARMING ARCTIC ch. 7 at 94 (Cambridge U. Press 2004) [hereinafter 2004 ARCTIC CLIMATE IMPACT ASSESSMENT]:

> Because ringed seals and polar bears are very unlikely to survive in the absence of summer sea ice, the impact on indigenous communities that depend upon these species is likely to be enormous.

The scientific endeavor that documented the rush of the Arctic towards deep environmental trouble is the ARCTIC CLIMATE IMPACT ASSESSMENT, IMPACTS OF A WARMING ARCTIC (Cambridge U. Press 2004) [hereinafter 2004 ARCTIC CLIMATE IMPACT ASSESSMENT]. This assessment was called for by the Arctic Council, which is described as follows in the preface of the document:

> The Arctic Council is a high-level intergovernmental forum that provides a mechanism to address the common concerns and challenges faced by arctic people and governments. It is comprised of the eight arctic nations (Canada, Denmark / Greenland/Faroe

Islands, Finland, Iceland, Norway, Russia, Sweden, and the United States of America), six Indigenous Peoples organizations (Permanent Participants: Aleut International Association, Arctic Athabaskan Council, Gwich'in Council International, Inuit Circumpolar Conference, Russian Association of Indigenous Peoples of the North, and Saami Council), and official observers (including France, Germany, the Netherlands, Poland, United Kingdom, non-governmental organizations, and scientific and other international bodies).

This 2004 Assessment survived a severe debunking treatment. CHRIS MOONEY, THE REPUBLICAN WAR ON SCIENCE 82 (Perseus Books 2005). The stature of the study has grown with time.

Here are a few of its findings and observations.

2004 ARCTIC CLIMATE IMPACT ASSESSMENT at 94:

As Indigenous Peoples perceive it, the Arctic is becoming an environment at risk in the sense that sea ice is less stable, unusual weather patterns are occurring, vegetation cover is changing, and particular animals are no longer found in traditional hunting areas during specific seasons. Local landscapes, seascapes, and icescapes are becoming unfamiliar, making people feel like strangers in their own land.

2004 ARCTIC CLIMATE IMPACT ASSESSMENT at 12–13:

Arctic Climate Trends

- Rising Temperatures
- Rising River Flows
- Declining Snow Cover
- Increasing Precipitation
- Thawing Permafrost
- Diminishing Lake and River Ice
- Melting Glaciers
- Melting Greenland Ice Sheet ("The area of melting in 2002 broke all previous records.")
- Retreating Summer Sea Ice ("declined by 15%–20% over the past 30 years").
- Rising Sea Level
- Ocean Salinity Change

2004 ARCTIC CLIMATE IMPACT ASSESSMENT at 16–17:

Impacts on Society

- Loss of Hunting Culture
- Declining Food Security
- Human Health Concerns
- Wildlife Herd Impacts
- Expanding Marine Shipping
- Increasing Access to Resources
- Enhanced Marine Fisheries
- Disrupted Transport on Land
- Decline in Northern Freshwater Fisheries
- Enhanced Agriculture and Forestry

2004 ARCTIC CLIMATE IMPACT ASSESSMENT:

Id. at 9: The impacts of climate change in the Arctic addressed in this assessment are largely caused from outside the region, and will reverberate back to the global community in a variety of ways.

Key findings of the 2004 ARCTIC CLIMATE IMPACT ASSESSMENT:

Id. at 10: The Arctic is now experiencing some of the most rapid and severe climate change on earth.

Disturbances such as insect outbreaks and forest fires are very likely to increase in frequency, severity, and duration, facilitating invasions by non-native species.

Reductions in sea ice will drastically shrink marine habitat for polar bears, ice-inhabiting seals, and some seabirds, pushing some species toward extinction.

As new species move in, animal diseases that can be transmitted to humans, such as the West Nile virus, are likely to pose increasing health risks.

Id. at 11: Reduced sea ice is very likely to increase marine transport and access to resources. Indigenous communities are facing major economical and cultural impacts.

Id. at 13: Global and Arctic sea level has risen 10–20 centimeters in the past 100 years.

The average extent of sea-ice cover in summer has declined by 15%–20% over the past 30 years.

2004 Arctic Climate Impact Assessment at 94:

Seals Become Elusive for Inuit in Nunavut, Canada

The ringed seal is the single most important food source for the Inuit, representing the majority of the food supply in all seasons. No other species is present on the land or in the waters of Nunavut in the quantities needed to sustain the dietary requirements of the Inuit. In recent decades, local people have observed that ringed seal pup production has suffered as increased temperatures have led to a reduction and destabilization of the sea ice. These ice changes have also affected the harvest of polar bear, another important food source, because ringed seals are central to a polar bear's diet and the bears are also directly affected by the observed changes in snow and ice.

To hunt, catch, and share these foods is the essence of Inuit culture. Thus, a decline in ringed seals and polar bears threatens not only the dietary requirements of the Inuit, but also their very way of life. Projections of sea-ice decline in the future spell further trouble....

2004 Arctic Climate Impact Assessment at 9:

One of the additional stresses in the Arctic that is addressed in this assessment results from increasing levels of ultraviolet radiation reaching the earth's surface due to stratospheric ozone depletion. As with many of the other stresses mentioned, there are important interactions between climate change and ozone depletion. The effects of climate change on the upper atmosphere make continued ozone depletion over the Arctic likely to persist for at least a few more decades. Thus, ultraviolet radiation levels in the Arctic are likely to remain elevated, and this will be most pronounced in the spring, when ecosystems are most sensitive to harmful ultraviolet radiation. The combination of climate change, excess ultraviolet radiation, and other stresses presents a range of potential problems for human health and well-being as well as risks to other arctic species and ecosystems....

D. Eyewitnesses to History: Loss of Ice

2007 Kolbert at 26–27:

The most precise measurements of Arctic sea ice have been made by NASA, using satellites equipped with microwave sensors. In 1979, the satellite data show, perennial sea ice covered 1.7 billion acres, or an area nearly the size of the continental United States. The ice's extent varies from year to year, but since then the overall trend has been strongly downward.... By now, though, the perennial sea ice has shrunk by roughly 250 million acres, an area the size of New York, Georgia, and Texas combined. According to mathematical models, even the extended period of a positive Arctic Oscillation can account for only a part of this loss.

———————

David Adam, *Loss of Arctic ice leaves experts stunned*, THE GUARDIAN FOR AMERICA, guardian. co.uk, Sept. 4, 2007 (*available at* http://www.guardian.co.uk/environment/2007/sep/04/ climate-change):

Figure 2. An iceberg melts in Kulusuk, Greenland, near the Arctic Circle. Photo: John McConnico/AP.

The Arctic ice cap has collapsed at an unprecedented rate this summer and levels of sea ice in the region now stand at record lows, scientists have announced.

Experts say they are "stunned" by the loss of ice, with an area almost twice as big as the UK disappearing in the last week alone.

So much ice has melted this summer that the Northwest passage across the top of Canada is fully navigable, and observers say the Northeast passage along Russia's Arctic coast could open later this month.

If the increased rate of melting continues, the summertime Arctic could be totally free of ice by 2030.

Mark Serreze, an Arctic specialist at the US National Snow and Ice Data Centre at Colorado University in Denver, said: "It's amazing. It's simply fallen off a cliff and we're still losing ice."

The Arctic has now lost about a third of its ice since satellite measurements began thirty years ago, and the rate of loss has accelerated sharply since 2002.

Dr Serreze said: "If you asked me a couple of years ago when the Arctic could lose all of its ice then I would have said 2100, or 2070 maybe. But now I think that 2030 is a reasonable estimate. It seems that the Arctic is going to be a very different place within our lifetimes, and certainly within our childrens' lifetimes."

The new figures show that sea ice extent is currently down to 4.4m square kilometres (1.7m square miles) and still falling.

The previous record low was 5.3m square kilometres in September 2005. From 1979 to 2000 the average sea ice extent was 7.7m square kilometres.

The sea ice usually melts in the Arctic summer and freezes again in the winter. But Dr Serreze said that would be difficult this year.

"This summer we've got all this open water and added heat going into the ocean. That is going to make it much harder for the ice to grow back."

Changes in wind and ocean circulation patterns can help reduce sea ice extent, but Dr Serreze said the main culprit was man-made global warming.

"The rules are starting to change and what's changing the rules is the input of greenhouse gases."

An Iñupiaq Reflection on "Ice"

Victoria Hykes Steere. The author is an Inupiaq from the village of Unalakleet. Her grandparents are Martha and Peter Nanouk; her parents are Ruth and Nelson Hykes. She has a JD from the University of Iowa College of Law, an LL.M from the University of Washington School of Law, and an economics degree from Colby College.

September 2008
Professor Rodgers,

I began putting together a legal argument on the right to sea ice based on international public law and human rights law and stopped after reading the first few chapters of Paul W. Kahn's book, THE CULTURAL STUDY OF LAW, including the following passage:

> We see here, in its earliest form, the problem of the colony for the practice of law's rule. This problem would plague the West for the next two hundred years. There were two patterns of thought about the long-term relationship of colony to colonizer. One believed that the end of the process would be incorporation of the colony into the metropolis such that the territory expanded into one extended nation.... Law overcame existing borders in the direction of empire. The other pattern understood colonization as a kind of trusteeship, which would end when the colony was capable of independent statehood under its own rule of law.... [This] envisioned multiple states under law's rule, joined loosely in the Commonwealth. The one thing that was not compatible with the rule of law was the fact of the situation: subordination of the colonial territory to the colonizing power as a permanent, structural relationship. This required an ideology of racism, not law. There has, for this reason, always been an air of lawlessness about the "law" with regard to Native Americans.... The act of dispossession set the modern agenda of revolution as decolonization.[†]

Kahn's words hit hard and true for they reflected my grandmother's question that led me to law school: "What happened to us? I was born free, why am I not going to die that way?"

This chapter is about our relationship to the sea ice, the animals and some of the communities being impacted by global warming/climate change. It is deeply personal as I wrestle with trying to take what is often seen as exotic and make it real. Just ice. That's all we need for our world to continue: sea ice in the early fall (October) rather than November/December as is currently occurring due to the impact of anthropogenic carbon emissions on the Arctic. Permafrost melt created by rising air temperatures endangers the very foundations of our world. Multi-year Arctic pack ice, essential for the well being of marine mammals—polar bears, bearded seals, walrus,

---

†. Paul W. Kahn, THE CULTURAL STUDY OF LAW 59–60 (Un. of Chicago Press 1999).

etc., is disappearing from our waters at an alarming rate. These animals are keystones to our subsistence in its fullest meaning, providing food, materials for shelter, crafts and forming part of our spiritual wellness.

Becoming Human: Memories from an Iñupiaq Life and Quest for Answers

Imagine being. Expand that thought to being and belonging. The limitless possibilities that arise are part of what makes us human. We are Iñupiat and our homeland is mapped in our faces, the way we laugh and interact with the world. The old-time people used words sparingly for we believe in the power of words. Words heal and it is my hope that all my grandparents, great-grandmother and so many others who taught me will be alive in this chapter and allow the world to understand our humanity. Our world will survive only if the rest of the world develops the political will and social conscience to lower drastically the greenhouse gases emissions that cause anthropogenic global warming.

Global warming and the accompanying change in climate are impacting our communities today! This is not some future scenario that might or might not happen. It is happening. Five out of seven immediately impacted villages identified by a 2004 General Accounting Office report are Iñupiat villages, including the village that I am from, Unalakleet, and the village closest to us, Shaktoolik. One hundred eighty four of Alaska's two hundred nineteen villages are or will be directly impacted by lack of sea ice, coastal erosion, sea level rise and/or melting permafrost. When telling stories in English, the old-time Iñupiat and their children would begin with, "This is a true story." Unfortunately, this is a true story. It impacts our very existence.

Learning about Ice and Snow

The balloons hung in the storm porch all winter long. First one, then another and another until the rafters were full. One day in what is our spring, my grandfather Peter took them down and packed them in his sled. He told me the balloons were seal bladders from the seals we'd eaten during the winter. He hitched up his dogs then bundled me in a reindeer skin and put me in the sled. We went onto the sea ice with a slight breeze off the ocean; bright sun reflecting off the white snow covered ice with bright blue sky. The snow sparkled clean as the team eagerly pulled us to a lead (a long linear area of open water created as sheets of sea ice are pulled apart). My grandfather took the seal bladders and laid them on the ice. He sang a song. It was beautiful. The song belonged to long ago before missionaries and the federal government made it almost impossible for our songs of thanksgiving to continue. While singing, my grandfather took the bladders and set them into the water and they floated in the open water. As the last two seal bladders (mostly bearded seals) entered the water, he prayed. We watched them until they disappeared. The dogs did not bark—we were silent, awake in a dream of pure joy.

"Always remember to give thanks to the animals for giving themselves to us," he said as he unhitched the dogs.

My grandfather sent me out to listen to the wind, the trees, and the ocean. In the late fall, he took me out on the sea ice, to feel it under my feet, to judge how thick it was, to hear it creak and groan, and to understand safe ice from unstable ice. He told me if I listened the right way, believing it possible, the elements would speak to me and teach me. Every day after school he asked what I learned and then in our dialect he would explain our own understanding of what was in the textbooks. The simplest example of what he taught me involved the five senses. He told me to write the five presented in class on the test, but explained that we have more than five senses. In our language, he explained a far more complex understanding of senses, which is part of our cosmology—our worldview. He said that our worldview allows us to have access to a greater range of senses because it doesn't restrict us to the obvious—taste, smell, hearing, seeing and touch. He also sent me to the slough, ponds and river to observe and sense in our way the difference in ice and notice how it reacted to the changing phases of the moon.

Why was it so important? In late April or early May, my cousins and I went to a birthday party. We were all either five or on our way to becoming five years old. We played a game we call bat introduced by the Sami herding families that brought reindeer (domesticated caribou) back to Western Alaska. Whalers, commercial fishers and miners had nearly exterminated all animals our villages relied on for food, clothing, kayaks, and umiaks. For thousands of years, caribou had been an important source of food and clothing for Western Alaska communities. After we left the party, the birthday girl went after her new ball and fell through the sea ice. Our language has no word for fair. Life isn't fair; we don't expect it to be, so we learn by watching and listening to those with more knowledge of the skills necessary for life in the Arctic.

The amount of information being generated about the changing climate in the Arctic and its impacts on communities, transportation, marine mammals, caribou etc. is overwhelming. We are quite literally facing the end of a relationship tens of thousands of years old with sea ice, marine mammals, reindeer, caribou, salmon and numerous tundra plants. We are losing our world. Everything that defines us is in crisis. The sea ice is no longer there in the fall to protect our villages from the raging storms that come out of Siberia, pounding our coastline. Storm surges are cutting away shorelines of five immediately impacted Iñupiat communities: Point Hope, Kivilina, Shishmaref, Shaktoolik and Unalakleet.

In our world time is not linear and we are the past, present and future interdependent on the actions of those alive now. We are responsible to those who lived before and who will live after to ensure we leave the animals, land, rivers, as though we had never been. My grandfather explained our monuments are the land and sea as they are. He taught me to read the clouds, sent me out alone to listen to the sea ice, water, trees and wind. One day, school was cancelled after lunch because of a blizzard. After playing with my cousins, I began my journey home. I started to panic when I could no longer see the outline of the houses—only snow blowing all around me. I moved my hand toward my face to see how close it would get before I saw it. I felt the mitten against my nose. I could not see it. I knew the wind blew the sea ice out because it was blowing from east to west. I stood still to fight the fear and swallowed snow. Praying, promising God I would be good if I lived, I shut my eyes and started walking. My feet moved. The way home became clear to me as I struggled up the first snow bank, using my feet to see. In the open area between one snow bank the next with the dip up then down and up again then down. I found my grandparents' house, but I could not open the porch door. The wind was too strong. Touching the house, I moved around the house and nearly lost hope when I came to the heating oil barrels but decided to crawl as close as I could to the house. I slowly made my way to the big porch door that opened inward and went inside. My grandfather asked me what I did. I told him, "I pressed my mittens toward my face to see how far I could see. I hit my nose and couldn't see so I prayed, promised God to be good, if I lived, shut my eyes and walked. When the porch door opened, I opened my eyes." He looked at me, raised his eyebrows and said, "Always remember, you come from people who didn't lay down and die."

I couldn't understand why the books and magazines described our world as wild, untamed, wilderness, desolate, barren, isolated, uninhabitable, bleak, unforgiving. My grandmother laughed and explained that our eyes see unending beauty in snow and ice; the land challenges us to be better people, work together, look after one another, become a part of it and makes our souls sing with joy. At eleven I read the book People of Kauwerak. It contains our oral history of who we are and how we became human beings. When snow and ice came to our ancestors, they learned to rely on one another, to be a communally-based society and to use their intelligence to survive. Snow and ice made us better people than we were before. We learned to be grateful for being alive and for the animals: ice seals, walrus, beluga, bowhead and humpback whales, salmon, caribou, black bears, grizzlies, polar bears, wolves, foxes, lemmings, etc., because their lives are as valuable as our own. They taught us how to take care of one another. As school children we left food out on the ice for ravens. My grandfather told me to leave fish on the river for the wolves when the rabbits were scarce so they'd leave the dogs in the village alone. When hunting, if an animal has fear in its eyes, it isn't to be killed. Always we are told to treat them with respect, to kill quickly and cleanly, put water in the mouth to release the spirit of the animal and give thanks for their willingness to give life to us.

There is a quiet dignity in the best hunters, skin sewers and the old. They are defined by their ability to be humble and generous with their gifts, and their memories of stories long ago. To be boastful and arrogant is to be small and incomplete. We are taught to shun anger. My grandmother said, "It is easy to be angry. It takes courage to love courage to forgive and courage to be alive. It is an honor and a privilege to carry our blood." So my brother and I grew up believing we were the luckiest people alive to be Iñupiat, to belong to a world that celebrated joy and laughter, that sent us to the ocean to deal with our raging as our worlds collided. We learned that each new day brought with it moments that belonged just to that day and if we were lucky, patient, aware we would carry those moments in our memory forever.

What does this have to do with climate change? I was packing salmon roe for the Japanese in twelve-hour shifts, and had just come home. My grandfather was sitting at his usual spot, on a stump with his cane. I looked up at the clouds, felt the wind, looked out into the horizon and told my grandfather that the rain was coming. He smiled, but did not lift up his eyes. I waited. His smile turned to sadness. I stood still, in hip boots, looking to the ground as he told me, "It doesn't work anymore. The clouds, the wind, everything is changing. What I taught you could get you killed." Only my eyes moved to his face. Slowly the tears escaped down the sides of my face. I nodded to him and left him to the silence of loss no words can express, comfort or fill.

Just Ice—Where My White Blood Breathes

Growing up, people in Unalakleet joked about needing tee shirts with the caption: Endangered Species! First the visitors came to buy furs, and then they came for the herring, whales, gold, salmon, land and oil. My own journey was set out by my great-grandmother when she told me: "Bunichai, you will go to college, university. You will learn how white people think and understand them better than they understand themselves. Always remember you are Iñupiat. If you fail, we will die." I stood looking up at her in the doorway with the sun shining on her, raised my eyebrows and looked down, to acknowledge that I understood and was showing respect for her.

The journey she set my life on—to explore the history, legal and economic system that allows people to righteously plunder the earth—has been extremely painful. I remember to let my white blood breathe and write only when the anger passes and the grace of our Creator, the beauty of the world and hope vibrates. Professor Palmer (Sir Geoffrey Palmer, former Prime Minister of New Zealand) assigned reading and lectured on global warming in his International Environmental Law class at the University of Iowa and sent me to the University of Washington School of Law.

This is an exciting time to be alive. It gives us a wonderful opportunity to join together to create solutions to problems created by our economic, social and political systems. Discover Card has an advertising campaign stating, "We are a nation of consumers...." Imagine a world economic and legal system based on recognizing the sacredness of all living creatures, plants and inanimate objects. What if we threw away the yoke of utility theory, the invisible hand of capitalism and created a world based upon honoring creation? I am dreaming. It's okay to laugh, but consider the consequences if we don't change. We are all, each and every one of us, in the process of destroying the earth's ability to deal with greenhouse gases, acidification of the oceans, overtaxing the planet for our constant need for more. Our laws protect corporations and the markets to an extent anyone can only envy. Our legal system requires harm before it acts. You must be a victim to assert a claim. International human rights standards are woefully inadequate and the mechanisms for addressing genocide, human trafficking, trafficking in endangered species, unjust wars and global warming/climate change save no lives.

Americans must come to terms with loss of international standing and the near total destruction of international public law in the name of national security. The Conventions regarding war and torture have been swept aside to bring democracy to a region of the world most Americans do not understand. International laws governing the markets function with just a hiccup now and again caused by the greed of the market in sub-prime mortgage lending, threatening a worldwide recession due to the bundling of mortgages sold to investors throughout the world.

America claims to have purchased Alaska but Russia never had dominion over us. Our villages are littered with formerly used defense sites loaded with toxic waste. A unilateral act of Congress created twelve, then thirteen, corporations making those of us born before Dec. 18, 1971 shareholders. The corporations must make a profit, even to the detriment of the shareholders at the village level. This venture genuinely destroyed the thousands of years of communal laws where we took care of one another. The corporate leaders are referred to as our leaders as if they are elected to govern our communities. The conflict is huge in villages being impacted by mining, offshore oil and gas lease sales and development. We are families and we love each other. We do not want to hurt each other, but values embraced or imposed create discord. Only one group has money, so only their voices are heard. Those of us who resist are labeled as "radicals." The truth is what my great-grandmother, grandfather and grandmother gave me: the courage to be willing to stand alone, for they told me this life of mine did not belong to me, but belonged to our ancestors and the future. I only hope that somehow my love for them and the world they so willingly made me a part of will flow into the consciousness of the world.

There is a glimmer of hope in Ecuador. It is voting on a Constitutional referendum that would protect the environment. After all my research: court cases, legal theory, climate change, scientific journal articles, and alternative energy, what gives me hope is that one by one the citizens of the world will pick up the banner for our world—whatever name you chose to call it— wilderness, nature or home. Polar bears, ice seals, walrus, and whales require sea ice to survive. Their story needs to be told. It is an incredible chance to rethink the culture wars and allow the places deemed wilderness, barren spaces to be.

Thank you, Professor Rodgers, for allowing me to assemble my thoughts on this new Alaskan import called "Climate Change."

———————

Notes

1. *Cracking up*, NEW SCIENTIST, Aug. 2–8, 2008, p.7 (with a photo of cracking summer ice):

Santa is skating on very thin ice. In 2007 the sea ice at the North Pole was at its thinnest since records began.

Christian Haas of the Alfred Wegener Institute for Polar and Marine Research in Brem - erhaven, Germany, and his team estimated the thickness of late summer ice at the North

Pole in 2001, 2004 and 2007. They found that the ice was on average 1.3 metres thick at the end of the summer in 2007. [While it] used to be thick "old" ice, much of it now is thinner first-year ice, which has had only a single winter to grow.

Earlier studies had already shown that the extent of Arctic sea ice reached its lowest level in 2007, 23 percent below the previous minimum set in 2005. Taken together, the studies suggest that the Arctic could soon be ice-free during summer.

2. Robert T. Anderson, *Alaska Native Rights, Statehood, and Unfinished Business*, 43 Tulsa L. Rev. 17 (2007) (contending that Congress could fix Alaska's problems regarding aboriginal access to fish and game and tribal sovereignty; emphasizing that the Marine Mammal Protection Act, enacted one year after the Alaska Native Claims Settlement Act, exempts Alaska Natives in coastal areas from the moratorium on the harvest of marine mammals. 16 U.S.C. § 1371(b)).

3. On Vickie Steere's reference to Ecuador, see *Forest Rights in Ecuador*, Multinational Monitor, Nov./Dec., 2008, p. 5:

Ecuador's vast environmental preserves now have inalienable legal rights. In a September referendum, Ecuadorian voters backed a new constitution for the country, which includes the right for nature to "exist, persist, maintain and regenerate its vital cycles, structure, functions and its processes in evolution." The new constitution grants legal standing to any person defending those rights in court.

....

[Specifically, the constitutional text reads]: "Any individual, people, community or nationality may demand the observance of the rights of the natural environment before public bodies."

E. The Polar Bear

2007 Tsosie on *Indigenous Environmental Justice* at 1641:

It is ironic that the most sustained attention to the impact of climate change in the Arctic has come not in relation to the Native peoples of the region, but in relation to the documented harm to polar bears in the region.

2008 Lynas at 96–97:

Retreating sea ice can only be bad news for polar bears—even if it is good news for oil companies and hard-nosed American entrepreneurs.

In the lower 48, melting in the Arctic has been summarized, articulated, and framed as an issue of the charismatic polar bear and the Endangered Species Act. Consider:

The petition to list the polar bear as threatened under the Endangered Species Act marks a seminal moment in climate change law as the first time that a species has been listed as threatened on the basis of global warming. This process has sparked extensive discussion, debate, and litigation.

The Executive Summary to the petition submitted by the Center for Biological Diversity on Feb. 17, 2005, is excerpted here:

Introduction

The polar bear (*Ursus maritimus*) faces likely global extinction in the wild by the end of this century as result of global warming. The species' sea-ice habitat is literally melting away. The federal Endangered Species Act ("ESA") requires the protection of a species as "Threatened" if it "is *likely* to become an endangered species within the *foreseeable future* throughout all or a significant portion of its range." 16 U.S.C. § 1532(20) (emphasis added). A species is considered an "endangered species" when it "is in danger of extinction throughout all or a significant portion of its range." 16 U.S.C. § 1532(6). Unfortunately, the endangerment of the polar bear and its likely extinction are all too foreseeable, as both polar bear and climate scientists agree that the species cannot survive the ongoing and projected loss of its sea-ice habitat in a warming Arctic. Absent substantial reductions in emissions of greenhouse gases, by century's end average annual temperatures in the Arctic will likely rise upwards of 7° C (13.6° F) and summer sea ice will decline by 50–100%. The polar bear cannot survive such changes and therefore meets the statutory criteria for protection as Threatened under the ESA.

. . . .

Scientists have been aware of global warming due to greenhouse gas emissions for over 30 years. That global warming is and will be more rapid and pronounced in the Arctic than in other areas of the world has been known and observed for nearly as long. Concern for the fate of the polar bear in a changing climate has been expressed for over a decade. However, in the past two years, with the release of the Arctic Climate Impact Assessment's ("ACIA's") report on *Impacts of a Warming Arctic* (ACIA 2004a), combined with a peer-reviewed analysis by three of the world's foremost experts on polar bears, *Polar bears in a warming climate* (Derocher, A.E., N.J. Lunn, and I. Stirling 2004), that the polar bear faces a very real likelihood of extinction in the foreseeable future cannot be dismissed as mere speculation. Rather, the "best available science" demonstrates that global warming is occurring, that Arctic sea ice is melting, and that absent significant reductions in human-generated greenhouse gases, such continued warming and consequent reduction of sea ice will occur [so] that the polar bear will face severe endangerment and likely extinction in the wild by the end of the century.

. . . .

Global Warming's Impact on the Arctic

Global warming is already having pronounced impacts on the Arctic. In November 2004 the Arctic Climate Impact Assessment's ("ACIA's") report on *Impacts of a Warming Arctic* (ACIA 2004a) was released. The ACIA is "a comprehensively researched, fully referenced, and independently reviewed evaluation of arctic climate change and its impacts for the region and for the world. It has involved an international effort by hundreds of scientists over four years, and also includes the special knowledge of indigenous people" (ACIA 2004a:v). The ACIA report concludes that greenhouse gas driven climate changes "are being experienced particularly intensely in the Arctic. Arctic average temperature has risen at almost twice the rate as the rest of the world in the past few decades. Widespread melting of glaciers and sea ice and rising permafrost temperatures present additional evidence of strong arctic warming" (ACIA 2004a:8). Significantly, "acceleration of these climatic trends is projected to occur during this century, due to ongoing increases in concentrations of greenhouse gases in the earth's atmosphere" (ACIA 2004a:8).

The ACIA's analysis and conclusions regarding Arctic temperature increases are dramatic. For example:

In Alaska and western Canada, winter temperatures have increased by as much as 3–4° C (5–7°F) in the past 50 years. Over the next 100 years, under a moderate emissions scenario, annual average temperatures are projected to rise 3–5°C (5–9°F) over land and up to 7° C (13°F) over the oceans. Winter temperatures are projected to rise by 4–7°C (5–9°F) over land and 7–10°C (13–18°) over the oceans. (ACIA 2004b:2).

This ongoing and projected warming has already and will continue to severely reduce the extent of sea-ice coverage:

> Over the past 30 years, the annual average sea-ice extent has decreased by about 8%, or nearly one million square kilometers (386,100 square miles), an area larger than all of Norway, Sweden, and Denmark (or Texas and Arizona) combined, and the melting trend is accelerating. Sea-ice extent in summer has declined more dramatically than the annual average, with a loss of 15–20% of the late-summer ice coverage. Additional declines of 10–50% in annual average sea-ice extent are projected by 2100. Loss of sea-ice during summer is projected to be considerably greater, with a 5-model average projecting more than a 50% decline by late this century, and some models showing near-complete disappearance of summer sea ice. (ACIA 2004b:3).

....

The Future of Polar Bears in a Warming Arctic

Polar bears are completely dependent upon Arctic sea-ice habitat for survival. Polar bears need sea ice as a platform from which to hunt their primary prey (ringed seals, *Phoca hispida*), to make seasonal migrations between the sea ice and their terrestrial denning areas, and for other essential behaviors such as mating. Unfortunately, the polar bear's sea-ice habitat is quite literally melting away.

Canada's Western Hudson Bay population, at the southern edge of the species' range, is already showing the impacts of global warming. Break-up of the annual ice in Western Hudson Bay is now occurring on average 2.5 weeks earlier than it did 30 years ago. Earlier ice break-up is resulting in polar bears having less time on the ice to hunt seals. Polar bears must maximize the time they spend on the ice feeding before they come ashore, as they must live off built-up fat reserves for up to 8 months before ice conditions allow a return to hunting on the ice. The reduced hunting season has translated into thinner bears, lower female reproductive rates, and lower juvenile survival. While population declines are not yet evident in Hudson Bay, polar bear scientists calculate that if sea-ice trends continue, most female polar bears in the Western Hudson Bay population will be unable to reproduce by the end of the century, and possibly as early as 2012 (Derocher *et al.* 2004). Without reproduction, this population is doomed to extinction.

....

The consequences of future sea-ice reductions for polar bears globally will be severe. According to the ACIA, "the reduction in sea ice is very likely to have devastating consequences for polar bears, ice-dependent seals, and local people for whom these animals are a primary food source." (ACIA 2004b:1). The ACIA concludes that "*polar bears are unlikely to survive as a species if there is an almost complete loss of summer sea-ice cover, which is projected to occur before the end of this century by some climate models.... The loss of polar bears is likely to have significant and rapid consequences for the ecosystems that they currently occupy.*" (ACIA 2004a:58) (emphasis added).

Even short of complete disappearance of sea ice, projected impacts to polar bears from global warming will affect virtually every aspect of the species' existence, in most cases leading to reduced body condition and consequently reduced reproduction or survival:

- The timing of ice formation and break-up will determine how long and how efficiently polar bears can hunt seals. A reduction in the hunting season caused by delayed ice formation and earlier break-up will mean reduced fat stores, reduced body condition, and therefore reduced survival and reproduction.

- Reductions in sea ice will in some areas result in increased distances between the ice edge and land. This will make it more difficult for female bears that den on land to reach their preferred denning areas. Bears will face the energetic trade-off of either leaving the sea ice earlier when it is closer to land or traveling further to reach denning areas. In either case, the result is reduced fat stores and likely reduced survival and reproduction.
- Reductions in sea-ice thickness and concentration will likely increase the energetic costs of traveling as moving through fragmented sea ice and open water is more energy intensive than walking across consolidated sea ice.
- Reduced sea-ice extent will likely result in reductions in the availability of ice-dependent prey such as ringed seals, as prey numbers decrease or are concentrated on ice too far from land for polar bears to reach.
- Global warming will likely increase the rates of human/bear interactions, as greater portions of the Arctic become more accessible to people and as polar bears are forced to spend more time on land waiting for ice formation. Increased human/bear interactions will almost certainly lead to increased polar bear mortality.
- The combined effects of these impacts of global warming on individual bears' reproduction and survival are likely to ultimately translate into impacts on polar bear populations. Impacts will be most severe on female reproductive rates and juvenile survival. In time, reduction in these key demographic factors will translate into population declines and extirpations.

....

Summarizing the various likely impacts of global warming on the polar bear, Derocher *et al.* (2004:172) come to the following sobering conclusion:

> In contrast to many terrestrial and most marine species that may be able to shift northward as the climate warms, polar bears are constrained in that the very existence of their habitat is changing and there is limited scope for a northward shift in distribution. Due to the long generation time of polar bears and the current pace of climate warming, we believe it unlikely that polar bears will be able to respond in an evolutionary sense. Given the complexity of ecosystem dynamics, predictions are uncertain but *we conclude that the future persistence of polar bears is tenuous.* (emphasis added).

In addition to the suite of impacts from global warming, polar bears also face additional threats such as increasing oil exploration and development and risk of oil spills throughout the Arctic, serious impacts to the immune system and reproductive system from exceptionally high levels of contaminants such as PCBs, unsustainable hunting and illegal poaching in some areas, and increased human activity in the Arctic. Global warming will likely interact with several of these additional threats in a synergistic and cumulative fashion, further increasing the polar bear's peril.

Existing Legal Mechanisms are Inadequate to Address Global Warming and Prevent the Likely Extinction of the Polar Bear

Global warming due to anthropogenic greenhouse gas emissions is the primary threat to polar bears, and also one of the most difficult threats to regulate. Despite the scientific consensus that global warming is in fact occurring, and will have dramatic effects across the world, greenhouse gas emissions continue to increase both globally and domestically. Existing regulatory mechanisms such as the United Nations Framework Convention on Climate Change and the Kyoto Protocol have to date been completely ineffective at actually reducing greenhouse gas emissions. At best, they have slowed the *rate of increase.* However, even if fully implemented (an unlikely scenario given the United States, the world's largest emitter of greenhouse gases, has officially renounced the Kyoto Protocol), these mechanisms will not reduce greenhouse gas emissions sufficiently to avoid the warming of the Arctic and consequent adverse impacts to polar bears that are *already occurring* or will occur by the end of the century. As such, it is clear that existing regulatory mechanisms are inadequate to prevent the polar bear from becoming an endangered species in the foreseeable future.

....

In 1997 the Kyoto Protocol became the first additional agreement added to the UNFCCC to set emissions targets. The Kyoto Protocol set goals for developed countries only to reduce their emissions to at least 5% below their 1990 levels (UNFCCC 2004). Over seven years passed before the Kyoto Protocol entered into force on February 16, 2005 (UNFCCC 2005). While the entry into force of the Kyoto Protocol is an important symbolic first step in the necessary global response to climate change, it is inadequate to prevent sufficient build-up of greenhouse gases to avoid significant warming of the Arctic and the consequent likely extinction of the polar bear. First, the Protocol's overall emissions targets are highly unlikely to be met, due in large part to the refusal of the United States to ratify the agreement. The United States accounts for approximately *24% of worldwide carbon dioxide emissions* (EIA 2004). The Kyoto target for the United States was a 7% reduction in greenhouse gas emission levels from 1990 levels by 2012 (EIA 2004). According to the U.S. Government Accounting Office ("GAO"), between 1990 and 2001, United States emissions have in fact *increased* by 13%. Total United States emissions are projected to grow a staggering additional *43.5% through the period 2025* (GAO 2003a). The United States simply will not meet Kyoto targets by the Protocol's 2012 deadline. Without United States compliance, global Kyoto targets are unlikely to be met. Overall, the EIA estimates that worldwide carbon emissions in 2025 will exceed 1990 levels by 72% (EIA 2004).

Moreover, even in the unlikely event that overall Kyoto targets were fully met by the year 2012, the reductions are far too small to substantially reduce Arctic warming and consequent sea-ice reduction sufficiently to protect the polar bear. Implementation of the Kyoto Protocol would only slightly reduce the rate of growth of emissions—it would not stabilize them (Williams 2002).

....

Most significantly, the ACIA projections of likely polar bear extinctions are based upon climate models that already assume future reductions in greenhouse gas emissions. Predictions of 50–100% loss of summer sea ice come from models using projected emissions levels that fall slightly *below* the average of possible scenarios. Actual impacts will likely be much greater. Only by implementing major cuts in greenhouse gas emissions in the very near future will a scenario be possible in which sufficient sea ice remains that the polar bear can persist as a species.

Conclusion

The future of the polar bear is indeed grim. While most populations are currently reasonably healthy and the global population is not presently endangered, the species as a whole faces the likelihood of severe endangerment and possible extinction by the end of the century. As such, it will be endangered in the foreseeable future and therefore meets the criteria for listing now as Threatened under the ESA. While the polar bear will likely not disappear for several decades, decisions made and actions taken over the next decade will likely dictate whether the species can survive. Only with prompt action to drastically reduce greenhouse gas emissions can the future of the polar bear be assured. The United States must play a leading role in this global effort. Listing the species under the ESA is a small but significant step in that direction.

Response to the Polar Bear Petition

The petition was filed on February 17, 2005, but the FWS response to the petition has been fraught with delay and avoidance. Although legally required to issue a proposed rule within one year from the receipt of a listing petition, the FWS failed to make a 12-month finding. Finally, after legal action taken by the Center for Biological Diversity, Greenpeace, and NRDC, the US Fish and Wildlife Service (FWS) published a proposed rule to list the polar bear as threatened on January 9, 2007. 72 Fed. Reg. 1064 (January 9, 2007). The FWS then had one year to publish a final rule. Yet, one year came and went with no rule. Once again, plaintiffs filed suit to compel publication of the final rule.

In *Center for Biological Diversity v. Kempthorne*, 2008 WL 1902703 (N.D.Cal. April 28, 2008) (Claudia Wilken, D.J.) the court granted plaintiffs' motion for summary judgment to compel the US Fish and Wildlife Service (USFWS) to publish a final listing determination on the polar bear, *Ursus maritimus*, by May 15, 2008. The decision outlines the USFWS's history of unexcused delays and the ample notice provided the agency as reasons for setting a short deadline for publication of the final listing decision. *Id.* at 3.

In compliance with the court's injunction, the FWS issued a final rule listing the polar bear as threatened under the Endangered Species Act. 73 Fed. Reg. 28212 (May 15, 2008). The reasons cited for the listing were the extensive and devastating loss of sea ice upon which polar bears depend for survival, from hunting to bearing young.

The cause for the unprecedented loss of sea ice is anthropogenic global warming. Nonetheless, the FWS excluded regulation of greenhouse gases from the protective measures available to polar bears under the ESA. By default, species listed as threatened receive the same protections as those listed as endangered. The Secretary, however, has the ability to curtail the protections for threatened species through a "4(d) rule." The FWS took advantage of this option to eviscerate the protections extended to the polar bear. 73 Fed. Reg. 28306 (May 15, 2008). The FWS determined that there was not a sufficient causal link between greenhouse gas emissions from a given federal action and harm to a listed species to require § 7 consultation. *Id.* at 28313.

This action catalyzed a number of legal challenges. Environmental organizations are challenging the validity of the 4(d) rule, while the State of Alaska and sport hunters are challenging the validity of the listing.

See Marsha Walton, *Polar bear now listed as "threatened" species*, CNN, May 14, *available at:* http://www.cnn.com/2008/TECH/science/05/14/polar.bears.listing/index.html (last visited August 9, 2008).

Notes

1. Meanwhile, as polar bear listing proceeds and as the ice disappears, it is the Alaska Natives that have taken on a fair share of the global warming litigation burden. The Hon. Ralph R. Beistline has been unsympathetic to a variety of NEPA, Marine Mammal Protection Act, Outer Continental Shelf Lands Act, and APA challenges. The State of Alaska has intervened in these lawsuits and is championing the cause of BP, Shell, the Minerals Management Service, and the National Marine Fisheries Service. *See, e.g., North Slope Borough and Alaska Eskimo Whaling Comm'n v. Minerals Management Service*, 2007 WL 1106110 (D.Alask. April 12, 2007) (Ralph R. Beistline, D.J.). In this case a 4-volume EIS was prepared in 2003 on three lease sales in the Beaufort Sea. Comments by plaintiffs "highlighted concerns about unprecedented industry interest in the Beaufort Sea, unrealistic single-filed development scenarios for Lease Sale 202, impacts from

seismic testing, and potentially significant cumulative impacts from seismic testing and climate change on subsistence and polar bears," p. 1. This NEPA challenge seeks supplementation of the 2003 EIS and argues that the 2003 picture has changed significantly due to "higher oil prices, more leases than expected sold in the far/ deepwater zones during lease sales 186 and 195, and the cumulative impact of climate change and increased industry interest in the Beaufort Sea on subsistence and polar bears," p. 3. Irreparable harm is alleged "from the effects of seismic testing on whales, seals, caribou, and waterfowl," p. 3. The court denies the motion for preliminary injunction, saying it is unlikely that plaintiffs could prevail on the merits, "especially in light of NEPA's purpose to ensure that environmental considerations are taken into account, but not necessarily elevated over other appropriate considerations," *citing Baltimore Gas & Elec. Co. v. Natural Resources Defense Council*, 462 U.S. 87, 97). Other decisions include *Native Village of Point Hope v. Minerals Management Service*, 564 F. Supp. 2d 1077 (D. Alask. July 2, 2008) (Ralph R. Beistline, D.J.) (granting state's motion to intervene and denying motion for preliminary injunction while dismissing the case), *later decision*, 2008 WL 2736040 (D. Alask. July 9, 2008) (denying motion for injunction pending appeal). This case was a NEPA / MMPA / OCSLA / APA challenge to the issuance of permits to oil companies for seismic surveys during the summer and fall of 2008 in the Chukchi and Beaufort Seas. The challenged agency action included an "incidental harassment authorization" authorizing Shell and its contractor to "take" marine mammals during these seismic surveys. *Id* at 1080: "Plaintiffs allege that a single survey may harm tens of thousands of marine mammals" and that this will adversely affect subsistence. The issue? *See id.* at 1081 (emphasis added): "whether NMFS and MMS violated NEPA by authorizing seismic surveys *before* completing the EIS currently underway to evaluate the impacts of, and alternatives to, the entire seismic survey program for the Beaufort and Chukchi Seas." There appears to be a clear violation of 40 C.F.R. § 1506.1(d) but this court boldly concludes, *id.* at 1084:

> The court agrees that the decision to prepare a Programmatic EIS on a hypothetical future level of seismic activity in the Arctic Ocean does not undermine the Agencies' issuance of the EAs / FONSIs for the specific activities in this case. Accordingly, the Court finds that it is consistent with NEPA's implementing regulations for the agencies to have issued EAs for the three G&G [geological and geophysical exploration] permits and one IHA [incidental harassment authorization] in question, notwithstanding the determination to conduct an EIS covering an anticipated increase in the level of seismic activity in the future.

Judge Beistline thus denies the motion for preliminary injunction and dismisses the case. This federal judge has become the "voice of the courts" for the great breakdown and melting in the Beaufort and Chukchi Seas. The case is an obvious "leap before you look" and represents all that NEPA denies. Environmental considerations are completely swamped by the State's arguments against "immediate and substantial harm," delay in development, the interference with "very long lead times," and "loss of production and income tax revenue, royalties, and an increase in the Trans-Alaska pipeline tariff rate." This is another important global warming ruling without mention of the phenomenon.

2. Judge Beistline's treatment of the NEPA / OSCLA issues is repudiated by the Ninth Circuit's ruling in *Alaska Wilderness League and REDOIL (Resisting Environmental Destruction on Indigenous Lands) v. Kempthorne*, 548 F.3d 815 (9th Cir. Nov. 20, 2008), discussed below in ch. 4 (p. 703).

3. *See* Marcilynn A Burke, *Green Peace? Protecting our National Treasures While Providing for Our National Security*, 32 Wm. & Mary L. & Pol'y Rev. 803 (2008).

4. Lloyd Miller, *Palin and Alaska Natives and Tribes*, Sept. 12, 2008:

Perhaps no issue is of greater importance to Alaska Native peoples as the right to hunt and fish according to ancient customary and traditional practices, and to carry on the subsistence way of life for future generations.

Governor Sarah Palin has consistently opposed those rights.

Once in office, Governor Palin decided to continue litigation that seeks to overturn every subsistence fishing determination the federal government has ever made in Alaska. (*State of Alaska v. Norton*, 3:05-cv-0158-HRH (D. Ak).) In pressing this case, Palin decided against using the Attorney General (which usually handles State litigation) and instead continued contracting with Senator Ted Stevens' brother-in-law's law firm (Birch, Horton, Bittner & Cherot).

The goal of Palin's law suit is to invalidate all the subsistence fishing regulations the federal government have issued to date to protect Native fishing, and to force the courts instead to take over the role of setting subsistence regulations. Palin's law suit seeks to diminish subsistence fishing rights in order to expand sport and commercial fishing.

Lloyd Miller is an Anchorage attorney with a specialty in Alaska Native issues.

5. *Carijano v. Occidental Petroleum Corp.*, 548 F. Supp .2d 823 (C.D. Cal. 2008) (25 members of the Achuar indigenous group who live along the Rio Corrientes River in the northern region of Peru and Amazon Watch sue Occidental Petroleum for oil exploration operations alleged to contaminate the Peruvian environment with hazardous substances, water pollution, etc. A wide-range of nuisance-plus theories are alleged, including trespass, medical monitoring, and the like. This motion to dismiss on *forum non conveniens* grounds is resisted by plaintiffs who want discovery on the functionality of the Peruvian legal system including corruption. But the court denies the discovery request; defendant consents to service in Peru and carries its burden of demonstrating that an adequate forum exists in Peru with an affidavit from a Peruvian attorney who attests to the bold tort theories available there. Plaintiffs counter with their own expert on Peruvian justice who says: "[w]ithin the Judiciary, there can be racism towards indigenous peoples on the part of guards, secretaries, officials, and the judges themselves," *id.* at 829; *id.* at 832: "Plaintiffs' evidence of corruption falls short of the 'powerful showing' of corruption necessary to defeat a *forum non conveniens* motion." Thus the motion to dismiss is granted).

Figure 3. *North of Arctic Circle, A High School Football Game*, ALL THINGS CONSIDERED, NPR (Oct. 2, 2008). This symbolic photo shows a lone polar bear presiding at a deserted high school football field in Barrow, Alaska.

Figure 4. Arctic sea ice is shrinking at an alarming rate, from THE ECONOMIST, Economist.com (August 29, 2008), http://www.economist.com/daily news/PrinterFriendly.cfm?story_id=12031918. This symbolic photo shows a healthy polar bear staring down above a map of the Arctic and its shrinking ice. For a less symbolic expression of the plight of the polar bear, see Anna T. Moritz, Kassie R. Siegel, Brendan R. Cummings, and William H. Rodgers, Jr., *Biodiversity Baking and Boiling: Endangered Species Act Turning Down the Heat*, 44 TULSA L. REV. 205 (2008).

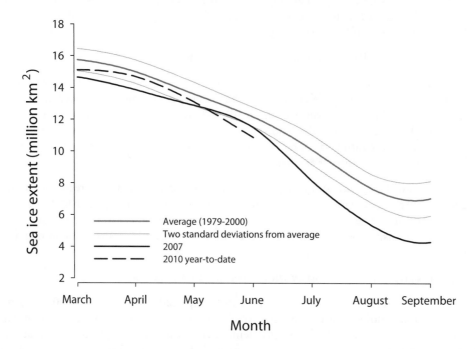

Figure 5. Extent of Arctic sea ice in precipitous decline. In recent years sea ice extent has fallen far below the normal range of sea ice extent between 1979 and 2000. The decline has been particularly marked at the summer minimum. Data source: Fetterer, F., K. Knowles, W. Meier, and M. Savoie. 2002, updated 2009. *Sea Ice Index.* Boulder, CO: National Snow and Ice Data Center. Digital media.

F. The New Grave-Robbers

No human or ecological catastrophe is sufficiently severe to dull the entrepreneurial response of the legally gifted or economically blessed. They raised the prices of lemonade in the wake of Katrina. Opportunity can swell the chests of ugly nationalism. Consider:

2008 Lynas at 95–96:

[On what the New York Times describes as "the Great Game in a cold climate."] Internationally, Arctic Ocean nations Canada, Denmark, the United States, Norway, and Russia are battling to establish undersea mineral rights to "their" sections of the seabed. In August 2007 Russian explorers mounted a particularly audacious land grab by piloting a submersible under the ice and planting a rustproof metal flag on the seabed 4,000 meters below the North Pole, thereby claiming the entire area, and its fossil fuel riches, for the motherland. "We are happy that we placed a Russian flag on the ocean bed, and I don't give a damn what some foreign individuals think about that," declared expedition leader Artur Chilingarov haughtily as he returned to a hero's welcome — complete with champagne and ranting pro-Kremlin youth groups — in Moscow. Stretching unintended irony to the breaking point, the triumphant Chilingarov was then handed a large furry toy polar bear — the emblem of the pro-Putin party United Russia (of which Chilingarov is a parliamentary deputy), as a military brass band played. The [U.S.] State Department was studiously unmoved....

Arctic Sovereignty: Cold Facts, Hot Issues

J. Ashley Roach. Captain, JAGC, U.S. Navy (ret'd), Office of the Legal Adviser (L/OES), U.S. Department of State.

It is my intention to provide an overview of the legal issues posed by melting of the ice in the Arctic.[1]

My specific charge is to help define and clarify the issues concerning sovereignty, territoriality and maritime passage in the Arctic Ocean that are coming into focus as large-scale navigation becomes feasible in these waters.

My first point is that consideration of these issues is timely now *before* large-scale navigation becomes feasible. It will take considerable time to identify and agree on the steps that will be needed to ensure the safety, security and environmental protection of the Arctic Ocean, and even more time to put them in place.

And we need to be aware that these issues are not just of concern to Canada and the United States. These issues are of concern to all five states bordering on the Arctic, the other states in the high north,[2] and flag states whose shipping might wish to ply these waters *when* they become suitable for commercial navigation.

1. Terminology

As a preliminary matter, it is important to be aware of the differences in "Arctic" terminology and definitions, which vary broadly:[3]

> Geographically, the Arctic consists of all land, submerged lands, and water north of the Arctic Circle (66° 33' 39" N).

> The U.S. Arctic Research Council statute includes a broader area, including the Bering Sea and a portion of the land area of Alaska below the Arctic Circle.[4]

> The Canadian Arctic Waters Pollution Prevention Act defines the Arctic as all Canadian land and waters north of 60° N (*i.e.*, the Northwest Territories).[5]

> Other definitions include where permafrost begins.[6]

Land territory north of the Arctic Circle includes northern Alaska, northern mainland Canada abutting the Bering Sea (the Northwest Territories), the Canadian Arctic islands (which

---

1. This paper updates and annotates a presentation by the author on March 7, 2008 for the Canadian Studies Program of the University of California, Berkeley, online at www.ias.berkeley.edu/ canada/icemelting/ roach.doc (17 August 2008). It also has been submitted in conjunction with a conference at the Southwestern Law School.

2. *See, e.g.*, report of 9–10 Sept 2008 Ilulissit Nordic Council Ministers' Arctic Conference *Common Concern for the Arctic*, to be published 29 Sept 2008, http://www.norden.org/conference.arctic20-8/Konference%20report.adsp (18 Sept. 2008); EU Commissioner for Fisheries and Maritime Affairs Jo Borg address to conference, 15 Sept. 2008, http://www.bymnews.com/news/newsDetails.php?id=42719 (15 Sept 2008); A. Arioldi, *The European Union and the Arctic: Policies and actions*, NORDIC COUNCIL OF MINISTERS, ANP 2008:729 (29 June 2008), online at http://norden.org/pub/miljo/miljo/sk/ANP2008729.pdf (30 August 2008).

3. *See* http://en.wikipedia.org/wiki/Arctic (17 August 2008).

4. 15 U.S.C. §4112 ("all United States and foreign territory north of the Arctic Circle and all United States territory north and west of the boundary formed by the Porcupine, Yukon, and Kuskokwim Rivers; all contiguous seas, including the Arctic Ocean and the Beaufort, Bering, and Chukchi Seas; and the Aleutian chain.").

5. Canadian Arctic Waters Pollution Prevention Act, as amended, section 2, online at http://www.tc.gc.ca/acts-regulations/general/a/awppa/act/awppa.htm (17 August 2008).

6. On melting permafrost and its positive feedback on climate change, see GABRIELLE WALKER AND SIR DAVID KING, THE HOT TOPIC AND WHAT WE CAN DO ABOUT GLOBAL WARMING 73–75 (Greystone Books 2008).

Canada calls the Canadian "arctic archipelago"[7]), Greenland (Denmark), Svalbard/Spitzbergen (Norway), northern Norway, northern Sweden, northern Finland, and the Russian territory of Franz Josef Land, Novaya Zemlya, North Land, Anjou Islands, Wrangel Island and northern Siberia.

Arctic submerged lands consist of the "continental shelf" and the "deep seabed." The "continental shelf" is the natural prolongation of the land mass, out to 200 nm automatically—and beyond where it meets the geological criteria of article 76 of the Law of the Sea (LOS) Convention. The "deep sea bed" is the sea floor beyond the continental shelf.[8]

Defining the Arctic Ocean is much like defining the Arctic; neither has a definitive and obvious extent.[9] As with the Arctic, the United States has an interest in not subscribing to one particular definition of the Arctic Ocean for all purposes. Rather each definition serves its own purpose.

There is a definition adopted by the International Hydrographic Organization (IHO) in 1953; it defines the Arctic Ocean by a series of segments that includes all the waters, whether or not frozen, seaward of the northern limits of the United States, Canada, Denmark (Greenland), Norway, and Russia. This definition includes several "seas," such as the Beaufort, Chukchi, Norwegian, Barents, Laptev, and Greenland Seas, as well as Baffin Bay.[10] As a member of the IHO, the United States agrees with this definition in the context of providing uniformity to mariners for navigational purposes (the primary purpose of this organization).

I make this point in part to recall that the entrance to the Arctic Ocean from the Pacific Ocean is through the Bering Strait. I suggest that consideration of issues concerning shipping in the Arctic Ocean need to begin to focus on that chokepoint rather than further north.

2. Maritime Zones

Next, let me briefly explain the different maritime zones in the Arctic Ocean: these are territorial seas, exclusive economic zones (EEZ), continental shelves, the deep seabed beyond the limits of national jurisdiction (*i.e.*, the Area) and high seas. These are the same zones found in other ocean areas, such as the Pacific and Atlantic.

Each of the five States bordering the Arctic Ocean has claimed an EEZ in the waters beyond and adjacent to its territorial sea, in which it enjoys sovereign rights for the purpose of exploring and exploiting, conserving and managing the natural resources, whether living or non-living, of the waters superjacent to the seabed and of the seabed and its subsoil, and in the same area, jurisdiction with regard to protection and preservation of the marine environment.[11]

The maximum breadth of the EEZ is 200 nm measured from baselines determined in accordance with the LOS Convention.[12]

Each of these five States has a continental shelf over which it has exclusive sovereign rights for the purpose of exploring it and exploiting its natural resources.[13]

---

7. While this area is an archipelago in the geographic sense, this area does not meet the definition of an archipelagic State in Part IV of the Law of the Sea Convention because Canada is not an island nation and therefore Canada is not entitled to draw archipelagic straight baselines enclosing these features.

8. Law of the Sea Convention, article 1(1)(1).

9. *See* http://en.wikipedia.org/wiki/Arctic_Ocean (16 August 2008).

10. http://www.iho-ohi.net/english/home/

11. *See* http://www.un.org/Depts/los/LEGISLATIONANDTREATIES/claims.htm (17 August 2008).

12. LOS Convention, article 57.

13. LOS Convention, article 77.

The continental shelf may extend more than 200 nm from properly established baselines if the geologic criteria set out in article 76 of the LOS Convention are met.[14]

For Parties to the LOS Convention (which includes the other four countries), the Convention sets forth a procedure for establishment of the outer limits of the shelf beyond 200 nm. If the coastal State establishes its outer limits on the basis of recommendations of the Convention's Commission on the Limits of the Continental Shelf (Commission), the limits are considered "final and binding."[15]

Russia and Norway have made submissions to the Commission but it has not yet made its recommendations on the outer limit of their extended shelves.[16] As is known, Russia is collecting additional data to substantiate its submission.[17]

Denmark,[18] Canada,[19] and the United States[20] are in the process of collecting the necessary scientific data to support their submissions/establishment. (The United States may not make a submission unless it is a party to the LOS Convention.) In that connection, earlier this year Canadian and U.S. scientists collected bathymetric and multi-channel seismic data of the sea floor in the northern and eastern portions of the Arctic where our shelves join. This involved both a United States and a Canadian icebreaker each doing what the other could not do.[21] Canada and Denmark did similar joint work last summer.[22]

The "Area" consists of the seabed and ocean floor and subsoil thereof beyond the limits of national jurisdiction (i.e., beyond the outer limits of the continental shelf). Under the LOS Convention, deep seabed mining in the Area is administered by the International Seabed Authority.[23]

The water column more than 200 nm from land in the Arctic Ocean, whether or not frozen, is "high seas" where: high seas freedoms apply, and no State may validly purport to subject any part of the high seas to its sovereignty.[24]

3. Maritime boundaries

In this area, not all the maritime boundaries have been agreed.

---

14. *See* Commission on the Limits of the Continental Shelf, Scientific and Technical Guidelines, online at http://www.un.org//Depts/los/clcs_new/commission_documents.htm#Guidelines, (document CLCS/11. as amended, 2000) (August 25, 2008); Continental Shelf Limits: The Scientific and Legal Interface (PJ Cook and CM Carleton, eds., Oxford Un. Press 2000); Division for Ocean Affairs and the Law of the Sea, Office of Legal Affairs, United Nations, The Law of the Sea: Definition of the Continental Shelf: An Examination of the Relevant Provisions of the United Nations Convention on the Law of the Sea (UN Sales No. E.93.V.16, 1993).

15. LOS Convention, article 76(8).

16. *See* http://www.un.org//Depts/los/clcs_new/clcs_home.htm (17 August 2008).

17. M. Benitah, *Russia's Claim in the Arctic and the Vexing Issue of Ridges in UNCLOS*, 11 ASIL Insight, issue 27, Nov. 8, 2007, *available at* http://www.asil.org/insights/2007/11/insights071108.html (2 September 2008); Sagalevitch, *Under the Ice Dome at the Geographic North Pole*, Sea Technology, Dec. 2007, at 10–13, http://www.sea-technology.com.

18. *See* http://a76dk (last visited August 18, 2008).

19. *See* http://www.international.gc.ca/continental/limits-continental-limites.aspx?lang=eng&menu_id= 20&menu=R (last visited August 18, 2008).

20. *See* http://www.state.gov/g/oes/continentalshelf/ (last visited August 18, 2008).

21. *See* http://www.state.gov/r/pa/prs/ps/2008/aug/108119.htm (last visited August 17, 2008).

22. *See* http://a76.dk/expeditions_uk/lomrog2007_uk/lomonosov_cma_2007.html (last visited August 18, 2008).

23. LOS Convention, article 1(1)(1); http://www.isa.org.jm/en/home (last visited August 17, 2008).

24. LOS Convention, articles 87, 89.

There are five maritime boundary situations in the Arctic Ocean where adjacent/opposite States have overlapping maritime claims: U.S.-Russia, U.S.-Canada, Canada-Denmark,[25] Denmark-Norway,[26] and Norway-Russia.[27]

The United States-Russia maritime boundary—running from the Bering Sea north to the Arctic—has been negotiated. The 1990 United States–USSR (now Russia) treaty is being applied provisionally pending ratification by the Russian Duma.[28] The U.S. Senate gave its advice and consent in 1992.[29] The treaty provides that the maritime boundary extends north along the 168° 58' 37" meridian through the Bering Strait and Chukchi Sea into the Arctic Ocean "as far as is permitted under international law."[30] The Russian submission to the Commission on the Limits of the Continental Shelf respects this boundary. Russia does not claim extended continental shelf on the US (east) side of this line.[31]

The United States and Canada disagree on the location of the maritime boundary in the Beaufort Sea and northward. Canada considers that the maritime boundary follows the 141st

---

25. Agreement between the Government of the Kingdom of Denmark and the Government of Canada relating to the Delimitation of the Continental Shelf between Greenland and Canada, signed Dec. 17, 1973, entered into force March 13, 1974, 950 UNTS 147, I INTERNATIONAL MARITIME BOUNDARIES 371–385 (Greenland) (J. Charney & L. Alexander eds, 1993); LIS 72; V. PRESCOTT & C. SCHOFIELD, THE MARITIME POLITICAL BOUNDARIES OF THE WORLD 527–528 (Nijhoff, 2d ed, Brill Academic Publishers 2005).

26. Agreement between the Government of the Kingdom of Denmark and the Government of the Kingdom of Norway concerning the delimitation of the continental shelf in the area between the Faroe Islands and Norway and the boundary between the fishery zone near the Faroe Islands and the Norwegian economic zone, signed June 15, 1979, entered into force June 3, 1979, 1211 UNTS 169, II INTERNATIONAL MARITIME BOUNDARIES 1711–1718 (J. Charney & L. Alexander eds. 1993); Agreement between the Kingdom of Denmark and the Kingdom of Norway concerning the delimitation of the continental shelf in the area between Jan Mayen and Greenland and concerning the boundary between the fishery zones in the area, signed December 18, 1995, entered into force May 27, 1998, 1903 UNTS 177, III INTERNATIONAL MARITIME BOUNDARIES 2507–2525 (Jan Mayen) (J. Charney & L. Alexander eds. 1998); Additional Protocol to the Agreement of December 18, 1995 between the Kingdom of Norway and the Kingdom of Denmark concerning the Delimitation of the Continental Shelf in the Area between Jan Mayen and Greenland and concerning the boundary between Fishery Zones in the Area, signed November 11, 1997, entered into force May 28, 1998, 2074 UNTS 58, IV INTERNATIONAL MARITIME BOUNDARIES 2913–2920 (J. Charney & L. Alexander eds. 2002); Agreement between the Government of the Kingdom of Norway on the one hand, and the Government of the Kingdom of Denmark together with the Home Rule Government of Greenland on the other hand, concerning the delimitation of the continental shelf and the fisheries zone in the area between Greenland and Svalbard, signed Feb. 20, 2006, entered into force June 2, 2006, PRESCOTT & SCHOFIELD 524.

27. Agreement between the Royal Norwegian Government and the Government of the Union of Soviet Socialist Republics concerning the sea frontier between Norway and the USSR in the Varangerfjørd, signed Feb. 15, 1957, entered into force April 24, 1957, 312 UNTS 323, II INTERNATIONAL MARITIME BOUNDARIES 1781–1789 (J. Charney & L. Alexander eds. 1993), LIS 17; 11 July 2007 agreement re Varangerfjord not in force; PRESCOTT & SCHOFIELD 524–526.

28. Agreement between the U.S. and the USSR to abide by the terms of the maritime boundary agreement of June 1, 1990, pending its entry into force, effected by an exchange of notes at Washington June 1, 1990, entered into force June 1, 1990, TIAS 11451.

29. Senate Executive Report 102–13; resolution of advise and consent approved 86–6, September 16, 1991, Cong. Rec. S13036–S13040, S13009, http://thomas.loc.gov/home/r102query.html (29 August 2008).

30. Senate Treaty Document 101-22, 26 Sept. 1990; 29 ILM 941 (1990); I International Maritime Boundaries 447–460 (J. Charney & L. Alexander eds. 1993). *See* John H. McNeill, *America's Maritime Boundary with the Soviet Union*, NAVAL WAR COLLEGE REVIEW, Summer 1991, at 46–57, *reprinted in*, *Readings on International Law from the Naval War College Review 1978–1994*, 68 INTERNATIONAL LAW STUDIES 219–230 (John Norton Moore and Robert F. Turner eds., 1995), *available at* http://www.nwc.navy.mil/cnws/ild/documents/Naval%20War%20College%20vol%2068.pdf (28 August 2008).

31. *See* http://www.un.org//Depts/los/clcs_new/submissions_files/submission_rus.htm (17 August 2008); PRESCOTT & SCHOFIELD 527.

meridian, which forms the land boundary between Alaska and the Northwest Territories. The United States rejects that the 1825 Anglo-Russian[32] and 1867 Russo-American[33] treaties establishing the land boundary also established the maritime boundary and considers that the boundary should be based on the "equidistance" methodology.[34]

Nevertheless, as described above Canadian and U.S. scientists cooperated this past summer in gathering seismic and bathymetric data related to establishment of the outer limits of their continental shelves in the Arctic.[35]

On February 6, 2008, the U.S. Minerals Management Service held a very successful lease sale of off-shore blocks for oil and gas exploration in the Chukchi Sea. These blocks were well off shore some 60–200 miles, thereby avoiding issues with protected species near-shore.[36]

Subsequently, on July 23, 2008, the U.S. Geologic Survey announced the first publicly available petroleum resources estimate of the entire area north of the Arctic Circle. The survey estimated the areas north of the Arctic Circle have 90 billion barrels of undiscovered, technically recoverable oil; 1,670 trillion cubic feet of technically recoverable natural gas; and 44 billion barrels of technically recoverable natural gas liquids in 25 geologically defined areas thought to have potential for petroleum.[37]

4. Northwest Passage

Then there is the Northwest Passage. Consider 2009 Pollack at 127:

> The Age of Exploration — roughly the sixteenth through the nineteenth centuries — coincided with the Little Ice Age cool interval. In the Arctic Ocean, ice formed in every nook and cranny, including in the many channels that wind their way through the archipelago of islands comprising the northern territory of Canada. This maze of waterways, were they to become ice-free, would allow a maritime shortcut from Europe to the trading nations of Asia, a route shorter by two-thirds compared to the alternative routes around either Africa or South America. This passage, more concept than reality, was called the Northwest Passage.

---

32. Convention between Great Britain and Russia concerning the Limits of the Respective Possessions on the North-West Coast of America and the Navigation of the Pacific Ocean, signed at St. Petersburg 16(28) Feb. 1825, 12 BFSP 38, 75 CTS 95 (article III provides: "The line of demarcation between the Possessions of the High Contracting Parties, upon the Coast of the Continent ... the line of demarcation shall follow the summit of the mountains situated parallel to the Coast, as far as the point of intersection of the 141st degree of West longitude (of the same Meridian); and, finally, from the said point of intersection, the said Meridian Line of the 141st degree, *in its prolongation as far as the Frozen Ocean,* shall form the limit between the Russian and British Possessions on the Continent of America to the North-West". The authentic French text reads " ... *dáns son prolongement jusqu'à la Mer Glaciale*").

33. Article I of the U.S.-Russia Convention ceding Alaska, signed at Washington March 30, 1867, entered into force June 20, 1867, 15 Stat. 539; TS 301; 11 BEVANS 1216; 134 CTS 331 (quoting article III of the 1825 treaty). *See* http://www.law.fsu.edu/library/collection/LimitsinSeas/IBS014.pdf (last visited August 28, 2008).

34. II CUMULATIVE DIGEST OF UNITED STATES PRACTICE IN INTERNATIONAL LAW 1981–1988, at 1889–1890 (M. Nash ed., 1994); PRESCOTT & SCHOFIELD 527–527; DIGEST OF UNITED STATES PRACTICE IN INTERNATIONAL LAW 2005, at 705–707 (S. Cummins ed. 2007).

35. *See* http://www.state.gov/g/oes/continentalshelf/ (last visited August 17, 2008); *Unexplored Arctic Region to be Mapped,* U.S.G.S. Press Release, Sept. 2, 2008, *available at* http://www.usgs.gov/newsroom/articlew.asp?ID=2013&from=rss (last visited Sept. 3, 2008).

36. *See* MMS Alaska News Release, Feb. 6, 2008, *available at* http://www.mms.gov/alaska/latenews/newsrel/News%20Releases%202008/News%20Release%20-%20193%20results%20_2_.pdf (last visited August 17, 2008).

37. *See* http://energy.usgs.gov/arctic/; http://www.usgs.gov/newsroom/article.asp?ID=1980 (last visited August 17, 2008).

The Northwest Passage connects Baffin Bay/Davis Strait in the Atlantic with the Beaufort Sea in the Arctic Ocean, through the waters of Canadian Arctic archipelago.[38] The commercial potential of the passage lies in the reduction, both in distance and time, of the transit between Asia and Europe or the eastern Atlantic.

The United States recognizes Canadian sovereignty over its Arctic islands.[39]

However, the United States—and many other countries—consider the Northwest Passage is a "strait used for international navigation," in which vessels and aircraft are entitled under the LOS Convention to the non-suspendable right of transit passage, in the normal mode, without the permission of, or prior notice to, the State bordering the strait.[40] Canada's right to enforce environmental requirements on transiting vessels in the strait is circumscribed by article 233 of the LOS Convention,[41] except to the extent article 234 on ice-covered areas applies.[42]

Article 234 (on ice-covered areas) of the LOS Convention was adopted following enactment of Canada's Arctic Waters Pollution Prevention Act.[43] One might question whether article 234

---

38. D. Pharand, Northwest Passage: Arctic Straits 2–21 (1984).

39. Remarks of President Bush, Montebello, Quebec, Canada, August 21, 2007, *available at* http://www.whitehouse.gov/news/releases/2007/08/20070821s3.html (" ... the United States does not question Canadian sovereignty over its Arctic islands, and the United States supports Canadian investments that have been made to exercise its sovereignty") (last visited August 29, 2008). *See* M. Carnaghan & A. Goody, Canadian Arctic Sovereignty, Parliamentary Information and Research Service PRB 05-61E, 26 January 2006, *available at* http://www.parl.gc.ca/information/library/PRBpubs/prb0561-e.pdf (last visited August 31, 2008).

40. Remarks of President Bush, Montebello, Quebec, Canada, August 21, 2007, *available at* http://www.whitehouse.gov/news/releases/2007/08/20070821-3.html ("Yes, we'll manage the differences—because there are differences on the Northwest Passage. We believe it's an international passageway.") (last visited August 29, 2008).

41. Article 233 provides the following safeguards with respect to the straits used for international navigation:

> Nothing in sections 5, 6 and 7 affects the legal regime of straits used for international navigation. However, if a foreign ship other than those referred to in section 10 [entitled to sovereign immunity] has committed a violation of the laws and regulations referred to in article 42, paragraph 1(a) and (b) [relating to safety of navigation, regulation of maritime traffic, and the prevention, reduction and control of pollution, by giving effect to applicable international regulations regarding the discharge of oil, oily wastes and other noxious substances in the strait], causing or threatening major damage to the marine environment of the straits, the States bordering the straits may take appropriate enforcement measures and if so shall respect *mutatis mutandis* the provisions of this section.

42. Article 234, which constitutes section 8 and therefore is excluded from the safeguards of article 233, permits coastal States to provide the following special protections for ice-covered areas:

> Coastal States have the right to adopt and enforce non-discriminatory laws and regulations for the prevention, reduction and control of marine pollution from vessels in ice-covered areas within the limits of the exclusive economic zone, where particularly severe climatic condition and the presence of ice covering such area for most of the year create obstructions or exceptional hazards to navigation, and pollution of the marine environment could cause major harm to or irreversible disturbance of the ecological balance. Such laws and regulations shall have due regard to navigation and the protection and preservation of the marine environment based on the best available scientific evidence.

Thus, article 234, to the extent it is applicable, permits the coastal State to take unilateral actions consistent with the article without seeking approval of the IMO. However, pursuant to article 236, article 234 does not apply to vessels entitled to sovereign immunity. *See* J.A. ROACH & R.W. SMITH, UNITED STATES RESPONSES TO EXCESSIVE MARITIME CLAIMS 339–353 (2d ed. 1996); IV UNITED NATIONS CONVENTION ON THE LAW OF THE SEA 1982: A COMMENTARY 392–398 (S. Rosenne & A. Yankov eds. 1991).

43. Canada's Arctic Waters Pollution Prevention Act was first enacted in 1970. Current text is codified in Chapter A-12 of the Revised Statutes of Canada, 1985, *available at* http://laws.justice.gc.ca/en/A-12/; http://www.tc.gc.ca/acts-regulations/general/a/awppa/act/awppa.htm (last visited August 28, 2008). Implementing regulations may be found at http://tc.gc.ca/acts-regulations/general/A/awppa/menu.htm (last visited

will continue to provide international legitimacy for that Act if or when Canada's arctic waters are no longer covered with ice "for most of the year" and no longer "create obstructions or exceptional hazards to navigation."[44]

Figure 6. How drastically has sea ice receded? For a daily image of sea ice extent, see the National Snow and Ice Data Center's Arctic Sea Ice News and Data Analysis website at http:// nsidc.org/arcticseaicenews/.

Canada claims the waters of the Northwest Passage are internal and that, therefore, Canadian consent is necessary for passage.[45] Canada also asserts the right to impose on vessels transiting the Northwest Passage environmental regulations of its choosing.[46] The United States rejects the Canadian claim—it does not meet the criteria for historic title, and article 35(a), which prevents drawing of straight baselines from altering the previous navigational rights, applies to the Canadian Arctic.[47]

In January 1988, Canada and the United States reached a pragmatic agreement (Agreement) applicable to a limited class of U.S. vessels, *i.e.*, icebreakers (all of which belong to the U.S. Coast Guard).[48] The Agreement, which was expressly without prejudice to either country's position on the status of the Northwest Passage, provides for U.S. icebreakers to conduct marine scientific research during the transit and, as such, for the United States to seek Canada's consent prior to such passage.[49] Subsequent transits by U.S. Coast Guard icebreakers of the Northwest Passage have all taken place in accordance with this Agreement.[50] The Agreement, however, does not cover transit of other types of ships.[51]

The U.S. Navy conducts submerged transits throughout the Northwest Passage and the Arctic region. The Arctic is a particularly advantageous pathway for shifting submarines between the Atlantic and Pacific fleets. Such transits are quicker, more covert, more fuel efficient, more cost effective, and provide greater force protection in comparison to alternative transits through the Panama Canal. In addition to these transits, U.S. naval forces conduct transits, training and op-

---

August 29, 2008). On August 27, 2008, Prime Minister Harper announced intentions to extend the act to 200 nm. Press release August 27, 2008, *PM Announces Government of Canada Will Extend Jurisdiction over Arctic Waters, available at* http://www.conservative.ca/EN/1091/101728 (last visited August 31, 2008).

44. These terms are not defined in the Convention, and the *traveaux preparatoire* are unrevealing.

45. M. Byers & Suzanne Lalonde, *Who controls the Northwest Passage?, available at* http://www.liu. xplorex.com/sites/liu/files/Publications/7Jun2006ArcticWatersDiscussionPaper.pdf (last visited August 31, 2008); Canada Senate Report, *The Coast Guard in Canada's Arctic: Interim Report,* June 2008, *available at* http://www.parl.gc.ca/39/2/parlbus/commbus/senate/com-e/fish-e/rep-e/rep04jun08-e.pdf (last visited August 31, 2008).

46. Article 234 only applies "within the limits of the exclusive economic zone," which on its face means from the outer limit of the territorial sea to 200 nautical miles measured from baselines determined in accordance with international law. LOS Convention, article 3, 55 & 57. The Virginia Commentary inexplicitly states that the zone "refers to that part of the sea extending from the outer limits of the coastal State's exclusive economic zone to that State's coastline". IV COMMENTARY 397 para. 234.5(d).

47. *See* ROACH & SMITH, UNITED STATES RESPONSES TO EXCESSIVE MARITIME CLAIMS 96–100, 340 n.93; ROACH & SMITH 351–353 and n.102; DIGEST OF UNITED STATES PRACTICE IN INTERNATIONAL LAW 2006, at 814–815 (S. Cummins ed. 2007).

48. Agreement on Arctic Cooperation, signed at Ottawa January 11, 1988, entered into force January 11, 1988, TIAS 11565, 1852 UNTS 59, *available at* http://untreaty.un.org/unts/60001_120000/30/4/00058175.pdf (last visited August 29, 2008), para. 3.

49. *Id.* paras. 3 and 4. Article 245 requires the express consent of the coastal State for the conduct of marine scientific research in its territorial sea.

50. ROACH & SMITH 351–353 and n.102; DIGEST OF UNITED STATES PRACTICE IN INTERNATIONAL LAW 2006, at 814–815 (S. Cummins ed. 2007).

51. Agreement on Arctic Cooperation, para. 3, limits the scope of the agreement to US and Canadian icebreakers.

erations in the Arctic region. U.S. force presence in other parts of the Arctic supports U.S. combatant commanders and strategic deterrence. The U.S. submarine force, in particular, is prepared to operate in and project maritime power from the Arctic.[52]

The U.S. Navy also maintains a training presence in the Arctic in order to evaluate tactics, platforms, weapons systems and associated equipment. For example, the submarine force operates temporary ice camps every two years. The most recent camp was in Spring 2007 with the next camp planned for Spring 2009. The U.K.'s Royal Navy shares the use of these camps and conducts cooperative training with U.S. Navy submarines.[53]

Since the early 1970s, the U.S. submarine force has collected Arctic data in support of the scientific community. These activities are conducted on a 'not to interfere' basis with military missions and requirements.[54]

However, rather than debating legal differences, it is much more useful to focus on the extensive, long-term common interests in security, environmental protection and safety of navigation shared between the United States and Canada in the Arctic.

5. Sources of law

In the view of the United States, there are many sources of international law that are applicable to the Arctic Ocean, and, more importantly, available to enhance the security, environmental protection and safety of navigation of the Arctic Ocean.[55] As a result, the United States does not believe it is necessary to develop a new regime of laws for the Arctic, as some have suggested.

The five circumpolar nations share this view. Meeting in Ilulissat, Greenland, 27–29 May 2008, they met at the political level, and adopted the following declaration:[56]

> The Arctic Ocean stands at the threshold of significant changes. Climate change and the melting of ice have a potential impact on vulnerable ecosystems, the livelihoods of local inhabitants and indigenous communities, and the potential exploitation of natural resources.

> By virtue of their sovereignty, sovereign rights and jurisdiction in large areas of the Arctic Ocean the five coastal states are in a unique position to address these possibilities and challenges. In this regard, we recall that an extensive international legal framework applies to the Arctic Ocean as discussed between our representatives at the meeting in Oslo on 15 and 16 October 2007 at the level of senior officials.[57] Notably, the law of the

---

52. R. Burgess, *Cold War?* Seapower Magazine, October 2007, at 15, 17 [hereinafter Seapower Magazine].

53. *See* Seapower Magazine, October 2007, *supra* note 52, at 14.

54. V. Kiernan, *The Big Thaw*, New Scientist, Nov, 2, 1996, *available at* http://www.newscientist.com/article/mg15220548.300-the-big-thaw—for-years-us-navy-scientists-have-been-the-envy-of-their-poorer-civiliancousins-now-the-caring-sharing-pentagon-is-unlocking-some-of-its-most-closelyguarded-secrets.html (2 September 2008).

55. Accord, H. Correll, *Reflections on the possibilities and limitations of a binding legal regime for the Arctic*, address to Arctic Frontiers Tromsø: Balancing human use and ecosystem protection, 22 January 2007, Tromsø, Norway, *available at* http://www.arctic-frontiers.com/index.php?option=com_remository&Itemid= 0&funcstartdown&id=61 (last visited August 31, 2008); D. Currie, Sovereignty and Conflict in the Arctic Due to Climate Change: Climate Change and the Legal Status of the Arctic Ocean, Aug. 5, 2007, http://www.globelaw.com/.

LawSea/arctic%20claims%20and%20climate%20change.pdf (last visited August 31, 2008); D. Rothwell & S. Kaye, *Law of the sea and the polar regions*, 18 Marine Policy 41–58 (1994).

56. Text of the Ilulissat Declaration, *available at* http://www.cop15.dk/NR/rdonlyres/BE00B850-D278-4489-A6BE-6AE230415546/0/ArcticOceanConference.pdf (last visited August 25, 2008).

57. The Norwegian Foreign Ministry issued the following press release describing this meeting:
   At the invitation of the Norwegian Government, representatives of the five coastal States of the Arctic Ocean—Canada, Denmark, Norway, the Russian Federation and the United States of America—met at the level of senior officials on 15 and 16 October 2007 in Oslo, Norway, to hold informal discussions.

sea provides for important rights and obligations concerning the delineation of the outer limits of the continental shelf, the protection of the marine environment, including ice-covered areas, freedom of navigation, marine scientific research, and other uses of the sea. We remain committed to this legal framework and to the orderly settlement of any possible overlapping claims.

This framework provides a solid foundation for responsible management by the five coastal States and other users of this Ocean through national implementation and application of relevant provisions. We therefore see no need to develop a new comprehensive international legal regime to govern the Arctic Ocean. We will keep abreast of the developments in the Arctic Ocean and continue to implement appropriate measures.

The Arctic Ocean is a unique ecosystem, which the five coastal states have a stewardship role in protecting. Experience has shown how shipping disasters and subsequent pollution of the marine environment may cause irreversible disturbance of the ecological balance and major harm to the livelihoods of local inhabitants and indigenous communities. We will take steps in accordance with international law both nationally and in cooperation among the five states and other interested parties to ensure the protection and preservation of the fragile marine environment of the Arctic Ocean. In this regard we intend to work together including through the International Maritime Organization to strengthen existing measures and develop new measures to improve the safety of maritime navigation and prevent or reduce the risk of ship-based pollution in the Arctic Ocean.

The increased use of Arctic waters for tourism, shipping, research and resource development also increases the risk of accidents and therefore the need to further strengthen search and rescue capabilities and capacity around the Arctic Ocean to ensure an appropriate response from states to any accident. Cooperation, including on the sharing of information, is a prerequisite for addressing these challenges. We will work to promote safety of life at sea in the Arctic Ocean, including through bilateral and multilateral arrangements between or among relevant states.

The five coastal states currently cooperate closely in the Arctic Ocean with each other and with other interested parties. This cooperation includes the collection of scientific data concerning the continental shelf, the protection of the marine environment and other scientific research. We will work to strengthen this cooperation, which is based on mutual trust and transparency, inter alia, through timely exchange of data and analyses.

The participants noted recent scientific data indicating that the Arctic Ocean stands at the threshold of significant changes, in particular the impact of melting ice on vulnerable ecosystems, livelihoods of local inhabitants, and potential exploitation of natural resources.

In this regard, they recalled the applicability of an extensive international legal framework to the Arctic Ocean, including notably the law of the sea. They discussed in particular application and national implementation of the law of the sea in relation to protection of the marine environment, freedom of navigation, marine scientific research and the establishment of the outer limits of their respective continental shelves. They discussed cooperative efforts on these and other topics. They also emphasized the commitment of their States to continue cooperation among themselves and with other interested States, including on scientific research.

Text of the news release is *available at* http://www.regjeringen.no/en/dep/ud/press/News/2007/The-Arctic-Ocean—meeting-in-Oslo-.html?id=486239 (last visited August 27, 2008).

The Arctic Council and other international fora, including the Barents Euro-Arctic Council, have already taken important steps on specific issues, for example with regard to safety of navigation, search and rescue, environmental monitoring and disaster response and scientific cooperation, which are relevant also to the Arctic Ocean. The five coastal states of the Arctic Ocean will continue to contribute actively to the work of the Arctic Council and other relevant international fora.

The sources of law applicable to the Arctic Ocean include, *e.g.*:

- the law of the sea, as reflected in the Law of the Sea Convention, which allows the coastal States to claim territorial seas, EEZs, shelf out to 200 nm,[58] shelf beyond 200 nm if it meets the Article 76 criteria,[59] passage rights for foreign flag vessels,[60] high seas freedoms,[61] the consent regime for marine scientific research;[62]
- various IMO agreements on safety of navigation and prevention of marine pollution clearly apply to the Arctic Ocean (*e.g.*, SOLAS,[63] MARPOL and its annexes on vessel source pollution,[64] the London Convention/Protocol on ocean dumping[65]); and
- various air-related agreements that indirectly protect the Arctic, such as the Montreal Protocol on the ozone layer,[66] the Framework Convention on Climate Change,[67] the PICs and POPs Conventions (to which the United States is not yet a party).[68]

There is also so-called "soft law" applicable to the Arctic Ocean, including the IMO guidelines and the Arctic Council guidelines.

IMO Guidelines for Ships Operating in Arctic Ice-Covered Waters (2002),[69] IMO's Enhanced Contingency Planning Guidance for Passenger Ships Operating in Areas Remote from SAR Facili-

---

58. Law of the Sea Convention, article 57.

59. Law of the Sea Convention, article 76.

60. Law of the Sea Convention, articles 17–26 (territorial sea); Part III, Straits Used for International Navigation.

61. Law of the Sea Convention, articles 58 & 87.

62. Law of the Sea Convention, articles 245–257.

63. International Convention for the Safety of Life at Sea, 1974, as amended, *available at* http://www.austlii.edu.au/au/other/dfat/treaties/1983/22.html.

64. Convention for the Prevention of the Ocean by Pollution from Ships, 1973/1978 as amended, http://www.austlii.edu.au/au/other/dfat/treaties/1988/29.html.

65. London Dumping Convention, *available at* http://www.admiraltylawguide.com/conven/dumping1972.html; London Convention Protocol, *available at* http://www.admiraltylawguide.com/conven/protodumping 1996.html.

66. Montreal Protocol on Substances that Deplete the Ozone Layer, with annexes, done at Montreal September 16, 1987, entered into force January 1, 1989, as amended, *available at* http://ozone.unep.org/Ratification_status/evolution_of_mp.shtml (last visited August 27, 2008).

67. United Nations Framework Convention on Climate Change, with annexes, done at New York May 9, 1992, entered into force March 21, 1994, *available at* http://unfccc.int/essential_background/ convention/items/2627.php (last visited August 27, 2008).

68. Rotterdam Convention on the Prior Informed Consent Procedure for Certain Hazardous Chemicals and Pesticides in International Trade, with Annexes, done at Rotterdam, September 10, 1998, Sen. Tr. Doc. 106-21, *available at* http://www.pic.int/home.php?type=t&id=49&sid=16 (last visited Sept. 2, 2008); Stockholm Convention on Persistent Organic Pollutants, with annexes, done at Stockholm May 22–23, 2001, Sen. Tr. Doc. 107-5, Sen. Ex. Rep, 108-8, *available at* http://chm.pops.int/Convention/tabid/54/language/en-US/Default.aspx (last visited Sept. 2, 2008).

69. IMO document MSC/Circ.1056 MEPC/Circ.399, 23 Dec. 2002, *available through links at* www.imo.org. Amendments to these guidelines are under consideration at the IMO. *See* IMO document DE 51/11/2, 27 Dec. 2007 (Finland); DE 51/28, paras. 11.1–11.8 (correspondence group established under Canadian leadership to propose revisions).

ties (2006),[70] the IMO's Guidelines on Voyage Planning for Passenger Ships Operating in Remote Areas (2007)[71] and the Arctic Council Guidelines on Arctic offshore oil/gas activities (1997/2002).[72]

The United States participated actively in the development of, and supports, the IMO Guidelines. The Guidelines for Ships Operating in Arctic Ice-Covered Waters was originally a Canadian initiative. They address construction, equipment, ship operation, and environmental protection and damage control. They are non-binding. They are presently being reviewed by the IMO for application in Antarctic waters.[73]

The United States also supports the Arctic Council Guidelines on off-shore oil/gas activities. They recommend voluntary standards, technical and environmental best practices, and regulatory controls for Arctic offshore oil and gas operators. The Guidelines were designed to be consistent with U.S. offshore regulations; Interior/MMS posts the Guidelines on its webpage, apparently applies them, and recommends their use to new operators in the Arctic. Greenland apparently requires that they be read by potential permit holders; Russia has said they suggest that leaseholders read them. In December 2007, an Arctic Council working group (PAME) began another round of updates to the Guidelines.

Another Arctic Council working group (the Arctic Monitoring and Assessment Program (AMAP))[74] recently released an Assessment of Oil and Gas Activities in the Arctic.[75] The Council is still considering the working group's policy recommendations.

Various institutions address the Arctic Ocean as well, whether as part of a global approach or specifically:

The Arctic Council[76] is the only diplomatic forum focused on the Arctic.[77] It is an intergovernmental forum of the eight countries with land territory about the Arctic Circle—Canada, Denmark (Greenland, Faroe Islands), Finland, Iceland, Norway, Russian, Sweden, and the United States. Six indigenous organizations serve as "permanent participants" in the Council and participate alongside the governments in the operation of the Council. There are six observer states (France, Germany, Netherlands, Poland, Spain, UK) and a number of non-governmental observers. China and Italy are seeking permanent observer status, and the EC is seeking ad hoc observer status.

The Council's focus is environmental protection and sustainable development.[78] With United States support, the Council's working groups have taken on increased responsibilities for studies and projects in recent years. The Council is not an international organization (IO); there are various proposals to either make it an IO or to give it certain attributes of an IO, such as mandatory assessments or a permanent secretariat.

---

70. IMO document MSC.1/Circ.1184, 31 May 2006, *available through links at* www.imo.org.

71. IMO Assembly Resolution A.999(25), 29 Nov, 2007, IMO document A 25/Res.999, 3 Jan. 2008, *available through links at* www.imo.org.

72. Arctic Council Protection of the Arctic Marine Environment Working Group, Arctic Offshore Oil & Gas Guidelines, October 10, 2002, *available at* http://old.pame.is/sidur/uploads/ArcticGuidelines.pdf (last visited August 27, 2008).

73. *See* IMO document DE 51/11, 14 Dec. 2007 (Australia); DE 51/11/1, 14 Dec. 2007 (Canada and others); MSC 79/8/2 (Secretariat on behalf of Antarctic Treaty Consultative Parties); MSC 79/INF.2; DE 51/28, paras. 11.3–11.4, 11.7.

74. http://arctic-council.org/working_group/amap (last visited Sept. 1, 2008).

75. *Arctic Oil and Gas 2007, available at* http://www.amap.no/oga/ (last visited Sept. 1, 2008).

76. http://arctic-council.org/article/about (last visited August 18, 2008).

77. E. Bloom, *Establishment of the Arctic Council*, 93 AJIL 712 (1999), online at http://www.state.gov/g/oes/ocns/arc/ac/ (last visited August 18, 2008). *See also* remarks of Evan Bloom, April 19, 2007, *available at* http://www.state.gov/g/oes/rls/rm/2007/85350.htm (last visited August 18, 2008).

78. *Participation in Arctic Council*, Digest of United States Practice in International Law 2001, at 741–742 (S. Cummins & D. Stewart eds., Oxford Un. Press 2002).

There are also various subsidiary bodies of the Council addressing Arctic scientific, environmental and social issues. The Arctic Monitoring and Assessment Program (AMAP) published the Arctic Climate Impact Assessment (2004),[79] a 2006 Assessment of Acidification and Arctic Haze, and a 2004 study of Persistent Toxic Substances, Food Security and Indigenous People in the Russian North.[80] AMAP also released the Assessment of Oil and Gas Activities in the Arctic in January 2008, as just mentioned.[81] The working group on Conservation of Arctic Flora and Fauna (CAFF)[82] launched an on-going Circumpolar Biodiversity Monitoring Program[83] in 2006 and a ten-year Arctic Biodiversity Assessment.[84] Publications include, for example, Arctic Flora and Fauna: Status and Conservation (2001);[85] Arctic Flora and Fauna: Recommendation for Conservation (2002);[86] Protected Areas of the Arctic: Conserving a Full Range of Values (2002);[87] and Vital Arctic Graphics.

The working group on Protection of the Arctic Marine Environment (PAME)[88] published the Arctic Offshore Oil and Gas Guidelines previously noted, and has recently begun an update of these guidelines to be completed during the Danish chairmanship of the Arctic Council (2009–2011). In 2004, it published Guidelines for Transfer of Refined Oil and Oil Products in Arctic Waters.[89]

The Sustainable Development Working Group[90] published the Survey of Living Conditions in the Arctic (2006); the Arctic Human Development Report (2004); Analysis of Arctic Children and Youth Health Indicators (2005); and International Circumpolar Surveillance: Prevention and Control of Infectious Diseases (2006).[91]

The U.S. experience with the Council has been positive overall, although we continue to resist calls to make it more like an international organization. The United States believes that the Council should remain a high-level forum devoted to issues within its current mandate. The United States does not support a transformation of the Council into a formal international organization, including one with assessed contributions. The United States is nevertheless open to updating the structure of the Council, including consolidation of or operational changes to its subsidiary bodies, to the extent such changes can clearly improve the Council's work and are consistent with the general mandate of the Council. Policy recommendations developed within the ambit of the Council's scientific reviews must be subject to policy review by governments.

6. Tools

Then, what specific tools are available to enhance the security, environmental protection and safety of navigation in the Arctic Ocean and its approaches? There are a number of international

---

79. http://www.amap.no/acia/index.html (last visited Sept. 1, 2008).

80. http://www.amap.no/ (last visited Sept. 1, 2008).

81. *Arctic Oil and Gas 2007*, http://www.amap.no/oga/ (last visited Sept. 1, 2008).

82. http://arctic-council.org/working_group/caff (last visited Sept. 1, 2008).

83. http://arcticportal.org/en/caff/cbmp (last visited Sept. 1, 2008).

84. http://arcticportal.org/en/caff/aba (last visited Sept. 1, 2008).

85. http://arctic-council.org/filearchive/AFF%20Status%20and%20Trends.pdf

86. http://arcticportal.org/uploads/na/1N/na1N7_icNSl-fguglMdO8g/CAFF-brochure.2002.pdf (last visited Sept. 1, 2008).

87. J. Pagnan & G. Legare, PROTECTED AREAS OF THE ARCTIC: CONSERVING A FULL RANGE OF VALUES (2002), *available at* http://arcticportal.org/uploads/WP/n5/WPn5BFu6Aq5YA5hdeYR0Fw/HCR-10—-Protected-Areas-of-the-Arctic—Conserving-a-Full-Range-of-Values-2002.pdf (last visited Sept. 2, 2008).

88. http://arctic-council.org/working_group/pame; http://arcticportal.org/en/pame/ (last visited Sept. 1, 2008).

89. http://arcticportal.org/en/pame/offshore-oil-and-gas (last visited Sept. 1, 2008).

90. http://arctic-council.org/working_group/sdwg (last visited Sept. 1, 2008).

91. http://portal.sdwg.org/ (last visited Sept. 1, 2008).

instruments available to do so. They relate to search and rescue, routing and reporting measures, vessel traffic services, ship identification, ISPS Code and MARPOL special areas.

Search and Rescue

The LOS Convention requires every coastal State to "promote the establishment, operation and maintenance of an adequate and effective search and rescue service regarding safety on and over the sea and, where circumstances so require, by way of mutual regional arrangements cooperate with neighboring States for this purpose."[92]

The Arctic nations are all party to the IMO's International Convention on Maritime Search and Rescue (1979).[93] The SOLAS Convention requires each party to provide search and rescue (SAR) services for the rescue of persons in distress at sea around its coasts.[94] The Arctic nations are also party to the Convention on International Civil Aviation (ICAO), Annex 12 of which addresses SAR.[95]

Figure 7. Arctic Aeronautical and Maritime Search and Rescue Regions. We have not included this map, but add the thought that geographies of jurisdiction always attend redefinitions of the boundaries of human behavior.

Both SAR Conventions require parties to establish SAR Regions (SRRs) and call on parties to cooperate in the establishment and provision of SAR services.[96] The United States has a number of bilateral SAR agreements and MOUs with other countries, including a maritime SAR agreement with Russia (1988)[97] and an aeronautical and maritime SAR MOU with Canada and the UK (1999).[98] The United States is also developing a multilateral SAR MOU for the North Atlantic SRR region.

In the Alaska region, the U.S. Coast Guard has been operating SAR aircraft from forward operating bases in Nome and Barrow since this past summer[99] and conducting patrols in the Arctic.[100]

---

92. LOS Convention, article 98(2).

93. International Convention on Maritime Search and Rescue, 1979, with annex, done at Hamburg April 27, 1979, entered into force June 22, 1985, as amended *available at* http://www.admiraltylawguide.com/conven/searchrescue1979.htm and http://www.admiraltylawguide.com/conven/amendsearch1998.html (last visited August 28, 2008).

94. SOLAS Convention, regulation V/7.

95. Convention on International Civil Aviation, done at Chicago December 7, 1944, entered into force April 4, 1947, 61 Stat. 1180, TIAS 1591, 3 Bevans 944, 15 UNTS 295; *available at* http://www.icao.int/icaonet/arch/doc/7300/7300_9ed.pdf. *See also* http://www.icao.int/eshop/annexes_list.htm and http://www.icao.int/icao/en/ro/apac/2005/ATM_AIS_SAR_SG15/ip04.pdf (last visited August 27, 2008).

96. IMO SAR Convention, annex para. 2.1.1; ICAO Annex 12, para. 2.2.1, 3.1.1.

97. U.S.-USSR Agreement on Maritime Search and Rescue, with exchange of letters, signed at Moscow May 31, 1988, entered into force July 3, 1989, TIAS 11440, 2191 UNTS 115.

98. Memorandum of Understanding for Co-operation among the Department of National Defence of Canada, the Department of Fisheries and Oceans of Canada, the United States Coast Guard, the United States Air Force, the United Kingdom Maritime and Coastguard Agency, the United Kingdom Civil Aviation Division of the Department of Environment, Transport and the Regions, and the United Kingdom Ministry of Defence Concerning Search and Rescue, signed at Ottawa, Washington and London 1 February–14 September 1999.

99. R. Boswell, *U.S. waking up to Arctic competition: Coast Guard chief, available at* http://www.canada.com/topics/news/story.html?id=9e1b3f2b-513a-4335-9be4-f3907adae7d7 (last visited August 8, 2008); M. Baldino, *Coast Guard warmly welcomed in Alaska's Arctic, available at* http://www.ktuu.com/ Global/story.asp?S=8816794 (last visited August 9, 2008); USCG Press Release, *Coast Guard Conducts First SAREX in the Arctic Ocean,* Aug. 27, 2008, *available at* http://www.uscgalaska.com/go/doc/780/222426 (August 28, 2008); A. Bailey, *Barrow welcomes Coast Guard presence,* 13 PETROLEUM NEWS No. 33, week of August 17, 2008, *available at* http://petroleumnews.com/pnarchpop/080815-15.html (August 28, 2008).

100. USCG press release, *Coast Guard Continues Operation Salliq Above Arctic Circle,* Aug. 8, 2008, http://www.uscgalaska.com/go/doc/780/220111/USCG press release (30 August 2008), *U.S. to Commence Homeland Security Patrols in the Arctic,* Aug. 21, 2008, *available at* http://www.uscgalaska.com/go/doc/780/

Routing and Reporting Measures, Vessel Traffic Services

The United States, Canada and Russia are party to the IMO's International Convention for the Safety of Life at Sea (1974, as amended) (SOLAS).[101] Chapter V of the annexed regulations provides for the establishment of ships' routing measures and ship reporting systems, which can be made mandatory if the IMO approves them (Regulations V/10 and 11). SOLAS regulation V/12 provides for the establishment by parties of vessel traffic services where the volume of traffic or the degree of risk justified such services.

On August 27, 2008, Canadian Prime Minister Harper announced plans to make the existing voluntary Arctic Ship Reporting System (NORDREG)[102] mandatory, and extend the geographic scope of its application to Canada's full Arctic 200 nm EEZ.[103] The U.S. Coast Guard is also considering the need for vessel traffic services in the Arctic waters off Alaska. The United States looks forward to working with Canada in developing appropriate submissions to the IMO in due course.

AIS and LRIT

SOLAS already requires all ships over 300 gross tons on international voyages and passenger ships irrespective of size to be equipped with automatic identification systems (AIS).[104] In a few months time, the IMO's system for long range identification and tracking (LRIT) of ships should become operational.[105] These systems, along with others in development, would enable coastal States to identify and track commercial ships heading for and in the Arctic Ocean if the appropriate shore-based receivers were in place.[106]

ISPS Code

Following 9-11, the IMO adopted special measures to enhance maritime security, as amendments to SOLAS (chapter XI-2) and the International Ship and Port Facility Security (ISPS) Code.[107] These are applicable to commercial ships that could be expected to traverse the Arctic Ocean, and will be applicable to ports on the rim.[108]

Review of the "Polar Code"

Consideration might be given to reviewing the IMO's Guidelines for Ships Operating in Arctic Ice-Covered Waters with a view to seeing if they need to be updated or strengthened.[109]

221596 (last visited August 26, 2008). *See* A. McCullough, *Assessing the polar problem*, Navy Times Aug. 25, 2008, and the United States Coast Guard, USCG Arctic Report to Congress, *available at* http://www.uscg.mil/hq/cg5/cg513/docs/FY08_OMNIBUS_Polar_Ops_Report.pdf (last visited June 10, 2009).

101. *Supra* note 94.

102. Arctic Ice Regime Shipping System Standards, Transport Canada publication TP 12259E (1988), *available at* http://www.tc.gc.ca/MarineSafety/tp/TP12259.htm (last visited August 29, 2008).

103. Press release 27 August 2008, *PM Announces Government of Canada Will Extend Jurisdiction over Arctic Waters*, *available at* http://www.conservative.ca/EN/1091/101728 (last visited August 31, 2008); http://www.pm.gc.ca (last visited August 27, 2008).

104. SOLAS regulation V/19.2.4. For USCG implementation of AIS, see http://www.navcen.uscg/ewnav/ais (5 September 2008). The USCG's nationwide AIS is described at http://www.uscg.mil/nais (last visited Sept. 5, 2008); *see also* USCG press release, *Coast Guard announces successful launch of Nationwide Automatic Identification System Satellite*, June 20, 2008, *available at* http://www.piersystem.com/go/doc /786/ 212499 (last visited Sept. 5, 2008).

105. SOLAS regulation V/19-1, entered into force 1 January 2008.

106. *Supra* note 104.

107. SOLAS Chapter XI-2, Special measures to enhance maritime security, and the International Ship and Port Facility Security Code, adopted 12 December 2002 by the Conference of Contracting Governments to the International Convention for the Safety of Life at Sea, 1974.

108. *Supra* note 107.

109. Supra note 73.

MARPOL Special Areas

Annex I to MARPOL 73/78 contains regulations for the prevention of pollution by oil. The Annex provides for the establishment of special sea areas where for recognized technical reasons in relations to its oceanographic and ecological condition and to the particular character of its traffic, the adoption of special mandatory methods for the prevention of sea pollution by oil is required.[110]

In respect of the Antarctic area, any discharge into the sea of oil or oily mixtures from any ship is prohibited.[111] A similar prohibition might be found to be appropriate for the Arctic Ocean as well.

Other possible steps

Other steps that might be considered include:

- entering into oil and other hazardous material pollution response agreements under the 1990 IMO International Convention on Oil Pollution Preparedness, Response and Cooperation (OPPRC)[112] and its 2000 Protocol on Preparedness, Response and Co-operation to Pollution Incidents by Hazardous and Noxious Substances (HNS Protocol);[113]
- consideration of ballast water rules under the 2004 IMO International Convention for the Control and Management of Ships' Ballast Water and Sediments;[114]
- review of air emission standards under MARPOL Annex VI;[115] and
- establishment of fishery conservation and management regimes to deal with future Arctic fish stocks.[116]

Conclusion

I hope this has been helpful to define and clarify the issues concerning sovereignty, territoriality and maritime passage in the Arctic Ocean. I've gone into some considerable detail because, as I said at the top, consideration of these issues is timely now *before* large-scale navigation becomes feasible.

Let me close by repeating myself: these issues are not just of concern to Canada and the United States. These issues are of concern to all five states bordering on the Arctic, to the other states in the high north, and to flag states whose shipping might wish to ply these waters *when* they become suitable for large-scale navigation.

I hope I have contributed in some small way to meeting those concerns.

---

110. MARPOL 73/78, Annex I, regulation I/1.11.

111. MARPOL 73/78, Annex I, regulation I/15.4.

112. International Convention on Oil Pollution Preparedness, Response and Cooperation, 1990, done at London November 30, 1990, text at http://fletcher.tufts.edu/multi/texts/BH981.txt and http://www.admiralty lawguide.com/
conven/polpolresponse1990.html.

113. Protocol on Preparedness, Response and Co-operation to Pollution Incidents by Hazardous and Noxious Substances, 2000, done at London March 15, 2000, text at http://www.admiraltylawguide.com/ con-ven/noxious1996.html.

114. International Convention for the Control and Management of Ships' Ballast Water and Sediments, done at London February 13, 2004, not in force.

115. Protocol of 1997 to amend the International Convention for the Prevention of Pollution fro Ships, 1973, as modified by the Protocol of 1978 relating thereto, Sen. Tr. Doc. 108-7, Sen. Ex. Rpt. 110-8. Amendments to be adopted during the October 2008 session of the Marine Environment Protection Committee (MEPC 58) include a revised regulation 14 on Sulphur Oxides (SO_2) and Particulate Matter that permits the establishment of Emission Control Areas. Appendix III provides the criteria and procedures for designation of Emission Control Areas. These amendments are expected to enter into force March 1, 2010.

116. More than one fisheries regime is likely to be needed. *See* U.S. Senate Joint Resolution, S.J. 17, Pub. L. 110–243, June 3, 2008, 122 Stat. 1569–1571.

As J. Ashley Roach suggests, concerns about sovereignty in the Arctic spread beyond the usual national "players."

Towards an Inuit Declaration on Arctic Sovereignty

Statement issued by Inuit Leaders at the Inuit Leaders' Summit on Arctic Sovereignty 6–7 November 2008

At the invitation of the Inuit Circumpolar Council (ICC) Canada, we Inuit leaders from Greenland, Alaska, and Canada gathered in Kuujjuaq on 6–7 November 2008 to discuss the issue of Arctic sovereignty.

We Inuit leaders, representing a broad constituency, came to Kuujjuaq with the awareness that an increasing focus on the Arctic is fostering unparalleled interest in, and claims over, our lands and seas from various sectors including governments and industry. We took note of various declarations and statements made by governments and industry regarding overlapping claims and assertions of Arctic sovereignty without full regard to Inuit concerns and rights. We further asserted that any claim of sovereignty that nation states may make is derived through the use and occupancy by Inuit of lands and seas in the Arctic.

We reviewed key aspects of international instruments recognizing the rights of indigenous peoples and shared among ourselves elements of various processes such as Inuit land claims agreements and self-government arrangements across the Arctic. We updated each other on the implementation status of these processes and informed each other of recent autonomy discussions between Inuit and Arctic governments, such as the Greenland-Denmark Accord on Self Rule, which Greenlanders will vote on in a referendum on 25 November 2008. We, the leaders present in Kuujjuaq, congratulated Greenland on its accord and pledged to fully support the choice Greenlanders will make.

Various aspects of what sovereignty means for Inuit were discussed. There was agreement among us that the foundation of Inuit sovereignty begins at home, and that only through Inuit well-being and the development of healthy and sustainable communities can meaningful sovereignty be achieved. To achieve these goals, we called upon Arctic governments to be active partners in creating such a foundation.

We, the Inuit leaders gathered in Kuujjuaq, reminded Arctic governments that they are obligated under various legal instruments—both national and international—to include Inuit in meaningful and direct ways in any and all discussions of sovereignty over the lands and seas we have lived on for thousands of years.

We expressed our concerns over potential environmental impacts on our seas as traffic through Arctic waters is sure to increase.

We recognized the value of the work of the Arctic Council and asked ICC, through its permanent participant status on the Council, to work especially hard to make Inuit concerns known at the April 2009 meeting of Arctic foreign ministers to be held in Tromsø, Norway.

We further noted the meaningful and direct role that indigenous peoples have at the Arctic Council, while at the same time expressing concern that the Council leaves many issues considered sensitive by member states off the table, including security, sovereignty, national legislation relating to marine mammal protection, and commercial fishing.

Concern was expressed among us leaders gathered in Kuujjuaq that governments were entering into Arctic sovereignty discussions without the meaningful involvement of Inuit, such as the

May 2008 meeting of five Arctic ministers in Ilulissat, Greenland. The Kuujjuaq summit noted that while the Ilulissat Declaration asserts that it is the coastal nation states that have sovereignty and jurisdiction over the Arctic Ocean, it completely ignores the rights Inuit have gained through international law, land claims and self-government processes. Further, while the ministers strongly supported the use of international mechanisms and international law to resolve sovereignty disputes, it makes no reference to those international instruments that promote and protect the rights of indigenous peoples.

We, as Inuit leaders, strongly committed ourselves to working both nationally and internationally reminding various actors about the rights of Inuit in matters of the Arctic and called upon the organizers of the December 2009 meeting in Copenhagen of the United Nations Framework Convention on Climate Change to directly and fully involve Inuit in their deliberations and give support to the associated Arctic Day. We called upon the parties to the UN Convention on the Law of the Sea to take into account the rights and interests of Inuit in any matter concerning the Arctic. We called upon the G-8 countries to centrally involve Inuit in their 2010 conference to be hosted by the Government of Canada.

We further committed ourselves to assert our rights and work collectively at the United Nations Permanent Forum on Indigenous Issues and through UN treaty bodies as well as, when necessary, through the office of the UN Special Rapporteur on the Rights and Fundamental Freedoms of Indigenous Peoples.

We called upon Arctic governments to include Inuit as equal partners in any future talks regarding Arctic sovereignty. We insisted that in these talks, Inuit be included in a manner that equals or surpasses the participatory role Inuit play at the Arctic Council through ICC's permanent participant status.

We agreed to continue the important Arctic sovereignty dialogue started here in Kuujjuaq at this first ever Inuit Leaders' Summit on Arctic Sovereignty and committed to developing a formal declaration on Arctic sovereignty within six months of the conclusion of this Inuit Leaders' Summit. We asked the Inuit Circumpolar Council to coordinate this activity.

While the Inuit leadership from Russia was unable to be present with us in Kuujjuaq, we were pleased to receive a written intervention from ICC Chukotka that stated that "the issue of sovereignty and self-determination is a very important issue for us, and while our path towards self-government has not matched the pace of some of your indigenous institutions in Greenland, Canada, and Alaska, we are pursuing our own path of self-determination, according to international norms and laws." We remained committed to strongly supporting the Inuit of Chukotka through ICC.

We pledged to continue to celebrate and strongly promote the unity of Inuit across the Arctic from Russia to Alaska to Canada to Greenland. We expressed our strong support for the Inuit Circumpolar Council, and wished to take special notice of the 7th of November as International Inuit Day, which was established at the last ICC General Assembly held in Barrow, Alaska in 2006. We also expressed our appreciation to ICC Greenland for hosting the next ICC General Assembly to be held in 2010. Finally, we thanked the people of Kuujjuaq and all of Nunavik for allowing us to have this leaders' summit in their region.

Kuujjuaq 7 November 2008.

G. Global Warming Remedies in the Arctic

The search for appropriate remedies to correct the extraordinary wrongs of climate change has drawn thousands of lawyers worldwide into energetic and creative imaginations of the legally possible. Consider:

NATIVE COMMUNITIES AND CLIMATE CHANGE: PROTECTING THE TRIBAL RESOURCES AS PART OF NATIONAL CLIMATE POLICY 1 (Sept. 19, 2007) (Natural Resources Law Center, U. Colo. School of Law) [hereinafter 2007 HANNA TRIBAL STUDY]:

> the effects of climate change will fall disproportionately on tribes. For example, Alaska Natives contribute very little to the anthropogenic drivers of climate change—warming temperatures, melting sea ice, coastal inundation and others—which are experienced most acutely in the Arctic region.

2007 HANNA TRIBAL STUDY at 1:

> the mitigation and adaptation efforts to address the disproportionate impact on tribes are going to require considerable funding to put into effect. The cost of relocating just one of the many Alaska Native villages threatened by flooding and erosion exacerbated by climate change is estimated to be as much as $400 million.

This 2007 HANNA TRIBAL STUDY mentions several legal theories on the question of damages from global warming in the Arctic. Consequently, we will follow this guide and briefly present these issues around the general legal headings of the Indian trust doctrine, Civil Rights Act / Environmental Justice, Aboriginal Rights, Subsistence Rights, Treaty Rights, Petitions to International Bodies, the Common Law, Muddling Through, and the Alien Tort Claims Act.

1. Indian Trust Doctrine

There is an extraordinary literature on the Indian trust doctrine. *See* 2005 COHEN'S HANDBOOK ON FEDERAL INDIAN LAW §§ 5.04–5.07. It has reached Alaska. DAVID S. CASE & DAVID A. VOLUCK, ALASKA NATIVES AND AMERICAN LAWS ch. 7 (2d ed., 2002, U. Alaska Press, Fairbanks). It threatens to reach Hawai'i. JON M. VAN DYKE, WHO OWNS THE CROWN LANDS OF HAWAI'I (U. Hawai'i Press 2008). It has recruited enthusiastic and articulate academic supporters. *E.g.*, Mary Christina Wood, Protecting the Attributes of Native Sovereignty: A New Trust Paradigm for Federal Actions Affecting Tribal Lands and Resources, 1995 Utah L. Rev. 109. It is grounded in the basic ideas "that it grew from the government-to-government relationship between the U.S. and the Indian people; it committed the U.S. to protection of Indian properties; and it constrained the U.S. in its dealings with Indian nations." WILLIAM H. RODGERS, JR., ENVIRONMENTAL LAW IN INDIAN COUNTRY § 1:9 at 218 (Thomson / West 2005).

Intuitively, one might suppose that U.S. policies that sweep the Natives from their lands or transform Indian properties into places unrecognizable would be fair game for retribution under the trust doctrine. But have no doubt that the U.S. will find many ways to say: "We are not the guardians of these people." Or: "They do not own the properties they think they own." Or: "The particular treacheries they object to are not technically ruled out by the trust doctrine."

But the questions should be asked.

Notes

1. Would the Indian trust doctrine serve to win recognition (not to mention compensation) for Alaska Native villages where "ice" has been removed by the very nations who scramble for pieces of the fossil-fuel pie made fortuitously available by their improvident development policies?

2. *See* 2007 Tsosie on *Indigenous Environmental Justice* at 1638–39 (footnotes omitted), responding to the question: "does the United States have any duty to protect the island peoples of the South Pacific?":

> In light of the environmental degradation the United States' actions have caused to these island communities, the answer to this question is clearly yes. The responsibility is particularly apparent in light of the United States' long history of exploiting the Pacific Islands, which extends beyond the nuclear testing of the 1950's. Notably, the United States was complicit in the overthrow of the Hawaiian Kingdom in 1893 by a group of American insurgents. In 1993, the United States Congress issued a Joint Resolution apologizing for this wrongdoing and promising to participate in a "reconciliation" process with the Hawaiian people. In 2000, Senators Akaka and Inouye sponsored a bill, a version of which is still pending in Congress, which would formalize a trust relationship with the Native Hawaiian people, in response to the United States promise of reconciliation. The United States has already established a separate political relationship with several SIDS [Small Island Developing States], including Guam and the Republic of Palau, both of which retain aspects of their original autonomous political status.

3. For further elaboration of the Indian trust doctrine, see ROBERT T. ANDERSON, BETHANY BERGER, PHILIP P. FRICKEY & SARAH KRAKOFF, AMERICAN INDIAN LAW: CASES & COMMENTARY 228–46 (Thomson / West 2008); W.H. RODGERS, JR., ENVIRONMENTAL LAW IN INDIAN COUNTRY § 1:9 (Thomson / West 2005).

---

2. Civil Rights Act / Environmental Justice

James M. Grijalva, *Introduction: Seeking Environmental Justice in Indian Country*, CLOSING THE CIRCLE: ENVIRONMENTAL JUSTICE IN INDIAN COUNTRY ch. 1 at 3–12 (2008, Carolina Academic Press, Durham, N.C.):

A growing body of scholarly literature offers a fascinating diversity of opinion on the theoretical and practical underpinnings of the contours, causes and challenges of environmental justice. Most commenters agree, however, that as a socio-political phenomenon the environmental justice movement in the United States blossomed in response to the appearance of various studies and reports in the 1980s and early 1990s suggesting the world's most progressive environmental regulatory nation was overlooking its more vulnerable populations.[1] People of color and those from low-income communities rallied around impassioned allegations of environmental racism, drawing strength from a variety of earlier movements challenging systemic inequities in the administration of government—civil rights, organized labor, American Indian self-determination, grassroots and anti-toxics—and some support from the mainstream environmental movement.[2] Policy and program actions taken in the 1990s by the federal executive branch and particularly the United States Environmental Protection Agency (EPA) in response to the growing public pressure for equity are typically cited as the first official governmental efforts confronting environmental injustice.[3]

---

1. *See, e.g.*, THE LAW OF ENVIRONMENTAL JUSTICE: THEORIES AND PROCEDURES TO ADDRESS DISPROPORTIONATE RISKS xxix (Michael B. Gerrard ed., ABA 1999).

2. *See generally* LUKE COLE & SHEILA FOSTER, FROM THE GROUND UP: ENVIRONMENTAL RACISM AND THE RISE OF THE ENVIRONMENTAL JUSTICE MOVEMENT (NYU Press 2001).

3. *See, e.g.*, CLIFFORD RECHTSCHAFFEN & EILEEN GUANA, ENVIRONMENTAL JUSTICE: LAW, POLICY AND REGULATION 3–4 (Clifford Rechtschaffen & Eileen Guana eds., Carolina Academic Press 2003).

Indian people are fairly accustomed to seeing social movements and federal initiatives come last to Indian country if at all. Too often its seems Indian concerns are at best an afterthought in the political, popular and scholarly dialogue on pressing national issues like civil rights, economic empowerment, criminal justice, health care, education and environmental protection. But that was not the case for the environmental justice movement or EPA's programmatic reactions to it. Though largely overlooked in the literature, Indian issues and indigenous activists were present at every stage of the modern movement's evolution, and EPA's environmental justice program responses consistently included specific strategies for seeking equitable protection of the Indian country environment.

The reason for the Agency's specific and separate attention to Indian country has been noted in a small but growing body of Indian environmental justice scholarship.[4] Indian tribes' status as sovereign governments under federal law and their strong cultural and spiritual connections with the natural environment uniquely distinguishes them from every other minority and low-income group affected by environmental injustice. To be sure, citizens of America's tribal nations often face a variety of disproportionately high health and environmental risks from multiple pollution sources just as members of other groups do. Yet, the existence of such risks may derive more from jurisdictional uncertainties hampering effective regulatory control than unfair program implementation, and their solution may lie in tribes' inherent powers over their territories.

EPA recognized both of those possibilities shortly after the first Earth Day and other significant developments in 1970 marked the beginning of the modern age of American environmental law and regulation. Tribes' homelands would simply be left out of the new federal programs being developed and implemented across the nation unless some creative action was taken. Scholarly commentary to the contrary notwithstanding, EPA's reaction to that threat some twenty years before the environmental justice movement began was the first time the federal government confronted the possibility of disproportionate environmental risks affecting minority communities.

The Environmental Justice Movement

Data collected in the 1980s and early 1990s by the federal government and independent organizations demonstrated disturbing correlations between race, income and environmental threats ostensibly controlled by the modern laws. Following the 1982 arrest of 500 protesters for civil disobedience in opposing the siting of a polychlorinated biphenyl waste disposal facility in a predominantly poor African-American community in North Carolina, the U.S. General Accounting Office surveyed the racial composition of communities surrounding four existing hazardous waste landfills in the southeastern United States and found African-Americans constituted the majority population in three of them. The United Church of Christ Commission for Racial Justice, which participated in the North Carolina protests, expanded the geographic focus in 1987, reporting a statistically significant correlation nationally between race and proximity to commercial hazardous waste facilities like landfills, lagoons and incinerators, and to closed or abandoned toxic waste sites.[5]

In early 1990, at the University of Michigan School of Natural Resources Conference on Race and the Incidence of Environmental Hazards, a coalition of social scientists, academics and civil rights activists formed and requested EPA initiate a series of actions addressing the mounting evidence of disproportionate environmental impacts on minority and low-income communities.

---

4. *See* Judith V. Royster, *Native American Law, in* THE LAW OF ENVIRONMENTAL JUSTICE: LAW, POLICY AND REGULATION 3–4 (Clifford Rechtschaffen & Eileen Guana eds., Carolina Academic Press 2003).

5. COMMISSION FOR RACIAL JUSTICE (United Church of Christ), TOXIC WASTES AND RACE IN THE UNITED STATES: A NATIONAL REPORT ON THE RACIAL AND SOCIO-ECONOMIC CHARACTERISTICS OF COMMUNITIES WITH HAZARDOUS WASTE SITES (1987).

EPA Administrator William Reilly responded by constituting within the Agency an Environmental Equity Workgroup charged with reviewing the evidence and considering how existing EPA programs, risk assessment and communication guidelines, institutional relationships and outreach might give rise to inequitable risk reduction and be adjusted to correct such instances. In 1991, Reilly announced by memorandum to his staff the Agency's first official position on the subject: "The consequences of environmental pollution should not be borne disproportionately by any segment of the population."

That same year the movement coalesced with an unprecedented First National People of Color Environmental Leadership Summit where community activists issued a set of seventeen principles under the terminology of environmental justice. The earlier term environmental racism's implicit focus on intentional discriminatory decisions arguably overlooked disproportionate impacts created inadvertently and seemed preoccupied with identifying problems rather than solutions, and EPA's term environmental equity implied a redistribution of risks among racial and economic groups rather than overall reduction and elimination of risks.

The Summit's principles and the movement they helped foment instead attacked the causes and consequences of disproportionate environmental impacts from four broad justice perspectives.[6] Distributive justice sought more equal protection through a lowering of environmental risks rather than a shifting or reallocation of existing risks. Corrective justice urged more equal governmental enforcement in minority and low-income communities, and sanctions and remedies on par with those routinely ordered in more affluent white communities. Procedural justice confronted the reality that the people most affected were often not included in the government's decision-making processes, or if they were, lacked the resources and information necessary to participate effectively. The broad concept of social justice tried to take account of both public health and economic opportunity as indispensable aspects of the quality of life in these communities; people should not be faced with choosing between an unsafe livelihood and unemployment.

The 1992 report of EPA's Workgroup retained the environmental equity term but incorporated much of the justice approach in focusing on the distribution and effects of environmental problems, the process for making environmental policy, and how environmental programs were being administered.[7] To no one's surprise, the Workgroup found a general lack of existing data on environmental health effects analyzed by race and income, and wide variation in the extent to which different Agency programs and regions accounted for environmental equity issues. Reilly responded to the Workgroup's suggestion for prioritizing those issues in a more centralized fashion by creating the Office of Environmental Equity in 1992.

Public pressure on the Agency for real action increased two months later with the publication of a special investigation by the National Law Journal that discovered significant inequities in the rates of environmental enforcement and hazardous substance cleanup in minority communities. EPA's responses to violations of several key regulatory programs and releases of hazardous substances under the Superfund program in those communities were generally slower, its cleanups less rigorous, and the enforcement sanctions levied lower or non-existent. A 1994 study updating the Church of Christ report concluded the disproportionate environmental impacts had grown to the point where people of color were forty-seven percent more likely than whites to live near a commercial hazardous waste facility, and

---

6. Robert R. Kuehn, *A Taxonomy of Environmental Justice*, 30 ELR 10,681 (2000).
7. ENVIRONMENTAL PROTECTION AGENCY, ENVIRONMENTAL EQUITY: REDUCING RISK FOR ALL COMMUNITIES (1992).

found sixty-three of sixty-four recent empirical studies documented environmental disparities by race and income for ambient air pollution, toxic exposures and environmental health
effects.[8]

That year environmental justice caught the attention of the White House. President Bill Clinton issued an executive order entitled "Federal Actions to Address Environmental Justice in Minority Populations and Low-income Populations," which directed every federal agency make
achieving environmental justice part of its mission, and develop a strategy for addressing any
disproportionately high and adverse human health or environmental effects of agency programs
on minority and low-income populations.[9] EPA's Office of Environmental Equity changed its
name to the Office of Environmental Justice, and drawing on the recommendations of the recently created National Environmental Justice Advisory Council, an independent body comprised of stakeholders from communities, organizations, industry and government, issued the
Agency's environmental justice strategy in 1995.[10]

The strategy was effectively the Agency's first official environmental justice policy, but it
echoed several key themes of the 1992 environmental equity report. Both documents reported a
lack of relevant data on the impacts of federal environmental programs on disenfranchised
groups and urged enhanced data collection and integration within existing information management systems. The equity report and strategy both sought more significant community involvement through improved public participation procedures, increased outreach to impacted communities, and additional partnerships with local and national organizations.

The strategy also followed the equity report's approach of using goals and principles in lieu of
defining the core concept. The Agency openly admitted in the 1992 report its difficulty in defining environmental equity, offering in its place Administrator Reilly's basic principle of allowing
no disproportionate effects of pollution on any population segment, supplemented by the stated
goals of making public health and environmental protection available to all groups, and implementing environmental programs in ways that equitably conferred benefits and risk reductions
on all groups. The 1995 strategy did not acknowledge its lack of a definition for environmental
justice but simply posited two goals—one a slightly refined version of Reilly's principle of no
disproportionate effects, and the other ensuring those affected by environmental decisions have
opportunities for participating in making them—and three guiding principles—engaging communities through a variety of communication means, helping them access pertinent information, and advocating environmental justice with other federal agencies.

Several years later the Agency folded these concepts into a definition of environmental justice
that continues to guide its policy and program actions today:

> Environmental Justice is the fair treatment and meaningful involvement of all people
> regardless of race, color, national origin, or income with respect to the development, im-
> plementation, and enforcement of environmental laws, regulations, and policies. Fair
> treatment means that no group of people should bear a disproportionate share of the
> negative environmental consequences resulting from industrial, governmental and com-
> mercial operations or policies. Meaningful involvement means that: (1) people have an
> opportunity to participate in decisions about activities that may affect their environment
> and/or health; (2) the publics [sic] contribution can influence the regulatory agency's de-

---

8. Benjamin A. Goldman *et al.*, Toxic Wastes and Race Revisited: An Update on the 1987 Report
on the Racial and Socio-Economic Characteristics of Communities with Hazardous Waste Sites
13–14 (1994).

9. Exec. Order No. 12989, 59 Fed. Reg. 2679 (Feb. 11, 1994).

10. *EPA Environmental Justice Strategy: Executive Order* 12898 (1995).

cision; (3) their concerns will be considered in the decision making process; and (4) the decision makers seek out and facilitate the involvement of those potentially affected.[11]

Achieving this vision of environmental justice, EPA recognized, would require new partnerships with a variety of stakeholders including grassroots organizations, local governments, business concerns and other federal agencies. The Agency's existing relationship with state environmental agencies was the most crucial, however, because they played the primary implementation role under the main federal environmental laws. States most often issued the operating permits required for lawful pollution discharges, monitored facility operations for compliance with environmental requirements, and determined whether and to what extent regulatory violations would be enforced. EPA's environmental justice strategy thus promised increased environmental justice emphasis, training and guidance directed at state implementation of federal programs.

Indian Country Environmental Justice

Indian country was the first place EPA applied its twin environmental justice themes of seeking fair treatment and enhancing the public involvement of disaffected groups, but it did so nearly twenty years before announcing them as the Agency's environmental justice policy in the late 1990s. The stimulus for EPA's early focus on environmental justice in the Indian country context was the unique characteristic that distinguishes Indian tribes from other minority groups affected by pollution and implicates a somewhat different source of and potential solution for environmental injustice in Indian country. Long political relations with the federal government and the resulting body of federal Indian law recognize in Indian tribes a pre-existing and continuing sovereignty as governments and impose on the federal government a trust responsibility for Indian welfare. The government-to-government and fiduciary relationships between tribes and the United States alters the constitutional concept of equal protection that underlies environmental justice; while American Indian citizens of the United States are entitled to fair treatment like other people of color, their dual citizenship in Indian tribes allows for different legal treatment, a sort of "measured separatism"[12] reflected in an entire title in the United States Code of federal laws devoted specifically and exclusively to Indians and Indian country.

EPA recognized the separateness of federal Indian law and Indian country when it first began implementing the modern environmental regulatory programs that two decades later would give rise to the environmental justice movement. Judicial decisions addressing federal power and tribal sovereignty over Indian reservations threw doubt on the comprehensiveness of federal-state partnerships emerging from the new federal environmental programs, leading the Agency to experiment with unprecedented federal-tribal partnerships and direct outreach to tribes in the 1970s.[13] Different creative approaches were necessary, the Agency announced in 1980, to address "the serious possibility" that the Indian country environment would otherwise be less effectively protected than environments elsewhere.[14] Or, in the language of the contemporary environmental justice movement, the risk that Indians might suffer disproportionate health impacts and lack meaningful involvement in environmental decision-making was unacceptable and required focused Agency attention.

EPA's efforts toward Indian country environmental protection through special relations with tribes expanded greatly in the 1980s alongside presidential policy statements favoring tribal self-determination and congressional amendments creating state-like regulatory roles for tribes in the environmental programs. So when the early studies on race and environmental risk com-

---

11. U.S. EPA Office of Environmental Justice, Background, http://www.epa.gov/compliance/basics/ejback ground.html (last visited July 27, 2007).

12. *See generally* CHARLES F. WILKINSON, AMERICAN INDIANS, TIME AND THE LAW (Yale Un. Press 1988).

13. James M. Grijalva, *The Origins of EPA's Indian Program*, 15 KAN. J.L. & PUB. POL'Y 191, 205–222 (2006).

14. EPA POLICY FOR PROGRAM IMPLEMENTATION ON INDIAN LANDS 1 (Dec. 19, 1980).

monly associated with the beginning of the environmental justice movement came out, parallel data for Indian country was also emerging. A 1985 survey of twenty-five Indian tribes indicated as many as 1,200 facilities generating or disposing of hazardous waste on or adjacent to their reservations.[15] A broader environmental survey of seventy-four reservations representing a combined human population of 369,500 and a landmass of forty-two million acres in 1986 reported twenty-one major sources of air pollution, fifty-two community dump sites, landfills or uncontrolled open dumps, and at least 130 sources of water pollution.[16] These and other sources contributed to a broad variety of environmental concerns expressed by tribes, including waterborne diseases, violations of drinking water standards, surface water quality impairment, uncontrolled dumping of solid waste, abandoned mine wastes, and violations of air quality standards.

The 1986 survey observed that an overall lack of comprehensive federal and tribal environmental infrastructure was contributing to the problems identified. It also noted nearly every responding tribe reported involvement in some form of broadly defined environmental management activity, lending additional credence to EPA's view that addressing environmental justice in Indian country required creative solutions utilizing tribes' governmental status. Shortly before the First People of Color Summit in 1991, EPA asserted:

> Indian tribes, for whom human welfare is tied closely to the land, see protection of the reservation environment as essential to preservation of the reservations themselves. Environmental degradation is viewed as a form of further destruction of the remaining reservation land base, and pollution prevention is viewed as an act of tribal self-preservation that cannot be entrusted to others. For these reasons, Indian tribes have insisted that tribal governments be recognized as the proper governmental entities to determine the future quality of reservation environments.[17]

The Agency's cultural generalizations and assumptions of tribal interest were strongly endorsed just months later at the Summit. The significant but typically unreported presence of indigenous advocates there succeeded in memorializing the tribal management approach in two of the seventeen principles announced:

> 5. Environmental justice affirms the fundamental right to political, economic, cultural and environmental self-determination of all peoples.
>
> ...
>
> 11. Environmental justice must recognize a special legal and natural relationship of Native Peoples to the U.S. government through treaties, agreements, compacts, and covenants affirming sovereignty and self-determination.[18]

Tribal environmental management, however, was not merely an exercise in political science and environmental health but was in fact perceived as fundamental to cultural survival. The Summit's

15. Council of Energy Resource Tribes, Inventory of Hazardous Waste Generators and Sites on Selected Indian Reservations (1985).

16. EPA Survey of American Indian Environmental Protection and Regulation of Reservation Environments 1 (July 10, 1991).

17. Environmental Protection Agency, Federal, Tribal and State roles in the Protection and Regulation of Reservation Environments 1 (July 10, 1991), *available at* http://www.epa.gov/Region4/indian/EPAStTri_relations.pdf (last visited June 11, 2009).

18. *Principles of Environmental Justice*, Proceedings, First National People of Color Environmental Leadership Summit xii (1991).

first Principle equated environmental justice with affirming "the sacredness of Mother Earth, ecological unity and the interdependence of all species." An Indigenous Environmental Statement of Principles prepared by the Native Lands Institute in 1995 noted the common native phrase "we are all related" reflects cultural and spiritual traditions of seeing all living things—insects, reptiles, fish, birds and mammals—as "peoples" having important relations with indigenous peoples. Professor Rebecca Tsosie more comprehensively explained in 1996 that traditional ecological knowledge is a culturally and spiritually based means by which indigenous groups relate to ecosystems built on perceptions of the earth as an animate being, land as essential to indigenous identity, human relations with other living beings, and balance and reciprocity between humans and the natural world.[19]

Recognizing such human connectedness naturally imposes special obligations of protection. Tribal environmental lawyer Dean Suagee characterizes the development of environmental programs by tribes as discharging part of a sacred trust born of cultural traditions with ancient roots in the land.[20] The ancient fundamental laws of the Diné or Navajo people, uniquely merged with contemporary tribal law in written format, embraces these views explicitly:

Diné Natural Law declares and teaches that:

A. The four sacred elements of life, air, light/fire, water and earth/pollen in all their foms must be respected, honored and protected for they sustain life; and

....

D. The Diné have a sacred obligation and duty to respect, preserve and protect all that was provided for we were designated as the steward of these relatives.[21]

Tribal management is doubly important because western environmental law as implemented by federal and state agencies is generally unable to account for Indian visions of environmental justice that include the physical, social and spiritual relations affected by various land development uses.[22] The Indigenous Environmental Statement of Principles offered as an example of that myopia western risk-based analysis that focuses primarily on acceptable rates of individual human harm and death, suggesting Indian country risk assessments must also account for the spiritual and psychological well being of the collective community as well as individuals. EPA's 1992 environmental equity report, which commendably devoted a separate section to Indian country issues, made some inroads in that vein, explicitly noting a need for incorporating cultural considerations like subsistence practices and higher than average wild food and fish consumption rates into the Agency's risk analyses.

EPA's first effort at that challenging task was a groundbreaking comparative risk project nearing completion as the equity report was issued. Between 1986 and 1992, EPA was involved in some twenty-five comparative analyses on environmental risks facing different states, regions and cities that, despite the growing concerns over environmental justice at the time, considered the entire population of the study areas without segregating data for minority groups. EPA broke new ground in 1992 with its first environmental justice comparative risk study, performed in Indian country. The study concluded the 20,000 to 30,000 American Indians constituting eleven tribes in Wisconsin faced different environmental risks than the population of the

---

19. Rebecca Tsosie, *Tribal Environmental Policy in an Era of Self-Determination: The Role of Ethics, Economics and Traditional Ecological Knowledge*, 21 Vт. L. Rev. 225 (1996).

20. Dean B. Suagee, *The Indian Country Environmental Justice Clinic: From Vision to Reality*, 23 Vт. L. Rev. 567 (1999).

21. Title I, ch. 1, §5, Navajo Nation Code (2002).

22. Robert Williams, Jr., *Large Binocular Telescopes, Red Squirrel Pi_atas, and Apache Sacred Mountains: Decolonizing Environmental Law in a Multicultural World*, 96 W. Vа. L. Rev. 1133 (1994).

northern Midwest as a whole.[23] The risk analyses EPA employed accounted for the different pathways of environmental contamination that Indians face, and interestingly, calculated economic damages to cultural and religious values as well as subsistence lifestyles. The project concluded that the disproportionately higher risks faced by Wisconsin Indians from both on and off-reservation pollution sources could be significantly reduced by the development of effective tribal environmental management infrastructure. Tribal programs could translate traditional cultural and spiritual values into the rubric of environmental quality standards affecting the substantive requirements of pollution permits issued under the modern federal environmental programs.

EPA's 1995 strategy adopted tribal program development as one of its primary objectives for Indian country environmental justice. Like the equity report, the strategy treated the issues unique to tribes separately, emphasizing their difference from environmental justice concerns elsewhere. In other areas of the country the Agency was focused on adjusting the federal and state programs already in place so they operated more fairly and with greater transparency. In Indian country, the disproportionately high environmental risks appeared more attributable to a surprising lack of operating programs. The perception of an environmental regulatory gap in Indian country had prompted EPA's early creative approaches to tribal partnerships, and its contemporary commitment to filling that gap manifested itself in 1994 with the creation of the American Indian Environmental Office. The Office of Environmental Justice's 1995 strategy also noted the need for filling jurisdictional gaps in national environmental protection and promised coordination with the Indian Office in developing and implementing Indian country programs in a government-to-government fashion consistent with tribal sovereignty and the federal trust responsibility.

―――――――

Notes

1. 1995 GREAT DOCUMENTS IN AMERICAN INDIAN HISTORY 166, 169 ("Fourth of July Address at Reidsville, New York, 1854"), *quoted in* WILLIAM H. RODGERS, JR., ENVIRONMENTAL LAW IN INDIAN COUNTRY 414 (Thomson / West 2005):

> Oh, what mockery to confound justice with law! Will you look steadily at the intrigues, bargains, corruptions and log rollings of your present legislatures, and see any trace of Justice?

> John Quinney, Mahican, July 4, 1854

2. 2007 Hanna Tribal Study at 38:

> tribes would not want to bring a stand-alone claim that disparate impacts of climate change, exacerbated by agency action or inaction, violate Title VI or the Executive Order, citing *Alexander v. Sandoval*, 532 U.S. 275 (2001) (there is no private right of enforcement under Title VI of the Civil Rights Act with regard to disparate impacts of agency regulations) and *South Camden Citizens in Action v. New Jersey Dep't of Environmental Protection*, 274 F.3d 771 (3d. Cir. 2001) (because Title VI proscribes only intentional discrimination, plaintiffs cannot sue under §1983 to enforce EPA's disparate impact regulations).

―――――――

―――――――

23. ENVIRONMENTAL PROTECTION AGENCY, TRIBES AT RISK: THE WISCONSIN TRIBES COMPARATIVE RISK PROJECT (1992).

3. Aboriginal Rights

The Alaska Native Claims Settlement Act (ANSCA) extinguishes:

[a]ll aboriginal titles, if any, and claims of aboriginal title in Alaska based on use and occupancy, including submerged land underneath all water areas, both inland and offshore, and including any aboriginal hunting or fishing rights that may exist.

43 U.S.C. § 1603(b)

Q. Are there any "ice rights" remaining? Can you extinguish A's aboriginal rights by making compensation available to B? *See* Robert T. Anderson, *Alaska Native Rights, Statehood, and Unfinished Business*, 43 TULSA L. REV. 17, 32–35 (2008).

4. Subsistence Rights

The subsistence rights of Alaska Natives are protected by federal law in various ways. See W.H. RODGERS, JR., ENVIRONMENTAL LAW IN INDIAN COUNTRY § 1:7 (Thomson/West 2005) [hereinafter 2005 RODGERS]; 16 U.S.C.A. § 1320(a). The hard question is whether this assemblage of mostly process-related "maybes" can be recruited to a level of legal concern over what amounts to a vast physical transformation of the region. *See* Sophie Theriault, *The Legal Protection of Subsistence: A Prerequisite of Food Security for the Inuit of Alaska*, 22 ALASK. L. REV. 35 (2005); Andrew P. Richards, *Aboriginal Title or the Paramountcy Doctrine?* Johnson v. McIntosh *Flounders in Federal Waters off Alaska in* Native Village of Eyak v. Trawler Diane Marie, Inc., 78 WASH. L. REV. 939 (2003) (unextinguished offshore hunting and fishing rights). Subsistence protection does win the day in *Alaska Wilderness League and REDOIL (Resisting Environmental Destruction of Indigenous Lands) v. Kempthorne*, 548 F.3d 815 (9th Cir. 2008).

5. Treaty Rights

The Northwest Indian tribes have reserved their treaty "rights of taking fish" and these have continued to show remarkable legal resilience. *E.g.*, 2005 RODGERS § 1:3; *United States v. Washington*, Civ. No. C-70-9213, Sub-Proceeding No. 01-01 (Phase II-Culverts), Decision on Cross-Motions for Summary Judgment (Martinez, J.), Aug. 22, 2007 (tribes prevail in initial ruling that treaty-protected fishing rights are impaired by fish-impassable culverts under highways and roads). If these classical treaties are violated by ejections, enclosures, violence, interceptions, and environmental destruction (all within the legal history of these measures), *see* J.C. DUPRIS, K.S. HILL & W.H. RODGERS, JR., THE SI'LAILO WAY: INDIANS, SALMON & LAW ON THE COLUMBIA RIVER (Carolina Academic Press 2006), global-warming related ousters and ruination appear to be treaty-vulnerable. *See* MICHAEL C. BLUMM, SACRIFICING THE SALMON: A LEGAL AND POLITICAL HISTORY OF THE DECLINE OF COLUMBIA BASIN SALMON 272–77 (Book World Publications 2002).

6. Petition to International Bodies

Considerable publicity and interest has attended the Petition of the Canadian Inuit to the Inter American Commission on Human Rights on Dec. 7, 2005. The petition alleges Violations Resulting from Global Warming Caused by the United States, *available at* http://www.inuit circumpolar.com/index.php?ID=316&Lang=En. The Request for Relief of the Petition reads as follows:

Petition to the Inter American Commission on Human Rights Violations Resulting From Global Warming Caused by the United States, Inuit Circumpolar Council (Canada), December 7, 2005:

IX. Request for Relief

For the reasons stated above, Petitioner respectfully requests that the Commission:

1. Make an onsite visit to investigate and confirm the harms suffered by the named individuals whose rights have been violated and other affected Inuit;
2. Hold a hearing to investigate the claims raised in this Petition;
3. Prepare a report setting forth all the facts and applicable law, declaring that the United States of America is internationally responsible for violations of rights affirmed in the American Declaration of the Rights and Duties of Man and in other instruments of international law, and recommending that the United States:
    a. Adopt mandatory measures to limit its emissions of greenhouse gases and cooperate in efforts of the community of nations—as expressed, for example, in activities relating to the United Nations Framework Convention on Climate Change—to limit such emissions at the global level;
    b. Take into account the impacts of U.S. greenhouse gas emissions on the Arctic and affected Inuit in evaluating and before approving all major government actions;
    c. Establish and implement, in coordination with Petitioner and the affected Inuit, a plan to protect Inuit culture and resources, including, *inter alia*, the land, water, snow, ice, and plant and animal species used or occupied by the named individuals whose rights have been violated and other affected Inuit; and mitigate any harm to these resources caused by US greenhouse gas emissions;
    d. Establish and implement, in coordination with Petitioner and the affected Inuit communities, a plan to provide assistance necessary for Inuit to adapt to the impacts of climate change that cannot be avoided;
    e. Provide any other relief that the Commission considers appropriate and just.

Notes

1. Commentary on the Inuit Petition has been voluminous. *See* SVITLANA KRAVCHENKO & JOHN E. BONINE, HUMAN RIGHTS AND THE ENVIRONMENT 557–573 (Carolina Academic Press 2008).

2. *See* R.N. CLINTON, C.E. GOLDBERG & R. TSOSIE, AMERICAN INDIAN LAW: NATIVE NATIONS AND THE FEDERAL SYSTEM: CASES & MATERIALS 121–134 (5th ed. Mathew Bender 2007) ("International Human Rights Law and Indigenous Peoples' Rights").

3. *See* Paul Arthur Berkman & Oran R. Young, *Governance and Environmental Change in the Arctic Ocean*, 324 SCIENCE 339, 340 (April 17, 2009):

> One useful approach in developing effective governance for a rapidly changing Arctic may be to treat the central Arctic as an international space and to draw a clear distinction between the overlying water column and the sea floor. Ecologically and legally distinct from the sea floor, the overlying water column and sea surface of the central Arctic can remain an undisputed international area ... in which the interest of Arctic and non-Arctic states alike play a role in the development of effective governance. This region involves the high seas, a sea zone universally accepted as beyond national jurisdictions. Focus on the high seas opens the door to treating the central Arctic as an international space subject to cooperative decision-making regarding a variety of issues (*e.g.*, fishing

and shipping) through regulatory arrangements articulated under the auspices of [Law of the Sea] and customary international law.

––––––––––

7. Common Law

David Fagan, *Multinational Corporations*,[1] in 2004 WATTERS, ch. 7, at 139–48:

Introduction

An indigenous person from a developing nation may tell the following story. She inhabited a land of inestimable worth. To her and her family, the land represented nothing less than life itself. It reared the children and received the elders; it sustained economic welfare; it embodied individual and collective spirituality and identity. The lushness of the land, however, contained resources that were in demand by others, including numerous foreign corporations. Eventually, one, or perhaps a few, of these corporations succeeded in either expropriating her land or having the land expropriated for them by the state that governs her tribe. She is not certain how it happened, nor does she care. She knows only that in the process of losing their land, members of her tribe have suffered, and with all or part of their land lost, they continue to suffer. She reports that they have lost their way of life, their spirituality, and their identity, and she says they have no domestic recourse.

In response to such exploitation, indigenous peoples have explored two avenues of judicial relief. First, indigenous groups have brought to international tribunals claims based on human rights, minority rights, and self-determination principles. Second, having little or no recourse in their own countries, indigenous plaintiffs have turned to the domestic courts of the countries in which multinational corporations (MNCs) are based in an attempt to hold these entities accountable for their actions overseas. Specifically, indigenous plaintiffs have brought lawsuits in the state and federal courts of the United States, asserting various state and common law tort claims, claims for violations of customary norms of international law, and claims seeking equitable relief for environmental damage. Thus far, indigenous plaintiffs have had little success, although this failure may be due more to prudential concerns or poor lawyering than to any substantive defect in the claims. Regardless of the outcome in these cases, there is a common current underlying and informing all the claims: the notion that the defendants have been enriched at the plaintiffs' expense. Yet, indigenous plaintiffs have not pursued unjust enrichment as an independent basis of liability.

Such a novel use of unjust enrichment in the indigenous context, while potentially controversial, finds support in the doctrine's heritage. Unjust enrichment originated as a theory of recovery in order to fill gaps left uncovered by traditional legal categories, such as contract, tort, and property law. For example, when there was a windfall benefit—such as money paid by mistake—in a noncontractual setting, courts invoked the fiction of a quasi-contract to provide recompense to the plaintiff and to deprive the defendant of an unjust enrichment. A similar, recent example has been the use of unjust enrichment as a substantive claim in the Holocaust litigation. In this way, unjust enrichment has developed as a moral check against the retention of a benefit that would violate "good conscience," if not another area of the law. Although the broad scope of this principle arguably has given rise to a rather muddled state of the law, it also has permitted the unique application of the doctrine, as in the Holocaust cases. Seen in this light, unjust en-

––––––––––

1. The publication from which the content in this chapter is adapted is *Achieving Restitution: The Potential Unjust Enrichment Claims of Indigenous Peoples Against Multinational Corporations*, 76 N.Y.U. L. REV. 626 (2001).

richment would appear to have a role for indigenous plaintiffs: The problem of indigenous exploitation is steeped in history and possibly not covered by other areas of law, thereby necessitating an exceptional solution.

Part I provides a more detailed overview of the problem of indigenous exploitation, using the experiences of Freeport-McMoRan Copper and Gold, Inc. (Freeport) and Unocal Corporation (Unocal) in Indonesia and Burma, respectively, as specific examples of MNC involvement in indigenous territory. In turn, the Freeport and Unocal cases serve illustrative purposes ... Part II examines the ability of indigenous plaintiffs to satisfy the substantive elements of an unjust enrichment claim against an MNC and to survive potential substantive defenses to the claim. Finally, Part III discusses the striking parallel between the concerns and goals of indigenous peoples and the considerations that underlie unjust enrichment and describes the equally significant remedial appeal of unjust enrichment for indigenous plaintiffs.

I. An Overview of the Problem of Indigenous Exploitation

A. Identifying the Plaintiffs: Defining Indigenous Peoples and the Problem of Exploitation

A single definition of "indigenous peoples" that succinctly incorporates all relevant or potentially relevant groups has proven elusive. Such a definition may be impossible. After all, the term "indigenous" is intended to include "a vast range of peoples with highly different life styles, living conditions and relations to their respective nation states." Outlooks and aspirations, means of subsistence, the degree of functional ability in dominant society, and even the level of adherence to traditional culture, all may vary among indigenous groups.

Despite these differences, broad unifying characteristics, experiences, and concerns exist among indigenous peoples. Generally, indigenous communities see themselves as cohesive peoples or nations that have been victims of foreign invasion and colonization. The legacy of colonialism ravaged indigenous "lands, sciences, ideas, arts and cultures" and left many indigenous communities "not only politically, but economically, culturally, and religiously dispossessed." The resulting social injustice has been borne out in stark terms as some of the world's highest rates of infant mortality, unemployment, alcoholism, disease, ill health, and incarceration pervade indigenous communities. Moreover, the colonial process continues in parts of the world, dimming the prospects of improvement for indigenous peoples in certain states. Specifically, in the rush to exploit untouched resources in remote regions, developing nations often trample on indigenous land and culture and commit atrocities against indigenous peoples.

The importance of indigenous land and the consequential significance of its exploitation cannot be overstated when identifying indigenous groups. First, the land is vital to the subsistence of many indigenous groups. Damage to indigenous land, therefore, may have a socioeconomic impact on indigenous groups that would exceed the effect of similar damage on nonindigenous peoples. Second, the land is sacred. It often is the source of indigenous worship and the object of indigenous return. Furthermore, specific sites, such as burial grounds, may have special ceremonial significance. In this way, the land becomes central to indigenous culture. In addition, the land may be inextricable from indigenous identity. For example, many indigenous peoples consider their relationship with the land to be the source of all knowledge and creativity. Thus, exploitation and appropriation of indigenous land is tantamount to an attack on the culture and identity of indigenous peoples.

Such exploitation nevertheless has endured, taking a public and a private form. On the public side, indigenous peoples remain vulnerable to exploitation by governing authorities. Indigenous groups tend to be underrepresented in critical elements of the national power scheme, including government, and they possess little leverage with governing authorities. Governmental prejudice against indigenous populations and a failure to recognize the rights of indigenous peoples persist in many states. Even constitutional provisions expressly protecting the rights of indigenous peoples do not always prevent the exploitation and destruction of indigenous land. Consequently, indigenous peoples continue to suffer a range of harms.

Certain injuries, such as the loss of cultural knowledge and the exploitation of indigenous property, have been exacerbated in recent years by the rapid internationalization of economies. On the private side in particular, the activities of MNCs in this economic process intensify indigenous concerns about exploitation, especially in developing nations where governments have shown little incentive to protect their indigenous communities. Developing nations often are attractive to MNCs because of the low production costs, including the absence of governmental regulation over the exploitation of natural resources. In turn, from the perspective of the developing nation, the high capital requirements of national development necessitate a large MNC presence. In some instances, the government may defer entirely to the MNC, which then serves as the de facto ruling authority and itself may pursue repressive and exploitative actions. In other cases, the MNC indirectly, if not directly, may support the ruling regime, which repays the MNC with concessions in indigenous areas and repression of dissent to MNC activities. Given the lack of consultation with the indigenous communities, the MNC's activities effectively assist governments in looting indigenous resources without regard for the needs and rights of indigenous owners.

B.   The Freeport and Unocal Case Studies

The investments of Freeport and Unocal in Indonesia and Burma, respectively, illustrate the typical MNC experience in indigenous settings and, therefore, are useful tools for examining the potential unjust enrichment claims of indigenous peoples against MNCs more generally. To begin with, each MNC forged a close relationship with the ruling authorities to help establish mutually attractive and lucrative operations. In 1966, Freeport became the first MNC to invest in Indonesia during the Suharto era, and the Indonesian government and Indonesian businesses have held minority interests in the subsidiary that runs Freeport's operations there. These operations, which are centered in the remote and indigenously populated Irian Jaya region, include the Grasberg mine, one of the richest mineral deposits in the world. These reserves, combined with those of the neighboring Ertsberg mines, have generated significant profits for Freeport. Given this return and the massive amount of investment that Freeport has put into its venture in Irian Jaya, the operations in the region are considered vital to Freeport's future.

Unocal presents, if possible, a more controversial example with similar dynamics. In 1993, Unocal joined a consortium of energy companies that had reached an agreement with the reviled ruling military junta of Burma, the State Law and Order Restoration Council (SLORC), to develop the offshore Yadana natural gas field. The project represented the largest foreign investment in Burma to date. As part of the project, SLORC had responsibility for clearing the pipeline route and providing security for the pipeline. The size of the investment and the nature of the agreement raised fears among critics of the regime that it would lend credibility to the rule of SLORC, which has been notorious for its brutal repression of prodemocracy forces and maltreatment of indigenous tribes.

Despite this criticism and numerous warnings and reports regarding SLORC's violent tactics, Unocal has persisted with its involvement in the project, presumably because it deems the risk of dealing with SLORC worth the reward. Although the Yadana project will produce significant income no earlier than 2001–02, it stands to provide a substantial annual revenue stream after capital expense and recovery for more than thirty years. Indeed, participation in the project already has provided dividends to Unocal. Specifically, Unocal signed a production sharing contract to exploit an important new gas field discovered by the consortium near the Yadana field. As the contract indicates, the Yadana project is significant not only for its riches, but also for its potential to facilitate future access to Burma's remunerative resources.

The Freeport and Unocal projects are typical of MNC investments in indigenous territory not only because of their profitability and their close association with governing authorities, but also because of their cost to the respective indigenous populations. Freeport's mining operations allegedly occur on expropriated land. Loss of their land has had tremendous cultural and social repercussions for the local indigenous peoples, including population resettlement and destruction of sacred religious and burial ground of the Amungme people. In addition, the mining activities have dumped over 114,000 tons of ground waste rock a day into local waterways. These untreated deposits have produced flooding and silting, destroyed miles of rain forest, and poisoned a regional lake. It is thus unsurprising that health problems among the indigenous peoples have become more prevalent. Finally, Freeport security forces in 1995 allegedly joined the Indonesian military in perpetrating various human rights abuses, including killing and kidnapping locals.

The allegations of human rights abuses in Irian Jaya resemble those that have arisen in the context of Unocal's Yadana project in Burma. In fulfillment of their contractual obligations, SLORC forces reportedly have used violence to relocate villages, enslave indigenous farmers, and steal property for the benefit of the pipeline. Indigenous farmers also assert that the presence of the consortium has led to the assault, rape, torture, and death of various members of the indigenous population in the Tenasserim region. As in Indonesia, the affected indigenous groups have been largely without domestic recourse.

The foregoing discussion points to some obvious distinctions between Freeport and Unocal. For instance, Freeport's venture has been of longer duration, has produced more tangible profits, and, arguably, is more directly responsible for the ensuing expense to the indigenous population. As a composite, however, the Freeport and Unocal cases present a firm basis to explore the elements of a potential unjust enrichment claim by indigenous plaintiffs against an MNC.

II. Making the Unjust Enrichment Claim

A claim for unjust enrichment must possess the following elements: (a) an enrichment must accrue to the defendant, (b) the enrichment must occur at the expense of the plaintiff, and (c) the enrichment must be unjust. In addition to these three elements, an unjust enrichment claim must survive any countervailing defenses or considerations. The following Sections will examine each element as it applies in the indigenous-MNC context and conclude with a discussion of potential MNC defenses to the unjust enrichment claim.

A.   Defining Enrichment

There must be some benefit flowing to a defendant MNC in order to initiate an unjust enrichment claim against it. The concept of enrichment, however, can be quite broad, and the ease with which an enrichment may be identified can vary. A common approach is to identify an enrichment as something positive—that is, as an accretion of wealth. Such enrichment is most obvious when there is an accumulation of assets or an acquisition of property by the defendant is the result of a subtraction from the plaintiff. This element is satisfied regardless of whether the defendant actually is responsible for the loss. A common example occurs when the defendant receives money due to the plaintiff's mistake of fact. In such a scenario, plaintiff's expense is the loss of money, and the defendant must disgorge the profit. In the indigenous context, Freeport serves as a potential example: If the loss of the land in Irian Jaya is considered the general expense to the indigenous people, then Freeport's enrichment resulted from this subtraction— after all, Freeport's profits derived from the land in question.

Of course, the expenses incurred by indigenous plaintiffs may not be easily identifiable. There may be disagreement over indigenous rights to the land at issue, and the loss of culture, identity, religion, and economic way of life that often accompanies MNC exploitation may be neither quantifiable nor translatable into the defendant's gain. The potential vagueness of these costs, however, does not defeat the expense element. The plaintiff's loss need not necessarily equate with the defendant's gain. Therefore, as long as the indigenous plaintiff incurs some loss, quantifiable or otherwise, the expense element can be satisfied.

When the loss to the plaintiff is not apparent, unjust enrichment theorists focus on the commission of a wrong against the plaintiff. Wrongdoing may include the breach of a duty owed the plaintiff or infringement of plaintiff's legal right, such as the right to exclude others from using a resource. Wrongful conduct typically associated with criminal, tort, or contract law may serve as evidence of an expense in a restitutionary setting. Moreover, claimants do not have to demonstrate a tangible loss if an offense has been committed. For example, if a defendant uses the property of another, there is an expense to the owner—the deprivation of the right to use the property—even if the owner did not intend to use it and therefore incurred no economic costs.

The foregoing discussion could be crucial to indigenous plaintiffs' unjust enrichment claims. The maltreatment that indigenous plaintiffs receive in connection with an MNC's venture into their territory may satisfy the second element of the plaintiffs' claim even though their greatest loss may not be captured in economic terms. Freeport provides a case in point: The duress imposed upon the indigenous people to give up their land and resettle reveals an expense. Thus, regardless of the ability of indigenous plaintiffs to state a claim under another area of law, such as tort, they could pursue an unjust enrichment claim without having to quantify the economic costs of the various physical, cultural, and other harms incurred.

. . . .

C.   Providing Content to Unjustness

The standard for injustice is whether a defendant's retention of the benefit at a plaintiff's expense would offend notions of fairness or equity. For a given set of facts, there may be benchmarks to suggest when this standard has been violated—namely, there may be a reason (such as a devious act or intent) or circumstance (such as the duress of the plaintiff) that makes the retention of an enrichment unjust.

In instances of a subtraction from the plaintiff, courts generally have found the enrichment to be legally unjust when it was achieved mischievously or, for lack of a better term, inequitably. For example, if a plaintiff is ignorant of the enriching qualities of an asset or does not have the capacity to protect the asset, the enrichment may be considered unjust. On the other hand, if a plaintiff voluntarily transfers an asset to a defendant who is free from misconduct, the defendant's enrichment will not be actionable. This latter scenario, however, is unlikely in the indigenous setting, where the benefits given up by indigenous people usually are conferred, if not entirely involuntarily, under significant duress. In such a case, the injustice element would be satisfied.

The ability to satisfy the element of injustice by pointing to the commission of a wrong makes the indigenous claim even stronger. Simply put, when the defendant commits a wrong, such as a tort, the ensuing enrichment may be unjust. Yet, the defendant does not have to commit an actionable civil wrong for the enrichment to be unjust. For example, a defendant who benefits through the unauthorized use of his neighbor's goods may be liable for unjust enrichment regardless of whether he would be liable as a converter. Similarly, circumstances resembling defenses to the enforcement of a contract, such as undue influence, duress, and unconscionability, also may make the retention of an enrichment unjust in a noncontractual setting. Perhaps most important in the indigenous context, the injustice element may be satisfied when the defendant in general has taken advantage of difficult circumstances confronting the plaintiff. Thus, indigenous plaintiffs can satisfy the requirement of injustice when an MNC or its government partner has committed tortuous conduct in violation of human rights norms, as in the Unocal setting; when the plaintiffs have been forced, without consultation, to give up their land for the benefit of an MNC, as in a Freeport-type case; or when it may be asserted that an MNC generally has taken advantage of an indigenous group's disadvantaged position.

That a third party most likely perpetrated the wrongful conduct against the indigenous plaintiffs does not preclude fulfillment of the unjustness element. The critical point is that the benefit resulted from some wrong to the plaintiff. Indeed, the relative innocence of a particular defendant may preclude the ability of a plaintiff to assert other claims and necessitate the claim of unjust enrichment. Put differently, "there are times when about all one can say in support of restitution is that it is just for the plaintiff rather than the defendant to have the benefit." Provided this background, indigenous plaintiffs may satisfy the final element of their claim not only because there is an identifiable act or situation that makes an MNC's retention of the benefit unjust, but also because they simply may have a superior right to the benefits derived from the land than does an MNC.

D.   Potential Defenses to Unjust Enrichment Claims of Indigenous Peoples

Substantive defenses to unjust enrichment claims generally seek either to deny the existence of an enrichment or to argue against any injustice in the enrichment. For instance, a defendant may argue that whatever benefit he may have received from the plaintiff has disappeared or that he relied upon the plaintiff's representation that the benefit was for the defendant to keep. While it is doubtful that these typical iterations of substantive defenses would bear upon indigenous claims against MNCs, the likely arguments to be offered by MNCs still may be categorized as enrichment and injustice defenses.

Note

1. An inspirational book on common law theories on global warming and other matters is CREATIVE COMMON LAW STRATEGIES FOR PROTECTING THE ENVIRONMENT (C. Rechtschaffen & D. Antolini eds., Environmental Law Inst. 2007).

----

8. Muddling Through with Partial Help from State and Federal Aid Programs

U.S. Army Corps of Engineers, 2006, speaking of the Alaska Village of Kivalina:[1]

> [W]ith global climate change the period of open water is increasing and the Chukchi Sea is less likely to be frozen when damaging winter storms occur. Winter storms occurring in October and November of 2004 and 2005 have resulted in significant erosion that is now threatening both the school and the Alaska Village Electric Cooperative (AVEC) tank farm.

Things are changing in the Arctic. Alaska is not what it used to be. Empirical reality has a relentless way of overcoming ideological insistence to the contrary. And whatever you hear about the U.S. government and its many bureaucratic "disguises," deep knowledge, vast experience, and creative response are not far beneath the surface. Consider the combined efforts of a "blind" Congress, an "unresponsive" bureaucracy, and the native "victims" of Alaska.

In 2003, Congress directed the United States General Accounting Office (GAO) to review Alaska Native villages affected by flooding and erosion. Specifically, Congress directed the GAO to determine the extent to which all Alaska Native villages are affected by flooding and erosion,

----

1. U.S. ARMY CORPS OF ENGINEERS, ALASKA VILLAGE EROSION TECHNICAL ASSISTANCE PROGRAM REPORT (AVETA) 23 (July, 2006).

identify federal and state programs, determine the status of efforts to respond to nine villages in need of immediate action, and identify alternatives Congress may wish to consider when providing assistance for flooding and erosion. This study resulted in the appropriately-titled report, *Alaska Native Villages: Most Are Affected by Flooding and Erosion, but Few Qualify for Federal Assistance.*[2] Figure 8[3] shows the 184 of the 213, or 86 percent of, Alaska Native villages affected by flooding and erosion to some extent and Figure 9[4] shows the nine villages determined to be in immediate danger due to flooding and erosion. By aligning the Map of Alaska by Native languages (Figure 10)[5] with the maps of Alaska villages affected by flooding and erosion, it appears that the two Native groups dealing most with the effects of global warming are the Iñupiaq and the Central Yup'ik.

The GAO reports that flooding and erosion in Alaska Native villages is due "in part to rising temperatures" at least eight times but does not identify what it considers the other contributing factors to be. Rising temperatures, impliedly attributed to global warming, are the cause of rising sea levels and loss of permafrost in Alaska and the surrounding seas. Of the nine villages studied it is important to note that two are the inland locations of Koyukuk and Bethel that were both identified as being in immediate danger. Coastal villages experience flooding and erosion due to rising sea levels and melting permafrost, but inland villages located on low-lying areas along river banks or in river deltas are susceptible to flooding and erosion caused by ice jams, snow and glacial melts and rising sea levels that drastically affect the river levels. Of the nine villages identified as being in immediate danger, four plan on relocating the entire village. Shishmaref, Kivalina, Newtok and Koyukuk are seeking new homes and locations, while the remaining five are taking other actions to prevent irreparable damage to infrastructure.

All is at risk for these villages. The response has been overwhelmingly proactive. None are sitting idly by while shorelines are stripped, sea levels rise, and ways of life snatched from them.

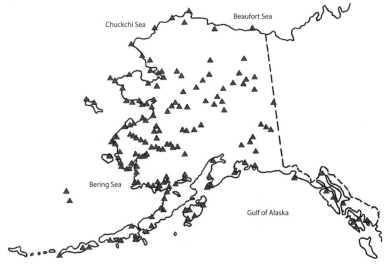

Figure 8. Alaska Native villages affected by flooding. Adapted from: U.S. General Accounting Office, Report 04-142, FLOODING AND EROSION IN ALASKA NATIVE VILLAGES Figure 4 (2003).

---

2. U.S. General Accounting Office, GAO-04-142 (Dec. 2003).
3. Borrowed from *id.* at 14.
4. Borrowed from *id.* at 28.
5. Borrowed from Alaska Native Language Center, *available at* http://www.uaf.edu/anlc/.

Shishmaref is located on a barrier island no wider than a quarter mile and three miles in length on the northwest coast of Alaska (*see* Figure 9). Similar to many other Alaska Native villages, the residents of the community are dedicated to maintaining traditional values and a subsistence hunting way of life. Most Alaska villagers practice this approach by choice and by necessity as the cost of transporting goods to the isolated locations is often impractical. In order to maintain the subsistence lifestyle, coastal villages have organized to cope with the vanishing shorelines in different ways.

Adaptive responses to protect what is theirs cover the legal landscape. The GAO's recognition that "Few Qualify for Federal Assistance" is partly a legal indictment of yesterday's disaster law and tomorrow's necessities in a remade world. The Shishmaref community has formed the Shishmaref Erosion and Relocation Coalition (SERC), which is comprised of the governing

Figure 9. Nine Alaska Native Villages in immediate danger of flooding. Adapted from: US General Accounting Office, Report 04-142, Flooding and Erosion in Alaska Native Villages Figure 7 (2003).

Figure 10. Alaska Native Language Map (20 Native Languages). Adapted from: Alaska Native Language Center, University of Alaska at Fairbanks. Available at: http://www.uaf.edu/anlc/.

members of the City, the Indian Reorganization Act (IRA) Council and the Shishmaref Native Corporation Board of Directors. This entity will act as the central organization in shaking loose funds to relocate the village to a more solid and permanent location.[6] The Village of Kivalina has brought a striking and creative lawsuit against oil and coal companies that are major sources of CO_2. (*See* ch. 1 p. 83 above). The lawsuit seeks $400 million to complete the planned relocation. The Village of Newtok is in a desperate race (with some success) to obtain funding (state, federal, or even private under the superfund law)[7] to allow a step-back to safety. No person in Newtok has reason to disbelieve or discount what the Corps of Engineers told them in 2006: "there are no geologic or channel geometry limitations evident that will slow down or stop the erosion before it reaches Newtok."[8] Public buildings in Newtok include a health clinic, school, armory, church, the Traditional Council Office, Post Office, and Community Hall. Some of these facilities could incur the significant cost of moving to a different location in town to temporarily avoid erosion, but erosion would reach the majority of these structures in ten to fifteen years.

"Removal," of course, is an ugly word in U.S. "Indian County,"[9] and it carries heavy burdens of things gone wrong. Virtually all law students know of the physical "relocation" of Japanese-Americans during World War II and of the privations and injustices that followed.[10] Far fewer know of the forced "relocation" of the Native Aleutian-islanders during World War II, and the deaths and destruction that followed.[11] Both of these campaigns earned official apologies from the U.S. government and won redress.[12] Only one was aimed at suspected enemies. The other was aimed at erstwhile friends and our own people at risk and in need.

Appreciation to Loren Hildebrandt, 2L, and to Aurora Lehr, 2L, for her paper entitled "Global Warming Hits Native Alaskan Villages," for the seminar, "Global Warming in Indian Country" (Prof. William H. Rodgers, Jr.), Law B584, University of Washington, School of Law, Spring 2008.

9. The Alien Tort Claims Act and the Small Island Nations

Ruth Gordon, Climate *Change and the Poorest Nations: Further Reflections on Global Inequality*, 78 U. Colo. L. Rev. 1559, 1623–24 (2007) (footnotes omitted):

The peoples of small island nations, the lowest-income nations, and the inhabitants of rapidly deteriorating habitats such as the Arctic region have no voice in this scen-

---

6. http://www.shishmarefrelocation.com/index.html (visited Aug. 18, 2008).

7. As suggested in the paper by Loren Hildebrandt for the seminar entitled, "Global Warming in Indian Country" (Prof. William H. Rodgers, Jr.), Law B584, University of Washington, School of Law, Spring 2008.

8. Alaska Village Erosion Technical Assistance Program Report 26 (AVETA), July 2006, *available at* http://www.iss.poa.usace.army.mil/akerosion/references/AVETA%20Report%20-%20Compressed.pdf (last visited August 18, 2008); *see* Kizzia, Tom, *State makes Erosion in Villages a Priority*, Anchorage Daily News, May 12, 2008, *available at* http://www.housemajority.org/coms/cli/cli_finalreport_20080301.pdf (last visited August 18, 2008):

The success of engineering projects is not strictly related to project costs. Expensive engineering structures have failed considerably sooner than the expected service life of the project in question … notably at Kivalina, where failed design and construction strategies cost millions, failed to protect citizens, and perpetuated threats to other village infrastructure.

9. *See* Indian Removal Act, 4 Stat. 411 (May 28, 1830), reproduced in Documents of United States Indian Policy 52 (2d ed. 1990, Francis Paul Prucha, U. Neb. Press, Lincoln).

10. Communication on Wartime Relocation and Internment of Civilians, Personal Justice Denied: Report of the Commission on Wartime Relocation and Internment of Civilians (Government Printing Office 1982).

11. John C. Kirtland & David F. Coffin, Jr., The Relocation and Internment of the Aleuts, vols. I-IV (Aleutian Pribilof Islands Ass'n 1981).

12. J.M. Lind, Sorry States: Apologies in International Politics (Cornell Un. Press 2008).

ario and will suffer until it is in the interests of the powerful to take a different path. Unfortunately, their distress is unlikely to influence this decision—it never has done so and it never will. The last factor, the climate, will eventually compel the revolution that must take place if we are to save our world, but by then the people at the bottom will be suffering the most horrific effects of what will be a much warmer world.

Five island nations will likely be destroyed by rising sea levels in the foreseeable future: Kiribati, Maldives, Marshall Islands, Tokalue, and Tuvalu (the "island-states").

One might think that complete and utter destruction of a nation by anthropogenic causes would give rise to a plausible claim under national or international law by the would-be "sacrificial" states. In 2002, Tuvalu threatened to bring a claim in the International Court of Justice ("the World Court" or "the Court") against the U.S. due to its overwhelming role in climate change.[1] But this lawsuit never happened. Nipped in the bud by discouraging prospects.[2]

The plight of the small island nations is a serious one. Due to their unique geography, these nations are particularly vulnerable to climate change. Furthermore, they are not responsible for the harms. The nations that make up the Alliance of Small Island States (AOSIS) constitute approximately 5% of the world population[3] yet they produce only about 0.5% of the world's carbon dioxide (CO_2) emissions in year 2002.[4] By contrast, the United States has a roughly equivalent population of 4.6% of the world, but it produced a shocking 23% of the world's CO_2 emissions in 2002.[5]

The small island states desperately need and deserve aid. These nations are generally considered "developing" and thus do not have the resources available to developed nations. The AOSIS has attempted international negotiations and accords without success, especially with regard to the United States.[6] Furthermore, international tribunals do not generally have enough authority to solve the problem. Thus recourse to the international courts may be a dead end. Luckily, the Alien Tort Claims Act of 1789 (ATCA)[7] affords a mechanism for obtaining justice through the U.S. courts. But getting into court is only the first step. There would be multiple hurdles to cross before a challenge could succeed.

Several law review articles have addressed aspects of environmental claims under ATCA,[8] and one Comment has suggested its application to small island states.[9]

Sea level rise may have the most devastating effect on small islands. Land-based ice and snow sequesters much of the Earth's water. As temperatures rise, these ice sheets melt and discharge their water to the ocean. The result is a rise in sea level. The IPCC predicts a sea level rise of only

---

1. Randall Abate, Climate Change, *The United States, and the Impacts of Arctic Melting: A Case Study in the Need for Enforceable International Environmental Human Rights*, 43A Stan. J. Int'l L. 3, 8 (2007).

2. Meghan Bowen, *Report on the Potential to Bringing a Claim Against the United States for Climate Change in the World Court: Pick Up Where Tuvalu Left Off*, for the seminar, "Global Warming in Indian Country" (Prof. William H. Rodgers, Jr.), Law B584, University of Washington, School of Law, Spring 2008.

3. http://www.sidsnet.org/aosis/index-2.html (visited Aug. 18, 2008).

4. Calculated by ATM based on statistics from this database: http://earthtrends.wri.org/index.php.

5. *Id.*

6. *See* description of activities on this website, Note 3, *supra*.

7. 28 U.S.C. § 1350 (2006).

8. Hari M. Osofsky, *Environmental Human Rights Under the Alien Tort Statute: Redress for Indigenous Victims of Multinational Corporations*, 20 Suffolk Transnat'l L. Rev. 335 (1997); Richard L. Herz, *Litigating Environmental Abuses Under the Alien Tort Claims Act: A Practical Assessment*, 40 Va. J. Int'l L. 545 (2000); Natalie L. Bridgeman, *Human Rights Litigation Under the ATCA as a Proxy for Environmental Claims*, 6 Yale Hum. Rts. & Dev. L.J. 1 (2003); *see* George P. Fletcher, Tort Liability for Human Rights Abuses (Hart Publishing 2008).

9. RoseMary Reed, Comment, *Rising Seas and Disappearing Islands: Can Island Inhabitants Seek Redress under the Alien Tort Claims Act?* 11 Pac. Rim L. & Pol'y J. 399 (2002).

20–43 cm this century.[10] But this estimate does not include the most important driver of sea level rise: the dynamics of ice sheet loss. There is abundant evidence that glaciers and ice sheets across the world are melting rapidly.[11] Careful analysis that takes into account ice sheet dynamics strongly suggests that sea level rise will be on the order of 5 meters in this century alone.[12] Meehl *et al.* emphasize the fact that there are still "in the pipeline" changes in temperature and sea level rise as a result of the increase in CO_2 concentration that has already occurred.[13] The authors point out that sea level rise will be approximately three times greater than the temperature increases.

Perceived or real limitations in international law might be overcome by the small-island states through use of the Alien Tort Claims Act. This statute gives jurisdiction to U.S. courts to hear alien claims: "The district courts shall have original jurisdiction of any civil action by an alien for a tort only, committed in violation of the law of nations or a treaty of the United States."[14] Thus, there are four main elements for a claim under the ATCA: alien plaintiff, defendant, tort, and violation of international law.

There are doctrinal hazards along the ATCA path of law. Courts will balk at being drawn into the "policy" waters and will be reluctant to take small bites out of problems that eventually will require vast investments in collective action.[15] Furthermore, it is difficult to prove that the emissions from any single actor are the proximate cause of damage, such as sea level rise at a remote island. Yet, a new meta-analysis has drawn close connections between human GHG emissions and the impacts of climate change.[16] Such an analysis coupled with a market theory that large emitters contribute a proportional amount to the impact could be used to show that the defendants were the cause of the harm to the small islands.[17] The sources of international norms will be at issue in ATCA cases[18] as will the nature of the rights asserted.[19] Human rights claims (piracy, torture, genocide, right to life, right to culture) are most common though an environmental claim in the infamous *Rio Tinto* case is still standing.[20]

ATCA is a remarkable relic of the U.S. lawmaking machine. It is a deep legacy whose own "tipping point" awaits a reconstituted U.S. Supreme Court. But litigators will continue to turn to it so long as U.S. climate-change policy favors drift, lack of purpose, and cynical denial.

Appreciation to Meghan Bowen, 3L and to Anna Moritz, 2L, for her paper, entitled "ATCA: Saving the Small Island States," for the seminar, "Global Warming in Indian Country" (Prof. William H. Rodgers, Jr.), Law B584, University of Washington, School of Law, Spring 2008.

Note

1. For more on the small island states, *see* ch. 3, § VI(B)(1).

---

10. IPCC, Climate Change 2007: Synthesis Report Summary for Policymakers (Cambridge Un. Press 2007).

11. *See, eg.,* Fred Pearce, With Speed and Violence (Beacon Press 2007).

12. James Hansen, *Scientific Reticence and Sea Level Rise,* 2 Environ. Res. Lett. 1 (2007).

13. Gerald A. Meehl *et al., How Much More Global Warming and Sea Level Rise?* 307 Science 1769 (2005).

14. 28 U.S.C. § 1350 (2006).

15. *See* Eric A. Posner, *Climate Change and International Human Rights Litigation: A Critical Appraisal,* 155 U. Pa. L. Rev. 1925 (2007).

16. Cynthia Roxenzweig *et al., Attributing Physical and Biological Impacts to Anthropogenic Climate Change,* 453 Nature 353 (2008); *see* Allen *et al., Scientific Challenges in the Attribution of Harm to Human Influence on Climate,* 155 U. Pa. L. Rev. 1353 (2007) (an attempt to "operationalize the attribution problem").

17. *E.g.,* Hymowitz v. Eli Lilly & Co., 73 N.Y.2d 487 (1989).

18. Filartega v. Pena-*Irala,* 630 F.2d 876 (2d Cir. 1980).

19. Natalie Bridgman, *Human Rights Litigation Under the ATCA as a Proxy for Environmental Claims,* 6 Yale Hum. Rts. & Dev. L.J. 1 (2003).

20. Sarei v. Rio Tinto, PLC, 487 F.3d 1193, 1213 (9th Cir. 2007).

Chapter Three

The Health of the Planet: The Atmosphere, the Earth, the Sea, the Residents

Chapter Three

The Health of the Planet:
The Atmosphere, the Earth,
the Sea, the Residents

I. Introduction

As one contemplates the rise in global fever and its multiple manifestations, it is important to remember that these "new" conditions are descending upon an earth already battered, stressed and compromised. James Gustave Speth, an experienced and astute observer of the world's environment and its legal scaffolding, begins his recent book (THE BRIDGE AT THE EDGE OF THE WORLD: CAPITALISM, THE ENVIRONMENT, AND CROSSING FROM CRISIS TO SUSTAINABILITY (Yale Un. Press 2008)) [hereinafter 2008 SPETH] with a series of "remarkable charts" that "reveal the story of humanity's impact on the natural earth." Speth continues (*id.* at 1) (footnote omitted):

> The pattern is clear: if we could speed up time, it would seem as if the global economy is crashing against the earth—the Great Collision. And like the crash of an asteroid, the damage is enormous. For all the material blessings economic progress has provided, for all the disease and destitution avoided, for all the glories that shine in the best of our civilization, the costs to the natural world, the costs to the glories of nature, have been huge and must be counted in the balance as tragic loss.

The "remarkable charts" were borrowed from W. Steffen *et al.*, GLOBAL CHANGE AND THE EARTH SYSTEM: A PLANET UNDER PRESSURE 15, 17 (Springer Verlag, Heidelberg 2005), Executive Summary, *available at* http://www.igbp.kva.se/documents/IGBP_Exec Summary.pdf (last visited 11/4/2008). These charts appeared at pages 132–33 of the Steffen book, with sources for the graphs cited in that book. There are no surprises. They show an exploding world population, rapidly rising Gross Domestic Product and Direct Foreign Investment, sharp increases in the damming of rivers, water use, fertilizer and paper consumption, and motor vehicles. Hand-in-hand with these developments come rising CO_2 concentrations, more ozone depletion (despite what you have read), hotter temperatures and added floods. The same package includes overexploited fisheries, run-away-pollution in the coastal zones, massive destruction of rain forest and woodland, and the unforgiveable and irreparable destruction of global biodiversity.

Pestilence

TIM FLANNERY, THE WEATHER MAKERS: HOW MAN IS CHANGING THE CLIMATE AND WHAT IT MEANS FOR LIFE ON EARTH 98 (Atlantic Monthly Press 2005) [hereinafter 2005 FLANNERY], *citing*

J. Whitfield, *Alaska's Climate: Too Hot to Handle*, NATURE NEWS, Oct. 2, 2003 http://www.nature.com/nature/journal/v425/n6956/full/425338a.html;jsessionid=1955B0D8B48B7EDE6AE84DACA82D1A0B (last visited Aug. 19, 2008):

> Among the most visible impacts of climate change anywhere on Earth are those wrought by the spruce bark beetle. Over the past fifteen years, it has killed some 40 million trees in southern Alaska, more than any other insect in North America's recorded history.

Fires

FRED PEARCE, WITH SPEED AND VIOLENCE: WHY SCIENTISTS FEAR TIPPING POINTS IN CLIMATE CHANGE 68 (Beacon Press 2007):

> This was late 1997, and the rainforest was burning. The most intense El Niño event on record in the Pacific Ocean had stifled the storm clouds that normally bring rain to Borneo and the other islands of Indonesia. Landowners took advantage of the dry weather to burn the forest and carve out new plantations for palm oil and other profitable crops. The fires got out of control, and the result was one of the greatest forest fires in human history. The smoke spread for thousands of miles. Unsighted planes crashed from the skies, and ships collided at sea; in neighboring Malaysia and distant Thailand, hospitals filled with victims of lung diseases, and schools were closed. The fires became a global news story. The cost of the fires in lost business alone was put at tens of billions of dollars.

Heatwave

GEORGE MONBIOT, HEAT: HOW TO STOP THE PLANET FROM BURNING 9 (South End Press 2007) (footnotes omitted):

> The summer of 2003 seems to have been the hottest in Europe since at least the year 1500. Thousands of people in Europe and India died as a result of the heatwave. According to a paper published in NATURE, human influence has at least doubled the chances of its recurrence. In northern Europe, however, the number of people dying because of extreme temperatures is likely to drop, as our winters become warmer.

Famine

MARK LYNAS, SIX DEGREES: OUR FUTURE ON A HOTTER PLANET 180–81 (National Geographic 2007):

> With structural famine gripping much of the subtropics [at ~ 2.5º C fever], hundreds of millions of people will have only one choice left other than death for themselves and their families: They will have to pack up their belongings and leave. The resulting population transfers could dwarf those that have historically taken place owing to wars or crop failures. Never before has the human population had to leave an entire latitudinal belt across the whole width of the globe.
>
> Conflicts will inevitably erupt as these numerous climate refugees spill into already densely populated areas. For example, millions could be forced to leave their lands in drought-struck Central American countries and trek north to Mexico and the United States. Tens of millions more will flee north from Africa toward Europe, where a warm

welcome is unlikely to await them; new fascist parties may make sweeping electoral gains by promising to keep the starving African hordes out.

Extinction

Stephen J. Culver & Peter F. Rawson, *The Biotic response to global change: a summary*, in BIOTIC RESPONSE TO GLOBAL CHANGE: THE LAST 145 MILLION YEARS 391, 392 (Cambridge Un. Press 2006):

> How do organisms react to environmental change of a rate or magnitude that precludes *in situ* adaptation? There are two possibilities; they can migrate or, if that is not possible or sufficient, they become extinct.

Chris D. Thomas, *Recent Evolutionary Effects of Climate Change*, in CLIMATE CHANGE AND BIODIVERSITY 75, 86, 79 (T.E. Lovejoy & Lee Hannah, eds. Yale Un. Press 2005):

> Something will live in these nonanalogue climates, but it is difficult to guess what.

> Climate change will bring with it massive changes in the composition of biological communities.

Disease

SIR JOHN HOUGHTON, GLOBAL WARMING: THE COMPLETE BRIEFING 178 (3d ed. Cambridge Un. Press 2004):

> A further likely impact of climate change on health is the increased spreading of diseases in a warmer world. Many insect carriers of disease thrive better in warmer and wetter conditions.... Under climate change scenarios, most predictive model studies indicate a net increase in the geographic range (and in the populations at risk) of potential transmission of malaria and dengue infections, each of which currently impinge on forty to fifty per cent of the world's population. Other diseases that are likely to spread for the same reason are yellow fever and some viral encephalitis. In all cases, however, actual disease occurrence will be strongly influenced by local environmental conditions, socio-economic circumstances and public health infrastructure.

II. A Human Future

WILLIAM H. CALVIN, GLOBAL FEVER: HOW TO TREAT CLIMATE CHANGE 4 (Un. Chicago Press 2008):

> What's the treatment? The obvious way to treat the fever is to remove the excess CO_2 from the air. Curiously, this is seldom mentioned today because "realists" have already scaled back their expectations—to merely slowing down the damage rather than fixing the problem.

We'll start with a trip to the doctor and a closer look at the diagnosis of CO_2 poisoning.

Climate Change and Human Health: The Likely Impact on the Human Community in the United States

Roger Rosenblatt, *Gregg Grunenfelder, J. Elizabeth Jackson, Catherine Karr, Rich Fenske. This paper was adapted from a report prepared for the State of Washington by the Human Health Preparation and Adaptation Work Group in December of 2007.*[1]

Introduction

Global climate change will have a major impact on the human community in the United States. From the standpoint of human health, the most significant aspects of climate change are rising temperatures, which will affect all components of our biological community. The Intergovernmental Panel on Climate Change (IPCC) estimates that by 2050 mean annual temperature will rise an average of 3 degrees F above late 20th century averages.[2] This increase will occur even if we are successful in stabilizing or reducing the production of greenhouse gases locally and world-wide.

Humans are an adaptable species, and we have already begun to anticipate the consequences of higher temperatures, more severe storms, and changing weather patterns on disease patterns and the built environment. The extent to which climate change will affect individuals and their communities depends to a large extent on the responses by public organizations, and on the vitality of our public health and public safety sectors. The purpose of this paper is to identify the most likely areas where climate change will impact human health directly, rather than to offer precise predictions of the scale of those impacts.

Key Human Health Impacts and Issues
1. Thermal stress
2. Degradation of air quality
3. Increase in vector-borne and other infectious disease
4. Impact of extreme weather events: storms, coastal erosion, flooding
5. Social and psychological impacts, and increases in social disparities

1. Thermal Stress

Annual average temperatures in the United States and globally are rising inexorably, although the effects vary from region to region. It is estimated that 400–700 people die from documented thermal stress, or hyperthermia, each year in the United States.[3] Because the actual cause of death is usually some form of cardiovascular failure, and hyperthermia is often not noted on the death certificate as an underlying factor, the number of heat-related deaths is underestimated.[4]

---

* Professor and Vice Chair of the Department of Family Medicine, School of Medicine; Adjunct Professor of Health Services and Global Health in the School of Public Health and Community Medicine; and Adjunct Professor of Foresty in the School of Forest Resrouces—University of Washington, Seattle, WA 98195. Tel.: (206) 543-9425; Fax: (206) 685-0610; rosenb@u.washington.edu.

1. Preparing for the Impacts of Climate Change in Washington: Draft Recommendations of the Preparation and Adaptation Working Groups, Preliminary Draft for Public Review (December 21, 2007), *available at* http://www.sboh.wa.gov/Meetings/2008/01-09/docs/Tab03g-DraftRec_ClimateChange PAWGs_122107.pdf.

2. G.A. Meehl *et al.*, *Global Climate Projections*, *in* Climate Change 2007: The Physical Science Basis. Contribution of Working Group I to the Fourth Assessment Report of the Intergovernmental Panel on Climate Change 747 (S.D. Solomon *et al.* eds., Cambridge Un. Press 2007).

3. S.M. Bernard & M.A. McGeehin, *Municipal heat wave response plans*, 94 American Journal of Public Health 1520 (2004).

4. M.I. Wolfe *et al.*, *Heat-related mortality in selected United States cities, summer 1999*, 22 The American Journal of Forensic Medicine and Pathology: Official Publication of the National Association of Medical Examiners 352 (2001); Centers for Disease Control and Prevention (CDC), *Heat-related deaths—United States, 1999–2003*, 55 Morbidity and Mortality Weekly Report 796 (2006).

The most devastating loss of life from weather events during the last 30 years has been due to relatively short but intense heat waves that led to hundreds of deaths in the United States and thousands of deaths in Europe.[5] Climate projections suggest that these events will become more frequent, more intense and longer lasting in the second half of the 21st century.[6] The greatest impacts will be in cities with milder summers, less air conditioning and higher population density.[7] An aging population also will put more people at risk.[8]

Retrospective epidemiological research allows us to identify the population groups most likely to be harmed by heat waves, and potentially to mitigate these harms through public interventions. The groups at greatest risk include:

- Children. Exercising children in particular are slower than adults to adapt to heat stresses.[9]
- The elderly. The physiological ability to maintain normal body temperature declines with advanced age. The elderly, especially if they have one of the other risk factors outlined in this list, account for the largest number of deaths during extreme weather events.[10]
- Poor, African-American, and isolated populations. As in the rest of our society, the most vulnerable groups are minority populations and the poor.[11]
- Urban dwellers, and those living in heat islands within cities. Not only do urban areas constitute heat islands within the larger landscapes, but poorer neighborhoods with fewer plants and more asphalt within cities are hotter than more affluent neighborhoods.[12]
- Outdoor laborers. Adults engaged in heavy outside labor during heat waves are at greater risk.[13]

---

5. T.S. Jones *et al.*, *Morbidity and mortality associated with the July 1980 Heat Wave in St Louis and Kansas City, Mo.*, 247 JOURNAL OF THE AMERICAN MEDICAL ASSOCIATION 3327 (1982); M.P. Naughton *et al.*, *Heat-related mortality during a 1999 heat wave in Chicago*, 22 AMERICAN JOURNAL OF PREVENTIVE MEDICINE 221 (2002); R. Kaiser *et al.*, *The effect of the 1995 heat wave in Chicago on all-cause and cause-specific mortality*, 97 Supp. 1 AMERICAN JOURNAL OF PUBLIC HEALTH S158 (2007); T. Karl & R. Knight, *The 1995 Chicago heat wave: How likely is a recurrence?* 78 BULLETIN OF THE AMERICAN METEOROLOGICAL SOCIETY 1107 (1997); S.A. Changon *et al.*, *Impacts and responses to the 1995 heat wave: A call to action*, 77 BULLETIN—AMERICAN METEOROLOGICAL SOCIETY 1497 (1996); S. Whitman *et al.*, *Mortality in Chicago attributed to the July 1995 heat wave*, 87 AMERICAN JOURNAL OF PUBLIC HEALTH 1515 (1997).

6. G.A. Meehl & C. Tebaldi, *More intense, more frequent, and longer lasting heat waves in the 21st Century*, 305 SCIENCE 994 (2004).

7. M. Medina-Ramon *et al.*, *Extreme temperatures and mortality: Assessing effect modification by personal characteristics and specific cause of death in a multi-city case-only analysis*, 114 ENVIRONMENTAL HEALTH PERSPECTIVES 1331 (2006).

8. K.E. Smoyer *et al.*, *Heat-stress-related mortality in five cities in Southern Ontario: 1980–1996*, 44 INTERNATIONAL JOURNAL OF BIOMETEOROLOGY 190 (2000).

9. American Academy of Pediatrics, Committee on Sports Medicine and Fitness, *Climatic heat stress and the exercising child and adolescent*, 106 PEDIATRICS 158 (2000).

10. C. Borrell *et al.*, *Socioeconomic position and excess mortality during the heat wave of 2003 in Barcelona*, 21 EUROPEAN JOURNAL OF EPIDEMIOLOGY 633 (2006); R. Basu *et al.*, *Temperature and mortality among the elderly in the United States: A comparison of epidemiologic methods*, 16 EPIDEMIOLOGY 58 (2005); Centers for Disease Control and Prevention (CDC), *Heat-related mortality—Arizona, 1993–2002, and United States, 1979–2002*, 54 MORBIDITY AND MORTALITY WEEKLY REPORT 628 (2005).

11. J.H. Greenberg *et al.*, *The epidemiology of heat-related deaths, Texas—1950, 1970–79, and 1980*, 73 AMERICAN JOURNAL OF PUBLIC HEALTH 805 (1983); C.R. Browning *et al.*, *Neighborhood social processes, physical conditions, and disaster-related mortality: The case of the 1995 Chicago heat wave*, 71 AMERICAN SOCIOLOGICAL REVIEW 66 (2006); M.A. McGeehin *et al.*, *The potential impacts of climate variability and change on temperature-related morbidity and mortality in the United States*, 109 Suppl. 2 ENVIRONMENTAL HEALTH PERSPECTIVES 185 (2001); Naughton, *supra* note 5.

12. C.S B. Grimmond & T.R. Oke, *Heat storage in urban areas: Local-scale observations and evaluation of a simple model*, 38 JOURNAL OF APPLIED METEOROLOGY 922 (1999); A.T. DeGaetano & R.J. Allen, *Trends in Twentieth-century temperature extremes across the United States*, 15 JOURNAL OF CLIMATE 3188 (2002); Smoyer, *supra* note 8.

13. Greenberg, *supra* note 11.

- People with chronic illnesses. Illnesses such as diabetes and heart disease — and the medications used to treat these diseases — increase vulnerability to sustained heat.[14]
- The mentally ill. People with severe mental illness are at higher risk, both because of behavioral factors and the effect of psychoactive medications.[15]

2.   Degradation of Air Quality

Climate change is likely to contribute to poorer air quality. As a result, air pollution issues are a major priority in the assessment of human health impacts of climate change.[16]

There is a direct relationship between ambient temperature and the key components of polluted air: ozone and fine particulate matter. Ozone and fine particulate matter already have a deleterious impact on humans. Ozone is produced through atmospheric reactions among precursors that include nitrogen oxides (NO_x) from industrial sources and fossil-fuel burning along with volatile organic compounds (VOCs) from manmade and natural sources. Levels of ozone are highest in the summer, when temperatures rise and accelerate these ozone-forming reactions.

Particulate matter (PM) is currently regulated in the Unites States as two size fractions, with the smaller or fine fraction (PM2.5) of greatest concern because of its impact on human well-being. Sources of PM2.5 include wood burning (woodstoves, field burning, and forest fires), as well as vehicle exhaust including cars, diesel trucks, and buses. Temperature inversions contribute to trapping of PM and cause localized peaks in concentrations. Higher temperatures, particularly in the American West, will almost certainly increase the frequency of wild fires.[17] Over the last two decades, a nearly fourfold increase in the incidence of large Western wildfires (*i.e.*, fires that burned at least 400 hectares) has been ascribed to increases in springtime temperatures.[18]

Epidemiological studies have identified a number of acute and chronic respiratory and cardiovascular (heart disease and stroke) health risks from exposure to these airborne contaminants. Increased exposure to ozone and PM air pollution have been implicated in premature death in adults, increased rates of infant mortality, worsened asthma or chronic obstructive pulmonary disease (COPD) in children and the elderly, low birth weight or prematurity in newborns, and serious respiratory infections, lung cancer, heart attack and stroke. Asthma and other allergic diseases such as seasonal allergic rhinitis ("hay fever") have increased in the population in the last decades and pollen—which is also likely to increase with climate change—is an important trigger for asthma and allergic symptoms. Ozone and PM are also asthma "triggers" and have been implicated in the development of asthma in children. It has been argued that the climate change that has already occurred may explain some of the rise in asthma incidence.[19] In ad-

---

14. Medina-Ramon, *supra* note 7.

15. R. Kaiser *et al.*, *Heat-related death and mental illness during the 1999 Cincinnati heat wave*, 22 THE AMERICAN JOURNAL OF FORENSIC MEDICINE AND PATHOLOGY: OFFICIAL PUBLICATION OF THE NATIONAL ASSOCIATION OF MEDICAL EXAMINERS 303 (2001).

16. *U.S. Climate Change Science Program Synthesis and Assessment Product 4.6 Draft*, available at http://www.climatescience.gov/Library/sap/sap4-6/public-review-draft/default.htm (last visited October 2, 2007).

17. D. McKenzie *et al.*, *Climatic change, wildfire, and Conservation*, 18 CONSERVATION BIOLOGY 890 (2004); J.S. Littell, *Climate Impacts to Forest Ecosystem Processes: Douglas-fir Growth in Northwestern U.S. Mountain Landscapes and Area Burned by Wildfire in Western U.S. Ecoprovinces*, UNIVERSITY OF WASHINGTON DISSERTATION (2006).

18. S.W. Running, *Is global warming causing more, larger wildfires?* 313 SCIENCE 927 (2006); A.L. Westerling *et al.*, *Warming and earlier spring increase western U.S. forest wildfire activity*, 313 SCIENCE 940 (2006).

19. P.J. Beggs & H.J. Bambrick, *Is climate change an early impact of anthropometric climate change?* 113 ENVIRON. HEALTH PERSPECT. 915 (2005).

dition, studies suggest co-exposure to allergens and air pollutants increase the potential for allergic symptoms to develop and may also increase the severity of response.[20]

These air pollution-related morbidities are important public health priorities. Heart disease is the leading cause of death for adults over 65 years of age, and prematurity and low birth weight are the second leading causes of infant mortality. Asthma rates remain unacceptably high in our country; for example 10.7% of adults and 12.7% of children have been diagnosed with asthma.[21] The direct costs of asthma in the United States are approximately $10 billion annually; the indirects costs due to lost productivity are an additional $8 billion annually.[22]

One of the anthropogenic ozone precursors is methane, which is also a potent greenhouse gas with a global warming potential that is approximately 21 times greater than that of carbon dioxide. One study has found that reducing anthropogenic methane emissions by approximately 20% would save over 30,000 lives in 2030 and approximately 370,000 lives between 2010 and 2030.[23] The monetized benefit of this reduction was approximately $240 per ton of methane. Furthermore, these authors found that there would be a reduction in PM-induced mortality as well due to chemical interactions with PM precursors.[24] Notably, these estimates did not take into account the secondary benefit of reducing the greenhouse effect.

The higher temperatures associated with climate change will increase ozone, PM, and pollen/fungal spore concentrations, and will thus adversely affect the cardiopulmonary health of United States residents. Specifically:

Ozone
- There will be an increase in the average summertime ozone concentration and the number of days where ozone concentrations exceed regulatory standards.
- The increased concentrations in ozone may result in ozone exposures that compromise human health, particularly for individuals with asthma, COPD, and those who work or play outside for extended periods of time.
- Climate change may undermine current and planned policy and regulatory efforts to improve air quality via reduced emissions and ozone precursors.

Pollen/Fungal Spores
- There will be an increase in concentrations of some aeroallergens (pollens, fungal spores), and the duration of the pollen season will increase.
- The allergenicity of some aeroallergens (due to biological factors and combined exposure with increased particulate matter) will increase.
- These may increase the number of individuals who develop allergic symptoms and worsen symptoms in those already affected.

Particulate Matter
- There will be an increase in wildfire-generated PM.
- PM2.5 associated with wildfires may yield a subsequent increase in the burden of both acute respiratory and cardiovascular effects in those exposed. This includes increased

---

20. C. Wyler *et al.*, The Swiss Study on Air Pollution and Lung Diseases in Adults (SAPALDIA) Team, *Exposure to motor vehicle traffic and allergic sensitization*, 11 EPIDEMIOLOGY 450 (2000).

21. Center for Disease Control, *Asthma Prevalence, Health Care Use and Mortality:*
United States, 2003–05 available at http://www.cdc.gov/nchs/products/pubs/pubd/hestats/ashtma03-05/asthma03-05.htm (last visited July 19, 2008).

22. *The Costs of Asthma*, Asthma and Allergy Foundation 1992 and 1998 Study, 2000 Update; *available at* http://www.aafa.org/display.cfm?id=6&sub=63&cont=252 (last visited July 19, 2008).

23. J.J. West *et al.*, *Global health benefits of mitigating ozone pollution with methane emissions controls*, 103 PROCEEDINGS OF THE NATIONAL ACADEMY OF SCIENCES 3988–3993 (2006).

24. *Id.*

physician, emergency department visits and hospitalizations for asthma, heart attacks and other cardiopulmonary conditions. Long-term increased exposure to PM2.5 may contribute to decreases in life expectancy and development of diseases such as asthma and lung cancer. It might also contribute to increased numbers of infants who die in their first year or who are born prematurely or of low birthweights.

In general, worsening air quality will have a greater impact on elderly, young, urban and rural poor (due to lack of access to chronic condition care and urban hotspots for ozone/particulate matter, rural hotspots for wildfire impacts). Also, there will be relatively higher exposure for individuals who spend more time outside such as the homeless, children active in sports, and outdoor laborers.

3.   *Increase in Vector-Borne and Other Infectious Disease*

Infectious diseases are potentially a major source of illness and death, and increased temperatures could influence infectious disease in several ways. First, global warming may increase the rate of reproduction of some pathogens, and may also have an effect on the immune response of the host— both animal reservoirs and humans. Also, temperature may affect exposure to infectious agents through changes in vector ranges and reservoir habitat, and via human behavior that may increase or decrease exposure to vector-borne, food-borne and water-borne diseases, *e.g.*, recreational water use, outdoor food preparation and consumption, and increased or decreased clothing coverage.

Extreme precipitation and flooding may increase exposure especially to water-borne pathogens that may contaminate surface and ground water supplies, and that may also alter the habitats of reservoir populations (*e.g.*, shellfish). The large number of climate-sensitive variables in vector-borne disease transmission makes the modeling of the effects of climate change very complex.[25] Moreover, there are a limited number of studies of the effects of climate change on ranges of vectors like ticks and mosquitoes, and at this point we do not know if we will experience an increased disease incidence with increased vector range.[26] The following are some of the diseases most likely to be affected by climate change in the United States.

Mosquito-Borne Diseases

Mosquito-borne viral illness such as malaria, dengue and West Nile (referred to collectively as arboviral diseases) are relatively rare diseases in the United States, but all occur sporadically and can cause severe illness and death. The disease vector for malaria exists widely in the U.S., and major outbreaks of malaria were common in both the nineteenth and twentieth centuries.[27] West Nile virus (WNV) has been detected in birds, horses and mosquitoes throughout the country,

---

25. National Research Council, Under the Weather: Climate, Ecosystems, and Infectious Disease (National Academy Press 2001).

26. J. Wegbreit & W.K. Reisen, *Relationships among weather, mosquito abundance, and encephalitis virus activity in California: Kern County 1990–98*, 16 Journal of the American Mosquito Control Association 22 (2000); S. Subak, *Effects of climate on variability in Lyme disease incidence in the northeastern United States*, 157 American Journal of Epidemiology 531 (2003); G.J. McCabe & J.E. Bunnell, *Precipitation and the occurrence of Lyme disease in the northeastern United States*, 4 Vector Borne & Zoonotic Diseases 143–148 (2004); A.T. DeGaetano, *Meteorological effects on adult mosquito (Culex) populations in metropolitan New Jersey*, 49 International Journal of Biometeorology 345 (2005); B.V. Purse *et al.*, *Climate change and the recent emergence of bluetongue in Europe*, 3 Nature Reviews Microbiology 171 (2005); K.E. Kunkel *et al.*, *Modeling the impact of variable climatic factors on the crossover of Culex restauns and Culex pipiens (Diptera: Culicidae), vectors of West Nile virus in Illinois*, 74 American Journal of Tropical Medicine & Hygiene 168 (2006); R.S. Ostfeld *et al.*, *Climate, deer, rodents, and acorns as determinants of variation in Lyme disease risk*, 4 PLoS Biology e145 (2006); S.M. Shone *et al.*, *Characterizing population dynamics of Aedes sollicitans (Diptera: Culicidae) using meteorological data*, 43 Journal of Medical Entomology 393 (2006).

27. R. Boyd, The coming of the spirit of pestilence: introduced infectious diseases and population decline among Northwest Coast Indians, 1774–1874 (Un. of British Columbia Press 1999).

and hundreds of human cases, with substantial mortality, have been reported in the last decade. Dengue is not currently endemic in the United States, but could become established if the vector were transported into the country and was able to reproduce in the wild. Other arboviral diseases that have occurred in the country and that may be sensitive to climate change are Western Equine Encephalitis and St. Louis Encephalitis.

Food- and Water-Borne Illnesses

Food-borne and water-borne illnesses are a significant source of morbidity throughout the United States and continue to be greatly underreported.[28] Most food- and water-borne pathogens are enteric pathogens transmitted via the fecal-oral route. Climate change may influence the pathogen directly (*e.g.*, growth, virulence, persistence) or indirectly through a combination of land use and climate events, for example, floods that contaminate food crops with animal waste.

One of the most commonly reported enteric diseases is campylobacteriosis, a bacterial food- and water-borne illness with tens of thousands of cases reported every year. This disease appears to have peak occurrence in warmer seasons but disease incidence cannot be reliably correlated with temperature. Gastroenteritis is also caused by a range of viruses (*e.g.*, norovirus, rotavirus, and enterovirus) and may be transmitted via food, drinking water or recreational water. Though seasonal in peak occurrence, no studies have linked temperature clearly to disease incidence. Gastroenteritis as such is not generally a reportable condition, so it is difficult to know just how great the impact of climate change is likely to be.

Vibriosis, caused by the pathogen Vibrio parahaemolyticus and other species, is primarily contracted through consumption of raw or undercooked shellfish. Washington State is the nation's leading producer of commercial oysters, and its experience with vibrio may presage the increased virulence and spread of other food-borne infectious diseases. Twenty cases of Vibriosis were reported in Washington in 2005[29] and 113 cases were found in 2006;[30] none were fatal. Although everyone survived in this instance, the outbreak crippled the oyster industry and caused severe and widespread economic damage.

Vibrio species are generally restricted to warmer waters, and in Washington most cases occur in summer months. Unusually warm weather and increased sun exposure in 2006 contributed to the outbreak. Washington oysters also infected at least 56 residents in nearby states between May and August.[31] Vibriosis is very likely to be an increasing threat to human populations with warmer summer temperatures. Vibrio vulnificus, a species found in warmer waters of the United States, is also known to cause infection through wounds and ingestion of infected shellfish. The fatality rate for V. vulnificus septicemia is above 50%.[32] As with V. parahaemolyticus, incidence of illness increases in warmer months.

Salmonellosis also appears to be directly influenced by climate change; of foodborne illnesses of known cause, 55% were traced to salmonella bacteria.[33] Thousands of cases of Salmonellosis are reported annually, and most cases go unreported. Salmonella cases peak in

---

28. P.S. Mead *et al.*, *Food-related illness and death in the United States*, 5 Emerging Infectious Diseases 607 (1999).

29. Washington State Department of Health, Communicable Disease Report (2005).

30. J.J. DeLoach & R.G. Lillie, *Crafting the Washington Vibrio parahaemolyticus Control Plan for 2007*, presented at Joint Conference on Health, Yakima, WA (October 2007).

31. *Id.*

32. *Vibrio vulnificus Infections Associated with Eating Raw Oysters*, 45 Morbidity and Mortality Weekly Report 621 (1996).

33. M.J. Lynch *et al.*, *Surveillance for foodborne-disease outbreaks—United States, 1998–2002*, 55 Morbidity and Mortality Weekly Reports 1 (2006).

summer months, though it is unclear if this occurs due to some intrinsic property of the bacterium or to seasonal eating habits and other human behaviors. Although salmonella is usually a self-limited disease in most people, it can be lethal in people with compromised immune systems.

Water-borne illnesses may also rise with increased frequency of flooding events. Outbreaks of water-borne diseases frequently follow heavy precipitation,[34] hurricanes[35] and flooding.[36] Both surface water and ground water used for drinking may be affected,[37] though generally surface water contamination is the greater risk. Campylobacter and E. coli have been found to contaminate drinking water supplies.[38] Although these diseases are primarily food-related,[39] flood events can result in contaminated crops that may transmit E. coli, Salmonella, or other enteric pathogens.

Cryptosporidiosis (Cryptosporidium parvum) and giardiasis (Giardia lamblia), both caused by parasites, are seasonal and are most frequently associated with recreational water use. As temperatures rise, increased use of water for recreation may lead to increased disease incidence.

Hantavirus Pulmonary Syndrome

Hantavirus, a zoonosis endemic in the western states, is carried by deer mice and other species, and humans are infected by inhalation of dust containing contaminated excreta. In this country, Hantavirus was first recognized during the spring of 1993 after a cluster of previously healthy individuals who lived in the Four Corners area of New Mexico acquired an acute cardiopulmonary illness. The disease has spread through many of the western states, with hundreds of confirmed cases nationwide. The disease is extremely dangerous, with a nationwide fatality rate of over 38 per cent.[40]

Incidence of the disease seems to be related to distribution and density of the rodent population,[41] which in turn is linked to the geospatial distribution of vegetation. Changing climate—in particular rising temperatures and increased rainfall in some places—may increase the extent of vegetation hospitable to the deer mouse. Washington provides a good example of the rate of spread of the disease once it has been diagnosed. Between its appearance in-state in 1994 and 2005, twenty-nine cases were reported, nine of which were fatal.[42] Three more cases, two fatal, were reported in 2006.[43]

Past experiences with these infectious diseases allow us to identify populations that are at elevated risk of illness and to develop interventions that may prevent or mitigate exposure to disease-causing pathogens.

The groups at greatest risk of climate-related infectious disease include:

---

34. F.C. Curriero et al., *The association between extreme precipitation and waterborne disease outbreaks in the United States, 1948–1994*, 91 AMERICAN JOURNAL OF PUBLIC HEALTH 1194 (2001); M.K. Thomas et al., *A role of high impact weather events in waterborne disease outbreaks in Canada, 1975—2001*, 16 INTERNATIONAL JOURNAL OF ENVIRONMENTAL HEALTH RESEARCH 167 (2006).

35. C. Setzer & M.E. Domino, *Medicaid outpatient utilization for waterborne pathogenic illness following Hurricane Floyd*, 119 PUBLIC HEALTH REPORTS 472 (2004).

36. T.J. Wade et al., *Did a severe flood in the Midwest cause an increase in the incidence of gastrointestinal symptoms?* 15 AMERICAN JOURNAL OF EPIDEMIOLOGY 398 (2004).

37. J.B. Rose et al., *Climate and waterborne disease outbreaks*, 92 JOURNAL OF THE AMERICAN WATER WORKS ASSOCIATION 77 (2000).

38. H. Auld et al., *Heavy rainfall and waterborne disease outbreaks: the Walkerton example*, 67 JOURNAL OF TOXICOLOGY AND ENVIRONMENTAL HEALTH, PART A 1879 (2004).

39. Washington State Department of Health, *supra* note 29.

40. http://www.montana.edu/wwwpb/pubs/mt9404.html (last visited January 24, 2008).

41. http://www.doh.wa.gov/Notify/guidelines/hantavirus.htm (last visited November 2, 2007).

42. Washington State Department of Health, *supra* note 29.

43. http://www.doh.wa.gov/Notify/nc/incidence/hanta.pdf (last visited October 3, 2007).

- Children under 5 years of age and infants are at greatest risk of contracting food-borne and water-borne illnesses, especially E. coli and Salmonella, and they may suffer serious complications from severe infections; children are also at elevated risk for dengue and malaria.
- The elderly also have increased risk with respect to food-borne and water-borne illnesses and dengue.
- Pregnant women have increased risk with respect to food-borne illnesses and malaria.
- Those with compromised immune systems are at greater risk for food-borne and water-borne illnesses, especially cryptosporidiosis and giardiasis, and also malaria.
- The rural poor and outdoor laborers have a higher risk of contracting Hantavirus and other vector-borne diseases.
- Socioeconomically disadvantaged groups are at elevated risk of contracting infectious disease in general; the increased psychological stress of living in poverty can impair proper function of the immune system.[44]

4.   Impact of Extreme Weather Events: Storms, Coastal Erosion, Flooding

Climate change research suggests that weather events will become more severe as increased terrestrial and oceanic heating increase the power of storms.[45] Coupled with rising sea levels from melting of ice world-wide, coastal erosion is expected to become severe.[46] Rain-on-snow events increase the likelihood of destructive river flooding. Coastal inundation, flooding, and landslides create direct hazards to humans who are living or traveling in harm's way.[47] In addition, flooding can spread toxins and infectious agents and contaminate water sources, and disrupt sewage systems, all of which threaten human health in the short and long term.

Many regions of the United States are susceptible to storm events that increase the chances of flooding and coastal erosion. As climate change progresses, the interaction of water and the human population will change. Rising temperatures globally will result in higher sea-levels, and potentially increase the intensity of storm events such as storm surges.[48] Higher temperatures will lead to more rain-on-snow events, a major trigger of the periodic river flooding that is already becoming more common.[49] Increasing population—many of whom will be tempted to settle near the coast or rivers—will increase the number of people affected by these forces.[50] And climate change may lead to increased precipitation in some parts of the country, although this is less certain.

Specifically, the likely increase in the severity of weather events will affect human health through the following mechanisms:

---

44. S. Cohen *et al.*, *Psychological Stress and Disease*, 298 Journal of the American Medical Association 1685 (2007).

45. G. Greenough *et al.*, *The potential impacts of climate variability and change on health impacts of extreme weather events in the United States*, 109 Supp. 2 Environmental Health Perspectives 191 (2001); R.M. Ashley *et al.*, *Flooding in the future—predicting climate change, risks and responses in urban areas*, 52 Water Science and Technology : A Journal of the International Association on Water Pollution Research 265 (2005).

46. S.C. Moser & J. Tribbia, *Vulnerability to inundation and climate change impacts in California: Coastal managers' attitudes and perceptions*, 40 Marine Technology Society Journal 35 (2006).

47. R.J. Nicholls *et al.*, *Increasing flood risk and wetland losses due to global sea-level rise: Regional and global analyses*, 9 Global Environmental Change-Human and Policy Dimensions S69 (1999).

48. R.J. Nicholls, *Coastal flooding and wetland loss in the 21st century: Changes under the SRES climate and socio-economic scenarios*, 14 Global Environmental Change-Human and Policy Dimensions 69 (2004).

49. W. Hoo & M. Sumitani, *Climate change will impact the Seattle department of transportation*, Seattle: Office of the City Auditor (2005).

50. H.E. Huppert & R.S. Sparks, *Extreme natural hazards: Population growth, globalization and environmental change*, 364 Philosophical Transactions. Series A, Mathematical, physical, and engineering sciences 1875 (2006).

- Slowly progressive coastal and estuarine inundation as sea-levels rise.[51]
- Acute flooding of coastlines as storms generate higher and more energetic storm surges on top of sea-level rise.
- Flooding of low-level inland areas as river flows increase during times of heavy precipitation and melting.

These geophysical changes in local weather patterns have the potential to cause direct human harm through the following mechanisms:

- Flooding—both coastal and inland—can hurt and kill people by destroying buildings, roads, and other portions of the built environment where humans reside during and after storm events.
- Landslides and avalanches can hurt and kill people through similar destruction of structures and roads.
- Flooding and coastal inundation can disrupt water supplies and sewage treatment facilities, and potentially lead to the spread of toxins, vectors of disease, and human pathogens.

Despite the current lack of specificity, it is clear that the physical impact of sea level rise and more intense storm events will place a greater proportion of the U.S. population in harm's way. The severe hurricanes of 2006, whether or not they were the direct consequence of climate change, demonstrated that destruction of natural barriers to storms coupled with more people living on the coasts led to tremendous destruction and loss of life. The extent of future damage is very sensitive to the extent to which public agencies prepare for and adapt to the inevitable changes in weather and its physical consequences.

5. *Social and Psychological Impacts, and Increases in Social Disparities*

The previous sections have focused on the effects of climate change on human health through mediating factors of the physical environment—that is, the heat island effect of urban settlements, worsening air quality, the increased range of disease vectors or persistence of zoonoses, and the immediate safety hazards of landslides and floods. In this section, we explore the links between climate change and a broader range of human welfare components that are mediated through social institutions. A thorough assessment of the disruptive effects of climate change at this level would encompass such phenomena as human migration patterns and population displacement; increased demand for social services; increased demand for energy; decreased employment, production and tax base; and disrupted delivery of essential services in the event of disasters (*e.g.*, floods) that impact infrastructure (transportation, communication).

Migration. Estimates place the number of global environmental refugees at 50 million by 2010[52] and 150 million by 2050.[53] Hurricane Katrina forced 1 million people from their homes, and one year later 250,000 people still had not returned.[54] Climate refugees are often adrift for

---

51. NATIONAL WILDLIFE FEDERATION, SEA-LEVEL RISE AND COASTAL HABITATS IN THE PACIFIC NORTH-WEST: AN ANALYSIS FOR PUGET SOUND, SOUTHWESTERN WASHINGTON, AND NORTHWESTERN OREGON (2007), *available at* http://www.nwf.org/sealevelrise/pdfs/PacificNWSeaLevelRise.pdf.

52. United Nations University, Institute for Environment and Human Security, Press release: *As ranks of "Environmental refugees" swell worldwide, calls grow for better definition, recognition, support* (2007), *available at* http://www.ehs.unu.edu/file.php?id=58 (last visited on November 14, 2007).

53. N. Myers, *Eco-refugees: A crisis in the making*, 3 PEOPLE & THE PLANET / IPPF, UNFPA, IUCN 6 (1994).

54. L.R. BROWN, GLOBAL WARMING FORCING U.S. COASTAL POPULATION TO MOVE INLAND: AN ESTIMATED 250,000 KATRINA EVACUEES ARE NOW CLIMATE REFUGEES (2006), *available at* http://www.earth-policy.org/Updates/2006/Update57.htm (last visited November 14, 2007).

years after an environmental disaster.[55] Incremental changes in climate also may lead to migration. Decreased agricultural and industrial production may contribute to job loss in some areas, leading residents to look for work elsewhere.[56] Sea level rise will displace others as low-lying settlements are abandoned. A flow of wealthy climate refugees from Europe to some areas of the United States may also occur.[57] Two streams of migration must be considered: inflows from outside the country, as immigrants from harder hit areas escape disasters or seek employment or less extreme weather conditions; and internal displacement within the country for the same reasons.

Social Services and Public Health. Displaced persons and migrants from outside the country will further encumber social services, requiring assistance with shelter, food, clothing, healthcare, and job placement. Those in poverty will lean more heavily on social services. Mitigation of the growing risks to health from climate change already discussed likely will require more resources to expand or improve public health infrastructure than are currently available. For example, the demands of increased maintenance and improvements to critical infrastructure due to climate change increase competition for public funding. The primary long-term factor cited in the inadequate response to hurricane Katrina was chronic understaffing of state and local agencies that plan for emergency response.[58]

Economic Impacts. The potential economic impacts of climate change are numerous. Higher temperatures, precipitation variability and runoff, and damage to infrastructure may result in reduced agricultural and industrial output, lower labor productivity, and reduced tax revenues.[59] Warmer temperatures likely contribute to outbreaks in disease-causing microorganisms, and costs to the industry are substantial when growing time and market share are lost because of these outbreaks.[60] Many industries are likely to be affected adversely by climate change, including forest products, fisheries, recreation, and agriculture, especially dairy and winemaking.[61] Also, the health impacts of climate change will exact an economic toll in public health costs as well as lost earnings and impaired productivity related to illness and death. Finally, in the case of disasters, insurance rates can rise dramatically in the aftermath as premiums are adjusted to match increased risk; those choosing to rebuild face much higher premiums and may have difficulty getting insurance at all.[62] On the individual level these factors add up to reduced employment, lower wages and lost earnings, and an increased cost of living; at the community level there are fewer resources for adaptation and recovery.

---

55. S.S. Morris *et al.*, *Hurricane Mitch and the livelihoods of the rural poor in Honduras*, 30 WORLD DEVELOPMENT 49 (2002).

56. U.K. DEPARTMENT FOR INTERNATIONAL DEVELOPMENT (DFID), IMPACT OF CLIMATE CHANGE ON PRO-POOR GROWTH (2004).

57. P. SCHWARTZ & D. RANDALL, AN ABRUPT CHANGE SCENARIO AND ITS IMPLICATIONS FOR UNITED STATES NATIONAL SECURITY (Department of Defense 2003).

58. U.S. Senate Committee on Homeland Security and Governmental Affairs, *Hurricane Katrina: A nation still unprepared*, No. 190-322 (109th Congress, 2d Session 2006).

59. DFID, *supra* note 56; Y. Bauman *et al.*, *Impacts of Climate Change on Washington's Economy*, Publication No. 07-01-010, Washington State Department of Ecology, Washington State Department of Community, Trade, and Economic Development (2006).

60. J.J. DeLoach & R.G. Lillie, *Crafting the Washington Vibrio parahaemolyticus control plan for 2007*, UNPUBLISHED MANUSCRIPT (2007).

61. Bauman, *supra* note 59.

62. J. LARSEN, HURRICANE DAMAGES SOAR TO NEW LEVELS: INSURANCE COMPANIES ABANDONING HOMEOWNERS IN HIGH-RISK COASTAL AREAS (2006), *available at* http://www.earth-policy.org/Updates/2006/Update58.htm (last visited November 14, 2007).

Energy Demand. While there is expected to be less demand for energy for heating during the winter as average temperatures climb, during the summer there may be increased demand for energy for cooling.[63] Many states rely on hydropower for generating electricity, and the predicted effects of climate change on snowpack and the timing of the snowpack melt will result in peak production of electricity occurring earlier in the spring and winter.[64] This may lead to supply shortfalls in the summer months. Heat waves already have resulted in temporary failure of electrical utilities, notably the 1995 Chicago heat wave, when unusually high demand for electrical power caused brownouts. Heat was directly implicated in 521 deaths in Chicago alone, many of which could have been avoided had cooling been available. In addition, the city's water supply was threatened as hundreds of fire hydrants were opened illegally by residents seeking relief from heat.[65] Energy constraints may have other effects on health; shortfalls in petroleum could jeopardize the ability of hospitals to use emergency generators if public utilities fail.[66]

Stress, Alienation and Health. Ultimately, the effects of migration, unemployment, cost of living, and reduced services is experienced by individuals in terms of their ability to cope in their daily lives; psychological stress has been defined as occurring when "an individual perceives that environmental demands tax or exceed his or her adaptive capacity."[67] The effects of stress on illness are well established; stress affects immune and inflammatory responses and is implicated in cardiovascular disease, depression, infectious and other diseases.[68] Public safety is another important component of wellbeing. Unemployment and perceptions of blocked opportunities are related to crime and social conflict.[69] Reduced public safety in turn becomes another source of stress. Weakening of the social and physical environment can undermine trust in government and policies; this lack of trust impairs civic engagement,[70] further alienating those most burdened by climate change. Finally, the same processes that increase business costs and reduce productivity and employment pose additional threats to health care access for the poor and underserved. The effect of these processes is to aggravate inequality, producing an underclass that is even sicker and more impoverished than before.

The following is an incomplete list of our Nation's key vulnerabilities to the effects of climate change on the social and economic institutions upon which our well-being depends:

- Employment and productivity in natural resource-dependent industries, including agriculture, fishing, hydroelectric power, and industries requiring reliable access to clean water may be threatened by warming temperatures and changes in precipitation patterns and runoff.

---

63. Bauman, *supra* at note 59.

64. *Id.*

65. E. KLINENBERG, HEAT WAVE: A SOCIAL AUTOPSY OF DISASTER IN CHICAGO (Un. of Chicago Press 2002).

66. H. Frumkin *et al.*, *Peak petroleum and public health*, 298 JOURNAL OF THE AMERICAN MEDICAL ASSOCIATION 1688 (2007).

67. S. COHEN *et al.*, *Strategies for measuring stress in studies of psychiatric and physical disorder*, *in* MEASURING STRESS: A GUIDE FOR HEALTH AND SOCIAL SCIENTISTS 3–26 (S. Cohen, R. C. Kessler & U. L. Gordon eds., Oxford Un. Press 1995).

68. S. Cohen *et al.*, *Psychological stress and disease*, 298 JOURNAL OF THE AMERICAN MEDICAL ASSOCIATION 1685 (2007).

69. P.R. Vowell & D.C. May, *Another look at classic strain theory: Poverty status, perceived blocked opportunity, and gang membership as predictors of adolescent violent behavior*, 70 SOCIOLOGICAL INQUIRY 42 (2000); S.W. Baron & T.F. Hartnagel, *Attributions, affect, and crime: Street youths' reactions to unemployment*, 35 CRIMINOLOGY 409 (1997).

70. E.M. Uslaner & M. Brown, *Inequality, trust, and civic engagement*, 33 AMERICAN POLITICS RESEARCH 868 (2005).

- State and local revenues from economic activities are vulnerable to climate change; declining revenues will be paired with increased demand for resources in many areas, including critical infrastructure, emergency preparedness, security and public health.
- Energy production and consumption, including projected peak consumption, will be challenged; the swings in the cost of energy will produce incremental changes, and the security of energy supplies will be critical to relief efforts during climate events like heat waves and floods.
- Increased costs of production (*e.g.*, agriculture, energy, transportation) will lead to increased cost of living for everyone.
- Migration, especially climate refugees from outside the country, will lead to increased demand for social services, employment, affordable housing and health care.
- Socioeconomically disadvantaged populations have fewer resources for adapting to a demanding environment; the poor are most vulnerable not only to the direct health impacts of warming but to indirect health impacts as well, namely increased economic pressures leading to worsened health care access and public safety, and increased stress and illness.

High Priority, Short-Term Recommended Strategies to Address the Health Implications of Climate Change

It is the responsibility of our public institutions to anticipate and respond to the threats posed by climate change. Although the most important state and national response for our country must be to reduce the local and global production of greenhouse gases, potentially disastrous climate change will occur even if we are successful in rapidly reducing the production of these atmospheric pollutants. The following preparation and adaptation priority strategies are recommended as initial steps that our country can take to minimize the potential human health impacts associated with climate change.

1.   *Enhanced Public Health Surveillance*

Climate change is anticipated to have impacts on the health of our communities in terms of increased communicable and vector-borne diseases, degraded air quality, and extreme weather events. Contributing to the magnitude of these changes is the possible immigration of "climate refugees" to the United States (*e.g.*, those individuals fleeing or forced from other countries due to severe climate change impacts), and possible internal displacement of U.S. citizens.

To prepare and adapt to the anticipated, as well as unanticipated, effects of climate change, critical public health surveillance systems will need to be enhanced. Public health surveillance is defined by the Centers for Disease Control and Prevention (CDC) as "the ongoing, systematic collection, analysis, interpretation, and dissemination of data about a health-related event for use in public health action to reduce morbidity and mortality and to improve health."[71] The ongoing and systematic collection of data is critical for monitoring changes in the magnitude of current public health threats and the early detection of new or emerging threats. Public health surveillance also will aid the development and monitoring of strategies to mitigate the impacts of these threats, including those related to climate change.

---

71. Centers for Disease Control and Prevention, Updated Guidelines for Evaluating Public Health Surveillance Systems: Recommendations from the Guidelines Working Group (July 27, 2001 / 40 (RR13), *available at* http://www.cdc.gov/mmwr/Preview/Mmwrhtml/rr5013a1.htm (last visited July 16, 2009).

To prepare for the projected public health impacts of climate change, near-term enhancements to the following existing surveillance systems are recommended:
- Zoonotic diseases,
- Air quality, and
- Notifiable disease conditions.

Zoonotic Disease Surveillance

Zoonotic diseases are diseases caused by infectious agents that can be transmitted from animals, directly or via a vector, to humans. Zoonotic disease spread is highly sensitive to climate change due to resulting ecological changes, or changes in human settlement. Surveillance for zoonotic diseases that may affect humans requires the ongoing collection, identification, testing, and reporting of disease among known vectors or animal hosts. State Departments of Health and Departments of Agriculture should collaborate on zoonotic disease surveillance improvements that include the following where they do not currently exist:

1. Enhance surveillance of vector mosquitoes and mosquito-borne diseases, including such diseases in animals;
2. Establish ongoing surveillance of vector ticks and tick-borne diseases;
3. Increase monitoring of vector fleas and plague in fleas and animals;
4. Establish long-term laboratory capacity and funding for identification and testing of potential arthropod disease vectors and zoonotic disease reservoirs;
5. Establish web-based notifiable conditions reporting for veterinarians;
6. Increase training of veterinarians on zoonotic diseases and disease reporting.

Air Quality Monitoring

Exposure to air pollutants including ground-level ozone, particulate matter, and allergens—all of which are likely to increase as a result of climate change—poses significant public health risks. Local climate warming is predicted to have a direct impact on air pollution levels due to increased air stagnation events and increased pollution from wild-fires, and indirectly from adaptation strategies such as the increased demand for electricity needed for cooling. Air quality monitoring varies enormously from state to state, and in many places is inadequate. We recommend that the federal government and the states should collaborate on improving air quality surveillance and outreach in the following ways:

1. Improve coordination and communication between regional air pollution control authorities, non-governmental health organizations, state and federal organizations responsible for air quality and local health jurisdictions;
2. Adopt standardized air health-risk communication strategies;
3. Improve health information dissemination strategies; and
4. Increase health-care provider outreach and education on air quality information sources and health implications.

Notifiable Conditions Surveillance

By law, hospitals, health care providers, laboratories, local health jurisdictions and veterinarians, are required to report various disease conditions to Health Departments nationwide within a defined period of time. The list of conditions varies from state to state, but generally includes: communicable and infectious diseases, environmental exposure-related diseases and conditions such as childhood lead poisoning, and water-borne and zoonotic diseases. States—with the assistance of the EPA and the Centers of Disease Control—should consider increasing the overall efficiency and sensitivity of the current surveillance systems to monitor for and respond to disease events, possibly to include:

1. Enhanced public health investigation and follow-up on emerging disease trends that may be caused by climate change;

2. Required electronic reporting to Health Departments of all notifiable conditions; and

3. Development of web-based training modules on notifiable conditions and reporting for health care providers, laboratories, veterinarians, and local health jurisdictions.

To prepare for and adapt to the public health impacts of climate change, it will be important to ensure that surveillance systems include a focus on sensitive populations (*i.e.*, individuals and communities of low socio-economic status, the elderly, and children). Such a focus not only includes data collection, but must also include methods of disseminating essential information to these populations in an appropriate and timely manner.

2. Enhanced Emergency Preparedness and Response Efforts

As previously described, climate change is predicted to contribute to severe weather events that may have dangerous and deleterious effects on the health of the citizens. State and federal government agencies should undertake concrete steps to mitigate and prepare for such events and to enhance emergency response preparedness. Initial recommendations for enhancing emergency preparedness and response efforts include the following:

- Emergency response systems should be developed in regions that may become prone to flooding and landslides, in conjunction with better land use planning to avoid future flood-related deaths.
- Emergency response systems at the local and state levels should convene a Heat Emergency Response Taskforce for the purpose of reviewing the emergency management planning requirements and guidelines for heat emergencies and emergency preparedness exercises. The Heat Emergency Response Taskforce membership should strive to improve cooperation across sectors and between agencies, and should include broad representation of state and local health, emergency response, and community agencies/associations.
- In conjunction with the efforts noted above, the Emergency Management Division should coordinate improvements to the state's ability to respond to heat-wave emergencies. Considerations for system improvements should include the following:
  - Enhancement of state-wide public awareness of the dangers of excessive heat and ways that individuals and the public can prevent health-related problems.
  - In close coordination with the National Weather Service, development of an effective state-wide early warning system for heat-wave emergencies.
  - Enhancement of public health infrastructure at the local level that will enable public health organizations to assume the role of Incident Command during heat-wave events and to assure effective coordination with state and federal resources (if needed) under National Incident Management System (NIMS) guidelines.
  - Improved collaboration among municipal agencies, hospitals, public safety, emergency medical services, industry and businesses, NGOs, and others.
  - Establishment of standards for public cooling centers for those without access to air conditioning.
  - Planning for response to extreme heat events accompanied by blackouts or power shortages.
  - Plans for providing transportation to at-risk persons to cooling centers or to triage and/or health care facilities.
  - A comprehensive system of training and exercises that enhances interagency coordination, that finds areas for plan improvement, and that revises the plan accordingly.

Summary

One of the critical impacts of climate change will be on human health, as discussed above. The extent of these impacts will depend upon how quickly climate change occurs, and the severity of the disruption of the climate under which our civilizations have arisen. Even if we are successful in rapidly reducing the production of greenhouse gases—and preparing for the antici-pated human health effects—the changes are likely to be pervasive and severe.

Climate change is the result of the activities of each of us, and of the social institutions of which we are a part. Reducing the production of greenhouse gases will require profound changes in personal and collective behavior. The fact that global warming will directly affect our health and the health of our children provides a powerful justification for making those changes as in-dividuals and as a society.

III. The Atmosphere, Oceans, and Climate: Supporting Services or Blanket of Life?

GABRIELLE WALKER, science writer, climate-change editor at NATURE, AN OCEAN OF AIR: WHY THE WIND BLOWS AND OTHER MYSTERIES OF THE ATMOSPHERE xi (Harcourt 2007) [hereinafter 2007 GABRIELLE WALKER]:

> This glow was the atmosphere, the single greatest gift our planet possesses. Earth's glorious blue color comes not from the oceans, but from the sky, and every astronaut who has seen that delicate halo has come back with the same tale: They couldn't believe how fragile it made Earth seem, and how beautiful.

> Back on the surface, robbed of that lofty perspective, we are inclined to take our at-mosphere for granted. Yet air is one of the most miraculous substances in the universe. Single-handedly, that thin blue line has transformed our planet from a barren lump of rock into a world full of life. And it is the only shield that stands between vulnerable earthlings and the deadly environment of space.

2007 GABRIELLE WALKER at xii:

> Every day, along with the warmth and light that allow us to live on Earth, the sun sends out x-rays and ultraviolet light from the deadly end of its rainbow.

> Thanks to our intervening sky [the ionosphere], this radiation never reaches the ground.

2007 GABRIELLE WALKER at xiii:

> [Our sky affords protection] from a force known as the solar wind. Electrically charged jets of particles from the sun were barreling toward Earth at more than a mil-lion miles an hour, ready to strip away our atmosphere and send it streaming out be-hind the planet like the tail from a giant comet.

> But to do so, it would first need to pass one of our staunchest defenders—Earth's magnetic field.... [Its] arching influence extends tens of thousands of miles above us, and it forces the solar wind to part around it like water around a ship's bow.

2007 GABRIELLE WALKER at xiii:

> ultraviolet rays that had slipped through the ionosphere were being soaked up by a dif-fuse cloud of invisible gas. Ozone is miraculous stuff. Near the ground it ... makes you choke. But high aloft it is both vigilant and resilient. Split asunder by ultraviolet rays, the ozone molecules around [Astronaut Kittinger] were calmly re-forming.

Discussions of justice often founder when the contemplated losses are not particularized as to persons, region, or enterprise. Professor Robin Kundis Craig brings the topic of ecosystem services to bear on the sober question of loss of "common resources" threatened by climate change.

A. Ecosystem Services

Borrowed from Thomas E. Graedel & Paul J. Crutzen, Atmosphere, Climate, and Change 3 (W.H. Freeman & Co. 1995). (See Figure 1.)

> Climate is perhaps most easily understood as what happens as a result of the atmosphere's and the oceans' combined efforts to redistribute heat from the Earth's equator to the poles. What happens at the atmosphere-ocean interface, therefore, is critical to climate, climate change, and the ecosystem services provided by every ecosystem on Earth.

This section reviews the basic processes of the atmosphere and the oceans, emphasizing their roles in climate regulation and other ecosystem services and paying particular attention to atmospheric-oceanic interactions. It concludes with a summary of how changes in these interactions contribute to climate change effects and the disruption of ecosystem services worldwide.

The Atmosphere, the Oceans, Climate, and Ecosystem Services

by Robin Kundis Craig, Attorneys' Title Insurance Fund Professor of Law and Co-Director, Program in Environmental and Land Use Law, The Florida State University College of Law, Tallahassee, FL 32306; Tel: (850) 644-0726; Fax: (850) 644-0576; rcraig@law.fsu.edu.

I. *The Atmosphere, the Oceans, and Ecosystem Services*

  A.   *What Are Ecosystem Services?*

The concept of "ecosystem services" acknowledges that functional ecosystems provide for human needs in ways that have real economic value.[1] The Millennium Ecosystem Assessment has broadly defined ecosystem services as "the benefits people obtain from ecosystems."[2] More specifically, according to Gretchen Daily, "*[e]cosystem services* are the conditions and processes through which natural ecosystems, and the species that make them up, sustain and fulfill human life."[3] In 1997, Robert Costanza and several colleagues estimated that the world's ecosystem services were worth US$16 to US$54 *trillion* each year,[4] emphasizing the economic importance of ecosystem services to human well-being.

While researchers classify ecosystem services in a variety of ways, their classification systems are broadly similar. This chapter adopts the Millennium Ecosystem Assessment's four categories of ecosystem services.[5]

---

1. Gretchen C. Daily, *Introduction: What Are Ecosystem Services?*, *in* Nature's Services: Societal Dependence on Natural Ecosystems 1, 3 (Island Press 1997) [hereinafter Nature's Services].

2. Millennium Ecosystem Assessment, Ecosystems and Human Well-Being: A Framework for Assessment 49, 53 (2003) [hereinafter MEA Framework].

3. Daily, *supra* note 1, at 3.

4. Robert Costanza, *et al.*, *The value of the world's ecosystem services and natural capital*, 387 Nature 253, 253 (15 May 1997).

5. MEA Framework, *supra* note 2, at 49, 56.

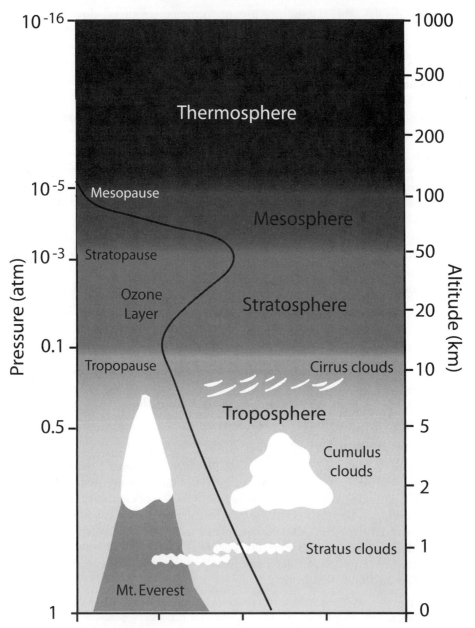

Figure 1. The variation of atmospheric pressure and temperature with altitude above Earth's surface. The regions of the atmosphere are noted, and the Himalayas are drawn in for perspective. Gabrielle Walker begins her splendid book entitled An Ocean of Air: Why the Wind Blows and Other Mysteries of the Atmosphere (Harcourt 2007) by describing the 13-minute, 45-second descent to earth by U.S. Air Force test pilot, Joe Kittinger, from a vast helium balloon above New Mexico. The date was August 16, 1960, and Kittinger was burdened with 150 pounds of survival gear, instruments, and cameras. Fifty miles above, in the ionosphere, Kittinger was protected from lethal x-rays by a few atoms of air. Above that, he was protected from the solar wind by the Earth's magnetic field. As he fell at a speed approaching sound, Kittinger tumbled through the ozone layer that soaked up invisible ultraviolet rays. At 60,000 feet Kittinger was below the point where a pinhole in his suit "would have allowed his blood to boil off into space." *Id.* at xiv. But the temperature had fallen to 98° below zero. A short time after he dropped past the altitude of Mt. Everest he hit the clouds and his parachute opened. He had reached the troposphere: "The air here isn't so much a protector as a transformer, a thick, life-giving blanket of air, wind, and weather that turns our planet into home." *Ibid.*

First are the *provisioning services*, or "the products obtained from ecosystems."[6] Sometimes referred to as "ecosystem goods,"[7] these services include food and fiber, fuel, fresh water, genetic resources, biochemicals, natural medicines, pharmaceuticals, and ornamental resources.[8]

Second, *regulating services* are "benefits obtained from the regulation of ecosystem processes...."[9] Regulating services are particularly relevant to climate change, because they include air quality maintenance, climate regulation, and storm control.[10] However, these services also include water regulation, erosion control, water purification and waste treatment, regulation of human diseases, biological control, and pollination.[11]

Third, ecosystems provide *cultural services*, which the Millennium Ecosystem Assessment defines as "the nonmaterial benefits people obtain from ecosystems through spiritual enrichment, cognitive development, reflection, recreation, and aesthetic experiences...."[12] Cultural services include cultural diversity, spiritual and religious values, knowledge systems, educational values, inspiration, aesthetic values, social relations, sense of place, cultural heritage values, and recreation and ecotourism.[13]

The last category of ecosystem services is the *supporting services*, the services that "are necessary for the production of all other ecosystem services" but which "are either indirect or occur over a very long time, whereas changes in the other categories have relatively direct and short-term impacts on people."[14] Given this definition, the Millenium Ecosystem Assessment considers the production of oxygen to be a supporting service, because such production occurs over centuries.[15] "Some other examples of supporting services are primary production, production of atmospheric oxygen, soil formation and retention, nutrient cycling, water cycling, and provisioning of habitat."[16]

Human changes to the world's ecosystems are already impairing the ecosystems' abilities to continue to provide their services. The Millennium Ecosystem Assessment concluded that "approximately 60% (15 out of 24) of the ecosystem services examined"... are being degraded or used unsustainably, "including fresh water, capture fisheries, air and water purification, and the regulation of regional and local climate, natural hazards, and pests."[17] Climate change will only increase this disruption of services, and change in the ways that the atmosphere and oceans interact will be important drivers of those disruptions.

B.   The Atmosphere's Role in the Provision of Ecosystem Services

Studies of ecosystem services often exclude the atmosphere as a *source* of ecosystem services,[18] and, indeed, it is difficult to think of the atmosphere as an "ecosystem," *per se*. Nevertheless, the atmosphere is considered part of the Earth's biosphere,[19] and the atmosphere is critically important to

---

6. *Id.* at 56.

7. Costanza *et al.*, *supra* note 4, at 253.

8. MEA FRAMEWORK, *supra* note 2, at 56–57.

9. *Id.* at 57.

10. *Id.* at 57–58.

11. *Id.* at 58.

12. *Id.*

13. *Id.* at 58–59.

14. *Id.* at 59.

15. *Id.* at 60.

16. *Id.*

17. MILLENNIUM ECOSYSTEM ASSESSMENT, ECOSYSTEMS AND HUMAN WELL-BEING: SYNTHESIS 1 (2005) [hereinafter MEA SYNTHESIS REPORT].

18. *See, e.g.,* Robert Costanza, *et al.*, *supra* note 4, at 253 (explicitly excluding the atmosphere from the study); MEA FRAMEWORK, *supra* note 2, at 3.

19. NEIL A. CAMPBELL, JANE B. REECE & LAWRENCE G. MITCHELL, BIOLOGY 1028 (Benjamin Cummings 1999).

ecosystems' abilities to provide ecosystem services. Most basically, atmospheric processes and phenomena, such as the ozone layer and the greenhouse effect, make life on Earth possible. In addition, the atmosphere plays an obvious role in weather and climate, affecting, among other things, water supply, food production, and many of the basic geochemical conditions (temperature, humidity, prevailing winds, oxygen and carbon dioxide circulation) that help to determine which ecosystems can exist where. Finally, many of the ecosystem services considered important for human well-being have a direct atmospheric component, including gas regulation and nutrient cycling.[20]

The atmosphere is the layer of gases that envelopes the Earth, held in place by Earth's gravity. In composition, the atmosphere is roughly 78 percent nitrogen (N_2), 21 percent oxygen (O_2), 1 percent argon, and 0.04 percent carbon dioxide (CO_2), with trace amounts of several other gases.[21] In addition, the atmosphere contains a varying amount of water vapor. Typically, water makes up about 0.25 percent of the entire atmosphere but accounts for 1 to 4 percent of the air near the Earth's surface.[22] The exact concentration of water in any particular location, in turn, plays an important role in determining weather, precipitation, and humidity.

This gas composition is important to ecosystems. As scientists note, "[o]ver billions of years the composition of the atmosphere has changed considerably."[23] In particular, over the eons, bacteria, algae, and plants have added oxygen to the atmosphere. This concentration of oxygen allows for both the existence of animal life and the formation of the atmosphere's ozone layer.[24] The ozone layer protects all life from damaging ultraviolet radiation,[25] one reason the entire world responded to the discovery of the ozone layer's deterioration and ozone "holes" in the atmosphere.[26] Finally, the presence of oxygen "also contributes to the self-cleansing ability of the atmosphere through oxidation processes."[27]

Focusing solely on the composition of the atmosphere, however, can imply that the atmosphere is uniform. Importantly, it is not.

First, the atmosphere consists of recognizable layers. Proceeding from the surface of the Earth to the edge of space, these layers are: (1) the *troposphere*, which contains roughly 80 percent of the mass of the atmosphere and varies in thickness from about 23,000 feet at the poles to 60,000 feet at the equator; (2) the *stratosphere*, which stretches from the troposphere out to about 160,000 feet above the Earth's surface and contains the Earth's protective ozone layer; (3) the *mesosphere*, which exists from 160,000 feet to approximately 265,000 to 280,000 feet above the Earth's surface and is where most meteors burn up; (4) the *thermosphere*, which extends from the mesosphere out to about 400 miles from the Earth's surface, with temperatures actually increasing the farther toward space one travels; (5) the *ionosphere*, lying beyond the thermosphere and so named because the gases are ionized by solar radiation, producing (among other effects) the Earth's auroras; and (6) the loosely organized *exosphere*, which extends 600 to 6,000 miles above the Earth's surface and interacts with the solar winds.[28]

---

20. Robert Costanza, *et al.*, *supra* note 4, at 254 tbl. 1.

21. WILLIAM K. PURVES, GORDON H. ORIANS & H. CRAIG HELLER, LIFE: THE SCIENCE OF BIOLOGY 1136 (W H Freeman & Co., 4d. 1995).

22. *Id.*

23. Susan E. Alexander, Stephen H. Schneider, & Kalen Lagerquist, *The Interaction of Climate and Life*, in NATURE'S SERVICES, *supra* note 1, at 71.

24. *Id.*

25. *Id.* at 72.

26. FRED PEARCE, WITH SPEED AND VIOLENCE: WHY SCIENTISTS FEAR TIPPING POINTS IN CLIMATE CHANGE 217–221 (Beacon Press 2007).

27. Alexander, Schneider, & Lagerquist, *supra* note 23, at 71.

28. NOAA, National Weather Service, http://www.srh.noaa.gov/srh/jetstream/atmos/layers.htm (last visited September 19, 2008).

The layering of the atmosphere combined with the presence of greenhouse gases in the atmosphere creates the greenhouse effect, which both keeps Earth warm enough for the life that currently exists here and provides the major mechanism for climate change. The atmosphere reflects about 30 percent of incoming solar radiation; the 70 percent that passes through warms the atmosphere, oceans, and land.[29] Much of this heat would re-escape into space, however, if the greenhouse gases—water vapor, carbon dioxide, methane, and nitrous oxide—in the troposphere and ozone in both the troposphere and stratosphere did not capture and re-radiate the heat energy. As a result, "[t]he natural greenhouse effect operating through clouds, water vapor, carbon dioxide, and other trace gases in the atmosphere keeps the earth's surface habitable. The surface temperature is about thirty-three degrees Celsius higher on average than if these gases or cloud particles were not present."[30]

Of course, the greenhouse effect and the greenhouse gases that can trap heat are also important to the processes of global climate change. In particular, researchers have emphasized that even though CO_2 makes up a relatively small percentage of the Earth's atmosphere, it "has a substantial effect on earth's heat balance by absorbing infrared radiation."[31] Measurements at the Mauna Loa observatory in Hawaii and from ice core samples indicate that concentrations of carbon dioxide in the atmosphere have been increasing rapidly since human societies began to industrialize,[32] increasing the atmosphere's heat-trapping potential.

Second, the gases in the atmosphere circulate in winds and currents, which are caused by differences in temperature and pressure in various parts of the atmosphere. For example, solar radiation heats air at the tropics. As its temperature increases, air at the equator expands and rises, creating a low-pressure belt. Cooler air from the high-pressure areas that exist around latitudes 30°N and 30°S then flows toward the equator, creating a general movement of surface air from these latitudes toward the equator.[33] Higher in the troposphere, air tends to move in the opposite direction, creating three-dimensional convection currents.[34] At the same time, the Earth's rotation deflects air flows to the west, a phenomenon known as the Coriolis effect, creating the northeast trade winds in the Northern Hemisphere and the southeast trade winds in the Southern Hemisphere.[35] Air also flows from the high-pressure areas at 30°N and 30°S toward the poles, creating the "Westerlies" in each hemisphere, which are strongest at about 40°N to 50°N and 40°S to 50°S.[36] Finally, air flows from high pressure areas at the poles toward the equator, creating the "Easterlies" in each polar region.[37]

The trade winds, Westerlies, and Easterlies are considered prevailing winds because they reflect consistent trends in the speed and direction of wind in particular regions of the Earth.[38] Local winds, of course, also exist, created as a result of more temporary and localized pressure

29. H. Le Treut *et al.*, *Historical Overview of Climate Change, in* Climate Change 2007: The Physical Science Basis. Contribution of Working Group I to the Fourth Assessment Report of the Intergovernmental Panel on Climate Change 94, 96 (S. Solomon *et al.* eds., Cambridge Un. Press 2007); Joe Kraynak & Kim W. Tetrault, The Complete Idiot's Guide to the Oceans 18 (Alpha Books 2003) [hereinafter Guide to the Oceans].

30. Alexander, Schneider, & Lagerquist, *supra* note 23, at 71–72.

31. Alexander, Schneider, & Lagerquist, *supra* note 23, at 77.

32. John T. Houghton, Global Warming: The Complete Briefing 30 (Cambridge Un. Press, 3d. 2004).

33. Guido Visconti, Fundamentals of Physics and Chemistry of the Atmosphere 245 (Springer 2001).

34. *Id.* at 246.

35. *Id.*; Dennis Pagen, Understanding the Sky 54–55 (Sport Aviation Publications 1992).

36. *Id.*

37. *Id.*

38. *Id.*

and temperature differentials. Both types of air movement, however, contribute to weather—the specific atmospheric conditions existing at a particular place at a particular time.[39] Most weather events occur in the troposphere, although the stratosphere also has weather that can influence Earth's surface through poorly understood mechanisms.[40]

At a longer temporal scale, the atmosphere's composition and currents also play a significant role in nutrient cycling. For example, atmospheric processes are an important part of the global nitrogen cycle. In this cycle, various soil, water, and plant processes take up atmospheric (N_2) and then "fix" it as ammonia (NH_3). Unlike gaseous nitrogen, ammonia can be used by living organisms.[41] As these organisms die and decay, bacteria re-convert the ammonia to nitrogen gas and nitrous oxides (N_2O).[42] The atmosphere also plays an important role in the sulfur cycle, involving sulfur dioxide (SO_2), sulfate (SO_4), and hydrogen sulfide (H_2S),[43] and in the carbon cycle, through its cycling of carbon dioxide (CO_2).[44]

C.   Ecosystem Services Provided by the Oceans

Unlike the atmosphere, the world's oceans *are* ecosystems—or, more specifically, a collection of interconnected ecosystems. In their 1997 article, Robert Costanza and his colleagues estimated that about 63 percent of the total world value of ecosystem services—about US $20.9 trillion—comes from marine environments.[45] These researchers emphasized that the oceans are particularly important for the gas regulation, disturbance regulation, nutrient cycling, biological control, habitat, food production, raw materials, recreation, and cultural services they provide.[46]

Thus, the oceans provide a variety of valuable ecosystem services, covering all four of the Millennium Ecosystem Assessment's categories. Starting with the longest-term of these services, the oceans provide supporting services in the form of oxygen production and the concentration of oxygen in both the atmosphere and the marine environment itself. Tiny plants that float near the oceans' surfaces throughout the world, known as phytoplankton, produce oxygen.[47] Some of this oxygen remains dissolved within the oceans themselves, where it is used by fish and other marine animals (but not marine mammals or sea turtles, which breathe atmospheric oxygen). Most of the oxygen, however, is released into the atmosphere. In fact, marine phytoplankton produce half of the world's atmospheric oxygen[48]—the oxygen upon which terrestrial animals, including humans, depend.

Oceans provide regulating services related to air quality maintenance. As the Millennium Ecosystem Assessment has noted, "[e]cosystems both contribute chemicals to and extract chemicals from the atmosphere, influencing many aspects of air quality."[49] With respect to the oceans more specifically, scientists have noted that "[g]iven time, the oceans can absorb most of what

---

39. AMERICAN HERITAGE DICTIONARY OF THE ENGLISH LANGUAGE 1948 (4th ed. 2000).

40. GLOSSARY OF METEOROLOGY. *Troposphere,* http://amsglossary.allenpress.com/glossary (last visited September 20, 2008); Cynthia O'Carroll, *Weather Forecasters May Look Sky-high For Answers,* GODDARD SPACE FLIGHT CENTER (NASA) (October 21, 2001) *available at* http://www.gsfc.nasa.gov/topstory/20011018wind surface.html (last visited September 20, 2008).

41. Alexander, Schneider, & Lagerquist, *supra* note 23, at 74.

42. *Id.* at 74–75.

43. *Id.* at 75–76.

44. *Id.* at 76–77; ch. 3, §IV.

45. Robert Costanza, *et al., supra* note 4, at 259.

46. *Id.* at 256 tbl. 2.

47. John Roach, *Source of Half Earth's Oxygen Gets Little Credit,* NATIONAL GEOGRAPHIC NEWS, http://news.nationalgeographic.com/news/2004/06/0607_040607_phytoplankton.html (June 4, 2004).

48. *Id.*

49. MEA FRAMEWORK, *supra* note 2, at 57.

we can throw into the atmosphere."[50] Ocean ecosystems, and especially coastal ecosystems, also contribute regulating services in terms of storm protection. For example, the Millennium Ecosystem Assessment recognized that "[t]he presence of coastal ecosystems such as mangroves and coral reefs can dramatically reduce the damage caused by hurricanes or large waves."[51] However, as it also recognized, "[a]pproximately 20% of the world's coral reefs were lost and an additional 20% degraded in the last several decades of the twentieth century, and approximately 35% of mangrove area was lost during this time (in countries for which sufficient data exist, which encompass about half of the area of mangroves)."[52]

The cultural services of the oceans—especially coastal areas such as beaches, coral reefs, and kelp forests—are obvious to anyone who has visited or lived in Hawaii, California, Florida, or Maine. Coastal and fishing communities have their own identities. In addition, ocean resources have particular cultural and religious significance for Native Hawaiians and many coastal Native American tribes.

Finally, oceans provide several kinds of provisioning services. The most obvious of these is food. In addition to producing oxygen, the phytoplankton form the basis of the extensive ocean food chain,[53] culminating in the fish, mollusks (clams, oysters, abalone), crustaceans (crab, lobsters), reptiles (sea turtles), and marine mammals (whales, seals, sea lions) that humans have depended upon and exploited throughout history. However, all evidence indicates resources are already being harvested unsustainably worldwide,[54] and this overuse is already having economic and cultural impacts on humans.[55]

II. Atmospheric-Oceanic Interactions

Oceans cover approximately 71 percent of the Earth's surface and are in continuous contact with the atmosphere. At this ocean-atmosphere interface, the two systems directly exchange gases, water and water vapor, particles, and energy, both kinetic and in the form of heat.[56] The most important point, however, is that ocean-atmosphere interactions go both ways: the atmosphere affects the oceans and their processes, but the oceans also affect the atmosphere and its processes.

Gas and chemical exchanges between the oceans and the atmosphere are important to life processes around the world. As noted, the phytoplankton in the oceans produce half of the world's oxygen and are the basis of many food webs. However, phytoplankton growth in the oceans is generally limited by lack of iron, an essential nutrient.[57] Most available iron reaches the oceans through wind-borne dust from the desert,[58] another important atmosphere-ocean interaction.

Gas and chemical exchanges between the atmosphere and oceans are also important to climate change processes. For example, phytoplankton "produce a chemical that affects the formation of clouds, which influence the amount of the sun's energy the earth retains."[59] In addition,

---

50. Pearce, *supra* note 26, at 86.

51. MEA Framework, *supra* note 2, at 58.

52. MEA Synthesis Report, *supra* note 17, at 2.

53. Guide to the Oceans, *supra* note 29, at 88.

54. MEA Synthesis Report, *supra* note 17, at 6. *See also generally* Callum Roberts, The Unnatural History of the Sea (Island Press 2007); C. Bruce Knecht, Hooked: Pirates, Poaching, and the Perfect Fish (Rodale Books 2006); Richard Ellis, The Empty Ocean: Plundering the World's Marine Life (Island Press 2003) (all describing over-exploitation of marine life).

55. *Id.*

56. Guide to the Oceans, *supra* note 29, at 18.

57. T.D. Jickells, *et al.*, *Global Iron Connections Between Desert Dust, Ocean Biochemistry, and Climate*, 308 Science 67, 67 (April 1, 2005).

58. *Id.*

59. Guide to the Oceans, *supra* note 29, at 88.

evaporation of water from the oceans contributes to the concentration of water vapor in the atmosphere, supporting the greenhouse effect and contributing to weather and precipitation patterns throughout the world.[60] Indeed, "[e]vaporation of ocean water is about six times as much globally as evapotranspiration on land...."[61]

Most importantly, the oceans are the world's largest carbon sinks, giving the oceans a direct and important role in regulating climate.[62] At least three ocean processes affect carbon dioxide concentrations in the atmosphere. First, carbon dioxide dissolves directly into ocean water.[63] Second, various animal species in the ocean use carbon dioxide to make their calcium carbonate shells.[64] Third, the phytoplankton in the oceans extract carbon dioxide from the atmosphere during photosynthesis[65] and "are responsible for converting 30 to 50 percent of the carbon dioxide in the atmosphere back into oxygen."[66]

The oceans' ability to sequester carbon dioxide has given rise to several climate change mitigation schemes. For example, after scientists discovered that adding iron to ocean waters could trigger the rapid growth of phytoplankton, known as phytoplankton blooms, ocean iron fertilization was proposed as a method for dealing with climate change,[67] and a dozen or so experiments to test this theory have been run.[68] However, recent reports indicate that these mechanisms don't work, although private companies have vowed to continue the efforts in the hopes of generating carbon credits to sell.[69]

Beyond carbon dioxide interactions, some of the most important atmosphere-ocean interactions with respect to climate involve currents. As Al Gore reported in AN INCONVENIENT TRUTH, "scientists say that the world's climate is best understood as a kind of engine for redistributing heat from the Equator and the tropics to the poles."[70] As was described for atmospheric winds, such redistribution arises because the regions surrounding the equator absorb far more solar energy than the polar regions. "The redistribution of heat from the Equator to the poles drives the wind and ocean currents, like the Gulf Stream and the jet stream."[71]

In the oceans, water circulates in both surface currents and in three-dimensional, globe-spanning, interconnected currents.[72] Ocean surface currents are driven by the prevailing winds[73] and account for 13 to 25 percent of all ocean water movement.[74] Near the equator, the trade winds push seawater from east to west; farther north and south, both the winds and the

---

60. Alexander, Schneider, & Lagerquist, *supra* note 23, at 73.

61. *Id.*

62. Pearce, *supra* note 26, at 86.

63. Alexander, Schneider, & Lagerquist, *supra* note 23, at 76.

64. *Id.*

65. GUIDE TO THE OCEANS, *supra* note 29, at 87.

66. *Id.* at 88.

67. World Resources Institute, *Scientists Doubt Ocean Iron Fertilization as a Climate Change Strategy*, http://earthtrends.wri.org/updates/node/282 (last visited Feb. 16, 2008); Environmental News Network, *Ocean Fertilization "Fix" for Global Warming Discredited by New Research*, http://www.enn.com/top_stories/article/29093/print (Jan. 11, 2008).

68. *Id.*

69. *Id.*

70. AL GORE, AN INCONVENIENT TRUTH: THE PLANETARY EMERGENCY OF GLOBAL WARMING AND WHAT WE CAN DO ABOUT IT 149 (Rodale Books 2006).

71. *Id.*

72. GUIDE TO THE OCEANS, *supra* note 29, at 13.

73. THE COLUMBIA ELECTRONIC ENCYCLOPEDIA at INFOPLEASE.COM, *Prevailing Winds and General Circulation Patterns* (Columbia Un. Press 2007) *available at* http://www.infoplease.com/ce6/weather/A0861968.html (last visited September 20, 2008).

74. GUIDE TO THE OCEANS, *supra* note 29, at 13.

ocean surface currents move from west to east.[75] Moreover, as was true with air currents, the Coriolis effect also applies to ocean surface currents, because the earth's rotation deflects ocean currents clockwise in the northern hemisphere and counterclockwise in the southern hemisphere.[76]

In contrast, the more three-dimensional ocean currents are driven by differences in temperature and salt concentration (salinity) and hence are known as the thermohaline circulation.[77] Nevertheless, while not wind-driven, this circulation still depends upon the oceans' interactions with the atmosphere. As Peter Ward has described it:

> When there are warm surface areas and cold surface areas of the ocean, cold water spontaneously flows toward the warm, and vice versa. But more than surface currents accomplish this. Cold seawater is denser than warm water of the same chemistry and thus sinks. Saline water is denser than less saline water of the same temperature and also sinks. In the heat of the tropical sun, water rapidly evaporates, making the surface saltier and thus denser. In the arctic, the melting of ice adds water to the sea, making it fresher. All of these factors create seawater bodies of different temperature and salinity that want to mix with others of different values, and in so doing produce conveyer currents throughout the world's oceans.[78]

As these powerful ocean currents redistribute heat, they also "stir [up nutrients, transport] food, mix [salt- and freshwater, and even influence] much of the weather and climate that we experience across continents."[79]

Thus, ocean currents play a large role in determining long-term climate patterns. The oceans can store far more heat than the atmosphere, and they transport this heat throughout the world in both the surface and thermohaline currents.[80] Heat transported north in the Gulf Stream, for example, keeps Eastern Europe temperate, while the occasional appearance of the strong El Niño current brings warm water to Peru and Ecuador and changes weather patterns throughout the world.[81] However, "[w]hen oceans have stored vast amounts of energy, typically near the equator during the summer months, they frequently release this energy in dramatic and sometimes very destructive ways through the creation of hurricanes (in the Atlantic Ocean), typhoons (in the Pacific Ocean), and cyclones (in the Indian Ocean)."[82]

Importantly for both humans and ecosystems, as both Peter Ward and Al Gore have pointed out, the oceanic thermohaline "conveyer system in its present configuration has ... been stable for a significant amount of the time that humans have had agriculture, and this stability has allowed both predictability of crop yields in Europe and Asia, as well as the biologically more important stability of ecosystems."[83] In other words, stable thermohaline circulation patterns produce predictable climates and predictable ecosystem services, including water and food supply.

Finally, the interaction of wind, surface currents, and the thermohaline circulation are also important to ocean food supplies because they produce upwellings of bottom nutrients in spe-

---

75. *Id.* at 13–14.

76. *Id.* at 14.

77. *Id.* at 14.

78. PETER C. WARD, UNDER A GREEN SKY: GLOBAL WARMING, THE MASS EXTINCTIONS OF THE PAST AND WHAT THEY CAN TELL US ABOUT OUR FUTURE 123 (Smithsonian Books 2007).

79. GUIDE TO THE OCEANS, *supra* note 29, at 10–11

80. *Id.* at 17.

81. *Id.* at 18.

82. *Id.*

83. Ward, *supra* note 78, at 153; *see also* GORE, *supra* note 70, at 149 ("These currents have followed much the same pattern since the end of the last ice age 10,000 years ago, since before the first human cities were built.").

cific and predictable places around the globe. Upwellings occur when the Coriolis effect deflects a surface current as it approaches a coast. As a result, "[d]eep nutrient-rich water rises up to replace the water carried away from the coast, causing an upwelling."[84] Because upwellings are nutrient-rich, they support plankton blooms and high concentrations of marine plants and animals, including commercially important species of fish.[85] Upwellings regularly occur off the coasts of California, Chile, and South Africa,[86] and these highly productive areas of the ocean support "20% of global fishery yield."[87]

III. Disruptions from Climate Change

As the very name suggests, climate change disrupts the climate, which in turn disrupts ecosystems and the services that they provide. Interactions between the atmosphere and the oceans both provide the mechanisms of climate change and reflect the fact that climate change is occurring. Both processes, moreover, impact existing ecosystems and ecosystem services.

Greenhouse gases like carbon dioxide accumulate in the atmosphere, and all indications are that atmospheric concentrations of these gases have been increasing since the Industrial Revolution, and particularly toward the end of the 20th century. One immediate consequence is that the oceans have been absorbing more carbon dioxide. As science writer Fred Pearce has observed, "[a]t any one time, there is fifty times as much carbon dioxide dissolved in ocean waters as there is the in atmosphere," and "the oceans currently absorb in excess of 2 billion tons more a year than they release."[88]

However, "since the beginning of the Industrial Revolution, the oceans have absorbed from the atmosphere something like 130 billion tons of carbon resulting from human activities."[89] The oceans have absorbed so much carbon dioxide, in fact, that their pH is changing.[90] Specifically, excess carbon dioxide dissolved in water transforms chemically into carbonic acid. This acid is corrosive enough to dissolve the calcium carbonate shells and skeletons of a variety of marine creatures—"coral, sea urchins, starfish, many shellfish, and some plankton."[91] Moreover, the presence of carbonic acid reduces the concentration of carbonate in the water, depriving these organisms of raw materials that they need to grow.[92] Both ocean acidification and effects on life have already been observed; as paleontologist Peter Ward reports, "in the Arctic Ocean, now so acidic that one group of mollusks, the pteropods, which are important in the food chain, are going extinct as their shells dissolve off their backs...."[93]

In addition, greater concentrations of greenhouse gases increase the atmosphere's ability to trap incoming solar radiation in the form of heat. The temperatures of both the atmosphere and the oceans increase.

One consequence of these increasing temperatures is that ecosystems begin to change. Perhaps most directly, increasing ocean temperatures can kill coral reefs, a phenomenon known as coral bleaching, and destroy or severely disrupt the ecosystems that coral reefs support.[94] More generally, the Intergovernmental Panel on Climate Change (IPCC) reported in 2007 that "[i]n

---

84. GUIDE TO THE OCEANS, *supra* note 29, at 15.

85. *Id.* at 16.

86. *Id.*

87. F. Chan, *et al.*, *Emergence of Anoxia in the California Current Large Marine Ecosystem*, 319 SCIENCE 920, 920 (Feb. 18, 2008).

88. Pearce, *supra* note 26, at 86.

89. *Id.* at 87.

90. INTERGOVERNMENTAL PANEL ON CLIMATE CHANGE, CLIMATE CHANGE 2007: SYNTHESIS REPORT: SUMMARY FOR POLICYMAKERS 9 (Cambridge Un. Press, Nov. 2007) [hereinafter IPCC 2007 SYNTHESIS SUMMARY].

91. PEARCE, *supra* note 26, at 87–88.

92. *Id.* at 88.

93. Ward, *supra* note 78, at 121.

94. IPCC 2007 SYNTHESIS SUMMARY, *supra* note 90, at 9, 10.

terrestrial ecosystems, earlier timing of spring events and poleward and upward shifts in plant and animal ranges are with *very high confidence* linked to recent warming. In some marine and freshwater systems, shifts in ranges and changes in algal, plankton and fish abundance are with *high confidence* associated with rising water temperatures, as well as related changes in ice cover, salinity, oxygen levels and circulation."[95]

Even more disturbing, "[s]cientists have found that as the oceans become warmer, they are less able to support the phytoplankton that have been an important influence on moderating climate change."[96] Specifically, toward the end of 2006, satellite data revealed that rising ocean temperatures are impeding marine phytoplankton growth.[97] In addition to taking up carbon dioxide from the atmosphere, phytoplankton, as noted, produce oxygen for both the oceans and the atmosphere and serve as the basis of the ocean food chain. Thus, reduced phytoplankton productivity as a result of climate change both results in a positive feedback loop, reducing the Earth's ability to compensate for increased levels of carbon dioxide, and threatens fundamental components of oceanic and terrestrial ecosystems worldwide.

In addition, increased temperatures in the air and water around the Equator will probably affect the frequency and strength of major storm events, such as hurricanes and typhoons. The IPCC reported in 2007 that "[t]here is observational evidence of an increase in intense tropical cyclone activity in the North Atlantic since about 1970, with limited evidence of increases elsewhere,"[98] and it considers it "likely" that tropical cyclone intensity will increase in the future.[99] In addition, it predicts a "poleward shift of extra-tropical storm tracks with consequent changes in wind, precipitation and temperature patterns."[100]

Less intensely but no less importantly, changes in wind patterns appear to already be changing ocean currents and ecosystems. For example, in May 2007, ocean researchers reported seeing "changes in ocean circulation in tropical regions as a result of a long-term weakening of the Pacific Ocean trade winds."[101] In February 2008, a group of marine specialists reported in *Science* that changes in the winds had changed upwelling patterns along the central Oregon continental shelf, resulting in oxygen deprivation (anoxia and hypoxia) in those waters.[102] The authors emphasized that "[s]trongly coupled atmospheric and oceanic circulation underpins ecosystem dynamics in wind-driven upwelling" systems and emphasized that these climate change effects could lead to "discontinuous ecosystem change."[103]

Another consequence of temperature increases is that polar ice begins to melt. All indications are that Arctic sea ice, Greenland glaciers, and Antarctic ice sheets are melting faster than anyone

---

95. *Id.* at 2. *See also id.* at 4, Fig. SPM.2 (providing a map that summarizes the effects of temperature changes on physical and biological systems and showing that by 2004, most areas of the ocean had warmed).

96. Steve Connor, *Climate Change is Killing the Oceans' Microscopic "Lungs,"* THE INDEPENDENT UK (Dec. 7, 2006), *available at* http://www.independent.co.uk/environment/climate-change/climate-change-is-killing-the-oceans-microscopic-lungs-427402.html (last visited September 19, 2008).

97. Michael J. Behrenfeld *et al.*, *Climate-driven Trends in Contemporary Ocean Productivity*, 444 NATURE 752 (2006).

98. IPCC 2007 SYNTHESIS SUMMARY, *supra* note 90, at 2.

99. *Id.* at 8.

100. *Id.*

101. *Climate Change Signal Detected in the Indian Ocean*, SCIENCEDAILY, http://www.sciencedaily.com/releases/2007/05/070530101024.htm (May 30, 2007).

102. F. Chan, *et al.*, *Emergence of Anoxia in the California Current Large Marine Ecosystem*, 319 SCIENCE 920, 920 (Feb. 18, 2008).

103. *Id. See also* Peter N. Spotts, *Climate Change Brews Ocean Trouble*, THE CHRISTIAN SCIENCE MONITOR, http://www.csmonitor.com/2007/0308/p13s01-sten.htm (Mar. 8, 2007) (offering an early reporting of the Oregon research).

expected,[104] and melting glaciers in the Himalayas are already threatening water supplies and grain harvests in China and India.[105] In addition, when land ice melts, sea levels begin to rise. The IPCC predicted in 2007 that sea levels would rise 0.18 meters to 0.59 meters by 2100.[106] However, its report did not account for the accelerating melting of glaciers.[107] Rising sea levels destroy coastal ecosystems and the ecosystem services that they provide.[108]

More potentially devastating, however, are the effects of melting ice on ocean currents. The thermohaline circulation pattern in the Atlantic Ocean appears to be particularly susceptible to change,[109] and "[t]he easiest way to cause this change, according to sophisticated computer models, is to pump fresh water into the northern part of the system."[110] The melting of Arctic and Greenland ice is accomplishing just that, and ocean currents do indeed appear to be changing as a result.[111] Specifically, researchers reported in SCIENCE that "[c]hanges in climate beginning in the late 1980s resulted in an enhanced outflow of low-salinity waters from the Arctic and a general freshening of" the North Atlantic Ocean.[112] "This freshening altered circulation and stratification patterns on the shelf and has been linked to changes in the abundances and seasonal cycles of phytoplankton, zooplankton, and fish populations."[113] The result has been a rapid shift in the North Atlantic ecosystem and its ecosystem services.[114]

Changes in atmospheric temperature, air currents, sea temperatures, and ocean currents all lead to changes in weather patterns, precipitation, and longer-term climatic states. While the movie "The Day After Tomorrow" exaggerated the immediacy of the threat, the possibility that increased heat in the atmosphere and melting ice will shut down or alter the current thermohaline circulation is real.[115] Such large-scale changes would alter climate patterns throughout the world.

Less dramatically, the IPCC reported in 2007 that "[i]t is *very likely* that over the past 50 years: cold days, cold nights and frosts have become less frequent over most land areas, and hot days and hot nights have become more frequent. It is *likely* that: heat waves have become more frequent over most land areas, the frequency of heavy precipitation events has increased over most areas, and since 1975 the incidence of extreme high sea level has increased worldwide."[116] For the future, the IPCC considered it "very likely" that the frequency of hot extremes, heat waves, and heavy precipitation would increase, "very likely" that precipitation would increase in high latitudes, and "likely" that precipitation would decrease in most subtropical land regions.[117] Researchers have already noted that trade winds in the Pacific Ocean are becoming weaker, while the Westerlies are becoming stronger.[118] These winds affect ocean currents and "'sea sur-

---

104. PEARCE, *supra* note 26, at 35–54.

105. Lester Brown, Earth Policy Institute, *Melting Glaciers Will Shrink Grain Harvests in China and India*, ENVIRONMENTAL NEWS NETWORK, http://www.enn.com/top_stories/article/33355/print (Mar. 21, 2008).

106. IPCC 2007 SYNTHESIS SUMMARY, *supra* note 90, at 8, Tbl. SPM.1.

107. *Id.* at 8.

108. PEARCE, *supra* note 26, at 55–59.

109. Ward, *supra* note 78, at 152.

110. *Id.*

111. Charles H. Greene & Andrew J. Pershing, *Climate Drives Sea Change*, 315 SCIENCE 1084, 1084 (Feb. 23, 2007).

112. *Id.*

113. *Id.* (citations omitted).

114. *Id.*

115. PEARCE, *supra* note 26, at 141–47.

116. IPCC 2007 SYNTHESIS SUMMARY, *supra* note 90, at 2.

117. *Id.* at 8.

118. *Climate Change Signal Detected in the Indian Ocean*, SCIENCEDAILY, http://www.sciencedailycom/releases/2007/05/070530101024.htm (May 30, 2007).

face temperature in regions relevant to the source and distribution of rainfall across southern Australia.'"[119] As the IPCC concluded, "Altered frequencies and intensities of extreme weather, together with sea level rise, are expected to have mostly adverse effects on natural and human systems."[120]

Finally, beyond actual changes to climate and weather, changes in ocean currents could have potentially profound implications for the survival of all life on earth. Paleontologist Peter Ward, investigating the causes of past mass extinctions, has emphasized that "[o]ur ocean, saturated with oxygen from top to bottom, is chemically far different, and far more benign, certainly to us animals, and even to most microbes," than oceans millennia ago.[121] This saturation results in great part from the global ocean circulation patterns, which prevent the oceans from becoming stratified into high-oxygen surface and low-oxygen bottom layers.

However, the addition of greenhouse gases such as carbon dioxide and methane to the atmosphere can eventually disrupt the ocean circulation system, resulting in warm, low-oxygen water being dumped into the bottom waters.[122] As Dr. Ward explains, "Warming continues, and the decrease of equator-to-pole temperature differences reduces ocean winds and surface currents to a near standstill. Mixing of oxygenated surface waters with the deeper, and volumetrically increasing, low-oxygen bottom waters decreases, causing ever-shallower water to change from oxygenated to anoxic."[123]

During these oceanic anoxic intervals, anaerobic bacteria proliferate in the oceans, producing deadly hydrogen sulfide.[124] According to Dr. Ward, "The horrific result would be great bubbles of highly poisonous hydrogen sulfide gas rising into the atmosphere,"[125] which both kills plants and animals on the surface and "rises into the high atmosphere, where it breaks down the ozone layer. [T]he subsequent increase in ultraviolet radiation from the sun kills much of the photosynthetic green plant phytoplankton."[126] Finally, "the combination of high heat and hydrogen sulfide creates a mass extinction on land. These," Dr. Ward emphasizes, "are the greenhouse extinctions,"[127] and he and his fellow researchers have theorized that several such extinctions have already occurred.

IV. Conclusion

Are we at the beginning of the next greenhouse extinction? The best answer is that it's probably too early to tell. As this chapter demonstrates, however, climate change may start in the atmosphere, but its effects arise largely from the atmosphere-ocean interface and changes to both systems' patterns of circulation.

Changes to these interactions as a result of changes in the atmosphere's capacity to absorb and retain heat will alter ecosystems and ecosystem services all over the planet, both marine and terrestrial. Even if mass extinction does not occur, therefore, climate change will alter the ecosystems that support human societies, perhaps, finally, drawing unavoidable attention to the ecosystem services that humans have come to take for granted.

---

119. *Id.*

120. IPCC 2007 SYNTHESIS SUMMARY, *supra* note 90, at 12.

121. Ward, *supra* note 78, at 113.

122. *Id.* at 137.

123. *Id.*

124. *Id.* at 117.

125. *Id.* at 117–18. This theory of mass extinctions is known as the Kump hypothesis, after Lee Kump of the Pennsylvania State University, who, with his colleagues Mike Arthur and Alexander Pavlov, first proposed it in 2005. *Id.* at 116–18.

126. *Id.*

127. *Id.* at 137–38.

Notes

1. For an introduction to this topic, see James Salzman, Barton H. Thompson, Jr., and Gretchen C. Daily, *Protecting Ecosystem Services: Science, Economics, and Law*, 20 Stan. Envtl. L. J. 309 (2001); Ezequiel Lugo, Ecosystem Services, *The Millennium Ecosystem Assessment, and the Conceptual Difference Between Benefits Provided By Ecosystems and Benefits Provided By People*, 23 J. Land Use & Envtl. L. 243 (2008); David R. Mongomery, Dirt: The Erosion of Civilizations (Un. of Cal. Press 2007). For the "creation story" of ecosystem services, see J.B. Ruhl & James Salzman, *The Law and Policy Beginnings of Ecosystem Services*, 22 J. Land Use & Envtl. L. 157 (2006–07).

2. *Natural Resource Damages and the Spill of the* Exxon Valdez. Professor Craig's typology (borrowed from The Millenium Ecosystem Assessment) includes provisioning services ("ecosystem goods"), regulating services, cultural services, and supporting services. Who can sue to protect these resources (or recover recompense for their loss or contributions for their restitution) under various natural resource damage regimes? Generally, federal, state, and tribal governments, under the examples of the Clean Water Act, Oil Pollution Act, and Superfund Law (Comprehensive Environmental Response, Compensation, and Liability Act), Section 311(f) of the CWA, 33 U.S.C. § 1311(f); Section 1006 of OPA, 33 U.S.C. § 2706; Section 107(f) of CERCLA, 42 U.S.C. § 9607(f). Of course, responsible parties always will say that "nobody owns" these ecosystem services and thus nobody can sue to preserve them. The 1989 *Exxon Valdez* oil spill gave us one bad example insisting that public nuisance law does not protect "cultural damages" sought by Alaska Natives. *See In re* Exxon Valdez, *Alaska Native Class*, 104 F.3d 1196 (9th Cir 1997) (Kozinsky, Leavy, and Schwarzer, C.J.s) (Alaska Native "subsistence lifestyle" claims arising out of the *Exxon Valdez* oil spill are not a sufficient "special injury" to support a public nuisance action; all Alaskans have these rights); Christopher V. Panoff, *In re the* Exxon Valdez *Native Class v. Exxon Corp.: Cultural Resources, Subsistence Living, and the Special Injury Rule*, 28 Envtl. Law 701 (1988). And of course the "trustees"—typically state and governments—will wish to monopolize any and all legal entitlements created as reparations for damages to the miraculous services that nature affords. The "nation states" of the world, whose cynical cautions have shaken the system to its foundations, will be first in line to collect their "dues." This strategy was evidenced, too, in the context of the 1989 *Exxon Valdez* oil spill and the consequent creation of the *Exxon Valdez* Oil Spill (EVOS) Trustee Council that excluded native voices. W.H. Rodgers *et al.*, *The* Exxon Valdez *Reopener: Natural Resource Damage Settlements and Roads Not Taken*, 22 Alask. L. Rev. 135 (2005). The United States and Alaska authorities gave every indication that they would "pass" on the availability of $100 million in "reopener" monies (available for restoration and rehabilitation of the spill-impacted Prince William Sound) and thus miss a June 1, 2006 deadline. This position was challenged in a legal petition prepared by students of the Kathy and Steve Berman Environmental Law Clinic at the University of Washington for the Alaska Inter-Tribal Council. It is excerpted below (Ch. 9, p. 1315). Note that the "subsistence" and "cultural" claims asserted can be described as "ecosystem service" claims, to use Professor Craig's categorizations.

3. *More on the Role of the Alaska Natives.* Over the years, the Natives have fought furiously (to little avail) for a stronger voice on the EVOS Trustee Council. A 2004 paper by the Chugach Regional Resources Commission[1] insists there have been no studies on the "impacts of this technological disaster to the Tribes and Native Communities from their perspective."[2] Disruption was enormous at

---

1. Patty Brown-Schwalenberg, The *Exxon Valdez* Oil Spill: Impacts and Responses from a Tribal Perspective (Jan. 2004) [hereinafter 2004 Tribal Study] (Chugach Regional Resources Commission) (representing the seven villages of Chenega Bay, Eyak, Nanwalek, Port Graham, Tatitlek, Qutekcak Native Tribe and Valdez Native Tribe).

2. 2004 Tribal Study, *supra* note 1, at 1.

the outset (harvest losses were up to 77% for some periods of time)[3] and the damage has not healed. "Community involvement" was mostly a canard that did not come to pass.[4] In 1999, the Council adopted a "recovery objective" for subsistence (that was not met then and has not been met now):[5]

> Subsistence will have recovered when injured resources used for subsistence are healthy and productive and exist at prespill levels. In addition, there is recognition that people must be confident that the resources are safe to eat and that the cultural values provided by gathering, preparing, and sharing food need to be reintegrated into community life.

The Gulf Ecosystem Monitoring ("GEM") program is the wind-down project for the EVOS Trustee Council.[6] Native "community involvement" has wound down with it. This lapse was identified in a review of GEM by the National Research Council, which recommended a strengthening of "community involvement" in the way it is understood by the Natives.[7] This recommendation of a prestigious science advisory committee, in turn, is viewed as a "window of opportunity for the tribes to pursue their idea of establishing their endowment titled Tribal Ecosystem Stewardship Program."[8] This tribal endowment has been formalized as follows:[9]

> The 20 communities affected by the *Exxon Valdez* Oil Spill are proposing that the EVOS Trustee Council establish an endowment of $20 million to ensure meaningful Tribal and community involvement in the GEM research and monitoring projects and programs. Such an endowment will assist in promoting community-based scientific research and monitoring of the traditional natural resources on a continuous long term basis. This program will also serve as a forum for western science to gain valuable traditional ecological knowledge about the resources, and for the community members to learn more about the language and intent of science and to receive certified technical on-the-job training in natural resource stewardship techniques.

The recommendation for a Perpetual Stewardship Council for Alaska Natives is not some impossible dream....

B. Biodiversity

E.O. Wilson, *quoted in* THOMAS L. FRIEDMAN, HOT, FLAT, AND CROWDED: WHY WE NEED A GREEN REVOLUTION—AND HOW IT CAN RENEW AMERICA 129 (Farrar, Straus & Giroux 2008) [hereinafter 2008 FRIEDMAN]:

---

3. *Compare.* 2004 TRIBAL STUDY, *supra* note 1, at 4 (discussing JAMES A. FALL, SUBSISTENCE USES OF FISH AND WILDLIFE BEFORE AND AFTER THE *EXXON VALDEZ* OIL SPILL, Alaska Dep't of Fish & Game (1996)) *and* Lee Stratton, *Resource Harvest and Use in Tatitlek, Alaska* (Alaska Dep't of Fish & Game Technical Paper No. 181, 1990) (a fortuitous "baseline" paper discussing pre-spill (1988) use of 75 kinds of resources in Tatitlek, a town that was a mere four miles from "ground zero" on Bligh Reef).

4. 2004 TRIBAL STUDY, *supra* note 1, at 8–14.

5. EVOS Trustee Council, 1999 at 27, quoted in 2004 TRIBAL STUDY, *supra* note 1, at 12.

6. Described in 2004 TRIBAL STUDY, *supra* note 1, at 14–16.

7. Committee to Review the Gulf of Alaska Ecosystem Monitoring Program (ROGEM), discussed in 2004 TRIBAL STUDY, *supra* note 1, at 17–18.

8. 2004 TRIBAL STUDY, *supra* note 1, at 18.

9. Chugach Regional Res. Comm'n, Tribal Ecosystem Stewardship Program: An Endowment for Tribal Involvement in the GEM Program (undated proposal, on file with authors).

> Destroying a tropical rain forest and other species-rich ecosystems for profit is like burning all the paintings of the Louvre to cook dinner.

2008 FRIEDMAN at 128:

> [W]e may be the first generation in human history that literally has to act like Noah—to save the last pairs of a wide range of species.... Unlike Noah, though, we—our generation and our civilization—are responsible for the flood, and we have the responsibility to build the ark.

E.O. WILSON, THE CREATION: AN APPEAL TO SAVE LIFE ON EARTH 29 (W.W. Norton 2006):

> With all the troubles that humanity faces, why should we care about the condition of living Nature? What difference will it make if a few or even half of all the species on Earth are exterminated, as projected by scientists for the remainder of this century? Many reasons exist fundamental to the human weal. Unimaginably vast sources of scientific information and biological wealth will be destroyed. Opportunity costs, which will be better understood by our descendants than by ourselves, will be staggering. Gone forever will be undiscovered medicines, crops, timber, fibers, soil-restoring vegetation, petroleum substitutes, and other products and amenities.

Id. at 31:

> Because wild natural ecosystems are in plain sight, it is also easy to take for granted the environmental services they provide humanity. Wild species enrich the soil, cleanse the water, pollinate most of the flowering plants. They create the very air we breathe.

Id. at 32:

> Living nature is nothing more than the commonality of organisms in the wild state and the physical and chemical equilibrium their species generate through interaction with one another. But it is also nothing less than that commonality and equilibrium. The power of living Nature lies in sustainability through complexity. Destabilize it by degrading it to a simpler state, as we seem bent on doing, and the result could be catastrophic. The organisms most affected are likely to be the largest and most complex, including human beings.

ELIZABETH KOLBERT, FIELD NOTES FROM A CATASTROPHE: MAN, NATURE, AND CLIMATE CHANGE 90 (Bloomsbury Publishing 2006) (quoting scientist Chris Thomas):

> If we are in the situation where a quarter of the terrestrial species might be at risk of extinction from climate change... if we've changed our biological system to such an extent, then we do have to get worried about whether the services that are provided by natural ecosystems are going to continue. Ultimately, all of the crops we grow are biological species; all the diseases we have are biological species; all the disease vectors are biological species. If there is this overwhelming evidence that species are changing their distributions, we're going to have to expect exactly the same for crops and pests and diseases.

One of the greatest victims of climate change will very likely be biodiversity. Biodiversity is defined as the "sum of the species, ecosystems, and genetic diversity of the Earth."[1] The IPCC estimates that upwards of 70% of the Earth's species could be at risk of extinction with a 3.5°C (6.3°F) rise in temperature, which could occur by the end of this century.[2] Furthermore, global

---

1. Lee Hannah, Thomas E. Lovejoy & Stephen Schneider, *Biodiversity and Climate Change in Context, in* CLIMATE CHANGE AND BIODIVERSITY 3 (Yale Un. Press 2005).

2. LENNY BERNSTEIN *et al.*, CLIMATE CHANGE 2007: SYNTHESIS REPORT OF THE INTERGOVERNMETAL PANEL ON CLIMATE CHANGE SUMMARY FOR POLICYMAKERS 7, 13–14 (2007).

warming will hasten extinction rates due to synergies with other stresses on species, such as disease, chemical pollution, and habitat fragmentation.[3]

The predicted loss in species could result in an extinction event on a scale second only to Earth's largest mass extinction, the Permian-Triassic event, which occurred 250 million years ago.[4] Another way of looking at species loss is as a rate of extinction between now and 2050: Conservation International estimates that in the "midrange" scenario one species will face extinction every 20 minutes, which could increase to one species every nine minutes.[5] The current extinction rate is a thousand times faster than the average during Earth's history.[6] Furthermore, a recent study indicates that most models used to predict future species losses do not properly account for certain population variables, resulting in underestimation of true extinction risk.[7]

There are two aspects to the risks posed by climate change. First, inexorable and relatively linear changes such as atmospheric and ocean temperatures, ocean pH, and sea level will result from the continual accumulation of anthropogenic carbon dioxide. These linear changes will be associated with a decrease in the viability of current habitat for a variety of species.

Second, as atmospheric carbon dioxide concentrations increase, there will be certain threshold events that trigger rapid and uncontrolled feedbacks within the system. These "tipping points" will be non-linear and could potentially induce large shifts in the environment. For example, rapid climate change already appears well underway in the Arctic, where sea ice hit a stunning record low in 2007,[8] with a similarly low level repeated in 2008.[9] Sea ice is important because its bright white surface reflects radiation from the sun back into the atmosphere, cooling the Earth. In contrast, the dark ocean that is exposed upon melt of sea ice is highly absorptive of incoming radiation. This shifts the balance of reflection and absorption toward greater absorption and heating, which in turn increases the rate of sea ice melt. This vicious cycle poses another problem: it increases the rate of permafrost melting, which releases methane. Methane is a greenhouse gas with a "global warming potential" that is approximately 25 times[10] that of the same volume of carbon dioxide over 100 years. Thus, releasing methane further amplifies the warming cycle.

There is no doubt that anthropogenic climate change is currently causing physical, *e.g.*, glacier loss and earlier peak spring water flow, and biological, *e.g.*, earlier leafing and flowering, changes. A recent study constructed a database from the scientific literature and found that 95 percent of 829 recorded physical changes and 90 percent of approximately 28,800 recorded biological changes are consistent with the direction expected with global warming.[11]

---

3. Thomas E. Lovejoy, *Conservation within a Changing Climate*, *in* Climate Change and Biodiversity 325, 325 (Yale Un. Press 2005).

4. Peter D. Ward, Under a Green Sky 177 (Smithsonian Books 2007).

5. Conservation International, *How Do We Set Our Clock?*, http://www.conservation.org/act/get_involved/Pages/stop-the-clock-methodology.aspx (last visited October 19, 2008).

6. Conservation International, http://www.conservation.org/LEARN/SPECIES/Pages/overview.aspx (last visited October 19, 2008).

7. Brett A. Melbourne & Alan Hastings, *Extinction Risk Depends Strongly on Factors Contributing to Stochasticity*, 454 Nature 100 (2008).

8. J. Stroeve *et al.*, *Arctic Sea Ice Extent Plummets in 2007*, 89 Eos 13 (2008).

9. National Sea Ice Data Center, Arctic Sea Ice News & Analysis (September 16, 2008), *available at* http://nsidc.org/arcticseaicenews/2008/091608.html.

10. P. Forster *et al.*, *Changes in Atmospheric Constituents and in Radiative Forcing Table 2.14*, *in* Climate Change 2007: The Physical Science Basis. Contribution of Working Group I to the Fourth Assessment Report of the Intergovernmental Panel on Climate Change 130, 211 Table 2.14 (S. Solomon *et al.* eds., Cambridge Un. Press 2007).

11. Cynthia Rosenzweig *et al.*, *Attributing Physical and Biological Impacts to Anthropogenic Climate Change*, 453 Nature 353 (2008).

In general, species are attempting to adapt to increased temperatures resulting from anthropogenic greenhouse gas emissions by moving pole-ward and to higher elevations.[12] This has been observed both in terrestrial and marine species.[13] Parmesan and Yohe quantified a "fingerprint" for the impacts of climate change by conducting a meta-analysis of studies that covered over 1700 species. The results of this analysis indicated that there was a significant pole-ward migration of species and that there was a significant increase in warm-adapted relative to cold-adapted species in the studied areas.[14] In a localized study, Craig Moritz and colleagues repeated an inventory of small mammals in Yosemite National Park 100 years after an initial inventory by Grinnell. Their results indicated that in the last century there has been a significant upward shift in a number of lower-elevation species, averaging about 500 meters (about 1640 feet) as well as contraction of the range of high elevation species.[15]

But there are significant hurdles facing species that attempt to adapt. First, humans have caused significant habitat fragmentation.[16] This means that it may be impossible for a species to migrate to new areas. Second, many species are already at the highest latitude or elevation possible. As a result, these species literally have nowhere to go. This is the plight of Arctic species and of high-elevation species such as the American pika. Third, species may simply not have time. While past changes in climate have occurred relatively slowly, current climate change due to human activity is occurring at a drastically accelerated pace. Unlike humans, a species cannot simply get in a moving van and travel 500 miles a day. Instead, species range migration is a gradual process, which often cannot keep pace with the rapidity with which temperatures are increasing and other habitat changes are occurring.

Marine species are facing even greater threats. Not only are oceans warming, but the pH of the oceans is dropping due to the absorption of atmospheric carbon dioxide. Furthermore, some of the greatest biodiversity in the world is found in coral reefs. Yet, coral are unable to migrate easily. But even those marine species that can potentially migrate to colder oceans cannot escape ocean acidification. In fact, the solubility of calcium carbonate is affected by temperature, with the result that colder waters tend to have lower carbonate concentrations.[17] This leaves marine species in a no-win situation, to say the least.

Coral species are the poster children for the ravaging effects of climate change. Coral reefs are both the most diverse and economically important ecosystems in the world. Coral reefs occupy a mere 0.1 to 0.5 percent of the ocean floor yet contain a third of all marine species; fish caught on reefs constitute approximately 10% of fish consumed by humans.[18] But the value of coral reef ecosystems extends to coastal protection, recreation/tourism, and aesthetic and cultural benefits. Peterson and Lubchenco explain the interdependence of coral reef species:

> [T]he complexity of interactions and degree of interrelatedness among component species is higher on coral reefs than any other marine environment. This implies that

---

12. *See generally* Camille Parmesan, *Biotic Response: Range and Abundance Changes, in* Climate Change and Biodiversity 41 (Thomas Lovejoy & Lee Hannah eds., Yale Un. Press 2005); Emma Marris, *The Escalator Effect*, 1 Nature Reports Climate Change 96 (2007).

13. Parmesan, *supra* note 12.

14. C. Parmesan & G. Yohe, *A Globally Coherent Fingerprint of Climate Change Impacts Across Natural Systems*, 421 Nature 37 (2003).

15. Craig Moritz *et al.*, *Impact of a Century of Climate Change on Small-Mammal Communities in Yosemite National Park, USA*, 322 Science 261 (2008).

16. Lee Hannah, Thomas Lovejoy & Stephen Schneider, *supra* note 1, at 4.

17. Scott Doney, *The Dangers of Ocean Acidification*, 294 Scientific American 58 (2006); Richard A. Feely *et al.*, *Impact of Anthropogenic CO_2 on the $CaCO_3$ System in the Oceans*, 305 Science 362 (2004).

18. Fredrik Moberg & Carl Folke, *Ecological Goods and Services of Coral Reef Ecosystems*, 29 Ecological Economics 215 (1999).

the ecosystem functioning that produces the most highly valued components is also complex and that many otherwise insignificant species have strong effects on sustaining the rest of the reef system.[19]

As Ove Hoegh-Guldberg and colleagues explain, the synergistic impacts of ocean acidification, ocean warming, and sea level rise spell disaster.[20] These authors identify an atmospheric carbon dioxide concentration of 500 ppm as the "tipping point" beyond which corals may be unable to survive.[21] This threshold leaves us little space to address climate change. The IPCC predicts that under conservative scenarios we will reach 500 ppm by the end of the century, with many scenarios predicting that atmospheric concentrations could be more than double this value. The Global Carbon Project recently released data for the year 2007. The staggering conclusions of this report were that (1) atmospheric carbon dioxide concentrations grew by 2.2 ppm in 2007, relative to 1.8 ppm in 2006, (2) anthropogenic carbon dioxide emissions are growing four times faster since 2000 than during 1990—2000 and (3) this rate of increase is *higher* than the worst case emissions scenario used by the IPCC![22]

Coral reef ecosystems are also an example of a "biodiversity hot spot."[23] Despite the global nature of climate change, the effects in some regions of the earth are more important for biodiversity than others. This is because certain isolated areas, such as tropical uplands, contain a higher proportion of range-restricted species that are unique to the region as well as widespread species.[24] E.O. Wilson describes the incredible richness of biodiversity hot spots:

> Thirty-four of the hottest spots, or more precisely the intact biologically rich habitats within them, cover a mere 2.3 percent of Earth's land surface, yet they are the exclusive homes of 42 percent of the planet's vertebrate species (mammals, birds, reptiles, and amphibians) and 50 percent of its flowering plants.[25]

Unfortunately, the same regions are often those under the greatest pressure from human development.[26] Furthermore, these areas are not only regions with highly concentrated biodiversity but also regions in which the species face the greatest danger of extinction.[27]

Why should we care that biodiversity is plunging at unprecedented rates? There are multiple reasons. One, species and biodiversity possess an intrinsic value. Ethically and morally it seems reprehensible for humans to determine that our existence is not only superior to that of other species but also that we have a right to annihilate species. Two, biodiversity and species have value to human well-being in providing enjoyment and potentially life-saving medications, for instance. Three, biodiversity provides "ecosystem services" such as filtering pollutants, erosion control, and natural carbon dioxide uptake.

The fact is that biodiversity is valuable. This value was codified by the United States Congress when it enacted the Endangered Species Act of 1973.[28] The Supreme Court recognized the Congressional understanding of the value of even a single species in *Tennessee Valley Authority v.*

---

19. Charles H. Peterson & Jane Lubchenco, *Marine Ecosystem Services, in* Nature's Services: Societal Dependence on Natural Ecosystems 177, 185 (Island Press 1977).

20. Ove Hoegh-Guldberg *et al.*, *Coral Reefs Under Rapid Climate Change and Ocean Acidification*, 318 Science 1737 (2007).

21. *Id.*

22. Global Carbon Project, Carbon Budget and Trends 2007 (2008), *available at* http://www.global carbonproject.org/carbontrends/index.htm (last visited October 19, 2008).

23. E.O. Wilson, The Creation: An Appeal to Save Life on Earth 97 (W.W. Norton 2006).

24. Lee Hannah, Thomas Lovejoy & Stephen Schneider, *supra* note 1.

25. Wilson, *supra* note 23, at 95.

26. Lee Hannah, Thomas Lovejoy & Stephen Schneider, *supra* note 1.

27. Wilson, *supra* note 23, at 96.

28. 16 U.S.C. § 1531 *et seq.*

Hill,[29] wherein it declared that a multimillion-dollar dam project must be halted because its completion threatened the existence of the snail darter. The value of biodiversity was also included in the influential STERN REVIEW OF THE ECONOMICS OF CLIMATE CHANGE estimates of the guaranteed costs of climate change, which it found are likely to be on the order of 5 percent of global GDP per year, with costs rising to 20 percent GDP per year.[30] In contrast, the STERN REVIEW estimates that these negative impacts could be mitigated for a mere 1 percent GDP.[31] Hsiung and Sunstein have argued that even under conservative estimates the costs of climate-change induced loss of biodiversity could run to the "hundreds of billions annually."[32]

Thomas Lovejoy and Lee Hannah conclude that while greenhouse gases must be stabilized to address the significant loss in biodiversity, the means by which this is accomplished is exceedingly important. They caution that "it makes little sense to trade one environmental problem for another."[33] The authors provide examples, such as the known problems with ocean carbon sequestration and ocean fertilization, which they consider "doomed as a viable option."[34] Furthermore, the authors consider that large-scale hydro and nuclear power carry environmental costs too high to be a major part of the solution. Another concern that Lovejoy and Hannah raise is that any system must offer a long-term solution; for if not the risk is that we would "trade one problem for another or merely delay impacts."[35]

The Convention on Biological Diversity,[1] introduced on June 5, 1992, is an international treaty aimed at protecting the Earth's biodiversity before it is too late. There are currently 191 countries on the list of parties, from which the United States is conspicuously absent.[2] Inspired by the influential STERN REVIEW: THE ECONOMICS OF CLIMATE CHANGE,[3] G8+5 countries adopted a proposal to issue a report on the economics and importance of biodiversity at the Heiligendamm Summit on June 6–8, 2007. Portions of the interim report are excerpted below.

THE ECONOMICS OF ECOSYSTEMS AND BIODIVERSITY, prepared by the German Federal Ministry for the Environment and the European Commission, with the support of several other partners at 9 (2008):[4]

> Current trends on land and in the oceans demonstrate the severe dangers that biodiversity loss poses to human health and welfare. Climate change is exacerbating this problem. And again, as with climate change, it is the world's poor who are most at risk from the continuing loss of biodiversity. They are the ones most reliant on the ecosystem services which are being undermined by flawed economic analysis and policy mistakes.

Id., Chapter 1: Biodiversity and Ecosystems Today, at 12 (references omitted):

---

29. TVA v. Hill, 437 U.S. 153 (1978).

30. Nicholas Stern, *Executive Summary, in* STERN REVIEW: THE ECONOMICS OF CLIMATE CHANGE (Cambridge Un. Press 2007).

31. *Id.*

32. *Id.* at 1699 (values given at 1740).

33. Thomas Lovejoy & Lee Hannah, *Global Greenhouse Gas Levels and the Future of Biodiversity, in* CLIMATE CHANGE AND BIODIVERSITY 387, 391 (Thomas Lovejoy & Lee Hanna eds., Yale Un. Press 2005).

34. *Id.*

35. *Id.*

1. Text and further information *available at* http://www.cbd.int/convention/.

2. Although the U.S. is not a party, it "signed" the Convention on June 4, 1993, see http://www.cbd.int/convention/parties/list/ for a current list of parties.

3. GERMAN FEDERAL MINISTRY FOR THE ENVIRONMENT AND EUROPEAN COMMISSION, THE ECONOMICS OF ECOSYSTEMS AND BIODIVERSITY 4 (2008).

4. Full report and supporting information *available at* http://ec.europa.eu/environment/nature/biodiversity/economics/index_en.htm (last visited November 1, 2008).

The well-being of every human population in the world is fundamentally and directly dependent on ecosystem services.

However, the levels of many of the benefits we derive from the environment have plunged over the past 50 years as biodiversity has fallen dramatically across the globe. Here are some examples:

- In the last 300 years, the global forest area has shrunk by approximately 40%. Forests have completely disappeared in 25 countries, and another 29 countries have lost more than 90% of their forest cover. The decline continues.
- Since 1900, the world has lost about 50% of its wetlands. While much of this occurred in northern countries during the first 50 years of the 20th century, there has been increasing pressure since the 1950s for conversion of tropical and sub-tropical wetlands to alternative land use.
- Some 30% of coral reefs—which frequently have even higher levels of biodiversity than tropical forests—have been seriously damaged through fishing, pollution, disease and coral bleaching.
- In the past two decades, 35% of mangroves have disappeared. Some countries have lost up to 80% through conversion for aquaculture, overexploitation and storms.
- The human-caused (anthropogenic) rate of species extinction is estimated to be 1,000 times more rapid than the "natural" rate of extinction typical of Earth's long-term history.

The effect of trends such as these is that approximately 60% of the Earth's ecosystem services that have been examined have been degraded in the last 50 years, with human impacts being the root cause.

Id., Chapter 2: Biodiversity, Ecosystems, and Human Welfare at 15:

Today's global consumption and production patterns are underpinned by ecosystems around the world. Many different types of policy can affect the resilience of natural as well as human-modified ecosystems. From transport to energy, agriculture to cultural well-being, policies and actions can have many unintended consequences. As demonstrated by the Millennium Ecosystem Assessment, the impacts of cumulative pressures on ecosystems may not be felt for many years, until some tipping points are reached leading to rapid non-linear changes.

Id. at 16–17, discussing the impacts on food availability "on land and at sea" (references omitted):

Rising food prices have provoked protests in many countries. In February 2007, tens of thousands of people marched through the streets of Mexico City, demonstrating against a 400% increase in the cost of corn used to make tortillas—blamed on increased demand for biofuels in the United States of America … There are many causes for the increase in food prices. They include rising demand for food and especially meat (which requires more land per calorie), the rising price of energy (which is an important input) and increasing demand for biofuels.

    ….

More than a billion people rely on fisheries as their main or sole source of animal protein, especially in developing countries. But half of wild marine fisheries are fully exploited, with a further quarter already overexploited. We have been "fishing down the food web."

    ….

This loss of biodiversity could have disastrous effects on the supply of seafood to the human population and on the economy. There is increasing evidence that species diversity is important for marine fisheries, both in the short term, by increasing productivity, and in the long term, by increasing resilience, while genetic diversity is important particularly for the latter. A 2006 study (Worm *et al.* 2006) concluded that all of the world's commercial fisheries are likely to have collapsed in less than 50 years unless current trends are reversed. It found that low diversity is associated with lower fishery productivity, more frequent "collapses", and a lower tendency to recover after overfishing than naturally species rich systems.

The security value of biodiversity can be compared with financial markets. A diverse portfolio of species stocks, as with business stocks, can provide a buffer against fluctuations in the environment (or market) that cause declines in individual stocks. This stabilizing effect of a "biodiverse" portfolio is likely to be especially important as environmental change accelerates with global warming and other human impacts.

Id. at 17–18, discussing water shortages:

There is also growing pressure on water resources—both the supply of water and its quality. Many parts of the world already live with water stress.... Climate change could accentuate the problems of chronic water shortage and drive the ecosystem service that provides a reliable supply of clean water beyond the breaking point.

In many areas, ecosystems provide vital regulating functions. Forests and wetlands can play an important role in determining levels of rainfall (at a regional and local level), the ability of land to absorb or retain that water and its quality when used. In other words, ecosystems play a part in determining whether we have droughts, floods and water fit to drink. The value of this role is often forgotten until it is lost.

Id. at 18–19, discussing impacts on human health (references omitted):

People have known the medicinal value of certain plants for thousands of years and biodiversity has helped our understanding of the human body. So ecosystems provide huge health benefits, and thus economic benefits. The corollary is that losing biodiversity incurs potentially huge costs, and our knowledge of these is growing.

There are significant direct links between biodiversity and modern healthcare:
- Approximately half of synthetic drugs have a natural origin, including 10 of the 25 highest selling drugs in the United States of America.
- Of all the anti-cancer drugs available, 42% are natural and 34% semi-natural.
- In China, over 5,000 of the 30,000 recorded higher plant species are used for therapeutic purposes.
- Three quarters of the world's population depend on natural traditional remedies.
- The turnover for drugs derived from genetic resources was between US$ 75 billion and US$ 150 billion in the United States of America in 1997.
- The gingko tree led to the discovery of substances which are highly effective against cardiovascular diseases, accounting for a turnover of US$ 360 million per year.

A recent global study reveals that hundreds of medicinal plant species, whose naturally occurring chemicals make up the basis of over 50% of all prescription drugs, are threatened with extinction. This prompted experts to call for action to "secure the future of global healthcare."

Id. at 20, discussing impacts on the poor:

A striking aspect of the consequences of biodiversity loss is their disproportionate but unrecognized impact on the poor.... The evidence is clear. The consequences of biodiversity loss and ecosystem service degradation—from water to food to fish—are not being shared equitably across the world. The areas of richest biodiversity and ecosystem services are in developing countries where they are relied upon by billions of people to meet their basic needs. Yet subsistence farmers, fishermen, the rural poor and traditional societies face the most serious risks from degradation. This imbalance is likely to grow. Estimates of the global environmental costs in six major categories, from climate change to overfishing, show that the costs arise overwhelmingly in high- and middle-income countries and are borne by low-income countries.

Id., *Chapter 3: Towards a Valuation Framework* at 40:

These are the key elements of our proposed framework:
- **Examine the causes of biodiversity loss:** designing appropriate scenarios to evaluate the consequences of biodiversity loss means incorporating information on the drivers of this loss. For example, loss of marine fisheries is driven by overfishing, so it would be appropriate to compare a scenario of business-as-usual (continued overfishing) with one where fisheries are sustainably managed. Evidence suggests that biodiversity is often being lost even where it would be socially more advantageous to preserve it. Identifying the market, information and policy failures can help us identify policy solutions.
- **Evaluate alternative policies and strategies that decision makers are confronted with:** the analysis needs to contrast two or more "states" or scenarios that correspond to alternative action (or inaction) to reduce biodiversity and ecosystem loss (World A and World B). This approach is also used in impact assessments and cost-benefit analyses to ensure that decisionmakers can make informed decisions on the basis of a systematic analysis of all the implications of various policy choices.
- Assess the costs and benefits of actions to conserve biodiversity: **the analysis will need to address both differences in benefits obtained from biodiversity conservation (*e.g.* water purification obtained by protecting forests) and in the costs incurred (*e.g.* foregone benefits from conversion of the forest to agriculture).**
- **Identify risks and uncertainties:** there is much that we do not know about how biodiversity is valuable to us, but that does not mean that what is not known has no value—we risk losing very important, but still unrecognized, ecosystem services. The analysis needs to identify these uncertainties and assess the risks.
- **Be spatially explicit:** economic valuation needs to be spatially explicit because both the natural productivity of ecosystems and the value of their services vary across space. Furthermore, benefits may be enjoyed in very different places from where they are produced. For example, the forests of Madagascar have produced anti-cancer drugs that save lives all over the world. Besides, the relative scarcity of a service, as well as local socio-economic factors, may substantially affect the values. Taking into account the spatial dimension also allows for better understanding of the impacts of conservation on development goals, and for the exploration of trade-offs between the benefits and costs of different options, highlighting regions that may be cost-effective investments for conservation.

Id., *Chapter 4: From Economics to Policies* at 47:

Society's defective economic compass can be repaired with appropriate economics applied to the right information. This will allow existing policies to be improved, new policies to be formed, and new markets to be created: all of which is needed to enhance human well-being and restore the planet's health.....

Here, we provide some examples to illustrate how the economic values of ecosystem benefits and costs can be internalized and used to help improve current policies or offer new options. The examples come from diverse policy fields but they convey four broad messages:
- rethink today's subsidies to reflect tomorrow's priorities;
- reward unrecognized benefits, penalize uncaptured costs;

- share the benefits of conservation;
- measure what you manage.

Notes

1. On the collapse of the salmon, the collapse of the cod and the pending collapse of the had-dock, *compare* Douglas W. Dompier, The Fight of the Salmon People: Blending Tribal Tradition with Modern Science to Save Sacred Fish (Slibrus Corp. 2005) (Columbia River) and David R. Montgomery, King of Fish: The Thousand-Year Run of Salmon (Westview Press 2003) *with* Michael Berrill, The Plundered Seas: Can the World's Fish Be Saved? 120–21 (Sierra Club Books 2007) and Mark Kurlasky, Cod: A Biography of The Fish That Changed the World (Penguin Books 1997) with *Fast-Food Fish Under Threat*, New Scientist, Nov. 29, 2008.

2. On biodiversity at the U.S. borders, see *Salmon Spawning & Recovery Alliance v. Basham*, 477 F. Supp. 2d 1301 (U.S. Ct. Int'l Trade 2007). This was an unsuccessful challenge to a failure to perform ESA-mandated duties in connection with the importation of threatened and endangered salmon from Canada into the U.S. Regulations say that importations of endangered fish are "to be refused Custom release." 19 C.F.R. § 12.26(g)(1). Plaintiffs documented the killing of endangered salmon (chinook from Puget Sound, the lower Columbia, and Snake River Fall Chinook) in Canadian waters and their subsequent import into the U.S. *Id.* at 1305: "In fact, in Canada an entire industry markets to U.S. sport fishermen the opportunity to hunt these protected salmon." But, says the court (*id.* at 1306): "The discretionary nature of Custom's exercise of its enforcement powers renders this Court incapable of redressing plaintiffs' § 9 claim," citing *Lujan*. This is therefore a discretionary action not enforceable under Section 11 of the ESA.

3. On stewardship abroad, see *United States v. 1866.75 Board Feet and 11 Doors and Casings, More or Less, of Dipteryx Panamensis Imported From Nicaragua*, 587 F. Supp. 2d 740 (E.D. Va. 2008). Two State Department employees stationed at Managua bring home 10,833 gross pounds of parquet floor squares made of *Dipteryx Panamensis* listed in App. III of CITES. This material is not exempt "household effects" and the court rejects a variety of other arguments (including due process, excessive penalty under the Eighth Amendment, and "innocent owner") on why this civil forfeiture was unfair to these people.

4. On "sustainable" trade in mahogany, see *Native Federation of the Madre de Dios River and Tributaries [of the Peruvian Amazon] v. Bozovich Timber Products, Inc.*, 491 F. Supp. 2d 1174, (Ct. Int'l Trade 2007) (Richard K. Eaton, J.). This is a challenge to trade in bigleaf mahogany from Peru without valid export permits, which would violate Section 9(c) of the ESA and CITES (Convention on International Trade in Endangered Species of Wild Fauna and Flora). This is a motion for preliminary injunction to restrain government defendants from permitting, and private defendants from pursuing, further importation. The issue is whether by honoring facially valid export permits (from Peru) the defendants violated U.S. law. Jurisdiction of the Court of International Trade extends to "embargoes or other quantitative restrictions on the importation of merchandise" (28 U.S.C.A. § 1581(i)(3)) and thus the court holds that Section 9(c) of the ESA does not provide for an embargo on the importation of Appendix II species. 491 F. Supp. 2d at 1182: "Section 9(c)) does not forbid trade in species protected under the Convention." 491 F. Supp. 2d at 1185: "By entering into the Convention, the United States did not agree to end trade in CITES-listed species, nor did it elect to do so by enacting Section 9(c) to implement the Convention. On the contrary, *the aim of CITES and the provisions of the ESA that implement it is to permit trade in certain species in a controlled,*

sustainable manner" (emphasis added, citing Proclamation of the Contracting States on "over-exploitation"). Thus the motion for preliminary injunction is denied because the court lacks jurisdiction.

***

Making Room for Nature's Refugees

Eric T. Freyfogle, Max L. Rowe Professor of Law, University of Illinois, 504 E. Pennsylvania Ave., Champaign, IL 61820; Tel: (217) 333-8713; Fax: (217) 244-1478; dfreyfog@illinois.edu.

Changes in the global climate will be hard on many life forms, not just humans, in the sense that they cannot keep living as they have and where they have. Due to climate change, many biotic communities will lose plant and animal species that can no longer survive in place. These losses of species will no doubt be offset by gains, as adaptable species expand in numbers and geographic ranges. But the gains are unlikely to match the losses. In most places local biodiversity is likely to decline. The species that disappear will often be ones that are carefully adapted to place; they will be species that can only exist in combination with certain other species or whose habitat needs are otherwise narrow. Collectively, these at-risk specialists add complexity and efficiency to community functioning. Thus, when communities lose members the communities themselves suffer, not just the at-risk species.[1]

These problems, in reality, are already upon us, whether due to climate change or the various other ways that humans have altered landscapes and rearranged biotic communities. A typical summary was recently offered by three scholars:

> The modern world is increasingly depauperate, with habitats that are increasingly species poor and increasingly homogeneous. Contemporary studies suggest that biodiversity loss is changing the way ecosystems function and the way our biota serves as repositories of phylogenetic content necessary for its evolution in the face of changing environments. This depauperate world may be less stable, lower in its rates of ecosystem functioning, and less capable of adapting to environmental change.[2]

How should we react to these biotic disturbances, caused importantly by human-induced climate changes? We could do nothing, allowing climate change slowly to sap the biologic composition and functioning of our landscapes. That option is familiar: many of our activities—plowing, paving, draining, grazing livestock—have had similar biotic effects and we have done little to counteract them. Or we could take affirmative steps to help species and other genetic variants move to better locations. We could work to increase local gains in biodiversity. Biotic communities would still lose species; we are unlikely to offset all climate-induced losses. But our interventions could help communities recruit new members, thereby retaining more ecological functioning. Landscapes would remain healthier in terms of efficiency in processing nutrients and abilities to respond to stress. As for the species themselves, our corrective interventions would create more winners than losers—just the outcome that nature prefers, to judge from normally prevailing evolutionary trends.

Let us say we want to take action to reduce the biological costs of climate change. Let us say we are willing to help sustain the complexity and functioning of our landscapes. What do we need to do, and what challenges would lie ahead?

---

1. The links between climate change and biological extinctions are considered in Peter D. Ward, Under a Green Sky (Smithsonian Books 2007).

2. Shahid Naeem, Robin S. Waples, and Craig Moritz, *Preserving Nature, in* The Endangered Species Act at 30: Conserving Biodiversity in Human-Dominated Landscapes, vol. 2 74 (J.M. Scott, D.D. Goble & F.W. Davis eds., Island Press 2006).

The question of what to do, in physical terms, is a matter for science. From scientists we need to hear about the needs of species, their abilities to migrate, and how we might intervene in landscapes to help biotic communities gain new members. The science here is difficult. There is much we do not know. Still, our knowledge is substantial and we can learn from real-world experiments through careful trial and error. We can learn what it takes for species to expand their territories and to thrive in landscapes that have become more suitable for them.

The science, though, is perhaps not the harder part of the challenge. Human behavior is at the root of the problem. It needs to change. And changing large-scale behavior, changing ourselves, is not all that easy.

I. Resettling the Land

Sometimes we could help species move by physically relocating individual plants and animals. It is hard to know how much work of this kind might prove useful, or who might do it and how. Many species though—the vast majority of them, surely—could not be relocated in this way. Most species are hardly visible if at all to the human eye. Many exist in interdependent webs of life and cannot live apart from these webs. For them, relocation would require movement of the community, not just the individual organism. Even in the case of macro species, they could have trouble surviving in new homes without the microspecies that interact with them. Moving a tree is not as easy as moving a living room sofa.

Whatever success we might have in such efforts, we will still need to find ways for species and biotic assemblages to migrate on their own. This means corridors of some sort along which species can travel or spread. Some of the corridors could be along waterways or riparian corridors. Others might follow coastal zones. Still others could traverse natural plains or parallel mountain ranges.

Merely to imagine such corridors is to confront the sizeable difficulty. People would need to get out of the way. People in many settings would need to alter their modes of using nature. This means halting or moving human activities. It will likely also mean reshaping landscapes to make them more useful and inviting to nature's migrants—by, for instance, removing levees and subsurface drainage tiles, providing passageways under roads, and, most of all, leaving more places where nature's forces, not human will, decide what will live and where. In the aggregate, this would amount to a new pattern of human occupation, a resettlement of the land.[3]

The basic idea behind such a resettlement is that our human activities should take place in natural settings that are ecologically suited for them. That is, we should look at the physical and biological nature in a place, consider larger ecological contexts, and then decide how we might use the place in ways consistent with its continued ecological health. It is a simple idea, yet one we have had grave difficulty implementing. Typically our land use decisions pay little or no attention to nature, except insofar as a land parcel's physical features make construction too expensive. We site roads, buildings, and factories in places that are convenient for us, with little regard for ecological disruption. In truth, we have a hard time restraining ourselves—or rather restraining one another—even when ecological ill-effects are obvious. The forces of development are simply too strong; our abilities to channel development, to places better suited for it, are too weak. These same weaknesses will confront us, looming tall and strong, should we try to make room for nature's refugees.

In sum, we will tax our scientific knowledge when trying to figure out the physical landscape changes needed to help nature respond to climate change. Even more we will tax our culture and our politics when we try to implement these changes.

---

3. A provocative vision for resettling the continent is proposed in DAVE FOREMAN, REWILDING NORTH AMERICA: A VISION FOR CONSERVATION IN THE 21ST CENTURY (Island Press 2004).

II. Needed: Large-Scale Planning

Many beneficial land-use changes could be undertaken by private parties acting on their own, by citizens and organizations that care about overall welfare and are prepared to sacrifice for it. Land trusts could pool money to buy land for restoration. Individual landowners might adopt land use practices that help species move or at least reduce obstacles. The problem with this approach is that it expects the virtuous few to repair the damage created by all. Economically, the overall benefits of such work could well exceed the costs. But the costs and benefits would not line up, just as they do not line up in conservation work or advocacy generally. The dedicated few who put in the time, money or land bear all the costs. The benefits, in contrast, are widespread. For the community, the effort makes economic sense. For the individuals who bear the costs it does not.

Voluntary action, though, will not be enough. We cannot expect citizen volunteers to perform this task, any more than we can expect them to fund the nation's defense. Indeed, it would be easier for virtuous citizens to shoulder the burden of national defense because they would only have to come up with the billions of dollars to pay the bills. In the case of land-use issues, though, money is not the only need. To allow species and biotic communities to migrate requires us to identify corridors and other migration routes. We then need to take steps to conserve or restore these lands and waters, modifying, removing, and restraining human activities that are inconsistent. But work of that type collides directly with the institution of private property and the presumed liberty of landowners to use their lands pretty much as they like. It runs into the swelling sentiment that government should refrain from exercising eminent domain. And it confronts the political fragmentation of our landscapes into countless legal jurisdictions, each with power to exert control over how pieces and parts of nature are put to use.

To allow nature's refugees to find new homes we will have to engage in land planning. We will need to pull out the maps and identify good places where nature's processes can push and pull life forms to compose new biotic communities. Some of this work will need to take place at quite large spatial scales, involving hundreds and thousands of square miles. Many of the land-use details, to be sure, can be filled out later, and by decision-makers working at much smaller spatial scales. But the broad brush strokes need to be set down at the large scale. The outlines need to be imposed; the basic goals and restrictions identified.

Large-scale land planning has not worked very well in the United States.[4] The few efforts at such planning mandated at the federal level have not done much, except here and there: in coastal zones due to the Coastal Zone Management Act;[5] in the Pinelands of New Jersey;[6] and in a few similar ecoregions. State-wide or regional planning has done only modestly better. State planning mostly pushes major developments away from places that are poorly suited for them. It is rare for a state to design and protect large-scale habitat as New York did with the Adirondacks.[7] Conservation work during the New Deal era did feature efforts to plant shelter-belts of trees up and down the Great Plains.[8] Regional development did take place in the Tennessee River valley and by reacquiring "submarginal" lands (constructing, in the process, some of today's most-used

---

4. See Todd A. Wildermuth, *National Land Use Planning in America, Briefly*, 26 J. Land Resources & Envtl. L. 73 (2005).

5. 16 U.S.C. §§ 1451–1466.

6. An overview of the multi-level governance scheme is offered in Gardner v. New Jersey Pinelands Commission, 125 N.J. 193, 593 A.2d 251 (1991). Background is presented in Jonathan Berge & John W. Sinton, Water, Earth, and Fire: Land Use and Environmental Planning in the New Jersey Pine Barrens (Johns Hopkins Press 1985).

7. Louise A. Halper, *The Adirondack Park and the Northern Forest: An Essay on Preservation and Conservation*, 19 Vt. L. Rev. 335 (1995).

8. Sarah T. Phillips, This Land, This Nation: Conservation, Rural America, and the New Deal (Cambridge Un. Press 2007).

national parks).[9] But instances of large-scale planning remain few. Americans just do not like the idea.

III. The Tragedy of Fragmentation

One common way to think about our environmental predicament is in terms of the well-known tale of the tragedy of the commons, most famously recounted by Garret Hardin. Hardin's best known example featured a grazing commons used by multiple livestock herders, each acting independently. Each herder has an economic incentive to add more animals to the pasture, even though, when other herders do the same, the pasture becomes overgrazed, its production declines, and everyone is harmed. Hardin termed his tale the tragedy of the *commons*, even though the commons was hardly to blame. The herders were to blame, and their behavior was motivated by selfish individualism. A better title for Hardin's article would have been the tragedy of selfish individualism. Or put otherwise, the tragedy arose because the herders failed to get together to set rules protecting their shared landscape. So Hardin could have called it the tragedy of no cooperation. Joint action was the solution.[10]

It is frequently said that the solution to the grazing-commons tragedy is to divide the commons into private parcels under separate management. In truth, this parcelization solution is more appealing to people who know little about grazing than to people who realize that confined grazing (rather than rotational grazing) is ill-suited for many landscapes. Setting that issue aside, the privatization solution typically skips over the work required to institute a regime of private property when none exists. Private property is a social institution that arises not automatically or by the acts of individuals in isolation but through collective means. It arises when people get together and decide what can be owned and what ownership shall mean.[11] Grazing parcels on separate landscapes are ecologically interdependent. Thus, the herders who craft a new private property regime would need to go beyond simply marking out boundaries, at least if they wanted to avoid degradation. They would need to prescribe limits on how each herder can use what he owns so as not to harm other herders or the community as a whole. Alternatively (and more wisely, in many landscapes), they could retain control of the commons and assign to one another limited rights to put animals on the commons, with rotational grazing then managed jointly. Even better, they would construct a governance regime through which they could periodically reconsider grazing conditions, modify grazing rights, and otherwise manage the commons collectively to enhance its productivity.

Work of this type, though, requires the herders to operate together. That is the key step. So long as they remain self-directed, caring only for themselves, the tragedy will continue. Or put otherwise, so long as the power to control the grazing resides at the individual level, with little or no managerial power at the collective level, then the tragedy will likely continue.

The tragedy of the commons does shed light on some of our environmental challenges, such as the plight of ocean fish stocks. But more of our environmental problems come not from common-pool resources that are undivided but instead from resources that are fragmented among owners, and among political jurisdictions, with too much power vested in these owners and jurisdictions to act with little regard for the welfare of larger wholes.[12] These power arrangements came about by means of collective action—setting up governments, prescribing laws, and allocating the resources. As this was done, too much authority over the resources was delegated to

---

9. *Id.*

10. I discuss Hardin's work, and elaborate on some of the points made here in THE LAND WE SHARE: PRIVATE PROPERTY AND THE COMMON GOOD 157–78 (Island Press 2007).

11. I consider the issue in ON PRIVATE PROPERTY: FINDING COMMON GROUND ON THE OWNERSHIP OF LAND 9–15 (Beacon Press 2007).

12. Eric T. Freyfogle, *The Tragedy of Fragmentation*, 36 VAL. U. L. REV. 307 (2002).

the individual owners and the smaller political jurisdictions. Not enough power was kept at the collective level to demand that individual behavior comport with the welfare of the larger community. We might term this the tragedy of fragmentation; the tragedy that comes when individuals and small-scale jurisdictions are empowered to pursue their own interests with little regard for the good of the whole.[13]

Whatever terminology we use, this is basically the challenge that we face when it comes to landscape planning. The individuals and small groups that manage the pieces wield too much power, with too little power maintained at larger spatial scales to formulate and implement large-scale land plans. The issue here is partially one of law and legal power. It is mostly, though, an issue of cultural values and political understandings. Our culture exalts the individual. We contend that people should be able to do what they want unless they cause obvious harm. We distrust government. We embrace a particular cultural understanding of private property that gives owners vast control over what they own. We view land use disputes as matters for resolution by local government, not at the state or federal level. The liberty we hold high is the negative, individual liberty of people to act free of governmental constraints. Of course, to say we want small government is to say we want as little collective action as possible. To say we want maximum landowner independence is to say that we are happy to allow individuals to pursue their self-interests, not the interests of the community.

Magnifying this constellation of values and preferences is our generally poor understanding of ecological processes. People do not really think, as alleged, that food comes from the grocery store. But too many people likely have little idea how food production methods have distorted fundamental ecological systems and deranged biotic communities.[14] Soil loss and degradation proceeds inexorably, and there is apparently nothing we can do about it given currenty farming methods. Our fertility cycles depend upon massive injections of inorganic fertilizers that create their own pollution problems. The world is awakening to the ill effects of emitting too much carbon dioxide into our environment. One day they will realize that we similarly emit too much nitrogen, and too much phosphorus, with grave consequences. Indeed, they will realize that any element or compound is a pollutant when it is too common or in the wrong places.

The solution to our ecological problems has long been on the table, but few people have noticed it and hardly any one takes it seriously. The solution is to revisit and alter significantly the ways we think about our places in nature. Our thinking on this issue should begin to sketch only a vague outline—not from our distinctness as individual, morally worthy human beings in a world of amoral physical stuff but instead from a recognition that we are living creatures embedded in and dependent upon a web of life. The land is a community of life, as Aldo Leopold put it in the middle of the last century.[15] By land Leopold meant the entire suite of plants, animals, soils, waters, and people living in a place. We can no longer see ourselves as conquerors of this community. We need to become responsible members of it, recognizing that our long-term welfare is aligned with the continued health and productivity of the community. What we need is not simply a new ethic. It is more fundamental than that. It is a new way of understanding our beings, a new ontology. We need to see our embeddedness in nature; we need to be aware of our constant, essential interactions with

---

13. I say "likely" because the herders might voluntarily get together and agree to rules or norms limiting their activities without any formal power residing at the collective level. On the other hand, social norms themselves carry social weight, which is to say they draw upon some reserve of collective power, even if not a formal law-making power.

14. The classic critique is WENDELL BERRY, THE UNSETTLING OF AMERICA: CULTURE AND AGRICULTURE (Sierra Club Books 1977).

15. ALDO LEOPOLD, A SAND COUNTY ALMANAC AND SKETCHES HERE AND THERE viii (Oxford Un. Press 1949).

the biotic and abiotic elements of our communities. Only in that way can we succeed at what Leopold termed "the oldest task in history"—to live on land without gradually destroying it.[16]

At its fullest, conservation poses a serious challenge to the constellation of values and understandings associated with the European era of the Enlightenment.[17] It challenges the wisdom of acting based on scientific facts when our scientific knowledge is woefully incomplete. It challenges the presumption that humans alone have moral value while the rest of the planet—including all life up to the top apes—is morally worthless. Mostly it challenges the implicit assumption that humans are really a different form of existence from all other life and that we can thrive, even as our surrounding landscapes decline. The educated among us typically pay homage to Darwin and evolution, ridiculing those who dissent. And yet our prevailing values and world views ignore Darwin's truths. We admit that we evolved from other life forms but act as though we were separately created. We deny that we differ in kind from other life forms yet presume that we alone have moral value and that we possess that moral value, not as interdependent parts of something larger, but as appropriately selfish individuals. Vice has become virtue. Climate change is one result.

IV. Looking Ahead

To get to the cultural roots of our environmental predicament is to gain a sense of what needs to change for us to help nature maintain its fertility, productivity, and biotic complexity in the face of a rapidly changing climate.

For starters, we need a sense of what good land use might entail. We need a sense of what our lands would look like if conservation succeeded. Such a vision of good land use could serve as a goal for the many forms of conservation work now taking place. One of the failings of our conservation movement in the United States is its failure to offer any sort of overall goal for its work.[18] We hear about clean water, clean air, and protecting rare species. But how does it all add up? Critics say environmentalists only care about nature, not about people or jobs. The charge is very wide of the mark, but it highlights the huge gap in environmental rhetoric. If the conservation cause is not out to protect nature from people, then what is it trying to accomplish? The vague, almost meaningless rhetoric of sustainability hardly begins to fit the bill.[19] Good land use is in fact quite hard to define. It is a normative ideal, derived by bringing together a large number of factors that seem relevant in evaluating the goodness and badness of the ways we interact with nature.[20] We have hardly made much effort to think through the idea clearly. Because we have not, we rush into questionable actions such as the push to grow biofuels to help meet energy needs, failing to note, in the rush, that biofuel production uses millions of acres of land with widespread ecological consequences.

In the attempt to deal with one particular aspect of our environmental plight, we implement measures that make other aspects of our plight worse. It is a familar story, and a long-standing object of complaint by our most thoughtful environmental observers. We need, soon, a clearer vision of how we ought to be living on land and interacting with nature. It is hard to know how we will get a vision, though, given the pernicious fragmentation of the environmental movement and our lack of even a single national environmental leader who is not better known in some other role. Can we move ahead without an environmental Martin Luther King? Could such

---

16. Aldo Leopold, *Engineering and Conservation, in* THE RIVER OF THE MOTHER OF GOD AND OTHER ESSAYS BY ALDO LEOPOLD 254 (S. Flader & J.B. Callicott eds., Un, of Wisconsin Press 1991).

17. A classic critique is DAVID EHRENFELD, THE ARROGANCE OF HUMANISM (Oxford Un. Press 1981).

18. ERIC T. FREYFOGLE, WHY CONSERVATION IS FAILING AND HOW IT CAN REGAIN GROUND 179–84 (SPI Publishers 2006).

19. *Id.* at 113–43.

20. *Id.* at 144–77.

a leader even arise given the reluctance of environmental groups to work together seriously and their collective failure to operate think tanks and to take normative ideas—as opposed to scientific facts—very seriously?

Setting aside the issue of overall goal, there is the equally daunting challenge of finding good ways for us to overcome the tragedies of fragmentation; the challenge of developing sound methods for citizens to make collective decisions about their shared homes. The challenge here, as noted, is chiefly cultural and only secondarily legal and political. Many governments enjoy public support when they provide basic services such as police and fire protection. Resistance rises when they attempt to deal with problems that some people see and others do not. If strong democracy prevailed, majority rule would carry more power. But special interests skew political processes, misinformation is rampant, ideology trumps reason, and rhetoric inflames passions and biases.

Somehow we need to come together to study our landscapes, to think about them in ways commensurate with their complexity, and to identify the basic terms on which we should interact with nature. None of this is easy work. Indeed, it is hard to imagine it happening without serious efforts to promote stronger democracy. Further, it will likely make sense to craft new types of governance mechanisms, ones that blur the line between public and private and that get land users more directly invested in decision-making about their natural homes.

Plainly, to reiterate, we also need to reconsider what private property means and how we might revise the norms of ownership—yet again, since our ancestors did it repeatedly—so that landowner rights are more consistent with the maintenance of healthy landscapes; so that, much more than in the past, they take nature into account.[21]

We need to foster new, more positive attitudes toward collective action and toward government by helping people realize that many goals are simply not achievable unless we work together. Liberty can be positive as well as negative; it can be collective as well as individual. We do not need less liberty. We need to balance individual, negative liberty with forms of liberty that allow us to get together and govern our natural homes—precisely the liberty that was most valued and most sought by the signers of our Declaration of Independence.

Perhaps above all, we need to reconsider our individualism and find new ways of talking about ourselves that recognize our embeddedness in nature and the many benefits of having healthy relations. We need to reconsider, that is, how the individual fits into the community—not just the human social community but the larger community of all life.

The basic challenge, then, can be distilled, and it has been, some time ago. In the fall of 1946, a fledgling political group, intended to start a new political party, approached Aldo Leopold and asked him, as the nation's leading conservationist, to prepare for the group a national conservation platform. He responded as he was prone to respond, by emphasizing the most important points. If these points were not achieved, the countless details were unimportant. Leopold's platform required only one half page of text and featured two items.

The second item of the platform was Leopold's claim that conservation could succeed only if it had an overall goal. That goal could not be, as people assumed, the promotion of flows of discrete valuable natural resources. Instead it had to be phrased in terms of the ecological functioning or health of whole landscapes. "The health of the land as a whole, rather than its constituent 'resources,' is what needs conserving."[22] In front of that item—the much-needed goal for all conservation—was a policy element even more important for conservation. Society had to rethink,

---

21. FREYFOGLE, *supra* note 18, at 203–53.

22. Aldo Leopold, "Conservation," unpublished manuscript, attached to manuscript letter, Horace S. Fries to Aldo Leopold, August 8, 1946, Aldo Leopold Papers, series 10-1, box 1, University of Wisconsin, Madison, archives.

Leopold stated, how the individual fit into the community and to develop a better sense of the individual as responsible community member. Leopold's first concept of conservation, therefore, was "that the average citizen, especially the landowner, has an obligation to manage land in the interest of the community, as well as his own interest." Or as Leopold put it a year later: "Conservation is getting nowhere because it is incompatible with our Abrahamic concept of land. We abuse land because we regard it as a commodity belonging to us. When we see land as a community to which we belong, we may begin to use it with love and respect."[23]

Human-induced climate change is simply the latest way, and one of the most severe, that we are altering nature without plan and with little regard for consequences. We are, in effect, conducting a huge, planetary experiment, posing risk to all peoples and other life forms, without any research protocol and without getting anyone's consent, informed or otherwise. If even the moderately dire predictions are true, the costs could be catastrophic.

This time, though, it will take more than money, blood, and technology to address the danger. It will also take a reassessment of the ways we understand the world and our place in it. It will require us to rethink our cleverness and our abilities to predict and control nature. It will require us to rethink the values we attach to individualism and negative liberty and to shift more value to the ways we form communities and to our needs to work together collectively. Perhaps it will help if we do come to love nature and if we do recognize moral value outside the human species. But we could continue to hold on to our anthropocentrism, we could continue to deny the moral implications of Darwin, and still take the steps we need to take.

A healthy planet is good for humans, without regard for its benefits for other life forms. We can protect the planet's health, if we choose, solely for the benefit of future generations of people. What is essential is that we see how we are in it together. Our fates are intertwined. Our tragedies are linked to an excessive faith in what we can do alone. We simply cannot respond well to climate change, we cannot sustain the planet's productivity and make room for nature's refugees, unless we readjust the ways we think and value. If we can do that, all else will likely follow.

————————

Notes

1. Cornelia Dean, *Thoreau is Rediscovered as a Climatologist*, N.Y. TIMES, Oct. 28, 2008:

CONCORD, MASS.—Henry David Thoreau endorsed civil disobedience, opposed slavery and lived for two years in a hut in the woods here, an experience he described in WALDEN. Now he turns out to have another line in his resume: climate researcher.

He did not realize it of course. Thoreau died in 1862, when the industrial revolution was just beginning to pump climate-changing greenhouse gases into the atmosphere. In 1851, when he started recording when and where plants flowered in Concord, he was making notes for a book on the seasons.

Now, though, researchers at Boston University and Harvard are using those notes to discern patterns of plant abundance and decline in Concord—and by extension, New England—and to link those patterns to changing climate.

Their conclusions are clear. On average, common species are flowering seven days earlier than they did in Thoreau's day, Richard B. Primack, a conservation biologist at Boston University, and Abraham J. Miller-Rushing, then his graduate student, re-

————————

23. LEOPOLD, *supra* note 15.

ported this year in the journal ECOLOGY. Working with Charles C. Davis, an evolutionary biologist at Harvard and two of his graduate students, they determined that 27 percent of the species documented by Thoreau have vanished from Concord and 36 percent are present in such small numbers that they probably will not survive for long. Those findings appear in the current issue of the PROCEEDINGS OF THE NATIONAL ACADEMY OF SCIENCES [Charles G. Willis *et al., Phylogenetic patterns of species loss in Thoreau's woods are driven by climate change*, 105 PNAS 17029 (Nov. 4, 2008)].

2. O. Hoegh-Guldberg *et al., Assisted Colonization and Rapid Climate Change*, 321 SCIENCE 345 (July 18, 2008):

> Rapid climate change has already caused changes to the distributions of many plants and animals leading to severe range contractions and the extinction of some species.... [R]esource managers must contemplate moving species to sites where they do not currently occur or have not been known to occur in recent history. This strategy flies in the face of conventional conservation approaches. The world is littered with examples where moving species beyond their current range into natural and agricultural landscapes has had negative impacts. Understandably, notions of deliberately moving species are regarded with suspicion. Our contrary view is that an increased understanding of the habitat requirements and distributions of some species allow us to identify low-risk situations where the benefits of such "assisted colonization" can be realized and adverse outcomes minimized.

3. K.E. Carpenter *et al., One-Third of Reef-Building Corals Face Elevated Extinction Risk from Climate Change and Local Impacts*, 321 SCIENCE 560 (July 25, 2008).

4. Margot Roosevelt, *Climate change threatens two-thirds of California's unique plants, study says*, LOS ANGELES TIMES, June 25, 2008, *available at* http://www.latimes.com/news/custom/scimedemail/la-me-speices25-2008jun25,0,638383 (last visited July 9, 2008):

> California's flora face a potential "collapse," said David Ackerly, an ecologist at UC Berkeley who was the senior author of the paper. "As the climate changes, many of these plants will have no place to go."
>
> Half of the plant species that are unique to the continental United States grow only in the Golden State, from towering redwoods to slender fire poppies. And under likely climate scenarios, many would have to shift 100 miles or more from their current range—a difficult task given slow natural migration rates and obstacles presented by suburban sprawl.
>
> The study, published Tuesday in the peer-reviewed on-line journal PLoS ONE, is the first to analyze the effect of climate change on all of the plants unique to one of the world's most biologically diverse areas. Previous models have focused on fewer species in areas such as the eastern United States, Europe, South Africa and Australia.
>
> "The climate is changing 10 times faster than it did during the last ice ages," said ecologist Scott Loarie, who has a doctorate from Duke University and who conducted the study over five years with Ackerly and other collaborators. "The first thing we need to do is to reduce the pace of change."
>
> The study, which was based on more than 80,000 specimens, was hailed as groundbreaking by leading scientists in the field. "It is a timely analysis of the likely fate of the plants of California in the face of climate change," Peter Raven, president of the Missouri Botanical Garden and coauthor of seminal texts on California flora, said in an e-mail.

And in Southern California, given water shortages and habitat disruption, he added, "lots of the populations are right on the edge.... The balance could easily be tipped so we could lose many of them in a very short period of time."

As California's unique species migrate, they could be separated from the creatures that pollinate them. Animals could be divided from the plants on which they depend, the researchers noted.

5. HENRY DAVID THOREAU, WALDEN 232–33 (Eyre & Spottis Woode 1952):

The Governor and his Council faintly remember the pond, for they went a-fishing there when they were boys; but now they are too old and dignified to go a-fishing, and so they know it no more forever. Yet even they expect to go to heaven at last. If the legislature regards it, it is chiefly to regulate the number of hooks to be used there; but they know nothing about the hook of hooks with which to angle for the pond itself, impaling the legislature for a bait. Thus, even in civilized communities, the embryo man passes through the hunter stage of development.

6. ANTHONY D. BARNOSKY, HEATSTROKE: NATURE IN AN AGE OF GLOBAL WARMING (Island Press 2009).

IV. The Carbon Cycle

Not only is carbon everywhere, but it is constantly moving. Carbon, the fundamental building block of life, exists in many forms, such as pure elemental carbons, sucrose or table sugar ($C_{12}H_{22}O_{11}$), calcium carbonate ($CaCO_3$), methane (CH_4), and carbon dioxide (CO_2). The diverse forms of carbon reflect the many ways that carbon is stored and used on Earth. The description of carbon storage and exchange is called the "carbon cycle."[1]

Within the carbon cycle, each major form of carbon, or reservoir, can be either a "sink" or a "source." A carbon sink is actively taking up and storing carbon; conversely, a carbon source is emitting or losing carbon. The main form in which carbon is exchanged is carbon dioxide.[2] With regard to global climate, the major sinks and sources include: the atmosphere, fossil fuels, the oceans, and terrestrial ecosystems. (See Figure 2.)

When atmospheric concentrations of carbon increase, so does temperature due to the greenhouse effect. Prior to the Industrial Revolution, the exchanges of carbon were balanced so that atmospheric carbon dioxide remained around 280 parts per million for approximately 1000 years. Since 1750, however, human activity has caused an unprecedented increase in carbon dioxide emis-

---

1. *See generally* K.L. Denman *et al.*, *Couplings Between Changes in the Climate System and Biogeochemistry*, *in* CLIMATE CHANGE 2007: THE PHYSICAL SCIENCE BASIS. CONTRIBUTION OF WORKING GROUP I TO THE FOURTH ASSESSMENT REPORT OF THE INTERGOVERNMENTAL PANEL ON CLIMATE CHANGE 499 (S. Solomon *et al.* eds., Cambridge Un. Press 2007).

2. JOHN HOUGHTON, GLOBAL WARMING: THE COMPLETE BRIEFING 29 (3d ed., Cambridge Un. Press 2004).

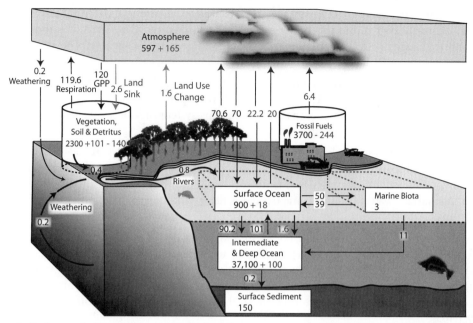

Figure 2. Carbon cycle from 1750 to 1994. Carbon fluxes are measured in Gigatons of carbon per year. The black numbers within each reservoir box indicate the natural carbon storage in Gigatons of carbon, while the gray numbers indicate post-Industrial revolution human additions or subtractions. The 140 GtC loss from "vegetation, soil, and detritus" reflects human-induced land use changes. "GPP" stands for annual gross primary production, which reflects the balance between photosynthesis and respiration. Adapted from Figure 7.3 of K.L. Denman *et al.*, *Couplings Between Changes in the Climate System and Biogeochemistry*, in CLIMATE CHANGE 2007: THE PHYSICAL SCIENCE BASIS, CONTRIBUTION OF WORKING GROUP I TO THE FOURTH ASSESSMENT REPORT OF THE IPCC 499, 515 (Cambridge Un. Press 2007).

sions that has resulted in a severe imbalance.[3] The major sources due to human activity are fossil fuel combustion and cement production (75%) and land use changes such as deforestation (25%).[4]

Despite the rapid rise in atmospheric carbon dioxide and resulting temperature, the result of human activity would have been much more drastic were it not for the absorption of carbon dioxide by the oceans and land-based plants. These two sinks have absorbed approximately 55% of human-released carbon dioxide since 1959.[5] Between 2000 and 2006, approximately 24% of emitted carbon dioxide was absorbed by the oceans, while 30% was taken up by terrestrial ecosystems.[6]

A. The Oceans

Oceans act as a carbon sink though two mechanisms: the "solubility pump" and the "biological pump." Because carbon dioxide dissolves in water, it is freely exchanged between the atmos-

3. *See, e.g.*, P. Falkowski *et al.*, *The Global Carbon Cycle: A Test of Our Knowledge of Earth as a System*, 290 SCIENCE 291 (2000).

4. *See* Denman, *supra* note 1, at 512, FAQ 7.1.

5. J.G. Canadell *et al.*, *Contributions to Accelerating Atmospheric CO_2 Growth from Economic Activity, Carbon intensity, and Efficiency of Natural Sinks*, 104 PROC. NATL. ACAD. SCI. 18866, 18867 Table 1 (2007).

6. *Id.*

phere and the waters on the ocean surface. The absorption of carbon dioxide is buffered by the oceans' carbonate system, but this buffer system has a limited capacity. Thus, if carbon dioxide were only exchanged with the upper ocean, it would not be a significant sink. The solubility and biological pumps vastly increase the ability of the ocean to store carbon.

The solubility pump involves cycling surface water down to deep layers of the ocean through the thermohaline circulation (THC) system. The THC depends on the temperature differential between bodies of water. As the oceans are heated, this system may be weakened, which would reduce the strength of the ocean sink.

The biological pump involves the uptake of carbon dioxide by seasonal phytoplankton "blooms" and subsequent sinking of the organisms after they die. These organisms only survive in the upper oceans. With increasing ocean temperatures and slowing of ocean circulation, there is a danger that surface waters could become oxygen deficient and unable to support the phytoplankton blooms.[7]

The absorption of carbon dioxide comes at a high price—ocean acidification. The buffering of carbon dioxide in the ocean results in an increase in bicarbonate and a decrease in carbonate ions, and consequently a reduction in ocean pH. Organisms such as phytoplankton, coral, and shell fish require calcium carbonate to build their shells. These organisms form the basis for virtually the entire ocean food web, so their loss could cause the collapse of the ocean ecosystem.

B. The Forests

Land-based plants and soil also exchange carbon with the atmosphere. This can be quantified as net ecosystem productivity, which is the balance between carbon dioxide uptake through photosynthesis and carbon dioxide release through respiration. Notably, the behavior of the terrestrial ecosystem can be either as a sink or a source. Furthermore, regional differences are substantial.

At present, the global terrestrial ecosystems act as a significant sink that helps offset anthropogenic carbon dioxide emissions, but this will likely change by mid-century.[8] The terrestrial ecosystem both influences climate and is influenced by climate. In the future, the impact of human activity and climate change will likely lead to a positive feedback effect whereby the balance is shifted towards production, as opposed to uptake, of carbon. The IPCC reports that the majority of climate models indicate that climate feedbacks on the carbon cycle will result in the addition of carbon to the atmosphere by 2100.[9]

There is already evidence that the major sinks, oceans and plants, are slowing down. One way to assess the function of carbon sinks is through the "airborne fraction," which is the amount of anthropogenic carbon dioxide that remains in the atmosphere. In recent years, this fraction has increased, which suggests that carbon sinks are absorbing less carbon dioxide.[10] Furthermore, most carbon cycle-climate models underestimate the observed increase in airborne fraction, suggesting that the predictions of the future switch from carbon sink to source may also be underestimations.

---

7. *See* James C. Zachos *et al.*, *An Early Cenozoic Perspective on Greenhouse Warming and Carbon-cycle Dynamics*, 451 NATURE 279, 281 (2008).

8. HOUGHTON, *supra* note 2, at 41, Figure 3.5.

9. Denman, *supra* note 1, at 535, Table 7.4.

10. Canadell, *supra* note 5.

The terrestrial ecosystem interacts with the climate in numerous ways. These can be broadly classified as biogeophysical, biogeographical, and biogeochemical.[11] Biogeophysical impacts includes changes in albedo and evapotranspiration. As the Arctic warms, the Boreal forest is migrating northward. Although one might think this will increase photosynthesis, the benefit is offset by the reduction in surface albedo.[12] Forests are much darker than the snowy surface that they are replacing. The white snow reflected solar radiation, but the forested land absorbs it, which increases the Earth's temperature. Similarly, evapotranspiration impacts climate by altering heat exchange as water vapor evaporates.

Biogeographical impacts include human land use and changes in species mix. This effect is particularly profound in the Amazon where deforestation is occurring at an alarming rate.[13] Loss of rainforest area reduces the amount of carbon storage, and it also puts direct stress on the viability of the ecosystem as a whole. Increased temperatures due to climate change will cause drying in portions of the rainforest. The forest has some natural resilience, but it is predicted that if 30% of more of the rainforest is lost, it will become unsustainable and dry out.[14] The edges of the rainforest are much more susceptible to drying out. This is exacerbated by the current fragmentation of the forest by clearing for agricultural uses. Finally, human land use creates a danger of fire. Fire is not a natural phenomenon in the Amazon, so the ecosystem is not adapted to withstand fire. Yet, fire is introduced by humans in the process of clearing land for agriculture, which creates an explosive situation when combined with the fragmentation and climate change-induced drying.[15]

Biogeochemical impacts refer to the carbon cycle and the exchange of carbon dioxide through photosynthesis and respiration. At one time it was hypothesized that increased atmospheric carbon dioxide would have a "fertilization" effect and increase photosynthesis, thereby creating a stronger sink. However, the fertilization effect appears to have been overrated. For instance, a hotter, drier Summer season in northern latitudes appears to offset the increased carbon dioxide uptake of an early Spring, even though temperature is considered the limiting factor in this region.[16] Similarly, Piao and colleagues found that the dry conditions of a warmer Autumn result in greater respiration, which offsets 90% of the benefit of the earlier Spring.[17]

One exciting new finding is that old growth forests may be much better carbon sinks than previously believed. A recent study performed a meta-analysis of carbon-flux measurements to find that in forests between 15 and 800 years old net ecosystem productivity is positive. The study found that old growth forests constitute approximately 15% of global forests and sequester approximately 1.3 Gigatonnnes of carbon each year.[18] These stands account for about 10% of the global ecosystem productivity.[19] This flies in the face of the traditional belief that only new,

---

11. Gordon B. Bonan, *Forests and Climate Change: Forcings, Feedbacks, and the Climate Benefits of Forests*, 320 SCIENCE 1444 (2008).

12. R.A. Betts, *Offset of the Potential Carbon Sink from Boreal Forestation by Decreases in Surface Albedo*, 408 NATURE 187 (2000).

13. *See* Yadvinder Malhi *et al.*, *Climate Change, Deforestation, and the Fate of the Amazon*, 319 SCIENCE 169 (2008).

14. *Id.*

15. *Id.*

16. A. Angert *et al.*, Drier *Summers Cancel Out the CO_2 Uptake Enhancement Induced by Warmer Springs*, 31 PROC. NATL. ACAD. SCI. 10823 (2005).

17. Shilong Piao *et al.*, *Net Carbon Dioxide Losses of Northern Ecosystems in Response to Autumn Warming*, 451 NATURE 49 (2008).

18. Sebastiann Luyssaert *et al.*, *Old-growth Forests as Carbon Sinks*, 455 NATURE 213 (2008).

19. *Id.*

rapidly growing forests sequester carbon. In fact, it may take several hundred years for a new tree to have the same amount of carbon as an old one.[20]

This finding has significant policy implications. Because it was believed that old growth forests did not sequester substantial levels of carbon, they are not included under the Kyoto Protocol accounting for carbon stock in the forests.[21] Given the significant potential for carbon storage in old growth, this may be a serious error of omission.

V. The Earth's Waters

A. The Oceans

Alan Carlin, *Global Climate Change Control: Is There a Better Strategy Than Reducing Greenhouse Gas Emissions?* 155 U. PA. L. REV. 1401, 1473 (2007):

> [D]ecreasing CO_2 emissions will be a difficult and at best a very slow undertaking. Reducing them by 98% does not appear to be within the realm of realistic possibility in the current world. But not reducing CO_2 emissions will result in the extinction of the world coral reefs, [Ken] Caldiera argues.

See Royal Society, *Ocean Acidification Due to Increasing Atmospheric Carbon Dioxide: Policy Document* 12/05 (2005), *available at* http://www.royalsoc.ac.uk/displaypagedoc.asp?id+13539.

Daniel Glick, National Geographic, quoted in TIM FLANNERY, THE WEATHER MAKERS: HOW MAN IS CHANGING THE CLIMATE AND WHAT IT MEANS FOR LIFE ON EARTH 189 (Atlantic Monthly Press 2005):

> Arguably, the largest oceanic change ever measured in the era of modern instruments is in the declining salinity of the subpolar seas bordering the North Atlantic.

Life History Trade-offs in Marine Organisms: Consequences of Climate Change

Felicia C. Coleman, Director, Florida State University Coastal & Marine Laboratory, http://www.marinelab.fsu.edu, 3618 Coastal Highway, St. Teresa, FL 32358-2702, Tel: (850) 697-4120, Fax: (850) 697-3822, coleman@bio.fsu.edu, and Laura E. Petes, Postdoctoral Associate, Florida State University Coastal & Marine Laboratory, St. Teresa, FL 32358-2702; Tel: (850) 697-4099, Fax: (850) 697-3822, lpetes@bio.fsu.edu.

I. Introduction

Climate can have profound influences on the life-history traits (*e.g.*, survival, growth, reproduction; Box 1.1) of marine organisms because of the influence that varying seasonal patterns of temperature, precipitation, and therefore oceanic circulation have on all aspects of their life cycle at a variety of spatial and temporal scales. In so doing, climate also affects the interactions among species within a given ecosystem, including their predator-prey (*i.e.*, trophic) and competitive relationships, as well as overall biodiversity. These features have piqued the interests of ecologists in the effects of climate change and particularly large-scale climatic events such as the North Atlantic Oscillation (NAO) and the El Niño Southern Oscillation (ENSO). However, the realities of climate change operating on so many different organizational levels, and at so many different scales, also

---

20. Emma Marris, *Old Forests Capture Plenty of Carbon*, NATURE NEWS online (September 10, 2008).
21. Luyssaert, *supra* note 18, at 215.

complicates our ability to readily predict the consequences.[1] Despite the fact that marine organisms, and indeed entire marine ecosystems, are being negatively impacted by multiple anthropogenic sources—including overfishing, invasive species, pollution, coastal development, and habitat destruction[2]—the climate signal continues to increase in strength. Evidence appears in temperature-induced shifts in community structure of fish populations in the North Sea[3] and in such marine habitats as coral reefs,[4] kelp forests,[5] and the rocky intertidal zone.[6] These shifts are largely attributable to declines in species that have low tolerance for temperatures outside their normal range, and, in contrast, expanded ranges of species that can tolerate warmer temperatures.

Box 1.1 A primer on the nature of trade-offs

All species have different strategies for increasing their survival and lifetime reproductive output. These strategies are shaped by both genetics and by the environment in which the species occurs. Thus, animals living in the deep sea—a harsh but relatively invariable environment where temperatures, light levels, and oxygen are extremely low and hydrostatic pressure is high—tend to be long-lived, slow to mature, and have low fecundities.[7] Conversely, animals living in highly-variable environments, such as estuaries, where salinity, temperature, and dissolved oxygen levels can change dramatically on a daily basis, tend to be relatively short-lived and highly fecund.

When the environment varies to produce either harsher or more benign conditions, organisms typically experience changes in life-history traits such as their age-specific mortality, growth, and fecundity schedules as they make energetic trade-offs of finite resources among competing metabolic needs. Perhaps the easiest way to envision these trade-offs is in the form of a metabolic pie composed of four pieces, each representing a competing function: maintenance, growth, storage, or reproduction. (See Figure 3.) The maintenance function relates to normal body function and repair, growth relates to increase in body size (typical for early life stages progressing towards maturity), reproductive effort is the production of gametes or offspring (typically a seasonal phenomenon in mature individuals), and the storage function refers to increasing lipid (fat) supplies prior to physiologically-costly activities such as reproduction or migration. Allocation of resources to one function diminishes the allocation available to another. This is the nature of the trade-off.

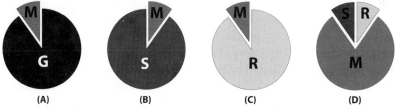

Figure 3. Metabolic Pie. (A) Juvenile; (B) Pre-spawn or migration; (C) Spawn; (D) Stress. G = growth; M = maintenance; R = reproduction; and S = storage.

1. B. Helmuth *et al.*, *Biophysics, Physiological Ecology, and Climate Change: Does Mechanism Matter?*, 67 ANNUAL REVIEW OF PHYSIOLOGY 177 (2005).

2. PEW OCEANS COMMISSION, AMERICA'S LIVING OCEANS: CHARTING A COURSE FOR SEA CHANGE. A REPORT TO THE NATION 144 (2003).

3. J.G. Hiddink & R. ter Hofstede, *Climate Induced Increases in Species Richness of Marine Fishes*, 14 GLOBAL CHANGE BIOLOGY 453 (2008).

4. O. Hoegh-Guldberg, *Climate Change, Coral Bleaching, and Future of the World's Coral Reefs*, 50 MARINE AND FRESHWATER RESEARCH 839 (1999).

5. D.R. Schiel *et al.*, *Ten Years of Induced Ocean Warming Causes Comprehensive Changes in Marine Benthic Communities*, 85 ECOLOGY 1833 (2004).

6. R.D. Sagarin *et al.*, *Climate-Related Change in an Intertidal Community over Short and Long Time Scales*, 69 ECOLOGICAL MONOGRAPHS 465 (1999).

7. Fecundity is the number of gametes or offspring produced by an organism over some period of time, usually during the spawning season for mass spawners and the birth event for live bearers.

The impacts of climate also include effects on trophic interactions from the bottom up through loss of primary productivity[8] and forage species[9] and from the top down through declines in top-level predators.[10] Yet another area of change is anticipated as warming trends allow expansion of the ranges of more tropical species towards the poles and compression of the ranges of species with limited thermal tolerances.

In this paper, we evaluate the projected[11] effects of climate change on a variety of marine habitats across major latitudinal gradients. In most cases, the habitats under consideration are formed from living organisms (*e.g.*, corals, mangroves, salt marshes, seagrass meadows, kelp forests) that serve as foundation species for the development of complex communities. Many of these habitats (*e.g.*, mangroves, estuaries, intertidal zones) also occur at the land-sea interface, where sea level rise will have its greatest effect. These habitats typically provide a number of ecosystem functions, ranging from protection of inland areas from storm surge and erosion, to provision of nursery habitat for economically-important fish and invertebrate species, and maintenance of water quality by sequestering pollutants. In the tropics, we discuss coral reef and mangrove habitats. In the temperate zone, we examine rocky intertidal, estuarine, and kelp forest habitats. We then evaluate climate change effects on polar habitats. Finally, we include a look at the impacts of large-scale climatic events on fisheries. Along the way, we provide life-history case studies as boxes, giving specific examples of life-history trade-offs affected by climate change. We end with a discussion of the implications of climate change for marine policy, management, and conservation.

II. Tropical Marine Habitats

A.   Coral Reefs

Coral reefs are among the more biologically diverse yet also most threatened habitats on the planet. Indeed, coral cover in the Caribbean has already declined by 80% in the last three decades.[12] Coral polyps, individuals that form the coral colony and make up the living reef structure, are sensitive to a number of stressors, including temperature, UV radiation, and pollution. Corals maintain a delicate mutual (or symbiotic) relationship with algae called zooxanthellae that live within their tissues and provide the coral colony with nutrition through photosynthesis. When corals experience stress, they respond by "bleaching," a phenomenon in which the relationship between the host coral and the symbiotic algae in their tissues breaks down. If corals have no algae for a prolonged period, they typically die because of lack of nutrients. Many environmental stressors can lead to bleaching, but the most common cause appears to be warm

---

8. K.A. Miller & D.L. Fluharty, *El Nino and Variability in the Northeastern Pacific Salmon Fishery: Implications for Coping with Climate Change*, in Climate Variability, Climate Change, and Fisheries 49 (Cambridge Un. Press 1992); G. Beaugrand *et al.*, *Plankton Effect on Cod Recruitment in the North Sea*, 426 Nature 661 (2003); A.J. Richardson & D.S. Schoeann, *Climate Impact on Plankton Ecosystems in the Northeast Atlantic*, 305 Science 1609 (2004).

9. S.A. Arnott & G.D. Ruxton, *Sandeel Recruitment in the North Sea: Demographic, Climatic, and Trophic Effects*, 238 Marine Ecology Progress Series 199 (2002).

10. R.R. Veit *et al.*, *Apex Marine Predator Declines Ninety Percent in Association with Changing Oceanic Climate*, 3 Global Change Biology 23 (1997).

11. We say "projected," because the effects of anthropogenically-induced climate change, with advances in modeling and forecasting, are becoming identifiable as substantively different from the normal oscillations in large-scale climatic events.

12. T.A. Gardner *et al.*, *Long-Term Region-Wide Declines in Caribbean Corals*, 301 Science 958 (2003).

water temperature.[13] The number of severe bleaching events globally has increased since the 1970s, concomitant with increases in seawater temperature.[14] For a group of organisms that has a narrow thermal tolerance, this is a disaster. The projection that these events will increase in both frequency and magnitude over the next century makes it unclear whether corals will be able to adapt. Corals can recover from bleaching by taking up new algal symbionts from the water if stressful conditions disappear quickly. However, resistance to and recovery from bleaching events appears to be species-specific,[15] and life-history trade-offs can occur in surviving corals (Box 1.2).

Box 1.2 Species-specific bleaching events in coral colonies on the Great Barrier Reef

Baird and Marshall[16] followed coral colonies after the Great Barrier Reef experienced a severe bleaching event due to warm water temperatures in 1998. Related species with different morphologies responded to this event quite differently. *Acropora hyacinthus*, a species that grows in a plate-like configuration, exhibited relatively high mortality (70% of all colonies), while *Acropora millepora*, a branching species, had significantly lower mortality (10% of colonies). Of the surviving colonies, 80% of the plating coral colonies suffered bleaching across the entire colony (all polyps), whereas in 70% of branching coral colonies, only a fraction of the polyps bleached. Many of the severely-bleached colonies eventually died, apparently from reduced ability to obtain nutrition. Species-specific differences in reproductive responses to bleaching were also observed: reproductive output was reduced more in severely-bleached colonies of plating corals than in severely-bleached colonies of branching corals. In addition, the more severe the bleaching, the greater the stress and the lower the reproductive output in plating corals.

There is also evidence that coral diseases show faster growth rates with warmer water temperatures,[17] increasing mortality rates on reefs throughout the world. Overall, the prevalence and severity of coral diseases are expected to increase under climate change, as the coral hosts become more stressed and less resilient, while pathogens increase in abundance and virulence.[18]

Another potential problem for corals under climate change is ocean acidification. As carbon dioxide concentration in seawater increases, the pH of the ocean becomes more acidic, decreasing the availability of the structuring material, carbonate ions, that are required for corals to build their calcium carbonate skeletons (Kleypas et al. 2006).[19] Oceans have already become more acidic (a 0.1 decrease in pH) since the Industrial Revolution (late 1800s to early 1900s). At current rates of ocean acidification under climate change scenarios, calcification will likely become

---

13. *See, e.g.*, Hoegh-Guldberg, *supra* note 4.

14. *Id.*

15. B.E. Brown *et al.*, *Bleaching Patterns in Reef Corals*, 404 NATURE 142 (2000).

16. *Mortality, Growth and Reproduction in Scleractinian Corals Following Bleaching on the Great Barrier Reef*, 237 MARINE ECOLOGY PROGRESS SERIES (2002).

17. *See, e.g.*, J.R. Ward *et al.*, *Temperature Affects Coral Disease Resistance and Pathogen Growth*, 329 MARINE ECOLOGY PROGRESS SERIES 115 (2007).

18. C.D. Harvell *et al.*, *Emerging Marine Diseases—Climate Links and Anthropogenic Factors*, 285 SCIENCE 1505 (1999); C.D. Harvell *et al.*, *Climate Warming and Disease Risks for Terrestrial and Marine Biota*, 296 SCIENCE (2002).

19. J.A. KLEYPAS *et al.*, IMPACTS OF OCEAN ACIDIFICATION ON CORAL REEFS AND OTHER MARINE CALCIFIERS: A GUIDE FOR FUTURE RESEARCH: A REPORT FROM A WORKSHOP SPONSORED BY THE NATIONAL SCIENCE

difficult for corals by the year 2100,[20] with up to a 35% decline in calcification from pre-Industrial levels.[21] Relatively little is known about the effects of ocean acidification on corals, but many research projects are currently underway to determine how this phenomenon will impact these animals.

B.   Mangroves

Mangroves, unique trees and shrubs bordering tropical estuaries worldwide, have lost ground at an alarming rate over the last 100 years due to coastal development in support of aquaculture,[22] agriculture and urbanization, tourism, and local uses for timber and fuel.[23] Their abundance has declined globally by ~35% since the 1980s[24] and in the United States in the Ten Thousand Islands region of Florida by 28% just between 1986 and 1997.[25] Duke et al.[26] raise concerns that the ecosystem services provided by mangroves could disappear within the next 100 years. Such losses lead to localized reductions in water quality and biodiversity, while releasing significant amounts of stored carbon.[27]

Climate change adds just one more pressure to an already overburdened system, with the greatest effects predicted to occur because of sea level rise. Ellison and Farnsworth,[28] for instance, demonstrated experimentally that mangroves would suffer reduced growth with sea level rise (Box 1.3). Other studies suggest that mangroves can keep pace with this phenomenon through increased sediment accumulation[29] or landward migration.[30] However, these assume that the rate of sediment accumulation exceeds the rate of sediment loss in the first case and that migration landward exceeds the rate of sea level rise in the latter.[31]

The species expected to be most impacted are those that depend on mangroves as nursery habitat and those that have reciprocal interactions with neighboring habitats, such as coral reefs. Koenig et al.[32] suggest that for goliath grouper (Epinephelus itajara)—a species listed as critically endangered on the IUCN Red List—the availability of mangrove habitat is essential for their recovery from the overfished state. Loss of mangroves through habitat change would likely sound

---

FOUNDATION, THE NATIONAL OCEANIC AND ATMOSPHERIC ADMINISTRATION, AND THE U.S. GEOLOGICAL SURVEY 88 (2006).

20. J.C. Orr et al., Anthropogenic Ocean Acidification over the Twenty-First Century and Its Impact on Calcifying Organisms, 437 NATURE 681 (2005).

21. J.A. Kleypas et al., Geochemical Consequences of Increased Atmospheric Carbon Dioxide on Coral Reefs, 284 SCIENCE 118 (1999).

22. I.A. Mendelssohn & K.L. Mckee, Saltmarshes and Mangroves, in NORTH AMERICAN TERRESTRIAL VEGETATION (Cambridge Un. Press 2000); I. Valiela et al., Mangrove Forests: One of the World's Threatened Major Tropical Environments., 51 BIOSCIENCE 807 (2001).

23. D.M. Alongi, The Ecology of Tropical Soft-Bottom Benthic Ecoystems, 28 OCEANOGRAPHY AND MARINE BIOLOGY ANNUAL REVIEW 381 (1990); D.M. Alongi, Present State and Future of the World's Mangrove Forests, 29 ENVIRONMENTAL CONSERVATION 331 (2002).

24. See supra note 22.

25. C. Koenig et al., Mangroves as Essential Nursery Habitat for Goliath Grouper (Epinephelus Itajara), 80 BULLETIN OF MARINE SCIENCE 567 (2007).

26. N.C. Duke et al., A World without Mangroves?, 317 SCIENCE 41 (2007).

27. E.L. Gilman et al., Threats to Mangroves from Climate Change and Adaptation Options: A Review, 89 AQUATIC BOTANY 237 (2008).

28. A.M. Ellison & E.J. Farnsworth, Simulated Sea Level Change Alters Anatomy, Physiology, Growth, and Reproduction of Red Mangrove (Rhizophora Mangle L.), 112 OECOLOGIA 435 (1997).

29. D.M. Alongi, Mangrove Forests: Resilience, Protection from Tsunamis, and Responses to Global Climate Change, 76 ESTUARINE, COASTAL, AND SHELF SCIENCE 1 (2008); C.J. Sanders et al., Recent Sediment Accumulation in a Mangrove Forest and Its Relevance to Local Sea-Level Rise (Ilha Grande, Brazil), 24 JOURNAL OF COASTAL RESEARCH 533 (2008).

30. Alongi (2002), supra note 23.

31. Gilman et al., supra note 27.

32. Koenig et al., supra note 25.

the death knell for this species. Similarly, Mumby *et al.*[33] demonstrate that rainbow parrotfish (*Scarus guacamaia*), among others, are so tightly linked to mangroves that habitat loss is a significant cause of population decline in this species.

Box. 1.3 Experimental response of red mangroves to sea level rise

Ellison and Farnsworth[34] raised Belizean mangrove plants in a greenhouse to study their responses at different life stages to changes in sea level, using current sea levels and those predicted to occur for the Caribbean over the next 50–100 years. Young mangroves exposed to high sea levels grew faster initially than those reared at low sea-level conditions. Once they reached the juvenile sapling stage, however, they experienced significantly slower growth rates. Indeed, the adult plants reared under the increased sea-level-rise scenario were smaller, had fewer stomata (tiny pores that function in gas exchange), and decreased photosynthetic rates compared to those reared at low sea level. In a classic energetic trade-off (Box 1.1), the mangroves invested more relative energy in flower production (a proxy for reproduction) and reproduced earlier than did the plants raised at current sea level. These results suggest that sea level rise could cause significant changes in life-history traits of mangroves that could lead to alterations in community structure.

III. Temperate Marine Habitats

A. Rocky intertidal zones

The intertidal zone is the region of the shore that is exposed to air at low tide and covered with water at high tide. Plants and animals that live in this zone are uniquely adapted to widely-fluctuating conditions. However, because this is a stressful environment, many species are already living close to or at their physiological tolerance limits. A major stressor for intertidal organisms, which are mostly ectotherms,[35] is exposure to extreme air and water temperatures, events predicted to increase in frequency with climate change.

Rocky intertidal zones occur in many temperate areas of the globe. Intertidal organisms are particularly vulnerable because they are exposed to air and water temperatures, which are both affected by climate change. In New Zealand, for instance, an extreme warm air temperature event that occurred at low tide led to mass mortality of intertidal mussels.[36] High air temperatures can also lead to sublethal effects for intertidal organisms (Box 1.4), such as reduced feeding rates in sea stars[37] and decreased growth and photosynthesis in algae.[38] Warm water temperatures can cause high metabolic rates in intertidal sea stars, increasing their feeding rate on mussels;[39] if seawater temperatures rise, the number of mussels could decline due to changes in this trophic relationship.

---

33. P.G. Mumby *et al.*, *Mangroves Enhance the Biomass of Coral Reef Fish Communities in the Caribbean*, 427 NATURE 533 (2004).

34. Ellison & Farnsworth, *supra* note 28.

35. An organism whose body temperature is primarily determined by the surrounding environment.

36. L.E. Petes *et al.*, *Environmental Stress Decreases Survival, Growth, and Reproduction in New Zealand Mussels*, 351 JOURNAL OF EXPERIMENTAL MARINE BIOLOGY AND ECOLOGY 83 (2007).

37. S. Pincebourde *et al.*, *Body Temperature During Low Tide Alters the Feeding Performance of a Top Intertidal Predator*, 53 LIMNOLOGY AND OCEANOGRAPHY 1562 (2008).

38. M.N. Dethier *et al.*, *Seaweeds under Stress: Manipulated Stress and Herbivory Affect Critical Life-History Functions*, 75 ECOLOGICAL MONOGRAPHS 403 (2005).

39. E. Sanford, *Regulation of Keystone Predation by Small Changes in Ocean Temperature*, 283 SCIENCE 2095 (1999).

Box 1.4 Effects of environmental stressors on intertidal mussels

Petes and colleagues[40] found that mussels on the central Oregon coast exhibit life-history trade-offs in response to thermal stress that differed depending on their vertical location within the rocky intertidal zone. Mussels found in the upper edge of the intertidal zone, where they experience greater exposure to high air temperatures, grew slowly and shifted their energetic investments from reproduction to the production of energetically-costly defense mechanisms (*e.g.*, production of heat shock proteins and antioxidant pigments) that protected them from heat stress. In contrast, mussels in the low edge of the intertidal zone, where there is less exposure to air, experienced significantly less stress and allocated more energy towards growth and reproductive output. As stress continues to increase due to climate change, it is likely that mussels will have to invest more energy into physiological defenses, and trade-offs will become manifest in reduced population sizes.

Species range shifts occur with warming water and air temperatures because species that are less resistant to warming temperatures gradually are replaced by species that prefer warm temperatures. Overall poleward movement of some species will occur as temperatures increase. Surveys conducted in central California revealed that between 1931 and 1996, most southern species (preferring warm water temperatures, such as the anemone *Corynactis californica*) increased in abundance, whereas most northern species (such as the anemone *Anthopleura xanthogrammica*) decreased in abundance.[41] In addition, the surveys revealed a dramatic (70%) decline in the cover of an algal species (*Pelvetia compressa*) that had dominated the central California rocky shores in the 1930s.[42] As species shift outside of their normal ranges, trophic interactions are altered due to the novel associations formed by the shifting roles of species within the ecosystem. The impacts of these new interactions could possibly cascade throughout the entire ecosystem.

Sea level rise will also affect intertidal zones, because these ecosystems occur at the land-sea interface. As sea level rises, species will likely move higher in the intertidal zone (upward shift) to avoid their predators, most of which live in the water and feed on intertidal prey during high tide. However, the extent to which organisms can survive in the upper intertidal zone is typically limited by their physiological tolerance to aerial exposure, as the higher an organism is in the intertidal zone, the longer it is exposed during low tide. Because extreme air temperatures are likely to increase in frequency, resulting mortality of intertidal organisms[43] at their upper limit could lead to a downward shift in the maximum height of the intertidal zone. Therefore, a "squeeze,"[44] or compression of the intertidal zone and the plants and animals that live there, is predicted to occur.

B.   Temperate Estuaries

Estuaries are bodies of water occurring where fresh water from rivers, streams, and runoff enters the ocean. The foundation plants of estuaries include intertidal species, such as salt marsh grasses, and subtidal species, like seagrasses. The organisms that live in estuaries are adapted to survive in environments that often have rapid changes in temperature, salinity, and dissolved oxygen levels. Many of these are juvenile stages of commercially-important fish species that use estuaries as nursery grounds. Estuarine wetlands are disappearing at a rapid rate due to coastal development, pollution, and habitat destruction. One of the major threats of climate change to the remaining estuarine habitats is sea level rise accompanied by salt water intrusion and flooding of intertidal habitats.

---

40. L.E. Petes *et al.*, *Intertidal Mussels Exhibit Energetic Trade-Offs between Reproduction and Stress Resistance*, 78 ECOLOGICAL MONOGRAPHS 387 (2008).

41. Sagarin *et al.*, *supra* note 6.

42. *Id.*

43. *See, e.g.*, Petes *et al.*, *supra* note 36.

44. Sensu C.D.G. Harley *et al.*, *The Impacts of Climate Change in Coastal Marine Systems*, 9 ECOLOGY LETTERS 228 (2006).

While estuarine plants and animals are adapted to environmental variability, prolonged exposure to high-salinity water can cause shifts in their distribution (Box 1.5), pushing some species up the estuary towards fresher water. These migrations may lead to overall shifts in community structure[45] and displacement of species living up-river. Increases in saline marsh types have already occurred in coastal Louisiana since the 1960s, with a concomitant decrease in less-saline marsh types.[46]

Box 1.5 A range shift in oyster disease

Oysters, in addition to serving as prey for humans and other organisms, create complex three-dimensional reefs that house hundreds of fish and invertebrate species, particularly vulnerable juveniles. Rising ocean temperatures[47] and salinities[48] have contributed to the spread of the oyster disease Dermo, caused by the protozoan parasite *Perkinsus marinus* that is already common throughout the U.S. Atlantic Coast and the Gulf of Mexico. Dermo infection can lead to reduced growth, poor body condition, and death in oysters, and it rapidly proliferates through host-to-host transmission at temperatures above 25° C.[49] From the time it was discovered in 1949 until the 1990s, the range of Dermo spread northward from Chesapeake Bay, Maryland, through Cape Cod, Massachusetts, likely due to warming waters.[50] Dermo is typically kept in check when salinity is low. Increased estuarine salinity from both sea level rise and regional drought could lead to greater infection intensity and disease-related mortality of oysters.[51] Loss of oyster reef habitat, from both adult mortality and reduced reproductive success of infected individuals, would mean a loss of local biodiversity and could negatively impact commercial fishing industries.

Compared to other marine habitats, salt marshes may be relatively resistant to the effects of climate change because of their ability to accumulate sediment.[52] Thus, they have some buffering capacity that may prove important as sea level continues to rise. This highlights the need to protect estuaries for both their ecological buffering capacity and as nursery habitat for commercially-important or threatened estuarine-dependent fish stocks.

C. *Kelp forests*

Giant kelp, *Macrocystis pyrifera*, spans a latitudinal range on the west coast of North America between Baja, Mexico and northern California. A severe El Niño event in 1997–1998 led to anomalously warm water temperatures in California and caused high mortality of giant kelp across its distribution.[53] Recovery of the kelp plants was much faster at its northern extent, where water temperatures are cool and nutrients are high, than at its southern boundary, where re-

---

45. R.S. Warren & W.A. Niering, *Vegetation Change on a Northeast Tidal Marsh — Interaction of Sea-Level Rise and Marsh Accretion*, 74 ECOLOGY 96 (1993).

46. D.F. Boesch *et al.*, *Scientific Assessment of Coastal Wetland Loss, Restoration and Management in Louisiana*, JOURNAL OF COASTAL RESEARCH 103 (1994).

47. Harvell *et al.*, *supra* note 18.

48. M.K. La Peyre *et al.*, *Environmental Significance of Freshets in Reducing Perkinsus Marinus Infection in Eastern Oysters* Crassostrea Virginica: *Potential Management Applications*, 248 MARINE ECOLOGY PROGRESS SERIES 165 (2003).

49. T. Cook *et al.*, *The Relationship between Increasing Sea-Surface Temperature and the Northward Spread of Perkinsus Marinus (Dermo) Disease Epizootics in Oysters*, 46 ESTUARINE, COASTAL, AND SHELF SCIENCE 587 (1998).

50. *Id.*; S.E. Ford, *Range Extension by the Oyster Parasite Perkinsus Marinus into the Northeastern United States: Response to Climate Change*, 15 JOURNAL OF SHELLFISH RESEARCH 45 (1996).

51. La Peyre *et al.*, *supra* note 48.

52. T. Simas *et al.*, Effects of Global Climate Change on Coastal Salt Marshes, 139 ECOLOGICAL MODELLING 1 (2001); P.M. Berry *et al.*, *Modelling Potential Impacts of Climate Change on the Bioclimatic Envelope of Species in Britain and Ireland*, 11 GLOBAL ECOLOGY AND BIOGEOGRAPHY 453 (2002).

53. M.S. Edwards & J.A. Estes, *Catastrophe, Recovery and Range Limitation in Ne Pacific Kelp Forests: A Large-Scale Perspective*, 320 MARINE ECOLOGY PROGRESS SERIES 79 (2006).

cruitment of juveniles was poor.[54] As water temperatures continue to rise due to climate change, this important species may no longer be found at its southern range limit.

Changes in the cover of dominant species, such as kelp plants, can have cascading effects on other levels of the food chain. For example, abalone species in southern California rely on kelp as their primary food source. Warm water temperature can increase the abalone disease "withering syndrome," and reduced food availability (kelp) causes decreased abalone growth and reproduction.[55] In another part of the food web, a reduction in California kelp forest fish species between the 1970s and 1990s (Box 1.6) also corresponds with increased water temperature and decreased nutrient availability.[56] These findings indicate that kelp forest ecosystems, and the species found within, are likely to be threatened by global climate change.

Box 1.6. Direct and indirect effects of climate change on kelp fish communities off the California coast

The coastal waters of California have warmed significantly over the last few decades, especially after a 1976–1977 climatic regime shift that raised the average ocean temperature in the eastern Pacific by 1°C. Holbrook and colleagues[57] studied kelp fish communities off the California coast to determine the direct and indirect effects of this temperature increase on the distribution and abundance of kelp fishes over a 14-year (1982–1995) period. What they found initially was that fish populations responded as expected: species' ranges shifted poleward, with cold-water associated species exhibiting range contractions and declining abundance, while warm-water species exhibited range expansions and increased abundance. By the 1990s, however, populations at all trophic levels collapsed simultaneously, with ~80% losses of adult surfperch (Family *Embioticidae*), their prey (benthic crustaceans such as crabs and amphipods), and the understory algal species that provided crustacean habitat and forage sites for the fish. In addition, declines in newborn[58] surfperch survival (linked tightly to the availability of their zooplankton prey) reached 80%.[59] Years of poor juvenile survival in surfperch (as in penguins) were immediately followed by years with reduced numbers of adults. These findings show that abundances of adult fishes are affected both by food supply and by recruitment success, phenomena that are tightly linked to climate.

IV. Polar Marine Habitats

Polar marine habitats are characterized by high ice cover, well-oxygenated water, and a narrow range of cold temperatures. Cold water temperatures prevent warmer-water animals from entering these marine systems to which resident animals are well-adapted. For example, polar fishes produce a type of antifreeze in their blood that allows them to withstand temperatures as low as -2°C.[60] However, as water temperatures warm, the physiological barriers preventing warmer-water species from inhabiting polar environments are removed, allowing species inva-

---

54. *Id.*

55. L.I. Vilchis *et al.*, *Ocean Warming Effects on Growth, Reproduction, and Survivorship of Southern California Abalone*, 15 ECOLOGICAL APPLICATIONS 469 (2005).

56. A.J. Brooks *et al.*, *Declines in Regional Fish Populations: Have Species Responded Similarly to Environmental Change?*, 53 MARINE AND FRESHWATER RESEARCH 189 (2002).

57. S.J. Holbrook *et al.*, *Changes in an Assemblage of Temperate Reef Fishes Associated with a Climate Shift*, 7 ECOLOGICAL APPLICATIONS 1299 (1997).

58. Surfperch species have live birth and nondispersing juveniles.

59. D. Roemmich, J.A. McGowan, *Climate Warming and the Decline of Zooplankton in the California Current*, 267 SCIENCE 1324 (1995).

60. *See, e.g.*, I.A. Johnston & A. Clarke, *Cold Adaptation in Marine Organisms*, 326 PHILOSOPHICAL TRANSACTIONS OF THE ROYAL SOCIETY OF LONDON SERIES B, BIOLOGICAL SCIENCES 655 (1990).

sions.[61] In turn, the cold-water species range is compressed, and local extinction could occur if suitable habitat completely disappears.

Polar marine ecosystems are particularly vulnerable to climate change because small changes in temperature can lead to large reductions in the cover of sea ice.[62] Sea-ice cover has a direct positive influence of the availability of a variety of crustaceans, important prey species in an extreme environment with simple food webs.[63] Therefore, sea-ice decline can either directly or indirectly have a dramatic domino effect on predator-prey interactions (Box 1.7). This could occur for groups like Arctic amphipods, which carry out their life cycle in sea-ice crevices, where they are preyed upon by a number of species, including cod and ringed seals.[64] Reductions in sea-ice cover could alter the availability of prey that use sea ice, ultimately leading to population declines in a suite of species, the most vulnerable of which include such marine mammals as hooded seals, narwhals, and polar bears, because of their specialized diets and feeding strategies.[65] Walruses are also affected by rapid break-up of sea ice, causing poor juvenile survival when calves become separated from their mothers.[66] In addition, stress related to food shortages and warmer temperatures is expected to lead to an increase in diseases of marine mammals, leading to poor body condition and reduced reproductive output.[67]

Box 1.7 A match-mismatch example for Atlantic cod in the North Sea

Year-class strength of fish populations is set at early life stages and varies in a way that is unrelated to adult population size. This seems counterintuitive to our expectations for mammals and birds but is standard for most exploited fish species. The relationship instead is between the timing of spawning—relatively fixed in time—and the availability of larval food supply trophically linked to seasonal phytoplankton blooms, which vary in response to key oceanographic features.[68] The "match" occurs when larval fish are in the water column at the same time that primary production (*i.e.*, phytoplankton availability) is high, leading to a relatively large year class, and the "mismatch" occurs when the food supply is low or absent, leading to poor year classes. Beaugrand and others[69] evaluated this hypothesis for Atlantic cod (*Gadus morhua L.*), a species overfished since the late 1960s, by comparing copepod plankton biomass to cod recruitment in the North Sea over three time periods: 1958–1962, 1963–1983, and 1984–1999. Larval cod occur in the North Sea during a 7-month period when plankton populations are the most variable. If the match-mismatch hypothesis operates effectively, then cod larvae should have relatively high survival rates when the plankton biomass is high and low survival when it is not. What Beaugrand et al. found was a strong positive correlation between cod year-class strength and conditions in the plankton ecosystem, suggesting not only tight tracking of cod populations to food availability, but also a significant decline in plankton biomass attributed to increasing water temperature in the North Atlantic. That is, in re-

---

61. R.B. Aronson *et al.*, *Climate Change and Invasibility of the Antarctic Benthos*, 38 ANNUAL REVIEW OF ECOLOGY, EVOLUTION, AND SYSTEMATICS 129 (2007).

62. V. Smetacek & S. Nicol, *Polar Ocean Ecosystems in a Changing World*, 437 NATURE 362 (2005).

63. J.M. Roessig *et al.*, *Effects of Global Climate Change on Marine and Estuarine Fishes and Fisheries*, 14 REVIEWS IN FISH BIOLOGY AND FISHERIES 251 (2004).

64. R.R. Gradinger & B.A. Bluhm, *In-Situ Observations on the Distribution and Behavior of Amphipods and Arctic Cod* (Boreogadus Saida) *under the Sea Ice of the High Arctic Canada Basin*, 27 POLAR BIOLOGY 595 (2004).

65. K.L. Laidre *et al.*, *Quantifying the Sensitivity of Arctic Marine Mammals to Climate-Induced Habitat Change*, 18 ECOLOGICAL APPLICATIONS S97 (2008).

66. L.W. Cooper *et al.*, *Rapid Seasonal Sea-Ice Retreat in the Arctic Could Be Affecting Pacific Walrus* (Odobenus Rosmarus Divergens) *Recruitment*, 32 AQUATIC MAMMALS 98 (2006).

67. K.A. Burek *et al.*, *Effects of Climate Change on Arctic Marine Mammal Health*, 18 ECOLOGICAL APPLICATIONS S126 (2008).

68. D.H. CUSHING, MARINE ECOLOGY AND FISHERIES (Cambridge Un. Press 1975).

69. Beaugrand *et al.*, *supra* note 8.

sponse to warmer temperatures, the average sizes of individual copepods had dropped significantly after 1980, leading to a lower overall food supply for cod and therefore poor cod recruitment. In this case, copepods responded to warming temperatures by having reduced growth rates, a direct effect of climate on the cod food source. Cod responded in a similar way: the higher temperatures led to increased metabolic rates that led to higher energetic costs (Box 1.1). The combination of higher energetic demands and lower food supply caused a reduction in growth rates and lower survival for larval and juvenile cod. Clearly, the effects of overfishing are compounded by effects of climate change.

Sea-ice declines have already had a direct, measurable effect on the ability of polar bears to forage. Polar bears depend on finding their air-breathing prey by locating small breathing holes in the ice. With sea-ice decline, they are instead faced with increased expanses of open water, making prey location uncertain. Under severe nutritional stress, the bears adopt strange and desperate feeding behaviors, including cannibalism.[70]

V. Climate Change Effects on Fisheries

Scientists have studied the effects of changes in ocean-atmosphere interactions on marine organisms for decades. Of particular interest is the influence of large-scale climatic events on population size,[71] the biological impacts of which have proved fairly predictable. Seasonal upwelling is a case in point. This phenomenon results from alongshore winds pulling surface water away from the coast, allowing deep, cold bottom water to well up to the surface, bringing with it nutrients that support local food webs, including productive fisheries. In years when upwelling is strong, for instance, this process supports enormous populations of small pelagic fish, such as anchovy (*Engraulis encrasicolus*), whereas in years when it is weak, there can be serious fisheries disasters. Thus, tracking the occurrence of large-scale events has implications not only for weather patterns but also for ecological and economic forecasting. The two most prevalent indices in the literature are the North Atlantic Oscillation (NAO), primarily influencing climate across the North Atlantic (affecting Europe and parts of Asia and Africa), and the El Niño Southern Oscillation (ENSO), influencing the Eastern Pacific, Atlantic, and Caribbean. The NAO causes patterns in the North Sea, for instance, to shift between relatively mild winters and summers accompanied by significant rainfall, to temperature extremes accompanied by drought. During El Niño years in the Eastern Pacific, marine waters are relatively warm and low in nutrients, caused by reduced upwelling, whereas during La Niña years, waters are cooler and have higher primary productivity. NAO events can affect community composition, year-class strength, growth, and predation for juvenile flatfish, smelt, codfish,[72] and sand eel[73] populations; ENSO events cause seasonal fluctuations in sardine (*Sardinops sagax*), anchovy (*Engraulis ringens*), skipjack tuna (*Katsuwonus pelamis*), and other pelagic fish populations.

Climate change can have a significant effect on these oceanic processes[74] by increasing the warming trend and shifting the timing (Box 1.8), duration, and magnitude of events. Indeed, it may be that anthropogenic forcing of the ocean-atmosphere processes could eventually cause sufficient changes in the NAO and ENSO as to render them poor indicators of biological impacts.[75] For instance, if ocean stratification (formation of discrete thermal layers in the water) increases in response to warming trends, then overall food availability could decline.

---

70. I. Stirling *et al.*, *Unusual Predation Attempts of Polar Bears on Ringed Seals in the Southern Beaufort Sea: Possible Significance of Changing Spring Ice Conditions*, 61 Arctic 14 (2008).

71. P. Lehodey *et al.*, *Climate Variability, Fish, and Fisheries*, 19 Journal of Climate 5009 (2006).

72. M.J. Attrill & M. Power, *Climatic Influence on a Marine Fish Assemblage*, 417 Nature 275 (2002).

73. Arnott & Ruxton, *supra* note 9.

74. *See* Craig paper: The atmosphere, the oceans, climate, and ecosystem services (p. 261 above).

75. Miller & Fluharty; *supra* note 8; C. Parmesan, *Ecological and Evolutionary Responses to Recent Climate Change*, 37 Annual Review of Ecology, Evolution, and Systematics 637 (2006).

Box. 1.8 Questions about tipping points

1. How do tipping points vary in magnitude among different regions of the globe?

2. How much change is necessary to push a system past its tipping point?

3. How long does it take to reach a tipping point, and how would this vary based on different climate change scenarios?

4. What are the effects of tipping points throughout the food chain?

5. How will community composition change after a tipping point has been reached?

There is widespread concern among scientists about the fall-out for fisheries.[76] For instance, Todd *et al.*[77] demonstrate reduced growth rates and stock size in Atlantic salmon (*Salmo salar L.*) that correlate with warming of the northeast Atlantic sea surface over the past 30 years. There is a strengthening view that climate change and exploitative processes are sufficiently intertwined to warrant their consideration together.[78] Fishing already affects marine organisms by causing dramatic demographic and geographic changes, eroding biodiversity, and causing serious imbalances in predator-prey relationships. Marine populations, already sensitized by these impacts, could respond to climate change with spectacular population collapses.

In addition to the direct effects of climate on fisheries, there are compelling examples of indirect effects through loss of habitat. Loss of coral reefs is a case in point. Many species of reef fishes and invertebrates depend on corals' three-dimensional structure for settlement sites during the larval stage, reproductive sites as adults, and shelter from predators throughout their lives. While reef fishes are more tolerant of temperature changes than corals, they will experience the effects of climate change directly through changes in metabolic processes and indirectly through loss of coral cover. Despite the thousands of fish species that inhabit coral reefs, relatively little is known about their response to climate change in this habitat.[79] Yet, we can be fairly certain that: (1) species diversity will decline as coral habitat disappears;[80] (2) species distributions will track changing temperature gradients, with warm-water species expanding their ranges poleward, while cold-water species may experience range compression or extinction;[81] (3) larval duration will be truncated;[82] and (4) reproductive output will decline.[83] Overfishing of coral reef species is already severe. Add to this direct anthropogenic impact the stress of climate change, and it becomes clear that a large contingent of the world's population living in the tropics could lose an important source of protein.

Historically, in the U.S. and around the world, there have been significant problems with fisheries management, and many of these problems are likely to be exacerbated by climate change. While the nation has outlined rebuilding plans for a number of species, few have been successful. Most plans remain either unimplemented, implemented ineffectively, or flawed from the start.

---

76. P.M. Cury *et al.*, *Ecosystem Oceanography for Global Change in Fisheries*, 23 Trends in Ecology & Evolution 338 (2008).

77. C.D. Todd *et al.*, *Detrimental Effects of Recent Ocean Surface Warming on Growth Condition of Atlantic Salmon*, 14 Global Change Biology 958 (2008).

78. K.M. Brander, *Global Fish Production and Climate Change*, 104 Proceedings of the National Academy of Sciences (USA) 19709 (2007).

79. P.L. Munday *et al.*, *Climate Change and the Future for Coral Reef Fishes*, 9 Fish and Fisheries 261 (2008).

80. *Id.*

81. Roessig *et al.*, *supra* note 63.

82. S. Sponaugle *et al.*, *Temperature-Mediated Variation in Early Life History Traits and Recruitment Success of the Coral Reef Fish Thalassoma Bifasciatum in the Florida Keys*, 308 Marine Ecology Progress Series 1 (2007).

83. B.I. Ruttenberg *et al.*, *Patterns, Causes and Consequences of Regional Variation in the Ecology and Life History of a Reef Fish*, 145 Oecologia 394 (2005).

Thus, many fisheries continue to operate in an unsustainable manner, and populations continue to be overfished. Grafton *et al.*[84] and others[85] argue that dramatic changes in ocean governance are required to deal with many of these problems.

VI.Climate Change and Ocean Policy

The challenge for those charged with the conservation and management of living marine resources is to determine ways to take climate change into consideration when developing policy. How are we doing so far? According to the Joint Ocean Commission Initiative's (JOCI) 2007 U.S. Ocean Policy Report Card, we are not doing very well. The U.S. government received a grade of "C" for policy and support of the "Links between Oceans and Climate Change." The areas of greatest concern included the government's failure to enact relevant legislation that includes oceans in a national initiative to better understand and mitigate climate change, lack of federal funding for ocean research and monitoring, and an increased need for support of state and regional (interjurisdictional) efforts to address the ocean-related impacts of climate change.[86]

Given the level of uncertainty about climate change impacts, the need to replace reactive management with proactive and adaptive management is acute. Adaptive management requires a combination of broad monitoring programs to gather new information, predictive modeling that can be updated with new information to inform policy decisions, characterization of uncertainty, reversal of the burden of proof to ensure accountability, and changing management strategies to test new hypotheses that reveal the benefits and pitfalls of particular policy measures.

JOCI[87] identified as a priority area the ability to determine where and when climate change will affect marine ecosystems. A promising approach for predicting the effects of short-range (20–50 year) climate change on species is ecological forecasting. Through a combination of mechanistic modeling of the effects of the environment on life-history traits, this approach explicitly forecasts relative ecological impacts across geographic regions.[88] This technique has been used successfully for intertidal species in Europe to document biogeographic range shifts in the barnacle *Semibalanus balanoides* and the polychaete worm *Diopatra neapolitana*,[89] and in the United States, to predict the ecological consequences of climate change on the intertidal mussel, *Mytilus californianus.*[90]

Can ecological forecasting be used to identify thresholds, or "tipping points"[91] in marine systems beyond which the system cannot recover? The likelihood is unclear,[92] leaving important questions about tipping points (Box 1.8) unanswerable at this time. In some marine ecosystems, tipping points may already have been reached, most notably in the Arctic due to

---

84. *Incentive-Based Approaches to Sustainable Fisheries*, 63 CANADIAN JOURNAL OF FISHERIES AND AQUATIC SCIENCE 699 (2006); *Positioning Fisheries in a Changing World*, 32 MARINE POLICY 630 (2008).

85. C. Walters & S.J.D. Martell, *Stock Assessments Needs for Sustainable Fisheries Management*, 70 BULLETIN OF MARINE SCIENCE 629 (2002).

86. JOINT OCEANS COMMISSION INITIATIVE, U.S. OCEAN POLICY REPORT CARD 2007 (2007).

87. *Id.*

88. B. Helmuth *et al.*, *Living on the Edge of Two Changing Worlds: Forecasting the Responses of Rocky Intertidal Ecosystems to Climate Change*, 37 ANNUAL REVIEW OF ECOLOGY, EVOLUTION, AND SYSTEMATICS 373 (2006).

89. D.S. Wethey & S.A. Woodin, *Ecological Hindcasting of Biogeographic Responses to Climate Change in the European Intertidal Zone*, 606 HYDROBIOLOGIA 139 (2008).

90. S.E. Gilman *et al.*, *Variation in the Sensitivity of Organismal Body Temperature to Climate Change over Local and Geographic Scales*, 103 PROCEEDINGS OF THE NATIONAL ACADEMY OF SCIENCES (USA) 9560 (2006).

91. Sensu R.W. Lindsay & J. Zhang, *The Thinning of Arctic Sea Ice, 1988–2003: Have We Passed a Tipping Point?*, 18 JOURNAL OF CLIMATE 4879 (2005).

92. M. Scheffer *et al.*, *Catastrophic Shifts in Ecosystems*, 413 NATURE 591 (2001); T.M. Lenton *et al.*, *Tipping Elements in the Earth's Climate System*, 105 PROCEEDINGS OF THE NATIONAL ACADEMY OF SCIENCES OF THE UNITED STATES OF AMERICA 1786 (2008).

the combined effects of melting sea ice and expanding areas of open water over the last 50 years,[93] and in the Eastern Pacific, where low-oxygen "dead zones" have appeared off the Oregon Coast.

We are facing an uncertain future for the oceans.[94] If we are serious about changing direction and taking steps towards conserving our living marine resources, then decisions must be made swiftly and without the luxury of perfect knowledge, while still grappling for a more thorough understanding of the ecological consequences of climate change. The real question is, what trade-offs are *we* willing to make?

Notes

1. *Marine Science "Under Resourced."* In a recent article, *Under-Resourced, Under Threat*, 320 SCIENCE 1294 (2008), Anthony Richardson and Elvira Poloczanska conclude that "marine ecosystems are undoubtedly under-resourced, overlooked, and under threat; our knowledge of impacts of climate change on marine life is a mere drop in the ocean compared with that for terrestrial organisms." The authors first explain the disproportionate representation of data on terrestrial ecology in the IPCC reports (references omitted):

> The recent IPCC (Intergovernmental Panel on Climate Change) FOURTH ASSESSMENT REPORT noted 28,586 significant biological changes in terrestrial systems but only 85 from marine and freshwater systems. Of these few observations from aquatic systems, 99% were consistent with global warming, which suggests that aquatic systems may be extremely vulnerable to climate change.

The authors then suggest that the reasons for this discrepancy likely include:
- the distribution of global science funding;
- the difficulty of disentangling multiple stressors from relatively poorly sampled systems;
- the disconnect between marine and terrestrial ecology;
- the way marine ecologists report research findings; and
- limitations in the existing IPCC process.

As Richardson and Poloczanska explain, the difficulty and expense of marine observation likely contributes to the fact that only 11% of published studies are related to marine systems. The authors also discuss the "profound disconnect" between marine and terrestrial ecology, based on the relative lack of contributions by marine science to general ecological theories. Part of the problem lies with the way that data is reported for marine and terrestrial systems, respectively (references omitted):

> Marine ecologists must also accept responsibility for the paucity of evidence of climate-driven impacts on marine species. Terrestrial studies state observed changes in distribution (as kilometer per degree celsius) and timing (as number of days earlier per degree celsius) explicitly for inclusion in meta-analyses and IPCC reports; these figures are rarely provided in the marine literature. The tendency for marine researchers to report bulk responses for functional groups rather than individual species also contributes to underestimates in the number of marine biological changes. Both marine and terrestrial ecologists must develop robust yardsticks against which climate-change impacts can be measured.

----

93. Lindsay & Zhang, *supra* note 91.

94. "SRES" scenarios are described in the FOURTH ASSESSMENT REPORT OF THE IPCC (Cambridge Un. Press 2007).

Although Richardson and Poloczanska acknowledge that there are some "general principles that transcend the division between these environments" that should be "embraced," they also warn against complacency (references omitted):

> The situation is made more urgent, as emerging evidence suggests that the response of marine organisms to climate change may be faster than on land, despite slower ocean warming. Range shifts of hundreds of kilometers in a few decades have been observed in phytoplankton, zooplankton, fish, and intertidal fauna.... Unfortunately, our greater knowledge of terrestrial climate impacts will not provide the means to understand marine impacts. Ocean and terrestrial (atmospheric) processes commonly operate over fundamentally different time and space scales.... Slow ocean dynamics also means that some changes will be essentially irreversible. For example, declines in ocean pH may impact calcifying organisms, from corals in the tropics to pteropods (winged snails) in polar ecosystems, and will take tens of thousands of years to re-equilibrate to preindustrial conditions. Understanding and adapting to climate impacts in the oceans will require some uniquely marine solutions.

2. *60 Seconds* column, NEW SCIENTIST, Nov. 1, 2008, p. 7:

Extra-salty sea

Increasing saltiness in parts of the Atlantic Ocean is down to us. Salinity is known to have risen in areas of the Atlantic in recent decades. Now a team led by Peter Stott at the UK's Hadley Centre for Climate Change has used climate models to show that anthropogenic warming is to blame, through increased evaporation and a decrease in rainfall. The study will appear in GEOPHYSICAL RESEARCH LETTERS.

3. J.C. Orr *et al.*, *Anthropogenic Ocean Acidification over the Twenty-First Century and Its Impact on Calcifying Organisms*, 437 NATURE 618 (2005).

4. The latest assaults on the oceans come atop fisheries management practices that leave something to be desired. For a grab sample, consider—

Agency-Industry Cooperation

Earth Island Institute v. Hogarth, 484 F.3d 1123, 1134 (9th Cir. 2007) (tuna / dolphins):

> a "compelling portrait of political meddling" (quoting district court opinion) "improperly influenced by political concerns" (conclusion of court of appeals)

Adaptive Management

National Wildlife Federation v. National Marine Fisheries Service, 481 F.3d 1224, 1239 (9th Cir. 2007) (Columbia River dams and salmon):

> the 2004 BiOp amounted to little more than an analytical slight of hand, manipulating the variables to achieve a "no jeopardy" finding.

Loyal and Faithful Monitoring

Natural Resources Defense Council v. Kempthorne, 506 F. Supp. 2d 322, 334 (E.D. Cal. 2007):

> The 2004 [Fall Midwater Trawl] index [for delta smelt], which was not discussed in the BiOp, was calculated to be ... the lowest ever recorded.

Rushing to Judgment: NOAA Fisheries and the Stock Rebuilding Plan for the Red Snapper

Coastal Conservation Ass'n v. Gutierrez, 512 F. Supp. 2d 896, 900 (S.D. Tex. 2007). This decision invalidates Amendment 22 to the Gulf of Mexico Reef Fishery Management Plan and repudiates its conclusion that no further regulatory action is needed to end overfishing and rebuild red snapper stocks by 2032. Amendment 22 "is inconsistent with the scientific data cited by the Gulf Council and has a less than fifty percent chance of rebuilding red snapper stocks by 2032."

This great fish in the Gulf of Mexico has been fished actively for at least a century. It has been adjudged "Overfished" with stocks at no more than 3% or 7% of historical abundance. Here are some dates in the management:

Year	Target Date to Achieve Stock Rebuilding
1990	2000
1991	2007
1993	2009
1996	2019
1997	Declared Overfished
2005	2032

Meticulous Due Process

United States v. Approximately 54,695 Pounds of Shark Fins, 520 F.3d 976 (9th Cir. 2008) (Reinhardt, C.J.). The 2000 Shark Finning Prohibition Act makes it unlawful to be in "custody, control, or possession" of a shark fin without the corresponding carcass aboard a "fishing vessel," 16 U.S.C.A. § 1857(l)(P). This forfeiture action against this at-sea buyer who is taking the fins to Guatemala fails because this ruthless operator did not have "fair notice" that it would be considered a "fishing vessel" when it facilitated and advanced this practice. Did the operator consider itself to be a "pirate ship"?

5. Elisabeth Rosenthal, *Rise in jellyfish swarms hints at oceans' decline*, SEATTLE TIMES, Aug. 3, 2008, p. A8, col. 1 (from NEW YORK TIMES) ("The explosion of jellyfish populations, scientists say, reflects a combination of severe overfishing of natural predators such as tuna, sharks, and swordfish; rising sea temperatures caused in part by global warming; and pollution that has depleted oxygen levels in coastal shallows"; references a National Science Foundation report).

While many of the effects of climate change are relatively obvious, some are more subtle. For example, a team of scientists, including renowned marine biologist Jane Lubchenco, recently determined that dead zones off the west coast of the United States are affected by climate change.[1] In a press release, reprinted below, the authors explained the significance of the finding:[2]

Communication Partnership for Science and the Seas (COMPASS), *Newly Discovered West Coast Arrhythmias Cause Marine Life Die-offs*, February 16, 2007, press release *available at* http://www.compassonline.org/pdf_files/AAAS2007PredictingPR.pdf (last visited Sept. 2, 2009):

San Francisco, CA—Oceanographers, climatologists, and ecologists at the American Association for the Advancement of Science meeting report that unusual ocean conditions and marine die-offs are changing the way scientists think about the future of ocean resources off the US West Coast. The researchers' new synthesis of decades of atmospheric and oceanographic data reveals that increasingly wild fluctuations in winds and currents appear to account for a series of recent anomalous ocean events—from repeated low oxygen zones larger than the size of Rhode Island to massive die offs of seabirds. The scientists say that the underlying swings in winds and position of the jet stream are consistent with climate change predictions.

---

1. John A. Barth, Bruce A. Menge, Jane Lubchenco, Francis Chan, John M. Bane, Anthony R. Kirincich, Margaret A. McManus, Karina J. Nielsen, Stephen D. Pierce, and Libe Washburn, *Delayed Upwelling Alters Nearshore Coastal Ocean Ecosystems in the Northern California Current*, 104 PROC. NATL. ACAD. SCI. 3719 (2007).

2. Full press release *available at* http://lucile.science.oregonstate.edu/lubchenco/Pages/PressRoom/News Release.cfm?id=141 (last visited October 18, 2008).

"There is no other viable suspect right now, no other obvious explanation," says Jane Lubchenco of Oregon State University. "We've entered new territory. These arrhythmias in the coastal ocean suggest we're observing a system that is out of kilter."

Understanding the interplay of warming, winds, and storms with ocean currents and biological productivity is a whole new area of study that is proving urgent. In 2002, when scientists first documented low-oxygen zones off the US Pacific Northwest coast, they thought it was a startling, once in a lifetime, event. But these "dead zones," which suffocate crabs, fish, sea stars, and anemones on the ocean floor, have continued, with 2006 now on the books as the largest, most severe and longest lasting dead zone on record for the west coast.

"It was unlike anything that we've measured along the Oregon coast in the past five decades," says Francis Chan of Oregon State University. "We're seeing more and more evidence that changing climate and changing currents can lead to big and surprising changes in something as fundamental as oxygen levels in the sea."

In 2005 and 2006, researchers also found tens of thousands of starving birds washing up on shore at times of the year when the birds should be healthiest. And scientists trying to predict salmon runs have recorded large swings in ocean temperatures at a much higher frequency than the past, a change that signals large shifts in the amount of food available for salmon, birds, and marine mammals. Scientists link the low oxygen zones and animal die offs to changes in the timing and strength of upwelling, a usually reliable and regular wind-driven process that brings cold, nutrient-rich waters up from the depths of the ocean and fuels productive coastal ecosystems.

"We are investigating the idea that dead crabs and sea stars at the bottom of the ocean are correlated with changes in coastal winds, which are in turn driven by changes in temperatures on land," says Lubchenco.

Around the globe, areas of coastal upwelling which include the waters off the west coasts of the US, Peru, and Chile, eastern New Zealand, southwest and northwest Africa, and the Arabian Sea, are known for their abundant sea life and account for nearly 50% of the world's fisheries landings. Upwelling on the US west coast typically begins during the spring, triggering growth of phytoplankton and fueling marine food webs from the bottom-up. Many marine animals time their breeding and migrations with this influx of nutrients and growth of prey populations. But in recent years, changes in wind patterns and the position of the jet stream have changed the timing and strength of upwelling, disrupting these long-standing patterns.

"These are not just little blips," says oceanographer Jack Barth of Oregon State University. "Winds in both 2005 and 2006 are outside the envelope of what we've seen in the last twenty to forty years. They are the two most anomalous years in the last two decades—and they are anomalous in opposite directions."

Starving Salmon

In 2005, relaxed winds delayed upwelling of cold water and nutrients by several months, resulting in water temperatures 6 degrees Celsius above normal and causing the typical boom in small, prey fish populations to occur too late for feeding salmon, seabirds, and whales.

"In 2005 we saw no upwelling in the spring, but then it came on so strong that we saw the same amount of upwelling in two months that we usually see in six," says Bill Peterson of NOAA. "The salmon go out to sea in mid-April to mid-May, that is when they always go out. But in 2005 they found nothing to eat—by the time upwelling started, they were dead, starved to death."

Then, in 2006, unusually strong winds doubled the typical amount of upwelling, and increased the influx of nutrients to the system, but these strong winds ebbed in the month of May, just when salmon went out to sea. These mismatches in timing of upwelling are critical for many salmon species whose return to spawning grounds has been only 2–4% in recent years, and Peterson predicts that 2007 will be another low year for salmon returns.

Sea-bird Die-offs

In the spring of 2005, the volunteers who work as citizen scientists patrolling beaches found tens of thousands of seabirds washing up dead on beaches in Washington, Oregon and California. Emaciated birds littered the beaches because the normal spring upwelling that fuels food production didn't occur until much later in the season.

"In Oregon, the volunteers would literally wade through 80 dead birds in a mile. They feared no birds would survive," says Julia Parrish of the University of Washington who leads the citizen scientist program. Murres' and cormorants' breeding cycles are timed to coincide with the boost in prey fish in the spring. Tied to coastal breeding colonies, they are not strong enough fliers to travel hundreds of miles to find new food sources.

In 2006, scientists have also documented unusual die-offs of migratory seabirds such as auklets that visit the US West coast during the winter months. "They appear to be starving to death at sea. It's not bird flu, not another disease, not oiling or some other chemical," says Parrish.

Increases in the severity or frequency of storms, a prediction from climate change models, may also be a major factor in the survival of these seabirds. Winter die-offs are linked to stormy weather conditions.

"The total number of wrecks (die-offs) is increasing over time, as is the severity of these events and their duration," says Parrish. "This year we are heading into a mild El Niño and we are sitting on pins and needles to see what happens."

Unprecedented Dead Zones

The supercharged upwelling in 2006 also created thick, green-brown waters off the coasts of Oregon and Washington. When these phytoplankton and zooplankton blooms sank to the sea floor and decayed, they consumed large amounts of oxygen, creating a 3,000 square kilometer "dead zone" that took up nearly two thirds of the water column and squeezed mobile animals like rockfish into shallow habitats and suffocated everything that could not swim away.

"Phytoplankton blooms are normally thought to be a good thing because they ultimately support the food webs that produce the crabs, salmon and tuna," says Bruce Menge of Oregon State University. "But too much of a good thing can be bad."

Two months into the dead zone, the scientists surveyed the sea floor. "We were shocked to see a graveyard," Chan said. "Frame after frame of carcass, carcass, carcass. Dead crabs, dead worms, dead sea stars." Two weeks later the scientists returned to the same place. This once biologically diverse habitat was covered with a white bacterial mass, indicating that the system had turned from low to no oxygen.

"The fact that we saw no fish—alive or dead—suggests that many were able to escape," says Lubchenco. "In previous years, fish that have escaped the low-oxygen area appear to have returned once the oxygen was renewed. This year may be different, however, because unlike earlier years, the living habitat was also suffocated. This year there was no home for them to return to."

Predicting the Unpredictable

"Climate change is upon us, there is no doubt about that, but what we don't know is exactly how it is going to affect upwelling," says Peterson. "What's catching us by surprise is the rate at which warming is hitting us. And, of course, how fast the ocean has changed—that is what amazes me."

The scientists hope that by better understanding the interplay of warming, winds, and storms with ocean currents and biological productivity, they will be able to help managers and fishermen plan for changing ecosystems. Predicting shifts in ocean ecosystems requires sustained observations. "We are poised to deploy a fleet of underwater robotic sensors to enable better understanding and useful predictions," says Barth. If scientists can predict the impact of dead zones or years of low salmon returns, for example, managers can adjust fishing quotas or regulations accordingly and fishermen can modify where and when they fish.

Scientists hope to get ahead of the curve on these surprises, but many mysteries remain. Despite intense hypoxic zones, for example, Dungeness crab catches in Oregon have been high in the last few years. In California, scientists are trying to understand why rockfish populations appear to be congregating in the northern and southern ends of their ranges. Future changes in the timing of upwelling may favor particular seabird or salmon species, changing the make up of animals along the coast. And animals that live their adult lives close to shore, like mussels and barnacles, are likely to react differently than fish that live further offshore.

"We need to think differently about using and managing these ecosystems," adds Lubchenco. "We should be expecting more surprises. Climate models predict increasing uncertainty, with wild fluctuations. And this is exactly what we are witnessing."

Penguins as Marine Sentinels

P. Dee Boersma, Wadsworth Endowed Chair in Conservation Science and Professor of Biology and Women's Studies, Department of Biology, University of Washington, Seattle, WA 98195; Tel: (206) 616-2185, Fax: (206) 221-7839, boersma@u.washington.edu.

From the tropics to Antarctica, penguins depend on predictable regions of high ocean productivity where their prey aggregate. Increases in precipitation and reductions in sea ice associated with climate warming are affecting penguins. The largest breeding colony of Patagonian (Magellanic) penguins, at Punta Tombo, Argentina, had approximately 200,000 breeding pairs in October 2006 — a decline of 22% since 1987. In the 1980s and 1990s, petroleum pollution was a major source of Patagonian penguin mortality. In 1994, tanker lanes were moved 40 kilometers (km) farther off the coast of Chubut, and the dumping of ballast water and the oiling of penguins are now rare. However, penguins are swimming 60 km farther north from their nests during incubation than they did a decade ago, very likely reflecting shifts in prey in response to climate change and reductions in prey abundance caused by commercial fishing. These temperate penguin species, marine sentinels for southern oceans, demonstrate that new challenges are confronting their populations.

Penguins are sentinels of the marine environment, and by observing and studying them, researchers can learn about the rate and nature of changes occurring in the southern oceans. As ocean samplers, penguins provide insights into patterns of regional ocean productivity and long-term climate variation. Having studied several species of temperate penguins for more than 30 years, I know firsthand how sensitive they are to their environment. I synthesize my observations to suggest that we have entered a new era of unprecedented challenges for marine systems.

The Antarctic Treaty protects living resources in Antarctica; the Convention on International Trade in Endangered Species of Wild Fauna and Flora regulates trade in endangered species, including the Peruvian (or Humboldt) penguin (*Spheniscus humboldti*) and African (or black-footed) penguin (*Spheniscus demersus*); and the International Union for the Conservation of Nature (*www.iucn.org*) regards 10 of 17 penguin species as vulnerable to extinction. Legal protections have been insufficient to halt penguins' decline, however. Penguins face a gauntlet of environmental challenges, from climate change to human take. The erect-crested penguins (*Eudyptes sclateri*) that breed on the Antipodes Islands, located over 800 kilometers (km) from the

South Island of New Zealand, numbered 50,000 breeding pairs in 1995—only half of what they were in 1978.[1] Temperate penguins and those that are inshore foragers, such as the yellow-eyed (*Megadyptes antipodes*) and African penguins, are in decline because they are the most likely to come into conflict with human activities such as commercial fishing, guano mining, and oil and gas development.[2]

Nonetheless, there are success stories. In New Zealand, penguin populations are growing in some areas after the removal of introduced predators. For example, rats were removed from more than 11,000 hectares of Campbell Island, the largest island in the world to be successfully cleared of rats. The island, declared rat free in 2003, is an important breeding ground for the rare endemic yellow-eyed penguin.[3] Erect-crested penguins, which used to breed on Campbell Island, may recolonize now that rats are gone. On New Zealand's South Island and in Australia, populations of the little blue penguin (*Eudyptula minor*) grew after nesting boxes were placed and predators trapped, resulting in new ecotourism businesses focused on penguins.

There are no safeguards to protect large breeding colonies of penguins, however, and it is these aggregations that people most wish to visit. Only 43 penguin "hotspots"—where at least 1% of the global penguin population aggregates to breed—are left in the world. (See Figure 4.)[4] Large colonies are important for the survival and health of each penguin species. Determining the status and trends of penguin populations at these 43 sites would provide insight into ocean ecosystem variability and viability, but these sites are rarely, and some almost never, counted. Population surveys twice every decade when penguins have eggs could reliably convey the state of the Southern Ocean. Ideally, each colony should be visited annually to determine six sentinel parameters: reproductive failure, adult mortality, foraging changes, reproductive success, breeding phenology, and demographic and range changes. Unfortunately, most of these colonies have not been counted even once a decade. When colonies have been counted more than once, it has been at different times in the breeding cycle, so the population trends of most of the large colonies remain unknown. Indeed, most of the sentinel parameters remain unknown.

Penguins of the world

Many people think of penguins as existing only in icy parts of the Southern Hemisphere, but only two species of penguins are restricted to Antarctica: the Adélie (*Pygoscelis adeliae*) and the emperor (*Aptenodytes forsteri*). There are 16 to 19 species of penguins, depending on the tools used in classification. The oldest penguin fossil dates to about 55 million years before the present.[5] Population genetic tools can distinguish differences that are not easily visible, thereby increasing the number of species recognized.[6] Using both genetic and morphological tools, and estimating divergence time among species, the evolutionary relationship can be shown as a family tree with five distinct branches.[7] One of these branches depicts the recent radiation of four species of penguins of the genus *Spheniscus* that occupy mid- to low-latitude temperate areas.

1. N. Peat, Subantarctic New Zealand: A Rare Heritage (Department of Conservation 2006).

2. P.D. Boersma & D.L. Stokes, *Conservation of Penguins: Threats to Penguin Populations, in* The Penguins: Spheniscidae 127 (T.D. Williams ed., Oxford Un. Press 1995); L.S. Davis & M. Renner, Penguins (Yale Un. Press 2003).

3. Peat, *supra* note 1.

4. P.D. Boersma & A. Van Buren, *Penguins, in* Wildlife Spectacles 149 (R.A. Mittermeier *et al.* eds., CEMEX, Agrupación Sierra Madre, Conservation International 2003).

5. R.E. Fordyce & C.M. Jones, *Penguin History and New Fossil Material from New Zealand, in* Penguin Biology 419 (L.S. Davis & J.T. Darby eds., Academic Press 1990).

6. J. Banks *et al.*, *Genetic Evidence for Three Species of Rockhopper Penguins*, Eudyptes Chrysocome, 30 Polar Biology 61 (2006).

7. Davis & Renner, *supra* note 2.

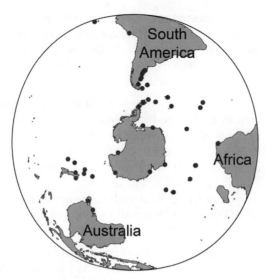

Figure 4. Map showing the 43 colonies that hold 1% or more of the global population for each species of penguin. These are the penguin hotspots of the world.

These species breed in coastal deserts on the Atlantic and Pacific oceans where they are relatively easily studied. The Galápagos penguin (*Spheniscus mendiculus*), the most northerly species, breeds in shady cracks, crevices, or lava tubes of the equatorial Galápagos Islands.

People travel from all over the world to spend a few hours with penguins. Each year, about 500,000 people visit Phillip Island, Australia, to see little blue penguins; over 100,000 tourists visit Punta Tombo, Argentina, the world's largest colony of Patagonian (or Magellanic) penguins (*Spheniscus magellanicus*); and about 50 cruise boats ply the waters in Antarctica, bringing 35,000 people to penguin colonies. (I use the location name, rather than the more widely used common name, for penguin species [*e.g.*, Patagonian, Galápagos, African, Peruvian] to clarify where most of the individuals for each species are found.) Immersion in a colony of hundreds of thousands of penguins is a profound experience. Emperor penguins on ice, or king penguins (*Aptenodytes patagonicus*) on bare ground, often stand nearly foot to foot among thousands of neighbors when incubating their one egg. To be surrounded by the expanse of their colony, the air filled with their strident calls and with the pungent odor of guano, leaves a lasting impression. In contrast, some species, such as yellow-eyed penguins, breed in forests or among large flax plants and never form dense aggregations. Although they may not be able to see their neighbors because of the vegetation, these penguins are in vocal communication. Their raucous yells and squeaks in the evenings are haunting.

Penguins are highly specialized for swimming and diving, and therefore reflect regional oceanic variation more completely than other seabirds.[8] They reflect changes in oceanographic productivity and human-induced changes in the environment, including fishing pressure, climate variation, and oil pollution. Like many other seabirds, penguins are long-lived, lay one or two eggs, and take months to rear their young. Penguins are central-place foragers. Some penguins, such as kings, take 14 to 16 months to successfully reproduce.[9] King penguins require 10 months to rear one chick because they may leave their chick for more than five months in the

---

8. P.D. Boersma *et al.*, *Following the Fish: Penguins and Productivity in the South Atlantic*, ECOLOGICAL MONOGRAPHS (In press 2008).

9. T.D. WILLIAMS, THE PENGUINS: *SPHENISCIDAE* (Oxford Un. Press 1995).

winter to forage.[10] The chicks overwinter on land, are fed frequently in the spring (September and October), and then fledge when food is abundant. Two king penguins tracked by satellite during winter foraging trips from Possession Island were gone more than 50 days and traveled 1600 to 1800 km away from their chicks.[11]

In contrast, Galápagos, Peruvian, and little blue penguins are gone less than a day when feeding chicks, and can rear their two chicks in only two months, because they find food close to their breeding sites and time their chick rearing for when prey is most available. The unpredictable nature of oceanographic productivity in the Galápagos archipelago has resulted in selection for molting before breeding, frequent nesting whenever conditions are favorable, and rapid chick growth.[12]

Impacts of climate change on Antarctic and sub-Antarctic penguins

The fourth report of the United Nations-sponsored International Panel on Climate Change concluded that there is an 80% probability that anthropogenic warming has influenced many physical and biological systems.[13] In the Northern Hemisphere, some butterflies[14] and intertidal invertebrates[15] have moved north. Plants bloom earlier as the climate warms.[16] Spring blooming in plants for temperate species is five days earlier than it was a decade ago.[17] The timing of breeding and hibernation for some birds and mammals is consistent with anticipated responses to global warming.[18] The impacts of global warming are predicted to be most severe at the poles, and they can already be seen in Antarctic and sub-Antarctic penguins.

In the heart of East Antarctica, far from the equator and El Niño, changes in the breakup of sea ice affect penguin reproductive success. Annual winter sea-ice cover has decreased over the last 50 years, and the regional warming has reduced krill abundance, altering the marine food web.[19] The geographic and oceanographic setting of colonies, and the differences in life-history patterns among penguins, can obscure population trends. This is why large colonies should be counted at least twice a decade during incubation. The East Antarctic ice sheet, the largest reservoir of ice on the planet, shows little variability in its mass balance,[20] but other glaciers and sea ice are retreating, and even small variations can have major consequences for penguins. I witnessed firsthand one colony's reproductive failure.

In 2006, I visited the French base at Dumont d'Urville in East Antarctica (Figure 5), where the movie *March of the Penguins* was filmed, in hopes of seeing the colony of emperor penguins that breeds there. This most Antarctic of species incubates its eggs in the middle of the South Polar

10. Davis & Renner, *supra* note 2.

11. K. Pütz et al., *Foraging Areas of King Penguins Aptenodytes Patagonicus Breeding at Possession Island, Southern Indian Ocean*, 27 Marine Ornithology 77 (1999).

12. P.D. Boersma, *An Ecological and Behavioral Study of the Galápagos Penguin*, 15 Living Bird 43 (1977).

13. R.A. Kerr, *Global Warming is Changing the World*, 316 Science 188 (2007).

14. C. Parmesan & G. Yohe, *A Globally Coherent Fingerprint of Climate Change Impacts Across Natural Systems*, 421 Nature 37 (2003).

15. J.P. Barry et al., *Climate-related, Long-term Faunal Changes in a California Rocky Intertidal Community*, 267 Science 672 (1995).

16. N.C. Stenseth et al., *Ecological Effects of Climate Fluctuations*, 297 Science 1292 (2002).

17. T.L. Root et al., *Fingerprints of Global Warming on Wild Animal and Plants*, 421 Nature 57 (2003).

18. D.W. Inouye et al., *Climate Change is Affecting Altitudinal Migrants and Hibernating Species*, 97 Proceedings of the National Academy of Sciences 1630 (2000).

19. V. Loeb et al., *Effects of Sea-ice Extent and Krill or Salp Dominance on the Antarctic Food Web*, 387 Nature 897 (1997); R.C. Smith et al., *Marine Ecosystem Sensitivity to Climate Change: Historical Observations and Paleoecological Records Reveal Ecological Transitions in the Antarctic Peninsula Region*, 49 BioScience 393 (1999).

20. A. Shepherd & D. Wingham, *Recent Sea-level Contributions of the Antarctic and Greenland Ice Sheets*, 315 Science 1529 (2007).

winter, and the chicks usually fledge in December and early January.[21] On 20 December 2006, as the ship anchored in front of the base, I saw no sea ice and fewer than a dozen small icebergs in the waters around the station. It was the first time Rodney Russ, Heritage Expeditions' founder and expedition leader, had seen the area free of sea ice since he started visiting the area in the 1980s.

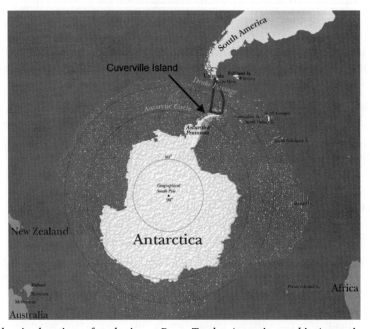

Figure 5. Map showing locations of study sites at Punta Tombo, Argentina, and in Antarctica.

The emperor penguin colony in 2006 bred in the same location as in other years, on the shore-fast sea ice behind two small islands. The ice here is protected from the open sea, and the winds howling off the ice cap blow the snow so it does not accumulate and destroy the eggs or chicks. In September, when the chicks were a little more than half grown, the adults started marching with their chicks across the ice. After several days, the colony had moved more than 5 km from where the eggs had hatched. Apparently the penguins sensed they were in danger and found more stable sea ice. In late September, a large storm hit, and the strong winds and waves broke up and blew out the remaining sea ice and the penguins. Although the penguins were where the ice had remained the longest, the ice was gone long before late November, when the chicks could be independent. Chicks in late September are downy, not waterproof, and are unable to survive in the sea for any period of time. The storm most likely caused the reproductive failure of the entire colony. The population trend for emperor penguins may not yet be clear, but it is apparent that global warming will be a problem for emperor penguins, which are dependent on stable sea ice to breed.

Some of the best-documented signals of regional warming come from the western Antarctic Peninsula (WAP).[22] In the WAP, the mean winter air temperature has risen more rapidly (6 degrees Celsius since 1950) than anywhere else in the world.[23] By the 1990s, a reduction in winter

---

21. WILLIAMS, *supra* note 9.

22. A.J. Cook *et al.*, *Retreating Glacier Fronts on the Antarctic Peninsula Over the Past Half-century*, 308 SCIENCE 541 (2005); Shepherd & Wingham, *supra* note 20.

23. E. Stokstad, *Boom and Bust in a Polar Hot Zone*, 315 SCIENCE 1522 (2007).

sea-ice cover caused shifts in penguin abundance and distribution.[24] Smith and colleagues[25] showed that the modern and paleo-climate records of these penguins are consistent with a rapid warming in the WAP during the past century.

Climate warming and sea-ice reduction have induced population responses among Adélie, chinstrap, and gentoo penguins and other seabirds.[26] Gentoo and chinstrap populations, which have expanded southward in the past 50 years with regional warming,[27] grew at a mean annual rate of 5.5% from 1979 to 2004.[28] In contrast, in the Antarctic Peninsula region, from King George Island to the South Shetlands, both Adélie and chinstrap populations have declined by 50% from the mid-1970s to the present.[29] The extensive ice cover in 1998 reduced reproductive success in chinstrap penguins.[30] Sea-ice reduction can benefit relatively ice-intolerant species such as chinstrap and gentoo penguins and cause ice-requiring species like Adélie and emperor penguins to decline.

Between 2003 and 2004, I visited Cuverville Island, a small island near the Lemaire Channel, and saw how global warming was affecting one of the most southerly colonies of gentoo penguins. (See Figure 6.) Cuverville Island has approximately 4000 pairs of gentoo penguins. On my three visits, 23 November 2003 and 15 and 26 January 2004, I observed that increased precipitation associated with global warming was affecting nesting times. Several meters of snow covered the island in November, and even the tops of rocky areas were snow covered. The penguins were milling, copulating, sleeping, and standing in the snow. (*See* Figure 7.) The ground in their nesting area, covered with more than a meter of snow, provided no exposed rock where they could lay eggs, so they waited. (*See* Figure 7a.) Some rested on the snow, melting a hollow and creating an ice platform, but they could not melt enough snow to reach the underlying rock. (See Figure 7b.)

Climate warming on the Antarctic Peninsula increases snowfall, a change that at first glance may appear counterintuitive. This happens because the warmer air holds more moisture, leading to more snow and rain. When I returned on 15 January, I expected to find chicks a few weeks old.

I enlisted tourists to look for chicks and report what they saw. One guest saw an egg and a tiny chick at the topmost peak. The wind exposed the peaks of islands, making these bare areas the first places where penguins laid their eggs. (See Figure 8a.)

The onset of egg laying in gentoo penguins, even at the same colony, can vary by three to five weeks from year to year. Cuverville Island is so far south that eggs are usually laid between late October and mid-November. The incubation period is 34 to 42 days, and chicks fledge in about 80 days.[31] During the period of my visits to Cuverville Island, the first egg was probably laid in early December 2003, about two weeks late.

---

24. W.R. Fraser *et al.*, *Increases in Antarctic Penguin Populations: Reduced Competition with Whales or Loss of Sea Ice Due to Environmental Warming?*, 11 Polar Biology 525 (1992); P.N. Trathan *et al.*, *Dynamics of Antarctic Penguin Populations in Relation to Inter-annual Variability in Sea Ice Distribution*, 16 Polar Biology 321 (1996); S. Nicol & I. Allison, *The Frozen Skin of the Southern Ocean*, 85 American Scientist 426 (1997).

25. Smith *et al.*, *supra* note 19.

26. J.P. Croxall *et al.*, *Environmental Change and Antarctic Seabird Populations*, 297 Science 1510 (2002); J. Forcada *et al.*, *Contrasting Population Changes in Sympatric Penguin Species in Association with Climate Warming*, 12 Global Change Biology 411 (2006).

27. S.D. Emslie *et al.*, *Abandoned Penguin Colonies and Environmental Change in the Palmer Station Area, Anvers Island, Antarctic Peninsula*, 10 Antarctic Science 257 (1998).

28. Forcada *et al.*, *supra* note 26.

29. J. Hinke *et al.*, *Divergent Responses of Pygoscelis Penguins Reveal a Common Environmental Driver*, 153 Oecologia 845 (2007).

30. A.S. Lynnes *et al.*, *Diet and Reproductive Success of Adélie and Chinstrap Penguins: Linking Response of Predators to Prey Population Dynamics*, 27 Polar Biology 544 (2004).

31. Williams, *supra* note 9.

Figure 6. Gentoo penguins on Culverville Island on the Antarctic Peninsula copulating in the snow, which has not yet melted to expose breeding sites. Photograph: P. Dee Boersma.

When I next returned on 26 January, I found that most of the nests had small chicks, but many nests still had unhatched eggs. To keep the eggs and chicks dry, gentoo penguins had gathered rocks and pebbles, sometimes more than a thousand, to build nests that acted as little islands (Figure 8b). To get to the snow-free ridges, penguins walked through deep snow, creating paths (Figure 8c). The oldest chicks I saw were probably 10 to 14 days old.

The heavy snow cover placed the gentoo chicks on Cuverville Island in a time squeeze. Could the chicks grow fast enough to fledge before their parents had to desert them to molt? A quick calculation suggested that fledging would be in April and May. Parents fattening for the molt would have to either desert their offspring before they were ready to fledge or die themselves.

Increases in rain or snowfall and reductions in ice cover (such as the early breakup of ice or blocking of entrances and exits to colonies by icebergs) can cause penguin nest failure. In addition, climate variation can cause timing mismatches between reproduction and prey

Figure 7. (a) Penguin group in the snow. (b) The penguin in the foreground has rested on the snow long enough to melt it but still has not reached the rocks beneath. Photographs: P. Dee Boersma.

Figure 8. (a) On the Antarctic Peninsula, the first place where the snow is blown away and melts is on the rocky peaks of islands. (b) Gentoo adults with their one- and two-week-old chicks are surrounded by melt-water on their nests. (c) Gentoo penguins breeding at the first exposed sites at the top of the island must make long treks, leaving deep paths in the snow that they use to reach nesting sites. Photographs: P. Dee Boersma.

availability.[32] Snow and rain affect penguin species differently. For chinstrap and gentoo penguins, the advantage conferred by sea-ice reductions may be negated by increases in snowfall that delay or prevent breeding. For Adélie penguins at Paulet Island in the Weddell Sea, increased rain causes chicks to die. Adélie chicks are adapted to cold weather and light snow. Snow can build up on their down, but beneath the feathers they are dry and warm. (See Figure 9a.) If they get wet in the rain, the chicks die from hypothermia. (See Figure 9b.) Adélie chicks need juvenile plumage under their chick down to tolerate rain. With global warming and increases in climate variation, some colonies and populations of penguins will do better and others worse. We can be confident that the changes will continue to be dramatic. (See Figure 9.)

Impacts of environmental cycles on temperate penguins

The first seabird reported to show the biological effects of El Niño farther west than the South American coast was the Galápagos penguin.[33] El Niño, with its warm, unproductive waters, caused adult Galápagos penguins to desert their eggs and chicks to search for food to save themselves while their chicks starved to death. One of the predicted results of climate warming is an increase in the frequency and severity of El Niño events. Galápagos penguin populations are now about 25% of what they were in the 1970s.[34] After the 1982–1983 and 1997–1998 events, Galápagos penguins declined by more than 65%.[35] In May 1998, both males and females weighed less

32. J.M. Durant *et al.*, *Climate and the Match or Mismatch Between Predator Requirements and Resource Availability*, 33 CLIMATE RESEARCH 271 (2007).

33. P.D. Boersma, *Galápagos Penguins as Indicators of Oceanographic Conditions*, 200 SCIENCE 1481 (1978).

34. P.D. Boersma, *Population Trends of the Galápagos Penguin: Impacts of El Niño and La Niña*, 100 THE CONDOR 245 (1998).

35. F.H. Vargas *et al.*, *Population Size and Trends of the Galápagos Penguin* Spheniscus Mendiculus, 147 IBIS 367 (2005); F.H. Vargas *et al.*, *Modeling the Effect of El Niño on the Persistence of Small Populations: The Galápagos Penguin as a Case Study*, 137 BIOLOGICAL CONSERVATION 138 (2007).

Figure 9. (a) Adélie penguin chicks may get covered in snow during storms, but beneath the snow their down is warm and dry. (b) When rain falls, downy Adélie chicks can get wet and, when soaked, can become hypothermic and die. Photographs: P. Dee Boersma.

than during the 1972 El Niño, reflecting the 1998 event's greater severity.[36] At the end of the 1998 El Niño, female penguins were only 80% and males 90% of their average body weight in the absence of El Niños.

Female penguins are probably more likely than males to die during El Niño because of poor body condition. If the sex ratio becomes skewed—and it was already biased toward males in the early 1970s and in 1998—population recovery will be slow, because many males will not find mates. So what will happen to Galápagos penguins if the climate warms and El Niños, as predicted, become more severe and frequent? Using population viability analyses, researchers estimate that the chance of Galápagos penguins' becoming extinct in the next 100 years is 30% without assuming more frequent and more severe El Niños.[37]

We now know that the impacts on seabirds from El Niños are global.[38] Peruvian penguins, like Galápagos penguins, show flexibility in breeding; if food is available, they can breed in any month of the year. Peruvian penguins have two peaks in reproduction—a large one in spring (October) and a smaller one in winter (May)—and, like Galápagos penguins, they molt before they breed. Although penguins show adaptations to environmental variability, environmental perturbations take a toll on their populations.

Climate variation is at least partly to blame for the decline of temperate penguins, but human impacts are also influencing their demise. All the temperate species of penguins are declining.[39] Populations of African, Peruvian, and Galápagos penguins have collapsed. In the past hundred years, African penguins have decreased from 1.5 million to 63,000 pairs,[40] with the harvest of guano and eggs the major reason for their decline. Oil spills slowed African penguins' recovery in 1994 and 2000, and then the penguins' distribution shifted eastward, apparently to follow their prey.[41] Commercial fishing has reduced the carrying capacity of the Benguela ecosystem for penguins to only 10% to 20% of what it was in the 1920s.[42]

Peruvian penguins show a similar pattern of decline—their population is only a fraction of what it once was. In the mid-1800s, about a million Peruvian penguins existed; by the 1930s, the population had precipitously declined because of fishing and guano harvest.[43] The current population may be only 30,000 birds or pairs, but the precise population size remains unknown. Estimates are as low as 10,000 to 30,000 Peruvian penguins in Peru and Chile.[44] Although human disturbance and fishing activities have caused colonies to be abandoned, in some protected sites, such as reserves, populations are stable or increasing.[45] Peruvian penguins, like

36. P.D. Boersma, *The 1997–1998 El Niño: Impact on Penguins*, 11 Penguin Conservation 10 (1998).

37. P.D. Boersma et al., *Living Laboratory in Peril*, 308 Science 925 (2005); Vargas et al., *supra* note 35.

38. R.W. Schreiber & E.A. Schreiber, *Central Pacific Seabirds and the El Niño Southern Oscillation: 1982–1983 Perspectives*, 225 Science 713 (1984); D.C. Duffy et al., *A Comparison of the Effects of El Niño and the Southern Oscillation on Birds in Peru and the Atlantic Ocean*, in Congressus Internationalis Ornithologici, vol II 1741 (H. Ouellet ed., Acta XIX Un. of Ottawa Press 1988).

39. Boersma & Stokes, *supra* note 2.

40. A. Roberts et al., Roberts' Birds of Southern Africa (Trustees of the J. Voelcker Bird Book Fund 2005).

41. R. Koenig, *African Penguin Populations Reported in a Puzzling Decline*, 315 Science 1205 (2007).

42. R.J. Crawford et al., *An Altered Carrying Capacity of the Benguela Upwelling Ecosystem for African Penguins* (Spheniscus Demersus), ICES Journal of Marine Science 570 (2007).

43. R.C. Murphy, Oceanic Birds of South America, Vol. I (Macmillan 1936).

44. *See* www.iucnredlist.org; C. Cheney, The *Current Situation of the Humboldt Penguin in Chile and Peru: A Report from the Population and Habitat Viability Analysis Meeting*, 11 Penguin Conservation 4 (1998); G. Luna-Jorquera et al., *Population Size of Humboldt Penguins Assessed by Combined Terrestrial and At-sea Counts*, 23 Waterbirds 506 (2000).

45. R. Paredes et al., *Status of the Humboldt Penguin in Peru, 1999–2000*, 26 Waterbirds 129 (2003).

Galápagos penguins, responded to El Niño periods by moving, dying from starvation, and raising no young.[46]

The most abundant of the temperate penguins is the Patagonian penguin. Living in Argentina, Chile, and the Falkland Islands, it has a population of more than one million breeding pairs.[47] Although the Patagonian penguin is more abundant than any other temperate penguin, judging from the serious threats this species faces, it also will most likely continue to decline. Expanding fisheries compete with these penguins for prey.[48] A new Argentinean anchovy fishery was announced in November 2007, to start in the Golfo San Matias near important breeding colonies of Patagonian penguins.

Focus on Patagonian penguins

The largest Patagonian penguin colony in the world is at Punta Tombo, where I have studied these temperate penguins for almost 25 years. The population probably peaked at nearly 400,000 pairs between the late 1960s and the early 1980s, declining to approximately 200,000 breeding pairs in October 2006. Climate is an important factor in the distribution and abundance of penguins, often playing a critical role in determining productivity and prey abundance. Penguins first colonized Punta Tombo around 1924, and their population expanded rapidly.[49] With the population increase, breeding colonies expanded north. Penguins colonized Peninsula Valdés in 1969. The most northern colony is now at the Complejo Islote Lobos (41°25'S, 65°01'W) in the province of Río Negro, Argentina, about 150 km north of Peninsula Valdés. When it was discovered in 2002, the colony had about 20 nests, but by November 2007, 200 to 300 penguins were present.[50]

Most penguins are faithful to their colony. Once they breed, they often return each year to the same nest site. One Patagonian penguin pair at Punta Tombo bred together for 16 years in the same nest. Out of the 54,361 penguins volunteers and I banded at Punta Tombo between 1982 and 2005, only 149 have been seen elsewhere. By far the majority of penguins sighted at least 25 km from Punta Tombo (48) were penguins banded as juveniles (one-year-olds) on the beaches at Punta Tombo. Although resting on the beach at Punta Tombo as yearlings, they may not have hatched at Punta Tombo. Juveniles must return to shore to molt their feathers, but they need not return to a colony until they breed. One banded juvenile, instead of molting at 15 months, waited until the following February when over two years of age to molt to adult plumage.

Patagonian penguins breed as young as four years of age, but most do not lay eggs or find a mate until they are five to eight years old. A few females wait until they are 12 or 14 years old and some males may never win a mate. Patagonian penguins have high fidelity to their colony, to their nest, and to the beaches closest to their nest site or the nest where they hatched. One young male returned to breed in a nest within a meter of where he hatched. A few penguins are seen in colonies other than where they hatched, but that is rare. Five adults out of 8712 adults banded at Punta Tombo were seen at another colony, 2 moved to the south, and 3 were sighted on Penin-

---

46. C. Hays, *Effects of the 1982–1983 El Niño on Humboldt Penguin* (Spheniscus Humboldti) *Colonies in Peru*, 36 BIOLOGICAL CONSERVATION 169 (1986); R. Paredes & C.B. Zavalaga, *Overview of the Effects of El Niño 1997–98 on Humboldt Penguins and Other Seabirds at Punta San Juan, Peru*, 11 PENGUIN CONSERVATION 5 (1998).

47. P. Gandini *et al.*, *Status and Conservation of Magellanic Penguins Spheniscus Magellanicus in Patagonia, Argentina*, 6 BIRD CONSERVATION INTERNATIONAL 307 (1996).

48. E. Skewgar *et al.*, *Anchovy Fishery Threat to Patagonian Ecosystem*, 315 Science 45 (2007).

49. P.D. Boersma *et al.*, *Reproductive Variability and Historical Change of Magellanic Penguins* (Spheniscus Magellanicus) *at Punta Tombo, Argentina*, *in* BIOLOGY OF PENGUINS 15 (L. Davis & J. Darby eds., Macmillan 1990).

50. P. García-Borboroglu, Consejo Nacional de Investigaciones Científicas y Técnicas, Puerto Madryn, Argentina, personal communication (November 7, 2007).

sula Valdés. Nine out of 40,322 chicks banded at Punta Tombo were seen in another colony, all on Peninsula Valdés, at locations closer to their foraging grounds. These data suggest that metapopulation dynamics are important in sustaining the species and may become more important in the face of greater climate variation. Punta Tombo is very likely a source population for other colonies and may be providing the individuals that are colonizing new sites and extending or shifting their breeding range northward.

About half of the Patagonian penguins at Punta Tombo live in burrows, and the other half live in bushes.[51] The best nest sites are those with the most cover from the elements. Small increases in nesting cover increase fitness.[52] My students and I followed the reproductive success of Patagonian penguins in the same two areas each year for 24 years. Reproductive success varied widely among years. When more than 60 millimeters of rain fell between 15 October and 15 December, reproductive success was unusually low. (See Figure 10.) Nests filled up with water; burrows collapsed; and chicks got wet, became cold, and died. In nests with a northern exposure, chicks were more likely to survive. Climate variation that brings more water to desert environments may benefit humans, but it will not help penguins, as our data on Patagonian penguins show. (See Figure 11.)

Each year since 1983, students and volunteers have helped me follow individual penguins; measure chick growth; determine reproductive success; attach satellite tags to determine where penguins forage; census the colony during incubation and the early chick-rearing period; and walk beaches to look for banded, recently dead, and oiled penguins. From the early 1980s until the early 1990s, many penguins died during their fall and spring migration. We estimated that petroleum from illegal ballast-water dumping killed approximately 20,000 adults

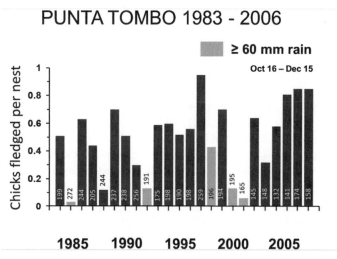

Figure 10. Reproductive success of Patagonian (Magellanic) penguins at their largest breeding colony, at Punta Tombo, Argentina. In years when at least 60 millimeters of rain fall between 15 October and 15 December (shown in gray), the penguin nests fill with water and young chicks get wet. Some burrows collapse, and many chicks become hypothermic and die.

---

51. D.L. Stokes & P.D. Boersma, *Effects of Substrate on the Distribution of Magellanic Penguins* (Spheniscus Magellanicus), 108 THE AUK 923 (1991).

52. D.L. Stokes & P.D. Boersma, *Nestsite Characteristics and Reproductive Success in Magellanic Penguins* (Spheniscus Magellanicus), 115 THE AUK 34 (1998); D.L. Stokes & P.D. Boersma, *Nesting Density and Reproductive Success in a Colonial Seabird, the Magellanic Penguin*, 81 ECOLOGY 2878 (2000).

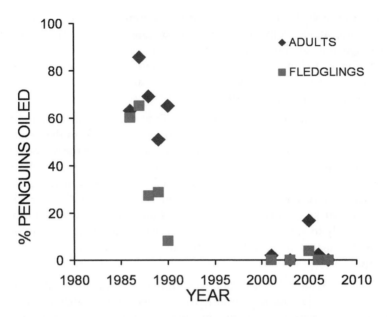

Figure 11. The percentage of dead penguins along two kilometers of coast at 6 to 15 locations along the coast of the Chubut province has declined significantly since the early 1980s. Tanker lanes were moved farther offshore in 1997, and illegal ballast water dumping is rare, so few penguins are encountering petroleum along the Chubut coast.

and 22,000 juveniles each year.[53] Petroleum pollution is an important factor in the decline of the penguin population because it kills adults that would not die otherwise. Even small amounts of petroleum can harm penguins, causing declines in breeding and increases in levels of stress hormones.[54]

For nearly a decade, the large number of penguins covered in petroleum each year drew the attention of newspapers, television, corporations, local environmental groups, and the general public. As a result of public concern, the provincial government of Chubut in 1997 moved tanker lanes 40 km farther offshore. In March 2001, 2003, 2005, and 2007, when Esteban Frere and I walked along the beaches in Chubut looking for dead birds, we were elated to find few dead penguins covered with petroleum (Figure 11). The oiled penguins we did find were feathered around the bill and very dry, which indicated that they probably died during migration between August and early October. Penguins have bare skin around the bill during the breeding season, but they are fully feathered following the molt, between April and early September. During the winter months, penguins are most likely to encounter petroleum between southern Brazil and northern Argentina. They probably become oiled while returning in the spring to their breeding colonies, because at Punta Tombo this is when we most often find penguins covered with petroleum.

There are 25 organizations dedicated to penguin rehabilitation from southern Brazil to northern Argentina. The first group began in northern Argentina in 1980, which suggests that

---

53. P. Gandini *et al.*, *Magellanic Penguins* (Spheniscus Magellanicus) *Are Affected by Chronic Petroleum Pollution Along the Coast of Chubut, Argentina*, 111 THE AUK 20 (1994).

54. G.S. Fowler *et al.*, *Hormonal and Reproductive Effects of Low Levels of Petroleum Fouling in the Magellanic Penguin* (Spheniscus Magellanicus), 112 THE AUK 382 (1995).

petroleum pollution is a long-standing problem.[55] The petroleum problem is much improved along the coast of Chubut province, but it is still a large problem north of Chubut to Southern Brazil. Although large spills are uncommon events, smaller, chronic leakages of petroleum can cause serious harm to a penguin that encounters the oil. One unlucky penguin, oiled in 2002 in Uruguay and cleaned and released in 2002, ran into petroleum a second time in 2007. He arrived onshore in July at Mar del Plata, Argentina, about 25% of his body covered in petroleum. How lucky he was to land below the Mar Del Plata aquarium, where he was rehabilitated a second time. The coast of northern Argentina and Uruguay appears to be an area where petroleum in the water is common. Rigorous ocean zoning and new marine parks can help keep penguins, petroleum, and fishers apart not only in Argentina but also throughout their range.

Although the population at Punta Tombo started declining in the early 1980s, it was not until 1987 that I placed 47 permanent stakes in the ground, 100 meters apart, along a transect at the colony. My students and I counted all the active nests within a 100-square-meter circle around 19 stakes that we surveyed each year. The pattern of decline at the 47 stakes that we counted irregularly showed the same trend as at the 19 stakes we counted annually. The colony declined nearly 22% between 1987 and 2006. (See Figure 12.) The biggest decline was in 1991 following an oil spill. After this spill, volunteers walked over 250 km of the Chubut coast, and we calculated that more than 20,000 penguins were killed in this one event. (See Figure 12.)

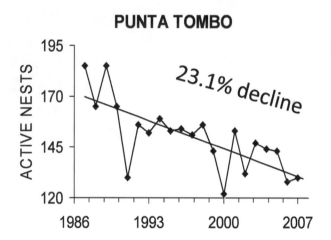

Figure 12. Patagonian penguins have declined by nearly 22% at Punta Tombo since 1987.

Petroleum is not the only thing causing the penguin population to decline; other human factors are taking a toll on the birds. Penguins are caught and killed in fishing nets. The collapse of some fisheries, and the development of others targeting the fish that penguins prey on, may do further harm to all temperate penguins. The large amount of small fish that humans remove from the productive system on which penguins depend is likely to diminish the prey available for penguins, thereby causing their populations to decline.

Close encounters with tourists may also have an impact on penguin populations, as these encounters affect the penguins' stress response. Although penguins become habituated to con-

---

55. P. García-Borboroglu *et al.*, *Chronic Oil Pollution Harms Magellanic Penguins in the Southwest Atlantic*, 52 MARINE POLLUTION BULLETIN 193 (2006).

trolled tourism, chicks in tourist areas develop their stress response much earlier than chicks in areas without tourists.[56] When people walk close to a penguin with small chicks, the adult often stands, exposing the chick to light, so that the chick peeps to be fed or burrows under the adult to be safe. These are physiological and probably energetic costs that penguins must pay because of human visitation.

Tourism is growing rapidly at Punta Tombo, and the number of people worldwide who visit penguin colonies will continue to grow. In the 1960s, before Punta Tombo became a provincial reserve, fewer than 100 people per year visited the colony. By the 1980s, visitors numbered in the thousands; by the 1990s, they reached the tens of thousands. In January 2007 more than 900 tourists walked into the reserve in one hour; that year, the number of visitors surpassed 105,000. (See Figure 13.)

Figure 13. Tourism at Punta Tombo has grown to more than 105,000 visitors per year and is overwhelming the very resource people come to see—penguins. Photograph. P. Dee Boersma.

The visitors who flock to Punta Tombo are loving the penguins to death. In September 2006, the provincial director of conservation started a tourist trail expansion that destroyed about 50 penguin nests before the season began and later caused penguins to desert existing nests adjacent to the new trail. The director planned to join the trail extensions in November 2006, making one large, circular trail. Our data showed the new trail would destroy 197 nests that had eggs close to hatching and would affect 10,000 more nests by forcing penguins to cross the new trail. Crossing the trail and dodging tourists would delay penguins returning from foraging from feeding their chicks.

---

56. B.G. Walker *et al.*, *Physiological and Behavioral Differences in Magellanic Penguin Chicks in Undisturbed and Tourist-visited Locations of a Colony*, 19 Conservation Biology 1571 (2005); B.G. Walker *et al.*, *Habituation of Adult Magellanic Penguins to Human Visitation as Expressed Through Behavior and Corticosterone Secretion*, 20 Conservation Biology 146 (2006).

In addition, in January 2007, five penguins were killed on the road by tourist traffic. The on-site warden at the provincial park responded responsibly by closing the road to vehicles—a request that the Wildlife Conservation Society and I had made for more than 20 years. With the evidence of damage to the penguins provided by our data, and following a change in leadership at the provincial level, the director of conservation was fired and the new trail extensions were removed, returning the trail to its 2005 configuration. In addition, a new bridge was built to allow penguins to move to and from their nests unhindered. In September 2007, the Punta Tombo Management Plan, a community-based project that had taken two years to produce (and the provisions of which the former director of conservation ignored), was formally adopted by the Province of Chubut and an oversight committee established.

Oceanic productivity and the locations where penguins find their prey vary among years. We know from tracking Patagonian penguins by satellite that the distance they must swim to find food affects their reproductive success. Penguins that forage close to the nest have greater reproductive success than those that must go farther. Penguins that swam 150 km or less from the nest had the highest probability of raising a chick. If a breeding adult penguin went more than 350 km, it had almost no chance of raising a chick. Breeding adults forage in roughly the same areas each year, but in some years they remain closer to the colony than in others. (See Figure 14.) When penguin prey is farther from the nest, reproductive success declines.

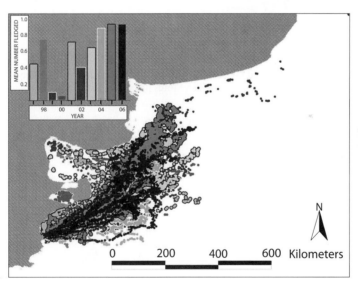

Figure 14. Each year during incubation, Patagonian penguins forage hundreds of kilometers north of their nest at Punta Tombo.

Penguin distribution and abundance in both the short and the long term are closely tied to their prey. In some years, such as 1987, 2000, and 2002, incubation trips were longer and adults went farther north, presumably to meet the returning migration of their prey, but the chicks starved to death before the adults returned to their nest. (See Figure 15.) Penguins are going about 60 km farther to find food than they did a decade ago. (See Figure 16.) Foraging grounds for penguins with chicks are well defined, making it possible to reduce conflicts between fishers and penguins by ocean zoning. For example, in the area "de veda de Isla Escondida"—appropriately 25,000 km^2, just offshore from Punta Tombo—large fishing boats are excluded from October to April to protect the spawning hake. A by-product of this restriction is that it affords protection to some of the foraging grounds of breeding penguins.

In years when prey is less available, ocean zoning could be used to exclude potential competition between fishers and penguins in the core area that penguins use. Penguins are following their prey and using areas of high productivity. How long a penguin is gone from its nest is closely related to how far it goes.[57] Thus, when penguins are gone longer, a larger area should be closed to fishers than when their foraging trips are short. As data have shown, Patagonian

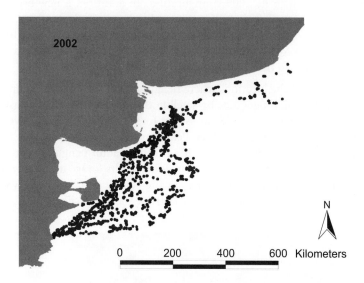

Figure 15. Patagonian penguins foraged farther north in 2002 than in other years. Many chicks died because penguin mates did not return in time to feed the hatchlings before they starved.

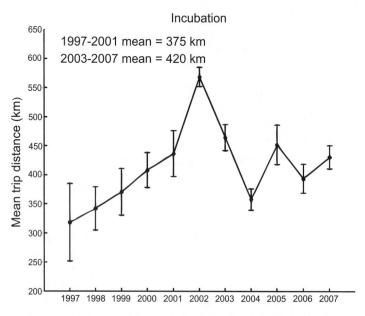

Figure 16. Patagonian penguins are traveling farther north during incubation than they did a decade ago. Climate variation is probably delaying the return of penguin prey, creating a mismatch between prey and predator.

57. P.D. Boersma *et al.*, *Oceans Apart: Conservation Models for Two Temperate Penguin Species Shaped by the Marine Environment*, 335 Marine Ecology Progress Series 217 (2007).

penguin populations are expanding at the northern part of their range in the Atlantic Ocean, as would be predicted if being closer to their prey is important. Unfortunately, data like these do not exist for other colonies of Patagonian penguins and are absent for other penguin species.

Penguins as marine environmental sentinels

Scientific knowledge of penguin population trends is meager. We know that many species and colonies are most likely in decline, but we have few systematic counts of colonies. Systematically monitoring the 43 penguin aggregations worldwide would provide the data necessary to determine the status and trend of all penguin species. With this information, scientists could identify trouble spots and intervene before populations crash. Furthermore, the status of penguin populations reflects the state of the oceans they inhabit. Penguins are sentinels, so why not use them? I recommend the formation of a nongovernmental organization dedicated to determining the population size, status, and trend of the major aggregations of penguin species. Such an organization could be supported by funds from a combination of the United Nations, national governments, private foundations, and the interested public. With international support, an organization focused on penguins could provide the data on penguin population trends needed to inform the public and policymakers of where penguins are in decline and what needs to be done.

Life is not likely to get easier for penguins. They have to withstand both climate variation and human development. They may not be able to follow their food as coastal development claims their breeding habitat, or their food may disappear as fishers take more and more of their prey. Climate warming is likely to shift prey species, reduce productivity, and make penguin life more difficult. Climate change, petroleum pollution, and changes in their prey distribution and abundance are causing Patagonian penguin populations to move and decline. A 10% decline per decade, in the biggest colony for this species, is simply not sustainable.

The changes in penguin populations reflect rapid changes in the marine environment and show that people are doing a poor job of managing the oceans. We are changing the world, the course of evolution, and the species with which we share the planet. Can people change to allow other species to persist and coexist? That is the real question: can we, and will we, manage ourselves?

Notes

1. *King Penguins in a Warmer World.* A recent study by Céline Le Bohec and others documents the threat of increased ocean temperatures to King penguins.[1] The authors of this study examined the influence of warm phases of the El Niño Southern Oscillation on breeding and survival. They used this as a predictor of the response to increased temperatures due to global warming. The striking finding of this study is that adult King penguins exhibit a 9% decline in adult survival with a mere 0.26°C (0.47°F) increase in sea surface temperature. The IPCC Fourth Assessment Report indicates average ocean surface temperature has increased by 0.13°C per decade between 1979 and 2005.[2] Penguins are clearly in trouble.

---

1. Céline Le Bohec *et al.*, *King Penguin Population Threatened by Southern Ocean Warming*, 105 PROCEEDINGS OF THE NATIONAL ACADEMY OF SCIENCES 2493 (2008).

2. K.E. Trenberth *et al.*, *Observations: Surface and Atmospheric Climate Change*, in CLIMATE CHANGE 2007: THE PHYSICAL SCIENCE BASIS. CONTRIBUTION OF WORKING GROUP I TO THE FOURTH ASSESSMENT REPORT OF THE INTERGOVERNMENTAL PANEL ON CLIMATE CHANGE 235, 243 (S. Solomon *et al.* eds., Cambridge Un. Press 2007).

2. *A Human Fingerprint in the Antarctic.* A recent study by an international team, Nathan Gillett *et al., Attribution of Polar Warming to Human Influence,* 1 NATURE GEOSCIENCE 750 (2008), has found evidence that the accelerated warming in both poles is due to human activity. It has been known for some time that Arctic warming is a consequence of anthropogenic greenhouse gases, but this is the first time that a study has indicated definitively that there is a measurable human influence on Antarctic warming. This result is important because it soundly refutes the IPCC's finding in the Fourth Assessment Report that Antarctica was the only continent where "anthropogenic temperature changes have not been detected so far."

3. *Krill.* 2005 FLANNERY at 96, 97–98 (footnotes omitted) but discussing A. Atkinson *et al., Long-Term Decline in Krill Stock and Increase in Salps within the Southern Ocean,* 432 NATURE 100 (2004):

> Indeed, so miraculous is the influence of sea ice on plankton, and therefore on krill and the creatures they feed [such as penguins, seals and great whales], that there is almost as much difference between the ice-covered and ice-free portions of the Southern Ocean as there is between the sea and the near sterile Antarctic continent itself.

> [Prior to 1976, krill populations in the Southern Ocean were stable]. But a very different pattern was seen in the years following 1976. Ever since that date, the krill have been in sharp decline, reducing at the rate of nearly 40 percent per decade.

> .... The reduction in krill numbers coincided so closely with the reduction of sea ice over time as to leave little doubt that climate change is a profound threat to the world's most productive ocean, and to the largest creatures that exist and feed there.

> To gain a sense of the magnitude and rate of change involved, imagine what it would mean for the beasts of the Serengeti if their grasslands had been reduced by 40 percent each decade since 1976.... Already, there are signs that some Antarctic fauna are feeling the pinch. The emperor penguin population is half what it was thirty years ago, while the number of Adelie penguins has declined by 70 percent.

4. *Penguins and the Endangered Species Act.* Recognizing the extreme danger posed by global warming, on November 28, 2006 the Center for Biological Diversity submitted a petition to list 12 species of penguins as endangered under the Endangered Species Act (ESA). The petition stated that penguins faced multiple threats:[3]

> Each of the petitioned penguin species faces unique and specific threats, ranging from introduced predators, disease, habitat destruction, disturbance at breeding colonies, oil spills, marine pollution, and in some cases, direct harvest. Additionally, most species are also impacted by fisheries, either directly, such as when individuals are caught and killed in trawls, nets and longlines, or indirectly, through the depletion of essential prey species such as krill. Cumulatively, these threats are for most of the petitioned species already of significant magnitude and impact such that listing under the ESA is warranted.

> Moreover, an additional overriding threat, affecting each species, makes listing under the ESA all the more urgent. Global warming has already been linked to past, on-going, and/or projected population declines in numerous species of penguins. Even under the most optimistic emission scenarios, continued warming over the next several decades will dramatically and irreversibly affect Antarctica, the Sub-Antarctic islands, the Southern Ocean, and the penguins dependant on these and adjoining ecosystems.

---

3. The full petition is *available at* http://biologicaldiversity.org/species/birds/penguins/action_timeline.html.

Global warming then represents the most significant and pervasive threat to the continued existence of penguins, and absent prompt action to cut United States and global greenhouse gas emissions, the march of the penguins will be a march towards extinction.

In response to the petition, the Fish and Wildlife Service (FWS) published a positive 90-day finding for ten of the species in the Federal Register,[4] although this finding was published nearly five months after the statutory deadline. Under the ESA, a positive 90-day finding triggers a requirement that the Secretary complete a 12-month review from the date of the petition. The FWS failed to do so, forcing the Center to file suit.[5] Pursuant to a court-ordered settlement agreement of this case, dated September 8, 2008, the Fish and Wildlife Service must publish its 12-month review by December 19, 2008.

5. *Penguins or People.* The justification for the destruction of the penguins described by Dee Boersma was written several years ago by William F. Baxter, PEOPLE OR PENGUINS: THE CASE FOR OPTIMAL POLLUTION 4–9 (1974, Columbia Un. Press, N.Y., London), ch. 1, *A 'Good' Environment: Just One of the Set of Human Objectives*:

> Recently scientists have informed us that use of DDT in food production is causing damage to the penguin population. For the present purposes let us accept that assertion as an indisputable scientific fact. The scientific fact is often asserted as if the correct implication—that we must stop agricultural use of DDT—followed from the mere statement of the fact of penguin damage. But plainly it does not follow if my criteria are employed.

> My criteria are oriented to people, not penguins. Damage to penguins, or sugar pines, or geological marvels is, without more, simply irrelevant. One must go further, by my criteria, and say: Penguins are important because people enjoy seeing them walk about rocks; and furthermore, the well-being of people would be less impaired by halting use of DDT than by giving up penguins. In short, my observations about environmental problems will be people-oriented, as are my criteria. I have no interest in preserving penguins for their own sake.

> It may be said by way of objection to this position, that it is very selfish of people to act as if each person represented one unit of importance and nothing else was of any importance. It is undeniably selfish. Nevertheless I think it is the only tenable starting place for analysis for several reasons,. First, no other position corresponds to the way most people really think and act—*i.e.*, corresponds to reality.

> Second, this attitude does not portend any massive destruction of nonhuman flora and fauna, for people depend on them in many obvious ways, and they will be preserved because and to the degree that humans do depend on them.

> Third, what is good for humans is, many respects, good for penguins and pine trees—clean air for example. So that humans are, in these respects, surrogates for plant and animal life.

> Fourth, I do not know how we could administer any other system. Our decisions are either private or collective. Insofar as Mr. Jones is free to act privately, he may give such preferences as he wishes to other forms of life: he may feed birds in winter and do with less himself, and he may even decline to resist an advancing polar bear on the ground that the bear's appetite is more important than those portions of himself that the bear may choose to eat. In short my basic premise does not rule out private altruism to com-

---

4. 72 Fed. Reg. 37695–37697 (July 11, 2007).
5. Center for Biological Diversity v Hall, Civ. No. 1:08-cv-00335-RMU (D.D.C. 2008).

peting life-forms. It does rule out, however, Mr. Jones' inclination to feed Mr. Smith to the bear, however hungry the bear, however despicable Mr. Smith.

Insofar as we act collectively on the other hand, only humans can be afforded an opportunity to participate in the collective decisions. Penguins cannot vote now and are unlikely subjects for the franchise—pine trees more unlikely still. Again each individual is free to cast his vote so as to benefit sugar pines if that is his inclination. But many of the more extreme assertions that one hears from some conservationists amount to tacit assertions that they are specially appointed representatives of sugar pines, and hence that their preferences should be weighted more heavily than the preferences of other humans who do not enjoy equal rapport with "nature." The simplistic assertion that agricultural use of DDT must stop at once because it is harmful to penguins is of that type.

Fifth, if polar bears or pine trees or penguins, like man, are to be regarded as ends rather than means, if they are to count in our calculus of social organization, someone must tell me how much each one counts, and someone must tell me how these life-forms are to be permitted to express their preferences, for I do not know either answer. If the answer is that certain people are to hold their proxies, then I want to know how those proxy-holders are to be selected: self-appointment does not seem workable to me.

Sixth, and by way of summary of the foregoing, let me point out that the set of environmental issues under discussion—although they raise very complex technical questions of how to achieve any objective—ultimately raise a normative question: what *ought* we to do. Questions of *ought* are unique to the human mind and world—they are meaningless as applied to a nonhuman situation.

I reject the proposition that we *ought* to respect the "balance of nature" or to "preserve the environment" unless the reason for doing so, express or implied, is the benefit of man.

I reject the idea that there is a "right" or "morally correct" state of nature to which we should return. The word "nature" has no normative connotation. Was it "right" or "wrong" for the earth's crust to heave in contortion and create mountains and seas? Was it "right" for the first amphibian to crawl up out of the primordial ooze? Was it "wrong" for plants to reproduce themselves and alter the atmospheric composition in favor of oxygen? For animals to alter the atmosphere in favor of carbon dioxide both by breathing oxygen and eating plants? No answers can be given to these questions because they are meaningless questions.

All this may seem obvious to the point of being tedious, but much of the present controversy over environment and pollution rests on tacit normative assumptions about just such nonnormative phenomena: that it is "wrong" to impair penguins with DDT, but not to slaughter cattle for prime rib roasts. That it is wrong to kill stands of sugar pines with industrial fumes, but not to cut sugar pines and build housing for the poor. Every man is entitled to his own preferred definition of Walden Pond, but there is no definition that has any moral superiority over another, except by reference to the selfish needs of the human race.

From the fact that there is no normative definition of the natural state, it follows that there is no normative definition of clean air or pure water—hence no definition of polluted air—or of pollution—except by reference to the needs of man. The "right" composition of the atmosphere is one which has some dust in it and some lead in it and hydrogen sulfide in it—just those amounts that attend to a sensibly organized society thoughtfully and knowledgably pursuing the greatest possible satisfaction for its human members.

The first and most fundamental step toward solution of our environmental problems is a clear recognition that our objective is not pure air or water but rather some optimal state of pollution. That step immediately suggests the question: How do we define and attain the level of pollution that will yield the maximum possible amount of human satisfaction?

———————

Response to Professor Baxter

This self-confident essay is expressive of the prevailing "law and economics" paradigm that has presided over the collapse of regulatory regimes and natural systems now marked by the arrival of global warming.

The conceit that leads the author to conclude humans are superior to all other animals and that humans will not suffer the same consequences illustrates how truly small-minded and short-sighted we as a species can be.

Baxter makes a series of assertions, each deeply flawed. This erroneous chain of premises can lead only to a fundamentally faulty conclusion. First, note that the author claims compatibility with the "way most people think and act," thereby alleging that this analysis "corresponds to reality" and any contrary view does not. Events at the time as well as today indicate that many people indeed do not share Baxter's view of the world.

Consider the destruction of penguins by DDT—an unfortunate event magnanimously conceded in the Baxter essay for sake of argument. This might mean that some growers of crops and makers of pesticides actually don't care whether they kill penguins as a sideline. A contrasting recollection is that this phenomenon was met by a flood of denials so that the growers and pesticides makers declared: "We do not kill penguins and people who say so are liars." Over time, this position succumbed to empirical reality and the defense of DDT changed accordingly: "We are sorry we kill penguins. These unfortunate circumstances can be avoided by greater care." A small number of misanthropes might stay with Baxter: "We kill penguins and are proud of it." We "have no interest in preserving penguins for their own sake."

Contrary to Baxter, we believe that the way "most people think and act" would be to condemn as normatively "wrong" the long-distance destruction of penguins by agricultural practices. What farmers in their right minds would believe they were morally justified to kill creatures (even if "incidentally") a continent away? In North America four centuries of common law would condemn this practice—on moral and then on legal grounds.

Dr. Boersma, we may suppose, begs to differ with Baxter. She might say that the penguin-sympathetic side of human nature lost out because the systems of decisionmaking made no allowance for it. Prof. Baxter might stand "corrected," perhaps, but only on the ground that the people didn't care about penguins as enthusiastically as he surmised.

But, says Baxter, the penguins must yet die in the interests of "optimal" pollution. If more "human" good is done than human "bad" by this deed of penguin-directed farming, then this deed must be allowed to go forward. It simply requires human judgment through human institutions to make the right ("the optimal") choice in the matter.

The arrogance to follow our own confusions and self-deceptions anywhere they might lead is certainly ambitious. And this view is well-represented in human history.

Professor Baxter was certain this was the way to go. This "attitude," he says, "does not portend any massive destruction of nonhuman flora and fauna, for people depend on them in many obvious ways, and they will be preserved because and to the degree that humans do depend upon them."

The presumptuousness of the author is astounding. He assumes that humans will always make good decisions, at least with regard to our own well-being. Yet, this is patently untrue. Witness increased cancer risks due to the ozone hole, which resulted from CFCs produced solely by human activity. How many times a week do we read of health hazards created by various human activities that were previously believed to be innocuous? It is ironic that Baxter uses DDT as an example of choosing humans over nature, given that DDT also can exert hormone-disrupting effects on humans and cause reduced fertility.

That many human societies have "collapsed" is an empirical caution against the conceit that every part of nature serves only us.

We were assured in 1974 that the humans would be worthy "surrogates" for penguins. That it didn't turn out that way is cause for regret. Prof. Baxter would say again that his only error was to overestimate the human attachment to penguins.

Baxter insists upon the assertion that we must decide all matters in an anthropocentric manner because it is impossible to "administer any other system." All collective decisions at some level reflect priorities of the people. It is just as easy to determine that a majority of people have a priority that includes protecting nature as a priority that includes protecting the right to choose a college.

As for the conundrum of human "proxies" for polar bears or penguins, says Baxter, "then I want to know how these proxy-holders are to be selected: self-appointment does not seem workable to me." But of course it was "self-appointment" by the DDT makers and agricultural operators in the first place that started the demise. They appointed themselves assailants of penguins. And now a new set of assailants is coming after the polar bear. Our climate is their collateral damage. And the only defense is a bevy of self-appointed protectors.

People or Penguins is an arrogant—and ultimately destructive—separation of humans from nature. The belief that there is no "normative definition" of the state of nature denies the origins of life, denies the conditions that sustain life, denies millions of years of evolution and the circumstances in which it was wrought, denies the multiple ways in which earth forces sustain life.

But it is a deft account of how global warming can happen.

Whales, Whaling and the Warming Oceans[1]

Alison Rieser, Dai Ho Chun Distinguished Chair in Arts and Sciences, Department of Geography, Director, Graduate Ocean Policy Program, University of Hawai'i at Manoa, Honolulu, HI 96822, Emeritus Professor Law, University of Maine School of Law, Portland, ME 04102; Tel: (808) 956-8467, Fax: (808) 956-3512, rieser@hawaii.edu.

Introduction

The great whales have long been a symbol of humanity's relationship to the oceans. In the 19th century, whales were the object of the first industrial fishery, and were hunted nearly to extinction.[2] After World War II, two decades of unrestrained factory-ship whaling in the Antarctic

---

1. An earlier version of this chapter was presented at a symposium on the great whales of the North Atlantic at Boston College Law School on October 16, 2008, sponsored by the MIT Sea Grant Program and the Boston College Environmental Affairs Law Review and published in the Review's volume 36, number 2. The author gratefully acknowledges the support of the sponsors and organizers who made possible her preparation of this chapter and their permission to reprint it in this volume.
2. *See* ANDREW DARBY, HARPOON INTO THE HEART OF WHALING (Da Capo Press 2008).

decimated the few populations the Yankee whaling ships had been unable to reach. The whales' survival then became a symbol of the early environmental movement of the late 20th century. The slogan 'Save the whales' was a call to arms to save the planet from humanity's folly. Now, in the 21st century, whales are sentinels for the large-scale changes that global warming and ocean industrialization are bringing to the seas.[3] They have also become a symbol of humankind's inability to find common ground and cooperate to protect the global environment.[4]

When nations agreed to a worldwide moratorium on the hunting of whales in the early 1980s, they fulfilled a central goal of the 1972 U.N. Conference on the Environment in Stockholm.[5] But the conservation movement behind the moratorium was never able to resolve a basic question: should whaling be banned permanently or, if and when whale populations recover, should they again be hunted for 'sustainable use'? As the climate crisis brings unprecedented changes to species, ecosystems and the access of different peoples to the Earth's resources, this unresolved question overshadows and undermines institutions we have established to address these changes.

In its first major undertaking in ocean diplomacy of the 21st century, the United States began a campaign to save one of the oldest elements of the public order of the oceans, the international regime for the regulation of whaling. The deliberations of the International Whaling Commission (IWC), the management body created by treaty in 1946, have deteriorated into an annual confrontation between the proponents of conflicting values: biodiversity preservation versus consumptive use of marine wildlife. The whaling regime has been verging on dissolution over the issue of commercial whaling for almost two decades. While this existential struggle has been waged, some State parties to the regime have sought quietly to turn its attention to the challenges cetaceans face from climate change, to position the IWC to engage with other international regimes to ensure whales survive the coming changes.[6]

U.S. whaling diplomacy appears to assume that the international regime for whale conservation is worth saving: an accommodation that removes the commercial whaling issue from the IWC's agenda will free that body to address the numerous environmental challenges that cetaceans face today, from climate change and marine pollution to collisions with vessels and fishing gear.[7] In this optimistic view, the IWC could become the keystone species in the "ecosys-

---

3. Thomas J. O'Shea and Daniel K. Odell, *Large-Scale Marine Ecosystem Change and the Conservation of Marine Mammals*, 89 J. MAMMALOGY 529 (2008).

4. *See* Cinnamon P. Carlarne, *Saving the Whales in the New Millenium: International Institutions, Recent Developments and the Future of International Politics*, 24 VA ENVTL L.J. 1, 48 (2005–06). *See also* CALESTOUS JUMA, THE FUTURE OF THE IWC: STRENGTHENING OCEAN DIPLOMACY, A REPORT TO THE IWC INTERSESSIONAL MEETING, May 2008, at 5, *available at* http://www.iwcoffice.org.

5. Carlarne, *supra* note 4, at 7.

6. *See* William C.G. Burns, *From the Harpoon to the Heat: Climate Change and the International Whaling Commission in the 21st Century*, 13 GEO. INTL. ENVTL L. REV. 335 (2001). The whaling treaty is formally known as the International Convention for the Regulation of Whaling, with Schedule of Whaling Regulations, Dec. 2, 1946, *entered into force* Nov. 10, 1948, 62 Stat. 1716, 161 UNTS 72 [hereinafter ICRW]. The ICRW is implemented in U.S. law by the Whaling Convention Act of 1949, 16 U.S.C. §§916–916l.

7. In 2007, a coalition of non-governmental organizations (NGOs) mounted a campaign to convince President George W. Bush to direct his administration to do everything it could to continue the global moratorium on the hunting of whales. By the time the campaign was launched, however, the chief U.S. official responsible for international whaling policy had already begun a campaign to broker a compromise to preserve the IWC and to keep the pro-whaling countries from abrogating the International Convention for the Regulation of Whaling (ICRW), the international whaling treaty. The NGO coalition feared that US delegates were so intent on reaching a compromise with pro-whaling nations that they may be tempted to agree to a new type of whaling, that of "small-type coastal whaling" by whaling vessels in Japan and Norway. *See* Patrick R. Ramage, International Fund for Animal Welfare, Testimony before Subcommittee on Fisheries, Wildlife and Oceans, U.S. House of Representatives, Committee on Natural Resources, June 10, 2008. U.S. diplomats believe the global whaling regime, based upon the ICRW, although dysfunctional for the past two decades,

tem" of international ocean institutions.[8] However, the norms that underlie ocean governance in the 21st century have been forged in an era of resource scarcity, declining ocean health, and recognition of the interdependence of governance institutions across temporal and spatial scales. Collectively referred to as the precautionary and ecosystem approaches, these principles and norms are almost diametrically opposed to those which underlie the 1946 International Convention on the Regulation of Whaling (ICRW), the IWC's constitutive document.[9]

For the last decade, one contracting government to the IWC, Japan, has presented legal and scientific arguments for lifting the moratorium on commercial whaling. Stressing the need for adherence to international law, this State relies upon the text of the ICRW to reinforce its view that ecosystem-based management of oceans prioritizes human needs.[10] As long as the ICRW remains in force, Japan is likely to continue to rely upon that treaty's approval of consumptive use of whales to support its view that whaling must be allowed as "sustainable use."[11] But as long as a majority of other parties to the treaty rejects this view, Japan is likely to continue to misuse the treaty's special permit provisions to support a growing consumptive take of whales and to characterize that unilateral 'harvest' as science- and ecosystem-based management.[12] It is not clear that a diplomatic agreement to put aside debates over commercial or 'scientific' whaling or anything short of international adjudication will be sufficient to prevent these legal and scientific claims from detracting from the ability of other ocean regimes to apply a truly precautionary and ecosystem approach to governance.

Over the course of the last two decades during which the collapse of the international whaling regime has been imminent, our understanding of marine ecosystems and how human activities affect them has advanced. Ocean governance institutions have been slow to incorporate this knowledge, choosing instead to focus on maximizing the extraction of marine wildlife for human consumption and appropriating ocean space and minerals for human use.[13] The need for reform of these institutions greatly surpasses the need for reform of the whaling regime, especially in light of climate change and its impacts on ecosystems. Any effort to maintain a role for the IWC in ocean governance must be part of the overall transformation of ocean institutions to precaution- and ecosystem-based management that emphasizes resource protection over exploitation. Otherwise, such effort risks being judged as the diplomatic equivalent of fiddling while Rome is burning.[14]

---

should be preserved, and that over time the treaty can be amended or finessed to allow the IWC to contribute to the conservation and management of cetaceans and other marine mammals. *See* William T. Hogarth, U.S. Commissioner to the IWC, Testimony before Subcommittee on Fisheries, Wildlife and Oceans, U.S. House of Representatives, Committee on Natural Resources, June 10, 2008.

8. JUMA, *supra* note 4, at 6 (uncertainties about the state of marine ecosystems represent an opportunity to position the IWC as a 'flagship' organization in ocean diplomacy and science-based conservation and management).

9. *See generally* Duncan Currie, *Whales, Sustainability and International Environmental Governance*, 16 RECIEL 45 (2007).

10. *See* Joji Morishita, *Multiple Analysis of the Whaling Issue: Understanding the Dispute by a Matrix*, 30 MARINE POLICY 802 (2006).

11. *Id.*

12. *See generally* Phillip J. Clapham *et al.*, *The Whaling Issue: Conservation, Confusion, and Casuistry*, 31 MARINE POLICY 314 (2007).

13. *See, e.g.*, Carl Safina and Dane H. Klinger, *Collapse of Bluefin Tuna in the Western Atlantic*, 22 CONS. BIOL. 243, 243–44 (2008) (the collapse of the bluefin tuna is only one of many examples of management failure, where scientific advice is ignored due to industrial lobbying, inability of parties to agree on common goals for shared resources, and interference with management by elected officials on behalf of their industrial constituencies).

14. The whaling industry was the first industrial fishery in the world, and its history should inform all policies on what the role of industrial fisheries should be in the new realities of altered marine ecosystems, global warming, and decreasing food and health security of coastal communities affected by global warming. If whaling were still being carried out by several nations, the IWC would be the most notoriously ineffective

This chapter begins with a brief review of the long-range challenges facing whales in light of ocean warming and what whales require from international governance. It then considers the recent efforts to reform the IWC and the premise that it could, if the moratorium stalemate were resolved, contribute to the protection of marine ecosystems that whales depend on as they face the unprecedented challenge of global climate change. A particularly troubling aspect of the current reform discussions is the assertion that 'normalization' of the regime is in fact consistent with an ecosystem approach, the emerging norm of international environmental governance. This rationale happens to coincide with the latest rationale the pro-whaling nations give for restarting commercial whaling, that culling top predators is needed in order to secure human food supplies. A brief look at the management regime for the burgeoning Antarctic krill fishery tests the premise that the IWC can function as an advocate for the whales in other ocean regimes.

I. Long-Term Threats to Cetaceans

A 2008 study published in the journal, SCIENCE, reveals the magnitude of the human footprint on the oceans.[15] Few if any areas of the oceans are free from human impacts. These impacts reduce the amount of habitat suitable for whales to live in, challenging their ability to recover from the factory whaling era. For example, shipping noise in the ocean increases exponentially with each decade, degrading the underwater acoustic environment whales depend on for communicating and locating prey.[16] Noise pollution may force whales out of the habitat where they are most likely to find prey, even as those prey fields are changing in response to ocean warming, further reducing the likelihood of population recovery.[17]

Ship strikes, entanglement in fishing gear and ecological interactions with fisheries pose additional challenges to whales. The number of cetaceans that die or are weakened by these forms of habitat degradation vastly outnumber the number of whales deliberately killed by whaling.[18] The North Atlantic right whale (*Eubalaena glacialis*), for example, occupies a greatly contracted range along the eastern seaboard of North America, and its population numbers in the few hundreds. Right whales use their baleen to strain large quantities of the copepod, *Calanus finmarchicus*, from the water. Mother whales and their calves migrate along the coast from the calving grounds off Georgia and Florida to find the dense swarms near Cape Cod and the Bay of Fundy in the spring and summer. These migrations, however, take them through some of the world's busiest shipping lanes and densest fields of stationary fishing gear, including millions of lobster traps and their associated lines and buoys. At least 18 right whales from a population of about 350 have been lost to the slow death from gear-entanglement injuries since 1986.[19] Since 1970,

---

regional fishery management body. Instead, in view of the moratorium and the impending collapse of the Atlantic bluefin tuna, that title would likely go to the International Commission for the Conservation of Atlantic Tunas. *See* Safina and Klinger, *supra* note 13.

15. Benjamin S. Halpern *et al.*, *A Global Map of Human Impact on Marine Ecosystems*, 319 SCIENCE 948, 951 (41% of the world's oceans are affected by multiple anthropogenic drivers of ecological change).

16. O'Shea and Odell 2008, *supra* note 3, at 531, citing Peter L. Tyack, *Implications for Marine Mammals of Large-Scale Changes in the Marine Environment*, 89 J. MAMMALOGY 549 (2008).

17. Tyack estimates that certain noises, like military and commercial sonar and seismic exploration, are especially damaging and could have a population-level effect equivalent to an increase in predation, *i.e.*, to a commercial whaling quota. *Id.*

18. The member states of the IWC have acknowledged that the great whales face a host of significant environmental challenges. Mortality from these sources far exceeds that of all whaling, including the commercial whaling carried out under objections to the moratorium, aboriginal subsistence whaling, and the special permit whaling under Article VIII whaling ("scientific whaling"). *See* Mike Iliff, *Normalization of the International Whaling Commission*, 32 MARINE POLICY 333, 335 (2008). The total harvest under all forms of whaling is about 3,000, including aboriginal subsistence whaling (300), Japan's Article VII whaling (2,000), Norway's EEZ commercial whaling under objection (650), and Iceland's EEZ commercial whaling (100). *Id.*

19. Andrew J. Read, *The Looming Crisis: Interactions Between Marine Mammals and Fisheries*, 89 J. MAMMALOGY 541(2008). It may take as long as several months for a large whale to die from entanglement injuries

another 24 right whales have been killed by ship strikes. As shipping intensifies with global trade, the percentage of unnatural mortality of great whales that is due to shipping is likely to grow.[20]

The human race's competition with whales for ocean space may soon be joined by its competition with whales for prey. Although there is currently no commercial fishery for *Calanus finmarchicus*, Norwegian companies are developing a *Calanus* fishery in the Barents Sea to produce fish meal for salmon farms.[21] Given the common pattern of boom-and-bust fishing from one species to another down and through the marine food web,[22] and the growing demand for sea-farmed salmon, it is not inconceivable that a similar fishery could develop in the Gulf of Maine. Or a *Calanus* fishery in the Eastern North Atlantic could affect the current-driven supply of copepods to U.S. waters.[23] On the other side of the world, the fishery for Antarctic krill (*Euphausia superba*), the most important prey species in Southern Ocean ecosystem, is on the verge of a major expansion, just as krill populations are decreasing, likely in response to climate change.[24]

The greatest long-term threat to the North Atlantic right whale and all cetaceans, however, is the synergistic effect of climate change with these sources of habitat alteration. Warming oceans will alter the conditions that make life in the oceans possible for whales, through acidification, changing oceanographic conditions, reduction in habitat for prey species and changes to processes upon which marine ecosystems depend.[25] Migratory species like whales may be required to travel greater distances to find areas where large quantities of their prey species aggregate.[26] Greater travel distances will affect the energetics of whales and could affect mating and reproductive success.[27]

---

and starvation, raising animal welfare issues as well as the risk of extinction. Michael J. Moore *et al.*, *Right Whale Mortality: A Message from the Dead to the Living*, in THE URBAN WHALE: NORTH ATLANTIC WHALES AT THE CROSSROADS 358–368 (Scott D. Kraus and Rosalind M. Rolland eds., Harvard Un. Press 2007).

20. Amy R. Knowlton and Moira W. Brown, *Running the Gauntlet: Right Whales and Ship Strikes*, in Kraus and Rolland, *supra* note 19, at 412. An examination of anecdotal records from the 1970s through the 1990s indicates that between 13 and 20% of all large whale strandings (where carcasses wash ashore) in the U.S., Italy, France, and South America were due to ship strikes. *Id.*, citing David Laist *et al.*, *Collisions Between Ships and Whales*, 17 MARINE MAMMAL SCIENCE 35 (2001).

21. *See* Rachel G. Tiller, *The Norwegian System and the Distribution of Claims to Redfeed*, 32 MARINE POLICY 928 (2008)(noting Norway's heavy investment in research on a potential *Calanus* fishery in the waters surrounding Norway as a replacement for dwindling populations of fish species used for fishmeal and fish oil). In March 2006, the Norwegian government put a moratorium on plankton harvesting in order to research the ecological effects of a fishery before it commences. *See also* Rachel G. Tiller, *New Resources and Old Regimes: Will the Harvest of Zooplankton Bring Critical Changes to the Svalbard Fisheries Protection Zone?* Paper presented at International Studies Assoc. 49th Annual Meeting, San Francisco, CA, March 2008, *available at* http://www.allacademic.com/meta/p252114_index.html. At least one commercial enterprise already exists and is marketing nutritional supplements made from *Calanus*. *See Calanus* AS, *available at* http://www.calanus.no/About.aspx.

22. *See* Daniel Pauly *et al.*, *Fishing Down Marine Food Webs*, 279 SCIENCE 860 (1998).

23. *See* Robert D. Kenney, *Right Whales and Climate Change: Facing the Prospect of a Greenhouse Future*, in Kraus and Rolland, *supra* note 19, at 448.

24. *See* Virginia Gascon and Rodolfo Werner, *CCAMLR and Antarctic Krill: Ecosystem Management Around the Great White Continent*, 7 SUST. DEVE. L. & POL'Y 14 (2003) (citing Stephen Nichol and Jacqueline Foster, *Recent Trends in the Fishery for Antarctic Krill*, AQUATIC LIVING RESOURCES, Aug. 13, 1999, at 107, and Angus Atkinson *et al.*, *Long-term Decline in Krill Stock and Increase in Salps Within the Southern Ocean*, 432 NATURE 100, 103 (2004)).

25. *See generally* Burns, *supra* note 6.

26. For example, the frontal zones in the Antarctic where krill are abundant are likely to move as the sea-ice coverage declines with warming seas. This will affect all baleen whale species in the Antarctic including humpback, blue, fin and minke whales. Cynthia T. Tynan and Joellen L. Russell, *Assessing the Impacts of Future 2°C Global Warming on Southern Ocean Cetaceans*, a paper presented to the IWC Scientific Committee, Document SC/60/E3 (2008).

27. *Id.* Despite the increasing certainty that surrounds the latest predictions of climate change, it is difficult to assess the global impacts of climate change on cetaceans. The scientific evidence indicates that climate change is likely to decrease or restrict the preferred habitat of all cetacean species listed as threatened on the

Acidification may make some species less abundant, especially the invertebrates that whales and other marine life consume. Like the reef-building corals that use carbonate to build their colonies, these prey species may find fewer carbonate ions with which to build their shells as the oceans absorb more and more carbon dioxide from the atmosphere and ocean pH rises.[28] This reduced availability of carbonate will be especially pronounced in the cold Arctic and Antarctic waters where many cetaceans live.[29] Beaked and sperm whales may find fewer squids as those species decline in acidified oceans.[30]

Climate change is especially challenging for whale species that are already at greatly reduced population levels.[31] *Calanus*, the right whale's prey, is swept into the Gulf of Maine from sub-polar regions because of the particular interplay of atmospheric and hydrologic conditions of the North Atlantic.[32] If these conditions change as is predicted with ocean warming and the melting of polar ice, the abundance and distribution of this zooplankton is likely to change as well. Scientists predict that *Calanus* will survive global warming.[33] But the ability of right whales, with such low population numbers, to find *Calanus* in concentrations adequate to support reproduction is in serious doubt.[34] Similarly, the blue whale (*Balaenoptera musculus*), reduced from a population of roughly half a million in 1900 to less than 5,000 today, may not be able to survive a reduction in Antarctic krill.[35]

The ability of cetaceans to adapt to warming-induced changes in the ocean may depend on whether we can improve the quality of their environments and thus enhance their resilience. This

---

IUCN Red List for which projections can be made. Because the polar regions are changing most rapidly, it is here that whales may experience the greatest impacts. For example, in the Southern Ocean, under a scenario of a 2°C warming, sea ice could be decreased by 10–15% with regional losses of up to 30%. The loss of sea ice will affect the extent and distribution of habitat of species like the Antarctic minke whale. With this level of ice loss, the remaining populations could be crowded into the remaining suitable sea-ice habitat, competing with other marine wildlife for food and space leading to further reductions in the availability of prey and in the size of these wildlife populations. Loss of the sea ice would also reduce the availability of Antarctic krill, *Euphasia superba*, the principal prey species for whales in the Southern Ocean. Loss of sea ice adversely affects krill in two ways: it can reduce the amount of its preferred habitat and the availability of its preferred food. A loss of up to 25% will increase by a corresponding amount the area of open ocean and of phytoplankton blooms, and greater blooms may lead to changes in the ecology of phytoplankton, reducing the amount of the large diatoms that krill like to eat and increasing the species (cryptophyes) that they do not.

28. *See* John Raven *et al.*, *Ocean Acidification Due to Increasing Atmospheric Carbon Dioxide*, Report of The Royal Society, London, UK, Policy Doct 12/05 (2008). *See also* WENDY ELLIOTT AND MARK SIMMONDS, WHALES IN HOT WATER? THE IMPACT OF A CHANGING CLIMATE ON WHALES, DOLPHINS, AND PORPOISES: A CALL FOR ACTION, WWF-International, Gland, Switzerland (2007), *available at* http://www.panda.org/species/.

29. ELLIOTT AND SIMONDS, *supra* note 28, at 5.

30. *Id.* at 10.

31. Again, the plight of the North Atlantic right whale illustrates the synergistic impacts of the transitory environmental change and climate change. Deaths from ship strikes and entanglement in fishing gear exceed the population growth rate and increase the likelihood of the species' extinction. If mortality from these sources stays at current levels or increases, mother whales will not be able to explore for and find the new places and timing of blooms of their zooplankton prey and pass on the knowledge of new feeding areas to their young. Charles H. Greene and Andrew J. Pershing, *Climate and the Conservation Biology of North Atlantic Right Whales: The Right Whale at the Wrong Time?* 2 FRONTIERS IN ECOL. & ENVT. 29 (2004).

32. *Id.*

33. Jim Provan *et al.*, *High Dispersal Potential Has Maintained Long-Term Population Stability in the North Atlantic Copepod* Calanus finmarchicus, PROC. R. SOC. B (2008), published online 23 Sept 2008 (*Calanus* has enough genetic diversity to be able to adapt).

34. *See* Kenney, *supra* note 23, at 453 (eliminating mortality from these immediate anthropomorphic threats will increase the number of mother-and-calf pairs that may stray into areas where they will encounter the new locations of *Calanus* and learn how to find them again).

35. Elliott and Simmonds, *supra* note 28, at 10.

requires that we use our governance institutions to reduce human-caused mortality from pollution, ship strikes, fishing gear entanglement, and ocean noise, and the reduced health of individuals and populations that these conditions can lead to.[36] Global, regional and national institutions that govern fisheries must take seriously the emerging norms requiring precaution and an
ecosystem approach. Merely paying them lip service through non-binding resolutions and action
plans will not be enough.[37] Unfortunately, while many cetacean species face increasing urbanization of the coastal and offshore waters they utilize for migration and calving, the willingness of
shipping, fishing and other marine industries and the military to alter their practices to reduce
these threats is not keeping pace, and institutions are not changing fast enough to require them to
do so.[38]

This institutional failure is particularly apparent with respect to marine fisheries. While the
oceans are being urbanized by a host of other industries,[39] fishing fleets have functioned as "roving bandits," responding to global markets and seafood demand with sequential depletion of virtually all marine resources, starting with the large predatory fish and moving down through the
marine food web to lower and lower trophic levels.[40] Because many nations and international
management bodies have not managed industrial fisheries effectively, fish populations around
the world have been depleted.[41] Collectively, we have removed both large quantities of fish and
entire trophic levels.[42]

The great whales were the first species to fall victim to the 'roving bandits' phenomenon,
and the IWC was the first ineffective fishery management body.[43] Member states used the IWC
as a whalers' club rather than a mechanism to constrain their factory whaling fleets and pro-

36. *See* Tynan and Russell, *supra* note 26.

37. Currie, *supra* note 9.

38. *See, e.g.*, Robbie Brown, *U.S. Requires Ships to Cut Speed in Waters Used by Right Whales*, New York
Times (Oct. 10, 2008). The final regulations setting speed limits on merchant shipping to and from U.S. ports
when right whales are present were published in late 2008. NOAA, Final Rule to Implement Speed Restrictions to Reduce the Threat of Ship Collisions with North Atlantic Right Whales, 73 Fed. Reg. 60173 (Oct. 10,
2008). The U.S. Navy's opposition to court-imposed restrictions on the use of sonar in military exercises to
prevent damage to whales was vindicated by the U.S. Supreme Court in Winter v. NRDC, 555 US ____, 129
S.Ct. 365 (2008) (invalidating lower court injunction imposing mitigation measures on Navy sonar exercises
to protect whales for giving inadequate weight to military readiness needs).

39. *See, e.g.*, Rachael E. Salcido, *Offshore Federalism and Ocean Industrialization*, 82 Tulane L. Rev. 1355
(2008).

40. F. Berkes *et al.*, *Globalization, Roving Bandits and Marine Resources*, 311 Science 1557 (2006).

41. The United Nations' Food and Agriculture Organization (FAO) estimates that in 2005, 25% of the
world's marine fisheries (the ones that rely on capturing wild stocks) were overexploited, depleted, or recovering from depletion; 52% were fully exploited; 20% were moderately exploited; and 3% were underexploited.
UN Food and Agriculture Organization, Status of World Fisheries and Aquaculture in 2005
(2006), *available at* http://www.fao.org.

42. Ransom A. Myers and Boris Worm, *Rapid Worldwide Depletion of Predatory Fish Communities*, 423
Nature 280 (2003) (in a fifteen-year period following World War II, industrialized fisheries removed 80–90%
of large predatory fish communities across a wide range of ecosystems). Many marine ecosystems have experienced a decline in the average trophic level of fish catches over the past 50 years, a sign that "fishing down marine food webs" is occurring. Pauly *et al.*, *supra* note 22.

43. The history of the IWC's management of the whaling industry has been recounted and analyzed from
various perspectives. *See, e.g.*, Patricia Birnie, International Regulation of Whaling: From Conservation of Whaling to Conservation of Whales and Regulation of Whale-Watching (1985); Phillip J.
Clapham *et al.*, *Modern whaling, in* Encyclopedia of Marine Mammals 1328–1332 (William F. Perrin *et al.*,
eds., Academic Press 2002); Michael Heazle, *Scientific Uncertainty and the International Whaling Commission:
An Alternative Perspective on the Use of Science in Policy Making*, 28 Marine Policy 361 (2004). *See also* Cinnamon P. Carlarne, *Saving the Whales in the New Millenium: International Institutions, Recent Developments
and the Future of International Politics*, 24 Va. Envtl L.J..1 (2005–06) (the IWC has undergone a normative
transition from a "whalers" club to an agent of conservation).

tect whale populations as called for in the whaling treaty. Acting together through the IWC, these fishing states set a precedent for international neglect in managing industrial fisheries that continues to this day at virtually all international fisheries bodies, a pattern of disregarding scientific evidence that catch rates are unsustainable and affording the industrial fishing sector a degree of political access and success disproportionate to its economic and social value.[44]

Even if commercial whaling does not recommence, whales will continue to be affected by roving bandit fishing fleets through their serial depletion of marine wildlife and the resulting ecological impacts that render ecosystems less resilient in the face of ocean warming.[45] To protect whales and other marine life from this fate, ocean governance institutions must begin to focus on the impact of ocean warming on whales' habitat and prey, to ratchet down fishing pressure on ecosystems, and to prevent new fisheries from developing that will compound the ecological challenges.

New fisheries for prey species that are critical to the functioning of marine food webs and ecosystems should be subject to the most precautionary and ecosystem-based approach. Krill and copepod harvesting, for example, are already increasing with the development of new technologies and new products.[46] These methods allow for the continuous extraction and near-simultaneous processing by very large fishing trawlers built by companies that manufacture feeds for aquaculture as well as products for the burgeoning consumer health products market.[47] As these new industries grow, the demands placed upon the oceans will grow even greater, just as whales need to adapt to the reduced abundance and changing spatial distribution brought about by ocean warming.[48] Fisheries for species that are prey for whales and other marine predators (*e.g.*, seabirds, sharks, and polar bears) are especially in need of a new norm for management, one based on estimates of the health of the entire ecosystem and not just the size of the exploitable biomass of the prey species.

II. New Ocean Governance Norms and the International Whaling Regime

Given the realities of a warming ocean and its projected ecological impacts, how likely are ocean governance bodies to break with past practice and begin to apply precaution- and ecosystem-based approaches to their mandates? More specifically, would resolution of the commercial whaling stalemate free the IWC to promote ecosystem-based management of fisheries and other ocean industries to improve the prospects for cetaceans? To consider this question we take a closer look at the ecological arguments that have been made in the context of the whaling stalemate including the rationale that pro-whaling member States give for seeking a resumption of whaling.[49] This shows, unfortunately, that the IWC's current characterization of the "ecosystem approach" is widely divergent from the emerging norm in international environmental law. It is therefore difficult to envision the IWC regime as an effective ambassador for cetaceans and their ecological requirements in other international governance bodies espe-

---

44. *See, e.g.*, Safina and Klinger, *supra* note 13; Carl Safina, *Bluefin Tuna in the West Atlantic: Negligent Management and the Making of an Endangered Species*, 7 CONS. BIOL. 229, 234 (2007).

45. For a discussion of the cumulative effects of human activities on the oceans, see Christian Nellerman *et al.*, *In Dead Water: Merging of Climate Change with Pollution, Over-Harvest, and Infestations in the World's Fishing Grounds*, UN Environment Program and GRID-Arendal (2008), *available at* http://www.unep.org/pdf/InDeadWater_LR.pdf.

46. *See* Nichols and Foster, *supra* note 24.

47. Gascon and Werner, *supra* note 24, at 16. *See also* text at notes 108–112, *infra*. Aker BioMarine, the company operating the new vessel technology in Atlantic sector of the Southern Ocean, has applied for eco-labeling certification from the Marine Stewardship Council. Marine Stewardship Council, *Antarctic Krill Fishery Enters Full Assessment*, Press Release (10 October 2008), *available at* http://www.msc.org/.

48. *See* discussion, *supra* at notes 24–27.

49. *See* discussion, *infra* at notes 82–84.

cially those involving fisheries. In management decisions for the growing Antarctic krill fishery, for example, if the IWC's contribution reflects the whaling regime's view of the ecosystem approach this will lay a very poor foundation for governing fisheries and other activities in the Southern Ocean.

A. The Law of the Sea and the Emerging Norms of Precaution and Ecosystem-Based Management

The Law of the Sea Convention created a new framework for ocean governance that sought to balance the interests of coastal States with broader community interests in the utilization of ocean space and resources.[50] Although it was negotiated before there was widespread recognition of climate change and the need for a precautionary, ecosystem approach, instruments negotiated since the Convention's entry into force adapt the Convention's framework principles to the current realities. The United Nations Fish Stocks Agreement of 1995, for example, acknowledges the limitations of the Convention's 'optimum use' paradigm for living marine resources. It codifies a precautionary approach in setting allowable catches and recognizes the impact of fishing on the health of the marine ecosystem.[51] Other instruments go even farther in making ecosystem health the central goal of international cooperation.[52]

Characterized as an 'implementing agreement' the 1995 Agreement directs nations that fish on the high seas to join and cooperate with regional ocean governance bodies. These bodies in turn must set fish conservation measures that take into account the needs of ecologically associated and dependent species and to protect the marine environment from adverse fishing impacts. The Agreement was the first international fisheries treaty to recognize the need to protect marine biological diversity.[53] It also borrowed some of the elements of the ecosystem approach to fisheries that was written into the fisheries treaty for the Southern Ocean under the Antarctic Treaty System known as CCAMLR.[54] Most notably, the 1995 Agreement broke with the standard risk-prone approach of single-species management to require a precautionary approach in limiting fisheries rates and biomass levels.[55]

---

50. United Nations Convention on the Law of the Sea, *opened for signature* Dec. 10, 1982, *entered into force* Nov. 16, 1994, 1833 U.N.T.S. 397, 21 I.L.M. 1261 [hereinafter UNCLOS].

51. Agreement for the Implementation of the Provisions of the United Nations Convention on the Law of the Sea of 10 December 1982 relating to the Conservation and Management of Straddling Fish Stocks and Highly Migratory Fish Stocks, entered into force Dec. 11, 2001, 34 I.L.M. 1542, *available at* http://www.un. org/Depts/los/convention_agreements/convention_overview_fish_stocks.htm. The 1995 Agreement fleshed out the obligations of fishing states with respect to certain high seas fish stocks. *See* Alison Rieser, *International Fisheries Law, Overfishing and Marine Biodiversity*, 9 GEO.INT. ENVTL. L. REV. 251 (1997). The UN Convention on the Law of the Sea guarantees the right of all nations to fish on the high seas (Article 116) as long as they cooperate in the conservation of fish, and it encourages coastal nations to make the fish stocks in their 200-mile EEZs available to foreign fishing fleets if the local population does not have the capacity to harvest the entire surplus of fish, determined in the process of setting total allowable catch levels (Articles 61, 62). The coastal nation has a duty to ensure "optimum utilization" of the fish stocks in its EEZ. States that fish on the high seas have a duty to cooperate in taking measures to ensure the conservation of high seas fish stocks that are highly migratory or that straddle the high seas and the EEZ. UNCLOS, *supra* note 50.

52. *See generally* Currie, *supra* note 9.

53. Rieser, *supra* note 51.

54. Gascon and Werner, *supra* note 24, at 14. CCAMLR Article II(c) and IX(2)(i), Convention on the Conservation of Antarctic Marine Living Resources, done at Canberra, May 20, 1980, entered into force April 7, 1982. Text *available online at* http://www.ccamlr.org/. Its members include Argentina, Australia, Belgium, Brazil, Chile, European Community, France, Germany, India, Italy, Japan, Republic of Korea, New Zealand, Norway, Poland, Russia, South Africa, Spain, Sweden, Ukraine, United Kingdom, United States, and Uruguay.

55. *See* Rieser, *supra* note 51. With respect to marine mammals, however, the Law of the Sea Convention does more than require international cooperation and precautionary management. It states that marine mammals are not subject to the principle of 'optimum utilization' and coastal nations, which have sovereign rights over marine mammals within their waters, are free to fully protect the whales in their EEZs and territorial wa-

While generally-agreed upon guidelines for implementing an ecosystem-based management of marine systems are lacking, there is consensus that the approach contains a number of elements that are not common in conventional fisheries management. Under an ecosystem approach, management is based on the properties of the relevant ecosystem rather than on the population dynamics of a single target species. Rather than "maximum sustainable yield" the goal of the ecosystem approach is to maintain the structure and function of ecosystems including their biodiversity and value as habitat.[56] In exploiting a fish species, measures are adopted to prevent fishing from adversely affecting populations of multiple species and their trophic interactions including predator-prey relationships. In addition to CCAMLR, the ecosystem approach is reflected in a number of multilateral environmental agreements, including the 1992 Convention on Biological Diversity, the Rio Declaration and Agenda 21, the Madrid Protocol, and the Convention on Migratory Species.[57]

Despite the normative advances of the 1995 U.N. Fish Stocks Agreement, the regional fisheries bodies have been very slow to adopt the new approaches, and fisheries managers have not yet developed widely agreed-upon guidelines.[58] Even CCAMLR, with its explicit ecosystem objective and management boundary (based on the Antarctic Convergence), is making very limited progress, especially in the ecologically significant krill fishery.[59]

B. The Impact of the Whaling Regime Stalemate on the Ecosystem Approach

As many commentators have noted, the mission and majority changed at the IWC in the early 1980s.[60] Long considered a whalers' club, it had seemingly presided over the demise of one whale stock after another. After the Stockholm conference on the environment (UNCED) in 1972 at which a nearly unanimous vote supported a global moratorium on whaling, the IWC began to entertain resolutions reducing the catch limits to zero. Several zero quotas were adopted as whale stocks fell to levels approaching extinction. The United States delegation, spurred on by environmental groups and the congressional policies of the Marine Mammal Protection Act of 1972, began introducing resolutions and campaigning for a total cessation of all whaling.[61] In 1974, the U.S. reluctantly accepted the Australian government's proposal that instead of a global moratorium, the IWC adopt a New Management Procedure, under which quotas would be set on a species-specific basis and would be driven by science rather than by the demands of the whaling industries of member states.

After several years in which new members were encouraged to join the IWC in order to support the moratorium, enough votes were present to achieve the three-fourths majority needed. In 1982 the IWC member states adopted a moratorium on all commercial whaling (in the form

---

ters. UNCLOS, Article 65. On the high seas, nations are obliged to cooperate through international bodies for the study, conservation and management of marine mammals. Again, they are free not to use the optimum utilization norm but to adopt a regime of total protection. UNCLOS, Article 64, 120. These last two provisions do not necessarily require that nations act through the International Whaling Commission; they could cooperate through another body, either existing or one that they bring into being through another instrument. *See* William T. Burke, *A New Whaling Agreement and International Law*, in Robert L. Friedheim, ed., Toward a Sustainable Whaling Regime (2001), at 75.

56. *See, e.g.,* Ellen K. Pikitch *et al.*, *Ecosystem-Based Fishery Management*, 306 Science 346 (2004).

57. *See generally* Duncan Currie, Ecosystem-Based Management in Multilateral Environmental Agreements: Progress Toward Adopting the Ecosystem Approach in the International Management of Living Marine Resources (March 2007), *available online at* http://www.globelaw.com/LawSea/Whales/Whales.html.

58. Anna Willock and Mary Lack, *Follow the Leader: Learning from Experience and Best Practice in Regional Fisheries Management Organizations*, a report by WWF and TRAFFIC International (2006), *available online at* http://assets.panda.org/downloads/rfmoreport06.pdf.

59. *See* Gascon and Werner, *supra* note 24, at 15.

60. For an extended examination of the changing role of the IWC, see Friedheim, *supra* note 55.

61. Hogarth, *supra* note 7.

of a zero catch quota for all whale species), effective in the 1986–87 season. Although several countries immediately announced an objection to the resolution, all but Norway were persuaded to withdraw their objections.[62]

Japan was persuaded by the U.S. to withdraw its objection through an agreement with the U.S. Department of Commerce.[63] That same year, however, Japan announced that it was beginning a program of scientific research that would require lethal takes of whales in the North Pacific and in the Antarctic.[64] This program provided a means of getting around the moratorium, using the chief rationale for the moratorium as justification: uncertainty surrounding estimates of whale population levels makes it difficult to regulate their hunting effectively.[65] Japan's research would improve the understanding of certain cetacean species' population dynamics so that sustainable catch limits could be defined. The improved information could be used by the IWC in the Revised Management Procedure which its Scientific Committee developed in order to set precautionary catch limits, and which the IWC formally adopted in 1994.[66]

Rejecting this justification and its premise, the U.S. and other IWC member states have consistently opposed the scientific whaling programs but have had little recourse under the terms of the ICRW.[67] The U.S. threatened to levy trade sanctions during the Clinton Administration but these measures were never invoked.[68] As Japan has grown increasingly frustrated by the IWC's failure to adopt the Revised Management Scheme and lift the commercial whaling moratorium,

---

62. Sean Murphy, *U.S. Sanctions Against Japan for Whaling*, 95 AMER J. INTL L. 149, 150 (2001). *See also* Carlarne, *supra* note 4, at 39–40.

63. *Id.* In exchange for its withdrawal, the Executive Branch would abstain from certifying Japan as a country whose actions undermined the decisions of international conservation bodies, potentially triggering an embargo on imports from Japan and the revocation of Japan's access to fishing in U.S. waters. After the U.S. Supreme Court upheld the agreement, Japan Whaling Ass'n v. American Cetacean Soc'y, 478 U.S. 221 (1986), Japan withdrew the objection, thereby relinquishing the right of its nationals to engage in commercial whaling. *See also* Howard S. Schiffman, *The International Whaling Commission: Challenges From Within and Without*, 10 ILSA J. INT'L & COMP. L. 367 (2003).

64. Article VIII of the ICRW allows State parties to issue special permits to their nationals to take whales for research purposes regardless of whether the cetacean species to be taken are subject to a zero commercial catch quota. *See* Walter K. de la Mare, *Problems of "scientific whaling,"* 345 NATURE 771 (1990); Dennis Normile, *Japan's Whaling Program Carries Heavy Baggage*, 289 SCIENCE 2264 (2000). Descriptions of Japan's plans for whaling under Article VIII, and the response of various national delegations, are contained in the reports of the IWC Standing Working Group on Scientific Permits, *available at* http://www.iwcoffice.org/_documents/sci_com/.

65. This rationale has been criticized by a number of scientists who work with the IWC's Scientific Committee. Clapham, *supra* note 12, at 314. *See also* Clapham et al., *Whaling as Science*, 53 BIOSCIENCE 210 (2003). Nevertheless, Japan has conducted continuous programs of 'scientific whaling' since shortly after the zero-quota moratorium went into effect in 1986. At almost every annual meeting of the IWC, Japan introduces a resolution to lift the moratorium and to set one or more commercial catch quotas. *See* Carlarne, *supra* note 4, at 3.

66. Carlarne, *supra* note 4, at 15.

67. ICRW Article VIII allows a contracting party to issue itself a special permit to take whales for scientific purposes. The Japanese government authorizes Japan-flagged whaling vessels under arrangements with the Institute for Cetacean Research to hunt for whales and to sell the whale meat once the samples are taken for analysis. Other features of the ICRW that contribute to the current stalemate include the requirement of a three-quarters majority for schedule amendments, the opting-out provision, the absence of a dispute settlement procedure, the absence of an independent scientific advisory body (members of the Scientific Committee represent member states rather than independent scientific institutions), the open membership, and the absence of a mechanism for amending the Convention. Together these provisions result in a "governance gap." Currie, *supra* note 9, at 48–52.

68. Murphy, *supra* note 62, at 152.

it has expanded the scope of its research whaling program in both the number and species of whales permitted to be killed.[69]

The reluctance of some anti-whaling states to sanction Japan for its scientific whaling program is likely due at least in part to the fear that Japan will withdraw from the IWC and abrogate the treaty, creating its own management body to set quotas for whaling.[70] Other observers take the view that Japan has more to lose than to gain by withdrawing from the Commission. Nevertheless, the commitment of the government of Japan to bringing about the resumption of commercial whaling is impressive in the face of such consistent opposition and disapproval. This is especially so given that Japan's whaling industry has never been and is unlikely to become a major contributor to the Japanese economy.[71]

Japan's determination to overturn the whaling moratorium and restore commercial whaling under the international regime is best understood when considered in the larger context of global fisheries and the emerging norms for their management. The government of Japan views the whaling moratorium as a bad precedent that if emulated by other regional fisheries organizations or governance bodies would threaten Japan's access to marine resources around the world.[72] Japan was one of the larger fishing states forced to stop large-scale high seas driftnet fishing under a U.N. General Assembly resolution and pressure from the US and other countries.[73] Supporters of the driftnet fishing moratorium justified it on the basis of the precautionary principle.[74] The driftnets' adverse ecological impacts were also used to support the ban despite the limited data then available on the ecological or species-population level impacts. Experience with this manifestation of the precautionary approach to fisheries has likely left Japan's fishery officials with a dim view of the benefits Japan would derive from broader application of the principle especially in the management of the lucrative international tuna fisheries.[75]

---

69. David Cyranoski, *Whaling Divisions Deepen as Japan Pushes for Credibility*, 435 NATURE 861(2005); Nicholas J. Gales, *et al.*, *Japan's Whaling Plan Under Scrutiny*, 435 NATURE 883 (2005).

70. Mike Iliff, *The International Whaling Regime post 2007*, 32 MARINE POLICY 522, 524 (2008). Under Article XI of the ICRW, for Japan to withdraw from the IWC, it would have to formally notify the United States, as the depository government for the ICRW, of its intentions by January 1 of the year of its withdrawal and that by June 30 it no longer intends to be bound by the Convention. *Id.* The Government of Iceland withdrew from the IWC in 1992 after the IWC voted not to lift the moratorium after its first ten years. It then entered into an agreement creating the North Atlantic Marine Mammal Commission with Denmark, Norway, the Faroe Islands and Greenland. Iceland "rejoined" in 2002 after a special meeting vote allowing Iceland to "readhere" to the ICRW with a reservation on the moratorium after 2006. *Id.*

71. For a range of views on Japan's reasons, see, *e.g.*, Amy L. Catalinac and Gerald Chan, *Japan, the West, and the Whaling Issue: Understanding the Japanese Side*, 17 JAPAN FORUM 133 (2005); Mike Danaher, *Why Japan Will Not Give Up Whaling*, 14 PACIFICA REVIEW 105 (2002); Sidney J. Holt, *Whaling: Will the Phoenix Rise Again?*, 54 MAR POLL. BULL. 1081 (2007). Holt argues that the only logical explanation for the Japanese government's actions is its firm commitment to have large-scale and profitable whaling in the distant future, allowing it to exploit its monopoly position in factory-ship whaling. *Id.* at 1084. Holt asserts that Japan increased the number and species in its scientific whaling program in the North Pacific to include large baleen whales in order to increase the pelagic whaling fleet's profitability so the government could reduce its subsidy. Sidney J. Holt, *Propaganda and Pretext*, 52 MAR. POLL. BULL. 363, 365 (2006).

72. Clapham *et al.*, *supra* note 12, at 318.

73. Large-Scale Pelagic Driftnet Fishing and Its Impact on the Living Marine Resources of the World's Oceans and Seas, U.N. G.A. Res. 44/225, 29 I.L.M. 1555 (1990).

74. *See, e.g.*, James Carr and Matthew Gianni, *High Seas Fisheries, Large-Scale Drift Nets, and the Law of the Sea*, in JON M. VAN DYKE, DURWOOD ZAELKE, AND GRANT HEWISON, FREEDOM FOR THE SEAS IN THE 21ST CENTURY 272 (Island Press 1993); Virginia M. Walsh, *Eliminating Driftnets from the North Pacific Ocean: U.S.-Japanese Cooperation in the International North Pacific Fisheries Commission*, 29 OCEAN DEVT. & INT'L L. 295 (1998).

75. *See, e.g.*, Kazuo Sumi, *The International Legal Issues Concerning the Use of Drift Nets, with Special Emphasis on Japanese Practices and Responses*, in JON M. VAN DYKE, DURWOOD ZAELKE, AND GRANT HEWISON, FREEDOM FOR THE SEAS IN THE 21ST CENTURY 272, 292 (Island Press 1993).

To hold the line on what it views as overly restrictive ocean governance norms that compete for legitimacy with the sustainable use principle, the government of Japan appears committed to restoring its commercial whaling industry. Some long-time observers of the whaling regime are convinced that Japan's long-range plan is to work with other member states to build the three-fourths majority necessary to lift the zero-catch quota provision that effectuates the moratorium and put in place the Revised Management Scheme that will be the basis for setting catch quotas.[76] Japan's goal is to keep the IWC focused on setting quotas for whaling. This narrow focus on the IWC as a bulwark against excessively conservation-oriented fisheries governance also helps explain why Japan's delegation has opposed efforts to expand the agenda of the IWC to include conservation issues and the effects of climate change.[77]

Most assessments of the state of fisheries take a very different view of current ocean governance regimes and attribute declining fish catches to overfishing and inadequate management of fisheries under the sustainable use paradigm.[78] Ocean diplomacy has begun to focus on reforming the regional management bodies through which member states coordinate their conservation and management of high seas fisheries. With increasing frequency, parties to multilateral agreements are expressing the view that fisheries can adversely affect marine biological diversity, including resolutions by parties to the Convention on Biological Diversity.[79] International trade is threatening some fish species with extinction either through directed fisheries or from incidental catch in industrial fisheries.[80] The consensus appears to be that ocean governance needs to be more, not less, precautionary and ecosystem-based.[81]

In contrast, Japanese delegates at the IWC and Japan's representatives on the IWC's Scientific Committee have suggested that depressed fish stocks may be a sign that recovering whale populations are taking the fish.[82] Japan and other pro-whaling states argue that it may be necessary to cull top predators to reduce their take of species that are needed for human consumption and food security, citing the drastic declines in world fisheries to advance a new rationale for commercial whaling. According to this view, whales eat fish from coastal waters where people would otherwise fish, leading to an imbalance in some marine ecosystems. In order to restore fish populations and ensure the food security of coastal nations, cetaceans should be hunted to reduce their numbers and thus make whales' prey species available to fish which can then be available for human consumption.[83]

Proponents of this view present it as the scientific rationale for the pro-whaling resolutions at the IWC. They argue that the opposition's insistence on maintaining the moratorium is a case of emotional attachment to whales blinding one's ecological and scientific judgment. This argument is disturbing to some fishery scientists as it seems to attribute the overexploitation of the

---

76. Holt, *supra* note 71, at 365.
77. *See generally* Iliff, *supra* note 70.
78. Holt *supra* note 71, at 365.
79. Currie, *supra* note 57, at 40–42.
80. Currie, *supra* note 57, at 46.
81. *See generally* Willock and Lack, *supra* note 58.
82. Clapham, *supra* note 12, at 315.
83. Wilf Swartz and Daniel Pauly, Who's Eating All the Fish? The Food Security Rationale for Culling Cetaceans, A Report to The Humane Society International, presented at the 60th Annual Meeting of the IWC, June 23, 2008, Santiago, Chile, *available at* http://www.hsus.org/web-files/PDF/hsi/daniel-pauly-paper-iwc-2008-pdf-doc.pdf, citing J. Morishita and D. Goodman, *Competition between fisheries and marine mammals: feeding marine mammals at the expense of food for humans*, in Proceedings of the Third World Fisheries Congress, Feeding the World with Fish in the Next Millenium— The Balance between Production and Environment 403–408 (B. Phillips, B. Megrey, and Z. Yingqi eds., American Fisheries Society, Symposium 38, Bethesda, MD, 2003).

world's fishery resources to marine mammals instead of to human fisheries.[84] This theory has emerged from scientific papers resulting from the Japanese program of Article VII whaling.

More than just a variation on the sustainable use argument used in the past, this view has a more sinister aspect, conveying as it does an over-simplification of our understanding of marine ecosystems and a likely deliberate distortion of the scientific evidence in order to advance the "sustainable whaling" agenda.[85] Some of the new members of the IWC recruited from the ranks of developing nations to support this view include small-island and coastal states from the Caribbean, West Africa and the Pacific. These states have concerns for the viability of their tuna and coastal fish stocks, the economic prospects of their domestic fishing industries and the food security of their citizens.[86] Misunderstanding the reasons behind these stocks' condition makes them even more vulnerable to changes brought by warming oceans.

The "whales-are-eating-our-fish" argument fails to explain why historically there were both higher fish biomass and marine mammal populations.[87] Moreover, there is often very little overlap between the food preferences of cetaceans and of commercial fisheries, nor do they overlap spatially. Most great whales, for example, feed in high latitude places for species that are not accessible to fishing gear and are not desirable for human consumption.[88]

This alternative view of the ecosystem approach reached its high water mark at the IWC in 2006. At the annual meeting that year, the Commission adopted a resolution acknowledging that ecosystem-based management is the new international standard and that whale stocks must be considered in a broader ecological context. But in a logic that appears to turn the ecosystem approach on its head, the resolution suggests that whales may need to be culled in order to ensure food security.[89] Or at the very least, nations should continue "scientific whaling" until such time as the ecological role of whales in fishery ecosystems is clarified.[90]

---

84. Swartz and Pauly, *supra* note 83, at 7.

85. *Id.* at 9–10.

86. *Id.* In an essay reprinted in the report's appendix, Daniel Pauly describes the chagrin expressed by members of the parliament of Senegal, when at a workshop on the issue, national fishery officials expressed the whales-eat-our-fish rationale. Pauly reports that the members said those views were contrary to the information they received from fishers in their communities on the causes of the decline of coastal fisheries and was also contrary to the nation's cultural admiration for cetaceans. DANIEL PAULY, WORRYING ABOUT WHALES INSTEAD OF MANAGING FISHERIES: A PERSONAL ACCOUNT OF A MEETING IN SENEGAL. *Id.* at 29–30.

87. It is likely that the historically large whale populations were in part responsible for the massive fish populations. Whales, if they eat fish at all, eat tiny, larval stages of fish, in addition to zooplankton and phytoplankton. This may have had the evolutionary effect of pushing fish populations to evolve into fast growing short-lived (high-fecundity) animals that could grow fast and avoid being eaten. Swartz and Pauly, *supra* note 83, at 6. This effect has been reversed by fisheries, which have targeted larger fish and thus exerted selective pressure on fish to grow slowly and mature later with lower productivity. *Id.*

88. *Id.* at 9.

89. This is despite the fact that several scientific studies dispute the value of culling to increase fish stocks. *See, e.g.*, Peter Yodzis, *Must top predators be culled for the sake of fisheries?* 16 TRENDS IN ECOLOGY & EVOL. 78 (2001); Peter Corkeron, *Fishery management and culling*, 306 SCIENCE 1891 (2004). Corkeron reports that the Norwegian Parliament, in May 2004, endorsed a new national policy for marine resources that would establish an ecosystem-based management regime for marine mammals in Norway's marine waters. In order to increase fisheries production, this policy will presumably be translated into larger quotas for the hunting of minke whales, harp seals and coastal seals in the sub-Arctic and Arctic waters in Norway's exclusive economic zone to reduce these populations' 'competition' with man for fish. *Id.*

90. A group of Caribbean nations introduced the Declaration in a resolution after Japan's proposed resolutions to amend the Schedule to set quotas for its four coastal whaling communities for North Pacific minke, Bryde's and sperm whales were voted down. The resolution included the following statement:

ACCEPTING that scientific research has shown that whales consume huge quantities of fish making the issue a matter of food security for coastal nations and requiring that the issue of management of whale stocks must be considered in a broader context of ecosystem management since ecosystem management has now become an international standard.

This interpretation of the ecosystem approach makes no mention of the need for ocean governance bodies to reduce human fisheries to maintain predator diversity and the predator-prey relationships characterizing healthy marine ecosystems. Nor does it suggest it may be necessary to reserve portions of prey species biomass for whales as their populations recover and they adapt to climate change, rather than simply assuming that the maximum amount of exploitable biomass can be taken for human use. The IWC's ecosystem approach resolution, moreover, in no way advances any of the ecosystem health needs of cetaceans by urging action to prevent habitat degradation from pollution, lost or active fishing gear, noise, ship strikes and climate change.[91] It merely asserts the ecosystem approach as justification for returning the IWC to the task of setting catch quotas for whaling.[92]

The culling hypothesis now serves as the scientific rationale for the extensive whaling carried out in the Southern Ocean under a special permit issued by the Government of Japan.[93] Although the value of these investigations has been challenged publicly by leading cetacean scientists,[94] the international whaling regime has no mechanism to force it to be terminated.[95] But, the longer the scientific whaling program continues, the harder anti-whaling proponents fight to defend the moratorium. The longer the moratorium stays in place, the bigger and more audacious the scientific whaling program becomes, despite the weaknesses in its ecosystem-based rationale. Meanwhile, the ability of the IWC to address ecological and environmental challenges to whales is stymied by the impasse.

The IWC's whales and ecosystems resolution may ultimately have little impact on the whaling moratorium at the IWC or, if the moratorium is ever lifted, on the setting of sustainable catch quotas under the Revised Management Procedure. But the possibility that some member states may actually accept the premise of the ecosystem resolution does not bode well for progress by other regional fishery management bodies. To keep their fleets fishing, fishing nations frequently look for ecological reasons to explain declining fish stocks, such as a reduction in the environment's carrying capacity. As in the case of western Atlantic bluefin tuna, whenever a marginally plausible ecological explanation is found, states can rationalize putting off decisions to reduce the size and capacity of their industrial fishing fleets or maintaining high catch rates of top predators.[96] States with large distant-water fishing fleets need only find one scientist who is will-

---

Of the thirty-three countries that voted for the St. Kitts and Nevis Declaration, 14 are classified as low-income, food-deficient countries by the FAO. This is cited as evidence that the argument based on food security as well as the financial assistance offered to domestic fisheries by Japan has influenced the size of the pro-whaling faction. It has been noted that some of the same countries that expressed concern for food security in voting for the Declaration have not joined the regional fishery body that manages tuna and other fish stocks in their EEZs even though its membership fee is lower than the IWC's. Swartz and Pauly, *supra* note 83, at 12.

91. Currie, *supra* note 57, at 4 (in Exec. Summ.).

92. *Id.* Others have suggested that the declaration lays the groundwork for setting whale catch quotas in the Antarctic that are higher than would otherwise result from the Scientific Committee's application of the highly precautionary Revised Management Procedure. *See, e.g.,* David M. Lavigne and S. Fink, *Whales and Fisheries*, Pamphlet, International Fund for Animal Welfare (2001) 4, *available at* http://www.ifaw.org.

93. D. Normile, *Japan's Whaling Program Carries Heavy Baggage*, 289 Science 2264, 2265 (2000). Japan's Institute of Cetacean Research operates a factory-whaling fleet in the Antarctic and each year kills hundreds of whales so that their stomach contents can be analyzed to determine if they compete with humans for marine resources. Under this rationale, Japan's researchers added Bryde's and sperm whales to the scientific whaling program. *Id.*

94. *Id. See also* Clapham, *et al.*, *Whaling as Science*, 53 Bioscience 210 (2006).

95. Because the whaling is carried out under the special permit provision of Article VIII, Japan believes that the activities of its fleet are not bound to observe the regulations contained in the IWC's Schedule, including the Southern Ocean Sanctuary and the ban on factory whale ships. Normile, *supra* note 93.

96. *See* Safina and Klinger, *supra* note 13.

ing to express the view that recovering whales or some other ecological phenomenon may be responsible for the poor conditions of certain fish stocks.[97] Scientific uncertainty, presented at the time when precautionary action is most needed, has often given cover to management officials who give greater weight to short-term economics than long-term ecosystem health and sustainability.[98]

III. The IWC and Precautionary Management of the Antarctic Marine Ecosystem

The best rationale for retaining the whaling regime is its potential to influence other governance regimes on behalf of whales.[99] The question is whether in order to reach the agreement needed to permit the whaling regime to perform this function, it will be necessary to compromise on principles in a manner that would make the whaling regime ineffective or, worse, counterproductive. For example, the pro-whaling member states' interpretation of the ecosystem approach may continue to be based on the premise that "whales are eating our fish."[100] If so, the IWC's contribution to management of fisheries targeting prey species will undermine rather than enhance efforts to ensure that dependent and ecologically associated species are not adversely affected, as required by the 1995 U.N. Fish Stocks Agreement.[101] Instead of ensuring that catch quotas are set low enough to protect foraging grounds for whales, the participation of whaling states holding this interpretation of the ecosystem approach, could lead to higher quotas for prey, to "cull" whale predators indirectly by reducing their food sources.

Developments in the management of Antarctic krill suggest that these concerns are not merely academic. Japan and Norway, fishing states that promote the culling hypothesis at the IWC and elsewhere, are also major participants in the developing Antarctic krill fishery.[102] Krill is managed by the regional body known as CCAMLR, the Commission for the Conservation of Antarctic Marine Living Resources, a body that has a reputation for being the most ecosystem-based and precautionary of all international fisheries regimes.[103]

CCAMLR is well-regarded because its treaty was the first international agreement to build ecosystem and precautionary principles into its management regime, serving as the model for the innovative provisions of the 1995 U.N. Fish Stocks Agreement.[104] CCAMLR incorporates these principles because it was founded for the purpose of managing fishing for krill in the

---

97. *Id.*

98. *See generally* Andrew A. Rosenberg, *Managing to the Margins: The Overexploitation of Fisheries*, 1 Fronteirs of Ecol. Environ. 102 (2003).

99. *See* Burns, *supra* note 6, at 354. As a regime that failed to achieve its basic objective of ensuring a sustainable fishery, the IWC can serve as a cautionary tale for other governance regimes, providing testament to the need for setting catch limits that are truly precautionary; for not disregarding scientific advice; for requiring verifiable and timely reporting of all catch and other data, supported by an effective compliance and infractions program; and for a mechanism for resolving disagreements over treaty interpretation that does not rely on an objection or opt-out clause.

100. *See* discussion, *supra* at notes 85–90.

101. Article 5, U.N. Fish Stocks Agreement, *supra* note 51.

102. Stephen Nichol and Jacqueline Foster, *Recent Trends in the Fishery for Antarctic Krill*, 16 Aquat. Living Resour. 42 (2003); Andrew Darby, *Ecologists fear huge rise in krill catch*, Sydney Morn. Herald, Nov. 5, 2007, *available at* http://www.smh.com.au/.

103. Philip Bender, *The Precautionary Approach and Management of the Antarctic Krill*, 18 J. Envtl. L. 229 (2006); Gascon and Werner, *supra* note 24, at 14.

104. Gascon and Werner, *supra* note 24, at 14. Living resources management in the Southern Ocean, however, has a somewhat checkered history. A.J. Constable, *Sustainable Fisheries in a High Latitude*, paper presented at symposium of the Australian Academy of Technological Sciences and Engineering, November, 2001, *available at* http://www.atse.org.au/. Both cetaceans and seals were hunted heavily and the result was extirpation and near extinction for many species despite the adoption of international conservation agreements. The Agreement for the Conservation of Antarctic Seals was adopted as part of the Antarctic Treaty System, as was

Southern Ocean. With such an ecologically significant species as the target for the fisheries, the CCAMLR treaty adopted an ecological boundary for its management area and standards requiring fisheries to be controlled in order to maintain the ecological relationships between harvested, dependent and related populations of Antarctic marine resources.[105]

Despite CCAMLR's advantages, in the face of pressure to expand fishing opportunities, states with fisheries operating in the Southern Ocean have resisted precautionary management, preventing the regime from fulfilling the promise reflected in its treaty provisions.[106] Fishing pressure in the Southern Ocean is on the rise as the decline of fish stocks in the Northern Hemisphere has sent vessels south in search of unexploited species to replace them. The Patagonian toothfish (*Dissostichus eleginoides*) is the most well-known of these quarries, becoming the target of rampant illegal fishing by vessels registered by CCAMLR member states or by open-registry states that may or may not be cooperating with CCAMLR.[107]

Fishing companies are also searching for abundant marine species that can be converted into fish feed. The international fish-farming industry has grown tremendously as catches in capture fisheries have plummeted due to poor management.[108] This has led to intense interest in the Antarctic krill (*Euphausia superba*), the species at the center of the marine food web in the Antarctic, and a key prey species for baleen whales and for the fishes that are preyed on by toothed whales.[109]

Under its mandate to manage fisheries with precaution and on an ecosystem basis, CCAMLR has adopted several well-conceived provisions for the krill fishery. These include a more conservative total catch quota than the conventional maximum sustainable yield model produces, subdivided into smaller areas. For example, the quota for the area around the Antarctic Peninsula and the islands of South Orkney and South Georgia is capped at four million metric tons per season.[110] Because krill fishing vessels tend to concentrate in areas where land-based predators such as penguins and seals need to forage, CCAMLR also created 15 smaller units, allowing quotas to be fine-tuned to prevent localized depletion of krill during the nesting season.[111]

CCAMLR, *supra* note 54, and was negotiated by the Antarctic Treaty Consultative Parties after entry into force of the Antarctic Treaty in 1959. *Id.*

105. Articles I and II(3)(b), CCAMLR, *supra* note 54. The boundary of the Convention area reflects the ecological boundary formed by the Antarctic Convergence (a frontal zone where currents carrying cold Antarctic waters and the warmer sub-Antarctic waters meet). These farsighted provisions are likely due to the low level of fishing pressure at the time it was negotiated and the significant role played by the international scientific research community in creating the Antarctic Treaty System. Growth in the krill fishery was anticipated, however, and the potential for a massive krill fishery was viewed as a threat to the entire Antarctic marine ecosystem. *See* Constable, *supra* note 104. It is somewhat ironic that the precautionary management procedures and methods for assessing the potential yield of exploited whale populations developed by the IWC's Scientific Committee in the late 1970s and 1980s inspired CCAMLR's approach. *Id.*

106. CCAMLR, *supra* note 54. *See generally* Gascon and Werner, *supra* note 24.

107. *See* Philip Bender, *A State of Necessity: Illegal, Unregulated, and Unreported Fishing in the CCAMLR Zone,* 13 Ocean & Coastal L.J. 233 (2008). *See also* C. Bruce Knecht, Hooked: Pirates, Poaching And The Perfect Fish (Rodale Books 2006).

108. The United Nations Food and Agriculture Organization (FAO) predicts that world aquaculture production will increase significantly and is already responsible for over 70% of the increase in fish production, with China and southeast Asian countries becoming the largest producers. FAO, The State of World Fisheries and Aquaculture 2004, *available at* http://www.fao.org/.

109. *See* Bender, *supra* note 103, at 234.

110. *Id.*

111. CCAMLR agreed to subdivide the Southwest Atlantic area (Area 48) into 15 small-scale management units around the Antarctic Peninsula and the islands of South Orkney and South Georgia in 2002. If the fishery in a given season ever reaches a 620,000 ton level, under CCAMLR's measures this will trigger further subdividing the quota among the smaller areas, to protect penguin and seal rookeries that depend on the availability of abundant krill. CCAMLR Conservation Measure 32/XIX, *available at* CCAMLR's website, http://www.ccamlr.org. However, while CCAMLR has not be able to reach consensus on how to allocate the

To meet the growing interest in krill-based products, a diversified maritime company based in Norway has now developed a technology that allows one krill fishing vessel to take as much as 120,000 tons per trip, as much as has been taken by all krill-fishing vessels in an entire season using the old methods.[112] New vessels are being constructed to replace the older, less efficient ones. As this happens, CCAMLR parties seem less willing to apply the ecosystem and precautionary approaches to the krill fishery. Krill is the only CCAMLR-managed fishery that is exempt from the requirement to board scientific observers on the vessels, contrary to the advice from CCAMLR's scientific committee that such information is crucial. The krill-fishing states have also blocked adoption of recommendations to expand the monitoring program which is designed to detect whether ecologically-related species are being adversely affected by exploitation of the krill.[113] Krill-fishing states like Japan blocked consensus approval of the observer requirement at the 2008 meeting of CCAMLR, despite a commitment in 2007 to adopt the program the following year. Likewise, fishing states have blocked a management procedure that would adjust control measures in response to the ecosystem monitoring program.[114]

Shortly after the IWC adopted a standing committee to address conservation issues, it also directed its Scientific Committee to work with the CCAMLR on its ecosystem approach. This work includes providing CCAMLR with the scientific information it needs to construct a model of the Antarctic marine ecosystem and to better manage the krill fishery.[115] The best mathematical models in the world, however, cannot compensate for a lack of data, especially if the goal is to model the effects of exploiting one population on other species. The joint IWC-CCAMLR modeling effort is hindered by the krill fishing states' unwillingness to submit catch and other data to CCAMLR and to require that scientific observers be placed on krill vessels. By depriving the modelers of the information they need, these states are acting more to protect their companies' competitive advantage than to protect the Antarctic marine ecosystem.

Conclusion

Despite the apparent willingness of IWC member states to cooperate with CCAMLR's ecosystem-based management, some are at the same time using CCAMLR to block measures aimed at minimizing the indirect effects of fishing on cetaceans and other krill predators.[116] Considering this contradiction, it is not immediately apparent how reform of the IWC could help. The whaling negotiators could use Japan's desire to restore commercial whaling in non-Antarctic waters as leverage

---

krill catch limit among these areas, the krill fishery continues to grow, with new vessels being identified for participation every year. Gascon and Werner, *supra* note 24, at 15. The idea behind precautionary measures is to have them in place before the industrial fishery develops its expectations for future seasons. Until these precautionary measures to protect dependent species can be agreed to, the Antarctic and Southern Ocean Coalition (ASOC), the leading NGO participating in CCAMLR scientific and plenary meetings, has urged CCAMLR to freeze the expansion of the krill fishery in these critical areas until models can help determine the level of krill exploitation the system can tolerate and appropriate measures put in place. Bender, *supra* note 103, at 234. The ASOC papers submitted to CCAMLR are *available at* http://www.asoc.org/.

112. Gascon and Werner, *supra* note 24, at 14. *See also* Marine Stewardship Council, *supra* note 47.

113. The monitoring program is one of the measures upon which CCAMLR's reputation for strong ecosystem-based management is based. Previously, Commission members agreed to research on the status of ecologically related species and to make changes in conservation and management measures for fisheries if the evidence showed they were being adversely affected. Gascon and Werner, *supra* note 24, at 15.

114. The Antarctic and Southern Ocean Coalition, *International Antarctic Meeting Falls Short of Providing Needed Protection to Antarctic Marine Ecosystems under Threat*, Press Advisory, *available at* http://www.asoc.org (last visited Dec. 1, 2008). In 2006, parties agreed to require their vessels to have Vessel Monitoring Systems so that they could keep track of them during the fishing season. *Id.*

115. CCAMLR-IWC Workshop to Review Input Data for Antarctic Marine Ecosystem Models, SC/59/EM1, *available at* www.iwcoffice.org/sci_com/workshops/IWC-CCAMLRworkshop.htm.

116. *See* ASOC, *supra* note 114.

for reform of CCAMLR's krill management. This kind of cross-regime horse-trading is probably not uncommon, but if it does exist, there is little evidence that it results in anything but larger quotas. If the negotiated compromise allows the pro-whaling states minority to prevail in exchange for progress in krill regulation, the whole enterprise of international cooperation in marine ecosystem management would suffer a huge setback. This seems an unnecessarily high price, especially given that Japan's claims of right under the ICRW to its scientific whaling program has such a weak legal foundation.[117] It seems that international adjudication would be better suited to clarifying what the legal obligations are of parties to the whaling regime. If diplomacy to resolve the whaling regime stalemate can only succeed by compromising norms that were earned the hard way, diplomacy, in that case, really is "not working." Indeed it may be better to litigate than accommodate.[118]

Obviously, the best way that U.S. ocean diplomacy can serve the long-range interests of cetaceans is to adopt a serious program to combat global warming by rapidly transitioning to a non-carbon based energy economy.[119] In addition, the U.S. can redouble its efforts to ensure that standards for international shipping require the construction of quieter vessels that burn cleaner fuels and that slow down, especially where shipping lanes cross whale migration routes, avoiding whale foraging grounds altogether. It should set a global example by scaling down commercial fisheries that deploy and leave fishing gear in whale habitat and insist that international regimes require the same. If, in the meantime, the new U.S. administration taking office in 2009 wants to resolve the impasse over commercial whaling it must be cognizant of the normative impact of such action. Any reform must advance and not set back the advances of the last 15 years. The need for reform is much greater in other regimes; a regime for whaling that is very costly to reform is not worth the price. Greater effort at other international bodies to advance precautionary and ecosystem approaches will in the long run do more for whales in a warming ocean than a less acrimonious IWC.[120]

---

117. The International Fund for Animal Welfare asked a committee of independent legal experts to prepare a legal analysis of the scientific whaling issue, including its legality under the ICRW and other international law. The panel concluded that a legal challenge to the scientific whaling program would likely succeed at the International Court of Justice or the International Tribunal on the Law of the Sea (ITLOS) under the international law theory of abuse of rights and several international treaties, including the ICRW, UNCLOS and CCAMLR. Report of the International Panel of Independent Legal Experts On: Special Permit ("Scientific") Whaling Under International Law, Paris, May 12, 2006, *available at* http://www.ifaw.org/ (link on IFAW, Press Release, June 1, 2006). The panel members were Laurence Boisson de Chazournes, Pierre-Marie Dupuy, Donald R. Rothwell, Philippe Sands, Alberto Székely, William H. Taft IV, and Kate Cook. The Australian Government has been under pressure by NGOs to pursue such litigation. *See, e.g.,* Donald R. Rothwell, *Time to end loophole "scientific" whaling,* Cosmos Magazine (July 31, 2007).

118. After Australia and New Zealand challenged Japan's experimental fishing for southern bluefin tuna under the UNCLOS dispute resolution provisions, the ITLOS concluded that the dispute was both legal and scientific and that the parties should take measures to avert further deterioration of the stock. ITLOS Order, paragraphs 79–80 (Aug. 27, 1999). The Arbitral Panel later found it had no jurisdiction due to the dispute settlement provision (Article 16) of the 1993 Convention for the Conservation of Southern Bluefin Tuna. New Zealand v. Japan; Australia v. Japan, 4 August 2000, 39 I.L.M. 1359 (2000). Despite the litigation, the working relationship among the litigants improved at the Commission for the Conservation of Southern Bluefin Tuna, even after Japan revealed that it had grossly underreported bluefin imports in the previous twenty years. For a scientific discussion of the dispute, see Tom Polacheck, *Experimental Catches and the Precautionary Approach: The Southern Bluefin Tuna Dispute,* 26 Marine Policy 283 (2002).

119. *See generally* Burns, *supra* note 6.

120. Just before the IWC's annual meeting in 2007, three NGOs hosted a workshop in Dakar, Senegal to discuss the claim that whales are responsible for declining fish catches. The workshop inspired one participant to later conclude:

> The most crucial reform would be moving from a situation where West African waters are seen as larder from which an endless supply of fish can be extracted to supply foreign markets to one where West African countries could build on export and processing of fish to strengthen their own econ-

Notes

1. *Whales and Patriotism*. On November 12, 2008, the United States Supreme Court decided that Navy sonar use during training was worth sacrificing the health of whales and other species of marine mammals The Ninth Circuit had upheld a preliminary injunction issued by a district court against the use of sonar until it decided whether an EIS was required under NEPA for the activity. This judgment was reversed in *Winter v. Natural Resources Defense Council*, 555 U.S. ____, 129 S.Ct. 365 (2008). Chief Justice Roberts begins the opinion with the statement that "To be prepared for war is one of the most effectual means of preserving peace." *Id.* slip op. at 1. This sets the tone for an opinion that at every turn heightens the importance of Navy training while disparaging the strong science behind the plaintiffs' claims on behalf of marine mammals of permanent hearing loss, decompression sickness, and major behavioral disruptions, including mass strandings. The Ninth Circuit applied the standard that a preliminary injunction could issue on evidence of the possibility of irreparable harm and that the balance of hardships and consideration of the public interest weighed in favor of the plaintiffs. *Id.* at 11. Yet, the Supreme Court in *Winter* admonished the Ninth Circuit, claiming the proper standard was that irreparable harm is "likely." *Id.* at 12. The Court continued that "great deference" should be given to the "professional judgment of military authorities concerning the relative importance of a particular military interest." *Id.* at 14. While the court spends many paragraphs discussing warfare and Navy training and use of sonar, it spends mere sentences here and there discussing the evidence of irreparable harm that sonar causes to marine mammals. In contrast, dissenting Justices Ginsburg and Souter emphasize that the Navy violated NEPA and does not dispute its obligation to prepare an EIS: "If the Navy had completed the EIS before taking action, as NEPA instructs, the parties and the public could have benefited from the environmental analysis—and the Navy's training could have proceeded without interruption. Instead, the Navy acted first, and thus thwarted the very purpose an EIS is intended to serve." *Winter*, dissenting slip op. at 1. The dissenting justices bring to light the fact that the Navy itself, in an EA, admitted that there would be definite harm caused by the training exercises: "use of MFA sonar in the SOCAL exercises will result in 564 instances of physical injury including permanent hearing loss (Level A harassment) and nearly 170,000 behavioral disturbances (Level B harassment), more than 8,000 of which would also involve temporary hearing loss." *Id.* at *10. It is hard to comprehend how the majority could deem that there is no credible evidence of injury on the record with the Navy itself having cataloged such instances.

The majority opinion (Roberts, C.J., joined by Scalia, Kennedy, Thomas, Alito, J.J.s) does read like a too-loud pledge of allegiance by men who had seen little service. Of the five, the only one claiming military service on the Supreme Court website is Anthony Kennedy who was a member "of the California Army National Guard in 1961." (Justice Alito's service in the National Guard is not mentioned on the Supreme Court website.) Associate Justice John Paul Stevens served in the U.S. Navy in World War II (1942–1945). This experienced sailor was content to join a separate opinion by Mr. Justice Breyer, concurring in part and dissenting in part. This Breyer opinion is missing the ruffles and flourishes of the majority pronouncement.

The day belonged to the summer soldiers and the sunshine patriots.

---

omy, and benefit their own people.... [But] such reforms are not being contemplated ... [T]op officials of West African countries appear to have thrown their lot in with Japanese advisors, and their "whales-eat-our-fish" mantra, for reasons that are either obscure or too obvious to mention. Pauly, *supra* note 86, at 29.

2. *Starving Orcas.* As reported by Robert McClure, *Are Orcas Starving?*, SEATTLE POST-INTELLI-GENCER (Oct. 24, 2008): *available at*: http://seattlepi.nwsource.com/local/384854_orcas25.html (*last visited* April 4, 2009), the Puget Sound Orca population suffered a devastating loss of seven members in 2008, including several females of reproductive age. This reduced the population to only 83, in contrast to estimates that the population originally numbered 100 to 200 members. The likely cause was starvation due to decreased Chinook salmon runs. As McClure notes: "Two of the orca families—L and K pods—have been seen in recent years feeding off the California coast in the winter. That was unheard of before early this decade, leading scientists to speculate they are driven to swim hundreds of miles just to meet their minimum nutritional requirements. Then last winter, they likely found many fewer salmon—even after an energy-draining swim to California."

The article also quotes Fred Fellerman, who has been studying these orcas since the 1980s, as explaining that food was once abundant: "We used to have whales that would rest in groups at the surface, flopping around like lions on the Serengeti sitting under a tree.... But now they are underwater hunting more and I've watched a steady progression over the years of the whales getting more and more dispersed.... As the prey became more diffuse, they had to spread out."

This depressing turn of events exemplifies the complex ecosystem interactions that lead to wide-ranging effects from climate change. As explained by Kyle Dittmer (this chapter, pp. 418–22), one of the impacts of climate change is increased water temperatures, which decreases salmon reproductivity. Thus, there will be a loss of a species higher in the food chain. Sadly, this is not an isolated example and the instances are only likely to multiply as global warming worsens.

3. *See Toxic Whales Off the Menu*, NEW SCIENTIST, Dec. 6, 2008:

> Chief medical officers of the Faroe Islands have announced that pilot whales are no longer fit for human consumption, because they are toxic—as revealed by research on the islanders themselves.

> The remote Atlantic islands between Scotland and Iceland have been one of the last strongholds of traditional whaling, with thousands of small pilot whales killed every year, and eaten by most Faroese.

> ....

> Anti-whaling groups have long protested, but the Faroese argue that whaling is part of their culture—an argument adopted by large-scale whalers in Japan and Norway.

> In a statement to the islanders last week, however, chief medical officers Pál Weihe and Høgni Debes Joensen announced that the meat and blubber contain too much mercury, PCBs and DDT derivatives to be safe for human consumption. "It is with great sadness that this recommendation is provided," they said. "The pilot whale has kept many Faroese alive through centuries."

> ....

4. Leah R. Gerber, Lyne Morissette, Kristin Kaschner & Daniel Pauly, *Should Whales Be Culled to Increase Fishery Yield?*, 323 SCIENCE 880, 881 (Feb. 13, 2009) ("For a wide range of assumptions about whale abundance, feeding rates and fish biomass, even a complete eradication of baleen whales in these tropical areas does not lead to any appreciable increase in the biomass of commercially exploited fish. In contrast, just small changes in fishing rates lead to considerable increases in fish biomas....").

5. *Humane Soc'y of the United States v. Guttierrez*, 625 F. Supp. 2d 1052 (D. Ore. 2008) (Mosman, J.). This was a challenge to an NMFS decision authorizing the lethal taking of sea lions preying on endangered Columbia River salmon at the Bonneville Dam; an EA / FONSI was

done; the case presents a table on "Observed Pinniped Predation on Salmonids at Bonneville Dam." The legal interest focuses on whether individually identifiable pinnipeds are "having a significant negative impact on the decline or recovery of salmonid fishery stocks," 16 U.S.C.A. § 1389(b)(1). NMFS elaborates on the meaning of "significant" ("measurable, growing, and could continue to increase," a "measurable effect" on productivity, "comparable" to mortality rates that have led to ESA "corrective action") and these factors are given deference. Section 120 does not require the agency to address "other reasons for the decline." A "significance" finding under Section 120 does not require a "significant" finding under NEPA. *Id.* at 1069: "the science behind NEPA's analysis is not controversial. Plaintiffs' argument is simply that killing sea lions is controversial." *Compare* W.H. Rodgers, Jr., *Defeating Environmental Law: The Geology of Legal Advantage*, 15 Pace Envtl. L. Rev. 1, 24–31 (1997–98) (an earlier tryst with "nuisance" pinnipeds).

6. *Strahan v. Holmes*, 559 F. Supp. 2d 161 (D. Mass. Jan. 30, 2009) (Gorton, D.J.). Here a *pro se* plaintiff sues a fisherman for entangling an endangered humpback whale in his lobster trawl gear. The whale survived and the fisherman thus did "capture" a humpback whale (though he did not "harass" it or "harm" it) but no injunction will be issued for this "take." The burden to the fisherman outweighs the benefits.

7. *Defenders of Wildlife v. Gutierrez*, 484 F. Supp. 2d 44 (D.D.C. 2007) (Friedman, J.). An ESA/MMPA/Ports and Waterways Safety Act challenge to denial of a petition seeking emergency regulations to reduce the risk of ships striking the North Atlantic right whale. It is not capricious for NMFS to deny petition in favor of a "more comprehensive strategy," nor for the Coast Guard that pled inability to affect the traffic separation schemes (TSSs) that were under the broader purview of the Int'l Maritime Organization. (Ed.) No rush to help this whale in "peril" that has been "listed as an endangered species since 1970—longer than the ESA itself has been in effect," *id.* at 47. *Compare* Cornelia Dean, *The Fall and Rise of the Right Whale*, N.Y. Times, March 17, 2009.

B. Freshwater Ecosystems

Fears for fish, New Scientist, Sept. 20, 2008, pp. 4–5:

North America's freshwater fish are in trouble—and we should have seen it coming.

A report commissioned by the American Fisheries Society has warned that the number of North American freshwater species in danger of extinction in at least part of their range has nearly doubled since 1989. As well as this, 33 per cent of fish have seen their conservation status grow more dire, while only 6 per cent have seen an improvement.

....

Habitat loss due to humanity's growing thirst for water is the root cause of the problem, says Noel Burkhead from the U.S. Geological Survey in Gainesville, Florida, and one of the report's lead authors.

Fish are not the first to feel the squeeze. Many freshwater mussel and snail species have previously become endangered for the same reasons, but the warning was ignored. "The pattern we observed in snails and mussels is now being observed in fishes," Burkhead says. "Unless we somehow change the way we interact with the landscape, fish extinctions are going to dramatically increase."

B.C. Bates, Z.W. Kundzewicz, S.W. and J.P. Palutikof, Eds, 2008: CLIMATE CHANGE AND WATER, TECHNICAL PAPER VI OF THE INTERGOVERNMENTAL PANEL ON CLIMATE CHANGE, IPCC Secretariat, Geneva, 210 pp., Executive Summary:

> *Observational records and climate projections provide abundant evidence that freshwater resources are vulnerable and have the potential to be strongly impacted by climate change, with wide-ranging consequences for human societies and ecosystems*

Observed warming over several decades has been linked to changes in the large-scale hydrological cycle such as: increasing atmospheric water vapour content; changing precipitation patterns, intensity and extremes; reduced snow cover and widespread melting of ice; and changes in soil moisture and runoff. Precipitation changes show substantial spatial and inter-decadal variability. Over the 20th century, precipitation has mostly increased over land in high northern latitudes, while decreases have dominated from 10°S to 30°N since the 1970s. The frequency of heavy precipitation events (or proportion of total rainfall from heavy falls) has increased over most areas (*likely*[1]). Globally, the area of land classified as very dry has more than doubled since the 1970s (*likely*). There have been significant decreases in water storage in mountain glaciers and Northern Hemisphere snow cover. Shifts in the amplitude and timing of runoff in glacier- and snowmelt-fed rivers, and in ice-related phenomena in rivers and lakes, have been observed (*high confidence*). [2.1[2]]

Climate model simulations for the 21st century are consistent in projecting precipitation increases in high latitudes (*very likely*) and parts of the tropics, and decreases in some sub-tropical and lower mid-latitude regions (*likely*). Outside these areas, the sign and magnitude of projected changes varies between models, leading to substantial uncertainty in precipitation projections.[3] Thus projections of future precipitation changes are more robust for some regions than for others. Projections become less consistent between models as spatial scales decrease. [2.3.1]

By the middle of the 21st century, annual average river runoff and water availability are projected to increase as a result of climate change[4] **at high latitudes and in some wet tropical areas, and decrease over some dry regions at mid-latitudes and in the dry tropics.**[5] Many semi-arid and arid areas (*e.g.*, the Mediterranean Basin, western USA, southern Africa and northeastern Brazil) are particularly exposed to the impacts of climate change and are projected to suffer a decrease of water resources due to climate change (*high confidence*). [2.3.6]

Increased precipitation intensity and variability are projected to increase the risks of flooding and drought in many areas. The frequency of heavy precipitation events (or proportion of total rainfall from heavy falls) will be *very likely* to increase over most areas during the 21st century, with consequences for the risk of rain-generated floods. At the same time, the proportion of land surface in extreme drought at any one time is projected to increase (*likely*), in addition to a tendency for drying in continental interiors during summer, especially in the sub-tropics, low and mid-latitudes. [2.3.1, 3.2.1]

---

1. *See* Box 1.1.

2. Numbers inside square brackets relate to sections in the main body of the Technical Paper.

3. Projections considered are based on the range of non-mitigation scenarios developed by the IPCC SPECIAL REPORT ON EMISSIONS SCENARIOS (SRES).

4. This statement excludes changes in non-climatic factors, such as irrigation.

5. These projections are based on an ensemble of climate models using the mid-range SRES A|B non-mitigation emissions scenario. Consideration of the range of climate responses across SRES scenarios in the mid-21st century suggests that this conclusion is applicable across a wider range of scenarios.

Water supplies stored in glaciers and snow cover are projected to decline in the course of the century, thus reducing water availability during warm and dry periods (through a seasonal shift in streamflow, an increase in the ratio of winter to annual flows, and reductions in low flows) in regions supplied by melt water from major mountain ranges, where more than one-sixth of the world's population currently live (*high confidence*). [2.1.2, 2.3.2, 2.3.6]

Higher water temperatures and changes in extremes, including floods and droughts, are projected to affect water quality and exacerbate many forms of water pollution — from sediments, nutrients, dissolved organic carbon, pathogens, pesticides and salt, as well as thermal pollution, with possible negative impacts on ecosystems, human health, and water system reliability and operating costs (*high confidence*). In addition, sea-level rise is projected to extend areas of salinisation of groundwater and estuaries, resulting in a decrease of freshwater availability for humans and ecosystems in coastal areas. [3.2.1.4, 4.4.3]

Globally, the negative impacts of future climate change on freshwater systems are expected to outweigh the benefits (*high confidence*). By the 2050s, the area of land subject to increasing water stress due to climate change is projected to be more than double that with decreasing water stress. Areas in which runoff is projected to decline face a clear reduction in the value of the services provided by water resources. Increased annual runoff in some areas is projected to lead to increased total water supply. However, in many regions, this benefit is likely to be counterbalanced by the negative effects of increased precipitation variability and seasonal runoff shifts in water supply, water quality and flood risks (*high confidence*). [3.2.5]

Changes in water quantity and quality due to climate change are expected to affect food availability, stability, access and utilisation. This is expected to lead to decreased food security and increased vulnerability of poor rural farmers, especially in the arid and semi-arid tropics and Asian and African megadeltas. [4.2]

Climate change affects the function and operation of existing water infrastructure — including hydropower, structural flood defences, drainage and irrigation systems — as well as water management practices. Adverse effects of climate change on freshwater systems aggravate the impacts of other stresses, such as population growth, changing economic activity, land-use change and urbanisation (*very high confidence*). Globally, water demand will grow in the coming decades, primarily due to population growth and increasing affluence; regionally, large changes in irrigation water demand as a result of climate change are expected (*high confidence*). [1.3, 4.4, 4.5, 4.6]

Current water management practices may not be robust enough to cope with the impacts of climate change on water supply reliability, flood risk, health, agriculture, energy and aquatic ecosystems. In many locations, water management cannot satisfactorily cope even with current climate variability, so that large flood and drought damages occur. As a first step, improved incorporation of information about current climate variability into water-related management would assist adaptation to longer-term climate change impacts. Climatic and non-climatic factors, such as growth of population and damage potential, would exacerbate problems in the future (*very high confidence*). [3.3]

Climate change challenges the traditional assumption that past hydrological experience provides a good guide to future conditions. The consequences of climate change may alter the reliability of current water management systems and water-related infrastructure. While quantitative projections of changes in precipitation, river flows and water levels at the river-basin scale are uncertain, it is *very likely* that hydrological characteristics will change in the future. Adaptation procedures and risk management practices that incorporate projected hydrological changes with related uncertainties are being developed in some countries and regions. [3.3]

Adaptation options designed to ensure water supply during average and drought conditions require integrated demand-side as well as supply-side strategies. The former improve water-use efficiency, *e.g.*, by recycling water. An expanded use of economic incentives, including metering and pricing, to encourage water conservation and development of water markets and implementation of virtual water trade, holds considerable promise for water savings and the reallocation of water to highly valued uses. Supply-side strategies generally involve increases in storage capacity, abstraction from water courses, and water transfers. Integrated water resources management provides an important framework to achieve adaptation measures across socio-economic, environmental and administrative systems. To be effective, integrated approaches must occur at the appropriate scales. [3.3]

Mitigation measures can reduce the magnitude of impacts of global warming on water resources, in turn reducing adaptation needs. However, they can have considerable negative side effects, such as increased water requirements for afforestation/reforestation activities or bio-energy crops, if projects are not sustainably located, designed and managed. On the other hand, water management policy measures, *e.g.*, hydrodams, can influence greenhouse gas emissions. Hydrodams are a source of renewable energy. Nevertheless, they produce greenhouse gas emissions themselves. The magnitude of these emissions depends on specific circumstance and mode of operation. [Section 6]

Water resources management clearly impacts on many other policy areas, *e.g.*, energy, health, food security and nature conservation. Thus, the appraisal of adaptation and mitigation options needs to be conducted across multiple water-dependent sectors. Low-income countries and regions are *likely* to remain vulnerable over the medium term, with fewer options than high-income countries for adapting to climate change. Therefore, adaptation strategies should be designed in the context of development, environment and health policies. [Section 7]

Several gaps in knowledge exist in terms of observations and research needs related to climate change and water. Observational data and data access are prerequisites for adaptive management, yet many observational networks are shrinking. There is a need to improve understanding and modelling of climate changes related to the hydrological cycle at scales relevant to decision making. Information about the water-related impacts of climate change is inadequate—especially with respect to water quality, aquatic ecosystems and groundwater—including their socio-economic dimensions. Finally, current tools to facilitate integrated appraisals of adaptation and mitigation options across multiple water-dependent sectors are inadequate. [Section 8]

———————

Rethinking Water Law in a Changing Climate

Robert W. Adler, Associate Dean for Academic Affairs, James I. Farr Chair and Professor of Law, University of Utah, S.J. Quinney College of Law and Wallace Stegner Center for Land, Resources and the Environment, 332 S. 1400 E., Salt Lake City, UT 84112; Tel: (801) 581-3791, Fax: (801) 581-6897, adlerr@law.utah.edu.[1]

————————

1. I am grateful to Megan DePaulis, University of Utah, S.J. Quinney College of Law Class of 2009, for her able research assistance contributing to this essay.

I. Introduction: Forces of Change in Water Law and Management

In late Eighteenth Century New England, a mill owner needed some assurance that an upstream riparian landowner could not diminish the flow of the stream so much that the wheels of the mill would not turn. The eastern United States borrowed the riparian rights doctrine of water law to provide that certainty, and the doctrine simultaneously served to provide some degree of protection to the stream itself.[2] In arid portions of the western United States a century later, settlers could not plow land and otherwise invest in agriculture without some reasonable assurance that they had a legal right to divert water to irrigate their crops, with protection against potential later users. To accommodate the very different conditions in the arid west, the western states developed the prior appropriation doctrine, a body of law that served more to dewater than to protect western aquatic ecosystems.[3] Public and private investments in water resources infrastructure have also rested on a platform of legal stability to support legal rights to use water stored behind dams, or to use property protected from flooding by levees and other engineered structures.

But no body of law, including water law, should remain rigid in the face of significant changes in physical or social conditions. In the context of climate change, more than three decades ago, water law expert Frank Trelease wrote: "While one function of law is to give stability to institutions and predictability to the results of action, often the strength of law will lie not in immutability but in capacity for change and flexibility in the face of new forces."[4]

Likewise, the scientific underpinnings on which water resources planning has rested for decades reflected an assumption of relative stability known as "stationarity."[5] Climate and hydrology reflect seasonal, annual, and multi-annual variability leading to patterns of relative aridity and humidity that have always posed challenges to civilizations around the world, and both water law and property law have responded in ways designed to mitigate the effects of those fluctuations. However, water resources engineers and planners have defined the concept of stationarity as "the idea that natural systems fluctuate within an unchanging envelope of variability."[6] Armed with adequate historical data and statistical methods of analysis, water resource managers could plan programs, investments and infrastructure with sufficient flexibility to account for that variability. Designers and operators of a dam, for example, could maintain enough reserve storage capacity to accommodate a predicted 100-year maximum flood. Similarly, lawyers developed rules of priority and rights of use to deal with inherent variability, but reasonably assumed that any change would remain within predictable bounds based on past hydrologic history.

Recent changes in global hydrologic conditions caused by human-induced climate change, however, have caused some scientists to "assert that stationarity is dead and should no longer serve as a central, default assumption in water-resource risk assessment and planning."[7] Although intensive land use and other artificial changes and disturbances in watersheds have already challenged the notion of stationarity in many regions, they argue that climate change is

---

2. *See* Part III.A, *infra*.

3. *See* Part III.B, *infra*.

4. Frank J. Trelease, *Climatic Change and Water Law*, in NATIONAL ACADEMY OF SCIENCES, CLIMATE, CLIMATIC CHANGE, AND WATER SUPPLY 70 (1977); *see, also*, ROBERT W. ADLER, RESTORING COLORADO RIVER ECOSYSTEMS: A TROUBLED SENSE OF IMMENSITY 17–25 (Island Press 2007); Joseph W. Dellapenna, *Adapting Riparian Rights to the Twenty-First Century*, 106 W. VA. L. REV. 539, 543–44 (2004) (asking whether existing legal regimes can accommodate major change without "unsettling uses and provoking resistance").

5. P.C.D. Milly, *et al.*, *Stationarity is Dead: Whither Water Management?*, 319 SCIENCE 573 (2008).

6. *Id.*

7. *Id. See also* Barnett, T.P., Malone, R., Pennell W., Stammer D., Semtner B, and Washington W., *The Effects of Climate Change on Water Resources in the West: Introduction and Overview*, 62 CLIMATIC CHANGE 1–11 (2004) (cannot assume that the future will look like the past).

now pushing the hydroclimate beyond the range of historic trends, and beyond the ability of existing water resources infrastructure to cope with those potential changes. Professor Trelease predicted this relationship between climate change and water law decades ago, urging that "we would be wise to plan for the unpredictable."[8]

It is time to plan—as best we can—for the unpredictable hydrological impacts of climate change. Because available computer models to predict the hydrological impacts of climate change are characterized by wider ranges of uncertainty than the models predicting changes in temperature,[9] both legal and technological institutions governing water law and management will have to respond in ways that are sufficiently flexible to address a wide range of possible future outcomes. However, although the exact nature and magnitude of changes in global water resources remain uncertain, there is a growing scientific consensus that those changes will be real, and that they will be significant. Therefore, "the time has come to move beyond the wait-and-see approach."[10] Although some argue that so-called "adaptation" responses to climate change may defer essential prevention or mitigation strategies,[11] it is now clear that prevention and mitigation will come too late to prevent significant water resource crises unless we also act soon to address those inevitable changes. At least with respect to water law and water resources, we cannot afford to wait for a reversal of human-induced climate change, but must adopt prevention and adaptation approaches simultaneously.[12]

This chapter begins with a review of the best available scientific predictions regarding the impacts of climate change on water resources. It then discusses potential changes in water law, policy and management that might be employed to respond to those challenges. Finally, it reviews the ability of existing legal systems to address those changes, at the state (U.S.), national (U.S.), and international levels.

II. The Effects of Climate Change on Water Resources

A. Global Hydrological Impacts of Climate Change

The scientific models available to forecast the range of possible hydrological impacts of climate change are relatively less certain than those designed to forecast changes in global temperatures over time.[13] However, basic physics suggests that adding more energy to the atmosphere will alter the movement of atmospheric moisture and therefore affect precipitation. There is significant agreement among a large number of models that those changes will be significant, but more uncertainty about the exact nature, timing, location, and magnitude of those changes.

Increased concentrations of greenhouse gases in the atmosphere cause increased levels of infrared radiation, which make more energy available for evaporation and therefore precipitation. However, the distribution of increased precipitation is not necessarily even, and the hydrological

---

8. TRELEASE, *supra* note 3, at 71; *see, also,* Denise Fort, *Climate Change and the Rio Grande: Throwing Gasoline on a Fire,* remarks at Water, Climate and Uncertainty: Implications for Western Water Law, Policy and Management, 24th Conference of the Natural Resources Law Center, University of Colorado, June 11–13, 2003 (discussing a "[n]ew realization" that the future will not necessarily resemble the past).

9. *See* Part II, *infra.*

10. Milly *et al., supra* note 5, at 573.

11. *See* Matthew D. Zinn, *Adapting to Climate Change: Environmental Law in a Warmer World,* 62 ECOL. L.Q. 61, 62 (2007) (reporting views of some environmentalists).

12. *See id.* at 63; A. Dan Tarlock, *Now, Think Again About Adaptation,* 9 ARIZ. J. INT'L & COMP. L. 169, 169–173 (1992).

13. *See* Wang, G., *Agricultural drought in a future climate: results from 15 global climate models participating in the IPCC 4th assessment,* 25 CLIMATE DYNAMICS 739, 740 (2005); Maurer, E.P., *Uncertainty in hydrologic impacts of climate change in the Sierra Nevada, California under two emissions scenarios,* 82 CLIMATIC CHANGE 309, 310 (2007) (DOI 10.1007/s10584-006-9180-9).

effects of those precipitation changes vary as well. Where increased precipitation is significantly greater than evaporation, it results in increased soil moisture and increased river runoff—and vice versa.[14]

Globally, for example, using the middle range of the Intergovernmental Panel on Climate Change (IPCC) potential future emissions scenarios,[15] models project a potential 2.3°C *average* temperature increase and a resulting 5.2% *average* increase in precipitation by the middle of the 21st Century.[16] But the geographic distribution of those impacts is not expected to be even.[17] The flow of arctic rivers such as the MacKenzie and the Ob are projected to increase by as much as 20 percent, and heavier precipitation is expected in areas such as eastern Brazil, the Northern Andes, Northern India and Tibetan Plateau, Indonesia, and parts of coastal Africa.[18] Although more water might be perceived as beneficial in some areas, it can also increase the risk of intense floods[19] that can strain the capacity of existing dams and flood control facilities, and lead to loss of life, dislocation of large populations, and extensive damage to property and other economic resources.[20] Evidence shows that the frequency of major floods already increased during the Twentieth Century, and that this trend is likely to continue, with flood rates increasing to as much as two to eight times greater than in the past.[21]

At the same time, both soil moisture and rainfall is expected to decline in already arid parts of the world, such as Southwestern North America, the Mediterranean coast, Northeastern China, the grasslands of Africa, parts of the Middle East, and Southern and Western Australia.[22] If temperatures continue to increase, arid regions are expected to expand, increasing the size of some of the world's largest deserts, such as the Sahara, Kalahari, Patagonian, Australian, Gobi and North American deserts.[23] Similarly, the arid portions of Europe are likely to expand northward.[24] That is likely to exacerbate water shortages in other regions, especially where crop water needs increase due to rising temperatures, increased evaporation, and lower soil moisture, causing what some experts predict will be "very acute" water shortages over the next few centuries.[25] Based on those hydrological predictions, other experts have suggested that we are likely to face a "worldwide agricultural drought."[26]

In short, rather than predicting that climate change will distribute increased precipitation evenly over the globe, or even redistribute water from wet to dry regions, available models pro-

---

14. *See* Manabe, Milly and Wetherald, *Simulated long-term changes in river discharge and soil moisture due to global warming*, 49(4) Hydrological Sciences 625, 626, 631 (2004).

15. *See* Chapter 1, this volume, for an explanation of the IPCC scenarios.

16. Manabe *et al.*, *supra* note 14, at 628, 631.

17. *Id.* at 631; *see, also*, Meehl, G.A., J.M. Arblaster, and C. Tebaldi, *Understanding future patterns of increased precipitation intensity in climate model simulations*, 32 Geographic Research Letters L18719 (2005); Milly, Dunne and Vecchia, *Global pattern of trends in streamflow and water availability in a changing climate*, 438 Nature: 347 (2005).

18. Manabe *et al.*, *supra* note 14, at 631.

19. *See* Milly, P.C.D., Wetherald, R.T., Dunne, K.A., and Delworth, T.L, *Increasing risk of great floods in a changing climate*, 415 Nature 514 (2002).

20. *See* Heather Cooley, *Floods and Droughts, in* The World's Water 2006–2007, The Biennial Report on freshwater Resources (Peter H. Gleick ed., Island Press 2006) (reporting that floods and droughts killed an estimated 17 million people and affected over 5 billion people between 1900 and 2005).

21. Milly *et al.*, *supra* note 19.

22. Manabe *et al.*, *supra* note 14, at 634; Milly *et al.*, *supra* note 17, at 347.

23. Manabe *et al.*, *supra* note 14, at 636.

24. Milly *et al.*, *supra* note 17, at 349.

25. Manabe *et al.*, *supra* note 14, at 639.

26. Wang, *supra* note 13, at 739, 752. *See also* Motha and Baier, *Impacts of Present and Future Climate Change and Climate Variability on Agriculture in the Temperate Regions: North America*, 70 Climatic Change 37 (2005).

ject that wet portions of the globe are likely to get wetter, and that arid portions of the globe are likely to get even drier, and to expand in size. Predicted changes in parts of the Western United States highlight the potential ramifications of those changes even for a wealthy region with per-haps the most extensively developed water resources infrastructure—both physically and insti-tutionally—anywhere in the world.

B.   A Regional Example: Hydrological Impacts of Climate Change in the Western United States

Because conflicts over water are already acute in the Western United States,[27] the potential impacts of climate change on water resources in that region are of particular concern and have been the subject of considerable analysis. Water storage in the West is particularly important because most of the annual precipitation falls in the form of winter snowfall in the moun-tains,[28] and the largest water storage is in snowpack (as opposed to artificial reservoirs), mak-ing western rivers vulnerable to changes in climate that affect snowfall and resulting winter snowpack and spring runoff.[29] In general, scientists expect that increasing temperatures in the West will increase the percentage of precipitation that falls as rain rather than snow, decrease snowfall in lower elevations, cause peak runoff to occur earlier in the spring, and increase the rate of evapotranspiration, the combined effects of which will decrease stream flows and reser-voir storage.[30]

Scientists have already identified trends in western hydrology since the middle of the Twenti-eth Century that reflect these changes in western precipitation. Shifts in western mountain pre-cipitation from 1950 to 1999 reflect all of the predicted changes discussed above.[31] Moreover, those changes diverge statistically from what might be expected due to natural climatic variabili-ty, in ways that have led researchers to conclude "with high confidence" that they have been caused by greenhouse gases and aerosols.[32] As a result, these trends in snowfall and other factors are likely to continue as the climate continues to warm, with "profound consequences for water use in a region already contending with the clash between rising demands and increasing alloca-tions of water for endangered fish and wildlife."[33]

As a result of these trends, as well as predictions from suites of linked climate change and hy-drology models, large portions of the western states are likely to face serious water shortages over the next century and beyond. One survey, for example, predicted that the Colorado River reser-voir system will not be able to meet demands placed on it by the middle of the 21st Century, in-cluding demands for hydroelectric power; California's Central Valley will experience reduced

---

27. *See, e.g.,* ADLER, *supra* note 4 (Colorado River basin); Reed D. Benson, *Giving Suckers (and Salmon) an Even Break: Klamath Basin Water and the Endangered Species Act,* 15 TUL. ENVTL. L.J. 197 (2002) (Klamath River); Harrison C. Dunning, *Confronting the Environmental Legacy of Irrigated Agriculture in the West: The Case of the Central Valley Project,* 23 ENVTL. L. 943 (1993) (California's Central Valley). *See generally* MARC REISNER, CADILLAC DESERT: THE AMERICAN WEST AND ITS DISAPPEARING WATER (Penguin 1986).

28. *See* Kalra, A., T.C. Piechota, R. Davies, and G. Tootle, *Changes in U.S. Streamflow and Western U.S. Snowpack,* 13(3) J.HYDROLOGIC ENGINEERING 156 (2008).

29. *See* Mote, P.W., *Climate-Driven Variability and Trends in Mountain Snowpack in Western North Amer-ica.,* 19 JOURNAL OF CLIMATE 6209 (2006); Mote *et al., Declining Mountain Snowpack in Western North Amer-ica,* 98 J. AM. METEOROLOGICAL SOC. 39 (January 2005).

30. *See* Barnett, Tim P. *et al., Human-Induced Changes in the Hydrology of the Western United States,* 319 SCIENCE 1080 (2008); Christensen, N. and D.P. Lettenmaier, *A multimodel ensemble approach to assessment of climate change impacts on the hydrology and water resources of the Colorado River Basin,* 11 HYDROLOGY AND EARTH SYSTEM SCIENCES DISCUSSION 1417 (2007); Mote, *supra* note 29, at 6209.

31. Barnett, *supra* note 30, at 1080; Mote, *supra* note 29, at 6209; Mote *et al., supra* note 29, at 39, 41–42, 47.

32. Barnett, *supra* note 30, at 1080, 1082.

33. Mote *et al., supra* note 29, at 48. *See also* Barnett, *supra* note 30, at 1082.

water deliveries, hydroelectric production and instream flows, with potentially serious ecosystem disruption; and the Columbia River system will not be able simultaneously to meet demands for hydroelectric power.[34] Drier conditions throughout the West are likely to increase the length and severity of the fire season, among other impacts.[35]

Certain regions appear to be particularly vulnerable, because of both existing problems of supply and demand and projected future reductions. There is a wide consensus that the Southwest will become drier in this century, and that the serious droughts of the past will become the norm and even more severe droughts are likely.[36] Although different model runs vary in the magnitude of predicted shortages, they all agree that Colorado River basin runoff will decline, by eight to eleven percent according to the most conservative models[37] and by as much as 45 percent in others.[38] "The Southwest appears to be entering a new drought era.... a near perpetual state of drought will materialize in the coming decades as a consequence of increasing temperature."[39] Especially given that the 1922 Colorado River Compact was negotiated on the basis of an overly optimistic understanding of long-term water supplies,[40] even lower projected flows are expected to result in significant "failures" in the reservoir system, meaning many years in which there will be insufficient water to meet delivery obligations under the Colorado River Compact and other established expectations.[41]

Similarly, water supplies in California may decline significantly due to climate change, in the face of rapid continuing population growth in that state. Models predict increasing river flows in winter and early spring, but earlier decreases in summer flows, reflecting more rain and less snow in the Sierra Nevada Mountains.[42] That may result in between 36 and 80 percent declines in the amount of water stored as snow in the Sierras, which will result in significant reductions in reservoir storage during summer months when demand is highest,[43] in part because of the need to reserve more reservoir storage space in the spring to prevent flooding.[44]

If stationarity is in fact dead, as these predictions tend to show, we will be wise to change water law and policy in ways that will minimize the impacts of a new but volatile set of hydrological conditions. Part III will survey the kinds of changes in water policy and management that

---

34. Barnett *et al.*, *supra* note 7, at 6–7.

35. *Id.* at 7. *See also* Robert B. Keiter, Climate Change and Wildfire Policy, p. 478 below.

36. Seager, R., M. Ting, I. Held, Y. Kushnir, J. Lu, G. Vechhi, H. Huang, N. Harnick, A. Leetma, N. Lau, C. Li, J. Velez, and N. Naik, *Model Projections of an Imminent Transition to a More Arid Climate in Southwestern North America*, 316 Science 1181 (2007).

37. *See* Christensen and Lettenmaier, *supra* note 30; McCabe and Wolock, *Warming may create substantial water supply shortages in the Colorado River Basin*, 34 Geophysical Research Letters L22708 (2007).

38. Hoerling and Eischeid, *Past Peak Water in the Southwest*, 6(1) Southwest Hydrology 18 (Jan/Feb. 2007). *See also* Bureau of Reclamation, Climate Technical Work Group, Review of Science and Methods for Incorporating Climate Change Information into Reclamation's Colorado River Basin Planning Studies, Final Report, August 21, 2007 (reviewing available models).

39. Hoerling and Eischeid, *supra* note 38, at 19.

40. *See* Adler, *supra* note 4, at 117–118.

41. McCabe and Wolock, *supra* note 37, at 4 (failure rates as high as 77 percent); Christensen and Lettenmaier, *supra* note 30, at 1428 (predicting "storage and hydropower decreases, compact violations, and delivery reductions"); Hoerling and Eischeid, *supra* note 38, at 35 (reliance on Colorado River Compact guarantees now risky).

42. Maurer, E.P., Uncertainty in hydrologic impacts of climate change in the Sierra Nevada, California under two emissions scenarios, 82 Climatic Change 309 (2007) (DOI 10.1007/s10584-006-9180-9).

43. *Id. See also* Miller, N.L., K.E. Bashford, and E. Strem, *Potential impacts of climate change on California hydrology*, 39 J. Amer. Water Resources Assn. 771 (2003).

44. T. Zhu, M.W. Jenkins, & J.R. Lund, *Estimated Impacts of Climate Warming on California Water Availability under Twelve Future Climate Scenarios*, 41(5) Journal of the American Water Resources Association 1027 (2005).

might be effective to help buffer the hydrological impacts of a changing climate on human economic needs and on ecosystems. Part IV will assess the ability of existing legal systems to accommodate or to facilitate those policy and management changes.

III. Changes in Water Policy and Management to Respond to Climate Change

The nature and magnitude of predicted hydrologic changes described above clearly have profound implications for national and international water resource policy and management. But potential responses will vary depending on the kinds and levels of impacts felt in different regions. Some areas will face increasing shortages, or mismatches in the timing of water supply and demand. Others regions will have to cope with the problems of too much water, especially in coastal areas and floodplains. Some places will have to build new or additional water resources infrastructure to cope with problems of both water scarcity and water excess, while others may find that existing facilities need to be used in very different ways. In other regions, more profound changes are needed in land use and other policies that affect water resources indirectly, but significantly.

A.   Responding to Problems of Scarcity

Areas that already strain existing water supplies, or that face significant expected growth or development, will face the most acute problems of increasing scarcity due to climate change. But because climate models predict that arid parts of the globe are likely to become even drier, and that arid zones will expand in size,[45] new problems will affect increasingly large regions, and more severely.

Logically, the categories of policy or management responses to water scarcity are limited. First, water users facing increasingly limited supplies can use the available water more efficiently by investing in technologies that achieve the same benefits with less water, such as sprinklers or drip irrigation systems instead of flood irrigation, or more efficient plumbing fixtures in homes and businesses.[46] Efficiencies might also be achieved in the water management system itself. For example, earthen canals might be lined to prevent seepage, although there are often tradeoffs where existing seepage contributes to groundwater recharge.[47] Similarly, evaporative losses might be reduced by changing from reservoir storage to aquifer storage and recovery, which might have the added benefit of restoring free-flowing river habitats, although at the potential expense of hydropower generation and flat water recreation on reservoirs.[48] Increased efficiency could allow some continued growth in the face of increasingly limited water supplies.

Second, the number of new users, or the degree to which existing users can increase usage, can be constrained. Some states, for example, have passed "assured supply laws" requiring developers to demonstrate sufficient water supplies to support new housing developments.[49] Even absent such formal requirements, however, one cannot use water that does not exist, and at some point limited supplies might act as a *de facto* constraint on growth in some regions, unless new

---

45. *See supra* Part II.A.

46. *See, e.g.*, U.S. Bureau of Reclamation, Lower Colorado Region, Water Conservation Report 1996–2001; Gleick *et al.*, Waste Not, Want Not: The Potential for Urban Water Conservation in California (Pacific Institute for Studies in Development, Environment, and Security, 2003); Western Resource Advocates, Smart Water: A Comparative Study of Urban Water Use Efficiency Across the Southwest (2003). On possible responses to supply shortages generally, see Trelease, *supra* note 4, at 71.

47. *See* U.S. Bureau of Reclamation, Pacific Northwest Region Water Conservation Center, Canal Lining Demonstration Project 10-Year Final Report (2002).

48. *See* R. David Pyne, Groundwater Recharge and Wells, A Guide to Aquifer Storage and Recovery (CRC 1994); Comprehensive Everglades Restoration Plan, Aquifer Storage and Recovery Program (2001); Doug McChesny, Washington State Dept. Ecology, 2001 Report to the Legislature: Artificial Storage and Recovery of Ground Water (2001).

49. *See* Lincoln Davies, *Just a Big, "Hot Fuss"? Assessing the Value of Connecting Suburban Sprawl, Land Use, and Water Rights Through Assured Supply Laws*, 34 Ecol. L. Q. 1217 (2007).

uses result in ongoing shortages to existing users as well.[50] Quotas or severe price incentives to curtail levels of use are the logical results of continued growth in the face of fixed or diminishing water supplies.

Third, existing supplies within a region can be reallocated among users, or groups of users, reflecting choices about the relative value of water devoted to particular uses. For example, water currently used to irrigate low value crops might be transferred to higher value crops or to municipal or industrial uses.[51] In the Western United States, for example, a very high percentage of water withdrawals are currently devoted to agriculture, including irrigated alfalfa and other feed for livestock, when the highest value use and fastest increase in demand is for urban growth.[52] Transferring water from agricultural to urban uses, therefore, is already a major innovation in western water policy, and that trend is likely to continue as urban populations grow and as regional water supplies shrink. As discussed in the next section, those choices could be made through market mechanisms, or through regulatory devices such as statutory preferences for municipal or domestic uses.[53] Ultimately, water shortages and transfers among uses might force a shift in the location of certain uses—especially agriculture—from some regions of the globe to others.

Fourth, regions facing increasing water shortages can try to augment water supplies, either by importing water from relatively wet regions or in other ways. There is a long history of transbasin water diversions, especially in the West, to move water from areas of excess to regions of scarcity. Most famous, perhaps, is the diversion of large amounts of Colorado River water to growing urban and agricultural regions from Colorado's Front Range to California's Imperial Valley and southern coastal megalopolis.[54] Even more dramatic inter-regional diversions have been proposed in the past, such as the North American Water and Power Alliance (NAWAPA), which would have diverted large amounts of water from the Columbia River Basin and even Alaska to the arid Southwest,[55] or proposals to divert Great Lakes water to the upper Mississippi River for navigational and other purposes.[56] Although those kinds of diversions have been rejected on environmental and economic grounds, such proposals are likely to resurface in the face of even larger regional imbalances between supply and demand, especially if climate change does cause currently wet regions to get even wetter, and currently arid regions to become even drier and to expand in size. A looming question is whether more pressing economic and other imperatives will be sufficient to overcome past environmental and other objections to such projects.

Increasing scarcity also might stimulate increased or renewed efforts to augment supplies through technological means, some of which have greater promise than others. Despite a questionable history of success in terms of long-term or significant increases in water supply, some areas continue the use of cloud seeding in an effort to increase precipitation, especially in drainage basins with storage reservoirs.[57] Other areas are mining groundwater to offset shortages

50. *See* A. Dan Tarlock, and Sarah B. Van de Weterling, *Western Growth and Sustainable Water Use: If There Are No "Natural Limits," Should We Worry About Water Supplies?*, 27 Pub. Land & Resources L. Rev. 33 (2006).

51. *See, e.g.*, B.M. Hadad, Rivers of Gold: Designing Markets to Allocate Water in California (Island Press 2000); Robert Glennon, *Water Scarcity, Marketing, and Privatization*, 83 Texas L. Rev. 1873 (2005).

52. *See* Adler, *supra* note 4, at 252–53; Tarlock, *supra* note 12, at 174.

53. *See infra* Part III.

54. *See* Adler, *supra* note 4, at 33–34; Reisner, *supra* note 27.

55. *See* Ludwik A. Teclaff, *The River Basin Concept and Global Climate Change*, 8 Pace Envt'l L. Rev. 355, 359 (1991) (describing NAWAPA as "[o]ne of the most ambitious and imaginative of these projects.").

56. *See* Mark Squillace, *Rethinking the Great Lakes Compact*, 2006 Mich. St. L. Rev. 1347, 1361–1362 (2006).

57. *See* Desert Research Institute, Nevada State Cloud Seeding Program, *available at* http://cloudseeding.dri.edu/ (including bibliography of research results on cloud seeding efficacy and methods).

in surface water supplies, but the sustainability of those practices is questionable as aquifer levels continue to decline faster than rates of recharge, and because of hydrological connections between surface and groundwater.[58] Decreased runoff in already arid basins will make those policies even more risky, because aquifer recharge rates may decline at the same time.

At least two other technological solutions have increasing promise for augmenting local and regional water supplies, although neither is free from environmental tradeoffs. More and more arid communities are turning to advanced wastewater treatment and reuse to stretch supplies by using water multiple times.[59] Although it may be more expensive to treat wastewater to higher standards deemed necessary to allow safe reuse,[60] especially where human contact is likely, it still may be cheaper than the marginal cost of new raw water supplies, although initial capital costs may be high.[61]

Public perceptions currently limit the use of reused water for human consumption,[62] but those psychological barriers could diminish over time, and there is ample demand to use treated wastewater to irrigate public parks, golf courses, and similar areas. For that matter, the modern urban paradigm of a single distribution system in which water treated to public drinking water quality is used for outside as well as inside human use is increasingly coming into question. As treatment and other costs increase, it may be more rational—especially for new developments— to provide separate water supplies for outside irrigation and inside domestic uses.[63] That would facilitate the reuse of "gray water" (drainage water from sinks and other sources of domestic water with only modest levels of contamination) for urban irrigation and other noncontact or low contact uses. One ironic problem with urban wastewater reuse, however, is that many rivers and streams in arid regions have been dewatered to such a degree that aquatic ecosystem maintenance and restoration may rely on return flows from municipal treatment plants to provide ecologically necessary instream flows.[64] Urban water reuse can therefore present communities with a difficult choice between stretching water supplies and aquatic ecosystem health.

Thirsty coastal communities are also turning increasingly to seawater desalination to augment water supplies.[65] If groundwater salinity in coastal areas continues to increase due to rising sea levels and resulting saltwater intrusion, more communities are likely to turn to desalination methods to make appropriate use of those groundwater supplies. In some parts of the world, such as Kuwait, where viable alternatives do not exist, desalination currently supplies the majority of fresh water.[66] The economic viability of desalination is also expected to increase as mem-

---

58. *See* ROBERT L. GLENNON, WATER FOLLIES, GROUNDWATER PUMPING AND THE FATE OF AMERICA'S FRESH WATERS (Island Press 2002).

59. *See* H. Furumai, *Reclaimed stormwater and wastewater and factors affecting their reuse, in* CITIES OF THE FUTURE: TOWARDS INTEGRATED SUSTAINABLE WATER AND LANDSCAPE MANAGEMENT (Vladimir Novotny and Paul Brown, eds. IWA 2007); Ginette Chapman, *Note, From Toilet to Tap: The Growing Use of Reclaimed Water and the Legal System's Response*, 47 ARIZ. L. REV. 773 (2005); Robert Bastian, *The Future of Water Reuse*, 47 BIOCYCLE 25 (2006).

60. *See* U.S. ENVIRONMENTAL PROTECTION AGENCY, GUIDELINES FOR WATER REUSE (2004), EPA/625/R-04/108.

61. *See* CRAIG BELL AND JEFF TAYLOR, WATER LAWS AND POLICIES FOR A SUSTAINABLE FUTURE: A WESTERN STATES' PERSPECTIVE 99–107 (2008), *available at* http://www.westgov.org/wswc/laws%20&%20policies%20report%20(final%20with%20cover).pdf.

62. *See* Bastian, *supra* note 59.

63. *See* TANG, S.L., YUE, D.P.T., AND KU, D.C.C., ENGINEERING AND COSTS OF DUAL WATER SUPPLY SYSTEMS (IWA 2007).

64. *See* V. Novotny, *Effluent dominated water bodies, their reclamation and reuse to achieve sustainability, in* Novotny and Brown, *supra* note 59, at 191.

65. *See* Bell and Taylor, *supra* note 61, at 141–150; JAMES E. MILLER, REVIEW OF WATER RESOURCES AND DESALINATION TECHNOLOGIES (Sandia National Laboratory, 2003).

66. *See* ADLER, *supra* note 4, at 251.

brane technologies and process methods improve. Some experts, in fact, predict that an imminent step-shift in membrane or other technologies will make desalination far more cost-effective relative to other water supply alternatives.[67] Efforts to increase coastal supplies through desalination might also alleviate shortages upstream, or due to current trans-basin diversions, by reducing or obviating the pressure for such inter-regional transfers. For example, if urban Southern California can meet more of its demand through desalination, current diversions that significantly dewater the lower Colorado River might be reduced.[68] Desalination, however, faces environmental as well as energy and economic barriers, related to the siting of desalination plants in sensitive coastal areas, and the need to dispose of brackish sediments from the treatment process.[69]

All of the above potential policy changes, moreover, assume that the dominant use of water involves diversion out of natural water bodies for human consumption and other uses. An important competing consideration, as suggested by the tradeoff between urban wastewater reuse and discharge to re-water rivers and streams, is the impact of increasing water shortages on instream flows for environmental and recreational purposes. Over the past several decades, Western states have redefined the concept of "beneficial use" to include instream flows for fisheries, wildlife, and other environmental purposes, and increasingly accepted the validity of water rights devoted to those uses.[70] As those uses compete more directly with cities, farmers, and other water uses under conditions of increased scarcity, public pressure to devote more and more water to human economic uses is likely to increase. Recent pitched water battles such as those that occurred in the Klamath River Basin may occur with increasing frequency and intensity, and in a growing number of regions nationally and internationally.

B.   Responding to Flooding and Other Problems of Excess Water

Although some regions in theory might benefit from an increase in water resources stimulated by climate change, whether more precipitation and more runoff is a blessing or a curse depends on timing and location. As discussed above,[71] most areas with predicted increases in precipitation already enjoy sufficient water resources, making more water less valuable incrementally (if at all). At the same time, the combination of more water and more intense storms can overwhelm existing storage and flood control facilities, or in less developed regions the natural buffering and storage capacity of riparian wetlands and floodplains, which can cause increased flooding of developed areas. Coastal rivers may face the duel threat of heavier and more concentrated flows from upstream, and rising sea level in downstream bays and estuaries. Even now, flooding is among the costliest form of natural disasters around the world, in terms of both property losses and human casualties.[72] Those problems could increase significantly if current model predictions about regional increases in storms and runoff are correct, and some sources indicate that those increased risks are already occurring.[73]

Responses to anticipated problems of flooding fit within an even smaller range of categories than is true for problems of aridity. Most of those responses are likely to be expensive, disruptive of existing development patterns, or both. Indeed, in some ways it is easier to deal with the ab-

---

67. Sandia National Laboratory and U.S. Bureau of Reclamation, Desalination and Water Technology Roadmap: Desalination and Water Purification Research & Development Program Report #95 (2003).

68. *See* Adler, *supra* note 4, at 251.

69. *See* California Coastal Comm., Seawater Desalination and the California Coastal Act (2004).

70. *See* Bell and Taylor, *supra* note 61, at 174–224.

71. *See* Part II, *supra*.

72. *See* Cooley, *supra* note 20.

73. *See* European Environment Agency, Climate Change and Water Adaptation Issues 13, EAA Technical Report 2/2007; Zinn, *supra* note 11, at 72.

sence of water than with excess water, the presence of which imposes a manifest physical reality with definite physical consequences.

The traditional, capital-intensive approach to flood control and management involves design and construction of artificial facilities designed to store and to contain flood waters.[74] Upstream storage reservoirs hold water from storm surges and winter snowmelt runoff, and release it more slowly into downstream rivers to prevent it from overflowing the banks in developed areas. Systems of levees or dikes can hold flood waters within artificially elevated and strengthened banks to protect developed areas beyond. At least initially, existing flood control structures might have to be managed differently to adapt to increased flow patterns. For example, more reservoir storage capacity might be reserved for expected flood waters during seasons of high predicted precipitation or runoff. Those practices, however, could reduce water storage for other purposes, such as hydroelectric power or agricultural or municipal use. Improved systems for flood prediction and early warning to downstream communities and the operators of storage dams and other facilities could increase our ability to manage existing infrastructure as prudently as possible.[75] But future storms and seasonal runoff may exceed the design assumptions made when existing facilities were built, and those structures could be overwhelmed by the increased magnitude or intensity of storms caused by climate change.

One response to that scenario is to build even larger storage dams and taller and stronger systems of levees. That strategy could be extremely expensive, however, especially on an international scale. Moreover, wealthy nations may be able to afford such investments, while poorer developing countries will face increasing risks to human life and property absent significant transfers of wealth or viable and less expensive alternative approaches. Sites for additional or larger storage dams or levees may also be limited or nonexistent, and their construction and operation is likely to cause significant environmental impacts on already stressed aquatic ecosystems. Finally, at least since the 1930s, some experts have questioned whether we can build our way out of flood control problems, *i.e.*, whether softer, land use-based approaches to flood control ultimately produce better results.[76]

Intensive development, especially development that increases the percentage of impervious surfaces (roads, parking lots, buildings), decreases the capacity of watersheds to absorb and release storm flows into waters slowly, thereby increasing the intensity of peak storm runoff. That both exacerbates storm water pollution and increases the probability and intensity of flash floods.[77] Similarly, filling or other impairment of wetlands, riparian habitats, and other areas that serve as natural hydrological buffers to storm flows can decrease the capacity of watersheds to accept higher flows without extensive flooding.[78] Changes in land use to mitigate those impacts may be less feasible for areas that are already highly developed. Land use planners in developing areas that are in the path of potentially increased patterns of runoff and intensive storms, however, would be wise to consider land use policies that preserve wetlands and floodplain habitats, and that retain sufficient open spaces and other pervious surfaces within the watershed to buffer the effects of more intense storms naturally.

---

74. *See* Robert W. Adler, *Addressing Barriers to Watershed Protection*, 25 Envt'l L. 973 (1994).

75. *See* European Environment Agency, *supra* note 73, at 44; Milly *et al.*, *supra* note 19, at 514.

76. *See* Adler, *supra* note 74, at 1023–35.

77. *See* Brown, L.R., Gray, R.H., Hughes, R.M. and Meador, M.R., *Introduction to Effects of Urbanization on Stream Ecosystems*, 47 Amer. Fish. Soc. Symp. 1 (2005); U.S. Dept. of the Interior, *Effects of Urbanization on Stream Ecosystems*, U.S. Geological Survey Fact Sheet FS-042-02 (2002).

78. *See, e.g.*, National Audubon Society, Valuing Wetlands: The Cost of Destroying America's Wetlands 22–25 (1994) (estimating flood control benefits of healthy wetlands in economic values from $4 billion to $31 billion annually in the United States); National Research Council, Riparian Areas: Functions and Strategies for Management 8–13 (2002).

A related issue is the human tendency to build as close to the water's edge as possible. Historically, communities developed along waterways for purposes of water supply, fish and other wild food resources, fertile soils fed by millennia of sediment deposits by the river, navigation, protection, and aesthetic values.[79] However, along with those benefits comes the danger inherent in being so close to potentially tempestuous bodies of water, which can do considerable damage to adjacent communities. That is true for both coastal communities and cities and other development in low-lying floodplains, both of which may become more vulnerable to flooding as sea levels rise and as runoff increases in increasingly wet regions of the world. In some cases, governments have permitted if not affirmatively encouraged those risks through land use policies and subsidized flood insurance programs.[80] Again, it will be more difficult for already built communities to adapt to increasing flood risks when extensive and sometimes expensive investments have been made in development at the water's edge. Developing communities should consider efforts to limit or prohibit new building in increasingly flood prone areas. Existing communities, however, still may find it more prudent—and more economically sound in the long run—to move even existing developments out of the path of future storms and floods.

C. Responding to Climate Change at a Watershed Level

For both situations discussed above—decreased water supplies in already arid areas and increased runoff and storm intensity in already wet regions—the hydrological problems that may come with climate change suggest an even greater emphasis on collaborative, coordinated, watershed-based management than has occurred or been proposed in the past.

Even absent the effects of climate change, for many decades analysts from virtually every relevant discipline have urged that water resources be planned and managed on a watershed or basin-wide scale, so that land use, water quality and quantity, aquatic ecosystem restoration and protection, and water resources infrastructure can be considered in an effective, coordinated way. Because watersheds almost always cross some geopolitical boundaries (whether local, state or provincial, or international), and often involve a very wide array of public and private parties and interest groups that manage, regulate, use or affect water resources, that level of coordination is often challenging.[81] Notwithstanding those challenges, there are many examples in which such efforts have produced results that are superior to previous, more fragmented approaches.[82]

As Professor Ludwik Teclaf suggested relatively early in the evaluation of climate change impacts, the predicted hydrological effects of climate change suggest even greater efforts to coordinate water resources policies and management on a watershed (or river basin) basis, especially where watersheds cross state and international borders.[83] Where water resources will become more scarce, especially relative to increasing demand, it will be desirable to promote increased efficiency of water storage, transportation, and use; to facilitate transfers from lower value to higher value uses; to assess and address environmental impacts on an ecosystem basis; and to plan, build, modify, and manage physical infrastructure in a coordinated way. Similarly, in regions that may expect more intense precipitation and runoff, flood control dams and other facil-

---

79. *See* Charles F. Wilkinson, *The Headwaters of the Public Trust: Some Thoughts on the Sources and Scope of the Traditional Doctrine*, 19 ENVTL. L. 425, 431–35 (1989) (describing the importance of waterways in the early United States).

80. *See* Robert W. Adler, *The Law at the Water's Edge: Limits to "Ownership" of Aquatic Ecosystems, in* WET GROWTH: SHOULD WATER LAW CONTROL LAND USE 201 (C. Anthony Arnold, ed. Environmental Law Institute 2005).

81. *See,* Adler, *supra* note 74; Dellapenna, *supra* note 4, at 1303.

82. *See, e.g.,* Robert W. Adler and Michele Straube, *Watersheds and the Integration of U.S. Water Law and Policy: Bridging the Great Divides*, 25 WM. & MARY ENVTL. L. & POL. REV. 1 (2000).

83. Ludwik A. Teclaf, *The River Basin Concept and Global Climate Change*, 8 PACE ENVT'L L. REV. 355 (1991); *see, also,* Zinn, *supra* note 11, at 87.

ities, as well as broader and potentially more effective land use strategies, are best designed and implemented in a coordinated way throughout large watersheds.

IV. Rethinking Water Law to Address Climate Change

Appropriate legal regimes and institutions are needed to accomplish the kinds of changes in water policy and management suggested above. A threshold question is thus whether the existing bodies of water law at the state, national, and international levels are sufficiently flexible to accommodate or to facilitate those changes. If not, a secondary question is what changes are necessary to do so. This analysis focuses first on the two predominant bodies of water law in the United States, where most aspects of water law are determined at the state level. It then examines the appropriate role of federal law in state and national water policy, and touches more briefly on principles of international water law. Finally, it suggests that there is a significant role for revised land use laws and policies in addressing the expected hydrological impacts of climate change.

A.   Rethinking Riparian Rights and Regulated Riparianism

The relatively humid eastern United States inherited the law of riparian rights from England. The original riparian rights doctrine developed in England as a system of property rights in which only riparian (waterside) land owners had the right to withdraw and use water from a stream or other water body.[84] The doctrine was based on a concept of "no harm," meaning that riparian landowners could use water so long as they did not substantially impair either the quantity or quality of water for downstream users. Although designed to protect the rights of downstream landowners rather than as a system for environmental protection, that system was inherently protective of aquatic ecosystems and ensured that neither upstream owners nor the earliest users could dominate water resources at the expense of others. This rights-based system also made sense in a country where most landowners had access to some supply of water, and at a time when water supply far exceeded demand. Courts reconsidered the pure riparian rights doctrine during early American history when mill users and others increased demand and competition for scarce water. As a result, American courts modified the doctrine to allow more significant stream depletions when justified to promote industry, agriculture, and other development.[85]

Under traditional riparian doctrine, domestic uses for culinary purposes, to cultivate gardens and other subsistence uses, enjoyed an absolute preference, but those uses typically were not large enough to cause significant depletions or harm. Other, more intensive uses, for example to run mills or other economic uses, are subject to the "reasonable use doctrine," in which uses are permissible if it is reasonable relative to the rights of other riparian landowners for other reasonable uses. The reasonable use doctrine requires courts to balance the rights of competing users based on factors such as the purpose of the use, the suitability of the use to the water body, the economic and social value of the use, the harm caused, ways to avoid the harm, etc.[86]

Under the balancing principles of riparian rights, courts seek to allocate shortages fairly among all legitimate users, so no single user is likely to be shut off completely. However, it does generate uncertainty for users because no fixed quantity of water is assured. Some courts, for example, have limited the ability of cities to withdraw water even for general public uses in violation of strict riparian doctrine.[87] To address this problem, state legislatures have often intervened by enacting special legislative preferences or authorities for certain uses, especially municipal

---

84. JOSEPH L. SAX, BARTON H. THOMPSON, JR., JOHN D. LESHY, AND ROBERT H. ABRAMS, LEGAL CONTROL OF WATER RESOURCES 20–97 (3d ed., Gale Cengage 2000).

85. *E.g.*, Snow v. Parsons, 28 Vt. 459 (Vermont, 1856).

86. AMERICAN LAW INSTITUTE, RESTATEMENT (SECOND) OF TORTS, §850A (1979).

87. SAX *et al.*, *supra* note 84, at 55–58.

water supply. For example, New York State's water supply law provides: "The acquisition, storage, diversion and use of water for domestic and municipal purposes shall have priority over all other purposes."[88] The inherent uncertainty of riparian rights law—along with practical issues of storage and distribution—also prompted cities to build reservoirs to store water during wet periods as a hedge against later shortages.

Riparian rights may function well as a system of allocation within areas that become wetter as a result of climate change. In regions where water is expected to become increasingly scarce, however, riparian rights pose several related problems. Most important, in times of shortages the basic remedy in the riparian rights system is to require all users to cut back equitably. That makes sense if it forces each of several users to reduce production marginally, but leaves all as profitable endeavors. But if the result is to bring all users below the minimum level required to remain viable (economically or otherwise) in an effort to share shortages equitably, the perverse result becomes no winners and all losers, rather than forcing difficult but necessary choices among competing uses and users.

Faced with such a perverse result, of course, under the somewhat general and flexible principles articulated in the Restatement Second of Torts or equivalent provisions of riparian state water statutes, courts more likely might choose certain users over others based on a variety of equitable factors.[89] That result more closely approximates the ramifications of prior appropriation doctrine, except that decisions about winners and losers need not follow a strict system of temporal priority (described in more detail below). Reliance on such tort-type litigation to resolve water disputes in riparian rights states, however, is itself extremely inefficient in conditions of severe shortages, in which disputes will occur with increasing frequency. Further, riparian rights disputes that are resolved judicially might have to be adjudicated anew as conditions change. Given the potential hydrologic volatility resulting from climate change, that system of dispute resolution and resource allocation is even less viable.[90]

Because of these problems with a system of riparian rights administered and enforced largely through judicial process, most eastern states have adopted a system of "regulated riparianism."[91] In this variation, state legislatures delegate to administrative agencies the task of allocating water rights through a permit system governed by a modified version of the substantive principles of riparian rights. Again, that system may work well when water supplies are reasonably sufficient, and when decisions about water permits are more likely to address issues of efficiency in water supply and distribution than basic choices among water uses and values. Regulatory systems for water allocation can also require minimum instream flows for ecosystem protection purposes, a notable benefit at times when scarcity might generate economic pressure to divert more water offstream at the expense of aquatic ecosystem health.[92] In times of increasing scarcity, however, especially absent very clear legislative guidance about which existing users should be curtailed or cut off entirely in times of shortage, the idea that unelected bureaucrats will make such fundamental questions about who will have access to fresh water might increasingly be questioned.

---

88. *Id.* at 58, quoting New York Environmental Conservation Law Title 15—Water Supply. Many riparian doctrine states also now have statutes and regulations that establish somewhat clearer rules governing municipal water rights, often modeled after the Regulated Riparian Model Water Code, *supra* note 86.

89. *See* Trelease, *supra* note 4, at 73–75; Dellapenna, *supra* note 4, at 561; Joseph W. Dellapenna, *Adapting the Law of Water Management to Global Climate Change and Other Hydropolitical Stresses*, 35 J. AMER. WATER RESOURCES ASS'N. 1301, 1305 (1999).

90. *See* Dellapenna, *supra* note 4, at 559–60 (key problem with riparianism is "vagueness and unpredictability" and laborious litigation process); Trelease, *supra* note 4, at 73–74, 81 (arguing that "riparian law has little to offer" in the face of climate change).

91. *See* Dellapenna, *supra* note 4, at 586 *et seq.*

92. *See id.* at 591.

Some analysts have suggested that marketability of water rights would allow scarce water resources to be allocated more efficiently from low value to high value uses.[93] Presumably, marketability would also serve efficiency goals because would-be sellers would have incentives to conserve as much water as possible to increase the amount they can sell, and would be buyers would reduce their costs of purchase by reducing their water needs for any given use. By contrast, under an administrative permit system users only have an incentive to reduce water uses or needs to the extent necessary to bring their use within the amounts allocated to them by permit, unless efficiency improvements are made conditions of administrative permits.

The fundamental problem with riparianism under conditions of increased climate change-induced scarcity, then, is that it lacks clear and efficient mechanisms to reach difficult choices among competing users, and as currently designed, does not aggressively promote efficiency or conservation. Judicial resolution appears to be the least efficient and least effective means of accomplishing those goals under traditional riparian doctrine. Regulated riparianism has the potential to address increasing conditions of scarcity, but the legitimacy of the resulting choices might be enhanced if the key value choices are adopted legislatively rather than administratively. Moreover, an administrative permit system might promote increased efficiency of water use by imposing conservation requirements as a condition of obtaining a permit, and can be used to ensure minimum flows necessary to sustain aquatic ecosystem health. Administrative systems, however, impose inherent barriers to efforts to transfer water among uses. Issuing water use permits that are freely transferable would cede some public control over the place, manner, and purpose of water use, but increase the degree to which water can be shifted to higher value uses over time.

B.   Rethinking Prior Appropriation

By the mid-nineteenth century, riparian rights principles did not serve the needs of water users in the arid west. Water was needed for mining, irrigation and other uses on non-riparian lands; greater certainty of water supply was needed to justify investments; and demand often exceeded supply, especially during droughts. To address those needs, western states developed the prior appropriation doctrine.[94] Under prior appropriation law, water rights are quantified specifically (x cubic feet per second (cfs) or y acre-feet (af)) and priority in times of shortage is determined in order of seniority ("first in time, first in right"). Priority dates are determined by the time at which water is first diverted and put to a legally "beneficial use," such as irrigation or municipal water supply, and during times of shortage senior water rights are honored in full before junior rights-holders receive any water at all. Prior appropriation law does not limit the place of use, meaning that large amounts of water can be—and are—transported out of the watershed of origin to distant locations where it is needed.

Unlike the riparian rights doctrine, in which water rights attach to ownership in land and continue whether or not water is used, appropriative rights are "usufructory" in nature. The public, through the state, owns the water but individuals are given the right to use it, at certain times and for certain purposes, and subject to various conditions. Thus, under the "use it or lose it" tenet of prior appropriation law, rights to use water can be forfeited if not exercised. This ostensibly ensures that water is not "wasted" or that water rights are not held purely for speculation. However, although in theory water must be used efficiently to prevent waste, the incentive is to use one's full water right so as not to lose it, and rules against inefficient waste are rarely enforced. Moreover, until relatively recently, traditional prior appropriation law has recognized as

---

93. *See* Tarlock, *supra* note 12, at 173–74; Trelease, *supra* note 4, at 73.
94. Sax *et al.*, *supra* note 84, at 98–279.

"beneficial uses" only offstream uses for human economic purposes, at the expense of instream and other environmental "uses."[95]

Potential water shortages due to climate change pose particularly acute problems for western states,[96] and hence for the prior appropriation doctrine. Most of the west is arid, and past growth has been accommodated through storage in reservoirs and related diversion facilities, as well as large-scale inter-basin transfers of water. Much of the west, however, and especially the arid southwest, has been growing at faster rates than most of the United States,[97] but faces the most severe expected future reductions in water supply. And much of that expected growth is in urban centers. As was true in riparian rights states, western legislatures recognized that domestic uses of water to sustain basic human needs warranted some priority over other uses, and that concept translated to some degree of preference for municipal water supply as well. Nevertheless, the fact that so much western water is held for agricultural and other non-municipal purposes, with very early priority dates, has created problems for rapidly growing western cities, especially in areas with inadequate proximate supplies of fresh water.

Growing western cities governed by prior appropriation law have tried to address water shortages in various ways. Cities in urban Southern California have facilitated water transfers from agricultural areas with superior water rights (such as the Imperial Valley) by paying those areas to implement more efficient water conveyance and use measures,[98] and are now beginning to use expensive desalination of ocean water. Las Vegas adopted aggressive water conservation measures, and is trying to augment existing supplies through groundwater from nearby basins. Denver and other cities along Colorado's Front Range import Colorado River water through tunnels beneath the high peaks of the Rockies. Many cities are reclaiming urban waste water to re-use for irrigation water. Despite all of those measures, however, each region faces shortages under the pressure of continued expected growth, especially if supplies decline significantly due to climate change.

In theory, the prior appropriation system is better equipped to address shortages than the riparian rights doctrine, but reality is another matter. Because the system gives full allocations to senior appropriators before junior appropriators get any, it is designed to avoid an "everyone loses" result.[99] However, other commentators have noted that this system "works" politically because there is usually enough water in most years to accommodate even the most junior appropriators to some degree, especially because of the large amounts of water stored behind the west's massive system of dams, and an efficient distribution system designed to deliver water when and where it is needed.[100] Thus, in reality there have been few losers throughout most of the history of the prior appropriation doctrine.

Stated differently, the harsh implications of the prior appropriation doctrine have yet to be tested in a significant way. That complacency may change if regional water supplies increasingly fail to keep up with demand. If senior appropriators stand on their absolute rights, the whole system could move from one of predominant winners to one of predominant losers. The most senior appropriators will continue to received full allocations, but many users could be cut off entirely, resulting in potentially serious economic and social consequences.

More important, as water scarcity increases, a system in which the winners are defined entirely by who got there first may become increasingly irrational. Although the concept of "first in time,

---

95. *See* BELL AND TAYLOR, *supra* note 61, at 173 *et seq.*

96. *See* Part II.B, *supra*.

97. *See* NATIONAL ACADEMY OF SCIENCES, COLORADO RIVER BASIN WATER MANAGEMENT (2007) (showing Arizona, Nevada, Utah, Idaho and Colorado as 5 of the 6 fastest growing states).

98. *See* note 51 *supra* and accompanying text.

99. *See* Trelease, *supra* note 4, at 72; Dellapenna, *supra* note 89, at 1305.

100. *See* Tarlock, *supra* note 12, at 175–76; Trelease, *supra* note 4, at 72–73.

first in right" bears a certain equitable appeal absent other, countervailing factors, it can freeze existing water uses that no longer reflect the highest and best use of an increasingly limited resource, or that reflect changing societal values about the value of aquatic ecosystems.[101] Moreover, when senior appropriators have a virtually guaranteed right to their share of water even during times of extreme scarcity, they have little incentive to conserve. Although the doctrine of "waste" theoretically prevents even senior appropriators from engaging in extremely inefficient practices, courts thus far have been very reluctant to enforce that concept except in extreme circumstances.[102] More serious shortages due to climate change, continued growth, or other factors, however, might well prompt more serious enforcement of the anti-waste tenet of prior appropriation law.

The tendency of prior appropriation law to freeze existing, potentially low value water uses, is especially problematic given traditional barriers to the marketability of appropriative rights, which can inhibit or prevent the transfer of water from lower to higher value uses. Although there is no formal barrier to the sale of appropriative water rights, especially relative to riparian rights that are tied more closely to specific lands and watersheds, such sales must take into account the rights of downstream users in an often complex set of relationships between appropriative rights from a particular water source. Those complexities can inject significant transaction costs and information costs into water rights transfers.

On the other hand, prior appropriation might function well in the face of climate change so long as impediments to marketability of water rights are overcome.[103] Critics argue that water marketing has been more theory than reality, and that most trades have involved relatively small, intrastate transactions among same or similar uses.[104] There are some notable exceptions, however, such as several major transfers of water from large agricultural districts to growing cities in Southern California.[105] And recent empirical studies suggest that water transfers may be on the rise in at least some parts of the west.[106] Increased marketability could both redirect available water to needed areas of growth, and inject the same kinds of incentives for conservation as would be true for marketable riparian rights.

Water marketing could also enable water rights to be purchased for environmental purposes via instream conservation easements or trusts or similar devices. Although protection of public aquatic ecosystems should be a public rather than a private responsibility, increased competition for scarce water may seriously test public commitment to instream protection, and private sector initiatives may become even more critical to aquatic ecosystem health in a changing climate. Of course, it will remain difficult for environmental uses of water to compete with the predominant existing agricultural uses so long as agricultural water in the west remains heavily subsidized. Phasing out those subsidies so that all users are required to bear the full cost of water supply and distribution will further contribute to more efficient water allocation, and increase incentives to invest in water efficiency.

Efforts by individual states to modify the prior appropriation doctrine, of course, will not increase water supplies. Those changes can only seek to improve the manner in which potentially dwindling supplies will be managed and used within western states. The fact that some parts of the country are likely to become even wetter while others become increasingly arid, however, suggests that interstate and national issues of water policy are likely to arise with increasing frequency.

---

101. *See* Tarlock, *supra* note 12, at 176; Dellapenna, *supra* note 4, at 573.
102. *See* Sax *et al.*, *supra* note 84, at 128 *et seq.*
103. For an analysis of those impediments, see Bell and Taylor, *supra* note 61, at 109 *et seq.*
104. *See* Dellapenna, *supra* note 4, at 573; Tarlock, *supra* note 12, at 174.
105. *See* Haddad, *supra* note 51.
106. *See* Glennon, *supra* note 51.

C. Rethinking Federal and State Roles in Water Law and Policy

Since at least the middle of the Nineteenth Century, state water law has reigned supreme as the primary authority governing the allocation and use of water resources.[107] To be sure, there is significant federal involvement in, and control of, various aspects of water resources management and protection. As a result, some prominent scholars have questioned whether the traditionally recognized dominance of state water law is more myth than reality.[108] Nevertheless, even those exercises of federal authority expressly or implicitly defer to state law in most key respects.[109]

The viability and absoluteness of this Nineteenth Century policy eroded as the Twentieth Century proceeded. Both the Supreme Court and Congress stepped in to help resolve interstate water disputes, although usually with significant continued deference to state law.[110] Federal dollars fueled massive dams and other water projects that allowed intrastate, interstate, and international allocation and diversion of water resources across both watershed boundaries and state lines, and those federal benefits came with some strings attached, but again with deference to state water law allocation regimes.[111] Large subsidies inherent in those national investments supported growing and changing economies, but also affected water resource allocation significantly through resulting market distortions rather than direct federal control. Federal regulatory statutes sought to protect water quality, aquatic ecosystems and biological diversity in the face of increasing use of water and waterways, but again, those laws expressly deferred to state water law on issues of allocation.[112]

The current balance between the traditional dominance of state water law and the growing federal financial and regulatory presence in the water resource arena will become considerably more tenuous if current scientific models are correct in their predictions about the effects of global warming on the nation's fresh water resources. As discussed above, state water law will have to adapt quickly to these changing climatic conditions, especially in areas in which water supplies are predicted to decline significantly, and even more so in areas already facing shortages due to rapid growth. Irrespective of those changes, however, significant redistribution of limited fresh water resources will increase pressure for interstate and trans-basin diversions. Purely intrastate remedies designed to re-allocate uses within regions, or to accommodate short-term droughts rather than longer-term or even permanent shifts in supplies, are not likely to prevent more serious interstate and international conflicts. Instream environmental uses may suffer in the face of political pressure to maintain local economies in the face of shortages. All of those limitations suggest that an increased federal role in water law is appropriate, and probably inevitable. Although these arguments will be developed in more detail in another source,[113] several factors suggest that an increased federal role in water law and policy is desirable if not inevitable in the face of climate change.

---

107. *See* California v. United States, 438 U.S. 645 (1978) (identifying a "consistent thread of purposeful and continued deference to state water law by Congress"); United States v. New Mexico, 438 U.S. 696 (1978) (indicating that Congress almost always defers to state water law, and identifying 37 statutes in which Congress had done so to some degree).

108. *See* Reed D. Benson, *Deflating the Deference Myth: National Interests vs. State Authority Under Federal Laws Affecting Water Use*, 2006 Utah L. Rev. 241 (2006); David H. Getches, *The Metamorphosis of Western Water Policy: Have Federal Laws and Local Decisions Eclipsed the States' Role?*, 20 Stan. Envtl. L. J. 3 (2001).

109. *E.g.*, 33 U.S.C. §1251(g) (Clean Water Act); 433 U.S.C. §383 (Reclamation Act §8).

110. *E.g.*, Kansas v. Colorado, 206 U.S. 46 (1907); New York v. New Jersey, 256 U.S. 296 (1921); Colorado v. New Mexico, 459 U.S. 176 (1982).

111. *See* California v. United States, *supra* note 107.

112. *See* 33 U.S.C. §1251 *et seq.* (Clean Water Act); 16 U.S.C. §1531 *et seq.* (Endangered Species Act).

113. Robert W. Adler, *Climate Change and the Hegemony of State Water Law* (in preparation).

First, states jealous of their rich water supplies have sometimes adopted protectionist attitudes toward interbasin water transfers,[114] while others have allowed such transfers to occur regardless of significant impacts to aquatic ecosystems.[115] Neither extreme will necessarily comport with the national interest in water use and allocation, as well as environmental protection, during times of extreme changes in the availability of water supplies across state lines. Clearly, the federal government has both legal authority and a manifest interest in those issues. The Supreme Court has ruled that water is a commodity,[116] and that at least navigable waters are channels of commerce for purposes of federal commerce clause authority.[117] The courts could invoke the dormant commerce clause to prevent states from adopting protectionist policies regarding water supplies that are not related to legitimate environmental, health or safety concerns, but history in similar areas such as interstate waste transport suggests that litigation is not necessarily the most effective and efficient way to regulate those kinds of commerce. A more viable solution might be federal regulation of interstate and international water markets, with rules to prevent protectionist policies, while also ensuring adequate protection of aquatic ecosystems and areas of origin.

Second, especially if regional water scarcity is likely to affect national economic interests as well as interstate and other nationally-important waterways and aquatic ecosystems, the federal government has a strong interest in promoting or requiring more efficient water use. In the past, the national taxpayer has borne the expense for significant federal investments in dams and other water infrastructure. Although the Supreme Court has upheld federal conditions on the use of those facilities despite Congress' general policy of deference to state water law,[118] those conditions typically have not involved water efficiency requirements. Such conditions certainly could be imposed on new or existing federal water facilities. For example, Congress could eliminate or phase out existing federal subsidies and create no new ones. It could establish federal efficiency standards as conditions of receipt of federal water or financial assistance for water projects. Or, it could require recipient states to develop their own efficiency standards tailored to regional climates, uses, and other factors.

Third, significant changes in the distribution of water resources is likely to stimulate more (and more intense) interstate, inter-regional, and international disputes over water use and allocation. The federal government has a strong interest and a useful role to play in resolving interstate and international water disputes fairly and efficiently. Indeed, that has been the most common reason for federal intervention in water resource issues historically, via equitable apportionment cases in Supreme Court, congressional approval of interstate compacts,[119] and in some cases direct federal legislation.[120] The federal government largely abandoned a national basinwide planning approach in the early 1980s when Congress eliminated funding for the Water Resources Development Act of 1965.[121] In the face of climate change, which is likely to pose serious challenges for interstate rivers,[122] it might be wiser for the federal government to anticipate broad regional water disputes and decisions with a more pro-active strategy, such as mandatory anticipatory negotiations on all major interstate river basins.

---

114. *See* Squillace, *supra* note 56; Teclaff, *supra* note 83.
115. *See* ADLER, *supra* note 4, at 33–35.
116. Sporhase v. Nebraska *ex rel.* Douglas, 458 U.S. 941 (1982).
117. United States v. Appalachian Electric Power Co., 311 U.S. 377 (1940).
118. *See* California v. United States, *supra* note 107.
119. *E.g.*, Colorado River Compact, 70 Cong. Rec. 324 (1928).
120. *E.g.*, Boulder Canyon Project Act, 43 U.S.C. §617 *et seq.* (1928).
121. *See* Teclaf, *supra* note 83.
122. *See id.*

Fourth, increased competition for scarce water resources, as well as efforts to control flooding in areas destined for more intense precipitation, will increasingly stress aquatic ecosystems. In efforts to provide adequate water supplies and to protect their citizens from floods, states might engage in a race to the bottom at the expense of aquatic ecosystem protection. The federal government currently intervenes in those choices between economic use and development of waterways and protection of aquatic ecosystem health through laws such as the Clean Water Act,[123] Endangered Species Act,[124] and National Environmental Policy Act.[125] That intervention is somewhat ambiguous, however, because all of them defer to state water law to some degree. At some point, climate change will force a critical value choice about value of water, as it will about many other resources. We will face key decisions about whether we are willing to leave sufficient water in our rivers, lakes, wetlands, and other waters to maintain their ecosystem integrity, in the face of intensified competition over water for economic uses. An obvious related issue is whether those kinds of decisions should be made at the national level, the state and local level, or both.

D.   Rethinking International Water Law

Although a full treatment of the impacts of climate change on international water law is beyond the scope of this analysis, changes in water distribution will have equally or more significant impacts on international water conflicts and agreements. Those disputes may be important because conflicts over water resources have the potential to degenerate into more serious military engagements around the globe, especially in areas where water scarcity leads to severe food shortages and other economic disruptions,[126] or in places such as the Middle East where international tensions are already acute.[127]

International water disputes can be resolved under general principles of customary international law, as reflected in multilateral conventions[128] as well as decisions by international tribunals.[129] Disputes are decided based on a flexible set of equitable criteria, similar to those used by the U.S. Supreme Court under the equitable apportionment doctrine. Although the source of considerable uncertainty until a decision is reached, that system may work reasonably well if conditions remain relatively consistent following a binding decision by the International Court of Justice or other decision making body. If water volumes, variability, seasonality, and other hydrological conditions change significantly due to climate change, the equitable factors underlying those decisions might change as well, causing one or more parties to seek relief from a decision that no longer reflects hydrological reality. That suggests that parties to international water

---

123. 33 U.S.C. §1251 *et seq.*

124. 16 U.S.C. §1531 *et seq.*

125. 42 U.S.C. §4321 *et seq.*

126. *See* Michael T. Klare, *The New Geography of Conflict,* 80(3) Foreign Affairs 49 (2001); Mark F. Giordano, Meredith A. Giordano and Aaron T. Wolf, *International Resource Conflict and Mitigation,* 42 Journal of Peace Research 47 (2005).

127. *See, e.g.,* Joseph W. Dellapenna, *Rivers as Legal Structures: The Examples of the Jordan and the Nile,* 36 Nat. Resources J. 217 (1996); Joseph W. Dellapenna, *The Two Rivers and the Lands Between: Mesopotamia and the International Law of Transboundary Rivers,* 10 BYU J. Pub. L. 213 (1996); James C. MacMurray and A. Dan Tarlock, *The Law of Later-Developing Riparian States: The Case of Afghanistan,* 12 N.Y.U. Envt'l. L.J. 711 (2005).

128. *E.g.,* The Helsinki Rules on the Uses of International Rivers (International Law Association, 1967); Convention on the Protection and Use of Transboundary Watercourses and International Lakes, 31 I.L.M. 1312 (1992); Convention on the Law of the Non-navigational Uses of International Watercourses, 36 I.L.M. 700 (1997).

129. *See* Ahshin A-Khavari and Donald R. Rothwell, *The ICJ and the Danube Dam Case: A Missed Opportunity for International Environmental Law?,* 22 Melb. U. L. Rev. 507 (1998).

disputes might better be served by more specific written agreements that take into account the kinds of variability anticipated due to climate change.

In fact, a large number of international water disputes have been resolved via bilateral or multilateral treaties that address the specific conditions in particular international water basins.[130] Treaties addressing water allocation (as opposed to water quality, infrastructure development, or other issues) follow two major patterns (or both). One specifies fixed volumes of water to which each country is entitled, or to which the downstream nation is entitled. Others establish proportionate allocations, resulting in variable allocations under changing hydrologic conditions.

One team of economists postulated that water allocation agreements must be stable to be effective, but that many existing agreements do not account at all for flow variability, including the expected increased degree of variability as well as declining flows in many rivers due to climate change.[131] Agreements with fixed flow allocations and no provisions for low flows or variability are the least stable, because declining flows obviously result in an inability to fulfill the treaty rights and obligations for all parties. Moreover, many existing water treaties have no provisions for dispute resolution, leaving retaliation as the most likely remedy for noncompliance by one or more parties.[132] Under those conditions, upstream nations with storage capacity or other necessary infrastructure might be expected to withhold water otherwise guaranteed by the treaty, leading to conflict or complete breakdown of the agreement. Treaties with proportional flow allocations, or agreements to share shortages proportionately or according to some other pre-negotiated formula, are likely to be more stable in times of shortage of extreme variability in flow.

The international community, and individual nations with shared water resources, should anticipate rather than react to the potential hydrological effects of climate change, especially in regions that are likely to face serious flooding or drought due to predicted changes in patterns of precipitation and water distribution. Fixed water allocation agreements should be renegotiated to provide for proportionate sharing or other allocation provisions that account for future flow variability. Existing agreements that lack dispute resolution provisions and institutions should be revised to do so. The best form of dispute resolution is likely to be watershed-based multilateral or bilateral commissions or other institutions that can assess and plan for water resources based on basin-wide assessments and solutions. Areas without any existing agreements, but where water distribution problems are likely to arise or worsen, should negotiate appropriate treaties or other agreements in advance of those problems, with sufficient flexibility to deal with changing conditions.

Even those measures, however, may be too narrowly-focused to address the global economic, social, and political impacts of the widespread flooding and droughts likely to occur due to climate change. Those events could be accompanied by severe famine, property damage, disease, and other secondary effects that will, in turn, lead to large populations of refugees and potentially political conflicts on a larger scale. That will affect countries well beyond the geographic regions in which specific hydrological changes occur. As such, the international community should

---

130. According to one source, various nations entered into 145 international agreements on water use in trans-boundary rivers during the Twentieth Century, about half of which address water allocation specifically. ERIK ANSINK AND ARJAN RUIJS, CLIMATE CHANGE AND THE STABILITY OF WATER ALLOCATION AGREEMENTS, Nota Di Lavoro 16.2007, *available at* http://www.feem.it/Feem/Pub/Publications/WPapers/default.htm.

131. *Id.*

132. *Id.*

plan for and address those expected events in advance. For example, it is possible to trade the benefits of water without transporting the water itself, which can be expensive, energy-consumptive (thus exacerbating the underlying issue of climate change), or physically impossible. Thus, a nation whose agricultural production remains less affected by climate change, or whose production may actually increase, can trade their surplus food for other resources in countries that are hydrologically less fortunate.

E. Rethinking the Linkage Between Water and Land Use

For reasons unrelated to climate change, scholars and practitioners from multiple disciplines have advocated better integration of land use and water laws and policies.[133] Benefits of that approach include improved water quality and public health protection; restored and protected aquatic, riparian and floodplain habitats; more sensible matching of water supply and demand; and improved flood control and property protection via natural rather than structural means.

The potential hydrological implications of climate change underscore the wisdom of integrated land use and water laws and policies, at both ends of the hydrological spectrum (drought and flood). High growth areas that are expected to face declining water supplies ultimately will face questions of limits. Unless urban water supplies can be stretched through greater efficiency or increased through agricultural transfers or other ways, communities may need to decide whether to restrict further urban or suburban growth through "assured supply laws"[134] or other means. Although growth limits are controversial, it may become essential to make difficult choices between two opposing strategies: either to transport more water from wet regions to areas in which more people want to live (and to bear the resulting economic and environmental costs), or to adopt policies that favor more people settling where water (and other) resources are adequate.

At the opposite (flood) end of the hydrological spectrum, the relationship between land use and water law and policy is equally or more controversial. Flood losses (to human life and property) do not occur simply because of natural cycles in which rivers naturally overflow their banks into their natural floodplains, or because coastal storms inundate low-lying coastal areas. They occur because of the historic human tendency to build homes, farms, and businesses in the path of those all too predictable events. In other sources I have critiqued laws and policies that allow and promote this extensive development "at the water's edge," and proposed that new concepts of property law should evolve to recognize more limited human development rights in the transition zone between terrestrial and aquatic areas.[135] The fact that so many developed communities in so many regions now face significantly increased threats to human life and property due to global warming-related flooding suggests even more strongly that we reconsider laws and policies that promote development at the water's edge.

V. Conclusion

Current water law regimes evolved during times of relative hydrological stability, at least compared to what scientists predict is likely to occur over the ensuing decades due to climate change. The stability that those legal systems sought to promote is now in jeopardy due to the "death of stationarity," that is, the significantly increased hydrological volatility predicted as a result of cli-

---

133. *See, e.g.* Adler, *supra* note 80; H. Furumai, *supra* note 59.

134. Assured supply laws require, with varying degrees of stringency, that new developments prove adequate water supplies before permits can be issued. *See* Davies, *supra* note 49.

135. *See* Robert W. Adler, *The Law at the Water's Edge: Limits to "Ownership" of Aquatic Ecosystems, in* WET GROWTH, *supra* note 80, at 201; Robert W. Adler, *Overcoming legal barriers to hydrological sustainability of urban systems, in* CITIES OF THE FUTURE, *supra* note 59, at 201.

mate change. It is foolish to wait for those changes to occur before rethinking water laws and policies to make them more adaptive to those expected changes.

———————

Notes

1. On the rethinking of water issues, pre- or post-climate change era, NEPA and its statutory relatives will be much in play. *See Center for Biological Diversity v. U.S. Dep't of Housing and Urban Development*, 541 F. Supp. 2d 1091 (D. Ariz. 2008) (Jorgenson, D.J.). This case was a challenge to actions of HUD, VA, and SBA that provide mortgage insurance, loan guarantees and loans to residential and commercial development in Sierra Vista, Arizona, which will pump groundwater to the detriment of the San Pedro River that is home to the ESA-listed umbel (a plant) and the southwestern Willow Flycatcher (a bird). These activities are alleged to violate NEPA and the ESA and cause "indirect effects" to the protected species. The court says that the actual federal funding here is "negligible or non-existent" and that "federal approval of a local plan does not become major federal action," citing *Rattlesnake Coalition v. U.S. EPA*, 509 F.3d 1095, 1102 (9th Cir. 2007). The court quotes 42 U.S.C.A. §4002(a)(2), which states:

> The Congress finds that the availability of Federal loans, grants, guarantees, insurance, and other forms of financial assistance are often determining factors in the utilization of land and the location and construction of public and private industrial, commercial, and residential facilities.

The district court says this statute "says nothing of environmental protection or discretionary authority over development." *Id.* at 1099. On the contrary, an understanding of NEPA—that expands the charter of all agencies—might find in this statute confirmation that federal funding is often the key or the "major Federal action" that clears the way for development that cries out for environmental analyses. The district court relies on *Ka Makani 'O Kohala Ohana Inc. v. Water Supply*, 295 F.3d 955 (9th Cir. 2002), for the proposition that HUD did not have discretionary control over the "entire" project. But of course there are scores of cases—under Section 404, for example—where the agency does not have discretionary control over the "entire" project but is obliged to discuss the environmental effects of projects they have set free. The court here says the defendants are not the "legal cause" of the harm and the actions do not "significantly affect" the environment. But of course this is why we require of agencies to undertake pre-NEPA analyses. This decision is so wrong that we are lucky the Supreme Court did not take it and declare it right.

2. See *Moss v. Cnty. of Humboldt*, 162 Cal. App. 4th 1041, 76 Cal. Rptr. 3d 428, _____ P.3d _____ (Ct. App. 1st Dist. 2008). This was a CEQA challenge to a long-debated subdivision project to develop 94 acres of former timberland on the north fork of Luffenholtz Creek upstream from the City of Trinidad. The major issues in the case are whether "substantial changes" and "new information" have appeared to require "supplementation" of the EIR. In this case, the County Board of Supervisors had issued a resolution identifying "two categories" of new information—impact on the city's water supply and on biological resources including the coho salmon and coastal cutthroat trout. The court says that new evidence of water use and the recognition that the capacity of the creek to provide water "to both the project and the City of Trinidad has *never actually been studied*" (*id.* at 1061) (emphasis in original) requires further study. The Board's finding that the project could impair fire-fighting capabilities and the threat of increasing forest fires either lacks support in the record or is not new. But the court says (*id.* at 1063): "the supplemental analysis of impacts on water sup-

ply should take account of and address Mayor Lin's concerns about the availability of sufficient water for the City of Trinidad to respond to fire hazards." Though the words "climate change" are not used, this court has acknowledged the possibility of a future with less water and more fire.

3. No-growth or slow-growth on water availability? See *In re Bay Delta Programmatic Environmental Impact Report Coordinated Proceedings*, 43 Cal.4th 1143, 77 Cal. Rptr. 3d 578, 184 P.3d 709 (2008) (Kennard, J.). This ruling reverses the Court of Appeals' determination that CAL FED's programmatic document was deficient for failure to consider an alternative of "smaller water exports" that in turn could curtail population growth. The court of appeals also erred in requiring CAL FED to identify where its future water would come from and what the effects of securing it would be. "[F]irst-tier" programmatic documents can omit the detail "appropriate for second-tier site-specific review." 77 Cal. Rptr. 3d at 597–98. *See id.* at 602: "Under CEQA's tiering principles, it is proper for a lead agency to use its discretion to focus a first-tier EIR on only the general plan or program, leaving project-level details to subsequent EIR's when specific projects are being considered." This is a manifestation of the contemporary debate in California on what Prof. Adler describes as assured supply laws.

4. Dave Owen, *Law, Environmental Dynamism, Reliability: The Rise and Fall of CALFED*, 37 Envtl L. 1145, 1214 (2007). Quotes the response of water managers to future severe droughts predicted by the models of climate change: "well, if that happens, forget it. There's just no way they could deal with that." The author: "those managers' attitude toward managing a different future — a future that will only be made more difficult if western water managers continue to subsidize and promote increased water consumption — suggests the inadequate paradigms informing much environmental management." Problems with "variable, scare resources" are "likely to recur over and over again." We are "inescapably in a world where management schemes must address dynamism and scarcity, no matter how difficult that task may be."

5. Climate change expert, Fred Pearce, has written a stirring and well-documented book, entitled When the Rivers Run Dry: Water the Defining Crisis of the Twenty-First Century (Beacon Press 2006). In it, he says (124):

> The U.S. government's Scripps Institution of Oceanography estimates that reservoir levels in the Colorado will fall by a third as declining rainfall and rising evaporation combine to reduce moisture by up to 40 percent across the southern and western states. The Niger River, which waters five poor and arid countries in West Africa, is expected to lose a third of its water, and the Nile, the lifeblood of Egypt and Sudan, could lose a fifth. Inland seas will be at special risk as many rivers in continental interiors lose flow. Lake Chad has almost succumbed and may suffer further in future. Also under threat are the Caspian Sea and Lake Balkhash in Central Asia, Lakes Tanganyika and Malawi in East Africa, and Europe's largest, Lake Balaton, in Hungary.
>
> In contrast, giant tropical rivers like the Amazon and the Orinoco in South America and the Congo in Africa will become even more bloated than today, the models predict. Similarly, the great Arctic rivers of northern Canada and Siberia will probably gain water as warmer air holds more moisture and more rain falls on their catchments. So the Mackenzie and the Yukon in Canada and the Ob, the Yenisei, and the Lena in Siberia will rage even more fiercely — 40 percent more, according to one big study.

6. On extravagant water withdrawal practices at home, *see Rangely Crossroads Coalition v. Land Use Regulation Comm'n*, 955 A.2d 223 (Me. 2008). A successful groundwater raid by Nestle Waters North America. Nestle submitted to the Maine Land Use Regulatory Commission an application for a development to permit Nestle to construct a commercial groundwater extraction and tanker-truck load-out facility that would move the water to bottling plants. Nestle has reached agreement with the Rangeland Water Dist. regarding use of the aquifer. Part of this deal is that "Nestle will negotiate a set of festival days with the Town of Rangely when Nestle's trucks will not be routed through the town." This use is permissible under Category 30 of the LURC rules (an open-ended invitation to act consistently with the plan and in ways "not detrimental to the resources or uses they protect.") Dissenters say: "Each day, up to one hundred trucks would transport 8,256 gallons each of water from the area."

7. For an ambitious, inspiring and well-documented overview, see Robert Glennon, Unquenchable: America's Water Crisis And What To Do About It (Island Press 2009).

8. Testimony of Dr. Jane Lubchenko, Under Secretary of Commerce for Oceans and Atmosphere and NOAA Administrator, National Oceanic & Atmospheric Administration, U.S. Department of Commerce, Hearing on Expanding Climate Services and Developing the National Climate Service, Before House Subcomm. on Energy & Environment, May 5, 2009, pp. 3–4:

> Until now, the systems and infrastructure that we as a nation have developed as the foundation of our water energy, transportation, agriculture, and other sectors have been designed and built based on what we know about local environmental conditions, and our understanding of the past. In the same way, our approaches to the management and conservation of ecosystems and species have largely relied upon our scientific, historical understanding of those systems.

> For example, water planning and management have been based on historical fluctuations in records of stream flows, lake levels, precipitation, temperature, and water demands. All aspects of water management including reservoir sizing, reservoir flood operations, maximum urban stormwater runoff amounts, and projected water demands have been based on these records. Because climate change will significantly modify aspects of the water cycle, the assumption of an unchanging climate is no longer appropriate for many aspects of water planning. To appropriately prepare their communities, decisionmakers will need to be supported with access to the best climate information science can provide, and tools to apply that data to guide their decisions.

Climate Change in Wetland Ecosystems:
Meeting the Needs and Welfare of the People and the Planet

Kim Diana Connolly, University of South Carolina School of Law

I. Introduction: Wetlands and Climate Change[1]

Wetlands are nifty. Biologically diverse systems that provide vital services to their local communities and the planet as a whole, wetlands of some sort are found in every one of the United States and in every nation in the world.[2] What we call a "wetland" differs greatly,[3] depending on local systemic factors including soil, topography, climate, hydrology, water chemistry, vegetation, and human impact.[4] Yet all wetlands provide various "functions and values"[5] (also known as ecosystem services)[6] that serve the needs and welfare of the people and the planet, including some combination of water quality improvement through the trapping and filtering of pollutants, flood water retention and storage, habitat for endangered and other species, recreational

---

1. Substantial portions of this chapter appeared as part of a document to fulfill the thesis requirement for an LL.M. from George Washington University Law School. The author is grateful for helpful comments from Prof. Arnold Reitze on an earlier draft.

2. *See* NATURESERVE, BIODIVERSITY VALUES OF GEOGRAPHICALLY ISOLATED WETLANDS IN THE UNITED STATES (2005), *available at* http://www.natureserve.org/publications/isolatedwetlands.jsp. For locations of wetlands of international importance throughout the world, see The Ramsar Convention on Wetlands, www.ramsar.org (last visited Aug. 23, 2008) and Wetlands International, Ramsar Sites Information Service, http://www.wetlands.org/RSDB/default.htm (last visited Aug. 23, 2008).

3. Hong Kong Ecotourism Society, Ltd., *Wetlands Definition/Delineation Controversy*, *available at* www.ecotourism.org.hk/other%20files/Wetlands%20Definition.doc ("Unfortunately, wetlands are difficult to reduce to a single definition, largely because their essential elements are so diverse and variable in character. Wetlands inhabit a transitional zone between terrestrial and aquatic habitats, and are influenced to varying degrees by both. They differ widely in character around the country because of regional and local differences in climate, soils, topography, landscape position, hydrology, water chemistry, vegetation, and other factors. Depth and duration of inundation, a key defining force, can differ greatly between wetland types and can vary from year to year within a single wetland type. Wetlands definition by vegetation is difficult, as some wetland species can live in either wetlands or uplands, while others are adapted to only a wet environment. Because wetland habitats are so diverse as to form a continuum connecting terrestrial to aquatic ecotypes, and because they can vary so significantly within a given type, no universally recognized wetland definition exists.")

4. U.S. Environmental Protection Agency, Wetlands Definitions, http://www.epa.gov/owow/wetlands/what/definitions.html (last visited Aug. 23, 2008). These differences in wetlands impact climate change analysis. As one group of scientists phrased it, "[t]he regional assessment revealed a wide variability in wetland responses to sea level rise, both within and among subregions and for a variety of wetland settings. This underscores both the influence of local processes on wetland elevation and the difficulty of scaling down regional/national scale projections of wetland sustainability to the local scale in the absence of local accretionary data. Thus regional or national scale assessments should not be used to develop local management plans where local accretionary dynamics may override regional controls on wetland vertical development." U.S. CLIMATE CHANGE SCIENCE PROGRAM, COASTAL SENSITIVITY TO SEA LEVEL RISE: A FOCUS ON THE MID-ATLANTIC REGION, draft at 137 (Feb. 12, 2008), *available at* http://climatescience.gov/Library/sap/sap4-1/public-review-draft/sap4-1-prd.pdf.

5. For a table summarizing wetland functions and values, see U.S. Army Corps of Engineers, *Wetland Functions and Values*, http://www.usace.army.mil/cw/cecwo/reg/wet-f-v.htm (last visited July 20, 2008).

6. United States Army Corps of Engineers and U.S. Army Corps of Engineers, Compensatory Mitigation for Losses of Aquatic Resources, 73 Fed. Reg. 19,594, 19,604 (Apr. 10, 2008), *available at* http://www.epa.gov/owow/wetlands/pdf/wetlands_mitigation_final_rule_4_10_08.pdf and http://www.usace.army.mil/cw/cecwo/reg/news/final_mitig_rule.pdf, *codified at* 33 C.F.R. pt. 325 and 40 C.F.R. pt. 230 (" ... we have eliminated the term 'values' from the final rule because the term 'services' is currently being used in the ecological literature to relate to the human benefits that are provided by an ecosystem. The concept of ecosystem services provides a more objective measure than 'values' of the importance of the functions performed by the ecosystem to human populations.").

and educational activities, and aesthetic values.[7] One increasingly recognized function for many wetlands is carbon sequestration,[8] a vital service as we consider how to mitigate for and adapt to climate change.[9] These services cross political boundaries in many cases.[10]

As complex biogeochemical systems,[11] wetlands, have been susceptible to human-induced[12] and non human-induced[13] impacts for many years. Most human impacts threaten ecosystems by decreasing associated functions and values.[14]

---

7. *See generally* NAT'L ACAD. OF SCIENCES, NAT'L RESEARCH COUNCIL, WETLANDS: CHARACTERISTICS AND BOUNDARIES (1995), *available at* http://www.nap.edu/books/0309051347/html/index.html; U.S. Army Corps of Engineers, *Technical and Biological Information*, http://www.usace.army.mil/inet/functions/cw/cecwo/reg/techbio.htm (last visited July 20, 2008); U.S. Envtl. Prot. Agency, *Functions and Values*, http://www.epa.gov/owow/wetlands/functions.html (last visited July 20, 2008). *See also* Brief of Ecological Society of America, Society of Wetland Scientists, American Society of Limnology and Oceanography, and Estuarine Research Federation As *Amici Curiae* in Support of Respondents, Rapanos v. United States, Carabell v. United States Army Corps Of Engineers, 126 S.Ct. 2208 (2006) (Nos. 04-1034, 04-1384), Supreme Court of The United States, Jan. 13, 2006, *available at* http://www.eswr.com/1105/rapanos/rapamicesa.pdf; Donald R. Cahoon, U.S. Geological Services, *Response of Coastal Ecosystems to Sea-Level Rise: Assessing Wetland Elevation Changes, Potential for Submergence, and Management Options* (2004), http://www.nrel.colostate.edu/projects/brd_global_change/proj_43_wetland_elev.html.

8. JON KUSLER, CLIMATE CHANGE IN WETLAND AREAS PART II: CARBON CYCLE IMPLICATIONS FROM ACCLIMATIONS (July–Aug. 1999), *available at* http://www.usgcrp.gov/usgcrp/Library/nationalassessment/newsletter/1999.08/Wet.html (" … there is broad agreement that wetland plants continue to convert atmospheric carbon into biomass and carbon-rich sediments continue to be deposited in wetlands. Net carbon sequestration occurs as long as rates of conversion exceed decomposition and external transport of materials from wetlands.… What is needed to better evaluate generically and in specific settings the roles of wetlands as carbon reservoirs and for carbon sequestering and to guide protection, enhancement, restoration or creation efforts. A combination of literature surveys, scientific consensus-building measures (workshops), field measures and laboratory studies are needed. Some priority topics for such evaluation efforts include: evaluating wetlands as carbon reservoirs; estimating sequestration rates in wetlands; and enhancing, restoring and creating wetlands.").

9. Watchwords of climate change policy are "adaptation" and "mitigation": in short, these terms are used to describe dealing with and planning for climate change impacts. *See generally* KIRSTIN DOW AND THOMAS E DOWNING, THE ATLAS OF CLIMATE CHANGE: MAPPING THE WORLD'S GREATEST CHALLENGE (2d ed. Un. of Calif. Press 2007).

10. *See, e.g.,* DR BRIAN GROOMBRIDGE, WORLD CONSERVATION MONITORING CENTRE, SHARED WETLANDS AND RIVER BASINS OF THE WORLD: PRELIMINARY FINDINGS OF A GIS ANALYSIS (report prepared in support of Ramsar COP7 Technical Session V), *available at* http://www.ramsar.org/cop7/cop7_doc_20.1_e.htm.

11. 8th INTECOL Wetland Conference website, Missions and Themes, http://www.cppantanal.org.br/intecol/eng/sections.php?id_section=5 (last visited Aug. 10, 2008) ("Wetlands play an important role in the biogeochemical cycles that affect the global climate, functioning, for instance, as carbon sinks but also as methane sources. Predictions about human-induced changes in the global climate include an increase in extreme climate events and changes in the amount and pattern of precipitation. These changes will strongly impact wetlands, because of their low hydrological buffer capacity.").

12. Royal C. Gardner, *Rehabilitating Nature: A Comparative Review of Legal Mechanisms That Encourage Wetland Restoration Efforts*, 52 CATH. U.L. REV. 573 (2003) ("In many parts of the world, people have long drained, filled, and otherwise destroyed vast areas of wetlands." *Id.* at 573).

13. *See, e.g.,* United States Fish and Wildlife Service, *Blackwater National Wildlife Refuge, Refuge at Risk*, http://www.fws.gov/blackwater/restore.html (last visited Oct. 9, 2008) ("Blackwater National Wildlife Refuge is a refuge at risk. Since the 1930s, over 8,000 acres—or 12 square miles—of marsh at Blackwater Refuge has been lost at a rate of 150 acres per year. Causes of this marsh loss include sea level rise, erosion, subsidence, salt water intrusion, and invasive species (such as the recently extirpated nutria).")

14. *See, e.g.,* Virginia R. Burkett, Chief, Forest Ecology Branch, National Wetlands Research Center, US Geological Survey, *Wetland Functions, Values and Vulnerability (Abstract)*, *available at* http://www.lanl.gov/projects/chinawater/documents/ecoabst.pdf ("Human settlements have historically been drawn to deltas, rivers, alluvial valleys, coastal zones, and other regions in which wetlands naturally occur due to the availability of water and other natural resources associated with these highly productive ecosystems. Population growth, coupled with man's increasing ability to manipulate the environment, has led to wetland deterioration and conversion to other uses. Wetlands have been drained and impounded for agricultural development;

Climate change ramps up these threats.[15] As Wetlands, the leading wetlands science text explains: "[w]etlands have significant yet generally under-appreciated roles in the global carbon cycle. They are also positioned in the landscape where climate change could affect them more than most other ecosystems."[16] Planning for climate change when dealing with wetlands thus requires us to acknowledge the roles of wetlands "both as players in and recipients of climate change...."[17] In short, development of short and long term climate change policy should include a more serious investment in assessing likely impacts on and opportunities from wetlands that will be associated with the shifting global climate. Managers and policymakers must develop scientifically sound and workable plans for adapting to and mitigating for change to wetland ecosystems.[18] The central role that wetlands play in the increasingly changing landscape of environmental law mandates no less.

This essay begins by exploring what science tells us about climate change and wetlands. It continues with an examination of how we govern wetlands (primarily on a federal level), both in terms of incentivizing preservation and wise management, and through regulation.[19] It goes on to discuss a new vision for federal wetland regulation in light of climate change, and reaches several conclusions. It concludes generally that serious and swift efforts to address climate overall will benefit all essential planetary resources including wetlands. On a wetland-specific level, it recommends that incentive programs to protect and restore wetlands be expanded, that drastically increased funding should be dedicated to relevant applied scientific research regarding wetlands and climate change, that broader climate change legislative efforts include wetland considerations, that fewer permits should be issued to allow wetland destruction by rigorously incorporating climate change considerations into existing regulatory program requirements, and that international efforts to address climate change and wetlands through the Ramsar Convention be increased. Wetlands deserve no less.

---

levees have been constructed around them to prevent flooding and rivers that provide essential water and nutrients have been channelized, dammed and diked. Approximately half of the wetlands that existed in the conterminous United States at the time of European settlement have been lost or converted to other uses.").

15. Deborah Zabarenko, *Wetlands could unleash "carbon bomb,"* Reuters UK (June 20, 2008) http://uk.reuters.com/article/environmentNews/idUKN1745905120080720 ("The world's wetlands, threatened by development, dehydration and climate change, could release a planet-warming 'carbon bomb' if they are destroyed, ecological scientists said on Sunday.") (last visited Aug. 10. 2008).

16. William J. Mitsch and James G. Gosselink, Wetlands 313 (4th ed. Wiley 2007).

17. *Id.*

18. For a terrific portal into research on climate change and wetlands, see Ass'n of State Wetland Managers, *Wetlands and Global Climate Change*, http://www.aswm.org/science/climate_change/climate_change. htm#1 (last visited Sept 5, 2008). *See also* the special issue of the National Wetlands Newsletter dedicated to climate change, http://www2.eli.org/nwn/nwnarchive/21-02articles.cfm. Interestingly, leading texts dedicated to climate change law do not invest much more than passing mention of wetlands. *See* Michael Gerrard, Global Climate Change and U.S. Law (American Bar Ass'n 2007). Likewise, leading wetlands law texts do not discuss climate change in any depth. *See, e.g.,* Kim Diana Connolly, Stephen M. Johnson and Douglas R. Williams, Wetlands Law and Policy: Understanding Section 404 (American Bar Ass'n 2005); William L. Want, Law of Wetlands Regulation (Westlaw 1989 and Supp. 2008).

19. The Corps is responsible for issuing permits pursuant to three statutes: Section 404 of the Federal Water Pollution Control Act, 33 U.S.C. §1344 (2000), Sections 9 and 10 of the Rivers and Harbors Acts of 1899, 33 U.S.C. 401, *et seq.* (2000), and Section 103 of the the Marine Protection, Research, and Sanctuaries Act, 33 U.S.C. §1413 (2000). *See generally* 33 C.F.R. Part 320 (General Regulatory Policies) (2008), 33 C.F.R. Part 321 (Permits for Dams & Dikes in Navigable Waters of the U.S.) (2008), 33 C.F.R. Part 322 (Permits for Structures in or Affecting Navigable Waters of the U.S.) (2008), 33 C.F.R. Part 323 (Permits for Discharges of Dredged or Fill Material Into Waters of the U.S.) (2008), 33 C.F.R. Part 324 (Permits for Ocean Dumping of Dredged Material) (2008), 33 C.F.R. Part 325 (Processing of Department of the Army Permits) (2008).

II. What Science Establishes About Climate Change and Wetlands

Climate change, also referred to in some literature as global warming,[20] has become a central part of national and international environmental policy in the past few years.[21] Wetlands (like other ecosystems) have been and will continue to be impacted by climate change.[22]

As the Intergovernmental Panel on Climate Change (IPCC) (a scientific intergovernmental body set up by the World Meteorological Organization (WMO) and by the United Nations Environment Programme (UNEP))[23] recently concluded, climate change is a serious worldwide crisis.[24] The 2003 Pew Commission report indicates that "scientists expect … climate change will result in … serious, if not catastrophic, damage to some ecosystems. Important coastal and ocean habitats, including coral reefs, coastal wetlands, estuaries, and mangrove forests will be particularly vulnerable to the effects of climate change. These systems are essential nurseries for commercial fisheries and support tourism and recreation."[25] Likewise, an IPCC 2008 Technical Paper on Climate Change and Water concluded that "[c]limate change will have its most pronounced effects on inland freshwater wetlands through altered precipitation and more frequent or intense disturbance events (droughts, storms, floods). Relatively small increases in precipitation variability can significantly affect wetland plants and animals at different stages of their life cycle.… Generally, climatic warming is expected to start a drying trend in wetland ecosystems. This largely indirect influence of climate change, leading to alterations in the water level, would be the main agent in wetland ecosystem change …"[26]

Like the panels and committees cited above, others have been warning for years that wetlands cannot escape the changing climate.[27] Scientific experts confirm that climate change[28] will affect

---

20. *See, e.g.*, An Inconvenient Truth, http://www.climatecrisis.net/ (last visited Oct. 10, 2008); U.S. Environmental Protection Agency, *Climate Change*, http://www.epa.gov/climatechange/ (last visited Oct. 10, 2008); Competitive Enterprise Institute, *Global Warming*, http://www.globalwarming.org/ (last visited Oct. 10, 2008); Union of Concerned Scientists, *Global Warming*, http://www.ucsusa.org/global_warming/ (last visited Oct. 10, 2008).

21. *See* PEW Center for Global Climate Change, *U.S. Federal*, http://www.pewclimate.org/federal (last visited Oct. 10, 2008).

22. As parties to the recent Ramsar Convention Conference of the Parties put it: "REAFFIRMING that integrative policies and planning measures need to be encouraged in order to address the influence of global climate change on the interdependencies between wetlands, water management, agriculture, energy production, poverty reduction and human health." 10th Meeting of the Conference of the Parties to the Convention on Wetlands (Ramsar, Iran, 1971); "Healthy wetlands, healthy people," Changwon, Republic of Korea, 28 October–4 November 2008, Resolution X.24 Climate change and wetlands, *available at* http://www.ramsar.org/res/key_res_x_index_e.htm (last visited Dec. 30, 2008).

23. Intergovernmental Panel on Climate Change, *About IPCC,* http://www.ipcc.ch/about/index.htm (last visited Oct. 10, 2008).

24. Intergovernmental Panel on Climate Change, Climate Change 2007: The Physical Science Basis, Summary for Policy Makers (Cambridge Un. Press 2007), *available at* http://www.ipcc.ch/SPM 2feb07.pdf.

25. Pew Oceans Comm'n, America's Living Oceans: Charting A Course For Sea Change 83 (2003), *available at* http://www.pewtrusts.com/pdf/env_pew_oceans_final_report.pdf.

26. B.C. Bates, Z.W. Kundzewicz, S. Wu and J.P. Palutikof, Eds., *Climate Change and Water, Technical Paper of the Intergovernmental Panel on Climate Change* (2008), *available at* http://www.ipcc.ch/pdf/technical-papers/climate-change-water-en.pdf [hereinafter *Climate Change and Water*].

27. *See, e.g.,* John Kusler & Virginia Burkett, *Climate Change in Wetland Areas Part I: Potential Wetland Impacts and Interactions*, Acclimations, Newsletter of the US National Assessment of the Potential Consequences of Climate Variability and Change (May–June 1999), *available at* http://www.usgcrp.gov/usgcrp/Library/nationalassessment/newsletter/1999.06/wet.html; James G. Titus, *Greenhouse Effect And Coastal Wetland Policy: How Americans Could Abandon An Area The Size Of Massachusetts At Minimum Cost*, 15 Env't Mgmt. 39 (1991); James G. Titus, *Sea Level Rise and Wetland Loss: An Overview, U.S. Environmental Protection Agency*, (1988) http://yosemite.epa.gov/oar/globalwarming.nsf/UniqueKeyLookup/SHSU5BNQKX/ $File/chap1.pdf.

28. For links to many excellent websites that address climate change generally, see NASA, *Global Warming*

wetlands.[29] Though the precise manner and extent of the effects are as yet unknown, scientists have presented some compelling data regarding a number of areas of impact. These include sea level rise, varying effects on coastal wetlands, unintended effects from biofuel production, hurricane-related effects, methane issuance, and ecosystem alteration.

In what is perhaps the most obvious impact, sea level rise will inundate coastal wetlands.[30] The IPCC 2007 WORKING GROUP II REPORT ON IMPACTS, ADAPTATION AND VULNERABILITY, for example, definitively concluded that "[s]ea-level rise and human development are together contributing to losses of coastal wetlands and mangroves and increasing damage from coastal flooding in many areas."[31] Accordingly, as one leading wetlands scientist put it, the future appearance of the coast "depends in part on how coastal wetlands respond. Will they keep up?"[32] Most experts agree that coastal wetlands are already experiencing negative climate change effects.[33] These effects are expected to escalate.[34]

Scientists have been studying the effect of climate change on coastal wetlands for decades. For example, a group of scientists began using one model in the 1980s, the Sea Level Affecting Marshes Model (SLAMM), which demonstrates that dominant processes involved in wetland conversions and shoreline modifications can be predicted during long-term sea level rise.[35] As it

---

and Climate Change Policy Websites, http://globalchange.nasa.gov/Resources/pointers/glob_warm.html (last visited July 20, 2008). One excellent website with an overview of the international policy issues associated with climate change generally is hosted by Climate Action Network, http://www.climatenetwork.org/climate-change-basics (last visited Aug. 15, 2008).

29. See supra notes 20–28 and accompanying text. See also A.E. Altor and W.J. Mitsch, Pulsing hydrology, methane emissions, and carbon dioxide fluxes in created marshes: A 2-year ecosystem study, 28 WETLANDS 423 (2008); A.E. Altor and W.J. Mitsch, Methane emissions and carbon dioxide fluxes in created wetland mesocosms: Effects of hydrologic regime and hydric soils, 18 ECOLOGICAL APPLICATIONS 1307 (2008). For a glimpse into some relevant science, see NASA, Global Change Master Directory, http://globalchange.nasa.gov/Keyword Search/Titles.do?Portal=GCMD&KeywordPath=Parameters|BIOSPHERE|AQUATIC+ECOSYSTEMS|WETLANDS&MetadataType=0&lbnode=mdlb2 (search BIOSPHERE > AQUATIC ECOSYSTEMS > WETLANDS). See also Mongabay, Destruction of wetlands worsens global warming (July 20, 2008) ("Destruction of wetland ecosystems will generate massive greenhouse gas emissions in coming years, warn experts convening at an international wetlands conference in Brazil."); U.S. Climate Change Technology Program, Technology Options for the Near and Long Term 3.2-11 (Aug. 2005), available at http://www.climatetechnology.gov/ library/2005/tech-options/tor2005-3216.pdf. ("Fire, permafrost melt, sea-level rise, and more frequent droughts will affect wetlands.").

30. WETLANDS, supra note 16, at 327; see also INTERGOVERNMENTAL PANEL ON CLIMATE CHANGE, CONTRIBUTION OF WORKING GROUP II TO THE FOURTH ASSESSMENT REPORT OF THE INTERGOVERNMENTAL PANEL ON CLIMATE CHANGE, Coastal Systems and Low-Lying Areas (2007), at 6, available at http://www.ipcc.ch/pdf/assessment-report/ar4/wg2/ar4-wg2-chapter6.pdf.

31. INTERGOVERNMENTAL PANEL ON CLIMATE CHANGE, CONTRIBUTION OF WORKING GROUP II TO THE FOURTH ASSESSMENT REPORT OF THE INTERGOVERNMENTAL PANEL ON CLIMATE CHANGE, Summary for Policymakers (Cambridge Un. Press 2007), available at http://www.ipcc.ch/pdf/assessment-report/ar4/wg2/ar4-wg2-spm.pdf.

32. James Morris, Climate Change and Coastlines, at 7, http://heinzhome.heinzctrinfo.net/Programs/SOCW/coastal_vision/charleston_forum_12_2006/presentations/Morris_Mepkin_and_Forum_Dec_5_and_6.pdf.

33. "It is virtually certain that the Nation's tidal wetlands already experiencing submergence by sea-level rise and associated high rates of loss (e.g., Mississippi River Delta in Louisiana, Blackwater River marshes in Maryland) will continue to lose area under the influence of future accelerated rates of sea-level rise and changes in other climate and environmental drivers." U.S. Climate Change Science Program, Coastal Elevations and Sensitivity to Sea Level Rise—Public Review Draft for Synthesis and Assessment Product 4.1 (2008) (emphasis deleted), available at http://climatescience.gov/Library/sap/sap4-1/public-review-draft/sap4-1-prd-exec-summary.pdf.

34. See Climate Change and Water, supra note 26.

35. SLAMM Version and Development History, http://www.warrenpinnacle.com/prof/SLAMM/Versions.html (last visited Aug. 1, 2008).

has evolved over the years, the SLAMM model looks at a variety of coastal wetlands as catego-rized by the U.S. Fish and Wildlife Services' National Wetlands Inventory,[36] and maps distribu-tions of wetlands under conditions of accelerated sea level rise, and subsequently presents results in tabular and interactive graphical form.[37] Depending on the rate of sea level rise, various sce-narios of inundation, erosion, overwash of barrier islands and saturation leading to the migra-tion of coastal swamps and fresh marshes play out.[38]

The production of biofuels has become very popular as a partial response to fossil fuel contri-butions to climate change.[39] There are, however, recognized impacts by biofuel production on wetlands.[40] As Wetland International's experts explain, "[r]esearch by Wetlands International showed that biofuels are responsible for huge carbon emissions due to peatland conversion and degradation."[41] Scientists are still studying the impacts,[42] but as energy policy evolves close atten-tion should be dedicated to this area as well.

In research on climate change and hurricanes, wetlands play a central part. The IPPC has con-cluded that "[i]n both developed and developing countries, the expected continuation of rapid population growth in coastal cities will increase human exposure to flooding and related storm damages from hurricanes and other coastal storms.... That very development is contributing to the loss of deltaic wetlands that could buffer the storm impacts."[43] Although this IPCC report and other sources[44] indicate that hurricanes can devastate wetlands, the relationship between hurricanes and climate change is not entirely clear. As one legal scholar wrote in 2006, "[t]he debate over the rela-tionship between global climate change and hurricane activity is unlikely to reach a definitive reso-lution any time soon."[45] Therefore, although the research regarding the relationship between wet-

---

36. The categories are: Dry Land (Developed and Undeveloped); Swamp (General, Cypress, & Tidal); Transitional Marsh (Occasionally Inundated, Scrub Shrub); Marsh (Salt, Brackish, Tidal Fresh, Inland Fresh, Tall Spartina); Mangrove (Tropical Settings Only); Beach (Estuarine, Marine, Rocky Intertidal) Flats(Tidal Flats & Ocean Flats); and Open Water (Ocean, Inland, Riverine, Estuarine, Tidal Creek). SLAMM Overview Powerpoint, linked from http://www.warrenpinnacle.com/prof/SLAMM/index.html (last visited Aug. 1, 2008). The National Wetlands Inventory homepage can be found at http://www.fws.gov/nwi/index.html.

37. SLAMM Model Overview, http://www.warrenpinnacle.com/prof/SLAMM/overview.html (last visited Aug. 1, 2008).

38. *Id.*

39. *See, e.g.*, U.S. Department of Energy, *Biofuels—A Solution for Climate Change* (Sept. 1999), *available at* http://www.nrel.gov/docs/fy99osti/24052.pdf (last visited Dec. 16, 2008); World Resources Institute, *Bio-fuels Production and Policy: Implications for Climate Change, Water Quality, and Agriculture*, http://www.wri. org/project/biofuels (last visited Dec. 16, 2008); Biofuels and Climate Change, http://biofuelsandclimate.word press.com/ (last visited Dec. 16, 2008).

40. As the Ramsar Conference of the Parties put it in its recent resolution, "biofuel can be manufactured from many different food and non-food crops, such as sugar cane, corn, beets, wheat and sorghum (grown for conversion to bioethanol) and rapeseed, sunflower, soya, oil palm, coconut and jatropha (grown for con-version to biodiesel), each with different potential impacts on wetlands, including differences between geno-types of the same crop type" 10th Meeting of the Conference of the Parties to the Convention on Wetlands (Ramsar, Iran, 1971) "Healthy wetlands, healthy people" Changwon, Republic of Korea, 28 October–4 No-vember 2008, Ramsar COP10 Resolution X.25, Wetlands and "biofuels," *available at* http://www.ramsar.org/ cop10/cop10_docs_index_e.htm#general (last visited Dec. 16, 2008).

41. *See* Wetlands International, *Wetlands and Biofuels*, http://www.wetlands.org/Whatwedo/Projects/ WetlandsandBiofuels/tabid/1253/Default.aspx (last visited Dec. 16, 2008).

42. *See, e.g.*, RL NAYLOR, AJ LISKA, MB BURKE, WP FALCON, JC, THE RIPPLE EFFECT: BIOFUELS, FOOD SE-CURITY, AND THE ENVIRONMENT (Heldref Publications, 2007).

43. *Climate Change and Water, supra* note 26, at 73.

44. *See, e.g.,* National Wildlife Federation, *Hurricanes and Global Warming: Hurricanes and Wetlands*, http://www.nwf.org/hurricanes/hurricanesandwetlands.cfm (last visited Oct. 5, 2008).

45. Robert L. Glicksman, *Global Climate Change and the Risks to Coastal Areas from Hurricanes and Rising Sea Levels: The Costs of Doing Nothing*, 52 LOY. L. REV. 1127, 1155 (2006) ("Although the question is certainly not free from doubt, there is evidence (regarded by some as merely suggestive, but by others as compelling)

lands loss and hurricanes is not yet conclusive,[46] we do know that "wetlands are valuable resources that moderate the impacts of coastal storms and hurricanes."[47] The fact that coastal wetlands can be severely damaged by hurricanes may in turn be exacerbated by other climate change impacts.

Science has also demonstrated that wetlands are being and will be impacted by climate change. As a leading wetlands conservation group, Wetlands International, urges, we must therefore build "international support and action to integrate wetland conservation and restoration in strategies to help people around the world to adapt to climate change."[48] Likewise, the International Union for Conservation of Nature (IUCN) has concluded that "there is a growing scientific understanding that the conservation and wise use of wetlands can no longer be achieved without taking climate change into account."[49]

In addition to being negatively impacted by climate change, wetlands may contribute to climate change. Many wetlands also have some level of methane emissions, which is a significant gas in terms of climate change.[50] Wetland disturbance may thus increase emissions of these gases,[51] and that means consideration should be given as to how to address such increased emissions and whether to limit disturbances to limit associated emissions. The U.S. Environmental Protection Agency estimates that "[n]atural wetlands are responsible for approximately 76% of global methane emissions from natural sources.... Wetlands provide a habitat conducive to methane-producing (methanogenic) bacteria that produce methane during the decomposition of organic material."[52] Some scientists point to wetland disturbance as a reason for the sharp 2008 increase in methane emissions worldwide, the first increase for over a decade.[53] Some scientists raise an even greater level of alarm about the role of wetlands in cli-

---

that increases in sea surface temperatures caused by anthropogenic global climate change, rather than only by natural climatic cycles, are correlated to increased hurricane severity." *Id.* at 1197.).

46. "Researchers appear to agree that there is no basis yet for asserting that anthropogenic climate change has affected or will affect the frequency of hurricanes that form in the North Atlantic." Rex Caffey, Louisiana Sea Grant College Program, *Lousiana Hurricane Resources*, http://www.lsu.edu/departments/laseagrant/ hurricane/archive/wetlands.htm (last visited Sept. 12, 2008) ("Was some of the damage from Hurricanes Katrina and Rita exacerbated by the loss of Louisiana's coastal wetlands? The answer is probably yes, although quantifying the additive hurricane damages caused by lost or highly deteriorated wetlands is a difficult, if not impossible task.").

47. Christine A. Klein, *The New Nuisance: An Antidote to Wetland Loss, Sprawl, and Global Warming*, 48 B.C. L. Rev. 1155, 1175 (2007).

48. Wetlands International, *Sustaining and Restoring Wetlands: An Effective Climate Change Response*, http://www.wetlands.org/Whatwedo/Wetlandsandclimatechange/Wetlandsandclimatechangeadaptation/tabid/ 836/Default.aspx (last visited Aug. 28, 2008).

49. Ger Bergkamp & Brett Orlando, IUCN—The World Conservation Union, Wetlands and Climate Change: Exploring Collaboration Between the Convention on Wetlands (Ramsar, Iran, 1971) and the UN Framework Convention on Climate Change (1999), *available at* http://www.ramsar. org/key_unfccc_bkgd.htm (last visited Aug. 28, 2008).

50. Harvey Augenbraun, Elaine Matthews & David Sarma, Goddard Institute for Space Studies, *The Global Methane Cycle*, http://icp.giss.nasa.gov/education/methane/intro/cycle.html ("Wetlands are most likely the largest natural source of methane to the atmosphere; their emissions are estimated to be about 100 Tg annually.").

51. *See, e.g.,* Huai Chen *et al., Determinants influencing seasonal variations of methane emissions from alpine wetlands in Zoige Plateau and their implications*, 113 Journal Of Geophysical Research 12303 (2008); Yanhua Wanga *et al., Influence of plant species and wastewater strength on constructed wetland methane emissions and associated microbial populations*, 32 Ecological Engineering 22 (2008).

52. U.S. Envtl. Prot. Agency, *Methane, Sources and Emissions*, http://www.epa.gov/methane/sources.html (last visited Aug 23, 2008).

53. Earth Science Research Laboratory, National Oceanic & Atmospheric Administration, *Annual Greenhouse Gas Index (AGGI) Indicates Sharp Rise in Carbon Dioxide and Methane in 2007* (Apr. 23, 2008), http://www.esrl.noaa.gov/news/2008/aggi.html (last visited June 22, 2009). ("Methane levels rose last year for the first time since 1998. Methane is 25 times more potent as a greenhouse gas than carbon dioxide, but

mate change, as summarized by a journalist in summer 2008: "[w]etlands are dangerous, scientists say, in the sense that they are ticking carbon bombs best left alone. To help stave off extreme climate change, existing wetlands should be enhanced and new wetlands created so they could capture more carbon."[54] Scientific research on methane, wetlands and climate change continues.[55]

In reviewing this scientific literature, it is important to remember that wetlands have been deemed vital to our people and the planet. As scientists and other experts who drafted the Millennium Ecosystem Assessment[56] summarized, wetlands provide "ecosystem services that contribute to human well-being, such as fish and fiber, water supply, water purification, climate regulation, flood regulation, coastal protection, recreational opportunities, and, increasingly, tourism."[57] Moreover, as that assessment continues, "[s]ome groups of people, particularly those living near wetlands, are highly dependent on these services and are directly harmed by their degradation."[58] Likewise, many non-human populations, including a high percentage of species listed under the United States Endangered Species Act,[59] depend on wetlands.[60]

Such vital wetland ecosystems worldwide are at the forefront of vulnerable areas in terms of the current and foreseen disruption of climate change. As the Ecosystems Interagency Working Group noted in 2006, in terms of planning scientific investigatory priorities, attention should be paid to the "most critical needs of society: food from the land and water; abundant, clean fresh water for consumption, industry, agriculture, recreation, and flow to coastal waters; clean air that minimizes health risks to humans and risks to ecosystems; healthy and productive estuaries and oceans bordering coastal regions where over half of all U.S. citizens live; security from diseases and environmental disasters; a healthy environment for recreation and enjoyment of nature; and wildlife and biodiversity."[61] Wetland ecosystems are an integral part of supporting such needs.[62] Therefore, as the Director of the U.S. Fish and Wildlife Service under

---

there's far less of it in the atmosphere.... Rapidly growing industrialization in Asia and rising wetland emissions in the Arctic and tropics are the most likely causes of the recent methane increase, said scientist Ed Dlugokencky from NOAA's Earth System Research Laboratory.")

54. Stephen Leahy, *Climate Change: Wetlands Loss Fuelling CO_2 Feedback Loop,* Interpress Service (July 22, 2008), *available at* http://www.ipsnews.net/news.asp?idnews=43254.

55. *See* Richard Black, *Methane rise points to wetlands,* BBC (May 23, 2008), http://news.bbc.co.uk/2/hi/science/nature/7408808.stm (last visited Oct. 9, 2008).

56. The Millennium Ecosystem Assessment ("MA") was "called for by the United Nations Secretary-General Kofi Annan in 2000. Initiated in 2001, the objective of the MA was to assess the consequences of ecosystem change for human well-being and the scientific basis for action needed to enhance the conservation and sustainable use of those systems and their contribution to human well-being." Overview of the Millennium Ecosystem Assessment, http://www.millenniumassessment.org/en/About.aspx#1 (last visited Aug. 1, 2008).

57. Ecosystems And Human Well-Being: Wetlands And Water, Synthesis, A Report of the Millennium Ecosystem Assessment, at *Key Messages,* Page 1, *available at* http://www.millenniumassessment.org/documents/document.358.aspx.pdf.

58. *Id.* at 1.

59. The Endangered Species Act of 1973, 16 U.S.C. §§ 1531–1544 (2006).

60. William Want, Law of Wetlands Regulation 2:3 (Thomson/West 2008); Jon A. Kusler, Our National Heritage: A Protection Guidebook 3 (1st ed. Environmental Law Institute 1983); Oliver A. Houck, *Reflections on the Endangered Species Act,* 25 Envtl. L. 689, 696 (1995) ("More than fifty percent of all listed endangered species occupy these same coastlines, floodplains, and wetlands.").

61. Alan Lucier *et al.,* Ecosystems and Climate Change: Research Priorities for the U.S. Climate Change Science Program—Recommendations from the Scientific Community 2–3 (2006), *available at* http://www.usgcrp.gov/usgcrp/Library/ecosystems/eco-workshop-report-jun06.pdf.

62. *See* Ger Bergkamp & Brett Orlando, IUCN—The World Conservation Union, Wetlands and Climate Change: Exploring Collaboration between the Convention on Wetlands (Ramsar, Iran, 1971) and the UN Framework Convention on Climate Change (1999), *available at* http://www.ramsar.org/key_unfccc_bkgd.htm#es.

President George W. Bush has asserted, "[t]he warming of the earth … could potentially have more far-reaching impacts on wildlife and wildlife habitat than any challenge that has come before us."[63]

It is not too late to call on scientists to help policy-makers reverse these trends. Scientists have transformed the way we view (and thus have influenced the way we govern) wetlands in the past. In 1956, the Fish and Wildlife Service published Samuel P. Shaw and C. Gordon Fredine's WETLANDS OF THE UNITED STATES.[64] This publication provided a new vocabulary—using the generic term "wetlands" in place of terms such as "swamp" or "bog"—that scholars have concluded "conveyed positive symbolic value born from trustworthy scientific expertise."[65] Shortly thereafter, the Fish and Wildlife Coordination Act[66] and other measures that provide some level of protection and oversight on wetland ecosystems were developed. Given what science already demonstrates regarding wetlands and climate change, stepped-up investment in efforts to mitigate and adapt to climate change in the wetlands context must be undertaken immediately. Like those scientists of the last century, appropriate science could lead to a change in direction on climate change policy as it impacts wetlands. As Wetlands International has phrased it: "strategies for adaptation to climate change that do not address the continuing crisis in wetlands loss and degradation, will have real limitations, and could result in maladaptation and reduced resilience."[67] We as a nation and a planet have much work to do.

III. How We Govern Wetlands in the United States

In the United States, the federal government has a number of laws it uses to manage our wetland resources.[68] Some federal programs encourage preservation of wetlands through financial incentives, outright acquisition, or other management techniques.[69] Two other federal programs regulate activities in wetlands: the Rivers and Harbors Act of 1899[70] and the Federal Water Pollu-

---

63. H. Dale Hall, Director, U.S. Fish and Wildlife Service, http://www.fws.gov/home/climatechange/dhall-public.html (last visited Aug. 30, 2008).

64. Samuel P. Shaw & C. Gordon Fredine, *Wetlands of the United States: Their Extent and Their Value to Waterfowl and Other Wildlife,* Fish and Wildlife Service Circular 39 (1956), *available at* http://www.npwrc.usgs.gov/resource/wetlands/uswetlan/index.htm.

65. ANN VILEISIS, DISCOVERING THE UNKNOWN LANDSCAPE: A HISTORY OF AMERICA'S WETLANDS 209 (Island Press 1997).

66. 16 U.S.C. §§ 661–667e (2006).

67. WETLANDS INTERNATIONAL, WETLANDS AND CLIMATE CHANGE ADAPTATION—SUSTAINING AND RESTORING WETLANDS: AN EFFECTIVE CLIMATE CHANGE RESPONSE, *available at* http://www.wetlands.org/ Portals/0/publications/Brochure/wetlands_adaptation_press19aug.pdf.

68. This section does not discuss wetlands regulation in other nations in much depth. For a more detailed discussion of international wetland protection measures, see RAMSAR SECRETARIAT, THE RAMSAR CONVENTION MANUAL: A GUIDE TO THE CONVENTION ON WETLANDS 44 (Ramsar, Iran, 1971, 4th ed. Gland, Switzerland 2006), *available at* http://www.ramsar.org/lib/lib_manual2006e.pdf. *See also* Royal C. Gardner and Kim Diana Connolly, *The Ramsar Convention on Wetlands: Assessment of International Designations Within the United States,* 37 ENVTL. LAW REPORTER 10089 (Feb. 2007), *available at* http://www.ramsar.org/ wurc/wurc_gardner_elr2007.pdf.

69. *See, e.g.,* the Coastal Wetlands Planning, Protection, and Restoration Act, 104 Stat. 4779, Title III of Pub. L. 101-646, 16 U.S.C. §§ 3951–3956 (2000), which established the National Coastal Wetlands Conservation Grant Program to acquire, restore, and enhance wetlands of coastal states and the Trust Territories. *See also* North American Wetlands Conservation Act, 103 Stat. 1968; Pub. L. 101-233, 16 U.S.C. §§ 4401–4412 (2000), which provides funding and administrative direction for implementation of the North American Waterfowl Management Plan and a Tripartite Agreement on wetlands between Canada, the U.S., and Mexico.

70. 33 U.S.C. §§ 401–418 (2006).

tion Control Act[71] (commonly known as the Clean Water Act).[72] Other nations have different regulatory approaches.[73] There is also regulation at state and local levels.[74]

Historically, humans invested much time and money in eliminating wetlands in the United States and worldwide.[75] Indeed, the U.S. Supreme Court even opined in 1900 that "swamps and stagnant waters are the cause of malarial and malignant fevers, and that the police power is never more legitimately exercised than in removing such nuisances."[76] Likewise, non-human causes have contributed to the loss of wetlands as well. As the authors of Coast 2050 wrote, "[d]irect losses can be quantified and attributed to specific causes with reasonable accuracy. Since the 1970s, direct losses have been reduced through a permitting program required by Section 404 of the Clean Water Act as well as state laws. Indirect losses, on the other hand, cannot be attributed to specific causes with any degree of accuracy. This is due to the natural variability of coastal processes and the complex way that human activities have altered these processes."[77] The result is that close to half of the wetlands originally in the United States no longer exist, and more than half (perhaps as much as 90 percent in some areas) are gone in other parts of the world.[78]

The United States shifted its approach to wetlands in recent decades. In terms of indirect federal governance in the United States provided through incentives, management support, and funding, several laws may come into play.[79] For example, the United States Department of Agriculture administers a Wetlands Reserve Program (WRP)[80] authorized by the Farm Bill.[81] The WRP is a voluntary program that provides technical and financial assistance to eligible landowners who wish to restore, enhance, and protect wetlands.[82] Landowners can enroll eligible wet-

---

71. Pub. L. No. 92-500, 86 Stat. 816 (1972), as codified in 33 U.S.C. §§ 1251–1387 (2006).

72. The Federal Water Pollution Control Act (FWPCA), is commonly referred to as the Clean Water Act following the 1977 amendments to the FWPCA. Pub. L. No. 95-217, 91 Stat. 1566 (1977) ("SEC. 518. This Act may be cited as the 'Federal Water Pollution Control Act' commonly referred to as the Clean Water Act.").

73. A compilation of some interesting regulatory approaches adopted by other nations can be found at The Ramsar Convention on Wetlands, The Wise Use Resource Centre, National Wetland Policies and Strategic Plans, http://www.ramsar.org/wurc/wurc_library.htm#nwps (last visited Aug. 15, 2008). *See also* Michael Bowman, The *Ramsar Convention on Wetlands: Has it Made a Difference? in* YEARBOOK OF INTERNATIONAL CO-OPERATION ON ENVIRONMENT AND DEVELOPMENT 61 (Olav Schram Stokke and Oystein B. Thommessen eds., Earthscan Publications 2002), *available at* http://www.ramsar.org/key_law_bowman2.htm.

74. *See generally* Assn of State Wetland Mgrs, State Wetland Programs, http://www.aswm.org/swp/statemainpage9.htm (last visited July 8, 2009). *See also* Leah Stetson, Assn of State Wetland Mgrs, *Understanding Federal, State and Local Dredge & Fill Permitting Programs* (July 2007), *available at* http://www.aswm.org/swp/design_wetlands/dredge_&_fill_0407.pdf.

75. *See generally* Kim Diana Connolly and Douglas R. Williams, Ch. 1, *Federal Wetlands Regulation: An Overview, in* KIM DIANA CONNOLLY, STEPHEN M. JOHNSON AND DOUGLAS R. WILLIAMS, WETLANDS LAW AND POLICY: UNDERSTANDING SECTION 404 (American Bar Ass'n, 2005).

76. Leovy v. United States, 177 U.S. 621, 626 (1900).

77. Denise J. Reed and Lee Wilson, *Coast 2050: A New Approach to Restoration of Lousiana's Coastal Wetlands*, 25 PHYSICAL GEOGRAPHY 4 (2004).

78. Environmental Protection Online, *Experts Review Wetlands in Climate Change Context* (July 24, 2008), http://www.eponline.com/articles/65640/ (last visited Aug. 1, 2008) ("Some 60 percent of wetlands worldwide—and up to 90 percent in Europe—have been destroyed in the past 100 years, principally due to drainage for agriculture but also through pollution, dams, canals, groundwater pumping, urban development, and peat extraction.").

79. A recent discussion of various incentive and funding programs that support wetlands can be found in COUNCIL ON ENVIRONMENTAL QUALITY, CONSERVING AMERICA'S WETLANDS 2008: FOUR YEARS OF PARTNERING RESULTED IN ACCOMPLISHING THE PRESIDENT'S GOAL, *available at* http://www.whitehouse.gov/ceq/ wetlands/2008/2008_wetlands.pdf.

80. *See generally* http://www.nrcs.usda.gov/Programs/WRP/.

81. Subtitle D, Title XII, Food Security Act of 1985 (16 U.S.C. §§ 3837–3837f); 7 C.F.R. Part 1467 (2008).

82. *See* Natural Resources Conservation Service, Wetlands Reserve Program Description (Apr. 2007), *available at* http://www.nrcs.usda.gov/Programs/WRP/2007_ContractInfo/2007WRPProgramDescription.pdf.

lands through permanent or long-term temporary easements or restoration cost-share agreements.[83] As of 2006, the WRP had enrolled 9,226 projects with a total of 1.744 million acres, and easements had been perfected on 1.37 million of those acres.[84] A related option through the Conservation Reserve Program's[85] Farmed Wetlands Program[86] provides incentive payments, and cost-sharing for installing necessary practices to farmers who own land containing farmed and prior converted wetlands annual rental payments.[87] Through 2006, the Farmed Wetlands Program had enrolled 166,000 acres through more than 10,000 contracts.[88] Additional incentives through the Wetland Restoration Initiative[89] of the Conservation Reserve Program have provided incentives for protecting larger tracts of land.[90]

---

83. *Id.*

84. Jeffrey A. Zinn, and Claudia Copeland, Congressional Research Service, Wetlands: An Overview of Issues, Summary at 14, (Dec. 11, 2006), *available at* http://www.ncseonline.org/NLE/ CRSreports/07Jan/RL33483.pdf. ("Under the Wetland Reserve Program (WRP), enacted in 1990, landowners receive payments for placing easements on farmed wetlands. All easements were permanent until provisions in the 1996 farm bill, requiring temporary easements and multi-year agreements as well, were implemented. The 2002 farm bill reauthorized the program through FY2007 and raised the enrollment cap to 2,275,000 acres, with 250,000 acres to be enrolled annually. In addition, in June 2004, NRCS announced a new enhancement program on the lower Missouri River in Nebraska to enroll almost 19,000 acres at a cost of $26 million, working with several public and private partners. Through FY2005, 9,226 projects had enrolled 1.744 million acres, and easements have been perfected on 1.37 million of those acres. A majority of the easements are in three states: Louisiana, Mississippi, and Arkansas. Most of the land is enrolled under permanent easements, while only about 10% is enrolled under 10-year restoration agreements, according to data supplied by NRCS in support of its FY2007 budget request. Prior to the 2002 farm bill, farmer interest had exceeded available funding, which may help to explain why Congress raised the enrollment ceiling in that legislation.").

85. Natural Resources Conservation Service, *Conservation Reserve Program*, http://www.nrcs.usda.gov/ programs/CRP/ (last visited Oct. 10, 2008) ("The Conservation Reserve Program (CRP) provides technical and financial assistance to eligible farmers and ranchers to address soil, water, and related natural resource concerns on their lands in an environmentally beneficial and cost-effective manner. The program provides assistance to farmers and ranchers in complying with Federal, State, and tribal environmental laws, and encourages environmental enhancement.... CRP is administered by the Farm Service Agency, with NRCS providing technical land eligibility determinations, conservation planning and practice implementation. The Conservation Reserve Program reduces soil erosion, protects the Nation's ability to produce food and fiber, reduces sedimentation in streams and lakes, improves water quality, establishes wildlife habitat, and enhances forest and wetland resources. It encourages farmers to convert highly erodible cropland or other environmentally sensitive acreage to vegetative cover, such as tame or native grasses, wildlife plantings, trees, filterstrips, or riparian buffers. Farmers receive an annual rental payment for the term of the multi-year contract. Cost sharing is provided to establish the vegetative cover practices.").

86. United States Department of Agriculture, Farm Service Agency, *Farmable Wetlands Program*, http:// www.fsa.usda.gov/FSA/webapp?area=home&subject=copr&topic=fwp (last visited Oct. 10, 2008). ("The Farmable Wetlands Program (FWP) is a voluntary program to restore up to 500,000 acres of farmable wetlands and associated buffers by improving the land's hydrology and vegetation. Eligible producers in all states can enroll eligible land in the FWP through the Conservation Reserve Program (CRP).").

87. *Id.*

88. Zinn & Copeland, *supra* note 84, at 14 ("The 2002 farm bill also expanded the 500,000-acre Farmable Wetlands Pilot Program within the Conservation Reserve Program (CRP) to a 1-million-acre program available nationwide. Only wetland areas that are smaller than 10 acres and are not adjacent to larger streams and rivers are eligible. This program may become more important to overall protection efforts in the wake of the *SWANCC* decision, discussed above, which limited the reach of the Section 404 permit program so that it does not apply to many small wetlands that are isolated from navigable waterways. Through September 2006, more than 166,000 acres had been enrolled in this program through more than 10,000 contracts, with about 70,000 of those acres in Iowa.").

89. United States Department of Agriculture, Farm Service Agency, Conservation Reserve Program—Wetlands Restoration Initiative, (Aug. 2004), *available at* http://www.fsa.usda.gov/Internet/ FSA_File/nonfloodwet04.pdf.

90. Zinn & Copeland, *supra* note 84, at 14 ("On August 4, 2004, the Administration announced a new Wetland Restoration Initiative to allow enrollment of up to 250,000 acres of large wetland complexes and

Similarly, the North American Wetlands Conservation Act (NAWCA) of 1989[91] provides matching grants to organizations and individuals who have developed partnerships to carry out wetlands conservation projects in the United States, Canada, and Mexico for the benefit of wetlands-associated migratory birds and other wildlife.[92] Likewise, the Coastal Wetlands Planning, Protection, and Restoration Act (CWPPRA),[93] enacted in 1990 and administered by the U.S. Army Corps of Engineers, funds wetland restoration projects, primarily in Louisiana.[94] Many of these programs have been identified as contributing to the no-net-loss concept of wetlands in the United States.[95] Given current realities, these programs should be expanded.

In terms of regulatory programs that govern some activities in wetlands, the oldest is that of the Rivers and Harbors Act of 1899.[96] Section 10 of that Act makes it unlawful "to excavate or fill, or in any manner to alter or modify the course, location, condition, or capacity of, any port, roadstead, haven, harbor, canal, lake, harbor of refuge, or inclosure [sic] within the limits of any breakwater, or of the channel of any navigable water" without the appropriate permit.[97] Since the century before last, the United States Army Corps of Engineers (Corps)[98] has been tasked with

---

playa lakes located outside the 100-year floodplain in the CRP after October 1, 2004. The Administration estimated that implementation of this initiative will cost $200 million. Participants receive incentive payments to help pay for restoring the hydrology of the site, as well as rental payments and cost sharing assistance to install eligible conservation practices.").

91. 103 Stat. 1968, 16 U.S.C. §§ 4401–2214 (2000). *See generally* U.S. Fish and Wildlife Service, North American Wetlands Conservation Act, http://www.fws.gov/birdhabitat/grants/nawca/index.shtm (last visited Aug. 31, 2008).

92. *See* Ducks Unlimited, *North American Wetlands Conservation Act Fact Sheet*, http://www.ducks.org/media/Conservation/Farm%20Bill/_documents/Fact%20Sheet%20-%20NAWCA%20(high%20res)%20June%202007.pdf (last visited Aug. 31, 2008).

93. 104 Stat. 4779, Title III of Pub. L. 101-646, 16 U.S.C. §§ 3951–3956 (2000).

94. *See* Council on Environmental Quality, Conserving America's Wetlands 2008: Four Years of Partnering Resulted in Accomplishing the President's Goal, Appendix I. Coastal Wetlands Planning, Protection and Restoration Act (CWPPRA), (Apr. 2008), *available at* http://www.whitehouse.gov/ceq/wetlands/2008/appendix-i.html.

95. *See* ENVIRONMENTAL PROTECTION AGENCY, THE UNITED STATES ARMY CORPS OF ENGINEERS, AND THE UNITED STATES DEPARTMENTS OF AGRICULTURE, COMMERCE, INTERIOR, AND TRANSPORTATION, NATIONAL WETLANDS MITIGATION ACTION PLAN 1 (Dec. 24, 2002), *available at* http://www.mitigationactionplan.gov/map1226withsign.pdf.

96. 33 U.S.C. §§ 401–418 (2000).

97. The full text of Section 10 of the Rivers and Harbors Act reads: "That the creation of any obstruction not affirmatively authorized by Congress, to the navigable capacity of any of the waters of the United States is hereby prohibited; and it shall not be lawful to build or commence the building of any wharf, pier, dolphin, boom, weir, breakwater, bulkhead, jetty, or other structures in any port, roadstead, haven, harbor, canal, navigable river, or other water of the United States, outside established harbor lines, or where no harbor lines have been established, except on plans recommended by the Chief of Engineers and authorized by the Secretary of War; and it shall not be lawful to excavate or fill, or in any manner to alter or modify the course, location, condition, or capacity of, any port, roadstead, haven, harbor, canal, lake, harbor of refuge, or inclosure [sic] within the limits of any breakwater, or of the channel of any navigable water of the United States, unless the work has been recommended by the Chief of Engineers and authorized by the Secretary of War prior to beginning the same." 33 U.S.C. § 403 (2000). The Corps' current regulations state in relevant part that "[t]he U.S. Army Corps of Engineers has been involved in regulating certain activities in the nation's waters since 1890." 33 C.F.R. § 320.1(a)(1) (2006).

98. *See* United States Army Corps of Engineers, Regulatory Program, http://www.usace.army.mil/cw/cecwo/reg/ (last visited Aug. 1, 2008). Congress created the United States Army Corps of Engineers in 1802. Act of Mar. 16, 1902, ch. 9, § 26, 2 Stat. 132, 137. Its duties eventually expanded to include regulatory functions. *See generally* Garrett Power, *The Fox in the Chicken Coop: The Regulatory Program of the U.S. Army Corps of Engineers*, 63 VA. L. REV. 503 (1977).

implementing the Rivers and Harbors Act of 1899, including its regulatory provisions.[99] Many modern activities that impact "navigable waters"[100] under that Act will require permits from the Corps.[101] These covered activities include many actions in or near wetlands.

Under the Rivers and Harbors Act of 1899, therefore, the Corps has been issuing permits for activities in the nation's waters since the century before last. In 1972, the Corps added to its regulatory regime when Section 404[102] of the Federal Water Pollution Control Act[103] (which came to be known as the Clean Water Act (CWA))[104] was enacted. Unlike the much older Rivers and Harbors Act of 1899, this law was one of a number of new laws evolving in the late 1960s through the early 1980s.[105] Through the CWA, Congress sought to "restore and maintain the chemical, physical and biological integrity of our nation's waters,"[106] in part through Section 404, "Permits for dredged or fill material."[107]

The CWA makes "the discharge of any pollutant by any person" without a permit unlawful.[108] The statute defines "discharge of a pollutant" as "any addition of any pollutant to navigable waters from any point source,"[109] then defines "pollutant" to include material such as "dredged spoil, ... rock, sand, [and] cellar dirt...."[110]

---

99. *See* UNITED STATES ARMY CORPS OF ENGINEERS, SUMMARY OF HISTORY, http://www.usace.army.mil/cw/cecwo/reg/reghist.pdf.

100. 33 C.F.R. Part 329 (2008). As defined in that part, "[n]avigable waters of the United States are those waters that are subject to the ebb and flow of the tide and/or are presently used, or have been used in the past, or may be susceptible for use to transport interstate or foreign commerce. A determination of navigability, once made, applies laterally over the entire surface of the waterbody, and is not extinguished by later actions or events which impede or destroy navigable capacity." § 329.4. Because the history and definition differ, there is significant debate about the term "navigable waters" as it pertains to the Clean Water Act. *See* Kim Diana Connolly, *Any Hope for Happily Ever After? Reflections on Rapanos and the Future of the Clean Water Act Section 404 Program*, *in* THE SUPREME COURT AND THE CLEAN WATER ACT: FIVE ESSAYS (VT. J. ENVTL. L. 2006), *available at* http://it.vermontlaw.edu/VJEL/Rapanos/7-Connolly.pdf.

101. Several other sections of the Rivers and Harbors Act of 1899 may be relevant to coastal activities. For example, Section 9 (codified at 33 U.S.C. § 401 (2000)) sets forth requirements for approval of dams, dikes, bridges or causeways to be constructed over or in navigable waters. Likewise, Section 11 (codified at 33 U.S.C. § 404 (2000)) gives the Secretary of the Army the power to establish harbor lines beyond which no structures may extend. Section 12 (codified at 33 U.S.C. § 406 (2000)) makes violations of sections 9, 10, and 11 criminal acts and imposes fines or imprisonment or both, and also provides for the removal or treatment of offending structures. Finally, Section 13, commonly known as "The Refuse Act" (codified at 33 U.S.C. § 407 (2000)) prohibits the discharge of "any refuse matter of any kind or description" into navigable waters.

102. 33 U.S.C. § 1344 (2000).

103. Pub. L. No. 92-500, 86 Stat. 816 (1972), *as codified in* 33 U.S.C. §§ 1251–1387 (2006), further amended in Pub. L. No. 95-217, 91 Stat. 1567 (1977); Pub. L. No. 100-4, 101 Stat. 45 (1987).

104. The Federal Water Pollution Control Act (FWPCA), is commonly referred to as the Clean Water Act following the 1977 amendments to the FWPCA. Pub. L. No. 95-217, 91 Stat. 1566 (1977) ("SEC. 518. This Act may be cited as the 'Federal Water Pollution Control Act' commonly referred to as the Clean Water Act.").

105. *See generally* RICHARD J. LAZARUS, THE MAKING OF ENVIRONMENTAL LAW (Un. Chicago Press 2004). *See also* ROBERT W. ADLER, JESSICA C. LANDMAN AND DIANE M. CAMERON, THE CLEAN WATER ACT 20 YEARS LATER (Island Press 1993).

106. 33 U.S.C. § 1251(a) (2006). To achieve this objective, Congress listed seven goals, each of which indicates concern for values other than navigability. *Id.* § 1251(a)(1)–(6). These broad goals of the law include "protection and propagation of fish, shellfish, and wildlife," "recreation in and on the water," elimination of "the discharge of toxic pollutants in toxic amounts," and "programs for the control of nonpoint source pollution." *Id.*

107. *Id* § 1344 (2006).

108. 33 U. S. C. § 1311(a).

109. *Id.* at § 1362(12).

110. 33 U.S.C. § 1362(6).

Under CWA section 404, the Corps may issue permits for the "discharge of dredged or fill material into the navigable waters."[111] Interpreting exactly when a permit is needed requires a case-by-case analysis.[112] Accordingly, for many permit applications the Corps assigns a project manager to evaluate the permit application.[113]

Pursuant to both CWA Section 404 and the Rivers and Harbors Act of 1899, Corps project managers consider thousands of permit requests for many different projects involving aquatic resources such as wetlands.[114] In recent years, Corps personnel[115] have reviewed close to 90,000 permit applications per year.[116] Available statistics demonstrate that the Corps denies only one quarter of one percent of submitted permit applications.[117] Furthermore, most permit applications proceed in an expedited manner[118] that does not involve a site-specific public interest review.[119] Only about 4,000 individual permits receive full assessment on a site-specific level of all

---

111. *Id.* at § 1344.

112. *See generally* KIM DIANA CONNOLLY, STEPHEN M. JOHNSON AND DOUGLAS R. WILLIAMS, WETLANDS LAW AND POLICY: UNDERSTANDING SECTION 404 (American Bar Ass'n 2005).

113. As the Corps explains on its website, "Corps districts operate under what is called a project manager system, where one individual is responsible for handling an application from receipt to final decision. The project manager prepares a public notice, evaluates the impacts of the project and all comments received, negotiates necessary modifications of the project if required, and drafts or oversees drafting of appropriate documentation to support a recommended permit decision. The permit decision document includes a discussion of the environmental impacts of the project, the findings of the public interest review process, and any special evaluation required by the type of activity such as compliance determinations with the Section 404(b)(1) Guidelines or the ocean dumping criteria." U.S. Army Corps of Engineers, Regulatory Program Overview, http://www.usace.army.mil/cw/cecwo/reg/oceover.htm (last visited Aug 20, 2008).

114. ExpectMore.gov, Detailed Information on the Corps of Engineers: Regulatory Program Assessment, http://www.whitehouse.gov/omb/expectmore/detail.10001130.2005.html (last visited June 29, 2006).

115. I have had the good fortune of becoming personally acquainted with dozens of Corps regulatory staff through my experience as an instructor in the Proponent-Sponsored Engineer Corps Training (PROSPECT) program. *See* U.S. Army Corps of Engineers, Professional Development Support Center, http://pdsc.usace. army.mil (last visited Sept 2, 2008). It has been incredibly rewarding to work with many dedicated regulatory and other Corps staff as an instructor in that program since 1998, teaching the Environmental Laws and Regulations course. Ground-level regulatory staff attempt each day to navigate applicable policy mandates the best they can, and are viewed in a very positive light by many members of the permitted community. *See* Kim Diana Connolly, *Survey Says: Army Corps No Scalian Despot*, 37 ENVTL. L. REP. 10317 (May 2007).

116. *See* U.S. ARMY CORPS OF ENGINEERS, US ARMY CORPS OF ENGINEERS REGULATORY PROGRAM, (2003) [hereinafter REGULATORY STATISTICS], http://www.usace.army.mil/inet/functions/cw/cecwo/reg/2003 webcharts.pdf (last visited Aug. 25, 2008).

117. The latest publicly available statistics are from FY 2002 and FY 2003. *Id.* They show that in 2002, there were 128 denials of the 81,302 permits applied for (0.16%), and in 2003, there were 299 denials of the 86,177 (0.35%) permits applied for. This is an average of 0.25%. To be fair, some permit applications for which applications are submitted may not ultimately result in development. Moreover, mitigation requirements and other conditions may be imposed as part of the Corps-issued permit. Yet as the Corps admits, "[t]hose few applicants who have been denied permits usually have refused to change the design, timing, or location of the proposed activity." U.S. Army Corps of Engineers, Frequently Asked Questions, http://www. usace.army.mil/cw/cecwo/reg/reg_faq.htm (last visited Sept. 2, 2008).

118. Most permits processed by the U.S. Army Corps of Engineers are those issued pursuant to Section 404(e), 33 U.S.C. § 1344(e). Regulatory Statistics, *supra* note 116, at 1 (showing that in FY 2003, 78,803 permits proceeded as nationwide or regional general permits).

119. U.S. Army Corps of Engineers, Regulatory Program, Overview, http://www.usace.army.mil/cw/ cecwo/reg/oceover.htm (last visited Aug. 25, 2008) ("Probably the single biggest safeguard of the program is the Corps public interest review, which also forms the main framework for overall evaluation of the project. This review requires the careful weighing of all public interest factors relevant to each particular case. Thus, one specific factor (*e.g.*, economic benefits) cannot by itself force a specific decision, but rather the decision represents the net effect of balancing all factors, many of which are frequently in conflict.").

impacts, while the rest are processed in a more expedited manner.[120] Most applicants who proceed through the process are very satisfied with the permitting experience.[121]

Corps permitting regulations acknowledge that wetlands have important functions, and states that because "[m]ost wetlands constitute a productive and valuable public resource, the unnecessary alteration or destruction of which should be discouraged as contrary to the public interest."[122] Wetlands that are recognized by the Corps to "perform functions important to the public interest include:

(i)   Wetlands which serve significant natural biological functions, including food chain production, general habitat and nesting, spawning, rearing and resting sites for aquatic or land species;

(ii)   Wetlands set aside for study of the aquatic environment or as sanctuaries or refuges;

(iii)   Wetlands the destruction or alteration of which would affect detrimentally natural drainage characteristics, sedimentation patterns, salinity distribution, flushing characteristics, current patterns, or other environmental characteristics;

(iv)   Wetlands which are significant in shielding other areas from wave action, erosion, or storm damage. Such wetlands are often associated with barrier beaches, islands, reefs and bars;

(v)   Wetlands which serve as valuable storage areas for storm and flood waters;

(vi)   Wetlands which are ground water discharge areas that maintain minimum baseflows important to aquatic resources and those which are prime natural recharge areas;

(vii)   Wetlands which serve significant water purification functions; and

(viii)   Wetlands which are unique in nature or scarce in quantity to the region or local area."[123]

In acknowledgement of this and other factors, before issuing a permit the Corps requires a formal "public interest review."[124] Characterized in 2000 by Corps Headquarters as "[p]robably the single biggest safeguard of the [Corps' regulatory] program,"[125] the public interest review process has been identified as providing "balancing" information on a White House website: "The CWA regulations … provide additional information on the 'public interest review' which is designed to balance both the protection and utilization of important natural and other resources, including aquatic resources."[126]

---

120. REGULATORY STATISTICS, *supra* note 116. For FY 2003, only 4,035 of the 86,177 permits processed by the Corps were individual (a.k.a "standard") permits. *Id.*

121. *See* Kim Diana Connolly, *Survey Says: Army Corps No Scalian Despot*, 37 ENVTL. L. REP. 10317 (May 2007).

122. 33 C.F.R. § 320.4(b)(1) (2008).

123. *Id.* § 320.4(b)(2).

124. 33 C.F.R. pt. 320 (2008). *See* generally Kim Diana Connolly, *Shifting Interests: Rethinking The U.S. Army Corps of Engineers Permitting Process and Public Interest Review in Light of Hurricanes Katrina and Rita*, 32 T. MARSHALL L. REV. 109, 115–119 (2006).

125. U.S. ARMY CORPS OF ENGINEERS HEADQUARTERS, REGULATORY DECISION SAFEGUARDS (Mar. 1, 2000), *available at* http://www.usace.army.mil/inet/functions/cw/cecwo/reg/press/safeguards.pdf. ("[p]robably the single biggest safeguard of the [Corps' regulatory] program… which also forms the main framework for overall evaluation of the project. This review requires the careful weighing of all public interest factors relevant to each particular case. Thus, one specific factor (*e.g.*, economic benefits) cannot by itself force a specific decision, but rather the decision represents the net effect of balancing all factors, many of which are frequently in conflict. The public interest review is used to evaluate applications under all authorities administered by the Corps.").

126. Expectmore.gov, Detailed Information on the Corps of Engineers: Regulatory Program Assessment, http://www.whitehouse.gov/OMB/expectmore/detail/10001130.2003.html (last visited Aug. 12, 2008).

The United States Supreme Court had the opportunity to examine the Corps' public interest review in another context in *United States v. Alaska*.[127] In that 1992 decision, the Court ruled unanimously in favor of the Corps' broad public interest review interpretation.[128]

Corps regulations set forth explicit requirements for its public interest review.[129] Specifically, current regulations entitled "General policies for evaluating permit applications" direct that "[t]he following policies shall be applicable to the review of all applications for [Corps] permits."[130] They go on to describe in subsection (a), the Public Interest Review, as follows:

> (1) The decision whether to issue a permit will be based on an evaluation of the probable impacts, including cumulative impacts, of the proposed activity and its intended use on the public interest. Evaluation of the probable impact which the proposed activity may have on the public interest requires a careful weighing of all those factors which become relevant in each particular case. The benefits which reasonably may be expected to accrue from the proposal must be balanced against its reasonably foreseeable detriments. The decision whether to authorize a proposal, and if so, the conditions under which it will be allowed to occur, are therefore determined by the outcome of this general balancing process. That decision should reflect the national concern for both protection and utilization of important resources. All factors which may be relevant to the proposal must be considered including the cumulative effects thereof: among those are conservation, economics, aesthetics, general environmental concerns, wetlands, historic properties, fish and wildlife values, flood hazards, floodplain values, land use, navigation, shore erosion and accretion, recreation, water supply and conservation, water quality, energy needs, safety, food and fiber production, mineral needs, considerations of property ownership and, in general, the needs and welfare of the people. For activities involving 404 discharges, a permit will be denied if the discharge that would be authorized by such permit would not comply with the Environmental Protection Agency's 404(b)(1) guidelines. Subject to the preceding sentence and any other applicable guidelines and criteria (see Section 320.2 and 320.3), a permit will be granted unless the district engineer determines that it would be contrary to the public interest.[131]

Accordingly, Corps personnel assess over twenty different factors in determining whether to issue a permit, including the catch-all concept of "the needs and welfare of the people."[132]

In addition to these factors, when undertaking its public interest review, the Corps is required to consider the following "general criteria" in the evaluation of every application:

> (i) The relative extent of the public and private need for the proposed structure or work;

> (ii) Where there are unresolved conflicts as to resource use, the practicability of using reasonable alternative locations and methods to accomplish the objective of the proposed structure or work; and

> (iii) The extent and permanence of the beneficial and/or detrimental effects which the proposed structure or work is likely to have on the public and private uses to which the area is suited.[133]

---

127. United States v. Alaska, 503 U.S. 569 (1992).
128. *Id.*
129. 33 C.F.R. §320.4.
130. *Id.*
131. 33 C.F.R. §320.4(a).
132. *Id.*
133. 33 C.F.R. §320.4(a)(2).

Decisions on individual permit applications must include results of the public interest review in the Statement of Findings, a document which must be prepared for many permit decisions.[134] The regulations are not, however, specific as to how Corps personnel undertaking a public interest review are to reach a final decision based on these varied and competing factors. In fact, the regulations leave a great deal of discretion to the Corps in reaching a public interest decision by directing only that "[t]he specific weight of each factor is determined by its importance and relevance to the particular proposal. Accordingly, how important a factor is and how much consideration it deserves will vary with each proposal. A specific factor may be given great weight on one proposal, while it may not be present or as important on another."[135] Under that same subsection, the Corps regulations direct that comments are to be given "full consideration and appropriate weight... including those of federal, state, and local agencies, and other experts on matters within their expertise."[136]

Given the science discussed above in section II, it is difficult to see why the public interest review would not require a thorough review of climate change. Moreover, permit issuance under the Clean Water Act also requires compliance with EPA's Section 404(b)(1) Guidelines.[137] These guidelines prohibit discharges of dredged or fill material (1) if a practicable alternative with less adverse impact is available;[138] (2) if such discharge would cause or contribute to violations of various related laws including those addressing water quality standards, toxic effluent standards, or endangered or threatened species;[139] (3) if such discharge would "cause or contribute to significant degradation of the waters of the United States";[140] or (4) "unless appropriate and practicable steps have been taken which will minimize potential adverse impacts of the discharge on the aquatic ecosystem."[141] Climate change factors should play a part in this analysis on a number of levels, including the determination of whether an alternative is practicable, whether it is the least damaging alternative, and whether a proposed action would negatively impact water quality or otherwise degrade waters of the United States.

At the same time, because of the high volume of approved permits,[142] the Corps and EPA use a process, commonly referred to as "mitigation," for those who apply for permits pursuant to Section 404 of the Clean Water Act.[143] Through this process successful permit applicants are often required to alleviate adverse impacts that their proposed activities may have on the aquatic environment.[144] An underlying theory of mitigation is the attempt to achieve a goal of "no net loss" of

---

134. 33 C.F.R. § 325.2(a)(6). *See* North Carolina v. Hudson, 665 F. Supp. 428, 435 (E.D.N.C. 1987).

135. 33 C.F.R. at 320.4(a)(3).

136. *Id.* Interestingly, if the Corps had its own environmental justice guidelines (which it doesn't) the public interest review would be a logical place in its own process to insert such an analysis. As it stands, however, a search for the term "environmental justice" on the Corps website turns up no useful hits (a search on June 28, 2006 using the phrase "environmental justice" in quotes on www.hq.usace.army.mil/ had two hits, neither of which provides any meaningful guidance). *See also* Jacalyn R. Fleming, *Justifying the Incorporation of Environmental Justice into the SEQRA and Permitting Processes*, 6 Alb. L. Envtl. Outlook J. 55, 60–61 (2002) (pointing to the Corps' public interest review as a process that may be useful to address environmental justice concerns).

137. 40 C.F.R. Part 230. The Corps requires full compliance with these guidelines before a permit can be issued. 33 C.F.R. § 323.6(a) ("a permit will be denied if the discharge authorized by such a permit would not comply with the 404(b)(1) guidelines").

138. 40 C.F.R. § 230.10(a).

139. *Id.* § 230.10(b).

140. *Id.* § 230.10(c).

141. *Id.* § 230.10(d).

142. *See supra* note 117 and accompanying text.

143. 33 U.S.C. § 1344 (2006).

144. *See generally* Royal C. Gardner, *Mitigation, in* Kim Diana Connolly, Stephen M. Johnson and Douglas R. Williams, Wetlands Law and Policy: Understanding Section 404 (American Bar Ass'n 2005).

wetlands,[145] a concept that President George W. Bush's Administration publicly embraced as recently as August 2006.[146] Recent amendments to the mitigation process were intended to increase the rigor of the mitigation process.[147] In fact, in the preamble to the final rule in response to comments regarding the role of wetlands in an era of climate change, EPA and the Corps stated that they "agree that protecting our Nation's existing aquatic resource base is an important way to help foster ecological and economic resilience as climatic patterns shift."[148] Although this text is phrased in optional language,[149] meticulous application of overall mitigation requirements should also trigger a climate change analysis associated with permitting activities in wetlands.

Furthermore, a number of other laws are triggered by the wetland permitting process under Clean Water Act Section 404.[150] For example, for coastal wetlands the Coastal Zone Management Act may apply.[151] If a state has adopted an approved coastal zone management program,[152] the Corps cannot issue a wetland permit for an activity that affects the coastal zone unless the state certifies that the proposed activity complies with the state's program.[153] CZMA has long recognized sea level rise issues[154] and thus should trigger a related assessment of climate change im-

145. *See* ENVIRONMENTAL PROTECTION AGENCY, THE UNITED STATES ARMY CORPS OF ENGINEERS, AND THE UNITED STATES DEPARTMENTS OF AGRICULTURE, COMMERCE, INTERIOR, AND TRANSPORTATION, NATIONAL WETLANDS MITIGATION ACTION PLAN, 1 (Dec. 24, 2002), *available at* http://www.mitigationaction plan.gov/map1226withsign.pdf.

146. Hearing Before The Subcommittee On Fisheries, Wildlife, And Water of the Committee On Environment And Public Works, United States Senate, 109th Cong. Aug. 1, 2006 (statements of Benjamin H. Grumbles, Assistant Administrator For Water, U.S. Environmental Protection Agency, and John Paul Woodley, Jr., Assistant Secretary of The Army For Civil Works, Department of The Army, *available at* http://www.epa.gov/water/speeches/060801bg.html ("President Bush established, on Earth Day 2004, a national goal to move beyond 'no net loss' of wetlands and to attain an overall increase in the quantity and quality of wetlands in America. Specifically, the President established a goal to increase, improve, and protect three million acres of wetlands by 2009. Since the President announced this objective, EPA, the Corps, the U.S. Department of Agriculture (USDA), and the Department of Interior (DOI) have restored, created, protected or improved 1,797,000 acres of wetlands. We now have 588,000 acres of wetlands that did not exist in 2004, we have improved the quality of 563,000 wetland acres that already existed, and we have protected the high quality of 646,000 acres of existing wetlands.").

147. United States Army Corps of Engineers *et al.*, Compensatory Mitigation for Losses of Aquatic Resources, 73 Fed. Reg. 19594 (Apr. 10, 2008), *available at* http://www.epa.gov/owow/wetlands/pdf/wetlands_mitigation_final_rule_4_10_08.pdf.

148. *Id.* at 19, 611. ("Today's rule reaffirms the existing requirement to avoid and minimize impacts to the nation's aquatic resources and to require, in cases where it is appropriate and practicable to do so, compensatory mitigation for impacts that cannot be avoided or minimized. Compensatory mitigation projects planned and designed using the watershed approach and the standards provided by today's rule are likely to provide ecosystem functions and services that, in addition to offsetting losses resulting from activities authorized by DA permits, also provide the ecological and economic resilience needed to address climate change. For example, the reestablishment of a forested wetland may also provide carbon sequestration benefits, over the long term, through the growth of trees. As another example, coastal wetland restoration projects could be designed to take into account reasonably foreseeable rises in sea level.")

149. A pervasive concern applying to the entire rule as noted by conservation groups. *See, e.g.*, Robin Mann & Jan Goldman-Carter, *Avoidance: Still the Best Solution to the Compensatory Mitigation Challenge*, NATIONAL WETLANDS NEWSLETTER, July–Aug. 2008.

150. For links to these and other "related laws" see U.S. Army Corps of Engineers, *Statutory, Administrative & Policy Materials*, http://www.usace.army.mil/cw/cecwo/reg/sadmin3.htm.

151. 16 U.S.C. § 1455. For state-specific coastal zone information, see NOAA Ocean and Coastal Resource Management, State and Territory Coastal Management Program Summaries, *available at* http://www.ocrm. nos.noaa.gov/czm/czmsitelist.html

152. Coastal zone management plans are reviewed and approved by the Secretary of Commerce. *Id.*

153. 16 U.S.C. § 1456(c)(3)(A). The Act places additional constraints on federal agencies when they are the permit applicant. *See* 16 U.S.C. § 1456(c); 33 C.F.R. § 325.2(b)(2)(i).

154. 16 U.S.C. § 1451 (l) ("Because global warming may result in a substantial sea level rise with serious adverse effects in the coastal zone, coastal states must anticipate and plan for such an occurrence.").

pacts before a consistency determination can be made.[155] Likewise, the National Environmental Policy Act (NEPA) requires preparation of an environmental impact statement (EIS) for any "major federal action significantly affecting the quality of the human environment,"[156] and consideration of environmental impacts of proposed actions and their alternatives in all cases.[157] Serious litigation is underway as to the obligations of climate change analysis under NEPA.[158]

EPA recognizes that climate change will impact those water resources it regulates.[159] But this has not yet been translated into regulatory reform. Moreover, while few prescient legal scholars have called for responses to climate change and impacts on wetlands for decades,[160] only a small minority of those who write on wetlands have focused on it yet. Upon further analysis in today's setting, existing statutory and regulatory requirements may well be interpreted to mandate rigorous climate change analysis.[161] If ultimately these existing tools are insufficient, rapid federal regulatory changes are definitely in order.

Other nations have different regulatory approaches to protecting wetlands that are beyond the scope of this essay.[162] However, many nations (including the United States) also join together to work on wetlands issues through the Convention on Wetlands of International Importance espe-

---

155. *See* Braxton Davis & Jena Carter, *The Role of CZM Programs in Adaptation to Climate Change,* http://usasearch.gov/search?v%3aproject=firstgov&v%3afile=viv_1033%4019%3a3BkQmx&v%3astate=root%7croot&opener=full-window&url=http%3a%2f%2fcoastalmanagement.noaa.gov%2fnews%2f archivedmtg-docs%2f2007SCRMarchives%2fczmclimatechange.ppt&rid=Ndoc1&v%3aframe=redirect&rsource=firstgov-msn&v%3astate=%28root%29%7croot&rrank=1& (last visited Oct. 10, 2008) (citing various relevant sections, including "302(l): "Because global warming may result in a substantial sea level rise with serious adverse effects in the coastal zone, coastal states must anticipate and plan for such an occurrence"; 303(b): "... the management of coastal development to minimize the loss of life and property ... in areas likely to be affected by or vulnerable to sea level rise, land subsidence, and salt water intrusion"; 303(k): "the study and development ... of plans for addressing the adverse effects upon the coastal zone of land subsidence and of sea level rise"; 303(3): "to encourage the preparation of special area management plans ... including those areas likely to be affected by land subsidence, sea level rise"; 309(a)(2): "Preventing or significantly reducing threats to life and destruction of property by ... anticipating and managing the effects of potential sea level rise and Great Lakes level rise." (emphasis deleted).).

156. 42 U.S.C. § 4332(2)(C).

157. *Id.* § 4332(2)(E). As part of the NEPA process, cumulative effects of the proposed activity, including its indirect effects, must be considered. 40 C.F.R. § 1508.8 (2008).

158. Michael B. Gerrard, *What the Law and Lawyers Can and Cannot Do About Global Warming,* 16 S.E. ENVTL. L.J. 33 (2007); the Gerrard essay, this book (ch. 9, p. 1190).

159. Letter from Benjamin H. Grumbles, Assistant Administrator for Water, to Interested Parties to Announce the Release of the Final National Water Program Strategy: Response to Climate Change (Sept. 30, 2008), *available at* http://www.epa.gov/water/climatechange/docs/interestedparties9.30.08.pdf.

160. *See, e.g.,* Robert L. Fischman, *Global Warming And Property Interests: Preserving Coastal Wetlands As Sea Levels Rise,* 19 HOFSTRA L. REV. 565 (1991) ("The problem of coastal wetlands migration is just one of many new challenges that climate change presents. Solving problems relating to the modification of agriculture, protection of endemic species, and supply of fresh water, will raise many of the same legal issues. An early, effective, and equitable response will not just save some of our dwindling coastal wetlands; it will set the tone for public reaction to the many other uncertainties and environmental perturbations presented by global climate change." *Id.* at 602.).

161. The observations in this essay are not unique. *See, e.g.,* Ellen Kracauer Hartig *et al.,* Ch. 5, *Wetlands, in* CLIMATE CHANGE AND A GLOBAL CITY: THE POTENTIAL CONSEQUENCES OF CLIMATE VARIABILITY AND CHANGE (Columbia Earth Institute July 2001), *available at* http://ccsr.columbia.edu/cig/mec/05_Wetlands.pdf ("While not originally intended for the purpose of increasing climate change preparedness, many of [federal and state] regulations may indeed be helpful. In many cases, stricter enforcement or changes in regulatory guidelines may increase the utility of the regulations already in effect.").

162. *See* The Ramsar Convention on Wetlands, The Wise Use Resource Centre, National Wetland Policies and Strategic Plans, http://www.ramsar.org/wurc/wurc_library.htm#nwps (last visited Aug. 15, 2008), *supra* note 73.

cially as Waterfowl Habitat (referred to as the Ramsar Convention).[163] The Ramsar Convention[164] began in Ramsar, Iran[165] on 2 February 1971.[166] As the Ramsar Secretary General remarked on World Wetlands Day 2008, "[w]hether we are talking about swamps and bogs, peatlands, rivers and lakes, estuaries and coastal zones, coral reefs or rice paddies, we understand that wetlands are essential for … mitigation of the effects of climate change … and so many other so-called 'ecosystem services.' …"[167] Thus climate change is very much on the agenda of the Ramsar Secretariat staff, and the recent Conference of the Parties adopted several resolutions related to climate change.[168] This may alter Ramsar Convention obligations over time and increase international wetland undertakings in light of climate change.

IV. Recommendations on Re-Envisioning Wetland Regulation to Address Climate Change?

As discussed above, science shows that wetlands are impacted by climate change. The regulatory structure may have existing tools to address this matter, but to date has done little. Accordingly, there are a number of wetland-specific recommendations to which the above discussion leads. First and foremost, general steps to mitigate for and adapt to global climate change impacts will almost certainly assist in wetlands protection. Wetlands, like other natural resources at the front lines of climate change impacts, will benefit from an aggressive plan to mitigate overall climate change, such as that proposed by Al Gore through the We Campaign.[169] Whether that particular approach can be achieved or another approach would be better is a matter for some debate … but rapid measures must begin now. As the heads of the national academies of ten nations explained in a joint 2005 declaration, "[w]e urge all nations … to take prompt action to reduce the causes of climate change, adapt to its impacts and ensure that the issue is included in all relevant national and international strategies."[170] Taking immediate steps to mitigate against further climate change generally will, of course, help wetlands indirectly.

Climate change itself has received deserved national and worldwide attention.[171] Journalistic coverage of the climate change crisis reflects journalistic values (including balance, accuracy, timeliness, proximity, prominence and impact, conflict, unusualness, and human interest).[172]

---

163. Convention on Wetlands of International Importance especially as Waterfowl Habitat (Feb. 2, 1971), T.I.A.S. No. 1084, 996 U.N.T.S. 245 (amended 1982 & 1987) [hereinafter Ramsar Convention].

164. Convention on Wetlands of International Importance especially as Waterfowl Habitat (Feb. 2, 1971), T.I.A.S No. 11084, 996 U.N.T.S. 245, *available at* http://www.ramsar.org/key_conv_e.htm.

165. The Convention's short form is derived from the name of the town where it was originally signed, and is not an acronym.

166. The 1971 version of the Convention can be found at http://www.ramsar.org/key_conv_e_1971.htm.

167. Anada Tiega, World Wetland Day 2008, A Message from the Secretary General, Maun, Botswana, 2nd February 2008, http://www.ramsar.org/wwd/8/wwd2008_rpts_botswana_tiega.htm.

168. *See* Ramsar, *Draft Resolutions,* http://www.ramsar.org/cop10/cop10_docs_index_e.htm#dr (last visited Oct. 14, 2008).

169. We Can Solve the Climate Crisis, http://www.wecansolveit.org (last visited Sept. 9, 2008) ("The We Campaign is a project of The Alliance for Climate Protection—a nonprofit, nonpartisan effort founded by Nobel laureate and former Vice President Al Gore. The goal of the Alliance is to build a movement that creates the political will to solve the climate crisis.").

170. http://www.nationalacademies.org/onpi/06072005.pdf (last visited Sept 10, 2008).

171. *See* Maxwell T. Boykoff and J. Timmons Roberts, Media Coverage of Climate Change: Current Trends, Strengths, Weaknesses, United Nations Development Programme, Human Development Report 2007, *available at* http://hdr.undp.org/en/reports/global/hdr2007-2008/papers/boykoff,%20maxwell%20and%20roberts,%20j.%20timmons.pdf.

172. The Missouri Group *et al.*, Telling the Story: The Convergence of Print, Broadcast and Online Media (Bedford/St. Martin's Press 2007).

Some analysts suggest the media have not gone far enough,[173] but there is no doubt that media have played a crucial role in the climate change saga.[174] When mentioning climate change, however, many media tend to mention wetlands only in passing, and focus on other issues.[175] Focus on non-wetland issues is warranted, because fossil fuel use and other activities not associated with wetlands do have a significant impact in terms of greenhouse gas emissions.[176] Yet wetlands cannot continue to play such a small role in our study of and planning for climate change.

To this end, I conclude this essay with five wetland-specific recommendations. First, we should expand incentive programs (and perhaps create new ones) that protect and enhance the nation's wetland resources. Second, we must invest in a dramatic increase in applied science surrounding multiple aspects of climate change and wetlands. Third, we must include wetland considerations in broader legislative fixes. Fourth, we must use existing United States federal wetland regulatory tools to account for climate change, and work toward amendments to the regulatory process that will directly integrate climate change into the wetlands permitting process. And finally, fifth, we must increase engagement on an international level, through the Ramsar Convention, working with other nations to ensure that those whose lives and livelihoods depend on wetland resources are equipped to deal (both in terms of adaptation and mitigation) with climate change. I discuss these recommendations in more depth below.

1. Expand Existing Incentive Programs (and Consider Creating New Ones)

As discussed in section III, the United States has in place a number of statutes and programs that provide incentives and investments in protecting and enhancing wetlands. These programs include the Wetlands Reserve Program (WRP),[177] the North American Wetlands Conservation

---

173. *See, e.g.*, Boykiff and Roberts, *supra* note 171, at 34 ("The difficult position of the media in capitalist society is that commercial news outlets require huge amounts of advertising to pay their salaries and other expenses, and the greatest advertisers are for automobiles, real estate, airlines, fast food, and home furnishings. To create demand for real mitigation of climate change emissions would require the media to repeatedly and insistently call for truly revolutionary changes in society, precisely away from consumption of the products of their advertisers.").

174. The Society of Environmental Journalists has compiled a page entitled *Outstanding climate coverage, available at* http://www.sej.org/resource/index18.htm.

175. There are thousands of articles and transcripts on climate change generally when one searches LEXIS. A number of press releases highlight issues related to wetlands (*see, e.g., Crucial Wetlands in Jeopardy According to International Climate Change Report*; *Report identifies climate change will impact wetlands that help to improve water quality and water storage, and provide critical wildlife habitat*, Canada NewsWire (Feb . 23, 2001); USGS *Scientists Present At 2008 International Meeting Of Society Of Wetland Scientists: MAY 26—30*, States News Service (May 23, 2008)) but few articles focus on wetlands impacts. *Cf.* Shauna Rempel, *Wetlands and the ecosystems; Arctic offers clues to sustainability in the face of climate variation*, Toronto Star L05 (Feb. 28, 2008).

176. United States Environmental Protection Agency, Inventory of U.S. Greenhouse Gas Emissions and Sinks: 1990—2006, (Apr. 15, 2008) 30, *available at* http://www.epa.gov/climatechange/emissions/downloads/08_CR.pdf ("The primary greenhouse gas emitted by human activities in the United States was CO_2, representing approximately 84.8 percent of total greenhouse gas emissions. The largest source of CO_2, and of overall greenhouse gas emissions, was fossil fuel combustion. CH_4 emissions, which have declined from 1990 levels, resulted primarily from enteric fermentation associated with domestic livestock, decomposition of wastes in landfills, and natural gas systems. Agricultural soil management and mobile source fossil fuel combustion were the major sources of N_2O emissions. The emissions of substitutes for ozone depleting substances and emissions of HFC-23 during the production of HCFC-22 were the primary contributors to aggregate HFC emissions. Electrical transmission and distribution systems accounted for most SF6 emissions, while PFC emissions resulted from semiconductor manufacturing and as a by-product of primary aluminum production.").

177. *See generally* http://www.nrcs.usda.gov/Programs/WRP/; Subtitle D, Title XII, Food Security Act of 1985 (16 U.S.C. §§ 3837–3837f); 7 C.F.R. Part 1467 (2008).

Act (NAWCA) of 1989[178] and the Coastal Wetlands Planning, Protection, and Restoration Act (CWPPRA).[179] These programs should be expanded,[180] and new programs considered that will have a climate-change focus. Such expansion or development of new programs may require more scientific information or action by Congress, which links this recommendation to the next two recommendations.

2.   *Dramatically Increase Investment in Applied Science*[181]

Scientists have reported a link between wetlands and climate change for decades.[182] Yet policy change evolves slowly,[183] even when facing a crisis.[184] In fact, calls for policy changes to re-

---

178. 103 Stat. 1968, 16 U.S.C. §§ 4401–2214 (2000). *See generally* U.S. Fish and Wildlife Service, North American Wetlands Conservation Act, http://www.fws.gov/birdhabitat/grants/nawca/index.shtm (last visited Aug. 31, 2008).

179. 104 Stat. 4779, Title III of Pub. L. 101-646, 16 U.S.C. §§ 3951–3956 (2006).

180. In light of President George W. Bush's commitment to No Net Loss there has been some limited expansion of these programs in recent years. COUNCIL ON ENVIRONMENTAL QUALITY, CONSERVING AMERICA'S WETLANDS 2007: THREE YEARS OF PROGRESS IMPLEMENTING THE PRESIDENT'S GOAL (2007), *available at* http://www.whitehouse.gov/ceq/wetlands/2007/index.html. For a criticism of the Bush administration's no net loss policy, see JULIE M. SIBBING, NATIONAL WILDLIFE FEDERATION, NOWHERE NEAR NO-NET-LOSS, *available at* http://www.nwf.org/wildlife/pdfs/NowhereNearNoNetLoss.pdf.

181. This recommendation is not intended to undercut the need for continued commitment to basic (or "pure") science. It is instead intended to acknowledge that, as discussed in earlier sections and elsewhere in this book, with climate change we are facing a practical problem of enormous dimension about which we need much information quickly. Applied science seems most likely to get us there. *See generally* the Academy of Applied Science website, http://www.aas-world.org/ (last visited Sept. 11, 2008). Of course, there will be political and other realities that must be grappled with, *see* DANIEL S. GREENBERG, SCIENCE, MONEY, AND POLITICS: POLITICAL TRIUMPH AND ETHICAL EROSION (Un. Chicago Press 2003), but that does not change the mandate facing wetland and related scientists in this era of increasing climate change.

182. *See, e.g.*, SCOTT W. NIXON, AND VIRGINIA LEE, WETLANDS AND WATER QUALITY — A REGIONAL REVIEW OF RECENT RESEARCH IN THE US ON THE ROLE OF FRESH AND SALTWATER WETLANDS AS SOURCES, SINKS, AND TRANSFORMERS OF NITROGEN, PHOSPHORUS, AND VARIOUS HEAVY METALS (1986), Report to the Waterways Experiment Station, *summarized at* http://www.osti.gov/energycitations/product.biblio.jsp?osti_id= 6577929 (last visited Aug. 30, 2008). More recently, in addition to the sources cited in Section II above, see Izaak Walton League, *Wetland Sights and Sounds*, May 2008, http://www.iwla.org/publications/enews/ss/volume4_issue1.htm (last visited Aug. 12, 2008) ("Across the United States, many people are already noticing some subtle — and some not so subtle — changes in their favorite hunting, fishing, bird-watching, and hiking spots. Both hunters and wildlife biologists are counting fewer ducks in North Dakota's prairie pothole region. Warmer water temperatures in the Great Lakes are causing declines in cold-water fish like lake trout, walleye, and cisco. Rising sea levels in the Chesapeake Bay have already swallowed vast expanses of tidal wetlands on the shores of its islands, some of which have entirely disappeared. Several states, including Maryland, Massachusetts, Georgia, and California, are losing their state birds as they migrate north in search of cooler temperatures. These are among the many signs that suggest climate change is already having serious impacts on our nation's wetland ecosystems.").

183. For an interesting timeline of EPA-based developments (starting from a legal memorandum in 1998 by then-General Counsel Jonathan Cannon), see E&E Publishing, *The long road to EPA climate regulations*, http://www.eenews.net/special_reports/domino_effect/timeline (last visited Sept. 8, 2008).

184. As part of a series of blog entries on why Congress should have implemented climate change legislation in 2008, the National Climate Campaign Director at Environmental Defense identified some political realities as reasons not to put off climate change legislation for a new administration, noting that "[t]he politics of climate change is as much regional as partisan, and that's not going to change.... Sixty votes are needed in the Senate to force a change, and no serious political observer believes we'll have 60 liberal environmental senators any time soon.... Climate change will not be at the top of the new president's agenda. A possible recession, the war in Iraq, and healthcare will take priority. It could be a year or more before attention shifts back to the climate, and that's a huge loss of time and momentum." STEVE COCHRAN, WHY A BILL IN 2008: SAME POLITICS IN 2009, http://environmentaldefenseblogs.org/climate411/2008/01/25/why-a-bill-in-2008-same-politics-in-2009/?gclid=CIm4ormmuJUCFQLBsgod8nrhQA (last visited Aug. 20, 2008). *See also* Marc Gunther, *Chances dim for climate-change legislation*, FORTUNE (May 30, 2008), *available at* http://money.cnn.com/2008/05/30/news/economy/gunther_legislation.fortune/ ("... the fact that businesses and senators are arguing

spond to climate change have been on-going for decades,[185] but no comprehensive solution has been put in place yet. The United States Congress has made progress on legislation to address climate change generally,[186] but progress on federal legislation is slow-going. Litigation efforts are underway using many existing statutes, but that is a challenging effort on many levels.[187] Many states have taken some steps toward climate change,[188] but in most cases those efforts have been limited and slow-going. Further, regulatory changes on every level have been slow or non-existent.[189]

Given this stagnation, policy efforts to address climate change have and will continue to focus on laws that do not govern wetlands.[190] Yet increased focus on wetlands ecosystems is necessary.[191] Wetland scientists have concluded that analysis cannot occur in isolation.[192] Yet "[w]etlands have properties that are not adequately covered by present terrestrial and aquatic ecology, making a case for wetland science as a unique discipline encompassing many fields, including terrestrial and aquatic ecology, chemistry, hydrology, and engineering."[193]

The end result is that much more scientific work in the climate change context is crucial. As one group of wetland scientists has eloquently explained, "[w]e will not be able to predict accurately the role of wetlands as potential positive or negative feedbacks to anthropogenic global change without knowing the integrative effects of changes in temperature, precipitation, atmospheric carbon dioxide concentrations, and atmospheric deposition of nitrogen and sulfur on the carbon balance of North American wetlands."[194] Likewise, another group of wetland scientists explains: "[t]o scale up site-specific model outputs to a national scale with high confidence, we need detailed data on the various local drivers and processes controlling wetland elevation across all the tidal geomorphic settings of North America. Obtaining and

---

about the details suggests that agreement is growing over the broader idea that Congress ought to regulate greenhouse gases.").

185. *See* Spencer Weart, The History of Climate Change Science (Jan. 2007), http://www. livescience.com/environment/070131_climate_change_history.html (last visited Aug. 15, 2008).

186. *See,* H.R. 2454, the American Clean Energy and Security Act, *available at* http://thomas.loc.gov/cgi-bin/bdquery/z?d111:H.R.2454.

187. *See* Arnold and Porter, *Climate Change Litigation in the U.S.,* http://www.climatecasechart.com/ (last visited Sept. 3, 2008); Michael B. Gerrard, *What the Law and Lawyers Can and Cannot Do About Global Warming,* 16 S.E Envtl. L.J. 33 (2007).

188. *See* Pew Center on Global Climate Change, *What's Being Done … In the States,* http://www.pewclimate.org/what_s_being_done/in_the_states (last visited Aug. 15, 2008).

189. Government Accountability Office, Climate Change: Agencies Should Develop Guidance for Addressing the Effects on Federal Land and Water Resources (Aug. 2007), *available at* http://www.gao.gov/new.items/d07863.pdf ("Resource managers are uncertain about what actions, if any, they should take to address the current effects of climate change and to plan for future effects on their resources. Agencies have not assigned climate change a priority among the other factors they must address and have not provided resource managers with direction on how or whether to address the effects of climate change. Without such guidance—and additional site-specific data—resource managers are constrained in their ability to address climate change in their planning and management activities." *Id.* at 9–10.).

190. *See, e.g.,* Environmental Protection Agency, Advance Notice of Proposed Rulemaking, Regulating Greenhouse Gas Emissions Under the Clean Air Act, 73 Fed. Reg. 44353 (July 20, 2008), *available at* http://www.epa.gov/climatechange/anpr.html.

191. One of the biggest initiatives begun in 2008 was the "We" campaign, a project of The Alliance for Climate Protection, which is a nonprofit, nonpartisan effort founded by Nobel laureate and former Vice President Al Gore. *See* http://www.wecansolveit.org/content/about (last visited Aug. 22, 2008). Yet a search on the "We" Campaign website on August 22, 2008 for the term "wetland" and its derivatives turned up no hits. *Id.*

192. Reed and Wilson, *Coast 2050, supra* note 77, at 4.

193. Wetlands, *supra* note 16, at 3.

194. Scott D. Bridgham, J. Patrick Megonigal, Jason K. Keller, Norman B. Bliss, and Carl Trettin, *The Carbon Balance of North American Wetlands,* 26 Wetlands 889, 889 (Dec. 2006).

evaluating the necessary data would be an enormous and expensive task, but not a totally impractical one."[195]

Coastal wetlands are of primary importance in terms of planning and thus in terms of research. As summarized in a 2007 Pew Foundation report entitled COASTAL WETLANDS & GLOBAL CLIMATE CHANGE, "[h]uman activities intended to reduce damage to life and property from climate extremes have unintentionally increased the vulnerability of coastal areas to climate change by altering the natural hydrologic functions of wetlands. For coastal wetlands to be sustained in a changing climate, therefore, restoration planning must account for the consequences of both climate change and human engineering of the environment."[196] Being ready to responsibly undertake such planning will require serious investment in applied science.

In addition, wetlands are possible, but challenging, options for carbon sequestration. As one scholar noted, "carbon sequestration is not likely to become a primary motive for wetland restoration projects for several reasons. First, there is currently no agreed methodology for measuring the carbon sequestration contribution of a restored wetland. Second, wetland restoration can be an expensive means of carbon sequestration; other, cheaper sinks, such as reforestation of uplands, are available. Moreover, the uncertainty of whether wetland restoration projects will be effective undercuts their attractiveness as tools for mitigating climate change. Although the carbon sequestration potential of wetlands may not be the most compelling reason to embark on a restoration project, such a benefit does provide a subsidiary reason to support such actions."[197] Most scientists in 2008 agree that sound methods for measuring carbon sequestration in wetlands are not yet available.[198] A review of the recent literature does demonstrate that scientists agree wetlands might play a role in a sequestration approach … but there is no agreement as to the specifics.[199]

---

195. U.S. CLIMATE CHANGE SCIENCE PROGRAM, COASTAL SENSITIVITY TO SEA LEVEL RISE: A FOCUS ON THE MID-ATLANTIC REGION, draft at 151 (Feb. 12, 2008), *available at* http://climatescience.gov/Library/sap/sap4-1/public-review-draft/sap4-1-prd.pdf.

196. ROBERT R. TWILLEY, COASTAL WETLANDS & GLOBAL CLIMATE CHANGE 2, *available at* http://www.pewclimate.org/docUploads/Regional-Impacts-Gulf.pdf (citations omitted). As mentioned in the conclusion to that report, "ultimately, sea-level rise will continue for centuries after human-induced greenhouse gases are stabilized in the atmosphere (IPCC, 2007). The benefits of coastal wetlands to society can only be secured by accounting for the long-term effects of climate change in the design of near-term restoration projects." *Id.* at 11.).

197. Gardner, *supra* note 12, at 586–587.

198. WETLANDS, *supra* note 16, at 316–319 ("Although soil carbon in wetland soils is recognized as an important component of global carbon budgets and future climate change scenarios, very little work has been done to consider the role of wetlands, particularly those in temperate and tropical regions of the world, in managing carbon sequestration." *Id.* at 316.) *See also* DAVID WYLYNKO, INTERNATIONAL INSTITUTE FOR SUSTAINABLE DEVELOPMENT, PRAIRIE WETLANDS AND CARBON SEQUESTRATION: ASSESSING SINKS UNDER THE KYOTO PROTOCOL (Sept 1999), *available at* http://www.iisd.org/wetlands/wrkshp_summ.pdf.

199. *See, e.g.,* Ned H. Euliss Jr. *et al., North American prairie wetlands are important nonforested land-based carbon storage sites,* 361 SCIENCE OF THE TOTAL ENVIRONMENT 179 (2006) (Calculated a regional estimate of the potential carbon storage in wetlands in a region within the zone thought to represent a large terrestrial carbon sink. "Wetland restoration has potential to sequester 378 Tg of organic carbon over a 10-year period. Wetlands can sequester over twice the organic carbon as no-till cropland on only about 17% of the total land area in the region. We estimate that wetland restoration has potential to offset 2.4% of the annual fossil CO_2 emissions reported for North America in 1990."); Yiqi Luo & James F. Reynolds, *Validity of Extrapolating Field CO_2 Experiments to Predict Carbon Sequestration in Natural Ecosystems,* 80 ECOLOGY 1568 (July 1999) (Concluding that results cannot be directly extrapolated to predict terrestrial sequestration in natural ecosystems responding to a gradual carbon increase. Predictive understanding requires improved experimental design and measurement plans and new approaches, such as deconvolution and inverse modeling, for data analysis and interpretation); GARY J. WHITING & JEFF CHANTON, GREENHOUSE CARBON BALANCE OF WETLANDS: METHANE EMISSION VERSUS CARBON SEQUESTRATION (Tellus B. 2001) (Examining the relationship between long-term carbon se-

Significant investment in scientific research with respect to sequestration options and other mitigation in the wetlands context is thus crucial.[200] There are other immediate needs for scientific research, including control of methane emissions. The reality is that we cannot realistically move forward on any front without knowing somewhat more. And the regulatory community will need to provide feedback to the scientists as this science is developed. "An increasing emphasis on adaptation demands greater efforts to understand the diversity of users and their evolving climate information needs, and to develop strategies for communicating risk and uncertainty."[201] The point is that we need to immediately increase research that is connected to decision-making without delay.

3. Legislative Reform Efforts

Some federal legislative efforts have included wetlands in the climate change calculus. For example, Senator Dianne Feinstein's proposed Electric Utility Cap and Trade Act of 2007 would have included avoided wetlands as part of the conversion matrix.[202] And back in 1993, the Technology Assessment Board of the 103rd Congress received a report entitled PREPARING FOR AN UNCERTAIN CLIMATE, VOLUME II,[203] with an entire chapter dedicated to wetlands and climate change.[204] It concluded that climate change would impact wetlands, and more study was needed

---

questration and the methane released by wetlands as a mitigating factor, and concludes that subtropical and temperate wetlands attenuate global warming but that northern wetlands may be perched on the "greenhouse compensation point"); Changsheng Li *et al.*, *Modeling Impacts of Management on Carbon Sequestration and Trace Gas Emissions in Forested Wetland*, ENVIRONMENTAL MANAGEMENT (2004) (Using modeling methods to determine how management practices affect the sequestration in wetlands with differing characteristics (climate, soil, vegetation, etc); concluded that process-based modeling used can be a powerful simulation to test management practices across varying circumstances, and that counting only carbon sequestration may not be adequate to assess impacts of management practices on global warming.); Eric C. Brevik & Jeffrey A. Homburg, *A 5000 year record of carbon sequestration from a coastal lagoon and wetland complex, Southern California, USA*, 57 CATENA 221 (2004) (Finding that the ability of coastal wetland systems to sequester at high rates now has been demonstrated on both the Pacific and Atlantic coasts of North America. Concluding that coastal wetlands are much more efficient per unit area than terrestrial soils at sequestering; suggests that preservation and restoration of coastal wetlands should be considered in a Kyoto-compliance strategy); Scott D. Brigham *et al.*, *The carbon balance of North American wetlands.* 26 WETLANDS 889 (2006) (Reviewing North American wetlands and proposing solutions to improve sequestration potential including wetland restoration and wetland conversion; authors concluded that "[e]stuarine wetlands sequester carbon at a rate about 10-fold higher on an area basis than any other wetland ecosystem due to high sedimentation rates, high soil carbon content, and constant burial due to sea level rise."); Yonghoon Choi & Yang Wang, *Dynamics of carbon sequestration in a coastal wetland using radiocarbon measurements*, GLOBAL BIOGEOCHEMICAL CYCLES (2004) (authors concluded that, "[b]ecause of higher rates of sequestration and lower CH_4 emissions, coastal wetlands could be more valuable carbon sinks per unit area than other ecosystem in a warmer world.").

200. *See, e.g.*, Eryn Gable, *Project eyes best ways to capture CO_2, rebuild Calif. delta's fragile peat islands*, LAND LETTER (Aug. 21, 2008). This article describes a grant-funded project with money from the California Department of Water Resources to U.S. Geological Survey and the University of California, Davis that will engage in a three-year multi-million dollar research undertaking intended "to take the concept of 'carbon-capture' farming to full-scale in the delta. Construction on the new wetlands, covering approximately 400 acres on a western delta island, is scheduled to start in the spring of 2009." However, as the article discusses, while related research documented significant sequestration of carbon dioxide by nearby wetlands, "wetlands can also be emitters of methane and nitrous oxide, two other greenhouse gases. Because of these emissions, researchers are still working to determine whether there is a net benefit from the wetlands." There is further concern about those particular wetlands insofar as potential for transport into water supplies of remnant methylmercury left over from California's Gold Rush. *Id.*

201. Kirstin Dow and Gregory Carbone, *Climate Science and Decision Making,* 1 GEOGRAPHY COMPASS 302, 309 (2007) *available at* http://www3.interscience.wiley.com/cgi-bin/fulltext/118529987/PDFSTART.

202. Electric Utility Cap and Trade Act of 2007, S. 317 ("SEC. 735. Offset Credits From the Avoided Conversion of Forested Land or Wetland. ").

203. U.S. CONGRESS, OFFICE OF TECHNOLOGY ASSESSMENT, PREPARING FOR AN UNCERTAIN CLIMATE, VOLUME II, OTA O-568 (1993).

204. *Id.* ch. 4.

to determine what the effects might be and how the federal government should react.[205] No immediate legislative results ensued.

Yet, surprisingly, none of the legislative initiatives on climate change with any serious momentum, including H.R. 2454, the American Clean Energy and Security Act of 2009, has a serious engagement with the need to address or intently study wetlands impacts. This too must change. Those drafting state level (and local) legislation should also consider wetlands as appropriate.

Policy decisions will depend on knowing much more about wetlands and their role in, and reaction to, climate change. "It is critically important for decision makers to explicitly account for global warming in prioritizing and developing meaningful land conservation and habitat protection and restoration strategies."[206] Moreover, "[t]he challenge before the scientific community is no longer to document whether climate is affecting nature, but rather to forecast where, when and how severe these impacts will be so that we can better prepare for the future."[207] "As scientists and diverse decisionmakers pursue closer collaborations to develop climate information for an operational context, they must effectively deal with probability and uncertainty present in the observed record, as well as future seasons and even decades."[208] Those drafting legislative fixes should incorporate serious measures to deal with impacts on wetlands in future efforts.

4. Employ Existing Wetland Regulatory Measures to Account for Climate Change, and Consider Developing New Ones

As discussed in section III, there are existing wetlands regulatory measures that can and should be addressing climate change directly. In particular, the requisite Public Interest Review[209] seems well-suited to incorporate climate change immediately. In fact, that regulation's use of the term "the needs and welfare of the people" as one of the factors that must be considered before a permit can issue, in light of the current state of scientific knowledge,[210] should be read to give those federal employees issuing permits no choice but to assess climate change impacts. Other required analyses in the permitting context, including that mandated under the National Environmental Policy Act,[211] should also include climate change implications.[212] Moreover, regulatory amendments (or at least guidance documents)[213] to directly acknowledge and provide guidance for assessment of climate change in the permitting process should be promulgated soon.

5. Expand International Cooperation through the Ramsar Convention Network

Wetlands of International Importance have been designated around the planet under the Convention on Wetlands of International Importance especially as Waterfowl Habitat (often

---

205. *Id.* at 172–179.

206. Patty Glick, Amanda Staudt, and Doug Inkley, Chesapeake Bay Foundation, The Chesapeake Bay and Global Warming: A Paradise Lost for Hunters, Anglers, and Outdoor Enthusiasts? (Sept. 2007), *available at* http://www.nwf.org/sealevelrise/pdfs/chesapeake_bay_final.pdf.

207. Brian Helmuth, Ph.D., Helmuth Lab, University of South Carolina, http://www.biol.sc.edu/~helmuthlab/ (last visited Sept 6, 2008).

208. Dow and Carbone, *supra* note 201, at 317.

209. 33 C.F.R. pt. 320.

210. *See supra* section II.

211. 42 U.S.C. §4321–4375 (2000).

212. *See* the Climate Change Case Chart, *supra* note 158, for a summary of the multiple cases that have considered climate change in the NEPA context.

213. The U.S. Army Corps of Engineers issues Regulatory Guidance Letters on a regular basis to help staff in the field address various issues. *See* U.S. Army Corps of Engineers, Regulatory Guidance Letters, http://www.usace.army.mil/cw/cecwo/reg/rglsindx.htm (last visited Sept. 10, 2008).

referred to as the Convention on Wetlands or the Ramsar Convention).[214] The Ramsar Convention provides support for worldwide wetland conservation and wise use.[215] The Convention obligates each Party to "formulate and implement ... planning so as to promote ... as far as possible the wise use of wetlands in their territory,"[216] which has been interpreted in concert with the concept of sustainable use.[217] The Scientific and Technical Review Committee to the Ramsar Convention issued a 2002 report on climate change and wetlands that concluded, among other things, that "adaptation is no longer an option: it is a necessity, given that climate changes and related impacts are already occurring. Adaptation options will vary with location and wetland types but have the potential to reduce many of the adverse impacts of climate change and to enhance beneficial impacts."[218] The Ramsar Convention network[219] is an appropriate vehicle to use for international cooperative efforts. The recent Conference of the Parties[220] in November 2008 in Korea provided an opportunity to move discussion forward on both adaptation and mitigation. At that session, the parties urged "Contracting Parties to manage wetlands wisely to reduce the multiple pressures they face and thereby increase their resilience to climate change and to take advantage of the significant opportunities to use wetlands wisely as a response option to reduce the impacts of climate change;"[221] and further urged "Contracting Parties to ensure that the necessary safeguards and mechanisms are in place to maintain the ecological character of wetlands, particularly with respect to water allocations for wetland ecosystems, in the face of climate driven changes and predicted changes in

---

214. Convention on Wetlands of International Importance especially as Waterfowl Habitat (Feb. 2, 1971), T.I.A.S. No. 1084, 996 U.N.T.S. 245 (amended 1982 & 1987) [hereinafter Ramsar Convention]; Royal C. Gardner and Kim Diana Connolly, *The Ramsar Convention on Wetlands: Assessment of International Designations Within the United States,* 37 Envtl. L. Rep. 10089 (Feb. 2007), *available at* http://www.ramsar.org/wurc/wurc_gardner_elr2007.pdf.

215. *See, e.g.,* United Nations Environment Programme, Note on the role of the Ramsar Convention and its role in global water supply, http://hqweb.unep.org/pdf/emgramsar.pdf (last visited Aug. 8, 2008) ("The Convention has increasingly recognized that wetlands not only play a vital role in the hydrological cycle, but that to secure their conservation and wise use it is essential that they are managed in the wider context of basin-scale and water resource management.").

216. Ramsar Convention, *supra* note 164, art. 3.1.

217. *See* Ramsar Manual at 48 (stating that through the "wise use" concept, Ramsar "continues to emphasize that human use on a sustainable basis is entirely compatible with Ramsar principles and wetland conservation in general"); *see also* Ramsar Secretariat, Resolution IX.1 Annex A: A Conceptual Framework for the Wise Use of Wetlands and the Maintenance of Their Ecological Character, *available at* http://www.ramsar.org/res/key_res_ix_01_annexa_e.htm ("Within the context of ecosystem approaches, planning processes for promoting the delivery of wetland ecosystem benefits/services should be formulated and implemented in the context of the maintenance or enhancement, as appropriate, of wetland ecological character at appropriate spatial and temporal scales.").

218. Ramsar, *Climate Change and Wetlands: Impacts, Adaptation and Mitigation,* Para. 294, http://www.ramsar.org/cop8/cop8_doc_11_e.htm (last visited Sept. 11, 2008).

219. The Ramsar Secretariat has strong working relationships with many related international organizations. *See* The Ramsar Convention on Wetlands, Memoranda of understanding and cooperation with other conventions and international organizations, http://www.ramsar.org/index_mou.htm (last visited Sept. 11, 2008).

220. *See* The Ramsar Convention on Wetlands, *10th Meeting of the Conference of the Contracting Parties,* http://www.ramsar.org/cop10/cop10_docs_index_e.htm#dr (last visited Oct. 13, 2008).

221. As parties to the recent Ramsar Convention Conference of the Parties put it: "REAFFIRMING that integrative policies and planning measures need to be encouraged in order to address the influence of global climate change on the interdependencies between wetlands, water management, agriculture, energy production, poverty reduction and human health," 10th Meeting of the Conference of the Parties to the Convention on Wetlands (Ramsar, Iran, 1971), "Healthy wetlands, healthy people," Changwon, Republic of Korea, 28 October–4 November 2008, Resolution X.24 Climate change and wetlands, *available at* http://www.ramsar.org/res/key_res_x_index_e.htm (last visited Dec. 30, 2008).

water distribution and availability due to the direct impacts of, and societal responses to, climate change...."[222]

V. Conclusion

This essay explores the wetland policy and regulation in the face of climate change. As discussed in the introduction, planning for the regulation of vulnerable wetland ecosystems must begin to seriously account for the impacts of (and potential impacts on) climate change.[223] As the United States Environmental Protection Agency has summarized it: "[w]etland habitats in particular are faced with unique challenges due to a number of factors including rising sea levels and variable temperature and precipitation patterns. The importance of wetland functions and ecosystem services will continue to grow as the climate changes."[224]

Part II of the chapter summarized the findings of scientists from different disciplines with respect to wetlands and climate change. From inundation due to sea level rise on coastal wetlands,[225] to hurricane impacts,[226] to ecosystem changes,[227] to opportunities for carbon sequestration,[228] to methane emissions,[229] scientists have studied wetlands and climate change for a number of decades. There is a direct connection between wetland ecosystems and climate change. Yet more study is needed.

Part III of the chapter examined existing wetland regulatory structures and identified some potential options under the existing approaches to adapt to and mitigate for climate change. On a federal regulatory level, a number of options under existing law were explored.[230] On a local and international level options may be less but there still may be opportunities to bring climate change into some analyses.[231]

In Part IV of the chapter, I offered five recommendations which propose serious undertakings if adopted, but even so may not be enough. These five recommendations are: (1) expand incentive programs (and perhaps create new ones) that protect and enhance the nation's wetland resources;[232] (2) invest in a dramatic increase in applied science surrounding multiple aspects of climate change and wetlands;[233] (3) include wetland considerations in broader legislative fixes for climate change;[234] (4) use existing United States federal wetland regulatory tools to account for climate change, and work toward amendments to the regulatory process that will directly integrate climate change into the wetlands permitting process;[235] and (5) engage on an international level, through the Ramsar Convention, with other nations to ensure consideration of those whose lives and livelihoods depend on wetland resources.[236]

The short story is that policymakers need to move forward now. As Prof. Lazarus has remarked, "ecological catastrophe and human tragedy can occur when the laws of humankind fictionalize or otherwise ignore the laws of nature. Humankind invariably fails to anticipate adverse

---

222. *Id.*

223. *See supra* section I.

224. U.S. Envtl. Prot. Agency Office of Wetlands, Oceans, & Watersheds, Watershed Academy, *Wetlands and Climate Change,* http://www.clu-in.org/conf/tio/owwcc_051308/ (last visited Oct. 8, 2008).

225. *See supra* notes 30–38 and accompanying text.

226. *See supra* notes 43–47 and accompanying text.

227. *See supra* notes 24–38, 48–49 and accompanying text.

228. *See supra* notes 8–10 and accompanying text.

229. *See supra* notes 50–55 and accompany text.

230. *See supra* Part III.

231. *See supra* Part III.

232. *See supra* Part IV(1).

233. *See supra* Part IV(2).

234. *See supra* Part IV(3).

235. *See supra* Part IV(4).

236. *See supra* Part IV(5).

environmental consequences that will in fact occur by failing to undertake necessary preventive actions and unwittingly promoting others with actions that affirmatively trigger or exacerbate such harmful consequences."[237] This is coupled with the reality that policy-makers are (perhaps understandably) nervous about adopting new requirements on climate change in the face of evolving science[238] and world-wide economic uncertainty.[239]

But the simple truth is this: without swift and serious action, nifty things like wetlands will be damaged or destroyed as climate change continues. Only expeditious engagement can meet the needs and welfare of the people and the planet in terms of wetlands ecosystems and the functions and values they provide.

Notes

As Professor Connolly makes clear, Section 404 is in the middle of huge development projects that have escaped any accounting for "global warming" or "climate change." Consider:

1. *Mountaintop Mining*

Bragg v. Robertson, 54 F. Supp. 2d 635, 646 (S.D. W. Va. 1999) (Hon. Charles H. Haden, II, J.) (issuing preliminary injunction upon finding irreparable harm), *quoted in Ohio Valley Envt'l Coalition v. U.S. Army Corps of Engineers*, 479 F. Supp. 2d 607, 614 (S.D. W. Va. 2007) (Chambers, J.):

> [M]ined sites were visible from miles away. The sites stood out among the natural wooded ridges as huge white plateaus, and the valley fills appeared as massive, artificially landscaped stair steps. Compared to the thick hardwoods of surrounding undisturbed hills, the mine sites appeared stark and barren and enormously different from the original topography.

Bragg v. West Virginia Coal Ass'n, 248 F.3d 275, 286 (4th Cir. 2001) (Paul V. Niemeyer, J.) (on mountaintop removal coal mining):

> Many valley fills bury intermittent and perennial streams and drainage areas that are near the mountaintop.

Ohio Valley Envt'l Coalition v. U.S. Army Corps of Engineers, 479 F. Supp. 2d 607, 629 (S.D. W. Va. 2007) (Robert Charles Chambers, J.) (remanding permits for reconsideration in an opinion strongly suggesting that EISs are required):

> The Corps' decision to issue these permits will allow the applicants to bury miles of streams and fill their valleys with excess spoil material.... The Corps candidly acknowledges ... that these valley fills will permanently bury the streams along with their ripar-

---

237. Richard J. Lazarus, *Environmental Law After Katrina: Reforming Environmental Law by Reforming Environmental Lawmaking*, 81 Tul. L. Rev. 1019, 1041 (2007).

238. Kirstin Dow and Gregory Carbone, *Climate Science and Decision Making*, 1 Geography Compass 302, 309 (2007) *available at* http://www3.interscience.wiley.com/cgi-bin/fulltext/118529987/PDFSTART ("For some regulators and sector decision-makers, interest and ability to adopt forecast information are limited by forecast uncertainties as these pose potential legal challenges in some regulatory situations, lack of correspondence with professional engineering standards, and face reluctance to modify current decision practices or models (Berkhout *et al.* 2006; Rayner *et al.* 2005). Differences among decision-makers' use of forecasts will also depend on their preferences about waiting for further information and their risk tolerance (Dempsey and Fisher 2005).").

239. The White House, *Fact Sheet: Taking Urgently Needed Action to Stabilize Our Markets—President Bush Lays Out Steps the Federal Government is Taking to Address the Financial Crisis*, http://www.whitehouse.gov/news/releases/2008/10/20081007-6.html (last visited Oct. 10, 2008).

ian areas, permanently alter the normal water flow within the area under the fill, and destroy or disrupt the living organisms and their habitats within the valley.

2. Environmental Creationism

In the *Ohio Valley Envt'l Coalition* case, Judge Chambers had before him a Clean Water Act/NEPA challenge to the issuance of four permits by the Corps of Engineers. These permits allowed the filling of West Virginia streams in conjunction with surface coalmining operations. As later explained by the court of appeals:[1]

> All together, the four challenged permits authorize the creation of 23 valley fills and 23 sediment ponds, and they impact 68,841 linear feet of intermittent and ephemeral streams, or just over 13 miles.

We will give you a taste of the to-and-fro between Judge Chambers and the Fourth Circuit Court of Appeals. We call this the "NEPA dialogue."

Judge Chambers said that filling streams with ripped-off mountains was destructive, wrong and illegal under the Clean Water Act and NEPA. The court of appeals said this technique was "pioneered in West Virginia."[2]

Speaking of the proposed mitigation, Judge Chambers said that it's not very easy to make a stream.[3] The court of appeals said that one stream might have been reestablished in Kentucky and that surely "the novelty of a mitigation measure alone cannot be the basis of our decision to discredit" the practice.[4]

Judge Chambers said that the Corps offered "only the conclusion that mitigation will offset the losses and simply no explanation for how the mitigation proposed will replace what will be lost."[5] The court of appeals embraced this dubious conclusion and said that "whatever the functional uniqueness of headwater streams, nothing in NEPA, the CWA, or the Corps' regulations prevents them from allowing mitigation of headwater stream destruction through enhancement, restoration, or creation of a downstream perennial system."[6]

Judge Chambers was tempted by the metaphor that it was a "Field of Dreams" approach to think you could make streams out of rocks.[7] The court of appeals said this attitude shows no respect for the "best professional judgment" of the Corps of Engineers.[8]

---

1. Ohio Valley Environmental Coalition v. Aracoma Coal Co., 556 F.3d 177, 187 (4th Cir. 2009) (Gregory and Shedd, C.J.s, with Michael, C.J., dissenting in part).

2. 556 F.3d at 186.

3. 479 F. Supp. 2d at 648–49 (footnote bracketed below):
   At trial, Plaintiffs offered Dr. Palmer as an expert in stream restoration. In her extensive participation in restoration projects and review of such projects across the United States, she explained that stream creation "has not succeeded and is not scientifically credible." [Dr. Palmer served as the lead of the National River Restoration Science Synthesis project, and in that capacity, stated that she had yet to learn of a single case of successful stream creation despite the compilation of over 30,000 stream and river restoration projects throughout the United States on behalf of the project.]

4. 556 F.3d at 205.

5. 479 F. Supp. 2d at 652.

6. 556 F.3d at 203.

7. 479 F. Supp. 2d at 648 (footnote bracketed below):
   Plaintiffs' experts characterized the Corps' position as a "Field of Dreams" approach [As in, "[i]f you build it, [the streams] will come" *Field of Dreams* (Universal 1989)] and explained that many obstacles make this theory of stream creation doubtful. The scientific community is skeptical of the likelihood that important headwater stream functions will actually be achieved in manmade streams. In addition, the USFWS, a sister federal agency with expertise in aquatic ecosystems, advised the Corps that there was no scientific support for the concept that these ditches could be considered even rough approximations biologically of a stream.

8. 556 F.3d at 204.

Judge Chambers said it was a "Federal" action for the Corps to issue permits for these valley fill projects. The court of appeals said that this was not so because "NEPA plainly is not intended to require duplication of work by state and federal agencies."[9]

Judge Michael did write a dissent in the court of appeals:[10]

> Today's decision will have far-reaching consequences for the environment of Appalachia. It is not disputed that the impact of filling valleys and headwater streams is irreversible or that headwater streams provide crucial ecosystem functions. Further, the cumulative effects of the permitted fill activities on local streams and watersheds are considerable. By failing to require the Corps to undertake a meaningful assessment of the functions of the aquatic resources being destroyed and by allowing the Corps to proceed instead with a one-to-one mitigation that takes no account of lost stream function, this court risks significant harm to the affected watersheds and water resources.

3. *California Native Plant Soc'y v. U.S. EPA*, 2007 WL 2021796 (N. D. Cal. July 10, 2007). This case was an ESA / NEPA challenge to a "June 2004 Conceptual Level Strategy for Avoiding, Minimizing & Preserving Aquatic Resources in the Sunrise-Douglas Community Plan Area." The planning area is in the City of Rancho Cordova, Sacramento County, and covers 6,042 acres. It overlaps areas within the recovery plan for vernal pool ecosystems. Several landowners within the area have applied to the Corps to fill vernal pools and the Corps has issued EAs / FONSIs on these projects. The court says the adoption of the Conceptual Strategy is not a final agency action and does not have to comply with NEPA. But the EAs / FONSIs for the individual projects are short on evaluation and are likely to fall short of the "hard look" on cumulative effects. The court enjoins "any further construction, groundbreaking, earthmoving, or other on-the-ground activity that may affect vernal pool habitat." *Id.* at 24: "Vernal pool habitat will be permanently destroyed in the development process. The risk of such permanent destruction absent the benefit of an adequate cumulative impacts or alternatives analysis under NEPA tips the balance of the hardships in Plaintiffs' favor. That, combined with the uncertainties associated with the probability of successfully offsetting the loss of natural vernal pools through vernal pool creation, reinforces the Court's conclusion that irreparable harm is sufficiently likely to warrant interim injunctive relief." No bond required in this public interest litigation.

4. In the famous phosphate mining case, Judge James Hoeveler found multiple violations of the ESA / CWA and NEPA in the Corps' issuance of Section 404 permits "for the destruction of approximately 5,400 acres of wetlands in order to remove the underlying limestone for processing into cement, concrete blocks, and other products." *Sierra Club v. Strock*, 495 F. Supp. 2d 1188, 1189 (S.D. Fla. 2007). He found that this Corps-permitted activity was the likely source of contamination of the Biscayne Aquifer. The court's opinion is strongly critical of the Corps and says this about the remedy (495 F. Supp. 2d at 1205) (footnote omitted):

> It appears that this Court's consideration of irreparable harm under the ABA's recommended guidelines [No. 107B (August 1997)] should weigh heavily against the continuation of activities currently resulting in substantial environmental damages that "cannot be remedied after such interim period" (*e.g.*, contamination of the Aquifer, the death of wood stork due to the destruction of their foraging habitat, and the continued devastation of wetlands).

The Eleventh Circuit remands on the curious ground that Judge Hoeveler mistakenly believed that NEPA was a substantive law. *Sierra Club v. Antwerp*, 526 F.3d 1153 (11th Cir. 2008) (Dub-

---

9. *Id.* at 196.
10. *Id.* at 226.

ing, J., joined by Coogler, J., with Kravitch, J., concurring in part and dissenting in part). *See id.* at 1361–62:

> We commend the District Court for his thorough analysis, [said the Court, while rephrasing the *Robertson* dictum that] it would not violate NEPA if the EIS noted that granting the permits would result in the permanent, irreversible destruction of the entire Florida Everglades, but the Corps decided that economic benefits outweighed that negative environmental impact.

See NEPA at 40: How a Visionary Statute Confronts 21st Century Impacts, 39 ELR 10575 (July 2009) (21 NEPA articles addressing a variety of issues including climate change).

————

Climate Change on Columbia Basin Tribal Lands

Kyle Dittmer, Hydrologist — Meteorologist, Columbia River Inter-Tribal Fish Commission.

You can't go far anymore without hearing about climate change and its effects on glaciers and rising sea levels. The impacts of climate change are not confined to specific regions of the earth. If you want examples of global warming, *all you have to do is look around you.* Look in your garden. Gardens are able to grow longer because of the warmer conditions. In my garden, the warming weather has pushed the harvest of raspberries back through November; twenty years ago I was done by late September.

While scientists have explored global warming impacts on a larger scale, few have considered the impacts we will have on a smaller level. In my role as the Oregon Chapter President of the American Meteorological Society, I've seen a strong interest in the issue among amateurs and professionals in recent years. Deeply involved in global warming issues, for the past seven years I have studied the impacts of global warming on Columbia Basin salmon and tribal lands. My findings don't bode well for salmon.

Impacts of Global Warming on Salmon

Over the past 100 years, the river and weather conditions of the Columbia River Basin have been extensively measured. Daily temperatures, precipitation and the amount of snowpack in the mountains has always been an important part of driving the ecosystem. Using this historical data to study the changes throughout the basin, I found that during the last century the average daytime and nighttime temperatures and annual precipitation for the region have increased. My analysis shows that over the past 100 years, watershed daytime temperatures have increased by 0.2° to 1.7°F and nighttime temperatures have increased by 0.6° to 4.1°F, or twice as fast as day temperatures. The annual precipitation has increased by 2% to 28%. While these changes may seem minor, they have considerable impacts on salmon.

Because of these changes, the timing of the spring snowmelt has shifted from 2 to 14 days earlier in the watersheds. The water that usually makes up the spring-summer runoff, when salmon need it the most, now flows during the autumn-winter. This means that there is less winter snow, earlier snowmelt, and less spring-summer flow. The warming winter temperatures cause the baby salmon to emerge from the river gravels weeks earlier than expected. The premature hatching means that late winter food supplies may be scarce for the young salmon. Even the inter-season volume of water has shifted. The spring-summer flows have declined 2% to 24% and the autumn-winter flows have increased 2% to 24%. (See Figures 17 and 18.)

The health and success of salmon populations in the Columbia River Basin are influenced by changing winter weather patterns and compounded by warming summer water temperatures. During the 1940s, it was rare for summer water temperatures to exceed 68°F at Bonneville Dam

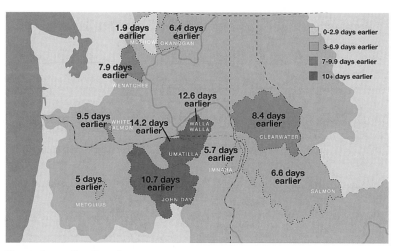

Figure 17. Change in median flow date.

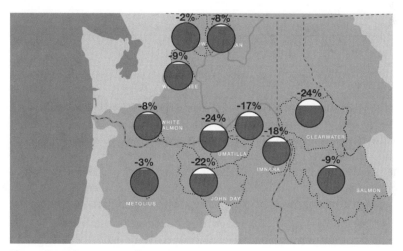

Figure 18. Change in spring/summer flow.

(which is the Oregon state water quality standard for salmon, the maximum water temperature tolerated for the survival of salmon). Today that critical threshold is exceeded half of the time. The rate of river warming during summer is twice as much as during spring-time (See Figure 19.)

In the last decade alone, the warming climate has not only influenced the juvenile salmon and their habitat, it has greatly altered the migratory behavior of adult salmon. Instead of seeing a gradual bell-shaped curve of migrating salmon in late August, the adult salmon are forced to linger in the cold water at the river bottom, then burst over the fish ladders at the dams when the river water temperature drops below 68°F. Salmon runs no longer follow a smooth progression over time, but now exploit sporadic opportunities to migrate when the cooler water temperatures allow for passage. As we move into the future, the lower Columbia hydro dams are becoming warm pools of death for returning fall Chinook in late summer.

Global Warming Impacts on Tribal Lands

I took my global warming research one step further. I asked the Columbia River Inter-Tribal Fish Commission (CRITFC) GIS specialist David Graves to explore the susceptibility of the ceded lands of CRITFC's four member tribes to climate change. Since research from the Univer-

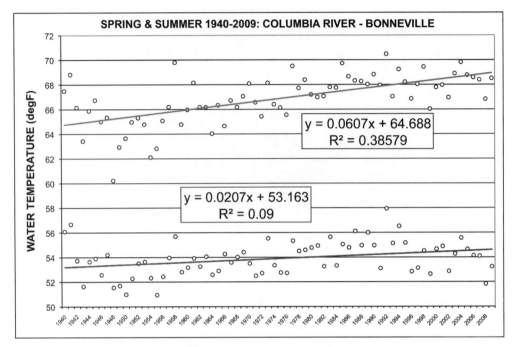

Figure 19. Spring and Summer 1940–2008: Columbia River-Bonneville.

sity of Washington's Climate Impacts Group (CIG) suggests that the effects of climate change are weaker above 4,000 feet and stronger below 4,000 feet, we used a GIS-based risk assessment model to evaluate the amount of tribal land above and below 4,000 feet in elevation. What we found is that the Yakama and Umatilla tribes face the highest risk of climate change, with 83% and 87% of their land below the 4,000 feet elevation mark. The Nez Perce Tribe faces a high risk of climate change, with 66% of its land below 4,000 feet while the Warm Springs faces a moder-ately-high risk of climate change, with 52% of its land below 4,000 feet.

In 2006, I traveled to Copenhagen, Denmark, and visited with researchers at the Danish Climate Center to find out about the Danish science perspective on global warming. I learned that Greenland in the north Atlantic may be the "canary in the coal mine" for early warning signs of rapid climate change. Greenland has been a part of Denmark for almost 300 years. The Danish scientists could provide insights on how future climate change may play out in North America. The Greenland glaciers of today have not melted this fast in 1000 years, since the early days of the Viking Era.

Addressing an Immediate Threat

According to research from the CIG, in the Pacific Northwest snow packs will continue to decline with a major loss of the low elevation snow and part of the mid-elevation snow; there will be lower spring and summer flows, causing summer water temperatures to continue to rise. The frequency of drought is expected to double, more extremes in weather patterns (such as the record breaking rains of November 2006 and December 2007) will occur. Forest fires and pest and disease infestations are becoming more common. The variability in the extremes is becoming more pronounced. The increased weather variability will hurt our ability to manage wisely natural resources.

The time to take action is growing short. Dr. James Hansen, of NASA, is considered to be the Federal Government's "Father of Climate Change." The spring of 2008 marked the 20-year anniversary of his testimony to Congress about the threat of climate change and the increased impacts of global warming. Hansen says we've squandered twenty years of lost opportunities to take significant action.

Hansen and others have warned that we're fast approaching a "tipping point" in the Earth's climate system. Once we exceed this tipping point, the Earth will experience runaway climate change and humans will be unable to stop that change. Think of being in a canoe that rocks back and forth. If you lean too much one way, then you'll immediately flip the canoe over and capsize. Now you know what a "tipping point" is.

When will we reach the "tipping point?" The research of Hansen and others suggests that when atmospheric carbon dioxide levels reach 450 parts per million (ppm), then we will hit "tipping point." We are at 385 ppm. I performed an analysis that models a best-fit curve of monthly carbon dioxide data from Mauna Loa, Hawaii, considered to be the most reliable gauging spot on Earth (*see* graph below). With 99% confidence, the curve suggests that we'll cross the 450 ppm threshold by 2026, or 18 years from now. (See Figure 20.)

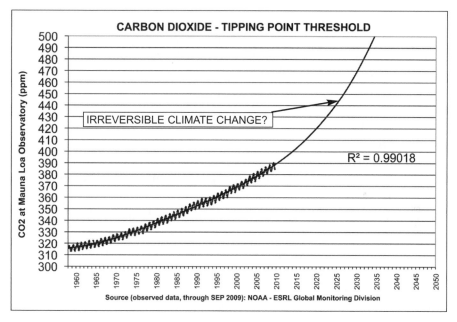

Figure 20. Carbon Dioxide—Tipping Point Threshold.

The potential impacts of global warming are staggering and the region must ask itself, what can be done to address a global problem? We should be proactive. By reducing greenhouse gas emissions and using green energy like wind and solar power, individuals can be part of the solution. But the response needs to go beyond that; there needs to be more resiliency and flexibility built into our hydropower system, society, and economies. New improvements in runoff forecasting can help to mitigate for a rapidly changing environment. By altering the refill and drawdown schedules of the hydro dams to reflect a more natural system, we are able to mitigate for the impacts of global climate change and provide adequate water for salmon. All these measures will help us to handle the unpredictability associated with climate change.

The legal implications for the region's tribes are equally staggering. The CRITFC serves as a science center for the Nez Perce, Umatilla, Warm Springs, and Yakama tribes. They have reserved treaty rights to hunt and collect their traditional foods—salmon, elk/deer, roots, and berries—at their "usual and accustomed places" as stipulated in the 1855 treaties. What happens, though, if the environmental baseline changes so fast and so radically that the tribe's natural resources migrate out of the region?

As scary as these prospects may be, don't give up and keep fighting the good fight. We, both individually and collectively, can make a difference. If we can make a difference, then we can make that change. If we can change the present, then we can alter the course of the future. Every one of us must do so, if we, and our children, and their children, are going to have any future worth having.

VI. The Earth's Terrestrial Surfaces

A. Public Lands

The practicing bar knows full well that NEPA obliges agencies to consider the effects of their actions and to analyze them. The appearance of "climate change" in future NEPA documents is a certainty. Therefore when courts tell agencies that they didn't consider "this or that" in their NEPA endeavors or locked out the public along the way, lawyers think: "These are NEPA precedents but soon to be climate change precedents."

Oregon Natural Desert Ass'n v. Bureau of Land Management, 531 F.3d 1114, 1124 (9th Cir. 2008) (Berzon, C.J.) (NEPA / FLPMA / Wilderness Act challenge to BLM land-use plan covering large portions of southeastern Oregon):

> [The BLM] explicitly disclaimed any general obligation to analyze the impacts of its Plan on wilderness values, or to consider management options for areas with those values, and took no action contrary to that statement.

> The BLM never considered closing a significant amount of land to ORVs.

Western Watersheds Project v. Kraayenbrink, 2007 WL 1667618 (D. Ida. June 2007) (Judge B. Lynn Winmill) (rejecting the embrace of grazing allotment monitoring requirements that would make most standards unenforceable for the foreseeable future):

> NEPA requires that the BLM take a hard look at the FEIS as to why public participation and [duties to consult, cooperate, and coordinate] should be more limited than those in the 1995 regulations.

> The FEIS violates NEPA because it improperly minimizes the negative side effects of limiting public input.

Facing Unprecedented Stewardship Challenges: Climate Change and Federal Land Management

Robert L. Glicksman,* Robert W. Wagstaff Distinguished Professor of Law, University of Kansas, Member Scholar and Member, Board of Directors of the Center for Progressive Reform, University of Kansas School of Law, 1535 W. 15th Street, Lawrence, KS 66045; Tel: (785) 864-9219, Fax: (785) 864-5054, r-glicksman@ku.edu.

----

    * The author thanks Christopher Steadham, Faculty Services & Research Librarian, University of Kansas School of Law, for his extremely valuable help in collecting the materials needed to write this essay.

The principal legislation that governs the approximately 650 million acres of the nation's land that is owned by the federal government was adopted before most scientists or policymakers became aware of the phenomenon of global climate change. It is now beyond reasonable dispute that, as a result of anthropogenic activities, the changes in climate that are already occurring and will continue to occur in coming decades will affect the environment in ways and to a degree that, until recently, could not have been imagined. The timing, nature, distribution, and severity of many of these effects remain uncertain. Clearly, though, the climate-related chemical, biological, and other physical changes, and the social and economic consequences that accompany them, present daunting challenges to the federal government's ability to manage its lands and resources in ways that contribute to the economic, ecological, and spiritual health of the present generation of Americans without sacrificing similar opportunities for future generations.

In some cases, the legislation that governs federal land and resource management is ill-equipped to confront climate change challenges that it was not designed to address. In other instances, existing statutory authority is sufficiently flexible and far-reaching to enable federal land management agencies to contribute to both mitigation of and adaptation to climate change. In many cases, however, the government is ignoring or mishandling that authority, with potentially catastrophic and irreversible consequences.

This paper addresses the potential impacts of climate change on federal lands and resources and the incalculable value they contribute to society. It first summarizes three categories of impacts climate change is having or is expected to have on federal lands and resources: physical, biological, and socio-economic. The second portion of the paper describes the existing statutory framework under which the federal government manages its rich natural resource heritage and the extent to which that framework may authorize the land management agencies to anticipate and respond to climate change. That discussion also highlights deficiencies in both the scope of existing legislation and the manner in which it has been implemented to date. The remainder of the paper reconceives the legal framework for managing the public lands. It makes ten general recommendations for changing either the statutes or the manner in which they are implemented. The recommendations are designed to ensure that the land management agencies have ample authority to protect the resources for which they are responsible by managing resources to mitigate and adapt to climate change. The paper concludes with a series of examples of protective measures the recommendations will facilitate.

The Impact of Climate Change on Federal Lands and Resources

Climate change has already begun to affect or is anticipated to affect all kinds of ecosystems represented on the federal lands, including forests, fresh water and wetlands ecosystems, grass and shrublands, and coastal and marine environments. These effects may be physical, biological, or socio-economic, although in many instances those categories overlap and the effects in one category cause or result from effects in another.[1]

Physical Effects

Anticipated changes in global weather patterns are likely to alter significantly the physical characteristics of federal lands and resources. One set of effects stems from changes in the timing, nature, and amount of precipitation. According to the Intergovernmental Panel on Climate Change (IPCC), rising global temperatures are very likely to increase precipitation in high lati-

---

1. This tripartite characterization of the effects of global climate change is used in U.S. Gov't Accountability Office, Climate Change: Agencies Should Develop Guidance for Addressing Effects on Federal Land and Water Resources, GAO-07-863 (Aug. 2007) [hereinafter GAO, Climate Change].

tudes and decrease it in lower latitudes. Daily heavy rainfall events may increase, even in regions in which mean rain decreases. In the United States, annual mean precipitation is very likely to increase in the northeast but decrease in the southwest.[2] These changes will affect conditions on the federal lands, perhaps dramatically. Rising temperatures have already caused noticeable changes in the western United States, where some winter precipitation has shifted from snow to rain. During the past half century, temperature increases have produced smaller late fall and early spring snowpacks and earlier melting in the western mountains, such as the Cascades and Sierra Nevadas, often despite increases in total winter precipitation. Scientists have measured a 15 to 30 percent reduction in April 1 snow water equivalent since 1950 in these areas.[3] Even under optimistic projections, snowpack will decline by 30 to 70 percent during the second half of the century in the Sierra Nevadas.[4] In addition, because snowmelt is occurring earlier, so is peak stream and river flow, causing dryer summers.[5] Studies have attributed as much as 60 percent of changes in river flows and snowpack in the western U.S. during the last 50 years to human-induced climate change.[6] Scientists predict that displacement of snow by rain and midwinter melting of snowpack caused by warmer winters in the mountainous west will increase winter flooding, which in turn will increase avalanches, soil erosion, sedimentation, and stream turbidity.[7]

A related phenomenon is glacial melting. Climate change is already causing glaciers to melt in places such as Glacier National Park, where the estimated number of glaciers has fallen from 150 to 26 in the last century and a half. Some scientists predict that if temperatures continue to rise, all of the glaciers in the park will be gone within 25 to 30 years.[8] Significant glacial attrition also has occurred in North Cascades, Mount Rainier, and Yosemite National Parks and on federal lands in Alaska.[9]

Coastal areas will experience different water-related problems.[10] Rising temperatures are causing sea levels to rise, both because heated water expands and because they contribute to the melting of ice sheets in places such as Greenland and Antarctica.[11] National wildlife refuges in Maryland, Florida, and Louisiana and Channel Islands National Park off the California coast are

---

2. Climate Change 2007: The Physical Science Basis, Contribution of Working Group I to the Fourth Assessment of the Intergovernmental Panel on Climate Change 87 (Cambridge Un. Press 2007), *available at* http://www.ipcc.ch/ipccreports/ar4-wg1.htm.

3. Kathleen A. Miller, *Climate Change and Water in the West: Complexities, Uncertainties, and Strategies for Adaptation*, 27 J. Land, Res. & Envtl. L. 87, 88–89 (2007).

4. Jon Gertner, *The Future Is Drying Up*, N.Y. Times Mag., Oct. 31, 2007, at 68, 70.

5. Stephen Saunders et al., *Losing Ground: Western National Parks Endangered by Climate Disruption*, 24 The George Wright F. 41, 42 (2007). *See also* Miller, *supra* note 3, at 89 (stating that "seasonal peak streamflow in the snowmelt-dominated rivers of western North America was occurring 1–4 weeks earlier by 2002 than in 1948"); Frederic H. Wagner, *Global Warming Effects on Climatically-Imposed Ecological Ingredients in the West*, 27 J. Land, Res. & Envtl. L. 109, 114 (2007) (reduced spring runoff peaks in California are occurring one to three weeks earlier); Noaki Schwartz, *Climate Changes Expected to Transform California*, Lawrence J.-World, Dec. 30, 2007, at 6A.

6. Tim P. Barnett et al., *Human-Induced Changes in the Hydrology of the Western United States*, 319 Science 1080 (Feb. 22, 2008).

7. GAO, Climate Change, *supra* note 1, at 21.

8. GAO, Climate Change, *supra* note 1, at 5, 18–19.

9. Saunders et al., *supra* note 5, at 43.

10. For a description of some of the areas of the United States at risk of inundation and erosion from rising sea levels, see James G. Titus & Charlie Richman, *Maps of Lands Vulnerable to Sea Level Rise: Modeled Elevations along the U.S. Atlantic and Gulf Coasts*, 18 Climate Research 205 (2000).

11. *See* Robert L. Glicksman, *Global Climate Change and the Risks to Coastal Areas from Hurricanes and Rising Sea Levels: The Costs of Doing Nothing*, 52 Loyola L. Rev. 1127, 1135–40 (2006).

among the areas that may be flooded.[12] Flooding may cause inundation and saltwater intrusion that destroy coastal wetlands and the freshwater ecosystems upon which freshwater aquatic species depend. If sea levels rise by two feet by the end of the 21st century, as the IPCC has projected, up to 50 percent of the Everglades' fresh water marsh would be transformed into a salt water system.[13] Coastal flooding and associated wetlands losses also could destroy storm buffers in low-lying areas.[14]

The problem in some federal land locations will be too little water, not too much. Drought is a source of stress for many native plant species found on the federal lands. Drought conditions due to reduced precipitation and rising temperatures linked to climate change are already adversely affecting resources at locations as diverse as the Cerbat Mountains of Arizona (where old growth pinyon-juniper pine trees are dying), the Colorado Plateau (where shrubs such as cliffrose are disappearing), and the Chugach National Forest (where lake levels have declined and former ponds have been transformed into grassy basins). When wet periods occur, invasive species such as annual grasses may fill gaps in native vegetation. These invasive species may be able to survive wildfires better than native species such as saguaro cacti and Joshua trees.[15] Among the areas most at risk of losing forests are Bandelier National Monument and Mesa Verde National Park.[16] Drought conditions have the potential to transform large expanses of woodlands into shrub or grasslands. According to the General Accountability Office (GAO), "some rare ecosystems, such as alpine tundra, California chaparral, and blue oak woodlands in California may become extinct altogether."[17]

Many of these changes have the potential to impair water quality. Severe storms following extended dry spells may accelerate soil erosion and sedimentation in lakes, rivers, and streams. In addition, reduced flow rates will increase concentrations of pollutants already in the water. Saltwater intrusion caused by coastal flooding could impair the quality of water essential to the survival of aquatic species or that used for drinking. Climate change is also predicted to increase acidification of coastal and ocean ecosystems because increases in CO_2 concentrations result in decreased concentrations of carbonate ion in seawater. Falling carbonate ion concentrations, in turn, reduce the biocalcification rate in corals and other marine organisms. The result could be compromised coral reefs and other changes in ocean chemistry in places such as the Florida Keys National Marine Sanctuary.[18]

The increasingly arid conditions that exist in areas starved of precipitation, runoff, and summer flows will create conditions amenable to an increase in wildfires. "Summer heat strongly correlates with fire increase," and larger and more frequent wildfires, and longer wildfire seasons, have occurred since the 1980s in the west and southwest. Increased wildfire activ-

12. *See* GAO, Climate Change, *supra* note 1, at 21–22; Sanders *et al.*, *supra* note 5, at 63.

13. Cornelia Dean, *The Preservation Predicament*, N.Y. Times, Jan. 29, 2008.

14. Allianz Group & World Wildlife Fund, Climate Change and Insurance: An Agenda for Action in the United States 16 (Oct. 2006), *available at* www.worldwildlife.org/news/pubs/allianzwwf.pdf [hereinafter, Allianz Group]. *See also* Elizabeth A. Stanton & Frank Ackerman, Florida and Climate Change: The Costs of Inaction 66, 68 (Nov. 2007), *available at* http://www.ase.tufts.edu/gdae/Pubs/rp/FloridaClimate.html.

15. GAO, Climate Change, *supra* note 1, at 18, 27.

16. *See* Saunders *et al.*, *supra* note 5, at 48 (stating that "[s]udden, widespread, climate-driven loss of forests is now occurring in the American Southwest, where semiarid conditions make even the hardy trees that can survive there susceptible to drought.").

17. GAO, Climate Change, *supra* note 1, at 26, 32–33.

18. *See* United Nations Environment Programme, In Dead Water: Merging of Climate Change with Pollution, Over-Harvest, and Infestations in the World's Fishing Grounds 35–37 (Feb. 2008); GAO, Climate Change, *supra* note 1, at 22.

ity in the northern Rockies is associated with increases in summer heat and earlier spring snowmelt.[19] Wildfires increase, sometimes for long periods, the amounts of sediment, debris, heavy metals, and nutrients that enter surface water bodies, adversely affecting water quality and aquatic species. Further, watersheds damaged by fires are more susceptible to flash floods.[20] Fire also decreases the capacity of affected forests to sequester carbon, at least until new growth emerges.[21]

Biological Effects

The biological effects of climate change are at least as dramatic as the effects discussed in the preceding section. Climate change will alter the habitat upon which myriad plant and animal species depend. In many cases, species will have to migrate to new areas as the ecosystems that previously sustained them become unsuited to their needs. A study of 130 species of trees in North America found that by the end of the 21st century, a massive migration of these species northward is likely to occur. Ranges of some species could shift by 400–500 miles. Ranges could decline by up to 58 percent if tree species cannot adapt to climate change by dispersing their progeny to more favorable areas (and thus survive only in areas that overlap with their current climatic range). The climate in much of the southern U.S. could be outside the known climatic tolerances for most of the 130 species studied.[22] As much as one-third of the land area of the eleven western states could experience a change in dominant vegetation type by 2100. High elevation areas are most likely to be affected.[23] Scientists have already verified tree-line changes and shifts in alpine vegetation.[24] Some animals are capable of shifting along with the vegetation that supports them.[25] But shifts in vegetation can be problematic for, if not fatal to, plant and animals species located at the northern and upper-elevational edges of their ranges that depend on low temperatures.[26] The rare ecosystems of alpine tundra, California chaparral, and blue oak woodlands in California are in this category.[27]

Seasonal variations in temperature and precipitation will affect phenology, the seasonal timing of biological events such as migration, reproduction, and leaf emergence. The changes could impair the viability of affected species. For example, studies have already documented the arrival of robins in Rocky Mountain National Park before the emergence of the food species they traditionally consume.[28] Similarly, due to earlier spring thaws, white-tailed

---

19. ALLIANZ GROUP, *supra* note 14, at 17–18. *See also* Miller, *supra* note 3, at 89–90 (documenting "a sudden and marked increase in wildfire activity beginning in the mid 1980s" in places that include the northern Rockies).

20. ALLIANZ GROUP, *supra* note 14, at 90.

21. *See* KRISTIE L. EBI *et al.*, REGIONAL IMPACTS OF CLIMATE CHANGE: FOUR CASE STUDIES IN THE UNITED STATES 29 (Dec. 2007), *available at* http://www.pewclimate.org/regional_impacts.

22. Daniel W. McKenney *et al.*, *Potential Impacts of Climate Change on the Distribution of North American Trees*, 57 BIOSCIENCE 939 (Dec. 2007).

23. According to one source, "[s]ubalpine forests could be replaced by temperate evergreen forests in North Cascades National Park; Boreal forests could be replaced by mixtures of temperate evergreen forests, shrub steppes, and savanna woodlands in Grand Teton, Rocky Mountain, and Yellowstone; shrub steppes could largely be replaced by savanna woodlands and grasslands across the many national parks of the Colorado Plateau." Saunders *et al.*, *supra* note 5, at 50.

24. Eric Bontrager, *Experts Weigh Warming's Effect on Wildfire*, Pests, GREENWIRE, Feb. 12, 2008.

25. The most chronicled, based on decades of observations, is the shift in the range of Edith's checkerspot butterfly (*Euphydryas editha*) from northern Baja California to southern British Columbia. Between the 1930s and 1990s, the species' distribution "shifted 92 km northward and 105 meters upslope." Wagner, *supra* note 5, at 100.

26. *Id.* at 100.

27. GAO, CLIMATE CHANGE, *supra* note 1, at 26. *See also* Wagner, *supra* note 5, at 47 (finding that rising temperatures "could eliminate all alpine tundra from Rocky Mountain national park").

28. *See* Wagner, *supra* note 5, at 112. If animals increase their metabolism before plant food sources have sprouted, they could die from starvation. *See* THE WILDLIFE SOCIETY, GLOBAL CLIMATE CHANGE AND

ptarmigan in the Park hatch much earlier, at a time when less food is available to them, than they did in the 1970s.[29] Animals who leave hibernation early could be vulnerable to predators they did not previously encounter.[30] Climate change may result in differential changes in development rates that create mismatches in timing between other predator and prey species, a phenomenon called phenological disjunction.[31] Phenological changes could disrupt the balance of entire ecosystems. Severe winter temperatures have helped to keep elk populations in Rocky Mountain National Park under control. As temperatures warm, that regulating effect may weaken, resulting in an overabundance of elk populations. Increased elk populations could adversely affect plant communities, reducing biological diversity.[32] Warming water temperatures may reduce food supplies, causing an increase in the intervals between reproduction events of aquatic species.[33] In short, "[t]here is already compelling evidence that species are shifting their ranges in response to on-going changes in regional climates, that species are altering their phenology, and that some species are facing extinction, or have become extinct."[34]

Climate change will increase damaging pest infestations, as pests move to and thrive in environments previously inhospitable to them or less frequently face the low winter temperatures that kill them. These scourges are likely to include species such as bark beetles, grasshoppers, fungi, and diseases transmitted by bacteria, parasites, and viruses. This phenomenon is already well underway. Southern pine beetles have migrated into red spruce territory in the southeast. Spruce bark beetles have infested the Chugach National Forest, causing high mortality rates on more than 400,000 acres of spruce forests.[35] Pine beetles have damaged the Great Smoky Mountains National Park and the Colorado forests, where warmer winters and drought conditions have facilitated the spread of the infestation.[36] Higher water temperatures may increase toxic algal blooms in both freshwater and ocean ecosystems. They will also facilitate the proliferation of pathogens, a phenomenon that has already occurred in the Yukon River as it flows through the Yukon Delta National Wildlife Refuge. Increased microbial activity attributable to warmer water could adversely affect fish and other aquatic life.[37]

Climate change is already responsible for the spread of invasive species in many federal lands areas. Invasive species are those that are not native to a particular ecosystem and whose introduction disrupts the invaded ecosystem and species that depend on it. Invasive species tend to be particularly adaptable, allowing them to accommodate to changed conditions more successfully

---

WILDLIFE IN NORTH AMERICA 7 (2004), *available at* www.nwf.org/nwfwebadmin/binaryVault/Wildlife_Society_Report2.pdf (stating that if rising temperatures cause migratory birds to change location at different times, their migrations may no longer match the availability of essential food sources such as invertebrates and plant seeds).

29. *See* Saunders *et al.*, *supra* note 5, at 57.

30. Eryn Gable, *Global Warming May Change Hibernation Patterns*, LAND LETTER, Feb. 7, 2008.

31. Humphrey Q.P. Crick, *Migratory Wildlife in a Changing Climate, in* MIGRATORY SPECIES AND CLIMATE CHANGE 41 (Robert Vaag & Helene Hepworht eds., United Nations Envrionment Program 2006).

32. Guiming Wang *et al.*, *Impacts of Climate Changes on Elk Population Dynamics in Rocky Mountain National Park, Colorado, U.S.A.*, 54 CLIMATIC CHANGE 205 (2002).

33. Crick, *supra* note 31, at 41. *See also* THE WILDLIFE SOCIETY, *supra* note 28, at 7 (discussing possibility that warmer temperatures will cause reductions in the size of amphibians, leading to reduced mating success, or will change sex ratios in some reptile species).

34. Wilfried Thuiller *et al.*, *Predicting Global Change Impacts on Plant Species' Distributions: Future Challenges*, 9 PERSPECTIVES IN PLANT ECOLOGY, EVOLUTION AND SYSTEMATICS 137, 137 (Mar. 2008) (citations omitted).

35. GAO, CLIMATE CHANGE, *supra* note 1, at 23–24.

36. Gable, *supra* note 30.

37. *See* GAO, CLIMATE CHANGE, *supra* note 1, at 25–26.

than native species. Once they enter a new area, they can displace native species either by competing for food and shelter or exposing native species to parasites or diseases for which they have built up no defenses. According to one estimate, invasive plants cause an estimated $20 billion each year in economic damage in the United States, and they already infest at least 2.6 million acres of the national parks. The culprits include Russian olive trees that destroy plant and animal habitat in national parks in New Mexico and Arizona; tamarisks that deplete water in national parks on the Colorado Plateau; weeds that take over stream corridors and degrade salmon spawning habitat in the northwestern national parks; and exotic grasses that threaten native cacti in desert national parks.[38] Invasive grasses on public lands in the Mojave Desert have helped transform some desert communities into annual grasslands. Warming temperatures in the Great Lakes have allowed nonnative zebra mussels to displace native species and rising water temperatures in the Chesapeake Bay may create conditions conducive to the spread of oyster predators.[39]

The array of physical and biological effects summarized here does not exhaust the list of potential adverse consequences of climate change. Hotter air, for example, may facilitate the formation of tropospheric ozone pollution, which may impair tree and other plant growth as well as contribute to respiratory problems for people and other animals.[40] In addition, the various stresses resulting from climate change may have synergistic effects. Forests damaged by fires spurred by droughts and hot weather, for example, may be more susceptible to pest infestations than healthy forests would.

The upshot of these changes is likely to be the extinction of some species that now inhabit the federal lands, with a resulting reduction in biodiversity. Among the species at greatest immediate risk are Joshua trees in Joshua Tree National Park, white-tailed ptarmigans in Rocky Mountain National Park, mountain yellow-legged frogs in the Sierra Nevadas, desert bighorn sheep across their entire range, and pikas in the lower elevations of their range.[41] One study projected that the extinction rate of immobile butterfly species may be as high as 37 percent by 2050.[42] The consequences of the resulting loss of biodiversity are impossible to predict.

Socio-Economic Effects

Significant adverse social and economic effects will accompany the physical and biological impacts of climate change discussed above. According to the U.S. Environmental Protection Agency (EPA), fishing opportunities may shrink significantly, especially at the southern boundaries of the habitat of cool and cold water species. The agency raised the possibility that cold water fish habitats could be lost entirely in certain states in the northeast and midwest.[43] The decline in fish species ill adapted to warm water conditions may affect not only recreational opportunities, but the economic vitality and lifestyle of communities dependent on the fishing industry, such as communities in Alaska that depend on subsistence fishing.[44] Climate change has the capacity to cause hardships to other segments of the economy. Ranchers, for example, could experience reduced incomes as drought conditions and shifting vegetation patterns make it harder to sustain range populations at their previous size.[45] Destruc-

---

38. Saunders *et al.*, *supra* note 5, at 52.

39. GAO, CLIMATE CHANGE, *supra* note 1, at 6, 26.

40. *See* ROBERT L. GLICKSMAN *et al.*, ENVIRONMENTAL PROTECTION: LAW AND POLICY 392 (5th ed. Aspen Publishers 2007).

41. Saunders *et al.*, *supra* note 5, at 48, 53, 56; GAO, CLIMATE CHANGE, *supra* note 1, at 27; Schwartz, *supra* note 5.

42. Wagner, *supra* note 5, at 113.

43. U.S. ENVTL. PROT. AGENCY, CLIMATE CHANGE AND COLD WATER FISH: IS TROUT FISHING AN ENDANGERED SPORT?, EPA-236-F-99-002 (May 1999).

44. GAO, CLIMATE CHANGE, *supra* note 1, at 33.

45. *Id.* at 34.

tion of forests by fire, pest infestation, or species migration may adversely affect the timber industry.

Industries that depend on recreational use of the federal lands, such as tourism, may be hard hit by the consequences of climate change. The federal lands may become less attractive places to spend leisure time as the decline of fish, waterfowl, and other species makes fishing and hunting more difficult to enjoy.[46] The seasons for winter sports such as skiing may shrink as temperatures rise and snowpacks decline.[47] Loss of beaches due to coastal flooding will eliminate additional recreational opportunities. Hiking and camping on the federal lands may become less popular as temperatures (particularly in the southwest) rise and bugs and other pests proliferate.

Climate change will almost certainly increase the operating costs of the federal land management agencies as climate-related events such as wildfires, severe storms, and flooding require resource rehabilitation. In some instances, the seasons for recreational use may expand as spring comes earlier and fall ends later. As a result, repair and maintenance costs in the national parks, forests, and other federal lands will need to increase to meet the demands imposed by heavier use. Storms and fires linked to climate change have already impaired the infrastructure at places such as Chugach National Forest and Glacier National Park.[48]

The impact of climate change on water quantity and quality will have significant economic effects.[49] Greater variability in runoff on the federal lands will reduce the reliability of storage of water used for drinking and other domestic and commercial uses both on and off the federal lands.[50] One study has predicted that Lake Mead, which is fed by the Colorado River and provides water to cities like Phoenix and Las Vegas, has a 50 percent chance of becoming unusable by 2021 under even moderate climate scenarios due to reduced snowpacks and runoff.[51] The problem is widespread. The GAO reported in 2003 that state water managers in 36 states anticipated water shortages in the next ten years. Assuming drought conditions, the number rose to 46.[52]

Current Statutory Authority to Address Climate Change

The federal land management agencies tend to have broad discretion to manage the lands and resources within their jurisdiction, although some have more significant constraints than others. The organic statutes of the agencies vest them with sufficient authority to begin addressing climate change. Other, cross-cutting statutes applicable to all federal agencies may require that they do so. Nevertheless, the land management agencies have responded slowly to the challenges of climate change for various reasons, including statutory constraints, inad-

---

46. *See id.* at 30.

47. *See* Saunders *et al.*, *supra* note 5, at 68–69 (discussing decline of opportunities for snow-dependent recreation in national parks in Colorado and Wyoming).

48. Heavier use also may generate more crime, more interactions between people and bears, and more frequent need for rescue operations. All of these will increase operating costs. *See* GAO, Climate Change, *supra* note 1, at 31–32.

49. For a description of the effects of climate change on water resources in the United States, see generally Katherine Jacobs *et al.*, Potential Consequences of Climate Variability and Change for the Water Resources of the United States 428 (2001), *available at* http://www.usgcrp.gov/usgcrp/Library/national assessment/foundation.htm.

50. *See* G. Tracy Meahan, III, *Energy, Climate Change, and Sustainable Water Management*, 38 Env't Rep. (BNA) 2637, 2641, Dec. 7, 2007.

51. Felicity Barringer, *Lake Mead Could Be Within a Few Years of Going Dry, Study Finds*, N.Y. Times, Feb. 13, 2008, at A14 (nat'l ed.).

52. U.S. Gov't Accountability Office, Freshwater Supply: States' Views of How Federal Agencies Could Help Them Meet Challenges of Expected Shortages, GAO-03-514 (July 2003).

equate information and resources, poor planning, leadership deficiencies, and lack of political will.

The Organic Acts

The organic acts that supply most of the authority for the National Park Service (NPS), the National Forest Service (NFS), the Bureau of Land Management (BLM), and the Fish and Wildlife Service (FWS) provide a foundation that enables those agencies to take steps to both mitigate the extent of climate change and adapt to its effects. The NPS, for example, is responsible for conserving the scenery, natural and historic objects, and wildlife found in the national parks and monuments in a manner that "leave[s] them unimpaired for the enjoyment of future generations."[53] That mandate requires that the agency manage for the future as well as the present, and that it take actions to ensure the long-term integrity of the natural resources it controls. It clearly authorizes the NPS to select management actions responsive to the threats posed by climate change.

Congress has directed the NFS to use multiple use, sustained yield management principles in managing the national forests.[54] The multiple use mandate requires "periodic adjustments in use to conform to changing needs and conditions," authorizes the agency to use some land for "less than all of the resources," and requires management that does not impair the productivity of the land.[55] These provisions empower the NFS to change its management approach in response to climate-related environmental changes and to limit or prohibit certain uses if their authorization in the face of climate change threatens permanent resource impairment. The sustained yield directive requires maintenance of the output of various renewable resources without impairment of land productivity.[56] The NFS therefore may take steps, such as increasing preservation efforts and restricting extractive or high-intensity recreational use, if necessary to prevent impairment of resources adversely affected by climate change. The National Forest Management Act (NFMA) requires that the NFS manage the national forests in accordance with land use plans, which are designed to protect forest resources (including watershed, wildlife, and fish) and provide for biodiversity of plant and animal communities.[57] Land use plans also must restrict timber harvests where necessary to prevent irreversible damage to soil, slope or watershed conditions or where harvesting is likely to adversely affect water conditions or fish habitat.[58] These provisions have obvious potential as means to abate activities that exacerbate the adverse effects of climate change on the national forests. If fires or flooding linked to climate change were to create a risk of soil erosion in a national forest, for example, the NFS would have the authority to halt timber harvesting that might exacerbate that risk.

The Federal Land Policy and Management Act (FLPMA) subjects the BLM to a multiple use, sustained yield management mandate similar to the one that governs the NFS,[59] although it may impose fewer constraints on the agency's management discretion than the NFMA and other multiple use laws do. Various FLPMA provisions seem well-suited to accommodating climate change. These include the mandate to manage the public lands under the BLM's control to protect scientific, scenic, ecological, environmental, "air and atmospheric," and water resource val-

---

53. 16 U.S.C. § 1.
54. 16 U.S.C. §§ 529, 1601(d).
55. 16 U.S.C. § 531(a).
56. 16 U.S.C. § 531(b).
57. 16 U.S.C. § 1604(g)(3), (i). *See generally* Robert L. Glicksman, Bridging Data Gaps through Modeling and Evaluation of Surrogates: *Use of the Best Available Science to Protect Biological Diversity Under the National Forest Management Act*, 83 Ind. L.J. 465 (2008).
58. 16 U.S.C. § 1604(g)(3)(E).
59. 43 U.S.C. § 1712(c)(1).

ues and to provide food and habitat for fish and wildlife.[60] Although the FLPMA planning provisions tend to be vaguer than the analogous NFMA provisions, they still allow the BLM to anticipate and respond to climate change. BLM land use plans, for example, must "give priority to the designation and protection of areas of critical environmental concern."[61] Those are areas where special management attention is required "to protect and prevent irreparable damage to ... fish and wildlife resources or other natural systems and processes."[62]

The FWS is responsible for administering the national wildlife refuges "for the conservation, management, and where appropriate, restoration, of fish wildlife, and plant resources and their habitats ... for the benefit of present and future generations of America."[63] The agency must ensure the "biological integrity, diversity, and environmental health" of the refuge system and "assist in the maintenance of adequate water quantity and water quality to fulfill the mission of the System and the purposes of each Refuge."[64] The organic statute governing administration of the refuge system requires that the FWS afford priority consideration to "compatible wildlife-dependent recreational uses" in refuge planning and management.[65] A "compatible use" is one that, in the FWS's judgment, "will not materially interfere with or detract from the fulfillment of the mission of the System or the purposes of the refuge."[66] These provisions authorize the FWS to control uses, including recreational uses, that threaten wildlife species or the ecosystems upon which they depend that have been or may be disrupted by climate change. The authorization to restore refuge resources is particularly significant.

Cross-Cutting Statutes

In addition to the organic statutes that supply the lion's share of the statutory authority of the federal land management agencies, several cross-cutting statutes supplement both the procedural and substantive obligations of these agencies to take steps to address climate change. The National Environmental Policy Act (NEPA) requires all federal agencies to prepare environmental impact statements when they propose major federal actions significantly affecting the quality of the environment.[67] The courts have begun to demand that agencies factor climate change considerations into their environmental impact evaluations under NEPA.[68] NEPA, however, only requires consideration and disclosure of potential climate change considerations. It may encourage and facilitate agency planning for projects that may affect or be affected by climate change, but it has no substantive clout.

The Endangered Species Act (ESA) includes both substantive and procedural mandates. Section 7 requires that federal agencies insure that their actions (including approval of private projects) are not likely to jeopardize the continued existence of endangered or threatened species or result in the destruction or adverse modification of the critical habitat of those species.[69] In fulfilling that mandate, the action agency must consult with either the FWS or the National Oceanic and Atmospheric Association (NOAA) Fisheries, depending on the species involved. In appropriate cases, the FWS or NOAA Fisheries must prepare a biological opinion that deter-

---

60. 43 U.S.C. § 1701(a)(8).
61. 43 U.S.C. § 1712(c)(3).
62. 43 U.S.C. § 1702(a).
63. 16 U.S.C. § 668dd(a)(2).
64. 16 U.S.C. § 668dd(a)(4)(B), (F).
65. 16 U.S.C. § 668dd(a)(4)(C).
66. 16 U.S.C. § 668ee(1).
67. 42 U.S.C. § 4332(2)(C).
68. *See, e.g.,* Center for Biological Diversity v. Nat'l Highway Traffic Safety Admin., 508 F.3d 508 (9th Cir. 2007), *opinion vacated and withdrawn* 538 F.3d 1172 (9th Cir. 2008) (modifying only the NEPA remedy).
69. 16 U.S.C. § 1536(a)(2).

mines, based on the best scientific and commercial data available, whether an agency proposal would contravene § 7 and, if so, recommend reasonable and prudent alternatives to avoid jeopardy or critical habitat destruction. These provisions have the potential to act as powerful constraints on the ability of the land management agencies to proceed with projects that might adversely affect listed species at risk due to climate change. The battle over whether to list the polar bear is illustrative.[70] Politicians in Alaska have fought the proposed listing, fearing that it would restrict the federal government's ability to issue oil and gas leases in polar bear habitat. In addition, § 9 of the ESA prohibits the taking of listed species, which includes habitat modification.[71] As with NEPA, climate change considerations have begun to emerge in ESA cases. In one case, a court found a biological opinion prepared by the FWS to be unlawful because it failed to acknowledge and analyze record low levels of the listed species at issue revealed by available studies, and neglected to consider the impact of climate change on the species and its habitat.[72]

The federal pollution control laws, which apply to all the land management agencies, may restrict their ability to pursue projects that risk exacerbating the adverse effects of climate change. The Clean Air Act (CAA) requires the agencies to protect the lands and resources under their charge against the adverse effects of air pollution. The extent to which the agencies' obligation to protect air quality-related values and visibility extends to pollutants, such as CO_2 and other greenhouse gases (GHGs), for which EPA has not adopted national ambient air quality standards, is not yet clear.[73] The Clean Water Act (CWA) requires all federal agencies engaged in activities resulting in the discharge or runoff of pollutants to comply with the Act's provisions to the same extent as private parties.[74] If flooding or erosion generated by climate change impairs the quality of streams or rivers that run through the national forests or BLM public lands, the CWA and state water quality standards adopted under it may prohibit authorization of road building, timber harvesting, and other activities that may exacerbate runoff.[75]

Climate Change Challenges to Federal Lands and Resources Under Existing Law

The statutes that govern the activities of the federal land management agencies seem to authorize them to pursue a wide range of actions that might help avoid ruinous climate change, mitigate its adverse effects, or restrict activities that might exacerbate those effects. The agencies' organic statutes, however, are known for the breadth of the discretion they afford the agencies.[76] As a result, there are likely to be many situations in which those statutes allow the agencies to pursue various measures but do not compel them to do anything. That discretion can be problematic because to date addressing climate change has not been a priority for any of the land management agencies. According to the GAO, the agencies tend to focus on "near-term activities they are required to take," at the expense of long-term problems such as climate change. The agencies have tended to use historical data to react to changes that have already occurred rather than anticipate potential future change.[77] That strategy is woefully inadequate to address the an-

---

70. Endangered and Threatened Wildlife and Plants; 12-Month Petition Finding and Proposed Rule To List the Polar Bear (*Ursus maritimus*) as Threatened Throughout Its Range, 72 Fed. Reg. 1064 (Jan. 9, 2007), 72 Fed. Reg. 56979 (Oct. 5, 2007) (reopening comment period in light of new information).

71. 16 U.S.C. § 1538(a)(1)(B); Babbitt v. Sweet Home Chapter of Communities for a Great Or., 515 U.S. 687 (1995).

72. NRDC v. Kempthorne, 506 F. Supp. 2d 322, 367–70 (E.D. Cal. 2007).

73. 42 U.S.C. §§ 7475(d), 7491–7492.

74. 33 U.S.C. § 1323(a).

75. *See, e.g.*, Nw. Indian Cemetery Protective Ass'n v. Peterson, 795 F.2d 688 (9th Cir. 1986), *rev'd on other grounds sub nom.* Lyng v. Nw. Indian Cemetery Protective Ass'n, 485 U.S. 439 (1988).

76. *See, e.g.*, Perkins v. Bergland, 608 F.2d 803, 806 (9th Cir. 1979) (describing the Multiple-Use, Sustained-Yield Act as a statute that "breath[es] discretion at every pore").

77. GAO, Climate Change, *supra* note 1, at 7–8.

ticipated impacts of climate change on federal lands and resources. Even when an organic act appears to require agencies to anticipate the manner in which their activities may affect the impact of climate change on the resources they control and to take appropriate steps to address the adverse effects, the agencies sometimes ignore that mandate or give it short shrift. The NFS, for example, has come close to gutting the provision of the NFMA that requires it to provide for and preserve biodiversity.[78]

In rare instances, existing statutes specifically require the agencies to address climate change. The NFMA, as amended in 1990, requires the NFS to include in the long-range planning program it is periodically required to transmit to the President recommendations that "account for the effects of global climate change on forest and rangeland conditions, including potential effects on the geographic ranges of species, and on forest and rangeland products."[79] The planning program is supposed to guide the formulation of land and resource management plans for individual forest units, which then constrain decisions on site-specific initiatives such as timber sales. Yet, few of those plans even mention climate change, no less make it a priority concern.[80] Similarly, the Secretary of the Interior issued an order in 2001 that requires that agencies within the Department "consider and analyze potential climate change impacts" in long-range planning, setting research priorities, and making major decisions concerning resource use. The order refers specifically to planning and management activities associated with energy resource and mineral development and water projects and resources.[81] Yet, more than six years after its issuance, Department headquarters had yet to provide guidance to resource managers about how to implement the order. NPS, BLM, and FWS officials all confirmed this lack of direction and stressed the importance of getting it.[82]

Some of the cross-cutting statutes constrain agency management discretion more significantly than the organic acts do. The "no jeopardy" and takings provisions of the ESA provide perhaps the best examples. But the ESA has long been criticized as a statute whose scope is too narrow in that it focuses on protecting particular species instead of biodiversity more generally.[83] On occasion, the FWS and the NOAA Fisheries have purported to incorporate into their ESA consultation documents analytical techniques such as adaptive management which, as described below, have the potential to enhance the land management agencies' ability to protect against the adverse effects of climate change. Even then, the courts have chastised them for doing so in ways that excuse the agency's failure to act in the face of uncertainty about future conditions rather than facilitate their ability to provide protective responses to changing conditions.[84]

---

78. 16 U.S.C. § 1604(g)(3)(B). For analysis of the history of the NFS's interpretation of the diversity provision, see generally Glicksman, *supra* note 57.

79. 16 U.S.C. § 1602(5)(F).

80. *See, e.g.*, GAO, Climate Change, *supra* note 1, at 7–8 (finding that NFS officials at the Chugach National Forest have not placed a priority on planning for climate change because it was not listed as a priority threat by the NFS Chief and is not considered to be a strategic issue by the agency).

81. Secretary of the Interior Order No. 3226, Evaluating Climate Change in Management Planning, § 3 (Jan. 19, 2001).

82. GAO, Climate Change, *supra* note 1, at 8–9.

83. *See, e.g.*, Holly Doremus, *Patching the Ark: Improving Legal Protection of Biodiversity*, 18 Ecology L.Q. 265 (1991); J.B. Ruhl, *Ecosystem Management, the ESA, and the Seven Degrees of Relevance*, 14-Wtr. Nat. Resources & Env't 156, 159 (2000). *But cf.* Oliver Houck, *Why Do We Protect Endangered Species, and What Does that Say About Whether Restrictions on Private Property to Protect Them Constitute Takings?*, 80 Iowa L. Rev. 297, 301 (1995) (describing the ESA as "very much a surrogate law for ecosystems").

84. *See, e.g.*, NRDC v. Kempthorne, 506 F. Supp. 2d 322 (E.D. Cal. 2007) (describing matrix incorporated in FWS biological opinion as nothing more than an organizational flow chart that prescribed meetings if certain criteria were exceeded, but that failed to define any quantified mitigation goals or specify any time for implementation of mitigation measures).

The absence of legal guidance on the role of climate change in planning and project-level decisionmaking has been exacerbated by the dearth of scientific information needed to make informed decisions on how best to ameliorate the potential adverse impacts of climate change. The land management agencies often lack adequate baseline data such as resource inventories that would enable them to determine whether the condition of plant and animal species found on federal lands are within the range of normal variability or have already begun to experience climate-related changes. The agencies often lack computer modeling programs capable of providing input needed to make site-specific decisions on activities potentially relevant to climate change.[85]

This brief discussion hardly exhausts the obstacles that current laws and practices pose to the ability of the federal land management agencies to deal effectively with climate change. Another is the fragmentation of responsibility for resource protection among multiple agencies. What makes this splintering of authority problematic is the likelihood that the scope of specific problems will outstrip the authority of any single agency to respond to them effectively. Agency jurisdictional boundaries and the ecological parameters of climate change impacts often do not correspond. Similarly, activities that take place outside the borders of federal lands may exacerbate resource problems linked to climate change, thereby limiting an agency's ability to provide a sufficient response. Savings clauses which preserve state authority to manage resources such as water and wildlife also limit the extent to which the federal land management agencies can implement holistic strategies for preserving resources found on the federal lands in the face of climate change and the risks with which it is associated.[86]

A Reconceived Stewardship Structure

It is perhaps unfair to place undue blame for the failure of the existing federal land management and cross-cutting statutes to specifically require agencies to address climate change, or even to prescribe decisionmaking techniques for land and resource management that are up the task of dealing with the phenomenon of climate change. The statutes by and large were adopted before climate change became a prominent concern. Further, the magnitude and complexity of the issues raised by climate change far exceed any resource management issue experienced by either Congress or the land management agencies. Similar excuses are not available to land managers who have buried their heads in the ground or failed to take advantage of the discretion they do enjoy to craft strong programs for anticipating climate change and laying the groundwork for dealing with its potential to put valuable federal lands and resources at risk.

This concluding section provides ten recommendations for better equipping the federal land management agencies to manage their resources in a way that minimizes the adverse effects of global climate change. The recommendations are relevant to both mitigation of and adaptation to climate change. Some of them require statutory amendments, while others can be implemented under existing law. After listing the recommendations and briefly describing the purpose of each, the chapter provides specific examples of the opportunities available to the agencies under a reconceived statutory and regulatory regime to manage federal lands and resources to contribute to worldwide efforts to avoid climate change and combat its adverse effects.

Recommendations for Resource Management in the Face of Climate Change

1. The federal land management agencies need to *adapt their planning processes* (with legislative directives, if necessary) to afford priority to climate change issues and to emphasize the long-term consequences of climate change. As Congress recognized when it adopted FLPMA, "the national interest will be best realized if the public lands and their resources are periodically

---

85. GAO, CLIMATE CHANGE, *supra* note 1, at 9.
86. *See* SUSAN HERROD JULIUS *et al.*, ADAPTATION OPTIONS FOR CLIMATE-SENSITIVE ECOSYSTEMS AND RESOURCES 5-31, 6-29, 7-36, 9-21 to 9-23 (Public Review Draft Aug. 2007).

and systematically inventoried and their present and future use projected through a land use planning process coordinated with other Federal and State planning efforts."[87] Similarly, Congress directed the NFS under the NFMA to "use a systematic, interdisciplinary approach [to planning] to achieve integrated consideration of physical, biological, economic, and other sciences."[88] Climate change represents the greatest and most sustained challenge that has ever faced federal land managers. Yet, climate change considerations are apparently not addressed at all, and certainly not in any depth, in many current planning efforts. In interviews with the GAO, planners from the NPS, NFS, and FWS confessed to confusion about the nature of their agencies' mandates to deal with climate change and to uncertainty about how to build climate change considerations into the planning and management process.[89] As one observer put it, land use plans are " an accountability tool.... What is not in a plan tends to be considered unimportant."[90] Top agency officials must make climate change a priority in the planning process and clearly convey that message throughout their organizations.

2. The land management agencies, in the planning process as well as in other contexts, must *rely heavily on* the management technique known as *adaptive management*. The Interior Department's proposed NEPA regulations define adaptive management as "a system of management practices based on clearly identified outcomes and monitoring to determine if management actions are meeting desired outcomes; and, if not, facilitating management changes that will best ensure that outcomes are met or re-evaluated. Adaptive management recognizes that knowledge about natural resource systems is sometimes uncertain."[91] Adaptive management is a planning and management device tailor-made for dealing with uncertainty.[92] The vast majority of scientists no longer disagree that climate change has begun or that human activities that generate GHG emissions are largely responsible for causing it. Yet major uncertainties remain over the timing, extent, and distribution of climate change and its associated impacts. The planning process must provide resource managers with sufficient flexibility to deal with unanticipated effects of climate change. Adaptive management provides that flexibility.

3. Planning and project level decisions are only as good as the information on which they are based. Resource managers have stressed the need for *better information*, both about baseline resource conditions on the federal lands and about the potential effects of climate change in particular ecosystems or federal land units. Agency officials have bemoaned the paucity of computational models capable of projecting small-scale climate-related changes.[93] Absent that information, it is difficult to anticipate problems or plan for their resolution. In addition, if agencies employ adaptive management techniques, they will need the resources to monitor conditions on an ongoing basis to allow them to adjust management approaches in light of prior successes or failures.

4. The effects of climate change are not bounded by human jurisdictional designations. If climate change exacerbates wildfire risks in a national park, it will also do so for adjacent National Forest

87. 43 U.S.C. § 1701(a)(2).

88. 16 U.S.C. § 1604(b).

89. *See* GAO, Climate Change, *supra* note 1, at 36–39.

90. David Welch, *What Should Protected Area Managers Do in the Face of Climate Change?*, 22 The George Wright F. 75, 86 (2005).

91. Department of the Interior, Implementation of the National Environmental Policy Act (NEPA) of 1969, 73 Fed. Reg. 126, 133 (Jan. 2, 2008) (proposed 43 C.F.R. § 46.30).

92. "Adaptive management is a methodology in which one can proceed with only limited or uncertain knowledge. It is an approach whereby an intervention is conducted as if it were a scientific experiment, with measurable, time-bound targets set in advance (policy = hypotheses), careful measurement of results as things happen (intervention = experiment), and approaches adjusted as new information becomes available (reporting, analysis, re-setting hypotheses)." Welch, *supra* note 90, at 87.

93. GAO, Climate Change, *supra* note 1, at 41–42.

System lands. Accordingly, land managers must *make greater efforts to coordinate management* of the nation's public lands and resources, both among themselves and with state and local resource managers. If they are not capable of doing so by themselves due to the fear of ceding jurisdiction and power to others, Congress should require that they do so and establish appropriate processes.

5. As indicated above, one of the most significant effects of climate change will be species migrations. As a result, what is desert today may be grassland tomorrow, and what is tundra this year may be temperate forests the next. Joshua Tree national park may soon be devoid of Joshua trees.[94] These kinds of shifts in the nature of the resources found in particular federal land units may require dramatic changes in the management directives that govern these units. Congress must establish a mechanism for *changing the status of particular land units* and for altering *the boundaries of adjacent units* (*e.g.*, a national wildlife refuge next to a national forest) to accommodate species migrations and other climate-related changes in the condition and location of resources such as wildlife.

6. Given the potential for climate change to cause resource devastation on a magnitude rarely seen to date, it may make sense to *change the balance of uses permitted* in the various federal land systems. If flooding, fire, or droughts linked to climate change result in soil erosion that significantly impairs water quality in streams or rivers, it may be appropriate to curtail uses that might exacerbate the risks of further erosion, such as grazing or off-road vehicle use. Agency discretion is probably broad enough under most of the organic acts to allow land managers to restrict or eliminate particular uses that are otherwise appropriate, at least in specific areas and until the threats have been reduced. But Congress should consider amending the statutes, particular the multiple use, sustained yield statutes, to provide explicit authorization.

7. Activities that threaten to create damaging synergies with adverse conditions resulting from climate change are not confined to the federal lands. Development outside a federal land unit, for example, may prevent wildlife or plant species whose natural habitat has migrated from relocating to areas suited to their needs. The land management agencies must have *enhanced authority to manage external threats* to the resources under their control. Agencies such as the NPS have some authority to address outside activities that create threats to federal lands and resources, but the scope of that authority is unclear and efforts to exercise it have achieved "mixed success."[95] Commentators have characterized federal interagency efforts in particular to abate external threats as inadequate.[96] Congress should reinforce and expand that authority.

8. In certain instances, regulation of external threats will be politically impossible or legally difficult because of the effects it would have on the property rights of neighboring landowners. The federal land management agencies have no inherent authority to exercise the power of eminent domain. They have some condemnation authority, either through specific statutory authorization or under the General Condemnation Act (GCA).[97] Congress also has authorized the land management agencies to engage in land exchanges.[98] But existing authority to condemn and acquire by exchange is limited. Under the GCA, for example, an agency's authority to condemn is only as broad as its authority under other laws to acquire lands through voluntary transactions.[99] Laws authorizing condemnation often restrict the purposes for which it is appropriate. The BLM, for ex-

---

94. *See* Schwartz, *supra* note 5.

95. 3 GEORGE CAMERON COGGINS & ROBERT L. GLICKSMAN, PUBLIC NATURAL RESOURCES LAW § 23:5 (2d ed. West / Thomson 2007).

96. *See, e.g.*, Joseph L. Sax & Robert B. Keiter, *Glacier National Park and Its Neighbors: A Study in Federal Interagency Relations*, 14 ECOLOGY L.Q. 207 (1987).

97. 40 U.S.C. § 257.

98. *E.g.*, 16 U.S.C. § 668dd(b)(3) (FWS); 43 U.S.C. § 1716 (NFS).

99. United States v. Kennedy, 278 F.2d 121 (9th Cir. 1960).

ample, may condemn land only to provide access to federal lands and then only in the amount necessary for reasonable access.[100] Congress should *expand the power of the land management agencies to acquire or exchange land* as a means of abating the adverse consequences of climate change.

9. The land management agencies must place *greater emphasis on protecting the integrity of entire ecosystems and protecting biodiversity* instead of focusing on the status of individual species deemed to be at risk due to climate change. Biodiversity strengthens the ability of an ecosystem to withstand stresses, including those caused by climate change. It is impossible to predict the precise impacts of climate change. The elimination of one species can trigger a cascade of changes in the ecosystem that supports it. Agencies should prioritize biodiversity protection rather than disable statutory and regulatory provisions designed to accomplish that, as the NFS has done in its shifting interpretations of the NFMA's biodiversity provisions.[101] If statutes such as the ESA focus too narrowly on preservation of individual species in isolation, Congress should amend them to allow the agency to broaden its focus.

10. Statutory and regulatory directives to plan for climate change, rely on adaptive management, regulate external threats, or protect biodiversity are meaningless if the land management agencies fail to abide by them. It is critical that the agencies be accountable. Judicial review is perhaps the most important avenue to ensure it. Individual statutes, such as the ESA,[102] and the Administrative Procedure Act[103] authorize judicial review of both agency actions and failures to act. But judicial decisions have narrowed opportunities for judicial review, making it more difficult to hold the land management agencies accountable for failing to abide by their statutory responsibilities.[104] Congress should *restore the ability of adversely affected or otherwise interested members so the public to seek judicial review of land management agency decisions*, to the extent that Article III of the Constitution permits it to do.

Specific Examples of Desirable Mitigation and Adaptation Measures

What kinds of initiatives to manage federal lands to mitigate and adapt to climate change might these ten general recommendations enable the land management agencies to pursue? The stewardship framework sketched out above would facilitate efforts to use the federal lands to minimize both the extent to which human activities contribute to climate change and the degree to which the climate change that cannot be prevented wreaks havoc on the nation's human and natural resources.

Mitigation Measures

The federal lands have the potential to mitigate climate change through carbon sequestration. Congress has already taken preliminary steps in that direction. The Energy Independence and Security Act of 2007 requires the Secretary of Interior to spearhead preparation of a multi-agency report to Congress on a framework for managing geological carbon sequestration activities on public lands. The report must include criteria for identifying candidate geological sequestration sites in operating and depleted oil and gas fields, unmineable coal seams, deep saline formations and systems used to extract heat from geothermal resources, and coalbeds used for methane recovery. The report also must include a proposed regulatory framework for the leasing of federal lands or interests for long-term CO_2 sequestration, and recommend additional legisla-

---

100. 43 U.S.C. § 1715(a).
101. *See* Glicksman, *supra* note 57.
102. 16 U.S.C. § 1540(g).
103. 5 U.S.C. §§ 702, 704, 706.
104. *See, e.g.,* Norton v. Southern Utah Wilderness Alliance, 542 U.S. 55 (2004) (restricting judicial review of agency inaction); Ohio Forestry Ass'n v. Sierra Club, 523 U.S. 726 (1998) (restricting judicial review of land use plans).

tion that may be required to ensure that public land management and leasing laws are adequate to accommodate long-term carbon sequestration.[105]

Congress and the land management agencies can provide additional opportunities for carbon sequestration through restrictions on timber harvesting. The capacity of federally owned forest lands to sequester carbon can also include forest preservation techniques such as limitations on road construction in forested areas and reducing the susceptibility of forests to destruction by fire or pest infestation. Reforestation of denuded areas should also be pursued.[106] Similarly, grasslands provide sinks for both carbon and methane. Restrictions on grazing capable of facilitating desertification can enhance the sequestration potential of these areas.[107]

Congress and the federal land management agencies can mitigate climate change by helping weaning America from its dependence on fossil fuels. Restrictions on leasing of federal lands for the extraction of fossil fuels is one way to contribute to that effort. Use of the federal lands to produce biofuels (such as through the conversion of dead trees into cellulosic ethanol) is another.[108] Finally, reducing the allowable degree of motorized recreation on federal lands can help reduce GHG emissions.

Adaptation Measures

Adaptation involves adjustments in management techniques in response to climate change and its effects. The function of adaptation is to reduce the risk that climate change will result in adverse changes to federal lands and resources by increasing the resilience of natural systems to withstand stresses caused by climate change.[109] Adaptation can be either anticipatory (or preventive) or reactive. *Anticipatory measures* to increase natural system resilience and integrity might include measures to protect natural systems that remain intact and relatively undisturbed.[110] Thinning of forests, prescribed burning, and the creation of fuel breaks can all contribute to minimizing the risk of damage from wildfires, insects, and air pollution. Prohibiting road construction and restricting developments such as ski area facilities can help prevent habitat fragmentation. Planting resistant species in multiple locations may reduce the risk that the species will be eliminated from a particular area. Similarly, efforts to preserve a diverse gene pool will tend to enhance protection of biodiversity.[111] The creation of habitat corridors for species threatened by species migration and the other adverse effects of climate change can remove impediments to species movement. So can installation of fish passages. Agencies can protect ecologically critical coastal areas by elevating land surfaces, modifying drainage systems, stabilizing dunes, and building dikes.[112]

---

105. Pub. L. No. 110-140, §714(b)(1), 121 Stat. 1492, 1715.

106. *See* Manuel Guariguata, *Interlinkages Between Biodiversity and Climate Change*, in United Nations Environment Programme and Secretariat of the Convention on Migratory Species of Wild Animals, Migratory Species and Climate Change: Impacts of a Changing Environment on Wild Animals 10 (2006) (urging planting a variety of native tree species instead of a monoculture to reduce the probability of pest incidence, restore key watershed functions, and promote ecological connectivity between forest fragments).

107. *See* Yamond P. Motha & Wolfgang Baier, *Impacts of Present and Future Climate Change and Climate Variability on Agriculture in the Temperate Regions: North America*, 70 Climatic Change 137, 160 (2005).

108. *See* Eryn Gable, *Can Dead Wood Fuel the Future?*, Land Letter, Feb. 28, 2008.

109. Julius *et al.*, *supra* note 86, at 2–3.

110. *See, e.g.*, Dean, *supra* note 13 (explaining that "environmentally intact salmon streams will undoubtedly be useful if new species move into them" and that "even if much of the Everglades is lost to a rise in sea level, preserving the rest will be crucial for maintaining fresh water supplies in South Florida").

111. *See* Welch, *supra* note 90, at 82.

112. *See* John C. Field *et al.*, Potential Consequences of Climate Variability and Change on Coastal and Marine Resources 475 (2001), *available at* http://www.usgcrp.gov/usgcrp/Library/national assessment/foundation.htm.

Proactive adaptive measures also might include restoring natural systems that have degraded for reasons unrelated to climate change to a healthier state so that they become more resistant to climate change. Agencies can buttress natural capacity to withstand climate change stresses by restoring flood plains and riparian buffers and augmenting low flows in rivers and streams that provide habitat for susceptible aquatic species. Agencies can reduce water withdrawals from rivers experiencing low flows that increase sediment and pollutant concentrations or otherwise threaten aquatic life. Finally, land managers should restrict activities occurring on federal lands or external activities over which they have jurisdiction that are likely to combine with climate-related stresses to produce unwanted synergies. These might include restricting fishing in overexploited areas or limiting air pollution that might weaken plant life and make it more susceptible to climate-related threats. To accomplish the latter, the agencies might restrict automobile off-road vehicle use on significant portions of the lands they supervise in order to cut emissions of ozone precursors. Federal land managers should use their CAA authority to block permitting of stationary sources that would emit pollutants that can contribute to acid rain that damages trees and acidifies surface waters.[113]

Adaptation also may take the form of *reacting to problems as they develop*. Land managers, for example, can facilitate migration to more suitable areas of species whose traditional habitat is no longer capable of sustaining them.[114] Acquisition of fee interests or conservation easements might help to accomplish that goal. Agencies can introduce species to areas they previously inhabited but no longer do as a result of human activities, provided the reintroduction sites are more capable of supporting the transplanted species than their current habitat is. The NPS's successful wolf reintroduction project in the Yellowstone National Park area might provide a model. Land managers might be able to provide food sources for species experiencing phenological disruptions until they are capable of migrating. Where feasible, they should control nonnative species that are able to invade formerly inhospitable terrain due to climate change and that threaten to crowd out native species. They should try to restore habitat degraded by fire, flooding, or drought to which climate change contributed. They should restrict or ban fishing and hunting of species that appear to be at risk, even if they are not listed under the ESA.

Anticipatory adaptive measures are generally preferable to reactive ones. The former are likely to be both more efficient and effective, just as preventing pollution tends to cost less and protect resource value better than after-the-fact remediation. Anticipation is particularly important when the consequences of acting too late may be irreversible, such as species extinctions. The precautionary approach to environmental protection has long been the hallmark of federal pollution control statutes such as the CAA. Congress should endorse its application in the natural resource management context more clearly than it has done and require federal land managers to use the expanded information at their disposal and the revised planning processes described above to minimize the vulnerability of federal lands and resources to climate change.

Notes

1. *See* BILL MCKIBBEN, THE END OF NATURE (Random House 2006). This book was published originally in 1989 and has been translated into twenty languages. Why did the author choose this title? *See Introduction* to the 2006 edition, *in id.* at xviii:

---

113. *See* LINDA JOYCE *et al.*, POTENTIAL CONSEQUENCES OF CLIMATE VARIABILITY AND CHANGE FOR THE FORESTS OF THE UNITED STATES 511 (2001), *available at* http://www.usgcrp.gov/usgcrp/Library/national assessment/foundation.htm.

114. *See, e.g.*, Dean, *supra* note 13 (describing assisted migration).

.... What mattered most to me was the inference I drew from [the] science: that for the first time human beings had become so large that they altered everything around us. That we had ended nature as an independent force, that our appetites and habits and desires could now be read in every cubic meter of air, in every increment on the thermometer.

This doesn't make the consequences of global warming any worse in a practical sense, of course—we'd be in as tough a spot if the temperature was going up for entirely "natural" reasons. But to me it made this historical moment entirely different from any other, filled with implications for our philosophy, our theology, our sense of self. We are no longer able to think of ourselves as a species tossed about by larger forces—now we *are* those larger forces. Hurricanes and thunderstorms and tornadoes become not acts of God but acts of man. That was what I meant by the "end of nature."

2. As Professor Glicksman points out, nonindigenous species enjoy advantages in a future world of climate change. The U.S. EPA is not unaware of this although the connections are slow to appear in agency reports. *See*, for example, the U.S. EPA's 2008 REPORT ON THE ENVIRONMENT at 6–23:

Non-indigenous species (NIS) are one of the greatest threats to aquatic ecosystems and can impact local and regional economies.... The number of invasive species in estuaries of the Pacific Northwest (including Puget Sound, Columbia Estuary, and Coos Bay) is rising, and these areas can become sources of invasives to other locales. Coastal waters are particularly vulnerable to NIS transported in ballast water and introduced via aquaculture.... It is becoming apparent that NIS are capable of impacting estuaries along the Pacific coast, even though they are rarely addressed in routine monitoring studies. One limitation is the lack of standardized invasion metrics and threshold values.

EPA's Environmental Monitoring and Assessment Program (EMAP) looked at this NIS problem in 1999–2001 by sampling estuaries from Camp Mendocino, Calif., north to the Strait of Juan de Fuca at the entrance to Puget Sound, Washington. The data showed (EPA's 2008 REPORT ON THE ENVIRONMENT at 6–24):

Approximately 15 percent of the stations in the Columbian Province were highly invaded (*i.e.*, abundance of NIS was greater than abundance of natives) and another 20 percent were moderately invaded (Exhibit 6-12). The EMAP survey showed that NIS were among the most frequently occurring anthropogenic stressors in this biogeographic region when compared to indicators of sediment contamination or eutrophication....

The extent of invasion was not uniform, however, among exposed and minimally exposed estuaries. Estuaries with greater exposure to these invasion vectors were more invaded; 44 percent of the stations in the exposed estuaries were moderately to highly invaded compared to only 21 percent of the stations in minimally exposed estuaries (Exhibit 5-12). Nonetheless, the observation that 21 percent of the stations in these "pristine" estuaries were at least moderately invaded indicates that NIS can disperse widely once they are introduced into a region, so even estuaries with no direct exposure to ballast water or aquaculture are at risk of invasion.

3. STEPHEN SAUNDERS & TOM EASLEY, LOSING GROUND: WESTERN NATIONAL PARKS ENDANGERED BY CLIMATE DISRUPTION (July 2006) (Dr. Jesse A. Logan, U.S. Forest Service (retired), Theo Spencer, NRDC, contributing authors) (The Rocky Mountain Climate Organization & Natural Resources Defense Council), is an excellent study. It presents the following graphic on climate change and the national parks (vii). (See Table 1.)

Table 1. Top 12 Western National Parks Most at Risk from Climate Disruption

	Loss of glaciers and snowfields	Closed parks due to fire	Loss of boating	Changes in vegetation	Loss of beaches	Loss of fishing	Wildlife extinction and other effects	Intolerable heat	Loss of winter recreation	Historical and archaeological losses	Overcrowding
Bandelier National Monument, NM				x						x	
Death Valley National Park, CA							x	x		x	
Glacier National Park, MT	x	x		x		x	x		x	x	
Glen Canyon Nat.Recreation Area, UT/AZ			x	x				x		x	
Golden Gate National Recreation Area, CA					x					x	
Grand Teton National Park, WY	x	x		x		x	x		x	x	x
Mesa Verde National Park, CO				x				x		x	
Mount Rainier National Park, WA	x			x					x		x
North Cascades National Park, WA	x			x		x			x		
Rocky Mountain National Park, CO	x			x		x	x		x	x	x
Yellowstone National Park, WY/ID/MT	x	x		x		x	x		x	x	x
Yosemite National Park, CA	x			x		x	x		x		

B. Forests

Understanding and Adapting to New Stress Complexes in Forest Ecosystems

David L. Peterson, Research Biologist, U.S. Forest Service, Pacific Northwest Research Station, Team Leader for the Fire and Environmental Research Applications Team, 400 N. 34th Street, Suite 201, Seattle, WA 98103, Tel: (206) 732-7812, Peterson@fs.fed.us, and Don McKenzie, Quantitative Ecologist, U.S. Forest Service, Pacific Northwest Research Station, Fire and Environmental Research Applications Team, 400 N. 34th Street, Suite 201, Seattle, WA 98103 (USA); Tel: (206) 732-7824, peterson@fs.fed.us.

Abstract

A warmer climate in western North America will affect forests directly through soil moisture stress and indirectly through increased extent and severity of disturbances. Interactions between climate and *stress complexes* in forests, combinations of biotic and abiotic stresses, will compromise the vigor and ultimate sustainability of forest ecosystems. Increased water deficit will increase the severity, spatial scale, and temporal scale of stress experienced in many forests, typically through the interaction of multi-year drought, insects, and fire. Four examples indicate how stress complexes are region-specific and are magnified under a warming climate. Symptoms of prolonged drought and insects have been documented in extensive dieback of pinyon pine in pinyon-juniper woodlands of the American Southwest, an area where only a few tree species can survive. Air pollution and high stand densities from fire exclusion have compromised mixed conifer forests of the Sierra Nevada. Bark beetles have proliferated and killed millions of hectares of dry forest in the northern interior of western North America, setting up the prospect of large and intense fires. High levels of fire and insect mortality in interior and southern Alaska have led to large-scale changes in species and functionality of boreal forest. Increased fire disturbance superimposed on forests with increased stress from drought and insects may rapidly alter growth, distribution, and abundance of forest species, and carbon dynamics. Managing forest ecosystems in the face of altered stress complexes will be challenging, but implementing *general adaptation strategies* at large spatial scales, and *specific adaptation options* at local scales, will enhance the ability of resource managers to maintain ecosystem functionality in the long term.

Introduction

The principal disturbance regimes of western North America, wildfire and insect outbreaks, respond to short-term weather and annual to decadal cycles in climate. For example, synchronous fire years are associated with the ENSO cycle in the Southwest and southern Rocky Mountains,[1] though less so in Oregon and Washington.[2] Short-term weather anomalies associated with atmospheric blocking ridges of high pressure are responsible for extreme wildfire years in the northwestern continental United States.[3] Outbreaks of insect defoliators are associated with years of high vegetation productivity,[4] whereas populations of cambium feeders such as bark beetles are typically promoted by drought years, in which tree defenses are compromised.[5]

Steadily increasing global temperatures are expected to change the frequency, severity, and extent of natural disturbances.[6] Large wildfires throughout the West, occurring during a cool phase of the Pacific Decadal Oscillation, portend a future in which wildfire will be an increasingly

---

1. T.W. Swetnam & J.L. Betancourt, *Mesoscale disturbance and ecological response to decadal climatic variability in the American Southwest*, 11 Journal of Climate 3128 (1998); T.T. Veblen *et al.*, *Climatic and human influences on fire regimes in ponderosa pine forests in the Colorado Front Range*, 10 Ecological Applications 1178 (2000).

2. A.E. Hessl *et al.*, *Drought and Pacific Decadal Oscillation linked to fire occurrence in the inland Pacific Northwest*, 14 Ecological Applications 425 (2004).

3. E.A. Johnson & D.R. Wowchuk, *Wildfires in the southern Canadian Rocky Mountains and their relationships to mid-tropospheric anomalies*, 23 Canadian Journal of Forest Research 1213 (1993); W.R. Skinner *et al.*, *The association between circulation anomalies in the mid-troposphere and area burned by wildfire in Canada*, 63 Theoretical and Applied Climatology 89 (1999); Z. Gedalof *et al.*, *Atmospheric, climatic, and ecological controls on extreme wildfire years in the northwestern United States*, 15 Ecological Applications 154 (2005).

4. T.W. Swetnam & A.M. Lynch, *Multicentury regional-scale patterns of western spruce budworm outbreaks*, 63 Ecological Monographs 399 (1993); U. Weber & F.H. Schweingruber, *A dendroecological reconstruction of western spruce budworm outbreaks* (Choristoneura occidentalis) *in the Front Range, Colorado, from 1720 to 1986*, 9 Tree 204 (1995).

5. G.T. Ferrell, *The influence of insect pests and pathogens on Sierra forests*, in Sierra Nevada Ecosystem Project: final report to Congress, v. II, Assessments and scientific basis for management options 1177 (Centers for Water and Wildland Resources, Un. of California, Davis 1996); Swetnam & Betancourt, *supra* note 1.

6. D. McKenzie *et al.*, *Climatic change, wildfire, and conservation*, 18 Conservation Biology 890 (2004); A.L. Westerling *et al.*, *Warming and earlier spring increase western U.S. forest wildfire activity*, 313 Science 940

dominant feature of Western landscapes. Similarly, mountain pine beetle (*Dendroctonus ponderosae*), whose life cycle is accelerated by increased temperatures, is causing extensive mortality across the West.[7] A third factor, air pollution, is less a function of increasing temperature than human-generated emissions from fossil fuel combustion, but can decrease physiological vigor of trees.

Fire and insect disturbance often interact, compounding rates of change in forest ecosystems.[8] For example, fire severity in subalpine forests, though usually associated with weather anomalies, can be altered by a combination of bark beetles and annual-scale drought.[9] In a warming climate, what will be the effects of increasing disturbance on forest ecosystems? Will disturbances continue to act synergistically, and in conjunction with direct climatic stress (*e.g.*, drought), air pollution, and perhaps pathogens and invasive species to cause rapid or irreversible changes in species composition and ecosystem function?

A conceptual model of tree pathology[10] can be used to assess interacting stresses on forest ecosystems. We define these interactions as *stress complexes*, and discuss how they may instigate rapid ecosystem changes in a warming climate, using examples from forests in western North America that may be on the cusp of directional changes induced by a warming climate. We conclude by identifying general adaptation strategies and specific adaptation options that can be used by land managers to promote desired resource conditions and reduce or delay unwanted changes.

Models of stress complexes

Climate provides an overarching control on the distribution of tree species[11] in that species do not establish or persist outside a characteristic bioclimatic domain, or *fundamental niche* (Pearson and Dawson 2003). Climate-induced stress occurs in low-suitability areas within a species-fundamental niche, and as a consequence, shifts in climatic regime lead to potential changes in species distribution and abundance. In forests with long-lived dominant species, compositional changes could be slow even in a rapidly warming climate, because mature individuals can survive at the edges of their ranges. Disturbance is therefore expected to be the principal agent of change, operating at shorter time scales than the direct influences of climate. (See Figure 21.)[12]

Limiting climatic factors operate mechanistically through the interface between organisms and their environment, and plant performance is compromised when one or more resources (*e.g.*, energy, water, nutrients) is limited. Forests of western North America can be coarsely partitioned into energy-limited vs. water-limited domains.[13] Energy-limiting factors are chiefly light (*e.g.*, productive forests where competition reduces light to most individuals) and temperature

---

(2006); J.S. Littell *et al.*, *Climate and area burned by fire in eco-provinces of the western U.S., 1916–2003*, 19-4 ECOLOGICAL APPLICATIONS 1003 (June 2009).

7. T.T. Veblen *et al.*, *The response of subalpine forests to spruce beetle outbreak in Colorado*, 72 ECOLOGY 213 (1991); Swetnam and Betancourt, *supra* note 1; J.A. Logan & J.A. Powell, *Ghost forests, global warming, and the mountain pine beetle* (Coleoptera: Scolytidae), 47 AMERICAN ENTOMOLOGIST 160 (2001).

8. T.T. Veblen *et al.*, *Disturbance regimes and disturbance interactions in a Rocky Mountain subalpine forest*, 82 JOURNAL OF ECOLOGY 125 (1994).

9. C. Bigler *et al.*, *Multiple disturbance interactions and drought influence fire severity in Rocky Mountain subalpine forests*, 86 ECOLOGY 3018 (2005).

10. P.D. MANION, TREE DISEASE CONCEPTS (2d ed. Prentice Hall 1991); P.D. Manion, *Evolution of concepts in forest pathology*, 93 PHYTOPATHOLOGY 1052 (2003).

11. F.I. WOODWARD, CLIMATE AND PLANT DISTRIBUTION (Cambridge Un. Press 1987); F.I. Woodward & I.F. McKee, *Vegetation and climate*, 17 ENVIRONMENTAL INTERNATIONAL 535 (1991).

12. McKenzie, *supra* note 6.

13. B.T. Milne *et al.*, *A scale-invariant coupling of plants, water, energy, and terrain*, 9 ECOSCIENCE 191 (2002); D. McKenzie *et al.*, *Climatic and biophysical controls on conifer species distributions in mountain forests of Washington State, USA.*, 30 JOURNAL OF BIOGEOGRAPHY 1093 (2003), J.S. Littell & D.L. Peterson, *A method for estimating vulnerability of Douglas-fir growth to climate change in the northwestern US*, 81 FORESTRY

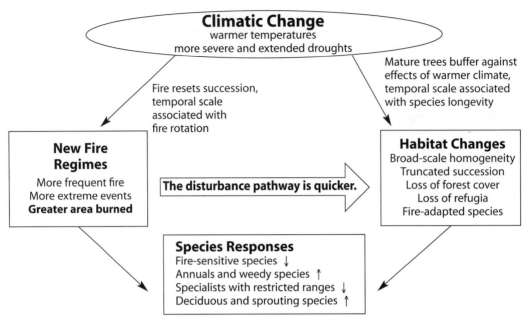

Figure 21. Conceptual model of the relative time scales for disturbance versus climatic change alone to alter ecosystems. Times are approximate. Adapted from McKenzie *et al.* (2004).

(*e.g.*, high-latitude or high-elevation forests). Energy-limited ecosystems in general appear to be responding positively to warming temperatures over the past 100 years.[14]

In contrast, productivity in water-limited systems is expected to decrease with warming temperatures, as negative water balances constrain photosynthesis across more of the West,[15] although this may be partially offset if CO_2 fertilization significantly increases water-use efficiency in plants.[16] For example, Littell *et al.*[17] found that most montane Douglas-fir (*Pseudotsuga menziesii*) forests across the northwestern United States are water limited; the area and magnitude of this limitation will increase as the climate continues to warm. Limiting factors can vary within a species range,[18] between seasons, and as water demands abate and energy needs increase.[19]

Manion[20] proposed a conceptual model of the multiple causes of tree death, termed the *disease spiral*. Earlier, Franklin *et al.*[21] proposed a *mortality spiral* that included competition, sup-

Chronicle 369 (2005); J.S. Littell *et al.*, *Douglas-fir growth in mountain ecosystems: water limits growth from stand to region*, 78 Ecological Monographs 349 (2008).

14. D.L. Peterson, Climate, *limiting factors and environmental change in high-altitude forests of western North America*, in Climatic Variability and Extremes: The Impact on Forests 191 (M. Beniston and J.L. Innes eds., Springer Berlin 1998); D. McKenzie *et al.*, *Recent growth in conifer species of western North America: assessing the spatial patterns of radial growth trends*, 31 Canadian Journal of Forest Research 526 (2001).

15. J.A. Hicke *et al.*, *Trends in North American net primary productivity derived from satellite observations*, 16 Global Biogeochemical Cycles 1018 (2002).

16. R.P. Neilson *et al.*, *Forecasting regional to global plant migration in response to climate change*, 55 Bioscience 749 (2005).

17. Littell, *supra* note 13.

18. D.W. Peterson & D.L. Peterson, *Mountain hemlock growth responds to climatic variability at annual and decadal scales*, 82 Ecology 3330 (2001).

19. N.L. Stephenson, *Climatic control of vegetation distribution: the role of the water balance*, 135 American Naturalist 649 (1990); N.L. Stephenson, *Actual evapotranspiration and deficit: biologically meaningful correlates of vegetation distribution across spatial scales*, 25 Journal of Biogeography 855 (1998).

20. Manion (1991), *supra* note 10.

21. J.F. Franklin *et al.*, *Tree death as an ecological process*, 37 Bioscience 550 (1986).

pression, insect attack, and finally pathogens. Manion's model separates the multiple causes into: *predisposing* factors, *inciting* factors, and *contributing* factors. An example relevant to forests of western North America would be:

- Predisposing: outside climatically adapted range
- Inciting: drought
- Contributing: wood and bark boring insects.

Although the terminology may be overlapping and imprecise, the concept of a disease spiral effectively illustrates the role of cumulative multiple stresses. This model can be extended to populations of a single species, because the same environmental stresses apply to each organism, although possibly exacerbated by competitive interactions. Where one or more stressed populations is a dominant component of an ecosystem, the pathological model translates to the idea of an *ecosystem-level* stress complex.

Temperature increase is a predisposing factor[22] causing potentially lethal stress in forest ecosystems of western North America, acting directly through increasingly negative water balance[23] and indirectly through increased frequency, severity, and extent of disturbances, chiefly fire and insect outbreaks.[24] Here we discuss examples of forest ecosystems whose species composition and stability are compromised by stress complexes precipitated by a warming climate. Two cases involve the loss of a single dominant species, and the other two involve two or more dominant species.

Effects of stress complexes in forests of western North America

Pinyon-juniper woodlands (American Southwest)

Pinyon pine (*Pinus edulis*) and various juniper species (*Juniperus* spp.) are among the most drought-tolerant trees in western North America. As such, pinyon-juniper ecosystems characterize lower treelines across much of the interior West. Although pinyon-juniper woodlands appear to be expanding in some areas, possibly due to fire suppression or cessation of Native American fuelwood harvesting,[25] they are clearly water-limited systems. At fine scales, pinyon-juniper ecotones are sensitive to feedbacks both from environmental fluctuations and existing canopy structure that may buffer trees against drought to some degree.[26] However, multi-year droughts can cause dieback of pinyon pines over large geographic areas, overwhelming resistance to low soil moisture.

Dieback of ponderosa pine (*Pinus ponderosa* var. *scopulorum*) and pinyon pine occurred during and before the 20th century,[27] but the current dieback is unprecedented in terms of the scale of response to a period of low precipitation and high temperature.[28] Figure 22 shows the stress complex associated with pinyon-juniper ecosystems. A warmer climate is a predisposing factor, pinyon pine mortality and fuel accumulations are inciting factors, and wood-boring insects that

---

22. Manion (1991), *supra* note 10.

23. Stephenson (1998), *supra* note 19; Milne, *supra* note 13; Littell, *supra* note 13.

24. Logan & Powell, *supra* note 7; McKenzie, *supra* note 6; C.N. Skinner & C. Chang, *Fire regimes, past and present, in* Sierra Nevada Ecosystem Project: Final report to Congress. Vol. II: Assessments and scientific basis for management options 1041 (Centers for Water and Wildland Resources, Un. of California, Davis 1996).

25. M.L. Samuels & J.L. Betancourt, *Modeling the long-term effects of fuelwood harvest on piñon-juniper woodlands*, 6 Environmental Management 505 (1982).

26. B.T. Milne et al., *Detection of critical densities associated with pinyon-juniper woodland ecotones*, 77 Ecology 805 (1996).

27. C.D. Allen & D.D. Breshears, *Drought-induced shift of forest-woodland ecotone: rapid landscape response to climate variation*, 95 Proceedings of the National Academy of Sciences 14839 (1998); D.D. Breshears et al., *Regional vegetation die-off in response to global-change-type drought*, 102 Proceedings of the National Academy of Sciences 15144 (2005).

28. Breshears, *supra* note 27.

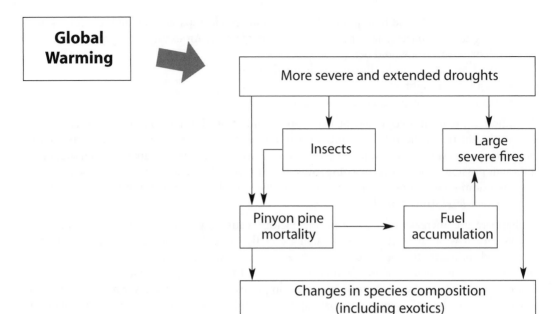

Figure 22. Stress complex in pinyon-juniper woodlands of the American Southwest. The effects of disturbance regimes (insects and fire) are exacerbated by a warmer climate. Stand-replacing fires and drought-induced mortality contribute to species changes and exotic invasions. Adapted from McKenzie *et al.* (in press).

can successfully attack weakened trees are contributing factors. Ecosystem change, possibly irreversible, comes from large-scale severe fires that lead to colonization of invasive species that further compromises the ability of pinyon pines to re-establish. (See Figure 22.)

Mixed conifer forests (Sierra Nevada, southern California)

Forests in central and southern California experience a Mediterranean climate with long dry
summers, and mild winters during which nearly all of the annual precipitation occurs. Fire frequency and extent have not increased with warmer temperatures[29] but have decreased due to decreased fuel loads from sheep grazing, decreased ignition from the demise of Native American
cultures, and fire exclusion.[30] Fire exclusion has led to increased fuel loadings[31] and competitive
stresses on trees as stand densities have increased.[32]

Elevated levels of ambient ozone affect the vigor of ponderosa pine (*Pinus ponderosa* var. *ponderosa*) and Jeffrey pine (*P. jeffreyi*) in the Sierra Nevada and southern California mountains[33] by

29. K.S. McKelvey *et al.*, *An overview of fire in the Sierra Nevada*, in Sierra Nevada Ecosystem Project:
final report to Congress, v. II, Assessments and scientific basis for management options 1033
(Centers for Water and Wildland Resources, Un. of California, Davis 1996).

30. T.W. Swetnam, *Fire history and climate change in giant sequoia groves*, 262 Science 885 (1993); S.
Stine, *Climate, 1650–1850*, in Sierra Nevada Ecosystem Project: final report to Congress, v. II, Assessments and scientific basis for management options 25 (Centers for Water and Wildland Resources, Un.
of California, Davis 1996).

31. McKelvey, *supra* note 29.

32. Ferrell, *supra* note 5; P.J. van Mantgem, *Effects of an introduced pathogen and fire exclusion on the demography of sugar pine*, 14 Ecological Applications 1590 (2004).

33. D.L. Peterson & M.J. Arbaugh, *Growth patterns of ozone-injured ponderosa pine* (Pinus ponderosa) *in
the southern Sierra Nevada*, 38 Journal of the Air Pollution Control Association 921 (1988); D.L. Peterson *et al.*, *Growth trends of ozone-stressed ponderosa pine* (Pinus ponderosa) *in the Sierra Nevada of California, USA* 1 The Holocene 50 (1991); A. Byternowicz & N.E. Grulke, *Physiological effects of air pollutants on
western trees*, in Response of Western Forests to Air Pollution 183–233 (R.K. Olson, D. Binkley, and M

reducing net photosynthesis, growth, and interannual accumulation of biomass.[34] Ozone that is synthesized from vehicular and industrial emissions in urban environments often concentrates at middle and upper elevations where forest ecosystems dominate.[35]

Sierra Nevada forests support endemic levels of a diverse group of insect defoliators and bark beetles, but bark beetles in particular have reached outbreak levels in recent years facilitated by protracted droughts.[36] Ferrell[37] refers to *biotic complexes* in which bark beetles interact with root diseases and mistletoes. Dense stands, fire exclusion, and the exotic fungus white pine blister rust (*Cronartium ribicola*) can exacerbate biotic interactions[38] and drought stress. Figure 23 shows the stress complex associated with Sierra Nevada forest ecosystems, and is likely applicable also to the mountain ranges east and north of the Los Angeles basin.

Lodgepole pine forest (western North America)

Lodgepole pine (*Pinus contorta* var. *latifolia*) is widely distributed across western North America. It is the dominant species over much of its range, often forming nearly monospecific stands that are maintained either because shallow soils preclude other species or through adapting to stand-replacing fires via cone serotiny.[39] Lodgepole pine is the principal host of the mountain pine beetle (*Dendroctonus ponderosae*), and dense stands that are stressed from low soil moisture are particularly vulnerable to mortality during beetle outbreaks.[40]

Recent beetle outbreaks have caused extensive mortality across millions of hectares in western North America,[41] with large mature cohorts (age 70–80 yr) contributing to widespread vulnerability.[42] Warmer temperatures facilitate insect outbreaks in two ways: (1) extended drought (and hence low soil moisture) weakens trees by lowering turgor pressure in the vascular tissue and thus reducing resistance to egg-laying beetles, and (2) beetle populations respond to increased temperatures by speeding up their reproductive cycles (*e.g.*, from two-year to one-year life cycles). (See Figure 23.)[43]

Figure 24 shows the stress complex for interior lodgepole pine forests. Warmer temperature in combination with accumulation of dead biomass (fuels) associated with beetle mortality sets up ecosystems for potential species conversion following stand-replacing fires, plus a favorable envi-

Böhm eds., Springer-Verlag Berlin and Heidelberg GmbH & Co. K 1992); P.R. Miller, *Mixed conifer forests of the San Bernardino Mountains, California, in* Response of Western Forests to Air Pollution 461 (R.K. Olson, D. Binkley, and M. Böhm eds., Springer-Verlag Berlin and Heidelberg GmbH & Co. K 1992).

34. P.B. Reich & R.G. Amundson, *Ambient levels of ozone reduce net photosynthesis in tree and crop species*, 230 Science 566 (1985): Peterson (1991), *supra* note 33.

35. S. Brace & D.L. Peterson, *Tropospheric ozone distribution in the Mount Rainier region of the Cascade Mountains, U.S.A*, 32 Atmospheric Environment 3629 (1998).

36. Ferrell, *supra* note 5.

37. *Id.*

38. van Mantgem, *supra* note 32.

39. USDA Forest Service, Silvics of North America: Volume 1. Conifers. Agriculture Handbook (R. M. Burns & B.H. Honkala coordinators, 1990).

40. J.A. Hicke *et al.*, *Changes in temperature influence suitability for modeled mountain pine beetle* (Dendroctonus ponderosae) *outbreaks in the western United States*, 111 Journal of Geophysical Research G02019 (2006).

41. Logan & Powell, *supra* note 7.

42. A. Carroll, *Changing the climate, changing the rules: global warming and insect disturbance in western North American forests*, paper presented at the 2006 MTNCLIM Conference, Timberline, OR (2006).

43. R.A. Werner & E.H. Holsten, *Factors influencing generation times of spruce beetles in Alaska*, 15 Canadian Journal of Forest Research 438 (1985); J.A. Logan & B.J. Bentz, *Model analysis of mountain pine beetle* (Coleoptera: Scolytidae) *seasonality*, 28 Environmental Entomology 924 (1999); Logan & Powell, *supra* note 7.

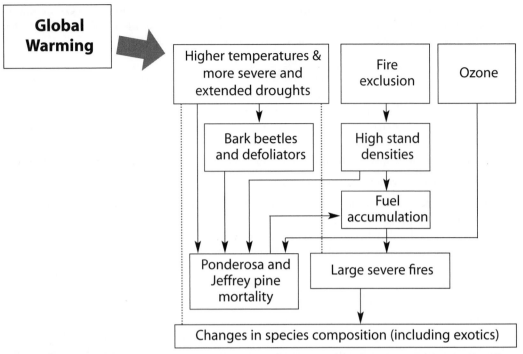

Figure 23. Stress complex in mixed-conifer forests of the Sierra Nevada and southern California. The effects of disturbance regimes (insects and fire) and fire exclusion are exacerbated by a warmer climate. Stand-replacing fires and drought-induced mortality contribute to species changes and exotic invasions. Adapted from McKenzie *et al.* (in press).

ronment for the establishment of species adapted to warmer temperatures, such as interior Douglas-fir or ponderosa pine. (See Figure 24.)

Boreal forest (central and southern Alaska)

Alaska has experienced historically unprecedented fires in the last decade, including the five largest fires in the USA;[44] over 2.5 million hectares burned in the interior in 2004. Concurrently (1990s), massive outbreaks of the spruce bark beetle (*Dendroctonus rufipennis*) occurred in white spruce (*Picea glauca*) forests on and near the Kenai Peninsula in southern Alaska.[45] Although periodic outbreaks have occurred throughout the historical record, both in southern Alaska and the southwestern Yukon, recent outbreaks may be unprecedented in mortality (>90% in many places) and extent.[46]

Fire and beetle outbreaks are likely associated with warmer temperatures in recent decades.[47]

---

44. *See* National Interagency Fire Center (NIFC), http://www.nifc.gov.

45. E.E. Berg *et al.*, *Spruce beetle outbreaks on the Kenai Peninsula, Alaska, and Kluane National Park and Reserve, Yukon Territory: relationship to summer temperatures and regional differences in disturbance regimes*, 227 Forest Ecology and Management 219 (2006).

46. D.W. Ross *et al.*, *Forest health restoration in south-central Alaska: a problem analysis*, USDA Forest Service General Technical Report PNW-GTR-523 (Pacific Northwest Research Station, Portland, OR 2001); Berg, *supra* note 45.

47. P.A. Duffy *et al.*, *Impacts of large-scale atmospheric-ocean variability on Alaskan fire season severity*, 15 Ecological Applications 1317 (2005); Berg, *supra* note 45; R.A. Werner *et al.*, *Spruce beetles and forest ecosystems in south-central Alaska: a review of 30 years of research*, 227 Forest Ecology and Management 195 (2006).

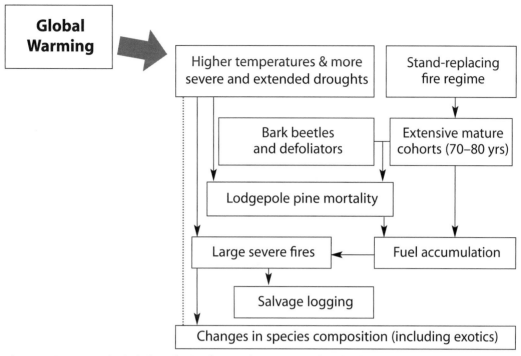

Figure 24. Stress complex in lodgepole pine forests of interior British Columbia and the western United States. The effects of disturbance regimes (insects and fire) are exacerbated by a warmer climate. Stand-replacing fires and beetle-caused mortality contribute to species changes. Adapted from McKenzie *et al.* (in press).

Summer temperatures in the Arctic have risen 0.3–0.4°C per decade since 1961.[48] Although fire-season length in interior Alaska is associated with the timing of onset of the late-summer monsoon, the principal driver of annual area burned is early summer temperature.[49] As with lodgepole pine, warmer temperatures can enhance beetle reproductive rates and outbreaks in spruce forests.

Disturbance regimes place unequal competitive stress on species most vulnerable to the particular disturbance. In interior Alaska, conifer species—white spruce and black spruce (*Picea mariana*)—are more flammable than their sympatric deciduous species (chiefly paper birch [*Betula papyrifera*]). Similarly, conifers are the target of bark beetles, so in southern Alaska they are disadvantaged compared to deciduous species. The stress complex for this forest ecosystem (Figure 25) predicts a potential transition to deciduous trees via more frequent and extensive disturbance associated with warmer climate. This transition would be unlikely without changes in disturbance regimes even under global warming, because both empirical and modeling studies suggest that warmer temperatures alone will not favor a life-form transition. (See Figure 25)[50]

Adapting to Altered Stress Complexes

Rapid climatic change and qualitative changes in disturbance regimes may send ecosystems across thresholds into dominance by different life forms with significant changes in productivity

48. F.S. Chapin *et al.*, *Role of land-surface changes in Arctic summer warming*, 310 SCIENCE 657 (2005).

49. Duffy, *supra* note 47.

50. J.F. Johnstone *et al.*, *Decadal observations of tree regeneration following fire in boreal forests*, 34 CANADIAN JOURNAL OF FOREST RESEARCH 267 (2004); D. Bachelet *et al.*, *Simulating the response of natural ecosystems and their fire regimes to climatic variability in Alaska*, 35 CANADIAN JOURNAL OF FOREST RESEARCH 2244 (2005); T.V. Boucher & B.R. Mead, *Vegetation change and forest regeneration on the Kenai Peninsula, Alaska, following a spruce beetle outbreak, 1987–2000*, 227 FOREST ECOLOGY AND MANAGEMENT 233 (2006).

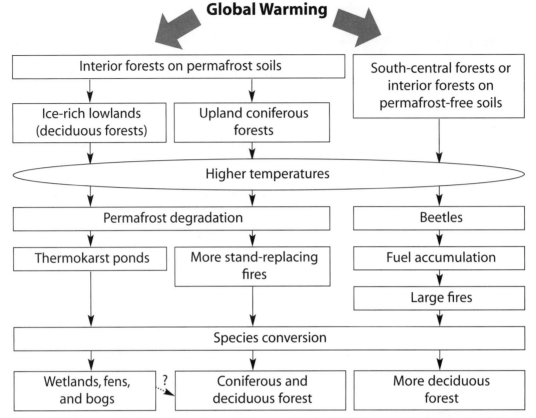

Figure 25. Stress complex in interior and coastal forests of Alaska. Rapid increases in the severity of distur-bance regimes (insects and fire) are triggered by a warmer climate. Stand-replacing fires, extensive mortality from insects, and stress-induced dieback contribute to species changes and conversion to deciduous species. Adapted from McKenzie *et al.* (in press).

and capacity for carbon storage. For example, in the American Southwest, stand-replacing fires are becoming common in what were historically low-severity fire regimes,[51] and protracted drought is killing species (ponderosa pine) that are adapted to low-severity fire.[52] If these trends continue, ponderosa pine may be lost from some of its current range in the Southwest, and productivity of these systems will decline. In contrast, if warming temperatures permit doubling of mountain pine beetle reproductive cycles[53] such that outbreaks are more frequent and more prolonged, lodgepole pine might be replaced by a more productive species such as Douglas-fir, at least on more mesic sites where conditions for establishment are favorable. We expect that more ecosystems will become water limited,[54] more sensitive to variability in temperature, and prone to more frequent distur-bance. Consequently, productivity may decline across much of the West,[55] and long-term carbon sequestration may be interrupted by the effects of high-severity fire and insect-caused mortality.

Adapting to climate-forced changes in forest ecosystems will be a major challenge for resource managers in coming decades; nevertheless it is critical to implement climate-smart management

---

51. C.D. Allen *et al.*, *Ecological restoration of southwestern ponderosa pine ecosystems: a broad perspective*, 12 ECOLOGICAL APPLICATIONS 1418 (2002).

52. Allen & Breshears, *supra* note 27.

53. Logan & Powell, *supra* note 7.

54. Milne, *supra* note 13; Littell (2008), *supra* note 13.

55. Hicke, *supra* note 15.

strategies as soon as possible to begin the process of adaptation before irreversible changes occur. Lack of fine-scale information on climatology and climate-change effects hinders decision making by resource managers, although the scientific basis[56] exists for recommending the following *general adaptation strategies* to maintain ecosystem resilience, where active management is prescribed, in response to multiple interacting stresses caused by a warming climate.

Manage for resilience, decrease vulnerability
- Reduce the vulnerability of resources to a changing climate while attaining specific management goals for the condition of resources and production of ecosystem services.
- Manage ecosystems to have structures and species assemblages that are resilient to disturbances such as fire and insects to ensure persistence of functional ecosystems in a warmer climate.

Manage dynamically and experimentally
- Implement adaptive management consistently over several decades, including feedback from resource monitoring to the decision-making process.
- Tolerate some failures within a broad experimental approach, then modify management accordingly.

Manage for process
- Use project planning and management to maintain or enhance ecological processes rather than to design structure or composition.
- Use novel mixes of species and spacing following large disturbances in order to reflect likely natural dynamic processes of adaptation.

Prioritize climate-smart treatments
- Prioritize treatments with the greatest likelihood of being effective in a warmer climate by anticipating landscape structures and composition in future disturbance regimes.
- Recognize that some projects may be somewhat detrimental in the short term but beneficial in the long term.

Consider tradeoffs and conflicts
- Consider how ecological and socioeconomic sensitivities to climate change might affect species conservation and other resource values, *e.g.,* preserving individual threatened species vs. increasing resilience by fostering new species.
- Explicitly incorporate tradeoffs and conflicts relative to climate-change adaptation in land management planning.

Manage for realistic outcomes
- Assess the viability of management goals and desired outcomes, recognizing that some projects will have a higher failure rate in a warmer climate.
- Abandon hopeless causes, *e.g.,* restoring mountain meadows with grasses and forbs if those meadows will inevitably become dominated by trees in a warmer climate.

It will also be necessary to focus adaptation efforts on operational activities and finer spatial scales. Based on scientific information in Joyce *et al.*[57] and Peterson *et al.*,[58] we recommend several *specific adaptation options* that can be applied to altered stress complexes in a warmer climate.

---

56. C.I. Millar *et al.*, *Climate change and forests of the future: managing in the face of uncertainty*, 17 ECO-LOGICAL APPLICATIONS 2145 (2007); L. Joyce *et al.*, *Chapter 3, National forests, in* PRELIMINARY REVIEW OF ADAPTATION OPTIONS FOR CLIMATE-SENSITIVE ECOSYSTEMS AND RESOURCES—A REPORT BY THE U.S. CLIMATE CHANGE SCIENCE PROGRAM AND THE SUBCOMMITTEE ON GLOBAL CHANGE RESEARCH 3.1–3.127 (S.H. Julius & J.M. West eds., 2008); D.L. Peterson *et al.*, *U.S. national forests adapt to climate change through science-management partnerships* (in review).

57. Joyce, *supra* note 56.

58. Peterson, *supra* note 56.

Increase landscape diversity
- Apply targeted forest thinning to increase variability in stand structure, increase resilience to stress by increasing tree vigor, and reduce vulnerability to disturbance.
- Implement thinning and harvest treatments appropriate at large spatial scales, manage for a variety of forest structures and vegetation composition, and avoid "one-size-fits-all" management prescriptions.
- Plan fuel reduction projects strategically by arraying treatments in patterns presumed to reduce fire spread, thus increasing tree vigor and resilience to more frequent fires.
- Maintain corridors that link habitat for animal species that migrate and have large home ranges.

Maintain biological diversity
- Diversify the phenotypic and genotypic template on which climate and competition interact, thus reducing the likelihood of widespread mortality at the regeneration stage.
- Plant multiple tree species rather than monocultures, including common local species and perhaps species common in adjacent warmer landscapes.
- Plant nursery stock from warmer, drier locations than what is prescribed in genetic guidelines based on current seed zones.

Increase resilience at large spatial scales
- Implement resilience management as a pathway to adaptation and to decrease the number of situations in which managers must respond in "crisis mode."
- Apply ecosystem-based management at large spatial scales and for multiple species and resource values to facilitate adaptability to a warmer climate.
- Increase management unit size to hundreds or thousands of hectares across logical biogeographic entities such as watersheds to decrease "administrative fragmentation" over space and time.
- Protect riparian areas in order to enhance biodiversity, provide corridors for animal and plant movement, and minimize fragmentation.
- Manage watersheds to maintain water quantity and quality, *e.g.*, by quickly revegetating areas burned by severe fires to minimize erosion and sediment loss.

Treat large-scale disturbance as a management opportunity
- Design and implement management experiments for adapting to climate change, and have plans in place in anticipation of large disturbances.
- Incorporate large disturbances in planning to encourage post-disturbance management that takes climate into account, rather than treating disturbance as an anomaly or crisis.
- Plan for and implement revegetation and silvicultural options appropriate for a warmer climate, *e.g.*, by planting tolerant genotypes, mixed genotypes, and mixed species of trees and possibly other vegetation that will likely survive over decades to centuries.

Implement early detection/rapid response
- Use proactive management to treat small problems before they become large unsolvable problems, *e.g.*, assertively eradicate exotic plants as soon as they are detected.
- Respond quickly to large disturbances with an eye towards adaptation, especially if a disturbance could lead to undesirable secondary effects, such as exotic plant invasion.

Promote education and awareness about climate change
- Conduct trainings to ensure that resource managers understand climate change science.
- Develop interpretive programs and materials that help educate visitors and stakeholders.
- Develop educational materials that document the role of active management in adaptation, and ensure that management is based on current scientific information.

Collaborate with a variety of partners on adaptation strategies
- Work closely with adjacent landowners to ensure compatibility of management objectives and adaptation options.
- Work with a diversity of local landowners, agencies, and stakeholders to develop support for adaptation options.

Some effects of climate change on forest ecosystems and natural resources in North America are already detectable,[59] and no historical analog exists for the combination of climate conditions, disturbance regimes, and land-use patterns expected for the 21st century. Adapting to those changes and sustaining ecosystem services is a priority, but adaptive capacity is limited by lack of fine-scale scientific information and uncertainty about outcomes of adaptive strategies. Tempering the idea of "desired future conditions" with "achievable future conditions" will facilitate more efficient allocation of resources to maintain forest resilience. Understanding how a warmer climate will affect stress complexes will improve the likelihood that general adaptation strategies and specific adaptation options will be successful.

Adaptive management—a general paradigm for all resource management—is the best way to detect and manage the effects of climate change on forest ecosystems. At the present time, there is often little legal flexibility in responding to dynamic ecosystem conditions, which limits the potential for using active management to adapt to climate change. However, given current knowledge, regulations, and levels of funding and personnel, resource managers can continue to emphasize management for diversity at all spatial scales as a "no regrets" strategy for building resilience to potentially adverse climate change effects.[60] A strong commitment to resource monitoring will be a key to successful adaptive management by detecting the effects of climate change, evaluating the effectiveness of management actions, and making appropriate revisions.

Acknowledgments

Research was funded by the U.S. Forest Service, Pacific Northwest Research Station, and the U.S. Geological Survey Global Change Research Program. This paper is adapted from McKenzie *et al.* (in press) and Peterson *et al.* (in review). It is a contribution of the Western Mountain Initiative.

C. Rangelands

Rangelands are in poor condition. This is a "whammy." Climate change on top of that is a "double whammy."

Recognition

U.S. Congress, 1978 (43 U.S.C. § 1901(a)(1)):

Vast segments of the public rangelands … are in unsatisfactory condition.

---

59. Intergovernmental Panel on Climate Change (IPCC), Climate Change 2007: The Physical Science Basis, in Summary for Policymakers, Contribution of Working Group 1 to the Fourth Assessment Report of the Intergovernmental Panel on Climate Change (Cambridge Un. Press 2007).

60. Peterson, *supra* note 56.

Grazing Lands

Western Watersheds Project v. Kraayenbrink, 2007 WL 1667618, pp. 17–18 (D. Ida. 2007) (ESA citizen suit, unlike APA, allows reference to extra-record material to show that BLM grazing rules "may affect" listed species and thus require ESA consultation):

> on over 23 million acres of public land, livestock grazing was a significant factor in standards violations.

> on tens of millions of acres, grazing is a significant factor in standards violations, and … tens of millions of acres remain unassessed.

> the revisions at issue here promote delay.

Dubious Progress: Grazing in the Streams

Oregon Natural Desert Ass'n v. Lohn, 485 F. Supp. 2d 1190, 1205, 1201 (D. Ore. 2007) (King, J.):

> In 2004, NMFS permitted [that] no more than two redds [salmon nests] could be taken from trampling [in the streams by cattle]. In 2006, NMFS permits a total of five redds to be trampled.

NMFS BiOps and the Doublespeak of Laying Down the Law

Oregon Natural Desert Ass'n v. Lohn, 485 F. Supp. 2d 1190, 1205, 1201 (D. Ore. 2007) (King, J.) (emphasis added):

> With *excessive*, *repeated* failures, "permit action" to remedy the situation *may be* warranted for resource protection, and "[f]ailure to meet / move indicators due to permittee lack of knowledge, effort or engagement *could* be rectified through firm, fair administration of the grazing permit and reflected in next year's annual operating instructions."

HIGH COUNTRY NEWS, June 23, 2008, p. 3 (emphasis dropped):

> Thirteen federal agencies, led by the Department of Agriculture, acknowledged reality in a thick May 28 report signed by three Bush cabinet secretaries. THE EFFECTS OF CLIMATE CHANGE ON AGRICULTURE, LAND RESOURCES, WATER RESOURCES, AND BIODIVERSITY IN THE UNITED STATES [published by the U.S. Climate Change Science Program] says the West has already been hit harder than other U.S. regions.

––––––––––

Climate Change and Livestock Grazing on Western Rangelands

Joseph M. Feller.[1] *Professor of Law, Sandra Day O'Connor College of Law, Faculty Fellow, Center for the Study of Law, Science, and Technology, Arizona State University. P.O. Box 877906, Tempe, AZ 85287-7906; Tel: (480) 965-3964, joseph.feller@asu.edu.*

One of the consequences of global warming is that, as temperatures rise, communities of plants and animals adapt by shifting their geographic ranges. As areas formerly occupied by a

––––––––––

1. In academic year 2008–09: On leave and serving as a Senior Counsel, National Wildlife Federation, 2260 Baseline Road, Suite 100, Boulder, CO 80302; Tel: (480) 441-5158, fellerj@nwf.org.

species become too warm or too dry, the species moves upwards in altitude or latitude to areas that are cooler or wetter.

Like plants and animals, human agricultural enterprises have natural climatic ranges to which they are best adapted. For these enterprises to remain viable they, too, may have to shift their geographic ranges as increasing temperatures render former locales less suitable. However, with respect to livestock grazing on western public lands, there is reason to doubt the willingness and ability of the governing legal and administrative systems to effectuate the necessary changes.

The "Life Zones" of Western Livestock Grazing

In the western United States, most lands that receive too little precipitation to support unirrigated crop production, and that cannot practically and economically be irrigated, are used for grazing of domestic livestock. The threshold separating croplands from grazing lands lies at an average annual precipitation of around twenty inches. This threshold corresponds to a geographic line at about the one hundredth meridian of longitude.

Conceptually, the broad region in which the climate is too dry for unirrigated crop production can be sub-divided into three grazing "life zones." Those areas that receive rainfall that is sufficient, and reliable enough, to support perennial grasslands that can sustain more-or-less permanent herds of livestock could be deemed the "perennial grazing life zone." A typical public land ranching business in the perennial life zone is a "cow-calf" operation in which a herd of mother cows is maintained as a capital asset that produces an annual crop of calves for sale.

More arid areas, where rainfall is less dependable, produce sufficient forage to sustainably feed livestock only in wetter years and seasons. Such areas, which could be deemed the "ephemeral grazing life zone" can be used to pasture livestock seasonally in years of good precipitation but they cannot support permanent herds. A typical grazing business in this life zone purchases "feeder" or "stocker" cattle in the winter of a wet year, places them on the range for a few months to fatten them up, then resells them at a higher price reflecting their increased weight. The third life zone, which could be termed the "no grazing" life zone, comprises those areas that are so arid that they cannot support any economically viable livestock production without unacceptable adverse environmental impacts.[2]

Pushing the Envelope

Historically, environmental and economic catastrophes have resulted from the expansion of agricultural enterprises out of their appropriate life zones into neighboring, drier life zones that cannot sustain them in the long run. Such attempts have sometimes been facilitated by unusually

---

2. *See, e.g.*, UNITED STATES GENERAL ACCOUNTING OFFICE, RANGELAND MANAGEMENT: BLM'S HOT DESERT GRAZING PROGRAM MERITS RECONSIDERATION 2–3, GAO-RCED-92-12 (1991) (concluding that grazing on nearly 20 million acres of hot desert lands in Arizona, California, Nevada, New Mexico, and Utah "risks long-term environmental damage while not generating grazing fee revenues sufficient to provide for adequate management" and that "the economic benefits derived from grazing on BLM lands in the hot desert areas are minimal").

In a thoughtful article published in 2004, Heitschmidt *et al.* argue that livestock grazing is sustainable on North American rangelands. R. K. Heitschmidt, L. T. Vermeire, and E. E. Grings, *Is rangeland agriculture sustainable?*, 82 J. ANIM. SCI. E138 (E. Supp. 2004). But livestock grazing may be sustainable on some, or even most, North American rangelands without being sustainable on all North American rangelands. Heitschmidt *et al.*'s research has been conducted on the northern Great Plains, an area with a long history of grazing by native ungulates (bison) and a climate far cooler and wetter than that of the desert southwest. Heitschmidt *et al.* argue that livestock grazing may be sustainable even in the southwest, but they recognize that the ecological effects of grazing in the two regions "are quite different," *id.* at E140. It is the premise of this article that, with global warming, more of the western United States will have a climate like that of the desert southwest and less of it like the northern Great Plains.

wet climatic periods that have rendered the drier zones temporarily suitable for land uses that, in more normal times, were undertaken only in wetter climes. Unfortunately, such attempts have also been encouraged by ill-advised government policies. For example, during wet periods in the late nineteenth and early twentieth centuries, "sod-busting" farmers, encouraged by the availability of free land under the Homestead Act, cultivated lands on the western Great Plains that had previously been considered too dry to farm. When drier, and more typical, days returned, many of these farms were abandoned, leaving a human legacy of shattered lives and an environmental legacy of tumbleweeds, catastrophic soil erosion, and permanent loss of grassland productivity.

A similar catastrophe, but on a longer time scale, has played out on millions of acres of public rangelands now managed by the United States Bureau of Land Management (BLM) in the far west. Livestock grazing on most of these lands began in the late nineteenth century, when hands-off government policy allowed, and effectively encouraged, the placement of livestock on virtually all public lands, including the most arid. The passage of the Taylor Grazing Act in 1934 imposed a regulatory permit system on these public rangelands, but it did not result in a rollback of livestock grazing. Rather, the Interior Department's Grazing Service and its successor agency, the BLM, issued permits that authorized grazing on virtually all of the lands under its administration, with no attempt made to discern whether any of those lands might be ill-suited to sustain livestock grazing in the long run. To this day, the BLM continues to renew these permits and generally refuses to consider the alternative of removing livestock from any of the lands that it manages.

The legacy of the BLM's "graze (almost) everywhere" tradition is that millions of acres of the BLM's more arid and sparsely-vegetated lands continue to be grazed inappropriately. Specifically, perennial grazing takes place in areas that are suitable only for ephemeral grazing, and ephemeral grazing is conducted in areas that really ought not be grazed at all. The folly of this inappropriate grazing is manifested in both economic and environmental consequences. Economically, the BLM and many of its permittees operate at a loss. The relatively small amount of livestock production that the BLM's land supports generates neither sufficient grazing fees to cover the BLM's costs nor, in many instances, sufficient income to make ranches profitable. Many of the permittees are hobbyists who operate money-losing ranches for the fun, relaxation, status, and lifestyle they provide rather than for profit. Environmentally, grazing in arid rangeland results in depletion or loss of the native plant species that are most favored by livestock and wildlife, invasion by exotic (non-native) and sometimes noxious plants, accelerated soil erosion, water pollution, degradation of wildlife habitat, destruction of archaeological sites, and degradation of the scenic and recreational value of the land, which in many arid areas far exceeds the value of the sparse livestock forage.[3]

Besides permitting grazing in areas where it is economically and environmentally unsustainable, the BLM permits perennial grazing (cow/calf operations) in areas where ephemeral grazing ("feeder" or "stocker" operations) would be more appropriate. In arid and semi-arid areas with highly variable annual precipitation, even where perennial grasses and shrubs are the predominant forage species, the productivity of these plants is "ephemeral" in the sense that is highly variable from year to year, depending on precipitation. A drier-than-average year results in reduced growth of both the roots and the above-ground parts of forage plants.[4] If the same num-

---

3. For a comprehensive treatments of the economic and environmental implications of livestock grazing on western public lands, see DEBRA L. DONAHUE, THE WESTERN RANGE REVISITED: REMOVING LIVESTOCK FROM PUBLIC LANDS TO PRESERVE NATIVE BIODIVERSITY (Un. of Oklahoma Press 1999).

4. *See, e.g.*, Larry Howery, *Rangeland Management Before, During, and After Drought*, University of Arizona Cooperative Extension Bulletin AZ1136, at 1–3 (1999), *available at* http://ag.arizona.edu/pubs/nat resources/az1136.pdf.

ber of livestock graze these smaller plants for the same period of time as in a normal or wet year, insufficient residual plant material may be left for the plants to survive and reproduce, for protection of soils from erosion, and for wildlife feed and cover. Therefore, the flexibility to promptly reduce the number of livestock on the range at the onset of drought is essential to sustainable range management.

Unfortunately, perennial cow-calf operations do not provide the needed flexibility. In a cow-calf operation, decisions about the size of the herd must be made before precipitation and forage conditions are known.[5] Moreover, reducing the size of the herd of mother cows during drought and then rebuilding it later, during wetter periods, is costly, and therefore many ranchers resist reductions in the hope that rainfall will soon return. It is these attempts to "hold on" at the beginning of a drought that typically cause the greatest damage to rangelands.[6] Even when a prolonged drought eventually results in severe reductions or even compete removal of herds, substantial damage may be done because these adjustments are made too late.

In principle, "stocker" or "feeder" operations offer greater flexibility. Such operations are more flexible and adaptable than cow-calf operations; the number of cattle purchased each year can be adjusted according to precipitation and forage conditions, and no cattle at all can be purchased in the driest years. Unfortunately, this flexibility is most often used not to mitigate the impacts of grazing on perennial grasslands but rather to extend grazing into the driest deserts, where the only forage available is annual or ephemeral plants, and where perennial grazing is impossible because there is simply no forage in dry years and seasons.[7] These are areas in which grazing is least economically and environmentally sustainable and in which the arguments are strongest for no grazing at all.

The Effects of Global Climate Change on Western Rangelands

The most important climatic factor affecting the condition of western North American rangelands is the water available to support plant life. And while there is little doubt that these rangelands will grow warmer as a result of anthropogenic global climate change, the effects of such change on water for vegetation are both less certain and more complex. Across the Colorado River basin, which encompasses virtually all of Arizona, most of Utah, large portions of Colorado, New Mexico, and Wyoming, and smaller parts of California and Nevada, the average annual surface air temperature has already increased by 2–3 degrees F over the last century.[8] Depending on the model chosen and the emissions assumed, temperatures across the basin are projected to further increase anywhere from 2 to 12 degrees F over the next century.[9] On the other hand, precipitation data reveal no obvious overall trend in the last century,[10] and model projections do not agree on whether average annual precipitation in the region will increase or decrease in the coming century.[11]

Even if average annual precipitation remains relatively constant, however, global climate change can be expected to have substantial impacts on the condition of western rangelands. First,

---

5. *Id.* at 3.

6. *See* Rex D. Pieper and Rodney K. Heitschmidt, *Is Short-Duration Grazing the Answer?* 43 J. Soil and Water Conservation, No. 2, at 133 (1988).

7. *See, e.g.,* 43 C.F.R. § 4100.0-5 (defining "Ephemeral rangelands" to mean "areas of the Hot Desert Biome (Region) that do not consistently produce enough forage to sustain a livestock operation, but from time to time produce sufficient forage to accommodate livestock grazing").

8. Committee on the Scientific Bases of Colorado River Basin Water Management, National Research Council, Colorado River Basin Water Management: Evaluating and Adjusting to Hydroclimatic Variability 82, fig. 3-2 (2007), *available at* http://www.nap.edu/catalog.php?record_id=11857.

9. *Id.* at 87, fig. 3-4.

10. *Id.* at 81, fig. 3-1.

11. *Id.* at 86.

higher temperatures will increase rates of evaporation and transpiration, so that less water will be available in the soil to support plant growth and reproduction. A measure of the combined effect of precipitation and temperature on water availability is the Palmer Drought Severity Index,[12] which is commonly used by range managers for purposes of adjusting livestock numbers and grazing practices to adapt to drought. Recently, Martin Hoerling of NOAA and Jon Eischeid of the University of Colorado used 18 different climate models to predict the Palmer Index in the Colorado River Basin for the 25-year periods 2006–2030 and 2035–2060.[13] These models project little change in precipitation as compared to the twentieth century average, but they predict that, as a result of a 2.5-degree increase in average temperature, the *average* value of the Palmer Index in 2006–2030 will be equal to its value during the southwest's drought of 2000–2003, which was generally agreed to be one of the worst droughts in the region's history. For 2035–2060, a predicted 5-degree increase in average temperature "drives the Palmer Index down to drought severity rarely witnessed during the 20th century." Hoerling and Eischeid concluded:

> In the 20th century, drought was principally precipitation driven, and enhanced by temperature. Indications from the simulations are that a near perpetual state of drought will materialize in the coming decades as a consequence of increasing temperature.[14]

Of equal concern for the management of western rangelands is a predicted increase in the *variability* of precipitation. Even if average precipitation remains relatively unchanged, the precipitation will be concentrated in fewer storms, with longer dry periods between.[15]

Implications for Rangeland Management

The effects of global climate change on western rangelands will exacerbate the problems already created by the extension of livestock grazing practices outside of their natural "life zones." Specifically, (1) increased temperatures and concomitant increases in evaporation and transpiration will expand the land area in which grazing is currently occurring but in which it is economically and environmentally unsustainable and (2) increased variability of precipitation will decrease the land area which can sustainably support permanent herds of livestock and increase the area which can support livestock only during wetter periods.

The logical response to these climatic changes would be for range managers and livestock producers, like communities of plants and animals, to shift their geographic ranges so as to remain within their life zones. Such a shift would involve retiring livestock grazing on the hotter and more arid lands that are currently grazed (including the drier parts of Arizona, California,

---

12. *See* WAYNE C. PALMER, METEOROLOGICAL DROUGHT (Weather Bureau, U.S. Dep't of Commerce, Research Paper No. 45) (1965).

13. Martin Hoerling and Jon Eischeid, *Past Peak Water in the Southwest*, 6 (1) SOUTHWEST HYDROLOGY 18 (January/February 2007).

14. *Id.* at 19. *See also* INTERGOVERNMENTAL PANEL ON CLIMATE CHANGE, CLIMATE CHANGE 2007: SYNTHESIS REPORT, SUMMARY FOR POLICYMAKERS 8 (Cambridnge Un. Press 2007), *available at* http://www.ipcc.ch/pdf/assessment-report/ar4/syr/ar4_syr_spm.pdf (expressing "high confidence" that many semi-arid areas, including the western United States, "will suffer a decrease in water resources due to climate change"); Jack A. Morgan *et al.*, *Management Implications of Global Change for Great Plains Rangelands*, 30 (3) RANGELANDS 18 (2008) (concluding that, even where precipitation increases, "[t]he dessicating effect of higher temperatures is expected to more than offset the benefit of higher precipitation, resulting in lower soil water content and increased drought throughout most of the Great Plains").

15. *See* Joel R. Brown and Jim Thorpe, *Climate Change and Rangelands: Responding Rationally to Uncertainty*, 30 (3) RANGELANDS 3, 5 (2008) (predicting that, in deserts and rangelands of the southwestern United States, rainfall "is likely to become more highly variable," with "[a]n increase in the number of extremely wet or dry years"). *See also* INTERGOVERNMENTAL PANEL ON CLIMATE CHANGE, CLIMATE CHANGE 2007: SYNTHESIS REPORT (Cambridge Un. Press 2007) 53, Table 3.2, *available at* http://www.ipcc.ch/pdf/assessment-report/ar4/syr/ar4_syr.pdf (predicting an increase in both "[h]eavy precipitation events" and in area affected by drought).

Nevada, New Mexico, and Utah) and changing from perennial to more flexible ephemeral grazing operations in many semi-arid areas. Unfortunately, historic and current attitudes, policies, and practices, of public land managers and livestock producers provide little hope that they will be willing to make such changes.

Retirement of grazing on any lands under its management is a policy option that is almost never seriously considered by the BLM, the agency that manages America's hottest and driest rangelands,[16] even though the BLM has ample legal authority to mandate such retirement where justified by economic and environmental circumstances.[17] One promising alternative to agency-mandated grazing retirements is the "buy-out" of public lands ranchers by conservation groups who either purchase ranches or pay ranchers not to graze livestock. Such buy-outs have been successful, at least temporarily, in relieving some areas of particularly important wildlife habitat or outstanding scenic beauty from the impacts of grazing. However, there is no evidence that conservation groups have sufficient money, or the willingness to spend it, to retire grazing on the tens of millions of acres necessary to adapt to a warmer and drier climate across the arid west.

Moreover, even in the relatively small areas where it has been pursued, this seemingly win-win strategy has sometimes run aground on the shoals of agency resistance. To be successful, a buyout requires the cooperation of the BLM to ensure that the BLM will not simply issue a grazing permit to another rancher, whose cows will replace those of the rancher who has been bought out. Such assurance can be provided by the BLM's amendment of an applicable land use plan to close the area in question to grazing. But, since the onset of the George W. Bush administration in 2001, the BLM has been unwilling to so amend its land use plans.

Like the retirement of lands from grazing, the conversion of perennial to ephemeral grazing operations is made very difficult by the administrative and economic practices that have developed around public land grazing permits. A perennial grazing permit is usually issued for a ten-year term, with the expectation that it will be renewed at the end of the term. Because of the lengthy term and the expectation of renewal, perennial grazing permits have developed an extra-legal but nonetheless very real economic value that is capitalized into the value of the private ranches that control the permits.[18] Ranches are priced according to the number of livestock authorized to graze by the associated permits. Ephemeral permits, on the other hand, are issued on an annual or seasonal basis, with no assurance of renewal. Therefore, the conversion of a perennial to an ephemeral permit can cause a substantial drop in the market value of the ranch that holds the permit. For this reason, public lands ranchers vigorously oppose the conversion of their perennial permits into ephemeral permits and the BLM, eager to avoid a fight with its ranching constituents, rarely undertakes such a conversion.

The administration in office in Washington from 1993 to 2001 made substantial efforts to reform public rangeland management, but it stopped short of the types of fundamental changes, such as retirement of grazing on the most arid and environmentally sensitive rangelands, that would be necessary to successfully adapt to the climatic changes expected to occur over the next

---

16. *See* Joseph M. Feller, *What is Wrong with the BLM's Management of Livestock Grazing on the Public Lands?*, 30 Idaho L. Rev. 555, 570–74 (1994).

17. *See id.* at 566–67. *See also* National Wildlife Fed. v. BLM, 140 I.B.L.A. 85, 101 (1997) ("Comb Wash" decision of the Interior Board of Land Appeals (IBLA) that the BLM must, in deciding whether to permit grazing in a particular area, "balance competing resource values to ensure that public lands are managed in the manner 'that will best meet the present and future needs of the American people'"(quoting 43 U.S.C. §1702(c) (definition of "multiple use"))); Joseph M. Feller, *The Comb Wash Case: The Rule of Law Comes to the Public Rangelands*, 17 Pub. Land & Resources L. Rev. 25, 34–35 (1996) (discussing the decision of an administrative law judge that was affirmed by the IBLA in the Comb Wash decision).

18. *See* Joseph M. Feller, *Back to the Present: The Supreme Court Refuses to Move Public Range Law Backward, but Will the BLM Move Public Range Management Forward?*, 31 Envtl. L. Rep. 10021, 10023 (2001).

century.[19] The administration in office from 2001 to 2009 was even less adaptable; it sought to reverse much of the modest progress that was made by the preceding administration, and to reinstate old regulatory provisions that reinforced the economic link between grazing permits and ranch values.[20] Reform of public rangeland management has never been a particularly high-profile topic on the national political agenda, and it is perhaps not surprising that it does not figure prominently in most discussions of the measures that ought to be taken to adapt to global change.

That's a shame because, whatever its political costs, changing public range policy is among the economically cheapest measures that ought to be taken to adapt to global warming. While retiring grazing on millions of acres of the driest public lands and converting perennial grazing operations to ephemeral ones on tens of millions more would be costly to individual public lands ranchers, those ranchers are relatively few in number, and the overall cost to the economy would be negligible.[21]

D. Farmlands

2008 FRIEDMAN at 179:

> Given the small net energy and CO_2 contribution made by corn ethanol, the whole craze reminds me of the late economist Ken Boulding's definition of suboptimal: Doing the best possible job at something that should not be done at all.

2008 FRIEDMAN at 179, quoting Rachid M. Rachid, Egypt's Ministry of Trade & Industry, Jan., 2008:

> "What are you guys doing? The average Egyptian family's food bill takes up about 60 percent of their total budget. We are the biggest importers of wheat in the world—six million tons a year!" So many American farmers were planting corn for ethanol, in place of wheat, that the price of wheat has gone up from $180 a ton at the end of 2006 to $390 a ton at the end of 2007. "It is a disaster. [It] is not over and the major reason is U.S. subsidies for biofuels," said Rachid. "I tell you, poor Egyptians hate biofuels. They don't know much about them, but they hate them."

WILLIAM F. RUDDIMAN, PLOWS, PLAGUES & PETROLEUM: HOW HUMANS TOOK CONTROL OF CLIMATE 5 (Princeton Un. Press 2005):

> Carbon dioxide concentrations began their slow rise 8,000 years ago when humans began to cut and burn forests in China, India, and Europe to make clearings for croplands and pastures. Methane concentrations began a similar rise 5,000 years ago when humans began to irrigate for rice farming and tend livestock in unprecedented numbers. Both of these changes started at negligible levels, but their impact grew steadily,

---

19. *See* Joseph M. Feller, *'til the Cows Come Home, The Fatal Flaw in the Clinton Administration's Public Lands Grazing Policy*, 25 ENVTL. L. 703 (1995).

20. *See* Joseph M. Feller, *Ride 'em Cowboy: A Critical Look at the BLM's Proposed New Grazing Regulations*, 34 ENVT'L. L. 1123 (2004). The proposed new regulations discussed in this article were promulgated into law on July 12, 2006, 71 Fed. Reg. 39,402 , but the new regulations were found unlawful and were enjoined in all respects by the United States District Court in Western Watersheds Project v. Kraayenbrink, 538 F. Supp. 2d 1302 (D. Idaho 2008). The district court's decision has been appealed to the United States Court of Appeals for the Ninth Circuit.

21. *See, e.g.*, Thomas M. Power, *Taking Stock of Public Lands Grazing: An Economic Analysis*, in WELFARE RANCHING: THE SUBSIDIZED DESTRUCTION OF THE AMERICAN WEST (George Weurthner and Mollie Matteson Eds., Foundations for Deep Ecology 2002), *available at* http://www.publiclandsranching.org/htmlres/wr_taking_stock.htm.

and they had a significant and growing impact on Earth's climate throughout the long interval within which civilizations arose and spread across the globe.

Global Warming and Non-Point Source Pollution in the Great Plains: What's Good for Agriculture Is Also Good for Planet Earth

Myrl L. Duncan, Professor of Law, Washburn University School of Law, Topeka, KS 66621; Tel: (785) 670-1630, Fax: (785) 670-3429, myrl.duncan@washburn.edu.

Introduction

The inextricable relationship between climate change and agriculture has been the subject of dozens, perhaps hundreds, of reports. Any short discussion thus necessarily must focus on a discrete issue as the vehicle with which to explore a numbingly complex set of interconnections; the trick is discovering the place to begin. I was asked to write about climate change as it relates to crop agriculture in the Farm Belt of the Great Plains, a logical choice given that region's importance to domestic and international food production. What will be the effects of global warming on agronomy in the region and how should policymakers address those effects? Initially, two almost polar opposite thoughts came to mind. First, what is the point in proposing solutions to a problem that many Midwesterners deny even exists? Second, as a student of water law, I asked where will we find the water in a drier climate for thirsty crops in a region that already relies heavily on irrigation? Initially, at least, the latter problem turned out to be the easier to tackle.

On first blush, one would intuitively expect that rising temperatures will make the Earth hotter and drier, and, indeed, that will be the effect in some regions. Paradoxically, however, a warmer climate will at the same time also produce more atmospheric moisture condensation, which in many areas will yield greater precipitation. Superficially, the moisture problem loomed less threateningly.

It soon became clear, however, that, as with nearly every climate change question, the answer is much more complex. It seems climatologists agree that much of this increased precipitation will not fall consistently but will come in the form of large, even extreme, precipitation events. As a teacher of the Clean Water Act, my thoughts turned quickly to soil erosion and nonpoint source pollution, the country's leading source of water pollution. Pollution from nonpoint sources has been the stepchild of the Clean Water Act from the beginning, and an effective remedy remains both logistically difficult and politically untenable. Could climate change be the catalyst that would cause the United States finally to get serious about addressing this insidious and pervasive form of environmental harm that has left our waterways polluted with sediment and chemicals? Even if that were to occur, would such a policy shift, notwithstanding its manifest water quality benefits, do anything to help abate global warming or would it be neutral in terms of climate change, simply a reaction to one of its consequences?

As it turns out, the matrix works both ways; land use practices that address global warming will also help clean up our rivers and streams. One much talked-about mechanism for reducing greenhouse gases (GHGs) is carbon sequestration, essentially locking up CO_2 in natural "sinks" to keep it from acting as a heat-trapping gas. Because plants contain large amounts of carbon, it is proposed that grasslands be used as a CO_2 depository. Perennial crops, increasingly the subject of cutting-edge research, would backhandedly accomplish the same result. In addition to helping to moderate global warming, storing carbon in plant matter would help to prevent nonpoint source pollution by addressing soil erosion, itself a natural resources disaster. The linkage between climate change and water pollution is obvious. Global warming will aggravate existing problems unrelated to climate: soil erosion and nonpoint source pollution; yet by addressing the phenomenon for its own sake—global warming *qua* global warming—we would end up attacking those pre-existing evils.

A somewhat different linkage is present with respect to a particular source of nonpoint pollution: the nitrogen fertilizer used in huge amounts by farmers on the Great Plains and everywhere else. Nitrogen fertilizer breaks down into various derivatives, including nitrate (NO_3) and nitrous oxide (N_2O). While much of the nitrate that is generated is taken up by the fertilized crop, unutilized amounts run off as a nonpoint source pollutant that is literally killing some of our waterways. Nitrous oxide, significant amounts of which are generated by nitrogen fertilizer, is a potent GHG, possessing far greater heat-trapping capacity than CO_2. Like pollution from sediments, fertilizer-induced nitrate pollution, will only get worse as the number of large precipitation events increases. And, of course, the elevated temperatures giving rise to those events will be in part caused by the nitrous oxide produced by that same fertilizer. It follows that finding more efficient ways to manage nitrogen fertilizer, perhaps using less of it, would result in reductions in both GHGs and in the level of nonpoint source pollution. Once again the connection between climate change and water pollution is clear, although the situation is more complicated than the relationship between CO_2 sequestration and soil erosion/water pollution. By attacking an existing practice—the use of nitrogen fertilizer—that is helping to cause global warming, we end up also enhancing water quality by reducing the level of nitrates.

Finally, and ironically, exploration of the climate change-water connection suggests a solution to my first dilemma: why global warming skeptics would take seriously proposals to address a problem they do not yet acknowledge. The answer is simple. By sequestering carbon and by better managing nitrogen fertilizer the agricultural community would be helping to sustain itself. Because carbon is a major component in soil, storing it in the roots of perennial grasses and crops would build up topsoil, benefitting future farmers—as well as society at large. Similarly, by employing fertilizer more sparingly, farmers would reduce costs and increase the efficiency of their operations.

The Problem

To most Americans global warming no doubt remains more of an abstraction rather than a reality. Even to those who live there, it is probably difficult to fathom that coastal areas are in danger of innundation from rising sea levels caused by melting of polar icecaps.[1] Similarly, far removed from such dramatic climate change consequences, many living in the Farm Belt of the Great Plains question the phenomenon's existence.[2] Some argue, incompletely, that rising CO_2 levels will benefit agriculture by enhancing crop yields.[3] Even to those willing to acknowledge the

---

1. *See* Massachusetts v. E.P.A., 127 S Ct. 1438, 1455, 1456 (2007) (references to reports predicting global rises in sea levels).

2. Fred Mullholland, Letter to the Editor, *So Much for Science*, Topeka Capital-Journal, Sept. 21, 2007, at A4, http://www.cjonline.com/stories/092107/opi_201451353.shtml (responding to statements of two local meteorologists that the existence of global warming lacks scientific support); Paul Post, Letter to the Editor, *Oil Resources Finite*, Topeka Capital-Journal, Sept.20, 2007, at A4, http://www.cjonline.com/stories/092007/opi_201130870.shtml (same).

3. "One of the really good things about CO_2 is that plants perform better under stress with increased levels of CO_2, said Rep. Larry Powell, R-Garden City." Tim Carpenter, *Expert: Sequestration Has Benefits: Governor Says Plan Could Provide a Boon for Kansas*, Topeka Capital-Journal, Dec. 30, 2007 at A, http://www.cjonline.com/stories/123007/kan_230136732.shtm; Rep. Larry Powell, Letter to the Editor, *CO_2 Isn't Villain*, Topeka Capital-Journal, Dec. 3, 200, at A4, http://www.cjonline.com/stories/120307/opi_222349285.shtml. (citing report stating that over the next 50 years "aerial fertilization effect of atmospheric CO_2 enrichment would boost world agricultural output by about 50 percent.") Studies do indeed suggest that when considered by itself, the level of CO_2 positively affects production, but those studies paint an incom-

problem, its long and short term consequences remain uncertain. It is easy enough to understand that changes in temperature will force shifts in the geographic zones in which food crops can or will be grown. More southern areas will experience crop reductions due to temperature increases while the extended growing seasons that will result in more northern climates may increase yields.[4] Other climate-related impacts on agriculture in general, and agronomy in particular, are not so apparent, however.[5]

Notably, rising temperatures will present both water quantity and water quality issues for the United States. According to some projections, some areas, such as the Southeast and Southwest, will probably become drier.[6] In addition, water for irrigation across the entire West will become more scarce, as warmer temperatures cause more winter precipitation to fall as rain, thus reducing snowpacks, which will also melt earlier, resulting in heavier spring runoff.[7] Because reservoirs have been engineered to hold gradual melt off, much of the front-loaded water supply generated by global warming will need to be released early in the growing season, leaving less water for irrigation in the heat of the summer.[8] A less obvious climate change-agriculture connection is the dramatic impact that elevated temperatures could have on water quality, particularly from agricultural nonpoint sources.

Not all regions will become drier. A warmer climate will also produce more atmospheric moisture condensation, which in many areas will yield greater precipitation.[9] Climatologists agree that much of this increased precipitation will come in the form of large, even extreme, precipitation events.[10] For example, of the two most commonly used climate models, one projects more than a twenty percent increase in the most intense rainfall events (the heaviest five percent); the other predicts a fifty-five percent rise.[11] Unless landowners have taken measures to prevent or reduce soil erosion, such abnormally heavy rainfalls will no doubt cause serious soil erosion, both depleting the land and polluting the waterways. Of course, soil itself will not be the only pollutant. In addition to sediment, nutrients, such as nitrates and phosphorus,

---

plete picture. When temperature increase is taken into account, the results are quite different. For example, temperature increases reduce the period of seed formation, resulting in lower biomass production. RICHARD M. ADAMS, et al., A REVIEW OF IMPACTS TO U. S. AGRICULTURAL RESOURCES, 33, n. 5 (Pew Center on Global Climate Change 1999), http://www.pewclimate.org/docUploads/env_argiculture.pdf. Increases in temperature also elevate the rate at which plants release CO_2, creating less than optimal growth conditions. Raymond Motha and Wolfgang Baier, *Impacts of Present and Future Climate Change and Climate Variability of Agriculture in the Temperate Regions: North America*, 70 CLIMATIC CHANGE 137, 154 (2005).

4. ADAMS, *et al.*, *supra*, note 3, at 12–13.

5. For example, shifts in frostlines may well result in changes in the incidence and distribution of pests and pathogens. *Id.* at 14. With respect to livestock, increased temperatures would likely cause appetite suppression and result in lower weight gains and decreased milk production. *Id.*

6. KENNETH D. FREDERICK, *et al.*, WATER & GLOBAL CLIMATE CHANGE: POTENTIAL IMPACTS ON U.S. WATER RESOURCES 5 (Pew Center on Global Climate Change 1999) http://www.pewclimate.org/docUploads/ clim_change.pdf; STEPHEN SAUNDERS, *et al.*, HOTTER AND DRIER: THE WEST'S CHANGED CLIMATE 10 (The Rocky Mountain Climate Organization/Natural Resource Defense Council 2008), http://www.nrdc.org/global Warming/west/west.pdf.

7. FREDERICK, *et al.*, *supra* note 6, at 8–9; SAUNDERS, *et al.*, *supra* note 6, at 8–10.

8. SAUNDERS, *et al.*, *supra* note 6, at 10.

9. SOIL AND WATER CONSERVATION SOCIETY, CONSERVATION IMPLICATIONS OF CLIMATE CHANGE: SOIL EROSION AND RUNOFF FROM CROPLAND 8 (2003), http://www.swcs.org/documents/Climate_changefinal_ 112904154622.pdf (hereinafter CONSERVATION IMPLICATIONS).

10. *Id.* at 10–12. *See also* U.S. CLIMATE CHANGE SCIENCE PROGRAM & THE SUBCOMMITTEE ON GLOBAL CHANGE RESEARCH, PRELIMINARY REVIEW OF ADAPTATION OPTIONS FOR CLIMATE ECOSYSTEMS & RESOURCES (Final Report Synthesis & Assessment 4.4) at §2.4.7 (June 2008), http://climatescience.gov/Library/sap/sap 4-4/final-report/default.htm.

11. CONSERVATION IMPLICATIONS, *supra* note 9, at 10.

animal wastes, salts and pesticides[12] will be transported directly to surface waters.[13] Climate change, it seems, has the potential to aggravate seriously existing levels of nonpoint source pollution.

The possibility of increased nonpoint pollution is reason for concern. Nonpoint source pollution is already the nation's most adamant water quality issue,[14] and agriculture, while not the sole culprit, is a major contributor.[15] Congressional attempts to address the problem have been half-hearted.[16] Unlike pollution from point sources, which can be identified and regulated, nonpoint source pollution is by definition diffuse, extremely difficult to pinpoint and thus to regulate.[17] Moreover, it stems not from industrial processes which have known a history of regulation but rather from land use practices, which have traditionally fallen within the purview of state control.[18] It is also a political reality that federal regulation of farming practices is simply unacceptable. States by and large have addressed the problem indirectly through farmer education programs and the promulgation of best management practices standards.[19] Given that nonpoint source pollution remains the country's dominant clean water shortcoming, it is fair to say the states have not been particularly successful.

We are left then with waterways chock full of levels of troublesome pollutants. Two, in particular, have unique relevance to a discussion of agronomy's relationship to global warming: sediments and nitrates. Both already cause serious environmental damage.

Sediment

Soil has been eroding from agricultural lands since the dawn of history; indeed soil erosion is now recognized as playing a role in the decline of historic civilizations.[20] In the United States, the most dramatic examples of erosion, the catastrophic wind-related losses that occurred during the Dust Bowl years of the 1930s,[21] served as the catalyst for the formulation of a broad-based array of conservation programs that still exist today.[22] Nonetheless, even into the 1980s erosion rates were still significant, 1,672 million tons per year—or an average of

---

12. U.S. EPA, NATIONAL MANAGEMENT MEASURES TO CONTROL NONPOINT POLLUTION FROM AGRICULTURE 2–9 (2003), http://www.epa.gov/owow/nps/agmm/chap2.pdf.

13. CONSERVATION IMPLICATIONS, *supra* note 9, at 9. Pollutants will also enter surface water via percolation into alluvia.

14. ROBERT PERCIVAL, *et al.*, ENVIRONMENTAL REGULATION: LAW, SCIENCE AND POLICY 703 (5th ed. Aspen Publishers 2006).

15. EPA reports that as of 2000, agriculture impacts forty-eight percent of rivers and streams and forty-one percent of lakes identified as impaired. U.S. EPA, NATIONAL MANAGEMENT MEASURES TO CONTROL NONPOINT POLLUTION FROM AGRICULTURE 2–9 (2003), http://www.epa.gov/owow/nps/agmm/chap2.pdf.

16. *See* George A. Gould, *Agriculture, Nonpoint Source Pollution and Federal Law*, 23 U. C. DAVIS L. REV. 461(1990).

17. *Contrast* §301(a) of the Clean Water Act which prohibits discharges from point sources except pursuant to the National Pollutant Discharge Elimination System established by §402. 33 U.S. C. §§1311, 1342 (2000).

18. Clean Water Act, §101(b), 33 U.S.C. §1251(b) (2000); Solid Waste Agency of Northern Cook County v. U. S. Army Corps of Engineers, 531 U. S. 159, 174 (2001).

19. *See, e.g.*, Press Release, *State Study Identifies Best Row Crop Pollution Controls*, Kansas Dept. of Health & Environment, Feb., 5, 1997, http://www.kdheks.gov/news/web_archives/1997/9019.html.

20. *See generally* DAVID R. MONTGOMERY, DIRT: THE EROSION OF CIVILIZATIONS (Un. of California Press 2007). Comparing inferred prehistoric natural rates of erosion to those caused by all agricultural activity, geologist Bruce Wilkinson estimates the latter to be twenty-eight times greater. Bruce H. Wilkinson, *Humans as Geologic Agents: A Deep-Time Perspective*, 33 GEOLOGY 161, 163 (March, 2005).

21. *See generally* MONTGOMERY, *supra* note 20, at 145–177; DONALD WORSTER, DUST BOWL: THE SOUTHERN PLAINS IN THE 1930S (Oxford Un. Press 1979); TIMOTHY EGAN, THE WORST HARD TIME: THE UNTOLD STORY OF THOSE WHO SURVIVED THE GREAT AMERICAN DUST BOWL (Houghton, Mifflin 2006).

22. Linda A. Malone, *A Historical Essay on the Conservation Provisions of the 1985 Farm Bill: Sodbusting, Swampbusting, and the Conservation Reserve*, 34 U. KAN. L. REV. 577, 578–79 (1986).

four tons per acre—for sheet and rill erosion.[23] While losses have dropped substantially (by 43%) since 1982,[24] due mainly to the Conservation Reserve Program (CRP) provisions in the 1985 Farm Security Act and the increased implementation of conservation tillage,[25] they are still significant: 971 million tons per year—or an average of 2.6 tons per acre—again for sheet and rill erosion.[26] Fifty-one percent of sheet and rill erosion occurs in the two Great Plains basins, the Missouri and the Souris-Red-Rainy/Upper Mississippi, the heartland of American agriculture.[27]

In addition to destroying one of our most vital natural resources, soil erosion—the archetype of non-point source pollution—affects the life of surface waters in two principal ways: by introducing suspended solids and increasing turbidity. Suspended solids, larger particles that remain in the column of moving water, reduce the amount of sunlight to aquatic vegetation and clog the gills of fish and the filtering mechanisms of filter feeders; as they settle out, for example in stagnant lakes and reservoirs, suspended solids also cover spawning areas and food supplies. Turbidity, the cloudiness of water due to finer particles which do not easily settle out, likewise interferes with the passage of sunlight to vegetation and thus interferes with the feeding habits of some species of fish who depend on aquatic plants.[28] Turbidity is also a concern of the standards for quality of drinking water.[29]

As injurious to aquatic health as this waterborne sediment is, it is only the beginning of the story; soil erosion's deleterious effects on water quality are not limited to suspended dirt. Sediment carried off the land also transports other pollutants. Because soil eroded by sheet, rill and ephemeral gully erosion comes mainly from the surface, or from the plow zone, it transports substances found there. This layer is, of course, the one in which fertilizers and other agricultural chemicals have been applied; accordingly, "eroding sediments generally contain higher concentrations of phosphorus, nitrogen, and pesticide than the parent soil (*i.e.*, they are enriched)."[30] The effects of one of those substances, nitrate nitrogen, can be disastrous.

Nitrates

Nitrates are a form of nitrogen, the most common element in the earth's atmosphere and one necessary to life.[31] Nitrogen takes many forms, three of which are relevant to a discussion of

---

23. U.S. Dep't Agric., Natural Resources Conservation Serv., National Resources Inventory (2003), http://www.nrcs.usda.gov/Technical/nri/2003/national_erosion.html. Wind erosion accounts for 3.3 tons per acre. *Id.* Highly erodible soils on 82.8 million acres were eroding above soil tolerance rates; on non-highly erodible soils, 86.3 million acres were eroding beyond tolerance rates. *Id.* Water erosion also takes the form of ephemeral and classic gully erosion and streambank erosion. U. S. EPA, *supra* note 12, at 2–15.

24. U.S.Dep't Agric., Natural Resources Conservation Serv., National Resources Inventory (2003), http://www.nrcs.usda.gov/Technical/nri/2003/nri03eros-mrb.html.

25. David R. Montgomery, 104 Proceedings of the National Academy of Sciences 13268, 13268 (2007), http://www.pnas.org/cgi/reprint/0611508104v1. The term conservation tillage covers practices which leave all or part of the stubble from the previous crop on the field, rather than plowing it under; the new crop is then planted into the stubble and weeds are controlled with herbicides. North Carolina State University, Conservation Tillage, http://www.cals.ncsu.edu/sustainable/peet/tillage/tillage.html.

26. U.S. Dept' Agric., *supra* note 23. In 1997, 65 million acres were eroding at rates beyond tolerance levels. Conservation Implications, *supra* note 9, at 8. Geologist Bruce Wilkinson estimates that combined with human construction activity, agriculturally-related soil reductions are approximately 18,000 times greater than the mass of material spewed by the 1880 eruption of Krakatoa and are enough to fill the Grand Canyon in approximately fifty years. Wilkinson, *supra* note 20.

27. U.S. Dep't Agric., *supra* note 24.

28. U.S. EPA, *supra* note 12, at 2–15. Background knowledge was also provided by Tony Stahl, in the Stream Chemical Monitoring Division of the Kansas Department of Health and Environment, June 24, 2008.

29. *See, e.g.*, 40 C.F.R. § 141–550 *et seq.* (2007).

30. U.S. EPA, *supra* note 12, at 2–16.

31. 8 The New Encyclopaedia Britannica 727 (Micropaedia 2002).

climate change. One form is used as agricultural fertilizer, a certain amount of which will end up polluting waterways as nitrate (NO_3). Another form, nitrous oxide (N_2O), is actually a potent GHG.

Nonpoint source pollution

Soil naturally contains nitrogen, though not in sufficient quantities to support modern agriculture.[32] Accordingly, farmers apply nitrogen-based fertilizers.[33] Soil bacteria convert the nitrogen in fertilizer to various other forms, including nitrate, that can be used by plants, as well as soil organic matter.[34] However, crops generally utilize less than seventy percent of applied nitrogen.[35] Consequently, excess nitrate not taken up by plants or transformed into other substances[36] often enters rivers and streams by way of direct surface runoff or indirectly by permeation through groundwater into base flow.[37] In addition, erosion releases nitrate that has become part of soil organic matter.[38]

Although background levels of nitrates are naturally present in surface water and marine ecosystems, the introduction of additional quantities can lead to calamitous scenarios. As a nutrient, nitrate serves as a food source for aquatic vegetation. Not surprisingly then, waters enriched with large quantities of nitrate experience eutrophication, dramatic increases in the growth of plants, for example large algae blooms. (These blooms, of course, will thrive and be most extensive in the summer heat). When the algae eventually die and drop to the river bottom or ocean floor, they are decomposed by oxygen-consuming bacteria. The result, hypoxia, or oxygen-depletion, can be catastrophic for aquatic creatures, which must have oxygen to live; marine life either dies out or moves elsewhere.[39] This drama has played out spectacularly in the Gulf of Mexico where scientists have been tracking a "dead zone" since 1974. In 1993, the year

---

32. U. S. EPA., *supra* note 12, at 2–11.

33. Anhydrous ammonia, an 82% nitrogen product, is the most commonly used nitrogen fertilizer. A liquid under pressure, anhydrous ammonia must be "injected" into the ground by a knife-bladed implement pulled behind a tractor. Because the breakdown required for the fertilizer to be usable by plants, note 34, *infra*, does not occur below 55°F., farmers often apply anhydrous ammonia in the late fall, to be taken up by, *e.g.*, corn, to be planted in the spring. Growing plants also require phosphorus which is applied as an additional fertilizer. Conversation with Arlen Wilcox, Agronomist, New Horizon Farm & Home Co-op, Paola, Kansas, March 19, 2008 (hereinafter Wilcox).

34. These processes are known as nitrification and denitrification; both processes produce nitrous oxide (N_2O), a dangerous GHG. U.S. Agriculture & Forestry Greenhouse Gas Inventory: 1990–2001, §3.1.3 at 45–46, http://www.usda.gov/oce/global_change/gg_inventory.htm (hereinafter Inventory). For discussion of N_2O, see text accompanying notes 94–106, *infra*. The process by which bacteria, in the presence of sufficient decomposable organic matter, convert nitrates into soil organic matter is known as immobilization. West Virginia University Extension Service, Agriculture practices and Nitrate Pollution of Water, http://www.caf.wvu.edu/—forage/nitratepollution/nitrate.htm.

35. Arvin Mosier, *et al.*, *An Overview of the Revised 1996 IPCC Guidelines for National Greenhouse Gas Inventory Methodology for Nitrous Oxide*, 2 Envt'l Sci. and Pol. §2.4, at 325 (1999), http://www.sciencedirect.com/science?_ob=ArticleURL&_udi=B6VP6-404RMM7-B&_user=784805&_rdoc=1&_fmt=&_orig=search&_sort=d&view=c&_acct=C000043292&_version=1&_urlVersion=0&_userid=784805&md5=95f7f34f47b3bc4811b282c480299577. Frequently, only about 20 % is taken up. *Id.*

36. Some nitrogen is also volitalized. *Id.*

37. U. S. EPA, *supra* note 12, at 2–12. Permeation through the alluvium is the "dominant pathway" by which nitrates enter waterways. Conversation with Jerry Glover, Agroecologist, The Land Institute, Salina, Kansas, Feb. 22, 2008. Nitrates also pollute groundwater, and concentrations are highest in agricultural areas. *Id.*

38. U. S. EPA, *supra* note 12, at 2–10.

39. For a description of this natural life cycle, see generally U. S. EPA, *supra* note 12, at 2–11; Carol Kaesuk Yoon, *A "Dead Zone" Grows in the Gulf of Mexico*, N. Y. Times, Mar. 19, 1998, http://query.nytimes.com/gst/fullpage.html?res=9B04E1DD1338F933A15752C0A96E958260&scp=1&sq=dead+zone%2C+hypoxia&st=nyt (hereinafter Yoon). *See also Dead Zones Emerging as Big Threat to 21st Century Fish Stocks*, UNEP press release 2004/14, http://www.unep.org/GC/GCSS-VIII/PressRelease_E2.asp.

of the huge Midwestern flood, nitrates pouring out of the Mississippi basin, America's agricultural heartland, caused the zone to double in size.[40] From 1993 to 1997, the hypoxic zone, ranged in size from 6,200 to 7,700 square miles, an area greater than the size of Chesapeake Bay.[41]

EPA has finally begun to address the situation in the Gulf.[42] But it is critical to recognize that it is only the very worst example of a scenario that is likely to become more common as the climate warms. Levels of nitrate, already a chronic nonpoint source pollutant, will increase with the temperature-driven frequency and intensity of precipitation events, more of which may be large enough and occur during the hottest part of already hotter years, to produce acute outbreaks of hypoxia not unlike that generated by the 1993 flood. Surely the specter of such nightmarish scenarios is enough to cause us finally to get serious about completing the work begun by the Clean Water Act.

Nitrous Oxide

The case for seriously attacking nonpoint source pollution is bolstered significantly by the fact that nitrogen also plays a far more sinister role in the global warming drama. As just discussed, sediments and nitrates present a common problem; both are nonpoint pollutants the levels of which will be increased by precipitation patterns altered by climate change. However, unlike the increased levels of sediments, which will be strictly the *product* of global warming, nitrates are associated with the *production* of the nitrous oxide (N_2O), the most potent of the primary greenhouse gases responsible for the phenomena.

Most discussion of global warming focuses on the ill effects of carbon dioxide (CO_2), the most ubiquitous and commonly identified of the three principal GHGs. Yet CO_2, on a per unit basis, possesses the least heat trapping capacity. Moreover, in terms of agricultural contributions to climate change, CO_2 is basically a non-factor; studies suggest that the changes which occur in agriculture because of global warming will not appreciably increase the amount of CO_2 in the atmosphere.[43] Two other gases, methane (CH_4) and nitrous oxide (N_2O), both of which are produced by agricultural activity, are actually far more destructive. One ton of methane is the

---

40. Yoon, *supra* note 39. By contrast, the dead zone was "almost absent" in 1988, the year of a major drought in the Midwest. *Id.*, quoting Dr. R. Eugene Turner, Director, Coastal Ecology Institute, Louisiana State University.

41. U. S. EPA, *supra* note 12, at 2–11. In 1997, the dead zone was the size of the state of New Jersey. Yoon, *supra*, note 39. Phosphorus also causes eutrophication, and it is estimated that the 55–66% of the phosphorus load which impairs Lake Champlain comes from agriculture. U. S. EPA, *supra*, note 12, at 2–13.

42. U. S. EPA, MISSISSIPPI RIVER/GULF OF MEXICO WATERSHED TASK FORCE, GULF HYPOXIA ACTION PLAN 2008 (Draft 2008), http://www.epa.gov/msbasin/taskforce/pdf/actionplan.pdf. *See also* William J. Mitsch, *et al.*, *Reducing Nitrogen Loading to the Gulf of Mexico from the Mississippi River Basin: Strategies to Counter a Persistent Ecological Problem,* 51 BIOSCIENCE 373 (May, 2001), http://0-proquest.umi.com.lib. wuacc.edu/pqdweb?index=6&did=74397013&SrchMode=1&sid=1&Fmt=6&VInst=PROD&VType=PQD& RQT=309&VName=PQD&TS=1217532050&clientId=536; MARY BOOTH, DEAD IN THE WATER: REFORMING WASTEFUL FARM SUBSIDIES CAN RESTORE GULF FISHERIES (Environmental Working Group 2006), http:// www.ewg.org/reports/deadzone.

43. *See* INTERGOVERNMENTAL PANEL ON CLIMATE CHANGE, FOURTH ASSESSMENT REPORT, WORKING GROUP III REPORT: MITIGATION OF CLIMATE CHANGE §8.3, at 503 (Cambridge Un. Press 2007), *available at* http://www.ipcc.ch/ipccreports/ar4-wg3.htm (hereinafter IPCC). In 2000, CO_2 emissions from agricultural soils accounted for less than 1% of human-generated CO_2 emissions. *Id.* Of course, considerable CO_2 is emitted by farm equipment powered by fossil fuel. New evidence gives some reason to question the base conclusion. Troubling new research suggests that groundwater contains CO_2, at concentrations 10–100 times higher than the Earth's atmosphere, which is released when the water is extracted; "outgassing of groundwater adds eight times more carbon dioxide to the atmosphere than the average yearly output from Earth's volcanoes." Radio broadcast: Carbon Dioxide and Groundwater (Kansas Public Radio, Jan. 28, 2008), http://research matters.ku.edu/2008/january/aquifersd.shtml. Drier conditions could, of course, result in greater reliance on groundwater resources.

equivalent (CO_2EQ) of 21 tons of CO_2, while one ton of N_2O equals 310 tons of CO_2. In other words, CH_4 and N_2O are, respectively, 21 and 310 times more effective at trapping heat than CO_2.[44] Of the two, N_2O is the more relevant to a discussion of crop agriculture.[45]

"[Nitrous oxide] N_2O from cropland soil amendments is the largest net source of U.S. GHG emissions from cropland agriculture."[46] Most of those emissions, 100 Tg CO_2EQ in 2001 for example,[47] are generated by the use of nitrogen fertilizers.[48] Although nitrogen is the main component in plant protein,[49] the natural nitrogen content of soil is inadequate to support modern agriculture.[50] Accordingly, farmers add chemical fertilizer.[51] Plants, however, cannot utilize the form of nitrogen applied as fertilizer; it must first be converted into ammonium and nitrates by microbial processes. It is during these conversions that N_2O is produced and directly reaches the air as a GHG.[52] "In most agricultural soils biogenic formation of N_2O is enhanced by an increase in available mineral N which, in turn increases nitrification and denitrification rates. Addition of fertilizer N, therefore, directly results in extra N_2O."[53]

Apropos to this discussion, N_2O is also produced from nitrogen that leaves the land. As noted previously, only about seventy percent of nitrogen is utilized by the crop.[54] The excess, which is not stored in the soil,[55] percolates into ground water or runs off into surface water, and a variable amount of it is later converted to N_2O.[56] These emissions are characterized as "indirect."[57] Significantly, these indirect emissions are but one stage (a temporary by-product) of the same ni-

---

44. Kenneth Paustian, *et al.*, Agriculture's Role in Greenhouse Gas Mitigation 3 (Pew Center on Global Climate Change 2006).

45. Methane is emitted as a byproduct of bovine digestion and rice production and from the decomposition of other organic matter that occurs, for example, when the permafrost melts or when peat bogs decompose. Inventory, *supra* note 34, at § 2.1, at 9–11; § 3.1, at 45–47.

46. *Id.* § 3.1.3, at 46. One study reports that from 1990 to 2003 approximately 80 MMT C-$_{eq}$ was emitted by in the U.S. in the form of N_2O from fertilizer and that almost 70% of U. S. N_2O emissions are from soils. Paustian, *et al.*, *supra* note 44, at 2, 14. Globally, in 2005, agriculture accounted for about 60% of N_2O emissions. IPCC, *supra* note 43, at 499.

47. One teragram (Tg) = 10^9 kg. M. U. F. Kirschbaum, *et al.*, Definitions of Some Ecological Terms Commonly Used in Carbon Accounting, http://www.greenhouse.crc.org.au/crc/ecarbon/publications/nee/chapter_definitions.pdf (last visited Mar. 28, 2008).

48. Inventory, *supra* note 34, at 57. N_2O is also generated by the addition of livestock manure and sewage sludge, by the plowing under of crop residue, the growing of legumes and the cultivation of highly organic soils. *Id.*, at 46, 59–62. Not all soil-produced N_2O is generated by agriculture; perhaps 6% of fertilizer in the U.S. is applied to lawns. *Id*, at 57. *See also* Arvin Mosier, *et al.*, *Closing the Global N_2O Budget: Nitrous Oxide Emissions Through the Agriculatural Nitrogen Cycle*, 52 Nutrient Cycling in Agriculture 225, 228–235 (1998).

49. Loraine Bailey and Cynthia Grant, *Efficient Nutrient Management for Quality Forages*, 13 Advances in Daily Technology 295, 296 (2001)

50. U.S. EPA 2003, *supra* note 12, at 2–11.

51. Prior to the advent of modern chemicals, farmers would have added manure or incorporated legumes, such as clover, into their crop rotations. *See generally* note 99, *infra*.

52. *See* note 34, *supra*. One of the processes, "denitrification, is the principal pathway by which N_2O enters the atmosphere." K. L. Weier, *et al.*, *Denitrification and the Dinitorogen/Nitrous Oxide Ratio as Affected by Soil, Water, Available Carbon and Nitrate*, 57 Soil Sci. Soc. Am. J. 66, 66 (1993). Also, waterborne nitrogen can later be converted to N_2O, resulting in indirect emissions. Inventory, *supra* note 34, at 46; *see also* text accompanying notes, 54–57, *infra*.

53. Mosier, *et al.*, *supra* note 48, at 228.

54. *See* note 35, *supra*.

55. Some is also volitalized. Mosier, *et al.*, *supra* note 35, at § 2.4.

56. *Id. See also* Inventory, *supra* note 34; Mosier, *et al.*, *supra* note 35, at § 2.4. Some is also volatilized. Mosier, *et al.*, *supra* note 35, at § 2.4.

57. *See generally*, sources cited in note 52, *supra*. Overall, indirect emissions account for one-third of all N_2O emissions. Mosier, *et al.*, *supra* note 35, at § 2.4.

trogen reduction process, denitirification, that produces the nitrates (another temporary by-product) which are responsible for nonpoint source water pollution, as outlined previously.[58] In other words, nitrogen fertilizer is double trouble. Its use pollutes our waterways, while at the same time setting in motion the production of a powerful GHG, that will, in a feedback loop, generate even more water pollution in the form of both sediments and nitrates.[59]

Possible Solutions

Land planted in grasses or other perennials is not prone to erosion; neither do such "crops" require much fertilization. Accordingly, by simply letting the Great Plains return to native vegetation, a Buffalo Commons,[60] much of the country's soil erosion and nonpoint source pollution problems could be eliminated. Such an approach would help also address global warming; plants would be storing carbon and fertilizer-generated N_2O levels would be diminished.

Obviously, such a "solution" is silly. It would put many of the nation's farmers out of business, lead to severe social upheaval and, of course, reduce world food supplies. On the other hand, hundreds of thousands of acres of highly erodible farmland are already enrolled in conservation reserve programs (CRP)[61] that remove them from crop production. Building on that concept, proposals for carbon sequestration on agricultural land offer the possibility of cutting back atmospheric CO_2 levels and at the same time reducing soil erosion. Also, while it is unrealistic to think anything resembling current crop yields can be maintained without the addition of significant amounts of nitrogen fertilizers, it may be possible through more effective management schemes to reduce both nitrate and N_2O production.

Carbon Sequestration

Numerous observers suggest carbon sequestration, essentially locking it up, as one strategy to reduce global warming. Possible geological receptacles include abandoned oil and gas wells,[62] coal deposits, and the basalt formations in the Columbia basin.[63] Two biological depositories that have been suggested are forests and trees and grasslands.[64] The theory is simple; trees and grasses remove CO_2 from the air, as all plants do, but instead of converting it to oxygen through photosynthesis, they act as carbon "sinks," storing the element in their roots and foliage. With respect to farm agriculture, instead of producing annual crops, fields could be al-

---

58. Conversation with Jerry Glover, Agroecologist, The Land Institute, Salina, Kansas, April 4, 2008.

59. It is also possible that global warming could create yet another feedback loop with respect to N_2O. Conversion of anhydrous ammonia to nitrates begins at about 55°F. Wilcox, *supra* note 33. Unless planting times are adjusted for warmer late winter/early spring temperatures, plants might not be ready to absorb released nitrates, which would be converted to N_2O and emitted directly into the air, or carried away by runoff and leaching to become indirect emissions. Water pollution also would be increased.

60. Deborah E. & Frank Popper, *The Great Plains: From Dust to Dust*, PLANNING 12 (1987). The Poppers' vision for the Great Plains set off a firestorm of outrage across the region but is now being reconsidered. Dave Ranney, *"Buffalo Commons" Gets a Second Look*, LAWRENCE J. WORLD, Feb. 9, 2004, http://www2.ljworld.com/news/2004/feb/09/buffalo_commons_idea/.

61. The program was established to protect highly erodible soils by paying farmers to leave them unplowed. Food Security Act of 1985, §§ 1231–1236, 99 Stat. 1509-1514 (1985). In 2001, USDA's Agricultural Research Service (ARS) estimated that 36 million acres of CRP land stored 10MMT of carbon per year. *Depositing Carbon in the Bank: The Soil Bank, That Is*, AGRICULTURAL RESEARCH 4, 6 (Feb., 2001), http://www.ars.usda. gov/is/AR/archive/feb01/bank0201.pdf.

62. U.S. Dept, of Energy, Geologic Sequestration Research, http://www.fossil.energy.gov/programs/sequestration/geologic/ (last visited June 27, 2008); *Demonstrating Carbon Sequestration*, GEOTIMES, March 2003, http://www.geotimes.org/mar03/feature_demonstrating.html.

63. Valerie Brown, *A Climate Change Solution?*, HIGH COUNTRY NEWS, Sept., 3, 2007, http://www.hcn.org/servlets/hcn.Article?article_id=17188.

64. *See generally* INVENTORY, *supra* note 34, ch. 4, at 80–93; Carol M. Rose, *From H_2O to CO_2. Lessons of Water Rights for Carbon Trading*, 50 ARIZ. L. REV. 91, 101–102 (2008).

lowed to return to native vegetation, as they do in the CRP program, could be used to produce hay or could be planted in perennials. It is important to note that agricultural carbon sequestration is not just a mechanism to reduce GHG. Because carbon, one of nature's primary building blocks, has been removed from the soil by plowing, restoring it would also replenish soil fertility.[65]

In 2003, it was estimated that over the previous twenty years grassland set aside programs, like CRP, had generated a sixteen percent increase in soil carbon stocks, roughly seven percent per year, and together with improved management practices accounted for twelve MMT of stored carbon per year.[66] Projecting forward, another study estimated potential sequestration at seventy to two hundred twenty-one MMT per year from a combination of land use practices that, in addition to set asides, included restoration of degraded lands and conservation tillage.[67] Other studies likewise indicate significant sequestration potential on agricultural lands,[68] especially in the northern Corn Belt and the Mississippi Delta.[69]

Although the sequestration theory makes sense logically, recent events and more sophisticated studies suggest the projections may be overly optimistic. First of all, the price of grain is driving thousands of farmers in precisely the opposite direction; they want to plant as much land as possible to take advantage of prices near ten dollars per bushel for wheat and eight dollars per bushel for corn.[70] Since October, 2007 over two million acres have been removed from federal set aside programs.[71] Driven by a demand for land on which to grow corn for ethanol production, in response to rapidly escalating energy costs, such record-breaking prices make it easy to decide to return land to crops rather than collect the average CRP payment of $51 per acre.[72] Obviously, making that choice means that no carbon is being sequestered; it also means that much of the carbon that was stored in the CRP vegetation is released into the atmosphere, as is that emitted by the agricultural equipment required to plant, cultivate and harvest the additional acreage and to process the biomass into fuel.[73]

---

65. John M. Baker, *et al.*, *Tillage and Soil Carbon Sequestration—What Do We Really Know?*, 118 AGRICULTURE, ECOSYSTEMS AND ENVIRONMENT 1,1 (2007), citing R. LAL, *et al.*, THE POTENTIAL OF U. S. CROPLANDS TO SEQUESTER CARBON AND MITIGATE THE GREENHOUSE EFFECT (CRC 1998).

66. PAUSTIAN, *et. al.*, *supra* note 44, at 3, 11, citing S. M . Ogle, *et. al.*, *Uncertainty in Estimating Land Use and Management Impacts on Soil Organic Carbon Storage for U. S. Agriculture between 1982 and 1997*, 9 GLOBAL CHANGE BIOLOGY 1521–1542 (2003). Data for the studies was limited to the top 30 cm. of soil, a fact that will be important to a subsequent discussion. *See* text accompanying notes 77–81, *infra*.

67. PAUSTIAN, *et al.*, *supra* note 44, at 12, citing R. Lal, *et. al.*, *Achieving Soil Carbon Sequestration in the United States: A Challenge to Policy Makers*, 168 SOIL SCIENCE 827–45 (2003).

68. Improved farm and range land management could store 180 MMT annually. *Depositing Carbon, supra* note 61. Potential storage from cropland, grasslands and land restoration amounts to approximately 200 MMT by 2030. IPCC, *supra* note 43, at 514, citing P. Smith *et. al.*, *Greenhouse Gas Mitigation in Agriculture*, PHILOSOPHICAL TRANSACTIONS OF THE ROYAL SOCIETY, B., 363. doi:10.1098/rtsb.2007.2184.

69. PAUSTIAN, *et al.*, *supra* note 44, at 12, *citing* M. Sperow, *et. al.*, *Potential Soil C Sequestration on U.S. Agricultural Lands*, 57 CLIMATIC CHANGE 319–339 (2003). Somewhat less potential exists in the Piedmont region of the Southeast and in the northern, central and southern Great Plains. *Id.*

70. On June 11, 2008, July wheat was priced at $9.09 per bushel on the Chicago Board of Trade; July corn was priced at $7.03. http://www.cbot.com/cbot/pub/page/0,3181,1322,00.html.

71. David Streitfeld, *As Prices Rise, Farmers Spurn Conservation*, N. Y. TIMES, April 9, 2008, A1, A16. CRP contracts are ten-year agreements which are difficult to break, but when five million acres expired in fall, 2007, only half were renewed. *Id.*

72. *Id.*

73. A 2006 study found that 74–95% of the energy in corn ethanol comes from fossil fuel inputs. ALMUTH ERNSTING, *et al.*, AGROFUELS THREATEN TO ACCELERATE GLOBAL WARMING, http://www.biofuelwatch.org.uk/docs/biofuels-accelerate-climate-change.pdf, *citing* Alexander Farrell *et al.*, *Ethanol Can Contribute to Energy and Environmental Goals*, 311 SCIENCE 27 (2006).

Conservation Tillage

In the face of this trend, is carbon storage by the agricultural community simply a non-starter, or is it possible to nonetheless mitigate carbon emissions through changes in farming practices? The previously discussed sequestration potential projections include a component of conservation tillage, a term covering numerous practices which leave all or part of the stubble from the previous crop on top of the field instead of plowing it under; the new crop is then planted into the stubble and weeds are controlled with herbicides or cover crops instead of through cultivation.[74] Introduced over fifty years ago because of their water conserving potential, such practices also help soils retain nutrients.[75] Likewise carbon which would be released from plowing under crop residues is retained in the soil and in the stubble—hence the practices' sequestration potential. "In fact, no-till is the most efficient management practice for sequestering C in cropland, when compared to cover crops, crop rotation, fertilizer strategies and manure applications."[76] In other words, even with a significant increase in planted acreage, it seems it may nonetheless be possible to reduce CO_2 emissions by sequestering significant amounts of agricultural carbon, while at the same time restoring the soil's vital carbon stocks, through the use of practices that would also retain nutrients, like nitrogen, all the while reducing soil erosion.

Unfortunately, like many win-win solutions that seem too good to be true, there is a fatal flaw in this proposition. The vast majority of studies suggesting the potential of conservation tillage to sequester carbon have been conducted on soil samples no deeper than thirty centimeters.[77] By contrast, when soils below that depth are included, recent studies reveal that the apparent near-gains in carbon levels relative to conventional tillage disappear; one study even shows a small net loss.[78] Because soil health and fertility are directly related to carbon levels, it follows that soils will be less productive when carbon is concentrated close to the surface. For example, no-till soils, which are effectively insulated, are cooler; they also are less penetrable and possess higher bulk density.[79] All these characteristics inhibit deeper root growth, as demonstrated by studies of both maize and winter wheat which reveal that soil root-length densities in no-till soil were greater near the surface than in plowed soil but that, deeper down, densities were greater in plowed soil.[80] In short, it appears that the widely-touted projections for carbon sequestration resulting from conservation tillage are, at best, "premature."[81] As previously discussed, conservation tillage has other advantages—and disadvantages, but it is unwise to urge its wide-spread adoption as a way to sequester carbon.

---

74. NORTH CAROLINA STATE UNIVERSITY, CONSERVATION TILLAGE, http://www.cals.ncsu.edu/sustainable/peet/tillage/tillage.html. By convention, the practices "leave at least 30% of the soil covered by crop residues." *Id.* The increased use of herbicides has made the practices controversial. *Id.*

75. *Id.* Untilled or partially tilled soil retains moisture more effectively than plowed soil; losses from runoff are also reduced. *Id.* Conservation tillage also saves the fossil fuel normally used to power cultivating equipment, although those gains must be offset against the increased fuel needed to produce the higher quantities of herbicides required.

76. Motha and Baier, *supra* note 3, at 163. One study suggests that broad-based adoption of conservation tillage in the U.S. could sequester 24-40 MMT per year. R. Lal, *et al.*, *Achieving Soil Carbon Sequestration in the United States: A Challenge to the Policy Makers*, 168 SOIL SCIENCE 827, 832 (2003).

77. Baker, *supra* note 65, at 2.

78. *Id.* at 3. Because the loss is within the margin of error, the researchers found it not to be significant; they conclude, however, that those results "agree qualitatively with other studies that have shown that in soils under no-till SOC [soil organic carbon] is concentrated near the surface." *Id.*

79. *Id.*

80. *Id.*

81. *Id.* at 5. The authors of the paper on which this discussion relies describe the projections as "artifact[s] of sampling methodology." *Id.* at 4.

Natural Systems Agriculture

If set aside land is being plowed up and hopes for conservation tillage are overly optimistic, are there other practices that can accomplish the goal of agricultural carbon sequestration, or is the idea simply a theory in search of reality? Those working on the cutting edge of agricultural research make a compelling argument that farming based on perennial crops—also known as Natural Systems agriculture—is the wave of the future.[82] Currently the vast majority of our food comes directly or indirectly (as animal feed) from annual crops such as cereal grains and legumes, which occupy eighty percent of the world's farmland.[83] Annual crops, of course, require huge expenditures of numerous resources—including petroleum-based products—year in and year out, and because they pour most of their biological energy into producing seeds, have shallow roots which often do little to hold soil in place or retain moisture. (It was such problems that originally gave rise to the conservation tillage movement). Neither do their root systems store much carbon, even when left in place.[84]

By contrast, perennial plants—eighty-five percent of North American species—renew themselves each year without replanting or cultivation and require no fertilizers, pesticides or herbicides; their denser and deeper roots also inhibit soil erosion, help retain moisture and increase carbon content by fifty percent or more over conventional annual crops.[85] Indeed, on a per acre basis, net carbon emissions (carbon emitted in the process of production minus carbon sequestered) for perennial crops are negative, *i.e.*, more carbon is stored than released. By contrast, net emissions from annual crops are positive in nature, more carbon is released than stored; furthermore, the disparity between the two is dramatic.[86] Clearly farming that mimics nature, Natural Systems Agriculture, offers many agriculturally and environmentally-friendly advantages, not the least of which is healthy soils that by definition sequester high levels of carbon.[87]

While certainly perennial crops are not yet viable food sources, research toward that goal is well-established. "Of the thirteen most widely grown grain and oil-seed crops, ten are capable of hybridization with perennial relatives," and trials are being conducted in a small number of breeding programs across the U.S. and Canada to develop perennial wheat, sorghum, corn, flax

---

82. One well-respected such researcher is geneticist Wes Jackson, founder of the Land Institute in Salina, Kan., author of New Roots for Agriculture (Un. of Nebraska Press 1980) and numerous other books. Wes is a prolific essayist, prominent nation-wide lecturer and winner of the coveted MacArthur Foundation Award. *See, e.g.,* Wes Jackson, *The Genome as an Ecosystem: The Good News/Bad News Implications,* 43 Washburn L. J. 533 (2004). The work of the Land Institute is often written up in major scientific journals. Information about the Land Institute and its work may be found at http://www.landinstitute.org/vnews/display.v/ ART/2000/08/10/37a747b43.

83. Jerry Glover, *et al., Future Farming: A Return to Roots?,* Scientific American, 81, 82 (Aug., 2007).

84. *See* text accompanying notes 77–81, *supra.*

85. Glover, *supra* note 83, at 83, 84; *cf.* David Tilman, *et al., Carbon-Negative Biofuels from Low-Input High-Density Grassland Biomass,* 314 Science 1598 (2006) (Biofuels produced from mixtures of native grassland perennials provide greater energy potential than those produced from annual crops such as corn and soybeans, with less agrichemical pollution).

86. Measured in kg of CO_2-equiv per hectare, the values for annual crops range from 140 to 1,140; values for perennial crops range from -1,050 to -200. Glover, *supra* note 83, at 86.

87. "The benefits of increasing soil carbon are well documented by soil scientists and agronomists. They include increasing soil fertility, improving the moisture-retaining capacity of the soil, improving nitrogen fertilizer use by crops, and making the soil more resilient to climatic stresses." Center for Rural Affairs, Climate Change: Report of a Center for Rural Affairs Task Force 5 (2007), http://www.cfra.org/files/ Climate_Change_and_Agriculture_Report.pdf. The Center for Rural Affairs, in Lyons, Neb., works "to strengthen small businesses, family farms and ranches, and rural communities." It is known for its pioneering work to help rebuild rural America. Information may be found at http://www.cfra.org/.

and oilseed sunflower.[88] At the Land Institute in Salina, Kansas, plant breeders are attempting to domesticate perennial wheatgrass,[89] and Green Lands, Blue Waters, an initiative based in St. Paul, Minnesota, is an advocate for perennial agriculture in the Mississippi River Basin.[90] A perennial wheat program already exists at the University of Western Australia.[91]

These programs exist not to combat global warming but rather to promote sustainable agriculture by fundamentally challenging the paradigm under which that enterprise currently operates. They do, however, also effectively address climate change—and one of its major consequences, increased soil erosion—by introducing farming systems that sequester carbon, thereby affirming the proposition that what is good global warming policy is also good for agriculture.[92] Because such a declaration is unlikely to convince a farming community skeptical about climate change, the proposition is perhaps best put the other around: agricultural practices—and the policies that support them—need foremost to be directed toward the long-term health of the land.

> [T]he national interest here is building quality soils in which carbon is not merely stashed, but in which it is stabilized as humus by living soil organisms that are part of a healthy, productive cycle of life. This process not only alters carbon from a relatively volatile condition in which it might be readily oxidized into the atmosphere, but it strengthens its role as an agent of healthy plant production. Soil must be more than just a carbon dump.[93]

In other words, what makes sense for agriculture will also help mitigate climate change.

Nitrous Oxide

The same may be said with respect to crop agriculture's contribution to N_2O emissions. Nitrogen in fertilizer is broken down by a process known as denitrificaction, the end result of which is a benign form of the element, molecular nitrogen (N_2).[94] Environmentally troublesome nitrates (NO_3) and nitrous oxide (N_2O) are byproducts of the process when it fails to run its full course. Although numerous factors affect whether denitrification continues to its end or terminates prematurely, it is generally true that the healthier the environment in which it occurs, the more likely it is that the process will produce N_2.[95] In particular, with respect to N_2O, the rate of escape (rN_2O) is lowest in high carbon environments—those found in healthy soils.[96]

Although results will be "highly dependent on environmental factors,"[97] numerous management practices can also reduce N_2O emissions; many of the same practices can also decrease NO_3 runoff.[98] Some such techniques are crop rotation that includes nitrogen-fixing legumes,

---

88. Glover, *supra* note 83, at 85, quoting T. Stan Cox, plant breeder at the Land Institute, Salina, Kan.

89. *Id.* For further information about the Land Institute, see note 82, *supra*, and accompanying text.

90. http://www.greenlandsbluewaters.org/.

91. Glover, *supra* note 83, at 85.

92. IPCC, *supra* note 43, at 526.

93. Center for Rural Affairs, *supra* note 87, at 7.

94. *See* note 34, *supra*.

95. Conversation with Jerry Glover, Agroecologist, The Land Institute, Salina, Kan., June 17, 2008.

96. Sasha Kramer, *et al.*, *Reduced Nitrate Leaching and Enhanced Denitrifier Activity and Efficiency in Organically Fertilized Soils*, 103 Proceedings of the National Academy of Sciences 4522, 4522 (2006), http://www.pnas.org/cgi/content/full/103/12/4522?maxtoshow=&HITS=10&hits=10&RESULTFORMAT=& fulltext=nitrate&searchid=1&FIRSTINDEX=0&volume=103&issue=12&resourcetype=HWCIT.

97. *Id.* at 4522.

98. Reduction of NO_3 emissions is normally addressed as a clean water/non-point source pollution issue. Though some management practices address both NO_3 and N_2O, and reducing NO_3 in surface water clearly would decrease indirect N_2O emissions (*see* text accompanying notes 55–58, *supra*), detailed discussion of the topic is generally beyond the scope of this paper. On nonpoint source pollution, see generally sources cited at note 42, *supra*; Dana L. Dinnes, *et al.*, *Nitrogen Management Strategies to Reduce Nitrate Leaching in Tile-Drained Midwestern Soils*, 94 Agron. J. 153 (2002).

with perennial legumes offering the soil health benefits discussed above;[99] precision farming, applying only the amount of fertilizer actually needed[100] (as opposed to using excess quantities as a kind of insurance hedge),[101] and at times when the nitrogen will be readily absorbed by the planted crop instead of being lost into the environment;[102]the use of slow-or controlled-release fertilizer formulations[103] or nitrification inhibitors which slow the breakdown process;[104] and injecting fertilizer into the ground so as to be more plant-accessible, as opposed to applying it to the surface.[105] Not surprisingly, the use of organic fertilizer, or a combination of organic and conventional, has been shown to reduce the rate of N_2O emissions.[106]

Many of these practices are no doubt already being implemented, in part because they are more efficient but mainly because they are dictated by economics: the price of fertilizer is skyrocketing.[107] Plainly, it is in farmers' overwhelming best interest to reduce nitrogen inputs. Doing so will in turn reduce N_2O emissions. In short, just as creating healthy soils reduces climate change by sequestering carbon, using nitrogen-based fertilizers more efficiently also combats one of the prime causes of global warming. Once again, what is good for agriculture, is likewise good for the planet.

Climate change skeptics, please take note.

USDA, Agriculture and Trade Reports: Food Security Assessment, 2007, pp. v, vi, 26, *available at* http://www.ers.usda.gov/Publications/GFA19/ (last visited Nov. 11, 2008):

Summary

The number of food-insecure people in 70 developing countries rose from 849 million to 982 million in 2006–07, USDA's Economic Research Service estimates in *Food Security Assessment,*

---

99. Text accompanying notes 85–87, *supra*. On nitrogen fixation, see generally GERALD W. EVERS, LEGUME NITROGEN FIXATION AND TRANSFER, http://overton.tamu.edu/clover/cool/nfix.htm (last visited Mar. 19, 2008). Deep-rooted, perennial cover crops such as alfalfa and sweet clover leave behind 120–150 pounds of nitrogen per acre. Conversation with Ed Reznicek, organic farmer and field organizer for the Clean Water Farm-Friendly Farm Project at the Kansas Rural Center, Whiting,, Kansas, June 18, 2008. The Kansas Rural Center promotes the long-term health of the land and its people through research, education and advocacy. Information about the organization may be found at http://www.kansasruralcenter.org/. Likewise, soy beans leave behind in the soil one pound of nitrogen per bushel of harvested beans, *id.*, although studies indicate high NO_3 runoff from soybeans (as much a 30–50 times greater than from perennial crops) and that switching from the current soybean-corn pattern to perennials on just ten percent of Mississippi River Basin farms could decrease NO_3 loading by 0.5MMT. Mitsch, *supra* note 42, at 375, 383.

100. IPCC, *supra* note 43, at 507.

101. PAUSTIAN, *et al.*, *supra* note 44, at 15; Mitsch, *et al.*, *supra* note 42, at 376.

102. Applying fertilizer in the fall to save time during spring planting results in nitrogen losses before any nutrients are taken up by the crop. Moreover, even after planting, crop uptake is slowest at the outset of the growing season, increases rapidly during the main growth spurt and then tapers off as the crop nears maturity. Applying fertilizer accordingly would greatly reduce unwanted emissions. PAUSTIAN, *et al.*, *supra* note 44, at 15. *See also* IPCC, *supra* note 43, at 507; Dinnes, *et al.*, *supra* note 98, at 156; Mitsch, *et al.*, *supra* note 42, at 376.

103. IPCC, *supra* note 43, at 507.

104. *Id.* at 507; Dinnes, *et al.*, *supra* note 98, at 159.

105. PAUSTIAN, *et al.*, *supra* note 44, at 15 (In 1997, fertilizer was applied to the surface on about 30 percent of corn, 60 percent of wheat and 70 percent of cotton and potatoes); IPCC, *supra* note 43, at 507.

106. Kramer, *et al.*, *supra* note 96, at 4523. Using strictly organic fertilizer resulted in the smallest nitrogen losses, strictly synthetic the largest; the combination resulted in intermediate losses. *Id.* at 4522. Although the study was conducted in orchards, the results are applicable to crop agriculture. *Id.* at 4526.

107. For example, the cost of anhydrous ammonia has gone from about $400/ton in the summer of 2007 to about $800/ton in the summer of 2008. Conversation with Arlen Wilcox, Agronomist, New Horizon Farm & Home Co-op, Paola, Kansas, June 20, 2008.

2007. Food-insecure people are defined as those consuming less than 2,100 calories a day, the nutritional target set by the United Nation's Food and Agriculture Organization (FAO).

What Is the Issue?

Over the next decade, a slowdown in worldwide economic growth is projected to combine with food and fuel price hikes to contribute to an ongoing deterioration in global food security. This will have a particularly negative impact on the developing countries that are already the most food-insecure—those in Sub-Saharan Africa. By 2017, SSA will account for more than half of the food-insecure people of the 70 countries while accounting for about a quarter of the population. The most significant regional change is occurring and will continue to occur in Asia. Previous projections had predicted long-term improvements in food security in Asia, but current analysis shows those improvements slowing to a halt.

The report, the latest in an ERS annual series, examines food prices and other factors that affect food security globally, regionally, and in 70 developing countries studied. Researchers also measure the food distribution gap (the amount of food needed to raise consumption of each income group to the nutritional requirement) and examine the factors that shape food security. Food security is defined as access by all people at all times to enough food for an active and healthy life.

What Did the Study Find?

In 2002, the declining commodity prices of the last few decades changed direction. Grain prices jumped about 50 percent from 2005–07. Based on USDA long-term projections, about 90 percent of that price shift will persist during the next decade. Low-income developing countries feel the price pressure even more than other countries because food expenditures make up such a large share of total household expenditures (more than 50 percent for many countries reviewed in this report). The recent oil price hikes add to the financial burden because the higher energy import bill can squeeze out the imports of necessities such as food and other raw materials. The financial pressure of price hikes is particularly overwhelming for those countries that were vulnerable to food insecurity at the outset.

The food distribution gap is estimated at about 44 million tons for 2007. That is almost three times the average national-level gap (the amount of food needed to meet the nutritional requirement at the aggregate, national level), reflecting the intensity and depth of the problem that is due to skewed income distribution within countries. By 2017, the distribution gap is projected to increase to more than 57 million tons. This is more than 7 times the amount of food aid received by these 70 countries in 2006.

As noted, earlier projections had predicted food security in Asia to move in a positive direction, but that progress has halted. Food security in Latin American and Caribbean (LAC) countries and the Commonwealth of Independent States (CIS) countries is projected to improve in the next decade. Sub-Saharan Africa's average calorie intake is not much higher than the daily requirement of 2,100 per day, and is by far the lowest in the world. Growth in production of grains, the main food group in the diet, was about 3 percent per year between 1990 and 2006, but on a per capita basis the gain was modest because of the 2.7-percent annual growth in population. ERS estimates that SSA had 457 million food-insecure people in 2007, nearly matching the total estimated for Asia. So, while SSA had nearly the same number of food-insecure people as Asia, the food security situation of SSA was far worse because SSA had only about a third of the total population of the Asian countries.

Asia, with more than 60 percent of the population of the 70 countries, accounted for less than half of the 982 million food-insecure people that ERS estimated for 2007. Although in absolute value the number of food-insecure people is projected to increase, Asia's share of the total population of the 70 countries is projected to decline slightly through 2017. Over the next 10 years, just over 20 percent of Asia's population will continue to be food-insecure. After averaging 2 percent per year through the 1990s, Asia's population growth is projected to slow to about 1.4 percent per year through the next decade, thereby reducing pressure on resources.

Food supplies in the LAC region increased during the last two decades, leading to improvements in food security. The role of food imports grew through time as domestic food production could not keep up with the growing food demand. Income growth has been the main force behind the increase in consumption. In terms of nutritional availability at the national level, all countries, with the exception of Haiti, had adequate food for their population in 2007. However, because of extremes in income from a small group of very wealthy consumers to a large group of very poor consumers at least 20 percent of the population in all countries (except for Jamaica) did not have access to adequate food to meet nutritional targets. The most severely affected countries were Haiti, where 80 percent of the population were food-insecure, the Dominican Republic, and Nicaragua, where 60 percent were food-insecure in 2007.

How Was the Study Conducted?

Food production estimates for 2007 are preliminary, based on USDA data as of January 2008, with supplemental data from the United Nations' Food and Agriculture Organization and World Food Program. Financial and macro economic data are based on the latest World Bank data. Projected macro economic variables are either extrapolated based on calculated growth rates for the 1990s and early 2000s or are World Bank projections / estimations. Projections/estimates of food availability include food aid, with the assumption that each country will receive the 2004–06 average level of food aid throughout the next decade.

....

Conclusions

The food-security indicators estimated for the study countries paint a bleak picture of not only the current situation, but also the intensifying of the problem over the next decade, assuming no significant changes in trends in production and financial situation of countries. Recent World Bank statements have been consistent with these findings and have indicated that high food prices are threatening recent gains in overcoming poverty and malnutrition and are likely to persist over the medium term. World Bank President Robert B. Zoellick, in the opening press briefing at the World Bank / International Monetary Fund meetings, addressed the challenges ahead: "This is not just about meals foregone today or about increasing social unrest. This is about lost learning potential for children and adults in the future, stunted intellectual and physical growth. Even more, we estimate that the effect of this food crisis on poverty reduction worldwide is in the order of seven lost years. So we need to address this not just as an immediate emergency but also in the medium term for development." (Washington, DC, April 10, 2008).

The situation in SSA is of major concern because of the deep poverty and food insecurity that existed prior to the food and fuel price hikes, particularly in countries that are struggling with political instability. According to FAO, the cereal import bill for low-income, food-deficit countries in Africa is estimated to increase by 74 percent 2007–08. This is happening at the same time these countries are facing a trade deficit. The IMF projects a slow-down in export earnings in SSA because of weak global growth, particularly in the United States and, to a lesser extent, in Europe (IMF, April 2008). Inflationary pressure is compounding the problem by raising production costs as well as reducing consumer purchasing power.

Official development assistance (ODA) plays a critical role in reducing the financial pressure on poor countries. ODA, excluding debt relief, rose only 2.4 percent in 2007. The aid to SSA increased by 10 percent in 2007, but remains far short of the 2005 donor commitment to double aid to Africa by 2010. Food aid, the major international safety net for these countries, has been trending downward during the last decade and its future path is not clear. Since food aid allocations are based on donors' cash donations, the higher grain prices mean a reduction in quantities unless major steps are taken to increase the budget to purchase grains and other commodity staples for delivery to food-insecure countries.

VII. Fire and Flood

A. Fire and the Health of the Lands

2005 FLANNERY at 86 (footnote omitted):

> The 1997–78 El Niño year has been immortalized by the World Wide Fund for Nature (now the WWF) as "the year the world caught fire." Drought had a stranglehold on a large part of the planet, and so fires burned on every continent, but it was in the normally wet rain forests of Southeast Asia that the conflagrations reached their peak. There, approximately 25 million acres burned, of which half was ancient rain forest. On the island of Borneo, 2 million acres were lost—an area almost the size of the Netherlands. Many of the burned forests will never recover on a time scale meaningful to human beings, and the impact that this has had on Borneo's unique fauna will, in all probability, never be fully known.
>
> Climatologist Kevin Trenberth and his colleagues believe that the 1997–98 event was an extreme manifestation of a more general impact on the El Niño–La Niña cycle by global warming....

J. MADELEINE NASH, EL NIÑO: UNLOCKING THE SECRETS OF THE MASTER WEATHER-MAKER 209 (Warner Books 2002):

> The great majority of the fires that occurred in 1997 and 1998 were related in some way to El Niño-inspired droughts, including the fires that seared at least eight million acres of forested land in the Brazilian Amazon. Actually, the damage was probably far greater than that. Most of the fires that spread along the forest floor went undetected, but the damaging wounds they inflicted, researchers noted, would make it easier for the fires the next time to cut into the forest more deeply.

JOHN HOUGHTON, GLOBAL WARMING: THE COMPLETE BRIEFING 250, 251 (3d ed. Cambridge Un. Press 2004):

> The total area covered by forest is almost one-third of the world's land area, of which ninety-five percent is natural forest and five percent planted forest. About forty-seven percent of forests worldwide are tropical, nine percent subtropical, eleven percent temperate and thirty-three percent boreal.
>
> At the global level, the net loss in forest area during the 1990s was an estimated 940,000 km^2 (2.4% of total forest area). This was the combined effect of a deforestation rate of about 150,000 km^2 per year and a rate of forest increase of about 50,000 km^2 per year. Deforestation of tropical forests averaged about one percent per year.
>
> ....
>
> Reducing deforestation can therefore make a substantial contribution to slowing the increase of greenhouse gases in the atmosphere, as well as the provision of other benefits such as guarding biodiversity and avoiding soil degradation.

Climate Change and Wildfire Policy

Robert B. Keiter, Wallace Stegner Distinguished Professor of Law, Director, Wallace Stegner Center for Land, Resources and the Environment, University of Utah, S.J. Quinney College of Law, 332 South 1400 East, Salt Lake City, UT 84112-0730; Tel: (801) 581-5035, Fax: (801) 581-6897, robert.keiter@law.utah.edu.

Global climate change is widely expected to alter existing wildfire regimes in many parts of the world. A warmer climate will likely mean longer and more severe fire seasons with increased property damages, suppression costs, and smoke pollution. Warmer temperatures and greater precipitation will facilitate vegetation growth, which will produce a ready source of combustible fuel for wildfire during drought periods. More fire will prompt changes in ecosystem structure and processes, creating new resource management challenges on both public and private lands. More burning will also mean more uncontrolled carbon emissions into the atmosphere that will only further exacerbate the global warming problem. In addition, more burning will destroy more vegetation, and thus reduce the effectiveness of forests and grasslands as a carbon sink. And because fire is an often unpredictable natural disturbance that has shaped terrestrial ecosystems for millennia, there are no easy fixes to the lurking problems.

Law and policy are just beginning to address the complex challenges that an expanded wildfire regime poses in the face of warming global temperatures. In the United States, until recently, federal fire policy was focused exclusively on extinguishing all fires in order to protect valuable resources and nearby communities. Fire was viewed as an evil or destructive force, not as a key ecological disturbance process necessary to sustain terrestrial ecosystems. Since the early 1970s, however, federal policy has begun to acknowledge a role for fire on the public lands, and it has shifted toward allowing some naturally ignited fires to burn in remote areas and to using fire as a management tool to curb the threat of runaway wildfires.[1] Federal fire policy is now largely directed toward reducing the fuel build-up from the suppression years, minimizing the legal hurdles involved in such projects, and increasing protection for the growing wildland urban interface zone.[2] The implications of global climate change have yet to factor into these policies in a meaningful way.

This essay will examine the relationship between global climate change and wildfire with a focus on legal policy developments in the United States. It begins with a description of the role that fire plays in the human environment, including how scientists perceive global warming will impact existing fire regimes and the predicted attendant consequences. Next it sets forth the legal regime and policy choices that govern wildfire management, emphasizing developments at the federal level, but also noting the role of state and local policies in fire management. The article concludes by examining whether current laws and policies are sufficient to address the challenges that wildfire will likely pose in an era of warmer temperatures and altered climatic patterns, including potential legal and policy revisions to address these looming challenges.

---

1. For a general overview of wildfire and fire management history, see STEPHEN J. PYNE, FIRE IN AMERICA: A CULTURAL HISTORY OF WILDLAND AND RURAL FIRE (Un. Of Washington Press 1982); DAVID CARLE, BURNING QUESTIONS: AMERICA'S FIGHT WITH NATURE'S FIRES (Praeger Trade 2002); ROCKY BARKER, SCORCHED EARTH: HOW THE FIRES OF YELLOWSTONE CHANGED AMERICA (Island Press 2005).

2. *See* Robert B. Keiter, *The Law of Fire: Reshaping Public Land Policy In an Era of Ecology and Litigation*, 36 ENVTL. L. 301 (2006).

A Warmer Climate Means More Fire

Fire has long been viewed as an important disturbance factor in most forest and grassland ecosystems, regularly serving as a cyclical source of ecological renewal. Long before European settlement in the United States, fires periodically burned across the continent, sparked by lightning and nourished by available fuel sources as well as prevailing weather conditions. In periods of drought, especially when combustible fuels had accumulated, these fires sometimes rampaged across the landscape destroying most everything in their path, not unlike the 1988 Yellowstone fires. At other times, the fire season might be more restrained and less destructive, particularly in those settings where wildfires occurred regularly at short intervals, as in the Ponderosa pine ecosystems in the Southwest where fire was historically confined to understory vegetation.[3] The Native Americans also frequently used fire as a tool for hunting, agricultural, and military purposes. Yet regardless of its origins, fire behavior on the landscape was primarily a function of local ecological and climatic conditions.

The arrival of European settlers in the new world changed the role that fire played across the continent. Fearing fire's destructive potential and intent on protecting human settlements and valuable resources, the settlers generally sought to control and suppress wildfires, though fire was also employed to clear forested lands and to help create fire-safe perimeters around vulnerable communities. As the country filled in with westward migration, the pressures to control wildfires intensified, eventually leading federal and state governments to institute an all-out fire suppression policy designed to extinguish any wayward wildfire.[4] Within a few decades, though, this suppression policy came under sharp attack as scientists recognized the salutary ecological role that wildfire had historically played on the landscape. But by then, suppression policies had proven successful enough that many locations—particularly the national forests and other public lands—were beginning to face a serious fuel accumulation problem. More fuel virtually guaranteed more severe and destructive fires during drought conditions.

Global climate change, of course, presages just such conditions in many locations across the United States and elsewhere in the world, where similar fire policies have held sway over the past century or longer. Indeed, the Intergovernmental Panel on Climate Change (IPCC), in its Fourth Assessment Report, anticipates much higher global temperatures, particularly in northern latitudes, noting that greenhouse gas emissions due to human activities have not only grown since pre-industrial times, but experienced a significant 70 percent increase from 1970–2004.[5] For the period 1955–2005, the greatest world-wide temperature increases were recorded in Alaska and northwestern Canada,[6] coincidentally also locations with expansive and potentially flammable forest cover. More precipitation is falling as rain rather than snow, and snowmelt (or the spring runoff) in the western North America mountains occurred 1 to 4 weeks earlier in 2002 than in 1948. Spring green-up is likewise beginning 10–14 days earlier, particularly in the temperate latitudes of the Northern Hemisphere. As a result, the IPCC expresses "very high confidence" that in North America "disturbances such as wildfire and insect outbreaks are increasing and are likely to intensify in a warmer future with drier soils and longer growing seasons."[7]

---

3. Stephen F. Arno and Steven Allison-Bunnell, Flames in Our Forest: Disaster or Renewal 68–70 (Island Press 2002).

4. *Id.* at 12–19; Carle, *supra* note 1, at 11–36.

5. Intergovernmental Panel on Climate Change Fourth Assessment Report, Climate Change 2007: Synthesis Report, Summary for Policymakers 2, 4 (Cambridge Un. Press 2007).

6. IPCC Fourth Assessment Report, Working Group II Report: Impacts, Adaptation and Vulnerability 620 (Cambridge Un. Press 2007) [hereinafter IPCC Fourth Rpt. W.G. II].

7. IPCC Fourth Rpt. W.G. II, *supra* note 6, at 619. These general findings follow closely those reached by the IPCC in its Third Assessment Report, which predicted the fire season was likely to lengthen and the area burned was likely to increase significantly. *Id.* at 620.

All of these global warming phenomena have implications for the incidence and severity of fire on the landscape. According to the IPCC, "warmer summer temperatures are expected to extend the annual window of high fire ignition risk by 10–30%, and could result in increased area burned of 74–118% in Canada by 2100."[8] One study reveals that during the last three decades the wildfire season in the western United States has already increased by 78 days, while the burn duration of larger fires has increased from 7.5 days to 37.1 days.[9] Another study reports that wildfires in the United States since 1980 have annually burned 22,000 square kilometers, compared to an average of 13,000 square kilometers burned annually from 1920–1980—a near doubling in size.[10] Scientists generally agree that these trends in the size and number of fires correspond closely to rising spring and summer temperature patterns over the past 35 years.[11]

Across the United States, wildfire regimes have historically varied in response to different regional ecological and climatic conditions. The West and Southeast tend to have more severe fire seasons than the Northeast and Midwest, where extensive settlement and forest cover removal have effectively limited wildfires. The western fire season occurs mostly during summer months,[12] while the southeastern fire season usually happens during the spring time. In Alaska, wildfires are typically larger than elsewhere in the country; the average fire in the lower 48 states will burn 48 acres, while the average Alaskan fire will consume 666 acres.[13] Scientists generally view wildfire as the most important natural ecological disturbance that occurs in western ecosystems, which have long been shaped by fire-related events.

Global climate change, with warmer temperatures and more precipitation, will plainly impact these fire-adapted ecosystems. Between 2040–69, the IPCC forecasts a temperature increase of 1.5–5.8°C, which is much greater than the 0.9°C temperature increase that the western United States has experienced over recent decades,[14] when wildfire activity has exceeded historic levels in many locations due to warmer springs and longer, drier summers. Any such increase in temperature will mean an earlier snowmelt and earlier drying of vegetation and soils, which will further increase the length and severity of the wildfire season. Several western states—particularly in the Southwest where drought conditions have recently prevailed—have already experienced the

---

8. *Id.* at 619.

9. Anthony L. Westerling *et al.*, *Warming and Earlier Spring Increase Western U.S. Forest Wildfire Activity*, 313 SCIENCE 940–43 (2006). *See also* B.J. Stocks *et al.*, *Large Forest Fires in Canada, 1959–1997*, 107 J. GEOPHYS. RES. 8149 (2002) (noting a similar annual increase in Canadian burned area since 1990); E.S. Kasischke and M.R. Turetsky, *Recent Changes in Fire Regime across the North American Boreal Region—Spatial and Temporal Patterns of Burning across Canada and Alaska*, 33 GEOPHYSICAL RESEARCH LETTER L09703 (2006) (finding that burned area in the North American boreal region increased from 6500 square kilometers annually during the 1960s to 29,700 square kilometers annually during the 1990s).

10. T. Schoennagel *et al.*, *The Interaction of Fire, Fuels, and Climate across Rocky Mountain Forests*, 54 BIOSCIENCE 661–76 (2004). *See also* Westerling *et al.*, *supra* note 9 (finding that the forested area burned in the western United States since 1986 is 6.7 times larger than the area burned from 1970–1986).

11. *See* Testimony of Thomas W. Swetnam and Anthony L. Westerling, Senate Energy and Natural Resources Comm., Hearing on Impacts of Global Climate Change on Wildfire Activity in the United States, Sept. 24, 2007 [hereinafter Swetnam and Westerling Testimony]; Westerling *et al.*, *supra* note 9.

12. In the Southwest, the fire season usually arrives during the spring months, and then moves northward following the rising temperatures. Summer monsoon rains often help dampen southwestern fires, though sometimes not in bad drought years.

13. Sonya Senkowsky, *A Burning Interest in Boreal Forests: Researchers in Alaska Link Fires with Climate Change*, 51 BIOSCIENCE 916, 920 (2001).

14. Anthony L. Westerling *et al.*, *Warming and Earlier Spring Increase Western U.S. Forest Wildfire Activity*, 313 SCIENCE 940, 943 (2006); *see also* Steven W. Running, *Is Global Warming Causing More, Larger Wildfires?* 313 SCIENCE 927, 928 (2006).

largest wildfires in recent history, including Arizona, Colorado, and Oregon in 2002, Texas in 2006, and Utah in 2007.[15] Several studies predict that the area burned across the western United States will at least double by the year 2100.[16]

These climate-related fire impacts will vary locally, with the Rocky Mountain region likely to be most heavily affected. In the northern Rockies, scientists project that earlier and warmer spring seasons will mean drier forests later during the summer months when the wildfire danger is greatest.[17] They also believe warmer temperatures will create biological changes: One study predicts that a 3.5°C temperature increase in the Rocky Mountains will cause a 2000 feet elevation change in vegetation patterns and shift existing vegetation over 200 miles northward, profoundly altering local fire regimes.[18] In savanna and chaparral ecosystems, like those that prevail across much of southern California, a warmer and drier climate will mean more frequent fires due to a shortened fire cycle and the invasion of weedy plant species better adapted to frequent fires.[19] Even in the arid Mojave Desert ecosystem, it is predicted that increased carbon in the atmosphere will stimulate plant growth in wet years and ultimately result in more frequent fires and corresponding changes in vegetation.[20] In contrast, the Pacific Northwest region is likely to become wetter and may thus experience fewer fires in the coastal forests.[21] Some scientists, though, note that large fires have recently occurred in relatively wet forest types, concluding that climate warming may be a more important factor in these fire regimes than precipitation, forest structure, and past fire suppression practices.[22] Similar variations are evident at the state level: One study predicts that fire regimes in Montana, Wyoming, and New Mexico will prove more sensitive to climate changes, while California and Nevada will prove less sensitive to these changes.[23]

As an ecological matter, fires change forest density and composition, which will then affect future fire regimes. By most estimates, drier conditions and more fires will render forests more susceptible to insects and diseases, and these blighted forests will in turn provide even more fuel for future wildfires. Severe insect-related tree mortality is already evident in Colorado, where beetles have devastated over 1.5 million acres;[24] extensive beetle-caused losses have also occurred

---

15. Swetnam and Westerling Testimony, *supra* note 11.

16. Donald McKenzie *et al.*, *Climatic Change, Wildfire, and Conservation*, 18 Con. Bio. 890, 897 (2004); Running, *supra* note 14, at 928; *see also* Yongqiang Liu *et al.*, *CO_2 Emissions from Wildfires in the U.S.: Present Status and Future Trends* 11 (available from author) (concluding that "wildfire emissions of CO_2 in the contiguous U.S. are expected to increase by 50 percent by 2050 and be doubled by 2100 due to the greenhouse effect").

17. Westerling *et al.*, *supra* note 9, at 943.

18. Testimony of John A. Helms, Scientific Assessment of Effects of Climate Change on Wildfire, Before Senate Comm. on Energy and Natural Resources, Sept. 24, 2007. Warmer temperatures have already increased growing seasons in many locations, enabling some tree species, such as the aspen in Colorado and the lodgepole pine in northern Canada, to expand their range while also being displaced elsewhere.

19. *See* James M. Lenihan *et al.*, The Response of Vegetation Distribution, Ecosystem Productivity, and Fire in California to Future Climate Scenarios Simulated by the MCi Dynamic Vegetation Model (Calif. Climate Change Center 2006); McKenzie, *supra* note 16, at 898.

20. Stanley D. Smith *et al.*, *Elevated CO_2 Increases Productivity and Invasive Species Success in an Arid Ecosystem*, 408 Nature 79 (2000); *see also* U.S. Govt. Accountability Office, Climate Change: Agencies Should Develop Guidance for Addressing the Effects on Federal Land and Water Resources 27 (2007).

21. U.S. Forest Service, Pacific Northwest Research Station, *Western Forests, Fire Risk, and Climate Change*, 6 Science Update 7 (2004).

22. *See* Liu *et al.*, *supra* note 16, at 8; Swetnam and Westerling Testimony, *supra* note 11; McKenzie *et al.*, *supra* note 16, at 893.

23. McKenzie *et al.*, *supra* note 16, at 897.

24. Eryn Gable, *Forests: Coloradans Try to Get Ahead of Beetles*, Land Letter, March 20, 2008.

among pinyon pine forests in the Southwest and lodgepole pine forests in British Columbia.[25] High tree mortality corresponds directly with more severe fires, enabling what might have been a surface fire to burn into the forest canopy to become a "crown fire" that has maximum destructive potential. Although forest ecosystems might be resilient enough to withstand one or two stressors, the cumulative impact of warmer temperatures, insect invasions, disease, and intensified fire will almost certainly alter these systems outside the range of historical variability and could render them ecologically unsustainable.[26] Moreover, these changes will reverberate throughout the ecosystem, affecting stream flow patterns and run-off conditions, as well as wildlife populations and habitat conditions.[27]

Forested landscapes can serve as a carbon sink to absorb atmospheric carbon, and thus help reduce global warming. In fact, northern boreal forests are widely regarded as the largest carbon sink in the world.[28] Although ecosystems in the United States released more carbon than they stored until 1977, they have since become a net carbon sink, due largely to forest expansion in the West and forest re-growth in the East.[29] But climate change could change this dramatically: Warmer and drier conditions will mean longer and more severe wildfires that will release more carbon into the atmosphere. These same fires will consume forested landscapes and thus reduce (or potentially eliminate) their carbon storage capacity.[30] Already wildfires on public lands in the West and Southeast release over ten tons of carbon dioxide per square kilometer.[31] In 2005, wildfires across the United States cumulatively released 140 million tons of carbon dioxide into the atmosphere.[32] At these levels, wildfires are annually adding atmospheric carbon equivalent to forty percent of fossil fuel carbon emissions.[33] Even more striking, one projection estimates that climate change will increase wildfire carbon emissions by almost 150 percent in the Southwest and by 100 percent in the northern United States, with an overall national increase of fifty percent.[34] It may therefore be difficult, in the face of global warming, to sustain the nation's forests as a net carbon sink.

Other factors, such as ocean water temperatures and related El Niño events, are also known to influence regional climatic patterns and wildfire behavior. These ocean-atmosphere oscillations, which include El Niño-Southern Oscillation (ENSO), the Pacific Decadal Oscillation (PDO), and the Atlantic Multi-decadal Oscillation (AMO), operate on a variable multi-year time scale to

---

25. John A. Helms Testimony, *supra* note 18 (noting that in British Columbia about 23 million acres of lodgepole pine were affected by bark beetles in 2006, and that in the Southwest about 3.8 million acres of pinyon pine were affected by bark beetles in 2003).

26. McKenzie *et al.*, *supra* note 16, at 898; Swetnam and Westerling Testimony, *supra* note 11.

27. McKenzie *et al.*, *supra* note 16; *see also* ch. 3, §§ III–IV above (discussing the water and wildlife impacts of climate change).

28. Senkowsky, *supra* note 13, at 916.

29. U.S. Forest Service, Pacific Northwest Research Station, *supra* note 21, at 8.

30. *Id.* at 8. In far northern regions, more severe forest fire events would likely increase permafrost melting, which could reduce carbon storage capacity in the soils and lead to even more carbon released into the atmosphere. *See* Senkowsky, *supra* note 13, at 919. A significant loss of carbon storage capacity in local "peatland" was observed during the large 1997 Indonesian fires, when a net release of carbon equivalent to 13–40 percent of the annual worldwide carbon emissions from fossil fuels occurred. *See* Susan E. Page *et al.*, *The Amount of Carbon Released from Peat and Forest Fires in Indonesia During 1997*, 420 NATURE 61 (2002).

31. Yon-Quiang Liu, *Wildland Fire and CO_2 Emissions*, SRS-4104 SCIENCE HIGHLIGHTS (fiscal year 2006).

32. Helms Testimony, *supra* note 18 (*citing* EPA, *Inventory of U.S. Greenhouse Gas Emissions and Sinks: 1990–2005* (2007), at www.epa.gov/climatechange/emissions/downloads06/07CR.pdf. *See also* Senkowsky, *supra* note 13, at 918 (estimating that greenhouse gases emitted annually from North American fires are equal to one third of the greenhouse gases emitted from the world's transportation sector).

33. Running, *supra* note 14, at 928.

34. Liu, *supra* note 31.

produce long lasting atmospheric high and low pressure systems that have been positively correlated to the frequency and severity of regional wildfire seasons. In the Southwest and Southeast, for example, the ENSO generally produces wetter conditions and less fire activity during cooler, rainier El Niño events, while the drier La Niña events will ordinarily produce more fire activity. Although these oscillation cycles appear to have triggered drought conditions and more fires in parts of the West, the historical evidence gleaned from similar periods in the past do not correspond with the large-scale fire events of recent years. This strongly suggests that global warming trends are playing an increasingly important role in recent large-scale wildfire patterns, which cannot be explained solely by El Niño and similar atmospheric events.[35]

The state of California, with its long history of destructive wildfire events and with its proactive approach to climate change, has sponsored several recent studies to better understand how warmer temperatures will affect local fire regimes. One modeling study concludes that increased temperatures will likely cause larger and more frequent wildfires in the state's forested and mountainous regions, which are less influenced by precipitation amounts, putting the state's growing wildland urban interface communities at heightened risk, particularly in the Sierra Nevada foothills outside Sacramento.[36] Another modeling study finds that climate change will most likely alter the composition of fuels, thus increasing the intensity of fires in grass and brush-dominated ecosystems and resulting in more fires escaping initial containment—a particularly troubling conclusion since several of the state's recent devastating fires have occurred in similar settings, namely the Berkeley-Oakland, Santa Barbara, San Diego, and Los Angeles areas.[37] Yet another modeling study found that warmer temperatures will cause significant changes in local vegetation patterns that could result in a 9–15 percent increase in the total area burned by the end of the century.[38] Researchers have also projected that warmer and windier conditions in northern California portend a fifty percent increase in the amount of acreage burned and will double the number of escaped fires.[39] In sum, these conclusions paint a picture of larger and more destructive fires that will further reshape the state's ecosystems and significantly increase the risk to human life and property.

Any substantial increase in the incidence and severity of wildfires will generate cascading environmental and economic impacts with important policy implications. A warmer climate and more fires will alter wildlife habitat and displace some species, which could be harmful or even fatal for those species with specific habitat needs. Many scientists believe that higher temperatures and more widespread fire activity could alter ecosystems in national parks and other nature reserves, and thus drive protected species from these sanctuaries. Displaced wildlife may not find suitable habitat on adjoining landscapes, many of which have been intensively developed and se-

---

35. *See* Westerling *et al.*, *supra* note 9, at 943; Swetnam and Westerling Testimony, *supra* note 11; Statements of Ann Bartuska, U.S. Forest Service, Deputy Chief, and Susan Conrad, U.S. Forest Service, Fire Ecology Research, National Program Leader, Before U.S. Senate Comm. on Energy and Natural Resources, Hearing on Scientific Assessments of the Impacts of Global Climate Change on Wildfire Activity in the United States, Sept. 24, 2007. *See also* Thomas Kitzberger *et al.*, *Contingent Pacific-Atlantic Ocean Influence on Multicentury Wildfire Synchrony over Western North America*, 104 PROCEEDINGS NATL. ACAD. SCIENCES 543 (2007).

36. ANTHONY WESTERLING AND BENJAMIN BRYANT, CLIMATE CHANGE AND WILDFIRE IN AND AROUND CALIFORNIA: FIRE MODELING AND LOSS MODELING 1, 24 (California Climate Change Center, 2006).

37. JEREMY S. FRIED *et al.*, PREDICTING THE EFFECT OF CLIMATE CHANGE ON WILDFIRE SEVERITY AND OUTCOMES IN CALIFORNIA: PRELIMINARY ANALYSIS 42–44 (California Climate Change Center, 2006).

38. JAMES M. LENIHAN *et al.*, THE RESPONSE OF VEGETATION DISTRIBUTION, ECOSYSTEM PRODUCTIVITY, AND FIRE IN CALIFORNIA TO FUTURE CLIMATE SCENARIOS SIMULATED BY THE MC1 DYNAMIC VEGETATION MODEL v (California Climate Change Center, 2006).

39. Jeremy S. Fried *et al.*, *The Impact of Climate Change on Wildfire Severity: A Regional Forecast for Northern California*, 64 CLIMATIC CHANGE 169–194 (2004).

verely fragmented, leaving the creatures stranded and subject to eventual extinction.[40] On the economic front, hotter temperatures and an expanded wildfire regime could adversely affect local businesses that depend on tourism by discouraging visitation and limiting recreational opportunities.[41] A charred landscape with little wildlife is rarely attractive to visit. More extensive fires will require additional financial resources for fire fighting efforts, which could reduce the level of funds devoted to fuel removal and other fire control efforts. In short, any assessment of the potential policy options for addressing wildfire in a warmer world must take into account the full range of potential ecological and economic costs, as well as those immediately associated with wildfire management.

Wildfire Policy and Law

Few natural resources policies have undergone such dramatic changes over the years as have those involving wildfire. Where fire was once seen merely as a destructive force that must be suppressed, it is now viewed as a vital ecological process that has historically shaped forest and grassland ecosystems. But decades of fire suppression have created highly flammable forests, and this has spawned a new interest in removing unnatural fuel accumulations, in part to protect burgeoning wildland urban interface communities. Until recently, these dramatic policy changes have had little impact on the legal framework governing fire, which has long given the federal land management agencies broad discretion to control fire, subject in recent years to compliance with the environmental laws. But Congress and the federal agencies have now adopted a more aggressive approach to controlling the fire threat and modified the environmental laws to do so. And Congress has even recently acknowledged a linkage between fire policy and carbon management.

Although the early settlers in North America regularly used fire as a productive tool, they soon came to fear runaway wildfires that threatened entire communities and nearby timber resources. But even as communities moved toward an aggressive fire suppression policy, it was apparent that few of them had the resources necessary to control large scale wildfires. Many of these fires originated on adjacent federally owned lands, often on the newly established forest reserves, which made the federal government the logical entity to take responsibility for fire control.[42] In 1905, the newly created Forest Service was ready to assume that role, as reflected in the new agency's first policy manual: "Probably the greatest single benefit derived by the community and the nation from forest reserves is insurance against the destruction of property, timber resources, and water supply by fire.... [N]o duty [is] more important than protecting the reserves from forest fires."[43] Congress gave its blessing to this policy by creating an open-ended funding process that handed the agency a blank check for its firefighting efforts.

During the devastating 1910 fire season, lightning-ignited blazes burned out of control across the northern Rocky Mountains, claiming 85 lives and leaving several towns in ashes. The 1910 fires traumatized the new Forest Service and impelled it to adopt an all-out fire suppression policy.[44] Congress responded too with legislation that provided federal funding to promote cooperative federal-state firefighting efforts.[45] Despite these initiatives, it was nearly impossible for the

---

40. *See* McKenzie *et al.*, *supra* note 16, at 898–99; *see also* chapter 3, § III(A), (B) above (discussing climate change and biodiversity).

41. IPCC Fourth Rpt. Wk. G. II, *supra* note 6, at 634.

42. *See* Keiter, *Law of Fire*, *supra* note 2, at 304–05.

43. U.S. Dept. of Agric., Forest Service, The Use of the National Forest Reserves: Regulations and Instructions 63 (1905).

44. Stephen J. Pyne, Year of the Fires: The Story of the Great Fires of 1910 (Mountain Press Publishing Company 2001).

45. *See infra* notes 59–61 and accompanying text for additional discussion of this legislation.

Forest Service or other federal agencies to mount effective fire suppression efforts in the remote backcountry, where fires continued to burn unabated.

That changed, however, when the New Deal brought the Civilian Conservation Corps (CCC) into existence. The CCC proceeded to construct hundreds of miles of new roads and trails that opened up the backcountry and thus facilitated more aggressive firefighting tactics. And it changed again in the aftermath of World War Two when the Forest Service and its sister agencies began acquiring surplus military aircraft to further extend their firefighting capacity. This heightened federal commitment to fire suppression was neatly captured in the Forest Service's well-publicized Smokey Bear national fire prevention campaign.[46] From 1946–1978, the amount of acreage burned annually by wildfires was cut in half, dropping from two million acres earlier in the century down to less than one million acres.[47]

But by mid-century, scientists were beginning to change their view of fire and its role on the landscape. Rather than seeing wildfires solely as a destructive force, they began to acknowledge that fire played an important role in shaping ecosystems and in reducing wildfire intensity.[48] It was also hard to justify spending large amounts of money to fight wildfires in remote locations far removed from where people lived. As a result, the National Park Service and the Forest Service revised their fire policies by eliminating their blanket full-suppression goal and allowing some wildfires to burn in the backcountry while also utilizing human-ignited blazes to begin restoring some fire-adapted ecosystems.[49] Though the expansive 1988 Yellowstone fires called this nascent effort to restore fire onto the landscape into question politically, the new fire policy survived mostly intact with the agencies agreeing to tighten how they implemented their let-burn strategies.[50] Scientists meanwhile were growing more alarmed about the accumulating fuel loads that were available to fuel ever larger and more intense fires.[51]

Another devastating fire season in 1994 prompted yet another review of federal fire policy and additional changes to address the new realities of increased fire risk and growing urban encroachment adjacent to publicly owned lands. The resulting 1995 Federal Wildland Fire Management Report reiterated that wildfire is "a critical natural process [that] must be reintroduced into the ecosystem," called for improved federal, state, and local coordination, particularly in at-risk urban-wildland interface zones, encouraged more public involvement in establishing fire management plans, and identified protecting human life as the principal priority while treating property and resource protection as secondary priorities.[52] Notwithstanding several subsequent bad fire years, these 1995 federal fire policies have remained in effect, though with some further refinement.[53] Most importantly, the changes have prioritized addressing unnatural fuel build-up levels, largely a product of earlier suppression efforts, that have contributed to the size and intensity of recent fires—all of which is directed toward reducing the fire risk for local communities.[54]

---

46. *See generally* Pyne, Fire in America, *supra* note 1, at 272–77.

47. Arno and Allison-Bunnell, *supra* note 3, at 20–21.

48. *See* Carle, *supra* note 1. *See also* Ashley Schiff, Fire and Water: Scientific Heresy in the Forest Service (Harvard Un. Press 1962).

49. *See* Pyne, Fire in America, *supra* note 1, at 295–315; Alfred Runte, America's National Parks: A History 201–08 (2d ed. Un. of Nebraska Press 1987).

50. *See* Keiter, *Law of Fire*, *supra* note 2, at 308–10.

51. *See* Assessing Forest Ecosystem Health in the Inland West (R. Neil Sampson & David L. Adams eds., CRS 1994).

52. U.S. Dept. of the Interior & U.S. Dept. of Agric., Federal Wildland Fire Management Policy and Program Review: Final Report (1995).

53. *See* Keiter, *Law of Fire*, *supra* note 2, at 308–313.

54. *See* U.S. Dept. of Agric. & U.S. Dept. of the Interior, Managing the Impact of Wildfires on Communities and the Environment: A Report to the President in Response to the Wildfires of 2000 (2000).

The early years of the 21st century brought even more catastrophic fire events: Over 8 million acres burned in 2000, including the escaped prescribed burn that nearly destroyed Los Alamos; over 7 million acres burned in 2002, as Colorado, New Mexico, Arizona, and Oregon experienced their worst fire seasons in modern history; and over 750,000 acres burned in 2003, which was southern California's worst-ever fire season.[55] In response, Congress and the Bush administration instituted a much more aggressive federal approach to controlling wildfire. For its part, the Bush administration adopted the Healthy Forests Initiative (HFI) in an effort to expedite the Forest Service's fuel removal efforts through more aggressive forest thinning, salvage logging, and prescribed burning efforts.[56] And for its part, Congress adopted the Healthy Forests Restoration Act of 2003,[57] which likewise focused on expediting hazardous fuel reduction projects in order to better protect at-risk wildland urban communities. Though fire is still acknowledged to be an important ecological process, these reforms send the unmistakable message that wildfire control is more a political and legal concern than an ecological one.

As federal fire policy evolved over the years, the law governing fire changed very little until recently. Congress early on gave the federal land management agencies broad discretionary authority to protect their lands and resources from wildfire. In the Organic Administration Act of 1897, Congress directed the Secretary of Agriculture to "make provisions for the protection against destruction by fire and depredations upon the public forests and national forests."[58] A similar 1922 statute authorized the Secretary of the Interior "to protect and preserve, from fire, disease, or the ravages of … insects, timber owned by the United States upon the public lands, national parks … or other lands under the jurisdiction of the Department of the Interior."[59] The Weeks Act of 1911[60] and the Clarke McNary Act of 1922[61] both sought to facilitate federal fire control efforts by providing federal funds to states and local communities to improve their fire fighting capacities and to strengthen federal-state-local cooperation. With only modest revisions, these laws still set the legal framework for federal fire policy.

But during recent years, federal fire policy has been shaped as much by key environmental laws—primarily the National Environmental Policy Act (NEPA) and the Endangered Species Act (ESA)—as by any other law. Under NEPA, federal agencies must undertake a preliminary environmental analysis before implementing any fire control projects, such as fuel thinning, salvage logging, or prescribed burning,[62] while the ESA mandates consultation with the U.S. Fish and Wildlife Service (FWS) before such projects may proceed if federally protected species might be

---

55. H.R. Rep. No. 108-96, pt. 1, at 2–3 (2003); Rocky Barker et al., A Challenge Still Unmet: A Critical Assessment of the Policy Response to Wildland Fire 2 (2004); U.S. Govt. Accountability Office, Wildland Fire Management: Important Progress Has Been Made, But Challenges Remain to Completing A Cohesive Strategy 3 (2005).

56. Office of the President, Healthy Forests: An Initiative for Wildfire Prevention and Stronger Communities (2002); U.S. Dept. of the Interior & U.S. Dept. of Agric., The Healthy Forests Initiative and Healthy Forests Restoration Act: Interim Field Guide (2004). See infra notes 66–73 and accompanying text for further discussion of the Healthy Forests Initiative.

57. Pub. L. No. 108-148, 117 Stat. 1887 (2004) (codified at 16 U.S.C.A. §§ 6501–6591).

58. Act of June 4, 1897, ch. 2, 30 Stat. 11, 34–36 (codified as amended at 16 U.S. C. §§ 473–482, 551 (2007). See also 16 U.S.C. § 551 (2007) (empowering the Secretary of Agriculture to make rules and regulations "to preserve the forests from destruction").

59. 16 U.S.C. § 594 (2007). This provision also authorizes the Secretary of the Interior to cooperate with other federal departments, the states, and private timber owners for fire protection and related purposes. Id.

60. Pub. L. No. 61-435, ch. 186, 36 Stat. 961 (codified as amended at 16 U.S.C. § 515 (2007).

61. Pub. L. No. 68-270, ch. 348, 43 Stat. 653 (repealed 1978).

62. 42 U.S.C. § 4332(2)(C) (2007; see also Keiter, Law of Fire, supra note 2, at 332–45.

affected.[63] The courts have vigorously enforced these laws, as reflected in the numerous injunctions entered in NEPA-based litigation designed to block allegedly ill-conceived fuel reduction and salvage logging projects.[64] Other federal laws, perhaps most notably the Federal Tort Claims Act, have had relatively little impact on federal fire policy; most FTCA claims have been dismissed summarily on the grounds that fire damage to private property is ordinarily the result of discretionary federal policy decisions, which render the agencies immune from liability.[65]

Significant legal changes, however, have occurred since the dawn of the new century. After the Bush administration took office and faced several bad fire years, it concluded that the environmental laws and related litigation were hampering federal efforts to contain the growing wildfire threat.[66] The principal vehicle for these changes has been the presidential Healthy Forests Initiative (HFI), which involved a series of new rules designed to change agency administrative appeals, as well as NEPA environmental analysis and ESA consultation requirements.[67] The HFI eliminated administrative appeal options for thinning, salvage, and other fire-related agency decisions,[68] introduced multiple categorical exclusions for fire-related projects into agency NEPA processes,[69] and reduced the FWS's ESA section 7 consultation role to further expedite such projects.[70] In response, the courts have been barraged by litigation challenging the legality of these revisions, which has led to injunctions blocking the administrative appeal revisions and some of the new NEPA categorical exclusions,[71] though the ESA revisions have survived intact.[72] At the same time, Congress responded to the growing fire danger by adopting the Healthy Forests Restoration Act of 2003 (HFRA),[73] which

63. 16 U.S.C. § 1536(a)(2) (2007); *see also* Keiter, *Law of Fire, supra* note 2, at 339.

64. *See, e.g.,* Blue Mountains Biodiversity Project v. Blackwood, 161 F.3d 1208 (9th Cir. 1998), *cert. denied,* 527 U.S. 1003 (1999); Sierra Club v. Bosworth, 199 F. Supp. 2d 971 (N.D. Cal. 2002); *see generally* Keiter, *Law of Fire, supra* note 2, at 334–37. More recent decisions enjoining timber salvage or fuel reduction projects include: Earth Island Inst. v. U.S. Forest Service, 442 F.3d 1147 (9th Cir. 2005); Ecology Center, Inc. v. Austin, 430 F.3d 1057 (9th Cir. 2005); Utah Envtl. Cong. v. Bosworth, 372 F.3d 1057 (10th Cir. 2004); Cascadia Wildlands Project v. Goodman, 393 F. Supp. 2d 1041 (D. Or. 2004); Northwest Ecosystem Alliance v. Rey, 380 F. Supp. 2d 1175 (W.D.Wash. 2005).

65. Miller v. United States, 163 F.3d 591 (9th Cir. 1998); McDougal v. United States, 195 F. Supp. 2d 1229 (D. Or. 2002); *see also* Keiter, *Law of Fire, supra* note 2, at 350–58.

66. *See* OFFICE OF THE PRESIDENT, HEALTHY FORESTS: AN INITIATIVE FOR WILDFIRE PREVENTION AND STRONGER COMMUNITIES (2002); U.S. DEPT. OF AGRIC., FOREST SERVICE, THE PROCESS PREDICAMENT: HOW STATUTORY, REGULATORY, AND ADMINISTRATIVE FACTORS AFFECT NATIONAL FOREST MANAGEMENT (2002).

67. *See* Keiter, *Law of Fire, supra* note 2, at 337–41; *see also* JACQUELINE VAUGHN & HANNA J. CORTNER, GEORGE W. BUSH'S HEALTHY FORESTS: REFRAMING THE ENVIRONMENTAL DEBATE (Un. Press of Colorado 2005); Jesse B. Davis, *The Healthy Forest Initiative: Unhealthy Policy Choices in Forest and Fire Management,* 34 ENVTL. L. 1209 (2004).

68. 36 C.F.R. pt. 215; Dept. of Agric., Forest Service, Notice, Comment and Appeal Procedures for National Forest System Projects and Activities, 68 Fed. Reg. 33,581 (June 4, 2003); 43 C.F.R. §4.410(b), §5003.1; U.S. Dept. of the Interior Bureau of Land Management, Special Rules Subject to Public Land Hearings and Appeals, 67 Fed. Reg. 77011 (Dec. 16, 2002); *see* Keiter, *Law of Fire, supra note* 2, at 339–40.

69. Dept. of Agric., Forest Service, and Dept. of the Interior, National Environmental Policy Act Determination Needed for Fire Management Activities; Categorical Exclusions: Notice, 68 Fed. Reg. 33814 (June 5, 2003); *see* Keiter, *Law of Fire, supra* note 2, at 338.

70. 50 C.F.R. pt. 402 (2007); Dept. of the Interior, Fish and Wildlife Service, and Dept. of Commerce, National Oceanic and Atmospheric Admin., Joint Counterpart Endangered Species Act Section 7 Consultation Regulations, 68 Fed. Reg. 68,254 (Dec. 8, 2003); *see* Keiter, *Law of Fire, supra* note 2, at 339.

71. Earth Island Inst. v. Ruthenbeck, 490 F.3d 687 (9th Cir. 2007), *cert. granted sub nom.* Summers v. Earth Island Inst., 76 U.S.L.W. 3391, 2008 WL 161477 (Jan. 18, 2008) (administrative appeal reforms and NEPA categorical exclusions); Sierra Club v. Bosworth, 510 F.3d 1016 (9th Cir. 2007) (NEPA categorical exclusions). *But see* Wildlaw v. U.S. Forest Service, 471 F. Supp. 2d 1221 (M.D. Ala. 2007) (sustaining new NEPA categorical exclusions).

72. Defenders of Wildlife v. Kempthorne, (D.D.C. 2006), 2006 WL 2844232.

73. 16 U.S.C. §§6501–6591 (2007); *see* Keiter, *Law of Fire, supra* note 2, at 344–50.

contained provisions that also altered NEPA compliance requirements and administrative appeal opportunities to expedite hazardous fuel reduction projects. Taken together, these HFI and HFRA revisions have refocused federal wildfire policy on controlling fires and reducing hazardous fuels.

In the states, fire law and policy is relatively straightforward. State law mostly focuses on suppression, though several western states recognize that fire plays an important role in forest ecosystems and permit prescribed burning as a management tool. Some states, including California, which probably has the most sophisticated laws governing fire, establish rigorous zoning, building, and property maintenance standards for the wildland-urban zone.[74] Under the Clean Air Act, the states also have legal primacy over air quality and smoke management, which can raise concerns either when controlled burning is contemplated or when a wildfire is allowed to burn.[75] But none of the states have yet instituted legal changes that address wildfire or forest management as an element of climate change.

Put simply, the existing laws and policies governing wildfire do not directly address the growing threat that climate change poses for intensifying the incidence and severity of wildfires over the coming years. But for the first time, in 2003, Congress inserted a provision in the Healthy Forests Restoration Act acknowledging that forest ecosystems are important "to enhance ... carbon sequestration,"[76] though the statute does not otherwise mention climate change as an issue. This statutory provision, however, could help sustain forested landscapes as important carbon sinks, so long as the related fuel reduction provisions do not foster a timber removal orgy that significantly reduces their carbon storage capacity. As we begin to confront the effects of climate change on forested landscapes and fire behavior, part of the challenge will be to design new legal and policy strategies to address warming-related threats.

Fire Policy and Law in a Warmer World

With global climate change upon us, we can expect longer and more severe fire seasons that will increase carbon emission levels and thus exacerbate the warming problem. A century of misguided suppression policies has already worsened our fire problem; increased temperatures and drought will only guarantee that even more combustible fuels are available for ignition. A warmer climate will also increase insect and disease problems on forested landscapes, leading to even more fuel accumulations, and it will facilitate invasion by non-native vegetation that is often more combustible. Such an expanded fire regime threatens the vitality and resilience of important terrestrial ecosystems, will put more property at risk, especially if home building continues apace in the wildland urban-interface zone, and could have heavy economic impacts, including increased fire-fighting expenses as well as lost tourism and other business revenues. It is imperative, therefore, to begin shaping policies and laws that will effectively integrate fire management and climate change concerns.

Plainly, the basic policy goals must be twofold: to reduce the wildfire risk in a warming climate and to store as much carbon as possible. These two goals—viewed through the lens of ecosystem restoration—should be seen as complimentary rather than contradictory. Controlling the risk of wildfire will reduce carbon emissions and help safeguard the forested landscapes that serve as carbon sinks. But since North American forest and grassland ecosystems have been

---

74. For a general overview of state law concerning wildfire, see Keiter, *Law of Fire*, *supra* note 2, at 358–65.

75. *Id.* at 361–62; *see also* Laura Sweedo, *Where There Is Fire, There Is Smoke: Prescribed Burning in Idaho's Forests*, 8 Dick. J. Envtl. L. & Pol'y 121 (1999).

76. 16 U.S.C. §6501(6)(C) (2007). This provision is found in the "Purposes" section of the statute and reads: "the purposes of this Act are ... to protect, restore, and enhance forest ecosystem components ... to enhance productivity and carbon sequestration." It is the only HFRA reference to global warming concerns, but it at least suggests that Congress views forests as one element in the federal portfolio for addressing climate change and greenhouse gas emissions.

significantly altered by past fire suppression practices, most scientists advocate aggressive fuel reduction strategies in order to restore fire-adapted ecological conditions, and thus reduce the risk of future catastrophic wildfires.[77] In the short term, these restoration efforts—based largely on prescribed burning and tree thinning—will not only produce additional carbon emissions, but could also reduce carbon storage capacity. Yet over the long term, restored and healthy forest and grassland ecosystems should experience fewer high-intensity fire events and have greater carbon storage capacity.

As a primary policy goal, an ecosystem restoration program raises several important threshold questions. First, how should we define the restoration goal: to recreate the same forest ecosystem that prevailed at pre-settlement times, to identify new and evolving forest conservation objectives, or to remove quickly as much fuel as possible? Second, which strategic approach is most appropriate to achieve this goal: should we let nature take its course without human intervention, or should we utilize more intensive management strategies to actively manipulate the ecosystem? Finally, assuming active management is necessary to restore fire-adapted ecosystems, should that intervention emphasize controlled burning or mechanical removal of accumulated fuel?

An evolving consensus is evident on the first two questions. Most observers, citing the dynamic and unstable nature of ecosystems, believe it is neither possible nor advisable to recreate pre-settlement ecological conditions, particularly in the face of ongoing climate change that well exceeds past experience. A feasible goal, instead, is to restore ecologically healthy and resilient forests that are sustainable over time and fall within the range of historical variability for that ecosystem. Because climate change will only exacerbate the already high fire danger in our fuel-choked forests, most observers also believe active intervention—mechanical forest thinning as well as prescribed burning—is required to reduce the risk of catastrophic fire events and to begin moving unbalanced forest conditions toward a more ecologically sustainable state.[78] In short, hazardous fuel reduction efforts are an essential aspect of an ecosystem restoration policy.

The next question, then, is where and how a hazardous fuel reduction policy should be carried out, which is fundamentally a risk management question. Federal and state officials have already identified the wildland-urban interface (WUI) zone as the initial target for these efforts, primarily to reduce the growing wildfire threat to human life and private property.[79] Given present excessive fuel loads, most observers believe WUI hazardous fuel reduction efforts will need to employ mechanical thinning rather than prescribed burning treatments.[80] This preference reflects concern that controlled burning under existing forest conditions could endanger nearby communities, as occurred during summer 2000 when a prescribed fire escaped containment in Bandelier National Park and consumed part of Los Alamos, New Mexico. Outside the WUI zone, most observers agree that fuel reduction efforts should focus on restoring fire-adapted ecosystems to minimize future fire danger. In these non-WUI settings, prescribed burning may be given preference over thin-

77. *See, e.g.*, STEPHEN F. ARNO & CARL E. FIEDLER, MIMICKING NATURE'S FIRES: RESTORING FIRE-PRONE FORESTS IN THE WEST (Island Press 2005); Wallace W. Covington & M.M. Moore, *Postsettlement Changes in Natural Fire Regimes and Forest Structure: Ecological Restoration of Old-Growth Ponderosa Pine Forests, in* ASSESSING ECOSYSTEM HEALTH IN THE INLAND WEST 154 (R. Neil Sampson & David L. Adams eds., CRC 1994).

78. *See* Assoc. for Fire Ecology and Third Intl. Fire Ecology and Management Cong., The San Diego Declaration on Climate Change and Fire Management (2006); Helms, *supra* note 18; Bartuska and Conrad Statements, *supra* note 35.

79. Because this WUI protective priority is driven as much by politics as by science, it may not represent the most ecologically sensitive fire management strategy. But once the WUI zone has been treated, agency officials can concentrate their efforts on controlling the fire danger through forest restoration in more ecologically important locations.

80. *See* ARNO AND FIEDLER, *supra* note 77, ch. 5 (*Restoration Objectives, Techniques, and Economics*).

ning, though high fuel levels and runaway fires are still a concern. However, it has been suggested that the enhanced fire danger attached to climate change may force a shift in fuel reduction priorities away from the WUI zone to more fire-prone parts of the forest, where the strategy should be to construct fuel breaks to steer future fires away from settled areas and toward fuel-choked areas.[81]

Selecting an appropriate fire control strategy must also account for the fact that different forest ecosystems have historically experienced quite different fire regimes. For example, southwestern Ponderosa pine forests typically supported frequent low intensity fires that consumed the understory vegetation and helped maintain an open park-like forest not susceptible to high-intensity crown fires that would consume the mature trees. In contrast, lodgepole pine forests in the northern Rockies usually experienced large-scale, stand-replacing fires at 200–400 year time intervals, much like occurred during the 1988 Yellowstone fires. In some forests, readily combustible insect-damaged or diseased trees are a potential hazardous fuel removal target. Although some scientists endorse salvage logging to remove the dead trees, others argue that these tree stands should be allowed to decompose as part of the natural ecological cycle or to burn if they present little risk to adjacent communities or other valuable resources.[82] These basic ecological concerns suggest that site-specific responses to climate-related wildfire threats are necessary, and must be carefully calibrated to match on-the-ground conditions.

At the federal level, the agency planning processes represent a logical point to begin addressing the relationship between climate change, fire, and other resource values. For the Department of the Interior, in January, 2001, then-Secretary Bruce Babbitt issued an order instructing "each bureau and office of the Department [to] consider and analyze potential climate change impacts when undertaking long-range planning exercises, when setting priorities for scientific research and investigations, when developing multi-year management plans, and/or when making major decisions regarding the potential utilization of resources under the Department's purview."[83] This order authorizes the Interior agencies to begin gathering needed data about the impact of warming temperatures on the incidence and intensity of wildfires in various ecosystems and to develop site-specific strategies through their planning processes to reduce the growing climate-related wildfire threat.

Nonetheless, the federal resource management agencies have not begun to address seriously the potential impact of climate change on fire policy. After meeting with officials from the Forest Service, Bureau of Land Management, U.S. Fish and Wildlife Service, National Oceanic and Atmospheric Administration, and National Park Service, the Government Accountability Office (GAO) concluded that "[the agencies] have not made climate change a priority, and the agencies' strategic plans do not specifically address climate change. Resource managers focus first on near-term, required activities, leaving less time for addressing longer-term issues such as climate change."[84] The GAO notes that "resource managers have limited guidance about whether or how

---

81. Richard Manning, Our Trial by Fire, On Earth 44, 49 (Winter 2008).

82. *Compare* J. Sessions *et al.*, *Hastening the Return of Complex Forests Following Fire: The Consequences of Delay*, J. of Forestry, April/May 2004, at 38 (supporting postfire logging for conifer restoration purpose) with D.C. Donato, *Post-Wildfire Logging Hinders Regeneration and Increases Fire Risk*, 311 Science 352 (2006) (concluding that "postfire logging … can be counterproductive to goals of forest regeneration and fuel reduction"). *See generally* Marc Fink, *Logging After Wildfire: Salvaging Economic Value or Mugging a Burn Victim?*, 19 Envtl. L. & Litig. 193 (2004); U.S. Forest Service, Postfire Logging: Is It Beneficial to a Forest? (2002).

83. U.S. Dept. of the Interior, Office of the Secretary, Order No. 3226 (January 19, 2001). As is evident from the date of this order, it was signed by Secretary Babbitt at the very end of the Clinton administration; thus it is not surprising that little has been done to implement it during the Bush administration's tenure given its overall reluctance to take any meaningful action on climate change.

84. U.S. Government Accountability Office, Climate Change: Agencies Should Develop Guidance for Addressing the Effects on Federal Land and Water Resources (2007).

to address climate change," including "incorporating climate change into their management actions and planning efforts."[85] Quoting the resource managers in attendance, the GAO suggests that "[the] agencies need an overall mandate and a coordinated approach to address the issue … [and] very strong direction from high-level officials to get agencies to address the effects of climate change."[86]

The federal resource agencies, however, seem to have adequate statutory authority to integrate climate change concerns into their planning efforts. The GAO concludes that "the agencies are generally authorized to plan and manage for changes in resource conditions, regardless of the cause that brings about the change. As a result, federal resource management agencies are generally authorized, but are not specifically required, to address changes in resource conditions resulting from climate change in their management activities."[87] The combination of their respective organic laws, planning mandates, and NEPA requirements not only obligate the agencies to manage their lands and resources in a sustainable manner, but empower them to take action, both through planning and management decisions. In fact, agency planning processes offer an ideal opportunity for officials to begin identifying and addressing the impacts that climate change, in combination with other environmental stressors,[88] could have on terrestrial ecosystems, whether those impacts take the form of more fires, insects, disease, or invasive species. These planning processes are designed to be forward looking and to assess how cumulative environmental impacts, including warming temperatures, will affect ecological conditions and critical resources.

But it is unclear whether the agencies have the necessary scientific tools or information to fully integrate climate change and fire concerns into their planning and decision processes. According to the GAO, the agencies lack the computational models necessary to make projections about the local effects of future climate change.[89] Most current global climate change models are useful at a national or regional scale, but have less utility or predictive capability at a more localized level, where conditions can vary greatly. These models typically focus on temperature and precipitation, but not on fire and potential future fire regimes. Thus, the present understanding of the relationship between climate change and fire is based largely on observations and conjecture.

In the face of such uncertainty, adaptive management offers a practical means to test current knowledge and experience against on-the-ground results. By acknowledging that nature is unpredictable and fosters much uncertainty, adaptive management allows officials to experiment with different management strategies and to modify their approach as necessary over time. The organic laws governing the federal public lands—most notably the National Forest Management Act and Federal Land Policy and Management Act—provide for adaptive management strategies, including monitoring, assessment, and adjustment to achieve desired resource conditions.[90] In the case of climate change and fire, an adaptive management approach would enable agency

---

85. *Id.*

86. *Id.* at 39. Notably, a bill has been introduced into the House of Representatives that would require the Secretary of the Interior to inform Congress on the steps being taken by the federal resource agencies to develop consistent protocols incorporating climate change impacts into land and water management decisions. Energy Policy Reform and Revitalization Act of 2007, H.R. 2337, 110th Cong. §441(b)(3).

87. U.S. Government Accountability Office, Climate Change: Agencies Should Develop Guidance for Addressing the Effects on Federal Land and Water Resources 2 (2007).

88. *See id.* at 9 (noting that "climate change-related effects can interact with and amplify the effects of other, preexisting environmental problems, such as nonnative species or fire on a given resource unit, making resource managers' jobs more difficult").

89. *Id.* at 41. *See also* Bartuska and Conrad Statements, *supra* note 35.

90. 16 U.S.C. §1604(g) (2)(B) (inventory data), §1604(g)(2)(C)(monitoring); 43 U.S.C. §1711(a) (ongoing inventory), §1712(c)(4) (inventory).

officials to monitor and adjust chosen ecological restoration, fire control, and carbon strategies to ensure they are achieving the desired results. At the very least, fire planning decisions that incorporate adaptive management protocols would enable the agencies to observe and respond to climate change impacts in a more timely fashion.

While the current legal framework empowers federal resource agencies to address climate change and related wildfire issues, the Bush administration has sought to alter existing environmental laws in an effort to expedite agency planning and decision making for fire management purposes. Knowledgeable observers worry that the changes, which were not driven by climate change concerns, have been designed primarily to increase timber harvest levels and to reduce public engagement in the decision process.[91] The most problematic changes involve NEPA and new categorical exclusions that effectively exempt hazardous fuel reduction and salvage logging projects from any environmental analysis, public comment, or judicial review.[92] However, given the uncertainties associated with climate change and potential wildfire management responses, the NEPA environmental review process appears more important than ever for planning and decision making purposes. It not only provides the agencies with a deliberate and scientifically credible method to understand and evaluate the climate-related wildfire threat, but it should enable them to assess potential fuel reduction strategies and reconcile them with carbon storage goals. The ultimate objective—as contemplated by NEPA and related environmental laws—should be a fully informed and technically defensible forest management response to the climate change threat, taking full account of the current state of knowledge about this emerging threat.

Because forests serve as an important carbon sink, it is becoming increasingly important to protect them for their carbon storage capacity. The implications of a protective forest management policy are significant. First, such a management objective calls into question any large-scale timber harvesting program, since wholesale removal of mature trees will inevitably eliminate much carbon storage capacity. Second, protecting green forests may mean curtailing wildfires that consume trees, as well as less use of controlled burning to restore altered ecosystems. Third, because most forest ecosystems have been altered by fire suppression, it may be necessary to remove accumulated fuels, which will reduce carbon storage capacity, at least in the short term. The solution is to devise a long term carbon storage management strategy, which may sacrifice some short term storage capacity for less fire prone forests with a greater long term carbon storage capacity.

One potential strategy for controlling carbon emissions from climate-related wildfires is to regulate emission levels. The Clean Air Act (CAA) already establishes extensive emission standards for various pollutants, including sulfur dioxide, nitrogen oxide, and particulates. And the states, through state implementation plans, utilize permitting requirements to set smoke pollution levels that officials must adhere to in deciding whether to set prescribed fires or to allow lightning-igniting fires to burn.[93] Most observers believe that either Congress or the EPA will soon set carbon emission standards.[94] Whether these standards will—or even can—effectively address wildfire carbon emissions is an open question. Unlike most other regulated air pollutant sources that are human-caused, fire is biogenic (not anthropogenic) in origin, and it is neither stationary nor particularly predictable. Rather, fire is spatially and temporally variable, and carbon emis-

---

91. *See* Keiter, *Law of Fire*, *supra* note 2, at 332–44, 365–78; Davis, *supra* note 67, passim.

92. *See supra* notes 67–73 and accompanying text.

93. Keiter, *Law of Fire*, *supra* note 2, at 361–62.

94. *See* Massachusetts v. Environmental Protection Agency, 549 U.S. 457, 127 S.Ct. 1438, 167 L.Ed.2d 248 (2007) (holding that the EPA has authority under the CAA to regulate greenhouse gas emissions as an "air pollutant" and can refuse to regulate only by finding "no endangerment" from these gases).

sions from wildfires are difficult to measure or anticipate, given the quite different ecosystems that prevail across the nation and the dramatic differences from one fire season to another.[95] Unlike fossil fuel emissions, fire induced carbon emissions will be off-set over time by the re-grown vegetation that inevitably follows a forest or range fire.[96] In the case of aging or dying forests, the re-growth may serve to capture more carbon and thus counterbalance the short term carbon losses stemming from fire, whether natural or man-made. Nonetheless, a CAA-based permitting system could help officials calibrate forests as potential carbon sinks and aid in measuring carbon emissions, which can then be used to incorporate fire-based carbon management into agency planning processes.

Other potential strategies for managing carbon emissions include incorporating forests into a cap and trade system or imposing a carbon tax. In a carbon cap and trade system, forests owners might offer carbon credits as an off-set to businesses that emit excessive carbon into the atmosphere. The forest owner, for example, could sell carbon storage credits and then use the payments to replant fast growing trees following a fire event or to create a new forest landscape.[97] As for a carbon tax on fire-induced carbon emissions, this approach seems problematic. Not only are wildfires an unpredictable natural phenomena usually beyond the control of anyone, but some carbon emissions should be encouraged in those cases where fire is essential to restore ecological systems and to deter more damaging future wildfires. Perhaps a carbon tax system could be fine-tuned sufficiently to address these concerns, but it seems more logical to experiment with this approach in an industrial setting, where these problems are not so evident.

Outside the federal government, state and local governments as well as the private sector might employ several strategies to address climate-related fire impacts. For the most part, these strategies should be viewed as complementary to federal efforts. With their inherent police powers, state and local governments should utilize their zoning and land use regulation authority to control housing development in the wildland-urban interface zone, including fire-proof construction standards, no-building zones, and landscaping requirements.[98] This would reduce the fire danger in the wildland-urban zone, which should then enable forest managers to concentrate their resources on ecological restoration efforts where they are most needed and most likely to enhance carbon storage opportunities. Government disaster aid programs, whether federal or state, generally should not provide assistance to homeowners who have suffered fire losses, but then insist on re-building in high-fire danger areas. Within the private sector, the insurance industry might use its financial power to require fire-proof home construction in the wildland-urban zone, fire-safe landscaping, and related research and educational efforts. When coordinated with similar governmental initiatives, these market-based strategies could help to reduce economic losses significantly, which should make more resources available to ameliorate the impact of climate change on forest and grassland ecosystems.

It is no surprise that the above-described legal and policy approaches to climate-related wildfire problems closely track those enumerated by the IPCC in its Fourth Assessment Report. In general, the IPCC advocates integrated adaptation and mitigation strategies to address global climate change. To control wildfire risks, the IPCC endorses public sector adaptation efforts that include community-based hazardous fuel reduction programs, as well as fire-wise zoning and building codes. In the private sector, the IPCC's adaptation recommendations focus on fire in-

---

95. Christine Wiedinmyer & Jason C. Neff, *Estimates of CO_2 from Fires in the United States: Implications for Carbon Management*, 2 CARBON BALANCE AND MANAGEMENT 10 (2007).

96. *Id.*

97. *See* Allen Best, *The Carbon Conundrum*, FOREST MAGAZINE 38 (Spring 2008).

98. *See* Keiter, *Law of Fire*, *supra* note 2, at 358–65.

surance risk-reduction incentives, research to prevent fire losses, and improved forest management practices.[99] The IPCC's carbon mitigation strategies include forestation and reforestation efforts, improved forest management practices, including more selectivity in tree species to enhance carbon storage capacity, and the use of forest products for bioenergy to replace fossil fuels.[100] For the most part, these IPCC recommendations can be readily squared with existing laws and policies, though the absence of clear national guidance on climate change has severely hampered implementation.

Conclusion

We are just beginning to understand and confront the significant threat that climate-related wildfires may present in the years ahead. Due to past ill-advised fire management policies, we already have a volatile mix of flammable fuels in our forest and grassland ecosystems, and these conditions will only worsen with warmer temperatures and more drought. Additional fire portends more carbon emissions, which will further exacerbate the global warming problem. There are no easy or quick fixes, but an aggressive ecological restoration effort designed to restore more fire-resistant ecosystems should pay long term dividends by reducing the catastrophic wildfire threat.

The current laws governing federal agency planning and decision making offer a viable framework for incorporating climate-related wildfire concerns and ecological restoration goals into a long range strategy designed to reduce the fire danger and emission levels. This approach should be carefully calibrated to maintain green forests for carbon storage by only removing vegetation selectively and then generally only in proximity to the WUI zone or when other valuable resources are at real risk. An adaptive management strategy, conceived and implemented with rigorous NEPA environmental analysis, should allow the agencies to address effectively the many uncertainties that lurk and to adjust their management strategies as necessary.

Of course, these federal fire management initiatives should be coordinated with similar state and private sector fire management initiatives designed to control the wildfire risk in politically sensitive WUI zones. Such a coordinated approach should make more resources available for broader-scale terrestrial ecosystem restoration efforts. Newly conceived emission control, cap and trade, and carbon tax schemes merit consideration, but they may prove difficult to implement initially in the wildfire emission context. If these strategies are not adequate to accomplish the restoration work ahead, then it may be necessary to consider new congressional mandates specifically designed to promote ecological restoration as an antidote to climate-related wildfire concerns.

Notes

1. *Forest Service Employees for Environmental Ethics v. U.S. Forest Service*, 530 F. Supp. 2d 1126 (D. Mont. 2008) was a NEPA / ESA challenge to Forest Service use of fire retardants in its many fire-fighting activities. Secretary Mark Rey was ordered to show cause why he should not be held in contempt and jailed. Chief District Judge Donald W. Molloy saw from the Forest Service:
   - *Id.* at 1127: "a strategy of circumventing, rather than complying with, NEPA and the ESA."
   - *Ibid.*: "In my view, the [FS] is in contempt of the law and the prior orders of this court."

---

99. IPCC FOURTH ASSESSMENT REPORT, IMPACTS AND ADAPTATION, *supra* note 6, at 636.
100. IPCC FOURTH ASSESSMENT REPORT, SYNTHESIS, *supra* note 5, at 18.

- *Id.* at 1131: "[The FS] had no real intention to comply with the law or the Court's Orders."
- *Id.* at 1134: The FS position is "duplicitous at best."
- *Id.* at 1135: "[The FS acted consistently] with its apparent strategy to feign compliance with the law while in reality disregarding it."

2. For a summary of the *Forests in Flux* Issue, see *The Future of Forests*, 320 SCIENCE 1435 (June 13, 2008):

Forests have had a pervasive influence on the evolution of terrestrial life and continue to provide important feedbacks to the physical environment, notably climate. Today, studies of the world's forests are taking place against a backdrop of unprecedented change, largely resulting either directly or indirectly from human activity. In this special issue, we focus particularly on the future of forests in light of these changes.

Current research on the relationships of forests and climate are considered in a Review by Bonan (p. 1444), which provides an overview of how climate and forests are connected through physical, chemical, and biological processes that affect the carbon cycle, the hydrologic cycle, atmospheric composition, and the flow of solar energy and heat through the Earth system.

For scientists interested in forest dynamics (the turnover of individual trees and species over time), long-term forest plots are yielding field data on processes that take place over time scales longer than a research career. Until recently, though, the development of predictive models of forest dynamics lagged behind observation. In a Perspective, Purves and Pacala (p. 1452) explain how advances in the mathematics of forest modeling and the ecological understanding of forest communities are generating exciting new possibilities for mapping future trajectories of forests over times from decades to centuries. At longer time scales, pollen and macrofossil records, along with genetic data, have revealed past movements of species as climates changed, which in turn provide pointers to the direction of future change, as discussed by Petit *et al.* in a Perspective (p. 1450).

Three further Perspectives deal with aspects of sustainable forest management. Miles and Kapos (p. 1454) consider the question of incentives for "avoided deforestation" in the context of the recent Bali conference on climate change; Canadell and Raupach (p. 1456) discuss how carbon sequestration can protect against the effects of climate change; and Chazdon (p. 1458) considers how forests and their ecosystem services can be restored on degraded lands. In another Perspective, Agrawal *et al.* (p. 1460) spotlight some recent trends in forest governance and ownership, which in effect define the limits and opportunities for sustainability.

The three News reports take a look at how humans have reshaped wooded landscapes across the globe. Stokstad (p. 1436) takes stock of a large-scale assessment of Amazonian biodiversity in regenerating forests and tree farms. Koenig (p. 1439) examines the precariousness of the extensive rainforests in the Democratic Republic of the Congo. Morell (p. 1442) reports on the success of preservation efforts in China's Hengduan Mountain Region, one of the richest temperate forest ecosystems.

Forests and trees have been intimately bound up with the emergence and cultural development of our own species. Their future, and that of human society, depends ever more on how humans treat them in the coming decades.

3. Erik Stokstad, *A Second Chance for Rainforest Biodiversity*, 320 SCIENCE 1436–37 (June 13, 2008):

As ever more of the Amazon falls under the ax, a large-scale project is helping to clarify how well various tropical species survive in recovering forests

In 1967, an American billionaire named Daniel Ludwig purchased 16,000 square kilometers of rainforest in Brazil—an area half the size of Belgium. Ludwig, who had made his fortune building supertankers, was betting on a paper shortage and hoped to boost his wealth by growing *Eucalyptus* trees for pulp.

Thinking big, Ludwig shipped a preassembled paper mill from Japan and floated it up the Jari River. He built a new town, and his workers chopped down about 1300 square kilometers of rainforest to make way for the plantations. The rest remained untouched. After a little more than a decade, however, the scheme failed. Stymied by rising energy costs and business setbacks, Ludwig pulled out. Logging continues in the area, but many of the clear-cuts have been returning to the wild.

Ludwig's losses have been science's gain. Given the rate at which rainforests are being cleared, some ecologists say there is a growing need to turn more attention to the woods that sprout up in their place. Whether the land is left to its own devices or managed by humans as tree farms, these second-generation ecosystems are coming to dominate the wooded landscape. Attracted by the Jari property's combination of intact rainforest, vast tree plantations, and regenerating forest, Carlos Peres recognized it was a perfect place to figure out which species persist where. "If you're trying to predict the future, this is what you need to do," says Peres. A wildlife biologist at the University of East Anglia in Norwich, U.K., he and his team have now published their follow-up of Ludwig's folly in a series of recent papers.

This research is by no means the first to look at the biodiversity of so-called secondary forests—those allowed to regrow on their own—and plantations, but it is one of the largest and most rigorous assessments in the tropics. "It's comprehensive enough that the results are convincing," says ecologist Robert Dunn of North Carolina State University in Raleigh. Whether those results are good news or bad news, however, is a matter of debate.

"The big take-home message is that there are a lot of species missing" from secondary forests and plantations, Dunn says. And for Peres's team, the findings reinforce the need to conserve the remaining old-growth tropical forests. "Primary forest is even harder to replace than many researchers expect," says Toby Gardner of the Federal University of Lavras in Brazil. "For many species, once these virgin forests have gone there is nowhere else to go."

Drawing on these and other findings, other ecologists accentuate the positive. They point to the species that can cope, even thrive, in secondary forests and plantations. "There is a huge opportunity for conserving forest ecosystem functions and biodiversity," says tropical ecologist Daniel Nepstad of the Woods Hole Research Center in Falmouth, Massachusetts. Ultimately, the amount of diversity that persists in the Amazon will be determined by how much land is set aside—and by how hard humans work the rest.

4. Elizabeth KOLBERT, FIELD NOTES FROM A CATASTROPHE: MAN, NATURE AND CLIMATE CHANGE 14 (Bloomsbury 2007):

The Fires of Fairbanks

In the summer of 2004, the fires started early in June, and were still burning two and a half months later; by the time of my visit, in late August, a record 6.3 million acres—an area roughly the size of New Hampshire—had been incinerated. The severity of the fires was clearly linked to the weather, which had been exceptionally hot and dry; the average summertime temperature in Fairbanks was the highest on record, and the amount of rainfall was the third lowest.

5. *See Utah Envt'l Congress v. Russell*, 518 F.3d 817 (10th Cir. 2008) (Seymour, C.J.). This was a NEPA / NFMA challenge to a FS FONSI on the Barney Top Project for timber harvesting and pre-scribed burning in Utah's Dixie National Forest. The stated purpose of the project (*id.* at 822) was "to suppress the spread of destructive spruce beetles among spruce and fir trees and to improve the distribution of age classes among spruce, fir, and aspens over a four-to-six-year period." There was adequate consideration of "firelines" and prescribed burns. As to old growth, the record shows the FS adequately examined the amount of old growth by drainage and the court does not allow a new argument on appeal that "these old growth classifications were not supported by adequate data" (*id.* at 828). This project will benefit not impair the situation for the goshawk and thus the court is not inclined to find a conflict between this endeavor and an earlier report recommending a habitat of 40% old growth trees ("the older the tree, the greater its susceptibility to spruce beetle infesta-tion"). There is not a word in this decision about global warming though "the spruce beetle infes-tation which was first discovered in 2000 has since reached epic levels." *Id.* at 831.

6. *See Sierra Club v. Bosworth*, 510 F.3d 1016 (9th Cir. 2007) (Thompson, Senior Circuit Judge). This case was a successful challenge to a Forest Service application of a NEPA CE ("Fuels CE") for all fuel reduction projects up to 1,000 acres and prescribed burn projects up to 4500 acres on all national forests in the U.S. The court notes that the year 2000 fire season was the worst in 50 years but there is no mention of climate change as a contributing factor. The chal-lenge arises in the context of three projects scheduled for 2004 in the Eldorado National Forest. The court says that the FS failed to demonstrate that it made a "reasoned decision" to promul-gate the Fuels CE (510 F.3d at 1026): "The service erred by conducting the data call as a post hoc rationale for its predetermined decision to promulgate the Fuels CE, failing to properly assess significance, failing to define the categorical exclusion with the requisite specificity, and therefore basing its decision on an inadequate record." There was a failure of scoping, and a failure to per-form a cumulative impacts analysis. *See* 510 F.3d at 1028: "The Forest Service's assertion that the Fuels CE is not a nationwide program that would necessitate a cumulative impacts analysis be-cause it has no immediate direct effects is disingenuous; the Fuels CE is precisely a nationwide program that was designed to implement the 10 year plan in a way that avoids the need for pro-duction of EISs or EAs." There was a failure to assess significance because of high controversy and uncertain risks. There is irreparable injury and the case is remanded "with instructions to enter an injunction precluding the Forest Service from implementing the Fuels CE pending its completion of an adequate assessment of the significance of the categorical exclusion from NEPA." 510 F.3d at 1034. Kleinfeld, C.J., concurs, expressing the opinion that this is a generous and well-meaning attempt to protect people from forest fires not a gruesome timber grab by op-portunistic beneficiaries.

7. Robert Glicksman, *Bridging Data Gaps through Modeling and Evaluation of Surrogates: Use of the Best Available Science to Protect Biological Diversity under the National Forest Management Act*, 83 Ind. L.J. 465 (2008).

8. See Dustin Till, U.S. Supreme Court Limits Rights of Environmental Groups to Challenge Federal Agency Decisions, http://www.martenlaw.com/news/?20090305-env=groups-rights-lim-ited (visited July 23, 2009):

> In a 5–4 decision issued on March 3, 2009, the United States Supreme Court limited the circumstances in which environmental groups can challenge federal agency regula-tions. *Summers v. Earth Island Institute*, No. 07-0463 (Mar. 3, 2009). The case was brought by Earth Island Institute and other environmental groups (collectively, Earth

Island), and challenged rules which exempt certain post-fire rehabilitation and salvage projects from public notice, comment, and administrative appeal procedures. Earth Island initially challenged the rules as applied to the Burnt Ridge Project in the Sequoia National Forest. It subsequently settled that claim, but sought to continue to pursue a facial challenge to the rules on grounds they violated requirements of the Forest Service Decisionmaking and Appeals Reform Act.

In the proceedings below, a federal District Court and the Ninth Circuit Court of Appeals agreed that Earth Island had standing to pursue its facial challenges to the rules, even though it settled the as-applied challenge to the Burnt Ridge Project after the complaint was filed. In an opinion authored by Justice Antonin Scalia, the Supreme Court reversed. Because the underlying project-specific challenge had settled, the Court held that affidavits submitted by Earth Island failed to sufficiently demonstrate that one of its members would imminently suffer a concrete and specific injury-in-fact—a mandatory requirement for Article III standing. In dissent, Justice Stephen Breyer countered that Earth Island's affidavits established a "reasonable likelihood" that an Earth Island member would suffer harm in the near future.

The Supreme Court insists in *Summers*: "The requirement of injury in fact is a hard floor of Article III jurisdiction that cannot be removed by statute." 129 S.Ct. 1142, 1151 (March 3, 2009). Prof. Joseph Feller reports that counterfeit versions of Article III, Section 2, clause 1 (the relevant clause) must be in wide circulation because his copy omits the operative language (injury, in, fact, is, a, hard, floor).

B. Floods & Storms

1. Small Island States

Because the effects of climate change vary by region, the greatest polluters may not feel the greatest impact, and vice versa. A prime example is the plight of small island nations. Due to their unique geography, these nations are particularly vulnerable to climate change. Furthermore, they are not responsible for the harms. The nations that make up the Alliance of Small Island States (AOSIS) constitute approximately 5% of the world population,[1] yet they produce only about 0.5% of the world's carbon dioxide (CO_2) emissions in year 2002.[2] In contrast, the United States has roughly equivalent population of 4.6% of the world, but it produced a shocking 23% of the world's CO_2 emissions in 2002.[3]

The AOSIS is an ad-hoc negotiating arm of the UN's Small Island Developing States.[4] The group comprises 43 island nations and low-elevation coastal nations, all of whom are in immediate threat due to sea level rise and climate change. In addition, these are developing nations that lack economic resources to address climate change themselves.

The average elevation of most of the countries is 1–4 meters. While there are a few isolated hills on some nations, other islands would be completely submerged with any measurable rise in sea level. Even those with isolated hills would likely become uninhabitable.

The AOSIS has been attempting international negotiations through the UN and through international processes such as the Rio Convention. In a recent declaration that resulted from a

---

1. http://www.sidsnet.org/aosis/index-2.html.
2. Calculated based on statistics from this database: http://earthtrends.wri.org/index.php
3. *Id.*
4. *See supra* note 1.

2005 conference in Mauritius, the AOSIS set out its goals for mitigation of climate change, which included international action. The Mauritius Implementation Strategy outlined the major impacts of climate change on the members' ecosystems, economy, health, and culture.[5]

One small island nation, the Maldives, has begun to plan for climate disaster by searching for land to purchase as a new "homeland."[6] The funds will be diverted from their income from tourism. Most of the Maldives, a chain of 1200 islands and coral atolls about 500 miles from the tip of India, is only 1.5 meters above sea level and the highest point is only 2.4 m above sea level. The newly-elected president, Mohamed Nasheed, states that: "We can do nothing to stop climate change on our own and so we have to buy land elsewhere. It's an insurance policy for the worst possible outcome."[7]

Climate Change on Small Island States

These islands will feel the brunt of climate change in many particulars. First, atmospheric temperature is rising. Over the last 100 years, global average temperatures have risen by 0.74°C.[8] Another 2°C (0.6°C due to fast feedbacks and 1.4°C due to slow feedbacks) are "in the pipeline" based on today's levels of CO_2.[9] This is particularly disconcerting given that the IPCC has stated that an increase of 2–3°C over pre-Industrial temperatures constitutes "dangerous climate change," while others argue that even less change will be dangerous.[10]

Associated with the increase in atmospheric temperatures, ocean temperature is also increasing. The oceans and atmosphere exchange heat. Thus, they will reach an equilibrium point over time.[11] This is part of the reason why atmospheric temperatures have risen relatively moderately. The problem is that the ocean ecosystem is adapted to a certain temperature. The current increase is jeopardizing the entire ocean food web. For example, coral bleaching has become a widespread phenomenon.[12]

Another impact on the oceans is the decrease in pH that results from absorption of carbon dioxide. This process is commonly referred to as ocean acidification. Like the temperature exchange between ocean waters and atmosphere, there is also an exchange of carbon dioxide until equilibrium is reached. So far, the oceans have absorbed about one third of anthropogenic CO_2 since the Industrial Revolution.[13] Ocean pH has already decreased by 0.11 units since the Industrial Revolution.[14] By the end of this century, ocean pH is expected to drop by another 0.4 units.[15] Unlike atmospheric climate change, there are no uncertainties in this process; it is driven by pure chemistry and is

---

5. *Available at* http://www.sidsnet.org/MIM.html.

6. Randeep Ramesh, *Paradise Almost Lost: Maldives Seek to Buy a New Homeland*, GUARDIAN.CO.UK (November 10, 2008), *available at* http://www.guardian.co.uk/environment/2008/nov/10/maldives-climate-change (last visited November 20, 2008).

7. *Id.*

8. LENNY BERNSTEIN *et al.*, CLIMATE CHANGE 2007: SYNTHESIS REPORT OF THE INTERGOVERNMETAL PANEL ON CLIMATE CHANGE SUMMARY FOR POLICYMAKERS (Cambridge Un. Press 2007).

9. James Hansen *et al.*, Target *Atmospheric CO_2: Where Should Humanity Aim?*, submitted to OPEN ATMOSPHERIC SCIENCE JOURNAL at 5 (2008), *available at* http://arxiv.org/abs/0804.1126 (last visited September 7, 2008).

10. *Id* at 1.

11. James Hansen *et al.*, *Dangerous Human-made Interference with Climate: A GISS ModelE Study*, 7 ATMOS. CHEM. PHYS. 2287 (2007).

12. TIM FLANNERY, *2050: The Great Stumpy Reef, in* THE WEATHER MAKERS (Atlantic Monthly Press 2005).

13. Richard A. Feely *et al.*, *Evidence for Upwelling of Corrosive "Acidified" Water onto the Continental Shelf*, 320 SCIENCE 1490 (2008).

14. C.L. Sabine *et al.*, *The Ocean Sink for Anthropogenic CO_2*, 305 SCIENCE 367 (2004).

15. J.C. Orr *et al.*, *Anthropogenic Ocean Acidification over the Twenty-first Century and Its Impact on Calcifying Organisms*, 437 NATURE 681 (2005).

highly predictable. Equally predictable is the catastrophic impact of the ocean acidification. Carbon dioxide in the ocean results in an increase in sodium bicarbonate and a decrease in carbonate.[16] Shellfish, coral, and planktonic creatures need calcium carbonate to build their shells and survive. The decrease in carbonate concentrations makes it impossible for these species to build shells. The decrease in oceanic pH also impacts the reproductive, immune, and metabolic systems in other marine species.[17] Loss of plankton would cause complete collapse of the ocean's food web.

Storm patterns will also likely change as a result of anthropogenic greenhouse pollutants. Several studies have reported on the 30-year trend for an increased number of strong, category 4 and 5, tropical cyclones.[18] Each study indicated that this trend agreed with the prediction of models of increased ocean surface temperature due to the enhanced greenhouse effect of CO_2. Likewise, increased intensity of land-based storms has also been predicted as a result of global warming.[19] Although two recent studies illustrate that prediction of climate change impacts on tropical storms is imprecise at this time, they underscore the fact that frequency of storms seems likely to decrease, although intensity may increase.[20]

Sea level rise may have the most devastating effect on small islands. Land-based ice and snow sequesters much of the Earth's water. As temperatures rise, these ice sheets melt and discharge their water to the ocean. The result is a rise in sea level. The IPCC predicts a sea level rise of only 20–43 cm this century.[21] But this estimate does not include the most important driver of sea level rise: the dynamics of ice sheet loss. There is abundant evidence that glaciers and ice sheets across the world are melting rapidly.[22] Careful analysis that takes into account ice sheet dynamics strongly suggests that sea level rise will be on the order of 5 meters in this century alone.[23] Meehl *et al.* emphasize the fact that there are still "in the pipeline" changes in temperature and sea level rise as a result of the increase in CO_2 concentration that has already occurred.[24] The authors point out that sea level rise will be approximately three times greater than the temperature increases.

Climate Impacts on Inhabitants

Sea level rise. Sea level rise will have drastic effects on inhabitants of small island states. First, as islands become submerged, the inhabitants will be forced to migrate. This will result in a disruption and even annihilation of the islands' individual cultures. On a larger level, this submersion may also result in endangerment of human health and life. Some individuals may lack resources to leave the islands, and thus may lose their lives.

Saline intrusion. Small islands often have high groundwater tables. As a result, any rise in sea level will cause saline intrusion and endanger the supply of fresh water. Furthermore, changes in precipitation may reduce the amount of freshwater that reaches the islands. Unlike larger, conti-

---

16. *See, e.g., supra* notes 13–15.

17. Hans O. Pörtner, *Synergistic effects of temperature extremes, hypoxia, and increases in CO_2 on marine animals: From Earth history to global change*, 110 J. OF GEOPHYS. RES. c9 (2005).

18. Kerry Emmanuel, *Increasing Destructiveness of Tropical Cyclones over the Past 30 Years*, 436 NATURE 686 (2005); P.J. Webster *et al.*, *Changes in Tropical Cyclone Number, Duration, and Intensity in a Warming Environment*, 309 SCIENCE 1844 (2005); Mark A. Saunders & Adam S. Lea, *Large Contribution of Sea Surface Warming to Recent Increase in Atlantic Hurricane Activity*, 451 NATURE 557 (2008).

19. Anthony D. Del Genio *et al.*, *Will Moist Convection Be Stronger in a Warmer Climate?*, 34 GEOPHYS. RES. LETT. L16703 (2007).

20. Kerry Emmanuel *et al.*, *Hurricanes and Global Warming*, BAMS 347 (March 2008); C. Wang & S-K Lee, *Global Warming and United States Landfalling Hurricanes*, 38 GEOPHYS. RES. LETT. L020708 (2008).

21. *See supra* note 8.

22. *See, e.g.,* FRED PEARCE, WITH SPEED AND VIOLENCE (Beacon Press 2007).

23. James Hansen, *Scientific Reticence and Sea Level Rise*, 2 ENVIRON. RES. LETT. 1 (2007).

24. Gerald A. Meehl *et al.*, *How Much More Global Warming and Sea Level Rise?*, 307 SCIENCE 1769 (2005).

nental nations, these countries can not simply turn to a bordering nation to have groundwater pumped in from elsewhere. Saline intrusion quite literally means that inhabitants will have no fresh water. The result needs no explanation: impossibility of survival.

Coastal erosion. Coastal erosion is related to sea level rise and storm patterns. Even if land is not being submerged, coastal areas may be diminished by erosion. This is problematic because most of the population is located on the coasts. Thus, a large proportion of citizens will be affected long before the island is submerged. The consequence will be loss of ecological habitat on which inhabitants rely, as well as forced migration of the residents. Coastal erosion will also cause a change in the character of surrounding bays and inlets due to the dumping of silt and earth into these fragile sea areas.

Increased temperature. The result of increased atmospheric temperatures will be a need for better cooling systems and thus energy infrastructure on the islands, which currently does not exist in many places. Furthermore, increased atmospheric temperatures will lead to increased disease. There may be increased incidence of heat stroke. More importantly, diseases that have previously been restricted to certain areas may spread as the vectors are able to survive in areas they could not do so before. Furthermore, certain species that can not tolerate warmer temperatures in many parts of the world are migrating towards higher elevations and northward. But that is not an option for species found on small islands. As a result, these species will go extinct and the island residents will suffer from the loss of biodiversity.

Coral bleaching. One of the disasters of ocean warming is coral bleaching. This not only destroys the ocean ecosystem, on which the island inhabitants depend for subsistence, but it also reduces tourism, one of the main sources of income for small islands, and finally coral reefs are extremely important for protecting coastal areas from erosion.

Stronger storms. Warmer sea waters seem to be related to stronger storms. Stronger storms are particularly dangerous on small islands where coastlines are a large proportion of the land area. Furthermore, as developing nations, these islands often do not have the infrastructure to withstand severe storms.

Ocean acidification. As discussed above, ocean acidification is advancing rapidly and inexorably. It will harm coral, and in addition has the ability to undermine the entire ocean food web. The catastrophic effects include: impairment of subsistence; loss of culturally significant ocean ecosystems; loss of tourism; and exacerbated coastal erosion and greater storm impacts due to the loss of protective coral reefs.

2. Hurricane Katrina

It is generally accepted among environmental geographers that there is no such thing as a natural disaster. In every phase and aspect of a disaster—causes, vulnerability, preparedness, results and response, and reconstruction—the contours of disaster and the difference between who lives and who dies is to a greater or lesser extent a social calculus.[1] Hurricane Katrina provides the most startling confirmation of that axiom.[2] This is not simply an academic point but a practical one, and it has everything to do with how societies prepare for and absorb natural events and how they can or should reconstruct afterward. It is difficult, so soon on the heels of such an unnecessarily deadly disaster, to be discompassionate, but it is important in the heat of the moment to put social science to work as a counterweight to official attempts to relegate Katrina to the historical dustbin of inevitable "natural" disasters.[3]

---

1. NEIL SMITH, THERE'S NO SUCH THING AS A NATURAL DISASTER, UNDERSTANDING KATRINA: PERSPECTIVES FROM THE SOCIAL SCIENCES (June 11, 2006), *available at* http://understandingkatrina.ssrc.org/Smith/.
2. In *re Canal Breaches Consolidated Litigation*, 627 F. Supp. 2d 656 (E.D. La. 2009).
3. Robert Kuehn, *A Taxonomy of Environmental Justice*, 30 ELR 10681 (2000).

Climate Change and Hurricane Katrina

Due to the likely link between rising ocean temperatures and the increased intensity and duration of hurricanes, these storms are likely to cause great havoc on coastal communities as global warming progresses. Hurricane Katrina may serve as the great warning bell for the impacts that climate change may bring in the future.

Making landfall on August 29, 2005 as a Category 3 hurricane, Katrina was one of the deadliest and most damaging storms in U.S. history, taking over 1,800 lives and causing over 81 billion dollars in damage.[4] According to news reports, New Orleans area residents drowned in fetid floodwaters, were swept out to sea, and died in collapsed homes. Many were killed less dramatically, in the form of "elderly and ill evacuees too fragile for grueling trips on gridlocked highways, infants stillborn to mothers who were shuttled to other cities when they should have been on bed rest and residents overcome with anxiety by 24-hour television broadcasts of the devastation back home."[5]

In addition to the human toll of the storm, Katrina had a devastating impact on the Gulf Coast environment. As a result of the storm, many coastal areas suffered erosion problems and over twenty percent of area marshes became permanently over-saturated with water.[6] In addition, sixteen wildlife refuges in the area, comprising about 365,000 acres, were closed by the storm. According to the Department of the Interior, several endangered or threatened species saw loss or alteration of habitat (including the Kemp's ridley sea turtle, the Alabama beach mouse, and a number of wading birds).[7]

The high toll of death and destruction in Katrina's wake has been further exacerbated by the federal government's inadequate preparation for, or response to, the disaster — the subject of numerous lawsuits being brought by citizens against the government. In 2008, three years after Katrina hit the Gulf Coast, the Federal Emergency Management Agency (FEMA) was still not prepared for "the next Katrina."[8] According to author Mike Tidwell:

> [T]here's been no meaningful new program on the ground to rebuild the barriers and wetlands in Southern Louisiana on the scale that's necessary. It's amazing how long it has taken to get a $7 billion program to adequately rebuild the levees of New Orleans, much less to rebuild the barrier islands and wetlands. The Army Corps and the Bush Administration have not revealed through their actions any serious commitment to treating the disease that led to Katrina and Rita being so catastrophic. The disease is catastrophic land loss that allows the hurricanes to come so far inland, whereas before, the natural speed bumps of barrier islands and wetlands slowed these hurricanes down.[9]

In addition to being blasted by the news media, the federal government's response to Hurricane Katrina has been lambasted in the courts.

---

4. U.S. Department of Health and Human Services. Retrieved on December 2, 2008. www.hha.gov. katrina/.

5. *Deaths of evacuees push toll to 1,577*, NEW ORLEANS TIMES-PICAYUNE. May 19, 2006 (last visited on December 2, 2008).

6. PERVAZE A. SHEIKH, THE IMPACT OF HURRICANE KATRINA ON BIOLOGICAL RESOURCES (Congressional Research Service, October 18, 2005), *available at* http://assets.opencrs.com/rpts/RL33117_20051018.pdf (last visited August 8, 2009).

7. *Id.*, citing U.S. Dept. of the Interior, *Fish and Wildlife Service, U.S. Fish and Wildlife Service Conducting Initial Damage Assessments to Wildlife and National Wildlife Refuges, available at* http://www.fws.gov/south east/news/2005/r05-088.html (last visited Sept. 17, 2005).

8. *Report: FEMA not ready for next Katrina*, USA TODAY, April 3, 2008 (last visited on December 4, 2008).

9. *When Will the Next Katrina Hit?* Interview with Mike Tidwell by MOTHER JONES, July 6, 2007, *available at* http://www.motherjones.com/arts/qa/2007/07/Tidwell.html

Katrina Litigation

Stanwood Duval, the U.S. District Court judge tasked with hearing the consolidated Katrina litigation, commented in his dismissal of the charges against the U.S. Army Corps of Engineers for their failure to protect hurricane victims from levee failures:[10]

> While the United States government is immune for legal liability for the defalcations alleged herein, it is not free, nor should it be, from posterity's judgment concerning its failure to accomplish what was its task. The citizens of each and every city in this great nation have come to depend on their government and its agencies to perform certain tasks which have been assigned to federal agencies by laws passed by Congress and overseen by the Executive Branch. It should not be unreasonable for those citizens to rely on their agents, whom they pay through their taxes, to perform the tasks assigned in a timely and competent way. However, because of § 702c, there is neither incentive, nor punishment to insure that our own government performs these tasks correctly. There is no provision in the law which allows this Court to avoid the immunity provided by § 702c; gross incompetence receives the same treatment as simple mistake.

> This story—fifty years in the making—is heart-wrenching. Millions of dollars were squandered in building a levee system with respect to these outfall canals which was known to be inadequate by the Corps' own calculations. The byzantine funding and appropriation methods for this undertaking were in large part a cause of this failure. In addition, the failure of Congress to oversee the building of the LPV and the failure to recognize that it was flawed from practically the outset—using the wrong calculations for storm surge, failing to take into account subsidence, failing to take into account issues of the strength of canal walls at the 17th Street Canal while allowing the scouring out of the canal—rest with those who are charged with oversight.

> The cruel irony here is that the Corps cast a blind eye, either as a result of executive directives or bureaucratic parsimony, to flooding caused by drainage needs and until otherwise directed by Congress, solely focused on flooding caused by storm surge. Nonetheless, damage caused by either type of flooding is ultimately borne by the same public fisc. Such egregious myopia is a caricature of bureaucratic inefficiency.

> It is not within this Court's power to address the wrongs committed. It is hopefully within the citizens of the United States' power to address the failures of our laws and agencies. If not, it is certain that another tragedy such as this will occur again.

According to Pierce O'Donnell, the lead attorney representing Hurricane Katrina victims in their case against the U.S. Army Corps of Engineers, the 2005 hurricane "caused 1,300 deaths (most of whom drowned in their homes), displaced more than 500,000 people and caused hundreds of billions of dollars of property damage over a hundred square mile area. Not a penny of compensation has been paid to the victims; nor has a single Army Corps official been disciplined, demoted or dismissed."

While the Flood Control Act of 1928 insulates the U.S. Government from legal liability for damages due to failed levees, the government may still be held liable for the Mississippi River Gulf Outlet (MRGO), a 76-mile-long navigation canal carved out of wetlands by the U.S. Army Corps of Engineers in the 1960s to create a shipping channel between New Orleans and the Gulf of Mexico. Credited by many for increasing the city's massive flooding and not maintained since the 2005 hurricane, the Army Corps officially de-authorized the channel in June 2008 through a report submitted to Congress.

---

10. *Available at* http://graphics8.nytimes.com/packages/pdf/national/20080130_Dismissal_Order.pdf.

In addition to the lawsuits against the federal government for levee breaks and MRGO damages, there are a number of other categories of litigation consolidated by the *In re: Katrina Canal Breaches Litigation.* According to the Web site of the U.S. District Court for the Eastern District of Louisiana:[11]

> On September 19, 2005, the first case, *Berthelot, et al. v. Boh Bros. Construction, et al.,* C.A. No. 05-4182 was filed in the Eastern District of Louisiana. This case began the stream of complaints that have been filed as a result of damages arising out of all levee breaches which occurred in the aftermath of Hurricane Katrina.... It was subsequently determined by the *en banc* court of the Eastern District of Louisiana that in order to avoid conflicting decisions among the various sections of the Court, the proper approach would be to consolidate all such filings for purposes of pretrial discovery and motion practice. As such, what is now captioned "*In re: Katrina Canal Breaches Consolidated Litigation,*" C.A. No. 05-4182, has become the umbrella for all cases which concern damages caused by flooding as a result of breaches or overtopping in the areas of the 17th Street Canal, the London Avenue Canal, the Industrial Canal, and the Mississippi Gulf River Outlet. The common factor among all of the claims in this umbrella is that the recourse sought involves a determination as to whether the failing of a specific levee or levees was caused by negligent design, construction or maintenance. A corollary to this issue is whether the water damage exclusion in all-risk insurance policies apply to these damages.
>
> There are six sub-categories established by Protocol No. 1 (Doc. 790) and Protocol No. 2 (Doc. 1403). They are: Levee, MRGO, Insurance, Responder, St. Rita and Dredging Limitation.

The trial between the plaintiff class and the U.S. federal government will commence on July 13, 2009 in U.S. District Court.[12] One important ruling is reported in In re Katrina Canal Breaches Consolidated Litigation, 674 F. Supp. 2d 644 (E.D.La. 2009.)

3. Flood Insurance

Justin R. Pidot, Coastal Disaster Insurance in the Era of Global Warming: The Case for Relying on the Private Market, Georgetown Environmental Law & Policy Institute, Georgetown University Law Center (2007):

EXECUTIVE SUMMARY

This report examines proposals before Congress for the federal government to take on an expanded role in providing insurance to property owners threatened by hurricanes and other coastal storms. Its basic conclusion is that most of the pending proposals are misguided and, to the extent possible, the United States should stay out of the insurance business and allow private companies to provide disaster coverage that reflects its true market cost.

Proposals for greater federal intervention in coastal insurance are being driven by citizens' concerns about affordability and availability of insurance along the Atlantic and Gulf coasts of the United States, particularly in Florida, and public officials' understandable efforts to address them. Recent rate hikes appear to partly reflect a normal cycle in the insurance business following severe disasters, and a response to the boom in coastal development and the corresponding increase in coastal real estate values. But longer-term causes also may be at work, including the commencement of a natural cycle of heavy hurricane activity, a realization by the insurance industry that it had systematically underestimated potential economic losses from hurricanes and

---

11. *Available at* http://www.laed.uscourts.gov/CanalCases/Intro.htm.
12. http://www.laed.uscourts.gov/CanalCases/Calendar.htm.

other storms, and the growing industry perception that global warming may produce more serious property damage in the future.

The current proposals before Congress to address the "crisis" in coastal insurance rates take three different forms. One proposal is to expand the forty-year-old federal flood insurance program to include coverage for wind damage from hurricanes and other storms. Another proposal is to make the United States a reinsurer (*i.e.*, an insurer of insurance companies) for coastal insurance. The third proposal is to expand the ability of private insurance companies to offer coastal insurance by eliminating taxation of premiums that companies dedicate to reserve funds to pay for future catastrophic losses.

Our analysis indicates that proponents of federal intervention have failed to make the case for a significantly larger federal role in coastal insurance or that coastal disaster insurance cannot continue to be provided largely, if not exclusively, by private companies. Contrary to the proponents of the proposals, there is no convincing evidence that hurricanes represent an inherently uninsurable risk or that private companies lack the capacity to handle coastal disasters. While many citizens and elected representatives are understandably concerned about higher insurance rates and market cycles that temporarily leave some property owners uninsured, at the end of the day these hurdles are not inherently problematic if they accurately reflect the risks associated with building in hazardous areas.

The report's analysis further indicates that a major new federal intervention in the private insurance market would likely have several unintended negative consequences, including imposing a potentially large financial burden on U.S. taxpayers, unfairly forcing those who live and own businesses in less hazardous areas to subsidize those in more hazardous areas, creating an incentive for additional coastal development that would increase the nation's long-term vulnerability to hurricanes and harm valuable coastal ecosystems, and displacing private insurance companies and stifling the development of new and innovative techniques to spread the risks posed by coastal hazards.

Policy makers could reasonably decide to provide some form of relief to some homeowners and certain other property owners who may have purchased property in hazardous coastal areas many years ago without understanding the risks involved. However, policy makers should draw a sharp distinction between long-time owners, on the one hand, and developers and new owners, on the other, to avoid subsidizing unwise decision making by those on notice about coastal hazards. In addition, this relief should take the form of targeted, direct payments to the intended recipients, not complex government insurance programs that would tend to distort the private marketplace.

In sum, the best federal policy appears to be one that does the least, that is, that largely leaves the business of providing insurance for hurricanes and other coastal storms to the private sector. Private insurance companies can generally provide appropriate coverage for the risks of property damage associated with hurricanes and other coastal storms while providing consumers reasonably accurate price signals about the dangers of building, living, and operating businesses in hazardous areas. Some states, Florida in particular, have arguably made reckless financial commitments to provide a short-term solution to the perceived crisis in insurance affordability and availability; many of the proposals before Congress would simply compound the problem by shifting responsibility for paying for these bad policy decisions to the federal taxpayer.

Our analysis shows that there are several useful, limited reforms that could be undertaken by the federal and state governments. The federal government could provide a valuable public service by generating maps and other information on how risks vary in different areas of the coast, which insurance companies could use to create more fine-grained rate structures that better match the hazards associated with particular properties. State insurance regulators should consider making wind-damage coverage mandatory in coastal areas. In view of the overwhelming evidence that the national flood insurance program has been a public policy disaster, Congress should consider phasing it out over time. Finally, Congress should consider eliminating taxation of insurance premiums that companies commit to dedicated reserve funds to pay future catastrophic losses.

Notes

1. The Endangered Species Act has found its way into U.S. flood insurance practice. *See Florida Key Deer v. Paulson*, 522 F.3d 1133 (11th Cir. 2008). The court explains a long administrative history on how FEMA's management of its flood insurance program encourages housing developments in the backyard of the 250–300 "meager" population of key deer. The court holds, first, that Section 7(a)(2) applies to FEMA's administrative activity because it has sufficient discretion to avoid the disaster, distinguishing *Public Citizen*; that FEMA need not conduct any independent analysis of the reasonable and prudent alternatives recommended by the F&WS; that under Subsection 7(a)(1) an agency "must in fact carry out a program to conserve, and not an 'insignificant' measure that does not, or is not reasonably likely to, conserve endangered or threatened species." The court declares that "total inaction" does not suffice, following *Pyramid Lake*, 898 F.2d at 1418 n.19 (O'Scannlain, C.J.): "[a]n 'insignificant' conservation measure in the context of [the] ESA is oxymoronic; if the proposed measure will be insignificant in its impact, how can it serve the ends of conservation, and thus be a 'conservation measure'?" The court of appeals concludes that the district court properly enjoined FEMA from issuing flood insurance for new developments in the "suitable habitats" of listed species in Monroe County.

2. For an administrative response to Endangered Species Act litigation, see letter to Donald Krupp, Chief Administrative Officer, Thurston, County, Washington from Dennis A. Hunsinger, Acting Regional Administrator, FEMA, U.S. Department of Homeland Security, Oct. 21, 2008:

> **U.S. Department of Homeland Security**
> **Region X**
> 130 228th Street, SW
> Bothell, WA 98021-9796

October 21, 2008

Mr. Donald Krupp, Chief Administrative Officer
Thurston County
2000 Lakeridge Drive SW
Olympia, Washington 98502

Dear Chief Administrative Officer Krupp:

In 2003 the National Wildlife Federation sued the U.S. Department of Homeland Security's Federal Emergency Management Agency (FEMA) for failure to consult under the Endangered Species Act (ESA) with respect to its administration of the National Flood Insurance Program (NFIP). On November 17, 2004, the United States District Court, Western District of Washington at Seattle agreed, and required FEMA to consult with the National Marine Fisheries Service (NMFS) on the impacts the NFIP was having on salmon. FEMA complied by submitting a Biological Evaluation on Feb 14, 2006 to NMFS, concluding that the NFIP affected salmon, but not adversely.

In September 2008 NMFS provided a Biological Opinion in which they concluded that development consistent with the NFIP jeopardizes threatened or endangered Chinook salmon, chum salmon, steelhead, and killer whales and adversely modifies critical habitat based on potential take of listed species. Federal agencies are prohibited by the Endangered Species Act (ESA) from causing Jeopardy or Adverse Modification.

Although the Biological Opinion determination is made for FEMA, the Endangered Species Act (ESA) is applicable to everyone, whether a federal agency, state agency, local jurisdiction or individual. We all have a legal responsibility to ensure our actions do not cause a take (harass, harm, pursue, hunt, shoot, wound, kill, trap, capture, or collect, or to attempt to engage in any such conduct) to threatened or endangered species. Under Section 9 of the ESA, actions or decisions enacted by you and your officials are subject to this prohibition regardless of federal involvement. Additionally, any person can be subject to criminal or civil penalties for causing a take. NMFS considers the issuance of floodplain development permits without addressing the impacts on listed species or their critical habitat as a take under the Endangered Species Act.

With a Jeopardy and Adverse Modification determination, NMFS is obligated to provide a Reasonable and Prudent Alternative, which are measures FEMA can do to avoid Jeopardy and Adverse Modification to critical habitat. These measures outline steps FEMA and communities participating in the NFIP can do to minimize harm to Puget Sound Chinook salmon, Puget Sound steelhead, Hood Canal summer-run chum and Southern Resident killer whales. For details on these measures, please see NMFS' Biological Opinion at http://www.nwr.noaa. gov/.

NMFS requires FEMA to modify implementation of the NFIP according to recovery priorities. The Biological Opinion requires FEMA to focus our efforts of assistance according to a tiered approach (see attached Appendix 3). We will focus our technical assistance efforts according to this tiered approach.

The Incidental Take section of the Biological Opinion authorizes a certain amount of harm to the species or their habitat during the time necessary for FEMA and participating NFIP communities to implement the Reasonable and Prudent Alternative (RPA). Thereafter, take is exempted in all county and municipal NFIP jurisdictions as soon as they implement the floodplain management criteria set forth in RPA Element 3 of the Biological Opinion, provided the activity resulting in take is carried out in conformance with RPA Element 3, including applicable mitigation requirements. In the interim, one immediate option suggested by NMFS is for your community to voluntarily implement a temporary moratorium on floodplain development that adversely impacts species or their habitat.

FEMA will be working on identifying other options or methods that your community can implement and will be sharing that with you as we develop them. Those options may include guidance, training, technical assistance, education tools, etc. One option we are working with NMFS on is the development of a model ordinance that would meet FEMA's minimum criteria while also avoiding or minimizing impacts to listed species. Once we've finalized this model ordinance, we will share it with you. Should your community adopt it, then you will have Endangered Species Act coverage under the Incidental Take Statement of the Biological Opinion.

During the interim, until full implementation of the Reasonable and Prudent Alternative, FEMA and its participating communities will be required to report our progress, including the extent of take that has occurred, mitigation that is utilized and any unmitigated actions. FEMA intends to develop a reporting tool to track activities that will help minimize the time and effort imposed upon your staff in meeting this requirement. Should communities issue floodplain development permits without mitigating for take on species or their critical habitat, FEMA will be bound, in coordination with NMFS acting under their own authority, to initiate appropriate enforcement action.

FEMA recognizes that many of you have already been implementing measures which pro-tect/mitigate floodplain development actions affecting listed species and their habitat. However, for others, these requirements may pose a burden on your community. We will work diligently with you, the state resource agencies and the NMFS to alleviate this burden as much as possible and to facilitate favorable opportunities for complying with the Endangered Species Act (ESA). We will keep you advised as we further develop our strategy for implementation. If you have any questions, please call Mark Carey, Mitigation Division Director at 425-487-4682.

Sincerely,

cc: Joseph W. Butler, Senior Plans Examiner, Thurston County Dan Sokol, NFIP Coordinator, W A State Dept. of Ecology

JG:bb

Chapter Four
Reconstructed Energy Futures

Chapter Four

Reconstructed Energy Futures

The significant problems we face today cannot be solved at the same level of thinking as when they were created.

Albert Einstein

I. Introduction

WORLD ENERGY COUNCIL, DECIDING THE FUTURE: ENERGY POLICY SCENARIOS TO 2050 (2007):

It is a myth that the task of meeting the world's energy needs while addressing climate change is simply too expensive and too daunting.

Stephen Pacala & Robert Socolow, *Stabilization Wedges: Solving the Climate Problem for the Next 50 Years with Current Technologie*s, 305 SCIENCE 968 (August 13, 2004):

Humanity already possesses the fundamental scientific, technical, and industrial know-how to solve the carbon and climate problem for the next half-century. A portfolio of technologies now exists to meet the world's energy needs over the next 50 years and limit atmospheric CO_2 to a trajectory that avoids a doubling of the preindustrial concentration. Every element in this portfolio has passed beyond the laboratory bench and demonstration project; many are already implemented somewhere at full industrial scale. Although no element is a credible candidate for doing the entire job (or even half the job) by itself, the portfolio as a whole is large enough that not every element has to be used.

JOSEPH ROMM, HELL AND HIGH WATER: GLOBAL WARMING—THE SOLUTION AND THE POLITICS—AND WHAT WE SHOULD DO 22–23 (Harper Collins 2007) (emphasis in original):

Imagine that from 2010 through 2060 the world achieves the following astonishing changes:

1. We replicate, nationally and globally, California's performance-based efficiency programs and codes for homes and commercial buildings. From 1976 to 2005, electricity consumption per capita stayed flat in California, while it grew 60 percent in the rest of the nation.
2. We greatly increase the efficiency of industry and power generation—and more than double the use of cogeneration (combined heat and power). The energy not lost as waste heat from U.S. power generation exceeds the energy used by Japan for all purposes.

3. We build 1 million large wind turbines (fifty times the current capacity) or the equivalent in other renewables, such as solar power.

4. We capture the carbon dioxide associated with 800 proposed large coal plants (four-fifths of all coal plants in the year 2000) and permanently store that CO_2 underground. This is a flow of CO_2 *into* the ground equal to the current flow of oil *out* of the ground.

5. We build 700 large nuclear power plants (double the current capacity) while maintaining the use of all existing nuclear plants.

6. As the number of cars and light trucks on the road more than triples to 2 billion, we increase their average fuel economy to 60 miles per gallon (triple the current U.S. average) with no increase in miles traveled per car.

7. We give these 2 billion cars advanced hybrid vehicle technology capable of running on electricity for short distances before they revert to running on biofuels. We take one-twelfth of the world's cropland and use it to grow high-yield energy crops for biofuels. We build another half-million large wind turbines dedicated to providing the electricity for these advanced hybrids.

8. We stop all tropical deforestation, while doubling the rate of new tree planting. (See Figures 1a. and 1b.)

A. Global Warming and the Resource Curse

Global warming can be conceptualized as fundamentally a symptom of resource exploitation. Developed nations have undeniably (over)used their own and other nations' natural resources. The result: run-away global warming.

Thomas Friedman, *First Law of Petropolitics*, FOREIGNPOLICY.COM (May/June 2006):

> You cannot be either an effective foreign-policy realist or an effective democracy-promoting idealist without also being an effective energy environmentalist.

Macartan Humphreys, Jeffrey D. Sachs & Joseph E. Stiglitz, Introduction: *What is the Problem with Natural Resource Wealth?*, *in* ESCAPING THE RESOURCE CURSE 1 (Columbia Un. Press 2007) (footnotes omitted) (emphasis in original):

> There is a curious phenomenon that social scientists call the "resource curse." Countries with large endowments of natural resources, such as oil and gas, often perform *worse* in terms of economic development and good governance than do countries with fewer resources. Paradoxically, despite the prospects of wealth and opportunity that accompany the discovery and extraction of oil and other natural resources, such endowments all too often impede rather than further balanced and sustainable development.

BP INC., BP STATISTICAL REVIEW OF WORLD ENERGY (June 2008), *available at* http://www.bp.com/productlanding.do?categoryId=6929&contentId=7044622:

> World primary energy consumption increased by 2.4% in 2007—down from 2.7% in 2006, but still the fifth consecutive year of above-average growth. The Asia-Pacific region accounted for two-thirds of global energy consumption growth, rising by an above-average 5% even though consumption in Japan declined by 0.9%. North American consumption rebounded after a weak year in 2006, rising by 1.6%—double the 10-year average. Chinese growth of 7.7% was the weakest since 2002, although still above

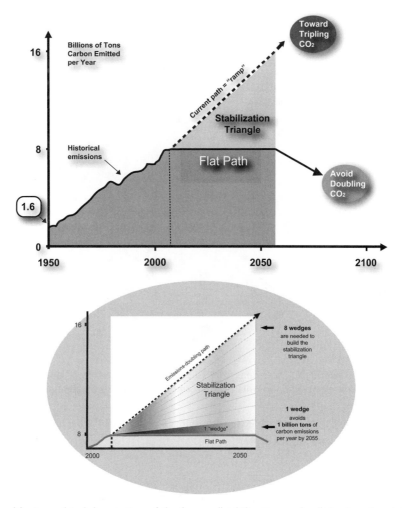

Figure 1, a and b. A graphical description of the famous "stabilization wedges" developed and described in Robert Socolow *et al.*, *Solving the Climate Problem: Technologies Available to Curb CO2 Emissions*, 46 ENVIRONMENT 8, 8, 11 (2004). Figure adapted from Princeton University's Carbon Mitigation Initiative at http://www.princeton.edu/wedges/presentation_resources/; earlier version depicted in John Dernbach and the Widener University Law School Seminar on Energy Efficiency, *Stabilizing and Then Reducing U.S. Energy Consumption: Legal and Policy Tools for Efficiency and Conservation*, 37 ELR 10003, 10013 (Jan. 2007).

the 10-year average (as was China's economic growth). China again accounted for half of global energy consumption growth. Indian consumption grew by 6.8%, the third-largest volumetric increment after China and the US. EU energy consumption declined by 2.2%, with Germany registering the world's largest decline in energy consumption.

U.S. Energy Information Administration, *Annual Energy Outlook 2008* 55 (June 2008), *available at* www.eia.doe.gov/oiaf/aeo [hereinafter AEO 2008], provides information on historical energy use as well as predicted use through 2030. Predictions use three models: reference, high growth, and low growth:

Total U.S. energy expenditures were $1.1 trillion in 2006. Energy expenditures rise to $1.3 trillion (2006 dollars) in 2030 in the *AEO2008* reference case and to $1.5 trillion in the high economic growth case.... For the economy as a whole, ratios of energy expenditures to GDP in 2006 were 8.6 percent for all energy, 5.1 percent for petroleum, and

Energy Profiles

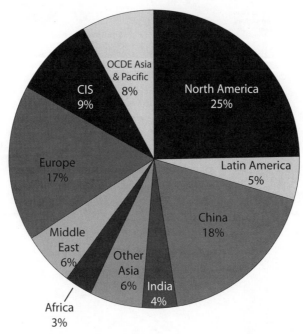

Figure 2. Distribution of World CO_2 Emissions from Energy Use in 2006. Adapted from: World Energy Council, Energy Efficiency Policies Around the World: Review and Evaluation (2008). Data source: ENERDATA.

1.4 percent for natural gas. Recent developments in the world oil market have pushed the energy expenditure shares upward[.]

AEO 2008 at 58:

> Total primary energy consumption, including energy for electricity generation, grows by 0.7 percent per year from 2006 to 2030 in the reference case.... Fossil fuels account for 55 percent of the increase. Coal use increases in the electric power sector, where electricity demand growth and current environmental policies favor coal-fired capacity additions. About 54 percent of the projected increase in coal consumption occurs after 2020, when higher natural gas prices make coal the fuel of choice for most new power plants under current laws and regulations, which do not limit greenhouse gas emissions. Increasing demand for natural gas in the buildings and industrial sectors offsets the decline in natural gas use in the electricity sector after 2016, resulting in a net increase of 5 percent from 2006 to 2030.

> The transportation sector accounted for more than two-thirds of all liquid fuel consumption in 2006, and 60 percent of that share went to light-duty vehicles (LDVs). Demand for liquid transportation fuels increases by 17 percent from 2006 to 2030, dominated by growing fuel use for LDVs, trucking, and air travel.

AEO 2008 at 58:

> *AEO 2008* also projects rapid percentage growth in renewable energy production, as a result of the Energy Independence and Security Act of 2007 Renewable Fuels Standard and the various State mandates for renewable electricity generation. Additions of new nuclear power plants are also projected, spurred by improving economics relative to plants fired with fossil fuels and by the Energy Policy Act of 2005 production tax credits.

B. The Fork in the Road

Thomas L. Friedman, Hot, Flat, and Crowded: Why We Need a Green Revolution — and How It Can Save America 13–14 (Farrar, Straus and Giroux 2008) [hereinafter 2008 Friedman]:

> [President Reagan] also slashed the budgets of most of President Carter's alternative energy programs, particularly the Solar Energy Research Institute and its four regional centers, which were just getting off the ground. Reagan's White House and the Democratic Congress also teamed up to let the tax incentives for solar and wind start-ups lapse, and several of these companies and their technologies, which were originally funded by American taxpayers, ended up being bought by Japanese and European firms — helping to propel those countries' renewable industries. Reagan even stripped off the solar panels Carter had put on the White House roof.
>
> They were eventually given away to a college in Maine, which later sold them in an online auction to history buffs.

2008 Friedman 154:

> [T]he human race can no longer continue to power its growth with the fossil-fuel-based system that has evolved since the Industrial Revolution and thrust us into the Energy-Climate Era. If we do, the earth's climate, forests, rivers, oceans, and ecosystems are going to be increasingly disrupted.

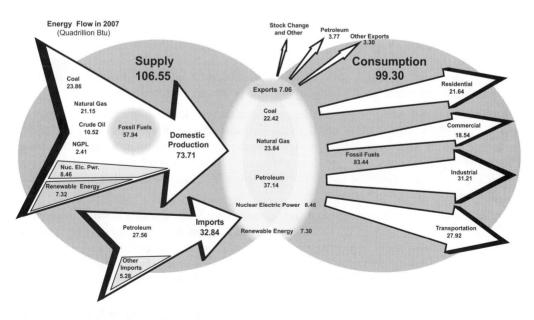

Figure 3. Energy Flow, 2007. Adapted from: U.S. Energy Information Administration, Annual Energy Outlook 2007. Full explanation of sources available at http://www.eia.doe.gov/overview_hd.html. NGPL stands for "natural gas plant liquids."

1. What We Did Not Do

The present state of energy and global warming policy is a product of a series of decisions, as laid out by Denis Hayes, founder, Earth Day, and past Director of the Solar Energy Research Institute.

Renewable Energy and the Reagan Revolution: An Unstoppable Force Derailed by an Immovable Object

Denis Hayes. Denis was National Coordinator of the first Earth Day in 1970, and he still chairs the international Earth Day Network. During the Carter administration, Denis was Director of the federal Solar Energy Research Institute (now the Renewable Energy Laboratory). Hayes is a graduate of Stanford Law School, and he spent six years as an adjunct professor of engineering at Stanford University. Hayes is now President and CEO of the Bullitt Foundation, a Seattle-based philanthropy dedicated to supporting the development of an ecologically sustainable economy in the Pacific Northwest. He was chosen by the National Audubon Society as one of the 100 most important conservation figures of the 20th Century. And TIME magazine named him as one of TIME's "Heroes of the Planet."

In the spring of 1981, I frequently found myself roaming the bleak corridors of the Forrestal Building in Washington, D.C.—headquarters of the U.S. Department of Energy. At the time, I was Director of the federal Solar Energy Research Institute just outside Denver, Colorado. With more than 1,000 scientists and others on its staff and a $125 million budget, SERI was then the world's premier renewable energy institute.

Ronald Reagan had just been inaugurated as President, having soundly defeated SERI's creator, Jimmy Carter. Prudence suggested I make frequent trips to headquarters to check the lay of the land as new political appointees arrived.

A friend had sent me the text of some commentaries Reagan had given as a syndicated radio broadcaster—praising solar and renewable energy sources as consistent with the conservative vision of a society in which power was decentralized. The election, my friend wrote, might prove to be a blessing in disguise. If so, as Winston Churchill responded when Lady Churchill said his 1945 election defeat might be a blessing in disguise, "It was certainly well-disguised."

Without exception, the political appointees I encountered knew nothing about energy, not even the most basic facts, figures, or vocabulary. As a candidate, Reagan had vowed to abolish the Department of Energy, so DOE was viewed as the booby prize among political appointees. The very last appointee to the Reagan Cabinet was Jim Edwards, a South Carolina politician and former dentist, who received the energy portfolio when Reagan was forcefully reminded that he had appointed no southerners at all.[1]

On one of my trips to Forrestal, I had an appointment scheduled with a thoroughly disagreeable man named Frank De George. DeGeorge was crude, dismissive, and way over his head. His lumpen awkwardness could have almost been endearing, in a Cabbage Patch Doll sort of way, were it not for his basic character—a mixture of fear and viciousness. He was terrified of anyone one step above him on the ladder, and he viewed anyone who was a half step beneath him as

---

1. Edwards, in his initial meeting with members of the National Petroleum Council, commented that while he didn't know much about energy, he too was from a profession where income was directly proportional to drilling. (He startled the crowd when he went on to say that he was never happier than when his hands were in a mouth full of warm spit.)

pond scum. Later, he would move on to other bureaucratic postings in the Department of Veterans Affairs and the Commerce Department before, predictably, his career ended badly.

At DOE, his title was "Acting Assistant Secretary for Energy Efficiency and Renewable Energy." That meant, to my deep regret, that the Solar Energy Research Institute reported to him.

As was my custom, I arrived at the Forrestal Building a couple of hours before the appointment and just hung out. Chatting casually with the permanent staff always yielded a mixture of data and rumors that I would later try to sort out with friends on Capitol Hill. That day, one of those staffers quietly told me exactly why DeGeorge had ordered me to Washington for the meeting.

As a result of this hushed conversation, I immediately left the building without waiting around for my appointment. (More on this later.) I called Colorado and asked my assistant to telephone DeGeorge's office to explain that I'd come down with stomach flu and wouldn't be able to meet with him. Then I called SERI's Assistant Director for Policy and Analysis with an urgent, confidential assignment. Two hours later, I caught a flight back to Denver.

Background

Today it is almost impossible to imagine the wildly optimistic mood among renewable energy proponents in 1980. Solar energy was in the ascendancy. Wind farms were sprouting up in the California hills. The photovoltaic industry was exciting Wall Street. Solar residential developments were becoming commonplace in some regions as new materials and innovative designs made passive solar technologies attractive and affordable. SERI was coordinating with four regional solar centers that, in turn, were working with fifty state energy offices to promote the best of the new technologies.

America had been through the Arab Oil Embargo of 1973–74, which caused oil prices to quadruple (from \$4/bbl to \$16/bbl). The Iran-Iraq War began on September 22, 1980—shortly before the Presidential election—causing oil prices to double yet again (to \$35/bbl). In addition to America's obvious vulnerability to foreign wars and foreign whims, we were shipping barges of dollars to the Middle East.

Four years earlier, President Jimmy Carter had focused his best-remembered speech on the energy crisis:

> With the exception of preventing war, this is the greatest challenge our country will face during our lifetimes. The energy crisis has not yet overwhelmed us, but it will if we do not act quickly.

> It is a problem we will not solve in the next few years, and it is likely to get progressively worse through the rest of this century. We must not be selfish or timid if we hope to have a decent world for our children and grandchildren....

> Our decisions about energy will test the character of the American people and the ability of the President and the Congress to govern. This difficult effort will be the "moral equivalent of war"—except that we will be uniting our efforts to build and not destroy.[2]

In responding to this crisis, the Carter Administration made some serious missteps. The worst of these was arguably the creation of the \$88 billion federal Synfuels Corporation to pro-

---

2. A televised talk given on April 18, 1977, http://www.pbs.org/wgbh/amex/carter/filmmore/ps_energy.html. This speech, which lifted the "moral equivalent of war" phrase from a famous talk that William James had delivered at Stanford, was cattily referred to by Carter's enemies by the acronym, "the MEOW speech."

duce liquid fuels from coal and oil shale, dramatically increasing the carbon footprint of fuel while consuming vast amounts of water in the parched West. (The Synfuels Corporation was swept away under Reagan, having accomplished nothing at all.)[3] President Carter, for all his decency and intelligence, was a conservative southern politician[4] who had done post-graduate work in nuclear physics and reactor technology. He often cited the architect of the nuclear navy, Admiral Hyman Rickover, as the most influential person in his life. An Annapolis graduate and a Korean War veteran, Carter selected the notable cold warrior James Schlesinger as his first Secretary of Energy.[5]

But President Carter also took some steps that were visionary and brave. Both Carter and Schlesinger believed that the energy crisis could only be solved with strong federal leadership within a market framework. Both understood that things like jet planes and computer chips would have never been developed without strong federal support. Both believed that a similar federal backing for renewable energy sources was necessary until they matured enough to compete with the heavily subsidized oil, gas, coal, and nuclear industries.

Therefore Carter pushed to create a Solar Energy Research Institute in Colorado as well as four regional solar centers across the country to commercialize technologies. At least 90 percent of the basic technologies being employed in the renewable energy field today were already under development at SERI during the Carter years. SERI developed or advanced every photovoltaic material currently in commercial use. SERI scientists were already employing enzymatic hydrolysis in the laboratory to convert cellulose into ethanol, and our internal goal was to displace all corn from ethanol production within five years using biotechnology. SERI headed the government's research into innovative wind technologies. We used our own discretionary funding to explore ultra-lightweight materials, like plastics and composites, for solar thermal applications (believing that heavy steel, concrete, and aluminum would never make economic or energetic sense). We pushed the frontiers of photoelectrochemistry to produce hydrogen directly from sunlight. We worked with homebuilders to dramatically reduce fuel use through passive solar design and new materials. We commissioned legal scholars to explore ways to create envelope zoning that would ensure that solar buildings and equipment would have guaranteed access to sunlight.

SERI had a true mission. Its goal was far more important than, say, NASA's effort to land a man on the moon. America, which had led the world into the age of oil, and then into a nuclear cul-de-sac, was now gearing up for a new transition: the transition to a super-efficient economy based directly and indirectly on energy received from the sun. The scientists, engineers, economists, policy wonks, architects, lawyers, and all the rest at SERI believed that they had a rendezvous with destiny.

---

3. Carter also promoted, unsuccessfully, an Energy Mobilization Board that would have effectively gutted environmental standards for all domestic energy projects.

4. Although Carter was a liberal in the context of Georgia politics, that was a pretty conservative context. His predecessor was Lester Maddox, the arch-segregationist. (Maddox also served as Carter's separately-elected Lieutenant Governor, although the two men disliked one another intensely.)

5. Schlesinger—former Chairman of the Atomic Energy Commission, former Director of the CIA, and former Secretary of Defense—was not the first choice of environmentalists. But in office, he defied the worst expectations of his opponents. He was a strong supporter of federal energy efficiency programs as well as of the development of all domestic energy sources, including renewables. One time, at my request, he personally intervened to save the solar photovoltaics program after his senior staff had recommended it be terminated. To be crystal clear, Jim Schlesinger personally acted to save one of the world's most important renewable energy options from oblivion.

The 20 Percent Goal

In 1979, after an educational campaign mostly orchestrated by the redoubtable Gus Speth, Chairman of the President's Council on Environmental Quality, President Carter had announced a 20 percent solar goal. By the year 2000, America was to get at least one-fifth of all its energy from renewable sources—mainly solar energy, wind, and biofuels.[6]

SERI was at the heart of this effort. Leading a team of distinguished scientists and analysts drawn from other national labs and major universities, SERI had been asked to prepare a detailed technical and policy blueprint to meet or surpass the 20 percent goal.[7]

By the day I was scheduled to meet with Frank DeGeorge, this two-year, multi-million-dollar effort was reaching completion. The analysis was finished, although the writing was what you'd expect from a collection of physicists, engineers, and economists.[8] We intended to translate it into compelling prose and release it within two months.

What I was told before I aborted my meeting was that Secretary Edwards had learned about the project and had ordered DeGeorge to bury it. I had been invited to Washington to receive an oral order to immediately stop the work, disband the team, shred the draft report, and return any unspent money. DeGeorge could easily have telephoned me. Presumably, he had ordered me to Washington for the simple pleasure of watching me react.

Instead, I skipped the meeting and called Henry Kelly. Kelly, SERI's wiry, brilliant Associate Director for Policy and Analysis, had spearheaded the study. No midwife ever attended any birth with more care than the eighteen months of 18-hour days that Henry lavished on this project. I had hired Kelly, holder of a Harvard Ph.D in physics, away from the Congressional Office of Technology Assessment, where he had been the senior official dealing with energy and natural resources. He was perfectly prepared to oversee the science, economics, and politics of this audacious venture. Together we'd recruited the smartest people we could find to work on it.

I told Henry on the phone to immediately make several dozen photocopies of everything he currently had in hand and mail the whole document to independent scientists, renewable industry leaders, and political champions. I made clear that anything that wasn't in the afternoon mail would very possibly never see the light of day.

Two days later, DeGeorge telephoned me in Colorado and inquired about my health. I said I was feeling much better.

Niceties over, DeGeorge cut to the chase. "We've decided that the report you started doing for the Carter Administration conflicts with the goals of the Reagan Administration. The Secretary has ordered me to instruct you to stop all expenditures immediately, and to destroy all drafts and background documents."

---

6. President Carter stated the 20 percent goal on numerous occasions. The first I have found was in an address on July 15, 1979.

7. *See* A NEW PROSPERITY, BUILDING A SUSTAINABLE ENERGY FUTURE: THE SERI SOLAR CONSERVATION STUDY (Brick House Publishing 1981). John Sawhill, the nation's first Deputy Secretary of Energy, provided us with political cover against attacks by the energy industry and from bureaucratic back-stabbing while he remained in office. Although the Reagan Administration refused to publish the report, it was read into the CONGRESSIONAL RECORD in its entirety by Representative Richard Ottinger, making it a "public record" that could then be published privately.

8. Our analysis found that the 20 percent goal was too low. With appropriate policies in place, the nation would be able to obtain nearly 30 percent of its energy from renewable sources by 2030. Crucial to this conclusion was a set of policies to promote all cost-effective investments in efficiency, thus making the denominator—total energy demand—much smaller.

"Well, we can certainly stop spending money," I said, "but I don't think it's physically possible to destroy the documents at this point. They've been circulated to experts all over the country for independent review."

"So what? Just order the reviewers to return them."

"I will if you tell me to, Frank. But most of these guys are tenured professors and independent businessmen, and they all have photocopy machines. Ordering them to bury the report could turn it into something like the Pentagon Papers."

"Shit. Let me check and get back to you. Don't send out any more!"

"We won't. But there are at least 50 or 60 of them out there already."

"God damn it."

That was the first overt move in what would evolve over the next couple of months into an elaborate, stylized drama that led, inexorably, to Black Monday.

The End

On June 22, 1981 — the bleakest day of my professional life — I resigned as Director of SERI, protesting the Reagan Administration's decision to slash SERI's staff by about 40 percent. In the next few months, the Reagan Administration formally abandoned the 20 percent solar goal, terminated all of the Institute's university and private contractors (including two who went on to obtain Nobel Prizes), terminated many more staff, and eventually reduced the Institute's budget by nearly 80 percent.[9]

Later, in a final, weird, gratuitous act of symbolic hostility, President Reagan ordered the Park Service to remove the solar water heaters that President Carter had installed on the White House.

My goodbye speech to the SERI staff, in which I condemned the Department of Energy as a collection of "dull gray men in dull gray suits roaming dull gray halls of dull gray buildings thinking dull gray thoughts that are consigning America's brightest energy hopes to oblivion," has become a foundation element of the Laboratory's creation myth.

Although the Reagan Administration attempted to completely dismantle SERI, the Institute hunkered down through the tough years and survived.[10] Over the last three decades, it has performed some useful research — particularly in photovoltaics.

SERI was eventually renamed the National Renewable Energy Laboratory. Unfortunately, as its name expanded its mission contracted. In 2008, NREL's budget, adjusted for inflation, finally

---

9. All this did not pass entirely unnoticed. THE LOS ANGELES TIMES, for example, decided that it warranted a banner headline across the front page. Robert A. Rosenblatt, *Solar Energy Research Slashed*, LOS ANGELES TIMES, June 24, 1981. And the television networks all covered it prominently — for one day. Then we disappeared, and the cuts kept coming. But the Reagan assault against the fruits of a half-century of liberal progress were so sharp and broadly focused that the decimation of the still-small renewable energy program quickly disappeared from sight as the media turned to, for example, the Department of Agriculture's decision to count ketchup as a "vegetable" in the school lunch program.

10. The late Harold "Hub" Hubbard, who succeeded me as director, deserves enormous credit. Under incredibly difficult circumstances, he kept the Institute alive. It was a truly brutal period, and SERI suffered numerous body blows. Leading SERI's remnants through this minefield was often a thankless task. He performed it gracefully, with intelligence, integrity, and courage.

climbed—for the first time—back to the level it had been 29 years earlier when I left.[11] It may not be entirely coincidental that in 2008, for the first time, the inflation-adjusted price of oil surpassed the record oil prices of 1980.[12]

Despite NREL's more robust budget, however, its aspirations to lead a renewable energy revolution were shattered in 1981. Indeed, America as a whole abandoned that quest—accentuated by our head-in-the-sand, anti-science approach to the mounting evidence of anthropogenic global warming.

The center of gravity for photovoltaic development shifted overseas, initially to Japan and more recently to Germany and now more broadly to Europe. Today, four of the ten largest photovoltaic companies in the world were German, four were Japanese, and two newcomers in the top ten were Chinese, one of which is on course to become the world's largest photovoltaic manufacturer by the end of 2008. None of the top ten companies was American.

During the same period, Denmark emerged as the global leader in wind power. Iceland became a world leader in geothermal. Brazil became the world's leading producer of ethanol—which it makes from sugarcane, a much better source than corn. In addition to its increasingly-important role in solar electricity, China, in 2007, produced more than half of all the world's solar water heaters. Other countries—including Australia, Spain, Taiwan, Britain, and South Korea—have recently moved aggressively into a variety of renewable energy fields.

America, which once led the world in every one of these technologies, is now scrambling to catch up. It is doing so—30 years late—with its most innovative funding coming almost entirely from private companies and from venture capitalists, now that basic concepts have been proven in other countries, and dramatic cost-reductions through mass production have been demonstrated abroad. As I write this, Congress has once again failed to renew its modest tax credits for renewable energy, even as other nations are pulling strongly ahead with rich incentives. Even most American-made solar devices are currently sold abroad.

The opportunity cost, in a nationalistic sense, was appalling. President Reagan's decision to decimate SERI marked the beginning of an incredibly painful period for proponents of renewable energy. In quick succession, federal and state renewable energy tax credits were abolished, as were many of the tax advantages encouraging private research and development. Peace was made with Iran; oil prices fell;[13] and America once again let its oil giants feed its addiction to overseas energy sources.

---

11. SERI's budget in 1981 was about $125 million. That equals about $277 million in today's inflated dollars. For 2008 NREL's budget will be nearly $300 million. This represents a big recent boost. As recently as 2006, NREL's budget had been cut to $174 million—down from about $200 million in 2005. But the Lab received a boost after the news media discovered that it had been forced to lay off 32 people the week before a visit by President Bush. http://www.rockymountainnews.com/drmn/energy/article/0,2777,DRMN_23914_5331081,00.html.

12. In April 1980, oil prices hit $39.50, which adjusted for inflation is equal to $103.76 in 2008. On March 3, 2008, oil prices on the New York Mercantile Exchange hit $103.76. Jan Mouawad, *Oil Tops Inflation-Adjusted Record set in 1980*, NEW YORK TIMES, March 4, 2008.

13. Ironically, President Carter's ill-advised Synfuels Corporation may have been partly responsible for this blow to renewable energy. Saudi Arabia had been alarmed by the degree to which America began reducing oil use in the wake of the 1978 price increases. A great many experts believe that if oil prices were stabilized at a price above $40/bbl (in 1978 dollars), liquid fuels from coal could be made competitive. So the Middle Eastern oil spigots were loosened to ensure that that did not happen. (Climate experts were already beginning to worry about global warming by then. I was sufficiently convinced by the work at NCAR and elsewhere that I devoted most of a keynote address to the American Association for the Advancement of Science to the role of renewable energy in avoiding climate change. *See* Denis Hayes, *Environmental Benefits of a Solar World: CO_2*

In 1980, SERI and its contractors employed more Ph.Ds than all other renewable energy research efforts in the world, combined. The next year, the United States walked away—sprinted away—from global leadership in the renewable energy field.

I had spent much of my time at SERI recruiting some of the brightest scientists, engineers, economists, lawyers, and policy analysts in the nation.[14] Even as we explored the cutting edge of photonics, molecular biology, wind turbine design, innovative architecture, and basic materials science, we also sought to create a policy context and financial framework in which renewable energy would blossom.

Then, on June 22, 1981, it was all smashed to smithereens. Former professors who had given up tenure in order to work on this "Manhattan Project for renewable energy" were fired with two weeks' notice and no severance pay.

Three decades later, the harsh truth is that the United States is in *worse* shape in the energy realm today than it was in 1980. And it is beyond dispute that, in the field of solar and renewable energy, the federal government has done far more harm than good.

It didn't need to be this way.

2. What We Did

MARK E. EBERHART, FEEDING THE FIRE: THE LOST HISTORY & UNCERTAIN FUTURE OF MANKIND'S ENERGY ADDICTION xiii, xv (Random House 2007):

> When [Ronald Reagan] declared that conservation meant "being too hot in the summer and too cold in the winter," America was back on track to being the most wasteful country of all time.
>
> ....
>
> Why is it that civilizations that faced collapse often could not take the necessary steps to conserve their energy resources? It is because they could not imagine an alternative energy future. We can.

ERIC ROSTON, THE CARBON AGE: HOW LIFE'S CORE ELEMENT HAS BECOME CIVILIZATION'S GREATEST THREAT 51 (Walker & Co. 2008):

> The law of conservation of matter frames the observation that tiny living things can alter the entire Earth. Little things, en masse and however defined—atoms, molecules, cyanobacteria, shelled algae, trees, cars—can cut pathways for carbon that over time change its global flow, and by extension, the conditions for life on Earth.

2008 FRIEDMAN at 33:

> [T]he story of the Energy-Climate Era doesn't stop with the perfect storm of hot, flat [expansion of global economy and players], and crowded. The convergence of global warming, global flattening, and global crowding is driving those five big problems— energy supply and demand, petrodictatorship, climate change, energy poverty, and biodiversity loss—well past their tipping points into new realms we've never seen before, as a planet or as a species.

---

and the Greenhouse Effect, VITAL SPEECHES, January, 1980, pp. 306–310. But there was no consensus on climate change sufficient to restrain a drive to produce liquids-from-coal.)

14. Many of us still meet for a weekend every few years under the auspices of a web-based, virtual organization called the "SERI Pioneers." But our hair is thinning. More sadly, our ranks are thinning. And, frankly, a lot of them are starting to look like geezers.

Rethinking Energy Law

Joseph P. Tomain, Dean Emeritus and the Wilbert & Helen Ziegler Professor of Law, University of Cincinnati College of Law, Cincinnati, OH, Tel: (513) 55-6-0067, Fax: (513) 556-5550, joseph.tomain@uc.edu.

Energy Law is the name given to a legal discipline that resulted from the energy crises and legislation in the 1970s. The first casebooks were published at that time, energy law treatises and journals were begun, and the organized bar began to treat energy law as an independent and recognized field. Energy law, though, has its predecessors and energy industries have been well regulated for over 100 years. Much of what today constitutes the field of energy law is based on the rationale and forms of public utility regulation first taken up by the states and later by the federal government in the first third of the 20th century. As a direct result of a long history of regulation, energy industries have embraced an identifiable structure and the country has developed an identifiable, but loosely coordinated, traditional energy policy. The regulated energy industries, the firms within those industries, and their regulators have developed a working and mutually supportive relationship over that period and that relationship has worked to inhibit a new, responsive energy policy. The entrenched relationship may be based on regulatory capture, or may, in fact, well serve the public interest.[1] Regardless of the degree of capture or of the public benefits enjoyed, global warming not only challenges the old ways, it demands new forms of regulation based on new assumptions about our energy future.

This paper describes the history and structure of our traditional and dominant energy policy and argues that the old policy has outlived its usefulness and must be changed. Change, in no small part in response to the challenges of global warming, is occurring as a new energy thinking takes hold, as new coalitions are formed, as new energy financing enters the market, and as a new energy politics develops. Going forward, our new energy policy must support those new ways for, as economist Jeffrey Sachs points out, a business-as-usual economic and environmental strategy will result in an "ecological crisis with calamitous results."[2] We, the world, he writes, have a narrow window of opportunity to redesign the way we do our energy business. Redesigning energy policy to effectuate the restructuring of our energy production and delivery systems is a central task that must be addressed.

What is Energy?

Most simply defined, energy is the ability to do work. Heating, cooling, lighting, and transportation are all examples of the types of work that energy does. In order to harness energy and make it operable in the world, natural resources must be transformed from their original state into their useful forms. It is during this transformation process that the key laws of physics take over. The First Law of Thermodynamics, the conservation of energy, holds that we do not "lose" energy; rather it changes from one state to the next—ice melts, water boils into steam vapor, plants decay. The Second Law of Thermodynamics, entropy, means that energy moves from a

---

1. Regulatory capture (a form of public choice) and public interest regulation are the dominant theories of government regulation and there is substantial evidence and examples to support both theories. For purposes of this paper, however, I am agnostic about which is the superior theory because the regulatory demands of global warming challenge both theories. Useful discussions of both theories can be found in George L. Priest, *The Origins of Utility Regulation and the "Theories of Regulation" Debate*, 36 J. Law & Econ. 289 (1993); Steven P. Croley, Regulation and Public Interests: The Possibility of Good Regulatory Government (Princeton Un. Press 2008); Sidney A. Shapiro & Joseph P. Tomain, Regulatory Law and Policy ch. 3 (3rd ed. Lexis 2003).

2. Jeffrey D. Sachs, Common Wealth: Economics for a Crowded Planet 5 (Penguin 2008).

more concentrated state to a less concentrated one; consequently, some of the useful energy is lost in the transformation process. Both laws are important for the use, and regulation, of the natural resources used to produce energy. If the potential energy in one ton of coal can provide electricity to 100 homes for one day, by the time that coal is burned, to heat water, to turn the rotors on an electric generator to generate electricity, and then to have that electricity distributed to a home, there will be energy loss throughout the cycle. After the transformation, and the operation of both laws of thermodynamics, roughly 31 out of the potential 100 homes will be served by that ton of coal.

The example of coal is instructive for several points. When we speak of energy, we are also speaking about the natural resources used in its production—energy and natural resources are inextricably linked. Consequently, energy laws and policies that are directed at the regulation of those resources from exploration and production through distribution and use, cannot ignore the environmental effects throughout the fuel cycle. Therefore, there are several reasons to regulate energy resources and industries. First, we should attempt to maximize the potential energy in each resource, to have it distributed most efficiently, and to have it consumed more sensibly. A second reason for energy regulation is that, like all resources, natural resources are subject to problems of scarcity and regulators must pay attention to price. The experience of the first few months in 2008 of oil trading at over $125 a barrel (and about $4 per gallon of gasoline) when just years before oil was priced was below $40 a barrel is illustrative of the problem of scarcity. Whether oil production worldwide has peaked or not, it is clearly the case that as demand increases, so will prices, and it is also clearly the case that further exploration and production is taking place in more expensive and delicate geographic areas. The third reason for energy regulation is to minimize the social and environmental costs of energy production and distribution.

The United States consumes roughly 100 quadrillion BTUs per year. The fossil fuels of petroleum, coal, and natural gas account for 85% of that energy. Nuclear power constitutes roughly 8% and alternative energy sources, such as biomass and hydroelectricity, constitute 6%. The remaining 1% of the energy that we use is comprised of renewable resources such as geothermal, solar, and wind power.[3] Fossil fuels, therefore, dominate our energy economy, and with 5% of the world's population, the United States consumes 25% of the world's fossil fuels and contributes 25% of the world's carbon emissions. A sound and environmentally sensitive fossil fuel policy, then, is essential for addressing climate change.

As we think through energy policies in the climate change era, another energy fact is significant. The energy profile of the United States can be divided roughly in half between oil and electricity. Most of the oil that is consumed in the United States is used in the transportation sector. Most of the electricity used in the United States is used for industrial, commercial, and residential purposes. In other words, these two sectors operate, for the most part, independently of each other. Hybrid cars are a counterexample and rely on both sectors but their overall role in our energy economy is negligible. Further, 50% of the electricity is generated by coal. This fact is significant because, depending on whose estimates one relies upon, the U.S. has either 50, 100, 250, 500, or more years of coal reserves available. Coal, the dirty burning fuel that it is, will continue to play a role in our energy future.[4] Still, while coal reserves are abundant with the increasing demand for electricity, as well as oil, by India and China, we are witnessing an escalation of coal prices, as well as oil prices.

---

3. The statistics in this section can be found in DOE, ENERGY INFORMATION ADMINISTRATION, ANNUAL ENERGY REVIEW 2006 (June 2007).

4. *See* JOHN DEUTCH & ERNEST J. MONIZ (co-chairs), THE FUTURE OF COAL: AN INTERDISCIPLINARY MIT STUDY 1 (2007).

The history of energy use is instructive as well. Since 1950, our energy consumption has more than tripled from 30 quads to 100 quads, but production has grown only from 30 quads to slightly over 60. Imports, particularly oil imports, make up the difference. Calls for independence from foreign oil are not new. In fact, they began in the Eisenhower Administration as oil consumption exceeded oil production for the first time. Our concern with oil independence, however, has been exacerbated since 1970. In 1970, domestic oil production peaked and has been declining continuously. The gap between oil production and consumption has grown dramatically since that time. Today, for example, we consume roughly 20 million barrels of oil per day (mbd). From that total, we consume approximately 15 mbd of crude oil, producing slightly over 5 mbd and importing the remainder.[5] Also since 1950, the use of renewable resources for energy production has remained essentially flat.

A last note on nomenclature. When we speak of alternative resources, we generally mean resources other than what are considered the conventional energy resources of oil, natural gas, coal, nuclear power, and hydropower. Alternative energy resources, then, are distinguished from conventional fuels and come in two forms. First, some alternative resources are fossil-fuel substitutes for the conventional resources and, as substitutes only, they also emit CO_2. Alternative energy resources such as oil shale, tar sands, coal gasification, and coal liquefaction, are substitutable alternatives to conventional fossil fuels. They are not renewable energy resources as the term is used. The second form of alternative resources are renewable energy resources such as solar, wind, biomass, and geothermal energy. As we confront the challenges of global warming, and as we consider the use of alternative resources in our energy mix, the distinction between conventional substitutes and renewable resources is significant.

A Brief History of Energy Policy

In the middle 19th century, our energy economy experienced a transition from wood and whale oil to coal and oil. In 1859, the first oil well was drilled in Titusville, Pennsylvania and in 1882, the first electric generating station was switched on by Thomas Edison on Pearl Street in New York City. The Pearl Street generating station served 59 customers. For the most part, the competitive era for oil, coal and electricity continued into the early decades of the 20th century and government regulation was largely nonexistent. The one notable exception was the antitrust case brought against the Standard Oil company that resulted in the breakup of John D. Rockefeller's oil monopoly.[6] Perhaps not so curiously, the breakup of Standard Oil doubled Rockefeller's wealth because he had stock in each of the subsidiary companies and all of his stock increased in value.[7]

What is notable about the tail end of the 19th century relative to energy policy, however, is that the modern administrative state was born. In 1887, the Interstate Commerce Commission was created and it served as the model for the modern administrative agency designed to monitor the economy through technical expertise. Earlier, in 1876, the Supreme Court decided the case of *Munn v. Illinois*,[8] which granted to the state the power to regulate prices. For a capitalist democracy, government price-setting may appear anathema and yet the *Munn* Court recognized that in the face of market failure, especially monopolies in industries affected with a public interest, government should set prices at competitive levels rather than at the supracompetitive levels

---

5. The difference between 20 mbd of petroleum consumption and the 15 mbd of crude oil consumption consists of blends, oil distillates and liquefied petroleum gases.

6. Standard Oil Co. of New Jersey v. United States, 221 U. S. 1 (1911).

7. Daniel Yergin, The Prize: The Epic Quest for Oil, Money and Power 113 (Simon & Schuster 1991).

8. Munn v. Illinois, 94 U.S. 113 (1876).

set by monopolists. Price regulation, then, was undertaken by government in the public interest and public utility regulation was set against this backdrop—price setting (to be later called ratemaking) by administrative agencies.

Rockefeller's Oil Trust was busted because it was a monopoly and a monopoly is the classic example of a market failure. Industry concentration and market power negatively affect the public because a monopolist can raise prices, reduce output, and reduce consumer choices in the market simultaneously. The Oil Trust manipulated rail rates and oil prices to the detriment of the public and was then dis-aggregated through antitrust litigation. The electricity industry also experienced consolidation but was regulated differently. Instead of breaking up the industry, electric utilities were given government-protected monopolies.

In the span of a few decades, Edison's Pearl Street Station went from a local to a regional monopoly. In 1896, for example, George Westinghouse harnessed the hydropower of Niagara Falls to serve the city of Buffalo 29 miles away. Shortly thereafter, another former Edison employee, Samuel Insull, created a complex holding company capable of manipulating electricity prices and stock holdings to his benefit and to the detriment of the public.[9] Just as the government stepped in to break up the oil trust, regulators stepped in to address the market abuses in the electric industry.

In the early decades of the 20th century, local and state regulators began to set electricity rates to avoid the monopoly abuses in the electric industry. The various monopoly sins of increased prices and reduced quantity could be corrected by setting prices at reasonable levels and state regulators engaged in ratemaking exactly for that purpose.

Around this time, state regulators also stepped in with laws to prop up the developing oil market. Oil, and natural gas, are fugacious, *i.e.* moveable, resources. The general common law rule was that whoever captured a fugacious resource, like someone capturing a hare running across a field, had legal title to that resource. The problem, known as the tragedy of the commons, should be obvious—the race goes to the swiftest. If the first captor wins the prize, then he who hesitates is lost and there will be more oil exploration companies than the market can reasonably suffer as multiple would-be captors attempt to be first in the ground to capture the oil or natural gas.

The tragedy in the tragedy of the commons is that it pays to consume rapidly and exhaust a resource before someone else does and this is exactly what happened in the flush fields of Texas, Louisiana, and Oklahoma in the 1920s and 30s. Oil exploration yielded vast quantities of oil to such an extent that oil could be purchased for less than 10¢ a barrel. The common law rule of capture had to be replaced by state regulation in order to sustain reasonable and competitive markets. Market stabilization was accomplished through state unitization and proration laws that limited the amount of oil that could be put on a market at any one time. Regulations also rewrote the rules of ownership by prorating fields.

The history of energy regulation in the early years, then, witnessed a transition from local common law regulation to state administrative regulation. As energy industries continued to expand and grow across state lines, federal regulation could not be, and was not, far behind. The first notable federal regulation was the Federal Power Act of 1920 under which the federal government exerted authority over hydroelectric projects because it had jurisdiction over navigable streams. With the coming of the New Deal, federal regulation expanded even more.

---

9. *See* Richard D. Cudahy & William D. Henderson, *From Insull to Enron: Corporate (Re)Regulation After the Rise and Fall of Two Energy Icons*, 25 ENERGY L. J. 35 (2005).

The challenge for FDR and his New Deal hotdogs,[10] was to stabilize the economy and provide a safety net for citizens generally. In the energy arena, the New Deal expanded public power projects and enacted two major statutes regulating private electric utilities. The Public Utility Holding Company Act of 1935[11] was enacted specifically to address the holding company abuses by Insull's electric utilities. In the same year, Part II of the Federal Power Act[12] was enacted to give the federal government ratemaking authority over interstate wholesale sales of electricity.

As the electricity industry expanded, it developed into three segments. Electricity is: (1) *generated* from a power plant at high voltage, (2) *transmitted* to local utilities then (3) *distributed* to end users. Private investor-owned utilities (IOUs) found it most profitable to integrate vertically and to engage in all three functions of generation, transmission, and distribution. As the vertically integrated electric IOUs grew in scale, they began to sell electricity across state lines and the transmission system began to exhibit monopoly characteristics. Thus, the federal government was justified in regulating interstate wholesale electricity rates and in leaving retail rate regulation to state regulators.

Similarly, in 1938, the Natural Gas Act[13] was passed to regulate the intestate sales of natural gas because of the concentration of ownership of interstate pipelines. The Natural Gas Act mimicked Part II of the Federal Power Act by regulating interstate sales through a ratemaking process intended to set rates which were just, reasonable, and nondiscriminatory.[14]

As energy industries moved from local to regional to national, transportation played an increasingly important role. Simply, private oil, natural gas, and electricity firms could most profitably operate at scale through interstate transportation of those resources before they were distributed to end users by local utilities. Each industry can be pictured as having multiple producers at one end of the transportation network, and millions of consumers at the other end. However, it makes no economic sense to have multiple and competing oil and natural gas pipelines or multiple and competing high voltage electric power lines constructed across the country. Neither producers nor consumers benefit from such wasteful expenditures. Because of economic necessity, then, the transportation system was limited to a handful of private owners creating a transportation bottleneck which gave private firms monopoly power which, in turn, demanded regulation by federal and state governments.

The form of regulation, in what has become known as the regulatory compact, was to give the private owners of these transportation systems a protected service territory in exchange for the government receiving ratemaking authority. These owners were protected from competition as, ironically, a private monopoly was exchanged for a government-protected one.

There are good economic reasons for the regulatory compact—to a point. Avoiding wasteful expenditures, achieving economies of scale, and providing service to customers were all justifiable. However, once the national infrastructure was completed and once new suppliers who do not own transportation facilities needed to get their product to market, then the reasons for granting a government monopoly to a private transportation firm lessen in importance and may be counterproductive, as happened in the last third of the 20th century.

---

10. Peter H. Irons, The New Deal Lawyers (Princeton Un. Press 1982); Joseph P. Lash, Dealers and Dreamers: A New Look at the new Deal (Doubleday 1988); Alan Brinkley, The End of Reform: New Deal Liberalism in Recession and War (Vintage 1995).

11. Public Utility Holding Company Act 1935, 15 U.S.C. §§ 79a *et seq.* (Repealed 2005).

12. Federal Power Act, 16 U.S.C. §§ 791a *et seq.*

13. Natural Gas Act of 1938, 15 U.S.C. §§ 717 *et. seq.*

14. Oil pipelines were similarly regulated by the then Interstate Commerce Commission under the 1906 Hepburn Act, 34 Stat. 589 (1906).

As the coal, oil, and natural gas industries grew and became concentrated during the first third of the century, the federal government played a promotive, as well as regulative, role. The U.S. Fuel Administration, the Federal Oil Conservation Board, the Petroleum Administration for War and the Solid Fuels Administration for War, all serve as examples of federal agencies that promoted fossil-fuel interests during the 1920s through World War II.[15]

During periods of abundance, with a national infrastructure being constructed, with economies of scale being realized, consumers did not confront rapidly escalating prices. In fact, oil, gas, coal, and electricity prices stayed relatively flat well past the Second World War. Economic prosperity and energy development went hand in hand during this period and as energy production and consumption increased, our economy expanded.

After WWII, our economy expanded in particular ways which increased the demand for both oil and electricity. As the interstate highway system developed, automobile use increased dramatically putting increasing demands on oil. As the suburbs added housing development after housing development, the demand for electricity grew with them. Fortunately, both electricity and oil were in abundance and even with increasing demand, relative prices were flat or declining. Expansion and flat prices in the electric industry continued until 1965. Expansion and flat oil prices continued until about 1970. Still, during this period troubling signs began to appear.

Through the post-WWII period, the fundamental economic assumption behind energy policy was the belief that there was a direct and positive relationship between energy production and consumption and the economy. In other words, the more energy that was produced and consumed, the healthier the economy would be. From the end of WWII looking into the future, it would seem that: (1) our demand for electricity would continue unabated at an annual rate of 7%; (2) coal, while a dirty-burning fuel, was abundant and cheap; and (3) nuclear power promised much—it was clean, abundant, and even cheaper than coal.

The development of commercial nuclear power, once touted as being "too cheap to meter," had the duel effect of transforming atomic energy from the destructive force witnessed at Hiroshima and Nagasaki to the peaceful "Our Friend the Atom." In 1954, the Atomic Energy Act[16] was passed with the intent of moving the control of nuclear power away from the hands of the military and into private, commercial uses—specifically electricity generation. Testifying in Congress in favor of commercial use, utility executives, however, were well aware of the potential danger of a catastrophic event and Congress responded with the Price Anderson Act of 1957[17] which limited the liability of utilities in case of such a disaster.

The beginning of our troublesome energy times began in the 1960's. In 1965, electric power production peaked with the result that marginal costs began to outstrip average costs for the first time. In other words, when economies of scale were no longer being realized and when power production technology hits its limits, then prices began to escalate. Additionally, in 1970, domestic oil production peaked and we began to rely on imported oil for most of our oil needs. Also around this time, we became aware of the environmental harms of unchecked resource use and began enacting environmental legislation like the National Environmental Policy Act of 1970 and other associated legislation to protect air, water, and land. So, although in 1970 the energy economy seemed fairly healthy, it would not be healthy for long.

From 1973 through 1980, a series of events throughout the energy sectors occurred to which we are still trying to respond. In 1973, the Arab Oil Embargo demonstrated our reliance on and our vulnerability to the Middle East oil states. Oil prices quadrupled, double-digit infla-

15. John G. Clark, Energy and the Federal Government: Fossil Fuel Policies, 1900–1946 (1987).
16. Atomic Energy Act, 42 U.S.C. §§ 2011 *et seq.*
17. Price-Anderson Act of 1957, 42 U.S.C. §§ 2011.

tion ensued, and energy became headline news as people waited in gas lines, on alternate days, to fill their tanks. President Nixon introduced a set of wage and price controls to address inflation and those controls extended to the oil industry in exceedingly complex ways as price controls were either manipulated or ignored.[18] President Nixon's Project Independence was continued by President Ford as oil price regulations continued through his WIN (Whip Inflation Now) Program. Neither program was successful, and neither led to any semblance of energy independence.

The economy of the mid-1970s was shaky at best and when President Jimmy Carter was elected, he quickly turned his attention to the matter of energy and the economy. In 1977, President Carter called the energy crisis the moral equivalent of war and was successful in having Congress pass the National Energy Act.[19] The National Energy Act is a series of five major statutes that attempted to reduce dependence on foreign oil, move fuel use from oil to coal, change the way utility prices were set, eliminate the duel market in natural gas that had developed (which, in turn, created a domestic shortage),[20] and generally attempted to promote conservation. For the most part, the National Energy Act addressed conventional energy resources as independent industries, and not in an overarching and coordinated way. In other words, the National Energy Act continued the traditional energy path on which the country had been traveling since the turn of the 20th century.

The National Energy Act had one great surprise—the Public Utilities Regulatory Policies Act (PURPA). PURPA provided for a new form of electricity generation. Going back to the second law of thermodynamics, to the extent that heat is produced in any process including manufacturing, that heat, if recaptured, can be used to produce energy. The idea of co-generation was born. If a company can recapture heat and use it to generate electricity, then that company would not require as much electricity from the local utility. In some instances, the company would generate more electricity than it needed and it could sell the excess electricity back to the local utility. Another portion of PURPA allowed small power producers (10 megawatts and under) to generate electricity which could also be sold to the local utility at a very favorable rate.[21] The surprise was that there was a greater amount of co-generation and small power production than anticipated. In fact, new companies were started under the theory that they could generate electricity at a much lower cost than that generated by the local utility and then sell that electricity to the utility for a tidy profit. Under the rules of PURPA, the local utility was obligated to purchase lower cost electricity at the higher cost of the utility's production.

In short, PURPA revealed that there were electricity providers other than traditional utilities that wanted to put cheaper electricity on the market. The problem was that since the traditional utilities were vertically integrated and owned the transmission lines, they were unwilling to have new providers use those lines at any rate that would threaten the price of their own product. The private transmission lines could be used but only at a price that was not competitive with the local utility. The matter of opening access to new sources of generation over the privately owned

18. *See, e.g.*, Robert Sherrill, The Oil Follies of 1970–1980 (Anchor Press 1983); David Glasner, Politics, Prices, and Petroleum: The Political Economy of Energy (Pacific Research Institute for Public Policy 1985); Joseph P. Kalt, Economics and Politics of Oil-Price Regulation: Federal Policy in the Post-Embargo Era (MIT Press 1983).

19. National Energy Act, P.L. 95-618 (1978).

20. *See generally* Paul W. MacAvoy, The Natural Gas Market: Sixty Years of Regulation and Deregulation (Yale Un. Press 2000).

21. The local utility was required to buy the electricity at the utility's cost of production, not at the supplier's cost. This was called the "fully avoided costs" and served to stimulate new producers of electricity to enter the market. *See* American Paper Institute, Inc. v. American Elec. Power Service Corp., 461 U.S. 402 (1983) (upholding the full avoided cost calculation).

lines of incumbent utilities has been a problem regulators have not solved since it was first revealed in the mid 1970s. We will return to this problem below.

The obituary for the nuclear power industry came in 1979 with the incident at Three Mile Island. Although the accident at Three Mile Island was attributable to human error,[22] it bore an uncanny and coincidental resemblance to a then current movie called *The China Syndrome*, which set public opinion against nuclear power in very vocal ways. The industry has gone through a very fallow period. Since 1978, no new nuclear plants have opened and all plants ordered since 1974 have been cancelled. Today, we are seeing some resurgence of interest in nuclear power because nuclear plants emit no carbon and there are 33 units in some stage of planning.[23]

Also in 1979, the Iranian oil embargo shot oil prices up and the Carter Administration responded with two more legislative efforts. The grander of the two was the enactment of the Energy Security Act.[24] The ESA, like the NEA before it, consisted of several major acts. The ESA was intended to move our energy economy in an alternative direction. It created the United States Synthetic Fuels Corporation that was supposed to extract oil from oil shale and tar sands. The ESA also aimed to increase the country's use of renewable energy and conservation. The ESA never achieved its goals. The Synfuels Corp was a $88 billion failure ended by Congress in 1986 and the renewable energy efforts yielded minimal results. Then in response to the run up in oil prices, Congress felt that consumers should not suffer while domestic oil companies profited from low-cost reserves that enjoyed the higher world prices. Congress enacted the Crude Oil Windfall Profits Tax[25] to take away windfall profits from oil companies and use that revenue for the development of alternative energy resources.

For all of his regulatory initiatives in the energy field, President Carter also believed in market forces and moved toward reducing price controls on oil and on natural gas. His experiment in energy reform ended in 1980 with the election of President Reagan whose first two acts in office were to accelerate oil price decontrols and eliminate the Crude Oil Windfall Profit Tax Act, both to the benefit of fossil-fuel interests.

After the Carter legislation, energy regulation moved out of the halls of Congress and into the hearing rooms of the Federal Energy Regulatory Commission (FERC), which attempted to address the deregulation and/or restructuring of the electric and natural gas industries by opening access to the distribution systems of both industries. Throughout the 1980's and 1990's, FERC sought to open access to the electricity grid, create regional electricity markets through an entity known as the Regional Transmission Organizations (RTOs), and redesign electricity markets through Special Market Design so that the electric industry would run more smoothly. Because FERC's jurisdiction was aimed at the wholesale level, retail regulation was seen as desirable but retail regulation had to be left to the states.

Recall that PURPA's surprise was that there was cheap electricity on the market that needed to get to customers. The thought behind these FERC initiatives, then, was that if an investor-owned utility (IOU) would divest itself of its transmission system, then that divestiture would remove the incentive to cheat in pricing the IOU's transmission service. Further, if regional producers could agree to participate under a common regulatory framework, then wholesale markets would open up and electricity would enjoy something closer to competitive pricing. Ideally, more producers would enter the market, prices would decline because more electricity was avail-

---

22. *See* REPORT OF THE PRESIDENT'S COMMISSION ON THE ACCIDENT AT THREE MILE ISLAND, THE NEED FOR CHANGE: THE LEGACY OF THREE MILE ISLAND (1979) (The Kemeny Commission Report).

23. *See* Nuclear Regulatory Commission chart at http://www.nrc.gov/reactors/new-licensing/new-licensing-files/expected-new-rx-applications.pdf.

24. Energy Security Act, P.L. 96-294 (1980).

25. Crude Oil Windfall Profit Tax Act, 26 U.S.C. §§ 1 *et seq.*

able, and the heavy hand of old command-and-control rate regulation could be reformed. Federal regulators, then, could monitor and charge for access at competitive prices allowing the cheaper electricity to reach customers.

To complete the cycle of deregulation, state regulators would adopt similar divestiture regulations in an effort to promote consumer choice for electricity in the same way that consumers could choose telephone service. Neither set of regulations have worked as electricity restructuring has stalled.

The federal regulations remain incomplete. Regional differences among utilities made RTOs unattractive for many utilities who did not want to raise prices to their customers. Electric market design was more technically complicated than anticipated[26] and these market regulations would be more cumbersome and costly to administer than the old rate hearings.

Just as the federal regulations stalled, state deregulation efforts imploded. The summer of 2000 witnessed an energy crisis in California caused, in no small part, by the manipulative practices by Enron traders at their trading desks.[27] There were other contributing factors to the crisis. The summer was drier than expected so adequate hydropower resources were not available. More electric units were down for rehabilitation than anticipated. And electricity demand was higher than estimated. However, the largest blunder was the fatally flawed deregulation scheme which resulted in utility bankruptcies and had a ripple effect throughout the whole country literally halting retail rate deregulation in particular and halting state restructuring efforts in general. In fact, several states are going back to the old form of rate regulation as deregulation efforts have resulted in increased consumer prices.[28]

California electricity restructuring failed in design and in execution. The basic assumption was that the deregulation of the electricity industry, like several other industries before it, would: (1) reduce the amount of regulation on the utilities; (2) result in more electricity being produced at lower prices; (3) eliminate the inefficient providers; and (4) make electricity a competitive product. To accomplish those goals, the deregulatory design: (1) capped retail rates; (2) forced a utility to divest its transmission segment; (3) maintained a utility's service obligations; (4) created a state transmission operating entity; and (5) made allowance for a utility to recover transition or stranded costs. Goal and design did not function together as utilities were required to buy electricity at the market price but could not sell that electricity to the consumers above the capped price leading to bankruptcy, price manipulation,[29] and the failure of electricity restructuring.

The Energy Policy Act of 1992 was the next major act that smoothed out some of rough bumps in the previous legislation. EPAct 1992 was also intended to be a response to the 1970s energy crises by reducing our country's growing dependence on foreign oil. The Act removed some of the impediments to investment in electric power and furthered the development of new sources of electricity generation that began under the National Energy Act. The 1992 Act also continued natural gas deregulation, provided tax relief to independent oil and gas producers and to synfuels producers, streamlined nuclear power regulation, authorized research into clean coal

26. *See, e.g.*, Peter Carstensen, *Creating Workably Competitive Wholesale Markets in Energy: Necessary Conditions, Structure, and Conduct*, 1 ENVT'L & ENERGY L. & POL. J. 85 (2005).

27. *See, e.g.*, Jacqueline Lang Weaver, *Can Energy Markets Be Trusted? The Effect of the Rise and Fall of Enron on Energy Markets*, 4 HOUSTON BUS. & TAX L. J. 1 (2004); NANCY RAPOPORT & JEFFREY D. VAN NIEL, ENRON AND OTHER CORPORATE FIASCOS: THE CORPORATE SCANDAL READER (2d ed. Foundation Press 2009).

28. GREGORY BASHEDA *et al.*, WHY ARE ELECTRICITY PRICES INCREASING?: AN INDUSTRY-WIDE PERSPECTIVE (June 2006) *available at* http://www.eei.org/industry_issues/electricity_policy/state_and_local_policies/rising_electricity_costs/Brattle_Report.pdf.

29. *See, e.g.*, Darren Bush & Carrie Mayne, *In (Reluctant) Defense of Enron: Why Bad Regulation Is to Blame for California's Power Woes (or Why Antitrust Law Fails to Protect Against Market Power When the Market Rules Encourage Its Use)*, 83 OR. L. REV. 207 (2004).

technologies, and initiated production tax credits for wind and biomass while extending production tax credits for solar and geothermal power. Yet, even with provisions for alternative and renewable resources, EPAct 1992 was heavily protective of fossil fuels.

The NEA, ESA, and EPAct 1992 were the precursors of the first energy legislation of the new century—the Energy Policy Act of 2005 and the Energy Independence and Security Act of 2007. Both acts largely continue traditional energy policies. Vice President Cheney's "secretive"[30] National Energy Policy (NEP), published May 2001, formed the basis for EPAct 2005. The NEP addressed the urgent need for more energy production arguing that we are facing the most significant energy shortage since the mid-1970s and that we will need a 32% increase in energy production by 2020.[31] The NEP also emphasized the preference for private sector energy production, the need for more oil refineries, the possibility of drilling in the Arctic National Wildlife Refuge, and the need for an improved electricity infrastructure. The NEP also spoke about the need for more nuclear power while giving a nod to conservation and to alternative and renewable energy resources.

Drawing on the NEP, EPAct 2005 was signed into law on August 8, 2005 just weeks before Katrina devastated New Orleans. Hurricanes Katrina and Rita should have served as wake-up calls to align more closely our energy and environmental policies, but they were not heard as such.[32] Instead, EPAct 2005 continues old ways. Upon signing the law, President Bush explicitly emphasized the key economic assumption behind traditional energy policy—the more energy we consume the healthier our economy will be "so people can realize their dreams."[33] The traditional economic assumption about a direct energy-economy link contained in EPAct 2005 shows no awareness of the need for a more dynamic energy policy in the face of global warming.

EPAct 2005 stayed true to traditional energy policies and while it does not authorize drilling in ANWR, it does streamline nuclear power plant licensing and construction, allows for the fast tracking of liquid natural gas (LNG) facilities, promotes clean coal projects, and mandates a survey for the outer continental shelf for further oil and gas exploration and production while giving a nod to conservation and to alternative and renewable energy resources.

The heart of EPAct 2005 is the Electricity Modernization Act that significantly amended the Public Utility Holding Company Act of 1935 and the Public Utility Regulatory Policy Act of 1978. The latter acts passed 70 and 30 years ago, respectively, were intended to put constraints on electric utilities. Those restraints were loosened in the 2005 Act with the intent of promoting the electricity market and lowering prices to consumers as new sources of electricity came on line. Such has not come to pass. The looser restrictions have enabled greater industry concentration,[34] and, as already noted, "deregulation" has been stalled as electricity prices remain high.[35] These statutory provisions support old ways of electricity regulation, which means increased coal consumption instead of promoting smarter, renewable alternatives.

---

30. The National Energy Plan published in the first year of the Bush Administration in May 2001, we now know, was the product of an energy study group headed by Vice President Cheney and dominated by fossil fuel industry participants even though the Administration prevailed in court to keep the list of participants secret. *See, e.g.*, John M. Broder, *New Glimpse at Players in Group Led by Cheney*, N. Y. Times (July 19, 2007). Also, when the Administration desired to peer into the future regarding our energy needs, it turned to the oil industry to tell us that we will need more energy, especially oil. *See* Jad Mouawad, *Big Rise Seen in Demand for Energy*, N. Y. Times (July 19, 2007). *See also* Cheney v. U.S. District Court for the District of Columbia, 542 U. S. 367 (2004).

31. National Energy Policy 1-1.

32. Joseph P. Tomain, *Katrina's Energy Message*, 20 Natural Resources & Env't 43 (Spring 2006).

33. *See* www.whitehouse.gov/news/releases/2005/08/20050808-6.html.

34. *See, e.g.*, Richard D. Cudahy, *Deregulation and Mergers: Is Consolidation Inevitable?*, 134 Pub. Util. Fort. 46 (October 15, 1996); Richard Stavros, *Merger Frenzy*, 145 Pub. Util. Fort. 22 (April 2007).

35. David Cay Johnston, *Competitive Era Fails to Shrink Electric Bills*, N.Y. Times A1 (Oct. 15, 2006).

On December 19, 2007, President Bush signed the Energy Independence and Security Act at the instigation of the Democrat-controlled Congress. The act does move the needle toward an alternative policy. The act established a mandatory renewable fuels standard requiring fuel producers to use at least 36 billion gallons of biofuels by 2022. Fortunately, Congress saw the need for a more aggressive approach to alternative fuels. Unfortunately, Congress set its sights on corn-based ethanol which is expensive, energy inefficient, and has the unwanted consequence of raising food prices.

Under the act, oil demand is intended to be reduced by setting national fuel economy standards at 35 miles per gallon by 2020. This is the first increase in fuel standards since 1975. The act also includes provisions to improve energy efficiency in lighting standards in federal buildings and setting new, higher efficiency appliance standards.

Fossil-fuel interests were heartened and frustrated by the act. They were heartened by the absence in the act of a set of proposed taxes, estimated at $12 billion, to be imposed on the oil industry. They were frustrated that the act did not open new public lands to oil exploration and development. Yet, on signing the legislation President Bush urged Congress to pass legislation opening the outer continental shelf and the Arctic National Wildlife Refuge for exactly that purpose. Environmentalists were also heartened and frustrated. They were heartened because Congress rebuffed automotive industry attempts to prevent higher fuel-efficiency standards. They were frustrated by the act because it did not include a national renewable portfolio standard requirement that at least 15% of a utility's electricity should be generated from non-fossil fuels thus reducing coal use.

Dominant Model of Energy Policy

From President Carter's Energy Security Act through President Bush's Energy Security and Independence Act, provisions have been made for alternative and renewable energy resources. However, the tendency to favor conventional, especially fossil, fuels over alternative resources is demonstrable. Throughout the period, energy R&D funding has declined steadily and government subsidies and financial incentives favor conventional resources by multiples.

The energy funding contained in EPAct 2005 is tilted heavily in favor of fossil fuels despite the calls for new initiatives favoring new energy sources. The text of EPAct 2005 itself stated that it would provide $14.5 billion for energy industries.[36] A House Minority Report indicated that 85% of the $14.5 billion would go to oil, coal, and nuclear power.[37] Other commentators, such as Bloomberg and the Public Interest Research Group, confirm the House Report that the bulk of the money would go to fossil fuel and nuclear power.[38] Production tax credits for wind, geothermal and some types of biomass fuel, that were established in the EPAct 1992, apply only to projects that are on line before January 1, 2008 and are not extended in EPAct 2005,[39] although they have been renewed in the past.

In his 2006 State of the Union message, President Bush recommended investment in zero-emission coal technologies as well as investments in solar and wind power. The message also sug-

---

36. Energy Policy Act of 2005 §§ 101–237.

37. U.S. House of Representatives Committee on Government Reform—Minority Staff Special Investigations Division, *Key Impacts of the Energy Bill—H. R., 6,* (July 2005); *see also* Robert L. Bamberger & Carl E. Behrens, *CRS Issue Brief for Congress: Energy Policy: Comprehensive Energy Legislation (H. R. 6) in the 109th Congress* (July 29, 2005).

38. Bloomberg News, *U.S. Energy Industry's Lobbying Pays Off With $11.6 Bln in Aid* (August 6, 2005) *available at* http://www.bloomberg.com/apps/news?pid=10000103&sid=agbeVimf04Ec&refer=us; U. S. PIRG & Friends of the Earth, Final Energy Tax Package Overwhelmingly Favors Polluting Industries (July 27, 2005) *available at* http://newenergyfuture.com/final2005energybilltaxanalysis.pdf.

39. DOE, Energy Information Administration, Annual Energy Outlook 2007: With Projections to 2030, at 16 (February 2007).

gested that the United States fund research and development for hybrid cars, batteries, and ethanol, and that we begin to wean ourselves from Middle East oil imports. If we go inside the numbers of the State of the Union, however, we find that it is estimated that its total investment would be about $236 million or 1/40th of the $10.8 billion quarterly profit that Exxon enjoyed in 2007. The energy message also recommended research and development of new batteries and allotted the miserly sum of $6.7 million for such investment.[40]

Legislation, regulations, and government funding all have contributed to creating a dominant model[41] of energy policy which favors conventional producers, disadvantages alternative resources, and has a negative effect on the environment.[42] Reforming energy policy requires understanding the dominant model and the assumptions behind it, then rethinking those assumptions.

The dominant model of energy policy is a paradigmatic example of how an idea, a particular version of free market ideology, has captured U.S. politics and markets to the benefit of industry interests and to the detriment of environmentally sensitive and economically valuable alternatives. Traditional energy industry actors, for over a century, have been successful in using free market rhetoric to frame the debate about energy. The language of the debate has been successful in ensuring that government institutions and policies are fossil-fuel friendly and serve to sustain a healthy economy while protecting national security.[43] Government should support, and lightly regulate, conventional energy resources, particularly fossil fuels, the argument goes, as good (and necessary) for our country to have and enjoy a healthy economy. More importantly, in a dangerous and troubled world, a sound fossil-fuel policy is also necessary (and good) for our country's domestic and global security.

This energy argument, and the free market rhetoric supporting it, would be unobjectionable except for three things: (1) the idea itself is flawed in theory and flawed in execution; (2) it ignores the extraordinarily inefficient social costs generated by pollution; and (3) it hampers the development of preferable, less costly, and more promising alternatives that will strengthen the economy and make our energy mix more self-sustaining. In short, this version of free market politics, especially as employed by the interests of conventional fuels, is insensitive to the changing economics that can stimulate innovation, open new markets, and bring new technologies on line all to the point of responding to the challenges of global warming.

The dominant model is based on three economic assumptions. The first assumption is that *More is Better*. The more energy that is produced and consumed, the healthier the economy will be. This assumption worked well for most of the 20th century. For most of the century, energy and the economy did move in tandem as a national energy infrastructure was built, as energy was abundant and reliable, and as prices remained stable. In the last decades of the century, however, price stability has eroded.

The second assumption is *Bigger is Better (and Cheaper)*. The idea behind this assumption is that economies of scale in energy production can be realized and that the more energy that is produced, the lower the unit costs. It is cheaper per barrel to produce 10,000 bpd rather than 1

---

40. *See* David B. Sandalow, *President Bush and Oil Addiction*, THE BROOKINGS INSTITUTION, Feb. 3, 2006, *available at* http://brookings.edu/views/op-ed/fellows/sandalow_20060203.htm.

41. Joseph P. Tomain, *The Dominant Model of United States Energy Policy*, 61 UNIV. OF COLO. L. REV. 355 (1990).

42. *See, e.g.*, DOUGLAS KOPLOW & AARON MARTIN, FUELING GLOBAL WARMING: FEDERAL SUBSIDIES TO OIL IN THE UNITED STATES ES-1 (Greenpeace 2005), *available at* http://www.greenpeace.org/usa/press-center/reports4/fueling-global-warming; NORMAN MYERS & JENNIFER KENT, PERVERSE SUBSIDIES: HOW TAX DOLLARS CAN UNDERCUT THE ENVIRONMENT AND THE ECONOMY 5–9 (Island Press 2001).

43. *See, e.g.*, Cutler J. Cleveland & Robert K. Kaufman, *Oil Supply and Oil Politics: Déjà Vu All Over Again*, 31 ENERGY POLICY 485 (2003) (further development of domestic oil will not significantly increase US production); Statement by the Center for Security Policy—*"Set America Free": A Blueprint for U. S. Energy Security*, *available at* http://www.setamericafree.org/blueprint.pdf.

bpd. Again, the arguing for economies of scale makes sense and scale economies were realized until the last third of the century. Nuclear plants were more expensive than anticipated; electricity plants reached excess capacity; the electric grid needs improvement; no new oil refineries were built since the 1970s; and, domestic natural gas supplies are declining. All of these factors mean that energy prices are increasing and that scale economies have been reached doing energy business the old way.

The final assumption is that *Markets are Good*. Instead of a fully coordinated and integrated plan, our energy policy assumes that private markets and private capital can best support independently operated energy firms and industries. In that way, competition can stimulate innovation among the sectors. Electric utilities, for example, do not use only one fuel to generate electricity; instead they have a portfolio of resources to economize on fuel costs.

The dominant model of energy policy was developed on these three assumptions with the following goals:(1) assure abundant supply; (2) at reasonable prices; (3) while limiting the market power of monopoly firms; (4) promoting inter-fuel competition; (5) supporting conventional, predominantly fossil, fuels; and (6) while relying on federal decision-making to guide national policy.

As a result of these assumptions, energy industries developed identifiable characteristics. Called the "hard path" by Amory Lovins over 30 years ago,[44] hard path energy industries were large-scale, capital-intensive, and centrally regulated. The oil, natural gas, coal, nuclear power, and electricity industries each have those characteristics. Consumers have grown familiar with these industries. Producers enjoy the competitive advantages of incumbency. And regulators understand the businesses that they regulate. The problem is that this coziness comes at too high a price. Consequently, the assumptions and the policy goals behind them must be reassessed for a sustainable energy future. We can recognize that each of these assumptions was true—to a point.[45] The problem of reaching that point is simply stated: The country cannot continue to pollute at the levels that we are experiencing and not realize negative economic effects.

An Energy Policy for the 21st Century

At the national level, the Energy Policy Act of 2005 and the Energy Independence and Security Act of 2007 largely continue the old ways as we await climate change legislation from the U.S. Congress. Nevertheless, there has been a new thinking about energy policy by broad-based and bipartisan groups of business, government, and academic leaders interested in the energy future.[46] This new energy thinking has led to new assumptions about energy, new energy politics, and new energy strategies.

Today, however, while we continue to believe energy is vital for the economy, we also assume that our future energy policy must be environmentally sensitive and must be sensitive to national and global security. Therefore, instead of just two variables—energy and the economy—future energy policy involves the four variables of energy, economy, environment, and security.[47]

---

44. AMORY B. LOVINS, SOFT ENERGY PATHS: TOWARD A DURABLE PEACE ch.2 (HarperCollins 1977).

45. *See* Joseph P. Tomain, *To A Point*, 52 LOYOLA L. REV.1201 (2007); Herman E. Daly, *Economics in a Full World*, SCI. AM., Sept. 2005 at 100; AMORY B. LOVINS, SOFT ENERGY PATHS: TOWARD A DURABLE PEACE chs. 1–2 (HarperCollins 1977); SACHS, *supra* note 2, at 29–30.

46. *See* ENERGY FUTURE COALITION, CHALLENGE AND OPPORTUNITY: CHARTING A NEW ENERGY FUTURE (2003), *available at* http://www.energyfuturecoaltion.org/pubs/EFCRreport.pdf; NATIONAL COMMISSION ON ENERGY POLICY, ENDING THE ENERGY STALEMATE: A BIPARTISAN STRATEGY TO MEET AMERICA'S ENERGY CHALLENGES (2004), *available at* http:\\www.nrel.gov\pv\thin_film\docs\energy_policy_report_2004 _for_ doe.pdf; WILLIAM J. CLINTON FOUNDATION, NEW THINKING ON ENERGY POLICY (2004), *available at* http:\\www.clintonfoundation.org\120604-nr-cf-gn-env-usa-fe-new-thinking-on-energy-policy.htm.

47. *See, e.g.*, Cutler J. Cleveland & Robert K. Kaufman, *Oil Supply and Oil Politics: Déjà Vu All Over Again*, 31 ENERGY POLICY 485 (2003) (further development of domestic oil will not significantly increase U.S. pro-

Designing a new energy policy comes with its own challenges. Aside from moving away from old policies and entrenched institutions and actors, it is also the case that the new energy variables are not always consonant and tradeoffs are inevitable.[48] There can be, for example, a trade-off between carbon reduction and security. A full-blown reduction strategy against carbon emissions would suggest an expansion of nuclear power. However, nuclear power, in turn, has its own security issues. In short, integrating energy, economy, environment and security requires a rethinking of the old assumptions as we develop a new policy and new approaches. If we combine these variables, then we can construct a new energy policy based on the following principles. Our future energy policy will: (1) use a *diversity* of energy resources; (2) in *efficient* and effective ways; (3) while being *environmentally* responsible; and, while (4) promoting domestic and global *security*.

New Energy Assumptions

Less is More. The core idea behind the dominant energy policy is that there was a direct energy-economy link so that the more energy we use, the healthier our economy would be. As we continue to pollute and consume the commons, we cannot expect continued economic growth. Jeffrey Sachs writes that "Anthropocentric climate change is the greatest of all environmental risks" and will "impose catastrophic hardships on many parts of the world." More to our point, "Markets alone, on a business-as-usual path, will not carry us to safety."[49]

The case of China, today, is instructive. The Chinese economy is growing at double digits, coal-fired electric plants are being constructed at the rate of two per week, and the World Bank estimates that there are upwards of three-quarter of a million premature deaths attributable to environmental pollution annually.[50] Pan Yue, a vice minister of China's State Environmental Protection Administration, has been quoted as saying the "the [economic] miracle will end soon because the environment can no longer keep pace."[51]

Instead of perpetual economic growth, there comes a point at which past policies must confront new realities and must change accordingly. We cannot continue to burn fossil fuels and expect to skip out on the environmental check when it becomes due. We will, of course, need more energy as the world population grows and as countries develop. Nevertheless, we cannot continue to use energy in the same ways; we must harness more of the potential energy in all resources while turning to resources which generate less pollution.

Small is Beautiful[52] *(And Cheaper).* There are instances, natural monopolies with scale economies is one example, in which the assumption *Bigger is Better (And Cheaper)* prevails — but not continuously. Electric power plants have reached a technological plateau. Not so many years ago, plants over 1000 megawatts were being constructed. Today, the optimum size is about 600MW even for nuclear plants.[53] Traditional power plants reached the peak of their capacities

---

duction); Statement by the Center for Security Policy—*"Set America Free:" A Blueprint for U. S. Energy Security, available at* http://www.setamericafree.org/blueprint.pdf.

48. John Holdren, *The Energy Innovation Imperative: Addressing Oil Dependence, Climate Change, and Other 21st Century Energy Challenges*, 2 INNOVATIONS 3 (Spring 2006).

49. SACHS, *supra* note 2, at 83 and ch. 5 *passim*.

50. Joseph Kahn & Jim Yardley, *As China Roars, Pollution Reaches Deadly Extremes*, N.Y. TIMES A1 (August 26, 2007).

51. Quoted in Elizabeth Economy, *The Great Leap Backward?*, FOREIGN AFFAIRS 38 (September/October 2007).

52. *See* E. F. SCHUMAKER, SMALL IS BEAUTIFUL: ECONOMICS AS IF PEOPLE MATTERED (Harper Perennial 1973).

53. *See, e.g.*, Jesse H. Ausbel, *Big Green Energy Machines: How Are we Going to Generate More Power and Decrease its Impact on the Environment?*, AMERICAN INSTITUTE OF PHYSICS (October/November 2004) *available at* http://www.aip.org/tip/INPHFA/vol-10/iss-5/p20.pdf.

and the cost of electricity began to rise. As noted above, PURPA demonstrated that alternative power producers were able and willing to put cheaper electricity on the market as the large utility behemoths are beginning to face competition from smaller competitors including wind farms and distributed generation.

The iPhone serves as model and metaphor for the new electric utility—the iUtility. The iUtility no more resembles a smoke-belching power plant than the iPhone resembles the heavy black rotary dial telephone of the past. Rather, the iUtility, like the iPhone, is technologically sophisticated, offers various services and products at various prices, and is adaptable, transparent, competitive and responsive to changing market demands.

The traditional IOU was vertically integrated, capital intensive, large-scale, centralized, depended on a wired network for transmission and distribution, and sold only one product—electricity. The traditional telephone company was integrated, capital intensive, large-scale, centralized, depended on a wired network for distribution, and sold only one product—telephony. The iPhone is not attached to any wall or desk, is not connected to a wired network, is not the product of an integrated firm, is small-scale, customizable, personalized, and sells music, videos, maps, internet access, PDA capabilities, photography, dictation and, as a byproduct—telephony. The iUtility will more resemble the iPhone than the IOU.

Regulation is Good. Private markets and private capital are good. Market competition creates wealth, stimulates innovation, allows producers to place all sorts of goods on the market while expanding consumer choice. Resource use is maximized and efficiency is achieved, the theory goes, through market competition. However, relative to energy industries there are two problems with this theoretical picture. First, none of the conventional energy industries operated in a completely unfettered free market. Instead, each has been the beneficiary of government largesse as the history of energy regulation demonstrated.

While the oil industry is relatively lightly regulated, oil has been and continues to be a centerpiece of our domestic and foreign policies. Domestically, the oil industry has had favorable royalty treatment,[54] benefitted from relaxed or ignored enforcement of price controls,[55] and has received generous tax treatment,[56] among other favors.[57] Internationally, blood for oil is not merely a metaphor, it is a harsh reality.[58]

---

54. *See, e.g.,* Edmund L. Andrews, *Inspector Finds Broad Failures in Oil Program,* N. Y. Times A1 (September 26, 2007); Office of the Inspector General, Department of the Interior, Minerals Management Service: False Claims Allegations (September 19, 2007); DOI Office of Inspector General, Audit Report: Mineral Management Service's Compliance Review Process 6 (December 6, 2006).

55. *See* Kalt, *supra* note 18.

56. *See* Mona Hymel, *The United States Experience with Energy-Based Tax Incentives: The Evidence Supporting Tax Incentives for Renewable Energy,* 38 Loy. U. Chi. L. J. 43 (2006); Salvatore Lazzari, CRS Issue Brief for Congress: Energy Tax Policy (April 22, 2005) *available at* http://kuhl.house.gov/UploadedFiles/energy%20tax.pdf; Salvatore Lazzari, CRS Issue Brief for Congress: Energy Tax Policy: An Economic Analysis (June 28, 2005) *available at* http://cnie.org/NLE/CRSreports/05jun/RL30406.pdf.

57. In EPAct 2005, the Secretary of the Interior was given discretion to forgive royalty payments and was required to map the outer continental shelf for oil and gas exploration. Both are financial benefits to the oil and gas industries. Royalty payments are not insubstantial. The Interior Department had dropped certain claims against oil companies that would forgive hundreds of millions of dollars of royalties. The announcement that Interior intended to drop those charges was quickly met with a request by the Republican-led House Government Reform Committee to ask the government accounting office to look into potential deficiencies in how the government collects billions of dollars in royalties. *See* Edmund L. Andrews, *U.S. Drops Bid Over Royalties from Chevron,* NY Times A1 (Oct. 31, 2006); *U.S. Agency To Review Oil Royalties,* NY Times C1 (Nov. 2, 2006).

58. *See, e.g.,* Daniel Yergin, The Prize: The Epic Quest for Oil, Money and Power (Free Press 1991); Toyin Falola & Ann Genova, The Politics of the Global Oil Industry (Praeger Publishers 2005);

By contrast, the coal industry is heavily regulated for environmental, health and safety concerns through such legislation as the Clean Air Act, the Clean Water Act, the Surface Mining Control and Reclamation Act, and the Black Lung Act. Nevertheless, the coal industry is twice blessed. In EPAct 2005 and in the Energy Independence and Security Act of 2007, there are substantial R&D earmarks for clean coal technologies and the Interior Secretary is directed to make more federal lands available for coal exploration.[59] And, regardless of the heavy-hand of government regulation, all of this health and safety legislation is under-enforced. Lands are not fully reclaimed, reclamation standards are slated to be relaxed, streams and valleys continue to receive the detritus from nearby coal mines, the industry continues to fight the imposition of the clean air standards,[60] and miners continue to work in unsafe conditions as the recent tragedies in the Crandall Canyon and Sago mines attest.

To round off the conventional energy industries, the natural gas industry has been favored in recent legislation by taking away the oversight roles of state and local governments in the siting process for LNG ports. The electricity industry has been given a freer rein to consolidate.[61] And, the nuclear power industry had received a set of financial incentives and a more streamlined licensing process in EPAct 1992 and EPAct 2005.

The point is a simple one. Free market rhetoric does not operate unfettered for our energy policy. Government financial and regulatory support, not the free market alone, has fortified the conventional energy industries and has not been as generous with alternative energy producers; now the government must rethink its financial policies in order to level the playing field as legislative and regulatory responses to global warming develop. This rethinking must also take into account the social costs of pollution which the dominant energy policy and the conventional energy industries have ignored.

Combined, our three reformulated policy assumptions led to a fourth assumption — inaction is unacceptable. We must acknowledge and accept the economic reality that the global commons is a public good. We must also acknowledge and accept that global warming cannot be ignored, that precaution,[62] not old habits, is a valuable perspective and that neither the competitive market nor the self-interested private actors in it can protect our commons if they operate only under free market principles. Instead, government regulation, including financial incentives, will play an indispensable role in a new energy policy addressing global warming.

MICHAEL T. KLARE, BLOOD AND OIL: THE DANGERS AND CONSEQUENCES OF AMERICA'S GROWING DEPENDENCY ON IMPORTED PETROLEUM (Holt Paperbacks 2004).

59. *See* KEVIN J. MCINTYRE, MARTIN V. KIRKWOOD & JASON F. LEIF, ENERGY POLICY ACT OF 2005: SUMMARY AND ANALYSIS OF THE ACT'S MAJOR PROVISIONS § 1.4 (LexisNexis 2006).

60. *See* Environmental Defense Fund v. Duke Energy Corp., 549 U.S. 561 (2007); *see also* United States v. New York (U.S. District Court S. D. Ohio Civil action No C2-99-1250) (Consent Decree Oct. 9, 2007) ($4.6 billion settlement of Clean Air Act "new source review" standards litigation between the US Environmental Protection Agency, nine states and seven utilities).

61. *See, e.g.,* Richard D. Cudahy, *Deregulation and Mergers: Is Consolidation Inevitable?,* 134 PUB. UTIL. FORT. 46 (October 15, 1996); Richard Stavros, *Merger Frenzy,* 145 PUB. UTIL. FORT. 22 (April 2007).

62. *See* John S. Applegate, *The Taming of the Precautionary Principle,* 27 WM. & MARY ENVT'L L. & POL. REV. 12 (2002). For a critical analysis of the precautionary principle, see CASS R. SUNSTEIN, WORST CASE SCENARIOS ch 3 (Harvard Un. Press 2007).

New Energy Politics

Together with the new energy thinking, there is a new energy politics. New energy research centers and institutes are proliferating,[63] new energy coalitions are forming,[64] and new energy markets are developing. Two examples should suffice. The Climate Action Partnership joins major utilities and environmental interest groups to discuss energy policy development. And, the Environmental Defense recruited Jon Anda, Vice Chairman of Morgan Stanley, to serve as president of the Environmental Markets Network—a new collaboration to engage business leaders to promote market-based economic solutions to climate change issues.[65]

Future energy policy will not be tied to old ways. Instead, future energy policy acknowledges and will be responsive to climate change, will develop new fossil-fuel policies, new utility policies, and, most importantly, will develop new markets and new technologies. To accomplish all of these goals, energy strategies move away from the traditional hard path structure of energy industries that are large-scale, capital intensive, and highly centralized, and significantly protected from competition. Future energy actors will face increased competition, energy production will be scaled-to-task, there will be greater energy diversity, and there will be greater decentralization.[66]

What is embedded in our new energy thinking and new politics is a new economics. In the last few years, a new energy actor, if not unanticipated, surprising nonetheless, has entered the energy stage—Wall Street. Commercial banks such as Citi and JP Morgan have agreed to a set of Carbon Principles which will guide their lending in the energy arena.[67] Investment banks, such as Goldman Sachs, have renewable energy investment units and major philanthropists, such as Richard Branson, is engaged in venture philanthropy specifically aimed at merging energy markets.

In 2006, over $100 billion of sustainable energy transactions took place and it was noted that "this is more than just interesting data, it is a powerful market signal to the arrival of an alternative future for today's fossil-fuel dominated energy markets ... this is full-scale industrial development, not just a tweaking of the energy system."[68] These new markets are directed at merging energy and the environment through such efforts as emissions trading, carbon investments, renewable investments, green technologies, and the like. These emerging markets involve capitalist

---

63. *See, e.g.*, Princeton Environmental Institute at http://web.princeton.edu/sites/pei/; Yale School of Forestry & Environmental Studies at http://environment.yale.edu/index.html; Harvard Electricity Policy Group at http://www.ksg.harvard.edu/hepg/; University of California Energy Institute at http://www.ucei.berkeley.edu/.

64. *See, e.g.*, U. S. Climate Action Partnership at www.uscap.org.; American Council on Renewable Energy at http://www.acore.org/.

65. *See* Environmental Defense Press Release, *Environmental Defense Announces Jon Anda as President of New Environmental Markets Network* (January 25, 2007), *available at* http://www.edf.org/pressrelease.cfm?contentID=6063.

66. *See, e.g.*, Eric Lambin, The Middle Path: Avoiding Environmental Catastrophe (Un. of Chicago Press 2007); Ted Nordhaus & Michael Shellenberger, Break Through: From the Death of Environmentalism to the Politics of Possibility (Houghton Mifflin 2007).

67. *See, e.g.*, *The Carbon Principles*—a statement by three leading commercial banks about lending practices which are carbon sensitive, *available at* http://www.morganstanley.com/global/CarbonPrinciplesFinal.pdf.

68. Chris Greenwood *et al.*, Global Trends in Sustainable Energy Investment 2008: Analysis of Trends and Issues in the Financing of Renewable Energy and Energy Efficiency in OECD and Developing Countries (2008), United National Environment Programme, *available at* http://www.ren21.net/pdf/Global_Trends_2008.pdf.

investment[69] and just reject traditional energy policy and rely, instead, on innovation and new technology for both a healthy environment and a healthy energy economy.[70]

New Energy Strategies

Predicting the future is always dicey and predicting the energy future has been more often wrong than right.[71] However, we should draw some comfort in the fact that sometimes predictions are correct[72] and that sometimes the signs are clear, at least about the general direction in which we must go. We can say, with a high degree of confidence, that we know the following about the future:

(1) climate change must be addressed;
(2) fossil fuels will continue to be primary fuels; and
(3) carbon reduction strategies will occur.

What is less clear, where future challenges lie, and what we cannot see with the clarity that we might desire is the precise shape of our energy future. The energy future we do not know consists of uncertainty about:

(1) the role of nuclear power;
(2) the timing and cost effectiveness of "clean coal" technologies;
(3) the proper mix of energy efficiency and renewable resources;
(4) the proper carbon reduction strategies; and
(5) the proper level of investments in new strategies and the financial risks involved with those new investments.

Nevertheless, we can make certain comments about the new energy politics and about future energy strategies. The federal government should continue to legislate in this area and should regain its former role as a national leader in energy policy formation and regulation. In addition to turning to the federal government for guidance, however, we can look to cities and states and regions for responsive climate control, policies, and regulations.[73] We can also look to new bipartisan coalitions for continued energy thinking and we can look to new players, new trade associations, and new research efforts to provide solid analysis and assessment. We can also look to new energy markets as old Wall Street meets new venture capital and new venture philanthropy. And, we can look to new energy strategies which would include redistribution of government subsidies, and increase in energy R & D, the use of multiple public actors, prolifer-

---

69. *See also* WORLDWATCH INSTITUTE, 2008 STATE OF THE WORLD: INNOVATIONS FOR A SUSTAINABLE ECONOMY (2008).

70. *See* WILLIAM J. BAUMOL, ROBERT E. LITAN & CARL J. SCHRAMM, GOOD CAPITALISM, BAD CAPITALISM, AND THE ECONOMICS OF GROWTH AND PROSPERITY (Yale Un. Press 2007); WILLIAM J. BAUMOL, THE FREE-MARKET INNOVATION MACHINE: ANALYZING THE GROWTH MIRACLE OF CAPITALISM (Princeton Un. Press 2002); DANIEL S. ESTY & ANDREW S. WINSTON, GREEN TO GOLD: HOW SMART COMPANIES USE ENVIRONMENTAL STRATEGY TO INNOVATE, CREATE VALUE AND BUILD COMPETITIVE ADVANTAGE (Wiley 2006); JASON FURMAN *et al.*, AN ECONOMIC STRATEGY TO ADDRESS CLIMATE CHANGE AND PROMOTE ENERGY SECURITY (October, 2007) (The Hamilton Project *available at* http://www.brookings.edu/papers/2007/10climatechange_furman.aspx); FLORIAN BRESSAND *et al.*, WASTED ENERGY: HOW THE US CAN REACH ITS ENERGY PRODUCTIVITY POTENTIAL (June, 2007); (McKensey Report *available at* http://www.mckinsey.com/mgi/publications/wasted_energy/index.asp).

71. *Compare* DONELLA H. MEADOWS, *et al.*, THE LIMITS TO GROWTH: A REPORT FOR THE CLUB OF ROME'S PROJECT ON THE PREDICAMENT OF MANKIND (Universe Books 1972) *with* MODELS OF DOOM: A CRITIQUE OF THE LIMITS OF GROWTH (H.S.D. Cole ed., Universe Publishing 1973).

72. *See* Amory B. Lovins, *Energy Strategy: The Road Not Taken?*, 55 FOREIGN AFFAIRS 65 (October 1976). Written nearly 30 years ago, Lovins' analysis is remarkably accurate today.

73. *See* the Regional Greenhouse Gas Initiative (RGGI): an initiative of the Northeastern and Mid-Atlantic State of the U.S., the multi-state effort to control carbon emissions *available at* http://www.rggi.org/.

ation of public-private partnerships, and willingness to sustain private investment in technology and innovation.

Conclusion

As in the past, we will rely on a mix of regulation and markets; we will not adopt a comprehensive energy policy aimed at coordinating energy industries; and we will not move dramatically away from the hard path of fossil fuels, large-scale producers, and a national energy infrastructure. Unlike the past, we must redesign the regulatory/market mix to assure more flexible market-based regulations which promote competition, innovation, and environmental protection; we must promote a diversity of resources while downsizing producers; and, we must diversify our energy portfolios with a greater investment in renewable and non-conventional energy resources. Let's assume for the moment that climate change is not a threat: Then a new, more efficient, more resource protective and more scaled-down energy system makes great sense as we move more rapidly into the 21st century.

Notes

1. Noam Chomsky, Failed States: The Abuse of Power and the Assault on Democracy 206 (Henry Holt & Co. 2006):

> The political system that is the subject of these critiques bears some resemblance to the initial design, though the framers would surely have been appalled by many subsequent developments, in particular the radical judicial activism that granted rights of persons to "collectivist legal entities" (corporations), rights extended far beyond those of persons of flesh and blood in recent international economic arrangements (mislabeled "free trade agreements"). Each such step is a severe attack against classical liberal principles, democracy, and markets. The enormously powerful immortal "persons" that have been created are, furthermore, required by law to suffer from moral deficiencies that we would regard as pathological among real people. A core principal of Anglo-American corporate law is that they must be dedicated single-mindedly to material self-interest. They are permitted to do "good works," but only if these have a favorable impact on image, hence profit and market share....

2. Amory B. Lovins, Soft Energy Parts: Toward a Durable Peace 3 (Penguin Books 1977):

> The energy problem, according to conventional wisdom, is how to increase energy supplies (especially domestic supplies) to meet projected demands. The solution to this problem is familiar: ever more remote and fragile places are to be ransacked, at ever greater risk and cost, for increasingly elusive fuels, which are then to be converted to premium forms—electricity and fluids—in ever more costly, complex, centralized, and gigantic plants. The side effects of these efforts become increasingly intolerable even as their output allegedly becomes ever more essential to our way of life and our very survival.

Compare id. at 218:

> Sunlight leaves an earth unravished, husbanded, renewed. It leaves a people unmutated, convivial, even illuminated. Above all, it respects the limits that are always with us on a little planet: the delicate fragility of life, the imperfection of human societies, and the frailty of the human design. We can still choose to live lightly, to live with light, and so choose life itself—by capturing the Hope left waiting at the bottom of Pandora's box.

3. *See* WILLIAM H. RODGERS, JR., ENVIRONMENTAL LAW IN INDIAN COUNTRY § 1:11 at 298–301 (Thomson / West 2005) (discussing the Federal Advisory Committee Act) (footnotes as in original, with sleight adaptations):

Case No. 83—Cheney v. United States District Court for the District of Columbia, 2001–present

The [National Energy Policy Development] Group recommends that the President issue an Executive Order to direct all federal agencies to include in any regulatory action that could significantly and adversely affect energy supplies, distribution, or use, a detailed statement on: (1) the energy impact of the proposed action, (2) any adverse energy effects that cannot be avoided should the proposal be implemented, and (3) alternatives to the proposed action.

> *Report to the President of the*
> *National Energy Policy Development Group*
> *[The Cheney Task Force], May, 2001*[78]

Few remember that the chief inspiration for FACA was President Nixon's National Industrial Pollution Control Council that brought industrialists to the helm of the administration's environmental policy under the auspices of Secretary of Commerce Maurice Stans.[79] Each industry met in sub-councils. Sub-council reports and minutes were made available to the public. Nobody mentioned executive privilege.

Times change. Executive privilege is now an important defense under FACA.

The National Energy Policy Development Group, headed by Vice President Dick Cheney, lists fourteen government officials as members. Its report that emerged in May 2001 is strongly pro-development. Tribes are barely mentioned. The Cheney report has 105 specific recommendations including the NEPA copy-cat, quoted above, that would extend process protections to agency actions that may affect adversely energy supplies. Even the beautiful pictures in this study have oil in them.

Figure 4. A striking image from 2001 Cheney Energy Report at 5-2. Although not shown here, this photo depicts the sun setting behind an offshore oil rig.

Suspecting the worst, two environmental groups, Judicial Watch and The Sierra Club, sued under FACA to get the minutes and working papers that might disprove their theory that industry (dressed up as subgroups, ad hoc or de facto groups, contractors or consultants) wrote the report or dictated its content. Attention focused on 24 boxes of documents that might answer this question.[80] The short of it was that the District Court ordered discovery and invited particularized executive privilege objections.[81] The government resisted all discovery, could not get an interlocutory order to appeal, and was obliged to seek mandamus in the court of appeals. It lost there[82] because, in usual times, mandamus is an extraordinary remedy and rarely granted.

---

78. RELIABLE, AFFORDABLE, AND ENVIRONMENTALLY SOUND ENERGY FOR AMERICA'S FUTURE 1–14 (May 2001) [2001 Cheney Energy Report].

79. William H. Rodgers, Jr., *The National Industrial Pollution Control Council: Advise or Collude?*, 13 B.C. IND. & COMM. L. REV. 719 (1972). Prof. Rodgers made a FOIA request for these so-called NIPCC documents. He received them, read them, and wrote about them.

80. Cheney v. United States District Court for the District of Columbia, 542 U.S. 367 n.5, 124 S.Ct. 2576, 159 L.Ed.2d 459, 487, 490 n.5 (2004) (Ginsburg, J., dissenting).

81. Judicial Watch, Inc. v. National Energy Policy Dev. Group, 219 F. Supp. 2d 20 (D. D.C. 2002) (other orders followed).

82. *In re* Cheney, 334 F.3d 1096 (D.C. Cir. 2003) (Randolph, C.J., dissenting).

In the Supreme Court, the issue thus became whether the court of appeals "may exercise its power to issue a writ of mandamus to modify or dissolve the orders when, by virtue of their overbreadth, enforcement might interfere with the officials in the discharge of their duties and impinge upon the President's constitutional prerogatives."[83] The court, in an opinion by Kennedy, J., answered this question in the affirmative. It thought that the extraordinary mandamus remedy should be available also to exert executive privilege above and beyond particularized separation-of-powers objections that had been disdained in the district court. It thus remanded the case to the court of appeals for an inquiry into whether the district court abused its discretion and took actions that "constituted an unwarranted impairment of another branch in the performance of its Constitutional duties."[84] The majority hints strongly that all this discovery trouble can be avoided if FACA is read as not reaching de facto committee participation such as that alleged.[85]

A Supreme Court cover-up. Simple enough. Easily understood. Wrapped in "executive privilege" and "mandamus."

4. For further comment on the Energy Policy Act of 2005, see GEORGE MONBIOT, HEAT: HOW TO STOP THE PLANET FROM BURNING 55 (South End Press 2007) (footnotes omitted) [hereinafter 2007 MONBIOT]:

> The Energy Policy Act the Bush administration pushed through Congress in 2005 handed a further $2.9 billion to the coal industry and $1.5 billion to oil and gas firms. According to the Democratic congressman Henry Waxman, the oil subsidy "was mysteriously inserted in the final energy legislation after the legislation was closed to further amendment." Most of the money, he discovered, would be administered by "a private consortium located in the district of Majority Leader Tom DeLay ... The leading contender for this contract appears to be the Research Partnership to Secure Energy for America (RPSEA) consortium ... Halliburton is a member of RPSEA and sits on the board, as does Marathon Oil Company ..."

> In short ... taxpayers will hire a private consortium controlled by the oil and gas industry to hand out over $1 billion to oil and gas companies. There is no conceivable rationale for this extraordinary largesse. The oil and gas industry is reporting record income and profits. According to one analyst, the net income of the top oil companies will total $230 billion in 2005.

5. *See* Robert N. Stavins, *A Meaningful U.S. Cap-and-Trade System to Address Climate Change*, 32 HARV. ENVTL. L. REV. 293 (2008).

6. "Cap-and-Trade" is an essential ingredient of all talked-about responses to global warming. Was the much celebrated acid rain program all trade and no cap? *See* BARBARA FREESE, COAL: A HUMAN HISTORY 170–71 (Penguin Books 2003):

---

83. Cheney v. United States District Court for the District of Columbia, 542 U.S. 367, 372–73, 124 S.Ct. 2476, 159 L.Ed.2d 459 (2004) (concurred in by five Justices; Thomas, J., joined by Scalia, J., would go farther and remand the case with instructions to issue the writ; Ginsburg, joined by Souter, JJs, dissent), *on remand* 406 F.3d 723 (D.C. Cir. 2005) (*en banc*) (issuing writ of mandamus directing district court to dismiss complaints and holding that the National Energy Policy Development Group and its subgroups are not FACA committees).

84. 542 U.S. 367, 159 L.Ed.2d at 484.

85. 542 U.S. 367, 159 L.Ed.2d at 485:
We note only that all courts should be mindful of the burdens imposed on the Executive Branch in any future proceedings. Special considerations applicable to the President and the Vice President suggest that the courts should be sensitive to requests by the Government for interlocutory appeals to reexamine, for example, whether the statute embodies the *de facto* membership doctrine.

Since 1990, when the acid rain issue disappeared from public view, there have been two big surprises. The first is that the SO_2 cuts have cost so much less than anyone thought—about twenty times less than some early industry estimates, and even less than environmentalists had predicted. SO_2 reductions have been a bargain thanks to cheaper-than-expected low-sulfur coal from the western United States, improving technology, and flexible regulations that allow the power industry to choose the cheapest means of compliance.

The second big surprise is less welcome: There is now evidence that the long-delayed and hotly debated cuts required by the 1990 law may not be enough. While acid rain has been reduced, average rainfall in many parts of the United States is still occasionally ten times more acidic than normal. After decades of being showered with acids, some areas have had the neutralizing minerals found naturally in the soils washed out, leaving them substantially more sensitive to newly arrived acids. The Canadian government has found that even after full implementation of the U.S. Acid Rain Program, thousands of Canadian lakes in an area the size of France and the United Kingdom combined will continue to acidify. Environmentalists point to studies showing acid-caused damage ranging from declining salmon stocks in Nova Scotia to the loss of trout in Virginia streams to the decline of red spruce and sugar maple in the Northeast, and are calling for additional SO_2 reductions of up to 80 percent beyond the 1990 requirements. Research suggests that even with cuts this deep, it will take up to a quarter of a century for some ecosystems to shake off the acidity accumulated over decades of pollution.

7. *See* 2007 Monbiot at 161:

The decision by governments in Europe and North America to pursue the development of biofuels is, in environmental terms, the most damaging they have ever taken. Knowing that the creation of this market will lead to a massive surge in imports of both palm oil from Malaysia and Indonesia and ethanol from rainforest land in Brazil; knowing that there is nothing meaningful they can do to prevent them; and knowing that these imports will accelerate rather than ameliorate climate change; our governments have decided to go ahead anyway.

8. Jeff Goodell, Big Coal: The Dirty Secret Behind America's Energy Future 242 (Houghton, Mifflin, 2006) [hereinafter 2006 Goodell, Big Coal]:

the sulfur dioxide trading program succeeded because there were precisely defined rules, firm caps, and significant penalties for exceeding the caps. In contrast, President George W. Bush's Clear Skies Initiative failed to attract much support. Not only did it not limit CO_2 emissions but it was poorly designed: it had loose caps, a long timetable for achieving goals, and it included a toxin, mercury, that accumulates in local "hot spots" and is therefore not suitable for a national trading program.

9. 2008 Friedman at 165:

No one designed this Dirty Fuels System, exactly. It just evolved from the eighteenth century until today, first powering the growth of the industrial West and more recently the soaring, trying-to-catch-up-as-fast-as-we-can growth of developing giants, like India, China, South Africa, Poland, and Egypt.

As systems go, it works quite efficiently. Coal, oil, and gas are extracted all over the world, tankers and trains and pipelines deliver these fossil fuels to power plants or refineries across the globe, and gasoline stations and power grids deliver their energy directly to consumers, who never think for a moment whether the lights will go on or a gas station will appear around the corner in the next few miles. The same is true for timber, water, and fish—it's all you can eat, all the time, until nothing is left. It is a system and it is deeply embedded.

But we cannot continue on with this Dirty Fuels System. If we do, the energy implications, the climate implications, the biodiversity implications, the geopolitical implications, and the energy poverty implications will undermine the quality of life for every person on this planet and eventually imperil life on earth itself.

10. Corporations and financial institutions appear to recognize that a new energy policy is necessary. As mentioned by Dean Tomain, one reflection of this awareness is the "Carbon Principles"[74] adopted by a number of major banks:

The Intent

We the adopting financial institutions have come together to advance a set of principles for meeting energy needs in the United States (US) that balance cost, reliability and greenhouse gas (GHG) concerns.[75] The principles focus on a portfolio approach that includes efficiency, renewable and low carbon power sources, as well as centralized generation sources in light of concerns regarding the impact of GHG emissions while recognizing the need to provide reliable power at a reasonable cost to consumers. The Carbon Principles ("the Principles") represent the first time that financial institutions, advised by their clients and environmental advocacy groups, have jointly committed to advance a consistent approach to the issue of climate change in the US electric power industry.

We advance these Principles to create an industry best practice for the evaluation of options to meet the electric power needs of the US in an environmentally responsible and cost effective manner. When evaluating the financing of new fossil fuel generation we will be guided by the Principles and employ the accompanying Enhanced Environmental Diligence Process (the "Enhanced Diligence Process") to assess project economics and financing parameters related to the uncertainties around current climate change policy in the US. The Enhanced Diligence Process will evaluate the ability of the proposed financing to meet financial requirements under a range of potential GHG emissions assumptions and parameters. These assumptions will include policies regarding CO_2 emission controls and potential future CO_2 emissions costs as well as the costs and feasibility of mitigating technologies or other mechanisms. Due to the uncertainties around many of these factors, the Enhanced Diligence Process will encourage consideration of assumptions that err on the side of caution until more clarity on these issues is available to developers, lenders and investors. Financial institutions that adopt the Principles will implement them with the accompanying Enhanced Diligence Process, while consulting with environmental groups and energy companies.

The Carbon Principle

Energy efficiency. An effective way to limit CO_2 emissions is to not produce them. We will encourage clients to invest in cost-effective demand reduction, taking into consideration the potential value of avoided CO_2 emissions. We will also encourage regulatory and legislative changes that increase efficiency in electricity consumption including the removal of barriers to investment in cost-effective demand reduction. We will consider demand reduction caused by increased energy efficiency (or other means) as part of the Enhanced Diligence Process and assess its impact on proposed financings of new fossil fuel generation.

---

74. *Available* for download *at* http://carbonprinciples.org/.
75. We consider all greenhouse gases but refer to CO_2 which is the most significant.

Renewable and low carbon energy technologies. Renewable energy and low carbon distributed energy technologies hold considerable promise for meeting the electricity needs of the US while also leveraging American technology and creating jobs. We will encourage clients to invest in cost-effective renewables, fuel cells and other low carbon technologies, taking into consideration the potential value of avoided CO_2 emissions. We will also support legislative and regulatory changes that remove barriers to, and promote such investments (including related investments in infrastructure and equipment needed to support the connection of renewable sources to the system). We will consider production increases from renewable and low carbon generation as part of the Enhanced Diligence Process and assess their impact on proposed financings of new fossil fuel generation.

Conventional or Advanced generation. In addition to cost effective energy efficiency, renewables and low carbon generation, we believe investments in other generating technologies likely will be needed to supply reliable electric power to the US market. This may include power from natural gas, coal and nuclear[76] technologies. Due to evolving climate policy, investing in CO_2-emitting fossil fuel generation entails uncertain financial, regulatory and environmental liability risks. It is the purpose of the Enhanced Diligence Process to assess and reflect these risks in the financing considerations for fossil fuel generation. We will encourage regulatory and legislative changes that facilitate carbon mitigation technologies such as carbon capture and storage (CCS) to further reduce CO_2 emissions from the electric sector.

New fossil fuel generation constructed with conventional technology, if not accompanied by mitigation measures, will increase the emission of CO_2 into the atmosphere at a time when federal and state level emissions controls seem likely and, in some regions of the country, are already mandated. An important aspect of the Enhanced Diligence Process will be to evaluate the mitigation strategy and plan of the developer to address the risks posed by the increased CO_2 emissions from new sources when future emissions controls are uncertain. For projects proposed in jurisdictions that already have controls on emissions in place, the developer will need to show how the new generation will be consistent with the existing rules and potential changes going forward. However, in the absence of regional or federal regulations, the development plan will need to account for the added risks due to the uncertainties around future emissions limits.

The Commitments

Adopters commit to:
- Encourage clients to pursue cost-effective energy efficiency, renewable energy and other low carbon alternatives to conventional generation, taking into consideration the potential value of avoided CO_2 emissions.
- Ascertain and evaluate the financial and operational risk to fossil fuel generation financings posed by the prospect of domestic CO_2 emissions controls through the application of the Enhanced Diligence Process. Use the results of this diligence as a contribution to the determination whether a transaction is eligible for financing and under what terms.
- Educate clients, regulators, and other industry participants regarding the additional diligence required for fossil fuel generation financings, and encourage regulatory and legislative changes consistent with the Principles.

---

76. It is recognized that nuclear plants carry a host of risks that financial institutions must consider, but which are outside the scope of these principles.

II. Finite-Resource Fuels

A. Coal

2006 JEFF GOODELL, BIG COAL, XXIV–XXV:

I spent three years researching and writing this book. I visited coal mines and power plants in ten states, as well as in China. I rode coal trains across the Great Plains, detonated 55,000 pounds of explosives in Wyoming, and spent a month on a research vessel in the North Atlantic with scientists who were studying climate change. As it turned out, the three years I spent on this book were three of the four hottest years on record. When I started my research, an energy industry consultant joked with me that a ferocious hurricane would have to wipe out New Orleans before America would wake up to the dangers of global warming. By the time I finished the book, that hurricane had arrived, although the awakening had not.

During those three years, about 3 billion tons of coal went up in smoke in America. They created light and heat for much of the nation (not to mention the glow on my computer screen even now as I write). But during those years, the American Lung Association calculates, about 72,000 people in the United States died prematurely from the effects of coal-fired power plant pollution—more than from AIDS, murder or drug overdose.

Obviously, there's no free power lunch: nukes can melt down, dams flood valleys, and wind turbines kill birds. Building the modern world is fraught with tradeoffs. But unlike in China or India, it's hard to argue that by burning coal to create electricity, America is lifting millions out of poverty and introducing them to hot showers and cold Cokes. Our affection for coal is essentially an old habit and an indulgence. At best, it's a short-term solution to a long-term problem. And the price of this indulgence may be higher than any economist can calculate. Wally Broecker, the great climatologist at Columbia University's Lamont-Doherty Earth Observatory, has compared the earth's climate to a dragon: when you poke it, you can never be sure how it's going to react. As Broecker says, "We're playing with the whole planet, dammit, just to get energy for a few hundred years."

Working on this book, I came to understand that when we talk about energy, what we are really talking about is how we live and what we value. Are we willing to put the earth's climate at risk to save ten bucks on our utility bills? To what degree do we want energy corporations to control our access to power? Is it more important to protect yesterday's jobs or to create a new industry for tomorrow? What degree of sacrifice are we willing to make in our lifestyles to ensure the well-being of our children and grandchildren? The coal industry, of course, would rather keep the conversation focused on the price of electricity per kilowatt-hour and the stockholders' return on investment. Coal is a commodity business, after all, one that is run mostly by number crunchers who see the world as a spreadsheet to conquer. Questions about the price of progress, and how we draw the line between what is acceptable to us as a rich, modern society and what is not, do not fit easily into these calculations.

The following testimony was delivered by Dr. James E. Hansen before the Iowa Utilities Board. The plaintiffs' coalition, which included Community Energy Solutions, Iowa Environmental Council, Iowa Farmers Union, Iowa Renewable Energy Association, and Physicians for Social Responsibility Iowa Chapter, was represented by the attorneys of Plains Justice. On August 25, 2008 the Board voted 2–1 to grant conditional approval. The Sutherland Generating Station Unit 4, without carbon controls, is well on its way to completion.

The editors were unable to include the amazing set of images that accompanied this written testimony and to which Dr. Hansen refers in his Q & A. We suggest that the reader visit Dr. Hansen's website to obtain a copy of the images and "follow along" as Dr. Hansen takes us on a tour of climate science. Iowa Coal Case slides (October 2007) available at: http://www.columbia.edu/~jeh1/ presentations.shtml.

Dr. James E. Hansen, 2007:

I am testifying here as a private citizen, a resident of Kintersville, Pennsylvania, on behalf of the planet, of life on Earth, including all species.[1]

Direct Testimony of James E. Hansen

Q. **Please state your name and business address.**

A. My name is James E. Hansen. My business address is 2880 Broadway, New York, New York 10025.

Q. **By whom are you presently employed and in what capacity?**

A. I am employed by the National Aeronautics and Space Administration (NASA) Goddard Space Flight Center (GSFC), which has its home base in Greenbelt, Maryland. I am the director of the Goddard Institute for Space Studies (GISS), which is a division of GSFC located in New York City. I am also a senior scientist in the Columbia University Earth Institute and an Adjunct Professor of Earth and Environmental Sciences at Columbia. I am responsible for defining the research direction of the Goddard Institute, obtaining research support for the Institute, carrying out original scientific research directed principally toward understanding global change, and providing relevant information to the public. I am testifying here as a private citizen, a resident of Kintnersville, Pennsylvania on behalf of the planet, of life on Earth, including all species.

Q. **What is your educational background?**

A. I was trained in physics and astronomy at the University of Iowa in the space science program of Professor James Van Allen. I have a bachelor's degree in physics and mathematics, a master's degree in astronomy, and a Ph.D. in physics, all from the University of Iowa. I also did research as a graduate student at the Universities of Kyoto and Tokyo, and I was a post-doctoral fellow of the United States National Science Foundation studying at the Sterrewacht, Leiden University, Netherlands, under Prof. Henk van de Hulst.

Q. **Please describe your professional experience.**

A. Upon graduating from the University of Iowa in February 1967 I joined the Goddard Institute for Space Studies, where I have worked ever since, except for 1969 when I was a post-doctoral fellow in the Netherlands. In my first ten years at the Goddard Institute I focused on planetary research. I was Principal Investigator for an experiment on the Pioneer Venus spacecraft to study the clouds of Venus and I was involved in other planetary missions. In the

---

1. *In Re* Interstate Power and Light, Docket No. GCU-07-1, *available at* www.columbia.edu/~jeh1/2007/ IowaCoal_20071105.pdf.

mid-1970s, as evidence of human-made effects on Earth's atmosphere and climate became apparent, I began to spend most of my time in research on the Earth's climate. I became director of the Goddard Institute in 1981, focusing the Institute's program on global change, while maintaining a broad perspective from planetary studies and the Earth's history.

Q. **What is the purpose of your testimony?**

A. My aim is to present clear scientific evidence describing the impact that coal-fired power plants (without carbon capture and storage) will have on the Earth's climate, and thus on the well-being of today's and future generations of people and on all creatures and species of creation.

Burning of fossil fuels, primarily coal, oil and gas, increases the amount of carbon dioxide (CO_2) and other gases and particles in the air. These gases and particles affect the Earth's energy balance, changing both the amount of sunlight absorbed by the planet and the emission of heat (long wave or thermal radiation) to space. The net effect is a global warming that has become substantial during the past three decades.

Global warming from continued burning of more and more fossil fuels poses clear dangers for the planet and for the planet's present and future inhabitants. Coal is the largest contributor to the human-made increase of CO_2 in the air. Saving the planet and creation surely requires phase-out of coal use except where the CO_2 is captured and sequestered (stored in one of several possible ways).

Q. **Coal is only one of the fossil fuels. Can such a strong statement specifically against coal be justified, given still-developing understanding of climate change?**

A. Yes. Coal reserves contain much more carbon than do oil and natural gas reserves, and it is impractical to capture CO_2 emissions from the tailpipes of vehicles. Nor is there any prospect that Saudi Arabia, Russia, the United States and other major oil-producers will decide to leave their oil in the ground. Thus unavoidable CO_2 emissions from oil and gas in the next few decades will take atmospheric CO_2 amounts close to, if not beyond, the level needed to cause dangerous climate change. The only practical way to prevent CO_2 levels from going far into the dangerous range, with disastrous effects for humanity and other inhabitants of the planet, is to phase out use of coal except at power plants where the CO_2 is captured and sequestered.

Q. **But why focus on a coal plant in Iowa? Coal-fired power plants are being built at a much faster rate in China.**

A. The United States is responsible for more than three times as much of the excess CO_2 in the air than any other country. The United States and Europe together are responsible for well over half of the increase from the pre-industrial CO_2 amount (280 ppm, ppm = parts per million) to the present-day CO_2 amount (about 385 ppm). The United States will continue to be most responsible for the human-made CO_2 increase for the next few decades, even though China's ongoing emissions will exceed those of the United States. Although a portion of human-made CO_2 emissions is taken up by the ocean, there it exerts a "back pressure" on the atmosphere, so that, in effect, a substantial fraction of past emissions remains in the air for many centuries, until it is incorporated into ocean sediments. Furthermore, even as China's emissions today approximately equal those of the United States, China's per capita CO_2 emissions are only about 20% of those in the United States.

China, India and other developing countries must be part of the solution to global warming, and surely they will be, if developed countries take the appropriate first steps. China and India have the most to lose from uncontrolled climate change, as they have huge populations living near sea level, and they have the most to gain from reduced local air pollution. Analogous to the approach of the Montreal Protocol, developing countries, with technical assistance, will need to reduce their emissions soon after the developed world reduces its emissions.

Furthermore, it makes economic sense for the United States to begin strong actions now to reduce emissions. Required technology developments in efficiency, renewable energies, truly clean coal, biofuels, and advanced nuclear power will produce good high-tech jobs and provide a basis for international trade that allows recovery of some of the wealth that the country has been hemorrhaging to China.

Q. How can one power plant in Iowa be of any significance in comparison with many power-plants in China?

A. The Iowa power plant can make an important difference because of tipping points in the climate system, tipping points in life systems, and tipping points in social behavior. A tipping point occurs in a system with positive feedbacks. When forcing toward a change, and change itself, become large enough, positive feedbacks can cause a sudden acceleration of change with very little, if any, additional forcing.

Arctic sea ice is an example of a tipping point in the climate system. As the warming global ocean transports more heat into the Arctic, sea ice cover recedes and the darker open ocean surface absorbs more sunlight. The ocean stores the added heat, winter sea ice is thinner, and thus increased melting can occur in following summers, even though year-to-year variations in sea ice area will occur with fluctuations of weather patterns and ocean heat transport.

Arctic sea ice loss can pass a tipping point and proceed rapidly. Indeed, the Arctic sea ice tipping point has been reached. However, the feedbacks driving further change are not "runaway" feedbacks that proceed to loss of all sea ice without continued forcing. Furthermore, sea ice loss is reversible. If human-made forcing of the climate system is reduced, such that the planetary energy imbalance becomes negative, positive feedbacks will work in the opposite sense and sea ice can increase rapidly, just as sea ice decreased rapidly when the planetary energy imbalance was positive.

Planetary energy imbalance can be discussed quantitatively later, including all of the factors that contribute to it. However, it is worth noting here that the single most important action needed to decrease the present large planetary imbalance driving climate change is curtailment of CO_2 emissions from coal burning. Unless emissions from coal burning are reduced, actions to reduce other climate forcings cannot stabilize climate.

The most threatening tipping point in the climate system is the potential instability of large ice sheets, especially West Antarctica and Greenland. If disintegration of these ice sheets passes their tipping points, dynamical collapse of the West Antarctic ice sheet and part of the Greenland ice sheet could proceed out of our control. The ice sheet tipping point is especially dangerous because West Antarctica alone contains enough water to cause about 20 feet (6 meters) of sea level rise.

Hundreds of millions of people live less than 20 feet above sea level. Thus the number of people affected would be 1000 times greater than in the New Orleans Katrina disaster. Although Iowa would not be directly affected by sea level rise, repercussions would be worldwide.

Ice sheet tipping points and disintegration necessarily unfold more slowly than tipping points for sea ice, on time scales of decades to centuries, because of the greater inertia of thick ice sheets. But that inertia is not our friend, as it also makes ice sheet disintegration more difficult to halt once it gets rolling. Moreover, unlike sea ice cover, ice sheet disintegration is practically irreversible. Nature requires thousands of years to rebuild an ice sheet.

Even a single millennium, about 30 generations for humans, is beyond the time scale of interest or comprehension to most people.

Because of the danger of passing the ice sheet tipping point, even the emissions from one Iowa coal plant, with emissions of 5,900,000 tons of CO_2 per year and 297,000,000 over 50 years, could be important as "the straw on the camel's back". The Iowa power plant also contributes to tipping points in life systems and human behavior.

Q. How can Iowa contribute to tipping points in life systems and human behavior?

A. There are millions of species of plants and animals on Earth. These species depend upon each other in a tangled web of interactions that humans are only beginning to fathom. Each species lives, and can survive, only within a specific climatic zone. When climate changes, species migrate in an attempt to stay within their climatic niche. However, large rapid climate change can drive most of the species on the planet to extinction. Geologic records indicate that mass extinctions, with loss of more than half of existing species, occurred several times in the Earth's history. New species developed, but that process required hundreds of thousands, even millions, of years. If we destroy a large portion of the species of creation, those that have existed on Earth in recent millennia, the Earth will be a far more desolate planet for as many generations of humanity as we can imagine.

Today, as global temperature is increasing at a rate of about 0.2°C (0.36°F) per decade, isotherms (a line of a given average temperature) are moving poleward at a rate of about 50–60 km (35 miles) per decade.[2] Some species are moving, but many can move only slowly, pathways may be blocked as humans have taken over much of the planet, and species must deal with other stresses that humans are causing. If the rate of warming continues to accelerate, the cumulative effect this century may result in the loss of a majority of existing species.

The biologist E.O. Wilson[3] explains that the 21st century is a "bottleneck" for species, because of extreme stresses they will experience, most of all because of climate change. He foresees a brighter future beyond the fossil fuel era, beyond the human population peak that will occur if developing countries follow the path of developed countries and China to lower fertility rates. Air and water can be clean and we can learn to live with other species of creation in a sustainable way, using renewable energy. The question is: how many species will survive the pressures of the 21st century bottleneck? Interdependencies among species, some less mobile than others, can lead to collapse of ecosystems and rapid nonlinear loss of species, if climate change continues to increase.

Coal will determine whether we continue to increase climate change or slow the human impact. Increased fossil fuel CO_2 in the air today, compared to the pre-industrial atmosphere, is due 50% to coal, 35% to oil and 15% to gas. As oil resources peak, coal will determine future CO_2 levels. Recently, after giving a high school commencement talk in my hometown, Denison, Iowa, I drove from Denison to Dunlap, where my parents are buried. For most of 20 miles there were trains parked, engine to caboose, half of the cars being filled with coal. If we cannot stop the building of more coal-fired power plants, those coal trains will be death trains—no less gruesome than if they were boxcars headed to crematoria, loaded with uncountable irreplaceable species.

So, how many of the exterminated species should be blamed on the 297,000,000 tons of CO_2 that will be produced in 50 years by the proposed Sutherland Generating Station Unit 4 power plant? If the United States and the rest of the world continue with "business-as-

2. J. Hansen *et al.*, *Global Temperature Change*, 103 Proc. Natl. Acad. Sci. 14288 (2006).
3. E. O. Wilson, The Creation (Norton 2006).

usual" increases in CO_2 emissions, a large fraction of the millions of species on Earth will be lost and it will be fair to assign a handful of those to Sutherland Generating Station Unit 4, even though we cannot assign responsibility for specific species. Moreover, the effect of halting construction of this power plant potentially could be much greater, because of the possibility of positive feedbacks among people.

Q. **What tipping points in human behavior are you referring to?**

A. As the reality of climate change becomes more apparent, as the long-term consequences of further climate change are realized, and as the central role of coal in determining future atmospheric CO_2 is understood, the pressures to use coal only at power plants where the CO_2 is captured and sequestered will increase. If the public begins to stand up in a few places and successfully opposes the construction of power plants that burn coal without capturing the CO_2, this may begin to have a snowball effect, helping utilities and politicians to realize that the public prefers a different path, one that respects all life on the planet.

The changes in behavior will need to run much broader and deeper than simply blocking new dirty coal plants. Energy is essential to our way of life. We will have to find ways to use energy more efficiently and develop renewable and other forms of energy that produce little if any greenhouse gases. The reward structure for utilities needs to be changed such that their profits increase not in proportion to the amount of energy sold, but rather as they help us achieve greater energy and carbon efficiency. As people begin to realize that life beyond the fossil fuel era promises to be very attractive, with a clean atmosphere and water, and as we encourage the development of the technologies needed to get us there, we should be able to move rapidly toward that goal. But we need tipping points to get us rolling in that direction.

Iowa, and this specific case, can be a tipping point, leading to a new direction. A message that "old-fashioned" power plants, *i.e.*, those without carbon capture and sequestration, are no longer acceptable, would be a message of leadership, one that would be heard across Iowa and beyond the state's borders.

Q. **Alleged implications of continued coal burning without carbon capture are profound and thus require proof of a causal relationship between climate change and CO_2 emissions. What is the nature of recent global temperature change?**

A. Figure 5(a) shows global mean surface temperature change over the period during which instrumental measurements are available for most regions of the globe. The warming since the beginning of the 20th century has been about 0.8°C (1.4°F), with three-quarters of that warming occurring in the past 30 years.

Figure 5. (*Image not shown*) (a) Global surface temperature relative to 1951–1980 base period mean, based on surface air measurements at meteorological stations and ship and satellite SST (sea surface temperature) measurements, (b) temperature anomaly for first six years of the 21st century relative to 1951–1980 base period.[4] Green vertical bars in (a) are estimated 2% error (95% confidence) of annual global mean temperature anomaly.

Q. **Warming of 0.8°C (1.4°F) does not seem very large. It is much smaller than day to day weather fluctuations. Is such a small warming significant?**

A. Yes, and it is important. Chaotic weather fluctuations make it difficult for people to notice changes of underlying climate (the average weather, including statistics of extreme fluctuations), but it does not diminish the impact of long-term climate change.

---

4. Update of figures of Hansen *et al.*, *supra* note 2.

First, we must recognize that global mean temperature changes of even a few degrees or less can cause large climate impacts. Some of these impacts are associated with climate tipping points, in which large regional climate response happens rapidly as warming reaches critical levels. Already today's global temperature is near the level that will cause loss of all Arctic sea ice. Evidence suggests that we are also nearing the global temperature level that will cause the West Antarctic ice sheet and portions of the Greenland ice sheet to become unstable, with potential for very large sea level rise.

Second, we must recognize that there is more global warming "in the pipeline" due to gases humans have already added to the air. The climate system has large thermal inertia, mainly due to the ocean, which averages 4 km (about 2.5 miles) in depth. Because of the ocean's inertia, the planet warms up slowly in response to gases that humans are adding to the atmosphere. If atmospheric CO_2 and other gases stabilized at present amounts, the planet would still warm about 0.5°C (about 1°F) over the next century or two. In addition, there are more gases "in the pipeline" due to existing infrastructure such as power plants and vehicles on the road. Even as the world begins to address global warming with improved technologies, the old infrastructure will add more gases, with still further warming on the order of another 1°F.

Third, eventual temperature increases will be much larger in critical high latitude regions than they are on average for the planet. High latitudes take longer to reach their equilibrium (long-term) response because the ocean mixes more deeply at high latitudes and because positive feedbacks increase the response time there.[5] Amplification of high latitude warming is already beginning to show up in the Northern Hemisphere. Figure 5(b) is the geographical pattern of mean temperature anomalies for the first six years of the 21st century, relative to the 1951–1980 base period. Note that warming over land areas is larger than global mean warming, an expected consequence of the large ocean thermal inertia. Warming is larger at high latitudes than low latitudes, primarily because of the ice/snow albedo feedback. Warming is larger in the Northern Hemisphere than in the Southern Hemisphere, primarily because of greater ocean area in the Southern Hemisphere, and the fact that the entire Southern Ocean surface around Antarctica is cooled by deep mixing. Also human-caused depletion of stratospheric ozone, a greenhouse gas, has reduced warming over most of Antarctica. This ozone depletion and CO_2 increase have cooled the stratosphere, increased zonal winds around Antarctica, and thus warmed the Antarctic Peninsula while limiting warming of most of the Antarctic continent.[6]

Until the past several years, warming has also been limited in Southern Greenland and the North Atlantic Ocean just southeast of Greenland, an expected effect of deep ocean mixing in that vicinity. However, recent warming on Greenland is approaching that of other landmasses at similar latitudes in the Northern Hemisphere. On the long run, warming on the ice sheets is expected to be at least twice as large as global warming. Amplification of warming at high latitudes has practical consequences for the entire globe, especially via effects on ice sheets and sea level. High latitude amplification of warming is expected on theoretical grounds, it is found in climate models, and it is confirmed in paleoclimate (ancient climate) records.

Q. **But those paleoclimate records show that the Earth's climate has changed by very large amounts many times in the past. For that reason, the NASA Administrator has suggested**

---

5. J. Hansen et al., *Climate Sensitivity: Analysis of Feedback Mechanisms, in* CLIMATE PROCESSES AND CLIMATE SENSITIVITY, GEOPHYS. MONOGR. SER. 29 (J.E. Hansen & T. Takahashi eds. American Geophysical Union 1984).

6. D.W.J. Thompson & S. Solomon, *Interpretation of Recent Southern Hemisphere Climate Change*, 306 SCIENCE 255 (2002); D.T. Shindell & G.A. Schmidt, *Southern Hemisphere Climate Response to Ozone Changes and Greenhouse Gas Increases*, 31 GEOPHYS. RES. LETT. L18209 (2004).

that we may not need to "wrestle" with human-made climate change. How do you reach a contrary conclusion?

A. Paleoclimate data, indeed, reveal large climate changes. But that history of ancient climate changes shows that modest forcing factors can produce large climate change. In fact, paleo-climate data provide our most accurate and certain measure of how sensitive global climate is to climate forcings, including human-made climate forcings.

Q. **What is a climate forcing?**

A. A climate forcing is an imposed perturbation to the Earth's energy balance, which would tend to alter the planet's temperature. For example, if the sun were to become 1% brighter, that would be a forcing somewhat more than $+2$ W/m^2, because the Earth absorbs about 238 W/m^2 of energy from the sun. An increase of greenhouse gases, which absorb terrestrial heat radiation and thus warm the Earth's surface, is also a positive forcing. Doubling the amount of atmospheric CO_2 is a forcing of about $+4$ W/m^2.

Q. **How large are natural climate variations?**

A. That depends on the time scale. A useful time scale to examine is the past several hundred thousand years. There is good data for the temperature, changes of atmospheric composition, and the most important changes on the Earth's surface. Specifically, we know the amount of long-lived greenhouse gases, CO_2, CH_4 and N_2O, as a function of time from air bubbles in the ice sheets. Ice sheets are formed by snowfall that piles up year by year and compresses into ice as the weight of snow above increases. The date when the snow fell is known accurately for about the past 15,000 years from counting annual layers marked by summer crusting. Annual layers can be clearly distinguished in the upper part of the ice sheet. Less precise ways of dat-ing ice layers are available for the entire depth of the ice sheets. The temperature when the snowflakes fell is inferred from the isotopic composition of the ice.

Figure 6 shows the temperature on the Antarctic ice sheet for the past 425,000 years. Simi-lar curves are found from Greenland and from alpine ice cores, as well as from ocean sedi-ment cores. Layered ocean sediments contain the shells of microscopic animals that lived in the ocean, the proportion of elements in these microscopic shells providing a measure of the ocean temperature at the time the animals lived. Swings of temperature from warm inter-glacial periods to ice ages occur worldwide, with the glacial-interglacial temperature range being typically 3–4°C in the tropics, about 10°C at the poles, and about 5°C on global average.

Figure 6. *(Image not shown)* **Temperature change in Antarctica over the past 420,000 as inferred from the isotopic composition of snow preserved in the ice sheet and extracted in the Vostok ice core.**[7]

We live today in a warm interglacial period, the Holocene, now almost 12,000 years in duration. The last ice age peaked about 20,000 years ago. Global mean temperature was about 5°C colder than today, with an ice sheet more than a mile thick covering Canada and reaching into the United States, covering the present sites of Seattle, Minneapolis, and New York. So much water was locked in this ice sheet, and other smaller ice sheets, that sea level was 110–130 meters (about 350–400 feet) lower during the ice age, thus exposing large areas of continental shelves.

Figure 7 shows that large changes of sea level are the norm as climate changes. Global sea level, global temperature, and atmospheric greenhouse gas amounts are obviously very highly correlated.

7. F. Vimeux *et al.*, *New Insights into Southern Hemisphere Temperature Changes from Vostok Ice Cores Using Deuterium Excess Correction*, 203 EARTH PLANET. SCI. LETT. 829 (2002).

Figure 7. *(Image not shown)* Temperature, CO_2, and sea level. *See* Hansen *et al.*[8] for original data sources.

Q.   The sea level changes are enormous. Is sea level always changing? What have the consequences been?

A.   On millennial time scales resolvable in this graph, sea level, CO_2 and global temperature change together. However, close examination shows that sea level has been stable for about the past 7000 years. In that period the planet has been warm enough to prevent an ice sheet from forming on North America, but cool enough for the Greenland and Antarctic ice sheets to be stable. The fact that the Earth cooled slightly over the past 8000 years probably helped to stop further sea level rise.

Sea level stability played a role in the emergence of complex societies. Day *et al.*[9] point out that when sea level was rising at the rate of 1 meter per century or faster biological productivity of coastal waters was limited. Thus it is not surprising that when the world's human population abandoned mobile hunting and gathering in the Neolithic (12,000–7000 years ago) they gathered in small villages in foothills and mountains. Day *et al.* note that within 1000 years of sea level stabilization, urban (>2500 people) societies developed at many places around the world (Figure 8). With the exception of Jericho, on the Jordan River, all of these first urban sites were coastal, where high protein food sources aided development of complex civilizations with class distinctions.

Modern societies have constructed enormous infrastructure on today's coastlines. More than a billion people live within 25 meter elevation of sea level. This includes practically the entire nation of Bangladesh, almost 300 million Chinese, and large populations in India and Egypt, as well as many historical cities in the developed world, including major European cities, many cities in the Far East, all major East Coast cities in the United States, among hundreds of other cities in the world.

Figure 8. *(Image not shown)* Distribution of early urban societies. Coastal mangroves and salt marshes shown by dark and light shades.[10]

Q.   How much will sea level rise if global temperature increases several degrees?

A.   Our best guide for the eventual long-term sea level change is the Earth's history. The last time the Earth was 2–3°C warmer than today, about 3 million years ago, sea level was about 25 meters higher. The last time the planet was 5°C warmer, just prior to the glaciation of Antarctica about 35 million years ago, there were no large ice sheets on the planet. Given today's ocean basins, if the ice sheets melt entirely, sea level will rise about 70 meters (about 230 feet).

The main uncertainty about future sea level is the rate at which ice sheets melt. This is a "nonlinear" problem in which positive feedbacks allow the possibility of sudden ice sheet collapse and rapid sea level rise. Initial ice sheet response to global warming is necessarily slow, and it is inherently difficult to predict when rapid change would begin. I have argued[11] that a "business-as-usual" growth of greenhouse gases would yield a sea level rise this cen-

---

8. J. Hansen *et al.*, *Climate Change and Trace Gases*, 365 PHIL. TRANS. ROYAL SOC. A 1925 (2007).

9. J.W. Day *et al.*, *Emergence of Complex Societies After Sea Level Stabilized*, 88 EOS TRANS. AMER. GEOPHYS. UNION 169 (2007).

10. *Id.*

11. J. Hansen, *A Slippery Slope: How Much Global Warming Constitutes "Dangerous Anthropogenic Interference"?*, 68 CLIM. CHANGE 269 (2005); J.E. Hansen, *Scientific Reticence and Sea Level Rise*, 2 ENVIRON. RES. LETT. 1 (2007).

tury of more than a meter, probably several meters, because practically the entire West Antarctic and Greenland ice sheets would be bathed in meltwater during an extended summer melt season.

The Intergovernmental Panel on Climate Change[12] calculated a sea level rise of only 21–51 cm by 2095 for "business-as-usual" scenarios A2 and A1B, but their calculation included only thermal expansion of the ocean and melting of alpine glaciers, thus omitting the most critical component of sea level change, that from ice sheets. IPCC noted the omission of this component in its sea level projections, because it was unable to reach a consensus on the magnitude of likely ice sheet disintegration. However, much of the media failed to note this caveat in the IPCC report.

Earth's history reveals many cases when sea level rose several meters per century, in response to forcings much weaker than present human-made climate forcings. Iceberg discharge from Greenland and West Antarctica has recently accelerated. It is difficult to say how fast ice sheet disintegration will proceed, but this issue provides strong incentive for policy makers to slow down the human-made experiment with our planet.

Knowledge of climate sensitivity has improved markedly based on improving paleoclimate data. The information on climate sensitivity, combined with knowledge of how sea level responded to past global warming, has increased concern that we could will to our children a situation in which future sea level change is out of their control.

Q. How can the paleoclimate data reveal the climate sensitivity to forcings?

A. We compare different climate states in the Earth's history, thus obtaining a measure of how much climate responded to climate forcings in the past. In doing this, we must define climate forcings and climate feedbacks clearly. Alternative choices for forcings and feedbacks are appropriate, depending on the time scale of interest.

A famous definition of climate sensitivity is from the "Charney" problem, in which it is assumed that the distributions of ice sheets and vegetation on the Earth's surface are fixed and the question is asked: how much will global temperature increase if the amount of CO_2 in the air is doubled? The Charney[13] climate sensitivity is most relevant to climate change on the decadal time scale, because ice sheets and forest cover would not be expected to change much in a few decades or less. However, the Charney climate sensitivity must be recognized as a theoretical construct. Because of the large thermal inertia of the ocean, it would require several centuries for the Earth to achieve its equilibrium response to doubled CO_2, and during that time changes of ice sheets and vegetation could occur as "feedbacks," *i.e.*, as responses of the climate system that engender further climate change. Feedbacks can either magnify or diminish climate changes, these effects being defined as positive and negative feedbacks, respectively.

Climate feedbacks include changes of atmospheric gases and aerosols (fine particles in the air). Gases that change in response to climate change include water vapor, but also the long-lived greenhouse gases, CO_2, CH_4 and N_2O.

Q. Is water vapor not a stronger greenhouse gas than these others?

A. Yes, and that is sometimes a source of confusion. Water vapor readily evaporates into and condenses out of the atmosphere. The amount of H_2O in the air is a function of the climate, primarily a function of temperature. The air holds more water vapor in the summer than in win-

---

12. IPCC, *Summary for Policy Makers, in* CLIMATE CHANGE 2007: SYNTHESIS REPORT, AN ASSESSMENT OF THE INTERGOVERNMENTAL PANEL ON CLIMATE CHANGE (Cambridge Un. Press 2007).

13. J. CHARNEY, CARBON DIOXIDE AND CLIMATE: A SCIENTIFIC ASSESSMENT (Nat. Acad. Sci. Press 1979).

ter, for example. Water vapor is a prime example of what we call "fast" feedbacks, those feedbacks that respond promptly to changes of climate. Because H_2O causes a strong greenhouse effect, and tropospheric H_2O increases with temperature, it provides a positive feedback.

The Charney climate sensitivity includes the effects of fast feedbacks such as changes of water vapor and clouds, but it excludes slow feedbacks such as ice sheets. We obtain an empirical measure of the equilibrium Charney climate sensitivity by comparing conditions on Earth during the last ice age, about 20,000 years ago with the conditions in the present interglacial period prior to major human-made effects. Averaged over a period of say 1000 years, the planet in each of these two states, glacial and interglacial, had to be in energy balance with space within a small fraction of $1 W/m^2$. Because the amount of incoming sunlight was practically the same in both periods, the 5°C difference in global temperature between the ice age and the interglacial period had to be maintained by changes of atmospheric composition and changes of surface conditions. Both of these are well known.

Figure 9 shows that there was a lesser amount of long-lived greenhouse gases in the air during the last ice age. These gases affect the amount of thermal radiation to space, and they have a small impact on the amount of absorbed solar energy. We can compute the climate forcing due to the glacial-interglacial change of CO_2, CH_4, and N_2O with high accuracy. The effective climate forcing,[14] including the indirect effect of CH_4 on other gases, is $3 \pm 0.5 W/m^2$.

Figure 9. *(Image not shown)* CO_2, CH_4, and temperature from the Vostok Antarctic ice core.[15]

Changes on the Earth's surface also alter the energy balance with space. The greatest change is due to the large ice sheets during the last ice age, whose high albedo ("whiteness" or reflectivity) caused the planet to absorb less solar radiation. Smaller effects were caused by the altered vegetation distribution and altered shorelines due to lower sea level during the ice age. The climate forcing due to all these surface changes is $3.5 \pm 1 W/m^2$.[16]

Thus the glacial-interglacial climate change of 5°C was maintained by a forcing of about $6.5 W/m^2$, implying a climate sensitivity of about ¾°C per W/m^2. This empirical climate sensitivity includes all fast feedbacks that exist in the real world, including changes of water vapor, clouds, aerosols, and sea ice. Doubled CO_2 is a forcing of $4 W/m^2$, so the Charney climate sensitivity is 3 ± 1°C for doubled CO_2. Climate models yield a similar value for climate sensitivity, but the empirical result is more precise and it surely includes all real world processes with "correct" physics.

Q. **This climate sensitivity was derived from two specific points in time. How general is the conclusion?**

A. We can check climate sensitivity for the entire past 425,000 years. Ice cores (Figure 9) provide a detailed record of long-lived greenhouse gases. A measure of surface conditions is provided by sediment cores from the Red Sea[17] and other places, which yield a record of sea level change (Figure 10a). Sea level tells us how large the ice sheets were, because water that was not in the ocean was locked in the ice sheets. Greenhouse gas and sea level records allow us to compute the climate forcings due to both atmospheric and surface changes for the entire 425,000 years.[18]

---

14. J. Hansen *et al.*, *Efficacy of Climate Forcings*, 110 J Geophys. Res. D18104 (2005).
15. Vimeux *et al.*, *supra* note 7.
16. Hansen *et al.*, *supra* note 5.
17. M. Siddall *et al.*, *Sea-level Fluctuations During the Last Glacial Cycle*, 423 Nature 853 (2003).
18. Hansen *et al.*, *supra* note 8.

When the sum of greenhouse gas and surface albedo forcings (Figure 10b) is multiplied by the presumed climate sensitivity of ¾°C per W/m^2 the result is in remarkably good agreement with "observed" global temperature change (Figure 10c) implied by Antarctic temperature change. Therefore this climate sensitivity has general validity for this long period. This is the Charney climate sensitivity, which includes fast feedback processes but specifies changes of greenhouse gases and surface conditions.

It is important to note that these changing boundary conditions (the long-lived greenhouse gases and surface albedo) are themselves feedbacks on long time scales. The cyclical climate changes from glacial to interglacial times are driven by very small forcings, primarily by minor perturbations of the Earth's orbit about the sun and by the tilt of the Earth's spin axis relative to the plane of the orbit.

Figure 10. *(Image not shown)* **(a) sea level records from three sources, (b) climate forcings due to greenhouse gases (CO_2, CH_4 and N_2O) and surface albedo from the Siddall *et al.* sea level record, (c) calculated and observed paleotemperature change. Calculated temperature is the product of the sum of the two forcings in (b) and ¾°C per W/m^2. Observed temperature is the Vostok temperature (Figure 6) divided by two.**

Q. Can you clarify cause and effect for these natural climate changes?

A. Figure 11 is useful for that purpose. It compares temperature change in Antarctica with the greenhouse gas forcing. Temperature and greenhouse gas amounts are obtained from the same ice core, which reduces uncertainty in their sequencing despite substantial uncertainty in absolute dating. There is still error in dating temperature change relative to greenhouse gas change, because of the time needed for ice core bubble closure. However, that error is small enough that we can infer, as shown in Figure 11b, that the temperature change tends to slightly precede (by several hundred years) the greenhouse gas changes. Similarly, although the relative dating of sea level and temperature changes are less accurate, it is clear that warming usually precedes ice melt and sea level rise.

These sequencings are not surprising. They show that greenhouse gas changes and ice sheet area changes act as feedbacks that amplify the very weak forcings due to Earth orbital changes. The climate changes are practically coincident with the induced changes of the feedbacks (Figure 11). The important point is that the mechanisms for the climate changes, the mechanisms substantially affecting the planet's radiation balance and thus the temperature, are the atmospheric greenhouse gases and the surface albedo. Earth orbital changes induce these mechanisms to change; for example, as the tilt of the spin axis increases both poles are exposed to increased sunlight. Changed insolation affects the melting of ice and, directly and indirectly, the uptake and release of greenhouse gases.

Figure 11. *(Image not shown)* **(a) Antarctic temperature from Vostok ice core[19] and global climate forcing (right scale) due to CO_2, CH_4 and N_2O. (b) Correlation (%) diagram showing lead of temperature over greenhouse forcing.**

Q. What is the implication for the present era and the role of humans in climate?

A. The chief implication is that humans have taken control of global climate. This follows from Figure 12, which extends records of the principal greenhouse gases to the present. CO_2, CH_4 and N_2O (not shown) are far outside their range of the past 800,000 years for which ice core records of atmospheric composition are available.

---

19. Vimeux *et al.*, *supra* note 7.

Figure 12. *(Image not shown)* Extension of Antarctic CO_2, CH_4 and temperature records of Figure 9 into modern era. Antarctic temperature is divided by two to make it comparable to global temperature extension.

Q. **Yet the global warming also shown in Figure 12 does not seem to be commensurate with the greenhouse gas increases, if we were to use the paleoclimate as a guide. Can you explain that?**

A. Yes. Observed warming is in excellent agreement with climate model calculations for observed greenhouse gas changes. Two factors must be recognized.

First, the climate system has not had enough time to fully respond to the human-made climate forcings. The time scale after 1850 is greatly expanded in Figure 12. The paleoclimate portion of the graph shows the near-equilibrium (~1000 year) response to slowly changing forcings. In the modern era, most of the net human-made forcing was added in the past 30 years, so the ocean has not had time to fully respond and the ice sheets are just beginning to respond to the present forcing.

Second, the climate system responds to the net forcing, which is only about half as large as the greenhouse gas forcing. The net forcing is reduced by negative forcings, especially human-made aerosols (fine particles).

Q. **But is not the natural system driving the Earth toward colder climates?**

A. If there were no humans on the planet, the long term trend would be toward colder climate. However, the two principal mechanisms for attaining colder climate would be reduced greenhouse gas amounts and increased ice cover. The feeble natural processes that would push these mechanisms in that direction (toward less greenhouse gases and larger ice cover) are totally overwhelmed by human forcings. Greenhouse gas amounts are skyrocketing out of the normal range and ice is melting all over the planet. Humans now control global climate, for better or worse.

Another ice age cannot occur unless humans go extinct, or unless humans decide that they want an ice age. However, "achieving" an ice age would be a huge task. In contrast, prevention of an ice age is a trivial task for humans, requiring only a "thimbleful" of CFCs (chlorofluorocarbons), for example. The problem is rather the opposite, humans have already added enough greenhouse gases to the atmosphere to drive global temperature well above any level in the Holocene.

Q. **How much warmer will the Earth become for the present level of greenhouse gases?**

A. That depends on how long we wait. The Charney climate sensitivity (3°C global warming for doubled CO_2) does not include slow feedbacks, principally disintegration of ice sheets and poleward movement of vegetation as the planet warms. When the long-lived greenhouse gases are changed arbitrarily, as humans are now doing, this change becomes the predominant forcing, and ice sheet and vegetation changes must be included as part of the response in determining long-term climate sensitivity.

It follows from Figure 11 that equilibrium climate sensitivity is 6°C for doubled CO_2 (forcing of 4 W/m^2) when greenhouse gases are the forcing, not 3°C. (Note: the Antarctic temperature change, shown in Figure 11, is about twice the global mean change.) To achieve this full response we must wait until ice sheets have had time to melt and forests have had time to migrate. This may require hundreds of years, perhaps thousands of years. However, elsewhere[20] we have discussed evidence that forests are already moving and ice sheet albedos are already responding to global warming, so climate sensitivity is already partially affected by these processes.

---

20. J. Hansen *et al.*, *supra* note 8.

Thus the relevant equilibrium climate sensitivity on the century time scale falls somewhere between 3°C and 6°C for doubled CO_2. The expected temperature change in the 21st century cannot be obtained by simply multiplying the forcing by the sensitivity, as we could in the paleoclimate case, because a century is not long enough to achieve the equilibrium response. Instead we must make computations with a model that includes the ocean thermal inertia, as is done in climate model simulations.[21] However, these models do not include realistically all of the slow feedbacks, such as ice sheet and forest dynamics.

Q. **The huge climate changes over the past few hundred thousand years show the dramatic effects accompanying global temperature change of only a few degrees. And you infer climate sensitivity from the documented climate variations. Yet the climate changes and mechanisms are intricate, and it is difficult for the lay person to grasp the details of these analyses. Is there other evidence supporting the conclusion that burning of the fossil fuels will have dramatic effects upon life on Earth?**

A. Yes. Climate fluctuations in the Pleistocene (past 1.8 million years) are intricate, as small forcings are amplified by feedbacks, including "carbon cycle" feedbacks. Atmospheric CO_2 varies a lot because carbon is exchanged among its surface reservoirs: the atmosphere, ocean, soil, and biosphere. For example, the solubility of CO_2 in the ocean decreases as the ocean warms, a positive feedback causing much of the atmospheric CO_2 increase with global warming. That feedback is simple, but the full story of how weak forcings create large climate change is indeed complex.

A useful complement to Pleistocene climate fluctuations is provided by longer time scales with larger CO_2 changes than those caused by orbital oscillations. Larger CO_2 changes occur on long time scales because of transfer of carbon between the solid earth and the surface reservoirs. The large CO_2 changes on these long time scales allow the Earth orbital climate oscillations to be viewed as "noise." Thus long time scales help provide a broader overview of the effect of changing atmospheric composition on climate.

A difficulty with long time scales is that knowledge of atmospheric composition changes is not as good. Samples of ancient air preserved in ice cores exist for only about one million years. But there are indirect ways of measuring ancient CO_2 levels to better than a factor of two beyond one million years ago. Atmospheric composition and other climate forcings are known well enough for the combination of Pleistocene climate variations and longer-term climate change to provide an informative overview of climate sensitivity and a powerful way to assess the role of humans in altering global climate.

Q. **What determines the amount of CO_2 in the air on long time scales?**

A. On long (geologic) time scales CO_2 is exchanged between the surface reservoirs (atmosphere, ocean, soil and biosphere) and the solid Earth. Two processes take CO_2 out of the surface reservoirs: (1) chemical weathering of silicate rocks, which results in the deposition of (calcium and magnesium) carbonates on the ocean floor, and (2) burial of organic matter, some of which eventually forms fossil fuels. Weathering is the more dominant process, accounting for ~80% of carbon removal from surface reservoirs.[22]

CO_2 is returned to the atmosphere principally via subduction of oceanic crustal plates beneath continents. When a continental plate overrides carbonate-rich ocean crust, the subducted ocean crust experiences high temperatures and pressures. Resulting metamorphism of the subducted crust into various rock types releases CO_2, which makes its way to the at-

---

21. J. Hansen et al., *Dangerous Human-made Interference with Climate: A GISS ModelE Study*, 7 ATMOS. CHEM. PHYS. 1 (2007); IPCC *supra* note 12.
22. R.A. BERNER, THE PHANEROZOIC CARBON CYCLE: CO_2 AND O_2 (Oxford Un. Press 2004).

mosphere via volcanic eruptions or related phenomena such as "seltzer" spring water. This return of CO_2 to the atmosphere is called "outgassing."

Outgassing and burial of CO_2, via weathering and organic deposits, are not in general balanced at any given time.[23] Depending on the movement of continental plates, the locations of carbonate-rich ocean crust, rates of mountain-building (orogeny), and other factors, at any given time there can be substantial imbalance between outgassing and burial. As a result, atmospheric CO_2 changes by large amounts on geologic time scales.

Q. How much do these geologic processes change atmospheric CO_2?

A. Rates of outgassing and burial of CO_2 are each typically 2-4 x 10**12 mol C/year.[24] An imbalance between outgassing and burial of say 2 x 10**12 mol C/year, if confined entirely to the atmosphere, would correspond to ~0.01 ppm CO_2 per year. However, the atmosphere contains only of order 10**(-2), *i.e.*, about 1%, of the total CO_2 in the surface carbon reservoirs (atmosphere, ocean, soil, biosphere), so the rate of geologic changes to atmospheric CO_2 is only about 0.0001 ppm CO_2 per year. This compares to the present human-made atmospheric CO_2 increase of ~2 ppm per year. Fossil fuels burned now by humans in one year contain the amount of carbon buried in organic sediments in approximately 100,000 years.

The contribution of geologic processes to atmospheric CO_2 change is negligible compared to measured human-made changes today. However, in one million years a geologic imbalance of 0.0001 ppm CO_2 per year yields a CO_2 change of 100 ppm. Thus geologic changes over tens of millions of years can include huge changes of atmospheric CO_2, of the order of 1000 ppm of CO_2. As a result, examination of climate changes on the time scale of tens of millions of years has the potential to yield a valuable perspective on how climate changes with atmospheric composition.

Q. What is the most useful geologic era to consider for that purpose?

A. The Cenozoic era, the past 65 million years, is particularly valuable for several reasons. First, we have the most complete and most accurate climate data for the most recent era. Second, climate changes in that era are large enough to include ice-free conditions. Third, we know that atmospheric greenhouse gases were the principal global forcing driving climate change in that era.

Q. How do you know that greenhouse climate forcing was dominant in the Cenozoic?

A. Climate forcings, perturbations of the planet's energy balance, must arise from either changes in the incoming energy, changes that alter the planetary surface, or changes within the atmosphere. Let us examine these three in turn.

Solar luminosity is growing on long time scales, at a rate such that the sun was ~0.5% dimmer than today in the early Cenozoic.[25] Because the Earth absorbs about 240 W/m^2 of solar energy, the solar climate forcing at the beginning of the Cenozoic was about -1 W/m^2 relative to today. This small growth of solar forcing through the Cenozoic era, as we will see, is practically negligible.

Changing size and location of continents can be an important climate forcing, as the albedo of the Earth's surface depends on whether the surface is land or water and on the

23. J.M. Edmond & Y. Huh, *Non-steady State Carbonate Recycling and Implications for the Evolution of Atmospheric PCO₂*, 216 Earth Planet. Sci. Lett. 125 (2003).

24. *Id.*; H. Staudigel *et al.*, *Cretaeous Ocean Crust at DSDP Sites 417 and 418: Carbon Uptake from Weathering Versus Loss by Magmatic Outgassing*, 53 Geochim. Cosmochim. Acta 3091 (1989).

25. L.J. Sackmann *et al.*, *Our Sun III: Present and Future*, 418 Astrophys. J. 457 (1993).

angle at which the sun's rays strike the surface. A quarter of a billion years ago the major continents were clumped together (Figure 13) in the super-continent Pangea centered on the equator.[26] However, by the beginning of the Cenozoic (65 million years before present, 65 My BP, the same as the end of the Cretaceous) the continents were close to their present latitudes. The direct (radiative) climate forcing due to this continental drift is no more than ~ 1 W/m^2.

In contrast, atmospheric CO_2 reached levels of 1000–2000 ppm in the early Cenozoic,[27] compared with values as low as $\sim$180 ppm during recent ice ages. This range of CO_2 encompasses about three CO_2 doublings and thus a climate forcing more than 10 W/m^2. So it is clear that changing greenhouse gases provided the dominant global climate forcing through the Cenozoic era.

We are not neglecting the fact that dynamical changes of ocean and atmospheric currents can affect global mean climate.[28] Climate variations in the Cenozoic are too large to be accounted for by such dynamical hypotheses.

Figure 13. *(Image not shown)* **Continental positions at four times.**[29]

Q. What caused atmospheric CO_2 amount to change?

A. At the beginning of the Cenozoic era, 65 My BP, India was just south of the Equator (Figure 13), but moving north rapidly, at about 15 cm/year. The Tethys Ocean, separating Eurasia from India and Africa, was closing rapidly. The Tethys Ocean had long been a depocenter for carbonate sediments. Thus prior to the collision of the Indian and African plates with the Eurasian plate, subduction of carbonate-rich oceanic crust caused outgassing to exceed weathering, and atmospheric CO_2 increased.

The Indo-Asian collision at $\sim$50 My BP initiated massive uplift of the Himalayas and the Tibetan Plateau, and subsequently drawdown of atmospheric CO_2 by weathering has generally exceeded CO_2 outgassing.[30] Although less important, the Alps were formed in the same time frame, as the African continental plate pushed against Eurasia. With the closing of the Tethys Ocean, the major depocenters for carbonate sediments became the Indian and Atlantic oceans, because the major rivers of the world empty into those basins.

For the past 50 million years and continuing today, regions of subduction of carbonate rich ocean crust have been limited. Thus, while the oceans have been a strong sink for carbonate sediments, little carbonate is being subducted and returned to the atmosphere as CO_2.[31] As a result, over the past 50 million years there has been a long-term decline of greenhouse gases and global temperature.

---

26. E.A. Keller & N. Pinter, *Active Tectonics: Earthquakes, Uplift, and Landscape, in* This Dynamic Earth: The Story of Plate Tectonics (J. Kious & R.I. Tilling eds. Prentice-Hall 1996), *available at* http://pubs.usgs.gov/publications/text/dynamic.html

27. M. Pagani *et al.*, *Marked Decline in Atmospheric Carbon Dioxide Concentrations During the Paleogene*, 309 Science 600 (2005); D.L. Royer, *CO2-forced Climate Thresholds During the Phanerozoic*, 70 Geochim. Cosmochim. Acta 5665 (2006).

28. D. Rind & M.A. Chandler, *Increased Ocean Heat Transports and Warmer Climate*, 96 J. Geophys. Res 7437 (1991).

29. Adapted from Keller & Pinter, *supra* note 26.

30. M.E. Raymo & W.F. Ruddiman, *Tectonic Forcing of Late Cenozoic Climate*, 359 Nature 117 (1992).

31. Edmond & Huh, *supra* note 23.

Q. Can you illustrate this long-term cooling trend?

A. Yes. Figure 14a shows a quantity, ^{18}O, that provides an indirect measure of global temperature over the Cenozoic era, with a caveat defined below. ^{18}O defines the amount of the heavy oxygen isotope ^{18}O found in the shells of microscopic animals (foramininfera) that lived in the ocean and were deposited in ocean sediments. By taking ocean cores of the sediments we can sample shells deposited over time far into the past. Figure 14a shows the average result from many ocean cores around the world obtained in deep sea drilling programs.[32]

The proportion of ^{18}O in the foraminifera shell depends on the ocean water temperature at the time the shell was formed, and thus ^{18}O provides a proxy measure of temperature. However, an ice sheet forming on the Earth's surface has an excess of ^{16}O in its H_2O molecules, because ^{16}O evaporates from the ocean more readily than ^{18}O, leaving behind a relative excess of ^{18}O in the ocean. As long as the Earth was so warm that little ice existed on the planet, as was the case between 65 My BP and 35 My BP, ^{18}O yields a direct measure of temperature, as indicated by the red curve and the temperature scale on the left side of Figure 14a.

The sharp change of ^{18}O at about 34 My BP was due to rapid glaciation of the Antarctic continent.[33] From 34 My BP to the present, ^{18}O changes reflect both ice volume and ocean temperature changes. We cannot separate the contributions of these two processes, but both increasing ice volume and decreasing temperature change ^{18}O in the same sense, so the ^{18}O curve continues to be a qualitative measure of changing global temperature, chronicling the continuing long-term cooling trend of the planet over the past 50 million years.

The black curve in Figure 14a shows the rapid glacial-interglacial temperature oscillations, which are smoothed out in the mean (red and blue) curves. Figure 14b expands the time scale for the most recent 3.5 million years, so that the glacial-interglacial fluctuations are clearer. Figure 14c further expands the most recent 425,000 years, showing the familiar Pleistocene ice ages punctuated by brief interglacial periods. Note that the period of civilization within the Holocene is invisibly brief with the resolution in Figure 14a. *Homo sapiens* have been present for about 200,000 years, and the predecessor species, *Homo erectus*, for about 2 million years, still rather brief on the time scale of Figure 14a.

Figure 14. *(Image not shown)* **(a) Global compilation of deep-sea benthic foraminifera ^{18}O isotope records from Deep Sea Drilling Program and Ocean Drilling Program sites (Zachos *et al.* 2001), temperatures applying only to icefree conditions, thus to times earlier than ~35 My BP. The blue bar shows estimated times with ice present, dark blue being times when ice was equal or greater than at present. (b) Expansion of ^{18}O data for past 3.5 My (Lisiecki and Raymo 2005). (c) Temperature data based on Vostok ice core (Vimeux *et al.* 2002).**

Q. Can you explain the nature of the global climate change illustrated in Figure 10?

A. The long-term cooling from 50 My BP to the present must be be due primarily to decreasing greenhouse gases, primarily CO_2, which fell from 1000–2000 ppm 50 My BP to 180–280

---

32. J. Zachos *et al.*, *Trends, Rhythms, and Aberrations in Global Climate 65 Ma to Present*, 292 SCIENCE 686 (2001).

33. *Id.*; C.H. Lear *et al.*, *Cenozoic Deep-sea Temperatures and Global Ice Volumes from Mg/Ca in Benthic Foraminiferal Calcite*, 287 SCIENCE 269 (2000).

ppm in recent glacial-interglacial periods. Full glaciation of Antarctica, at about 34 My BP,[34] occurred when CO_2 fell to 500 ± 150 ppm.[35]

Between 34 and 15 My BP global temperature fluctuated, with Antarctica losing most of its ice at about 27 My BP. Antarctica did not become fully glaciated again until about 15 My BP. Deglaciation of Antarctica was associated with increased atmospheric CO_2,[36] perhaps due to the negative feedback caused by reduction of weathering[37] as ice and snow covered Antarctica as well as the higher reaches of the Himalayas and the Alps.

Cooling and ice growth resumed at about 15 My BP continuing up to the current Pleistocene ice age. During the past 15 My CO_2 was at a low level, about 200–400 ppm[38] and its proxy measures are too crude to determine whether it had a long-term trend. Thus it has been suggested that the cooling trend may have been due to a reduction of poleward ocean heat transports, perhaps caused by the closing of the Isthmus of Panama at about 12 My BP or the steady widening of the oceanic passageway between South America and Antarctica.

We suggest that the global cooling trend after 15 My BP may be due to continued drawdown of atmospheric CO_2 of a degree beneath the detection limit of proxy measures. Little additional drawdown would be needed, because the increasing ice cover on the planet makes climate sensitivity extremely high, and the logarithmic nature of CO_2 forcing[39] makes a small CO_2 change very effective at low CO_2 amounts. There are reasons to expect CO_2 drawdown in this period: the Andes were rising rapidly in this period,[40] at a rate of about 1 mm per year (1 km per My). The mass of the Andes increased so much as to slow down the convergence of the Nazca and South American plates by 30% in the past 3.2 My.[41] Increased weathering and reduced subduction both contribute to drawdown of atmospheric CO_2. Finally, a suggestion that CO_2 has been declining over the relevant period is provided by the increase of C4 plants relative to C3 plants that occurred between 8 and 5 My BP.[42] C4 plants are more resilient to low atmospheric CO_2 levels (C4 and C3 photosynthesis are alternative biochemical pathways for fixing carbon, the C4 path requiring more energy but being more tolerant of low CO_2 and drought conditions). However, given the high climate sensitivity with large ice cover, other small forcings could have been responsible for the cooling trend without additional CO_2 decline.

In summary, there are many uncertainties about details of climate change during the Cenozoic era. Yet important conclusions emerge, as summarized in Figure 15. The dominant forcing that caused global cooling, from an ice free planet to the present world with large ice sheets on two continents, was a decrease in atmospheric CO_2. Human-made rates of change of climate forcings, including CO_2, now dwarf the natural rates.

Q. Is this relevant to the question of whether we need to "wrestle" with climate change?

---

34. *Id.*

35. J. Hansen & M. Sato, *Global Warming: East-West Connections* (2007) *available at* www.columbia.edu/~jeh1/2007/EastWest_20070925.pdf; J. Hansen & M. Sato, *Climate Forcings in the Cenozoic* (in preparation).

36. Pagani *et al.*, *supra* note 27.

37. C.H. Lear *et al.*, *Late Eocene to Early Miocene Ice Sheet Dynamics and the Global Carbon Cycle*, 19 Paleooceanography PA4015 (2004).

38. Pagani *et al.*, *supra* note 27; Zachos *et al.*, *supra* note 32.

39. *See* formulae in J. Hansen *et al.*, *Global Warming in the Twenty-first Century: an Alternative Scenario*, 297 Proc. Natl. Acad. Sci 9875 (2000).

40. C.N. Garzione *et al.*, *Rapid Late Miocene Rise of the Bolivian Altiplano: Evidence for Removal of Mantle Lithosphere*, 241 Earth Planet. Sci. Lett. 543 (2006).

41. G. Iaffaldano *et al.*, *Mountain Belt Growth Inferred From Histories of Past Plate Convergence: A New Tectonic Inverse Problem*, 260 Earth Planet. Sci. Lett. 516 (2007).

42. T.E. Cerling *et al.*, *Expansion of C4 Ecosystems as an Indicator of Global Ecological Change in the Late Miocene*, 361 Nature 344 (1993).

Summary: Cenozoic Era	
1. Dominant Forcing: Natural ΔCO_2	– Rate ~100 ppm/My (0.0001 ppm/year) – Human-made rate today: ~2 ppm/year
Humans Overwhelm Slow Geologic Changes	
2. Climate Sensitivity High	– Antarctic ice forms if CO2 <~500 ppm – Ice sheet formation reversible
Humans Could Produce "A Different Planet"	

Figure 15. Principal inferences from Cenozoic Era relevant to present-day climate.

A. Yes, it may help resolve the conundrum sensed by some lay persons based on realization that the natural world has undergone huge climate variations in the past. That is true, but those climate variations produced a different planet. If we follow "business as usual" greenhouse gas emissions, putting back into the air a large fraction of the carbon that was stored in the ground over millions of years, we surely will set in motion large climate changes with dramatic consequences for humans and other species.

Q. Why are climate fluctuations in the past few million years (Figure 14b) so regular?

A. The instigator is the distribution of sunlight on the Earth, which continuously changes by a small amount because of the gravitational pull of other planets, especially Jupiter and Saturn, because they are heavy, and Venus, because it comes close. The most important effect is on the tilt of the Earth's spin axis relative to the plane of the Earth's orbit (Figure 16). The tilt varies by about 2° with a regular periodicity of about 41 Ky (41,000 years). When the tilt is larger it exposes both polar regions to increased sunlight at 6-month intervals. The increased heating of the polar regions melts ice in both hemispheres.

The 41 Ky climate variability is apparent in Figure 14b and is present in almost all climate records. However, glacial-interglacial climate variations became more complex in the most recent 1.2 My, with large variations at ~100 Ky periodicity, as well as ~41 Ky and ~23 Ky periods. As the planet became steadily colder over the past several million years, the amplitude of glacial-interglacial climate swings increased (Figure 14b) as ice sheet area increased. Ice sheets on Northern Hemisphere continents, especially North America, extended as far south as 45N latitude. Similar ice sheets were not possible in the Southern Hemisphere, which lacked land at relevant latitudes.

Hemispheric asymmetry in ice sheet area allows two additional Earth orbital parameters, which work in concert, to come into play. Gravitational tugs of the planets cause the eccentricity of the Earth's orbit about the sun to vary from near zero (circular) to an eccentricity of about 0.06. When the orbit is significantly non-circular, this allows another orbital parameter, axial precession, to become important. Precession, which determines the date in the year at which the Earth in its elliptical orbit is closest to the sun, varies with a periodicity of ca. 23 Ky. When the Earth is closest to the sun in Northern Hemisphere winter, thus furthest from the sun in summer, ice sheet growth in the Northern Hemisphere is encouraged by increased winter snowfall and cool summers. The effect of eccentricity + precession on ice sheet growth is opposite in the two hemispheres, so the effect is important only when the area of high albedo ice and snow is much different in the two hemispheres, as it has been in the past million years. Climate variations then include all three periodicities, ~23 Ky precession, ~41 Ky tilt, and ~100 Ky eccentricity, as has been demonstrated for the recent ice age cycles.[43]

---

43. J.D. Hays *et al.*, *Variations in the Earth's Orbit: Pacemaker of the Ice Ages*, 194 SCIENCE 1121 (1976).

Figure 16. *(Image not shown)* Increased tilt of Earth's spin axis exposes both poles to greater melt of high latitude ice.

Q. **What are the current Earth orbital parameters?**

A. Precession has the Earth closest to the sun in January, furthest in July, which would favor growth of Northern Hemisphere ice. But eccentricity is small, about 0.016, so the precession effect is not large. Tilt is about midway between its extremes headed toward smaller tilt, the next minimum tilt occurring in ~10 Ky. Smaller tilt favors ice sheet growth, so, if it were not for humans, we might expect a trend toward the next ice age. But the trend may have been weak, because, by the time tilt reaches its minimum, the Earth will be closest to the sun in Northern Hemisphere summer. Thus in this particular cycle the two mechanisms, tilt and eccentricity + precession, will be working against each other, rather than reinforcing each other. In any event, this natural tendency has become practically irrelevant in the age of fossil-fuel-burning humans.

Q. **Why is the natural glacial-interglacial cycle irrelevant?**

A. Earth orbital changes were only pacemakers for glacial-interglacial climate change, inducing changes of ice area and greenhouse gases. Changes of surface albedo and greenhouse gases were the mechanisms for climate change, providing the immediate causes of the climate changes. We showed in Figure 10 that these two mechanisms account for the glacial-interglacial climate variations.

Now humans are responsible for changes of these climate mechanisms. Greenhouse gases are increasing far outside the range of natural glacial-interglacial variations (Figure 12) and ice is melting all over the planet. The weak effect of slow orbital changes is overwhelmed by the far larger and faster human-made changes.

Humans are now entirely responsible for long-term climate change (Figure 17). However, it would be misleading to say that humans are "in control." Indeed, there is great danger that humans could set in motion future changes that are impossible to control, because of climate system inertia, positive feedback, and tipping points.

Q. **Can we finally finish with this paleoclimate discussion?**

A. Please allow one final comment. For the record, since I could only estimate broad ranges for CO_2 in the Cenozoic era, I should show at least one estimate from the proxy CO_2 data. Figure 18A shows estimated CO_2 for the entire Phanerozoic eon, the past 540 million years. I show this longer time interval, because it includes CO_2 changes so large as to make the errors in the proxies less in a relative sense.

Implications of Pleistocene Climate Change
1. *Chief instigator* of climate change was earth orbital change, a very weak forcing.
2. *Chief mechanisms* of Pleistocene climate change are GHGs & ice sheet area, *as feedbacks*.
3. Climate on long time scale is *very sensitive* to even small forcings.
4. *Human-made forcings dwarf natural forcings* that drove glacial-interglacial climate change.
5. *Humans now control the mechanisms for global climate change*, for better or worse.

Figure 17. Principal inferences from Pleistocene climate variations.

Geologic evidence for ice ages and cool periods on this long time frame (Figure 18B) shows a strong correlation of climate with CO_2. Climate variations were huge, ranging from ice ages with ice sheets as far equatorward as 30 degrees latitude to a much warmer planet without ice. Although other factors were also involved in these climate changes, greenhouse gases were a major factor.

Figure 18. *(Image not shown)* (A) Estimates of CO_2 in the Phanerozoic based on proxy CO_2 data and GEO-CARB-III model of Berner and Kothavala (2001), (B) Intervals of glacial (dark) or cool (light) climates, (C) Latitudinal distribution of direct glacial records (tillites, striated bedrock, etc., from Crowley 1998). Figure is from Royer *et al.* (2004).

Q. Are climate models consistent with paleoclimate estimates of high climate sensitivity and with observed global warming in the past century?

A. Yes. Climate models yield equilibrium sensitivity (the response after several centuries) of typically about 3°C for doubled CO_2. Figure 19B shows the resulting global warming when such a climate model (one with ~3°C sensitivity for doubled CO_2) is driven by climate forcings measured or estimated for the period 1880–2003 (Figure 19A). The calculated and observed warmings are similar. Good agreement might also be obtained using a model with higher sensitivity and a smaller forcing or using a model with lower sensitivity and a larger forcing. But the sensitivity of this model[44] agrees well with the empirical sensitivity defined by paleoclimate data.

Q. I am confused. Did you not say earlier that climate sensitivity is about 6°C for doubled CO_2?

A. Yes. That is an important point that needs to be recognized. We showed that the real world climate sensitivity is 6°C for doubled CO_2, when both fast and slow feedback processes are included, based on data that covered climate states ranging from interglacial periods 1°C warmer than today to ice ages 5°C cooler than today. That 6°C sensitivity is also the appropriate estimate for the range of warmer climates up to the point at which all ice sheets are melted and high latitudes are fully vegetated.

This higher climate sensitivity, 6°C for doubled CO_2, is the appropriate sensitivity for long time scales, when greenhouse gases are the specified forcing mechanism and all other slow feedbacks are allowed to fully respond to the climate change. The substantial relevant slow feedbacks are changes of ice sheets and surface vegetation.

Q. Yet you employed a climate model with 3°C sensitivity, a model excluding these slow feedbacks. Does this cause a significant error?

A. No, not in simulations of the 20th century climate change as in Figure 19. Feedbacks come into play not in response to climate forcing but in response to climate change. Ocean thermal inertia introduces a lag, shown by the climate response function in Figure 19c. The response function is the fraction of the equilibrium surface response that is achieved at a given time subsequent to introduction of the forcing. About half of the equilibrium response occurs within a quarter century, but further response at the Earth's surface is slowed by mixing of water between the ocean surface layer and the deeper ocean. Nearly full response requires several centuries.

Furthermore, the response time to a climate forcing increases in proportion to the square of climate sensitivity,[45] so the response time for 6°C climate sensitivity is about four times greater than that shown in Figure 19C. The explanation for this strong dependence of re-

---

44. Hansen *et al.*, *supra* note 21.

45. J. Hansen *et al.*, *Climate Response Times: Dependence on Climate Sensitivity and Ocean Mixing*, 229 SCIENCE 857 (1985).

sponse time on climate sensitivity is simple: the rate of heating is fixed, so to warm the ocean mixed layer would take twice as long for 6°C sensitivity as for 3°C sensitivity. But this additional time allows more mixing of heat into the deeper ocean. For diffusive mixing it follows analytically, as shown in the referenced paper, that the response time goes as the square of climate sensitivity.

In addition, some climate feedback processes can increase response time above that associated with ocean thermal inertia alone. A fast feedback such as atmospheric water vapor amount occurs almost instantly with temperature change. However, ice sheets require time to disintegrate or grow, and vegetation migration in response to shifting climate zones also may require substantial time.

Ice sheet and vegetation responses were not important factors affecting the magnitude of 20th century global warming, so simulations of 20th century global temperature change were not compromised by exclusion of those feedbacks. However, with a substantial and almost monotonic global warming now in place (Figure 5a), the ice sheet and vegetation feedbacks should begin to contribute significantly to climate change in the 21st century. Ice sheet and vegetation changes will continue to alter the planetary energy balance over century time scales and must be accounted for in projecting future climate change.

Figure 19. *(Image not shown)* **(A) Climate forcings since 1880, relative to the forcings in 1880. The largest forcing is the positive (warming) forcing due to greenhouse gases, but human-made aerosols and occasional volcanoes provide significant negative forcings. (B) Observed global temperature and temperature simulated with the GISS global climate model, which has climate sensitivity 2.8°C for doubled CO_2, using the forcings in (A). (C) Climate response function (% of equilibrium response) obtained with GISS atmosphere modelE connected to the Russell ocean model.[46]**

Q. Can we move on from this technical discussion of feedbacks and response time?

A. Please allow one final comment. The 6°C sensitivity (for doubled CO_2) is valid for a specified change of greenhouse gases as the climate forcing. That is relevant for human-made change of atmospheric composition, and this sensitivity yields the correct answer for long-term climate change if actual greenhouse gas changes are used as the forcing mechanism. However, climate model scenarios for the future usually incorporate human-made emissions of greenhouse gases. Atmospheric greenhouse gas amounts may be affected by feedbacks, which thus alter expected climate change.

Greenhouse gas feedbacks are not idle speculation. Paleoclimate records reveal times in the Earth's history when global warming resulted in release of large amounts of methane to the atmosphere. Potential sources of methane include methane hydrates "frozen" in ocean sediments and tundra, which release methane in thawing. Recent Arctic warming is causing release of methane from permafrost,[47] but not to a degree that has prevented near stabilization of atmospheric methane amount over the past several years.

Hansen and Sato[48] have shown from paleoclimate records that the positive feedbacks that occur for all major long-lived greenhouse gases (carbon dioxide, methane, and nitrous oxide) are moderate for global warming less than 1°C. However, no such constraints exist for still larger global warming, because there are no recent interglacial periods with global

---

46. Hansen *et al.*, *supra* note 21.

47. T.R. Christensen *et al.*, *Thawing Sub-arctic Permafrost: Effects on Vegetation and Methane Emissions*, 31 Geophys. Res. Lett. L04501 (2004); K.M. Walter *et al.*, *Methane Bubbling from Siberian Thaw Lakes as a Positive Feedback to Climate*, 443 Nature 71 (2006).

48. J. Hansen & M. Sato, *Greenhouse Gas Growth Rates*, 101 Proc. Natl. Acad. Sci. 16109 (2004).

warming greater than about 1°C. Based on other metrics (avoiding large sea level rise, extermination of species, and large regional climate disruption) we argue that we must aim to keep additional global warming, above the level in 2000, less than 1°C. Such a limit should also avert massive release of frozen methane.

Q. **Observed (and modeled) global warming of 0.8°C in the past century seems small in view of the large changes of greenhouse gases shown in Figure 12. Why is that?**

A. There are two reasons.

First, there is the large thermal inertia of the ocean. It takes a few decades to achieve just half of the global warming with climate sensitivity of 3°C for doubled CO_2, as shown in Figure 19C. And the slow feedbacks that contribute half of the paleoclimate change are now just beginning to come into play.

Second, the greenhouse gases are not the only climate forcing. Human-made tropospheric aerosols, Figure 19A, are estimated to cause a negative forcing about half as large as the greenhouse forcing, but opposite in sign.

Q. **There must be some uncertainty in the climate forcings, especially the aerosol forcing. Can you verify that the estimated forcings are realistic?**

A. Yes. The aerosol forcing is difficult to verify directly, but there is an exceedingly valuable diagnostic that relates to the net climate forcing. Given that the greenhouse gas forcing is known accurately, the constraint on net forcing has implications for the aerosol forcing, because other forcings are either small or well-measured (Figure 19A). The diagnostic that I refer to is the planetary energy imbalance.[49]

The Earth's energy imbalance, averaged over several years, is a critical metric for several reasons. First and foremost, it is a direct measure of the reduction of climate forcings required to stabilize climate. The planetary energy imbalance measures the climate forcing that has not yet been responded to, *i.e.*, multiplication of the energy imbalance by climate sensitivity defines global warming still "in the pipeline."

A good period to evaluate the Earth's energy imbalance is the eleven-year period 1995–2005, because this covers one solar cycle from solar minimum to solar minimum. A climate model with sensitivity ~3°C for doubled CO_2, driven by the climate forcings in Figure 19A, yields an imbalance of 0.75 ± 0.15 W/m^2 for 1995–2005. Observations of heat gain in measured portions of the upper 700 m of the ocean yield a global heat gain of ~0.5 W/m^2. Measured or estimated heat used in sea ice and land ice melt, warming of ground and air, and ocean warming in polar regions and at depths below 700 m yield a total estimated heat gain of 0.75 ± 0.25 W/m^2.[50]

The observed planetary energy imbalance thus supports the estimated climate forcings used in the climate simulations of Figure 19. This check is not an absolute verification, because the results also depend upon climate sensitivity, but the model's sensitivity is consistent with paleoclimate data. Indeed, the existence of a substantial planetary energy imbalance provides confirmation that climate sensitivity is high. Climate response time varies as the square of climate sensitivity, so if climate sensitivity were much smaller, say half as large as indicated by paleoclimate data, it would not be possible for realistic climate forcings to yield such a large planetary energy imbalance.

49. J. Hansen *et al.*, *Earth's Energy Imbalance: Confirmation and Implications*, 308 SCIENCE 1431 (2005).

50. J. Hansen, presentation at American Geophysical Union Fall Meeting in San Francisco (December 2007).

Comment: The planetary energy imbalance is the single most critical metric for the state of the Earth's climate. Ocean heat storage is the largest term in this imbalance; it needs to be measured more accurately, present problems being incomplete coverage of data in depth and latitude, and poor inter-calibration among different instruments. The other essential measurement for tracking the energy imbalance is continued precise monitoring of the ice sheets via gravity satellite measurements.

Q. How much is global warming expected to increase in the present century, and how does this depend upon assumptions about fossil fuel use?

A. We can project future global warming with reasonable confidence, for different assumed scenarios of greenhouse gases, by extending the climate model simulations that matched well the observed global temperature change in the past century. Figure 20 shows such a projection based on the GISS global climate model, which has climate sensitivity close to 3°C for doubled CO_2. The model excludes slow climate feedbacks such as changes of ice sheet area and global vegetation distributions, but the effects of those slow feedbacks on global mean temperature should be small during the next several decades.

"Business-as-Usual" climate scenarios, such as IPCC scenarios A1B and A2, yield additional global warming of at least 2°C in the 21st century. Actual warming for "business-as-usual" climate forcing could be larger because: (1) slow climate feedbacks such as ice sheet disintegration, vegetation migration, and methane release from melting permafrost are not included, (2) atmospheric aerosols (small particles, especially sulfates) that have a cooling effect are kept fixed, but it is expected that they could decrease this century, (3) CO_2 emissions as high as in business-as-usual scenarios may have climate effects large enough to alter the ability of the biosphere to take up the assumed proportion of CO_2 emissions.

The "alternative scenario" is defined with the aim of keeping additional global warming, beyond that of 2000, less than 1°C. This requires that additional climate forcing be kept less than about 1.5 W/m^2, assuming a climate sensitivity of about 3°C for doubled CO_2, and in turn this requires that CO_2 be kept from exceeding about 450 ppm, with the exact limit depending upon how well other climate forcings are constrained, especially methane.[51] Figure 20 shows that additional global warming in the alternative scenario is about 0.8°C by 2100, and it remains less than 1°C under the assumption that a slow decrease in greenhouse gas forcing occurs after 2100.

Q. How do these levels of global warming relate to dangerous climate change?

A. That is the fundamental issue, because practically all nations, including the United States, have signed the Framework Convention on Climate Change, agreeing to stabilize greenhouse gas emissions at a level that prevents "dangerous" anthropogenic interference with the climate system (Figure 21). In just the past few years it has become clear that atmospheric composition is already close to, if not slightly beyond, the dangerous level of greenhouse gases. In order to understand this situation, it is necessary to define key metrics for what constitutes "danger", to examine the Earth's history for levels of climate forcing associated with these metrics, and to recognize changes that are already beginning to appear in the physics of the climate system.

Principal metrics defining dangerous include: (1) ice sheet disintegration and sea level rise, (2) extermination of species, and (3) regional climate disruptions (Figure 22). Ice sheet disintegration and species extinction proceed slowly at first but have the potential for disastrous non-linear collapse later in the century. The consequences of ice sheet disintegration

---

51. Hansen *et al.*, *supra* note 39.

Climate Simulations for IPCC 2007 Report
• Climate Model Sensitivity 2.7–2.9°C for 2xCO_2 (consistent with paleoclimate data & other models)
• Simulations Consistent with 1880–2003 Observations (key test = ocean heat storage)
• Simulated Global Warming < 1°C in Alternative Scenario
Conclusion: Warming < 1°C if additional forcing ~1.5W/m^2

Figure 20. *(Image not shown)* Extension of climate simulations through the 21st century. A1B (dark blue line) is a typical "business-as-usual" scenario for future greenhouse gas amounts. The "alternative scenario" has CO_2 peaking near 450 ppm, thus keeping additional warming beyond that in 2000 less than 1°C.

and species extinction could not be reversed on any time scale of interest to humanity. If humans cause multi-meter sea level rise and exterminate a large fraction of species on Earth,

United Nations Framework Convention on Climate Change
Aim is to stabilize greenhouse gas emissions …
"… at a level that would prevent dangerous anthropogenic interference with the climate system."

Figure 21. Practically all nations in the world, including the United States, have signed the Framework Convention on Climate Change. The problem is that "dangerous anthropogenic interference" in not defined.

they will, in effect, have destroyed creation, the planet on which civilization developed over the past several thousand years.

Regional climate disruptions also deserve attention. Global warming intensifies the extremes of the hydrologic cycle. On the one hand, it increases the intensity of heavy rain and floods, as well as the maximum intensity of storms driven by latent heat, including thunderstorms, tornados and tropical storms. At the other extreme, at times and places where it is dry, global warming will lead to increased drought intensity, higher temperatures, and more and stronger forest fires. Subtropical regions such as the American West, the Mediterranean

Metrics for "Dangerous" Change
Ice Sheet Disintegration: Global Sea Level
1. Long-Term Change from Paleoclimate Data
2. Ice Sheet Response Time
Extermination of Animal & Plant Species
1. Extinction of Polar and Alpine Species
2. Unsustainable Migration Rates
Regional Climate Disruptions
1. Increase of Extreme Events
2. Shifting Zones / Freshwater Shortages

Figure 22. Suggested principal metrics for defining the "dangerous" level of climate change.

region, Australia and parts of Africa are expected to be particularly hard hit by global warming. Because of earlier spring snowmelt and retreat of glaciers, fresh water supplies will fail in many locations, as summers will be longer and hotter.

Q. Is it possible to say how close we are to deleterious climate impacts?

A. Yes. I will argue that we are near the dangerous levels for all three of these metrics.

In the case of sea level, this conclusion is based on both observations of what is happening on the ice sheets today and the history of the Earth, which shows how fast ice sheets can disintegrate and the level of warming that is needed to spark large change.

Figure 23 shows that the area on the Greenland ice sheet with summer melt has been increasing over the period of satellite observations, the satellite view being essential to map this region. The area with summer melt is also increasing on West Antarctica.

Figure 23. *(Image not shown)* Area on Greenland with summer surface melt fluctuates from year to year, but has been increasing during the period of satellite observations. Recent years, not shown, have broken the record set in 2002.

Figure 24 shows summer meltwater on Greenland. The meltwater does not in general make it to the edge of the ice sheet. Rather it runs to a relative low spot or crevasse on the ice sheet, and there burrows a hole all the way to the base of the ice sheet. The meltwater then serves as lubrication between the ice sheet and the ground, thus speeding the discharge of giant icebergs to the ocean (Figure 25).

Figure 24. *(Image not shown)* Summer surface melt-water on Greenland burrows a hole in the ice sheet, more than a mile thick, that carries water to the base of the ice sheet. There it serves as lubrication between the ice sheet and the ground beneath the ice sheet.

Figure 25. *(Image not shown)* The rate of discharge of giant icebergs from Greenland has doubled in the past decade.

Q. Is it not true that global warming also increases the snowfall rate, thus causing ice sheets to grow faster?

A. The first half of that assertion is correct. The inference drawn by "contrarians," that global warming will cause ice sheets to become bigger, defies common sense as well as abundant paleoclimate evidence. The Earth's history shows that when the planet gets warmer, ice sheets melt and sea level increases. Ice sheet size would not necessarily need to decrease on short time scales in response to human-made perturbations. However, we now have spectacular data from a gravity satellite mission that allows us to evaluate ice sheet response to global warming.

The gravity satellite measures the Earth's gravitational field with sufficient precision to detect changes in the mass of the Greenland and Antarctic ice sheets. As shown by Figure 26, the mass of the ice sheet increases during the winter and decreases during the melting season. However, the net effect is a downward trend of the ice sheet mass. In the past few years Greenland and West Antarctica have each lost mass at a rate of the order of 150 cubic kilometers per year.

Figure 26. *(Image not shown)* The GRACE satellite mission measures the Earth's gravitational field with such high precision that changes of the mass of the Greenland and Antarctic ice sheets can be measured. The ice sheet mass grows with winter snowfall and decreases during the melt season. Overall Greenland and West Antarctica are each now losing mass at rates of the order of 150 cubic kilometers of ice per year.

Q. Is sea level increasing at a significant rate?

A. Sea level is now increasing at a rate of about 3.5 cm per decade or 35 cm per century, with thermal expansion of the ocean, melting of alpine glaciers, and the Greenland and West Antarctic ice sheets all contributing to this sea level rise. That is double the rate of 20 years ago, and that in turn was faster than the rate a century earlier. Previously sea level had been quite stable for the past several millennia.

Q. **Is the current level of sea level rise dangerous?**

A. This rate of sea level rise is more than a nuisance, as it increases beach erosion, salt water intrusion into water supplies, and damage from storm surges. However, the real danger is the possibility that the rate of sea level rise will continue to accelerate. Indeed, it surely will accelerate, if we follow business-as-usual growth of greenhouse gas emissions.

Q. **How fast can sea level rise and when would rapid changes be expected?**

A. Those questions are inherently difficult to answer for a non-linear process such as ice sheet disintegration. Unlike ice sheet growth, which is a dry process limited by the rate of snowfall, ice sheet disintegration is a wet process that can proceed rapidly and catastrophically once it gets well underway.

Some guidance is provided by the Earth's history. When the Laurentide ice sheet, which covered Canada and reached into the northern edges of the United States, disintegrated following the last ice age, there were times when sea level rose several meters per century. The Greenland and West Antarctic ice sheets are at somewhat higher latitudes than the Laurentide ice sheet, but West Antarctica seems at least as vulnerable to rapid disintegration because it rests on bedrock below sea level. Thus the West Antarctic ice sheet is vulnerable to melting by warming ocean water at its edge as well as surface melt. In addition, if we follow business-as-usual, the human-made climate forcing will be far larger and more rapid than the climate forcings that drove earlier deglaciations.

I have argued[52] that business-as-usual greenhouse gas growth almost surely will cause multi-meter sea level rise within a century. High latitude amplification of global warming would result in practically the entire West Antarctic and Greenland ice sheets being bathed in meltwater for a lengthened melt season. A warmer ocean and summer rainfall could speed flushing of the ice sheets. If we wait until rapid disintegration begins, it will be impossible to stop.

Q. **What consequences would be expected with multi-meter sea level rise?**

A. Most of the world's large cities are on coast lines (Figure 27). The last time that global mean temperature was 2–3°C warmer than now was in the Pliocene, when sea level was about 25 meters higher than today. About one billion people live within 25-meter elevation of sea level. As shown by Figure 28, most East Coast cities in the United States would be under water with a sea level rise that large, almost the entire nation of Bangladesh, the State of Florida, and an area in China that presently contains about 300 million people. There are historical coastal cities in most countries. A sea level rise of 5–7 meters, which could be provided by West Antarctica alone, is enough to displace a few hundred million people.

Figure 27. *(Image not shown)* **A majority of the world's 100 largest cities are located on coast lines.**

Figure 28. *(Image not shown)* **A sea level rise of 25 meters would displace about 1 billion people. Even a 5–7 meter sea level rise would affect a few hundred million people, more than 1000 times greater than the number of people in New Orleans affected by the Katrina hurricane disaster.**

---

52. Hansen, *supra* note 11.

Q. Does sea level provide a precise specification of "dangerous" warming?

A.   I suggest that it is useful to look at prior interglacial periods, some of which were warmer than our current interglacial period. In some of these periods, *e.g.*, the interglacials ~125 and ~425 thousand years ago, sea level was higher than today by as much as a few meters, but sea level did not approach the level in the Pliocene. Although we do not have accurate measurements of global mean temperature for the earlier interglacial periods, we do have local measurements at places of special relevance.

Figure 29a is the temperature in the Western Pacific Warm Pool, the warmest ocean region on the planet, a region of special importance because it strongly affects transport of heat to higher latitudes via both the atmosphere and ocean. Figure 29b is the temperature in the Indian Ocean, the place that has the highest correlation with global mean temperature during the period of instrumental data, the period when an accurate global mean temperature can be calculated.[53] Figure 29 concatenates modern instrumental temperatures with proxy paleo measures. In both of these regions it appears that the warming of recent decades has brought recent temperatures to within about 1°C or less of the warmest interglacial periods.

Tropical ocean temperature change is only moderately smaller than global mean temperature change in both recent times and glacial-interglacial climate change. For this reason, I assert that it would be foolhardy for humanity to allow additional global warming to exceed about 1°C.

Figure 29. *(Image not shown)* **Paleo and Modern Temperatures in Critical Global Regions. Temperatures in the Pacific Warm Pool (a) and Indian Ocean (b), regions of special significance for global climate. Warm Pool temperature affects the transport of heat to much of the world via ocean and atmosphere; the Indian Ocean has the highest correlation with global mean temperature. In both regions warming of recent decades has brought the temperature within less than 1°C of the temperature during the warmest interglacial periods.**

Q. But if additional global warming is kept less than 1°C that does not seem to guarantee that sea level rise of a few meters would not occur, given the changes that occurred in the previous interglacial periods, does it?

A.   You are right, and I am not recommending that the world should aim for additional global warming of 1°C. Indeed, because of potential sea level rise, as well as the other critical metrics that I will discuss, I infer that it is desirable to avoid any further global warming.

However, I also note that there is an enormous difference between global warming less than 1°C and global warming of 2–3°C. The latter warming would have the global climate system pointed toward an eventual sea level rise measured in the tens of meters. In that case we should expect multi-meter sea level rise this century and initiation of ice sheet disintegration out of our control with a continually rising sea level and repeated coastal disasters unfolding for centuries. Economic and social consequences are difficult to fathom.

With global warming less than 1°C it is possible that sea level rise this century would be less than 1 meter. Ice sheet changes would likely unfold much more slowly than with 2–3°C global warming. If the maximum global warming is kept less than 1°C, it may be practical to achieve moderate adjustments of global climate forcings that would avert the occurrence of large sea level change. Human-made gases in the air will decrease when sources are reduced sufficiently, so as events unfold and understanding improves, it may prove necessary to set goals that yield a declining global temperature beyond the human-induced maxi-

---

53. Hansen *et al.*, *supra* note 2.

mum temperature. However, considering the 1000-year lifetime of much of the CO_2, if the additional warming is 2–3°C, it will be impractical to avoid disastrous consequences.

Q. **What other ghosts of climate future can be seen?**

A. Another potential consequence that would be irreversible is extermination of species. Animal and plant species can survive only within certain climatic zones. As climate changes, animals and plants can migrate, and in general they deal successfully with fluctuating climate. However, large climate changes have caused mass extinctions in the past. Several times in the Earth's history global warming of five degrees Celsius or more led to extinction of a majority of species on the planet. Of course other species came into being over many thousands of years. But mass extinctions now would leave a far more desolate planet for as long as we can imagine.

Global warming of 0.6°C in the past three decades has initiated a systematic movement of climatic zones, with isotherms moving poleward at a rate of typically 50–60 km per decade.[54] As this movement continues, and as it would accelerate with business-as-usual increases of fossil fuel use, it will add a strong climatic stress to the other stresses that humans have placed on many species. Species at high latitudes (Figure 30) and high altitudes (Figure 31) are in danger of, in effect, being pushed off the planet by global warming. Many other species will be threatened as the total movement of climatic zones increases, because some species are less mobile than others. Interdependencies of species leave entire ecosystems vulnerable to collapse.

Figure 30. *(Image not shown)* **Unchecked global warming will, in effect, push polar species off the planet.**

It can be argued, as E.O. Wilson has suggested, that the world beyond the 21st century, post fossil fuel domination and post the human population peak, could have an environment that is more tolerant of all species. It is difficult to project how many of the species of creation will survive the bottleneck in the 21st century (Figure 32), but surely the number will be much smaller if the stresses include business-as-usual climate change.

Realization that we are already near "dangerous" climate change, for sea level rise and other effects, has a bright side. It means that we must curtail atmospheric CO_2 and other climate forcings more sharply than has generally been assumed. Thus various problems that had begun to seem almost inevitable, such as acidification of the ocean, cannot proceed

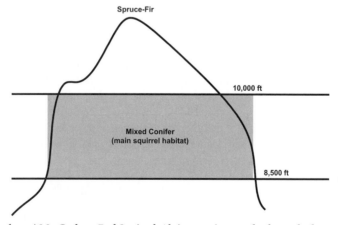

Figure 31. *(Photo not shown)* **Mt. Graham Red Squirrel. Alpine species can also be pushed to extinction as global warming causes isotherms to move up the mountains. The Mt. Graham red squirrel is an example of a threatened species. Impacts of climate change occur in bursts; forest fires in the lower reaches of the forested region cause permanent change, as the forests are unable to recover. Figure re-drawn from original Hansen testimony.**

---

54. *Id.*

much further, if we are to avoid other catastrophes. If the needed actions are taken, we may preserve most species.

Q. Are there other criteria, besides sea level and species extinction, for "danger"?

A. There are many regional effects of global warming. Large natural weather and climate fluctuations make it difficult to identify global warming effects, but they are beginning to emerge. If

Survival of Species	
1. "Business-as-Usual" Scenario	– Global Warming ~3°C – Likely Extinctions ~25–50 percent
2. "Alternative" Scenario	– Global Warming < 1°C – Likely Extinctions < 10 percent
How Many Species to Survive Bottleneck?	
Climate Feedbacks → Scenario Dichotomy	

Figure 32. The millions of species on the planet are being stressed in several ways, as humans have taken over much of the planet. Based on prior global warmings in the Earth's history, much slower than the present human-induced climate change, it is expected that the added stress from the large global climate change under business-as-usual scenarios would lead to eventual extinction of at least several tens of percent of extant species.

we follow business-as-usual, the southernmost parts of our country are likely to have much less tolerable climate. Fresh water shortages could become a frequent problem in parts of the country, especially those dependent on snowpack runoff, as spring comes earlier and summers are longer, hotter and drier, and forest fires will be an increasing problem. Other parts of the country, and in some cases the same places, will experience heavier rain, when it occurs, and greater floods. The tier of semi-arid states, from West Texas through the Dakotas, is subject to the same expected increase of hydrologic extremes, but overall they are likely to become drier and less suited for agriculture, if we follow business-as-usual and large global warming ensues.

Given that effects of global warming on regional climate are already beginning to emerge, the regional climate criterion also implies that further global warming much above the present level is likely to be deleterious.

Q. Is it still possible to avoid dangerous climate change?

A. It is possible, but just barely. Most climate forcings are increasing at a rate consistent with, or even more favorable (slower), than the "alternative scenario" which keeps warming less than 1°C. CO_2 is the one climate forcing that is increasing much more rapidly than in the alternative scenario, and if CO_2 emissions continue on their current path CO_2 threatens to become so dominant that it will be implausible to get the net climate forcing onto a path consistent with the alternative scenario. Furthermore, as I have discussed, there are reasons to believe that even the smaller warming of the alternative scenario may take us into the dangerous range of climate change. It is likely that we will need to aim for global warming even less than 1°C.

Q. Why are CO_2 and coal the focus of climate concerns?

A. Figure 33a shows one crucial fact. When a pulse of CO_2 is added to the atmosphere by burning fossil fuels, half of the CO_2 disappears from the air within about 25 years, being taken up by carbon sinks, principally the ocean. However, uptake then slows as the CO_2 added to the ocean exerts a "back pressure" that inhibits further uptake. About one-fifth of the initial increase is still present in the atmosphere after 1000 years. Complete removal of the pulse depends upon formation of carbonate sediments on the ocean floor, a very slow process. It is this long atmospheric lifetime that makes CO_2, on the long run, the principal climate forcing for human-made climate change.

Figure 33. *(Image not shown)* **Critical carbon cycle facts. (a) A pulse of CO_2 added to the atmosphere by burning fossil fuels decays rapidly at first, with about half of the CO_2 taken up by sinks, principally the ocean, within the first quarter century. However, uptake slows as the CO_2 added to the ocean exerts a back-pressure on the atmosphere. Even after 1000 years almost one-fifth of the increase due to the initial pulse is still in the atmosphere. (b) Fossil fuel reservoirs are finite. Oil and gas proven and estimated reserves are sufficient to take atmospheric CO_2 to the neighborhood of 450 ppm. Coal and unconventional fossil fuels, if exploited without carbon capture, have the potential to at least double or triple the pre-industrial atmospheric CO_2 amount of 280 ppm.**

Q. Why do you focus especially on coal?

A. Part of the reason is the size of the coal carbon reservoir, shown in Figure 33b. The coal reservoir is larger than either oil or gas. The amount of CO_2 already emitted to the atmosphere, shown by the purple portions of the bar graphs, is about 50% from coal, 35% from oil and 15% from gas. On the long run, coal will be even much more important.

Proven and estimated reserves of these fossil fuels are uncertain, and the amounts shown in Figure 33b for oil and coal both could be substantially over-estimated. Many experts believe that we are already at a point of having used approximately half of the economically recoverable reserves of oil. In that case we are already at approximately the point of "peak oil" production and oil use will soon begin to noticeably decline because of resource constraints.

Uncertainties in the oil and gas reserves have little qualitative effect on the climate discussion, however. The reasons are, first, that remaining oil and gas, used at any feasible rate, can at most only take atmospheric CO_2 to approximately 450 ppm. Second, it is impractical to avoid the use of readily extractable oil and gas, and most of the CO_2 resulting from that oil and gas will be emitted to the atmosphere, because it is emitted by small sources where it is impractical to capture the CO_2.

Coal reserves are also uncertain and it is likely that the estimates in Figure 33b, even the smaller estimate of EIA (Energy Information Agency), are too high. Nevertheless, there is more CO_2 in coal than in the other conventional fossil fuels. Indeed, there is enough CO_2 in coal to take the Earth far into the "dangerous" zone of climate change, to doubled atmospheric CO_2 and even beyond.

The second critical fact about coal is that it is possible to imagine coal being used only at power plants to generate electricity, with the CO_2 emissions captured and sequestered, with the carbon put back underground where it came from. Indeed, the elementary carbon cycle facts summarized in Figure 33 dictate the solution to the global warming problem.

Q. Can a solution to global warming be defined?

A. An outline of a practical solution can be defined readily (Figure 34). By far the most important element in this solution, indeed 80% of the solution, is phase-out of coal use except at power plants where the CO_2 is captured and sequestered. This requirement is dictated by the fundamental facts of the carbon cycle summarized in Figure 33.

The steps needed to achieve termination of CO_2 emissions from coal use are: (1) a moratorium in developed countries on construction of new coal-fired power plants until the technology is ready for carbon-capture and sequestration, (2) a similar subsequent moratorium in developing countries, (3) a phase-out over the next several decades of existing old-technology coal plants, with replacement by coal-fired plants that capture and sequester the CO_2, energy efficiencies, renewable energies, or other sources of energy that do not emit CO_2.

Figure 35 defines a specific scenario: developed countries halt construction by 2012 of any coal-fired power plants that do not capture and sequester CO_2, developing countries

Outline of Solution	
1. Coal only in Powerplants w Sequestration	Old Technology "Bulldozed" in Decades
2. Stretch Conventional Oil & Gas	Via Incentives (Cap of Tax) & Standards No Unconventional F.F. (Tar Shale, etc.)
3. Reduce non-CO_2 Climate Forcings	Methane, Black Soot, Nitrous Oxide
4. Draw Down Atmospheric CO_2	Agricultural & Forestry Practices Biofuel-Powered Power-Plants

Figure 34. CO_2 can be kept below 450 ppm only if coal and unconventional fossil fuels are used only where the CO_2 is captured and sequestered. If there is a near-term moratorium in developed countries on new coal-fired power plants that do not sequester CO_2, a similar moratorium 10 years later in developing countries, and if over the period 2025–2050, existing coal-fired power plants are phased out linearly, CO_2 can be kept below 450 ppm. It will also be necessary to stretch conventional oil and gas supplies via economic incentives (a price on carbon emissions) that drive technology development needed for improved energy efficiency and renewable energies. A moderate gradually rising price on emissions can be achieved by a variety of means including individual emission allowances, cap-and-trade or taxes, but for maximum effectiveness it must be accompanied by standards, for example on building and vehicle efficiencies, and barriers to efficiency should be removed, *e.g.*, by decoupling utility profits from the amount of energy sold. Important supplementary actions that will help stabilize climate sooner are reduction on non-CO_2 climate forcings and actions that draw down atmospheric CO_2, especially improved agricultural practices that sequester carbon in the soil, better preservation of forests, and perhaps power plants that burn biofuels and capture and sequester the CO_2.

halt such construction by 2022, and all existing coal-fired power plants without sequestration are "bull-dozed" by 2050 (linear decrease of their emissions between 2025 and 2050). The 10-year delay of the moratorium for developing countries is analogous to that allowed by the Montreal Protocol in chlorofluorocarbon phase-out and it is justified by the primary responsibility of developed countries for the current excess of greenhouse gases in the atmosphere as well as by the much higher per capita emissions in developed countries.

Figure 36 shows that continued business-as-usual emission of CO_2 will more than double the pre-industrial amount of CO_2 (280 ppm) in the air, even though we have neglected feedbacks that would likely accompany such large emissions and we have included no emissions from unconventional fossil fuels (tar shale, tar sand, heavy oil, etc.). Figure 37 shows that this specified phase-out of coal emissions keeps the maximum future atmospheric CO_2 level at about 450 ppm.

Is Alternative Scenario Feasible?
Example: Phase-Out of "Dirty" Coal
• CO_2 Sequestered at New Coal Power Plants after 2012 / 2022 in Developed / Developing Countries
• Coal Power Plants w/o Sequestration Bull-Dozed During 2025–2050 (Decision required by ~2020)
• Analogous to Montreal Protocol: Extra Time & Technology Assistance for Developing Countries
• Incentives for Developing Countries: Clean Air & Water, avoidance of Climate Catastrophes

Figure 35. The most difficult aspect of the alternative scenario is stabilization of CO_2 at a level of, at most, about 450 ppm. Given that it is impractical to capture CO_2 produced by mobile and other small sources burning oil or gas, and given the magnitude of potential emissions from coal, it is apparent that the one practical way to limit atmospheric CO_2 is to limit future coal use to places where CO_2 is captured and sequestered.

Figure 36. *(Image not shown)* Business-as-usual use of all three conventional fossil fuels yields a doubling of pre-industrial CO_2 levels. This estimate does not include unconventional fossil fuel use or potential positive biosphere feedbacks that might accompany large climate response to doubled CO_2.

Figure 37. *(Image not shown)* Phase-out of coal use, except where CO_2 is captured and sequestered, yields maximum CO_2 under 450 ppm, even with oil and gas reserves used entirely, including anticipated oil and gas discoveries.

Q. **Is it plausible for coal-fired power plants without carbon capture to be phased out?**

A. The time scale for action used in calculations for Figures 36 and 37, with moratoria in developed countries by 2012 and in developing countries by 2022, are conservative, our aim being to show that it is practical to keep CO_2 below 450 ppm. However, because it is becoming increasingly likely that an additional 1°C global warming will cause substantial climate impacts, it is highly desirable to take action sooner.

I believe that the plausibility of obtaining actions in time depends upon whether citizens become informed and place pressure on the decision-making process. It seems highly unlikely that national governments, which are under the strong influence of fossil fuel special interests, will exercise the required leadership. Even Germany, among the "greenest" of all nations, is making plans to build coal-fired power plants without carbon capture. Clearly decision-makers do not yet "get it." The public must become more involved, if they hope to preserve creation.

Those who argue that it is implausible to "bulldoze" old technology power plants, while energy efficiency and clean energy sources are expanded, might compare the task with the efforts put into World War II. It is a feasible undertaking.

Q. **If coal is 80% of the solution, what is the other 20%?**

A. There must be a gradually increasing price on carbon emissions. A carbon price is essential to wean us off of our fossil fuel addiction. Without such a phased withdrawal we will soon begin to exhibit the behavior of a desperate addict, attempting to squeeze carbon fuels out of unconventional or remote sources, *e.g.*, "cooking" the Rocky Mountains to drip oil out of tar shale and traveling to extreme environments such as the Arctic National Wildlife Refuge to extract every last drop of oil from the ground.

The irrationality of this behavior is apparent from the realization that fossil fuels are finite. We must learn to live without them as they dwindle. If we begin sooner, we can live with cleaner air and water, preserve creation, and pass on to our children a healthy planet with almost all of the species that we found when we arrived. (See Figure 38.)

Q. **A carbon price? Does that mean a tax?**

A. It could be a tax, but there are various options, and it does not need to increase the amount of money extracted from citizens by the government. It might include rations that could be bought and sold, cap and trade emission quotas for industries, and other alternatives that stimulate energy and carbon efficiencies, including renewable energies and other forms of energy that do not produce greenhouse gases. This price can start small, the key requirement being certainty that it will continue to rise, because this is the stimulus that the business community needs to make the essential long-term investments. The price must promise to be large enough that it stimulates technology development, but it must not be so large or rise so rapidly that it harms the economy.

It is a truism that a strong economy is needed to afford the investments needed for a clean environment and stable climate. It is desirable to separate the decisions on altering the carbon price from short-term political considerations. One way to achieve this would be via

Why Stretch Supplies—Carbon Price
Wean from Fossil Fuel Addiction
• Fossil fuels finite—future energies cleaner—advantageous to get there sooner, good hi-pay jobs in U.S. → gradually increasing carbon price
• Carbon price can be fair & revenue neutral: cap & trade, carbon rations, carbon tax, etc.
• Irrational drunken addict: squeeze every drop from tar shale, Arctic nature preserves, decapitate mountains—some FF should be left in the ground!
• Even addicts have a brain—our behavior suggests special role of special interests—our addiction will not be solved by politicians w/o encouragement—our democracy still functions—let's use it!

Figure 38. Stretching of conventional fossil fuel supplies is essential to prevent irrational behavior of a drunken addict. The future beyond fossil fuel addiction is an attractive world, provided we do not damage the Earth irreparably in the transition. The only way to do that successfully is to wean ourselves off fossil fuels now, before we pass the climate tipping points. Environmental destruction, for the sake of squeezing every drop of black stuff from the Earth, does not make sense.

a "Carbon Tsar", analogous to the Chairman of the Federal Reserve, who would carefully adjust the carbon price so as to optimize economic and environmental gain.

Q. **Can coal phase-out and a gradually rising carbon price solve the climate problem?**

A. These would need to be accompanied by sensible actions. A gradually rising price is not sufficient for the demand reductions that will be needed to phase off the fossil fuel addiction fast enough. There need to be improved efficiency standards on buildings, vehicles, appliances, lighting, electronic devices, etc. Regulations on utilities need to be modified so that profits grow when the utilities help consumers waste less energy, rather than profits being in proportion to amount of energy sold. The government should be supporting more energy research and development, and more effectively, than it is now.

However, the coal phase-out and carbon price are the essential underpinnings. Without these, other actions are nearly fruitless, only yielding a modest slowing of emissions growth.

Q. **But are even these enough, if we are so close to a dangerous greenhouse gas level?**

A. There are additional actions that could close the gap between where we are and where we need to be to stabilize climate, even if we are slightly overshooting the dangerous level. However, these other actions can close the gap only if we get onto a path to stabilize CO_2 in the near future. Without getting onto a downward path of CO_2 emissions, these other actions provide little respite.

The planet is now out of energy balance by something between 0.5 and 1 W/m^2. If we reduced human-made climate forcings by that amount, the warming "in-the-pipeline" would be eliminated, the forcing leading to a continual warming tendency would be eliminated. Figure 39 shows that there is a large enough climate forcing in pollutant forcings, specifically, tropospheric ozone, especially its precursor methane, and black soot, to offset the present planetary energy imbalance, if we should make major reductions of these pollutants.

Some of these non-CO_2 forcings are particularly effective in the Arctic,[55] so it may even be possible to save the Arctic from further ice loss by means of special efforts to reduce these forcings, coupled with stabilization of atmospheric CO_2. There are other benefits of such an effort: these pollutants are harmful to human health, being a primary cause of asthma and other respiratory and cardiovascular problems, and they reduce agricultural productivity.

Figure 39. *(Image not shown, but see Chapter 1, Figure 7)* Pre-industrial to Present Climate Forcings with Primary Indirect Effects. There is approximately enough potential for reduction of methane, tropospheric ozone, CFCs and black soot to restore planetary energy balance, the present imbalance being in the range 0.5-1 W/m^2. There would be large side benefits in reduction of these air pollutants, which are damaging to human health and agricultural productivity, especially in the developing world. In evaluating the potential to reduce non-CO_2 forcings to mitigate climate change, it is important to include the "efficacy" of each forcing.[56] Thus, for example, although the efficacy is low for black soot on global average, limitations on soot emissions in the Arctic would be very effective, suggesting the importance of placing constraints on ships and other sources within the Arctic.

Q. Even if these forcings are reduced, will not the benefits soon be erased by inevitable increases of CO_2? It is said that even a 450 ppm limit on CO_2 is inconceivable.

A. It is said by whom? Fossil fuel companies, and government energy departments, take it as a god-given fact that all fossil fuels will be burned because they are there. That may almost be true for the readily mined oil and gas. However, we have shown above[57] that even with generous estimates for undiscovered oil and gas reserves, CO_2 never exceeds 450 ppm if coal use is phased out except at power plants that capture and sequester the CO_2. Old technology coal-fired power plants must be replaced by 2050, but the pressure for doing so will mount as climate change and its consequences become more apparent, especially the consequences for China, India and Bangladesh.

Q. But CO_2 is already 385 ppm and increasing about 2 ppm per year. Does not simple arithmetic say that we will pass 450 ppm within a few decades?

A. Yes, if we keep increasing fossil fuel CO_2 emissions. But that is not a god-given fact.

Q. But even if emissions from coal use are reduced, today's oil plus gas emissions exceed coal emissions. How can coal be so important?

A. Phasing out coal emissions will reduce the annual growth rate of atmospheric CO_2. Today, and for the period of accurate CO_2 data, the annual increase of CO_2 in the air averages 57% of the fossil fuel emissions (Figure 40), despite the fact that we (the world) have not done a good job of limiting deforestation and we have not done a good job of encouraging agricultural practices that would sequester CO_2 in the soil. If we reduce CO_2 emissions from coal, the airborne fraction of CO_2 will decrease in the near and medium term, so there would be a more than proportionate decrease of the annual growth in atmospheric CO_2.

Figure 40. *(Image not shown)* Ratio of annual increase of CO_2 in the atmosphere divided by annual fossil fuel CO_2 emissions. The long-term mean is ~57% with negligible trend.

Q. But will not a decrease in emissions of CO_2 from coal be offset by a continuing increase in emissions of CO_2 from oil?

A. On the contrary, oil production is going to peak and CO_2 emissions from oil will inevitably decline, if not now then surely within the next few decades. And there is considerable potential, via improved forestry and agricultural practices, to do much better at sequestering CO_2 in soil and in forests, as opposed to the loss (emission) of CO_2 from forests and soils in the past.

---

55. Hansen *et al.*, *supra* note 21.
56. Hansen *et al.*, *supra* note 14.
57. Hansen *et al.*, *supra* note 8; *see also* P.A. Kharecha & J.E. Hansen, *Implications of "Peak Oil" for Atmospheric CO_2 and Climate, submitted* (2007).

Q. But you admit that we are likely to pass the dangerous level of CO_2. Is there anything that can be done in that case?

A. In the short-term we only have to reduce CO_2 emissions by more than 57% for atmospheric CO_2 to begin to decline (in the long run the reduction must be larger). However, there is at least one feasible way to draw CO_2 from the atmosphere. As summarized in Figure 37, if biofuels were burned in power plants, with the CO_2 captured and sequestered, atmospheric CO_2 could be drawn down.[58] The growing vegetation would take in CO_2 from fossil fuel-elevated atmospheric levels, and this CO_2 would then be captured at the power plant. In effect, fossil fuel CO_2 would be put back underground, where it had come from.

    The biofuels should be extracted from natural grasses or other cellulosic fibers farmed in a way that promotes soil conservation and carbon storage in the soil. Such an approach contrasts with production of corn-based ethanol, which in net is ineffective at reducing atmospheric CO_2.

Figure 41. *(Image not shown)* Power plants that burn biofuels could be used to draw down atmospheric CO_2, with the CO_2 sequestered locally in appropriate geologic formations or piped to the coast where it could be injected beneath ocean sediments where it is inherently stable. The biofuels should be natural grasses or other cellulosic fibers farmed in a way that promotes soil conservation and carbon storage in the soil, *e.g.*, using no till practices.

Q. Rather than go to this trouble, can we not adapt to the impacts of climate change?

A. Yes, leaving aside the effects of large changes in regional climate extremes and the extermination of species, we could deal with a one meter rise of sea level by making a lake large enough to hold that much water. Two hundred meter dams at the locations indicated in Figure 42 could hold that much water. A large number of people would be displaced by this lake. It may require difficult negotiations with Canada. And if we allow ice sheets to disintegrate to the point of one meter sea level rise, we can be quite sure that another meter is on the way.

Figure 42. *(Image not shown)* Lake Wobegone. The water contributing one meter of sea level rise could be stored in a lake formed by placing 200 meter high dams at the indicated locations in Canada. This lake would cover a substantial area that is presently inhabited, providing an example of how difficult it would be to adapt to substantial disintegration of ice sheets.

Q. Is there not a good place for another lake?

A. Yes, it would require higher dams (242 meters), but one meter of sea level could be stored in Russia (Figure 43). This also displaces a large number of people. And if we let the ice sheets go that far, there is probably two more meters of sea level on the way. There are no remaining geological candidates for storing that much water. So the historic coastal cities are sunk. It seems that the adaptation path is a lot like appeasement; it just gets you into deeper trouble.

Figure 43. *(Image not shown)* Lake Wobegone II. The water contributing one meter of sea level rise could be stored in a lake formed by placing a 242-meter-high dam at the indicated location in Russia. This lake would cover a substantial area that is presently inhabited, providing an example of how difficult it would be to adapt to substantial disintegration of ice sheets.

Q. Well then, is there still time to avoid the climate problems?

---

58. J. Hansen, *How Can We Avert Dangerous Climate Change?* (2007).

A. Yes, there is still time (Figure 44). As shown above, we can just barely still avoid 450 ppm by phasing out coal use except at power plants that capture and sequester CO_2. It requires an almost immediate moratorium on new coal-fired power plants in the West, and, within a decade later, a moratorium in the developing world.

Q. **Isn't this going to cause energy shortages and blackouts?**

A. Not if we exploit the potentials in energy efficiency, renewable energies, nuclear power, or other energy sources that do not produce greenhouse gases. We are going to have to learn to do that someday anyhow, and it is an enormous economic advantage to us if we learn it sooner rather than later. Others, including China, will need better technologies. If we get

Summary: Is There Still Time?
Yes, But:
• Alternative Scenario is Feasible, yielding a healthy, clean planet.
− But It Is Not Being Pursued
• Action needed now.
A decade of Business-as-Usual eliminates Alternative Scenario

Figure 44. It is still feasible to keep atmospheric CO_2 well below 450 ppm and to keep additional global warming well below 1°C, but only if actions are taken quickly to get onto a new pathway. Business-as-usual growth of emissions, for even another decade, eliminates that possibility: atmospheric CO_2 will reach 400 ppm by 2015, and with a further 20% increase of CO_2-producing infrastructure, it becomes infeasible to avoid dangerous climate change. The principal action required to achieve the alternative scenario is a moratorium on new coal-fired power plants without sequestration in the West, followed by a similar moratorium in developing counties within a decade.

there first, we will have something to sell them. We might get some of the money back that we have been sending over there.

Q. **Why take the first step? Why not demand that China act at the same time?**

A. I already mentioned the economic reason. In addition, we are responsible for the problem. China has just passed us in current emissions, but the climate change is due to cumulative emissions, not current emissions.[59] The United States is responsible for more than three times as much of cumulative CO_2 emissions as any other country, and we will continue to be most responsible for decades. Even with China's high current emissions, our per capita emissions are five times as great as China's. (See Figures 45 and 46.)

Q. **Is there any evidence that such an approach would work?**

A. Certainly. The prior global atmospheric threat, destruction of the ozone layer, was solved with just such an approach. When the science suggested that chlorofluorocarbons (CFCs) had the potential to destroy the stratospheric ozone layer, there was an immediate moratorium on building of more CFC factories. Consumers played a big role in reducing demand, and immediately annual CFC production stabilized (Figure 47). Later, when the Antarctic Ozone hole was discovered, the Montreal Protocol was adopted and later strengthened several times, phasing out production of these chemicals. A key aspect of this protocol was that developing countries should have an extra ten years to implement the phase-out, and they should be provided with technical assistance to achieve it.

---

59. Hansen *et al.*, *supra* note 21.

1751 - 2006 Cumulative Fossil Fuel Carbon Dioxide Emissions

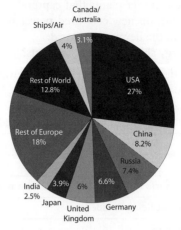

Figure 45. Responsibility for current climate change is proportional to cumulative emissions of long-lived greenhouse gases, not current emissions (Hansen *et al.* 2007b). Thus the United States has a responsibility more than a factor of three greater than any other country, and will continue to be most responsible for decades even though China is passing the United States in current emissions. Europe is responsible for more than 30% and the U.S. plus Canada and Australia are responsible for another 30%. Figure re-drawn from original Hansen testimony.

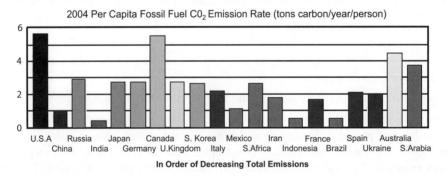

Figure 46. Per capita CO_2 emissions, with countries ranked in order of total emissions. Figure re-drawn from original Hansen testimony.

Figure 47. *(Image not shown)* Production of CFCs stabilized (no new factories) immediately after the first warning that they may affect stratospheric ozone. Production began to increase in the 1980s for refrigeration in developing countries, but after the Montreal Protocol and its subsequent tightenings production fell rapidly. Developing countries were allowed 10 years longer than developed countries to phase out CFC use.

The ozone story was a success story (Figure 48), as scientists transmitted a clear message, the media informed the public, the public responded in a positive way, and the United States government exercised strong leadership. Special interests, the chemical companies producing CFCs, denied the science for several years, but they cooperated once it become clear that they could make money producing substitute chemicals.

Q. Why has the global warming story not followed a similar path?

A. The blame can be spread around. I believe that we scientists have not done as good a job in making clear the threat to the planet and creation. Special interests have been extremely effective in casting doubt on the science. Moreover, they have managed to have a great impact

Ozone Success Story	
↑	1. Scientists: Clear warning
↑	2. Media: Transmitted the message well
	3. Special Interests: Initial opposition, but forsook disinformation, pursued advanced technologies
↑↑	4. Public: quick response; spray cans replaced; no additional CFC infrastructure built
↑	5. Government: U.S. / Europe leadership; allow delay & technical assistance for developing countries

Figure 48. All parties deserve credit for the success in avoiding ozone catastrophe. Scientists provided a clear message, the media reported it, the public was responsive by reducing frivolous uses of CFC for spray cans, and governments, led by the United States, took leadership roles in defining solutions. Special interests, specifically Dupont Chemical company, initially disputed the science, but eventually focused upon substitute chemicals.

on the media, demanding that the story be presented as "fair and balanced" even when the evidence became "clear and unambiguous." I also infer, based on numerous observations, that special interests have had undue influence (exceeding the one person one vote concept) on governments, especially in Washington.

Although the responsibility can be spread widely (Figure 50), the consequences of our profligate use of resources will be borne primarily by young people, today's children and grandchildren, and later generations.

Q. Are you saying that the blame belongs on past generations?

Global Warming Story	
↓	1. Scientists: Fail to make clear distinction between climate change & BAU = A Different Planet
↓	2. Media: False "balance," and leap to hopelessness
↓↓	3. Special Interests: Disinformation campaigns, emphasis on short-term profits
↓	4. Government: Seems affected by special interests; fails to lead—no Winston Churchill today
↓	5. Public: understandably confused, uninterested

Figure 49. The global warming story differs markedly from the ozone story. Scientists have perhaps not made clear the emergency that is upon us. Special interests have been particularly effective in affecting the media and governments so as to avoid actions needed to stem global warming.

A. No. They can genuinely say "we did not know." The blame will fall squarely on today's adults, if we do not act. We can no longer feign ignorance. Scientific consensus has been reached. If we stay on the business-as-usual course that our energy departments take for granted, when climate events unfold in the future it is not likely that our children and grandchildren will look back on our generation with equanimity, nor should they. If we allow climate to deteriorate and creation to be destroyed, we will be the generation that knew enough and still had time, but for selfish reasons declined to take actions. Instead, we built more coal-fired power plants. In that event, rather than the "greatest generation", how will our epitaph read?

Q. I am the one asking questions. Is there still time?

A. There is still time (Figure 51). However, it is clear that Congress does not "get it." They stand ready to set a goal of 60% reductions, 80%, 90%! Horse manure. Those are meaningless numbers, serving nothing but their campaign purposes. Before you cast a vote for a politician

As it appears that the world may pass a tipping point soon, beyond which it will be impossible to avert massive future impacts on humans and other life on the planet:
Who Bears (Legal / Moral) Responsibility?
1. Scientists?
2. Media?
3. Special Interests?
4. Politicians?
5a. Public?
5b. Children / Grandchildren?
Who Will Pay?

Figure 50. Responsibility for the current situation rests, in my opinion, with all of the parties 1 through 5a. Unfortunately it is the younger and future generations, bearing little if any responsibility, who will be faced with most of the consequences and will need to pay for our profligate use of natural resources.

ask whether they will support actions that can actually solve the problem. Specifically, I suggest that you ask them whether they will support the Declaration of Stewardship (Figure 52).

The most important question, by far, is the moratorium on new coal-fired power plants in the United States and Europe, the places that have created the climate problem. Until we take that action, we have no basis for a successful discussion with China, India, and other developing countries.

Q. **So you think that replacing some people in Congress can solve the problem?**

A. It is important to replace members of Congress who place the profits of special interests above the future of our children and grandchildren, but even with personnel changes I would not expect Congress to solve the climate crisis without more direct help from the public. Strong specific messages are needed. Rejection of a coal-fired power plant that does not capture CO_2 is such a message.

Of course such an action then places obligations on various parties. Steps must be taken to promote greater energy efficiency and acquisition of alternative energy sources. These are challenges that can be met and that will yield benefits in the future.

Q. **Do you see reason for optimism if such steps are taken?**

A. Yes. CO_2 is the main problem. Figure 53d shows that the growth of CH_4 is falling below even the alternative scenario, far below all IPCC scenarios. Figure 53e shows that the growth of N_2O is close to the alternative scenario and below most IPCC scenarios. Figure 49f shows that the growth of Montreal Protocol trace gases and other trace gases is falling below all IPCC scenarios and is approaching the alternative scenario. So the growth of the non-CO_2 climate forcings is encouraging.

Indeed, if we look at the growth rate of the sum of all long-lived greenhouse gases (Figure 54), we see that is it falling between the IPCC scenarios and the alternative scenario. The reason that the net forcing is higher than in the alternative scenario is that the actual CO_2 growth rate has exceeded the growth rate for CO_2 assumed in the alternative scenario. Actual recent CO_2 increases have averaged close to 2 ppm per year, while the alternative scenario requires the growth rate of the late 1990s (1.7 ppm) to decline to ~1.3 ppm per year by

Urgent Action Needed:
Moratorium on New Coal Powerplants
Plant Lifetime ~ 50–75 Years
Sequestration Technology ~ 10 Years Away
Efficiency, Renewables in Interim
Need to Remove Barriers to Efficiency
Citizens Must Stand Up
Coal Industry is Very Powerful
Congress Unlikely to Act Decisively

Figure 51. By far the most important action needed to get the world onto a track that will stabilize climate is an immediate moratorium on new coal-fired power plants in the developed world, to be followed by a similar ban in developing countries within a decade.

Declaration of Stewardship for the Earth and all Creation	
1. Moratorium on New Coal Powerplants	I will support a moratorium on coal-fired power plants that do not capture and sequester CO_2.
2. Price on Carbon Emissions	I will support a fair, gradually rising, price on carbon emissions, reflecting costs to the environment. Mechanisms to adjust price should be apolitical and economically sound.
3. Energy and Carbon Efficiency Incentives	I will support legislation to reward utilities and others based on energy or carbon efficiencies rather than the amount of energy sold.

Figure 52. Failure of governments to take actions needed to preserve creation, and the priority that governments have given to special interests over the common good, make it clear that citizens need to place greater priority on preservation of creation in exercising their electoral prerogatives. Candidates for office have begun to make note of the climate issue and utter fuzzy words in support of the planet and the environment. However, actions proposed are, in most cases, ineffectual, not incorporating the two essential needs for stabilizing climate: phase-out of dirty coal and a gradually rising price on carbon emissions.

mid century. (If it turns out that 1°C additional global warming is dangerous, then an even steeper decline may be needed.)

Clearly a much more promising future than in IPCC business-as-usual scenarios is possible. The issue is CO_2 and more specifically it is coal. It is still possible to get on the alternative scenario track, and even do better than that scenario, but only if coal emissions begin to decline. Once the CO_2 emissions are in the air we cannot get them back—a large fraction will stay in the air more than 1000 years.

Figure 53. *(Image not shown)* Climate Forcing by Long-Lived Greenhouse Gases. CO_2 emissions are increasing at a rate at or above IPCC "business-as-usual" scenarios. Other greenhouse gases are increasing at slower rates.

Figure 54. *(Image not shown)* Climate forcing by all long-lived greenhouse gases is increasing at a rate that falls below all IPCC scenarios, about half-way between the IPCC and alternative scenarios. The last two points (2005 and 2006) on the observations may be somewhat misleading, as they are 3-year and 1-year means, while the other points are 5-year means. Because the 2006 CO_2 increase was relatively small, that decreases the 2005 and 2006 results, which may be modified when 2007 and 2008 allow full 5-year means to be calculated.

Q. Can you summarize the status of the matter?

A. Figures 55 and 56 are my summary and my personal observations, my personal opinion. The climate surely is approaching tipping points, with the potential for us to lose control of the consequences. A solution is feasible and the required actions would have many side benefits. Opposition, it seems to me, stems primarily from short-term special financial interests, whose effective misinformation campaigns make the struggle to inform difficult.

This is a matter which should unite those of conservative and liberal bents. The core issue is one of generational inequity. Younger people can help by making clear that they recognize the difference between words and deeds. Stalling and misinformation may help keep short-term profits flowing, but the legacy that it leaves on the planet will not be erased or forgotten. (See Figures 55 and 56.)

Q. Do you have any final comments for the Board?

Status of the Matter	
1. Climate Situation Clear, not Communicated Well	Positive Feedbacks Coming into Play, Tipping Points are Near, Real Potential to Lose Control
2. Solution is Feasible	Peak Oil will occur, Coal Moratorium in West now, Moratorium in 10 years in Developing Countries, Dirty Coal Phase-Out by 2050 → CO_2 <450 ppm Carbon Price, Reduce Pollution, Draw Down CO_2
3. Side Benefits are Great	High-Tech, High-Pay Jobs Energy Independence Clean Atmosphere, Clean Water

Figure 55. We have reached a climate crisis, but there are feasible actions that could defuse the global warming time bomb, and these actions have many ancillary economic and environmental benefits.

Personal Observations (opinions)	
1. Struggle Against Greed	Special Interests Guard Short-Term Profits
2. Struggle Against Ignorance/Misinformation	Modest Progress Recently Misconceptions are Shocking Should be a Conservative Issue
3. Best Hope	Draw Attention to Generational Inequity Watch Deeds, not Words

Figure 56. Based on experience, I believe that the difficulty in communication about global warming and the lack of success in obtaining actions needed to reduce global warming are, at least in part, a consequence of the role of special interests who seem to place inordinate priority on short-term profits. Although global warming has received much attention of late, there remains a large gap between what is understood by the relevant scientific community and what is known by those who need to know, the public and policy-makers. I find it puzzling that conservatives, and I consider myself to be a moderate conservative, are not more concerned about preserving creation. I believe that the best hope for achieving the actions needed to preserve climate for the benefit of all residents of the planet is to draw attention to the generational inequity, the burden that we could leave for our children and grandchildren. For this purpose it is desirable that young people themselves become educated on the matter and help communicate with their elders. One word of caution: when fossil fuel companies start putting "green" advertisements in the newspaper, throw those in the waste bin straightaway and instead check what fraction of their earnings are being invested in energy sources that do not produce greenhouse gases.

A. Yes. I would like to express my gratitude to the State of Iowa, which has always been so generous in providing educational opportunities to its people, even as many graduates go on to
careers in other states across the nation. I was extremely fortunate to be able to attend the
University of Iowa, and especially to learn in the Department of Physics and Astronomy of
Prof. James Van Allen. I thank Bruce Johansen and Ines Horovitz for comments on this testimony, and Makiko Sato for technical scientific assistance and my wife Anniek for her tolerance of inordinate obsessions.

Notes

1. *Iowa's Decision.* The following is a posting from the Iowa Utility Board's website.

On August 25, 2008, the Iowa Utilities Board (IUB) issued its written order
(http://www.iowa.gov/iub/docs/orders/2008/0825_gcu071.pdf) in this case. Subject to
certain conditions, the order grants Interstate Power and Light Company's (IPL) request
for an electric generating certificate to construct and operate a 630-megawatt coal-fired
power plant in Marshall County. This includes a requirement that IPL burn biomass
fuels at the plant, as IPL says the plant is designed to do, and a requirement that IPL
add new renewable energy sources (in addition to 200 megawatts of new wind resources
already proposed) to its generation mix over the next 20 years. These requirements are
intended to mitigate the company's future greenhouse gas emissions and the exposure
of IPL and its customers to cost risks associated with those emissions. On April 30,
2008, the Board held public deliberations before voting 2–1 to grant this conditional
approval for the plant. For background information about this proceeding, please visit
the GCU-07-1 information page (http://www.iowa.gov/iub/energy/gcu071.html) (last
visited April 13, 2009).

2. *Coal in Kansas.* On October 18, 2007 the Kansas Department of Health and Environment
(KDHE) denied Sunflower Electric's application for an air permit to construct a coal plant
based on the adverse health and environmental effects of carbon dioxide emissions. This was
the first time a coal plant was denied on the basis of CO_2 emissions and global warming. This
quickly led to a nasty dispute, including newspaper ads put out by Sunflower Electric that
compared Governor Sebelius and her administration to Vladimir Putin, Hugo Chavez, and
Mahmoud Ahmadinejad (November 5, 2007). Sunflower Electric sued, and the Kansas
Supreme Court agreed to hear the case (November 30, 2007). At the start of 2008, several
Kansas state legislators introduced a bill that would allow the coal plant to be built with very
weak restrictions. The bill was heavily influenced by Sunflower Electric. Even more damaging,
the bill would also remove the KDHE's ability to impose stricter standards than the federal
Clean Air Act without state legislative approval. Sebelius as well as at least one Republican
Kansas legislator voiced opposition to the bill. Nonetheless, the bill passed. Governor Sebelius,
however, vetoed the bill and offered a compromise including a smaller plant and a commitment to some renewable energy (March 23, 2008). The attempt to override the veto failed by
two votes. Then on April 7, 2008 the Kansas legislature passed another bill that would have allowed the coal plant to be built, and again Sebelius vetoed. A third bill was sent to the Governor on April 25, 2008. That bill included a smaller plant, but still limited the KDHE authority
to impose stricter standards than the CAA. Sebelius vetoed the third bill as well, and again the
attempt to override her veto failed. Although this marks the end of the Kansas legislative session and likely the end of this legislative battle, it remains to be seen what the Kansas Supreme
Court will choose to do with the lawsuit filed by Sunflower Electric.

3. *Hansen Testimony in the Kingsnorth Six Case.* Dr. Hansen recently submitted testimony[1] in the prosecution of six Greenpeace activists who were painting a message on a coal plant in the U.K. during a protest. The defendants were acquitted of criminal charges by a jury on September 10, 2008.[2] Dr. Hansen's testimony stated that a number of facts were known—and ignored—by the government, the utility, and the fossil fuel industry:

- *Tipping points:* The climate system is dangerously close to tipping points that could have disastrous consequences for young people, life and property, and general well-being on the planet that will be inherited from today's elders.
- *Coal's dominant role:* Coal is the fossil fuel most responsible for excess CO_2 in the air today, and coal reserves contain much more potential CO_2 than do oil or gas. Coal is the fossil fuel that is most susceptible to either (a) having the CO_2 captured and sequestered if coal is used in power plants, or (b) leaving the coal in the ground, instead emphasizing use of cleaner fuels and energy efficiency.
- *Recognized responsibilities:* The U.K. is one of the nations most responsible for human-made CO_2 in the air today; indeed, on a per capita basis it is the most responsible of all nations that are major emitters of CO_2. This fact is recognized by developing countries, making it implausible that they would consider altering their plans for coal use if the U.K. plans to continue to rely on coal-fired power.
- *Recognized impacts of climate change:* The U.K. government, [utility company] EON, and the fossil fuel industry were aware of the likely impacts of continuation of coal emissions, specifically impacts on future sea levels, extinctions of animal and plant species, and regional climate effects, *i.e.,* they were all aware that their actions would contribute to these adverse impacts, leaving a more impoverished planet for today's young people and the unborn.
- *Greenwash:* Governments, utilities, and the fossil fuel industry have presented public faces acknowledging the importance of climate change and claiming that they are taking appropriate actions. Yet the facts, as shown in this document, contradict their claims. Construction of new coal-fired power plants makes it unrealistic to hope for the prompt phase-out of coal emissions and thus makes it practically impossible to avert climate disasters for today's young people and future generations.

Hansen avers that "Recognition of these basic facts by the defendants, realization that the facts were also known by the government, utility, and fossil fuel industry, and realization that the actions needed to protect life and property of the present and future generations were not being taken undoubtedly played a role in the decision of the defendants to act as they did."[3]

4. *See* 2006 JEFF GOODELL, BIG COAL at 229:

Depending on what statistics you cite, China may or may not be the fastest growing economy in the history of the world. But it is without question the world's premier coal junkie. The Chinese burn less coal per capita than the Americans, but in terms of sheer tonnage, they burn twice as much. Seventy percent of the nation's energy comes from coal, and Chinese leaders have made it clear that economic growth is their number one priority. They see themselves as following essentially the same development path that the West took: get rich first, clean up later.

For China, this strategy represents an enormous gamble. Workers die every day in unsafe Chinese coal mines. Outdoor air pollution kills hundreds of thousands of people

---

1. Full testimony *available at* http://www.columbia.edu/~jeh1/mailings/20080910_Kingsnorth.pdf.
2. Reuters U.K., *Greenpeace Protestors Cleared Over Coal Protest*, http://uk.reuters.com/article/topNews/idUKLA34747320080910 (September 10, 2008).
3. James Hansen post, *Trumping Old King Coal*, GRISTMILL, Grist.org (September 11, 2008).

each year. Acid rain is falling on a third of the country, crippling agricultural production. Not surprisingly, pollution is becoming a source of political turmoil.

5. On the "straw that broke the camel's back" and related matters, see Myles Allen, Pardeep Pall, Darthi Stone, Peter Stott, David Frame, Seung-Ki Min, Toru Nozawa, & Seiji Yukimoto, *Scientific Challenges in the Attribution of Harm to Human Influence on Climate*, 155 U. PA. L. REV. 1353, 1393–94 (2007):

> [in the context of United States tort law,] plaintiffs … must show that, more probably than not, their individual injuries were caused by the risk factor in question, as opposed to any other cause. This has sometimes been translated to a requirement of a relative risk of at least two. If the risk factor in question were human influence on area-averaged summer temperature in southern Europe in 2003, it would appear that this threshold has already been passed.

Quoting David A. Grossman, *Warming Up to a Not-So-Radical Idea: Tort-Based Climate Change Litigation*, 28 COLUM. J. ENVTL. L. 1, 23 (2003) (footnote omitted).

6. On "coal trains as death trains," see *Sierra Club v. U.S. EPA*, 499 F.3d 653 (7th Cir. 2007) (Posner, C.J.) (EPA permit approves construction of a 1,500-megawatt coal-fired electrical generating plant (Prairie State Generating Co.) near St. Louis. The plant is "mine-mouth" (meaning ample supplies of high-sulfur coal are at hand) and the question is whether BACT requires low-sulfur coal that must be transported from more than 1,000 miles away. We learn (*id.* at 654) from EPA that BACT "does not include redesigning the plant proposed by the permit applicant" unless it "intentionally designs the plant in a way calculated to make measures for limiting the emission of pollutants ineffectual." *Id.* at 655: on the elusive difference between "control technology" and facility "redesign." "[T]his opens the further and crucial question where control technology ends and a redesign of the 'proposed facility' begins. As it is not obvious where to draw that line either, it makes sense to let the EPA, the author of the underlying distinction, draw it, within reason." *Id.* at 657: the court thus upholds the Environmental Appeals Board decision, believing "that it granted the permit not because it thinks that *burning* low-sulfur coal would require the redesign of Prairie State's plant (it would not), but because *receiving* coal from a distant mine would require Prairie State to reconfigure the plant as one not co-located with a mine, and this reconfiguration would constitute a redesign" (emphasis in original). (ed.) *Note should be made also of the fact that on August 24, 2007, a new power plant burning high-sulfur coal breezes through the U.S. Court of Appeals for the Seventh Circuit without notice, mention, or acknowledgement of global warming*).

7. Who discusses "coal trains" in law school? *See Mid States Coalition for Progress v. Surface Transportation Board*, 345 F.3d 520 (8th Cir. 2003).

Figure 57. *Although not shown here,* this symbolic figure depicts a map of several central states with a rail line stretching from the eastern border of Minnesota nearly to the western border of South Dakota.

This was the "largest and most-challenging rail construction project" ever to come before the Surface Transportation Board (or its predecessor the Interstate Commerce Commission).[1] It gave approval to the Dakota, Minnesota & Eastern Railroad Corporation's proposal to construct 280 miles of new rail line to reach the coal mines of Wyoming's Powder River Basin and to upgrade 600 miles of existing rail line in Minnesota and South Dakota. The proposal had conspicuous environmental losers (the City of Rochester and the Mayo Clinic) that would suffer from con-

---

1. 345 F.3d 520, 550 (8th Cir. 2003), *later decision* Mayo Foundation v. Surface Transportation Bd., 472 F.3d 575 (8th Cir. 2006).

struction and traffic and was supported by a long list of ag shippers. It is also another great push by commercial America into Sioux country.

These plans were resisted strongly by the Natives. In November of 2000, members of the Oceti Sakowin, the Lakota Tribes from North and South Dakota, met with Victoria Ruston of the Surface Transportation Board and other federal officials to confirm their opposition in the "official government-to-government consultation" that is the norm today.[2] The Lakota tribes in North and South Dakota still consider western South Dakota (and the Powder River Basin of Wyoming from which the coal will be taken) to be part of the Great Sioux Reservation outlined in the 1851 and 1868 Fort Laramie treaties. Attending this consultation were approximately 100 Native American people from the Pine Ridge, Rosebud, Crow Creek, Lower Brule, Standing Rock and Wind River reservations. One of the highlights of the three-day meeting occurred, according to Charmaine White Face, "when Black Hills Sioux Nation Treaty Council representatives made a motion opposing the railroad and asked for a vote from all the people rather than just representatives of the six Lakota bands present. The whole room stood up in support of the motion."[3]

Obviously, the NEPA process for this unimaginatively massive project was writ large—5,000-page draft EIS, 8,600 public comments, four years in the making. In the NEPA-plus litigation enveloping the project, the agency was sent back to do further study on the effects of train whistle / vibration noises and to consider what would appear to be a somewhat urgent question of how granting access to 100-million tons of low-sulfur coal might affect emissions of NO_x, CO_2, particulates, and mercury (SO_2 is "capped" by the 1990 amendments to the Clean Air Act). The "nature of the effect" of the air pollution "is far from speculative," the court wrote. It is "reasonably foreseeable—indeed—it is almost certainly true—that the proposed project will increase the long-term demand for coal and any adverse effects that result from burning coal." When "the nature of the effect is reasonably foreseeable, but its extent is not," said the court, "we think that the agency may not simply ignore the effect."[4]

The Reagan administration made much of its 1986 change in the CEQ rules when it banished the "worst case" analysis in favor of a more flexible "scientific uncertainty" approach.[5] In this Black Hills train case, the Surface Transportation Board did not pretend to comply with either approach.

Despite these fundamental errors in approach, the court applauds the agency for its wonderful work—"on the whole the Board did a highly commendable and professional job in evaluating an enormously complex proposal."[6] Thus the attitude on this next expression of manifest destiny is that it is certain to happen with a few details to be worked out later.

This leave-it-to-later posture was the approach to this project under the National Historic Preservation Act. The major legal issue is whether the statutory mandate to take effects into account "prior to the issuance of any license"[7] can head off the inevitable tendency to treat historical and cultural calculations as end-of-the-line apple-polishing to be handled by minor traffic controls. The court approves not a sequential approach to NHPA issues (identification, assessment, mitiga-

---

2. Charmaine White Face, *Oceti Sakowin meets over railroad*, NATIVE NEWS, Dec. 18, 2000, http://www.escribe.com/culture/nativenews/m4379.html (last visited March 5, 2004).

3. *Ibid.*

4. 345 F.3d at 549–50, quoting 40 C.F.R. § 1502.22; the Board's Section on Environmental Analysis "has completely ignored the effects of increased coal consumption, and it has made no attempt to fulfill the requirements laid out in the CEQ regulations."

5. 40 C.F.R. § 1502.22.

6. 345 F.3d at 556.

7. 16 U.S.C.A. § 470f.

tion) but a phased-approach where large areas are under consideration as alternatives.[8] But the court points out approvingly that "[b]y requiring that agencies identify and assess individual properties as project alternatives become more concrete, the regulations assure that the agency will be in a position to proceed to the mitigation step."[9] The decision in *Mid States Coalition for Progress* reads the NHPA rules as forbidding the prolonged deferral of mitigation until after license approval:[10]

> The ACHP's regulations, when read in their entirety, thus permit an agency to defer completion of the NHPA process until after the NEPA process has run its course (and the environmentally preferred alternatives chosen), but require that NHPA issues be resolved by the time that the license is issued. In this case, the Board's final decision contains a condition requiring [DM & E] to comply with whatever future mitigation requirements the Board finally arrives it. We do not think that this is the type of measure contemplated by the [Advisory Council on Historic Preservation] when it directed agencies to "avoid, minimize, or mitigate" adverse effects.

The Court pointed out that the ACHP regulations offer an "alternative" to the customary approach—namely, "a programmatic agreement to govern the implementation of a particular program or the resolution of adverse effects from certain complex situations."[11] Such a programmatic agreement was not finalized here before issuance of the license, and it should have been, according to the Eighth Circuit:[12]

> If the programmatic agreement had been executed, the Board could have finalized the NHPA details at a future date according to the terms of the agreement, just as it wished. Not willing to delay publication of its decision until after a consensus could be reached on the terms of the programmatic agreement, the Board instead issued the license having neither secured a programmatic agreement nor completed the alternate NHPA process. On remand, it must do one or the other.

The most interesting issue in *Mid States Coalition for Progress* was the position of the Sioux who maintained that the Board violated the Fort Laramie Treaty of April 29, 1868,[13] and its fiduciary duty to Indians when it licensed the construction of DM & E's new extension without Sioux consent. The Sioux tribes obviously were not part of this Coalition and had a different view of progress. They were in a position to veto the project because the famous art. XII of the 1868 treaty requires that cessions of reservation land be approved by at least three-fourths of the adult male Sioux population. The railroad and the court avoided this legal dagger by saying that the "proposed line does not pass through any present-day reservation, [and thus because] no cession of reservation land is required before the proposed line can be built, the Fort Laramie Treaty does not apply."[14] The rail route did cross land taken from the Sioux by act of 1877 (for which compensation was paid) and still more land taken by act of 1889 (that was approved by three-fourths of the male population as a whole not band-by-band).[15] Thus, the legal barriers of the twentieth and twenty-first centuries were no more helpful to the Sioux than their military barriers of the nineteenth century.

---

8. 345 F.3d at 553–54, citing and approving 36 C.F.R. §800.4(b)(2).

9. *Id*. at 554.

10. *Ibid*, quoting 36 C.F.R. §800.8(c)(4).

11. *Ibid*, quoting 36 C.F.R. §800.14(b).

12. *Id*. at 555.

13. 15 Stat. 635.

14. 345 F.3d at 555.

15. This is all that was required according to the court. *Id*. at 555–56.

This case is an amazing and bland business-as-usual approach in the face of global warming, long-range acid transport, and waning fossil-fuel reserves. Once again the tribes are set apart in distinct and radical ways.

8. James Hansen reminds us that "sea level has been stable for about the past 7000 years." p. 555 above. He says (p. 556): "we could will to our children a situation in which future sea level change is out of their control." This would be a "future interest" worth discussion in first-year property courses.

9. William H. Calvin, Global Fever: How to Treat Climate Change 120 (Un. Chicago Press 2008), quoting glaciologist Richard Alley:

> These [rapid Greenland ice] flows completely change our understanding of the dynamics of ice sheet destruction. We used to think that it would take 10,000 years for melting at the surface to penetrate down to the bottom of the ice sheet. But if you make a lake on the surface and a crack opens and the water goes down the crack, it doesn't take 10,000 years, it takes ten seconds. That huge lag time is completely eliminated.
>
> The way water gets down to the base of glaciers is rather the way magma gets to the surface in volcanoes—through cracks. Cracks change everything. Once a crack is created and filled, the flow enlarges it and the results can be explosive. Like volcanic eruptions. Or the disintegration of ice sheets.

10. Steven Ferrey, *Why Electricity Matters, Developing Nations Matter, and Asia Matters Most of All*, 15 N.Y.U. Envtl. L.J. 113, 115 (2007):

> Global warming has been called a number of things: A pending environmental Armageddon, the cause of catastrophic ecological devastation of the planet, and even an overblown tempest in a teapot. In January 2007, the Bulletin of the Atomic Scientists moved their Doomsday Clock forward two minutes closer to midnight, where midnight on the clock symbolizes the annihilation of civilization. This move, intended to reflect the threat of global warming, marks the first time that the Clock has been moved to reflect an environmental instead of a military risk.

Citing Board Statement, Bulletin of the Atomic Scientists, *5 Minutes to Midnight* (Jan. 17, 2007), *available at* http://www.thebulletin.org/minutes-to-midnight/board-statements.html ("Global warming poses a dire threat to human civilization that is second only to nuclear weapons.")

11. Jared Wiesner, *A Grassroots Vehicle for Sustainable Energy: The Conservation Reserve Program & Renewable Energy*, 31 Wm. & Mary Envtl. L. & Pol'y Rev. 571 (2006–07) (on amending the Conservation Reserve Program to create incentives to produce biomass and wind energy).

12. *North Carolina v. EPA*, 531 F.3d 896 (D.C. Cir. 2008) (Sentelle, C.J., Rogers and Brown, C.J.s) (*per curiam*) (34 pp.) This is a complete demolition of the Clean Air Interstate Rule that is vacated and remanded in its entirety. There is much discussion of the amount of emissions from one state that would "contribute significantly" to nonattainment in another state. 531 F.3d at 908: "It is unclear how EPA can assure that the trading programs it has designed in CAIR will achieve section 110(a)(2)(D)(i)(I)'s goals if we do not know what each upwind state's 'significant contribution' is to another state." 531 F.3d at 910: "All the policy reasons in the world cannot justify reading a substantive provision out of a statute"; and here, "[a]reas that find themselves barely meeting attainment in 2010 due in part to upwind sources interfering with that attainment have no recourse under EPA's interpretation of the interference prong of" Section 110(a)(2)(D)(i)(I). EPA's choice of SO_2 budgets for trading violates Section 110. EPA's boasting about the "highly successful" Title IV trading program doesn't explain how its choice of emission caps based on Title IV allowances will achieve the CAIR goals. 531

F.3d at 919: "EPA's interpretation cannot extend so far as to make one state's significant contribution depend upon another state's cost of eliminating emissions." 531 F.3d at 920: "Yet that is exactly what EPA has done." "In essence, a state having mostly coal-fired EGUs gets more credits because Louisiana can control emissions more cheaply" [with its higher dependence on oil and gas]. 531 F.3d at 921: "The net result will be that states with mainly oil- and gas-fired EGUs will subsidize reductions in states with mainly coal-fired EGUs." This violates Section 110. 531 F.3d at 922: "no statute confers authority on EPA to terminate or limit Title IV allowances, and EPA thus has none." Title IV allowances are "fixed currency." (ed.) This reference to "fixed currency" should be kept in mind when Congress goes down the cap-and-trade trail on global warming.

13. *Northern Cheyenne Tribe v. Norton*, 503 F.3d 836 (9th Cir. 2007) (Kleinfeld, C.J.). This is a NEPA attack on coal-bed methane leasing. "Coal bed methane is a natural gas generated by coal deposits and trapped in coal seams by groundwater. Coal bed methane is extracted by pumping the groundwater out of the land and into the rivers," *id.* at 839. The court mentions three environmental problems associated with this process—aesthetics, pollution of the rivers, lowering of the water table; there is a fourth—methane is a potent greenhouse gas. The court approves a partial injunction and says the plaintiffs are getting the very phased development they wanted BLM to examine in the EIS. Chief Judge Schroeder says plaintiffs are entitled to injunctive relief preserving the status quo, *id.* at 846, 847: "We are ... bound by NEPA, and allowing the agency to take new action without adequate environmental study creates a serious threat of irreparable harm under NEPA."

14. Life-extension of older coal-burning powerplants is one of the deeper embarrassments in the administration of the Clean Air Act. Here is Judge McKinney's opinion that this phenomenon was not simply a "confusion of law":

What Did They Know and When Did They Know It?

United States v. Cinergy Corp., 495 F. Supp. 2d 892, 903 (S.D. Ind. 2007) (Larry L. McKinney, C.J.):

> Cinergy, though apparently professing confusion over the meaning of the [Routine Maintenance, Repair or Replace Exclusion] [RMRR], [did not seek] an applicability determination [and did not inquire] about the meaning of the RMMR exclusion. This factor is particularly compelling when one considers the evidence that suggests Cinergy's actual knowledge of the standards and what could arguably be construed as industry's attempt to subvert enforcement efforts. Specifically, Cinergy was aware that whether a project was considered "routine" was based on viewing both the industry as a whole and a particular unit.... Further, a memo presented at the August 1985 EPRI conference advised industry that life extension projects might not be considered routine by the EPA and so efforts should be made to identify those projects as "upgraded maintenance programs" or "plant restoration" and to deal with state and local authorities in order to avoid elevating a project "to the status of a national environmental issue." ... Cinergy should have known that its projects were irregular or unusual, and therefore far from what could be considered "routine." The only reasonable inference from this evidence is that Cinergy had actual knowledge of the standards for determining whether a project met the RMRR exclusion.

15. *EPA Environmental Appeals Board's Bonanza decision.* On November 13, 2008 the EPA Environmental Appeals Board overturned a permit for the Bonanza coal-fired plant in Vernal, Utah on the basis that the Bush administration had provided an invalid reason why greenhouse gas emissions from the plant could not be regulated in light of the Supreme Court's decision in

Massachusetts v. EPA. Bryan Walsh, *Environmentalists Win Big EPA Ruling*, TIME.COM HEALTH & SCIENCE (November 13, 2008), http://www.time.com/time/health/article/0,8599,1859049,00. html?iid=tsmodule:

> Thursday's decision means that any new air pollution permits for coal plants will require that Best Available Control Technology (BACT) be used to reduce CO_2 emissions, the same criteria currently used for other pollutants, like sulfur dioxide or soot. BACT requires companies involved in power plants to use the best available technology to control pollutants—it's a tool to keep pollution controls up to date as both safety technology and our understanding of pollution improves. In the past, CO_2 wasn't affected by BACT because the EPA didn't recognize it as a pollutant. This decision changes that.
>
> Right now, however, there is no definition of BACT for CO_2, and environmentalists estimate it will take six months to a year to figure that out. In the meantime, all other coal plants in the permitting process, or stuck in the courts, will be frozen. Over the longer term, it's possible that new coal plants may be impossible to certify at all until a technology exists to greatly reduce or sequester carbon emissions from coal plants— and currently none has been proven....
>
> That effectively punts the future of coal in America to President-elect Barack Obama's incoming Administration. It's not yet clear how he'll act, but his renewable energy advisor Jason Grumet has said that Obama would be willing to use the EPA to directly regulate CO_2—something President George W. Bush has refused to do.

16. *See* RICHARD ELLIOTT BENEDICK, OZONE DIPLOMACY: NEW DIRECTIONS IN SAFEGUARDING THE PLANET (Enlarged ed., Harvard Un. Press 1998).

Climate Change and Coal: Exploring the Dark Side

Patrick Charles McGinley, Judge Charles H. Haden II Professor of Law, College of Law, West Virginia University, Morgantown, WV 26506, Tel: (304) 293-6823 & (304) 522-2631, Fax: (304) 293-6891 & (304) 292-9822, patrick.mcginley@mail.wvu.edu.

> To see coal purely as a gift from God overlooks the many dangerous strings attached to that gift. Similarly, to see it as just an environmental evil would be to overlook the undeniable good that accompanies that evil. Failing to recognize both sides of coal—the vast power and the exorbitant costs—misses the essential heartbreaking drama of the story.[1]
>
> BARBARA FREESE, COAL: A HUMAN HISTORY

I. Introduction

The shadow cast by the threat of climate change clouds the world's path to a sustainable energy future. In a relatively short time hundreds of millions of people around the world have recognized global warming as a threat of potentially catastrophic proportions. This paper seeks to provide a small measure of illumination to facilitate informed decision-making as future energy options are explored. Informed decisions are necessary if the potential disasters attendant upon climate change are to be avoided. Ignorance is no longer an option. Careful, objective consideration of the full range of costs and benefits of each option will effectively serve the public interest. It is imperative that public policy decision-makers accurately address the true range of costs and benefits of

---

1. COAL: A HUMAN HISTORY 12–13 (Penguin 2004).

all energy options—including those relating to coal. However, such a cost-benefit analysis could easily overlook the externalities of coal mining and burning as those costs have, historically, been obscure.

Therefore, the following discussion recognizes "both sides of coal" with an emphasis on those aspects of coal mining and burning that falls on what coal historian Barbara Freese calls "the dark side."[2] Her book, COAL: A HUMAN HISTORY acknowledges the extraordinary contribution coal has made to modern civilization, observing that "[l]ike a good genie, coal has granted many of our wishes enriching most of us in developed nations beyond our wildest pre-industrial dreams."[3] Importantly, Freese also acknowledges the costs of coal, asserting that "also like a genie, coal has an unpredictable and threatening side.... although we have always known that, we are just beginning to realize how far reaching that dark side is."[4]

The modern coal and power industries—"Big Coal"—have no difficulty being heard by public policy decision-makers.[5] Coal, power generation interests and those associated with them, have millions at their disposal to promote and spread the positive side of coal's story.[6] However, the "dark side" of coal—its obscured externalities—is little appreciated or understood by the public. These externalities are the primary focus of this paper. Even while recognizing coal's contributions to world industrialization this paper identifies and discusses coal's history in the United States of socio-economic, environmental, workplace safety and public health externalities. No argument is made here for or against coal's use in meeting the world's demand for energy. The modest hope is that public policy decision-makers will weigh in the balance both the costs and the benefits of coal as the climate change debate focuses on future energy options.

II. Coal at the Millennium

The International Energy Agency's Coal Industry Advisory Board ("IEA") has concluded that "[d]iverse, secure, affordable and environmentally acceptable energy supplies are essential to sustainable development."[7] The IEA Advisory Board emphasized that "[r]esponding effectively to the risks of global climate change while continuing to meet the high energy demands of mature economies and the rapidly increasing energy demands of developing economies is a significant international challenge."[8]

---

2. *Id.* at 12.

3. *Id.* at 13.

4. *Id.*

5. The term "Big Coal" was coined by author Jeff Goodell who defined it as "shorthand for the alliance of coal mining companies, coal-burning utilities, railroads, lobbying groups, and industry supporters that make the coal industry such a political force in America." Goodell is highly critical of these interests. J. GOODELL, BIG COAL, THE DIRTY SECRET BEHIND AMERICA'S ENERGY FUTURE (First Mariner Books Ed. 2007). Goodell emphasizes that the term is not meant to suggest the industry is monolithic or that its proponents meet in secret to plan grand strategies. Rather, he posits, the coal industry like many other industries "can be identified by certain common goals and pursuits" and thus, he uses the term to suggest that commonality as well as to remind the reader of the power and influence of "the players involved." It is in this specific sense the term "Big Coal" is used in this paper. Throughout this paper the term is used interchangeably with "Coal," each term intended to have the same meaning.

6. As explained below, climate change concerns constitute an enormous concern of Big Coal. Coal's strategic response has been to tout its affordability, availability and adaptability, arguing that these benefits should guarantee coal's share of future energy markets. Indispensable to Coal's strategy is the promise that "clean coal" technology is just around the proverbial corner.

7. INTERNATIONAL ENERGY AGENCY, REDUCING GREENHOUSE GAS EMISSIONS: THE POTENTIAL OF COAL 9 (2005) [hereinafter IEA COAL INDUSTRY ADVISORY BOARD].

8. *Id.* at 9.

In meeting this challenge, fuel choices will no doubt include some mix of coal and its competitors including oil, natural gas, solar, hydro, wind, biomass and nuclear. The composition of the future mix is presently unclear. What is clear is the contribution coal currently makes to the world energy market and to the greenhouse gas emissions that contribute to climate change concerns.

In the last two decades of the Twentieth Century, world coal production increased by thirty eight percent to four billion tons.[9] Coal production has steadily increased in Asia while European production has declined steadily.[10] World coal production increased one and a half times as much from 2003 to 2007 as it did over the previous twenty-three years.[11] By 2030 annual world coal production is projected to grow to seven billion tons, China accounting for half of the increase.[12] The United States reserves amount to thirty percent of the world's coal. China is by far the largest producer but possesses only half the reserves of the U.S. which is the number two producer.[13]

In 2006 Big Coal had plans to build as many as 150 new coal-burning power plants in the United States.[14] None of these proposed facilities had concrete plans for carbon capture and sequestration.[15] Chinese plans for constructing new facilities for generating electricity by coal combustion are even more ambitious. China is planning to construct the equivalent of two five-hundred megawatt, coal-fired power plants *per week* with a capacity comparable to the entire power grid of the United Kingdom *each year*.[16] Worldwide, hundreds of new coal-fired power plants are currently under construction or are in various stages of planning that will put them on-line in the next few decades.[17]

---

9. The geographic extent of mineable coal reserves is reflected in statistics identifying leading coal producing nations. Thirty-four countries produce one million tons of coal per year. The leading coal producers are China (1119.8); United States (595.1); India (209.7); Australia (203.1); South Africa (144.8); Russia (144.5) (numbers represent million tons oil equivalent). *See* The GeoHive, http://www.geohive.com/charts/en_coal prod.aspx (last visited Nov. 12, 2008).

10. Asia is the source of fifty-four percent of current global coal production. INTERNATIONAL ENERGY AGENCY REPORT, INTERNATIONAL COAL PRODUCTION 1980–2007, http://www.eia.doe.gov/emeu/international/coalproduction.html (2008) (last visited on November 2, 2008) [hereinafter IEA PRODUCTION REP'T].

11. *Id.*

12. WORLD COAL INSTITUTE, THE COAL RESOURCE: A COMPREHENSIVE OVERVIEW OF COAL 13 (2005), http://www.worldcoal.org/pages/content/index.asp?PageID=37 (last visited Nov. 30, 2008) [hereinafter THE COAL RESOURCE].

13. *See* ENVIRONMENTAL WORKING GROUP, COAL: RESOURCES AND FUTURE PRODUCTION (2007), *available at* http://www.energywatchgroup.org/fileadmin/global/pdf/EWG_Report_Coal_10-07-2007ms.pdf (last visited on Nov. 12, 2008) [hereinafter EWG COAL RESOURCES AND PRODUCTION]. The EWG reports that the
[l]argest coal producers in descending order are: China, USA (half of Chinese production), Australia (less than half of US production), India, South Africa, and Russia. These countries account for over 80 percent of global coal production. Coal consumption mainly takes place in the country of origin. Only 15 percent of production is exported, 85 percent of produced coal is consumed domestically.
Id.

14. *See* Mary Wood, *Nature's Trust: A Legal, Political and Moral Frame for Global Warming*, 34 B.C. ENVTL. AFF. L. REV. 577, 590 (2007), citing News Release, Nat'l Energy Tech. Lab., *Department of Energy Tracks Resurgence of Coal-Fired Power Plants* (Aug. 2, 2006), *available at* http://www.netl.doe.gov/publications/press/2006/06046-Coal-Fired_Power_Plants_Database.html ("Updated Database Shows 153 New Plants Proposed by 2025.").

15. More than twenty proposed coal-fired power plants were cancelled in 2007 and more than three dozen other plants were delayed, primarily because of financing concerns. *See* INTERFAITH CENTER ON CORPORATE RESPONSIBILITY, DON'T GET BURNED: THE RISKS OF INVESTING IN NEW COAL-FIRED GENERATING FACILITIES 9 (2008), http://www.synapse-energy.com/Downloads/SynapseReport.2008-02.GRACE.Don't-Get-Burned-Risks-of-New-Coal.07-014.pdf (last visited Sept. 10, 2008) [hereinafter SYNAPSE REPORT].

16. MASSACHUSETTS INSTITUTE OF TECHNOLOGY, THE FUTURE OF COAL, OPTIONS FOR A CARBON CONSTRAINED WORLD ix (2007) (hereinafter FUTURE OF COAL) *available at* http://web.mit.edu/coal/ (last visited Sept. 10, 2008).

17. Mark Clayton, *Global boom in coal power—and emissions*, THE CHRISTIAN SCIENCE MONITOR (March 22, 2007), *available at* http://www.csmonitor.com/2007/0322/p01s04-wogi.html (last visited on April 3, 2008).

Today coal produces thirty-nine percent of the world's electricity with natural gas, hydro and oil far behind.[18] Ninety-three percent of South Africa's electricity is produced by coal, in China seventy-eight percent, Australia eighty, India sixty-nine, the United States fifty, and Germany forty-seven percent.[19] Fifty percent of the electricity generated in the United States is from coal.[20] The average age of the more than five hundred coal-burning power plants in this country is thirty-five years.[21]

Just one five-hundred megawatt coal-fired power plant produces approximately three million tons of carbon dioxide ("CO_2") per year.[22] As of 2008, the United States' coal-burning power plants were producing CO_2 at an annual rate of about one and a half billion tons.[23] Coal contributes more climate change inducing CO_2 greenhouse gas than any other fossil fuel. Coal burning is the world's largest source of carbon dioxide emissions, accounting for 40.3 percent of the total.[24] Moreover, as far as perceptions go, coal has a well established reputation in the public eye as a "dirty" fuel, long synonymous with smoke and air pollution.[25] Thus, in making its case for future energy market share, Big Coal starts with major disadvantages even without factoring in the other serious externalities discussed below.

III. History of Coal

A. Early History

Coal is a natural resource found in seams in underground layers throughout the world. Coal underlies every continent—including Antarctica.[26] Coal has been exploited as an energy source

---

18. IEA PRODUCTION REP'T, *supra* note 10. Coal generates electricity in many nations across the globe. Thirty-four countries consume more than a million tons oil equivalent per year. The biggest coal consumers are: China (1191); United States (567.3); India (237.7); Japan (119.1); Russian Federation (112.5); South Africa (93.8); Germany (82.4); Poland (58.4); South Korea (54.8); Australia (51.5); United Kingdom (43.8); Ukraine (39.6); Taiwan (39.5); Canada (35.0); Kazakhstan (29.7); Turkey (28.8); Indonesia (27.7); (numbers represent million tons oil equivalent). *See* http://www.xist.org/charts/en_coalcons.aspx (last visited July 1, 2008). Percentages of market share of other fuels are natural gas (19%), nuclear (17%), hydro (16%), and oil (7%). *Id.*

19. *See* M. DEISENDORF, COAL-FIRED ELECTRICITY AND ITS IMPACT ON GLOBAL WARMING 6, World Wildlife Fund, www.wwf.org.au/publications/australias_polluting_power.pdf (last visited on Sept. 10, 2008).

20. FUTURE OF COAL, *supra* note 16.

21. *Id.* These power plants produce, on average, five hundred megawatts.

22. *Id.*

23. *Id.*

24. World carbon dioxide emissions from the consumption of coal totaled 11.4 billion metric tons of carbon dioxide in 2005, up 38.6 percent from the 1995 level of 8.2 billion metric tons. China and the United States were the two largest producers of carbon dioxide from the consumption of coal in 2005 accounting for 38 and 19 percent, respectively, of the world total. India, Russia, and Japan together accounted for an additional 15 percent. U.S. ENERGY INFORMATION ADMINISTRATION, WORLD ENERGY OVERVIEW (2007), http://www.eia.doe.gov/iea/overview.html (last visited Sept. 10, 2008). Petroleum ran a close second to coal as a source of CO_2 emissions from the consumption and flaring of fossil fuels. In 2005 petroleum accounted for 39.0 percent of the total. *Id.*

25. *See, e.g.,* Editorial, *Clean Power or Dirty Coal?,* N.Y. TIMES (Feb. 10, 2008); Craig Whitlock, *Dependent on a Dirty Fuel, German Coal Mines Thrive Despite Push for Cleaner Energy,* WASHINGTON POST at D1 (Feb. 8, 2008), *available at* http://www.washingtonpost.com/wp-dyn/content/article/2008/02/07/AR2008020703755. html (last visited September 12, 2008). Coal combustion produces significantly greater CO_2 emissions than oil and natural gas. FUTURE OF COAL, *supra* note 16, at 5. CO_2 emissions from coal-fired electricity generation comprise nearly 80 percent of the total CO_2 emissions produced by the generation of electricity in the United States. Fifty-one percent of electricity generation is fueled by coal. *See* CARBON DIOXIDE EMISSIONS FROM THE GENERATION OF ELECTRIC POWER IN THE UNITED STATES 3 (U.S. Dept. of Energy & U.S. E.P.A.) (July 2000). http://www.eia.doe.gov/cneaf/electricity/page/ co2_report/co2emiss.pdf (last accessed September 12, 2008).

26. Coal is found in significant if not necessarily mineable quantities in many countries. The nations with the most estimated reserves (in million tons) are: United States (246,643); Russian Federation (157,010); China (114,500); India (92,445); Australia (78,500); South Africa (48,750); Ukraine (34,153); and Kazakhstan

for millennia.[27] It is mentioned in the annals of Roman occupiers of the British Isles in the third to fifth centuries A.D.[28] Three centuries before colonization of the Americas began, coal use in Europe began on an ascending path leading, several centuries later, to its supplanting wood as the fuel of choice in England.[29] By the start of the Fourteenth Century, coal use had become common as well as problematic in English cities. London streets in the summer of 1306 were filled with coal smoke from blacksmith and artisan fires, leading to laws in the reign of Edward I banning coal burning and imposing "great fines and ransoms" on violators.[30]

B. Coal and the Industrial Age

Two centuries later, population had significantly increased and the great forests of the British Isles had been decimated to provide wood for heating, cooking and other domestic uses. England turned to coal as its primary source of fuel.[31] Elizabethan England's transition from wood to coal has been identified as a pivotal turning point in world history.[32] It is seen by one commentator as a transformational event of enormous magnitude:

> [The English] went on to spark a coal-fired industrial revolution that would transform the planet. The industrial age emerged literally in a haze of coal smoke, and in that coal smoke we can read much of the history of the modern world.[33]

Coal-fired industrialization expanded in the late eighteenth and the early nineteenth centuries with the market for coal increasing dramatically following perfection of steam engine technology.[34]

The coal market in England and industrializing European nations continued to expand exponentially to meet the increasing demands of iron and later of steel production, train transporta-

---

(31,279). *See* Energy.eu Europe's Energy Portal, http://www.energy.eu/#non-renewable (European Commission). *See also* World Energy Council, *Survey of Energy Resources*, http://www.worldenergy.org/documents/coal_1_1.pdf. (last visited Oct. 3, 2008).

27. Mining in northeastern China provided coal for a copper smelter and casting coins around 1000 B.C. The World Coal Institute asserts that "one of the earliest known references to coal was made by the Greek philosopher and scientist Aristotle, who referred to a charcoal like rock." The Coal Resource, *supra* note 12, at 19.

28. There is evidence of use of coal by Roman occupiers of the British Isles from 300–500 A.D. Barbara Freese, Coal, A Human History 15–17 (Penguin 2003) [hereinafter Freese], citing J.U. Nef, 1 The Rise of the British Coal Industry 2 (1933, *reprinted*, Frank Cass & Co., 1966).

29. *See* Freese, *supra* note 1, at 15–42 (discussing use of coal in the British Isles from the time of Roman occupation *circa*. 300 B.C until the end of the reign of Queen Elizabeth I).

30. *Id.* at 1, citing Robert Galloway, 1 Annals of Coal Mining and the Coal Trade 10 (1898, *reprinted*, 1999).

31. By the end of the Sixteenth century coal use increased dramatically as sources of wood for fuel were depleted. Before the end of the reign of Elizabeth I in 1603, coal surpassed wood as the primary source of English fuel. Robert Galloway, *Id*, citing, John Hatcher, 1 The History of the British Coal Industry, Before 1700: Towards The Age of Coal (Oxford Un. Press 1993).

32. *Id.* at 2, 30–32. Robert Galloway explained:

> Had the coal ban held up ... human history would have been radically different. As it happened, though, in the late 1500s the English faced an energy crisis ... they learned to tolerate what had been intolerable, becoming the first western nation to mine and burn coal on a large scale. In so doing, they filled London and other English cities with some of the nastiest urban air the world had yet seen.

Freese, *supra* note 1, at 2, 230–32, citing Robert Galloway, 1 Annals of Coal Mining and the Coal Trade 10 (1898, *reprinted*, 1999).

33. Freese, *supra* note 1, at 2.

34. Sally B. Gentille, Reinventing Energy: Making the Right Choices 3 (Diane Pub. Co. 1996). The steam engine was patented in 1769; coal-fired steam energy jump-started the industrial revolution.

tion and steamships.[35] Capitalizing on domestic coal, coal-fueled industrialization boosted Great Britain to global commercial and military power lasting the better part of two centuries.

C. Coal and Industrialization in the United States

Beyond the far-flung British Empire, the industrial revolution took root most quickly in the coal-rich United States. America's vast coalfields contained more coal than all of England, and were the largest, easiest to access and highest quality coal reserves in the world.[36] It was near the end of the nineteenth century in the United States that invention and ingenuity led to another surge in world demand for coal.

Tinkering at his Menlo Park, New Jersey, laboratory, Thomas A. Edison produced ideas and inventions crucial to propel forward worldwide industrialization. Yet, alone, Edison's light bulb was of little value. To fulfill its promise the bulb required stimulation by electric current.

Edison pioneered in the development of an efficient electricity generation and transmission system.[37] Edison designed and oversaw the construction of an electric generating station that began commercial operation in New York City in 1882.[38] To fuel his system, Edison turned to coal—which was readily available, found in seemingly limitless quantities and in convenient locations reachable by rail and water.

Coal's entrepreneurs, politicians, laborers and financiers sprang into action. The agrarian economic base that had been the defining characteristic of the nation since colonial times rapidly declined in importance as engines whirred and factories spewed out mass produced goods into the markets of the new American industrial age.

Thus, at the turn of the twentieth century, Edison's genius brought coal and electric generation together effectively triggering an inexorable expansion of the market for coal that continues today. Comfort was no longer strictly the province of the wealthy. The lives of many Americans improved dramatically. From Atlantic to Pacific, coal was the fuel providing light to America's cities and farms and powering her factories. Coal's time had come in America.

IV. Coal's Dark Side: Examining its Externalities

Air pollution caused by coal combustion is only one of many externalities produced by coal mining and burning adversely impacting the environment and coalfield communities.[39] These

---

35. *Id.* Coal was also used extensively to fuel gas lights in many urban areas. Coal gasification triggered exponential growth in gas lighting in urban areas in the early nineteenth century, especially in London. Electricity eventually replaced coal gas street lighting at the end of the century as electric generation and transmission became common. *See* http://www.worldcoal.org/pages/content/index.asp?PageID=37.

36. Today, after well over a century of mining billions upon billions of tons of coal, the United States coal reserves are still greater than that of any other nation of the world. Estimates of the remaining minable coal in the nation run between one and two hundred years. There is a measure of controversy concerning the accuracy of world and national coal reserve estimates. *See, e.g.,* EWG Coal Resources and Production, *supra* note 13.

37. The genius of Thomas Edison was aimed not only at electric lighting, but necessarily at designing an efficient mechanism for generating electricity and transmitting current long distances to activate his invention. *See* Francis Rolt-Wheeler, Thomas Alva Edison, 125–136 (The MacMillan Co. 1915), *available at* http://books.google.com/books?id=ZKIDAAAAYAAJ&pg=PA125&dq=edison+%22light+bulb%22&lr=&num=100&as_brr=1&ei=45ngR5vrN4-KzQTWtIyPDw#PPP10,M1.

38. *Id.* The Edison plant generated electricity that was transmitted around the city to provide residential lighting. The Coal Resource, *supra* note 12, at 19.

39. The externalities discussed in this chapter are limited to those experiences in the Appalachian coalfields in the United States. Other coal mining regions of the world, notably China, also have experienced similar serious adverse impacts from coal mining and burning. China consumes more coal than any other nation and it consumes one fourth of the world's total production. Half the increase of world coal consumption is contributed by China. *See, e.g.,* He Youguo, China's Coal Demand Outlook for 2020 and Analysis of

consequences of coal are little known nor understood outside the world's coal mining regions. Most people in developed nations have long been unaware of the connection between coal's costs and the simple act of flipping a light switch to illuminate a room. They are generally oblivious to coal's worker safety and environmental externalities: soil erosion, landslides, sulfuric acid water pollution, stream sedimentation, loss of potable water supplies, workplace injuries, diseases and fatalities.[40] Nor is the public aware of coal's socio-economic impacts including family and community disruptions, economic stagnation and accompanying lack of educational, employment and economic development opportunities. Sadly, many or all of these burdens are often borne by coalfield communities.[41]

A. The Socio-Economic Costs of Coal Mining and Burning

1. Industrial Awakening in the Coalfields

The coming of the industrial age impacted the awakening coalfields of Appalachia quite differently than it did the distant cities. As Edison innovated in Menlo Park, the vast underground coalfield of Appalachia rested largely undisturbed as it had for millennia. The industrial activities of America's burgeoning cities lay in sharp contrast with the solitude of Appalachia's mountains:

> Great forests of oak, ash, and poplar, covered the hillsides with a rich blanket of deep hues, and clear, sparkling streams rushed along the valley floors. No railroad had yet penetrated the hollows. The mountain people lived in small settlements scattered here and there in the valleys and coves. Life on the whole was simple, quiet, and devoted chiefly to agricultural pursuits.[42]

Within three decades the quiet rural life in the coal-laden mountains of the region had vanished. Young men and their families fled hard-scrabble subsistence farming, flocking to work in underground coal mines and live in a multitude of "coal camps"—coal company-built and owned towns tucked up remote valleys and hollows in West Virginia, Kentucky, and Pennsylvania.[43] From sun up to sun down, miners wielded picks and shovels loading coal into mule and horse drawn carts that hauled coal to the surface and on to industrial markets.[44] Miners spent

---

COAL SUPPLY CAPACITY, International Energy Agency, *available at* http://www.iea.org/Textbase/work/2003/beijing/4Youg.pdf (last visited Nov. 14, 2008). For articles discussing China's coal-related externalities, see Simon Elegant, *Zhangjiachang, Where The Coal Is Stained With Blood*, TIME MAGAZINE (Mar. 2, 2007), *available at* http://www.time.com/time/magazine/article/0,9171,1595235,00.html (last visited Mar. 3, 2008) ("... 20,000 miners die in accidents each year. And that count doesn't include tens of thousands more of the country's estimated 5 million miners who die of lung afflictions and other work-related diseases every year."); Keith Bradsher, David Barboza, *Pollution From China Casts a Global Shadow*, N.Y. TIMES (June 11, 2006), *available at* http://www.nytimes.com/2006/06/11/business/worldbusiness/11chinacoal.html (last visited Mar. 2, 2008) ("The sulfur dioxide produced in coal combustion poses an immediate threat to the health of China's citizens, contributing to about 400,000 premature deaths a year. It also causes acid rain that poisons lakes, rivers, forests and crops."); YANG YANG, A CHINA ENVIRONMENTAL HEALTH PROJECT RESEARCH BRIEF: COAL MINING AND ENVIRONMENTAL HEALTH IN CHINA, Woodrow Wilson Center (April 02, 2007), *available at* http://www.wilsoncenter.org/topics/docs/coalmining_april2.pdf (last visited Oct. 14, 2008).

40. *See generally* P. McGinley, *From Pick and Shovel to Mountaintop Removal: Environmental Injustice in the Appalachian Coalfields*, 34 ENVTL. L. 23 (2004). *Cf.* KYM ANDERSON, WARWICK J. MCKIBBIN, REDUCING COAL SUBSIDIES AND TRADE BARRIERS: THEIR CONTRIBUTION TO GREENHOUSE GAS ABATEMENT 3–4 (The Brookings Institution, July 1997). http://www.brookings.edu/~/media/Files/rc/papers/1997/11globaleconomics_anderson/bdp135.pdf (last visited October 1, 2008) [hereinafter REDUCING COAL SUBSIDIES].

41. *See generally* P. McGinley, *supra* note 40.

42. RONALD D. ELLER, MINERS, MILLHANDS, AND MOUNTAINEERS: INDUSTRIALIZATION OF THE APPALACHIAN SOUTH, 1880–1930 161 (1982) [hereinafter MINERS AND MILLHANDS].

43. *Id.*

44. A history of the Pennsylvania bituminous coalfields explains the work performed by men and boys:
   Coal mining was arduous work, especially before mechanization. Miners labored in coal seams ...

long hours underground engaged in back-breaking underground work. They found solace and refuge above ground in the coal camp homes rented from their employer.

New coal camp communities sprouted throughout the remote wilderness overlying the vast coal deposits.[45] The great virgin forest was clear-cut with a vengeance and pristine mountain streams, only a few decades earlier teeming with native trout, were polluted by coal mine drainage.[46]

In short order, coal mining transformed the Appalachian landscape and "civilized" the region's inhabitants:

> [E]vidence of change was to be found on every hand. Coal-mining village after coal-mining village dotted the hollows along every creek and stream. The weathered houses of those who worked in the mines lined the creeks and steep slopes, and the black holes themselves gaped from the hillsides like great open wounds. Mine tipples, headhouses, and other buildings straddled the slopes of the mountains. Railroads sent their tracks in all directions, and long lines of coal cars sat on the sidings and disappeared around the curves of the hills.
>
> ....
>
> The once majestic earth was scarred and ugly, and the streams ran brown with garbage and acid runoff from the mines. A black dust covered everything. Huge mounds of coal and "gob" piles of discarded mine waste lay about. The peaceful quiet of three decades before had been replaced by a cacophony of voices and industrial sounds.[47]

Historian David Alan Corbin observed that "[o]wnership of the land and resources gave coal companies enormous social control over the miners. 'You didn't even own your own soul in those damnable places,' recalled one elderly miner. 'The company owned everything, the houses, the schools, churches, the stores—everything.'"[48] Indeed, the coal camp came to symbolize the rapid industrialization of rural Appalachia. Historian Ron Eller observed:

---

two- to twenty-feet thick, many spent the work day hunched over in narrow seams. Before mechanization they used crude hand tools and explosives to break coal from the vertical face. A skilled miner, usually lying on his side, used his pick and wedges to remove chunks of coal without shattering them. If he could not dislodge coal with his hand tools, a skilled miner drilled holes into the rock face with a hand-powered auger, placed explosives in the holes, and detonated the explosives.... Laborers ... shoveled dislodged coal into wooden cars, which ... animals ... pulled along rails to the surface or to a mine elevator in a shaft. Boys often led the draft animals, and opened and closed tunnel doors to regulate the flow of fresh air through mines. The wooden cars delivered coal to ... the surface....

ExplorePAhistory.com, *King Coal: Mining Bituminous*, ch. 2, http://www.explorepahistory.com/story.php?storyId=30&chapter=3 [hereinafter *Pennsylvania History*] (last visited September 12, 2008).

45. U.S. Senate Reports and Bureau of the Census information indicate that at the zenith of the early twentieth century coal boom, almost four-fifths of southern West Virginia mine workers and more than two-thirds of mining families in southwestern Virginia and eastern Kentucky lived in nearly 500 company towns. *Id.* at 162–63. In contrast, less than 100 independently incorporated towns existed in the same region. *Id.* at 163.

46. *See generally* MINERS AND MILL HANDS, *supra* note 42, at 161. *See also* Patrick C. McGinley, *supra* note 40, at 24–46.

47. MINERS AND MILL HANDS, *supra* note 42, at 161–162. Professor Eller dedicates an entire book chapter to an examination of life in coal company towns. *See id.* at 161–98.

48. THE WEST VIRGINIA MINE WARS: AN ANTHOLOGY 1 (David Alan Corbin ed., Un. Pittsburgh Press 1990) [hereinafter W. VA. MINE WARS]. In the coal camps, "company rule included the company police in the form of mine guards, who would toss the miners in jail when they got disruptive, or administer the company beating when they attempted to unionize." *Id.* The coal company towns provided a complete cradle to grave system which provided a company doctor to deliver babies, the mines in which boys and men worked and cemeteries where camp inhabitants were eventually buried. *Id.*

[C]ompany town[s] became for thousands of mountaineers the dominant institution of community life—a vital social center around which the miners' world revolved. Not only was the coal camp the site of one's work, the source of one's income, and the location of one's residence, but for many it also provided an
introduction to organized community life and the setting in which new attitudes,
values, and social institutions evolved. Completely owned and tightly dominated by
the coal companies, the mining towns also reflected the underlying transition in land
ownership and social power which had swept the region with the coming of the industrial age.[49]

With ownership of the towns came coal company administrative responsibilities for providing
public services.[50] Only two percent of company towns possessed a sewer system; the vast majority
simply dumped community wastes into nearby creeks.[51] Streams running through coal camps
were often polluted by a combination of raw sewage and acid mine runoff that completely eliminated all biological life.[52] Water pollution affected human health. During hot, humid summers
the polluted stream stank and diseases like typhoid ravaged the children of the coal camps.[53] "Civilization [had] come into the mountains" Professor Eller noted—with no small hint of irony.[54]

2. Early Labor-Management Coalfield Conflicts

Industrial strife was common in the coalfields from 1900 to the 1930s when the onset of the
"New Deal" Administration of President Franklin Delano Roosevelt began to level the playing
field between labor and management.[55] Unionization played a central role in coal camp residents' struggle for economic and social justice during repeating cycles of coal market-related
boom and bust. While miners engaged in strikes both in support of unionization and higher
wages they also struck "for their dignity and freedom."[56] For decades miners battled anti-union
coal operators who dominated the Southern Appalachian coalfields.

In West Virginia, during the decade from 1912 to 1921, a virtual war existed between coal
company forces and miners.[57] On several occasions martial law was declared and the state militia
was summoned. Miners were arrested and tried by military tribunals.[58] Once, in September
1921, President Warren G. Harding sent federal troops to intervene in the conflict.[59]

---

49. *Id.* at 162.

50. Winthrop D. Lane, The Denial of Civil Liberties in the Coal Fields 2 (1924).

51. Miners and Mill Hands, *supra* note 42, at 184.

52. *Id.* at 186.

53. *Id.* (*citing* Jerry Bruce Thomas, *Coal Country: The Rise of the Southern Smokeless Coal Industry and Its
Effect on Area Development, 1872–1910* (1971) (unpublished Ph.D. dissertation, University of North Carolina
at Chapel Hill)). At the time coal companies' responded to criticism "arguing that coal could not be mined
economically if they concerned themselves with ecology." *Id.*

54. *Id.*

55. Conflicts between company and Union continued on a slowly diminishing scale until the 1990s where
an era of rapprochement between coal industry and labor brought relative peace to coal field labor relations.

56. Jerry Bruce Thomas, An Appalachian New Deal: West Virginia in the Great Depression
91–106 (Un. Press of Kentucky 1998) [hereinafter Appalachian New Deal].

57. *See generally* W. Va. Mine Wars, *supra* note 48, at 1.

58. Arthur Warner, *Fighting Unionism with Martial Law*, The Nation, Oct. 12, 1921, at 395, 396. Local
newspapers referred to this conflict as an "industrial controversy." *Id.* at 395. Warner reminds us, however,
that "the home folks resent the words 'civil war' as describing the situation, but they seem to forget that the
phrase is that [of West Virginia's] Governor ... in proclaiming martial law in Mingo County on May 19
[1921], [who] said that 'a state of war, insurrection, and riot and bloodshed is and has been for some time in
existence.' ..." *Id.*

59. *The War in West Virginia*, Independent, Sept. 17, 1921, *reprinted in* W. Va. Mine Wars, *supra* note
48, at 106.

Contemporaneously, a political battle raged across the region's coalfields as miners fought for the right to unionize.[60] Appalachian historian and sage Harry Caudill observed that:

> In 1931, for all practical purposes, the only law for the miners … was the mining companies' law as interpreted by deputies sheriff selected and paid directly by the companies…. The system was simply law enforcement stripped of any pretense of impartiality, and it is difficult to imagine a more effective device for promoting violence and engendering resentful hatred among a people bred in the free air of the Kentucky hills.[61]

The 1932 election of President Franklin D. Roosevelt and the advent of his "New Deal" administration did not end coalfield violence nor the terrible poverty and oppression of the coal camps. Labor unrest and strikes continued to pit miners against nonunion coal operators during the 1930s. Some coal operators recognized the United Mine Workers Union, but others "resolved to fight the menace so long as they had a shot to fire."[62] Historian Caudill chronicled the tactics of those coal operators who resisted unionization:

> [T]hey proceeded step by step along the road to intimidation and coercion. Miners suspected of joining the union, harboring its agents or spreading its propaganda were summarily ordered out of company houses and off company property. The detailed leases covering the camp residences, as interpreted by the docile courts, authorized such summary evictions. Many unfortunate coal diggers found their possessions and families thrust out of doors when they were practically without funds and with no place to go. If another miner took such a dangerous family into his own house for even the shortest period he risked the same fate.[63]

Aggravating existing management-labor conflicts was the onset of the Great Depression which further distressed an already depressed coal market.[64] Widespread bankruptcies hit banks and coal operators alike.[65] Coal company managers slashed miners' already meager wages and then reverted to paying workers on a "piecework" basis.[66] Miners were permitted to stay underground for as long as they wished, resulting in ten-to twelve-hour workdays.[67]

---

60. James M. Cain, *The Battle Ground of Coal*, ATLANTIC MONTHLY, Oct. 1922, *reprinted in* W. VA. MINE WARS, *supra* note 48, at 151, 157.

61. HARRY M. CAUDILL, NIGHT COMES TO THE CUMBERLANDS: A BIOGRAPHY OF A DEPRESSED AREA 195–96 (Jesse Stuart Foundation 1962) (quoting Russell Briney of the COURIER-JOURNAL (Louisville, Kentucky)) [hereinafter NIGHT COMES].

62. *Id.* at 195.

63. *Id.* Coal Company owners contradicted these reports. One operator testified before a federal commission that "In all cases, regard has been paid to the health and comfort of those persons whom it was found necessary to evict…." *See* W.VA. MINE WARS, *supra* note 48, at 9 (quoting BITUMINOUS OPERATORS' SPECIAL COMMITTEE, THE COMPANY TOWN: REPORT SUBMITTED TO THE U.S. COAL COMMISSION 36–37 (1923)). In W.VA. MINE WARS, Corbin also cites other evidence from an early effort to unionize coal camps in Kanawha County, West Virginia that contradicts coal operator denials:

> [M]ine guards arrived in the early morning and threw breakfasts out with the furniture. During the process the mine guards destroyed over $40,000 worth of furniture. In the town of Banner, the mine guards came to the house of Tony Seviller, whose wife was pregnant. The head of the squadron shouted, "Get out!" Mrs. Seviller, in bed and in labor when ordered out, responded, "My God! Can't you see I am sick; just let me stay here until my baby is born." The guard leader replied, "I don't give a damn, get out or I'll shoot you out." Mrs. Seviller gave birth to her baby two hours later, in a tent furnished by the UMWA.

W.VA. MINE WARS, *supra* note 48, at 10.

64. It was not until war clouds gathered over Europe prior to World War II that the coalfield economy began to revive.

65. *Id.* at 171–174.

66. *Id.* at 170.

67. *Id.* at 170–71.

The Depression's effects were bad for most American workers, but even more devastating to Appalachian coal miners and their families. "People who have never lived in mining communities cannot comprehend the feeling of captivity and helplessness that lay so heavy in the coal camps through these years."[68] Although aided by New Deal labor legislation granting rights to organize and strike, it was not until the late 1930s that unions gained a semblance of parity with coal industry management.[69]

3. Economic Boom—Bust Cycle in Coalfield Communities: 1940–2009

By 1940, ninety percent of the nation's coal came from union mines.[70] The federal government nationalized and ran coal mines during World War II and its negotiations with the union produced an agreement to pay miners generous wages.[71] The war-time demands for coal-fired industrial production stoked coal production and a coalfield economic boom.[72] "Empty camps filled again and the ghastly, painted houses swarmed with new brigades of ragged irrepressible children.... [t]he coal camps had been rejuvenated by 1945, and union miners and their families were enjoying unparalleled freedom and prosperity."[73]

The government relinquished control of the mines to their owners following the war. However, as the country welcomed returning veterans of battle the coal market collapsed. Prices plummeted. A glut of coal stockpiled for wartime consumption collided with the severely contracting demand of a peacetime economy.[74] Adding greatly to the dysfunctional coalfield economy, coal began to lose its traditional market share as railroads and home furnaces increasingly were fueled by cheaper and cleaner-burning oil and natural gas.[75]

A new period of labor-management conflict followed in the wake of this coalfield "bust" economy. Eventually, after a long, hostile strike in 1950 and 1951, coal companies and the union agreed to a revolutionary contract that significantly increased miner wages and benefits in return for union acquiescence to mine mechanization.[76] By the beginning of the 1960s, the new mining machines had greatly increased coal production while drastically reducing the need for skilled and unskilled labor.[77]

By 1960 coal industry consolidation, a poor coal market, loss of mining jobs and a concomitant immigration from coalfield communities "made for a severe and chronic economic predica-

---

68. *Id.* at 174–75.

69. *See* JOHN ALEXANDER WILLIAMS, APPALACHIA: A HISTORY 272 (Un. North Carolina Press 2001) [hereinafter APPALACHIA HISTORY]. The New Deal Congress enacted the National Labor Relations Act, 29 U.S.C. §§ 151–169 (2000) ("NLRA") (§ 157 of the NLRA guaranteed employees "the right to form, join, or assist labor organizations").

70. Richard A. Couto, *The Memory of Miners and the Conscience of Capital, in* FIGHTING BACK IN APPALACHIA: TRADITIONS OF RESISTANCE AND CHANGE 165, 167 (Stephen L. Fisher ed., Temple Un. Press 1993) [hereinafter *Memory of Miners*]. UMWA membership grew from a few thousand in 1931 to almost 300,000 in 1940. APPALACHIA HISTORY, *supra* note 69, at 280.

71. *Memory of Miners*, *supra* note 70, at 167.

72. NIGHT COMES, *supra* note 61, at 220–21.

73. *Id.*

74. *Id.* at 247.

75. *Id.*; *Memory of Miners*, *supra* note 70, at 168.

76. APPALACHIA HISTORY, *supra* note 69, at 318; *Memory of Miners*, *supra* note 70, at 168–69. *See also* NIGHT COMES, *supra* note 61, at 258–64 (describing the mechanization of coal mining). *See generally* KEITH DIX, WHAT'S A COAL MINER TO DO? THE MECHANIZATION OF COAL MINING (Un. Pittsburgh Press 1988).

77. OTIS K. RICE, STEPHEN W. BROWN, WEST VIRGINIA: A HISTORY 280 (2d ed. Un. Press of Kentucky1993) [hereinafter W.VA. HISTORY]. Coal production per man-day increased from 5.57 tons in 1945 to 10.05 tons in 1957. In 1948, 117,104 miners were at work in West Virginia. In 1957, only 58,732 miners were employed; by 1961 the number of miners had shrunk to only 42,557 in West Virginia and less than 200,000 nationwide. *Id.* at 280, 284. *See also* APPALACHIAN NEW DEAL, *supra* note 56, at 238.

ment" for West Virginia's coalfield communities.[78] The depressed job market drove up unemployment in mining communities. West Virginia's unemployment rate was the nation's highest—triple that of the nation.[79] As the coal-based economy continued to collapse, tens of thousands left the coalfields in search of work in the industrial plants of the Northeast and the nonunion textile and manufacturing plants of the Sunbelt.[80] Some miners and their families elected to stay and hope for better times. One man described the quandary faced by unemployed coal miners:

> "It's rough, buddy.... This is home. This is where we were both born and raised. We like it here. Until I can find work, we stay. If the program I'm on runs out, well, then I guess we'll have to think about moving on. Where to? Where can a man with a family go with no place to set out for and no money to get there? Hard as it is, we want to stay here. This hollow is home."[81]

The beleaguered, poverty-stricken coalfield communities of Central Appalachia did receive a measure of assistance via the food stamp and public assistance programs launched by the administration of Presidents John F. Kennedy and Lyndon Johnson.[82]

The future of the coal regions appeared brighter by 1970 when a new, coal "boom" took hold. The United States faced an "energy crisis" brought on by a Middle-Eastern cartel's oil price fixing.[83] In the coalfields of Appalachia the hiring call went out for miners for the first time in decades as electric generating power companies shifted from more expensive oil to coal which was not only cheaper but a more reliable source of fuel not subject to international political intrigue and terrorism. Thousands of miners were hired or re-hired and the region sprang back to life:

> During those fabulous days in the mid-seventies, thousands of men who had left the mountains came home from distant cities to dig coal. In West Virginia, Virginia, Kentucky, and Tennessee, small truck mines that had been abandoned for years were re-opened. Nearly anybody who had or could borrow money to buy a dump truck and a road grader could become a strip mine operator. Bootleggers mined without permits

---

78. *See* Appalachian New Deal, *supra* note 56, at 239 (1998). During this period of economic distress the character of the company town relationship between company and residents changed. *See generally* McGinley, *supra* note 40, at 35–36. Many houses were sold to their occupants and others were rented to anyone who could pay the meager rent (in 1987, as little as $15 per month) for the dilapidated structures. Indeed, this relationship continues today in some former coal camps. *See id.* citing Jules Loh, *The Longstanding Paradox of Eureka Hollow*, Charleston Gazette, Jan. 4, 1987, at A4 [hereinafter *Longstanding Paradox*]; Jules Loh, *Despite Billions In Aid, Poverty Still Plagues Appalachia*, The Dallas Morning News 6A, 1987 WLNR 1943627 (January 4, 1987).

79. *Id.* at 239.

80. *See* W.Va. History, *supra* note 77, at 280 ("Thousands of young men, who normally would have entered the mines ... left for Pittsburgh, Cleveland, Akron, Chicago, Detroit, and other cities."); Appalachia History, *supra* note 69, at 394 (recounting the southward exodus to the "sunbelt"). *See generally* Chad Berry, Southern Migrants, Northern Exiles (Un. of Illinois Press 2000) (describing Appalachian migration during times of economic distress); Harry K. Schwartzkeller *et al.*, Mountain Families in Transition: A Case Study of Appalachian Migration (Pa. State Un. Press 1971) (describing the "exodus" of residents from Beech Creek, Ky.).

81. *Longstanding Paradox, supra* note 78.

82. *See generally* Appalachia History, *supra* note 69, at 339–52, 366–79. Professor Williams quotes Harry Caudill as expressing the concern that the Kennedy-Johnson Administration's "War on Poverty" threatened to "turn Appalachia into a giant welfare reservation." *Id.* at 369, *citing* Harry Caudill, The Watches of the Night (Little Brown 1976).

83. *See generally* David Yergin, The Prize: The Epic Quest for Oil, Money, and Power 607–09 (Free Press 1993). The per barrel cost of oil quickly escalated as the Organization of Petroleum Exporting Countries (OPEC) ratcheted up prices in response to the "Yom Kippur War" and the shut-down of oil fields of Iran after the country's leader was overthrown in a 1978 coup. *Id.* at 607–609, 635, 685.

and got good money for gray mixtures of coal, slate, and rock. Spot market prices soared to nearly $100 a ton and suddenly-rich independent operators lived in opulence, bought luxury cars for their wives, and concluded business deals on the golf course.[84]

The 1970s coal boom was short-lived. By 1980, the boom subsided and economic hard times returned once again to the coalfields. For example, by 1984, West Virginia experienced the nation's highest unemployment rate and "economic indicators pointed to continuing difficulties, with recovery trailing far behind that of the other states."[85]

In 1987 a journalist described the condition of the old coal camp in Eureka Hollow, West Virginia:

> The village on its trash-strewn banks at the mouth of the hollow is Eckman. You won't find it on a road map. Eckman consists of a grocery store, filling station and a one-room post office. Wooden planks thrown over a ditch at the uphill edge of town mark the start of the road up Eureka Hollow. Woebegone wooden houses, many of them falling down, dot the hillsides along the road. Tree limbs, like crutches, prop up porches. Abandoned houses crumble alongside inhabited mobile homes. Coal dust trodden into black gum replaces grass. Red dog, a rust-colored mine waste turned into coarse gravel, paves driveways. Automobile carcasses rot beneath clotheslines burdened with patched jeans and faded shirts.[86]

The streets of Whitesville, West Virginia, were clogged with shoppers and traffic during the 70s boom; by 2002 they were usually empty. A reporter described the town: "[v]acant stores dot the town's main drag and windows are covered with dust from coal trucks that rumble through night and day. Traffic lights work intermittently. Parking meters were removed long ago."[87]

During the period from 1982–2008 the Appalachian coalfield economy has continued to experience an extended decades long bust phase. Midwestern utility companies eschewed Appalachian coal for cheaper western coal and loss of mining jobs in Appalachian underground mines continued as a result of further mechanization.[88]

West Virginia's coal economy typified that of the Central Appalachian coal region. In 1980, coal jobs in the State had dropped by 7,000 from the boom high of almost 63,000 in 1978; five years later only 35,813 miners were at work in West Virginia.[89] Ten years later, in 1990, coal

---

84. Rudy Abramson, *New Coal Isn't Old Coal*, 20 APF Reporter 1 (2001), *available at* http://www.alicia patterson.org/APF2001/Abramson/Abramson.html (last visited Sept. 10, 2008) [hereinafter Abramson].

85. W.Va. History, *supra* note 77, at 238. *See also* Ry Bearak, *Numbers Worsen Poverty: Toll Grows Amid Aid Cutbacks*, Los Angeles Times at 1A, 1985 WLNR 947120 (July 28, 1985).

86. *Longstanding Paradox*, *supra* note 78. Reporter Loh's description of Eureka Hollow cannot be generalized to all former coal camps. Some coal company lessors maintained their properties and often remodeled houses they owned keeping them in good repair. *See* Night Comes, *supra* note 61, at 263–268; Gerald M. Stern, The Buffalo Creek Disaster: How the Survivors of One of the Worst Disasters in Coal-Mining History Brought Suit Against the Coal Company—and Won 41–42 (Vintage Books ed. 1977) [hereinafter Buffalo Creek Disaster].

87. Abramson, *supra* note 84.

88. *See* McGinley, *supra* note 40, at 44.

89. *Id.*

miner employment dipped to less than 29,000; today less than 20,000 miners are at work in the state.[90]

Appalachian coal production, boosted by more efficient mining technologies and methods, reached record levels at the beginning of the millennium. During the same period, the numbers of miners employed dropped to the lowest level since the nineteenth century.[91] Ironically, high levels of coal production and unemployment coincide—a paradox explained by new technologies and large scale mining methods that utilize far fewer workers than ever.[92]

Dan Radmacher, now editor of the Roanoke (Virginia) Times, has examined this paradox, finding the coal-producing counties in West Virginia, Kentucky, and Virginia are much poorer than coal-producing counties in western states.[93] In Mingo County, West Virginia, the heart of the so-called "Billion Dollar Coalfields," Radmacher found that the median household income is $12,000 less than the national average and the area is filled with "empty houses and businesses ... which has to be a psychological burden as well as a barrier to economic development."[94] A local bank's profile of the area observed that "[t]oday, a large percentage of the coal mined in West Virginia is from strip [mining], requiring fewer people. This means fewer jobs, lack of a well-planned infrastructure for communities and an educational system that suffers from all of these factors."[95]

B. Environmental Impacts of Coal

1. Limited Public Awareness of Coal's Externalities

The contribution of coal burning to global warming has increasingly been the focus of intense scientific study and growing public concern. The enormous consumption of billions of tons of coal for electric generation pollutes the Earth's atmosphere with green house gases including sulfur dioxide, carbon dioxide and ozone.[96] Other constituents of coal-fired power plant emissions including mercury, arsenic and dioxin raise serious public health concerns.[97]

---

90. *Id.*

91. *Id.*

92. *Id.*

93. Dan Radmacher, *The Curse of Coal: Out West, Counties Fare Better*, Sunday Gazette-Mail (Charleston, W. Va.), June 10, 2001, at 1C, *available at* 2001 WL 6672917.

94. *Id. See also* Amy K. Glasmeier, *Living in Coal Country: A Profile of Upshur County* (Jan. 8, 2006), *available at* http://www.povertyinamerica.psu.edu/2006/01/08/living-in-coal-country-a-profile-of-upshur-county/ (last visited Nov 2, 2008) ("In Upshur County, labor force participation rates are low by state and national standards. Almost half of the working-age population is not in the labor force.")

95. *See Coalfield Counties Rich in Potential: Bank President Says Tourism Vital to Growth*, Discover: The Real West Virginia Found., Summer 2002, at 6, *available at* http://www.drwvfoundation.org/pdf/Discover Summer02.pdf (last visited Nov. 3, 2008).

96. In addition, underground coal mining operations release into the atmosphere enormous amounts of methane gas from strata adjacent to buried coal seams. Methane Gas is more than 20 times as effective as CO_2 at trapping heat in the atmosphere. U.S.E.P.A., Inventory of U.S. Greenhouse Gas Emissions and Sinks: 1990–2006 ES-9 (2008), *available at* http://epa.gov/climatechange/emissions/downloads/08_CR.pdf (last visited Nov. 2, 2008).

97. *See generally* Office of Air Quality Planning and Standards, USEPA, Study of Hazardous Air Pollutant Emissions from Electric Utility Steam Generating Units—Final Report to Congress (EPA-453/R-98-004b) (February 1998), http://www.epa.gov/ttn/caaa/t3/reports/eurtc1.pdf (last visited October 30, 2008). *See also* Robert B. Finkelman, Harvey E. Belkin, Baoshan Zheng, *Health impacts of domestic coal use in China*, 96 Proc. Natl. Acad. Sci., 3427–3431 (1999), *available at* ES-26, http://www.epa.gov/ttn/caaa/ t3/reports/utilexec.pdf (last visited Sept. 14, 2008).

However important coal burning's contribution to global warming, generation of greenhouse gases is not the fuel's only adverse environmental consequence. Coals' adverse effects on natural resources and coal-related human health effects have long been documented, if not generally recognized by the public. As discussed below, there many other serious adverse environmental and socio-economic consequences of coal. These adverse externalities have failed to gain major traction in public discourse on the world's energy future.

2. Environmental Impacts of Early Coal Mining

When coal was first mined in the United States its impact on the environment was minimal. American coal was hand-mined underground from the late nineteenth century to the nineteen twenties by men with the help of animals including mules, ponies, oxen goats and even dogs.[98] Mine tunnels originally were dug by pick and shovel, aided by use of explosives to clear the path through rock layers to the coal.[99]

Because most of the coal mined prior to World War II came from underground pits,[100] the environmental impacts of coal mining were limited to surface subsidence and water pollution.[101] Mines and the number of miners grew in size and tunnels dug deeper and deeper underground. The industry's footprint grew as did the severity of its environmental effects.

2. Post-World War II Impacts of New Mining Technologies and Methods

At the conclusion of World War II, mining technology evolved quickly as did the adverse impacts of coal. Strip mining accelerated as equipment grew larger and more efficient. In the late nineteen-forties, highly productive "continuous mining" machines were introduced and rapidly adopted as the mining equipment of choice.[102] These new mining methods and technologies dramatically boosted production per man/hour. Correspondingly, coal mining required substantially less manual labor than it had only a decade earlier.[103]

During the next two decades, the most visible adverse impacts of the new mining technologies appeared on the surface as a consequence of the growing use of strip mining. Surface mining gashed scars in Appalachian mountainsides stripping away the forest on thousands of acres and caused erosion and attendant stream sedimentation and siltation. Stripping was almost completely unregulated so coal operators rarely reclaimed disturbed land. Surface mining smothered stream aquatic life.

In some coalfield regions, iron-laden sulfuric acid mine drainage pollution from underground and strip mining created ecologically sterile watercourses while staining stream beds red

---

98. *See, e.g.*, GeoFacts, History of Coal mining in Ohio, Ohio Geological Survey, Ohio Dep't Natural Res., http://www.dnr.state.oh.us/Portals/10/pdf/GeoFacts/geof14.pdf (last visited October 11. 2008).

99. *See* Pennsylvania History, *supra* note 44.

100. Steam engines and improved mechanization made strip mining of coal feasible from 1940 onward. Appalachia History, *supra* note 69, at 257.

101. Of course mining coal did cause some serious air pollution in industrial cities. Pittsburgh earned the sobriquet "the smoky city" because it was common for streets to be lit at mid-day due to the smoked-filled air.

102. Kentucky Coal and Energy Education Project, Mechanization of the Coal Industry in Appalachia, (1999) http://www.coaleducation.org/coalhistory/Jenkinshis.htm (last visited October 27, 2008).

103. *See, e.g.*, W.Va. History, *supra* note 77, at 280. In 1940 130,457 miners produced 126,619,825 tons of coal. In 1955, 54,321 miners produced 137,073,372 tons. West Virginia Office of Miners' Health, Safety and Training, Production of Coal and Coke in West Virginia 1863–2007, *available at* http://www.wv minesafety.org/historicprod.htm (last visited April 14, 2009).

and orange with iron and manganese precipitants.[104] Underground and strip mining fractured strata and depleted aquifers. Wells and springs used by many coalfield families were contaminated or went dry with severe effects on domestic home life.[105]

Loud noise and dust from blasting and earth-moving activities disturbed nearby communities and wildlife.[106] During mining, dust and debris often filled the air as soil and underlying rock strata were blasted apart, coal extracted.[107] Indiscriminate dumping of mine spoil down-slope on steep mountainsides caused landslides and buried cars, homes, and sometimes killed people.[108]

On occasion, mine site coal-slurry impoundments, containing wastes generated by coal processing and cleaning have been breached or collapsed, causing loss of life and severe economic and ecological damage.[109] The most poignant example is the totally avoidable 1972 collapse of a huge coal waste impoundment at Buffalo Creek, West Virginia.[110] A towering flood wall created by a succession of upstream collapsing huge waste impoundments hurtled 132 million gallons of slurry down a narrow valley killing 125 people, and injuring thousands more. The flood totally destroyed 17 coal camp communities, leaving 4000 homeless.[111]

After two decades of protests, the enormous harm caused by unregulated surface and underground coal mining throughout the Appalachian coalfields generated support for a national strip mining regulatory law. After several years of debate and two Presidential vetoes, Congress passed and a new President, Jimmy Carter, signed the Federal Surface Mining Control and Reclamation Act of 1977 ("SMCRA").[112] Professor Mark Squillace described the breadth of the damage that led to the enactment of the SMCRA:

---

104. *See* CHAD MONTRIE, TO SAVE THE LAND AND PEOPLE: A HISTORY OF OPPOSITION TO SURFACE COAL MINING IN APPALACHIA 3 (Un. of North Carolina Press 2003) [hereinafter HISTORY OF OPPOSITION]. For a brief technical explanation of Acid Mine Drainage, see U.S. GEOLOGICAL SERVICE, ACID MINE DRAINAGE: AN INTRODUCTION, *available at* http://energy.er.usgs.gov/health_environment/acid_mine_drainage/ (last visited Nov. 2, 2008).

105. *See* Committee on Ground Water Recharge in Surface-Mined Areas, NAT'L RESEARCH COUNCIL, SURFACE COAL MINING EFFECTS ON GROUNDWATER RECHARGE 4 (1990) (describing destruction of aquifers in Kentucky caused by surface mining); U.S. ARMY CORPS OF ENGINEERS *et al.*, DRAFT PROGRAMMATIC ENVIRONMENTAL IMPACT STATEMENT ON MOUNTAINTOP MINING/VALLEY FILLS IN APPALACHIA III.E-6 (2003) ("[Coal mine drainage] can adversely affect human populations by impairing surface and ground water used for drinking water...."), *available at* http://www.epa.gov/region03/mtntop/pdf/III.%20Affected%CC20 Environment%CC20and%CC20Consequences%CC20of%CC20MTM%CF.pdf. (last visited on November 15, 2008).

106. J. BARTIS, F. CAMM, DAVID ORTIZ, PRODUCING LIQUIDS FROM COAL: PROSPECTS AND POLICY ISSUES, Rand Corp., 78–79 (2008) http://www.rand.org/pubs/monographs/2008/RAND_MG754.pdf (last visited, Dec. 12, 2008) [hereinafter Rand Corp. Report], citing U.S. Environmental Protection Agency, *Mountaintop Mining/Valley Fills in Appalachia: Final Programmatic Environmental Impact Statement*, EPA Region 3, EPA 9-R-05002, October 2005. http://www.epa.gov/region3/mtntop/ (last visited Nov. 3, 2008).

107. *Id.*; *see also* H.R. Rep. No. 95-218, at 58–59 (1977) (detailing the devastating impacts of surface mining which inspired Congress to pass SMCRA), reprinted in 1977 U.S.C.C.A.N. 539, 596–97.

108. HISTORY OF OPPOSITION, *supra* note 104, at 3.

109. Rand Corp. Report, *supra* note 106, at 79, citing I. Frazier, *Coal Country*, ONEARTH, Spring 2003. http://www.nrdc.org/onearth/03spr/coal1.asp (last visited, October 28, 2008).

110. *See generally* BUFFALO CREEK DISASTER, *supra* note 86. *See also* Rand Corp. Report, *supra* note 106, at 79, citing, I. Frazier, *Coal Country*, ONEARTH, Spring 2003, *available at* http://www.nrdc.org/onearth/ 03spr/coal1.asp (last visited Oct. 28, 2008). Three and a half decades after the Buffalo Creek disaster, serious questions continue to be raised about impoundments' physical integrity in the near and long terms.

111. *Id.*

112. *See generally* P. McGinley, *The Surface Mining Control And Reclamation Act of 1977: New Era of Federal-State Cooperation or Prologue to Future Controversy?*, in EASTERN MINERAL LAW FOUNDATION INSTITUTE 16, Chapter 11 (1997) (with E. Green, L. Price, D. Michael Miller and G. M. McCarthy). A primary author of

Over the past twenty years, coal mining has disturbed almost two million acres of land; only half of that has been reclaimed even to minimum standards. More than 264,000 acres of cropland, 135,000 acres of pasture, and 127,800 acres of forest have been lost. In a 1977 report, Congress estimated the cost of rehabilitating these ravaged lands at nearly $10 billion.... more than 11,000 miles of streams have been polluted by sediment or acid from surface and underground mining combined. Some 29,000 acres of reservoirs and impoundments have been seriously damaged by strip mining. Strip mining has created at least 3000 miles of landslides and left some 34,500 miles of highwalls. [By 1977] two-thirds of the land that had been mined for coal had been left unreclaimed.[113]

3. New Technologies and Mining Methods Create New Environmental Hazards

Coal mining technology took a spectacular leap forward in the decades after the 1977 enactment of the SMCRA.[114] Like the post World War II technology burst, new equipment and technology facilitated a quantum leap forward in worker efficiency and coal production capacity. As in the earlier post-war technology revolution, the number of coal miners again dropped precipitously.[115] With new surface mining and underground mining technologies and equipment came the potential for new and often more extensive environmental damage than that caused by older mining methods.

Increased coal mine productivity coincided in the late 1970's with an oil shortage orchestrated by a Middle-Eastern oil cartel. Electricity generating power plants switched from burning oil to coal with an unintended byproduct—"acid rain." Acid rain was caused primarily by emissions from high-sulfur coal burning electricity-generating plants in the Ohio River Basin, extending from Missouri east to West Virginia and south to Georgia.[116] Scientists confirmed what hunters and anglers were reporting. Vast forested regions of the Northeastern United States as well as lakes and streams were feeling serious adverse impacts of "acid precipitation" or "acid rain."[117]

SMCRA, Congressman Morris K. Udall (D-Ariz.) observed: "[The] Act was passed after years of struggle by people in the coal fields—people who have lived with the mutilated mountainsides, spoiled streams, landslides and destruction of their homes. The voices of those people were heard on that August day [when SMCRA was enacted]." Morris K. Udall, *Foreword* to M. SQUILLACE, THE STRIP MINING HANDBOOK: A COALFIELD CITIZENS' GUIDE TO FIGHT BACK AGAINST THE RAVAGES OF STRIP MINING AND UNDERGROUND MINING 1 (Environmental Policy Institute & Friends of the Earth 1990) [hereinafter Coalfield Citizens' Guide].

Recently, the National Research Council confirmed that "[a]dverse safety and environmental impacts of coal mining—*even with regulation*—are well documented and include mine drainage, mine fires, waste piles, ground movements (subsidence), and hydrological impacts." JAMES T. BARTIS *et al.*, PRODUCING LIQUID FUELS FROM COAL: PROSPECTS AND POLICY ISSUES 78 (Rand Corporation 2008) (citing NATIONAL RESEARCH COUNCIL, COAL: RESEARCH AND DEVELOPMENT TO SUPPORT NATIONAL ENERGY POLICY (2007)).

113. COALFIELD CITIZENS' GUIDE, *supra* note 112, at 10–11 (1990). Squillace lamented: "Grossly underregulated coal mining in the 1960's and 1970's spawned one of the greatest abuses of the environment in the history of the United States. The statistics of strip mine abuse numb the mind and overwhelm the spirit."

114. *See* Udall, *supra* note 112, at 1 ("Overall [SMCRA] has produced a vast improvement in mining methods and reclamation compliance in much of the coalfields. Nevertheless, in some regions—too often the very regions which compelled the passage of the law—abuses continue at an alarming rate."). Notwithstanding improvements in mining and enforcement, SMCRA has not proven a panacea. SMCRA's strict regulatory regime has been muted by a combination of forces including industry lobbyists, state politicians inured to industry positions for political reasons, and government regulators who have been cowed by external pressures.

115. For example, in West Virginia, 55,256 coal miners were employed in 1975. By 2007 the number of working miners dropped by almost two thirds to 19,175. In contrast, coal production increased by more than fifty percent during 1975–2007—from 109,048, 898 to 160,043,930 tons.

116. The high-sulfur coal was produced in Northern Appalachia and the Mid-West coalfields of Ohio, Illinois and Indiana.

117. Acid precipitation occurs when sulfur dioxide and nitrogen oxides from coal-fired power plants and other sources of carbon fuel combustion react in the upper atmosphere with water, oxygen, and other chemicals to form sulfuric acid and nitric acid. The resulting acid-laced rain and snowfall damages forests and acidification of lakes limits their ability to support fish and other aquatic life. Acid precipitation damage has been

As in the more recent climate change debate, late 1970s governmental inaction on acid rain became a significant environmental and political issue. The issue pitted Mid-Western and Northern Appalachian high-sulfur coal producing states against conservationists and the downwind northeastern states whose forests and streams were suffering damage.[118] And, as with climate change controversy, scientific findings were ignored or minimized by Big Coal and its political allies.[119] The acrimonious debate lasted for more than a decade until a Congressional stalemate was finally overcome by the enactment of Title IV of the Clean Air Act Amendments of 1990, which included an Acid Rain Program to address both sulfur dioxide ("SO_2") and nitrogen oxide ("NO_X") emissions from coal-fired power plants.[120]

Underground, "longwall mines" cut vast swaths under the earth—often 1000 feet wide and a mile or more long—through thick coal seams.[121] Only a fraction of the miners required for continuous miner operations are employed in longwall mining.[122] On the surface, strip miners using high explosives blasted apart mountain ridge tops in Kentucky, West Virginia and Virginia.[123] The blasts, part of the new extraordinarily large-scale "mountaintop removal" mining method, allow coal to be scooped from the broken mountaintops by twenty story tall "draglines."[124] Dragline booms may extend 300 feet or more and their buckets are big enough to hold five Jeep Cherokees or more at a time.[125] An enormous amount of rock and debris—the remains of what

---

most experienced in the northeastern United States and Canada where the forests and lakes are lightly buffered and thus more sensitive to acidic deposition. Byron Swift, *How Environmental Laws Work: An Analysis Of The Utility Sector's Response To Regulation Of Nitrogen Oxides And Sulfur Dioxide Under The Clean Air Act*, 14 TUL. ENVTL. L.J. 309, 314 (2001), citing JAMES L. REGENS & ROBERT RYCROFT, THE ACID RAIN CONTROVERSY 35–58 (Un. Pittsburgh Press 1989); NATIONAL ACID PRECIPITATION ASSESSMENT PROGRAM, 1990 INTEGRATED ASSESSMENT REPORT (1991); Richard L. Revesz, *Federalism and Interstate Environmental Externalities*, 144 U. PA. L. REV. 2341, 2351–52 (1996).

118. *Id.*, citing BRUCE A. ACKERMAN & WILLIAM T. HASSLER, CLEAN COAL AND DIRTY AIR: OR HOW THE CLEAN AIR ACT BECAME A MULTIBILLION-DOLLAR BAILOUT FOR HIGH-SULFUR COAL PRODUCERS (Yale Un. Press 1981); RICHARD COHEN, WASHINGTON AT WORK, BACK ROOMS AND CLEAN AIR 152–66 (Longman 1990).

119. Swift, *supra* note 117, at 315.

120. Clean Air Act Amendments of 1990, Pub. L. No. 101-549, 104 Stat. 2399 (1990) (codified at 42 U.S.C. §§ 7401–7700 (1994)).

121. Longwall and other methods of underground mining release 13% of the methane gas emitted annually by industrial sources into the earth's atmosphere. See REDUCING COAL SUBSIDIES, *supra* note 40, citing WORLD RESOURCES REPORT 1996–1997 328, *available at* http://pdf.wri.org/worldresources1996-97_bw.pdf (last visited Nov. 22, 2008).

122. For a brief explanation of longwall mining technology see McGinley, *supra* note 40, at 55–56 n. 179, 180. *See also* BARLOW BURKE, JR. *et al.*, MINERAL LAW: CASES AND MATERIALS 316 (Anderson Pub. Co. 1994) [hereinafter BURKE]. Longwall mining removes huge chunks of a coal seam that lies horizontally hundreds of feet beneath the earth's surface. BURKE at 316. A huge longwall shear cuts coal from the seam. *Id.* The longwall equipment is protected by hydraulic roof jacks ("roof supports") that also shield the miners operating the longwalling machine. *Id.* The roof supports move forward as the shears cut into the coal. *Id.* As the supports move forward, the strata they support cave in causing overlying rock to subside. *Id.* at 316–17. Longwall mining under rural coalfield communities has caused widespread significant subsidence damage to homes and other structures. Similarly longwall subsidence has triggered pervasive loss or contamination of rural domestic well and spring water supplies. *See id.* ("After the subsidence, water supplies may be affected....").

123. *See, e.g.*, McGinley, *supra* note 40, at 54–57.

124. Abramson, *supra* note 84 ("[t]he efficiency of [Appalachia's] most productive mines pales beside that of mines in the West."). Strip mining operations use draglines that take 200 cubic yard bites and dump coal or rock into 400-ton trucks. *Id.*

125. *See* Ken Ward Jr., *Strip-Mining Battle Resurfaces in State*, SUNDAY GAZETTE-MAIL (Charleston, W. Va.), Mar. 22, 1998, at 1A [hereinafter *Strip-Mining Battle Resurfaces*], *available at* 1998 WL 5940942 (the "valley fills" contain huge amount of waste rock, "enough ... to fill 1.1 million railroad cars, a train that would stretch from Charleston [W. Va.] to Myrtle Beach, S.C., and back a dozen times."). *See also* Ken Ward Jr., *Industry, Critics Look for Mountaintop Removal Alternative: Is There Another Way?*, SUNDAY GAZETTE-MAIL

were high mountain ridges—are shoved into valleys burying headwater streams creating "valley fills."[126]

In reflecting on the impacts of MTR mining one commentator observed:

> Trucks and power shovels have grown to gargantuan sizes.... Mountaintop mines that reduce ridges and peaks by hundreds of feet now sprawl across more than 2,000 acres. An estimated 400 square miles of southern West Virginia mountains and ridges have been leveled and 1,000 miles of streams buried.... The move to the use of large-scale mountaintop removal operations would make mining in Appalachia more efficient, productive, and—most importantly for coal operators—much less labor-intensive. Mechanization and concomitant massive job losses attendant stripping operators' embrace of mountaintop removal were paralleled by the underground operators' adoption of new deep mining technology.[127]

In 1979, 58,565 miners produced 112.3 million tons of coal in West Virginia; two decades later 15,000 miners produced almost 170 million tons.[128]

In 1999, a federal district court judge presiding over a challenge to state agency permitting of mountaintop removal ("MTR") operations in West Virginia flew over all of the MTR mines. The flight

> .... revealed the extent and permanence of environmental degradation this type of mining produces.... the ground was covered with light snow, and mined sites were visible from miles away. The sites stood out among the natural wooded ridges as huge white plateaus, and the valley fills appeared as massive, artificially landscaped stair steps. Some mine sites were twenty years old, yet tree growth was stunted or non-existent. Compared to the thick hardwoods of surrounding undisturbed hills, the mine sites appeared stark and barren and enormously different from the original topography.[129]

Chief Judge Haden continued:

> If the forest canopy ... is leveled, exposing the stream to extreme temperatures, and aquatic life is destroyed, these harms cannot be undone. If the forest wildlife are (sic) driven away by the blasting, the noise, and the lack of safe nesting and eating areas, they cannot be coaxed back. If the mountaintop is removed, even [coal company] engineers will affirm that it cannot be reclaimed to its exact original contour. Destruction of the unique topography of southern West Virginia, and of Pigeonroost Hollow in particular, cannot be regarded as anything but permanent and irreversible.[130]

The newest generation of technology and mining methods has also magnified the scale of coal waste impoundments which are bigger than ever and continue to pose threats to downstream communities. More than three decades after the 1972 Buffalo Creek disaster, an even larger coal waste lake in Eastern Kentucky gave way allowing 306 million gallons of watery sludge to reach a

---

(Charleston, W. Va.), June 6, 1999, at 1A *available at* 1999 WL 6730006 ("By the end of the 1990s, mountaintop removal mines used 240-ton trucks. Valley fills sometimes measured 100 million cubic yards or more.").

126. *See* Bragg v. Robertson, 72 F. Supp. 2d 642, 646 (S.D.W. Va. 1999) (describing mountaintop removal and the creation of valley fills), *rev'd sub nom.* Bragg v. W. Va. Coal Ass'n, 248 F.3d 275 (4th Cir. 2001). *See also Strip-Mining Battle Resurfaces, supra* note 125.

127. Abramson, *supra* note 84, at 74.

128. Abramson, *supra* note 84, at 74.

129. *Id.*

130. 54 F. Supp. 2d 635, 646 (S.D. W.Va. 1999) (Haden, J., granting preliminary injunction).

nearby stream.[131] The waste travelled more than one hundred miles downstream from Kentucky into West Virginia, burying and destroying stream life.[132] In 2008 a Tennessee Valley Authority coal-fired power plant impoundment containing liquid fly ash waste from coal combustion broke through a dam wall allowing 525 million gallons of ash sludge containing unknown amounts of mercury, arsenic and lead, to escape damaging a dozen homes and flowing into a tributary of the Tennessee River.[133]

As related above, the externalized environment and associated socio-economic costs of coal mining and burning have been incalculable. Much of the harm of the past, however, can be prevented by responsible mining practices and strict government enforcement of the SMCRA, the Clean Water Act and the Clean Air Act. With the exception of untested CO_2 capture and sequestration, technology is available to allow coal to be mined and burned at a profit with limited environmental and related impacts. However, the history of lax enforcement and regulatory politicization under those laws does not engender confidence that coal's environmental externalities will be effectively minimized as Congress intended.[134]

C. Miner Safety and Public Health Impacts of Coal

1. A Century-Long Trail of Workplace Injuries and Deaths

Early on the morning of January 2, 2006, almost a century after the single worst industrial accident occurred in United States history in Monongah, West Virginia, an explosion ripped

---

131. To provide scale, in contrast, the *Exxon Valdez* oil tanker spill of twenty years ago, often called one of the worst environmental disasters in U.S. history, involved 11 million gallons of crude.

132. The impoundment collapse occurred on October 11, 2000. *See* U.S. Dep't of Labor, MINE SAFETY AND HEALTH ADMINISTRATION, INTERNAL REVIEW OF MSHA's ACTIONS AT THE BIG BRANCH REFUSE IMPOUNDMENT, MARTIN COUNTY COAL CORPORATION, Inez, Martin County, Kentucky (2003), http://www.msha.gov/MEDIA/PRESS/2003/Report20030113.pdf (last visited Nov. 1, 2008). *See also* KY. ENVNTL. QUALITY COMM., MARTIN COUNTY COAL SLURRY SPILL: THREE YEARS LATER, http://www.eqc.ky.gov/NR/rdonlyres/78642226-A465-4EDC-9D2C-8F673DCECC84/0/coalslurrytour.pdf (last visited Nov. 1, 2008). Kentucky officials reported that twenty miles of streams and floodplains were buried in 8 feet of slurry. The sludge contaminated water supplies of riverside communities in Kentucky and West Virginia with measurable amounts of heavy metals including arsenic, mercury, lead, cadmium, copper, and chromium. Four municipal drinking water intakes were shut down. All aquatic life was eliminated in Wolf and Coldwater creeks and severely damaged in approximately 70 miles of streams. The cleanup cost was estimated to be at least $58 million. *Id.*

133. Anne Paine and Colby Sledge, *Flood of sludge breaks TVA dike: Collapse poses risk of toxic ash*, THE TENNESSEAN A1 (December 23, 2008), *available at* http://www.tennessean.com/article/20081223/ GREEN02/8 12230370 (last visited Dec. 23, 2008) (THE TENNESSEAN reported that "[m]illions of yards of ashy sludge broke through a dike at TVA's Kingston coal-fired plant Monday, covering hundreds of acres ... [a]bout 2.6 million cubic yards of slurry—enough to fill 798 Olympic-size swimming pools"). Environmental organizations have been lobbying for more regulation of power plant production ash. *See, e.g.,* http://www.environ mentalintegrity.org/news_reports.php (last visited Aug. 30, 2010).

134. Pervasive laxness in enforcement of the SMCRA in some coal producing states is well documented. In W. Va. Highlands Conservancy v. Norton, the Court stated that:

a climate of lawlessness [exists], which creates a pervasive impression that continued disregard for federal law and statutory requirements goes unpunished, or possibly unnoticed. Agency warnings have no more effect than a wink and a nod, a deadline is just an arbitrary date on the calendar and, once passed, not to be mentioned again. Financial benefits accrue to the owners and operators who were not required to incur the statutory burden and costs attendant to surface mining; political benefits accrue to the state executive and legislators who escape accountability while the mining industry gets a free pass. Why should the state actors do otherwise when the federal regulatory enforcers' findings, requirements, and warnings remain toothless and without effect?

161 F. Supp. 2d 676, 684 (S.D. W.Va. 2002) (Commenting on two decades-long failure of federal and state regulators to enforce reclamation bonding requirements of the SMCRA).

through the depths of a coal mine in rural north-central West Virginia.[135] For forty hours an international television audience watched with growing trepidation as coal company officials and government regulators periodically reported on efforts to rescue 13 coal miners trapped deep in the Sago mine.[136] During around-the-clock cable news coverage of the rescue efforts, network talking heads and mining experts discussed whether the men could continue to survive in a mine that had filled with poisonous gasses liberated by the explosion.[137]

Ultimately, the truth was revealed as morning dawned on the third day after the explosion: one miner had died at the time of the blast and 11 others died hours later of asphyxiation when thick toxic fumes overwhelmed them as they lay barricaded deep in the mine. One miner, although overcome by fumes, was found lying among his comrades, unconscious, but alive. The Sago tragedy was neither unique nor was it the worst of our nation's coal mine disasters. It ranks as but one of more than 600 mine disasters that have visited American coal mining communities over the last century.[138]

For those familiar with coalfield history, Sago joins a long list of names synonymous with death, injury, shattered families and devastated communities stretching back to the 1800's.[139]

Over the course of a century, more than one hundred thousand coalminers died from mine roof falls, cave-ins, fires, explosions and other causes in American coal mines. Several million miners suffered injuries, many of them serious and disabling.[140] The deadliest year in the nation's

---

135. The December 6, 1907, explosion at a coal mine in Monongah, West Virginia, is thought to have killed over 500 miners. Almost a century later, the Sago Mine disaster occurred a scant seventy miles from Monongah.

136. For general information regarding the Sago mine explosion see: http://www.msha.gov/sagomine/sagomine.asp.

137. *See* Transcript of CNN News, http://transcripts.cnn.com/TRANSCRIPTS/0601/04/acd.02.html (last visited Nov 1, 2008). For a discussion of media coverage of the events at the Sago Mine, see, *e.g.*, James Dao, Maria Newman, *False Report of 12 Survivors Was Result of Miscommunications*, N.Y. TIMES (January 4, 2006), *available at* http://www.nytimes.com/2006/01/04/national/04cnd-mine.html (last visited Nov. 3, 2008).

138. Regulators and historians arbitrarily define a mine "disaster" as an incident involving at least five deaths. *See* Centers for Disease Control, Coal Mining Disasters (1839–2007), *available at* http://www.cdc.gov/niosh/mining/statistics/discoal.htm (accessed Aug. 3, 2008).

139. Among the disasters that gained the most public notoriety were: Monongah (500), Stag Canyon No. 9 (263), Cherry Mine (259), Mather (195), Centralia (111), Pond Creek No. 1 (91), Farmington (78), Willow Grove (72), Scotia (26), Finley Coal Nos. 15 & 16 (38), Wilberg (27), Jim Walter Resources No. 5 (13), Dutch Creek No. 1 (15), Grundy Mining No. 21 (13), Robena No. 3 (37) and Blacksville No. 1 (9) (The numbers in the parentheticals represent the number of deaths reported).

140. 605 mine disasters have occurred in American coal mines since 1876 (defined as accidents in which five or more workers were killed). United States Department of Labor, Mine Safety and Health Administration Fact Sheet. (hereinafter MSHA Fact Sheet), *available at* http://www.msha.gov/MSHAINFO/FactSheets/MSHAFCT8.HTM. The MSHA website documents the history of the carnage in America's coal and other mines from 1936 through 2007:

Fatalities and Injuries for All Mining (Coal & Noncoal)

Years	Average Annual & Total Deaths for Period	Average Annual Injuries	Total Injuries During Period
1936–1940	1,546 / 7730	81,342	406,710
1941–1945	1592 / 7960	82,825	415,125
1946–1950	1,054 / 5270	63,367	316,835
1951–1955	690 / 3450	38,510	192,550
1956–1960	550 / 2750	28,805	144,025
1961–1965	449 / 2245	23,204	116,020
1966–1970	426 / 2130	22,435	112,175
1971–1975	322 / 1610	33,963	169,815
1976–1980	254 / 1270	41,220	206,100
1981–1985	174 / 870	24,290	121,450
1986–1990	122 / 610	27,524	137,620
1991–1995	99 / 495	24,201	121,005

coal mining history was 1907, when 3,242 deaths were recorded.[141] Coal mine deaths then declined from 1910 to the present.

In the aftermath of the tragic events at Sago, as every other coal mine disaster, familiar pledges were made. Indeed, time after time for a century coal mine operators, government regulators and union leaders have asserted that they have "learned from" these disasters. They have also made commitments that similar events would "never happen again" and have solemnly vowed that miners have not "died in vain."

Time after time, these pledges have rung hollow as coal miners, their families and coalfield communities suffered from death and injuries in the nation's mines. Following the deaths of 111 miners at the Centralia Illinois mine in 1947, legendary United Mine Workers Union President John L. Lewis captured the sense of *déjà vu* accompanying death and loss in America's coal field communities:

> There is public sorrow at the moment, but we know from harsh experience that it is only a momentary feeling of pity on the part of the public, and this sacrifice, like others before, will soon be forgotten. Shortly after the mine workers bury their dead, the feeling of sorrow will remain only in the breasts of the loved ones who survived: and the mine workers can look forward to the next catastrophe.[142]

History documents a demonstrable mine disaster leading to new laws cause and effect cycle. In this repeating cycle, a coal mine disaster is followed by strengthening of mine safety laws and enforcement, a lax enforcement phase that includes industry resistance to regulation followed by another mine disaster, and so on. The causal connection between mine disasters involving multiple fatalities and enactment of mine safety laws should, however, not lead one to ignore the *far greater number of injuries and loss of lives suffered in isolated accidents* involving only one or two individuals.[143]

2. Mine Safety In The Twenty-First Century

The cycle continues today although a century has passed between the 1906 Monongah and the 2006 Sago explosions. Following Sago, miners died needlessly in Massey Energy's Aracoma Mine in southern West Virginia and the Darby Mine in eastern Kentucky in 2006. A year later in late summer of 2007, at a mine at Crandall Canyon, Colorado, another drama unfolded before an international television audience and ended, like Sago, in unnecessary death and

---

1996–2000	86 / 430	17,500	87,500
2001–2005	62 / 310	12,952	64,625
2006–2007	69 / 138	11,800	23,600
	Total: 37,268		**Total: 2,803,970**

See U.S. Mine Safety Administration, MSHA Fact Sheets, *available at* http://www.msha.gov/MSHAINFO/FactSheets/MSHAFCT2.HTM (hereinafter MSHA Fact Sheets). While these numbers include "metal and non-metal" mine statistics, the great majority reflect coal mine injuries and fatalities. It is fair to assume that for the period 1880 to 1935 for which there are not reliable statistics, far more deaths and injuries occurred than in the period from 1936 to the present.

141. *Id.*

142. *Text of Lewis Order Calling Stoppage,* THE NEW YORK TIMES (March 30, 1947), *see* http://select.ny-times.com/gst/abstract.html?res=F40E10F63B5F1A7A93C2AA1788D85F438485F9&scp=1&sq=text+of+lewis+order+calling+stoppage&st==, [hereinafter *Text of Lewis Order*] (last visited March 13, 2011). Lewis' letter to all United Mine workers members calling for a week's holiday in memorial to the victims of the Centralia mine disaster was printed in full in the *Times*.

143. *See* Ken Ward Jr., *Beyond Sago: One by One: Disasters make headlines, but most miners killed on the job die alone,* THE CHARLESTON GAZETTE (November 5, 2006), *available at* http://wvgazette.com/News/Beyond+Sago/200611050006. *See also All Mining Fatalities by State,* U.S. Dep't. of Labor Fact Sheet, http://www.msha.gov/stats/charts/allstatesnew.asp.

heartache.[144] Once again Congress passed a new law in the wake of promises of "never again."[145] It is fair to say that every significant advance in coal mine safety has been written in the blood of coal miners.[146]

Improvements in mine safety have reduced deaths and serious injuries over time. Records of the federal Mine Safety and Health Administration show that in each decade of the twentieth century the number of mining deaths and serious injuries reported have slowly declined.[147] As the chart in footnote 140 indicates, annual coal mine fatalities numbered more than 1,500 a year from the late 1930's to an average of about 450 in the 1950s, and dropped to 140 in the 1970s. By 2001–2005 the yearly average of coal miner deaths dropped to 30 per year.[148] The safest year in American coal mining history occurred in 2005 which experienced an all-time low of 23 coal mining deaths, bettering the previous record low of 28 fatalities recorded in 2002. Thirty-three miners died in 2007.[149] Even as the number of fatalities in U.S. mines dropped, MSHA loosened federal mine safety law enforcement in favor of giving "compliance assistance" to coal companies.[150] MSHA documented more than one hundred seventy thousand miner injuries from 1995–2007.[151]

---

144. *See* CNN News, http://transcripts.cnn.com/TRANSCRIPTS/0708/22/acd.02.html (last visited Nov 2, 2008). Mine Safety and Health Administration Investigation Report, Crandall Canyon Mine, *available at* http://www.msha.gov/Fatals/2007/CrandallCanyon/FTL07CrandallCanyonNoAppendix.pdf (last visited Sept. 11, 2008).

145. Mine Improvement and New Emergency Response Act of 2006 (MINER ACT), P.L. 109-236. *See also* Supplemental Mine Improvement and New Emergency Response Act of 2007 (S-MINER Act), H.R. 2768, (110th Cong., 2007–2008). The bill passed the House by a vote of 214–199, but died in the Senate due to industry and administration opposition.

146. *Text of Lewis Order, supra* note 142. "The American people must be aroused to the stark realities of the situation and the casualties of the coal industry. Coal is already saturated with the blood of too many brave men and drenched with the tears of too many surviving widows and orphans." *Id.* The irony is emphasized by J. Davitt McAteer, lawyer, scholar, and former MSHA chief:

> In 1940, mine explosions claimed 91 miners at Bartley, West Virginia; 72 miners at St. Clairsville, Ohio; and 63 miners at Portage Pennsylvania. Coal mine safety legislation was passed the next year. In 1951, 119 miners died in a West Frankfort, Illinois explosion, and 1952 brought a new law. In 1968, 78 coal miners were killed in Farmington, West Virginia. Congress acted in 1969. In 1972, 91 miners were killed at Kellogg, Idaho in a silver mine fire; and in 1976 26 miners died in back-to-back coal mine explosions in Scotia, Kentucky. The Mine [Federal Mine Safety and Health] Act was passed in 1977.

J. McAteer, *The Federal Mine Safety and Health Act of 1977: Preserving a Law that Works*, 98 W. Va. L. Rev. 1105, 1113 (1996) (bracketed words added; footnotes omitted). *See* Ken Ward Jr., *Beyond Sago: One by One: Disasters make headlines, but most miners killed on the job die alone*, The Charleston Gazette (November 5, 2006). *See also*, Mining Fatalities by State, U.S. Dep't of Labor Fact Sheet, *available at* http://www.msha.gov/stats/charts/allstatesnew.asp (last visited Sept. 11, 2008).

147. MSHA's averages are based upon measuring the numbers of miner injuries against hours worked. *See* MSHA Facts, *supra* note 140 (last visited Sept. 10, 2008).

148. *Id.* According to the MSHA website data, the coal miner death rate decreased from about .20 fatalities per 200,000 hours worked by miners (or one death per million production hours) in 1970 to about .07 fatalities in 1977 and dropped still lower to an average of .03 fatalities for the 2001–2005 period. *Id.*

149. *Id.*

150. Christopher W. Shaw, Undermining Safety: A Report on Coal Mine Safety 24 (Center for The Study of Responsive Law, 2008), *available at* http://www.csrl.org/reports/UnderminingSafety.pdf (last visited April 16, 2009). *See generally* Democratic Staff, Committee on Education and the Workforce, House of Representatives, Review of Federal Mine Safety and Health Administration's Performance from 2001 to 2005 Reveals Consistent Abdication of Regulatory and Enforcement Responsibilities, (109th Congress, 2nd Sess., January 31, 2006), *available at* http://edlabor.house.gov/publications/minesafetyreport.pdf (last visited Dec. 10, 2008).

151. MSHA Fact Sheets, *supra* note 140.

Clearly, efforts to protect coal miners' health and safety have not stood still since the 500 or more lives were lost in the Monongah explosion in 1907.[152] Regulation, Union persistence and more responsible coal mining management have now greatly reduced the number of miners killed and maimed in American mines. It is fair to say that extraordinary progress has been made over time in advancing mine safety and reducing coal miner deaths and injuries.

Nevertheless, preventable deaths and injuries continue to externalize the costs of coal mining and burning at an unacceptable rate. That tragic deaths in mine disasters are the primary, indeed the only, impetus for stimulating politicians to enact legislation to protect miners lives and health speaks volumes about the coal industry and the governments that regulate it. The American public is ignorant of the significant externalized costs of coal.

D. Coal's Externalized Health-Related Costs: Black Lung Disease

While a century of coal mine accidents and disasters have claimed thousands of lives and injured more than two million miners, a more insidious and obscure health hazard has caused many more deaths and disabilities. Medically known as coal workers' pneumoconiosis, "black lung" disease is the common name for any lung disease developing from inhaling coal dust. The term "black lung" relates to the lungs of diseased victims whose lungs appear black instead of pink.[153] The inhalation and accumulation of coal dust into the lungs increases the risk of developing emphysema and chronic bronchitis.[154] Coal dust can also increase the risk of developing chronic obstructive pulmonary disease or "COPD."[155] Black lung is a respiratory disease that develops over a fairly long period of exposure.[156]

Black lung disease was first identified in the mid-Nineteenth Century by doctors treating British coal miners.[157] For many years, the disease was called "miner's asthma" or "miner's consumption" and medically labeled "anthracosis."[158] Miners' symptoms include progressive dyspnea, chest discomfort, and cough, sometimes dramatically accompanied by the expectoration of copious quantities of black, inky sputum.[159] Black lung can be very debilitating and often fatal. In the early days of coal mining, men and boys worked for a pittance in extraordinarily dusty places in mines where the process of contracting black lung would often begin. Throughout the history of coal mining, miners have been exposed to and have contracted black lung disease.

---

152. *See* J. DAVITT MCATEER, MONONGAH (W.Va. Un. Press 2007).

153. There are two forms of black lung: simple, which is known as coal workers' pneumoconiosis ("CWP"), and complicated, which is known as progressive massive fibrosis (PMF). The disease develops over a fairly long period of exposure to inhaled coal dust and can be very debilitating or even fatal.

154. *See, e.g.*, WebMD, Black Lung Disease, *available at* http://www.webmd.com/a-to-z-guides/black-lung-disease-topic-overview (last visited Sept. 15, 2008).

155. *Id.*

156. Facing South, Institute for Southern Studies, *As Black Lung Rises Among Appalachian Coal Miners, Industry and Regulators Block Action*, *available at* http://southernstudies.org/2008/09/as-black-lung-rises-among-appalachian.html (last visited April 16, 2009).

157. *See* ALAN DERICKSON, BLACK LUNG: ANATOMY OF A PUBLIC HEALTH DISASTER 6 (Cornell Un. Press 1998) [hereinafter BLACK LUNG]. Black lung was not officially recognized as a compensable occupational disease in Great Britain until 1937. *See* BARBARA ELLEN SMITH, DIGGING OUR OWN GRAVES: COAL MINERS AND THE STRUGGLE OVER BLACK LUNG DISEASE 4 (Temple Un. Press 1987).

158. *See* FREDERIC GOMES CASSIDY, JOAN HOUSTON HALL, 3 DICTIONARY OF AMERICAN REGIONAL ENGLISH 607 (Belknap Press 1996), *available at*: http://books.google.com/books?id=eEB0YFR2EowC&pg=PA607&lpg=PA607&dq=%22miner's+asthma%22++%22miner's+consumption%22&source=bl&ots=S7NGQy9u88&sig=UeiFWYW2BKdW_C0Ym_7FkzWpJD4&hl=en&sa=X&oi=book_result&resnum=2&ct=result (last visited Dec. 1, 2008).

159. Greg Wagner, Book Review, *Black Lung: Anatomy of a Public Health Disaster*, 340 NEW ENGLAND J. OF MEDICINE 1770 (June 3, 1999).

Even today, modern coal mining technologies continue to expose miners to black lung disease, notwithstanding a federal regulatory regime intended to minimize such exposure.

It would surprise most Americans to learn that black lung disease has claimed "far more lives than do catastrophic cave-ins and explosions."[160] "Perhaps even worse ... black lung "condemn[s] thousands of miners to live out their days crippled by the devastating effects of progressive, chronic lung disease."[161] The statistics of black lung's costs are staggering. While 104,659 miners died in coal mine accidents from 1900 to 2005,[162] four times more miner deaths during the same period are attributable to black lung.[163] By 1969, at least 365,000 miners died of black lung disease; another 120,000 miners died between 1969 and 2000.[164]

For a century in the United States, coal industry and governments generally refused to recognize the existence of the disease.[165] Bizarrely, some coal industry officials, politicians and even medical doctors claimed that inhalation of coal dust posed no health threat.[166] A noted public health historian has observed that "it is clear in retrospect that denial of the dangers of mine dust shortened the lives of hundreds of thousands of anthracite and bituminous coal miners."[167]

It was not until a huge public outcry resulting from the 1968 Farmington, West Virginia mine disaster and a grassroots uprising of coal miners' widows forced a reluctant Congress and President to address the disease and its cause. The Federal Coal Mine Safety and Health Act of 1969 included limits on miners' workplace exposure to black lung-causing ambient coal dust.[168]

---

160. David C. Vladeck, *The Failed promise of Workplace Health Regulation*, 111 W. Va. L. Rev. 15, 19 (2008) [hereinafter *Failed promise*], citing an April, 1998, Louisville Courier Journal series focusing on the devastating impact of black lung disease on miners and their families. The series is *available at* http://www.courier-journal.com/cjextra/dust/ (last visited Nov. 2. 2008). Articles in the series focusing on the victims of black lung can be found at http://www.courier-journal.com/cjextra/blacklung/index.html (last visited Nov. 2, 2008).

161. *Id.*

162. *Id.*, citing MSHA, Coal Fatalities for 1900 through 2007, http://www.msha.gov/stats/centurystats/coalstats.asp (last visited Nov. 2, 2008).

163. *Id.*, citing MSHA, Coal Fatalities for 1900 through 2007, http://www.msha.gov/stats/centurystats/coalstats.asp (last visited Nov. 2, 2008).

164. *See* Christopher W. Shaw, Undermining Safety: A Report on Coal Mine Safety 7–8, Center for the Study of Responsive Law, *available at* http:// www.csrl.org/reports/UnderminingSafety.pdf (last visited Nov. 2, 2008).

165. Brian C. Murchison, *Due Process, Black Lung, And The Shaping Of Administrative Justice*, 54 Admin. L. Rev. 1025, 1038–1048 (2002).

166. *Id.* at 1040. Murchison explains:

> By 1930, the "denial of coal workers' respiratory difficulties had triumphed in the United States," due to a host of factors that historians are still trying to understand. One factor was the stance of company physicians that inhaling coal mine dusts was harmless because the body was naturally equipped to expectorate "deposits of carbon" and thus purify itself. Another claim was that inhaling carbonaceous dusts was in fact *beneficial* to miners' health because it caused fibrotic formations which supposedly prevented tubercular bacilli "from getting a foothold" in the lungs. A third industry position was that the only real danger posed by either anthracite or bituminous mining was inhalation of "silicious dusts associated with sandstone, slate, and other minerals that occurred with coal deposits." According to industry doctors, miners with dust-induced lung disease must have inhaled dust containing rock dust, since inhaling particles of coal "posed no hazard at all." This effort to equate all mine dust disease with silicosis became the conventional wisdom; the only conceded effect of inhaling coal particles without significant silica was anthracosis, which coal interests insisted was not a disease but a discoloration of the lung.

Id. at 1040–1041 (citations omitted).

167. Black Lung, *supra* note 157, at xii.

168. Federal Mine Safety and Health Act of 1977, Pub. L. No. 91-173, 83 Stat. 760 (respirable dust standard codified at 30 U.S.C. §842(b)(2) (2000) ("each [mine] operator shall continuously maintain the average concentration of respirable dust in the mine atmosphere during each shift to which each miner in the active

One widow put the impact of black lung disease in perspective:

> My father was killed by black lung. I lost four brothers to black lung. My first husband had black lung when he died, and my second husband died of black lung ... women and children live in the coal fields, too, and they breathe coal dust just like the men do, and they end up with asthma.[169]

The 1969 legislation, however, did not end the nightmare experienced by black lung riddled coal miners and their families. For almost four decades coal operators and their lawyers have continued to challenge miners' and widows' black lung claims in a tortuous U.S. Department of Labor administrative adjudicatory system.[170] A law professor who directs a black lung clinic representing coal miners in black lung administrative cases described the agency's scandalous black lung claims system in testimony before a Congressional subcommittee:

> I have argued cases before the United States Supreme Court as well as the Supreme Courts of several states. I have also represented people before Justices of the Peace and Small Claims Courts. And I can say without hesitation that the most unfair process I have ever run into is that which I found in the Federal black lung system. It defies due process of law, it defies reason and it is just simply unreasonable.[171]

It is true that government mandated dust mitigation measures have resulted in a significant decline in black lung fatalities since 1970.[172] However, while the incidence of black lung disease among miners dropped substantially from the tragic numbers inflicted before government regulation, "the numbers are on the rise again."[173] Recent government statistics showed that coal

---

workings of such mine is exposed at or below 2.0 milligrams of respirable dust per cubic meter of air.") Federal Law also requires miners and their widows/families to receive compensatory benefits if it can be proven that a miner contracted the disease while working in coal mines. Black Lung Benefits Act ("BLBA"), 83 Stat. 792, as amended, 30 U.S.C. § 901 *et seq.*

169. W. Davis, *Out Of The Black Hole: Reclaiming The Crown Of King Coal*, 51 Am. U. L. Rev. 905, 952 (2002), citing Randall Norris & Jean-Phillipe Cypres, Women of Coal (Un. Press of Ky. 1996); Carol A.B. Giesen, Coal Miner's Wives: Portraits of Endurance 56 (Un. Press of Ky. 1995).

170. *See generally* Brian C. Murchison, *Due Process, Black Lung, And The Shaping Of Administrative Justice*, 54 Admin. L. Rev. 1025 (2002), *citing, inter alia*, Ron Nixon, *Benefits Claims Process is as Slow, Painful as the Disease, Miners Say*, Roanoake Times & World News, Nov. 24, 2000 at A13 (reporting anger of black lung claimants at slowness of the process and lack of finality); Ron Nixon, *A Coalfield Legacy: Black Lung—As Court Battles for Disability Benefits Drag On, Miners Slowly Suffocate*, Roanoake Times & World News, Nov. 24, 2000 at A1 (reporting black lung claims can last for decades); Ron Nixon, *Lawyers Are Few and Far Between for Black Lung Plaintiffs*, Roanoake Times & World News, Nov. 25, 2000 at A9 (reporting fee restrictions are a disincentive to claimants' attorneys). Murchison recites the history of one shocking convoluted case, typical of numerous others, in which a coal miner suffering serious disability from black lung fought a circuitous route through hearing after hearing for more than a decade seeking benefits to which he was clearly entitled.

171. *Id.* at 1032.

172. M.D. Attfield, J. M. Wood, V.C. Antao, G.A. Pinheiro, Changing Patterns of Pneumoconiosis 627–32 (2004) (U.S. Center for Disease Control, Morbidity and Mortality Mortality Weekly Report July 23, 2004), *available at* http://www.cdc.gov/MMWR/preview/mmwrhtml/mm5328a1.htm (last visited Nov. 15, 2008).

173. Joby Warrick, *Into the Darkness*, Washington Post Magazine, January 21, 2007, http://www.washingtonpost.com/wp-dyn/content/article/2007/01/16/AR2007011601066.html?nav=emailpage (last visited Nov. 3. 2008). *See also Failed promise, supra* note 160, at 17, *citing*, MSHA, Controlling Respirable Coal Mine Dust In Underground Coal Mines: Introductory Remarks, at Slide 4, *available at* Slide 4, http:// www.msha.gov/s&hinfo/BlackLung/ControlDust2007/CTD2007.asp (last visited Sept. 8, 2008) (mortality chart showing miner deaths from black lung 1968–2004). Louisville Courier-Journal reported in 1998:

> Every year, black lung disease kills almost 1,500 people who have worked in the nation's coal mines. It's as if the Titanic sank every year, and no ships came to the rescue. While that long-ago disaster continues to fascinate the nation, the miners slip into cold, early graves almost unnoticed.

Dust, Deception and Death: Why Black Lung Has Not Been Wiped Out, Louisville Courier-Journal, at A1 (April 19, 1998), *available at* http://courier-journal.com/cjextra/dust/. The National Black Lung Association mines in the United States were logging more than six thousand violations of ambient coal dust regulations annually over a five year period.[174]

Unlike the externalized socio-economic and environmental costs of coal, it is possible to put a monetary price on coal mine operators' externalization of black lung costs. Since 1969, the federal government has administered a compensation program for victims of black lung paid in part by coal company fees.[175] In addition to the price paid by miners themselves, their families and their communities, the American people have had to bear some of the costs. As Professor Vladeck emphasizes, mine "owners have managed to cap and partially off-load their liability for black lung disease on both the companies that buy coal and the American people."[176] From 1969 through 2004 black lung benefits paid to almost one million miners have totaled more than $41 billion.[177]

The externalization of environmental harm, mine safety injuries and deaths and the socio-economic damage attendant coal mining and burning have long been obscured from public view. Coal's externalized blight of black lung disease similarly has escaped public attention notwithstanding the enormous documented financial costs of the black lung compensation program.

V. Climate Change and Coal: A Burning Question

A. Coal's Market Share in The New Energy Future

Electricity generated by burning coal fuels industrialization and improves living standards in developed and developing countries. Electricity from coal brings historically unparalleled personal comfort and convenience to peoples of developed nations and promises the same in the future for populations of poorer countries. Now, coal faces what is, for the industries and interests involved, a crisis of unprecedented proportions.

Big Coal appears to accept the conclusion of most scientists that carbon capture and storage (or "CCS") is apparently "the only viable option for making significant CO_2 emission reductions from coal-fired power."[178] Indeed, the influential Massachusetts Institute of Technology

---

similarly estimates that black lung claims the lives of 1,500 coal miners each year. *See* Press Release, Mine Safety and Health Administration, *Nation's Coal Miners Take Advantage of Labor Department's Free Chest X-Rays* (June 9, 2000) *available at* http://www.msha.gov/media/press/2000/nr000609.htm (last visited Nov. 15, 2008).

174. Ken Ward Jr., *Beyond Sago: Coal dust most common violation; Mines averaging 6,000 citations for it each year*, THE CHARLESTON GAZETTE (December 17, 2006), *available at* http://wvgazette.com/News/Beyond+Sago/200612170006 (last visited Nov. 2, 2008).

175. For a discussion of the origins of the black lung program and the system it creates, see Usery v. Turner Elkhorn Mining Co., 428 U.S. 1 (1976). *See also* Donald T. DeCarlo, *The Federal Black Lung Experience*, 26 How. L. J. 1335 (1983).

176. *Failed promise*, *supra*, note 160, at 40.

177. *Id.* at 41, *citing*, GAO, FEDERAL COMPENSATION PROGRAMS: PERSPECTIVES ON FOUR PROGRAMS FOR INDIVIDUALS INJURED BY EXPOSURE TO HARMFUL SUBSTANCES 1–8, GAO-08-628-T (Apr. 1, 2008).

178. *See* THE ecoENERGY CARBON CAPTURE AND STORAGE TASK FORCE, CANADA'S FOSSIL ENERGY FUTURE, THE WAY FORWARD ON CARBON CAPTURE AND STORAGE 8 (Rept. To the Minister of Alberta Energy & The Minister Natural Resources Canada, 2008), *available at* http://www.energy.gov.ab.ca/Org/pdfs/Fossil_energy_e.pdf (last visited Nov. 2, 2008). "Carbon sequestration" is defined as "the capture and secure storage of carbon that would otherwise be emitted to, or remain, in the atmosphere." The goal of carbon capture and sequestration ("CCS") is the removal of CO_2 directly from industrial or utility facilities and storing it in secure reservoirs. The rationale for carbon capture and storage is to facilitate use of fossil fuels thereby reducing release of CO_2 into the atmosphere and mitigating global climate change. HOWARD HERZOG, DAN GOLOMB, CARBON CAPTURE AND STORAGE FROM FOSSIL FUEL USE (2004) (Massachusetts Institute of Technology, Laboratory for Energy and the Environment) *available at* http://sequestration.mit.edu/pdf/enclyclopedia_of_energy_article.pdf (last visited Nov. 2, 2008).

report *The Future of Coal* recently concluded that "CO_2 capture and sequestration (CCS) is the critical enabling technology that would reduce CO_2 emissions significantly while also allowing coal to meet the world's pressing energy needs."[179] Moreover, the MIT report is clear that "[a]t present government and private sector programs to implement on a timely basis the required large-scale integrated demonstrations to confirm the suitability of carbon sequestration are completely inadequate."[180]

Further, a report of The Union of Concerned Scientists emphasizes that while CCS is still an emerging technology "it has the potential to substantially reduce CO_2 emissions from coal plants."[181] However, the Union contends, for CCS to play a major role in reducing CO_2 emissions "an enormous new infrastructure must be constructed to capture, process, and transport large quantities of CO_2."[182]

In addition, although CCS has been the subject of considerable research and analysis, it has yet to be demonstrated in the form of commercial-scale, fully integrated projects at coal-fired power plants.[183] No existing or proposed CCS pilot project sequesters more than 1.5 million tons of CO_2 annually.[184] In fact, to make CCS technology practical, it would have to capture and transport immense amounts of the gas to a storage site.

Just one 600 megawatt supercritical coal plant emits approximately four million metric tons of CO_2 per year,[185] and the U.S. produces about 1.5 billion tons of CO_2 annually from power plants that burn coal.[186] MIT scientists relate that "if all of this CO_2 is transported for sequestration, the quantity is equivalent to three times the weight and, under typical operating conditions, one-third of the annual volume of natural gas transported by the U.S. gas pipeline system."[187] "If 60% of the CO_2 produced from U.S. coal-based power generation were to be captured and compressed to a liquid for geologic sequestration," the MIT analysis indicates, "its volume would about equal the total U.S. oil consumption of 20 million barrels per day."[188]

Thus, for CCS to make a major contribution to long-term CO_2 emissions reductions (*i.e.*, 3.6 billion metric tons per year by 2050),[189] the world would need 3,600 sites each sequestering one million metric tons per year.[190] The Union of Concerned Scientists suggests that "[m]eeting the challenge of scale requires considerable research simply to identify potential sequestration sites.... [I]dentifying specific sites that can be counted on to store the CO_2 indefinitely represents a massive undertaking."[191]

---

179. THE FUTURE OF COAL, *supra* note 16, at x.

180. *Id.*, *supra* note 16, at xii.

181. BARBARA FREESE, STEVE CLEMMER, ALAN NOGEE, COAL POWER IN A WARMING WORLD: A SENSIBLE TRANSITION TO CLEANER ENERGY OPTIONS 1 (Union of Concerned Scientists' Rept., 2008), *available at* http:// www.ucsusa.org/assets/documents/clean_energy/Coal-power-in-a-warming-world.pdf (last visited Nov. 15, 2008) [hereinafter COAL POWER].

182. *Id.*

183. *Id.*

184. COAL POWER, *supra* note 181, at 53.

185. *Id.*

186. THE FUTURE OF COAL, *supra* note 16, at ix.

187. *Id.*

188. *Id.*

189. This level of CO_2 reduction represents one of seven emission reduction "wedges" necessary to stabilize global emissions, according to Pacala and Socolow. *See* S. Pacala and R. Socolow, *Stabilization wedges: Solving the climate problem for the next 50 years with current technologies*, 305 SCIENCE 968, 969–972 (August 13, 2004), *available at* http://carbonsequestration.us/Papers-presentations/htm/Pacala-Socolow-ScienceMag-Aug2004.pdf (last visited Nov. 15, 2008).

190. THE FUTURE OF COAL, *supra* note 16, at 43.

191. COAL POWER, *supra* note 181, at 53, citing INTERGOVERNMENTAL PANEL ON CLIMATE CHANGE ("IPCC"), IPCC SPECIAL REPORT ON CARBON DIOXIDE CAPTURE AND STORAGE, chapter 5 (Working Group

B. "Clean Coal"

Big Coal has embraced CCS technology as its Holy Grail—science's best hope for substantially reducing greenhouse gas emissions from coal-fired power plants.[192] Indeed, it argues that the research and development of the technology should be partially funded by tax dollars. The National Mining Association "supports the timely adoption of comprehensive federal legislation that incorporates the priorities" including "sufficient funding and incentives to accelerate the development, demonstration and broad commercial deployment of affordable advanced carbon management technologies … including CCS."[193]

Big Coal obviously faces no small undertaking as it seeks public funding for clean coal initiatives and struggles to maintain its global energy positioning. In addition to worldwide fears of climate change catastrophe, Coal's mission is further complicated by a looming national and international financial meltdown not experienced since the Great Depression. Coal must explain to a skeptical public why the largest single contributor to atmospheric greenhouse gasses should receive public funding to enable it to maintain its share of the world energy market.

The current global climate change debate presents the biggest challenge Big Coal has yet faced—and—it presents a great opportunity. How Big Coal responds to the challenge will determine its future. Big Coal must effectively make its case. The industry risks losing all credibility if it were to continue its decades-long campaign of denial of responsibility for the many externalities its mining and burning creates—including its enormous contribution to greenhouse gas emissions that feed global climate change.

There is evidence that Big Coal's leadership is internally conflicted. On one hand, many responsible leaders of Big Coal seem to agree that protecting the environment, miner health and safety and communities constitutes a public good—and that environmental pollution and other coal externalities are bad. For example, CONSOL Energy President and CEO Brett Harvey has staked out a refreshingly enlightened position on coal mine safety, arguing to other industry leaders that zero injuries in U.S. coal mines is a realistic goal.[194] In a speech to the Utah Mining Association in August, 2007, Brett Harvey stated:

> We need to change the paradigm and we need to change it now.… What industry must change is our incremental approach to safety improvement because it creates an unintended level of tolerance to accidents.… We will start with the premise that our normal state of operation is no accidents. An accident is an abnormality that is unacceptable. Accidents are an exception to our core values. Our approach means safety trumps everything else we do. It trumps production, it trumps profits, it trumps all other rules,

III of the IPCC, B. Metz, O. Davison, H.C. de Coninck, M. Loos, and L.A. Meyer, eds. 2005), *available at* http://www.ipcc.ch/ipccreports/srccs.htm. (last visited Nov., 17, 2008).

192. Signaling significant progress in making "clean coal" a reality, industry lobbyists list more than 100 "carbon capture and storage research projects, predominately underway in the U.S.… proving that the coal-based electricity sector is moving aggressively towards bringing advanced clean coal technologies to the marketplace domestically and abroad." *See* statement, American Coalition for Clean Coal Electricity ("ACCCE") (Dec. 22, 2008), *available at* http:/www.americaspower.org/News/Press-Room-Releases/ACCCE-Details-More-than-80CO2-Capture-and-Storage-Projects (last visited Dec. 23, 2008) [hereinafter ACCCE Statement]. (ACCCE "is a non-partisan partnership of companies involved in producing electricity from coal … [it] supports energy policies that balance coal's vital role in meeting our country's growing need for affordable reliable electricity with the need to protect the environment … [and] … advance clean coal technologies that will produce electricity with near zero emissions.")

193. NATIONAL MINING ASSOCIATION (NMA) POSITION ON CLIMATE CHANGE POLICIES 2 (July, 2008), *available at* http://www.nma.org/pdf/073108_climate_change.pdf (last visited Nov. 15, 2008).

194. Consol ranked fifth among U.S. coal producers in 2007 according to the U.S. Energy Information Administration, http://www.eia.doe.gov/cneaf/coal/page/acr/table10.html (last visited Nov. 23, 2008).

policies or procedures.... I firmly believe it is possible for CONSOL to achieve "zero-accidents" performance at every CONSOL facility and we intend to achieve those results within the next five years.[195]

The Vice President of the American Coalition for Clean Coal Energy, a trade association representing both the electric power generating industry and many of America's leading coal producers, has indicated that his members support reducing greenhouse gas emissions and protecting the environment:

> Our industry supports President-elect Obama's plan to invest in five full-scale carbon capture and storage demonstration projects. By investing in energy infrastructure projects like advanced clean coal projects, we can create jobs, promote domestic energy security, ensure access to affordable and reliable electricity, and promote continued progress in reducing emissions and protecting the environment.[196]

The National Mining Association, the leading American trade association representing the coal industry, also has officially recognized the critical importance of addressing climate change:

> Any meaningful effort to achieve long-term, sustainable reductions in global greenhouse gas emissions will depend on the development and deployment of new energy technologies, including advanced clean coal technologies and carbon capture and storage (CCS). The rapid development, demonstration and widespread deployment of such technologies are of paramount importance in any reasoned and effective effort to address climate change concerns.... [T]he need to address U.S. climate and energy policies and to move forward aggressively toward the broad, worldwide commercial deployment of CCS and other advanced clean-coal technologies is both urgent and imperative.[197]

The National Mining Association publicly supports the principle that "[c]limate change and energy policies are inextricably linked with each other and with other economic, environmental and social issues. None can be properly or successfully addressed in isolation, nor without consideration given to their direct and indirect costs and benefits."[198]

In contrast, other Big Coal leaders have adopted a strategy that involves continuing to obfuscate the fact of the industries' externalities while stridently attacking critics.[199] In a 2008 speech to mining industry people, Don Blankenship, chairman and CEO of Massey Energy, emphatically dismissed concerns about climate change asserting that "they can say what they want about

---

195. Brett Harvey, Keynote Address, Utah Mining Association 92nd Annual Meeting Park City, Utah (August 23, 2007), *available at* http://www.consolenergy.com/Newsroom/Speech5.aspx (last visited Nov. 16, 2008).

196. ACCCE Statement, *supra* note 192.

197. NATIONAL MINING ASSOCIATION POSITION ON CLIMATE CHANGE POLICIES, http://www.nma.org/pdf/ 073108_climate_change.pdf (last visited Nov. 2, 2008). *See also* NATIONAL MINING ASS'N, CARBON CAPTURE AND STORAGE, *available at* http://www.nma.org/pdf/fact_sheets/ccs.pdf (last visited Nov. 2, 2008).

198. *Id.*

199. Julia R. Goad, *Coal CEO calls environmentalists crazy*, WILLIAMSON (WV) DAILY NEWS (Nov. 22, 2008), *available at* http://www.williamsondailynews.com/articles/2008/11/22/news/doc49281e3eb9f80 1504 69491.prt (last visited Nov. 30, 2008). A video of Mr. Blankenship's remarks to members of the Tug Valley Mining Institute is *available at* http://wonkroom.thinkprogress.org/2008/12/13/blankenship-greeniacs/ (last visited Nov. 30, 2008) [hereinafter Blankenship Speech]. *See also* Steven Mufson, *Coal-Funded Ad Is Called Misleading*, WASHINGTON POST, Nov. 7, 2007, at A09 (Big Coal entities use newspaper ad campaign in Kansas attacking Kansas Governor for blocking air permits for two coal-fired electricity plants because of carbon dioxide emissions, asserting action jeopardized U.S. national security and made happy foreign leaders including Russian President Vladimir Putin, Venezuelan President Hugo Chavez and Iranian President Mahmoud Ahmadinejad).

climate change.... But the only thing melting in this country that matters is our financial system and our economy."[200]

Blankenship also suggested that the official public positions of both the National Mining Association and the United States Chamber of Commerce recognizing the dangers of climate change conceal the organizations' real views: "How many times have the people in this room heard, at the US Chamber of Commerce or at the National Mining Association, 'I don't believe in climate change, but I'm afraid to say that because it is a political reality.'"[201] Blankenship is a member of the Board of Directors of both organizations.

Whether Big Coal actually accepts the challenge of reducing greenhouse gas emissions from coal combustion or in the privacy of its corporate boardrooms denies the prevailing climate change science is yet to be determined. What is clear is that Big Coal has launched a multi-million dollar national public relations campaign trumpeting a new generation of "clean coal" technology that will capture earth-warming greenhouse smoke and prevent it from reaching the atmosphere.[202] A litany of television spots, newspaper advertisements and roadside billboards drive home a theme to consumers in the United States: "Coal Keeps The Lights On," and "Coal: Clean, Green, Affordable Energy." The advertiser's mantra, "Coal Keeps the Lights On," is intended to emphasize coal's positives — to make consumers think of light, security, comfort when they turn a light on or power up a computer.

There is certainly nothing wrong with publicizing these CO_2 capture/sequestration research projects. However, the thrust of Coal's strategy seems to imply that "clean coal" technology is already proven and available for use in the near future. The public may not be buying. A Los Angeles Times editorial opined:

> [T]here is no such thing as "clean coal." The phrase is an Orwellian marketing slogan invented by coal interests.... Coal producers are similarly trying to head off future greenhouse-gas regulation by marketing so-called clean coal, which relies on the notion that we eventually will be able to liquefy carbon emissions from coal-fired power plants and pump the waste underground, a process called carbon sequestration.... Coal backers rightly point out that even without carbon sequestration, new technologies have reduced some emissions. But this is sort of like tobacco companies claiming that filtered cigarettes are "safe"; just because it's cleaner doesn't make it clean.[203]

---

200. *Id.* Massey Energy ranks sixth among the nation's coal producers.

201. In the same speech, Blankenship also accused a newspaper editor of being a communist, and asserted that former Vice President Al Gore, U.S. House of Representatives Speaker Nancy Pelosi and U.S. Senate President Harry Reid are "totally wrong" and "absolutely crazy." Blankenship also warned that "[t]he greeniacs are taking over the world ... and that ... [i]f [U.S. House of Representatives Speaker] Pelosi thinks that decreasing CO_2 in this country is going to save the polar bears, she's crazy. If CO_2 emissions are going to kill the polar bears, it's going to happen. What we do here [in the U.S.] is not going to do it." Blankenship Speech, *supra* note 199.

202. *See, e.g.*, American Coalition for Clean Coal Electricity website focusing almost exclusively on broadcasting the American power and coal industries commitment to advancing clean coal technology, *available at* http://www.americaspower.org/ (last visited Dec. 3. 2008).

203. Editorial, *Coal and Votes*, The Los Angeles Times (October 7, 2008), *available at* http:// www.latimes.com/news/opinion/la-ed-coal7-2008oct07,0,2673112.story (last visited Nov. 3, 2008). In the Virginia coalfields, a Roanoke Times editor similarly observed that:

> the technology seems like a stretch. Massive amounts — hundreds of millions of tons — of carbon dioxide would have to be diverted from emissions stacks, using technology only recently implemented commercially. Then it would have to be transported to sites where it could be efficiently, safely and permanently stored underground. Researchers are still trying to determine what sites will work best.

The TIMES did more than ridicule Big Coal's "clean coal" mantra. It specifically called the industry out on its long obscured but significant negative externalities:

> From extraction to combustion, coal is an environmental catastrophe. It is the most carbon-intensive fossil fuel, the top source of mercury pollution and among the top causes of global warming. Particles and soot from burning coal kill thousands of Americans every year. And its extraction ruins ecosystems as mountains are blown apart and the rubble is tossed into streams.[204]

There are many arguments supporting Big Coal's desire to continue to play an important role in the new energy future of the United States and the world. There are national security benefits of having coal provide a substantial part of a nation's energy needs. The world's largest reserves of oil and gas are located in the politically unstable Persian Gulf region. Petroleum use raises serious issues of stability of supply as well as price manipulation by the international oil cartel. In contrast the world's coal reserves are distributed in many regions, most notably the United States, China and India. For them, as well as European and East Asian coal importers, security of supply and economics provide significant incentives for continuing use of coal.[205]

Moreover, as Big Coal asserts, coal has the potential to reduce national reliance on oil whose market price-per-barrel spiked to stratospheric levels in 2008, before dropping precipitously as world economies felt the effects of a world financial crisis. Finally, under many scenarios, coal may be cheaper and more readily available in the foreseeable future, at least if all of coal's previously obscure externalities are not included in the calculation. It is these and other pragmatic considerations and not slick advertising campaigns touting "clean coal" technology that will most likely influence public policy decision-makers.

VI. Conclusion

If coal is to play an important role in the world's new energy future, pragmatism and demands of rational decision-making should lead to an inclusion of a full calculation of all of Coal's costs, not just its benefits. As demonstrated above, in the United States at least, these enormous externalized costs have been reduced significantly by government regulation, more enlightened management and by labor union and public pressures. Nevertheless, coal mining and burning continues to exact a huge demonstrable price from miners and their families, coalfield communities, taxpayers and the environment. In considering coal's future, the externalized socio-economic, environmental, and health and safety costs must be fully considered. The climate change crisis provides a historic opportunity to open the dark side of coal to the light of reasoned public decision-making. To the refrain "coal keeps the lights on" one must ask "at what cost?"

Editorial, *Cleaning up coal*, ROANOKE TIMES (June 22, 2008), *available at* http://www.roanoke.com/editorials/wb/166819 (last visited Dec. 4, 2008).

204. *Id.* Similarly, THE SAN ANTONIO TIMES also reported on a Texas utility's decision to build a new coal burning power plant:

> Coal is also, despite a public relations campaign to clean up its image, the dirtiest and most carbon intensive of all major fuel sources. When burned, it produces mercury and other pollutants that help create smog. It's also a chief source of carbon dioxide, the main culprit in global warming. This makes the [utilities'] decision, in many eyes, a big gamble for a future almost certain to include a new regimen of global-warming regulations that punishes those who add to the problem. "We've known for a long time that coal is the dirtiest way to produce power," said Alice McKeown of Worldwatch Institute. "You've got to ask how they justify the risk they are taking here."

Anton Caputo, *A Greener City: Powering the future*, THE SAN ANTONIO NEWS (Sept. 27. 2008), *available at* http://www.mysanantonio.com/news/local_news/29851924.html (last visited Sept. 30, 2008).

205. THE FUTURE OF COAL, *supra* note 16, at 5.

Notes

1. 2008 FRIEDMAN at 185:

> Coal companies are going green by renaming themselves "energy" companies and stressing how sequestration of CO_2, something none of them has ever done, will give us "clean coal."

2. *Ohio Valley Environmental Coalition v. Aracoma Coal Co.*, 556 F.3d 177 (4th Cir. 2009) (Gregory and Shedd, C.J.s, with Michael, C.J., dissenting in part). This dreadful decision by the Fourth Circuit restores mountaintop mining to the category of legal and proper under NEPA and the Clean Water Act. It draws this dissent from Michael, C.J. (556 F.3d at 226):

> Today's decision will have far-reaching consequences for the environment of Appalachia. It is not disputed that the impact of filling valleys and headwater streams is irreversible or that headwater streams provide crucial ecosystem functions. Further, the cumulative effects of the permitted fill activities on local streams and watersheds are considerable. By failing to require the Corps to undertake a meaningful assessment of the functions of the aquatic resources being destroyed and by allowing the Corps to proceed instead with a one-to-one mitigation that takes no account of lost stream function, this court risks significant harm to the affected watersheds and water resources.

For commentary, see William H. Rodgers, Jr., *NEPA's Insatiable Optimism*, 39 ENVTL. L. RPTR. 10618, 10620–22 (2009).

3. *Appalachian Voices v. Bodman*, 587 F. Supp. 2d 79 (D. D.C. 2008) (Ricard M. Urbina, D.J.). This is a NEPA / ESA challenge by a group concerned about the "air quality crisis in the Smoky Mountains" alleging that the defendants DOT and DOE have "erroneously failed to consider the environmental consequences" of the tax credits for "clean coal technology" established by the Energy Policy Act of 2005. The IRS has allocated $1 billion in credits to nine clean coal projects, including the Duke Energy Cliffside Modernization Project, in North Carolina. One of the claims is that an EIS should be done on these tax credit programs and another claim is that Endangered Species Act consultation is required before implementation of the tax credit programs. These plaintiffs fail the "traceability" test for standing; (ed.) and, of course, "climate change" is a remote unmentionable.

4. *Southern Alliance for Clean Energy v. Duke Energy Carolinas, LLC*, 2008 WL 5110894 (W.D. N.C. Dec. 2, 2008). This is a challenge to the construction of Duke's new 800 megawatt coal-fired power plant (Cliffside Unit 6) without satisfaction of the MACT requirement; the main issue in the case is whether the requirements of Section 112(g)(2)(B), 42 U.S.C.A. §7412(g)(2)(B), which has the BACT rule ("maximum achievable control technology emission limitation"), apply to the ongoing construction of unit 6. Duke got its permit to construct and operate Unit 6 ten days before the court ruled in *New Jersey v. EPA*, 517 F.3d 574 (D.C. Cir. 2008) that the rule seeking to remove power plants from the Section 112(c) list regarding MACT controls for Hazardous Air Pollutants was invalid. Duke says construction began on Jan. 30, 2008, while plaintiffs say it began on Feb. 9, 2008. Plaintiffs have standing and the doctrine of abstention does not apply. The court rules in favor of plaintiffs, with these comments on remedy, *id*; p. 10:

> Plaintiffs request the Court grant immediate injunctive relief in the form of a halt to further construction of Unit 6 until a MACT process, conducted in accordance with current legal requirements, is completed. While such a drastic measure is justified by Defendant's refusal to comply with the plain requirements of current law, the Court concludes that Defendant should be given the opportunity to comply with CAA and DAQ [North Carolina Division of Air Quality] requirements within a limited period of time, after which injunctive relief may be granted, if necessary.

5. *North Carolina ex re. Cooper v. Tennessee Valley Authority*, 593 F. Supp. 2d 812 (W.D. N.C. 2009) (Lacy H. Thornburg, D.J.). This is a public nuisance action by the State of North Carolina against TVA. It is alleged that airborne particles from TVA plants "enter North Carolina in unreasonable amounts, thereby threatening the health of millions of people, the financial viability of an entire region, and the beauty and purity of a vast natural ecosystem." 593 F. Supp. 2d at 815. Costs in the amount of billions of dollars every year are claimed for "health care expenses, sick days, and lost tourism revenue" plus less quantifiable costs for environmental damage. Costs of abating this pollution are estimated by North Carolina experts to be $5 billion while TVA says it would be $3 billion. The court has held earlier that the Clean Air Act does not preempt state remedies, *see North Carolina v. TVA*, 549 F. Supp. 2d 725, 729 (W.D. N.C. 2008). This case is mostly about the primary pollutants of SO_2, NOx, and mercury; and the secondary pollutants of O_3 and $PM_{2.5}$. There are substantial findings on the effects of these various pollutants and the four 100-mile plants within 100 miles of North Carolina—John Sevier, Bull Run in North Carolina, Kingston in Tennessee and Widows Creek in Alabama. The court explores public nuisance law of Alabama, Kentucky, and Tennessee and concludes (as to Alabama) that "an injunction requiring prompt installation and year-round use of appropriate pollution control technologies at Widows Creek is a necessary outcome of this litigation." 593 F. Supp. 2d at 830. The same relief is indicated for Kingston, Bull Run, and John Sevier; the two Kentucky plants are too remote to significantly impact air quality in North Carolina.

6. *Palm Beach County Environmental Coalition v. Florida*, 587 F. Supp. 2d 1254 (S.D. Fla. 2008) (Donald M. Middlebrooks, D.J.). This is a challenge to construction of a new powerplant called the West Cnty. Energy Center that promises to emit, among other things, 12.5 million tons of greenhouse gasses per year, "which will greatly exacerbate global warming," id. at 1255. This court denies the motion for a preliminary injunction because plaintiff has failed to show a substantial likelihood of success on the merits.

Professor Parenteau addresses the question of carbon capture and sequestration in a thought-provoking paper.

Go Back, It's a Trap!
The Perils of Geological Sequestration of CO_2

Patrick Parenteau, Professor of Law and Senior Counsel, Environmental and Natural Resources Law Clinic, Vermont Law School, pparenteau@vermontlaw.edu.

Background

What do Peabody Coal, Exxon-Mobil, American Electric Power Corp., the World Resources Institute, the Union of Concerned Scientists, the Natural Resources Defense Council, and President George W. Bush all have in common? They all support rapid development and deployment of commercial-scale carbon capture and storage (CCS), also called geological sequestration, to allow continued use of coal and other fossil fuels while mitigating climate change and buying time to "de-carbonize" the energy system. This is a classic American approach to environmental problems: an unwavering faith that technology will bail us out of any jam. Only this time the stakes have never been higher.

CCS involves capturing CO_2 from coal-fired power plants and other fossil-fuel sources, transporting and injecting it into deep (>800m) underground geologic formations, and closely monitoring it to see that it stays put for centuries. Though CCS technology has been used in many small scale projects around the world, mainly for secondary recovery in natural gas and oil fields, it has not been demonstrated at anywhere near the scale that would be required to permanently store all the CO_2 from the burning of coal and other fossil fuels at projected rates of energy consumption here and abroad.

It is not too surprising that coal companies and their allies in the utility industry support CCS, especially if the government covers much of the R&D costs to make it feasible. Smart CEO's understand that if coal is to have a future in a carbon-constrained world the CO_2 has to go somewhere other than the atmosphere. Somewhat more surprising is the zeal with which major environmental organizations and charitable foundations are pushing CCS.[1] Undoubtedly, it reflects a pragmatic view that coal is abundant, cheap, available, and will be burned somewhere, if not in the U.S then in China, India, and other fast-developing nations. Politicians, especially those from coal-rich regions, are happy to join this unusual coalition of business and environmental interests to keep coal in the energy mix. With energy demands projected to grow by forty percent by 2030, and with fuel prices hurting the economy and squeezing consumers, any option advertised as cheap, climate friendly, and free of foreign entanglements looks like a "win-win" solution.[2]

Industry, of course, has been busy trying to convince the public of the virtues of "clean coal." In the heat of the 2007–08 presidential primary season, a coalition of coal and utility industries launched a thirty-five million dollar ad campaign touting coal as the "the fuel that powers our way of life," featuring a power cord plugged into a lump of coal.[3] But the pictures on the ground tell a different story: Appalachian watersheds devastated by "mountaintop removal" mining;[4] alpine lakes and forests damaged by acid rain;[5] aquatic ecosystems contaminated with mercury;[6] National Parks shrouded in haze;[7] groundwater polluted by toxic leachate from combustion waste;[8] and increased rates of human mortality and morbidity from exposure to fine particulates and other contaminants in soot and smog.[9] In terms of life cycle impacts, coal is easily the dirtiest and most destructive form of energy on the planet. Add the fact that coal is the most carbon intensive fuel and accounts for 40% of the CO_2 emissions causing global warming, and the "clean" label becomes a parody.[10] Coal combustion can certainly be made cleaner and more efficient through use of "best available control technologies" such as integrated gasification com-

---

1. For example, the Joyce Foundation has committed $7 million over three years to the development of "clean coal" technologies including CCS at Midwest coal plants. Information *available at*: http://www.joyce fdn.org/News/NewsDetails.aspx?newsid=55.

2. Organization for Economic Cooperation and Development (OECD) and the International Energy Agency (IEA), World Energy Outlook (2006) [hereinafter World Energy Outlook (2006)].

3. Steven Mufson, *Coal Industry Plugs Into the Campaign*, Washington Post, January 18, 2008, at D01.

4. More than 450 mountains, 2000 miles of headwater streams and one million acres of forests have been destroyed by mountaintop removal. The devastation can be seen on Google Earth: http://www.gearthblog.com/blog/archives/2006/10/end_mountain_top_rem.html.

5. Hubbard Brook Experimental Forest, Acid Rain Revisited, (2001), *available at* http://www. hubbardbrookfoundation.org/article/view/12940/1/2076/.

6. USGS, Mercury Contamination of Aquatic Ecosystems, *available at* http://water.usgs.gov/wid/FS_216-95/FS_216-95.html.

7. National Parks and Conservation Association, Dark Horizons (June, 2008), *available at* http://www.npca.org/darkhorizons/pdf/Dark_Horizons_Report.pdf.

8. Natural Resources Defense Council, Dangerous Disposal: Keeping Coal Combustion Wastes Out of Public Water Supplies (2007), *available at* http://www.nrdc.org/health/effects/coal/coalwater.pdf.

9. Studies by the Harvard School of Public Health and the American Cancer Society have found strong links between high levels of small particles (2.5 microns) and a rise in death rates. *See* Andrew Revkin, *Tiny Bits of Soot Tied to Illness*, New York Times, April 21, 2001.

10. Coal combustion produces about 1.9 billion tons of CO_2 per year in the U.S., roughly equivalent to all CO_2 emissions from U.S. transport per annum. A typical coal-fired power plant will produce about one ton of CO_2 for every megawatt hour of electricity that it generates, while a natural gas-fired power plant will produce about one-half ton of CO_2 per megawatt hour.

bined cycle (IGCC),[11] but in terms of its cradle to grave impacts coal will never be clean, or environmentally acceptable. Indeed, the best way to sequester carbon, protect human health and safeguard ecosystems is to leave the coal in the ground.

Of course, that is not likely to happen. The reality is that the world is becoming ever more dependent on coal as a primary source of fuel to power economic growth particularly in the fast developing nations of China and India. Coal produces over half of the electricity used in the U.S.[12] Globally, coal accounts for eighty percent of the electricity produced.[13] Prior to the release of the IPCC's Fourth Assessment, concluding that the evidence of climate change is "unequivocal" and that humans are "very likely" (i.e. to a 90% certainty) responsible for it,[14] the utility industry was projecting a surge in construction of conventional pulverized coal (PC) plants. In 2007, the National Energy Technology Laboratory (NETL), a division of the U.S Department of Energy, forecast the construction of 151 new coal plants by 2020, representing a total capacity of 90 GW.[15] However, scores of these plants have been canceled or delayed due to permit denials, cost overruns, regulatory uncertainties and concerns regarding CO_2 emissions.[16] Nevertheless a number of coal plants are under construction and many more are in various stages of planning and permitting.[17] The reasons are obvious: coal is cheap, abundant and relatively accessible compared to, say, oil from the Persian Gulf.[18] With an estimated 275 billion tons of coal in the ground, the U.S is considered the "Saudi Arabia" of coal.[19] If all of this coal could be economically and safely mined it would be enough to meet domestic demand for 250 years at current rates of consumption.[20] Other nations, notably China and India, rely even more heavily on coal. Coal accounts for eighty percent and seventy percent of electricity production in China and India, respectively.[21] China is adding about one coal plant per week to the national grid.[22] Aided by a $4.2 billion grant from the World Bank, India is build-

---

11. The National Energy Technology Laboratory (NETL) within the U.S. Department of Energy has this to say about IGCC: "Integrated gasification combined cycle (IGCC) is an exciting and emerging technology for coal power, offering the potential for higher efficiency and reduced cost of pollutant emissions control." *Available at* http://www.netl.doe.gov/technologies/carbon_seq/core_rd/co2capture.html. Others are not so sanguine, pointing out that there are only two IGCC plants operating in the U.S. and that there are many unanswered questions about the technology including what to do with the CO_2 once it is separated. *See, e.g.,* Energy Justice website: http://www.energyjustice.net/coal/igcc/factsheet-long.pdf.

12. Energy Information Administration (EIA), Annual Energy Outlook (2007), *available at* http://www.eia.doe.gov/oiaf/archive/aeo07/index.html.

13. World Energy Outlook (2006), *supra* note 2.

14. IPCC, Climate Change 2007 Synthesis Report: Summary for Policymakers 2–4, *available at* http://www.ipcc.ch/pdf/assessment-report/ar4/syr/ar4_syr_spm.pdf.

15. NETL, Tracking New Coal-Fired Power Plants: Coal's Resurgence in Electric Power Generation, May 2007., *available at* http://www.netl.doe.gov/publications/press/2007/07030-DOE_Updates_Power_Plants_Report.html. A gigawatt is one thousand megawatts (1,000 MW) or one million kilowatts (1,000,000 kW) or one billion watts (1,000,000,000 watts) of electricity. One gigawatt is enough to supply the electric demand of about one million average California homes. Energy Glossary http://www.energyquest.ca.gov/glossary/glossary-g.html.

16. Information *available a*t SourceWatch, http://www.sourcewatch.org/index.php?title=Coal_moratorium.

17. NETL, Tracking New Coal-Fired Power Plants, (Update) February 2008, *available at* http://www.netl.doe.gov/coal/refshelf/ncp.pdf.

18. Energy Information Administration (EIA), Annual Energy Outlook, 2007, *available at* http://www.eia.doe.gov/oiaf/archive/aeo07/index.html.

19. Source: *Clean Energy USA, available at* http://www.clean-energy.us/facts/coal.htm.

20. *Id.*

21. Source: Pew Center on Global Climate Change at http://www.pewclimate.org/global-warming-basics/coalfacts.cfm.

22. Peter Fairly, *China's Coal Future,* Technology Review (MIT) January, 2007. India has about 90,000 MW installed capacity for electricity generation, of which more than 70% is produced by coal-based thermal power plants. Information *available at* http://cat.inist.fr/?aModele=afficheN&cpsidt=15539972.

ing a massive new 4000 MW "supercritical" Tata Mundra coal plant in Gujarat state.[23] Even climate-conscious Europe has proposed a significant expansion in coal-fired electrical generation.[24] Coal is now a highly mobile global commodity with prices rising sharply, largely in response to demands from Asia.[25]

The irony of ramping up coal production in the face of mounting evidence that climate change is proceeding much faster than IPCC models have predicted,[26] and that the window of opportunity to take action to prevent the worst consequences of climate disruption is closing fast has not been lost on the scientific community. Prominent climatologists such as James Hansen of the NASA Goddard Institute for Space Studies have called for a moratorium on building new coal plants without CCS, starting in 2012 for developed countries and by 2022 for developing countries.[27]

Concerns have also been raised about diverting badly needed investments in efficiency and conservation, which offer the quickest, cheapest and cleanest way to reduce GHG.[28] According to a recent report by McKinsey & Company, a leading management consulting firm, the world could cut energy use in half by 2020 through a series of targeted policies and investments that would pay a handsome return in energy savings over a relatively short period of time.[29] The Electric Power Research Institute, an industry-funded think tank, estimates that the U.S. could cut its energy demand by forty-five percent by 2030 with the "aggressive development and deployment of several advanced technologies."[30]

Others worry that funding for CCS will come at the expense of badly needed investments in solar, wind, geothermal and other renewables.[31] Greenpeace argues that the preoccupation with CCS raises "false hopes" and diverts attention from the more pressing need to accelerate the conversion to a low-carbon economy.[32] The Sierra Club has launched a nationwide and so far very successful campaign to block construction of conventional coal plants "without CCS capacity."[33]

23. Information *available at* http://www.enn.com/business/article/34296.

24. Elisabeth Rosenthal, *Europe Turns to Coal*, NEW YORK TIMES, April 23, 2008.

25. Source: World Coal Institute at http://www.etftrends.com/2008/05/coal-has-had-a.html.

26. IPCC FOURTH ASSESSMENT, SUMMARY FOR POLICYMAKERS (Cambridge Un. Press 2007), *available at* http://www.ipcc.ch/pdf/assessment-report/ar4/syr/ar4_syr_spm.pdf.

27. James Hansen, *The Need for an International Moratorium on Coal Power*, Bulletin of the Atomic Scientists, *available at* http://www.thebulletin.org/web-edition/features/the-need-international-moratorium-coal-power.

28. *See* Peter Montague, *The Basket Our Eggs Are In*, RACHEL'S DEMOCRACY & HEALTH NEWS #939, December 27th, 2007 [hereinafter *The Basket Our Eggs Are In*], *available at* http://www.rachel.org/en/newsletters/rachels_news/939. It is important to distinguish between energy efficiency, which means doing more with less, and energy conservation, which means preventing waste. *See* Gill Owen, *Energy Efficiency and Energy Conservation: Policies, Programmes and their Effectiveness*, ENERGY AND ENVIRONMENT, Vol. 11 No 5 (2000), *available at* http://www.iea.org/Textbase/work/2004/eewp/owen_paper. pdf.

29. MCKINSEY & COMPANY, CURBING GLOBAL ENERGY DEMAND GROWTH: THE ENERGY PRODUCTIVITY OPPORTUNITY, (May 2007), *available at* www.mckinsey.com/mgi. Energy productivity is defined as the amount of energy obtained from every unit of energy used. In a subsequent study, McKinsey reports that an average investment of $180 billion a year for the next thirteen years would yield savings of $900 billion by 2020 in all end-use sectors (housing, transportation, etc). MCKINSEY GLOBAL INSTITUTE, THE CASE FOR INVESTING IN ENERGY PRODUCTIVITY, February, 2008, *available at* http://www.mckinsey.com/mgi/rp/energy markets/index.asp.

30. EPRI, THE POWER TO REDUCE CO_2 EMISSIONS: THE FULL PORTFOLIO (Summer, 2007), *available at* http://mydocs.epri.com/docs/public/DiscussionPaper2007.pdf.

31. *See* Edward Mazria and Kristina Kirschner, *The 2030 Blueprint: Solving Climate Change Saves Billions*, ARCHITECTURE 2030 (April 7, 2008), *available at* http://www.architecture2030.org/pdfs/2030Blueprint.pdf.

32. GREENPEACE INTERNATIONAL, FALSE HOPES: WHY CARBON CAPTURE AND STORAGE WON'T SAVE THE PLANET (2008), *available at* http://www.greenpeace.org/raw/content/international/press/reports/false-hope. pdf.

33. Sierra Club, *Frequently Asked Questions*, *available at* http://www.sierraclub.org/coal/faq/.

Even more centrist groups like the Union of Concerned Scientists express ambivalence about support for development of CCS:

> Within the full portfolio of domestic and international approaches to manage carbon comprehensively, UCS views geologic carbon sequestration as one potentially viable option to achieve reductions in carbon dioxide emissions and atmospheric concentrations. In no way, however, should geologic carbon sequestration be seen as a "silver bullet" to reducing emissions, nor should it be researched and developed at the expense of other environmentally sound, technologically feasible, and economically affordable solutions to climate change.[34]

However, given a shaky economy, budget deficits as far as the eye can see, mounting pressure to expand domestic sources of oil and develop corn ethanol and other ill-advised "biofuels,"[35] it is unrealistic to think that there will be no trade-offs between funding CCS and funding green energy alternatives.[36] In a letter to Congress signed by over fifty grassroots environmental organizations, many from the coalfields of Appalachia, the groups opposed public funding for CCS and argued that every available dollar was needed for investments in efficiency and clean energy technologies.[37] However, the political constituency for efficiency and renewables is not as strong as the coal and electric utility industries when it comes to divvying up the federal pie. CCS demonstration projects are very expensive. The cost estimates for the FutureGen project, billed as "a public-private partnership to build a first-of-its-kind coal-fueled, near-zero emissions power plant," have doubled, causing the Bush Administration to pull the plug on further federal participation.[38] The current price tag of $1.8 billion is almost twice the entire DOE FY 09 budget for efficiencies and renewables.[39]

Nevertheless, CCS faces formidable barriers that analysts believe may take a decade or more to overcome.[40] Ultimately, of course, there is no way to insure that CO_2 will remain sequestered in perpetuity with no leakage or other unintended environmental consequences. Human society has not been around long enough to know whether such a thing is even possible. We are conducting a planetary experiment on a grand scale. Some say the choice is obvious: better to put the carbon in the ground rather than in the atmosphere. But that may be a gross oversimplification of the dilemma we face. The science is telling us quite clearly that we are fast running out of time to stabilize atmospheric loadings of CO_2 before certain "tipping points" are reached and

---

34. UCS position statement on geologic sequestration, *available at* http://www.ucsusa.org/global_warming/solutions/geologic-carbon-sequestering.html.

35. In a study published in SCIENCE researchers concluded that widespread use of ethanol from corn could result in nearly twice the greenhouse gas emissions as the gasoline it would replace because of expected land-use changes. Searchinger *et al.*, *Use of U.S. Croplands for Biofuels Increases Greenhouse Gases Through Emissions from Land-Use Change*, 319 SCIENCE 1238 (2008).

36. According to the McKinsey Global Institute, an investment of $38 billion per year in the U.S. would cut energy demand in half and yield a seventeen percent return by 2030. McKINSEY & COMPANY, THE CASE FOR INVESTING IN ENERGY PRODUCTIVITY, February, 2008, *available at* http://www.mckinsey.com /mgi/publications/Investing_Energy_Productivity/. By contrast, the FY '09 federal budget calls for only $1.2 billion for the combined DOE Energy Efficiency and Renewable Energy Programs. Source: *Climate Progress, available at* http://climateprogress.org/2008/02/05/details-on-bushs-anti-efficiency-budget/.

37. *Available at* http://understory.ran.org/2008/05/06/public-interest-groups-oppose-carbon-capture-scam/.

38. *See* DOE press release at http://www.energy.gov/news/5912.htm. Nevertheless, DOE's FY 09 budget still contains $149 million for the project. PLATT's NEWS SERVICE http://www.platts.com/Nuclear/News/6920585.xml.

39. FutureGen Alliance, http://www.futuregenalliance.org/about.stm.

40. *Compare* J. ANDREW HORNER AND NIA ROBINSON, A CLIMATE OF CHANGE: AFRICAN AMERICANS, GLOBAL WARMING AND A JUST CLIMATE POLICY FOR THE U.S. (July 2008) [hereinafter HORNER & ROBINSON], *available at* http://www.ejcc.org/ *with* IPCC, SPECIAL REPORT ON CARBON DIOXIDE CAPTURE AND STORAGE 60–61 (Cambridge Un. Press 2007) [hereinafter SRCCCS], *available at* http://archrivm.nl/env/int/ipcc/pages_media/SRCCS-final/IPCCSpecialReportonCarbonddioxideCaptureandStorage.htm.

catastrophic consequences become inevitable, and there is almost no margin of error. The world cannot afford to lock in a whole new generation of carbon intensive coal-fired power plants that will be operating for 40–50 years without a fairly high level of confidence that the CO_2 emissions from these plants can in fact be safely and permanently stored in geological formations. Further, even if sequestration was a sure thing, the broader human health and environmental impacts of coal raise troubling ethical and environmental justice issues. Technologies that enable continued reliance on coal may exact disproportionate burdens on poor and minority communities, the same ones that are bearing the brunt of climate change impacts.[41] Politically, it may be true that coal plus CCS is the best we can do at the moment. But if that is true then perhaps the answer is to work harder to change the politics, at home and abroad, rather than accept a flawed strategy.

With this in mind, the balance of this paper will describe the difficult technology, economic, regulatory, public acceptance, and long term liability issues that must be resolved if CCS is to play a significant role in climate mitigation within the narrow window of opportunity available to avoid irreversible consequences of climate change. The essay concludes with some observations on the broader policy and ethical dimensions of relying on CCS as a climate mitigation strategy.

Technology Issues

CCS is not a single technology like a scrubber on a smokestack. Rather it is a combination of processes involving three integrated steps: first, CO_2 must be "captured" from process or exhaust gases at a power plant, oil refinery, cement plant, ethanol plant, or other source; second the CO_2 must be cleaned, dried, and compressed for transportation by pipeline or other means; and third, the compressed CO_2 must be injected as a supercritical (liquid-like) fluid for efficient storage in deep, secure geologic formations.[42] Each of these steps is discussed below.

Capture

Capture is the easy part.[43] The chemistry is straightforward. Carbon dioxide reacts with a group of chemicals called amines. At higher temperatures these chemicals separate. Power plants can be purged of CO_2 by running their exhaust through an amine bath before it is vented, and the amine can be warmed to release the gas. Better still, the coal can be reacted with water to produce a mixture of CO_2 and hydrogen, which makes it much easier to scrub out the CO_2, leaving pure hydrogen to be burned.

There are currently three options for capturing CO_2. Post combustion capture, the one most in use today, involves separation of the CO_2 from the flue gas. CO_2 can also be separated and captured from fuel before burning in pre-combustion de-carbonization. Integrated gasification combined-cycle (IGCC) power plants use this approach. Post-combustion capture, although it is the most mature technology, is expensive and energy-intensive. Pre-combustion capture (IGCC) is estimated to have the lowest overall costs, but there are only two IGCC plants in operation in the U.S. and more operational experience is needed to judge its commercial efficacy.[44] Oxy-fuel

---

41. *See* HORNER & ROBINSON, *supra* note 40.

42. IPCC, SPECIAL REPORT ON CARBON DIOXIDE CAPTURE AND STORAGE 60–61 (2007) [hereinafter, IPCC SPECIAL REPORT], *available at* http://arch.rivm.nl/env/int/ipcc/pages_media/SRCCS-final/IPCCSpecialReport onCarbondioxideCaptureandStorage.htm; THE FUTURE OF COAL, OPTIONS FOR A CARBON-CONSTRAINED WORLD, an Interdisciplinary MIT Study 1 (2007) [hereinafter, 2007 THE FUTURE OF COAL], *available at* http://web.mit.edu/coal/.

43. Information on carbon capture is available on the Department of Energy website at http:// www.fossil.energy.gov/programs/sequestration/capture/.

44. FUTURE OF COAL, *supra* note 42, at xiii.

combustion is a third, emerging option to achieve a relatively pure stream of pressurized CO_2. This process uses oxygen instead of air for combustion, and produces a concentrated CO_2 exhaust stream. Oxy-fuel technology is still in the demonstration phase, and large scale testing is needed to assess its commercial potential.

Transport

Most CO_2 is transported by pipeline, although trucks and ships can also be used.[45] Since the early 1970s, oil companies have been transporting CO_2 through pipelines for use in secondary oil recovery. Today, over 3600 miles of dedicated pipeline—most of it in the United States— carries more than 40 million metric tons of CO_2 per year.[46] The Cortez pipeline, for example, delivers CO_2 over a distance of 500 miles from natural CO_2 deposits in Southwest Colorado to the Denver City hub in Texas. Most of the Enhanced Oil Recovery (EOR) projects in the U.S. are in the Permian Basin of West Texas and tap naturally occurring CO_2 sources, which is easier than capture from plants.[47]

A whole new pipeline system dedicated to CO_2 shipments over long distances will be required to handle the output from an expanding coal sector. A variety of agencies will need to coordinate these developments. State oil and gas commissions, the Federal Energy Regulatory Commission, and the Departments of the Interior, Energy, and Transportation may all play a role in siting, approving, and maintaining new CO_2 pipelines. How long it will take and how much it will cost to put this infrastructure in place is anyone's guess. One way to cut costs and expedite deployment might be to create a pipeline "hub" system to which multiple power plants and priority storage sites can be connected. The feasibility and extent of these systems will be determined by the availability of suitable underground storage capacity and cost of construction and operation of long pipelines.[48]

Storage

Here is where things get interesting. Storage of CO_2 must be permanent if it is to an effective climate mitigation strategy.[49] Given the enormous amount of CO_2 that must be stored, even tiny amounts of leakage could prove disastrous for the climate.[50] To be a successful burial site, a geologic formation must be more than 1 km underground.[51] That depth provides enough pressure to turn CO_2 from a gas into what is known as a supercritical fluid, a form in which the CO_2 is more likely to stay put. The rock formation also has to have enough pores and cracks to hold the CO_2. Lastly, it needs to be covered with a layer of non-porous rock to provide a leak-proof cap.

---

45. World Resources Institute, Capturing King Coal: Deploying Carbon Capture and Sequestration in the United States at Scale 12, June 2008 [hereinafter 2008 Capturing King Coal], *available at* http://www.wri.org/publication/capturing-king-coal.

46. Congressional Budget Office, The Potential for Carbon Sequestration in the United States, 15 September, 2007 [hereinafter 2007 Potential For Carbon Sequestration].

47. Paul Parfomak and Peter Folger, Carbon Dioxide (CO_2) Pipelines for Carbon Sequestration: Emerging Policy Issues, April 2007, Congressional Research Service (CRS), *available at* http://www. assets. opencrs.com/rpts/RL33971_20070419.pdf.

48. 2008 Capturing King Coal, *supra* note 45, at 12.

49. Carbon remains in the atmosphere for centuries. Direct Testimony of James E. Hansen, p. 587 above.

50. Peter Montague, editor of Rachel's Environmental News, calculates that if only twenty-five percent of the world's coal, oil and gas reserves was burned and the carbon sequestered, leakage of only 0.8 percent of the total per year would exceed the current annual human contribution to atmospheric carbon of eight billion tons. *See The Basket Our Eggs Are In*, *supra* note 28.

51. Information on carbon storage available from the Carbon Mitigation Initiative at Princeton University: http://www.princeton.edu/~cmi/events/Geological%20Storage%20Workshop.htm.

Deep saline formations offer the most promising places to store CO_2, followed by oil and gas fields, and coal beds that cannot be mined economically because of their depth or the thickness of the seam.[52] Analysts estimate that in the United States and Canada combined, such reservoirs could hold a total of 1.2 trillion to 3.6 trillion metric tons of CO_2 emissions.[53] Deep saline formations, filled with water unfit for agricultural or industrial use, account for 80 percent of the low-end estimate of geologic storage capacity in the United States and Canada. Oil and gas reservoirs—both those in production and those that are or will soon be abandoned—account for about 7 percent of the low-end estimate of geologic storage capacity in the United States and Canada. Carbon dioxide is already injected into oil fields as part of a process called enhanced oil recovery (EOR). Un-minable coal seams account for the other thirteen percent of the low-end estimate of geologic storage capacity in the United States and Canada. Coal seams might be able to store several times more CO_2 than natural gas reservoirs of the equivalent volume because of the large surface area of the coal.

Capture and injection of carbon dioxide into oil, gas, and coal reserves have been integral parts of EOR for several decades, but long-term storage underground has yet to be demonstrated. Moreover, while technical feasibility has been demonstrated for some technologies already, there are still significant economic costs (*e.g.*, for capture/separation and compression technologies, transportation) and energy efficiency losses involved. Efficiency losses of 10–20% with currently available separation technologies result in higher fuel input per unit of delivered energy. Energy penalties of this magnitude are particularly serious if safe, long-term underground carbon storage cannot be assured, *i.e.*, if the CO_2 was quickly returned to the atmosphere (on the order of years or decades) so as to increase future greenhouse gas concentrations. A number of current research and development efforts focus on ways to lower costs, *e.g.* through improving the capture and compression technologies, increases in energy efficiency and increases in opportunities for economic benefits from capturing, recycling/reusing, or permanently storing CO_2.

Commercial stage sequestration projects include a project in Sleipner, Norway where Statoil operates a commercial gas platform in the North Sea to separate CO_2 from gas and re-inject it 1,000 meters beneath the seabed.[54] Another project operates through a joint venture between British Petroleum, Statoil, and Sonatrach (Algeria's state-owned energy company). The In Salah project in Algeria also removes CO_2 from gas. Finally, in the Weyburn oil field in Saskatchewan, Canada, the CO_2 produced by a coal gasification plant in North Dakota is piped across the border for an EOR operation in a partly depleted oil field. Collectively, however, these projects represent only a tiny fraction of the amount of CO_2 that would need to be permanently stored from existing and new coal-fired powerplants.[55]

In sum, CCS is a complex process that poses daunting challenges for scaling up to the levels that would be required to safely store the trillions of tons of CO_2 produced by an expanding fleet of coal-fired plants around the world. There is no integrated CCS system operating anywhere else in the world today. The following statement from Entergy sums up where things stand from a utility perspective:

> To date, carbon capture and sequestration has not been demonstrated commercially on any power plant in the United States. Even today, pilot scale projects are only now being

---

52. 2007 Potential For Carbon Sequestration, *supra* note 46, at 12.

53. *Id.*

54. 2007 Potential For Carbon Sequestration, *supra* note 46; 2008 Capturing King Coal, supra note 45.

55. These three projects each sequester about 1.5 million tons per year. But America's electricity industry alone produces 1.5 *billion* tons per year. It would take 1500 sites like the three pilot projects to store that much CO_2. *See Dig Deep, Special Report: The Future of Energy*, The Economist, June 19, 2008, *available at* http://www.economist.com/specialreports/displaystory.cfm?story_id=11565676.

developed in the United States. The Company does not believe that this technology is commercially and reliably viable on a utility scale at the current level of technology development. Significant research and development in the performance, cost, and reliability of carbon capture technology remains to be completed. In addition, further research is also required on underground sequestration of carbon, including costs, permitting, and technological advancement such as appropriate geological formations and appropriateness for long term storage of carbon dioxide and the transportation of CO_2 gas.[56]

Economic Issues

No matter how it's done, CCS is going to be a very expensive process.[57] A number of studies have estimated the costs under different scenarios. In a 2007 report, an interdisciplinary team of experts at the Massachusetts Institute of Technology (MIT) estimated that the cost of carbon capture and sequestration for a new PC plant that was designed and built to include carbon capture technology at the outset would be about \$28/ton.[58] The cost for a more efficient "supercritical" plant would be \$37 per ton. The MIT study concluded that it would be much more expensive to retrofit carbon capture technology onto existing coal-fired power plants.[59] Moreover, these cost figures only represent the cost of capture. Costs for the transportation and sequestration of the captured CO_2 would further increase the overall cost of CCS regardless of which combustion technology was employed.

The largest cost associated with CCS is the energy penalty, also called the "parasitic load," required to run the system. A 2007 NETL study calculated that a 580 MW gross supercritical coal plant that would generate 550 MW net of power without CO_2 capture technology would produce only 463 MW with CO_2 capture.[60] Stated differently, in order to get 550 MW net output with carbon capture, a company would have to increase the size of the plant to 663 MW. Thus, CCS actually increases the amount of coal that must be mined, the emissions that result from burning and the wastes that must be disposed of.

In a 2008 report prepared for the Interfaith Center on Corporate Responsibility, Synapse Energy Economics Inc. surveyed a number of independent economic studies of CCS and concluded that adding and operating CCS equipment will raise the cost of generating electricity at new coal-fired power plants by perhaps as much as 60 percent to 80 percent.[61] While noting that new technologies being studied, such as aqueous ammonia and chilled ammonia, might lower carbon capture and sequestration costs to perhaps as low as \$20/ton of CO_2 avoided, Synapse warned that these technologies have only been evaluated in very small scale tests and the associated results are very preliminary.[62] Finally, Synapse noted that "even if or when the technology for CO_2 capture matures, there will always be significant regional variations in the cost of the

---

56. Entergy Louisiana's Response to Question No. LPSC 1–18 in Louisiana Public Service Commission Docket No. U-30192.

57. IPCC estimates that the incremental cost to the consumer of electricity produced from plants equipped with CCS has been estimated at 1–5 cents per kilowatt hour. IPCC SPECIAL REPORT, *supra* note 42. The Bush administration pulled the plug on the very expensive FutureGen project. *See* DOE press release at http://www.energy.gov/news/5912.htm. The FY 09 Omnibus Spending Bill passed by Congress does not contain funding for FutureGen but does include \$218 million for the "Clean Coal Power Initiative." *See* GREENWIRE (3/11/09), *available at* http://www.eenews.net/EEDaily/2009/03/11/archive/2?terms=futuregen.

58. 2007 THE FUTURE OF COAL, *supra* note 42, at 28–29.

59. *Id.*

60. NETL, COST AND PERFORMANCE BASELINE FOR FOSSIL ENERGY PLANTS 4, revised August 2007.

61. SYNAPSE ENERGY ECONOMICS, INC., DON'T GET BURNED: THE RISKS OF INVESTING IN NEW COAL-FIRED GENERATING FACILITIES 31 (2008) [hereinafter DON'T GET BURNED], *available at* http://www.iccr.org/news/press_releases/pdf%20files/DontGetBurned08.pdf.

62. *Id.* at 32.

transportation and storage of the captured CO_2 due to the proximity and quality of storage sites."[63]

Given these costs, firms are not likely to build coal plants with CCS unless forced to do so by rising carbon prices, or "incentivized" to do so with taxpayer subsidies or some other revenue stream.[64] For CCS to be economically feasible, the price of CO_2 would have to be high enough to cover the incremental costs of CO_2 capture and compression (at power plants designed for that purpose), transport, and storage. According to the Congressional Budget Office (CBO), that price may vary from \$15 to \$90 per metric ton of CO_2.[65] Analysts generally compare the costs of producing electricity at similar plants with and without CO_2 capture, taking into account the added greenhouse-gas emissions that result from the energy required for the capture and compression processes. Then they add estimates of transport costs, based on the distance to a potential storage site, and storage costs, based on the type of storage reservoir. Estimates of the economic potential of CCS typically do not include the effects of the regulatory system that might be set up to implement carbon dioxide capture and storage.

According to CBO, "the additional cost of carbon dioxide capture and storage will depend on the types of plants that would be built in the absence of limits on CO_2 emissions, which would vary with the relative cost of producing electricity at different types of plants at different points in time."[66] In a recent report, CAPTURING KING COAL, the World Resources Institute (WRI) estimates that it will cost "hundreds of billions of dollars" to install CCS systems capable of "decarbonizing" 76 gigawatts (GW) of new coal plants (the amount WRI believes is necessary to achieve one "wedge" of carbon reduction).[67] As WRI points out, it is not going to be easy to find investors willing to put up this kind of money on an unproven technology, let alone a complex, integrated system like CCS with technological challenges at each step in the process. Socially conscious institutional investors commanding over \$1.5 trillion in assets are already backing away from coal,[68] and major banks such as JP Morgan and Citibank have adopted "Carbon Principles" and strict screening criteria to assess the risks of coal.[69] As WRI puts it:

> In terms of financing an eventual clean coal build-out, the major challenge to capital formation around low-carbon technologies is that the technologies are relatively new and untested. This poses a fresh set of risks for construction firms, which may be unwilling to extend the same performance guarantees for them. Therefore, deployment of advanced coal technologies may require innovative approaches to risk and reward struc-

---

63. *Id.*

64. One proposal would be to sell the captured CO_2 to oil and gas companies for EOR to replace the natural CO_2 that would otherwise have to be extracted at greater expense. Proponents claim this would result in a net reduction of CO_2 to the atmosphere. However, this fails to take into account the fact that cheaper sources of CO_2 would simply increase the rate of EOR leading to a net increase in CO_2 emission from the gas fuel cycle. *See* Climate Progress blog at http://climateprogress.org/2007/08/23/rule-four-of-offsets-no-enhanced-oil-recovery.

65. 2007 POTENTIAL FOR CARBON SEQUESTRATION, *supra* note 46, at 15.

66. CBO concluded that IGCC plants represent the most likely baseline for measuring the incremental cost of CCS. *Id* at 17.

67. 2008 CAPTURING KING COAL, *supra* note 45, at 3.

68. On September 17, 2007 a coalition of institutional investors and environmental organizations, led by CERES, filed a petition with the Securities and Exchange Commission calling for more rigorous guidelines requiring publicly traded corporations to disclose the risks of climate change in their securities filings and prospectuses.

69. *See* Press Release issued by Citigroup: *Leading Wall Street Banks Establish The Carbon Principles*, February 4, 2008, *available at* http://www.citigroup.com/citigroup/press/2008/080204a.htm.

tures to make financiers comfortable with investing in promising new technologies. This may require, for example, exploring increased government participation.[70]

WRI proceeds to outline a series of government policies designed to "push" CCS by means of, for example, a federal cap and trade program; and polices designed to "pull" CCS forward by means of government sponsored R&D programs, subsidies and other incentives.[71] For example, for post-combustion capture WRI recommends accelerating research on using chilled ammonia to reduce the energy penalty of capture.[72] For pre-combustion capture, WRI suggests funding research to develop membrane technologies for separating the CO_2 from syngas, which may have the potential to reduce power requirements by 50 percent.[73]

Other commentators have suggested the need for new legislation to spur adoption of CCS. In Global Warming and the Future of Coal, Ken Berlin and Bob Sussman, two experienced environmental practitioners, recommend that Congress mandate a power emission performance standard that effectively requires all new coal plants to control emissions to the level achievable by CCS systems.[74] The authors recommend that this standard should be implemented in conjunction with an emissions cap-and-trade system for existing power plants.[75] The standard would apply to all new plants for which construction is commenced after a date certain (say 2010), although flexibility would be allowed in the timing for CCS implementation so that the power industry can gain more experience with capture and sequestration technologies.

Capture-ready Plants

Given the long lead time facing development and deployment of CCS at scale, the question becomes what to do about the raft of new coal plants that are either under construction or working their way through the permit process. One idea is to make the plants "capture-ready."[76] While sounding good, the concept is meaningless without content.[77] Unless plants are designed with CCS in mind it may not be economical to retrofit them, and it could be cheaper to scrap the plant and build a new one from scratch.[78] Moreover, a "capture-ready site" isn't worth much without a proven transportation and storage system. A more detailed definition is provided by the International Energy Agency (IEA) GHG Program, which proposes that the aim of building plants that are capture-ready is to reduce the risk of stranded assets or "carbon lock-in." IEA goes further and gives examples of what needs to be considered and included — sufficient space for the capture equipment, access to the additional facil-

---

70. 2008 Capturing King Coal, *supra* note 45, at 26.

71. *Id.*

72. *Id* at 27.

73. *Id.*

74. Berlin & Sussman, Global Warming and the Future of Coal: The Path to Carbon Capture and Storage 49 (Center for American Progress 2007), *available at* http://www.americanprogress.org/issues/2007/05/coal_report.html (last visited Nov. 5, 2008) [hereinafter 2007 Berlin & Sussman].

75. The DC Circuit recently struck down the Clean Air Interstate Rule (CAIR) which would have established a cap and trade program for NO_x and SO_2. North Carolina v EPA, 531 F.3d 896 (D.C. Cir. 2008). The court found numerous flaws with the rule, particularly with respect to its impact on downwind states, and remanded it to EPA with instructions to "redo its analysis from the ground up." *Id.* at 929. Given the undisputed need to reduce power-plant emissions to achieve NAAQS for NO_x and SO_2, it is likely that CAIR will be resurrected, and even strengthened, by the next administration. CAIR provides a model for how a cap and trade program could be implemented for CO_2 under existing CAA authority.

76. 2007 Berlin & Sussman, *supra* note 74, at 26.

77. As David Hawkins of NRDC quipped regarding the vagaries of the capture-ready concept: "My garage is Ferrari-ready."

78. 2007 The Future of Coal, *supra* note 42, at 38.

ities, and reasonable routes to storage sites. WRI recommends that a working definition of "capture readiness" should cover all system parts for capture readiness — design and construction elements of the plant itself as well as elements of the transport and storage facilities and define the full range of technical options a plant or a facility has to have in order to be considered ready.

IGCC plants are already capturing carbon, mercury, sulfur, nitrogen oxides and other pollutants. In IGCC plants, coal is partially combusted and gasified into syngas. Carbon dioxide and other impurities are filtered from the syngas through absorption or membrane technologies, and the remaining hydrogen is fired in a combustion turbine that produces electricity.[79] Current carbon capture technologies can potentially reduce an IGCC facility's carbon dioxide emissions by 95% if the emissions are properly sequestered. But IGCC plants are expensive and very few are in operation worldwide. Still, IGCC plants may look like a bargain when compared to the cost of retro-fitting PC plants. A study by MIT found that a baseline PC plant is the most economical choice under low CO_2 prices, and IGCC plants are preferable at higher CO_2 prices (*e.g.*, an initial price of about \$22/ton CO_2 starting in 2015 and growing at 2%/year).[80]

Utilities, not to mention their bankers, are understandably reluctant to commit large capital outlays to IGCC plants where there is a risk that these costs may not be recoverable.[81] In states where utilities are still regulated cost recovery must be approved by state utility commissions. In unregulated states, utility companies must rely on a steady revenue stream to recoup their investments over the 40–60 year life of a coal plant.[82]

Finally, the capture-ready debate fails to address an even more pressing problem: what to do with all the existing dirty coal plants, many of which have escaped installing modern pollution control equipment for conventional and hazardous air pollutants for decades, never mind CO_2 emissions. In two recent licensing decisions, the states of Indiana and North Carolina conditioned approval of new coal units on the retirement of existing units.[83] These decision also required that the new units be "capture-ready," but without imposing any specific requirements or timetables for actually installing CCS systems. As Berlin & Sussman observe:

> Unless emissions by existing plants are reduced, a stringent emissions standard for new plants might simply prolong the useful life of older plants and discourage new power generation — much as existing New Source Performance Standards under the Clean Air Act have encouraged continued operation of older power plants beyond their expected useful life.[84]

Regulatory Issues

There is currently no comprehensive regulatory framework within the U.S. to deal with CCS. Rather, there is a patchwork of state and federal laws that deal with various parts of the CCS system.[85] The transport of CO_2 from capture to storage reservoir is technically established but issues

---

79. For a diagram and description of the Shell Global Solutions IGCC technology burning bituminous coal, see http://www.netl.doe.gov/energy-analyses/pubs/deskreference/B_IG_Shell_051507.pdf.

80. BOHM *et al.*, CAPTURE-READY COAL PLANTS — OPTIONS, TECHNOLOGIES AND ECONOMICS (Laboratory for Energy and the Environment, Massachusetts Institute of Technology 2007).

81. *See* Richard J. Pierce, *The Regulatory Treatment of Mistakes in Retrospect: Canceled Plants and Excess Capacity*, 132 U. PA. L. REV. 497 (1984) (discussing the "prudent investment" rule); Paul Rodgers and Charles D. Gray, *State Commission Treatment of Nuclear Power Plant Costs*, 13 HOFSTRA L. REV. 443 (1985).

82. DON'T GET BURNED, *supra* note 61, at 3.

83. *See* Parenteau, *Lead, Follow or get Out of the Way: The States Tackle Climate Change with Little Help from Washington*, 40 U. CONN. L. REV. No. 5 (2008).

84. 2007 BERLIN & SUSSMAN, *supra* note 74, at 42.

85. *Id.*, *passim*.

around regulatory responsibility, classification of CO_2, right-of-way, and eminent domain remain. While the safety aspects of interstate pipelines constructed for transporting CO_2 fall under the jurisdiction of the Department of Transportation (DOT), there is no regulatory oversight over rates, access, and siting of CO_2 pipelines. Oversight by DOT is somewhat limited as compared to regulation by Federal Energy Regulatory Commission (FERC) over oil and natural gas pipelines.

FERC presently has no legislative authority to regulate CO_2 as an article of interstate commerce.[86]

One issue that will need to be resolved is the legal status of CO_2—is it a commodity or a pollutant, or both? When used in enhanced oil recovery (EOR), CO_2 is classified as a commodity.[87] However, in light of the U.S. Supreme Court decision in *Massachusetts v EPA*, CO_2 is also an "air pollutant" under the Clean Air Act.[88] Though it is still dragging its feet on making the endangerment finding, the day of reckoning is fast approaching when EPA will have to begin actual regulation of CO_2 and other GHGs under the CAA.[89] With the advent of regional cap and trade programs such as the Regional Greenhouse Gas Initiative (RGGI),[90] and the prospect of a national program being enacted by Congress following the November election, CO_2 is expected to become a more widely tradable commodity.

For CCS, the major permitting issues revolve around injection and storage. Geologic sequestration of CO_2 through well injection meets the definition of "underground injection" in section 1421(d)(1) of the Safe Drinking Water Act (SDWA). EPA has authority for underground injection of carbon dioxide (CO_2) under the SDWA Underground Injection Control (UIC) program. EPA and states, territories, and tribes that have primacy for UIC programs ("Primacy States") act as co-regulators to protect drinking water supplies from any potential endangerment from underground injection of CO_2. Underground injection of CO_2 for purposes such as enhanced oil recovery (EOR) and enhanced gas recovery (EGR) is a long-standing practice. CO_2 injection specifically for geologic sequestration involves different technical issues and potentially much larger volumes of CO_2 and larger scale projects than in the past.

In May, 2007, EPA issued a guidance document under the SDWA for CO_2 injection at geological sequestration (GS) sites.[91] This guidance is intended to address only pilot GS projects (*i.e.*, the limited number of experimental projects anticipated to be brought online in advance

---

86. 2008 CAPTURING KING COAL, *supra* note 45, at 22.

87. Source: DOE, *available at* http://www.fossil.energy.gov/programs/oilgas/eor/index.html.

88. Massachusetts v. EPA, 549 U.S. 497, 500, 127 S. Ct. 1438, 1462 (2007) ("Because greenhouse gases fit well within the Clean Air Act's capacious definition of 'air pollutant,' we hold that EPA has the statutory authority to regulate the emission of such gases from new motor vehicles.") EPA has yet to make the "endangerment finding" which is the necessary predicate for regulation of GHG under section 202 of the CAA. The D.C. Circuit recently issued a *per curiam* order rejecting a Petition for Mandamus filed by the original petitioners in Mass v EPA trying to force EPA to make a decision. Commonwealth of Massachusetts v EPA, No. 03-1361 (June 26, 2007). Judge Tatel filed an opinion concurring in part and dissenting in part in which he agrees that mandamus was not appropriate at this point, but urged the court to hold the case in abeyance and require EPA to file progress reports every four months to hold the agency's feet to the fire.

89. As recently reported in the national media, the White House apparently tried to block attempts by EPA staff to transmit a proposed endangerment finding to the Office of Management and Budget. Juliet Eilperin, *White House tried to Silence EPA proposal on Car Emissions*, WASHINGTON POST, June 26, 2008. According to Jason Burnett, the former Associate Deputy Administrator who resigned in protest, his email messages were returned unopened and he was instructed by OMB officials to "recall" the email, which he refused to do. Burnett reportedly told the WASHINGTON POST: "The White House made it clear they did not want to address the ramifications of that finding and have decided to leave the challenge to the next administration. Some [at the White House] thought that EPA had mistakenly concluded that climate change endangers the public. It was no mistake."

90. Information on RGGI is *available at* http://www.rggi.org/.

91. CYNTHIA DOUGHTERY (Office of Ground Water and Drinking Water) and BRIAN MCLEAN (Office of Atmospheric Programs), USING THE CLASS V EXPERIMENTAL TECHNOLOGY WELL CLASSIFICATION FOR PILOT

of commercial-scale operations over the next several years). The guidance calls for a two phase program. The first phase—the "validation" phase—is slated to begin in 2008 and will provide *in situ* tests of GS technology by injecting low volumes of CO_2. The validation phase projects include 25 field tests where CO_2 will be injected and its fate and transport will be monitored. The second phase—"deployment"—would follow, beginning around 2009. Drawing on the knowledge gained in the validation phase, these projects will involve higher volumes of CO_2. Full, commercial-scale deployment of GS technology is expected to commence around 2012.

EPA anticipates that pilot projects will have a variety of objectives, including testing the effectiveness of various well materials and injection practices, assessing the usefulness of geophysical survey and monitoring techniques, testing failure scenarios, and/or validating models of the fate and transport of CO_2 in the subsurface. EPA has identified a number of technical issues to be addressed:

- Potential impacts of CO_2 injection on ground water and underground sources of drinking water (USDWs);
- Potential impacts of CO_2 injection on human health and the environment;
- Integrity of CO_2 injection wells and other wells in the area of review;
- Potential to induce seismic activity;
- Remediation technologies;
- Land surface deformation;
- Potential for large-scale CO_2 releases;
- Measurement, monitoring, and verification tools applicable to GS of CO_2;
- Potential impacts of CO_2 injection on geologic media (reservoir and seals); and
- Geochemical and geomechanical effects.[92]

On July 2008, EPA published a proposed rule under the SDWA for the underground injection of CO_2 for the purpose of long term underground storage or geologic sequestration (GS).[93] In the fact sheet accompanying the proposed rule EPA explained the purpose as follows:

> While the elements of today's proposal are based on the existing regulatory framework of EPA's Underground Injection Control (UIC) Program, modifications address the unique nature of CO_2 injection for GS. The relative buoyancy of CO_2, its corrosivity in the presence of water, the potential presence of impurities in captured CO_2, its mobility within subsurface formations, and large injection volumes anticipated at full scale deployment warrant specific requirements tailored to this new practice.[94]

EPA's proposed rule would establish a new class of injection well—Class VI—and technical criteria for geologic site characterization; area of review and corrective action; well construction and operation; mechanical integrity testing and monitoring; well plugging; post-injection site care; and site closure for the purposes of protecting underground sources of drinking water. The proposal also discusses the long term liability issue of GS and requests public comments, but gives no indication of how those issues might be treated in a final rule. In earlier

---

GEOLOGIC SEQUESTRATION PROJECTS—UIC PROGRAM GUIDANCE (UICPG #83.) (March 1, 2007), *available at* http://www.epa.gov/safewater/uic/pdfs/guide_uic_carbonsequestration_fi nal-03-07.pdf.

92. *Id*. at 2.

93. U.S. Environmental Protection Agency, Proposed UIC Regulations for Geologic Sequestration of Carbon Dioxide (December 3–4, 2007); *available at* http://www.epa.gov/ogwdw/uic/pdfs/summary_uic_carbosequestration_meeting_december3-2007.pdf (last visited April 19, 2009).

94. Fact sheet *available at* http://www.epa.gov/OGWDW/uic/pdfs/fs_uic_co2_proposedrule.pdf (last visited April 19, 2009).

statements, EPA has made it clear that it will be up to Congress to address long term liability issues.[95]

Congress has only begun to consider some of these issues. A recent proposal "Carbon Dioxide Pipeline Study Act of 2007" introduced by Senators Coleman (R Minn.) and Salazar (D Colo.) directs the Secretary of Energy to conduct a feasibility study related to construction and operation of plants with carbon capture and pipelines for CO_2 transport. The proposal outlines a myriad of issues that must be resolved to advance the development of a CO_2 pipeline infrastructure.[96]

Several states are already moving forward with legislative and regulatory proposals for carbon dioxide sequestration programs. In May 2007, Montana adopted a CO_2 emissions performance standard for electric generating units in the state with the enactment of HB 25.[97] The bill prohibits the state Public Utility Commission from approving electric generating units primarily fueled by coal unless a minimum of 50 percent of the CO_2 produced by the facility is captured and permanently geologically sequestered. The standard applies only to electric generating units constructed after January 1, 2007. In Iowa, a bill has been introduced to require new power plants to achieve carbon neutrality—meaning that the facility could not contribute to any increase in statewide emissions of greenhouse gases.[98] The applicant for a new power plant would have to obtain preconstruction approval of its carbon-neutral plan, which could rely upon energy conservation, demand-side management, renewables, or carbon sequestration. The Washington Department of Ecology has proposed rules that would amend its UIC regulations to support geologic carbon sequestration.[99] A recent report by the Interstate Oil and Gas Compact Commission ("IOGCC") concluded that states are best suited to regulate geologic sequestration based on their experience with enhanced oil and gas recovery wells.[100] In spite of this flurry of activity at the state level, federal preemption via EPA rulemaking or new legislation remains a distinct possibility.

Long Term Liability Issues

The fate of geologic sequestration of CO_2 could well depend on what type of liability regime is chosen to deal with the long term risks of accidents.[101] CCS projects will face different kinds of liability issues but the two that are most significant are climate liability and *in situ* liability. Climate liability results from any CO_2 leakage from the storage sites that may affect the global climate by contributing to CO_2 concentrations in the atmosphere. Given the large volumes of CO_2 that are involved even tiny amounts of leakage are problematic. In one study, for example, the authors concluded that a seepage rate of 1% would offset any gain from sequestration.[102] These authors proposed a performance standard of less than 0.01% per year.

---

95. *EPA Begins Discussions on Rulemaking for Underground Storage of Carbon Dioxide*, BNA Environment Reporter (Dec. 7, 2007).

96. 2008 Capturing King Coal, *supra* note 45, at 22–23.

97. Montana HB 25, 60th Leg., Reg. Sess. (Mt. 2007) (amending MCA § 15-72-103); *available at* http://www.pewclimate.org/docUploads/montanaHB0025%20(2).pdf (last visited April 19, 2009).

98. Iowa S.F. 391, 82nd General Assembly, Regular Session (Ia. 2007); *see also* Richard Cowart and Shanna Vale, State Options for Low-Carbon policy (Pew Center on Climate Change 2007), *available at* http://www.pewclimate.org/docUploads/StateOptions-02-20-08.pdf (last visited April 19, 2009).

99. A copy of the draft rule is *available at* http://www.ecy.wa.gov/laws-rules/activity/wac173407_218.html (last visited April 19, 2009).

100. The Interstate Oil and Gas Compact Commission, Storage of Carbon Dioxide in Geologic Structures—A Legal and Regulatory Guide for States and Provinces, 10, *available at* http://www.iogcc.state.ok.us/docs/MeetingDocs/Master-Document-September-252007-FINAL-(2).pdf).

101. *See generally* Alexandra B. Klass and Elizabeth J. Wilson, Climate Change and Carbon Sequestration, Assessing a Liability Regime for Long Term Storage of Carbon Dioxide (2008) [hereinafter, 2008 Klass & Wilson], *available at* http://works.bepress.com/alexandra_klass/4.

In situ liability is associated with leakage or migration that could result in public health, environmental, or ecosystem damage. Carbon dioxide can be sequestered in different ways. When CO_2 is compressed it can be injected via deep wells into oil and gas production zones deep underground. Under layers of impermeable "cap rock," oil and gas has been held in porous rock reservoirs for millions of years. As the oil and gas is produced, it travels through the porous rock to a well and then to the surface, essentially freeing space between the grains of rock where CO_2 can be injected to replace the produced oil and gas.

Another option is to pump CO_2 into saline aquifers where it dissolves in salty water. The water with dissolved CO_2 is heavier than the water around it and so it sinks to the bottom of a rock formation, theoretically trapping the CO_2 indefinitely. Another form of sequestration takes place when CO_2 reacts with the minerals in the surrounding rocks and forms new minerals on the rocks, much like shellfish use calcium and carbon from seawater to form their shells. Depending on the chemistry of the rocks and water, this process can be very rapid or very slow, but its effect is to bind the CO_2 to the rocks.

Commentators have pointed out several kinds of risks associated with these processes including the fact that buoyancy flow could drive CO_2 upward through pathways in undetected faults or abandoned well bores.[103] Although large surface releases are unlikely, they could pose health risks to humans, both in the form of immediate death from asphyxiation or effects from prolonged exposure to high concentrations of CO_2. Slow CO_2 seepage into the near subsurface could harm flora and fauna, and potentially cause local disruptions of ecology or agriculture. Induced seismic activity is another risk.[104] There are also a number of potential risks associated with injected CO_2 even if it remains underground, including displacement of saline groundwater into potable aquifers, contamination of hydrocarbon resources, and pressure changes causing seismic events.

A major issue with long-term liability is simply the timeframe itself. CO_2 must be sequestered for hundreds, perhaps thousands of years, longer than corporations—or the United States itself, for that matter—have existed.[105] This poses unprecedented challenges to design a monitoring, measurement and verification (MMV) program to develop and deploy technologies that can provide an accurate accounting of stored CO_2, and a high level of confidence that the CO_2 will remain permanently sequestered. Effective application of these MM&V technologies must ensure the safety of sequestration projects with respect to both human health and the environment, and provide the basis for establishing carbon credit trading markets for sequestered CO_2.[106]

There are a number of theories of liability that could apply to CCS. Tort theories include trespass, negligence, nuisance (public and private), strict liability and product liability. Contract theories include breach of implied warranty of fitness under the Uniform Commercial Code and breach of contractual provisions related to the purchase and sale of emission credits under a cap and trade program. These theories have been thoroughly explored elsewhere and need not be re-

---

102. ROBERT P. HEPPLE AND SALLY M. BENSON, IMPLICATIONS OF SURFACE SEEPAGE ON THE EFFECTIVENESS OF GEOLOGICAL STORAGE OF CARBON DIOXIDE AS A CLIMATE CHANGE MITIGATION STRATEGY (2002), *available at* http://www.osti.gov/bridge/servlets/purl/802042-vzNwYO/native/802042.pdf.

103. 2008 KLASS & WILSON, *supra* note 101, at 7.

104. Mark Anthony de Figueirido, *The Liability of Carbon Dioxide Storage*, Ph.D Dissertation, MIT (2007) [hereinafter, *de Figueirido Dissertation*], *available at* http://sequestration.mit.edu/pdf/GHGT8_deFigueiredo.pdf.

105. The Hudson's Bay Company, chartered on May 2, 1670, is one of the oldest companies in the world; yet it is has been in existence less than 400 years. WIKIPEDIA.

106. NETL, CARBON SEQUESTRATION TECHNOLOGIES, *available at* http://www.netl.doe.gov/technologies/carbon_seq/index.html.

peated here.[107] A good case can be made that a standard of strict, joint and several liability similar to Superfund ought to apply.[108] Although the courts have held that oil and gas recovery is not an "abnormally dangerous" activity, the injection of massive quantities of CO_2 underground is an entirely new kind of undertaking with an as yet unknown potential to do irreversible harm to drinking water supplies and to the atmosphere from leakage.[109] Courts have applied strict liability principles to the dangers posed by radon, a naturally occurring radioactive substance.[110] There is a parallel between the unknown risk of radon and the unknown risks of carbon sequestration. Leakage of CO_2 could be viewed as a defect in the CCS system, akin to product defects.[111]

In the absence of federal preemption or a uniform rule of liability established under federal common law, state laws would govern. This raises the spectre of inconsistent or conflicting liability rules across the country, which has led to calls for some form of government indemnification.[112] Though Congress has considered indemnification provisions none have passed as yet.[113] As discussed below, there is a risk that efforts to cap or limit liability will undermine public confidence in CCS.

Financial Responsibility

Various mechanisms have been suggested to provide financial assurances for long term monitoring and verification, as well as a source of funds to take corrective actions and provide compensation for damages. One option is to create a trust fund financed by a generation charge on coal-fired power plants. One study calculates that a fee of 0.04–0.05 cents per kWh would support a program of $7–10 billion per year, providing the incremental CCS costs for both new plants and retrofits of existing plants in a 10-plant test program.[114] Questions raised by this proposal include who should administer the trust fund, and whether including the fees in customer bills require approval by each state's public utility commission or can be authorized by federal legislation.

Bonding is another tool that is widely used in a variety of environmental contexts including municipal landfills, transport and storage of hazardous waste, and underground injection and disposal. Bonding requires upfront commitment of resources such as cash, letters of credit, surety bonds, or escrow accounts to offset the costs of potential future costs of pollution. However, as explained by Klass & Wilson, there are problems with trying to use bonding in the context of CCS:

> Bonding is costly in terms of imposing liquidity constraints on firms and transaction costs, and becomes more costly as complexity increases. A problem for both liability rules and bonding is the potentially long lag time between the operators' activity (injection of CO_2) and the potential harm (leakage to the surface or resource damage). Also, over long time horizons, the responsible firm may go out of business, or surety

---

107. *de Figueirido Dissertation*, *supra* note 104; 2008 KLASS & WILSON, *supra* note 101.

108. *See* information on EPA website at http://www.epa.gov/oecaerth/cleanup/superfund/liability.html.

109. *See* RESTATEMENT (SECOND) OF TORTS, §§519–520. To determine what is "abnormally dangerous," §520 sets forth several factors including: (1) "the existence of a high degree of risk of some harm to person, land or chattels of others;" (2) "the inappropriateness of the activity to the place where it is carried out;" and (3) "the extent to which its value to the community is outweighed by its dangerous attributes." Thus, the factors incorporate a kind of risk-utility concept.

110. *See* C. K. Hoyden, *Indoor Radiation: Regulating a Blameless Cause*, 181 BUFFALO L. J. 3 (1995).

111. M.A. de Figueirido, *et al.*, *Towards a long-term Liability Framework for Geologic carbon Sequestration*, paper presented at the Second Annual Conference on Carbon Sequestration, Alexandria Va. (May, 2003), *available at* http://sequestration.mit.edu/pdf/defigueiredo_et_al_MIT_paper.pdf.

112. 2008 KLASS & WILSON, *supra* note 101, at 34–35.

113. *Id.*

114. E. S. Rubin, *Accelerating Deployment of CCS at U.S. Coal-Fired Power Plant*, Proceedings of the 6th Annual Conference on Carbon Capture and Sequestration, Pittsburgh, PA, May 7–10, 2007.

providers are unlikely to underwrite bonds with such uncertainties. Thus, for bonding to be effectively utilized within CCS projects regulators must explicitly define periods of responsibility.[115]

Pollution liability insurance is another potential tool that is used in regulation and cleanup of hazardous wastes under RCRA and CERCLA.[116] Again, however, the unique challenges posed by CCS will require specialized insurance coverage to deal with the site-specific nature of sequestration and the difficulty of assessing the long term risks of releases to the atmosphere. As noted by Klass & Wilson, the International Risk Governance Council has determined that all of the risks posed by CCS could be covered by conventional environmental impairment liability (EIL) clauses with the notable exception of risks to the climate from leakage.[117]

Given the vagaries of tort law and the length of time it takes to litigate cases and collect damages, there is a need for some form of federal compensation system, perhaps loosely modeled on the one used for the nuclear power industry under the Price-Anderson Act.[118] The *quid pro quo* for a publicly financed system would probably involve damage caps and federal preemption of tort actions, which could prove contentious. Klass and Wilson propose a hybrid system modeled on the Trans-Alaska Pipeline Liability Fund ("TAPL Fund"), now part of the funding available under the Oil Pollution Act ("OPA"):

> This system provides information analogs for CCS for at least two reasons. First, the OPA reconciles existing regulatory standards and incorporates approaches to liability and risk management depending on the location of the damage. Second, it creates a significant fund for quick payout of claims in case of harm but allows claimants to seek damages in excess of the fund's maximum from liable parties under state or federal tort law. These features make the liability structure for claims associated with the Trans-Alaska Pipeline (and now oil spills in general) particularly relevant for CCS.[119]

Finally, there is the question of what to do about post-closure liability and financial responsibility, once the capacity of any given storage site has been reached. To achieve the benefits of CCS and justify its high front end costs, CO_2 must remain sequestered for hundreds to thousands of years. To deal with these long time frames, Klass & Wilson recommend a phased approach to post-closure responsibility:

> Over the first post-closure phase, the project operator would bear full responsibility for all liability and be required to provide some type of financial assurance. Over the longer-term, stewardship of CCS projects—and funds to ensure remediation—would be transferred to a public or private organization with a pool of resources to ensure public and environmental health are managed over the long term. Bonds, insurance, and selective damage caps (for early pilot projects and the long-term stewardship periods only) could all play a role to ensure CCS risk is managed over the long-term.[120]

Any way you cut it, CCS poses complex, novel questions of liability and financial responsibility that have no clear answers at the moment. That is not to say that the obstacles are insur-

---

115. 2008 KLASS & WILSON, *supra* note 101, at 36.
116. Martin T. Katzman, *Pollution Liability Insurance and Catastrophic Environmental Risk*, 55 JOURNAL OF RISK & INSURANCE 75 (1988).
117. 2008 KLASS & WILSON, *supra* note 101, at 38.
118. *Id.* at 39–40.
119. *Id.* at 42.
120. *Id.* at 44.

mountable, but rather that they are formidable and will take a long time to sort out, and time is a precious commodity given the onrushing threat of climate change.

Public Acceptance

Even the best designed projects can run aground on the fickle shoals of public opinion. Already a new term has been coined—NUMBY (Not Under My Backyard)—to describe the expected reaction to proposals to sequester CO_2 underground.[121] Proponents of CCS should avoid the mistake that the nuclear industry made decades ago in dismissing concerns about the risks of low-level radioactive waste disposal by calling it a public relations problem rather than acknowledging the very real technological and geological challenges, not to mention political obstacles that have yet to be overcome.[122] It may well be true, as some scientists have said,[123] that carbon sequestration, if properly done, poses no insurmountable obstacles or serious risks to public health or the environment, but it does not necessarily follow that the public will simply accept the views of experts far removed from the site. The public has heard the "risks are manageable" refrain many times, only to see the best laid plans go terribly wrong. The environmental justice community is already mobilizing to oppose sequestration projects in California.[124] It will take more than the soothing assurances of the experts to persuade the public that sequestration is both a necessary and safe option for mitigating climate, and that the site selection process will be demonstrably fair and well-grounded on verifiable experience. As Dr. Granger Morgan, Director of the Climate Decision Making Center at Carnegie Mellon University, puts it:

> We need to do this right. During the initial field experiences, a single major accident, resulting from inadequate regulatory oversight, anywhere in the world, could seriously endanger the future viability of [geologic sequestration].[125]

Currently, CCS is not even on the public radar. A 2006 study by MIT found that less than 5 percent of people in the U.S. had even heard of CCS.[126] A major study by the Tyndall Centre for Climate Change Research in the UK reached this conclusion:

> On first hearing about carbon storage in the absence of information as to its purpose, we found that the majority of people either do not have an opinion at all or are somewhat skeptical. Once (even limited) information is provided on the role of carbon storage in reducing CO_2 emissions to the atmosphere, opinion shifts considerably towards slight support for the concept. Support depends, however, upon concern about human-caused climate change, plus recognition of the need for major CO_2 emission reductions. It also

---

121. 2008 CAPTURING KING COAL, *supra* note 45, at 25.

122. The effort to license a nuclear waste repository at Yucca Mountain Nevada has been underway since Congress passed the Nuclear Waste Policy Act in 1982, but has been blocked in the courts and by the fierce opposition by the State of Nevada, Indian tribes and environmentalists. *See Why Does the State Oppose Yucca Mountain?*, *available at* http://www.state.nv.us/nucwaste/yucca/state01.html.

123. In a letter dated July 2, 2007 to the Honorable Loni Hancock, Chair of the California Assembly Natural Resources Committee, five distinguished scientists conclude that "CCS is not a technology of the distant future—it is available to us today, and it can be perfectly safe"; *available at* http://www.rachel.org/lib/nrdc_defends_carbon_sequestration.070501.pdf.

124. Valerie J Brown, *Of Two Minds: Groups Square off on Carbon Mitigation*, ENVIRONMENTAL HEALTH PERSPECTIVE, November 2007, *available at* http://www.pubmedcentral.nih.gov/articlerender.fcgi?artid=2072838. The article decries the formation of an environmental justice group to oppose a bill in the California legislature designed to set standards for siting CCS projects in their communities around Los Angeles.

125. Wilson, *et al.*, *Regulating the Geologic Sequestration of CO_2*, ENVIRONMENTAL SCIENCE AND TECHNOLOGY, April 15, 2008, *available at* http://pubs.acs.org/subscribe/journals/esthag/42/i08/html/041508viewpoint_morgan.html.

126. D. REINER *et al.*, AN INTERNATIONAL COMPARISON OF PUBLIC ATTITUDES TOWARDS CARBON CAPTURE AND STORAGE TECHNOLOGIES (2006), *available at* http://sequestration.mit.edu/pdf/GHGT8_Reiner.pdf.

depends upon CCS being seen as one part of a wider strategy for achieving significant cuts in CO_2 emissions. A portfolio including renewable energy technologies, energy efficiency and lifestyle change to reduce demand, was generally favoured. CCS can be part of such a portfolio but wind, wave, tidal, solar and energy efficiency were generally preferred as options. As a stand-alone option, it was felt that CCS might delay more far-reaching and necessary long-term changes in society's use of energy. The notion of CCS as a "bridging strategy" to a hydrogen-based energy system was welcomed.[127]

Other studies have shown that the public does not view risk the same way the experts do, and is skeptical of quantified assessments that downplay risks as negligible or "acceptable."[128] The public is also suspicious of new technologies and impatient for straight answers to hard questions even when those answers are not readily available. The suspicion deepens when a new technology is strongly supported by industries having an economic stake in it and government offers to provide liability shields, as it did for the nuclear industry under the Price-Anderson Act.[129] All of these considerations do not augur well for ready public acceptance of CCS.

Nevertheless, the public might be won over through a concerted effort to provide accurate, timely and honest information with a high degree of transparency in the regulatory processes, and meaningful opportunities for public participation (*i.e.* beyond routine notice and comment). Of course, actions speak louder than words, and nothing succeeds like success. Care must be taken in the selection and execution of the pilot projects to demonstrate how potential hazards will be avoided or minimized. History teaches us to expect the unexpected when tinkering with the environment. Mistakes and surprises are inevitable and adaptive management and contingency plans are essential to respond quickly and effectively when things don't go as planned. The level of public trust in government oversight is not very high at the moment given the sorry record of the Bush Administration on environmental matters.[130] The coal industry in particular faces an uphill battle convincing the public it is trustworthy given the awful legacy it has compiled.[131]

Various "stakeholder" processes have been initiated to promote better public understanding and acceptance of CCS. In its "Carbon Sequestration Roadmap" the Department of Energy acknowledges that: "It is imperative, therefore, that the relevant government and private entities engage the public to explain the technology and address environmental, health, and safety concerns as they arise.[132] To this end, DOE has established seven "regional partnerships" to study and test carbon sequestration throughout the country. The Big Sky Carbon Sequestration Partnership (BSCSP's) is one of these regional partnerships covering Montana, Idaho, South Dakota,

127. Simon Shackley, Carly McLachlan and Clair Gough, *The Public Perceptions of Carbon Capture and Storage*, Tyndall Centre Working Paper 44, January 2004, *available at* http://www.tyndall.ac.uk/publications/working_papers/wp44_summary.shtml.

128. Gregory R. Singleton, *Geologic Storage of Carbon Dioxide: Risk Analyses and Implications for Public Acceptance*, Master's Thesis MIT (2007).

129. 42 U.S.C. §2210. The main purpose of the Act is to partially indemnify the nuclear industry against liability claims arising from nuclear incidents while still ensuring compensation coverage for the general public. The Act establishes a no-fault insurance-type system in which the first $10 billion is industry-funded and any claims above the $10 billion would be covered by the federal government. The Supreme Court upheld the constitutionality of the Act against a due process challenge in Duke Power Co. v. Carolina Environmental Study Group, 438 U.S. 459 (1978).

130. *See* Parenteau, *Anything Industry Wants: Environmental Policy under Bush (II)*, 14 Duke Envtl. L. & Pol'y F. 363 (2004).

131. *See* David Hawkins, Stick It Where?? — Public Attitudes towards Carbon Storage, Natural Resources Defense Council (2001), *available at* http://www.netl.doe.gov/publications/proceedings/01/carbon_seq/1c2.pdf.

132. NETL, Carbon Sequestration Technology Roadmap and Program Plan (2007) ("By cost-effectively capturing CO_2 before it is emitted to the atmosphere and then permanently storing or sequestering it, fossil fuels can be used in a carbon constrained world and without constraining economic growth."), *avail-*

Wyoming, and the Pacific Northwest.[133] The purpose of the BSCSP is to "prepare its member organizations for a possible carbon-constrained economy and enable the region to cleanly utilize its abundant fossil energy resources and sequestration sinks to support future energy demand and economic growth." The BSCSP seeks to "demonstrate and validate the region's most promising sequestration technologies and create the supporting infrastructure required to deploy commercial scale carbon sequestration projects." This supporting infrastructure includes "a geographic information system (GIS)-based economic and risk assessment tool to help determine optimal energy development strategies, regulatory and permitting approaches, and enhanced public understanding and acceptance." BSCSP acknowledges that "the environmental acceptability and safety of CO_2 storage in geologic formations is a key issue and is a major component of the research being done worldwide." The goal of the demonstration project is to show that CO_2 will not escape from geologic formations or contaminate drinking water supplies.

In 2006, WRI launched the "CCS Initiative" with the objective of building "stakeholder consensus around guidelines for the safe and effective deployment of the technology and to inform and engage the public on CCS."[134] WRI plans on issuing guidelines in 2008 that will cover each phase of a CCS project lifecycle, including CO_2 capture, transport, site characterization and assessment, operations, and site closure. According to WRI, the goal of the process is "to protect human health and safety, and underground sources of drinking water and other natural resources while facilitating cost-effective and timely deployment of CCS technologies."

The Carbon Sequestration Leadership Forum is an international climate change initiative that is focused on development of improved cost-effective technologies for the separation and capture of carbon dioxide for its transport and long-term safe storage.[135] The purpose of the CSLF is to make these technologies broadly available internationally; and to identify and address wider issues relating to carbon capture and storage. This could include promoting the appropriate technical, political, and regulatory environments for the development of such technology. The CSLF is currently comprised of 22 members, including 21 countries and the European Commission. Membership is open to national governmental entities that are significant producers or users of fossil fuel and that have a commitment to invest resources in research, development and demonstration activities in carbon dioxide capture and storage technologies. Anyone can register online to become a stakeholder and participate in the process.[136]

Policy and Ethical Implications of Geologic Sequestration

The conventional wisdom is that geologic sequestration is the only hope we have of mitigating climate impacts over the next few decades while the world gradually weans itself from fossil fuels and transitions to a low-carbon economy. The lifeboat metaphor is frequently invoked to express the dilemma we face: the sequestration lifeboat may leak, but it's better than going down with the ship. Despite all the unknowns and the unprecedented challenges facing the successful commercial scale deployment of CCS, we are told, there is no choice but to take the chance and hope it all works out.

---

able at http://www.netl.doe.gov/technologies/carbon_seq/refshelf/project%20portfolio/2007/2007Roadmap.pdf.

133. Information *available at* http://www.bigskyco2.org/.

134. 2008 Capturing King Coal, *supra* note 45, at 25.

135. The CSLF website states: "We value the perspectives and potential contributions of stakeholders and express commitment to include them in CSLF work." *Available at* http://www.cslforum.org/cslfstake/ (last visited April 19, 2009).

136. http://www.cslforum.org/membership.htm.

But of course we do have a choice, and there are risks no matter what we decide to do or not do. There is a certain fatalistic quality to this conventional wisdom. It is based on the assumption that, like a drug addict, we are hooked on fossils and cannot go "cold turkey." To extend the drug metaphor, we have to move from heroin to methadone before we can really kick the habit. Given the realpolitik[137] of the moment, it may be true that continued dependence on coal and other fossil fuels seems inevitable. But, as Einstein once famously observed, "We can't solve problems by using the same kind of thinking we used when we created them."[138]

Climate change is not just another environmental problem in search of wonky policy solutions. In bold relief, climate change highlights all that is wrong is with market economics. As Sir Nicholas Stern, author of the influential Stern Review[139] on the economics of climate change has observed: "This is the greatest example of market failure the world has seen."[140] This failure cannot be cured by tweaking the capitalist model that is driving the global economy. The biosphere is too big an externality to be internalized in a benefit-cost analysis. Neither altruism nor profit are sufficient incentives for the fundamental changes that are needed. There is no technological fix—no silver bullet—for climate change; not even "silver buckshot" will do the trick.[141] We need a paradigm shift in the way that the human economy is conceptualized. Briefly stated, the human economy is a subset of nature's economy, not the other way around. The climate change crisis is a direct result of an economic system that operates with complete disregard for the natural systems that sustain life on earth. The roots of the crisis go deep into an economic model based on limitless consumption of resources and waste disposal. Humans are not only changing the climate and altering the course of evolution.[142] Human activity is disrupting every major ecological process, from the carbon cycle to the nitrogen cycle to the hydrological cycle to ocean chemistry.

The real message of climate change has yet to sink into the body politic: we have to stop burning fossils fuels *yesterday*. Not only must we start thinking outside the box, we have to build a new box altogether, a box that looks a lot like what nature has already built. There is a rich and growing body of literature from the fields of economics,[143] business,[144] conservation biology,[145]

---

137. "Politics based on practical and material factors rather than on theoretical or ethical objectives." Merriam Webster's Online at http://www.merriam-webster.com/dictionary/realpolitik.

138. Collected Quotes from Albert Einstein *available at* http://rescomp.stanford.edu/~cheshire/Einstein Quotes.html.

139. The Stern Review is *available at* http://www.hm-treasury.gov.uk/sternreview_index.htm (last visited April 19, 2009).

140. New Economist at http://neweconomist.blogs.com/new_economist/2006/10/stern_review_2.html.

141. The term "silver buckshot" is attributed to Bill McKibben, whose prescient book The End of Nature (Random House 2006) first drew public attention to the climate change issue. *See* Bill McKibben, *Welcome to the Climate Crisis*, New York Times, May 27, 2006, at A25, *available at* http://www.washingtonpost.com/wp-dyn/content/article/2006/05/26/AR2006052601549.html (last visited April 19, 2009).

142. *See* E.O. Wilson, The Future of Life (Vintage 2005).

143. *See, e.g.*, Herman Daly, Beyond Growth: the Economics of Sustainable Development (Beacon Press, 1996); Robert Costanza, The Science and Management of Sustainability (Columbia Un. Press 1991).

144. *See, e.g.*, Paul Hawkins, Amory Lovins and Hunter Lovins, Natural Capitalism: Creating the Next Industrial Revolution (Back Bay Books 1996); Michael Braungart and William McDonough, Cradle to Cradle: Remaking the Way We Make Things (North Point Press 2002).

145. *See, e.g.*, E.O. Wilson, The Diversity of Life (W.W. Norton & Company 1992); The Creation: An Appeal to Save Life on Earth (W.W. Norton & Company 2006); Jared Diamond, Collapse: How Societies Choose to Fail or Succeed (Viking 2005); Peter Ward, Under a Green Sky: Global Warming, the Mass Extinctions of the Past and What They Can Tell us about the Future (Harper Collins 2007).

engineering,[146] ethics,[147] and law[148] from which to draw the principles necessary to immediately undertake the task of remaking the economic and social institutions that are required for humanity to survive and prosper this century and beyond.

The most immediate burden of change must necessarily and rightly fall upon the industrialized nations that are principally responsible for this crisis. The developing nations cannot be expected to forego the economic development their populations so desperately need and deserve.[149] Nor can they be expected to pioneer the green technologies, sustainable land use policies and other reforms needed to transform the global economy. After being AWOL from the community of nations for the past eight years, the United States must re-assert the progressive leadership it once had on solving environmental problems. This leadership does not include finding new ways to keep mining and burning coal, or drilling for oil in Alaskan wilderness and coastal waters, or growing crops to burn in automobiles. True leadership means cutting our energy demand in half in less time than it will take to demonstrate the commercial viability of carbon sequestration, while at the same time creating good paying jobs, cutting energy costs, putting more money into the economy, saving habitat, improving air and water quality, and in general improving the quality of life in communities from Appalachia to Brooklyn. True leadership means launching a "man on the moon" scale program, funded by an economy-wide carbon tax or the auction of allowances under a cap and trade program to achieve a carbon-free energy system as fast as possible. Al Gore has called for a national commitment to produce 100% of our electricity from renewable energy and other clean sources within ten years.[150] It didn't take the critics in the blogosphere long to denounce the idea as unrealistic and un-American.[151] But there are plenty of studies laying out blueprints for how the nation could actually achieve such a feat, if not in ten years then perhaps twenty.[152] We have been talking about the need to invest in solar and renewable energy since the Arab oil embargo of the 1970's; and yet here we are thirty years later still talking, still making excuses, and still looking for the easy way out. There is no easy way out. If it was easy we would have done it by now. It does not take a rocket scientist to figure out that the reason we have made so little progress on breaking our fossil addiction is because there was nothing forcing our hand. Now there is.

We need a game-changing set of policies to deal with climate change, and carbon sequestration is not one of them. The main purpose of sequestration is not climate protection; it is

---

146. *See, e.g.*, Amory Lovins, Small is Profitable: The Hidden Economic Benefits of Making Electrical Resources the Right Size (Rocky Mountain Institute 2003).

147. *See, e.g.*, Stephen M Gardner, *A Perfect Moral Storm: Climate Change, Intergenerational Ethics and the Problem of Moral Corruption*, 15 Environmental Values 397 (August 2006).

148. *See, e.g.*, J.B. Ruhl, Steven E. Kraft, and Christopher L Lant, The Law and Policy of Ecosystem Services (Island Press 2005); Edith Brown Weiss, *Climate change, intergenerational equity and international law: An introductory note*, 15 Climatic Change 327 (2004).

149. *See* Jeffrey D. Sachs, The End of Poverty: Economic Possibilities for Our Time (Penguin 2003).

150. Audio and text of the speech available on NPR at http://www.npr.org/templ ates/story/story.php?storyId=92638501.

151. *See* Andrew Revkin, *The (Annotated) Gore Energy Speech*, New York Times (July 17, 2008).

152. Worldwatch Institute, American Energy: The Renewable Path to Energy Security (September 2006), *available at* http://www.worldwatch.org/files/pdf/AmericanEnergy.pdf; InterAcademy Council, Lighting the Way: Toward a Sustainable Energy Future (study commissioned by the governments of China and Brazil) (October, 2007), *available at* http://www.interacademycouncil.net/?id=12161; American Council for Energy Efficient Economy, The Twin Pillars of Sustainable Energy: Synergies between Energy Efficiency and Renewable Energy Technology and Policy (May, 2007), *available at* http://aceee.org/pubs/e074.pdf?CFID=1257125&CFTOKEN=88003749; *The Power and the Glory: A Special Report*, The Economist, June 21, 2008.

to keep using coal, which is continuing down the wrong path, albeit at a slower speed. Granted, China and India are going to burn coal no matter what we do, and they will be only too happy to buy U.S. coal if the price is right. Given that, it makes sense for the U.S. to develop, in partnership with China, India, Europe and other nations, carbon sequestration technologies that might actually work in the places where coal must be burned because there is no alternative. But it does not follow that the U.S. must build a whole new fleet of coal plants in order to demonstrate the feasibility of sequestration. For one thing, what works in the saline aquifers of South Texas may not work in Guangdong Province. China and India may not have the option of forgoing coal as a major source of energy for the foreseeable future, but the U.S. clearly does have a choice. The U.S. and other industrialized nations of the world have a vested interest in what happens in China, and should be willing to develop and sell, or even give away, technology that will enable China to reduce its carbon footprint, much of which is the result of U.S. outsourcing of its manufacturing base.[153] But the best way that the U.S. can help itself as well as China and other developing nations is by focusing like a laser on the main task of de-carbonizing *our* energy sector, putting our best and brightest people to work on the effort, and not spreading our resources too thin by trying to prolong the day of reckoning on coal.

The quantities of CO_2 that must be sequestered are, in the words of one expert, "stupefying."[154] As described by Dr. Wallace S. Broecker, long time researcher at Columbia University's Lamont-Doherty Earth Observatory:

> If the twenty-nine gigatons produced by the world's fossil-fuel burning in a single year were liquefied and spread over Manhattan, they would bury the island to about the eighty-fifth floor of the Empire State Building. In a little over sixteen years, the CO_2 would fill Lake Erie.[155]

No doubt we have the skill and intelligence to inject vast quantities of CO_2 into the ground, but can we say with confidence that it will stay there and not cause any serious unintended consequences? A performance standard of .01%, as has been recommended by some experts, leaves precious little room for error. The engineers who are working on this problem are some of the best in the business, and their motivation and integrity is unquestioned. But there is also an element of hubris not unlike what we have seen in other environmental contexts. Our experience with burying wastes underground does not justify the kind of unbridled confidence that characterizes much of the technical assessments that have been done.[156] The seemingly intractable problems of finding a suitable and publicly acceptable site for disposal of low-level radioactive waste ought to temper expectations that a massive new system of pipelines, injection wells and monitoring equipment can be deployed within the time frame necessary to achieve the climate stabilization objectives demanded by the science.

Finally, even if carbon sequestration was a sure thing that could be implemented in record time, there remains the question whether a strategy designed to prolong the use of coal, given its horrific track record of damaging public health and the environment, is the "right" thing to do. This is not simply a choice of policy instruments. There are moral questions that have not been fully explored in the rush to find ways of mitigating climate. What do we say, for example, to the

---

153. *See* Mongabay.com, *Industrialized countries outsource CO_2 emissions to China*, June 2, 2007, *available at* http://news.mongabay.com/2007/0622-china.html.

154. WALLACE S. BROECKER AND ROBERT KUNZIG, FIXING CLIMATE: WHAT PAST CLIMATE CHANGES REVEAL ABOUT THE CURRENT THREAT — AND HOW TO COUNTER IT 213 (Hill and Wang 2008).

155. *Id.* at 213.

156. *See, e.g.*, Earle A. "Rusty" Herbert, *The Regulation of Deep-well Injection: A Changing Environment Beneath the Surface*, 14 PACE ENVT'L. L. REV. 169 (Fall 1996).

people of Appalachia whose homes and communities are, quite literally, being blown to pieces to get at the coal? What do we say to the communities whose water supplies are being contaminated by disposal of combustion waste? What do we say to the families of individuals whose health has been ruined and whose lives have been shortened from exposure to soot and smog? What do we say to the women of child-bearing age whose fetuses have been damaged by mercury exposure *in utero*? Or to the minority communities that consume a disproportionate amount of mercury-contaminated fish? We cannot honestly tell those at risk that technology will make all these "side effects" of coal go away.

So, we are at a crossroads. We can continue down the path of building "cleaner" coal plants and gamble on our ability to safely store carbon underground until cleaner sources can be brought online at some indeterminate future date. Or we can choose a different path that commits to ending the coal era now and gamble on our ability to radically reduce energy demand and accelerate the replacement of coal with cleaner sources, perhaps even including nuclear. Either path is fraught with uncertainty, obstacles and the risk of failure. But to say that we have no choice is simply a cop-out. The United States can meet its energy needs without building more coal plants, and we have the chance to show the world how to do it.

To those thinking this is political naiveté at its worst my only response is that it is equally naïve to believe that technology alone will solve climate change. Climate change is the product of too many humans consuming too many resources and putting too much waste into systems that can no longer handle the load. Our actions indicate that we value material goods more than healthy ecosystems. Unless and until that changes, we cannot hope to prevail in this epic challenge to human civilization.

Notes

1. *Another View.* Appendix C of David Hawkins' testimony before the Senate Committee on Environment and Public Works regarding the Climate Security Act summarizes carbon capture and sequestration. He states that "we need to begin capturing CO_2 from new coal plants without delay in order to keep global warming from becoming a potentially runaway problem. Given the pace of new coal investments in the U.S. and globally, we simply do not have the time to build a coal plant today and think about capturing its CO_2 down the road." David Hawkins, Testimony at 33 (November 13, 2007). *See* Chapter 6, Section II(A)(2) this volume for complete testimony. Hawkins also poses the question: "Despite this conclusion by recognized experts there is still reason to ask about the implications of imperfect execution of large scale injection projects, especially in the early years before we have amassed more experience. Is the possibility of imperfect execution reason enough to delay application of CO_2 capture systems to new power plants until we gain such experience from an initial round of multi-million ton 'demonstration' projects?" *Id.* at 35. Hawkins answers: "I believe that any objective assessment will conclude that allowing new coal plants to be built without CO_2 capture equipment on the ground that we need more large scale injection experience will always result in significantly greater CO_2 releases than starting CO_2 capture without delay for new coal plants now being designed." *Id.*

2. *William Calvin* comments in *Turning Around by 2020, in* GLOBAL FEVER: HOW TO TREAT CLIMATE CHANGE ch. 19 (Un. Chicago Press 2008), reproduced below in Chapter 6, Section V:

> Such capture-and-storage talk may be another example of Big Coal trying to buy time by delaying action while, of course, getting yet another tax break from Congress to increase their record profits. Worst of all, even if practical, carbon capture and storage is not going to help very much for decades. I can think of better ways to spend our climate makeover money.

3. *See* WALLACE S. BROECKER & ROBERT KUNZIG, FIXING CLIMATE: WHAT PAST CLIMATE CHANGES REVEAL ABOUT THE CURRENT THREAT — AND HOW TO COUNTER IT 214 (Three Books Publishing 2008):

> A better solution than watching [the demise of organisms that make shells of carbonate such as coral] would be to capture atmospheric CO_2 and pipe it directly into the deep sea — putting it where it will eventually go, but without letting it do damage at the surface first....

> What happens to the liquid CO_2 itself is clear: it quickly reacts with the water to form a solid called a clathrate, with seven water molecules forming a cage around each molecule of CO_2. The clathrate is denser than either water or liquid CO_2; it forms a kind of slush on the sea floor....

These are the same "clathrates," of course, that figure in the disaster scenarios of Dr. Peter Ward (Chapter One, §I).

4. For developments post-*Massachusetts v. EPA*, see Chapter One, §III(D) above.

B. Oil & Natural Gas

PAUL ROBERTS, END OF OIL: ON THE EDGE OF A PERILOUS NEW WORLD 6 (Houghton Mifflin 2005) [hereinafter 2005 ROBERTS]:

> The oil industry is among the least stable of all business sectors, tremendously vulnerable to destructive price swings and utterly dependent on corrupt, despotic "petrostates" with uncertain futures. Natural gas, though cleaner than oil, is hugely expensive to transport, while coal, though abundant and easy to get at, produces so much pollution that it is killing millions of people every year.

2005 ROBERTS at 122 (emphasis in original):

> Because hydrocarbons provide 85 percent of the world's energy today and, given current trends, will play a dominant role for decades to come, substantially reducing CO_2 emissions would entail more or less chucking the existing energy system and finding something new. Not surprisingly, this hasn't been an especially easy package to sell. Despite widespread understanding of the links between energy and climate, and despite broad consensus on the need to move *eventually* to a carbon-free energy economy, most governments, companies, and individuals are not yet ready to commit to such a radical program.

Thomas Friedman, *First Law of Petropolitics*, ForeignPolicy.com (May/June 2006):

> The price of oil and the pace of freedom always move in opposite directions.

2008 FRIEDMAN at 99 (quoting Professor Vladimir Mau, Director, Russia's Academy of National Economy, 2007):

> The more oil you have, the less policy you need.

2008 FRIEDMAN at 72, 100, 8 (emphasis in original):

> Our addiction to oil makes global warming warmer, petrodictators stronger, clean air dirtier, poor people poorer, democratic countries weaker, and radical terrorists richer. *Have I left anything out?*

>   ....

That is why going green is no longer simply a hobby for high-minded environmentalists or some "personal virtue," as Vice President Dick Cheney once sneered. It is now a national security imperative. Any American strategy for promoting democracy in an oil-rich region that does not include a plan for developing renewable energy alternatives that can eventually bring down the price of oil is doomed to fail.

....

During the 2008 presidential primary campaign, Senators John McCain and Hillary Clinton both actually proposed suspending the federal excise tax on gasoline, 18.4 cents a gallon, for the summer's travel season, to give American drivers "a break," even though they knew — because every expert in the country said so — that it would only increase demand for summer driving and therefore keep gasoline prices high and further contribute to the global warming that both senators claimed to have plans to mitigate. That proposal was the epitome of "dumb as we wanna be" politics.

KENNETH S. DEFFEYES, BEYOND OIL: THE VIEW FROM HUBBERT'S PEAK 7 (Hill & Wang 2005):

So the big news is: World oil production has ceased growing, and by the year 2019 production will be down to 90 percent of the peak level.

The Future of the Petroleum Industry in a World of Global Warming©

Jacqueline Lang Weaver is the A.A. White Professor of Law at the University of Houston Law Center. She graduated from the Law Center magna cum laude *in 1975 after working as an energy economist in corporate planning for Exxon Co. USA. Her teaching and research interests cover oil and gas law, energy law and policy, international energy, and environmental and natural resources law. Professor Weaver's reputation as an outstanding teacher is reflected in her many teaching excellence awards. She has recently taught international petroleum transactions to CNPC and Sinopec managers in Beijing and to law students in Cairo, Egypt. She has co-authored, with Professor Ernest Smith at the University of Texas, the three-volume treatise,* TEXAS LAW OF OIL AND GAS. *She is also a co-author of the nationally used casebook titled* ENERGY, ECONOMICS AND THE ENVIRONMENT *and has written articles on energy markets, sustainable development in the international energy industry, comparative unitization laws in energy-producing nations, energy policy, and traditional oil and gas law topics. She was the Director of the Russian Petroleum Legislation Drafting Project, which drafted model laws for Russia's petroleum sector in 1990–91. Professor Weaver holds a B.A. in Economics from Harvard University, a Ph.C (Candidate of Philosophy) degree in Economics from the University of California at Los Angeles, and a J.D. degree from the University of Houston. This essay is adapted from a longer draft working paper in progress on the same topic.*

"[I]f automobiles are going to run on milk, then we'll be in the milk business."

Chairman of Chevron, 1999[1]

"We need to meet our customers' need for energy, even if that means leaving hydrocarbons behind."

Chairman, Royal Dutch/Shell Group, Sir Mark Moody-Stuart, 2001[2]

---

1. BOSSELMAN, EISEN, ROSSI, SPENCE AND WEAVER, ENERGY, ECONOMICS & THE ENVIRONMENT 1200 (2d ed., Thomson / West 2006) (quoting from 49 OIL DAILY #60, Mar. 30, 1999) [hereinafter 2006 ENERGY, ECONOMICS & THE ENVIRONMENT].

2. *A Survey of Oil: Consider the Alternatives,* THE ECONOMIST, Apr. 30, 2005.

"The U.S. government must make conserving energy the 'American thing to do.'"

Chevron, 2008[3]

"Drive Smarter: [It] doesn't just save money. It reduces gasoline consumption, … and strengthen[s] U.S. energy security. And it reduces greenhouse-gas emissions."

"Keep your tires properly inflated. This improves gas mileage by about three percent."

ExxonMobil, 2008[4]

I. Introduction

Most industries want you to buy more of what they sell. Like ExxonMobil, the 175 members of the National Petroleum Council (NPC)[5] also want you to buy less oil and gas and become more energy efficient. The NPC's first recommendation to President Bush's Secretary of Energy in its 2007 report HARD TRUTHS: A COMPREHENSIVE VIEW TO 2030 OF GLOBAL OIL AND NATURAL GAS[6] is to "moderate demand by increasing energy efficiency" through higher fuel economy standards on vehicles, more energy-efficient building codes and appliance standards, and better industrial sector efficiency through tax credits and more funding for R&D.[7]

What is the future of the petroleum industry that seems set on such an idiosyncratic course? And what is triggering this searching inquiry into the industry's future through 2030? Is it recognition of the reality of global warming? Or of Peak Oil? Or of geopolitical conflicts around the world, almost too numerous to count? Or is it just electoral politics tied to higher gasoline prices? And why is T. Boone Pickens, the epitome of the hard-boiled, straight-shootin' Texas oil man urging us to lobby for wind and natural gas vehicles in a massive media campaign?

This article looks at the future of the petroleum industry in an era of globalization and global warming. Warning: the future is not for the squeamish either on the petroleum producers' side or the consumers' side.

First a few basics.

A. What is Petroleum?

Petroleum is a chemically complex substance composed of carbon and hydrogen with trace amounts of oxygen, nitrogen and sulfur. It occurs in underground reservoirs either as a liquid

---

3. Brett Clanton, *An Industry in Flux*, HOUSTON CHRONICLE, Mar. 26, 2008, at D1.

4. ExxonMobil advertisement, NEW YORK TIMES, Aug. 7, 2008, at A25 (one of a series of "advertorials" that run opposite the editorial page, on the OpEd page of the TIMES).

5. The National Petroleum Council (NPC) is a federally chartered and privately funded advisory committee to the executive branch, created by President Truman in 1946 to advise, inform and recommend policy options to the Secretary of Energy. Its 175 members are chosen by the Secretary of Energy to assure balanced views from all segments of the oil and gas industry in all regions of the country. While its membership list is overwhelmingly corporations in the oil industry and its related sectors, a few universities, such as Stanford (through its Energy Modeling Forum) and the University of Texas (through its Bureau of Economic Geology) and some accounting, financial and consulting firms that service the industry are also members.

6. The report is *available at* www.npc.org [hereinafter NPC 2007 REPORT]. In October 2005, Secretary Bodman requested that the NPC address the implications of peak oil and growing world demand for oil and gas, by studying "What does the future hold for global oil and natural gas supply?" and then what strategies should be pursued to ensure greater economic stability and prosperity. NPC 2007 REPORT, *id.* at App. A. Unlike the Bush/Cheney national energy plan developed in 2001 in virtual secrecy without participation from those outside the industry, the NPC 2007 REPORT was drafted in an open process with input from Congressional staffs, environmental NGOs, international energy organizations, and others. *Id.* at App. C.

7. *Id.* at 15–16, 241–42. John Hofmeister, the retiring president of Shell Oil Co., blasted the profligate use of energy in the U.S. after oil prices of $120/barrel seemed to have no effect on Americans' addiction to megamansions supercooled to 72 degrees. *Shell President Criticizes U.S. Energy Use*, GREENWIRE, May 7, 2008 (reporting on Hofmeister's speech to the National Ass'n of Attorneys Generals).

(commonly called crude oil) or as a gas[8] (consisting largely of methane), depending on the temperature and pressure at which it is found. Oil and gas are sometimes found together in a reservoir, with a lighter gas "cap" sitting on top of the heavier oil stratum. Some fields produce only natural gas; other fields produce mostly oil, although some gas production inevitably accompanies oil production. If no market or pipeline connection exists for the gas which is brought up with the oil (called casinghead gas), it is either flared or reinjected into the reservoir.

B. Oil versus Gas

The future of oil is different from the future of natural gas, especially in a world of global warming. One way of reducing greenhouse gas (GHG) emissions is to shift from coal to natural gas to generate electricity. By contrast, almost no oil is used to make electricity. Oil is used almost exclusively in the transport sector. Boone Pickens is plugging a shift to natural-gas powered vehicles to decrease our dependency on foreign oil imports. The shift requires that wind energy replace the natural gas now being used in power plants so that the freed-up natural gas can go into cars. The shift would coincidently reduce GHG emissions.[9]

Thus, oil and gas serve different markets, have different chemical compositions and properties, impact the environment differently in significant ways, and have different supply profiles for the future. For these reasons, this chapter will discuss the two fuels separately before looking at the future of the industry as a whole. A brief historical overview of oil and gas markets and prices also provides context for the future and a caution about the accuracy of forecasts.

II. Is the World Running Out of Oil? The Peak Oil Debate[10]

A. The Geopolitics of Oil

In recent years, discussions of "Peak Oil" have flooded the media waves, industry conferences, and the trade press. While often blended together, the Peak Oil discussions reflect three different, although related, concerns: The "true" Peak Oil debate is about when world-wide, long-term oil production will follow the famous "Hubbert curve" and thereafter inevitably decline, as has already occurred in the United States and the North Sea. This debate is independent of short-term spikes in prices due to geopolitical events or natural disasters. A second, related discussion involves why oil and gas prices have shot up to such near-record levels since 2001, reaching price levels not even imagined as late as 2003.[11]

The third track focuses largely on the long-term national security implications of the Western world's dependence on oil (and increasingly, natural gas) from hostile and unstable countries,

---

8. In this article, "gas" is not the gasoline that you put in your car and which has been refined from crude oil. Gas is natural gas or methane.

9. In his $50-million media campaign, Pickens touts natural gas as a "patriotic" fuel that can reduce dependence on dangerous foreign oil suppliers and create jobs for Americans in windy, rural areas. Global warming is not the motivation. Pickens is building a 2,000-megawatt (MW) wind farm in Texas and is planning the world's largest windfarm of 4,000 MWs in the Texas Panhandle. *Energy Markets: Texas Oilman Makes Big Push for Wind Power*, Greenwire, July 8, 2008. His Mesa Power company is investing $12 billion in the Pickens Plan, *available at* www.pickensplan.com.

10. Part II of this article is adapted from Jacqueline Lang Weaver, *The Traditional Petroleum-Based Economy: An "Eventful Future,"* 36 Cumberland L. Rev. 505, 508–514 (2005–2006) [hereinafter Weaver, *An Eventful Future*].

11. In 2003, a Goldman Sachs energy analyst warned that "super spikes" could shoot oil prices to $100 a barrel. Andy Serwer, *Are Oil Prices Headed for a 'Super Spike'?*, Fortune, May 2, 2005, at 51. By definition, spikes are not permanent. The price of oil averaged about $140/barrel in July 2008 and was above $100/barrel for several months in 2008. *See* data at the Energy Information Administration website, *available at* http://tonto.eia.doe.gov/dnav/pet/pet_pri_wco_k_w.htm.

regardless of when Hubbert's peak might occur globally. The geopolitical implications of this third track are profound. After all, it doesn't matter to the consumer whether oil and gas supplies are scarce because Mother Nature has run out of them or because the few countries which hold the vast majority of remaining reserves of oil and gas simply refuse to produce the underground resource or invest in the capacity to do so. The bulk of remaining reserves of conventional crude oil are in the Mideast.[12] Chevron ran a large series of advertisements in 2006, asking the public disquieting questions like the following:[13]

> *Over half the world's oil lies in 5 countries. So where do you live?*
>
> *Russia, Iran and Qatar have 58% of the world's nature gas reserves. The U.S. has 3%. So what does that mean for us?*

The use of an oil embargo by Mideastern producers as a weapon against the West in 1973 was a watershed event which transformed the international energy industry. The oil price shocks of 1973 (the embargo year) and 1978 (the year of the overthrow of the U.S.-backed Shah of Iran) caused profound dislocations in importing nations, as prices of crude oil climbed from $3/barrel to almost $40/barrel. In the U.S., unemployment rose from 4.7 percent in the fall of 1973 to over 8.5 percent by the end of 1974. Inflation jumped from an annual rate of 6.1 percent to 11.4 percent over the same period, resulting in a new vocabulary word, stagflation. The oil shocks of 1973 and 1978 had two enormous effects on oil markets. First, higher prices led producers to discover many more sources of oil in many countries around the globe, from the North Sea to Africa, so importing nations could diversify their sources of supply. Secondly, consumers reacted to the price increases by conserving energy in unprecedented amounts. Although it took a few years, by 1981, a combination of fuel switching (to coal, nuclear and gas) and technological improvements in energy efficiency led to a third "oil shock"—the shock of a price plunge in early 1981. By 1985, the U.S. was 25 percent more energy efficient and 32 percent more oil efficient than it had been in 1973. By 1983, oil consumption in the entire noncommunist world was about 6 million barrels less than daily consumption had been at its peak in 1979.[14] The collapse of world oil prices in 1981 then sent the economies of many oil-exporting nations (and of many producing states like Texas) into a tailspin, causing distress in these regions.

International crude oil markets are still subject to control by the large exporting countries. In December 1998, world oil prices had fallen to $10/barrel, a near-historic low (if adjusted to constant dollars) because of weakened demand due to the Asian financial crisis and Venezuela's push to produce more oil (with the help of foreign investment which had been welcomed by the then Western-friendly leadership of Venezuela). OPEC export revenues fell by 35 percent in just one year. In March 1999, OPEC ministers, joined by non-OPEC producing countries like Mexico, Norway and Russia that also faced steep budgetary losses, agreed to reduce output. By July 1999, prices had risen to almost $20/barrel. By March 2000, the price of a barrel of crude oil reached more than $30 and soaring gasoline prices have become a serious political issue in many importing countries since then. Saudi Arabia has had little excess capacity to add to world oil supplies in response to booming Chinese and Indian demand for crude. The personal visit to Saudi Arabia and entreaties of President Bush to the Saudi ruling family to increase supplies accomplished little.[15]

---

12. *See* BP Statistical Review of World Energy 6, 22 (June 2008) for the distribution of proven oil and gas reserves globally, *available at* http://www.bp.com/statisticalreview.

13. Print advertisements in author's files.

14. Bosselman, Rossi & Weaver, Energy, Economics & the Environment 1098–1101 (Thomson / West 2000).

15. Sheryl Gay Stolberg & Jad Mouawad, *Saudis Offer Little in Response to Bush Plea for More Oil Production*, N.Y. Times, May 17, 2008, at A5. However, Saudi Arabia has pledged to make investments to increase ca-

Moreover the events of September 11 illustrate starkly the Faustian bargain of crude oil dependency. Oil can finance terrorism and weaponry. Few Mideastern nations are democracies. Even the rulers of moderate oil-rich nations are constrained by the need to appease radical extremists in their own countries. Both Europe and the United States have sought to diversify their sources of oil imports to reduce the geopolitical risk of oil embargoes, but despite discoveries of oil in many new areas around the world, the continued global dependence on crude oil from Mideast reserves is a fact of life in virtually every projection of future energy supply and demand over the next few decades.[16]

The rest of this article will focus largely on the first track which asks: Is the world running out of oil because the earth contains only a limited physical endowment of this depleting resource and we have used much of it?

B. Hubbert's Curve and Peak Oil—The Geologists' View

The true Peak Oil debate involves the application of Hubbert's curve to global oil production. In 1956, geologist M. King Hubbert of Shell Oil forecast that U.S. oil production would peak in the early 1970s—and it did. The Peak Oil proponents extend Hubbert's model, or variants of it, to global oil production today. Hubbert's model is based on the following pattern: Oil discoveries will peak at some point because oil is a finite resource and the big fields that are easy to find are found first. Once discoveries peak, oil production will peak some years later as these new discoveries are exploited and depleted over time. In short, when discoveries start falling, production will ultimately fall too, around 40 years later. At that point, we will not have "run out of oil," but we will be on an irreversible declining curve. (Picture a bell curve that first rises, peaks at the top of the bell, and then declines.) Another Chevron ad from 2006 captures this aspect of the Peak Oil debate:

> *The world consumes 2 barrels of oil for every barrel discovered. So, is this something you should be worried about?*

Here is where geological pessimism confronts economic and technological optimism, as best shown by juxtaposing two sets of competing books whose titles are self-explanatory. On one shelf rest:

- DAVID GOODSTEIN (a physicist and vice provost at the California Institute of Technology), OUT OF GAS: THE END OF THE AGE OF OIL (W. W. Norton 2003).
- PAUL ROBERTS, THE END OF OIL: ON THE EDGE OF A PERILOUS NEW WORLD (Mariner Books 2004).

---

pacity. Margaret Coker & Neil King Jr., *Saudis Promise More Oil to Curb World-Wide Fears: Kingdom Raising Output this Year and Capacity Later*, WALL ST. J., June 23, 2008, at A6.

16. *See* NPC 2007 REPORT, *supra* note 6, at 120–21, 252–56 (summarizing the long-term forecasts of 29 international oil companies and private consultants and 5 forecasts by the U.S. Energy Information Administration (EIA) and the International Energy Agency (IEA) of the OECD countries, in addition to other studies, such as THE STERN REPORT, all showing increased production expected from OPEC by 2030). In 2000, two-thirds of the crude oil trade to industrialized countries came from Persian Gulf exports. To guard against future embargos, the United States has created strategic petroleum reserves that store crude oil underground in large salt dome caverns along the Gulf Coast for use in an emergency. Europe also has stockpiled strategic reserves. The cost of maintaining these stockpiles and of keeping a military presence to defend friendly oil-exporting countries can validly be recognized as an externality unique to crude oil use. In December 2004, Osama Bin Laden's tape-recorded message to followers commanded them to take the jihad (holy war) to the Mideast oil fields to stop Americans from getting the oil. Eric Watkins, *Oil's Terrorist Threats*, OIL & GAS J., Jan. 10, 2005, at 27. In May, 2004, al-Qaeda terrorists attacked oil contractors in Saudi Arabia, killing six Westerners and a Saudi; a second terrorist shooting spree at an oil company's residential compound in Saudi Arabia killed 22 people, 19 of them foreigners.

- MATTHEW SIMMONS, TWILIGHT IN THE DESERT: THE COMING SAUDI OIL SHOCK AND THE WORLD ECONOMY (Wiley 2005).

On the second shelf sit:

- PETER W. HUBER AND MARK P. MILLS, THE BOTTOMLESS WELL: THE TWILIGHT OF FUEL, THE VIRTUE OF WASTE, AND WHY WE WILL NEVER RUN OUT OF ENERGY (Basic Books 2005).
- PETER R. ODELL, WHY CARBON FUELS WILL DOMINATE THE 21ST CENTURY'S GLOBAL ENERGY ECONOMY (Multi-Science Publishing Co. 2004).

Geological pessimism is best displayed in the Simmons' book which focuses in detail on the Saudi oil fields. After surveying more than 200 technical papers on these fields, Mr. Simmons, a respected Houston-based investment banker in the energy industry, disputed the Saudi claim that it has enough oil to fuel the world for 70 more years. About 90% of its oil output comes from seven huge fields, including three that have pumped for more than 50 years.[17] When U.S. output peaked in 1970, Saudi Arabia ramped up production from its fields — from 3 million barrels per day (bpd) in 1970 to an astounding 8 million bpd just four years later.[18] However, this surge had a big downside: some wells were produced above their proper engineering rate, so pressures dropped in parts of the field, creating "water cuts" which allowed saltwater to invade the wells prematurely. From 1974 onward, the Saudis have struggled with unsustainable water injection programs that will ultimately result in rapid declines in these giant fields within the next 5 to 10 years. When Saudi production peaks, the age of oil ends.[19]

The anti-Peak Oil proponents argue that energy comes from human ingenuity — a bottomless well. Anything is possible — surely bacteria will be invented to ferment tar sands. The cost of extracting oil will go up slowly, but we will always find more. Prices are high today because the actual current costs of producing Saudi oil are so low that the Saudis could wipe out any private investments in tar sands, shales, and alternate energy sources, using oil as a weapon. Thus, private capital will not develop unconventional oil and gas sources or other fuels unless their price is very high, offsetting the high market risk. Also, the Peak Oil theorists do not properly account for the often-negative role of government policies in restricting access to petroleum reserves, both in the U.S. and around the world. Governments, not Mother Nature, create the "geological" shortages.

The two camps see very different oil scenarios in our future. One foresees the possibility of Oil War III, abrupt recessions in oil-consuming countries, and continuous global conflicts to secure oil supplies unless consumers adapt to a more frugal lifestyle. The other camp says "keep the lights on" and enjoy the use of energy as technology, human intelligence and markets bring good things to life.

Any reader is understandably confused by the jarring dissonance between the competing brainpower on both sides of the Peak Oil issue. However, the "disconnect" may not be quite so large when framed as follows: Much of the Peak Oil debate is about conventional oil, although this is not always clear from the material. And the debate is not about living without oil completely; it is about living with oil when global supplies are declining, not increasing. All players recognize that the world has large supplies of unconventional oil locked in tar sands and shales,

---

17. MATTHEW SIMMONS, TWILIGHT IN THE DESERT: THE COMING SAUDI OIL SHOCK AND THE WORLD ECONOMY xv (Wiley 2005).

18. *Id.* at 47–52; 161–79. The Saudis rebut Simmons' analysis, but their reserve data is treated as a state secret, making it difficult to assess their claims. *See* Weaver, *An Eventful Future*, *supra* note 10, at 510, n. 10.

19. PAUL ROBERTS, THE END OF OIL: ON THE EDGE OF A PERILOUS NEW WORLD 64 (Mariner Books 2004).

and similarly larger amounts of unconventional natural gas. (The world also has hundreds of years of coal and ample uranium for nuclear power, although air pollution, global climate change, and nuclear security issues make these sources less than ideal; and neither coal nor nuclear can be used directly in the transportation sector.) The heart of the geological debate reflects this question: When will the peak in conventional global oil (particularly Saudi output) occur as a definitive stage in this transition?

If you want to "bet on the future," here are the dates when oil production will peak and then begin an inexorable decline, according to some leading experts:[20]

- Kenneth Deffeyes (geologist and author of BEYOND OIL: THE VIEW FROM HUBBERT'S PEAK) — 2006.
- Richard Heinberg (author of THE PARTY'S OVER: OIL, WAR, AND THE FATE OF INDUSTRIAL SOCIETIES) — 2007–08.
- Matthew Simmons (author noted *supra* and at note 17 *supra*) — 2007–2009.
- Colin Campbell (author of THE ESSENCE OF OIL AND GAS DEPLETION (Multi-Science Publishing Co. 2003))[21] — between now and 2010.
- PETROLEUM REVIEW (a respected trade publication) — 2007.
- David Goodstein (author noted *supra*) — 2010.
- Daniel Yergin (Cambridge Energy Research Associates) — not before 2010.
- Francis Harper (oil company consultant) — between 2010 and 2020.
- PFC Energy (a well-known energy consulting firm) — 2010 to 2015.

The Peak Oil debunkers include Michael Lynch and Peter Odell who dispute that Hubbert's curve can be applied globally. Yet, importantly, they do think that oil supplies may ultimately peak in 2025 or 2030 — but the long time-frame gives the world plenty of time to adapt slowly to other sources of supply. So scenarios of doom and gloom featuring $5-a-gallon gasoline and crashing economies are unwarranted.[22]

Our own government is an optimistic player in this debate. The Energy Information Administration (the EIA is the statistical arm of the Department of Energy) used data on global reserves amassed in an extensive study in 2000 by the U.S. Geological Survey (USGS) to project a series of twelve possible Peak Oil scenarios.[23] The mean scenario (*i.e.,* the one with the highest expected value, based on a 2% growth rate in global demand for oil) projects a peak in conven-

---

20. The listed data appear in various publications, notably Jeffrey Ball, *As Prices Soar, Doomsayers Provoke Debate on Oil's Future,* WALL ST. J., Sept. 21, 2004, at A1; Matt Creson, *Experts Ponder Oil's Peak,* HOUSTON CHRONICLE, May 29, 2005, at D2; Lynn J. Cook, *No Consensus on Future of Oil,* HOUSTON CHRONICLE, June 23, 2005, at D1. THE OIL & GAS JOURNAL has run many articles devoted to Peak Oil and "Hubbert Revisited," starting in July 2003.

21. This is a collection of articles by members of the Association for the Study of Peak Oil (ASPO) and the Oil Depletion Analysis Center. It has a good bibliography of both sides of the debate. Campbell's data show that oil production is reaching a plateau or declining in 33 of 48 major oil producing countries, including 6 of the 11 OPEC countries. He states that since the early 1980s, the world has been pumping more oil out than finding oil. By 2005, the world will have produced half of the total that exists — the peak of Hubbert's curve. We would have oil for another century, but we will never again have cheap oil.

22. In late 2000, when gasoline prices had soared in Europe, protestors, especially farmers and truck drivers, took to the streets and blockaded fuel depots in several European countries. One OPEC response to consuming countries' concerns about high gasoline prices was to urge the consuming countries to use their self-help remedy of reducing fuel taxes in their own countries. *OPEC Suggests Countries Adjust Fuel Taxes,* GREENWIRE, Dec. 2, 2005.

23. John H. Wood *et al., Long-Term World Oil Supply Scenarios* (posted on August 18, 2004 on the Energy Information Administration website at http://www.eia.doe.gov/pub/oil_gas/petroleum/feature_articles/2004/worldoilsupply/oilsupply04.html (last visited Sept. 7, 2008).

tional world crude oil in 2037,[24] leading the EIA to conclude that Peak Oil is unlikely to be "right around the corner."

Given the range of possibilities, dependent on demand growth and technological advances, one must wonder whether the Peak Oil "date debate" is more conjecture than forecast. Nonetheless, regardless of date, no one doubts that Peak Oil is a legitimate way to look at the future of a depleting resource base like conventional oil. The only question is when the peak will hit, whether a plateau exists at the top rather than a sharp point, and how smooth the ride up and down will be. The oil industry's own view of future supplies appears in section IV of this article, after a discussion of the other part of petroleum—natural gas.

III. Are We Running Out of Gas?[25]

A. Natural Gas

Methane is nature's most pervasive hydrocarbon. Cows belch it and swamps bubble with it. Mix organic waste with water in an airtight tank, add anaerobic bacteria, and the microbes will digest the waste and produce methane.[26]

Methane is a potent greenhouse gas (GHG). Each unit of methane released into the atmosphere has about 20 times the heat-trapping potency of a unit of CO_2. However, the carbon content per British Thermal Unit (BTU) of gas is only 55% of that for coal and 70% of that for oil, so its use as a substitute for the other fossil fuels significantly reduces CO_2 emissions from combustion. If China had the same mix of fossil fuels as the Netherlands, its CO_2 emissions would be reduced 30%.[27] While methane stays in the atmosphere for a decade or so, this is short compared to the hundreds of years that CO_2 emissions stay. Natural gas is by far the cleanest burning of the three major fossil fuels. It is virtually free of sulfur and toxic metals such as mercury. When economies shift from coal to gas to generate electricity in power plants, emissions of CO_2, sulfur and nitrogen oxides (NO_x) are reduced substantially. England took this path many decades ago and eliminated the killer fogs that once smothered London.

Because natural gas is such a "golden" fuel compared to oil and coal under current technology, its projected price is the key variable determining the degree to which energy users will shift away from alternative fuels into natural gas. The stakes in the coal v. gas battle are huge. For example, in its environmental impact statement on the restructuring of wholesale electricity markets in the U.S., the Federal Energy Regulatory Commission (FERC) projected that competitive pricing conditions would favor gas over coal, and therefore the move to competitive markets in electricity would have beneficial rather than adverse environmental effects.[28] Another study by the Environmental Law In-

---

24. *Id.* at Fig. 2 and Table 1. The soonest that the peak might arrive is 2021 and the latest is 2112, although neither of these extremes is very probable.

25. This section of the article is adapted from Jacqueline Lang Weaver, *Sustainable Development in the Petroleum Sector, in* ENERGY LAW AND DEVELOPMENT (Adrian J. Bradbrook & Richard L. Ottinger eds.) (Int'l Union for the Conservation of Nature (IUCN) Envt'l Policy and Law Paper No. 47, 2003) and from 2006 ENERGY, ECONOMICS & THE ENVIRONMENT, *supra* note 1, at 525–37, and Weaver, *An Eventful Future, supra* note 10, at 515–25.

26. Methane from landfills is produced anaerobically.

27. China is 67% dependent on coal and 3% on gas; the Netherlands is 8% coal and 53% gas. James M. Griffin, *Introduction: The Many Dimensions of the Climate Change Issue, in* GLOBAL CLIMATE CHANGE: THE SCIENCE, ECONOMICS AND POLITICS 11–12 (James M. Griffin ed., Cambridge Un. Press 2003).

28. The Environmental Protection Agency (EPA) disagreed with FERC, projecting instead that competition would result in increased generation at older, high-polluting, coal-fired power plants which had often been exempted through "grandfathering" from Clean Air Act requirements. These coal plants have a low, depreciated cost basis and use relatively low-cost coal, against which the new gas turbine plants would not be able to compete, especially if environmental regulations did not force the older plants to install additional pollution control equipment.

stitute analyzed the benefits and costs of reducing by 50 percent the use of coal in electric generation in the U.S. by the year 2010, using natural gas turbines and a small increase in wind power and other sources as substitutes for coal. The transition would lower pollution levels dramatically: SO_2 emissions would fall by 50 percent, NO_x by 40 percent, mercury by 60 percent, and CO_2 by 25 percent. The price of electricity would rise about six-tenths of a cent per kilowatt hour, but the total health benefits of the emissions reductions would offset the increased cost of electricity.[29]

Natural gas has gone from the Cinderella of fuels, the unwanted stepchild of oil, to the golden fuel of the 21st century.[30] The passage of the Clean Air Act in 1970 elevated gas to a premium fuel. Unfortunately, at that time, federal price controls on natural gas had begun to create shortages in gas supplies. When the OPEC oil embargo hit in 1973, natural gas was already in short supply and the U.S. had a full-blown energy crisis on its hands.[31] At that time, both industry and government experts estimated that the U.S. had about 208 trillion cubic feet (TCF) of gas reserves, about a ten-year supply at then-current consumption rates.[32] However, the gas shortages of the 1970s stemmed in significant degree from bad regulatory policies. We had large reserves of "unconventional" natural gas that could be tapped if the price was right.[33] These included:

- **Deep reservoir gas.** This gas is found at depths between 15,000 and 30,000 feet where drilling is technically difficult because of high pressures and temperatures.
- **Tight sands gas.** These concrete-hard sandstones could contain some 800 TCF of gas.
- **Coalbed methane or coal seam gas.** At least 850 TCF of gas existed in the nation's coalbed seams.[34]

---

29. Environmental Law Institute, Cleaner Power: The Benefits and Costs of Moving from Coal Generation to Modern Power Technologies, ELI Research Report (May 2001).

30. From 1935 to 1951, the average price of gas on a BTU basis was about 6 cents per million BTUs, while the price of crude oil rose from 18 cents to 43 cents on the same BTU basis. Thus, gas sold for 1/3 to 1/7 of the equivalent heating value of oil. Natural gas is measured either by volume (such as thousands of cubic feet or MCFs) or by its heat value in BTUs (British Thermal Units). One BTU is roughly the amount of energy produced by a match tip. One million BTUs of energy is about one thousand cubic feet (MCF) of gas.

31. In 1978, interstate pipelines were forced to curtail and ration gas to end users along the East coast, and Congress was finally prompted to pass a huge National Energy Policy Act, a good part of which involved policies to solve natural gas shortages.

32. For comparison, the U.S. currently uses about 23 TCF (trillion cubic feet) of gas per year.

33. On the eve of passage of the Natural Gas Policy Act of 1978, an issue of the National Geographic featured the many new technologies that could be used to access new reserves of natural gas, considered too difficult or costly to exploit at the prices which had prevailed in the past. Bryan Hodgson, *Natural Gas: The Search Goes On*, Nat'l Geographic, Nov. 1978, at 632–51.

34. Producing natural gas from coal seams, called coalbed methane (CBM), is one of the hottest plays in Wyoming and Montana today. CBM is produced when plant matter, CO_2 and water are transformed into peat, lignite, and then higher quality coal grades. This coalification process produces large volumes of methane which is stored in porous coal in three states: as free gas, as gas dissolved in the water in coal, and as gas "adsorbed" on the surface of coal, *i.e.*, held to the surface by weak forces. Because of the large surface area of coal pores, much methane is adsorbed. When coal mining reduces the pressure on the coalbed, the gas in the coal formation is released. CBM may also be found in thin reservoirs adjacent to the coal seam and in fractures within the coal where methane has accumulated. Historically, coal miners considered CBM a hazard because it caused explosions and deaths of workers.

In the early 1980s, new research and technology and substantial federal tax credits led to the growth of the CBM industry. To release CBM from the coal, pressure in the underground coal seam must be reduced by removing water from the coalbed. The dewatering process requires drilling a relatively shallow well and pumping large amounts of water from depths of 350 to 1200 feet. Dewatering an average CBM well in Wyoming pumps up 21,000 gallons of water per day. The Bush/Cheney energy strategy projected 51,000 new CBM wells drilled in this area by 2010. The dewatering process can result in lowering the water table of local aquifers and in land subsidence. Dewatering can also pollute surface waters because of the dissolved salts and sodium in the produced water, unless the water is reinjected into disposal aquifers or contained in surface reservoirs (which have their own environmental problems). The disposal cost of wastewater from CBM production is

- **Devonian shales.** More than 1,000 TCF could be trapped in dense rock underlying 90,000 square miles of Appalachia.
- **Geopressurized methane.** Located largely in the Gulf Coast region, this is gas dissolved at high temperatures in deep aquifers of saline water that may contain 60,000 TCF of natural gas.
- **Methane hydrates.** Methane and water form a lattice-like, solid substance beneath permafrost and in deep-ocean seabeds. Discovered only in the late 1960s, hydrates may have trapped almost unlimited quantities of gas thought to have dissipated millennia ago.

As price controls were gradually lifted on natural gas production after 1978, the optimism expressed in the article seemed accurate. At higher prices, producers drilled more wells and invested in newer technologies to develop deeper gas, tight-sands gas and coalbed methane. Indeed, a surplus of natural gas (called the natural gas "bubble") developed in the early 1980s and gas producers urgently sought new markets for their gas, especially in the electric power industry.

By the decade of the 1990s, natural gas prices had settled at about $2.00 per MCF (thousand cubic feet), a relatively low price considering the clean air benefits of burning gas versus coal. Gas was eagerly sought by the new generation of independent power plants sprouting up to compete in deregulated electricity markets and also by traditional utilities that found siting or operating coal-fired power plants to be increasingly difficult. Between 2000 and 2004, 200,000 megawatts of gas-fired power plants were added to the electricity sector in the U.S.—the functional equivalent of 245 nuclear units (of the size built at Calvert Cliffs).[35] Of the new power plants built between 2000 and 2004, 90% were powered with natural gas and many had no alternative fuel capability.[36] Improved gas turbine design and the low gas prices of the 1990s reduced the price of electricity derived from gas to levels below that of coal, oil and sometimes even hydropower sources.[37]

Thus, at the beginning of the 21st century, gas seemed poised for a bright and sunny future, from both the demand and supply sides. Environmental think-tanks (interested in gas as a less carbon-intensive fuel than coal) and the industry's own National Petroleum Council conducted studies of the long-term outlook for natural gas and found no major problems ahead for the increased use of gas. The Environmental Law Institute (ELI) concluded, based on its survey of many other studies, that gas could be used as an abundant energy source for centuries, depend-

---

much greater than the costs from a conventional gas well. In the arid west, aquifer recharge is unlikely to occur for hundreds of years. While dewatering ratios and the salinity of produced water from CBM wells can vary significantly in different geographic areas, the externalities of CBM production in some Western states have led to a boomlet in local moratoria on well permitting by town officials.

Released methane can also migrate away from wellbores and vent into the atmosphere through natural fractures, endangering residential communities (methane is colorless and odorless) and contributing to GHG emissions. Coal reserves are plentiful in many parts of the world. If CBM production develops abroad without strong environmental controls, methane releases and dewatering pose serious threats to the environment.

35. Frank Clemente, *The Problem with Natural Gas*, July 14, 2005, at 2 (EnergyPulse ECP Online).

36. *Id.* at 3.

37. Natural gas power plants have other advantages. Both small- and large-scale gas power plants are equally feasible. The smaller scale plants can be built relatively cheaply and quickly compared to nuclear and coal plants, and they can be turned on and off quickly as sources of "peaking" power for times of high electricity demand. The mechanics are simple: gas is burned in the functional equivalent of an airplane's jet engine which turns the wheels of an electric generator. The latest generation of advanced Combined Cycle Gas Turbines (CCGTs) now has efficiency rates of 58%. These plants include both a gas turbine and a steam turbine that uses the excess heat thrown off by the gas turbine to create steam which turns a second generator. Such plants are able to produce energy efficiencies higher than competing technologies using other fuel sources. A new "H System" turbine developed by a public-private research and development effort between the Department of Energy (DOE) and GE can operate at a 60% efficiency rate, a breakthrough touted as the equivalent of running the four-minute mile.

ing on technology and one other key factor: price.[38] If the price of gas dropped significantly below $2 per MCF, technology advances would be slow and supply would fall below even the official reserve estimate of 1,331 TCF.[39] On the other hand, a price of $4 per MCF would trigger major new supplies around the world and would allow liquefied natural gas (LNG) from large foreign reserves to enter U.S. coastal markets. This price would also make large Alaskan gas reserves, now trapped at Prudhoe Bay, marketable via a gas pipeline to the lower 48 states.

The National Petroleum Council's December 1999 study shared the same basic conclusions as the ELI report. As its title proclaimed, the industry was capable of "Meeting the Challenges of the Nation's Growing Natural Gas Demand." Gas demand could climb from about 23 trillion cubic feet a year to 30 TCF a year by 2010 because domestic supplies were amply available at about $3/MCF.[40] "30 at $3" was a catchphrase often heard.

No sooner had the ink dried on the reports described above than the price of natural gas began a steep, almost relentless climb to heights unanticipated by anyone. In April 2000, the price was already at $3/MCF and it soared to $8 in a cold snap in late 2000. At this price, industrial users with switching capability turned off the gas taps. Between 2000 and 2002, industrial demand for gas dropped from 17.1 billion cubic feet (bcf) per day to 10.3 bcf/day and many ammonia and methanol plants that produced fertilizers along the Gulf Coast closed. Gas-fired power plants took the gas released from the industrial sector. Mild weather moderated prices in 2002, although $4 gas was becoming the norm by fall 2002. Then, in an abnormally cold period in late February 2003, gas prices on one day rose to an astounding $22/MCF, although they dropped again fairly quickly. Nonetheless, since the end of 2003, natural gas prices have stayed high in a range of $7 to $8 per MCF and have regularly peaked at levels far above this.[41] Trying to look on the bright side, the Energy Department reported that growth in natural gas demand would moderate in the U.S. as our industries moved overseas, taking jobs with them.[42]

"Peak Gas" appeared to be more of a problem than Peak Oil. What had happened?

Beneath the sunny outlooks of late 1999 lay some disturbing trends. The production of natural gas from conventional domestic sources in the U.S. had peaked in 1973, just two years after the peak in domestic oil. The new, domestic production of natural gas in response to deregulated prices had never increased the total amount of gas produced above its 1973 peak.[43] Gas wells in existing fields had experienced accelerated and rapid rates of decline in production. Pro-

---

38. ENVIRONMENTAL LAW INST., HOW ABUNDANT? ASSESSING THE ESTIMATES OF NATURAL GAS SUPPLY (1999), ELI Research Report *available at* http://www.eli.org/bookstore/rrgas99.htm.

39. *Id.* Compare this estimate of domestic gas reserves of 1,331 TCF to the 1978 estimate of 203 TCF in the NATIONAL GEOGRAPHIC article discussed in the text *supra* at note 33. The 1999 Environmental Law Institute study surveyed both government and industry gas supply forecasts to assess the nation's ability to switch from dirty coal to cleaner gas. Official estimates of recoverable gas reserves, based on then-current prices and little technological growth, totaled 1,331 TCF or about 60 years of supply. Technical progress measured by the historical trend would add another 100 years to future gas supplies. If technological progress instead advanced at the rapid rate of the 1990s, this would unlock even greater gas resources considered economically unrecoverable at the price of $2 per MCF, such as coalbed methane (300 TCF), tight sands (6,600 TCF), deep gas deposits (3,200 TCF), and geopressurized aquifers (5,700 TCF). The potential gas stored in methane hydrates could add an astounding 200,000 TCF of gas to the resource base.

40. NATIONAL PETROLEUM COUNCIL, MEETING THE CHALLENGES OF THE NATION'S GROWING NATURAL GAS DEMAND (1999), *available at* http://www.npc.org/reports/ng.html.

41. Natural gas wellhead prices in the U.S. are *available at* http://tonto.eia.doe.gov/dnav/ng/ng_pri_sum_dcu_nus_m.htm.

42. Editorial, *Volatile*, HOUSTON CHRONICLE, Dec. 19, 2003, at 46A.

43. Clemente, *supra* note 35, at 5. For example, 23,500 gas wells in Texas produced 9.5 billion cubic feet (bcf) of gas in 1970; by 2004, about 70,000 gas wells produced only 5.8 BCF, a significant drop in well productivity.

duction from new fields discovered on the Outer Continental Shelf and in the Rockies could not offset the declines in the old fields nor could increased production from tight sands or coal seams. Throughout the 1990s, the United States increased its imports of natural gas from Canada to meet the growing gap between domestic supply and demand. Successful exploration in both western and eastern Canada (onshore and offshore) had made Canada eager to export gas to the U.S. market. By 2000, Canadian gas supplied about 20 percent of the U.S. market. But such pipelines were constrained by their capacity levels, and when bitter cold hit New England, there was no more natural gas to route to the region quickly.

In 2003, the National Petroleum Council issued a gloomy report stating that a "fundamental shift" in gas supply and demand had occurred in just three years.[44] An energy analyst summarized the new report's major findings.[45]

- The 1999 NPC study greatly underestimated the explosion in construction of gas-fired power plants and their demand for gas.
- The drilling boom simply could not replace rapidly depleting supplies from existing wells, especially when technological advances in drilling slowed. In 1999, 10,877 gas wells were completed in the U.S.; by 2001, the drilling boom resulted in 22,083 completed gas wells. Still, the U.S. could not drill itself out of the shortage because supplies were depleting about 29% a year and, in the NPC's words, there was "a lower average production response to higher prices from new wells."
- Access to leasing areas became further restricted as Outer Continental Shelf (OCS) moratoria continued and new areas were classified as national monuments and closed to future leasing. The OCS held 80 TCF of technically recoverable reserves subject to leasing moratoria. Another 56 TCF in the Rockies was suffering added costs and development delays because of access-related restrictions.

The NPC 2003 REPORT presented Americans with a choice: the "Reactive Path" or a "Balanced Future." The Reactive Path assumed continued conflict between policies that encouraged gas use but discouraged supply development. It would result in long-term gas prices of $5 to $7 through 2025. The Balanced Future scenario, built on policies such as phased lifting of moratoria and better demand-response technologies, projected long-term prices in the $3 to $5 range. Even this "balanced" future path set aggressive production goals. It would require that deepwater OCS gas and Rocky Mountain supplies (largely coalbed methane) offset decline rates of 25% in existing wells. And even the Reactive Path would require overcoming obstacles to building an Alaskan gas pipeline, siting LNG terminals and leasing federal lands. If these obstacles were not hurdled, long-term prices would average 18% more. An analyst warned that the industrial sector had made all of the easy demand reductions it could make.[46] We had "bet the ranch" on natural gas at a time when about 55% of current global gas production was in terminal decline and when Arctic gas supplies were at least 10 years away.[47]

---

44. NATIONAL PETROLEUM COUNCIL, BALANCING NATURAL GAS POLICY—FUELING THE DEMANDS OF A GROWING ECONOMY (2003), *available at* http://www.npc.org/reports/ng.html.

45. Matthew R. Simmons, *U.S. Natural Gas Crisis: Is It Real?*, National Research Council Workshop, Apr. 21, 2003, Washington D.C. (copy of Powerpoint slide presentation in author's files).

46. In April 2004, Dupont, a large chemical company, announced it was laying off 3,500 workers in order to reduce costs and stay competitive against companies with much lower gas prices abroad. Thaddeus Herrick, *Dupont to Eliminate 3,500 Jobs As High Gas Prices Take a Toll*, WALL ST. J., Apr. 15, 2004, at A16.

47. President Bush had long pushed for a national energy act that would provide incentives to oil and gas operators to spur more drilling; reduce restrictions on access to public lands for leasing; and diversify the nation's energy portfolio by encouraging nuclear and clean coal. Just before its 2005 summer recess, Congress passed such an act and the President signed it into law. (A loan guarantee for an Alaskan Natural Gas Pipeline

In short, in a few short years, the sunny optimism about natural gas supplies that had been voiced at the start of the new century had turned to gloom. With domestic natural gas prices now perpetually far above $3/MCF, importing LNG from abroad was the quickest "bridge" supply source, although the necessary liquefaction plants, special LNG tankers, and regasification terminals were multi-billion dollar ventures with 3- to 4-year lead times. Utilities started building coal-fired plants rather than natural-gas generating units.[48]

Despite the stunning run-up in natural gas prices, little discussion of "peak gas" on a global scale occurred. Why not? Perhaps because several new sources of gas exist in our future, as follows:

Stranded gas: LNG and gas-to-liquids (GTL). In 2000, about half of the world's proven gas reserves of about 6,200 TCF were stranded in the sense that they had no access to transportation.[49] In the past decade, striking technological improvements in engineering and construction of liquefaction plants and tankers have decreased the costs of LNG shipments by as much as 30%. In 1999, recall that forecasters predicted LNG would be profitable if the price of natural gas rose above $3.00/MCF, a 50% increase over its then norm of about $2.00, but a price that today seems unbelievably low.[50] A single tanker cargo of LNG can deliver the equivalent of 5% of U.S. gas consumption on an average day.[51]

Gas can also become "unstranded" by converting it to a liquid product that can move overland by pipeline. In 2000, Conoco announced plans to build a $35- to $50-million plant to test its technology for converting gas to synthetic petroleum which could then be economically shipped by pipeline, tanker, barge, or truck. It estimated that its "gas-to-liquids" (GTL) technology would be profitable at oil prices of about $25 a barrel.[52] The virtue of GTL technology is that the synthetic liquid can be used as clean-burning transportation fuels.[53] The small Mideast nation of Qatar has launched an enormous GTL industry to turn its large reserves of natural gas into clean diesel fuel that will be priced competitively with crude oil on the export market. ExxonMobil, Shell and Chevron have pledged $20 billion to build GTL facilities in an industrial park in Qatar that is twice the size of Manhattan.[54]

Coal gasification and carbon sequestration. The integrated gasification combined-cycle (IGCC) power plant can turn coal into a gas to be used to generate electricity. Capturing CO_2 emissions from the plant and sequestering the CO_2 in depleted reservoirs creates a near "zero-emissions" power plant. Because the U.S. has very large reserves of coal (about one-quarter of the world's total reserves), this source of energy can also diminish our dependence on unstable imports of either oil

---

to bring gas from Prudhoe Bay to the lower 48 states had already been enacted in 2004.) Within days, the Energy Information Administration released an analysis of the House version of the sweeping energy bill: It would have only a "modest impact" on energy production, imports, oil prices, overall energy consumption and economic growth. In particular, it would provide no improvement in lower-48 natural gas production through 2025. Because the act neither opened ANWR to development nor lifted the OCS moratoria, little additional domestic supply of oil and gas would result from its passage. Energy Information Administration, *Impacts of Modeled Provisions of H.R. 6*, at vii (Aug. 2005).

48. Rebecca Smith, *After Long Taking Its Lumps, Coal Is Suddenly Hot Again*, WALL ST. J., Apr. 1, 2004, at A1.

49. Iraj Isaac Rahmim, *Stranded Gas, Diesel Needs Push GTL Work*, OIL & GAS J., Mar. 14, 2005, at 20. For example, Conoco has identified 1,200 stranded fields around the world which have no pipeline access.

50. A price of $3/MCF is about $3.00 per million BTUs.

51. Daniel Yergin & Michael Stoppard, *The Next Prize*, 82 FOREIGN AFF. 103, 107 (Nov./Dec. 2003).

52. Monica Perin, *Is it Gas? Is It Liquid? It's Both and It's Big*, HOUSTON BUS. J., Feb. 18–24, 2000, at 1A.

53. Syntroleum Corporation in Tulsa, Oklahoma has a GTL technology that produces ultra-clean synthetic gasoline and diesel fuels (which can also be used in fuel cells). Many energy giants, like BP, are testing new GTL technologies that promise to bring down costs. Lynn J. Cook, *Plan To Convert Gas to Diesel Advances*, HOUSTON CHRONICLE, Sept. 3, 2004, at D4.

54. Russell Gold, *In Qatar, Oil Firms Make Huge Bet on Alternative Fuel*, WALL ST. J., Feb. 15, 2005, at A1.

or gas. However, capital costs are about 20% higher than conventional coal plants and utilities face higher operating costs and risks, especially if carbon capture and sequestration (CCS) is part of the IGCC plant's gasifying process. Without CCS, CO_2 emissions from IGCC plants remain high.

Methane hydrates. An enormous source of methane lies at the outer edges of the ocean's continental shelf, just beneath the ocean floor. A methane hydrate is a cage-like lattice of ice in which molecules of methane are trapped. Geologists now estimate that the amount of methane trapped inside hydrates is about twice the amount of carbon held in all fossil fuels on the planet. However, the instability of the carbon-hydrate cycle poses many issues. Even minor changes in ocean temperatures and currents might trigger massive releases of methane from the oceans, with profound implications for global climate change. While hydrates produce relatively small amounts of CO_2 and particulates (and no sulfur) when burned, uncontrolled releases of methane from the hydrate's cage into the atmosphere could result in a massive injection of a greenhouse gas which is 20 times more potent than CO_2 in trapping heat. Much research is required to determine if methane can be captured from hydrates with minimal venting into the atmosphere. For this reason, methane hydrates, while abundant, are unlikely to compete with LNG, GTL or coal gasification as a viable source of gas in the next few decades. R&D on these hydrates is occurring, however, because the potential gas stored in them is such an astonishing resource base.

Over the last 200 years, methane concentrations in the atmosphere have more than doubled, largely due to human-related activities.[55] Rural areas of West Texas, Oklahoma and Kansas have "urban smog" from the formation of ozone. The precursors of ozone are the hydrocarbons from oil and gas wells and processing plants.[56] An EPA National Methane Emissions Inventory estimated that gas processing plants in the U.S. emitted 37 billion cubic feet of methane in 2000, most of which (70%) came from fugitive emissions from leaks and the remainder from venting and combustion during normal operations. Simple "best management practices" such as closing valves more tightly could save significant amounts of methane.[57]

B. A Note on Renewables versus Oil and Gas

The relative price of renewable energy sources (wind, solar, geothermal, hydropower and biomass) compared to oil and gas is also a key determinant of the shift in use between these two fuel groups. A Resources for the Future study of the performance of renewables in penetrating the market for electricity generation in the United States in the 30 years before 1999 showed that renewables performed quite well in reducing their costs of production and reliability. However, the costs of generating electricity using fossil fuels fell relatively more (due to the deregulation of natural gas prices, technological change reducing the costs of finding and producing oil and gas, more diverse and competitive world oil markets, dramatic cost reductions for rail transportation of coal, and the rise of competitive wholesale generators under the Energy Policy Act of 1992).

---

55. Before the 1950s, vast quantities of unwanted gas—trillions of cubic feet—were vented or flared into the atmosphere as a waste byproduct of oil production in the United States. Today, flaring in the U.S. is rare. Natural gas is far too valuable as a fuel source, state conservation commissions have largely prohibited the practice, and a network of pipelines exists to bring the gas to market. However, large-scale flaring still occurs in some places, *e.g.*, Nigeria, Brazil and Siberia, where oil production began without requirements for gas reinjection and where inadequate domestic infrastructure and markets exist to use the gas. Astronauts report that the gas flaring in Siberia outrivals Paris as the "greatest light show" on the Eurasian continent. Gas flaring around the world is easy to see in a National Oceanic & Atmospheric Administration (NOAA) satellite video *available at* http://web.worldbank.org/WBSITE/EXTERNAL/TOPICS/EXTOGMC/EXTGGFR/0,,menuPK:578075~pagePK:641684 27~piPK:64168435~theSitePK:578069,00.html (last visited August 26, 2009).

56. Aaron Katzenstein *et al.*, *Extensive Regional Atmospheric Hydrocarbon Pollution in the Western United States*, 100 PROCEEDINGS OF THE NAT'L ACADEMY OF SCIENCES 11,975–979 (Oct 14, 2003).

57. Roger Fernandez *et al.*, *Study Comparison Reveals Methane-Emissions Reduction Opportunities in Gas Processing*, OIL & GAS J., June 13, 2005, at 53–59.

Thus, while renewable technologies performed well on an absolute scale, their relative growth in penetrating electric markets was quite small. The study concludes: "The ultimate impacts of these changes in the regulation, technology and market structure of fossil fuels have been mostly favorable for electricity consumers; they have also been frustratingly disappointing for the fate of renewable technologies."[58]

IV. The Future of the Petroleum Industry with Global Warming: to 2030

A. Introduction

At this point, with adequate background and some historical perspective about the oil and gas resource bases, markets, and physical characteristics, we are ready to look at the future of the petroleum industry, particularly in a time of global warming. A huge number of studies projecting world oil and gas supplies to the year 2030 exist. They are often several hundred pages long and spew forth a bedazzlement of variant futures based on different assumptions about relative fuel prices and carbon constraints, resulting in a mind-numbing display of multi-hewed wedges, lines, and acronyms. Yet most of the leading reports, whether by industry or by government agencies (the Energy Information Administration in the U.S. and the International Energy Agency in the European Union, and even OPEC's own 2030 report)[59] end up in much the same place, at least through 2030. The National Petroleum Council's 2007 Report collected more than 35 forecasts, including both government and proprietary forecasts of the large international oil companies and petroleum consultants. Its graphics neatly depict the differences among the many studies, including "outlier" forecasts.[60]

A few brave souls have tackled the future out to 2050, largely through the use of scenarios rather than detailed econometric modeling of data, and some offer a brief glimpse of the energy world in 2100. This article can only give broadbrush treatment to all of these studies, but that is all that is needed for its purpose. The National Petroleum Council's comparative analysis of the many different forecasts provides a ready way of viewing the range of uncertainty inherent in any attempts to crystal ball the future. And some key outcomes appear in virtually all the forecasts.

B. The ExxonMobil 2007 Annual Energy Outlook

First up is ExxonMobil's annual Energy Outlook. This recent convert to the belief that global warming is real[61] publishes an annual projection 25 years into the future. It has the virtue

---

58. James McVeigh et al., *Winner, Loser, or Innocent Victim? Has Renewable Energy Performed as Expected?*, Resources for the Future (RFF) Discussion Paper No. 99-28 at p. iii (1999), *available at* www.rff.org. In addition, environmental laws and technological change improved the environmental performance of new fossil fuel plants quite dramatically over the same 30 years, reducing the relative advantage of renewables in this sphere as well.

59. OPEC, World Oil Outlook 2008 (2008) [hereinafter OPEC Outlook 2008], *available at* http://www.opec.org/library/World%20Oil%20Outlook/WorldOilOutlook08.htm.

60. Perhaps the lesson of past forecasts is that "outlier" projections should not be lightly dismissed. The uncertainty in Peak Oil dates among experts has already been noted, as have the major mistakes made in forecasting natural gas supplies for the U.S. alone by the National Petroleum Council between its 1999 and 2003 reports. Furthermore, no one, whether in or outside the energy industry, appears to have accurately accounted for the massive rise in demand from China and India in the 21st century in forecasts done a few years ago.

61. In February 2006, ExxonMobil released a report, Tomorrow's Energy: A Perspective on Energy Trends, Greenhouse Gas Emissions and Future Energy Options, *available at* http://www.exxonmobil. com/Corporate/Files/Corporate/tomorrows_energy.pdf. After acknowledging that the concentrations of CO_2 in the atmosphere have increased about 30% and methane has doubled since the 1800s, the report states (at page 10): "Human activities have contributed to these increased concentrations, mainly through the combustion of fossil fuels for energy use, land use changes (especially deforestation); and agricultural, animal husbandry and waste-disposal practices."

of being short and direct, despite the extensive data behind its analysis.[62] ExxonMobil is known in the industry as the leanest and meanest of the majors, relentless in cost-cutting, an erstwhile skeptic on global warming,[63] a technically based company with little PR charm, but with an indefatigable belief in markets and the highest return on capital invested in the industry.[64] How does it see the future in terms of Peak Oil, global gas markets, and global warming?

In short, ExxonMobil projects that through the year 2030, traditional fossil fuels—coal, oil and gas—will continue to supply the vast majority of energy needs, just as they do today. By 2030, the world's population will have increased from 6 billion people in 2000 to 8 billion people, with 90% of this increase in the developing countries.[65] The global economy will almost double in size with the fastest growth again in developing countries. China, India, Indonesia and Malaysia will become a block of non-OECD Asian-Pacific countries whose combined output approaches that of Europe.[66] This rapid economic growth is a key driver of growing world energy demand, as follows:

- The world will use about 40 percent more energy in 2030 than in 2005, even though the projected rate of energy demand growth from 2005–2030 (1.3% a year) is considerably slower than the historical growth rate between 1980–2005 (1.8%), largely because of strong improvements in energy efficiency.
- Oil and gas combined will continue to supply 60 percent of world energy use, which is the share they hold today. Coal, oil and gas will continue to supply about 80% of energy demand.

Exxon spent $16 million between 1998 and 2005 to fund 43 nonprofit groups that questioned the science behind global warming. ExxonMobil's Vice President of Public Affairs said the company has stopped this funding because "there is no question that human activity is the source of carbon dioxide emissions." *Exxon-Mobil Changes Position on Global Warming*, Greenwire, Feb. 9, 2007. In this 2006 Report, ExxonMobil states that the accumulation of GHGs in the atmosphere "poses risks that may prove significant for society and ecosystems. We believe that these risks justify action now."

62. ExxonMobil, The Outlook for Energy: A View to 2030 (Nov. 2007) [hereinafter ExxonMobil Outlook 2007], *available at* http://www.exxonmobil.com/Corporate/Files/energy_outlook_2007.pdf. The Outlook first assesses energy demand projections for nearly 100 individual countries and then covers the rest of the world in groups of 15–20 countries. It looks at the major drivers of energy demand, mainly economic growth and population growth. ExxonMobil also considers efficiency improvements and current trends and future expectations in consumption patterns (including interfuel competition, especially in electric power generation) to project the demand outlook into 2030. The company then evaluates the supply outlook, using its own experts and the company's vast experience in geology and engineering in many parts of the world. It models production profiles for key countries and also uses external data to establish resource estimates for both oil and gas in individual countries. In analyzing both the supply and the demand side, ExxonMobil divides the world into regions in two ways: first, the western, developed countries (represented by OECD membership) are contrasted with the developing, non-OECD countries; and second, large geographic regions are grouped together as North America, Russia/Caspian, Mideast, and Asian-Pacific. Unless otherwise noted, the data discussed in the text is from the 2007 Outlook, released in November 2007.

63. In considering its response to global warming, Exxon saw little value in improving its image, according to one of its spokesmen: "If we appear more green, it might get us a better seat at the policy table, but the real question is whether it would improve our access to resources and markets." Congress couldn't "ignore us anyway; we are the big elephant at the table." Ans Kolk & David Levy, *Multinationals and Global Climate Change: Issue for the Automotive and Oil Industries*, 9 Research in Global Strategic Management 171, 183 (2004).

64. ExxonMobil has the reputation of being "bruising, hard-bitten capitalism exemplified," respected but not much liked in the industry. Anthony Bianco, *Exxon Unleashed*, Bus. Week, Apr. 9, 2001, at 58, 60–61.

65. Non-OECD countries are the developing countries. OECD countries are in the Organization for Economic Cooperation and Development and include Australia, Austria, Belgium, Canada, Czech Republic, Denmark, Finland, France, Germany, Greece, Hungary, Iceland, Ireland, Italy, Republic of Korea, Japan, Luxembourg, Mexico, the Netherlands, New Zealand, Norway, Poland, Portugal, Spain, Sweden, Switzerland, Turkey, the UK, and the United States.

66. ExxonMobil, The Outlook for Energy: A View to 2030 (2005 version), *available at* www.exxonmobil.com [hereinafter ExxonMobil Outlook 2005].

- Energy efficiency gains will continue in both the developing countries and the OECD countries. The energy intensity of producing a unit of Gross Domestic Production (GDP) will decrease by 1.6 percent a year between 2005 and 2030, a rate which is significantly greater than the 1 percent improvement in efficiency between 1980 and 2005. By 2030, energy intensity globally is almost 50 percent below the 1980 level.[67]
- Global demand for transportation fuel is the fastest growing sector, but has a striking pattern. In OECD countries, demand for fuel (mostly oil) for light-duty vehicles has almost reached a plateau and will actually decline around 2015 due to better fuel economy in cars (although demand for air, marine and truck traffic will result in a small rate of growth of 0.6%/year). In non-OECD countries, fuel demand for transportation will soar at a rate of 3.1% a year in all transport sectors.[68] By 2030, oil demand in developing countries will exceed that in the OECD countries.
- The largest (by volume) growth in energy demand is fuel for electric power generation. Per capita consumption of electricity in non-OECD countries will more than double, driving the demand for natural gas, coal, and nuclear. Without a price on CO_2 emissions, coal is the cheapest fuel to use. If a cost of $30/tonne for CO_2 emissions to the atmosphere is assumed, then coal plants are significantly disadvantaged. The cost of gas-fired plants also rises, but not as much, making gas competitive with coal. Nuclear emerges as a strong economic alternative for new baseload capacity.
- OECD countries will price carbon and use less carbon-intensive fuels in power generation. Renewables will grow most rapidly in the OECD, followed by natural gas and nuclear for power generation. Coal use and oil use will decline.
- In non-OECD countries, coal demand will grow at 1.8%/year and retain its 50% share of power generation. Gas demand for power will grow even faster at 2.3%; nuclear at 4.2% and renewables at 3.5%. Still, by 2030, coal still powers 40% of all electricity plants, with large effects on CO_2 emissions.
- Integrated Gasification Combined Cycle (IGCC) plants that convert coal to gas and then use carbon capture and sequestration (CCS) are not widely applied by 2030 because of added complexity, cost and risk.
- Energy for the industrial sector will stay essentially flat in OECD countries while it grows at almost 2% in non-OECD countries. Almost all growth in heavy manufacturing and the chemical industry will occur in developing countries—a hard lesson in globalization that Americans in the rust belts of Ohio and Pennsylvania have already learned.
- Similarly, there is virtually no growth in demand in the residential and commercial sectors of OECD countries. The 80% of the world's population in non-OECD countries will drive virtually all growth in these sectors.
- In meeting global energy demand through the year 2030, oil use will grow at 1.2% annually, gas at 1.7%, coal at 0.9%,[69] and nuclear at 2%.
- Renewables will grow at 1.5%/year, but this figure masks another striking pattern. Traditional biomass (wood, charcoal, dung) grows at 0.7% a year. Modern renewables—solar, wind and biofuels (mainly ethanol)—grow at remarkably high rates of 9–10% per year

---

67. By 2030, the Mideast is projected to have the highest energy intensity (energy consumption per unit of GDP) in the world, even though its intensity is projected to decline relative to the year 2000. NPC 2007 REPORT, *supra* note 6, at 54.

68. Tata Motors, an Indian company, manufactures the $2,500 Nano mini-car, the world's cheapest car. Eric Bellman & Santanuy Choudhury, *Tata Chairman Threatens to Move Mini-Car Plant*, WALL ST. J., Aug. 23–24, 2008, at A5.

69. This low (0.9%) rate for coal growth is markedly different from the 1.8% growth rate projected in ExxonMobil's 2005 Outlook. Nuclear energy, on the other hand, grows much faster in the 2007 Outlook than in the 2005 one.

(which ExxonMobil notes reflects "government subsidies and mandates"). Even at these rates, wind and solar combined will account for only about 1% of global energy demand in 2030 and biofuels will add another 1%.

- Not surprisingly, the pattern of growth in energy demand outlined above inexorably leads to the following: CO_2 emissions will increase at a rate of almost 2% per year in non-OECD countries, which is almost 95% of all emissions over the Outlook period.

So—with the world still dependent on oil and gas for 60% of its energy, where will the supply come from? The 2005 ExxonMobil Outlook addressed the issue of Peak Oil more directly than its 2007 Outlook by presenting a single graphic of the world's seven major regions: North America, Latin America, Europe, Africa, Asia-Pacific (including Australia), the Middle East, and the Russia/Caspian area. The world as a whole has conventional oil resources totaling 3.2 trillion barrels of which one trillion barrels have been produced from the beginning of history through today. In other words, more than 2 trillion barrels remain to be produced from the original resource endowment of 3.2 trillion barrels. If non-conventional "frontier" resources such as heavy oil were added in, global oil resources total over 4 trillion barrels.[70]

Only the North American continent (the U.S. and Canada) have peaked in terms of having already produced more than half of its oil resources. All other regions have more conventional crude oil and condensate[71] remaining than has yet been produced, with the Middle East and the Russia/Caspian regions having the largest remaining resources (and markedly so). Europe is close to the 50% ratio signaling Peak Oil and its North Sea reserves are depleting fairly quickly.

So where will the additional oil and gas come from to fuel the world's energy demand through 2030? The 2005 Outlook reassuringly declared that hydrocarbon liquids production will increase over the next 25 years, both from new discoveries and from increases in known reserves, based on past experience showing that technology advances and reserves grow steadily over time.[72] New gas developments will be further from markets and thus more costly and challenging, but the world has the gas. Long-distance natural gas imports by LNG tankers or pipelines (some stretching more than a thousand miles) will become increasingly important to North America, Europe, and Asia.

ExxonMobil is not alone among the majors or among government and other forecasters in projecting the continuation of a petroleum- and fossil fuel-based economy through 2030. Its projections can be viewed as a mainstream "business as usual" (BAU) outlook.[73] However, this BAU future is in many ways unusual compared to the past. The 2007 ExxonMobil Outlook builds in a higher factor for increased energy efficiency;[74] it builds in technical advances on both

---

70. These numbers include both discovered and undiscovered resource estimates and use a "growth" component that reflects the well-documented trend of resource estimates to increase over time.

71. Condensate is a liquid hydrocarbon similar to crude oil which drips out of natural gas when the gas is brought to the surface where pressures and temperatures are lower than they were in the reservoir.

72. The NPC 2007 Report presents graphs and data showing how estimates of oil and gas reserves in many different studies over the years have generally increased over time. See NPC 2007 Report, supra note 6, at pp. 98–100.

73. NPC 2007 Report, supra note 6, at 35 (review of 35 forecasts concludes that by 2030, fossil fuels will account for 83% to 87% of world energy demand). See also the International Energy Agency's World Energy Outlook 2006 projection in the NPC 2007 Report, id. at 8. It should be noted that ExxonMobil's Outlook differs in significant details from others in the NPC Report. E.g., almost all projections collected in the NPC 2007 Report see demand for coal growing faster than in the past in the U.S. and in the world. Id. at 35. ExxonMobil's 2007 Outlook sees a slower growth in coal, as noted supra at n. 69.

74. By contrast, Shell Oil's forecasts see a relinking, not a delinking, in economic growth and energy demand. Shell states that the year 2004 will go down in history as a watershed in global energy because of what the International Monetary Fund (IMF) calls the "permanent oil shock" of the global middle class. China's manufacturing sector, churning out appliances and other goods for the growing middle classes of many developing countries, will make global economic growth more energy intensive again. When countries reach about

the supply and demand sides; it builds in very slow growth in demand in OECD economies, especially for oil, and a commitment to pricing carbon as a pollutant. It projects coal as the slowest growing fuel globally, anticipates a renaissance in nuclear energy, and sends modern renewables soaring upwards in power generation in both OECD and non-OECD countries. Still, the world will warm dangerously as CO_2 emissions climb.

C. Other Forecasts: The National Petroleum Council 2007 Report

While ExxonMobil's Outlooks do not discuss Peak Oil as such, the NATIONAL PETROLEUM COUNCIL'S 2007 REPORT presents an analysis of data on oil and gas endowments and future production levels collected from many different reputable sources, and it does speak to Peak Oil.[75] The NPC REPORT summarizes its overall findings on oil and gas as follows:[76]

> The natural gas resource appears more than adequate to meet the increased natural gas production typically anticipated by energy outlooks over the study period.[77]

> There is uncertainty about the potential of the oil resource base to sustain growing oil production rates.... The study observed a range of oil [supply] projections from less than 80 to 120 million barrels per day in 2030. The wide range results from differing assumptions about [many] uncertainties.

The lowest projection of only 80 million barrels per day (bpd) of production in 2030 belongs to the Association for the Study of Peak Oil (ASPO).[78] The U.S. government's EIA Reference Case is one of the highest, at close to 120 million bpd in 2030. The average of the major international oil companies forecasts lands at 107 million bpd. And where does ExxonMobil's Outlook place? It projects global oil supplies to be 116 million barrels per day.[79] ExxonMobil is betting that OPEC crude production, including that from Iraq, will rise from about 30 million bpd today to about 47 million bpd by 2030. As its 2005 OUTLOOK states: "We are assuming that OPEC countries will make investments in a timely manner to meet rising demand."[80] In almost all forecasts of oil growth, OPEC, and the Mideast countries in particular, are projected to increase production by a significant amount.[81]

The uncertainties alluded to in the NPC REPORT include not only the question of how much oil the Saudis or others may have in reserves, but also whether investments in increased capacity will be made in the countries (such as Iran, Iraq and Venezuela) which own the world's largest shares of remaining reserves. The range of uncertainty is staggeringly large, and the NPC RE-

---

$3,000 in per capita income, energy demand explodes as personal mobility takes off. At $15,000 per capita, energy demand slows because services begin to replace goods in family budgets. At $25,000, countries can have economic growth without significant energy increases if they choose the Japanese path rather than the U.S. path. SHELL SCENARIOS TO 2025, at 191 (discussed further in Part V *infra*). A critical uncertainty in future energy forecasts is what path the new middle classes will choose.

75. NPC 2007 REPORT, *supra* note 6, at Ch. 1 on *Energy Demand* and Chapter 2 on *Energy Supply*, esp. 89–143 on oil and gas endowments, recoverable resources and production forecasts. Peak Oil is addressed at 127–130. The forecasts collected in the NPC 2007 REPORT generally do not consider major new policies constraining carbon beyond those existing today, so to this extent they may be considered "business as usual" forecasts.

76. *Id.* at 9.

77. Recall that the study period is through 2030.

78. NPC 2007 REPORT, *supra* note 6, at 93.

79. EXXONMOBIL ENERGY OUTLOOK 2007, *supra* note 62, at 20.

80. Sam Fletcher, *ExxonMobil President Sees Long-Term Energy Changes*, OIL AND GAS J., Jan 3, 2005, at 28; and EXXONMOBIL OUTLOOK 2005, *supra* note 66, also reproduced in Weaver, *An Eventful Future*, *supra* note 10, at 538. EXXONMOBIL'S 2007 OUTLOOK projects the same increase in OPEC liquids production as its 2005 OUTLOOK.

81. NPC 2007 REPORT, *supra* note 6, at 120–22.

PORT recommends a "new assessment of global oil and gas endowments and resources to provide more current data for the continuing debate."[82] (The last USGS assessment of global resources was in 2000.) It is not clear, however, how a new global assessment can be accurate without major oil-exporting states adopting more transparent reserve data.

Two other summary results from the NPC analysis of many forecasts will suffice for purposes of assessing the petroleum industry's future:

- The year 2015 marks a point of "increasing risks" because of production declines in many of the world's mature fields and lack of adequate access to or investment in resources.[83] (In other words, 2015 seems a good year to pick for Peak Oil.)
- In most outlooks, natural gas grows more quickly than total energy demand through 2030.[84] In a carbon-constrained world, natural gas is likely to grow significantly more than in a BAU future.[85]

The NPC 2007 REPORT dispassionately reviews the reasons why Peak Oilers think that oil supplies will not grow significantly from current levels and will not keep pace with global demand. It presents the reasons why other forecasts differ, based on different expectations for new discoveries, increased recovery rates from existing fields, and technological advances that bring unconventional liquids into the market.[86] In short, Peak Oil forecasts do not see unconventional resources as offsetting declines in existing conventional production. The NPC REPORT then shows, as an illustrative example of future oil supplies, a graphic which appears several times in the report:[87]

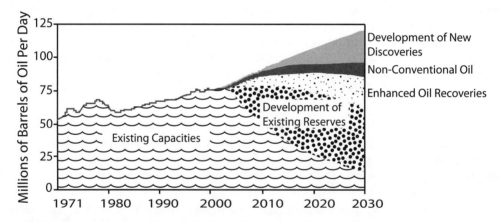

Figure 58. World oil production past, present, and future divided by sources of oil. Adapted from International Energy Agency, WORLD ENERGY OUTLOOK 2004 Figure 3.20 (2004).

This graphic starkly depicts the nature of an industry based on a depleting resource: One must constantly find and develop more, just to stay in place as existing production declines.[88]

---

82. *Id.* at 18.

83. *Id.* at 109, 127.

84. *Id.* at 35, 106.

85. *Id.* at 131

86. *Id.* at 127–130.

87. *Id.* at 9, 92, 104 and 130. The NPC REPORT took the graphic from the IEA's WORLD ENERGY OUTLOOK 2004.

88. Global output from existing oil fields is declining by 4.5% per year, according to a Cambridge Energy Research Associates (CERA) study. *Global Output Declining by 4.5% Annually, Study Finds*, GREENWIRE, Jan.17, 2008.

The section then concludes rather oddly by showing two different production profiles.[89] Profile A is the typical profile for a well or field or a country's aggregate of these: After discovery, production climbs quickly to a peak and then almost immediately starts falling. Profile B is a "plateau" that looks like a southwestern butte rather than the Matterhorn's peak. Like Profile A, production rises quickly in Profile B, but then stays high and flat for a period of time. However, on the far side of the plateau is a cliff that drops rapidly to zero where the plateau ends. Both profiles are worrisome. Both profiles herald the end of an age of conventional oil. It is just a matter of time and how long the world can rest on a plateau before production drops precipitously. The NPC REPORT then shows, for the third time, the graphic reproduced above and states that much of the world's existing oil production will need to be replaced by 2030.[90]

As to gas, the mid-range projections of the collected forecasts expect less than 50 percent of estimated conventional gas reserves to be produced by 2030. However, if the lower-range reserve estimates of the major oil companies prove more accurate, global gas production will exceed 50 percent of the technically recoverable resource by 2030.[91] (The same effect would occur if carbon constraints raise the demand for gas.) While the NPC REPORT does not use the term "peak gas," this 50% marker is one way of identifying this event. Implicitly recognizing this, the NPC RE-PORT continues: "Whether or not global natural gas production reaches a plateau during the study time frame, the possibility becomes greater within the next 50 years, unless a major technical breakthrough allows economic production of significant volumes of unconventional gas and gas hydrates."[92] And if that wasn't scary enough, the report reminds us that current proved reserves of gas are highly concentrated in four countries: Russia, Iran, Qatar, and Saudi Arabia.

In the end, despite the neutral and non-alarmist language of the NPC 2007 REPORT, there is a tough future ahead for oil and gas consumers. The producing companies are in a declining industry.[93] The only hope seems to be for a bit of rest on a plateau, perhaps giving unconventional oil and gas or other sources of energy time to replace what we have run out of.

Indeed, some of the participants in the industry, including those involved in the NPC study, have used more alarmist language. The CEO of Total (the large French major) stated that he thought the world's production was already near its peak and that the International Energy Agency's projections were far too high to be realistic.[94] The CEO of ConocoPhillips stated that he did not think world oil supply will ever exceed 100 million barrels per day. ConocoPhillips cut its long-term growth projections for oil and gas production and announced that it would rely heavily on enhanced oil recovery (EOR) technology in existing fields to achieve that growth.[95] Shell foresees that production of conventional oil and gas in non-OPEC countries will plateau in a

---

89. NPC 2007 REPORT, *supra* note 6, at 129–30.

90. *Id.* at 130.

91. *Id* at 132.

92. *Id.* at 132.

93. ExxonMobil has bought back an astounding $102 billion of its own stock between the end of 2004 and June 30, 2008. Jason Zweig, *With Buybacks, Look Before you Leap*, WALL STREET J., Aug. 30, 2008, at B1. It has no place else to put its money because of lack of access to much of the world's oil reserves with the rise of resource nationalism and national oil companies. ExxonMobil is the largest of the Western majors, but it is still only a distant 14th on the list of largest oil companies in the world in terms of reserves. The top companies are state monopolies like Saudi Aramco, the National Iranian Oil Co, Gazprom of Russia, Pedevesa of Venezuela and the Nigerian National Petroleum Co. Weaver, *An Eventful Future*, *supra* note 10, at 544–45.

94. EUROPEAN TRIBUNE blog by Jerome a Paris, *Panic Gripping Our Oil Elites*, Nov. 10, 2007, *available at* www.eurotrib.com/story/2007/11/10/71327/177.

95. *Conoco Sees Constraints on Long-term Output Growth*, GREENWIRE, Mar. 12, 2008. Conoco projects that it can replace its reserves over the next 5 years, but only with more capital spending on expensive non-conventional oil and gas recovery, including Canadian tar sands. Conventional oil and gas production is "mostly gone."

decade or so and warns that a number of producer countries may find it in their interests to keep production at a lower plateau for a longer period.[96] Fatih Birol, the chief economist for the IEA, was interviewed by the FINANCIAL TIMES in November 2007 and said about the global energy system that "the wheels may fall off."[97]

D. To 2030 with Carbon Constraints

Some forecasts have looked at the implications of the projected increases in energy demand and supply growth in terms of global warming. All are pessimistic. For example, even with aggressive assumptions for energy intensity improvements, ExxonMobil projects that global energy-related CO_2 emissions will increase at 1.2% a year to 2030. The final graphic in its 2007 ENERGY OUTLOOK lists some possible options to reduce CO_2 emissions and estimates their effects, if enacted.[98] The options include:

- Doubling biofuels production with a breakthrough in cellulosic ethanol would have virtually no impact on reducing CO_2 emissions in 2030.
- Doubling the expected rate of increase in vehicle fuel economy would reduce CO_2 emissions by only about 1% by 2030 because the turnover in the car fleet is so slow.
- Replacing half of the growth in coal for power generation with either nuclear or IGCC-CCS (integrated gas combined-cycle power plants with carbon capture and sequestration) would reduce CO_2 emissions by 3% and would require adding 125 more nuclear plants to the 170 already projected to be built.
- Retiring all existing coal plants at 40 years and replacing them with nuclear or IGCC-CCS would reduce CO_2 emissions by 10% in 2030.
- Combining all of these, unlikely as each is, would eliminate CO_2 growth within the next decade, but would not decrease the stock of existing CO_2 in the atmosphere.

In sum, the world is going to get warmer. Shell's expert scenario-builder also concludes that the odds of rapid climate change are quite substantial by 2050.[99] BP says that we will have to "catch up" after 2050.[100] In its view, the technology is available, but so many vested interests exist that it is difficult for policymakers to create the framework to catalyze them.[101]

---

96. SHELL INT'L LTD., SHELL GLOBAL SCENARIOS TO 2025 at 189 (2005). Some producer countries have no need to maximize immediate revenues; they are awash with cash surpluses.

97. Ed Crooks & Javier Blas, *Financial Times Interview with Fatih Birol*, FT.COM, Nov. 7, 2007, at 1. Dr. Birol explained the alarmist statement as follows: The level of CO_2 emissions seems to be on an irreversible trend and there appears to be a 12.5 million barrel-per-day gap between demand and supply at the end of the next 7 to 8 years. The IEA looked at all of the 230 existing projects in OPEC and non-OPEC countries that are projected to bring in 25 million bpd of oil around 2015. Yet, the world will be demanding 37.5 million bpd. Hence the gap. Either demand must come down or more investment in capacity in the oil-producing countries must occur quickly. Prices above $100/barrel will cause users to conserve, but the three big demand centers of China, India and the Middle East subsidize the price of oil and gas to their consumers, so market forces do not work here. Dr. Birol expressed greater pessimism about non-OPEC production because its decline rates were so high. On the other hand, he was more optimistic about unconventional supplies, such as tar sands, because oil prices will be high enough to make such sources profitable when there is such a large gap to fill.

98. EXXONMOBIL OUTLOOK 2007, *supra* note 62, at 23. The Outlook's base case projects energy-related CO_2 emissions totaling 37 billion tonnes in 2030. If all four options presented as sensitivities were implemented within the next decade, energy-related CO_2 emissions would total about 33 billion tonnes in 2030.

99. SHELL INT'L LTD., SHELL GLOBAL SCENARIOS TO 2025, at 216 (2005) [hereinafter SHELL SCENARIOS 2025], *available at* www.shell.com/scenarios.

100. *World Unlikely to Cut CO_2 Significantly before 2050*, CLIMATEWIRE, June 4, 2008.

101. *Id.*

V. 2050 and Beyond

2050 may well be remembered as the year when what is known as the "energy industry" be-came the "energy-and-carbon industry." While a genuine "hydrogen economy" may take decades to materialize — if it ever does — economists can make the case that we have already moved from the age of hydrocarbons to that of hydrogen and carbon, as both commodities now carry a price tag. Atoms of carbon are convenient "vehicles" to deliver hydrogen into the world's billions of combustion chambers. Until Kyoto, what happened to the atoms of carbon was of concern to ecologists, but not to economists. This is no longer the case.

SHELL GLOBAL SCENARIOS TO 2025[102]

By 2100, the world's energy system will be radically different from today's. Renewable en-ergy will make up a large share of the energy mix, and nuclear energy too will have a place. Humans will have found ways of dealing with air pollution and GHG emissions.

Two Energy Futures, Shell[103]

It is time for some good news. By 2050 we may have muddled our way through a treacherous landscape and the world is on its way to lowering GHG emissions in the atmosphere. By 2100, we have solved the problem. The technologists and economists are right. Put a price on carbon and energy markets will evolve to non-carbon emitting forms. So how do we get there?

This is the futurist world of Shell's highly regarded Global Scenarios. The Scenarios are not so much forecasts as they are possible narratives about the future, although Shell uses economic forecasting models to project economic growth, energy demand, and other key variables for each narrative.[104] One shelf of books listed at the start of this article depicts a rather brutish, "us versus them" view of a polarized world in which nations fight for access to increasingly scarce supplies of petroleum. Yet, global flows of capital, people, and goods also bind the world together in peaceful ways that can foster cooperation and mutual economic growth among nations. After all, the economies of producing nations are just as dependent on sales of petroleum as the economies of the Western nations are on the use of petroleum. ExxonMobil's Outlooks clearly see an expanding world of global trade in oil and gas sufficient to fuel economic growth in both developing and de-veloped nations, assuming that governments allow access to their reserves and that timely invest-ments are made to expand capacity. But, what if these assumptions are not realized?

The 2005 issue of the SHELL GLOBAL SCENARIOS focuses on the dual crises of security and trust, sparked by the fallout from the 9-11 terrorist attacks (and those in Spain and London) and widespread lapses in corporate governance following the Enron scandal. Peoples' beliefs are shaped by these events. States respond to these dual crises with different mixes of market incen-tives, coercion and regulation. Communities seek social cohesion and physical and economic se-curity. Distrust brings greater sectarianism; trust opens doors to trade and international ex-changes of people, goods, and services. Shell projects trends in beliefs and values through 2025, using three different scenarios briefly described thus:

The first of these "possible futures" is called *Low Trust Globalization*. This is a legalistic world where the emphasis is on security and efficiency, even at the expense of social co-hesion. The second, *Open Doors*, is a pragmatic world that emphasizes social cohesion and efficiency, with the market providing "built-in" solutions to the crises of security

---

102. SHELL SCENARIOS 2025, *supra* note 99, at 208.

103. Speech by Jeroen van der Veer, CEO of Royal Dutch Shell, dated Jan. 1, 2008, *available at* http://www.shell.com/home/content/media/news_and_library/speeches/2008/jvdv_two_energy_futures_25012008.html.

104. This section of the article is adapted from Weaver, *An Eventful Future*, *supra* note 10, at 561–63. Most footnotes and sources therein have been deleted in this adaptation.

and trust. The third, called *Flags,* is a dogmatic world where security and community values are emphasized at the expense of efficiency.[105]

After developing the assumptions and trends underlying each of the three possible futures, patterns of economic growth are projected for each scenario, reflecting the differences in incentives, market structures, socio-political trends and degree of global integration. In short, by 2025, global economic prosperity is 40% higher in Open Doors than in Flags[106] because of integrated capital markets, cross-border regulatory harmonization, transparency initiatives in corporate governance, technology sharing, educational exchanges and the like.[107] There is a downside to Open Doors: Because economic growth is higher in this scenario and because the world embraces free trade rather than indigenous renewable energy sources, Open Doors produces the most rapid increase in CO_2 emissions.

While it is difficult to summarize the SHELL SCENARIOS in a meaningful way in a short space, three points can be made:

- First, uncertainty is pervasive, even if the sources of the uncertainty are well-analyzed and understood. This uncertainty has large effects on future economic growth paths, energy prices, and energy policies.
- Second, leaders in government, business and civic society have the power to promote and steer the choice of scenarios.
- Events such as 9-11 and the war in Iraq drive these scenarios. The world is a difficult place to navigate, even if governments work to promote Open Doors.

Shell's three-scenario framework provides a useful way of filtering current events and putting them into a pattern that points to which narrative is most likely to prevail in the future. For example, the negative response of the United States to the Chinese national oil company's bid to acquire Unocal was clearly a Flags reaction to the issues of security and trust. It is an approach of national preferences, insider advantages, gated communities, patronage and fragmentation.[108] Similarly, federal support of indigenous biofuels to reduce dependence on Mideast imports is a large Flag. It is contrary to the Open Doors approach advocated by ExxonMobil in one of its advertorials on U.S. energy policy: "Interdependence, not independence, is key to America's future energy security."[109]

In 2007, Shell released "Signposts," a short supplement to its 2005 GLOBAL SCENARIOS, summarizing which of the three paths the world seemed to be traveling along after the passage of two years.[110] The answer: Low Trust Globalization with a goodly amount of Flags behavior. While globalization and economic growth were proceeding apace (reflecting a degree of trust in markets), the Doha trade talks had collapsed, Iran and the EU could not reach a compromise over Iran's nuclear program, NATO expansion to Ukraine and Georgia was being

---

105. SHELL SCENARIOS 2025, *supra* note 99, at *Foreward.*

106. *Id.* at 19.

107. *Id.* at 21.

108. The Flags scenario is summarized in the Executive Summary of the SHELL SCENARIOS, *supra* note 99, at 13 and explored in depth in Chapter 5.

109. Headline title of ExxonMobil advertisement placed on Op-Ed page of N.Y. TIMES, Nov. 3, 2005 (further explaining that the U.S. will be an oil importer for decades to come, so we must be smarter buyers by maintaining diverse sources of global supplies, and our government must promote durable global trade relationships). The oil industry's reaction to President Bush's State of the Union pledge to reduce U.S. imports from the Mideast by 75% is reflected in an editorial in the Oil & Gas Journal titled *Bush Botches Energy,* which then called the speech "bluster." Editorial, OIL & GAS J., Feb. 6, 2006, at 21.

110. SHELL INT'L LTD., SIGNPOSTS: SUPPLEMENT TO GLOBAL SCENARIOS TO 2025 (Feb. 2007), *available at* http://www-static.shell.com/static/aboutshell/downloads/our_strategy/shell_global_scenarios/supp_glo_sc.pdf.

fought by the Kremlin,[111] and resource nationalism was on the rise in Bolivia and Venezuela. In Europe, tensions between Christian and Muslim communities persisted. In short, security and social cohesion seemed to be greater political imperatives than market efficiency, even though the world economy was proving to be resilient to higher energy prices and the sub-prime credit crisis in the U.S. The terrain to be traversed moving forward would be hard to navigate.

Then, how does the bright future envisioned in 2050 and 2100 come about? In 2008, at Davos, Shell released SHELL ENERGY SCENARIOS TO 2050, centered on energy alone.[112] Two scenarios lead us to 2050.

In Scramble, nations rush to secure resources for themselves, fearing that energy security is a zero-sum game played by winners and losers. Local coal and biofuels increase fast. Patchy controls are placed on GHG emissions until severe weather events are blamed on lack of climate action. Then governments react with stringent policies imposed on industry, and markets experience price spikes and shortages. Life is volatile and uncertain. The world learns its lesson the hard way. By 2050, having started so slowly and then overreacted so severely, GHG emissions are being moderated, but the level of CO_2 in the atmosphere is still far above the safety point of 550 parts per million (ppm).[113]

The alternate scenario is Blueprints—a less painful path in which actions outpace events. It starts with a motley group of people in California—venture capitalists, politicians and NGOs—who build smart investments to improve energy efficiency and reduce GHG emissions in ways that pay for themselves. Local actions are linked by coalitions of mayors and others, sharing good practices with different tools of taxes, mandates, and voluntary reporting of emissions. Carbon-emissions trading starts regionally, but coalesces into a critical mass. With carbon pricing, peoples and businesses improve efficiency and invest in new technologies. After 2020, CCS begins in earnest. By 2040, renewables compete on price against fossil fuels which are managed with CCS. By 2050, cooperation, harmonized policies across the globe, and faster technology deployment have set a sustainable course for the future. CO_2 levels are still above the safe level, but there is a much smaller gap to close and living standards are higher and more secure.

Shell considers both scenarios to be equally plausible, and in only a short time (by 2012 when the Kyoto Protocol must be renewed) we will know whether the Bali declaration in late 2007 (that developed nations would halve CO_2 emissions by 2050) was "rhetoric or a real start." Much will depend on the U.S., China and India.

Time is of the essence. Blueprints assumes CO_2 is captured and sequestered at 90% of all coal- and gas-fired power plants in developed countries by 2050 and 50% of them in non-OECD countries.[114] Today, none do so.

Blueprints aligns best with the globalization and market economy of Open Doors. Under Open Doors, "the Kyoto Protocol rises like a phoenix from the ashes."[115] GHG controls are ramped up slowly and steadily over two decades, with an emphasis on global emissions trading. Developing countries are induced to participate by the promise of subsidized projects to reduce GHGs, like Germany's decision in 2004 to subsidize production of Brazilian cars running on

---

111. The Signposts were indeed prescient about the Russia-Georgia conflict that erupted in August 2008.

112. SHELL INT'L LTD., ENERGY SCENARIOS TO 2050 (2008), *available at* http://www.shell.com/home/content/aboutshell/our_strategy/shell_global_scenarios/shell_energy_scenarios_2050/shell_energy_scenarios_02042008.htm [hereinafter SHELL ENERGY SCENARIOS 2050].

113. At 550 ppm, climate models project that global temperature rise will be no more than 2 degrees Centigrade.

114. SHELL ENERGY SCENARIOS 2050, *supra* note 112, at 32.

115. SHELL SCENARIOS 2025, *supra* note 99, at 210.

biofuels. In spite of these developments, CO_2 concentration surpasses the 550 ppm level after 2015, but more radical policy changes can now be implemented, such as mandatory CCS for all new powerplants. Eventually, a mix of new technology, mandates and global carbon pricing will bring emissions within the safe zone.[116] The alternative of Flags will keep CO_2 below 550 ppm, but only because the global economy grows so slowly.

VI. Effect of Global Warming on Petroleum Operations

Before looking at what the petroleum industry is actually doing about global warming today rather than 50 years from now, this section surveys the effects of warmer temperatures on the industry's operations, followed by a section which reviews the likely economic impacts of climate change legislation on the industry.

The U.S Geological Survey (USGS) released a report in July 2008 estimating that the Arctic holds 90 billion barrels of undiscovered oil, 1,670 TCF of technically recoverable gas and 44 million barrels of technically recoverable natural gas liquids.[117] This represents 22% of the world's undiscovered, technically recoverable petroleum resource. The best place to find oil is off Alaska; Siberia is best for gas.

Ironically, the Arctic is the region being most seriously affected by global warming today. In certain regions of the Arctic temperatures are warming at twice the rate as the rest of world and additional warming of 4 to 7 degrees Centigrade is projected over the next 100 years.[118] The higher temperatures have already had profound effects on Arctic life and on the petroleum industry. First, the sea ice is disappearing rapidly, allowing marine transport (might LNG tankers have an Arctic future?) and greater access to Arctic resources, including offshore oil and gas—a good thing for industry, a bad thing for polar bears. Second, when the ground thaws, transportation infrastructure and buildings crack and sag as the ground shifts underneath them. The Trans-Alaskan Pipeline which carries crude oil 800 miles from Prudhoe Bay in the Arctic to the southern port of Valdez incurred substantial additional costs to counter this effect. Pilings with thermal siphons are used to carry heat away from the ground around the pipeline supports and in some places, the ground is artificially chilled.[119]

---

116. The World Energy Council in 2007 released Energy Policy Scenarios to 2050, using four scenarios for tackling climate changes. One of its findings is that the cost per ton of CO_2 captured and stored must fall to about $30, which is 2/3 less than the current cost, if CCS is to be used for power generation and creating synthetic liquids from coal with zero emissions. See http://www.worldenergy.org/publications/energy_ policy_scenarios_to_2050/default.asp and the accompanying short video of the lion, giraffe, elephant and leopard, each depicting one of the scenarios. The "lion scenario" is best for the world because lions are social and plan their hunts carefully, the analogy being a world with both strong government leadership and strong cooperation on global warming.

117. The USGS report is *available at* http://energy.usgs.gov/arctic.

118. Arctic Council, Impacts of a Warming Arctic: Arctic Climate Impact Assessment 994 (Cambridge Un. Press 2004) (report of the Arctic Council, an intergovernmental forum that addresses issues faced by Arctic people and governments; the International Arctic Science Committee and academies of science are part of the Council), *available at* http://www.acia.uaf.edu [hereinafter cited as Arctic Council]. Chapter 18 summarizes the 1,000-plus page study. *See also Arctic: Loss of Sea Ice Could Accelerate Permafrost Melting*, Greenwire, June 11, 2008 (in fall 2007, sea ice was 43% below the average ice extent existing in 1979 and temperatures were more than 4 degrees Fahrenheit warmer than the 30-year average; Arctic soil is estimated to hold a third of all carbon stored in soil worldwide and thawing of the permafrost would have dramatic impacts).

119. U.S. Climate Change Science Program, Effects of Climate Change on Energy Production and Use in the United States, Synthesis and Assessment Product 4.5, at 58 (Oct. 2007) [hereinafter SAP 4.5], *available at* http://www.climatescience.gov/Library/sap/sap4-5/final-report/default.htm.

The Alaskan permafrost has already begun to thaw in recent decades.[120] Tundra travel days on the North Slope have shrunk from 200 days a year in 1970 to 100 days in 2004. Because the oil industry only drills in the winter when ice roads and ice pads for the rig and equipment allow use of the surface, this smaller window has significant impacts on the drilling season. It is unlikely that the industry can conduct exploration and development plans with a winter work season less than 120 days.[121]

When peat bogs unfreeze, organic matter in the top layer decomposes, releasing methane and CO_2 which causes further warming in a pernicious feedback loop. Were methane hydrates trapped below the permafrost to thaw, a massive release of methane would have very serious global warming impacts. Some Arctic vegetation may grow faster with warmer temperatures and take up more carbon, but methane hydrate releases, should they occur, would swamp any vegetation effect.

A substantial percentage of U.S. oil and gas currently comes from the Gulf of Mexico. Hundreds of offshore platforms are in Hurricane Alley in the Gulf. Many large refineries and a huge network of oil and gas pipelines criss-cross the coastal areas and the seabeds of the Gulf. Hurricanes Katrina and Rita in 2005 amply showed the destructive power of nature unleashed against these man-made structures. The 2005 hurricanes caused direct losses to the energy industry of about $15 billion; 100 platforms were destroyed and 558 pipelines damaged.[122] Hurricane Gustav in 2008 passed directly over the Louisiana Offshore Oil Port (LOOP) that unloads tankers carrying 10% of U.S. oil imports. About 40% of U.S. refining capacity is located along the Gulf Coast; Rita knocked out about 25% of this total capacity for a period of time.[123] Henry Hub, the largest gas transmission interconnection site in the U.S. was out of service briefly in Katrina and for some weeks after Rita. The impact on energy markets from the loss of oil and gas due to the 2005 hurricane damage lingered for eight months.[124] Many experts forecast that extreme weather events will occur more often with global warming. Industry and government have prepared guidelines to harden infrastructure against winds and waves and to develop better ways of repairing undersea pipelines, all of which will add to costs. Insurance prices have soared.

Global warming is also projected to cause sea level rise. The rise is not likely to affect offshore platforms (although higher wave heights will), but would affect onshore refineries, LNG terminals, gas processing plants, wells and pipelines.[125] The Strategic Petroleum Reserve (our emergency supply of crude oil) is also susceptible to sea level rise and extreme weather. In short, flooding, erosion and storm surges accompany hurricane winds and can have large effects on the petroleum industry and its consumers.

On the demand side, global warming will affect patterns of using oil and gas. A small change in system reliability can have very large effects because of the scale of the energy industry. Warming will decrease the demand for gas and fuel oil for space heating in colder climates, but increase the demand for gas to generate electricity for more air conditioning, especially in the south where demand for energy for cooling could increase by 20%. One robust finding of the U.S. Climate Change Science Program is that climate change would cause a significant increase in the demand for electricity in the U.S. and would require building billions of dollars of new

---

120. Arctic Council, *supra* note 118, at 991 (summarizing Ch. 2 which discusses observed changes in the Arctic climate in recent decades).

121. SAP 4.5, *supra* note 119, at 58.

122. *Id.* at 59–63. Section 3.1.4 of SAP 4.5 discusses "Extreme Events."

123. Dan Fitzpatrick & Robert Lee Hotz, *Hurricane Gustav: Scientists Remain Divided Over Issue of Changing Patterns in Storms*, Wall St. J., Sept. 2, 2008, at A16.

124. SAP 4.5, *supra* note 119, at 48.

125. *Arctic Wells Could Disappear with Erosion*, Greenwire, July 26, 2008. The Bureau of Land Management (BLM) has identified at least 30 coastal wells in Alaska that must be plugged before erosion accelerates. A USGS study found that warming temperatures could send more Alaskan wells into the Arctic ocean as the coastline is eaten away by erosion which dissolves the permafrost, accelerating land loss. *Id.*

generation and transmission.[126] Power plants become less efficient (by about 1%) when ambient temperatures rise, requiring replacements for that small but significant drop in supply.[127] As demand for oil, gas and coal adjusts regionally to changing temperatures, the petroleum industry's markets also change. For example, running the air conditioner in a car reduces fuel efficiency by 12% at highway speeds.[128] As temperatures rise, more cars will use air conditioning and more gasoline or alternative fuels will be sold.

Another unfortunate feedback loop appears: Pipeline performance degrades with increased ambient temperatures. The network of existing pipelines and the thousands of miles of new pipelines that may be built to move CO_2 for enhanced oil recovery or sequestration will experience this negative effect.[129]

VII. Effect of Climate Change Legislation on the Petroleum Industry

Given the significant costs that global warming imposes on the oil industry in the United States today, will the industry welcome legislation that ultimately reduces GHG emissions? Many effects such as sea level rise and extreme weather will occur in other parts of the world as well, especially in Arctic and coastal areas where petroleum operations are located. The answer, of course, depends on how the legislation affects the bottom line. And that depends largely on how a carbon trading system will be set up and what other legislation, such as renewable fuels standards, might be enacted.

A large number of studies have modeled the effect of pricing carbon on the overall world economy, on energy prices, and on GHG reductions.[130] Suffice it to say that pricing carbon will move the economy to greater energy efficiency, the use of more nuclear and renewables, and the deployment of new technologies, and that the costs and ultimate effect on energy prices and on Gross Domestic Product (GDP) will depend on how rapidly technology advances, especially CCS technology. With carbon pricing, the studies generally find that GDP will be lower than otherwise because energy prices absorb a greater share of the consumer's purchasing power.

The narrower question of how such legislation may affect the petroleum sector has been addressed in a few studies, most of which have been commissioned by the industry. Shell's SCENAR-IOS depict a world of opportunity for energy companies in the active management of carbon, most notably by companies creating emission credits which are then sold to others at a profit in their own operations. Alternatively, the credits can be created through investments in projects with other companies (such as reinjecting CO_2 into depleted reservoirs) or projects implemented through the Clean Development Mechanism of the Kyoto Protocol to reduce GHG emissions in a developing country.[131] While these opportunities do exist, it does seem likely that

---

126. SAP 4.5, *supra* note 119, at 27, 43. Greater energy efficiency and smaller house sizes can offset this effect. If additional electricity needs come from coal plants, GHG emissions are increased.

127. *Id.* at 48. Without technological advances in cooling system efficiency, overall generation efficiency will fall. *Id.* at Sec. 3.1.1. Ambient temperature increases have immediate negative impacts on gas turbine performance. *Id.* at 53.

128. *Id.* at 40.

129. *Id.* at 56.

130. *See* James A. Edmonds & Ronald D. Sands, *What Are the Costs of Limiting CO_2 Concentrations?*, *in* GLOBAL CLIMATE CHANGE: THE SCIENCE, ECONOMICS, AND POLITICS 140–156 (James M. Griffin ed. Edward Elgar 2003).

131. SHELL SCENARIOS 2025, *supra* note 99, at 207. The Clinton administration's optimism that the U.S. could meet its Kyoto targets at modest cost to the domestic economy was premised on being able to meet 75 to 85 percent of the nation's obligations through purchasing credits from other nations or doing offset projects abroad. George (Rock) Pring, *The United States Perspective, in* KYOTO: FROM PRINCIPLES TO PRACTICE 210 (Peter D. Cameron and Donald Zillman eds. Kluwer Law International 2001) (in association with the Int'l Bar Ass'n Section on Energy & Nat. Res. Law).

the petroleum industry will take a hit if a bill such as Lieberman-Warner's S.2191 were passed because the industry is itself energy-intensive.

The Energy Policy Research Foundation (EPRINC) issued a report in July 2008 on the IMPACT OF A NATIONAL CARBON EMISSION CAP AND TRADE PROGRAM ON THE U.S. PETROLEUM INDUSTRY.[132] On balance, the impact is projected to be adverse because refineries and petrochemical plants will not be able to fully pass along to consumers the rising costs of energy inputs, especially when competitors abroad are not burdened with GHG controls.[133] Also, petroleum companies may be required to obtain allowances, not just for their own energy use, but for the CO_2 emitted by their customers when their products are combusted. The transportation sector accounts for 28% of U.S. greenhouse gas emissions, so petroleum firms would have to submit allowances for this large percentage of allowances.[134] A cap-and-trade program would also increase energy price volatility, adversely affect demand, and hinder investment. Two opportunities are obvious though. First, if Congress allocates some free allowances to emit CO_2 to industry, then companies will receive something of value for free. (Of course, the companies will have to pay their lobbyists to win the freebies.) Second, if Congress decides to spend monies raised by allowance auctions on alternative energy or energy R&D, some companies can benefit. Those industry members in the natural gas business may also see a relative increase in demand for gas in power generation, but their costs will also rise.[135]

If the emissions targets in S.2191 are to be met, per capita GHG emissions in the U.S. will have to drop 30% by 2020 and 50% by 2030. Without the near-term viability of large-scale CCS, the drop in the use of fossil fuels must be steep and must be replaced by nuclear and renewables. Otherwise, "fairly dramatic changes in lifestyle" would be required to reach the targets.[136]

Acknowledging that cap-and-trade programs may vary on matters such as the banking of allowances, a price safety valve or floor, the distribution of allowances and revenues, and the use of offsets through the Clean Development Mechanism or in domestic agriculture (using soils and crops or forests as carbon sinks), the EPRINC REPORT hypothesizes that trading will become international in scope, so that the price of an allowance in the U.S. will be close to that in Europe. Prices for petroleum products sold to users are estimated to rise between 20 cents and 60 cents a gallon at the start, and will probably rise further as allowances are reduced.[137] S.2191

---

132. ENERGY POLICY RESEARCH FOUNDATION (EPRINC), IMPACT OF A NATIONAL CARBON EMISSION CAP AND TRADE PROGRAM ON THE U.S. PETROLEUM INDUSTRY (July 2008) [hereinafter EPRINC REPORT]. EPRINC is a think-tank funded by 35 companies in the petroleum industry, but its research in energy economics is fairly objective. See http://www.eprinc.org. EPRINC concludes that a carbon tax would be superior to a cap-and-trade program because there would be no volatility in the price of allowances and some of the taxes may be used to reduce income taxes.

133. The American Petroleum Institute (API) commissioned an analysis of S.2191 which concluded that the bill would send refining and other industries overseas, with a consequent loss of jobs at home. Imports of refined products from abroad would increase, although these imports would have to bear increased transport costs. See AMERICAN PETROLEUM INST., ADDENDUM TO IMPACT ASSESSMENT OF MANDATORY GHG CONTROL LEGISLATION ON THE REFINING AND UPSTREAM SEGMENTS OF THE U.S. PETROLEUM INDUSTRY at pp. ES2, ES10-13 (ICF Consulting, April 2008).

134. EPRINC REPORT, *supra* note 132, at 16.

135. The API study estimates that drilling for natural gas would decrease in the U.S under S.2191 because the cost of allowances to emit methane will be high relative to well operating costs, so domestic gas production will be reduced. *Id. See also* WOOD MACKENZIE, IMPACT ASSESSMENT OF CONSUMER EMISSION ALLOWANCE COSTS UNDER THE LIEBERMAN-WARNER CLIMATE SECURITY ACT OF 2007 ON U.S. NATURAL GAS PRODUCTION (May 29, 2008) (domestic gas production will fall).

136. EPRINC REPORT, *supra* note 132, at 15.

137. *Id.* at 13–15. The EPRINC report notes that the recent increase in the price of gasoline by about a dollar a barrel is equivalent to a $100 per ton increase in the cost of emitting CO_2. This shows the effect that a cap-and-trade program would have. The price of an emission allowance for CO_2 in Europe was about $40 per ton in July 2008.

does not return any of the monies raised from the sale of allowances to taxpayers or consumers. Thus, the program acts like a tax of sufficient magnitude (about $100 billion) to cause considerable adverse effects on the economy.

All members of the energy industry must learn how to manage allowances, including the strategic use of hedging and forward purchases. In large energy companies, managing allowances will be a major activity. If a company can create an offset at less cost than the price of an allowance, then emissions trading can be a profit center in its own right.

Aside from S.2191, the Energy Independence and Security Act (EISA), passed in 2007, has significant impacts on the industry. It raises fuel economy standards significantly by 2020 and mandates a huge increase in ethanol. In addition, California is running its own GHG program (much to the delight of the Blueprint scenarists) and has proposed a Low Carbon Fuel Standard which requires sellers of motor fuels to steadily decrease the life-cycle carbon content of fuels they sell.[138] With so much ethanol replacing gasoline and the likely use of more natural gas-powered vehicles and hybrids in California, there is less need for crude oil refining capacity in the U.S.[139] Most alternatives to gasoline cost more and have lower energy content. Thus, sellers of gasoline and diesel will be "taxed" by having to subsidize the alternative fuels which they must offer to meet mandated targets. Ever larger subsidies will flow over time from high carbon to low carbon fuels.

In short, a future under carbon constraints does not seem particularly sunny for the petroleum industry, at least at the start.

VIII. "Can the Oil and Gas Industry Save the Planet?"[140]

> A vision without resources is a hallucination. (Pentagon saying). Right now we are having a green hallucination.
>
> **Thomas Friedman 2008**[141]

> Imagine a power plant that captures and buries its CO_2 that then, as a by-product, makes clean hydrogen for transport fuel, and also by combusting biomass, generates negative CO_2 emissions (as biomass absorbs CO_2 while it grows). This is not science fiction. It could be reality if we work together to make it happen and if enough governments—starting with the G8 Leaders' Hokkaido Summit in July—agree to a long-range global policy framework with the right mix of regulation and stable incentives.
>
> We welcome the call by the G8 Energy Ministers for the launch of 20 large-scale CCS projects globally by 2010.... In our view of the future, CO_2 could be captured and stored at 90% of all coal- and gas-fired power plants in developed countries by 2050, and at least 50% of plants in developing countries. Today, none use CCS because it adds extra costs, uses more energy, and because permit requirements and liability for the CO_2 are not yet clear.

---

138. *Id.* at 17. Similarly, a committee amendment to S.2191 would mandate a 5% decrease in the carbon content of transportation fuels by 2015 and a 10% cut by 2020. *Id.* at 8.

139. *See also* IMPACTS OF POTENTIAL CLIMATE CHANGE POLICIES ON THE REFINING AND PETROCHEMICAL SECTORS, a study prepared by NERA Economic Consulting for the National Petrochemical and Refiners Ass'n (April 2008) (finding greater negative effects on refining from the implementation of the EISA and the ethanol mandate than from S.2191; gasoline and refined product prices would rise by an average of 48 cents per gallon by 2030 (in constant 2007 dollars)).

140. This is the title of a speech by Dr. Steven L. Bryant who directs the Geological CO_2 Storage Joint Industry Project at the University of Texas where he holds the J.H. Herring Centennial Professorship in Petroleum Engineering. The speech was presented at the 54th Annual Rocky Mtn. Min. L. Inst., July 17–19, 2008, in Snowmass, Colorado and will be published in 54 ROCKY MTN. MIN. L. INST. 2-1 (2008).

141. As quoted in Stephen Kotkin, *A Call to Action for Earth and Profit*, N.Y. TIMES, Sept. 7, 2008, at BU8 (reviewing Thomas Friedman's latest book titled HOT, FLAT AND CROWDED).

There is no time to lose, especially as more energy will come from more carbon-intensive types of fossil fuels. Consider Canada's vast reserves of oil sands.... [I]ts CO_2 emissions are higher than conventional petrol—about 15% more. Yet the world needs this oil to meet rising demand.... CCS could be an effective way of mitigating these higher emissions.

Shell: A Climate Plan for the G8 Leaders, July 5, 2008[142]

The U.S. Congress seems to want the oil companies to save the planet by investing in renewables. After yet another quarter of record profits, the House Select Committee on Energy Independence and Global Warming summoned the executives of the major western oil companies—BP, Shell, Chevron, ConocoPhillips and ExxonMobil—to appear and explain why they were not investing more in renewables.[143] The Committee was considering raising taxes on the oil industry to offset the costs of extending tax credits for renewables.

Some of the majors are investing in green energy. One study found that the oil and gas industry in North America had put about $3.4 billion into non-hydrocarbon investments between 2000 and 2006, mainly in wind and biomass, but also in solar, geothermal and landfill gas.[144] This is a tiny amount in both absolute and relative terms. The industry spent much more on other GHG mitigation strategies, such as improving energy efficiency (through cogeneration and developing advanced technology for vehicles), reducing natural gas flaring and fugitive methane emissions, substituting lower carbon fuels (*e.g.*, by importing more LNG), and engaging in research on "enabling technologies" such as CCS projects and second-generation biofuels. These types of projects constituted 92% (or $38.7 billion) of the companies' total reported investments in GHG mitigation projects of $42.1 billion. Thus renewables were a mere 8% of the industry's efforts on GHG reduction. Almost all of the GHG mitigation investments would have been done in response to higher energy prices, regardless of pending legislation or global warming concerns.

Yes, some of the major oil companies do have a toe in the renewable pool. Chevron is the world's largest geothermal producer. BP and Shell both produce solar panels. Shell has a 50% stake in Iogen, a leading Canadian biotech firm, doing commercialization of cellulosic ethanol.[145] Chevron has teamed up with Weyerhaeuser, the timber company, in a joint venture called Catchlight Energy to convert cellulose and lignin into biofuels.[146] Outside of the U.S., Statoil-Hydro, the Norwegian oil company, has built the world's first full-scale floating wind turbine, combining its offshore experience with advanced wind power technology. The wind turbine sits atop a giant spar buoy which loads oil from platforms to tankers and feeds electricity to land through underwater cables.[147]

As for ExxonMobil, R&D and relentless cost-cutting are its thing.[148] It constantly promotes its funding of the launch of Stanford University's Global Climate and Energy Project (GCEP),

---

142. Shell advertisement, appearing in THE ECONOMIST, July 5, 2008 (copy in author's files). *See* the data in n. 167 *infra* on the CO_2 emissions from oil sands development versus conventional oil production.

143. *Executives Defend Profits, Warn against Tax Hikes*, E&E NEWS PM, Apr. 1, 2008. The testimony of the five major oil companies appears at *Hearing Before the House Select Committee on Energy Independence and Global Warming*, FED. NEWS SERVICE, Apr. 1, 2008.

144. THOMAS TANTON, T-SQUARED & ASSO., KEY INVESTMENTS IN GREENHOUSE GAS MITIGATION TECHNOLOGIES BY ENERGY FIRMS, OTHER INDUSTRY AND THE FEDERAL GOVERNMENT 7 (May 2008) (reviewing data reported in over 300 company annual reports and other public sources). Much of the reported investment was probably made for reasons of enhancing profitability, not for GHG mitigation.

145. *Cellulosic Ethanol: Shell Will Increase Investment in Canadian Biotechnology Venture*, CLIMATE WIRE, July 16, 2008. Iogen has a demonstration commercial plant using wheat straw as feedstock.

146. *Biofuels: Weyerhaeuser, Chevron Team Up for Biofuels Venture*, GREENWIRE, Mar. 5, 2008. Chevron reported that it would spend $2.5 billion between 2007 and 2009 on renewables and end-use efficiency.

147. *Wind Power: Oil Company Develops First Floating Turbine*, GREENWIRE, May 23, 2008.

148. ExxonMobil's cost of finding oil dropped from about $4 per barrel in the 1980s to 65 cents per barrel in 2000. Bianco, BUS. WEEK, *supra* note 64, at 62. Its finding costs then dropped to about 44 cents per barrel

which conducts energy research and climate modeling, but the money involved is trivial relative to ExxonMobil's budget, no matter the high quality of the project.

The company's former CEO, Lee Raymond, was characteristically blunt about renewable energy: It is a "complete waste of money."[149] One Exxon manager, remembering the company's experience in the late 1970s and 1980s, put it this way: "We are not looking to get into any business supported by government subsidies. We lost more than $500 million on renewables and learnt a lot of lessons."[150]

The Exxon manager's comment reflects the inconsistent federal policy of the post-OPEC embargo era. Congress under President Carter initiated a large federal program to wean Americans off imported oil, but it was abruptly cut by President Reagan when oil and gas shortages disappeared, bringing an era of low oil and gas prices that lasted more than 20 years. The most notable federal effort for "Project Independence" was the Synthetic Fuels Corporation (SFC), an $88-billion program of expenditures—the largest peacetime industry effort ever made by America—to produce 2 million barrels a day of synthetic fuel.[151] The SFC was designed to be the investment-banker catalyst of a huge new industry.[152] The scope of the project was greater than the sum total of monies spent on the interstate highway system, the Marshall Plan and the space program combined, at the time the program was announced.[153] In 1980, as the SFC was being launched, Exxon characterized it as offering "some of the most significant business and employment opportunities in modern history."[154] At the same time, cautionary voices asked what would prevent these federal subsidies from creating hundreds of industrial plants that would be the most costly "white elephants" in history (with elephant-sized environmental impacts).[155] And spokesmen from other major oil companies warned that the SFC program, even if successful, would not make a major dent in the fuel-supply problem, given the world's appetite for oil and gas.[156] The backbone of the program was to be giant coal and oil shale conversion projects,

---

in 2004. *ExxonMobil Exploration Strategy to Pursue All Quality Opportunities*, OIL & GAS J. Oct. 3, 2005, at 32–33. ExxonMobil is the industry leader in energy efficiency in its refineries.

149. *Survey: Consider the Alternatives*, THE ECONOMIST, Apr. 30, 2005, at 24. The text that follows on the Synthetic Fuels Corporation is adapted from Weaver, *An Eventful Future*, *supra* note 10, at 565–66.

150. Ans Kolk & David Levy, *Multinationals and Global Climate Change: Issue for the Automotive and Oil Industries*, in 9 RESEARCH IN GLOBAL STRATEGIC MANAGEMENT: MULTINATIONALS, ENVIRONMENT AND GLOBAL COMPETITION 171, 179 (Sarianna M. Lundan ed., JAI Press 2004). Other oil companies invested in solar photovoltaics in the 1970s, but most posted losses and exited, as did GE and Westinghouse. CHRISTOPHER FLAVIN & NICHOLAS LENSSEN, POWER SURGE: GUIDE TO THE COMING ENERGY REVOLUTION 161 (World Watch Inst. 1994).

Of course, the oil and gas industry has received a goodly share of tax incentives over the years. U.S. tax credits for unconventional gas have spurred its growth to equal 30% of U.S. gas production today. The success of these incentives is used to argue for more federal R&D monies for oil and gas research, even though it may be viewed as "corporate welfare" by some. Scott W. Tinker & Eugene Kim, *Oil and Gas in Energy Research Spending: A Call for Balance*, OIL & GAS J., Sept. 27, 2004, at 18–24, esp. Figs. 5 to 8. A study by the General Accounting Office (now called the General Accountability Office) found that federal tax breaks for the oil industry had totaled almost $150 billion in the three decades before the year 2000, far outpacing the tax breaks of $11.5 billion accorded to corn-based ethanol since 1979. General Accounting Office, GAO/RCED-00-301R, Letter to Senator Tom Harkin with Enclosure I, titled *Tax Incentives for Petroleum and Ethanol Fuels*. The cover letter contains Table 1 summarizing the data cited above.

151. Robert D. Hershey Jr., *Blessing or Boondoggle? The $88 Billion Quest for Synthetic Fuels*, N.Y. TIMES, Sept. 21, 1980, at sec. 3, p. 1.

152. Robert D. Hershey Jr., *Congressional Conferees End Financing of Synthetic Fuels Program*, N.Y. TIMES, Dec. 16, 1985, at B11.

153. *Id.* The program would have required the employment of 80% of all the pipefitters, electricians, boilermakers, and welders then existing in the U.S., according to the Department of Energy.

154. *Id.*

155. *Id.* Synthetic fuels covered many different projects, ranging from huge plants to extract oil from oil shale or turn coal into gas to smaller-scale ventures that produced alcohol fuels from grain, wood or garbage.

156. *Id.* (citing chief economist of Standard Oil of Indiana).

brought into being with incentives such as price and loan guarantees, direct loans and purchase agreements. A few months after its launch, oil and gas prices dropped precipitously, President Reagan withdrew support for the program and in 1985, the SFC was effectively killed, having provided funding for only four plants in its five-year history, all of them uneconomic at world energy prices.[157]

Instead of relying on what it considers to be fickle government largesse, ExxonMobil invents products and processes that it hopes will strengthen its bottom line. It developed a Fast Drill Process that reduces the time to drill oil and gas wells by 35%;[158] the R3M "listening" device to pick up electromagnetic signals to detect undersea deposits; and technology that can double the capacity of LNG liquefaction plants and increase by 80% the LNG carried by a single tanker, substantially reducing LNG costs.[159] Its 14,000 scientists and engineers (of whom more than 1,000 have Ph.Ds) conduct research totaling $1 billion a year, including items like advanced vehicle and fuel technologies. In recent advertisements, it touts its better plastic film separator based on hydrocarbon polymers which prevents lithium ion batteries from overheating and short circuiting, thus improving hybrid vehicle performance.[160] And remember that car tire that ExxonMobil recommends you keep properly inflated? ExxonMobil has started manufacturing a new inner liner for tires made with its trademarked "Exxcore" that significantly improves the retention of tire pressure.[161] If all tires retained air pressure better, it would reduce GHG emissions by 6 million tons per year, equivalent to taking a million cars off the road.

It is clear that the major oil companies see a petroleum-based economy providing the vast preponderance of the world's energy needs for at least the next quarter century. Only by 2050 has the energy mix changed significantly, and only by 2100 has the world been weaned off of its petroleum dependence. We have seen that almost all serious long-term projections through 2030 of our energy future agree with these profiles.

If renewables, already expected to grow at very high rates, and energy efficiency (also projected to improve more quickly than its historical average) will not alone save the planet, what will? The oil companies are betting on one technology near and dear to them: carbon capture and sequestration (CCS).

Oil companies already handle CO_2 in large quantities in enhanced oil recovery. For example, a 400-mile pipeline carries large volumes of naturally occurring CO_2 from an underground deposit in Colorado to West Texas where it is pumped into large, mature oil fields. The CO_2 acts as a good solvent that "cleans" the oil out of the pore spaces in the reservoir rock, in addition to repressuring the field. A significant percentage of additional oil can be recovered from these CO_2-EOR projects. While the CO_2 is now vented or sold for reuse, it can instead be permanently sequestered when the EOR operation is over. The NPC 2007 REPORT notes: "The oil industry has

157. Robert D. Hershey Jr., *Congressional Conferees End Financing of Synthetic Fuels Program*, N.Y. TIMES, Dec. 16, 1985, at B11; *U.S. Synthetic Fuel Corporation Shuts Down*, NEW YORK TIMES, April 19, 1986, at sec. 1, p. 46.

158. *ExxonMobil Advancement Cuts Drilling Time Up to 35 Percent*, BUS. WIRE, Nov. 1, 2005 (Energy Central Professional Online).

159. EXXONMOBIL, TOMORROW'S ENERGY: A PERSPECTIVE ON ENERGY TRENDS, GREENHOUSE GAS EMISSION AND FUTURE ENERGY OPTIONS 7 (Feb. 2006), *available at* http://www.exxonmobil.com/Corporate/Files/Corporate/tomorrows_energy.pdf.

160. ExxonMobil announced in October 2008 that it would test its new battery separator film in a joint project with battery-maker EnerDel which plans to become the first company to mass produce lithium ion batteries for vehicles. ExxonMobil broke ground on a plant in South Korea which will manufacture commercial quantities of the separator film. Brett Clanton, *Charging Ahead on Batteries*, HOUSTON CHRONICLE, Oct. 14, 2008, at D1.

161. *See* www.businesswire.com/news/exxonmobil/20080827005059/en.

extensive experience with pumping liquids into subsurface formations and evaluating the security of these formations for storage."[162] With "relative ease," the industry could store the CO_2 permanently.[163] And, in a carbon-constrained world, oil companies will have a financial incentive to use anthropogenic CO_2 from power plants in EOR.

Review the graphic presented earlier in this article depicting the profile of future liquids supply. One big wedge of future supply is enhanced oil recovery, or EOR. The oil companies will be key players in CO_2-EOR, followed by the permanent sequestering of the CO_2. A table in the NPC REPORT provides a summary of how the industry sees CCS technologies developing over time from 2010 to 2030.[164] By 2030, a new process of "rig-site or subsurface hydrocarbon processing" keeps most of the carbon in or near the reservoir, simplifying CCS logistics and costs, and providing low-carbon fuels to consumers.

Here is ExxonMobil's latest CCS invention: A $100 million commercial demonstration plant in Wyoming will remove CO_2 from natural gas wells near the field.[165] The plant will use a patented "controlled freeze zone" technology which passes the natural gas through the plant and cryogenically freezes the gas, removing the CO_2, hydrogen sulfide and other pollutants from the gas stream. The clean, low-carbon natural gas is transported to utilities for sale. The CO_2 can be reinjected into the ground on site or sold to developers for enhanced oil recovery (EOR). The process will lower the costs of CCS because the CO_2 is pumped back into the ground on site rather than compressed and transported. And the process makes business sense because it lowers the risks from pending federal legislation that will regulate CO_2 emissions by eliminating the emissions.

This is what the oil industry is good at: Big, complex projects that crack molecules of carbon, hydrogen and oxygen and rearrange them, move them, store them, and sell them. This is what its thousands of petroleum and chemical engineers do while its civil engineers design iceberg-proof platforms for the Arctic, ultra-large LNG tankers, and directional wells that extend horizontally for 8 miles to reach an offshore reservoir from land.

Another wedge in the graphic is unconventional oil, *i.e.*, heavy and extra-heavy oil and bitumen (tar sands) which do not flow easily or are in solid form. Heavy oils are so thick that they will not move up a wellbore unless they are treated or diluted. Large quantities of steam or natural gas are injected in them to "lighten" them so that the oil will flow. The resulting product must then be upgraded before the crude oil can enter a normal refinery. "Tar sands" is an apt name for the enormous deposits of heavy oil intermixed with sand in huge deposits in Canada. (Imagine pouring tar into a sandbox and then digging up the black, oily mixture and processing it to separate the sand from the tar-like oil.)

It takes more energy and creates more GHG emissions to produce and process unconventional oil than conventional oil. Alberta, Canada has created a $2 billion fund to promote "clean" tar sands by building a large-scale CCS project to store some of the GHG emissions.[166] Compa-

---

162. NPC 2007 REPORT, *supra* note 6, at 237.

163. *Id.* at 249. *See also* Table 3-1 on p. 179 (about one million tons of CO_2 are injected for EOR today and the industry has experience with many other types of storage and fluid projects listed in the table).

164. NPC 2007 REPORT, *supra* note 6, at 181, Table 3-3. OPEC's 2008 WORLD OIL OUTLOOK also speaks approvingly of CCS as a technology that could make a "significant contribution to abate the growth of CO_2 emissions." OPEC OUTLOOK, *supra* note 59, at 2.

165. ExxonMobil press release *available at* http://www.businesswire.com/portal/site/exxonmobil/index.jsp?ndmViewId=news_view&ndmConfigId=1001106&newsId=20080505006145&newsLang=en. The plant has a projected start-up date in 2009.

166. Steven Poruban, *Alberta Keeps Oil Sands' Environmental Impacts in Check,* OIL & GAS J., July 28, 2008, at 29 (Alberta's climate change plan expects to reduce GHG emissions by 50% by 2050, largely through the use of CCS). Shell is testing ways to take CO_2 from its upgrader and inject it into saline aquifers for storage. Norval Scott, *Shell Launches Carbon-Capture Project,* THE GLOBE AND MAIL, July 9, 2008, at B6.

nies can either make actual CO_2 reductions in their operations or pay \$15 per ton of CO_2 emitted into the fund to use in other projects that will reduce emissions.[167] If the price of CCS falls and the price of emitting CO_2 rises over time, tar sands production will become cleaner. If neither happens, then the world is likely to warm considerably as conventional oil declines and is replaced with unconventional oil, unless nuclear power, renewables, and electric vehicles surge spectacularly to rescue the earth.

One patch of western Colorado, a 1,200-square mile tract, holds as much oil as the entire world's proven oil reserves.[168] It is in the form of oil shale or kerogen. Kerogen needs a few million more years of natural heat and pressure to cook its way into becoming conventional crude oil. The oil shale plant that Exxon started in Rifle, Colorado (before President Reagan pulled the rug out from underneath it), would have dug up the shale rock by surface mining, crushed it, and put it into a retort (a huge furnace) to drip out the oil. At the end of the process, vast quantities of spent rock would have to be stored in valleys somewhere.

Today the oil companies are experimenting with *in situ* processing that heats the ground and cooks the kerogen in place.[169] Shell has inserted electric heaters hundreds of feet into the ground to heat the kerogen to 650–700 degrees for two years. It simultaneously chills the surrounding area with a "freeze wall" so that groundwater does not flow into the heated space. Schlumberger is using radiowaves, like a microwave instead of Shell's toaster oven approach, to heat the kerogen. ExxonMobil is applying electric currents directly to heat the rock. Chevron is experimenting with a chemical process rather than heat.

Coal-to-liquids, coal-to-gas, large-scale, high-tech biofuels from non-food sources, hydraulic fracturing of tight sands formations, cooking kerogen to crude, producing hydrogen from natural gas—these are projects that the petroleum industry can do and wants to do. With CCS, the projects can be low-carbon emitting. The future of the petroleum industry is in chapter 3 of the National Petroleum Council's 2007 Report titled "Technology."[170] Its tables of time frames to commercialize new technologies that are at least well enough known to be listed and envisioned through 2030 are a geek's delight and will provoke a "gee whiz" from any reader.[171] In addition to the *in situ*, subsurface processing of hydrocarbons into low-carbon feedstocks (using recycled CO_2 within the reservoir for EOR followed by CCS in 2030), the NPC Report envisions that accelerated R&D on processing water produced from unconventional gas wells will convert what is

---

167. Canada has signed the Kyoto Protocol, although it seems unlikely that it will meet any near-term targets when it is tripling output from the tar sands. Producing a barrel of oil from oil sands generates three times as much GHG emissions as producing a barrel of conventional oil, although on a well-to-wheels basis (considering production, transportation, refining and use in engines), oil sands are only 10% to 20% more GHG intensive. This data illustrates the large impact that the end-use of gasoline in combustion engines has on the GHG life-cycle analysis. *See Climate, Security Concerns Clash as Canada Boosts Oil-Sands Production*, Greenwire, Oct. 14, 2008, and *Climate: Alberta, Canada to Cap Emissions but Continue to be Key Oil Supplier*, Greenwire, Jan. 25, 2008.

168. James T. Bartis *et al.*, Oil Shale Development in the United States: Prospects and Policy Issues 6 (RAND Corp. 2005) (prepared for the National Energy Technology Laboratory of the U.S. Dep't of Energy).

169. David Ivanovich, *Oil Shale: A Hard Sell*, Houston Chronicle, July 13, 2008, at A1. While the Energy Policy Act of 2005 contained provisions encouraging oil shale development, in 2007, Congress placed a one-year moratorium on publishing final regulations for commercial oil shale leasing. The moratorium was imposed to allow more time for completion of a programmatic environmental impact statement and for comments from governors of the affected states, especially regarding the massive energy and water requirements for oil shale development. Nick Snow, *Oil Shale Debate Becomes "Chicken-or-the-Egg" Question*, Oil & Gas J., May 26, 2008, at 27. The Draft EIS for oil shale development on federal lands is now available at http://ostseis.anl.gov/documents/fpeis/index.cfm.

170. NPC 2007 Report, *supra* note 6, at 171–211.

171. *Id.* at 180–81, 185, 188, 190, 197, 198, 200–201.

now a waste stream into water that can be used in agriculture, industry, and well drilling and completion by 2020.[172] Another item on a table's list, with a time frame between 2020 and 2030, is the development of "fit-for-purpose," small-scale nuclear power plants for use in the production of unconventional petroleum and hydrogen.[173]

Readers interested in climate change are usually familiar with the "stabilization wedges" conceptualized by two scientists, Robert Socolow and Stephen Pacala. Each wedge represents 25 billion tons of carbon that must be cut from future carbon emissions over the next 50 years to avoid the doubling of atmospheric CO_2 concentration from pre-industrial levels.[174] The two scientists list 15 wedge strategies that are based on existing technologies, not uncertain breakthroughs. At least 7 wedges are needed to reach the target.

Four of the wedges deliver lower carbon through efficiency and conservation, such as doubling vehicle fuel efficiency from 30 miles per gallon (mpg) to 60 mpg, doubling coal plant efficiency, and insulating buildings better. Six wedges are renewables and biostorage: wind, solar, wind-generated hydrogen, biofuels, forest carbon sinks, and soil carbon storage. Nuclear is one wedge—and if oil shale is going to be cooked *in situ*, considerable additional electricity will be needed, with nuclear energy as a possible low-carbon base source.[175]

And then there are four fossil-fuel based wedge strategies, three of which use CCS: Switching from coal to gas (*i.e.*, replacing 1,400 coal plants with natural gas plants); generating electricity with CCS; converting coal to liquids or gas with CCS; and producing hydrogen from fossil fuels with CCS.

The oil companies would like to play in the future of the fossil-fuel wedges, with some time spent scoping out the potential of second-generation biofuels and a bit of dabbling with renewables, if for no other reason than it is good PR. And might nuclear be in their future if CCS turns out to be less profitable than expected and nuclear plants are used for *in situ* processing of hydrocarbons or to create hydrogen by splitting water molecules as the world shifts to a hydrogen economy? But if cars run on milk, the industry will not invest in dairy farms. Instead, their labs will turn to ways of creating artificial milk by cracking molecules and catalyzing and fermenting chemicals that speed the process of converting grass or algae to milk without a cow in sight. That is what they like to do and what they are good at.

---

172. *Id.* at 198 (Table 3-12).

173. *Id.* at 201 (Table 3-15). *See* Energy Info. Admin., The Impact of Increased Use of Hydrogen on Petroleum Consumption and Carbon Dioxide Emissions (Aug. 2008) (while hydrogen-fueled vehicles have the potential to dramatically decrease CO_2 emissions and the use of petroleum in the transportation sector, the production of the hydrogen itself is energy-intensive and new distribution and storage systems for hydrogen are highly capital-intensive, so overall energy demand and GHG emissions are not reduced unless fossil fuels with CCS, nuclear or renewables are used).

174. Stephen Pacala & Robert Socolow, *Stabilization Wedges: Solving the Climate Problem for the Next 50 Years with Current Technologies*, 305 Science 968–72 (Aug. 13, 2004). The wedges have been made into a game. *See* Socolow & Pacala, Stabilization Wedges: A Concept & Game, *available at* the Carbon Management Initiative, Princeton University. One problem with the wedge strategy is that there are no comparative cost analyses to evaluate one wedge strategy (say, wind) against another (like CCS).

175. *See* Judy R. Clark, *Nuclear Heat Advances Oil Shale Refining in Situ*, Oil & Gas J. 22 (Aug. 11, 2008) (reporting on a study by MIT Professor Charles W. Forsberg which proposed the use of nuclear reactors to generate heat to perform underground refining of heavy oils, tar sands, oil shale and coal, converting them *in situ* into light distillates which need little additional refining for use as gasoline, diesel or jet fuel). The Draft EIS for oil shale development on federal lands is *available at* http://ostseis.anl.gov/documents/fpeis/index.cfm. The massive amounts of energy and water required by its development are problematic no matter how "gee whiz" the *in situ* inventions are.

"We are a technology company that produces energy."

Chevron, March 26, 2008[176]

More than 80% of the world's oil reserves are now owned by state-controlled companies. The Western majors like ExxonMobil and Shell are finding it increasingly difficult to gain access to conventional oil reserves in the Mideast, Russia, Venezuela, and other countries where resource nationalism prevails. They now compete against Chinese, Indian and Malaysian oil companies for contracts to develop reserves in the countries that still welcome foreign investment, such as Angola, Colombia or Nigeria. One can cynically argue that Shell's ardent entreaty to the G8 ministers for carbon pricing is designed to make CCS an attractive business opportunity for the Western oil industry, as its members see both geopolitics and the natural decline curves in conventional oil shrink their traditional petroleum base.[177] Successful CCS projects should be able to make money in a world of carbon pricing, unless nuclear and renewables can beat them out, which appears unlikely at the scale required through 2050.[178]

Will citizens be happy that the petroleum industry is uniquely positioned to help save the planet by profiting from CCS? Many readers are apt to lament the entirety of the energy outlook profile presented here by so many experts from government, industry, think tanks and consulting firms. The energy future depicted is a "hard path" of massive capital-intensity and infrastructure development, routed on top of an existing fossil-fuel based global economy of tremendous scale. Where is the "soft path" envisioned by thinkers like Amory Lovins whose 1970s article on *Energy Strategy: The Road Not Taken?* is familiar to all who lived through that decade of energy shortage and turmoil?[179] This article outlined the contrasting paths that the U.S. might follow over the next 50 years (to 2025). The hard path extrapolated past policy and practice from "trend into destiny:"[180] the expansion of large, centralized energy facilities, especially electric power plants, including nuclear; the expanded use of coal and its conversion to liquids; and oil and gas production from increasingly expensive areas such as the Arctic and offshore. The soft path combined conservation with the rapid development of renewables, often deployed on a small scale, such as neighborhood-sized solar collectors.

The hard path followed the consensus forecast forged by the federal government, Exxon, and the Edison Electric Institute at that time.[181] Its formidable capital costs, especially for coal con-

---

176. Peter Robertson, Vice Chair of Chevron, as quoted in Brett Clanton, *An Industry in Flux*, Houston Chronicle, Mar. 26, 2008, at D1.

177. The use of CO_2 for EOR, followed by sequestration of the CO_2 in the now-depleted oil reservoir, has a possible downside: That the worst (*i.e.*, most likely to leak) sites for CO_2 storage will be used first. Because CO_2 injection practices are currently based on petroleum industry techniques, regulatory frameworks and risk assessment for the long-term sequestration of CO_2 may follow the deployment strategy that views EOR as the primary goal and CO_2 sequestration as a mere afterthought. Yet, CO_2 storage in deep saline reservoirs should be safer than storage in depleted oil and gas reservoirs where many production and injection wellbores penetrate the surface, increasing the risk of leakage. *See* Alexander J. Bandza & Shalini P. Vajjhala, *Long-Term Risks and Short-Term Regulations: Modeling the Transitions from Enhanced Oil Recovery to Geologic Carbon Sequestration* (Resources for the Future Discussion Paper DP 08-29, Sept. 2008) *available at* http://www.rff.org/Publications/Pages/PublicationDetails.aspx?PublicationID=20595 *or at* http://ssrn.com/abstract=1272668.

178. The IPCC found that CCS implementation can reduce the overall costs of GHG mitigation. Intergovernmental Panel on Climate Change, Intergovernmental Panel of Climate Change (IPCC), Special Report on Carbon Dioxide Capture and Storage (Cambridge Un. Press 2005) *available at* www.ipcc.ch, a finding duly noted in the NPC's 2007 Report. *See* NPC 2007 Report, *supra* note 6, at 238 (in Chapter 5 on *Carbon Management*). *See also* Edmonds & Sands, in Griffin (ed.), *supra* note 130, at 173–74.

179. Amory B. Lovins, *Energy Strategy: The Road Not Taken?*, 55 For. Affairs 65 (1976–77).

180. *Id.* at 86.

181. *Id.* at 68–71.

version which would be necessary because oil and gas would continue to be in short supply, had led Shell's futurists to conclude that many countries would not be able to afford large-scale centralized technologies. This path also threatened a doubling of atmospheric CO_2 early in the 21st century, with irreversible changes in global climate. Energy conservation was treated more as rhetoric than a realistic option.

Juxtaposed against this hard path were soft fixes: better car mileage, more efficient appliances, building codes and designs, cogeneration of heat and power in industrial processes, long-run marginal cost pricing of electricity, life-cycle costing and removing subsidies.[182] These would decrease energy demand while soft supply technologies such as solar, wind, and biomass entered the market as "flexible, resilient, sustainable and benign" sources.[183] These dispersed technologies (which we would call "distributed generation" today) would produce jobs for workers and avoid massive infrastructure building. Advanced coal technologies and fluidized-bed combustion systems (even at the household furnace level) would provide a transitional bridge to a future of soft energy.[184] By the year 2000, oil and gas would be an increasingly small "wedge" of energy for the U.S. economy.

Dr. Lovins contrasted the two paths as follows:

> The [soft energy] innovations required, both technical and social, compete directly and immediately with the incremental actions that constitute a hard energy path: fluidized beds vs. large coal gasification plants and coal-electric stations, efficient cars vs. offshore oil, roof insulation vs. Arctic gas, cogeneration vs. nuclear power. These two directions ... are mutually exclusive: the pattern of commitments of resources and time required for the hard energy path and the pervasive infrastructure which it accretes gradually make the soft path less and less attainable.[185]

The geopolitical implications of soft vs. hard were profound. If the U.S. asserted its technological leadership in the development of soft technologies with a pledge to share it with Europe and developing countries, the threat of nuclear proliferation would diminish.[186] A complex, centralized electricity grid would be vulnerable to both deliberate terrorist attacks and simple mistakes that could plunge whole regions into cascading blackouts. By contrast, the dispersion of soft technologies would bring electricity to rural villages around the world.

Dr. Lovins presciently ended his article with the warning that wherever we transitioned to, "once we arrive we may be stuck there a long time."[187]

Readers may rue the fact that we seem to have mostly traveled the hard path since 1976 and that fossil fuels are projected to continue to dominate the world's energy future through 2030, with even more massively capital-intensive projects required in order to capture and sequester carbon. Looking back, the greatest roadblock to the soft path appears to be the mistaken assumption, made in virtually all forecasts in the 1970s, that oil and gas prices would stay high because these fuels would be in short supply through the year 2000 and beyond. Also, the discovery of new global sources of oil and gas in so many countries outside the Persian Gulf was not expected on the scale at which it happened. Yet, by the early 1980s, oil and gas prices had fallen, ushering in almost two decades of low-priced fossil fuels to serve American consumers' appetite for larger cars, larger houses, more appliances, and vacation travel. Many of the softer fixes espoused by Dr. Lovins have

---

182. *Id.* at 71–76

183. *Id.* at 77. Directly storing solar energy at the point of use of the individual household would be done with low-tech water tanks, rock beds or possibly fusible salts.

184. *Id.* at 84–85.

185. *Id.* at 86. Also, the high-tech, hard technologies amass influential lobbying power with disproportionate influence on government and mission-oriented agencies. *Id.* at 93.

186. *Id.* at 89–90.

187. *Id.* at 96.

come to pass on a modest-to-significant scale: cogeneration, better fuel economy in cars, electricity pricing reforms, technological advances in wind and solar, and less energy use per unit of GDP. However, soft fixes were handicapped by the falling prices of its hard competitors. (Also, fossil fuel prices were not required to reflect the externalities of global warming or national security.)

The Lovins' article focused on U.S. energy policy with nary a word about a possible surge in demand from developing countries with emergent middle class consumers, eager to share the American dream. However, even in forecasts dating from only a few years ago, no one, whether in or outside the energy industry, appears to have accurately accounted for the massive rise in demand from China and India in the 21st century.

Perhaps, then, the lesson about forecasting the energy future is that only one thing is certain—uncertainty. An ancillary lesson is that "outlier" projections should not be lightly dismissed. The uncertainty in Peak Oil dates among experts has already been noted, as have the major mistakes made in forecasting natural gas supplies for the U.S. by the National Petroleum Council between its 1999 and 2003 reports. Perhaps, then, this is why the petroleum industry recommends that we follow both the hard and the soft paths today. We must use less, invest in a wide range of renewable sources of energy, and pursue unconventional hard technologies that will power us beyond 2050 to a low-carbon future.

Yes, a breakthrough technology may startle us as we travel into the future. Google has released a Clean Energy 2030 proposal that would wean the U.S. (but not the world) off of coal for electricity and reduce oil use in cars by 38%.[188] Geothermal energy is Google's "sleeping giant" and merits its own acronym "EGS" for Enhanced Geothermal Energy Systems. But, Google's plan, like any other, depends on many actions being taken: a long-term national commitment to renewables, a carbon price, tax credits, adequate transmission capacity and grid resources to handle intermittent generation, and—most importantly—R&D to bring renewables and breakthrough technologies to cost parity with fossil fuel generation in the next several years.[189]

If these actions do not materialize and consumers crank up their air conditioning in the years ahead as global temperatures warm, where will the electricity come from? In 2100, dancing electrons on window solar film may power an off-grid A/C unit in the backyard behind the garage where an electric vehicle is parked. But, first we have to make it to 2030 and then to 2050. Only one thing is certain: It will be a scramble.

For an excellent article on the intersection of human rights and oil exploitation, see Thomas L. Friedman, *The First Law of Petropolitics*, FOREIGN POLICY (May/June 2006), available at www.ForeignPolicy.com.

------

188. Jeffrey Greenblatt, *Clean Energy 2030: Google's Proposal for Reducing U.S. Dependence on Fossil Fuels* (released Oct. 2, 2008), *available at* http://knol.google.com/k/-/-/15x31uzlqeo5n/1#. Renewable sources would replace all coal-fired electricity generation and about half of that from natural gas. Solar and wind (both onshore and offshore) grow at very high rates, in addition to EGS. Plug-in hybrids, increased fuel efficiency in conventional cars, and a quicker turnover of the vehicle fleet reduce oil consumption. Aggressive efficiency standards for appliances and buildings and a "smart" energy grid conserve electricity. The Google plan would require about $4.4 trillion in investment over the next 22 years.

189. The need for public investment in R&D to achieve breakthroughs in technology is dramatically presented in Michael Shellenberger *et al.*, *Fast, Cheap & Clean: Cutting Global Warming's Gordian Knot*, 2 HARV. L. & POL'Y REV. 94 (2008) (recommending that public funds raised by auctioning CO_2 allowances be poured into R&D and technological innovation to create a new energy infrastructure that makes green energy cheaper than high-carbon energy. Without breakthrough technologies, the price of carbon would have to be so high to spur clean energy alternatives that consumers would revolt. The article does not consider fossil-fuels with CCS as a clean energy alternative).

Oil producing nations fully recognize the danger that reduced oil dependence poses to their economic welfare, as evidenced by their obstructionist tactics in various forums.[1] In an interesting attack on attempts to mitigate greenhouse gas emissions, the following excerpts are from a document (TN/TE/W/9) that Saudi Arabia submitted to the World Trade Organization Committee on Trade and Environment on September 23, 2002. Appreciation is expressed to Cheryl Nyberg, Reference Librarian, Marian Gould Gallagher Law Library, University of Washington, for tracking down this document.

Energy Taxation, Subsidies and Incentives in OECD Countries and their Economic and Trade Implications on Developing Countries, in Particular Developing Oil Producing and Exporting Countries

Introduction

1. In the light of the responsibility of the Committees on Trade and Environment (CTE) and Negotiating Group on Market Access, we present this initial contribution identifying the impact on energy producing and exporting countries as well as recommendations. The adoption of measures to mitigate the impact and alleviate the trade implications on developing countries, particularly energy producing and exporting among them, and improve their market access is at the heart of the Doha Work Programme that will be negotiated by WTO member countries. Given the nature of this issue, we are submitting this paper to both Committees on Trade and Environment (in Special and Regular sessions) and the Non-Agricultural Market Access Negotiating Group.

     ....

4. There are a number of ways in which environmental mitigating actions of one country may impact the economic interests of another country. However, there are a number of areas in which countries pursuing environmental objectives (such as climate change policy) may *contravene* their WTO obligations and seek to protect their domestic interests. [And] these actions may have significant implications for energy (and related) exports from developing countries.

5. This paper summarizes the current relationship between trade and environment. In particular, it examines the implications of the WTO trade and environment agenda for energy and oil and contemplates how developed countries' energy and environmental policies could affect developing countries by provisions relating to energy and environmental taxes, and domestic subsidies. The paper also covers the economic implications on developing countries, the spillover effects on developing countries and proposes actions to be taken by developed countries to minimize the impacts.

WTO and the Environment

The WTO

6. The agreements govern trade in goods and services establishing legal responsibilities and rights of WTO member states and imposing consequences on members who are found to have acted in a manner inconsistent with WTO obligations.

---

1. See Ross Gelbspan, The Heat Is On: The Climate Crisis, The Cover-Up, The Prescription 119–123 (Updated Edition, Perseus Books 1998) (discussing obstructionism of Saudi, Kuwait, and US oil interests at Climate Convention meetings); see also Paul Roberts, The End Of Oil 287 (First Mariner Books 2005).

7. Basic obligations include the duty to refrain from imposing quantitative restrictions on trade or raising tariffs beyond bound levels. Basic rights include the principle of non-discrimination, which is incorporated in the national treatment and most-favoured nation status.

Trade and Environment in the WTO

8. In this context, it should be noted that the development and policing of trade-related environmental policies is not part of the WTO's remit. Such a task falls under the jurisdiction of other multilateral frameworks, such as the United Nations Framework Convention on Climate Change (UNFCCC). The WTO's involvement is limited to the settlement of disputes between contracting and non-contracting parties to multilateral environmental agreements (MEAs).

. . . .

OECD Countries' Energy Policies

10. OECD countries rely on a mixture of policy instruments in particular connection to reduction of CO_2 emissions that will have trade implication on developing oil-producing countries. The following schematic summarizes the major policies:

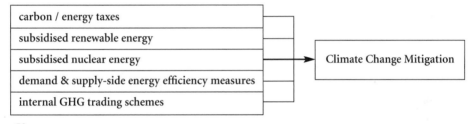

Figure 59.

11. This section outlines the use of energy-carbon taxes and subsidies policies, and discusses the potential interaction (or conflict) between these domestic environmental policies and WTO rules. The UNFCCC is considered as the most relevant MEA to this paper and reference is made to direct trade-related impacts upon developing energy producers and exporters such as Saudi Arabia where necessary.

Energy—Carbon Taxation

12. With carbon taxes, governments are able to tax goods in commerce based on how much those goods contribute to greenhouse gas emissions. The main thrust of this policy for OECD governments is to limit emissions at the same time creating additional and guaranteed government revenues. However, the introduction of such taxes has raised concerns over associated trade effects on developing countries.

13. At present, OECD countries apply different rates of tax on fossil fuels, with oil being heavily discriminated against compared to other fuels. The following schematic represents the different rates of taxation that are applied across fossil fuels:

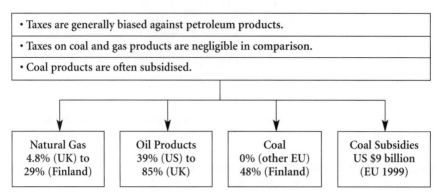

Figure 60.

....

15. Furthermore, the following table indicates the different fossil fuel consumption tax percentages between the EU, USA and Japan. The range of taxes runs between 4.8% up to 82%.

Fossil Fuel Consumption Taxes Percentage of End-Use Prices			
	EU	USA	JAPAN
Gasoline	66%–81%	30.6%	55.8%
Diesel	62%–82%	42.3%	42.7%
HFO	0%–31.2%	0%	4.8%
Nat. Gas	0%	0%	4.8%

Figure 61.

16. In addition to the use of consumption taxes, several EU members are currently employing carbon and energy taxes to lower their carbon emissions (for example, the UK climate levy). Although most of these taxes have the stated aim of reducing CO_2 emissions, they are generally biased against already highly taxed petroleum products. The only immediate impact of this approach has been to increase government revenues. It has not, as was intended, led to a decrease in overall emissions.

....

18. Most Annex B Parties also provide some form of incentive—either as investment credits or tax offset—for petroleum exploration and development. Removal of these policies would drive up costs of producing oil in OECD countries, leaving a higher share of the demand to be supplied from lower cost fossil fuel exporters such Saudi Arabia.

Coal Subsidies

19. Another major existing market distortion within OECD countries energy markets is the continued subsidisation and tax-exemption of domestic coal. A paper prepared by the Annex I Experts Group in 1996 concluded that the removal of subsidies in coal and electricity could both

substantially reduce CO_2 emissions—and stimulate economies with revenues that had previously been tied up in subsidies.

20. According to the IEA's 1998 publication Coal Information, approximately 5.5 % of the coal produced by IEA member countries received state aid, primarily in Japan, Germany, Turkey, Spain and France. Of these, only France is committed to end all subsidised production. Given that the primary use of coal is in power generation, removal of such subsidies would promote the use of other fuels (most likely natural gas), reducing the impacts on hydrocarbon-exporting countries such as Saudi Arabia.

....

Nuclear Subsidies

21. Significant subsidies for OECD nuclear power stations also remain (although are generally being phased out), despite the significant environmental and political problems associated with their operational safety and decommissioning. Figure 62 shows that a number of OECD countries have high implicit subsidies.

Renewable Subsidies

22. The increased use of renewable energy has become a major aspect of most OECD countries as a climate change strategy. The EU and its member States are at the forefront of proposing policies and measures aimed at securing an increased place for renewable power production within liberalizing energy markets. For example, as part of its Climate Change Strategy the UK has set itself a goal of increasing renewable energy as a share of total energy consumption from around 2% to 10% by the year 2010. EU policies and measures aimed at promoting and developing renewable forms of energy include:

- Increased financial support for renewable projects

IMPLICIT SUBSIDY FOR NUCLEAR

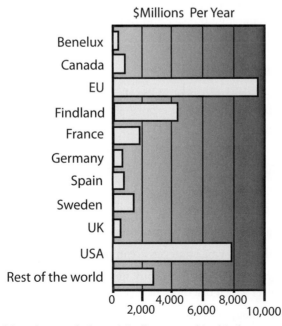

Figure 62. Adapted from bar graph that originally appeared in this document.

- Increased technological research and demonstration schemes
- National commitments to increasing renewable energy production
- Legislation to ensure a foothold for renewable energy in a liberalizing energy market (preferential grid access, guaranteed shares of supply etc.)

23. As technology improves, wind, solar, hydro and geothermal energy [are] predicted to rise as a share of global energy use. The IEA forecasts renewables share will reach 3% of total primary energy use by 2020 (WORLD ENERGY OUTLOOK 2000). However, financial supports are given at the expense of other energy forms and are discriminatory in nature.

Energy Efficiency Measures

24. Actions to increase energy efficiency have long been seen as perhaps the most obvious approach to reducing greenhouse gas emissions. Therefore, improvements in energy efficiency from power plant performance levels to household appliances have been a key focus in climate policy discussions.

....

26. Despite the EU adopting a wide-ranging and fairly strict regulatory approach to encouraging energy efficiency along with employing an extensive range of national carbon and energy taxes, sustained lobbying from industrial groups has resulted in a gradual shift towards more flexible policy forms.

27. The US approach to energy efficiency policies and measures is generally less regulatory, with a preference for voluntary, least-cost options. The US is continuing to invest in greater efficiency in power generation, and is seeking continued voluntary agreements with various energy-using groups.

28. A major issue is that many of the policies and measures suggested by the EU such as energy taxes and the use of optimal technology are aimed at reducing domestic energy use, rather than encouraging potential investors to invest in less-costly energy efficient projects in developing countries. This will have a significant effect on developing oil-producing countries and will reduce the opportunities for technology transfer and private investment in both oil producing and developing countries will be less than otherwise.

Economic Implications on Developing Countries

29. This section will highlight the assessment of the effects of environmental policies, in particular Climate Change, and measures upon oil exporting and developing countries in light of the WTO trade dimension.

....

31. The section identifies two main areas of concern for developing oil-producing and exporting common to developing countries as well. These are:

- Reduction of global demand for developing energy producers; and

- adverse effects upon the economic development of developing countries.

32. The analysis finds that the following strategies are in the long-term interests of all:

- Removal of existing energy market distortions such as coal subsidisation and existing OECD taxation structures which discriminate against developing energy producers;

- encouragement of technology transfer, investment and research, especially in technologies that promise to improve the efficiency and emissions performance of oil products.

33. It is in the interest of both energy exporting and energy importing countries to pursue environmental policies, which minimise the adverse effects on producing countries' economies, and seek the least-cost flexible solutions.

. . . .

Impacts on Developing Energy Producing Countries

. . . .

35. The main areas of impact on developing energy—oil producers—are:

- Adverse tax policies leading to reduced demand for oil, and lower revenues;
- reduced global growth in industry and GDP;
- loss of trade by oil producers to other fuels; and
- replacement of fossil fuels by renewable and nuclear energy sources.

. . . .

Impactions on Welfare

39. The rationale for carbon taxation is provided by the theoretical assumption that a cost-effective outcome in aggregate economic terms can be obtained if all countries equalize their marginal cost of emission reduction.

40. However, numerous studies on carbon taxation have shown that it can have significant macroeconomic effects and produce substantial welfare losses in practice.

. . . .

43. Despite differences in model assumptions and parameters, an analysis of the modelling results offers some powerful indications of the impact of carbon taxation. The models essentially agree that in the short to medium-term, the introduction of carbon taxes will have economic implications and [will lead] to global welfare losses and reduced GDP growth. This will result in negative trade to developing countries due to lower growth.

Distributional Impacts

. . . .

45. A carbon tax could have the following distributional effects:

- A tax on CO_2 emissions will reduce demand for fossil fuels. This will tend to reduce both the overall volume of exports from energy producers and, by reducing pressure on reserves, the price that can be commanded on the world markets. For countries that have large fossil fuel reserves and are dependent on fossil fuel exports, this will lead to declining fossil fuel rents with resulting implications for their national economies.
- If domestic action taken in response to a carbon tax is sufficient to significantly depress overall economic consumption, this may lead to a decline in levels of imports. This is likely to be very country-specific and will particularly affect those developing countries whose economies are based upon a small range of exported commodities.
- Even with equal marginal costs of abatement, total costs of reducing emissions would differ from country to country. A large burden would fall on OECD countries and economies in transition in the early years, shifting to developing nations in later years.

. . . .

Spillover Effects

49. Damages to developing countries could be significantly reduced if developed countries phase out and eliminate existing energy and fuel taxes and subsidies. Spillover effects on developing countries would be reduced, and impacts on developing oil-exporting countries would be cut at least in half.

50. There are four important changes in the terms of trade that account for these spillover effects:

- Imports from developed countries will rise in price due to higher energy costs;
- energy exports will fall in price because of decreasing demand;
- exports of less energy-intensive goods to developed countries will fall in price because of a drop in demand for all imports by developed countries; and
- exports of energy-intensive goods from all countries will rise in price.

. . . .

53. Other trade spillovers will also harm developing oil-producing countries. A general reduction in levels of economic activity in developed countries, compared to baseline levels, will reduce demand for other exports. Oil-exporting countries will also face higher costs for imports from developed countries, especially energy-intensive imports. Specialized oil-exporting countries, such as Saudi Arabia, that are more heavily dependent on oil export revenues will be harmed the most through changes in oil prices.

. . . .

Conclusions and Recommendations

. . . .

57. There are a number of ways in which environmental mitigating actions of one country may impact the economic interests of another country. However, there are a number of areas in which countries pursuing environmental objectives (such as climate change policy) may contravene their WTO obligations and seek to protect their domestic interests. As these actions may have significant implications for energy (and related) exports from developing countries.

Market Imperfections and Market Instruments

58. The reduction of market imperfections and distortions with regard to global and domestic energy markets would generally benefit developing countries, in particular oil producing. At present, the use of energy taxes within OECD countries discriminates unfairly against oil and petroleum products. A reform of these taxation policies ... based on carbon content would be less damaging to the developing oil producing and exporting economies. The extensive subsidization policies concerning both coal and nuclear energy should also be discouraged, as these protectionist approaches are inefficient [and] environmentally unsound. Also the financial support and incentives of other energy forms needs to be removed. Therefore, the main areas of market distortion in global and domestic energy markets are through the use of subsidies and the structure of existing and planned OECD country energy taxes, subsidies and incentives need to be addressed.

. . . .

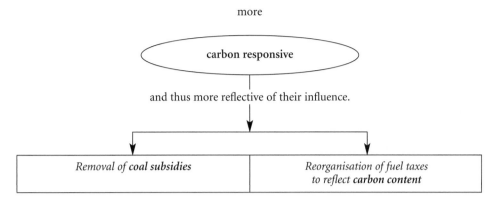

Figure 63.

. . . .

William Pentland, *Alaska's Waters Quietly Reopen to Drilling, August 5, 2008*, FORBES.COM, *available at* http://www.forbes.com/home/2008/08/04/alaska-oil-energy-biz-energy-cx_wp_0805 alaska.html:

In a recent appearance on *The Daily Show*, House Majority Speaker Nancy Pelosi quipped that in the congressional battle over offshore drilling, if the Republicans "want Alaska, we'll give them Alaska."

Too late. Even if she's as good as her word, she'll find there's not much left to give.

In 2004, Congress quietly lifted the moratorium on oil drilling in the ecologically sensitive Northern Aleutian Basin. On Aug. 1, the U.S. Interior Department's Mineral Management Service completed the first major step toward selling the leasing rights to oil and gas drilling companies by publishing a notice in the Federal Register calling for public comments.

Slightly north of the Aleutian Islands in the Bering Sea on the southwestern tip of Alaska, the North Aleutian Basin straddles the Gulf of Alaska and Bristol Bay. The environmental and safety dangers posed by drilling in the North Aleutian Basin seem hard if not impossible to rival. But while Alaska boasts of having nearly half of the 88,633 miles of tidal shoreline that surround the U.S., not a single mile of it will be affected by Congress' decision on offshore oil drilling.

Often described as Alaska's breadbasket, the Aleutian Basin has abundant stocks of pollock, cod, red-king crab, halibut and salmon, which supply 40% of the entire U.S. seafood catch. Commercial fishing generates more than $100 million a year in revenues for the region. Sport fishing and related tourism throughout southwest Alaska provides an additional $90 million a year to local economies.

"The Aleutian Islands are home to natural resources found nowhere else in the world, and the regional economy is dominated by commercial fishing," the nonpartisan National Research Council, a part of the National Academy of Sciences, recently said in a report about the risks posed by oil spills. "Protection of the region's natural resources is therefore a paramount public concern."

Former Interior Secretary James Watt first leased federal offshore drilling rights in the Aleutian Basin in the 1980s over the fishing industry's objections. A subsequent bipartisan congressional drilling ban was placed on the region as a result of the 1989 *Exxon Valdez* oil spill in Prince William Sound.

In 1990, President George H.W. Bush declared a moratorium on oil drilling projects in the Aleutian Basin by executive order. In 1998, President Clinton extended the offshore oil drilling ban until 2012. The moratorium remained unchanged for more than a decade until Alaskan Sen. Ted Stevens spearheaded a successful effort to suspend the moratorium in 2003. In January 2007, President George Bush lifted Clinton's moratorium on leasing the drilling rights in the Aleutian Basin.

Unlike other offshore areas off the coast of northern Alaska, the Aleutian Basin has relatively small amounts of estimated oil, and some of the worst weather in the nation. It's in the cross hairs of a major Pacific storm track, and three to five storms batter the area a month.

But it does have one thing none of the others do: shallow waters. The Aleutian Basin is the only shallow-water leasing area currently offered by the Interior Department. Roughly 80% of the area's waters are less than 200 feet deep. The most promising drilling prospects are located in water depths of about 300 feet.

The cost of developing deep water oil fields is an order of magnitude larger than the costs of developing fields in shallow water. It costs about $600,000 a day to rent an offshore oil rig capable of drilling in the deeper waters of the Gulf of Mexico. Shallow water rigs cost only a quarter of that price, or about $150,000, to rent daily. The total cost of a large shallow-water project would be roughly $200 million, while a big deep water field would cost closer to $3 billion to develop.

In fact, the Aleutian Basin is so shallow in many places that Congress allows oil transport in small single-hull vessels—banned after the *Exxon-Valdez* investigation revealed the design flaw in those vessels—to operate in the area. Currently, the Aleutian Basin is among the few places where single-hull tank barges weighing less than 1,500 gross tons, which can carry nearly a million gallons of cargo capacity, continue to operate.

Ironically, oil isn't the only energy to be found in the area. The Aleutian Islands have the best wind-power resource potential in the U.S., according to the U.S. Department of Energy. In every season but summer, wind speeds exceed 50 mph and frequently rise above 100 mph. The westernmost Aleutian Islands experience wind speeds too high to measure—most measurement devices cannot record wind speeds higher than 128 mph. Not even Congress can top that.

———

Offshore Oil Drilling— ## Fact vs. Fiction[1]

- The United States burns 24 percent of the world's oil, yet we only have 3 percent of the world's oil reserves.

Energy Information Administration, U.S. Crude Oil, Natural Gas and Natural Gas Liquid Resources, 1999 Annual Report, DOE / EIA-0216 (99) (December 2000).

- There is no correlation between increased drilling and lower gas prices. The number of drilling permits increased by 361 percent from 1999 to 2007. And yet gas prices more than doubled in that time.

The Truth About America's Energy: Big Oil Stockpiles Supplies and Pockets Profits, A Special Report by the Committee on Natural Resources Majority Staff, June 2008 (A

———

1. From a fact sheet produced by GreenPeace and *available at* http://www.greenpeace.org/usa/ Global/usa/binaries/2008/8/ocs-fact-sheet.pdf; *see also* GreenPeace, *Offshore Drilling—It's NOT the Answer to High Gas Prices at the Pump* (August 4, 2008), *available at* http://www.green peace.org/usa/en/news-and-blogs/news/ offshore-drilling-it-snot-t/.

new investigative report from the House Committee on Natural Resources *available at* http://www.resourcescommittee.house.gov/images/stories/Documents/truth_about_americas_energy.pdf, studied the current system of drilling permits on federal lands and in federal waters).

- Drilling for more oil in the U.S. won't result in lower gas prices because oil prices are set on the global market. This means that all oil produced around the world is sold all at the same price. As U.S. citizens we wouldn't get a discount just because we drilled for it on U.S. soil.

How World Oil Markets Work, Natural Resources, Canada, *available at* http://fuelfocus.nrcan.gc.ca/fact_sheets/oilmarket_e.cfm. This site explains why crude oil prices are similar all around the world. Prices vary only to reflect the cost of transporting crude oil to that market and the quality differences between the various types of oil:

- By requiring all automobiles in the U.S. to achieve 35 mpg by 2020 we will save 1.2 million barrels of oil per day.

Edmund L. Andrews, *Senate Adopts Energy Bill Raising Mileage for Cars*, THE NEW YORK TIMES, June 22, 2007, *available at* http://www.nytimes.com/2007/06/22/us/22energy.html, citing The Union of Concerned Scientists.

Notes

1. GEORGE MONBIOT, HEAT: HOW TO STOP THE PLANET FROM BURNING 55 (South End Press 2007), discussing NORMAN MYERS & JENNIFER KENT, PERVERSE SUBSIDIES: HOW TAX DOLLARS CAN UNDERCUT THE ENVIRONMENT AND THE ECONOMY (Island Press 2001) (footnote omitted):

As well as the annual $362 billion the thirty richest governments were paying their farmers when PERVERSE SUBSIDIES was published, they were spending some $71 billion on fossil fuels and nuclear power and a staggering $1.1 trillion on road transport. Worldwide, governments pay companies $2.5 billion a year to destroy the earth's fisheries, and $14 billion to wreck our forests.

2. As for subsidies to the U.S. domestic petroleum industry, consider the performance of the U.S. Supreme Court in *Exxon Shipping v. Baker*, ___ U.S. ___, 128 S.Ct. 2605, 171 L.Ed.2d 570 (June 25, 2008). The court reduced a $5 billion jury verdict for punitive damages arising out of the 1989 *Exxon Valdez* Oil Spill by an order of magnitude. It reasoned that a departure from a 1:1 ratio between actual damages awarded and punitive damages would be unfair under the maritime law.

3. Challengers to the recent rush to develop Alaska's offshore oil resources had difficulty getting past the Hon. Ralph Beistline, U.S. District Court, Alaska. Judge Beistline's treatment of the NEPA / Outer Continental Shelf Lands Act (OCSLA) issues was repudiated by the Ninth Circuit in *Alaska Wilderness League and REDOIL (Resisting Environmental Destruction of Indigenous Lands) v. Kempthorne*, 548 F.3d 815 (9th Cir. Nov. 20, 2008) (Opinion by D.W. Nelson, Senior Circuit Judge, with a dissent by Circuit Judge Bea) (opinion vacated and withdrawn in *Alaska Wilderness League v. Kempthorne*, 559 F.3d 916 (9th Cir. March 6, 2009); appeal dismissed as moot in *Alaska Wilderness League v. Salazar*, 571 F.3d 859 (9th Cir. June 30, 2009)). The major holdings under NEPA are that the Mineral Management Service's approval of Shell Offshore Inc's exploration plan proceeded without an adequate "hard look" at the impacts of drillship and ice breaker activities on bowhead whaling and other subsistence activities at the *specific sites* identified for exploration. These lease-block "prospects" included the Cornell Prospect that is "fifteen to twenty miles offshore of the Colville River Delta, north of the Inupiat Eskimo village of Nuigsut." Additionally, the "Sivullig Prospect is ten miles offshore in Camden Bay between the

villages of Nuiqsut and Kaktovik. The Olympia Prospect is located north of Kaktovik. The Fosters and Fireclaw Prospects are located farther east, between Kaktovik and the Canadian border." 548 F.3d at 818.

The major NEPA error was the familiar problem of agency "tiering" to an earlier and generalized analysis that did not answer the specific questions at hand. Thus, said Judge Nelson, the agency may not "hide behind the cloak of its generalized multi-sale EIS." 548 F.3d at 825. The agency's EA left too much unknown, unpursued, and unresolved about how the bowhead whale population (an endangered species) would respond to this three-year exploration plan. There were NEPA errors in the agency's reliance on monitoring being equated with mitigation, on its use of generalities rather than analysis of the "specific parameters and potential dangers of Shell's project" (548 F.3d at 828), on its assumption that the Inupiat could adequately protect their own "subsistence" by working out a private (albeit unenforceable) "conflict avoidance" agreement with Shell ("too vague and uncertain as a mitigation measure to justify the agency's decision not to engage in further analysis" (548 F.3d at 830)), in its "cursory glance" accorded other subsistence activities such as beluga whales, caribou, and fishing (the "biggest gap" in the NEPA tale is the analysis of impacts on "fish populations" (548 F.3d at 831)), and in the "unsubstantiated conclusion" that impacts will be insignificant. 548 F.3d at 831–32. The NEPA remand anticipated either a revised EA or the preparation of a full EIS.

There were OCSLA violations too. Most obviously was a clear violation of 30 C.F.R. § 250.211(b), which says that an exploration plan must include "[a] map showing the surface location and water depth of each proposed well and the locations of all associated drilling unit anchors." (548 F.3d at 834). Shell identified drilling sites in 2007 but did not specify where it wished to drill in 2008–2009. The court said (548 F.3d at 835):

> Without specific information about future well locations, the agency cannot meet its obligation to "review and approve proposed well location and spacing" in accord with 30 C.F.R. § 250.203. As a result, the agency erred by approving an EP for 2007–2009 without knowing where Shell would be drilling for the last two years.

Additionally, said the court (548 F.3d at 835):

> MMS acted in contravention of the regulations by approving Shell's three-year plan without determining the locations of the wells that would be drilled in that period. In order to comply with the regulations, the agency needs to consider the location of the proposed wells before it can approve the project for all three years.

This case underscores that "regulation" of offshore oil development is a misnomer. Descriptions of the Mineral Management Service as a "regulator" is an exaggeration and a misnomer.

4. PAUL ROBERTS, THE END OF OIL 311, 313 (Houghton Mifflin Co. 2005):

> Were the United States to move deeper into a traditional hydrocarbon economy, and further away from even a pretense of reducing CO_2 emissions, analysts fear that European governments might be pressured into delaying their own aggressive CO_2 reduction goals.... China and India, too, could feel less pressure from the West to modernize their own energy economies and might resume the rapid expansion of conventional coal-fired power plants. If these developments occurred, energy analysts say, keeping atmospheric concentrations of CO_2 below the 550 parts-per-million threshold would prove impossible and catastrophic warming would become all but inevitable.
>
>   ....
>
> To encourage this transitional stage, the policy would focus on three near-term objectives designed to jump-start the process: first, an immediate move to expand natural gas

imports; second, the rapid deployment of a carbon tax; and third, dramatically improved automotive fuel efficiency.

5. Jacqueline Lang Weaver, *The Federal Government as a Useful Enemy: Perspectives on the Bush Energy / Environmental Agenda from the Texas Oilfields*, 19 Pace Envtl. L. Rev. 1, 9 (2001) (footnote omitted):

> In the first week of January 1901, the largest gusher the world had ever seen spewed 800,000 barrels of oil across the coastal plain just southeast of Houston. Oil in unimaginable torrents flowed from this well. Thousands of people traveled to see this sensation, many pressing close enough to feel the black mist on their faces.
>
> Within five years of its discovery, the Spindletop field had gone from boom to bust....

6. Jay Inslee & Bracken Hendricks, Apollo's Fire: Igniting America's Clean Energy Economy 34 (Island Press 2007) (footnote omitted):

> Oil survives, thrives and dominates because it is the biggest protection racket and the biggest subsidy in the solar system. Up to a quarter of the country's defense budget is dedicated to our massive capability to "intervene" to protect the sanctity of precious oil fields and shipping lanes. When oil's century-old gravy train is eliminated, new clean-energy sources will thrive on a level playing field.
>
> But this is chump change compared to the greatest subsidy the fossil-fuel energy system has enjoyed since its inception: treating the world's atmosphere as a dump for emissions free of charge. Every ton of coal and every gallon of gas we use sends CO_2 into our atmosphere, gratis, with absolutely no tribute, no cost, no payment of any kind. We can no longer afford this luxury.

7. Lester R. Brown, Plan B 3.0: Mobilizing to Save Civilization 7 (W.W. Norton & Co. 2008) (Earth Policy Institute) [hereinafter 2008 Lester Brown] (footnote omitted):

> One of the best examples of this massive market failure can be seen in the United States, where the gasoline pump price in mid-2007 was $3 per gallon. But this price reflects only the cost of discovering the oil, pumping it to the surface, refining it into gasoline, and delivering the gas to service stations. It overlooks the costs of climate change as well as the costs of tax subsidies to the oil industry (such as the oil depletion allowance), the burgeoning military costs of protecting access to oil in the politically unstable Middle East, and the health care costs for treating respiratory illnesses from breathing polluted air.

8. 2008 Lester Brown at 7–8 (footnotes omitted):

> Another market distortion became abundantly clear in the summer of 1998 when China's Yangtze River valley, home to nearly 400 million people, was wracked by some of the worst flooding in history. The resulting damages of $30 billion exceeded the value of the country's annual rice harvest.
>
> After several weeks of flooding, the government in Beijing announced a ban on tree cutting in the Yangtze River basin. It justified this by noting that trees standing are worth three times as much as trees cut: the flood control services provided by forests were far more valuable than the lumber in the trees. In effect, the market price was off by a factor of three.

9. David Shearman & Joseph Wayne Smith, The Climate Change Challenge and the Failure of Democracy 122–23 (Praeger Publishers 2007) (footnotes omitted):

> Consider but one of the problems that we have discussed: the end of cheap oil. Suppose that the school of thought of the oil limitationists is right. Some estimates of the date of peak oil production put this at the year 2008, others at 2012, still others some-

what later, but many experts believe that this date will be before the end of the second decade of this century.

Although the oil optimists hope that rising oil prices will make other fuels competitive and that by market forces other substitutes will replace oil, this process will only occur if there really are substitutes. There are limits to all other forms of energy, such as nuclear fission and solar energy. Even if there was an oil substitute, there would need to be a replacement of the oil infrastructure—and our civilization could not exist without oil....

Without a replacement of the oil infrastructure, social chaos is likely. For example, the globally connected information economy depends upon an abundant and secure supply of electricity. Without it, the security of the power grid is threatened, and with it goes the information economy.... The problem of depletion is made much worse of course by the vested interest in the oil society not to seek alternatives with the same level of anxiety that one would approach a war. Even from an optimistic viewpoint, oil reserves will decline and the price of oil will soar.... [There] is an inertia in liberal democracies that prevents governments [from] dealing with long-term threats. Any government that acted to curb even one use of oil by the voting citizens of a liberal democracy would be thrown out of office. If we are realistic and honest we must conclude that the inertia of liberal democracies will ensure that the problem of oil depletion is not solved before it is too late.

10. The short-term move to natural gas has brought its own environmental conflicts. Section 313(b) of the Energy Policy Act of 2005 amended the Natural Gas Act to afford United States Courts of Appeals "original and exclusive jurisdiction over any civil action for the review of an order or action of a Federal agency ... or State administrative agency acting pursuant to Federal law to issue, condition, or deny any permit, license, concurrence or approval ... required under Federal law" for the construction of a natural gas facility. 15 U.S.C.A. §717r(d)(1). This brings to the courts of appeals the "veto" or "knock-out" measures in the various environmental laws. Most conspicuous here will be the state water quality certifications under Section 401 of the Clean Water Act. *See Islander East Pipeline Co., LLC v. McCarthy*, 525 F.3d 141 (2d Cir. 2008), upholding denial of water quality certification as regards 22.6-mile section of a natural gas pipeline that would cross Long Island Sound; the state denial focuses largely on the protection of shellfish beds. June A. Restani, J., dissents, as she did in *Islander East Pipeline Co. v. Conn. Dep't of Envt'l Protection*, 482 F.3d 79 (2006).

11. *Wilderness Workshop v. U.S. Bureau of Reclamation*, 531 F.3d 1220 (10th Cir. 2008) (Briscoe, C.J.). This is a challenge to an authorization to construct a national gas pipeline through roadless national forest land. This court affirms an appeal from a denial of a motion for a preliminary injunction; this pipeline right-of-way is not a "road" within the meaning of the Roadless Rule. Will the 55–60 natural gas wells that will come later be "connected actions" requiring discussion in the EIS on the pipeline? No, because there is an "immediate purpose" of this pipeline that has "nothing to do with future gas well development." 529 F.3d at 1230. (ed.) Nobody mentions global warming in the discussion of the "public interest" regarding this sought-after preliminary injunction.

12. *Weaver's Cove Energy, LLC v. Rhode Island Dep't of Environmental Management*, 524 F.3d 1330 (D.C. Cir. 2008) (Ginsburg, C.J.). File this under the heading of aggressive action to pursue natural gas development. In a petition under the Natural Gas Act, the court holds that the energy company lacks standing to claim that Rhode Island and Massachusetts administrative inaction on CWA Section 401 "certifications" (unfortunately the norm in this business) were waived to free up the dredge-and-fill ambitions of the developer. *Id.* at 1333: WCE was not "injured" by the states' inaction. "On the contrary, WCE's theory of the case is that it benefited from the agencies' inaction; that is, the agencies, by failing to issue timely rulings on WCE's applications, waived their rights to deny the certifications WCE seeks." The company might be aggrieved by the denial of a certification (but this hasn't happened yet). The inaction might result in a denial

by the Corps (but that injury would be caused by a nonparty); or the inaction might cause delay in the Corps' response but this wouldn't be redressed by a holding that the Corps is not bound by a state decision.

13. *See Pennaco Energy, Inc. v. Montana Board of Envt'l Review*, 199 P.3d 191, 347 Mont. 415 (2008). This was a challenge by natural gas companies to numerical standards for water-sodium adsorption ratio (SAR) and electrical conductivity (EC) of coal bed methane-produced water. This is an effort to regulate this "salty" produced water; the major holdings are that the District Court did not apply an excessively deferential standard of review, the pollutants were properly designated as "harmful" within the meaning of Montana's nondegradation policy, and this rule was not "more stringent than a federal standard" and thus did not trigger the necessity for more written findings.

14. *See Western Organization of Resource Councils v. Bureau of Land Management*, 591 F. Supp. 2d 1206 (D. Wyo. 2008) (Alan B. Johnson, D.J.). This was a challenge to the decision of the BLM approving the development of up to 51,000 coalbed methane wells in the Powder River Basin. *See* 591 F. Supp. 2d at 1208–09:

> The project would also authorize construction of 17,000 miles of road and 26,000 miles of pipeline; it would permit up to 1.0 trillion gallons of water to be pumped from groundwater aquifers onto the surface; allow for excavation of 3,100 unlined reservoirs of waste pits to hold some of the produced water and authorize the discharge of the remainder of the water, untreated, onto the ground. Plaintiffs contend that almost 200,000 acres of surface resources including soils and vegetation, will be affected.

Three river basins (the Powder, Little Powder, and Tongue) "will receive discharges of hundreds of billions of gallons of coalbed methane produced water over the life of the project." *Id.* at 1209.

It is alleged that

> the [NEPA] process was completed under political pressure to complete the project speedily and hasten development in accordance with the administration's national energy plan. The BLM.... decided critically important questions, such as whether to prepare a single EIS for the entire basin or two, and whether to include alternatives or a supplemental EIS, on the basis of whether delay would be caused. Plaintiffs assert that the FEIS still proposed development of the same exact number of CBM wells the companies wanted, with the same water handling methods, infrastructure and mitigation measures analyzed by the DEIS.

591 F. Supp. 2d at 1210.

All claims are rejected.

15. Robert Kunzig, *Scraping Bottom*, NATIONAL GEOGRAPHIC, March 2009, *available at* http://ngm.nationalgeographic.com/2009/03/canadian-oil-sands/kunzig-text/1:

> One day in 1963, when Jim Boucher was seven, he was out working the trap-line with his grandfather a few miles south of the Fort McKay First Nation reserve on the Athabasca River in northern Alberta. The country there is wet, rolling fen, dotted with lakes, dissected by streams, and draped in a cover of skinny, stunted trees—it's part of the boreal forest that sweeps right across Canada, covering more than a third of the country. In 1963 that forest was still mostly untouched. The government had not yet built a gravel road into Fort McKay; you got there by boat or in the winter by dogsled. The Chipewyan and Cree Indians there—Boucher is a Chipewyan—were largely cut off from the outside world. For food they hunted moose and bison; they fished the Athabasca for walleye and whitefish; they gathered cranberries and blueberries. For income they trapped beaver and mink. Fort McKay was a small fur trading post. It had no gas, electricity, telephone, or running water. Those didn't come until the 1970s and 1980s.

....

Where the trapline and the cabin once were, and the forest, there is now a large open-pit mine. Here Syncrude, Canada's largest oil producer, digs bitumen-laced sand from the ground with electric shovels five stories high, then washes the bitumen off the sand with hot water and sometimes caustic soda. Next to the mine, flames flare from the stacks of an "upgrader," which cracks the tarry bitumen and converts it into Syncrude Sweet Blend, a synthetic crude that travels down a pipeline to refineries in Edmonton, Alberta, Ontario, and the United States. Mildred Lake, meanwhile, is now dwarfed by its neighbor, the Mildred Lake Settling Basin, a four-square-mile lake of toxic mine tailings. The sand dike that contains it is by volume one of the largest dams in the world.

Nor is Syncrude alone. Within a 20-mile radius of Boucher's office are a total of six mines that produce nearly three-quarters of a million barrels of synthetic crude oil a day; and more are in the pipeline. Wherever the bitumen layer lies too deep to be strip-mined, the industry melts it "*in situ*" with copious amounts of steam, so that it can be pumped to the surface. The industry has spent more than $50 billion on construction during the past decade, including some $20 billion in 2008 alone. Before the collapse in oil prices last fall, it was forecasting another $100 billion over the next few years and a doubling of production by 2015, with most of that oil flowing through new pipelines to the U.S. The economic crisis has put many expansion projects on hold, but it has not diminished the long-term prospects for the oil sands. In mid-November, the International Energy Agency released a report forecasting $120-a-barrel oil in 2030—a price that would more than justify the effort it takes to get oil from oil sands.

Nowhere on Earth is more earth being moved these days than in the Athabasca Valley. To extract each barrel of oil from a surface mine, the industry must first cut down the forest, then remove an average of two tons of peat and dirt that lie above the oil sands layer, then two tons of the sand itself. It must heat several barrels of water to strip the bitumen from the sand and upgrade it, and afterward it discharges contaminated water into tailings ponds like the one near Mildred Lake. They now cover around 50 square miles. Last April some 500 migrating ducks mistook one of those ponds, at a newer Syncrude mine north of Fort McKay, for a hospitable stopover, landed on its oily surface, and died. The incident stirred international attention—Greenpeace broke into the Syncrude facility and hoisted a banner of a skull over the pipe discharging tailings, along with a sign that read "World's Dirtiest Oil: Stop the Tar Sands."

The U.S. imports more oil from Canada than from any other nation, about 19 percent of its total foreign supply, and around half of that now comes from the oil sands. Anything that reduces our dependence on Middle Eastern oil, many Americans would say, is a good thing. But clawing and cooking a barrel of crude from the oil sands emits as much as three times more carbon dioxide than letting one gush from the ground in Saudi Arabia. The oil sands are still a tiny part of the world's carbon problem—they account for less than a tenth of one percent of global CO_2 emissions—but to many environmentalists they are the thin end of the wedge, the first step along a path that could lead to other, even dirtier sources of oil: producing it from oil shale or coal. "Oil sands represent a decision point for North America and the world," says Simon Dyer of the Pembina Institute, a moderate and widely respected Canadian environmental group. "Are we going to get serious about alternative energy, or are we going to go down the unconventional-oil track? The fact that we're willing to move four tons of earth for a single barrel really shows that the world is running out of easy oil."

....

The Alberta government estimates that the province's three main oil sands deposits, of which the Athabasca one is the largest, contain 173 billion barrels of oil that are economically recoverable today. "The size of that, on the world stage—it's massive," says Rick George, CEO of Suncor, which opened the first mine on the Athabasca River in 1967. In 2003, when the Oil & Gas Journal added the Alberta oil sands to its list of proven reserves, it immediately propelled Canada to second place, behind Saudi Arabia, among oil-producing nations. The proven reserves in the oil sands are eight times those of the entire U.S. "And that number will do nothing but go up," says George. The Alberta Energy Resources and Conservation Board estimates that more than 300 billion barrels may one day be recoverable from the oil sands; it puts the total size of the deposit at 1.7 trillion barrels.

Getting oil from oil sands is simple but not easy. The giant electric shovels that rule the mines have hardened steel teeth that each weigh a ton, and as those teeth claw into the abrasive black sand 24/7, 365 days a year, they wear down every day or two; a welder then plays dentist to the dinosaurs, giving them new crowns. The dump trucks that rumble around the mine, hauling 400-ton loads from the shovels to a rock crusher, burn 50 gallons of diesel fuel an hour; it takes a forklift to change their tires, which wear out in six months. And every day in the Athabasca Valley, more than a million tons of sand emerges from such crushers and is mixed with more than 200,000 tons of water that must be heated, typically to 175°F, to wash out the gluey bitumen. At the upgraders, the bitumen gets heated again, to about 900°F, and compressed to more than 100 atmospheres—that's what it takes to crack the complex molecules and either subtract carbon or add back the hydrogen the bacteria removed ages ago. That's what it takes to make the light hydrocarbons we need to fill our gas tanks. It takes a stupendous amount of energy. *In situ* extraction, which is the only way to get at around 80 percent of those 173 billion barrels, can use up to twice as much energy as mining, because it requires so much steam.

Most of the energy to heat the water or make steam comes from burning natural gas, which also supplies the hydrogen for upgrading. Precisely because it is hydrogen rich and mostly free of impurities, natural gas is the cleanest burning fossil fuel, the one that puts the least amount of carbon and other pollutants into the atmosphere. Critics thus say the oil sands industry is wasting the cleanest fuel to make the dirtiest—that it turns gold into lead. The argument makes environmental but not economic sense, says David Keith, a physicist and energy expert at the University of Calgary. Each barrel of synthetic crude contains about five times more energy than the natural gas used to make it, and in much more valuable liquid form. "In economic terms it's a slam dunk," says Keith. "This whole thing about turning gold into lead—it's the other way around. The gold in our society is liquid transportation fuels."

Most of the carbon emissions from such fuels comes from the tailpipes of the cars that burn them; on a "wells-to-wheels" basis, the oil sands are only 15 to 40 percent dirtier than conventional oil. But the heavier carbon footprint remains an environmental—and public relations—disadvantage. Last June Alberta's premier, Ed Stelmach, announced a plan to deal with the extra emissions. The province, he said, will spend over $1.5 billion to develop the technology for capturing carbon dioxide and storing it underground—a strategy touted for years as a solution to climate change. By 2015 Alberta is hoping to capture five million tons of CO_2 a year from bitumen upgraders as well as from coal-fired power plants, which even in Alberta, to say nothing of the rest of the world, are a far larger source of CO_2 than the oil sands. By 2020, according to the plan, the province's carbon emissions will level off, and by 2050 they will decline to 15 percent below their 2005 levels. That is far less of a cut than scientists say is necessary. But it is more than the U.S. government, say, has committed to in a credible way.

One thing Stelmach has consistently refused to do is "touch the brake" on the oil sands boom. The boom has been gold for the provincial as well as the national economy; the town of Fort McMurray, south of the mines, is awash in Newfoundlanders and Nova Scotians fleeing unemployment in their own provinces. The provincial government has been collecting around a third of its revenue from lease sales and royalties on fossil fuel extraction, including oil sands — it was expecting to get nearly half this year, or $19 billion, but the collapse in oil prices since the summer has dropped that estimate to about $12 billion. Albertans are bitterly familiar with the boom-and-bust cycle; the last time oil prices collapsed, in the 1980s, the provincial economy didn't recover for a decade. The oil sands cover an area the size of North Carolina, and the provincial government has already leased around half that, including all 1,356 square miles that are minable. It has yet to turn down an application to develop one of those leases, on environmental or any other grounds.

. . . .

16. *See* RICHARD HEINBERG, POWER DOWN: OPTIONS AND ACTIONS FOR A POST-CARBON WORLD 49–50 (New Society Pub. 2004), which asks about policy "options" for confronting impending shortages of natural gas:

> One would be simply to tell the people of these nations [U.S. and Canada] the truth — that natural gas supplies are in decline and will never recover; to conserve what remains of this important resource; and to fund a transition to renewable alternatives.

> But the solution actually being proposed is quite different, consisting of three strategies:

> • Increase the exploitation of coal-bed methane, a source of natural gas that is expensive and environmentally destructive (the production process entails a waste stream of saline, toxic water that pollutes water tables and streams).
> • Open up access to lands not now accessible because of environmental and other restrictions.
> • Import more liquefied natural gas (LNG) from suppliers overseas, including countries like Russia, Bolivia, Iran, Egypt, Algeria, Nigeria, and Venezuela.

17. *See* JAMES HOWARD KUNSTLER, THE LONG EMERGENCY: SURVIVING THE END OF OIL, CLIMATE CHANGE, AND OTHER CONVERGING CATASTROPHES OF THE TWENTY-FIRST CENTURY 102–10 (Grove Press 2006) (on why the U.S. will not be rescued by natural gas; a pipeline would take too long and wouldn't make much difference; the liquid natural gas receiving terminals for imports (a dozen recommended by the U.S. Department of Energy) would be slow to arrive, vulnerable to price, and subject to political vulnerabilities similar to those brought to bear by heavy reliance on oil imports).

C. Nuclear

2006 LOVELOCK at 11:

> I am a green and would be classed among them, but I am most of all a scientist; because of this I entreat my friends among greens to reconsider their naïve belief in sustainable development and renewable energy, and that this and saving energy are all that

need be done. Most of all, they must drop their wrongheaded objection to nuclear energy. Even if they were right about its dangers, and they are not, its use as a secure, safe and reliable source of energy would pose a threat insignificant compared with the real threat of intolerable and lethal heatwaves and sea levels rising to threaten every coastal city of the world. Renewable energy sounds good, but so far it is inefficient and expensive. It has a future, but we have no time now to experiment with visionary energy sources: civilization is in imminent danger and has to use nuclear energy now, or suffer the pain soon to be inflicted by our outraged planet. We must follow the good green advice to save energy, and we must all do this whenever we can, but I suspect that, like losing weight, it is easier said than done. Significant energy saving comes from improved designs, and these take decades to reach the majority of users.

I am not recommending nuclear fission energy as the long-term panacea for our ailing planet or as the answer to all our problems. I see it as the only effective medicine we have now. When one of us develops late-onset diabetes as a consequence of overeating and insufficient exercise, we know that medicine alone is not enough; we have to change our whole style of living. Nuclear energy is merely the medicine that sustains a steady secure source of electricity to keep the lights of civilization burning until clean and everlasting fusion, the energy that empowers the sun, and renewable energy are available. We will have to do much more than just rely on nuclear energy if we are to avoid a new Dark Age later in this century.

Overcoming the Loneliness of the Long-Distance Runner: Nuclear Power for 2020

Fred Bosselman, Professor of Law Emeritus, Chicago-Kent College of Law, Illinois Institute of Technology, Room 853, 565 West Adams Street, Chicago, IL 60661-5000, Tel: (312) 906-5351, Fax: (312) 906-5280, fbosselm@kentlaw.edu.

It's a treat, being a long-distance runner, out in the world by yourself with not a soul to make you bad-tempered or tell you what to do ..."[1]

The most fortunate electric utility executives are those who inherited nuclear power plants built 30 years ago. Today those plants produce low-cost power reliably over 90% of each year, emit no dangerous pollution or radiation, have a safety record unmatched by any other source of electricity, provide a variety of jobs that community residents enjoy, and will be passed over by any future government demands for new taxes or allowances.[2]

How did this happen? In 2000, when we wrote the first edition of our energy law casebook, opinion in the business community was unanimous that nuclear power was an expensive relic of a past era. A survey of utility executives found no one who thought new nuclear power plants would be built in this country, and Wall Street investors were equally negative, so we gave the issue short shrift.[3]

Some economists were so sure that the existing nuclear plants would be unprofitable that they demanded government compensation for the utilities because the government approved the utilities' applications to build these plants. They devised the idea of a regulatory contract

---

1. Alan Sillitoe, The Loneliness of the Long-Distance Runner 11 (Plume 1992).
2. My views on *The Ecological Advantages of Nuclear Power* can be found at 15 NYU Envt'l L. J. 1 (2007).
3. Bosselman, Rossi & Weaver, Energy, Economics and the Environment 955–56 (Foundation Press, 1st ed. 2000). The second edition in 2007 included more coverage.

based on these approvals and claimed that the available of newer, more economical technologies meant that the government had "taken" the utilities' property by saddling them with "stranded costs."[4] Although this theory gained no traction in the courts, it persuaded a number of state legislatures to allow utilities to use transition charges to recover some of these supposedly stranded costs.

The more economical technology to which the economists referred was the natural gas-fired turbine, particularly those using new combined-cycle technology. And it was not just economists that thought natural gas was the future of electric generation. Bankers, utility executives and regulators all were enthusiastic about the lower costs this technology was going to provide. This led to a wave of construction at the turn of the millennium that produced a massive amount of new generating capacity.[5] Only a few perspicacious observers noted that this cheerleading was reminiscent of the exuberant overoptimism that greeted the first nuclear power plants decades earlier.[6]

As I write this, natural gas that you could buy for about $2.00 when you began to construct your power plant now will cost you over $12.00. Moreover, analysts predict that our future supplies of natural gas will be heavily dependent on the international market for liquefied natural gas, increasing amounts of which are being shipped by tanker around the world. Japanese and Korean importers are paying $18.00 to $20.00 for such gas, and the U.S. importers are scrambling for supplies.[7]

Meanwhile, the old nuclear power plants kept turning out increasingly cheap and reliable power. As the century turned, owners of these supposedly obsolete plants began to seek extensions of their licenses; they uprated the capacity of existing reactors, and increased efficiency by following new performance-based regulations of the Nuclear Regulatory Commission (NRC).[8] In 2007, the average nuclear reactor provided power continuously 91.8% of the time, continuing a steady trend of improved reliability.[9] Although these improvements were common knowledge in the industry, they largely escaped the attention of the media and the public, and nuclear power continued its quiet operations without attracting a great deal of public interest.

Then Al Gore made a movie.[10] Polls found that the American public thought that global warming was one of our most serious environmental problems.[11] College students began taking five-minute showers and creating algorithms to demonstrate their carbon neutrality. (And I bought a hybrid car and compact florescent light bulbs).

This issue was not news to the Europeans, who had been following the climate much more closely than Americans. The Europeans had established targets for the reduction of greenhouse gases, and set up a mechanism to allow anyone to trade allowances to emit greenhouse gases ei-

---

4. J. Gregory Sidak and Daniel F. Spulber, Deregulatory Takings and the Regulatory Compact (Cambridge Un. Press 1997).

5. http://www.eia.doe.gov/neic/speeches/howard020906.pdf.

6. The most perceptive has been Judge Cudahy. See, e.g., Richard D. Cudahy, Commentary: The Folklore of Deregulation (with Apologies to Thurman Arnold), 15 Yale J. on Reg. 427, 435–436 (1998).

7. Arjun N. Murti, What Mr. Crude Oil Sees Ahead, Barrons online, June 9, 2008. http://online. barrons.com/article/SB121279317214553377.html?mod=googlenews_barrons&page=3.

8. Through improvements in existing plants, nuclear power operators increased output in an amount equivalent to adding 18 new 1000 MW plants. Building New Nuclear Plants: The Utility Decision, EIA 2008 Energy Conference, April 8, 2008. Eugene S. Grecheck, Vice President Nuclear Development, Dominion Energy.

9. http://www.eia.doe.gov/cneaf/nuclear/page/nuc_generation/gensum.html.

10. Al Gore, An Inconvenient Truth (Rodale Books 2006).

11. "Americans now rank climate change as the country's most pressing environmental concern, a new MIT survey reveals. This is a dramatic shift from just three years ago, when climate change ranked only sixth out of 10 environmental problems." http://www.foxnews.com/story/0,2933,227457,00.html (Nov. 3, 2006).

ther directly or by creating "offsets" that would reduce emissions somewhere else.[12] The prospect of profits from trading attracted high rollers, who formed an International Emissions Trading Association (IETA), whose members included units of the major investment banks and multinational corporations, among others.[13]

Analysis of the EU's experience with carbon trading would stray beyond the point of this paper. What is important is that the idea of reducing greenhouse gases had the attention of well-financed people around the world, and that American business interests believed that some form of tradable penalty for emitting such gases was likely to become law in the United States.[14] Now the fact that nuclear power plants emitted no greenhouse gases began to have potential dollar signs attached to it. People began to recognize that the earlier generation of utility executives and investment bankers who built the existing nuclear power plants were either prescient or very lucky.

Was it just luck that nuclear power plants finally became a gold-plated investment? Or were their backers an example of determined followers of a long-range strategy who stuck to their principles in a society that focused exclusively on short-range gains and losses? In other words, were they examples of Alan Sillitoe's metaphorical lonely long-distance runner who runs to satisfy inner goals rather than public approval?

Whether the daring pioneers of nuclear power were extremely far-sighted or just stubborn fools can be debated by others. The bottom line is that their willingness to pursue long-range goals paid off in a big way. Those nuclear plants join a vast array of other infrastructure that we have inherited from past generations: highways, schools, pipelines, railroads, transit systems. We tend to take the value of these assets for granted, and rarely recall how risky their original construction seemed.

A change in attitudes toward long-term investment has increased the difficulty of raising funds for big projects that will take a long time and a lot of money to build. The business community now tends to demand quick returns on investments, and focuses on quarterly profits rather than long-range potential.[15] In addition, energy has increasingly become traded in international markets, which adds a new layer of risk to investment decisions.[16]

At a 2008 conference, MIT's Paul Joskow listed some of the competitive risks that builders of nuclear or coal-fired power plants must navigate: (1) uncertainties about future U.S. CO_2 policies and associated CO_2 prices (including international linkages), (2) uncertainties about the cost and availability of carbon capture and storage (CCS) for existing and (primarily) new coal generating capacity, (3) uncertainties about the application of financial incentives and load guarantee policies to new nuclear plants, (4) uncertainties of state and local restriction of nuclear capacity, (5) dramatic increases in construction costs for all technologies and uncertainties about whether this is a short-run "bubble" or long-run adjustment to large increase in demand for infrastructure investments, (6) uncertainties about regulatory treatment of construction costs in "regulated" states, (8) uncertainties about the future of competitive wholesale and retail markets in "competitive" states, and (9) limited balance sheet capacity of many U.S. utilities and independent power producers absent regulatory recovery and/or loan guarantees.[17]

---

12. http://europa.eu/press_room/presspacks/climate/index_en.htm.

13. www.ieta.org.

14. Anne Moore Odell, *Concerned Investors and Businesses Call for Congress to Pass a Carbon-Cap or Wear a Dunce Cap*, http://www.socialfunds.com/news/article.cgi/2260.html (March 27, 2007).

15. *See, e.g.*, Coke, *Quarterly Estimates and "The Numbers Game*," KNOWLEDGE@WHARTON, January 29, 2003.

16. Andrew Ross Sorkin, *Sewing the Energy Loopholes Shut*, http://dealbook.blogs.nytimes.com/2008/05/30/sewing-the-energy-loopholes-shut/?hp (May 30, 2008).

17. Paul L. Joskow, *Investing in New Base Load Generating Capacity*, National EIA Conference, April 8, 2008.

In addition to these risks that worry investors, the general public is frequently hearing from various commentators who argue that we can stop climate change solely by short term improvements in energy efficiency and conservation and by the quick development of renewable resources.[18] The appeal of "small is beautiful" is very real for young people who would like to feel that they can make a contribution with their own hands.

Nuclear power promoters must also deal with arguments about nuclear waste. I have summarized elsewhere the view that current systems of dry cask storage provide safe handling of spent fuel for 50 to 100 years during which new ways for using the material may evolve,[19] a view that has received the support of the National Research Council, the National Commission on Energy Policy, the Interacademy Council, the Union of Concerned Scientists and even Greenpeace.[20] Nevertheless, the battle-hardened positions of the opposing sides in long quarrel over Yucca Mountain's safety and cost continues to preclude agreement on sensible alternatives.[21]

But climate change is a long-range issue. Most unbiased analyses of ways to mitigate climate change see a need to make huge capital investments in projects that will take many years to complete. In June, 2008, the International Energy Agency released a study showing that to reach the IPCC's goal of cutting greenhouse gas emissions in half by 2050 the world would need to build 32 new nuclear power plants every year in addition to increasing energy efficiency, building new windpower, and implementing carbon capture and storage.[22]

How can we motivate people to make long-range risky investments on this kind of scale? I am not confident that we can, but we might succeed if we approach the problem from a number of different fronts.

First, we should continue to remind people that their own descendants will suffer the consequences if we fail to take action. If the IPCC's projections are correct, adverse impacts will be felt by the next few generations—people who we will learn to know and love before we die. They will not be an abstract concept involving the distant future, but real people who might be thought to have value even at the University of Chicago.[23] People's love of their descendants is a strong emotion, but they need to be reminded of it.

Some scientists believe that the appropriate emotion to motivate people is the fear of disaster. Although the IPCC's 2007 reports play down the likelihood of sudden and dramatic effects of climate change, some very reputable scientists disagree. Some argue that shifts in ocean circulation might occur suddenly in ways that would cause drastic changes in the climate of various re-

---

18. *See, e.g.*, Amory B. Lovins and Imran Sheikh, The Nuclear Illusion, http://www.rmi.org/images/PDFs/Energy/E08-01_AmbioNuclIllusion.pdf

19. Fred Bosselman, *Resolving the Spent Fuel Issue for New Nuclear Power Plants*, 35 Ecology Law Currents 13 (2008).

20. *See Id.* "NRC Commissioner Gregory Jaczko said May 13 that NRC should consider a rulemaking to encourage utilities to move spent fuel from their storage pools into dry storage casks." Maureen Conley, Nucleonics Week, May 22, 2008.

21. *See generally* Robert Vandenbosch and Susanne E. Vandenbosch, Nuclear Waste Stalemate (Un. of Utah Press 2007).

22. In the IEA's scenario: "A substantial switch to nuclear contributes 6% of CO_2 savings, based on the construction of 32 GW of capacity each year between now and 2050." International Energy Agency, Energy Technology Perspectives 2008, page 4. http://www.iea.org/Textbase/techno/etp/ETP_2008_Exec_Sum_English.pdf.

23. Eric Posner, *Agencies Should Ignore Distant-Future Generations*, 74 U. of Chi. L. Rev. 139, 142 (2007) (arguing that analysts could give the next generation, and perhaps the generation after, the same weight as they give current generations).

gions.[24] Others fear that melting of Antarctic and Greenland ice sheets will cause rapid sea level rise in a short time.[25]

Economists tend to think that the best way to motivate support for new nuclear power plants is through market forces—if the price of competing sources of base-load power rise substantially, nuclear power will thrive. They often advocate some form of carbon tax, operating either directly or in the form of a cap-and-trade program for greenhouse gas emission allowances.[26] At the time of writing, market conditions have already been increasing the cost of competing fuels. Oil and natural gas cost much more than anyone predicted a few years ago, and even coal is being shipped around the world to take advantage of high demand and high prices.[27]

Other observers believe that the issue that should most convincingly motivate the American public is national security. They cite a study done for the Central Intelligence Agency that argues that climate change will create social and economic disruption throughout the world in ways that threaten America's security.[28] Dislocation, migration, starvation might breed anarchy that would affect both developing and developed nations. And many actions that reduce climate change would also lessen America's dependence on imported fossil fuels, which many believe would improve our security.[29]

Another way to reduce the fear of long-range investment is to make the long range shorter through incremental reductions. For example, some companies want to use modular technologies that would allow "package plants" to produce smaller increments of nuclear power than existing plants, but would be designed so that additional modules could be added relatively quickly. South Africa's Eskom is developing a pebble-bed reactor that will test this idea,[30] and Toshiba has suggested construction of a small reactor for a small Alaskan community.[31] In addition, the NRC has attempted to shorten the time for approving new nuclear power plants by the use of certified plant designs, early site permits and a combined operating license.[32]

The utilities that are poised to build new plants have focused much of their attention on government guarantees covering the risks associated with building such plants. The Energy Policy Act of 2005 endorsed the idea of a loan guarantee program to support low-emission energy projects, including nuclear power plants, but the industry says the program has not been adequately funded.[33] The estimated costs of construction have increased so significantly—from around $2500 a kW in 2003 to around $6000 a kW in 2007—that many utilities lack the assets to justify private financing for a new plant.[34]

---

24. *See* scientists quoted in Eugene Linden, The Winds of Change 210–243 (Simon & Schuster 2006).

25. Jim Hansen, presentation at PACON International, Honolulu HI, June 3, 2008. http://www.columbia.edu/~jeh1/2008/HawaiiPACON_20080603.pdf.

26. For a summary of the arguments for a carbon tax, see http://www.carbontax.org/.

27. http://www.eia.doe.gov/cneaf/coal/quarterly/html/t7p01p1.html.

28. *See* Mark Townsend and Paul Harris, *Now the Pentagon tells Bush: climate change will destroy us*, The Observer, February 22, 2004. http://www.guardian.co.uk/environment/2004/feb/22/usnews.theobserver.

29. Alan M. Herbst and George W. Hopley, Nuclear Energy Now 165–186 (John Wiley and Sons 2007).

30. http://www.pbmr.com/index.asp?Content=216.

31. http://www.iser.uaa.alaska.edu/Publications/Galena_power_draftfinal_15Dec2004.pdf#search='Toshiba 4S'.

32. htttp://www.nrc.gov/reactors/new-reactor-licensing.html.

33. For a concise summary, see Alan M. Herbst and George W. Hopley, Nuclear Energy Now 4–7 (John Wiley and Sons 2007).

34. *Building New Nuclear Plants: The Utility Decision*, EIA 2008 Energy Conference, April 8, 2008. Presentation by Eugene S. Grecheck, Vice President Nuclear Development, Dominion Energy.

Another motivation that would encourage a utility to invest in nuclear power would be to set the company up as a guaranteed monopoly free from effective regulation by federal and state agencies and even the voters. An unlikely prospect, one might say, but look who is leading the way in the revival of nuclear power: the Tennessee Valley Authority, an entity that fits that model rather closely. On May 19, 2008, the TVA approved a plan to ensure that at least half of its generating plants will be carbon-free by 2020.[35] CEO Tom Kilgore told the media that "we all believe that nuclear is the way to reduce our carbon footprint" in the near term.[36]

TVA has already taken the lead by renovating a nuclear reactor at its Browns Ferry generating plant, and beginning construction of a second reactor at its Watts Barr plant.[37] It has license applications pending before the NRC for two other reactors to be added to its Bellefonte site.[38] The TVA still operates numerous hydroelectric power facilities that it was authorized to build when it was created in 1933 by President Franklin Roosevelt, and these plants now produce cheap electricity. But when it ran out of feasible hydropower sites, TVA began to build coal-fired plants, which now provide 60% of its power supply.[39] Although socialized power production in the deep South might seem anomalous, TVA's low rates effectively protect it from most forms of oversight.

But TVA is one-of-a-kind, and it would probably take another great depression to bring back the Keynesian economic theories that supported its creation. For the rest of us, we must depend on the private sector to find the courage to move forward with long-term planning. We can help by providing both legal and psychological backing, but we will need to find decision makers who have stamina and determination to last the long distance. And these same character traits will be needed if we are to make the other major changes that could mitigate climate change, such as the "hydrogen highway," the rebirth of the electric car, the expansion of public transit systems, the perfection of cellulosic ethanol, and the construction of green buildings.

Notes

1. On the substantial "law" of nuclear energy, see FRED BOSSELMAN, JOEL B. EISEN, JIM ROSSI, DAVID B. SPENCE, & JACQUELINE WEAVER, CASES & MATERIALS ON ENERGY, ECONOMICS AND THE ENVIRONMENT Ch. 13 (3d ed. Thomson/Reuters 2010).

2. For an example of procedural "twists" in a new information context, see *Massachusetts v. United States*, 522 F.3d 115 (1st Cir. 2008) (Lynch, C.J.). This case answers "no" to the question of whether Massachusetts can participate directly in relicensing proceedings for the Pilgrim Plant and the Vermont Yankee plant to press its concerns about new information on the safe storage of spent fuel rods. The court describes the EIS methodology of the agency. *Id.* at 126: "The Commonwealth's principal argument in these petitions is that by refusing to take into account its alleged new and significant information regarding pool fires in the Pilgrim and Vermont Yankee license renewal proceedings, whether by admitting the Commonwealth as a party to the licensing proceedings or by promising to apply the results of the rulemaking to those proceedings, the NRC violated NEPA and the [APA]." The Commonwealth is obviously worried that a rulemaking cannot beat the two ongoing relicensings to the finish line. Ostensibly, there is a stay procedure that would

---

35. http://www.tva.gov/environment/pdf/environmental_policy.pdf.
36. Charles Davis, *TVA's Climate Plan Boosts Nuclear Power, Energy* WASHINGTON WEEK, May 28, 2008.
37. http://www.tva.gov/power/nuclear/nuclear_fact_sheet.pdf.
38. http://www.nrc.gov/reactors/new-licensing/new-licensing-files/new-rx-licensing-app-legend.pdf.
39. http://www.tva.com/power/ ("Fossil-fuel plants produce about 60 percent of TVA's power, nuclear plants about 30 percent, and hydropower dams about 10 percent. Green power also contributes to the generation mix.").

allow this to happen. But this case appears to be an example of another appellate court bamboozled by the agency's shell games that prevent true opposition from gaining leverage in an agency proceeding.

3. For a particularly devious avoidance of NEPA, see *Natural Resources Defense Council, Inc. v. Dep't of Energy*, 2007 WL 1302498 (N.D.Cal. May 2, 2007) (Samuel Conti, U.S. D.J.). This is a NEPA / CERCLA / ESA challenge to DOE's decision regarding remediation of Area IV of Santa Susana Field Laboratory in Simi Valley. Most of the 2400-acre site is the property of the Rocketdyne Propulsion & Power Division of the Boeing Co. It is a testing area for nuclear energy, solar energy and geothermal energy. It includes ten nuclear research reactors, etc. There were nine nuclear accidents, tritium is in the groundwater, and there is a substantial chemical contamination. *Id.*, p. 3: "The EPA was highly critical of the Rocketdyne Survey, faulting its methodology on several accounts and ultimately calling for it to be scrapped and redone." The EPA was in—then quickly out—of the evaluation process. The DOE deigned to do a draft EA in response to criticisms by a "few outspoken individuals." But the court says (*id.*, p. 14): "After a thorough, probing, in-depth review of the [Administrative Record], the Court finds that Plaintiffs have established, as a matter of law, that the DOE's decision to issue a FONSI rather than prepare an EIS was not in accordance with the law and constituted a clear error of judgment." *Id.*, p. 16: "The DOE's argument that the remediation is categorically excluded from the requirement to prepare an EIS by virtue of being a cleanup fails for several reasons." See p. 17: the agency cannot avoid NEPA by declaring that the overall remediation will have a "positive effect." This is "highly controversial." The court enters a permanent injunction against transfer of ownership over any portion of Area IV until completion of an EIS and ROD.

4. *See* Fred Bosselman, *The Ecological Advantages of Nuclear Power*, 15 N.Y.U. Envtl. L. J. 1, 25 (2007):

> The Ecological Impacts of Every Stage of the Use of Coal Are Disastrous.

Id. at 44:

> Significant Releases of Radiation Caused by Terrorist Attacks or Accidents at Modern Nuclear Power Plants Are Highly Unlikely.

5. On developments post-Chernobyl, see Mary Mycio, Wormwood Forest: A Natural History of Chernobyl (Joseph Henry Press 2005).

6. *See* Helen Caldicott, Nuclear Power Is Not The Answer ch. 5 at 107–11 (New Press 2006):

> Never in its sixty-five-year history has the nuclear industry taken responsibility for the massive amounts of profoundly lethal radioactive waste that it has continued to produce at an ever-increasing pace. As it is impossible for mere mortals to fathom the concept of infinity of time and space, so it is impossible to comprehend the true gravity of mutagenic carcinogens lasting for half-a-million years.

> Radioactive waste comes in various forms and guises, classified according to concentration of isotopes, types of isotopes, and origins of the material. Of these, the most dangerous is high-level waste, extremely concentrated waste, pulsing with intensely energetic radioactive elements emanating both from the production of plutonium for nuclear weapons (91 million gallons in total) and from radioactive spent fuel from nuclear power reactors (52,000 metric tons in 2006).[1]

---

1. Other kinds of nuclear waste include transuranic waste, low- and mixed low-level waste, and tailings. Transuranic waste is material contaminated with plutonium or its deadly alpha emitting relatives—neptunium, americium, curium, einsteinium and others—consisting of tools, clothing, filters, and other polluted

Initially, the Department of Energy proposed in the early 1970s to store high-level waste in salt domes in Lyons, Kansas, but it was discovered that the domes had been accidentally punctured by gas exploration holes. Other sites were explored and ruled out, largely in response to political pressures from an aroused public. In 1982, Congress passed the Nuclear Waste Policy Act, promising to take responsibility for the radioactive waste from nuclear power plants, and in 1987 Congress designated Yucca Mountain in Nevada as the primary repository.

Initially, it was thought that the Yucca site would be simple and that the geology and site characterization would be easy. Yet in retrospect, Yucca Mountain, a volcanic remnant composed of pumice or layers of volcanic ash, with a complex geology, was a particularly poor choice. To this day, Yucca Mountain has yet to receive a single shipment of nuclear waste.[2]

The stated requirement of a geological storage site is to prevent the leakage and seepage of waste for at least 500,000 years. The EPA standards require storage to the time of the peak dose. This may be as many as 500,000 years in the future.[3] That mandate will never be achieved at Yucca Mountain site for several reasons:

- Contaminated water from corroded casks could seep into the groundwater and spread to Amargosa Valley, which may communicate via a hydrological pathway to Death Valley, and spread to nearby farming areas and protected species habitat, and produce radioactive springs.[4]
- A volcanic event may lead to magma intrusion into the tunnels where the waste is stored, melting the canisters. If the volcanic event opened a path to the surface, radioactivity could be spread around the landscape.
- Radioactive chlorine 36 has been found deep inside the so-called waterproof mountain. This isotope could have come only from atmospheric nuclear testing performed in the 1950s and 1960s, meaning that water penetrated the mountain in fewer than fifty years, thousands of times faster than was estimated by the DOE.[5]
- Much more water was discovered inside the mountain than originally estimated—conditions were supposed to be relatively dry so the metal casks containing the radiation would not corrode over time. It is expected that the climate will become much wetter in the future. This will likely increase infiltration.[6]

---

matter. A salt mine [has] been opened in Carlsbad, New Mexico, to receive some of this transuranic waste, but 11.3 million tons remain buried at numerous government sites.

Low- and mixed low-level waste includes hospital, industrial, research, and institutional waste and polluted materials from air filters, clothing, decommissioned power plants, and tools, which amounts to approximately 472 million cubic feet. Tailings from uranium mining and milling amount to 265 million tons.

TIME magazine encompassed this waste problem in an article published in July 2002 written by Peter Essick when he wrote, "Load these tailings into railroad cars, then pour the 91 million gallons of waste into tank cars, and you would have a mythical train that would reach around the equator and then some" (Peter Essick, *Half Life NRC, NUREG-1350, The Lethal Legacy of America's Nuclear Waste,* TIME, http://www.nrc.gov/reading-rm/doc-collections/nuregs/staff/sr1350, July 2002).

2. Dr. Paul P. Craig, former member of the U.S. Nuclear Waste Technical Review Board, *Yucca Mountain—Time to Slow Down,* August 14, 2005.

3. *Ibid.*

4. *Background Status of High-Level Nuclear Waste Management,* Nuclear Information and Resource Service, August 1992; *Stop the Yucca Mountain Nuclear Waste Dump,* GREENPEACE, c/o Nuclear Information and Resource Service; and personal e-mail communication with Paul Craig, January 17, 2005.

5. Personal e-mail communication with Paul Craig, January 17, 2005.

6. Presentation to the California Energy Commission, energy.ca.gov/2005_energypolicy/documents/2005-08-16_workshop/presentations/panel-1/Craig_Yucca_Mountain.pdf, August 14, 2005.

- Yucca Mountain is located in an active earthquake zone, and at least thirty-three known active faults pass within twenty miles of the Mountain, some within the proposed repository itself. In June 1992, an earthquake measuring 7.4 on the Richter scale hit Yucca Valley in Southern California.[7] Two days later, an earthquake measuring 5.2 caused $1 million of damage to the DOE building located six miles from Yucca.
- Part of Yucca Mountain is below the Nellis Air Force Base flight training region. This is where new military jets and pilots are tested. It is also used for war exercises involving both U.S. pilots and pilots from other countries. Crashes are not unusual.[8]

Some scientists have compared the Yucca Mountain Program to "NASA before the Challenger."[9]

In such an inadequately chosen mountain, huge quantities of radioactive waste will need to be stored for thousands of years. Temperatures inside the repository will be above boiling point for 1,250 years, with temperatures reaching 662 degrees Fahrenheit inside the canisters and 527 degrees or far above boiling point in the rock holding the canister. One spent fuel assembly contains ten times the amount of long-lived radiation released by the Hiroshima bomb; the mountain is to house 140,000 assemblies.[10] However this data is subject to revision as the whole project is currently (January 2006) under revision.

The following information is gleaned from the Nevada State web site titled "Chronology of Selected Yucca Mountain Emails." The DOE, under the 1982 Nuclear Waste Policy Act, was obliged to report to Congress the bad news that Yucca Mountain's geology is inappropriate to contain the nuclear waste. But by the time these derogatory assessments had been made, the DOE, commercial nuclear industry, and many members of Congress were clearly intent on just making the Yucca Mountain repository work no matter what.[11] Rather than end this venture for the DOE Yucca Mountain bureaucracy and its contractor, the project had taken on a life of its own. The DOE shifted from assessing geological storage to designing a man-made waste package that would prevent water from reacting with the radioactive waste—even though it is a golden rule that radioactive waste storage facilities require "defense in depth"—that is, when the containers fail and radiation escapes, the geological environment must prevent further radioactive escape. DOE engineers developed a bizarre scheme, consisting of a titanium "drip shield" to be placed by remote control over the canisters some hundred years hence by our descendents, just before the repository is finally closed—when the tunnels themselves may well have collapsed. The DOE then decided to ignore the troublesome site selection geological guidelines.[12]

As the DOE decided to rely on the waste package and drip shield instead of geological integrity, the problems with corrosion became crucial to the exercise. But the DOE does not have long-term corrosion data on C22, the nickel-based alloy used for the containment canisters, as it has been in existence for only a few decades. It is impossible to extrapolate from a few decades to tens of thousands of years when the fundamental corrosion mechanisms are not well understood. Nevertheless, glossing over the science, in

---

7. HELEN CALDICOTT, NUCLEAR MADNESS (W.W. Norton 1994).

8. Personal e-mail communication with Judy Treichel, Executive Director, Nevada Nuclear Waste Task Force, January 22, 2006.

9. Direct quote from Paul Craig, used by Treichel.

10. CALDICOTT, *supra* note 7; and personal e-mail communication with Treichel, *supra* note 8.

11. Nevada State web site, *Chronology of Selected Yucca Mountain Emails*, http://www.state.nv.us/nucwaste/ September 9, 2005.

12. *Ibid.*

typical fashion, and relying on inadequately supported models, the DOE publicly reassured everyone that the integrity of these materials would be maintained for tens of thousands of years.[13]

Meanwhile, no matter how the DOE manipulated its computer codes, because the site was so poor, the peak dose to the public once the canisters failed was too high to meet the EPA guidelines. So late in the time frame that these decisions were being made, the NRC and the EPA decided to change the guidelines limiting the period of regulatory compliance to 10,000 years (down from hundreds of thousands of years), which then allowed the DOE to qualify for a license on the basis of its flawed corrosion-resistant packages.[14]

    ....

7. Some commenters are not as sanguine regarding the wisdom of relying on nuclear power. Amory Lovins and Imran Sheikh in *The Nuclear Illusion* in the November 2008 issue of Ambio provide a comprehensive analysis of the pitfalls of nuclear energy. They first comment on the poor economics of nuclear energy at page 2 of the draft paper (footnotes omitted):

> During the nuclear revival now allegedly underway, no new nuclear project on earth has been financed by private risk capital, chosen by an open decision process, nor bid into the world's innumerable power markets and auctions. No old nuclear plant has been resold at a value consistent with a market case for building a new one. And two strong global trends—greater transparency in governmental and energy decision-making, and wider use of competitive power markets—are further dimming nuclear prospects.

These authors provide evidence that nuclear power is much more expensive than other renewables, such that:

> Nuclear power's potential climate solution is further restricted by its inherent slowness of deployment (in capacity or annual output added per year), as confirmed by market data below. And its higher relative cost than nearly all competitors, per unit of net CO_2 displaced, means that *every dollar invested in nuclear expansion will worsen climate change by buying less solution per dollar. Id.* at 15 (draft).

In fact, Lovins & Sheikh estimate that every dollar spent making and delivering new nuclear power will result in 1.4 to 11 times *less* climate solution than cheaper options such as wind-power, cogeneration, or end-use efficiency. *Id.* at 19. The authors next point to the fallacy of comparing the constant availability of nuclear power to the putative variability of renewable sources such as wind and solar. They explain that the proper comparison is to the aggregate renewable portfolio, in which the variability of individual sources averages out when combined. *Id.* at 22–26. The authors also provide data indicating that new capacity added in 2007 and projected to 2010 from nearly all other alternative energy sources far out-paced the added capacity of nuclear. *Id.* at Figure 8.

8. *Nuclear's Carbon Footprint.* A recent report by Kurt Kleiner, *Nuclear Energy: Assessing the Emissions*, 2 Nature Reports Climate Change 130 (2008) compares the carbon footprint of nuclear to other that of renewables. It finds that the life-cycle carbon emissions per kilowatt-hour produced is six times greater than that for wind energy and at least double that of solar photovoltaic.

---

13. *Ibid.*
14. *Ibid.*

9. *See* ARJUN MAKHIJANI, CARBON-FREE AND NUCLEAR-FREE: A ROADMAP FOR U.S. ENERGY POLICY (IEER Press 2007) (A Joint Research Project of the Nuclear Power Research Institute and the Institute for Energy and Environmental Research).

III. Renewables

Patrick R. Jacobi, *Renewable Portfolio Generator Applicability Requirements: How States Can Stop Worrying and Learn to Love the Dormant Commerce Clause*, 30 VT. L. REV. 1079, 1133 (2005–06):

> Current dormant Commerce Clause jurisprudence indicates that the Court will not reach the environmental benefits of an [Renewable Portfolio Standard] if the legislation includes a geographic limit.

Sanya Carleyolsen, *Tangled in the Wires: An Assessment of the Existing U.S. Renewable Energy Legal Framework*, 46 NAT. RES. J. 759, 761–62 (2006) (footnote omitted):

> Much of the existing RE [Renewable Energy] legislation was passed in the late 1970s and early 1980s in response to the global oil crisis. When the United States realized that restricted supplies could not meet increasing demands spurred by advanced industrial development, suburbanization and the increase in automobile ownership and miles traveled, and rising demands for electricity, policy makers understood that Americans needed to change their consumption habits. Political efforts were made to respond to these social crises through the research and development of RE technologies, while individuals endeavored to limit household electricity demand. Regulatory codes were also adopted to diversify electricity mixes and to open the electricity market to non-utilities.

GEORGE MONBIOT, HEAT: HOW TO STOP THE PLANET FROM BURNING 100 (South End Press 2007):

> There are many things I dislike about renewable energy, or—to be more precise—about the industry that promotes it. I dislike the misleading claims its advocates make. I dislike the tokenism that attends it: a petrol company might put a wind turbine beside a filling station (because it is too far from the grid to make a connection worthwhile) and its customers think it has gone green.

Christopher Flavin, *Stimulating a Clean Energy Revolution, in* SUDDEN AND DISRUPTIVE CLIMATE CHANGE 241 (M.C. MacCracken, F. Moore, J.C. Topping, Jr. eds. Earthscan Publications Ltd. 2008) [hereinafter 2008 Flavin]:

> In an absolute sense, the world is heavily dependent on fossil fuels, which currently provide over 80 percent of the energy on which global society depends. However, the annual growth rates of various energy sources show that change is on the way. Since 2001, the growth rates of solar photovoltaic (30 percent), wind (26 percent), and biofuel sectors have been much larger than for traditional sectors of coal (4.4 percent), oil (1.6 percent), natural gas (2.5 percent) and even nuclear (1.1 percent).

2008 Flavin at 244:

> In contrast to those in Europe, US renewable energy policies over the past two decades have been an uneven and ever-changing patchwork of regulations and subsidies. Abrupt changes in direction at both the state and federal levels have deterred investors and led

dozens of companies into bankruptcy. Embracing the path of renewable energy is not only an environmental necessity, but also makes good economic sense, allowing both companies and individuals to save money, and generating high-wage jobs in a rapidly growing technological industry.

A. Energy Efficiency

Joseph Romm, Hell and High Water: Global Warming—The Solution and the Politics—and What We should Do 159–160 (Harper Perennial 2007) [hereinafter 2007 Romm]:

> Energy efficiency remains by far the single most cost-effective strategy for achieving these goals, for minimizing carbon dioxide emissions in the air.

> Most buildings and factories can cut electricity consumption by more than 25 percent right now with rapid payback (under four years).

2007 Romm at 230:

> The enabling strategy is energy efficiency—since that generates the savings that pays for the zero-carbon sources, like wind power and coal with carbon sequestration.

John Houghton, Global Warming: The Complete Briefing 279 (3d ed. Cambridge Un. Press 2004) (footnotes omitted):

> Assessments have been carried out across all energy uses comparing actual energy use with that which would be consumed by ideal devices providing the same services. Although there is some difficulty in defining precisely the performance of such 'ideal' devices, … assessments of this kind come up with world average end-use energy efficiencies of the order of three percent. That sort of figure suggests that there is a large amount of room for improvement in energy efficiency, perhaps by at least threefold.

Nature News team, *Electricity Without Carbon*, 454 Nature 816 (2008):

> The easiest way to cut the carbon released by electricity generation is to increase efficiency. But there are limits to such gains, and there is the familiar paradox that greater efficiency can lead to greater consumption.

Thomas R. Casten, *Recycling Energy to Reduce Costs and Mitigate Climate Change*, in Sudden and Disruptive Climate Change 247 (M.C. MacCracken *et al.* eds. Earthscan Publications Ltd. 2008):

> Conventional wisdom holds that battling climate change will cost enormous sums of money. Yet, this assertion rests on the questionable assumption that all present generation of [electric] power, which accounts for 68 percent of present fossil carbon emissions, is already economically optimal. Put another way, it assumes no possible investments to improve energy efficiency can yield a profit. This standard assumption, however, is wrong.

Worldwatch Institute, American Energy: the Renewable Path to Energy Security 21 (2006):

> Improving energy efficiency represents the most immediate and often the most cost effective way to reduce oil dependence, improve energy security, and reduce the health and environmental impact of our energy system. By reducing the total energy requirements of the U.S. economy, improved energy efficiency will make increased reliance on renewable energy sources more practical and affordable.

Energy efficiency has played a critical role in the U.S. energy supply in recent decades, reducing total energy use per dollar of gross national product (GNP) by 49 percent since the 1970s. Compared to a 1973 baseline, America now saves more energy than it produces from any single source, including oil. Efficiency improvements stabilize energy prices by reducing demand, while also delivering the same services we value—whether hot showers or cold drinks—at lower cost.

The potential for additional energy savings is vast: U.S. energy use per dollar of GNP is nearly double that of other industrial countries. More than two-thirds of the fossil fuels consumed are lost as waste heat—in power plants and motor vehicles.

The fuel economy of new U.S. motor vehicles advanced rapidly, from 14 miles per gallon in the mid-1970s to 21 miles per gallon in 1982, driven by rising fuel prices and government-mandated fuel economy standards. But in 2006, new U.S. vehicles still averaged just 21 miles per gallon; for over two decades, automakers have put most of their engineering efforts into building larger vehicles with more powerful engines, offsetting the potential fuel economy gains from new technologies.

The time is ripe for another great leap in vehicle efficiency. New technologies such as hybrid drive trains, clean-burning diesel engines, continuously variable transmissions, and lightweight materials could allow vehicle fuel economy to double over the next two decades.

Significant efficiency gains are also possible in the electricity sector. Americans spend $200 billion annually on electricity, but current demand could be halved with cost-effective technologies already available on the market. Furthermore, decreasing electricity demand reduces the need for new, large power plants, allowing smaller, distributed, renewable generation to play a greater role in meeting our energy needs.

Past experience demonstrates that strong government policies can spur the private sector to invest in efficiency improvements. Since national home appliance efficiency standards were enacted in 1987, manufacturers have achieved major savings in appliance energy use.

Refrigerator efficiency nearly tripled between 1972 and 1999, and dishwasher efficiency has more than doubled in the last eight years.

California's "Flex Your Power" campaign, enacted in response to the state's 2001 energy crisis, immediately reduced power demand by 5,000 megawatts by replacing millions of standard light bulbs with compact fluorescent lights (CFLs), installing light-emitting diode (LED) traffic lights, and replacing inefficient appliances. Because of robust efficiency policies, California has the lowest per capita energy consumption in the nation, without sacrificing comfort or valued services.

Technologies available today could increase appliance efficiency by at least an additional 33 percent over the next decade, and further improvements in dryers, televisions, lighting, and standby power consumption could avoid more than half of the projected growth in demand in the industrial world by 2030.

The integration of efficiency with renewable energy maximizes the benefits of both. For example, the correct building orientation can save up to 20 percent of heating costs; those savings can jump to 75 percent when renewable energy and appropriate insulation are integrated into the building.

A national commitment to improved efficiency can transition the U.S. energy economy in ways that will yield dividends for all Americans.

John C. Dernbach, *Overcoming the Behavioral Impetus for Greater U.S. Energy Consumption*, 20 GLOBAL BUS & DEVELOP. L. J. 15 (2007).

This article references ALFRED W. CROSBY, CHILDREN OF THE SUN: A HISTORY OF HUMANITY'S UNAPPEASABLE APPETITE FOR ENERGY (W.W. Norton & Co. 2006), and discusses the mysteries of human behavior and incentives. He points out (*id*. at 19) that U.S. energy efficiency efforts have focused on three areas within the reach of individual purchasing decisions — appliances and related equipment, buildings, and motor vehicles. These big three account for 56% of the nation's overall energy consumption.

The state of the law on appliances? *Id*. at 19 (footnotes omitted):

Federal efficiency standards for appliances and other equipment were first required by the National Appliance Energy Conservation Act of 1987. [Pub. l. 100-12, 101 Stat. 103]. The Act establishes energy efficiency standards for certain consumer products and authorizes the [Department of Energy] to set new or amended energy conservation standards for a variety of consumer products, including refrigerators, washing machines, and clothes dryers.

Buildings? *Id*. at 22 (footnotes omitted):

State energy-efficiency standards for buildings are prompted to some degree by federal legislation. The Energy Policy Act of 1992 required each state to review the energy-efficiency provisions of its residential and commercial building codes, and to determine within two years whether it should adopt model energy-efficiency codes prepared by third parties.... About half of the states have the most recent and energy efficient residential codes, and the rest have the less-recent codes or none at all.

Corporate average fuel economy (CAFE) standards? *Id*. at 24 (footnotes omitted):

These standards are established by the Department of Transportation under the Energy Policy and Conservation Act, which was first adopted in 1975 in the wake of the 1973–74 Arab oil embargo....

The mandated average fuel economy for automobiles increased from 18.0 to 27.5 miles per gallon ("mpg") between 1978 and 1990, a level that has remained unchanged. The required average fuel economy for light trucks, which at least until recently represented a large and rapidly growing share of the motor-vehicle market, is much lower. From the 1996 to 2004 model years, the average required fuel economy for light trucks has been 20.7 miles per gallon, rising to 21.0 miles per gallon for 2005 and 22.5 miles per gallon for the 2007 model year. From the late 1980s to the present, light trucks gained market share and began to slowly pull the mpg-combined-average rating for cars and light trucks below the 1988 peak. As a result, average fuel economy was 24.7 mpg for cars and 18.2 mpg for light trucks.

This article makes reference (*id*. at 27) (footnote omitted) to the fact that "[s]everal different types of human behaviors are relevant to environmental protection, including committed activism, financial and other support for environmental causes and policies, and influencing the organizations to which individuals belong." Useful to the framework of mobilizing human behavior in the campaign to reduce U.S. energy consumption are plausible goals, public information, readily available choices, financial incentives, and regulatory requirements.

See also John Dernbach and the Widener University Law School Seminar on Energy Efficiency, *Stabilizing and Then Reducing U.S. Energy Consumption: Legal and Policy Tools for Efficiency and Conservation*, 37 ELR 10003 (2007, Environmental Law Institute) ("No energy policy choices available to the United States are as attractive and necessary as energy efficiency and conservation").

Notes

1. JAY INSLEE & BRACKEN HENDRICKS, APOLLO'S FIRE: IGNITING AMERICA'S CLEAN ENERGY ECONOMY 66–67 (Island Press 2007) [hereinafter 2007 INSLEE & HENDRICKS] (footnote omitted):

> In early 2005 China passed landmark renewable energy legislation pledging to produce 10 percent of the country's total energy from renewable sources by 2020. This legislation is set to create a huge market demand for renewable energy products, including solar technologies. China already has a burgeoning domestic solar industry, ready to compete for its market share.

2. 2007 INSLEE & HENDRICKS at 74:

> Where is the American government as Germany, Japan, and China aid investment to maximize this vast economic potential [of solar energy]? The sad answer is that Congress is in the thrall of the old energy industries. Federal research in solar power is now one-fourth what it was, adjusted for inflation, in 1975.

3. 2007 INSLEE & HENDRICKS at 101–102:

> [U]tilities around the country have discovered that it is much cheaper to "buy" power by funding conservation efforts that free up energy that would otherwise be wasted than to buy additional power to feed into the system or build additional plants. Is it too much to ask, then, that a utility be required to show that it cannot obtain savings through efficiency before it builds new plants? Shouldn't a utility have to explore programs to help its consumers pay for better lighting or pumps before it spends billions on more expensive nuclear or other large-scale generation that takes years to come on line?

These are the same questions asked of the U.S. Supreme Court thirty years ago. The court gave a retrogressive reading of NEPA to declare that "energy conservation" was not one of those alternatives that had to be discussed in an Environmental Impact Statement on a nuclear power plant. *See Vermont Yankee Nuclear Power Plant v. Natural Resources Defense Council, Inc.*, 435 U.S. 519 (1978), discussed in William H. Rodgers, Jr., *A Hard Look at* Vermont Yankee: *Environmental Law Under Close Scrutiny*, 67 GEORGE. L. J. 699 (1979).

4. 2007 INSLEE & HENDRICKS at 53, quoting Amory Lovins, on automobiles (footnote omitted):

> He rages at the machine. His rage is justified, he says, because the technology of the car has made such modest improvements in one hundred years. 'After more than a century of devoted engineering effort, today's cars use less than 1 percent of their fuel energy to move the driver. Only 13 percent of the fuel energy reaches the wheels, and just 6 percent accelerates the vehicle — 95 % of the weight it pushes is its own, not the driver's.'

5. 2007 INSLEE & HENDRICKS at 58–59:

> our fleet of private vehicles today gets lower gas mileage than it did in 1982. During the time we invented the Internet, mapped the human genome, and saw into the farthest reaches of the universe, Congress did not move a muscle to break America's dependence on oil.

6. 2007 INSLEE & HENDRICKS at 45, quoting Mike Walsh, formerly, U.S. EPA, now an advisor to several nations on their auto industries:

> Once America removed its signals that we need to conserve fuel [— and stopped raising standards —]the SUV began to emerge as the only real profit center for the domestic manufacturers.

7. On the so-called CAFE standards litigation, see Ch. 9, §III(D).

8. PAUL ROBERTS, THE END OF OIL 15–16 (Houghton Mifflin Co. 2004):

[T]he United States has made only theatrical gestures over alternative fuels, improved efficiency, or policies that would harness the markets to reduce carbon. As a result, the energy
superpower has not only surrendered its once-awesome edge in such energy technologies
as solar and wind to competitors in Europe and Japan but made it less and less likely that
an effective solution for climate change will be deployed in time to make a difference.

Critics place much of the blame on a political system corrupted by big energy interests—companies desperate to protect billions of dollars in existing energy technologies
and infrastructure. An equal measure of blame, however, must fall on the "average"
American consumer, who each year seems to know less, and care less, about how much
energy he or she uses, where it comes from, or what its true costs are. Americans, it
seems, suffer profoundly from what may soon be known as energy illiteracy: most of us
understand so little about our energy economy that we have no idea that it has begun
falling apart.

9. Norman Myers & Jennifer Kent, The New Consumers: The Influence of Affluence on the
Environment (Island Press 2004).

10. JAMES HOWARD KUNSTLER, THE LONG EMERGENCY: SURVIVING THE END OF OIL, CLIMATE
CHANGE, AND OTHER CONVERGING CATASTROPHES OF THE TWENTY-FIRST CENTURY 101 (Grove
Press 2005) (footnote omitted):

The belief that "market economics" will automatically deliver a replacement for fossil
fuels is a type of magical thinking like that of the cargo cults of the South Pacific.

11. *See* PAUL R. EHRLICH & ANNE H. EHRLICH, THE DOMINANT ANIMAL: HUMAN EVOLUTION
AND THE ENVIRONMENT 296–97, esp. 297 (Island Press 2008) ("Energy: Are We Running Out of
It?") (describing John Holdren's "best plausible" scenario for the global population-energy-envi-
ronment-economic future):

As the table also illustrates, the carbon efficiency of the global economy (roughly the
amount of carbon emitted per unit of gross domestic product in the form of CO_2 from
fossil fuel burning) would increase some twenty-five-fold, through switching almost entirely to non-carbon-emitting technologies and sequestering substantial amounts of CO_2.

———

One method of increasing energy efficiency is through "energy recycling" in which waste heat
produced during generation of conventional electricity and thermal energy is captured and used.
Both waste energy and heat can be recycled. Waste energy in the form of unused gas or steam
produced by industrial applications is converted into electrical power. Waste heat from an electrical power plant can also be recycled by on-site industrial processes that use the thermal energy
for heating, cooling, or industrial processes.

———

B. Dismantling the Grid

Before we "dismantle" the grid or "abandon it" or "go around it" or "replace it," we would be
well advised to understand it. This task is undertaken by a balanced and insightful book by
PHILLIP F. SCHEWE, THE GRID: A JOURNEY THROUGH THE HEART OF OUR ELECTRIFIED WORLD
(Joseph Henry Press 2007). Schewe begins his tale as follows (*id.* at 1):

The electrical grid goes practically everywhere. It reaches into your home, your bed-room, and climbs right up into the lamp next to your pillow. It's there while you sleep, and it's waiting for you in the morning. Taken in its entirety, the grid is a machine, the most complex machine ever made. The National Academy of Engineering called it the greatest engineering achievement of the 20th century. It represents the largest industrial investment in history.

Schewe finds plenty of room in his book for Amory Lovins (seven references, twelve pages) and closes in a teasing way with a series of rhetorical questions (*id.* at 268) (emphasis in original):

China catching up to Western levels of electrification—this might be a logical place to end the story. Or how about finishing with a quick summary of the latest inven-tions, the proposed technical fixes for all those billion-dollar blackout problems? Well, this is not how the book will end. I am not going to profile some promising new thermo-electric turbine design since, anyway, it is likely to be overtaken soon by yet another model. Nor am I going to specify how and when minimum electricity goals will be met in poor countries. Nor speculate on when or how the American Congress will seriously address the grave connection between energy use and climate change.

Instead the book will end with a search for more meaning. What does the grid *mean* for the human race? We haven't exactly avoided this question. We've looked at some of the best things the electrical grid does. It helps yield more food per acre, it helps scan for tumors, it makes possible cheap aluminum and kerosene-less lamps for reading after dark. We have also had occasion to look, sometimes with the help of Lewis Mumford, at the social compromises brought on by electrical equipment (with much help from other fossil-fuel-burning technologies, such as automotives): not quite clear skies, no more Milky Way, and less self-made musical entertainment. No more piano.

When will we know if we got the right mixture of benefit and compromise? Does the grid serve any purpose other than bringing convenient energy by wire? We can't fully answer....

2007 Monbiot at 124:

But there is an entirely different way of responding to the question of how our en-ergy might be generated. It's generally described as "micro generation" or "the energy internet." In its pure form, it involves scrapping the national grid.

Instead of producing a large amount of power in a few places, the energy internet produces small amounts of power everywhere.

The total cost of electricity includes both costs of generation and transmission and distribution. Similarly, energy may be lost or wasted during each portion of the process between raw source and end-user. The traditional view is that large centralized facilities are more efficient than small, local plants or on-site power generation.[1] This assumption appears to be wrong.

The costs of transmission and distribution for centralized facilities are extremely high, with the result that the cost per kilowatt of power is 170% higher for centralized than decentralized facilities.[2] Second, the further the electricity is transmitted, the more energy is lost. This means that a centralized plant must produce 1.44 kilowatts per 1.0 kilowatt delivered to the end-user; a

---

1. See generally Thomas R. Casten, Recycling Energy to Reduce Costs and Mitigate Climate Change, in Sudden and Disruptive Climate Change 247–257 (M.C. MacCracken *et al.* eds. Earthscan Publications Ltd. 2008).

2. *Id.* at 251, Table 20.1.

decentralized facility must produce only 1.07 kilowatts per 1.0 delivered.[3] The final result is that the cost per kilowatt delivered to the user is 228% higher for centralized than decentralized power generation.

Power facilities must have extra generating capacity to accommodate failures in the system. A large, centralized power plant must have approximately 18 percent extra capacity to achieve system reliability.[4] In contrast, a local decentralized facility must have only 3 to 4 percent spare capacity.[5]

All the excess electricity that must be produced by centralized facilities translates into wasted carbon dioxide emissions that could be avoided without asking consumers to change their habits or electric usage.

Given these benefits, why isn't decentralized power generation the dominant system? Thomas Casten points to the policies and regulations of utility companies that create subsidies and monopolies, which protect utility companies from the free market.[6]

––––––––––––

The Renewable Policy Network for the 21st Century report, RENEWABLES 2007: A GLOBAL STATUS REPORT[1] summarizes current trends in renewable energy:[2]

- Renewable electricity generation capacity reached an estimated 240 gigawatts (GW) worldwide in 2007, an increase of 50 percent over 2004. Renewables represent 5 percent of global power capacity and 3.4 percent of global power generation. (Figures exclude large hydropower, which itself was 15 percent of global power generation.)

- Renewable energy generated as much electric power worldwide in 2006 as one-quarter of the world's nuclear power plants, not counting large hydropower. (And more than nuclear counting large hydropower.)

- The largest component of renewables generation capacity is wind power, which grew by 28 percent worldwide in 2007 to reach an estimated 95 GW. Annual capacity additions increased even more: 40 percent higher in 2007 compared to 2006.

- The fastest growing energy technology in the world is grid-connected solar photovoltaics (PV), with 50 percent annual increases in cumulative installed capacity in both 2006 and 2007, to an estimated 7.7 GW. This translates into 1.5 million homes with rooftop solar PV feeding into the grid worldwide.

- Rooftop solar heat collectors provide hot water to nearly 50 million households worldwide, and space heating to a growing number of homes. Existing solar hot water/heating capacity increased by 19 percent in 2006 to reach 105 gigawatts-thermal (GWth) globally.

- Biomass and geothermal energy are commonly employed for both power and heating, with recent increases in a number of countries, including uses for district heating. More than 2 million ground-source heat pumps are used in 30 countries for building heating and cooling.

- Production of biofuels (ethanol and biodiesel) exceeded an estimated 53 billion liters in 2007, up 43 percent from 2005. Ethanol production in 2007 represented about 4 percent

––––––––––––

3. *Id.*

4. H. Zerriffi, *Electric Power Systems Under Stress: An Evaluation of Centralized vs. Distributed Systems Architectures*, Ph.D. thesis, Carnegie Mellon University (2004).

5. *Id.*

6. *Id.* at 252.

1. www.ren21.net.

2. http://www.ren21.net/globalstatusreport/#download.

of the 1,300 billion liters of gasoline consumed globally. Annual biodiesel production increased by more than 50 percent in 2006.

- Renewable energy, especially small hydropower, biomass, and solar PV, provides electricity, heat, motive power, and water pumping for tens of millions of people in rural areas of developing countries, serving agriculture, small industry, homes, schools, and community needs. Twenty-five million households cook and light their homes with biogas, and 2.5 million households use solar lighting systems.

- Developing countries as a group have more than 40 percent of existing renewable power capacity, more than 70 percent of existing solar hot water capacity, and 45 percent of biofuels production. (See Figures 64, 65, and 66.)

IPCC WG3 CH. 4 at 272:

Renewable-energy systems can contribute to the security of energy supply and protection of the environment. These and other benefits of renewable energy systems were defined in a declaration by 154 nations at the Renewables 2004 conference held in Bonn (Renewables, 2004).

IPCC at 272:

Renewable-energy technologies can be broadly classified into four categories:

- *technologically mature with established markets in at least several countries:* large and small hydro, woody biomass combustion, geothermal, landfill gas, crystalline silicon PV solar water heating, onshore wind, bioethanol from sugars and starch (mainly Brazil and US);

- *technologically mature but with relatively new and immature markets in a small number of countries:* municipal solid waste-to-energy, anaerobic digestion, biodiesel, co-firing of biomass, concentrating solar dishes and troughs, solar-assisted air conditioning, mini- and micro-hydro and offshore wind;

- *under technological development with demonstrations or small-scale commercial application, but approaching wider market introduction:* thin-film PV, concentrating PV, tidal range and currents, wave power, biomass gasification and pyrolysis, bioethanol from ligno-cellulose and solar thermal towers; and

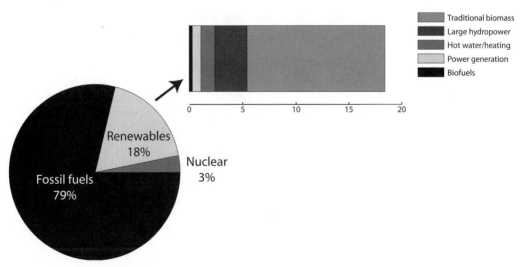

Figure 64. Renewable Energy Share of Global Final Energy Consumption in 2006. Adapted from REN21, Renewables 2007 Global Status Report Figure 1, *available at* www.ren21.net.

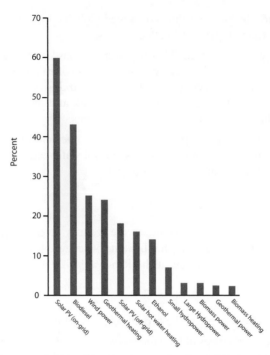

Figure 65. Annual Growth Rates of Renewable Energy Capacity (2002-2006). Adapted from REN21, Renewables 2007 Global Status Report Figure 3, *available at* **www.ren21.net. See** *Id.* **endnotes 4–17 for sources of data values.**

- *still in technology research stages*: organic and inorganic nanotechnology solar cells, artificial photosynthesis, biological hydrogen production involving biomass, algae and bacteria, biorefineries, ocean thermal and saline gradients, and ocean currents.

C. Wind Power

World Energy Council, *2007 Survey of Energy Resources: Executive Summary* 18 (2007):

> Wind energy capacity has grown rapidly since 1990, doubling every three and a half years.

Id.:

> The world's wind resources are vast: it has been estimated that if only 1% of the land area were utilized, and allowance made for wind's relatively low capacity factor, wind-power potential would roughly equate to the current level of worldwide generating capacity.

Wind energy is an ancient source of power, with the first windmills invented in Persia in the ninth century.[1] Windmills can be located either inland or offshore. Offshore locations are sometimes preferable because these locations have higher average wind speeds and the public is generally less resistant. Wind energy is particularly well-suited to areas that are remote and difficult to connect to the power grid.

---

1. Ahmad Y Hassan & Donald Routledge Hill, Islamic Technology: An Illustrated History 54 (Cambridge Un. Press 1986).

Country/region	Existing share (2006)	Future target (by 2010)	Country/region	Existing share (2006)	Future target
World	18%	—			
EU-25	14%	21%	**Other Developed/OECD Countries**		
			Australia	7.9%	—
Selected EU Countries			Canada	59%	—
Austria	62%	78%	Israel	—	5% by 2016
Belgium	2.8%	6.0%	Japan	0.4%	5% by 2016
Czech Republic	4.2%	8.0%	Korea	1.0%	7% by 2010
Denmark	26%	29%	Mexico	16%	—
Finland	29%	31.5%	New Zealand	65%	90% by 2025
France	10.9%	21%	Switzerland	52%	—
Germany	11%	12.5%	United States	9.2%	—
Greece	13%	20.1%			
Hungary	4.4%	3.6%	**Developing Countries**		
Ireland	10%	13.2%	Argentina	1.3%	8% by 2016
Italy	16%	25%	Brazil	5%	—
Luxembourg	6.9%	5.7%	China	17%	—
Netherlands	8.2%	9.0%	Egypt	15%	20% by 2020
Poland	2.6%	7.5%	India	4%	—
Portugal	32%	45%	Malaysia	—	5% by 2005
Slovak Republic	14%	31%	Morocco	10%	12% by 2012
Spain	19%	29.4%	Nigeria	—	7% by 2025
Sweden	49%	60%	Pakistan	—	10% by 2015
United Kingdom	4.1%	10%	Thailand	7%	—

Figure 66. Share of Electricity from Renewables, Existing in 2006 and Targets. From REN21 *Renewables 2007 Global Status Report*, **Table R8, www.ren21.net.**

Notes

1. *Kerncrest Audubon Soc'y v. City of Los Angeles Dep't of Water & Power*, 2007 WL 2208806 (Cal. App. 5th Dist. Aug. 2, 2007). This was an unsuccessful CEQA challenge to a project to construct and operate a wind farm consisting of eighty 1.5 megawatt wind turbine generators plus eight miles of transmission line in the southern Sierra Nevada Mountains in Kern County. The environmental documents confirmed that "direct impacts to sensitive raptors and bats could result from collisions with rotating turbine blades" but that *populations* would not be affected. Bird surveys were adequate. Night surveys were unnecessary. An avian monitoring condition in the approval of the project by the Board of Water and Power Commissioners was adequate, citing *Irritated Residents v. County of Madera*, 107 Cal. App. 4th 1383 (5th Dist. 2003) for the proposition that an EIR is not required "to conduct every suggested test or field study."

2. JAMES LOVELOCK, THE VANISHING FACE OF GAIA: A FINAL WARNING 26–27 (Perseus Books 2009) [hereinafter 2009 LOVELOCK]:

It is absurd to think that we can alter the Earth's response in our favor by using wind or solar voltaic energy at its present stage of development. A wind farm of twenty 1 mega-watt turbines requires more than ten thousand tons of concrete. It would require two hundred of these wind farms covering an area of one thousand square miles to equal the constant power output of a single coal-fired or nuclear power station. Even more absurd, a full-sized nuclear or coal-fired power station would have to be built for each of these monster wind farms to back up the turbines for the 75 percent of time when the wind was either too high or too low. As if this were not enough to damn wind energy, the construction of a 1 giga-watt wind farm would use a quantity of concrete, 2 million tons, sufficient to build a town for one hundred thousand people living in thirty thousand homes; making and using that quantity of concrete would release about 1 million tons of carbon dioxide into the air. For us to survive as a civilized nation, our cities need that safe, secure, and constant supply of electricity that only coal, gas, or nuclear can provide, and only with nuclear can we be assured of a constant supply of fuel. We have already seen how vulnerable gas supplies are to the continued integrity of pipelines perhaps a thousand miles long, and to the aggressive politics of autocrats.

3. Jonathan Thompson, *Modern-day La Mancha: Two Weeks in the West*, HIGH COUNTRY NEWS, June 22, 2009, p. 5 (Special Report on Alternative Energy), quoting Miguel de Cervantes (in the early 1600s) on the response of Don Quixote to the sight of thirty or forty windmills rising from the plain:

> Do you see over yonder, friend Sancho, thirty or forty hulking giants? I intend to do battle with them and slay them … for this is a righteous war and the removal of so foul a brood from off the face of the earth is a service God will bless.

D. Solar Power

R.E.H. Sims *et al.*, *Energy supply*, *in* CLIMATE CHANGE 2007: MITIGATION. CONTRIBUTION OF WORKING GROUP III TO THE FOURTH ASSESSMENT REPORT OF THE INTERGOVERNMENTAL PANEL ON CLIMATE CHANGE 251, 278 (B. Metz *et al.* eds. Cambridge Un. Press 2007) [hereinafter R.E.H. Sims, *Energy supply*]:

> The proportion of solar radiation that reaches the Earth's surface is more than 10,000 times the current annual global energy consumption.

There are two main types of solar power: thermal and photovoltaic. Thermal solar involves heating a liquid so that it produces steam, which then rotates a turbine and produces energy. Photovoltaic (PV) solar power is produced through the use of semiconductors. When photons in sunlight hit a semi-conducting material, such as silicon, they cause atoms in the material to lose atoms, which flow through the material creating electricity. Concentrating solar plants use large arrays of mirrors to focus light on a thermal solar installation.

Technology Around the Corner

Thin-film solar uses non-silicon semi-conducting materials to create photovoltaic cells. The benefit is that these materials are less expensive and can be rolled or printed on flexible or lightweight materials. A number of nanotechnology companies have developed thin-film applications; it is expected that some will be market ready as early as 2009. Thin-film technology is predicted to reduce the cost of solar to 1$/watt, which would make solar power competitive with traditional energy sources.

Note

1. OLIVER MORTON, EATING THE SUN: HOW PLANTS POWER THE PLANET 231–32 (Harper Collins 2008):

> This great difference [between plants and animals] stems from the fact that sunlight is, at the efficiencies photosynthesis is capable of, a rather dilute source of energy. To appreciate how insufficient it would be to animal needs, imagine the Green Man of forest folklore. Let us assume that his greenness is due to chlorophyll through which he feeds himself. Given the surface area of his skin—and the fact that at any given time

some of it will inevitably be averted from the sun—such a green man would have about as much energy on which to run his metabolism as someone restricted to a diet grown in a couple of square metres of garden. All he could eat in a day would be what his little plot could grow in a day. A few leaves for breakfast, maybe a morsel of root for supper: berries for Sunday lunch.

On the sunshine equivalent of this meager diet, our Jack of the Forest has no energy for moving, or for thinking—nerves and muscles use a lot of energy. He lacks the energy to breathe in or out, or to keep his body any warmer than the outside air. He's not good for much except sitting there repairing the daily entropic wear and tear to his body. Indeed he doesn't really have enough energy for that; quite a lot of him will rot away. The prognosis for the Green Man is vegetable.

E. Geothermal

MIT study 2007, *The Future of Geothermal Energy,* at 1–9:

In general terms, geothermal energy consists of the thermal energy stored in the Earth's crust. Thermal energy in the earth is distributed between the constituent host rock and the natural fluid that is contained in its fractures and pores at temperatures above ambient levels. These fluids are mostly water with varying amounts of dissolved salts; typically, in their natural *in situ* state, they are present as a liquid phase but sometimes may consist of a saturated, liquid-vapor mixture or superheated steam vapor phase. The amounts of hot rock and contained fluids are substantially larger and more widely distributed in comparison to hydrocarbon (oil and gas) fluids contained in sedimentary rock formations underlying the United States.

MIT study 2007, at 1–8:

Although geothermal energy has provided commercial base-load electricity around the world for more than a century, it is often ignored in national projections of evolving U.S. energy supply. This could be a result of the widespread perception that the total geothermal resource is often associated with identified high-grade, hydrothermal systems that are too few and too limited in their distribution in the United States to make a long-term, major impact at a national level. This perception has led to undervaluing the long-term potential of geothermal energy by missing an opportunity to develop technologies for sustainable heat mining from large volumes of accessible hot rock anywhere in the United States.

For further discussion of the mechanics and potential of geothermal energy, see William Calvin, *Turning Around by 2020*, this volume Chapter 6, § V.

F. Hydrogen

IPCC Ch. 4 at 283:

Realizing hydrogen as an energy carrier depends on low-cost, high-efficiency methods for production, transport and storage. Most commercial hydrogen production today is based on steam reforming of methane, but electrolysis of water (especially using carbon-free electricity from renewable or nuclear energy) or splitting water thermo-chemically may be viable approaches in the future.

IPCC at 283–4:

The prospects for a future hydrogen economy will depend on developing competitively priced fuel cells for stationary applications or vehicles, but fuel cells are unlikely to become fully commercial for one or two decades.

2007 ROMM at 185:

The promise of hydrogen cars as a simple techno-fix, a *deus ex machina* to solve our environmental problems painlessly, and without regulations, is a cornerstone of the Bush administration's climate policy.... The president didn't tell the public that more than 98 percent of the hydrogen made in this country today must be extracted from fossil fuel hydrocarbons—natural gas, oil, and coal—and that process releases huge amounts of carbon dioxide.

2007 ROMM at 186:

Study after study has shown that it makes no sense to squander renewable power to make hydrogen for cars until the electric grid is itself virtually greenhouse gas free—and that is at least four decades away.... And this analysis assumes that hydrogen cars will actually become practical for consumers any time soon. But that is highly unlikely. They simply require too many scientific breakthroughs.

G. Biofuels

IPCC WG3 ch. 4 at 275:

Biomass sources include forest, agricultural and livestock residues, short-rotation forest plantations, dedicated herbaceous energy crops, the organic component of municipal solid waste (MSW), and other organic waste streams.

IPCC at 276:

Prior to conversion, biomass feedstocks tend to have lower energy density per volume or mass compared with equivalent fossil fuels. This makes collection, transport, storage and handling more costly per unit of energy.

IPCC at 276:

A wide range of conversion technologies is under continuous development to produce bioenergy carriers for both small- and large-scale applications. Organic residues and wastes are often cost-effective feedstocks for bioenergy conversion plants, resulting in niche markets for forest, food processing and other industries.

2009 LOVELOCK at 19:

I think it unlikely that serious harm can come from the small-scale use of biofuels made from agricultural waste, recycled cooking oil, or a modest harvest of ocean algae. But planting crops of sugarcane, beetroot, maize, oilseed rape, and other plants solely for fuel production is almost certainly one of the most harmful acts of all.

H. Ocean Energy

R.E.H. Sims *et al.*, *Energy supply*, in CLIMATE CHANGE 2007: MITIGATION. CONTRIBUTION OF WORKING GROUP III TO THE FOURTH ASSESSMENT REPORT OF THE INTERGOVERNMENTAL PANEL ON CLIMATE CHANGE 251, 280 (B. Metz *et al.* eds., Cambridge Un. Press 2007):

The potential marine-energy resource of wind-driven waves, gravitational tidal ranges, thermal gradients between warm surface water and colder water at depths of >1000 m, salinity gradients, and marine currents is huge, but what is exploitable as the economic potential is low.

The ocean can provide for two types of energy: tidal and wave kinetic energy. Tidal energy can be captured using submerged turbines. Several such installations exist: the Severn Barrage and a plant on the Rance estuary off the coast of Brittany.[1] Wave energy capture is still in the development phase, but designs include mechanisms by which the flow of water causes a turbine to turn.

I. Hydropower

NatureNews, *Electricity Without Carbon*, 454 NATURE 816 (2008):

> The world has a lot of dams—45,000 large ones, according to the World Energy Council, and many more at small scales.... As a source of electricity, dams are second only to fossil fuels ... One reason for hydropower's success is that it is a widespread resource—160 countries use hydropower to some extent.

NatureNews at 817:

> Hydroelectric systems are unique among generating systems in that they can, if correctly engineered, store the energy generated elsewhere, pumping water uphill when energy is abundant.

Notes

1. The "downsides" of hydroelectric energy are enormous, within the U.S. and elsewhere. *E.g.*, JIM LICHATOWICH, SALMON WITHOUT RIVERS: A HISTORY OF THE PACIFIC SALMON CRISIS (Island Press 1999); FRED PEARCE, WHEN THE RIVERS RUN DRY: WATER—THE DEFINING CRISIS OF THE TWENTY-FIRST CENTURY (Beacon Press 2006).

2. Adell Louise Amos, *Hydropower Reform and the Impact of the Energy Policy Act of 2005 on the Klamath Basin: Renewed Optimism or Same Old Song?*, 22 J. ENVTL. L. & LIT. 1, 43 (2007):

> Overall, the Klamath Basin remains a complicated and dynamic system. This Article sets out some of the reasons behind the tentative, but revived, sense of optimism for settlement in the Basin that has developed over the past several years. Certainly the new hydropower regulations, while decried as a detriment to river restoration, have resulted in a solid factual record for fishway prescriptions, and potentially for dam decommissioning and removal in the Klamath Basin. The Skokomish decision and PacifiCorp's experience with the Condit Dam in Washington may also represent significant influences as the relicensing proceeding moves forward. Outside the hydropower context, the ESA and takings litigation over the past decade may help to set the table for settlement. In the end, however, the issues remain contentious, and livelihoods and cultural traditions are on the line.

---

1. NatureNews, *Electricity Without Carbon*, 454 NATURE 816 (2008).

IV. Energy Security

Richard Pierce, *Energy Independence and Global Warming*, 21 NAT. RESOURCES & ENV. 68, 68 (2007):

> The pursuit of energy independence is one of the few national goals that attract near unanimous support from politicians of both parties, as well as from virtually all journalists and members of the public. Yet, I know of no expert on energy policy who thinks that pursuit of energy independence makes any more sense than pursuit of automobile independence, tomato independence, or underwear independence ...

CHRISTOPHER FLAVIN *et al.*, AMERICAN ENERGY: THE RENEWABLE PATH TO ENERGY SECURITY, (Report for Worldwatch Institute and Center for American Progress 2006), *available at* http://americanenergynow.org/:

> Many of the new technologies that harness renewables are, or soon will be, economically competitive with the fossil fuels that meet 85 percent of U.S. energy needs. With oil prices soaring, the security risks of petroleum dependence growing, and the environmental costs of today's fuels becoming more apparent, the country faces compelling reasons to put these technologies to use on a large scale ...

> Improving efficiency and diversifying fuel choices will take the pressure off energy prices, while enabling the country to make diplomatic and security decisions based on American interests and values rather than the relentless need to protect access to oil ...

> America's current energy system undermines national security in other ways as well. The centralized and geographically concentrated nature of the country's power plants, refineries, pipelines, and other infrastructure leaves it vulnerable to everything from natural disasters to terrorist attacks. One year after Hurricane Katrina crippled approximately 10 percent of the nation's oil refining capacity, oil and gas production and transportation in the Gulf of Mexico still had not been fully restored.

> Security experts believe that a well-orchestrated physical or electronic attack on the U.S. electricity grid could cripple the economy for an extended period. It is estimated that the 2003 Northeast blackout cost between $4 billion and $10 billion over the course of just a few days.

> The country's 104 nuclear power plants and their associated pools of high-level radioactive waste present another U.S. security threat. If one of the planes that struck the World Trade Center on September 11, 2001, had instead hit the Indian Point nuclear plant just north of New York City, the human and economic toll of that fateful day could have been vastly greater.

> The distributed nature of many renewable energy technologies helps reduce the risk of accidental or premeditated grid failures cascading out of control. An analysis of the 2003 Northeast blackout suggests that solar power generation representing just a small percentage of peak load and located at key spots in the region would have significantly reduced the extent of the power outages ...

> As with oil dependence, the broader energy security threats cannot be eliminated overnight. But immediate steps to invest in a diverse, decentralized energy system that relies more heavily on domestic renewable resources will allow the United States to steadily enhance its security in the years ahead.

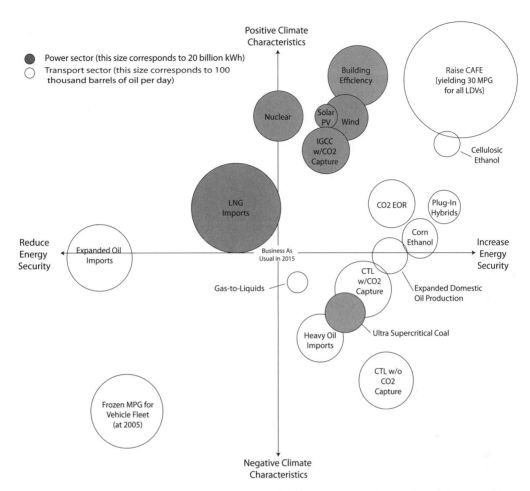

Figure 67. Energy security and climate impacts in 2025 of different energy options. Adapted from: World Resources Institute, bubble chart available at http://www.wri.org/stories/2007/07/weighing-u-s-energy-options-wri-bubble-chart. Bubble size corresponds to the incremental energy provided or avoided in 2025. The reference point is "business as usual" for 2025. The horizontal axis includes sustainability as well as traditional aspects of sufficiency, reliability, and affordability. The vertical axis illustrates lifecycle greenhouse gas intensity. Bubble placements are based on quantitative analysis and WRI expert judgment. Gray represents the power sector and white represents the transportation sector. For more information on underlying assumptions, visit www.wri.org/usenergyoptions.

Chapter Five
Framing the Climate Change Debate

Chapter Five

Framing the Climate Change Debate

Framing Global Climate Change

Howard Latin, Professor of Law and Justice Francis Scholar, Rutgers University School of Law, Newark, N.J.

People are now faced in varying degrees by the worst pollution problem of all time, the worst environmental problem of all time, and likely the worst human problem of all time. Yet, the greenhouse gas (GHG) polluting nations have not agreed on sensible policies for overcoming global climate change, and nearly all current mitigation programs are now headed in the wrong direction. As the U.N. Secretary-General, Ban Ki-moon, noted in June 2008: "The bottom line is that our climate is changing fast, and the world has been too slow in response."[1] Conflicting values and priorities as well as economic self-interest have undermined possible climate change solutions, but distorted or deceptive "framing" of the critical issues has also been a barrier to the creation of successful precautionary programs. As a result of inaccurate framing, most policymakers do not realize that they lack a clear understanding of global warming and climate change problems, and consequently they are bound to continue making serious mistakes. In response to misguided perceptions and counter-productive policies, this Chapter explains why climate change program failures are inevitable if we remain on the current path, and it offers an overview of the strategies we should be adopting instead.

Daniel Kahneman and Amos Tversky, two giants in the field of cognitive psychology, showed that the way in which information about risks is presented or "framed" can be highly influential in determining how people respond to the information.[2] For example, people may be willing to spend more to avoid a risk of *n* deaths than they would spend to save *n* lives. In a famous experiment, Kahneman and Tversky found that whether risks are framed in terms of *lives lost* or *lives saved* can shift the attitudes of the information recipients from risk-avoiding to risk-preferring (or the reverse) despite identical risks under consideration.[3] The strength of framing effects was demonstrated by the reluctance of the research subjects to give up this "preference reversal" even when their inconsistency was explained to them.[4] Framing effects can be created by deliberate or

---

1. UNA-UK address on "Securing the Common Good: The United Nations and the Expanding Global Agenda," U.N. News Service (June 13, 2008, downloaded from www.un.org on 06/14/ 2008).

2. Amos Tversky & Daniel Kahneman, *Rational Choice and the Framing of Decisions, in* RATIONAL CHOICE: THE CONTRAST BETWEEN ECONOMICS AND PSYCHOLOGY 67 (Robin M. Hogarth & Melvin W. Reder eds., Un. Chicago Press 1987) [hereinafter Tversky & Kahneman, *Rational Choice*]; Daniel Kahneman & Amos Tversky, *Choices, Values, and Frames,* 39 AM. PSYCHOLOGIST 341 (1984); A. Tversky & D. Kahneman, *The Framing of Decisions and the Psychology of Choice,* 211 SCIENCE, Issue 4481, 453–458 (1981).

3. Daniel Kahneman & Amos Tversky, *Choices, Values, and Frames,* 39 AM. PSYCHOLOGIST 341, 343 (1984).

4. Tversky & Kahneman, *Rational Choice, supra* note 2, at 76.

accidental manipulation of information formats and may be just as important as the content of the information in shaping people's choices.

Professors Kahneman and Tversky surely never imagined that two decades after their research on framing effects, the whole world would be engaged in an unanticipated, unplanned, uncontrolled experiment on framing potential responses to global climate change. The ways in which competing approaches for overcoming global warming and resulting climate changes are being framed, more than the substance of the information on mitigation and adaptation measures, have been leading to the adoption of ineffectual policies that may have tragic consequences for centuries. The inability of national and international leaders to understand the full dimensions of global climate change is exposing billions of people to unprecedented ecological and economic hazards—exposures occurring every day and growing worse every year. Unfortunately, most climate policymakers, scientists, and environmental activists, like most lay people, are seldom conscious of the negative influences that inappropriate frames may have on their decisions.[5]

Frame One: Reducing Greenhouse Gas Emissions

At its most basic, the greenhouse effect arises from the retention of heat-trapping gases in the atmosphere. This "blanket" of greenhouse gases prevents a variable percentage of the heat absorbed by the earth from being radiated back into space or the upper atmosphere.[6] Increasing the amount of GHGs in the atmosphere will worsen the greenhouse effect by trapping more heat, which means that the *concentration of greenhouse gases in the atmosphere* is the primary determinant of the extent of global warming.[7] One might suppose, then, that the climate-policy focus would be on reducing the atmospheric GHG concentration that causes greenhouse effects and related climate changes. Yet, virtually all pollution control programs have focused instead on reducing existing or predicted GHG emissions by some percentage rate over several decades, not on reducing the atmospheric concentration. The core framing problem arises because these two kinds of program targets—GHG emissions reductions and atmospheric concentrations—seem to be equivalent, and many people treat them as the same, but they definitely are not the same.

The widely-accepted Frame One requests every government, organization, business, and consumer to cut greenhouse gas emissions each year, which supposedly would correspondingly decrease the harms from global climate change. We could shift to more fuel-efficient vehicles that discharge fewer GHGs per thousand miles driven. We could reduce emissions from electricity generation by requiring utilities to switch to cleaner fuels and to increase their use of renewable energy sources. We could design more energy-efficient buildings and turn out the lights more often. We could compel or implore all corporations to identify their GHG discharges and to find ways to reduce their emissions. We could ask millions of consumers to buy hybrid cars instead of gas guzzlers, fluorescent lights instead of incandescent bulbs, paper bags instead of plastic bags,

---

5. *See generally* James R. Bettman and Mita Sujan, *Effects of Framing on Evaluation of Comparable and Noncomparable Alternatives by Expert and Novice Consumers*, 14 J. of Consumer Res., No. 2, 141 (Sept. 1987).

6. *See* Intergovernmental Panel on Climate Change, Climate Change: The Physical Science Basis, Contribution of Working Group I to the Fourth Assessment Report 129–234, 755–759 (2007); Intergovernmental Panel on Climate Change Fourth Assessment Report, Climate Change 2007: Synthesis Report, Summary for Policymakers 4–6 (Cambridge Un. Press 2007) [hereinafter IPCC Synthesis]; Kerry Emanuel, What We Know About Climate Change 15–21 (The MIT Press 2007).

7. *See* J. Canadell *et al.*, *Contributions to Accelerating Atmospheric CO$_2$ Growth from Economic Activity: Carbon Intensity, and Efficiency of Natural Sinks*, Proc. Natl. Acad. Sci. (Early Edition Approved Sept. 17, 2007, downloaded from www.pnas.org on 11/14/2007); U.S. EPA, Climate Change Science: State of Knowledge (2007, downloaded from www.epa.gov on 04/29/2007); Environment Canada, *The Science of Climate Change-Part I: Introduction/GHG/Radiative Forcing* (April 2001); *Climate Panel Reaches Consensus on the Need to Reduce Harmful Emissions*, NY Times On-line (May 4, 2007).

locally grown vegetables instead of agricultural produce from distant locations, and to make a host of other behavioral changes cumulatively aimed at reducing GHG pollution.

Many climate experts and other concerned people feel comfortable with this Frame One vision—we are all vulnerable to climate change risks; we all have a stake in minimizing the harmful effects; and we can all help to reduce climate change by adopting a broad range of emissions-reduction practices. As an illustration of the Frame One vision, an environmental law professor recently wrote:

> I tell anyone who asks (my students, friends, etc.) that everything they do to reduce their own carbon emissions immediately helps. I do this because I think part of the answer is to flip the "intractable collective action problem" view of the issue around in the following way. Yes, everyone everywhere has to be part of the zero-emissions plan or it will not succeed. But this same fact means that every single one of us can contribute to the solution (unlike many conventional pollution problems, where our "help" is at best indirect ...) This is empowering to people, and also has the benefit of being true. And then [I] add immediately, so as not to be misunderstood, that contributing to the solution also means pressing those in government to ensure that our individual reductions ARE part of a larger, effective global solution.[8]

Another participant in this academic exchange of views agreed: "I second [the] comment that everyone can do something about this problem. Carbon (or at least CO_2-equivalent units) in the atmosphere are truly fungible. Even if individuals can each do only a small amount, multiply that by millions."[9] The Dean of Princeton's Woodrow Wilson School recently stated: "[A]s any climate scientist will tell you, it's going to take a wide array of solutions, big and small, to begin reversing the damage we have already done, much less avoiding even greater catastrophe."[10]

Most American politicians, including the 2008 presidential candidates, have accepted this Frame One conception of reducing GHG emissions through many thousands of diverse industrial and consumption changes. Senators McCain and Obama are supporting cap-and-trade systems that would allow major and medium-sized polluters to decide whether to reduce GHG emissions or to purchase pollution reduction credits (or allowances or shares) created when other GHG sources cut their discharges more than the amount required under the regulatory cap.[11] Even President Bush, despite his opposition to mandatory GHG pollution control targets, has proposed improving fuel-efficiency standards for cars to reduce their GHG emissions; and he recently signed into law a federal energy act aimed partly at that purpose.[12]

On the international plane, the Kyoto Protocol provides that developed nations should cut their GHG emissions on average to about five percent below 1990 discharge levels,[13] and only the United States among affluent countries has not agreed to meet this modest target. The U.N.'s Clean Development Mechanism and Joint Implementation programs have enabled the European Union nations to sponsor hundreds of projects that are meant to reduce net GHG emissions by

---

8. Sarah Krakoff, Comments on Envlawprofessors E-Mailing List, Novermber 12, 2007.

9. Debra L. Donahue, Comments on Envlawprofessors E-Mailing List, Novermber 12, 2007.

10. Anne-Marie Slaughter, *Real Action on Climate Change*, NY TIMES ON-LINE (Dec. 7, 2007, Guest Commentary, "On the Ground" Blog of Nicholas D. Christoff, downloaded on 12/07/2007).

11. *See* Carbonpositive Carbon News and Info, *US Presidential Race Narrows to Climate Candidates* (February 7, 2008), downloaded from www.carbonpositive.net on 02/08/2008.

12. *See Bush Sets Greenhouse Gas Emissions Goal*, NY TIMES ON-LINE (April 17, 2008); Associated Press, *Senate Approves New Fuel-Economy Standards, Bill Requires Average 35 miles Per Gallon Over the Next 13 Years* (Dec. 13, 2007, downloaded from MSNBC.com on 12/14/2007); *Crossing a Threshold on Energy Legislation*, NY TIMES ON-LINE (Dec. 5, 2007).

13. Kyoto Protocol to the United Nations Framework Convention on Climate Change, Art. 3(1) (Dec. 10, 1997), *reprinted in* 37 I.L.M. 22.

taking advantage of the lower pollution control costs in developing countries.[14] Kyoto Protocol member-states are now evaluating more stringent but essentially similar measures to reduce GHG emissions in the decades after the treaty expires in 2012.[15] Reflecting the Frame One conception, the various existing and proposed measures to restrict GHG pollution are based on a central presumption—that *reducing GHG discharges in a myriad ways in a myriad places will generate corresponding reductions in the harms caused by global climate change.*

This emphasis on promoting countless decentralized public and private efforts to reduce GHG emissions undoubtedly can be inspirational. On the other hand, this approach is not cost-free and may detract from the efforts and funding needed for more substantial mitigation or adaptation measures. The crucial question is whether a multitude of largely uncoordinated emissions-reduction efforts—some voluntary and others compelled by law—can be sufficiently effective to overcome impending climate change harms.

My conclusion, as explained throughout this Chapter, is that reliance on conventional emissions-reduction programs to cut GHG pollution in thousands of contexts cannot succeed well enough, soon enough, to overcome predicted climate change risks. Contrary to the Frame One viewpoint, the attempts of millions of people to reduce GHG emissions are not really helping because they are being negated by the choices of countless other people and institutions. To paraphrase a previous comment: "even if individuals can each do only a small amount [of harm], multiply that by millions."[16] Overcoming the difficult collective-action problems requires shifting our mitigation efforts and investments from a *GHG emissions-reduction strategy* to a *GHG-free technology-replacement strategy*. We cannot cut out all GHG pollution, which would be especially hard to do in poor nations whose highest priority is increasing their economic and social development,[17] but a GHG-free technology-replacement strategy would be the best, most realistic, approach for removing the greenhouse gases that can feasibly be eliminated.

Frame Two: Reducing the Increases in Greenhouse Gas Concentrations

In an assessment of the scientific knowledge on global warming, the U.S. Environmental Protection Agency (EPA) concluded: "The major greenhouse gases emitted by human activities remain in the atmosphere for periods ranging from decades to centuries. It is therefore virtually certain that atmospheric concentrations of greenhouse gases will continue to rise over the next few decades."[18] The U.N. Intergovernmental Panel on Climate Change (IPCC), the largest, most influential association of scientists studying climate change issues, similarly concluded: "The consequences of greenhouse gas emissions changes, and CO_2 emissions changes in particular,

---

14. *See, e.g.*, Craig A. Hart, *The Clean Development Mechanism: Considerations for Investors and Policymakers*, 7 Sustainable Dev. L. & Policy, Issue 2, 41 (Spring 2007); Florens Flues, Axel Michaelowa & Katharina Michaelowa, *UN Approval of Greenhouse Gas Emission Reduction Projects in Developing Countries: The Political Economy of the CDM Executive Board*, Working Paper 35, Center for International and Comparative Studies (2008); Anna Korppoo and Arild Moe, *Russian JI Procedures: More Problems Than Solutions?*, Briefing Paper for the Fridtjof Nansen Institute of Norway (June 2007).

15. *See, e.g.*, J.G.J. Olivier *et al.*, *Consequences of the European Policy Package on Climate and Energy*, Report to Netherlands Environmental Assessment Agency (2008); Aaron Cosbey, Deborah Murphy & John Drexhage, *Market Mechanisms for Sustainable Development: How Do They Fit in the Various Post-2012 Climate Efforts?* Report to the Int'l Inst. for Sustainable Development (July 2007, downloaded from www.iisd.org on 07/19/2007); Daniel Bodansky, *International Sectoral Agreements in a Post-2012 Climate Framework*, A Working Paper Prepared for the Pew Center on Global Climate Change (May 2007).

16. *See* text accompanying note 9, *supra.*

17. For a similar conclusion, see Jeffrey D. Sachs, *Keys to Climate Protection*, 298 Sci. Amer., Issue 4, 40 (April 2008); Jeffrey D. Sachs, *Climate Change after Bali*, 298 Sci. Amer., Issue 3, 33–34 (March 2008).

18. U.S. EPA, Climate Change-Science: State of Knowledge (2007, downloaded from www.epa.gov on 04/29/2007).

take decades to centuries to manifest themselves fully in the climate system."[19] Given this high degree of persistence, GHGs discharged in recent years are already in the global warming "pipeline"[20] and will continue to increase global warming for decades or centuries to come.

Frame Two reflects the view that the great majority of existing and proposed emissions-reduction programs will never decrease the level of GHGs in the atmosphere. Rather, these pollution control initiatives will only *reduce the increases* in atmospheric GHG concentrations each year. The claimed "reductions" come from comparisons with the amount of GHGs that will be discharged if no pollution restrictions are imposed, not from comparisons with the amount of GHGs *already in the air*. In the literature on climate change, the do-nothing or no-regulation baseline is described as the "business-as-usual" scenario. An emissions-reduction target that cuts business-as-usual pollution from a country or company by 50 percent would allow the remaining 50 percent of persistent GHG emissions to be discharged into the air every year, constantly increasing the atmospheric GHG concentration. The following graph may help explain the "reducing the increases" residual pollution problem:

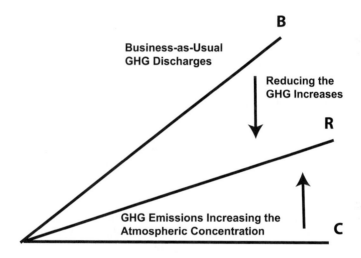

Figure 1.

A GHG source may generate high business-as-usual emissions at level B that could be reduced to level R by voluntary or mandatory pollution control programs. However, at level R this pollution source would still be adding substantial amounts of residual GHGs to the existing atmospheric GHG concentration at level C, thereby expanding the greenhouse effect and global warming. In essence, the GHG "reductions" from B to R would leave residual pollution that increases, not decreases, atmospheric GHG levels and related climate changes. Contrary to the Frame One conception, reducing level B pollution to level R pollution will not result in any corresponding improvements to global warming and climate change. Instead, the persistent GHG concentration in the atmosphere will be growing worse every year. We could spend many billions of dollars annually on "reducing the increases" emissions-reduction programs that will not produce any meaningful benefits because these efforts only reduce business-as-usual GHG discharges (B to R), while their residual pollution emissions (C to R) continue to increase the crucial atmospheric GHG concentration and related global climate change hazards.

19. IPCC, Implications of Proposed CO$_2$ Emissions Limitations 3 (Oct. 1997).

20. James Hansen, *Guest Opinion: Global Warming Twenty Years Later*, Worldwatch Mag. (June 23, 2008, downloaded from www.worldwatch.org on 06/27/2008).

Contrary to Frame One, all nations, businesses, consumers, and other GHG sources could reduce their business-as-usual pollution by a large percentage—perhaps considerably more than 50 percent—and yet their remaining GHG emissions would continue to increase the atmospheric GHG concentration, causing more human and environmental harms. To properly evaluate the climate change dangers, policymakers must consider not only the amount of existing or projected business-as-usual emissions and the amount that could be cut from these GHG pollution discharges by emissions-reduction programs, but also the residual volume of GHGs that an emissions-reduction program will allow to be discharged into the air every year. The greater the residual GHG pollution, the worse the greenhouse effect will be.

As our first Frame Two example, California adopted motor vehicle regulations to reduce GHG emissions from new cars and trucks 30 percent by 2016.[21] People who accept the Frame One vision likely believe this state initiative is a triumph, while Frame Two analyses should treat this regulatory program as a climate change disaster. The California rules provide that new vehicles will be limited to discharging 70 percent of the GHG emissions they would have put out each year if there were no regulations, which means the residual allowable GHG pollution will be more than twice as much as the contemplated reductions. For every 10 million tons of GHGs that new vehicles would have discharged under the business-as-usual scenario, the permissible emissions after the California standard takes effect in 2016 would be "reduced" to pumping seven million tons of *additional GHG discharges* into the atmosphere each year.

The California emissions-reduction program would induce a 30 percent smaller *increase* in GHG pollution from new vehicles in comparison with the business-as-usual baseline, but this cutback cannot achieve any reduction or stabilization of the atmospheric GHG concentration and resulting climate effects because new vehicles will be allowed to discharge millions more tons of GHGs into the air every year. Moreover, after the California regulations take effect, the claimed GHG emissions reductions could be counter-balanced by an increase in the number of motor vehicles, an increase in the number of miles driven, or an increase in engine idling and pollution discharges resulting from interminable traffic jams.

In September 2007, many environmental lawyers were jubilant because the Federal District Court of Vermont interpreted the federal Clean Air Act to hold that Vermont, and by implication more than a dozen other states, could adopt the California regulations as their vehicle standards for GHG emissions.[22] I wonder how many of these environmental law proponents understand that this legal "victory" means Vermont and other states will *reduce the increases* in new vehicle GHG emissions by 30 percent while allowing the vehicles to add 70 percent of the business-as-usual discharges to the atmosphere each year. As a result of GHG persistence, the residual 70 percent of vehicle emissions reaching the air annually is certain to increase the atmospheric GHG concentration and to degrade rather than improve global warming problems. If the California and similar state regulations operate perfectly for hundreds of years, they will never reduce climate change risks because they allow substantial *annual increases* in persistent GHG discharges that will constantly raise the atmospheric concentration.

The California motor vehicle standards cannot take effect unless the U.S. EPA approves the state regulations, which the federal agency thus far has refused to do. In December 2007, Congress enacted an energy conservation law that, among other provisions, mandates a 35 percent

---

21. Central Valley Chrysler-Jeep, Inc. v. Goldstene, 529 F. Supp.2d 1151 (E.D. Calif., Dec. 11, 2007), as corrected March 26, 2008; Associated Press, *Judge Backs Calif. On Emissions Rules*, NY TIMES ON-LINE (Dec. 12, 2007); *Automakers Attack Proposal to Address Global Warming*, NY TIMES ON-LINE (Sept. 23, 2004). The California Law is commonly referred to as Assembly Bill 1493.

22. Green Mountain Chrysler Plymouth v. Crombie, 508 F. Supp. 2d 295 (D. Vt. 2007); Reuters, *U.S. Automakers Challenge Vermont Emissions Law*, NY TIMES ON-LINE (April 10, 2007).

fuel efficiency improvement that will achieve about the same GHG emissions reductions by 2020 as the California regulations would require by 2016. EPA cited this federal energy statute as the basis for its decision that the California regulations should be preempted to impose a uniform national standard for motor vehicle fuel-efficiency requirements.[23] When the federal energy statute was adopted, the Senate Majority Leader Harry Reid called the new law "a step to fight global warming"[24] and Senator Inouye said it "demonstrates to the world that America is a leader in fighting global warming."[25] Regrettably, these political claims were completely wrong despite the sincerity of the speakers. These Senators and probably all other politicians do not understand the difference between Frame One (reducing GHG emissions) and Frame Two (reducing the increases in atmospheric GHG levels), and in this instance they were celebrating large Frame Two *residual increases* in the atmospheric GHG concentration that cannot possibly improve climate change risks.

The federal energy statute is indeed similar to the California regulations because it would only *reduce the increases* in GHG discharges into the atmosphere roughly 30 percent by 2020 while allowing the remaining 70 percent of business-as-usual vehicle emissions to be discharged into the air every year. The politicians quoted above and their colleagues have accepted the invalid Frame One presumption that all GHG pollution "reductions" would comparably reduce climate change harms, when the vital issue is what the ramifications would be for atmospheric GHG levels that cause the greenhouse effect and global warming. It should be indisputable that we cannot overcome climate change problems by constantly increasing the atmospheric GHG levels that exacerbate global warming, which means both the California and federal laws on vehicle emissions would be totally ineffective means to help combat global climate change.

As another example, a recent WASHINGTON POST story reported that: "Maryland joined seven states yesterday in a Regional Greenhouse Gas Initiative aimed at reducing carbon dioxide pollution from power plants 10 percent by 2019 in the absence of tougher federal emissions standards."[26] Maryland's Governor was quoted as announcing that: "The fight to reduce global warming crosses state lines, and Maryland is proud to join its neighbors in reducing greenhouse gas emissions while protecting our electric industry."[27] The Frame One unintentional distortion could not be more striking here: This multi-state regulatory program is not reducing the amount of persistent GHGs in the atmosphere and thus cannot "reduce global warming," as Maryland's Governor claimed. Instead, these regulations are only *reducing the increases* in GHGs that will remain in the atmosphere after the utilities' residual discharges. Under this regulatory standard, the fossil fuel-based generators will be allowed to discharge the remaining 90 percent of business-as-usual GHG emissions into the air each year. After these multi-state regulations take effect, the utilities will continue to discharge thousands or millions of tons of additional GHGs into the atmosphere annually, which is hardly a cause for environmental celebration. Energy production based on fossil fuel combustion has been the largest source of GHG pollution since the industrial revolution began, and yet this regional regulatory initiative will only be *re-*

---

23. U.S. EPA, California State Motor Vehicle Pollution Control Standards, Notice of Decision Denying a Waiver of Clean Air Act Preemption for California's 2009 and Subsequent Model Year Greenhouse Gas Emission Standards for New Motor Vehicles, 73 Fed. Reg., No. 45 (March 6, 2008); William W. Buzbee, *Let California Experiment*, Op-ed column in ATLANTA JOURNAL-CONSTITUTION (Dec. 28, 2007, downloaded from http://AJC.com on 01/07/2008); *E.P.A. Says 17 States Can't Set Emission Rules*, NY TIMES ON-LINE (Dec. 20, 2007).

24. Associated Press, *Senate Approves New Fuel-Economy Standards—Bill Requires Average 35 Miles Per Gallon over the Next 13 Years* (Dec. 13, 2007, downloaded from http://MSNBC.com on 12/15/2007).

25. *Id.*

26. *Maryland Joins Pact: Montgomery Plan Announced*, WASHINGTON POST ON-LINE (April 21, 2007).

27. *Id.*

ducing the increases of GHGs discharged into the atmosphere by a very minimal if not trivial amount.

The only arguable benefit of emissions-reduction programs that "reduce the increases" in GHG levels in the atmosphere is that climate changes would eventually become even worse if we do absolutely nothing to curtail them. However, a lesser "bad" does not make a "good" or a good climate policy. All "reducing the increases" emissions-reduction programs cannot serve as climate change solutions because every year, year after year, they will continue contributing to higher atmospheric GHG concentrations and worse greenhouse effects. The "reducing the increases" emissions-reduction programs—the great majority of present and proposed climate change mitigation efforts—cannot even keep us *where we are now* in terms of their greenhouse effects, to say nothing of their inability to reduce future damages. The Frame One climate-policy mistake is occurring because politicians and climate experts are focused on reducing existing business-as-usual emissions, and they have not been considering the residual pollution impacts of emissions-reduction programs that constantly increase the atmospheric GHG concentration.

When the 1990 emissions-level target was chosen under the Kyoto Protocol, many people thought it was too little too late, but other climate-policy experts believed the Kyoto emissions-reduction plan was the best agreement the developed nations would accept and it could become a platform for further GHG reductions in the future.[28] However, the Kyoto Protocol negotiators were influenced by the Frame One unintentional distortion and did not acknowledge or probably understand that compliance with the treaty's emissions targets would substantially worsen, not improve, GHG levels in the atmosphere. Meeting the Kyoto target at best would only *reduce the increases* in business-as-usual emissions from the participating nations by a little. In 1990, all of the major developed countries were discharging large quantities of GHGs into the atmosphere, constantly making global warming worse, and they are still pumping large amounts of persistent GHGs into the air every year.[29] If the Kyoto Protocol target had been attained by *reducing the increases* in GHG annual emissions to five percent below 1990 levels, the member-states would still have continued discharging *additional* GHGs into the atmosphere every year equal to 95 percent of the allowable 1990 emissions, thus increasing rather than decreasing atmospheric GHG levels. The only "reduction" would come from slowing the annual *increases* in business-as-usual GHG pollution and GHG levels in the air by a very small proportion.

The same inadequacy applies to a European Union plan for "reducing" GHG discharges to between 25 and 40 percent below 1990 levels by 2020.[30] If this plan is successful in the sense that all E.U. nations meet their pollution control targets, these nations would still be putting out at least 60 percent to 75 percent as much business-as-usual GHGs as in 1990. The E.U. nations would

---

28. *See* Tim Stephens, *Kyoto is Dead, Long Live Kyoto! A New Era for International Climate Change Law*, Univ. of Sydney Legal Studies Research Paper 08/45 (April 2008, downloaded from www.ssrn.com on 04/30/2008); John Browne, *Beyond Kyoto*, NY Times On-line (August 2, 2004, condensed from July/August 2004 issue of Foreign Aff., downloaded from www.nytimes.com on 08/10/2004); Richard N. Cooper, *The Kyoto Protocol: A Flawed Concept*, research paper for Fondazione Eni Enrico Mattei (2001, downloaded from www.ssrn.com on 09/28/2001).

29. *See, e.g.,* CO_2 and Energy: France & Worldwide, 2007 Edition (French Ministries of Ecology and Economy, 2007); Lauren Sorkin, *Climate Change Impacts Rise, in* Vital Signs 42–43, 133–34 (Worldwatch Inst., 2006–2007).

30. *See* Nicholas Stern, Key Elements Of A Global Deal On Climate Change (May 2008); M.G.J. den Elzen, P.L. Lucas & A. Gijsen, Exploring European Countries' Emission Reduction Targets, Abatement Costs and Measures Needed Under the 2007 EU Reduction Objectives, MNP Report 500114009/2007 (2007); European Energy: A Plan to Cut Hot Air, Economist.com (Jan. 23, 2008, downloaded from economist.com on 01/24/2008). This 20 percent reduction target conforms to recommendations in the 2007 report of IPCC Working Group 3.

still be discharging high volumes of persistent GHGs each year that can only increase, not decrease, atmospheric GHG concentrations. In response to recent scientific findings about the severity of global warming risks and trends, the E.U. has apparently now modified its plan to focus on the target of reducing GHG pollution 60 to 80 percent by mid-century when compared to discharges in 2000.[31] This more stringent emissions-reduction target would nonetheless allow substantial residual GHG discharges to continue, which in turn would increase the atmospheric levels of persistent GHGs. The well-meaning E.U. nations cannot legitimately claim that their emissions-reduction programs will help decrease global warming in any meaningful way because meeting their targets for percentage reductions will constantly *increase* the volume of GHGs in the air. *Reducing the increases* in GHG emissions each year, while allowing significant annual increases in the atmospheric GHG concentration, cannot possibly curtail the greenhouse effect and global warming.

In July of 2008, the leaders of the G8 developed nations agreed to cut GHG emissions 50 percent by 2050,[32] without being precise about any intermediate pollution control targets. This is a perfect example of "reducing the increases" motivated by the Frame One fallacy that any reductions in business-as-usual GHG emissions will have corresponding benefits for improving global warming and climate change. Assuming that the G8 countries do meet the 50 percent reduction target by 2050, which is doubtful based on past regulatory history, they will still be discharging the remaining 50 percent of persistent GHGs into the atmosphere every year and increasing the annual GHG concentrations. In the 40 years before the G8 nations hypothetically meet their 50 percent emissions-reduction target, they will be discharging even larger residual GHG emissions into the air. This agreement reflects Frame One at its worst: How could anyone believe this international initiative will help overcome global warming when it authorizes billions of tons of persistent GHGs to be discharged into the air every year for four decades and beyond? The only dubious virtue of this emissions-reduction program is that it may help prevent even worse climate conditions if there were no GHG pollution control at all. But this emissions-reduction agreement is not a long-term climate change solution or the beginning of a solution.

The U.N. Clean Development Mechanism allows affluent nations to claim that they are reducing net GHG emissions by paying developing countries to eliminate a designated amount of pollution that would otherwise be discharged by sources in the beneficiary nations. A full evaluation of the CDM process and related practices is outside the scope of this Chapter,[33] but I can illustrate the effects on atmospheric GHG concentrations by copying diagrams from a CDM manual published by Japan's Ministry of the Environment.[34]

---

31. *Carbon Output Must Near Zero To Avert Danger, New Studies Say*, Washington Post A01 (March 10, 2008, downloaded from http://washingtonpost.com on 04/10/2008); *see also* Nicholas Stern, *supra*, note 30.

32. *After Applause Dies Down, Global Warming Talks Leave Few Concrete Goals*, NY Times On-line (July 10, 2008); *G-8 Leaders Pledge to Cut Emissions in Half by 2050*, NY Times On-line (July 9, 2008).

33. *See, e.g.*, Christina Voigt, *Is the Clean Development Mechanism Sustainable? Some Critical Aspects*, 7 Sustainable Dev. L. & Policy, No. 2, 15–21 (Winter 2008); Joyeeta Gupta *et al.*, An Evaluation of the Contribution of the Clean Development Mechanism to Sustainable Development in Host Countries, Report to the Policy and Operations Evaluation Dept. of the Netherlands (IOB), No. 310 (April 2008); Michael Wara, *Measuring the Clean Development Mechanism's Performance and Potential*, Stanford Program on Energy & Sust. Dev. Working Paper No. 56 (2006); M. Germain, A. Magnus & V. van Steenberghe, *Should Developing Countries Participate in the Clean Development Mechanism under the Kyoto Protocol? The Low-Hanging Fruits and Baseline Issues*, Research Paper for the Belgian Federal Science Policy Office (December 22, 2004).

34. CDM/JI Manual for Project Developers and Policy Makers, Japan Ministry of the Environment, Figure 1-1 at 2 (2007).

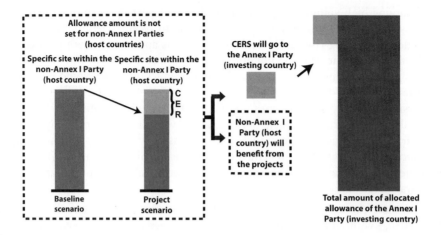

Figure 2.

In the left panel, GHG emissions from the "Baseline scenario" or business-as-planned project design will be reduced in the "Project scenario" in response to payments or technology transfers from an investor nation, leading to the designation of "Certified Emissions Reductions" (CERs) equal to the "reductions" reflected in the Project scenario's lower GHG emissions. The right panel shows that the CERs credited to the developed sponsor state will allow that nation to claim a comparable reduction against the annual GHG emissions-reduction target it is committed to meet under the Kyoto Protocol. Because the CDM project takes place in a developing country that has no national GHG emissions cap or other limits under the Kyoto treaty, the beneficiary nation may accept payments for "reducing the increases" from this project's GHG emissions while building dozens of coal-burning power plants further down the road or river. This is more than conjecture because China, for example, in 2008 "approved 51 more projects under the clean development mechanism (CDM) with the capacity to generate 7.7 million UN-regulated carbon credits per year …"[35] although China is currently building more coal-burning power plants at a more rapid rate than any other developing or developed country.[36]

The CDM process indisputably is a "reducing the increases" initiative: Reduced GHG discharges from the Project scenario still leave a large volume of residual GHG emissions that will increase atmospheric GHG concentrations. Look at the dark area of the Project scenario column in the table's left panel—that area represents persistent GHG discharges that will be pumped into the atmosphere every year by this prototypical project. In essence, the CDM process allows wealthy nations to avoid cutting their own emissions by paying developing countries to construct new GHG-polluting projects, and then they must "reduce" some of the increased emissions to yield a comparable amount of CER offset credits. The net result would normally be an overall increase in cumulative GHG discharges rather than any actual reduction.

The only rationale for why the CDM process may lead to claimed emissions reductions is that the developing countries might construct business-as-planned polluting Baseline scenario projects anyway, with no GHG reductions unless CDM payments persuade them to "reduce the in-

---

35. *China Approves 51 CDM Projects in Latest Update*, Carbon Market News Service (July 10, 2008); *see also Outsized Profits, and Questions, in Effort to Cut Warming Gases*, NY Times On-line (Dec. 6, 2006).

36. Worldwatch Inst., *Coal Use Rises Dramatically Despite Impacts on Climate and Health*, Vital Signs On-line (2007, downloaded from www.worldwatch.org on 11/30/2007); *see generally* Michael P. Vandenbergh, *Climate Change: The China Problem*, 81 S. Cal. L. Rev. 905 (2007–2008).

creases" resulting from these projects. CDM consulting companies are now swarming through more than a hundred developing nations to assist the beneficiary states in qualifying for various CDM projects and payments, while giving the consultants a hefty commission and allowing the developed investor nations to claim they are "offsetting" their GHG discharges. Everybody wins from CDM initiatives: everybody except global climate change victims, who will suffer from the greater greenhouse effects of higher atmospheric GHG concentrations.

As an extreme illustration, Norway recently announced that it will become the first "carbon-neutral" nation by 2030, which means its CO_2 generation will be counterbalanced by the CO_2 emissions it has eliminated.[37] However, the reductions would come primarily from Norwegian purchases of GHG offset credits issued under the CDM plan and other international programs,[38] and these offsets will mostly entail paying for "reducing the increases" projects in developing nations. Norway does not plan to make substantial cuts in its own CO_2 emissions and, in a minor irony, its CERs or offset credit purchases will be financed by revenues derived from its North Sea oil production.[39] What is happening to Norway's on-going GHG emissions? They are consistently increasing the atmospheric GHG concentration despite the CDM offsets.

The CDM conception is a generous way to pay for international development assistance and to redistribute wealth from developed nations to less affluent countries. But the asserted global warming benefits arise from many duplicitous Frame One claims about "reducing" GHG emissions that may never have been generated in the first place without the availability of CDM subsidies. Under the CDM system, the project sponsors always have an incentive to exaggerate Baseline scenario pollution levels in order to expand the potential pollution reductions and CERs resulting from foreign CDM investments. At the same time, the project creators always have incentives to overstate the CERs that can be gained because this will offset more of the actual GHG pollution in the sponsor nations. For example, one assessment of CO_2 tax proposals noted that "in the case of Norway, emissions have actually increased by 43 percent per capita."[40] Yet Norway claims it is on the road to carbon neutrality. Even when the CDM process represents a sincere attempt to reduce climate change harms, rather than mainly paying developing nations to help wealthy states avoid cutting their GHG pollution, the CDM initiative and similar north-south redistributive efforts are normally promoting "reducing the increases" projects that cannot help diminish or stabilize atmospheric GHG concentrations.

The CDM project sponsor must show that additional GHG emissions will be reduced in comparison to the initial Baseline project—otherwise the investor nation would simply be paying for an international development project without getting any GHG pollution reduction benefits. To explain this concept of *additionality*, the Japanese CDM Manual included U.N. guidelines providing that a "CDM project activity is additional if anthropogenic emissions of greenhouse gases by sources are reduced below those that would have occurred in the absence of the registered CDM project activity."[41] This definition is reflected in the following table:

---

37. *Lofty Pledge to Cut Emissions Comes With Caveat in Norway*, NY Times On-line (March 22, 2008).

38. *Id.*

39. *Id.*; Andrew C. Revkin, *DOT EARTH: Norway's Green Plans—and Carbon Reality*, NY Times On-line Blog (March 22, 2008).

40. Monica Prasad, *On Carbon, Tax and Don't Spend*, Op-Ed column, NY Times On-line (March 25, 2008).

41. CDM/JI Manual, *supra* note 34, Figure 1–2 at 3; *see* Emily Boyd *et al.*, *The Clean Development Mechanism: An Assessment of Current Practice and Future Approaches for Policy*, The Tyndall Centre for Climate Change Research Working Paper No. 114, at 4 (October 2007).

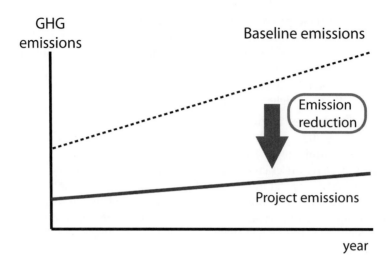

Figure 3.

The "Emission reduction" area in Figure 3, showing *additionality* that allows this project to qualify for CDM assistance and its sponsors to obtain CERs, corresponds precisely to my "reducing the increases" diagram in Figure 1. The Baseline design here would discharge a relatively large amount of GHGs. After the projected CDM "Emission reduction," the project would still discharge significant residual "Project emissions" into the atmosphere. The asserted "reductions" would only occur in comparison with the unregulated Baseline scenario pollution, and in practice the residual Project emissions would increase the annual GHG concentration in the atmosphere. This hypothetical CDM project—as is true for most actual CDM projects—will only be "reducing the increases" in residual GHG emissions and will typically exacerbate global climate change problems, not help to resolve them.

Cap-and-trade pollution credits (or allowances or shares) programs are the preferred approach of many economists, businesses, and politicians who advocate flexible market-based pollution control strategies.[42] Although somewhat different cap-and-trade models are advocated by various economists and politicians,[43] this widely-held but not universal preference among climate experts presumes that there is one "most efficient" pollution control instrument no matter how deep (or shallow) the GHG pollution cuts must be. I question this one-size-fits-all treatment and contend that the most effective method for achieving a 50 percent GHG reduction is not necessarily the same method that will be best for achieving an 80 or 90 percent GHG reduction.

A cap-and-trade program cannot set the GHG cap close to zero emissions, or the claimed innovation and flexible trading benefits of economic incentive mechanisms would be unlikely to

---

42. *See, e.g.,* U.S. EPA, CAP-AND-TRADE ESSENTIALS (downloaded from www.epa.gov/airmarkets on July 6, 2008); Robert Stavins, *Addressing Climate Change with a Comprehensive U.S. Cap-and-Trade System*, Faculty Research Working Paper RWP07-053 (Nov. 2007); *Sizing Up the Utilities, if Carbon Caps Take Hold*, NY TIMES ON-LINE (April 13, 2008); *but see* Zhongxiang Zhang, *Why has China Not Embraced a Global Cap-and-Trade Regime?*, 7 CLIM. POLICY, No. 2, 166–70 (2007); *Robert Baldwin, Regulation Lite: The Rise of Emissions Trading*, London School of Economics Working Papers 3/2008 (downloaded from http://ssrn.com/ on 06/06/2008); *The $100 Billion Windfall: Why Utilities Love Cap-and-Trade*, WALL STREET J. BLOG (downloaded from http://www.wsj.com on 04/07/2008).

43. *See* Sergey Paltsev *et al.*, *Assessment of U.S. Cap-and-Trade Proposals*, National Bureau of Economic Research Working Paper 13176 (June 2007).

materialize.[44] The incentive for firms to participate in a cap-and-trade program arises from their ability to choose whether to purchase additional pollution credits or to develop cheaper pollution control methods that would allow the firms to become profitable sellers of their pollution credits. It is hard to see what business gains would stem from this market system tool if the cap is set near zero and all firms will have to come very close to phasing out all of their GHG pollution. How much will any given business invest in innovation to create more efficient GHG pollution controls when there will be little permissible pollution—a very low cap—and a limited market with few tradable pollution credits? I have not found a single thoughtful analysis of the benefits of cap-and-trade systems under conditions in which the regulatory cap must be set at a very stringent level, and yet the need for drastic GHG reductions verging on total elimination is increasingly accepted by many climate scientists.[45]

If the cap is set at roughly a 50 percent "reduction" level, as it was for the Clean Air Act's acid rain precursor program, this means the GHG polluters will possess a legal right in the form of tradable emissions-reduction credits to discharge the remaining 50 percent of business-as-usual GHG pollution into the air each year. Under this approach, polluting firms are allowed to discharge substantial residual GHGs into the atmosphere annually based on the number of GHG pollution credits or allowances they own, which would lead to another ineffectual "reducing the increases" outcome from the perspective of combating global warming.

Cap-and-trade programs are faced with a dilemma: If the GHG cap is set near zero emissions, there will be few business incentives to promote pollution control innovation and flexibility, which are the reputed market system benefits of cap-and-trade systems; but if the cap is set substantially above zero emissions, the program will become a "reducing the increases" mechanism that would allow continuous residual discharges leading to higher atmospheric GHG concentrations. We could design a cap-and-trade program in which the credits or shares shrink by a specified percentage each year to reduce the allowable amount of GHG discharges over the life of the program. Yet, the faster and further the GHG pollution cap decreases, the less incentive there will be for dischargers to participate in the economic incentives program. And the slower the cap decreases, the more residual GHGs will be lawfully discharged into the atmosphere, compounding the greenhouse effect. It is important to stress that a 50 percent cap established for a GHG cap-and-trade program, precisely the same as a 50 percent direct regulation cutback, will authorize the discharge of large residual quantities of persistent GHGs that will increase rather than reduce atmospheric GHG levels each year.

The sad thing is that the diplomats, politicians, environmental lawyers, economists, and other climate experts devoting their efforts to creating "reducing the increases" pollution control programs sincerely believe that they have been helping to overcome global warming and climate change—the Frame One unintentional distortion—when they are actually *authorizing substantial annual increases* in persistent GHG levels and greenhouse effects. From the perspective of climate science, any program that allows significant annual increases in the atmospheric GHG concentration cannot be reducing global warming. Unfortunately, all of the familiar GHG emissions-reduction models summarized above, and every conventional GHG pollution control program similar to those above, are creating the Frame One illusion of progress while they are actually aggravating the climate change problems we are now experiencing. Global climate change harms undoubtedly will get worse every year if we continue to rely on "reducing the increases" emissions-reduction programs.

---

44. For critiques arguing that cap-and-trade mechanisms are not as effective at eliciting technological innovation as the alternative of direct regulation, *see* David M. Driesen, *Does Emissions Trading Encourage Innovation?*, 33 ELR 10094-108 (Jan. 2003); David M. Driesen, *Free Lunch or Cheap Fix?: The Emissions Trading Idea and the Climate Change Convention*, 26 B.C. ENVTL. AFFAIRS L. REV. 1–87 (1998).

45. *See* text accompanying notes 49–68, *infra*.

When President Bush in April 2008 announced his lame-duck goal of reducing the growth in U.S. GHG emissions 18 percent by 2012 and stopping the emissions growth by 2025,[46] a columnist for the New York Times, Gail Collins, cleverly observed that if President Bush had adopted an equivalent "reducing the growth rate" approach to his body weight when he first took office, he would weigh 332 pounds in 2008, 400 pounds in 2012, and 486 pounds in 2025 when further American GHG pollution growth is supposed to cease.[47] This satirical image of the "fat Bush"[48] becoming progressively more corpulent while "reducing" his obesity growth rate is essentially the same as the "reducing the increases" Frame Two vision I have been describing, except Ms. Collins did not mention that this counter-productive practice applies to almost all climate change programs now advocated by climate policymakers and environmental groups.

When faced with potentially catastrophic human and environmental harms from global climate change, *reducing the increases* of GHG discharges into the atmosphere in comparison with business-as-usual pollution discharges is clearly not good enough. Adopting ineffectual emissions-reduction measures on the rationales that they are "better than nothing" or "conditions would be even worse without them" is a losing approach regardless of the "feel good" satisfactions that some people may get from being part of the supposed solution. Most present climate change programs are *actually harmful* because they authorize or allow large amounts of residual GHGs to be discharged into the atmosphere in return for limited reductions in the amount of business-as-usual pollution. Invalid Frame One praise for conventional emissions-reduction programs cannot show that they are confronting climate change in any meaningful way or are creating the conditions needed for future reductions in climate change risks.

Many climate experts who accept Frame One conceptions have difficulty grasping this vital point: A constellation of emissions-reduction efforts may cut business-as-usual pollution to an appreciable degree while continuing to discharge large amounts of residual pollution that increase the atmospheric GHG concentration. Contrary to Frame One, these cuts will not help curtail global warming and climate change. Rather, these "reducing the increases" emissions-reduction programs are a climate change disaster, not a solution. The atmospheric GHG level, not the business-as-usual pollution level, is the central factor in causing the greenhouse effect and resulting climate change. This is basic climate science, and no human rationalizations can alter the equation. The atmospheric GHG concentration determines the extent of the greenhouse effect, which makes it hard to imagine how the world's nations could continue to discharge billions of tons of persistent GHGs into the air every year without compounding global warming harms. Unarguably, they cannot! If the atmospheric GHG concentration keeps growing, the greenhouse effect, global warming, and climate change harms will also keep growing—not necessarily at a linear rate. This is the inescapable reality in which the merits of GHG emissions-reduction programs and of GHG-free technology-replacement strategies must be compared.

Frame Three: Drastic Reductions to Avoid Climate Tipping Points

Many scientists have recently warned that the harmful consequences of global warming may not be proportional to the increasing volume of GHG emissions, and instead may occur sooner with more severe damages than has been predicted. These climate experts are concerned that a further increase in global temperatures of more than one degree Centigrade beyond current average temperatures or two degrees Centigrade above pre-Industrial Revolution levels may lead to passing global warming "tipping points" that will create irrevocable disastrous consequences.

---

46. *Bush Sets Greenhouse Gas Emissions Goal*, NY Times On-line (April 17, 2008).
47. Gail Collins, *The Fat Bush Theory*, Op-Ed Column, NY Times On-line (April 19, 2008).
48. *Id.*

The most commonly-cited tipping point involves the rapid melting of the western Antarctica and Greenland ice sheets, which would cause major sea level rises, shifts in regional weather patterns, and other harmful results.[49] Another tipping point involves the rate of species extinctions arising from the limited capacities of many species to adapt to rapid changes in climatic conditions.[50] A third tipping point involves the rapid melting of glaciers and mountain snow packs that provide the primary fresh water supplies for hundreds of millions of people.[51] From the Ganges to the Colorado, historical river flows will diminish because the snow and ice that constitute mountain reservoirs have been vanishing. A fourth potential discontinuity is cited by the author of a book about tipping points who describes "an email out of the blue from a Siberian scientist alerting me to drastic environmental change in Siberia that could release billions of tons of greenhouse gases from the melting permafrost in the world's biggest bog."[52] Another book emphasized climate tipping points that could catastrophically affect worldwide agricultural production and freshwater scarcity.[53] A marine scientist in Oregon reported that the "severe low-oxygen events" off the Pacific Northwest coast during the past few years indicate "[i]n this part of the marine environment, we may have crossed a tipping point."[54] The list of potential tipping points keeps growing as scientists discover rapid environmental transformations in the historical record and unexpectedly fast changes in current environmental conditions.

The central concern about tipping points is not only that severe harms will occur — which applies to more frequent hurricanes, tornados, wildfires, droughts, ocean acidification, and other climate change hazards — but that a relatively small increase in average global temperatures could unleash a series of irreversible climate-related catastrophes that we must do everything possible to prevent while we still can. Scientists and environmental groups concerned by the proximity of rapid climate changes are calling for developed nations to take immediate draconian actions that would sharply reduce GHG emission levels to avoid passing climate tipping points.[55] Dr. James Hansen, the NASA scientist who courageously resisted attempts of the Bush Administration to muzzle his statements, is the most widely-known advocate of the need for

---

49. *See* Mark Serreze, Scott B. Luthcke & Konrad Steffen, *Arctic Sea Ice Melt and Shrinking Polar Ice Sheets: Are Observed Changes Exceeding Expectations?*, Presentation for the American Meteorological Society (Nov. 26, 2007); Andrea Thompson, *Ice Shelf on Verge of Collapse: Latest Sign of Global Warming's Impact Shocks Scientists*, MSNBC LiveScience Blog (March 25, 2008, downloaded from http://MSNBC.com on 03/31/2008); *No Place to Hide*, NY Times On-line Editorial (Jan. 20, 2008); *Arctic Melt Unnerves Experts*, NY Times On-line (Oct. 2, 2007).

50. *See* Peter D. Ward, Under a Green Sky (Collins 2007); Luiz Eduardo O. C. Aragao *et al.*, *Interactions Between Rainfall, Deforestation and Fires During Recent Years in the Brazilian Amazonia*, 363 Phil. Trans. R. Soc. B (2008) 1779–1785 (Feb. 11, 2008); *IUCN Red List 2008 for birds: Climate change and continental drift*, IUCN News Press Release (May 19, 2008); *The Preservation Predicament*, NY Times On-line (Jan. 29, 2008).

51. *See* J.A. Marengo *et al.*, *Hydro-Climatic and Ecological Behaviour of the Drought of Amazonia in 2005*, 363 Phil. Trans. R. Soc. B 1773–1778 (Feb. 12, 2008); Pradeep Kurukulasuriya and Robert Mendelsohn, *Endogenous Irrigation: The Impact Of Climate Change On Farmers In Africa*, World Bank Research Paper 4278 (July 2007); *Governor Declares Drought in California and Warns of Rationing*, NY Times On-line (June 5, 2008).

52. Fred Pearce, With Speed and Violence xxiv–xxv (Beacon Press 2007).

53. Lester R. Brown, Plan B: 3.0 (WW Norton Co. 2008).

54. *Ocean Dead-Zones May Be Linked to Global Warming*, Science Daily (Feb. 15, 2008), quoting Professor Jane Lubchenco.

55. *See, e.g.,* George Monbiot, Heat: How to Stop the Planet from Burning (South End Press 2007); Lester R. Brown, *supra* note 53; Fred Pearce, *supra* note 52; *Debate on Climate Shifts to Issue of Irreparable Change: Some Experts on Global Warming Foresee "Tipping Point" When It Is Too Late to Act*, Washington Post A01 (Jan. 29. 2006, downloaded from http://washingtonpost.com on 10/04/2007); Union of Concerned Scientists, Global Warming 101: A Target for U.S. Emissions Reductions (downloaded from www.ucs.org on 02/20/2008).

dramatic GHG reductions to avoid climate tipping points.[56] In recent testimony before Congress, Dr. Hansen observed that passing the tipping points will "set in motion irreversible changes to the detriment of nature and humanity."[57] In another recent public comment, Dr. Hansen emphasized that: "We have at most ten years—not ten years to decide upon action, but ten years to alter fundamentally the trajectory of global greenhouse emissions."[58]

At the Bali conference on global climate change in December 2007, a group of more than 200 scientists issued a joint statement urging government leaders to take radical action to slow global warming because "there is no time to lose."[59] A *Washington Post* article reported that the central scientific "debate has shifted to whether climate change is progressing so rapidly that, within decades, humans may be helpless to slow or reverse the trend."[60] This story continued: "While scientists remain uncertain when such a [tipping] point might occur, many say it is urgent that policymakers cut global carbon dioxide emissions in half over the next 50 years or risk the triggering of changes that would be irreversible."[61] Although the IPCC Synthesis in November 2007 of its Fourth Assessment Report did not identify specific tipping points, it acknowledged the possibility that they may occur: "Anthropogenic warming could lead to some impacts that are abrupt or irreversible, depending upon the rate and magnitude of the climate change."[62]

George Monbiot, the journalist-author of a book on global warming hazards, described a cornucopia of disasters that could occur if average global temperatures increase another couple of degrees, and he claimed that developed nations must reduce GHG emissions 90 percent on average by 2030 to avoid climate tipping points.[63] A well-known environmental forecaster, Lester R. Brown, similarly warned that we must reduce GHG emissions levels at least 80 percent by 2050 to avoid tipping point disasters.[64] The Union of Concerned Scientists (UCS), using "research from climate scientists at Stanford and Texas Tech," publicized another catalog of potential catastrophes from climate tipping points and contended that "the world's industrialized nations will have to reduce their emissions an average of 70 to 80 percent below 2000 levels by 2050" to prevent the destructive effects from global warming.[65] The UCS plan calls for sharp reductions in GHG emissions by all developed nations in the next few decades and also for large reductions by developing nations, which are more problematical.[66]

As scientific knowledge about global warming hazards and climate tipping points has accumulated in recent years, the extent of GHG emissions reductions believed necessary to preserve acceptable climate conditions has become progressively larger in scientific circles. Two separate papers published in 2008 concluded that GHG emissions must be almost entirely eliminated in

---

56. Dr. Hansen has several dozen articles, research papers, presentations, speeches, and other climate change-related materials available on his professional Web Site at http://pubs.giss.nasa.gov/authors/jhansen. html.

57. James Hansen, *How Can We Avert Dangerous Climate Change?* (2007), at 3. Dr. Hansen described this paper, which he has been distributing on his web site, in the following manner: "This paper consists of written testimony that I delivered as a private citizen to the Select Committee on Energy Independence and Global Warming, United States House of Representatives, on 26 April 2007. I have added to that testimony: this abstract, references for several statements in the testimony, and some specificity in the final section on solutions."

58. Jim Hansen, *The Threat to the Planet*, 53 New York Rev. Books, No.12, 13 (July 13, 2006).

59. Associated Press, *Scientists Beg for Climate Action*, NY Times On-line (Dec. 5, 2007).

60. *Debate on Climate Shifts to Issue of Irreparable Change: Some Experts on Global Warming Foresee "Tipping Point" When It Is Too Late to Act*, Washington Post On-line (Jan. 29. 2006, downloaded from washingtonpost.com on 10/04/2007).

61. *Id.*

62. IPCC Synthesis, *supra* note 6, at 13.

63. George Monbiot, *supra* note 55, at 5–17.

64. Lester R. Brown, *supra* note 53, at 64–67.

65. Union of Concerned Scientists, *Scientists Weigh In at Climate Negotiations in Bali*, email from UCS to author, from ssi@ucsusa.org (Dec. 11, 2007).

66. *Id.*

the next few decades to keep average global temperatures and atmospheric GHG concentrations only a little above the present level.[67] These papers reflect climate research finding that GHGs are significantly more persistent than previously conceived and that additional GHG emissions could remain in the atmosphere for thousands of years while compounding the greenhouse effect.[68]

Assuming the scientific validity of these catastrophic global warming predictions, which appear to be supported by recent climate-history studies, I nonetheless believe Frame Three—*immediate drastic GHG reductions to avoid climate tipping points*—is deceptive and dangerous from a policy perspective because it is constructed on the quicksand of wishful thinking. The fact that we urgently *need* to do something to avoid human and environmental harms in no way demonstrates that we can or will achieve this difficult objective in practice. As another NASA climate scientist noted: "People aren't reducing emissions at all, let alone debating whether 88 percent or 99 percent is sufficient."[69] A representative of an environmental group similarly complained: "The current debate over global warming policy tends to focus on long-term goals, like how to reduce greenhouse gas emissions by 80 percent over the next 50 years [but] while we debate, carbon dioxide emissions from power plants keep rising, making an already dire situation worse."[70]

I can see no politically palatable and economically feasible way in which sufficiently stringent GHG emissions reductions could be implemented within a timeframe that would enable the world's nations to avoid passing the projected climate tipping points. It is probably already too late to prevent irreversible consequences by employing any socially acceptable, economically practicable, and technically feasible precautionary means; and the idealistic claim that we can all work miracles together to prevent climate tipping point disasters would require precisely that ... genuine miracles.

Not one major polluting nation is now on the path towards implementing the required draconian GHG emissions reductions. Most large nations with growing economies, including the U.S. and China, are expected to increase their conventional energy production and GHG emissions in the next decade.[71] Not one highly-populated developing country has agreed to establish firm numerical targets for reducing GHG emissions. There is no reason to believe that most citizens of affluent countries would be willing to accept substantial restrictions on their lifestyles to avoid the possibility of climate tipping points, and it is even less likely that the governments and people of developing countries would give up their intense pursuit of more economic and social development. Unless we can actually avoid passing climate tipping points through the adoption

---

67. *Carbon Output Must Near Zero To Avert Danger, New Studies Say*, WASHINGTON POST ON-LINE (March 10, 2008, downloaded from http://washingtonpost.com on 04/10/2008), *citing* H.D. Matthews & K. Caldeira, *Stabilizing climate requires near-zero emissions*, GEOPHYSICAL RESEARCH LETTERS (in press, published on-line on Feb. 14, 2008); Andreas Schmittner *et al.*, *Future changes in climate, ocean circulation, ecosystems, and biogeochemical cycling simulated for a business-as-usual CO_2 emission scenario until year 4000 AD*, 22 GLOBAL BIOGEOCHEM. CYCLES (14 February 2008).

68. *Carbon Output Must Near Zero To Avert Danger, New Studies Say*, WASHINGTON POST ON-LINE (March 10, 2008, downloaded from http://washingtonpost.com on 04/10/2008).

69. *Id.*

70. TIEMPO CLIMATE NEWSWATCH, quoting Eric Schaeffer of the Environmental Integrity Project (March 30, 2008).

71. *See, e.g.*, J. Canadell *et al.*, *Contributions to Accelerating Atmospheric CO_2 Growth from Economic Activity, Carbon Intensity, and Efficiency of Natural Sinks*, PROC. NATL. ACAD. SCI. (Early Edition Approved Sept. 17, 2007, downloaded from www.pnas.org on 11/14/2007); F. Gerard Adams and Yochanan Shachmurove, *Projections of Chinese Energy Demands in 2020*, Penn Institute for Economic Research Working Paper 07-012 (2007); Worldwatch Inst., *Coal Use Rises Dramatically Despite Impacts on Climate and Health*, VITAL SIGNS ON-LINE (2007), downloaded from www.worldwatch.org on 11/30/2007; *U.S. Predicting Steady Increase for Emissions*, NY TIMES ON-LINE (March 3, 2007); *Pollution from Chinese Coal Casts a Global Shadow*, NY TIMES ON-LINE (June 11, 2006).

of politically and economically acceptable GHG emissions-reduction measures, which appears very doubtful if not impossible, the adage "haste makes waste" is likely to apply to emergency emissions-reduction measures advocated by climate scientists and environmentalists who want every nation and person to make drastic behavioral changes in order to avoid drastic climate changes.

There are many reasons why emergency programs meant to forestall passing the climate tipping points are unrealistic and very likely to fail. The United States has more than 200 million GHG-discharging vehicles and nearly 100 million energy-inefficient homes as well as millions of other buildings that were not constructed with GHG pollution control in mind. These investments cannot be abandoned overnight or replaced in one decade. Our suburban sprawl and coastal-strip development practices are not conducive to emergency improvements in energy distribution and land use patterns. American corporations have invested hundreds of billions of dollars in coal-burning power plants and other fossil-fuel combustion facilities that they, and their employees, will not give up without a fierce political struggle. Reducing GHG emissions by a very high percentage would require innumerable changes in our economy and lifestyles, which cannot realistically be implemented in less than several decades unless the American people and their political leaders make overcoming global climate change their highest, if not only, national priority. Yet, recent polls have shown that the U.S. electorate may be concerned about global warming and climate change but generally did not consider these problems among the most pressing issues in the recent Presidential campaign.[72]

The U.S. is the world's largest GHG polluter on a per capita basis and either the largest or second-largest (after China) on an aggregate basis, which means that converting America into a very-low-emissions nation on an emergency timeframe would be difficult, expensive, and controversial.[73] Any rapid emissions-reduction programs would probably require reliance on improving already-available technologies and adopting variants of widely-accepted practices that may not be adequate to meet the draconian GHG emissions-reduction challenge.

Another important impediment is the unwillingness of many American people to make major sacrifices in their lifestyles in order to reduce their share of global GHG emissions. For every hybrid vehicle purchaser, there are people who prefer more powerful, less fuel-efficient cars.[74] For every green consumer who leaves an automobile behind and begins commuting by bicycle, there are many people who choose to own second cars and some who would be happy to own a Lamborghini[75] or giant SUV. Millions of Americans have bought second homes and paid for expensive vacations to far-away places, reflecting their personal priorities regardless of the negative effects on GHG emissions. The exceptionally high price of gasoline and falling housing prices this year may temporarily reduce consumer demand for long-distance driving or distant vacation homes, but there is no reason to believe that most American consumers would give up

---

72. *Why Bother*, NY TIMES (April 20, 2008); Charles Blow, *All Atmospherics, No Climate*, Op-Ed column, NY TIMES (April 19, 2008) (indicating that less than 2/3ds of Americans considered the environment a crucial issue during the Gore Presidential Campaign, and the percentage has dropped to under 60 percent despite global warming concerns); *Global Warming and Your Wallet*, NY TIMES ON-LINE (July 6, 2007); *Growing Number of Americans See Warming as Leading Threat: Most Want U.S. to Act, But There Is No Consensus on How*, WASHINGTON POST ON-LINE (April 20, 2007).

73. *See* EIP Report: *U.S. Power Plant Carbon Dioxide Emissions Rose 3 Percent In 2007, Biggest One-Year Jump In Nearly A Decade*, Environmental Integrity Project Press Release (March 18, 2008).

74. *Detroit Auto Show: An Unconvincing Shade of Green*, NY TIMES ON-LINE (Jan. 20, 2008); *One Billion Cars: It Won't Be Long Before the World Hits that Number. Here's What It Means for the Consumer, the Industry—and the Planet*, WALL STREET JOURNAL R1 (April 17, 2006, downloaded from http://wsj.com on 02/27/2008).

75. *Around the Block: 2008 Lamborghini Gallardo Superleggera—Trim and Ready to Rumble*, NY TIMES ON-LINE (Feb. 3, 2008).

these amenities in the future if they can afford them, or that recent purchasing patterns reflect a strong global warming consciousness on the part of most American consumers. The NEW YORK TIMES recently published an unintentionally amusing story about a concerned "eco-mom" who made numerous "green" improvements to her home and homemaking purchases while she continued driving the SUV parked in her driveway.[76] Undoubtedly, there has been a groundswell of public concern about global climate change[77] with many voluntary behavioral changes ranging from minimal to radical, but that is altogether different from nearly universal consumer commitments to accept major lifestyle sacrifices required as a means to help avoid the unseen perils of climate tipping points.

The Union of Concerned Scientists' emissions-reduction proposal contends that: "If we assume the world's developing nations pursue the most aggressive reductions that can reasonably be expected of them, the developed nations will have to reduce their GHG emissions an average of 70 to 80 percent below 2000 levels by 2050."[78] This idealistic assumption is completely implausible: We should expect that most developing nations will refuse to accept *any* significant GHG emissions reductions, as they have done in recent international negotiations, and instead they will continue to increase their national emissions in pursuit of greater economic and social welfare.

Many commentators from poor and affluent nations alike have argued on ethical grounds that developing countries should not be expected to undertake substantial efforts to reduce GHG emissions at the cost of improving the living conditions and welfare opportunities of their people.[79] One common argument is that their nations' historical contributions to GHG levels in the atmosphere were miniscule compared to the vast discharges from developed nations.[80] The per capita GHG pollution discharges from countries with many poor people and rapidly growing GHG emissions, such as China and India, still remain substantially lower than the per capita discharges from most developed nations. As a matter of equity and economics, why should poor countries have to reduce their GHG emissions drastically or even minimally to help people in wealthy nations maintain their profligate lifestyles? Many advocates of assisting economically and socially disadvantaged peoples contend that they should have a right to exploit inexpensive fossil-fuel combustion technologies to attain greater development, just as affluent nations have

---

76. *For "EcoMoms," Saving Earth Begins at Home*, NY TIMES ON-LINE (Feb. 16, 2008).

77. *See* Ariel Malka, Jon A. Krosnick & Gary Langer, *The Association of Knowledge With Concern about Global Warming: Trusted Information Sources Shape Public Thinking*, Stanford University Research Paper (June 2008); Jon A. Krosnick et al., *The Origins and Consequences of Democratic Citizens' Policy Agendas: A Study Of Popular Concern about Global Warming*, CLIMATE CHANGE DOI: 10.1007/s10584-006-9068-8 (2006).

78. UNION OF CONCERNED SCIENTISTS, GLOBAL WARMING 101: A TARGET FOR U.S. EMISSIONS REDUCTIONS (downloaded from www.ucs.org on 02/20/2008).

79. *See* U.N. ECOSOC ECONOMIC COMMISSION FOR AFRICA & AFRICAN UNION COMMISSION, CLIMATE CHANGE: AFRICAN PERSPECTIVES FOR A POST-2012 AGREEMENT (March 5, 2008); *Developing World Must Be Able to Lift Emissions: Nobel winner*, AGENCE FRANCE-PRESSE (Dec. 8, 2007, downloaded from www.afp.com/ english/home/ on 12/09/2007); PAUL BAER, TOM ATHANASIOU & SIVAN KARTHA, THE RIGHT TO DEVELOPMENT IN A CLIMATE CONSTRAINED WORLD: THE GREENHOUSE DEVELOPMENT RIGHTS FRAMEWORK (Nov. 2007); *but see* David Wheeler & Kevin Ummel, *Another Inconvenient Truth: A Carbon-Intensive South Faces Environmental Disaster No Matter What the North Does*, Center for Global Development Working Paper 134 (Dec. 2007).

80. *See* ANCHA SRINIVASAN et al., THE CLIMATE REGIME BEYOND 2012: RECONCILING ASIAN DEVELOPMENTAL PRIORITIES AND GLOBAL CLIMATE INTERESTS, Institute for Global Environmental Strategies (2008); JOHN C. DERNBACH, ENERGY EFFICIENCY AND CONSERVATION AS ETHICAL RESPONSIBILITIES: SUGGESTIONS FOR IPCC WORKING GROUP III (Jan. 27, 2008, downloaded from http://ssrn.com on June 13 (2008); BENITO MÜLLER, NIKLAS HÖHNE & CHRISTIAN ELLERMANN, DIFFERENTIATING (HISTORIC) RESPONSIBILITIES FOR CLIMATE CHANGE, Oxford Inst. for Energy Studies Summary Report (Oct. 2007); Axel Gosseries, *Historical Emissions and Free Riding*, 11 ETHICAL PERSPECTIVES 1, 36 (2004); *Developed Nations Asked to Take Lead in Climate Conservation*, HINDUSTAN TIMES (June 17, 2007).

done for two centuries and are still doing. Recent international laws and United Nations proceedings have recognized the special status of developing states and have accepted their justifications for putting poverty alleviation and social welfare improvements, including better education and health care, above other national priorities.[81] In light of these influential political arguments and social considerations, proponents of emergency GHG reductions by developing countries are not being at all realistic.

The thrust of these comments is that attempts to undertake draconian emissions-reduction programs on an emergency timeframe in response to climate tipping points would be extremely likely, if not certain, to fail abjectly. I do not see how we can reach the required GHG emissions-reduction levels until after we have designed and deployed affordable GHG-free technologies able to avoid many social sacrifices that would otherwise be required. The development of effective GHG-free replacement technologies and clean energy processes probably cannot be achieved without a transition period that is incompatible with adopting emergency timeframes. Implementing an effective transition to a GHG-free technology-replacement strategy will require decades of smart, well-funded efforts—we cannot reliably predict how long this transition might take—but if this transformation is reasonably successful, it would reduce GHG pollution levels and atmospheric GHG concentrations more than any current emissions-reduction programs possibly could, and it would offer technology transfers that would enable developing states to improve their economic and social welfare without discharging ever-increasing amounts of GHGs.

It is conceivable though unlikely that massive GHG emissions reductions could combine with natural or human-made processes to remove more GHGs from the atmosphere than are added in a given year—this hypothetical stringent pollution control would reduce atmospheric GHG levels. However, this reversal of the imbalance between atmospheric GHG increases and decreases is not close to occurring now, and I see no credible political or economic reason to expect that the necessary drastic GHG emissions reductions will occur in the foreseeable future.

Natural removal processes, including plant photosynthesis and ocean absorption of CO_2, have been unable to counterbalance the present atmospheric GHG concentration, and they may become less effective GHG absorbers in the future due to global factors such as widespread deforestation, increased urbanization, and further warming and acidification of marine waters. In short, we cannot count on natural processes to remedy or overcome a much higher level of GHG pollution. It is conceivable that scientists might develop techniques that can directly reduce atmospheric GHG concentrations, including sub-surface CO_2 sequestration[82] ("carbon capture and storage" projects), reforestation,[83] and chemical methods to capture GHGs directly from the

---

81. *See* Benito Müller and Harald Winkler, *One Step Forward, Two Steps Back? The Governance of the World Bank Climate Investment Funds*, Oxford Energy & Environment Comment (Feb. 2008); Ancha Srinivasan, *supra* note 80 (many references to meeting the U.N. Millennium Development Goals despite climate change problems); Piet Buys *et al.*, *Country Stakes in Climate Change Negotiations: Two Dimensions of Vulnerability*, World Bank Policy Research Working Paper 4300 (Aug. 2007); Working Group on Climate and Development, Up in Smoke? (2004), downloaded from the New Economic Foundation, www.nef.org on 07/23/2008).

82. *See, e.g.*, International Petroleum Industry Envtl. Conservation Ass'n, Oil and Natural Gas Industry Guidelines for Greenhouse Gas Reduction Projects (March 2007); Olawuyi Damilola Sunday, Enlisting Carbon Dioxide Capture And Storage As A Clean Development Mechanism Project: Legal And Regulatory Issues Considered (2006); Bert Metz, *et al.*, IPCC Special Report on Carbon Dioxide Capture and Storage (2005); *Running in Circles Over Carbon*, NY Times On-line (June 8, 2008).

83. *See, e.g.*, Katia Karousakis & Jan Corfee-Morlot, Financing Mechanisms To Reduce Emissions From Deforestation: Issues In Design And Implementation (OECD, Dec. 2007); Leo Peskett & Zoe Harkin, *Risk and Responsibility in Reduced Emissions from Deforestation and Degradation* (Overseas Dev. Inst. Forestry Briefing No. 15, Dec. 2007); Michael Dutschke & Reinhard Wolf, Reducing Emissions from Deforestation in Developing Countries: The Way Forward (April 2007).

air.[84] The effectiveness of these technological GHG-removal possibilities remains speculative at this time, with no evidence that they could be implemented fast enough on a worldwide scale to achieve the rapid deep GHG reductions sufficient to avoid the identified climate tipping points.[85]

The Frame Three vision of drastic emergency GHG pollution reductions to avoid tipping points could succeed in decreasing global warming and climate change only if the reductions are politically acceptable, technically practical, and economically feasible on a global scale, which does not seem to be a realistic prospect. Proponents of draconian measures to prevent passing climate change tipping points emphasize the environmental and social consequences of failing to adopt rapid emissions reductions, but I have not seen any discussion of the political, economic, and psychological ramifications if developed nations attempt to attain massive GHG reductions and these emergency emissions-reduction efforts fail miserably, as they probably would. The failure to resolve global warming risks on an emergency basis may erode the willingness of nations, businesses, and people to undertake the difficult, expensive steps required to overcome global warming over a longer but more practical timeframe. A long-term program focus may not be responsive to urgent climate tipping point problems, but neither is wishful thinking that cannot be translated into effective, affordable, politically acceptable mitigation measures.

Attempting to meet a rapid emissions reduction timeframe would limit the available technological choices in many ways that may lead to ineffectual or excessively costly pollution control measures—for example, we might have to rely on hybrid vehicles that will still discharge significant amounts of GHGs instead of switching to all-electric or hydrogen fuel-cell vehicles. Nations have limited financial, technical, and personnel resources available to create successful climate change action programs, and we cannot waste these resources on inadequate, unproven, or impracticable methods that may never yield any tangible global warming benefits. We cannot wait for scientific or economic certainty before launching ambitious programs to combat global climate change problems, but we do need to have a good idea of what we are undertaking before expending billions on speculative programs that may turn out to be more harmful than beneficial. As a pointed example, the world's nations are now proposing to waste many billions of dollars on "reducing the increases" emissions-reduction programs that will never produce any tangible climate change benefits.

Alternative Strategies for Climate Solutions

The main purpose of the following sections is to present information and arguments for preferring a GHG-free technology-replacement strategy to the current emphasis on "reducing the increases" emissions-reduction programs that cannot succeed in overcoming climate change hazards but nevertheless have been praised and promoted by most climate experts. Before we can develop realistic approaches that respond effectively to climate problems, policymakers must understand the objectives and limitations of alternative strategies for attaining better mitigation results. In my opinion, the adoption of technologies that can eliminate GHG emissions in many industrial and consumption contexts, though not all, and the adoption of carbon capture and storage (CCS) or other sequestration technologies that remove GHGs from the air offer more promising approaches than reliance on percentage GHG emissions-reductions programs and consumer behavioral changes that leave substantial residual discharges to compound atmospheric GHG concentrations.

When GHG-free technologies are not available in specific contexts, policymakers will have to choose between investing limited financial and administrative resources in improving emissions-

---

84. *See, e.g.,* S. Pacala & R. Socolow, *Stabilization Wedges: Solving the Climate Problem for the Next 50 Years with Current Technologies*, 305 Science No. 5686, 968–72 (Aug. 13, 2004); *For Carbon Emissions, A Goal of Less Than Zero*, NY Times On-line (March 26, 2008).

85. *See Running in Circles Over Carbon*, NY Times On-line (June 8, 2008); *A "Bold" Step to Capture an Elusive Gas Falters*, NY Times On-line (Feb. 3, 2008).

reduction programs or attempting to devise innovative replacement technologies. These decisions cannot be uniform for all sectors and will depend on the technical and economic characteristics of particular GHG-generating activities. We may never be able to produce GHG-free cow patties, but we can engineer GHG-free cars if we put our minds to it. There is a point of diminishing returns in emissions-reduction investments where the cost of cutting out the next percentage of GHG pollutants (and the next few percent after that) will become prohibitively expensive; and a transition to GHG-free technologies will become more cost-effective in the long run. Whether we will reach this point, or will need to surpass it, depends to a great degree on how much and how soon we need to reduce the level of GHGs in the atmosphere. The greater the extent of GHG reductions that must be achieved to resolve climate change problems, the more appealing the development of GHG-free technologies and processes will be.

Changing Consumer Behaviors

Most large environmental groups and many other climate-change organizations publicize lists of actions that consumers should take to reduce their energy usage and "carbon footprints." WWF advocates purchasing high-fuel-efficiency cars; choosing an electric utility company that uses renewable energy resources; switching to lower-energy fluorescent light bulbs; replacing inefficient household appliances; replacing windows to reduce heating and air conditioning needs; wrapping the water-heater in an "insulating jacket" and using low-flow showerheads to reduce energy and water requirements; insulating building walls and ceilings; and walking, biking, or using mass transit to cut energy consumption.[86] The Nature Conservancy advocates some of these same measures and also asks consumers to use teleconferencing instead of flying; to buy locally grown foods; to inflate vehicle tires to improve mileage per gallon of fuel; to recycle wastes and to use products made from recycled materials; to turn down the heat and air conditioning in homes; and to plant native trees.[87] The Natural Resources Defense Council, in addition to recommending many of the changes above, advocates keeping vehicle engines tuned-up; driving less; "buying 'wind certificates' or 'green tags,' which represent clean power you can add to the nation's energy grid in place of electricity from fossil fuels;" and calculating the "global warming pollution associated with your everyday activities, then buy enough [clean energy] certificates to offset them and become climate neutral."[88] And the Union of Concerned Scientists suggests, among many recommended measures, that Americans should give up using private cars to a large extent and should rely instead on carpooling whenever possible.[89]

This emphasis on utilizing voluntary or mandatory consumer behaviors to reduce GHG pollution stems not only from the direct effects of lower consumption of harmful goods and services,[90] but also from the presumption that businesses will change their production and distribution methods in efforts to evoke positive consumer responses. Some academicians have espoused more extreme reliance on consumption choices to reduce GHG emissions: for example, the Uni-

---

86. *See* www.wwfus.org/climate/ for a discussion of these and other proposed consumer behavior changes.

87. *See* www.nature.org/initiatives/climatechange/activities/art19630.html ("What You Can Do"); www.nature.org/initiatives/climatechange/activities/ & www.nature.org/activities/everydayenv.html.

88. *See* www.nrdc.org/air/energy/genergy.asp & www.nrdc.org/globalWarming/gsteps.asp.

89. *See* www.ucsusa.org/global_warming/solutions/what-you-can-do-about-global-warming.html; Union of Concerned Scientists, 10 Earthwise, No. 2, 1–4 (Spring 2008).

90. *See, e.g.,* Michael P. Vandenbergh & Brooke A. Ackerly, *Climate Change: The Equity Problem*, 26 Va. Envtl. L.J. 55 (2008); Andrew Green, *Self Control, Individual Choice, and Climate Change*, 26 Va. Envtl. L.J. 77 (2008); John C. Dernbach, *Harnessing Individual Behavior to Address Climate Change: Options for Congress*, 26 Va. Envtl. L.J. 107 (2008); Deborah L. Rhode & Lee D. Ross, *Environmental Values and Behaviors: Strategies to Encourage Public Support for Initiatives to Combat Global Warming*, 26 Va. Envtl. L.J. 161 (2008); Albert C. Lin, *Evangelizing Climate Change* (July 21, 2008 draft, downloaded from http://ssrn.com/abstract= 1142919 on 08/20/2008).

versity of Surrey law faculty recently sponsored a conference to advocate shifting the responsibility for reducing GHG emissions from production to consumption activities;[91] and a European scientist suggested that countries should switch from a production-based inventory of GHG sources to a national inventory of consumption-based emissions.[92] Professor John Dernbach has similarly written several articles that discuss various legal approaches that might be employed to require American consumers to reduce the amount of energy they are now using.[93]

For many reasons, I believe we would be making a very serious climate-policy mistake by imposing substantial responsibilities or expectations for overcoming global climate change on billions of consumers worldwide with different capacities and desires. Given the diversity and complexity of climate change issues and the intrinsic cognitive limitations on consumer decisionmaking, it would be a more realistic approach to "fix" GHG-producing technologies and processes than to try to "fix" the consumption choices of a myriad dissimilar people by trying to persuade them to sacrifice important aspects of their lifestyles and chosen behaviors.

It is well-established in the fields of cognitive psychology and behavioral economics that human beings have only limited time, attention spans, and cognitive abilities, which constrain the effectiveness of decisionmaking in innumerable contexts.[94] Each consumer must face hundreds or thousands of choices every day with significant implications for global warming effects. As one consumer is deciding what kind of "eco-conscious" underwear to purchase,[95] another may be examining dozens of ways publicized on the Angie's List web site to make houses "greener."[96] A third consumer may be considering unusually benign snowmobile conditions in Vermont, and weighing the love of outdoors activities against GHG emissions from this pastime.[97] Another consumer might be considering the argument against consuming meat offered by PETA (People for the Ethical Treatment of Animals) derived from a U.N. Food and Agricultural Organization claim "that the livestock business generates more greenhouse gas emissions than all forms of transportation combined."[98] In order to reduce the rapid growth in Japanese energy usage, one government report proposed that Japanese families take shorter baths.[99] A suburban "soccer mom" with green inclinations could be rationalizing her purchase of a GHG-spouting SUV under the mistaken impression that it will safeguard her family better than ordi-

91. Workshop on Production and Consumption at the University of Surrey, Guildford, UK (downloaded workshop announcement on March 21, 2008).

92. *See* Glen P. Peters, From *production-based to consumption-based national emission inventories*, 65 ECOLOGICAL ECON. 13 (March 2008); *see also* Glen P. Peters, *Post-Kyoto greenhouse gas inventories: production versus consumption*, 86 CLIMATE CHANGE, Nos. 1–2, 51–66 (Jan. 2008).

93. *See* John C. Dernbach, *Amending the Lieberman-Warner Climate Security Bill to Harness Individual Behavior*, Widener Law School Research Paper Series No. 08-42 (2008); John C. Dernbach, *supra* note 80; John C. Dernbach, *Stabilizing and Then Reducing U.S. Energy Consumption: Legal and Policy Tools for Efficiency and Conservation*, 37 ELR 10003 (2007); John C. Dernbach, *Overcoming the Behavioral Impetus for Greater U.S. Energy Consumption*, Widener Law School Research Paper Series No. 08-16 (2007).

94. For some of my previous writing on the intersections of law and cognitive psychology, see Howard Latin, *"Good" Warnings, Bad Products, and Cognitive Limitations*, 41 UCLA L. REV. 1193 (1994), *reprinted in* A. BERNSTEIN, ED., A PRODUCTS LIABILITY ANTHOLOGY (1995); Howard Latin, *Behavioral Criticisms of the Restatement (Third) of Torts: Products Liability*, 16 J. PRODUCTS AND TOXICS LIABILITY 209 (1994); Howard A. Latin, *Problem-Solving Behavior and Theories of Tort Liability*, 73 CALIF. L. REV. 677 (1985).

95. Marisa Belger, *Organic, Sustainable, Renewable ... Undies? It May Be Time to Question What Fabrics You Place Near Your Nethers* (March 31, 2008, downloaded from http://MSNBC.com on 03/31/2008).

96. Angie's List, Special Edition: Turning Homes Green (downloaded from http://angieslist.com on 04/04/2008).

97. *Vermont Highways of Snow*, NY TIMES ON-LINE (Feb. 1. 2008).

98. *Trying to Connect the Dinner Plate to Climate Change*, NY TIMES (Aug. 27, 2007).

99. *Japanese Urged to Bathe Faster: Families Asked to Cut a Minute Off, and Speed Up Move from Shower to Tub*, MSNBC NEWS SERVICES (June 3, 2008, downloaded from http://MSNBC.com on 05/05.2008).

nary passenger sedans would.[100] An advertisement near the beginning of a recent issue of *Wildlife Conservation* magazine shows a thriving coral reef ecosystem and lists several coastal regions the Wildlife Conservation Society is helping protect so that people can enjoy "incredible experiences" on Royal Caribbean International cruise ships with smokestacks belching GHGs from fossil fuels.[101]

These are random selections among millions of consumer choices made by people every day, people who cannot possibly evaluate all of the environmental and climate ramifications of their behaviors even if they want to help reduce global climate change. The "green consumer" lists offered by environmental groups on beneficial and harmful consumer choices do not recognize that people can only assess the climate effects of a tiny fraction of the decisions they must make. If millions of consumers thoroughly assess 20 potential products or services per day with regard to their GHG ramifications, which is an unduly optimistic expectation, this commitment would mean that these consumers are not considering the climate impacts of a much larger number of daily choices that might be equally or more important. No one, not even climate experts, can afford to devote the time and attention necessary to assess the global warming effects of the great majority of their personal choices. As a consequence, putting the primary responsibility or substantial responsibility on consumers for limiting GHG discharges would ensure many millions of bad choices by many millions of good people.

When interested consumers do have time available to consider global warming effects, they often would not have the knowledge and expertise necessary to assess vital circumstances or to make complicated tradeoffs. Switching to compact fluorescent light bulbs, for example, is among the most common environmental group recommendations for how consumers can save energy and cut GHG pollution, but most people cannot evaluate these messages on the back of a GE 60-watt CFL package: "Hg—Lamp Contains Mercury" and "Manage in Accord with Disposal Laws." This product warning does not say how much mercury is present in the fluorescent bulb; how harmful the mercury could be, especially in the case of fetal exposures; what the health effects would be of breaking a bulb in a house with young children or a pregnant woman; and what the aggregate environmental effects of persistent mercury from these bulbs might be after improper waste disposal. Hundreds of millions of these compact fluorescent bulbs must be sold each decade to realize the desired energy-conservation benefits, and yet consumers would not have any informed idea about how many compact fluorescent bulbs will be recycled and how many will be discarded in the trash causing an unknown amount of long-term harm.

I find it rather mind-boggling that environmentalists have fought for decades to reduce the mercury pollution from coal-burning power plants and other common sources, and yet they are now encouraging consumers to buy compact fluorescent bulbs that will definitely add to the cumulative mercury residues in the environment.[102] This recommendation seems to reflect a "*we*

---

100. *See* Howard Latin & Bobby Kasolas, *Bad Designs, Lethal Profits: The Duty to Protect Other Motorists Against SUV Collision Risks*, 82 B.U. L.Rev. 1161 (Dec. 2002).

101. The cited ad appears on an unnumbered page following page two of Wildlife Conservation (June 2008).

102. The environmental groups are minimizing the dangers of the mercury in compact fluorescent light bulbs (CFLs) by looking at the low mercury content of each bulb in isolation, rather than in aggregate terms with all other sources of mercury contamination in the environment. The discussion of CFL bulbs on the Environmental Defense web site, for example, tells consumers not to "worry" about the mercury. But the ED discussion provides these instructions to users if a bulb breaks in a house: "First, open nearby windows to disperse any vapor that may escape. Sweep up the fragments (do not use your hands) and wipe the area with a disposable paper towel to pick up all glass fragments. Do not use a vacuum. Place all fragments in a sealed plastic bag and follow the disposal instructions below," which told the user to locate the "nearest mercury recycling or disposal facilities." This sounds like a cause to "worry" to me because hundreds of millions of CFL bulbs will be used each year. The quoted text was downloaded on April 15, 2008 from www.climate411.org, a

have to do something" crisis mentality that advocates emergency behavioral changes before the consequences of those behaviors can be carefully evaluated. Alternative lighting products, such as light-emitting diodes (LEDs), organic light-emitting diodes (OLEDs), and other GHG-free lighting technologies could be produced in the near future that will not increase mercury contamination as a negative side-effect.[103] But in the rush to do something *now*, the failure to consider the harmful long-term effects of alternative technologies and processes may lead to mistakes that have dangerous consequences for decades or centuries.[104] The main point of this critique, however, is that most consumers could not assess the risks and energy-conservation benefits of fluorescent light bulbs, to say nothing of alternative energy production methods, improved transportation technologies, and many other ways to reduce GHG pollution in contexts where climate change impacts are a major factor, but not the only factor, that must be examined.

Another well-established finding from cognitive psychology is that most people are more opposed to losing what they already have than they are concerned about giving up opportunities for potential gains.[105] Once people become accustomed to having particular possessions or entitlements, attempts to deprive them of these goods and amenities are likely to meet stronger resistance than would result from depriving them of opportunities to possess things they have never had. Yet, most efforts to elicit consumer behavioral changes to reduce GHG emissions and energy usage are telling many millions of consumers that they must cut down on, or give up, diverse products and amenities they are used to enjoying and will not want to lose.

We can be quite confident that a great many Americans will not voluntarily give up their large houses, vacation homes, SUVs, second cars, long-distance air travel and vacations, HDTV televisions, NASCAR racing,[106] ski resorts, snowmobiles, fireplaces, campfires, Disney World visits, night baseball games, fast food burgers, air conditioning, and innumerable other familiar goods and services. Where do we draw the line? Attempts to tell tens of millions of American consumers that they should sacrifice valued aspects of their lifestyles, even if many high-GHG purchases could be characterized as "luxuries," are not likely to gain widespread political support for programs to overcome climate change. Similar attempts to tell the people in developing countries that they must limit the "carbon footprints" associated with attaining greater economic growth, improved health care, better access to education, and other forms of increased welfare are bound to be wholly ineffectual.

We must also acknowledge that some people do not believe global climate change will be personally harmful, and other people will choose to put short-term gratification above concerns about long-term climate hazards. Millions of Americans evidently will not put a high priority on thinking about the climate change effects of their behavior. For example, a recent article in the NEW YORK TIMES reported: "Pollsters and communications experts have noted that the public remains deeply divided along party lines over global warming and that the issue rarely shows up

---

web site Environmental Defense has devoted to climate issues. See *also* Worldwatch Inst. Eye on Earth, *Lighting an Efficient Future, Minus the Mercury* (May 30, 2008, downloaded from www.worldwatch.org on 06/05/2008).

103. *Fans of L.E.D.'s Say This Bulb's Time Has Come*, NY TIMES ON-LINE (July 28, 2008); *Solid State Steps Out of the Shadows*, NY TIMES (April 9, 2008); *see also* WORLDWATCH INSTITUTE EYE ON EARTH, *Lighting an Efficient Future, Minus the Mercury* (May 30, 2008).

104. There is little reason to believe that most CFL bulbs will actually be recycled after they stop working or are broken. *See* Reuters, *U.S. Consumers Still Slow to Recycle Gadgets*, NY TIMES ON-LINE (April 17, 2008).

105. This is one of the central propositions of "prospect theory," a psychology-based behavioral theory inconsistent with the economics theory of rational utility maximization. *See* Amos Tversky & Daniel Kahneman, *Advances in Prospect Theory: Cumulative Representation of Uncertainty*, 5 J. RISK & UNCERTAINTY, No. 4, 297–323 (Oct. 1992); Jack S. Levy, *An Introduction to Prospect Theory*, 13 POLITICAL PSYCH. 171–86 (June 1992).

106. *See Fast Cars, Full Tanks*, NY TIMES ON-LINE (June 3, 2008).

on voters' lists of worries."[107] According to a 2006 survey conducted by the Pew Research Center: "Barely half of the Americans who have heard of global warming say they personally worry about the issue a great deal (19%) or a fair amount (34%). Nearly as many say they worry only a little (26%) or not at all (21%)."[108] If roughly half of American voters are not especially concerned about the potentially disastrous consequences of global warming, why should anyone expect that these same people in their capacities as consumers will devote appreciable attention to the climate change impacts of their purchases in the course of their daily lives? The point of these observations is that we can appeal to many millions of consumers with disparate preferences and values to decrease the GHG impacts of their behavior, but we cannot rely on more than a small fraction of these people to make consistent choices that will reduce more than a small fraction of GHG pollution.

Reliance on various attempts to modify consumption behaviors around the world is also unrealistic because many people will consciously or unintentionally become "free riders."[109] Why should consumers make significant lifestyle sacrifices when they cannot be prevented from enjoying any climate benefits that result from the lifestyle changes other consumers may decide to undertake?[110] Many people will participate in collective actions despite the presence of free riders in order to feel they are part of the "solution," but many other people will undoubtedly choose to continue their present behaviors because these individual actions cannot make a major climate-change difference and they can still gain whatever benefits arise from the public-spirited behaviors of others. As is generally true in free-rider contexts, some people who do want to help resolve global climate change problems will nonetheless decide not to participate in mitigation efforts because they feel it would be unfair for them to bear significant burdens while other people can benefit equally without paying for the benefits or changing their harmful actions.

In sum, I do not agree with the environmental groups and other climate organizations that are trying to persuade millions of consumers to modify their behaviors as a primary means to reduce GHG emissions and energy usage in as many contexts as possible. This strategy cannot function effectively on a wide-enough scale as a result of human cognitive and time limitations, and its focus on asking for countless individual sacrifices will doubtless evoke a great deal of public hostility and political opposition in developed and developing nations. There is no reason to doubt that most American and European consumers want to keep what they now have, while billions of people in developing nations want to attain higher levels of prosperity. The idealistic message that everyone must make many personal sacrifices to avoid climate change disasters may convince some people to change some of their consumption behaviors, but not nearly enough people often enough to overcome global warming harms. This message is also bound to antagonize many people who are unwilling or unable to make the necessary changes and bear the necessary burdens. People do not like to be told that they have to do something they do not want to do. Yet, the current reliance on percentage-rate emissions-reduction approaches in effect is asking innumerable people to accept one loss after another.

---

107. *Gore Group Plans Ad Blitz on Global Warming*, NY TIMES ON-LINE (April 1, 2008); *see* Ariel Malka, Jon A. Krosnick & Gary Langer, *The Association of Knowledge With Concern about Global Warming: Trusted Information Sources Shape Public Thinking*, unpublished Stanford University research paper (June 2008).

108. PEW RESEARCH CENTER, PEW GLOBAL ATTITUDES PROJECT REPORT (June 13, 2006).

109. *See, e.g.*, Nicholas Stern, *What Is the Economics of Climate Change?*, 7 WORLD ECON. No. 2, 4, 10 (April–June 2006); Michael Hoel, *Efficient Climate Policy in the Presence of Free Riders*, 27 J. ENVTL. ECON. & MGT., No. 3, 259–74 (1994); Robert Albanese & David D. van Fleet, *Rational Behavior in Groups: The Free-Riding Tendency*, ACAD. OF MGT. REV. 244–55 (April 1985); Oliver Kim & Mark Walker, *The Free Rider Problem: Experimental Evidence*, 43 PUBLIC CHOICE, No. 1, 3–24 (Jan. 1984).

110. *Why Bother*, NY TIMES ON-LINE (April 20, 2008).

Instead of trying to change the consumption patterns of billions of people, we should adopt a more realistic policy aimed at confronting climate change through reliance on GHG-free replacement technologies while modifying consumer behaviors to the least extent possible. One way to achieve this objective is to implement a series of programs to fully electrify as many production and consumption processes as possible in developed nations initially and later in the developing states—and to put intense efforts into producing a great deal more electrical power using GHG-free methods. In this way, most people will be able to continue doing what they want to do and what they have done in the past, although they will have to pay the costs of achieving their desired goals through greater reliance on electrical power generated without damaging the Earth's climate.

In place of fossil-fuel consumption for industrial heating purposes, we could mandate the adoption of electrical ovens or other electrical heating elements. In place of fossil-fuel based home heating, we could require the installation of electric furnaces with possible subsidies to help homeowners undertake the necessary conversions. The same GHG-free requirement could be imposed on all commercial buildings. We could replace all gas-consuming appliances with electric appliances during a transition period of a couple of decades. Instead of continuing to rely on internal combustion engines, we could mandate the development of all-electric vehicles, hydrogen fuel-cell cars, or other GHG-free vehicles. We could require the adoption of electrical-powered tractors and other GHG-free farm machinery to reduce emissions from agricultural activities. We could replace many aircraft flights with zeppelins (or blimps). We could mandate the adoption of electric lawnmowers, go-karts, railroad engines, barbecue grills, fireplace inserts, and a host of other products that can meet existing consumption desires to a great degree while replacing GHG-polluting equipment. In some instances, such as airplanes and commercial vessels, we may have to accept reliance on energy-efficient hybrid engines for safety reasons that preclude eliminating all GHG emissions. However, after a progressive transition period of a few decades, we should be able to enable most consumers to do what they want and live how they want without requiring major lifestyle sacrifices and without adding substantial GHG emissions to the atmosphere, as we are now doing every year.

GHG-free technology replacements may not be perfect substitutes in many contexts, but they are certainly far more realistic than asking millions of consumers in developed nations to give up their inefficient cars, houses, and vacations, or to ask billions of people in poor nations to give up their aspirations for the same amenities and opportunities as consumers in wealthy nations now enjoy. The technology-replacement strategy would place the primary burden for making constructive behavioral changes not on decentralized consumers but on governments and businesses to expand GHG-free electricity generation. Aiming to electrify America and the other developed nations completely, and then the developing states, will require a great expansion in GHG-free electrical capacity at an affordable price, which will take a significant amount of time, effort and money to accomplish.[111] On the other hand, once this transformation is accomplished, most nations will not need to spend vast amounts of money annually to purchase harmful fossil fuels. Converting to GHG-free energy production will not be easy or cheap, but it is a realizable goal over several decades, unlike reforming the myriad choices of billions of consumers. Nearly all climate experts would agree that the world will need to achieve this transition to abundant GHG-free energy sources under any realistic climate change mitigation strategy.

The central argument here is that adopting GHG-free replacement technologies, including an array of familiar and innovative clean-energy methods, likely could succeed over time if we in-

---

111. *See* Richard G. Richels & Geoffrey C. Blanford, *The Value of Technological Advance in Decarbonizing the U.S. Economy*, AEI-Brookings Joint Center For Regulatory Studies Working Paper 07-19 (Nov. 2007).

vest enough resources and effort in pursuing this strategy. In contrast, trying to impose a climate policy dependent on the compliance of billions of consumers making billions of decentralized consumption choices is a utopian fantasy that cannot possibly succeed in attaining actual climate change progress or even in helping us to remain where we are now.

I am sure many concerned people believe we need to adopt both approaches concurrently, but reliance on widespread modifications of consumer behaviors is certain to prove expensive, confusing, often alienating, and ineffectual in comparison with minimal climate change benefits, if any. It follows that we should be putting the overwhelming majority of our research efforts and investments into creating affordable GHG-free energy and industrial technologies rather than into public relations campaigns asking consumers to make numerous behavioral changes that can never be sufficiently effective.

I have no reservations about *asking* consumers to try to reduce their energy demand before and after comprehensive electric power networks are created. An advantage of many renewable energy technologies, such as wind turbines and most solar energy methods, is that they can be implemented where needed, when needed, in developing nations without requiring the construction of expensive nationwide electrical power grids like the ones in developed nations.[112] While asking decentralized consumers to conserve energy may be useful during the transition from fossil-fuel combustion to GHG-free energy technologies and beyond, we cannot realistically rely on substantial public compliance with these requests. Most people will normally do what they regard as best for their personal interests and lifestyles. Utopian thinking about miraculous changes in consumer behaviors around the world, which unfortunately seems quite common in climate-policy analyses, cannot serve as a pragmatic basis for addressing global climate change problems.

Changing Industrial Behaviors and Interim Pollution Control Targets

Despite countless pronouncements asking consumers to reduce their "carbon footprints," almost all proposals for mandatory emissions-reductions, including cap-and-trade systems and other economic incentive mechanisms, have been directed at GHG polluting production activities and industrial sectors. As previously discussed, for example, several laws have recently been enacted that require automobile manufacturers to improve the fuel efficiency of their vehicles or to reduce GHG emissions, but I am not aware of any laws requiring vehicle purchasers to drive less or to buy smaller cars. This differential treatment arguably is a political confirmation of my view that we can ask millions of consumers to lessen their GHG impacts, but it would be politically unpalatable as well as ineffective in practice to try to force innumerable consumers to make major personal sacrifices in GHG emissions-reduction contexts.

In contrast to the relative dearth of regulations imposed on consumer behaviors, we have a long history of mandating increasingly strict pollution controls on industrial dischargers and other large-scale commercial pollution sources. This regulatory pattern has induced industrial polluters to increase their prices and pass the regulatory costs on to consumers when they can, which means the dichotomy between production-based and consumption-based pollution-control approaches is not as clear as it may initially appear. Nevertheless, requiring sharp reductions or complete elimination of GHG emissions from only a few categories of industrial products and processes—notably energy generation and transportation—could go a long way toward resolving climate change problems and would appreciably reduce administrative burdens in comparison with programs that try to designate, monitor, and enforce pollution cutbacks by many millions of decentralized consumers.

---

112. I thank my colleague, Professor Louis Raveson, for emphasizing this point.

The World Business Council for Sustainable Development recently noted that: "changes toward a low-carbon economy will be required in power generation, industry and manufacturing, transport and buildings & commerce, four key sectors of the economy that need specific and different policy approaches."[113] Some climate experts have advocated a more detailed sectoral approach that would focus on the best pollution control strategies for each different industry or major pollution source.[114] However, the greater the detailed information and distinctive efforts required to implement effective solutions in many disparate GHG pollution contexts, the more expensive and time-consuming the regulatory process is certain to be. Difficult comparisons and trade-offs will have to be made between sectoral approaches that require a great deal of specific information about diverse GHG production sources and the lesser implementation burdens of general percentage-rate emissions-reduction programs that treat all industrial GHG sources approximately equally.[115]

Before we can decide how to reduce industrial GHG pollution, we would have to decide how low the allowable national emissions cap must be set—entirely different industrial changes would usually be necessary to achieve a cap equal to half of the existing GHG discharges in comparison to a regulatory cap that imposes the lowest feasible level of discharges or eliminates them entirely. Various climate organizations and experts contend that America must reduce GHG emissions by 25 to 40 percent, 50 percent, 60 to 80 percent, 70 percent, 80 percent, 90 percent, or eliminate all discharges because of their persistent character. Various timeframes have also been identified for the achievement of these emissions-reduction targets, including 2012, 2020, 2030, 2050, and the end of the 21st century. It is important to recognize that the relative effectiveness of alternative approaches for reducing GHG pollution will be dependent on which of these criteria are chosen.

Some environmental groups have proposed setting comparatively strict middle-of-the-century emissions-reduction targets combined with less demanding interim targets. For example, NRDC advocates emissions cuts of "25 percent by 2020 and 80 percent by 2050";[116] and Environmental Defense asked people to support the *Lieberman-Warner Climate Security Act,* which would have cut GHG pollution "almost 20 percent below current levels by 2020, while setting us on the path to the 80 percent emissions reductions scientists say we need by mid-century."[117] We must consider whether the choice of interim emissions-reduction targets and escalating stringency in pollution control programs will help establish more cost-effective industrial pollution control, or will the adoption of sliding interim targets impede realistic GHG pollution control decisions?

Policymakers should recognize that the numerical targets listed in the previous two paragraphs are speculative numbers imagined for a single moment in time—economists call this a *static* perspective—although global activities and climate conditions are changing *dynamically* every year. If the GHG discharges from an activity are reduced by 50 percent, cutting pollution

---

113. World Business Council for Sustainable Development, The Sectoral Approach Debate (international meeting announcement, June 7, 2008).

114. *See, e.g.,* Michel Colombier & Emmanuel Guerin, *Sectoral Agreements, Breaking the Climate Deadlock Briefing Paper* (2008, downloaded from www.breakingtheclimatedeadlock.com on 08/03/2008); Richard Baron et al., Sectoral Approaches to Greenhouse Gas Mitigation: Exploring Issues for Heavy Industry (report to International Energy Agency, Nov. 2007); Daniel Bodansky, *International Sectoral Agreements in a Post-2012 Climate Framework,* Pew Center on Global Climate Change Working Paper (May 2007).

115. *See generally* Howard A. Latin, *Ideal Versus Real Regulatory Efficiency: Implementation of Uniform Standards and "Fine-Tuning" Regulatory Reforms,* 37 Stanford L. Rev. 1267–1332 (1985); *reprinted in* R. Fischman, M. Lipeles & M. Squillace (eds.), An Environmental Law Anthology (1996); *reprinted in* 1987 Land Use & Environment Law Review.

116. Natural Resources Defense Council Solicitation Letter, received by the author on April 2008, at 3.

117. Environmental Defense Solicitation Letter, 2008 Climate Action Plan, February 29, 2008, at 1.

in half for each unit of the activity, while the number of units doubles over time, there will be no net gain in GHG emissions reduction. This is a vital consideration because world population is expected to grow to about nine billion people by 2050[118] and many of the people in developing nations have rising aspirations that will require significantly improving their economic and social welfare. In effect, we may have to run as hard as we can just to stand still in terms of atmospheric GHG levels.

Viewed in this light, the mitigation measures sufficient to achieve an 80 percent GHG reduction by 2050 in comparison with current business-as-usual discharges will no longer be good enough in 2051 or thereafter. We cannot ever *stop* reducing GHG pollution levels if we intend to meet any of these arbitrary numerical targets. As an outcome of emissions-reduction efforts for decades, perhaps one moment will occur when the atmospheric GHG level is counterbalanced by the results of natural and human-made processes that remove GHGs from the air—this is called a "stabilization point" in the climate change literature[119]—but the next moment someone somewhere will decide to go for a long drive or take a distant vacation, and the atmospheric GHG stability will be upset. GHG pollution control programs must continuously improve their performance to meet the increasing GHG emissions from expanding development activities benefiting more people in more places and from growing populations in many regions. I believe it will be impossible to keep up with this dynamic growth unless nearly all GHG-based technologies and industrial processes can be replaced by equivalent GHG-free production and consumption methods that can be scaled upwards to accommodate population growth and higher economic and social development while still remaining GHG-free.

It is also important to acknowledge that some GHG-producing activities cannot feasibly be eliminated in the foreseeable future. Until the whole world is electrified using various energy technologies, for example, hundreds of millions of indigent people will go on burning wood or charcoal for heating and food preparation purposes. We cannot expect these people to behave otherwise until low-cost GHG-free heating technologies are available to them that achieve comparable subsistence functions. Harmful GHG emissions cannot be completely eliminated from agriculture, some forms of transportation, some existing buildings, and other common pollution sources within a timeframe of several decades, which means these continuing sources of GHGs must be accommodated within whatever long-term emissions-reduction goal is chosen.

Many recreational, cultural, or lifestyle activities attract people with strong preferences who will not give up these cherished behaviors even when there are reasonable GHG-free alternatives. Some of these "dirty" but satisfying activities include auto racing, whaling and sport fishing, recreational flying, aesthetic wood fires and campfires, mountain climbing in remote ranges, vacations to Disney World or beach resorts, beef consumption, whisky distilling, and outer space exploration, to name only a few choices among millions of pastimes with dedicated adherents and significant GHG emissions. Because GHGs are persistent, emissions from these diverse activities must also be included in all plans to reach percentage emissions-reduction goals this century. These observations indicate that we are not going to approach zero GHG pollution in the foreseeable future no matter what long-term goals or targets may be set.

In recognition of the difficult impediments to overcoming global climate change and the recognition that we will never be able to eliminate all GHG emissions, I see only one long-

---

118. U.S. Census Bureau International Data Base, Predicting a World Population of 9.3 Billion in 2050 (June 18, 2008); U.N. News Centre, *World Population to Reach 9.1 Billion in 2050*, UN Projects (Feb. 24, 2005).

119. *See, e.g.,* U.S. EPA, FUTURE CLIMATE CHANGE (2007, downloaded from www.epa.gov on 04/23/2007); IPCC, STABILIZATION OF ATMOSPHERIC GREENHOUSE GASES: PHYSICAL, BIOLOGICAL AND SOCIO-ECONOMIC IMPLICATIONS (Feb. 2007); Govinda R. Timilsina, *Atmospheric Stabilization of CO_2 Emissions: Near-term Reductions and Intensity-based Targets*, World Bank Policy Research Working Paper 4352 (Sept. 2007).

term target that appears suitable for developed nations: *We need to eliminate as much GHG pollution as feasible as soon as feasible in as many contexts as feasible.* In other words, the target should be to eliminate GHG pollution to the greatest practical extent because we cannot cut out all GHG emissions in any realistic timeframe. Aiming for less-stringent emissions-reduction targets cannot be sufficient to combat dynamic global warming problems successfully, and even the standard of eliminating all GHG emissions to the greatest extent feasible will not be enough unless the large GHG polluting developing nations can be persuaded to join these efforts. It is unlikely that developing nations will accept any restrictions on their GHG emissions until they become convinced that the developed states, which to an overwhelmingly degree have caused the global warming problem, are doing everything they can to prevent further climate change.

If climate policymakers accept the conclusion that developed nations will have to make extreme reductions in GHG emissions, coming as close to zero discharges as they feasibly can despite many activities that continue generating some GHG pollution, perhaps climate experts will stop debating arbitrary percentage-reduction targets and will agree that deploying GHG-free replacement technologies must be the primary strategy for meeting GHG mitigation goals. The conventional emissions-reduction programs, including economic incentive mechanisms, that would be suitable means for a 50 percent reduction in atmospheric GHG levels, cannot attain sufficiently low GHG concentrations to meet the more stringent target levels approaching GHG elimination. In the words of several scholars who have reached similar conclusions, society must create "transformative technologies" able to replace GHG polluting sources that have caused, and are still causing, increasing climate change perils.[120]

After recognizing that climate change mitigation programs must cut out as much GHG pollution as they feasibly can, the next vital question is whether we should consider modest emissions-reduction targets as useful "interim" or "first step" measures on the way to attaining comprehensive GHG elimination goals. American politicians and environmental groups have supported various first steps on the rationale that we need to *do something now* and that any kind of reduction in GHG discharges would be beneficial, which is definitely a Frame One mistake. When the Senate defeated the Lieberman-Warner Climate Security Act in June of 2008, a *New York Times* editorial described the Bill as "short of what most climate scientists believe is necessary but an important first step."[121] I disagree: A first step is only valuable if it is heading in the right direction, and this editorial failed to consider several persuasive reasons why efforts to implement interim or first-step mitigation measures may prove more harmful than helpful.[122]

The technology needed to achieve an interim emissions-reduction target will often be wholly different from the technology required to attain a carbon-free standard. Motor vehicles, for example, can reduce GHG discharges in non-radical ways by using less powerful engines and lighter materials, by substituting biofuels for high-CO_2 petroleum, or by producing hybrid engine designs.[123] Vehicles with these modifications will continue to discharge large amounts of GHGs into the air and cannot approach the carbon cleanliness of all-electric or hydrogen fuel-cell vehicles. Indisputably, the money and efforts invested in first-step auto technology modifica-

---

120. Roger Pielke, Jr., Tom Wigley & Christopher Green, *Dangerous Assumptions*, 452 Nature 531–32 (April 3, 2008); Nicholas D. Kristoff, *Our Favorite Planet*, Op-Ed column, NY Times On-line (April 20, 2008).

121. Editorial: *Another Failure on Climate Change*, New York Times On-line (June 11, 2008).

122. *See generally* Cary Coglianese & Jocelyn D'Ambrosio, *Policymaking under Pressure: The Perils of Incremental Responses to Climate Change*, University of Pennsylvania Law School Research Paper No. 08-30 (2008).

123. *See, e.g.*, Joseph M. Crabb & Daniel K.N. Johnson, *Fueling the Innovative Process: Oil Prices and Induced Innovation in Automotive Energy-Efficient Technology*, Colorado College Working Paper 2007-04 (May 2007); 2009 *Acura TSX: A Redesign Waiting for Diesel*, NY Times On-line (April 20, 2008); Jim Motavalli, *Getting There: A Guide to Planet Friendly Cars*, E—The Environmental Magazine (July–Aug. 2004).

tions will no longer be available to finance the expensive but essential transition to GHG-free vehicles.

As a case in point, General Motors ran a detailed series of on-line advertisements in May 2008 that said their employees also live on planet Earth and they are working concurrently on several new ways to reduce the global warming pollution from their vehicles. The GM efforts include engine and materials improvements, modified diesel engines, flex-fuel engines using a low percentage of ethanol, more ambitious biofuel designs, hybrid gas and electric engines, all-electric cars, and hydrogen fuel-cell vehicles.[124] The GM ad did not predict specific dates for the widespread deployment of any of these alternative design improvements, but it did indicate that GHG-free designs are bound to be expensive and would not be broadly available until a long time in the future, if ever.[125] This auto manufacturer—and all American auto companies—is putting much more money and engineering personnel into near-term design modifications that can meet the modest fuel-efficiency and emissions-reduction targets imposed by the California regulations and federal energy law mentioned above, but these modest design "improvements" cannot come close to eliminating GHG emissions from future models. GM is not going all-out to develop GHG-free electrical or hydrogen-fueled vehicles, and instead is making relatively small investments in the more innovative clean technologies because the applicable laws have only imposed first-step requirements for compliance.

If we spend many billions of dollars on interim technology improvements, this political and economic choice will reduce the funding available for clean carbon-free vehicles and it will create an aura of legitimacy for vehicles that in the aggregate will still be discharging large quantities of GHGs each year. If the auto manufacturers adopt first-step technological changes at relatively high costs, they will be more likely to resist replacing their interim design measures with carbon-free vehicles.[126] Indeed, GM apparently is already planning for this kind of political resistance by claiming that their customers want "affordable" vehicles.[127]

If first-step improvements reach the point of diminishing returns in design efficiencies—there is an intrinsic limit on how GHG-clean an internal combustion engine burning fossil fuels or biofuels can be made—it is not clear that the costs of interim changes would be less than the costs of a direct transition to carbon-free vehicles during the next few decades. Under the defeated Lieberman-Warner Bill, and under the recent California and federal regulations, vehicle purchasers would have to pay the cumulative costs of "first step" improvements, probable "second step" improvements, and the eventual "third step" of conversion to carbon-free automotive technologies that will be essential over the long run. This is not a cost-effective approach in my opinion and is especially wasteful because the first-step vehicle modifications will not yield any tangible climate change benefits and instead will only *reduce the increases* in GHG emissions from motor vehicles to a modest degree.

The same kind of contrast can be drawn in energy industries among first-step investments for end-of-the-pipe pollution controls,[128] coal liquefaction or gasification projects,[129] and power

---

124. *See* the examples of five alternative vehicle technologies discussed in the 2008 GM web site advertisement at http://chevy.nytimes.com.

125. *Id.*

126. The American auto manufacturers are already challenging the federal energy act requirement that they cut GHG emissions by 30 percent by 2020. The companies are using the interesting argument that they invested heavily in large gas-guzzling vehicles that have become unpopular because of rapidly increasing gas prices, and as a result they cannot afford to build future vehicles efficient enough to meet the new regulatory standards. *See Big Carmakers Say Fuel Rule Plan Too Strict*, NY TIMES ON-LINE (July 1, 2008).

127. *See* the 2008 advertisement at http://chevy.nytimes.com.

128. *See* U.S. DEPT. OF ENERGY, CLEAN COAL TECHNOLOGY & THE PRESIDENT'S CLEAN COAL POWER INITIATIVE (downloaded from www.doe.gov on 01/ 31/2008).

129. *See, e.g.,* WORLD COAL INSTITUTE, COAL MEETING THE CLIMATE CHALLENGE: TECHNOLOGY TO REDUCE GREENHOUSE GAS EMISSIONS (2008); U.S. DEPT. OF ENERGY, HYDROGEN & CLEAN FUELS RESEARCH (downloaded from www.doe.gov on 01/31/2008); U.S. Dept. of Energy, ALTERNATIVE FUELS AND ADVANCED

plant conversion from coal to natural gas as fuel[130] in contrast to "carbon capture and storage" (CCS) technologies that could inject large quantities of C02 underground instead of allowing the persistent gases to reach the atmosphere.[131] This year a major CCS demonstration project was canceled[132] because neither the federal government nor the private coal-power company was willing to bear the "public goods" project costs,[133] while less effective first-step approaches are being developed that will lock us into *reducing the increases* in GHG discharges from energy production for decades to come. Once we develop new first-step technologies, such as "clean coal" gasification, they will gain substantial political support from coal-producing states as well as coal companies and affected labor unions;[134] and it will become more difficult to abandon these expensive first steps that can never achieve sufficient GHG emissions reductions.

Even if fossil-fuel industry efforts could attain fairly significant emissions reductions, they would still use carbon-based production processes that discharge persistent GHG pollution every year and increase the atmospheric GHG concentration. As one widely-criticized example, the World Bank is funding an Indian project to build a large "supercritical" coal-burning power plant—the high-temperature combustion process reduces GHG pollution by about 10 percent per unit of energy output in comparison to ordinary "subcritical" coal-based power plants. This new coal-combustion facility will discharge more than 20 million tons of GHGs per year for decades, an irreversible "reducing the increases" GHG pollution mistake, when India could be moving toward solar power generation and other GHG-free replacement technologies instead.[135] Billions of dollars spent on first-step or interim pollution controls, economic incentive programs, and other "reducing the increases" emissions clean-up measures for marginally cutting GHG pollution from the energy industries will not be available for replacing carbon combustion-based power generation with clean carbon-free energy technologies. The industries forced to absorb substantial emissions-reduction costs will make strong equity claims that they should not have to *pay twice* when we later attempt to make them eliminate their carbon-based technologies. It is true that the transition to a carbon-free economy will take a few decades, but it will also take several decades for interim or first-step GHG emissions-reduction programs to im-

---

VEHICLES DATA CENTER, ENERGY EFFICIENCY AND RENEWABLE ENERGY (downloaded from www.doe.gov on 11/16/ 2007); WORLDWATCH INST. EYE ON EARTH, *U.S. Government Dumping $100 Million Into Filthy Fuels Project* (Nov. 9, 2007, downloaded from www.worldwatch.org on 11/16/2007); *Lawmakers Push for Big Subsidies for Coal Process*, NY TIMES ON-LINE (May 29, 2007).

130. *See The Energy Challenge: Utilities Turn from Coal to Gas, Raising Risk of Price Increase*, NY TIMES ON-LINE (Feb. 5, 2008).

131. *See, e.g.*, Manfred Fischedick *et al.*, *CO_2-Capture and Geological Storage as a Climate Policy Option*, Wuppertal Inst. Special No. 35e (2007); Daniel Valentin, *Inducing the International Diffusion of Carbon Capture and Storage in the Power Sector*, Wuppertal Papers No. 162 (April 2007); U. DEPT. OF ENERGY & NATL. ENERGY TECHNOLOGY LAB., ROADMAP: CARBON SEQUESTRATION TECHNOLOGY AND PROGRAM PLAN (2007, downloaded from www.doe.gov on 01/31/2008); Heleen de Coninck, *The International Race for Carbon Capture and Storage: And the Winner is ... ?*, Forum for Atlantic Climate and Energy Talks, FACET Commentary No. 12 (June 2008).

132. *See Running in Circles Over Carbon*, NY TIMES ON-LINE (June 8, 2008); *A "Bold" Step to Capture an Elusive Gas Falters*, NY TIMES ON-LINE (Feb. 3, 2008).

133. *See generally* Geoffrey Heal, *New Strategies For the Provision of Global Public Goods: Learning from International Environmental Challenges*, PaineWebber Working Paper Series in Money, Economics and Finance (Dec. 1998).

134. *See, e.g.*, Roberta Mann, *Another Day Older and Deeper in Debt: How Tax Incentives Encourage Burning Coal and the Consequences for Global Warming*, 20 GLOBAL BUSINESS & DEVEL. L.J. 111 (2007); *Lawmakers Push for Big Subsidies for Coal Process*, NY TIMES ON-LINE (May 29, 2007).

135. *See* Ted Nace, *The World's Dumbest Project: Tata Ultra Mega*, GRISTMILL ON-LINE (March 20, 2008, downloaded from http://gristmill.grist.org/story/2008/3/19/155929/151 on 07/20/ 2008); David Wheeler, *Tata Ultra Mega Mistake: The IFC Should Not Get Burned by Coal* (March 13, 2008, downloaded from http://carma.org/blog/tata-ultra-mega-mistake-the-ifc-should-not-get-burned-by-coal/#comment-863 on 07/20/ 2008).

pose strict controls on distinctive carbon-based energy sources, such as "clean coal" projects. These alternative climate policy approaches—GHG technology-replacements or emissions-reduction programs—will use entirely different pollution control technologies, and any program that requires making large investments in GHG-based emissions reductions from power plants will impede the diffusion of carbon-free energy production technologies.

When we do begin the expensive conversion to a carbon-free economy, there will be little residual value from many billions of dollars expended on interim emissions-reduction measures that will be phased out along with the associated carbon-based energy technologies; and there will be strong political opposition from fossil-fuel energy companies and other constituencies that have been required to make the interim investments. Under first-step or interim emissions-reduction approaches, the American public will be asked to expend billions of dollars and to accept diverse lifestyle sacrifices or inconveniences in return for no tangible climate change benefits. Nearly all emissions-reduction measures now involve *reducing the increases* outcomes that cannot improve atmospheric GHG concentrations and therefore cannot provide relief from global warming. The absence of climate change benefits commensurate with first-step or interim expenditures raises the prospect that a plethora of emissions-reduction measures may weaken both short-term and long-term public support for essential technology-replacement programs. Environmental regulatory history has shown that fiscal support for expensive environmental protection programs is erratic over time,[136] and we should not dissipate the present support on a multitude of interim measures that will never substantially reduce climate change impacts.

The international ramifications of reliance on first-step or interim emissions-reduction measures may be even worse. There is widespread agreement among climate experts that the developed nations cannot resolve global warming problems without the cooperation of the major GHG-polluting developing states, primarily China and India, which now rank among the world's worst GHG dischargers. Yet, these developing countries and most others will never agree to mitigation measures that would significantly impede their economic growth and prosperity. A "first step" that consists of paying these nations to adopt the same kinds of emissions-reduction programs that developed states are employing would not facilitate greater economic and social welfare for poor nations, which is what they want most, and it also would not avoid "reducing the increases" results that will not lower atmospheric GHG levels.

Even remarkable reductions in U.S. and E.U. greenhouse gas emissions could not reduce global climate change impacts enough to achieve real climate change progress as long as China, India, and other developing countries continue using fossil fuels and carbon-based technologies to propel their expanding economies. However, the developing nations want increased economic growth more than GHG emissions reductions, and it is hard to condemn them for this priority. The only things we could transfer to the developing nations that would meet *their objectives and ours* are GHG-free technologies that could increase their economic and social welfare without causing any more global warming.

Tragically, the developed nations have focused almost all of their GHG pollution control efforts on various emissions-reduction programs and have not produced GHG-free technologies that would enable effective technology transfers to developing states. To the extent we continue to view improved emissions-reduction programs as viable first-step or interim measures, we will not be creating the tools and methods suitable for technology transfers that can help developing states reduce their GHG pollution without sacrificing any welfare improvements. If we cannot

---

136. For example, the public concern for the rising price of gasoline is now dominating global warming concerns, and other hazards may have the same kind of diversionary effect in the future. *See, e.g.,* Editorial: *The Gas-Guzzler Gambit*, NY TIMES ON-LINE (May 1, 2008); *Are We Ready to Track Carbon Footprints?*, NY TIMES ON-LINE (March 25, 2008); *Global Warming and Your Wallet*, NY TIMES ON-LINE (July 6, 2007).

gain the cooperation of large developing nations on climate change mitigation except through technology transfers, trade preferences, or other international subsidies, it is in our own long-term interest and theirs to help them adopt carbon-free technologies suitable for their economic and social needs. But the interim measures most climate experts now advocate focus on "reducing the increases" emissions-reduction programs rather than putting the primary emphasis on GHG-free technology innovations. Typically expensive but futile interim emissions-reduction programs in affluent nations will not promote GHG-free technologies and technology transfers that are our most realistic hope for enlisting the cooperation of developing nations in confronting worldwide climate changes.

Changing International Behaviors

Successful global warming solutions will require commitments by all major polluting nations, including the U.S., E.U., and the heavily polluting developing nations, such as China and India. We must recognize that an effective international treaty will be extremely difficult to negotiate because global climate change is the *mother of all collective-action problems*: No legally acceptable means exist to force non-participating sovereign states to reduce their GHG emissions; and no physical or legal means can prevent non-participating nations from enjoying whatever climate benefits the treaty member-states may gain from their pollution control efforts. Given the indisputable need for international cooperation to overcome global warming risks, one might conclude that a comprehensive international agreement is a prerequisite for any realistic chance of success. However, there are serious disagreements among developed and developing nations that are not close to resolution, and an ambiguous international legal agreement that avoids rather than resolves climate change problems would not be useful. Indeed, a treaty that masks critical disagreements may be actively harmful by creating the illusion of cooperation and progress without any commensurate accomplishments in practice. At present, the leading economic and social priorities of the GHG polluting nations are predominately incompatible[137] and any effective international agreement to overcome global climate change will not be forthcoming without divine intervention or radically changed perceptions of national interests.

In December 2007, the Conference of the Parties (COP13) held in Bali to strengthen the U.N. Framework Convention on Climate Change (UNFCCC)[138] and Kyoto Protocol[139] produced a "roadmap" agreement to negotiate a meaningful substantive agreement in the next two years before the planned meeting in Copenhagen. Indonesia's Minister of the Environment and the President of the Bali meeting, Rachmat Witoelar, claimed that "the decisions in Bali have launched a new process for reaching agreement by 2009."[140] He also described the meeting as "a 'break-

---

137. *See, e.g.*, U.N. Economic Comm. for Africa & African Union Comm., Climate Change: African Perspectives for a Post-2012 Agreement (March 5, 2008); Ancha Srinivasan *et al.*, The Climate Regime Beyond 2012: Reconciling Asian Developmental Priorities and Global Climate Interests, Institute for Global Environmental Strategies (2008); Andrew Stevenson & Christine Loh, Bali's Hope and Asia's Future (2007, downloaded from www.chinadialogue.net on 01/22/2008); Piet Buys *et al.*, *Country Stakes in Climate Change Negotiations: Two Dimensions of Vulnerability*, World Bank Policy Research Working Paper 4300 (Aug. 2007); William A. Pizer, *A U.S. Perspective on Future Climate Regimes*, Resources for the Future Discussion Paper (2007); *Bitter Divisions Exposed at Climate Talks*, NY Times On-line (Dec. 14, 2008).
138. United Nations Framework Convention on Climate Change, U.N. Doc. A/AC.237/18 (1992), *reprinted in* 31 I.L.M. 849 (1992).
139. Kyoto Protocol to the United Nations Framework Convention on Climate Change, Dec. 10, 1997, U.N. Doc. FCCC/CP/197/L.7/Add. 1, art. 3.1 & Annex B, *reprinted in* 37 I.L.M. 22 (1998).
140. *Bali Conference Ends With Agreement on Roadmap*, Intl. Inst. for Sustainable Dev., Reporting Services (Dec. 15, 2007).

through' where delegates demonstrated leadership to create a sustainable future" and as "a tribute to delegates' solidarity" in facing the "defining challenge of the century."[141]

This "breakthrough" reflects a consensus that developed nations must provide financial and technological assistance to help developing states reduce their greenhouse gas emissions and adapt to climate change hazards, but the roadmap agreement does not specify when, where, how, and how much the developing states will be obliged to cut back their pollution discharges, or how much foreign aid must be given by affluent nations to particular developing countries under which terms and conditions.[142] If nebulous idealized principles with absolutely no specificity could overcome global warming problems, the world undoubtedly would be safe from future climate change harms. Most people at the Bali meeting were pleased that the UNFCCC states-parties agreed to try to reach an action-oriented agreement in 2009 after the Bush Administration has left office. Yet, this political sea change will probably not be sufficient to overcome entrenched North-South disputes and the lack of an international consensus on mitigation priorities and adaptation commitments among states with dissimilar national interests.

The aspect I found most disappointing about the Bali conference was that nearly all proposed action plans were rehashes or limited extensions of Kyoto Protocol measures that have made little progress in the past decade. For example, instead of the Kyoto target for developed nations to cut their GHG emissions to about five percent below 1990 levels, which most treaty members have not attained, the E.U. advocated progressively larger percentage reductions by 2020 and 2050 while relying on the same kinds of emissions-reduction programs and carbon trading programs that have been ineffectual for years under the Kyoto treaty.[143] Most of the resolutions, position papers, press releases, and technical reports coming out of the Bali meeting showed little imagination and ignored the vital question of whether familiar emissions-reduction mechanisms, including cap-and-trade systems, can succeed well-enough, soon-enough by cutting GHG emissions deeply enough to overcome the climate change risks we must confront today and tomorrow. The diplomats and climate policymakers in Bali focused on debating differential GHG percentage emissions-reduction targets for developed nations and developing states in comparison to business-as-usual discharges and also on differential fiscal commitments from affluent nations and poor countries, rather than addressing the effects of alternative mitigation policy choices on critical atmospheric GHG concentrations.

There is no international consensus on the trade-offs between expanding development and GHG emissions reduction. For example, China and India, with about a third of the world's population, have hundreds of millions of poor people despite their remarkable economic progress in the past decade. These nations rely extensively on coal-burning power plants to generate ever-increasing amounts of electricity and ever-increasing amounts of GHG pollutants because they lack oil and natural gas deposits; and coal, which they do have, is the least expensive fossil fuel that can meet their growing energy demand. Both nations plan to continue expanding reliance on coal-combustion technologies, which will be a GHG pollution disaster compounding global climate change problems.[144]

---

141. *Id.*

142. *See Agreeing Upon a Timetable: A Deal is Finally Struck in Bali*, Economist.com (Dec. 15, 2007); *Deadlock Stymies Global Climate Talks*, NY Times On-line (Dec. 12, 2007); *Battleground Bali: Developing Countries Take on Industrialized Countries*, ETN Global Travel Industry News (Dec. 9, 2007).

143. *See* text accompanying notes 30–31, *supra.*

144. *See, e.g.*, Gwyn Prins, *The Road from Kyoto*, The Guardian (April 4, 2008); David Wheeler & Kevin Ummel, *Another Inconvenient Truth: A Carbon-Intensive South Faces Environmental Disaster No Matter What the North Does*, Center for Global Development Working Paper 134 (Dec. 2007); *China, U.S. Face Off on Climate Policies*, Associated Press (Dec. 7, 2007, downloaded from http://msnbc.com on 12/12/2007); *Cuts Urged in China's and India's Energy Growth*, NY Times On-line (Nov. 7, 2007).

The Chinese and Indian governments surely understand that their reliance on increasing coal combustion for energy production and for other GHG-producing industrial practices will substantially worsen global warming and will cause significant harms to their own people. Yet, the governments of both nations regard increasing economic and social development as their highest priority and they have refused to accept any numerical limits on their GHG discharges or to promise any specific future emissions reductions.[145] In essence, they will not compromise their drive for greater development by agreeing to restrain GHG discharges from their rising production and consumption activities.

The continuing development of relatively poor countries is the U.N.'s highest priority,[146] with the possible exception of peace-keeping efforts, and the right to increased development has been incorporated into numerous international treaties. Rather than accepting any GHG emissions-reduction commitments that may impede greater development, the developing nations argue based on the equitable and distributional reasons summarized above that developed nations should pay for whatever GHG emissions-reduction or adaptation programs the developing states may choose to run.[147] For example, one report contended China's position is that "the West is responsible for rising temperatures, because it has been pumping climate-changing gases into the air for centuries."[148]

Dr. Rajendra K. Pachauri, the leader of the IPCC who recently accepted their half of the 2008 Nobel Peace Prize, has argued that: "Developing nations must be allowed to boost carbon emissions to lift millions out of poverty."[149] Jeffrey Sachs, a Nobel-prize winning economist, similarly contended: "If we try to restrain emissions without a fundamentally new set of technologies, we will end up stifling economic growth, including the development prospects for billions of people."[150] Regardless of whatever normative principles people may embrace, the current "real world" position is that most GHG polluting developing nations will not accept stifled development prospects resulting from emissions-reduction commitments.

At the other extreme, the U.S. Senate unanimously rejected the Kyoto Protocol a decade ago partly because China and other GHG-polluting developing nations were not required to cut their emissions commensurately or to select specific target levels for limiting future GHG discharges.[151] This rejection was partly based on concerns about competitive disadvantages if Amer-

---

145. *See, e.g.,* Michael P. Vandenbergh, *Climate Change: The China Problem*, 81 S. Cal. L. Rev. 905 (2007–2008); Zhong Xiang Zhang, *China, the United States and Technology Cooperation on Climate Control,* 10 Environmental Sci. & Pol., Nos. 7–8, 622 (2007); Zhong Xiang Zhang, *Can China Afford to Commit Itself to an Emissions Cap? An Economic and Political Analysis,* 22 Energy Economics 587 (2000); Cass R. Sunstein, *The Complex Climate Change Incentives of China and the United States* at 2, n.4, Univ. of Chi. Olin Working Paper No. 352 (Aug. 7, 2007); *India Plans Non-Targets Climate Action,* Carbon News and Info (Feb. 11, 2008); Sunita Narain, *The Mean World of Climate Change,* Down to Earth: Science and Environment On-line (Aug. 5, 2008).

146. *See* United Nations Millennium Development Goals, adopted by the U.N. General Assembly (Sept. 2000); Global Monitoring Report 2006, Millennium Development Goals: Strengthening Mutual Accountability, Aid, Trade and Governance, Intl. Bank for Reconstruction and Development/World Bank (2006); World Bank, The Road to 2050: Sustainable Development for the 21st Century (2006).

147. *See* text accompanying notes 78–81, *supra.*

148. *U.S. "Not Ready" to Commit to Bali,* The Associated Press, *reprinted* by NY Times On-line (Dec. 9, 2007).

149. *Developing world must be able to lift emissions: Nobel winner,* Agence France-Presse (Dec. 8, 2007).

150. *A Shift in the Debate Over Global Warming,* NY Times On-line (April 6, 2008); *see* Jeffrey D. Sachs, *Climate Change after Bali,* 298 Sci. Amer., Issue 3, 33–34 (March 2008).

151. *See* Donald A. Brown, *The U.S. Performance in Achieving Its 1992 Earth Summit Global Warming Commitments,* 32 Envtl. L. Rep. 10741 (July 2002); Alan S. Manne and Richard G. Richels, *U.S. Rejection of the Kyoto Protocol: The Impact on Compliance Costs and CO_2 emissions,* AEI & Brookings Joint Center for Regulatory Studies Working Paper 01-12 (Oct. 2001).

ican businesses have to bear the costs of reducing GHG emissions while competing foreign firms do not. The Bush Administration also claimed that voluntary GHG pollution control initiatives will prove sufficient,[152] a position most climate experts regard as nonsense. At the Bali meeting, Al Gore acknowledged that the U.S. was "principally responsible" for the lack of global warming progress.[153] Michael Bloomberg, the New York City Mayor, observed: "There's a belief that the United States should not do anything until all the other governments are willing to go along and do it at the same time.... [but we] should be doing this regardless of whether the world is following or not."[154]

Although U.S. diplomats eventually accepted the Bali "roadmap" commitment to provide fiscal and technological assistance to developing states, the U.S. rejected the European-supported proposal to reduce GHG emissions 25 to 40 percent by 2020 and other proposals for numerical GHG emissions-reduction targets.[155] A Worldwatch Institute staff member reported that Bali produced no progress on resolving the two most controversial issues: "Whether a process to add emission-reduction commitments of developing countries will be on the negotiating agenda; and whether a range of industrial countries' emission-reduction commitments will be referred to in the text."[156] In practice, the large developing countries would not agree to accept any definite commitments for GHG emissions reductions, and the U.S. along with several other developed nations would not agree to specific numerical targets for how much they must cut their GHG emissions. In short, there was almost perfect disagreement about the most fundamental issues.

The Bali debate took the form of "how much will they reduce their GHGs" in comparison to "how much will we have to reduce our GHGs" and "how much will we pay them to limit their GHG pollution," with no satisfactory consensus emerging. There is no reason to expect any resolution because the conflicting concerns of the opposing states have not been harmonized or circumvented in any practical way. Despite well-publicized commitments by the Bali delegates to work towards a concrete action plan during the two years before the next scheduled climate conference in Copenhagen, there cannot be significant progress until the conflicting priorities and ethical claims have been resolved.

To the extent that the developed nations genuinely want to overcome climate change problems, these nations must change their focus or frame of reference away from emissions-reduction targets by asking how they can persuade developing countries to reduce their GHG discharges, because climate change cannot possibly be contained or reversed unless both groups of nations undertake effective pollution control measures. Most developing states will not accept pollution restrictions that preclude exploitation of "dirty" energy-producing and manufacturing technologies currently necessary to expand their development. These nations would regard any request to sacrifice increasing development as another attempt by wealthy states to prevent less advantaged countries from "catching up" to the comparable level of economic and social welfare they feel entitled to attain. As long as the developing nations follow in our "dirty" industrial development and consumption footsteps by using the same GHG-polluting industrial and con-

---

152. *Bush Sets Greenhouse Gas Emissions Goal*, NY Times On-line (April 17, 2008); *Bush Splits With Congress and States on Emissions*, NY Times On-line (April 4, 2007).

153. *Nations Agree on Steps to Revive Climate Treaty*, NY Times On-line (Dec. 16, 2007).

154. *Id.*

155. *See U.S. "Not Ready" to Commit to Bali*, The Associated Press, *reprinted* by NY Times On-line (Dec. 9, 2007); Tiempo Climate Newswatch: The Bali Roadmap (Dec. 2007, downloaded from http://www.tiempocyberclimate.org on 01/19/2008).

156. James Russell, Bali Conference Day 9: Brackets, [Friend][Foe] of the Consensus Process, Worldwatch Inst. (Dec. 11, 2007).

sumption methods the developed nations created,[157] any attempts to mitigate climate risks will be hopeless and more international meetings on global climate change will be pointless.

I am arguing that developed nations and multilateral institutions must modify their climate change strategy to include fostering development in less affluent nations while at the same time reducing GHG pollution and atmospheric concentrations. The only realistic course of action that can meet both requirements is offering the developing nations GHG-free technologies that would enable them to increase their prosperity without discharging large quantities of GHGs. Consistent with the negotiated Bali "roadmap," the wealthy nations will have to pay a large proportion of the costs for these clean technology transfers.

Even meeting a stringent GHG emissions-reduction target in the affluent nations—perhaps a hypothetical 80 percent decrease in GHG pollution—would not give the developing countries what they want most, which is more international aid to foster greater economic growth and social welfare. If the affluent states offer developing nations improved emissions-reduction technologies, such as more fuel-efficient vehicle engines, these technology transfers may help reduce GHG emissions compared to unrestricted business-as-usual pollution, but they would not promote greater development in many countries that regard development as their highest priority. In contrast, the provision of GHG-free replacement technologies, especially clean energy technologies, could promote development and eliminate GHG pollution at the same time. A carbon-free electric power generating plant, for example, can provide the energy required for further economic development without discharging the residual GHG pollution that would remain in the atmosphere after adoption of GHG emissions-reduction programs.

As noted above, the fly-in-the-ointment is that the developed nations have not yet designed and deployed feasible replacement technologies that could achieve improvements in the welfare of poor nations without producing harmful GHG emissions. We do not now have the technology they need, and we need, for there to be any realistic chance of effectively reducing the GHG concentration in the atmosphere. There is no point in conducting expensive, time-consuming, controversial, ultimately fruitless international climate change conferences when the fundamental requirements for meaningful agreements do not exist. After the developed nations are able to create suitable GHG-free replacement technologies that could be transferred to developing states without requiring them to make economic sacrifices, international meetings will be necessary for negotiations on how much financial aid and technology transfer assistance should be provided by the affluent nations. At that time, the technical ability to eliminate or drastically reduce GHGs while enabling greater development will be demonstrated, as it has not been today, and the debate would turn to which nations should pay how much to combat more global climate change.

If effective GHG replacement technologies can be devised in the next several decades, which I regard as more of a political and economic challenge than an engineering problem, the developing states would gain the economic and social welfare enhancement assistance they urgently want while the developed nations would get tangible global warming progress without having to give up anything but a modest amount of their capital. In contrast, endless demands from the U.S. and other wealthy states for emissions-reduction commitments by developing nations will continue to be ignored because they conflict with these states' welfare-improvement goals. In the same vein, transfers of interim emissions-reduction technologies, such as dual-fuel vehicle engines, may be better than nothing but they cannot reduce GHGs nearly as effectively as all-electric or hydrogen fuel-cell cars, and they will not be attractive to developing nations because they

---

157. *See China Grabs West's Smoke-Spewing Factories*, NY TIMES ON-LINE (Dec. 27, 2007); Thomas L. Friedman, *No, No, No, Don't Follow Us*, Op-Ed column, NY TIMES ON-LINE (Nov. 4, 2007).

do little or nothing to promote more prosperity. Until affluent states have created affordable replacement technologies, the transition to a GHG-free economy that would also facilitate increased development in poor countries will be impossible.

Implementation Choices and Institutions

If the volume of persistent GHGs in the atmosphere must be stabilized and then cut back to the greatest extent feasible to minimize climate change hazards, this can only be achieved by developing GHG-free technologies that enable people to maintain or improve their standards of living without generating harmful greenhouse gases. It would require an entire book or possibly a shelf-full of books to analyze in detail all of the regulatory institutions and technological innovations needed to implement successful clean-technology programs in many contexts and places around the world. Given space limitations and my limited technological expertise, I can only offer a broad overview of the social initiatives that have a good chance to attain the goal of promoting GHG-free technologies to mitigate climate change. If readers find these arguments and conclusions persuasive, the next step would be to work out the implementation plans in a more rigorous manner and to generate more political and financial support. But first we need to consider the "big picture."

I believe no single initiative or institutional regime could address all complex dimensions of a technology-replacement strategy for combating global climate change. The essential tasks are to design effective GHG-free technologies and to ensure their widespread deployment, which would require economic affordability and political palatability. Effective implementation of this technology-replacement strategy will involve four overlapping implementation mechanisms: (1) the creation of a government-sponsored "Technology Development and Dissemination Fund" (TDD Fund) that could support the design, production, and marketing of competing GHG-free technologies; (2) the imposition of a direct regulation program that would force industrial dischargers to reduce their GHG emissions by a specified percentage rate each year, which would create incentives for polluting firms to reduce their GHG emissions and to develop clean technologies and processes outside the sponsorship of the TDD Fund; (3) the imposition of a progressive carbon tax to create an additional inducement for polluting firms to reduce their GHG discharges and to generate the substantial revenues needed to finance the Fund's research and development programs, technology transfers to developing nations, and retraining programs or social dislocation assistance to make the transition more acceptable for fossil-fuel producing areas; and (4) the imposition of national or international GHG emissions-monitoring and disclosure programs applicable to all major GHG dischargers.

Many climate experts have advocated one or another of these approaches as their primary regulatory mechanism for overcoming global warming in the U.S., and subsequently in the world, but I believe we will need all of them working simultaneously and reinforcing each other to maximize the chances for successful GHG mitigation outcomes.

The Technology Development and Dissemination Fund

The TDD Fund conception reflects my view that we cannot depend on market forces to produce and distribute sufficient effective GHG-free technologies in the next few decades. Many economists and other climate experts have claimed that we must identify the "correct market price" for GHG discharges; we must impose pollution taxes equal to the harm caused by GHG discharges; we must promote a "level playing ground" that allows clean technologies to compete against established GHG polluting processes; and we must try to prevent climate change effects only when the aggregate benefits of mitigation actions exceed the costs.[158] The implication of

---

158. *See, e.g.,* Nicholas Stern, The Stern Review: The Economics of Climate Change (2007 Cambridge Univ. Press, Cambridge); Marilyn A. Brown & Benjamin K. Sovacool, *Promoting a Level Playing Field for Energy Options: Electricity Alternatives and The Case of the Indian Point Energy Center,* 1 Energy Effi-

these economic recommendations is that, after tweaking GHG markets and market prices in suitable ways, we could rely on decentralized market system forces to determine how much of our scarce resources should be expended to overcome climate change risks and how much of the resulting damages should be regarded as acceptable or unavoidable.

Every economist with any interest in environmental and energy issues is doubtless aware of the massive subsidies, widespread externalized damages, price supports or other interventions by many nations, economies of scale in production and distribution, and other aspects of current energy and manufacturing markets that would make it virtually impossible for GHG-free technologies to compete against fossil-fuel combustion technologies under existing market conditions.[159] What would the energy industries look like today without long-standing tax depletion allowances; relatively minor penalties not yet paid for the *Exxon Valdez* oil spill 20 years ago and many other externalized ecological harms; the give-away of coal and mineral deposits on public lands compared to the costs of mining on private lands; the frequent dislocation and sometimes poisoning of indigenous peoples in developing countries, and a great many other lucrative subsidies and externalities? The idea that we can readily repair these market imperfections and return to business as usual — using the same "free market" mechanisms that have brought us to the climate change precipice — seems wholly unrealistic because we do not know how much harm will be caused by global climate change in the future[160] or what the costs will be of successful prevention. And we also have no persuasive market-based means to overcome difficult collective-action problems.

Without a comprehensive understanding of the potential benefits and dangers of all the polluting activities contributing to the greenhouse effect, which is far beyond the state of current scientific and economic knowledge, there is no reliable way that energy prices and GHG pollution prices can be "corrected." Moreover, market prices depend equally on demand choices by consumers; achieving the "correct" demand and resulting market prices for GHG-polluting activities would require billions of individuals with limited information and cognitive restrictions to make countless "correct" purchases reflecting their preferences about energy availability, industrial processes, and harmful climate change impacts that they would very rarely understand. Typically uninformed consumption choices would be further degraded by enormous transac-

---

ciency 35–48 (2008); U.S. Climate Change Science Program, Reducing U.S. Greenhouse Gas Emissions: How Much at What Cost? Executive Summary (May 2008); Nicholas Stern, *Key Elements of a Global Deal on Climate Change*, London School of Economics and Politics Working Paper (May 2008); Equal Exchange: Determining a Fair Market Price for Carbon, UNEP Perspectives Series (Glenn Hodas & Sami Kamel eds., 2007); Martin Altemeyer-Bartscher, Dirk T. G. Rübbelke & Eytan Sheshinski, *Policies To Internalize Reciprocal International Spillovers*, CESIFO Working Paper No. 2058 (July 2007); Kenneth J. Arrow, *Global Climate Change: A Challenge to Policy*, Economists' Voice (June 2007, downloaded from www.bepress.com/ev/ on 11/01/2007); Sheila M Olmstead & Robert N. Stavins, *An International Architecture for the Post-Kyoto Era*, Harvard Kennedy School of Government Working Paper RWP06-009 (March 2006); *The Carbon Calculus*, NY Times On-line (Nov. 7, 2007).

159. *See, e.g.*, David R. Hodas, *Ecosystem Subsidies of Fossil Fuels*, Widener Law School Research Paper Series No. 08-37 (2008); Thomas L. Friedman, *Dumb As We Wanna Be*, Op-Ed column, NY Times On-line (April 30, 2008); Roberta Mann, *Another Day Older and Deeper in Debt: How Tax Incentives Encourage Burning Coal and the Consequences for Global Warming*, 20 Global Business & Devel. L.J. 111 (2007); *Lawmakers Push for Big Subsidies for Coal Process*, NY Times On-line (May 29, 2007); *Pollution From Chinese Coal Casts a Global Shadow*, NY Times On-line (June 11, 2006); Axel Gosseries, *Historical Emissions and Free-Riding*, 11 Ethical Perspectives, No. 1, 36 (2004); Doug Koplow & John Dernbach, *Federal Fossil Fuel Subsidies and Greenhouse Gas Emissions: A Case Study Of Increasing Transparency For Fiscal Policy*, 26 Annual Rev. Energy & Envt. 361 (2001).

160. *See* Martin L. Weitzman, *On Modeling and Interpreting the Economics of Catastrophic Climate Change*, Harvard REStat Working Paper, Final Version (July 5, 2008); *Climate Experts Tussle Over Details, Public Gets Whiplash*, NY Times On-line (July 29, 2008).

tions costs resulting partly from the vast number of affected individuals and partly from widespread free-rider and coordination problems and the "public goods" quality of climate change problems that would be impossible to resolve in practice through decentralized market choices.[161]

Of course, pro-market ideologues would contend that government decisions will always be even worse. Yet, coordinated actions supported or mandated by government is the generally-accepted means in conventional economic theory to overcome public goods and collective-action problems.[162] In response to the market advocates who believe government can do no good, I would point to the Eisenhower Interstate Highway Program, the Publicly-Owned Treatment Works construction program under the Clean Water Act, and the Apollo program as instances where the American government has undertaken multi-billion-dollar projects with considerable success. The potential harms from global climate change are certainly as pressing as the public needs that inspired these ambitious government programs, which are still providing valuable public benefits, and the need for collective action on climate problems is at least as urgent.

Many GHG-free technologies, including renewable energy alternatives, already exist but are not necessarily in mature forms that can support widespread diffusion at affordable costs. An incomplete list would include several different types of solar energy processes, wind turbines, wave and tidal power, geothermal energy, hydropower generation, nuclear energy, hydrogen fuel cells, plasma gasification (a thermal chemical process to convert garbage and industrial wastes into "clean" fuels), methane combustion from waste disposal sites and feed lots, and diverse biofuels made from nearly every biological material. In addition to various energy production technologies, carbon capture and storage methods could be extremely important by allowing the use of fossil fuels without the pernicious atmospheric effects, and carbon sequestration through reforestation could also be useful up to a point. I cannot choose which one(s) of these potential technologies will become effective substitutes for GHG-polluting methods, and I predict that different alternative HG-free technologies will prove desirable in different places under different conditions. The central point, though, is that we should be developing and deploying whichever GHG-free technologies emerge as most effective and affordable; and we should not be wasting administrative resources on ineffectual, counter-productive emissions-reduction programs.

Some experts claim that existing technologies are sufficient to overcome global warming if they are widely adopted, while other experts contend that adequate GHG-free technologies have not yet been demonstrated in many contexts.[163] I am inclined to agree with the latter assessment because carbon capture and storage technologies are likely to be vital, and their feasibility has

---

161. *See* Thomas C. Schelling, *Climate Change: The Uncertainties, the Certainties, and What They Imply About Action*, ECONOMISTS' VOICE (July 2007, downloaded from www.bepress.com/ev/ on 11/01/2007); Agnar Sandmo, *Global Public Economics: Public Goods And Externalities*, Norwegian School of Economics and Business Administration Working Paper (July, 2006); Axel Gosseries, *Historical Emissions and Free-Riding*, 11 ETHICAL PERSPECTIVES, No. 1, 36 (2004).

162. *See* Thomas C. Schelling, *Climate Change: The Uncertainties, the Certainties, and What They Imply About Action*, ECONOMISTS' VOICE (July 2007, downloaded from www.bepress.com/ev/ on 11/01/2007); Robert N. Stavins & Scott Barrett, *Increasing Participation and Compliance in International Climate Change Agreements*, Harvard Kennedy School of Government Working Paper No. RWP02-031, 18–20, 26 (2002).

163. *Compare* Quirin Schiermeier, *Climate Challenge Underestimated? Technology Will Not Automatically Come to Our Aid, Experts Warn*, NATURE ON-LINE (April 2, 2008) and Roger Pielke, Jr., Tom Wigley & Christopher Green, *Dangerous Assumptions*, 452 NATURE 531–32 (April 3, 2008) *with* Stephen Pacala & Robert Socolow, *Stabilization Wedges: Solving the Climate Problem for the Next 50 Years with Current Technologies*, 305 SCIENCE., No. 5686, 968–72 (Aug. 13, 2004).

not yet been shown on a commercial scale.[164] Rather than guessing about which potential clean technologies would be best, with a high likelihood of mistakes, I propose that the TDD Fund should be guided by a Commission whose members would be chosen mainly from the National Academy of Sciences and National Academy of Engineering, perhaps with a couple of American participants in the IPCC. There is no question that politics, money, and private interest-group lobbying will influence the technological and fiscal choices of the Commission, as these forces have affected all dimensions of American political life, but the Commission should strive to rise above political machinations through the informed recommendations of experienced scientists, engineers, and economists who have been assessing GHG-free technologies and climate change issues for a considerable time.

Because we cannot yet predict which GHG-free technologies will prove most effective in different contexts, the TDD Fund will need to sponsor numerous design, production, and pilot projects that would enable various clean technologies to compete against each other. However, it is crucial that these GHG-free technologies must not be required to compete against GHG-based technologies, such as energy, transportation, and manufacturing processes that rely on fossil fuel combustion. In light of the rapid increase in recent energy prices, the fossil fuel production countries and companies now possess extraordinary financial resources and cannot be allowed to under-price or underbid nascent clean technologies, as they arguably did in the aftermath of the oil crisis of 1973. We must not forget that long-established fossil fuel-based technologies have been the leading cause of global climate change, and we cannot allow the producers and beneficiaries of fossil fuels to undermine efforts to create GHG-free replacement technologies. The functions of the TDD Fund would be to assess, compare, sponsor, and subsidize an array of potential GHG-free technologies while promoting greater market penetration and insulating clean technologies from the distorted market prices and often corrupt practices associated with established GHG-based processes.

As much as I respect Dr. Hansen's scientific knowledge and admire his passionate and courageous public advocacy, I cannot agree with his primary recommendations for addressing climate change problems. For two decades, he has argued that the first steps in avoiding global warming disasters should be to impose a moratorium on new coal-burning power plants and to phase out existing coal-burning generators unless carbon capture and storage methods can be perfected.[165] Yet, international energy demand has sharply increased during the same period and hundreds of new coal-burning power plants have been built to meet this growing demand. Coal combustion is the single worst contributor to GHG emissions, but it is also the least expensive fuel for expanding power generating capacity. There is no question which conflicting factor has been dominant in the policies of GHG polluting nations, with the result that coal-burning power plants and factories are still being constructed frequently in many places.

The problem with Dr. Hansen's recommendations is that he did not present a compelling discussion of feasible alternative energy sources. We must develop adequate energy alternatives before asking the nations of the world to give up proven GHG-based technologies that promote more development despite causing global warming. If we cannot provide satisfactory, feasible alternatives, the request to abandon coal-burning power plants and other "dirty" pollution sources is an unrealistic appeal for nations and people to *sacrifice* the development they want most. The

---

164. *See* Roger Pielke, Jr., Tom Wigley & Christopher Green, *Dangerous Assumptions*, 452 NATURE 531–32 (April 3, 2008); *Running in Circles Over Carbon*, NY TIMES ON-LINE (June 8, 2008); *The Energy Challenge: Mounting Costs Slow the Push for Clean Coal*, NY TIMES ON-LINE (May 30, 2008).

165. *See* James Hansen, *How Can We Avert Dangerous Climate Change?* (congressional testimony given in 2007, downloaded from http://publs.giss.nasa.gov/authors/jhansen.html on 09/27/2007); Jim Hansen, *The Threat to the Planet*, 53 N.Y. REV. BOOKS, no.12, 13 (July 13, 2006).

mission of the TDD Fund is critically important because I do not believe that climate change campaigns based on pleas for broad public sacrifices can prevail in competition with intensely-felt economic and social welfare aspirations.

As Professor Jeffrey Sachs has emphasized,[166] we cannot expect poor countries and their people to sacrifice economic and social development opportunities even when their activities produce GHG pollution, and therefore we must show them that a better way exists to achieve the same development objectives. Instead of telling countless millions of people in developed and developing nations to reduce this and cut out that, and to give up other desired amenities and activities, as many environmentalists have advocated, a more realistic strategy must be grounded on the dissemination of affordable GHG-free technological alternatives that people will find satisfactory because they would still be able to do what they want to do while they are helping to confront global warming.

Dr. Hansen has blamed the lack of progress in promoting his recommendations on the influence of powerful private interest groups and lack of government vision, which are serious concerns, but I believe there is a more fundamental reason—the lack of broad popular support for self-sacrificing measures. Most Americans do not appear willing to give up their plans and hopes for the future despite the risks from global climate change, which many people do not feel are personally relevant or urgent. Environmentalists must recognize that they need to persuade a large portion of the entire population, not just each other, to take appropriate actions despite inevitable opposition from affected businesses and interest groups. If we cannot create clean GHG-free technological alternatives, I see no realistic way to prevent the atmospheric GHG concentration from growing worse every year. The TDD Fund to guide the development of clean replacement technologies and processes is the lynchpin of my plan—meeting this vital need is not going to happen by accident or wishful thinking or as a by-product of conventional emissions-reduction efforts.

In the same vein, Al Gore recently challenged the U.S. to supplant all GHG-based energy sources with GHG-free alternative energy methods within the next decade.[167] This is an inspirational goal and not entirely impossible to meet, but Gore did not describe the potential costs if America embarks on this difficult mission and is not successful for a variety of political and economic reasons. It seems highly improbable that our society would put its entire economy and employment base at risk by demanding radical technological and behavioral changes before we are reasonably certain that suitable energy sources, industrial processes, product designs, governance institutions, and political support exist that could achieve the required technology transformations at an affordable cost. We do not definitely possess any of these core requirements now, and we surely need to invest more time, efforts, and money in meeting them.

In recent years, quite a few Funds have been created or proposed with various global climate change missions. For example, the World Bank is participating in the financing of a dozen climate-related Funds, including one with about five billion dollars to help developing countries adapt to climate change hardships and another Fund to help these states achieve cleaner energy production.[168] However, the latter efforts have been sharply criticized by environmental groups because the World Bank has been willing to support "clean coal" projects and other fossil-fuel energy technologies that will produce large amounts of greenhouse gases.[169] The United King-

---

166. *See* Jeffrey D. Sachs, *Keys to Climate Protection*, 298 Sci. Amer., Issue 4, 40 (April 2008); Jeffrey D. Sachs, *Climate Change after Bali*, 298 Sci. Amer., Issue 3, 33–34 (March 2008).

167. *Gore Urges Change to Dodge an Energy Crisis*, NY Times On-line (July 18, 2008).

168. *See* World Bank, Carbon Finance at the World Bank: List of Funds (2008, downloaded from www.carbonfinance.org on 08/10/2008).

169. *Climate Change: Greens, Lawmakers Assail World Bank Funds*, Inter Press Service News (July 11, 2008).

dom has created a Fund of 400 million pounds (about $800 million) to promote the development of clean technologies, but this relatively small Fund will remain secondary to the British involvement with emissions-reduction programs featuring cap-and-trade mechanisms.[170] The Premier of Alberta recently announced two Funds with about four billion Canadian dollars to promote public transportation systems and to support carbon capture and storage programs, which may be a public relations response to the Province's large oil-shale development projects that are sure to worsen GHG emissions unless CCS programs can be implemented effectively.[171] The government of Pennsylvania recently announced their "Energy Independence Fund" with 850 million dollars intended to support rebates for efficient household appliances, to provide capital loans for alternative energy companies, and to pay for some of the "development or equipment costs for specific energy economic development projects."[172] I found descriptions of these Funds with their diverse purposes while writing this material, and undoubtedly there are many other current or proposed institutional funding programs addressing climate change issues.

None of these Funds, or any comparable fiscal proposals I have seen, embody the single-objective clean-technology focus and extensive financial resources of my TDD Fund proposal, which will be needed to support competitive evaluations of more than a dozen potential replacement technologies and to promote the design, development, marketing, and protective nurturing of feasible GHG-free technologies that can replace harmful polluting methods in many contexts. Thus far, nearly all governments and international institutions appear to be spreading their limited climate change funds across an array of tasks, including research and development, mitigation, adaptation, compensation, and often fruitless negotiation. In my opinion, expending a few billion dollars here and a few billion dollars there on many different missions and implementation tasks is unlikely to produce significant progress anywhere. I am arguing that we must put the great majority of our climate change "eggs" into a technology-replacement "basket" because diffuse and ambiguous mandates cannot succeed in dealing with the difficult real-world problems arising from global warming and climate change.

Shrinking-Cap Direct Regulation of GHG Pollution

There will be many opponents of the transition to a GHG-free technology-replacement economy, including major fossil-fuel producing nations and companies; people concerned that competitive pressures from large developing nations, especially China, will undermine the value of American innovation if we have to pay the business costs of creating and distributing clean technologies while less prosperous states do not; other people who do not want to pay high pollution control costs when most climate change mitigation benefits ostensibly will mostly help poor people in vulnerable regions of developing countries; and still other people who would rather avoid the fiscal burdens and become free-riders. These formidable opponents are not likely to give up their existing economic and social advantages without a knock-down, drag-out political fight that will continue for years or decades.

Under these political conditions, I am concerned that the budgetary support for the TDD Fund or any comparable funding mechanism will gradually fade away unless it is perceived as the least onerous measure among several regulatory programs imposed on GHG polluters, con-

---

170. U.K. Dept. for Environment, Food and Rural Affairs, Funding for Low Carbon Technologies: The Environmental Transformation Fund (April 2, 2008).

171. *Alberta Premier Promises $4B in Green Cash*, Canwest News Service (July 11, 2008, downloaded from www.canada.com on 07/11.2008).

172. *Governor Rendell Unveils Energy Independence Strategy to Save Consumers $10 Billion over 10 Years, Reduce Reliance on Foreign Fuels*, Pennsylvania Government Press Release (Feb 1, 2007).

sumers, and taxpayers. In other words, continuing support for the TDD Fund may be dependent not only on replacement-technology successes, but also on the public perception that putting more reliance on alternative regulatory approaches will be even more objectionable and expensive for climate change program opponents. If this concern appears speculative,[173] it might be useful to ask what has happened to the funding commitments for hundreds of publicly-owned sewage-treatment plants and hundreds of Superfund cleanups.

The U.S. government could mandate the adoption of particular technologies to reduce GHG pollution in particular contexts or sectors, as Congress did by requiring motor vehicle fleets to burn a percentage of ethanol-based biofuels produced largely from American corn.[174] However, this agricultural-subsidy choice turned out to be mistake for numerous reasons,[175] and it calls into question the desirability of regulations that impose specific pollution control technologies rather than adopting a shrinking emissions cap that would allow polluters to choose their own means for progressively decreasing GHG discharges. The biofuels legislation is another example of the "*we have to do something now*" mentality without a careful assessment of the potential downside of risky innovations.[176] Despite the urgency resulting from climate tipping points and the persistence of greenhouse gases, we cannot afford to waste billions of dollars and years of irreplaceable time on supposed remedial measures that in practice may prove more harmful than beneficial.

The purpose of a shrinking regulatory cap is not only to reduce the volume of GHG pollution, but also to encourage regulated firms to look for innovative ways to cut their emissions by creating clean technologies specific to their industries and practices. The TDD Fund will proba-

---

173. *See* Daniel M. Kammen & Gregory F. Nemet, *Real Numbers: Reversing the Incredible Shrinking Energy R & D Budget*, Issues in Sci. and Tech. 84–88 (Fall 2005).

174. *See, e.g.*, Arnold W. Reitze, Jr., *Should the Clean Air Act Be Used to Turn Petroleum Addicts into Alcoholics?* Envtl. Forum 50–60 (July/Aug. 2007); *As Ethanol Takes Its First Steps, Congress Proposes a Giant Leap*, NY Times On-line (Dec. 18, 2007); *see generally* Raya Widenoja, Destination Iowa: Getting to a Sustainable Biofuels Future, Sierra Club & Worldwatch Inst. Report (Oct. 2007); Nathanael Greene, Growing Energy: How Biofuels Can Help End America's Oil Dependence, Natural Resources Defense Council Report (Dec. 2004).

175. *See, e.g., Another Problem with Biofuels?*, Time Magazine & CNN (March 12, 2008, downloaded from http://www.time.com on 04/18/2008); *Biofuels Deemed a Greenhouse Threat*, NY Times On-line (Feb. 8, 2008); Deepak Rajagopal & David Zilberman, *Review of Environmental, Economic and Policy Aspects of Biofuels*, World Bank Policy Research Working Paper No. 4341 (Sept. 2007); *Food and Fuel Compete for Land*, NY Times On-line (Dec. 18, 2007); Bart Mongoven, *The Biofuel Backlash*, Stratfor Public Policy Intelligence Report (Sept. 13, 2007, downloaded from https://www.stratfor.com on 09/21/2007); *Paved With Good Intentions*, Time Magazine & CNN (April 19, 2007, downloaded from http://www.time.com on 01/19/2008); Richard Doornbosch and Ronald Steenblik, *Biofuels: Is the Cure Worse than the Disease?*, OECD Roundtable Paper (Paris, Sept. 11–12, 2007).

176. One consistent problem is that many environmental groups and many well-intentioned scientists presume idealistically that every step in a complex process will go perfectly and every involved party will behave properly based on social needs rather than private incentives. In the context of biofuels, for example, the utopian analysis assumed that producers would only use biological waste material and cellulosic ethanol made from twigs and dead leaves, rather than employing readily accessible corn and soy crops that would compete with food production. And the idealists assumed that farmers would continue to produce food crops as before, while growing suitable biofuel materials on marginal lands. However, as long as the prices of fossil fuels remain high, the prices of biofuels are likely to exceed the price of food crops per pound, and many farmers would prefer to get the higher prices for their work even if that choice may create national and international food shortages. The moral is that complexity, uncertainty, short-sightedness, and private interests or greed will always affect and degrade complicated efforts to produce desirable environmental conditions and public goods. Only a stargazing dreamer would support a program with as many obvious weakness and externalities as biofuels proliferation without carefully examining the negative aspects as well as the hypothetical good ones. *See As Prices Rise, Farmers Spurn Conservation*, NY Times On-line (April 9, 2008); *Studies Deem Biofuels a Greenhouse Threat*, NY Times On-line (Feb. 8, 2008).

bly focus primarily on sponsoring GHG-free technological alternatives in the energy and transportation industries, which are the leading sources of GHG emissions and are also critically important to economic development efforts. However, many other industries, such as building construction, livestock production, forestry, and agriculture, combine to produce substantial annual GHG discharges. A steadily decreasing GHG emissions cap would create an on-going incentive for these polluting firms to devise cleaner methods. The imposition of a progressively decreasing regulatory cap should also improve the market penetration of GHG-free technologies, whether sponsored by the TDD Fund or by private entrepreneurs, because it will be cost-effective for many polluting firms to adopt GHG-free methods that enable them to stay beneath the shrinking regulatory cap. Adopting clean industrial processes may also offer a competitive advantage over firms that do not choose to employ GHG-free replacement technologies.

We have a great deal of regulatory experience in trying to devise and enforce different pollution control standards for different industries that discharge different mixes of pollutants—these "technology-based standards" are the central regulatory instruments in the Clean Water Act and are almost equally important in the Clean Air Act—which required the promulgation of thousands of detailed regulations based on the technological and economic characteristics of hundreds of classes and categories of polluting industries.[177] I believe this sector-by-sector approach would be too complicated and would require too much time and administrative resources in the many contexts in which dissimilar GHG polluters are discharging essentially fungible emissions. As a matter of implementation practicality rather than theoretical efficiency, imposing the same shrinking percentage emissions cap on all types of major GHG dischargers would be much more administrable than adopting a sector-by-sector regulatory approach.

Several variations on the shrinking regulatory cap approach are worth consideration. We could, for example, impose a 10-percent reduction mandate for the first decade and three-percent shrinkage rate per year thereafter (using compound, not simple, interest) on the rationale that the less stringent initial rate would allow firms facing the "shock" of mandated pollution controls more time to identify their best options and would give the TDD Fund more time to bring an array of GHG-free technologies to market maturity. Conversely, we could make the near-term shrinkage rate more stringent than in later years on the rationale that most firms will be able to choose their least expensive pollution-control options during the initial period, while the marginal cost of further GHG reductions is likely to increase after the cheap, easy ways have already been adopted. Or we could choose a two-percent or three-percent annual shrinkage rate and impose it throughout the duration of the shrinking cap regulatory program. I do not have a strong feeling about which of these choices is better, but it will take several years for the government regulations and TDD Fund to get up to speed and for polluting industries to assess various GHG-free pollution control options. As a result, the approach imposing a lower initial shrinkage rate may be the most realistic and the least likely to result in surprises and wasteful mistakes. There can be no doubt that we must expect, and plan for, serious implementation problems when we try to run a complex, controversial regulatory program affecting almost every aspect of our economic and social welfare.

From an international perspective, it would be desirable if the U.S., the E.U., and other developed nations could cooperate in operating the TDD Fund and adopting the same GHG shrinking cap approach, but this seems to be an unlikely prospect. Disputes about which Fund expenditures should promote which technological developments in which countries would be difficult to resolve, and competitive tensions will arise from the ramifications of patenting GHG-free replacement technologies supported at least in part by financing from a coalition of nations with

---

177. *See., e.g.,* Wendy E. Wagner, *The Triumph of Technology-Based Standards,* 2000 U. Ill. L. Rev. 83; Howard A. Latin, *supra* note 115.

partly conflicting economic interests. A uniform shrinking GHG cap also appears unlikely to be widely accepted in Europe because the E.U. nations have been focusing almost exclusively on emissions trading schemes in which mandatory regulatory shrinkage may reduce the value of the emissions allowances and trades. The U.S. will probably have to take the lead under the new Administration to develop effective GHG-free replacement technologies in competition with European and Asian countries. At the same time, we need to design clean technologies suitable for technology transfers to developing nations as a means to reduce the GHG pollution levels in these countries without sacrificing economic and social welfare opportunities. The shrinking cap regulatory program would probably not be accepted by developing countries, but it would help show those states that the American government and people have become serious about cutting their own greenhouse gas emissions before asking the people of poor nations to do the same.

Progressively Increasing GHG Pollution Tax

The most important function of this pollution tax or pollution charges system is to raise substantial revenues for climate change programs, which would be essential in financing the transition to a GHG-free economy and society. The proposed TDD Fund will need several tens of billions of dollars at least to facilitate its mission to assess, develop, promote, and nurture a variety of GHG-free replacement technologies and processes. It will also require large fiscal resources to pay for technology transfers to developing nations, which almost certainly will be essential for the affluent states to persuade poor nations to curtail their GHG discharges.

I predict that we will also need to offer dislocation assistance programs for retraining and adaptation in some U.S. regions to attain sufficiently broad political support for the regulatory and clean-technology initiatives. In the utopian world occupied by many environmentalists and climate experts, everyone will pitch in voluntarily to overcome the potentially catastrophic effects of global warming—all we have to do is explain the need for long-term collective action. But in the frustrating real world of divergent human interests and priorities, many people will not vote, or voluntarily pay, to support GHG pollution control efforts that threaten their jobs and incomes, their lifestyles, or other undesired losses. Plenty of politicians will doubtless emerge to "serve" these antagonistic constituencies. Remember the cognitive psychology finding that many people would rather avoid a loss than pursue a commensurate gain.[178] Effective programs to combat climate change are certainly going to result in losses for many communities as well as businesses, and we need to plan to provide some form of dislocation assistance to help overcome the resulting political hostility.

The Interstate Highway System and Publicly-Owned Treatment Works construction programs, though they provided large net social benefits, both contained redistributive provisions to soften the dislocation costs and burdens imposed on the people in relatively unfortunate areas. I predict that the sponsors of GHG-free technology-replacement programs, adaptation programs, and other GHG pollution control efforts will need to consider very carefully the political dimensions of national and international redistributive effects. There will be many perceived "losers" if we are able to create programs that can overcome global climate change; and there will be many perceived "losers" if we are not able to implement effective mitigation programs. The losers are likely to expect compensation or redistribution in any case.

In addition to the revenue benefits from gradually increasing the GHG taxes or charges, the prospect of imposing progressively higher GHG taxes on polluting firms would strengthen their economic incentives to adopt GHG-free technologies and other clean methods. The predictable increases in GHG taxes each year will probably encourage some firms to undertake a more rapid

---

178. *See* text and citations accompanying notes 2–4, 105, *supra*.

conversion to pollution-free methods, and many other firms to try to improve the relative clean-liness of their industrial processes even if they are not prepared to go completely GHG-free. The progressively increasing tax should have a particularly strong effect because it will be imposed in addition to the shrinking regulatory cap program, and therefore will not allow firms to maintain or expand their GHG emissions even if they are willing to pay higher pollution taxes indefinitely.

There has been an on-going debate about the effectiveness of greenhouse gas tax schemes in comparison to cap-and-trade systems,[179] which I cannot duplicate in this Chapter. The propo-nents of cap-and-trade programs have somehow convinced both Presidential candidates and many other American politicians that this is the best climate protection approach, though I would gladly wager that none of the politicians have a solid grasp on the details and pitfalls of GHG emissions credit trading programs in practice. What I find disturbing is that comparable trading programs have not performed very well in Europe,[180] where they have been the core of the E.U. Kyoto Protocol and Emissions Trading Scheme (ETS) compliance strategy for years,[181] and yet I have not found any American cap-and-trade proponent specifically explaining why our future GHG cap-and-trade programs will be implemented more effectively or perform better than the cap-and-trade experiences of the E.U. As a result of background political cultures, it is likely that political opposition and interest-group pressures will be even stronger here than in Europe.

The E.U. ETS has been degraded by political wrangling among E.U. states, regional protec-tionism, special-interest lobbying, inadequately trained and financed personnel, ambiguous legal provisions, national fears of creating competitive disadvantages, and determination to avoid imposing regulatory costs that cause significant social dislocation even if those costs are legally mandated. There is no reason to doubt that the same common regulatory and lobbying problems will arise in U.S. attempts to implement GHG emissions trading systems; yet nearly everything written by emissions trading proponents' claims these programs can be implemented effectively in most contexts and locations. It seems likely that cap-and-trade advocates find the theory of economic incentive schemes appealing and have not invested sufficient effort in under-standing the multiple factors that have degraded emissions trading systems in other developed countries.

Imposing progressively higher GHG pollution taxes fits better with the other parts of my plan than a cap-and-trade system would because it is simpler to implement and administer a tax plan

---

179. *See, e.g.,* Ian W.H. Parry & William A. Pizer, *Combating Global Warming: Is Taxation or Cap-and-Trade the Better Strategy for Reducing Greenhouse Emissions?,* REGULATION 18–22 (Fall 2007); Carol M. Rose, *Hotspots in the Legislative Climate Change Proposals,* Arizona Legal Studies Discussion Paper No. 07-36 (2007); *Ecotaxes: Are Taxes the Best Means to Cut Greenhouse Emissions?,* ECONOMIST.COM (April 23, 2007); Thomas Eichner & Ruediger Pethig, *Efficient CO_2 Emissions Control with National Emissions Taxes and International Emissions Trading,* CESifo Working Paper No. 1967 (April 2007); Monica Prasad, *On Carbon, Tax and Don't Spend,* Op-Ed column, NY TIMES ON-LINE (March 25, 2008).

180. *See, e.g.,* PAULA CASTRO & AXEL MICHAELOWA, CLIMATE STRATEGIES REPORT: EMPIRICAL ANALYSIS OF PERFORMANCE OF CDM PROJECTS (2008); *Europe Turns Back to Coal, Raising Climate Fears,* NY TIMES ON-LINE (April 23, 2008); BEN BLOCK, EU BEHIND IN MEETING KEY ENVIRONMENTAL TARGETS, Worldwatch Inst. (March 10, 2008, downloaded from www.worldwatch.org on 03/13/2008); *The Climate Challenge. Same as it Ever Was?,* NY TIMES ON-LINE (Jan. 21, 2008); *Europe's Problems Color U.S. Plans to Curb Carbon Gases,* WASHINGTON POST A01 (April 9, 2007, downloaded from http://washingtonpost.com on 04/09/2007).

181. *See, e.g.,* POINT CARBON ADVISORY SERVICES, A REPORT FOR WWF: EU ETS PHASE II—THE POTEN-TIAL AND SCALE OF WINDFALL PROFITS IN THE POWER SECTOR (March 2008); CHRISTIAN EGENHOFER *et al.,* THE EU EMISSIONS TRADING SCHEME: TAKING STOCK AND LOOKING AHEAD, European Climate Platform Re-port (July 2006); Angus Johnston, *Free Allocation of Allowances under the EU Emissions Trading System: Legal Issues,* 6 CLIMATE POLICY (May 2006); ALANA HERRO, KYOTO: IMPOSSIBLE GOAL OR ECONOMIC OPPORTU-NITY?, Worldwatch Inst. (July 17, 2006, downloaded from www.worldwatch.org on 09/27/2006).

applicable to all major GHG dischargers, and because the taxes and direct regulations will create a continuing incentive for firms to reduce their GHG pollution even when a firm, such as an oil company or electric utility, could easily afford to buy the necessary number of pollution shares or allowances under a trading program.[182] Some opponents of trading schemes have also expressed the concern that wealthy firms—such as the major oil procuring companies—could buy most of the available emissions allowances as a means to restrict market entry or competition. In the context of the E.U. Emissions Trading System, many speculators have emerged who appear more interested in the daily fluctuations of market prices for carbon allowances than in the goal of GHG pollution reduction.

In any case, imposing a progressively increasing tax on GHG emissions appears to be easier to understand and implement than any comparably extensive emissions credit trading program. In economic theory, the cost of the emissions allowance, which is a prerequisite for lawful pollution, is just as much of a tax on polluting activities as a pollution taxes scheme would be, and politicians can call my proposal a greenhouse gas emission charges scheme if they want to stay away from the dreaded word "tax." Some cap-and-trade proponents claim that the American population has come to hate all "taxes" and therefore is more likely to approve a trading system than a pollution taxes program. I am simply making the point that a cap-and-trade program would impose just as much of a tax on polluters, and we can call a pollution tax program a "pollution charges" scheme or any other semantic formulation people find acceptable.

The Interstate Highway System was financed by higher gas taxes that did not evoke much public opposition because people could see the construction of new highways and the practical benefits arising from improved transportation. In contrast, the proposed cap-and-trade systems are likely to lose their degree of public tolerance much sooner because cap-and-trade programs, as much as conventional emissions-reduction programs, are "reducing the increases" fiascos that will not yield any significant climate change benefits. Taxpayers and consumers will hear about numerous trades of GHG allowances, and they will hear about many consultants and speculators who populate the GHG allowance trading field, but concerned people will not be able to identify any discernible global warming benefits.

Exactly the same criticisms could be directed at a GHG tax program, which could show that companies are paying the taxes—just as cap-and-trade proponents could show some firms are buying GHG allowances—but the affected people would not find that the taxes or trades are achieving any demonstrable progress in reducing climate change harms. The crucial difference is that the GHG taxes are only one component of my multi-institution plan with the primary mission of raising revenues to fund GHG-free technology development rather than overcoming global warming hazards. The proponents of cap-and-trade systems have "sold" their economic incentives approach to climate policymakers as *THE* mechanism for solving climate change problems, and yet these pollution-credit trading schemes are almost certain to produce "reducing the increases" results that are not useful solutions at all.

---

182. The cap-and-trade advocates contend that their approach will achieve the same continuing incentives to reduce emissions because firms with low pollution control costs will be able to make a profit by selling their excess shares or allowances to firms with higher control costs. I am skeptical about this claim in practice because it is based on the dubious premise that most firms try to maximize their profits at all times, while I believe that many firms put a higher priority on ensuring income consistency and steady growth rather than profit maximization. The cap-and-trade system would require periodic auctions or distributions of the pollution shares, and many firms will hold onto their shares to increase their fiscal safety under conditions of uncertainty arising from evolving knowledge about global warming risks. In other words, the firms that can afford to buy the allowances may hold onto them for security and predictability reasons, or possibly to impede market entry by other firms, rather than following the idealized profit maximization behavior that the cap-and-trade proponents assume will occur.

One of the most serious constraints on participation in international GHG pollution control initiatives has been the fear that domestic firms will not be able to compete against products and services from countries that are not required to bear the costs of cutting their GHG emissions.[183] This competitive disadvantage problem could be partly ameliorated from the U.S. perspective by imposing a GHG tax, which has sometimes been called a "border tax adjustment,"[184] on imported products or services from foreign providers that have not undertaken comparable GHG emissions-reduction efforts to ours. This treatment would undoubtedly be resented by developing countries, which will claim with some justice that they should be entitled to produce any goods and services for international trade without paying for GHG emissions-reduction programs. I cannot resolve here the ethical issues and conflicting perceptions of fairness implicit in this disputed practice, but I do want to emphasize that a GHG import tax would be easier to graft onto an existing GHG pollution tax system than onto a pollution-credit trading system.

Under a market-based trading scheme, would we make international exporters purchase enough GHG credits to cover their entire output, even if only part of their output is exported to the U.S. or developed nations? How could we monitor and enforce the volume of GHGs the exporting state is discharging in their home nations to ensure they do not exceed the amount of GHG emissions authorized by their purchased pollution credits? How will the trading program proceed if the governments of some producing nations claim this program is a scheme for compromising their sovereignty and penalizing their current production efforts despite their lack of GHG pollution in the past? Fortunately, I do not need to resolve these controversial issues and instead I am only supporting my claim that a GHG tax system would be somewhat easier to implement and enforce than a GHG cap-and-trade system.

Mandatory GHG Pollution Disclosure Programs

This approach would be modeled on the Toxic Release Inventory (TRI) mandated by the Clean Air Act[185] and on comparable E.U. programs such as the "European Pollutant Release and Transfer Register."[186] These "shaming" programs do not impose regulatory limits on pollution, which must be done through other legal provisions, but instead they seek to embarrass polluters through mandated public disclosure and to adversely affect their reputations as good corporate citizens. Though I do not believe we could depend primarily on consumers to reduce GHG emissions resulting from their daily choices and behaviors, a GHG Disclosure program would enable people who are seriously or casually concerned to make selective purchasing decisions that may influence the practices of polluting businesses whose perceived "good will" is at stake.

The government agency responsible for this GHG disclosure program could require more detailed disclosures, such as the annual GHG pollution volume as a function of the company's production output or natural resources exploitation, which would enable concerned consumers to make more informed choices about which goods and services to choose. This kind of pollution disclosure program should be regarded as another overlapping mechanism to create incentives

---

183. *See, e.g., Senate Opens Debate on Politically Risky Bill Addressing Global Warming*, NY Times On-line (June 3, 2008); *EU Climate Policy "Too Negative,"* BBC News (January 18, 2008, downloaded from http://www.news.bbc.co.uk/ on 01/31/2008).

184. *See* Katrin Jordan-Korte & Stormy Mildner, Climate Protection and Border Tax Adjustment: Economic Rationale and Political Pitfalls of Current U.S. Cap-and-Trade Proposals, FACET Analysis No.1 (June 2008).

185. U.S. EPA, What is the Toxics Release Inventory (TRI) Program (March 31, 2008, downloaded from www.epa.gov on 08/11/2008).

186. *See* Karen E. Macdonald, *The European Pollutant Release and Transfer Register: A Case Study of Bosnia-Herzegovina*, 10 European J. of Law Reform, No. 1, 21–49 (2008).

for polluting firms to adopt GHG-free technologies in the near future.[187] The same kinds of implementation, monitoring, and enforcement prerequisites will be required as under the TRI program, which have not been insurmountable in the past, and the agency may impose a fee or fine on polluters above the disclosure limit to finance the program and its enforcement.

It has recently been suggested that U.S. regulations should require the compilation and dissemination of an "individual carbon release inventory" that would inform American citizens about their personal effects on GHG pollution and would encourage or require them to reduce their impacts to a degree.[188] I cannot imagine the administrative burdens and costs of imposing compliance with this disclosure mandate;[189] or the hostility resulting from behavioral changes by some people that are rejected by many others. This initiative is an attempt to impose a large share of the responsibility for overcoming climate change on individual consumers and other decentralized persons, which I regard as a fundamentally unrealistic and ineffectual approach for the numerous reasons previously given.

As another example, it would be far more effective to adopt regulations eliminating all fossil-fuel and biofuel-combustion vehicle engines during the next two or three decades while replacing them with GHG-free engine technologies, rather than disclosing what kind of vehicles more than 200 million Americans own and telling or forcing them to buy smaller, more fuel-efficient cars, and to drive less. It is merely sophistry to refer to current GHG transportation emissions as the result of "individual behaviors" when they can be constrained by better technological options to a much greater extent than by trying to change the separate behaviors of countless people with many divergent preferences and priorities.

Overcoming global warming and climate change hazards will affect almost all facets of human life and will require many complicated and controversial pollution control choices. Under these constraints, there is no reason to expect that only one type of regulatory regime or institution will be sufficient to undertake all of the necessary mitigation and adaptation measures.[190] To the contrary, several overlapping preventive measures are likely to be more effective than any single approach. Nevertheless, my critique of "reducing the increases" emissions-reduction programs leads me to put much greater emphasis on the development and diffusion of GHG-free technologies than on any other climate change strategy. If we can develop effective, affordable clean replacement technologies and processes, the remaining political and economic hurdles will probably be overcome in the near future as climate change risks become ever more apparent.

Conclusion

Every GHG emissions-reduction program imposes a cap or target that specifies how much pollution must be cut from business-as-usual discharge levels; and every GHG emissions-reduction program allows the remaining residual pollution below the cap to be discharged into the air each year. If the cap requires a 30 percent pollution cutback, as the recent California and federal motor vehicle regulations do, the annual residual GHG pollution will be 70 percent of the business-as-usual discharges. This is a climate change disaster, not a success: Because GHGs are highly persistent, the residual discharges will increase the atmospheric GHG concentration and

---

187. *See* David Wheeler, *Moving Toward Consensus on Climate Policy: The Essential Role of Global Public Disclosure*, Centre for Global Development Working Paper No. 132 (Nov. 2007).

188. *See* Michael P. Vandenbergh & Anne C. Steinemann, *The Carbon-Neutral Individual*, 82 N.Y.U. L. Rev. 1673 (2007); Albert C. Lin, *Evangelizing Climate Change*, Draft Working Paper (July 21, 2008, downloaded from http://ssrn.com/abstract=1142919 on 08/20/2008).

189. *See* Daniel A. Farber, *Controlling Pollution by Individuals and Other Dispersed Sources*, 35 Envtl. L. Rep. 10,745 (2005).

190. *See* Lawrence H. Goulder & Ian W.H. Parry, *Instrument Choice in Environmental Policy*, Resources for the Future Discussion Paper No. 08-07 (April 2008).

worsen the greenhouse effect, global warming, and climate change. By not addressing the long-term consequences of residual GHG discharges, emissions-reduction programs intended to help overcome global climate change will contribute to higher atmospheric GHG concentrations and resulting climate change harms.

The fundamental flaw underlying these counter-productive pollution control programs is the invalid Frame One presumption that any GHG emissions cutbacks will lead to corresponding climate change improvements. The recent 50 percent cutback OECD agreement, for example, presumes that reducing twenty billion tons of GHG emissions per year to ten billion tons of residual GHG discharges will somehow reduce the greenhouse effect and global warming. However, adding 10 billion tons every year (or 10 tons) of persistent GHGs to atmospheric GHG levels that are already too high cannot reduce climate change dangers. The central problem is that nearly all politicians and climate policymakers are focusing on the *emissions cuts* from business-as-usual discharges and not on the *residual GHG emissions* and their atmospheric effects.

The world's nations are now discharging vast quantities of residual GHG pollution that will progressively increase atmospheric concentrations until they reach the level at which climate change catastrophes are inescapable. As a result, all present and proposed emissions-reduction programs that allow large residual GHG discharges will be climate change failures, not climate change solutions. This dire conclusion applies regardless of whether the emissions-reduction program uses direct regulation, cap-and-trade systems, or some other economic incentives plan. As long as emissions-reduction approaches authorize substantial annual discharges of residual GHGs into the atmosphere, they cannot possibly overcome global warming and climate change.

If emissions-reduction programs are incapable of reducing climate change to a tolerable level, the only sensible alternative is to stop using the processes and methods that are generating GHG pollution and increasing the atmospheric GHG concentration. GHG-free replacement technologies and processes would not exacerbate the residual GHG pollution problem because they will not generate any more GHGs; and carbon capture and storage programs will prevent additional GHGs from reaching the atmosphere and compounding the greenhouse effect. It will not be easy or cheap to convert a myriad production and consumption activities to clean GHG-free methods, but there is no other practical way to succeed in stabilizing and eventually rolling back the critical atmospheric GHG levels and related climate change hazards.

Overcoming global climate change will probably be the most difficult, controversial, expensive task the human race has ever undertaken on a collective basis. We need to attain two ambitious goals concurrently: eliminating as much GHG pollution as feasible, while promoting economic and social development in nations that otherwise will continue pumping destructive GHGs into the atmosphere. Yet, the world's climate policymakers are still engrossed in debating whether to reduce GHG pollution 30, 50, 60, 70, or 80 percent by relying on emissions-reduction programs, including economic incentive schemes, which cannot achieve either essential function. We urgently need a better understanding among climate policymakers and experts of residual GHG pollution and its atmospheric effects, and we need to build a consensus that a GHG-free technology-replacement strategy is far more likely than any emissions-reduction program to overcome global climate change during this century under many difficult real-world conditions and constraints.

Chapter Six

United States' Response to Climate Change

Chapter Six

United States' Response to Climate Change

James E. Hansen *et al.*, *Target Atmospheric CO$_2$: Where Should Humanity Aim?*, 2 OPEN ATMOSPHERIC SCIENCE JOURNAL 217, 217 (2008):

> If humanity wishes to preserve a planet similar to that on which civilization developed and to which life on Earth is adapted, paleoclimate evidence and ongoing climate change suggest that CO$_2$ will need to be reduced from its current 385 ppm to at most 350 ppm. The largest uncertainty in the target arises from possible changes of non-CO$_2$ forcings. An initial 350 ppm CO$_2$ target may be achievable by phasing out coal use except where CO$_2$ is captured and adopting agricultural and forestry practices that sequester carbon. If the present overshoot of this target CO$_2$ is not brief, there is a possibility of seeding irreversible catastrophic effects.

Robert N. Stavins, *What is the Future of U.S. Coal?*, 24 ENVT'L FORUM 16, 16 (July/Aug. 2007):

> CO$_2$ emissions from coal consumption accounted for 30 percent of U.S. greenhouse gas emissions in 2005, and nearly all resulted from coal's use in generating electricity.

> Potential climate policies can be grouped into four major categories: standards, subsidies, or credit-based programs, carbon taxes, and cap-and-trade.

GEORGE MONBIOT, HEAT: HOW TO STOP THE PLANET FROM BURNING 46 (South End Press 2007) [hereinafter 2007 MONBIOT] (footnote omitted):

> [discussing] the European Union's Emissions Trading Scheme. This system, which has been running since the beginning of 2005, began by handing out carbon dioxide emission permits, free of charge, to big European companies. By and large, those who produced the most carbon emissions were given the most permits; the polluter was paid. This handout was so generous that, in May 2006, the British government's consultants calculated that power firms would be making a windfall profit from the scheme of around [1 billion pounds], while doing nothing to reduce their emissions. The Emissions Trading Scheme is a classic act of enclosure. It has seized something which should belong to all of us—the right, within the system, to produce a certain amount of carbon dioxide—and given it to the corporations.

2007 MONBIOT at 210 (footnotes omitted) (on the deep fictions of "carbon offsets" and a return to the "sale of absolutions"):

> Today you can find the tariffs for crimes about to be committed on noticeboards erected throughout cyberspace. "Carbon offset" companies promise to redeem the environmental cost of your carbon emissions by means of intercession with the atmosphere: planting trees, funding renewable energy projects in distant nations and doubtless, somewhere, helping Andean villagers to build bridges. Just as in the fifteenth and sixteenth

centuries you could sleep with your sister, kill and lie without fear of eternal damnation, today you can leave your windows open while the heating is on, drive and fly without endangering the climate, as long as you give your ducats to one of the companies selling indulgences. There is even a provision of the Kyoto Protocol permitting nations to increase their official production of pollutants by paying for carbon-cutting projects in other countries [the Clean Development Mechanism]. I will not attempt to catalogue the land seizures, conflicts with local people, double counting and downright fraud that has attended some of these schemes. That has been done elsewhere. My objections are more general.

DAVID SHEARMAN & JOSEPH WAYNE SMITH, THE CLIMATE CHANGE CHALLENGE AND THE FAILURE OF DEMOCRACY 161 (Praeger 2007) [hereinafter 2007 SHEARMAN & SMITH]:

[English common law systems are strongly individualistic and property-based. These concepts] form the conceptual basis of capitalism. For this reason alone we doubt whether any sort of legal challenge could achieve substantial changes to the present social system. Legal challenges may produce some useful stopgap measures, but this is not enough. Outside of constitutional interpretations, governments can always make new laws to trump any court decision they don't like. Finally, justice through the courts is expensive and very slow, which is far from ideal. Nevertheless in a desperate situation it is worthwhile exercising every option, and limited reforms and changes are better than nothing at all.

I. The Political Environment: The Deep History of Denial

See also Chapter 1, § III, for a further discussion of governmental suppression of climate science.

2007 MONBIOT at 214:

Governments will pursue this course of inaction — irrespective of the human impacts — while it remains politically less costly than the alternative. The task of climate-change campaigners is to make it as expensive as possible. This means abandoning the habit of mind into which almost all of us have somehow slumped over the past ten years or so: the belief that someone else will do it for us.

James E. Hansen, *A Last Chance to Avert Disaster*, MULTINATIONAL MONITOR, Nov. / Dec., 2008, pp. 52, 54:

these CEOs [of fossil energy companies know what they are doing] and should be tried for high crimes against humanity and nature.

A. The Rejection of Kyoto

U.S. involvement in the Kyoto Protocol was effectively halted by Senate Resolution 98, the so-called Byrd-Hagel Resolution, on July 25, 1997. The resolution states that the U.S. should not sign the treaty unless (1) developing nations will be held to the same standards and (2) there are no substantial economic costs to the U.S.:

Resolved, That it is the sense of the Senate that—

(1) the United States should not be a signatory to any protocol to, or other agreement regarding, the United Nations Framework Convention on Climate Change of 1992, at negotiations in Kyoto in December 1997, or thereafter, which would—

(A) mandate new commitments to limit or reduce greenhouse gas emissions for the Annex I Parties, unless the protocol or other agreement also mandates new specific scheduled commitments to limit or reduce greenhouse gas emissions for Developing Country Parties within the same compliance period, or

(B) would result in serious harm to the economy of the United States[.]

Who Killed Kyoto? Sharon Beder, Paul Brown, and John Vidal argue that the passage of this Senate Resolution was a resounding victory for Big Oil in their article *Who Killed Kyoto?,* THE GUARDIAN at 4 (October 29, 1997):

> The champagne corks are popping in the boardrooms of BP, Shell, Esso, Mobil, Ford, General Motors, and the coal, steel and aluminium corporations of the US, Australia and Europe. Last week's announcement by President Clinton that realistic targets and timetables for cutting greenhouse gas emissions should be put off for 20 years has effectively maintained corporate business as usual.
>
> In a stunning example of raw backroom power and political manipulation, the "death-row" industries showed who rules the economic world by effectively killing any hope of combatting global warming at the Kyoto climate conference in December.
>
> For a decade now, the fossil fuel industries in the US, Australia and Europe have led a vicious and ever more intense campaign to prevent any treaty being signed that involves greenhouse gas reduction targets.
>
> It has taken billions of pounds of co-ordinated lobbying effort and media manipulation by some of the world's largest corporations, PR companies, legal teams and think-tanks. As more and more scientific evidence emerged that global warming was not just happening but that it was man-induced, the intention was to systematically subvert science and the political process.
>
> The public has had little appreciation of the epic struggle to deny science. It was only last month, when a US consortium of 20 organisations launched a pounds 10 million campaign of TV ads designed to scupper the climate treaty with dire warnings that jobs would be lost and taxes would rise if a meaningful treaty went ahead, that it really surfaced.
>
> But the TV campaign was only the most overt and last act of the campaign to discredit scientific predictions and undermine the political will to prevent a treaty that would realistically limit global warming.
>
> The campaign, one of the most successful and vicious of all time, never tried to disprove the consensus of the 2,500 world scientists who had concluded that man-made greenhouse gases were contributing to a dangerous ecological situation that threatened to impact ... everyone. The aim was to sew enough doubt that the politicians would not feel that they needed to act.
>
> Using corporate PR, psychology, mass media manipulation techniques and political muscle to get to the politicians and opinion formers, they set up a series of front groups, funded "independent scientists," nurtured politically conservative and far-right think-tanks, and sought to discredit individuals and, especially, environment groups at every turn. With money no object, they could run rings around their opponents.

B. Denial by the Bush II Administration

Professor Patrick Parenteau, *Anything Industry Wants: Environmental Policy under Bush II*, 6 Vt. J. Envtl. L. 2, 2 (2005) (footnotes omitted):

> From day one, the Bush Administration has set about the task of systematically and unilaterally dismantling over thirty years of environmental and natural resources law. It started with the "Card Memo" and the Anything But Clinton ("ABC") rule, which first quarantined and then quietly put to sleep, scores of regulations issued by the previous administration [on] everything from arsenic in drinking water, to fuel efficiency standards, to snowmobiles in Yellowstone National Park. Since then, the anti-Clinton reaction has grown into a full-fledged ideological crusade to deregulate polluters, privatize public resources, limit public participation, manipulate science, and abdicate federal responsibility for tackling national and global environmental problems.

Since 1997, obstruction and denial by the federal government has continued, notably by the Bush Administration. In 2000, George W. Bush campaigned on a pledge to regulate carbon dioxide emissions as a central component of his energy policy.[1] His administration's relentless opposition to such regulation, nonetheless, began immediately after he took office. In a March 13, 2001 letter, President Bush proclaimed: "I do not believe, however, that the government should impose on power plants mandatory emissions reductions for carbon dioxide, which is not a 'pollutant' under the Clean Air Act."[2] Vice President Cheney said of the President's campaign pledge, "It was a mistake because we aren't in a position today to … cap emissions."[3] Eight years after this about-face, the Bush Administration continued to exhibit its willingness to ignore climate science and interfere with agency activity and legal processes.

For instance, the Bush Administration attempted to suppress periodic climate assessment reports required by the Global Change Research Act of 1990.[4] It was only following an injunction from a district court in California[5] that these assessment reports were released. More recently, the Administration used delay tactics and censorship to avoid complying with the Supreme Court's order in *Massachusetts v. EPA*[6] to make an endangerment finding under the Clean Air Act.

———

Rather than make an endangerment finding, the Environmental Protection Agency merely issued an advance notice of proposed rulemaking[7] (ANPR), which requested comments regarding regulation of greenhouse gases under the Clean Air Act. OMB Watch[8] reported on the censorship and interference that occurred prior to this official release:

> In May 2007, the White House ordered the EPA, along with other agencies, to prepare regulatory responses by the end of the year. According to EPA officials, the agency's draft finding and recommendations on the dangers of CO_2 emissions, entitled, "Control of Greenhouse Gas Emissions from Motor Vehicles," were sent to the White House

———

1. For example, on Sept. 29, 2000, while campaigning in Saginaw, Mich., President Bush said: "We will require all power plants to meet clean-air standards in order to reduce emissions of carbon dioxide within a reasonable period of time." http://thinkprogress.org/2006/07/07/co2-pledge/.

2. http://www.whitehouse.gov/news/releases/2001/03/20010314.html.

3. CNN, *Cheney urges "fresh look" at nuclear power*, CNN.com (May 8, 2001).

4. 15 U.S.C. §§ 2921–2961.

5. Center for Biological Diversity v. Brennan, No. 4:06-cv-07062-SBA (August 21, 2007) (granting motion for summary judgment).

6. Massachusetts v. EPA, 549 U.S. 497, 127 S. Ct. 1438, 1463 (2007).

7. 73 Fed. Reg. 44354 (July 30, 2008).

8. http://www.ombwatch.org/node/3741 (July 22, 2008).

Office of Management and Budget (OMB) in a December 2007 e-mail.[9] Since the Clean Air Act requires EPA to regulate emissions that endanger the public, the so-called endangerment finding carries a legal obligation that the agency take action. Officials at OMB refused to open the e-mail or the draft document, knowing that it may trigger regulatory action on climate change. Climate change is being caused by high concentrations of greenhouse gases in the earth's atmosphere.

Investigations conducted by two committees in the House found that the administration delayed acting on the EPA findings. In fact, despite repeated requests for the EPA information, the White House refused to share any related documents until the records were subpoenaed in April by the House Select Committee on Energy Independence and Global Warming.

After reviewing the subpoenaed records, Rep. Edward Markey (D-MA), Chair of the House Select Committee, charged the administration[10] with discarding EPA's science and legally based recommendations to address climate change. Markey reported that the EPA documents supported scientific conclusions that greenhouse gas emissions may "endanger public welfare" and that motor vehicle emissions do contribute to global warming.

Rep. Henry Waxman (D-CA), Chair of the House Oversight Committee, declared[11] the administration's lack of action to be "in violation of the Supreme Court's directive." According to his committee, the draft was the product of about 500 comments from internal EPA review, external federal expert review, and other interagency comments.

Changing Facts

The WALL STREET JOURNAL, which claimed to have obtained a copy of the original EPA documents, reported[12] that the White House had done more than delay the information—it appeared the administration had attempted to remove entire findings. According to anonymous officials quoted by the paper, the White House pressured EPA to remove conclusions that greenhouse gases endanger public welfare, information on how to regulate the gases, and an analysis of the cost of regulating greenhouse gases. The draft of EPA's findings affirmed "the agency's authority to tackle climate change, and suggest[ed] a variety of regulatory avenues" and concluded that the "net benefit to society" of regulating automobile emissions "could be in excess of $2 trillion." However, the cuts the White House pushed were reportedly intended to rework EPA's findings to indicate that the Clean Air Act is a flawed vehicle for regulating greenhouse gas emissions and that separate legislation is needed.

On July 11, EPA released an Advance Notice of Proposed Rulemaking (ANPR) on climate change that appears to confirm that the White House changes had been made. The ANPR included conclusions that differed starkly from those listed by the JOURNAL and congressional committees....

Despite the Supreme Court ruling that the administration has the authority to regulate greenhouse gas emissions, the administration continued to deny the Clean Air Act should be used. Unlike the original draft, the ANPR was accompanied by 85 pages from other department secretaries aimed at attacking the act and included no finding of endangerment or regulatory recommendations. The Department of Energy called[13] the act

---

9. Felicity Barringer, *White House Refused to Open Pollutants E-Mail*, NEW YORK TIMES (June 25, 2008).
10. http://globalwarming.house.gov/tools/2q08materials/files/0064.pdf.
11. http://oversight.house.gov/documents/20080312110250.pdf.
12. http://online.wsj.com/article/SB121578600530545953.html.
13. http://online.wsj.com/public/resources/documents/anpr20080711.pdf.

a flawed vehicle for regulating greenhouse gas emissions, stating that it was "unilateral and extraordinarily burdensome." ...

C. Interference with Government Scientists

Perhaps the best-known instance of interference is the censorship of Dr. James Hansen, NASA's leading climate expert,[14] although this is clearly not an isolated example. A 2006 study by the Union for Concerned Scientists, VOICES OF FEDERAL CLIMATE SCIENTISTS: GLOBAL WARMING SOLUTIONS DEPEND ON UNIMPEDED SCIENCE, quantified the extreme level of political interference with government science:

> In summer 2006, the Union of Concerned Scientists distributed surveys to more than 1,600 climate scientists working at seven federal agencies and the independent National Center for Atmospheric Research (NCAR), asking for information about the state of climate research. Scientists' responses indicated a high regard for the quality and integrity of federal climate research itself, but also identified broad and substantial interference in their work.

> *Political Interference with Climate Science*

> Large numbers of federal climate scientists reported various types of interference, both subtle and explicit:
> - 73 percent of all respondents perceived inappropriate interference with climate science research in the past five years.
> - 58 percent of all respondents personally experienced interference with climate science research in the past five years. This number increased to 78 percent among scientists whose work always or frequently touches upon sensitive or controversial topics. In contrast, only 22 percent of NCAR scientists personally experienced interference with climate science research.
> - Nearly half of all respondents (46 percent) perceived or personally experienced pressure to eliminate the words "climate change," "global warming," or other similar terms from a variety of communications. This number increased to nearly three in five (58 percent) among respondents from the National Oceanic and Atmospheric Administration (NOAA).
> - 46 percent of all respondents perceived or personally experienced new or unusual administrative requirements that impair climate related work.

> *Scientific Findings Misrepresented*

> Federal climate scientists reported that their research findings have been changed by non-scientists in ways that compromise accuracy:
> - Two in five respondents (43 percent) perceived or personally experienced changes or edits to documents during review processes that changed the meaning of scientific findings.
> - 25 percent perceived or personally experienced situations in which scientists have actively objected to, resigned from, or removed themselves from a project because of pressure to change scientific findings.
> - 37 percent of respondents perceived or personally experienced instances in which their agency misrepresented scientists' findings.

---

14. *See* Mark Bowen, CENSORING SCIENCE: INSIDE THE POLITICAL ATTACK ON DR. JAMES HANSEN AND THE TRUTH OF GLOBAL WARMING (Penguin Group Publishers 2008).

Barriers to Communication

Agency scientists are not free to communicate their research findings to the media or the public:

- 52 percent of respondents said their agency's public affairs officials always or frequently monitor scientists' communications with the media. In contrast, only seven percent of NCAR respondents reported that same level of monitoring.
- Two in five respondents (39 percent) have perceived or personally experienced "fear of retaliation for openly expressing concerns about climate change outside their agency."
- 38 percent of respondents perceived or personally experienced "disappearance or unusual delay of websites, reports, or other science-based materials relating to climate."
- A majority of NASA respondents (61 percent) agreed with the statement, "Recent changes to policies pertaining to scientific openness at my agency have improved the environment for climate research," in sharp contrast to the 12 percent of non-NASA respondents who agreed with the statement. The high percentage among NASA respondents is most likely the result of a recent policy implemented at the agency that affirmed that the role of public affairs officers was not "to alter, filter or adjust engineering or scientific material produced by NASA's technical staff."

Climate Scientists are Disheartened

While a large majority of respondents (88 percent) agreed with the statement, "U.S. federal government climate research is of generally excellent quality," respondents reported decreasing job satisfaction and a worsening environment for climate science in federal agencies:

- Two-thirds of respondents said that today's environment for federal government climate research is worse compared to five years ago (67 percent) and 10 years ago (64 percent). Among scientists at NASA, these numbers were nearly four in five (79 percent and 77 percent, respectively).
- 45 percent of all respondents said that their personal job satisfaction has decreased over the past few years. At NASA, three in five (61 percent) reported decreased job satisfaction.
- More than a third of respondents from NASA, and more than one in five (22 percent) of all respondents, reported that morale in their office was "poor" or "extremely poor." Among NCAR respondents, only seven percent reported such low levels of morale.
- Insufficient resources are a source of concern among respondents. More than half (53 percent) disagreed with the statement, "The U.S. government has done a good job funding climate research."

D. President Obama's Plans

On November 4, 2008, Barack Obama was elected as the next President of the United States. One of the focuses of President Obama's election campaign was the need to address climate change through a new energy plan. The following is an excerpt from the New Energy for America plan[1] on which President Obama and Vice President Biden campaigned:

Mid-to-Longterm Solutions: New Energy for America

Our nation is confronted by two major energy challenges — our dependence on foreign oil and global climate change — both of which stem from our current dependence on fossil fuels for energy. Barack Obama and Joe Biden believe we have a moral, environ-

---

1. The energy plan outline is *available at* http://my.barackobama.com/page/content/newenergy (last visited Nov. 8, 2008).

mental, economic, and security imperative to address our dependence on foreign oil and tackle climate change in a serious, sustainable manner.

Tackle Climate Change

As a result of climate change, the polar ice caps are shrinking causing sea levels to rise; extreme weather is wreaking havoc across the globe; droughts are becoming more severe, tropical diseases are migrating north and numerous species are being threatened with extinction.

- Implement Cap and Trade Program to Reduce Greenhouse Gas Emissions
- Make the U.S. a Leader on Climate Change

Invest in Our Secure Energy Future and Create 5 Million New Jobs

Barack Obama and Joe Biden will use a portion of the revenue generated from the cap-and-trade permit auction to make investments that will reduce our dependence on foreign oil and accelerate deployment of low-carbon technologies. The investments will focus on three critical areas: 1) Basic Research; 2) Technology Demonstration and 3) Aggressive Commercial Deployment and Clean Market Creation

- Invest In A Clean Energy Economy and Help Create 5 Million New Green Jobs
- Create a "Green Vet Initiative"
- Convert our Manufacturing Centers into Clean Technology Leaders
- Create New Job Training Programs for Clean Technologies

Make our Cars, Trucks and SUV's Fuel Efficient

Last year, oil provided more than 96 percent of the energy in our vehicles. It is an economic, national security and environmental imperative that this near-total dependence comes to an end. To achieve this goal, Barack Obama and Joe Biden will implement a strategy that will—within 10 years—allow us to reduce our consumption of oil by more than we currently import from the Middle East and Hugo Chavez's Venezuela combined. In order to do that, he will:

- Increase Fuel Economy Standards
- Invest in Developing Advanced Vehicles and Put 1 Million Plug-in Electric Vehicles on the Road by 2015
- Partner with Domestic Automakers
- Mandate All New Vehicles are Flexible Fuel Vehicles
- Develop the Next Generation of Sustainable Biofuels and Infrastructure
- Establish a National Low Carbon Fuel Standard

Promote the Supply of Domestic Energy

With 3 percent of the world's oil reserves, the U.S. cannot drill its way to energy security. But U.S. oil and gas production plays an important role in our domestic economy and remains critical to prevent global energy prices from climbing even higher. There are several key opportunities to support increased U.S. production of oil and gas that do not require opening up currently protected areas.

- A "Use it or Lose It" Approach to Existing Leases
- Promote the Responsible Domestic Production of Oil and Natural Gas
- Prioritize the Construction of the Alaska Natural Gas Pipeline
- Getting More from our Existing Oil Fields

Diversify Our Energy Sources

There are no silver bullet solutions to our energy crises. Our economy, security and environment will be best served through a sustained effort to diversify our energy sources. Barack Obama and Joe Biden will:

- Require 10 Percent of Electricity to Come from Renewable Sources by 2012
- Develop and Deploy Clean Coal Technology
- Safe and Secure Nuclear Energy

Commitment to Efficiency to Reduce Energy Use and Lower Costs

According to the United Nations, America is only the 22nd most energy efficient country among the major economies in the world, which means we spend more on energy than we need to because our lifestyle and our built environment are wasting too much excess energy. Since 1973, the average amount of electricity each of us uses has tripled. We can do better. An Obama administration will strive to make America the most energy efficient country in the world.

- Deploy the Cheapest, Cleanest, Fastest Energy Source — Energy Efficiency
- Set National Building Efficiency Goals
- Overhaul Federal Efficiency Standards
- Reduce Federal Energy Consumption
- Flip Incentives to Energy Utilities
- Invest in a Smart Grid
- Weatherize One Million Homes Annually
- Build More Livable and Sustainable Communities

In hopes of getting the Obama Administration off to a good start, the CENTER FOR PROGRESSIVE REFORM issued a report entitled PROTECTING PUBLIC HEALTH AND ENVIRONMENT BY THE STROKE OF A PRESIDENTIAL PEN: SEVEN EXECUTIVE ORDERS FOR THE PRESIDENT'S FIRST 100 DAYS (2008). Here is the Executive Summary of that document (*id.* at 1–5). Nothing of this sort happened.

Executive Summary

Since the great whirlwind of policymaking that defined President Franklin Roosevelt's first 100 days in office, new Presidents have recognized the importance of launching their administrations with a series of steps that reflect their top policy priorities and that set a tone for their administrations. Those initial weeks offer an opportunity to draw distinctions with the previous occupant of the Oval Office, to demonstrate that campaign commitments were more than empty rhetoric, and to seize and even generate political momentum.

But more than those things, the first 100 days offer an opportunity to do the people's business. In a broad sense, presidential campaigns are about Americans' hopes and aspirations, and they give voters a chance to choose someone to champion their cause for the next four years. Once in office, Presidents want a fast start, and voters want to know that their choice is staying true to the values and objectives that won their votes. Those first 100 days in office are therefore a time of great significance, not just for the new President but for the voters who sent him there.

A new President's first 100-day agenda is often imagined largely in legislative terms. And the new President's legislative agenda, and that of the new Congress, is of obvious importance. But the President's broad authority over the executive branch can be far-reaching, as well. By directing federal agencies to focus on particular priorities, and by reshaping the internal processes by which agencies do their business, the new President can effect great change.

As this white paper demonstrates, the new direction the next President gives to the agencies of his administration can be vitally important in both substantive and symbolic terms. He can make important headway on issues of great concern, reversing some destructive policies of his predecessor, and sending a clear message to the public—the electorate—that the change they voted for is under way.

This white paper recommends a series of seven Executive Orders to the new Administration, all in the areas of health, safety, and the environment. Each of the suggested Executive Orders directs agencies of the government to take specific steps that would make a real-world difference and simultaneously send a signal to the public, Congress, the business community, and others that a new course has been charted and that change has arrived.

The Orders cover a range of health, safety, and environmental issues, and are detailed in the pages that follow. In summary:

1) Executive Order on Climate Change, Part One: Reducing the Federal Government's Carbon Footprint

Few issues that will confront the new President have an impact as far-reaching as climate change. Legislation to address the nation's disproportionate emissions of greenhouse gases is sorely needed. But the President need not wait for Congress to act to make a difference, or to send a message to the public and the world that the new occupant of the White House means business on the issue. According to one estimate, federal government operations in its 2005 fiscal year generated approximately 100 million metric tons of carbon dioxide-equivalent, around 1.4 percent of all U.S. greenhouse gas emissions that year.

The new President should issue an Executive Order requiring each federal agency to measure, report, and reduce its carbon footprint. Not only would the Executive Order have a meaningful impact on the federal government's carbon emissions, it could also lead to the creation of uniform, practical standards for measuring such footprints, standards that could be applied government-wide and beyond. Each of the provisions of this proposed Order is consistent with the goals of the National Environmental Policy Act.

2) Executive Order on Climate Change, Part Two: Considering Climate Change in Agency Decisionmaking

On an almost daily basis, federal agencies make decisions that have a major effect on climate change. For example, a 2006 decision by the National Highway Traffic Safety Administration (NHTSA) not to establish more aggressive Corporate Average Fuel Economy (CAFE) standards for light trucks was a monumental lost opportunity for great progress—a choice delegated to NHTSA by Congress, and therefore made entirely on NHTSA's authority, without need of congressional approval. In that instance, the Bush Administration simply gave scant attention to the issue of climate change when deciding whether a more ambitious set of CAFE standards would have been more appropriate.

The next President should issue a new Executive Order clarifying that all federal agencies are obligated to consider the global climate change-related implications of their actions. This proposed Order is consistent with the goals of the National Environmental Policy Act.

3) Executive Order on Children and Toxics: Taking Children into Account

Children are not merely "little adults," especially when it comes to health issues. With that in mind, Congress wrote all of the major environmental laws to allow agencies to craft protections that take the special vulnerabilities of children into account. But the Bush Administration and some of its predecessors have generally ignored those provisions, with the result that the federal government does a poor job of protecting children from environmental harms. One example: the federal government has refused to require agribusiness to protect the young children of farm workers from exposure to inordinately high levels of pesticides, from which they suffer disproportionately.

The next President should amend Executive Order 13045 (issued initially by President Clinton and then amended by President Bush) to mandate that agencies establish an affirmative agenda for protecting children from lead, mercury, perchlorate, phthalates, fine particulate matter, ozone, and pesticides; require the reform of risk assessment policy so that children are accounted for as a vulnerable group; and end the use of discounting the value of children's lives in cost-benefit analysis. As is the case with the provisions of the existing Order on Protecting Children, each of these recommendations is consistent with the goals of the various environmental, safety, and public health statutes.

4) Executive Order on Environmental Justice: Keeping America's Promise

U.S. environmental laws have dramatically improved the quality of the nation's air, water, and wilderness, while saving countless lives. But these efforts continue to produce radically unequal results among various populations. For example, African Americans have the highest asthma rate of any racial or ethnic group in the country, and poor children and children of color are eight times more likely to have elevated levels of lead in their blood than other children. The nation's environmental laws also produce inequalities based on diversity in culture and lifeways. Some Native American tribes in the Great Lakes region rely on subsistence fishing, and are therefore disproportionately harmed when fish are contaminated with mercury or other pollutants. Similarly, cap-and-trade proposals for addressing climate change could actually intensify local concentrations of particulate matter and other pollutants that accompany carbon emissions in poor cities, if polluters there choose to buy extra permits to pollute.

President Clinton's Executive Order 12898 promised to reshape federal agency action toward achieving environmental justice for minority and low-income communities, but is in dire need of overhaul. The next President should amend or replace the original Executive Order on Environmental Justice. The new Order should require a meaningful analysis of the environmental justice impacts and implications of all major new rules; impose on agencies a substantive obligation to take affirmative steps to ameliorate environmental injustice; launch an affirmative Environmental Justice agenda; hold agencies accountable for carrying out their environmental justice obligations; and clarify key terms from the current Order, including "environmental justice communities" and "subsistence," to avoid the kind of narrow interpretation of the terms applied by the Bush Administration. As is the case with the existing Executive Order on Environmental Justice, these recommendations are consistent with the goals of Title VI of the Civil Rights Act.

5) Executive Order to Restore Open Government: Promoting Transparency Under FOIA and FACA and During Regulatory Review

Open government is a cornerstone of American democracy. While secrecy is occasionally necessary, government should be biased toward transparency, so that the public can fairly evaluate what is done in its name. Under the Bush Administration, the vital concept of transparency has been replaced by a presumption of secrecy.

The new President should issue an Executive Order restoring open government in three areas where unwarranted secrecy has developed. The Order should restore the presumption of disclosure concerning exemptions from the Freedom of Information Act (FOIA) so that political appointees and career government employees cannot operate free of scrutiny; forbid agencies from taking advantage of loopholes that limit the transparency provisions of the Federal Advisory Committee Act (FACA) so that the public can be assured that special interests do not have undue influence on agency decisionmaking; and improve the transparency of regulatory review by the Office of Information and Regulatory Affairs (OIRA) so that efforts by political appointees in the White House to override the judgment of scientists and other experts in regulatory agencies can at least be transparent to the public. All of the proposed Order's provisions are consistent with the goals of FOIA and FACA.

6) Executive Order to Prevent Preemption: Shielding Protective State Laws from a Federal Power Grab

The U.S. Constitution makes clear that when federal laws conflict with state laws, federal laws take precedence. The Framers, however, could not have anticipated that, 220 years after the drafting of the Constitution, federal agencies would seek to preempt state laws not by act of Congress, but by federal regulation. That is precisely what regulatory agencies of the Bush Administration—the National Highway Traffic Safety Administration, the Food and Drug Administration, and the Environmental Protection Agency—have done, often in the absence of statutory language to support preemption. Not surprisingly, given the Bush Administration's ideological bent, such preemptions have invariably been aimed at state laws that protect citizens from various harms, putting the profits of polluters or manufacturers of dangerous products ahead of the interests of innocent victims.

The next President should issue an Executive Order halting the practice. Specifically, it should amend the existing Executive Order on Federalism to strengthen provisions setting forth a presumption against preemption; require agencies to provide a written justification for preemption; and require that, when a federal statute allows states to adopt more stringent standards or seek a waiver of statutory preemption (as in EPA's denial of California's Clean Air Act waiver), agencies must provide a written justification to the White House before denying the state's regulatory authority or waiver request. As is the case with the existing Executive Order on Federalism, these recommendations are consistent with the goals of the various statutes under which the environmental, safety, and public health agencies operate, including the National Environmental Policy Act.

7) Executive Order on Stewardship of Public Lands: Promoting Ecological Integrity and Public Participation

The United States owns approximately 28 percent of the nation's land area. This immense trove of resources requires careful stewardship to ensure that current demands and short-term priorities do not degrade the long-term value of this heritage for the future. Over the past few years, however, the federal government has failed miserably at its stewardship responsibilities, permitting overexploitation and encouraging the commodification of resources, causing long-term damage to biodiversity and ecosystems. Climate change will only exacerbate the challenges ahead.

The next President should issue a new Executive Order declaring a national policy of promoting ecological integrity as a baseline requirement for sustainable public land use. The President should also revoke two Bush Administration Executive Orders issued in 2005 (Executive Orders 13211 and 13212) that made it easier to develop energy resources on public lands, even at the risk of causing long-term degradation of natural resource values. In addition, the President should amend a third Bush Order (Executive Order 13443) by providing equal opportunities for public participation in federal land use decisionmaking to a wide variety of constituencies, in addition to those promoting hunting. All of these measures are consistent with the goals of the various public lands statutes.

By CPR Member Scholars
Rebecca M. Bratpies, David M. Driesen, Robert L. Fischman,
Sheila Foster, Eileen Guana, Robert L. Glicksman, Alexandra B. Klass,
Catherine A. O'Neill, Sidney Shapiro, Amy Sinden,
Rena Steinzor, Robert R.M. Verchick, and Wendy Wagner,
and CPR Policy Analyst James Goodwin

II. Congressional Action

A. Past Proposals: Lieberman-Warner Climate Security Act

The 110th Congress saw a prodigious number of climate bill proposals—over 235 as of July 2008—up from 106 in the previous term.[1] Of these, eight were comprehensive climate change bills.[2] Despite the large number of proposals, the Boxer-Lieberman-Warner Climate Security Act[3] was the first climate legislation to make it to the floor of the Senate since 2005.[4] Once on the floor, however, it failed to garner the needed 60 votes to invoke cloture and close debate.[5] An update on activities of the 111th Congress appears at p. 834, *infra*.

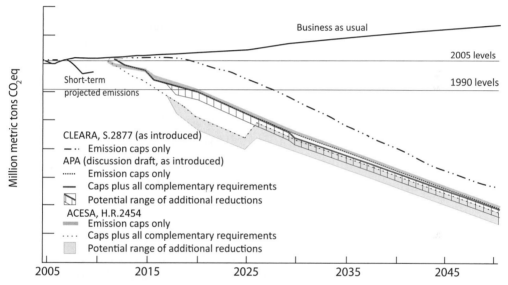

Figure 1. Net estimates of emissions reductions through 2050 that would be achieved with climate and energy bills proposed in the 111th Congress. Adapted from: World Resources Institute Report, Comparison of Legislative Climate Change Targets (updated June 8, 2010). Footnotes from the original figure have been omitted. "Short-term projected emissions" are based on EIA's estimates for 2008–2010. Reductions from Carbon Limits and Energy for America's Renewal Act (CLEARA) would require additional acts of Congress. American Power Act (APA) and American Clean Energy and Security Act (ACESA) reductions depend on offsets, which, if not real, verifiable, additional, and permanent, would reduce the net emissions reductions achieved. Visit http://www.wri.org/usclimatetargets for further information regarding methods and assumptions.

---

1. *See* Pew Center on Global Climate Change website, *available at* http://www.pewclimate.org/what_s_being_done/in_the_congress/110thcongress.cfm.

2. See WORLD RESOURCES INSTITUTE ANALYSIS, COMPARISON OF LEGISLATIVE CLIMATE CHANGE TARGETS (September 9, 2008), *available at* http://www.wri.org/publication/usclimatetargets.

3. S. 3036, substituted for S. 2191 on May 20, 2008. Reported by Senator Boxer of the Committee on Environment and Public Works.

4. In 2005, Senate re-considered the McCain-Lieberman Climate Stewardship Act. The Act was defeated by a vote of 38–60. A number of Senators opposed the bill because it offered subsidies for construction of nuclear power plants.

5. 48 senators voted in favor, and 36 voted to reject. In addition, six senators were absent but indicated on the record that they would have voted in favor had they been present. *See* Pew Center discussion, *available at* http://www.pewclimate.org/analysis/l-w/updates.

1. Viewpoints on the Act

The Climate Security Act was criticized by a number of groups, including some environmental organizations who believe the bill does not do enough to address global warming. For instance, Friends of the Earth provides a comprehensive analysis at its website,[6] including a statement of the major shortcomings of the Climate Security Act:

> The Lieberman-Warner bill gives hundreds of billions of dollars to corporate polluters over 38 years. The giveaways come in two forms. First, pollution permits (worth up to $489 billion) will be handed to the fossil fuel industry for free. Instead of this approach, polluters should be required to pay for all emissions through a 100 percent auction of pollution permits. Second, the revenues raised by the bill's auctions should be invested wisely; instead, much revenue is directed to polluters through billions of dollars of subsidies to coal and potentially to nuclear power (worth up to $105 billion).

On the other hand, the Climate Security Act was viewed by a substantial portion of the environmental community as an important step towards addressing global climate change.

David Hawkins testified to this effect before the U.S. Senate Committee on Environment and Public Works (November 13, 2007).

Testimony of David Hawkins, Director, Climate Center, Natural Resources Defense Council, Before the Committee on Environment and Public Works, United States Senate Hearing on America's Climate Security Act of 2007, S. 2191

David Hawkins

Chairwoman Boxer, I would like to thank you for the opportunity to testify and share NRDC's views on the America's Climate Security Act (S. 2191) and for your leadership in addressing the critical challenge posed by global warming. I also want to thank Senator Lieberman and Senator Warner for all of your work to develop this legislation and improve it in Subcommittee. We view favorable Committee action on this measure as an important, initial step toward enactment of comprehensive global warming legislation and we look forward to working closely with you, and the other members of the Committee, as you act to report legislation to the full United States Senate.

On October 24th NRDC President Frances Beinecke testified before the Subcommittee on Public and Consumer Solutions to Global Warming and Wildlife Protection on America's Climate Security Act (ACSA).[1] In her testimony she stated that the time for action on global warming is now. Climate scientists warn us that we must act now to begin making serious emission reductions if we are to avoid truly dangerous global warming pollution concentrations. Failure to pursue significant reductions in global warming pollution very soon will make the job much harder in the future—both the job of stabilizing atmospheric pollution concentrations and the job of avoiding the worst impacts of climate chaos.

A growing body of scientific research indicates that we face extreme dangers to human health, economic well-being, and the ecosystems on which we depend if global average temperatures are

---

6 http://action.foe.org/content.jsp?content_KEY=3820&t=2007_Global-Warming.dwt.
1. Frances Beinecke, Testimony Before the Subcommittee on Public and Consumer Solutions to Global Warming and Wildlife Protection, Committee on Environment and Public Works, "America's Climate Security Act", October 24, 2007. http://docs.nrdc.org/globalwarming/glo_07102401A.pdf.

allowed to increase by more than 2 degrees Fahrenheit from today's levels. We have good prospects of staying below this temperature increase if atmospheric concentrations of CO_2 and other global warming gases are kept from exceeding 450 ppm CO_2-equivalent and then rapidly reduced. To make this possible requires immediate steps to reduce global emissions over the next several decades, including action to halt U.S. emissions growth within the next few years and then cut emissions by approximately 80% by mid-Century.

This goal is ambitious, but achievable. It can be done through an annual rate of emissions reductions that ramps up to about a 4% reduction per year. But if we delay and emissions continue to grow at or near the business-as-usual trajectory for another 10 years, the job will become much harder. In such a case, the annual emission reduction rate needed to stay on the 450 ppm path would double to 8% per year. In short, a slow start means a crash finish, with steeper and more disruptive cuts in emissions required for each year of delay, or if insufficient action is taken a seriously disrupted climate.

Costs of Inaction

The claim that climate protection is "too expensive" treats it like a discretionary expense — perhaps like a luxury car or exotic vacation that is beyond this year's budget. No harm is done by walking away from a high-end purchase that you can't quite afford.

But if we walk away from climate protection, we will be walking into danger. Unless we act now, the climate disruption will continue to worsen, with health, economic, and environmental costs far greater than the price of protection.

Scholars and economists have only begun a serious assessment of the costs of inaction but it is clear from their work that it is climate disruption, *not* climate protection programs, which will wreck the economy.

- THE STERN REVIEW, sponsored by the British government and directed by Sir Nicholas Stern, formerly the chief economist at the World Bank, estimated that 5% of world economic output would be lost, given a narrowly defined estimate of economic damages. Add in an estimate for environmental damage and for the increased chance of an abrupt climate change catastrophe, and Stern's estimates of losses from climate disruption climb to 11% or more of world economic output.[2]
- A recent study from the University of Maryland reviews the extensive research literature on the costs due to plausible climate change in the U.S., including coastal property losses from sea level rise, increased damages from intensified hurricanes, drought and wildfire risks in the west, disruption of water supplies, decreased agricultural yields in most of the country, and many more harmful impacts.[3]

This extended excerpt from the report provides a sobering summary of how high the economic stakes are:

The effects of climate change will be felt by the entire nation:
- all sectors of the economy — most notably agriculture, energy, and transportation — will be affected;

---

2. SIR NICHOLAS STERN, STERN REVIEW: ECONOMICS OF CLIMATE CHANGE (January 2007) *available at* http://www.hm-treasury.gov.uk/independent_reviews/stern_review_economics_climate_change/stern_review_report.cfm.

3. MATTHIAS RUTH, DANA COEHLO, DARIA KARETNIKOV, THE US ECONOMIC IMPACTS OF CLIMATE CHANGE AND THE COSTS OF INACTION, A REVIEW AND ASSESSMENT by the Center for Integrative Environmental Research (CIER) at the University of Maryland, October 9, 2007) *available at* http://www.cier.umd.edu/climateadaptation/index.html.

- essential infrastructures that afford us reliable services and high standards of living (such as water supply and water treatment) will be impacted; and
- ecosystems, on which quality of life relies (such as forests, rivers, and lakes), will suffer.
- **In the West and Northwest**, climate change is expected to alter precipitation patterns and snow pack, thereby increasing dry fuel loads and the risk of forest fires. Forest fires cost billions of dollars to suppress, and can result in significant loss of property. The Oakland, California fire of 1991 and the fires in San Diego and San Bernardino Counties in 2003 each cost over $2 billion. Every year for the past four years, over 7 million acres of forests in the National Forest System have burned with annual suppression costs of $1.3 billion or more.
- **The Great Plains and the Midwest** will suffer particularly from increased frequency and severity of flooding and drought events, causing billions of dollars in damages to crops and property. For example, the North Dakota Red River floods in 1997 caused $1 billion in agricultural production losses, and the Midwest floods of 1993 inflicted $6–8 billion in damages to farmers alone.
- **The Northeast and Mid-Atlantic** regions will see increased vulnerability to sea level rise and storms. Depending on the category of the event, evacuation costs for the Northeast region may range, for a single event, between $2 and $6.5 billion. Since 1980, there have been 70 natural weather-caused disasters, with damages to coastal infrastructure exceeding $1 billion per event. Taken together, their combined impact surpassed $560 billion in damages.
- Decreased precipitation levels in **the South and Southwest** will strain water resources for agriculture, industry and households. For the agriculturally productive Central Valley in California alone, the estimated economy-wide loss during the driest years is predicted to be around $6 billion per year. Net agricultural income for the San Antonio Texas Edwards Aquifer region is predicted to decline by 16–29% by 2030 and by 30–45% by 2090 because of competing uses for an increasingly scarce resource — water.
- The true economic impact of climate change is fraught with "hidden" costs. Besides the replacement value of infrastructure, for example, there are real costs of re-routing traffic, workdays and productivity lost, provision of temporary shelter and supplies, potential relocation and re-training costs, and others. Likewise, the increased levels of uncertainty and risk brought about by climate change impose new costs on the insurance, banking, and investment industries, as well as complicate the planning processes for the agricultural and manufacturing sectors and public works projects. Since the early 1990s, and especially during the 21st century, significant progress has been made in understanding the impacts of climate change at national, regional, and local scales.
- States particularly vulnerable to climate change are likely to suffer considerable negative economic impacts. Florida, a prime example, can expect large revenue losses due to decreases in tourism as the climate worsens, losses to coastal residential property from sea level rise, intensified hurricane damages, and increased electricity costs for air conditioning. Those categories of damages will significantly affect the gross state product. In addition, Florida, like many other states, will face a water crisis, as hotter temperatures increase the demand for water but decrease the usable supply.

Inaction on climate change also increases the chance of an abrupt, irreversible catastrophe, which would be much worse than the predictable costs of inaction discussed above. This point is emphasized in the Stern Review, and the economic analysis behind it is supported by recent research by Harvard University economist Martin Weitzman.[4] The collapse and complete melting

---

4. *See, e.g., On Modeling and Interpreting the Economics of Catastrophic Climate Change* (November 2007), where Weitzman argues that conventional cost-benefit analyses of climate change are misleading because they ignore nontrivial risks of genuine disaster. "Standard conventional cost-benefit analysis (CBA) of climate change does not even come remotely close to grappling seriously with this kind of potential for disasters.

of either the Greenland or West Antarctic ice sheets would cause sea levels to rise by 20 feet or more, causing devastation of coastal cities and regions where a large fraction of the American population lives. No one can say for certain at what temperature this will occur, but it becomes more likely as the world warms. We are taking a gamble, where the stakes are unbelievably high and the odds get worse the longer we stay on our current course.

No sensible person bets his or her home on a spin of the roulette wheel. But inaction on climate change is betting the only home humanity has. Who knows, we might get lucky and win the bet; a few scientists still doubt that hurricanes are getting worse. But the consequences of a bad bet are enormous. Without arguing that Katrina was "caused" by global warming, the misery it caused the people of Louisiana and Mississippi and the continuing economic turmoil it produced are wake-up calls that show how much harm a disrupted climate can produce.

A catastrophe, such as 20 feet or more of sea level rise, is not certain to occur; we don't know enough today to say how quickly we may lock in these catastrophic events with current emission paths. But homeowners buy fire insurance although they are not likely to have a fire next year; healthy young parents buy life insurance to protect their children, although they are not likely to die next year. The most catastrophic dangers from climate change are so immense that even if we believe the chance of catastrophe is small, it is irresponsible to ignore them. Taking action against climate change is life insurance for our home planet, needed to protect everyone's children.

Costs and Benefits of Action

The debate on global warming in Washington has turned decisively from "Is it a problem?" to "What are we going to do about it and how much is it going to cost?" In fact, we can't afford not to solve global warming. Economic analyses of the cost of reducing global warming pollution do not attempt to tally the benefits of preventing global warming. As the studies just discussed make clear, the costs of inaction are far higher than the costs of reducing emissions.

Even considering only the direct economic implications, it is clear that action to reduce global warming pollution presents opportunities as well as costs, as recognized by the leading business and environmental leaders that have formed the US Climate Action Partnership. We need only look to California as a prime example of how aggressive implementation of climate friendly energy efficiency measures has been accompanied by strong economic growth. Due to these measures, California's per capita electricity consumption has been level over the last 30 years while that of the US as a whole has steadily increased. Per capita electricity consumption in California is now more than 40 percent lower than in the rest of the country. Meanwhile, from 1990 to 2005 the California economy grew by more than 50 percent in real terms, an average annual growth rate of 2.9 percent.[5] And from 2003–2006 California has had an average annual real growth rate of 4 percent, while nationally the growth rate was 3.1 percent per year.[6]

The results of recent economic studies analyzing the costs of global warming cap and trade bills have shown that we can cut our global warming pollution substantially in a manner that is affordable for consumers and the US economy as a whole.

When CBA is done correctly, by including reasonable probabilities of (and reasonable damages from) catastrophic climate change, the policy implications can be radically different from the conventional advice coming out of a standard economic analysis that (essentially) ignores this kind of potential for disasters." http://www.economics.harvard.edu/faculty/Weitzman/papers/Modeling.pdf.

5. California Department of Finance, http://www.dof.ca.gov/html/FS_DATA/STAT-ABS/TABLES/d1.xls.

6. Bureau of Economic Analysis, U.S Department of Commerce, http://www.bea.gov/national/xls/gdplev.xls.

A useful starting point is EPA's analysis of the "Climate Stewardship and Innovation Act of 2007" (S.280), introduced by Senators Joe Lieberman (I-CT) and John McCain (R-AZ) in January of this year.[7] This bill is similar to ACSA in its cap levels and overall structure. The bottom line from this EPA analysis is that solving global warming is affordable.

EPA finds that reducing global warming pollution will have an imperceptible effect on economic output overall. If we take no action to cut emissions, GDP is projected to grow at 2.61–2.72 percent per year from 2010 to 2050, which of course ignores the prospect that climate disruption in this period would harm the economy. With S. 280, GDP grows between 2.54–2.69 percent per year. EPA's analysis, which we consider to be conservative, finds that the reduction in GDP growth from enacting the Climate Stewardship Act is a mere 0.03–0.07 percent per year. If S. 280 were enacted, consumption of goods and services by U.S. households would increase 103% between 2005 and 2030, according to the *Applied Dynamic Analysis of the Global Economy* (ADAGE) model used by EPA, which is virtually indistinguishable from the 105% increase projected without the legislation. Of course, household consumption is not the same as welfare. It does not include the value we place on reducing the risk of catastrophic storms, preserving our favorite beaches and alpine meadows, and preventing polar bears and countless other species from being driven to extinction.

What about energy prices? Changes would be far smaller and less disruptive than those consumers have experienced in recent years. According to EPA's analysis, S. 280 would have modest impacts on electricity and gasoline prices, and natural gas prices would not be significantly affected. The ADAGE model projects that the price of CO_2 allowances will be $27/ton in 2030, which would add 23 cents per gallon to the price of gasoline. But unlike recent, much larger, price increases, the money won't go to OPEC or national oil-producing economies under laws like ACSA. The money we spend on global warming solutions will be spent in the U.S., creating new jobs and economic opportunities. ACSA helps ensure this result by directing over time the entire economic resource created by the emission allowance program to public benefits, such as helping finance more fuel-efficient vehicles, homes, and appliances for American consumers and promoting the deployment of climate-friendly technologies here at home.

EPA projects that S. 280 would increase electricity prices somewhat (less than 1 cent per kilowatt-hour), but we don't write checks for *prices*, we write them for *energy bills*. EPA concludes that under S. 280 the total cost of generating electricity would decrease 7 percent in 2025 because energy efficiency measures will reduce total electricity consumption. Along with lower power production come significant health benefits from lower particulate and mercury emissions from power plants.

Using a version of the ADAGE model employed by EPA, the Nicholas Institute at Duke University just completed an analysis of the August 2nd version of ACSA.[8] Their results were very similar to EPA's results for the Climate Stewardship Act. In particular, the Duke study found that compliance with the targets has a small effect on rising GDP. By 2030 GDP is projected to increase 112% from 2005 levels in the Reference Case, and by 2050 the projected increase in GDP from 2005 levels is 238%. Under ACSA, GDP is projected to increase 111% by 2030 and 236% by 2050.

---

7. UNITED STATES ENVIRONMENTAL PROTECTION AGENCY'S ANALYSIS OF SENATE BILL S.280 IN THE 110TH CONGRESS, THE CLIMATE STEWARDSHIP AND INNOVATION ACT OF 2007 (July 2007), *available at* http://www.epa.gov/climatechange/economicanalyses.html#s280.

8. B.C. MURRAY & M.T. ROSS, THE LIEBERMAN-WARNER AMERICA'S CLIMATE SECURITY ACT: A PRELIMINARY ASSESSMENT OF POTENTIAL ECONOMIC IMPACTS (October 2007) *available at* http://www.nicholas.duke.edu/institute/econsummary.pdf.

In reality, the opportunities to cost-effectively reduce total energy demand are greater than considered in EPA's or Duke's analysis. Stronger building and appliance efficiency standards, a national Renewable Electricity Standard, and higher vehicle fuel economy standards are all part of a sound energy policy designed to increase energy security and lower consumer costs by overcoming market barriers that are slowing the adoption of these technologies. These policies would also help achieve the global warming pollution reductions required by ACSA, reducing compliance costs. EPA's analysis of S.280 does not consider these complementary energy policies. As a result it understates the role that renewable energy and vehicle efficiency improvements can play in achieving the emission reductions required by the bill, and overstates the role of other low-emission electricity generating technologies, offsets, and international credits. Several such complementary energy policies are included in ACSA and Congress can act even more quickly to adopt these policies by enacting this year a strong energy bill incorporating the best elements of the House- and Senate-passed bills.

It bears highlighting that no economic model can fully anticipate the advances in technology likely to be spurred by a policy package that caps and reduces emissions and uses allowances and performance standards to promote innovation. For example, prior to enactment of the cap on SO_2 emissions in the 1990 Clean Air Act amendments, EPA projected that the price of SO_2 allowances would be \$500–\$1000 per ton.[9] In fact, prices have been far lower, generally in the range of \$100 to \$200 per ton until it became clear that emission limits would be tightened further than originally enacted by Congress.

To ensure the affordability of a global warming cap and trade bill the legislation must be designed smartly. That means establishing a firm pollution cap that will spur innovation, allowing trading such that emission reductions can be made at least-cost, and using the value of emission allowances in the public interest making it possible to offset any increases in energy costs for low and middle-income consumers. A recent MIT analysis of the Lieberman-McCain Climate Stewardship Act found that a family of four could receive in 2015 more than \$3500 in revenue from the auction of allowances under this legislation, increasing over the years of the program.[10]

Some economic analyses estimate much higher costs. In particular, during the hearing last Thursday (November 8, 2007) you heard testimony from Dr. Anne Smith of CRA International and Dr. Margo Thorning of American Council for Capital Formation. We believe their analyses are seriously flawed. The attached memorandum from several well respected economists who have worked and published in the field of climate economics and energy economics for over three decades identifies some of the most serious defects, including the failure to examine the economic benefits of protecting the climate and the unjustified assumption that the business as usual economy operates in a perfect welfare-maximizing fashion. The memo's purpose is to promote understanding of the issue of abatement cost studies by pointing out the economic logic, assumptions, and deficiencies of the CRA and ACCF analyses in relation to best-practice in this field. This is especially important because these analyses have been privately produced and have not appeared in the peer-reviewed literature.

Focusing briefly on Dr. Smith's testimony, her analysis suggests that most of the emission reductions will occur in the electricity sector, neglecting opportunities to reduce emissions in industry and the transportation sector. Further, the CRA model limits the amount of ad-

---

9. ACID RAIN PROGRAM: 2005 PROGRESS REPORT, http://epa.gov/airmarkets/progress/docs/2005report. pdf.

10. S. PALTSEV, J.M. REILLY, H.D. JACOBY, A.C. GURGEL, G. E. METCALF, A.P. SOKOLOV, AND J.F. HOLAK, ASSESSMENT OF U.S. CAP-AND-TRADE PROPOSALS, MIT Joint Program on the Science and Policy of Global Change, Report No. 146, p. 25 (April 2007) *available at* http://web.mit.edu/globalchange/www/MITJPSPGC_Rpt146.pdf.

vanced technology that can come into the electricity sector in the future—for example, constraining deployment rates for carbon capture and disposal systems and assuming less penetration of renewable energy than Energy Information Administration's Annual Energy Outlook.

Other issues with CRA modeling include an artificially high emissions "baseline" (what would happen without a cap), which results in much higher costs for complying with emission caps. For example, the Energy Information Administration estimates additional lower carbon energy capacity will come on board even without a climate policy. EIA assumes that in coming decades if new coal plants are built they will probably be IGCC plants. However, CRA assumes business as usual coal technology and therefore factors in the full cost of new advanced technologies like IGCC with CCS when only the incremental costs of CCS should be included, thereby significantly increasing the overall cost estimates.

As a result of these and other assumptions, the cost impacts predicted by CRA are much higher than EPA's or Duke University's Nicholas School's recent modeling, which find that compliance with the emissions targets has only a small effect on GDP.

Finally, CRA's suggestion that delaying emission reductions would reduce costs ignores the primary driver of innovation. Entrepreneurs will only invest in developing and deploying the low-emission technologies we need if a market for these innovations is established by capping global warming pollution now. Delaying action will only delay progress in further reducing the costs of the many technology options available today.

When all is said and done, solving global warming is not only affordable, it is likely to be beneficial to the economy as well as our environment and public health. But even if it costs several times as much as EPA's or Duke's estimates, it is still a much better choice than gambling our future through inaction. (*See* attached "Economists' Statement on Climate Change").

We have the solutions—cleaner energy sources, new vehicle technologies and industrial processes and enhanced energy efficiency. What we lack is the policy framework to push business investments in the right direction and to get these solutions in the hands of consumers. America's Climate Security Act is a solid start on a policy framework that will trigger the necessary technological innovation in a manner that will strengthen our economy and lower the risk of catastrophic climate disruption.

Global Warming Pollution Reductions under ACSA (as amended in Subcommittee)

NRDC appreciates that ACSA was amended in the Subcommittee last week to expand its coverage of natural gas emissions. The bill covers all sources of global warming pollution that emit more than 10,000 tons of carbon dioxide equivalent per year in the electric power and industrial sectors as well as all transportation fuel providers whose products will produce more than 10,000 tons per year when consumed, and as amended in the Subcommittee, all emissions from natural gas consumption in the United States.

The expanded coverage adopted in Subcommittee significantly increases the emission reductions that ACSA would achieve. A recent analysis by the World Resources Institute (WRI) estimates that the bill, as amended, covers 84% of U.S. emissions, up from 75% as originally introduced.

The impact of the bill on total greenhouse gas emissions depends on assumptions made about state action, emissions from non-covered sources, and changes in biological carbon sequestration. The bill includes incentives for states to adopt climate policies that are more stringent than the federal program, to adopt and enforce model building codes, decouple electric and gas utility revenue from sales, and make energy efficiency investments as profitable as increasing energy supplies. The bill also includes energy efficiency standards for residential boilers and provisions requiring regular updates to residential and commercial building codes. Finally, the bill sets aside

5% of the total allowance pool to promote increased biological sequestration in domestic farms and forests and an additional 2.5% for similar international efforts.

These provisions will reduce emissions from non-covered sources below business as usual levels but the magnitude of these benefits is difficult to quantify. NRDC has constructed an Optimistic and Pessimistic case to bound the likely range of total greenhouse gas emission reductions under the bill.

- State Programs:
  - The Optimistic case assumes that any states that enact climate programs more stringent than the federal program retire the bonus allowances allocated to them (2% of the total allowance pool). While the bill makes clear that states have the authority to enforce global warming pollution standards more stringent than federal requirements currently there is no clear mechanism by which these state programs would result in reductions in national emissions other than by retiring their bonus allowances. Further elaboration of the state authority provisions could allow for greater national benefits from state programs.
  - The Pessimistic case assumes that these state programs help achieve the emission caps specified in the bill but do not achieve additional environmental benefits.
- Emissions from non-covered sources:
  - In the Optimistic case non-covered emissions from the residential and commercial sectors and non-covered methane emissions are assumed to decline at the same annual rate as they did from 2000 to 2005 (0.7% and 1.2%, respectively). Emissions of nitrous oxide and other non-covered greenhouse gases are assumed to remain constant at 2005 levels. In addition, the 7.5% allowance set aside for biological sequestration is assumed to generate one ton of benefits for each ton of allowances devoted to this purpose.[11]
  - In the Pessimistic case emissions from all non-covered sources are assumed to increase at the rate projected by EPA in its analysis of S.280 using the ADAGE model (0.3% per year) and the 7.5% allowance set aside for biological sequestration is assumed to generate 0.5 tons of benefits for each ton of allowances devoted to this purpose.

Based on these assumptions, we estimate that ACSA, as reported by the Subcommittee, would reduce total U.S. greenhouse gas emissions by 18 to 24 percent in 2020 compared to 2005 levels. By 2050 the bill would reduce total emissions by 59 to 66 percent. More detailed results are provided in the table below.

Year	Emissions of Covered Sources	Estimated Total Emissions Optimistic Case (MMTCO2e)	Estimated Total Emissions Pessimistic Case (MMTCO2e)	Reductions in Emissions from Covered Sources (2005 Baseline)	Estimated Range of Reductions in Total Greenhouse Gas Emissions (2005 Baseline)
2012	5,773	6,359	6,715	6%	8–12%
2020	4,920	5,538	5,923	20%	18–24%
2030	3,854	4,517	4,933	37%	32–38%
2040	2,789	3,501	3,945	54%	45–52%
2050	1,732	2,499	2,966	72%	59–66%

Figure 2.

---

11. While some "anyway" tons are likely to be promoted through these programs the cost per ton to reduce emissions through biological sequestration is expected to be less than the market price for allowances within the cap. The assumption here is that price differential between the incentives for biological sequestration and the price of allowances sold compensates for the anyway tons.

Coverage of Emissions

The cap and trade program should cover as much of the economy's GHG emissions as is possible. We commend the Subcommittee for expanding the bill's coverage to include all emissions from the use of natural gas. Similar to the transportation sector, it is not feasible to cover emissions from natural gas use in homes and offices at the point of emission due to the very large number of small sources. It is, however, feasible to include these emissions within the cap by moving the point of regulation upstream. We believe the most straightforward way to implement full coverage of natural gas is to keep coverage in the electric power and industrial sector at the point of emission as in ACSA as introduced, and to make all natural gas distributors above a given size threshold responsible for managing allowances for emissions by their residential and commercial customers (*e.g.*, all distributors that sell natural gas to residential and commercial customers, the combustion of which generates more than 10,000 tons of carbon dioxide equivalents).[12]

Alternatively, allowances could be managed by interstate and intrastate pipelines or by a combination of natural gas processors, importers, and pipelines for gas that is not processed. Downstream sources would not be required to submit allowances for emissions associated with their use of natural gas. This option is only acceptable if it is implemented in a way that prevents bypass of the point of regulation. Furthermore, this option moves the point of regulation further away from the actors who have direct control or influence over emissions. This could reduce the responsiveness of emitters to the cap, increasing compliance costs.

Allowance Allocations and other Policies under ACSA

ACSA would implement its cap and reductions through an allowance trading system. NRDC agrees that—combined with complementary policies, some of which are contained in this bill and in other legislation, such as the pending energy bill—this is the most effective and efficient approach to curbing global warming pollution. As the sponsors are aware, a cap and trade system requires attention to how the emissions allowances are allocated, and for what purposes. It is important to distinguish between the abatement cost of a cap and trade system and its distributional implications. The abatement cost will be significant, but far less than the cost of inaction. At the same time, the value of the pollution allowances created by the law will be higher than the abatement costs: some estimates place their value between $30 and 100 billion per year.

NRDC believes these pollution allowances are a public trust. They represent permission to use the atmosphere, which belongs to all of us, to "dispose of" global warming pollution. As such, they are not a private resource owned by historical emitters and such emitters do not have a permanent right to free allowances. The value of the allowances should be used for public purposes including promoting clean energy solutions, protecting the poor and other consumers, ensuring a just transition for workers in affected industries, and preventing human and ecosystem impacts both here and abroad, especially where they can lead to conflicts and threats to security.

ACSA embraces the principle that these pollution allowances should be used for public purposes but it implements the principle too slowly. NRDC believes that over the first 25 years of the program the bill gives away more allowances to the biggest emitting firms than is needed to fully compensate such firms for the effects of their compliance obligations on the firms' economic values. The result is that there are not enough allocations available to fully meet public needs. As discussed more fully below, the allowance allocations in the bill can be substantially improved.

---

12. 10,000 tons of CO_2 corresponds to 183 million cubic feet of natural gas. There are about 500 entities that distribute this volume of natural gas or more to residential and commercial customers.

ACSA also allows the owner or operator of a covered facility to satisfy up to 15 percent of a given year's compliance obligation using "offsets" generated within the United States. These offsets would come from activities that are not covered by the emissions cap. The 15 percent limitation is essential to ensure the integrity of the emissions cap in the bill and to spur technology innovation. The total amount of offsets allowed should not be increased. In addition, as discussed below, further changes to the bill should be made regarding the types of offsets that should be allowed and the conditions for such offsets.

We are pleased to note that ACSA includes "cost containment" provisions that protect the integrity of the emissions cap and preserve incentives for technology innovation. In particular, we commend your rejection of the misnamed "safety valve" concept that would allow the government to print unlimited pollution allowances at a set price.

The fundamental problem with the safety valve is that it breaks the cap without ever making up for the excess emissions. Simply put, the cap doesn't decline as needed or, worse, keeps growing. "Safety valve" is actually a misleading name. In boiler design, the role of a safety valve is to allow pressures to build within the vessel to working levels, well above atmospheric pressure. A safety valve's function is to open on the rare occasion when the boiler is pressured beyond its safe operating range, to keep it from exploding. In the life of a well-run boiler, the safety valve may never open.

Imagine, however, a boiler designed with a valve set to open just slightly above normal atmospheric pressure. The valve would always be open, and the boiler would never accomplish any useful work. That is the problem with the safety valve design in other legislative proposals. The valve is set at such a low level that it is likely to be open virtually all the time.

In addition to breaking the U.S. cap, a safety valve also would prevent U.S. participation in international trading systems. If trading were allowed between the U.S. and other capped nations, a major distortion would occur. Firms in other countries (acting directly or through brokers) would seek to purchase U.S. lower-priced allowances. Their demand would almost immediately drive the U.S. allowance price to the safety valve level, triggering the "printing" of more American allowances. Foreign demand for newly-minted U.S. safety valve allowances would continue until the world price dropped to the same level. The net result would be to flood the world market with far more allowances—and far less emission reduction—than anticipated.

Although NRDC believes that the primary and most effective cost containment device in any mandatory legislation will be the cap and trade system itself, NRDC also supports other means of providing flexibility. Banking has long been a feature of cap and trade systems. We also support the bill's provisions allowing firms to borrow allowances with appropriate interest and payback guarantees. The bill includes a further provision, nicknamed the Carbon Fed, based upon a proposal developed by Senators Warner, Graham, Lincoln and Landrieu. The board created under this provision is charged with monitoring the carbon market and is authorized to change the terms of allowance borrowing, including the interest rate and the time period for repayment. Crucially, however, the Carbon Fed does not have the authority to change the cumulative emissions cap. Under such a proposal, the environment is protected and cost volatility is minimized.

Areas for Additional Improvement

While ACSA provides a solid framework for sound global warming legislation, there are some significant areas in which it can and should be substantially improved. A more detailed discussion of these areas follows:

Scientific Review of Targets

The bill as introduced includes a provision under which the National Academy of Sciences would assess the extent to which emissions reductions required under the Act are being achieved, and would determine whether such reductions are sufficient to avoid dangerous global warming. However, unlike the similar provisions of the Sanders/Boxer legislation, ACSA does not authorize the Environmental Protection Agency to respond to the NAS assessments and reports by adjusting the applicable targets. The bill should be revised to allow EPA to take all necessary actions to avoid dangerous global warming by requiring additional reductions, including by changing applicable targets or through increasing the coverage of the bill.

Complementary Performance Standards

Performance standards for key sectors are an important complement to the comprehensive cap on emissions. The bill recognizes the importance of performance standards for building codes and appliance efficiency and contains standards for these energy consuming activities. But energy producers also need performance standards to avoid counterproductive investments in the early years of the program.

Carbon Capture and Disposal:

Perhaps the most important performance standard for the energy production sector is for coal-fired electric generation. It is critical to recognize that continued investments in old technology will "lock in" high carbon emissions for many decades to come and create a tremendous economic burden. This is particularly so for the next generation of coal-fired power plants. Power plant investments are large and long-lasting. A single plant costs around $2 billion and will operate for 60 years or more. If we decide to do it, the United States and other nations could build and operate new coal plants that return their CO_2 to the ground instead of polluting the atmosphere. With every month of delay we lose a piece of that opportunity and commit ourselves to 60 years of emissions. The International Energy Agency (IEA) forecasts that more than 20 trillion dollars will be spent globally on new energy technologies between now and 2030.

It is critical that we stop building new coal plants that release all of their carbon dioxide to the air. The Sanders-Boxer bill contains two complementary performance standards for coal plants and we recommend the Committee incorporate these concepts into ACSA. The first standard is a CO_2 emissions standard that applies to new power investments. California enacted such a measure in SB1368 last year. It requires new investments for sale of power in California to meet a performance standard that is achievable by coal plants using CO_2 capture.

The second standard is a low-carbon generation obligation for coal-based power. The low-carbon generation obligation requires an initially small fraction of sales from coal-based power to meet a CO_2 performance standard that is achievable with carbon capture. The required fraction of sales would increase gradually over time and the obligation would be tradable. Thus, a coal-based generating firm could meet the requirement by building a plant with carbon capture, by purchasing power generated by another source that meets the standard, or by purchasing credits from those who build such plants. This approach has the advantage of speeding the deployment of carbon capture systems while avoiding the "first mover penalty." Instead of causing the first builder of a commercial coal plant with carbon capture to bear all of the incremental costs, allowance incentives and the tradable low-carbon generation obligation would spread those costs over the entire coal-based generation system.

With such performance standards included, the bill could — at no added cost — prevent construction of new uncontrolled coal power plants and free up some of the incentive allowances for other purposes.

The bill contains several incentive provisions to reward developers who incorporate carbon capture and geologic disposal systems for new coal plants. NRDC supports such incentives though we believe that the bill currently overallocates to carbon capture and disposal (CCD) projects. In particular, the program for advanced coal under the auction is limited to 20 GW, but is allocated more revenue than it would need to deploy this capacity. As a result this amount could be reduced significantly without reducing the number of projects that are supported. In addition, the bonus allowance program for CCD provides more of an incentive than is needed given the caps in the bill. These revenues and allowances could be put toward other public benefits such as the adaptation needs of disadvantaged peoples and communities in the U.S and internationally who will be adversely affected by global warming impacts.

Some have argued that key technologies, such as carbon capture and disposal (CCD), are not yet available or are only available now at exorbitant cost. Such arguments are incorrect. All the elements of CCD systems are actually in use today but not are used in an integrated fashion. Arguments that claim full CCD systems are not ready because they are not in use today, under today's market conditions, fundamentally miss the point that sound global warming legislation will create the market conditions for deployment of such systems going forward from today.

Expert studies have concluded that we have the knowledge base now to proceed safely with geologic disposal of carbon dioxide in the amounts produced by the typical coal fueled power plant.[13]

Taking a frozen snapshot of the cost of carbon control technologies today is also misleading. Think how wrong such an assessment would have been if applied to computer technology at any point in the last thirty years. Speed and capacity have increased by orders of magnitude as costs plummeted. We now carry more computing power in our cell phones than the Apollo astronauts carried to the moon. Once market signals are in place, it will be the same for technologies such as carbon capture and disposal.[14]

Low-Carbon Fuels Standard:

Other complementary policies should also be considered for sectors such as the transportation area. NRDC supports a Low Carbon Fuel Standard, which would cut greenhouse gas emissions from fuels by 10% from today's levels by 2020 and spur development and use of cellulosic ethanol and other low carbon fuels. We support inclusion of such a performance standard in ACSA. It is also important to note that other ongoing efforts in the Senate, such as the Corporate Average Fuel Economy measures included in the Senate energy bill, could lead to substantial reductions in greenhouse gas emissions and, if enacted, will provide another important complement to the provisions in ACSA.

---

13. *See, e.g.,* the SPECIAL REPORT ON CARBON DIOXIDE CAPTURE AND STORAGE of the INTERGOVERNMENTAL PANEL ON CLIMATE CHANGE discussed in Appendix C. *See also* MIT's REPORT ON THE FUTURE OF COAL (2007). The MIT report's lead authors, Professors John Deutch and Ernest Moniz, had this to say about the safety of multi-million ton injection projects to the Senate Energy and Natural Resources Committee in March 2007: "Each plant will need to capture millions of metric tonnes of CO_2 each year. Over a fifty-year lifetime, one such plant would inject about a billion barrels of compressed CO_2 for sequestration. *We have confidence that megatonne scale injection at multiple well-characterized sites can start safely now,* but an extensive program is needed to establish public confidence in the practical operation of large scale sequestration facilities over extended periods and to demonstrate the technical and economic characteristics of the sequestration activity." (Deutch, emphasis supplied); "I think the important thing to emphasize, so there's no confusion, is that we feel very, very confident about the wisdom of going ahead now with those mega-ton per-year projects." (Moniz). U.S. Senate, Energy and Natural Resources Committee, "Future of Coal," March 22, 2007, S. Hrg. 110-69 at 9, 11.

14. Appendix C contains a more thorough discussion of the readiness of carbon capture and disposal systems.

Offsets:

ACSA allows the owner or operator of a covered facility to satisfy up to 15 percent of a given year's compliance obligation using "offsets" generated within the United States. These offsets would come from activities that are not covered by the emissions cap.

While there are many emission reduction activities outside the cap that are worth encouraging, many experts have worked for more than 30 years in an attempt to produce reliable, workable offset programs in both the clean air and global warming contexts but there is little reason for satisfaction with the results. Even if criteria for measurability and enforceability are met, offsets still have the potential to break the cap because of difficulties in assuring that actions being credited are actually "additional" — *i.e.*, that they are not simply actions that would have taken place anyway in the absence of credit.

The additionality problem is not readily soluble, because it is extraordinarily difficult to devise workable rules for determining business-as-usual baselines at the project level. In some areas, credits may leverage new actions that would not have occurred, with a minimum of credit bestowed on "anyway" actions. But far more often, "anyway" actions make up a large — even dominant — fraction of the reductions credited. If offsets represent even a small percentage of "anyway" tons, climate protection actually moves backwards. A full ton is added to the cap in exchange for an action that may represent only 0.9 ton of reduction — or worse, 0.1 ton of reduction. With each offset, net emissions increase.

Offsets also can delay key industries' investments in transformative technologies that are necessary to meet the declining cap. For instance, unlimited availability of offsets could lead utilities to build high-emitting coal plants instead of investing in efficiency, renewables, or plants equipped with carbon capture and storage.

For these reasons, NRDC has proposed setting aside a portion of the allowances from *within* the cap to incentivize mitigation actions from sources, like agriculture, that are outside the cap. Since the allowances would come from within the cap, they do not run the risk of expanding actual emissions as a result of rewarding this activity. Another acceptable approach would be to allow only a limited quantity of offsets in the cap-and-trade design.

The Lieberman/Warner bill takes both approaches. The bill includes a "set aside" for agricultural reductions which would provide allowances from within the cap, and the bill also limits domestic offsets from outside the cap to 15 percent of a facility's annual compliance obligation.

NRDC believes that there are some additional changes needed in the offset provisions to remove offsets for forest management activities, where additionality fundamentally cannot be guaranteed. Moreover, forest management activities focused on maximizing carbon storage could result in ecological damage to forests, which have many functions in addition to carbon storage. The authority of the Carbon Market Efficiency Board to expand the use of offsets should also be constrained. A number of other safeguards need to be strengthened. We will be glad to continue working with your staff regarding these provisions.

Allocation of Allowances:

The Lieberman/Warner bill recognizes that allowances can and should be used to achieve important public purposes, but the bill provides too many allowances for free to emitters in the early years of the program.

The bill provides allowances for public purposes in two ways:
1) auctioned allowances, with the proceeds of the auction going for such purposes as climate-friendly technologies, low income energy consumers, wildlife adaptation, national security/global warming measures and worker training.

2) free allowances to electricity consumers, state and tribal governments, and U.S. farmers and foresters, for a range of designated public purposes.

But the bill also initially gives 40 percent of the allowances for free to emitters in the electric and industrial sectors with no requirement that these allowances be used for public purposes. These free allowances to emitters continue at gradually reduced rates until 2036 when they are terminated. The amount of allowances that are auctioned for public purposes grows from 24 percent in 2012 to 73 percent in 2036.

NRDC appreciates the substantial changes that have been made to ACSA since the bill outline was released in August. These changes include eliminating the perpetual free allocation to industrial emitters and removing free allowances to oil and coal companies.

The current bill's allocation to electric power and industrial emitters, however, is still much higher than justified under "hold-harmless" principles and will result in windfall profits to the shareholders of emitters. For example, an economic analysis by Larry Goulder of Stanford University suggests that in an economy-wide upstream cap and trade program, only 13% of the allowances will be needed to cover the costs that fossil-fuel providers would not be able to pass on to their customers. Similar analyses, with similar results, have been conducted by Resources for The Future and the Congressional Budget Office.

As a result, NRDC believes that the bill should be improved substantially by reducing the starting percentage of free allowances to emitters and phasing them out faster—within 10–15 years of enactment. This would allow a greater percentage of the allowances to be devoted to public purposes initially and in later years. In particular, reducing the free allocations to emitters would allow for more resources to be directed to states, to low-income consumers in the United States, and to the most vulnerable among us both here and abroad.

International Cooperation:

The bill includes a provision to encourage other nations to join in action to reduce greenhouse gas emissions, and to protect American businesses and workers from unfair competition if specific nations decline to cooperate. Under this provision, the United States would seek to negotiate for "comparable emissions reductions" from other emitting countries within 8 years of enactment. Countries failing to make such commitments would be required to submit greenhouse gas allowances for certain carbon intensive products. NRDC supports this provision, while bearing in mind that the U.S., as the world's greatest contributor to the burden of global warming pollution already in the atmosphere, needs to show leadership in meeting the global warming challenge.

Adaptation Issues:

The sad truth is that if we do our utmost to cut global warming pollution starting tomorrow, people and sensitive ecosystems we depend on will still suffer serious impacts due to the emissions that are already in the air and those "in the pipeline." We must do what we can now to ensure that communities and natural ecosystems are best prepared to withstand and adapt to ongoing and expected change.

The impacts of global warming will be felt to a much greater extent by vulnerable communities abroad, particularly those in the least developed countries that bear the smallest share of responsibility for increases in greenhouse gas concentrations.

The average American is responsible for many times more emissions than an average citizen of most African countries. Providing assistance for international adaptation is not only the right thing to do, it is also in our national interest. Global warming is a destabilizing force that will act against our hopes for the advancement of human rights and democracy. It will elevate the risk of displacement, famine, and poverty—the kind of conditions in which violence, oppression, and radical ideologies can flourish. Providing support for adaptation will also help advance international negotiations toward an effective global agreement for the period beyond 2012.

But our motive for providing help should not rest solely on whether these countries are a "security" threat, but also because this is the right thing to do, and because we have a crucial opportunity to ameliorate worldwide suffering by assisting these nations in adopting more sustainable energy and development paths.

————————

Note

1. *Appendices.* David Hawkins' testimony included three appendices. The first two (Appendices A & B) address the economics of climate change mitigation. They have been reproduced in part below in Section H of this Chapter. Appendix C addresses the technological feasibility of carbon capture and disposal; it is reproduced in part in Section II(A) of Chapter 4. The full testimony may be retrieved at: docs.nrdc.org/globalWarming/glo_07111301A.pdf.

2. Climate Principles

On October 2, 2008, Congressmen Waxman, Markey, and Inslee submitted a letter to Speaker of the House Pelosi outlining "climate principles" that should guide all future climate change legislation.[1] The letter was co-signed by an impressive 152 members of the U.S. House of Representatives:

The following are the principles we have developed to guide the creation of comprehensive global warming legislation.

Comprehensive legislation to address global warming must achieve four key goals:
- Reduce emissions to avoid dangerous global warming;
- Transition America to a clean energy economy;
- Recognize and minimize any economic impacts from global warming legislation; and
- Aid communities and ecosystems vulnerable to harm from global warming.

To meet each of these goals, climate change legislation must include the following key elements.

Reduce Emissions to Avoid Dangerous Global Warming
- Review and respond to advancing climate science
- Make emissions targets certain and enforceable
- Require the United States to engage with other nations to reduce emissions through commitments and incentives

Transition America to a Clean Energy Economy
- Invest in the best clean energy and efficiency technologies
- Include and encourage complementary policies
- Preserve states' authorities to protect their citizens

Recognize and Minimize Any Economic Impacts from Global Warming Legislation
- Use public assets for public benefit in a fair and transparent way
- Return revenues to consumers
- Return revenues to workers and communities

————————

1. The letter and more information about the Climate Principles is *available at* http://globalwarming.house.gov/mediacenter/pressreleases_2008?id=0047#main_content (last visited November 21, 2008).

- Protect against global trade disadvantages to U.S. industry

Aid Communities and Ecosystems Vulnerable to Harm from Global Warming
- Assist states, localities, and tribes to respond and adapt to the effects of global warming
- Assist developing countries to respond and adapt to the effects of global warming
- Assist wildlife and ecosystems threatened by global warming

B. Future Proposals: A Framework for Evaluating U.S. Climate Change Policy

Whether similar to the Lieberman-Warner proposal or divergent from it, it is certain that climate change legislation will continue to be introduced and debated in Congress. Professor Victor Flatt provides a framework for assessing climate change legislation.

Evolving Trends in Federal Climate Change Legislation[1]

Victor B. Flatt, Tom & Elizabeth Distinguished Professor of Environmental Law at the University of North Carolina Chapel Hill School of Law. He also has an appointment as a Distinguished Scholar in Carbon Markets and Carbon Trading at the Global Energy Management Institute at the University of Houston's Bauer College of Business, and is a member scholar of the Center for Progressive Reform. Before joining UNC Chapel Hill, Prof. Flatt served as the first A.L. O'Quinn Chair in Environmental Law at the University of Houston Law Center, where he was also director of the Center for Environment, Energy, and Natural Resources Law; Tel. (919) 962-4118, flatt@email.unc.edu.

The United States will almost certainly enact federal legislation designed to reduce emissions of greenhouse gases within the next two years. But it is uncertain what final form this legislation will take, and what variables will be in play in the discussion. At this stage, even the ultimate target in greenhouse gas reductions is not yet known. The legislation could have economy-wide effects, or could only affect certain industries. It might allow the use of offsets or not. It may integrate with existing pollution-control regimes or stand on its own. It will likely create new wealth for certain segments of the economy, but may put others out of business. How these and other policy choices are resolved could turn out to be the most important legislative question that our country addresses in the foreseeable future.[2] At the time this is written, we do not have a crystal ball. However, we already know enough about the problem to tell us what questions the ultimate bill must address as well as how it is likely to do so.

---

1. Some of this paper is condensed from Victor B. Flatt, *The Legislative Temperature for Climate Change*, 102 Nw. U. L. Rev. Colloquy 123 (2007), at http://www.law.northwestern.edu/lawreview/colloquy/prior-colloquies/climate-change.html. It should also be noted that this was prepared in early April to meet the deadline for written materials; this is a fast moving area, and particular attention will be paid to any updates since this went to press.

2. The Congressional Budget Office estimates that the value of carbon allocations in a U.S. cap and trade system could approach hundreds of billions of dollars. *See* http://www.eenews.net/features/documents/2007/04/25/document_gw_02.pdf.

The cost of avoided harm by controlling climate change is more uncertain, but has been estimated in the trillions. *Climate Change Fight Can't Wait*, BBC News, Oct. 31, 2006, *available at* http://news.bbc.co.uk/2/hi/business/6096084.stm.

In April, 2008, there were at least eleven legislative proposals in Congress that address climate change.[3] As identified by their primary sponsors, these include Lieberman-Warner, Bingaman-Specter, Udall-Petri, Lieberman-McCain, Kerry-Snowe, Waxman, Sanders-Boxer, Feinstein-Carper, Alexander-Lieberman, Stark, and Larson. In addition, other politicians, such as John Dingell, have announced "plans" for legislation, hold their own goals for climate change, and/or have endorsed various components of the filed bills.[4] However, as debate on bills and ideas have progressed, it seems that the Lieberman-Warner Bill is the template from which other bills are working. Lieberman-Warner was re-introduced with important changes in May 2008 (S. 3036), and was debated by the Senate in June. The amendments as well as the contours of the debate (the bill was defeated) also give us some guidance and suggestions as to how the important questions of any comprehensive climate change legislation will be answered.

1. What is the Goal of Climate Change Legislation?

To a casual observer, the goal of climate change legislation might seem to be simple—stop climate change. But one quickly sees that expense, cost allocation and harm distribution are equally important.

A climate change legislative goal must, at a minimum, address the harmful effects that it seeks to avoid—the "effects target." An effects target will guide how much we want to avoid temperature rise and other associated effects of climate change. This goal must also specify how that change can be translated into actual reductions of CO_2 or other gases that affect climate change. This requires us to determine how much harm we are willing to endure, whose harm we are concerned about, and how much we are willing to pay to avoid this harm.

Since Carbon Dioxide ("CO_2") is the primary gas which contributes to the greenhouse effect, which is driving a rise in temperatures and other associated climate change effects, most discussion of climate change avoidance since its inception has focused on the amount of annual reductions in the emission of CO_2 (and CO_2 equivalents)[5] that we will need to make to avoid the harms that are associated with climate change. The Rio Framework on Climate Change and the later Kyoto protocol focused on the reductions in CO_2 emissions of industrialized countries in a relatively short time frame, as a first step towards later reductions.[6] Recent new targets in reductions have been proposed and offered by countries around the world as the next step in fighting climate change.[7]

---

3. www.rff.org/climatechangelegislation. (One of the bills, Udall-Petri, is a draft that has not been introduced but retains elements of prior Udall and Petri bills in the 109th Congress. Discussion of this bill is based on an analysis of what is currently expected to be proposed.) A specific date is noted due to ongoing alterations in proposed legislation.

4. http://www.eenews.net/Greenwire/2007/03/21/#2.

5. CO_2 provides about 70% of the heat retention associated with the greenhouse effects at play in the Earth's atmosphere. Other gases, such as methane, water vapor, and HCFCs also have greenhouse forcing capabilities. Generally, when greenhouse gas amelioration is discussed, it is done with respect to CO_2 reductions. Nevertheless, it is clearly recognized that reductions in other greenhouse gases may have the same effect as a different amount of CO_2 reduction, and therefore many discussions of greenhouse gas reductions are in terms of CO_2 or amounts of other gases that would be equivalent to an amount of CO_2 reduction. These equivalent gases are very important in any climate change legislation and will be considered explicitly, *infra*. However, for ease of discussion I will drop the parenthetical regarding CO_2 equivalents, and one should assume that discussion of CO_2 reductions may include reduction of other gases that can be equated to CO_2 reductions.

6. *See* UN Kyoto Protocol, Article III (limits until 2012), at http://unfccc.int/resource/docs/convkp/kpeng.html.

7. EU Climate Change statement, at http://ec.europa.eu/environment/climat/future_action.htm; Darren Samuelsohn, *Congress Has Its Eye on International Warming Talks*, E&E DAILY, Sept. 24, 2007.

However, the simplicity of such percentage reductions masks huge complications in estimating the actual effects of these reductions. A reduction in atmospheric CO_2 lags the greenhouse effects of the gas by 40 years or more, meaning that temperatures will rise and we will see more effects even if all greenhouse gas emissions were stopped now.[8] Reductions in one jurisdiction must be compared to reductions or increases in others to ascertain the worldwide reductions that will occur. Moreover, "targets" may not translate into actual reductions. With these caveats, however, there is some scientific consensus about the effects of CO_2 concentrations on temperature change and associated climate change effects. Moreover, there is some consensus on what reductions from historic emissions must occur worldwide to avoid the worst climate change harms.

Current CO_2 concentrations are at about 377 parts per million (ppm) (higher than pre-industrial levels by 40%) and projections indicate that CO_2 concentrations will grow by 63% to 235% by 2050, depending on programs to reduce CO_2.[9] There is consensus that if average global warming is kept lower than 2 degrees Celsuis, the effects of that temperature rise, while harmful, would not be catastrophic.[10] There is also consensus that CO_2 emissions must be reduced by 50% to 80% of 1990 CO_2 production levels to achieve this lower level of warming.[11]

It is from these scientific analyses that we choose reduction targets, and it is with these scientific analyses that we compare legislative choices. The uncertainty in the science of these predictions, what warming is acceptable (with respect to the entire world, a nation, or some identified group), what technological changes may exist in the future to address energy production or climate change harms, and what costs a jurisdiction is willing to accept, presumably drive any legitimate variance in CO_2 reduction targets in legislation. While uncertainty clearly still exists as to the effects of average temperature rise, most nations have embraced the notion that reductions in annual output of CO_2 must be made to stabilize the atmospheric concentrations at a level to keep average global temperature rise under 2 degrees Celsius.

In keeping with the above consensus, most of the legislative proposals analyzed in this essay target an average worldwide temperature rise no greater than 2 degrees C (3.8 F). Most then translate this temperature rise limitation into goals for reductions in annual CO_2 emissions.[12] Ten of the current legislative proposals: Lieberman-Warner, Bingaman-Specter, Udall-Petri, Lieberman-McCain, Kerry-Snowe, Sanders-Boxer, Waxman, Feinstein-Carper, Alexander-Lieberman, and Stark have either CO_2 reduction targets or estimates of CO_2 reductions in a specified time frame.[13] The reductions are made in comparison to historical emissions data and are at least theoretically designed to limit all or most U.S. emissions by this percentage in the

---

8. STERN REVIEW ON THE ECONOMICS OF CLIMATE CHANGE, [hereinafter STERN REPORT], Part I, *The Science of Climate Change*, at 1.4, p. 10, *available at* http://www.hm-treasury.gov.uk/media/3/6/Chapter_1 _The_Science_of_Climate_Change.pdf. (While many of the economic assumptions of the STERN REPORT have been criticized and challenged, its discussion of the scientific basis of climate change and the effects resulting from that are widely accepted).

9. T.J. BLASING AND CARMEN SMITH, CARBON DIOXIDE INFORMATION ANALYSIS CENTER, RECENT GREENHOUSE GAS CONCENTRATIONS, *available at* http://cdiac.ornl.gov/pns/current_ghg.html; PEW CENTER, KEVIN BAUMART, JONATHAN PERSHING, CLIMATE DATA, INSIGHTS AND OBSERVATIONS, p. 15, *available at* http://www. pewclimate.org/docUploads/Climate%20Data%20new.pdf.

10. The irreversible melting of the Greenland and Antarctic ice sheets is considered catastrophic and may occur with temperature rise above 2 degrees C. Other impacts have also been described as catastrophic.

11. PEW CENTER, CLIMATE CHANGE 101: SCIENCE AND IMPACTS, at 7, *available at* http://www.pewclimate. org/docUploads/101_Science_Impacts.pdf.

12. *See* Sanders-Boxer (S. 309), at 10, *available at* http://frwebgate.access.gpo.gov/cgi-bin/getdoc.cgi? db-name=110_cong_bills&docid=f:s309is.txt.

13. www.rff.org/climatechangelegislation.

time frame specified.[14] The Larson proposal, one of the tax proposals, does not reference a specified reduction goal in greenhouse gas emissions.

Most of the economy-wide CO_2 reductions target at least a 50% reduction in CO_2 from 1990 levels by mid-century, though there are some outliers.[15] The largest reduction is anticipated to come from the Waxman and Boxer-Sanders proposals (80%).[16]

While each of the proposed statutes reference the importance of avoiding climate change harm, these percentage reductions are not defined with respect to what variables could affect such a choice, such as community considered, allocation of costs and benefits, and expectations of other reductions or future technological changes or solutions. From the press releases of the legislative sponsors, it appears that all believe that their reductions are just enough to avoid the worst harm, while inflicting minimal damage to the economy. Though these "Goldilocks" targets all claim to be "just right," a distinction in target levels ostensibly to reach the same result brings these suppositions into question. Without valid supporting studies, we cannot be sure if these targets accomplish climate change mitigation as the legislative sponsors claim. It is true that scientists themselves may not be sure of the probability of temperature rise associated with certain reductions or the distribution and effects of that rise, but failure to be more specific leaves the focus on direct economic impacts to the detriment of the other concerns. Moreover, details on what sectors the percentage reductions cover may be critical; lack of reductions in certain areas will reduce the supposed overall reduction and thus the possibility of avoiding the worst climate change harms. Thus, bills such as the Lieberman-McCain proposal which target a 50% reduction in CO_2 from 1990 levels by mid-century (without applying to all sectors and with the possibility of a safety valve, *see infra*) may be less "costly" to the economy in one sense, but the costs associated with harms that occur from not setting the target reduction high enough means that such a bill may in fact be more costly to our society and economy in the long run than the Waxman or Boxer-Sanders bills, which target an 80% reduction in CO_2 from 1990 levels by mid-century. It is of course possible to revisit reduction targets as new scientific information comes in, and this is proposed in the Boxer-Sanders legislation, but this same strategy has not worked well in revisiting human health effects and residual risk in the Clean Air Act's control of Hazardous Air Pollutants.[17]

The newest science (much of it since the original proposals) continues to emphasize that the reductions of developed countries need to be towards the 80% range from 1990 levels by mid-century. This seems to be where the EU is heading, and has been embraced by the post-Kyoto climate change treaty discussions. Legislators supporting a comprehensive bill will have a hard time facing down this increasing certainty. Both Lieberman and Warner have indicated that they would be receptive to higher targets.

---

14. www.rff.org/climatechangelegislation (*see* Timeline of Emissions Targets Bills). The legislative proposals vary in what percentage of sources the CO_2 emissions reductions will apply to. The Lieberman-Warner proposal will only affect 80% of US CO_2 sources, and doesn't cover residential or commercial buildings, or the agricultural sector. Darren Samuelsohn, *Lieberman-Warner plan tighten emissions cap, limits credits*, GREENWIRE, Oct. 16, 2007. Similarly, the current legislative proposals do not address all CO_2 or other greenhouse gas reductions despite many being touted as economy-wide.

15. Direct comparison is difficult in the text since some proposals refer to reductions from CO_2 amounts produced in years other than 1990. Note also that some sectors may not be covered. A graphical representation that takes some of this into account has been published by Resources for the Future, comparing reductions across proposals. This can be found at: www.rff.org/climatechangelegislation. A version taking into account the possibility of escape valves and business assistance (*see infra*) is found at World Resources Institute, at http://www.wri.org/climate/pubs_description.cfm?pid=4343.

16. *Id.*

17. Victor B. Flatt, *Gasping for Breath: The Administrative Flaws of Federal Hazardous Air Pollution Regulation and What We Can Learn from the States*, 34 ECOL. L. Q. 107,118 (2007).

But even a strict reduction to affect worldwide average temperature stabilization does not tell the whole story. The newest studies indicate that the Western United States will continue to warm at twice the average global warming level.[18]

Alaska will also face extreme warming. This indicates that the target may not be equally as helpful across the country, and also brings up the issue of compensation or adaptation.

2. How to Reach the Goal

Interestingly, all of the climate change legislative proposals would be considered to be market-based control regimes, with Lieberman-Warner, Bingaman-Specter, Udall-Petri, Lieberman-McCain, Kerry-Snowe, Waxman, Feinstein-Carper, and Alexander-Lieberman, all envisioning a cap-and-trade scheme for CO_2, and Stark and Larson proposing an economy wide tax.

A tax system can control pollution by setting a tax on emissions (such as for CO_2) at a high enough level to discourage such emissions. For instance, one could presumably set a tax on CO_2 emissions (or energy production associated with CO_2 emissions) that would discourage emissions enough to reach a CO_2 reduction target. Cap-and-trade systems adopt the target first and then allocate the overall amount allowed by the target to parties in the market to use, sell, or buy (trade) as they please. Cap-and-trade can be an efficient pollution reduction mechanism because the trading allows the private sector to control emissions at the lowest possible cost (to the private sector) and also encourages innovation.

Currently, none of our environmental laws attempt to control pollution through a tax and we have only one cap and trade system, the one for sulfur dioxide (SO_2), to control acid rain that was passed in 1990.[19] That all of the climate change legislative proposals embrace a tax or cap-and-trade system shows just how much these systems have gained in respectability in the last seventeen years.

Most of the public discussion has assumed that we will have a cap-and trade bill rather than a tax. The environmental community supports this because it requires that a certain level be reached. Although a tax could do this as well, it would require ever increasing taxes to keep reducing CO_2 use, the political palatability of which seems more difficult. However, cap-and-trade could have problems with administrative costs. One of the unique features of the cap and trade market in SO_2, which is the model on which our environmental cap and trade systems are based, is that those sources involved in the market (large coal-fired power plants) are relatively limited in number and already regulated.[20] This means that enforcement and administration costs are relatively low for the benefit that can be derived from the system.[21] CO_2 regulation would be a different animal altogether. First, CO_2 (and other greenhouse gases) are not limited to coal-fired power plants, though these are a major source. Mobile sources play a large role, and if a system were to include offsets (*see* discussion, *infra*), the entities that must be monitored and regulated mushroom exponentially.

The difficulty with enforcement may be why two of the proposals (Feinstein-Carper and Alexander-Lieberman) only apply to the electricity sector. Feinstein-Carper and Alexander-Lieberman could be seen as compromise proposals that anticipate further legislation in other sectors, but propose the electricity generation sector first because of the ease of regulation.

---

18. NRDC, HOTTER AND DRIER, THE WEST'S CHANGED CLIMATE, *available at* http://www.nrdc.org/global Warming/west/contents.asp (last visited April 9, 2008).

19. 42 U.S.C. Sec. 7651c *et seq.*

20. Victor B. Flatt, *The Enron Story and Environmental Policy,* ELR NEWS & ANALYSIS, 10485, 10494 (2003).

21. *Id.*

Nevertheless, the very concept of proceeding in sectors raises concern. First, there is no guarantee that future legislation will occur after one sector is brought in. Moreover, as discussed above, experience with cap-and-trade in the electricity generating sector may not be applicable to all industries, requiring individual sector systems in any future legislation. Sector-by-sector regulation might reduce cheating because trading within sectors will likely be easier to monitor, but the lack of inter-sector trading or offsets would defeat many of the benefits of a market system in the first place. Economy-wide proposals may be considered the most efficient and the most fair, but this consideration must be balanced against the enforceability of economy-wide limits.[22]

3. Offsets

Any cap and trade system for CO_2 must also address the question of offsets. An offset is anything that will actually reduce CO_2 production (or sometimes future CO_2 production) at one location, which can then be credited against CO_2 production at another location. For instance, if a party has 100 credits which allow the production of 100 tons of CO_2, but wishes to emit 110 tons, instead of buying 10 more credits under the cap-and-trade system, that person might "offset" the extra ten tons of CO_2 by eliminating ten tons of CO_2 production elsewhere. This could be done through retiring a source, creating a physical system to absorb CO_2, or (more controversially) avoiding an increase in future CO_2 production by providing alternate methods of energy that do not produce CO_2. This is essentially a "purchase" of offsets that takes place outside a cap-and-trade system.

Offsets are very complex, but would add greatly to the efficiency of a system, allowing for faster and cheaper reductions. They are also a mechanism for transferring some of the benefits of compliance to developing countries. The main concern with offsets is which ones should be allowed. Presumably, we wish offsets to actually do what they are intended to do. This means that any offsets will require proper measurement systems, verification systems, scientific consensus and consideration of possible unintended consequences. With respect to verification, the current state of the CO_2 trading system in the EU is under critical evaluation.[23] The EU has recently discovered that its initial CO_2 allocations and some offsets were improperly reported by the CO_2 producers, which inflated the number of credits in the system. Because the EU did not have any mechanism in place to verify what sources were actually producing, the system was improperly designed.

Some proposals for carbon offsets may be scientifically suspect. Biological carbon sinks, which—theoretically, at least—absorb CO_2, are under increased scientific scrutiny and criticism[24] because some, such as tree planting in the far northern hemisphere, may contribute to warming rather than offsetting it.[25] Others, such as a plan to seed the ocean with iron filings near the Galapagos Islands to spur plankton, have been blasted as not being based on sound science, harmful, and motivated by nothing but profit.[26] Lastly, offsets purchased in developing countries

---

22. Darren Samuelsohn, *Sanders Shifts Warming Debate With Power Plant Only Bills*, E&E DAILY, April 25, 2007.

23. Question Marks over EU CO_2 Trading Scheme, May 16, 2006, EurActiv.com, *available at* http://www.euractiv.com/en/sustainability/question-marks-eu-co2-trading-scheme/article-155349.

24. *Critics Attack Offsetting Plan Near Galapagos Islands*, GREENWIRE, August 17, 2007, *available at* http://www.eenewsnet/Greenwire/2007/08/17/12/#12.

25. S.G. Gibbard, K. Caldeira, G. Bala, T.J. Phillips, M. Wicket, *Climate Effects of Global Land Cover*, Lawrence Livermore National Laboratory, Global Research Letter, UCRL-JRNL-215046, *available at* http://www.llnl.gov/tid/lof/documents/pdf/324200.pdf; *see also* Gustavo A. B. da Fonseca, Carlos Manuel Rodriguez, Guy Midgley, Jonah Busch, Lee Hannah, Russell A. Mittermeier, *No Forest Left Behind*, PLOS BIOLOGY, *available at* http://biology.plosjournals.org/perlserv/?request=get-document&doi=10.1371/journal.pbio.0050216.

26. Wall Street Journal Blog, *available at* http://blogs.wsj.com/energy/2007/08/16/upset-about-an-offset/.

under the Kyoto Protocol's clean development mechanism are not required to be sustainable or environmentally beneficial, and may only enrich the traders themselves.[27]

Moreover, verifying trades and offsets can be a daunting problem. It is difficult to track small sources, such as the CO_2 from the 300 million automobiles in the United States, meaning that mobile source usage intensity will not be a reliable offset.[28] Offsets in foreign countries present particular difficulties. Although most economists agree that avoiding or reducing CO_2 production in developing countries is more efficient than reductions in the developed world, which supports the idea of international trading and offsets, verifying these reductions over international borders will be difficult.[29] The Kyoto Protocol's Clean Development Mechanism (CDM) program, which allows the purchase of offsets in foreign countries, has been roundly criticized for the questionable validity of the offsets purchased.[30]

Eight of the current legislative proposals: Lieberman-Warner, Bingaman-Specter, Udall-Petri, Lieberman-McCain, Kerry-Snowe, Sanders-Boxer, Feinstein-Carper, and Alexander-Lieberman, specifically allow the use of offsets.[31] The Waxman proposal does not specify the validity of particular offsets, but does state that the goals of a GHG reduction program should encompass "enhanced sequestration of carbon in the forest and agricultural sectors."[32] The Stark and Larson tax system proposals do not allow offsets per se but do propose tax credits (which can be seen as an "offset" in taxes) for certain sequestration or GHG destruction projects.[33] Therefore all of the proposals trigger the issues of concern with offsets.

The original Lieberman-Warner Bill brought forward a particularly important innovation with respect to offsets. It required that all U.S. biological offsets be analyzed not only for purposes of whether they are genuine and whether they will continue (Secs. 2404–07); but also whether they will cause other environmental effects (Sec. 2410), bringing the question of "co-goods" and "co-bads" into the leading legislative template.

The May 2008 revision contained even more details on offsets. A focus on tighter verification rules suggests that the suspicion of offsets is deep and that we will have a rigorous vetting and possible limitation of offsets in the final federal bill. The 2008 revision specifically proposed that offsets be reduced by "leakage"—defined as ineffectiveness—change outside boundaries. Also, the environmental analysis is still included in the offset analysis, with the EPA to consider impacts on the environment and health (Sec. 310(a)). In addition, the new iteration of the bill would exclude offsets that undermine the "integrity of [the trading] program," such as conversion or clearing of land—Sec. 314(e)(1); and favor a use of "native" plant species. Sec. 310 (c). All of these rules are also to be applied to foreign offsets. Sec. 321(c)(2)(A).

This means that before an offset could be approved and given credit, it would be adjusted based on an administrative analysis of whether the proposed offset created other environmental harms or benefits. For instance, planting an even-aged forest might absorb CO_2, but it might also destroy habitat. The Lieberman-Warner Bill indicates that this should get less credit, but how much less?

---

27. *London Profits, While Africa Awaits Kyoto Benefits*, REUTERS, August 13, 2007, *available at* http://www.reuters.com/article/environmentNews/idUSL137011320070813.

28. *Trading Foes Hail EPA Region IX Report Criticizing RECLAIM Program*, INSIDE EPA, Nov. 22, 2007, at 7.

29. Kyoto Protocol website, Clean Development Mechanism, *available at* http://unfccc.int/kyoto_protocol/mechanisms/clean_development_mechanism/items/2718.php.

30. Dag Hammarskjold Foundation, press release, *New Book Exposes Scandal of Carbon Trading*, http://www.dhf.uu.se/documents/Press_release_carbon_trading.pdf.

31. www.rff.org/climatechangelegislation.

32. Waxman proposal (H.R. 1590), 110th Congress, at 13, *available at* http://frwebgate.access.gpo.gov/cgi-bin/getdoc.cgi?dbname=110_cong_bills&docid=f:h1590ih.txt.

33. www.rff.org/climatechangelegislation.

This additional environmental review, though important, reduces the predictability of offsets and trades, and makes it harder to integrate a system with other systems, such as the EU ETS system. If US offsets are subject to additional administrative analysis concerning whether more or less credit should be given per trade, then credits not subject to this or a similar evaluation could not be freely traded in the U.S. market. Moreover, the principle could also be applied to trades themselves. Trading between coal fired power plants might concentrate mercury emissions in a particular locale, which could be more environmentally damaging than spreading it out.

In terms of the kind of legal practice such a bill would create, it suggests that a cap and trade regime would not be a purely business enterprise, but would require environmental attorneys to conduct the administrative analysis of offsets and preparation of offset projects for the market.

4. How Would Credits be Allocated?

Due to the popularity of the cap and trade option, the allocation of credits may be one of the biggest of all questions for climate change legislation. Many of the current legislative proposals seem to take a "cut the baby in half" approach to this question, where some allowances are auctioned while others are awarded based on historic CO_2 or energy output for free.[34] The Bingaman Bill, for instance, gives out 55% of the allocations free to industry, and reserves the rest to encourage low carbon coal development and for auction.[35] The original Lieberman-Warner Bill suggested that only 33% be given away to industry, reduced to 32% in the next iteration. Because we have had quite a long time to consider climate change legislation, due to President Bush's unwillingness to sign legislation, the trend is towards less and less giveaway. It does seem clear that even if a significant amount is auctioned, some provision will be made to offset fast rising costs for consumers and businesses associated with carbon intensive energy production, like coal-fired power plants.[36] The Lieberman-Warner substitute Bill indicates more money to these areas than the original Lieberman-Warner Bill.

5. Clean Technology R&D, Safety Nets, and Pre-emption

Many of the legislative proposals set aside money (or the money from selling CO_2 allocations) for research and development, and grants for "clean energy."[37] In the cap and trade systems, these grants are to be funded from the money received from the portion of CO_2 allocations that are to be auctioned.[38] In one of the tax proposals, 6 billion dollars of carbon tax receipts would go to research and development.[39] The Bingaman proposal seems to go as far as any in terms of specifications. It identifies categories (including coal-fired plant efficiency, zero emission electricity production, coal sequestration, cellulosic biomass, and lower vehicle emis-

---

34. www.rff.org/climatechangelegislation.

35. http://energy.senate.gov/public/_files/END07842_xml1.pdf.

36. What hasn't received as much publicity is how the allocation of any free credits will be determined. The Bingaman bill primarily allocates based on historic CO_2 output. Though described as a "heat input" allocation, the Alexander-Lieberman bill (which only applies to the electricity sector) also gives free CO_2 allocations based on CO_2 output. The Feinstein-Carper bill, on the other hand, primarily allocates its credits based on energy output rather than historic CO_2 production.
    What is most surprising is that this critical question of allocation based on energy output or historic CO_2 output has not received more attention. In many of the bills, it takes careful attention to decipher which method is being used, and the legislative press reports do not seem to focus on this distinction. Even major environmental organizations have been more likely to focus on the "safety valve" issue as the environmental bugaboo rather than the impact that allocation of credits based on historic CO_2 emissions might have on encouraging clean energy.
    http://www.environmentaldefense.org/pressrelease.cfm?ContentID=6606.

37. ww.rff.org/climatechangelegislation.

38. Id.

39. Id.

sion technology) that may receive grants, and even specifies a rudimentary formula for awards in certain instances.[40] While this may be about the best that can be done if one must do R&D grants, we must recognize that the large amounts of money at stake, and the prior identification of favored technologies, increases the probability of lobbying for financial gain as opposed to finding a way to really spur development of the most promising technologies.[41]

The "safety net" mechanisms which would cap the amount charged for a CO_2 allocation credit may also be more of an economic windfall for certain businesses, and even if it were administered without any favoritism, it does not contribute to an effective CO_2 control strategy. Though some commentators believe that such a mechanism is politically necessary to gain Republican votes on any bill, the tide may be changing. Senator Bingaman has indicated his willingness to temper or alter a safety net mechanism in response to criticisms about such a program, and Senators Lieberman and Warner have eschewed a safety net, though they would create a committee to step in if prices of allocations rise too high or too quickly.[42] Lieberman-Warner has proposed a competitive "safety" provision if developing countries fail to make binding CO_2 reductions, but this may face problems with the WTO. I believe that this issue will be re-visited when costs are looked at more closely, but the policy problems will be no different.

There has been some legislative discussion about the pre-emption of state programs that have their own binding CO_2 limits.[43] However, none of the current bills explicitly pre-empt state programs. Of course, it would still be possible for a court to find implicit pre-emption in certain circumstances. With respect to common law pre-emption of litigation, the Bingaman bill includes a provision for financial assistance to those specifically affected by climate change, with particular provisions governing the state of Alaska. While this may have been solely to secure the support of Alaska's Republican Senators, or may in fact, be good policy, the fact that there is a statutory compensation scheme may mean possible common law pre-emption.

Because they would be weaker than a likely federal cap-and-trade bill, both the Western States Greenhouse Gas Initiatives and the Regional Greenhouse Gas Initiatives in the Northeast (RGGI), would likely be implicitly pre-empted. Nevertheless, it is likely that participants in these Initiatives as well as the voluntary Chicago Climate Exchange will be given credit for prior reductions, something mentioned explicitly in most proposed legislation.

The new Lieberman-Warner bill gives more thought to how a federal cap-and-trade bill would interact with state bills. In particular it offers recognition of previous efforts and CO_2 credits to states with mandatory limitations (such as California and Washington) if these states "opt in" to the federal program. There is strong resistance to this, particularly since the federal bill would probably take several years to begin operation.

6. Adaptation Funding

The new Lieberman-Warner Bill is much more explicit in recognizing the costs associated with adapting to the effects of climate change, and provides large amounts of money, via the granting of CO_2 allocation rights, to various states and other groups that would be affected. The

---

40. http://energy.senate.gov/public/_files/END07842_xml1.pdf, at 59–75.

41. For example, the much touted hydrogen car in President Bush's 2003 State of the Union address, which has received large amounts of federal funding, is no closer to reality than it was in 2003. Brett Clanton, *So, When Do We Get Hydrogen Vehicles*, HOUSTON CHRONICLE, Sept. 5, 2007, at A1.

42. Katherine Ling, *Senator Bingaman calls his CO_2 allocation a First Attempt*, E&E DAILY, July 17, 2007; Darren Samuelsohn, *Lieberman, Warner eye new cost proposal, shy away from "safety valve,"* E&E DAILY, July 27, 2007.

43. Alex Kaplun, *Senior Dems Break with Committee Chairs on Energy Bill*, GREENWIRE, June 7, 2007.

state of Alaska, which has seen the most extensive effects from climate change, is offered the lion's share at 20% of state funding, with 40% being reserved for other coastal states. Indian tribes are eligible for a large amount of adaptation funding, recognizing their unique dependence on water and resources. This shows the increasing recognition of the costs of adaptation and that the government should take some responsibility in doing the funding.

CONCLUSION

With so many proposals and so many possible ways these proposals can go, what can be taken away from the current state of climate change legislative proposals? The most important thing is that some kind of binding limitation on CO_2 is highly likely, and this should factor into business and regulatory decisions. One can already see this in the marketplace as over half of the recently proposed coal-fired power plants have been stopped by state energy regulators because of climate change considerations. It is important for clients to understand this reality. Because the legislation credits prior reductions, it makes sense to get clients used to inventorying and thinking of ways to reduce emissions.

Moreover, activity at the state and sub-regional level is still important and will likely survive federalization. It should be recognized that understanding and participating in local climate change initiatives may bring economic benefits to those who participate. These local initiatives have been shown to increase the knowledge of CO_2 impacts and of ways to reduce. They can also change public and business opinion, which will be important if climate change mitigation is to be successful.

Because it will likely be a cap-and-trade system, the climate change bills should be seen as the business and economic bills they are. Opportunities exist in engaging in trade, setting up offsets and offset verification mechanisms, and in many Research and Development possibilities. The Lieberman-Warner bill recognizes the use of biological and land use offsets. This will probably survive into any final bill. Opportunities for absorbing CO_2 could provide economic benefits for other conservation decisions. In fact, it is these business opportunities that have provided much of the impetus for progress on the bills so far.

Because of complexity, there is also a lot that can go wrong inadvertently. Proposing legislative alterations that are not necessarily policy-based, but that can be seen as easing administration of a system, should be paid attention to.

An update, as reported by the Pew Center on Climate Change:[1]

The U.S. House of Representatives passed the American Clean Energy and Security Act of 2009 (ACES Act), H.R. 2454, on June 26 by a vote of 219 to 212. This comprehensive national climate and energy legislation would establish an economy-wide, greenhouse gas (GHG) cap-and-trade system and critical complementary measures to help address climate change and build a clean energy economy. The House Energy and Commerce Committee voted 33–25 to approve the ACES Act on May 21. Committee Chairman Henry Waxman (D-California) and Rep. Edward Markey (D-Massachusetts), chairman of a key subcommittee, introduced the bill on May 15, after floating a discussion draft in March.

Now that the House has passed the ACES Act, it will be sent to the U.S. Senate for consideration. The Senate Energy and Natural Resources Committee, chaired by Sen. Jeff Bingaman (D-New Mexico) passed on June 17 an American Clean Energy Leadership Act (S.1462). This bill addresses several energy issues, including many addressed under the

---

1. The American Clean Energy and Security Act (Waxman-Markey Bill) http://www.pewclimate.org/acesa. *See also* http://www.pewclimate.org/docUploads/Waxman-Markey-short-summary-revised-June26.pdf (providing a two-page summary).

ACES Act. Several Senate Committees will be addressing aspects of a clean energy and climate bill in September. These measures will likely be combined to create the Senate counterpart to the ACES Act. If the Senate passes this combined bill, differences between the Senate and House bills would have to be reconciled, with the final bill passed by both houses, before the bill could be sent to President Obama and signed into law.

Notes

1. *Providing Context.* In a companion article to the one written by Professor Flatt, Professor Hari M. Osofsky addresses "how does the possibility of U.S. legislative action fit within a broader picture of transnational climate change governance?" *Climate Change Legislation in Context,* 102 Nw. U. L. Rev. Colloquy 245 (2007) (footnotes omitted):

> I focus on three main types of pressures on the legislation. First, the legislation faces vertical pressures from "above" (international negotiations for the post-2012 regime) and "below" (state and local efforts). Second, the legislation is influenced horizontally by activity in the other two branches of the U.S. government, namely climate change litigation and executive policy, as well as advocacy efforts by a range of nongovernmental actors. Moreover, many interactions that ultimately influence legislation are simultaneously horizontal and vertical, such as when states and cities use federal courts to push executive branch agencies to regulate. Finally, and perhaps most importantly given the looming Presidential election, the shifting public awareness of climate change creates an impetus for Congress to take meaningful action or at least to appear to do so.

> ....

> [Discussing vertical pressures] Professor Flatt provides a version of "best" that allows legislative efforts to move forward in tandem with initiatives at other levels of governance. He explains that the statutory regime should neither wait for agreement on the 2012 replacement for the Kyoto Protocol nor develop in a way that would be incompatible with its likely targets. Similarly, Flatt acknowledges the importance of subnational efforts on climate change, and urges that the legislation not be structured in a manner that preempts those innovative efforts.

> I agree with Professor Flatt's analysis, but would like to develop it further through reference to geography and, more specifically, to issues of regulatory scale. Climate change is a multiscalar problem that demands multiscalar solutions. In other words, both emissions and impacts take place at personal, local, state, national, and international levels, and regulation at the national level likely cannot address all of these aspects effectively. Legislative proposals should include the flexibility to adapt to vertical pressures because the problem cannot be regulated at only one level of governance, even a very powerful national one.

> Although there has been broad acknowledgment across the political spectrum of the value of addressing climate change at a global scale, more skepticism exists about state and local initiatives. Some argue that the problem is too large both spatially and temporally to manage at smaller levels of governance. These types of antiregulatory arguments are potentially dangerous, whether made in the context of legislation or litigation for three primary reasons.

> First, neither international nor national efforts seem likely to go far enough to get this problem under control, so smaller scale efforts are needed to spur innovation and action.... Second, however the balance between centralization and decentraliza-

tion of governmental power is struck in this area of law, effective climate policy should provide opportunities to draw from state and local expertise and core competences.... Finally, and most importantly, privileging larger-scale regulation potentially prevents holistic regulatory solutions necessary to manage cross-cutting problems....

[Discussing horizontal pressures]. The horizontal pressures from the executive and judicial branches also deeply influence the legislative debate and the possibilities for achieving meaningful regulation. Our two-term presidency means that not only do the current congressional proposals occur in the context of the Bush Administration's longstanding recalcitrance on this issue—which is reflected in both macro-level White House statements and decisions and in micro-level agency decisionmaking—but also that Executive Branch policy soon will change, almost certainly in the direction of additional regulatory efforts. Although this electoral context initially appears to create a more positive environment for legislation, it more likely delays congressional action for at least another year....

Moreover, the increasing willingness of the judicial branch to engage climate change creates another complicated horizontal force influencing the legislative environment. The Supreme Court's decision in *Massachusetts v. EPA*, though it bears upon executive agency decisionmaking directly, has been part of the conversation on Capitol Hill; it thus has both formal and informal horizontal influences on the other two branches of the federal government.... Any version of the legislation will alter the litigation environment, which will in turn impact the overall efforts to regulate climate change in the United States.

As with the smaller-scale efforts discussed above, litigation plays a crucial role in the regulation of climate change and the legislation should not attempt to preempt access to courts too broadly. Rather, the statutory scheme should provide a clear basis for concerned individuals and organizations to address inadequate regulation by government and failures by major emitters to reduce their production of greenhouse gases. Such a structure will insure that litigation can continue to play its crucial role in the push and pull of the complex formal and informal regulatory dance over climate change.

Furthermore, these horizontal forces have vertical dimensions, and vice versa. As elections involve individuals and communities in political decisionmaking, they become part of a vertical conversation....

[Discussing sociocultural pressures]. This formal and informal regulatory dance is deeply shaped by the sociocultural discourse over climate change. The awarding of a Nobel Peace Prize to Al Gore and the Intergovernmental Panel on Climate Change (IPCC) symbolizes the increased focus on this problem. Opinion polls show a growing public recognition of and concern with the problem of climate change, and the legal academic world has seen an explosion in the past two years of public conversation and scholarly discourse over this issue, as exemplified by this colloquy.

This sudden interest and activity, like the election environment, probably will have a mixed impact on the proposed legislation. The science that suddenly captivates people is not new; the recent Fourth IPCC Assessment—the most widely recognized compilation of the state of climate science and policy responses to the problem—synthesizes studies by leading scientists and provides policy summaries, which reflect stances that those involved in crafting it are willing to take publicly. Public opinion polling shows increasing concern with climate change, but not necessarily the will to make the hard choices necessary to get this problem under control....

As Congress and commentators debate the specifics of legislative proposals, the interaction between sociocultural forces and political decisions shapes what is possible.

The public's view of the problem influences how far politicians dependent on an election cycle are willing to go, and Congress's approach to the problem in turn impacts public opinion. And yet all of this interaction occurs against the backdrop of a multiscalar ecological phenomenon we do not fully understand....

[Concluding remarks]. Returning to the question of "best" that Professor Flatt raised, my view is that the broader context in which legislative proposals occur suggests cause for guarded optimism. National-level legislation, even in a major emitter like the United States, cannot solve the problem of climate change. Current and future proposals will always be buffeted by international negotiations and smaller-scale land use policy choices, executive and judicial decisionmaking, and the broader sociocultural discourse over this problem.

But even in this context, our national-level legislative choices matter deeply. From a practical perspective, as Professor Flatt analyzed, they have the potential to reduce U.S. greenhouse gas emissions substantially and, in the process, significantly bring down the global total. As part of transnational regulation of climate change, they are arguably even more critical. During his announcement of the decision not to participate in the Kyoto Protocol, President Bush acknowledged that almost 20 percent of the world's human-made greenhouse gases originate from within this country's borders; furthermore, the United States' official climate action report from 2002 indicated that its emissions will rise by 42.7 percent between 2000 and 2020. This focus on legislative action, even if it does not bear fruit until after the 2008 elections, opens up the potential for a national-level policy in the United States that takes climate change more seriously. Such a policy—if constructed with sensitivity to vertical, horizontal, and sociocultural dynamics—may help to foster other regulatory progress; for example, it could help to support constructive international negotiations and dynamic local initiatives.

2. *Framing*. Professor Howard Latin's paper (ch. 5, *supra*) offers another framework for assessing comprehensive climate change legislation. His formulation of "reducing the increases" should not be ignored.

3. J.R. De Shazo & Jody Freeman, *Timing and Form of Federal Regulation: The Case of Climate Change*, 155 U. Pa. L. Rev. 1449 (2006–07).

4. Benjamin Somers & Becky Ham, *Climate Change Already Dramatic in U.S, Experts Warn Congress*, 323 Science 1182 (Feb. 27, 2009).

5. John M Broder, *Democrats Unveil Climate Bill*, N.Y. Times, April 1, 2009 (the Waxman-Markey bill "requires that emissions be reduced 20 percent from 2005 levels by 2020, while [President] Obama's plan calls for a 14 percent reduction by 2020. Both would reduce emissions of carbon dioxide, methane, and other greenhouse gases by roughly 80 percent by 2050;" "the bill has no Republican support."

III. Climate Policy Architecture

A. Public Opinion

As Professor Osofsky notes above, one of the greatest impacts on the structure of climate policy may indeed be the perception of climate risks in the general public and among decisionmakers. A recent article by John Sterman, *Risk Communication on Climate: Mental Mod-*

els and Mass Balance, 322 SCIENCE 532 (2008), discusses why the public can remain stubbornly complacent in the face of the scientific consensus regarding climate change (references omitted):

Effective risk communication is grounded in deep understanding of the mental models of policy-makers and citizens. What, then, are the principal mental models shaping people's beliefs about climate change? Studies show an apparent contradiction: Majorities in the United States and other nations have heard of climate change and say they support action to address it, yet climate change ranks far behind the economy, war, and terrorism among people's greatest concerns, and large majorities oppose policies that would cut greenhouse gas (GHG) emissions by raising fossil fuel prices.

More telling, a 2007 survey found a majority of U.S. respondents (54%) advocated a "wait-and-see" or "go slow" approach to emissions reductions. Larger majorities favored wait-and-see or go slow in Russia, China, and India. For most people, uncertainty about the risks of climate change means costly actions to reduce emissions should be deferred; if climate change begins to harm the economy, mitigation policies can then be implemented. However, long delays in the climate's response to anthropogenic forcing mean such reasoning is erroneous.

Wait-and-see works well in simple systems with short lags. We can wait until the teakettle whistles before removing it from the flame because there is little lag between the boil, the whistle, and our response. Similarly, wait-and-see would be a prudent response to climate change if there were short delays in the response of the climate system to intervention. However, there are substantial delays in every link of a long causal chain stretching from the implementation of emissions abatement policies to emissions reductions to changes in atmospheric GHG concentrations to surface warming to changes in ice sheets, sea level, agricultural productivity, extinction rates, and other impacts. Mitigating the risks therefore requires emissions reductions long before additional harm is evident.

....

Obviously, few people are trained in climatology or nonlinear dynamics, and public understanding of these topics is poor. But there is a deeper problem: poor understanding of stocks and flows—the concept of accumulation. Accumulation is pervasive in everyday experience: Our bathtubs accumulate the inflow of water through the faucet less the outflow through the drain, our bank accounts accumulate deposits less withdrawals, and we all struggle to control our weight by managing the inflows and outflows of calories through diet and exercise. Yet, despite their ubiquity, research shows that people have difficulty relating the flows into and out of a stock to the level of the stock, even in simple, familiar contexts such as bank accounts and bathtubs. Instead, people often assess system dynamics using a pattern-matching heuristic, assuming that the output of a system should "look like" — be positively correlated with — its inputs.

....

Poor understanding of accumulation leads to serious errors in reasoning about climate change. Sterman and Booth Sweeney gave 212 graduate students at the Massachusetts Institute of Technology (MIT) a description of the relationships among GHG emissions, atmospheric concentrations, and global mean temperature. The description was excerpted from the IPCC's "Summary for Policymakers" (SPM), a document intended for nonspecialists. Participants were then asked to sketch the emissions trajectory required to stabilize atmospheric CO_2. To highlight the stock-flow structure, participants were first directed to estimate future net removal of CO_2 from the atmosphere (net CO_2 taken up by the oceans and biomass), then draw the emissions path needed to stabilize atmospheric CO_2.

Knowledge of climatology or calculus is not needed to respond correctly. The dynamics are easily understood using a bathtub analogy in which the water level represents the stock of atmospheric CO_2. Like any stock, atmospheric CO_2 rises when the inflow to the tub (emissions) exceeds the outflow (net removal), is unchanging when inflow equals outflow, and falls when outflow exceeds inflow. Participants were informed that anthropogenic CO_2 emissions are now roughly double net removal, so the tub is filling.

Yet, 84% drew patterns that violated the principles of accumulation.... Nearly two-thirds of the participants asserted that atmospheric GHGs can stabilize even though emissions continuously exceed removal—analogous to arguing a bathtub continuously filled faster than it drains will never overflow. Most believe that stopping the growth of emissions stops the growth of GHG concentrations.

....

Training in science does not prevent these errors. Three-fifths of the participants have degrees in science, technology, engineering, or mathematics (STEM); most others were trained in economics. Over 30% hold a prior graduate degree, 70% of these in STEM. These individuals are demographically similar to influential leaders in business, government, and the media, though with more STEM training than most.

It is tempting to respond to these discouraging results by arguing that poor public understanding of climate change is unimportant because policy should be informed by scientific expertise. Many call for a new Manhattan Project to address the challenge.

....

But a Manhattan Project cannot solve the climate problem. The bomb was developed in secret, with no role for the public. In contrast, reducing GHG emissions requires billions of individuals to cut their carbon footprints by, *e.g.*, buying efficient vehicles, insulating their homes, using public transit, and, crucially, supporting legislation implementing emissions abatement policies. Changes in people's views and votes create the political support elected leaders require to act on the science. Changes in buying behavior create incentives for businesses to transform their products and operations. The public cannot be ignored.

The civil rights movement provides a better analogy for the climate challenge. Then, as now, entrenched interests vigorously opposed change. Political leadership and legislation often lagged public opinion and grass-roots action. Success required dramatic changes in people's beliefs and behavior, changes both causing and caused by the courageous actions of those who spoke out, registered voters, and marched in Washington and Selma.

Building public support for action on climate change is in many ways more challenging than the struggle for civil rights. Science is not needed to recognize the immorality of racism but is critical in understanding how GHG emissions can harm future generations. The damage caused by segregation was apparent to anyone who looked, but the damage caused by GHG emissions manifests only after long delays....

When "common sense" and science conflict, people often reject the science. Even if people sincerely wish to mitigate the risks of climate change, wait-and-see will seem prudent if they misunderstand basic concepts of accumulation and erroneously believe that stopping the growth of emissions will quickly stabilize the climate. The implications go beyond the failure to understand accumulation. People's intuitive understanding of dynamics, including stocks and flows, time delays, and feedbacks, is poor. Analogous to common biases and errors in probabilistic reasoning, these errors are unlikely to be corrected merely by providing more information.

We need new methods for people to develop their intuitive systems thinking capabilities. Bathtub analogies and interactive "management flight simulators" through which people can discover, for themselves, the dynamics of accumulation and impact of policies have proven effective in other settings and may help here. [C]limate scientists should partner with psychologists, sociologists, and other social scientists to communicate the science in ways that foster hope and action rather than denial and despair.

....

Of course, we need more research and technical innovation—money and genius are always in short supply. But there is no purely technical solution for climate change. For public policy to be grounded in the hard-won results of climate science, we must now turn our attention to the dynamics of social and political change.

B. Economic Considerations

JOSEPH ROMM, HELL AND HIGH WATER: GLOBAL WARMING—THE SOLUTION AND THE POLITICS—AND WHAT WE SHOULD DO 134 (Harper Perennial 2007) [hereinafter 2007 ROMM]:

It is hard to imagine that people will use low-carbon technologies on the vast scale needed until they see a financial return for cutting carbon, and that will not happen until spewing out carbon has a significant financial cost. But for carbon to have a cost, the government must either tax carbon dioxide emissions or create a market that establishes a price for emitting carbon dioxide.

2007 SHEARMAN & SMITH at 114:

[T]he economic rationalist writers in our daily papers are essentially relativists in their approach to the environment. For them the world can only be seen through the vision of economics. This explains why the STERN REVIEW—THE ECONOMICS OF CLIMATE CHANGE—had more impact than the voluminous scientific reports of the Intergovernmental Panel on Climate Change (IPCC).

JAY INSLEE & BRACKEN HENDRICKS, APOLLO'S FIRE: IGNITING AMERICA'S CLEAN ENERGY ECONOMY 21–22 (Island Press 2008) (quoting 2006 STERN REPORT) (emphasis added) [hereinafter 2008 INSLEE & HENDRICKS]:

[THE STERN REVIEW was a] seminal report that put hard numbers to the question of how climate change will affect the economy. Unlike many past studies on the issue, it did not make the baseless assumption that inaction on climate change has no cost. While some have taken issue with the precise analytical methods and how costs were measured, this report finally compared the costs of preventing climate change to the likely negative economic and social impacts of a warming planet and chaotic environment. It did not minimize the difficulty of the path ahead, stating, "*Climate change presents a unique challenge for economics. It is the greatest and widest-ranging market failure ever seen.*"

The startling finding of the STERN REPORT is that far from being a death knell for the economy, compared to the costs of inaction, dealing with climate change will provide substantial benefits to the economy....

The report concludes that a 5 to 20 percent loss of economic output globally could occur due to global warming. These findings are staggering. Yet for an investment of only 1 percent of GDP we can head off those costs. Put simply, we have the opportunity to make low-cost and economically productive investments now in new technology that yields substantial benefits, instead of accepting a much larger reduction in our overall prosperity through such real costs as lost agricultural productivity and increased harm to human health.

Economic considerations arguably underlie virtually every aspect of decisionmaking with regard to climate change. The growth of fields such as environmental justice suggests that there is hope that moral and ethical considerations are becoming more important. To date, however, economics remain a fundamental consideration.

The Economics of Climate Change

Richard O. Zerbe, Daniel J. Evans Distinguished Professor, Daniel J. Evans School of Public Affairs, Associate Dean, Vice President and President Elect of The Society for Benefit Cost Analysis; Director, Center for Benefit Cost Analysis; Co-Editor, Journal of Research in Law and Economics, University of Washington, The Evans School, Box 353055, Seattle, WA 98195, Tel: (206) 616-5470, Fax: (206) 543-1096, zerbe@u.washington.edu; and Nancy Garland, Ed.M., a graduate student in public administration and law at the Evans School of Public Affairs and University of Washington School of Law.

Nearly all climate scientists agree that anthropogenic emissions are forcing changes in the earth's climate.[1] Perhaps the most important decisions of our time, or of other times, will be decisions affecting climate change. From an economic point of view, formal analysis of government project decisions involves benefit-cost analysis. Numerous models of the economic effects of climate change have been advanced,[2] each with its own variations. These variations and the consequent differences in predictions of environmental and economic damage in turn have led to a wide range of suggested policies. The first benefit-cost analysis of climate change issued with the imprimatur of a major government was the STERN REVIEW of October 2006.[3] THE REVIEW itself has been the object of numerous other reviews.[4] These models and their accompanying reviews and criticisms furnish both substantive information about the economics of climate change and lessons about the process and conduct of policy economics and benefit-cost analyses.

This paper serves as an introduction to the economics of climate change, and briefly discusses four issues: (1) The nature of benefit-cost analysis and its relationship to law; (2) benefit-cost analysis as currently practiced in economic climate change analysis; (3) the particular challenge posed by the uncertainty about catastrophic climate change; and (4) the collective action diffi-

---

1. *See, e.g.,* INTERGOVERNMENTAL PANEL ON CLIMATE CHANGE, CLIMATE CHANGE 2007: SYNTHESIS REPORT 39 (Cambridge Un. Press 2007) ("Most of the observed increase in global average temperatures since the mid-20th century is *very likely* due to the observed increase in anthropogenic GHG concentrations."); Daniel H. Cole, *Climate Change and Collection Action* 1(2007) (unpublished manuscript on file with the author) [herinafter Cole, *Collection Action*].

2. *See, e.g.,* R.O. Mendelsohn, *et al., Country-specific market impacts of climate change,* 45 CLIMATIC CHANGE 553 (1998); R.S.J. Tol, *Estimates of the damage costs of climate change—Part II: dynamic estimates,* 21 ENVTL. & RESOURCE ECON. 135 (2002); W.D. NORDHAUS & J.G. BOYER, WARMING THE WORLD: THE ECONOMICS OF THE GREENHOUSE EFFECT (MIT Press 2000); NICHOLAS STERN, THE ECONOMICS OF CLIMATE CHANGE: THE STERN REVIEW (Cambridge Un. Press 2007).

3. STERN, *supra* note 2.

4. *See, e.g.,* Martin L. Weitzman, *A Review of the* STERN REVIEW OF THE ECONOMICS OF CLIMATE CHANGE, 45 J. ECON. LITERATURE 703 (2007); William D. Nordhaus, *A Review of the* STERN REVIEW ON THE ECONOMICS OF CLIMATE CHANGE, 45 J. ECON. LITERATURE 686 (2007).

culties in arriving at a solution, including how distributional issues exacerbate the collective action challenge. The article presumes, in accord with evidence, that climate change is happening and that we can do something, though not everything, about it.

Benefit-Cost Analysis

Benefit-cost analysis compares the social costs and benefits of an action. In practice, the analysis generally gives standing only to certain interests, *e.g.*, the costs to particular groups of people or the benefits to a set of or other people or countries. Economic theory offers no rationale for limiting standing in this way, though as a practical matter, limiting standing is necessary. Benefits are measured by the willingness to pay (WTP) for them; costs by the willingness to accept payment (WTA). WTP is bounded by the ability to pay, WTA can be infinite. The analysis represents a sort of vote in which the votes are weighted by the intensity of sentiments and the ability to pay or willingness to accept payment.

Costs and benefits are calculated from a legal status quo position defined by established rights. In considering a government action that affects whether or not you live or die, the government could ask, "What would you pay to preserve your life," a question that presupposes you have no right to live. Your WTP would represent the value of your gain of a right to live. Alternatively, the question could be "What amount would you accept to give up your life?" This amount would represent the value of the loss of your life, and presupposes you have a right to life. As this example suggests, where the good in question is important and unique the difference between the WTP and WTA measures can be very large. Where there are no established rights the cost-benefit approach measures all parties' willingness to pay, essentially auctioning that right. Though most of us thankfully do not face the question of life or death in such a stark way, we regularly face increases or decreases in risk. The relevant questions remain the WTP to reduce risk and the WTA to bear it.

In making comparisons of the costs and benefits of a project, the value of future benefits and costs is reduced to what amount would be invested now to yield these future amounts at current relevant interest rates. Discounted benefits and costs are referred to as *present values,* so that the benefit-cost comparison is between the present value of benefits (PVB) and the present value of costs (PVC). The result of the comparison is the net present value or NPV = PVB − PVC. In very simple terms, if the NPV is positive—if the present value of benefits is larger than the present value of costs—then a project is worthwhile from a BCA perspective.

Though there are many critics of benefit-cost analysis, the reality is that some form of benefit-cost analysis is used in nearly every decision in business and policy. Government contracts explicitly require those submitting bids to specify their costs, and agencies in turn are required to contract with the lowest reasonable bidder. The Environmental Protection Agency, the Army Corps of Engineers, and other federal, state and local agencies make regular use of benefit-cost analysis to justify their projects to legislators, taxpayers and constituents.[5] Judges also balance costs and benefits, either implicitly or explicitly. For example, due process cases require an explicit cost-benefit analysis as promulgated by the Supreme Court in *Matthews v. Eldridge.*[6] Balancing relative benefits and costs is also a part of the civil

---

5. *See, e.g.,* Exec. Order No. 12,866, 3 C.F.R. 58 Fed. Reg. 51,735 (Sept. 30, 1993) (reforming and making more efficient the regulatory review process, and requiring agencies to assess the costs and benefits of an intended regulation); Envtl. Protection Agency, *Guidelines for Preparing Economic Analyses,* http://yosemite. epa.gov/EE/Epa/eerm.nsf/vwSER/DEC917DAEB820A25852569C40078105B?OpenDocument (last visited Oct. 13, 2008); Dept. of the Army Corps of Engineers, Civil Works Strategic Plan 2004–2009 13 (Mar. 2004).

6. 424 U.S. 319 (1976). *See also* Van Harken v. City of Chicago, 103 F.3d 1346 (1997).

discovery process,[7] and increasingly plays a part in the rising discussion of rights surrounding electronic discovery.[8]

Benefit-Cost Analysis Applied to Climate Change

The economic analysis of climate change begins with a climate science model that simulates the effects of climate change. Values are then assigned to various effects, creating an integrated assessment model (IAM). An IAM measures impacts in terms of differential economic growth rates under different climatic scenarios. The fact that there is considerable uncertainty[9] about long-term effects of climate change presents a challenge to all IAMs. Among the uncertainties is the possibility of a non-linear damage function resulting from extreme temperature changes and climate feedback mechanisms.[10] These uncertainties are exacerbated by debate about the values that should be attached to various effects. As a result, wildly disparate predictions of the costs and benefits of combating climate change and of climate change itself emerge, ranging from advising sharp and immediate reductions to advocating slower "ramp-up" policies with little present change.[11]

Though there are numerous models of climate change and climate change economics, this paper considers two in depth, THE STERN REVIEW of 2006, and Nordhaus' 2007 response. The IAM used in the STERN REVIEW was developed by Chris Hope and is called PAGE2002.[12] PAGE2002 deals with uncertainty by using a Monte Carlo simulation[13] of the effects of 79 different key parameter variables. PAGE2002's parameters effectively summarized scientific and economic literature on climate change, as the parameters were calibrated to underlying research studies.[14] The model was flexible enough to include market and non-market impacts, as well as to account for the possibility of catastrophic climate change through its incorporation of non-

---

7. FED. R. CIV. P. 26(b)(2).

8. *See, e.g.*, Zubulake v. UBS Warburg LLC, 217 F.R.D. 309, 318 (2003) ("The burden or expense of discovery is, in turn, 'undue' when it 'outweighs its likely benefit, taking into account the needs of the case, the amount in controversy, the parties' resources, the importance of the issues at stake in the litigation, and the importance of the proposed discovery in resolving the issues.")

9. In economics, uncertainty is distinct from risk or probability. A risk carries a known probability; uncertainty carries an unknown probability.

10. *See* CASS R. SUNSTEIN, WORST-CASE SCENARIOS 93 (Harvard Un. Press 2008) ("If climate change is abrupt, the harm will be far higher than otherwise; abrupt climate change may lead to worldwide catastrophe."); Elisabeth Rosenthal & Andrew C. Revkin, *Science Panel Calls Global Warming "Unequivocal"*, N.Y. TIMES, Feb. 2, 2007. An example of a climate feedback mechanism can be seen with Arctic sea ice. Ice, because of its color, reflects heat, but as more ice melts due to rising global temperatures, white ice is replaced by dark water. The dark water in turn absorbs heat and increases the speed of melting ice.

11. *Compare* STERN, *supra* note 2, *with* William Nordhaus, *The Challenge of Global Warming: Economic Models and Environmental Policy* (July 24, 2007) (unpublished manuscript on file with the author).

12. STERN, *supra* note 2, at 173. Hope developed the model in Chris Hope, *The Marginal Impacts of CO_2, CH_4 and SF_6 Emissions* (Judge Institute of Management Research Paper No.2003/10, 2003). PAGE is an acronym for Policy Analysis of the Greenhouse Effect.

13. A Monte Carlo simulation assigns probabilities and a distributional form to key parameters, and develops a calculating equation in which the parameters are inputs. The simulation varies the value of the parameters according to the assigned probabilities to produce a probability distribution of outcomes.

As an oversimplified example of a Monte Carlo simulation, consider if we were to simulate the probabilities of accidents on a highway as a function of rainfall and vehicle speed, we might initially be able to assume that rainfall followed a normal distribution, and speed was a normal distribution with truncations at either end. We could develop an equation that expressed the probability of an accident as a function of speed and rainfall, and using Monte Carlo simulation we could then estimate the number of accidents under various conditions of speed and rainfall. The cost of accidents would then be considered along with reductions in speed limits. The costs of speed limit reductions would then be compared with the gains from fewer accidents to determine what the speed limit should be in sunny and in wet weather.

14. STERN, *supra* note 2, at 174.

linearity.[15] Incorporating non-linearity allows consideration of feedback effects that could produce major impacts at extreme conditions. This aspect of the model was crucial and provided a new perspective, since, as Daniel Cole noted, earlier analyses looked "where the light was better"[16] and avoided the situations with potentially the greatest damage because the impacts in these conditions involved the greatest scientific uncertainty.

Nordhaus' model, DICE-2007, aggregates countries into single global output of capital stock, technology and emissions values.[17] Through this aggregation model, basic trends and tradeoffs can be reasonably accurately captured, though it is not able to capture regional variations in output.[18] The model is based in neoclassical economics that recognizes a single commodity that can be used for either consumption or investment, and takes into account current regional stocks, population and growth, and technological change. The model then includes several geophysical relationships that connect the economy with climate change, including the carbon cycle and a radiative forcing equation, among others.[19]

No single model will account for all aspects of climate change economics or be entirely without controversy. Controversy will particularly arise regarding treatment of the discount rate and uncertainty, and on the degree of regionalization of the model.[20] Regardless of model, what simple economic analysis requires is that we know the value of risks reduced as we spend to reduce global warming. This analysis proceeds by determining at what point the additional costs of reducing greenhouse gases equal the additional benefits from the reduction in global warming.

The Stern Review supports international, strong, prompt action, in part because the actions of the coming decades will have a profound effect on the climate going forward, and could contribute to or minimize major disruptions to social and economic activity. The Review advocates reducing GHG emissions to three quarters of current levels based on a multi-pronged strategy that reduces demand for emissions-intensive goods and services, promotes efficiency gains, and reduces non-fossil fuel emissions, such as those that are a result of deforestation. The costs of action are projected to be around $1 trillion in 2050, 1% of global GDP.[21] The Stern Report's model includes flexible policies that price carbon through taxes, trading or regulation; promotes the development and deployment of new technologies; and depends on understanding of problems to change preferences and behavior.[22]

Nordhaus finds that an "ideal" efficient climate change policy is relatively inexpensive and would have a substantial impact on long-run climate change.[23] This model considers the ideal model one that sets emissions reductions to maximize the economic welfare of humans. This model would have a net present-value benefit of $3.4 trillion, but reduce the global temperature increase relative to 1900 temperatures to 2.8 °C in 2100, and to 3.4 °C by 2200. This optimal plan is projected to avoid $5.3 trillion of climatic damages compared to doing nothing.[24] Nordhaus

---

15. *Id.*

16. Daniel H. Cole, *The Stern Review and its Critics: Implications for the Theory and Practice of Benefit-Cost Analysis*, 48 Nat. Res. J. 53(2008) [hereinafter Cole, *Stern Review*].

17. Nordhaus, *supra* note 11, at 39.

18. *Id.* at 15, 39. DICE-2007 is an acronym for Dynamic Integrated model of Climate and the Economy. Regional variations are being researched by Nordhaus and Yang through the Regional Integrated model of Climate and the Economy (RICE).

19. *Id.* at 41.

20. *Id.* at 60.

21. Stern, *supra* note 2, at 260.

22. *Id.* at 641.

23. Nordhaus, *supra* note 11, at 171.

24. *Id.*

also estimates the costs of the ambitious proposals of Gore and the Stern report and recent proposals from the German and Japanese governments. These are about ten times as expensive, overly expensive says Nordhaus, as they involve substantial reductions in greenhouse gases at significantly earlier stages of mitigation.[25]

The Challenge of Determining Discount Rate

Future benefits and costs, as mentioned, are normally reduced to present value using some interest (discount) rate. The rationale is that returns now are more valuable than those later as those now can be invested and will grow to be greater in the future. Some argue, however, that it is immoral to discount the returns to future generations and especially to discount the value of future lives.[26] However, the failure to discount, including the failure to discount future human lives, will lead to inefficiencies and can make both the current and the future generation worse off.[27] In addition, uncertainties about benefits, costs and timing of projects may be incorporated into the discount rate. Zerbe suggests that a better approach to moral concerns is to directly count the current generations' WTP to support future generations.[28] Similarly it is more informative to treat uncertainty directly rather than to incorporate it into the discount rate. With respect to climate change, the WTP to prevent or reduce global warming would directly measure current sentiments towards future generations. This, in fact, is the purpose and goal of CBA: to measure current preferences, including current preferences for future generations, given that future generations are unavailable.

There is a range of interest or discount rates that economists regard as reasonable.[29] The choice of rate within this range can have dramatic consequences for which policies are found to be economically efficient. Suppose that we believe the discount rate is (absent inflation) either 2% or 5% with equal probability. The usual practice has been to use the average of the two rates as the best point estimate. That is, the best estimate would have been found by using 3.5% which is the simple average of 2% and 5%. This is incorrect. What one wishes is the average of the two present values found by using 2% and 5% respectively. Mathematically, averaging the discount rates before computing the present value is not the same as averaging the present values; this difference becomes more pronounced when the time period is long. The present value of $100 to be received in one year's time will be $98 at 2% and $95 at 5%. The average present value will be $96.64. The single discount rate that yields this result is 3.48%. This is close to the average of the two discount rates which is 3.5%. This difference in discount rate does not make a large difference when the time period for discounting is short.

When dealing with longer time periods, a rate closer to the lowest rung of the range becomes the best single estimate of the correct discount rate. Consider discounting $100 over 100 years. At 2% the present value is $13.80 and at 5% it is $0.76. The average present value is then $6.86. The single discount rate that will yield this result is 2.7%, much closer to 2% than to 5%. This result occurs because the average of the discount factors, not the average discount rate, should be used. For example the discount factor for a $100 return in one hundred years

---

25. *Id.* at 177.

26. *See, e.g.,* RICHARD L. REVESZ & MICHAEL A. LIVERMORE, RETAKING RATIONALITY 111 (Oxford Un. Press 2008).

27. Richard O. Zerbe & Jonathan Lesser, *What Can Economic Analysis Contribute to the "Sustainability" Debate,* 13 CONTEMPORARY ECON. POL'Y 88 (1995).

28. Richard O. Zerbe, *The Legal Foundation of Cost-Benefit Analysis,* 2 CHARLESTON L. REV. 93 (2007); Richard O. Zerbe, *Should moral sentiments be incorporated into benefit-cost analysis? An example of long-term discounting,* 37 POL'Y SCI. 305 (2004).

29. Mark A. Moore, *et al., "Just Give Me a Number!" Practical Values for the Social Discount Rate,* 23 J. POL'Y ANALYSIS & MGMT. 789 (2004).

using a 2% discount rate is $[1/(1.02)100]$ or 0.1380 so that the present value of the future $100 is $13.8. At a 5% discount rate the discount factor is $[1/(1.05)100]$ or 0.0076 so that the present value is $0.76 dollars. The average of these discount factors is 0.1456 which corresponds to a discount rate of 2.7% as noted above. The discount factor is $(1/(1+r))^t$, where r is the discount rate and t is time. The smaller of two rates dominates the average discount factors increasingly as time increases. The smaller fraction for the larger rate will more quickly approach zero. If the smaller of a range of discount rate is close to zero, the average discount factor will then tend towards zero for a very long term project for outcomes reaching out to 100 years or beyond.

THE STERN REPORT used a discount rate very near zero.[30] For this it has been extensively criticized. Stern asserts "the only ethical sound basis for placing less value on the utility of future generations was the uncertainty over whether or not the world will exist, or whether those generations will all be present."[31] THE STERN REVIEW starts with a discount rate of zero—equally valuing the welfare and utility of generations currently alive and those in the future. It then considers the probability that the human race will drive itself to extinction, and thus that there will be no future generations' welfare to consider after a certain point in time. THE STERN REVIEW uses a pure time discount rate of 0.1 percent per year, reasoning that although this may seem to result in a high probability of human extinction within the next 100 years, dire consequences are possible yet hard to forecast, and there is some support for even more certain extinction.[32]

In contrast, Nordhaus finds his discount rate by solving for it as a function of the underlying parameters. Nordhaus considers the discount rate a function of two parameters, the time discount rate and a measure of consumption elasticity. The time discount rate—measuring the importance of future generations' welfare relative to present—is 1.5%. Utility elasticity measures society's aversion to inequality between generations. Nordhaus combines a time discount rate of 1.5% and utility elasticity of 2, to establish an effective rate of real return on capital of approximately 5.5% for the first half-century of projections.[33] As a result of the discount rate being based on other parameters, this rate can change as parameters are affected. Choosing different discount rates changes the implications of the model drastically, though Nordhaus asserts that in the near-term, these choices are largely immaterial.[34] This model specifically assumes there will be no catastrophic outcomes that would result in human extinction or serious harm to civilization.[35] An effect of this variable discount rate is little confidence in this model's projections beyond 2050.[36]

Regardless of the theoretical challenge posed by choosing a discount rate, both models suggest climate change is substantial but not something we couldn't handle with a modicum of political will and coordination. However, the climate change problem is analytically more difficult than others because of five considerations: (1) today's decisions have difficult or impossible to reverse consequences that will be felt in the far future,[37] (2) deep uncertainty exists within science over the extent and timing of changes, (3) non-negligible probabilities of facing a catastrophic loss exist, (4) calculating the value of avoiding a catastrophic loss is difficult, and (5) co-

---

30. STERN, *supra* note 2, at 35.

31. *Id.* at 51.

32. *Id.* at 53.

33. Nordhaus, *supra* note 11, at 62.

34. *Id.*

35. *Id.* at 34.

36. *Id.*

37. Martin L. Weitzman, *On Modeling and Interpreting the Economics of Catastrophic Climate Change,* 91 REV. ECON. & STAT. 1 (2009).

ordination among nations and different peoples poses a logistical and diplomatic challenge. These five issues fall broadly into two categories: the possibility of catastrophic loss and the coordination problem.

The Challenge Posed by Potential Catastrophic Loss

Current emissions trends predict a rise in average global temperatures of 2–3°C relative to pre-industrial levels over the next fifty years.[38] Some scenarios in the International Panel on Climate Change's report predict possible changes as large as 6.9°C before the end of the century.[39] An even larger rise is possible or even predicted if feedback systems amplify the warming effect.[40] The effects of a change of temperature this drastic in such a short period of time are very uncertain. There is a probability of extreme weather events, and even more drastic effects due to abrupt and large-scale changes, such as the loss of the Amazon rain forest. With most probability analyses, events with very low probability are treated as extremely unlikely, and even if they hypothesize dire consequences, are largely ignored. Though mathematically logical, this approach is questioned by our acceptance of another principle: the Precautionary Principle.

Though not universally accepted, the Precautionary Principle is currently used in many documents and policies, including those of the United Nations and the United States government.[41] The One-Percent Doctrine promulgated by Vice President Cheney and our invasion of Iraq following 9/11 are examples in our government's policies; significantly "weaker" versions of the principle show up in our taking a cab home to avoid walking at night or buckling our seat belts.[42] A strong version of the principle suggests we should regulate even in instances with speculative evidence and high economic costs, if there are possible risks to health, safety or the environment. Riding this principle to the extreme results in paralysis in decision making, for there are always risks, and alternate courses of action will often conflict. Regardless of this potential for paralysis, the precautionary principle does have merit when consequences of particular low-probability events are dire.

The catastrophic events in the right-hand tail of the distribution suggest sinister possibilities. Martin Weitzman uses 22 peer-reviewed studies encompassing a wide range of methodologies to estimate a 5% chance over the next two centuries of a 10°C temperature rise and a 1% chance of a 20°C rise.[43] This rise in temperature could result in drastic effects, including mass extinctions, sea levels rising 30 meters or more, extreme changes in weather patterns.[44] Yet such estimates are wildly uncertain. Weitzman gives equal weight to the various studies, when in fact some will be better than others. Regardless, however, there is a possible powerful amplification of warming from greenhouse gases sequestered in Arctic permafrost and other soggy soils, and the more remote possibility of heat-induced releases of even vaster offshore deposits of CH_4. In classic economics and statistics, the small probabilities of these catastrophes ensures they are largely ignored. However, non-negligible probabilities of extreme events, that is, the 5% and 1% probabilities that Weitzman estimates, have the potential to eliminate human life and much of life as we know it. As a result, Weitzman notes, "other things being equal, the more speculative and fuzzy are the tiny tail probabilities of extreme events, the less ignorable and the more serious

---

38. STERN, *supra* note 2, at 68.
39. INTERGOVERNMENTAL PANEL ON CLIMATE CHANGE, *supra* note 1, at 45.
40. STERN, *supra* note 2, at 68.
41. SUNSTEIN, *supra* note 10, at 118, 123.
42. *Id.* at 123.
43. Weitzman, *supra* note 37, at 7. Weitzman acknowledges these are crude ballpark estimates, but asserts that does not affect the situation he is describing.
44. *Id.* at 9.

is the impact on present discounted expected utility for a risk-averse agent."[45] We ignore these fat-tailed[46] distributions at great peril.

What is the value of lowering the risk and uncertainty associated with the extreme tail? How much peril is acceptable? The values in consideration here are nothing less than those associated with the loss of life, civilization, and the human species. The normal economic way of thinking about this would be similar to thinking about a person reducing her consumption to reduce the probability of her early death. The person's estimate would depend on the initial level of consumption and her relative risk aversion. Risk reflects known probabilities—as with the flipping of a coin. Uncertainty arises when we do not know the probabilities. Risk aversion is a concept in economics, finance, and psychology related to the behavior of consumers and investors under uncertainty. Risk aversion is the reluctance of a person to accept a fair bet. A risk averse person would not pay $0.50 to take a 50% change of winning or losing $1.00. The value placed on risky choices will reflect risk preferences, and risk preferences will be affected by the level of uncertainty. One may be risk averse, risk neutral, or risk preferring and one can change from one risk state to another depending on the situation. Relative risk aversion simply normalizes risk aversion using consumption so that it is a more convenient parameter.

The economic question is then how much are we willing to pay to reduce the chance of catastrophic climate change. We do not know the answer to this. Alternately, we could also ask how much we would be willing to accept to bear various levels of risk and uncertainty. To ask this latter question presupposes that we have a right to avoid some levels of risk. One person's right, however, is another person's duty. Who has the duty? Do more developed nations have a moral obligation or duty to take the lead and bear much of the costs, since they have been the primary beneficiaries of growth that has been the source of global warming? Does the duty rest with those who are now contributing more to greenhouse gases in the atmosphere, the rising nations such as China and India? What is rational based on the costs and benefits for a particular nation is crucially affected by our obligations to other nations. If we perceive no duty based on our past emissions, for example, other countries should pay the United States for the benefit they will receive when we reduce our output.[47] However, if we have bought our obligation with our prior emissions, then we will likely pay handsomely to programs that will ultimately benefit those outside our nation.[48]

The divergence between the WTP and WTA increases with the uniqueness of the good and with uncertainty. Since the good we are considering here, survival, is both unique and uncertain, this divergence will be very great. If we grant ourselves the right to survive, then the relevant measure is the WTA which is potentially infinite. Thus there is an economic argument that suggests that we should be willing to spend any amount we can as long as we are lowering the probability of catastrophe. This argument is conditional, weak, uncertain and could stand for any number of other nightmare scenarios that face us: biological weapons, rogue nanotechnology, asteroids, strangelets,[49] pandemics, runaway computer systems, and nuclear war. As a matter of practicality, our resources are finite, and we cannot lower the possibility of all potential catastrophes.

---

45. *Id.*

46. In traditional economics, the "tail" of a probability distribution is "narrow" or very small, and extends to infinity. Weitzman describes these low-probability high-uncertainty events as residing in a "fat" right-hand tail of the statistical distribution, reasoning that despite their low probability, the potentially dire consequences suggest we ignore them at our peril.

47. Eric A. Posner & Cass R. Sunstein, *Climate Change Justice*, 96 GEO. L.J. 1565, 1589 (2008).

48. *Id.* at 1570.

49. Strangelets are theorized cosmological objects composed of an exotic form of matter known as strange matter or quark matter. This form of matter is created in the cores of particularly massively neutron stars. This may be regarded as a phase change, like changing from a liquid to a solid, only at densities many orders of magnitude greater than those occurring in this solar system. It has been hypothesized that strangelets (sub-

Even though we may not be able to completely counteract climate change, current analyses suggest that some action to mitigate climate change is in fact justified by benefit-cost analysis.[50] Given the potential for catastrophic consequences, we need to relatively quickly invest to increase knowledge about what level of risk we face and if needed to take more extensive action. In any case, there appears little or no justification to just sit back and do nothing; not if we care about future generations or about the evolution of the planet.

Collective Action

A collective action issue is one that requires the cooperation of disparate persons or groups to address. Collective action problems arise when the costs of market exchange to address a problem are too high, often when there are public goods involved,[51] or when the best choice overall is not the most efficient choice for an individual. The famous prisoners' dilemma is one example of a collective action problem.[52]

Public goods issues often involve a "bad"; clean air is the good and pollution the bad. Economists often approach mitigating public "bads" by either taxing the bad or creating a limit on the amount of the bad and creating a market in which rights to the bad may be bought and sold. This is the approach of the Kyoto Protocol.[53] These are attractive approaches to reducing the production of GHG, but they do not solve the collective action problem.

Climate change promises to be a difficult collective action problem. First, effective action requires participation of many countries. Second, the stake in the outcome is dramatically different for varying countries. Third, there is considerable scientific uncertainty about key issues. Fourth, any solution is likely to be expensive.

Effective action to combat climate change will require multi-country participation. Any single nation acting alone is unlikely to have a meaningful effect slowing climate change. This holds

---

stellar agglomerations of strange matter) may be able to exist independently from the quark stars which created them. If so, there may be many strangelets in this universe, a possible explanation for the dark matter problem. Since strangelets maintain such deep gravity wells for objects of their size, calculations show that strangelets coming in contact with ordinary matter would overwhelm this matter with their gravitational fields, breaking down the ordinary matter into strange matter. If strangelets exist and keep coming into contact with ordinary matter indefinitely, it may be only a matter of time (albeit a cosmologically long duration of time) before strangelets swallow all the conventional matter in the universe. Edited from *What is a Strangelet?*, http://www.wisegeek.com/what-is-a-strangelet.htm (last visited Oct. 13, 2008).

50. *See, e.g.*, STERN, *supra* note 2; Nordhaus, *supra* note 11.

51. Public goods are usually defined to have two characteristics, non-rivalry and prohibitive exclusion costs. Often, however, they are defined simply by the latter characteristic.

52. The basic Prisoner's Dilemma problem involves two conspirators caught and questioned separately from one another. If one criminal confesses and the other does not, the confessor gets a light sentence and the non-confessor receives a heavy one. If neither confesses, both get moderate sentences. If both confess, they each receive somewhat heavier sentences. The structure of the problem is as follows:

	Prisoner B Stays Silent	Prisoner B Betrays
Prisoner A Stays Silent	Each serves 4 months	Prisoner A: 12 years
		Prisoner B: goes free
Prisoner A Betrays	Prisoner A: goes free	Each serves 5 years
	Prisoner B: 12 years	

No matter what the prisoner B does, it pays prisoner A to confess and vice versa. This leads to the non-optimal solution in which each serves 5 years. In a Prisoner's Dilemma game, each player always receives a higher payoff (lesser sentence) by betraying; betrayal is therefore the dominant strategy. Rational self-interested decisions result in each prisoner's being worse off than at their joint optimum. Collective action problems arise because self interest conflicts with group interest. The more players, the more divergent the interests, the less the ability to communicate, the fewer the iterations of the particular game, the smaller the empathy for others, the greater is the cost of a solution.

53. SUNSTEIN, *supra* note 10, at 89.

true even for the largest contributors to greenhouse gases, the United States and China. Even if these countries could be convinced to take unilateral action at great economic cost to themselves, the change in greenhouse gases overall would be minimal.[54] This is in part because current emissions are only part of the problem for greenhouse gases. Effective action in fact requires participation of a majority of countries, including those in both the developing and developed world.

Coming to an agreement regarding curbing greenhouse gases is particularly challenging because each country's benefits and costs are different. Some countries, notably Russia, are projected to benefit from climate change in terms of increased arable land for agriculture.[55] Many of the countries with the greatest projected costs are projected to receive very minimal benefits. The United States, for example, is responsible for the largest portion of the current greenhouse gases in the atmosphere and continues to be a leading producer. Any agreement will come at substantial cost to the United States, which will likely receive little benefit. Other countries will have marginal costs and receive substantial benefits. In addition, developing countries, who currently contribute little to greenhouse gas stores, are wary of having their progress limited by restrictions on emissions. A common proposal is to grant developing countries carbon rights and make them tradable with other nations, ensuring that developing countries continue to progress economically while still limiting emissions. The problem as Cole points out is to reduce greenhouse gases while allowing developing countries to develop and ensuring that developed counties have sufficient energy to maintain production.[56]

Even with trading in carbon rights, combating climate change is expected to be expensive. There currently exist no reliable and cost-effective substitutes for the fossil fuels that contribute to GHG emissions. Ethanol, for example, requires 29% more energy from fossil fuels to produce than the final product contains.

Conclusion

It is reasonable to conclude that we should at least control greenhouse gases to the extent it is fairly cheap to do so. After all, if we can benefit from doing something relatively minor, we likely should. Yet once the cheap controls are used, how much further, if at all, should we go? Right now we do not have enough information to determine this, and yet, we cannot wait around to be one hundred percent certain of what will occur. It appears that the policy focus for climate change should not just be on the costs and benefits of controlling GHG, but on the costs and benefits of gathering more and better information. In particular it appears imperative that we come to a better understanding of the uncertainty and risk of catastrophe and of ways to reduce both.

C. The Astonishing Stern Review

The following is an excerpt from a comprehensive economic analysis contained in THE STERN REVIEW: THE ECONOMICS OF CLIMATE CHANGE (Cambridge Un. Press 2007). The full report is *available at* http://www.hm-treasury.gov.uk/independent_reviews/stern_review_economics_climate_change/sternreview_index.cfm.

---

54. SUNSTEIN, *supra* note 10, at 1580.
55. *Id.* at 1582.
56. Cole, *supra* note 16.

Stern Review: The Economics of Climate Change, Summary of Conclusions

Sir Nicholas Stern, Head of the Government Economic Service and Adviser to the U.K. Government on the economics of climate change and development.

There is still time to avoid the worst impacts of climate change, if we take strong action now.

The scientific evidence is now overwhelming: climate change is a serious global threat, and it demands an urgent global response.

This Review has assessed a wide range of evidence on the impacts of climate change and on the economic costs, and has used a number of different techniques to assess costs and risks. From all of these perspectives, the evidence gathered by the Review leads to a simple conclusion: the benefits of strong and early action far outweigh the economic costs of not acting.

Climate change will affect the basic elements of life for people around the world—access to water, food production, health, and the environment. Hundreds of millions of people could suffer hunger, water shortages and coastal flooding as the world warms.

Using the results from formal economic models, the Review estimates that if we don't act, the overall costs and risks of climate change will be equivalent to losing at least 5% of global GDP each year, now and forever. If a wider range of risks and impacts is taken into account, the estimates of damage could rise to 20% of GDP or more.

In contrast, the costs of action—reducing greenhouse gas emissions to avoid the worst impacts of climate change—can be limited to around 1% of global GDP each year.

The investment that takes place in the next 10–20 years will have a profound effect on the climate in the second half of this century and in the next. Our actions now and over the coming decades could create risks of major disruption to economic and social activity, on a scale similar to those associated with the great wars and the economic depression of the first half of the 20th century. And it will be difficult or impossible to reverse these changes.

So prompt and strong action is clearly warranted. Because climate change is a global problem, the response to it must be international. It must be based on a shared vision of long-term goals and agreement on frameworks that will accelerate action over the next decade, and it must build on mutually reinforcing approaches at national, regional and international levels.

Climate change could have very serious impacts on growth and development

If no action is taken to reduce emissions, the concentration of greenhouse gases in the atmosphere could reach double its pre-industrial level as early as 2035, virtually committing us to a global average temperature rise of over 2°C. In the longer term, there would be more than a 50% chance that the temperature rise would exceed 5°C. This rise would be very dangerous indeed; it is equivalent to the change in average temperatures from the last ice age to today. Such a radical change in the physical geography of the world must lead to major changes in the human geography—where people live and how they live their lives.

Even at more moderate levels of warming, all the evidence—from detailed studies of regional and sectoral impacts of changing weather patterns through to economic models of the global effects—shows that climate change will have serious impacts on world output, on human life and on the environment.

All countries will be affected. The most vulnerable—the poorest countries and populations—will suffer earliest and most, even though they have contributed least to the causes of climate change. The costs of extreme weather, including floods, droughts and storms, are already rising, including for rich countries.

Adaptation to climate change—that is, taking steps to build resilience and minimise costs—is essential. It is no longer possible to prevent the climate change that will take place over the next two to three decades, but it is still possible to protect our societies and economies from its impacts to some extent—for example, by providing better information, improved planning and more climate-resilient crops and infrastructure. Adaptation will cost tens of billions of dollars a year in developing countries alone, and will put still further pressure on already scarce resources. Adaptation efforts, particularly in developing countries, should be accelerated.

The costs of stabilising the climate are significant but manageable; delay would be dangerous and much more costly.

The risks of the worst impacts of climate change can be substantially reduced if greenhouse gas levels in the atmosphere can be stabilised between 450 and 550ppm CO_2 equivalent (CO_2e). The current level is 430ppm CO_2e today, and it is rising at more than 2ppm each year. Stabilisation in this range would require emissions to be at least 25% below current levels by 2050, and perhaps much more.

Ultimately, stabilisation—at whatever level—requires that annual emissions be brought down to more than 80% below current levels.

This is a major challenge, but sustained long-term action can achieve it at costs that are low in comparison to the risks of inaction. Central estimates of the annual costs of achieving stabilisation between 500 and 550ppm CO_2e are around 1% of global GDP, if we start to take strong action now.

Costs could be even lower than that if there are major gains in efficiency, or if the strong co-benefits, for example from reduced air pollution, are measured. Costs will be higher if innovation in low-carbon technologies is slower than expected, or if policy-makers fail to make the most of economic instruments that allow emissions to be reduced whenever, wherever and however it is cheapest to do so.

It would already be very difficult and costly to aim to stabilise at 450ppm CO_2e. If we delay, the opportunity to stabilise at 500–550ppm CO_2e may slip away.

Action on climate change is required across all countries, and it need not cap the aspirations for growth of rich or poor countries.

The costs of taking action are not evenly distributed across sectors or around the world. Even if the rich world takes on responsibility for absolute cuts in emissions of 60–80% by 2050, developing countries must take significant action too. But developing countries should not be required to bear the full costs of this action alone, and they will not have to. Carbon markets in rich countries are already beginning to deliver flows of finance to support low-carbon development, including through the Clean Development Mechanism. A transformation of these flows is now required to support action on the scale required.

Action on climate change will also create significant business opportunities, as new markets are created in low-carbon energy technologies and other low-carbon goods and services. These markets could grow to be worth hundreds of billions of dollars each year, and employment in these sectors will expand accordingly.

The world does not need to choose between averting climate change and promoting growth and development. Changes in energy technologies and in the structure of economies have created opportunities to decouple growth from greenhouse gas emissions. Indeed, ignoring climate change will eventually damage economic growth.

Tackling climate change is the pro-growth strategy for the longer term, and it can be done in a way that does not cap the aspirations for growth of rich or poor countries.

A range of options exists to cut emissions; strong, deliberate policy action is required to motivate their take-up.

Emissions can be cut through increased energy efficiency, changes in demand, and through adoption of clean power, heat and transport technologies. The power sector around the world would need to be at least 60% decarbonised by 2050 for atmospheric concentrations to stabilise at or below 550ppm CO_2e, and deep emissions cuts will also be required in the transport sector.

Even with very strong expansion of the use of renewable energy and other low-carbon energy sources, fossil fuels could still make up over half of global energy supply in 2050. Coal will continue to be important in the energy mix around the world, including in fast-growing economies. Extensive carbon capture and storage will be necessary to allow the continued use of fossil fuels without damage to the atmosphere.

Cuts in non-energy emissions, such as those resulting from deforestation and from agricultural and industrial processes, are also essential.

With strong, deliberate policy choices, it is possible to reduce emissions in both developed and developing economies on the scale necessary for stabilisation in the required range while continuing to grow.

Climate change is the greatest market failure the world has ever seen, and it interacts with other market imperfections. Three elements of policy are required for an effective global response. The first is the pricing of carbon, implemented through tax, trading or regulation. The second is policy to support innovation and the deployment of low-carbon technologies. And the third is action to remove barriers to energy efficiency, and to inform, educate and persuade individuals about what they can do to respond to climate change.

Climate change demands an international response, based on a shared understanding of long-term goals and agreement on frameworks for action.

Many countries and regions are taking action already: the EU, California and China are among those with the most ambitious policies that will reduce greenhouse gas emissions. The UN Framework Convention on Climate Change and the Kyoto Protocol provide a basis for international co-operation, along with a range of partnerships and other approaches. But more ambitious action is now required around the world.

Countries facing diverse circumstances will use different approaches to make their contribution to tackling climate change. But action by individual countries is not enough. Each country, however large, is just a part of the problem. It is essential to create a shared international vision of long-term goals, and to build the international frameworks that will help each country to play its part in meeting these common goals.

Key elements of future international frameworks should include:

- *Emissions trading:* Expanding and linking the growing number of emissions trading schemes around the world is a powerful way to promote cost-effective reductions in emissions and to bring forward action in developing countries: strong targets in rich countries could drive flows amounting to tens of billions of dollars each year to support the transition to low-carbon development paths.
- *Technology cooperation:* Informal co-ordination as well as formal agreements can boost the effectiveness of investments in innovation around the world. Globally, support for

energy R&D should at least double, and support for the deployment of new low-carbon technologies should increase up to five-fold. International cooperation on product standards is a powerful way to boost energy efficiency.

- *Action to reduce deforestation:* The loss of natural forests around the world contributes more to global emissions each year than the transport sector. Curbing deforestation is a highly cost-effective way to reduce emissions; large-scale international pilot programmes to explore the best ways to do this could get underway very quickly.
- *Adaptation:* The poorest countries are most vulnerable to climate change. It is essential that climate change be fully integrated into development policy, and that rich countries honour their pledges to increase support through overseas development assistance. International funding should also support improved regional information on climate change impacts, and research into new crop varieties that will be more resilient to drought and flood.

Notes

1. *Cost of Carbon.* THE IPCC's FOURTH ASSESSMENT REPORT provides an overview of the varied estimates of the social cost of carbon, which is "an estimate of the economic value of the extra (or marginal) impact caused by the emission of one more tonne of carbon (in the form of carbon dioxide) at any point in time; it can, as well, be interpreted as the marginal benefit of reducing carbon emissions by one tonne." G. Yohe *et al.*, *Perspectives on climate change and sustainability, in* CLIMATE CHANGE 2007: IMPACTS, ADAPTATION AND VULNERABILITY. CONTRIBUTION OF WORKING GROUP II TO THE FOURTH ASSESSMENT REPORT OF THE INTERGOVERNMENTAL PANEL ON CLIMATE CHANGE 812, 821–824 (M.L. Parry *et al.* eds., Cambridge Un. Press 2007). The IPCC panel indicates that a comparison of peer-reviewed analysis resulted in an average cost of 43 US$/tonne C. *Id.* at 822. THE STERN REVIEW estimates the social cost of carbon to be US$ 310/tonne C. *Id.* One of the largest influences on the cost of carbon is discount rate. *Id.* Nicholas Stern has argued persuasively regarding the inappropriateness of pure-time discounting in which future generations are valued less than the current generation. N. Stern, *Climate Change: Costs of Inaction, Targets for Action*, Testimony before the U.S. House of Representatives Committee on Energy & Commerce (June 26, 2008). He goes on to distinguish between current market rates, which reflect only near-term benefits, versus the value of "young or unborn" generations. *Id.*

2. *World Bank: Climate Profiteer.* The World Bank's carbon finance program began in 1999 with the development of its Prototype Carbon Fund. According to a news release by the Bank, "[t]he World Bank's overall mission of reducing poverty and promoting long-term development is … inextricably linked to climate change and efforts to alleviate it. Action will require development of policy as well as regulatory, fiscal, and financial instruments across sectors to provide countries with effective incentives to reduce GHG emissions. It will also require the deployment of a broad mix of low-carbon technologies together with the development of innovative technologies." The Bank's work on climate change has not gone without some degree of controversy.

The April 2008 report, WORLD BANK: CLIMATE PROFITEER, released by the Sustainable Energy and Economy Network,[1] declares that "[t]he global fossil fuel financier and emissions trader has

---

1. The Sustainable Energy and Economy Network is a project of the Institute for Policy Studies (based in Washington, D.C.).

little to show in the way of reduced emissions, sustainable development or benefits for the poorest communities of the developing world.... The World Bank irresponsibly and recklessly continues to perpetuate the world's dependence on climate-altering fossil fuels while profiting from carbon-trading...."[2]

The report's key findings reveal:

- a lack of transparency in the World Bank's carbon finance programs,
- the Bank doesn't appear to have made much progress on emissions reductions in its carbon trading deals,
- clean energy has been shortchanged,
- the carbon finance portfolio is dominated by dirty industries,
- the carbon finance portfolio has been of little benefit to the poor, even though poverty alleviation is one of its priorities,
- the Bank has a conflict of interest, as it has loaned over $1.5 billion to oil, gas, and coal projects between 2005 and 2007 alone,
- the carbon finance program creates perverse incentives for other kinds of pollution to replace greenhouse gas emitting industries,
- the equity issues associated with the forest-related efforts of the BioCarbon fund are not addressed,
- the Bank's carbon fund is creating significant risks for developing countries,
- and the Bank's new Climate Investment Funds transfer power away from developing countries.

D. Other Views

1. Lomborg

Bjorn Lomborg, controversial author of COOL IT: A SKEPTICAL ENVIRONMENTALIST'S GUIDE TO GLOBAL WARMING (Knopf 2007), argues that cap-and-trade is not an appropriate response in *A Better Way Than Cap and Trade*, WASHINGTON POST, A19 (June 26, 2008):

Sen. Barbara Boxer (D-Calif.), a co-sponsor of the bill, has called it "the world's most far-reaching program to fight global warming." It is indeed policy on a grand scale. It would slow American economic growth by trillions of dollars over the next half-century. But in terms of temperature, the result will be negligible if China and India don't also commit to reducing their emissions, and it will be only slightly more significant if they do. By itself, Lieberman-Warner would postpone the temperature increase projected for 2050 by about two years.

Politicians favor the cap-and-trade system because it is an indirect tax that disguises the true costs of reducing carbon emissions. It also gives lawmakers an opportunity to control the number and distribution of emissions allowances, and the flow of billions of dollars of subsidies and sweeteners.

Many people believe that everyone has a moral obligation to ask how we can best combat climate change. Attempts to curb carbon emissions along the lines of the bill now pending are a poor answer compared with other options.

---

2. WORLD BANK: CLIMATE PROFITEER 3 (Sustainable Energy and Economy Network 2008), *available at* http://www.ips-dc.org/reports/.

Consider that today, solar panels are one-tenth as efficient as the cheapest fossil fuels. Only the very wealthy can afford them. Many "green" approaches do little more than make rich people feel they are helping the planet. We can't avoid climate change by forcing a few more inefficient solar panels onto rooftops.

The answer is to dramatically increase research and development so that solar panels become cheaper than fossil fuels sooner rather than later. Imagine if solar panels became cheaper than fossil fuels by 2050: We would have solved the problem of global warming, because switching to the environmentally friendly option wouldn't be the preserve of rich Westerners....

The United States has an opportunity to lead the world on research and development, which would give it the moral authority to demand that everyone else do the same. The world's sole superpower could finally provide the leadership on climate change that has been lacking in the White House.

Even if every nation spent 0.05 percent of its gross domestic product on research and development of low-carbon energy, this would be only about one-tenth as costly as the Kyoto Protocol and would save dramatically more than any of Kyoto's likely successors.

2. Hodas

Professor David Hodas argues that to the contrary, addressing climate change is fundamentally economically feasible in *Imagining the Unimaginable: Reducing U.S. Greenhouse Gas Emissions by Forty Percent*, 26 VA. ENVTL. L. J. 271, 273 (2008):

The perception that reducing GHG emissions is impossible without seriously damaging the national economy is premised on a fundamentally incorrect underlying assumption about the cost of reducing GHG emissions. Most economic models predicting future environmental compliance costs seriously overestimate such costs.[1] These models reflect a mistrust of the market's ability to innovate and invent solutions not imagined before the relevant environmental controls are in place. This is a serious flaw because until the market is required to innovate to meet a mandate, there is little economic incentive for businesses to invest in technology to meet that mandate.[2] On the other hand, once a mandate is in place, competition to meet that new demand becomes fierce, innovation is rapid, and costs often plummet.[3] Remov-

---

1. Frank Ackerman & Lisa Heinzerling, *Pricing the Priceless: Cost-Benefit Analysis of Environmental Protection*, 150 U. PA. L. REV. 1553, 1580 (2002). The article notes that there is a "tendency, as a matter of practice, to overestimate the costs of regulation in advance of their implementation." *Id.* It goes on to state that this premise is wrong "because regulations often encourage new technologies and more efficient ways of doing business.... [G]iven the technology-forcing character of environmental regulations, it is not surprising to find a marked propensity to overstate the cost of such rules." *Id.*

2. *See* Lisa Heinzerling & Frank Ackerman, *The Humbugs of the Anti-Regulatory Movement*, 87 CORNELL L. REV. 648, 669 (2002) ("Perhaps most absurdly, ... [is the assumption] that money spent on regulation simply vanishes—it creates no jobs, no business, no productive gains whatsoever. This assumption, too, is in error: environmental protection is big business in this country, employing people who make and install the complicated, expensive pollution-control technologies (even though the costs of these technologies are, in fact, frequently exaggerated when estimated in advance of regulation).").

3. *See* RUTH RUTTENBERG AND ASSOC., INC., NOT TOO COSTLY, AFTER ALL: AN EXAMINATION OF THE INFLATED COST-ESTIMATES OF HEALTH, SAFETY AND ENVIRONMENTAL PROTECTIONS (2004), *available at* http://www.citizen.org/documents/ACF187.pdf (reviewing, in a report prepared for the Public Citizen Foundation, the many factors that lead to cost overestimations).

ing lead from gasoline,[4] controlling benzene in the workplace,[5] eliminating CFCs use to protect stratospheric ozone,[6] and reducing sulfur emissions to mitigate acid precipitation[7] are a few examples of seemingly unimaginable reductions achieved at remarkably low costs.

3. Pierce

In the following excerpt, Professor Richard Pierce comments on the varied estimates of the costs of climate change mitigation in *Energy Independence and Global Warming*, 21 NAT. RESOURCES & ENV. 68–69, 70 (Winter 2007):

Let me begin this discussion with a few estimates of the economic effects of global warming by two Yale economists. Robert Mendelsohn estimates that global warming will reduce annual global output by only 0.1 percent, an amount so small that it would justify only modest efforts to address the problem. His colleague, William Nordhaus, estimates that global warming will reduce annual global output by 3 percent, a staggering economic effect that would justify an aggressive and costly response.

When you disaggregate the estimates of Nordhaus and Mendelsohn geographically, you begin to recognize the difficulty of choosing an appropriate response even if you accept Nordhaus's estimate of the devastating effects of global warming on the global economy. Both Mendelsohn and Nordhaus predict that some regions and countries will lose and others will gain as a result of global warming. Thus, for instance, both predict that India and Africa will be major losers, while Russia will gain as a result of global warming....

Both Mendelsohn and Nordhaus predict only modest changes in U.S. GDP as a result of global warming—Nordhaus predicts a 0.5 percent decline in U.S. GDP, while Mendelsohn predicts a 0.3 percent increase in U.S. GDP. Both also predict large variations in effects within the United States, with some regions and states losing a lot and others actually gaining. Ironically, support for action to address global warming is much stronger in New England than in Oklahoma, even though global

---

4. Alan S. Miller, *Cleaning the Air While Filling Corporate Coffers: Technology Forcing and Economic Growth*, 1990 ANN. SURV. AM. L. 69, 73–74 (1990).

5. Hart Hodges, *Falling Prices: Cost of Complying With Environmental Regulations Almost Always Less Than Advertised* 3 (Econ. Policy Inst., Briefing Paper No. 69, 1997), *available at* http://www.epinet.org/briefing papers/bp69.pdf ("In the late 1970s, chemical production plants predicted that controlling benzene emissions would cost $350,000 per plant. Shortly after these predictions were made, however, the plants developed a process that substituted other chemicals for benzene and virtually eliminated control costs.").

6. Alan S. Miller, *Environmental Policy in the New World Economy*, 3 WIDENER L. SYMP. J. 287, 295 (1998): Environmental necessity proved to be the mother of invention. Industry responded to the clear determination of a need for substitutes. In a remarkably short period of time, industry developed substitutes that were less costly and performed better than had been predicted. The Environmental Protection Agency (EPA) estimates of costs and benefits evaluated after each change in international policy showed a steady trend of projected costs declining each time, despite the faster schedule and wider range of chemicals and applications being regulated. This phenomenon is not unique but reflects the powerful incentives for technological innovation created by environmental regulation. Prior to regulation, environmental gains were an insufficient spur to action, but once mandated, industry could respond with surprising effectiveness.

Id. at 296.

7. Heinzerling & Ackerman, *supra* note 2, at 1580 ("Before the 1990 Clean Air Act Amendments took effect, industry anticipated that the costs of sulfur reduction under the amendments would be $1500 per ton. In 2000, the actual cost was under $150 per ton.").

warming is likely to have net beneficial effects in New England and terrible effects in Oklahoma.

Estimates of the costs of taking the kinds of actions that would avoid global warming span a range as large as the range of estimates of the cost of global warming. Thus, for instance, Britain's House of Lords estimates that the cost of avoiding global warming would be a reduction of 0.2 percent to 3.2 percent of global output. If you accept the high end of the British estimate of the cost of avoiding global warming and the Mendelsohn estimate of the cost of global warming, it would be economically rational to do nothing and allow global warming to take place. Even if you accept the relatively low Mendelsohn estimate of the economic cost of global warming and the high end of the British estimate of the cost of avoiding global warming, however, you might still support an aggressive and expensive effort to avoid global warming because of some of the noneconomic costs of global warming. Thus, for instance, a recent study by a prestigious team of scientists predicts that global warming will eliminate 30 percent to 60 percent of the species now on the planet, and many studies predict that global warming will displace scores of millions of impoverished residents of the coastal areas of Bangladesh and Indonesia....

So what can, and should, we do about global warming? There is a broad consensus on two issues. First, an effective global warming effort must be global in scope. We may not have to persuade Malawi and Mauritius to participate actively, but no effort can be successful unless it involves the active participation of all major nations, including the United States, China, India, and Russia. Any effort that excludes major nations would be an expensive exercise in futility. It would yield more geographic redistribution of emissions than reduction of emissions.

Second, command-and-control regulation would not be effective for this purpose. An effective command-and-control system would be prohibitively expensive to implement. We must choose instead between a global cap-and-trade system of the type that presently is being pioneered by the Kyoto participants and a globally coordinated carbon tax.

Nordhaus has argued persuasively that a globally coordinated carbon tax is far more promising than a global cap-and-trade system. Nordhaus anticipates several serious problems with any global cap-and-trade program. Such a program would require nations to make coordinated decisions about emissions baselines that would be difficult or impossible to make. It would create so much uncertainty about the future prices of emissions permits that trade in permits would be severely impaired. A global cap-and-trade system would also produce highly volatile energy prices and would be characterized by transaction costs so high that they would impair its efficacy. Finally, Nordhaus fears that a global cap-and-trade system would be impossible to enforce effectively and would be plagued by pervasive corruption.

Nordhaus also points out that a globally coordinated carbon tax has the additional advantage of responding to each nation's fiscal needs. This is a particularly important advantage to the United States. The Federal Reserve Board has identified our present large structural budget deficit as our most serious long-term economic problem. No one knows how much longer we can sustain our present level of deficit spending, but everyone agrees that we must reduce the deficit soon. That can be accomplished only through some combination of increased taxes and reduced spending. A large carbon tax would allow us to get our fiscal house in order without having to make the politically and economically painful decisions to increase income taxes or reduce spending.

4. Driesen

David M. Driesen, *Sustainable Development and Market Liberalism's Shotgun Wedding: Emissions Trading Under the Kyoto Protocol*, 83 IND. L. J. 21, 68–69 (2008):

> The question of how to design institutions to make wise fundamental technological changes presents a puzzle, a puzzle that lies sadly buried under much simplistic rhetoric about "economic incentives" and "command-and-control" regulation. The puzzle arises from market actors' systematic tendency to view such choices too narrowly, coupled with the tendency of governments to avoid visible short-term costs and offense to special interests. It's likely that the proper solution to this puzzle will vary from country to country and will involve some mixture of government choices and private initiative. In contexts like climate change, where we ultimately need major technological changes, the appropriate choices will recognize and address the tradeoff between market liberalism's preference for cost effectiveness and the need for investments that advance sustainable development to protect future generations.
>
> ....
>
> The emissions trading experience under the Kyoto Protocol suggests that weak market liberalism might manage to co-exist with weak sustainability. Either a strong preference for markets (as opposed to economic concepts) or a strong concept of sustainability, however, tends to sever the union. Liberal markets, even markets designed for environmental protection, often fail to encourage expensive investments leading to long-term benefits because of positive spillovers.
>
> This implies that environmental law must address a tension between cost effectiveness maximization and long-term technological capability. This tension should influence both instrument choice and design.
>
> The problem of the proper role of collective decision-making in technological change poses a puzzle requiring much closer attention. Emissions trading's tendency to undermine CBA suggests that neoliberalism's institutional direction conflicts with its analytical predilections and with sustainable development. On the other hand, collective decision-making does not provide a panacea either, as shortsightedness can infect both public and private spheres. Study of the emissions trading experience under the Kyoto Protocol yields fascinating insights about the relationship between sustainable development and market liberalism. We can only hope that the nations of the world will build on these insights as they move forward in addressing climate change and other major global challenges.

E. Alternatives to Cap and Trade

Thomas D. Peterson, Robert B. McKinstry & John C. Dernbach, *Developing a Comprehensive Approach to Climate Change Policy in the United States that Fully Integrates Levels of Government and Economic Sectors*, 26 VA. ENVTL. L. J. 227, 246–247 (2008) (footnotes omitted):

> [Discussing five comprehensive climate change bills before Congress as of April 1, 2007.] Furthermore, the bills' almost exclusive focus on emissions trading is driven by a number of assumptions that are founded upon the successful record of the acid deposition program in achieving reductions at minimal cost. This success has contributed to a popular belief that command and control regulation found in the major environmental

laws enacted between 1969 and 1990 does not work, and it assumes that the next generation of pollution controls should be managed via cap and trade. This conclusion is based on assumptions that (1) the measures employed in environmental laws before cap and trade do not achieve success in a cost-effective manner, (2) the acid rain cap and trade program applicable to a single, highly regulated sector can readily be applied to emissions of GHGs across the whole economy, and (3) the cap-and-trade program was successful as a "stand alone" venture. The strategy of relying wholly or largely on cap and trade may also be based on the additional assumption that future economic growth is closely tied to historically low energy prices, and that energy prices will rise due to climate policy, creating irreconcilable conflicts.

None of these assumptions ultimately holds up under scrutiny. Most notably, while the acid deposition cap-and-trade program established by Subchapter IV-A of the CAA succeeded in achieving very significant reductions of acid rain precursors at a minimal cost, its success was due to a number of unique circumstances. While a number of the characteristics of GHG emissions suggest that a trading system may be an effective tool to address climate change, there are important limitations that militate towards limiting the use of such a system to particular circumstances.

Id. at 251:

A second group of assumptions that underlie other federal proposals, such as those putting a cap on costs of emissions control or those basing their approach on the questionable concept of GHG intensity, are also flawed. Specifically, the assumptions that economic growth is closely tied to energy prices and that energy prices will rise due to climate policy are incorrect. State actions provide substantial evidence on the economic benefits of climate change mitigation. Recent state plans show net economic savings from the combined effects of specific, proven actions at the state level when combined with long-term transitions toward new technologies, systems, and practices. The economic performance of these plans is driven both by the new energy economy and by opportunities to save energy and diversify supply through a host of reform actions.

———————

Dr. James Hansen endorses Peter Barnes'[1] plan for a carbon tax and 100% dividend:[2]

A tax on coal, oil and gas is simple. It can be collected at the first point of sale within the country or at the last (*e.g.*, at the gas pump), but it can be collected easily and reliably. You cannot hide coal in your purse; it travels in railroad cars that are easy to spot. "Cap," in addition, is a euphemism that may do as much harm as good. The public is not stupid.

The entire carbon tax should be returned to the public, with a monthly deposit to their bank accounts, an equal share to each person (if no bank account provided, an annual check—social security number must be provided). No bureaucracy is needed to figure this out. If the initial carbon tax averages $1200 per person per year, $100 is deposited in each account each month. (Detail: perhaps limit to four shares per family, with child shares being half-size, *i.e.*, no marriage penalty but do not encourage population growth).

———————

1. *See* Peter Barnes, Who Owns the Sky? Our Common Assets and the Future of Capitalism (Island Press 2001).

2. *See* June 4, 2008 posting titled *Carbon Tax and 100% Dividend—No Alligator Shoes!*, *available at* http://www.columbia.edu/~jeh1/.

A carbon tax will raise energy prices, but lower and middle income people, especially, will find ways to reduce carbon emissions so as to come out ahead. Product demand will spur economic activity and innovation. The rate of infrastructure replacement, thus economic activity, can be modulated by how fast the carbon tax rate increases. Effects will permeate society. Food requiring lots of carbon emissions to produce and transport will become more expensive and vice versa—it is likely, *e.g.*, that the UK will stop importing and exporting 15,000 tons of waffles each year. There will be a growing price incentive for life-style changes needed for sustainable living.

The present political approach is to set carbon emission reduction goals for 2025 or 2050. The politicians do not expect the goals to be reached, and they define escape hatches that guarantee they will not. They expect to be retired or become lobbyists before the day of reckoning. The goals are mainly for bragging rights: "mine is bigger than yours!"

The worst thing about the present inadequate political approach is that it will generate public backlash. Taxes will increase, with no apparent benefit. The reaction would likely delay effective emission reductions, so as to practically guarantee that climate would pass tipping points with devastating consequences for nature and humanity.

Carbon tax and 100% dividend, on the contrary, will be a breath of fresh air, a boon and boom for the economy. The tax is progressive, the poorest benefitting most, with profligate energy users forced to pay for their excesses. Incidentally, it will yield strong incentive for aliens to become legal; otherwise they receive no dividend while paying the same carbon tax rate as everyone.

F. Energy Subsidies

Christopher Flavin, *Stimulating a Clean Energy Revolution, in* Sudden and Disruptive Climate Change: Exploring the Real Risks and How We Can Avoid Them 246 (M.C. MacCracken, F. Moore, J.C. Topping, Jr. eds., Earthscan Publications Ltd. 2008):

> The current situation, in which the US trails both Europe and Asia in the implementation of renewable technology, can be reversed with a consistent and coherent energy policy that embraces renewables through long-term subsidies and the removal of perverse fossil fuel subsidies. This move is the first step on the long journey to the carbon-free economy that the US will inevitably have to adopt for the future[.]

On the role of perverse subsidies favoring conventional energy industries and of uncalculated and uncollected spillover costs, see Congressman Nick Lampson (D-TX), *Government's Role in Promoting Renewable Energy Solutions*, 2 Envtl. & Energy L. & Pol'y J. 319, 322–23 (2008).

Energy Information Administration, *Federal Financial Interventions and Subsidies in Energy Markets 2007*, SR/CNEAF/2008-1 (2008):

> Federal energy subsidies and interventions discussed in the body of this report take four principal forms:
> - **Direct Expenditures.** These are Federal programs that directly affect the energy industry and for which the Federal government provides funds that ultimately result in a direct payment to producers or consumers of energy.

- **Tax Expenditures.** Tax expenditures are provisions in the Federal tax code that reduce the tax liability of firms or individuals who take specified actions that affect energy production, consumption, or conservation in ways deemed to be in the public interest.
- **Research and Development (R&D).** Federal R&D spending focuses on a variety of goals, such as increasing U.S. energy supplies, or improving the efficiency of various energy production, transformation, and end-use technologies. R&D expenditures do not directly affect current energy production and prices, but, if successful, they could affect future production and prices.
- **Electricity programs serving targeted categories of electricity consumers in several regions of the country.** Through the Tennessee Valley Authority (TVA) and the Power Marketing Administrations (PMAs), which include the Bonneville Power Administration (BPA) and three smaller PMAs, the Federal government brings to market large amounts of electricity, stipulating that "preference in the sale of such power and energy shall be given to public bodies and cooperatives." The Federal government also indirectly supports portions of the electricity industry through loans and loan guarantees made by the U.S. Department of Agriculture's Rural Utilities Service (RUS). (See Tables 1 and 2.)

United Nations Environment Programme, *Reforming Energy Subsidies: Opportunities to Contribute to the Climate Change Agenda* (2008):

Energy subsidies have important implications for climate change and sustainable development more generally through their effects on the level and composition of energy produced and used. For example, a subsidy that ultimately lowers the price of a given fuel to end-users would normally boost demand for that fuel and the overall use of energy. This can bring social benefits where access to affordable energy or employment in a domestic industry is an issue, but may also carry economic and environmental costs. Subsidies that encourage the use of fossil fuels often harm the environment through higher emissions of noxious and greenhouse gases. Subsidies that promote the use of renewable energy and energy-efficient technologies may, on the other hand, help to reduce emissions.

. . . .

There is enormous confusion about what is meant by an energy subsidy. The narrowest and perhaps most common definition is a direct cash payment by a government to an energy producer or consumer to stimulate the production or use of a particular fuel or form of energy. Broader definitions attempt to capture other types of government interventions that affect prices or costs, either directly or indirectly.

. . . .

The assumed baseline level of costs and prices is crucial, whatever the chosen definition. The assumption of market costs and prices as suggested by the above definitions implies that any attempt by a government to address market failures by reducing the price or cost of energy to internalise an external environmental or social benefit would constitute a subsidy. On the other hand, if baseline costs and prices are assumed to take account of external costs and benefits, a failure by the government to address a market failure involving an external cost could be considered a subsidy. In practice, assessing quantitatively the magnitude of externalities is extremely difficult so empirical studies of subsidies often use a conventional definition that simply assumes market prices and costs.

. . . .

Governments like to keep subsidies "off-budget" for political reasons, since "on-budget" subsidies are an easy target for pressure groups interested in reducing the overall

Beneficiary	Direct Expenditures	Tax Expenditures	Research & Development	Federal Electricity Support	Total
Coal	—	290	574	69	932
Refined Coal	—	2,370	—	—	2,370
Natural Gas and Petroleum Liquids	—	2,090	39	20	2,149
Nuclear	—	199	922	146	1,267
Renewables	5	3,970	727	173	4,875
Electricity (Not fuel specific)	—	735	140	360	1,235
End Use	2,290	120	418	—	2,828
Conservation	256	670	—	—	926
Total	2,550	10,444	2,819	767	16,581

Table 1. Energy Subsidies and Support by Type and Fuel, FY2007 and FY1999 (million 2007 dollars). Source: Table ES1 from EIA, FEDERAL FINANCIAL INTERVENTIONS AND SUBSIDIES IN ENERGY MARKETS 2007 (2008).

Fuel End Use	Direct Expenditures	Tax Expenditures	Research & Development	Federal Electricity Support	Total
Coal	—	264	522	68	854
Refined Coal	—	2,156	—	—	2,156
Natural Gas and Petroleum	—	203	4	20	227
Nuclear	—	199	922	146	1,267
Renewables	3	724	108	173	1,008
Transmission and Distribution	—	735	140	360	1,235
Total	3	4,281	1,696	767	6,747

Table 2. Fiscal Year 2007 Electricity Production Subsidies and Support (million 2007 dollars). Source: Table ES4 from EIA, FEDERAL FINANCIAL INTERVENTIONS AND SUBSIDIES IN ENERGY MARKETS 2007 (2008).

tax burden. For this reason, subsidies often take the form of price controls that set prices below full cost, especially where the energy company is state-owned, or of a requirement on energy buyers to take minimum volumes from a specific, usually domestic, supply source.

. . . .

Worldwide, energy subsidies might amount to $300 billion per year, or around 0.7 percent of world GDP, most of which go to fossil fuels.

. . . .

Subsidies reduce incentives to use energy efficiently, act as a drain on government finances and hold back economic development.

. . . .

The key to determining whether a subsidy is good or bad for mitigating climate change is whether the energy source it supports is more or less carbon-intensive than the alternative. Various empirical studies provide strong evidence that the large subsidies to fossil-fuel consumption worldwide in place today contribute to higher greenhouse-gas emissions and exacerbate climate change. A study by the OECD in 2000, for instance, showed that global CO_2 emissions would be reduced by more than 6 percent and real income increased by 0.1 percent by 2010 if all subsidies that lower the prices of fossil fuels used in industry and the power sector were removed everywhere in the world. An earlier study by the IEA revealed that the removal of consumption subsidies in eight of the largest non-OECD countries would reduce primary energy use by 13 percent, lower CO_2 emissions by 16 percent and raise GDP by almost 1 percent in those countries as a whole. Because coal is the dirtiest fuel, removing coal subsidies generally yields the biggest environmental benefits.

. . . .

Subsidies to support renewable energies and energy-efficient technologies may help reduce noxious and greenhouse-gas emissions depending on how they are structured as well as on prevailing market conditions. In some cases, subsidies to renewables need to be big to make those technologies competitive with existing ones based on fossil fuels. If renewable energy replaces fossil fuels and the amount of fossil fuel-based energy consumed in building plants and equipment is not too high, then the net effect on emissions will generally be positive. However, some types of renewables may also have adverse environmental consequences[.]

. . . .

The *way* in which governments subsidise fuels is all-important, regardless of their objectives. A good subsidy is arguably one that enhances access to sustainable modern energy or has a positive impact on the environment, while sustaining incentives for efficient delivery and consumption. There is no single right approach or model.

. . . .

———————

Note

1. For more material on energy subsidies, see Chapter 4, § II(B) at 694–711, *supra*.

G. Rethinking Today's Market Economy

2007 SHEARMAN & SMITH at 91 (footnote omitted):

As held by Milton Friedman, there is but one social responsibility of the corporation and this is to make as much money as possible for [its] shareholders. This is a moral imperative, and to choose environmental goals instead of profits is immoral. We believe that this is the rock upon which the leaking ship of democracy steered by Plato's savages will finally flounder.

2007 SHEARMAN & SMITH at 96:

[C]onsumerism has become the engine of capitalist society, consuming the earth's limited resources and creating jobs to stoke it. This fundamental nature of democracy is unsustainable.

JAMES GUSTAVE SPETH, THE BRIDGE AT THE EDGE OF THE WORLD: CAPITALISM, THE ENVIRONMENT, AND CROSSING FROM CRISIS TO SUSTAINABILITY 46 (Yale Un. Press 2008) [hereinafter 2008 SPETH]:

Is anything in our society more faithfully followed than economic growth? Its movements are constantly watched, measured to the decimal place, deplored or praised, diagnosed as weak or judged as healthy and vigorous. Newspapers, magazines, and cable channels report endlessly on it.

Id. at 47 (footnote omitted):

Promoting growth—achieving ever-greater economic wealth and prosperity—may be the most widely shared and robust cause in the world today. Economic growth has been called the "secular religion of the advancing industrial societies."

Id.:

When one wants to kill a proposal for government action, the most effective argument is that it will hurt the economy, exactly what President Bush said when he rejected the international climate treaty's Kyoto Protocol early in his administration.

Id. at 49–50:

The relation between economic gains and environmental losses is close, as McNeill notes. The economy consumes natural resources (both renewable and nonrenewable resources), occupies the land, and releases pollutants. As the economy has grown, so have resource use and pollutants of great variety.

Id. at 52:

Economist Wallace Oates has provided a clear description of "market failure," one reason the market does not work for the environment: "Markets generate and make use of a set of prices that serve as signals to indicate the value (or cost) of resources to potential users. Any activity that imposes a cost on society by using up some of its scarce resources must come with a price, where that price equals the social cost."

Id. at 53 (continuing to quote Wallace Oates):

Many of our environmental resources are unprotected by the appropriate prices that would constrain their use. From this perspective, it is hardly surprising to find that the environment is overused and abused. A market system simply doesn't allocate the use of these resources properly.

Id. at 107:

Economic growth is modern capitalism's principal and most prized product. The idea that there are or should be limits to growth is typically met with derision.

Id. at 111–112:

In the recent past and in the present, the economic growth actually experienced has been and remains the principal source of our major environmental problems.

Id. at 118–119:

Ecological economists contend that for any given ecosystem setting, there is an optimum scale of the economy beyond which physical growth in the economy (throughput) starts costing more than it is worth in terms of human welfare. They see diminishing returns to growth as consumers' more basic needs are met; at some point the limit of consumer satiation is reached. Meanwhile, the costs of extra growth increase, environmental costs prominent among them. Eventually a society reaches a point where more growth is not worth it. Practically, Daly and others would maintain we have already reached or passed this point[.]

Id. at 126:

> Has America's pursuit of growth and ever-greater material abundance brought true happiness and satisfaction in life?

Id. at 130 (footnotes omitted):

> A good place to begin is with studies that compare levels of happiness and life satisfaction among nations at different stages of economic development. They find that the citizens of wealthier countries do report higher levels of life satisfaction, although the correlation is rather poor and is even poorer when such factors as quality of government are statistically controlled. Moreover, this positive relationship between national well-being and national per capita income virtually disappears when one looks only at countries with GDP per capita over ten thousand per year. In short, once a country achieves a moderate level of income, further growth does not significantly improve perceived well-being. (See Figure 3.)

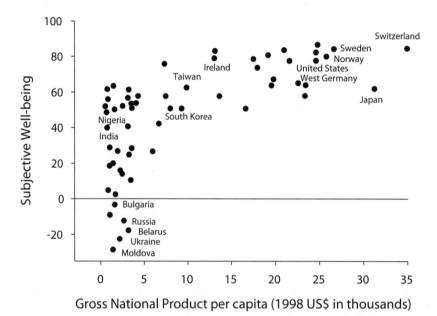

Figure 3. Subjective well-being as a function of gross national product. Adapted from: Anthony Leiserowitz *et al.*, Sustainability Values, Attitudes and Behaviors: A Review of Multinational and Global Trends, 31 AnnuAL Review of Environment and Resources 413 at C-1, Figure 1 (2006), as used by James G. Speth, The Bridge at the Edge of the World: Capitalism, the Environment, and Crossing from Crisis to Sustainability 131, Figure 1 (2008).

Id. at 130:

> Diener and Seligman report that peoples with the highest well-being are not those in the richest countries but those who live where political institutions are effective and human rights are protected, where corruption is low and mutual trust is high.

———————

James Galbraith, Predator State: How Conservatives Abandoned the Free Market and Why Liberals Should Too 130 (Free Press 2008):

> While the causes of occupational safety, consumer product safety, fair competition, living wages, and the environment have all enjoyed the backing of spirited and often effec-

tive public interest groups, these groups cannot by themselves account or take credit for the pervasiveness of the late-twentieth-century regulatory system. Regulation emerged, reached its high point in the Nixon administration, and survived thereafter because a large part of the business community was prepared to support it. And this was so because while regulation is a burden for some businesses, it is a competitive blessing for others. A functioning structure of regulation is the competitive instrument of the most progressive part of the business community, which wishes—for its own advantage—to force everyone to play by a common set of rules.

Id. at 146–147:

The Predator State is an economic system wherein entire sectors have been built up to feast on public systems built originally for public purposes and largely serving the middle class. The corporate republic simply administers the spoils system. On a day-to-day basis, the business of its leadership is to deliver favors to their clients. These range from coal companies to sweatshop operators to military contractors.

Id. at 152:

[I]n area after area, the pursuit of "market-friendly" policy solutions is the search for measures that have the virtue of being politically innocuous and moderately useful and have the defect of being ineffective. The perfectly functioning market is a will-o'-the-wisp in most areas to which the concept is applied, and in a good many of them the "market" itself barely exists. What does not exist cannot be perfected by minor adjustments. In many cases, the right policy requires limiting, restricting, regulating, disciplining, defeating, or bypassing markets, or even shutting them down.

Id. at 160:

Like all other market-based policies, cap-and-trade assumes that the sum of decentralized decisions, taken by thousands of businesses and millions of individuals, is the same as the best achievable result. But the existence of interdependence and externalities and asymmetric information and transactions costs is sufficient to show that there is no reason to believe this. As Joseph Schumpeter wrote of technological change, you may add up as many carriages as you please, but you will not get a railway thereby. Carbon dioxide is a global problem. The fact that Europeans emit about half, per capita, as do Americans for a similar quality of life is not a matter of market choices but of the way their lives are organized, of the housing patterns and transportation networks and power grids designed in part by the European states. Changing masses of individual driving decisions in America will not transform our systems into the efficiency equivalent of theirs, and the attempt to do so by prices alone could put the economy in such a slowdown that the ordinary course of progress toward more efficient patterns of energy use might stop.

Id. at 164–165:

[Discussing the need for planning.] [I]n a properly designed system, planning and markets do not contradict each other. They are not mutually exclusive. Rather, the choice of one or the other for any particular problem is what works best for the purpose: it's a question of a social and political division of labor, of what tools are needed for what goal.

Id. at 165:

Planning, properly conceived, deals with the use of today's resources to meet tomorrow's needs. It specifically tackles issues markets cannot solve: the choice of how much in the aggregate to invest (and therefore to save), the directions to be taken by new technology, the question of how much weight and urgency are to be given to environmental issues, the role of education, and of scientific knowledge, and culture. Decisions on these matters involve representing the interests of the future—interests that are poorly represented by markets. And in the modern world, planning happens: it is what corporations exist to do. The only issue, therefore, is whether the planning function is to be left entirely in the hands of private corporations … or whether the government and the larger public are entitled to play a role.

Id. at 169–70 (reference omitted):

New Orleans encapsulates the dilemma of planning writ small. Global warming raises the same issues writ large. The publication in 2007 of the FOURTH ASSESSMENT REPORT OF THE INTERGOVERNMENTAL PANEL ON CLIMATE CHANGE (IPCC) makes clear, in a way that cannot be gainsaid, that the problem of technological planning and disaster management will soon enough become the central security issue facing every part of the planet. And it will become so in a way that must necessarily remove a central element of economic life—control over the sources and uses of energy—from the purview of private corporations and place it under public administration. Indefinitely. That is the reality of climate change if we are going to manage climate change and not merely succumb to it.

Id. at 171–172:

The path to survival of the existing human way of life requires acting now, in ways that the political system can support, to achieve goals within three or four decades that can avert a catastrophe that is, at a reasonable guess, somewhere between six decades and two centuries off. Nothing quite like it has ever been attempted.

Achieving the goal will require something far more than compulsion. It will require the agreement and the cooperation, plus the active insistence, of a mobilized population—a population that must be not only willing to change its patterns of economic life, but also willing to demand that the choices offered to it by the planning system comport, practically above all other priorities, with the larger goal of reducing greenhouse gas emissions. In other words, it must be a population that is aware of the danger, conscious of the need to act, and mobilized to act in ways that promote rather than obstruct the objective.

What are the elements of such a plan? A rough template can be drawn from the only major example of successful planning in the history of the United States: the economic mobilization for World War II. That mobilization doubled GDP within four years, reduced unemployment to zero, placed an army of 11 million men and women in the field, controlled inflation, and established both the technical and financial foundation for a generation of stable prosperity and social progress—albeit founded on ever-increasing use of fossil fuels.

Id. at 177–178:

[Discussing the need for standards.] What was (and is) the function of the form of business regulation known as selective price control? A first answer is simple and obvious: in most cases, price controls are put in place in order to reduce economic inequalities—that is, inequalities in real living standards. They are by far the simplest, most direct, most effective way of achieving this objective. This is true of subsidies for tortillas in Mexico, fertilizer in Malawi, and milk historically in the United States.

Id. at 178–179:

What the critiques [of regulation and price control] all share is a frame of reference. For every good, there is, in principle, a competitive market price. The actual price under regulation can be above, below, or (in rare cases) just at the competitive norm. But why control things if competition will give you the right result without the controls?

The problem with this argument lies in the presumption of the existence of a competitive market price. As economic theorists know, the real world is necessarily devoid of any such thing. If there is just one administered, or controlled, or monopolistic price in the system—an oil price or an interest rate—then even if all the other markets are perfectly competitive, all of them will be "distorted" by the presence of the one monopolistic price. Deregulating all the other markets does not help. The idea that social welfare is enhanced by moving individual markets from controlled or monopolized toward a competitive position is simply wrong; for the theory to work, even in principle, you have to go all the way. All of the markets have to be competitive, as well as free of externalities and public goods.

But in the real world of complex organizations and advanced technologies, as we have seen, this is never the case. The fact is that monopoly and market power are not only pervasive; they are at the center of economic life.

Id. at 196:

We turn to a final set of questions. How to pay?

Does the United States face a financial limit on its ability to implement a plan? Can it afford to deal with the core deficiencies of infrastructure, social development, and the environment? Could it set and enforce standards to raise pay and incomes at the bottom while limiting them at the top? Can it, by these and other measures, should it choose to do so, bring the Predator State to heel?

Id. at 205:

Here is the key question: What would be the impact on the dollar of a major change in American policy, away from predation and toward collective international security, toward domestic full employment and infrastructure renewal, and toward renewed technological leadership in the areas most needed by the world, such as climate change? Could and would the world react to this by extending to this country the financial backing required to pull off this transition?

Id. at 206–207:

The ideology of free markets behind which [conservatives] hid is bankrupt, but the country is not. The underlying stability and versatility of the quasi-public institutions in the United States have not disappeared. Our universities and research centers remain the leading technical and scientific institutions that the world has. Our government can be repaired. Mechanisms for creating new institutions as they are needed, and for forging new directions for those that we already have, exist. The way forward is to use them. At the same time we must come to grips with the need for effective and enforced regulation and break the power of the predatory elements—of the culture of predation— over the government and major corporations.

H. Regulated Entities

1. Federalism

One of the issues raised with respect to climate change legislation is the appropriate distribution of regulatory authority between state and federal governments. From the time of the framing of the Constitution, federalism has been a point of tension and debate. Climate change presents a novel federalism challenge. States have been at the forefront of climate action to date in large part to fill the utter void of federal action. Yet, now that federal legislation may be enacted the role of state actions is in question. Potential constitutional challenges may be raised under the Dormant Commerce Clause, the Supremacy Clause, the Compacts Clause, and Article II powers over foreign affairs.[1]

Adelman and Engel argue that "environmental federalism" always has involved role reversals where federal regulations reach areas of local concern and state regulations affect polices at national levels as well as local levels.[2] Traditional theory holds that regulatory authority should correlate to the geographical scope of a problem.[3] Yet, Adelman and Engel reject this "static" conceptualization in favor of "dynamic federalism," which accounts for the multifaceted nature of environmental problems and the fact that environmental policy is constantly shifting due to "natural processes and human interventions."[4] A similar concept is "cooperative federalism," which seeks to take advantage of the respective strengths of state and federal action.[5]

Legal scholars have proposed a variety of conceptual architectures to address the tension between state and federal legislation. Several general factors arise repeatedly:[6]

- Federal regulation is necessary to create consistency and avoid leakage, or the race to the bottom;
- There should be a presumption *against* federal preemption to allow for state innovation and stricter state standards;
- Although there is a role for market-based approaches, direct regulation, such as is achieved under the Clean Air Act, is necessary.

These issues are explored further in Chapter Eight, *infra*.

2. Individuals & Big Emitters

WILLIAM CALVIN, *Turning Around by 2020*, in GLOBAL FEVER: HOW TO TREAT CLIMATE CHANGE, ch. 19 at 239 (Un. Chicago Press 2008) (re-excerpted below):

The standard green answers (compost, carpool, eat locally grown foods rather than ones that require long-haul transport, become a vegetarian, and so forth) are all important. But, as James Lovelock likes to say, they may prove no more effective than dieting.

What we need are sure-fire solutions that stop the CO_2 pollution from all of those tailpipes and smokestacks.

Once the appropriate regulatory body has been determined, the next question is to what degree climate legislation should be targeted at individuals as opposed to major emitters. Professor

---

1. *See* Robert K. Huffman & Jonathan M. Weisgall, *Climate Change and the States: Constitutional Issues Arising from State Climate Protection Leadership*, 8 SUSTAINABLE DEV. L. & POL'Y 6 (2008).

2. David E. Adelman & Kirsten H. Engel, *Adaptive Federalism: A Case against Reallocating Environmental Regulatory Authority*, 92 MINN. L. REV. 1796, 1796 (2008).

3. *Id.*

4. *Id.* at 1799–1800.

5. Alice Kaswan, *A Cooperative Federalism Proposal for Climate Change Legislation: The Value of State Autonomy in a Federal System*, 85 DENV. U. L. REV. 791 (2008).

6. *See id.*; Adelman & Engel, *supra* note 2; Robert L. Glicksman, *Balancing Mandate and Discretion in the Institutional Design of Federal Climate Change Policy*, 102 NW. U. L. REV. 196 (2008); Kirsten H. Engel, *Harnessing the Benefits of Dynamic Federalism in Environmental Law*, 56 EMORY L.J. 159 (2006).

Latin, ch. 5, *supra*, argues that global warming reduction efforts aimed at individuals cannot be successful. On the other hand, Professor John Dernbach argues that individuals as consumers and citizens are important to the success of greenhouse gas reduction strategies.

John C. Dernbach, *Harnessing Individual Behavior to Address Climate Change: Options for Congress*, 26 Va. Envtl. L.J. 107, 111 (2008) (footnotes omitted):

> These [five comprehensive climate] bills [introduced as of April 1, 2007] are comprehensive because they address all six gases that are subject to reduction under the Kyoto Protocol, not simply carbon dioxide. They also apply to all sectors of the economy rather than only electrical generation or transportation. The five bills tend to cover the largest direct emitters of GHGs as well as those entities indirectly responsible for the largest share of emissions. This approach makes considerable sense because it focuses on a discrete set of sources that contribute significantly to the problem. The bills, however, do not provide individuals with a serious role in the national effort to address climate change, either as citizens or as consumers. This is a significant omission because large emitting facilities and individuals each have a role to play in reducing GHG emissions and these roles can be mutually reinforcing. Individual engagement, moreover, is not just an add-on feature for legislation once the legal design work is done; it must be part of the design itself.

Id. at 114 (footnotes omitted):

> The magnitude of the climate change challenge suggests not only that individuals need to be engaged in all of their relevant roles. Two roles are particularly important—the individual as citizen and the individual as consumer. Congress should engage individuals because of the importance of ensuring that the legislation is properly implemented, the international significance of the legislation, and the substantial role that individuals play in contributing to GHG emissions. Additionally, this engagement is essential because the only way to address some important sources of emissions is by changing the behavior of individuals.

Id. at 114–115 (discussing "Individuals as Citizens") (footnotes omitted):

> One key feature of U.S. environmental law is public participation in implementation and administration. American environmental laws tend to address large institutional sources of pollution, but individuals and citizen groups are necessary to ensure that these laws are properly implemented. Public participation provisions are thus directed at ensuring the effectiveness and responsiveness of government regulation of large institutional sources.

Id. at 116 (footnotes omitted):

> Citizen participation in the various administrative processes will operate as a counterweight to the influence of affected corporate interests. As a consequence, citizen participation will enhance the likelihood that a statute will be carried out more or less as written, reduce the ability of regulated entities to weaken the effect of the legislation, and ensure that decisions involving particular facilities or companies are more responsive to the concerns of citizens. The significant economic power of the affected entities, their history of previous opposition to climate change legislation, and their willingness to work together to advance their own interests are all factors that support an argument in favor of a high level of citizen participation.

Id. at 117 (discussing "Individuals as Consumers") (footnotes omitted):

> Climate change legislation should also engage individuals as consumers. The magnitude of the challenge, the significant role that individuals in the United States now play in contributing to GHG emissions, and the substantial constructive role that individuals can play in reducing such emissions all support this conclusion.

Id. at 118–119 (footnotes omitted):

> In important ways, engaging individuals as consumers is tantamount to harnessing the power of the market. Ordinarily, market incentives are understood as applying to corporations and other large entities, but there is no reason to limit such incentives to them. Individuals participate in the market as consumers and therefore shape the market. Market-based approaches that harness human creativity and ingenuity can apply to both individuals and corporations. In each case, the effect of incentives is to enable and reward individual initiative.

Id. at 120 (footnotes omitted):

> In the context of individual responses to climate change, two types of behaviors are especially relevant. The first is efficiency—the substitution of a more energy-efficient appliance, motor vehicle, or other device for a less energy-efficient one. Efficiency tends to require a financial investment, not an alteration, in daily behavior. The second is curtailment of energy use—for example, taking the bus to work rather than driving. Curtailment tends to require changes in daily behavior without a financial investment. Because the overall contribution of individual Americans to GHG emissions is so significant, however, almost any reduction from either approach would be of value.

Id. at 128 (footnotes omitted):

> The two roles [of citizen and consumer], taken together, are likely to be more effective than either role by itself. The citizen who is initially interested or engaged in the effective implementation of a regulatory program will more likely be interested in what he or she can do to contribute to solving the problem addressed by that program. Similarly, the consumer who is initially concerned with her product choices may often become engaged in how the regulatory program for those products is being administered.

Id. at 128 (footnotes omitted):

> Arguably, individual responsibility detracts from or weakens the case for the responsibility of large polluters, which is where, according to this objection, sole attention should be drawn. Corporations and other large polluters, in fact, often seek to deflect attention from their environmental damage by trying to focus on individual behavior. The need to seriously address climate change, however, is so great that both large emitters and citizens must be engaged. Of course, it is necessary to ensure that the failure of individuals to act does not provide an excuse for large emitters to fail to act, and vice versa.

Another impressive effort on the role of individuals and climate change is that of Michael P. Vandenbergh & Anne C. Steinemann, *The Carbon Neutral Individual*, 82 N.Y.U. L. Rev. 1673 (2007).

3. Revisiting the Politics of Regulation

a. The Elusiveness of Truth: The Example of Offshore Oil Drilling

The Truth About America's Energy:
Big Oil Stockpiles Supplies and Pockets Profits

A Special Report by the Committee on Natural Resources Majority Staff†
June 2008

Introduction

While the oil industry and some Members of Congress argue that opening more federal lands and waters would lead to lower gasoline prices, the facts prove otherwise. The fact is that the Nation simply cannot drill its way to lower prices at the pump. Other options, from greater energy efficiencies to the development of alternative fuels, are essential to reducing dependency on petroleum fuels and lowering fuel costs.

Increased Domestic Drilling Activity Has Not Led To Lower Gasoline Prices

Since the 1990s, the federal government has consistently encouraged the development of its oil and gas resources and the amount of drilling on federal lands has steadily increased during this time. The number of drilling permits has exploded in recent years, going from 3,802 five years ago to 7,561 in 2007.

Between 1999 and 2007, the number of drilling permits issued for development of public lands increased by more than 361%, yet gasoline prices have also risen dramatically (Figure 4) contradicting the argument that more drilling means lower gasoline prices. There is simply no correlation between the two.

Energy Companies Not Using Federal Lands Already Open to Energy Development

Even if increased domestic drilling activity could affect the price of gasoline, there is yet no justification to open additional federal lands because oil and gas companies have shown that they cannot keep pace with the rate of drilling permits that the federal government is handing out.

In the last four years, the Bureau of Land Management has issued 28,776 permits to drill on public land; yet, in that same time, 18,954 wells were actually drilled. That means that companies have stockpiled nearly 10,000 extra permits to drill that they are not using to increase domestic production.

Further, despite the federal government's willingness to make public lands and waters available to energy developers, of the 47.5 million acres of on-shore federal lands that are currently being leased by oil and gas companies, only about 13 million acres are actually "in production", or producing oil and gas (Figure 5). Similar trends are evident offshore as well (Figure 6), where only 10.5 million of the 44 million leased acres are currently producing oil or gas.

Combined, oil and gas companies hold leases to nearly 68 million acres of federal land and waters that are not producing oil and gas (Figure 7). Oil and gas companies would not buy leases to this land without believing oil and gas can be produced there, yet these same companies are not producing oil or gas from these areas already under their control.

---

† This report has not been officially adopted by the Committee on Natural Resources and may not therefore necessarily reflect the views of its Members.

If we extrapolate from today's production rates on federal land and waters, we can estimate that the 68 million acres of leased but currently inactive federal land and waters could produce an additional 4.8 million barrels of oil and 44.7 billion cubic feet of natural gas each day.

That would nearly double *total* U.S. oil production, and increase natural gas production by 75%. It would also cut U.S. oil imports by more than a third, and be more than six times the estimated peak production from the Arctic National Wildlife Refuge (ANWR).[1]

Vast Majority of Federal Oil and Gas Resources Already Available for Development

Proponents of opening additional lands to oil and gas leasing assert that vast quantities of oil and gas are closed to energy development. In fact, according to the Minerals Management Service, of all the oil and gas believed to exist on the Outer Continental Shelf, 82% of the natural gas and 79% of the oil is located in areas that are currently open for leasing.

The Department of the Interior recently released a report[2] that the Administration is using to delude Americans into believing that vast tracts of federal land with large concentrations of oil and gas are off-limits to oil and gas development. In actuality, the report shows that only 38% of the oil and 16% of the natural gas are excluded from leasing—largely because those resources are underneath National Parks and wilderness areas that have significant scenic, recreational, and wildlife values. The rest is either fully accessible under standard lease stipulations designed to protect lands and wildlife, or will be accessible pending the completion of land-use planning or environmental reviews.

Alaska

Proponents of drilling in Alaska are most often focused on a 1.5 million acre area in the 19.2 million acre Arctic National Wildlife Refuge (ANWR). Established in 1960 and expanded in 1980, ANWR includes a 1.5 million acre area of the coastal plain known as the "1002 area" which requires Congressional authorization before oil drilling may proceed there.

However, in addition to ANWR, there are another nearly 91 million acres currently open to leasing in the Arctic region of Alaska, including onshore and offshore lands. Oil and gas companies have leased only 11.8 million of the 91 million acres.

Within the National Petroleum Reserve-Alaska (NPR-A), oil companies have leased 3 million acres of 22.6 million acres available to lease. No production has occurred on any of those lands and industry has drilled only 25 exploratory wells there since 2000.

The Energy Information Administration (EIA) estimates that it will require 8 to 10 years after opening ANWR before oil is produced from any new leases. Furthermore, it would be 20 years after opening ANWR before oil production reached its peak of only 780,000 barrels per day. Production at that level would start to drop within a short time.

According to the EIA, opening ANWR would reduce U.S. crude oil imports, but not until 2022–2026 and only by a few percentage points. Further, it would not significantly increase total world oil production, nor would it significantly affect world oil prices.

In a Nutshell

- On the Outer Continental Shelf, 82% of federal natural gas and 79% of federal oil is located in areas that are currently open for leasing.

---

1. Energy Information Administration, *Analysis of Crude Oil Production in the Arctic National Wildlife Refuge*, May 2008.

2. *Inventory of Onshore Federal Oil and Natural Gas Resources and Restrictions to Their Development*, U.S. Departments of the Interior, Agriculture, and Energy, May 2008.

- Onshore, 62% of oil and 84% of natural gas resources are either fully accessible under standard lease stipulations designed to protect lands and wildlife, or will be accessible pending the completion of land-use planning or environmental reviews.
- Between 1999 and 2007, drilling permits for oil and gas development on public lands increased more than 361%.
- Since 2004, the Bureau of Land Management has issued 28,776 permits to drill on public land; in that same time, only 18,954 wells were actually drilled.
- Oil and gas companies have stockpiled nearly 10,000 extra permits to drill that they are not using to increase domestic production.
- Onshore, of the 47.5 million acres of federal lands leased by oil and gas companies, only about 13 million acres are actually producing oil and gas.
- Offshore, only 10.5 million of the 44 million leased acres are currently producing oil or gas.
- Combined, oil and gas companies hold leases to nearly 68 million acres of federal land that are not producing oil and gas.
- The 68 million acres of leased, inactive federal land could produce an additional 4.8 million barrels of oil and 44.7 billion cubic feet of natural gas each day.
- That would nearly double *total* U.S. oil production, and increase natural gas production by 75%.
- 4.8 million barrels of oil equals more than six times the estimated peak production from the Arctic National Wildlife Refuge.
- Development of and production from the 68 million acres currently under lease but not in production would cut US imports of oil by one-third. (See Figures 4–9.)

———————

Greenpeace, *Take Action! Say "No to offshore drilling"*, August 19, 2008:

Gas prices have been jumping over and under the $4 mark all summer, your grocery bills are soaring, and campaign ads are blasting you about the benefits of offshore drilling. So what's an average Joe or Jane supposed to believe? Will offshore drilling really make things better for you?

What you're hearing on the news is pretty one-sided, and most reporters are talking about this issue like it makes perfect sense. Well, it doesn't.

What can I say, sometimes dumb ideas get a lot of attention. That's exactly what's happening right now as President Bush has lifted the executive moratorium on offshore drilling, and Congress is being pushed to do the same.

Let me take just a second to review the top 10 reasons offshore drilling is such a dumb idea:
   10. Offshore oil drilling won't impact gas prices today, and it won't have a significant impact on gas prices in the future.
   9. This is nothing more than a money grab by the oil companies—who are already making record-breaking profits.
   8. We burn 25% of the world's oil here in the U.S., but we have only 3% of the world's oil reserves. So even if all offshore oil magically came to market today, the vast majority of our oil would continue to be imported, and we wouldn't see price relief at the pump.
   7. The current moratorium was put in place decades ago to protect us from the danger of oil spills along our coastlines and beaches.
   6. Burning fossil fuels like oil causes global warming, which causes stronger hurricanes, which will threaten the very offshore drilling rigs being proposed, which will contribute to even more global warming.
   5. To avoid the worst impacts of global warming, we need to switch from fossil fuels to renewable energy within the next 10 years. The billions of dollars that would be spent on

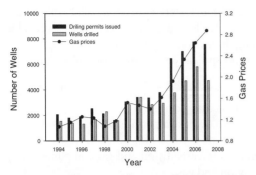

Figure 4. Drilling more does not lower gas prices. Adapted from: A Special Report by the Committee on Natural Resources Majority Staff, THE TRUTH ABOUT AMERICA'S ENERGY: BIG OIL STOCKPILES SUPPLIES AND POCKETS PROFITS Figure 1 (June 2008).

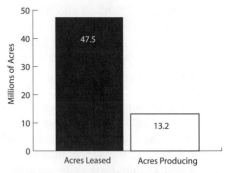

Figure 5. Onshore federal acres leased and in production in 2007. Adapted from: A Special Report by the Committee on Natural Resources Majority Staff, THE TRUTH ABOUT AMERICA'S ENERGY: BIG OIL STOCKPILES SUPPLIES AND POCKETS PROFITS Figure 2 (June 2008).

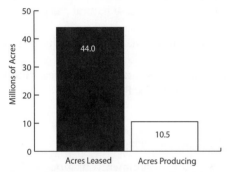

Figure 6. Offshore federal acres leased and in production in 2007. Adapted from: A Special Report by the Committee on Natural Resources Majority Staff, THE TRUTH ABOUT AMERICA'S ENERGY: BIG OIL STOCKPILES SUPPLIES AND POCKETS PROFITS Figure 3 (June 2008).

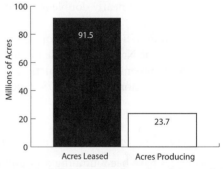

Figure 7. Total federal acres leased and in production in 2007. Adapted from: A Special Report by the Committee on Natural Resources Majority Staff, THE TRUTH ABOUT AMERICA'S ENERGY: BIG OIL STOCKPILES SUPPLIES AND POCKETS PROFITS Figure 4 (June 2008).

Figure 8. The majority of natural gas is currently open to leasing. Adapted from: A Special Report by the Committee on Natural Resources Majority Staff, THE TRUTH ABOUT AMERICA'S ENERGY: BIG OIL STOCKPILES SUPPLIES AND POCKETS PROFITS Figure 5 (June 2008). Offshore Undiscovered Technically Recoverable Reserves as determined by the Minerals Management Service, 2006.

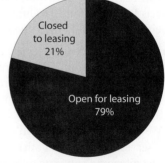

Figure 9. The majority of oil is currently open to leasing. Adapted from: A Special Report by the Committee on Natural Resources Majority Staff, THE TRUTH ABOUT AMERICA'S ENERGY: BIG OIL STOCKPILES SUPPLIES AND POCKETS PROFITS Figure 6 (June 2008). Offshore Undiscovered Technically Recoverable Reserves as determined by the Minerals Management Service, 2006.

Prepared by Subcommittee on Energy and Mineral Resources

offshore oil drilling just postpones the inevitable transition from fossil fuels to renewable energy.

4. Oil exploration requires massive seismic testing—which threatens whales and dolphins.

3. Oil prices are set on the global oil market, so American oil is no cheaper than Saudi oil. We won't get a discount for oil drilled in the U.S.

2. We can't solve the world's energy problems with the same drilling that created them.

1. Renewable energy is available now, so it's time to walk away from fossil fuels and toward a clean energy future.

....

b. The Importance of Process: Conducting a Hearing

Natural gas pipelines are not pre-ordained, in design or location. For an account of one of the world's most famous natural gas pipeline hearings, see WILLIAM H. RODGERS, JR., ENVIRONMENTAL LAW IN INDIAN COUNTRY § 1:16 at 437–39 (Thomson / West 2005) (footnotes as in original):

Case No. 99 — A Berger Inquiry, 1983–1985

Contrasts between mainstream and Native environmental law are drawn sharply around the topic of public hearings. In the mainstream there is considerable evidence that in the public forum manners decline, bullies appear, and factions rule.[72] The typical show-up-and-say-something public display is avoided by the cooler heads and often serviced by agency novices doing initiation duty. A frequent spectre is wild and boastful talk spinning freely until 2:00 a.m.—fueled by rumor, resentments, and intimidation.

By contrast, the show-up-and-say-something hearing in Native forums is quite different and much emulated. It is more austere and dignified. It has a name—the "Berger Inquiry"—after Thomas R. Berger, who served on the British Columbia Supreme Court and later resigned to do work on various royal commissions of inquiry. Judge Berger fixed the contours of his "Berger Inquiry" when he headed up the Mackenzie Valley Pipeline Inquiry to determine social, environmental, and economic impact of the proposed Arctic Gas pipeline to be built from Prudoe Bay, Alaska, down through the Mackenzie Valley in western Canada. In 1977, the government of Canada rejected the pipeline proposal on Berger's recommendation. The 1977 report resulting from the inquiry, *Northern Frontier, Northern Homeland*, became the best-selling book ever published by the government of Canada.[73]

Berger took his inquiry to the Natives and let them talk to him. They could speak in their own languages, at their own pace, and with ground rules that encouraged participation. All were invited to talk without the restraints of formality, relevance, status, or admissible evidence. All statements were recorded so that archival value would be maintained. Something magical happened at this "Berger inquiry." It became a fount of keen observation, passionate advocacy and moving eloquence.

Berger refined his efforts in a second inquiry that was published as the Report of the Alaska Review Commission entitled *Village Journey*.[74] This gave rise to strong recommendations on

---

72. *See* Jim Rossi, *Participation Run Amok: The Costs of Mass Participation for Deliberative Agency Decision-making*, 92 NW. U. L. Rev. 173 (1997).

73. *See* Thomas R. Berger, NORTHERN FRONTIER, NORTHERN HOMELAND: THE REPORT OF THE MACKENZIE VALLEY PIPELINE INQUIRY (1988 ed. Douglas & McIntyre, originally published in 1977).

74. Thomas R. Berger, *Village Journey: A Report of the Alaska Native Review Commission*, insert page in back of volume 5 (Hill & Wong 1985) (Inuit Circumpolar Conference) [hereinafter *Village Journey*].

tribal sovereignty, retribalization of ANSCA lands, self-government, exclusive tribal management of hunting and fishing on Native lands, and subsistence.

Eloquence and insight fills these pages. Consider the failure of law to limit access by nonnative users (statement of Sheila Aga Theriault, Larsen Bay):[75]

> You can't go out into our bays and walk on a beach without worrying about a bullet go zinging past your head. We have so many hunters here from the mainland, from down below—and how come they're coming here to our land? Have we invited them? We depend upon that land. You go out there now, the deer is scarcer now and with each year, more scarce. People come down for a weekend, for two days, come in their planes. They land on our [beaches]—on the shoreline. They go walk up and shoot the deer and, with the snow level coming down, that is the only place for the wildlife to live, down by the shore, and it's just duck soup for them. They just go and pick them off. And then where are we left when they go back home again? …

Thomas R. Berger concludes his *Village Journey* with these observations:[76]

> Governments build castles in the air. They want to believe that building schools in the bush and establishing corporations on the tundra will modernize rural Alaska. But there is no real prospect of wages or salaried employment except for a few persons in each village. The only possibilities for any measure of self-sufficiency lie in access to fish and wildlife. At present, state and federal policies seem designed to limit access to these resources. Is it any wonder that Native peoples are bitter because the promises held out, under the rubrics of education and development, have not been fulfilled? And that now, as they see their land and subsistence rights in jeopardy, they should be insisting on facing truths that others will not face? Who are the realists? Who are the sentimentalists?

The Berger inquiry is a variation of the talking circles that are familiar in Indian country. These are used successfully to explore popular opinion because they have rules of decorum, priority, and participation that are widely subscribed to.

c. Memories of Deregulation

While "regulation" brought its own backlash and recruited its own army of resistance, the same can now be said for "deregulation." The latest assailants of the public interest marched under this banner. Pledges of allegiance to the "wisdom of the market" are not quite as shrill as they were a few years ago. Consider:

Jay Inslee, *When Energy Markets Go Wrong: Surviving Enron, in* APOLLO'S FIRE: IGNITING AMERICA'S CLEAN ENERGY ECONOMY 89–92 (Jay Inslee, Bracken Hendricks eds., Island Press 2008):

> It took a while, but the truth finally dawned on me: Enron owned the White House. One would think I would have figured that out earlier. After all, the White House had refused to help solve the western energy crisis, even though electricity prices had gone up sometimes 1,000 percent in my congressional district in Washington State. This had happened because Enron and its fellows had figured out a way to constrict the supply of electricity in the West, both by literally turning off generators and by creating transmission bottlenecks that produced artificial shortages. The fine folks at Enron were later caught on tape describing their plans under such colorful names as "Death Star" and

---

75. *Village Journey* at 68–69.
76. *Village Journey* at 185 (Epilogue).

"Throw Momma from the Train." I had fought for a year with every tool at my disposal to get the Bush administration to rein in Enron, to no avail. Obviously, Enron had some sway over them.

But it took a meeting with Dick Cheney to realize how malignant that conspiracy of inaction was.

That morning, a bipartisan group of congressmen were to meet with the vice president in HC-5, one of the general-purpose meeting rooms in the basement of the Capitol Building. It was my first meeting with Mr. Cheney, and an important one, since we were there to try to talk him into lifting a finger, any finger, to stop Enron from bleeding our constituents dry.

On walking into the room, my first impression was that Mr. Cheney was on time and I was not. I felt a little embarrassed but quickly recovered when I remembered that he had kept my constituents waiting for about four months already in trying to get relief from Enron's gouging.

After Mr. Cheney had shaken hands with the twenty assembled members of Congress and engaged in the usual pleasantries, we got down to the business at hand. Several members gently described the dire circumstances caused by the 1,000 percent increases in the spot power market—for example, the elderly having to go without heat during power shortages and the stoplights going out in California. These were down-home stories that one would think would appeal to a man who once served as the congressman for Wyoming.

It quickly became apparent, however, that the stories of suffering had about as much effect in melting the vice president's heart as the arctic blasts that scour the high plains of Wyoming have on the frozen ice fields of the Grand Teton Mountain. He wasn't merely unmoved, he was so unresponsive and callously indifferent that I half expected him to say, "Let them eat Sterno."

So I decided to take a more economically demonstrable approach, using facts and figures. Surely, facts and figures would appeal to this former CEO of Halliburton. I launched into the facts regarding the energy market. The market had never experienced such volatility. The price explosions were unprecedented. Fully 32 percent of the generators in the western market were turned off, creating huge price hikes, when typically only 2 percent were down for maintenance at any one time. I told him only one conclusion could be drawn from this data—someone was consciously diminishing supply to drive up prices, and was succeeding, given the vertical climb of prices on the spot market. The evidence was incontrovertible, and he and the president were the only people in America standing between my constituents and fiscal ruin. I asked him to help us.

He looked straight at me, and his reply had all the subtlety of being slapped in the face with a flounder. He said, in a voice dripping with arrogance, "You know what your trouble is? You just don't understand economics."

I came close to responding, "You're right, Mr. Vice President, I don't understand economics, but I do understand a rip-off when I see one." But, given the dignity of our respective offices, I did not. Neither did I say that I would match my degree in economics from the University of Washington with what was probably his in ballistics from the University of Wyoming any day. Instead, I simply responded that the facts were clear, and that when the truth emerged, what Enron was doing would be a scandal.

The vice president did not tell me to "go [expletive deleted]," as he once told a colleague on the floor of the Senate, but the message was the same. Of course, this was a vice president who had gone into a room with a hundred oil and gas lobbyists and written an energy policy that basically deeded the nation's crown jewels to the oil and gas industry. But given the obvious chicanery being committed by Enron, it was still disappointing when the vice president of the United States ignored an economic emergency and topped it off by suggesting that I was dumber than a post.

So when Mr. Cheney's own Federal Energy Regulatory Commission (FERC) finally examined the evidence three years later, in 2005, and reached the obvious conclusion that Enron had been stealing the West blind, it should have been satisfying to know that my constituents and I did, indeed, know something about economics. We just did not understand "Enronomics." It should have been a tasty dish, a lightly salted serving of Enron crow presented on the vice president's finest china at his lushly appointed home in the U.S. Naval Observatory. Instead, with the exception of a few convictions, little has changed. Ratepayers, shareholders, and retirees have been left holding the bag, and the American people remain vulnerable to future manipulation.

The Enron scandal was the crowning jewel of a school of thought that hoped to place the private sector beyond all public controls. Enron CEO Ken Lay, nicknamed "Kenny Boy" by the president himself, was a top donor to the president's campaign, served on the transition team for the Department of Energy, and was even responsible for the selection of two nominees to FERC who would oversee the regulation of his industry.[1]

In truth, the Enron scandal and the energy crisis that came along with it were the result of a systematic scheme that dismantled the rules and incentives that protected the public interest in a market where power is concentrated in the hands of industry. Not only is the concentration of power we've seen over the past six years antithetical to democracy, it's also bad for business and bad for the climate.

The clean-energy revolution will not succeed if power is concentrated, for the simple reason that there are no silver bullets. No one industry has the answer, or even half of the answer. In Dick Cheney's worldview, concentration among a few favored companies is the way the game is played. The future belongs to different ideas.

IV. Adaptation

Richard M. Burian, *Adaptation: Historical Perspectives, in* KEYWORDS IN EVOLUTIONARY BIOLOGY 7 (E.F. Keller & E.A. Lloyd eds., Harvard Un. Press 1992):

> the term "adapted" and its cognates meant apt, or suited to, some particular purpose or other.... The term has other biological uses, covering, for example, physiological and biochemical adaptations of organisms to stress, altitude, nutrition, and so on.

WORKING GROUP III contribution to the FOURTH ASSESSMENT REPORT OF THE INTERGOVERNMENTAL PANEL ON CLIMATE CHANGE, CLIMATE CHANGE 2007: MITIGATION OF CLIMATE CHANGE, Preface (Cambridge Un. Press 2007):

> "Mitigation of Climate Change" aims to answer essentially five questions relevant to policymakers worldwide:

---

1. Joel Connelly, *In the Northwest: Enron's Real Obscenity Is Continuing Cost of "Crisis,"* SEATTLE POST-INTELLIGENCER, June 9, 2004, http://seattlepi.nwsource.com/connelly/176931_joe109.html.

- What can we do to reduce or avoid climate change?
- What are the costs of these actions and how do they relate to the costs of inaction?
- How much time is available to realize the drastic reductions needed to stabilize greenhouse gas concentrations in the atmosphere?
- What are the policy actions that can overcome the barriers to implementation?
- How can climate mitigation policy be aligned with sustainable development policies?

One must be careful with technical definitions. As Professor Verchick explains below, adaptation is aimed at coping. Mitigation is directed at fixing.

Some amount of investment must be made to adapt to a warmer world. But what measures are the best? How should investment be distributed between adaptation and mitigation measures?

2007 ROMM at 151:

> Many Delayers use the idea of adaptation to argue against action now, to create the false hope that global warming will be of a pace and scale that our children and their children can deal with—which, ironically, would be true only if we ignored their advice and took aggressive mitigation action now. After all, how do you adapt to sea levels rising a foot or more a decade until oceans are 80 feet higher or more?

Id. at 151:

> Of course we should develop drought-resistant crops and new levee technology and better desalinization technology. But for the foreseeable future, avoiding global warming should receive ten to one hundred times the funds of any adaptation effort.

––––––––––

Professor Verchick argues below that we can and must hold two concepts at once in our minds: mitigation of greenhouse gases—necessary for the long-term; and adaptation to a warmer world—necessary for the short-term.

Adaptive Justice

Robert R.M. Verchick, Gauthier-St. Martin Chair in Environmental Law, Loyola University New Orleans. This chapter draws from an earlier essay of mine, "Adaptation, Economics, and Justice," in CLIMATE CHANGE AND THE NEOLIBERAL MODEL *(David Driesen ed., MIT Press 2008). For helpful comments on this draft, I thank Vicki Arroyo, Director of Policy Analysis at the Pew Center on Global Climate Change.*

Efforts to combat climate change correctly emphasize reducing greenhouse gases, or GHGs. But for those unfortunate populations that could be wiped out by one sustained draught or misplaced hurricane, the long road to reduction is not enough. No matter how successful we are with pollution markets and electric cars, the world appears locked into a pattern of rising temperatures for at least another 40 to 50 years. Communities in the crosshairs, whether in the United States or abroad, must start *adapting* to climate change—now. But in the United States, the federal government has done little to help regions that are particularly vulnerable to climate change, like drought-prone states in the west or coastal communities on the Gulf and along the Atlantic seaboard. And the United States and other wealthy nations have done little to help the world's poorest and most vulnerable countries, many of whom can't afford to erect the levees, insurance markets, and health clinics that adaptation requires. We are like Phoebe, in the television show, "Friends," who, when asked by a neighbor to help move furniture replies, "I wish I could, but I don't want to."

Why is this so? Why, when faced with a coming plague of drought, famine, and souped-up storms do Americans and (and many others in the developed world) appear so blasé? And what, if anything, can we do about it? This chapter examines those questions. My tentative conclusion is that the timid response to adaptation in the United States and abroad is connected to a misguided view of government responsibility and justice. On the domestic level, many Americans have bought into the idea that large federal programs are ideologically inappropriate and, in practice, inefficient. We have forgotten that Americans, at their best, sink or swim together.

On the global level, a political divide between "northern" industrialized countries and "southern" developing countries, which was instigated in part by the United States, has encouraged both sides to approach international climate policy from a very short-term, instrumentalist perspective. Thus while the North recognizes the practical need to engage the South in reducing GHGs, the North sees little advantage in helping the South protect against calamities that may never leave southern shores. This instrumentalist view has prevented the North from acting justly and from building trust with its neighbors to the south. Equally important, this view has deprived the North of a crucial opportunity to engage the South in stronger efforts to reduce GHGs for the benefit of all. While global warming is surely "the biggest market failure in the world," it is about more than markets.[1] Global warming is also about inequality—inequality based on wealth, race, geographic location, and political power. Understanding this inequality is the key to understanding the moral and practical justifications for helping needy communities adapt to climate change and to imagine what a comprehensive world-wide adaptation program might look like.

To that end, the first part of this paper briefly reviews anticipated climate-based changes, with an emphasis on national and global inequality and the need for adaptive measures. The second part shows how federal adaptation efforts in the United States and in the international community fail to address the need. The efforts fall short, in large part, because they are based on a market-based approach to problem-solving that steers leaders away from higher moral obligations and long-term strategies of international cooperation. Part three calls for a stronger moral foundation for adaptation aid, which market economics cannot provide. The fourth part offers a moral justification for adaptation aid. Drawing from international relations literature on fairness and trust, this section finds both philosophical and practical reasons for supporting a moral view beyond what the market perspective alone can justify. Based on that discussion, the section then begins to speculate about what a "serious" global adaptation initiative might look like.

Before moving on, I should define two terms, *mitigation* and *adaptation*. *Mitigation* refers to actions taken either to reduce GHG emissions or to enhance the sequestation of such gases in "carbon sinks." Mitigation includes energy conservation, use of renewable energy, forest enhancement, and carbon capture and storage. *Adaptation* refers to the responses a society takes to better cope with or adjust to climate change impacts. Such responses could include building seawalls, restoring barrier islands, or improving the regional insurance system. Some initiatives, like better zoning near shore, address dangers of exposure. Others, like malaria prevention and micro-lending programs, seek to reduce vulnerability and enhance social resilience. As one example of the term's breadth, the U.N. Development Programme catalogs global adaptation programs under headings ranging from "Agriculture/Food security," to "Public Health," to "Disaster Risk Management."[2]

According to the United Nations' Intergovernmental Panel on Climate Change (IPCC), adaptation by itself will never be enough to cope with all climate change effects, particularly the loss

---

1. NICHOLAS STERN, THE ECONOMICS OF CLIMATE CHANGE: THE STERN REVIEW 1 (Cambridge Un. Press 2007) [hereinafter THE STERN REVIEW].

2. Programming Climate Change Adaptation, *UNDP's Adaptation Portfolio*, United Nations Development Programme, www.sdnhq.undp.org (last visited June 3, 2008).

of biodiversity and the disintegration of ice sheets and glaciers.[3] The effectiveness of any given strategy is highly particularized and will depend on geographic risk, the social capital of the community involved, and political and financial constraints. No one knows what "full" adaptation, however defined, would actually cost. Estimating the cost of an effective levee—as residents of New Orleans are now finding—is hard enough. How do you predict the cost of agricultural reform in drought-prone Africa? Or the relocation of millions of people in Bangladesh? In one of the few estimates available, the World Bank speculates that it would cost $10–40 billion annually for the world to substantially adapt to climate change.[4] When you consider that the cost of restoring Louisiana's coast, alone, might cost $1 billion annually over the next thirty years, this estimate seems low.

A. Mapping Vulnerability

As other chapters in this book show in more detail, climate change threatens the basic elements of human welfare across the globe.[5] An average global temperature rise of 2–3 degrees Celsius could lead to many severe impacts including melting glaciers, declining crop yields, ocean acidification, sea-level rise, and loss of ecosystems.[6] As the planet warms, these impacts are expected to become disproportionately more damaging. But the predicted exposure of societies to such damage is not uniform. Countries in tropical areas are more likely to be hit harder. Tropical nations already endure climatic disturbances like cyclones, monsoons and the El Niño and La Niña cycles. There is persuasive evidence that global warming could extend or intensify these events.[7] Agricultural productivity in the tropics has always presented special geographic challenges, a fact that has contributed to overall slower economic growth. Such challenges include extreme weather, poorer soils, the presence of pests, and higher crop respiration rates. Climate change will augment these problems. In the blunt words of the 2007 Stern Review: "[C]limate change will have a disproportionately damaging impact on developing countries, due in part at least, to their location in low latitudes, the amount and variability of rainfall they receive, and the fact that they are already too hot."[8]

As the 2004 Asian Tsunami demonstrated, people in the developing world are least able to cope with sudden disasters when they do occur because of substandard infrastructure, poor emergency response, and insufficient medical services. Indeed, research suggests that deaths from natural disaster are generally linked to a nation's economic welfare and its degree of income inequality.[9] Developing countries will also show greater sensitivity to climate change because of their economic reliance on agriculture and fragile ecosystems. In Sub-Saharan Africa, for instance, 64% of people are employed in the rural farming sector.[10] The percentage is nearly the same in South Asia.[11] People in developing countries also rely more heavily on subsistence goods and services drawn from the environment, such as fish, vegetables, firewood, fiber, and drinking water.

---

3. INTERGOVERNMENTAL PANEL ON CLIMATE CHANGE, CLIMATE CHANGE 2007: CLIMATE CHANGE IMPACTS, ADAPTATION AND VULNERABILITY, CONTRIBUTION OF WORKING GROUP II TO THE FOURTH ASSESSMENT REPORT OF THE INTERGOVERNMENTAL PANEL ON CLIMATE CHANGE 781 (Cambridge Un. Press 2007).

4. *Id.* at 734 (*citing* WORLD BANK, CLEAN ENERGY AND DEVELOPMENT: TOWARDS AN INVESTMENT FRAMEWORK, Annex K (World Bank 2006)).

5. Chs. 2, 4, *supra.*

6. THE STERN REVIEW, *supra* note 1, at 13–16, 56–57.

7. *Id.* at 56.

8. *Id.* at 94–95 (internal quotation marks omitted).

9. *See* Matthew E. Kahn, *The Death Toll From Natural Disasters: The Role of Income, Geography, and Institutions,* 87, no. 2, THE REVIEW OF ECONOMICS AND STATISTICS 271 (2005).

10. THE STERN REVIEW, *supra* note 1, at 32, 52.

11. *Id.*

In developing countries, climate victims will be mainly people of color. A large share will be infants and children, elderly people, and the disabled.[12] This means more work for women and girls, who generally care for the children, the elderly, and the infirm.[13] Women and girls, who in many cultures also grow the food and collect the water, will find these chores consuming more and more of their time, leaving less time for education and vocational training.[14] By pushing girls out of school, climate change is expected to increase female illiteracy.[15]

Wealthy countries, like the United States, Japan, and the original members of the European Union, will also face serious climate-related problems, including sea-level rise and more intense droughts and storms. In the United States, state governments and private research centers have begun documenting an array of climate-induced harms expected in California, the Pacific Northwest, and the Northeast. Bowing to a court order, the Bush administration in 2008 released a summary report on the anticipated effects of climate change in the United States. The document warns of devastating water shortages in the Southwest, thousands of miles of washed-out highways and sunken railroad lines in the East, and an alarming increase in heatstroke, smog-induced asthma, and post-traumatic stress disorder.[16] If protective action is not taken in the next fifty years, hundreds of miles of storm buffering wetlands in the Gulf and along the Atlantic coast could be swallowed up by sea-level rise, along with recreational beaches, coastal spits, and barrier islands.[17] Hurricane Katrina reminds us that even in rich countries weather-related violence visits particular harm on vulnerable classes—the poor, the infirm, the elderly, and children.[18] The government's own reports on climate change emphasize this fact, warning that vulnerable classes will likely bear the brunt of increased heat waves, flooding, and drought.[19]

B. Current Efforts to Address Adaptation

1. International Efforts

From the very beginning, the U.N. Framework Convention on Climate Change (FCCC) acknowledged the need for adaptation strategies, although it was short on details. Article IV, for instance, requires parties to "cooperate in preparing for adaptation to the impacts of climate change."[20] Article III urges parties to expand development assistance to foster "sustainable economic growth and development in ... developing country Parties, thus enabling them better to address the problems of climate change."[21]

---

12. *Id.*, pp. 110, 114.

13. *Id.*, p.114.

14. *Id.*

15. *Id.*

16. *See generally* COMMITTEE ON ENVIRONMENT AND NATURAL RESOURCES, NATIONAL SCIENCE AND TECHNOLOGY COUNCIL, SCIENTIFIC ASSESSMENT OF THE EFFECTS OF GLOBAL CHANGE ON THE UNITED STATES, *available at* www.climatescience.gov (last visited June 03, 2008).

17. *See* U.S. CLIMATE CHANGE SCIENCE PROGRAM, COASTAL ELEVATIONS AND SENSITIVITY TO SEA LEVEL RISE 21–23 (2008).

18. *See* Robert R.M. Verchick, *Risk, Fairness, and the Geography of Disaster*, ISSUES IN LEGAL SCHOLARSHIP, Symposium on Catastrophic Risks: Prevention, Compensation, and Recovery (2007); Article 6, www.bepress.com (last visited May 28, 2008).

19. COMMITTEE ON ENVIRONMENT AND NATURAL RESOURCES, NATIONAL SCIENCE AND TECHNOLOGY COUNCIL, SCIENTIFIC ASSESSMENT OF THE EFFECTS OF GLOBAL CHANGE ON THE UNITED STATES 14, 165, 167–68 (May 2008), *available at* www.climatescience.gov (last visited May 29, 2008) (noting vulnerability of poor and other groups to heat waves, flooding, drought).

20. United Nations Framework Convention on Climate Change, art. IV, opened for signature May 29, 1992, S. Treaty Doc. No. 102-38 (1992), 1771 U.N.T.S. 107.

21. *Id.*, art. III.

Convention parties have since created four programs to promote adaptation. Two specifically target the poorest countries. The Least Developed Countries Fund (LDC Fund) assists needy countries in preparing National Adaptation Programmes of Action (NAPAs), reports that identify actions and priorities important to adaptation efforts. A second fund, the Adaptation Fund, will provide more significant funding for projects in poor countries. This program, which comes on line in 2010, is partially funded by the sale of certified emissions reduction units to richer countries. Two other programs are nominally open to all member nations. One, the Strategic Priority on Adaptation (SPA) fund, supports projects that enhance vulnerable ecosystems and produce "global environmental benefits."[22] The other, the Special Climate Change Fund (SCC Fund), supports adaptation, disaster-risk management, coastal zone planning, and other long-range activities.

The programs are nothing if not ecumenical. There is something for nations with globally important eco-assets and for those scraping by on almost nothing. Some, like the LDC Fund and the SCC Fund, focus on institutional and developmental needs; others, like the SPA fund, want to see change in the physical landscape. All suggest that need and geographic diversity are important. But however broad in scope, these programs are at most a drop in a very big ocean. All programs require the recipient nation to share costs, sometimes on a 50-50 basis, a non-starter for some poor countries. And while the U.N. optimistically puts the annual cost of climate adaptation at "tens of billions of dollars," the sum of all pledged adaptation funds tops out at only a few hundred million dollars.[23]

2. National and Local Efforts

In the United States, federal adaptation policy makes for short discussion. The American Bar Association's 2007 book on American climate change policy—which is nearly 800 pages long—covers adaptation in two pages, with room for photos.[24] On the international side, U.S. behavior has obstructed multi-national adaptation efforts more than it has helped. The U.S. decision to quit Kyoto pulled at an already sensitive rift between North and South that to this day threatens cooperation on issues of mitigation and adaptation. To its credit, the United States does contribute to FCCC adaptation funds. Over the last decade, it has pledged hundreds of millions of dollars to the Global Environmental Facility (GEF), the financial organization that manages the LDC and SCC Funds.[25] Unlike the European Union, which has proposed generating more adaptation funds by further tapping the market for emissions reduction credits, the United States has urged that adaptation funds rely instead on voluntary contributions.[26]

In addition, the U.S. government has been criticized for trying to steer the GEF away from a need-based allocation system and toward a "performance-based" system. That model would favor aid to countries that are judged to be political, economic, and environmental reformers while limiting aid to those that are not.[27] At the 2004 conference in Buenos Aires—the so-called "Adaptation COP"—the United States fiercely resisted a progressive adaptation "work plan" of-

---

22. *Programming Climate Change Adaptation*, Strategic Priority on Adaptation (SPA), United Nations Development Programme, www.undp.org (accessed June 3, 2008).

23. OXFAM INTERNATIONAL, FINANCING ADAPTATION: WHY THE U.N.'s BALI CLIMATE CONFERENCE MUST MANDATE THE SEARCH FOR NEW FUNDS 5, Table 1 (Dec. 4, 2007), *available at* www.oxfam.org (last visited June 3, 2008).

24. *See* John C. Dernbach, *U.S. Policy*, Chap. 3 *in* GLOBAL CLIMATE CHANGE AND U.S. LAW 61-100, 80–82 (Michael B. Gerrard ed., American Bar Association 2007).

25. SUSAN R. FLETCHER, GLOBAL ENVIRONMENT FACILITY (GEF): OVERVIEW, CRS Report for Congress (March 2007), *available at* http://leahy.senate.gov/issues/foreign%20policy/Environment/GEF2007.pdf (last visited April 29, 2009).

26. Michael Casey, *Poor Nations Demand Global Warming Deal*, IRRAWADDY (Chiang Mai), April 2, 2008, *available at* www.irrawaddy.org (last visited May 28, 2008).

27. J. TIMMONS ROBERTS AND BRADLEY C. PARKS, A CLIMATE OF INJUSTICE: GLOBAL INEQUALITY, NORTH-SOUTH POLITICS, AND CLIMATE POLICY 227–28 (MIT Press 2007) [hereinafter 2007 ROBERTS & PARKS].

fered by Argentina, although the plan did eventually pass. Also in Buenos Aires, the United States raised hackles when it supported Saudi Arabia's plea that adaptation funds be made available to oil-producing nations whose economies would be harmed by green technologies.[28] That proposal temporarily derailed negotiations at the Adaptation COP, although aid for oil producers was eventually incorporated into the SCC Fund.

On the domestic side, U.S. adaptation efforts lag significantly behind those of other countries. Unlike Great Britain, for instance, whose ambitious Climate Impacts Program establishes new construction guidelines and aids communities in future planning, the U.S. federal government has no national adaptation policy. Some federal agencies have begun to factor climate change into their projects. One of the most dramatic examples concerns the rebuilding of New Orleans after Hurricane Katrina. Having acknowledged serious flaws in the construction and design of the federal levee system, the U.S. Army Corps of Engineers is now combining stricter design standards with state-of-the-art computer models that aim to project the effects of global warming on storm surge, storm frequency, and sea-level rise. The Corps's long-term efforts to restore Louisiana's endangered coastal wetlands (some of the most productive in the world) will similarly include ongoing assessments of climate change effects.

While there is not yet a national adaptation policy, it's possible that in the next few years something like that will emerge. Several bills already introduced in Congress address adaptation concerns to various degrees. These proposals, considered either on their own or in combination, suggest the range of possibilities now under discussion.

Some of the proposed cap-and-trade programs—such as the Lieberman-Warner Climate Security Act or the Bingaman Low-Carbon Economy Act—would use money from permit auctions to support regional adaptation efforts. The Lieberman-Warner bill would divide adaptation funds among federal agencies, to be used for preserving wildlife, protecting forests, and restoring coastal wetlands.[29] The Bingaman bill, sensitive to the need for political buy-in, would allocate funds according to geography, allocating a quarter of funds to coastal areas in the Lower 48, a quarter to Alaska, and the remaining half to other natural resource projects throughout the country.[30]

Several bills specifically seek to protect ecosystem services and wildlife from the stress of a hotter world. One would enlist the EPA and Army Corps of Engineers in protecting the nation's "water resources, water sheds, and water quality."[31] Another would require a national strategy for wildlife protection.[32] In solidarity with the Arctic's favorite big-eyed mammal, Representative Jay Inslee's Polar Bear Protection Act would bravely end imports of "sport-hunted polar bear trophies" from Canada.[33] It is, I suppose, a start.

As with mitigation efforts, more progress is being made at the state and local levels than at the federal level. That is not all bad. Much more so than mitigation, adaptation requires a parochial view. By nature adaptation measures must be tailored to regional geography and land-use patterns. And the implementation is usually local.[34] But the complexity and expense of adding new

---

28. Hermann E. Ott, Bernd Brouns, Wolfgang Sterk, and Bettina Wittneben, *It Takes Two To Tango — Climate Policy at COP 10 in Buenos Aires and Beyond*, 2 JOURNAL FOR EUROPEAN ENVIRONMENTAL & PLANNING LAW 84, 86 (2005).

29. America's Climate Security Act of 2007, S. 3036 (formerly S. 2191), 110th Cong., 2nd Sess.

30. Low Carbon Economy Act of 2007, S. 1766, 110th Cong., 2nd Sess., Sec 204.

31. Transportation Energy Security and Climate Change Mitigation Act of 2007, HR 2701, 110th Cong., 2nd Sess.

32. Global Warming Wildlife Survival Act of 2007, HR 2338,110th Cong., 2nd Sess.

33. Polar Bear Protection Act of 2007, HR 2327, 110th Cong., 2nd Sess.

34. Robert R.M. Verchick, *Why the Global Environment Needs Local Government: Lessons from the Johannesburg Summit*, 35 URBAN LAWYER 471, 471–494 (2003) (noting that most environmental initiatives in urban areas require some local implementation).

infrastructure like dams and bridges will require federal involvement, as will resource projects that span many jurisdictions. According to the Pew Center on Global Climate Change, at least seven states have some policy on adaptation, focusing on everything from developing salt-tolerant crops to stabilizing river banks.[35] City building codes in New Orleans, informed by federal flood maps, now also incorporate the effects of climate change. And California has launched a major initiative to study the state's vulnerability to drier weather, shrinking aquifers, and rising tides.[36]

Washington's King County and its largest city, Seattle, have become national leaders in adaptation policy. Faced with the prospects of disappearing beaches, shrinking snow pack, increased flooding, and explosive wildfires, the county government created an interdepartmental adaptation team to inform all decision making. With the help of scientists and policy experts, everything from land-use planning to capital investment is viewed through the lens of climate change.[37] The City of Seattle has also adopted a climate plan, which, in addition to mitigation efforts, calls for recommendations for adaptive measures, particularly those related to sea-level rise, storm water management, urban forestry, building codes, and heat waves.[38]

On the opposite coast, New Yorkers are defending themselves from global warming too. They had better. According to a report on port cities released by the Organization for Economic Cooperation and Development, New York's metropolitan area ranks *second in the world* in terms of economic assets threatened by coastal flooding and sea-level rise.[39] (Miami is first, for those keeping track; New Orleans ranks third.)[40] New York's new climate plan, which Mayor Michael Bloomberg introduced in 2007, acknowledges the tremendous risk the city faces from hurricanes, flooding, wind storms, and heat waves. The mayor's plan calls for new emergency response systems, an assessment of all infrastructure, and a system for incorporating climate policy into all investment and planning decisions.[41] It is said that New York is a city that never sleeps. But unfortunately too many American cities do. Despite the work of exceptional places like Seattle and New York, in general local and regional adaptation efforts are modest at best and trail significantly behind the efforts of many European cities and Canadian provinces.[42]

C. An Ideological Barrier

There are several reasons for America's slow response to adaptation needs at home and abroad. Auto makers, Big Oil, and the coal industry have all helped subdue public calls for more aggressive climate policy nationally and internationally. President George W. Bush's personal distrust of climate science and sometimes abrasive style has also stymied progress on this topic. But another barrier concerns an ideology premised on limited government and free-market solu-

---

35. Pew Center on Global Climate Change, Adaptation Planning—What U.S. States and Localities Are Doing 4–15, Table 1 (undated), *available at* www.pewclimate.org (last visited May 28, 2008).

36. California Environmental Protection Agency, Climate Action Team Report to Gov. Schwarzenegger and the Legislature (March 2006), *available at* www.climatechange.ca.gov (last visited June 4, 2008).

37. *See* 2007 King County Climate Change Plan, Feb. 2007, *available at* www.metrokc.gov (last visited June 4, 2008).

38. *See* City of Seattle, Climate Action Plan 34, Sept. 2006, *available at* www.seattle.gov (last visited June 4, 2008).

39. *Warming Risks Listed by Population, Costs*, MSNBC News, Dec. 4, 2007, www.msnbc.msn.com (last visited June 4, 2008); *see generally* R.J. Nicholls *et al.*, *Ranking Port Cities with High Exposure and Vulnerability to Climate Extreme*, OECD Environment Working Paper No. 1, pp. 7–8 (2007), *available at* www.oecd.org (last visited June 4, 2008).

40. *Id.*

41. NYC.Gov, A Greener, Greater New York, PLANYC, *available at* www.nyc.gov (last visited May 28, 2008).

42. *See* Beth Daley, *U.S. Lags on Plans for Climate Change*, Boston Globe, April 5, 2007, p. 1A.

tions, a view often associated with "neo-liberalism." Neo-liberalism favors market-based solutions and distrusts government-based ones. It measures desirable outcomes in terms of "objective" indicators of combined social wealth, without formal concern for less measurable values like distributional fairness or restorative justice. In addition, we might add that neo-liberalism promotes an ethic—some would say "virtue"—of self-sufficiency and the stoic acceptance of unfortunate consequences. That is, individuals are expected to assume the risk of participating in the market and to adapt to changing landscapes. This ideology has influenced ideas about adaptation on both the national and international level, and has obscured for many the need for a more coordinated approach to adaptation that is based on stronger moral principles.

On the domestic side, these views have hampered even the most basic improvements in the areas of health care, resource protection, and public infrastructure. As for disproportionate effects on the poor and other vulnerable groups, the idea seems to be that if the economy grows enough, vulnerable people will develop the resources to protect themselves without special federal help. I will not go into detail here. But it should be obvious that the federal government must play a primary role in restoring and protecting important natural and artificial infrastructures like biodiversity, coastal wetlands, levees, and bridges. Similarly, economic expansion in the United States has also produced a troubling wealth gap that has increased the vulnerability of many people; the federal government has a moral obligation to protect and empower those people.

On the international side, one can see the neo-liberal influence in the U.S. calls for "performance-based" rather than "need based" adaptation aid, or in its view that U.N. adaptation funds should be supported by voluntary donations rather than emissions-based trades. But neo-liberalism's most significant influence may be that it has led many economists to suggest that targeted adaptation funds should be replaced by (or subordinated to) general development aid.

Recall that poor people, because they lack basics like medical care and safe shelter, are much more likely to suffer from environmental disaster than rich people. Economists Gary Yohe and Richard Tol estimate that "for every percent of economic growth [in a country] vulnerability falls by a percent."[43] For this reason, many have begun to follow the lead of economist and Nobel laureate, Douglass North, who contends that general and targeted development aid to poor countries should be the highest priority in international adaptation policy.[44] The Copenhagen Consensus Center, an economics-based think tank in which North participates, goes even further. In a highly publicized report, the group suggested that liberalizing trade was more important than responding to global warming at all, whether through mitigation or adaptation.[45] Such prescriptions are appealing to a market view because they minimize governmental involvement (which neoliberals distrust) and purport to maximize social utility.

But as the international leaders ponder the next stage of adaptation policy, it would be a mistake to substitute either aid or trade for a comprehensive adaptation strategy. Sure, prosperity is good. But general advancement does not necessarily serve the same constituency as more tailored adaptation programs. The millions of farmers in flood-prone deltas or African dustbowls need lifesaving infrastructure *now*, in the form of dikes, reservoirs, greenbelts, insurance networks, and other projects. Development aid, nearly by design, has a longer time line. It could take generations for such aid to translate into the kinds of infrastructure most needed to combat

---

43. Gary Yohe & Richard S.J. Tol, *Indicators For Social and Economic Coping Capacity: Moving Toward a Working Definition of Adaptive Capacity*, 12 GLOBAL ENVIRONMENTAL CHANGE 25, 29 (2002).

44. DOUGLASS C. NORTH, INSTITUTIONS, INSTITUTIONAL CHANGE, AND ECONOMIC PERFORMANCE 80–82 (Cambridge Un. Press 1990).

45. Copenhagen Consensus 2004, Press Release, *HIV/AIDS, Hunger, Free Trade and Malaria Top Experts' List* (undated), *available at* www.copenhagenconsensus.com (last visited May 28, 2008); HOW TO SPEND $50 BILLION TO MAKE THE WORLD A BETTER PLACE (Bjørn Lomborg ed., Cambridge Un. Press 2006).

climate change. As for more liberalized trade, it is true that pulling down trade barriers will lead to larger aggregate growth. But the benefits and costs of globalization have always been unevenly distributed. Even with today's relatively free markets, just 6% of foreign investment goes to Africa, while the 47 poorest countries receive only 2%.[46]

From a market-based perspective, these distributional differences do not matter so much. Because neoliberalism focuses on combined social welfare, an aggregate rise in wealth is a success regardless of which rice farmers are helped in what poor country. But to those with a more holistic view, distribution matters very much. If one of the goals of adaptation policy is to help people in the South whose lives are endangered by energy policies in the North, the proposals of aid and trade fall short. In addition to these arguments, there is one last objection to using general aid as a substitute for a more ambitious adaptation policy. The idea dangerously confuses the concepts of charity and justice. The remainder of this chapter develops this idea within the context of international policy.

D. Adaptation and Justice

Over two centuries ago, early feminist Mary Wollstonecraft roared, "[i]t is justice, not charity, that is wanting in the world!"[47] While many recognize some need for adaptation in climate change policy, world leaders tend to view adaptation funding as a charity, rather than a requirement of justice. Wealthy nations—looking through a neoliberal lens—do not see global adaptation as an urgent need or at least do not see it as benefiting them in any important economic way, and so tend to treat it like an inefficient charity. Thus they underfund it. Viewing adaptation funding as a moral obligation grounded in justice principles would lead to a more robust response to the global adaptation needs. We need a broader sense of national purpose anchored in a theory of global justice. The move from "charity" to "justice" requires a reframing of the issues. Charity is what a Samaritan does when she feels sorry for you and wants to help. Justice is what a society owes to you because of your membership in a shared community.

Justice is important for both philosophical and practical reasons. In many philosophical traditions, the point of identifying shared ethical values is to bring people and societies together. This end is inherently good, as it fulfills an innate human need to connect to others, to care for others, and to be cared for. On the practical side, justice promotes altruism, reciprocity, and cooperation. All of these things promote community and enable long-term survival. To ground an adaptation strategy in something more durable than market preference will require a commitment to a model of justice that appeals both to philosophical principles and realistic concerns. In the remainder of this chapter, I hope to start a discussion about an appropriate model of justice to guide adaptation policy.

1. Justice for Philosophers

Adaptation strategy should begin with the moral commitment that society owes to the least advantaged. In political theory the idea is perhaps best expressed as a version of distributive justice, made famous by philosopher John Rawls. Seeking a standard of wealth distribution among members of a single society, Rawls imagined how members would define their interests at the formation of a hypothetical "social contract." He concluded that members of this new society, if shorn of information about their eventual "class position or social sta-

---

46. *See* James Gustave Speth, *Development Assistance and Poverty,* Chap. 7 *in* STUMBLING TOWARD SUSTAINABILITY 163–72, 167–168 (John C. Dernbach ed., Environmental Law Institute 2002).

47. MARY WOLLSTONECRAFT, A VINDICATION OF THE RIGHTS OF WOMEN 71 (Carol H. Poston ed., Norton 1975).

tus,"[48] would choose distributional principles that maximize the position of the persons least well-off.

Years later, Rawls modified the theory to apply it to distributions of wealth among different societies. There, Rawls declined to extend his earlier rule in full, but instead argued that privileged societies have the duty to aid their poorer neighbors at least up to the point that their neighbors can "manage their own affairs reasonably and rationally and eventually ... become members of the Society of well-ordered Peoples."[49] Once the target is reached, "further assistance is not required, even though the now well-ordered society may still be relatively poor."[50] Significantly, redistributions of wealth may be unequal (the poorest get more). For Rawls, the principles of allocation are based in a theory of international community.

Rawls's views are concerned with a strand of theory called "distributional justice." But it is also possible to justify aid to the world's poor in terms of "compensatory justice," which addresses how those inflicting harm should compensate those that they injure. Under this theory, LDCs would argue that their need for adaptation aid arises from historical injury visited on them by their more industrialized neighbors.

There is truth in this charge. Recent empirical studies using materials-flow analysis show that natural capital in southern countries is sacrificed to feed consumption in the North. Pointing to such analyses, economists J. Timmons Roberts and Bradley Parks argue that "from both an import and export perspective ... core economies are draining ecological capacity from extractive regions by importing resource-intensive products and have shifted their environmental burdens to the South through the export of waste."[51] In one example they note that the original fifteen E.U. nations import, in *physical terms*, more than *four times* what they export; but that the *money value* of what they export is *four times* that of what they import.[52] This unequal exchange of natural capital, what some call "environmental imperialism," is fueling enormous resentment among developing countries and has become a significant stumbling block in climate negotiations.

2. Justice for Realists

When put into practice, a sound theory of justice leads to practical improvements in individual and political life. Justice helps define human goals and adds muscle to flabby social policies. In times of crisis—a war, disaster, or social upheaval—a commitment to justice can unite those with shared interests and stiffen resolve. Today the world faces a series of existential red alerts, from global warming, to nuclear proliferation, to Islamist jihad. The challenges are too broad for any regional bloc or even hemisphere to address. They require cooperation among nations in the North and South.

There are many ways to encourage poor countries to join industrialized countries in efforts to address important global problems. The use of "soft" power through the practice of justice is one important element. Sometimes powerful countries enlist other countries into global initiatives through moral suasion and "leading by example." Since World War II, such strategies were significant to human rights initiatives, including the official rejection of torture by most thoughtful nations. The importance of setting a just example explains the alarm expressed by many Americans upon hearing reports of abusive CIA interrogation tactics under the second Bush administration. Nations also attempt to encourage cooperation among nations through trade and aid

48. JOHN RAWLS, A THEORY OF JUSTICE 302–03 (Oxford Un. Press 1973).
49. JOHN RAWLS, THE LAW OF PEOPLES 111 (Harvard Un. Press 1999).
50. *Id.*
51. 2007 ROBERTS & PARKS, *supra* note 27, at 168 (citations omitted).
52. *Id.*, citing Stefan Giljum and N. Eisenmenger, *North-South Trade and The Distribution of Environmental Goods and Burdens: a Biophysical Perspective*, 13 JOURNAL OF ENVIRONMENT & DEVELOPMENT 84 (2004).

programs. The strategy can be successful if targeted correctly. One could imagine encouraging nations like Indonesia or Brazil to participate in mitigation efforts in return for, say, adaptation aid. The philosopher will object that aid, if already justly deserved, should not be conditioned on future acts. But such carrot-dangling is nearly inevitable in real-world politics. It may be defended on pragmatic grounds *if* such policies produce a significant net benefit for receiving countries and *if* local governments and civil society are included in the development of those policies.

A sometimes overlooked benefit of practicing justice is the fostering of community through trust. Today the bonds of trust between rich and poor nations are badly frayed. A significant reason is that the South believes the North has built its flashy culture and plus-sized economy on the backs of equatorial peoples. Half a millennium ago, the North enriched itself by stealing the South's labor and natural resources. Today it has stolen the climate, and shows comparatively little concern for tropical and sub-tropical nations left to resist rising tides and sun-baked fields.

This lack of concern was exemplified in the second televised presidential debate in 2000, when then-candidate George W. Bush had this to say about what he would do in response to climate change: "I tell you one thing I'm not going to, [sic] is I'm not going to let the United States carry the burden of cleaning up the world's air, like the Kyoto treaty would have done. China and India were exempted from that treaty. I think we need to be more even-handed."[53] Years earlier, Bush's father, George H.W. Bush, had caused considerable stir at the Rio Earth Summit when, as president, he expressed a similar skepticism for targets and timetables by insisting that "the American lifestyle is not open to negotiation."[54]

These statements reveal important points about fairness and community, respectively. George W. Bush's concern for an "even-handed" approach suggests a theory of justice based on straight egalitarianism, without regard to a nation's resources or culpability. His father's refusal to consider any concession that might threaten "the American lifestyle" suggests that fairness has its limits. Specifically, the elder President Bush appeared to suggest that these needier nations lay *outside* the community to which the United States owes much responsibility. He appeared to question the very existence of a Rawlsian social contract among nations.

But the elder Bush, a veteran of World War II, surely understood the necessity of a social contract among today's nation states. Neoliberals, riding on the comet's tail of globalization, promote the role of institutional togetherness through the World Trade Organization, the World Bank, the European Union, and other entities. Even President George W. Bush, typically seen as a go-it-alone president, speaks persuasively for a world committed to global security, where countries fight terrorism, not only for their own national security, but for the national security of others.

Climate change is likewise a serious threat to global security that requires extraordinary cooperation among nations. Everyone agrees that stabilizing GHG emissions cannot happen without help from the largest developing countries. Even if the North were capable of completely adapting to climate change (a goal it could never approach), it would still be wise to attend to the South. As a U.N. development report noted earlier this decade, "In the global village, someone else's poverty very soon becomes one's own problem: of lack of markets for one's products, illegal immigration, pollution, contagious disease, insecurity, fanaticism, terrorism."[55]

---

53. Transcript of Second Gore-Bush Presidential Debate, Winston-Salem, NC, Oct. 11, 2000, *available at* www.cnn.com (last visited June 4, 2008).

54. 2007 ROBERTS & PARKS, *supra* note 27, at 3 (quoting President Bush).

55. UN General Assembly, Fifty-fifth Session, Official Records, Agenda item 101, HIGH-LEVEL INTERNATIONAL INTERGOVERNMENTAL CONSIDERATION OF FINANCING FOR DEVELOPMENT: FINAL REPORT, prepared by THE UNITED NATIONS SECRETARY-GENERAL 3, A/55/10002001, *available at* www.un.org (last visited June 4, 2008).

It is tempting to hope that enlightened self-interest will push even poor countries to enlist in the struggle to mitigate GHGs, but this does not appear to be the case. At a recent U.N. conference on a post-Kyoto treaty, developing countries pushed hard on the need for aggressive adaptation aide. "Adaptation is critical to our very survival," said a delegate from Barbados, speaking for the Alliance of Small Island States. "If a deal on adaptation is not part of this agreement, we have no incentive to be part of it."[56]

In fact, one month later—to the day—Cyclone Nargis raked over Myanmar's sprawling delta, killing tens of thousands, an event many news agencies soon linked to climate change.[57] "Nargis is a sign of things to come," warned the head of India's Center for Science and the Environment in an interview, later referring to those harmed as "climate change victims."[58] As with Katrina, we'll never know what role if any climate change played in the Nargis tragedy, but the level of distrust for the North is exceedingly high and continues to be fueled by a range of perceived injustices, from carbon emissions to inequalities in resource exchange to the history of colonialism.

In short, anyone thinking that climate risk, alone, will lead poor, populous countries to negotiate GHG reductions had better think again. "No matter how important a nation is ecologically or how vulnerable it currently is," write Roberts and Parks, "other factors tend to lead to adoption of environmental treaties."[59] Those "other factors," which include democratic structures and meaningful foreign assistance, challenge the current American approach, which under-funds initiatives and rhetorically appeals to "even-handedness." Overtures to the developing world may someday have strings attached. But a successful approach must also acknowledge the moral dimension of the global-warming debate. This will mean moving away from some market-based ideas like "voluntary contributions" and "self sufficiency" and toward agreements favoring aid to "the least advantaged" or the "least culpable."

3. A Marshall Plan for the South?

Climate change now demands an unprecedented political and economic commitment. It suggests the need for a kind of 21st century Marshall Plan. Economist Thomas Schelling has thoughtfully argued that global reductions of GHG emissions require strategies reminiscent of America's successful effort to revive war-torn Europe.[60] But perhaps the more compelling application is to *adaptation* rather than mitigation.

As in the era following World War II, we face a group of nations that have an aching need for technical and economic assistance. Their plight is not the result of war, but of another destructive force that, while less direct, threatens to erode the economic, political, and cultural stability of billions of people. The moral imperative is there. To stand by while a generation of innocents slips into chaos cannot be justified. Similarly, the rehabilitation and protection of this vulnerable community is essential for the long-term political and economic stability of the rest of the world.

What would a "serious" adaptation program, patterned after the Marshall Plan, look like? For starters it would be bold and well funded. The Marshall Plan, begun in 1947 and bankrolled by the

---

56. Michael Casey, *Poor Nations Demand Global Warming Deal*, IRRAWADDY (Chiang Mai), May 2, 2008, *available at* www.irrawaddy.org (last visited May, 28, 2008) (quoting Selwin Hart).

57. *Cyclone in Burma Due to Climate Change: CSE*, HOWRAH NEWS SERVICE, *available at* www.howrah.org (last visited May 28, 2008); Michael Casey, *Is Global Warming to Blame for Burma Cyclone?*, USA TODAY, May 8, 2008, *available at* www.usatoday.com (last visited May 28, 2008); Sai Soe Win Latt, Opinion, *Cyclone Nargis Has Never Been "Natural,"* IRRAWADDY (Chiang Mai), May 2, 2008, *available at* www.irrawaddy.org (last visited May, 28, 2008).

58. *Cyclone in Burma Due to Climate Change: CSE*, *supra* note 57.

59. 2007 ROBERTS & PARKS, *supra* note 27, at 209.

60. Thomas C. Schelling, *What Makes Greenhouse Sense?* 81 FOREIGN AFFAIRS 2–9 (May/June 2002).

United States, eventually distributed more than $12 billion in technical and economic assistance to nearly 20 European countries.[61] A serious adaptation plan must over the course of a decade be expected to distribute tens of billions of dollars to perhaps 50 of the neediest countries. Like the Marshall Plan, a serious adaptation plan would go for the deep pockets. In 1947, the United States correctly understood that while it had not caused the war, its booming economy had put it in a unique position to help dress the wounds. It also understood that European markets and political stability were an important part of the national interest. Today OECD nations are similarly in a position of enormous comparative wealth, and have a compelling interest in global environmental, economic, and political stability. In addition, they have all profited immensely from the carbon economy and thus should be expected to contribute to global adaptation efforts.

Like the Marshall Plan, a serious adaptation program would focus on allocating funds quickly. In the first years of the Marshall Plan, the American government did not bother with highly uncertain cost-benefit surveys. Indeed, in the latter years of the program, the United States required receiving nations, themselves, to allocate American funds, which they eventually did with the help of arbitration. (As it turns out, the final allocation of Marshall Plan funds roughly tracked a per capita distribution pattern.) Adaptation funds should not be allocated this loosely, but should ideally target need and population base, while including a strong role for participants in major allocation decisions.

But the new approach to adaptation would also differ from the Marshall Plan in important ways. Unlike the Marshall Plan, which focused only on Europe and excluded Japan and Hong Kong, a new adaptation fund would be geographically diverse and focus primarily on need. Targeting the 50 poorest nations would be a good start. A serious adaptation plan would emphasize physical infrastructure and a more precise targeting of programs to make sure that money reached the neediest people within countries. In this way, the adaptation program would differ from the Marshall Plan, which was more concerned with developing trade and consumer markets than it was with promoting environmentally sustainable economies.

The details will require a balance between the philosophical and realist notions of global justice. The philosophical side argues for aid with few conditions, premised either on one's membership in the global community or on one's subjection to unjust harm. The side of the realist is concerned not only with justice as an *end*, but also with justice as a *means*—in this case, a means toward cooperative efforts to fight climate change. This suggests the eventual need for development assistance with real strings attached in order to nudge countries like India, China, and Brazil toward serious mitigation and adaptation efforts.

The ideal adaptation plan would include a mix of methodologies. But the overriding goal would be to build trust between North and South. Industrial countries must promote policies that show concern for the real threats now facing developing countries. In the beginning, this may mean transfers of need-based aid without concern for political or economic policies. Eventually, aid must be tied to reform; but those reforms should be targeted primarily to enhance the conditions that make poorer nations most amenable to engaging in environmental cooperation. Future aid would thus help poor nations diversify resource-based economies and encourage a strengthening of civil liberties and an acceptance of civil society.

"Climate change," write Roberts and Parks, "is fundamentally an issue of inequality."[62] Addressing that inequality is fundamental to any future progress on climate change. As long as the

---

61. Herbert Giersch, Karl-Heinz Paque and Holger Shmieding, *Openness, Wage Restraint, and Macroeconomic Stability: West Germany's Road to Prosperity 1948–1959*, Chap. 1 *in* Postwar Economic Reconstruction and Lessons for the East Today 15 (Rudiger Dornbusch, Wilhelm Nölling and Richard Layard eds., MIT Press 1993).

62. 2007 Roberts & Parks, *supra* note 27, at 23.

North views southern desperation as largely irrelevant to its own interest, adaptation aid will continue to be a mission of charity only—help that we wish we would give, but don't want to. Seeing climate threats as issues of inequality and unfairness enables us to move from charity to justice and, as it turns out, from altruism to long-range self interest.

Notes

1. For more on U.S. adaptation, see the Pew Center's excellent report: ADAPTATION PLANNING: WHAT U.S. STATES AND LOCALITIES ARE DOING, *available at* http://www.www.pewclimate.org/ working-papers/adaptation.

2. The State of California recently unveiled for public comment a multi-sector strategy guide to help guide California's efforts to adapt to climate change: *2009 California Climate Adaptation Strategy Discussion Draft, available at* http://www.ecy.wa.gov/climatechange/adaptation.htm. Similarly, the State of Washington commissioned a study led by the University of Washington's Climate Impacts Group in 2009 which provides a detailed examination of how climate change is likely to affect that state, including an examination of adaptation: THE WASHINGTON CLIMATE CHANGE IMPACTS ASSESSMENT: EVALUATING WASHINGTON'S FUTURE IN CHANGING CLIMATE, *available at* http://cses.washington.edu/db/pdf/wacciareport681.pdf.

V. Technology: Do We Have What It Takes?

As the dizzying array of climate proposals make clear, global warming will require substantial changes in the way that we produce and use energy. Less evident is the extent to which this will require new discoveries and innovations. Or do we just need to be creative with the technology that already exists?

2007 ROMM at 8:

> Energy is a subject with as many myths as climate science. The most destructive one is that we cannot tackle global warming until we develop new breakthrough technologies. In fact, the reverse is true. We have cost-effective technologies today that can sharply reduce global-warming pollution.

FRED KRUPP & MIRIAM HORN, EARTH: THE SEQUEL—THE RACE TO REINVENT ENERGY AND STOP GLOBAL WARMING 3 (W.W. Norton & Co. 2008) (Environmental Defense Fund):

> This book is about the kinds of inventors who will stabilize our climate, generate enormous economic growth, and save the planet. It is also about the near certainty that unless the United States acts as a nation to give these innovators the chance to compete fairly in the world's biggest business, they will fail to avert the crisis in time.

See ROBERT ZUBRIN, ENERGY VICTORY: WINNING THE WAR ON TERROR BY BREAKING FREE OF OIL, esp. ch. 6 (Promethus Books 2007) ("The Technology to Break OPEC's Chains") (urges "flex-fuel" autos; hydrogen is a "hoax," conservation a "losing strategy," nuclear and the renewables cannot produce the necessary "liquid fuel").

Ray Kurzweil, *Optimism on the Continuum Between Confidence and Hope, in* WHAT ARE YOU OPTIMISTIC ABOUT? TODAY'S LEADING THINKERS ON WHY THINGS ARE GOOD AND GETTING BETTER 297 (J. Brockman ed., Harper Collins 2007):

Consider energy. We are awash in energy (10,000 times more than required to meet all our needs falls on Earth) but we are not very good at capturing it. That will change with the full nanotechnology-based assembly of macro objects at the nano scale, controlled by massively parallel information processes, which will be feasible within twenty years. Even though our energy needs are projected to triple within that time, we'll capture that .0003 of the sunlight needed to meet our energy needs with no use of fossil fuels, using extremely inexpensive, highly efficient, lightweight, nano-engineered solar panels, and we'll store the energy in highly distributed (and therefore safe) nanotechnology-based fuel cells. Solar power is now providing 1 part in 1,000 of our needs, but that percentage is doubling every two years, which means multiplying by 1,000 in twenty years.

In a call for more aggressive technology research, Martin Hoffert and 17 other leading scientists wrote in *Advanced Technology Paths to Global Climate Stability: Energy for a Greenhouse Planet,* 298 SCIENCE 981, 981 (2002) (abstract of article):

Stabilizing the carbon dioxide-induced component of climate change is an energy problem. Establishment of a course toward such stabilization will require the development within the coming decades of primary energy sources that do not emit carbon dioxide to the atmosphere, in addition to efforts to reduce end-use energy demand.... Here we survey possible future energy sources, evaluated for their capability to supply massive amounts of carbon emission-free energy and for their potential for large-scale commercialization.... We conclude that a broad range of intensive research and development is urgently needed to produce technological options that can allow both climate stabilization and economic development.

———————

David Battisti & the Tamaki Foundation, *Geo-engineering Climate Change, available at* http://www.atmos.washington.edu/~david/geo.htm (last visited April 29, 2009):

On our present course, carbon dioxide will increase in the atmosphere to such an extent that by the middle of this century the global food supply will be diminished by global warming through reductions in crop yields (due to increasing temperature) and decreased water security (for irrigation and consumption). These climate stresses will be greatest in the tropics and subtropics — places where today over a billion people already suffer from food insecurity, and where population is expected to almost double by 2050.

The real solution to global warming is to dramatically reduce the amount of fossil fuel that is burned, but that solution involves a level of international cooperation that would be unprecedented in human history and key statesmen and governments do not consider this a realistic scenario. As such, engineers and scientists in the US (who developed the Star Wars Defense System and the scenarios for how climate would be affected by a global nuclear war) are seriously considering "geoengineering" solutions to global warming, ranging from fertilizing the ocean to increase the marine food chain so that it takes up more carbon dioxide from the atmosphere (thereby disrupting the very foundation of the global food chain) to space-based mirrors that would deflect enough sunlight away from the Earth to cancel out the warming due to the increased carbon dioxide in the atmosphere.

The most popular geoengineering solution among this group of engineers and scientists is to have regular (*e.g.,* monthly) launches of missiles that would fly to the stratosphere and deploy tiny particles that would be mixed throughout the atmosphere and block just enough sunlight to cancel the warming of the planet due to the increased carbon dioxide in the atmosphere. I and many other scientists believe this is an extremely dangerous proposition. Many scientists believe it isn't a solution at all — that there would be drastic changes in global climate if you allowed carbon dioxide to increase in the atmosphere and deployed this geoengineering technology to try and cancel the impact of carbon dioxide. For example, it is highly likely that the net effect of increased carbon dioxide and stratospheric aerosols will make the tropics drier; it is highly likely that everyone living in the mid and high latitudes will still experience warming, and everywhere winters would still be very, very warm compared to today. Carbon dioxide will continue to be dissolved into the ocean, so the ocean will become more and more acidic (estimates suggest by the end of the century, coral reefs will not be able to form). Additional sulfur dioxide in the stratosphere will expand the ozone hole, and when the sulfur dioxide falls from the stratosphere, the plants on the land will be exposed to more acidic rains. Perhaps the most disturbing feature of this "solution" is that if carbon dioxide continues to increase, more sulfates will need to be deployed and if the system failed (by, for example, sabotage), the world would warm at a rate that would devastate the fabric of global society and it would be the greatest shock to the global ecology since the asteroid impact 65 million years ago, that led to mass extinctions.

Injections of sulfate aerosol into the stratosphere is the most popular and most likely geoengineering option implemented because—compared to a global shift to alternative sources of energy than fossil fuel—this option is simple and inexpensive: it could be deployed in less than two years by existing government contractors, such as Boeing and Lockheed Martin, who would vie for lucrative contracts to control the Earth's climate.

Though most scientists are quite sure that the combination of increasing carbon dioxide and stratospheric aerosols would lead to profound changes in the climate (including those listed above), the research studies to quantify these changes have not yet been done. With inadequate science to inform a debate on this extremely dangerous proposal for a geoengineering solution to global warming, it is difficult to imagine that governments won't take the seemingly easy out and deploy this last-gasp technology to mitigate some of the global warming problem, rather than shift the global economy away from fossil to alternative clean fuels.

We are using state-of-the-art climate models to simulate and quantify the impact of this geoengineering "solution" on the regional and global climate, and to further quantify the impact that these climate changes will have on global food security. Our hope is that our findings will catalyze an informed debate on whether we should pursue this "solution" before it becomes an uninformed *fait accompli.*

William Calvin lays out a vision of addressing climate change in an excerpt from his book GLOBAL FEVER: HOW TO TREAT CLIMATE CHANGE ch. 19 (Un. of Chicago Press 2008). Published in SKEPTIC (Altadena CA, March 22, 2008), with modifications.

Turning Around by 2020: How to Solve the Global Warming Problem

William H. Calvin is professor emeritus at the University of Washington in Seattle and the author of fourteen books, including A BRAIN FOR ALL SEASONS: HUMAN EVOLUTION AND ABRUPT CLIMATE CHANGE, published by the University of Chicago Press.

Time has become so short that we must turn around the annual emissions growth before 2020 to avoid saddling today's students with the world of refugees and genocides that will result if we're too slow. That means not waiting for a better deal on some post-Kyoto treaty. It means immediately scaling up technologies that we know will work, not waiting for something better that could take decades to debug.

The standard green answers (compost, carpool, eat locally grown foods rather than ones that require long-haul transport, become a vegetarian, and so forth) are all important. But, as James Lovelock likes to say, they may prove no more effective than dieting. What we need are sure-fire solutions that stop the CO_2 pollution from all of those tailpipes and smokestacks. And do it quickly, which means not relying on efficiency improvements or new rapid transit systems that take decades to implement. Our problem has now become too big and too immediate to rely on reforming people's habits.

The Manhattan Project of 1942 to 1945 shows us how we have quickly turned recent science discoveries into major engineering projects. Going to the Moon was a major national effort that, while expensive, did not require a wartime economic restructuring. I once had lunch with George Mueller, who ran the Apollo Project for NASA in those critical years from 1963 to 1969. I asked him what it would take to stage, on an urgent basis, our energy makeover and climate restoration. First, he said, simply banning certain energy uses would not work any better than the U.S. experiment with banning alcohol, which simply created a bootlegging industry. (Imagine cheap Chinese incandescent bulbs smuggled into California, Australia and Canada when they decide to ban the old-fashioned bulbs.)

For an Apollo-scale project to create non-carbon energy alternatives, Mueller said that we needed a goal that is easy to understand (something like putting a man on the moon and returning him safely). And the goal needs a time frame (President Kennedy's "this decade") to persuade the public to act now. I propose "Turning Around" by 2020 as our goal and time frame, followed up by two more.

- The 2020 target would be stopping the annual growth in emissions to keep the eventual fever below 2°C. But we'd still be growing the CO_2 blanket, year after year, just at a constant rate.
- The 2040 target would be to stop the annual CO_2 growth altogether. This means that increased sinks would have to balance out any remaining fossil carbon emissions, including the delayed ones. Note that we still haven't reduced CO_2 concentration, only stopped its growth. Then we begin removing more CO_2 from the air each year than we add. That makes it a matter of adding sinks, not merely controlling emission sources. Call it "Sinking CO_2 by 2040."
- Restoring CO_2 concentrations to 1939 levels would be my third goal. Call it "Restoration by 2080."

We may well need to double power production in order to clean up CO_2, double again for worldwide modernization, and with another step up if we are to go to electric cars. This expansion only makes sense with Carbon-free (C-Free) energy—lots of it. Let me now evaluate the various candidates for accomplishing the 2020 turnaround.

Alternative Automobiles

There are two versions here. The relatively painless one is increasing efficiency. A modern refrigerator uses one-fourth the power of a 1975 model. And so we replace incandescent light bulbs with compact fluorescents or LEDs. Same lumens, fewer watts. Better gasoline mileage and more carpools also achieve the same end use, but using less power.

The more painful version is the diet that requires shedding the end uses themselves—say, turning off the all-night street lights or hanging the clothes out to dry instead of using the clothes dryer. Such banished end uses tend to creep back on stage within a few years. Furthermore, both versions are local or regional solutions that won't produce global solutions in time. Developing countries won't forego modernization just because we say so.

Better for 2020 to assume that those end uses will stay the same and even expand. And so we must focus on substituting C-free power sources and finding ways to create new carbon sinks.

Figure 10. (*Photograph not shown.*) **This satellite image shows North America at night. The United States and other populated areas are glowing.**

We already know the scenario for reducing our use of oil—converting to hybrid vehicles and alternative fuels. If plug-in hybrid electric vehicles (PHEVs) were to replace the 198 million cars, vans, SUVs, and light trucks in the U.S., it would cut oil imports by half.

Though I wouldn't recommend it, 84% of the recharging job could be done with excess overnight capacity in America's coal-fired plants. Even though burning coal to replace oil, it would nonetheless reduce overall CO_2 emissions. Such is the wasted energy from using 198 million inefficient internal combustion engines that must be kept idling in congested traffic.

But this has to be done globally. A fleet of PHEVs requires much mining to make the batteries. Poorer countries would have to import them. "Air cars" that run on compressed air would be easier for a developing country to manufacture from local materials.

No, it's not a rocket. No electric motor, either. It's an engine where compressed air runs a piston. Refilling the air tank can be done overnight by plugging in the onboard compressor. So air cars also run on electricity, just one step removed. It's the same for hydrogen fuel cell cars.

	Ability to Expand	Public View	Down Side	Ups & Downs	Enough by 2020?
Hybrids	large	very good	mining battery	—	•••
Compressed Air Car	large	none yet	air tanks	—	•
Improve Efficiency	good	in favor	slow grind	—	•
Dieting	limited	a pain	easy to fail	yo-yo	no

Figure 11.

The Coal Conundrum

Coal fired power plants are the big actors on the fossil carbon scene (in the U.S., more than half of the electricity comes from burning dirty coal) and if we don't address them immediately, the long run considerations will be irrelevant.

Coal-fired power plants are large, what with the ash heaps and settling ponds for the parts of coal that aren't carbon. Their footprint also includes those sawed-off mountains and terraformed landscapes left behind.

Though some new coal plants do a better job of capturing the metals which fall out locally, and the sulfuric acid that can travel much farther downwind, capturing the invisible CO_2 and methane is talk rather than action. The so-called "clean coal" is, at present, just trapping more ash and sulfur from going up the smokestack.

Coal-fired power plants throughout the world are the major source of radioactive materials released to the environment. Thorium and uranium may only be a tiny fraction of the coal but we burn a lot of coal. These trace amounts add up to far more than the entire U.S. consumption of nuclear fuels for electricity. About 10% is carried aloft on fly ash, made airborne for us to breathe.

For all the talk of capturing CO_2 and storing it down deep somewhere, it looks like such technology will suck up 40% of the power generated. Let's see, retrofitting the 403 existing U.S. coal plants would create a need for another 269 coal plants. Big Coal's sales would go up 67%. (It's odd that no one ever mentions that.)

Figure 12. (*Photograph not shown.*) **This image shows a coal power plant with each part of the equipment labeled.**

The Zimmer power plant in Ohio was supposed to be a nuclear power station but, in the middle of construction, they switched to coal, abandoned the expensive containment dome next door, and now truck the ash to what will become the highest mountain in southern Ohio. Dumping the finer stuff in the air we breathe is "free."

Over a 50-year lifetime, each retrofitted 500-megawatt coal plant would produce a billion barrels of liquid CO_2 to be stored underground. No one knows how safe such storage would be. An earthquake could fracture the well's casing, allowing the stored CO_2 to escape. Clearly, this is experimental technology, not ready for prime time.

Such capture-and-storage talk may be another example of Big Coal trying to buy time by delaying action while, of course, getting yet another tax break from Congress to increase their record profits. Worst of all, even if practical, carbon capture and storage is not going to help very much for decades. I can think of better ways to spend our climate makeover money.

Figure 13. (*Aerial photograph of the Zimmer power plant not shown*). **In 1992, Zimmer set the world record for the most coal burned by a single generating unit, consuming four million tons of coal that year and venting thirteen million tons of CO_2.**

Figure 14. *Although this figure is not shown,* **it is a map of the United States with filled circles for coal plants and open circles for plants that had scrubbers; the open circles are few and far between. Most U.S. coal plants have not bothered to retrofit acid rain scrubbers. Even using low-sulfur coal, there is the problem of uranium and thorium in the fallout.**

Figure 15. Planned number of additional 500 mw coal-fired power plants before 2030. 2007 list at www.netl. doe.gov/coal/refshelf/ncp.pdf.

It's grossly irresponsible, but U.S. power companies are planning on doubling coal consumption by 2030. The U.S. Department of Energy 2007 report is entitled "Coal's Resurgence in Electric Power Generation." It contains not a single word about the impact on climate change.

Here's my subjective evaluation of coal.

	Ability to Expand	Public View	Down Side	Ups & Downs	Footprint	Storage Needed	Enough by 2020?
Coal as usual	huge	dirty	huge	no	very large	no	n/a
Coal but capture the CO_2	large	caution	storage burp, leaks	no	67% more coal	huge	very little

Geothermal

Hot Rock Energy is the most attractive possibility I know for quickly expanding an alternative energy source. Drill a 5 km deep well into hot granite, feed it water, harvest the rising steam to spin the usual old technology steam turbine, and you get electricity.

Though still in the demonstration project stage, it doesn't suffer from nuclear fears, 15-year permit delays, and 5-year construction times. It is an alternative energy solution that is C-free, doesn't fade as the sun sets, isn't fickle like the wind, doesn't require lots of space like biofuels, and doesn't require mining heavy metals that are radioactive. It's nice and steady without needing storage like hydro. It's immune to droughts.

There's nothing equivalent to coal trains and supertankers, not even trade deficits. There are no big questions hanging over it as with carbon capture and sequestration. A Hot Rock plant's footprint is no bigger than a two-story parking garage, with no runoff or air pollution or trucks hauling stuff—indeed, it would fit atop an old oil platform offshore or inside a large barn (except when cooling condensers are needed).

If you haven't heard of Hot Rock Geothermal it's because "geothermal" has an image problem rather like electric cars once had. It took the success of a 1997 gasoline-electric hybrid called the Prius to help people think ahead to an all electric car without defaulting to an image of a golf cart of limited utility.

Hearing geothermal, we often pop up a mental image of a sulfurous hot spring and wrinkle our nose. Too many people think that geothermal is just piping near surface hot water around to heat some buildings. This in turn makes you think that geothermal electrical power is a special case, nice for Iceland but not more generally. That, however, is your grandfather's notion of geothermal.

And a heat pump might be your father's. That's a different principle—the one that has long led people to build underground cellars to store food. A few feet down, the soil doesn't change temperature very much between winter and summer—and so by running a pipe through it, a heat pump can get it to cool water (which then cools air) in the summer and to provide heat in the winter. Just think of burying a sprinkler system without the sprinklers.

Many countries have good traditional geothermal resources that have yet to be exploited for generating electricity. Shallow wells are the most common. That's the "geothermal" implied in most mentions of alternative fuels.

Figure 16. (*Figure not shown.*) **This is a map of the US indicating the best areas for geothermal energy at 6 km depth (Blackwell, SMU 2004).**

The deep version now coming on stage is Hot Rock Energy with two or three adjacent wells. The idea is not to find hot water but rather hot rock that is dry. Then apply water to make steam. Though the U.S. has been lagging behind, the Hot Dry Rock concept was invented by scientists working at the Los Alamos National Laboratory in 1972.

Below the sedimentary layers is usually granite that's hot and dry. The farther down you drill into granite, the hotter it gets. Drilling 6 km below the surface is often sufficient to get 200°C (about 400°F, oven temperature) in the western U.S. The 100°C you'd get elsewhere works too, though it produces lesser amounts of electricity. (So you drill twice as many wells.) It usually takes the deep drilling technique used by the oil industry, which can go 7 km down.

Unlike the hot springs version of geothermal, you have to provide your own water. But after you prime the well, you just recirculate. What comes up as dry steam is pumped right back down again as water, via a second well nearby. It forces through cracks in the granite, heats back up, flashes into steam, shoots up the other well to the steam turbine, which spins the electrical generator, which feeds the great electrical grid, which keeps your domestic climate comfortable and your car recharged.

And how do these two wells connect? Such deep rock is already fractured along onion-like sheets, ancient planes of stress from bending. Mineralization has filled those cracks—but high pressure injection can force water into them, opening up passages. When the high pressure is released, many do not reseal. Sometimes the layers shift a little, and the noise from such little earthquakes serves to locate the newly opened crack. A map of the enhanced fracture zone is built up and, when it is several km across, the second (and sometimes a third) well is drilled into it to harvest the steam.

Gushers and mud eruptions don't come up out of the granite layers. If a sizeable earthquake fractures the well shaft, nothing happens—you just drill a new well nearby. That makes it much safer than drilling for oil or natural gas—or for storing CO_2.

Figure 17. (*Figure not shown.*) **This is a schematic cross-section of the earth showing a geothermal well and parts. Adapted from a 2006 MIT panel report.**

Hot Fractured Rock is drought proof and does not involve a perpetual stream of truck traffic as biofuels and fossil fuels do. It is perhaps the least demanding on industry, except for manufacturing enough tall drill rigs and training enough crews. What's above ground is mostly modern steam plant gear, manufactured in many countries and quite reliable. Operating it is well within the competence of all developing countries.

How extensive a resource is deep geothermal? For the U.S., the experts said it could yield a thousand times more than our present overall energy use. How polluting? Close to zero.

> Geothermal energy from EGS [enhanced geothermal systems = Hot Rock Energy with engineered fracturing] represents a large, indigenous resource that can provide base-load electric power and heat at a level that can have a major impact on the United States, while incurring minimal environmental impacts. With a reasonable investment in R&D, EGS could provide 100 GWe or more of cost-competitive generating capacity in the next fifty years. Further, EGS provides a secure source of power for the long term that would help protect America against economic instabilities resulting from fuel price fluctuations or supply disruptions. Most of the key technical requirements to make EGS work economically over a wide area of the country are in effect, with remaining goals easily within reach.
>
> —The MIT panel's 2006 report, entitled THE FUTURE OF GEOTHERMAL ENERGY: IMPACT OF ENHANCED GEOTHERMAL SYSTEMS (EGS) ON THE UNITED STATES IN THE 21ST CENTURY.

Hot Rock Energy, unfortunately, has been on the back burner for decades, along with most other alternative energy sources, kept there by cheap and dirty coal and the small budgets for government R&D. Nonetheless there have been various research projects around the world that have demonstrated the deep heat mining techniques over the last three decades.

Serious power production, however, is only getting started. In northern France, they are getting near commercial-sized yields at depths of 4 to 5 km. There are some projects in southern Germany, northern Switzerland, and Japan. Australia has quite a few proof-of-concept projects limping along on private money.

Figure 18. (*Photograph of a 125 mW two-well geothermal power station in the Philippines not shown.*) **A modern two-well geothermal plant, though using shallow wells and a heat exchanger (thus requiring 178 condensers) not needed for dry steam. Nothing is more than two stories high. It was operating 15 months after the ground-breaking ceremony in Lyete.**

The only hesitation that I have about Hot Rock Energy for 2020 is that there is simply not enough experience with it yet, compared with the experience of running hundreds of nuclear plants over 50 years time. Even though merely combining two tested techniques, steam power plant and deep drilling/stimulation, there will be beginners' errors to discover.

The capital costs per megawatt hour are similar to those of a new coal plant. They are mostly drilling costs. Indeed, until opening up those fractured rocks in the depths with the initial high pressure injection, you don't know what size power plant to order for the well head. That might cause private capital to hesitate, suggesting a proper role for government money to fund the initial steam farms.

As demand increases, improvements will likely drive down drilling costs. Hot Rock power plants could be rather simple compared to shallow geothermal plants today, where the well's output contains a lot of things that you wouldn't want to inflict on a steam turbine sensitive to corrosion. Protecting it means a heat exchanger and that requires a hundred condensers to cool the secondary fluid before it recirculates through the steam turbine.

So a lot of customizing attends most geothermal today. But continuing further down to 150°C dry granite would allow mass production techniques for simplified power plants. Each installation can tie up a deep drilling rig for the better part of a year, so we are going to need to clone those tall rigs.

If I were the 2020 czar, I'd place an order for twenty deep drilling rigs and fund 50 small heat farms in order to find the beginner's errors and the efficient combinations. We urgently need to know if Hot Rock Energy can be ramped up worldwide to thousands of units.

	Ability to Expand	Public View	Down Side	Ups & Downs	Footprint	Storage Needed	Enough by 2020?
Hot Rock Energy	huge	Just another well?	Month of small EQs?	very stable	very small	none	•••• to ••

Figure 19. (*Figure not shown.*) **This is world map of the location of nuclear reactors.**

Nuclear Power

Nuclear power generation is currently the major C-free energy source. It is over 50 years old, with an excellent safety record. It took three decades before the efficiency doubled. Unlike the other expandable C-free sources, the beginner's mistakes have already been made.

France has nearly quadrupled electricity production using 78% nuclear. It sounds as if nuclear power is cheap in such quantities. So much for arguments that nuclear power is expensive and that reform of our dependence on fossil fuels is impractical, can't be done, will damage the economy, and other excuses heard for maintaining the status quo. Why are so many countries denying themselves this C-free power source, while allowing growth in the hazardous fossil fuels?

Let me briefly discuss the downside of nuclear power. Our view of it—including my own view, until recently—tends to focus on fuel diversion into nuclear weapons or dirty bombs, reactor accidents, and the long term management of nuclear waste.

Some things have changed since the heyday of the antinuclear power movement in the 1970s. Since the Soviet Union's political meltdown, the cat may already be out of the bag for illicit nuclear fuel, so that avoiding additional reactors may not gain us much. New issues have also emerged. There is now the problem of suicide aircraft attacks with a full fuel load, which might scatter radioactivity downwind. There may be undergrounding solutions to this if the containment walls cannot be strengthened enough, but again, pause and note that additional reactors do not really increase this problem; there are sufficient targets already. Indeed, chemical plants of many types are vulnerable. In Bhopal, India, all it took was a gas leak at a pesticide plant to kill 8,000, injure a half million people, and contaminate an entire city.

There is much data on the safety and environmental problems of all the power sources. Nuclear electricity generation has proven far safer than fossil fuels of all sorts, and even safer than hydro. Dams fail. Per megawatt generated, the hydro fatality rate around the world is a hundred times higher than for nuclear electricity, largely because towns grow up on the old flood plains of the river.

That is startling enough. The production and storage of the fossil fuels is far more deadly. Counting only the major disasters (each big enough to kill 300 or more) between 1979 and 2006, there were more than 2,400 deaths from oil and 1,800 from natural gas. For coal—well, China alone has 6,000 miner deaths each year. Coal mining in the Ukraine is even more deadly.

The worldwide fatalities from nuclear power generation average out to one per year. For commercial nuclear power in all countries except one, there has never been a fatality. Two workers at a small, badly designed nuclear reprocessing plant in Japan were killed in 1999 in a flash of radioactivity. No radiation was released into the environment. It was not at a reactor site. The plant was a small specialty operation, not part of the commercial fuel cycle for electricity. They were processing a batch of fuel that had been enriched about four times more than allowed in any commercial nuclear power plant and—the fatal error—they didn't dilute it properly.

The Chernobyl reactor meltdown in 1986 is the only major meltdown accident with fatalities. The operators had violated the rules by disabling major safety features and, when the power surged and popped the lid, it had—incredible as it now seems—no containment to trap the radioactive gases. In the first few weeks, 32 Ukrainian staff and fire-fighters died.

Immediate fatalities are the only number for which easy comparisons can be made between energy sources. So that's less than 50 killed in the first 50 years of nuclear power reactors, all in one accident.

What about Three Mile Island in Pennsylvania? This accident occurred in 1979 (just 13 days after a star-laden movie opened, a nuclear reactor control room drama, The China Syndrome). The steam explosion killed no one. (No injuries, either.) Anyone living nearby got a one time dose less than what they got every day from the rocks beneath their house. The analysis of the TMI accident completely changed things: now reactors automatically shut down when trouble threatens and even experienced control room operators train 240 hours a year on simulators.

Delayed deaths are often difficult to attribute to a single cause, making comparisons between power plant types even more problematic. But for Chernobyl, we can safely say that another 25 died later, including nine children from thyroid cancer, but that the feared spike in leukemia did not materialize. Guessing farther out into delayed effects, perhaps 1% of the 200,000 workers exposed in the accident and during its cleanup may die from their radiation exposure, suggesting that 2,000 eventual deaths from the accident are possible.

Of course, mining coal has similar delayed effects, such as black lung disease. It involves many more people, including nonminers who simply live downwind of coal-burning power plants (in the U.S., that's almost everyone in the eastern half of the country) and breathe the ash and sulfur aerosols. Similarly, petroleum causes many delayed deaths from air pollution.

Figure 20. (*Figure not shown.*) **This is a map showing the number of deaths due to fatal respiratory disease and cancer as a result of fine particles from coal-fired power plants.**

Three Mile Island had a huge impact on the future of nuclear power in the U.S. and in other countries, creating a gap that has been largely filled by coal. No new nuclear plants have been started in the U.S. since 1978, though new nuclear plants are common enough in the rest of the world (31 countries now generate nuclear power).

We already know how to make safe nuclear reactors, even for the traditional style that uses water to both cool the reactor and to slow down the neutrons so they don't trigger additional, unwanted nuclear fissions. The danger here is that if the water leaks out or the pumps fail or the water boils off, the reaction speeds up and heats up. And so you get a meltdown of the core and a radioactive slag heap in the basement.

There is not an explosion as with a nuclear bomb. These are steam explosions, the same as when the lid of a pressure cooker pops and coats the kitchen with hot food. The reactor may also catch on fire. Any steam or ash that escapes from an overheated reactor can create radioactive fallout downwind (hence the containment dome, which kept Three Mile Island from being a problem offsite).

There is now, 50 years after the first nuclear power station was built, a much safer third generation reactor design that uses a water tower above the reactor. Water floods the reactor if it overheats, all without relying on pumps or operator actions.

Given that we need something surefire, we have no choice but to start expanding nuclear. Clearly, nuclear is capable of being a big part of the solution but I doubt whether permit obstacles will be hurdled in time.

For the long run of 2025, there's a design for a fourth generation reactor that doesn't rely on water for slowing down the neutrons. Like a fast-breeder reactor, it runs on fast neutrons and thus generates all manner of radioactive isotopes. It extracts 24 times as much energy from its fuel pellets as conventional reactors do. This leaves the fuel exhausted and unsuitable for bomb manufacture, licit or illicit. That may handle the traditional worries about fuel diversion into nuclear weapons, as we saw in 1974 when India illicitly made a bomb using a research reactor donated by Canada, with heavy water supplied by the U.S.

Furthermore, the fourth generation nuclear waste decays to ordinary levels in only centuries, not the 10,000-year time scale of the current nuclear waste, which has only had 4% of its binding energy extracted. The isotopes with the long half lives are broken up by the fast neutrons. So the time scale for managing stored nuclear waste shrinks by 96%.

In principle, we know how to solve the recycling aspect as well. Because the fourth generation plants are so much more efficient at extracting megawatts from uranium, they can run on the accumulated "spent" fuel of the last 50 years, solving our storage dilemma for high level nuclear waste. And when the fourth generation fuel's output drops off because of accumulating lighter elements that soak up neutrons, the fuel pebbles can be reprocessed on site rather than being shipped long distances (South Africa, for example, ships its spent fuel to France; oddly, U.S. commercial nuclear plants are not allowed to reprocess fuel, period.)

Much of our traditional rationale for opposing expansion of nuclear power (or even, as Germany plans to do, retiring all nuclear power plants) needs reevaluating. One of the great hurdles is the public's perennial confusion of nuclear electricity generation with nuclear bombs.

I have a suggestion: let us rename the fourth generation reactors as, say, binding energy extractors (BEEs) on the model of what medical equipment manufacturers did about 1979. Magnetic resonance imaging (MRI) avoided the long-standing scientific name, nuclear magnetic resonance (NMR), probably because the marketing people warned that including the word "nuclear" was a downer.

	Ability to Expand	Public View	Down Side	Ups & Downs	Footprint	Storage Needed	Enough by 2020?
Third Generation Nuclear	10X	caution	many	steady	mining	spent fuel	••• to ••

Renewables

Even if the developed countries bring their addiction under control, fossil fuel use has soared in the rest of the world. Unless we can provide an alternative to burning coal and oil, they won't change their ways fast enough. If we can convert them to using electric or compressed-air vehicles, then the issue becomes clean and cheap electrical power. In the long run, in-country deep geothermal might be best. For 2020, we need an additional, sure-fire strategy.

Figure 21. (*Figure not shown.*) **This schematic depicts the fact that it takes 15 wires to move 10 gigawatts with high-voltage AC, with losses of 10% over 1300 km, but it takes 4 wires to move 10 gigawatts with high-voltage DC, with losses of 10% over 2100 km.**

One way of solving this would be connecting all countries to regional power grids constructed with efficient DC transmission lines. It's an old technology commonly used for underwater and underground power lines; the aerial versions of DC are now used for power lines over 1,300 km long. (That's the length of the DC line from the Washington-Oregon border down to Los Angeles.) The longest DC transmission line in the world, completed in 1983, spans 1,700 km in the Congo. A 3,000 km DC line from Spain would cover all of northern Africa; one from Johannesburg would cover all of southern and eastern Africa plus Madagascar; one from Mexico could cover the Caribbean and into South America; one from Hong Kong or Australia could cover southeast Asia. This would enable nuclear power plants to be restricted to the present thirty-one countries. That's important if, rather than waiting for the fourth generation BEEs, we are to use the current generation reactor designs that incidentally yield bomb material. The architects' sensible plans for green buildings are long-term only, unable to help much in closing The Gap by 2020. It's the same for rapid transit. I'm inclined to encourage their growth but put the big money elsewhere for now. Our enthusiasm for long-term thinking is, sad to say, short-sighted given the 2020 emergency. What we do for 2020 will re-frame the problem, and new science and technology by then will hopefully show us a better path.

Figure 22. (*Photo not shown.*) **This photograph shows rooftops in Japan, virtually all covered with solar panels.**

Solar

The growth in solar panels since 1995 has been impressive. Solar currently provides about 1% of world electricity (much less in the U.S.). The photovoltaic version is especially suitable for off grid use in modernizing countries.

"Concentrating solar" heats a fluid that runs the usual steam turbine. It's being tried out in sunny Spain with mirrors that track the sun, keeping sunlight focused on the top of the tower. Both solar versions have unpredictable ups and downs as clouds move by. Solar is also used for direct (no electric middleman) heating, such as rooftop hot water heating.

Figure 23. *Photo not shown* **of a massive solar array near Seville, Spain.**

Hydropower

Hydropower is the current big item after nuclear in the C-free power portfolio and efficiency improvements can be made by modernizing turbines at existing dams. The number of dams in the world grew from 5,000 in 1950 to more than 45,000 today—that's two dams a day for 50 years—but it is close to saturated. Low rise and stream flow hydro are not going to be big players for 2020.

Biofuels

Biofuels, however green in small amounts, turn out to be a bad idea when scaled up. First, a serious drought (and in the coming decades, they are very likely) would impact both food supply and transportation fuel simultaneously. All prices would soar and the economy would stagger. As any investment advisor will tell you, spread your bets to avoid simultaneous downturns. Hydro power is already at risk in a drought and we should be adding drought resistant alternative power, not biofuels.

Biofuels in developing countries will also require more land clearing, reducing the world's carbon sinks and depleting poor tropical soils—as is already happening with "deforestation diesel." European subsidies prompted an enormous boom in planting palm oil trees in Indonesia and Malaysia. Cutting the forests and draining the swamps emitted far more carbon than could ever be saved from using biodiesel.

	Ability to Expand	Public View	Down Side	Ups & Downs	Footprint	Storage Needed	Enough by 2020?
Solar	lots	OK	few	night clouds	multi use	some	··
Wind	lots	ugly	noise, bird kills	fickle, unstable grid	multi use	some	··
Biofuels	compete with food	organic fuel	not C-neutral	drought	huge	some	·
Flow & Tidal Hydro	some	caution	ecology	drought	large		unlikely
High-Rise Hydro	nearly full	nice lakes	dam failure	drought	large	lakes	none

Diagnosis, Prognosis, Treatment

My father ran a medium sized insurance company in Kansas City in the 1950s, back when fire departments fought a lot more home and building fires than they currently do. When we were driving around town in my youth, he was always pointing out everyday situations that had gotten some people into big trouble. (Indeed the reason that there aren't as many fires these days is because society has incorporated into building codes and regular inspections what the fire chiefs and insurance executives had noticed over the years.)

Later, twenty years of talking shop with the neurosurgeons at my university every day helped to form my notions about when you can afford to wait and when prompt intervention is needed. James Lovelock, Jared Diamond, and I are all Ph.D physiologists who, during decades of medical research en route to looking at things more broadly, also learned to think like physicians.

Note that both my father and my neurosurgical colleagues were at the top of a pyramid of information. For example, few people in medicine 40 years ago really suspected how dangerous it was to ride a motorcycle without a helmet. But the neurosurgeons were the ones who had to cope with the broken heads and they realized the protection that the helmet conferred. This gave them the responsibility to do something, to try and prevent the ruined lives. So they pushed for better helmet designs and for laws that required helmets to be worn.

It used to be that you had to be a scientist in order to realize how serious the climate problem was becoming. You needed the view from the top of that pyramid of information. Now anyone who can read a book on global warming or watch a documentary film can gain much of that formerly rarified view.

Consider for a moment your present situation. You are now better informed about climate than thousands of your neighbors. What can you do with that knowledge? For myself, I recall the moment that led to this book—a sinking feeling when it finally became clear that there was a 2020 emergency developing. It felt like what many have described for the eve of a great war, where future plans have to be put on hold, superseded by civic duty. It becomes payback time. I realized, as Tim Flannery put it, that "in the years to come, this issue will dwarf all the others combined. It will become the only issue."

Even the well informed politicians, who understand the actions needed, will require reassurance that starting a major makeover won't result in budget conscious voters throwing them out of office at the next opportunity. My advice would be to set a good long term example for the kids and developing nations, but don't count on it solving our big 2020 problem in time. Remember that the real focus needs to be on political action to stop this runaway train, real soon.

Ranking the Major C-Free Candidates for Stopping Emissions Growth by 2020

Energy	Ability to Expand	Public View	Down Side	Ups & Downs	Footprint	Storage Needed	Enough by 2020?
Hot Rock Energy	huge	Just another well?	Year of small EQs?	very stable	very small	none	•••• to ••
Nuclear	10x	caution	many	steady	mining	spent fuel	••• to ••
Solar	lots	OK	few	night clouds	multi use	some	••
Wind	lots	ugly	noise, bird kills	fickle, unstable grid	multi use	some	••
Biofuels	compete with food	organic fuel	not C-neutral	drought	huge	some	•
High-Rise Hydro	nearly full	nice lakes	dam failure	drought	large	lakes	no
Coal but Capture the CO_2	large	caution	storage burp	steady	67% more coal	huge	no

Others	Ability to Expand	Public View	Down Side	Ups & Downs	Footprint	Storage Needed	Enough by 2020?
Plankton Iron Blooms	large	caution	side effects?	likely	fleet of ships	some	•
Plug-In	hybrid cars	large	very good	mining battery			•••
Compressed	air car	large	none yet	air tanks			•
Improve Efficiency	good	in favor	slow grind	—			•
Energy Diet	limited	a pain	easy to fail	yo-yo			no

Not comprehensive. Opinionated. Likely outdated (updates at http://global-fever.org/).

The International Law and Policy of Climate Change

Chapter Seven

The International Law and Policy of Climate Change

Cinnamon Pinfion Carlarne, *Good Climate Governance: Only a Fragmented System of International Law Away?*, 30 LAW & POLICY, 450, 451 (October 2008) [hereinafter 2008 Carlarne]:

Efforts to develop a system of global climate governance reveal a fundamental flaw that challenges not just international climate governance, but also the creation of an integrated system of international environmental governance. That flaw is the fragmentation—both issue compartmentalization and institutional disjunction—that defines international environmental law today. Fragmentation is the hallmark of modern international environmental law; it is both the key to its success and the possible pathway to its unraveling.

International environmental law is defined largely by and through the many multilateral environmental agreements (MEAs) that now exist. Rarely, if ever, do these MEAs cross issue-specific lines to address more cross-cutting questions, except at the periphery. Further, MEAs often impact other areas of international law, from human rights, to trade, to the law of the sea without directly or indirectly addressing these inter-linkages. The international legal regime for climate change epitomizes the fragmented nature of international environmental law, with both its positive and negative points.

I. Introduction to International Climate Change Policy

A. Establishment of the Intergovernmental Panel on Climate Change (IPCC)

Following a request by the UN General Assembly to the Executive Heads of the World Meteorological Organization (WMO) and the United Nations Environment Program (UNEP), the IPCC was established in 1988 by the 40th Session of the WMO Executive Council to provide independent scientific advice on the complex and important issue of climate change. The Panel was asked to prepare, based on available scientific information, a report on all aspects relevant to climate change and its impacts and to formulate realistic response strategies. The first assessment report of the IPCC, issued in late 1990, clearly stated that human activity was likely the cause of unprecedented warming. It served as the basis for negotiating the United Nations Framework Convention on Climate Change (UNFCCC).

Even after entry into force of the UNFCCC Convention, the IPCC remained the most important source for the Convention's scientific, technical and socio-economic information and continued to have a strong impact on its further development. The relationship between the UNFCCC and the IPCC has become a model for interaction between science and decisionmakers. Several attempts have been made to establish a similar assessment process for other environmental issues. Some of the most important principles of the IPCC are to be policy-relevant but not policy-prescriptive and to adhere to scientific integrity, objectivity, openness and transparency. This is achieved through a rigorous review process for all IPCC reports and an adoption and approval process that is open to all member governments.[1]

The initial mandate and terms of reference for the IPCC can be examined below.[2] The IPCC's fundamental ongoing requirements and goals include:

1. Undertaking and periodically updating the assessments of the available scientific information on climate change, the resulting environmental and socio-economic impacts, and various response options from near and long-term perspectives. (*e.g.*, WMO EC-XL, Res. 4; UNEP GC, decision SS II/3; WMO Cg 11, Res. 11; WMO EC-XLIV, Res.1; UNEP/GC, decision 21/9).

2. Evaluating the special problems of developing countries and small island states and ensuring their effective participation in IPCC work (*e.g.*, UNEP GC decision SSII/3; WMO 11th Cg, Res.11).

3. Providing scientific and socio-economic information and advice, initially for the development and negotiations of a UN Framework Convention on Climate Change (UNFCCC) and after entry into force of the Convention to continue to work closely with the UNFCCC and to provide scientific, technical and socio-economic information and advice (*e.g.*, UNEP GC decision 15.3; WMO EC-XLI, Res. 4; UNEP GC decision SSII/3; WMO EC-XLIV, Res. 1; WMO Cg 12, Res. 8; UNEP GC decision 18/20; WMO EC-L, Res. 3; WMO EC-LVI, Res. 1; WMO EC-LVII, Res.1; WMO Cg-XIV, Res. 8).

4. Reporting to the governing bodies of the parent organizations and communicating the results of the assessments broadly (*e.g.*, UNEP GC SSII/3; WMO 11th Cg Res. 11; WMO EC-XLIV Res. 1; WMO 12th Cg Res. 8; UNEP GC 18/20).

1988 Res. 4 (EC-XL) — INTERGOVERNMENTAL PANEL ON CLIMATE CHANGE

THE EXECUTIVE COUNCIL,

NOTING:

(1) Resolution 42/184 (UN General Assembly) — International co-operation in the field of the environment,

(2) Resolution 9 (Cg-X) — Global Climate Change,

(3) Paragraphs 3.2.0.4 and 3.2.0.5 of the general summary of the abridged report of Tenth Congress,

(4) Paragraphs 3.3 and 3.4 of the general summary of the abridged report of EC-XXXIX,

(5) The decision of the XIVth Session of the Governing Council of the United Nations Environment Programme,

---

1. http://www.ipcc.ch/pdf/10th-anniversary/anniversary-brochure.pdf.
2. http://www.ipcc.ch/meetings/session26/doc4.pdf.

BEING AWARE OF:

(1) The results of recent international meetings that produced an updated assessment of possible climate change and suggested actions towards developing policies for responding to climatic change,

(2) A need to:

(a) Maintain and develop further an efficient long-term monitoring system, making it possible to diagnose accurately the current state of the climate system, the trends, and the factors having an influence on climate,

(b) Improve our knowledge of the sources and sinks of the major radiatively important trace gases ("greenhouse gases"), and develop more reliable methods for predicting their future atmospheric concentrations,

(c) Promote research aimed at closing gaps in our ability to understand and predict the climate system, including reliable projections of the regional distribution of the expected climatic change,

CONSIDERING:

(1) That there is a growing international concern about the possible socio-economic consequences of the increasing atmospheric concentrations of radiatively active trace substances (greenhouse gases and particulates),

(2) That several nations have undertaken scientific assessments of this issue during the last few years,

(3) The current and potential involvement of national meteorological and hydrological agencies in comprehensive integrated national and regional studies of the consequences of a climatic change on natural and human eco-systems, taking into account sociological and economic factors, and in developing strategies for adjustment to a climatic change, especially regarding agriculture and water resources,

CONSIDERING FURTHER that there is an urgent need to evaluate to what extent a climatic change can be delayed by appropriate national/international actions,

AGREES that an Intergovernmental Panel on Climate Change should be established,

AGREES FURTHER:

(1) That the activities of the Intergovernmental Panel on Climate Change (IPCC) should be aimed at (i) assessing the scientific information that is related to the various components of the climate change issue such as emissions of major greenhouse gases and modification of the Earth's radiation balance resulting therefrom, and that needed to enable the environmental and socio-economic consequences of climate change to be evaluated; and (ii) formulating realistic response strategies for the management of the climate change issue,

(2) That the panel should report on its activities to the governing bodies of WMO and UNEP,

RECOMMENDS:

(1) That, while the choice of the nominated representative to the IPCC is the sole prerogative of sovereign governments, they take into consideration the importance of such representation being at as high a level as possible and include persons knowledgeable of science, environment and related policy issues;

(2) That, for example, should the nominee be from the meteorological/hydrological service, he/she should preferably be at the level of the Permanent Representative of the country with WMO;

(3) That to ensure adequate expert advice to the nominated representative, the governments consider appointing advisor(s) to the representative as needed, who should also be at as high a level as possible.

B. The United Nations Framework Convention on Climate Change (UNFCCC)

Signed at the Earth Summit in 1992, the United Nations Framework Convention on Climate Change (UNFCCC) is an international treaty aimed at evaluating what can be done to reduce global warming and to cope with its inevitable temperature increases. Beginning in 1997, a number of nations approved an addition to the treaty: the Kyoto Protocol, which has more powerful and legally binding emission reduction requirements. The UNFCCC secretariat continues to be the primary support center for institutions involved in international climate change policy.[3]

1. The Kyoto Protocol

The Kyoto Protocol[4] is an optional addition to the UNFCCC. The Kyoto Protocol was adopted in Kyoto, Japan, on December 11, 1997 and entered into force on February 16, 2005. 182 Parties of the Convention have ratified its Protocol to date. The detailed rules for the implementation of the Protocol were adopted at COP 7 in Marrakesh in 2001, and are called the "Marrakesh Accords."

The major feature of the Kyoto Protocol is that it sets binding targets for 37 industrialized countries and the European Community for reducing greenhouse gas (GHG) emissions. These amount to an average of five percent reduction below 1990 levels over the five-year period 2008–2012. The major distinction between the Protocol and the Convention is that while the Convention encouraged industrialized countries to stabilize GHG emissions, the Protocol commits them to do so.

Recognizing that developed countries are principally responsible for the current high levels of GHG emissions in the atmosphere as a result of more than 150 years of industrial activity, the Protocol places a heavier burden on developed nations under the principle of "common but differentiated responsibilities."

The Kyoto Protocol is generally seen as ineffective in practice but an important first symbolic step towards a truly global emission reduction regime to stabilize GHG emissions. To many, the Protocol also provides the essential architecture for any future international agreement on climate change.

By the end of the first commitment period of the Kyoto Protocol in 2012, a new international framework must be negotiated and ratified to deliver the stringent emission reductions the Intergovernmental Panel on Climate Change (IPCC) has clearly indicated are needed.

2. The Bali Roadmap

The Bali Roadmap outlines a two-year process for the creation of a legally binding international climate agreement to follow the Kyoto Protocol after its expiration in 2012. At the 2007

---

3. http://unfccc.int.
4. *See* http://unfccc.int/kyoto_protocol/.

Climate Change Conference in Bali, Parties to the UNFCCC decided to launch formal negotiations on a strengthened international agreement on climate change. These negotiations are scheduled to culminate at 2009 at the Climate Change Conference in Copenhagen. To facilitate this process, a subsidiary body under the UNFCC was set up, named the Ad Hoc Working Group on Long-term Cooperative Action under the Convention (AWG-LCA).

Mr. Rachmat Witoelar, President, U.N. Climate Change Conference, The Bali Roadmap, address to closing plenary, December 15, 2007:[5]

Closing of Joint High-Level Segment, Bali, 15 December 2007

I am delighted to say that we have finally achieved the breakthrough the world has been waiting for: the Bali Roadmap! The decisions we have taken in Bali together create the world's road map to a secure climate future. The governments assembled here have responded decisively in the face of new scientific evidence and significant advances in our thinking to collectively envision, and chart, a new climate-secure course for humanity.

The Bali Roadmap consists of a number of forward-looking decisions adopted today. These decisions represent various tracks that are essential to reaching a secure climate future.

At this meeting we have launched a new negotiation process, designed to tackle climate change, with the aim of completing this by 2009.

We have also addressed the AWG negotiations, setting a 2009 deadline, firmly launched the Adaptation Fund, and defined the scope and content of the Art. 9 review of the Kyoto Protocol—all of these on the Kyoto track.

Similarly we have charted a course forward on reducing emissions from deforestation and on technology transfer, including an exciting new strategic programme. As we begin our work for the future, we should not forget that we are only a few weeks away from the start of the first commitment period. And whilst we have made an excellent start in Bali towards a secure climate future, we must also ensure that existing commitments are fully implemented. The road from Bali to Poznan and Copenhagen must be paved not with good intentions but concrete actions and rigorous implementation.

The Bali Roadmap is a testament to the remarkable spirit of cooperation that Parties have displayed in these last two weeks. It is also a tribute to the solidarity with which we have come together to address climate change—the defining human development challenge of the 21st century.

The world was expecting us to show true vision and leadership and I have no doubt that we have proven equal to that task. It is said that leaders are those who create the future. Here in Bali, you have demonstrated the leadership needed to create a sustainable future for us all.

C. The 2007 Nobel Peace Prize: Al Gore and the IPCC

The 2007 Nobel Peace Prize was jointly awarded to Al Gore and the IPCC for spreading awareness of and encouraging solutions to global climate change.

Albert Arnold Gore, Jr., is perhaps best known for serving as the forty-fifth Vice President of the United States from 1993–2000. Prior to his role in the Clinton-Gore Administration, Gore

---

5. http://unfccc.int/meetings/cop_13/.

served as an Army journalist in Vietnam, a member of the U.S. House of Representatives, and a U.S. Senator.

Al Gore became interested in climate change in 1967 after taking a course at Harvard from pioneering climate scientist and oceanographer Roger Revelle. He took his passion for the environment to Congress, inviting Professor Revelle to be the leadoff witness at the first congressional hearing on climate change. While a Senator, Gore wrote the 1992 bestselling book, *Earth in the Balance: Ecology and the Human Spirit*, outlining his agenda for environmental reform.

After a controversial failed attempt at the Presidency in 2000, Gore turned his attention full time to the climate crisis. In 2004, Gore launched the sustainable investment management company, Generation Investment Management in London, with former Goldman Sachs executive, David Blood. In 2006, Gore founded The Alliance for Climate Protection, a nonpartisan effort whose mission is "to persuade the American people—and people elsewhere in the world—of the importance and urgency of adopting and implementing effective and comprehensive solutions for the climate crisis." The Alliance is focused on "undertaking an unprecedented mass persuasion exercise based on scientific facts."[6] The Alliance is responsible for creating the "We Campaign," a public outreach and media effort dedicated to achieving 100 percent clean energy within ten years.[7]

Gore also starred in the 2006 documentary film, "An Inconvenient Truth," which won two Academy Awards, and showcased his lifelong journey to educate leaders and citizens around the world about the climate crisis. Building off of the public's warm reception of the film, Gore founded The Climate Project, a group that has trained over two thousand volunteers to give his public presentations about climate change.

Below are the acceptance speeches of both Gore and R.K. Pachauri, the IPCC Chairman.

1. Al Gore Nobel Peace Prize Lecture, Oslo, December 10, 2007[8]

Your Majesties, Your Royal Highnesses, Honorable Members of the Norwegian Nobel Committee, Excellencies, Ladies and Gentlemen.

I have a purpose here today. It is a purpose I have tried to serve for many years. I have prayed that God would show me a way to accomplish it.

Sometimes, without warning, the future knocks on our door with a precious and painful vision of what might be. One hundred and nineteen years ago, a wealthy inventor read his own obituary, mistakenly published years before his death. Wrongly believing the inventor had just died, a newspaper printed a harsh judgment of his life's work, unfairly labeling him "The Merchant of Death" because of his invention—dynamite. Shaken by this condemnation, the inventor made a fateful choice to serve the cause of peace.

Seven years later, Alfred Nobel created this prize and the others that bear his name.

Seven years ago tomorrow, I read my own political obituary in a judgment that seemed to me harsh and mistaken—if not premature. But that unwelcome verdict also brought a precious if painful gift: an opportunity to search for fresh new ways to serve my purpose.

Unexpectedly, that quest has brought me here. Even though I fear my words cannot match this moment, I pray what I am feeling in my heart will be communicated clearly enough that those who hear me will say, "We must act."

---

6. http://www.climateprotect.org/about/alliance.
7. http://wecansolveit.org/.
8. http://nobelprize.org.

The distinguished scientists with whom it is the greatest honor of my life to share this award have laid before us a choice between two different futures—a choice that to my ears echoes the words of an ancient prophet: "Life or death, blessings or curses. Therefore, choose life, that both thou and thy seed may live."

We, the human species, are confronting a planetary emergency—a threat to the survival of our civilization that is gathering ominous and destructive potential even as we gather here. But there is hopeful news as well: we have the ability to solve this crisis and avoid the worst—though not all—of its consequences, if we act boldly, decisively and quickly.

However, despite a growing number of honorable exceptions, too many of the world's leaders are still best described in the words Winston Churchill applied to those who ignored Adolf Hitler's threat: "They go on in strange paradox, decided only to be undecided, resolved to be irresolute, adamant for drift, solid for fluidity, all powerful to be impotent."

So today, we dumped another 70 million tons of global-warming pollution into the thin shell of atmosphere surrounding our planet, as if it were an open sewer. And tomorrow, we will dump a slightly larger amount, with the cumulative concentrations now trapping more and more heat from the sun.

As a result, the earth has a fever. And the fever is rising. The experts have told us it is not a passing affliction that will heal by itself. We asked for a second opinion.

And a third. And a fourth. And the consistent conclusion, restated with increasing alarm, is that something basic is wrong.

We are what is wrong, and we must make it right.

Last September 21, as the Northern Hemisphere tilted away from the sun, scientists reported with unprecedented distress that the North Polar ice cap is "falling off a cliff." One study estimated that it could be completely gone during summer in less than 22 years. Another new study, to be presented by U.S. Navy researchers later this week, warns it could happen in as little as 7 years.

Seven years from now.

In the last few months, it has been harder and harder to misinterpret the signs that our world is spinning out of kilter. Major cities in North and South America, Asia and Australia are nearly out of water due to massive droughts and melting glaciers. Desperate farmers are losing their livelihoods. Peoples in the frozen Arctic and on low-lying Pacific islands are planning evacuations of places they have long called home. Unprecedented wildfires have forced a half million people from their homes in one country and caused a national emergency that almost brought down the government in another. Climate refugees have migrated into areas already inhabited by people with different cultures, religions, and traditions, increasing the potential for conflict. Stronger storms in the Pacific and Atlantic have threatened whole cities. Millions have been displaced by massive flooding in South Asia, Mexico, and 18 countries in Africa. As temperature extremes have increased, tens of thousands have lost their lives. We are recklessly burning and clearing our forests and driving more and more species into extinction. The very web of life on which we depend is being ripped and frayed.

We never intended to cause all this destruction, just as Alfred Nobel never intended that dynamite be used for waging war. He had hoped his invention would promote human progress. We shared that same worthy goal when we began burning massive quantities of coal, then oil and methane.

Even in Nobel's time, there were a few warnings of the likely consequences. One of the very first winners of the Prize in chemistry worried that, "We are evaporating our coal mines into the air." After performing 10,000 equations by hand, Svante Arrhenius calculated that the earth's average temperature would increase by many degrees if we doubled the amount of CO_2 in the atmosphere.

Seventy years later, my teacher, Roger Revelle, and his colleague, Dave Keeling, began to precisely document the increasing CO_2 levels day by day.

But unlike most other forms of pollution, CO_2 is invisible, tasteless, and odorless—which has helped keep the truth about what it is doing to our climate out of sight and out of mind. Moreover, the catastrophe now threatening us is unprecedented—and we often confuse the unprecedented with the improbable.

We also find it hard to imagine making the massive changes that are now necessary to solve the crisis. And when large truths are genuinely inconvenient, whole societies can, at least for a time, ignore them. Yet as George Orwell reminds us: "Sooner or later a false belief bumps up against solid reality, usually on a battlefield."

In the years since this prize was first awarded, the entire relationship between humankind and the earth has been radically transformed. And still, we have remained largely oblivious to the impact of our cumulative actions.

Indeed, without realizing it, we have begun to wage war on the earth itself. Now, we and the earth's climate are locked in a relationship familiar to war planners: "Mutually assured destruction."

More than two decades ago, scientists calculated that nuclear war could throw so much debris and smoke into the air that it would block life-giving sunlight from our atmosphere, causing a "nuclear winter." Their eloquent warnings here in Oslo helped galvanize the world's resolve to halt the nuclear arms race.

Now science is warning us that if we do not quickly reduce the global warming pollution that is trapping so much of the heat our planet normally radiates back out of the atmosphere, we are in danger of creating a permanent "carbon summer."

As the American poet Robert Frost wrote, "Some say the world will end in fire; some say in ice." Either, he notes, "would suffice."

But neither need be our fate. It is time to make peace with the planet.

We must quickly mobilize our civilization with the urgency and resolve that has previously been seen only when nations mobilized for war. These prior struggles for survival were won when leaders found words at the 11th hour that released a mighty surge of courage, hope and readiness to sacrifice for a protracted and mortal challenge.

These were not comforting and misleading assurances that the threat was not real or imminent; that it would affect others but not ourselves; that ordinary life might be lived even in the presence of extraordinary threat; that Providence could be trusted to do for us what we would not do for ourselves.

No, these were calls to come to the defense of the common future. They were calls upon the courage, generosity and strength of entire peoples, citizens of every class and condition who were ready to stand against the threat once asked to do so. Our enemies in those times calculated that free people would not rise to the challenge; they were, of course, catastrophically wrong.

Now comes the threat of climate crisis—a threat that is real, rising, imminent, and universal. Once again, it is the 11th hour. The penalties for ignoring this challenge are immense and growing, and at some near point would be unsustainable and unrecoverable. For now we still have the power to choose our fate, and the remaining question is only this: Have we the will to act vigorously and in time, or will we remain imprisoned by a dangerous illusion?

Mahatma Gandhi awakened the largest democracy on earth and forged a shared resolve with what he called "Satyagraha"—or "truth force."

In every land, the truth—once known—has the power to set us free.

Truth also has the power to unite us and bridge the distance between "me" and "we," creating the basis for common effort and shared responsibility.

There is an African proverb that says, "If you want to go quickly, go alone. If you want to go far, go together." We need to go far, quickly.

We must abandon the conceit that individual, isolated, private actions are the answer. They can and do help. But they will not take us far enough without collective action. At the same time, we must ensure that in mobilizing globally, we do not invite the establishment of ideological conformity and a new lock-step "ism."

That means adopting principles, values, laws, and treaties that release creativity and initiative at every level of society in multifold responses originating concurrently and spontaneously.

This new consciousness requires expanding the possibilities inherent in all humanity. The innovators who will devise a new way to harness the sun's energy for pennies or invent an engine that's carbon negative may live in Lagos or Mumbai or Montevideo. We must ensure that entrepreneurs and inventors everywhere on the globe have the chance to change the world.

When we unite for a moral purpose that is manifestly good and true, the spiritual energy unleashed can transform us. The generation that defeated fascism throughout the world in the 1940s found, in rising to meet their awesome challenge, that they had gained the moral authority and long-term vision to launch the Marshall Plan, the United Nations, and a new level of global cooperation and foresight that unified Europe and facilitated the emergence of democracy and prosperity in Germany, Japan, Italy and much of the world. One of their visionary leaders said, "It is time we steered by the stars and not by the lights of every passing ship."

In the last year of that war, you gave the Peace Prize to a man from my hometown of 2000 people, Carthage, Tennessee. Cordell Hull was described by Franklin Roosevelt as the "Father of the United Nations." He was an inspiration and hero to my own father, who followed Hull in the Congress and the U.S. Senate and in his commitment to world peace and global cooperation.

My parents spoke often of Hull, always in tones of reverence and admiration. Eight weeks ago, when you announced this prize, the deepest emotion I felt was when I saw the headline in my hometown paper that simply noted I had won the same prize that Cordell Hull had won. In that moment, I knew what my father and mother would have felt were they alive.

Just as Hull's generation found moral authority in rising to solve the world crisis caused by fascism, so too can we find our greatest opportunity in rising to solve the climate crisis. In the Kanji characters used in both Chinese and Japanese, "crisis" is written with two symbols, the first meaning "danger," the second "opportunity." By facing and removing the danger of the climate crisis, we have the opportunity to gain the moral authority and vision to vastly increase our own capacity to solve other crises that have been too long ignored.

We must understand the connections between the climate crisis and the afflictions of poverty, hunger, HIV-Aids and other pandemics. As these problems are linked, so too must be their solutions. We must begin by making the common rescue of the global environment the central organizing principle of the world community.

Fifteen years ago, I made that case at the "Earth Summit" in Rio de Janeiro. Ten years ago, I presented it in Kyoto. This week, I will urge the delegates in Bali to adopt a bold mandate for a treaty that establishes a universal global cap on emissions and uses the market in emissions trading to efficiently allocate resources to the most effective opportunities for speedy reductions.

This treaty should be ratified and brought into effect everywhere in the world by the beginning of 2010—two years sooner than presently contemplated. The pace of our response must be accelerated to match the accelerating pace of the crisis itself.

Heads of state should meet early next year to review what was accomplished in Bali and take personal responsibility for addressing this crisis. It is not unreasonable to ask, given the gravity of our circumstances, that these heads of state meet every three months until the treaty is completed.

We also need a moratorium on the construction of any new generating facility that burns coal without the capacity to safely trap and store carbon dioxide.

And most important of all, we need to put a price on carbon—with a CO_2 tax that is then rebated back to the people, progressively, according to the laws of each nation, in ways that shift the burden of taxation from employment to pollution. This is by far the most effective and simplest way to accelerate solutions to this crisis.

The world needs an alliance—especially of those nations that weigh heaviest in the scales where earth is in the balance. I salute Europe and Japan for the steps they've taken in recent years to meet the challenge, and the new government in Australia, which has made solving the climate crisis its first priority.

But the outcome will be decisively influenced by two nations that are now failing to do enough: the United States and China. While India is also growing fast in importance, it should be absolutely clear that it is the two largest CO_2 emitters—most of all, my own country—that will need to make the boldest moves, or stand accountable before history for their failure to act.

Both countries should stop using the other's behavior as an excuse for stalemate and instead develop an agenda for mutual survival in a shared global environment.

These are the last few years of decision, but they can be the first years of a bright and hopeful future if we do what we must. No one should believe a solution will be found without effort, without cost, without change. Let us acknowledge that if we wish to redeem squandered time and speak again with moral authority, then these are the hard truths:

The way ahead is difficult. The outer boundary of what we currently believe is feasible is still far short of what we actually must do. Moreover, between here and there, across the unknown, falls the shadow.

That is just another way of saying that we have to expand the boundaries of what is possible. In the words of the Spanish poet, Antonio Machado, "Pathwalker, there is no path. You must make the path as you walk."

We are standing at the most fateful fork in that path. So I want to end as I began, with a vision of two futures—each a palpable possibility—and with a prayer that we will see with vivid clarity the necessity of choosing between those two futures, and the urgency of making the right choice now.

The great Norwegian playwright, Henrik Ibsen, wrote, "One of these days, the younger generation will come knocking at my door."

The future is knocking at our door right now. Make no mistake, the next generation will ask us one of two questions. Either they will ask: "What were you thinking; why didn't you act?"

Or they will ask instead: "How did you find the moral courage to rise and successfully resolve a crisis that so many said was impossible to solve?"

We have everything we need to get started, save perhaps political will, but political will is a renewable resource.

So let us renew it, and say together: "We have a purpose. We are many. For this purpose we will rise, and we will act."

2. Acceptance Speech for the Nobel Peace Prize Awarded to the Intergovernmental Panel on Climate Change (IPCC), Delivered by R.K. Pachauri, Chairman, IPCC, Oslo, December 10, 2007 (excerpt)[9]

The IPCC produces key scientific material that is of the highest relevance to policymaking, and is agreed [to] word-by-word by all governments, from the most skeptical to the most confident. This difficult process is made possible by the tremendous strength of the underlying scientific and technical material included in the IPCC reports.

The Panel was established in 1988 through a resolution of the UN General Assembly. One of its clauses was significant in having stated, "Noting with concern that the emerging evidence indicates that continued growth in atmospheric concentrations of 'greenhouse' gases could produce global warming with an eventual rise in sea levels, the effects of which could be disastrous for mankind if timely steps are not taken at all levels." This means that almost two decades ago the UN was acutely conscious of the possibility of disaster consequent on climate change through increases in sea levels. Today we know much more, which provides greater substance to that concern.

. . . .

Honouring the IPCC through the grant of the Nobel Peace Prize in 2007 in essence can be seen as a clarion call for the protection of the earth as it faces the widespread impacts of climate change. The choice of the Panel for this signal honour is, in our view, an acknowledgement of three important realities, which can be summed up as:

1) The power and promise of collective scientific endeavour, which, as demonstrated by the IPCC, can reach across national boundaries and political differences in the pursuit of objectives defining the larger good of human society.

2) The importance of the role of knowledge in shaping public policy and guiding global affairs for the sustainable development of human society.

3) An acknowledgement of the threats to stability and human security inherent in the impacts of a changing climate and, therefore, the need for developing an effective rationale for timely and adequate action to avoid such threats in the future.

These three realities encircle an important truth that must guide global action involving the entire human race in the future. Coming as I do from India, a land which gave birth to civilization in ancient times and where much of the earlier tradition and wisdom guides actions even in modern times, the philosophy of "Vasudhaiva Kutumbakam," which means the whole universe is one family, must dominate global efforts to protect the global commons. This principle is crucial to the maintenance of peace and order today as it would be increasingly in the years ahead, and as the well-known columnist and author Thomas Friedman has highlighted in his book THE WORLD IS FLAT.

Neglect in protecting our heritage of natural resources could prove extremely harmful for the human race and for all species that share common space on planet earth. Indeed, there are many lessons in human history which provide adequate warning about the chaos and destruction that could take place if we remain guilty of myopic indifference to the progressive erosion and decline of nature's resources. Much has been written, for instance, about the Maya civilization, which flourished during 250–950 AD, but collapsed largely as a result of serious and prolonged drought. Even earlier, some 4000 years ago a number of well-known Bronze Age cultures also crumbled extending from the Mediterranean to the Indus Valley, including the civilizations

---

9. http://www.ipcc.ch/graphics/speeches.

which had blossomed in Mesopotamia. More recent examples of societies that collapsed or faced chaos on account of depletion or degradation of natural resources include the Khmer Empire in South East Asia, Easter Island, and several others.

Changes in climate have historically determined periods of peace as well as conflict. The recent work of David Zhang has, in fact, highlighted the link between temperature fluctuations, reduced agricultural production, and the frequency of warfare in Eastern China over the last millennium. Further, in recent years several groups have studied the link between climate and security.

These have raised the threat of dramatic population migration, conflict, and war over water and other resources as well as a realignment of power among nations. Some also highlight the possibility of rising tensions between rich and poor nations, health problems caused particularly by water shortages, and crop failures as well as concerns over nuclear proliferation.

One of the most significant aspects of the impacts of climate change, which has unfortunately not received adequate attention from scholars in the social sciences, relates to the equity implications of changes that are occurring and are likely to occur in the future. In general, the impacts of climate change on some of the poorest and the most vulnerable communities in the world could prove extremely unsettling. And, given the inadequacy of capacity, economic strength, and institutional capabilities characterizing some of these communities, they would remain extremely vulnerable to the impacts of climate change and may, therefore, actually see a decline in their economic condition, with a loss of livelihoods and opportunities to maintain even subsistence levels of existence.

Since the IPCC by its very nature is an organization that does not provide assessments that are policy prescriptive, it has not provided any directions on how conflicts inherent in the social implications of the impacts of climate change could be avoided or contained. Nevertheless, THE FOURTH ASSESSMENT REPORT provides scientific findings that other scholars can study and arrive at some conclusions on in relation to peace and security. Several parts of our reports have much information and knowledge that would be of considerable value for individual researchers and think tanks dealing with security issues as well as governments that necessarily are concerned with some of these matters. It would be particularly relevant to conduct in-depth analysis of risks to security among the most vulnerable sectors and communities impacted by climate change across the globe.

Peace can be defined as security and the secure access to resources that are essential for living. A disruption in such access could prove disruptive of peace. In this regard, climate change will have several implications, as numerous adverse impacts are expected for some populations in terms of:

- access to clean water,
- access to sufficient food,
- stable health conditions,
- ecosystem resources,
- security of settlements.

Climate change is expected to exacerbate current stresses on water resources. On a regional scale, mountain snowpack, glaciers, and small ice caps play a crucial role in fresh water availability. Widespread mass losses from glaciers and reductions in snow cover over recent decades are projected to accelerate throughout the 21st century, reducing water availability, hydropower potential, and the changing seasonality of flows in regions supplied by meltwater from major mountain ranges (*e.g.*, Hindu-Kush, Himalaya, Andes), where more than one-sixth of the world's population currently lives. There is also high confidence that many semi-arid areas (*e.g.*, the Mediterranean Basin, western United States, southern Africa, and northeastern Brazil) will suffer a decrease in water resources due to climate change. In Africa by 2020, between 75 and 250 million people are projected to be exposed to increased water stress due to climate change.

Climate change could further adversely affect food security and exacerbate malnutrition at low latitudes, especially in seasonally dry and tropical regions, where crop productivity is projected to decrease for even small local temperature increases (1–2°C). By 2020, in some African countries, yields from rain-fed agriculture could be reduced by up to 50%. Agricultural production, including access to food, in many African countries is projected to be severely compromised.

The health status of millions of people is projected to be affected through, for example, increases in malnutrition; increased deaths, diseases, and injury due to extreme weather events; increased burden of diarrheal diseases; increased frequency of cardio-respiratory diseases due to higher concentrations of ground-level ozone in urban areas related to climate change; and the altered spatial distribution of some infectious diseases.

Climate change is likely to lead to some irreversible impacts on biodiversity. There is medium confidence that approximately 20%–30% of species assessed so far are likely to be at increased risk of extinction if increases in global average warming exceed 1.5–2.5 degrees C, relative to 1980–99. As global average temperature exceeds about 3.5 degrees C, model projections suggest significant extinctions (40%–70% of species assessed) around the globe. These changes, if they were to occur, would have serious effects on the sustainability of several ecosystems and the services they provide to human society.

As far as security of human settlements is concerned, vulnerabilities to climate change are generally greater in certain high-risk locations, particularly coastal and riverine areas, and areas whose economies are closely linked with climate-sensitive resources. Where extreme weather events become more intense or more frequent with climate change, the economic and social costs of those events will increase.

Some regions are likely to be especially affected by climate change.

- The Arctic, because of the impacts of high rates of projected warming on natural systems and human communities,
- Africa, because of low adaptive capacity and projected climate change impacts,
- Small islands, where there is high exposure of population and infrastructure to projected climate change impacts,
- Asian and African mega deltas, due to large populations and high exposure to sea level rise, storm surges, and river flooding.

THE IPCC FOURTH ASSESSMENT REPORT concludes that non-climate stresses can increase vulnerability to climate change by reducing resilience and can also reduce adaptive capacity because of resource deployment towards competing needs. Vulnerable regions face multiple stresses that affect their exposure and sensitivity to various impacts as well as their capacity to adapt. These stresses arise from, for example, current climate hazards, poverty, and unequal access to resources, food insecurity, trends in economic globalization, conflict, and incidence of diseases such as HIV/AIDS.

Within other areas, even those with high incomes, some people (such as the poor, young children, and the elderly) can be particularly at risk.

Migration and movement of people is a particularly critical source of potential conflict. Migration, usually temporary and often from rural to urban areas, is a common response to calamities such as floods and famines. But as in the case of vulnerability to the impacts of climate change, where multiple stresses could be at work on account of a diversity of causes and conditions, so also in the case of migration, individuals may have multiple motivations and they could be displaced by multiple factors.

Another issue of extreme concern is the finding that anthropogenic factors could lead to some impacts that are abrupt or irreversible, depending on the rate and magnitude of climate change. For instance, partial loss of ice sheets on polar land could imply metres of sea level rise, major changes in coastlines, and inundation of low-lying areas, with greatest effects in river deltas and low-lying islands.

Global average warming above about 4.5°C relative to 1980–99 (about 5 degrees C above pre-industrial) would imply:

- Projected decreases of precipitation by up to 20% in many dry tropical and subtropical areas.
- Expected mass loss of Greenland's ice if sustained over many centuries (based on all current global climate system models assessed) leading to sea level rise up to 4 metres and flooding of shorelines on every continent.

The implications of these changes, if they were to occur, would be grave and disastrous. However, it is within the reach of human society to meet these threats. The impacts of climate change can be limited by suitable adaptation measures and stringent mitigation of greenhouse gas emissions.

Societies have a long record of adapting to the impacts of weather and climate.

But climate change poses novel risks often outside the range of experience, such as impacts related to drought, heat waves, accelerated glacier retreat, and hurricane intensity. These impacts will require adaptive responses such as investments in storm protection and water supply infrastructure, as well as community health services. Adaptation measures essential to reduce such vulnerability are seldom undertaken in response to climate change alone but can be integrated within, for example, water resource management, coastal defence, and risk-reduction strategies. The global community needs to coordinate a far more proactive effort towards implementing adaptation measures in the most vulnerable communities and systems in the world.

Adaptation is essential to address the impacts resulting from the warming which is already unavoidable due to past emissions. But, adaptation alone is not expected to cope with all the projected effects of climate change, and especially not in the long run as most impacts increase in magnitude.

There is substantial potential for the mitigation of global greenhouse gas emissions over the coming decades that could offset the projected growth of global emissions or reduce emissions below current levels. There are multiple drivers for actions that reduce emissions of greenhouse gases, and they can produce multiple benefits at the local level in terms of economic development and poverty alleviation, employment, energy security, and local environmental protection.

The Fourth Assessment Report has assessed the costs of mitigation in the coming decades for a number of scenarios of stabilization of the concentration of these gases and associated average global temperature increases at equilibrium. A stabilization level of 445–590 ppm of CO_2 equivalent, which corresponds to a global average temperature increase above pre-industrial at equilibrium (using best estimate climate sensitivity) of around 2.0–2.4 degrees C would lead to a reduction in average annual GDP growth rate of less than 0.12% up to 2030 and beyond up to 2050. Essentially, the range of global GDP reduction with the least-cost trajectory assessed for this level of stabilization would be less than 3% in 2030 and less than 5.5% in 2050. Some important characteristics of this stabilization scenario need careful consideration:

- For a CO_2-equivalent concentration at stabilization of 445–490 ppm, CO_2 emissions would need to peak during the period 2000–15 and decline thereafter. We, therefore, have a short window of time to bring about a reduction in global emissions if we wish to limit temperature increase to around 2 degrees C at equilibrium.

- Even with this ambitious level of stabilization the global average sea level rise above pre-industrial at equilibrium from thermal expansion only would lie between 0.4–1.4 meters. This would have serious implications for several regions and locations in the world.

A rational approach to management of risk would require that human society evaluates the impacts of climate change inherent in a business-as-usual scenario and the quantifiable costs as well as unquantifiable damages associated with it against the cost of action. With such an approach the overwhelming result would be in favour of major efforts at mitigation. The impacts of climate change even with current levels of concentration of greenhouse gases would be serious enough to justify stringent mitigation efforts. If the concentration of all greenhouse gases and aerosols had been kept constant at year 2000 levels, a further warming of about 0.1 degrees C per decade would be expected. Subsequent temperature projections depend on specific emission scenarios. Those systems and communities, which are vulnerable, may suffer considerably with even small changes in the climate at the margin.

Science tells us not only that the climate system is changing, but also that further warming and sea level rise is in store even if greenhouse gases were to be stabilized today. That is a consequence of the basic physics of the system. Social factors also contribute to our future, including the "lock-in" due, for example, to today's power plants, transportation systems, and buildings, and their likely continuing emissions even as cleaner future infrastructure comes on line. So the challenge before us is not only a large one, it is also one in which every year of delay implies a commitment to greater climate change in the future.

It would be relevant to recall the words of President Gayoom of the Maldives at the Forty Second Session of the UN General Assembly on the 19 October 1987: "As for my own country, the Maldives, a mean sea level rise of 2 metres would suffice to virtually submerge the entire country of 1,190 small islands, most of which barely rise 2 metres above mean sea level. That would be the death of a nation. With a mere 1 metre rise also, a storm surge would be catastrophic, and possibly fatal to the nation."

On 22 September 1997, at the opening of the thirteenth session of the IPCC at Male, the capital of the Maldives, President Gayoom reminded us of the threat to his country when he said, "Ten years ago, in April 1987, this very spot where we are gathered now, was under two feet of water, as unusually high waves inundated one third of Male, as well as the Male International Airport and several other islands of our archipelago." Hazards from the impacts of climate change are, therefore, a reality today in some parts of the world, and we cannot hide under global averages and the ability of affluent societies to deal with climate-related threats as opposed to the condition of vulnerable communities in poor regions of the globe.

The successive assessment reports published by the IPCC since 1990 demonstrate the progress of scientific knowledge about climate change and its consequences. This progress has been made possible by the combined strength of growing evidence of the observations of changes in climate, dedicated work from the scientific community, and improved efforts in communication of science. We have now more scientific evidence of the reality of climate change and its human contribution. As stated in the Fourth Assessment Report, "warming of the climate system is unequivocal," and "most of the global average warming over the past 50 years is very likely due to anthropogenic greenhouse gases increases."

Further progress in scientific assessment needs however to be achieved in order to support strong and adequate responses to the threats of climate change, including adaptation and mitigation policies.

There is also notable lack of geographic data and literature on observed changes, with marked scarcity in developing countries. Future changes in the Greenland and Antarctic ice sheet mass are another major source of uncertainty that could increase sea level rise projections. The need for further scientific input calls for continued trust and cooperation from policymakers and society at large to support the work needed for scientific progress.

How climate change will affect peace is for others to determine, but we have provided scientific assessment of what could become a basis for conflict. When Mr. Willy Brandt spoke at the acceptance of the Nobel Peace Prize in 1971, he said, "... we shall have to know more about the origins of conflicts.... As I see it, next to reasonable politics, learning is in our world the true credible alternative to force."

At a fundamental level the world now has to create knowledge and practice on a path of development, which is not resource degrading and carbon intensive. Human ingenuity and strength are capable of meeting this challenge. Dr. Gro Harlem Brundtland told us 20 years ago of the importance of sustainable development as the path to peace and prosperity. We need to commit ourselves to that path today before it is too late.

The thirteenth Conference of the Parties to the UN Framework Convention on Climate Change is being held in Bali right now. The world's attention is riveted on that meeting and hopes are alive that unlike the sterile outcome of previous sessions in recent years, this one will provide some positive results. The work of the IPCC has helped the world to learn more on all aspects of climate change, and the Nobel Peace Prize Committee has acknowledged this fact. The question is whether the participants in Bali will support what Willy Brandt referred to as "reasonable politics." Will those responsible for decisions in the field of climate change at the global level listen to the voice of science and knowledge, which is now loud and clear? If they do so at Bali and beyond then all my colleagues in the IPCC and those thousands toiling for the cause of science would feel doubly honoured at the privilege I am receiving today on their behalf.

II. Kyoto: Too Little, Too Soon

The Legal Dilemmas of the Kyoto Protocol for Carbon Control

Steven Ferrey. Professor of Law, Suffolk University Law School in Boston; former Visiting Professor of Law at Harvard Law School; since 1993, legal advisor to the World Bank and the U.N. on carbon control and renewable energy in various developing nations; author of 6 books and numerous articles on the energy-environmental legal/policy interface; Tel: (617) 573-8103, sferrey@suffolk.edu.

I. Introduction

The Kyoto carbon mechanism is struggling to meet its potential. It terminates by its own terms after 2012, and it will not meet either its own targets or the much more ambitious targets that many climate scientists believe are necessary to prevent ecological catastrophe. One leading climate scientist gives the world less than a decade to significantly reduce our increasing Greenhouse Gas (GHG) emissions.[1] Climate scientist James Hansen notes that merely waiting a decade until 2018 to stop the "growth of greenhouse gas emissions" reduces the probability to near no chance to avoid catastrophic effects of warming.[2] According to Dr. John Holdren, Director of the

---

1. Jim Hansen, *The Threat to the Planet*, N.Y. Rev. Books, July 13, 2006, at 12; Jim Hansen, *et al.*, *Global Temperature Change*, Proc. Nat'l Acad. Sci. U.S. AM, Sept. 26, 2006, at p. 14288.
2. Robin Chase, *Get Real on Global Warming Goals*, Boston Globe, April 22, 2008, at A15.

Woods Hole Laboratory, even if U.S. greenhouse emissions plateau in 6 years in 2015, the citizens of the world already will have reduced our chances by 50% to avoid climate catastrophes.[3] The forecasts by international energy agencies and the U.S. EIA offer no assurance that there will be even a plateau by 2015 under combined Kyoto and U.S. actions.

The Framework Convention on Climate Change treaty was agreed at the Rio de Janeiro U.N. Conference on Environment and Development in 1992 and the Kyoto convention was entered in 1997. The Kyoto Protocol received the required 55% ratification of Annex I (developed country) signatories by February 2005, and then became binding. Its first implementation year was 2008. Set in motion in 1992, it took 5 years to negotiate details and an additional decade to reach first implementation. The world does not have another 16 years as was afforded originally.

The U.S., India and China, three of the five largest carbon emitters, are not limited in the Kyoto 2008–2012 period or beyond, nor are more than 80% of the world's countries. There are at least four primary problems with the Kyoto Protocol as a method to control world carbon emissions:

Legally Covered Countries:

Three out of five of the largest carbon emitters are not part of the Kyoto Protocol. They need to be included; at least two fundamental changes are required to bring in developing nations: adding forest preservation and GHG chemicals of concern in developing countries.

Zero-CO_2 Technology-Transfer:

There is no Kyoto requirement that developed economies make any shift to zero-or low-carbon renewable power. The Kyoto Protocol has navigated in another less effective direction.

Volume of In-Developed-Country Compliance:

There must be incentives for Annex 1 In-Country zero-emission compliance options rather than reliance on non-CO_2 Clean Development Mechanism (CDM) external compliance default options.

Enforcement Issues:

Time is a critical dimension, given approaching possible tipping points in CO_2 emissions. The Kyoto Protocol contains no enforcement mechanism.

Each of these elements and their legal implications are discussed below.

II. The Number of Participating Countries

Progress in universal control of carbon has been slow. Even the most recent December 2007 compromise guidelines from the Kyoto conference in Bali backed away from: specific targets for Annex 1 developed countries to cut GHGs by 2020; any binding commitments; and any requirements for developing countries. It also set in motion the "Bali Roadmap" of two years of discussions aimed at cutting GHGs by 2050, rather than by 2020 as originally proposed.

The New Math of Kyoto

The quantitative goals in the Kyoto Protocol—although they have been accused of being too modest—are not the core problems with Kyoto; it is their application to only 20% of the nations that ratified the Protocol. Three-dozen countries are covered, while more than 80% of

---

3. *Id.*

countries have no required GHG reductions under the Kyoto Protocol. Numerators are critical in the equation of Kyoto. The denominator of participating carbon contributors is a known operand of 175 world countries. The numerator of the Kyoto Protocol is the critical operand to determine the participation of emitters. However, that numerator within the Kyoto Protocol only includes 35 Annex I countries, and in this fact lays a major shortcoming of the Protocol as an ineffective legal instrument on an international scale.

The non-Annex 1 developing nations can host CDM offset projects sponsored by industry or speculators in carbon from outside their borders. The 40% of world GHG emissions emitted just by the U.S. and China, neither of which are covered by limits under the Kyoto Protocol, dwarf the cumulative 28% of world GHG emissions from all 35 Annex 1 Kyoto signatory parties.[4] Without inclusive active involvement of more countries, there is no way to stabilize, let alone decrease, atmospheric carbon concentrations.

Ninety-eight percent of anthropogenic CO_2 emissions are from the combustion of fossil fuels.[5] More than one-third of CO_2 emissions are attributable to the electric power sector. Global CO_2 emissions are rising at the rate of approximately 10% per year.[6]

Energy use, and the construction of fossil fuel fired power generation facilities, is increasing as population growth and development continue, especially in developing nations.[7] The majority of energy and power generation expansion will occur primarily in Asia over the coming decades.[8] Unabated, this exponential increase in power demand in developing nations will tip the global environment thermostat to run-away global warming risk, regardless of what the U.S. and other developed nations do to reign in their carbon emissions.[9] If not addressed, the annual increase in GHG emissions in India, China, Brazil, Indonesia, or any one of several dozen fast-growing nations, cumulatively will swamp all of the collective GHG reductions of the developed nations complying with the relatively modest requirements of the Kyoto Protocol.

While world CO_2 emissions (25 gigatons annually) are slightly dominated by OECD nations[10] the cross-over point is projected to be no later than 2020 when OECD countries and developing countries each are projected to emit roughly comparable amounts of CO_2 into the atmosphere. By 2030, the dominance of developed and developing nations will have reversed, with developing countries' emissions increasing as a percentage of the total over time into the foreseeable future.

The trend is important. Developing nations are expected to emit a majority of CO_2 emissions within 10 years, while China has surpassed the U.S. as the largest CO_2 emitter in the world. China had the highest emissions in the world per unit of GNP by a factor more than double other nations. The critical reality: developing nations represent the geographic core of expected exponential increase in CO_2 emissions, and where new global warming architecture and law

---

4. Jeffrey Ball, *Kyoto's Caps on Emissions Hit Snag in Marketplace*, WALL STREET JOURNAL, Dec. 3, 2007, at A-1, 19.

5. U.S. Dept. of Energy, EIA, *Emission of Greenhouse Gases in the United States, 1998* (1999).

6. *See* Ray Purdy, *The Legal Implications of Carbon Capture and Storage under the Sea*, SUSTAINABLE DEVELOPMENT LAW & POLICY, Fall 2006, at 22.

7. World Bank Statement, Ministerial Segment—COP11—Montreal 4, *available at* http://siter.esources. worldbank.org/ESSDNETWORK/Resources/MINISTERIALSEGMENTCOP11Montreal.pdf.; INTERNATIONAL ENERGY AGENCY, WORLD ENERGY OUTLOOK (2004) [hereinafter 2004 IEA WORLD ENERGY OUTLOOK], *available at* www.worldenergyoutlook.org.

8. 2004 IEA WORLD ENERGY OUTLOOK, *supra* note 7.

9. INTERGOVERNMENTAL PANEL ON CLIMATE CHANGE, UNITED NATIONS ENVIRONMENT PROGRAMME, CLIMATE CHANGE 2007: THE PHYSICAL SCIENCE BASIS, SUMMARY FOR POLICY MAKERS 17, *available at* http://www.ipcc.ch/SPM2feb07.pdf.

10. Ray Purdy, *supra* note 6, at p. 23, Table 1.

must effectively focus. To bypass or ignore developing country carbon emissions, as the Kyoto Protocol does, is to invite broad policy failure in the near-term future.

World population is not abated and could reach eight billion people by 2020 and nine to ten billion by 2050.[11] East and South Asia now contain more than three billion of the world's six billion people.[12] By 2025, one quarter of the world's population will be living in Asian cities.[13] The average annual growth rate in primary energy use in developing countries grew from 1990 to 2001 by 3.2% per year, compared to industrialized countries where growth over the same period even with immigration was 1.5% annually.[14]

Two-thirds of all future energy demand will emanate from just China and India, which are not covered by the Kyoto Protocol carbon restrictions.[15] Projections estimate that by 2030, China's GHG emissions will quadruple and Asia alone will emit 60% of the world's carbon emissions.[16] To cope with the increased electrification that accompanies the substantial increase in per capita energy use, which will occur in developing nations in the next decades, the world may have to achieve a reduction of CO_2 of up to 50% during the 21st century. The very countries that the Kyoto Protocol does not cover are the critical missing link.

Forests and Kyoto

Leading carbon scientists have submitted that the only way to reduce carbon concentrations to even 90% of current levels is to adopt "forestry practices that sequester carbon" or there will be "... irreversible catastrophic effects."[17] Rainforests in the Brazilian Amazon, Indonesia and the Philippines are seeing soaring rates of deforestation.[18] Between the years of 2000–2005, there was a loss of 7.3 hectares of forest per year, which is a loss of 18 percent of the world's forests annually.[19] Two billion tons of carbon are released each year due to deforestation.[20] About half of the mature tropical forests, between 750 to 800 million hectares of the original 1.5 to 1.6 billion hectares that once covered the planet, have already fallen.[21]

Developing countries harbor some of the great forests of the world, such as the rainforests of South America and Indonesia. The net concentration of CO_2 in the environment is a function not only of the output of CO_2, but the conversion of CO_2. Forests are an opportunity to sequester CO_2 in the atmosphere, rather than the proposed and controversial sequestration experiments underground in mines or in the ocean.

---

11. Uwe R. Fritsche and Felix Chr. Matthew. Matthes, *Changing Course: A Contribution to a Global Energy Strategy* (GES), Heinrich Böll-Foundation, Paper No. 22, at 1314 (2002 World Summit, Johannesburg 2003) (First Edition March 2003) (Printed in Berlin, März), *available at* http://www.boell.org/docs/changing_course.pdf.

12. *Id.* (utilizing IEA 2002 data).

13. Susan Sim, *Overtaking the West: Asia's Teeming Urbanites,* The Straits Times (Singapore), December 9, 1996 at 41.

14. 2004 IEA World Energy Outlook, *supra* note 7, at 31.

15. *Id.*

16. Deborah E. Cooper, *The Kyoto Protocol and China: Global Warming's Sleeping Giant*, 11 Geo. Int'l Envtl. L. Rev. 401, 405 (1999).

17. James Hansen, *et al.*, Target Atmospheric CO_2: Where Should Humanity Aim? (NASA Goddard Institute for Space Studies June 2008 monograph).

18. R. Houghton, D. Skole, & C. Nobre, *Annual Fluxes of Carbon from Deforestation and Regrowth in the Brazilian Amazon*, 403 Nature 301 (2000).

19. Food and Agriculture Organization, *Deforestation Continues at an Alarming Rate*, November 15, 2005, *available at* http://www.fao.org/newsroom/en/news/2005/1000127/index.htm.

20. *Id.*

21. Ron Nielsen, The Little Green Handbook: Seven Trends Shaping the Future of Our Planet (Picador 2006).

When deforestation accounts for 18–25% of global annual carbon emissions, forests become a tremendous resource, especially in developing countries.[22] Annually, there are depletions of forests equal to the size of Portugal, or half the size of England. Half of this destruction is from illegal logging that is not effectively policed. A World Bank report found that 83% of Indonesia's annual greenhouse gas emissions, as well as 60% of Brazil's greenhouse gas emissions, come from the destruction of their forests rather than emissions. Collectively, these emissions from two countries account for almost 10% of the world's total net emissions of greenhouse gases.

Yet, the most recent news from Indonesia features not forest protection, but a crash program to build by 2010 a significant number of new coal-fired power plants without sequestration of their carbon emissions. In spring 2008, Indonesia invited banks to participate in financing five new coal-fired power plants worth more than $2 billion, representing the first part of an effort by the world's fourth most populous country to almost double its generating capacity, primarily utilizing coal-fired generation.[23]

Under the Kyoto Protocol, offset carbon credits can be obtained for planting trees but not for preserving existing forests. The Kyoto CDM offset program only counts projects that involve planting forest in areas that were deforested before 1990, as well as afforestation (planting forest in areas where there was previously no forest vegetation for at least 50 years).[24] Even the EU ETS carbon program excludes forestry credits, including those from forestation and reforestation projects.[25] It is estimated that purchasing and policing existing forest preservation could be accomplished at a price of approximately $4 per ton of carbon saved, much cheaper than the cost of purchasing EU ERU carbon credits.

Efforts of some developing countries to include avoiding deforestation as a Kyoto CDM project ultimately were tabled in 2005 Kyoto meetings, and not resolved at the Bali Kyoto meetings in late 2007. Thus, the Kyoto parties have tabled the conservation of forests until after 2012. In the June 2008 United States Lieberman-Warner climate legislation, 15% of compliance would be allowed to involve international carbon offsets. U.S. Senator Craig offered a forest management amendment to the Lieberman-Warner bill because he stated that the bill "would give money to Brazil to save the rain forest," but would not do enough for domestic forest conservation, where 10 million acres of forest in the U.S. burn each year, releasing CO_2.[26] Moreover, Senator Saunders would have banned the use of international offsets altogether in any U.S. system.[27] Other bipartisan-supported amendments in the U.S. Senate sought to eliminate the import of offsets created overseas.[28]

Natural biologic forest systems are the natural, ecological, carbon control mechanism. However, they receive limited attention in the Kyoto Protocol. This is a glaring deficiency that must be remedied.

---

22. A. Mitchell *et al.*, *Forests First in the Fight Against Global Climate Change*, GLOBAL CANOPY PROGRAMME, June 2007, *available at* http://globalcanopy.org/themedia/file/PDFs/forests%20First%20June%20 2007.pdf.

23. *Banks Invited to Bid for Financing 5 Indonesia Power Projects*, ASIA PULSE PTY LTD., March 19, 2008.

24. *Id.*

25. *See* Stuart E. Eizenstat, *Seeing the Climate Policy for the Trees*, Opinion Piece, THE NEW YORK TIMES, Nov. 4, 2006, *available at* http://www.nytimes.com/2006/11/04/opinion/04eizenstat.html.

26. *Climate Bill Amendments Roundup*, www.carboncontrolnews.com, June 4, 2008.

27. *Id.*

28. *Senate Climate Debate's Focus on Costs Poses Political Risks for both Sides*, WWW.CARBONCONTROLNEWS. COM, June 2, 2008.

Emissions in Developing Countries

The majority of Kyoto CDM projects, which all must be sited in (Non Annex 1) developing countries, have been projects to reduce HFC-23, a refrigerant. HFCs constitute less than 1% of GHGs, but they have received almost half of the investment in mitigation of GHG emissions.[29] This disparity occurred because of the 11,700 times greater CO_2e of HFC; for an investment of 100 million Euros, because of this carbon multiplier it generates Kyoto CDM credit revenues worth 4.6 billion Euros.[30] Ironically, HFC emitters earned almost twice as much from these HFC by-product reduction activities than they did from selling their refrigerant gases produced as the saleable commodity in the process.[31]

The problem is that HFC capture and destruction projects do nothing to reduce CO_2 nor to shift the energy base of the world's economies to sustainable, renewable power technologies. The necessary structural energy sector transformations to low-carbon generating technologies are not occurring. It is of note that CDM programs were originally a late minor add-on to the original Kyoto Protocol.[32] However, they have been the conduit for altering the key carbon-emitting activity of world economies.

Black carbon, commonly known as soot, is an unaddressed and Kyoto Protocol-ineligible significant GHG emission of concern, especially in the Arctic and the Himalayas including Greenland and the West Antarctic ice sheets. Black carbon particulate emissions were recently identified as the second most important climate changing chemical agent, trapping heat as an aerosol, and changing albedo of snow and ice.[33] Simultaneously, reducing black carbon emissions would save up to three million lives a year that otherwise would be lost to air pollution.[34]

Black carbon is not covered in any way under the Kyoto Protocol, nor did it appear on the late 2007 Bali conference Kyoto agenda. Addressing black carbon "particularly from fossil-fuel sources, is very likely to be the fastest method of slowing global warming" in the immediate future, according to Dr. Mark Jacobson at Stanford University, who notes that major cuts in soot emissions could slow the effects of climate change for a decade or two,[35] giving policymakers more time to address CO_2 emissions.[36]

There is an important locational component to black carbon. Today, unlike CO_2, the overwhelming majority of black carbon emissions is from developing countries[37] and is expected to

---

29. Jeffrey Ball, *supra* note 4, at A-1.

30. Ari Bessendorf, *Understanding Carbon Project Deal Structure*, Houston, Texas, Nov. 14, 2007, at 6.

31. *Id.*

32. Jeffrey Ball, *supra* note 4, at A-1, 19.

33. James Hansen & Larissa Nazarenko, *Soot Climate Forcing Via Snow and Ice Albedos*, 101 Proceedings of the National Academy of Sciences 423, 425 (2004).

34. Mark Jacobson, *Control of Fossil-Fuel Particulate Black Carbon and Organic Matter, Possibly the Most Effective Method of Slowing Global Warming*, 107(D19) J. Geophysical Research 4410, at 19 (2002) (citing C. A. Pope III and D. W. Dockery, *Epidemiology of particle effects*, in Air Pollution and Health 673–705 (S. T. Holgate *et al.*, eds., Academic Press 1999) and statistics from the World Health Organization).

35. V. Ramanathan, Testimony for the Hearing on Black Carbon and Climate Change, U.S. House Committee on Oversight and Government Reform 12 (October 18, 2007), at 3 ("Thus a drastic reduction in BC has the potential of offsetting the CO_2 induced warming for a decade or two").

36. Mark Z. Jacobson, Testimony for the Hearing on Black Carbon and Climate Change, U.S. House Committee on Oversight and Government Reform 12 (October 18, 2007) *available at* http://oversight.house.gov/story.asp?ID=1550 [hereinafter 2007 Jacobson Testimony]; V. Ramanathan and G. Carmichael, *Global and Regional Climate Changes due to Black Carbon*, Nature Geoscience 222 (23 March 2008), at 226.

37. Tami Bond, Testimony for the Hearing on Black Carbon and Climate Change, U.S. House Committee on Oversight and Government Reform 2–3 (October 18, 2007) *available at* http://oversight.house.gov/story.asp?ID=1550.

increase.[38] The largest sources of ambient black carbon emissions are in Asia, Latin America, and Africa.[39] China and India alone account for 25–35% of total worldwide black carbon emissions, with emissions from China having doubled between 2000 and 2006,[40] yet control of black carbon is totally unrecognized in any Kyoto carbon controls.

III. The Power Bases in Developing Countries

The Power Generating Sector

Renewable power is the long-term, win-win development scenario for developing nations. Renewable energy can provide opportunities for poverty alleviation, supply energy, and enhance energy security by relying on domestic resources.[41] Unlike fossil fuels, renewable resources are widely disseminated across the globe. While many nations, particularly developing nations, have no significant fossil fuel reserves of oil, coal or natural gas, every nation has significant renewable energy in some form—hydropower, sunlight, wind, agricultural biomass waste, wood, ocean wave power, etc.

Developers of Kyoto CDM projects in developing nations are often trapping methane and flaring it, without turning it into free electric power in the process.[42] These easy solutions create the most cost-effective reductions of GHGs for the investor, but perpetuate the need for electricity for the community derived from other conventional fossil-fuel sources. Therefore, while the Kyoto Protocol CDM process encourages carbon reduction in developing countries, it does not always result in a substitution of renewable power for conventional fossil-fuel power.

The world stands at a crossroad because in the next decade, there will be a massive investment in electrification of developing nations.[43] Once installed, those facilities will remain in place, contributing to global warming for 40 years or longer.[44] According to Rajendra Pachauri, IPCC Chairman, "What we do in the next two to three years will determine our future." These choices in energy technology made now will be the signature of the world carbon footprint for the remainder of this century, during which we may pass the point of no return in terms of warming.

But under the current Kyoto Protocol, proper incentives are not present: "The CDM has, for a variety of reasons, been largely unsuccessful in encouraging real and significant changes in developing countries," according to the June 2008 report of an independent task force of the Council on Foreign Relations.[45] CDM "has been disappointingly ineffective at achieving its goal of effecting fundamental shifts toward cleaner energy production …"[46]

---

38. Jacobson Testimony, *supra* note 36, at 5.

39. Tami Bond, "Summary C. Aerosols, Air Pollution as a Climate Forcing: A Workshop," Honolulu, Hawaii, April 29–May 3, 2002, *available at* http://www.giss.nasa.gov/meetings/pollution2002.

40. Ramanathan and Carmichael, *supra* note 36, at 226.

41. M.T. El-Ashry, *Framework for a Post-Kyoto Climate Change Agreement*, SUSTAINABLE DEVELOPMENT LAW & POLICY, Winter 2008, at 2, 3.

42. Author's observation from his extensive work around the world advising international organizations and developing countries on carbon policy. *See Environmental Impacts of Gas Flaring, Venting Add Up*, ENVIRONMENTAL SCIENCE AND TECHNOLOGY, Dec. 14, 2004, at 480A, *available at* http://pubs.acs.org/doi/pdf/10.1021/es0406886 (last visited May 4, 2009); *see also* GOVERNMENT ACCOUNTABILITY OFFICE, NATURAL GAS FLARING AND VENTING: OPPORTUNITIES TO IMPROVE DATA AND REDUCE EMISSIONS, *available at* www.gao.gov/cgi-bin/getrpt?GAO-04-809 (last visited May 4, 2009).

43. *See* Section II above.

44. National Energy Foundation, *Fuel Consumption Statistics*, *available at* http://www.nefl.org/ea/eastats.html.

45. Council on Foreign Relations, Independent Task Force, *Confronting Climate Change: A Strategy for U.S. Foreign Policy*, June 2008, at p. 21.

46. *Id.* at p. 46.

Now, China and India are building almost a new coal plant each week.[47] China and India harbor around one-quarter of the world's coal reserves, and are deploying these reserves rapidly to fire electric power plants.[48] India has targeted 100,000 MW in new capacity over the next ten years.[49] China is currently installing 1,000 MW of coal power generation each week and predictions are that by the year 2030, coal-fired power in India and China will add 3,000 million extra tons of CO_2 to the atmosphere every year.[50] Therefore, just these *additional* CO_2 emissions from Chinese and Indian electric power sectors will constitute approximately 10% of all world CO_2 emissions from all sources.[51] While aware of renewable possibilities, instead, each year China adds 40 times more new coal capacity than new wind power capacity.[52]

The single-point nature of power plants' emissions, the very centralized nature of most power plant sector decisions in developing nations, and the fast increasing demand for electricity, make new electricity generating plants the logical frontal assault on GHG emissions. There needs to be a proven format that developing nations can deploy to achieve the right kind of renewable energy power projects. Fortunately, the proven model for the new post-Kyoto architecture exists.

The Successful Model in Developing Nations

There is hard evidence of the model for success in developing nations deploying renewable power.[53] For the past decade, since the original decision to implement international carbon controls, five nations in Asia were among the first developing nations to develop small power producer (SPP) programs to promote renewable energy development in their countries.[54] These programs create an important model of best practices.

These renewable SPP programs have made, in just a few years, a substantial contribution to their growing national energy supplies. Almost four percent of the power supply in Sri Lanka, Thailand, and states in India are from SPP independent renewable energy initiatives.[55] This is the appropriate laboratory, as approximately sixty percent of all new power generation capacity financed in developing countries is in Asia. These five Asian nations feature very different forms of government and have different predominant fuel sources in their power generation bases (hydro, coal, gas, oil). Some of their national electric sectors have an integrated high-voltage transmission system, whereas others have a disaggregated or island system. These successes in Asia are the architecture for developing countries of every type to initiate win-win participation in the post-Kyoto carbon reduction scheme, based on renewable energy investments. Table 1 displays key comparative elements of program design and implementation in these leading five non-Annex 1 nation carbon-mitigation programs.

---

47. *Id.*

48. Lord Ronald Oxburgh, *Capturing the Moment*, Parliamentary Monitor, July 21, 2006.

49. U.S. Dept. of Energy, India Country Analysis Brief, at http://www.eia.doe.gov/cabs/india.html.

50. House of Commons, Science and Technology Committee, *Meeting UK Energy and Climate Needs: Role of Carbon Capture and Storage*, First report of Session 2005-06, Vol. I, HC-578-1 (2006), as related in Ray Purdy, *The Legal Implications of Carbon Capture and Storage under the Sea*, in Sustainable Development Law & Policy, 23 Fall 2006.

51. Ray Purdy, *supra* note 50, at 23, Table 1.

52. *Id.*

53. *See* Steven Ferrey, *Power Paradox: The Algorithm of Carbon and International Development*, 19 Stanford Law & Policy Review 510 (2008).

54. Professor Ferrey was the legal advisor to the host country and to the World Bank and/or United Nations on the majority of these programs.

55. For statistics on the Thai and Sri Lanka programs, see EGAT (2003) and Energy Services Delivery Project (2002), respectively; http://www.boi.lk lists incentive investment details for Sri Lanka. A review of programs, tender notices, and a series of reports on the India program is *available at* www.MNES.nic.in.

Country Program	Year Begun	Maximum Size (MW)	Premium for Renewable Energy	Primary Fuel	Eligible PPA Solicitation
Thailand	1992	<60 or <90	Yes, competitive bid	Gas	Controlled period
Indonesia	1993	<30 Java <15 other island grids	No	Renewable Energy	Controlled period
Sri Lanka	1998	<10	No	Hydro	Open offer
India: Andhra Pradesh	1995	<20 Prior <50	Yes, in tariff	Wind	Open offer
India: Tamil Nadu	1995	<50	No	Wind	Open offer

Table 1. Comparative Developing Nation Renewable Program Overview.

These programs provide lessons for carbon and renewable energy policy in developing nations.[56] There is a proven model for successfully shifting to a renewable power base in fast-electrifying developing nations. The model has been demonstrated in developing countries with very different forms of government and different power generation and transmission infrastructure bases. It has worked across the spectrum of developing countries.

Shifting Generation Technology in Developed Countries

Only those Annex 1 developed nations are regulated under the Kyoto Protocol. The Protocol requires 35 developed nations by 2012 to reduce CO_2 emissions an average of 7% below 1990 baseline levels, which is substantially below business-as-usual scenarios. The other GHGs must be reduced by them to 5 to 7% below either their 1990 or 1995 baseline levels by 2012. Industrial emitters in each country are able to trade emission credits or create new credits through offset mechanisms.

The Kyoto Clean Development Mechanism (CDM) allows projects that reduce greenhouse gases in developing nations to earn Certified Emission Reductions (CERs) for each ton of CO_2-equivalent of GHG reduced.[57] Those CERs are then traded or sold to carbon emitters in Annex I developed countries and that increases that country's emission cap allocated under the Protocol. Under the Kyoto Protocol CDM CERs and JI ERUs can be used in future compliance to satisfy up to 2.5% of a party's annual allowed emissions. The Kyoto CDM architecture is maximizing creation of imported credits, while not effecting necessary rapid structural change in the carbon-intensity of the energy production base of either developed or developing nations.

In 2005, U.S. monitored carbon emissions rose 0.6% while EU (Annex 1) emissions fell 0.4%, while in 2006 U.S. monitored but unregulated carbon emissions fell 1.3% and EU regulated emissions fell 0.3%.[58] On balance, both U.S. and the Annex 1 EU nations experienced the same 0.7% net carbon emissions change during 2005–2006. Emissions of carbon dioxide in the E.U. actually rose 1.1% in 2007 compared to 2006.[59]

---

56. Steven Ferrey, *Power Paradox: The Algorithm of Carbon and International Development*, 19 STANFORD LAWS & POLICY REVIEW 510 (2008).

57. *See* Art. 12, Kyoto Protocol to the United Nations Framework Convention on Climate Change, Dec. 10, 1997, 37 I.L.M. 22 (1998).

58. *EU and US greenhouse gas Emissions fell in 2006*, REUTERS NEWS, April 18, 2008.

59. *Analysis Shows Increase in EU Carbon Emissions*, BNA ENVIRONMENT REPORTER, April 11, 2008, at 706; *see also* http://ec.europa.eu/environment/ets/.

Internal trading of limits has occurred in the EU carbon control system. Among EU countries that were reallocated credits from other EU countries so as to provide generous increases in their limits, rather than reductions from 1990 levels, such as Spain, Ireland, Portugal, and others, these nations will not achieve even their generous levels allowing such substantial increases. Kyoto has not facilitated any significant CO_2 reduction in the bulk of Annex 1 countries. It is difficult to conclude that the E.U. carbon system, which parallels and implements the Kyoto Protocol, resulted in any carbon reductions that would not have occurred in the absence of the cap-and-trade system, according to Rachel Miller, director of federal affairs for BP.[60]

Kyoto has allowed increases in Annex 1 developed country CO_2 emissions through the CDM mechanism. There are almost a thousand CDM projects, with twice that many in the project development pipeline. The existing projects have generated 117 million issued CERs, with an estimated 2.6 billion CERs to be generated by 2012.[61] This would equate to almost 10% of all monitored emissions. Each CER generated in a developing country increases the GHG emissions allowed in an Annex 1 country to which it is exported through the Kyoto registration process.

There is an obvious connection between renewable power options and carbon reduction strategies.[62] At current rates of energy development, energy-related CO_2 emissions in 2050 would be 250% of their current levels under the existent pattern.[63] Unprecedented deployment of renewable energy generation alternatives will be required to alter this trend.

Annex 1 countries were anticipated to shift a significant percentage of their power generation bases to typically more expensive renewable energy options.[64] CDM projects to date have been located in a limited number of countries and involve only a few gases, with "little contribution to sustainable development."[65] As of the end of 2006, the World Bank reports that CDM offset projects were located 61% in China, 12% in India, 7% in other Asian countries, 10% in Latin America (most significantly Brazil), and 3% in Africa.[66] A report by the World Wildlife Fund found that the production of a large quantity of cheap carbon credits allows businesses and developed countries to avoid a fast shift to renewable resources and/or to keep emitting carbon.[67]

How this can be done legally will vary in each jurisdiction. There is no uniform model as with renewable energy investments in developing countries. Although allowed and significantly used in Europe, attempts by U.S. states indirectly or directly to promote higher wholesale energy prices or feed-in tariffs for certain renewable energy projects have been stricken by the federal courts of appeals in the U.S. as legally impermissible under U.S. law.[68] The U.S. Federal Energy Regulatory Agency, FERC, also held that states legally cannot set higher prices for renewable

---

60. *Id.*

61. Christine Voigt, *Is the Clean Development Mechanism Sustainable?* 8 Am. U. Sustainable Dev. L. & Pol'y 15 (Winter 2008).

62. Neal J. Cabral, *The Role of Renewable Portfolio Standards in the Context of a National Carbon Cap-and-Trade Program*, Sustainable Development Law & Policy, Fall 2007, at pp. 13, 14–15.

63. International Energy Agency, Energy-Technology Perspectives—Scenarios and Strategies to 2050 (2006).

64. Neal J. Cabral, *supra* note 62, at pp. 13, 14.

65. M.T. El-Ashry, *supra* note 41, at pp. 2, 5.

66. Lauren Etter, *In China, a Plan to Turn Rice into Carbon Credits*, Wall Street Journal, October 9, 2007, at A1, A15.

67. *Id.* at p. 39.

68. Independent Energy Producers Ass'n v. California Pub. Utilities Comm'n, 36 F.3d 848 (9th Cir. 1994) (the court found no separate basis for the state PUC to act to establish a premium price for renewable low-carbon power projects).

wholesale power.[69] The European feed-in tariff incentives would be unconstitutional if applied in the United States. Therefore, careful attention to legal requirements is imperative.

Creating International Enforcement Mechanisms

Enforceability is a key element to the success of international carbon policy. A significant problem with Kyoto is that it is a wholly voluntary agreement.[70] There is no provision in the Kyoto Protocol to ensure compliance of any nation that fails to achieve its reductions or violates any provision. There is no effective international organization with any effective power over the carbon-emitting practices of nations. Achievement, at the end of the day, is voluntary and unenforceable.

With most countries slated to miss their Kyoto goals, there is no sanction, no penalty, and no accountability in the international architecture. Unlike some international legal disputes, there is not even an international court to which to take Kyoto disputes.

The failure to impose penalties for national non-compliance stands in contrast to other E.U. and U.S. emission penalty provisions. There is very high compliance with required emissions levels with the SO_2 and NOx trading programs because the U.S. cap-and-trade system has an automatic penalty for non-compliance that is significantly higher than the market price for acquiring allowances, coupled with a liquid market for trading allowances. In ten years of operation, there have been only 21 excess emission penalties, plus nine additional civil penalties for other violations such as failure to monitor and report emissions. The EU provides compliance penalties of 100 Euros per ton between January 2008 and December 2012 for failure to have enough AAU allowances.[71]

However, in contrast, violation of the Kyoto carbon pollutant targets carries no penalty. This recourse to enforcement tools is important because of projected slippage between the carbon goals and the achievements. Even with penalties, European GHG emissions in industrialized European countries are increasing.[72] Most E.U. countries are forecast to miss their Kyoto targets, with the exception of two former Soviet countries:[73] Only Russia and Poland among the Annex 1 countries covered by the Kyoto Protocol are expected to easily satisfy their 2010 targets, and this is because of industrial collapse in those countries shutting many existing CO_2 emission sources. Canada and Japan are projected to miss their interim 2010 targets by 500 million tons each of CO_2; Japan's emissions are rising, and Canada has backed away from its target obligations.[74]

Even if all developed countries could achieve a Herculean reduction of 80% of their GHGs by 2050, this would not achieve Kyoto goals without vigorous participation by non-Annex 1 developing countries to shift the foundation and vectors of their fast-growing energy use.[75] CO_2 emissions remain in the atmosphere for approximately a century. Therefore, the global warming of the next century is already sewn in the molecular tapestry of Earth's atmosphere. Ultimately, there needs to be an international enforcement mechanism to ensure significant carbon reduc-

---

69. S. Ferrey, *Goblets of Fire: State Programs on Global Warming and the Constitution*, 34 ECOLOGY L.Q. 835 (2009).

70. IPCC, THIRD ASSESSMENT REPORT: CLIMATE CHANGE 2001 (2001), *available at* www.ipcc.ch/pub/online.htm.

71. Council Directive 2003/97-EC, *Establishing a Scheme for Greenhouse Gas Emission Allowance Trading Within the Community and Amending Council Directive 96/61/EX*, 2003, O.J. 275/32.

72. UNFCCC, GREENHOUSE GAS DATA, 2006 (Oct. 2006) (showing 11 ton increase in GHG emissions from 1990–2004, excluding the former Soviet countries).

73. *See* Ray Purdy, *supra* note 50, at 22; www.ipcc.ch.

74. Jeffrey Ball, *supra* note 4, at A-1, 19.

75. M.T. El-Ashry, *supra* note 41, at 2.

tions. The law and regulation must catch up with the scientific reality of the residence time of these GHG molecules.

VI. CONCLUSION

James Hansen stated two years ago that "[W]e have at most ten years—not ten years to decide upon action, but ten years to alter fundamentally the trajectory of global greenhouse emissions."[76] To do so, at least four significant shortcomings of the Kyoto Protocol must be remedied in the next round of international carbon control agreements: developing countries must be included in carbon mitigation, there must be a fundamental shift to renewable energy technologies rather than just the abatement of industrial HFCs, Annex 1 developed countries must make changes in-country, and an effective enforcement mechanism must be adopted. All of these are legal deficiencies that can and must be remedied to combat climate change.

Notes

1. Kyoto: A Fresh Approach?

GEORGE MONBIOT, HEAT: HOW TO STOP THE PLANET FROM BURNING v (South End Press 2007) (references omitted) [hereinafter 2007 MONBIOT]:

George Bush's government has sought to sabotage every effective international effort to prevent global warming. It recruited China and India to an "alternative Kyoto" (the Asia Pacific Partnership on Clean Development and Climate), without targets or sanctions, in order to prevent them from signing a binding treaty. Then it has announced that as India and China haven't signed a binding treaty, neither can the United States. It has all but wrecked the talks attempting to replace the Kyoto Protocol when it expires in 2012.

But the inconvenient truth we seek to forget is that the Clinton-Gore administration did even greater damage. Bush might have pulled the US out of the Kyoto Protocol, but the Clinton administration destroyed the Protocol as an effective instrument—for everyone. It insisted on measures which allow countries to trade hot air and launder fake cuts. It encouraged other countries to reduce their targets (and thereby allow a higher level of emissions). In his speech to the Kyoto conference in December 1997, Al Gore used the same mendacious formula George Bush now employs, claiming that limiting carbon emissions the US might otherwise have produced in a hypothetical future equates to real cuts in actual emissions. It was one of the most disgraceful moments in the Clinton presidency, and is impossible to reconcile with the subsequent career of the former next president of the United States. Clinton failed to submit the protocol to the Senate, Bush refused to do so. There is little practical difference.

In other words, the china had already been smashed when Bush took office: he simply ground it into dust. I admire Al Gore's film and Bill Clinton's Climate Initiative, but they also stick in the throat. Like many former leaders, they do a much better job of governing when out of office.

2. 2007 MONBIOT at 40:

---

76. James Hansen, *The Threat to the Planet*, N.Y. REV. BOOKS, July 13, 2006, at p. 16, *available at* www.ny books.com/articles/19131.

We have chosen to believe that the targets set by some of the more progressive governments form realistic means of dealing with [global warming]. The United Kingdom,
for example, intends to cut carbon emissions by 60 percent by 2050. This is one of the
world's most ambitious objectives. It is also, as I hope the previous chapter demonstrated, next to useless. But most of the climate-change reports produced by the major
environmental groups seek to demonstrate that this target can be met without major
economic loss. Whether or not it can be met is irrelevant: it is the wrong target. None
of them has yet stepped forward to say that we need a cut of the magnitude the science
demands.

3. DAVID SHEARMAN & JOSEPH WAYNE SMITH, THE CLIMATE CHANGE CHALLENGE AND THE
FAILURE OF DEMOCRACY 163 (Praeger 2007):

[T]here needs to be major reform to the legal systems within nations and to international law if environmental damage is to be arrested. We are highly skeptical of the ability of the legal system to lead the way. Only when the larger political battle has been
won or when the ecological crisis is visible to all will legal reform follow. The law is in-
trinsically a slow-moving, conservative beast, constructed for personal and property
protection, and we cannot expect much assistance from that source. Nevertheless that is
not a reason for defeatism and as environmental and human rights lawyers contrive to
address these problems in the courts, we wish them well.

4. JAMES GUSTAVE SPETH, RED SKY AT MORNING: AMERICA AND THE CRISIS OF THE GLOBAL
ENVIRONMENT 97 (Note Bene ed., Yale Un. Press 2005) [hereinafter 2005 SPETH]:

Right track or wrong track, it is a frightening thought to conclude that either way we
have wasted much of the twenty years we could have spent preparing for action. It
would be comforting to think that all of the international negotiations, summit meetings, conference agreements, conventions, and protocols at least have taken the international community to the point where it is prepared to act decisively—comforting but
wrong. Global environmental problems have gone from bad to worse, governments are
not yet prepared to deal with them, and, at present, many governments, including some
of the most important, lack the leadership to get prepared.

2005 SPETH at xi–xii:

I hope this short book will be a wake-up call to those of us, including many in the environmental community, who may believe that all the international negotiations, treaties,
and other agreements of the past two decades have prepared us to deal with global environmental threats. They haven't. The current system of international efforts to help the
environment simply isn't working. The design makes sure it won't work, and the statistics keep getting worse. We need a new design and to make that happen, civil society
must take the helm.

5. ANN RAPPAPORT & SARAH HAMMOND CREIGHTON, DEGREES THAT MATTER: CLIMATE
CHANGE AND THE UNIVERSITY 19–20 (MIT Press 2007) (footnote omitted and table included):

The Kyoto Protocol uses 1990 emissions as the baseline and establishes reduction targets from that point....

....

Other approaches might have been used. For example, Anil Agarwal argued that instead of starting with total emissions as a point of departure, it is more equitable to establish a per capita emission target that will reduce global CO_2 to an agreed level. The
effect of a per capita target would be to allow developing countries to increase emis-

sions, while developed countries would have to decrease theirs, dramatically in some cases.

Country	CO_2 Emissions (kt)	CO_2 Emissions (metric tons per capita)	GDP (constant 2000 US $ millions)	GDP per Capita (constant 2000 US $)
Bangladesh	29,253	0.22	$455,244	$347
China	2,790,451	2.21	$1,080,741	$856
Philippines	77,530	1.01	$75,912	$991
Thailand	198,647	3.27	$122,725	$2,021
Peru	29,543	1.14	$53,086	$2,047
Brazil	307,520	1.81	$601,732	$3,538
Costa Rica	5,423	1.42	$15,946	$4,185
Hungary	54,161	5.40	$46,680	$4,657
Mexico	423,972	4.33	$581,428	$5,935
New Zealand	32,067	8.31	$52,175	$13,524
Finland	53,428	10.33	$119,905	$23,184
Canada	435,858	14.17	$713,796	$23,198
United Kingdom	567,843	9.64	$1,439,348	$24,445
Denmark	44,606	8.35	$158,226	$29,630
United States	5,601,509	19.85	$9,764,800	$34,599
Japan	1,184,502	9.34	$4,746,068	$37,409

Table 2. GDP and Emissions for Select Countries. Source: World Bank, *World Development Indicators* (online) (Washington, D.C.: World Bank, 2006), *available at* http://www.devdata.worldbank.org/dataonline/.

6. This preface was written by Donald M. Zillman, Godfrey Professor of Law, University of Maine, in December 2000, and appears in Kyoto: From Principles to Practice xix (Kluwer Law 2001) (in association with the International Bar Association Section on Energy and Natural Resources). The book has several essays anticipating the trajectory Kyoto would take. Prof. Zillman included these comments on the November 2000 election in his introduction:

> The contrast between the two major candidates' positions on climate change issues was stark. A joint interview with Vice President Gore and Governor Bush in the September–October issue of Audubon magazine queried: "Do you support the Kyoto Protocol, under which developed countries would reduce greenhouse gas emissions by 5 percent compared with 1990 levels?"
>
> Vice President Gore responded: "I am proud of my role in negotiating the Kyoto Protocol—a historic first step in the effort the world must undertake to curb the tremendous threat to our way of life from climate change. I will strongly advocate the ratification. The protocol includes a legally binding emissions-reduction target for the United States of 7 percent below 1990 levels by the years 2008–2012. That target represents a reduction on the order of 25 percent that I believe the United States should pursue."
>
> Governor Bush responded: "[Efforts] to improve our environment must be based on sound science, not social fads. Scientific data shows average temperatures have increased slightly during this century, but both the causes and the impact of this slight warming are uncertain. Changes in the earth's atmosphere are serious and require much

more extensive scientific analysis. I oppose the Kyoto Protocol; it is ineffective, inadequate, and unfair to America because it exempts 80 percent of the world, including major population centers such as China and India, from compliance. America must work with business and other nations to develop new technologies to reduce harmful emissions."

III. The Significance of Copenhagen

The most widely anticipated modern development in international climate policy was perhaps COP 15—the fifteenth conference of the parties to the United Nations Framework Convention on Climate Change (UNFCCC), which took place from December 7–18, 2009, in Copenhagen, Denmark. While the major goal of the two-week session was to create a legally binding set of mitigation targets as a post-2012 follow-up to the 1997 Kyoto Protocol, climate justice issues such as adaptation policy and technology transfer were also featured on the agenda. Many commentators consider the negotiations a catastrophe because the process failed to produce any kind of legally binding outcome. But this result may be more an appraisal of the UNFCCC's governance process, which requires consensus among its 193 member countries, than a commentary on the overall state of international climate policy.

Notably, a small group of powerful countries including the United States, Brazil, India, South Africa, and China were able to bypass successfully the official COP 15 process and pull together a nonbinding Copenhagen Accord. This agreement creates a timetable for countries to follow in making formal emission reduction targets; but perhaps more importantly, it outlines a bold proposal for "new multilateral funding for adaptation" that will "be delivered through effective and efficient fund arrangements, with a governance structure providing for equal representation of developed and developing countries." (Copenhagen Accord, Paragraph 8.) It is unclear what impact the Copenhagen Accord will have on the international climate policy agenda or the entire UNFCCC process, which will continue with its next major meeting (COP 16) in November, 2010, in Cancun, Mexico. Until then, many climate policy advocates have their eyes on the U.S. Senate and the multitude of NGOs working to establish comprehensive climate policy at the national level.

IV. What Comes Next?
The New Geopolitics of Climate Change

A. National Security Concerns

"We will pay for this one way or another. We will pay to reduce greenhouse gas emissions today ... or we will pay the price later in military terms. And that will involve human lives. There will be a human toll. There is no way out of this that does not have real costs attached to it. That has to hit home."[1]

---

1. General Zinni, former Commander of U.S. Central Command, quoted by Sherri Goodman, General Counsel of the Center for Naval Analysis, Testimony before the Committee on Energy & Commerce, Subcommittee on Energy & Air Quality, U.S. House of Representatives, June 26, 2008, *available at* http://security andclimate.cna.org/testimony/transcripts/Goodman%20Testimony%20Jun%2026%2008%20final.pdf.

"Environmental changes caused by global warming will not only affect human living conditions but may also generate larger societal effects, by threatening the infrastructures of society or by inducing social responses that aggravate the problem. The associated socio-economic and political stress can undermine the functioning of communities, the effectiveness of institutions, and the stability of societal structures. These degraded conditions could contribute to civil strife, and, worse, armed conflict."[2]

The Center for Naval Analysis brought together eleven three-star and four-star retired generals and admirals to analyze the impacts of climate change on U.S. national security in THE CNA CORPORATION, NATIONAL SECURITY AND THE THREAT OF CLIMATE CHANGE (2007) (excerpts from the Executive Summary):[3]

Projected climate change poses a serious threat to America's national security. The predicted effects of climate change over the coming decades include extreme weather events, drought, flooding, sea level rise, retreating glaciers, habitat shifts, and the increased spread of life-threatening diseases. These conditions have the potential to disrupt our way of life and to force changes in the way we keep ourselves safe and secure.

In the national and international security environment, climate change threatens to add new hostile and stressing factors. On the simplest level, it has the potential to create sustained natural and humanitarian disasters on a scale far beyond those we see today. The consequences will likely foster political instability where societal demands exceed the capacity of governments to cope.

Climate change acts as a threat multiplier for instability in some of the most volatile regions of the world. Projected climate change will seriously exacerbate already marginal living standards in many Asian, African, and Middle Eastern nations, causing widespread political instability and the likelihood of failed states.

Unlike most conventional security threats that involve a single entity acting in specific ways and points in time, climate change has the potential to result in multiple chronic conditions, occurring globally within the same time frame. Economic and environmental conditions in already fragile areas will further erode as food production declines, diseases increase, clean water becomes increasingly scarce, and large populations move in search of resources.

Weakened and failing governments, with an already thin margin for survival, foster the conditions for internal conflicts, extremism, and movement toward increased authoritarianism and radical ideologies.

The U.S. may be drawn more frequently into these situations, either alone or with allies, to help provide stability before conditions worsen and are exploited by extremists. The U.S. may also be called upon to undertake stability and reconstruction efforts once a conflict has begun, to avert further disaster and reconstitute a stable environment.

Projected climate change will add to tensions even in stable regions of the world. The U.S. and Europe may experience mounting pressure to accept large numbers of immigrant and refugee populations as drought increases and food production declines in Latin America and Africa. Extreme weather events and natural disasters, as the U.S. experienced with Hurricane Katrina, may lead to increased missions for a number of U.S. agencies, including state and local

---

2. Jürgen Scheffran, a research scientist in the Program in Arms Control, Disarmament and International Security and the Center for Advanced BioEnergy Research at the University of Illinois, quoted in *Climate Change Could Be Impetus For Wars, Other Conflicts, Expert Says*, SCIENCE DAILY, August 22, 2008. http://www.sciencedaily.com/releases/2008/08/080821164304.htm.

3. http://securityandclimate.cna.org/report/.

governments, the Department of Homeland Security, and our already stretched military, including our Guard and Reserve forces.

Climate change, national security, and energy dependence are a related set of global challenges. As President Bush noted in his 2007 State of the Union speech, dependence on foreign oil leaves us more vulnerable to hostile regimes and terrorists, and clean domestic energy alternatives help us confront the serious challenge of global climate change. Because the issues are linked, solutions to one affect the other. Technologies that improve energy efficiency also reduce carbon intensity and carbon emissions.

Recommendations of the Military Advisory Board:[4]

1. *The national security consequences of climate change should be fully integrated into national security and national defense strategies.*

As military leaders, we know we cannot wait for certainty. Failing to act because a warning isn't precise enough is unacceptable. The intelligence community should incorporate climate consequences into its National Intelligence Estimate. The National Security Strategy should directly address the threat of climate change to our national security interests. The National Security Strategy and National Defense Strategy should include appropriate guidance to military planners to assess risks to current and future missions caused by projected climate change. The next Quadrennial Defense Review should examine the capabilities of the U.S. military to respond to the consequences of climate change, in particular, preparedness for natural disasters from extreme weather events, pandemic disease events, and other related missions.

2. *The U.S. should commit to a stronger national and international role to help stabilize climate change at levels that will avoid significant disruption to global security and stability.*

Managing the security impacts of climate change requires two approaches: mitigating the effects we can control and adapting to those we cannot. The U.S. should become a more constructive partner with the international community to help build and execute a plan to prevent destabilizing effects from climate change, including setting targets for long term reductions in greenhouse gas emissions.

3. *The U.S. should commit to global partnerships that help less developed nations build the capacity and resiliency to better manage climate impacts.*

As President Bush noted in his State of the Union speech, "Our work in the world is also based on a timeless truth: To whom much is given, much is required." Climate forecasts indicate countries least able to adapt to the consequences of climate change are those that will be the most affected. The U.S. government should use its many instruments of national influence, including its regional commanders, to assist nations at risk build the capacity and resiliency to better cope with the effects of climate change. Doing so now can help avert humanitarian disasters later.

4. *The Department of Defense should enhance its operational capability by accelerating the adoption of improved business processes and innovative technologies that result in improved U.S. combat power through energy efficiency.*

Numerous Department of Defense studies have found that combat forces would be more capable and less vulnerable by significantly reducing their fuel demand. Unfortunately, many of

---

4. The Military Advisory Board is comprised of: General Gordon R. Sullivan, USA (Ret.), Admiral Frank "Skip" Bowman, USN (Ret.), Lieutenant General Lawrence P. Farrell Jr., USAF (Ret.), Vice Admiral Paul G. Gaffney II, USN (Ret.), General Paul J. Kern, USA (Ret.), Admiral T. Joseph Lopez, USN (Ret.), Admiral Donald L. "Don" Pilling, USN (Ret.), Admiral Joseph W. Prueher, USN (Ret.), Vice Admiral Richard H. Truly, USN (Ret.), General Charles F. "Chuck" Wald, USAF (Ret.), and General Anthony C. "Tony" Zinni, USMC (Ret.).

their recommendations have yet to be implemented. Doing so would have the added benefit of reducing greenhouse gas emissions.

5. *The Department of Defense should conduct an assessment of the impact on U.S. military installations worldwide of rising sea levels, extreme weather events, and other projected climate change impacts over the next 30 to 40 years.*

Many critical defense installations are located on the coast, and several strategically important ones are on low-lying Pacific islands. Sea level rise and storm surges will threaten these facilities. Planning and action can make these installations more resilient. Lack of planning can compromise them or cause them to be inundated, compromising military readiness and capability.

Notes

1. On national security implications of climate change, see P.H. Liotta & Allan W. Shearer, Climate Change and Humanity's Loss (Praeger 2007).

2. Richard A. Matthew, *Climate Change and Human Security, in* Climate Change? What It Means for Us, Our Children and Our Grandchildren 161 (Joseph F.C. Dimento & Pamela Doughmen eds., MIT Press 2007) (with chapters on likely impacts, the scientific consensus, how the world is responding, and communicating environmental science as news, among others).

3. Kyoto: From Principles to Practice (Peter D. Cameron & Donald Zillman eds., Kluwer Law Int'l 2001) (discussing implementation of Kyoto around the globe, with sections on Europe, North America, Latin America, North and South Asia, and Africa).

4. Klaus Bosselman, *Carbon Neutrality and the Law, in* Carbon Neutral by 2020: How New Zealanders Can Tackle Climate Change 258, 259 (Niki Harre & Quentin D. Atkinson eds., Craig Potton Pub. 2007) ("The Current Situation"):

> New Zealand has the world's most advanced environmental law, the Resource Management Act, but it is not used for reducing our greenhouse gas emissions. In 2004, the government deliberately exempted greenhouse gases from the Act. Therefore, no legislation is in place, at present, to reduce carbon emissions. The recently announced emission-trading system and other proposed policies are insufficient to meet our Kyoto target, let alone to achieve carbon neutrality. The sad reality is that, per person, New Zealand is among the highest emitting countries in the world and our government has done nothing to change that. In the absence of guiding laws, policies or tax incentives, it is entirely up to each of us to reduce our carbon footprint.

5. Prue Taylor, *The Role of Ethics in Climate Change Strategies, in* Carbon Neutral by 2020: How New Zealanders Can Tackle Climate Change 199, 206 (Niki Harre & Quentin D. Atkinson eds., Craig Potton Pub. 2007) (footnotes omitted):

> The essence of the *Earth Charter* can perhaps best be understood by reading the first four core principles, upon which all the other supporting principles are based:
> 1.   Respect Earth and life in all its diversity;
> 2.   Care for the community of life with understanding, compassion, and love;
> 3.   Build democratic societies that are just, participatory, sustainable, and peaceful;
> 4.   Secure Earth's bounty and beauty for present and future generations.

App. 2 in this book sets forth the *Earth Charter*. *See* http://www.EarthCharter.org.

V. The Role of Developing Nations in Climate Change

Amy Sinden, *Climate Change and Human Rights*, 27 J. Land Res. & Envtl. L. 255, 256 (2007) (footnotes omitted):

> In one sense, all of humanity is in this together. But in another sense this crisis divides us both in terms of culpability and vulnerability. The haves of the world are responsible for the vast majority of the greenhouse gases that have already accumulated, and yet it is the have-nots who are likely to bear the brunt of its effects. The U.S., for example, with less than five percent of the world's population, is responsible for more than 28 percent of GHGs. But many of the areas most vulnerable to sea level rise and debilitating drought are in the developing world. Additionally, throughout the world, the poor are generally less likely to have the resources to cope with calamity when it strikes.

Thomas L. Friedman, Hot Flat and Crowded: Why We Need a Green Revolution— And How It Can Renew America 141 (Farrar, Straus & Giroux 2008):

> It is hard to believe in this day and age, but the World Bank estimates that roughly 1.6 billion people—one out of every four people on the planet—don't have regular access to an electricity grid. Every night is a blackout for 1.6 billion people. In sub-Saharan Africa, excluding South Africa, according to the World Bank, 75 percent of households, or 550 million people, have no access to network electricity. In South Asia— places like India, Pakistan, and Bangladesh—700 million people, 50 percent of the overall population and 90 percent of the rural population, are not on the grid. And under business-as-usual scenarios, the International Energy Agency projects that 1.9 billion people will still lack access to electricity in 2030.
>
> Meanwhile, indoor air pollution caused by the smoke emitted from cooking over open fires with inefficient stoves and pots—the most common alternative to grid electricity—is responsible for 1.6 million deaths per year, mostly of young children and mothers. That means that this biomass cooking as a cause of death ranks just behind malnutrition, unsafe sex, and lack of clean water and sanitation, according to the World Health Organization.

A. India

Energy Justice

Lakshman D. Guruswamy, Ph.D., Nicholas Doman Professor of Law and Director, Center for Energy & Environmental Security (CEES), University of Colorado at Boulder. Email: guruswam@colorado. edu; www.colorado.edu/law/eesi; Tel. 303-735-0181.

Introduction

The attention given to the energy-based problems of global warming caused by carbon dioxide emissions and peak oil has tended to ignore another immediate and pressing energy-based problem afflicting a third of the world's population. This problem cries out for energy justice for three compelling, interconnected reasons. First, indoor pollution, one manifestation of this other problem, is exacting a horrendous toll of death and sickness, especially among women and children. It blights the 2.5 billion energy-oppressed poor (EOP) who rely on fire as their sole source of energy for cooking, illumination and heating. The EOP burn animal dung, waste, crop residues, rotted wood, other forms of "bad" biomass, and raw coal for their energy needs. Cooking on an open fire, or with a traditional stove, using biomass results in inefficient combustion that releases dangerous quantities of carbon monoxide, particulate matter, and other pollutants. These indoor pollutants result in the premature death every year of between 1.3 and 1.6 million women and children from pneumonia, chronic obstructive pulmonary diseases, lung cancer and asthma. They also cause chronic respiratory ailments and debilitating sickness for many more millions.[1]

Second, recent scientific investigations published in peer-reviewed journals of the highest standing conclude that the black carbon emitted by the burning of biomass makes the second strongest contribution to current global warming after carbon dioxide emissions.[2] According to these studies, the particulates in black carbon absorb reflected solar radiation, as well as direct solar radiation, thus warming the atmosphere more severely than other greenhouse gases like methane, halocarbons and tropospheric ozone.[3] Moreover, black soot can travel potentially thousands of miles from its sources on air currents, and eventually settle out of the air, onto land and water, and ice. Black soot may lower the albedo, or reflectivity, of polar ice that covers vast stretches of the Arctic and Antarctica. The presence of overlying black soot may result in ice retaining more heat, leading to increased melting, and eventually a warmer Earth.[4]

Scientific assessments demonstrate that global warming disproportionately afflicts the EOP because they are unable to adapt to changes in climate, increased droughts or rising seas. Millions of EOP, particularly in Africa, face some of the biggest risks from drought and disrupted water supplies. As the oceans swell with water from melting ice sheets, it is the crowded river deltas in Asia and Egypt, along with small island nations, which are most at risk. While rich countries and peoples are hardly immune from drought and flooding, their wealth will largely insulate them from severe harm, at least for the next generation or two. Not so the EOP. The double envelopment of the EOP in this manner makes their position exceptionally perilous. Their situation is intolerable under any canon of justice, and cries out for redress.[5]

Third, geopolitically, developing peoples[6] have the right to develop, and developed countries have a duty to help them do so. Energy is a prerequisite to sustainable development and to addressing issues of poverty, hunger, education, gender equality, child and maternal health, sanitation, and environmental protection. It is important, however, that economic and social development be forged in a manner that avoids the major mistakes and costly problems created by the developed world. High among such problems is electricity generated by large, centralized dirty fossil fuel power plants, and transmitted through expensive, long-distance power distribution and transmission grids, comprised of transmission and power substations, high voltage lines, and transformers.

---

1. *See infra* Section I (C).

2. *See infra* Section I (C).

3. *See infra* Section I (C).

4. NASA/GODDARD SPACE FLIGHT CENTER CONCEPTUAL IMAGE LAB, ICE ALBEDO: BLACK SOOT AND SNOW 5 *available at* http://svs.gsfc.nasa.gov/goto?10023 (last visited Nov. 12, 2008).

5. UNITED NATIONS DEVELOPMENT PROGRAM, HUMAN DEVELOPMENT REPORT 2007/2008, Foreword (Palgrave 2007).

6. The reference here to "peoples" rather than countries anticipates the adoption (*see infra* Section 2) of the Rawlsian hypothesis of the law of peoples in preference to an analysis based on the law of nations.

A better—more enlightened—way of addressing the struggles of the EOP, beginning with indoor air pollution, is through intermediate technologies, for which there may be markets if corresponding financing systems are put in place. Appropriate sustainable energy technologies (ASETs) are on-the-shelf technologies which fall within the economic, cultural and technological grasp of the rural and urban EOP. The daunting prospect of adding the energy demand and polluting emissions of 2.5 billion developing people to a global environment groaning under the load of traditional, centralized, fossil fuel energy generation can be avoided with ASETs. More importantly, ASETs can lay the foundation for a new socio-political developmental path that not only avoids the mistakes of centralized fossil power generation, but also creates indigenous developmental opportunities that enable burdened societies, and especially the women within them, to make genuine sustainable economic and social progress.

This article will be divided into three sections. The first section will focus on the particularly horrendous problem of indoor air pollution, and the resulting public health and global warming repercussions. The second section will examine energy justice and demonstrate why the broader socio-political and legal responses to the problems of the EOP must be predicated on energy justice. The energy dominant two-thirds of the world should recognize and remedy the afflictions of the EOP, based on the foundational concepts of international justice developed by John Rawls in his *Law of Peoples*. The third section argues that energy justice calls for action in the form of dissemination and distribution of ASETs to the EOP, and the mainstreaming of women. It further delineates why addressing the problem of indoor pollution caused by burning biomass is only one step toward creating a more comprehensive basis for the energy-based sustainable development of the EOP. This important first step, along with the mainstreaming of women, should become part of an unbroken sustainable energy continuum spanning indoor pollution, agriculture, cottage industries, distributed energy, public health, and education to address the needs of the EOP.

I. Negative Effects of Indoor Energy Air Pollution

Humans are constantly engaged in energy conversions—processes that transform one form of energy into a more useful form. Because energy is necessary for meeting basic needs like cooking, sanitation, lighting, and heating, efficient human organization bears a strong correlation to effective energy conversion. The extent to which good organization can convert human labor to produce energy of the kind unimaginable before the industrial revolution is offered by the building of the Great Pyramid of Khufa.[7] Technological innovations help convert fossil fuels, solar radiation, or nuclear fuels into other, more useful energy forms such as electricity, mechanical energy, or heat. The fossil fuel based civilization of the more prosperous two-thirds of the contemporary world has developed by exploiting the rich energy endowment embodied in fossil hydrocarbons. The very high energy density of these sources, along with the technological systems that have been fashioned to harness them, has created an enormously effective development subsidy for the prosperous.

In contrast, the world's remaining one-third, comprising 52% of the total population in developing countries, relies on biomass such as agricultural waste, animal dung, fuel wood, and char-

---

7. The Great Pyramid of Khufu at Giza has been described as perhaps the most colossal single building ever erected on the planet. *See* ENCYCLOPAEDIA BRITANNICA ONLINE, PYRAMIDS OF GIZA, http://www. britannica.com/eb/article-9036944/Pyramids-of-Giza (last visited June 19, 2008). It was built by humans using slave labor or human energy converted by innovative social organization and management without the use of modern technology. Many archaeologists now believe that the Egyptian Pharaohs did not use slaves to build the pyramids, but rather conscripted peasants or even paid workers. *See, e.g.*, Jonathan Shaw, *Who Built the Pyramids?*, HARVARD MAGAZINE, July–Aug. 2003. Regardless, the enormity of the Pharaohs' organizational achievement stands whether the workers involved were enslaved or free, and is perhaps more incredible if the workers were not coerced.

coal, as their primary fuel source.[8] Using biomass for fuel, the process of cooking over an open fire, or even with a traditional stove, results in inefficient combustion. For instance, when using a traditional biomass-burning stove, only about 18% of the energy from the fire goes into the pot. This inefficiency means that more biomass must be burned to cook meals, creating more pollution.[9] Depending on the type of fuel and stove being used, indoor air pollution can contain a variety of dangerous pollutants, such as carbon monoxide, nitrous oxides, sulphur oxides, formaldehyde, carcinogens (such as benzene), and small particulate matter.[10] This section will discuss the effects of burning biomass on human health, local economics, and global warming.

A. Effects on Human Health

Reliance on biomass as a primary source of energy leads to many adverse consequences for human health.[11] The poverty that results in biomass dependence usually also means that kitchens are small and poorly ventilated, causing extremely elevated concentrations of dangerous indoor air pollution. For instance, whereas the U.S. Environmental Protection Agency (EPA) sets a limit of 150 $\mu g/m^3$ for small particulates in the U.S., the World Health Organization (WHO) reports that a typical 24-hour mean level for homes burning biomass fuels is around 1,000 $\mu g/m^3$.[12] This results in pollution far more deadly than the atmospheric pollution experienced by the developed world.

The concentration of indoor air pollution is not the sole factor in determining its negative health effects. Instead, negative health effects are also a function of the exposure level, based on the amount of time an individual spends inhaling the polluted air.[13] As women are traditionally responsible for cooking and childcare in the home, women and children have the highest exposure to indoor air pollution and thus disproportionately suffer from the associated negative health effects.[14]

In addition to possible burns and injuries associated with cooking over an open fire, the time spent by EOP women cooking greatly increases their health risks.[15] Depending on the demands of the local cuisine, women who cook over biomass fires generally spend between three and seven hours each day near the stove preparing food.[16] Not only do these women spend more total time around the fire, but they are also exposed to the most intense pollution which occurs during short peaks when fuel is added or moved, the stove is lit, the cooking pot is placed on or removed from the fire, or food is stirred.[17] Because these factors are generally not considered

---

8. INTERNATIONAL ENERGY AGENCY, WORLD ENERGY OUTLOOK 2006 (OECD/IEA 2006), *available at* http:// www.worldenergyoutlook.org/2006.asp.

9. PRACTICAL ACTION, SMOKE'S INCREASING CLOUD ACROSS THE GLOBE (ITDG Publishing June 16, 2006), *available at* http://practicalaction.org/docs/smoke/itdg%20smoke%20-%20part%202.pdf [hereinafter PRACTICAL ACTION].

10. WORLD HEALTH ORGANIZATION, FUEL FOR LIFE (WHO Press 2006), *available at* http://www.who.int/indoorair/publications/fuelforlife.pdf [hereinafter WHO, FUEL FOR LIFE]; KIRK SMITH, INDOOR POLLUTION AND HEALTH IN DEVELOPING COUNTRIES (Feb. 8, 2005), http://www.energyandenvironment.undp.org/undp/index.cfm?module=Library&page=Document&DocumentID=5827 (last visited Nov. 28, 2008).

11. Martin Donohoe & Emily P. Garner, *Health Effects of Indoor Air Pollution From Biomass Cooking Stoves*, MEDSCAPE PUBLIC HEALTH & PREVENTION, May 19, 2008, http://www.medscape.com/viewarticle/572069 (last visited July 7, 2008) [hereinafter 2008 Donohoe & Garner].

12. WHO, FUEL FOR LIFE, *supra* note 10.

13. 2008 Sandy Cairncross *et al.*, *Health, Environment and the Burden of Disease: A Guidance Note*, DEPARTMENT FOR INTERNATIONAL DEVELOPMENT (DFID) 24 (Feb. 2003), *available at* http://www.dfid.gov.uk/pubs/files/healthenvirondiseaseguidenote.pdf [hereinafter 2003 Cairncross *et al.*]

14. 2008 Donohoe & Garner, *supra* note 11.

15. 2003 Cairncross *et al.*, *supra* note 13, at 25.

16. World Health Organization, Indoor Air Pollution and Health Fact Sheet No. 292 (June 2005), http://www.who.int/mediacentre/factsheets/fs292/en/index.html (last visited July 8, 2008) [hereinafter WHO, Indoor Air Pollution and Health].

17. 2003 Cairncross *et al.*, *supra* note 13, at 24.

when calculating exposure from average pollution levels, the exposure of women to indoor air pollution may be underestimated by more than 50%.[18]

Children are also particularly susceptible to the hazards of burning biomass, and often suffer from burns or injuries from interactions with open fires in addition to indoor air pollution effects. To provide childcare, mothers usually must carry their infants on their backs as they work and keep young children inside for supervision. As a result, children spend many hours breathing indoor air pollution during the first few years of their lives. Infants and young children are particularly vulnerable to indoor air pollution because their airways are still developing; thus 56% of all indoor air pollution-attributable deaths occur in children under five years of age.[19]

Children may also be affected by indoor air pollution in utero. There is emerging evidence that pregnant women exposed to indoor air pollution may increase the risk of low birth weight and prenatal mortality, or stillbirths and deaths in the first week of life.[20] Exposure to tobacco smoke is known to be a significant factor in decreased birth weight, and the combustion of wood and other biomass is qualitatively similar to burning tobacco in terms of health effects.[21] A study in Guatemala found that pregnant women using wood fuel gave birth to babies with a lower mean birth weight than women using cleaner fuels, even when socioeconomic status was taken into consideration.[22] Low birth weight is a factor in infant mortality and morbidity, and puts children at further risk of developing respiratory illnesses if they survive past infancy.[23]

Indoor air pollution is responsible for approximately 1.3 to 1.6 million deaths per year in developing countries, which amounts to one life lost every twenty seconds.[24] Most of these deaths take place in eleven countries—Afghanistan, Angola, Bangladesh, Burkina Faso, China, the Democratic Republic of the Congo, Ethiopia, India, Nigeria, Pakistan, and the United Republic of Tanzania—where indoor air pollution kills a total of 1.2 million people each year.[25] According to the WHO, exposure to high concentrations of indoor air pollution presents one of the ten most important threats to public health worldwide.[26] Exposure to indoor pollution results in acute lower respiratory infections (ALRI), chronic obstructive pulmonary disease (COPD), lung cancer, tuberculosis, and asthma. Each of these conditions deserves brief mention.

The WHO estimates that 35.7% of all instances of ALRI worldwide, such as pneumonia, are caused or worsened by exposure to biomass smoke.[27] Indoor air pollution can also increase the incidence of ALRI by affecting the body's defense systems, such as the ability to filter and remove particles in the upper airways. ALRI is the most important single cause of death in children under age five, responsible for three to five million deaths in this age group annually.[28] There is consistent evidence that exposure to indoor air pollution can lead to ALRI in young children.[29] A series of studies in developing countries have indicated that young children living in homes

---

18. 2003 Cairncross *et al.*, *supra* note 13, at 24.

19. WHO, Indoor Air Pollution and Health, *supra* note 16.

20. WHO, Indoor Air Pollution and Health, *supra* note 16.

21. PRACTICAL ACTION, *supra* note 9.

22. 2003 Cairncross *et al.*, *supra* note 13, at 26.

23. 2003 Cairncross *et al.*, *supra* note 13, at 24.

24. World Health Organization, Indoor Air Pollution—the Killer in the Kitchen (Oct. 14, 2004), http://www.who.int/mediacentre/news/statements/2004/statement5/en/index.html (last visited July 8, 2008) [hereinafter WHO, Killer in the Kitchen].

25. World Health Organization, Indoor Air Pollution Takes Heavy Toll on Health (Apr. 30, 2007), http://www.who.int/mediacentre/news/notes/2007/np20/en/index.html (last visited July 8, 2008) [hereinafter WHO, Indoor Air Pollution Takes Heavy Toll on Health].

26. WHO, Indoor Air Pollution Takes Heavy Toll on Health, *supra* note 25.

27. PRACTICAL ACTION, *supra* note 9.

28. 2003 Cairncross *et al.*, *supra* note 13, at 26.

29. WHO, Indoor Air Pollution and Health, *supra* note 16.

dependent on biomass have a two to three times greater risk of suffering from ALRI than unexposed children. This figure was reached even after other factors, such as socioeconomic status, had been taken into consideration.[30] Although ALRI deaths have been declining in the industrialized world with improvements in vaccines and antibiotics, such remedies are often unavailable to the EOP.[31]

Indoor air pollution is also considered a risk factor for chronic obstructive pulmonary disease (COPD), such as chronic bronchitis.[32] In industrialized countries, tobacco smoking accounts for over 80% of COPD cases. However, this disease also occurs in the developing world in areas where tobacco smoking is rare. The United Nations Development Programme (UNDP) states that the use of poorly ventilated, inefficient stoves "can have the same adverse health impacts as smoking two packs of cigarettes a day."[33] A person who is exposed to a biomass fire on a daily basis is two to four times more likely to suffer from COPD than a person who remains unexposed. The WHO estimates that 22% of all COPD cases worldwide are caused by exposure to indoor air pollution from biomass fires.[34]

Smoke inhalation is also associated with lung cancer. In developing countries, women who do not smoke tobacco form an unexpectedly high proportion of lung cancer patients.[35] For instance, approximately two-thirds of women with lung cancer in China and India are non-smokers.[36] While a clear link between lung cancer and biomass smoke has yet to be demonstrated, the International Agency for Research on Cancer (IARC) concluded that indoor emissions from household combustion of biomass is probably carcinogenic to humans.[37] Furthermore, after a thorough review of published scientific evidence, the IARC concluded that indoor emissions from household combustion of coal are, in fact, carcinogenic to humans.[38]

There are several additional negative health effects associated with the daily inhalation of biomass smoke. Three published studies suggest that people in homes using wood for cooking are at 2.5 times greater risk of active tuberculosis than those who do not.[39] Growing evidence suggests that indoor air pollution also causes cataracts.[40] Furthermore, there is some evidence that wood smoke pollution may be a trigger for asthma or exacerbate it when combined with other ambient pollutants.[41]

B. Economic Effects

In addition to the disproportionate health burden placed on women and children, biomass fuel collection also imposes a serious economic burden on the EOP. The average amount of time spent by a family collecting fuel falls between thirty minutes and two hours each day. Where bio-

---

30. PRACTICAL ACTION, *supra* note 9.
31. PRACTICAL ACTION, *supra* note 9.
32. WHO, Indoor Air Pollution and Health, *supra* note 16.
33. PRACTICAL ACTION, *supra* note 9.
34. PRACTICAL ACTION, *supra* note 9.
35. Press Release, Int'l Agency for Research on Cancer, Indoor Emissions From Household Coal Combustion Carcinogenic: Women in Low- or Medium-Resource Countries Most Exposed (Nov 29, 2006), *available at* http://www.iarc.fr/en/Media-Centre/IARC-Press-Releases/Archives-2006-2004/2006/Indoor-emissions-from-household-coal-combustion-carcinogenic-women-in-low-or-medium-resource-countries-most-exposed (last visited July 8, 2008).
36. *Id.*
37. *Id.*
38. *Id.*
39. PRACTICAL ACTION, *supra* note 9.
40. PRACTICAL ACTION, *supra* note 9.
41. PRACTICAL ACTION, *supra* note 9.

mass has become scarce, fuel collection can take much longer.[42] Children, particularly girls, may be kept out of school in order to assist their mothers with collecting fuel.[43] There are significant risks associated with collecting large amounts of biomass. Transporting large loads of fuel exposes women and children to injuries and, when women are pregnant, to miscarriages.[44] In areas of war and civil unrest, women and children may be exposed to violence and injury as they search away from their homes for fuel.[45]

This perpetual chore of collecting fuel is both a cause and a result of poverty. Poor households often do not have the resources to obtain cleaner, more efficient fuels and appliances. These families are not faced with a choice, but a fact: they must cook using biomass or they will not eat.[46] Women in these circumstances tend to have limited decision-making power in the home, which decreases their ability to change the system, making household energy needs a lower priority than women might wish.[47] Reliance on biofuels denies EOP women and children the opportunity for education and income-generating activities that could increase their family's standard of living.[48] Other consequences of poverty, such as malnutrition, deprivation, poor sanitation, and low standards of available medical services, further intensify the negative health effects of indoor air pollution.[49] Thus, dependence on biomass contributes to a vicious cycle of poverty.

C. Environmental and Climate Change Effects

In addition to perpetuating poverty and negatively affecting the health of women and children, there are also severe environmental impacts of biomass dependence. The reliance on wood as a fuel source puts considerable pressure on local forests, particularly in areas where fuel is scarce and demand for wood outstrips natural re-growth.[50] Depletion of woodland can lead to soil erosion and loss of a carbon sink.[51] Furthermore, it has been well established that burning dung and agricultural residues emits carbon dioxide and methane.[52] Arresting new research findings, which have been well-received though have not yet garnered universal consensus among the scientific community, have now identified emissions from the burning of biomass as a significant cause of anthropogenic global warming.

According to an article in NATURE GEOSCIENCE,[53] which was discussed in SCIENCE,[54] black carbon emitted by burning biomass makes the second strongest contribution to current global warming after carbon dioxide emissions. The authors conclude that black carbon warms the atmosphere more severely than other greenhouse gases such as methane, halocarbons, and tropos-

---

42. PRACTICAL ACTION, *supra* note 9.

43. WHO, Indoor Air Pollution and Health, *supra* note 16.

44. PRACTICAL ACTION, *supra* note 9.

45. PRACTICAL ACTION, *supra* note 9.

46. WHO, Killer in the Kitchen, *supra* note 24.

47. 2003 Cairncross *et al.*, *supra* note 13, at 25.

48. World Health Organization, Indoor Air Pollution-Broader Impacts of Household Energy (2008), *available at* http://www.who.int/indoorair/impacts/en/ (last visited July 8, 2008) [hereinafter WHO, Broader Impacts].

49. 2003 Cairncross *et al.*, *supra* note 13, at 25.

50. WHO, Broader Impacts, *supra* note 48.

51. 2003 Cairncross *et al.*, *supra* note 13, at 25.

52. *See, e.g.*, Ambuj D. Sagar, *Alleviating Energy Poverty for the World's Poor*, 33 ENERGY POL'Y 1367, 1368 (2005). Sagar notes that burning crop residue and dung also degrades local farmland, as this biomass is not allowed to decompose and enrich the soil.

53. V. Ramanathan & G. Carmichael, *Global and Regional Climate Changes Due to Black Carbon*, 1 NATURE GEOSCIENCE 221 (2008).

54. Robert F. Service, *Study Fingers Soot as Major Player in Global Warming*, 319 SCIENCE 1745 (2008).

pheric ozone. It does so by absorbing both direct and reflected solar radiation, contributing to a significant enhancement of lower atmosphere solar heating.[55]

Unlike carbon dioxide, the primary cause of anthropogenic global warming, which has a life cycle of 50 to 200 years, black carbon, remains in the atmosphere for less than one year, and perhaps only one week.[56] Although black carbon leaves the atmosphere much more quickly than carbon dioxide, its global warming capacity stays intact as long as its ambient concentrations remain high, which happens so long as newly emitted black carbon replenishes what is removed. On the other hand, if emissions were to cease today and were not replenished, the existing ambient concentrations of black carbon would be gone in as little as one week. Thus, helping to move one-third of the global population away from biomass burning will have the effect of reducing global warming more efficiently than merely reducing carbon dioxide emissions. Furthermore, black carbon has also been implicated in interfering with the albedo effect of ice cover. Snow and ice are very reflective, and albedo refers to a specific form of reflectivity which allows between 70 to 80 percent of the sun's rays that hit snow and ice to bounce back into space. It has been concluded by two credible scientists that black soot on snow impairs its albedo and may amount to a quarter of global warming.[57]

II. Energy Justice

This section examines energy justice and demonstrates why the broader socio-political and legal responses to the problems afflicting the EOP, which extend beyond indoor pollution, must be predicated on energy justice. The energy dominant two-thirds of the world should recognize and remedy the afflictions of the EOP. The call to action based on the moral imperative to take national and international measures to meet the energy needs of the EOP is embodied in numerous international political declarations as well as reports from science academies.[58]

It is important, however, to go beyond assertion and conceptualize the jural foundations or predicates for acting to remedy the condition of the EOP. One approach to this is based on the foundational concepts of international justice developed by John Rawls in his LAW OF PEOPLES.[59] Rawls' conclusion underlining the duty of liberal democratic and decent hierarchical peoples to assist "burdened societies," and his further elucidation that they do so to the point where burdened peoples are enabled to join the society of peoples, is of particular pertinence. In this context, international consensus has coalesced around the United Nations Millennium Declaration[60] and the the Millennium Development Goals (MDGs).[61] They are buttressed by the principle of Common But Differentiated Responsibility (CBDR) which

---

55. "Lower atmosphere" exists between the Earth's surface and an altitude of roughly 3 km. In atmospheric "hotspots," regions with 15 W m^{-2} forcing, black carbon can increase solar heating by as much as fifty percent.

56. This results from the amplification of black carbon's warming effect when mixed with other aerosols such as sulfates. The removal of black carbon from the ambient air removes a significant cause of pollution.

57. James Hansen & Larissa Nazarenko, *Soot climate forcing via snow and ice albedos*, 101 PNAS 425 (2004).

58. For example, the InterAcademy Council concluded recently that meeting the basic energy needs of the poorest people on this planet is a moral and social imperative. In May 2000 all of the world's science academies created the IAC to mobilize the best scientists and engineers worldwide to provide high quality advice to international bodies — such as the United Nations and the World Bank — as well as to other institutions. INTERACADEMY COUNCIL, LIGHTING THE WAY (2007), *available at* http://www.interacademycouncil.net/Object. File/Master/12/096/First%20half.pdf [hereinafter 2007 INTERACADEMY COUNCIL].

59. JOHN RAWLS, THE LAW OF PEOPLES (Harvard Un. Press 1999) [hereinafter 1999 RAWLS].

60. United Nations General Assembly Resolution 18th September 2000, A/RES/55/2.

61. Road map towards implementation of the Millennium Development Goals, Report of the Secretary General, A/56/326.

places primary responsibility for remedial action pertaining to climate change and environmental degradation on the developed world. However, Rawls also demonstrates why the responsibility of developed nations does not absolve developing country governments from taking appropriate action.

This section first explains Rawls' theory of justice, and then delineates how Rawls' theory of justice provides a rational jurisprudential and philosophical foundation for dealing with the EOP as burdened societies or peoples as distinct from countries or nations. As burdened societies, the EOP are denuded of human capital by sickness and death and lacking the knowledge-based, monetary or technological resources necessary to break free from their energy bondage and become fulfilled members of a well ordered society. The prosperous peoples in the developed world *have a duty to assist burdened societies*[62] to reduce their burden, and to raise them to a position where they make intelligent and effective use of their unburdened status, and lead reasonable and worthwhile lives. Rawls of course discusses the idealistic world of the future and his ideas need to be reconciled to present realities. Still, energy justice calls for decisive and specific measures that will help the EOP overcome their energy plight.

A. Rawls' Theory of Justice

The moral and jural bases for the provision of modern energy services to the EOP are best encapsulated in the work of John Rawls. Rawls' unique contribution to moral and political philosophy lay in the manner in which he unites moral philosophy (intuitionism) and social philosophy (contractarianism) to formulate principles that are constructive and rational for liberal democratic societies. According to Noah Feldman, "Rawls's historical importance thus derives from his extraordinary accomplishment of grafting a Kantian-inspired moral theory onto a familiar — yet modified — discourse of social contract and then using the resulting product to justify the Western welfare state, and thus welfare capitalism itself."[63]

Rawls' "original position," a thought experiment expounded in *A Theory of Justice* (1971) and developed in numerous other works,[64] envisioned a collection of negotiators from liberal democratic societies. The negotiators were assembled behind a veil of ignorance and shorn of any knowledge that might be the basis of self-interested bias — such as knowledge of their gender, wealth, race, ethnicity, abilities and general social circumstances. Rawls explained that the purpose of such a negotiation was to arrive at legitimate principles of justice under fair conditions — hence "justice as fairness."[65] He further stipulated two governing principles for any fair negotiation. First, each person is to have equal rights to the most extensive system of basic liberties. Second, (the difference principle) social and economic inequalities are to be re-arranged so that they are to be of the greatest benefit to the least advantaged, and attached to offices and positions open to all under conditions of equality and liberty.[66]

---

62. 1999 RAWLS, *supra* note 59, at 106.

63. Noah Feldman, *Cosmopolitan Law?*, 116 YALE L.J. 1022, 1038 (2007).

64. JOHN RAWLS, A THEORY OF JUSTICE (rev. ed., Harvard Un. Press 1999) (1971); POLITICAL LIBERALISM (Columbia Un. Press 1993); THE LAW OF PEOPLES (Harvard. Un. Press 1999); JUSTICE AS FAIRNESS: A RESTATEMENT (Harvard Un. Press 2001); *Justice as Fairness*, 67 PHIL. REV. 178 (1958); *Justice as Fairness: Political Not Metaphysical*, 14 PHIL. & PUB. AFF. 223 (1985).

65. JOHN RAWLS, JUSTICE AS FAIRNESS: A RESTATEMENT (Harvard Un. Press 2001).

66. JOHN RAWLS, POLITICAL LIBERALISM 5–6 (Columbia Un. Press 1993) [hereinafter 1993 RAWLS]. According to Rawls persons in an original position agree that all basic liberties such as political freedom and freedom of choice in occupations, opportunity, income, wealth, and self-respect will be distributed equally unless an unequal distribution of any or all of these goods is to the advantage of the least favored. Rawls thus depicts justice as an issue of fairness permitting an unequal distribution only to the extent that the weakest members of society benefit from that inequality. To Rawls, therefore, redistribution is justified where it would improve the situation of the disadvantaged.

In his *Law of Peoples*, concerning justice and international law, Rawls extended his theories from liberal democratic states to "decent" peoples living in non-democratic international societies. Rawls envisioned such "well-ordered hierarchical societies" to be "... nonliberal societies whose basic institutions meet specified conditions of political right and justice (including the right of citizens to play a substantial role, say through associations and groups in making political decisions) and lead their citizens to honor a reasonably just law for the Society of Peoples."[67] Well-ordered societies must satisfy a number of criteria: they must eschew aggressive aims as a means of achieving their objectives, honor basic human rights dealing with life, liberty, and freedom, and possess a system of law imposing bona fide moral duties and obligations, as distinct from human rights. Moreover, they must have law and judges to uphold common good ideas of justice.[68]

Rawls emphasized the crucial importance of peoples rather than states because a peoples' capacity for "moral motives" is lacking in the bureaucratic machinery of a state.[69] Rawls is not talking then about a people regarded as an ethnic or religious group (*e.g.*, Slavs, Jews, Kurds) who are not members of the same society. Rather, a people consists of members of the same well-ordered society who are united under, and whose relations are governed by, a political constitution and basic structure. Comprised of members of a well-ordered society, a people is envisioned as having effective political control over a territory that its members govern and within which their basic social institutions take root. In contrast to a state, however, a people has a "moral nature" that stems from the effective sense of justice of its individual members. A people's members may have "common sympathies" for any number of non-requisite reasons, including shared language, ethnic roots, or religion. The most basic reason for members' common sympathies, however, lies in their shared history as members of the same society and consequent shared conception of justice and the common good.

Rawls' concept of "peoples" has been criticized. Among his more cogent critics, Pogge[70] and Nussbaum[71] question the validity of the distinction between peoples and states, and the difficulties of defining peoples. They claim their criticisms assume importance in any attempt to realize the 'society of Peoples' Rawls envisions as his realistic utopia. Such criticisms have actually been anticipated by Rawls, who pointed out that he eschewed the "state" as a polity because of its historical Hobbesian connotations in "realist" international political theory, which suggests that the power of states can be limited only by the power of states, and not by moral or legal constraints.[72] Samuel Freeman correctly observes that a "people" for Rawls is a philosophical construct; it is an abstract conception needed to work out principles of justice for a particular subject — in this case, relations among different well-ordered liberal and "decent" societies. Rawls demonstrated how the law of peoples may be developed out of liberal ideas of justice similar to, but more general than, the idea of "justice as fairness" presented in A THEORY OF JUSTICE (1971).[73] Just as individuals in the first original position were shorn of knowledge about their attributes and placed behind a veil of ignorance to create principles for a just domestic society, the bargainers in the so-called second original position are representatives of peoples who are shorn of knowledge about their peoples' resources, wealth, power, and the like. Behind the veil of igno-

---

67. 1999 RAWLS, *supra* note 59, at 3.

68. 1993 RAWLS, *supra* note 66, at 64–67.

69. 1999 RAWLS, *supra* note 59, at 17.

70. Thomas W. Pogge, *The Incoherence Between Rawls' Theories of Justice*, 72 FORDHAM L. REV. 1739, 1743 (2004).

71. MARTHA P. NUSSBAUM, FRONTIERS OF JUSTICE: DISABILITIES, NATIONALITY, SPECIES MEMBERSHIP 236–244 (Harvard Un. Press 2006).

72. 1999 RAWLS, *supra* note 59, at 23–30.

73. 1999 RAWLS, *supra* note 59, at 3–4.

rance, the representatives of peoples — not states, since states lack moral capacity — develop the principles of justice that will govern relations between them: the Law of Peoples.

The law of peoples would be a kind of higher law, creating rights and duties for peoples and States. It would impose moral duties and obligations on all persons and States living in well-ordered hierarchical societies. Rawls now arrives at a critical conclusion. Well-ordered peoples *"have a duty to assist burdened societies"*[74] to reduce their burden, and to raise them to a position where they may join the ranks of well-ordered peoples.[75] According to Rawls, "burdened societies" do not fall within the category of well-ordered societies because they may have become denuded of human capital by sickness and death or lack the knowledge-based, monetary or technological resources needed to be a well-ordered society.

Rawls seeks to determine the principles of cooperation for such "well-ordered peoples." Rawls thinks non-ideal conditions cannot adequately be addressed unless principles of justice are determined for ideal conditions. Otherwise, it is impossible to know what kind of just society to aim to establish and the necessary means to do so.[76] A "realistic utopia," as Rawls prefers to call his theory, is aspirational and does not reflect the existing reality of international law and relations. It is, however, possible to relate the Rawlsian ideal, and square it with social reality in a functional manner that concentrates on those areas of the existing international framework that lend themselves to the Rawlsian ideal.[77] There are a variety of international instruments, referred to below, attributable to a new association or social contract giving expression to Rawls' law of peoples.

B. Applying Rawls' Theory to the EOP

A starting point for analyzing the international phenomena of the EOP must begin with the fact that the EOP should be identified primarily as "burdened societies"[78] in the Rawlsian sense. Furthermore, their special status as burdened societies must be highlighted rather than hidden. Unfortunately, the EOP has for too long been glossed over or lost in the sometimes misleading categorization of their predicament simply as problems of the developing world, or else painted with the same socio-political and economic brush as the States in which they are located. For example, the EOP tend to be seen primarily as a problem of India or China or Afghanistan and not perceived as a burdened society apart from the geopolitical entities in which they reside. Such classification is unhelpful, however, because the EOP in any given country are effectively precluded from any meaningful participation in the society that has political control over their geographical location.

All developing countries tend to be conceptualized within a single typology, based on the binary division of the world into developing and developed countries. Thus the differences between the least developed countries (LDCs), located primarily in sub Saharan Africa and parts of Asia, and the advanced developing countries (ADCs), like China, India, the Asian Tigers[79] and Brazil, have only fitfully been recognized. It is therefore necessary at the outset to acknowledge at

---

74. 1999 RAWLS, *supra* note 59, at 106 (emphasis in original).

75. 1999 RAWLS, *supra* note 59, at 111.

76. 1999 RAWLS, *supra* note 59, at 128.

77. David Mitrany pioneered in conceiving of need-based responses by international organizations, which linked scientific knowledge, expertise and technology, and created its own dynamic to provide a "functional" supra-national authority and basis for action. DAVID MITRANY, THE FUNCTIONAL THEORY OF POLITICS (St. Martin's Press 1976).

78. 1999 RAWLS, *supra* note 59, at 106.

79. Originally called the Four Asian Tigers or East Asian Tigers, the term referred to the economies of Taiwan, Singapore, Hong Kong, and South Korea, but the term has been extended to include Thailand and Indonesia.

least two major categories among the developing countries: LDCs and ADCs. The commonalities, differences, and variegated energy needs, uses and demands of ADCs and LDCs call for complex, nuanced and demanding responses that would vary on a case-by case basis as much for ADCs as for LDCs.

The LDCs consist of fifty countries and 767 million people located largely in Africa and Asia.[80] The LDCs have been officially identified by the United Nations as "least developed" in the light of their low income (GDP of less than $7500); weak human assets (low nutrition, high mortality, lack of school enrollment, and high illiteracy); high economic vulnerability; exposure to natural shocks and disasters; prevalence of trade shocks; economic smallness; and economic remoteness.[81] They do not share the economic or technological strengths of the ADCs. It is worth noting in this context that the push for more energy and specifically for coal-powered energy arises from the ADCs not the LDCs. The problems facing the LDCs and the predominantly rural EOP located within them, unlike those of ADCs, arise from their woeful lack of energy and suboptimal energy conversions. In contrast, most ADCs use fossil fuel energy, and hunger for more of it to satisfy their industrial appetite.

Furthermore, the differences between the energy rich and the EOP in the ADCs have not been recognized. The fact that the EOP reside in the same country as the energy rich should not obscure the monumental disparities between them. While the top echelons of the economic pyramid in ADCs are inhabited by high energy users, similar to those in developed countries, the much larger lower parts of the economic pyramid are populated by the EOP who have no access to power or electricity.[82] Indeed, as the middle classes of China and India rapidly approach lifestyles comparable to the middle classes in Europe and North America, the EOP in these countries remain hidden in the toxic haze of windowless huts, cut off from the attention of their governments and the wider world.

ADCs like China and India have been treated as monoliths, when in reality the developed parts of those countries are dramatically different from the rural and urban EOP. Such mega-sovereign states may count as single nations under international laws and relations, but in fact consist of a plurality of socio-political, economic, cultural and geographical entities or societies. The similarity between the EOP in LDCs and the EOP in ADCs has generally been ignored. The socioeconomic condition and lack of technological knowledge among the 500 million EOP in China and India are analogous to the 750 million EOP in the LDCs. These EOP form distinct burdened societies, and justice calls for them to be treated separately from the richer segments of ADCs.

Given the widespread existence of energy poverty, the services provided by energy could save millions of EOP lives in any type of developing country. Ideally, energy services could power

---

80. UN Office of the High Representative for the Least Developed Countries, Landlocked Developing Countries and Small Island Developing States, List of Least Developed Countries, *available at* http://www.un.org/special-rep/ohrlls/ldc/list.htm (last visited Oct. 19, 2008).

81. The Criteria for the Identification of the LDCs. *Id.*

82. Each year since 1990, the Human Development Report (HDR) of the United Nations Development Program (UNDP) publishes the Human Development Index (HDI). This index looks beyond gross domestic product (GDP) to a broader definition of well-being. The HDI seeks to capture three dimensions of human development: a long and healthy life (measured by life expectancy at birth); being educated (measured by adult literacy and enrollment in primary, secondary and tertiary education). And third: GDP per capita measured in U.S. dollars at Purchasing Power Parity (PPP). United Nations Development Programme, Human Development Report 2007–2008, 355–357 (Palgrave Macmillan 2007), *available at* http://hdr.undp.org/en/media/HDR_20072008_EN_Complete. pdf. According to a recognized Indian commentator India rose in the dollar billionaire rankings, from rank eight in 2006 to number four in the Forbes list 2007, but slipped from 126 to 128 in human development of the United Nations Development Programme (UNDP). P. Sainath, *India 2007: High growth, low development*, The Hindu, Dec. 24, 2007, http://www.india together.org/2007/dec/psa-i2007.htm (last visited Nov. 14, 2008).

pumps and filters to supply relatively safe drinking water, and help provide sanitation to reduce water-borne diseases. Cooking devices powered by solar, kerosene, gas or electricity would shrink indoor pollution responsible for millions of premature deaths from pulmonary diseases, primarily of women and children, caused by the need to collect and use wood and other biomass for cooking and heating. Energy would free young girls from the drudgery of fuel collection and enable them to go to school. Energy is the key component of a functional health system, providing lights for operating rooms, refrigeration for life saving vaccines and life saving drugs, and power for communication systems.[83] Cheap accessible energy would decrease deforestation, reduce air borne pollutants, and prevent injuries and desertification arising from the search for fuel, food and water in semi-desert climates.

Ideally, the availability of modern energy services would promote income generation in developing countries. Electricity can provide illumination to permit longer working hours, and power for irrigation in order to yield better high-value crops. The use of process heat for grinding, milling, husking, and preserving can create value-added products from raw agricultural commodities. Refrigeration can enable sales to higher value markets. Computers, internet and telephone can provide access to information and markets and facilitate greater trade.[84] But, as will be demonstrated in Section III below, the true costs of and collateral damage caused by modern fossil fuel energy outweighs its benefits. Consequently, reliance should instead be placed on appropriate sustainable energy technologies (ASETs) to produce energy that satisfies the energy needs of the EOP while avoiding the damage caused by hydrocarbons.

It then becomes important to draw attention to Rawls' suggestion on how the duty of assistance should be discharged, bearing in mind his particular conclusion that merely dispensing funds will not suffice to rectify basic and political injustice.[85] Here, Rawls' duty of assistance finds resonance in principles and rules of international law dealing with human, social, economic and environmental rights. These principles and rules have been negotiated by the representatives of nation states within the framework of traditional international law, but are consistent with the Law of Peoples. To the extent that many of these instruments create obligations for developed liberal democratic and decent hierarchical countries, they could also be seen as an approximation of the laws made by those representatives in the first original position—the THEORY OF JUSTICE version—of the Rawlsian social contract.

These human, social, economic and environmental rights are referred to in numerous quasi-legal documents[86] such as the Universal Declaration of Human Rights (1948),[87] the Declaration

---

83. CHRISTOPHER FLAVIN & MOLLY HULL AECK, ENERGY FOR DEVELOPMENT: THE POTENTIAL ROLE OF RENEWABLE ENERGY IN MEETING THE MILLENNIUM DEVELOPMENT GOALS 23 (WorldWatch Institute 2005) [hereinafter 2005 ENERGY FOR DEVELOPMENT]; R.M. Shrestha, et al., Application of Productive Uses of Renewable Energy for Small, Medium and Micro Enterprises, UNITED NATIONS DEV. PROGRAMME EXPERT MEETING ON PRODUCTIVE USES OF RENEWABLE ENERGY 2 (2005), available at http://www.serd.ait.ac.th/ep/epkas/ (follow "3.1 Keynote Paper" hyperlink) (last visited Nov. 14, 2008).

84. GLOBAL NETWORK ON ENERGY FOR SUSTAINABLE DEVELOPMENT, REACHING THE MILLENNIUM DEVELOPMENT GOALS AND BEYOND: ACCESS TO MODERN FORMS OF ENERGY AS A PREREQUISITE 5 (Global Network on Energy for Sustainable Development 2007) [hereinafter GNESD PREREQUISITES].

85. RAWLS, supra note 59, at 108.

86. It is possible for governments to begin the process of creating customary law (which is based on the two requirements of state practice and opinio juris) by the act of voting for declarations and resolutions within international organizations such as the United Nations. After being passed such aspirational resolutions and declarations could evolve, first, into quasi-legal or "soft law" instruments, and subsequently develop into legally binding (hard law) by attracting state practice and opinio juris.

87. Universal Declaration of Human Rights, G.A. Res. 217A, at Art. 21, 23, 24, 25, 26 and 27, U.N. Doc. A/810 (Dec. 12, 1948), available at http://www.un.org/Overview/rights.html.

on the Right to Development (1986),[88] the Rio Declaration on Environment and Development (1992),[89] and the Millennium Development Declaration and Millennium Development Goals.[90] Additionally, they appear in a number of legally binding treaties such as the International Convention on Elimination of All Forms of Racial Discrimination (1965),[91] the International Covenant on Economic, Social and Cultural Rights (1966),[92] Convention on the Elimination of Discrimination Against Women (1979),[93] Convention on the Rights of the Child (1989),[94] and Convention (No.169) concerning Indigenous and Tribal Peoples in Independent Countries (1989).[95]

From the standpoint of energy justice perhaps the most important of these treaties is the United Nations Framework Convention on Climate Change (UNFCCC).[96] Its Preamble affirms and recognizes that:

> responses to climate change should be coordinated with social and economic development ... with a view to avoiding adverse impacts on the latter, taking into full account the legitimate priority needs of developing countries for the achievement of sustained economic growth and the eradication of poverty.... In order for developing countries to progress toward that goal their *energy consumption will need to grow....* (emphasis added).

In so stating, the treaty expresses a conclusion reiterated and embodied in many other multilateral treaties between developed and developing parties. A succinct articulation of this conclusion is found in the Convention on Biological Diversity, which affirmed that *economic and social development and eradication of poverty are the first and overriding priorities of the developing countries.*[97]

In this context, the most notable of the five principles embodied in Art 3 of the UNFCCC is the conclusion that the Parties have a right to and should promote sustainable development, and that economic development is essential for adopting measures to address climate change. So too is the affirmation that full consideration be given to the special circumstances of developing countries. This principle is tied to the obligation of the Parties to protect the climate system on the basis of equity and in accordance with their common but differentiated responsibilities and respective capacities. The principle of common but differentiated responsibility (CBDR) affirms

---

88. Declaration on the Right to Development, G.A. Res. 41/128, 48 U.N. GAOR Supp. (No. 49), U.N. Doc. A/41/53 (Dec. 4, 1986), *available at* http://www.unhchr.ch/html/menu3/b/74.htm.

89. The United Nations Conference on Environment and Development, Rio de Janeiro, Braz., June 13–14, 1992, *available at* http://www.unep.org/Documents.Multilingual/Default.asp?DocumentID=78& ArticleID= 1163.

90. The 8 MDGs dealt with the eradication of extreme poverty and hunger, gender equality and empowerment of women, reduction of child mortality, improved maternal health, combating HIV/AIDS, malaria and other diseases, environmental sustainability, and a global partnership for development. *Supra* notes 60 and 61.

91. International Convention on the Elimination of All Forms of Racial Discrimination, G.A. Res. 2106 (XX), Annex, at Art. 1, 5, 6, 7, 11, 12 and 13, 20 U.N. GAOR Supp. (No. 14), U.N. Doc. A/6014 (Dec. 21, 1965).

92. International Covenant on Economic, Social and Cultural Rights, G.A. Res. 2200A (XXI), at Art. 24, 27, 28, 29 and 32, 21 U.N. GAOR Supp. (No. 16), U.N. Doc. A/6316 (Dec. 16, 1966).

93. Convention on the Elimination of Discrimination Against Women, G.A. Res. 34/180, at Art. 3, 7, 10, 11, 13 and 14, 34 U.N. GAOR Supp. (No. 46), U.N. Doc. A/34/46 (Dec. 18, 1979).

94. Convention on the Rights of the Child, G.A. Res. 44/25, Annex, 44 U.N. GAOR Supp. (No. 49), U.N. Doc. A/44/49 (Nov. 20, 1989), *available at* http://www.unhchr.ch/html/menu3/b/k2crc.htm.

95. 72 ILO Official Bull. 59 (1989), *available at* http://www.unhchr.ch/html/menu3/b/62.htm.

96. United Nations Framework Convention on Climate Change, 1771 UNTS 107, S. Treaty Doc. No. 102-38, U.N. Doc. A/AC.237/18 (Part II)/Add. 1 (May 9, 1992), *available at* http://unfccc.int/resource/docs/ convkp/conveng.pdf.

97. The Convention on Biological Diversity, G.A. Res. 49/117, at Art. 20(4), 49 U.N. GAOR Supp. (No. 49), U.N. Doc. A/49/49 (June 5, 1992), *available at* http://www.cbd.int/convention/convention.shtml.

the responsibility of the developed country parties to take the lead in combating climate change and the adverse effects thereof.

Rawls provides a conceptual template for extending these principles to the EOP. While the duty of assistance at an international level requires the extension of the CBDR principle to the EOP, Rawls' warning that the mere distribution of funds will not rectify the targeted problems now becomes of special relevance. Many rulers, Rawls points out, have been callous about the well-being of their own peoples,[98] and transferring resources to national governments does not ensure that they will be applied to the problems of the EOP. For this reason Rawls advocates that assistance be tied to the advancement of human rights. Tying assistance to human rights will also embrace the status of women who often are oppressed. It has, moreover, been proven that the removal of discrimination against women has resulted in major economic and social progress.[99]

Such measures almost certainly will be resisted by authoritarian regimes that will argue this approach amounts to an intrusion into the national sovereignty of a country and violates international law. These rulers might fear that establishing human rights as a condition for helping the EOP will expose their own corruption and lack of good governance. Such rulers have reason to fear the granting of human rights where they have not confronted their problems or have demonstrated weak governance. As an example of this, Rawls cites to the works of Amartya Sen and Partha Das Gupta who have demonstrated that the main cause of famine in Bengal, Ethiopia, Sahel and Bangladesh was government mismanagement rather than shortage of food.[100]

Corruption remains a major problem in many developing countries, where large numbers of complex, restrictive regulations are coupled with inadequate controls.[101] In both ADCs and LDCs, people have learned to live with corruption, even considering it, fatalistically, as an integral part of their culture. Not only are official decisions—for instance, the award of government contracts or the amount of tax due—bought and sold, but very often citizens must pay for access to a public service or the exercise of a right, such as obtaining civil documents. The process of allocating political and administrative posts—particularly those with powers of decision over the export of natural resources or import licenses—is influenced by the gains that can be made from them.[102] And the political foundations are cemented as these exchanges of privileges are reciprocated by political support or loyalty.[103] Corruption in turn takes its toll on the countries as a whole. It has been estimated, for example, that moving from a relatively "clean" government like that of Singapore to one as corrupt as Mexico's would have the same effect on foreign direct investment as an increase in the marginal corporate tax rate of 50%.

---

98. 1999 RAWLS, *supra* note 59, at 109.

99. MUHAMMAD YUNUS, A WORLD WITHOUT POVERTY: SOCIAL BUSINESS AND THE FUTURE OF CAPITALISM (Public Affairs 2008); BANKER TO THE POOR: MICRO-LENDING AND THE BATTLE AGAINST WORLD POVERTY (Public Affairs 2003).

100. AMARTYA SEN, POVERTY AND FAMINES, AN ESSAY ON ENTITLEMENT AND DEPRIVATION (Oxford Un. Press 1981); JEAN DREZE & AMARTYA SEN, HUNGER AND PUBLIC ACTION (Clarendon Press 1989); PARTHA DAS GUPTA, AN INQUIRY INTO WELL-BEING AND DESTITUTION (Oxford Un. Press 1995).

101. Corruption refers to the use of public office for private gain where an official entrusted with a public task engages in some sort of malfeasance for private gain. Pranab Bardhan, *Corruption and Development, A Review of Issues, in* POLITICAL CORRUPTION: CONCEPTS AND CONTEXTS 322 (Arnold J. Heidenheimer & Michael Johnston eds., Transaction Publishers 2002).

102. The link between political and economic power can be direct, such as in the system of patrimonialism in Morocco, or indirect too, such as in the Philippines where political position in a patronage-based system can be bought and sold.

103. Irene Hors, *Fighting Corruption in the Developing Countries,* OECD OBSERVER No 220, April 2000, *available at* http://www.oecdobserver.org/news/printpage.php/aid/291/Fighting_corruption_in_the_developing_countries.html.

What this proves is that the task of addressing the EOP does clearly invoke concepts of justice, international law and CBDR that calls upon developed countries to play a dominant part in alleviating the condition of the EOP. It also invokes the need for action by national governments. Justice requires both that assistance be given and that such assistance be properly administered. The failure of foreign aid has been debated,[104] and better ways of granting assistance must be found. Justice also requires that national governments take on the task of addressing the EOP. It is not possible to lay the blame on avaricious rich countries alone.

As burdened societies, the EOP are owed assistance by both developed and developing countries until they are capable of integrating into the liberal democratic or well-ordered hierarchical society that controls their geographical area. Of course, the amount and type of assistance required from developed and developing countries will differ from one segment of the EOP to another depending upon the needs of the EOP and the capabilities of the developing state. Like responsibility for climate change, the responsibility for assistance to the EOP is common to all peoples, but differentiated by ability to help.

Rapidly developing ADCs such as Brazil, China, and India must mobilize their governments to provide administrative support to internationally-based sustainable energy programs from developed countries and the United Nations to the EOP. Indeed, without action from the domestic government to promote the rule of law and provide a framework for organization of labor, capital, and energy (through markets or otherwise) to the EOP, international technological and financial assistance such as disseminating ASETs or microfinancing will fall flat. The primary concern of ADC governments is development for their populations; that development must, according to the law of peoples, include not only their rising middle classes, but the impoverished burdened society they have hitherto left behind.

While the EOP may reside within the borders of the ADCs, the obligation of the liberal or decent peoples in the ADC to assist them resides in the law of peoples. The division of responsibility here is relatively clear. Developed nations should provide resources that facilitate the advancing of knowledge and the adoption of intermediate energy technologies that improve the energy conversions of the EOP. For their part, the ADCs should provide the administrative, managerial and legal frameworks advancing the behavioral changes leading to the adoption of those technologies, and thereby raising the EOP out of poverty so that they might integrate into the larger society. The importance of managerial and administrative assistance by the ADCs to the EOP, cannot be ignored.

But because LDCs lack the financial resources of ADCs, and the EOP constitute a far larger proportion of the population of LDCs, developed nations bear a greater responsibility for ensuring that the assistance they provide actually reaches the EOP in LDCs. Such a responsibility is a corollary to the primary duty of liberal and decent peoples to assist burdened societies. Merely providing cookstoves, treadle-pumps, and bio-intensive agriculture plans to the governments of LDCs, based on the assumption that those governments have the resources and knowledge to publicize, organize and administer the technologies in ways that both reach and impact the EOP is a prescription for failure. This kind of aid does not satisfy the duty of assistance to burdened societies, because it may never reach those who need it, or may not be effectively implemented into their lives.

Developed nations providing sustainable energy assistance must not only promote ASETs, but also work with the LDC governments to create the administrative, managerial and legal frameworks for publicizing, educating, and training the EOP on how to utilize them. Developed na-

---

104. *E.g.*, William Easterly, The White Man's Burden: Why the West's Efforts to Aid the Rest Have Done So Much Ill and So Little Good (Penguin Group 2006).

tions must work sensitively with LDC governments to create and maintain these frameworks in a way that does not challenge the self respect or sovereignty of the LDCs. Furthermore, administrative and legal frameworks for mainstreaming energy technologies to the EOP must be crafted in ways that comport with the culture, religion, and values of the burdened EOP. A developed country's stipulation of administrative requirements attached to technological aid extends only to advance the "common institutions and practices of all liberal and decent societies," with the "final aim of assistance: freedom and equality for the formerly burdened societies."[105]

Rawls concluded that the law of peoples "will restrict a state's internal sovereignty or (political) autonomy, its alleged right to do as it wills with people within its own borders.... [W]e must therefore reformulate the powers of sovereignty in light of a reasonable Law of Peoples and deny to states the traditional rights to war and unrestricted internal autonomy."[106] As discussed, sovereignty cannot be a shield thwarting measures to address the crushing toll of death and suffering borne by the EOP.

This view of diminished importance of absolute sovereignty stems directly from Rawls' focus on peoples rather than states. States are instrumentalities for carrying out the rights and duties of peoples. They are not sacrosanct in their authority if that authority is being used in violation of the law of the peoples. While it would be unduly imperialistic for a developed nation to require an LDC to import a governmental framework that does not comport with its political culture, a state has no right to accept technological or financial assistance on behalf of a burdened society living within its borders and then fail to implement it. The moral conscience of the liberal democratic or decent hierarchical people cannot permit a state to act in such a way.

III. The Path Not Taken

This article has addressed the plight of the EOP and demonstrated why they should be treated as burdened peoples to whom we owe a duty of assistance. Such a duty demands mitigatory actions. The mortality and morbidity caused by indoor air pollution, arising from the use of biomass burning, vividly illustrates why the EOP should move up the energy ladder by using more efficient energy conversions, such as cookstoves, that save lives and help to facilitate an improved quality of life. It is also very clear that the developmental path of the EOP should not be based on the kind of hydrocarbon energy that has fueled the perilous prosperity of the other two-thirds of the world. Instead, a significant quotient of the energy required to address issues of poverty, hunger, education, gender equality, child and maternal health, and sanitation, should be derived from ASETs. Doing so makes sense pragmatically, and is predicated on the philosophical/moral framework established in Part II.

A. Conventional Energy

In general, modern development in Advanced Developing Countries (ADCs) like China, India, the Asian Tigers, Mexico and Brazil is based on electricity generated by huge centralized power plants, and transmitted through expensive, long distance power distribution and transmission grids, comprised of transmission and power substations, high voltage lines, and transformers. The proposal of China and India to expand this network and build between 750 and 1,000 pulverized coal low technology power plants, along with the accompanying grids, in the next eight to ten years will lock those countries into unsustainable development for a number of reasons.

First, these coal plants are resulting, and will continue to result, in huge public health problems arising from air, water, and solid waste pollution caused by pollutants ranging from sulfur

---

105. 1999 RAWLS, *supra* note 59, at 111.
106. 1999 RAWLS, *supra* note 59, at 26.

dioxide, nitrogen oxides, particulate matter, carbon monoxide and heavy metals such as mercury and lead. In China alone coal combustion contributes to over 400,000 premature deaths a year.[107] Of course, the harmful emissions of coal plants do not merely contribute to the mortality and morbidity of people in the countries in which they are located. Emissions also migrate to other countries. For example, experts estimate that up to 50% of mercury pollution and significant parts of ozone pollution worldwide originate in China.[108]

Second, conventional energy generation comes with a heavy price tag. Energy systems relying on centralized coal-fired generation require huge capital investments, extensive transmission grids, and large budgets for research, development and demonstration. They impose large debts on developing countries that have to be repaid,[109] and remain largely out of reach to the 1.3 billion people worldwide living on less than a dollar a day.[110] In many instances the prohibitive expense of extending power grids to remote rural areas also prevents access to energy for the remote rural poor. According to a World Bank study of several developing countries, grid extension to rural areas typically ranges from $8,000–$10,000 per kilometer, excluding the cost of materials, which adds roughly another $7,000. This high cost, coupled with very low capacity utilization of such grids due to very small loads, makes extension economically unviable to many utilities.[111] Certainly, there have been some successes in rural electrification such as the program in Bangladesh,[112] but they reach only a small segment of rural EOP worldwide. Similarly, the hundreds of millions of shanty-dwelling urban poor have also been unable to afford the costs of such electricity.[113] Some of them engage in illegal connections which are also very costly.[114]

Third, coal-based energy systems will dramatically increase emissions of carbon dioxide, potentially exacerbating global warming past a point of no return. Coal's share of world carbon dioxide emissions grew from 39 percent in 1990 to 41 percent in 2005 and is projected to increase to 44 percent in 2030.[115] Coal is the most carbon-intensive of the fossil fuels, and it is the fastest-growing energy source.[116] Together, China and India account for 79 percent of the projected increase in the world's coal-related carbon dioxide emissions from 2005 to 2030. For China alone, coal-related emissions are projected to grow by an average of 3.2 percent annually, from 4.3 billion metric tons in 2005 to 9.6 billion metric tons (51 percent of the world total) in 2030. India's carbon dioxide emissions from coal combustion are projected to total 1.4 billion metric tons in 2030, accounting for more than seven percent of the world total.[117] The emissions of the fossil fuel dependent two-thirds of the world is set to double carbon dioxide in the atmos-

107. Keith Bradsher & David Barboza, *Pollution from Chinese Coal Casts a Global Shadow*, N.Y. Times, June 11, 2006, at 11.

108. *The Dark Side of Coal Dependence*, Daily Camera, Nov.5, 2007, 8A.

109. 2005 Energy for Development, *supra* note 83, at 5–6.

110. Of the 1.3 billion people living on less than a dollar a day, approximately 800 million are in rural locations, and 500 million in urban areas. These numbers are changing with the growing exodus to cities. 2005 Energy for Development, *supra* note 83, at 9.

111. Joint United Nations Development Programme/World Bank Energy Sector Management Assistance Programme, Reducing the Cost of Grid Extension for Rural Electrification, 8 Report No. ESM 227 (2000), *available at* http://www.club-er.org/upload/DOC207.pdf (last visited Nov. 15 2008).

112. GNESD Prerequisites, *supra* note 84, at 19.

113. Global Network on Energy for Sustainable Development (GNESD), Can Renewable Energy Make a Real Contribution? 6 (Global Network on Energy for Sustainable Development, 2006) [hereinafter GNESD Contribution].

114. *Id.* at 7, 46.

115. Energy Information Administration, International Energy Outlook 2008, ch. 7 (Energy Information Administration 2008), *available at* http://www.eia.doe.gov/oiaf/ieo/pdf/0484(2008).pdf [hereinafter EIA, International Energy Outlook].

116. *Id.*

117. *Id.*

phere by 2050,[118] with possibly catastrophic consequences.[119] The Energy Information Agency (EIA) forecasts world energy increasing by 50% in 2030, while consumption by developing non-OECD[120] countries will increase by 84%.[121] Hydrocarbons, which are primarily responsible for climate change, are projected to continue to supply almost 85% of energy in 2030. If coal is to additionally supply the unmet energy needs of one-third of the world, the results will be devastating. The EOP cry out for energy, and the climate challenge demands that it be environmentally friendly energy.

B. Technology Transfers

The well-intentioned actions of some ADCs who plan on using cheap coal and old technology simultaneously could cause massive health problems for their people, adversely affect other countries, and seriously aggravate global warming. A significant number of scientists and engineers in ADCs have expressed alarm at the decisions taken by their governments to build coal-fired power stations using old technology and pulverized coal.[122] These ADC scientists and engineers share the technological optimism of their colleagues in developed countries. They believe that clean energy will displace the old coal-powered plants when advanced, climate-friendly technology is transferred.[123] According to them, research and discoveries that transcend national boundaries offer solutions to many critical issues ranging from climate change and genetically modified organisms to the crucial challenge of achieving sustainability.[124] Many believe that developing countries can leapfrog pollution-producing energy.

A striking recent expression of international consensus between scientists and engineers is found in the blue ribbon report of the InterAcademy Council entitled *Lighting the Way*.[125] The product of a transnational effort among elite scientists, the report calls for more R&D on low carbon technologies including carbon capture and sequestration, energy storage and conversion, enhancing long distance electric transmission capability and advances in molecular and systems biology. Predictably, it also recommends greater resources for research, development and demonstration, and technology transfers between developed and developing countries so that developing countries may adopt more advanced technology.[126] It appears that to these scientists and engineers, the frontiers of new knowledge and technology could be rolled out over all sec-

---

118. In pre-industrial times, the concentration of carbon dioxide in the atmosphere was about 280 parts per million (ppm). The atmospheric concentration of carbon dioxide at present is about 380 ppm, and according to the *International Energy Outlook 2008* reference case projections, by 2030 it would be about 450 ppm. If the growth of world carbon dioxide emissions continues unabated, the concentration of carbon dioxide in the Earth's atmosphere could reach 560 ppm by the middle of the 21st century. *Id.*

119. INTERGOVERNMENTAL PANEL ON CLIMATE CHANGE [IPCC], WORKING GROUP I, *2007 Summary for Policymakers, in* CLIMATE CHANGE 2007 (Solomon *et al.* eds., Cambridge Un. Press 2007).

120. The Organization for Economic Co-operation and Development (OECD) was established by treaty in 1960 and was a rich country club consisting only of the developed economies of the world. The membership has now been expanded and includes Australia, Austria, Belgium, Canada, Czech Republic, Denmark, Finland, France, Germany, Greece, Hungary, Iceland, Ireland, Italy, Japan, Korea, Luxembourg, Mexico, the Netherlands, New Zealand, Norway, Poland, Portugal, Slovak Republic, Spain, Sweden, Switzerland, Turkey, United Kingdom, United States.

121. EIA, INTERNATIONAL ENERGY OUTLOOK, *supra* note 115.

122. 2007 INTERACADEMY COUNCIL, Conclusions, 1, 2 and 3, *supra* note 58.

123. Global Environment Facility, *Catalyzing Technology Transfer*, GLOBAL ACTION ON CLIMATE CHANGE (July 2006), *available at* http://www.gefweb.org/Projects/focal_areas/climate/documents/Insrt_4_Catalyzng. pdf (last visited November 14, 2008).

124. Caroline S. Wagner & Loet Leydesdorff, *Network Structure, Self-Organization and the Growth of International Collaboration in Science*, 34 RESEARCH POL'Y 1608 (2005).

125. 2007 INTERACADEMY COUNCIL, *supra* note 58.

126. *Id.* at conclusions 2 & 3.

tions of developing countries regardless of their technological proficiency. Pursuant to these beliefs, a number of international bodies including the Expert Group on Technology Transfer (EGTT) under the UNFCCC,[127] the Global Environmental Facility (GEF), and the Clean Development Mechanism (CDM) under the Kyoto Protocol have been charged with figuring out how technology transfer might work.

The technological optimism of the science academies has not gone unchallenged. A recent insightful report of the United Nations Conference on Trade and Development (UNCTAD) cogently deconstructs this view.[128] It points out that such a worldview erroneously treats knowledge in static terms, as a universally transferable commodity without geography or history. At its most simplistic level, that perspective assumes that knowledge has almost instantaneous transformative properties that can be transferred from one context to another quickly and with little cost. According to the report, the complex dynamics of knowledge accumulation and adaptation are essentially excluded from the picture altogether. In assuming that knowledge is socially disembodied and universally transferable, the technological optimists ignore the fundamentally dynamic character and plural aspects shaping knowledge production and generation. The report tellingly points out that in practice, it is clear that the assimilation and the absorption of foreign technology will involve substantial costs and risks, and that success will depend on major sociocultural changes and technological learning. Such an observation is of special application to the EOP living in LDCs.

Despite the rhetoric, the fact remains that advanced technologies have not been transferred. It is now becoming evident to UN-affiliated organizations and some NGOs working in the fields of energy and environment and development that the current path is incompatible with sustainable development.[129] State-led intergovernmental efforts have failed to yield effective technology transfer by private firms who own patents and intellectual property rights. This is because private owners of intellectual property rights will not transfer them without guarantees of favorable returns, and governments cannot force them to do so.[130] Furthermore, as explained above, a substantial portion of the rural poor live in areas where the cost of extending the grid would be prohibitive due to isolating terrain or remoteness. Many of the urban poor also find that connecting to the modern style grid is prohibitively expensive and some resort to stealing electricity.[131]

Although some intermediate sustainable energy technologies such as small-scale PV installations are not widespread due to high initial costs, leapfrogging to advanced renewable energy technologies is sometimes justified despite its initial cost, depending on local factors such as reliance on energy imports and domestic job growth.[132] For example, Brazil has more than recouped its costly initial investment in sugarcane ethanol.[133] And given the current volatility of world energy prices, developing nations without domestic coal and petroleum reserves might be better served by minimizing their use. Rapid increases in oil prices have a disproportionate effect

---

127. Some like the EGTT have only played a largely analytical role, studying a wide range of technology-related issues and helping countries assess technology needs and options. *See* PEW CENTER ON GLOBAL CLIMATE CHANGE, SUMMARY OF COP 12 AND COP/MOP 2 (2006), *available at* http://www.pewclimate.org/doc Uploads/COP%2012%20Report.pdf (last visited Nov. 17, 2008).

128. UNITED NATIONS CONFERENCE ON TRADE & DEVELOPMENT, THE LEAST DEVELOPED COUNTRIES REPORT: KNOWLEDGE, TECHNOLOGICAL LEARNING AND INNOVATION FOR DEVELOPMENT (2007).

129. GNESD PREREQUISITES, *supra* note 84, at 13.

130. *See* Keith E. Maskus, *Intellectual Property Challenges for Developing Countries: An Economic Perspective*, 2001 U. ILL. L. REV. 457, 462–66 (2001).

131. GNESD CONTRIBUTION, *supra* note 113, at 4.

132. VIJAY MODI, SUSAN MCDADE, DOMINIQUE LALLEMENT & JAMAL SAGHIR, ENERGY SERVICES FOR THE MILLENNIUM DEVELOPMENT GOALS 32 (U.N. Millennium Project 2005).

133. *Id.* at 32.

on the economies of developing countries, with one study estimating that the GDPs of the poorest countries contract around 1.5% for every sustained $10 increase in the price of a barrel of oil.[134]

The good news is that even small increases in per capita energy consumption can net big benefits for the EOP. Martínez calculates that as little as 400 kilograms of oil equivalent (kgoe) (about seven percent of the modern world's current total energy consumption)[135] for the EOP would be sufficient to double their Human Development Index (HDI) to 0.7.[136] Although larger increases, on the order of 2500 kgoe per capita, would be needed to support a further increase in HDI to about 0.9 (the level of most developed countries),[137] this demonstrates that large-scale, centralized energy production is not necessary to improve the lives of the EOP, and may even be harmful if it diverts funds from more beneficial projects without addressing the needs of the EOP.[138]

Promoting only the adoption of advanced clean technologies at national and international levels is a flawed response. High-end, top-down technologies that lie beyond the economic, cultural and technological grasp of the EOP cannot effectively ease the plight of the EOP in the foreseeable future. By contrast, the adoption of intermediate technologies as energy conversion mechanisms could give rise to distributed sustainable energy systems that promote sound economic and social development. ASETs can also more satisfactorily alleviate suffering among the EOP, without creating the problems spawned by oil, gas and coal-powered economic development.

C. ASETs

The importance of appreciating and institutionalizing virtues of "mundane science" has been compellingly and authoritatively demonstrated.[139] Decentralized intermediate renewable energy technologies represent a more affordable way to extend modern energy. Appropriate sustainable energy technology (ASETs) consist of on-the-shelf technologies that, with adaptation, fall within the technological and cultural comfort zone of the 2.5 billion rural and urban EOP. The ASETs, developed according to engineering best practices, will span a spectrum of distributed energy solutions, encompassing both distributed electricity generation and proven non-electricity based mechanical and thermal devices and products. Examples of electricity generating ASETs include solar thermal generators, photovoltaics, micro hydropower generators and small non-grid connected wind turbines. Renewable energy technologies need not produce electricity to be effective, however. Energy solutions for the EOP could also come in the form of small-scale biogas anaerobic digesters, gel fuels, treadle pumps, solar cookers, passive solar desalination, fog collectors, rainwater harvesting equipment, improved ploughs and harnesses, hand-held solar lamps, better-designed carts, composting, and pit latrines. A recent study highlights how intermediate and appropriate technologies such as treadle and wind pumps, improved biomass stoves, biodiesel, solar water heaters, wind energy systems, vegetable oil, PVs, and biomass gasification

---

134. *Id.* at 22. While oil prices are subject to fluctuation, the cost of oil will remain very costly for less developed countries. The reference case scenario of the Energy Information Agency has oil dropping to around $70 in 2015 and rising again to $113 by 2030. ENERGY INFORMATION ADMINISTRATION, INTERNATIONAL ENERGY OUTLOOK 2008, ch.2 (2008), *available at* http://www.eia.doe.gov/oiaf/ieo/liquid_fuels.html.

135. About 1000 kgoe is equal to 43 gigajoules (GJ).

136. Daniel M. Martínez & Ben W. Ebenhack, *Understanding the Role of Energy Consumption in Human Development through the Use of Saturation Phenomena*, 36 ENERGY POL'Y 1430, 1433–34 (2008).

137. *Id.* at 1434.

138. José Goldemberg, *What Is the Role of Science in Developing Countries?*, 279 SCIENCE 1140 (Feb. 20, 1998).

139. Daniel M. Kammen, Michael R. Drove, *The virtues of mundane science*, 39 ENVIRONMENT 10 (July/Aug. 1997).

have worked in East Africa, Tunisia, Senegal, South Africa, Lebanon, Argentina, Brazil, China, Cambodia and India.[140]

The more modest energy services provided by intermediate sustainable energy technologies are more than sufficient to start the EOP on the path to sustainable development, and may be more appropriate for their needs than centralized electricity generation.[141] For example, many of the EOP suffering from indoor pollution live in rural areas where they depend on agriculture and draught animals for their subsistence. Glaringly, many of the EOP do not presently use relatively inexpensive intermediate energy conversion technologies such as improved harnesses, yokes, and ploughs for draught animals. The application of these energy conversion technologies would significantly improve their productivity and quality of life.

Perhaps the most promising potential remedy for biomass-created indoor pollution is to design and apply simple cookstoves capable of maintaining higher heat and greater combustion, along with some form of venting. In this case, cookstoves would allow ordinary fire to be used more effectively and efficiently. Additional energy conversion remedies include switching to cleaner-burning, low-smoke fuels, such as liquid petroleum gas, kerosene, ethanol, or biogas, or, ideally, substituting solar-powered stoves. Moreover, adding more windows around cooking areas to improve ventilation, and keeping children, especially infants, away from cooking areas as much as possible, would be helpful in addressing the devastating health effects of indoor pollution.

IV. Conclusion

The application of the Rawlsian paradigm will ensure first that the duty of assistance be exercised in a manner conferring direct benefit to the EOP, as distinct from their governments, or the nation states in which they reside. Second, a Rawlsian duty of assistance will provide for energy conversions that advance sustainable development, and forswears unsustainable development of the kind relied on by the other two-thirds of the world. Consequently, the socioeconomic development of the EOP resulting from such assistance will avoid fouling the planet with more pollutants, or inflicting disease and death in the way that traditional coal-based power plants do. Third, such assistance will advance technologies that are sympathetic to the cultural mores and technological knowledge baseline of the EOP. Finally, such technologies should empower women to take the vanguard in economic development, and the generation of income.

The adoption of ASETs, and not high technology, will satisfy the Rawlsian predicates for action. For example, the most practicable and enlightened approach toward alleviating the EOP suffering from indoor air pollution is through intermediate and appropriate technologies such as more efficient cookstoves, along with the advance of behavioral changes that will lead to their widespread use. Necessary responses to indoor air pollution should include educating women about the health risks of biomass smoke inhalation, providing access to quality healthcare and reproductive options, and improving the overall status of women by enhancing their access to capital and increasing their participation in domestic decisions.

Moreover, we have seen that the abatement of black soot emitted by the burning of biomass is the second most significant cause of global warming. The elimination or reduction of black soot by using an ASET such as a cookstove has the extraordinary co-benefit of reducing global warming. A dollar spent on eliminating black soot will have the double benefit of improving human health as well as of mitigating global warming, thereby benefiting not only the EOP but the entire world. Even those developing countries driven by rational self-interest alone may find it ad-

---

140. GLOBAL NETWORK ON ENERGY FOR SUSTAINABLE DEVELOPMENT, RENEWABLE ENERGY TECHNOLOGIES AND POVERTY ALLEVIATION: OVERCOMING BARRIERS AND UNLOCKING POTENTIALS (2007).

141. MODI et al., supra note 132, at 28; Sagar, supra note 52, at 6.

vantageous to finance such an efficient way of mitigating global warming. But other problems afflicting the EOP such as poor sanitation, lack of drinking water, absence of education or gender inequality do not possesses such epiphenomenal consequences. This fact alone means that they should be addressed on the basis of Rawlsian principles.

Using ASETs to address the devastating effects of burning biomass only represents the beginning of a journey. It is a first step toward creating a more comprehensive basis for the energy-based sustainable development of the EOP. The daunting prospect of adding the energy demand and polluting emissions of 2.5 billion developing people to a global environment groaning under the load of traditional, centralized fossil fuel energy generation can be avoided with ASETs. In other words, helping one-third of the world to address the public health crisis posed by indoor air pollution can also embark the EOP on a different developmental pathway that bypasses the problems created by the other two-thirds of the world.

Unfortunately, intermediate energy conversion technologies, and ASETs more generally, often escape the notice of policymakers some of whom look to more costly high-tech solutions. In the field of agriculture, for example, there has been a push toward the use of tractors and mechanization, as contrasted with improving the productivity of draft animals, which could be accomplished by better designed harnesses. The introduction of expensive oil or electricity-driven machinery for de-husking, and grinding of grain diminishes the role of women who could use microfinance to purchase much cheaper mechanical ASETs that could perform the same functions, and create small businesses that generate income. In short, the use of cookstoves and other ASETs should become part of an unbroken sustainable energy continuum spanning indoor pollution, agriculture, cottage industries, distributed energy, public health, and education.

More importantly, ASETs can lay the foundations for a new socio-political developmental path that not only avoids the mistakes of centralized power generation, but also creates indigenous developmental opportunities that enable burdened societies, and women and children, to make genuine sustainable economic and social progress.

––––––––––

Notes

1. Eli Kintisch, *New Push Focuses on Quick Ways to Curb Global Warming*, 324 SCIENCE 323 (April 17, 2009):

> .... Carbon dioxide may get all the attention, Shindell says, but black carbon—a component of soot—is also an important factor in global warming.... [R]educing emissions of black carbon and other short-lived pollutants that contribute to global warming could buy the world crucial time while governments begin the slow overhaul of global energy systems that will be required to reduce emissions of CO_2, which comprise 77% of all greenhouse gas emissions.

> Dirtier air has slowed global warming over the past century by blocking solar radiation. But the four short-lived pollutants that scientists are targeting actually warm the atmosphere. Methane and hydrofluorocarbons (HFCs) are greenhouse gases like CO_2, trapping radiation after it is reflected from the ground. Black carbon and tropospheric ozone, an element of smog, are not greenhouse gases, but they warm the air by directly absorbing solar radiation. Compared with CO_2, which can persist in the atmosphere for up to 3000 years, black carbon remains for only 2 weeks and methane for no more than 15 years.

2. *See* 323 SCIENCE 1273 (March 2, 2009) (atmospheric scientist V. Ramanathan and glaciologist Richard Alley share the $200,000 Tyler Prize for Environmental Achievement):

Ramanathan, of the Scripps Institution of Oceanography at the University of California, San Diego, says the prize will help him get "back to my roots." As a child in India, he watched his grandmother cook over a smoky fire of dung and wood. As a climate researcher, he documented the "brown cloud" blowing off India from such fires and burning fossil fuels. He then showed how the cloud warmed the upper atmosphere, reduced monsoon rainfall and rice harvests, and led to the retreat of Himalayan glaciers supplying drinking water to billions of people. Now he is organizing a project in north India to show how much using more efficient stoves and cleaner fuels could thin the brown cloud.

3. Western Environmental Law Center, News Release, April 9, 2009:

The Western Environmental Law Center (WELC) today sent an urgent letter to Lisa Jackson, Administrator of the U.S. Environmental Protection Agency, urging her to speed issuance of regulation aimed at restricting greenhouse pollution and to include black carbon, or soot, among climate forcing events to be regulated.

B. Africa

Jo Timmons Roberts & Bradley C. Parks, A Climate of Injustice: Global Inequality, North-South Politics, and Climate Policy 145–46 (MIT Press 2007) (footnote omitted):

[Cambridge University economist Michael] Grubb and his colleagues describe one telling interaction between rich and poor nations at the Kyoto negotiations that lasted late into the night. At 3 o'clock in the morning, amidst heated debate over global emissions trading, China, India, and the Africa Group of Nations expressed their strong support for a per capita allocation of global atmospheric property rights. Chairman Raul Estrada and a representative of the U.S. delegation responded that the contraction and convergence proposal was a political nonstarter, and negotiations were immediately brought to a close.

Joseph Romm, Hell and High Water: Global Warming — The Solution and the Politics — and What We Should Do 93 (Harper Collins 2007):

Imagine what will happen in Africa, a continent already afflicted with persistent, widespread drought and a shortage of safe drinking water. One 2006 study reported in Science found that by 2100, climate change could dry up lakes and streams in one-quarter of the African continent.

The "Curse" of Ecological Interdependence: Africa, Climate Change and Social Justice

Joel M. Ngugi. * *Professor Ngugi is an Associate Professor of Law at the University of Washington. His research interests include the role of law in economic development, the role of governments in market regulation and wealth allocation, and legal reforms in transition and developing economies; Tel: (206) 543-7611, jngugi@u.washington.edu.*

While the world's poor walk the Earth with a light carbon footprint they are bearing the brunt of unsustainable management of our ecological interdependence. In rich countries, coping with climate change to date has largely been a matter of adjusting thermostats, dealing with longer,

* I would like to thank Anna "Mickey" Moritz and Jeni Krencicki Barcelos for their research assistance, and Professor Bill Rodgers for his insistence and persistence. All errors are, of course, mine.

hotter summers, and observing seasonal shifts. Cities like London and Los Angeles may face flooding risks as sea levels rise, but their inhabitants are protected by elaborate flood defense systems. By contrast, when global warming changes weather patterns in the Horn of Africa, it means that crops fail and people go hungry, or that women and young girls spend more hours collecting water.[1]

Introduction

All nations and all people share the same atmosphere, the only one we have—so states the 2007 Human Development Report—as if that fact is an exciting discovery.[2] Greenhouse Gas (GHG) emissions by *any* country and *anybody* threaten the climate for *all* the countries and *everybody*. Yet, the Report also solemnly reminds us about the inverse relationship between responsibility for climate change and vulnerability to its impacts. "The World's poor," it announces, "will suffer the earliest and most damaging impacts [of climate change]. [While] [r]ich nations and their citizens account for the overwhelming bulk of the greenhouse gases locked in the Earth's atmosphere ... poor countries and their citizens will pay the highest price for climate change."[3]

This paper considers the moral and legal dilemma posed by the ironic figures and facts of climate change which are the attributes of our ecological interdependence: those most responsible for causing climate change will suffer the least; those least responsible could pay the most to rectify the situation; and finally, that non-action will punish the least responsible the most— hence creating powerful disincentives for those most responsible to act. In sum, ecological interdependence can rightfully be viewed as a "curse" by the vulnerable segments of the world's population who bear least responsibility for the emissions causing climate change but who will bear the greatest risks and costs because they share a planet with those most responsible for harming it.

The paper makes four points. First, it makes the argument that the only way for Africa and African people to get a voice on the climate change issue is to urgently re-frame the climate change issue as a social justice issue. Second, it outlines the difficulties in this re-framing.[4] Unsurprisingly, the chief structural problem is the powerlessness of African countries in the global governance system—a powerlessness that is both evidenced and highlighted by the way the climate change and other international environmental discourses have progressed. The chief chal-

---

1. UNITED NATIONS DEVELOPMENT PROGRAM, HUMAN DEVELOPMENT REPORT 2007: FIGHTING CLIMATE CHANGE—HUMAN SOLIDARITY IN A DIVIDED WORLD 3 (2007).

2. *Id.* at 2.

3. *Id.* at 3.

4. It is important to flag my conceptual use of "Africa" and "Africans" in this Chapter. Of course, in reality, there is no such place as "Africa" as a monolith—except in the Eurocentric conception of the world which homogenizes and erases great diversity and differences. "Africa" is a multiplicity of places, voices, interests and perspectives. Indeed, the very word "Africa" can "never entirely escape its bondage to the idea of Africa in the European imagination" which might be the only sense in which Africa is singular. (Bill Ashcroft, *Globalism, Postcolonialism and African Studies*, 512 *in* A COMPANION TO RADICAL AND ETHNIC STUDIES (David Theo Goldberg & John Solomos eds., Blackwell Publishers 2002)). However, I use "Africa" and "Africans," despite their diversity and incoherence as analytical constructs, here for two reasons. Conceptually, I use the term "Africa" as an analytical category to denote a continent, and a people, who are systematically marginalized by international legal discourses that use global Europe as the frame of reference of which the climate change discourse provides an excellent example. Also, pragmatically, on climate change issues, perhaps more than on any other issue, there appears to be an "African" position because of the adverse effects to the geographical place we can metaphorically call "Africa" where the earliest and most severe effects of climate change will be felt. In this sense, the "Africa" of which I speak here is "one of the places [that] get erected as permanencies within the flux and flow of capital circulation" and hence becomes a "real" place. (*See* DAVID HARVEY, SPACES OF HOPE 295 (Un. California Press 2000)).

lenge, therefore, is to highlight, in a meaningful way, that there are winners and losers in climate change—and African countries and African people constitute the latter group. Third, the chapter describes implications for such a rendering of Climate Change in social justice terms—principally, the distributive effects or stakes of climate change on African countries and African people. Finally, the chapter adumbrates a number of strategies for this re-framing.

A. Africa, International Law and Climate Change Regime

To re-conceptualize climate change as social justice from an African perspective, one must negotiate two conflicting if seemingly valid impulses to the still-emerging climate change regime. On the one hand, there is the view that international law in general is a predatory system that produces authoritative knowledge which legitimizes the asymmetrical power relations between the West and Africa.[5] From this perspective, international law is viewed as "a predatory system that legitimizes, reproduces and sustains the plunder and subordination" of African countries by the West.[6] In this trope, international environmental law, including the nascent climate change regime, is the latest chapter in this history (which includes regimes regulating economic, trade and financial matters) of induced consensus, domination, and oppression of Africa by the West. From this perspective, international law is undergirded by a system of production of knowledge that is decidedly Western, which is used to construct the regulative concepts that frame the discourse, govern and delimit its parameters, and, ultimately, determine its outcomes.[7]

On the other hand, there is the view that climate change is a truly global concern that will, first and foremost, harm Africa and Africans in more profound and debilitating ways than the West. For example, William Cline has concluded that "the composition of agricultural effects is likely to be seriously unfavorable to developing countries, with the most severe losses occurring in Africa, Latin America, and India."[8] At the same time, the effects on wealthy nations will be far more modest.[9]

From the first viewpoint, international environmental law—including climate change regime—is a regime and discourse of domination and subordination: regulative and authoritative knowledge is produced in the West, and then deployed to govern the Rest (including Africa). From the second viewpoint, international environmental law, and climate change law in particular, holds the potential to be a regime and discourse of resistance and liberation: if Africa has contributed the least to creating the problem of climate change, has the least regulatory, technological, and financial capacity to adapt to the adverse effects climate change will wrought, and yet it would suffer the most, it behooves the legal system to craft a regime that would fairly allocate costs and burdens of climate change impacts. From this perspective, climate change regime can be a discourse of resistance and liberation: African countries and Africans can use the climate change regime and the interstices it produces as a site for emancipation.

While this chapter concludes that the discourse on regulating and managing climate change has, so far, become the latest chapter in Africa's powerlessness and subordination in international affairs, and thus, has the potential to become the next phase of the West's intervention in Africa's affairs, climate change regime has the potential to found an international jurisprudence

---

5. *See, for example,* Makau wa Mutua, *What is TWAIL?* 94 A.S.I.L. Proc. 31 (2000) [hereinafter 2000 Mutua].

6. *Id.*

7. Sally Falk Moore, *The International Production of Authoritative Knowledge: The Case of Drought-Stricken West Africa,* 2 Ethnography 161 (2001) [hereinafter 2001 Moore].

8. William Cline, Global Warming and Agriculture: Impact Estimates by Country 2 (Peterson Institute 2007).

9. *Id.* at 2.

and discourse of resistance and emancipation. This creates both the need and the urgency of rendering the climate change issue as a social justice issue.

B. The Power of Framing: Sahel, Grazing and the Desertification Convention

The Sahel is a wide stretch of land that lies south of the Sahara Desert in North Africa. It runs about 2,400 miles from the Atlantic Ocean in the West to the Red Sea in the East—an area that covers nine countries (Burkina Faso, Cape Verde, Chad, Gambia, Guinea-Bissau, Mali, Mauritania, Niger, and Senegal) and more than forty-nine million people. Ecologically, the Sahel is a semi-arid tropical savanna; it is a transition zone between the arid Sahara and the wooded, wetter tropical area to the South.[10] Although typically semi-arid and unstable climatically, in the 1960s, evidence began emerging that the rainfall the Sahel was receiving was rapidly decreasing: From an average of about 284 millimeters in 1968 to about 44 millimeters of rainfall in 1972.[11] This decrease in rainfall led to severe and widespread drought.

In the late sixties to early eighties, the Sahelian drought led to a dramatic famine which is thought to have claimed hundreds of thousands of lives and affected millions of people. It is estimated that more than 25 million people were exposed to starvation, malnutrition, and disease during the Sahelian drought.[12] Most scientists and ecologists explained the drought and resulting famine in terms of "desertification"—the degrading of lands in arid and semi-arid regions due to human activities such as overgrazing, deforestation, surface land mining and poor irrigation techniques that put undue pressures on land.[13] Scientists warned that unless concerted efforts were undertaken to reverse the situation, the process of desertification would continue apace.

As a response to the Sahelian tragedy, the United Nations Environment Program (UNEP) convened the UN Conference on Desertification (UNCOD) in September, 1977 to "initiate concerted international action to combat desertification."[14] The conference adopted a Plan of Action to Combat Desertification (PACD) which had three central aims: to increase the global awareness of desertification, to collect together all knowledge on the problem of desertification and its possible solutions, and to commence a program to combat desertification.[15] Despite its ambitious twenty-eight recommendations which were subsequently adopted by the General Assembly in a resolution, PACD is widely considered an "abject failure."[16] Commentators have attributed this failure to at least four factors. First, the ambitious PACD anti-desertification program has been severely underfunded with both industrialized and African governments paying scant attention to their responsibilities to mobilize resources for the program.[17] Second, anti-desertification measures were inadequately integrated into national development plans, and ultimately had little substantive im-

---

10. Serigner Tacko Kandji, Louis Verchot, & Jens Mackensen, Climate Change and Variability in the Sahel Region: Impacts and Adaptation Strategies in the Agricultural Sector 2 (World Agroforestry Center/United Nations Environment Programme 2006), *available at* http://www.unep.org/Themes/Freshwater/Documents/pdf/ClimateChangeSahelCombine.pdf (last visited May 12, 2009).

11. *Desertification: An Overview*, UN Conference on Desertification, Provisional Agenda Item 4, at 5, UN Doc. A/CONF.74/1 (1977).

12. Dept. of State, Pub. No. 8906, Desertification: A Global Challenge 2 (1977).

13. *See, for example,* Harold Dregne, *Desertification of Arid Lands*, 53 Econ. Geography 322, 328 (1977).

14. G.A. Res. 3337, U.N. GAOR 2nd Comm., 29th Sess., Supp. No. 31, at 64, U.N. Doc. A/9631 (1975).

15. *See* Leena Ninan, *Fighting Against Ourselves: Efforts to Combat Desertification and Land Degradation*, 10 Currents Int'l Trade L.J. 65, 71 (2005).

16. William Burns, *The International Convention to Combat Desertification: Drawing A Line in the Sand?*, 16 Mich. J. Int'l L. 831, 852 (1995).

17. *Id.* at 853.

pact on development activities on the ground.[18] To this extent, PACD's emphasis on the establishment of national and sub-regional action plans resulted in "over-production of plans."[19] Third, and related, PACD contained no binding obligations on the governments. Fourth, the recommendations represented a "top-down approach to addressing desertification."[20]

During the United Nations Conference on Environment and Development (UNCED) in Rio de Janeiro (largely dubbed the "Earth Summit") in 1992, African governments forcefully put desertification on the agenda. These countries felt "the attention of the developed world was too focused on problems of climate change and biodiversity, whereas the challenges to sustainable development that they faced, including food insecurity and poverty, were being overlooked."[21] Many industrialized countries stiffly resisted the idea of an international anti-desertification convention for two reasons—one conceptual and one pragmatic. Conceptually, many industrialized countries argued that desertification was not a "global" problem:

> The OECD countries did not accept the idea of a convention. They felt that desertification was not a global problem of the same kind as, for example, climate. It was certainly a problem of global significance, but that would not necessarily warrant a global arrangement.[22]

The pragmatic objection by the industrialized countries was related to the conceptual problem: the industrialized countries did not want to establish any binding financial or technology transfer mechanisms for dealing with desertification—partly because they felt that the problem was not "global" but a "cumulative result of desert populations' decisions and actions."[23] As such, they objected to a global response that bound industrialized countries to commit financial resources in a global response.

The resolution of these two key issues involved compromises reflected in the ensuing UN Convention to Combat Desertification (UNCCD) (the "Desertification Convention). In the end, the Desertification Convention settled for the following language: "that [the parties acknowledge that] desertification and drought are problems of *global dimension* in that they affect all regions of the world and that joint action of the international community is needed to combat desertification and/or mitigate the effects of drought."[24] On the question of technology transfer, the Desertification Convention vaguely required the parties to "undertake, as mutually agreed and in accordance with their respective national legislation and/or policies, to promote, finance and/or facilitate the financing of the transfer, acquisition, adaptation and development of environmentally sound, economically viable and socially acceptable technologies relevant to combating desertification and/or mitigating the effects of drought, with a view to contributing to the achievement of sustainable development in affected areas. Such cooperation shall be conducted bilaterally or multilaterally, as appropriate, making full use of the expertise of intergovernmental and non-governmental organizations."[25]

---

18. L.C. Stringer, *Reviewing the International Year of Deserts and Desertification 2006: What Contribution Towards Combating Global Desertification and Implementing the United Nations Convention to Combat Desertification?*, 72 J. Arid Env. 2065, 2066 (2008) [hereinafter 2008 Stringer].

19. Camila Toulmin, Combating Desertification: Setting the Agenda for a Global Convention 20 (International Institute for Environment and Development 1993).

20. 2008 Stringer, *supra* note 18, at 2066.

21. *Id.*

22. Bo Kjellen, *The Saga of the Convention to Combat Desertification: The Rio/Johannesburg Process and the Global Responsibility for the Drylands*, 12 Reciel 127, 128 (2003).

23. 2008 Stringer, *supra* note 18, at 2066.

24. Text of the United Nations Convention to Combat Desertification, *Prologue, available at* http://www.unccd.int/convention/text/convention.php?annexNo=0 (1994) (last visited May 12, 2009).

25. *Id.* art. 18.

On the key issue of financing, the Desertification Convention settled for the equally vague exhortatory language wherein the parties pledged to "promote the availability of financial mechanisms and shall encourage such mechanisms to seek to maximize the availability of funding for affected developing country Parties, particularly those in Africa, to implement the Convention."[26]

As expected, the Desertification Convention has been an ineffective vehicle to respond to the widespread desertification going on in much of Africa.[27] In the next section, I briefly put the Desertification Convention in the context of climate change as an attempt to explain the neglect of the anti-desertification crusade globally.

C. A Tale of Two Conventions: The Desertification and Climate Change Conventions

The difference in approach between the Desertification Convention and the United Nations Framework Convention for Climate Change (UNFCCC) (the "Climate Change Convention") is striking in quite a few ways. First, the Desertification Convention is hailed as representing "progressive development in the tools and doctrines of international environmental law" because of its "bottom-up" approach.[28] As Kyle Danish has written:

> The hallmark of the Desertification Convention is its "bottom-up" approach. Other international environmental conventions obligate states to centralize and expand their powers or regulation. The Desertification Convention, however, obligates states to channel authority and resources down to local land users and particularly to non-governmental organizations (NGOs). The Convention does not mandate new regulations; instead, it mandates new alliances and new partnerships that link international institutions, states, NGOs, and communities.[29]

As various commentators have remarked, this approach to international law-making with its focus on "participatory policy-making at decentralized policy levels" is unprecedented and innovative.[30] Hans Bruyninckx argues that these innovative elements in the Desertification Convention can be "interpreted as emanations of policy discourses which have been gaining in importance since the introduction and the fairly broad acceptance of sustainable development and Agenda 21 as guiding conceptual frameworks for international environmental and development initiatives."[31] Bruyninckx breaks down these policy discourses into three specific discourses. First, the participation discourse obligates stakeholder involvement in policy-making.[32] Second, the decentralization discourse mandates the dispersal and devolution of political, institutional and policy responsibilities to local governments.[33] Third, the local knowledge discourse encour-

---

26. *Id.* art 21.

27. *See* Section C below.

28. Kyle Danish, *International Environmental Law and the Bottom-Up Approach: A Review of the Desertification Convention*, 3 IND. J. GLOBAL LEGAL STUD. 133 (1995).

29. *Id.* at 134.

30. Hans Bruyninckx, *The Convention to Combat Desertification and the Role of Innovative Policy-Making Discourses: The Case of Burkina Faso*, 4 GLOBAL ENV. POL. 107, 108 (2004) [hereinafter 2004 Bruyninckx].

31. *Id.* at 109.

32. *For example*, Art. 9(1), Desertification Convention stipulates that national action programs "shall be updated through a continuing participatory process on the basis of lessons from field action, as well as the results of research." Similarly, Art 10(2) requires National action programs to "specify the respective roles of government, local communities and land users and the resources available and needed" and in sub-paragraph (f) calls for "effective participation at the local, national and regional levels of non-governmental organizations and local populations, both women and men, particularly resource users, including farmers and pastoralists and their representative organizations, in policy planning, decision-making, and implementation and review of national action programs."

33. For example, Art. 4(2)(b), Desertification Convention obligates affected African countries to "sustain and strengthen reforms currently in progress toward greater decentralization."

ages countries to take into account local traditional knowledge and experience-based knowledge of the dynamics of desertification in policy-making.[34]

The Climate Change Convention, on the other hand, is a more "normal, standard" regime.[35] The Climate Change Convention has "few procedural or institutional innovations" and lies between a framework convention (a procedural instrument that aims to establish a basis for future action) and a substantive convention (one that presently commits states to specific measures and policies).[36] The treaty therefore established an "ultimate objective" to stabilize emissions at a level which would no longer interfere in a harmful way with the global climate, but did not specify emission reduction targets.[37] While states make few concrete commitments in the Climate Convention, there is an unmistakable view that the state (and not the local government) is the locus of the Convention. For example, among the commitments states undertake is to "take climate change considerations into account, to the extent feasible, in their relevant social, economic and environmental policies and actions, and employ appropriate methods, for example impact assessments, *formulated and determined nationally*, with a view to minimizing adverse effects on the economy, on public health and on the quality of the environment, of projects or measures undertaken by them to mitigate or adapt to climate change."[38] Indeed, the focus on traditional "top-down" regulation in the Climate Change Convention is so severe that some commentators have suggested that there is an "assumption that only extensive government regulation will generate substantial reductions from the [individual and household] sector [which] is a barrier to change."[39] The point is that the Climate Change Convention is decidedly state-centric. Where, for example, it requires parties to "formulate, implement, publish and regularly update" programs to reduce global warming, it envisages that these plans would be national in orientation, and, where appropriate, regional.

Though the Climate Change Convention was negotiated around the same time as the Desertification Convention (both are the products of the Earth Summit), it makes no attempt to use the "innovative" participatory discourses mandated by the Desertification Convention. What accounts for this radical difference in approach?

One response would be to point to the differences in subject-matter. The Desertification Convention directly implicates land use strategies by local populations:

> Soil degradation often has strong and specific local impacts on farmers and other groups. In terms of concrete policy measures, the local level is therefore important because these measures tend to be based on actions that are implemented at the level of the individual farmer and/or locally embedded organizations.[40]

However, as many environmental commentators have pointed out, local action and decision-making is equally important in climate change mitigation and adaptation.[41] Hence, while partic-

---

34. For example, Art. 16(g) Desertification Convention state parties agree to "exchange information on local and traditional knowledge, ensuring adequate protection for it and providing appropriate return from the benefits derived from it, on an equitable basis and on mutually agreed terms, to the local populations concerned."

35. United Nations Framework Convention on Environment and Development: May 9, 1992, 31 I.L.M. 849 (entered into force Mar. 21, 1994) (hereinafter "UNFCCC").

36. DANIEL BODANSKY, *THE U.N. FRAMEWORK CONVENTION ON CLIMATE CHANGE: A COMMENTARY*, 18 YALE J. Int'l L. 451, 494–95 (1993).

37. Art. 2, UNFCCC.

38. Art. 4(1)(f), UNFCCC (emphasis added).

39. Michael P. Vandenbergh, Jack Barkenbus & Jonathon Gilligan, *Individual Carbon Emissions: The Low-Hanging Fruit*, 55 UCLA L. REV. 1701 (2008) [hereinafter 2008 Vandenbergh].

40. 2004 Bruyninckx, *supra* note 30, at 111.

41. *See, for example,* Paula J. Schauwecker, *Land Use To Address Global Climate Change,* 23-Fall NAT. RESOURCES & ENV'T 48 (2008); 2008 Vandenbergh, *supra* note 39.

ipatory discourses are, generally, good, even progressive, the context in which this innovation was foisted onto African countries through the Desertification Convention seems curious. First, it seems to align with the industrialized countries' views that desertification was indeed a "local" not "global" issue. This is in turn aligned with the categorical notion that desertification was primarily caused by local human activities (overgrazing and over-cultivation) as opposed to broader biophysical processes especially climatological controls. If desertification is blamed on local environmental mismanagement and local human impact on the environment, it makes more sense to focus on the local in devising mitigation measures.

The scientific explanation of Sahelian desertification that implicates improper land use as the main driver is based on the feedback (between atmospheric circulation and land surface processes) hypothesis (also called the Charney thesis).[42] Under this paradigm, changes in land use and/or land cover are believed to be the major cause of climate perturbations in the Sahel: Land denudation resulting from poor agricultural practices of the local population translates into an increase of the reflectivity of the Earth's surface (albedo) to which the atmosphere responds with downward motion of air parcels. This downward motion of air parcels counteracts the upward motion that produces rainfall resulting in a biogeophysical feedback: an increase in albedo resulting from reduced plant cover leads to a decrease in rainfall, which further reduces vegetation naturally.[43]

The science that blames the desertification of the Sahel on local environmental mismanagement has, however, been impugned by recent studies on global climate change. Recent evidence suggests that the Sahelian drought has been caused, in large part, by variations in global sea surface temperature and not by regional or local environmental mismanagement.[44] Hence, global emissions of greenhouse gases and aerosols mainly from industrialization are directly implicated in the Sahelian desertification. According to this alternative theory, variability of rainfall in the Sahel results from the response of the African summer monsoon to oceanic forcing, amplified by land-atmosphere interaction. Therefore, the recent drying trend in the semiarid Sahel is attributed to warmer-than-average low-latitude waters around Africa, which, by favoring the establishment of deep convection over the ocean, weaken the continental convergence associated with the monsoon and engender widespread drought from Senegal to Ethiopia.[45] From this perspective, then, global climate change is the main driver of desertification in the Sahel because drought in the Sahel is related to a generalized pattern of warming of the global tropical oceans, especially in the Indian Ocean.

Another likely factor implicated in the Sahelian desertification is "global dimming."[46] While most climate change discussion focuses on carbon dioxide, there are a number of other compounds that affect atmospheric temperature. One of these influences is aerosols. Aerosols comprise a diverse array of particles, from dust to sulfates, which are suspended in the air. Some of these components, such as dust, tend to scatter radiation and thus usually reflect light away from the earth. This leads to a slight cooling effect. In contrast, other particles like black carbon, the black component of soot, absorb radiation and heat up the atmosphere. The particles that scatter light lead to a decrease in surface radiation and resulting "global dimming." Although this might at first seem like a good thing, it causes severe hydrological impacts. Rainfall results from

---

42. Jule Charney, *et al.*, *Drought in the Sahara: A Biogeophysical Feedback Mechanism*, 187 SCIENCE 434–435 (1975).

43. *Id.*

44. *See, for example*, Alessandra Giannini *et al.*, *Oceanic Forcing of Sahel Rainfall on Interannual to Interdecadal Time Scales*, 302 SCIENCE 1027 (2003).

45. *See* A. Giannini *et al.*, *Oceanic Forcing of Sahel Rainfall on Interannual to Interdecadal Time Scales*, 302 SCIENCE 1027 (2003); N. Zeng, *Atmospheric Science: Drought in the Sahel*, 302 SCIENCE 999 (2003).

46. *See* TIM FLANNERY, THE WEATHER MAKERS 125–127 (Grove Press 2005).

the evaporation of surface moisture, which requires surface heating. If surface radiation is reduced, less evaporation occurs, and less precipitation falls in the area.[47] Studies indicate that there are large amounts of scattering aerosols over the Sahel.[48] Increased dust loading as a result of drought would exacerbate the problem.

Both the Giannini thesis (positing that changes in the surface temperature of the oceans are a major factor in the Sahelian desertification) and the "global dimming" thesis powerfully lay much of the blame for the Sahelian desertification on climate change and global warming. This, in turn, implies that the single most important objection that industrialized countries had to helping out African countries to combat desertification—namely that the causes of desertification are local (*i.e.* human-induced reduction in vegetation cover due to poor agricultural practices)—are unfounded. Rather than supplying an excuse for non-involvement in the managing of desertification, the new evidence on the effects of climate change on dry-lands suggests that industrialized countries, as the main emitters of both greenhouse gases and aerosols, bear responsibility for the desertification as well.

The contestable science (Charney thesis) that influenced the substantive content of the Desertification Convention (through the global/local distinction) also influenced the procedural content as well. As intimated above, the foregrounding of local human factors in desertification justified the "bottom-up" approach to the Desertification Convention. While, of course, there is nothing inherently wrong with a "bottom-up" participatory approach, in the case of the Desertification Convention, the participatory discourse appears to have been driven by deep mistrust of African states to manage environmental matters rather than a genuine desire to move environmental governance in the path of participatory democratic governance. That this is so is reflected by the Climate Change Convention's reversion to the top-down mechanism. It would seem, therefore, the real reason for preferring the participatory discourses in the Desertification Convention was to keep with the main message of Neoliberal reforms sweeping through Africa at the behest of the World Bank and the International Monetary Fund (IMF). This required "smaller" governments and privatization. Hence, as Bruyninckx writes:

> The text of the [Desertification Convention], however, implicitly suggests an even stronger argument for decentralization. It reflects the general idea that decentralization in developing countries will provide more fertile ground for more participatory and more effective policy-making, through the spreading of a more democratic political context. This same discourse can be found in documents and policy programs conducted by the World Bank and the International Monetary Fund. It is often (partially) translated as good governance in the conditions for financial support and loans.[49]

As Sally Falk Moore writes, the design of the Desertification Convention, despite its "populist rhetoric about rural populations and decentralization of government," was "Northern-generated."[50] Rather than expand the processes of participatory decision-making by local population within African countries, it expanded opportunities for Northern "donors" and Northern-funded NGOs to intervene in African affairs.[51] It comes as no surprise, therefore, that the rhetoric of decentralization has not been very effective or useful in combating desertification. The problem, though, is not just the ineffectiveness of the sloganized idea of decentralization. The more worrying problem, as Sally Falk Moore astutely points out, is the way the asymmetri-

---

47. *See* V. Ramanathan & G. Carmichael, *Global and Regional Climate Changes Due to Black Carbon*, 1 NATURE GEOSCI 221 (2008).

48. *Id.*

49. 2004 Bruyninckx, *supra* note 30, at 111.

50. 2001 Moore, *supra* note 7.

51. *Id.* at 179.

cal relationship between Africa and the West is embedded in a "predefined conception of authoritative knowledge that has a particular content."[52] As an instrument of international environmental law, hence, the Desertification Convention, despite its good intentions and potential, easily becomes a "medium for the creation and perpetuation of a racialized hierarchy of international norms and institutions that subordinate non-Europeans to Europeans."[53] Though the Desertification Convention's participatory, decentralization, and local knowledge's discourses could putatively transform environmental law and subject it to participatory and substantive democracy, its specific context makes it yet another site for maintaining the dichotomy between the civilized West and the uncivilized Africa, demarcating the former as 'universal' and the latter as 'particular', and seeking to bridge the gap between the two by developing techniques to normalize the aberrant society.[54] In this case, decentralization as a "regulative" concept provides the doctrinal and textual basis for "normalizing" the African state through the intervention of Northern "donors" and NGOs. Community-based approach, then, becomes a reflection of domination rather than a genuine belief that participatory democracy is an antidote to environmental mismanagement and ecological deterioration. In this rendition, top-down approach is a merely populist sloganized version of the Neo-liberal agenda to "reduce" the size of the (African) government.

In this way, rather than the Desertification Convention becoming a useful tool to address the adverse global effects of climate change that are manifesting themselves in Africa, the Desertification Convention fitted well into the mold of regulative and authoritative knowledge produced to intervene in, and manage, Africa.

D. Climate Change Regime and Africa: Subordination or Emancipation?

What, then, is the fate of Africa under the Climate Change regime? The short answer is that it depends. It depends on how vigilant African countries, African people, and advocates of social justice will be in demanding action to protect Africa and its people from the adverse effects of climate change. The present climate regime, like international law architecture generally, is not perfect but it might provide some wiggle room through which transformative projects can be undertaken both to mitigate GHG emissions while helping African people adapt to the expected adverse effects of climate change. This section will first briefly sketch out the adverse effects of climate change in Africa. It will then parse out Africa's powerlessness and lack of influence as reflected in the present regime of climate change before it considers the interstices of liberation presented by the regime.

1. Effects of Climate Change in Africa

Let's begin with some three perturbing truths that should frame this section. *First,* Africans have contributed the least to climate change caused by humans. *Second,* Africa is the most vulnerable continent to the likely effects of climate change. *Third,* Africa has the least capacity to adapt to the effects of climate change. An equitable climate change regime or a social justice perspective to the climate change regime will have to take these three truths into account in fashioning effective responses to climate change and allocating responsibilities to state parties. It is doubtful that the current climate change regime has achieved this. Before considering this question and suggesting recommendations, let's briefly substantiate each of the "truths" first.

---

52. *Id.* at 184.
53. 2000 Mutua, *supra* note 5.
54. Antony Anghie, Imperialism, Sovereignty and the Making of International Law 6 (Cambridge Un. Press 2005).

According to the World Resources Institute, Africa's historical cumulative emissions of CO_2 between 1800 and 2000 were just 1.7% of the world's total.[55] Africa has very low carbon dioxide emissions because of its lack of a large transportation sector, combined with relatively low rates of electrification, appliance penetration, and industrialization. Only five African countries have per capita CO_2 emissions higher than the global average (1.23 metric tons of carbon per year): Equatorial Guinea (2.86), South Africa (2.68), Libya (2.55), the Seychelles (1.84), and Algeria (1.50). Based on 2004 per capita emission rates, 28 of the 54 African nations for which data are available have per capita emissions less than 0.1 metric ton of carbon per person per year.[56] Africa represents only a small fraction, 3.6%, out of the total carbon dioxide (CO_2) emissions per year, yet 14% of the population of the world lives here.[57] To put it starkly, on a per capita basis, CO_2 emissions in Africa average approximately 0.4 metric ton per year per person while the United States CO_2 emissions averages about 19.5 tons per person.[58] Hence, the average per capita emission by an American is almost 50 times greater than that of an African. Or, as the 2007 Human Development Report starkly put it: The state of Texas (population 23 million) in the United States registers CO_2 emissions of around 700 Mt CO_2 or 12 percent of the United States' total emissions. That figure is greater than the total CO_2 footprint left by sub-Saharan Africa—a region of 720 million people.[59]

While Africans have the lightest carbon footprint, their continent will be most impacted by the adverse effects of climate change—and the impacts seem almost apocalyptic. Worse still, primary effects (such as desertification) are likely to lead to secondary effects (such as war and conflict) exacerbating the adverse consequences. The authoritative Intergovernmental Panel on Climate Change (IPCC) report concludes that Africa is one of the most vulnerable continents to climate change because of multiple stresses.[60] It identifies five separate drivers which, in concert, make Africa extremely vulnerable to climate change:

Water stress and water insecurity. Global warming will increase the rate of evaporation and re-duce soil moisture. At the same time, a decrease in run-off will lead to reservoirs with less water.[61] It is projected that by 2020, between 75 million and 250 million people in Africa alone will be exposed to increased water stress due to climate change.[62] It is also estimated that the area of the continent suitable for agriculture is likely to decrease, particularly along the edges of semi-arid and arid regions; and that by 2020, yields from rain-fed agriculture in some countries could decrease by as much as 50%, exacerbating malnutrition and food security problems.[63] This water shortage and its attendant pasture shortage coupled with food insecurity can easily lead to vio-lent conflict as water becomes scarce, farm and grazing land gets lost to the desert, and food be-

55. WORLD RESOURCES INSTITUTE (WRI), WORLD RESOURCES 2002–2004: DECISIONS FOR THE EARTH BALANCE, VOICE AND POWER (2003) Data Table 7, 258–9 [hereinafter 2003 WORLD RESOURCES INSTITUTE].

56. G. MARLAND, T.A. BODEN, AND R.J. ANDRES, GLOBAL, REGIONAL, AND NATIONAL CO_2 EMISSIONS, TRENDS: A COMPENDIUM OF DATA ON GLOBAL CHANGE (2007), Carbon Dioxide Information Analysis Center, Oak Ridge National Laboratory, U.S. Department of Energy, Oak Ridge, Tenn., U.S.A.

57. UNEP/GRID Arendal Maps and Graphics Library, Emissions of carbon dioxide, in Africa and selected OECD countries, available at http://maps.grida.no/go/graphic/emissions_of_carbon_dioxide_in_africa_and_selected_oecd_countries (last visited October 25, 2008).

58. 2003 WORLD RESOURCES INSTITUTE, *supra* note 55, Data Table 7.

59. UNITED NATIONS DEVELOPMENT PROGRAM, HUMAN DEVELOPMENT REPORT 2007: FIGHTING CLIMATE CHANGE: HUMAN SOLIDARITY IN A DIVIDED WORLD 43 (2007).

60. M. Boko *et al.*, *Africa*, in CLIMATE CHANGE 2007: IMPACTS, ADAPTATION AND VULNERABILITY. CONTRIBUTION OF WORKING GROUP II TO THE FOURTH ASSESSMENT REPORT OF THE INTERGOVERNMENTAL PANEL ON CLIMATE CHANGE 435 (M.L. Parry *et al.* eds., Cambridge Un. Press 2007).

61. *Id.*

62. UNFCCC 2007.

63. *Id.*

comes scarce. Indeed, commentators have described the Darfur conflict as the first climate change conflict.[64]

Food insecurity and agricultural production. Since most African countries are net food importers, changes in local climate conditions (which will result in lower crop productivity) will combine with the expected rise in world food prices to increase food insecurity in the region.[65] A recent UN Report has warned that some African countries could experience a reduction of yields from rain-fed agriculture by up to 50 percent by 2020.[66] It has already been reported that the number of food emergencies encountered each year in Africa has tripled since the mid-1980s.[67]

Health. The projected increases in temperature will extend the habitats of vectors of diseases such as malaria and cholera while extreme weather events will result in increased frequency of epidemics and enteric diseases especially because of inadequate infrastructure.[68] Recent research has, for example, found a link between climate change and malaria: it concluded that even a half-degree centigrade warming can increase mosquito abundance by 30–100%.[69] Also, the reduction in the quantity of water in a continent where 250 million people have no access to potable water and 300 million people do not have adequate sanitation will only lead to further reduction in water quality which could lead to further deterioration in human health.[70] Increased flooding could facilitate the breeding of malaria carriers in formerly arid areas.[71] Heat stress and drought are likely to have a negative impact (both directly due to increased heat, and indirectly through lack of pastures and fodder) on animal health, and, consequently, the production of dairy and meat products. This could, in turn, result in protein deficiency, malnutrition, and its associated diseases.[72]

Desertification. As argued above, evidence has emerged that climate change and desertification are inextricably linked through feedbacks between land degradation and precipitation.[73] Climate change is, also, expected to lead to increased frequency of droughts and other extreme weather events.

Settlements and Ecosystems. According to the IPPC, an increase in extreme weather events, especially floods and dust storms, would result in damage to settlements and infrastructure and af-

---

64. Scott Baldauf, *Africans are Already Facing Climate Change*, CHRISTIAN SCI. MONITOR, Nov. 6, 2006, at 4. Baldauf quotes British Home Secretary John Reid as saying: "[Climate] changes make the emergence of violent conflict more rather than less likely. The blunt truth is that the lack of water and agricultural land is a significant contributory factor to the tragic conflict we see unfolding in Darfur. We should see this as a warning sign."

65. Text accompanying notes 44–48 above.

66. UN General Assembly Background Paper, *Climate Change and the Most Vulnerable Countries: The Imperative to Act* (July 8, 2008).

67. *Id.*

68. *Id.*

69. J.A. Patz & S.H. Olson, *Malaria Risk and Temperature: Influences from Global Climate Change and Local Land Use Practices*, 103 PROC NATL ACAD. SCI USA 5635 (2006) (discussing findings of M. Pascual *et al.*, *Malaria Resurgence in the East African Highlands: Temperature Trends Revisited*, 103 PROC NATL ACAD SCI USA 5829 (2006)). The possibility that global warming is causing the spread of malaria is also acknowledged by the IPCC in the FOURTH ASSESSMENT REPORT, contribution of Working Group 2, Chapter 9: *Africa, available at* http://www.ipcc.ch/ipccreports/ar4-wg2.htm.

70. Mahmoud Medany, *et al.*, *Background Paper on Impacts, Vulnerability and Adaptation to Climate Change in Africa, available at* http://unfccc.int/files/adaptation/adverse_effects_and_response_measures_art_48/application/pdf/200609_backgroun_african_wkshp.pdf.

71. *Id.* (citing M. Warsame, *et al.*, *An epidemic of* Plasmodium falciparum *malaria in Balcad Somalia, and its causation*, 98 TRANSACTIONS OF THE ROYAL SOCIETY OF TROPICAL MEDICINE AND HYGIENE 142–145 (1995)).

72. *Id.*

73. Text accompanying notes 44–48 above.

fect human health. The situation is made extremely dire by the fact that most of Africa's largest cities are along the coast, and a large population is land-locked.[74] Also, sea-level rise, coastal erosion, salt water intrusion, and flooding will have significant impacts on African communities and economies.[75]

2. The Latest Chapter in Africa's Powerlessness and Marginalization

As briefly documented above, climate change will not only have drastic environmental, economic and social impacts on Africa, it will also have implications for peace, security and migration in the region. One would therefore expect Africa to be a powerful voice in the climate change negotiations, and in shaping the climate change regime. However, this has not been the case. As Dr. Albert Mumma has complained, Africa has, so far, failed to articulate an "African position" in the Climate Change Convention negotiations, and has, as a result, failed to influence the emerging regime in a direction that serves Africa's unique interests in the negotiations.[76] The two chief and inter-related reasons for this failure are lack of resources ("financial, technical and human—to develop, popularize and consistently articulate a position")[77] and the extant and entrenched pattern of marginalization in the international legal system.[78] Dr. Mumma has dramatically demonstrated the asymmetrical negotiating abilities between Western countries and African countries. Typically, African countries can only afford to send very small delegations of officials while industrialized countries can send extraordinarily large contingents complete with experts and backed by Northern-based NGOs and private sector representatives. This allows industrialized countries to be dominant during the negotiations and to drive the process. As Dr. Mumma dramatically illustrates:

> Taking the example of the 4th Conference of the Parties at Buenos Aires, the United States delegation was a contingent of eighty-three people and the European Union forty-five, excluding the national delegations of EU member states. The "developed country viewpoint" was supported by a whole array of publications distributed by "think tanks"— from the government, business sector and non-governmental organizations alike—which had been at work for months (perhaps years) developing and clarifying their positions on the pertinent issues. This was reinforced by the presence of hundreds of "manned stands" and "side events" at the Conference venue at which these viewpoints were explained and argued, and by daily newsletters on the issues of the day as the writers saw them.

> In contrast, the typical African delegation had two to four people. Most countries were able to attend only because they could rely on the two air tickets availed to developing country delegates by the Secretariat. African countries had no stands and no side events, and only rarely was an African to be found speaking on a panel at an event organized by others, even where the event had advertised itself as presenting "the Southern perspective." There was a similar scarcity at the Conference of African non-governmental organizations or business sector representatives. Lacking a pre-existing network African government delegates relied on meetings organized at the venue to try and come up with a position. On the whole, the meetings were poorly attended by African delegates and the discussion desultory.[79]

---

74. *Id.*

75. *Id.*

76. Albert Mumma, *The Poverty of Africa's Position at the Climate Change Convention Negotiations*, 19 UCLA J. Envtl. L. & Pol'y 181, 198 (2001–2002) [hereinafter 2001 Mumma].

77. *Id.* at 202.

78. Ruth Gordon, *Climate Change and the Poorest Nations: Further Reflections on Global Inequality*, 78 U. Colo. L. Rev. 1559, 1618–22 (2007) [hereinafter 2007 Gordon].

79. 2001 Mumma, *supra* note 76, at 202–203 (footnotes omitted).

However, the marginalization of Africa is not just because of resource constraints. Rather, the resource constraints only make the domination more acute with representatives from industrialized countries setting the agenda and driving the process.[80] Indeed, some representatives of developing countries have complained that the climate change negotiations are not "negotiations" but a forum in which the rich nations tell the South what is and is not going to happen.[81]

Yet, while Africa's equity arguments (based on historical responsibility for emissions and the legitimate need to industrialize) and marginalization arguments (based on resource constraints and structure of international relations generally) are compelling, Africa must work to develop "a vision about its interests on the issue of climate change."[82] For this to happen, African countries must, first, seriously address the structural impediments that make it hard or impossible for it to forcefully articulate its position on climate change issues. These include improving the profile of its negotiators at the climate change conferences, but also retaining experts, and creating awareness domestically and abroad about the vulnerabilities and opportunities presented by climate change. This must begin with the first step of taking climate change seriously. While African countries must, of necessity, promote their development imperatives, they must realize that climate change poses the greatest threat to the promise of sustainable economic development. Hence, they must more effectively link sustainable development with climate change concerns. At the same time, they must forcefully interject the social justice argument into the climate change discourse.

3. Transforming Climate Change Discourse into a Social Justice Discourse

Social justice, in the context of climate change, refers to the application of substantive and procedural norms and policies that promote fairness and equity in the distribution of the burdens and benefits of the global ecology—including principles of corrective justice, deterrence and inter- and intra-generational equity—in the use of shared global environmental resources.[83] Apart from meaningful participation in shaping the climate change regime as argued for above, the social justice perspective in the climate change discourse would have to take into account the following four factors in fashioning rights and obligations of states in the climate change regime:

> *First*, historical and current responsibility for emissions causing climate change (the "Responsibility Principle");
>
> *Second*, vulnerability to adverse effects of climate change, *i.e.*, both the projected degree of exposure to shocks, and capacity to cope with the adverse effects expected from climate change including both preparedness (land and building codes and better forecasting) and response to disasters (such as financing mechanisms and post-disaster relief) (the "Vulnerability Factor");[84]
>
> *Third*, the financial and technological capacity to adapt to the adverse effects of climate change and the relative opportunity to reduce GHG emissions cost-effectively (the "Capacity and Opportunity principle"); and,

---

80. 2007 Gordon, *supra* note 78, at 1621–22.

81. Anil Agarwal, *A Southern Perspective on Curbing Global Climate Change, in* CLIMATE CHANGE POLICY: A SURVEY 375, 378–9 (Schneider *et al.*, eds., Island Press 2002).

82. 2001 Mumma, *supra* note 76, at 207.

83. David Miller writes: "When we talk and argue about social justice, what exactly are we talking and arguing about? Very crudely, I think, we are discussing how the good and bad things in life should be distributed among the members of a human society." DAVID MILLER, PRINCIPLES OF SOCIAL JUSTICE 1 (Harvard Un. Press 1999).

84. *See* WORLD BANK, DISASTERS, CLIMATE CHANGE, AND ECONOMIC DEVELOPMENT IN SUB-SAHARAN AFRICA: LESSONS AND FUTURE DIRECTIONS 1 (Evaluation Brief 3, 2007).

Fourth, the standard of living of the population, *i.e.*, the legitimate welfare needs of populations in developing countries. This means that the ultimate objective of stabilizing greenhouse gas concentrations in the atmosphere at a level that would prevent dangerous anthropogenic interference with the climate system must be achieved within a time frame sufficient to allow ecosystems to adapt naturally to climate change and with the goal of ensuring that food production is not threatened while enabling economic development to proceed in a sustainable manner (the "Special Needs Principle").

One could plausibly argue that these four social justice principles are already incorporated (but not fore-grounded) in the UNFCCC and the Kyoto Protocol through the principle of common but differentiated responsibilities, and that it behooves Africa to push for specific commitments and mechanisms to vivify them in designing a post-Kyoto Protocol operational regime. In particular, the principle of common but differentiated responsibilities, read in context and brought to life, could be used as the basis for transforming the climate change discourse into a social justice discourse. The recipe for action is already in place. The preamble to UNFCCC has the following stipulations:

- It acknowledges climate change as an issue of ecological interdependence and calls for concerted action from all states "in accordance with their common but differentiated responsibilities and respective capabilities and their social and economic conditions."[85]
- It notes "that the largest share of historical and current global emissions of greenhouse gases has originated in developed countries, that per capita emissions in developing countries are still relatively low and that the share of global emissions originating in developing countries will grow to meet their social and development needs."[86]
- It recognizes the "leadership principle," *i.e.*, the need for developed countries to take the first actions towards comprehensive response strategies "with due consideration of their relative contributions to the enhancement of the greenhouse effect."[87]
- It recognizes the special development needs of developing countries and especially that "in order for developing countries to progress towards that goal, their energy consumption will need to grow taking into account the possibilities for achieving greater energy efficiency and for controlling greenhouse gas emissions in general, including through the application of new technologies on terms which make such an application economically and socially beneficial."[88]

The principle of common but differentiated responsibilities is also specifically mentioned in Articles 3 and 4 of UNFCCC, and became the major premise of the Kyoto Protocol where developing countries do not have to make any binding reductions of their emissions. The real question remains, however, how to transform this general concept of common but differentiated principles into a series of operational and effective rules, principles or policies that simultaneously mitigate climate change, increase the capacity of African countries to adapt to the adverse effects of climate change, and promote sustainable economic development.

The scope of this chapter does not allow an exhaustive elaboration of all such operational rules but we would like to briefly suggest four here. The aim is to demonstrate that foregrounding social justice in the climate change regime yields different substantive rules that are fairer, more equitable, and more favorable to Africa.

---

85. UNFCCC, Preamble.
86. *Id.*
87. *Id.*
88. *Id.*

a. Rethinking Mitigation Strategies

African countries must, first, transcend the sterile position that the fact that they bear little responsibility for historical emissions of GHGs and the fact that they need to fuel their social and economic development means that they should not take any binding commitments to mitigate GHG emissions.[89] This is a self-defeating position for at least three reasons.

First, if all developing countries (including China and India) continue increasing their GHG emission rates at the current rates, it will completely dwarf any reduction commitments by developed countries leading to an increase in GHG emissions, and, hence, global warming. If, as outlined above, Africa will suffer earliest and the most from global warming, any mitigation regime that leads to an increase in GHG emissions overall is bad for Africa even if Africa does not have to take any present commitments to reduce or limit its emissions.

Second, a generalized position that all developing countries should not make binding commitments to reduce emissions lumps together countries like China and India (with significant and ever-rising emissions) with African countries (with insignificant emissions) in complete disregard to the common but differentiated standards principle.

Third, a blanket application of the common but differentiated responsibilities standard (that comprehends only the developed and developing countries categories) creates a grid-lock as some developed countries (especially the United States and Australia) insist that an acceptable climate change regime must impose emissions reduction/avoidance obligations on all countries.[90] Sadly, a "no binding regime" is bad news for Africa precisely because it will suffer most from the adverse effects of climate change.

This, then, means that the current Climate Change regime including the Kyoto Protocol is not satisfactory from an African point of view. A new post-Kyoto Protocol regime must explicitly take into consideration the Responsibility Principle, the Vulnerability Factor, the Capacity and Opportunity Principle, and the Special (Development) Needs Principle in fashioning a new GHG emissions reduction/avoidance. In other words, the Post-Kyoto Protocol regime for allocating emission entitlements must be "equitable" and not "be based simply on a party's negotiated position."[91] As Dr. Mumma has suggested, such a regime would include allocating GHG emission entitlements and caps to *all* countries under a formula that involves three criteria: responsibility (both past and future responsibility for emissions), standard of living (as a proxy for ability to pay for mitigation), and opportunity (*i.e.*, the differing cost of reducing emissions be-

---

89. Under Article 3.1 of the Kyoto Protocol, all developing countries have no binding obligations to reduce GHG emissions. *See* Non-Annex I position paper on the Kyoto Protocol, *available at* http://www-geology.uc davis.edu/~GEL10/Warming/DevelopingPosition.pdf. ("The Kyoto Protocol does not impose restrictions on developing countries. However, nations included in Annex I must limit their GHG emissions while countries that are not part of the annex have no limitations: We find this justified by the fact that developed countries are the major producers of carbon dioxide.... We find this quite fair, as we cannot escape the damage already done by the developed nations. It is unconscionable that we are expected to contribute to the damage already done by developed nations.")

90. In 1997, the United States Senate unanimously passed the Byrd-Hagel Resolution asking that "the United States should not be a signatory to any protocol to, or other agreement regarding, the United Nations Framework Convention on Climate Change of 1992, at negotiations in Kyoto in December 1997, or thereafter, which would ... mandate new commitments to limit or reduce greenhouse gas emissions for the Annex I Parties, unless the protocol or other agreement also mandates new specific scheduled commitments to limit or reduce greenhouse gas emissions for Developing Country Parties within the same compliance period." S. Res. 98, 105th Cong. (1997); Press Release, White House Office of the Press Secretary, President Bush Discusses Global Climate Change (June 11, 2001), *available at* http://www.whitehouse.gov/news/releases/2001/06/2001 0611-2.html. ("The world's second-largest emitter of greenhouse gases is China. Yet, China was entirely exempted from the requirements of the Kyoto Protocol.... India was also exempt from Kyoto.")

91. 2001 Mumma, *supra* note 76, at 204.

tween countries) to reduce emissions).[92] Such a regime would be "equitable" and a function of social justice from an African perspective for three reasons. One, it would lead to overall reduction of GHG emissions and hence reduce the doomsday scenarios that threaten Africa if the current rates of emissions continue. Two, it would create incentives to depart from the current paths to economic development (that have relied on low fossil fuel energy use) and incentivize developing countries (including Africa) to invest in renewable sources of energy.[93] Three, if coupled with a flexible trading mechanism, such a system would create real opportunities for technology transfer and environmentally-sound investments.

b. Rethinking the Clean Development Mechanism and Technology Transfer

The Clean Development Mechanism (CDM) permits Annex I countries to meet a portion of their agreed emission reduction targets through certified emission reductions (CERs) in developing countries. Article 12 of the Kyoto Protocol defines the dual objectives of the CDM:

- to assist non-Annex I parties to achieve sustainable development and in contributing to the ultimate objective of the Convention; and
- to assist Annex I parties in achieving compliance with their quantified emission limitation and reduction commitments under Article 3.

There is a real question, however, whether the "sustainable development" objective of CDM is a serious one or whether it was merely included as a "clever political move" to gain the acceptance of developing countries.[94] The CDM can, as a concept, provide a powerful mechanism for promoting climate change mitigation strategies that simultaneously provide local benefits through sustainable development. For the CDM to play this virtuous role (as opposed to a role of merely subsidizing industrialized countries by providing them with free "ecological space")[95] it must be re-designed to re-orient it towards sustainable development and sharpen it as a tool of social justice.

Two specific problems can be identified. First of all, the CDM is too narrow in its focus and orientation. Article 12 of the Kyoto Protocol creates the CDM as a project-based mechanism. As Spalding-Fecher and Simmonds write, in the drafting of Kyoto Protocol, developing countries presented a proposal to replace "projects" in Article 12 of the Protocol with the text "programs and policies" but the proposal was rejected.[96] Hence, the CDM mechanism has been interpreted as tethered to project-level implementation efforts as opposed to more sector-wide strategies to finance cleaner technologies to fuel development.[97] As a result, CDM projects are conceived very narrowly, and in ways that cannot address the real needs and obstacles to sustainable economic development in Africa.

Moreover, as currently conceived, the current CDM mechanism "punishes" Africa for its low GHG emissions. As structured, the primary factor influencing CDM investment is the capacity

---

92. *Id.* at 204–05.

93. *See* David R. Hodas, *Climate Change and Land Use in Africa, in* LAND USE LAW FOR SUSTAINABLE DEVELOPMENT 45 (Nathalie J. Chalifour *et al.*, eds., Cambridge Un. Press 2006).

94. Agus P. Sari and Stephen Meyers, *Clean Development Mechanism: Perspectives From Developing Countries,* (June 1, 1999), Lawrence Berkeley National Laboratory (Paper LBNL-43418), *available at* http://repositories.cdlib.org/lbnl/LBNL-43418. ("The inclusion of a provision to foster sustainable development in Article 12 was a clever political move. This provision is considered by developing countries as what, first and foremost, CDM is about. Indeed, the entire name juggling from JI to CDM is a brilliant political move; no one can disagree with clean development.")

95. Randall Spalding-Fecher & Gillian Simmonds, *Sustainable Energy Development and the Clean Development Mechanism: African Priorities in the Negotiations, in* CLIMATE CHANGE FOR AFRICA: SCIENCE, TECHNOLOGY, POLICY, AND CAPACITY BUILDING 126 (P.S. Low ed., Cambridge Un. Press 2005).

96. *Id.*

97. *Id.*

for cheap emissions reductions. Since African countries account for a very small portion of GHG emissions, it follows that they present few opportunities to reduce emissions. Many ordinary Africans engage in activities that sink rather than emit CO_2 and hence replenish rather than degrade the environment.[98] Hence, with low levels of industrialization, and since CDM projects must reduce GHG emissions below a measurable baseline level, there is absolutely no incentive to invest CDM projects in African countries: such an investment is not only unlikely to qualify under the CDM narrow eligibility criterion, but it would also cost more. As Ruth Gordon writes:

> CDM projects must reduce GHG emissions below a baseline level, which creates an incentive for investors to forgo investment in the poorest countries, even though these nations are most in need of development and are at risk of developing as inexpensively as possible and thus often without regard to environmental concerns. Private investors are more likely to invest in nations such as China or India, where there are substantial emissions problems that can be improved with readily available technology requiring only a modest investment and little or no research. Where GHG emissions are low because of lack of industrialization, there are few incentives for private companies to invest because this kind of innovation is not rewarded. In sum, the CDM assumes a level of industrialization that is conspicuously absent in most of sub-Saharan Africa, a quandary that applies to most countries in Africa with the exception of South Africa.[99]

It should come as no surprise, then, that CDM has not been able to deliver sustainable development in Africa.[100] For example, of 1191 registered projects, Africa accounts for 27 only or 2.27% of the total.[101] The narrow conceptualization of the CDM mechanism is directly traceable to the dominant orientation of the climate change regime: prioritizing mitigation and de-emphasizing distributive effects of climate change (as a function of the inverse relationship between responsibility for emissions and the degree of adversity resulting from climate change). Foregrounding social justice arguments would, at a minimum, call for a rethinking of the CDM. African countries must not be called upon to sacrifice the welfare needs of their people and sustainable economic development. This means that for sustainable development to occur, since the international community cannot assume away the energy needs of developing countries, there is a need to decouple emission growth from economic growth, by, for example, requiring industrialized countries to provide technological and financial resources to produce more efficient and lower GHG-emitting technologies and processes in developing countries. This will enable these countries to leapfrog the GHG-intensive development path taken by industrialized countries.[102] Rather than narrowly focus on the mitigation targets of industrialized countries, the CDM should be oriented towards creating incentives for investors to "entirely omit fossil fuels 'leapfrog effect' where countries would adopt clean energy technologies at the outset of their industrialization."[103]

---

98. A.B. Sebitosi & P. Pillay, The Kyoto Protocol: A sub-Sahara African Perspective, *available at* http://ieeexplore.ieee.org/stamp/stamp.jsp?arnumber=01611828.

99. 2007 Gordon, *supra* note 78, at 1614–15 (footnotes omitted).

100. Karen Olsen, The *Clean Development Mechanism's Contribution to Sustainable Development: A Review of the Literature, available at* http://www.cd4cdm.org/Publications/CDM&SustainDevelop_literature.pdf (concluding that CDM has not been able to deliver sustainable development as earlier planned).

101. http://cdm.unfccc.int/Statistics/Registration/RegisteredProjByRegionPieChart.html

102. Jiahua Pan, Common but Differentiated Commitments: A Practical Approach to Engaging Large Developing Emitters Under L20 3 (2004), *available at* http://www.l20.org/publications/6_5c_climate_pan1.pdf.

103. 2007 Gordon, *supra* note 78, at 1615.

c. Prioritizing Adaptation

Viewing climate change issues only through the lens of mitigation (that is "how to reduce greenhouse gas levels and by how much, so as to limit future increases in global temperatures")[104] leaves neglected and unexplored the important question of adaptation, and the related question of who should bear the costs of such adaptation. A primary focus on mitigation of global warming on pragmatic grounds (that focusing on adaptation to global warming could undermine the political pressure for mitigation) is crowding out the issue of social justice by postponing or avoiding altogether the vital question of who pays for the adaptation.[105] In reality, a non-decision on the question of adaptation is a decision that is structurally unfair to Africa for two primary reasons. First, it ignores the question of culpability in causation or unjust enrichment in the distribution of the benefits of activities that resulted in the historical emissions of GHGs. From a fairness stand-point, countries and peoples that benefited most from the emission of GHG and/or emitted most GHG should bear a greater proportionate burden in climate change adaptation either as a matter of corrective justice or as a deterrence mechanism.[106] Since African countries emitted the least amount of GHG and industrialized countries emitted the greatest amounts historically, it follows that industrialized countries should be obligated to pay more for adaptation under a tort-like regime that advances corrective justice or behavioral effects as its goals. Second, a non-decision on adaptation regimes also ignores the fact that African countries are least likely to have the financial or technological means of developing infrastructure for mitigating the impacts of climate change. As the STERN REPORT has concluded:

> The poorest in society are likely to have the least capacity to adapt.... Given that the greatest need for adaptation will be in low-income countries, overcoming financial constraints is also a key objective. This will involve transfers from rich countries to poor countries. The argument is strongly reinforced by the historical responsibility of rich countries for the bulk of accumulated stocks of GHGs.[107]

Hence, there is an urgent need to feature adaptation as an integral and core part of the climate change regime. While mitigation is imperative, adaptation is equally important both as a matter of corrective justice as well as fairness in sharing the benefits and burdens of environmental interdependence.[108] One could say that the Kyoto Protocol is, at the core, a mitigation protocol: it aims, primarily, to meet the objectives of UNFCCCC by creating a regime that obligates certain countries to reduce their GHG emissions. Its flexible mechanisms—including CDM—are vehicles for the reduction of GHG emissions. To this extent, the technology transfer and adaptation properties of the Kyoto Protocol are merely incidental to the objective of reducing GHG emissions. An equitable post-Kyoto climate change regime must, however, have a consciously designed regime for increasing the adaptive capacity of African countries through funding and technology transfer. Participation by industrialized countries in the regime must be obligatory, and not as incidence to their emission-reduction obligations.

d. Linking Desertification Convention to the Climate Convention

Africa has already suffered the earliest adverse effects of climate change through desertification and its concomitant drought, water stress, and food insecurity. Yet, global anti-desertifica-

---

104. Daniel A. Farber, *Adapting to Climate Change: Who Should Pay?*, 23 FLA. ST. U. J. LAND USE & ENVTL. L. 1, 2 (2007) [hereinafter 2007 Farber].

105. *Id.*

106. *Id.*

107. NICHOLAS STERN, THE ECONOMICS OF CLIMATE CHANGE: THE STERN REVIEW 42 (Cambridge Un. Press 2007).

108. 2007 Farber, *supra* note 104.

tion measures taken so far have been ineffective and underfunded—derailed by the mistaken belief that the desertification problem is a local environmental mismanagement problem. The Desertification Convention obligates parties to the Convention to make "every effort to ensure that adequate financial resources are available for programs to combat desertification and mitigate the effects of drought," and, especially, to "promote the mobilization of adequate, timely and predictable financial resources."[109] However, funding has not been forthcoming for anti-desertification measures. While the United Nations Environment Program (UNEP) estimates that an effective 20-year global effort would cost US$ 10–22 billion per year,[110] the total funding so far averages less than $3 billion per year.[111] Alon Tal has described the disappointing financial investment in anti-desertification measures thus:

> Combating desertification has never really been a major money maker. Other international environmental challenges—from whaling to ozone holes—have always offered a better sell. For example, the Global Environmental Facility (GEF), the world's largest fund for support of international environmental challenges, did not identify desertification as part of its agenda for years. Support for projects addressing challenges associated with climate change and biodiversity has been plentiful—the other two UN-sponsored Rio Conventions enjoyed support between 1991 and 2005 of roughly $2 Billion each; land degradation received only $91 million in grants from GEF.[112]

The UNCCD Secretariat gives three reasons for the financing gap for desertification measures. First, it explains that developed country parties to the Desertification Convention "have not made a clear commitment to provide stable resources to UNCCD implementation."[113] Second, developing country parties have failed to harmonize their anti-desertification objectives with their national development plans and in mobilizing national resources.[114] And third, "development partners" have failed to mainstream UNCCD programs and activities into their programs and projects.[115]

One result of this disconnect is that anti-desertification efforts proceed in completely parallel tracks from climate change mitigation and adaptation efforts—with developed countries more willing to fund climate change issues.[116] Developing countries, including African countries, as a result, have a huge disincentive to de-prioritize anti-desertification measures. Hence, the best way to address both desertification and climate change is to harmonize efforts towards both goals.

There are two principal reasons to aggressively seek synergies between anti-desertification and climate change efforts. First, the linkages between climate change and desertification means that anti-desertification measures need to be seen as part of adaptation measures to climate change—a responsibility that industrialized countries should bear as part of their climate regime responsibilities. Second, it makes economic sense to link anti-desertification and climate change measures since most of the measures required to restore dry-land productivity would, at the same time, mitigate climate change by sequestering carbon over very large areas.[117]

---

109. Desertification Convention, Art. 20.

110. UNCCD, *Fact Sheet 8: Financing Action to Combat Desertification, available at* http://www.unccd.int/publicinfo/factsheets/showFS.php?number=8.

111. Alon Tal, *Degraded Commitments: Reviving International Efforts to Combat Desertification*, 13 BROWN J. WORLD AFFAIRS 187, 192–3 (2002).

112. *Id.* at 192.

113. UNCCD Secretariat, Follow-up to the Joint Inspection Unit report and strategy development to foster the implementation of the Convention. Situational analysis, ICCD/COP(8)/INF.5 (12 July 2007), para. 24.

114. *Id.*

115. *Id.*

116. *Id.* at paras. 17–19.

117. Lennart Olsson & Jonas Ardö, *Soil Carbon Sequestration in Degraded Semiarid Agro-Ecosystems: Perils and Potentials*, 31 AMBIO 471 (2002).

Conclusion

The ravages of global warming will entrench the existing "geographies of injustice" in the global distribution of resources unless the challenge of climate change is taken seriously and new innovative approaches are pursued.[118] Africa, as a place connoting material deprivation through structural marginalization, is the epicenter of these "geographies of injustice." Its denizens will pay the dearest for climate change—yet they bear the slightest responsibility for its causes. Because of the existing "geographies of injustice," Africa, also, has the least adaptive capacity to insulate its people from the expected ravages of climate change. This inverse relationship between responsibility for causation on the one hand, and burdens for corrective action and adversities suffered on the other hand, is only vaguely reflected in the current climate change regime. To obtain climate justice, Africa must move beyond the general position where it views climate change as a "development problem" and then contradistinguishes its view with that of industrialized countries which primarily frame climate change as an "environmental problem." Instead, African countries must re-frame the climate change discourse as one of social justice, equity and fairness, and actively aim to re-work the specific rules, mechanisms and policies of the climate change regime with a clear sense of the four social justice principles discussed in this chapter: Responsibility Principle, the Vulnerability Factor, the Capacity and Opportunity Principle, and the Special (Development) Needs Principle.

Notes

1. Thomas L. Friedman, Hot Flat, and Crowded: Why We Need a Green Revolution And How It Can Renew America ch. 7 at 141–42 (Farrar, Straus & Giroux 2008) ("Energy Poverty"):

> How will we know when Africa as a continent stands a chance to climb sustainably out of poverty? My metric is very simple: It's when I see Angelina Jolie posing next to a vast field of solar panels in Ghana or a wind farm crowded with turbines in Zimbabwe. In recent years, Jolie and other celebrities have done a great service by drawing attention to Africa's travails. In highlighting the issues of poverty and disease, they have brought some much-needed global aid and debt relief. But there is one problem in Africa that almost never gets the spotlight, and that is Africa's shortage of light. If you look at satellite pictures of earth at night, it is quite stunning. Little lights flicker across Europe, the America's and Asia, while vast swaths of Africa are simply pitch-black.

> AIDS relief has its champions, as do water purification, forest preservation, malaria treatment, and the alleviation of poverty. But the problem of "energy poverty" has no champion. It's not sexy; it has no international constituency, no buzz, no wristband, no human face. No one wants to embrace power plants, which are either dirty politically or just plain dirty. Worse, they take years to finance and build, and you can't see the results of your investment for a long time.

> Energy, in fact, is Africa's oldest orphan. But how, one wonders, will the tides of poverty, HIV/AIDS, unsafe drinking water, and malaria be turned back in Africa for good without enough energy to turn on the lights? According to the World Bank, the Netherlands today produces as much electrical power annually as all of sub-Saharan

----

118. Upendra Baxi, *Geographies of Injustice: Human Rights at the Altar of Convenience*, in Torture As Tort: Comparative Perspectives on the Development of Transnational Human Rights Litigation 197 (Craig Scott, ed., Hart Publishing 2001).

Africa, excluding South Africa: 20 gigawatts. Every two weeks or so China adds as much power—1 gigawatt of electricity—as the forty-seven countries of sub-Saharan Africa, excluding South Africa, add every *year*.

But despite this staggering power gap, the problem of energy poverty rarely gets discussed. Universal access to electricity was not even one of the eight Millennium Development Goals that were set out by the UN and the world's leading development institutions in 2000. Those goals range from halving extreme poverty to providing universal primary education, all by 2015. How are we going to eradicate poverty without eradicating energy poverty?

C. China

New Scientist, Aug. 2–8, 2008, p. 6:

CO_2 blame game

Could developed nations be to blame for China's greenhouse gas emissions? A study of the source of these emissions suggests so.

Economists say that one-third of China's human-made emissions are pumped into the atmosphere while manufacturing goods for export. Climatologists have long thought this was likely, but few had tried to quantify the effect until now.

Christopher Weber of Carnegie Mellon University in Pittsburgh, Pennsylvania, and colleagues combined a standard model of the Chinese economy, which reflects how much money flows in and out of different sectors, with nationally produced emissions data. They calculated that in 2005 the export industry generated 1.7 billion tonnes of carbon dioxide—33 percent of China's total emissions.

How to apportion the liability for emissions due to China's exports is "the million dollar question," says Weber. "It's just like narcotics," says Benito Muller of the Oxford Institute for Energy Studies, UK. "Who is responsible, the drug baron or the junkies?"

Elizabeth C. Economy, Forcing Affairs, Sept. 7–Oct. 7, 2007, quoted in Thomas L. Friedman, Hot, Flat, and Crowded: Why We Need a Green Revolution—And How It Can Renew America 53 (Farrar, Straus & Giroux 2008):

Chinese developers are laying more than 52,700 miles of new highways throughout the country. Some 14,000 new cars hit China's roads each day. By 2020, China is expected to have 130 million cars, and by 2050—or perhaps as early as 2040—it is expected to have even more cars than the United States ... China's grand-scale urbanization plans will aggravate matters. China's leaders plan to relocate 400 million people—equivalent to well over the entire population of the United States—to newly developed urban centers between 2000 and 2030. In the process, they will erect half of all the buildings expected to be constructed in the world during that period. This is a troubling prospect considering that Chinese buildings are not energy efficient—in fact, they are roughly two and a half times less so than those in Germany. Furthermore, newly urbanized Chinese, who use air conditioners, televisions, and refrigerators, consume about three and a half times more energy than do their rural counterparts.

Poisoned Air: The Negotiating State and the Changing Climate in China

Dongsheng Zang. Assistant Professor of Law, University of Washington School of Law, Box 353020, Seattle, WA 98195-3020; Tel: (206) 543-0830, zangd@u.washington.edu. I wish to thank University of Washington School of Law Professors William H. Rodgers, Jr., and Michael Robinson-Dorn for their generosity with their time and wisdom. I am also deeply indebted to Lester Ross, Bill Alford, Hongjun Zhang, and Bill Andersen, for their works and insights. All errors are mine. Sources in Chinese are used in this chapter. Any such source is provided twice: first by an English translation in the footnotes, and then in its original Chinese form at the end of the chapter.

In its recently published *World Energy Outlook 2007*, the International Energy Agency (IEA) projects that, without any major policy change (the Reference Scenario in IEA terms), China will overtake the United States as the largest consumer of energy soon after 2010.[1] With the increased energy consumption comes a price—air pollution. The IEA reports that from 2000 to 2006, an "astonishing 58% of the global increase in emissions" of carbon dioxide (CO_2)—the main greenhouse gas (GHG)—came from China.[2] A report by the Netherlands Environmental Assessment Agency, published in June 2008, suggests that China overtook the United States in 2007 as the largest emitter of CO_2.[3] Concerns over the environment cast a big cloud over the Beijing Olympic Games in the summer of 2008,[4] which was supposed to be a showcase of China's economic miracle.

There are at least two structural elements plaguing China's environment: energy structure and economic structure. In terms of energy structure, coal has been a main source of energy,[5] which results in emissions of CO_2, sulfur dioxide (SO_2), and particulates. In 2005, coal accounted for 68.9% of the primary energy consumption,[6] down from the 1990's 76%; oil accounted for 23.4% in 2002, up from 16.6% in 1990.[7] The Energy Institute of the National Development and Reform Commission (NDRC) estimates that coal will nevertheless occupy 62.3% of all energy consumption by 2020.[8] Switching to oil is not an easy solution, given the size of China's demand. It poses

---

1. International Energy Agency, *World Energy Outlook 2007: China and India Insights*, Paris: OECD/IEA 2007 at 3 [hereinafter, *WEO 2007*].

2. IEA, *WEO 2007*, id, at 55. Among GHGs, the focus of the Kyoto Protocol is on the six following: carbon dioxide, methane (CH_4), nitrous oxide (N_2O), hydrofluorocarbons (HFCs), perfluorocarbons (PFCs), sulfur hexafluoride (SF_6).

3. Elisabeth Rosenthal, *China Increases Lead as Biggest Carbon Dioxide Emitter*, N.Y. Times, Jun. 14, 2008, A05.

4. Jim Yardley, *Beijing's Olympic Quest: Turn Smoggy Sky Blue*, N.Y. Times, December 29, 2007; *Consultant Questions Beijing's Claim of Cleaner Air*, N.Y. Times, Jan. 10, 2008, A3; *Don't Drink the Water and Don't Breathe the Air*, Economist (Jan. 24, 2008); Maureen Fan, *Beijing's Water Policies Add to Crisis, Report Says*, Wash. Post, Jun. 27, 2008, at A13.

5. Ni Weidou & Nien Dak Sze, *Energy Supply and Development in China*, in Energizing China: Reconciling Environmental Protection and Economic Growth 67–117, especially, Figure 2, Coal Dependence of China, at 74 (Michael B. McElroy, Chris P. Nielsen & Peter Lydon, eds., Harvard Un. Press 1998) [hereinafter 1998 Ni Weidou & Nien Dak Sze].

6. *Id.* at 77. From 2000 to 2005, the portion of coal in China's energy consumption was: 67.7%, 66.7%, 66.3%, 68.4%, 68.0%, and 68.7%, respectively. In 1959, coal represented 95% of China's primary energy sources.

7. Wang Jinnan & Cao Dong, *et al.*, *Energy and Environment: China 2020*, Beijing: China Environmental Science Press 2004 (Wang & Cao, 2004), Table 1-5, at 11 (showing China's statistics on energy consumption from 1990 to 2002) and 86–87 [hereinafter Wang & Cao]; Frank Wang & Hongfei Li, *Environmental Implications of China's Energy Demands: An Overview*, in China's Environment and the Challenge of Sustainable Development 180–200 (Kristen A. Day ed., Armonk 2005) [hereinafter 2005 Wang & Li].

8. Wang & Cao, *id.* at 86.

challenges to the world energy market: in 2003, China surpassed Japan as the second biggest consumer of oil. China's switch to oil contributes to the global demand for oil,[9] and has all the problems (including CO_2 emissions) of hydrocarbon.

China's addiction to coal is aggravated by the way coal is consumed in the economic system. In the United States, which is also a heavy consumer of coal, coal is used for electric power generation, and is more concentrated; in China the use of coal is spread across different industries (chemical, cement, paper, steel, etc.) of various scales, and is used in millions of households for heating and cooking.[10] This has its sociopolitical roots in China's recent industrialization. Environmental issues were largely ignored during the 1950s–1970s period. One notorious example is the Great Leap Forward (1958) when a large number of primitive steel mills were set up (though the steel they made was useless).[11] The other example comes from the 1960s "Third Front" movement. Large-scale industrial complexes were built in remote areas for strategic reasons. They proved to be environmental disasters.[12] The environmental situation deteriorated during the economic reform of the 1980s–1990s, as a key policy was to encourage so-called "township and village enterprises" (TVEs) throughout the country. These millions of TVEs became a major source of pollution.[13]

These two elements—the proportion of coal and the dispersion of its use—are formidable obstacles for the environmentalists in China. One is a material condition dictated by mother-nature, the other—though admittedly man-made—is a product of state policy set by the paramount leaders on the top. Environmentalists have neither the financial resources nor the political muscle to challenge either. They can only negotiate—sometimes through seeking temporary alliance with the State, sometimes with the international environmental movement, sometimes through self-help. And the State will negotiate back. Both sides engage in this process through the vocabulary of "rule of law," or, the departure from it. Environmental crisis, in China as elsewhere, is a result of failure in political representation. But the failure, as a whole, is not static; it is rather a dynamic one—the result of ongoing contentions and suppressions. The point is not to be fatalist,[14] but to understand the dirty secret of the structure, and to see that cracks are already visible.

Overview of the Legal System

The Regulatory Bodies

On the national level, the structure of the environmental regulatory system has three elements: the legislatures, the executive branch and the judiciary. Under the Constitution, the high-

---

9. The IEA projects that around 42% of the increase in oil demand in 2006–2030 comes from China and India. India's demand for oil is projected to grow faster, but China's accounts for the biggest increase in oil demand in absolute terms of any country or region. IEA, *WEO 2007, supra* note 1, at 79.

10. 2005 Wang & Li, *supra* note 7, at 181–82.

11. Yu Cheung-Lieh, *Economic Reform and Its Impact on the Environment in China, in* LEARNING FROM CHINA? DEVELOPMENT AND ENVIRONMENT IN THIRD WORLD COUNTRIES 120–21 (Bernhard Glaeser ed., Allen & Unwin 1987).

12. JUDITH SHAPIRO, MAO'S WAR AGAINST NATURE: POLITICS AND THE ENVIRONMENT IN REVOLUTIONARY CHINA (Cambridge Un. Press 2001).

13. ELIZABETH ECONOMY, THE RIVER RUNS BLACK: THE ENVIRONMENTAL CHALLENGE TO CHINA'S FUTURE 63 (Cornell Un. Press 2004).

14. ROBERTO M. UNGER, FALSE NECESSITY: ANTI-NECESSITARIAN SOCIAL THEORY IN THE SERVICE OF RADICAL DEMOCRACY ((revised ed.), Cambridge Un. Press 2001 (first published in 1987)).

est legislative body is the National People's Congress (NPC). But because it has more than three thousand delegates and only meets for two weeks a year, its routine legislative work is managed by its Standing Committee, which acts more like a regular legislative body. The NPC Standing Committee has a specialized sub-committee, the Environment and Natural Resources Protection Committee (ENRPC), set up in 1993, which is in charge of drafting and reviewing statutes on the environment and natural resources. The Chinese People's Political Consultative Conference is a national forum for political deliberation by the smaller political parties and ethnic groups. Though it does not have the power to make or amend statutes, it has been gaining political influence in recent years.

The highest executive office is the State Council, led by the Prime Minister. The State Council makes rules and regulations to implement statutes passed by the NPC and its Standing Committee. It makes important policy decisions on substantive issues such as energy policy and environmental protection policy. The State Council is composed of ministries, commissions, and agencies. Since March 2008, the department in charge of the environment is the Ministry of Environmental Protection (MEP),[15] elevated to the status of ministry from what was formerly known as the State Environmental Protection Administration (SEPA).[16] As will be discussed shortly, MEP enjoys a wide range of statutory authority and powers in regulating the environment. Because environmental policies are often related to other departments in charge of energy, water resources, etc., the State Council set up an Inter-Agency Joint Meeting on Environment on July 4, 2001 in order to facilitate policy coordination. It convenes ministers from relevant departments once a year. On June 12, 2007, the State Council established the Leadership Group on Climate Change (LGCC), chaired by the Prime Minister himself, and with over thirty members who are mostly minister-level officials.[17]

I. The Legal Framework

In a speech in 1982, Qu Geping, then head of the Environmental Protection Office, had declared a fundamental transformation in China's environment protection through the establishment of "rule of law."[18] Qu was able to present an impressive list of statutes and regulations, more than a dozen of them, passed by the legislature or the State Council between 1979 and 1982.[19] This was a period of time in which the idea of "law" was displacing Maoist ideology. Many of China's fundamental laws were passed during this period,[20] including the 1982 Constitution, and the first Environmental Protection Act (For Trial Use) of 1979.[21] Tremendous efforts

---

15. Wu Jiao & Fu Jing, *Ministry Will Give More Weight to Green Issues*, CHINA DAILY, Mar. 13, 2008, at 5.

16. Abigail R. Jahiel, *The Organization of Environmental Protection in China*, 156 CHINA QUARTERLY 757 (Dec. 1998).

17. The State Council, *Circular on the Establishment of Leadership Group on Climate Change and Energy Conservation and Emission Reduction*, June 12, 2007, Decree No.18 (2007) (State Council, 2007).

18. QU GEPING, ENVIRONMENT PROBLEMS IN CHINA AND RESPONSES 99 (3rd ed. Beijing: China Environmental Science Press 1989 (first published in 1984)) [hereinafter Geping]. For the early development of environmental law in China, see, LESTER ROSS & MITCHELL A. SILK, ENVIRONMENTAL LAW AND POLICY IN THE PEOPLE'S REPUBLIC OF CHINA (Quorum Books 1987).

19. Geping, *id.* at 100–01.

20. Jerome A. Cohen, *The Year of the Law, in* A NEW LOOK AT LEGAL ASPECTS OF DOING BUSINESS WITH CHINA: DEVELOPMENTS A YEAR AFTER RECOGNITION 139–56 (Howard M. Holtzmann & Walter Sterling Surrey eds., Practicing Law Institute 1980).

21. Passed on September 13, 1979 by the Fifth NPC Standing Committee, full-text English translation, *Environmental Protection Law (for Trial Implementation) of the People's Republic of China* (1979), 37 CHINESE LAW AND GOVERNMENT 51–57 (May/Jun. 2004, No.3) ["EPA of 1979"].

were devoted to building up the legal system, and enhancing the "rule of law."[22] By the end of 2006, China had 26 environmental statutes, more than 50 regulations issued by the State Council, more than 200 rules issued by regulatory agencies, and more than 800 national standards; local laws and regulations numbered more than 1600.[23] The ENRPC is contemplating more statutes in the near future.

At the top of the legal system lies the Constitution passed in 1982.[24] Article 26 of the Constitution makes a general policy statement on the environment: "The State protects and improves the living environment and the ecological environment, and prevents and remedies pollution and other public hazards." Article 26, however, is more inspiring than practical, as it neglects to offer any legal remedy and does not grant citizens a cause of action when their environmental rights are violated.[25] They must look to the statutes for legal remedies. Statutes on the basic environment law framework and air pollution include:

- Environmental Protection Act (EPA) of 1989;[26]
- Air Pollution Prevention and Control Act (APPCA) of 2000;[27]
- Environmental Impact Assessment Act (EIAA) of 2003.[28]

The EPA of 1989 establishes a general legal framework, which includes a regulatory framework with civil and criminal liabilities. The statute contemplates a regulatory agency in charge of environmental protection on a national level. The regulatory agency has the following powers: (1) rulemaking, including the power to establish emission standards; (2) monitoring of environmental quality through a national monitoring network; (3) licensing, including the authority to approve environmental impact assessments; and (4) supervisory powers, such as inspections, collecting discharge fees, and imposing fines and other penalties. In the past three decades, one of the focuses of reform in environment protection was the status, resources and powers of the regulatory agency. As the following table suggests, there has been a steady improvement in all aspects. The elevation from SEPA to MEP is part of a bigger plan of the State Council to restructure the government and to establish the so-called "super ministries."[29]

---

22. Richard J. Ferris, Jr. & Hongjun Zhang, *Reaching Out to the Rule of Law: China's Continuing Efforts to Develop an Effective Environmental Law Regime*, 11 Wm. & Mary Bill Rts. J. 569 (2003). For an earlier critique, see William P. Alford & Yuanyuan Shen, *Limits of the Law in Addressing China's Environmental Dilemma*, 16 Stan. Envtl. L.J. 125 (1997).

23. Mao Rubo, *Environment Problems and Environmental Legislation in China*, 148 L. Rev. 3 (2008, No.2). The author is a ranking member of the ENRPC, also a member of the NPC Standing Committee.

24. *Constitution of the People's Republic of China*, 9 Rev. Socialist L. 183 (1983) [hereinafter, the "Constitution"].

25. Shen Kui, *Is it the Beginning of the Era of the Rule of the Constitution? Reinterpreting China's "First Constitutional Case"*, 12 Pac. Rim L. & Pol'y J. 199 (2003) (discussing two decrees issued by the Supreme People's Court on this issue).

26. Passed by Seventh NPC Standing Committee on Dec. 26, 1989, *Environmental Protection Law of the People's Republic of China (1989)*, 37 Chinese Law and Government 58–65 (May/Jun. 2004, No.3) [hereinafter, "EPA of 1989"]. The EPA of 1989 replaces the earlier EPA of 1979, *supra* note 21.

27. Passed by Ninth NPC Standing Committee on Apr. 29, 2000, full-text of English translation, *Law of the People's Republic of China on the Prevention and Control of Atmospheric Pollution (2000)*, 37 Chinese Law & Government 24–38 (May/Jun. 2004, No.3) [hereinafter, "APPCA of 2000"]. APPCA was first enacted in September 1987, and amended in August 1995, both *available at* 37 Chinese Law & Government 8–23 (May/Jun. 2004, No.3). The amendment of 1995 was discussed in great detail in William P. Alford & Benjamin L. Liebman, *Clean Air, Clear Processes? The Struggle over Air Pollution Law in the People's Republic of China*, 52 Hastings L. J. 703 (Mar. 2001, No.3) [hereinafter 2001 Alford & Liebman].

28. Passed by the Ninth NPC Standing Committee on October 28, 2002, took effect from September 1, 2003 [hereinafter, EIAA of 2003].

29. Jim Yardley, *China Retools Its Government in Efficiency Push*, N.Y. Times, March 12, 2008, at A01.

Year	Name of Regulatory Agency	Remarks
1974	State Council Environmental Protection Small Leadership Group	
1982	Environmental Protection Office, under the Ministry of Urban and Rural Construction and Environmental Protection.	It was promoted to the status of a "bureau," though still under control of the Ministry; its size (personnel) was increased from 30 to 60.
1984	National Environmental Protection Bureau (NEPB), under the Ministry of Urban and Rural Construction and Environmental Protection.	More under the leadership of SC-EPC, so it became relatively independent from the Ministry; its personnel was increased from 60 to 120.
1988	National Environmental Protection Agency (NEPA)	It became an independent agency, with a rank only half-notch below a ministry; personnel increased from 120 to 321.
1998	State Environmental Protection Agency (SEPA)	It was granted ministerial status; its functional domain expanded. In the meantime, since the SC-EPC was abolished, the SEPA now could submit its legislative proposals directly to the NPC Standing Committee.
2008	Ministry of Environmental Protection (MEP)	Full ministry status, with personnel of 311.

The EPA statutes also establish some fundamental principles of environmental law in China. The EPA of 1979 adopted the "polluters pay" rule;[30] the EPA of 1989 made this rule more specific: "A party who has caused an environmental pollution hazard shall eliminate the hazard and be liable to other work units or individuals directly impacted for the damages incurred as a consequence of the hazard."[31] Furthermore, Article 41 of the EPA of 1989 provided a cause of action to work units or individuals. This general civil liability rule is replicated in the APPCA of 2000.[32] The EPA of 1989 also imposed criminal liabilities on anyone directly responsible for a serious environmental pollution accident leading to heavy losses of public or private property or human injuries or deaths.[33]

II. Negotiating Power

In 1984, the State Council decided through its "Resolution on Environment Protection" to set up an Environment Protection Commission (SC-EPC).[34] Thus, from 1984 to 1998, the SC-EPC was the highest policymaker on the environment in the executive branch. Its stated mission was to formulate policies on the environment, and lead and coordinate the nation's environmental

---

30. Article 6 of the EPA 1979, *supra* note 21.

31. Article 41 of the EPA 1989, *supra* note 26.

32. Article 62, APPCA of 2000, *supra* note 27. This rule had appeared as Article 45 of the 1995 APPCA and Article 36 of the 1987 APPCA, supra note 27.

33. Article 43 of the EPA 1989, *supra* note 26; Yang Chun-xi, John W. Head & Liu Sheng-rong, *China's Treatment of Crimes against the Environment: Using Criminal Sanctions to Fight Environmental Degradation in the PRC*, 8 J. OF CHINESE L. 145 (Fall 1994, No.2). This is similar to Article 61 of APPCA 2000. In 1997, when the Criminal Code was completely revised, a section on environment and natural resources was added to the chapter on crimes against social order. Criminal Code of the People's Republic of China, passed by the 8th NPC on March 14, 1997 [Criminal Code of 1997], English translation *available at* http://www.cecc.gov/pages/newLaws/criminalLawENG.php (last visit on July 23, 2008).

34. "Resolution of the State Council on Environment Protection Work," May 8, 1984 (State Council 1984a), pp. 1–4.

protection work.[35] Unlike some more powerful departments or commissions, the SC-EPC was seen more as a roundtable for policy deliberation than a ministerial entity. Its members included mostly ministers from relevant departments who met on a quarterly basis.[36] The SC-EPC was chaired by Li Peng, then the Vice Prime Minister from 1984 to 1988; Song Jian, a State Counselor, succeeded Li Peng in 1988.

In 1988, an environmental crisis occurred in Benxi city, Liaoning province, northern China. For many years, heavy air pollution and solid waste created by its steel, cement, and coal industries had plagued Benxi. In 1988, the air pollution had become so severe that, reportedly, the city became invisible to satellites. In January 1988, the SC-EPC formed a task force consisting of the NEPB, the Ministry of Metallurgical Industry, the Ministry of Coal Industry, the State Construction Materials Bureau, and the Liaoning Provincial People's Government to Benxi, to investigate the situation.[37] In March, it was estimated that Rmb 5 million yuan (US$) would be needed for a cleanup. Thus, from April to July, NEPA lobbied the Ministry of Metallurgical Industry, the Ministry of Coal Industry, and the State Construction Materials Bureau (SCMB) for financial resources for the cleanup project. No entity was willing to contribute funds. From July 9–July 11, the NEPA mobilized major media groups that included the People's Daily, the Central Radio Station, the Central Television Station, Xinhua News Agency, Economic Daily, China Environment Daily, etc., to visit Benxi and report on the pollution in Benxi. This proved to be an effective strategy. In August, an internal report by Xinhua News Agency caught the attention of the Party's senior leader Chen Yun. Chen Yun was shocked by the pollution and instructed that money be allocated to clean up the city.[38] On September 12, Song Jian, made Chen Yun's instruction public at a press conference at the NEPA.[39]

On October 8, Song Jian chaired the meeting of the SC-EPC, where the Benxi cleanup project was discussed. Having received support from Chen Yun, the purpose of the meeting was to put more pressure on the industry ministries to make financial contributions. The NEPA invoked the Constitution and the fundamental principle of "polluters pay."[40] Here the "polluters pay" principle, imported from the West as a private law doctrine, was transformed into a public law doctrine as a negotiating tool between the NEPA on one side, and those powerful industry ministries on the other. After the SC-EPC meeting, the SCMB finally agreed to reduce 40,000 tons of cement from its mandatory production plan, which meant that factories in Benxi could sell that amount of cement on the market and use the proceeds to fund the cleanup project. On November 28, Song Jian praised the SCMB for its support, and continued to press the Metallurgy Ministry to negotiate with Benxi Steel Co., and the Energy Ministry to negotiate with the coal company. The Benxi City Government was also committed to raise Rmb 160 million yuan (US$).[41] By mid-December 1988, the ministries were finally able to settle on the funds for the cleanup project and the SC-EPC issued an official resolution on Benxi pollution cleanup on December 18. Having nailed down the financial resources, SC-EPC instructed the Provincial Government to coordinate and manage the cleanup project.[42] In his speech at the SC-EPC meeting on Decem-

---

35. Qu Geping, *A Brief History of the SC-EPC and Statement on Several Draft Documents* 11–12 (Sep. 1988).

36. "Vice Prime Minister Li Peng's Speech at the First Meeting of the State Council Environment Protection Commission," Jul. 10, 1984 (Li Peng 1984), at 8–9.

37. Wang Yangzu, Vice Director of the SEPA, *Statement on the Decision on Funding of Cleaning Benxi's Pollution* 37 (Wang Yangzu 1989).

38. Wang Yangzu, *id*, at 37 (on Chen Yun's instruction); *NEPA, Review of the Environmental Protection Work in 1988*, Mar. 17, 1989 (NEPA 1989), at 42–43 (on Chen Yun's instruction).

39. Wang Yangzu, *supra* note 37, at 37 (on Song Jian's press conference).

40. Wang Yangzu, *supra* note 37, at 38.

41. Wang Yangzu, *supra* note 37, at 38.

42. SC-EPC, *Resolution on Benxi City Environment Pollution Cleanup*, Dec. 18, 1988 (SC-EPC 1988b), pp. 28–29.

ber 29, Song Jian felt encouraged by the result of the negotiations, and praised the ministries for their efforts to cooperate.[43]

Here, the SC-EPC and the NEPA were playing the role of the negotiating state. In this process, powerful ministries on a national level represented manufacturers' interests. SC-EPC had to solicit the support from the top leadership in order to bargain with those ministries. In this case, the Party's senior leader, Chen Yun's, intervention was crucial.[44] Chen Yun was among the most powerful leaders in the Party apparatus after 1978, as "he was the only person who spoke to Deng [Xiaoping] as an equal."[45] Also, Chen Yun had been in charge of the economy for many years;[46] thus he had the authority and persuasive power over those industry ministries. It is also interesting to note that the NEPA strategically publicized the environmental pollution to mobilize political support. The Benxi incident coincided with some important legal developments that helped the NEPA to make its case: the APPCA had been passed by the NPC Standing Committee in September 1987 and was planned to take effect in June 1988; and the EPA Bill was under deliberation at the national legislature. Mass media was used to bring pressure to the negotiation table. However, top officials from behind the scenes managed the whole process, and the local residents in Benxi were not assigned any role in this process! Local people would not even qualify as spectators in this drama featuring a spectacular art of negotiation among bureaucratic masters.

Negotiation with these powerful ministries, however, is rarely a winning strategy. Again, the Benxi case is illuminating. Three years after the SC-EPC's deal, the Benxi City People's Government came back to report the progress of the cleanup project.[47] While the report showed impressive progress, it also asked for more financial input—millions of yuan every year. This time, the SC-EPC noted the progress, but remained silent about the financial request.[48] Benxi, however, was not an isolated case during the 1980s. While recognizing that air pollution was the priority in environmental protection in 1988, the SC-EPC had to prioritize 32 cities for cleaning up smoke and particulates, and Benxi was only one of them.[49] In its official self-assessment of its work in 1988, the SC-EPC admitted that its success in curbing air pollution was limited and that air pollution was "very serious."[50] It recognized that, in 1988, China's CO_2 emissions totaled more than 14 million tons, and particulates 110 milligrams per cubic meter—1.83 times that of international standards.[51]

III. Negotiating Developments

A. International Norms in the Making of China's Environmental Policy

China has taken part in a number of international conferences and has signed and ratified all major environmental treaties and agreements related to climate change since 1972, when China first took part in the United Nations Conference on Man and the Environment in Stockholm.[52]

---

43. Song Jian, "Speech at the Fourteenth Session of the SC-EPC," Dec. 29, 1988 (Song Jian 1988).

44. Lester Ross has shown that support from senior leaders such as Vice-Premier Wan Li was important for the initial formation of the environmental regulatory structure in the early 1980s; *see* LESTER ROSS, ENVIRONMENTAL POLICY IN CHINA 143, 147 (Indiana Un. Press 1988).

45. Ezra F. Vogel, *Chen Yun: His Life*, 14 J. OF CONTEMPORARY CHINA 741 (Nov. 2005).

46. DAVID BACHMAN, CHEN YUN AND THE CHINESE POLITICAL SYSTEM (Institute of East Asian Studies and Center for Chinese Studies, University of California, Berkeley, 1985).

47. BENXI CITY PEOPLE'S GOVERNMENT, REPORT ON IMPLEMENTATION OF BENXI ENVIRONMENT POLLUTION CLEANUP PROJECT, Aug. 6, 1992.

48. "Minutes of the 23rd Session of the SC-EPC," Aug. 6, 1992 (SC-EPC 1992), at 527.

49. NEPA, 1989, *supra* note 38, at 45.

50. NEPA, 1989, *supra* note 38, at 48.

51. NEPA, 1989, *supra* note 38, at 48.

52. Lester Ross, *China: Environmental Protection, Domestic Policy Trends, Patterns of Participation in Regimes and Compliance with International Norms*, 156 CHINA QUARTERLY 809 (1998); Elizabeth Economy,

On August 30, 2002, then Premier Zhu Rongji announced China's ratification of the Kyoto Protocol at the UN World Summit on Sustainable Development in Johannesburg.[53] Thus, "environmental diplomacy" was a term that became popular in China during the early 1990s.[54]

International Treaty	Taking Effect	China's Participation
Vienna Convention for the Protection of the Ozone Layer	Adopted on March 22, 1985, 1513 U.N.T.S. 324 (1988), 26 ILM 1516 (1987); entered into force on September 22, 1988.	Signed on September 1, 1989.
The Montreal Protocol on Substances that Deplete the Ozone Layer, 1987	Adopted on September 16, 1987, 1522 U.N.T.S. 3, 26 ILM 1550 (1987).	
London Amendment	Adopted on June 29, 1990; entered into force on August 10, 1992.	Signed on June 14, 1991.
Copenhagen Amendment	Adopted on November 25, 1992; entry into force on June 14, 1994.	
The United Nations Framework Convention on Climate Change ("UNFCCC")	Adopted on May 9, 1992, Doc. No. 102-38 (1992), 1771 U.N.T.S. 108; entered into force on March 21, 1994.	Signed on June 1, 1992; ratified on January 5, 1993.
Kyoto Protocol to the United Nations Framework Convention on Climate Change (the "Kyoto Protocol")	Adopted at the Third Conference of the Parties to the UNFCCC (COP 3) in Kyoto, Japan, December 10, 1997, UN Doc. FCCC/CP/1997/7/Add.2, 37 ILM 22 (1998). It entered into force on February16, 2005.	Signed on May 29, 1998; ratified on September 3, 2002.

There are a few reasons for China to participate in international environmental agreements. First, the immediate political and historical context of the Tiananmen massacre in June 1989 resulted in widespread condemnation and economic sanctions from the West. As a consequence, Beijing fell into a difficult diplomatic isolation, and the environment became a perfect area for it to "break the ice." Second, as can be seen from the Benxi incident discussed earlier, the political center in Beijing was well aware of its environmental crises and was looking for financial support and technology transfer through environmental diplomacy. Third, environmental engineers and scientists started seeking alliance with the international environmental movement, intellectually and financially, from the late 1980s. An ambitious research program called the Chinese National Committee for the International Geosphere-Biosphere Program (CNCIGBP) had been started in 1988, with members from China's most prestigious research institutes.[55] Another channel of en-

---

Chinese Policymaking and Global Climate Change: Two Front Diplomacy and the International Community, in THE INTERNATIONALIZATION OF ENVIRONMENTAL PROTECTION 19–41 (Miranda A. Schreurs & Elizabeth Economy, eds., Cambridge Un. Press 1997) [hereinafter, 1997 Elizabeth Economy, *Chinese Policymaking and Global Climate Change*]; Cai Shouqiu & Mark Voigts, *The Development of China's Environmental Diplomacy*, 3 PAC. RIM L. & POL'Y J. 17 (1993).

53. *China Approves Kyoto Protocol*, CHINA DAILY, Sep. 4, 2002.

54. *E.g.*, CAI SHOUQIU, INTRODUCTION TO ENVIRONMENTAL DIPLOMACY (China Science and Technology Press 1992).

55. In 1991, the United States National Science Foundation (NSF) established a Panel on Global Climate Change Sciences in China. The Panel visited China in 1991 and interviewed members of the Chinese scientific community to learn about research projects in China. The Panel issued a report based on these interviews and data collected during the trip. *See* PANEL ON GLOBAL CLIMATE CHANGE SCIENCES IN CHINA, CHINA AND GLOBAL CHANGE: OPPORTUNITIES FOR COLLABORATION (National Academy Press 1992) [hereinafter PANEL].

gagement was the scientific discussions under the auspices of the United Nation's Intergovernmental Panel on Climate Change (IPCC), also started in 1988. As research funding in these institutes was largely dependent on the State's grants, the scientific community increasingly looked to international sources. During their visit to China in 1991, a group of American experts observed that there "has been ever increasing pressure on Chinese institutions to seek international cooperation to carry out research projects, to gain access to expertise, training opportunities and equipment."[56]

B. The Climate Group

In March 1989, China sent a delegation — led by the Vice Chair of the SC-EPC — to London's International Conference to Save the Ozone Layer. In its report to the State Council back at home, the delegation concluded that climate change needed leadership from the State Council and the involvement of multiple departments; efforts from meteorological and environmental bureaus were not good enough. The delegation proposed that a planning group should be established.[57] Another delegation, which attended UNEP's Fifteenth Meeting from May 15–26, 1989 in Nairobi, Kenya, made two proposals back at home: first, environmental issues have become major political issues in the world, so the SC-EPC should set up a coordinating group on the international environment. Second, in order to change its "awkward position" (*beidong diwei*) in the international arena, the delegation suggested that China should improve its air quality and accelerate its adjustment of energy policy, so that CO_2 would be reduced effectively.[58] In January 1990, the proposals led to the creation of the Coordinating Group on Climate Change under the SC-EPC. The head of the SC-EPC, Mr. Song Jian, chaired the Group.

From October 29 to November 7, 1990, China sent another delegation to take part in the Second World Climate Change Conference in Geneva.[59] Song Jian led the Chinese delegation, and its members included Qu Geping. In its report to the State Council, the delegation proposed four points: first, it was reiterated that climate change was a serious issue, thus must be handled seriously. "Since we are the third largest country in terms of energy consumption and our emission high, and both energy consumption and emissions are growing rapidly, ... we are getting a lot of attention."[60] Second, it noted that China still lacked adequate scientific data on climate change issues and thus suggested that the State Planning Commission and State Science and Technology Commission allocate more funds to support research and monitoring equipment. Third, it called for more efforts to be dedicated to preparation for the climate change negotiations at Rio de Janeiro. Fourth, it proposed making policy changes that would promote clean energy and energy efficiency, so as to reduce emissions. It reiterated, "Since our per capita energy consumption and emissions are still low, the international community cannot blame us. But once we have signed the climate change treaty, the general trend would still be to reduce emissions, sooner or later."[61]

---

56. PANEL, *id.* at 39. According to Elizabeth Economy, "... agencies such as NEPA and the SMA [State Meteorological Administration], which traditionally had been concerned with issues linked to the debate on global climate change (for example, energy conservation or pollution monitoring), were especially driven to access the ideas of the foreign scientific community." 1997 Elizabeth Economy, *Chinese Policymaking and Global Climate Change*, *supra* note 52, at 24.

57. LUO JIBIN, REPORT ON THE ISSUE OF GLOBAL WARMING 64–65, Mar. 17, 1989.

58. REPORT ON THE 15TH SESSION OF THE UNITED NATIONS ENVIRONMENT PROGRAMME GOVERNING COUNCIL MEETING 134–35, Jul. 5, 1989 (SC-EPC 1989).

59. REPORT ON THE SECOND WORLD CLIMATE CHANGE CONFERENCE, Dec. 30, 1990 (SC-EPC 1990).

60. SC-EPC 1990, *id.* at 255.

61. SC-EPC 1990, *id.* at 255–56. Qu Geping also gave a speech at a meeting of SEPA officials on December 1, 1990, promoting the idea of taking advantage of the international environment movement. *See* HOW TO PUSH FORWARD OUR ENVIRONMENT WORK BY TAKING ADVANTAGE OF THE INTERNATIONAL ENVIRONMENT

These proposals, however, should not be read alone, as they were written either in response to the strong opposition from those powerful industry ministries or with those industries in mind. Those departments typically included the Ministry of Energy and the State Planning Commission, as well as the political hardliner—the Ministry of Foreign Affairs.[62] In this process, the SC-EPC and NEPA gradually reinforced themselves by bringing in more members of the scientific community. When preparatory work for the Rio de Janeiro Conference was started in September 1990, the Climate Group invited a large number of scientists and engineers to serve as advisors on technical issues.[63] One year later, Song Jian made two suggestions at a SC-EPC meeting to further reinforce the influence of the scientific community.[64] One was to set up a Scientific Advisory Group under the SC-EPC, thus formalizing the channel between the Climate Group and the scientific community. The second was to set up a "China Council for International Co-operation on Environment and Development" in order to facilitate communication between China and international organizations, foreign foundations, and specialists. The Council was formed on April 22, 1992 in Beijing, with support from the Canadian International Development Agency.[65] It is composed of more than 40 experts and publicists from both China and abroad, and has become a bridge between China and the international environmental movement.

During the Kyoto Protocol negotiations, China fiercely opposed a mandatory cap on emissions for China and other developing countries. However, it did not want to jeopardize the whole framework, so it softened its opposition during the first Conference of Parties (COP1), held in Berlin in March and April 1995.[66] The scientific community was also quickly rewarded by joint research projects with the United States, Germany, Japan and Great Britain,[67] as well as environmental loans from the World Bank, Asian Development Bank, and private foundations.[68] However, one should not overstate the role of the environmental engineers. During this period of time, discourse on the environment rarely happened beyond a small circle of scientists and engineers from the most privileged institutions such as the Chinese Academy of Science, Chinese Academy of Environmental Science (CAES) and Tsinghua University. *Huanjing Baohu* (*Environmental Protection*), a journal published by China Environmental Science Press (which is under the CAES), had very little discussion between 1988 and 1992. Insiders wrote most of the articles that touched on environmental diplomacy.

Tide, Part I Environmental Protection 2–4 (1991, No.6), and How to Push Forward Our Environment Work by Taking Advantage of the International Environment Tide, Part II Environmental Protection 2–4 (1991, No.7).

62. 1997 Elizabeth Economy, *Chinese Policymaking and Global Climate Change, supra* note 52, at 28 (discussing the positions of the Ministry of Energy and the State Planning Commission); Lester Ross, *The Politics of Environmental Policy in the People's Republic of China*, 20 Policy Studies Journal 628 (Winter 1992, No.4) (noting the positions of the State Planning Commission and the Ministry of Finance in the debate on global warming).

63. "Song Jian's Speech at the 20th Session of the SC-EPC," Sep. 6, 1991, at 285 [hereinafter Son Jian 1991]; Report on the Preparatory Work for the Negotiation of the Climate Change Treaty (Jan. 15, 1991), prepared by the Fourth Working Group, Coordinating Group on Climate Change (SC-EPC 1991a), at 256.

64. Song Jian 1991, *id.* at 285.

65. Environmental Protection and Sustainable Development in China 282–85 (Zhu Tan ed., Science Pub. 2007) [hereinafter Zhu Tan 2007].

66. Abram Chayes & Charlotte J. Kim, *China and the United Nations Framework Convention on Climate Change, in* Energizing China 503–40 (Michael B. McElroy, *et al.*, eds., Harvard Un. Pres 1998), *supra* note 5 (noting that between the eleventh Intergovernmental Negotiating Committee meeting (INC-XI) in New York in February 1995 to the first Conference of Parties (COP1), the Chinese delegation shifted to a low profile position while India took the lead for the majority of the developing countries).

67. SEPA, Twenty Years of Environment Protection in China 335–38 (China Environmental Science Press 1994); *see also* Zhu Tan 2007, *supra* note 65, at 240–51.

68. SC-EPC, Review of Environmental Protection Work in the Year of 1992 614 (Apr. 7, 1993).

C. Translation into a Domestic Agenda

Through the "environmental diplomacy" of the early 1990s, the notion of climate change was gradually translated into a domestic policy-making process. In January 1991, the SC-EPC convened a meeting with a focus on climate change.[69] Following the Rio Conference's Agenda 21, in July 1992, with the support from the UNDP, the SC-EPC decided to organize more than 300 experts from more than 50 ministries under the State Council to work on a large-scale project called *China's Agenda 21*,[70] which was eventually finished in 1994. With the soft loan support from the International Development Association of the World Bank, the NEPA worked on an *Action Plan for China's Environmental Protection, 1991–2000*,[71] also finalized in 1994. In 1993 the Asian Development Bank provided technical assistance to the newly established ENRPC.[72] One of the major legislative initiatives of the ENRPC and the NEPA during this period was to strengthen air pollution control by amending the APPCA.[73] During the drafting and deliberation debate processes, as Alford and Liebman suggested, the ENRPC and NEPA used international agreements to justify stronger measures and higher standards.[74]

The idea of total emission control is a good example showing how this key notion was translated into domestic environmental law through "environmental diplomacy." China's pollution control had been based on concentration of pollutants, not a total emission control, like the cap outlined in the FCCC and Kyoto Protocol.[75] However, total emission control was introduced into the legislative process in the second half of 1993, when ENRPC and NEPA started working on amending the Water Pollution Prevention and Control Act (WPPCA), which was finalized in May 1996.[76] The WPPCA allowed the provincial governments to control the total discharge of major pollutants. In June 1996, the State Council's Information Office published a white paper on environmental protection,[77] where it was declared as a "strategic move" that pollution control be changed from focusing on concentration control of specific pollutants to a combination of concentration and "total quantity control." In August, the State Council issued a "Decision on Several Issues in Environment Protection,"[78] where the term "total emission control" was put at the center of the overall rethinking of pollution control in China. As a hybrid of the notion of a

---

69. "Minutes of SC-EPC's Meeting on Climate," Jan. 15, 1991 (SC-EPC 1991b).

70. *China's Agenda 21: White Paper on China's Population, Environment, and Development in 21st Century China* (approved by the State Council on Mar. 25, 1994), China Environmental Science Press 1994 English edition. The project was a comprehensive discussion of economy, society, energy and environmental issues from the vantage point of sustainable development. On greenhouse gas emissions, *id.* pp. 208–10.

71. Action Plan for China's Environmental Protection, 1991–2000 (China Environmental Science Press 1994 SEPA 1994b).

72. Asian Development Bank (Environmental Division, Office of Environment and Social Development), *Reform of Environmental and Land Legislation in the People's Republic of China, Manila*: ADB 2000.

73. 2001 Alford & Liebman, *supra* note 27 (discussing the role of the ENRPC in the making of the 1995 APPCA, *supra* note 31).

74. In response to the fierce opposition from the industry ministries, "… at least some in the ENRPC and NEPA argued that China's growing engagement with the international community in the years following the original air pollution law's development provided further rationale for its revision." Alford & Liebman, *supra* note 27, at 714.

75. Article 4:2(b) of the Convention sets a target for the Annex I member countries to reduce their emission of greenhouse gases to the 1990 level by 2000. Article 3 of the Kyoto Protocol sets the targets of reducing Annex I member countries' overall emissions by at least 5 percent below 1990 levels in the commitment period 2008 to 2012.

76. First enacted on May 11, 1984, amended 1996. "Law of the People's Republic of China on Prevention and Control of Water Pollution (1996)," 37 *Chinese Law & Government* 88–100 (May/Jun. 2004, No.3).

77. State Council Information Office, "Environmental Protection in China," (Jun. 1996), English translation is available from the website http://www.china.org.cn/e-white/environment/index.htm.

78. State Council, "Decision on Several Issues in Environment Protection," Aug. 3, 1996 (State Council 1996).

cap and concentration control, the Decision announced that the nation's goal was to bring all pollution discharged to the national standards by 2000, and that every province should bring major pollutants within the total discharge amount allocated to the province. Total emission control was written into the APPCA 2000,[79] under which the State may take measures to control the total amount of major atmospheric pollutants discharged in different areas.

D. Bargain Beyond Kyoto

However, in those domestic environment programs, total emission control is only applied to the control of SO_2 and chemical oxygen demand (COD) in water, but not greenhouse gases (GHGs). The 1996 Decision, discussed above, only instructed local governments to prioritize air pollution caused by coal-burning, SO_2 and acid rain; it was silent on GHGs. From 1996 on, China has formulated three five-year-plans (FYP) on the environment; the Ninth FYP (1996–2000),[80] the Tenth FYP (2001–2005),[81] and the Eleventh FYP (2006–2010)[82] all have set targets on emissions reductions for COD and SO_2, but none has specified any target for GHGs. Similarly, in June 2007, the NDRC issued a National Climate Change Program,[83] which announced that China would adopt a variety of measures to improve energy efficiency and reduce energy consumption per unit of output value in GDP by 20%, which would result in a cut in emissions of carbon dioxide. But even this program focused on climate change didn't contain any specific reduction targets for GHGs.

Admittedly, having the targets set in the FYPs does not guarantee that emissions will be reduced as planned. The Eleventh FYP (2006–2010) set a target for the year 2010 for reducing major emissions by 10% from the 2005 baseline. In March 2007, Premier Wen Jiabao admitted in his annual report to the national legislature that the emissions reduction plan for the year 2006—the first year of the 11th FYP—was not met.[84] Not until June 2008 could the newly formed MEP announce that the total emissions in 2007 declined.[85] Either up or down, SO_2 and COD are the focus of national campaigns. Emissions trading is similarly focused on SO_2 and COD. Pilot projects were launched by the SEPA in 1999 with help from Environmental Defense, an NGO based in the United States.[86]

In terms of GHG emission control, China seems happy with the Clean Development Mechanism (CDM) under the Kyoto Protocol. Article 12 of the Kyoto Protocol permits Annex I (developed) countries to invest in emission control facilities in non-Annex I countries. The emission reductions, once certified by a special procedure, will be counted as a contribution to compliance with the investing country's overall commitments under Article 3.[87] For example, a recent

---

79. APPCA (2000), *supra* note 27.

80. NEPA, *The Ninth Five-Year-Plan for China's Environmental Protection and the Long-Term Development Plan* (1996–2010) (Dec. 1997) (NEPA 1997).

81. SEPA, *The Tenth Five-Year-Plan for China's Environmental Protection* (Dec. 2001) (SEPA 2001).

82. SEPA & NDRC, *The Eleventh Five-Year-Plan for China's Environmental Protection* (Nov. 2007) (SEPA 2007).

83. NDRC, China's National Climate Change Program (Jun. 2007), *available at* http://www.china. org.cn/english/environment/213624.htm. The Program continues to reject the idea of a mandatory reduction plan on the international level. Jim Yardley & Andrew C. Revkin, *China Issues Plan on Global Warming, Rejecting Mandatory Caps on Greenhouse Gases*, N.Y. Times, Jun. 5, 2007.

84. Jim Yardley, *Chinese Premier Focuses on Pollution and the Poor*, N.Y. Times, Mar. 5, 2007.

85. Keith Bradsher, *China Reports Declines in 3 Major Pollutants, Reversing Trend*, N.Y. Times, Jun. 6, 2008, A12.

86. Richard D. Morgenstern, *et al.*, *Emissions Trading to Improve Air Quality in an Industrial City in the People's Republic of China*, *in* China's Environment and the Challenge of Sustainable Development 150–79 (Kristen A. Day ed., M.E. Sharpe 2005), *supra* note 7.

87. Article 12, Kyoto Protocol.

deal was reached on February 5, 2007, between ICECAP, a British firm, and Guangzhou Huijing Environmental Protection Co., on a landfill gas recovery and electricity generation project.[88] Under the CDM, ICECAP would invest US $50 million dollars to build emission control facilities. In return, 500 tons of CO_2—the expected emission reduction—will be counted as Great Britain's compliance with the latter's commitment under the Kyoto Protocol. China has been a major beneficiary of the CDM schemes in the world. It is reported that China accounted for 61% of carbon-credit trading under the CDM. In 2006, China captured $3.2 billion of that $4.8 billion in subsidies for dozens of projects.[89]

Since half of the CDM projects in China are from the European Union, the EU is eager to woo China to commit itself to a mandatory cap under the Kyoto Protocol.[90] However, this did not seem to be able to convince President Hu Jintao to change his position at the Group of Eight (G8) summit in July 2008 in Japan.[91] In his speech, President Hu made two points at the summit: the developed countries should take responsibility for curbing climate change; and financial support to developing countries is still the key issue for China.

IV. The State, Society and the Environment

As environmental degradation continues, the political center in Beijing finds itself being forced to make promises repeatedly on environment issues, while its legitimacy is increasingly threatened by its failures to live up to those promises. In response, relentless national campaigns characterize environmental protection in China today: from well publicized lawmaking and rulemaking, to high profile law enforcement campaigns,[92] to all the fanfare around the recent elevation of the SEPA to MEP. However, the national campaigns, like the SC-EPC in the Benxi case, or "environmental diplomacy," are also merely a negotiating tool with different tactics. The Benxi case is a closed-door political negotiation between different departments of the government; its politics are not for public consumption. By contrast, the politics of "environmental diplomacy" is for public consumption, but with no channel for popular participation. National campaigns are supposedly politics for public consumption, though their main function is to silence discontent and suppress resistance. These campaigns have a crucial weakness: resistance can turn politics against the ruling elites—through political use of the law itself. It is here that the ruling elites finally meet their ultimate counterparts in the negotiations—ordinary citizens. One illuminating area is environmental impact assessment (EIA).

---

88. The UNFCCC makes the project documentation available online. Project 1075: Guangzhou Xingfeng Landfill Gas Recovery and Electricity Generation CDM Project, *available at* http://cdm.unfccc.int/Projects/DB/JCI1175576815.21.

89. *Knowing Which Way Wind Blows: Handful of Nations Get Most Subsidies*, Int'l Herald Tribune, May 10, 2007, at 1; *Clean Power That Reaps a Whirlwind*, N.Y. Times, May 9, 2007, at 1.

90. Jos Manuel Barroso, President of the European Commission, visited China in April 2008. Serge Abou, the EU Ambassador to China, wrote an article for the China Daily Serge Abou, *China, Europe Together in Kyoto Action*, China Daily, Apr. 23, 2008, at 9.

91. Gao Zugui, *Joint Efforts Needed for a New, Just Global Order*, China Daily, Jul. 16, 2008, at 8 (reporting on President Hu Jintao's speech on July 9, 2008 at the summit). Xie Zhenhua, former head of the SEPA, now Deputy Director of the NDRC, urged the United Nations on transfer of technology, saying: "The core of the mechanism must be technology transfer, and it should have sufficient funding to support such transfers." Sun Xiaohua & Wang Shanshan, *UN Urged to Lead on Tech Transfers*, China Daily, Apr. 25, 2008, at 5.

92. Benjamin van Rooij, *Implementation of Chinese Environmental Law: Regular Enforcement and Political Campaigns*, in China's Limits to Growth: Prospects for Greening State and Society 55–72 (Peter Ho & Eduard B. Vermeer eds,. Blackwell Publishers 2006).

The EPA of 1979 had already required EIAs.[93] Ten years later, the EPA of 1989 made the EIA requirement clearer.[94] However, Article 13 doesn't prescribe any opportunity for the public to be involved in the EIA process; rather, the EIA under Article 13 was solely dependent on the local EPB's review of the EIA report.[95] In order to prescribe rules for public participation, the EIAA was enacted in October 2002.[96] Article 21 of the EIAA explicitly requires that public hearings or other forms of consultation be held to seek comments from the general public, interested parties and experts before an EIA report is submitted for approval. In order to publicize the EIAA, the SEPA launched a national campaign, promoting EIA as an institution to curb pollution. In December, 2004, it hosted an international conference focused on EIA in southern China.[97] In January 2005, the SEPA surprised the nation by issuing an order to suspend construction of thirty large projects in the electricity industry on the ground that the EIA was not proper. The action was hailed by the media as the "environmental storm."[98] In November, the SEPA even issued a specific regulation on EIA approval process,[99] which allows the SEPA, when a construction project that may have serious impact on local living conditions, or when a construction project is very controversial, to hold public hearings.[100] In February 2006, the SEPA issued procedural rules,[101] detailing procedures for the public to participate in the EIA process.

An incident in Xiamen city, southern China, occurred right in the midst of SEPA's "environmental storm." In November 2007, Xiamen residents broke their silence by a quiet and yet revolutionary protest by text messaging through cell-phones to oppose a chemical factory being constructed in their city.[102] The chemical factory was to produce paraxylene, which is used in plastics, polyester and other synthetic products, with total investment of more than Rmb 10 billion yuan (US $1.5 billion). The protest was led by Zhao Yufen, a U.S.-trained chemistry professor at Xiamen University. Professor Zhao also holds membership in two important institutions: she is a member of the Chinese Academy of Science—a distinguished and well respected position in the Chinese scientific community, and a delegate of the Chinese People's Political Consultative Conference (CPPCC)—a politically powerful position for a non-Party member. Early in 2006, she had tried to contact local officials in vain.

In March 2006, when the CPPCC was in session in Beijing, Zhao and her colleagues motioned an inquiry of the matter; Zhao and her group also contacted SEPA for help. On March 14, 2007, SEPA's top official in charge of EIAs met Zhao and her group, but told them that the SEPA did not have the authority to change the project since it had been approved by the NDRC. On May 15, the NDRC finally responded to the CPPCC's inquiry, but insisted that it did not have

---

93. Article 7 of EPA of 1979, *supra* note 21.

94. Article 13 of EPA of 1989, *supra* note 26.

95. Wang Jin, *A Study of Public Participation in Environmental Impact Assessment Process*, 124 L. Rev. 107, at 108 (2004, No.2) (Wang Jin 2004).

96. EIAA 2003, *supra* note 28.

97. Pan Yue, the Vice Minister of SEPA, gave a keynote speech at the international conference on December 13, 2004. Pan Yue, *Several Opinions on Strengthening Environment Impact Assessment Administration*, Environmental Protection 14 (2005, No.2).

98. Xiong Zhihong, *"Environmental Impact Assessment"—A Storm Stirs in 2005*, in The China Environment Yearbook (2005): Crisis and Breakthrough of China's Environment 3–18 (Liang Congjie & Yang Dongping eds., Brill 2007).

99. SEPA, *Approval Procedures for Construction Projects Environmental Impact Assessment Documentation*, Nov. 23, 2005 (SEPA 2005).

100. Article 13, SEPA 2005.

101. SEPA, *Provisional Procedures for the Public Participation in the Environment Impact Assessment*, Feb. 14, 2006 (SEPA 2006).

102. Edward Cody, *Text Messages Giving Voice to Chinese: Opponents of Chemical Factory Found Way Around Censors*, Wash. Post, Jun. 28, 2007, at A01.

any reason to change the plan that it had approved. Frustrated by the lack of support from SEPA and NDRC, the local residents in Xiamen started sending complaints to more officials as well as research institutions. The City government not only used locally controlled media to justify the project, it even tried to cover up the controversy by confiscating copies of a Hong Kong-based journal covering the story. However, on May 24, the Outlook East Weekly, a Beijing-based national journal, broke the censorship by a report with a sensational title: *A Hundred CPPCC Delegates Cannot Stop the Xiamen Multi-billion Chemical Project.*[103] The report told the story of Zhao and her colleagues at CPPCC. It raised legal issues about the project, particularly with the environmental impact assessment. It pointed to the EIAA of 2003, asking that if the general public had been informed of this chemical project through the EIA process, why did few people know about it? Local residents were encouraged, but since they had no access to the local media, they could only use text messaging to express their discontent, using national law as a means of their "rightful resistance."[104] On May 28 alone, around a million text messages were sent throughout Xiamen city. The City government did not give in easily. They announced that the project would be postponed on May 30 though public hearings were not held until December 13 and 14. As they continued to play tricks, the local residents kept up the pressure. Within China's authoritarian regime, a break of silence is often considered a disruption of order, thus a political challenge to the regime. But at the same time, politicized resistance also signals widespread discontent with the local government, which would invite the leadership in Beijing to step in. The story made a decisive turn when on December 19, 2007, the People's Daily — the mouthpiece of the Party — published a detailed report sympathetic to the residents in Xiamen.[105] Eventually, the residents won the battle and the chemical factory was relocated.

Throughout the process, the SEPA did not lend its support to the residents in Xiamen, despite the national campaign to promote public awareness of EIA. It chose to shy away from the crowds. However, the Xiamen residents quickly learned to turn the logic of authoritarianism into their own weapon — they used collective action as leverage in their negotiation with the local officials and forced them to follow the rules of law.[106] Unlike the SC-EPC in the Benxi incident and the "environmental diplomacy" outlined above, the 2007 Xiamen incident marked a significant change. The negotiating State had monopolized politics in the past, but now it must face its ultimate negotiation counterparts — the people.

V. Conclusion

In their grand negotiations with the State, elite environmentalists in post-Mao China have adopted an array of different strategies: temporary alliance with the State's top leadership, alliance with the international environment movement, and finally, national campaigns. In the process, they have achieved temporary and limited success, but none of these efforts have been able to help them gain strength or independence. In the Benxi incident, support from the top leadership was extremely important. In the "environmental diplomacy" context, environmental scientists and engineers helped bring new ideas and technology to China, but their influence in setting the State's agenda remained marginal. The Xiamen incident proved that the "environmental storm" in 2005

---

103. *A Hundred CPPCC Delegates Cannot Stop the Xiamen Multi-billion Chemical Project*, Outlook East Weekly (May 26, 2007).

104. Kevin J. O'Brien & Lianjiang Li, Rightful Resistance in Rural China (Cambridge Un. Press 2006).

105. *The Xiamen PX Project: Stay or not to Stay?*, People's Daily, Dec. 19, 2007, at 5.

106. Kevin J. O'Brien & Lianjiang Li, *supra* note 104, at 51–63. Professor Hualing Fu has documented the role of agitation politics in dispute resolution in rural China. *See* H. L. Fu, *The Politics of Mediation in a Chinese County: The Case of Luo Lianxi*, 5 Austl. J. of Asian L. 107 (2003, No.2).

also failed to offer any real solution. Over time, environmentalists have become more dependent on State power—thus moving closer to becoming part of the State apparatus.

This is the political backdrop of China's environmental degradation. But it doesn't have to be this way. The Xiamen incident points to a different direction. The Xiamen residents' political use of national environmental law turns the logic of authoritarianism against itself. This is not to advocate an unwarranted optimism, because the negotiating State will not stop suppressing any effort to challenge its authority. But China's elite environmentalists should choose their tactics carefully.

References in Chinese:

Benxi City Government

1992:

本溪市人民政府，《关于本溪市环境污染治理规划实施情况的汇报》，载《国务院环境保护委员会文件汇编（二）》，北京：中国环境科学出版社1995年，第543-46页。

Cai Shouqiu:

1992:

蔡守秋，《环境外交概论》，香港：香港中华科技出版社1992年。

Li Peng:

1984: 李鹏，《一定要提倡干实事的好风气》（1984年7月10日），载，国务院环境保护委员会办公室编《国务院环境保护委员会文件选编》，北京：中国环境科学出版社1988年，第8-9页；

1985:《要特别重视强化乡镇企业的环境管理—李鹏副总理在国务院环境保护委员会第三次会议上的讲话》（1985年3月26日）.

Luo, Jibin:

1989: 骆继宾，《关于全球气候变暖问题的汇报》（1989年3月17日），载《国务院环境保护委员会文件汇编（二）》，北京：中国环境科学出版社1995年，第59-65页.

Mao Rubo:

2008: 毛如柏，《我国的环境问题和环境立法》，载《法学评论》2008年第2期第3-9页.

Outlook:

2007:《百名政协委员难阻厦门百亿化工项目》，《瞭望东方周刊》2007年5月26日.

NEPA (National Environmental Protection Agency):

1989: 国家环境保护局，《1988年环境保护工作总结》（1989年3月17日），载载《国务院环境保护委员会文件汇编（二）》，北京：中国环境科学出版社1995年，第42-50页.

Pan Yue:

2005: 潘岳，《加强环境影响评价管理的几点意见》，载《环境保护》2005年第2期第14页.

People's Daily:

2007:

《厦门PX项目 续建、停建还是迁建》，《人民日报》2007年12月19日第5版.

Qu Geping:

1988: 曲格平，《关于国务院环境保护委员会历史情况介绍及对几个文件的简要说明》，载，国务院环境保护委员会秘书处编《国务院环境保护委员会文件汇编（二）》，北京：中国环境科学出版社1995年，第11-12页；

1989: 曲格平，《中国环境问题及对策》（第3版），北京：中国环境科学出版社1989年（1984年初版）；

1991: 曲格平，《如何利用国际环境浪潮推动我国的环保工作（上）》，载《环境保护》1991年06期第2-4页；《如何利用国际环境浪潮推动我国的环保工作（下）》，载《环境保护》1991年07期第2-4页；

SC-EPC (State Council Environment Protection Commission):

1988a: 国务院环境保护委员会办公室编《国务院环境保护委员会文件选编》，北京：中国环境科学出版社1988年；

1988b: 国务院环境保护委员会《关于治理本溪市环境污染的决定》（1988年12月18日），载《国务院环境保护委员会文件汇编（二）》，北京：中国环境科学出版社1995年，第28-29页；

1989: 出席联合国环境规划署第十五届理事会的中国代表团，《关于参加联合国环境规划署第十五届理事会的情况报告》（1989年7月5日），载《国务院环境保护委员会文件汇编（二）》，北京：中国环境科学出版社1995年，第131-35页；

1990: 出席第二次世界气候大会代表团，《出席第二次世界气候大会的报告》（1990年12月30日），载《国务院环境保护委员会文件汇编（二）》，北京：中国环境科学出版社1995年，第250-56页；

1991a: 国家气候变化协调小组第四工作组，《关于气候变化公约谈判准备情况的汇报》（1991年1月15日），载《国务院环境保护委员会文件汇编（二）》，北京：中国环境科学出版社1995年，第256-62页；

1991b: 《国务院环境保护委员会气候专题会议纪要》（1991年1月15日），载《国务院环境保护委员会文件汇编（二）》，北京：中国环境科学出版社1995年，第246-48页；

1992: 《国务院环境保护委员会第二十三次会议纪要》（1992年8月6日），载《国务院环境保护委员会文件汇编（二）》，北京：中国环境科学出版社1995年，第524-28页；

1993: 《1992年全国环境保护工作总结》（1993年4月7日），载《国务院环境保护委员会文件汇编（二）》，北京：中国环境科学出版社1995年，第597-616页；

1995: 国务院环境保护委员会秘书处编《国务院环境保护委员会文件汇编（二）》，北京：中国环境科学出版社1995年.

SEPA (State Environmental Protection Agency):

1992: 国家环保局、国家物价局、财政部和国务院经贸办《征收工业燃煤二氧化硫排污费试点方案》1992年9月14日；

1994a: 编委会，《中国环境保护行政二十年》，北京：中国环境科学出版社1994年；

1994b: 《中国环境保护行动计划

1991-2000:

年》，北京：中国环境科学出版社1994年；

1995: 国家环境保护局自然保护司，《中国乡镇工业环境污染及其防治对策》，北京：中国环境科学出版社1995年；

2001: 国家环保局，《国家环境保护"十五"计划》（2001年12月）；

2005: 国家环境保护总局《建设项目环境影响评价文件审批程序规定》，2005年10月27日第二十次局务会议通过；

2006: 国家环保总局，《环境影响评价公众参与暂行办法》（2006年2月14日）；

2007: 国家环保总局、国家发展改革委员会，《国家环境保护"十一五"计划》（2007年11月）.

Song, Jian:

1988:《大家分工合作共同努力环保就有希望—宋健同志在国务院环境保护委员会第十四次会议上的讲话》（1988年12月29日），载《国务院环境保护委员会文件汇编（二）》，北京：中国环境科学出版社1995年，第26-28页；

1991： 《宋健同志在国务院环境保护委员会第二十次会议上的讲话（摘要）》（1991年9月6日），载《国务院环境保护委员会文件汇编（二）》，北京：中国环境科学出版社1995年，第285-87页.

State Council:

1984a: 国务院《关于环境保护工作的决定》1984年05月08日，载，国务院环境保护委员会办公室编《国务院环境保护委员会文件选编》，北京：中国环境科学出版社1988年，第1-4页；

1984b:

国务院《关于加强乡镇、街道企业环境管理的规定》，国发[1984] 135 号；

1990:

国务院《关于进一步加强环境保护工作的决定》，1990年12月5日；

1996: 国务院《关于环境保护若干问题的决定》（1996年8月3日）；

2007a: 国务院《关于成立国家应对气候变化及节能减排工作领导小组的通知》，国发〔2007〕18号；

2007b: 国务院新闻办公室，《中国的能源状况与政策》，二〇〇七年十二月.

Wang Jin

2004:

汪劲，《环境影响评价程序之公众参与问题研究—兼论我国《环境影响评价法》相关规定的施行》，载《法学评论》2004年第2期第107-18页.

Wang & Cao:

2004: 王金南、曹东等，《能源与环境：中国2020》，北京：中国环境科学出版社2004年.

Wang Yangzu:

1989: 国家环保局副局长王扬祖，《关于《关于解决本溪市治理污染资金问题的决定》的说明》，载《国务院环境保护委员会文件汇编（二）》，北京：中国环境科学出版社1995年，第36-37页.

World Bank:

2007: 世界银行东亚和太平洋地区基础设施局、国务院发展研究中心产业经济部，《机不可失：中国能源可持续发展》，北京：中国发展出版社2007年。

Zhu Tan

2007:

朱坦主编，《中国环境保护与可持续发展》，北京：科学出版社2007年.

Notes

1. Timo Koivurova, *International Legal Avenues to Address the Plight of Victims of Climate Change: Problems and Prospects*, 22 J. Envtl. L. & Lit. 301 (2007).

2. *See* Elizabeth C. Economy, The Environmental Challenge to China's Future: The River Runs Black ix (Cornell Un. Press 2004) (A Council on Foreign Relations Book):

> For more than two decades, I along with the rest of the world, have watched as the Chinese people have transformed their country from a poverty-stricken nation into an economic power-house. Equally striking, however, has been the terrible price China's environment has paid for this impressive transformation. Today, the environment is beginning to exact its toll on the Chinese people, impinging on continued economic development, forcing large-scale migration, and inflicting significant harm on the public's health.

3. Daniel A. Farber, *Apportioning Climate Change Costs*, 26 UCLA J. Envtl. L. & Pol'y 21, 53 (2007–08):

> Cost apportionments should be based on "excess" emissions, determined to be whatever limited degree of precision is feasible. The climate change costs at any given time should be allocated on the basis of an emitter's current share of total atmospheric loadings at that time (meaning the use of average rather than marginal harm, and of historic rather than current emissions). To minimize the risks due to future insolvencies, emitters should also be required to purchase insurance covering their projected future share of costs.

4. Christine J. Lee, *"Pollute First, Control Later" No More: Combating Environmental Degradation in China Through an Approach Based in Public Interest Litigation and Public Participation*, 17 Pac. Rim L. & Pol'y J. 795 (2008).

VI. The Search for a New International Law That Works

Paul G. Harris, *Climate Change and Global Citizenship*, 30 Law & Policy 481, 481 (2008):

> The international climate change regime has failed. Even the most optimistic assessment of action to limit greenhouse pollution in the coming few decades will not prevent calamitous changes in Earth's climate. Arguments for international—that is, interstate—justice that have permeated international negotiations on climate change have been insufficient in fostering robust action by states.

James Gustave Speth, The Bridge at the Edge of the World: Capitalism, the Environment, and Crossing from Crisis to Sustainability 71–72 (Yale Un. Press 2008):

> Although there has been strong progress in protecting the ozone layer and some improvement on acid rain, most of the threatening environmental trends highlighted a quarter century ago have worsened. As we saw in Chapter 1, global-scale problems are

now deeper and more urgent than ever. It would be nice to think that the international treaties and action plans, the main focus of efforts to date, have given us the policies and programs we need, so that we could at last get on with it. But that is not the case. Despite all the conferences and negotiations, the international community has not laid the foundation for rapid and effective action.

The result of two decades of international environmental negotiations are deeply disappointing. The bottom line is that today's treaties and their associated agreements and protocols cannot drive the changes needed. In general, the issue with the major treaties is not weak enforcement or weak compliance; the issue is weak treaties. Typically, these agreements are easy for governments to slight because the treaties' impressive—but nonbinding—goals are not followed by clear requirements, targets, and timetables. And even when there are targets and timetables, the targets are often inadequate and means of enforcement are lacking. As a result, the climate convention is not protecting climate, the biodiversity convention is not protecting biodiversity, the desertification convention is not preventing desertification, and even the older and stronger Convention on the Law of the Sea is not protecting fisheries. The same can be said for the extensive international discussions on world forests, which never have reached the point of a convention.

In sum, global environmental problems have gone from bad to worse, governments are not yet prepared to deal with them, and at present, many governments, including some of the most important, lack the leadership to get prepared.

Considerable interest has centered upon the question of whether international human rights law or U.S. tort law offers a route for breaking out of the "Cycle of Failure" and the "Lowest Common Denominator" that International Environmental Law has become.

Thus, *see* Noah Sachs, *Beyond the Liability Wall: Strengthening Tort Remedies in International Environmental Law*, 55 UCLA L. Rev. 837, 900–01 (2008) (footnotes omitted), quoting from Harold Hongju Koh, Address, *Bringing International Law Home*, 35 Houst. L. Rev. 623 (1992) and citing David A. Grossman, *Warming Up to a Not-So-Radical Idea: Tort-Based Climate Litigation*, 28 Colum. J. Envtl. L. 1 (2003):

> Climate change has emerged as one of the most active areas of international environmental litigation, and norms regarding transboundary environmental damage and the transnational procedures for seeking a remedy could emerge through these cases. The past five years have seen an explosion of litigation in domestic and international fora....
>
>   ....
>
> The bodies hearing these suits may become "law-declaring fora" that strengthen international norms on transboundary pollution through "defining, elaborating, and testing the definition of particular norms and opining about their violation." If U.S. courts begin to rule that greenhouse gas emissions can constitute a nuisance and provide a remedy in injunction or money damages, then a wave of domestic climate change suits will likely follow, as well as transnational suits in U.S. courts and elsewhere, brought by foreign entities against U.S. firms. As firms distinguish themselves as leaders or laggards on addressing their emissions of greenhouse gases, advocates can begin to select defendants and argue that laggards are deviating from a standard of ordinary care regarding the global impact of their emissions.
>
> The current wave of climate litigation is a classic bottom-up legal strategy that is occurring in tandem with the public law process of implementing the Kyoto Protocol (outside the United States) and negotiating a successor convention. Transnational cli-

mate litigation will test the current robustness of liability walls, as courts will undoubtedly confront novel questions of jurisdiction, remedies, enforcement of judgments, and
forum non conveniens. Even if these suits are unsuccessful, they will nevertheless have a
political impact that could be helpful in strengthening international legal norms related
to transboundary pollution. The suits focus public attention on the fact that climate
change has real victims who can be located thousands of miles away from the major
emissions sources. Climate change may come to be viewed not just as an issue of governance of the global commons, but rather as a series of increasingly severe transboundary impacts, some of which will be suitable for private law remedies.

Compare ch. 2 above *with* ch. 8 below on various "litigation" initiatives regarding climate change.
Many are skeptical about whether it is possible to "sue" one's way to a better world. *See* Michael
B. Gerrard, *What the Law and Lawyers Can and Cannot Do About Global Warming*, 16 S.E.
Envtl. L. J. 33, 51 (2007–08).

A. The Enforcement of International Climate Change Law

Expanding the Jurisdiction of the International Court of Justice as a Means of Addressing Climate Change: Lessons from the Global Trade Regime

*Andrew Strauss. Distinguished Professor of Law, Widener University School of Law; Tel: (302) 477-
2254, andrewl.strauss@law.widener.edu. I would like to thank Mary Ellen O'Connell for her enthusiastic response to my questions regarding this project and Michael Hubbard for his very able research assistance.*

I. Introduction: The Under Utilization of the International Court of Justice

The World Trade Organization's dispute settlement mechanism, now in its second decade,
stands as one of the crowning achievements of the international legal system. That mechanism,
which includes binding dispute resolution that no member can opt out of, allows trade conflicts
to be resolved peacefully and authoritatively. Disputing parties are no longer left to make their
own line calls without the benefit of a referee.

Now that we have significant evidence that the WTO system succeeds in settling the law and
encouraging compliance, the time is right to consider extending the model to conflicts over
global warming and other matters of international contention. One way this can be done is by
expanding the jurisdiction of the International Court of Justice (ICJ). As the only tribunal designed to hear disputes generally, it is the closest institution we have to a high court of the
world.[1] Presently, however, the power of the Court to exercise compulsory jurisdiction, which
requires states to submit to the authority of the Court, is optional,[2] and many states, in particular some of the most powerful, have not been willing to cede the Court such power.[3] In the absence of compulsory jurisdiction, the Court is foreclosed from presiding over a contentious case
unless all of the states agree *ad hoc* to give the Court jurisdiction[4] or a treaty that governs a dispute happens to contain a "compromisory clause" allowing for dispute resolution by the Court.[5]

Because of the Court's limited ability to exercise jurisdiction in contentious cases, the great majority of disputes cannot be adjudicated. In the area of climate change specifically, developing a
plausible theory for the Court to exercise jurisdiction over countries that do not accept the Court's
compulsory jurisdiction is extremely difficult, and this difficulty has no doubt contributed to the
absence of climate change cases.[6] Without cases, the Court has been deprived of the opportunity

to apply the rules of customary international law dealing with state responsibility for harming the environment. Because there is no other tribunal within the international system capable of rendering an authoritative decision on the matter, the law of climate change remains underdeveloped.

This underdevelopment has significant implications for future generations. Some of the more extreme yet credible scenarios suggest a global climate that could make civilization as it has developed over the past five thousand years unsustainable.[7] Even less dramatic scenarios that have been predicted by climate scientists with much higher degrees of certainty will dramatically alter the natural environment with significant implications for future generations.[8] While the effort to deal seriously with the climate problem will involve far more than the application of law, international law is clearly necessary for both constraining and coordinating state action. Climate change is only one of the more pressing examples of global problems whose amelioration could be furthered through involvement of the International Court of Justice. If jurisdictional barriers could be overcome, the Court could play a significantly enhanced role in both settling international law generally and resolving individual disputes.

II. A Legal Strategy to Expand the Role of the Court

Unfortunately, securing the necessary political support for amending the Court's treaty, the Statute of the International Court of Justice, to provide universal binding jurisdiction in contentious cases is most likely not politically viable now or in the foreseeable future. Article 69 of the Court's Statute incorporates by reference the formidable barriers to amendment contained in Articles 108 and 109 of the United Nations Charter.[9] Article 108 requires that an amendment be approved by two-thirds of the United Nations General Assembly and subsequently ratified by two-thirds of the members of the United Nations, including all of the permanent members of the Security Council.[10] Getting each and every one of the permanent members of the Security Council to go along is particularly unlikely as these permanent members are presently (except for Great Britain) declining to accept the compulsory jurisdiction of the Court.[11]

---

1. *See generally* NAGENDRA SINGH, THE ROLE AND RECORD OF THE INTERNATIONAL COURT OF JUSTICE (Springer 1989) (discussing the influence of the International Court of Justice); *see also* Robert Y. Jennings, *The United Nations at Fifty: The International Court of Justice After Fifty Years*, 89 A.J.I.L. 493 (1995).

2. *See* Statute of the International Court of Justice, art. 36 (2), Oct. 24, 1945, 59 Stat. 1031, 1060, T.S. No. 993 [hereinafter ICJ Statute], *reprinted in* 1 INTERNATIONAL LAW AND WORLD ORDER: BASIC DOCUMENTS I.A.2 (Burns H. Weston & Jonathan C. Carlson eds., 1994) [hereinafter 1994 Weston & Carlson].

3. Of the five permanent members of the United Nations Security Council, for example, Russia never accepted the compulsory jurisdiction of the Court. The acceptance by the Chinese nationalist government was later repudiated by the Communist regime and the United States and France withdrew their acceptance of compulsory jurisdiction. Only the United Kingdom currently accepts the compulsory jurisdiction of the Court subject to certain reservations. *See* International Court of Justice, Declarations Recognizing the Jurisdiction of the Court as Compulsory, http://www.icj-cij.org/jurisdiction/index.php?p1=5&p2=1&p3=3 (last visited February 27, 2008).

4. *See* ICJ Statute, *supra* note 2, art. 36(1).

5. *Id.*

6. For a discussion of possible jurisdictional theories upon which a global warming case might be presently brought before the Court, *see generally* Andrew Strauss, *Climate Change Litigation: Opening the Door to the International Court of Justice, in* ADJUDICATING THE CLIMATE: INTERNATIONAL AND NATIONAL CAUSES OF ACTION ON CLIMATE CHANGE (William C.G. Burns & Hari Osofsky eds., Cambridge Un. Press 2008).

7. *See, for example,* PETER SCHWARTZ AND DOUG RANDALL, AN ABRUPT CLIMATE CHANGE SCENARIO AND ITS IMPLICATIONS FOR UNITED STATES NATIONAL SECURITY (Environmental Defense Fund 2003), *available at* http://www.edf.org/documents/3566_AbruptClimateChange.pdf (last visited May 16, 2009) (suggesting that a climate change induced slowing of the ocean's thermohaline conveyor could cause changes in global weather patterns significantly reducing food supplies and the carrying capacity of the earth's environment).

8. *See* INTERGOVERNMENTAL PANEL ON CLIMATE CHANGE (IPCC), WORKING GROUP II, CLIMATE CHANGE 2007: IMPACTS, ADAPTATION AND VULNERABILITY, SUMMARY FOR POLICYMAKERS 1–3 (2007).

Under Article 109 of the Charter, a Charter review conference can be called into session by a two-thirds vote of the General Assembly and an affirmative vote of any nine members of the fifteen member Security Council with no provision for permanent member veto.[12] Any alteration of the Charter coming out of the review conference, however, must be approved by two-thirds of the conference and ratified by two thirds of the United Nations membership, again including all of the permanent members of the Security Council.[13]

Though the current prospects for universalizing the Court's compulsory jurisdiction by way of amendment are bleak, there is a practical solution that would allow the Court to render advisory opinions on conflicts between states without the requirement of state consent. In addition to exercising binding jurisdiction over contentious cases, the Court's statute empowers it to render advisory decisions of a nonbinding nature. Thus far, in accordance with the original scheme of the Court's Statute and the United Nations Charter, such opinions have only been given in response to requests by either the Security Council, the General Assembly or other international organizations. A creative use by the General Assembly of its powers under the Charter, however, would allow it to establish a mechanism for states to request advisory opinions.

Pursuant to Article 65 of the Court's Statute, the Court is empowered "to give an advisory opinion on any legal question at the request of whatever body may be authorized by or in accordance with the Charter of the United Nations to make such a request."[14] Article 96 of the United Nations Charter provides that in addition to the General Assembly and the Security Council, other organs of the United Nations and specialized agencies may request advisory opinions of the Court on any legal question so long as they arise within the scope of their activities and they are authorized to make such requests by the General Assembly.[15] If the General Assembly, therefore, had the legal authority to establish a "Judicial Organ" and empower it to request advisory opinions from the Court upon the application of states, then under the terms of Article 96 such requests would be within the scope of the organ's activities and authorized by the General Assembly.

The General Assembly, it so happens, does have this authority under Article 22 of the United Nations Charter, which empowers the General Assembly to establish such subsidiary organs as it deems necessary to perform its functions.[16] The Judicial Organ could be structurally independent, and any state that wanted to pursue a legal complaint against another state could petition the Judicial Organ, and upon certain criteria of justiciability, or no criteria, it could refer the case to the Court for an advisory opinion.[17] Though probably not necessary for consistency with the requirements of the United Nations Charter or the Statute of the Court, the Security Council as a matter of policy should have the ability to defer the referral. Under the Charter, the Security Council has primary responsibility for international peace and security, and if the Council believes that the Court might interfere with, rather than further, the political resolution of a conflict, it should be able to secure the suspension of a case. A similar deferral scheme has been adopted as a way of coherently institutionalizing the relationship between the International Criminal Court and the Security Council.[18] Perhaps a similar power should also be granted to

---

9. ICJ Statute, *supra* note 2, art. 69.

10. Charter of the United Nations, art 108. June 26, 1945, 1976 Y.B.U.N. 1043, 59 Stat. 1031, T.S. 993, S. Ex. F/79-1 [hereinafter "UN Charter"], *reprinted in* 1994 1 Weston & Carlson I.A.1, *supra* note 2.

11. *See supra* note 3.

12. *See* UN Charter, *supra* note 10, art. 109, para. 1.

13. *Id.*, art. 109, para. 1.

14. ICJ Statute, *supra* note 2, art. 65.

15. UN Charter, *supra* note 10, art. 96 ("1. The General Assembly or the Security Council may request the International Court of Justice to give an advisory opinion on any legal question; 2. Other organs of the United Nations and specialized agencies, which may at any time be so authorized by the General Assembly, may also request advisory opinions of the Court on legal questions arising within the scope of their activities.").

the General Assembly which enjoys a subsidiary responsibility for the maintenance of international peace and security under the Charter.[19]

Of course, in theory there is nothing to stop a state now from petitioning the General Assembly to request an advisory opinion regarding that state's legal dispute with another state, and this has been done on rare occasion.[20] In practice, however, the process of getting the General Assembly to request an advisory opinion has been slow and politically cumbersome. In addition, while the General Assembly has requested fourteen advisory opinions since its inception in 1945,[21] the requests, with some notable exceptions,[22] have generally been limited to clarifying matters of internal United Nations governance or legal issues otherwise directly involving the United Nations. By taking the bureaucracy and politics out of the ability of states to secure advisory opinions, the proposed Judicial Organ would provide a regularized process for the Court to hear cases that would never otherwise come before it.

While opponents could likely come up with arguments challenging the General Assembly's powers to create such an organ, its competence to do so rests on a legally sound reading of the Charter, and as a practical matter, the Court would be unlikely to want to stand against such an expansion of its powers from a resolute General Assembly.[23] The real question is one of politics within the General Assembly. Could the General Assembly muster the political will to create such a body? Certainly, the political barriers to action by the Assembly are far less than to amending the Court's Statute. The members of the Security Council could not veto the creation of the Judicial Organ, the requisite vote would either be a majority or two-thirds[24] of the General Assembly instead of three quarters, and there would be no requirement of national ratification.

Relatively less powerful developing countries that constitute a majority of the General Assembly might look with favor on the instigation of a mechanism for allowing cases to be brought

---

16. *Id.*, art. 22 ("The General Assembly may establish such subsidiary organs as it deems necessary for the performance of its functions.").

17. In the mid 1970's the late Paul Szasz proposed a *specialized tribunal* similar to what I have dubbed the Judicial Organ. Although he did not comprehensively work out the basis for the tribunal's legality, he did elaborate upon its composition: "For [the task of transmitting requests for advisory opinions to the Court] the General Assembly might establish a specialized tribunal whose sole function would be the evaluation of proposals for the submission of questions to the ICJ, against criteria established by the General Assembly, and perhaps the Court itself, for such submissions. Similar to other international tribunals, its members would be politically/geographically distributed but chosen on the basis of individual qualifications for relatively long terms to ensure maximum independence; they would not necessarily function full-time in that capacity, though they would have to avoid inconsistent employment." Paul C. Szasz, *Enhancing the Advisory Competence of the World Court, in* THE FUTURE OF THE INTERNATIONAL COURT OF JUSTICE 499, 527 (Leo Gross ed., Oceana 1976).

18. Rome Statute of the International Criminal Court, June 15–17, 1998, United Nations Diplomatic Conference of Plenipotentiaries on the Establishment of an International Criminal Court, U.N. Doc A/CONF.183/9, (hereinafter "ICC Statute") *reprinted in* 1994 1 Weston & Carlson I.H.13., *supra* note 2, art. 16 ("No investigation or prosecution may be commenced or proceeded with under the Statute for a period of 12 months after the Security Council in a resolution adopted under Chapter VII of the Charter of the United Nations, has requested the Court to that effect; that request may be renewed by the Council under the same conditions.").

19. UN Charter, *supra* note 10, arts. 10, 11, 12, 35.

20. *See* Western Sahara Advisory Opinion, 1975 I.C.J. 12, 32 (Oct. 16).

21. A complete list of ICJ advisory opinions can be found at http://www.icj-cij.org/docket/index.php?p1=3&p2=4.

22. In recent years these have been the Nuclear Weapons and Israeli Wall requests for advisory opinions. *See* Legality of the Threat or Use of Nuclear Weapons, Advisory Opinion, 1996 I.C.J.226 (July 8); Legal Consequences of the Construction of a Wall in the Occupied Palestinian Territory, Advisory Opinion, 2004 I.C.J. 131 (July 9).

against dominant countries that enhances the role of law as a force for constraining raw power. In particular, concerns about the effects of climate change, which have been disproportionately caused by wealthy countries,[25] and are likely to disproportionately impact both present and future generations of residents in poor countries,[26] might encourage the General Assembly to act.

The establishment of what I am calling *universal advisory jurisdiction* is, in fact, a political compromise between the restrictions that presently allow the Court to exercise binding jurisdiction only with consent and a system of binding jurisdiction obligatory for all countries. An incremental progression toward expanding the jurisdiction of the Court is an approach modeled on the formula for success at the World Trade Organization. The WTO's system of compulsory and binding dispute resolution was not created out of whole cloth in the Marrakesh Agreement which formally established the WTO.[27] Rather, in the early days of the trade regime, the parties to the GATT came to the conclusion that some process for authoritatively determining the respective rights and obligations of conflicting parties would help resolve trade disputes.

With very little textual authority from the GATT treaty,[28] the original approach of referring disputes to "working parties" consisting of the disputing parties and any other interested GATT parties gave way to the establishment of three- or five-member neutral panels.[29] Over time, these panels became more legalistic in their approach and their processes became more formalized by subsequent agreements and understandings.[30] Wary of ceding too much of their political autonomy, and consistent with the fact that panels had no independent legal authority under the GATT, the parties originally allowed that the panel reports would only be advisory unless all of the parties to the GATT (including the losing party) agreed by adopting them to make them binding.[31] Over many years, and based on a slowly gained comfort with the GATT system, the parties took the step of instituting compulsory and binding dispute resolution[32] in the 1994 Marrakesh Agreement.[33] While the issues surrounding trade and the trade regime are in many ways

---

23. If this proposal were to be seriously considered by the General Assembly, it would, of course, be important to consult with the Court before proceeding and to gain assurance from the Court that it would be favorably received. One matter of concern is that in the Status of Eastern Carelia case the Court's predecessor, the Permanent Court of International Justice, rejected a request for an advisory opinion concerning Russia, a country that had refused to accept any form of that court's jurisdiction. The Permanent Court ruled that advisory opinions may not be used "for circumventing the principle that a state is not obliged to allow its disputes to be submitted to judicial settlement without its consent." *See* Eastern Carelia 1923 P.C.I.J. 29 (Ser. B) No. 5 (Reply of the Court of July 23, 1923 to Request for an Advisory Opinion). The International Court of Justice has never directly contradicted this holding, but it has likewise never let it stand in its way of accepting requests for advisory opinions. To get around the Permanent Court's holding, it has distinguished between directly deciding contentious cases between parties and honoring requests to provide a UN organ with legal advice that on the circumstances of each case it has found to be necessary for that organ's own purposes. This distinction, however, would not well support the Court's accepting requests for advisory opinions instigated by individual countries, but it would seem past time to explicitly put to rest the Permanent Court's basic proposition that states have a right to consent to whether the Court can issue a decision which they are not bound to follow.

24. The requisite vote depends upon whether the decision at hand should be regarded as an "important question" requiring a two-thirds as opposed to majority vote under Article 18 of the United Nations Charter. While Article 18 specifies certain voting matters as important questions, additional unspecified matters are also according to its terms important questions. There is, however, little precedent on which other matters generally qualify, and, as most subsidiary organs have been approved by consensus, the requisite vote required for their establishment is unclear. *See* UN Charter, *supra* note 10, art. 18.

25. *See* World Resources Institute Chart of Total Greenhouse Gas Emissions in 2000, *available at* http://cait.wri.org/cait.php?page=yearly (last visited 22 March 2008).

26. *See generally* INTERGOVERNMENTAL PANEL ON CLIMATE CHANGE, CLIMATE CHANGE 2007: IMPACTS, ADAPTATION AND VULNERABILITY, Contribution of Working Group II to the Fourth Assessment Report of the Intergovernmental Panel on Climate Change (2007).

unique, the general principle holds that a system of advisory dispute resolution could eventually give states enough familiarity with the Court as a stalwart of international conflict resolution to make them comfortable with moving toward a universal system of binding dispute resolution.

In the interim, the difference between advisory and binding decisions is not as great as it might appear. Presently, the International Court of Justice has no adjunct international administrative structure to enforce even its binding decisions. In theory, the United Nations Security Council is empowered under Article 94[34] to enforce the Court's decisions, but it has never done so.[35] One reason compliance with the Court's decisions have generally been quite high is because of the moral pressure it places on the losing country, and, of course, even advisory decisions are important in helping settle the law.

III. The Case for Universal Advisory Jurisdiction

Both the GATT and WTO dispute resolution systems were instituted, at least in theory, with the consent of the states involved. Under the proposal being advanced, the institution of *universal advisory jurisdiction* is realized through the authorization of the requisite majority of the General Assembly rather than by the individual consent of each state that could be the subject of an advisory opinion. Some would no doubt claim that allowing for states to be the subject of decisions, even advisory ones, without their consent is normatively illegitimate. In a system based on the fundamental principle of state sovereignty each state, they would argue, should be free to determine which international regimes it wishes to join and which international processes it should be subject to.

---

27. *Marrakesh Agreement Establishing the World Trade Organization, in* WORLD TRADE ORGANIZATION, THE LEGAL TEXTS: THE RESULTS OF THE URUGUAY ROUND OF MULTILATERAL TRADE NEGOTIATIONS (1999). *Reprinted also in* 1994 4 Weston & Carlson IV.C.2a, *supra* note 2.

28. What authority exists is found in Articles XXII dealing with consultation and XXIII, dealing with "nullification and impairment." Under Article XXIII:1 if a contracting party considered that a benefit accruing to it under the GATT was being nullified or impaired by another party, it could complain in writing to that other party. If this did not lead to a satisfactory resolution of the situation, the complaining party was Authorized by Article XXIII:2 to refer matters to the Contracting Parties, who were then to investigate and make recommendations.

29. For further discussion, *see generally* DAVID PALMETER AND PETROS C. MAVROIDIS, DISPUTE SETTLEMENT IN THE WORLD TRADE ORGANIZATION, PRACTICE AND PROCEDURE 7 (2d ed., Cambridge Un. Press 2004).

30. Most significantly the Tokyo Round (1973–1979) resulted in the adoption of the Understanding Regarding Notification, Consultation, Dispute Settlement and Surveillance (Nov. 28, 1979) GATT B.I.S.D. (26th Supp.), at 210 (1980).

31. For further discussion of this process, see G. Richard Shell, *Trade Legalism and International Relations Theory: An Analysis of the World Trade Organization*, 44 DUKE L.J. 829, 831–33 (1995). For a listing of those panel reports which were adopted as binding, see THE WORLD TRADE ORGANIZATION, ADOPTED PANEL REPORTS WITHIN THE FRAMEWORK OF GATT 1947, *available at* http://www.wto.org/english/tratop_e/dispu_e/gt47ds_e.htm.

32. Decisions are now binding unless all of the parties, including the winning party, agree that they are not binding.

33. Understanding on Rules and Procedures Governing the Settlement of Disputes, *Marrakesh Agreement Establishing the World Trade Organization*, Annex 2, 1869 U.N.T.S. 401, 33 I.L.M. 1226 (Apr. 5, 1994).

34. UN Charter, *supra* note 10, art. 94(2) ("If any party to a case fails to perform the obligations incumbent upon it under a judgment rendered by the Court, the other party may have recourse to the Security Council, which may, if it deems necessary, make recommendations or decide upon measures to be taken to give effect to the judgment.").

35. A resolution calling for the United States to comply with the Court's judgment in the Nicaragua case referred to in note 37 *infra* was introduced into the Security Council, but it was vetoed by the United States. *See* S/PV.2718 October 1986, p. 51 (UN Doc. S/18428).

The international community has, however, already departed from the principle of state consent in the area of conflict resolution such as with the Security Council's establishment of tribunals to try individuals from the former Yugoslavia and Rwanda without the consent of the relevant states. Of perhaps greatest recent institutional relevance is that the United Nations Security Council can refer cases to the International Criminal Court (ICC) involving individuals from countries that have not consented to that court's competence.[36] This departure from consent should not just be limited to the discretion of the politically-driven Security Council. To maintain that states should continue to be able to unilaterally decide the extent to which their compliance with international law can be authoritatively reviewed is to inhibit the evolution toward an international system based on the rule of law. Certainly, it is universally recognized in domestic societies, from the most simple to the most complex, that minimal public order (including the interests of future generations) requires that members of the community not be allowed to opt out of institutions for identifying infractions of community law. The mechanism for establishing this review, authorization by the requisite majority of the General Assembly, would also be a positive development on the road to a more law-based international system. After all, there are few areas in international society where the General Assembly can implement its decisions as a proto-legislature. This could be one of them.

A more pragmatic argument against the proposal is that the alienation of states, and especially powerful states who might find themselves the unwilling subjects of the Court's decisions, could damage the Court and by extension the international system. Unlike the normative defense of states' ability to preclude authoritative review of their actions, this claim should give pause to those who support strengthening the rule of international law. At least some countries committed to the world order status quo would object and do what they could to undermine the innovation. In particular, as with the International Criminal Court, the United States might actively oppose this innovation, as very likely would the other permanent members of the Security Council who are not currently accepting the binding jurisdiction of the Court.

Even more than with the International Criminal Court, however, it is difficult to see what these countries could practically do to stop such an innovation. They could threaten to cut off funding for the Court, but if the political will is there, other countries could make up the relatively small (in national budgetary terms) difference. They could decline to conform their practices to the advisory opinions of the Court thereby undermining its legitimacy by making it appear impotent, but this potentiality is not unique to advisory cases. In fact, when the Court has exercised compulsory jurisdiction under the optional clause or has taken jurisdiction pursuant to a compromisory clause in a treaty, respondent parties usually contest jurisdiction and are unhappy when they lose. At times they have even refused to appear in the merits phase of the decision.[37] Indeed, securing compliance with the Court's judgments has been one of the central challenges that the Court has faced in its continuing growth and evolution. Recent empirical evidence suggests, however, that compliance is generally forthcoming,[38] and there is no reason to believe the compliance problems associated with the proposal would be of a different order.

---

36. *See* ICC Statute, *supra* note 18, art. 13(b). The ICC has competence also to try individuals who hail from countries that have not joined that Court but who commit offenses within the territory of states that have. Some argue that this power to prosecute non-party nationals is a form of universal jurisdiction that contradicts the principle of state consent. (*See i.e.* statement of Senator Jesse Helms, Hearing on the United Nations International Criminal Court Before the Senate Foreign Relations Comm., July 23, 1998, *available in* 1998, FEDERAL DOCUMENT CLEARING HOUSE CONGRESSIONAL TESTIMONY, July 23, 1998.) Such claims notwithstanding, the power to prosecute non-party nations who commit offenses within the territory of states parties is consistent with the principle of state consent in as much as it provides that states can agree to delegate their territorially based jurisdictional right to try individuals (even if they be non-nationals) who commit offenses within their territory.

In fact, if the Court were to become more ubiquitous, it might well be that acceptance of its judgments would grow over time as was the case with the GATT panel decisions.

Finally, opposing countries and their supporters in the press and the academy might unleash a public relations assault designed to undermine the Court's legitimacy. While this potentiality needs to be taken seriously, recent history suggests the limited effectiveness of such assaults. The U.S. did this after the *Nicaragua* case, and the Court's influence actually grew. The International Criminal Court, which has not garnered the support of the U.S., China or Russia, has been subject to considerable criticism by U.S. government officials and their ideological allies. At least so far, their efforts to derail that court have largely failed. In fact, recent experience has shown that powerful countries are as dependent on the legitimacy they derive from being supported by the international system as the other way around. The Bush administration attempted to undermine the credibility of the United Nations when the Security Council refused to authorize its invasion of Iraq only to immediately return to the organization to seek approval for its occupation of that country. If history is any guide, once the institution of *universal advisory jurisdiction* is established, even opposing countries will find resort to the Court's chambers in strategically important cases where they have the legal upper hand all but irresistible. The United States has already acquiesced to allow the Security Council to refer the Darfur situation to the International Criminal Court.[39] If, for example, the U.S. could now secure an ICJ advisory judgment regarding Iran's pursuit of nuclear technology that would significantly help it secure UN sanctions and otherwise isolate that country, its temptation to do so would be extremely strong.

Another serious and related argument against the establishment of universal advisory jurisdiction is that it will interfere with the political settlement of disputes. This is already a common claim that countries make in both contentious and advisory cases.[40] It is currently being leveled in a powerful way against the International Criminal Court,[41] and it was for a long time an argument against moving toward a more legalized system of dispute resolution at the GATT.[42]

No doubt, in the world as it exists today there are times when disputes might be more easily settled without judicial involvement, just as there are times when they might be more easily settle with judicial involvement. As I suggest above, the Security Council should have the ability to defer the referral of cases to the Court, and the Court itself is, of course, sensitive to real world political dynamics. While it is constrained by the boundaries of international law, such dynamics no doubt play a role in influencing the formulation of its decisions. If the Court's ability to hear cases were to be expanded in the way suggested here, it could, if necessary, introduce judicial preclusion devices to limit further its adjudication in cases of intractable hostilities where its intervention would be counterproductive. Conveniently, the Court was given the unqualified discretion to decline to hear an advisory case.[43]

---

37. In four instances one of the parties in a contentious case refused to appear before the Court: Fisheries Jurisdiction (Gr. Brit. v. Ice.), 1974 I.C.J. 3 (July 25) *and* Fisheries Jurisdiction (F.R.G. v. Ice.), 1974 I.C.J. 175 (July 25) (deciding case without Iceland's participation); France in Nuclear Tests (N.Z. v. Fr.), 1974 I.C.J. 457 (Dec. 20) (deciding case without France); United States Diplomatic and Consular Staff in Tehran (U.S. v. Iran), 1980 I.C.J. 3 (May 24) (deciding case without Iran); Military and Paramilitary Activities in and Against Nicaragua, (Nicar. v. U.S.), 1986 I.C.J. 14 (June 27) (deciding case without the United States).

38. *See* CONSTANZE SCHULTE, COMPLIANCE WITH DECISIONS OF THE INTERNATIONAL COURT OF JUSTICE (Oxford Un. Press 2004).

39. *See* Marlise Simons, *Sudan Poses First Big Trial for World Criminal Court*, N.Y. TIMES, April 29, 2005, at 12.

40. For example, the Israeli's made this claim in the Israeli Wall advisory case and the United States made this claim in the Nicaragua case. The legal basis for the claim is grounded in the meaning of "legal dispute" under Article 36 and "legal question" under Article 65 of the Court's statute.

In the final analysis, since at this point in history we are not in a political position to create a functioning world judiciary out of whole cloth, the key determination we must make is whether we are committed to working through the anomalies that will naturally arise on the path to a more law-based international system. Currently we are caught in the contradiction between a global order that is partially based on raw power politics and even violence and one that is partially based on the rule of law. The path to a more rule-based system will not happen overnight, and it will not be easy to achieve. If we proceed with that end in sight, however, such contradictions will gradually diminish.

Finally there are a variety of practical and logistical problems that need to be resolved if the Court's ability to hear advisory cases is to be expanded in the way suggested here. If a relevant party refuses to participate, what should be done to ensure that the Court fairly considers all the legal and factual questions? In what ways could the Court adapt to the inevitable and probably dramatic increase in its caseload? Are there procedures that could preclude the Court from taking on an essentially law-making function? These kinds of questions are inevitable in the development of any judicial system, and there is no reason to believe they cannot be successfully resolved. In fact, the Court has already dealt with many of them in contentious cases or in advisory opinions.

IV. Conclusion: Universal Advisory Jurisdiction and Climate Change

Establishing a mechanism for the Court to obtain universal advisory jurisdiction would benefit the global system in ways that go well beyond helping to ameliorate climate change and its impact on future generations. The increasing recognition of global warming and its tremendous social costs may, however, provide a concrete reason for the General Assembly to establish the judicial organ. Both the remediation of and adaptation to climate change is likely to be enormously expensive, and the Court could help establish equitable principles grounded in law—defining the rights and obligations of individual states as well as obligations towards future generations.

Carefully crafted opinions applying international environmental rules of state responsibility to climate change could have additional salutary benefits. It could positively influence the interstate dynamics of negotiation over the future of the post-Kyoto treaty regime. Those states that are significant producers of greenhouse gases and wish to stay out of a treaty regime or otherwise free ride would have greater reason to concern themselves with the uncertain legal environment this could create. Apprehension that gaps in the law will be filled by courts is a reason those who face potential legal exposure in domestic systems often support regulation.[44]

To the extent that corporations face a credible threat of exposure to climate change litigation, corporate managers are likely to want to reduce that potential by encouraging constructive par-

---

41. Joseph Kony, the commander of the Lord's Resistance Army, a Ugandan rebel organization alleged to be responsible for serious human rights abuses, including abducting more than 25,000 children to serve as soldiers and sex slaves, has been indicted by the International Criminal Court. As a condition for signing a permanent peace accord with the government of Uganda, Kony has demanded that the ICC withdraw the indictment against him and two deputies. Thus far, despite pressure from the Ugandan government, eager to see the conclusion of the peace treaty, the prosecutor has refused. *See* Nora Boustany, *Ugandan Rebel Reaches Out to International Court; Kony's Legal Team Explores an Exit that Could Seal Peace Pact*, Wash. Post, Mar. 19, 2008, at A12.

42. *See generally* William J. Davey, Symposium: *International Economic Conflict and Resolution: The World Trade Organization's Dispute Settlement System*, 42 S. Tex L. Rev. 1099 (2001).

43. The language of Article 65 of the Court's statute providing that the Court "may give" an advisory opinion has always been interpreted to mean that the Court has discretion to comply with a request. *See Interpretations of Peace Treaties with Bulgaria, Hungary and Romania, First Phase, I.C.J Reports 1950*, p. 65, at 71. *Reservations to the Convention on the Prevention and punishment of the Crime of Genocide, I.C.J Reports 1951*, p. 15 at 19.

ticipation by their governments in a post-Kyoto regime that contains clearly identifiable limits on greenhouse gases to which they can comply.[45] While the Court would likely rule on state responsibility under international law rather than corporate responsibility under domestic law, such rulings would carry liability implications for corporations. In potential domestic nuisance or negligence cases against corporations for causing harm, it is necessary to establish that the defendant corporation's contribution to climate change contravened some community-wide standard of behavior.[46] A decision by the Court could help to establish the existence of such standards and perhaps serve as a guide to the limits on corporate greenhouse gas emissions they require.

The problem of global warming is perhaps only the most salient today of the many areas that could benefit from expanding the advisory jurisdiction of the Court. As discussed in this paper, Court involvement in other domains of conflict between states would offer different advantages and different challenges. Common to all, however, is the opportunity for the Court to expand its role in promoting an international system based on the rule of law.

B. A Theory of Atmospheric Trust Litigation

Atmospheric Trust Litigation

Mary Christina Wood. Philip H. Knight Professor of Law, Founding Director, Environmental and Natural Resources Law Program, former Morse Center Resident Scholar and Luvaas Faculty Fellow, University of Oregon School of Law, Eugene, OR 97403-1221; Tel: (541) 346-3842, Fax: (541) 346-1564, mwood@law.uoregon.edu. Part of this chapter is based on material published in Mary Christina Wood, Atmospheric Trust Litigation, chapter in ADJUDICATING CLIMATE CHANGE: SUB-NATIONAL, NATIONAL, AND SUPRA-NATIONAL APPROACHES (William C.G. Burns & Hari M. Godowsky, eds.) (Cambridge Un. Press 2009), available at https://www.law.uoregon.edu/faculty/mwood/docs/atlpaper.pdf.

I. The Stakes

Leading climate scientists warn that Earth is in "imminent peril," on the verge of runaway climate heating that will impose catastrophic conditions on generations to come.[1] In their words, continued carbon pollution will cause a "transformed planet"[2]—an Earth obliterated of its major fixtures, including the polar ice sheets, Greenland, the coral reefs, and the Amazon forest. The annihilatory trajectory launched by humans over the past century threatens to trigger the planet's Sixth mass extinction—the kind that hasn't occurred on Earth for 65 million years.[3] Should Business as Usual continue even for a few more years, our children and their descendants—future Humanity for untold generations—will be pummeled by floods, hurricanes, heat waves, fires, disease, crop losses, food shortages, and droughts as part of a hellish struggle to survive within a deadly greenhouse of our own making.[4] In a world of runaway climate heat-

---

44. *See* GABRIEL KOLKO, THE TRIUMPH OF CONSERVATISM; A REINTERPRETATION OF AMERICAN HISTORY, 1900–1916 (Free Press 1977).

45. *See* David A. Grossman, *Warming Up to a Not-So-Radical Idea: Tort-Based Climate Change Litigation*, 28 COLUM. J. ENVTL. L. 1 (2003); J. Kevin Healy and Jeffrey M. Tapick, *Climate Change: It's not Just a Policy Issue for Corporate Counsel—It's a Legal Problem*, 29 COLUM. J. ENVTL. L. 89 (2004).

46. *See generally* DAN D. DOBBS, THE LAW OF TORTS 393–403 (Thomson West 2000).

ing, these unrelenting disasters would force massive human migrations and cause staggering numbers of deaths—ultimately resulting in Humanity's "self-destruction."[5] As author Fred Pearce states: "Humanity faces a genuinely new situation.... a crisis for the entire life-support system of our civilization and our species."[6]

In face of this unprecedented "planetary emergency,"[7] environmental law hasn't changed that much.

When it comes to saving civilization, law should have a role to play. The very essence of the law is allocating responsibility for harm. Americans contribute nearly 30% of greenhouse gases to the atmosphere, but remarkably, U.S. law has not taken even modest steps towards assigning liability for greenhouse gas pollution. The scope and pervasiveness of carbon pollution is so vast that it slips through established legal paradigms. The time lag inherent in the future infliction of cruelty, deprivation, and death through pollution unleashed today defies causal linkages familiar to the law. Yet, law is a creative institution and, to be of any use at all, must mold to new and urgent circumstances. Climate crisis demands broad, system-changing solutions and doctrines. Tinkering around the edges with approaches that have failed in the past holds no more promise than throwing a rescue rope that is too short.

This chapter proposes an organizing legal framework based on the public trust doctrine to define government responsibility in climate crisis.[8] The public trust doctrine imposes a fundamental limitation on the power of government over natural resources.[9] Government holds crucial natural resources in trust for its citizens and bears the fiduciary obligation to protect such resources for present and future generations.[10] Broadly viewed, the trust is embedded in the law as an attribute of sovereignty itself.[11] An ancient and enduring principle, it has roots and reasoning that put it on par with the highest liberties of citizens living in a free society. Yet, the principle has all but been obfuscated in a mudflow of regulations and statutes that have oozed thickly across the legal landscape during the past three decades of environmental law.

---

1. James Hansen *et al.*, *Climate Change and Trace Gases*, PHIL. TRANS. R. SOC. A, 1925, 1949 (2007) [hereinafter *Climate Change and Trace Gases*], *available at* http://www.planetwork.net/climate/Hansen2007.pdf. *See also* Steve Connor, *The Earth Today Stands in Imminent Peril*, THE INDEPENDENT, June 19, 2007, *available at* http://environment.independent.co.uk/climate_change/article2675747.ece.

2. Jim Hansen, *The Threat to the Planet*, 53 N.Y. REV. BOOKS, July 13, 2006, at 12, *available at* http://pubs.giss.nasa.gov/docs/2006/2006_Hansen.pdf.

3. John Boitnott, *Berkeley Scientists: World in "Mass Extinction Spasm"—Scientists: Humans to Blame*, NEWS REPORT NBC, Aug. 12, 2008, *available at* http://www.nbc11.com/news/17171725/detail.html.

4. *See* Geoffrey Lean, *A World Dying, But Can We Unite to Save It?*, THE INDEPENDENT UK, Nov. 18, 2007.

5. *See* Joseph Romm, *Is 450 ppm (or less) Politically Possible? Part 0: The Alternative is Humanity's Self-Destruction*, *available at* http://climateprogress.org/2008/04/26/is-450-ppm-or-less-politically-possible-part-0-the-alternative-is-humanitysself-destruction. Joseph Romm is the author of HELL AND HIGH WATER (William Morrow Publishers 2007).

6. FRED PEARCE, WITH SPEED AND VIOLENCE: WHY SCIENTISTS FEAR TIPPING POINTS IN CLIMATE CHANGE (Beacon Press 2007); *see also* Al Gore, *Moving Beyond Kyoto*, N.Y. TIMES, July 1, 2007 ("This is a moral issue, one that affects the survival of human civilization.... Put simply, it is wrong to destroy the habitability of our planet and ruin the prospects of every generation that follows ours.").

7. *See* James Hansen, *Dangerous Human-Made Interference with Climate*, Testimony Before Select Committee on Energy Independence and Global Warming, U.S. House of Representatives 3 (April 26, 2007), *available at* http://www.columbia.edu/~jeh1/testimony_26april2007.pdf; Felicity Barringer & Andrew C. Revkin, *Al Gore Warns of 'Planetary Emergency,'* INTERNATIONAL HERALD TRIBUNE, Mar. 21, 2007, *available at* http://www.iht.com/articles/2007/03/21/america/web.0321goresub.php.

This paper seeks to bring definition to the trust framework as a paradigm of responsibility for addressing climate crisis. Section One presents the basic elements of the trust doctrine. Section Two introduces six attributes of legal responsibility necessary for controlling carbon pollution, discusses why existing environmental law does not measure up to the task ahead, and suggests the trust paradigm as a galvanizing legal principle in face of climate crisis. Section Three describes atmospheric trust litigation as a tool for waking a sleeping judiciary to the unfolding climate catastrophe. It maps out a remedy by which courts can invoke their injunctive powers to impose life-saving restraints on deadly carbon excesses of industrialized society.

II. The People's Natural Trust

The public trust has been described in depth elsewhere and will only be sketched here. Deriving from the common law of property, the doctrine is evident in hundreds of judicial decisions, including landmark Supreme Court opinions.[12] Arguably an implied, inherent constitutional limit on legislative power,[13] the principle asserts that government holds vital natural resources in "trust" for the public.[14] As trustee, government must protect the natural assets for the beneficiaries of the trust, which are present and future generations of citizens.[15]

Under this doctrine, government may not allow private interests to cause irrevocable harm to critical public trust resources. As the Supreme Court said in *Geer v. Connecticut*:

> [T]he power or control lodged in the State, resulting from this common ownership, is to be exercised, like all other powers of government, as a trust for the benefit of the people, and not as a prerogative for the advantage of the government, as distinct from the people, or for the benefit of private individuals as distinguished from the public good.... [T]he ownership is that of the people in their united sovereignty.[16]

---

8. For a fuller description of the proposed framework and additional citations to authority supporting the principles described herein, *see* Mary Christina Wood, *Atmospheric Trust Litigation*, chapter *in* Adjudicating Climate Change: Sub-National, National, and Supra-National Approaches (William C.G. Burns & Hari M. Osofsky eds., Cambridge Un. Press 2009) [hereinafter 2009 Wood *Atmospheric Trust Litigation*], *available at* https://www.law.uoregon.edu/faculty/ mwood/docs/atlpaper.pdf. This article does not delve into private liability for carbon pollution, which is the subject of ongoing climate nuisance suits.

9. For sources and materials on the public trust doctrine, see Jan G. Laitos, Sandra B. Zellmer, Mary C. Wood & Dan H. Cole, Natural Resources Law Chapter 8.II (Thomson West 2006). For discussion of the public trust doctrine, see Joseph L. Sax, *The Public Trust Doctrine in Natural Resource Law: Effective Judicial Intervention*, 68 Mich. L. Rev. 471, 558–66 (1970); Harrison Dunning, *The Public Trust: A Fundamental Doctrine of American Property Law*, 19 Envtl. L. 515 (1989); Mary Christina Wood, *Advancing the Sovereign Trust of Government to Safeguard the Environment for Present and Future Generations* (Parts I and II), 39 Envtl. L. 43 and 91 (2009), *available through request at* http://www.law.uoregon.edu/faculty/mwood/publications.php.

10. Illinois Cent. R. Co. v. Illinois, 146 U.S. 387, 455 (1892); Arizona Ctr. for Law in the Pub. Interest v. Hassell, 837 P.2d 158, 169 (Ariz. Ct. App. 1991) ("The beneficiaries of the public trust are not just present generations but those to come."); *see also* source cited in *infra* note 19.

11. *See* Jan S. Stevens, *The Public Trust: A Sovereign's Ancient Prerogative Becomes the People's Environmental Right*, 14 U.C. Davis. L. Rev. 195, 196 (1980) (noting jurisprudence "in the form of declarations that the public trust is inalienable as an attribute of sovereignty no more capable of conveyance than the police power itself."). Professor Douglas Grant ties the public trust doctrine to the Constitutional reserved powers doctrine, which prevents any one legislature from taking acts that would compromise a future legislature's ability to exercise sovereignty on behalf of the people. *See* Douglas L. Grant, *Underpinnings of the Public Trust Doctrine: Lessons from* Illinois Central Railroad, 48 Ariz. St. L.J. 849 (2001) [hereinafter 2001 Grant].

12. *See discussion* at Allen Kanner, *The Public Trust Doctrine*, Parens Patriae, *and the Attorney General as the Guardian of the State's Natural Resources*, 16 Duke Envtl. L. & Pol'y F. 57, 71–72 (2005); Gerald Torres, *Who Owns the Sky?* 19 Pace Envtl. L. Rev. 515 (2002).

13. *See* 2001 Grant, *supra* note 11, at 872.

The lodestar public trust opinion is *Illinois Central Railroad Co. v. Illinois*, where the Supreme Court announced that the shoreline of Lake Michigan was held in public trust by the State of Illinois and could not be transferred out of public ownership to a private railroad corporation. In broad language expressing the public's fundamental right to natural resources, the Court stated:

> [T]he decisions are numerous which declare that such property is held by the state, by virtue of its sovereignty, in trust for the public. The ownership of the navigable waters of the harbor, and of the lands under them, is a subject of public concern to the whole people of the state. The trust with which they are held, therefore, is governmental, and cannot be alienated....[17]

While traditionally applied to water-based resources, the public trust doctrine logically encompasses air and atmosphere as assets in the people's trust. In defining the scope of the trust endowment, courts have looked to the needs of the public as the primary guiding factor. At the time of the *Illinois Central* case, lakebeds served a vital function in supporting fishing, navigation and commerce. Describing the lakebed as property in which "the whole people are interested," the Court reasoned: "The trust with which they are held, therefore, is governmental.... This follows necessarily from the *public character of the property*."[18]

As Professor Charles Wilkinson explains, "[The public trust doctrine is rooted in the precept that some resources are so central to the well-being of the community that they must be protected by distinctive, judge-made principles."[19] Not surprisingly, courts have expanded the assets constituting the res of the public trust on the rationale that such assets are necessary to meet society's changing needs.[20] The doctrine, for example, has pushed beyond the original societal interests of fishing, navigation and commerce to protect modern concerns such as biodiversity, wildlife habitat, aesthetics and recreation.[21]

Guided by the essential doctrinal purposes expressed by courts in public trust cases, it is no great leap to recognize the atmosphere as one of the crucial assets of the public trust. The public interests at stake in climate crisis are unfathomable leagues beyond the traditional fishing, navigation and commerce interests at the forefront of *Illinois Central*. Atmospheric health is essential to all civilizations and to human survival across the globe. As one climate analyst put it, carbon reduction is necessary for averting "the end of life as we know it."[22] There is no question that treating the atmosphere as a public trust asset is consistent with the central purpose of the trust doctrine.

---

14. *See supra* note 11.

15. Geer v. Connecticut, 161 U.S. 519, 534 (1896) ("The ownership of the sovereign authority is in trust for all the people of the state; and hence, by implication, it is the duty of the legislature to enact such laws as will best preserve the subject of the trust, and secure its beneficial use in the future to the people of the state."). While *Geer* was later overruled for its treatment of commerce clause issues, the underlying trust basis of the decision holds force today. For discussion, see Mary Christina Wood, *The Tribal Property Right to Wildlife Capital (Part 1): Applying Principles of Sovereignty to Protect Imperiled Wildlife Populations,* 37 IDAHO L. REV. 1 (2000).

16. *Geer,* 161 U.S. at 529. *See also* Lake Michigan Federation v. U.S. Army Corps of Engineers, 742 F. Supp. 441, 445 (D. Ill. 1990) ("[T]he public trust is violated when the primary purpose of a legislative grant is to benefit a private interest.").

17. *Illinois Cent. R. Co.,* 146 U.S. at 455 (but noting that parcels could be alienated "when parcels can be disposed of without detriment to the public interest in the lands and waters remaining."). *Id.* at 453.

18. *Id.* at 452–456 (emphasis added). *See also id.* at 455 ("It would not be listened to that the control and management of the harbor of that great city—*a subject of concern to the whole people of the state*—should thus be placed elsewhere than in the state itself....") (emphasis added).

19. Charles F. Wilkinson, *The Public Trust Doctrine in Public Land Law,* 14 U.C. DAVIS L. REV 269, 315 (1980).

20. *See, e.g.,* Matthews v. Bay Head Improvement Association, 471 A.2d 355, 365 (N. J. 1984). As the New Jersey Supreme Court said, "[W]e perceive the public trust doctrine not to be 'fixed or static,' but one to be

It should be noted that, while air has not previously been the subject of trust litigation, the Roman origins of the public trust doctrine classified air—along with water, wildlife and the sea—as "*res communes.*"[23] In a landmark public trust decision, *Geer v. Connecticut,* the Supreme Court relied on this ancient Roman classification of "*res communes*" to find the public trust applicable to wildlife.[24] Since then, the Court has also recognized the states' sovereign interests in air as a basis upon which to bring an interstate nuisance suit. In *Georgia v. Tennessee Copper Co.,* the Court upheld an action brought by the state of Georgia against Tennessee copper companies for discharging noxious gas that drifted across state lines, stating: "[T]he state has an interest independent of and behind the titles of its citizens, in all the earth and air within its domain."[25] Given the essential nature of air, it is unsurprising that numerous state court decisions, constitutions, and codes have recognized air as part of the *res* of the public trust,[26] and commentators have urged that characterization as well.[27] In sum, courts have a solid legal rationale from which to draw in designating the atmosphere as a public trust asset.

III. Legal Requirements for Saving the Planet

Three decades ago, Congress passed a set of ambitious environmental statutes, such as the Clean Air Act, the Clean Water Act, the Endangered Species Act, and many others. States and local governments also enacted a suite of environmental statutes. Most climate litigation strategies rely on claims deriving from these laws. Before relying exclusively on these statutes, however, it is worth isolating the legal requisites necessary to achieving sufficient carbon reduction in the short window of time remaining before irrevocable climate thresholds are passed. This section suggests six basic criteria for such a legal formulation and contrasts existing environmental statutory law with the trust approach in terms of their capacity to satisfy the criteria.

'molded and extended to meet changing conditions and needs of the public it was created to benefit.'" (citation omitted).

21. *Matthews,* 471 A.2d at 363; National Audubon Society v. Superior Court, 658 P.2d 709, 719–22 (Cal. 1983).

22. *See* Joseph Romm, post, *Study: Water-Vapor Feedback is "Strong and Positive," So We Face "Warming of Several Degrees Celsius,"* CLIMATE PROGRESS BLOG (A "'warming of several degrees Celsius" = the end of life as we know it.'"), *available at* http://climateprogress.org/2008/10/26/study-water-vapor-feedback-is-strong-and-positive-so-we-face-warming-of-degrees-celsius.

23. *See Geer,* 161 U.S. at 525 ("These things are those which the jurisconsults called '*res communes*'—the air, the water which runs in the rivers, the sea and its shores ... [and] wild animals."). *See also* Torres, *supra* note 12, at 529–30 (discussing *res communes*).

24. *See Geer,* 161 U.S at 523.

25. State of Ga. v. Tennessee Copper Co., 206 U.S. 230, 237 (1907). The passage was cited in Massachusetts v. U.S. Environmental Protection Agency, 549 U.S. 497, 127 S.Ct. 1438, 1454 (2007).

26. *See, e.g.,* Her Majesty v. City of Detroit, 874 F.2d 332, 337 (6th Cir. 1989) (citing Michigan act that codifies public trust to include "air, water, and other natural resources"); Haw. Const., art. XI, §1 (stating, "All public natural resources are held in trust by the State for the benefit of the people," and "the State and its political subdivisions shall conserve and protect Hawaii's ... natural resources, including land, water, air, minerals and energy resources...."); LA. Const., art. IX, §1 ("natural resources of the state, including air and water ... shall be protected...."); R.I. Const., art. I, §16 (duty of legislature to protect air), interpreted as codification of Rhode Island's public trust doctrine in State ex. Rel. Town of Westerly v. Bradley, 877 A.2d 601, 606 (R.I. 2005); National Audubon Society v. Superior Court of Alpine County, 658 P.2d 709, 720 (1983) ("purity of the air" protected by the public trust).

27. *See* Torres, *supra* note 12, at 533, 526 ("Properly understood ... the traditional rationale for the public trust doctrine provides a necessary legal cornerstone ... to protect the public interest in the sky."); PETER BARNES, WHO OWNS THE SKY: OUR COMMON ASSETS AND THE FUTURE OF CAPITALISM (Island Press 2006).

A. Protecting Nature's Assets as a Matter of Obligation, Not Discretion

The most glaring and inexcusable deficiency of modern environmental law is the apparent lack of governmental obligation to protect natural resources. Ironically, while the vast body of statutory law was designed to safeguard natural resources for the American public, instead, the law itself has become a major engine of environmental destruction.[28] Nearly all existing environmental and land use statutes give agencies authority to issue permits to allow the very damage that the statutes were designed to prevent. The permit systems were never intended to subvert the goals of the statutes, but the vast majority of agencies use their permit discretion to allow nearly unending damage.[29] Agencies are subject to intense political pressure by developers, industrialists, private property owners, and politicians to issue permits.[30] Internal political drivers are rarely exposed, concealed by a strong bureaucratic façade of neutrality and nearly impenetrable technical regulatory language.

Because of this dysfunction, government squandered years of precious time in which it could have controlled carbon pollution to avert the crisis society now faces. The federal agency in charge of regulating air pollution, the U.S. Environmental Protection Agency, has been the target of political subversion from the highest appointees over the past eight years. While the agency has ample tools and expertise to regulate carbon and holds a clear statutory duty to the American public to protect it from endangerment as a result of air pollution,[31] the Bush II EPA—particularly Administrator Steve Johnson—persistently resisted regulating carbon under the Clean Air Act and rejected California's efforts to increase motor vehicle fuel efficiency standards.[32] Considerable evidence suggests that these EPA decisions, along with other high-level Bush II administration decisions, were made to favor the fossil fuel industries with which the administration had a close political alliance.[33] Elevating the interests of political cronies over the general public welfare is a hallmark of governmental corruption. Remarkably, however, the point seems to have been lost in the highly technical statutory litigation challenging the actions.[34]

Such politicization of agency decision-making undermines the very premise of administrative law—namely, that agencies are constituted to carry out statutory objectives in neutral fashion. The systemic corruption of agencies—and society's passive acceptance of it—represents one of the most consequential breakdowns in administrative law. Legal reform must be geared towards

---

28. For discussion, see Wood, *Advancing the Sovereign Trust, supra* note 9, at Part I, Section II.

29. See *id.* at note 63 and sources cited therein. *See also* JAMES GUSTAVE SPETH, THE BRIDGE AT THE END OF THE WORLD: CAPITALISM, THE ENVIRONMENT, AND CROSSING FROM CRISIS TO SUSTAINABILITY 84 (Yale Un. Press 2008); ROBERT F. KENNEDY JR., CRIMES AGAINST NATURE 32–33 (HarperCollins 2004) (Federal agencies in the Bush II administration "have given quick permit approvals and doled out waivers that exempt campaign contributors and polluters from rules or regulations.").

30. *See generally* KENNEDY, *supra* note 29; SPETH, *supra* note 29, at 85 (also citing William Greider, WASHINGTON POST writer: "The regulatory state has become a deeply flawed governing mess.... Many of the enforcement agencies are securely captured by the industries they regulate....") For a discussion of politicized agency decision-making, see Holly Doremus, *Scientific and Political Integrity in Environmental Policy*, 86 TEX. L. REV. 1601 (2008).

31. *See* 42 U.S.C. §7521(a)(1), *discussed in* Massachusetts v. U.S. Environmental Protection Agency, 549 U.S. 497, 127 S.Ct. 1438 (2007).

32. *See generally* Jonathan S. Martel & Kerri L. Stelcen, *Clean Air Regulation, in* GLOBAL CLIMATE CHANGE AND U.S. LAW 133 (Michael B. Gerrard ed., ABA 2007) [hereinafter GLOBAL CLIMATE CHANGE].

33. *See* H. Joseph Herbert, *EPA Scientists Complain about Political Pressure*, ASSOCIATED PRESS, Apr. 23, 2008, *available at* http://www.cnn.com/2008/TECH/04/23/epa.scientists.ap/index.html; GENERAL ACCOUNTING OFFICE, TOXIC CHEMICAL RELEASES: EPA ACTIONS COULD REDUCE AVAILABILITY OF ENVIRONMENTAL INFORMATION TO THE PUBLIC, GAO-08-128 (2007), *available at* http://www.gao.gov/new.items/d08128.pdf (discussing political factors influencing denial of California waiver by Stephen Johnson, head of EPA); Richard Simon, *Lawmaker Alleges Whitehouse Role in Stopping California Emissions Law*, L.A. TIMES, May 20, 2008, *available at* http://www.latimes.com/news/nationworld/washingtondc/la-na-epa20-2008may20,0,113 981.story; Jody Freeman & Adrian Vermeule, Massachusetts v. EPA: *From Politics to Expertise*, 2007 SUPREME COURT RE-

producing a firm, abiding obligation to protect natural resources. Engineering such reform need not entail changing the environmental laws themselves, but rather changing the way such laws are construed, applied, and enforced.[35] In holding government accountable for greenhouse gas pollution, the political discretion model of administrative law must yield to fixed restraints on government actors.

In contrast to statutory law, trust principles infuse obligation into governmental management of natural resources. Under well-established principles of private trust law, trustees may not sit idle and allow damage to occur to the trust.[36] Unlike principles of administrative discretion, the governmental trustee bears a strict fiduciary obligation to protect the people's trust assets from damage.[37] Scores of cases emphasize this duty of protection.[38]

Moreover, public trust jurisprudence makes clear that government is not at liberty to disclaim its fiduciary obligation to protect crucial natural resources. As the Court said in *Illinois Central*: "The state can no more abdicate its trust over property in which the whole people are interested ... than it can abdicate its police powers in the administration of government and the preservation of the peace.... Every legislature must, at the time of its existence, exercise the power of the state in the execution of the trust devolved upon it."[39] Litigation strategy to force government to reduce carbon will face an uphill battle as long as it is based on a system of laws premised on administrative political discretion. By emphasizing strict obligation, the trust represents a fundamentally different and potentially more promising legal approach.

B. Carbon Math in a Minute Glass: It All Must Add Up in Time

A legal formulation of carbon responsibility must comport with ecological reality. In order to stem global warming, the law must recognize and calibrate to the physical, chemical, and biological requirements for achieving climate equilibrium. Such requirements are set by Nature, not politicians. Stated another way, averting climate disaster is a matter of carbon math, not carbon

---

VIEW 54–61 (2008) (compiling accusations of politicized decision-making by EPA surrounding global warming regulation within the context of the Clean Air Act, noting broad allegations of "an unprecedented degree of politicization of agency expertise under the George W. Bush administration"); Doremus, *supra* note 30, at 1632–33 (reviewing politicization of Bush II agencies and noting, "Political appointees throughout the administration have proved willing to substitute the least attractive form of politics for principles.").

34. *See* Massachusetts v. U.S. Environmental Protection Agency, 549 U.S. 497, 127 S.Ct. 1438 (2007).

35. The trust doctrine can operate as an interstitial duty of protection that is compatible with statutory law. Most environmental statutes provide agencies with ample authority and administrative mechanisms to protect the environment. What is lacking is the clear obligation to exert such authority. The EPA, for example, has broad authority under its statutory emergency powers to bring a suit against sources of pollution that pose an "imminent and substantial endangerment to public health or welfare, or the environment," 42 U.S.C. §7603, a provision that could support action against carbon polluters. Professor Robert L. Glicksman has analyzed the statutory authority to regulate under statutory endangerment provisions in his article, *Coal-Fired Power Plants, Greenhouse Gases, and State Statutory Substantial Endangerment Provisions: Climate Change Comes to Kansas*, 56 U. Kansas L. Rev. 517 (April 2008). While the interface between the trust doctrine and statutory law is well beyond the scope of this chapter, it is considered in Wood, *Advancing the Sovereign Trust*, *supra* note 9, at Part I, Section III.

36. *See* George T. Bogert, Trusts §99, at 358 (6th ed. West Pub. Co., 1987) ("The trustee has a duty to take whatever steps are necessary ... to protect and preserve the trust property from loss or damage."); Am. Jur. 2d Trusts §656 (noting the "power, and a duty of the trustee, to initiate actions ... for the protection of the trust estate").

37. *See, e.g., Geer*, 161 U.S. at 534 ("[I]t is the duty of the legislature to enact such laws as will best preserve the subject of the trust, and secure its beneficial use in the future to the people of the state."); State v. City of Bowling Green, 313 N.E.2d 409, 411 (Ohio 1974) ("[W]here the state is deemed to be the trustee of property for the benefit of the public it has the obligation to bring suit ... to protect the corpus of the trust property.").

38. For sources, see Wood, *Advancing the Sovereign Trust, supra* note 9, at notes 30–32.

39. *Illinois Central*, 146 U.S. at 460.

politics. Moreover, it's math in a minute glass. Scientists warn that the world has only a short time to begin reversing global emissions of carbon before the planet passes a "tipping point,"[40] at which point dangerous feedback loops will unravel the planet's climate system—despite any subsequent carbon reductions achieved by Humanity.[41] While just a year ago scientists believed the "tipping point" would be triggered at 450 parts per million of carbon in the atmosphere, some now believe the threshold is at 350 parts per million.[42] Present levels are at 387 parts per million and climbing at an unprecedented pace.[43] Analysts are repeatedly warning in the clearest terms possible that the Earth is now in a danger zone—a state of planetary emergency[44]—and that, if Humanity follows Business As Usual for even another few years, it will "lock in" future catastrophic global heating.[45] The head of the UN's climate panel recently told the world, "What we do in the next two to three years will determine our future. This is the defining moment."[46] Legal strategies must account for this time frame.

For the law to have any chance at being effective, it must be tied to a carbon prescription set by leading climate scientists. The prescription must have immediate, short-term targets that create sufficient carbon reduction in the near future to avert the tipping point. The prescription

---

40. *See* Pearce, *supra* note 6; David Spratt & Philip Sutton, Climate Code Red: The Case for a Sustainability Emergency (Friends of the Earth 2008), *available* at http://www.climatecodered.net/ [hereinafter Climate Code Red] (summarizing science). The tipping point concept has been recognized by the Ninth Circuit in a recent climate case. *See* Center for Biological Diversity v. Nat'l Highway Traffic Safety Admin., 508 F.3d 508, at slip op. 34 (9th Cir. 2008) ("Several studies also show that climate change may be non-linear, meaning that there are positive feedback mechanisms that may push global warming past a dangerous threshold (the 'tipping point')").

41. *See* Hansen, *Testimony*, *supra* note 7, at 5 ("In the past few years it has become clear that the Earth is close to dangerous climate change, to tipping points of the system with the potential for irreversible deleterious effects."); Hansen, *Threat to the Planet*, *supra* note 2, at 14 ("[B]ecause of the global warming already bound to take place as a result of the continuing long-term effects of greenhouse gases and the energy systems now in use, ... it will soon be impossible to avoid climate change with far-ranging undesirable consequences. We have reached a critical tipping point."); *Climate Change and Trace Gases*, *supra* note 1, at 1925, 1949 (discussing positive feedback loops); James Hansen et al., *Dangerous Human-Made Interference With Climate: A GISS Model Study*, 7 Atmos. Chem. Phys. 2287, 2303 (2007) [hereinafter *Dangerous Human-Made Interference*], *available at* http://www.atmos-chem-phys.net/7/2287/2007/acp-7-2287-2007.pdf (discussing tipping point: "[W]e must be close to such a point, but we may not have passed it yet."). While the term "tipping point" is often used, in actuality there are many dangerous feedback loops, each representing a destabilizing tipping point. For discussion of the many tipping points, see Pearce, *supra*, note 6.

42. James Hansen, Makiko Sato, Pushker Kharecha, David Beerling, Valerie Masson-Delmotte, Mark Pagani, Maureen Raymo, Dana L. Royer & James C. Zachos, *Target Atmospheric CO_2: Where Should Humanity Aim?*, 2 The Open Atmospheric Sciences Journal 217 (Nov. 2008), *available at* http://arxiv.org/abs/0804.1126 [hereinafter Hansen, *350 Target Paper*]; *see* Bill McKibben, *Remember This: 350 Parts Per Million*, Washington Post, Dec. 28, 2007, http://www.washingtonpost.com/wp-dyn/content/article/2007/12/27/AR2007122701942.html.

43. David Adam, *World Carbon Dioxide Levels Highest for 650,000 Years, Says US Report*, The Guardian, May 13, 2008, at 16, *available at* http://www.guardian.co.uk/environment/2008/may/13/carbonemissions.climatechange. While the 350 target has been exceeded, climate scientists still offer hope of atmospheric stability if the "overshoot" is brief. *See* Hansen, *350 Target Paper*, *supra* note 42, at 1 ("If the present overshoot of this target CO_2 is not brief, there is a possibility of seeding irreversible catastrophic effects.").

44. *See* Climate Code Red, *supra* note 40, at chapters 23, 24; Speth, *supra* note 29, at 27 (quoting Jim Hansen: "The crystallizing scientific story reveals an imminent planetary emergency. We are at a planetary tipping point.").

45. *See* Hansen, *Testimony*, *supra* note 7 ("[I]gnoring the climate problem at this time, for even another decade, would serve to lock in future catastrophic climatic change and impacts that will unfold during the remainder of this century and beyond...."); James Hansen, *Why We Can't Wait*, The Nation, May 7, 2007 ("If we do follow that [Business as Usual] path, even for another ten years, it guarantees that we will have dramatic climate changes that produce what I would call a different planet...."); Jim Hansen, *Climate Change: On the Edge*, The Independent, Feb. 17, 2006, *available at* http://environmentindependent.co.uk/article345926.ece

must also have regularly spaced longer-term targets geared towards achieving a zero-carbon society over the next few decades. Many current climate policy initiatives are exactly backwards, governed by how much politicians are willing to give, not by the actual carbon reduction needed to recover the atmosphere.[47]

The present body of environmental statutory law is not geared to achieving overall carbon reduction necessary for climate equilibrium. The laws are micro in orientation, focusing on specific governmental actions. Any carbon reduction they accomplish will be incremental and haphazard in the aggregate. The trust approach, by contrast, is designed as a macro level legal strategy to enable enforcement of scientific prescriptions for carbon reduction.[48] It does so by characterizing the atmosphere in its entirety as a defined trust asset. A trustee's primary fiduciary obligation is to ensure overall health of the asset—a standard defined by objective criteria. Scientific prescriptions for achieving climate equilibrium amount to, in essence, the yardstick of fiduciary obligation for protecting the atmosphere. This formulation is both designed to create a uniform approach to climate responsibility and also to divest the politicians of their assumed prerogative to take action only if consistent with their political ambition.

Of course, defining the fiduciary obligation by reference to science involves hurdles, not the least of which is that climate scientists are often reticent to provide prescriptions for action, be-

---

("How long have we got? We have to stabilize emissions of carbon dioxide within a decade, or temperatures will warm by more than one degree. That will be warmer than it has been for half a million years, and many things could become unstoppable."). A disturbing United Nations IPCC report indicates that the planet has already reached the danger point of atmospheric carbon dioxide equivalent concentrations, indicating that a decade is far too long to achieve significant greenhouse gas reduction. *See* Gregory M. Lamb, *A Key Threshold Crossed*, Christian Sci. Monitor, Oct. 11, 2007, *available at* http://www.csmonitor.com/2007/1011/p11s01-wogi.html (quoting climate scientist Tim Flannery, "[A]lso we have really seen an unexpected acceleration in the rate of accumulation of CO_2 itself, and that's been beyond the limits of projection ... beyond the worst-case scenario. We are already at great risk of dangerous climate change—that's what the new figures say.... It's not next year, or next decade; it's now.").

46. Elizabeth Rosenthal, *U.N. Chief Seeks More Climate Change Leadership*, N.Y. Times, Nov. 18, 2007, *available at* http://www.nytimes.com/2007/11/18/science/earth/18climatenew.html?scp=1&sq=UN%20Panel:%20avert%20climate%20disaster&st=cse.

47. State and regional climate initiatives are emerging, and many incorporate reduction targets. But such targets are widely variable, and many create a shortfall of carbon reduction in comparison to the atmospheric requirements established by scientists. *Compare infra* notes 52–58 and accompanying text (scientific targets) and Western Climate Initiative Statement of Regional Goal 4, *available at* http://www.western climateinitiative.org/ewebeditpro/items/O104F13006.pdf (chart summarizing widely varied state goals). The Western Climate Initiative, for example, announced a regional, economy-wide greenhouse gas emissions target of only 15 percent below 2005 levels by 2020. *See id.* at 1. The first compliance period does not even begin until 2012 under the current design. *See* Western Climate Initiative, Design Recommendations for the WCI Regional Cap-and-Trade Program 4 (Sept. 23, 2008), *available at* http://www.westernclimateinitiative.org/ewebeditpro/items/O104F19866.PDF. This is two years after the scientific targets call for arresting the growth of U.S. emissions. *See infra* note 56 and accompanying text.

48. *See* Torres, *supra* note 12, at 532 ("The public trust doctrine supplies a broad framework that supports the establishment of a mechanism ... to supervise the government dealings in relationship to the carrying capacity of the atmosphere."). It should be noted, however, that a carbon prescription standing alone, even if faithful to the best science, will likely not solve our global warming crisis. As Professor Howard Latin notes, society must deploy multiple strategies to arrive at carbon reduction. *See* Ch. 5, above. He points out that climate policy should focus on carbon-replacement, rather than carbon-reduction, and to this end he advocates for a Fund to finance new carbon-replacing technology. The idea has considerable merit. For every unit of carbon replaced by green energy, a unit of doubt is eliminated from a deeply flawed legal system, which relies on administratively-forced pollution reduction. In the long term, a carbon-replacing strategy will no doubt prove far more effective, efficient, and enduring. But it is entirely possible that such strategy will not come to fruition in time without a clear framework of legal responsibility that forces carbon reduction. A carbon prescription mandating regular cuts on a path to a zero-carbon endpoint seemingly reinforces the other strategy by mandating the transition sooner rather than later.

cause doing so has the appearance of treading into the policy realm.[49] Such reluctance leaves a treacherous gulf between science and the law. Officials, judges, and citizens need to have scientific information expressed in terms that they can translate into mandates. While scientists have been forthright as to dangerous atmospheric carbon loads and average temperature increases resulting from such loads,[50] these numbers alone do not provide meaningful parameters for legal or policy initiatives. A mayor, county commissioner, or state legislator, for example, would have no idea how much carbon reduction to achieve for his or her particular jurisdiction merely by knowing that 350 parts per million may be the climate threshold for runaway heating as recently projected by some climate scientists. There is a need to *extrapolate* planetary carbon levels into numeric reduction targets that leaders and policy-makers can implement through legal mechanisms. Much like a doctor would offer a heart patient a cholesterol reduction regime, scientists—not politicians—are qualified to map out a quantitative carbon reduction regime for restoring atmospheric health.

The Union of Concerned Scientists has detailed a cleanup prescription for industrialized nations in its report, *Targets for U.S. Emissions Reduction*.[51] The report represents a major advancement, because it distills an extensive body of climate science into reduction targets that lawmakers can implement on the ground. The Target delineates a "reasonable emissions pathway" for the United States[52] calibrated to the goal of not exceeding 450 parts per million (ppm) carbon equivalent in the atmosphere.[53] Establishing separate assumptions and targets for the industrialized world and the developing world,[54] the report sets forth the following trajectory of U.S. greenhouse gas emissions reduction: 1) arrest the rise of greenhouse gas emissions by 2010;[55] 2) reduce emissions by 4% each year thereafter; and 3) ultimately bring emissions down to 80% below 2000 levels by 2050.[56] Even this path may not be sufficiently ambitious, as the climate threshold is now thought by some scientists to be 350 parts per million.[57] Nevertheless, the UCS

---

49. Moreover, as different scientific prescriptions emerge, there will be inevitable choice-making. In this regard, courts may invoke the precautionary approach to define the fiduciary obligation. Reasonable guesses on the part of qualified, independent scientists as to a precautionary approach will carry weight in the climate context as they do in any other trial proceeding involving science. While beyond the scope of this chapter, courts may invoke several procedural tools to gain the scientific expertise necessary to define the fiduciary standard of care. Increasingly, judges use court-appointed experts, technical advisors, and special masters to resolve difficult scientific questions in environmental, toxic torts and product liability cases. *See* FEDERAL JUDICIAL CENTER, REFERENCE MANUAL ON SCIENTIFIC EVIDENCE (Federal Judicial Center 1994); THE CARNEGIE COMMISSION ON SCIENCE, TECHNOLOGY, AND GOVERNMENT, SCIENCE AND TECHNOLOGY IN JUDICIAL DECISION MAKING: CREATING OPPORTUNITIES AND MEETING CHALLENGES (1993).

50. *See* HANSEN, *350 Target Paper, supra* note 42 (suggesting 350 parts per million of carbon as the threshold).

51. A. LUERS, M. D. MASTRANDREA, K. HAYHOE & P. C. FRUMHOFF, HOW TO AVOID DANGEROUS CLIMATE CHANGE: A TARGET FOR U.S. EMISSIONS REDUCTIONS 5 (Union of Concerned Scientists 2007) [hereinafter UCS TARGET], *available at* http://www.ucsusa.org/assets/documents/global_warming/emissions-target-report.pdf.

52. *Id.* at 14. Of course, the developing world and the industrialized world are not similarly situated in terms of their carbon pollution. Recognizing this, the UCS TARGET provides separate assumptions and timelines for the developing world. It should be noted that the UCS TARGET, in establishing essentially uniform goals for the industrialized world (with some minor adjustment for the United States, because of its dominating polluter status), embraces a "cleanup" approach to carbon reduction. Under this approach, each sovereign reduces from a baseline of historic levels. The cleanup liability operates according to proportionate shares of pollution. There is another, arguably more equitable, approach called "contraction and convergence" that sets carbon quotas among nations based on population. *See* PEARCE, *supra* note 6, at 246. While there may be much merit in such an approach, it is doubtful a court would enforce it in domestic lawsuits. The advantage of the cleanup approach is that it grows out of a legal tradition of holding parties responsible for their proportionate share of the damage incurred. Because time is of the essence, a straightforward approach that can be implemented through judicial decrees at any level of government carries advantage over an international approach that, while in some sense more equitable, is still uncertain. The judicial approach set forth herein in no way precludes other regimes or international agreements. It is simply a domestic form of liability imposed to spur action towards carbon reduction within the United States.

53. UCS TARGET, *supra* note 51, at 3, 8, 14.

TARGET is a model for the type of clear, quantitative prescription that scientists should develop and continually revise as necessary. While its long-term goal might be inadequate to bring about climate equilibrium, the short-term goal of arresting the growth of emissions by 2010 is justifiable in terms of avoiding shorter-term climate tipping points.[58]

Casting a prescription in terms of percentage carbon reduction from current levels creates a "scale-up/scale-down" method transferable to any jurisdictional level.[59] Every jurisdiction, in theory, has the ability to measure its carbon footprint, however rough around the edges such measurement may be. The carbon reduction formula such as that developed in the UCS TARGETS can apply to any city, county, state, or national government in the industrialized world. Tied into a fiduciary obligation applicable to government trustees, the standard has a mechanism of judicial enforcement through atmospheric trust litigation.

Some will criticize any reduction regime on the basis that its mileposts are inherently random. To be sure, there is no scientific assertion that the prescribed 4% annual reduction is materially different from a 3.99% reduction. Such criticism, however, could apply to any pollution reduction regime. There are, of course, no absolutes in climate science or any other field of science.[60] But society and law would be paralyzed if it could not draw lines or set quantitative goals, despite the inherent random nature of the details of such an exercise. The well-established precautionary approach gives a basis for scientists to designate reasonable mileposts and to err on the side of caution.[61] It is predictable that there will be scientific disputes over carbon reduction targets, but courts, as in other areas of the law, have the fact-finding ability to judge scientific adequacy and adopt a cautionary course of action. Judicial enforcement of scientific targets as a fiduciary obligation in no way precludes more ambitious action by any jurisdiction — though such action is highly unlikely given that most climate initiatives likely arise from the lowest common denominator of political acceptability.

---

54. *Id.* at 9–12. The report groups the U.S. with other industrialized nations and then sets forth specific U.S. targets. The report assumes that developing nations like China and India are going to take more time to arrest emissions.

55. *Id.* at 14. The call for arresting U.S. emissions growth by 2010 is in line with a call by the United Nations to arrest the growth of world-wide emissions by 2015. *See* Cahal Milmo, *"Too Late to Avoid Global Warming," Say Scientists*, THE INDEPENDENT UK, Sept. 19, 2007, *available at* http://www.independent.co.uk/environment/climate-change/too-late-to-avoid-global-warming-say-scientists-402800.html. The Kyoto Protocol established a short term reduction goal of 5% emissions reduction by 2012. Kyoto Protocol to the United Nations Framework Convention on Climate Change, United Nations, Dec. 11, 1997, *available at* http://unfccc.int/resource/docs/convkp/kpeng.pdf.

56. The UCS TARGET delineates a "reasonable emissions pathway" for the United States calibrated to the goal of not exceeding 450 parts per million (ppm) carbon equivalent in the atmosphere. UCS TARGET, *supra* note 51, at 3, 8, 14.

57. *See supra* note 42 and accompanying text.

58. For discussion of the need for an emergency response by government, see CLIMATE CODE RED, *supra* note 40.

59. *See* Hari M. Osofsky, *The Geography of Climate Change Litigation Part II: Narratives of* Massachusetts v. EPA, 8 CHICAGO J. INT'L L. 573, 583 (2008) (concept of "scaling up and down" in climate strategies).

60. *See* James E. Hansen, *A Brighter Future*, 52 No. 4 CLIMACTIC CHANGE 438 (2002) ("There is no fixed 'truth' delivered by some body of 'experts.' Doubt and uncertainty are the essential ingredients in science.").

61. The UNFCCC sets forth the precautionary approach as a principle to guide climate policy. *See* UNFCCC, Principle 3.3: "The Parties should take precautionary measures to anticipate, prevent or minimize the causes of climate change.... Where there are threats of serious or irreversible damage, lack of full scientific certainty should not be used as a reason for postponing such measures...." In the area of private trust law, courts expect a trustee to use caution in choosing investments and avoid "new, speculative, or hazardous ventures" that could risk depleting the trust. *See* BOGERT, *supra* note 36, § 102, at 367.

C. The Inexcusability of Orphan Shares

In hazardous waste cleanups, there is a concept of "orphan shares."[62] If 20 different companies contribute waste to a toxic dump, all 20 are liable for the cleanup costs. If one company has gone bankrupt, it leaves an orphan share. In order for the site to be totally cleaned up, there can be no orphan shares. All must be adopted.

Carbon pollution should be analyzed in similar terms. The carbon load on the atmosphere can be viewed as one pollution "pie," with each government having a current emissions share of that pie. In order for the *aggregate* industrialized share of the carbon pie to shrink by the amount it needs to, the law must not excuse any orphan shares of liability. This is because any unaccounted share could provide a critical deficit in the overall reduction needed to meet the carbon math. The orphan share concept is particularly important for the United States, which, through its sheer failure to act, has abdicated responsibility for its nearly 30% emissions in the global carbon pie.[63] The orphan share principle scales down to the state and local level as well. If any city, county, or state fails to reduce carbon sufficiently, it leaves an orphan share or partial orphan share that could sink overall efforts.

For any legal framework of carbon responsibility to work, it must respond to this macro level of necessary carbon reduction by imposing across-the-board obligations on the local level. In order to avert orphan shares, the law must impose an organic responsibility on virtually each government to reduce carbon. Orphan shares must be wholly inexcusable.[64]

There is a second reason for imposing an organic obligation to reduce carbon on all levels of government. As a practical matter, different types of government have different tools to bring to the task. They also have different sources of carbon within their jurisdictions. A county government has control over local transportation infrastructure, while a state environmental agency has authority over air pollution permits, and a federal agency manages timber harvest on public lands. Because the required carbon reduction is so steep, it cannot be achieved through the efforts of just a handful of agencies. It will require all of the mechanisms of government across all sectors. Taxes, regulations, infrastructure projects, finance, programs, public lands management, government operations, and education must all be geared to carbon reduction at every level of government in order to meet the steep climate prescriptions advised by scientists.

Again, the statutory body of environmental law alone will not create sufficient progress towards overall carbon reduction goals. Largely procedural, it is geared towards specific, discrete government actions. Present statutorily-based climate litigation concerns the listing of polar bears under the Endangered Species Act, fuel efficiency standards under the Clean Air Act, environmental analysis requirements for specific federal actions under the National Environmental Policy Act, and a host of other claims tailored towards individual actions. None of these suits creates a macro framework of obligation that reaches to all governments and captures all orphan shares.

The trust principle can be tapped as a source of governmental obligation that creates a macro approach designed to leave no orphan shares of responsibility. Viewed organically, the trust is a fundamental limit on sovereignty itself, arguably generic to all states and the federal govern-

---

62. *See* Arkema, Inc. v. ASARCO, 2007 U.S. Dist. LEXIS 45511, 65 ERC (BNA) 1952 (W.D. Wash. 2007).

63. Hansen, *Testimony, supra* note 7, at 16 (depicting emissions of various nations, showing U.S. emissions as 27.8 % of the world's total emissions).

64. It should be noted that cap and trade programs for carbon that rely on financial tools to shift carbon pollution among various emitters do not represent a manner of excusing orphan shares. Rather, they are mechanisms by which states carry out their share of carbon reduction while allowing as much financial flexibility as possible. Whether they will work or not is yet to be determined. Their sheer complexity presents a time drag on the expediency called for in face of climate urgency.

ment.[65] As one federal district court said in applying the doctrine to both the federal and state governments, "The trust is of such a nature that it can be held only by the sovereign, and can only be destroyed by the destruction of the sovereign."[66] The atmospheric trust approach characterizes the United States as a trustee, and each of the 50 states as co-trustees, of the atmosphere. All share the basic fundamental obligation to protect the asset for their present and future generations of citizens. Each agency or sub-jurisdiction of government is as agent of the trustee, held to the same fiduciary standards. By applying the trust as an inherent limitation on government and invoking a uniform fiduciary obligation for all, the trust presents a holistic approach designed to leave no orphan shares of carbon in the United States.

D. A Framework of Obligation for the Whole World

On a global level, the traditional means of allocating responsibility for trans-border or planetary pollution has been through reliance on international law mechanisms such as treaties. The Kyoto Protocol, for example, provides a framework for carbon pollution. While the hope is that all culpable nations will accept and carry out their responsibilities under the treaty, the Kyoto experience has demonstrated that this is not the case. The U.S., for example, never ratified the commitment. Due to the autonomy of nations and the lack of any world "super-power," there is no certain way of forcing direct accountability for orphan shares left by deadbeat sovereigns. The bottom line for international "law" is, unfortunately, voluntary compliance.

Climate law must develop alternative, yet complementary, strategies to spur carbon reduction across the globe.[67] One promising approach is to design legal models for climate responsibility that are transferable to domestic legal systems of other nations. Many nations share similar doctrinal principles for addressing environmental problems. Climate solutions should tap the deepest roots of such approaches to find a generic obligation of carbon reduction that that can be invoked by citizens against their own governments, worldwide. The goal should be to develop a construct of liability that is applicable to governmental institutions despite differences in nationality and culture. There is, of course, no assurance that citizens of other nations will be equipped to hold their own governments accountable,[68] but this reality should not diminish the effort. A framework that pursues uniformity in defining carbon obligation among nations in the industrialized world may have political sway with even recalcitrant governments.

Some of the ongoing climate litigation in the United States arguably advances domestic efforts in other nations. The carbon nuisance lawsuits draw on principles that are likely common to

---

65. *See Geer,* 161 U.S. at 528 (referring to the trust over wildlife as an "attribute of government" and tracing its historical manifestation "through all vicissitudes of government."). While most public trust cases involve states, the doctrine logically applies to the federal government as well. *See* Complaint of Steuart Transp. Co., 495 F. Supp. 38, 40 (E.D. Va. 1980) (applying doctrine to federal government); U.S. v. 1.58 Acres of Land, 523 F. Supp. 120, 124 (D. Mass. 1981); *see also* Zygmunt J.B. Plater *et al.*, Environmental Law and Policy: Nature, Law, and Society 1103 (3d ed. Aspen Publishers 2004) ("In several cases, courts have asserted that the federal government is equally accountable and restricted under the terms of the public trust doctrine....").

66. 1.58 Acres of Land, 523 F. Supp. at 124. Within the United States, layered sovereign interests in natural resources arise from the constitutional configuration of states and the federal government. Where the federal government has a national interest in the resource, it is a co-trustee along with the states. For an extensive discussion of these co-trustee interests, see *id.*

67. *See* Jennifer M. Gleason & Bern A. Johnson, *Environmental Law Across Borders,* 10 J. Envtl. L. & Litig. 67, 76 (1995) [hereinafter 1995 Gleason & Johnson] (advocating transference of legal principles across national borders to augment international law). The organization, Environmental Law Alliance Worldwide, is dedicated to promoting such a strategy. *See* http://www.elaw.org/.

68. Barriers such as standing may prove insurmountable bars in some nations. In other nations, sheer corruption of the judiciary may impede legal recourse. Needless to say, tyrannical governments will likely not be held accountable by citizens through any legal procedure.

many countries. The NEPA lawsuits reflect an approach that may have transferability to other nations having NEPA-like statutes. But none of the litigation brought so far establishes a clear framework of government responsibility on a macro level that may be exported to other legal systems worldwide.

A notable strength of the trust doctrine's property framework is that it creates logical rights to shared assets that are not confined within any one jurisdictional border. The trust both provides a framework of international obligation and a liability principle that is potentially transferable to other nations through domestic legal systems. It is well established that, with respect to transboundary trust assets, all sovereigns with jurisdiction over the natural territory of the asset have legitimate property claims to the resource.[69] In this vein, all nations on Earth may be viewed as trustees of the global atmosphere.[70] This conception is reinforced by the United Nations Framework Convention on Climate Change, which essentially declares an atmospheric trust obligation by calling upon nations to "protect the climate system for the benefit of present and future generations of humankind...."[71]

Shared interests in the common asset are best described as a sovereign co-tenancy. A co-tenancy is "the ownership of property by two or more persons in such manner that they have an undivided ... right to possession."[72] Courts have used the co-tenancy model to describe shared sovereign interests in other natural resources. In landmark treaty litigation, the Ninth Circuit invoked the model to describe shared tribal and state sovereign rights to migrating salmon.[73] The court also recognized the bedrock principle that a co-tenancy relationship gives rise to correlative duties not to waste the common asset.[74] Thus, in addition to a fiduciary obligation owed to their own citizens to protect the atmosphere, all nations have duties to prevent waste arising from their co-tenancy relationship to one another.

---

69. States that share a waterway, for example, have correlative rights to the water. State of Ariz. v. State of Cal., 373 U.S. 546, 601 (1963). Similarly, states and tribes have co-existing property rights to share in the harvest of fish passing through their borders. Washington v. Washington State Commercial Passenger Fishing Vessel Ass'n, 443 U.S. 658, 676–79 (1979). *See also* Idaho *ex rel.* Evans v. Oregon, 462 U.S. 1017, 1031 n.1 (1983) (O'Connor, J., dissenting) (noting "recognition by the international community that each sovereign whose territory temporarily shelters [migratory] wildlife has a legitimate and protectable interest in that wildlife").

70. For the concept of a "planetary trust," see Edith Brown Weiss, *The Planetary Trust: Conservation and Intergenerational Equity*, 11 Ecol. L.Q. 495 (1984); Peter H. Sand, *Sovereignty Bounded: Public Trusteeship for Common Pool Resources*, 4 Global Environmental Politics 47, 57–58 (2004), *available at* http://www.mit pressjournals.org/doi/pdfplus/10.1162/152638004773730211?cookieSet=1 (suggesting trust principles as framework for international law and stating, "[A] transfer of the public trust concept from the national to the global level is conceivable, feasible, and tolerable.... the essence of transnational environmental trusteeship ... is the democratic accountability of states for their management of trust resources in the interest of the beneficiaries—the world's 'peoples'....").

71. United Nations Framework Convention on Climate Change, Article 3, Principle 1 (1992).

72. 20 Am. Jur. 2d Cotenancy and Joint Ownership § 1 (1995); Joseph William Singer, Property Law: Rules, Policies, and Practices 711 (2d ed. Aspen Publishers 1997).

73. Puget Sound Gillnetters Ass'n v. U. S. Dist. Court, 573 F.2d 1123, 1126 (9th Cir. 1978) (holding that the treaty established "something analogous to a co-tenancy, with the tribes as one cotenant and all citizens of the Territory (and later of the state) as the other."); United States v. Washington, 520 F.2d 685, 686, 690 (9th Cir. 1975) (applying co-tenancy construct, by analogy, to Indian fishing rights).

74. Acts that amount to permanent damage to the common property are held to constitute waste. E. Hopkins, Handbook on the Law of Real Property § 214, at 342 (West 1896); 2 W. Walsh, Commentaries on the Law of Real Property § 131, at 72 (West 1947). *See also Washington*, 520 F.2d at 685 (stating, in context of fisheries shared between states and tribes):

> Cotenants stand in a fiduciary relationship one to the other. Each has the right to full enjoyment of the property, but must use it as a reasonable property owner. A cotenant is liable for waste if he destroys the property or abuses it so as to permanently impair its value. A court will enjoin the commission of waste.... By analogy, neither the treaty Indians nor the state on behalf of its citizens may permit the subject matter of these treaties to be destroyed.

These principles, applied to the international context, frame the liability for carbon pollution by defining respective sovereign obligations. Trust principles, or close legal cousins, are found in the legal systems of many other countries on Earth.[75] Indeed, one of the strongest judicial iterations of the public trust came from the Philippines Supreme Court in a case brought on behalf of children.[76] India, one of the world's fastest growing carbon polluters, has a robust public trust doctrine in its jurisprudence.[77] Trust principles reflect a shared human understanding that ecological heritage essential to human survival is inviolate.[78] With a fundamental basis that can transcend many national and cultural differences, a trust approach provides a potential strategy for citizens of other nations to establish carbon liability against their own governments.

E. Restoring the Role of the Courts

It is highly unlikely that, absent judicial intervention, the political branches will achieve the requisite carbon reduction—in the short time remaining before irrevocable climate thresholds are passed. Straight-jacketed by political concerns, the legislative and executive branches and their representative agencies continue to permit actions that drive runaway greenhouse gas emissions.[79] In both the legislative and executive arenas, lobbyists for huge carbon industries viciously fight climate legislation and regulation.[80]

For several reasons, the American public is a weak political counterweight to these dynamics. Global warming is a complex phenomenon and not readily understood by the average citizen. Attempts by the fossil fuel industries to obfuscate the threat, combined with outright suppression of scientific conclusions by the Bush II administration,[81] has engendered climate confusion among citizens.[82] Moreover, as leading psychologists observe, humans are hard-wired by evolution to ignore long-term threats like global warming.[83] Until Americans actually feel the consequences of global heating on a daily basis, the issue may not become salient enough to create the political pressure for a national carbon reduction effort—and by then it may be too late. Finally,

---

75. *See* 1995 Gleason & Johnson, *supra* note 67, at 76 ("The public trust doctrine, having roots in ancient Roman law, appears in many legal systems."); Ved P. Nanda & William K. Ris, Jr., *The Public Trust Doctrine: A Viable Approach to International Environmental Protection,* 5 Ecol. L. Q. 291, 306 (1976) (inventorying trust concepts in other countries and concluding, "The principles of public trust are such that they can be understood and embraced by most countries of the world.")

76. Juan Antonio Oposa v. Fulgencio S. Factoran, Jr., G.R. No. 101083 (Sup. Ct. Phil. 1993), *as excerpted in* Laitos, Zellmer, Wood & Cole, *supra* note 9, at 443–44.

77. *See, e.g.,* M.C. Mehta v. Kamal Nath, 1 SCC 388 (India 1997); Karnataka Industrial Areas Development Board v. C.Kenchappa, AIRSCW 2546 (India 2006).

78. The petitioners in *Oposa*—children and their parents—characterized their right to self-preservation and perpetuation as "the highest law of humankind—the natural law." *Oposa, supra* note 76. For discussion of a natural law basis for the public trust, see Victor John Yannacone, Jr., *Agricultural Lands, Fertile Soils, Popular Sovereignty, The Trust Doctrine, Environmental Impact Assessment and the Natural Law,* 51 N. D. L. Rev. 615 (1975).

79. Two-thirds of the greenhouse gas pollution emitted in this country is pursuant to government-issued permits. *See* Laura H. Kosloff & Mark C. Trexler, *Consideration of Climate Change in Facility Permitting, in* Global Climate Change, *supra* note 32, at 259.

80. For investigative journalism into the lobbying against climate legislation, see PBS Documentary, HEAT, *available at* http://www.pbs.org/wgbh/pages/frontline/heat/.

81. *See Rewriting the Science,* CBS News, July 30, 2006; Seth Shulman, Undermining Science: Suppression and Distortion (Un. of California Press 2006); Mark Bowen, Censoring Science: Inside the Political Attack on James Hansen and the Truth of Global Warming (Dutton Adult 2007).

82. James Hansen, *Why We Can't Wait,* The Nation, May 7, 2007 (noting "gap between what the relevant scientific community understands and what the public and policy-makers know.").

83. *See* Daniel Gilbert, Op-Ed., *If Only Gay Sex Caused Global Warming: Why We're More Scared of Gay Marriage and Terrorism Than a Much Deadlier Threat,* L.A. Times, July 2, 2006, at M1, *available at* http://www.latimes.com/news/opinion/commentary/la-op-gilbert2jul02,0,7539379.story?coll=la-news-comment-opinions.

even when Americans demand climate action, they are easily misled to believe that small measures will achieve climate stability. Citizens are accustomed to addressing social problems through progressive, incremental policy that creates building blocks to larger transformation. Few citizens understand the concept of "carbon math" or deadlines imposed by Nature.

While these political encumbrances are classic to natural resource issues, they are dangerously amplified in the present situation, because the imminence of the climate tipping point forecloses many of the standard political processes that would normally provide solutions over the years. "Educational and democratic initiatives mounted by citizens may be too slow moving to force government to take responsibility for carbon pollution within the narrow window of time remaining." Professor Joseph Sax, a leading scholar on public trust law, pointed to these "insufficiencies of the democratic process" as reason to invoke judicial power over crucial natural resources that are irrevocably jeopardized by legislative or executive action—or in this case, inaction.[84] A legal strategy for holding government accountable for carbon pollution should invoke the power of the judiciary as an enforcement arm of government. Courts hold the power to order swift and decisive injunctive relief necessary to address urgent problems.[85]

Unfortunately, over the past few decades, courts have significantly diluted their role in environmental law, primarily by invoking the administrative deference doctrine which allows judges to give undue weight to agency decisions. At the heart of this deference principle is an abiding faith in administrative expertise and a corresponding perception that courts are no match for agencies in the scientific and technical realm.[86] As noted earlier, however, agency neutrality is often a myth. While there are many good reasons behind the deference doctrine, they are now offset by the realities of administrative practice, which often respond to inappropriate internal or external political drivers. Judges have not innovated any standards for applying the deference doctrine to sift out politically-driven decisions from neutral ones.

A trust approach has potential to overcome the deference doctrine that characterizes the statutory setting. Courts approach traditional trust cases with strong judicial scrutiny. Public trust jurisprudence in particular reflects a judicial suspicion towards legislative or administrative actions that cause permanent impairment of the corpus of natural resources needed for public welfare and survival. As an Arizona court explained, "The check and balance of judicial review provides a level of protection against improvident dissipation of an irreplaceable *res*."[87] A federal district court said in the submersible lands context: "The very purpose of the public trust doctrine is to police the legislature's disposition of public lands."[88]

---

84. Sax, *supra* note 9, at 521, noting also:

   Public trust problems are found ... in a wide range of situations in which diffused public interests need protection against tightly organized groups with clear and immediate goals. Thus, it seems that the delicate mixture of procedural and substantive protections which the courts have applied in conventional public trust cases would be equally applicable and equally appropriate in controversies involving air pollution.... Of course, the insufficiencies of the democratic process do not mean that efforts to mobilize the citizens should not advance with as much momentum possible, but only that the courts must intervene to protect the natural status quo while environmental democracy struggles to keep up with the threats on the horizon.

85. While litigation is notoriously time-consuming, judges have the ability to expedite hearings and arrange their calendars to prioritize urgent matters.

86. *See, e.g.,* Marsh v. Oregon Natural Resources Council, 490 U.S. 360, 378 (1989); Mt. Graham Red Squirrel v. Espy, 986 F.2d 1568, 1575 (Ariz. 1993); Ronald A. Cass *et. al.*, Administrative Law, Cases and Materials 216–17 (2d ed. Aspen 1994).

87. Arizona Ctr. for Law in the Pub. Interest v. Hassell, 837 P.2d 158, 169 (Ariz. Ct. App. 1991).

88. Lake Michigan Federation v. U.S. Army Corps of Engineers, 742 F. Supp. 441, 446 (D. Ill. 1990).

F. Finding Moral and Economic Fortification for the Law

Finally, in order for society to accomplish massive carbon reduction in the window of time remaining, a legal framework must engage other realms of society in pursuit of the same goals. Legal principles should reflect a strong moral culture that can inspire massive political support, and they should dovetail with a new sustainable vision of the economy. No legal framework can accomplish these ends if it is detached from a common well-spring of human thought and experience, or too complex to engage political coalitions comprised of ordinary citizens.

Statutory environmental claims typically gain little fortification from the economic, moral, or political realms. This is largely because they are mired in complexity and beyond the understanding of most ordinary people. Citizens are removed from the value-core of the statutes by several impenetrable layers of procedure understood only by lawyers and judges. The acronyms and techno-jargon embedded in the regulations and their endless iterations cast a mind-numbing pall over the moral hazards of environmental harm. They readily obfuscate the ethical abomination of creating a world of runaway heating that would subject the children living today, at some point during their life spans, to unthinkable natural damage and social calamity.

To exacerbate the problem, the environmental laws have no corollary vision in economics that affords hope of prosperity consistent with ecological protection. Typically the statutes operate at cross grains to economic objectives, as captured by the "jobs versus environment" dichotomy that so often demolishes environmental advocacy in the courts of public opinion. In trying to control some of the ill effects of the industrial pollution economy, the environmental statutes nevertheless sanction that same economy. Rarely do system-changing economic alternatives emerge from environmental statutory litigation. Relying on a set of laws so detached from the moral and economic facets of civic life and far removed from the realm of popular understanding, the environmental movement has hemorrhaged its own political base.[89] A synergistic relationship between law, morality, economics, and politics must materialize rapidly in order to force necessary carbon reduction.

Atmospheric trust litigation has seemingly greater potential as a legal vessel for moral and economic reasoning. On a moral level, trust principles reflect a primeval ethic towards children. A trust approach underscores the strong urge of human beings to pass estates along to future generations.[90] The atmosphere is an endowment to which future generations have a legitimate moral claim: failure to safeguard it amounts to generational theft. Litigation that takes shape around this moral structure draws from a wellspring of human understanding that is instinctive, passion-bound, and deeply shared among citizens of distant cultures.

In economic terms, the trust dovetails with principles of natural capitalism, which leading thinkers present as a paradigm of business and industrial reform.[91] Natural capitalism urges

---

89. *See* Michael Shellenberger & Ted Nordhaus, *The Death of Environmentalism: Global Warming Politics in a Post Environmental World* (2004), *available at* http://www.thebreakthrough.org/images/Death_of_Environ mentalism.pdf.

90. Civic and religious leaders have framed climate crisis in terms of a moral obligation towards future generations. *See* Al Gore, Op-Ed., *Moving Beyond Kyoto*, New York Times (July 1, 2007) *available at* http://www.nytimes.com/2007/07/01/opinion/01gore.html?ex=1341115200&en=be0b465c91dbcaaf&ei=5124 &partner=permalink&exprod=permalink ("Our children have a right to hold us to a higher standard when their future—indeed, the future of all human civilization—is hanging in the balance."); Colin Woodard, *In Greenland, An Interfaith Rally for Climate Change*, Christian Science Monitor (Sept. 12, 2007), *available at* http://www.csmonitor.com/2007/0912/p06s01-woeu.html?page=1 (Shiite, Buddhist, Hindu, Jewish, Christian, and Shinto leaders join in commitment at Greenland inter-faith climate rally to leave the planet "in all its wisdom and beauty to the generations to come.").

91. *See* Paul Hawken, Amory Lovins, L. Hunter Lovins, Natural Capitalism: Creating The Next Industrial Revolution (Little Brown 1999); Speth, *supra* note 29; Peter Barnes, Capitalism 3.0: A Guide to Reclaiming the Commons (Berrett Koehler Publishers 2007). Perhaps the best example of government pursuing a natural capital approach to both its fiscal and environmental policy comes from Ireland, a country

business to structure operations using the Earth's interest, not its capital. Emphasis on renewable energy is an example of this approach. Commentators increasingly point to the prospect of millions of new green jobs and increased domestic security by converting from fossil fuels to wind, solar, tidal, and geothermal sources.

There is no silver bullet to solving climate crisis, in the law or elsewhere. But if the criteria of legal responsibility outlined above make any sense at all, clearly a shift from conventional legal strategies has to occur with all urgency. In the context of climate crisis, which threatens "life as we know it,"[92] the public trust doctrine can function as a judicial tool to ensure that the political branches of government protect the people's basic right to survival and their expectations of civilizational stability.

IV. Atmospheric Trust Litigation

Like any novel litigation strategy, atmospheric trust litigation has many unknowns. A number of defenses and legal issues may prove insurmountable in some courts. Nevertheless, climate litigation strategy must take shape around the magnitude of the threat facing society and the short window of time in which to address it. Whether an ATL claim will succeed depends largely on individual judges' perception of the urgency of climate crisis, their belief as to whether the political system will address it, and their view of the judicial function. This section only briefly outlines the litigation strategy, as fuller treatment is provided elsewhere.[93]

The ATL claim characterizes government as a sovereign trustee of natural resources with an organic fiduciary obligation to protect the atmosphere in order to ensure the survival and prosperity of present and future generations of citizen beneficiaries. Positioned along with other sovereigns, government is a co-tenant of the atmosphere and therefore holds a correlative duty to prevent waste to the asset. The fiduciary obligation of protection and the duty against waste are substantially the same, as quantified by reference to leading scientific prescriptions for carbon reduction, such as the one put forth by the Union of Concerned Scientists.

The trust framework presents two causes of action, available to different classes of parties. The first is an action by citizen beneficiaries against their governmental trustees to enforce the fiduciary obligation owed to them. It is well settled that beneficiaries may sue the trustee to protect their property.[94] Public trust cases have recognized citizen standing to enforce the trust.[95] Citizens are seemingly positioned to bring trust actions against their cities, counties, states, or the federal government.[96] The most compelling action may be a class action brought by children and their parents for breach of fiduciary duty that impairs the atmosphere and other natural re-

---

that has enacted a carbon "budget." *See infra* note 110 and accompanying text. In a statement announcing the budget, Minister John Gormley said:

> As I am speaking in a Budget debate, let me put it this way: all these activities are vital to protect our environmental capital into the future, and ensure that this most irreplaceable asset is not depreciated by damage to the different environmental media.

Gormley Delivers Carbon Budget, Dec. 6, 2007 (statement of John Gormley, Minister for the Environment, Heritage and Local Government), *available at* http://www.greenparty.ie/news/latest_news/gormley_delivers_carbon_budget.

92. *See supra* note 22.

93. *See* 2009 Wood *Atmospheric Trust Litigation, supra* note 8.

94. *See* Bogert, *supra* note 36, § 154 at 551 ("If the trustee is preparing to commit a breach of trust, the beneficiary need not sit idly by and wait until damage has been done. He may sue in a court of equity for an injunction against the wrongful act.").

95. Marks v. Whitney, 491 P.2d 374, 381 (Cal. 1971) (private citizens have standing to sue under public trust though a court may raise the issue on its own).

96. Of course issues of sovereign immunity may arise in such suits, and general Constitutional requirements of standing apply.

sources needed for survival and prosperity later in the children's life spans. One of the most stirring public trust opinions ever written was in response to a case brought by children in the Philippines opposed to logging the last of that nation's old growth forest. The Court found the claim compelling and awarded relief, stating:

> [T]he right to a balanced and healthful ecology ... belongs to a different category of rights altogether for it concerns nothing less than self-preservation and self-perpetuation ... the advancement of which may even be said to predate all governments and constitutions. As a matter of fact, these basic rights need not even be written in the Constitution for they are assumed to exist from the inception of humankind. If they are now explicitly mentioned ... it is because of the well-founded fear of its framers that unless the right to a balanced and healthful ecology and to health are mandated as state policies by the Constitution itself ... the day would not be too far when all else would be lost not only for the present generation, but also for those to come— generations which stand to inherit nothing but parched earth incapable of sustaining life.[97]

The second possible cause of action is a one brought by one sovereign trustee against another for waste to common property—the atmosphere. Co-tenants have a right against other co-tenants for waste and for failure to pay necessary expenses.[98] States may bring an action for waste against other states or the federal government. Tribal sovereigns may also bring actions.[99] Notably, both the waste and breach of trust claims find grounding within the same basic property framework.

As with any claim, a myriad of issues may bar recovery. Litigants must navigate potential barriers such as standing, sovereign immunity, preemption, political question doctrine, causation, ripeness, jurisdiction, intervention, and others. While this chapter does not delve into such issues, it should be noted that courts recognizing the enormity of the climate crisis, and the crucial role of the judiciary, may approach these barriers with a leniency that is not characteristic of past decisions. At its core, the unparalleled force of the public trust doctrine lies in its mandate to preserve survival resources for future generations—and the role of the court in policing the legislature and agencies in their management of such trust assets. Procedural barriers to meaningful relief may leave citizens without a remedy, a result that at least some courts will find unacceptable in view of the extraordinary stakes in climate crisis.[100]

The remedy for an ATL claim consists of a declaratory judgment and injunctive measures. A declaratory judgment carries enormous importance for its potential impact beyond the courtroom, as it could be transmitted internationally through news feeds that reach thousands of climate professionals and activists in other countries. By clarifying a framework of carbon responsibility, a declaratory judgment could become a yardstick for political action worldwide and provide citizens with the conceptual tools they need to hold their own governments accountable in quantifiable terms at all jurisdictional levels. As such, the judgment should clearly iterate the following princi-

---

97. *Oposa, supra* note 76.

98. Willmon v. Koyer, 143 P. 694, 695 (Cal. 1914); 63C AM. JUR. 2d PROPERTY §31; Chosar Corp. v. Owens, 370 S.E.2d 305 (Va. 1988) (co-tenants who allowed mining without consent of all other co-tenants were liable for waste); *see also supra* note 74 (discussing waste in context of sovereign co-tenancy in migrating fishery).

99. Tribes may be precluded in bringing actions against states under principles of sovereign immunity. *See* Seminole Tribe v. Florida, 116 S.Ct. 1114 (1996). Tribes, however, may have additional trust claims against federal agencies arising out of their unique trust relationship with the federal government. *See generally* Mary Christina Wood, *Indian Land and the Promise of Native Sovereignty: The Trust Doctrine Revisited*, 1994 UTAH L. REV. 1471 (1994).

100. While procedural issues are beyond the scope of this chapter, they are being considered in a work-in-progress by the author, *Courts as Guardians of the Global Atmospheric Trust*.

ples: 1) all governments have a fiduciary obligation, as trustees, to protect the atmosphere as a commonly shared asset; 2) all governments bear liability for reducing carbon; 3) the fiduciary obligation among industrialized nations and sub-jurisdictions is to comply with scientific prescriptions to reduce carbon sufficiently to avert runaway heating and restore climate equilibrium; 4) this fiduciary obligation is organic to government and permits no orphan shares or partial orphan shares.[101]

Declaratory relief should be accompanied by suitable injunctive relief that allows courts to provide a remedy on a macro level without invading the province of the political branches.[102] By drawing on traditional relief available against co-tenants and trustees for misuse of property, courts may require carbon accountings and enforceable carbon budgets as procedural remedies for sovereign breach of the atmospheric fiduciary obligation without reaching into the law-making purview of the other branches.

An accounting is a traditional remedy springing from the equitable powers of the court in both the co-tenancy and trust contexts.[103] It is a judicial process whereby co-tenants or trustees must account for expenses and/or profits in connection with the property.[104] The basic premise of an accounting in the co-tenancy context is that each co-tenant is responsible for his share of the expenses, and is due his share of the profit from the property.[105] An accounting is the procedural method by which this "fair share" principle is enforced by courts. In the trust context, an accounting is the method by which beneficiaries may ensure proper management of their property.[106] Accordingly, courts have held that "any beneficiary, including one who holds only a present interest in the remainder of a trust, is entitled to petition the court for an accounting."[107]

In the context of atmospheric trust litigation, an accounting would take the form of quantifying carbon emissions and tracking their reduction over time. Modern modeling is capable of quantifying a carbon footprint on virtually any scale, from individual to global.[108] Several cities, such as Seattle, Washington, have already quantified their carbon footprint.[109]

---

101. However, a declaratory judgment should not be a "'general admonition,'" but must be narrowly crafted to define a duty according to "concrete facts presented in a particular dispute." United States v. Washington, 2007 U.S. Dist. LEXIS 61850 *23 (W.D. Wash. 2007). Courts have rejected overly broad declaratory judgments. *See id.*

102. Weinberger v. Romero-Barcelo, 456 U.S. 305, 312 (1982) (the basis for injunctive relief is a finding of irreparable injury and the absence of an adequate legal remedy) (citations omitted).

103. *See, e.g.*, Evans v. Little, 271 S.E.2d 138, 141 (Ga. 1980) (co-tenancy); *Koyer*, 143 P. at 695 (same); Zuch v. Conn. Bank & Trust Co., 500 A.2d 565, 568 (Conn. App. 1985) ("As a general matter of equity, the existence of a trust relationship is accompanied as a matter of course by the right of the beneficiary to demand of the fiduciary a full and complete accounting at any proper time.") (citations omitted); Cobell v. Norton, 240 F.3d 1081 (D.C. Cir. 2001) (*Cobell VI*) (accounting against federal government for mismanagement of Indian trust funds).

104. *Evans*, 271 S.E.2d at 141.

105. *See, e.g.*, Garber v. Whittaker, 174 A. 34, 37 (Super. Ct. Del. 1934); *Koyer*, 143 P. at 695–96; *see also* WILLIAM B. STOEBUCK & DALE A. WHITMAN, THE LAW OF PROPERTY 205 (3d ed. West Publishing 2000) (where a cotenant derives income from a use of property that permanently reduces its value, the cotenant must account to the other cotenants).

106. *See Zuch*, 500 A.2d at 567 ("The fiduciary relationship is in and of itself sufficient to form the basis for the [accounting].") (citations omitted).

107. *In re* Estate of Ehlers, 911 P.2d 1017, 1021 (Wash. App. 1996) (citation omitted).

108. *See, e.g.*, UNFCCC, COUNTING EMISSIONS AND REMOVALS: GREENHOUSE GAS INVENTORIES UNDER THE UNFCCC, available at http://unfccc.int/resource/docs/publications/counting.pdf; Seth Borenstein, *Texas, Wyoming Take Lead in Emissions*, USA TODAY, June 2, 2007, *available at* http://www.usatoday.com/weather/climate/globalwarming/2007-06-02-emissions_N.htm (chart depicting state emissions); The Climate Registry, *available at* http://www.theclimateregistry.org/index.html (last visited Sept. 18, 2007) (tracks emissions from private industry).

109. CITY OF SEATTLE, CLIMATE CHANGE ACTION PLAN, *available at* http://www.seattle.gov/climate/carbonfootprint.htm (last visited Sept. 18, 2007); CITY OF SEATTLE, OUR CARBON FOOTPRINT, *available at*

Carbon accounting allows co-tenants and beneficiaries of the trust to evaluate government's measures to protect the atmospheric asset. The accounting would determine jurisdictional compliance with the Target for U.S. Emissions Reductions or other scientific prescription which, as explained previously, may express a quantitative standard of government's fiduciary obligation. This fiduciary obligation must be carried out through a "budget" for carbon reduction over time that sets forth clear mileposts, as well as a portfolio of measures designed to achieve the requisite reduction.[110] Developing such a portfolio is, by its very nature, a political matter, but courts can supervise the process to ensure that the measures add up to the required carbon math. A court must maintain on-going jurisdiction over the case to receive periodic progress reports, a common procedure in accounting cases. The narrow window of time remaining before climate thresholds are crossed seemingly justifies carbon accounting reports every quarter.

Coordination in the carbon accounting ordered in various atmospheric trust litigation cases is made possible using the "nested jurisdiction" concept. Greenhouse gas reductions achieved on a sub-jurisdictional level (*i.e.*, cities and counties) are readily and easily attributable to the umbrella jurisdiction (the state). For the same reason, reductions at the sub-national (state) level are easily accounted for at the federal level. Through open accounting processes, carbon reduction can simultaneously be attributed to the most immediate jurisdictional level as well as the broadest jurisdictional level.

Procedural relief alone is insufficient for jurisdictions that fail to carry out their budgets. Substantive injunctive relief, therefore, is necessary as a possible judicial "hammer" for carbon reduction. Such judicial enforcement likely cannot extend to every measure contained in a carbon reduction portfolio, as they are likely to contain a set of measures beyond the power of courts to enforce—measures such as carbon taxes, infrastructure projects and transfer of public investment. Nevertheless, courts have it well within their power to force carbon reduction through discrete injunctive measures tailored towards obvious carbon sources. An injunction may contain "backstops" that consist of measures the court will mandate if the budget is not carried out. Injunctions might prohibit, for example, new coal-fired plants,[111] large-scale logging, recreational vehicle use on public lands, airport expansions, sewer hook-ups, issuance of air pollution permits, and a myriad of other activities.[112] Of course, perhaps the most effective enforce-

---

http://www.seattle.gov/climate/PDF/Our_Carbon_Footprint.pdf ("Any serious initiative to reduce global warming pollution must begin with a very challenging first step: A greenhouse gas emissions inventory that establishes the baseline against which progress will be measured, and identifies the major sources of pollution that will be the focus of the program.").

110. Ireland instituted a carbon budget that is in its second year. *See* Gormley Delivers Carbon Budget (Dec. 6, 2007) (statement of John Gormley, Minister for the Environment, Heritage and Local Government), *available at* http://www.greenparty.ie/news/latest_news/gormley_delivers_carbon_budget; Dail Statement by Mr. John Gormley TD, Oct. 15, 2008, *available at* http://www.google.com/search?hl=en&client=safari&rls=en&q=protocol+for+carbon+budget&start=10&sa=N. Climate analysts have also developed a British carbon budget. *See* ECOFYS, *Developing a Carbon Budget for the UK: With Opportunities for EU Action* (2006), *available at* http://www.foe.co.uk/resource/reports/carbon_budgetting.pdf. By focusing on the actual bottom-line carbon reduction set by a budget, courts would not interfere with emerging regional and local initiatives such as carbon taxes and cap and trade schemes. Such climate measures are tools to achieving the requisite carbon reduction. *See id.* at 11 ("A budget refers to the actual amount of carbon that is available—be it to a nation, firm or individual. A trading mechanism is a way in which division of this budget can be made more flexible.").

111. *See* Hansen, *Testimony, supra* note 7, at 18 ("Thus the most critical action for saving the planet at this time, I believe, is to prevent construction of additional coal-fired power plants without CO_2 capture capability.").

112. Many of these injunctions have occurred in the statutory context. *See, e.g.,* Jeffery J. Matthews, *Clean Water Act Citizen Suit Requests for Municipal Moratoria: Anatomy of a Sewer Hookup Moratorium Law Suit*, 14 J. ENVTL. L. & LITIG. 25 (1999); American Motorcyclist Ass'n v. Watt, 543 F. Supp. 789, 798 (C. D. Cal. 1982) (enjoining off-road vehicle use); Pacific Rivers Council v. Thomas, 30 F.3d 1050 (9th Cir. 1994) (enjoining the U.S. Forest Service from proceeding with projects under land resource management plans); Lane County

ment mechanism is to hold government officials personally in contempt of court for failure to carry out court-ordered fiduciary duties.[113]

V. Conclusion

Inevitably, atmospheric trust litigation will encounter criticism that it invites courts to overstep their function whereas the matter of carbon reduction should be handled by the political branches. In a functioning democracy, that much would probably be true. We would expect legislatures and agencies to respond with all due speed to climate crisis, rendering litigation altogether unnecessary. But critics must take a step back and engage in a reality check. The political branches have not responded to the threat of runaway heating. Instead, their sluggishness has left a deadly vacuum, putting the future of human civilization worldwide at stake over the coming century. Government has squandered any further opportunity for slow, incremental policy. Comprising a legitimate third branch of government, courts are a last resort—but a resort nonetheless.

At a time in history when thinkers across the world are calling for new, innovative technologies and practices to address climate crisis, lawyers should pioneer promising, if untested, legal constructs to address carbon loading of the atmosphere. Exclusive reliance on statutory claims for imposing climate responsibility is treacherous. The body of statutory environmental law is a product of an altogether different era, formulated to respond to circumstances far less urgent, less dangerous, and less pervasive than those now confronting society. The environmental statutes were never crafted to address a planetary emergency.

Atmospheric trust litigation challenges lawyers and judges to take fundamental principles of public trust law and apply them in coherent fashion to a new and urgent context so as to arrive at a uniform, quantifiable measure of governmental responsibility to reduce carbon. While unprecedented, the task is made easier by the fact that these principles are logical, compelling, and seemingly organic to all states and the federal government. The trust claim defines a binding fiduciary obligation that is calibrated mathematically to scientific understanding. In that way, it is perhaps the only claim that speaks directly to the sovereign's full duty to protect the atmosphere from greenhouse gas pollution.

Judges have it well within their ability to issue decisions that would force carbon reduction. In past eras, judges have called forth logic and principled reasoning to formulate common law in response to unprecedented circumstances. As Justice Holmes wrote, the common law is "[t]he felt necessities of the times."[114] Unfortunately, after three decades of interpreting statutory law, most judges are now so accustomed to issuing rulings within detailed confines of legislation or regulations that they have lost their imagination to construct meaningful remedies using their traditional common law prerogatives. Nevertheless, history tells us that conditions of impossibil-

---

Audubon Soc'y v. Jamison, 958 F.2d 290, 294 (9th Cir. 1992) (enjoining the BLM from new timber sales); Thomas v. Peterson, 753 F.2d 754 (9th Cir. 1975) (enjoining construction of road); Oregon Natural Desert Assn v. Singleton, 75 F. Supp. 2d 1139 (9th Cir.1999) (permanently enjoining grazing).

113. Two Secretaries of Interior and one Secretary of Treasury have been held in contempt of court in an Indian case alleging breach of trust obligation. *See* Pierre Thomas, *Federal Judge Holds Babbitt and Rubin in Contempt,* CNN, Feb. 22, 1999, *available at* http://www.cnn.com/ALLPOLITICS/stories/1999/02/22/cabinet. contempt/; *Interior Secretary Cited for Contempt of Court,* NPR, Sept. 17, 2002, *available at* http://www.npr. org/templates/story/story.php?storyId=1150178. One district court threatened U.S. Agriculture Undersecretary Mark Rey with contempt of court and jail time for his agency's "systematic disregard of the rule of law." *See* Matt Gouras, *Judge: Ag Undersecretary Avoids Jail Time,* Associated Press, *available at* http://hosted.ap. org/dynamic/stories/B/BUSH_OFFICIAL_CONTEMPT?SITE=AP&SECTION=HOME&TEMPLATE= DEFAULT&CTIME=2008-02-28-00-41-37.

114. O.W. Holmes, Jr., The Common Law 1 (Dover Publications 1881).

ity often inspire heroic imagination and courage. Handed the right complaint, there will be judges who recognize this epochal moment in the course of human civilization and exert their common law authority to protect the globe's atmosphere—and the billions of people dependent on it for all time to come.

Notes

1. Professor Wood's message does not reach the court in *Sierra Club v. Tennessee Valley Authority*, 592 F. Supp. 2d 1357 (N.D. Ala. 2009) (Virginia E. Hopkins, D.J.) (extended Findings of Fact on operations of the Colbert Fossil Fuel Plant in Tuscumbia, Ala.). The court concludes that plaintiffs have failed to prove any "injury in fact" from the operation of this facility. Plaintiffs have failed to show that "any non-exempt exceedances" since Jan. 1, 2008 "are preventable, were numerous, are likely to recur, or were of long duration." 592 F. Supp. 2d at 1375. The balance of hardships does not warrant an injunction. The public interest would be disserved by a permanent injunction. This case is "moot" in any event by reason of a change in law. This is either the cleanest power plant in the world or some strange misfiring occurred during the course of the litigation. There is no mention of climate change.

2. Indian law and environmental law frequently merge. In this context, the Supreme Court has reminded us recently that "two wrong claims do not make one that is right."[1]

But the high court has made clear in *United States v. Navajo Nation* (*Navajo II*)[2] that two wrong decisions make one that is right. The background is as follows:[3]

> The Tribe launched the present lawsuit in 1993, claiming that the Secretary's actions in connection with the approval of the coal lease amendments constituted a breach of trust. In particular, the Tribe alleged that the Secretary, following upon improper *ex parte* contacts with Peabody, had delayed action on Peabody's administrative appeal in order to pressure the economically desperate Tribe to return to the bargaining table. This, the complaint charged, was in violation of the United States' fiduciary duty to act in the Indian' best interests. The Tribe sought $600 million in damages, invoking the Indian Tucker Act to bypass sovereign immunity.

The tribe proved the *ex parte* contact, the trickery in the interference in the administrative process, and the deception that was worked on the economically desperate tribe. What they couldn't demonstrate, according to Justice Ginsburg's opinion in *United States v. Navajo Nation* (*Navajo I*), was "a substantive source of law that establishes specific fiduciary or other duties."[4] That limitation of the Indian trust doctrine to a tight version of codified deception was mistake No. 1. The high court simply extends this rule in *Navajo II*. It still could not discover any duty

---

1. Pacific Bell Telephone Co. v. Linkline Communications, Inc, 555 U.S. ___, 129 S.Ct. 1109, 172 L.Ed.2d 836 (Feb. 25, 2009), *quoted in* Hawai'i v. Office of Hawaiian Affairs, 556 U.S. ___, ___, 129 S.Ct. 1436, 1444, 173 L.Ed.2d 333 (March 31, 2009).

2. 556 U.S. ___, 129 S.Ct. 1547, 173 L.Ed.2d 429 (April 6, 2009) (7:2, Opinion for the Court by Scalia, J., Souter, J., concurs, joined by Stevens, J.).

3. 556 U.S. ___, 129 S.Ct. at 1552–53.

4. 537 U.S. 488, 506 (2003), criticized in William H. Rodgers, Jr., *The Tenth Supreme Court Justice (Crazy Horse, J.) and Dissents Not Written—The Environmental Term of 2003–2004*, 34 ELR 11033, 11040 (2004) ("The Court's insistence upon codification cheapens the Secretary's trust duties into legalistic corner-cutting. No code of moral conduct on earth would meet the stingy precision the majority demands.... This Court should expect more of a Secretary who understands 'Thou Shalt Not Steal' to mean 'But You Can Take Economic Advantage by Deception, by Secret Consultation With Adversaries, and by Secret Veiled Threat.'")

that the tribe could enforce in any action for damages under the Tucker Act. That ruling is mistake No. 2. These two wrongs do make a right, as the Supreme Court now declares: "This matter should now be regarded as closed."[5]

This matter might be closed. But the memory of it will never be closed. And the injustice of it must await correction at a later date.

VII. International Environmental Law

As we have seen throughout this compilation, climate change is truly a "world" problem and effective responses to it must reach around the globe. The paper following demonstrates that expectations of effectiveness (from which international environmental law have been long immune) will rush to meet international institutions that are in place.

Sites for Sore Eyes: The World Heritage Convention and the Specter of Climate Change

Dr. William C.G. Burns. Senior Fellow, Santa Clara University School of Law, Santa Clara, California, wburns@scu.edu. The author would like to acknowledge the helpful comments of Stephen Leonard of the Australian Climate Justice Program.

1. Introduction

The disheartening record over past few decades at both the international and national levels to confront climate change in a meaningful fashion is likely to have dire implications for many of the world's most vulnerable States in this century and beyond. The most recent assessment by the Intergovernmental Panel on Climate Change (IPCC) concluded that global average surface temperatures have increased by 0.8°C over the last century, with the linear warming trend over the past fifty years twice that of the past century.[1] Despite this alarming trend, the drafters of the United Nations Framework on Climate Change,[2] in the face of pressure from the United States and other States, resorted to "constructive ambiguities" and "guidelines," rather than establishing strict legal commitments to reduce greenhouse gas emissions.[3] Thus, the UNFCCC merely calls on the Parties in Annex I (developed countries and economies in transition) to "aim" to return their emissions back to 1990 levels.[4]

---

5. 556 U.S. ___, 129 S.Ct. at 1551.

1. S. Solomon, *et al.*, *Technical Summary, in* INTERGOVERNMENTAL PANEL ON CLIMATE CHANGE, CLIMATE CHANGE 2007: THE PHYSICAL SCIENCE BASIS 5 (2007), http://www.ipcc.ch/ipccreports.ar4-wg1.htm (last visited May 25, 2008) [hereinafter THE PHYSICAL SCIENCE BASIS]. Atmospheric temperatures have been rising at a rate of approximately 0.2°C per decade over the past thirty years. James E. Hansen, Green Mountain Chrysler-Plymouth-Dodge-Jeep v. Thomas W. Torti, Case Nos. 2:05-CV-302 & 2:05-CV-304 (Consolidated), *Declaration of James E. Hansen*, (Vt. 2007), http://www.columbia.edu/~jeh1/case_for_vermont.pdf (last visited May 25, 2008).

2. United Nations Framework Convention on Climate Change, May 9, 1992, 31 I.L.M. 849 [hereinafter UNFCCC].

3. Ranee Khooshie Lai Panjabi, *Can International Law Improve the Climate? An Analysis of the United Nations Framework Convention on Climate Change Signed at the Rio Summit in 1992*, 18 N.C. J. INT'L L & COMM. REG. 491, 404 (1993).

4. UNFCCC, *supra* note 2, at art. 4(2)(b).

The Kyoto Protocol[5] to the UNFCCC did establish targets and timetables for reducing the greenhouse gas emissions of industrialized States. However, the modest nature of these commitments, coupled with the fact that neither the United States nor rapidly growing developing States such as China and India are participating, ensures that the Protocol will have a *de minimis* impact on projected climatic trends during this century.[6] While negotiations are taking place to develop a successor agreement to Kyoto under the rubric of the "Bali Action Plan,"[7] it is difficult to be hopeful in face of continued resistance by the United States and major developing countries.[8]

Indeed, the rate of increase in greenhouse gas emissions has leapt in the first decade of the new century to more than two and half times the rate in the 1990s,[9] outstripping even the IPCC's most intensive emissions scenario.[10] As a consequence, even limiting projected temperature increases to below 4°C above pre-industrial levels may require a "radical reframing of both the climate change agenda, and the economic characterization of contemporary society."[11] This is an extremely foreboding development, as most scientists and policymakers now believe that even a 2°C increase from pre-industrial levels will result in serious impacts on human institutions and ecosystems.[12]

This combination of the urgency of the problem and complexity of politico-legal solutions has caused many State and non-State actors to look beyond traditional international treaty mechanisms and national legislation for solutions to anthropogenic climate change.[13] In this context, litigation and other legal actions at sub-national, national, and international levels have evolved from innovative ideas to an emerging practice area over the last several years.[14] Some of

---

5. Kyoto Protocol to the United Nations Framework Convention on Climate Change, Dec. 10, 1997, FCCC/CP/1997/L.7/Add. 1, 37 I.L.M. 22.

6. Overall, climate researchers have estimated that full implementation of Kyoto would reduce projected warming in 2050 by only about *one twentieth of one degree* and projected sea level rise by a mere *5 millimeters*. Martin Parry *et al.*, *Buenos Aires and Kyoto Targets Do Little to Reduce Climate Change Impacts*, 8(4) GLOBAL ENVTL. CHANGE 285, 285 (1998). *See also* Mustafa H. Babiker, *The Evolution of a Climate Regime: Kyoto to Marrakesh and Beyond*, 5 ENVTL. SCI. & POL'Y 195, 202 (2002).

7. UNFCCC, 13th Conference of the Parties, *Bali Action Plan*, CP.13 (2007), *available at* http://unfccc.int/ files/meetings/cop_13/application/pdf/cp_bali_action.pdf (last visited May 25, 2008).

8. David Adam, *U.S. Balks at Bali Carbon Targets*, GUARDIAN UNLIMITED, Dec. 10, 2007, http://www.guardian.co.uk/environment/2007/dec/10/climatechange.usnews (last visited May 25, 2008); Joydeep Gupta, *Developed Countries Declarations on Climate Change "Make No Sense,": India*, INDIA ENEWS, July 2, 2008, http://www.indiaenews.com/business/20080702/129150.htm (last visited Oct. 22, 2008).

9. Kevin Anderson & Alice Bows, *Reframing the Climate Change Challenge in Light of Post-2000*, PHILOSOPHICAL TRANSACTIONS ROYAL SOC'Y A, Aug. 29, 2008, at 15 [hereinafter Anderson & Bows].

10. Juliet Eilperin, *Carbon is Building Up in the Atmosphere Faster than Predicted*, WASHINGTONPOST.COM, Sept. 26, 2008, *available at* http://www.washingtonpost.com/wp-dyn/content/article/2008/09/25/AR200809 2503989.html?hpid=moreheadlineshttp://www.washingtonpost.com/ (last visited Oct. 22, 2008).

11. Anderson & Bows, *supra* note 9, at 18.

12. Many climatologists and policymakers have identified temperature increases of 1–2°C above pre-industrial levels as the threshold for dangerous anthropogenic interference with the atmosphere. German Advisory Council for Global Change, *New Impetus for Climate Policy: Making the Most of Germany's Dual Presidency*, Germany Advisory Council on Global Change, WBGU Policy Paper 5 (2007); Commission of European Communities, *Communication from the Commission to the Council, the European Parliament, the European Economic and Social Committee and the Committee of the Regions, Limiting Global Climate Change to 2°C the Way Ahead for 2020 and Beyond* (2007); James Hansen, *et al.*, *Dangerous Human-Made Interference with Climate: A GISS Model Study*, 7 ATMOSPHERIC CHEMISTRY & PHYSICS 2287–2312 (2007), *available at* http://pubs.giss.nasa.gov/docs/2007/2007_Hansen_etal_1.pdf (last visited Oct. 21, 2008).

13. *See* Hari M. Osofsky, *The Geography of Climate Change Litigation: Implications for Transnational Regulatory Governance*, 83 WASH. U. L.Q. 1789, 1795–1800 (2005); Eric A. Posner, *Climate Change and International Human Rights Litigation: A Critical Appraisal*, 155 U. PA. L. REV. 1925 (2007).

14. *See* Eric Torbenson, *Lawyers Preparing for Explosion of Climate-Related Work*, THE DALLAS MORNING NEWS, Business Section, June 24, 2007.

these actions have been filed in domestic courts, including in the United States. These include a challenge to the U.S. Environmental Protection Agency's denial of a petition to regulate greenhouse gas emissions from new motor vehicles under section 202(a)(1) of the Clean Air Act,[15] an action alleging that climate change constitutes a "public nuisance,"[16] and petitions to list species allegedly threatened by climate change under the Endangered Species Act.[17]

Two actions have also been initiated in international fora. In 2005, a petition was filed with the Inter-American Commission on Human Rights on behalf of Inuit in Canada and the United States requesting relief for human rights violations associated with climate change "caused by actions and omissions of the United States."[18] The Commission rejected the petition a year later. However, it subsequently agreed to a hearing to more closely examine the nexus of human rights and climate change, which took place in March 2007.

This paper will focus on the other climate change action initiated to date at the international level: the efforts of several petitioners to secure designation of several sites listed under The Convention Concerning the Protection of World Cultural and Natural Heritage[19] (World Heritage Convention) as "In Danger" as a consequence of climate threats. In this pursuit I will: 1). Outline the key provisions of the World Heritage Convention; 2). Describe the climate change petitions to the World Heritage Committee; and 3). Proffer a critique of the Committee's disposition of these petitions.

2. Causes of Action

2.1 Overview of the World Heritage Convention

The Convention concerning the Protection of World Cultural and Natural Heritage[20] (hereinafter the Convention) grew out of increasing recognition in the 1950s and 1960s of serious anthropogenic threats to both cultural sites and natural areas.[21]

The General Assembly of the United Nations Educational, Scientific and Cultural Organization (UNESCO) adopted the World Heritage Convention at its seventeenth session on Nov. 16, 1972, and it entered into force in December of 1975.[22] It is one of the more widely adopted multilateral agreements, with 185 Parties as of September of 2008.[23]

Noting "that deterioration or disappearance of any item of the cultural or natural heritage constitutes a harmful impoverishment of the heritage of all the nations of the world,"[24] the World Heritage Convention calls on its Parties to identify and delineate cultural and natural heritage of "outstanding universal value" within their respective borders.[25] As of September of 2008,

---

15. Massachusetts v. EPA, 549 U.S. 497, 127 S. Ct. 1438 (2007).

16. State of Connecticut v. Am. Elec. Power Co., 406 F. Supp. 2d 265, 273 (S.D.N.Y. 2005).

17. Ctr. for Biological Div., Petition to List Acropora Palmata (Elkhorn Coral), Acropora Cervicornis (Staghorn Coral), and Acropora Prolifera (Fused-Staghorn Coral) as Endangered Species Under The Endangered Species Act (2004), *available at* http://www.biologicaldiversity.org/swcbd/SPECIES/coral/petition.pdf (last visited May 25, 2008).

18. Petition to the Inter American Commission on Human Rights Seeking Relief from Violations Resulting from Global Warming Caused by Acts and Omissions of the United States 1, Dec. 7, 2005, *available at* http://www.inuitcircumpolar.com/files/uploads/icc-files/FINALPetitionICC.pdf (last visited May 25, 2008).

19. 11 ILM 1358 (1972) [hereinafter World Heritage Convention].

20. *Id.*

21. UNESCO WORLD HERITAGE CENTRE, WORLD HERITAGE INFORMATION KIT 7 (2008), *available at* http://whc.unesco.org/documents/publi_infokit_en.pdf (last visited Oct. 12, 2008).

22. *See* http://whc.unesco.org/en/169/ (detailing history of the World Heritage Convention) (last visited Aug. 25, 2006).

23. *See* http://whc.unesco.org/en/statesparties/ (last visited Sept. 15, 2008).

24. World Heritage Convention, *supra* note 19, at Preamble.

25. *Id.* at art. 1–3.

the Parties to the Convention have inscribed 679 cultural sites, 174 natural sites, and 25 mixed properties.[26]

Each Party to the Convention acknowledges its duty to ensure the protection and conservation of heritage sites within its national borders so that they may be transmitted to future generations.[27] To facilitate this, each Party pledges to take measures to protect sites that they have designated under the Convention, including integration of site protection in comprehensive planning processes, the provision of adequate staffing and infrastructure, appropriate scientific research, development of effective laws and adequate financing of protection and conservation programs.[28] Under Article 13 of the Convention, the Parties are authorized to request assistance with respect to World Heritage properties within their respective territories,[29] including the World Heritage Fund, which consists of compulsory and voluntary contributions made by the Parties, and other sources, including contributions from inter-governmental organizations, non-governmental organizations, and individuals.[30]

While each State Party is the primary protector of its respective World Heritage sites, the Convention also ascribes responsibilities to other Parties. The Convention states that "such heritage constitutes a world heritage for whose protection it is the duty of the international community as a whole to co-operate."[31] Under Article 6 State Parties agree "to give their help in the identification, protection, conservation and presentation of the cultural and natural heritage ... if the States on whose territory it is situated so request."[32] Moreover, the Convention requires that all Parties avoid any deliberate measures that might directly or indirectly damage cultural or natural heritage situated in the territory of another Party.[33]

The Convention also established the World Heritage Committee, composed of 21 Parties, and elected by the Parties.[34] The Committee's responsibilities include: establishing the List of World Heritage, monitoring the state of conservation of World Heritage properties, establishing the terms for use of the World Heritage Trust, a fund to help protect World Heritage sites, and allocation of financial assistance upon requests from Parties.[35]

The World Heritage Committee is also tasked with establishing a "list of World Heritage in Danger" when circumstances require it.[36] The List of World Heritage in Danger is reserved for World Heritage sites "threatened by serious and specific dangers ... for the conservation of which major operations are necessary and for which assistance has been requested under this Convention."[37] Only sites "threatened by serious and specific dangers" may be included on the list.[38] However, the Operational Guidelines of the Convention, developed by the World Heritage Com-

---

26. UNESCO, World Heritage Convention, *World Heritage List,* http://whc.unesco.org/en/list/ (last visited Sept. 16, 2008).

27. UNESCO, World Heritage Convention, *supra* note 19, at art. 4. *See also* Budapest Declaration on World Heritage, 26th Session of the World Heritage Committee, WC-02/CONF.202/25, 9 (2002), at para. 2 ("The properties on the World Heritage List are assets held in trust to pass on to generations of the future as their rightful inheritance"), *available at* http://whc.unesco.org/en/budapestdeclaration/ (last visited Sept. 23, 2008).

28. *Id.* at arts. 4–5.

29. *Id.* at art. 13(1).

30. *Id.* at art. 15.

31. *Id.* at art. 6(1).

32. *Id.* at art. 6(2)

33. *Id.* at art. 6(3).

34. *Id.* at art. 8(1).

35. *Id.* at arts. 8–14

36. *Id.* at art. 11(4).

37. *Id.* at art. 11(4).

38. *Id.*

mittee to prescribe precise criteria for inscription of properties of the World Heritage List and the provision of international assistance under the World Heritage Fund, provide that a site may warrant listing on the List of World Heritage in Danger for both ascertained and potential dangers.[39] Examples of such dangers include:

> ... the threat of disappearance caused by accelerated deterioration, large-scale public or private projects or rapid urban or tourist development projects; destruction caused by changes in the use or ownership of the land; major alterations due to unknown causes; abandonment for any reason whatsoever; the outbreak or the threat of an armed conflict; calamities and cataclysms; serious fires, earthquakes, landslides; volcanic eruptions; changes in water level, floods and tidal waves.[40]

Article 13 of the Convention authorizes the Committee to entertain requests for assistance for sites on the List of World Heritage in Danger and to decide on the actions to be taken. If the Committee determines that a site should be listed as "in danger," it will define a program of corrective actions and propose that the Party in which the site is found immediately implement the program.[41] A "significant" portion of the World Heritage Fund is also allocated for financing assistance for sites on the List.[42]

2.2 The World Heritage Climate Change Petitions

Between 2004 and 2006, 37 non-governmental organizations and individuals from several countries[43] filed 5 petitions[44] with the World Heritage Committee, requesting that it add several World Heritage sites to the Convention's List of World Heritage in Danger.[45] Four of the petitions

---

39. UNESCO, Intergovernmental Commission for the Protection of the World Cultural and Natural Heritage, Operational Guidelines for the Implementation of the World Heritage Convention, U.N. Doc. WHC Doc. 08/01 (Jan. 2008), at paras. 178–180, http://whc.unesco.org/archive/opguide08-en.pdf (last visited Sept. 23, 2008) [hereinafter Operational Guidelines].

40. UNESCO World Heritage Convention, *supra* note 19, at art. 11(4).

41. Operational Guidelines, *supra* note 39, at para. 186.

42. UNESCO World Heritage Convention, *supra* note 19, at art. 13(1); Operational Guidelines, *supra* note 39, at para. 189.

43. For a full list of the petitioners, see Climate Justice Programme, Briefing for the UNESCO World Heritage Committee, 31st Session, World Heritage and Climate Change: Complying with International Law 5 (2007), http://www.climatelaw.org/cases/country/intl/case-documents/unesco/unozblmtns/report.june.2007.pdf (last visited Sept. 19, 2008).

44. Technically, one of the filings with the World Heritage Committee was a report (Sydney Centre for International & Global Law, Global Climate Change and the Great Barrier Reef: Australia's Obligations under the World Heritage Convention (2004), http://www.law.usyd.edu.au/scigl/SCIGL FinalReport21_09_04.pdf (last visited Sept. 28, 2008), which analyzed the potential impacts of climate change on a natural heritage site in Australia, the Great Barrier Reef, and the legal obligations of Parties to the Convention to prevent harm to the site. However, the report was classified by the Committee as a danger-listing petition. Climate Justice, *UNESCO: World Heritage Committee Debate and Decision* (July 2005), http://www.climatelaw.org/cases/country/intl/unescoglacier/2005Jul13/ (last visited Sept. 16, 2008).

45. *See* the Climate Justice site for the text of the petitions, http://www.climatelaw.org. The United States in its position paper on the climate change petitions contended that non-States were not authorized under the Convention to file in-danger petitions. United States, Position of the United State [sic] of America on Climate Change with Respect to the World Heritage Convention and World Heritage Sites, at 4, http://www.elaw.org/assets/word/u.s.climate.US%20paper.doc (last visited Sept. 26, 2008). While the World Heritage Convention does not expressly authorize petitions of this nature by non-governmental organizations and individuals, one of the climate change petitions cited a UNESCO World Heritage Centre publication, the *World Heritage Information Kit*, http://whc.unesco.org/documents/publi_infokit_en.pdf (last visited Oct. 1, 2008). The publication indicates that private individuals, non-governmental organizations and other groups may draw the Committee's attention to existing threats. *Id.* at 18. Petition to the World Heritage Committee Requesting Inclusion of the Huascaran National Park in the List of World Heritage in Danger 17–37 (2004), http://www.climatelaw.org/cases/country/intl/unescoperu/ (last visited Sept. 17, 2004). The other petitions simply cited the authority of the World Heritage Committee to add sites to the List of World Heritage in Danger. Stephen

were filed in 2004, for Sagarmatha National Park in Nepal, Huascaran National Park in Peru, the Great Barrier Reef in Australia, and Belize's Barrier Reef Reserve System, and the fifth in 2006 by non-governmental organizations in the United States and Canada, seeking to add the Waterton-Glacier International Peace Park to the List.[46]

All five petitions alleged that climate change posed a primary threat to the sites in question, with the principal impacts linked to glacial melt[47] and coral bleaching associated with rising sea surface temperatures.[48] Petitioners seeking "in-danger" listings in the past have almost always contended that the requisite "major operations" to protect the sites must be conducted by the State in which the endangered site is found. However, notably in three of the five climate change in-danger petitions (with the exception of the petition for Waterton-Glacier International Peace Park in the United States and Canada and the Great Barrier Reef in Australia), the petitioners argued that third party States are also obligated to engage in major operations to control the greenhouse emissions that are precipitating climate change.

For example, in the Belize Barrier Reserve System petition, petitioners contended that Belize, with assistance from other Parties, needed to enhance the resilience of coral reef ecosystems through corrective measures, such as better protection of marine protected areas, enhanced monitoring and responses to coral reef bleaching events, and increased research and educational outreach efforts.[49] However, the petition also contended that any effective management plan for the reefs must include measures to reduce greenhouse gas emissions, especially by major emitting Parties.[50] The petition contended that Article 6(3) of the Convention arguably imposed the greatest obligation in this context on those Parties whose "deliberate emission(s) of high levels of

---

Leonard of the Australian Climate Justice Program has also suggested that Article 13(7) of the Convention, which provides that the World Heritage Committee will cooperate with international and national governmental and non-governmental organizations that have objectives concordant with the Convention, as additional authority for the right of non-States to submit in-danger petitions. Personal correspondence with Stephen Leonard, Sept. 26, 2008. The Committee appears to have sided with the petitioners on this issue. At its Thirtieth Session in 2006, the Committee indicated that it "takes note of the four petitions," and launched an initiative to assess the impacts of climate change on World Heritage sites and potential Party responses. UNESCO World Heritage Committee, Thirtieth Session, Vilnius, Lithuania, July 8–16, 20006, WHC-06/30.COM/7.1. Additionally, the Committee recently considered the petition of a private citizen, seeking an in-danger listing for La Amistad International Peace Park in Panama and Costa Rica. Erica Thorson et al., International Environmental Law Project, Petition to the World Heritage Committee requesting inclusion of Talamanca Range La Amistad Reserves La Amistad National Park on the list of World Heritage in danger (2007) *available at* http://www.law.lclark.edu/org/ielp/objects/LaAmistadPetition_4-23-07_english.pdf (last visited Sept. 26, 2008).

46. Climate Justice, http://www.climatelaw.org/cases/topic/unesco/ (last visited Sept. 26, 2008).

47. Petition to the World Heritage Committee Requesting Inclusion of the Huascaran National Park in the List of World Heritage in Danger, *supra* note 45, at 49–55 (2004) (glacial melting associated with warming trends posed human hazards, including ice and rock avalanches, glacial lake flooding and glacier surges, as well as threats to biodiversity); Petition to the World Heritage Committee Requesting Inclusion of Waterton-Glacier International Peace Park 8–15 (2004) (snow and snowmelt may adversely affect many hydrological and ecosystem processes, as well as the scenic appeal of the Park), http://www.climatelaw.org/cases/country/intl/unescoglacier/ (last visited Sept. 26, 2008); Petition to the World Heritage Committee Requesting Inclusion of Sagamatha National Park in the List of World Heritage in Danger as a Result of Climate Change and for Protective Measures and Actions 21–24 (2004) (glacial melting can cause glacial flooding and surges, resulting in potential bursting of dams, and threats to property, including critical energy infrastructure), http://www.climatelaw.org/cases/country/intl/unesconepal/ (last visited Sept. 26, 2008).

48. Petition to the World Heritage Committee Requesting Inclusion of Belize Barrier Reef Reserve System 16–17 (2004) (bleaching events associated with higher temperatures and greater frequency and intensity of storms linked to climate change will "devastate" Belize Barrier reef), http://www.climatelaw.org/cases/case-documents/unesco/belize-petition.doc (last visited Sept. 23, 2008).

49. *Id.* at 26–9.

50. *Id.* at 29.

greenhouse gases" threatened the Belize Barrier Reef.[51] The other four petitions similarly called for the Committee to consider the imposition of such measures.[52]

2.3 The World Heritage Committee/Parties' Response to the Petitions

The World Heritage Committee responded to the first four climate change-related petitions in a decision at its 29th Session in 2005. While acknowledging the "genuine concerns" of the petitioners and the impacts of climate change on World Heritage natural and cultural sites, the Committee opted not to inscribe the sites in question on the In Danger list. Rather, the Committee commissioned the establishment of a working group of experts to work in conjunction with the Petitioners, other Parties, and advisory bodies to assess the potential impacts of climate change on World Heritage sites and to assist the Parties in developing appropriate management responses.[53] Moreover it requested that the group of experts and other relevant bodies prepare a report on predicting and managing the effects of climate change on World Heritage sites for the Committee's consideration at its 30th Session.[54]

The United States, which had been elected a member of the Committee in 2005,[55] filed a position paper with the Committee opposing the petitions in advance of the Meeting of Experts in 2006.[56] The U.S. advanced five arguments in favor of its position: 1). While not specifically articulated in Article 11(4) of the Convention, a World Heritage Site could not be included on The List of World Heritage In Danger absent the consent of the State in which the site is found; 2). Failure to take an action, such as not reducing greenhouse gases, did not constitute a "deliberative [sic] measure which might damage a site" under Article 6(3); 3). The Operational Guidelines for the inscription of properties on the List of World Heritage in Danger required that the factors affecting the sites must be amenable to human action; yet it could not be established that climate change is caused only by anthropogenic emissions; this fact also contravened Guideline requirements that most threats posed to natural heritage sites must be of human origins; 4). The confrontational nature of the Petitions threatened to undermine "the camaraderie created by the unified spirit of conservation;" and 5). The most appropriate role for the Committee is to collect and share scientific information on potential impacts of climate change and provide examples of management actions that could be taken to mitigate these impacts.[57]

The Meeting of Experts drafted a "Strategy to assist States Parties to implement appropriate management responses in 2006."[58] The Strategy focused on three sets of actions to safeguard

---

51. *Id.* at 30.

52. *See* Petition to the World Heritage Committee Requesting Inclusion of Sagarmatha National Park in the List of World Heritage in Danger as a Result of Climate Change and for Protective Measures and Actions 40 (2004), http://www.climatelaw.org/cases/country/intl/unesconepal/ (last visited Sept. 26, 2008); Petition to the World Heritage Committee Requesting Inclusion of the Huascaran National Park in the List of World Heritage in Danger, *supra* note 45, at 40 (2004); Petition to the World Heritage Committee Requesting Inclusion of Waterton-Glacier International Peace Park, *supra* note 47, at 17–26; Sydney Centre for International & Global Law, *supra* note 44, at 20–30.

53. UNESCO, World Heritage Committee, Examination of the State of Conservation of World Heritage Properties: State of Conservation Reports of Properties Inscribed on the World Heritage List, Decision 29 COM 7B.a (2005), http://whc.unesco.org/download.cfm?id_document=5941 (last visited Sept. 29, 2008).

54. *Id.*

55. UNESCO, World Heritage Convention, *World Heritage Committee, 2007–2009,* http://whc.unesco.org/en/committeemembers/ (last visited Oct. 7, 2008).

56. Position of the United State [sic] of America on Climate Change with Respect to the World Heritage Convention and World Heritage Sites (2006), *available at* http://www.elaw.org/node/1603 (last visited Oct. 7, 2008).

57. *Id.* at 1–6.

58. UNESCO, World Heritage Committee, Issues Relating to the State of Conservation of the World Heritage Properties: The Impact of Climate Change on World Heritage Properties, WHC-

heritage: preventive actions, including monitoring, reporting and mitigation of climate change impacts; corrective actions, with a focus on global, regional and local adaptation strategies; and the sharing of knowledge, including best practices, education, and capacity building.[59]

Most notably, the Strategy's section on mitigation severely circumscribed the role of the Convention in mitigating greenhouse gas emissions. The Strategy emphasized that global and national mitigation strategies were being formulated by the United Nations Framework Convention on Climate Change (UNFCCC). While concluding that the World Heritage community had "a role" to play in mitigation, the Strategy restricted this to providing information to the UNFCCC and the Intergovernmental Panel on Climate Change, as well as encouraging site-based reductions of greenhouse gas emissions.[60]

Per the request of the World Heritage Committee, the expert working group also drafted a joint report entitled "Predicting and Managing the Effects of Climate Change on World Heritage."[61] The report included a detailed assessment of the potential impacts of climate change on World Heritage natural and cultural properties.[62] Moreover, it presented a detailed strategy for site-based mitigation and adaptation responses, as well as cooperation with other regimes.[63]

The World Heritage Committee at its 30th Session in 2006 endorsed the working group's Strategy and called for Party implementation to the fullest extent possible. It also took note of the Joint Report.[64] Finally, the Committee requested that the World Heritage Center prepare a policy document on the impacts of climate change on World Heritage properties for discussion at the General Assembly of States Parties[65] in 2007.[66]

The Policy Document was endorsed by the World Heritage Committee and adopted by the 16th General Assembly of State Parties in 2007.[67] The Document echoed the World Heritage Committee's characterization of the UNFCCC and the IPCC as the primary international institutions to address climate change, and indicated that the World Heritage Convention should focus on its "comparative advantage" of management of outstanding cultural and natural properties.[68] While the Document did advert to the obligation of the Parties under Article 6(3) to address climate change, it merely emphasized the need for a "collaborative approach."[69] The Document also amplified the Joint Report and Strategy's prescriptions for future research needs, including monitoring and adaptation strategies.[70]

06/30.COM/7.1 (June 26, 2006), http://whc.unesco.org/archive/2006/whc06-30com-07.13.pdf (last visited Sept. 29, 2008) [hereinafter WORLD HERITAGE COMMITTEE].

    59. *Id.* at 3.
    60. *Id.* at 4–5.
    61. UNESCO, WORLD HERITAGE COMMITTEE, *supra* note 58, at Annex 4.
    62. *Id.* at 20–33.
    63. *Id.* at 34–55.
    64. UNESCO, WORLD HERITAGE COMMITTEE, ISSUES RELATED TO THE STATE OF CONSERVATION OF WORLD HERITAGE PROPERTIES: THE IMPACTS OF CLIMATE CHANGE ON WORLD HERITAGE PROPERTIES, Decision 30 COM 7.1 (2006), http://whc.unesco.org/en/activities/471/ (last visited Sept. 29, 2008).
    65. The General Assembly of States Parties to the Convention meets during the sessions of the General Conference of UNESCO. UNESCO World Heritage Convention, *supra* note 19, at art. 8(1).
    66. *Id.*
    67. UNESCO WORLD HERITAGE CENTRE, POLICY DOCUMENT ON THE IMPACTS OF CLIMATE CHANGE ON WORLD HERITAGE PROPERTIES, http://whc.unesco.org/uploads/activities/documents/activity-397-2.pdf (last visited Sept. 29, 2008).
    68. *Id.* at 4.
    69. *Id.* at 7.
    70. *Id.* at Annex 1.

3. The World Heritage Convention Decisions: A Mixed Bag ... but Mostly Empty

3.1 The Positive Aspects of the Committee's Decisions

There were some praiseworthy elements of the Committee's decision-making in this matter. First, by acknowledging the petition for inscription of the Waterton-Glacier International Peace Park on the In Danger list, the Committee at least implicitly rejected the contention of the United States that sites cannot be inscribed without the consent of the States in which such sites are found. The World Heritage Convention's fundamental tenet is that it is important to protect natural and cultural sites "for all the peoples of the world ... safeguarding this unique and irreplaceable property, to whatever people it may belong."[71] To have accepted the position of the United States would have permitted it, or other States Parties, to make a unilateral decision to refuse to take measures to protect properties of great value to all of mankind when those sites became imperiled.

Interpretation of the World Heritage Convention's text on listing procedures also supports this position. While the Convention does bow to principles of State sovereignty in Article 11(3) by providing that "the inclusion of a property on the World Heritage List requires the consent of the State concerned,"[72] Article 11(4) simply directs the World Heritage Committee to "maintain" the "List of World Heritage in Danger." As Thorson argues, the drafters of the Convention clearly knew how to craft language requiring State consent when they deemed it necessary; however, they chose not to require such consent for inclusion of sites on the In Danger list.[73]

Another positive outgrowth of the Committee's deliberative process was its clear rejection of the increasingly anachronistic position of the United States that there is not a clear link between anthropogenic greenhouse gas emissions and climate change. This may make it increasingly difficult for the United States to advance such a position in international fora, perhaps engendering more cooperation in the future to confront climate change. Even more helpful, perhaps, has been the assessment of the Committee and its supporting bodies of the impacts of climate change on individual World Heritage sites, including detailed case studies for 26 sites.[74] Micro-scale impacts analyses of this nature can assist the UNFCCC in ascertaining the appropriate stabilization level of atmospheric greenhouse gas concentrations to "prevent dangerous anthropogenic interference with the climate system."[75]

Perhaps the most salutary aspect of the Committee's response to the petitions has been its commitment to developing effective adaptation strategies for protecting natural and cultural world heritage sites. While the emphasis for most of the first decade after the UNFCCC was opened for signature was on mitigation research and strategies,[76] adaptation has emerged in the past few years as an "urgent priority."[77] This is true for two primary reasons. First, as indicated in the introductory section of this essay, the world community's wholly inadequate re-

---

71. UNESCO World Heritage Convention, *supra* note 19, at Preamble.

72. *Id.* at art. 11(3).

73. Erica J. Thorson, *On Thin Ice: The Failure of the United States and the World Heritage Committee to Take Climate Change Mitigation Pursuant to the World Heritage Convention Seriously*, 38 Envtl. L. 139, 173 (2008) [hereinafter Thorson].

74. UNESCO, World Heritage Centre, Case Studies on Climate Change and World Heritage (2007), http://whc.unesco.org/documents/publi_climatechange.pdf (last visited Oct. 7, 2007).

75. UNFCCC, *supra* note 2, at art. 2.

76. Ian Burton & Bo Lim, *Achieving Adequate Adaptation in Agriculture*, 70 Climatic Change 191, 191 (2005); Richard J.T. Klein, *et al.*, *Portfolio Screening to Support the Mainstreaming of Adaptation to Climate Change into Development Assistance*, Tyndall Centre for Climate Change Research, Working Paper 102 (2007), at 1.

77. United Nations Department of Economic & Social Affairs, Division for Sustainable Development, *Adaptation to Climate Change in the Context of Sustainable Development*, Climate Change and Sustainable Development: A Workshop to Strengthen Research and Understanding, Apr. 7–8 (2007), at 1.

sponse to climate change virtually ensures that many World Heritage sites will be imperiled during this century,[78] necessitating efforts to ameliorate potential impacts. Second, there is a "timescale mismatch"[79] between mitigation measures and results. As a consequence, even if the world community were to stir from its slumber and implement effective measures to reduce emissions, it will be many decades before there are discernible effects of even meaningful efforts to reduce greenhouse gas emissions because of the inertia of the climatic system.[80] Indeed, a recent study concluded that even if greenhouse gas concentrations were held constant at 2005 values, we would have already committed the planet to temperature increases of 2.4°C above pre-industrial levels.[81] As outlined above, this increase is above the temperature threshold that most scientists and policymakers believe will visit serious impacts on human institutions and ecosystems,[82] emphasizing the need for adaptive responses over the next thirty years.

Yet, there are daunting challenges ahead in developing effective adaptive responses to climate change. Financial constraints are perhaps the most imposing barrier that the most vulnerable States in the world face in seeking to implement adaptation programs. It has been estimated that developing countries will require something on the order of $28–86 billion annually within the next few decades to adapt to climate impacts, most of which will need to come from developed countries.[83] By contrast, it's been estimated that the current international financial stream for meeting these needs is in the order of a mere $13 million per annum over the next five years,[84] though it's anticipated that future flows will be more substantial.[85] The commitment to developing adaptation programs in the World Heritage regime may help to bolster funding for such programs, as well as attract funding from other members of the world community to protect some of the world's most spectacular natural and cultural properties.

Moreover, at this point there is little concrete experience in implementing adaptation strategies, including "analysis of alternative adaptation strategies that could be applied to particular systems, their cost, or their likely effectiveness."[86] The World Heritage regime's adaptation blueprint includes several components that most experts believe will be critical for obtaining this experience and implementing effective adaptation strategies, including development of effective monitoring systems,[87] application of adaptive management responses,[88] and creation of a clear-

---

78. *See* Introduction, *supra* note 12, and accompanying text.

79. Roger Pielke, Jr., *et al.*, *Lifting the Taboo on Adaptation*, 445 NATURE 597, 597 (2007).

80. *Id.*

81. V. Ramanathan & Y. Feng, *On Avoiding Dangerous Anthropogenic Interference With the Climate System: Formidable Challenges Ahead*, 105(38) PROC. NAT'L ACAD. SCI. 14245, 14246 (2008).

82. *See supra* note 12, and accompanying text.

83. Sven Harmeling, *Adaptation to Climate Change—Where Do We Go From Bali?*, TIEMPO CLIMATE NEWSWATCH, Oct. 20, 2008, http://www.tiempocyberclimate.org/newswatch/comment080321.htm (last visited Oct. 21, 2008).

84. BENITO MÜLLER, INTERNATIONAL ADAPTATION FINANCE: THE NEED FOR AN INNOVATIVE AND STRATEGIC APPROACH 7 (Oxford Institute for Energy Studies, June 2008), *available at* http://www.oxfordenergy.org/pdfs/EV42.pdf (last visited Oct. 21, 2008).

85. *Adapt or Die*, ECONOMIST.COM, Sept. 11, 2008, http://www.economist.com/world/international/displaystory.cfm?story_id=12208005 (last visited Oct. 21, 2008).

86. Australian Government, Department of the Environmental and Heritage, AUSTRALIAN GREENHOUSE OFFICE, CLIMATE CHANGE RISK AND VULNERABILITY 107 (2005); *see also* United Nations Department of Economic & Social Affairs, *supra* note 77, at 2; GLOBAL ENVIRONMENT FACILITY, FINANCING ADAPTATION ACTION 8 (2007), http://www.energyandenvironment.undp.org/undp/indexAction.cfm?module=Library&action=GetFile&DocumentAttachmentID=2366 (last visited Oct. 22, 2008).

87. UNESCO, WORLD HERITAGE COMMITTEE, *supra* note 64, at 54.

88. *Id.*

inghouse mechanism for best-case adaptation practices.[89] Moreover, natural World Heritage sites are distributed around the world and represent a variety of ecosystems; they are exposed to impacts from climate change of different kinds, magnitudes and rates.[90] Thus, adaptation projects for these sites may serve as highly effective laboratories for ascertaining optimal adaptive strategies for the global community.

3.2 The Problematic Aspects of the Committee's Decision

The World Heritage Convention regime's response to the five climate change petitions is disheartening. All five petitioners provided compelling evidence that the World Heritage sites in question warranted In Danger listings, as they were all "threatened by serious and specific [climatic and non-climatic] dangers."[91] Moreover, the petitioners made a clear case for invoking Article 6(3) of the Convention to require major greenhouse gas emitters to control their emissions given their potential serious impacts on natural and cultural heritage properties.

Yet, despite the fact that the World Heritage Committee has inscribed 30 sites to date on the In Danger list,[92] most of which appear to face dangers no more pressing than those set forth in the climate petitions, the World Heritage Committee opted for an extremely tepid alternative to inscribing the sites, a climate change "strategy" with no binding components. This approach is particularly distressing given the Committee's conclusion that climate change poses a growing threat to World Heritage sites,[93] and the finding in a survey that revealed that 72% of responding World Heritage States discerned climatic impacts on their World Heritage properties.[94]

The primary rationale advanced by the Committee for this approach appears to be the alleged primary role of the UNFCCC in addressing mitigation of greenhouse gas emissions at the international and national level.[95] It is unclear if the Committee's position is based on legal or policy considerations, but in either case, I would suggest it is misguided.

The Committee may have believed that its approach was dictated by a generally-accepted principle for interpretation or conflict-solution in public international law, *lex specialis*.[96] The

---

89. UNESCO World Heritage Centre, *supra* note 67, at 6.

90. UNESCO, *Climate Change and World Heritage,* 22 World Heritage Rep. 27 http://whc.unesco.org/documents/publi_wh_papers_22_en.pdf (last visited Sept. 27, 2008).

91. UNESCO World Heritage Convention, *supra* note 19, at art. 11(4).

92. UNESCO World Heritage Convention, *List of World Heritage in Danger,* http://whc.unesco.org/en/danger/ (last visited Oct. 3, 2008).

93. Document on the Impacts of Climate Change on World Heritage Properties, *supra* note 67, at 3. *See also* UNESCO World Heritage Centre, *Climate Change and World Heritage,* 22 World Heritage Rep. 40 (2007), http://whc.unesco.org/documents/publi_wh_papers_22_en.pdf (last visited Sept. 27, 2008). ("As far as natural heritage is concerned, the vast majority of biomes may be adversely impacted by the effects of climate change").

94. UNESCO, World Heritage Committee, *supra* note 58, Annex 4, at 16. *See also* Convention on Biological Diversity, Proposals for the Integration of Climate Change Activities within the Programmes of Work of the Convention, Options for Mutually Supportive Actions Addressing Climate Change within the Rio Conventions and a Summary of the Findings of the Global Assessment on Peatlands, Biodiversity and Climate Change, UNEP/CBD/SBSTTA/12/7, http://www.cbd.int/doc/meetings/sbstta/sbstta-12/official/sbstta-12-07-en.doc (last visited Sept. 19, 2008) ("the negative impacts of climate change on protected areas are manifested within at least 79 Natural and Mixed World Heritage Sites identified as being threatened by climate change").

95. *Supra* note 60; UNESCO World Heritage Centre, *Climate Change and World Heritage,* 22 World Heritage Rep. 37 (2007), http://whc.unesco.org/documents/publi_wh_papers_22_en.pdf (last visited Sept. 27, 2008).

96. United Nations General Assembly, International Law Commission, 58th Session, *Fragmentation of International Law: Difficulties Arising from the Diversification and Expansion of International Law,* A/CN.4/L.682, April 13, 2006, at 37. While the principle was not incorporated into the Vienna Convention on the Law of Treaties, May 23, 1969, Art. 53, 1155 UNTS 331, it was observed during the drafting process that a treaty

principle of *lex specialis* is "grounded in the idea that the 'most closest, detailed, precise or strongest expression of state consent,' as it relates to a particular circumstance, ought to prevail."[97] *Lex specialis* may be applicable in the context of provisions within a single treaty, between provisions within two or more treaties, between a treaty and a non-treaty standard, or between two non-treaty standards.[98] In considering the climate change In-Danger petitions, the World Heritage Committee may have held the position that: 1). The United Nations Framework Convention on Climate Change[99] was specifically established to mitigate anthropogenic greenhouse gas emissions that precipitate climate change; and 2). As such, it constitutes a *lex specialis* regime, and thus should be the forum in which States address this issue.

I would argue that this conclusion is not dictated by the principle of *lex specialis*. First, under international law there is a strong presumption that when creating new obligations, States will not to derogate from their current obligations, including multilateral treaties.[100] Under the well recognized international legal principle of harmonization, "[w]hen two States have concluded two treaties on the same subject-matter, but have said nothing of their mutual relationship, it is usual to first try to read them as compatible ..."[101] This same rule applies with multilateral treaties, unless the parties have expressed their intent to supplant the obligations of the earlier treaty with those of the latter.[102] This principle has been incorporated into the Vienna Convention on the Law of Treaties (VCLT).[103] Article 59 provides that prior treaties are not terminated between States who have entered into a subsequent treaty, absent evidence that the Parties intended that the subsequent treaty should govern a particular matter, or the provisions of the two treaties are so incompatible that they can't be applied simultaneously.

The International Tribunal for the United Nations Convention on the Law of the Sea also applied the principle of harmonization in the *MOX Plant Case*.[104] In *MOX*, Ireland brought an action against the United Kingdom under UNCLOS, alleging that the U.K.'s plan to site a mixed oxide fuel plant on the eastern shore of the Irish Sea threatened the Sea with nuclear contamination.[105] In finding that an ad hoc arbitral tribunal had prima facie jurisdiction over the dispute,

---

might be "special" in relation to another treaty. Statement of the Expert Consultant (Waldock), United Nations Conference on the Law of Treaties, Second Sess., Vienna, Apr. 9–22, Official Records 270 (1970).

97. Joost Pauwelyn, Conflict of Norms in Public International Law: How the WTO Law Relates to Other Rules of International Law 388 (Cambridge Un. Press 2003).

98. United Nations General Assembly, International Law Commission, Fragmentation of International Law: Difficulties Arising from Diversification and Expansion of International Law, A/CN.4/L.702 (2006), at 8.

99. *Supra* note 2.

100. International Law Commission, *supra* note 96, at 26. *See also In the Case Concerning the Right of Passage over Indian Territory (Portugal v. India) (Preliminary Objections)*, 1957 I.C.J. Rep. 142 ("It is a rule of interpretation that a text emanating from a government must, in principle, be interpreted as producing and is intended to produce effects in accordance with existing law and not in violation of it"); Joost Pauwelyn, *The Role of Public International Law in the WTO: How Far Can We Go?*, 95 Am. J. Int'l L. 535, 550 (2001); Oppenheim's International Law 1275 (9th ed., Robert Jennings & Arthur Watts eds., Oxford Un. Press 1992).

101. V. Czaplinkski & Gl Danilenko, *Conflict of Norms in International Law*, XXI Netherlands Y.B. Int'l L. 20-1 (1990); United Nations General Assembly, International Law Commission, 58th Sess., *Conclusions of the work of the Study Group on the Fragmentation of International Law: Difficulties arising from the Diversification and Expansion of International Law* (2006), at 2, http://untreaty.un.org/ilc/texts/instruments/english/draft%20articles/1_9_2006.pdf (last visited Oct. 6, 2008) [hereinafter Czaplinski & Danilenko].

102. Czaplinkski & Danilenko, *supra* note 101, at 20-1.

103. *Supra* note 96.

104. *The Mox Plant Case* (Ireland v. United Kingdom), 126 Int'l Law Rep. 260 (Dec. 3, 2001) (Int'l Tribunal for the Law of the Sea; *Request for Provisional Measures*).

105. United Nations Convention on the Law of the Sea, Arbitral Tribunal, In the Dispute Concerning the MOX Plant, International Movements of Radioactive Materials, and the Protection of the Marine Environment of the Irish Sea, *Ireland v. United Kingdom*, Memorial of Ireland, Vol. 1

the Tribunal emphasized the fact that multiple treaty regimes may have authority to address the same environmental issue:

> ... even if the OSPAR Convention, the EC Treaty and the Eurotom treaty contains rights or obligations similar to or identical with the rights set out in [UNCLOS], the rights and obligations under these agreements have a separate existence from those under [UNCLOS].[106]

In context of the climate change issues, then, the presumption should be that the World Heritage Committee has the authority to craft measures to protect World Heritage properties imperiled by climate change, including mandating greenhouse gas emissions reductions by major emitting States under Article 6(2). The issue, then, is whether the world community, in establishing the UNFCCC, effectively supplanted the authority of the World Heritage Committee in this context under the principle of *lex specialis*.

There is no language in the text of the UNFCCC that evinces the intent of the Parties to displace potentially parallel mandates under other regimes to address climate change when this is deemed necessary to effectuate the objectives of those regimes. We must presume that the Parties would have included such language if this was their intent, because States have done so in numerous other international environmental regimes where they wished to define the relationship of two or more regimes. For example, Article 311 of the United Nations Convention on the Law of the Sea (UNCLOS)[107] provides that UNCLOS prevails between its Parties over the Geneva Conventions on the Law of the Sea. Conversely, Article XIV(4) of the Convention on International Trade in Endangered Species (CITES)[108] provides that its Parties are relieved of their trade obligations for marine species under Appendix II of the Convention if they are also Parties to a marine conservation agreement in force at the time that CITES entered into force. To the extent that similar language was not included in the UNFCCC, the World Heritage Committee should not have felt compelled to defer to the climate regime in considering the climate change In-Danger petitions.

Second, even assuming, *arguendo* that the maxim of *lex specialis* were apposite in this matter, international law recognizes the right of a State to avail themselves of alternative remedies in the face of "regime failure":

> Special regimes or the institutions set up by them may fail. Failure might be inferred when the special laws have no reasonable prospect of appropriately addressing the objectives for which they were enacted. It could be manifested, for example, by the failure of the regime's institutions to fulfill the purposes allotted to them, persistent non-compliance by one or several of the parties, desuetude, withdrawal by parties instrumental for the regime, among other causes ... In the event of failure, the relevant general law becomes applicable.[109]

As set forth in the introduction to this chapter, the UNFCCC might be characterized as a quintessentially failed regime, with burgeoning global greenhouse gas emissions and critical

---

(2002), at paras. 1.65–169, http://www.pca-cpa.org/upload/files/Ireland%20Memorial%20Part%20I.pdf (last visited Oct. 8, 2008).

106. *MOX Plant case, Request for Provisional Measures Order* (Ireland v. the United Kingdom) (3 Dec. 2001), *International Tribunal for the Law of the Sea*, 126 INT'L L. REV. 273 (2005), at para. 50.

107. U.N. Convention on the Law of the Sea, 10 Dec. 1982, U.N. Doc. A/Conf. 62/121, 21 I.L.M. 1261 [hereinafter *UNCLOS*].

108. Mar. 3, 1973, 27 U.S.T. 1087, T.I.A.S. No. 8249, 993 U.N.T.S. 243, ELR Stat. 40336.

109. United Nations General Assembly, *supra* note 98, at 13. *See also* Gaetano Arangio-Ruiz, *Fourth Report on State Responsibility*, Doc. A/CN.4/444, II(1) Y.B. INT'L L. COMM'N 40–1 (1992), http://untreaty.un.org/ilc/publications/yearbooks/Ybkvolumes(e)/ILC_1992_v2_p1_e.pdf (last visited Oct. 5, 2008).

thresholds for severe impacts looming for both human institutions and ecosystems. Thus, it would be reasonable for the World Heritage Convention to step into the vacuum created by the UNFCCC to fashion remedies to protect the sites within its trust.

Third, a tenable argument can certainly be made that the UNFCCC is the *lex specialis* regime in this matter, given its focus on mitigating greenhouse gas emissions. However, an equally defensible argument could be made that the World Heritage Convention is the more "specialized" agreement in the matter at hand because the regime focuses on the protection of individual sites from threats such as climate change, rather than the more generalized mandate of the UNFCCC to mitigate the adverse effects of climate change,[110] "protect the climate system,"[111] and prevent "dangerous anthropogenic interference with the climate system."[112]

Alternatively, in characterizing the UNFCCC as "the preferred international tool to address mitigation,"[113] the World Heritage Committee might have also believed that deferring to the UN-FCCC in the context of mitigation of greenhouse gas emissions was salutary from a policy perspective given that regime's focus and expertise. In the best of all worlds, this would assuredly be the case. However, while the UNFCCC ostensibly seems to be optimally positioned to address the issue of climate change, empirically, it has not fulfilled its promise to date. There is a very real threat that if the World Heritage Committee waits for the UNFCCC to "solve" this problem, much of the world's cultural and natural heritage may be lost. Given this very real threat, the most judicious approach would be for the World Heritage Convention to concomitantly address climate change in the context of the sites that it is committed to protect. As one commentator observed recently, "[r]ather than engage in a wholly unrealistic attempt to create a hierarchy within the fragmentation of global law, efforts should thus instead be focused on the intraregime responsiveness to the immediate human and natural environment; that is, functional regimes must each evolve their own *ius non dispositivum*."[114]

Of course, the Committee did call for site-specific mitigation measures "where appropriate,"[115] as well as at the Committee's Headquarters.[116] However, even stringent measures in these limited venues would do virtually nothing to slow or reverse greenhouse gas emissions trends.[117]

Ultimately, the Committee's decision may have reflected regime *realpolitik*. Should the Committee have chosen to list the five sites in question on the In-Danger List, it may have felt compelled to include among its corrective measures a call for large greenhouse gas emitting States to significantly reduce their greenhouse gas emissions.

However, should a large greenhouse gas emitting State, such as the United States, have chosen to flout such corrective measures, the Committee's authority could have been substantially undermined. As Andrew Strauss observes, international tribunals carefully marshal their political capital in an effort to preserve and enhance their legitimacy:

> While the official function of international tribunals is to find the pre-existing law, in reality, for judges to have their decisions so accepted, they must engage in the creative

---

110. UNFCCC, *supra* note 2, at art. 3(3).

111. *Id.* at art. 3(1).

112. *Id.* at art. 2.

113. UNESCO World Heritage Centre, *Climate Change and World Heritage*, 22 World Heritage Rep. 37 (2007), http://whc.unesco.org/documents/publi_wh_papers_22_en.pdf (last visited Sept. 27, 2008).

114. Andreas Fischer-Lescano & Gunther Teubner, *Regime-Collisions: The Vain Search for Legal Unity in the Fragmentation of Global Law*, 25 Mich. J. Int'l L. 999, 1037 (2004).

115. UNESCO, World Heritage Committee, *supra* note 53, at 4.

116. UNESCO World Heritage Centre, *supra* note 67, at 9.

117. Thorson, *supra* note 73, at 13.

process of negotiating the differing global interests to formulate results that are in accord with the international community's normative center of gravity. In arriving at politically viable legal standards, in addition to formally reviewing submitted briefs and memoranda and informally reading other legal commentary, judges engaged in a pragmatic assessment of the political situation, by factoring in the relative power of the protagonists and the interests of other important international actors.[118]

Indeed, State non-compliance with the orders of a regime body is always a possibility,[119] and there are instances in the past where this has occurred.[120] The Committee may have simply opted to avoid this prospect by taking a wholly non-confrontational stance. Of course, one must ask the question as to whether a regime such as the World Heritage Convention can deem itself to be "legitimate" if it fails to address an issue that may already be having substantial impacts on the vast majority of the sites it seeks to protect, and will have far more serious ramifications in the future.[121]

4. Conclusion

The World Heritage Committee's failure to take the opportunity to address the potential effects of climate change in a meaningful fashion is lamentable given the virtual abdication of responsibility by the Parties to the UNFCCC to confront one of the most pressing issues of this generation, and many more to come. In June 2007, four non-governmental organizations filed a petition with the World Heritage Committee, requesting that the eucalypt forests of the Blue Mountains in Australia be placed on the List of World Heritage in Danger because of the threat of climate change.[122] This filing accords the Committee another opportunity to galvanize the Convention's Parties to address an issue that is likely to pose a graver and graver threat to the world's precious heritage in the future.

VIII. Adaptation to Climate Change

PEW CENTER ON GLOBAL CLIMATE CHANGE, ADAPTATION TO CLIMATE CHANGE: INTERNATIONAL POLICY OPTIONS 13–14 (November 2006):[1]

In principle, adaptation was established as a priority at the very start of the international climate effort. In the UNFCCC, all parties committed generally to undertake national adaptation measures and to cooperate in preparing for the impacts of climate change.[2] The Convention also calls for full consideration of the specific needs and concerns of developing countries—espe-

---

118. Andrew Strauss, *Toward an International Law of Climate Change: Utilizing a Model of International Tribunals as Law-Makers, in* ADJUDICATING CLIMATE CHANGE: SUB-NATIONAL, NATIONAL, AND SUPRA-NATIONAL APPROACHES 107 (William C.G. Burns & Hari Osofsky, eds., Cambridge Un. Press 2009).

119. Deborah Horowitz, Southern Bluefin Tuna Case (Australia And New Zealand v. Japan) (Jurisdiction And Admissibility); *The Catch of Poseidon's Trident: The Fate of High Seas Fisheries in the Southern Bluefin Tuna Case,* 26 MELBOURNE U. L. REV., http://www.austlii.edu.au/au/journals/MULR/2001/26.html (last visited Sept. 17, 2008).

120. Richard J. Silk, Jr., *Nonbinding Dispute Resolution Processes in Fisheries Conflicts: Fish Out of Water?,* 16 OHIO ST. J. ON DISP. RESOL. 791, 800–01 (2001).

121. *See supra* note 94 and accompanying text.

122. Climate Justice, *UNESCO 6th Danger-Listing Petition Filed (22 June 2007),* http://www.climatelaw.org/cases/country/intl/unescoozbmtns/unesco/ (last visited Oct. 22, 2008).

1. *Available at* http://www.pewclimate.org/docUploads/PEW_adaptation.pdf.

2. UNFCCC, Article 4.1.

cially the least developed—arising from the adverse effects of climate change.[3] More concretely, developed countries committed to help "particularly vulnerable" countries meet the costs of adaptation.[4] Nearly 15 years after the Convention's negotiation, however, the international adaptation effort is more an irregularly funded patchwork of multilateral and bilateral initiatives than a fully conceived and functioning regime.

At the first Conference of the Parties (COP) to the Convention, in 1995, the parties established a three-stage framework for addressing adaptation. Stage I, to be carried out in the "short term," was to focus on identifying the most vulnerable countries or regions and adaptation options. Stage II was to involve measures, including capacity building, to prepare for adaptation. Stage III was to entail implementing measures to facilitate adaptation. The latter two stages were to be implemented over the "medium and long term."[5]

Broadly speaking, the effort to date has centered primarily on Stage I- and Stage II-type activities, more often simultaneously than sequentially. Multilateral and bilateral support has focused on building the capacity of developing countries to assess their vulnerability to climate change and examine adaptation needs and options. For example, with assistance provided under the Convention, Bangladesh and small island states in the Caribbean and the Pacific have examined their vulnerabilities to climate change and are assessing options for adaptation. The U.N. Environment Programme has worked with about half a dozen countries on in-depth assessments of vulnerability, while the U.N. Development Programme is assisting scores of countries in assessing adaptation needs. In addition, several countries, including the United States, Britain, the Netherlands, Japan, Germany, and Canada, have provided bilateral assistance. By one recent accounting, bilateral programs have committed $110 million to more than 50 adaptation projects in 29 countries.[6]

Recently, the emphasis has shifted to setting priorities among adaptation options. More than 40 least developed countries have received funding under the Convention to prepare National Adaptation Programmes of Action (NAPAs) addressing urgent needs.[7] The NAPAs are meant to draw on existing information and community-level input to assess vulnerability to current climate variability and areas where risks will be heightened by climate change, and to identify priority actions. The Global Environment Facility (GEF), which administers adaptation funding under the Convention, recently approved the first allocations for implementation projects through a $50 million Strategic Priority on Adaptation (SPA) initiative.[8]

Arguably, one significant constraint on adaptation efforts to date has been limited funding. At COP 7, in 2001, parties established three GEF-managed funds dedicated fully or in part to supporting adaptation.[9] However, not all funds pledged by developed countries have yet been made available, and some developing countries cite difficulties in accessing what funds are available. The World Bank reported in 2006 that its support for adaptation had been "on the order of approximately $50 million over about five years," mainly through the GEF.[10] Parties

---

3. UNFCCC, Article 3.

4. UNFCCC, Article 4.4.

5. UNFCCC, Decision 11/CP.1.

6. Frankel-Reed, Jennifer. 2006. "Emerging Approaches in Climate Change Adaptation from Theory and Practice." Unpublished Master's thesis.

7. GEF (2006).

8. GEF was established in 1992 to channel financing to developing countries to address environmental problems of global concern. It operates through three implementing agencies—the World Bank, the U.N. Environment Programme, and the U.N. Development Programme.

9. The three funds are the Least Developed Countries Fund, the Special Climate Change Fund, and the Adaptation Fund. The first two are supported by voluntary contributions from donor countries; the third by a share of the proceeds from credits generated through the Kyoto Protocol's Clean Development Mechanism.

10. The World Bank GEF (2006). In addition, the GEF has provided approximately $170 million for the preparation of national communications, which address both mitigation and adaptation. *See* Assistance to

decided at COP 7 that, to supplement donor country contributions, one of the three new funds will be supported by a levy of two percent on proceeds from emission credits generated through the Kyoto Protocol's Clean Development Mechanism (CDM). Future CDM flows, however, are highly uncertain; the Bank projects they could generate from "a few tens of millions" to $1 billion for adaptation purposes by 2012. Within the negotiations, administration of the Adaptation Fund remains highly contentious, with many developing countries maintaining that as the funds are not from donor countries, they should be managed by an entity other than the GEF.

Funding levels aside, the adaptation effort has suffered from ambiguities in the regime. One concerns the very definition of adaptation, which is nowhere explicit in the Convention. In that adaptation is referenced only in the context of climate change, the implication is that support under the Convention must be directed to activities addressing primarily if not exclusively human-induced impacts. Yet, as noted earlier, and in expert meetings convened under the Convention, adaptation strategies often are most effective when addressing the full continuum of climate risk. In addition, there appears significant confusion over the terms for adaptation funding through the GEF. As the GEF was established to address global environmental issues, projects supported through its principal trust fund must deliver a "global environmental benefit." In the area of adaptation, most funding flows through the separate dedicated funds established under the Convention and the Kyoto Protocol. Although guidance from the parties is not explicit on the point, the GEF's position is that the "global environmental benefits" test does not apply to these funds.[11] Yet there remains a widespread perception among potential recipients that it does:[12]

> ... [T]he international effort to date has delivered some information, resources, and capacity building, but has yet to facilitate significant on-the-ground implementation, technology development or access, or the establishment of robust national institutions to carry the adaptation agenda forward. Even if significant new resources were forthcoming, it appears improbable that existing arrangements under the Convention could alone serve as an adequate basis for a strengthened adaptation effort.

A. Climate Refugees

See Chapter Six above, §IV, for Professor Robert R.M. Verchik's paper on "Adaptive Justice." Professor Verchik observes:[1]

> As long as the North views Southern desperation as largely irrelevant to its own interest, adaptation aid will continue to be a mission of charity only—help that we wish we would give, but don't want to.

Statement by the Honorable Dr. Feleti Vaka'uta Sevele, Prime Minister of Tonga:[2]

Address Adaptation, GEF/C.23/Inf.8/Rev.1 of May 11, 2004; and Status Report on the Least Developed Countries Fund For Climate Change and The Special Climate Change Fund, GEF/C.25/4/Rev.1 of May 2, 2005.

11. *See* Working Draft GEF Climate Change Strategy, Meeting on the Fourth Replenishment of the GEF Trust Fund, GEF/ R.4/Inf.7. *Also see* Decision 7/CP.7 on funding under the Convention and Decision 10/CP.7 on funding under the Kyoto Protocol in FCCC/CP/2001/13/Add.1. *Also see* Decision 5/CP.9 on further guidance for the financing mechanism to operate the SCCF and Decision 6/CP.9 on further guidance for the operation of the LDCF in FCCC/CP/2003/6/Add.1.

12. Personal communications with developing country officials engaged in adaptation efforts.

1. Ch. 6 at §IV.

2. Speech to the United Nations General Assembly, September 26, 2008.

[T]he prospect of climate refugees from some of the Pacific Island Forum countries is no longer a prospect but a reality, with relocations of communities due to sea level rise already taking place. Urgent Action must be taken now.

Statement by U.N. General Assembly President Srgjan Kerim:[3]

The topic of climate refugees is no longer a concept—it is a sad fact.... Each nation, each city, each town, each community and individual has a stake.

Angela Williams, *Turning the Tide: Recognizing Climate Change Refugees in International Law*, 30 LAW & POL'Y 502, 502 (2008):

There has been much ink spilled in recent years over legal and policy initiatives regarding climate change. While debate continues to rage over the most responsive, appropriate, and equitable method of addressing our changing climate, there is quickly developing a subsidiary problem. Increasingly, climate change is seen as being responsible for the displacement of individuals, communities, and, in some cases, entire nations, as the impacts of our changing climate are more widely and intensely felt. However, the plight of so-called "climate change refugees" continues largely unrecognized and mostly devoid of support by the international community.

---

3. Speech to the Global Humanitarian Forum, June 24, 2008.

Chapter Eight

Local, State, Regional, Tribal and Private Climate Change Initiatives

Chapter Eight

Local, State, Regional, Tribal and Private Climate Change Initiatives

CONGRESSIONAL RESEARCH SERVICE, CLIMATE CHANGE: ACTION BY STATES TO ADDRESS GREENHOUSE GAS EMISSIONS, CRS-4 (2008) (footnotes included):

> In the late 1980s, Vermont[13] and Oregon[14] were the first states to set greenhouse gas reduction goals, but during the subsequent decade (1990–2001), both states increased their greenhouse gas emissions: Vermont by 18% and Oregon by 30%.[15] However, a majority of states have more recently begun to develop their own climate change strategies or policies, with a small but increasing number of states adopting or proposing more significant provisions, including mandatory greenhouse gas reductions.

I. Introduction

Given the void in federal action, the state and local response to climate change presents a complex picture. States have made astounding and impressive attempts to address the problem. The question remains, however, whether state or local authorities will choose to—or be capable of—implementing their plans. Furthermore, as with any political action, there is always the question: is this enough? The sections below explore this dynamic.

A. The Impossibility Theorem

From some perspectives, it may be difficult to see why local or state initiatives on global warming would ever happen. DANIEL R. ABBASI, AMERICANS AND CLIMATE CHANGE 17 (Yale School of Forestry and Environmental Studies 2006) calls climate change the "perfect problem." What he means is that it appears to be close to insolvable. Here's why: The topic has

- complex and inaccessible scientific content;

---

13. Vermont Executive Order 79 (October 23, 1989) called for a 15% reduction below 1989 levels by 2000. *See* U.S. Congress, Office of Technology Assessment, 1991, *Changing by Degrees: Steps to Reduce Greenhouse Gases*, p. 327.

14. Oregon Senate Bill 576 (1989) set a goal of 20% reduction of 1988 levels by 2005. *See* U.S. Congress, Office of Technology Assessment, *Changing by Degrees: Steps to Reduce Greenhouse Gasses*, p. 327 (1991).

15. *See* World Resources Institute, *Climate Analysis Indicators Tool*, at http://cait.wri.org/ (last visited Nov. 14, 2008).

- a substantial (and uncertain) time lag between cause and effect;
- inertia in all the key drivers of the problem, from demographic growth to long-lived energy infrastructure to ingrained daily habits at the household level;
- psychological barriers that complicate apprehension and processing of the issue, due in part to its perceived remoteness in time and place;
- partisan, cultural, and other filters that cause social discounting or obfuscation of the threat;
- motivational obstacles, especially the futility associated with what is perhaps the quintessential "collective action problem" of our time;
- mismatches between the global, cross-sectoral scope of the climate change issue and the jurisdiction, focus, and capacity of existing institutions;
- a set of hard-wired incentives, career and otherwise, that inhibit focused attention and action on the issue.

See also Jedediah Purdy, *Climate Change and the Limits of the Possible*, 18 Duke Envtl. L. & Pol. F. 289 (2008).

The factors suggest that some legal or social "impossibility theorem" would bar any serious local or state initiatives to combat global warming. Grave objections of "can't-be-done" would steer local governments away from temptations to butt the municipal skull against this immovable brick wall. But, of course, hard science, entrenched interests, timid leaders and wavering law doesn't add up to "impossible." Unprecedented and daunting doesn't mean "impossible." The fact is that many state and local laws are being enacted. So many people are optimistic enough to attempt "the impossible."

B. The "Faking-It" Theorem

Another way of explaining the explosion in local and state laws on global warming is that they are not intended or designed to solve serious problems. They are, instead, largely political gestures meant to give the *appearance* of revolutionary change, the *example* of doing good, and the *attitude* that new policies will soon swing into action.

If actually overcoming the multiple threats of climate change is a journey of 1000 miles, the first few miles conceivably might be the least painless. A tad of planning, a touch of process, an aspirational utterance, a distant goal might well suffice. High political awards could attend small and tentative political initiatives.

Environmental law is steeped in the experience of deception, pretense, and indirection. The breakthrough of the Clean Air Act has been modeled convincingly as a credit-claiming competition between Presidential aspirants, Richard Nixon and Edmund Muskie. Elliott, Ackerman & Millian, *Toward a Theory of Statutory Evolution: The Federalization of Enviornmental Law*, 1 J.L. Econ. & Org. 313 (1985). Aspirational laws—short on substance, wanting in forceful direction—have come under sustained criticism. John P. Dwyer, *Pathology of Symbolic Legislation*, 17 Ecology L.Q. 233 (1990). Enforcement has long been recognized as a discordant quartet of appearances, limited knowledge, retaliation, and incentive-adjustment. *Compare* David R. Hodas, *Enforcement of Environmental Law in a Triangular Federal System: Can Three Not be A Crowd when Enforcement Authority is Shared by the United States, the States, and Their Citizens?*, 54 Md. L. Rev. 1552 (1995) *with* Clifford Rechtschaffen, *Competing Visions: EPA and the States Battle for the Future of Environmental Enforcement*, 30 Envtl. L. Rep. 10803 (2000) and Joel A. Mintz & Clifford Rechtschaffen, Environmental Enforcement: Cases & Materials (Carolina Academic Press 2007) and *Ass'n of Irritated Residents v. EPA*, 494 F.3d 1027 (D.C. Cir. 2007).

(This case is a challenge to "agreements" between EPA and animal feeding operations (AFOs). Petitioners argue that these are "rules" disguised as "enforcement actions." The majority (Sentelle, Cavanaugh, C.J.s) dismisses the petitions because exercises of EPA's enforcement discretion are not reviewable in court. *See* Animal Feeding Operations Consent Agreement and Final Order, 70 Fed. Reg. 40,016 (July 12, 2005); "several thousand AFOs have signed Agreements." Rogers, C.J., dissents, arguing that the agency's enforcement discretion disappears "when an agency veers far afield of Congress's enforcement regime.... By replacing the enforcement scheme in three congressional statutes with an unauthorized system of nominal taxation of regulated entities, EPA has promulgated a reviewable regulation." 494 F.3d at 1042).

State and local lawmaking (whether it be in executive, legislative, or judicial form) certainly is not immune from a phenomenon identified by Noam Chomsky, in Failed States: The Abuse of Power and the Assault on Democracy 103 (Henry Holt & Co. 2006):

> Mother Nature doesn't provide the answers on a silver platter, but at least she does not go out of her way to set up barriers to understanding. In human affairs, such barriers are the norm. It is necessary to dismantle the structures of deception erected by doctrinal systems, which adopt a range of devices that flow very naturally from the ways in which power is concentrated.

There is an obvious—and perhaps justified—skepticism whether any law (whatever its source) is up to the challenge of herding humanity towards realization of its better and collective interests. But this is a commentary on all law not just state or local law. Indeed, the "locals" and the "states" can claim a closer-to-the-people, bottom-up legitimacy that the United States or the "nations of the world" cannot.

Thomas L. Friedman, in his book, Hot, Flat, and Crowded: Why We Need A Green Revolution—and How It Can Renew America (Farrar, Straus, & Giroux 2008), has touched on the question of "faking it." In a chapter entitled *205 Easy Ways to Save the Earth*, Friedman asks (at 185) (emphasis in original):

> "Really? Really? A green revolution? Have you ever seen a revolution where no one got hurt? That's the green revolution we're having." In the green revolution we're having, everyone's a winner, nobody has to give up anything, and the adjective that most often modifies "green revolution" is "easy." That's not a revolution. That's a party. We're actually having a green party. And, I have to say, it's a lot of fun. I get invited to all the parties. But in America, at least, it is mostly a costume party. It's all about *looking* green—and everyone's a winner. There are no losers. The American farmers are winners. They're green. They get to grow ethanol and garner huge government subsidies for doing so, even though it makes no real sense as a CO_2-reduction strategy. Exxon Mobil says it's getting green and General Motors does too. GM put yellow gas caps on its cars that are flex-fuel, meaning they can run on a mix of gasoline and ethanol. For years, GM never bothered to highlight that its cars were flex-fuel, or use it as a selling point with customers, because the only reason GM made a certain number of cars flex-fuel was that, if it did so, the government would allow it to build even more gas-guzzling Hummers and pickup trucks and still remain under the CAFÉ fuel economy standard mandated by Congress—but why quibble?
>
> Coal companies are going green by renaming themselves "energy" companies and stressing how sequestration of CO_2, something none of them has ever done, will give us "clean coal." I am sure Dick Cheney is green. He has a home in Wyoming, where he goes hunting, and he favors liquefied coal. We're all green. "Yes, step right up, ladies and gentlemen, in the green revolution we're having in America today, everybody gets to play, everybody's a winner, nobody gets hurt, and nobody has to do anything hard."

As I said, that's not the definition of a revolution. That's the definition of a party.

And Friedman has this to say about empty law (whether it be local, state, federal, or international) (*id.* at 186):

> Pentagon planners like to say: "A vision without resources is a hallucination." Right now we are having a green hallucination, not a green revolution. Because we are offering ourselves and our kids a green vision without the resources—without a systemic response shaped by an intelligent design and buttressed by market forces, higher efficiency standards, tougher regulations, and an ethic of conservation that might have a chance of turning that vision into reality. We have willed the ends, but not the means.

Friedman also comments on "easy" law (*id.* at 188–89) (emphasis in original):

> The truth is: Not only are there not 205 easy ways to *really go green*, there isn't *one easy way to really go green*! If we can pull this off, it will be the biggest single peacetime project humankind will have ever undertaken. Rare is the political leader anywhere in the world who will talk straight about the true size of this challenge.

Aspirational, hortatory, and not-all-that-serious legal utterances will not suffice. Once again, Friedman puts it powerfully (*id.* at 188) (emphasis in original):

> For starters, let's remember what we're trying to do: *We're trying to change the climate system—to avoid the unmanageable and manage the unavoidable*! We are trying to affect how much the rain falls, how strong the winds blow, how fast the ice melts. In addition to all that, *we're trying to preserve and restore the world's rapidly depleting ecosystems*— our forests, rivers, savannahs, oceans, and the cornucopia of plant and animal species they contain. Finally, we are trying to break a collective addiction to gasoline that is having not only profound climate effects, but also geopolitical ones. It doesn't get any bigger than this. This is not something you do as a hobby, and the adjective "easy" should never—ever, ever—accompany this task.

Thus Thomas Friedman might test any "Faking-It" theories of local and state law by asking such questions as the resources put behind the scheme, the severity of the directional change, the boldness of the impositions, the comprehensiveness of the exercise, and the futurist visions that guide it.

C. The "Futility" Theorem

Another reason for anticipating a slow start by state and local governments on matters of climate change is not only that progress cannot be made (the "Impossibility" theorem) but that meaningful initiatives cannot be started (we will call this the "Futility" theorem). The principal legal driver of the "Futility Theorem" that discourages state and local law is some version of what is often called Defensive Preemption. The history of environmental law is littered with examples of useful law being displaced by a dumbed-down, wrung-out, and deflated version of "higher," albeit weaker, law. This game of preempting something with nothing races up the sovereignty food chain with strong local laws being preempted by weaker state laws that are displaced by weaker-yet national laws that are overcome by the weakest-of-all international laws.

A workable description of Defensive Preemption Theory appears in J.R. De Shazo & Jody Freeman, *Timing and Form of Federal Regulation: The Case of Climate Change*, 155 U. PA. L. REV. 1499, 1506 (2006–07) (footnotes omitted):

Yet what will industry demand from Congress? It will demand a federal standard that preempts inconsistent state regulation and eliminates regulatory uncertainty. Uniformity is not enough, however. Industry will also try to undercut the most aggressive state standards by seeking a lower federal ceiling. States thus establish the boundaries within which the federal negotiation over standards takes place—the more stringently states regulate at the outset, the more leverage they create for a compromise at the end. If the federal standard turns out to be weaker than the most aggressive state standard, and if preemption prevents any deviation, then industry achieves a double win.

There is already a healthy literature on the issue of preemption and related doctrines. See, for example, the appropriately titled article by Allison A. Davis and Craig Gannett, with assistance from S. Joshua Davidson and Mathew Gordon, all of Davis Wright Tremaine, LLP. The article is entitled *State and Regional Approaches to Climate Change: Precocious or Preempted?* (Rocky Mountain Mineral Law Foundation, 2008 Mineral Law Series No. 3 (2008)). *See, e.g.*, Cinnamon Carlarne, *Notes From a Climate Change Pressure-Cooker: Sub-Federal Attempts at Transformation Meet National Resistance in the USA*, 40 Conn. L. Rev. 1351 (2008); Cary Coglianese & Jocelyn D. Ambrosio, *Policymaking Under Pressure: The Perils of Incremental Responses to Climate Change*, 40 Conn. L. Rev. 1411 (2008); David A Dana, *Democratizing the Law of Federal Preemption*, 102 NW. U.L. Rev. 507 (2008); Daniel A. Farber, *Climate Change, Federalism, and the Constitution*, 50 Ariz. L. Rev. 879 (2008); Robert L. Glicksman & Richard E. Levy, *A Collective Action Perspective on Ceiling Preemption By Federal Environmental Regulation: The Case of Global Climate Change*, 102 Nw. U.L. Rev. 579 (2008); Joseph Allan MacDonald, *Why Climate Law Must Be Federal: The Clash Between Commerce Clause Jurisprudence and State Greenhouse Gas Trading Systems*, 40 Conn. L. Rev. 1431 (2008); Jonas Monast, *Integrating State, Regional, and Federal Greenhouse Gas Markets: Options and Tradeoffs*, 18 Duke Envtl. L. & Pol'y F. 329 (2008).

"Futility" is a wonderful reason for not trying. And it is a satisfactory excuse for defecting from any collective action endeavor. A decision giving voice to this view is *Okeson v. City of Seattle*, 159 Wash. 2d 436, 150 P.3d 556 (2007), which was a successful challenge to the City of Seattle's program to mitigate effects of Seattle City Light's greenhouse gas emissions to a "net zero" by paying public and private entities to reduce their emissions. By a sharply divided 5:4 vote the Washington Supreme Court held that Seattle City Light lacked authority to use ratepayer revenues to enter into offset contracts. In questioning from the bench during oral argument, Justice James M. Johnson heaped sarcasm on the utility's arguments that purchasing offsets was its most economic option. He reminisced about the City of Seattle's plan in the 1970s to increase its hydropower by raising the height of the Ross Dam:

> By the way, the factual background they were then claiming that they were facing the next ice-age, in the mid-70's, so I am not always so reliant on the factual background that you have here either.

See http://www.tvw.org/media/mediaplayer.cfm?evid=2006050048D&TYPE=V&CFID=29640&CFTOKEN =32579981&bhcp=1.

Justice Johnson joined in the concurrence written by Justice Richard Sanders. This gives full voice to the "impossibility" theorem for resisting state and local initiatives on global warming (159 Wash. 2d at 453, 454, 150 P.3d at 565):

> On this record Seattle City Light's program of paying others not to emit greenhouse gases has about as much effect on global warming as making a bonfire out of ratepayers' hard-earned dollars. Let us consider the following:

There are uncertainties about whether warming will really be bad (think longer growing seasons), but let's assume that cutting carbon dioxide emissions is a desirable goal.

The nations that signed the Kyoto Protocol on global warming agreed to cut their emissions in the future. If each of them made the sacrifices of full compliance (the betting is that few will even come close), and those measures worked as expected, the world would end up only a tenth of a degree cooler.

And if that big an effort gets no results, state and local government policies can only be empty gestures. Economic activity will shift away from them toward other areas or nations—remember that China and India are exempt from the agreement.

Quoting Robert Michaels Commentary, *Renewable Electricity "Creating" Jobs, Destroying Wealth*, Env't & Climate News, Dec. 2006, at 2. (ed.). Thus does "contrarian" policy climb into the chairs of appellate courts in the United States.

––––––––––

Notes

Examples of international law in recent times reaching (and influencing) U.S. domestic environmental and climate change law in a retrogressive fashion include—

1. *Nat'l Ass'n of Clean Air Agencies v. EPA*, 489 F.3d 1221 (D.C. Cir. June 1, 2007). This is a challenge to an EPA rule increasing the stringency of the NOx emission standards applicable to newly certified commercial aircraft gas turbine engines under Section 231 of the Clean Air Act. The state regulators say the rule "did not go far enough" and improperly strayed from a "technology-forcing" result. The 1944 Chicago Convention on International Civil Aviation puts the mild rules of the International Civil Aviation Organization (ICAO) in the prominent background. The standing of NACAA is established because weaker NOx regulations for aircraft make it "more difficult for state air pollution control agencies to establish SIPs." State agencies "have no choice but to impose greater restrictions on other sources of NOx." 489 F.3d at 1227. On the merits, NACAA challenged the final rule as allowing "codification of current practices rather than requiring a technology-forcing approach" and as imposing standards that "almost all aircraft already satisfy." But the court, like the EPA, could see no technology-forcing in this law. Section 231 did not oblige the agency to give subordinate status to cost, safety, and noise, *citing and following George E. Warren Corp. v. EPA*, 159 F.3d 616, 623–24 (D.C. Cir. 1998) (rejecting claim that "the maintenance or improvement of air quality is the sole focus" of the anti-dumping provisions of the CAA).

2. *Pacific Merchant Shipping Ass'n v. Cackette*, 2007 WL 2492681 (E.D. Cal. Aug. 30, 2007) (William B. Schubb, D. J.). CARB regulations establishing limitations for emissions of diesel PM, SO_x and NO_x from diesel-electric engines on ocean-going vessels are preempted by title II of the CAA. Any ship with a noncomplying diesel engine was forbidden from operating within 24 miles of a large portion of the California coast. *Id*. at *5: "the implied preemption [under subsection 209 (e)(2)] for non-road vehicles and engines is broader than the express preemption of road vehicles and engines [under Subsection 209 (a)—the latter applying only to new sources"], *discussing Engine Mfs. Ass'n ex rel*. Certain of its *Members v. EPA*, 88 F.3d 1075, 1087–93 (D. C. Cir. 1996). The court says these regulations are not "in-use requirements" and they directly affect international commerce. They are therefore preempted.

This ruling is a very green light for very dirty fuel, including the infamous Bunker Fuel No. 7.

3. *Defenders of Wildlife v. Gutierrez*, 484 F. Supp. 2d 44 (D.D.C. 2007) (Friedman, J.). This is an ESA / MMPA / Ports and Waterways Safety Act challenge to denial of a petition seeking emergency regulations to reduce the risk of ships striking the North Atlantic right whale. It is not capricious for NMFS to deny the petition in favor of a "more comprehensive strategy"; nor for the Coast Guard to plead inability to affect the traffic separation schemes (TSSs) that were under the broader purview of the Int'l Maritime Organization. There is no rush to help this whale in "peril" that has been "listed as an endangered species since 1970—longer than the ESA itself has been in effect." *Id.* at 47.

4. *See* Leticia M. Diaz & Barry Hart Dubner, *Environmental Damage and the Destruction of Life—Problems That Add a New Balancing Dimension to International Port Access vs. Efficient Trade Under International Law*, 10 Barry L. Rev. 1 (2008).

D. No-Regrets Policy

Small steps to fight hopeless odds are often justified as useful in and of themselves. Sips of water for the defenders of the Alamo might not have presaged eventual victory but they certainly were comforting to the embattled few.

This sentiment is explicit in Jeff Goodell, Big Coal: The Dirty Secret Behind America's Energy Future ch. 10, esp. 245 (Houghton Mifflin Co. 2006), discussing the *local* work in China of Dan Dudek, economist with the Environmental Defense Fund:

> Dudek isn't bothered by these numbers [showing that any particular strategy is a "hopelessly small solution to a very big problem."] He often talks about what he calls a "no regrets" strategy for dealing with global warming. That strategy entails finding solutions that can be implemented now to reduce greenhouse gas emissions, that don't require billions of dollars of investments, and, most of all, that have ancillary benefits that are worthwhile in and of themselves: poverty alleviation, ecosystem restoration, increased energy efficiency. These are all small steps and easy to write off as ineffectual given the enormity of global warming, but as the rise of China itself demonstrates, many people taking small steps can have a big impact. "I'm for anything that helps us think differently about global warming," he says. "A lot of people are fixated on cutting carbon dioxide emissions, which is fine, but it also narrows the conversation. Ultimately, what matters is what happens in the atmosphere, not what happens at any particular power plant."

E. The "Laboratory" Theorem

Mark Pagel, *The Limits of Democracy, in* What Are You Optimistic About? Today's Leading Thinkers on Why Things are Good and Getting Better 319, 320–21 (John Brockman ed., Harper Perennial 2007):

> Some nations, and especially some American states, are researching new, low-carbon-footprint technologies and voluntarily committing to expensive climate-change targets. In most cases, they are doing so without any democratic mandate. They realize that there may be larger and longer-term stakes to play for than the "right" to behave as one pleases or to have what one wants.

Disraeli, quoted in *id*. at 32:

> The world is wearied of statesmen whom democracy has degraded into politicians.

The simplest—and perhaps most convincing—account of the virtual explosion of state and local law on climate change is that the federal government has thwarted developments on the international scene, undermined its own science, warred against its special environmental laws, and fallen prey to the self-interested pleas of the merchants of backward technologies. Consider the biting comments of George Monbiot, in HEAT: HOW TO STOP THE PLANET FROM BURNING iv–v (South End Press 2007):

> Under the Bush administration, the science of climate change has been treated much as the Catholic Church, during Galileo's lifetime, handled the science of planetary motion.... Contempt for science often goes hand in hand with contempt for democracy.
>
>   ....

Shortcomings of the federal government certainly figure in the accounts of why state and local governments have taken action to combat climate change. But there are a host of other motivations stemming from desires to advance their citizens' economic and environmental interests. David Hodas, for one, identifies a range of state objectives justifying attention to climate change, including environmental goals, efficiency gains, helping in energy infrastructure replacement cycles, and escaping from the raging fluctuations of gasoline prices. *State Initiatives*, *in* GLOBAL CLIMATE CHANGE AND U.S. LAW ch. 10 (Michael B. Gerrard ed., ABA Section on Environment, Energy & Resources 2007).

Rumors of "green" depressions are greatly overrated. Consider:

———————

See Felicity Barringer, *Green Policies in California Generated Jobs, Study Finds*, THE NEW YORK TIMES online, Oct. 20, 2008.

A comprehensive summary of state actions was done by the Congressional Research Service. *See* JONATHAN L. RAMSEUR, CLIMATE CHANGE: ACTION BY STATES TO ADDRESS GREENHOUSE GAS EMISSIONS, Congressional Research Service, November 23, 2007, *available at* http://www.cnie.org/NLE/CRS/abstract.cfm?NLEid=1849- (visited Nov. 15, 2008). [hereinafter 2007 CRS STUDY ON STATE ACTIONS]. This study gives voice to "States as Policy Laboratories" (CRS-23) (footnote included):

> **States as Policy Laboratories.** A central argument in support of state climate change action is that states can serve as laboratories for policymaking. States can test different ideas and policies on a smaller scale, and help determine which climate change solutions are most effective. For example, there has been some debate regarding how a cap-and-trade program might work on a national level. Although the federal acid rain program, which involves sulfur dioxide emissions trading, is generally considered a success, emissions trading programs for other purposes have encountered problems during implementation.[99] State programs offer the opportunity to iron out logistical details that are crucial in a cap-and-trade system:

———————

99. For example, the Southern California's Regional Clean Air Incentives Market (RECLAIM), which was implemented in 1994 to reduce emissions of nitrogen oxides (NOx) and sulfur dioxide (SO_2), saw a 50-fold increase in NOx allowance prices during the 2000–2001 California energy crisis. The European Union's GHG trading system has also experienced drastic swings in allowance prices during its start-up years, making planning and decision-making difficult for participating entities. For additional information on the EU trading system, see CRS Report RL33581, *Climate Change: The European Union's Emissions Trading System (EU-ETS)*, by Larry Parker.

- How high to set the emissions cap.
- Which sources to regulate.
- How to allocate emissions allowances.
- When to allow offsets instead of actual reductions.
- Whether to include a safety valve and, if so, how high to set it.

State programs can inform federal policymakers in other ways. The political process by which states create climate change policy can be enlightening and perhaps adaptable on the federal level. For instance, by examining the development and passage of state legislation, federal policymakers may better understand the motivations of different stakeholders and learn how best to frame the issues.

....

II. Local Initiatives

Asking a local mayor in the U.S. to "solve" or "address" the "global warming problem" is like asking a small child to hold back the North Sea. Why have these mayors nonetheless given it a go?

A. Mayors' Climate Protection Agreement

http://www.mayors.org/75thAnnualMeeting/pressrelease_062207a.pdf (visited Nov. 15, 2008) (see list of 902 participating mayors as of 11/4/2008 at http://www.usmayors.org/climate protection/list.asp):

The U.S. Mayors' Climate Protection Agreement
(As endorsed by the 73rd Annual U.S. Conference of
Mayors meeting, Chicago, 2005)

A. We urge the federal government and state governments to enact policies and programs to meet or beat the target of reducing global warming pollution levels to 7 percent below 1990 levels by 2012, including efforts to: reduce the United States' dependence on fossil fuels and accelerate the development of clean, economical energy resources and fuel-efficient technologies such as conservation, methane recovery for energy generation, waste to energy, wind and solar energy, fuel cells, efficient motor vehicles, and biofuels;

B. We urge the U.S. Congress to pass bipartisan greenhouse gas reduction legislation that 1) includes clear timetables and emissions limits and 2) a flexible, market-based system of tradable allowances among emitting industries; and

C. We will strive to meet or exceed Kyoto Protocol targets for reducing global warming pollution by taking actions in our own operations and communities such as:
   1. Inventory global warming emissions in City operations and in the community, set reduction targets and create an action plan;
   2. Adopt and enforce land-use policies that reduce sprawl, preserve open space, and create compact, walkable urban communities;

3. Promote transportation options such as bicycle trails, commute trip reduction programs, incentives for car pooling and public transit;

4. Increase the use of clean, alternative energy by, for example, investing in "green tags", advocating for the development of renewable energy resources, recovering landfill methane for energy production, and supporting the use of waste to energy technology;

5. Make energy efficiency a priority through building code improvements, retrofitting city facilities with energy efficient lighting and urging employees to conserve energy and save money;

6. Purchase only Energy Star equipment and appliances for City use;

7. Practice and promote sustainable building practices using the U.S. Green Building Council's LEED program or a similar system;

8. Increase the average fuel efficiency of municipal fleet vehicles; reduce the number of vehicles; launch an employee education program including anti-idling messages; convert diesel vehicles to bio-diesel;

9. Evaluate opportunities to increase pump efficiency in water and wastewater systems; recover wastewater treatment methane for energy production;

10. Increase recycling rates in City operations and in the community;

11. Maintain healthy urban forests; promote tree planting to increase shading and to absorb CO2; and

12. Help educate the public, schools, other jurisdictions, professional associations, business and industry about reducing global warming pollution.

B. Mayors' Climate Performance Initiative

Kevin McCarty, *Bloomberg, Palmer Lead USA and World Mayors on Climate Protection*, U.S. Mayor Newspaper (May 21, 2007), *available at* http://www.usmayors.org/usmayornewspaper/documents/05_21_07/pg1_NYC_climate.asp (visited Nov. 5, 2008):

Mayors who stand before you here today represent one quarter of a billion people on the face of this planet. What has brought us together is the need to give leadership. We can't wait for all of our governments to make up their minds.

. . .

All that is required to tackle climate change is to use what we have already invented and devised. All that is required is political will. These mayors represent an expression of that political will.

Kristen H. Engel & Barak Y. Orbach, *Micro-Motives for State and Local Climate Change Initiatives*, 2 Harv. Law & Pol. Rev. 119, 122 (2008), *available at* http://ssrn.com/abstratct=1014749 (footnotes included):

In June 2005, the U.S. Conference of Mayors adopted the Mayors Climate Protection Agreement that urges cities to adopt measures designed to meet or exceed the target and timetable for reducing greenhouse gases established by the Kyoto Protocol—a reduction of 7 percent below 1990 levels by the year 2012.[8] As of Nov 5, 2008, the

---

8. U.S. Conference of Mayors, *The U.S. Mayors Climate Protection Agreement* (As endorsed by the 73d Annual U.S. Conference of Mayors meeting, Chicago, 2005), *available at* http://www.usmayors.org/climate protection/documents/mcpagreement.pdf (last visited Nov. 5, 2008).

mayors of over 902 cities had joined the Agreement.[9] Participating cities are instituting programs to reduce greenhouse gas emissions by installing energy-efficient lighting; developing and enforcing building codes incorporating energy-efficient designs; investing in mass transit, carpooling and bicycle commuting programs; and switching over to solid waste management programs that use less energy and recover landfill gases.[10] Actions at the city level have generated political capital for several mayors. Two prominent examples are Greg Nickels of Seattle and Michael Bloomberg of New York City. Nickels spearheaded the U.S. Conference of Mayors [Climate Protection Agreement].

Figure 1. For an interactive map of member cities, see http://www.usmayors.org/climate protection/map.asp.

Under the Agreement, participating cities commit to take the following three actions:

- Strive to meet or beat the Kyoto Protocol targets in their own communities, through actions ranging from anti-sprawl land-use policies to urban forest restoration projects to public information campaigns;
- Urge their state governments, and the federal government, to enact policies and programs to meet or beat the greenhouse gas emission reduction target suggested for the United States in the Kyoto Protocol—7% reduction from 1990 levels by 2012; and
- Urge the U.S. Congress to pass the bipartisan greenhouse gas reduction legislation, which would establish a national emission trading system.

Hari M. Osofsky and Janet Koven Levit, *The Scale of Networks? Local Climate Change Coalitions*, 8 Chicago J. Intl Law, 409, 410 (2008) *available at* http://ssrn.com/abstract=1018310, observe (footnotes included):

Urban leadership on climate change in the United States, however, began well before the federal government withdrew from the Kyoto Protocol. Many US cities and counties have played a crucial role in international coalitions of localities attempting to make progress on emissions. Portland, Oregon, for example, has long been at the forefront of these issues, including being the first US city to develop a carbon reduction plan back in 1993.[7] Portland's 2001 Local Action Plan on Global Warming aimed to reduce its carbon emissions to 10 percent below its 1990 levels by 2010.[8]

And, much of the work to be done may well involve the local level. Transportation and zoning constitute a large portion of GHG emissions in many states. These sources will need to be

---

9. For an up-to-date list of the mayors who have signed the Agreement, see U. S. Conference of Mayors, Mayors Climate Protection Center, Participating Mayors, http://www.usmayors.org/climateprotection/list.asp. (last visited Nov. 5, 2008).

10. *See generally* Harriet Bulkeley & Michele M. Betsill, Cities and Climate Change (2003) (describing Denver and Milwaukee's climate protection initiatives); Michele M. Betsill, *Mitigating Climate Change in U.S. Cities: Opportunities and Obstacles,* 6 Loc. Evn't 393, 397–98, 404 (2001), *available at* http://www.colostate.edu/Depts/PoliSci/fac/mb/Local%20Environment.pdf (examining municipal action under the Cities for Climate Protection Initiative).

7. *See* Joan Laatz, *City Council Hears Plan to Cut Air Pollution*, Oregonian C6 (Mar 4, 1993); ICLEI— Local Governments for Sustainability, *CCP Participants, available at* http://www.iclei.org/index.php?id=809 (last visited Nov 17, 2007); Timothy Grewe, Susan Anderson, and Laurel Butman, *Portland, Oregon: A Case Study in Sustainability*, 18 Govt. Fin. Rev. 8 (Feb 2002).

8. *See* City of Portland and Multnomah County, *Local Action Plan on Global Warming* 1 (April 2001), *available at* http://www.portlandonline.com/shared/cfm/image.cfm?id=25050 (last visited Nov 17, 2007); Local Action Plan on Global Warming: Binding City Policy BCP-ENN-5.01, Portland City Council Res 35995 (Apr 25, 2001), *available at* http://www.portlandonline.com/Auditor/index.cfm?a=cfaej&c=cjbfb (last visited Nov 17, 2007).

addressed at a state and local level. Similarly new building codes will be adopted and enforced at the local level.

As explained by John C. Dernbach & Seema M. Kakade, *Climate Change Law: An Introduction*, 29 ENERGY L.J. 1, 16–17 (2008), *available at* http://ssrn.com/abstract=1033467 (footnotes omitted):

> *Energy efficiency provisions in building codes.* Energy efficiency standards for buildings are primarily a matter of state law, though prompted to some degree by federal legislation. The Energy Policy Act of 1992 required each state to review the energy efficiency provisions in its residential building codes and to determine within two years whether it should adopt the 1992 Model Energy Code published by the Council of American Building Officials. The Act contains a similar requirement for the review of energy efficiency standards in commercial building codes....
>
> ....
>
> These codes do not, however, apply to existing residential and commercial buildings. As a consequence, broadly speaking, newer buildings tend to be more energy efficient than older buildings, and often substantially more efficient. Sixty percent of residences are not well insulated, for example, and 70% or more of commercial buildings lack roof or wall insulation. Retrofitting and upgrading existing structures and their heating, ventilation, and air conditioning systems offers a considerable opportunity to improve energy efficiency. This is especially true because existing residential and commercial buildings will be around for a long time.

During April and May 2007 the U.S. Conference of Mayors surveyed the mayors of the 430 cities which at that time had signed The U.S. Conference of Mayors Climate Protection Agreement to identify the kinds of climate protection activities that were underway or under consideration in their cities. Responses, representing over 25 million people, were received from 134 cities in 36 states; populations of these cities ranged in size from Los Angeles, the largest at 3,694,820, to Milan, Minn., the smallest at 326. Note that these projects, in Goodell's words, all "have ancillary benefits that are worthwhile in and of themselves."

Here is a press release containing key findings, *available at* http://www.mayors.org/75th AnnualMeeting/pressrelease_062207a.pdf (last visited Nov. 5, 2008):

For Immediate Release Contact: Lina Garcia/Mayors Climate Protection Center
(Embargoed until 6:00 am EST, 202.341.6113/lgarcia@usmayors.org
Friday, June 22, 2007)

Mayors Proactive in Curbing Greenhouse Emissions
*New Survey Shows Four out of Five Cities Now Use Renewable
Energy or Expect to By Next Year, Among Key Findings*

Los Angeles, CA—According to a new survey released by the Mayors Climate Protection Center during The U.S. Conference of Mayors' 75th anniversary meeting, mayors are acting on many fronts to enhance climate protection, without significant support from their state and federal partners.

The survey indicates that cities throughout the country, regardless of size, have initiated a multitude of actions aimed at reducing carbon emissions. Surveying the 400 mayors who at that time had signed The U.S. Conference of Mayors Climate Protection Agreement, 134 of them provided data for this first-ever assessment of city climate protection efforts. Among the survey's key findings are:

- *More than four out of five of the survey cities now use renewable energy,* or are considering beginning by next year.
- *All but four of the survey cities (97 percent) are using more energy-efficient lighting technologies in public buildings, streetlights, parks, traffic signals,* and other applications, or expect to by next year.
- *Seventy-two percent of the responding mayors stated that their city fleets now run on alternative fuels* and/or use hybrid-electric technology.
- *Nearly nine in ten of the cities require, or anticipate requiring in the next year, that new city government buildings be more energy efficient* and environmentally sustainable.
- *More than three out of four of the cities are undertaking efforts to encourage the private sector to construct buildings that are energy efficient* and use sustainable building techniques.

"This survey clearly shows that mayors are acting decisively to curb global warming, helping fill the void left by federal inaction," said Conference President Trenton Mayor Douglas H. Palmer. "Mayors are leading the way by implementing successful strategies to change human behavior and help protect the planet."

Conference Executive Director Tom Cochran added: "This survey demonstrates the high level of innovation and creativity that U.S. mayors are employing to create more sustainable communities. This is not a new phenomenon, since mayors are often at the forefront of positive change."

Additional key findings:

- **More than nine out of ten cities consider efforts to reduce greenhouse gas emissions to be part of their broader efforts to address public health concerns,** such as improving air quality or encouraging active living.
- *In nearly three in four of the cities, mayors have reached out to other mayors,* elected county officials, or other leaders in the region to encourage them to sign on to the U.S. Conference of Mayors Climate Protection Agreement and/or take action on climate protection.
- **If the Energy and Environmental Block Grant now pending in Congress is enacted, half of the cities will use the funds provided through it to improve community energy efficiency.** Instituting and/or encouraging green building practices leads the list of specific activities for which resources are currently not available that cities would undertake if block grant funds became available.

As of June 21, 540 mayors have signed The U.S. Conference of Mayors Climate Protection Agreement, committing to reduce carbon emissions in cities below 1990 levels, in line with the Kyoto protocol and due to an absence of federal leadership.

For the past few months, mayors have been working closely with Congressional leaders to enact new legislation to support local government efforts to reduce greenhouse gases. Called the Energy and Environment Block Grant program, similar to the popular HUD Community Development Block Grant (CDBG) program, this initiative would supply formula-based grants to cities, counties, and states to reduce energy dependence and promote greater energy efficiency. The United States Senate is currently debating its energy legislation which includes a block grant program; a key House energy panel will be considering this proposal next week during action on its energy package.

To view the full survey results released by the Mayors Climate Protection Center, please visit: www.usmayors.org.

III. State Initiatives

Carol M. Rose, *Federalism and Climate Change: The Role of the States in a Future Federal Regime—An Introduction*, 50 Ariz. L. Rev. 673, 675 (2008) (introducing a symposium on the topic):

> The Symposium authors are remarkably sanguine about the possibilities for [subnational actors] to contribute relevant and useful knowledge.

Q. How many state laws use the terms "Global Warming" or "Climate Change" in the title of an enactment?

A. Sixteen, representing nine states—California, Connecticut, Iowa, Massachusetts, New Jersey, New York, Oregon, Rhode Island and Washington.

> — Westlaw Search of State Statutes—Unannotated Database, for William H. Rodgers, Jr., by Melia Cossette, Intern Reference Librarian, Marian Gould Gallagher Law Library, University of Washington, School of Law, Oct. 12, 2008.

> Students will want to reflect upon why states have acted, what they have done, and how they did it.

A. Why the States?

David Hodas, *State Initiatives*, *in* Global Climate Change and U.S. Law 343 (Michael Gerrard, ed., ABA Section on Environment, Energy, and Resources 2007):

> Just as nature "abhors a vacuum," so too, in human society, political actors abhor a power vacuum. In nature, air rushes in to fill the space; in society, political entities inevitably move to fill a power void. In the absence of federal leadership on global warming, state and local governments have moved into this void. The scope of state legal and policy initiatives over the past decade has been truly remarkable; it is sufficiently significant to warrant serious attention by any lawyer working in the field.

Governor Gray Davis, *Governor Davis Signs Environmental Legislation to Protect California's Air and Water*, Sept. 9, 2002, press release *available at* http://www.climateregistry.org/resources/docs/press-releases/sb812_gov_press_release_090802.pdf (last visited Nov. 5, 2008), upon signing a series of environmental bills including AB 1493 (the Pavely Bill):

> "Nothing is more fundamental than protecting the air we breathe and the water we drink," Governor Davis said. "These bills will protect our environment and our quality of life."

California Governor Arnold Schwarzenegger, *Gov. Schwarzenegger Signs Bills to Take Additional Steps to Reduce State's Carbon Emissions* (Sept. 25, 2006), *available at* http://gov.ca.gov/press-release/4074/ (visited Nov. 15, 2008), in advance of signing AB 32, California's landmark Global Warming Solutions Act:

> We simply must do everything we can in our power to slow down global warming before it is too late. The science is clear. The global warming debate is over.

California Governor Arnold Schwarzenegger, *Leading the Fight Against Global Warming*, Transcript of Governor Schwarzenegger's June 11, 2005 Weekly Radio Address, *available at* http://gov.ca.gov/radio-address/3404/ (visited Nov. 15, 2008):

> As of today, California is going to be the leader in the fight against global warming. We know the science, we see the threat, and we know the time for action is now.

California Governor Arnold Schwarzenegger, *Gov. Schwarzenegger, British Prime Minister Tony Blair Sign Historic Agreement to Collaborate on Climate Change, Clean Energy* (July 31, 2006), *available at http://gov.ca.gov/index.php/press-release/2770/* (visited Nov. 15. 2008):

> "California will not wait for our federal government to take strong action on global warming," said Gov. Schwarzenegger after an hour-long roundtable focused on clean energy and climate issues with the Prime Minister and more than a dozen CEOs. "Today, we are taking an unprecedented step by signing an agreement between California and the United Kingdom. International partnerships are needed in the fight against global warming and California has a responsibility and a profound role to play to protect not only our environment, but to be a world leader on this issue as well."

Thomas D. Peterson, Robert B. McKinstry, Jr., & John C. Dernbach, *Developing a Comprehensive Approach to Climate Change Policy in the United States That Fully Integrates Levels of Government and Economic Sectors*, 26 Va. Envtl. L.J. 226, 237–240 (2008) (footnotes omitted):

> In the midst of this stalemate state governments are attempting to help close the United States' emissions reduction gap through an array of climate change mitigation actions. Since 2000, twenty-six states have developed and implemented a variety of comprehensive climate action plans covering all emitting sources and sectors. These states recently established, or will establish, statewide emissions reduction targets.
>
> ....
>
> The magnitude of existing state actions that reduce GHGs is underappreciated. In combination, states undertake or plan well over 250 different actions across all sectors to reduce GHG emissions.
>
> ....
>
> State experience identifies the following six key action areas that are critical to achieving national GHG emissions reductions targets:
> * Energy efficiency and conservation,
> * Clean and renewable energy,
> * Transportation and land use efficiency,
> * Agriculture and forestry conservation,
> * Waste management and recycling,
> * Industrial process improvements.

See, e.g., Cinnamon Carlarne, *Notes from a Climate Change Pressure-Cooker: Sub-Federal Attempts at Transformation Meet National Resistance in the USA*, 40 Conn. L. Rev. 1351 (2007–2008) (chronicling a series of recent "sub-federal" legal decisions and policy developments responding to global climate change as important steps on the path to "inevitable" federal regulation).

Compare Kirsten H. Engel & Scott R. Saleska, *Subglobal Regulation of the Global Commons: The Case of Climate Change*, 32 Ecology L.Q. 183, 232 (2005), who challenge the conventional wisdom that unilateral regulation by subglobal governments is irrational:

> Our overall goal in this Article has been to explore policy options for addressing a global commons environmental problem in the absence of a comprehensive binding international agreement. More narrowly, using climate change as the quintessential global commons problem, we have (1) questioned the prevailing wisdom that unilateral action by individual countries to restrain despoliation of the global commons is presumptively irrational, and have shown that despite the existence of free-riding by nonregulating commons-users and the "leakage" of benefits, unilateral regulation can still result in a net-benefit to the subglobal regulator; and (2) probed the reasons for the failure of subglobal actors to implement unilateral action more aggressively to at least reduce green-

house gases to levels considered optimal under noncooperative equilibrium models. We have suggested that unilateral subglobal regulation is a viable, if not optimal, approach to global commons environmental problems.

See further David E. Adelman & Kirsten H. Engel, *Adaptive Federalism: The Case Against Reallocating Environmental Regulatory Authority*, 92 MINN. L. REV. 1796, 1847–48 (2007–2008) (footnotes omitted):

> Global climate change policy illustrates the power of the bottom up dynamics that are characteristic of adaptive systems. Although the "wrong" jurisdictions from a static economic perspective, state and local initiatives can play an instrumental role in generating innovative policies and propelling change at higher levels of government. First, state actions bring much-needed public and media attention to climate change and its local effects. Second, state and local governments prompt, albeit on a small scale, critical technological, social, and economic changes essential to mitigating climate change. Third, state and local governments, as the old saying goes, function as "laboratories of democracy" for parallel testing of initiatives in a range of contexts that then can serve as models for other jurisdictions. Finally, action at the state and local level can feed back to the national level, as the threat of fifty distinct state laws regulating a single industry has, as in the past, the potential to prompt congressional action.

B. What Have the States Done?

1. Introduction

For an excellent introduction for teachers, see John C. Dernbach & Seema Kakade, *Climate Change Law: An Introduction*, 29 ENERGY L.J. 1 (2008):

> The law of climate change is being constructed at the intersection of several areas of law, including environmental law, energy law, business law, and international law. Any effort to address climate change also raises issues about the proper role of state, local, and federal governments, as well as their relationship to one another. This article is intended to serve as an introduction to this complex and rapidly changing subject.

The following article puts state initiatives in context and gives a brief outline to the content of this collective law-making.

Robert B. McKinstry, Jr., John C. Dernbach & Thomas D. Peterson, *Federal Climate Change Legislation as if the States Matter*, 22 NAT. RES. & ENVIRON. No. 3, pp. 3–4 (Winter 2008):

> [As a result of the explosion of environmental laws in the early 1970s], state environmental protection and natural resource agencies have become larger, better funded, more professionally staffed, and more effective than they were in 1970. For climate change, by contrast, the federal government has delayed taking action far beyond the time in which it acted [on environmental matters.] State and regional action greatly exceed in both scope and number those seen on other environmental issues prior to major federal legislation.
>
> The federal government's failure to take significant action has not been due to any desire to allow states to pursue independent action without federal interference. But the states have responded to climate change because they believe their shorelines, water resources, key industries, and people are at risk....

....

Based on these practical and legal considerations, one would think that the climate change bills introduced in Congress in 2007 would assign an important role to the states. One would be wrong. Six comprehensive climate change bills are now pending in Congress, and all are focused predominantly on the role of the federal government....

....

What the comprehensive climate change bills do not do, and what amended or future bills need to do, is enable or encourage states to play a substantial and constructive role in the newly developed federal regime. To be sure, the bills do envision a state role, but it is a limited one. Many explicitly or implicitly allow more stringent programs....

....

State experience has produced significant data and experience that can inform development of a more effective federal program. The majority of states have now implemented comprehensive planning processes involving stakeholders from all sectors of the economy to identify a portfolio of measures and policies for achieving significant emissions reductions.

These processes have been initiated by both executive order and legislation, and they frequently establish reduction goals. The planning processes begin with a GHG emissions inventory that calculates current GHG emissions, projects future emissions under a business-as-usual (BAU) scenario, and determines the net emissions reductions from BAU that will be required to achieve the necessary reductions. A portfolio of policy actions is then selected from a menu of more than 250 measures.... These measures cover a wide range, including (1) energy efficiency and conservation, (2) clean and renewable energy, (3) transportation and land use efficiency, (4) agriculture and forestry conservation, (5) waste management and recycling, (6) industrial process improvements, and (7) cross cutting issues. Each state typically selects a portfolio of forty or more measures tailored to the needs of the state and calculated to achieve the emissions reduction goals. These measures are based on an equally wide variety of legal tools, including codes and standards, incentives, market mechanisms, such as taxes and cap and trade, monitoring, education, and technical assistance, voluntary agreements, and demonstration projects. For an overview of state activities as well as maps depicting state use of specific legal and policy tools, see Pew Center on Global Climate Change, What's Being Done ... in the States, www.pewclimate.org/what_s_being_done/in_the_states./

———————

Pew Center on Global Climate Change, Learning from State Action on Climate Change, May 2008 Update, *available at* http://www.pewclimate.org/docUploads/States%20 Brief%20(May%202008).pdf (last visited Nov. 15, 2008) (illustrations adapted to black and white from color in the original):

Learning from State Action on Climate Change

May 2008 Update

While U.S. federal policy on climate change has not been forthcoming, states have taken the lead on developing climate policies and initiatives. States are setting emission reduction targets, mandating investment in renewables and energy efficiency, developing plans to mitigate climate change, and designing greenhouse gas cap and trade programs. State governments cite a variety of reasons for action, including promoting economic development, reducing vulnerability to fluctuating energy prices, and preventing damages to the states' resources from climate change.

In the absence of federal leadership to reduce greenhouse gas (GHG) emissions, many U.S. states and regions have begun taking actions to address the issue of climate change. States, for a variety of motives, have taken a broad range of actions that reduce greenhouse gases. While confronting the challenge of climate change will require a national and international regime, the states and regions have a valuable role to play.

States often function as "policy laboratories," developing initiatives that serve as models for federal action. This has been especially true with environmental regulation—most federal environmental laws have been based on state models. In addition, state actions can have a significant impact on emissions, because many individual states emit high levels of greenhouse gases. Texas, for example, emits more than France, while California's emissions exceed those of Brazil. State actions are also important because states have primary jurisdiction over many areas—such as electric generation, agriculture, and land use—that are critical to addressing climate change.

It is important to understand that states have limited resources to devote to the climate issue, and their strict budget requirements can put long-term climate policies in jeopardy. States also lack certain powers that would be crucial to a comprehensive climate change policy, such as the authority to enter into international agreements. Finally, when states take individual approaches to an issue, a "patchwork quilt" of policies can result across the nation. This patchwork of policies may be inefficient for complying businesses and may result in some states duplicating the work done in other states. While some states are delivering real reductions of GHG emissions, only in a few cases are the reductions commensurate with what will be needed on a global scale.

Ultimately, climate change is a global problem that will demand global action, including national action in the United States. State and regional action cannot substitute for a coordinated national response, but it can help provide the foundation for that response.

Motivation for Action

States that enact climate change policy almost always do so with long-term economic well being in mind. Many states are concerned with the toll climate change is projected to take on their economies, many of which are closely tied to their natural resources. Coastal states consider the impact of rising sea levels, agricultural states worry about lost productivity, and the dry Western states are alarmed by the prospect of worsening droughts. Many states, however, are looking at policies that address climate change as economic opportunities: to produce and sell alternative fuels, to become renewable energy exporters, to attract high-tech business, or to sell carbon emission reduction credits. Some states will be better able to take advantage of these opportunities than others, and many are concerned about the economic impacts of climate policy.

But economic development is just one motivator. In fact, multiple drivers lead to state policies that address climate change. Efforts to improve air quality, lessen traffic congestion, secure energy supply and reliability, or even to reduce odors from livestock feedlots often indirectly result in GHG reductions. Likewise policies designed explicitly to reduce GHG emissions often bring about benefits in these other areas.

In part because reducing GHG emissions can deliver multiple benefits, it has often been possible to build broad coalitions around GHG reduction policies. Climate change has, in fact, often been a bipartisan issue in the states, with Democratic, Republican, and Independent governors signing climate change legislation. Even when governorships have changed hands, policies have remained in place. Policymakers at the national level may be able to learn from the states how to find common ground on this issue.

Regional Initiatives

Regional programs can be more efficient than programs at the individual state level, as they encompass a broader geographic area, eliminate duplication of work, and create more uniform regulatory environments. Regional initiatives across the U.S. are addressing climate change and clean energy (*see* Figure 2). As of mid-2008, a total of 23 states are participating in the design of three separate regional cap-and-trade systems to reduce greenhouse gas emissions.

On November 15, 2007, six states and one Canadian Province established the Midwestern Regional Greenhouse Gas Reduction Accord. Under the Accord, members agree to establish regional greenhouse gas reduction targets, including a long-term target of 60 to 80 percent below current emissions levels, and develop a multi-sector cap-and-trade system to help meet the targets. Participants will also establish a greenhouse gas emissions reductions tracking system and implement other policies, such as low-carbon fuel standards, to aid in reducing emissions. The Governors of Illinois, Iowa, Kansas, Michigan, Minnesota, and Wisconsin, as well as the Premier of the Canadian Province of Manitoba, signed the Accord as full participants; the Governors of Indiana, Ohio, and South Dakota joined the agreement as observers. The Accord represents the first Midwestern regional agreement among U.S. states to collectively reduce greenhouse gas emissions, and will be fully implemented within 30 months.

In February 2007, Governors Janet Napolitano of Arizona, Arnold Schwarzenegger of California, Bill Richardson of New Mexico, Ted Kulongoski of Oregon, and Christine Gregoire of Washington signed an agreement establishing the Western Climate Initiative, a joint effort to reduce greenhouse gas emissions and address climate change. In the spring of 2007, Utah and the Canadian Provinces of British Columbia and Manitoba joined the agreement. In November, 2007, Montana joined, and the Canadian province of Quebec joined in mid-2008. Under the agreement, the WCI states and provinces jointly set a regional emissions target of a 15 percent reduction below 2005 levels by 2020, and by August 2008 the members will design a market-based system to aid in meeting the target. The states will also set up an emissions registry and tracking system. The initiative builds on work already undertaken individually by the participating states, each of which has already set its own emissions reductions goals, as well as two existing regional agreements (*see* below): the Southwest Climate Change Initiative of 2006, which includes Arizona and New Mexico, and the West Coast Governors' Global Warming Initiative of 2003, which includes California, Oregon, and Washington.

Ten Northeastern and Mid-Atlantic states have agreed to the Regional Greenhouse Gas Initiative (RGGI), the first cap-and-trade system in the nation to cover carbon dioxide (CO_2) emissions from regional power plants. RGGI sets a cap on emissions of carbon dioxide from power plants, and allows sources to trade emissions allowances. The program will begin by capping emissions at current levels in 2009, and then reducing emissions 10 percent by 2019. In December 2005, the governors of seven of the states signed a Memorandum of Understanding agreeing to adopt the program. Maryland joined RGGI in mid-2007, and Massachusetts and Rhode Island joined in January 2007. To facilitate compliance with reduction targets, RGGI will provide flexibility mechanisms that include credits for emissions reductions achieved outside of the electricity sector. The successful implementation of RGGI is an interesting model for federal policy makers. It will also set the stage for other states to join or form their own regional cap and trade systems and may encourage the program to expand to other greenhouse gases and other sectors.

Regional Initiatives

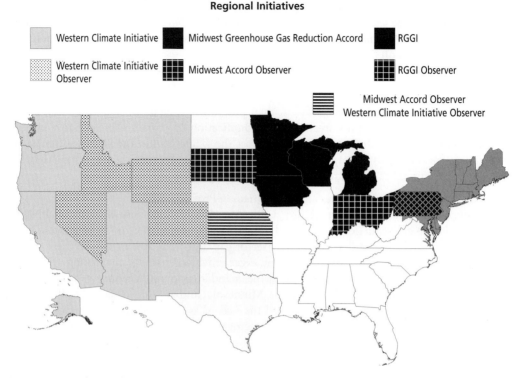

Figure 2. Regional Initiatives.

The Western Governors' Association (WGA) Clean and Diversified Energy Initiative, including 18 western states, investigated strategies to increase efficiency and renewable energy sources in their electricity systems. To meet its goals, the Initiative's advisory committee (CDEAC) appointed eight technical task forces to develop recommendations based on reviews of specific clean energy and efficiency options. In mid-2006, the CDEAC made recommendations to the Western Governors' Association that include strategies to increase energy efficiency, expand the use of renewable sources in the region, and incentivize carbon capture and sequestration technologies. Additionally, the WGA and the California Energy Commission are creating the Western Renewable Energy Generation Information System (WREGIS). WREGIS is a voluntary system for renewable energy credits that tracks renewable energy credits (RECs) across 11 western states in order to facilitate trading to meet renewable energy portfolio standards.

In 2001 six New England states committed to the New England Governors and Eastern Canadian Premiers (NEG-ECP) climate action plan, including short- and long-term GHG emission reduction goals. Powering the Plains, launched in 2002, is a regional effort involving participants from the Dakotas, Minnesota, Iowa, Wisconsin and the Canadian Province of Manitoba. This initiative aims to develop strategies, policies, and demonstration projects for alternative energy sources and technology and climate-friendly agricultural development.

On May 8, 2007, more than 30 states signed on as charter members of The Climate Registry, a collaboration aimed at developing a common system for entities to report greenhouse gas emissions. As of May 2008, the Registry has 39 members. The Registry will serve as a tool to measure, track, verify and publicly report greenhouse gas emissions consistently and transparently between states. Voluntary, market-based and regulatory greenhouse gas emissions reporting programs are all supported under the Registry. In addition to the states shown in the map below, the Campo Kumeyayy Nation and the Canadian provinces of British Columbia and Manitoba have also joined the Registry. This collaboration is the largest national effort to date to track greenhouse gas emissions. (See Figure 3.)

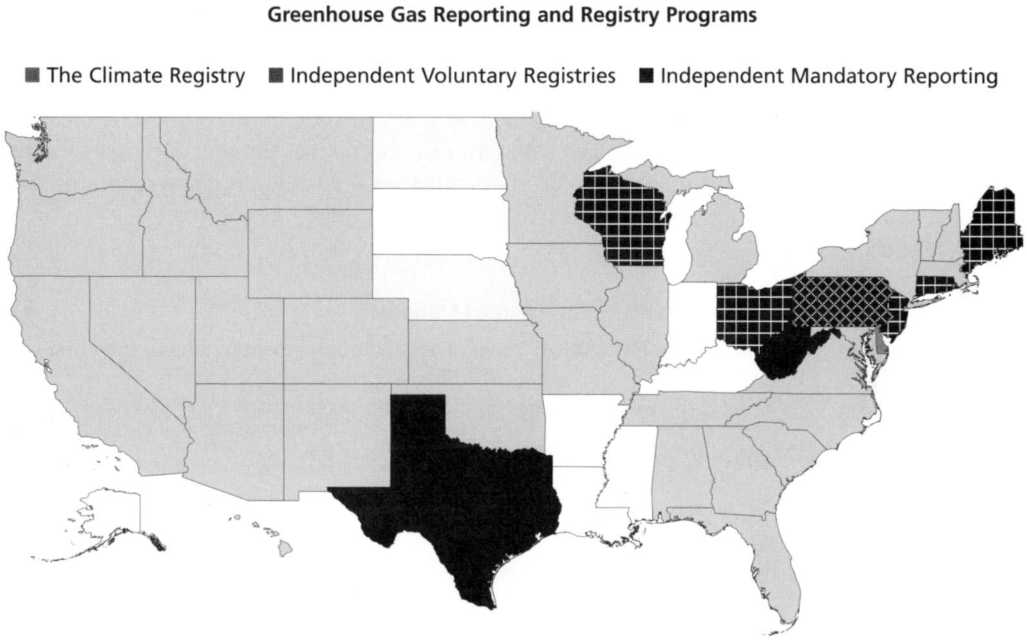

Greenhouse Gas Reporting and Registry Programs

■ The Climate Registry   ■ Independent Voluntary Registries   ■ Independent Mandatory Reporting

Figure 3. GHG Reporting and Registry Programs.

Many of the regional initiatives in the U.S. center around cap and trade systems to reduce greenhouse gas emissions. On October 29, 2007, a number of governments from around the world who have or are in the process of designing cap and trade systems announced the formation of the International Carbon Action Partnership (ICAP). The Partnership will provide a forum for members to share experiences, research, and best practices on the design of trading schemes. This will help the different trading systems develop in a compatible manner to facilitate the transition to a potential global carbon market in the future. The 10 U.S. state members are Arizona, California, Maine, Maryland, Massachusetts, New Jersey, New Mexico, New York, Oregon, and Washington. The other members of ICAP are nine European Union countries, the European Commission, two Canadian provinces, New Zealand and Norway.

Low-Carbon Electricity Policies

The generation of electricity accounts for approximately 38 percent of all carbon dioxide emissions in the United States. States have considerable authority over the production of electricity within their borders, and many options are available to them to promote low-carbon energy production.

Twenty-seven states and the District of Columbia have mandated that electric utilities generate a specified amount of electricity from renewable sources (*see* Figure 4). Most of these requirements take the form of "renewable portfolio standards," or RPSs, which require a certain percentage or amount of a utility's power plant capacity or generation to come from renewable sources by a given date. The standards range from modest to ambitious, and definitions of renewable energy vary. While the use of renewable energy does deliver significant GHG reductions, climate change is only one of several motivations behind these standards. Other advantages include job creation potential, energy security, and improved air quality. Most recently, Ohio became the 27th state to adopt a renewable electricity standard, mandating that by 2025, at least 25 percent of all electricity sold in the state come from alternative energy resources. At least half of the standard, or 12.5 percent of electricity sold, must be generated by renewable sources such as wind, solar (which must account for at least 0.5 percent of electricity use by 2025), hydropower, geothermal, or biomass. At least half of this renewable energy must be generated in-state. In addition to renewables, the additional 12.5 percent of the overall 25 percent standard can also be met through alternative energy resources like third-generation nuclear power plants, fuel cells, energy-efficiency programs, and clean coal technology that can control or prevent carbon dioxide emissions.

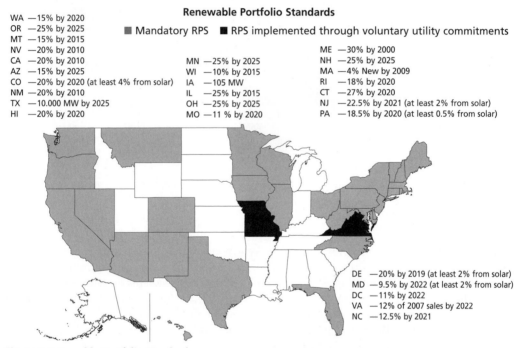

Renewable Portfolio Standards

WA —15% by 2020
OR —25% by 2025
MT —15% by 2015
NV —20% by 2010
CA —20% by 2010
AZ —15% by 2025
CO —20% by 2020 (at least 4% from solar)
NM —20% by 2010
TX —10.000 MW by 2025
HI —20% by 2020

■ Mandatory RPS   ■ RPS implemented through voluntary utility commitments

MN —25% by 2025
WI —10% by 2015
IA —105 MW
IL —25% by 2015
OH —25% by 2025
MO —11 % by 2020

ME —30% by 2000
NH —25% by 2025
MA —4% New by 2009
RI —18% by 2020
CT —27% by 2020
NJ —22.5% by 2021 (at least 2% from solar)
PA —18.5% by 2020 (at least 0.5% from solar)

DE —20% by 2019 (at least 2% from solar)
MD —9.5% by 2022 (at least 2% from solar)
DC —11% by 2022
VA —12% of 2007 sales by 2022
NC —12.5% by 2021

Figure 4. Renewable Portfolio Standards.

Almost half of all states have funds, often called "public benefit funds," dedicated to supporting energy efficiency and renewable energy projects (*see* Figure 5). The funds are collected either through a small charge on the bill of every electric customer or through specified contributions from utilities. The charge ensures that money is available to fund these projects. Publicly managed clean energy funds from eighteen of these states have formed the Clean Energy States Alliance to coordinate public benefit fund investments in renewable energy.

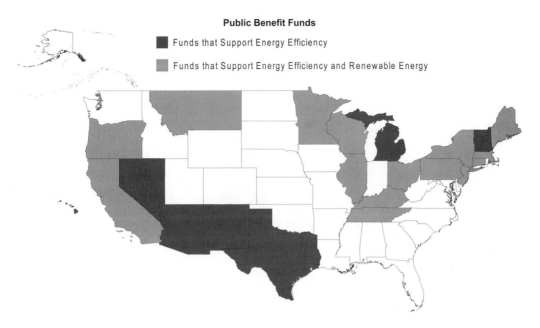

Figure 5. Public Benefit Funds.

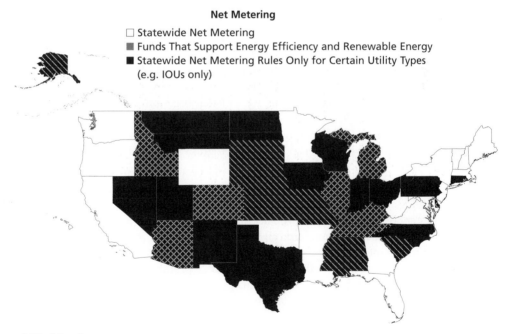

Figure 6. Net Metering.

Forty-two states have at least one utility that permits customers to sell electricity back to the grid, referred to as net metering. Twenty of these states offer net metering state-wide (*see* Figure 6). Forty-four states have utilities which offer green pricing, allowing customers the option of paying a premium on their electric bills to have a portion of their power provided from designated renewable sources. Six of these states—Colorado, Washington, New Mexico, Montana, Minnesota, and Iowa—have made green pricing options mandatory for electricity generators (*see* Figure 7).

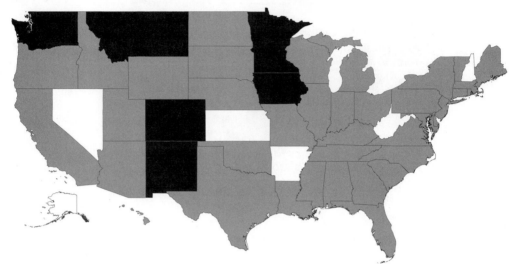

States with Green Pricing Programs

■ Green Pricing Programs   ■ Mandatory Green Pricing Programs

Figure 7. Green Pricing.

Both Washington and Oregon require that new power plants offset a certain portion of their anticipated CO_2 emissions, by either undertaking emission reduction or mitigation projects themselves, or by paying a specified fee to a designated organization that will then select and fund offset projects. Massachusetts and New Hampshire have gone even further by requiring CO_2 emissions reductions from existing power plants. The California Public Utilities Commission is developing a greenhouse gas cap and trade program for the electric sector.

Some states also require that new power plants meet a CO_2 performance standard. To date, California, Oregon, Washington, and Montana have enacted emissions performance standards. Washington and Montana have most recently established new standards in May 2007. Washington's SB 6001 establishes a GHG performance standard for all new, long-term baseload electric power generation. Under the standard, all baseload generation for which utilities enter into long-term contracts must meet a greenhouse gas emissions standard of 1,100 pounds per megawatt-hour beginning in July 2008. Montana's HB 25 prohibits the state Public Utility Commission from approving electric generating units primarily fueled by coal unless a minimum of 50 percent of the CO_2 produced by the facility is captured and sequestered.

In October 2007, Secretary of the Kansas Department of Health and Environment Roderick Bremby rejected an air permit for a proposed coal-fired power plant based on the threat to public health and the environment of carbon dioxide emissions. In the past, air permits have been denied over emissions such as sulfur dioxide, nitrogen oxides, and mercury, but this marks the first rejection based on impacts from carbon dioxide emissions. The decision was based in part on an April Supreme Court decision that greenhouse gasses should be considered pollutants under the Clean Air Act.

Many states provide incentives for the development of technologies that may make carbon capture easier, such as IGCC (integrated gasification combined cycle), and some are also investigating the potential to store carbon in geologic formations within their borders. West Virginia and Ohio, two major coal producers, are supporting a pilot project to sequester carbon in a deep underground rock formation on the border between the two states. The ability to capture and store carbon would facilitate the continued use of coal, a vital economic resource in many states.

The federal government has established minimum efficiency standards for approximately 20 kinds of residential and commercial products, including washers and dryers, refrigerators and freezers, dishwashers, and air conditioners. Numerous states, including Arizona, New York, Rhode Island, Washington, Maryland, Connecticut, California, and New Jersey have set standards on products not covered by federal standards.

Transportation Policies

Transportation accounts for 27 percent of all GHG emissions in the United States; therefore, any successful strategy to address climate change must include the transportation sector. States have many options to address GHG emissions from transportation. California has adopted a requirement to reduce GHG emissions from new light-duty vehicles; this requirement is pending a legal challenge from the automobile industry. If upheld by the courts, California estimates that its standard will reduce annual greenhouse gas emissions by 30 million tons of CO_2 equivalent by 2020, and the potential for reductions is higher if additional states adopt California's standards. California has unique authority among states to set vehicle emissions standards, because of a special provision in the federal Clean Air Act. Other states have the option of either following federal standards or adopting California's. In September, 2007, the U.S. District Court for the District of Vermont upheld Vermont's decision to adopt the California standards by deciding against a group of automobile manufacturers charging that the costs to industry will be too high. EPA denied California's waiver request in December 2007; California and several other states have sued to have the decision overturned. Sixteen states have announced their intention to follow California's vehicle standards: Arizona, Colorado, Connecticut, Florida, Maine, Maryland, Massachusetts, New Jersey, New Mexico, New York, Oregon, Pennsylvania, Rhode Island, Utah, Vermont, and Washington.

Numerous states have mandates or incentives for biofuel production and use. Biofuels can have better GHG emissions performance than gasoline on a life-cycle basis, but the GHG emissions depend on how the fuel is made. This fact has sparked interest in adoption of low-carbon fuel standards (LCFS). In January 2007, Governor Schwarzenegger of California announced that his state would establish the world's first Low Carbon Fuel Standard (LCFS). It will apply to all transportation fuels sold in California, with the goal of reducing the carbon intensity of California's passenger vehicle fuels at least 10 percent by 2020. The LCFS includes provisions for market-based mechanisms—such as carbon credit trading—that will allow fuel providers to meet the new requirements in the most cost-effective manner. The standard is expected to substitute low-carbon fuels for up to 20 percent of current vehicle gasoline consumption and greatly expand the number of alternative and hybrid vehicles in the state.

Numerous states have policies requiring that a certain percentage of state-owned vehicles run on alternative fuels, such as ethanol or natural gas, or that the state fleet meet a fuel efficiency standard. Some states offer tax breaks for alternative fuels, gasoline/ethanol blends, alternative fuel vehicles, low-emission vehicles, or for converting traditional vehicles to run on alternative fuels.

Agricultural Policies

Agriculture contributes approximately 7 percent of total U.S. GHG emissions, with nitrous oxide (N_2O) accounting for two-thirds and methane (CH_4) for one-third of agricultural emissions. In addition to reducing these emissions, there are opportunities in agriculture to offset emissions from other sectors by sequestering greenhouse gases in biomass. In doing so, farmers may be able to tap additional revenue sources.

Biomass, as a low-carbon energy source, provides an opportunity for the agricultural sector to address climate change in a profitable way. For example, Iowa has pilot programs to improve production of switch grass to co-fire with coal in power plants.

Soil conservation techniques increase the amount of carbon stored in soil while improving soil quality. Compared to conventional tilling techniques, soil conservation techniques such as "no till" reduce fuel use, time, and cost of farmland preparation. Alaska, Idaho, Illinois, Nebraska, North Dakota, Oklahoma, South Dakota, and Wyoming have formed carbon sequestration advisory committees to investigate the potential for in-state agricultural carbon sequestration.

Emissions Targets and Climate Action Plans

Comprehensive climate plans combined with enforceable GHG emissions targets provide the highest certainty of significant emissions reductions. Thirty-eight states have climate action plans completed or in development; eighteen have state-wide emission targets (*see* Figures 8 and 9).

In September 2006 Governor Schwarzenegger signed AB 32, the Global Warming Solutions Act. The Act caps California's greenhouse gas emissions at 1990 levels by 2020. This legislation represents the first enforceable state-wide program in the U.S. to cap all GHG emissions from major industries that includes penalties for non-compliance. It requires the State Air Resources Board to establish a program for statewide greenhouse gas emissions reporting and to monitor and enforce compliance with this program. The Act authorizes the state board to adopt market-based compliance mechanisms including cap-and-trade, and allows a one-year extension of the targets under extraordinary circumstances. AB 32 builds on California Governor Arnold Schwarzenegger's 2005 Executive Order committing the state to GHG reduction targets equivalent to reaching 2000 emissions levels by 2010, 1990 levels by 2020, and 80 percent below current levels by 2050.

Governor Bill Richardson of New Mexico also signed a 2005 executive order to set GHG targets at achieving 2000 emissions levels by 2012, 10 percent below 2000 levels by 2020, and 75 percent below 2000 levels by 2050. These goals supplement both California's and New Mexico's existing climate-friendly policies including renewable portfolio standards, renewable energy tax credits, and energy efficiency goals. New Mexico is the first major coal, oil, and gas-producing state to set targets for cutting GHG emissions.

Notable actions include announcements in early 2007 by the Governors Blagojevich of Illinois, Corzine of New Jersey, and Gregoire of Washington setting new emissions targets for their respective states, and a September 2006 executive order by Arizona Governor Janet Napolitano to implement recommendations included in her state's Climate Change Advisory Group's Climate Action Plan and to establish a statewide goal to reduce Arizona's GHG emissions to 2000 levels by 2020, and 50 percent below this level by 2040.

Other actions include new target announcements in mid-2007 by Governors Ted Kulongoski of Oregon, Linda Lingle of Hawaii, and Tim Pawlenty of Minnesota. Oregon's HB 3543 directs the state to stop the growth of greenhouse gas emissions by 2010 and to reduce GHG emissions to 10 percent below 1990 levels by 2020 and to 75 percent below 1990 levels by 2050. Hawaii's Act 234, the Global Warming Solutions Act of 2007, mandates that statewide greenhouse gas emissions be reduced to 1990 levels by 2020. Finally, Minnesota's Next Generation Energy Act established statewide GHG emission reduction goals of 15 percent by 2015, 30 percent by 2025, and 80 percent by 2050, based on 2005 levels.

The process of developing a climate action plan can identify cost-effective opportunities to reduce GHG emissions that are relevant to the state. The individual characteristics of each state's economy, resource base, and political structure provide different opportunities for dealing with climate change. However, without strong incentives, climate action plans will not achieve real reductions in GHG emissions. A number of states have set up advisory boards or commissions to develop and/or implement climate action plans. For example, North Carolina established a Legislative Commission on Global Climate Change to address the threats posed by global warming and determine the costs and benefits of the various mitigation strategies adopted by state and national governments, as well as to assess the state's potential economic opportunities in emerging carbon markets. Most recently, Governor Kathleen Sebelius of Kansas signed Executive Order 08-03, establishing the Kansas Energy and Environmental Policy Advisory Group.

.... On July 13, 2007, Florida Governor Charlie Crist signed three climate change related executive orders. EO 07-126 sets GHG emission reduction targets for state agencies and departments of 10 percent below current levels by 2012, 25 percent below by 2017, and 40 percent below by 2025. The order adopts the U.S. Green Building Council's LEED standards for all new state government facilities and all existing buildings owned by the Department of Management Services. EO 07-126 requires state-owned vehicles to be more fuel efficient and to use ethanol and biodiesel fuels when available. EO 07-127 sets statewide GHG emission reduction targets of 2000 levels by 2017, 1990 levels by 2025, and 80% below 1990 levels by 2050. The order directs the Florida Secretary of Environmental Protection to immediately develop rules to adopt the California motor vehicle GHG emission standards. The Florida Energy Code for Building Construction will be revised to increase the energy performance of new construction by at least 15 percent from the 2007 Energy Code. EO 07-127 requests that the Florida Public Service Commission initiate rulemaking to 1) require that utilities produce at least 20 percent of their electricity from renewable sources and 2) to authorize statewide net metering. Executive Order 07-128 creates the Florida Governor's Action Team on Energy and Climate Change to develop an Energy and Climate Change Action Plan to recommend ways to meet the new GHG reduction targets. (See Figures 8 and 9.)

States with Climate Action Plans

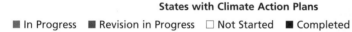

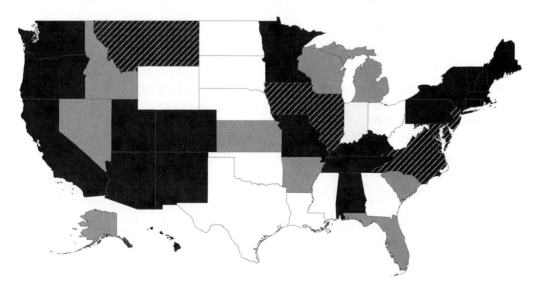

Figure 8. States with Climate Action Plans.

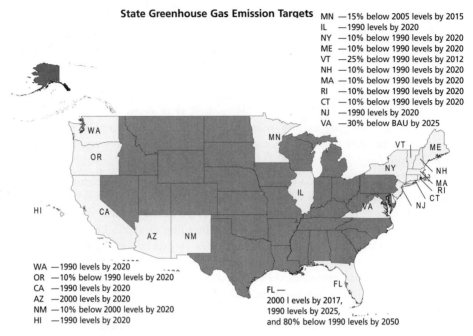

Figure 9. State GHG Emission Targets.

Conclusion

While most state climate change efforts have been implemented relatively recently, some lessons are already emerging for future state, regional and federal efforts. State programs such as emissions reporting and cap-and-trade systems should be designed so that they can easily be expanded or integrated into other programs. Design foresight and flexibility will help facilitate future policies at the state, regional, and federal level. Although garnering support for mandatory goals is sometimes difficult, these policies are generally more effective at achieving significant reductions than voluntary measures. States considering their options to effectively deal with climate change may consider beginning or joining a regional initiative in order to reduce climate impacts more efficiently while avoiding a regulatory patchwork and helping businesses more easily adapt to new policies.

As states move forward, they should be guided by a specific long-term emissions goal and a commitment to minimizing costs to achieve that goal. States may want to move toward a comprehensive approach incrementally, focusing first on policies that are relatively easy to implement and yield multiple benefits.

The actions undertaken by states to reduce GHG emissions are a collective first step on the United States' path to confronting climate change. The policy and technology lessons taken from these efforts should do much to inform future efforts at the national and international levels.

The Pew Center on Global Climate Change is a non-profit, non-partisan, independent organization dedicated to providing credible information, straight answers, and innovative solutions in the effort to address global climate change.

Notes

1. A comprehensive summary of state actions was done by the Congressional Research Service. *See* JONATHAN L. RAMSEUR, CLIMATE CHANGE: ACTION BY STATES TO ADDRESS GREENHOUSE GAS EMISSIONS, Congressional Research Service, November 23, 2007, available at http://www.cnie.org/NLE/CRS/abstract.cfm?NLEid=1849- (visited Nov. 15, 2008) [hereinafter 2007 CRS STUDY ON STATE ACTIONS]. Here is the "Summary" from that report:

Summary

In the absence of a federal climate change program, a number of states have taken actions that directly address greenhouse gases (GHGs). States' efforts cover a wide range of policies. Although much of the early activity was largely symbolic, the more recent state actions have been more aggressive.

Twenty-three states have joined one of the three regional partnerships that would require GHG (or just carbon dioxide) emission reductions. Set to take effect in 2009, the Regional Greenhouse Gas Initiative (RGGI) is a partnership of 10 Northeast and Mid-Atlantic states that creates a cap-and-trade system aimed at limiting carbon dioxide emissions from power plants. Seven western states (and two Canadian provinces) have formed the Western Climate Initiative, which set an economy-wide GHG emissions target of 15% below 2005 levels by 2020. In addition, six states (and one Canadian province) signed the Midwestern Greenhouse Gas Reduction Accord, which would establish a multi-sector, GHG cap-and-trade program in the Midwest. The latter two programs are still in the early development stages, while many of RGGI's logistics have been decided by the participants.

Three states — California, Hawaii, and New Jersey — have passed laws establishing mandatory, economy-wide GHG emission limits. However, the critical elements of these programs are still being developed.

California has addressed GHG emissions on several fronts. To complement its statewide emissions reduction regime, California established GHG performance standards that would effectively limit the use of coal-generated electricity in California. In 2004, California issued regulations to reduce greenhouse gases from motor vehicles. At least 14 other states have indicated they intend to follow California's new vehicle requirements. In addition, the state has also taken action to reduce the carbon intensity in its transportation fuels.

Predicting the precise consequences of the state-led climate change actions is difficult. Some actions, particularly the mandatory emission reductions, may create economic effects, especially in the automotive manufacturing and electricity-generating sectors. Industry stakeholders are especially concerned that the states will create a patchwork of climate change regulations across the nation. This prospect is causing some industry leaders to call for a federal climate change program. If Congress seeks to establish a federal program, the experiences and lessons learned in the states may be instructive.

Although some states are taking aggressive action, their possible emission reductions may be offset by increased emissions in states without mandatory reduction requirements. This is perhaps the central limitation of state climate change programs in actually affecting total greenhouse gas emissions. Legal challenges represent another obstacle for state programs, particularly for the more aggressive, mandatory programs.

---

2. This 2007 CRS STUDY ON STATE ACTIONS organizes this sprawling topic around "direct" and "indirect" initiatives, described as follows (CRS-3 to CRS-4) (footnotes as in original):

Direct Action Versus Indirect Action

Direct state actions that address greenhouse gas emissions include laws, regulations, or policies that are established explicitly to reduce GHG emissions. In some cases, it is difficult to draw a line between direct and indirect actions, because a specific policy may be undertaken for multiple purposes, including GHG reduction. One of the best examples of this ambiguity is a Renewable Portfolio Standard (RPS). An RPS requires that a certain amount or percentage of electricity is generated from renewable energy resources (*e.g.*, solar, biomass). Twenty-eight states have implemented or are developing some type of RPS.[8] Although greenhouse gas reduction is not the primary driver for an RPS in most states, some states list their RPS as part of a comprehensive strategy to reduce greenhouse gases.

Indirect actions are often characterized as "no regrets" approaches, providing net benefits regardless of the magnitude of their impacts on climate change. For the purposes of this report, indirect actions are those developed primarily to address other concerns, such as improvements in energy efficiency, energy security, or air quality. Examples of indirect actions include:

- Building codes: A majority of states have building codes that promote energy efficiency in commercial and residential structures; many of these states' standards are more stringent than federal policy.[9]
- Appliance Standards: Twelve states have set energy efficiency standards for appliances that are not covered under the federal program.[10]
- Agricultural policies: Several states promote agricultural practices that may indirectly reduce GHG emissions. For example, a "no-till" farming technique saves fuel and man hours, while keeping carbon stored in the soil.[11]

This report, however, does not attempt to discuss the extremely wide variety of such indirect actions.

––––––––––

3. "Voluntary" markets and undefined "carbon offsets" and "renewable energy certificates" have drawn the attention of the Federal Trade Commission and critics of dubious business practices. *See* Anna Liese Bulley, "The Government and Greenwashing: A Critical Analysis of the Proposed Amendments to the FTC's Green Guides," University of Washington School of Law, Global Warming and Justice Seminar (Winter 2009); Annie Vithayathil, "Companies Making Carbon Offset and Renewable Energy Certificate Claims Should Be Penalized By the FTC, Not Legitimated," University of Washington School of Law, Global Warming and Justice Seminar (Winter 2009) (footnotes renumbered). The latter article makes the following points (pp. 7–9):

––––––––––

8. *See* EPA, Summary of State Clean Energy-Environment Policy Data Table (current as of 1/1/2007), at http://www.epa.gov/cleanenergy/stateandlocal/activities.html. *See also* the Pew Center on Global Climate Change, Map: States with Renewable Portfolio Standards at http://www.pewclimate.org.

9. EPA data indicate that 26 states have commercial codes more stringent than federal energy efficiency standards; 22 states have residential codes more stringent than federal energy efficiency standards. See EPA, Summary of State Clean Energy-Environment Policy Data Table (current as of 1/1/2007).

10. *See* EPA, Map: State Energy Efficiency Actions—State Appliance Efficiency Standards (as of 1/1/2007), at http://www.epa.gov/cleanenergy/stateandlocal/activities.htm.

11. Georgia promotes this technique through its No-Tillage Assistance Program (NTAP), which provides equipment and funding assistance. *See* Pew Center on Global Climate Change, State and Local Net Greenhouse Gas Emissions Reduction Programs, at http://www.pewclimate.org.

The voluntary markets, and the over-the-counter markets in particular, are a rough frontier with unclear standards. In particular, carbon offsets within the market are known to suffer from the following uncertainty variables:[1]

- **Additionality**: Was the carbon reduction of the offsetting project a true reduction, or just a "business as usual" reduction? Additionality "has the function of maintaining scarcity in the marketplace";[2] without it, an "offset" is meaningless. Unfortunately, "no test for additionality can provide certainty about what would have happened otherwise."[3]
- **Verification**: Did the reduction actually occur after money had changed hands? As of November 2007, "there [was] no agreed standard for monitoring methods or the appropriate frequency and requirements for verification."[4]
- **Vintage**: Did the reduction occur when it was supposed to? Due to the time-value of money, and the unabated march of a changing climate, a carbon reduction today is not equivalent to a carbon reduction next year.[5]
- **Ownership**: Who gets to "claim" the credit? What prevents a seller or buyer from re-selling a credit repeatedly? "Legal mechanisms are not yet in place to disallow two parties from selling the same reduction or to prevent a single party from selling a reduction to multiple buyers."[6]

In light of this uncertainty, it is unsurprising that an industry insider noted that "[a] lot of people have called this [over-the-counter] market the wild west or have considered it a buyer beware market."[7] As Gillenwater notes, "a host of independent 'standards' operating in a regulatory vacuum has the potential to discredit market-based environmental policies with the public as a means of addressing climate change."[8] Unfortunately, with low consumer literacy about the uncertainties of carbon offsets, the consumption choices of individuals may be unduly influenced by "carbon neutral" claims. This could even result in a net increase of carbon emission, as consumers, absolved from guilt by illusory carbon offsets, spend more. Unfortunately, given the size, growth and diversity of the market and the disinterested nature of its primary corporate customers, many people stand poised to profit from the continued chaos of the voluntary carbon markets.

---

2. Particulars of State Programs

Consider the following elaborations of these huge and interlocking policy landscapes: (a) State Climate Action Plans, (b) Renewable Portfolio Standards, (c) Regulation of Coal-Fired Power Plants, (d) State Auto Emission Standards; and (e) the California Experience.

---

1. Michael Gillenwater *et al.*, *Policing the Voluntary Carbon Market*, NATURE REPORTS, Nov. 2007, pp. 85, 86 [hereinafter 2007 Gillenwater].

2. *Id.*

3. *Id.*

4. *Id.*

5. Letter from Timothy Stumhofer, Climate Clean, to U.S. Federal Trade Commission regarding Comment No. P074207 (2008), available at http://www.ftc.gov/os/comments/carbonworkshop/.

6. 2007 Gillenwater, *supra* note 1, pp. 85, 85–86.

7. Transcript of Session 1 of Federal Trade Commission public workshop on Carbon Offsets & Renewable Energy Certificates at 35–36 (January 8, 2008), *available at* http://www.ftc.gov/bcp/workshops/carbonoffsets/transcript/session 1.pdf.

8. 2007 Gillenwater, *supra* note 1, at 86.

a. State Climate Action Plans

2007 CRS STUDY ON STATE ACTIONS at CRS-4-9 (footnotes as in original):

―――――――

State Action Plans

At least 36 states have either completed or are in the process of preparing climate change action plans (see Figure 10). Typically, state action plans are drafted by a climate change task force, composed of members with diverse backgrounds and expertise. In general, task force members examine their state's sources of greenhouse gases, and identify and rank the policy options that are most appropriate (*i.e.*, cost-effective, politically feasible, etc.) for controlling emissions in their state. Often the state action plan is made available for public comment, revised if necessary, and then submitted for approval to state officials.

Figure 10. *Map not shown.* **States with Completed and Under-Development Climate Change Action Plans. Source: Prepared by the Congressional Research Service with data from U.S. EPA Climate Change Division and Pew Center on Global Climate. Online links to individual state action plans are available through EPA's website, at http://www.epa.gov/climate change.**

Reflecting the fact that states have different economic sectors, natural resources, and political structures, state climate change action plans can vary substantially. Some state action plans focus more on indirect, "no regrets" strategies, such as improved energy efficiency, which will likely yield benefits irrespective of climate change effects. Other state action plans are more comprehensive and recommend a portfolio of direct efforts that address GHG emissions. Although the state climate change action plans may *recommend* an array of policy options, the plans do not necessarily result in direct actions to reduce GHG emissions. However, the number of completed state plans indicates the interest that a majority of states have in addressing climate change mitigation on some level.

Greenhouse Gas Emissions Targets

State emissions targets are goals by which a state can measure its progress in achieving greenhouse gas emissions reduction. By themselves, state emissions targets do not directly reduce greenhouse gases. The targets are often established by the executive branch of state government (*e.g.*, through an executive order) and may not have the support of the state's legislative branch. However, a target signals that state officials, at least from one branch of the government, consider climate change an important issue.

Seventeen states have established *statewide* targets for greenhouse gas emissions (see Table 1).[15] Three of the state targets—California, Hawai'i, and New Jersey—are mandatory (discussed below). Considering the GHG limits and targets set on the international stage in past years, these state targets are relatively modest.[16] Nearly all of these states are in either the Northeast or on the west coast of the United States. The New England states' targets are similar, if not identical, because they are part of a cooperative plan developed in 2001.[17] Of the 17 states in Table 1, New Mexico and Illinois stand out because they have substantial coal production.[18]

―――――――

15. Several states have also developed more narrow targets, either for industry or electricity generation or only for carbon dioxide emissions.

16. The U.S. Kyoto target was 7% below 1990 levels, averaged over the commitment period 2008 to 2012. For more on international climate agreements and U.S. involvement, see CRS Report RL33826, CLIMATE CHANGE: THE KYOTO PROTOCOL AND INTERNATIONAL ACTIONS, by Susan R. Fletcher and Larry Parker.

17. New England Governors/Eastern Canadian Premiers, *Climate Change Action Plan 2001*, August 2001, at http://www.negc.org.

18. In 2005, Illinois and New Mexico ranked 9th and 11th, respectively, in coal production. New Mexico ranked 3rd in natural gas production, a fuel that releases significantly less GHG than coal or oil when

Table 1 compares the states' GHG emissions in 1990 with emissions from the most recent three years of available data.[19] The emissions data show the reductions states would need to make to meet their established targets. Although some of the states appear within reach of their 2010 targets, the most recent data from many of these states suggest that emissions are not decreasing, but at best are leveling off. More years of data are needed to evaluate progress, primarily because many of the states issued their greenhouse gas targets after 2003, and state-level data after 2003 are not yet available. Moreover, the emissions targets were typically created in conjunction with greenhouse gas reduction policies—some of them mandatory limits on specific industries or segments of state activities—whose implementation is not reflected in the available emissions data.

Table 1. Statewide Greenhouse Gas Targets Compared with Emissions Data from 1990 and Recent Years of Available Data.

State	Greenhouse Gases Target(s)	Greenhouse Gas Emissions (million metric tons of CO2 equivalent)				
		1990	2000	2001	2002	2003
AZ[20]	2000 levels by 2020; 50% below 2000 levels by 2050	70	93	95	94	96
CA[21]	2000 levels by 2010; 1990 levels by 2020; 80% below 1990 levels by 2050	412	442	449	447	453
CT[22]	1990 levels by 2010; 10% below 1990 levels by 2020	44	47	45	44	46
FL[23]	2000 levels by 2017; 1990 levels by 2025; 80% below 1990 levels by 2050	208	264	263	267	271
HI[24]	1990 levels by 2020	23	21	21	22	23
IL[25]	1990 levels by 2020; 60% below 1990 levels by 2050	231	277	266	268	269
MA[26]	1990 levels by 2010; 10% below 1990 levels by 2020	89	88	88	89	92

burned. *See* U.S. Department of Energy, Energy Information Administration Statistics, at http://www.eia.doe.gov/.

19. The emissions data in Table 1, particularly the 1990 levels, may differ from the official estimates provided by individual states. The objective of the table is to compare emission levels over time, and assess the challenge of meeting emissions targets. Because some states only have estimates for 1990 levels, this report uses data from the World Resources Institute for a consistent comparison.

20. Arizona Executive Order 2006–13 (September 7, 2006).

21. California Executive Order S3-05 (June 1, 2005) set the 2010 and 2020 targets; AB 32 (discussed below) made the 2020 target mandatory.

22. Connecticut Public Act No. 04-252 (June 14, 2004).

23. Florida Executive Order 07-127 (July 13, 2007).

24. Hawai'i Governor Lingle signed the Global Warming Solutions Act of 2007 (Act 234) into law June 30, 2007. The act mandates statewide GHG emission reductions.

25. Announcement from Illinois Governor Blagojevich (February 13, 2007), related to Executive Order 2006-11 (October 5, 2006).

26. Massachusetts Climate Protection Plan of 2004 (Spring 2004).

Table 1. Statewide Greenhouse Gas Targets Compared with Emissions Data from 1990 and Recent Years of Available Data (*continued*)

ME[27]	1990 levels by 2010; 10% below 1990 levels by 2020	21	25	25	26	26
MN[28]	15% below 2005 levels by 2015; 30% below 2005 levels by 2025; 80% below 2005 levels by 2050	99	118	114	117	120
NH[29]	1990 levels by 2010; 10% below 1990 levels by 2020	16	19	18	19	22
NJ[30]	1990 levels by 2020; 80% below 2006 levels by 2050	124	137	135	135	137
NM[31]	2000 levels by 2012; 10% below 2000 levels by 2020; 75% below 2000 levels by 2050	58	66	66	64	66
NY[32]	5% below 1990 by 2010; 10% below 1990 levels by 2020	233	244	236	230	244
OR[33]	Stabilize by 2010; 10% below 1990 levels by 2020; 75% below 1990 levels by 2050	39	52	52	50	51
RI[34]	1990 levels by 2010; 10% below 1990 levels by 2020	10	13	14	13	13
VT[35]	1990 levels by 2010; 10% below 1990 levels by 2020	7	8	8	8	8
WA[36]	1990 levels by 2020; 25% below 1990 levels by 2035; 50% below 1990 levels by 2050	84	99	100	93	95

Source: Prepared by the CRS with data from the following: state targets compiled by Pew Center on Global Climate Change, at http://www.pewclimate.org; GHG emissions data from World Resources Institute, Climate Analysis Indicators Tool, at http://cait.wri.org/ (GHG data excludes land use changes).

In addition to the individual state targets discussed in this section, two multi-state partnerships—the Western Climate Initiative and the Midwestern Greenhouse Gas Reduction Accord—have established (or proposed to establish) regional, economy-wide targets to reduce GHG emissions. Another regional agreement in the Northeast and Mid-Atlantic regions—the Regional Greenhouse Gas Initiative—covers carbon dioxide emissions from power plants....

---

b. Renewable Portfolio Standards

THOMAS L. FRIEDMAN, HOT, FLAT AND CROWDED: WHY WE NEED A GREEN REVOLUTION—AND HOW IT CAN RENEW AMERICA 322 (Farrar, Straus & Giroux 2008) [hereinafter 2008 FRIEDMAN]:

On January 1, 2006, China instituted a national renewable energy mandate—of the sort the U.S. Congress rejected in 2007—that requires China's provincial governments to develop and adopt renewable energy for their localities. China's target is to increase renewable energy—particularly wind, hydro, and biomass—to 16 percent of its total

---

27. Maine LD 845 (HP 622) (effective September 13, 2003).
28. Minnesota Governor Pawlenty, signed into law the Next Generation Energy Act May 25, 2007.
29. The Climate Change Challenge (December 2001).
30. New Jersey Governor Corzine signed into law the Global Warming Response Act (A3301) July 6, 2007, which requires mandatory emission reductions.
31. New Mexico Executive Order 05-033 (June 9, 2005).
32. New York State Energy Plan (June 2002).
33. Oregon Governor Kulongoski signed HB 3543 into law August 6, 2007.
34. Rhode Island Greenhouse Gas Action Plan (July 2002).
35. This target is discussed in Vermont's state plan, *Fueling Vermont's Future: Vermont Comprehensive Energy Plan and Vermont Greenhouse Gas Action Plan* (July 1998).
36. Washington Governor Gregoire signed SB 6001 into law May 3, 2007.

energy production by 2020. Today it is 7 percent. China also adopted world-class mileage standards for its cars.

FRED KRUPP & MIRIAM HORN, EARTH: THE SEQUEL—THE RACE TO REINVENT ENERGY AND STOP GLOBAL WARMING 57 (W.W. Norton & Co. 2008) (emphasis in original):

> [A renewable portfolio standards approach] focuses on the wrong thing: on process (how utilities generate power) rather than on *performance* (how much pollution they emit), which is what ultimately counts. In essence, renewable standards, subsidies, and other mandates assume that the government has all the answers, rather than letting the market figure out the best way to produce clean energy at the lowest cost.

STEVEN FERREY with ANIL CABRAAL, RENEWABLE POWER IN DEVELOPING COUNTRIES: WINNING THE WAR ON GLOBAL WARMING 35 (PennWell Corp. 2006), *quoting* Richard Smalley, Nobel Laureate, 2002:

> Energy is the single most important problem facing humanity today. We must find an alternative to oil ... [T]he cheaper, cleaner, and more universally available this new technology is, the better we will be able to avoid human suffering, and the major upheavals of war and terrorism.

PAUL ROBERTS, THE END OF OIL: ON THE EDGE OF A PERILOUS NEW WORLD 291 (Houghton Mifflin Co. 2004):

> In 2000 [in Germany], the so-called red-green coalition government enacted a Renewable Energy Law (REL), repealing the 5 percent cap [that had decreed that renewable energy could rise no higher than 5% of the total power market] and offering generous subsidies to renewable energy producers, to be financed by a small tax on all energy sales. Utilities, arguing that the subsidies violated European Union free trade requirements, challenged the REL. The German government, however, countered that subsidies were intended simply to "internalize" the long-unpaid external costs of coal-fired and other polluting energy. The law stood.

JAMES LOVELOCK, THE REVENGE OF GAIA: EARTH'S CLIMATE IN CRISIS AND THE FATE OF HUMANITY 66–67 (Basic Books 2006):

> If it is perverse and dangerous to gain energy by burning fossil carbon in fossil oxygen, it may be equally so to imagine that comparable quantities of energy are freely and safely available from the so-called "renewable" resources.

2008 FRIEDMAN at 355:

> Eleven years to fully connect one wind farm. I don't think that timetable is going to cut it in a world where every two weeks China opens new coal-fired power plants big enough to serve all the households in my hometown of Minneapolis. Yes, you say, it's relatively easy to build dirty coal plants—and you are right. It's much more difficult to build power plants that are clean and superefficient. Right now China is mainly putting up dirty ones. But soon they will be putting up wind farms, solar facilities, and nuclear plants with the same relentless efficiency. You can bet your house on it. It will take time, but they will eventually try to outgreen us. They'll have to, or they won't be able to breathe.

> And what about us? Will we step up our game? We can't be China for a day, and we should not have to and we should not want to. But it is a measure of how incoherent, ad hoc, and asystematic American energy policy is right now that such fantasies flash into your mind. If we cannot find a way to overcome all of these weaknesses and chart an intelligently designed energy strategy, our generation had better brace itself for a rocky retirement—and some really unpleasant questions from our kids.

No one doubts that achieving a significant presence for "renewable" energy sources is somewhat more complicated than declaring this to be so by law. *See* Joseph P. Tomain & Richard D. Cudahy, Energy Law in a Nutshell ch. 11 (Thomson/West 2004). And no one doubts, as James Lovelock hints, that "renewables" will contain their own sad stories of environmental damage and cast-off costs. The Chinese people know this about the Three Gorges Dam. *See* Elizabeth C. Economy, The River Runs Black: The Environmental Challenge to China's Future 82 (Cornell Un. Press 2004) ("One estimate is that 300 million farmers will be resettled, some forcibly"; projects that include Three Gorges Dam). Indian tribes of the U.S. Pacific Northwest have looked to law for 150 years to save their worlds and their fish from the "blessings" of hydroelectric development on the Columbia River. *E.g.*, Michael C. Blumm, Sacrificing the Salmon: A Legal and Policy History of the Decline of Columbia Basin Salmon (BookWorld Publications 2002); Joseph C. Dupris, Kathleen S. Hill & William H. Rodgers, Jr., The Si'lailo Way: Indians, Salmon and Law on the Columbia River (Carolina Academic Press 2006).

But with this said, the renewable portfolio laws are pronounced "changes of course." Ships of state are cumbersome things and they have built up enormous inertia in pursuit of what is and what has been. Turning away from fossil-fuel may be easier said than done. But if it is not said, it will not be done.

c. Regulation of Coal-Fired Power Plants

Barbara Freese, Coal: A Human History 170 (Penguin Books 2004):

> As the evidence linking acid rain to coal poured in, the response of the electric and coal industries was to deny the link, to question the motives of those investigating the connection, and always to call for more research. In October 1980, the head of the National Coal Association dismissed acid rain as "a campaign of misleading publicity which seems designed to gain public support for new legislative and regulatory measures."

So, too, with global warming though the tide is turning.

2007 CRS Study on State Actions at CRS-16 to CRS-17 (footnotes as in original):

Individual State Efforts. Two states have already established emission reduction requirements at *existing* power plants:

- Massachusetts: In 2001, Massachusetts became the first state to take formal action on carbon dioxide emissions at operational power plants. As part of a multi-pollutant strategy, which went into effect in 2006, the state's six largest power plants must reduce carbon dioxide to levels consistent with those produced in the late 1990s. In 2008, this cap is lowered further.[66] The program allows the plants to either make the reductions, demonstrate offsite reductions, or purchase emissions credits from other verifiable sources. Note that the carbon dioxide components of this program will be superceded when RGGI goes on-line in 2009. RGGI will require reductions from 32 power plants in the state.
- New Hampshire: In 2002, the state enacted multi-pollutant legislation[67] requiring its three fossil fuel power plants to reduce carbon dioxide to 1990 levels by the end of 2006.

---

66. 310 Massachusetts Code of Regulations 7.29.
67. New Hampshire Clean Power Act (May 9, 2002), codified in New Hampshire Statute, Title X, Chapter 125-O (Multiple Pollutant Reduction Program).

In order the meet the cap, the law allows sources to bank early reductions or buy credits through other programs deemed acceptable by state officials. The carbon dioxide elements of this program will be superceded by RGGI.

Both Oregon and Washington have programs that require *new* power plants to reduce carbon dioxide emissions or purchase offsets. In 1997, Oregon became the first state to regulate carbon dioxide emissions by passing legislation[68] requiring new power plants to equal or exceed carbon dioxide levels that are 17% below the best natural gas-fired plant in the nation. Plants can either reduce emissions directly or purchase offsets from a nonprofit organization (the Oregon Climate Trust) that was established with the 1997 law. This organization helps develop various projects that will reduce or sequester GHG emissions. These projects generate the pool of offsets available (by purchase) to the power plants. So far, all of the new facilities have chosen to purchase offsets instead of reducing onsite emissions.[69] Washington passed similar legislation in 2004, requiring new power plants to offset 20% of their carbon dioxide emissions.[70]

Professor Glicksman provides more detail on the legal basis for the denial of a permit for KDHE's coal power plant in Kansas.

Robert L. Glicksman, *Coal-Fired Power Plants, Greenhouse Gases, and State Statutory Substantial Endangerment Provisions: Climate Change Comes to Kansas*, 56 KAN. L. REV. 517 (2008).

Id. at 517–20 (footnotes omitted):

On October 17, 2007, the Bureau of Air and Radiation, Air Permitting Section of the Kansas Department of Health and Environment ("KDHE") recommended the issuance of an Air Quality Construction Permit under state air quality legislation to the Sunflower Electric Power Corporation ("Sunflower"). The permit would have allowed Sunflower to construct two new 700 megawatt coal-fired steam generating units and associated ancillary equipment at the site of its existing generating station located in Holcomb, Kansas. The very next day, Roderick Bremby, the Secretary of KDHE, announced that the agency was denying Sunflower's application for a construction permit for the two plants.

… While the denial of the Sunflower application might have stoked the fury of the project's supporters no matter what its basis, Secretary Bremby's justification for refusing to license the two new units was the real headline grabber. Bremby based his denial on the "substantial endangerment" to health and the environment in Kansas that would result.…

… Part IV analyzes the legality of KDHE's denial of the Sunflower application. It addresses not only the relevant Kansas statutes, but also the case law construing the federal environmental statutes that mirror the Kansas statute primarily relied upon by KDHE. I conclude that the denial of air quality permits for the Sunflower units is within KDHE's authority to take actions to prevent the substantial endangerment to public health and the environment arising from GHG emissions. I reach this conclusion even though the denial was based on projected as opposed to ongoing emissions and even though, at the

---

68. HB 3283, codified in Oregon Administrative Rules, Chapter 345, Division 24.
69. Point Carbon, 2006, *Carbon Trading in the US: The Hibernating Giant*, CARBON MARKET ANALYST, September 13, 2006.
70. HB 3141 (signed into law on March 31, 2004).

time of the decision, neither Kansas nor the federal government had designated GHGs as air pollutants for air quality regulatory purposes. Part V briefly assesses the implications of KDHE's decision for the future of coal-fired electricity generation and the development of an energy policy for Kansas in the climate change era.

Id. at 560–62 (footnotes omitted):

KDHE Secretary Ronald Bremby announced his decision on October 18, 2007, the day after the release of the staff recommendation (and nearly a month after the issuance of the Attorney General's Opinion). In his brief letter, Bremby began by referring to his duty as KDHE Secretary under the Kansas Air Quality Act "to protect the public health and environment from actual, threatened or potential harm from air pollution." Bremby interpreted the Act and KDHE's implementing regulations as vesting in the Secretary broad authority to protect health and the environment, including the denial of an air quality permit under section 65-3008a. Bremby also cited section 65-3012. He read that statute to authorize the Secretary to take actions necessary to protect health and the environment from the emission of air pollutants that present a substantial endangerment, which "may be a threatened or potential harm as well as an actual harm." Bremby noted the Supreme Court's decision in April 2007 in *Massachusetts v. EPA*, in which the Court held that CO_2 qualifies as an air pollutant under the federal CAA. He reasoned that "the Kansas air quality act similarly has a broad definition of what constitutes air pollution." The Secretary also referred to the Supreme Court's recognition of the "deleterious impact of greenhouse gases on the environment in which we live." Similarly, Bremby concluded that the information gathered during the Sunflower permit proceeding "provides support for the position that emission of air pollution from the proposed coal fired plant, specifically carbon dioxide emissions, presents a substantial endangerment to the health of persons or to the environment." Based on that information, Secretary Bremby denied the permit.

KDHE issued a press release the same day, quoting Bremby and reiterating the basis for his decision. The release quoted Bremby as stating that he decided to deny the Sunflower permit "after careful consideration of my responsibility to protect the public health and environment from actual, threatened or potential harm from air pollution" under sections 65-3008, 65-3008a, and 65-3012. Bremby added that "it would be irresponsible to ignore emerging information about the contribution of carbon dioxide and other greenhouse gases to climate change and the potential harm to our environment and health if we do nothing." The release characterized Bremby's decision as "a first step in emerging policy to address existing and future carbon dioxide emissions in Kansas." It noted that the two new Sunflower units would have released a projected eleven million tons of CO_2 each year, and quoted Bremby to the effect that "denying the Sunflower air quality permit, combined with creating sound policy to reduce carbon dioxide emissions[,] can facilitate the development of clean and renewable energy to protect the health and environment of Kansans."

Notes

1. Kan. Stat. Ann. §62-3012(a) (2002) reads:

[n]otwithstanding any other provision of this Act, the [S]ecretary may take such actions as may be necessary to protect the health of persons or the environment: (1) Upon re-

ceipt of information that the emission of air pollution presents a substantial endangerment to the health of persons or to the environment ...

2. Similar conflicts over proposed coal-fired plants have occurred in Washington, Florida, North Carolina, and Texas. *See* Glicksman, 56 KAN. L. REV. at 538–52.

3. Prof. Glicksman describes the law's most dramatic moratorium on the construction of certain kinds of electrical generating facilities. 56 KAN. L. REV. at 538 (footnotes omitted but citing Cal. Pub. Res. Code § 25524.2(a) (West 2008) and *Pac. Gas & Elec. Co. v. State Energy Res. Conservation & Dev. Comm'n*, 461 U.S. 190 (1983)):

> In 1976, the California legislature amended the Warren-Alquist Act to bar the construction of nuclear fission thermal power plants pending issuance by a state agency of a finding "that there has been developed and that the United States through its authorized agency has approved and there exists a demonstrated technology or means for the disposal of high-level nuclear waste." Because the federal Nuclear Regulatory Commission was in no position to approve such technology, either at the time the statute was amended or in the foreseeable future, the statute in effect amounted to a state-wide moratorium on the construction of nuclear power plants for the indefinite future. In 1983, the Supreme Court upheld the Warren-Alquist Act, holding that it was not preempted by the Atomic Energy Act.

In conclusion, Prof. Glicksman writes (*id.* at 607):

> There is little question that KDHE's denial of the Holcomb air quality permit on the basis of the plants' potential to contribute to climate change was unprecedented in Kansas. It is also legitimate to question the agency's authority to issue that decision in light of the absence of judicial interpretation of the applicable statutes. Nevertheless, there are strong arguments to support the conclusion that KDHE had ample authority to do exactly what it did. If the text of the state's air quality statute does not dictate the conclusion that KDHE acted within the scope of its authority in denying the Sunflower permit application, the statute certainly is reasonably interpreted to support that conclusion. KDHE's interpretation and application of the statute are also consistent with the policies underlying precautionary environmental legislation such as the Kansas substantial endangerment provision. Finally, the deference typically afforded agency policy determinations of the sort involved here makes it very difficult to characterize KDHE's action as an illegitimate "administrative fiat" that somehow threatens the legislature's primacy in fashioning energy, environmental, and economic policy for the state.

4. Prof. Glicksman also explains how the so-called CAFE standards (for corporate average fuel economy standards) figure in the CO_2 regulatory dance set loose by *Massachusetts v. EPA* (56 KAN. L. REV. at 530 n. 74):

> Late in 2007, President Bush signed the Energy Independence and Security Act of 2007. Pub. L. No. 110-140, 121 Stat. 1492 (2007). That Act raised the corporate average fuel economy standards for passenger automobiles to 35 miles per gallon by 2020. *Id.* § 102(a)(2) (to be codified at 49 U.S.C. § 32902(b)(2)(A)). EPA Administrator Stephen Johnson hinted that the energy bill makes it unnecessary for EPA to adopt mandatory controls on GHG emissions from motor vehicles, despite *Massachusetts v. EPA. See* Dawn Reeves, *Environmentalists Eye Suit to Force EPA GHG Endangerment Finding*, INSIDE EPA WEEKLY, Jan. 4, 2008, at 1, 1 ("Johnson suggested that the fuel economy mandates may satisfy [*Massachusetts v. EPA*]"); Stephen D. Cook, *Waxman Opens Investigation into Denial of California's Greenhouse Gas Limit Waiver*, 39 ENV'T REP. (BNA) 12, 12–13 (Jan. 4, 2008) (quoting Johnson as stating that the energy bill amounts to a "comprehensive solution" for motor vehicles).

See Bryan C. Banks, *High Above the Environmental Decimation and Economic Domination of Eastern Kentucky, King Coal Remains Firmly Seated on Its Gilded Throne*, 13 Buffalo Envtl. L.J. 125 (2006); Amy Williams, *Review of Big Coal: The Dirty Secret Behind America's Energy Future*, 46 Nat. Res. J. 1090 (2006).

d. State Automobile Emission Standards

Patrick Parenteau, *Lead, Follow, or Get Out of the Way: The States Tackle Climate Change With Little Help From Washington*, 40 Conn. L. Rev. 1453, 1466 (2008) (footnotes omitted):

> The transportation sector is the second largest source of CO_2 emissions in the United States. Almost all of the energy consumed in the transportation sector is petroleum based, including gasoline, diesel and jet fuel. Automobiles and light-duty trucks account for almost two-thirds of emissions from the transportation sector, and emissions have grown steadily since 1990. Reducing GHG emissions from the transportation sector requires three distinct strategies: (1) increased fuel efficiency, (2) developing cleaner "biofuels", and (3) promoting "smart growth" through compact development and mass transportation.

Raymond B. Ludwiszewski, Esq. & Charles H. Haake, Esq., *Cars, Carbon, and Climate Change*, 102 Nw. U.L. Rev. 665, 666 (2008) (footnotes omitted):

> California's history of regulating mobile source emissions of smog-forming pollutants has been cited as a classic example of the "race to the top." Generally, motor vehicle emissions are regulated exclusively by the federal government, and states are expressly preempted from enacting their own emissions standards. The state of California, however, may obtain a waiver from this preemption under a special provision in the Clean Air Act (provided certain preconditions are met), and pursuant to this provision has long taken the lead in reducing motor vehicle emissions of pollutants that cause smog and unhealthful air such as carbon monoxide, hydrocarbons, and oxides of nitrogen. Recently, the state has expanded on this body of mobile source regulation and attempted to regulate greenhouse gas emissions from automobiles, principally carbon dioxide (CO_2), which do not cause localized smog or unhealthful air, but rather are attributed to global climate change. Another eleven states have taken advantage of a provision of the Clean Air Act that allows them to adopt California emissions standards that have received a Clean Air Act waiver and have adopted California's greenhouse gas emissions requirements for new automobiles.

———————

Notes

1. Professor Daniel Farber picks up the story of California's role in stricter auto emission standards in Daniel A. Farber, *Climate Change, Federalism, and the Constitution*, UC Berkeley Public Law Research Paper No. 1081664 at 6 (January 9, 2008) *available at* http://papers.ssrn.com/sol3/papers.cfm?abstract_id=1081664 (footnotes included) (visited Dec. 12, 2008). (This article appears under the same title in 50 Ariz. L. Rev. 879, 887–90 (2008) with slight variations in text):

> ....

> The transportation sector is a critical part of climate change regulation. California has taken the lead. Beginning with the 2009 model year, the California Air Resources Board has a mandate to reduce CO_2 emission from new car models by 30 percent on a

fleet average basis.[1] A statute known as A.B. 1493 directs the California Air Resources Board to adopt regulations that achieve "the maximum feasible and cost-effective reduction of greenhouse gas emissions regulations from motor vehicles." The CARB may not, however, impose fees or taxes, ban SUVs or light trucks, or impose speed limits.[2] California is also moving toward adoption of a low-carbon fuel standard.[3]

Federalism has been a significant issue in terms of vehicle regulation, particularly regarding the new car regulations authorized by A.B. 1493. The state's regulatory scheme has been challenged on several grounds. To begin with, the Clean Air Act prohibits any state from adopting regulations concerning emissions from new vehicles. The sole exception is for California, which can be granted a waiver from preemption if the EPA determines that the state standards are at least as stringent as the federal standards. Before the Supreme Court rejected its position, EPA contended that CO_2 was not an "emission" within the meaning of the statute, creating some puzzles about the application of the preemption and California waiver provisions.[4] Those issues have now been resolved, but the statute allows EPA to reject the waiver application on the ground that California had failed to establish the existence of "compelling and extraordinary circumstances."[5]

California also faces claims that its regulations are preempted by the federal CAFE (fuel efficiency) standards. The statute establishing the federal standards also preempts states from issuing any regulations that "relate to fuel economy standards."[6] Reducing CO_2 from automobiles requires burning less gasoline; the question is whether CARB can craft regulations that may indirectly have this effect without falling into the forbidden category. The state may once again take some cheer from *Massachusetts v. EPA*, where the federal government used a similar argument in support of its claim that EPA lacked jurisdiction over CO_2 under the Clean Air Act. The Court responded:

> EPA finally argues that it cannot regulate carbon dioxide emissions from motor vehicles because doing so would require it to tighten mileage standards, a job (according to EPA) that Congress has assigned to DOT. But that DOT sets mileage standards in no way licenses EPA to shirk its environmental responsibilities. EPA has been charged with protecting the public's "health" and "welfare," a statutory obligation wholly independent of DOT's mandate to promote energy efficiency. The two obligations may overlap, but there is no reason to think the two agencies cannot both administer their obligations and yet avoid inconsistency.[7]

---

1. Engel & Saleska, *Subglobal Regulation of the Global Commons: The Case of Climate Change*, 32 ECOLOGY L.Q. 183, 221 (2005). The statutory mandate is A.B. 1493, also called the Pavley Act, which requires the state to issue regulations achieving the "maximum feasible and cost-effective reduction of greenhouse gas emissions" from vehicles. Cal. HSC §433018.5(a).

2. Ann E. Carlson, *Federalism, Preemption, and Greenhouse Gas Emissions*, 37 U.C. DAVIS L. REV. 281, 294 (2003).

3. *See* DeShazo and Freeman, *infra* note 6, at 1527 [J.R. DeShazo and Jody Freeman, *Timing and Form of Federal Regulation: The Case of Climate Change*, 155 U. PA. L. REV. 1499 (2007).]. For the relevant gubernatorial executive order, see Executive Order S-01-07 (January 18, 2007), *available at* http://gov.ca.gov/index.php?/print-version/executive-order/5172/.

4. Carlson, *supra* note 2, at 295–296.

5. *Id.* at 296–297.

6. *Id.* at 304.

7. 127 S.Ct. 1438, 1451–62 (2007).

Obviously, this does not speak directly to the issue of state preemption, but it does suggest that the Court views fuel efficiency rules and limitations on CO_2 emissions as two very different matters.[8]

The first ruling on the validity of the California program came in *Green Mountain Chrysler Plymouth Dodge Jeep v. Crombie*.[9] The court considered that the federal agencies involved could work out any tensions between federal fuel economy standards and California's right to a waiver from EPA.[10] The court also found that the greenhouse gas regulations encompassed much more than a fuel economy mandate, particularly as concerned hydrocarbon and carbon monoxide emissions, and also because the regulations encompassed upstream emissions from refineries and other fuel sources.[11] The court also found that the challengers had failed to prove that the rules were technologically or economically infeasible.[12] Finally, the court rejected the argument that the California rules improperly intruded into the field of foreign affairs.[13] The court noted that the State Department had in fact praised state and local efforts in its reports to international agencies.[14]

California's program also passed muster in a separate challenge, *Central Valley Chrysler-Jeep, Inc. v. Goldstene*.[15] Relying heavily on *Massachusetts v. EPA* for guidance about the relationship between the Clean Air Act and CAFÉ standards, a California district court ruled that if the California standards were approved by EPA, the Department of Transportation would have a duty to harmonize the CAFÉ standards with the California requirements. The district court also relied on *Massachusetts v. EPA* in concluding that an executive branch policy could not override the congressionally mandated standards for California's waiver request. The district court held that a claim of foreign policy preemption would require a showing that the state law conflicted with an international agreement or at least a program that derived from international regulations, neither of which were present.

From the state's point of view, *Green Mountain Chrysler Plymouth Dodge Jeep* and *Central Valley Chrysler-Jeep* were promising rulings. Shortly after the latter decision, however, the EPA administrator rejected California's waiver request.[16] The state immediately announced its intention to litigate the refusal. Obviously, the federalism issues will not be settled in the immediate future.

Even if the CARB turns out to be unable to adopt across-the-board restrictions on CO_2 from vehicles, it may still be able to do so on a more limited basis. The Ninth Circuit recently upheld a requirement that the state and local governments with large vehicle fleets purchase only low-emission vehicles, even though the Supreme Court had previously struck down a similar rule that covered private buyers.[17] ...

---

8. The Congressional Research Service concluded that California should qualify for a waiver, particularly in light of Massachusetts v. EPA. *See Report Finds California Has Strong Case to Get Approval of Vehicle Emission Rules*, 38 ENVTL. REP. (Sept. 7, 2007). The Bush Administration later denied the waiver....

9. 508 F. Supp. 2d 295 (D. Vt. 2007).

10. *Id.* at 356.

11. *Id.* at 352.

12. *Id.* at 357.

13. *Id.* at 395.

14. *Id.* at 396.

15. 529 F. Supp. 2d 1151 (E.D. Cal 2007) (CV F 04-6663 AIW LJO).

16. *See* EPA, *America Receives a National Solution for Greenhouse Gas Emissions* (Dec. 19, 2007), *available at* http://yosemite.epa.gov/opa/admpress.nsf/eebfaebc1afd883d85257355005afd19/41b4663d8d380c5852573b 6008141e5!OpenDocument (visited Nov. 15, 2008).

17. Engine Mfrs. Ass'n v. South Coast Air Quality Maint. District, 498 F.3d 1031 (9th Cir. 2007). The court relied on precedent holding that state proprietary activities are not preempted in the absence of a contrary indication from Congress. *Id.* at 1041. The court also remarked that "[i]t is possible that some aspects of

....

2. After an election, some things change. Juliet Eilperin, *EPA Presses Obama to Regulate Warming Under Clean Air Act*, WASHINGTON POST, March 24, 2009, p.1, col. 1.

3. Did environmental law create the electric car or did administrative law kill it? *See The resurrection*, NEW SCIENTIST, Sept. 20, 2008, p. 33:

> Industry's first modern-day foray into the electric car market was a controversial one. In 1996, General Motors launched its EV1 all-electric car. The EV1's development was triggered by Californian laws demanding that car makers in the state start producing zero-emission vehicles, but a legal challenge mounted by the manufacturers followed as quickly as the cars appeared. Critics allege that GM was never enthusiastic about the project. Only 800 EV1s ever hit the road, all of them leased rather than sold, and the company retained the right to withdraw them.
>
> Many leaseholders loved the sleek, quiet EV1s and made overtures to GM to buy them. The car giant rebuffed most of these offers and in 2003 the vehicles were withdrawn and crushed.
>
> In 2006, Sony Pictures released the film *Who Killed the Electric Car?* In it, GM was accused of conspiring with oil companies to sink electric-vehicle technology. In response, GM put a statement on its website which said in part: "When GM launched the EV1, gas was cheap, there wasn't a war in Iraq, and there was less discussion about global warming. There were far fewer reasons for people to make the trade-offs in their transportation lifestyle to make the EV1 work for them. The good news is that both the technology and the GM team who developed the EV1 live on. We didn't kill the electric car; electric vehicle technology is far from dead."

4. For a well thought-out position, see Daniel A. Farber, *Climate Change, Federalism, and the Constitution*, 50 ARIZ. L. REV. 879, 879 (2008), summarized as follows:

> Federal climate change legislation seems increasingly likely, but at least some states are likely to continue pursuing independent initiatives. Courts, state governments, and EPA will then be faced with the question of how much room remains for state climate regulations. This Article argues for a bifurcated approach to the constitutional authority of states to pursue climate change mitigation. Courts should reject regulations that violate clear statutory preemption clauses, discriminate against interstate commerce, ban transactions under federal cap-and-trade schemes, or directly interfere with international agreements. In the remaining cases, this Article advocates adoption of a strong presumption of validity for state climate change regulation.

e. More on the California Experience

Alice Kaswan, *The Domestic Response to Global Climate Change: What Role for Federal, State, and Litigation Initiatives?*, 42 U. SAN. FRAN. L. REV. 39 (2007) (summary of a March 31, 2007 Sym-

---

the [market participant] doctrine have a constitutional dimension, protecting certain sovereign activities by the states from unconstitutional interference by the federal government." *Id*. at 1042. This seems to be a dubious proposition in light of Garcia v. San Antonio Metro. Transit Authority, 459 U.S. 557 (1985). The primary issue in the case was whether the market participant exception applied even though the rule applied to local governments as well as the state government itself. The court's conclusion that the doctrine did apply seems well-founded, since the federal constitution does not speak to the division of authority between state and local governments.

posium). *Id*. at 46–73 (summarizing the "most far-reaching state initiatives taken to date") including (*id*. at 46):

- The July 2002 California "AB 1493" or the "Pavley Bill" that requires the California Air Resources Board (CARB) to develop "regulations that achieve the maximum feasible and cost-effective reduction of greenhouse gas emissions from motor vehicles." Cal. Health & Safety Code §43018.5(a) (West 2006). The regulations, promulgated in 2004, "seek to reduce automobiles' greenhouse gas emissions by 30 percent below 2002 levels when fully implemented by 2016." *Id*. at 49.
- AB 32 or California's 2006 Global Warming Solutions Act, implemented by Governor Schwarzenegger's 2005 Executive Order that "established the goal of reducing California's greenhouse gas emissions to 2000 levels by 2010, to 1990 levels by 2020, and, even more dramatically, to 80 percent below 1990 levels by 2050." *Id*. at 53. The Global Warming Solutions Act "provides few directions about how the state is to achieve its reductions. The statute does not specify particular sectors to be regulated. It does, however, contemplate direct regulation of at least some sectors or industries: it requires CARB to adopt regulations 'to achieve the maximum technologically feasible and cost-effective greenhouse gas emission reductions from sources or categories of sources....' [*citing* Cal. Health & Safety Code §38560]. The law authorizes the CARB to consider a wide variety of potential mechanisms, including direct controls, market measures, and incentive systems. AB 32 also requires the state to consider a wide range of equitable and policy concerns in designing its regulations," *id*. at 54–55 & n. 85 [*citing* the "environmental justice" criterion in Cal. Health & Safety Code §38562(b)(2) (rules must "not disproportionately impact low-income communities")]. "While AB 32 merely states that CARB 'may' adopt a market mechanism, California is very likely to adopt a cap-and-trade program." *Id*. at 55.

Professor Kaswan concludes that state initiatives on climate change are fitting and proper if ultimately an insufficient substitute for a federal-state package. *See id*. at 71 (footnotes omitted):

> Moreover, the states are fulfilling all the desired functions of state-level regulation. States such as California and the Northeastern states are establishing emission reduction goals that address the particular urgency these states perceive. The states are serving as laboratories of invention for each other, and ultimately, for federal legislation if and when it emerges. California is exploring various regulatory options, and both California and the Northeastern states are exploring how best to reconcile numerous competing objectives in designing cap and trade programs. Given the relatively low level of state regulatory action to date, the potential problem of disparate state standards has not yet significantly materialized. Moreover, the federal government has embraced the states' active role. Rather than perceiving state efforts as a threat to federal power, the federal government has touted state efforts as part of the nation's overall approach to climate change.

> In light of the importance of state initiatives, courts should be reluctant to imply federal preemption, and policymakers exercising discretion over state initiatives, like EPA in connection with California's waiver request, should resolve that discretion in favor of the states. More broadly, in light of all the potential impediments to a robust federal response, states considering action should not defer on the expectation of imminent federal legislation.

Notes

1. Global Warming Solutions Act (AB 32), published on Pew Center on Global Climate Change (http://www.pewclimate.org), visited Nov. 16, 2008:

Update on AB 32: California Air Resources Board Releases Proposal for Implementing Global Warming Law

On October 15, 2008, the California Air Resources Board (ARB) released a final Proposed Scoping Plan for implementing A.B. 32, the Global Warming Solutions Act of 2006. The Scoping Plan provides recommendations for reducing the state's greenhouse gas emissions to 1990 levels by 2020. Key elements of the plan include expanded energy efficiency programs and higher efficiency standards, increased use of renewable energy sources, the creation of a California cap-and-trade program that can be integrated with the Western Climate Initiative cap-and-trade program, and efforts to decrease transportation-related emissions.

The document builds on a draft plan, released in June 2008, and incorporates public and stakeholder input. While modifications to the final proposal were minimal, important changes include more aggressive transportation-related emissions targets, detailed recommendations for a cap-and-trade program covering 85 percent of California's emissions by 2020, and a focus on the health, economic, and job-related benefits of climate action. The plan was created by the ARB in collaboration with the state's Climate Action Team. Members of the ARB will vote on the Proposed Scoping Plan in December, and measures will be developed and implemented by 2012.

Update on AB 32: California Market Advisory Committee Releases Final Report

On June 29, 2007, California's Market Advisory Committee (MAC) released its final report and recommendations for the design of a greenhouse gas cap and trade system in the state. The report addresses the major questions and challenges involved in program design. The California Air Resources Board will ultimately decide whether and how to implement a market-based system as part of the state's efforts to reduce greenhouse gases under AB 32, the Global Warming Solutions Act. The 14-member Committee was formed in December 2006 to support the state with implementation of AB 32. Among its members is Judi Greenwald, Director of Innovative Solutions for the Pew Center on Global Climate Change. Josh Bushinsky, Western Policy Coordinator for the Pew Center, serves on the staff to the committee.

Background on the Global Warming Solutions Act (AB 32)

On September 27, 2006, Governor Schwarzenegger signed AB 32, the Global Warming Solutions Act. The Act caps California's greenhouse gas emissions at 1990 levels by 2020. This legislation represents the first enforceable state-wide program in the U.S. to cap all GHG emissions from major industries that includes penalties for non-compliance. It requires the State Air Resources Board to establish a program for statewide greenhouse gas emissions reporting and to monitor and enforce compliance with this program. The Act authorizes the state board to adopt market-based compliance mechanisms including cap-and-trade, and allows a one-year extension of the targets under extraordinary circumstances.

Statement by Eileen Claussen, President, Pew Center on Global Climate Change:

"California has achieved the right balance, the goals they have established are reasonable enough to meet, and ambitious enough to spur innovation. This is a big deal and a beautiful example of leadership and bi-partisanship at work."

2. Kimberly Kobo, *California Global Warming Solutions Act of 2006: Meaningfully Decreasing Greenhouse Gas Emissions or Merely a Set of Empty Promises?*, 41 LOYOLA OF L.A. L. REV. 447, 475 (2008):

> Although the California Global Warming Solutions Act of 2006 has the potential to lead the country and spur further action, it now becomes a waiting game to see how CARB will decide to proceed. Until CARB decides on a plan of action, the bill is virtually

meaningless. AB-32 is certainly a step in the right direction, but because it lacks any real guidelines to ensure its success, its potential impact on the environment and on California businesses will be unknown for several more years. So while Governor Schwarzenegger continues to laud the bill as a revolutionary piece of environmental legislation that does not hinder California's thriving economy, it remains a mystery as to whether or not these promises will actually come true.

3. *California Climate Policy Update.* On December 11, 2008, after an eighteen month planning process, the California Air Resources Board (ARB) approved a "Scoping Plan" for fulfilling the greenhouse gas emissions targets articulated by the state's landmark climate legislation, AB 32 (The Global Warming Solutions Act of 2006). According to Mary Nichols, ARB Chair, "[t]his plan is California's prospectus for a more secure and sustainable economy. It will guide capital investments into energy efficiency to save us money, into renewable energy to break our dependence on oil, and promote a new generation of green jobs for hundreds of thousands of Californians."[1]

The Scoping Plan articulates the methods that California will use to reduce its emissions to 1990 levels by 2020, which include a comprehensive cap and trade program (in conjunction with the Western Climate Initiative), a "clean cars" program, and a mandate for smart growth.[2] In particular, the Plan creates: an emissions cap on utilities, refineries and other large industrial sources of greenhouse gases, a requirement that fuel companies reformulate fuels so they are a combined 10 percent less carbon-intensive by 2020, incentives for local governments to curb urban sprawl and reduce how far people drive to work or school, requirements for utilities to generate one-third of their electricity from renewable sources such as wind, solar and geothermal by 2020, and strengthened energy-efficiency standards for appliances and for existing and new buildings.

3. Other State Responses on Urgent Issues of Climate Change

There follows an account by Professor Denise Antolini who describes the climate change trek of the island State of Hawai'i.

————————

Drowning Hawai'i:
Island Resiliency and Climate Change

Denise Antolini is an Associate Professor of Law at the William S. Richardson School of Law, University of Hawai'i at Mānoa and Director of the Environmental Law Program. She is a member of the University of Hawai'i at Mānoa Climate Change Commission and a founding advisor of the University of Hawai'i's new Center for Island Climate Adaptation and Policy (ICAP). The author acknowledges the research assistance of law students Nathaniel Noda and George White; the inspiration from Professor Mingyuan Wang (Director, Center for Environmental, Natural Resources, and Energy Law at Tsinghua University, Beijing); the much-appreciated contributions of University of Hawai'i faculty including Chip Fletcher, Gordon Grau, Kem Lowry, Steve Meder, Makena Coffman, and Maxine Burkett; the leadership of Hawai'i environmental colleagues Jeff Mikulina, Josh Stanbro, Henry Curtis, Kat Brady, and Doug Codiga; the vision of Hawai'i legislators Hermina Morita and Gary Hooser; and the support from her husband Ken and boys Tate and Conrad. Professor Antolini can be reached at: antolini@hawaii.edu.

————————

1. California Air Resources Board Press Release. *Available at* http://www.arb.ca.gov/newsrel/nr121108.htm.
2. For more information on California's smart growth mandate, see Senate Bill 375.

Introduction

In late 2007, a Sunday edition of the Honolulu Star-Bulletin published a front-page story on the future impacts of climate change on Hawai'i.[1] To dramatize the risks of rising ocean waters, a large photograph showed turquoise waves drowning the iconic statue of Duke Kahanamoku in Waikiki. In another photograph, University of Hawai'i scientist Charles Fletcher held a yardstick on the sand amidst sunbathing tourists to illustrate the "slowly emerging catastrophe" of sea-level rise.[2] Fletcher predicted that, in 100 years, Hawai'i's ocean waters would rise over one meter, inundating the state's key coastal areas.[3] To further drive home the point, the article showed a bird's-eye graphic with Waikiki's famous seaside hotels as fragmented islets, helpless against the rising sea.[4]

For the vast majority of Hawai'i residents, the article was likely the first time they read anything specific to Hawai'i about the implications of climate change and global sea-level rise. Many readers were probably shocked to see the islands' beloved Duke[5] appear so helpless and wearing a cheap pink plastic "floatie." For over half a century, Waikiki has been Hawai'i's world-renowned golden egg, anchoring the state's tourism-dependent economy by attracting millions of visitors annually.[6] The widespread loss of precious beaches and coastal areas in Hawai'i—given their critical role in the islands' lifestyle, tourism, culture, ecosystems, and infrastructure—is far beyond the wildest imagination of residents. Out of sincerity, ignorance, or fear, some completely dismiss the idea that anything will change. Yet, the evidence of the risk of severe disruption to Hawai'i's future is increasing. Adapting to climate change and building the islands' resiliency deserves immediate attention from policymakers and all sectors of our economic, environmental, and academic communities. The Star-Bulletin article and its daring images helped to spark public awareness about the need to act now, not later, so Hawai'i can adapt—as seamlessly as possible—to its uncertain future.

The isolated[7] Hawaiian islands had a historic opportunity to speed up local and global public awareness about the risks of climate change when, in January 2008, Honolulu hosted the George W. Bush Administration's post-Bali "major economies meeting."[8] Similar to the U.S.'s national

---

1. Diana Leone, *The Drowning of Hawaii*, Honolulu Star-Bulletin, Sept. 23, 2007, http://starbulletin.com/2007/09/23/news/story01.html (photograph by Kip Aoki and Dennis Oda) [hereinafter Leone]. This chapter title is derived from the article title and used with permission of the Star-Bulletin.

2. *Id.*

3. *Id.*

4. *Id.* The graphic was produced by the University of Hawai'i at Mānoa School of Ocean and Earth Science and Technology.

5. Affectionately known as "Duke," Hawai'i's favorite son Duke Kahanamoku was a 1912 Olympian champion swimmer, pioneer of Hawai'i surfing, and an international celebrity. *See* Duke Kahanamoku, http://www.co.honolulu.hi.us/cameras/waikiki_beach/duke.htm. His statue represents the unique cultural history of Hawai'i and symbolizes the physical prowess of its ocean-recreation culture.

6. Mary Vorsino, *Can Waikiki handle growth?*, Honolulu Advertiser, Mar. 10, 2008, http://the.honoluluadvertiser.com/article/2008/Mar/10/ln/hawaii803100358.html (noting that, on any given day, there are 75,000 tourists in Waikīkī and more than 30,000 workers, and that it has a capacity of 30,000 hotel rooms). In 2007, Hawai'i attracted 7.4 million visitors statewide, with approximately 4.6 million of these visiting Oahu. State Department of Business, Economic Development and Tourism (DBEDT), *News Release, Total Visitor Spending in 2007 Reached $12.2 Billion, Up $103.2 Million*, Jan. 29, 2008, at 1. This compares to the estimated resident population in Hawai'i of 1.285 million (in 2006), DBEDT, *Residents*, State of Hawaii Data Book Time Series, Table 1.04 (2008), and about 900,000 residents on Oahu. *Id.* Table 1.06.

7. The Hawaiian Islands are the most geographically isolated chain on the planet (2,390 miles from California and 3,850 miles from Japan). G.A. Macdonald *et al.*, Volcanoes in the Sea: The Geology of Hawaii (2d ed. 1984, Univ. Hawai'i Press).

8. The George W. Bush Administration convened the Major Economies Meeting on Energy Security and Climate Change (dubbed "MEM") on January 30–31, 2008 at the East-West Center adjacent to the University of Hawai'i at Mānoa campus. Seventeen of the world's major countries, or major emitters, participated along with United Nations' representatives in closed-door talks. Paul Berry, *Cool It 2.0*, Honolulu Weekly, Feb. 6–12, 2008, at 6 [hereinafter Berry]. The MEM countries represented 80% of the world's energy use and 80%

position on climate change at that time, however, this event was almost entirely disconnected from its real-world island context. Media access was restricted, coverage was sparse, and the delegates met entirely behind closed doors. After the lack of progress at the Bali Conference of Parties only a month before, the international delegates were probably hoping only to get to the beach after their meetings. Seeking to draw public attention to the local-global connection, locked-out local activists drew a "blue line" on neighborhood sidewalks to represent the risk of rising waters,[9] and University of Hawai'i faculty and students held a packed teach-in at the law school.[10] The warning to a Hawai'i reporter by French delegate Brice LaLonde that "Global warming is the most important and terrifying thing facing mankind"[11] seemed unrelated to Hawai'i given the lack of mainstream coverage of the event and any local context. For years, the Hawai'i newspapers had ignored the crescendo in global media attention to climate change.[12] Not even the plea of Hawai'i's Pacific Island relatives in tiny Tuvalu, who have been sounding the alarm for years about their island's vulnerability to rising waters,[13] had roused much local media interest. The 2008 meeting of global climate change negotiators in Honolulu seemed similarly to be of little meaning to Hawai'i residents.[14]

Yet, to those paying attention, the specter of gloom potentially caused by climate change—severe drainage problems, exacerbated erosion, increased flooding by high waves, ocean acidification, extreme weather, and economic-social isolation—as LaLonde warned, should be alarming. Perhaps it is *too* alarming for the average reader. Do people in Hawai'i think it just will not happen, believe that they will remain unaffected, or simply feel powerless? Out of sight, out of

---

of its greenhouse gas (GHG) emissions. *Id.* at 7. The very low expectations for the MEM meeting were met, just barely. By most accounts, the meeting was a policy failure. No new initiatives were announced or even hinted. The chief U.S. negotiator, John Connaughton, "sat silent and deadpan, looking like he'd just been dealt a lousy poker hand." *Id.* "Weary delegates at the final press meeting issued the *pro forma* thanks ... followed by a round of clichéd diplomatic euphemisms about candid, frank and constructive talks...." *Id.*

9. When the MEM talk came to Honolulu in January 2008, the Hawai'i Chapter of the Sierra Club joined with other local environmental groups and school children to "draw the line on climate change" by chalking blue lines and climate-awareness messages on sidewalks in a neighborhood that would be reached by Professor Fletcher's predicted one-meter rise in sea level. Sierra Club Hawai'i Chapter, NEWSLETTER, Mar. 28, 2008, at 1 (on file with author). The demonstration was "eye-popping," drawing the attention of international reporters gathered in Honolulu. *Id.* The *China News* quoted a 16-year-old Hawai'i girl as saying: "I didn't realize everything I knew would be underwater." *Id.* (at enclosed flyer). *See also* Associated Press, *Leaders Talk Climate Change in Hawaii*, Jan. 31, 2008, *available at* www.summitdaily.com/article/20080131/NEWS/785058700.

10. Berry, *supra* note 8.

11. *Id.*

12. *See, e.g.,* Madeleine Brand, National Public Radio, *Resource-Rich Hawaii Depends on Fossil Fuel*, May 27, 2007, http://www.npr.org/templates/story/story.php?storyId=10512492 (noting the surprising lack of concern among Hawai'i residents about their dependence on fossil fuels).

13. *See* http://www.tuvaluislands.com/warming.htm. Tuvalu is a small island country about mid-way between Hawai'i and Australia with no islands over 15 feet above sea level. Leslie Allen, *Will Tuvalu Disappear Beneath the Sea?*, SMITHSONIAN MAGAZINE, Aug. 2004, http://www.smithsonianmag.com/travel/tuvalu.html. Tuvalu's problems may be caused both by rising seas and extreme weather conditions; its plight has become a cause célèbre for island nations and climate change advocates. *Id.*

14. Few in Hawai'i even know that the islands have played a critical role in global climate science. A few weeks before the MEM meetings were occurring in Honolulu, scientists from around the world gathered on the Island of Hawai'i (known informally as the "Big Island") to celebrate the 50th Anniversary of the Mauna Loa Observatory's readings of carbon dioxide in the atmosphere. *See* Rod Thompson, *Manhattan Project to save climate urged*, HONOLULU STAR-BULLETIN, Dec. 3, 2007, http://starbulletin.com/2007/12/03/news/story 04.html. The measurements, called the Keeling Curve after Scripps scientist Dr. Charles Keeling, began in 1957 and formed the core foundation for the IPCC reports on temperature increase. *See* NOAA, Earth System Research Laboratory, Atmospheric Carbon Dioxide—Mauna Loa, http://www.esrl.noaa.gov/gmd/ccgg/trends/co2_data_mlo.html; IPCC, IPCC Data Distribution Center, Carbon Dioxide Projected Emissions and Concentrations, Figure 1 http://www.ipcc-data.org/ddc_co2.html.

mind? For many scientists, advocates, and policymakers in Hawai'i, however, the risk of climate change is very real and rapidly becoming the most urgent priority on their professional and personal agendas.[15] The need to drastically accelerate action on local and global climate change mitigation efforts and the equally urgent need to address adaptation and build resiliency in the face of this risk is just beginning to dawn on Hawai'i. Not a moment too soon.

Under the pessimistic scenario, when my two sons, now nine and thirteen years old, reach my age in about 2050, the sea-level rise predicted by Fletcher—say a foot or so by then—will be regularly cutting off Hawai'i's numerous low-lying coastal roadways at high tide and during high wave events that happen a dozen times each year, severely eroding the most popular beaches, threatening to undermine beachfront communities, flooding the storm drainage system in downtown Honolulu and Waikiki, lapping at the airport runways, and dislocating key industrial zones. By then, they and many others may have, with heavy hearts, left the islands for the continental U.S., which will be facing its own set of adaptation challenges. Or they may feel, like many others, that leaving Hawai'i is not a moral or economic option; they may "choose" to live in a chaotic, stressed, and isolated society far different from our comfortable connected island lifestyle of today.

Under the optimistic scenario, by 2050, my sons will still happily be in Hawai'i, with their own families, contributing to and enjoying a "sustainable paradise." At a very large cost, Hawai'i will have prepared itself for a resilient future through massive smart investment—moving people, industry, and infrastructure away from the shoreline, creating sustainable communities, and protecting diverse ecosystems. Under the best case scenario, Hawai'i will have also become a leader not just in adaptation but also mitigation, by shifting to a locally sustainable economy and embracing indigenous renewable energy sources to gird against further climate change and escalating fossil fuel costs. Perhaps my Hawai'i-born sons and their millennial generation will repay their debt to the islands better than their parents have by figuring out between now and then how to make the islands truly resilient and sustainable. As a professor of environmental law, this is my intellectually preferred scenario; as a resident of Hawai'i and as a mother, this is my private hope. But, hope must be joined with action. For my sons' generation to succeed, my generation must as well. Now, not later.

This chapter discusses the emerging consensus among policymakers, activists, and academics in Hawai'i about the stark risks and vibrant opportunities presented to the islands by climate change—the state's new initiatives to address mitigation and the growing discussions about adaptation. The potential for a positive future for Hawai'i is enormous. The islands possess all of the natural resources, talent, and multi-cultural wisdom necessary to build a resilient future and to become a global model of a community that fully accepts its responsibility to shape a sustainable future. As the NEW YORK TIMES editorialized in early 2008, "It's almost embarrassing how green things could be in blue Hawaii."[16]

In the past four years, Hawai'i's Republican Governor Linda Lingle and the Democratic-majority Hawai'i Legislature have both shown increasingly strong leadership in addressing the State's energy dependence and greenhouse gas emissions. Yet, even though mitigation is far from solved, no visionary political leader in Hawai'i has turned the public's attention from mitigation to resiliency. The window of time for creating sustainable islands is already quickly passing but the discussion on adaptation is just beginning. The challenges may seem too large, the impacts too remote, or the scenarios too speculative. But waiting is risky. Some good news is that Hawai'i's legislative effort in 2007 to address emissions mitigation has now sparked a new effort

---

15. This is based on the author's personal experience among environmental law professors nationwide, environmental advocates, the legal profession, and university colleagues in Hawai'i.

16. Lawrence Downes, *Editorial, Languid Hawaii Looks to be an Energy Leader*, N.Y. TIMES, Feb. 2, 2008, http://www.nytimes.com/2008/02/08/opinion/08fri4.html.

to (at least) study adaptation. In May 2009, the State Legislature passed a proposal endorsed in an earlier draft of this chapter—a two-year state task force to study and recommend statewide adaptation measures.[17] Although under-funded, this task force is a critical step forward that can catalyze parallel efforts to move the issue higher on the public agenda. In addition, the University of Hawai'i recently established a new inter-disciplinary Center for Island Climate Adaptation and Policy (ICAP)—which was also only a pipe dream of the author and other collaborators just a year ago—to bring the best science, law, and policy to island communities in need of adaptation guidance. These initiatives are major steps forward, but more needs to be done. The next few years are the critical policy window for the islands to attack this thorny issue from multiple, not just two, fronts. Will Hawai'i languidly choose to go "underwater" or will it boldly conquer the rising waves? In just a few years, we will likely all know.

I. Hawai'i's "Luau Carbon Feet"[18] and Addiction to Fossil Fuels

Hawai'i's contribution to climate change, by some accounts, may seem miniscule but, upon further examination, is surprisingly large. Year 1990 emissions in Hawai'i (18 million metric tons (MMT) of CO_2 equivalent) were only 0.3% of U.S. greenhouse gas (GHG) emissions.[19] But the state's footprint may not actually be so quaint and two recent inventories indicate that emissions have increased in the past decade.[20] The islands' geographic isolation, residents' expectations of a high standard of living, and modern local and global transportation systems all add up to a big carbon appetite. According to the *Honolulu Weekly*,

> Hawaii ranks 43d among the states and 32d in per capita emissions per resident. But our real carbon footprint—the releases of carbon dioxide, methane and nitrous oxide we're responsible for—is a lot bigger. That's because the rankings don't take into account Hawaii's reliance on goods made elsewhere. The gases released in producing the food, fuel and building supplies we import are not counted against us. Nor are the fossil fuels burnt in transporting all this stuff to our shores.... Yes, we're islands. Hungry islands. And we've got big fat luau carbon feet.[21]

---

17. SB266, SD2, HD2, CD1, 25th Leg. (Hawai'i 2009) http://www.capitol.hawaii.gov/session2009/bills/SB266_CD1_.pdf (one of the welcome changes to the original bill was the addition of the new Director of ICAP to the task force). The Governor may still veto the bill, but the legislature could then over-ride the veto or re-introduce the bill again next year.

18. The term "luau feet" means big feet in pidgin, the local Hawai'i dialect. *See* Pat Sasaki *et al.*, Pidgin to Da Max (25th Anniv. Ed. 2005).

19. State of Hawai'i Dep't Business, Economic Development & Tourism, Hawaii Energy Strategy 2000, 2–8 (2000).

20. Two recently released independent emissions inventories reached somewhat similar conclusions with updated but differing methodologies and time frames. *See* ICF International, *Draft Hawaii Greenhouse Gas Inventory: 1990 and 2007* (Oct. 2008) (indicating a "modest" increase in emissions of 3% from 1990 to 2007, *id.* at 9, but including out of state air travel, the increase was 32%, *id.* at 8); *cf.* University of Hawai'i Economic Research Organization, *Energy and Greenhouse Gas Solutions: Hawai'i Greenhouse Gas Emissions Profile 1990 and 2005* (Jan. 30, 2009), http://www.uhero.hawaii.edu/eggs/EGGS_GHG_2009_1.pdf (indicating an increase of 23% in 15 years, to 26.4 MMT, primarily due to a "surge" in ground transportation, excluding air travel, *id.* at 8 & Table 2).

21. *Hawaii's carbon footprint*, Honolulu Weekly, Jan. 23–29, 2008, at 6. Hawai'i's total emissions of CO_2 (measured in metric tons) as of 2003 was 21.5, tiny compared to Texas's 670.2 (ranked No. 1 nationally) and surprisingly higher than Vermont's 6.5 (ranked 50th). *Id.* at (inset). Our annual per capita emissions of CO_2 in 2003 were 17.78 metric tons, not much lower than the U.S. average of 20.4 metric tons per capita, and about twice that of the average Italian (7.69 tons per capita). *Id.* Hawai'i uses about 263.0 million BTU per capita annually, about five times less than the highest consuming states (Alaska has a 1,193.9 million BTU per capita usage). Hawaiian Electric Company, 2007 Corporate Sustainability Report 17 (2007) (hereinafter Hawaiian Electric 2007 Report).

In fact, air transportation accounts for about 25% of all of Hawai'i's emissions,[22] but this source is left out of the national rankings calculations.

Even if small, the emissions trend in Hawai'i is bad. A preliminary review of the change in emissions between the baseline year 1990 and 2005 showed a 7.5% increase over 15 years.[23] A closer look is even more disconcerting. Emissions from residential, commercial, and industrial power generation *increased 118%*; municipal solid waste emissions increased by 46.5%; and, electricity generation (roughly one-third of the total) grew by nearly 15%.[24] One area that showed major improvement resulted from the loss of Hawai'i's historic sugarcane industry, the reduced acreage used by large agricultural enterprises,[25] and the closure of Hawai'i's cement industry. Although these declines are helpful to Hawai'i's carbon bottom line, none of these downward shifts resulted from intentional climate change policy efforts, and they indicate decreasing economic self-sufficiency for the state in these sectors. These major transitions in Hawai'i's economy were also outside the state's control due to the rising land values in the state and increasing global pressures on its traditional exports such as sugar and pineapple. No reason for pride here.

The story from the state's transportation sector is equally discouraging. Ground transportation (accounting for about one-fifth of all emissions) increased by 28%.[26] Part of this increase resulted from people in Hawai'i buying *less* fuel efficient cars in recent years, even while national CAFE standards were increasing.[27] Air transportation showed a decrease of 26%, largely because aircraft have become more efficient.[28] Even though the decline in air transportation emissions was good news, the total transportation sector still accounted for the lion's share of Hawai'i's GHG emissions, both in 1990 (international = 25.81%; domestic = 15.57%; ground = 15.63%, totaling 57.01%) and in 2005 (international = 17.62%; domestic 13.87%; ground = 18.63%, totaling 50.12%).[29] The 2008 spike in gas prices in Hawai'i (consistently the highest in the nation) may have minimized the problem of people driving inefficient cars.[30] However, the air transportation issue will need maverick leadership not easily found in a state whose economy is addicted to carbon-based transportation.

Considering how millions of sun-seeking visitors get to Hawai'i each year and realizing that the state has an unusually large military presence, it is not surprising that Hawai'i's lead-

---

22. Makena Coffman, *Preparing for Climate Change Mitigation in Hawaii*, Presentation to the Natural Resources Section, Hawai'i State Bar Ass'n, May 20, 2008 (slides on file with author).

23. Patricia Tummons, *Greenhouse Gas Emissions in Hawaii Grew 7.5 Percent from 1992 to 2005*, ENVIRONMENT HAWAII, Jan. 2008, at 6 (citing John Tantlinger, retired manager of DBEDT's energy policy and planning branch).

24. *Id.*

25. The rapid decline in Hawai'i's agricultural sector tells part of the tale as well. Emissions from domestic animals dropped about 30%; "manure management" emissions declined 56%; emissions from sugarcane burning (now a nearly dead industry after 100 years of success) slid 66%; only "fertilizer use" emissions grew at a low 2.4%. *Id.*

26. *Id.*

27. *Id.* On the other hand, the economic and cultural connections of Hawai'i to Japan mean that the more efficient Toyota, Honda, and Nissan cars are tops among car sales in the state for many years. *See, e.g.,* Howard Dicus, *While mainland vehicle sales fall, Hawaii sales rise*, PACIFIC BUSINESS NEWS, Mar. 1, 2004, http://www.bizjournals.com/pacific/stories/2004/03/01/daily6.html. Along with the limited driving range in the islands, this should make it one of the lowest emitters per capita in the ground transportation category. Higher gas prices in 2008 may have also sparked a reversal of the inefficiency trend in Hawai'i; demand for hybrid cars began outstripping supply, with sales of the Prius, for example, shooting up 41% over the prior year. Lynda Arakawa, *Hawaii motorists flock to gas sippers*, HONOLULU ADVERTISER, May 27, 2008.

28. Tummons, *supra* note 23.

29. HAWAIIAN ELECTRIC 2007 REPORT, *supra* note 21, at 10 (chart).

30. Alexandre de Silva, *Isle Drivers Cut Time on Road to Save Gas*, HONOLULU STAR-BULLETIN, May 30, 2008, http://starbulletin.com/print/2005.php?fr=/2008/05/30/news/story01.html (reporting 46% of Hawai'i drivers were driving fewer miles because of high gas prices).

ing energy consuming sector is "heavy jet fuel use by military installations and commercial airlines."[31] Indeed, these two issues—air transportation and military use—may be the most difficult emissions issues to address politically. Even many environmental advocates consider them untouchable. The 2007 "climate change solutions" legislation in Hawai'i (Act 234, addressed below) simply avoided these issues, carving them completely out of the scope of the legislation that has otherwise boldly set Hawai'i on the path to mandatory emissions limits.[32] Jet fuel usage must become a legitimate part of the discussion about climate change in Hawai'i,[33] even at the risk of further social-economic isolation. A head-in-the-sand approach to this major emissions sector simply makes the problem harder to address in the future and is unfair to the other economic sectors that will soon be asked to respond to state emissions targets.

Hawai'i's numbers are even less flattering considering that the islands' mild climate eliminates the need for home heating and, relying on natural tradewinds and ceiling fans, almost all Hawai'i homes can forego air conditioning. Yet, new tract and luxury homes built in hotter zones (such as the rapidly growing "second city" in 'Ewa, O'ahu) include, or beg for, fossil-fuel-intensive air conditioning. The percentage of Hawai'i households with air conditioning rose from only 16% in 1990 to 57% in 2006.[34] The new preference for air conditioning, secondary refrigerators and freezers, larger home entertainment systems, big-box store consumption patterns, and scads of personal electronics are also factors that are pushing usage upward.[35] Changes in building codes, stronger green building incentives, reduction in wasteful vampire loads, and re-orienting the homeowner mindset toward efficiency will certainly be important to decreasing emissions from current households and to creating wedges that cut into the always upward pressure from new housing development.

This complex picture of emissions also indicates how vulnerable the state's economy is to the global fossil fuel markets. Hawai'i imports over 80% of its food and virtually all of its consumer goods.[36] Shockingly, Hawai'i imports of tropical fruits have more than tripled since the 1960s.[37] Hawai'i now brings in four avocadoes and one banana for each one grown locally.[38] Local bananas consistently cost about 20–30% *more* than imported bananas.[39] Imports get to Hawai'i in only two ways: ships and airplanes. Both methods completely depend on fossil fuels. The 2008 surge in oil prices almost immediately sparked higher fuel surcharges in transportation, which were quickly passed to already stretched consumers.[40] In 2008, in Hawai'i, a half-gallon of milk cost $5.00 compared to $3.99 in 2007; green grapes cost $2.99 per pound compared to $1.28 in 2007.[41] The is-

---

31. HAWAIIAN ELECTRIC 2007 REPORT, *supra* note 21, at 17.

32. *See* Tummons, *supra* note 23, at 6 (quoting Sierra Club's Jeff Mikulina as stating that the Attorney General put airplanes outside the bill because of concerns about interstate commerce and federal supremacy, whereas Senior Vice President for Hawaiian Electric Robbie Alm reportedly noted the purpose of the exclusion was to avoid burdening the tourism industry).

33. The European Union recently reached a landmark controversial agreement to include air transportation emissions in its climate trading scheme. James Kanter, EU reaches landmark deal to cap airline emissions, INT'L HERALD TRIBUNE, June 26, 2008, http://www.iht.com/bin/printfriendly.php?id=14026434.

34. HAWAIIAN ELECTRIC 2007 REPORT, *supra* note 21, at 23.

35. *Id.*

36. Coffman, *supra* note 22.

37. Sean Hao, *Imports tip island produce scale*, HONOLULU STAR-BULLETIN, May 7, 2007, http://the. honoluluadvertiser.com/article/2007/May/07/ln/FP705070359.html.

38. National Agricultural Statistics Office, Statistics of Hawaii Agriculture 20006, Market Supply: Fresh Fruits 2002–2006, http://www.nass.usda.gov/hi/stats/t_of_c.htm.

39. Author's observation.

40. Staff, *Young Brothers Raising Fuel Fee*, HONOLULU ADVERTISER, Feb. 22, 2008, http://the.honolulu advertiser.com/article/2008/Feb/22/bz/hawaii802220335.html.

41. B.J. Reyes, *Rising Oil Prices Spread Beyond Gas*, HONOLULU STAR-BULLETIN, Mar. 16, 2008, http://star bulletin.com/print/2005.php?fr=/2008/03/16/news/story01.html.

lands' two major barge companies increased the fuel surcharge to a record 33.75%.[42] Hawai'i's over-reliance on imported food and goods makes it triply vulnerable to rising fossil fuel costs.

For energy itself, blue Hawai'i relies on black fossil fuels more so than any other state in the U.S. Fossil fuels constitute more than 96% of its energy needs.[43] Making matters worse, the vast majority of Hawai'i's fossil fuels are imported (as of 2007, about 89%).[44] Of Hawai'i's imported foreign crude oil in 2006, which represents 91% of state demand,[45] 23% came from Vietnam, 20% from Saudi Arabia, 10.7% from Brunei, 10% from Indonesia, 9% from China, 5.2% from Thailand, and less than 5% from Libya, Ecuador, Angola, U.A.E., Oman, and other countries.[46] Of the imported coal (about 5% of state fossil fuel demand), most comes from Indonesia.[47] The estimated economic "outflow" from Hawai'i for these fossil fuel purchases is more than $4 billion per year, leaving a huge hole in the state's economy.[48]

In addition to the same concerns that dependence on foreign sources causes the U.S. in general, Hawai'i has the added problem of being a fly-speck on the international market. As one commentator stated, "Think India and China. In this context, the needs of tiny, out-of-the-way Hawaii will hardly be of major concern to the global oil industry."[49] With its high rate of dependence, Hawai'i is completely at the mercy of the volatile global oil market and, some would say, particularly vulnerable to price gouging.[50] Characterizing the vulnerability more vividly, if the daily oil tankers and coal barges stopped arriving, Hawai'i's fossil fuel supplies would last about a week.[51] Equally scary, if the ships and planes bringing consumer goods stopped coming, Hawai'i's basic store supplies would also run out in a few days, quickly putting residents in dire straits.[52]

Not surprisingly, gasoline historically also costs way more in Hawai'i than on the continental U.S. As of August 2008, the average gas price for regular on O'ahu was $4.44, compared to the average price in California of $4.17 and the national average of $3.81.[53] The price of regular gas on the remote luxury resort island of Lana'i is typically the highest in the nation, and has regu-

---

42. *Id.*

43. Rocky Mountain Institute, POLICY RECOMMENDATIONS FOR HAWAII'S ENERGY FUTURE, prepared for DBEDT (Mar. 2008), at 68 & Fig. 11, http://hawaii.gov/dbedt/info/energy/publications/HEPR-Full-Report-080407.pdf [hereinafter RMI].

44. STATE OF HAWAI'I DBEDT, ENERGY RESOURCES COORDINATOR, ANNUAL REPORT 2007, http://www.hawaii.gov/dbedt/info/energy/publications/erc07.pdf (from 1992–2006, Hawai'i's dependence on foreign oil has increased as Alaska imports have declined dramatically from about 30% to zero).

45. RMI, *supra* note 43, at 68.

46. *Id.* (cover chart).

47. *Id.*

48. RMI, *supra* note 43, at 43 Fig. 3 & n.38 (Hawai'i energy costs totaled $4.26 billion in 2005, about 10% of personal income).

49. Editorial, *Energy future must be built here at home,* HONOLULU ADVERTISER, at 2B, July 23, 2006.

50. Hawai'i enacted a controversial "gas cap" law in 2004, H.R.S. 486H (2004), based on the premise that the state was paying unfairly high gas prices compared to continental U.S. states. Associated Press, *Honolulu caps gas prices,* USA TODAY, Aug. 24, 2005, http://www.usatoday.com/money/industries/energy/2005-08-24-hawaii-gas_x.htm. That law was, however, repealed in the 2007 session and currently only tracking of prices is undertaken by DBEDT. *See* State of Hawai'i Dep't of Commerce and Consumer Affairs, Hawaii Gas Cap Law, http://hawaii.gov/dcca/areas/dca/gascap.

51. Hawaiian Food Sovereignty: Ho'ea Ea, http://www.localharvest.org/newsletter/20070824/food-sovereignty.jsp (estimating supplies would last three to ten days).

52. This vulnerability is well known to those who have lived through dock strikes in Hawai'i, like the one in 1971 and the ones threatened in 1999 and 2002 when rice, spam, and toilet paper flew off the store shelves. *See* June Watanabe, *Hawaiians worried over dock strike, stockpile goods,* S.F. CHRON., Oct. 2, 2002, http://www.sfgate.com/cgi-bin/article.cgi?file=/chronicle/archive/2002/10/02/BU172405.DTL&type=business.

53. American Automobile Association, Daily Fuel Gauge Report, National Average & State by State Average, http://www.fuelgaugereport.com/index.asp (visited Aug., 2008).

larly topped $5.00.[54] Like electricity, gasoline fuels the state's daily economy and higher prices are causing substantial reverberations in the cost of goods, transportation patterns, and individual habits.

Hawai'i pays the price for its geographic isolation and lack of developed indigenous fuel sources in innumerable ways. Electricity costs are a key indicator of how the price signal echoes loudly through the local economy, with all prices ramping up even higher on the "neighbor islands," which have smaller grids and fewer sources of fuel. Hawai'i consumers pay the highest prices in the country for electricity. As of 2006, the national residential average was about 10¢ per kWh.[55] That year, the Hawai'i average was 21¢.[56] As of early 2008, the official Hawai'i electricity rates had tripled: 30¢ kWh for residential customers, up from the official prices of 22¢ kWh the prior year.[57] My family's recent utility bill, with fuel surcharges included, was 32¢ kWh. The upward trend is likely to continue, even with some slippage due to the current economic downturn.

When Hawai'i's electricity production is viewed by fuel source, the data further reveal Hawai'i's "dirty secret":[58] despite abundant natural energy sources and years of policy initiatives to support alternatives, the state is still almost completely reliant on non-renewable sources of energy. As of December 2007, Hawaiian Electric Company (Hawaiian Electric) (which provides 93% of the Hawai'i electricity market through its separate utilities on O'ahu, Mau'i, and the Big Island) and the handful of independent producers relied on oil for 78% of their fuel source, coal for another 18%, and solid waste another 4%.[59] A measly percentage of Hawaiian Electric's energy comes from renewables: out of 6,478.67 Gigawatts (GW), only 1.42 GW come from biofuels (on Maui), 14.73 GW comes from hydropower (on the Island of Hawai'i, commonly called "the Big Island"), and 0.44 GW from wind (on the Big Island).[60] Even Hawai'i's "independent" power producers (IPPs) depend primarily on fossil fuels, using renewables for only a small portion of their contribution to the grid. Out of a total of 4,227.89 GW put on the Hawaiian grid by all IPPs, only 57.47 GW comes from biomass,[61] 229.89 GW from geothermal, 37.29 GW from hydro, 2.26 GW from solid waste, and 241.54 GW from wind, totaling 568 GW or 13%.[62]

Alternative energy sources have enjoyed more success on the Big Island (where wind contributes about 10%, hydro 4%, and geothermal 18%) and on Maui (where wind is 9%, hydro 1%, and biomass/fuel 5%)[63] than on the most populated island O'ahu. On O'ahu, for example, all three power plants use imported oil, generating a total of 1,263 Megawatts (MW).[64] IPPs on O'ahu produce another 434 Megawatts: 46 MW from Honolulu's "H-Power" garbage-to-energy

---

54. Joe Benton, *Relentless Gas Price Increase Continues*, CONSUMER AFFAIRS (June 10, 2008), http://www.consumeraffairs.com/news04/2008/06/gas_prices253.html.

55. U.S. Energy Information Administration, Annual Energy Review, Table 8.10 (Average Retail Prices of Electricity, 1960–2007), http://www.eia.doe.gov/emeu/aer/txt/ptb0810.html.

56. U.S. Energy Information Administration, HAWAII ELECTRICITY PROFILE 2006, http://www.eia.doe.gov/cneaf/electricity/st_profiles/hawaii.html.

57. U.S. Energy Information Administration, Official Energy Statistics from the U.S. Government, Average Retail Price of Electricity to Ultimate Customers by End-Use Sector, by State (statistics cited are for April 2008), http://www.eia.doe.gov/cneaf/electricity/epm/table5_6_a.html.

58. *See* Sierra Club, Hawai'i Chapter, Chart "Hawaii's Dirty Secret," derived from 2000 DBEDT data, http://www.risingtidehawaii.com/.

59. HAWAIIAN ELECTRIC 2007 REPORT, *supra* note 21, at 18. Whether to count solid waste (*e.g.,* so-called garbarge-to-energy plants as "renewable") is itself controversial.

60. *Id.*

61. Aside from controversy about the wisdom of burning forest products in tropical climates, the potential for biomass in Hawai'i appears small. Hawaiian Electric projects a total of 25 MW from two forestry projects on the Big Island. *Id.* at 28.

62. *Id.* (chart).

63. *Id.* at 19 (charts).

64. *Id.* at 20.

plant (municipal solid waste),[65] 180 MW from the AES-Hawai'i coal-powered plant, and 208 MW from the private Kalaeloa Partners oil-powered plant.[66] Kaua'i has its own utility cooperative (not part of the Hawaiian Electric companies), which also relies on fossil fuel imports.[67] The small islands of Moloka'i and Lana'i survive only on single power sources—oil-powered plants operated by Maui Electric Company (a HECO subsidiary).[68] The state's dependency on oil is deep and pervasive, but rising state renewable standards portend aggressive shifts in this picture in the future, *if* the standards can be enforced and *if* the renewables market is supported by high oil prices.

The State's Renewable Portfolio Standards (RPS)[69] established in 2004 set a solid "20 by 2020" goal for renewable and energy efficient sources.[70] According to Hawaiian Electric's 2007 data, 16.1% of its electricity currently comes from renewable energy sources.[71] Hawaiian Electric believes it is exceeding the interim RPS goals and is well on its way to meeting the 20/2020 goal.[72] Critics question, however, Hawaiian Electric's definition of "renewables" and the enforceability of the law.[73] More than one-third of the renewables amount counted by Hawaiian Electric comes from a category it calls "biomass," which, on O'ahu, is the municipal garbage-to-energy plant.[74] Many would disagree that garbage is a renewable resource.[75] Furthermore, Hawaiian Electric's solar hot water program, while laudable,[76] is counted as a "displacement" value of 66 GW, or 6.7% of the total RPS claimed.[77] And, "energy efficiency" equals 36.8%.[78] Thus, when reduced to

---

65. The likelihood of Hawai'i burning more of its garbage to generate energy is increasing, even while Honolulu considers shipping bundled garbage to the Northwest landfills on barges. HAWAIIAN ELECTRIC 2007 REPORT, *supra* note 21, at 28. The City and County of Honolulu is considering increasing the size of its H-Power plant with a third boiler by 2011. *Id.* at 29. The County of Hawai'i is considering a 3.5 MW municipal incineration plant. *Id.*

66. HAWAIIAN ELECTRIC 2007 REPORT, *supra* note 21, at 20.

67. *See* Kaua'i Independent Utility Cooperative, http://www.kiuc.coop/.

68. HAWAIIAN ELECTRIC 2007 REPORT, *supra* note 21, at 21. The small private island of Ni'ihau is completely off the grid, with no electricity except solar power, and now boasts the state's first fully solar-power school. Staff, Niihau school now powered entirely by solar energy, HONOLULU ADVERTISER, Dec. 12, 2007, http://the.honoluluadvertiser.com/article/2007/Dec/12/br/br8463025197.html.

69. H.R.S. § 269-91 (2004) (Act 95, http://www.capitol.hawaii.gov/session2004/Bills/SB2474_HD1_.htm).

70. *See* Gordon Pang, *New law to require use of renewable energy*, HONOLULU STAR-BULLETIN, June 3, 2004, http://the.honoluluadvertiser.com/article/2004/Jun/03/ln/ln38a.html. Act 95 (SB2474) mandated that the state's utility companies establish a renewable energy portfolio standard showing 8 percent renewable energy sales by 2005, 10 percent by 2010, 15 percent by 2015, and 20 percent by 2020. *Id.* Renewable energy is defined in the Act as "wind, solar, ocean, geothermal, waves and conversion of agricultural and other waste to energy." *Id.* At that time, the percentage of renewables was only 7%. *Id.* Prior to 2004, Hawai'i had only renewable portfolio "goals." *See* Act 272 (2001).

71. HAWAIIAN ELECTRIC 2007 REPORT, *supra* note 21, at 25.

72. *Id.*

73. Prabha Natarajan, *Sparks fly over new energy law*, PAC. BUS. NEWS, June 14, 2004, http://www.bizjournals.com/pacific/stories/2004/06/21/focus1.html?t=printable (according to energy activist Henry Curtis, "It's ineffective and a giant step backward.").

74. HAWAIIAN ELECTRIC 2007 REPORT, *supra* note 21, at 26 (compare chart on page 26 to chart on page 18, showing 326 Gigawatts).

75. Henry Curtis, *Life of the Land 10-Point Energy Plan*, http://www.lifeofthelandhawaii.org/Ten_Point_Energy_Plan.html.

76. Hawaiian Electric's Demand Side Management (DSM) programs are also laudable but not very substantial upon examination. Hawaiian Electric states that it has "paid out nearly $75 million for energy efficiency projects for businesses and residents, reducing demand by more than 152 MW and avoiding the use of 1.2 million barrels of oil a year," but this is the total amount over an 11-year period, roughly only $6.8 million a year, or about the cost of a single luxury Hawai'i beachhouse in Lanikai each year. HAWAIIAN ELECTRIC 2007 REPORT, *supra* note 21, at 26 (author calculations).

77. *Id.*

78. *Id.*

"pure" renewables, the "truly green" power percentage of Hawai'i's 2007 portfolio may only be about 6%—much farther away from the 20% goal than some may think.[79]

Related vulnerability factors that compound this dim assessment include the lack of competition, the uncoordinated grid, and the highly centralized nature of energy utilities in Hawai'i. Ninety-three percent of Hawai'i's electricity services comes from one company—Hawaiian Electric.[80] Although monopolies may be inevitable in small island environments, even the Republican Governor of Hawai'i has criticized Hawaiian Electric for its recalcitrance on renewables and lambasted its self-interested management of a $19 million demand-side-management fund, which the Legislature reluctantly agreed to shift to the Public Utilities Commission even if not the independent utility suggested by the Governor.[81] The grid itself is also under more scrutiny. Although proposals for inter-island deepwater energy cables have failed in the past[82] and are now being partially re-proposed, each of the Hawaiian Islands has always had a "stand-alone grid," connected only by shipments of oil.[83] This makes Hawai'i's utility grid particularly vulnerable compared to the inter-connected systems in the continental U.S.

Recognizing the state's embarrassingly large lag, and equally ripe opportunity, on renewables, in early 2008, Governor Lingle announced a unique partnership with the U.S. Department of Energy and Hawaiian Electric—called the Hawai'i Clean Energy Initiative—to make Hawai'i a model for renewables. She set a high target of 70% renewables by 2030[84]—"one of the most ambitious targets in the world."[85] Although the goal is just that—a goal that is not yet part of the state's hard law[86]—the Governor's initiative grabbed attention from New York to China[87] and soon attracted international interest in renewable projects in Hawai'i.[88] Another major goal of

---

79. Author calculations based on HAWAIIAN ELECTRIC 2007 REPORT, *supra* note 21, at 26 (charts).

80. HAWAIIAN ELECTRIC 2007 REPORT, *supra* note 21, at 3.

81. Kevin Dayton, *Lawmakers defer to utilities agency*, HONOLULU ADVERTISER, Sept. 8, 2008, http://the.honoluluadvertiser.com/article/2006/May/04/ln/FP605040337.html; HAWAIIAN ELECTRIC 2007 REPORT, *supra* note 21, at 26 (author calculations).

82. *See* Blue Ocean Preservation Society v. Watkins, 767 F. Supp. 1518 (D. Haw. 1991) (commenting that plaintiffs had submitted "substantial evidence" on the impact of the proposed deep-water cable on Hawai'i's marine environment).

83. HAWAIIAN ELECTRIC 2007 REPORT, *supra* note 21, at 3.

84. *Feds Help Hawaii Move to 70% Renewables by 2030*, ENV'T NEWS SERVICE, Jan. 28, 2008, http://www.ens-newswire.com/ens/jan2008/2008-01-28-091.asp [hereinafter *Feds Help Hawaii*]. Under the agreement, DOE is gaining a state "showcase" and laboratory, and will commit to "technical and policy expertise and capabilities to help demonstrate reliable, affordable and clean energy technologies in Hawaii." *Id.*

85. Jim Carlton, *Hawaii the Alternative State*, W.S.J., June 30, 2008, http://sopogy.com/blog/2008/06/30/wall-street-journal-alternative-state [hereinafter Carlton].

86. The details of the agreement, which emerged in late 2008, include: integration of 1100 MW of additional renewable energy on the Hawaiian Electric companies' grids; an undersea cable connecting Maui, Moloka'i, and Lāna'i to support 400 MW of wind generation for transmission to O'ahu; doubling the RPS standard to 40% renewables by 2030; a "feed in tariff" to accelerate renewable power providers; development of a "smart grid" that allows customers greater control over usage and rates; changing the business model of Hawaiian Electric to de-link energy sales and profits; encouraging Hawaiian Electric to retire older fossil fuel plants; converting existing fossil fuel generators to renewable biofuels, ideally locally and sustainably grown crops; prohibiting new coal plants in Hawai'i; expanding pay-as-you-save for residential solar hot water; eliminating system caps on net metering; establishing "lifeline" rates for certain low income customers; and encouraging electric vehicles incentives and usage by government and utility fleets. *See* State and Hawaiian Electric Strike Sweeping Agreement for Hawai'i's Energy Future, Governor's Press Release, Oct. 20, 2008.

87. *Hawaii to be "world model" for clean energy economy*, CHINA DAILY, Jan. 31, 2008, http://chinadaily.com.cn/world/2008-01/31/content_6432098.htm.

88. Carlton, *supra* note 85. For example, Royal Dutch Shell PLC has started an algae biofuel venture in Kona. *Id.* Australian Oceanlinx has the backing of the Governor to install wave energy platforms on Maui. B.J. Reyes, *Ocean of Energy*, HONOLULU STAR-BULLETIN, Feb. 5, 2008, http://starbulletin.com/2008/02/05/news/story09.html.

the Governor's initiative is improving the overall strength of the grid, especially its ability to utilize variable sources (*e.g.*, wind) and its inter-connectedness.[89] As a result of the initiative, Hawai'i could also be the first state in the country to find "the Holy Grail"—a "feed-in-tariff" system that could fire up the renewable energy market.[90] As further discussed below, the Governor's bold announcement built on several years of positive policy initiatives by the Legislature; if the two branches work together, they could indeed turn "the most energy-insecure state in America,"[91] into "one of the world's leading incubators of alternative energy."[92] The state seems to have finally chosen a positive course for its future although much of the policy rubber has yet to hit the road. In addition to alacrity, however, the state's energy independence initiatives must work hand-in-hand with its other nascent efforts to mitigate the growing threats of climate change.

II. Climate Change Threats to Hawai'i

The physical threats of climate change to Hawai'i are likely to be numerous but are still hard to predict with much confidence. The science on local impacts is rapidly emerging but still evolving. The concomitant social, cultural, economic, and political consequences of climate change in Hawai'i are equally varied and unpredictable but here too the picture is becoming a bit clearer. The attention to climate change by Hawai'i's academic, consulting, advocacy, and policy communities has crescendoed in the past two years and the "coconut wireless" is now buzzing with conferences, papers, research groups, new information, and more media coverage. Indeed, the urgent challenge now on mitigation and energy independence is not just creating new information but coordinating it and disseminating it quickly and effectively for public and policymaker consumption.[93] This section synthesizes some of the current science on the threats to Hawai'i posed by the four best understood and potentially worst micro-threats to the islands: sea-level rise, ocean acidification, severe weather impacts, and terrestrial ecosystem disruption.

A. Sea-Level Rise

Hawai'i is not alone in its concern about sea-level rise, but it is especially vulnerable as an island state.[94] The United Nations' Intergovernmental Panel on Climate Change (IPCC) 2007 report put sea-level rise at the top of the list of potentially severe climate change impacts to small islands: "Sea-level rise is expected to exacerbate inundation, storm surge, erosion and other coastal hazards, thus threatening vital infrastructure, settlements and facilities that support the

---

89. *Feds Help Hawaii, supra* note 84.

90. Mark Niesse, *Hawaii gets to work on energy independence*, USA TODAY, Apr. 18, 2009, http://content. usatoday.net/dist/custom/gci/InsidePage.aspx?cId=indystar&sParam=30576831.story (describing the optimism generated by recent hearings before the State Public Utilities Commission on adoption of a feed-in-tariff and the challenge of finding the appropriate rate).

91. Dennis Camire, *Isles most energy "insecure" state in the U.S., Lingle says*, HONOLULU ADVERTISER, Feb. 25, 2008, http://the.honoluluadvertiser.com/article/2008/Feb/25/ln/hawaii802250332.html.

92. Carlton, *supra* note 85.

93. The author is involved with many others in two such coordinating efforts at the University of Hawai'i at Mānoa: the Mānoa Climate Change Commission and the new inter-disciplinary Center for Island Climate Policy and Adaptation.

94. Island communities worldwide are increasingly banding together to raise their unique concerns about sea-level rise and adaptation. *See* Small Island Developing States Network, http://www.sidsnet.org. Hawai'i's connection to other island states appears to be growing even if not yet in the area of adaptation. In July 2008, the U.S. Department of Energy announced a joint "clean energy" initiative with New Zealand and other countries called the International Partnership for Energy Development in Island Nations (EDIN). U.S. Dep't of Energy, Press Release, *U.S. and New Zealand Take Steps to Launch International Partnership to Further the Development of Clean Energy on Island Nations*, July 24, 2008, http://energy.gov/print/6429.htm.

livelihood of island communities."[95] The IPCC further pointed out that human-influenced sea-level rise has already begun to occur in recent decades, and that "sea-level rise under warming is inevitable."[96]

Estimates of future global sea-level rise vary considerably and are less predictable by region. The IPCC's 2007 report projected sea-level rise of .18 meters to .59 meters by the end of this century.[97] Others have predicted much higher levels, including up to over 5 meters.[98] The IPCC estimate is admittedly conservative (some said "sugarcoated") because it did not consider the then-recent bad news about the rapid increase in the melting of the Greenland and Antarctica ice sheets.[99] The IPCC did indicate, however, that, if these events materialized, sea-level rise would likely be much, much higher—on the magnitude of "several metres."[100] Professor Robin Bell, a leading climate change scientist, is more blunt. She predicts that, if these two huge sheets melt, the rise could be 213 feet.[101] Skeptics say it will be far less.[102] But even 1% of that extreme level would be highly problematic for Hawai'i.

According to University of Hawai'i Professor Charles Fletcher, the current accumulation of carbon dioxide concentrations in the atmosphere means that a meter-plus amount of sea-level rise is inevitable, even if immediate mitigation measures are put into place globally.[103] Combined with high surf, high tides, and ongoing beach erosion,[104] highways and coastal infrastructure will be at risk.[105] The State of Hawai'i's 2007 MULTI-HAZARD MITIGATION PLAN pointed out that the islands are already experiencing small amounts of sea-level rise, which, interestingly, vary by island due to differences in the islands' geological age and stability.[106] The increase for O'ahu, for example, has been .6 inches/decade, compared to .7 on Kauai, .98

---

95. INTERGOVERNMENTAL PANEL ON CLIMATE CHANGE (IPCC), CLIMATE CHANGE 2007: SYNTHESIS REPORT, SUMMARY OF POLICYMAKERS, at 12, Table SPM.2 (Small Islands) [hereinafter IPCC 2007 SPM].

96. *Id.* at 6 ("Human influences have: *very likely* contributed to sea-level rise during the latter half of the 20th century") & 20 ("inevitable").

97. *Id.* at 8, Table SPM.1.

98. STATE OF HAWAII, MULTI-HAZARD MITIGATION PLAN, at 3–74 (Table 3-24, *citing* Hansen, unpublished 2007) [hereinafter MULTI-HAZARD MITIGATION PLAN].

99. IPCC 2007 SPM, *supra* note 95, at 19 ("the risk of additional contributions to sea-level rise from both the Greenland and possibly Antarctic ice sheets may be larger than projected by ice sheet models and could occur on century time scales. This is because ice dynamical processes seen in recent observations but not fully included in ice sheet models assessed in the AR4 could increase the rate of ice loss.") *See also Melting ice means global warming report all wet, say some experts*, AP, Jan. 1, 2007, http://www.usatoday.com/weather/climate/2007-01-28-ice-sheets-ipcc_x.htm [hereinafter AP, *Melting ice*].

100. IPCC 2007 SPM, *supra* note 95, at 20.

101. This frightening scenario of "rapid change" caused by global warming is suggested by Professor Robin Bell of the Columbia Earth Institute, in the February 2008 issue of SCIENTIFIC AMERICAN, based on her observations of slippage and cracks in the Arctic ice sheet. http://www.sciam.com/article.cfm?id=the-unquiet-ice&print=true ("If the West Antarctic ice sheet were to disappear, sea level would rise almost 19 feet; the ice in the Greenland ice sheet could add 24 feet to that; and the East Antarctic ice sheet could add yet another 170 feet to the level of the world's oceans: more than 213 feet in all.").

102. AP, *Melting ice*, *supra* note 99 (quoting University of Alabama at Huntsville Professor John Christy, "a prominent so-called skeptic" who is a member of the IPCC).

103. Leone, *supra* note 1.

104. *Id.* (Eileen Shea, director of the National Oceanic and Atmospheric Administration (NOAA) Integrated Data and Environmental Applications Center, commented: "'You and I aren't going to feel the average sea-level rise,'.... 'What we're going to see is how they're going to affect extreme events,' because even a few inches of higher sea level can magnify the bad effects of hurricanes and high surf.")

105. Leone, *supra* note 1 (coastal highways will start to be flooded more often by high surf, according to Cheryl Anderson, director of the Hazards, Climate and Environment Program at the UH's Social Science Institute).

106. MULTI-HAZARD MITIGATION PLAN, *supra* note 98, at 3-111 & 3-114 (Figure 3-36).

on Maui, and 1.6 on the Big Island.[107] Recent unpublished studies suggest, however, that "oceanographic factors and not geological factors" are responsible for the increase in Hawai'i.[108]

Some people may laugh at the idea that sea-level rise threatens Hawai'i, thinking that it could only mean "surf's up!" However, the dynamic relationship between sea-level rise and coastal erosion suggests that it may really mean "where's my beach?" The Hawai'i mitigation plan states that "[s]tudies show a *150 times erosion multiplier* for sea-level rise on sandy shorelines."[109] Thus, with the predicted mean .24 meter rise by 2050, vulnerable Hawai'i beaches could recede 36 meters (118 feet).[110] Many of the state's popular beaches, including in Waikīkī, are already shrinking about a foot a year, have become alarmingly narrow, or even given way to bare rock, causing economic consternation and prompting costly restoration plans.[111] As a popular Hawai'i publication recently stated: "our shoreline is disappearing—fast."[112] Sea-level rise can be buffered by an adequate supply of sand,[113] but compared to continental coasts, tropical shorelines are notoriously short of sand supply and many of Hawai'i's already besieged beaches will be particularly vulnerable.

Sea-level rise that hastens the destruction of the state's famous sandy beaches is a serious economic, cultural, environmental, and social threat. For the state's 750-plus miles of coastline,[114] sea-level rise, combined with other ongoing threats like seawalls and natural erosion, could mean huge losses of the most scenic, usable, and popular beaches let alone infrastructure (such as coastal roads) that depends on sandy beach barriers. Erosion impacts seem increasingly evident in recent years. On the Windward side of O'ahu, storm surge regularly covers the low parts of the "circle island" Kamehameha Highway with sand and water, creating a constant battle between asphalt and the sea.[115] The cost of adaptation to the double-whammy of erosion and sea-level rise will only increase over time. The Hawai'i mitigation report concludes that "[t]he impact of rising sea level in the Hawaiian Islands will be severe unless planners and resource managers incorporate sea-level rise scenarios into their coastal management efforts."[116] Potentially, that means moving (or giving up) highways, drainage and sewage systems, water and utility lines, as well as homes and recreational areas.

At a recent workshop of University of Hawai'i faculty involved in climate change issues, the participants agreed that, above all, sea-level rise poses an urgent threat to the islands.[117] In the

---

107. *Id.* at 3-116 (Maui figure of .25 cm converted to inches by author) & at 119 (Big Island). *See also* CHARLES FLETCHER *et al.*, ATLAS OF NATURAL HAZARDS IN THE HAWAIIAN COASTAL ZONE (2002).

108. DENNIS J. HWANG, HAWAII COASTAL HAZARD MITIGATION GUIDEBOOK, §4.1.4, at 63 (2005) [hereinafter HWANG, GUIDEBOOK].

109. MULTI-HAZARD MITIGATION PLAN, *supra* note 98, at 3.9.7 (Sea-level rise and Erosion) (emphasis added), http://www.scd.state.hi.us/HazMitPlan/chapter_3.pdf ("Studies show a 150 times erosion multiplier for sea-level rise on sandy shorelines. For a mean 0.24 m rise by 2050, beaches will recede 36 m (118 ft).... The following diagram shows the rise of sea level in Hawaii State, such that: • Hawaiian tide gauges document a history of local sea-level rise; • Sea Level is rising around the world at 1.5 to 2.2 cm per decade; • Sea-level rise is projected to accelerate over the next century.") (citation omitted).

110. *Id.* (citation omitted).

111. Ron Mizutani, *The Disappearing Sands of Waikiki*, MID-WEEK CURRENTS, Aug. 13, 2008, http://www.midweek.com/content/columns/currents_article/the_disappearing_sands_of_waikiki/. *See also* HWANG, GUIDEBOOK, *supra* note 108, 98 at Ch. 1 & Figures 1-1 through 1-11 (giving current examples of beach loss).

112. Ron Mizutani, *supra* note 111.

113. HWANG, GUIDEBOOK, *supra* note 108, at 65.

114. HAWAII STATE DEPARTMENT OF BUSINESS, ECONOMIC DEVELOPMENT AND TOURISM, STATE OF HAWAII DATA BOOK 1995 (October 1996), Table 5.05.

115. Leone, *supra* note 1 (State Department of Transportation says it is looking at: "trouble spots on the Kamehameha Highway on Oahu's Windward side.").

116. MULTI-HAZARD MITIGATION PLAN, *supra* note 98, at 3-112.

117. Mānoa Climate Change Commission, Strategic Planning Session (Jan. 17, 2008), in which the author participated.

U.S., about 25% of all Americans live within 300 feet of the coastline.[118] In Hawai'i, the entire state is considered to be within the "coastal zone" and 90% of all people live within a few miles of the ocean.[119] Many major highways and roads have key portions at or near sea level. The Honolulu airport is built on artificial "reef," only a few feet above sea level and unshielded by ocean barriers. Hawai'i's busy harbors are all built to current sea levels. The major sewage plants are near the coast just enough above sea level to gravity feed the ocean outfalls. Oahu's largest industrial park and gasoline refineries are only a few feet above sea level. The Hawai'i Legislature agrees that sea-level rise is a top threat to the state and sees these broad implications, and has just started to think seriously about directly addressing adaptation. When legislators passed landmark global warming mitigation legislation in 2007, they described the nature of the risk of climate change to the state:

> [C]limate change poses a serious threat to the economic well-being, public health, natural resources, and the environment of Hawaii. The potential adverse effects of global warming include a rise in sea levels resulting in the displacement of businesses and residences and the inundation of Hawaii's freshwater aquifers, damage to marine ecosystems and the natural environment, extended drought and loss of soil moisture, an increase in the spread of infectious diseases, and an increase in the severity of storms and extreme weather events.[120]

While still uncertain, any one of these impacts would itself be a disaster. Mitigation will be costly. Ten years ago, EPA suggested that "the cumulative cost of sand replenishment to protect the coast of Hawaii from a 20-inch sea-level rise by 2100 is estimated at $340 million to $6 billion."[121] Six years ago, the state's estimate of the cost of a (temporary) sand replenishment project for all of Waikiki was $25 million.[122] The value of the lost tourism from the disappearing beach could mount to $2 billion.[123]

Some predict that the future may resemble a scary movie. As Professor Fletcher explains, many areas along Hawai'i's coasts "are highly vulnerable to inundation by seawater during high waves, storms, tsunami and extreme water levels. Hotel basements will be flooded, ground floors will be splashed by wave run-up, and seawater will come out the storm drains on most of the streets in Waikiki and along Ala Moana," even if waves themselves might not be "rolling down the streets."[124] He continued: "Beaches will be gone, and we'll have built large seawalls, but most of the buildings will probably still be [habitable]. Residents will time their movement in and out of buildings between the tides, just as they do today in Mapunapuna."[125] He added:

> In McCully and Waikiki, they will see the wetlands of the 19th century reemerging, as the water table rises above ground level in some areas (not all areas). Under these conditions, when it rains, we will have a real problem. The runoff will raise the water table, the storm drains will be full of seawater except at the very lowest state of tide (perhaps even then?) and standing pools of water will accumulate throughout the region with no

---

118. *Why Are Rising Sea Levels a Threat?*, E MAGAZINE, June 2, 2008, http://www.enn.com/ecosystems/article/37337.

119. Author's observation.

120. Act 234, Section 1(a), codified at HAW. REV. STAT. § 342B-71 (Supp. 2007)].

121. U.S. EPA, Office of Policy, *Climate Change and Hawaii*, EPA 236-F-98-007e, at 3 (Sept. 1998) [hereinafter EPA *Climate Change*], http://yosemite.epa.gov/oar/GlobalWarming.nsf/UniqueKeyLookup/SHSU5 BUNQM/$File/hi_impct.pdf.

122. Associated Press, *Where's Waikiki's sand?*, CCN.COM, July 5, 2003, http://www.cnn.com/2003/US/West/07/05/waikiki.sand.ap/index.html.

123. Mary Vorsino, *Erosion of Waikiki beach would cut Hawaii tourism by $2 billion*, HONOLULU ADVERTISER, Dec. 8, 2008, www.honoluluadvertiser.com.

124. Berry, *supra* note 8, at 7 (inset).

125. *Id.*

place to drain. Travel will be limited and many lands will turn to wetlands; there may be some areas of permanently standing water.[126]

And this frightening scenario is for just the main Hawaiian Islands, which do have substantial topographical relief. However, in the Northwestern Hawaiian Islands, a spectacular 1,200-mile-long archipelago of mainly low-lying atolls stretching toward Japan now protected by state and federal law, sea-level rise could wipe out a large part of the chain.[127] In a 2006 study, "A team of Hawaii-based scientists calculate[d] that two-thirds of some islands in the Northwestern Hawaiian Islands (NWHI) could be submerged by 2100."[128] With the federal waters designated by President George W. Bush in 2008 as the Papahānaumokuākea Marine National Monument, the area is now the largest marine protected area in the world.[129] Yet, despite the paper protection, the chain is particularly vulnerable to all of the factors discussed above, and the impacts will be on a globally treasured ecosystem, not directly on humans. The islands host only a few government employees and scientists, but are the critical home for many endemic and indigenous species of wildlife, including some of Hawai'i's most notable native species such as the Hawaiian monk seal and the charismatic green sea turtle, the mid-Pacific population of which nests almost exclusively on a single atoll.[130] Will the resources be available to protect *both* the populated main Hawaiian islands *and* the unpopulated Northwestern Hawaiian Islands from sea-level rise? Unlikely.

Compounding the potentially dire consequences of sea-level rise for both the main and Northwestern Hawaiian Islands is the risk of ocean acidification, which threatens global marine ecosystems.

B. Ocean Acidification

Scientists are still seeking to understand the potential impacts of climate change to the world's oceans and coral reefs but, increasingly, the risk of ocean acidification is grabbing the headlines in the emerging science. Ocean acidification occurs "when carbon dioxide in the air is absorbed by the ocean at a rate faster than the ocean can assimilate it."[131] A major effect of ocean acidification is bleached coral reefs, and therefore the destruction of fish habitat, but acidification also disrupts the physiology, reproduction cycles, and distribution of marine life.[132] The effects may be particularly harsh in Hawai'i, where coral reefs are not just critically important to the state's marine ecosystems, the economy, recreation, and lifestyle, but also a fundamental part of the Native Hawaiian culture.[133]

The ocean acidification science seems to be converging. Stanford University chemical oceanographer Ken Caldeira suggests that high levels of carbon dioxide will adversely affect the world's coral reefs and other calcium carbonate-reliant organisms. "Caldeira and other scientists with the Carnegie Institution's Department of Global Ecology have calculated that if current emission trends continue, by 2050, 98% of the reef habitats will have become too acidic for reef

---

126. *Id.*

127. James Owen, *Global Warming May Swamp Hawaiian Wildlife, Study Warns*, NATIONAL GEOGRAPHIC NEWS, June 5, 2006, http://news.nationalgeographic.com/news/2006/06/060605-hawaii.html.

128. *Id.*

129. *See* Papahānaumokuākea Marine National Monument web site, http://hawaiireef.noaa.gov/.

130. *Id.*

131. Teresa Dawson, *Declaring War on Climate Change*, ENV'T HAWAII, Aug. 2008, at 7 [hereinafter Dawson].

132. *Id.*

133. *See* Mary Simms, *Global Warming Threatens Hawaii's Coral Reefs*, KHNL8, July 26, 2007, http://www.khnl.com/Global/story.asp?S=6847592. *See also* MARTHA W. BECKWITH (TRANS.), THE KUMULIPO: A HAWAIIAN CREATION CHANT, http://www.sacred-texts.com/pac/ku/index.htm ("The coral was the first stone in the foundation of the earth mentioned in the chant.").

growth."[134] In the July 2008 issue of SCIENCE, Richard Zeebe of the University of Hawai'i and his colleagues reported on the major threat posed by ocean acidification. Zeebe stated: "If we continue with business as usual and don't cut carbon dioxide emissions, carbonate reefs will ultimately start to dissolve."[135] In the past two centuries, the pH levels in the oceans, which naturally absorb carbon dioxide, have increased, pointing toward larger levels of pH in the future.[136] Even changes "as small as 0.2 to 0.3 units of surface pH can harm corals and some plankton and other marine organisms that build their skeletons from pH-sensitive carbonate minerals."[137] Zeebe's research team concluded that, by 2050, the levels of pH in the Northwestern Hawaiian Islands are in danger of exceeding acceptable levels,[138] possibly leading to coral reef ecosystem collapse.

A recent report on the risk of ocean acidification to Hawaiian fisheries painted a similarly grim picture. At the June 2008 meeting of NOAA's Western Pacific Fishery Management Council in Honolulu, Australian coral reef expert John "Charlie" Veron reported that "acidification is [already] affecting plankton in the southern ocean" and "moving toward the equator."[139] In a highly acidic ocean environment, he said, corals cannot recover from other heat stressors such as El Nino.[140] He commented: "This is not a cheerful talk, but it's based on the best science available."[141] He concluded: "Things are looking very nasty for our planet."[142] In another sign of the increasing attention to the issue, an environmental advocacy group recently petitioned the State of Hawai'i Department of Health to "declare Hawaii's ocean waters to be impaired under the Clean Water Act due to ocean acidification."[143] The Center for Biological Diversity contends that CO_2 absorption is already degrading Hawai'i's waters.[144]

These vignettes of cutting edge science and advocacy indicate that ocean acidification will soon become a high-profile issue that commands Hawai'i's attention in the discussion of the global and local implications of climate change. But again the prospects may be too frightening to be taken seriously. It is indeed hard to imagine that, in less than fifty years, Hawai'i's reefs (60% of the U.S. stock)[145] will be severely damaged or gone. The loss is unfathomable on many levels, but especially considering that coral reefs have been developing on earth for millions if not billions of years,[146] provide 25% of the habitat for all marine species globally,[147] and that corals grow so slowly, at only a few millimeters per year.[148] Can Hawai'i even exist without its

---

134. Dawson, *supra* note 131, at 11.

135. Helen Altonn, *Carbon dioxide buildup creating crisis in oceans*, HONOLULU STAR BULLETIN, July 7, 2008, http://starbulletin.com/2008/07/07/news/story03.html.

136. *Id.*

137. *Id.*

138. *Id.*

139. Dawson, *supra* note 131, at 7.

140. *Id.*

141. *Id.*

142. *Id.*

143. Douglas A. Codiga, *Act 234: Hawaii's climate change law*, HAWAII B.J., May 13, 2008 [hereinafter Codiga].

144. Codiga, *supra* note 143, at 13–14 (*citing* Center for Biological Diversity, *Seven Coastal States Petitioned to Address Ocean Acidification: Clean Water Act Requires Regulation of Carbon Dioxide That Could Drive Ocean Species Extinct*, Aug. 15, 2007, http://www.biologicaldiversity.org/news/press_releases/ocean-acidification-08-15-2007.html).

145. MICHAEL FIELD et al., Abstract, U.S. Geological Survey, U.S. CORAL REEFS-IMPERILED NATIONAL TREASURES, http://pubs.usgs.gov/fs/2002/fs025-02/.

146. *Id.*

147. *Id.*

148. U.S. Coral Reef Task Force, *What Are Corals and Coral Reefs?*, http://www.coris.noaa.gov/about/what_are/ ("Massive corals tend to grow slowly, increasing in size from 0.5 cm to 2 cm per year.").

coral reefs? In a cultural, economic, and environmental sense, the answer may be no. Extreme weather and ecosystem disruption predictions indicate similarly serious concerns for terrestrial Hawai'i.

C. Extreme Weather Events

Climate models have a difficult time predicting localized changes in weather. The models used by the IPCC are not refined enough to predict small-scale changes for sub-grid areas like Hawai'i;[149] however, preliminary modeling for the mid-Pacific by the IPCC indicates that Hawai'i will experience an "increase-decrease dichotomy," that is, "a decrease in precipitation north of the island chain, and increase to the south, but directly over the islands, the models don't agree on what will happen."[150]

Local science is rapidly developing. The University of Hawai'i's International Pacific Research Center (IPRC) is conducting groundbreaking climate change work with an increasing focus on Hawai'i.[151] UH researchers Tom Giambelluca and Oliver Timm, along with NOAA scientists, are working on ways to better predict micro-climate impacts in Hawai'i, where local variation in rainfall historically ranges from 10 to 200 inches and most rainfall comes from major storm events.[152] Despite the lack of predictability, some indications of changes in Hawai'i weather are consistent with the global models. For example, Giambelluca found that high-elevation night-time temperatures have increased by .79 degrees Fahrenheit per decade over the past thirty years in Hawai'i.[153] He also found that "trade wind inversion," associated with less precipitation, has also become more frequent in the past twenty-five years and "may become more so with global warming."[154]

The U.S. Environmental Protection Agency (EPA) Office of Policy suggested ten years ago that Hawai'i's mild climate and dependable rainfall may be permanently changing.[155] "In Honolulu, Hawaii, the average temperature has increased 4.4°F over the last century, and precipitation has decreased approximately 20% over the last 90 years.... Over the next century, climate in Hawaii may change even more."[156] According to EPA, a warmer climate means greater variability in the weather, with the range of micro-climate impacts including flooding, high surf, polluted runoff, prolonged droughts, groundwater salinity, agricultural losses, water-use restrictions, changes in pests, and stresses on forests and native species.[157]

---

149. Teresa Dawson, *Conservation Alliance Holds Forum on Climate Predictions for Hawaii*, ENV'T HAWAII, May 2008, p. 10 (quoting NOAA climatologist Henry Diaz, commenting that global models typically have a resolution of 150–300 kilometers, and "Hawaii almost fits inside *one* box."). *See also* Kevin Hamilton, *Analyses of IPCC Climate Model Data at IPRC*, 7 IPRC CLIMATE 3, 7 (2007) ("A major limitation of the IPCC assessments has been the horizontal resolution of the models.... Such low resolution prevents the representation of many aspects of the atmospheric circulation. This problem is particularly acute for Hawai'i. Hawaiian weather is strongly affected by the steep mountains. The typical models in the AR4 might represent all the Hawaiian islands as a single land grid box or even ignore Hawai'i entirely!"); *see also id.* at 8–9 (describing the IPRC's more realistic new models for the main Hawaiian islands that should result in better information on "the global warming signal in temperature, rainfall, and wind").

150. *Id.*

151. *See* International Pacific Research Center (IPRC), http://iprc.soest.hawaii.edu. *See also* Thomas Giambelluca *et al.*, *Secular Temperature Changes in Hawaii*, 35 GEOPHYS. RSCH. LETTERS L12702 (June 2008) ("Results show a relatively rapid rise in surface temperature in the last [approximately] 30 years, with stronger warming at the higher elevations.").

152. *Id.*

153. *Id.*

154. *Id.*

155. *EPA Climate Change, supra* note 121.

156. *Id.*

157. *Id.*

One of the most frightening but still uncertain risks is increased hurricane activity. Late Stanford University scientist and IPCC member Professor Steve Schneider said he could not predict increased frequency of hurricanes in Hawai'i but he did foresee that hurricanes in the islands will be stronger with climate change.[158] Schneider said that "Conditions likely will spawn 'perfect storms' much more frequently."[159] Although hurricanes are relatively "rare" in Hawai'i, with five major hurricanes since 1950, when they do hit, the damage can be severe, particularly given the islands' isolation.[160] Hurricane 'Iniki in 1992 caused $2.3 billion in property damage, wreaking major destruction on Kaua'i that displaced thousands of people and killed the island's economy for a decade.[161] For those who "survived 'Iniki, the risk of warmer global waters spawning stronger hurricanes in Hawai'i is not hard to comprehend."[162]

D. Native Ecosystem Disruption

The fourth major area of likely impact to Hawai'i's natural environment from climate change is terrestrial ecosystem disruption. U.S. Fish and Wildlife Service (FWS) biologist Stephen Miller gave the plenary address to the 2008 Hawai'i Conservation Conference, the state's largest gathering of conservation stakeholders, on the topic of how natural resource managers must be ready to respond to climate change in the islands. Miller stated bluntly that the "basic life zones" in Hawai'i are going to change:

> The places where today you find wet, mesic, and dry conditions are going to be different in the future. Current communities of species may disassemble and novel communities may appear. Species and populations may go extinct, and ranges may shrink. And invasive species may begin to come into play and occupy many of these new regimes.[163]

Miller added that climate change will make current management plans obsolescent.[164] He called for education, better modeling, and "anticipatory adaptation."[165] He pointed out that high elevation temperature changes were the most rapidly changing, and this is the current refuge of many of Hawai'i's native species.[166] This will have a "profound effect on plant and bird species ... [and] warm night temperatures will undoubtedly affect the distribution of malaria in Hawaiian forests and its impact on birds."[167] (The cooler temperature in the islands' high-elevation native forests may be one of the last barriers of protection for some of Hawai'i's rare native forest birds against the deadly avian malaria carried by mosquitoes.)[168] University of Hawai'i geography professor Jonathan Price noted that Hawai'i's native species are at a disadvantage against aggressive invasive

---

158. *Climate Change Expert Predicts Hawaii Hurricanes to Get Stronger*, Ins. J., Sept. 18, 2007, http://www.insurancejournal.com/news/west/2007/09/18/83574.htm?print=1.

159. *Id.*

160. *Hurricanes in Hawaii*, University of Hawai'i School of Ocean and Earth Science and Technology (SOEST), http://www.soest.hawaii.edu/MET/Faculty/businger/poster/hurricane/.

161. *Id.*

162. University of Hawai'i hurricane expert Professor Thomas A. Schroeder believes that although the "jury is still out" on specific scenarios for the islands, the increased "maximum potential intensity" of hurricanes for Hawai'i is "a logical future." Thomas A. Schroeder, *The Hurricane Future: Science and Policy* (Sept. 2008 power point, on file with author). For an excellent resource on Hawai'i's hurricane hazards, see Dennis Hwang & Darren Okimoto, Homeowner's Handbook To Prepare for Natural Hazards (2007) (Chapter 2.2, *Hurricane Hazards in Hawai'i*).

163. Patricia Tummons, *Hawai'i Natural Resource Managers Confront Challenges of Global Warming*, Env't Hawaii, Sept. 2008, at 3.

164. *Id.*

165. *Id.*

166. *Id.*

167. *Id.*

168. *See* U.S. Geological Survey, Pacific Islands Ecosystem Research Center, *Avian Malaria*, http://biology.usgs.gov/pierc/Native_Birds/Avain_Malaria.htm.

species, stating that, "in the next 100 years, elements of Hawai'i's ecosystems will be lost, I hate to say, but there will be overlap between what we have in the future and what we have today."[169]

Thus, in addition to being battered by sea-level rise, ocean acidification, and extreme weather, Hawai'i's fragile native species will feel the effects of climate change from its marine surroundings to its shores and mountaintops. A warmer climate will push the "endangered species capital of the world" even more toward a future of permanent degradation and diminish hope for restoring protected species and rare ecosystems. Yet, if Hawai'i gets moving now, there is cause for optimism. As Professor Price concluded: "'We are NOT doomed.' We have a number of tools necessary right now to cope with climate change."[170] All of these risks need to be part of the discussion of why Hawai'i must, despite its small size, contribute to the global effort to mitigate emissions (the next section) but, more importantly, why the state needs to move even more quickly on local adaptation (the last section).

III. Hawai'i Energy Policy and Mitigation: The Growing Consensus for Action

Even if the awareness of climate change risk among most Hawai'i residents lags strangely behind the citizens of many developed countries,[171] Hawai'i policymakers, scientists, and other professional communities have increasingly stepped up to the plate in recent years to start to tackle the enormous tasks of mitigation. The rate of policy response began to rise in 2006 and 2007 when Hawai'i passed solid energy and climate legislation, and again in 2008 with the shocking[172] rise in oil prices. The response must also now include adaptation as the scenarios of potential economic dislocation and isolation for our islands, akin to all the Hawai'i miserable hurricanes of the past put back-to-back, become more real to ordinary people through daily media coverage and community discussion.

Fortunately, some of the same factors that lead to a bleak future can also lead to solutions. Particularly for Hawai'i, energy independence, economic security, and climate change responses go hand-in-hand. As former Vice President Al Gore recently stated, there is a positive "common thread" to the convergence in responses to the oil price crisis and the climate change challenge.[173] He added: "[I]f we grab hold of that common thread and pull it hard, all of these complex problems begin to unravel and we will find that we're holding the answer to all of them right in our hand. The answer is to end our reliance on carbon-based fuels."[174] Similarly, by seriously addressing mitigation, the best answers for adaptation will also emerge.

The following section examines whether Hawai'i is ready to pull that critical thread of change. The prognosis is positive, but cautious. Some of the initiatives are bold, but the State has had some "energy independence" policies in place for many years with discouraging results. As noted above,

---

169. Note 163 *supra*.

170. *Id.*

171. This conclusion is based on the author's experiences living and teaching in Italy for a year and a half since 2003, where climate change and energy policy frequently dominated the news and daily conversation, particularly during the unusually warm European winter of 2006–2007. *See, e.g., Piazze e terrazzi sono già in fiore Così Milano anticipa la primavera*, LA REPUBBLICA, Feb. 27, 2007 (discussing the earliest spring on record in Milan and the surprising flowering of many plants), http://ricerca.repubblica.it/repubblica/archivio/repubblica/2007/02/27/piazze-terrazzi-sono-gia-in-fiore-cosi.html.

172. Although shocking to many, 2008's major shift toward higher oil prices was "as expected" for those who are familiar with the Peak Oil theory. *See* Keith Johnson, *Peak Oil: IEA Inches Toward the Pessimists' Camp*, WALL STREET J. BLOG, July 1, 2008, http://blogs.wsj.com/environmentalcapital/2008/07/01/peak-oil-iea-inches-toward-the-pessimists-camp. For more on peak oil, see Association for the Study of Peak Oil and Gas, http://www.peakoil.net/.

173. Al Gore, *A Generational Challenge to Repower America*, July 17, 2008, http://www.wecansolveit.org/content/pages/304. In his speech, Gore called for a carbon-free electricity future within ten years.

174. *Id.*

greenhouse gas emissions and the state's dangerous dependence of imported fossil fuels have *increased*. Yet, there is cause for optimism in this close-knit island state. Recently, Republican Governor Lingle, the Democratic-controlled Legislature, key businesses, and policy leaders have cooperated and supported new initiatives that, if fully implemented, will make a big difference. Some more innovative measures (such as a ban on energy inefficient light bulbs and a "right to dry" clothes outside) have thus far failed to gain sufficient political support but will likely resurface in future legislative sessions. Major Hawai'i businesses and landowners are starting to take action but still seem tentative about investing in an alternative future. Hawai'i leaders relish talking a lot about becoming a "model" in energy policy. But the true test will be in the next few years. Will the talk result in action? Will laws be fully enforced? Will initiatives get fully funded despite the state's fiscal crisis? So far, the policies adopted have not required major lifestyle or economic changes. Change will only get tougher as Hawai'i, along with the U.S. continent, experiences an economic downturn. Time will soon tell whether Hawai'i has the fortitude and vision to change and to be a leader—"fo' real."

Hawai'i's response to energy dependence and climate change has taken many forms. The section below highlights a few of the more unique and most recent developments in Hawai'i related to mitigation, including energy policy, greenhouse gas reductions, and installations of clean renewable energy such as solar, wind, and wave energy. It also discusses the obstacles encountered by some controversial energy sources such as geothermal and biofuels.

A. Hawai'i's Recent Energy Policy Legislation

Hawai'i's energy efficiency and independence policy efforts started with a banner year in 2006. Catalyzed by an innovative, multi-year collaborative project led by the University of Hawai'i's Hawai'i Energy Policy Forum[175] and backed by staff from the progressive Rocky Moun-

---

175. The Hawai'i Energy Policy Forum (HEPF) was started in 2002 by the University of Hawai'i, in partnership with Hawaiian Electric, DBEDT, and many other key stakeholders, *see* Hawai'i Energy Policy Forum, Minutes, June 10, 2002, http://www.hawaiienergypolicy.hawaii.edu/pages/minutes_02/061002.html, after a major HECO transmission line project (Wa'ahila Ridge) was defeated by strong public opposition. *See, e.g.,* Mālama O Mānoa, *The Kamoku-Pukele 138Kv Project—A Brief History*, http://www.malamaomanoa.org/138kv/rfeis.html; *see also* Ben DiPietro, *Next Round Begins in Scuffle Over HECO Line*, Pac. Bus. News, Nov. 2, 2001, http://www.bizjournals.com/pacific/stories/2001/11/05/story5. html. The forum is a collection of high-level, diverse members from the legislature, executive, industry, labor, and local government, with a few community/ environmental advocates. HEPF, Forum Members, http://www.hawaiienergypolicy.hawaii.edu/pages/forum_members.html. Its mission and vision has been to find "smart energy solutions to sustain a healthy, prosperous, and secure Hawaii." *Id.* at Mission & Vision. Its activities involve reports but also key legislative briefings and support for innovative legislation. *Id.* at Legislative Briefings. Part of its brain trust was Kyle Datta, at that time a staff member of Rocky Mountain Institute. *Id.* at 2003 Reports. Led by co-founder Mike Hamnett (Director of the Research Corporation of the University of Hawai'i (UH) and UH's Sharon Miyashiro, Associate Director of the Public Policy Center), HEPF created a "10-Point Plan" in 2006 that started with key support from its business and legislative members and ultimately spurred effective legislative action. *Id.* at *Ten-Point Plan* (revised for 2007–2008). That plan calls for: 1. Expand renewable opportunities, using indigenous resources; 2. Energy efficiency in public buildings, new and old; 3. Increase solar water/energy efficient appliances (via financing); 4. Adopt policies and regulations to encourage energy efficiency and renewables; 5. Preserve regulatory protections, support the Public Utilities Commission and the Consumer Advocate; 6. Invest in planning for sustainable communities; 7. Improve transportation energy efficiency and options, decrease fossil fuels for ground, sea, and air transportation; 8. Support research and development of alternative fuels (including hydrogen); 9. Encourage development, production, and use of biofuels (from agriculture); 10. Ensure secure systems for fuel and electricity grid to decrease risk of disasters." *Id.* HEPF's track record in encouraging legislation in each of these areas is remarkable. Not surprisingly, the 2006 Legislature approved Act 163 (HB 2848) appropriating $200,000 to allow HEPF to: develop an action plan, timeline, and benchmarks; to further engage Hawai'i's leaders and stakeholders in implementing the forum's visions, concepts, and recommendations for Hawai'i's preferred energy future; and to assess the feasibility of the State participating in the Chicago Climate Exchange. Act 163 (HB 2848), http://www.capitol.hawaii.gov/ session2006/bills/HB2848_cd1_.htm.

tain Institute (RMI),[176] the state's Republican Governor pushed for, and the Democrat Legislature adopted, four major bills as an "Energy for Tomorrow" package.[177] The new wave of legislation revealed interesting political bedfellows. In a watershed moment in Hawai'i's political history, the powerful Sierra Club publicly supported the Governor and criticized the Legislature for watering down her revolutionary proposals.[178]

The first bill, Act 96 (HB 2175), provided a new state framework for energy self-sufficiency, focusing on energy efficiency and use of renewable resources in state facilities, vehicles, and equipment; put $5 million into solar power for the public schools; set increasing standards for alternative fuel usage by and efficiency of the state fleet; and set up priority permitting for green building projects at the county level.[179] For example, it adopted a minimum green building standard of silver "LEED" certification or equivalent for all new or renovated state buildings.[180] The act also required a new State Energy Resources Coordinator to evaluate the state's progress toward efficiency and conservation goals, and gave authority to conduct audits.[181]

A second piece of the "Energy Tomorrow" package was Act 162 (SB 3185), through which the Governor tried to wrest some control over Hawai'i's energy future from the major utility company Hawaiian Electric.[182] The act strengthened the Renewable Portfolio Standards law by requiring "20 by 2020," although ironically the Democratic-controlled Legislature was not willing to go as far as the Republican Governor. For example, Governor Lingle had proposed that utilities be required to generate 20% from renewables *excluding efficiency*. The Legislature passed a compromise that allowed a utility to get half of the 20% from renewables and half from efficiency, but added penalties for non-compliance. The bill also allowed the Public Utilities Commission (PUC) to redirect the demand side management (DSM) surcharge into a new independent Public Benefits Fund for energy efficiency and DSM programs, eliminating the conflict of interest of having utilities run their own programs. The bill further required the fuel rate adjustment surcharge (at the PUC's discretion) to be shared by the utility to incentivize greater use of renewables. These major changes are still "in progress,"[183] and the jury is out on whether they will have the desired impact of closing some loopholes in the prior approach.

---

176. *See* News from Rocky Mountain Institute, *Comprehensive Energy Bill to Radically Reduce Hawaii's Energy Dependence*, Jan. 12, 2006, http://healthandenergy.com/renewable_energy_in_hawaii.htm.

177. *See* U.S. Dep't of Energy, Energy Efficiency and Renewable Energy, State Activities & Partnerships, *Hawaii's New Energy Bills To Boost Efficiency, Renewable Energy*, June 28, 2006, http://apps1.eere.energy.gov/states/state_news_detail.cfm?news_id=10100/state=HI. For current information on the Governor's energy initiatives, see http://hawaii.gov/gov/energy.

178. *See* Governor's E-Newsletter, Jan. 7–13, 2006, http://ploneadmin.hawaii.gov/gov/news/enewsletters/2006/January%207-13,%202006.pdf (quoting Jeff Mikulina: "We haven't heard such a comprehensive, solid package, I think, from anyone in this state until today.").

179. Act 96 (HB 2175), http://www.capitol.hawaii.gov/session2006/bills/GM626_.PDF, codified at H.R.S. §46-19 (2006) [hereinafter Act 96].

180. LEED stands for Leadership in Energy Efficiency and Design, and is a popular voluntary certification program of the U.S. Green Building Council. For more on LEED, see http://www.usgbc.org. The State of Hawai'i enacted mandatory greening of new state buildings (to LEED "silver" or equivalent standards) in 2006. Act 96 (HB2175), http://www.capitol.hawaii.gov/session2006/bills/HB2175_cd1_.htm. The City and County of Honolulu requires "all new City and County of Honolulu facilities larger than 5,000 square feet to meet a minimum LEED standard of environmentally sensitive design when feasible or appropriate, beginning in fiscal year 2008." Codiga, *supra* note 143, at 12.

181. Act 96, *supra* note 179.

182. Act 162, SB 3185, SD2 HD2 CD1, http://www.capitol.hawaii.gov/session2006/bills/SB3185_cd1_.htm.

183. The Hawai'i Public Utilities Commission (PUC) established the Public Benefits Fund in March 2007; it was scheduled to take effect in January 2009. PUC, Press Release, Mar. 2007, http://hawaii.gov/budget/puc/pr/NR-Energy_Efficiency_Public_Benefits_Fund.PDF.

The third bill, Act 240 (SB 2957),[184] provided another framework for energy self-sufficiency by focusing on a multitude of programs: made permanent the tax credits for renewable energy (solar hot water, wind, and photovoltaic); established a pilot pay-as-you-save program for solar hot water systems; established a bio-diesel preference in the state procurement law and mandated a state biofuels assessment; created a Hawai'i Renewable Hydrogen Program and hydrogen investment capital special fund of $10 million; and established state support for alternative fuels standards (setting a goal of 10% of highway alternative fuel demand by 2010, 15% by 1015, and 20% by 2020).[185]

Fourth, Act 163 (HB 2848) appropriated $200,000 to reconvene the Hawai'i Energy Policy Forum to develop an action plan, timeline, recommendations, and benchmarks to meet the state's energy self-sufficiency goals.[186] (Act 163 also asked HEPF to examine whether Hawai'i should become part of the Chicago Climate Exchange, which the group later recommended against.[187])

The strong leadership of the Governor and Legislature continued in 2007. The landmark bill of the 2007 session, Act 234, sometimes called the Hawai'i Global Warming Solutions Act, is described in Section B below. In addition, Act 159 (SB 1943) encouraged the further production and use of biofuels in Hawai'i.[188] It authorized biofuel processing facilities, for private, public, or commercial use, to be a permitted use in designated agricultural districts. It also established an energy feedstock program within the Department of Agriculture to encourage production and to establish milestones and objectives for feedstock in Hawai'i.[189] Act 253 (HB 1003)[190] established the Hawaii Natural Energy Institute (HNEI) at the University of Hawai'i to research and develop renewable energy in coordination with government and private agencies; created an energy systems development special fund for the development of renewable energy and energy efficient technologies; and charged DBEDT with creating a bioenergy master plan for the 2009 Legislature.[191]

The 2008 legislative session was also very active in the area of energy policy. The Legislature passed Act 90,[192] again to encourage biofuels. Act 188 (SB 3001) clarified that the utility's DSM funds would now go into the independent public benefits fund.[193] Act 151 (SB 988) authorized the PUC to establish a rate-payer funded PV rebate program of the public benefits fund.[194] The most stunning piece of legislation was Act 204 (SB 644), a mandatory solar hot water law, discussed further below. Act 207 (HB 2863) established a streamlined renewable energy siting

---

184. Act 240, SB 2957, SD2 HD2 CD1, http://www.capitol.hawaii.gov/session2006/bills/GM770_.PDF.
185. *Id.*
186. Act 193, HB 2848 CD1, http://www.capitol.hawaii.gov/session2006/bills/HB2848_cd1_.htm.
187. *See* Hawai'i Energy Policy Forum, Final Report on Chicago Climate Exchange, http://www.hawaiienergypolicy.hawaii.edu/pages/ccx.html.
188. Act 159, SB 1943 HD2 SD2 CD1, http://www.capitol.hawaii.gov/session2007/bills/SB1943_cd1_.htm.
189. *Id.*
190. Act 253, HB 1003, HD3 SD1 CD1, http://www.capitol.hawaii.gov/session2007/bills/HB1003_cd1_.htm.
191. *Id.*
192. Act 90, HB 3179, http://www.capitol.hawaii.gov/session2008/bills/GM732_.PDF. The new law "expands the definition of renewable energy producer to include growers and producers of organic materials used primarily for the production of biofuels. This allows the energy producer to enter into direct negotiations to lease public lands where they may grow their crops or raise livestock, then transport the materials to a biofuel conversion facility located in an industrial or commercial zone. The bill also clarifies that the byproducts from the organic materials may be used for other beneficial purposes such as mulch, feed or feedstock, and still qualify for the directly negotiated leases." http://hawaii.gov/gov/news/events/2008/may/bill-signed-to-encourage-biofuel-production.
193. Act 188, SB 3001, SD2 HD2 CD1, http://www.capitol.hawaii.gov/session2008/bills/GM760_.PDF.
194. Act 151, SB 988 SD2 HD3 CD1 http://www.capitol.hawaii.gov/session2008/bills/GM793_.pdf.

process (discussed below)[195] and Act 208 created a new "renewable energy coordinator" position within DBEDT.[196] Act 31 (HB 2502) expressly allowed solar facilities on low-quality agricultural land.[197]

Complementing the legislative push, the Governor threw down the gauntlet early in the 2008 session (coinciding with the attention from the Bush Administration related to the Major Economies Meeting in Honolulu) to up the ante on the state's clean energy goals. She announced the Hawai'i Clean Energy Initiative, in partnership with the U.S. Department of Energy (DOE), setting a state goal of 70% "clean energy" by 2030.[198] Hawai'i, they said, was well positioned to change course and lead the country. The national energy consultant, McKinsey Co., hired by DOE to examine the Hawai'i situation, optimistically stated that the state "can go farther and faster than the rest of the country" in reaching its emissions reductions and clean energy goals.[199] McKinsey reported that Hawai'i can meet its targets using "top ten technologies."[200] The good news is that most of those "technologies" are familiar and not terribly difficult to implement — they are the well-known "low hanging fruit" of mitigation, including energy-efficient commercial and residential lighting, appliances, and electronics; efficient transportation; solar; geothermal; biofuels; gas recovery from landfills; hydropower; afforestation and reforestation.[201] The other good news is that the study was based on oil prices of $60 barrel, about half of the 2008 spike so the technology revolution could move faster than anticipated if high prices stuck.

On the other hand, the bad news was that the study may have used some overly optimistic assumptions about the feasibility of these new technologies and may have unduly shrunk the estimate of Hawai'i's carbon footprint by deliberately omitting from the analysis emissions from international and marine travel and "imported carbon" (emissions from production of goods imported to Hawai'i).[202] As mentioned above, this omission appears to be politically expedient but painfully short-sighted.

The McKinsey report also seems to have assumed a too-rosy scenario for sugarcane ethanol for the islands. The report assumed a maximum acreage production scenario of about 36,000 acres, which Hawai'i has not seen since 1969, and it assumes all prior sugarcane land would be devoted to production of ethanol, which is highly doubtful.[203] It also assumes the construction of a new undersea cable from Maui to O'ahu, but marine energy cables have encountered strong

---

195. Act 207, HB 2863, HD2 SD2 CD1 http://www.capitol.hawaii.gov/session2008/bills/GM850_.pdf.

196. Act 208, HD 2505 HD2 SD2 CD1, http://www.capitol.hawaii.gov/session2008/bills/GM851_.pdf.

197. Act 31, HD 2502, HD2 http://www.capitol.hawaii.gov/session2008/bills/GM662_.PDF.

198. *Feds Help Hawaii Move to 70% Renewables by 2050*, Env't News Service, Jan. 28, 2008, http://www.ens-newswire.com/ens/jan2008/2008-01-28-091.asp.

199. Teresa Dawson, *Economists Attempt to Quantify Potential For Greenhouse Gas Reduction in Hawai'i*, Env't Hawai'i 19 (2008), at 6 (citing report entitled Reducing Hawaii's Oil Dependence and Greenhouse Gas Emission stating that Hawai'i "can go farther and faster than the rest of the country.") [hereinafter Dawson *Economists Attempt to Quantify*].

200. *Id.*

201. *Id.* at 5 (chart from McKinsey & Co.).

202. *Id.* at 1.

203. *Id.* at 5 & 7 (citing the concerns of Hawai'i Department of Health (DOH) Deputy Director Larry Lau). One of the environmental problems with sugarcane cultivation is the enormous water requirements, which was the subject of the landmark Waiāhole public trust litigation in Hawaii. *See generally* D. Kapua'ala Sproat & Isaac Moriwake, *Ke Kalo Pa'a o Waiāhole: Use of the Public Trust as a Tool for Environmental Advocacy*, in Creative Common Law Strategies for Protecting the Environment (Denise Antolini & Cliff Rechtschaffen eds., Environmental Law Institute 2007). With the demise of sugar and the intensive litigation over the issue, it is difficult to imagine that the "freed up" water will easily be available for ethanol production.

opposition in the past[204] and are not proven technology in Hawai'i.[205] The ability of the State's aging harbors to handle ethanol is another impediment to this ambitious goal; although the 2008 Legislature passed a bill for $618 million in port upgrades,[206] there are no specific provisions yet for making the upgrades friendly to these new technologies (*e.g.*, ethanol-related facilities),[207] or, for that matter, integrating climate change science into the infrastructure changes.

Moreover, in Hawai'i, environmental concerns or permitting issues are very real obstacles to development (even of "friendly" energy facilities), undermining the "friction-free environment" assumption made by McKinsey.[208] For example, the renewal of massive sugarcane for ethanol raises a host of environmental permitting and infrastructure issues. Substantial investment (estimated at $20 million) would also be needed to restore the deteriorating irrigation systems that have fallen into decay since the demise of Big Sugar.[209] A lot of former sugarcane land has been creeping and leaping toward urbanization or is being used for diversified agriculture, which would be politically impossible (and undesirable) to displace.[210] In Central O'ahu, for example, thousands of acres of former sugarcane land that have lain fallow for years are "available" for agriculture but, absent substantial economic incentives, the major landowners will avoid commitment to long-term agriculture and seek better investment opportunities such as urbanization.[211]

With a substantially strengthened advocacy effort from the Hawai'i-based Blue Planet Foundation,[212] directed by former Sierra Club leader Jeff Mikulina, the 2009 legislative session also proved active on clean energy initiatives, passing several key bills that now await the Governor's signature. The House initiated three important bills. First, HB 1464, an omnibus clean energy bill, fortifies the state's renewable portfolio standards (to 25% by 2020, and 40% by 2030, with a stronger definition of "renewable energy"), directs the PUC to establish energy *efficiency* portfolio standards of 30% of anticipated demand in 2030; and provides funding for an energy effi-

---

204. In the early 1990s, the author was involved in litigation on behalf of several Hawai'i environmental groups against fourteen federal agencies to require an environmental impact statement for a massive geothermal project on the Island of Hawaii. *See* Blue Ocean Preservation Society v. Watkins, 767 F. Supp. 1518 (D. Hawai'i 1991) (EIS required for $5 million geothermal power plant on the slopes of Kilauea crater, an active volcano). Part of that project involved a proposed undersea cable from Maui to O'ahu, which engendered substantial public opposition. *Id.*

205. Dawson, *supra* note 199, at 5.

206. Act 200, SB 3227 CD1 (2008), http://www.capitol.hawaii.gov/session2008/Bills/SB3227_CD1_.htm. *See also* Derrick DePledge, *$842M in Hawaii harbor upgrades pending OK*, HONOLULU ADVERTISER, Dec. 19, 2007, http://the.honoluluadvertiser.com/article/2007/Dec/19/ln/hawaii712190386.html.

207. Dawson *Economists Attempt to Quantify*, *supra* note 199, at 5.

208. *Id.* at 5–6. An example of the friction that can often accompany biofuels projects is the recent controversy over a renewable energy project on Kaua'i involving afforestation. *See id.* at 11 (*Farmers Make Room for Green Energy*). The project had to switch tree species (from the invasive fast-growing albizia to the more stable eucalyptus) due to environmental objections, and then ran into vocal objections from displaced diversified farmers who faced the loss of acreage and irrigation water to the biofuel project. *Id.*

209. *Id.* at 5.

210. *Id.* (quoting Davito).

211. *See, e.g.,* Rick Daysog, *New Galbraith Broker*, HONOLULU ADVERTISER BLOGS, http://bizbites.honadvblogs.com/2008/07/08/new-galbraith-broker (describing pending sale of 2,100 acres of prime agricultural land in Central O'ahu that could be slated for housing of up to 1000 homes).

212. Blue Planet Foundation's primary mission is to "end the use of fossil fuel on Earth by making Hawai'i a role model for energy independence within a decade," and legislative action is a top priority. *See* www.blue-planetfoundation.org. The NEW YORK TIMES hailed Mikuluina's new leadership at Blue Planet, editorializing: "Advances like these, plus a concerted push for conservation, may be just the steps needed to complete the state's transformation from blue to green. Hawaiians have a long tradition of self-sufficiency, community action and a deep attachment to the land that sustains them—leadership in a clean-energy movement could powerfully reaffirm those values and perhaps spread them to the rest of the nation." Editorial, *Hawai'i's Moon Shot*, N. Y. TIMES, Dec. 1, 2008, http://www.nytimes.com/2008/12/02/opinion/02tue2.html?_r=1.

ciency loan program for buildings.[213] The second important bill passed—HB 1271 for "food and energy security"—could be transformational. Essentially "carbon tax lite," it proposes a $ 1 fee on every barrel of imported oil in order to raise funds for energy security, food independence, the clean energy initiative, and renewable energy projects.[214] The surcharge may raise about $40 million annually, a huge boost for these programs especially given the poor economy. The Legislature also passed HB 1270, already signed by the Governor into law as Act 50, allowing the PUC to approve the purchase of renewable electricity at a "just and reasonable cost," even when the cost exceeds that produced by fossil fuel sources, which should stabilize the renewable energy markets.[215] The Senate was similarly pro-active with four successful bills:[216] SB 1202, increasing incentives for electric vehicles by requiring parking set asides and setting up a grant and loan program for infrastructure; SB 464, enhancing the tax credit for solar and wind energy systems for households; SB 1338, re-passing the earlier "right to dry" bill, which would prohibit codes and covenants from banning clotheslines; and SB 1260, eliminating the "loophole" that allows major emitters of air emissions over 4,000 tons annually from paying fees under the state clean air law.[217]

Whether the accumulated strength of these strong 2006–2009 legislative initiatives and the McKinsey report are on target remains to be seen, but together they create strong signals that Hawai'i's policy efforts are gaining momentum. The media coverage has also dramatically shifted, touting clean energy issues as "one of the very few issues on which voters can see … legislative-executive collaboration … it's easy to see why energy independence has become a motherhood-and-apple-pie value."[218] The state is beginning to attract businesses to harvest its powerful unique natural assets of wind, solar, and wave energy. Innovative entrepreneurs— like the electric car system purveyor Better Place[219]—have been attracted to Hawai'i's unique setting. Public support is still passive, however, and there are strong voices of resistance to the "streamlining" efforts that may unduly trample Hawai'i's longstanding environmental laws and sensibilities. Nonetheless, these initiatives paint a positive picture for Hawai'i, especially when added to the major greenhouse gas emissions cap passed in 2007. As the ADVERTISER optimistically editorialized, "the Legislature deserves praise for much of its energy package that appears to have solid support even in a difficult year.... The goals do seem a long way off, but that should harden the resolve for staying the clean-energy course, toward a future other than enslavement by imported oil, a commodity with supplies that are dwindling, day by day."[220]

---

213. HB 1464, HD3 SD2 CD1, was enrolled to the Governor on May 11, 2009; http://www.capitol.hawaii.gov/session2009/lists/measure_indiv.aspx?billtype=HB&billnumber=1464.

214. HB 1271, HD3 SD2 CD1, http://www.capitol.hawaii.gov/session2009/Bills/HB1271_CD1_.HTM; the bill is currently awaiting signature by the Governor and may be vetoed because she is opposed to "new" taxes.

215. HB 1270, HD1 SD2, http://www.capitol.hawaii.gov/session2009/lists/measure_indiv.aspx?billtype=HB&billnumber=1270.

216. The text and status of each of these bills can be viewed at: http://www.capitol.hawaii.gov under "Bill Status and Documents."

217. *See* Blue Planet Foundation, *Major clean energy bills pass legislature,* Legislative Review (Newsletter), May 2009. A bold proposal by Blue Planet Foundation, which was (amazingly) endorsed by the Governor and numerous organizations, that did *not* pass was the "no new coal or oil plants" amendment to HB 1464. *See* http://blueplanetfoundation.org/bpf/whathappened.html.

218. Editorial, *Isles making steady shift to clean energy,* HONOLULU ADVERTISER, at B2, Apr. 12, 2009.

219. *See* Ben Mack, *Hawaii Is a Better Place for EVs,* Dec. 5, 2008, http://www.wired.com/autopia/2008/12/hawaii-becomes (noting "Hawaii is the latest place to fall in love with EV evangelist Shai Agassi's plan to bring electric cars to the masses, inviting his startup to build as many as 100,000 charging spots across the state by 2012 and bring EVs into the mainstream.").

220. *Id.*

B. Mitigation: Greenhouse Gas Emissions Cap (Act 234)

The centerpiece of the 2007 Legislature's efforts on energy policy was passage of a "second in the nation" statewide legislative mandate to reduce greenhouse gas emissions.[221] Hawai'i represents only 0.3% of U.S. GHG emissions, but despite its small contribution, the State made a strong commitment to being a leader in mitigation by initiating a framework for reducing emissions to 1990 levels by 2020. Hawai'i announced its ambition to serve as "an example to other states, the federal government, and other countries to protect our fragile environment,"[222] and to "position its economy, technology centers, financial institutions, and businesses to benefit from national and international efforts to meet this important policy."[223]

Act 234 received surprisingly broad support in the Legislature and from Governor Lingle.[224] Modeled after California's law,[225] the act established a ten-member task force to create a plan, by the end of 2009, to recommend how Hawai'i can meet the emissions target.[226] The task force includes two members of the University of Hawai'i faculty, two leading environmental advocates, four representatives of the energy and transportations industries, and two cabinet members.[227] The State of Hawai'i Department of Health (DOH) is charged with establishing limits that must be met by each emission source, with rules and penalties to take effect by 2012.[228] The State Department of Business, Economic Development and Tourism (DBEDT) also plays a strong role in the development of the emissions reduction scheme. Despite that the Act did not include within its scope the largest emissions sector (transportation),[229] the law sets a strong foundation for future regulation and expansion. Most importantly, it passed.

The first step under Act 234 was for DOH and DBEDT to update a 1997 inventory of emission sources, categories, or sources.[230] The second step is for the task force to create a "work plan" and a "regulatory scheme" before December 1, 2009 for "implementing the maximum practically and technically feasible and cost-effective reductions in greenhouse gas emissions from sources or categories of sources."[231] The act also requires DOH to adopt rules regarding the reporting and verification of statewide GHG emissions.[232] The task force contracted with Washington D.C's ICF International to update the inventory and develop the regulatory scheme.[233]

---

221. For a good summary of Hawai'i's new climate change law, *see* Codiga, *supra* note 143 (noting that other states to pass similar initiatives in 2007 include Washington State, New Jersey, and Florida).

222. Act 234, § 1, http://www.capitol.hawaii.gov/sessioncurrent/bills/hb226_cd1_.htm.

223. *Id.*

224. *Id. See also* Sea Change Hawaii (Sierra Club), Global Warming Solutions Act of 2007, http://www.seachangehawaii.org/learn/hawaii-s-carbon-cap.

225. Act 234, *supra* note 222.

226. *Id.*

227. *Id.*; Codiga, *supra* note 143, at 9.

228. Act 234, *supra* note 222.

229. As of 2005, about half (50.12%) of all of Hawai'i's GHG emissions were attributable to "transportation," including ground, domestic, and international aviation and marine transportation. HAWAII ELECTRIC REPORT, *supra* note 21, at 11. (This contribution is larger than the 33.74% attributed to the electric utilities and independent power producers sector, which will be regulated by Act 234.) *Id.*

230. The inventory update was produced in draft in December 2008. *See supra* note 20. Alongside this state effort, the University of Hawai'i (the second largest energy consumer in the state after the military) is launching parallel initiatives as part of its participation in the American College and University Presidents Climate Commitment, including its inaugural emissions inventory submitted in September 2008. Personal communication from Prof. Denise Konan, Sept. 16, 2008 (on file with author); UH Mānoa emissions report *available at* http://www.aashe.org/pcc/reports/ghg-report.php?id=340.

231. Act 234, *supra* note 222.

232. *Id.*

233. Greenhouse Gas Emissions Reduction Task Force Meeting Agenda for Aug.7, 2008, at http://calendar.ehawaii.gov/calendar/html/event/2008/8/7.

The task force is also examining the market-based options as directed by the Act, struggling with the pros and cons of cap and trade, and whether it should join in regional initiatives and at what level, as well as the option of a more even-handed but potentially less aggressive carbon tax.[234] According to Hawaiian Electric, even though the market mechanisms being examined by the Act 234 task force allow flexibility, the application of cap and trade, in particular, to Hawai'i "may be problematic."[235] The proof will be in the pudding—the task force now has a few more months to come up with the regulatory scheme. Not an easy task, but if it gets weak-kneed, it may be fatal for the mitigation effort and for any similar kind of sweeping attempt to address adaptation. Conversely, if Act 234 succeeds, it will boost the significance of the new companion legislation on adaptation.

C. Harnessing Hawai'i's Natural Energy Assets: Wind, Solar, Wave

When it comes to certain clean energy assets, Hawai'i does seem to have it all: wind, solar, and waves. Development of each of the sectors is tantalizingly close to moving beyond experimental to the medium- or large-scale commercial phase. Market forces and governmental greenlights are now moving projects along more quickly, testing the state's and island communities' commitment to renewables "in my front yard."

1. Harvesting the Wind

Wind energy is still small but growing rapidly in Hawai'i. As of 2007, Hawai'i had several major wind farms in place or proposed on: the Big Island (a 21 MW expansion at Pakini Nui, operated by Tawhiri Power LLC); Maui (a 20 MW plant proposed by Shell Wind Energy at Ulupalakua Ranch and a 30 MW proposed expansion at Kaheawa by UPC wind); O'ahu (proposals for more than 40 MW on the North Shore by UPC (now "First") Wind and others); and Moloka'i/Lana'i (>300 MW).[236] Hawaiian Electric itself has an ambitious goal of 100 MW from wind in the "next 5 to 10 years."[237] Recently, as part of the Clean Energy Initiative, the Governor, Castle & Cooke, First Wind, and Hawaiian Electric announced a "Big Wind" initiative to coordinate and capture a total of 400 MW from the Lana'i and Moloka'i projects.[238]

As important, the public attitude about wind farms in Hawai'i seems to be changing as the operations become visible (and as gas prices soared in 2008). Wind in Hawai'i had a fitful start in the 1980s in Kahuku, on the North Shore of O'ahu, where the world's largest turbine died not long after launch. The prominent site quickly became a white elephant and set back public perception about the viability of wind power. When Hawaiian Electric proposed a $70 million 39 MW wind farm for the Kahe Point area on the west side of O'ahu in 2005, it was met with strong cultural and environmental justice objections and ultimately killed by the Mayor of Honolulu who told the company to move it to Kahuku.[239] And, there are still objections to wind farms based on aesthetics and flight paths for endangered birds. But, as one pro-

---

234. Coffman, *supra* note 22.

235. Hawaiian Electric Report, *supra* note 21, at 15: "Hawaii's size, isolation and relatively simple energy economy means that local emissions permit trading opportunities are extremely limited. The result of these limited trading opportunities could be that financial resources from Hawaii's energy consumers leave the state to purchase emissions permits elsewhere. This could be a severe economic blow for a capital poor state that already spends billions of dollars externally for food and fuel." *Id.*

236. *Id.* at 28.

237. *Id.*

238. Press Release, *Governor Lingle Announces Agreement To Advance "Big Wind" Projects*, Mar. 17, 2009, http://hawaii.gov/gov/news/releases/2009-news-releases/governor-lingle-announces-agreement-to-advance-big-wind-projects.

239. Crystal Kua, *Mayor rejects Kahe wind farm*, Honolulu Star-Bulletin, Sept. 27, 2005, http://archives.starbulletin.com/2005/09/27/news/story4.html.

gressive ex-legislator commented: "Environmentalists have to get over the ugly objection to wind."[240]

Today, there are two large wind farm proposals for Kahuku, and there seems to be strong (but not full) community support, spilling over from a successful project on Maui. The new Kaheawa Wind plant with eighteen very visible new turbines on the windy hills above Ma'alaea harbor on Maui added 30 MW of capacity (about 9% of the island's demand) and seems to have warmed part of the community to wind.[241] Appropriate siting, cultural sensitivity, and community relationships will continue to be the key that unlocks the future of renewables, including wind, in Hawai'i, but visible success stories and indications of direct community benefit will be particularly powerful in a small island state.

To boost wind and similar renewable projects even more, in mid-2008, Governor Lingle signed a controversial piece of streamlining legislation.[242] Act 207 (HB 2863)[243] encountered substantial opposition because many believed it was special interest legislation to benefit a particular project proposed by David Murdoch, the owner of Castle & Cooke and the "private" luxury-hotel island of Lana'i.[244] According to Life of the Land's Henry Curtis, the act ran roughshod over standard public input and governmental approval processes; he called it the "worst bill of the session."[245] The Act gives DBEDT authority to shepherd "large" (>200 MW projects) through the federal, state, and county approval process, and makes DBEDT the accepting authority for the projects' environmental impact statements.[246] Although many of the most objectionable provisions of the bill were deleted during legislative hearings, the new law still greatly concerns environmental groups, proponents of good government, and even some wind proponents.[247]

2. Capturing Solar Energy

Hawai'i can justly brag about having the best opportunities for harnessing solar energy among all U.S. states. According to the Sierra Club Hawai'i Chapter, "The most populated parts of the state receive between 450 and 500 calories of solar radiation per square centimeter every day. To put [that] into perspective, an average rooftop space of 1100 square feet receives the energy equivalent of approximately 15 gallons of gasoline daily."[248] Yet, only with rising oil prices in 2008 has Hawai'i been shocked into making solar a standard rather than a novel way to achieving energy independence and reducing greenhouse gas emissions. The 2008 Legislature passed several bills

---

240. Comment by former State Representative Brian Schatz to author (May 26, 2006).

241. For more information on the project, go to: www.kaheawa.com.

242. See Act 207, HB 2863, http://www.capitol.hawaii.gov/session2008/bills/GM850_.pdf.

243. Alongside Act 207, the Legislature passed Act 208, which established the DBEDT energy facilitator position. Act 207 (HB 2505), http://www.capitol.hawaii.gov/session2008/bills/GM851_.pdf [hereinafter Act 207].

244. According to opponents, the true purpose of the bill was to expedite the plans of land mogul David Murdoch (owner of Castle & Cooke) for a 300–400 MW wind farm on the small "private island" of Lana'i, which includes a controversial proposal to run an undersea energy cable to O'ahu. Patricia Tummons, *Renewable Energy Bills Take Center Stage at '08 Legislature*, ENV'T HAWAI'I, June 2008, at 8 [hereinafter Tummons, *Renewable*].

245. *Id.*

246. *Id.* The coordinator, attorney Joshua Strickler, was hired with unusual fanfare. Governor Linda Lingle, Press Release, Aug. 27, 2008, http://hawaii.gov/gov/news/releases/2008/governor-lingle-names-joshua-strickler-as-energy.

247. Tummons, *Renewable, supra* note 244, at 8. Two other minor related bills passed to increase DBEDT's capacity to handle renewable energy projects (Act 207, *see supra* note 242) and staff the greenhouse gas emissions task force (Act 235, HB 2507). *Id.*

248. Jeff Mikulina, Executive Director, Sierra Club, Hawai'i Chapter, Testimony on SB 644 (Solar Hot Water), Mar. 26, 2008, before the House Finance Committee (on file with author) [hereinafter Mikulina].

aimed at enhancing homeowner and industrial solar hot water and photovoltaic installation.[249] Reflecting a growing consensus among the Governor, the Legislature, business, utilities, and environmental advocates, an impressive number of steps have been taken toward a brighter solar future for the state.

In 2008, with Act 204, Hawai'i became the first state in the nation to mandate solar hot water on new residential homes, starting in 2010.[250] Although Hawai'i already boasts the highest rate of solar hot water systems in the U.S., coverage is only about 20%, far below the state's capacity.[251] The goal of the recent legislation is to take solar hot water out of the novelty stage and make it a "basic amenity" in Hawai'i.[252] The move makes basic economic sense even to non-tree-huggers. In Hawai'i, solar hot water systems can reduce a home's utility bill by 30–35%.[253]

The incentives for installing solar hot water (and photovoltaic panels and wind) in Hawai'i come from federal and state tax credits, as well as a utility rebate.[254] On O'ahu, HECO began giving rebates for solar hot water systems in 1996, and as of 2007, had paid out nearly $35 million in rebates to support the installation of more than 39,000 systems.[255] Initiated in 1990,[256] the Hawai'i state tax credit for solar hot water systems is now 35% or $2,250, whichever is less (for single family homes); 35% or $350 per unit, whichever is less, for multi-family residential property; and 35% or $250,000, whichever is less, for commercial property.[257] The federal credit was 30% in 2008 (up to $2000).[258] Maui County and the City and County of Honolulu have partnered with utilities to offer zero-interest loans to certain homeowners (on O'ahu, low-income).[259] Thus, on average, a $5,000 solar hot water system currently would ultimately cost the

---

249. One innovative solar bill introduced by the Sierra Club as part of the national "right to dry" movement, www.laundrylist.org, would have allowed homeowners to install outdoor clotheslines despite private covenants. The bill "sailed through" the Legislature, Tummons, *Renewable, supra* note 244, at 8, but was successfully vetoed by Governor Lingle, who was concerned about trampling the existing rules of homeowner associations. *See* Richard Borreca and B.J. Reyes, *Veto Overrides create 13 laws,* HONOLULU STAR-BULLETIN, July 9, 2008, http://starbulletin.com/2008/07/09/news/story01.html. The bill is once again on the Governor's desk. *See supra* note 217.

250. Part of the inspiration for the Hawai'i bill came from countries like Spain that have mandated solar hot water for new residential units since 2007. Mikulina, *supra* note 248, at 2.

251. *Id.* Some statistics suggest a much larger "penetration" of solar hot water in Hawai'i, but this number appears to be inflated with the inclusion of thousands of federal military housing units, which have been far ahead of the game in Hawai'i for many years thanks to the leadership of Army Garrison Hawai'i and solar company Actus Lend Lease. *See* Dan Nakaso, *Massive solar project to power army homes,* HONOLULU ADVERTISER, Aug. 3, 2005, http://the.honoluluadvertiser.com/article/2005/Aug/03/bz/508030328.html [hereinafter Nakaso] (announcing plans to power 3,000 Army homes with solar hot water and photovoltaic energy). According to Richard Reed, representative of the Hawaii Solar Energy Association, 5500 solar hot water units were installed in 2007, with 37% of those units on new homes. Extended Testimony of Richard Reed, Hawaii Solar Energy Association, on SB 644, Mar. 26, 2008, before the House Finance Committee, at 3, available from author.

252. Mikulina, *supra* note 248, at 1.

253. *See* Act 204, SB 644, § 1 (2008), http://www.capitol.hawaii.gov/session2008/bills/GM847_.pdf. The personal experience of the author, whose family installed a residential solar hot water system in 2006, was even better, with a reduction of approximately 40% of the base electricity consumption.

254. Currently, the utility rebate is substantial. For example, the HECO raised its rebate in 2007 from $750 to $1000. *See* www.heco.com at "solar hot water" page.

255. HAWAIIAN ELECTRIC REPORT, *supra* note 21, at 27.

256. H.R.S. § 235-12.4 (amended 2003, 2004, 2006, 2007).

257. H.R.S. § 235-12.5.

258. 26 U.S.C. § 25D (2008). *See* Database of Incentives for Renewables & Efficiency (DSIRE), Federal Incentives for Renewable Energy, http://www.capitol.hawaii.gov/session2008/bills/GM847_.pdf.

259. *See* www.heco.com at "Interest Free Solar Loans" (Maui) and "HECO Solar Hot Water Heating Loan" (Honolulu) for low-income families or landlords who rent to them.

homeowner only about $1500,[260] with a pay-back of three to seven years (a period that shortens as fossil fuel prices rise).[261] Yet, most homeowners still struggle with putting the cash up front needed to obtain the long-term benefits.

Act 204 will pick the "low hanging fruit" of solar hot water both "backward" (that is, through continuing tax credits for existing homes[262]) and "forward," that is, for all new homes in Hawai'i that pull building permits starting in January 2010 (roughly 5,000 new homes a year, or 60,000 new homes over the next twenty years).[263] The purpose of the bill was to shift, for new homes (with some variances allowed), from a system of state tax credits that were being claimed by housing developers to a broad mandate for builders. Compared to a retrofit by individual homeowners, the built-in system is more readily and cheaply absorbed as a marginal cost of all new homes.[264]

Ironically, the solar hot water industry and many land use and tax organizations in Hawai'i strongly opposed the solar hot water bill, concerned that it would put the existing tax credits at risk, would reduce the industry's opportunities to market their individual services to new homes, and result in shoddy mass installations.[265] The bill endured many amendments, a major tug-of-war in numerous legislative hearings, and 11th hour behind-the-scenes negotiations between the industry and grassroots advocates. Its success was uncertain right up to the Governor's signing, but she ultimately signed the bill, setting a new national standard for residential solar hot water and, its proponents hope, forcing a shift in attitudes about the role of solar in our everyday lives.

Photovoltaic energy systems have also long been supported by limited tax credits in Hawai'i[266] but have been slow to catch on because of the much larger up-front costs to homeowners. The State passed a net metering law in 2004, and extended that in 2005 to projects over 10 kW (requiring interconnection standards) (Act 69).[267] The potential for PV is large, if the price can become more affordable. For example, the author's family recently installed five panels (an 875-watt package) on their home, generating approximately 3 kWh a day, about 25% of their family's energy needs (already reduced by solar hot water and other energy saving measures). The up-

---

260. *Id.*

261. The payback period varies, of course, with utility prices, but was estimated in 2008 by Mikulina at three to seven years. Mikulina, *supra* note 248, at 2.

262. Hawai'i's state tax credit for solar hot water was originally enacted in 1976 (Act 189), H.R.S. §235-12, legislative history http://www.capitol.hawaii.gov/hrscurrent/Vol04_Ch0201-0257/HRS0235/HRS_0235-0012.htm. The original Act has been amended more than a dozen times, with changes in credit rates, applicability, and duration, demonstrating that past progress and prior accomplishments in energy sustainability confer no license for complacence.

263. Figures from Mikulina, *supra* note 248, at 2. The author and students in her Fall 2007 Environmental Law class were involved in reviving interest in this residential mandate bill, sponsored by Senator Gary Hooser of Kaua'i; the bill had failed early in the 2007 session, *see* SB 644 (2007) status sheet, http://www.capitol.hawaii.gov/session2007/status/SB644.htm, sparking its adoption as a class project, *see* http://www2.hawaii.edu/~elp/bills/, for discussions with Senator Hooser and Representative Hermina Morita of Kaua'i. Students following the bill through to passage in the 2008 Session.

264. With an average home price on O'ahu of over $600,000 in May 2008, Kristen Consillio, *Oahu home prices show a mixed trend*, Honolulu Star-Bulletin, May 2, 2008, http://starbulletin.com/2008/05/02/news/story06.html, the cost of an average solar hot water system ($5,250), HECO, Hawai'i's Energy Future, http://www.hawaiisenergyfuture.com/SolarWaterHeating/index.html, would be even lower on a mass-install basis and is ultimately marginal (less than 1%), easily folded into the mortgage.

265. *See, e.g.,* Extended Testimony of Richard Reed, Hawaii Solar Energy Association, Mar. 26, 2008, before the House Finance Committee, available from author.

266. Under H.R.S. §235-12.5 (2008), the current PV state tax credit is 35% or $5,000, whichever is less, for single-family residential; 35% or $350 per unit, whichever is less, for multi-family residential; and 35% or $500,000, whichever is less, for commercial property. The federal credit, at least through the end of 2008, is 30%. *See* http://www.hawaiisenergyfuture.com/Images/pv-tax-credit.jpg.

267. Act 69, HB 606 (2005) (amending H.R.S. §269-11), http://www.capitol.hawaii.gov/session2005/bills/HB606_cd1_.htm.

front cost was about $8,000, and the tax credits totaled $4,700 ($2,700 state and $2,000 federal), leaving us a net cost of $3,300. At our current electricity price, with surcharges, of 35¢ kW, we save about $31.5 a month, or $378 a year, giving us a payback period of 9–10 years.[268] The bright side of likely higher oil prices in the future is an accelerated payback period.

The Legislature and Governor also found common ground during the 2008 session in a bill (Act 31) that allows solar energy facilities on Hawai'i's agricultural lands of "marginal" value (class D or E).[269] Wind farms and biofuel production were already considered allowable uses on certain agricultural lands, making the inclusion of solar fairly noncontroversial.[270] The bill passed with only limited concern expressed by farming advocates that solar might be incompatible with or displace diversified agriculture or ranching that does well on marginal lands.[271] Another bill that passed into law in 2008 with little fanfare, Act 151, took a new step toward encouraging the installation of photovoltaic (PV) systems by authorizing the Public Utilities Commission to establish a ratepayer-funded PV rebate program.[272]

One very bright spot in the PV landscape in Hawai'i has been the aggressive installation of residential PV by the U.S. Army Garrison Hawai'i, which manages the logistics of the very large Army population in Hawai'i. Under the strong leadership of Lt. Col. Howard Killian, the Garrison installed approximately 7 MW at Schofield Barracks alone by 2006.[273] This momentum increased dramatically because of recent federal legislation, leading to a joint military effort in Hawai'i to reduce fossil fuel use, including the Marines' recent announcement that it would install the state's largest PV and bio-fuel project at the Kāne'ohe Marine Corps Air Station, projected to produce all of the base's electricity needs by 2015.[274] Given the large military presence in Hawai'i, the military's leadership on renewable energy can influence both minds and markets.

Commercial interest in PV is low but growing rapidly. The famous Mauna Lani resort pitches itself as the luxury resort with the largest solar capacity "in the world," using a 500 KW PV "sun tracking" installation and even solar-powered golf carts.[275] A major Harley-Davidson store near the Honolulu airport put a highly visible PV installation on its roof.[276] On Lana'i, Castle & Cooke installed a $19 million, 10-acre, 7,400-panel installation, now the largest in the state.[277] On O'ahu, commercial PV is completed or near-completion by the State of Hawai'i, Wal-Mart, Costco, and the James Campbell Company.[278] The innovative firm Sopogy Inc. is proposing a

---

268. Information available from author, based on August 2008 HECO bill.

269. HB 2502, Act 031 (signed April 23, 2008), amending H.R.S. Ch. 205-2.

270. *See* Tummons, *Renewable*, *supra* note 244, at 8.

271. *See, e.g.,* Testimony of Sandra Kunimoto, Chair, Hawaii Board of Agriculture, Before Energy and Environmental Protection Committee, on HB 2505 (Feb. 5, 2008) (on file with author).

272. SB 988, Act 151 (2007) (amending H.R.S. Ch. 269), http://www.capitol.hawaii.gov/session2008/bills/GM793_.pdf. The act allowed the PUC to delegate this program to the new "public benefits fund administrator," established pursuant to H.R.S. § 269-122 in 2006 (Act 162). *Id.*

273. *See* Nakaso, *supra* note 251.

274. William Cole, *Bold energy plans for Corps in Hawaii*, HONOLULU ADVERTISER, Dec. 3, 2008, http://www.navytimes.com/news/2008/12/gns_marine_energy_plan_hawaii_120108w/ (noting that the military represents 15% of O'ahu electricity demand and is Hawaiian Electric's biggest customer).

275. *See* Mauna Lani web site, http://www.maunalani.com/r_hc_solar.htm.

276. Pat Bigold, *Solar Pays Off for Cycle City Showroom*, PACIFIC BUS. NEWS, Apr. 15, 2005, http://www.bizjournals.com/pacific/stories/2005/04/18/story8.html (noting that, with 11,000 square feet of rooftop solar panels, the Harley-Davidson showroom saves about $10,000 on its monthly utility bill).

277. HAWAIIAN ELECTRIC REPORT, *supra* note 21, at 28. *See also* RenewableEnergyaccess.com, *Castle & Cooke to build 1.5 MW solar farm on Lanai*, June 6, 2007, http://www.renewableenergyworld.com/rea/news/story?id=48828; Jennifer Sudick, *Lanai's la ola solar farm is dedicated*, HONOLULU STAR-BULLETIN, Jan. 7, 2009, http://www.starbulletin.com/business/20090107_Lanais_la_ola_solar_farm_is_dedicated.html (noting that the farm will supply 30% of the island's needs).

278. HAWAIIAN ELECTRIC REPORT, *supra* note 21, at 28.

10MW "concentrated solar" project on O'ahu and 1 MW demonstration plant at the Natural Energy Lab in Kona.[279] Hawaiian Electric itself plans to enter into a purchase power agreement with Hoku Solar for a 167 kW PV system on its own facility at Ward Avenue to begin service in 2009.[280] Especially if additional tax credits and power purchase agreements can address some of the lagging sectors (such as the large rental housing stock, educational facilities, and commercial buildings with large roofs), the solar future for Hawai'i does indeed look bright.

3. Riding Waves and Cooling with Seawater Air Conditioning

Hawai'i is world famous for its beautiful and massive waves, and the great promise of wave and seawater energy is just starting to show in Hawai'i. The islands have "one of the world's best and most consistent wave regimes."[281] A 1992 study showed that "annual wave energy resources off northern shores of the Hawaiian islands far exceeds the energy demands of all but one of the major islands,"[282] and, for that island (O'ahu), wave power could meet two-thirds of its needs.[283] A 2004 study by the Electric Power Research Institute identified 1,500 MW of annual energy output from potential wave sites in Hawai'i.[284]

The first foray into wave energy in Hawai'i began in 2004 with a demonstration project in Kāne'ohe Bay sponsored by the U.S. Navy, which produced 20 kW.[285] In 2008, the Australian company Oceanlinx announced a 2.7 MW project on Maui, to be operational by 2009, that will use a compressed air method and units anchored more than a mile offshore to power 2,700 homes.[286] Each platform will be about the size of a three-bedroom house, sit above the water, and use the air forced back and forth in a vertical column to power a turbine. Maui Senator J. Kalani English urged support for the plan, saying the aesthetic impacts were "a very small speck in the ocean" and that "[i]t should provide the beginning of some very good and clean energy from the ocean for us."[287] In 2008, the State Legislature readily passed a $20 million special purpose revenue bond to support the project,[288] and it may also qualify for Hawai'i's unique 100% tax credit as a high-technology investment.[289]

---

279. *Id.*

280. *Id.* at 29.

281. DBEDT, WAVE ENERGY IN HAWAII (Apr. 2006), http://hawaii.gov/dbedt/info/energy/publications/wave2006.pdf.

282. *Id. See* George Hagerman, SEASUN Power Systems, WAVE ENERGY RESOURCE AND ECONOMIC ASSESSMENT FOR THE STATE OF HAWAII (1992).

283. DBEDT, WAVE ENERGY, *supra* note 281.

284. HAGERMAN *et. al*, E21 EPRI SURVEY AND CHARACTERIZATION OF POTENTIAL OFFSHORE WAVE ENERGY SITES IN HAWAII, Electric Power Research Institute (June 2004), http://oceanenergy.epri.com/attachments/wave/reports/003_Hawaii_Site_Report_Rev_1.pdf.

285. Sean Hao, *Wave Energy May Soon Light Up Maui Homes*, HONOLULU ADVERTISER, Jan. 28, 2008, http://the.honoluluadvertiser.com/article/2008/Jan/28/bz/hawaii801280319.html [hereinafter Hao] ("Pennington, N.J.-based Ocean Power Technologies Inc. has worked with the Navy for several years with buoys deployed off Marine Corps Base Hawaii at Kāne'ohe Bay. Ocean Power Technologies plans to test a 150 kilowatt, or .15 megawatt, buoy in Hawai'i this year, according to a filing with the Securities & Exchange Commission"); *see also* B.J. Reyes, *Ocean of energy*, HONOLULU STAR-BULLETIN, Feb. 5, 2008, http://starbulletin.com/2008/02/05/news/story09.html [hereinafter Reyes].

286. HAWAIIAN ELECTRIC REPORT, *supra* note 21, at 29 & 30; Hao, *supra* note 285; Reyes, *supra* note 285.

287. Reyes, *supra* note 285.

288. SB 2304 (Act 103), § 1 (2008) ("to assist Oceanlinx Hawaii LLC, in planning, designing, and constructing a wave energy, or hydrokinetic, power facility and supplying electric energy generated from that facility to an electric utility for resale to the general public"), http://www.capitol.hawaii.gov/session2008/bills/GM745_.PDF.

289. Hao, *supra* note 285. In 2001, Hawai'i became the only state with a 100% high technology tax credit (up to $2 million) for qualified businesses, which covers many types of renewable energy projects from hydrogen to biomass. H.R.S § 235-110.9 (2008).

But companies interested in Hawai'i's wave and wind resources will have to demonstrate special sensitivity to environmental concerns. An ambitious $400–600 million proposal by a Seattle company to install 100 offshore wind-wave platforms with 1000 MW potential in an area off Maui called Penguin Banks—smack dab in the middle of the Hawaiian Islands Humpback Whale National Marine Sanctuary—raised a storm of criticism and ended in a bust in April 2009 with the company acknowledging "game over" because the federal government had moved to prohibit wind projects in marine sanctuaries.[290] The Penguin Banks flurry shows that Hawai'i will always need to be vigilant about separating the truly innovative proposals that complement the indigenous context of the islands from the merely speculative that seek only to exploit them.

An innovative system of using local seawater for air conditioning is a good example of a novel proposal that seems to suit the islands well and consequently is gaining support in Hawai'i. Honolulu Seawater Air Conditioning LLC (HSWAC) expects to start construction of its system in 2009.[291] The company estimates the benefits from the 25,000-ton downtown project will save nearly 65 million kWh/year, "equivalent to more than 25,000 residential solar water heating systems,"[292] and avoid 17 MW of new generation.[293] Adding greater legitimacy to the project, Hawaiian Electric is one of HSWAC's signed clients.[294]

D. Pushing Biofuels and Reviving Geothermal: Dead Ends?

The merits of renewables are highly contextual. Place, culture, tradition, and trade-offs matter, considerably. Two often-touted renewable energy solutions for Hawai'i—biofuels and geo - thermal—may encounter too many obstacles to be viable green alternatives for the islands. Or, their progress may be at the expense of splitting otherwise allied partners in the environmental and energy communities.

Biofuels in Hawai'i have generated several major controversies in recent years. First, the state requirement of ethanol in gasoline has proven controversial for consumers and failed to spur any local ethanol feedstock. Second, a proposal by HECO to import palm oil for a new power plant on O'ahu has encountered substantial objections from environmental advocates concerned about harmful palm oil farming practices in Indonesia and Malaysia.

The driving, boating, and yard-clearing public in Hawai'i has been very unhappy with the State's commitment to imported ethanol as a 10% additive to gasoline. Even though the law requiring 10% ethanol in at least 85% of gas supplies, known as the "E10" requirement, had been on the books since 1994, it had not been enforced because there were no Hawai'i producers.[295] Caught up in the early 2000s national rush toward corn-based ethanol, Governor Lingle's DBEDT pushed out long-delayed rules enforcing the E10 requirement as of April 2006.[296] Hawai'i began importing tankers of ethanol from the continental U.S.[297] Aside from the irony of using fossil

---

290. Rob Perez, *Penguin Bank project called off*, HONOLULU ADVERTISER, Apr. 21, 2009, http://www.honoluluadvertiser.com/apps/pbcs.dll/article?AID=/20090421.

291. HAWAIIAN ELECTRIC REPORT, *supra* note 21, at 29. For more about HSWAC, go to: http://honoluluswac.com.

292. *Id.* at HSWAC "Benefits" page.

293. *Id.*

294. HAWAIIAN ELECTRIC REPORT, *supra* note 21, at 28.

295. Rachel Gantz, *Rule implementing Hawaii ethanol mandate signed into law*, Sept. 27, 2004, http://www.allbusiness.com/energy-utilities/renewable-energy-biofuels-ethanol/11461833-1.html.

296. Theodore E. Liu, Director, DBEDT, Ethanol Fuel and Hawaii's Energy Policy, Feb. 9, 2006, slide presentation: http://hawaii.gov/dbedt/ert/new-fuel/files/01-dbedt-liu.pdf.

297. Sean Hao, *Hawaii ethanol law falls short of goal*, HONOLULU ADVERTISER, June 25, 2007, http://the.honoluluadvertiser.com/article/2007/Jun/25/bz/FP706250322.html (Hawai'i imported 55 million gallons of ethanol in first twelve months of the law, all from foreign sources, and had yet to break ground on any local projects).

fuels to carry ethanol thousands of miles across the Pacific Ocean to Hawai'i, complaints quickly started to surface, not only about decreased gas mileage (which also directly undermined the very point of adding ethanol) but also about "gunk" causing failure in small engines including boats.[298] Moreover, three years later, the mandate had still not inspired any local production of ethanol.[299] When fuel prices rose in 2008, plans began progressing for a cellulosic sugarcane plant on Kaua'i, otherwise stalled by financial and technical barriers, which promised to supply 30% of state demand.[300] As noted above, the dream of revitalizing the once-dominant sugarcane industry in Hawai'i may no longer be feasible given the conversion of the land in recent years to alternative uses, large owners' inclination toward land banking, and community objections to the massive diversion of water to sugarcane lands from native streams and traditional taro agriculture.[301]

Another ongoing controversy over biofuels in Hawai'i was sparked by HECO's plan to use imported palm oil to generate electricity at its recently approved Campbell Industrial Park Generating Station, a new 110-MW biodiesel-only power plant slated to open in 2009.[302] Environmental groups Life of the Land and Environmental Defense strongly oppose the plan, arguing that importing biofuels is bad public policy for a number of reasons, particularly since the plant would rely on palm oil from Malaysia and Indonesia, where the plantations create environmental harm to native forests and foment social dislocation.[303] At the moment, the opposition and financial problems of HECO's palm oil refining partner Imperium LLC (which planned to build a $91 million processing plant on O'ahu) seems to have stalled the controversial plan.[304] To many, the very idea of *importing* renewables is inherently a losing proposition. Although they replace fossil fuels, they do not further the state goal of energy or economic independence.

The state is trying to bring some order to the biofuels chaos. Act 253 in 2007 required DBEDT to develop and prepare a bioenergy master plan that would help to develop a bioenergy industry in Hawai'i.[305] In May 2008, the state launched its Bioenergy Master Plan, with a host of stakeholders and grand promises of public consultation.[306] The study is now nearing completion

---

298. Gina Mangieri, *Action Line: What's breaking auto engines*, KHON2 News, Apr. 20, 2007, http://www.khon2.com/features/actionline/7129541.html.

299. Lynda Arakawa, *Still no ethanol production in Hawaii*, Honolulu Advertiser, July 5, 2008, http://www.honoluluadvertiser.com/apps/pbcs.dll/article?AID=/20080705/NEWS01/807050313/1001/LO-CALNEWSFRONT. In fact, from 2006 through 2008, Hawai'i "imported about 87.6 million gallons of foreign ethanol," primarily from El Salvador. *Id.*

300. *Id.* ("The company that appears to be the furthest along in its plans for an ethanol facility is Kauai Ethanol, a partnership between sugar producer Gay & Robinson Inc. and Pacific West Energy LLC. Kauai Ethanol's goal is to open a $40 million, 15 million gallon facility at Kaumakani in the fourth quarter of next year," said William Maloney, president of Pacific West. "The project, which would supply more than 30 percent of the state demand, was supposed to break ground last year and begin operating later this year.")

301. Tummons, *Renewable*, *supra* note 244, at 5 & 7 (citing the concerns of DOH Deputy Director Larry Lau). Sugarcane cultivation requires large amounts of freshwater, an increasingly fought-over commodity in Hawai'i. *See, e.g., supra* note 203.

302. Hawaiian Electric is also proposing a 200MW biodiesel plant on Maui, possibly also powered by palm oil, starting in 2009. Hawaiian Electric Report, *supra* note 21, at 28.

303. Berry, *supra* note 8, at 1. *See also* www.lifeoftheland.org and http://www.lifeofthelandhawaii.org/Palm_Oil_for_Electricity_Generation.html.

304. Greg Wiles, *Biodiesel plant in doubt as firm closes isle office*, Honolulu Advertiser, Aug. 11, 2008 ("Imperium[, which] has a contract to be the exclusive biodiesel supplier for the HECO plant through 2011," was reported to be laying off staff, backing off a public stock offering, and closed its Hawai'i office), http://www.honoluluadvertiser.com/apps/pbcs.dll/article?AID=/20080811/BUSINESS/808110330/1071. Due to the company's financial difficulties, the Board of Land and Natural Resources waived its rent and, upon payment of a $100,000 fee, extended by one year the start date of the lease of state land needed for the facility at Barbers Point Harbor. *Board Waives Rent for Biofuel Plant*, Environment Hawaii, at 12, May 2009.

305. Act 253, http://www.capitol.hawaii.gov/session2007/bills/HB1003_cd1_.htm.

306. *See* http://hawaii.gov/dbedt/info/energy/renewable/bioenergy/kickoff/index_html.

under the leadership of the new Hawai'i Natural Energy Institute at the University of Hawai'i, but it is too early to tell if this will be just another splashy plan bedecked with flower lei or whether it will truly make locally and sustainably grown biofuels a major part of Hawai'i's energy future.[307]

Outside observers often query why Hawai'i does not utilize the vast geothermal resources of its famous active volcanoes. The Mauna Loa and Kilauea volcanoes and the recent venting at Hale'ma'uma'u Crater on the Island of Hawai'i draw over 1.5 million visitors a year to Hawai'i Volcanoes National Park.[308] Some of the objections to geothermal drilling in Hawai'i are based on a Native Hawaiian religious belief that drilling violates the spirit and body of the Hawaiian Volcano Goddess Pele.[309] Other objections arise because early geothermal ventures on the Big Island were too aggressive, violated environmental laws, proposed to industrialize the last intact low-lying native rainforest in Hawai'i, and endangered public health.[310] Today, a geothermal plant run by Puna Geothermal Venture (PGV) accounts for 229.89 Gigawatts a year, or roughly 2% of statewide generation.[311] PGV's proposed expansion of 8 MW,[312] only a slight increase, will likely encounter substantial opposition but the facility is much smaller than the controversial 500 MW plant supported by the federal government in the early 1990s.[313]

In short, Hawai'i is making progress toward a green energy future. Particularly for wind, solar, and wave, many good policy building blocks are in place. Yet, the effort seems dilettantish at times and, despite the large potential return on investment, the business and financial sector do not yet seem fully engaged in the huge private efforts needed to complement the policy initiatives. As former Sierra Club director Jeff Mikulina commented, "the financing structure for such an investment at this scale isn't in place.... So where are Hawai'i's heavy investors? Where are Hawai'i's 'local' banks, moneyed institutions like Kamehameha Schools and private investors putting their money? Is it helping local folks in Hawai'i? Are they getting a better yield than 50 percent? What do we need to do to focus serious money on vastly improving Hawai'i's energy efficiency in the short term?"[314] The creative response of international and local businesses to the policy signals in Hawai'i, despite the currently bleak state economy, and the Governor's Clean Energy Initiative that would "de-couple" Hawaiian Electric's current incentives to depend on fossil fuel generation,[315] will be among the keys to unlocking the future of renewables. Policies on paper alone do not generate green energy.

---

307. B.J Reyes, *Bioenergy plan in works*, Honolulu Star-Bulletin, May 22, 2008, http://starbulletin.com/print/2005.php?fr=/2008/05/22/news/story04.html; *see also* story comments ("sounds like lip service").

308. *Partners working to preserve Hawaii Volcanoes National Park and promote sustainable tourism*, July 23, 2008, http://www.nps.gov/havo/parknews/upload/havo_pr_20080721_wha_wrkshp.pdf.

309. *See* Blue Ocean Preservation Soc'y v. Watkins, 767 F. Supp. 1518 (D. Haw. 1991); *see also* Pele Defense Fund v. Paty, 837 P.2d 1247, 1260 (Haw. 1992), *cert. denied*, 113 S. Ct. 1277 (1993). *See also* Jeremiah Johnson et al., Hawaii County Baseline Energy Analysis (May 2006), http://www.hawaii-county.com/rd/hawaii_county_ baseline_energ.pdf (*see especially* Section 4.2 Case Study in Multi-Stakeholder Process: Geothermal).

310. *See, e.g.*, Wao Kele O Puna, Sacred Lands Film Project, http://www.sacredland.org/historical_sites_pages/wao_kele.html; *and* Kristine Kubat, *Here we go again*, Big Island Weekly, June 25, 2008 ("The subterranean steam found in Puna is one of the world's most toxic resources, under more pressure, heated to a higher degree and located in an area more prone to catastrophe than most."), http://www.bigislandweekly.com/articles/2008/06/25/read/comment/comment01.txt.

311. Hawaiian Electric Report, *supra* note 21, at 19 (author calculation based on charts).

312. *Id.* at 28.

313. *See* Blue Ocean Preservation Soc'y v. Watkins, 767 F. Supp. 1518 (D. Haw. 1991).

314. Jeff Mikulina, *A Brighter Idea*, Honolulu Star-Bulletin, Aug. 24, 2008, http://starbulletin.com/2008/08/24/editorial/special.html.

315. Mark Niesse, *Hawaii dreams to be renewable, plugged-in islands*, USA Today, Mar. 28, 2009, http://www.usatoday.com/news/nation/states/hawaii/2009-03-28-3851541379_x.htm (according to Ted Peck, the

IV. Conclusion: Time to Address Adaptation

For the past few years, Hawai'i has begun seriously to address a more independent energy future. Act 234, the bold framework law to address mitigation, is encouraging. Yet, the twin concern of how to address *adaptation* has only begun to surface, and even then only among a few government agencies, academics, and environmental advocates. The public concern about adaptation is non-existent. This chapter concludes by discussing two new developments and a third proposal that, together, can dramatically enhance the State's capacity to address adaptation to climate change in the immediate future.

A. Enacting New Adaptation Planning Legislation

Adaptation legislation to kick-start a new statewide planning process in the islands (SB 266)[316] was first proposed in the 2008 session and, fortunately, passed in the 2009 session. Despite the low funding for the task force (only $100,000 for two years), the bill appropriately puts the advisory effort under the State Office of Planning and provides for an inclusive membership, essential for a coordinated, collaborative approach to the problem. The legislation had a rocky start. The 2008 bill (SB 2016) quickly stumbled and died,[317] with only a non-binding resolution (SCR 126) passing the Senate.[318] However, rarely does the Hawai'i Legislature act on new ideas in one

---

state energy administrator, "Everything depends on decoupling. Everything.... It gets HECO agnostic about where the power is coming from.").

316. SB 266, SD2 HD2 CD1, passed the House and Senate with only two "no" votes and, as of May 8, 2009 was awaiting the Governor's signature. *See* SB 266 Status sheet, at http://www.capitol.hawaii.gov/session2009/lists/measure_indiv.aspx?billtype=SB&billnumber=266.

317. The bill was originally co-introduced as SB 2016 by Senators Nishihara and Espero with no companion house bill. *See* SB 2016 Status Sheet, at http://www.capitol.hawaii.gov/site1/docs/getstatus2. asp?billno=SB2016. After second reading, the bill was expanded at the suggestion of The Nature Conservancy to include impacts on native species and ecosystems. *See* SB 2016 SD1, at Senate Standing Committee Report 2364, http://www.capitol.hawaii.gov/session2008/CommReports/SB2016_SD1_SSCR2364_.htm. The bill died shortly after the Senate committees passed it, as amended, on February 15, 2008, because the fiscal committee, Senate Ways and Means (WAM), declined to schedule it for hearing. *See* SB 2016 Status Sheet, *supra*. About one month later, on March 19, 2008, Senate Majority Leader Gary Hooser helped revive the bill by allowing two Senate committees to gut another environmental bill, HB 2510 (by then no longer needed as a vehicle to fund a University of Hawai'i EIS study), *see* HB 2510, SD2 HD1, http://www.capitol. hawaii.gov/session2008/Bills/HB 2510_SD1_.htm and Senate Standing Committee Report No. 3128, http://www.capitol. hawaii.gov/session2008/CommReports/HB2510_SD1_SSCR3128_.htm. By that late in the session, however, the window for any fiscal momentum was greatly diminished and the bill again died on referral to WAM. *See* HB 2510 SD1 Status Sheet, http://www.capitol.hawaii.gov/site1/docs/getstatus2.asp? billno=HB2510.

The state's environmental impact state law must of course also adapt to climate change. Proposals to modify Chapter 343 have already been made and will likely result from an ongoing University of Hawai'i study for the Legislature on the state's environmental impact law and policies, for which the author serves as a co-investigator. Interestingly, in the 2008 session, only one other bill (HB 2103) grazed the issue. It would have required the state environmental impact statement process to consider the impacts of a project *on* contributing to climate change, but did not focus on how projects might themselves be affected by climate change. *See* HB 2103, 24th Leg, 2008, http://www.capitol.hawaii.gov/session2008/Bills/HB2103_.htm (proposing to add that an EIS would consider the "effects of a proposed action as a contributor to climate change").

318. SCR 126 easily passed the Senate by a 23-1 vote. *See* SCR 126 Status Sheet, http://www.capitol. hawaii.gov/site1/docs/getstatus2.asp?billno=SCR126. See SCR 126, http://www.capitol.hawaii.gov/session 2008/Bills/SCR126_.htm. The Senate Committee on Energy and Environment supported the task force idea, stating: "Your Committee finds that Hawaii, as an island state, is particularly vulnerable to rising ocean levels and other consequences of global warming; and therefore, the State must take action to address the near-term and long-term effects of global warming. However, before action may be taken, efforts must be made to fully predict and evaluate the effects that rising ocean levels and other consequences of climate change will have upon Hawaii." Senate Standing Committee Report 3466, http://www.capitol.hawaii.gov/session2008/Comm Reports/SCR126_SSCR3466_.htm. The House versions of the resolution did not even manage to get a first

session, and the Senate resolution laid the hopeful groundwork for the more concerted effort in the 2009 session to enact the task force bill.

As is typical for the soft-start legislative approach to new issues in Hawai'i, where consensus and stakeholder processes are highly valued, the 2008 (and initial version of the 2009) Senate bill requested the State Department of Health (DOH) to establish a 29-member task force "to assess the impacts of global warming on the state," particularly sea-level rise.[319] The task force would be charged with making recommendations to the Legislature and the Governor on measures that would address or mitigate the near- and long-term effects of climate change, including: (A) Preventing shoreline erosion; (B) Preserving the visitor industry; (C) Improving or relocating transportation infrastructure such as airports and shipping terminals; (D) Implementing restrictions on construction in affected areas; (E) Improving or hardening utilities infrastructure; (F) Preparing for health emergencies; and (G) Maintaining the health and resilience of native species and ecosystems.

In 2008, the bill and resolution flew under the radar in the Senate and testimony was sparse. The Sierra Club, the Hawaii Hotel & Lodging Association, The Nature Conservancy, Hawai'i Interfaith Power and Light (HIPL), and the Windward Ahupua'a Alliance supported the measure.[320] Many testifiers criticized the task force as too big or too narrow in membership.[321] The State Department of Health opposed the bill and the resolution on several grounds. (Those objections undoubtedly prompted the Legislature to move the task force to the Office of Planning.) First, DOH stated that the task force could be costly, outside of the proposed executive budget; second, it would conflict with or duplicate the results of the Act 234 effort; third, it covered too many topics and was "unwieldy"; fourth, it was unclear on funding and method; and fifth, the "task force approach" was questionable.[322] Oddly, DOH concluded: "[a]ll businesses, agencies, and organizations should be working now to assess potential impacts of climate change on their operations and the effect of their greenhouse gas emissions. We all need to integrate such concerns into ongoing operations, rather than relying solely on a panel of experts."[323]

DOH is, of course, correct that everyone should be concerned about adaptation and that those concerns should be integrated into "ongoing operations." There are scattered signs of increasing concern about adaptation among various federal, state, and county agencies. However, there is neither evidence of much awareness among businesses and other organizations nor much coordination among all of these entities. The testimony of HIPL's David Turner on SB 2016 made the case for synthesizing scattered research on adaptation in Hawai'i and creating a single state roadmap: "What is needed is a single document that summarizes the present research in a clear and concise manner, and is presented in a way that is accessible to those entrusted with planning responsibilities as well as the general public. Done properly, such a document can serve as a key component for any future planning for the state of Hawaii which takes seriously the re-

reading. See HCR 179 (Status Sheet, http://www.capitol.hawaii.gov/site1/docs/getstatus2.asp?billno=HCR179) and HR152 (same).

319. SB 2016 SD1, *supra* note 318.

320. *See* Senate Standing Committee Report 2364 on SB 2016 SD1, http://www.capitol.hawaii.gov/session 2008/CommReports/SB2016_SD1_SSCR2364_.htm *and* Testimony of David Turner, Hawaii Interfaith Power and Light, on SB2016 (Feb. 12, 2008), http://www.capitol.hawaii.gov/session2008/Testimony/SB2016_ENE_ 02-12-08_late.pdf [hereinafter Turner testimony].

321. *See, e.g.*, Testimony of Robert Harris, Director, Sierra Club Hawai'i Chapter, Mar. 19, 2009, at http:// www.capitol.hawaii.gov/session2009/Testimony/SB266_SD2_TESTIMONY_EEP_03-19-09_LATE_.pdf.

322. DOH Testimony on SB 2016, http://www.capitol.hawaii.gov/session2008/Testimony/SB2016_ENE-TSG_02-12%20%20-08_.pdf, and DOH Testimony on SCR 126, http://www.capitol.hawaii.gov/session2008/ Testimony/SCR126_SR65_ENE_4-01-08_.pdf.

323. DOH Testimony on SCR 126, *supra* note 322.

ality of global climate change. Without such a summary document, Hawaii faces the prospect of traveling into … uncertain waters without even the semblance of a roadmap."[324]

Pieces of that synthesis document can be found in the 2007 draft revision of the *State Hazard Mitigation Plan*, a document required by the Federal Emergency Management Agency for the state to get federal disaster aid, which has a new section on climate change, including sea level changes.[325] As University of Hawaiʻi researcher Cheryl Anderson commented, "Government agencies are in the early stages of 'working with development plans to think about what these changes might mean.' "[326] The State Department of Transportation (DOT) is "aware of the sea-level rise trend, but is dealing with it by addressing coastal highways that are suffering from high surf erosion now."[327] DOT has several highways "on the drawing board for possible movement inland."[328]

State resource agencies are also increasingly engaged. The head of the State's Office of Conservation and Coastal Lands stated: "We don't want to create a panic, but we need to make everyone aware that it's something we need to plan for in the future."[329] There are "[s]ome signs that Hawaii government officials are beginning to take action," including studies of coastal erosion trends and building setbacks on Maui, Oʻahu, and Kauaʻi; acknowledgement by the Hawaii Ocean Resources Management Plan Policy Group that sea-level rise and climate change are critical areas of need; the possibility that Congress will consider requiring states to conduct climate change planning; and handbooks published by state and federal agencies that include information about sea-level rise, such as coastal hazard mitigation, coastal erosion, and what to look for when buying coastal real estate.[330]

Even if preliminary, these agency efforts are important. Unfortunately, there is no evidence that a laissez-faire approach will generate an appropriately strong direction, which can come only from unified governmental policy. Strong leadership is needed at all levels, but especially at the state government level. Therefore, it is encouraging that the 2009 Legislature did reconsider the adaptation task force bill, moved its oversight out of DOH to the Office of Planning, gave it a bit of funding,[331] revamped its membership structure, and passed the bill to the Governor for her signature.[332] Depending on the independence and tenacity of the task force members, and their ability to pull along the state's political leadership, this new legislation can be another watershed moment for Hawaiʻi.

B. Pulling Together Science, Law, and Policy: Introducing ICAP

Another important recent development in Hawaiʻi to address climate adaptation is the new University of Hawaiʻi at Mānoa's Center for Island Climate Adaptation and Policy (ICAP). This interdis-

---

324. Turner testimony, *supra* note 320.

325. Leone, *supra* note 1 (quoting Cheryl Anderson, director of the Hazards, Climate and Environment Program at the UH's Social Science Institute).

326. *Id.*

327. *Id.*

328. *Id.*

329. *Id.* (quoting Sam Lemmo, administrator of the State Office of Conservation and Coastal Lands).

330. *Id.*

331. In DOH's 2009 testimony, again opposing the bill, the agency estimated that the task force would realistically need about a $1 million budget. *See* Testimony of Chiyome Fukino, Director, DOH, Mar. 19, 2009, http://www.capitol.hawaii.gov/session2009/Testimony/SB266_SD2_TESTIMONY_EEP_03-19-09_LATE_.pdf.

332. A more laser-like (but non-collaborative) approach would be simply to require that the state planning process immediately start focusing on adaptation. Hawaiʻi might learn from its Pacific Island neighbor New Zealand, which in 2004 passed a simple amendment to its comprehensive Resource Management Act requiring regional and local planning to "plan for the effects of climate change." Section 7(i), Resource Management (Energy and Climate Change) Amendment Act of 2004, http://gpacts.knowledge-basket.co.nz/gpacts/public/text/2004/se/002se5.html.

ciplinary center was collaboratively designed in 2008 by a group of campus faculty seeking to connect the university's expertise with the needs of government agencies and communities grappling with adaptation challenges.[333] ICAP's mission is to "facilitate a sustainable, climate-conscious future for Hawai'i, the Pacific, and global island communities through innovative research and real-world solutions to island decision-makers in the public and private sectors."[334] After only a few months of existence, ICAP has already prepared a white paper for state legislators concerned about shoreline erosion, attracted media and congressional attention, and has a large portfolio of projects.[335]

ICAP is building on the growing number of U.S. domestic and international efforts focused on adaptation, including the work of California and the United Kingdom, which are synthesizing the science on adaptation both to drive policy and to serve the broader community. In California, the Governor's Climate Adaptation Strategy (CAS) "will synthesize the most up-to-date information on expected climate change impacts to California for policy-makers and resource managers, provide strategies to promote resiliency to these impacts and develop implementation plans for short and long term actions."[336] The CAS has six different action groups (oceans and coastal resources, water, biodiversity and habitat, public health, working landscapes (forestry and agriculture), and infrastructure).[337] The CAS will also incorporate peer reviewed research from "around the world." It is currently working on drafts in each Working Group's sector and anticipates releasing a report in 2009, after public workshops.[338] Similarly, the U.K. already has an advisory service called the Climate Impacts Programme that provides advice on adaptation, offers a web-based "wizard" to guide adaptation approaches, assists with research, maintains a database of case studies, and produces climate change scenarios for public planning.[339]

Hawai'i's ICAP can lead a similar approach, with the key addition of a critically important "cultural" sector to those already listed in the California CSA. The need for, and power of information, regarding adaptation in the local context cannot be under-estimated. Hawai'i already has many excellent researchers, organizations, and institutions working on climate change science (from hard to soft), but, until ICAP, had not yet developed a body to pull those key threads together in order to shape state policy or provide a reliable one-stop shop for the private sector. The valuable cross-fertilization taking place for the past few years between agencies and academia needs to grow exponentially. A 2001 workshop called the *Pacific Regional Assessment on the Consequences of Climate Variability and Change*, sponsored by NOAA and the East West Center,[340] focused on sectoral impacts and made six general adaptation recommendations including: 1) enhancing water resources; 2) protecting marine and coastal resources; 3) protecting infrastructure and ensuring public safety; 4) protecting public health from more prevalent infectious diseases and increased risk of water-borne illnesses; 5) protecting agricultural resources by increasing water availability,

---

333. The author was among the group of faculty who helped to form the new Center and select the new Director, Associate Professor and Sea Grant Extension Specialist Maxine Burkett, who has a split appointment between the UH Law School and UHM Sea Grant faculty.

334. ICAP is a partnership of the UH Law School's Environmental Law Program, Sea Grant, the College of Social Sciences, the Hawai'inuiakea School of Hawaiian Knowledge, and the School of Ocean and Earth Sciences and Technology.

335. Christine Donnelly, *Maxine Burkett*, Honolulu Star-Bulletin, Apr. 24, 2009, http://www.starbulletin.com/editorials/20090424_Maxine_Burkett.html.

336. *Id.*

337. *Id.*

338. *Id.*

339. DEFRA, Climate Impacts Programme, http://www.defra.gov.uk/environment/climatechange/adapt/adaptation/ukcip.htm#ukciptools.

340. Eileen Shea *et al.*, Preparing for a Changing Climate: The Potential Consequences of Climate Variability and Change (Executive Summary) (2001), http://www.eastwestcenter.org/publications/search-forpublications/ and browse-alphabetic-list-of-titles/?class_call=view&pub_ID=1299&mode=view).

improving informational tools and forecasts to help in seasonal planting, and developing drought resistant food crops; and 6) protecting tourism by incorporating risk managers, hotel associations, and the visitors bureau in planning ways to accommodate tourism, which is vital to local economic viability, and to ensure that there are adequate resources and safety for the residents of Hawai'i. This valuable collaborative effort needs to move forward and not be left on the table. In collaboration with the University of Hawai'i Mānoa Climate Change Commission, ICAP will also soon be embarking on a "mini-IPCC" initiative that aims to coalesce the University-centered science on adaptation.[341]

C. Placing the Third Cornerstone: A Proposal for an Executive Order To Require Agency Planning

Independent executive action is the third cornerstone needed to complement the recent legislative and University initiatives on adaptation. Wrangling reluctant agencies into the planning process can happen quickly through an executive order. Although Governor Lingle has not issued many executive orders during her tenure, she has done so for similar high priority state initiatives.[342] To address adaptation, she should consider a Hawai'i Climate Action Strategy (HCAS) executive order. She does not need to wait for the adaptation task force report in 2011 to act.

The proposed executive order could follow the lead of California Governor Arnold Schwarzenegger who, in 2005, issued an executive order addressing both mitigation and adaptation. With regard to adaptation, he followed a "reporting" model and ordered: "That the Secretary shall also report to the Governor and the State Legislature by January 2006 and biannually thereafter on the impacts to California of global warming, including impacts to water supply, public health, agriculture, the coastline, and forestry, and shall prepare and report on mitigation and adaptation plans to combat these impacts."[343]

The California Resources Agency has taken the lead on developing California's Climate Adaptation Strategy (CAS).[344] Even though the agency acknowledges "[s]ome uncertainty remains regarding exactly how these impacts will occur, ... there is enough information now to increase our resiliency to these impacts."[345] Further, the agency noted that "Billions of dollars are spent annually to build infrastructure, purchase sensitive habitat and fight wildfires. Implementing adaptation strategies will improve these efforts and will be cheaper than acting at the last minute."[346]

This kind of "mandatory risk assessment" approach, beginning with agency reporting, may be the most effective short-term approach. Reaching further around the world, Hawai'i could borrow from the experience of the United Kingdom, which is considering comprehensive climate legislation, including on adaptation.[347] The UK bill would also take a reporting approach: require national risk assessments every five years; create a national adaptation program, updated every five years; allow the government a sweeping mandate to require public authorities (from schools to prisons) and utilities to report on their adaptation efforts; and establish an indepen-

---

341. The author is a member of the Mānoa Climate Change Commission and the chair of the "Impacts Committee," which is currently working with ICAP on developing an IPCC-like process in the Hawai'i context.

342. *See* State of Hawaii, Executive Order 07-01, Establishing the Hawaii Innovation Council, http://hawaii.gov/gov/news/executive-orders/HawaiiInnovationCouncil.71.pdf/view.

343. State of California, Office of the Governor, Executive Order S-3-05, http://gov.ca.gov/index.php?/print-version/executive-order/1861/.

344. *See* State of California State Resources Agency, Climate Adaptation Strategy, http://www.climatechange.ca.gov/adaptation/index.html.

345. *Id.*

346. *Id.*

347. U.K. Department of Environment, Food, and Rural Affairs, Adaptation in the Climate Change Bill, http://www.defra.gov.uk/environment/climatechange/adapt/bill/.

dent committee to oversee the effort.[348] This information-driven approach can create an effective carrot and stick dynamic, possibly avoiding resort to a command-and-control regulatory model.

The U.K.'s "mandatory risk assessment" approach is not a foreign concept and is, in fact, very similar to the U.S. environmental impact statement approach—requiring information that then drives decision-making. Although this approach can be criticized as too soft because it produces "only" information, it is precisely this type of information that is needed in Hawai'i so that solutions to adaptation are wisely considered and not hastily or haphazardly adopted. Once the information is more refined, it can be fed into the adaptation task force process, coordinated with ICAP's work, and be transformed into specifically targeted changes in policy and planning.

By the end of 2009, Hawai'i's Governor should take the bold step of requiring state agencies under her control to begin reporting in 2010 on their understanding of impacts within their sector and possible strategies for adaptation. An iterative process that generates public information and a risk assessment approach throughout all agencies, statewide, from bottom to top, from prisons to agriculture, will trigger both early awareness and provide a strong foundation for the most cost-effective early action.

The state adaptation task force, ICAP, and the Governor's efforts to address adaptation will all need staff, research funding, and technical support, not unlike the levels provided to the Act 234 Task Force and the Hawai'i Energy Policy Forum. Where would the funding come from? Given the very tight state budget,[349] it is hard to imagine major new funding from the general budget. But there are three reasons why a new funding mechanism based on some kind of energy fee should be created to support this effort. First, the sooner we begin, the cheaper adaptation will be. Second, the benefits are statewide, diffuse, and ubiquitous. Third, the problem directly relates to energy consumption. The funding could come from a fee on utility usage, gasoline, or fossil fuel imports. In California, the funding comes through the utility commission (the California Energy Commission under its Public Interest Energy Research Program);[350] in Hawai'i, it could be under the Public Utilities Commission and tied into the new Public Benefits Fund. Such an initiative would be in line with the Governor's recently successful efforts to take DSM funds away from the utilities and create an independent fund to more strongly support alternative energy initiatives and a sustainable energy future.[351] Or, the funding could come from an eventual carbon tax, which is only just on the discussion table by the Act 234 task force. The recently passed $1 barrel tax (HB 1271, discussed above) is another well-suited potential source of funding, if the bill survives and if the amount and purpose can be broadened in the future. Hawai'i needs a combination of all of these approaches, and fast. As a relatively small social laboratory with a cohesive social fabric, Hawai'i has major natural advantages in meeting global adaptation challenges. On the other hand, adaptation will require major public education and shifts in priorities to address obvious vulnerabilities. It will not be easy or cheap, but the longer we wait, the worse it will be. The pol-

---

348. *Id.*

349. Governor Lingle recently asked all state agencies to develop budget-cutting scenarios at 10-15-20% reduction levels, in response to a projected state budget deficit of $903 million by mid-2011. Richard Borreca, *Lingle and Unions Talk Budget*, Honolulu Star-Bulletin, Sept. 24, 2008, http://www.starbulletin.com /news/hawaiinews/20080924_Lingle_and_unions_talk_budget.html?page=all&c=y.

350. *See* PIER web site: http://www.energy.ca.gov/research/index.html. PIER is funded by a variety of sources, including executive orders and 2006 legislation (Bill 1250 (Peralta, Chapter 512, Statutes of 2006)) and awards up to $62 million annually. *Id.* It recently announced grants of about $3 million for adaptation research. http://www.energy.ca.gov/contracts/2008-09-02_CLIMATE_CHANGE_NOPA.PDF.

351. Public Utilities Commission, Press Release, Mar. 6, 2007, http://hawaii.gov/budget/puc/pr/NR-Energy_Efficiency_Public_Benefits_Fund.PDF (the PUC was authorized to take jurisdiction under Act 162).

icy changes that the islands' leaders initiate in the next few years will be the key to avoiding the drowning of Hawai'i.

4. Scholarship: State Action and Beyond

Obviously, legal scholarship has touched all parts of the "climate change" monster—from local to domestic to international law and from many conceivable vantage points. But the separate law of the U.S. states is heavily addressed. So far that is where the action can be found.

Q. How many law review articles with "Global Warming" or "Climate Change" in the title have been published between 1980 and the present?

A. 140 or 222, depending on data base searched.

— Search of Westlaw—Journals & Law Reviews (JLR) (140 results) and Westlaw—Legal Resource Index (LRI, Electronic Comparison to Current Law Index) (222 results), for William H. Rodgers, Jr., by Ann Hemmens, Reference Librarian, Marian Gould Gallagher Law Library, University of Washington School of Law, Oct. 12, 2008.

Among the early articles on the topic was one by Earl Finbar Murphy, *The Necessity to Change Man's Traditional View of Nature*, 48 NEB. L. REV. 299 (1968–1969). Professor Murphy argued that the "common man" must "not come to see nature as a mine and his future salvation as a rocket ride to Mars where all the old worldly mistakes can be repeated." He urged, instead, a "vision of man as the giver to nature, the warden of himself and his environment, the planner who encompasses his present and provides for the future relation of human demands and the natural resources which must meet them." *Id.* at 323–24 (footnote omitted).

An article by James N. Corbridge, Jr. & Raphael J. Moses, entitled *Weather Modification: Law and Administration*, 8 NAT. RES. J. 207 (1968), is an anticipatory primer for our new world of modified weather. Corbridge and Moses summarized the legal response. This was detectable in private law, and in state and federal legislation. As to private law, Corbridge and Moses wrote (id. at 213):

> Whatever the situation, fundamental questions of private law are raised by the unusual source of the harm. Suppose the action is grounded on allegedly illegal diversion of cloud formations, which, if left undisturbed, would have benefited the plaintiff's property. What is the nature of that plaintiff's property right, if any, in the clouds? Is there some "natural right" in the use of the atmosphere or in preventing detrimental uses? What if, by design or miscalculation, modification operations produce undesired precipitation on plaintiff's property and result in flooding, hail damage, or interference with a specific land use? Has there been a trespass? Can liability be grounded on negligence? Nuisance?

Corbridge and Moses point out that twenty-three states have statutes dealing specifically with the subject of weather modification. *See* 217-18 n. 65. This law contains measures on licensing, public notice of operations, collection of data and public disclosure, and liability. Several statutes assert "the state's right to, or the use of, the moisture in the atmosphere over the state." *Id.* at 218 n. 68 (identifying Colorado, Louisiana, Nebraska, New Mexico, North Dakota, South Dakota, and Wyoming).

Corbridge and Moses identify 1953 as marking the appearance of the first federal legislation on the topic. Congress created an Advisory Committee on Weather Control "to study and evaluate public and private experiments in weather modification." Following the recommendations of the Advisory Committee, Congress in 1958 amended the National Science Foundation Act to authorize the Foundation to initiate and support a program of study, research, and evaluation in the field of weather modification, giving particular attention to areas that have experienced floods, drought, hail, lightning, fog, tornadoes, hurricanes, or other weather phenomena, and to report annually to the President and the Congress thereon.

Id. at 220 (citations omitted including 42 U.S.C. § 1862(a)(9) (1964)).

Other articles relatively early in time include Charles F. Cooper, *What Man-Induced Climate Change Might Mean?*, 56 FOR. AFF. 500 (1977–1978) and Robert C. Seamans, Jr., James Liverman, & Frederick I. Ordway, *National Energy Planning and Environmental Responsibility*, 6 ENVTL. AFF. L. REV. 283, 291 (1977–1978) ("the danger exists that widespread use of coal and other fossil fuels may release sufficient carbon dioxide into the atmosphere to result in a potentially hazardous global warming trend" (citation omitted)).

One of the founders of environmental law, A. Dan Tarlock, shares with us some personal recollections of his meetings with the concepts of "global warming" or "climate change":

I think that the first mention, at least that I can remember of global climate change, appears at pp. 621–22 of the 1979 CEQ Report—the last real report before the Reagan revolution. My files tell me that I participated in a workshop on water and climate change as part of an [Office of Technology Assessment] report, PREPARING FOR AN UNCERTAIN CLIMATE, Vol. 2, 1993. I have zero recollection of the workshop. The first time I appear in print is *Western Water Law, Global Climate Change, and Risk Allocation, in* MANAGING WATER RESOURCES IN THE WEST UNDER CONDITIONS OF CLIMATE UNCERTAINTY AND WATER RESOURCES MANAGEMENT 239 (National Research Council, Commission on Geosciences, Environment and Resources, 1991). I recycled and broadened this paper twice: *Western Water Law, Global Warming, and Growth Limitations*, 24 LOYOLA OF LOS ANGELES L. REV. 979 (1991) and *Now, Think Again About Adaptation*, 9 ARIZ, J. INT. AND COMP. L. 169 (1992)—very good early symposium.

E-mail communication to William H. Rodgers, Jr., Oct. 8, 2008.

IV. Regional Initiatives

Regional initiatives on global warming are popping up in the four corners of the U.S. and all over the world. We will focus on the one known as "RGGI."

Alice Kaswan, *The Domestic Response to Global Climate Change: What Role for Federal, State, and Litigation Initiatives?* 42 U. SAN. L. REV. 39, 58 (2007):

The Northeastern States' Regional Greenhouse Gas Initiative (RGGI) is a "cap and trade program targeting the electricity sector. RGGI could provide important lessons to Congress and to other states or regions considering cap and trade programs."

Kirsten H. Engel, *Mitigating Global Climate Change in the United States: A Regional Approach*, 14 N.Y.U. ENVTL. L.J. 54, 58 (2005):

This essay argues that, because a regional interstate cooperative approach will likely lead to greater emissions reductions, it constitutes a more effective and efficient approach to climate change than leaving the matter to individual states.

Note, *State Collective Action*, 119 HARV. L. REV. 1855, 1876 (2006):

This Note's description of the potential for state collective action is only the beginning of a larger inquiry into how dynamic interactions between groups of states affect national welfare. On the positive side, agreements between states could develop flexible, intermediate governmental structures between federal and state actors that are better equipped to handle certain types of challenges. On the negative side, the obvious worry is that these intermediate governmental structures would impose costs on other states or the nation as a whole, and thus the challenge is to delineate exactly when such intermediate regulation is appropriate. But as this Note demonstrates, identifying these boundaries is a complicated task without clear solutions. The potential solution proposed above is to use a more vigorous Compact Clause jurisprudence to force groups of states to contract with other states to ensure that socially suboptimal policies are not adopted. But although this solution represents an improvement over the status quo, it is not a first-best solution, and thus future work might discover a superior approach that allows society to capture more fully the benefits of state collective action while better avoiding the potential costs.

2007 CRS STUDY ON STATE ACTIONS at CRS-12 to CRS-14 (footnotes in original):

> *Regional Greenhouse Gas Initiative.*[60] One of the more significant climate change developments at the state level is the Regional Greenhouse Gas Initiative (RGGI). RGGI is a market-based effort by 10 states—Connecticut, Delaware, Maine, Maryland,[61] Massachusetts,[62] New Hampshire, New Jersey, New York, Rhode Island, and Vermont—to reduce carbon dioxide emissions from power plants. RGGI would set up the nation's first mandatory cap-and-trade program for carbon dioxide.[63] The initial objective of RGGI is to stabilize current carbon dioxide emissions from power plants in RGGI states, starting in January 2009, followed by a 10% reduction by 2019. A primary strategy of RGGI is to create a program with flexibility, so that in the future other emission sources/sectors, GHGs, or states could be included.
>
> Some observers consider RGGI to be a possible test-case for a federal cap-and-trade program, and thus several of RGGI's design elements are generating interest and debate. For example, one specific feature—the emission allocation scheme—is drawing both praise and criticism. In both RGGI's Memorandum of Understanding and its Model Rule, states agreed that at least 25% of emission allowances will be allocated for a "consumer benefit or strategic energy purpose."[64] Several states have indicated that they intend to allocate 100% of their states' allowances for that purpose. This action would re-

---

60. For a more in-depth analysis, see CRS Report RL33962, *Greenhouse Gas Reductions: California Action and the Regional Greenhouse Gas Initiative*, by Jonathan L. Ramseur.

61. Maryland Governor O'Malley signed RGGI's Memorandum of Understanding on April 20, 2007, making Maryland the first state that was not an original RGGI participant to join the regional initiative.

62. Massachusetts and Rhode Island were involved in RGGI's development from the beginning. However, both states' governors declined to sign the Memorandum of Understanding in 2005, citing costs as their primary rationale for not participating. Massachusetts and Rhode Island joined RGGI as participants in January 2007.

63. In a cap-and-trade system, regulators set a cap (or limit) on the overall emissions of a given gas from a specified group of sources, such as power plants. The emissions allowed under the new cap are then allocated in the form of credits (or permits) to individual sources. Sources that emit more than their allowance must buy credits from those who emit less than their allowance, thus creating a financial incentive for sources to reduce their own emissions. For more information on cap-and-trade systems, see EPA's website at http://epa.gov/airmarkets/cap-trade/index.html.

64. *See* RGGI Model Rule, issued August 15, 2006, p. 42; and RGGI Memorandum of Understanding, Section G(1), signed by participating state governors December 20, 2005, both *available at* http://www.rggi.org/modelrule.htm.

quire power plants to purchase the set-aside allowances, most likely through an auction, instead of receiving them at no charge.[65]

Although RGGI is one of the more aggressive state programs addressing climate change, the program will likely face several obstacles. For example, RGGI proponents expect the program to face legal challenges, which could delay program initiation. In addition, a critical design detail—electricity imports from non-RGGI states—is unresolved. This is often described as the "leakage" problem. Leakage can occur when an emissions reduction program does not include all sources contributing to the environmental problem. For example, if a RGGI state lowers its emissions by importing more power from a non-RGGI state, the emissions reductions in the RGGI state may be offset by an emission increase in the exporting state.

Notes

1. *See* Michael H. Wall, *The Regional Greenhouse Gas Initiative and California Assembly Bill 1493: Filling the American Greenhouse Gas Regulation Void*, 41 U. Rich. L. Rev. 567, 574 (2006–07):

> Because the northeast states produce relatively little CO_2, the CO_2 reductions realized through the [Regional Greenhouse Gas Initiative] will not markedly decrease CO_2's atmospheric content. The real value of the RGGI, however, lies not in its contributions to global CO_2 reductions but in the prototype it provides for other regional trading programs.

2. *See* Regional Greenhouse Gas Initiative, Model Rule & Amended Memorandum of Understanding, http://www.rggi.org/modelrule.htm (last visited Dec. 12, 2008).

V. Tribal Initiatives

A. Introduction

*The World We Used to Live In**

* Vine Deloria, Jr., Title of the Danz Lecture, University of Washington, April 17, 2003.

> the women made a formal procession through the trees, surrounding their abandoned cabins, stroking the leaves of the oak and elm trees in silent farewell**

** Upon the occasion of the Choctaw removal from their ancestral home in Mississippi, Native American Testimony: A Chronicle of Indian-White Relations From Prophecy to the Present, 1492–1992, at 145, 151 (Peter Nabokov ed., Penguin 1992) (*Exiles in Their Own Land*).

These two quotations are used to introduce a text (by William H. Rodgers, Jr.) on Environmental Law in Indian Country § 1.1 at 4.5 (Thomson / West 2005) ("Theory and Values"). It is there asserted that differences in sovereignty, law (including the trust relationship), properties, and ethical stance (particularly as regards the "land ethic") give the tribes an insistent—and in-

---

65. For more discussion regarding these issues, see CRS Report RL33799, *Climate Change: Design Approaches for a Greenhouse Gas Reduction Program*, by Larry Parker.

fluential—voice in matters of the environment. If true, would this not also be so on the basic life-and-death questions of climate change? Consider:

· *The proclivity to experiment and break free of historic patterns*

Jay Inslee & Bracken Hendricks, Apollo's Fire: Igniting America's Clean Energy Economy 325–26 (Island Press 2008) (Pat Spears and Bob Gough, Rosebud, South Dakota) (emphasis in original) [hereinafter 2008 Inslee & Bracken]:

> The wind energy potential on reservations across the country is over 535 billion kilowatt-hours annually, with the bulk of that found on the two dozen large reservations on the northern Great Plains. Since 1995, the Rosebud Sioux and the other Intertribal Council on Utility Policy (COUP) tribes have sought to transform these gifts into sustainable reservation economies through a series of distributed utility-scale tribal-owned wind projects arrayed along the federal transmission grid built to carry hydroelectric power from mainstream Missouri River dams.

> Indian reservation households are ten times more likely *not* to be electrified than elsewhere in the United States, and those that are pay a higher portion of their household incomes to power extremely energy-inefficient structures. The COUP intertribal energy vision begins with making tribal housing more efficient and affordable to create local jobs, save energy and incomes, and enhance the quality of life.

See also Fred Krupp & Miriam Horn, Earth: The Sequel—The Race to Reinvent Energy and Stop Global Warming ch. 6 at 115 (W.W. Norton & Co. 2008) (Environmental Defense Fund) (on the travails of the Makah Indian Tribe to win a FERC license for a wave-energy project at Makah Bay; "It's all about the motion in the ocean").

· *Familiarity with the effects of global warming and an inclination to respond*

2008 Inslee & Bracken at 5 (speaking of Essay Note, president of the Marshall Islands):

> The people of the island nation of Tuvalu have already agreed to move to New Zealand when their home becomes uninhabitable. President Note sees the United States as a more likely destination for his island's climate refugees due to political ties. We put Katrina refugees in the Astrodome. Where will we put the Marshall Islanders?

2008 Inslee & Bracken at 11:

> The first American homes to be destroyed by global warming have already been lost to the sea in Shishmaref, Alaska.

See Chapter 1, section III(E)(3) (on the lawsuit that seeks removal costs for the Village of Kivalina).

· *Successful litigation to protect endangered natural resources*

Court Finds in Favor of Miccosukee Tribe in Everglades
Clean Water Act Case
Says EPA Avoided Its Duty to Protect the Everglades

Today the Miccosukee Tribe of Indians of Florida, whose members have lived in the Everglades since time immemorial, announced that they have won a major legal victory toward protecting their ancestral homeland. In 2004, the Tribe filed a lawsuit against the Environmental Protection Agency ("EPA") in federal court claiming that the federal agency was arbitrary and capricious for not finding that the State of Florida's 2003 Everglades Forever Act, and 2004 Phosphorus Rule, violated the federal Clean Water Act ("CWA"). The Tribe contended that the

Amended EFA, and the Rule, contained loopholes that allowed dischargers to continue to pollute the fragile Everglades until 2016 and beyond.

In a 101-page order issued today by Judge Gold in Case No.04-21448-CIVGOLD, the Court found that by adopting the Long Term Plan the Florida Legislature "violated its fundamental commitment and promise to protect the Everglades by extending the December 31, 2006 compliance deadline for meeting the phosphorus criterion for at least ten more years." Order at 2. The Court further found that the EPA turned a "blind eye" by concluding it did not extend the deadline. *Id.* The Order states that: "Federal law does not authorize anything like a twenty-two year compliance schedule, which is what the 1994 EFA, the Amended EFA and the Phosphorus Rule now allow with regard to achieving the narrative and numeric phosphorus criterion (the original EFA took effect in 1994 but compliance is not contemplated until 2016)." Order at 92. The Court remanded the Amended EFA back to EPA to review it as a change in water quality standards. The Order states that: "The EPA also violated 40 C.F.R. § 131.10(b) by failing to consider the effects on the downstream water user, the Miccosukee Tribe, since a significant portion of the impacted areas lie directly above the Tribe's lands." Order at 89, FN 70. The Court remanded the Phosphorus Rule to EPA to require the State of Florida to meet the requirements of the CWA.

The Order concluded that "any further delay through endless, undirected rounds of remands to EPA to do its duty, which it steadfastly has refused to do, is alone insufficient, and that it is imperative that this Court exercise its equitable powers to avoid environmental injury to the Everglades through the implementation of the Amended EFA and the Phosphorus Rule as a result of the use of blanket exemptions." Order at 93. The Court enjoined the Florida Department of Environmental Protection ("DEP") "from issuing permits pursuant to those sections of the Phosphorus Rule that I have set aside, and enjoin DEP from considering blanket exemptions or variances under the current Phosphorus Rule pending compliance with the CWA and its regulations." Order at 97.

According to Dexter Lehtinen, the Tribe's attorney on the case, "this ruling puts a halt to the conspiracy of evasion of cleaning up the Everglades by the State, the SFWMD, and the EPA. The Tribe, whose members live in the Everglades, has been a victim of this evasion and is thankful that a federal Judge has stood up for both the Everglades and the Tribe."

Federal Court Finds in Favor of Miccosukee Tribe

Preliminarily Enjoins Corps on Its Tamiami Trail Bridge

The members of the Miccosukee Tribe of Indians have lived in the Florida Everglades since time immemorial. *In a November 13, 2008, Order in Case No. 08-21747-CIV-UNGARO, Federal District Court Judge Ursula Ungaro preliminarily enjoined the Army Corps of Engineers from taking further steps to implement its Tamiami Trail bridge project due to the irreparable injury faced by the Tribe and its members.*

The Tribe filed its lawsuit against the Corps in June 2008. In its lawsuit, the Tribe contended that the Corps violated the National Environmental Policy Act (NEPA), and other federal law, in devising its Tamiami Trail plan for the Modified Water Deliveries Project (MWDP). The Tribe contended that the Corps violated NEPA by not analyzing the environmental impacts of its plan, including potential flooding to the Tribal Everglades and private property in Miami-Dade County.

The Court's Order recognizes that the Corps has been repeatedly criticized for its delay in implementing the MWDP, but found: "*[i]t is of paramount importance that all federal laws, especially those, such as NEPA, that focus on the environment, are followed in the implementation of this pro-*

ject." [28] The Order further finds: "[t]he *Court can fairly assume that Congress desires that other federal statutes, such as NEPA, are properly followed in the implementation of the long-awaited MWDP."*[30]

According to Dexter Lehtinen, the Tribe's attorney who argued the preliminary injunction motion before the Court: "*The bridge is a strawman designed to avoid addressing real restoration issues.* In its haste to pour concrete to look like it was finally doing something, the Corps turned a blind eye to environmental laws necessary to protect the Tribe and the Everglades. It is time for the Corps to address the serious problems facing the Everglades and its restoration. Failure to do so could *risk wasting mega-bucks of taxpayer money."*

The Order states: "From the testimony at the hearing, *it appears the Corps may not have done an intellectually honest analysis of the relative merits of the different alternatives* considered in the LRREA." [23] The Order also recognizes that other components of the MWDP need to be completed before the Tamiami Trail project can operate. The Order states: "Without those additional MWDP components, the TT component is no more than the construction of an '*environmental bridge to nowhere'* that accomplishes (and harms) nothing but which would be a *complete waste of taxpayer dollars."* [20] The Court finds that *any delay "would really be attributable to the Corps itself,* for it could have avoided this lawsuit (and others like it) by scrupulously following all relevant federal laws." [30].

Says Dexter Lehtinen: "The Corps does not now in any year move as much water as the structures can handle because of potential flooding in Miami-Dade County. Until the flooding impacts of the project are analyzed, and addressed, the Everglades can not be restored."

The Order concludes: "Defendants are PRELIMINARILY ENJOINED from taking any further steps toward implementing the Recommended Plan (Alternative 3.2.2.a), unless and until the Corps … properly analyzes all relevant factors to determine whether to issue an SEIS or FONSI in connection with its chosen plan for the Tamiami the Trail component of the Modified Water Deliveries Project." [31].

- *Status as Natural Resource "Trustees" Under the Clean Water Act, Oil Pollution Act, and CERCLA*

See the Petition of the Alaska Intertribal Council on the Exxon Valdez Reopener, May 2006, ch. 9 below; JUDITH V. ROYSTER & MICHAEL C. BLUMM, NATIVE AMERICAN NATURAL RESOURCES LAW ch. V (Carolina Academic Press 2002).

- *Flexibility and Disposition to Settle Important Matters of Natural Resource Management*

William McCall, *BPA, tribes reach $900 million deal to help Columbia River salmon*, Associated Press *in* THE SEATTLE, TIMES, April 7, 2008, *available at* http://seattletimes.nwsource.com/html/localnews/2004332803_webtribes07m.html (visited Dec. 12, 2008):

PORTLAND—Federal officials have reached a settlement with four of five Northwest tribes that would leave hydroelectric dams in the Columbia Basin intact and commit federal agencies to spend $900 million on improving conditions for endangered salmon.

Regional tribes and federal agencies that manage 24 dams and irrigation projects along the Columbia and Snake rivers have been legal adversaries for years over balancing fishing rights, salmon runs and power demands.

Under the settlement announced today by the Bonneville Power Administration, the tribes would end lawsuits they have filed against the federal agencies over management of the power-producing system and agree not to file further lawsuits for 10 years.

During that time, the federal agencies would expand their efforts to protect endangered and threatened fish in the Columbia Basin, spending the $900 million for hatchery improvements, stream restoration work, screens to protect fish and additional spillway weirs on some of the dams.

However, the settlement may still face some hurdles.

Another regional tribe, the Nez Percé, has not signed on.

And environmental groups and fishing groups were critical of the agreement because it would take the possibility of dam-breaching off the table.

"This agreement doesn't change the law, it doesn't change the science," said Todd True, attorney for Earthjustice, representing a number of environmental groups.

"It addresses issues that may be important to the tribes, but it doesn't address the critical issue of river operations," True said.

Environmentalists have argued that salmon populations cannot recover without removing some dams.

It is unclear whether a federal judge who has been holding hearings on the lawsuits will give his blessing to the agreement.

U.S. District Judge James Redden has rejected several plans from the Bonneville Power Administration for balancing the conflicting demands on the Columbia Basin. In 2005 he ordered the agency to negotiate with regional tribes, Oregon and Washington state on ways to better protect fish.

Negotiations with the states are continuing.

Before the agreement can be implemented, federal agencies will first have to persuade Redden that they have a workable scientific plan for protecting fish. That plan, separate from the agreement announced today, is called a biological opinion.

Redden has given federal officials until May 5 to present him with a new biological opinion.

The BPA and the four tribes that announced the settlement hope it will give impetus to resolving disputes that have been raging for years over how to protect endangered and threatened fish in the Columbia and Snake rivers.

The tribes have taken the agency to task for what they felt were inadequate responses to their treaty rights, cultural and religious beliefs that have strong ties to fishing, said John Ogen of the Confederated Tribes of the Warm Springs Reservation.

"There have been improvements and gains secured" in this agreement, Ogen said. "It's a real action plan for fish."

The groups say the agreement makes specific commitments to action that haven't been seen in other plans, including more than 200 specific projects across the basin, ranging from fixing degraded streams and riparian areas to putting in screens and irrigation systems that allow agriculture to move forward but protect fish.

"We have spent decades arguing with each other," said Steve Wright, BPA administrator. "Today these parties are saying let's lay down the swords, let's spend more time working collaboratively to implement measures that help fish and less time litigating."

The tribes that signed on to the agreement are the Confederated Tribes of the Umatilla Indian Reservation, the Confederated Tribes of the Warm Springs Reservation, the Confederated Tribes and Bands of the Yamaka Nation and the Confederated Tribes of the Colville Indian Reservation.

Note

1. Don't believe for a moment that the Nez Perce are indifferent to the future of the North-west Salmon. *See Nez Perce Tribe v. NOAA Fisheries*, 2008 WL 938430 (D. Ida. April 7, 2008) (B. Lynn Winmill). This was a successful challenge to a NOAA Bi-Op on BOR's operation of the Lewiston Orchard Project (LOP) that is a series of reservoirs, dams, and canals fed by water from creeks that are designated as critical habitat for the Snake River Basin steelhead. *Id.* at *3: "the continued operation of a project that degraded designated critical habitat and threatened recovery of the species cannot be justified merely on the basis that the species will persist or survive during the project's operation"; "primary effects" on the Sweetwater, Webb, and Lapwai creeks. *Id.* at *9: "NOAA's finding that connectivity is 'likely' is not based on any scientific data or observational studies. It is more of a guess than a reasoned estimate." There must be a process "to quickly detect errors through monitoring and change flows to ensure connectivity." BOR will do the one but not the other: "Thus, the 'guess' that these flows will be enough for connectivity will be enshrined, right or wrong, for a decade. Habitat could continue to be degraded and the action area continue to be a population sink, all in violation of the ESA. Having spent much of the Bi-Op describing the importance of connectivity, NOAA ignores it as a goal without explanation in its final approval." Also, there is no analysis of the flows necessary for recovery.

B. Tribes and Climate

See the remarkable article by Professor Rebecca Tsosie, *Indigenous People and Environmental Justice: The Impact of Climate Change*, 78 U. Colo. L. Rev. 1625 (2007), which appears with this summary:

> The international dialogue on climate change is currently focused on a strategy of adaptation that includes the projected removal of entire communities, if necessary. Not surprisingly, many of the geographical regions that are most vulnerable to the effects of climate change are also the traditional lands of indigenous communities. This article takes the position that the adaptation strategy will prove genocidal for many groups of indigenous people, and instead argues for recognition of an indigenous right to environmental self-determination, which would allow indigenous peoples to maintain their cultural and political status upon their traditional lands. In the context of climate change policy, such a right would impose affirmative requirements on nation-states to engage in a mitigation strategy in order to avoid catastrophic harm to indigenous peoples. This article argues for a new conception of rights to address the unique harms of climate change. An indigenous right to environmental self-determination would be based on human rights norms in recognition that "sovereignty claims" by indigenous groups are not a sufficient basis to protect traditional ways of life and the rich and unique cultural norms of such groups. Similarly, tort-based theories of compensation for the harms of climate change have only limited capacity to address the concerns of indigenous peoples.

See Jane Braxton Little, *Dust Settles in the Owens Valley*, 32 High Country News No. 8 (April 24, 2000) ("Los Angeles vows to return some water to a parched lakebed"):

KEELER, Calif.—Owens Lake lies barren and dry between the Sierra Nevada and the Inyo Mountains. For nearly a century, the winds sweeping down from 12,000-foot peaks have stirred up the parched lakebed, sending clouds of caustic dust across the eastern California valley from

Bishop to Ridgecrest. A single windstorm can kick up an 11-ton swirl of particles laden with arsenic, cadmium and other toxins. The people who breathe that air regularly have suffered from asthma, bronchitis and other, often deadly, respiratory problems.

"When it's blowing real bad, you have to go inside. That dust collects on your hair, your clothes, everything," says Sam Wasson, a retiree who has lived in Owens Valley most of his life. He's now the unofficial mayor of Keeler, a town of 100 residents on the eastern edge of the dry lake. "It's enough to make your eyes and nose sting until you get out of it."

This year, however, a promise of change is in the particle-filled air. Under an agreement between Los Angeles and Owens Valley officials, the lake will get some of its water back, enough to dampen its salty crust and decrease the dust (HCN, 2/17/97: Who wins when a river returns?). The agreement is too little, too late for many of the 40,000 people who have been breathing the arsenic-tainted dust, but it is a start, says Wasson. He's unabashedly optimistic about the future.

"This town will grow once the dust settles. It's going to be the garden spot of Owens Valley," he says.

. . . .

The 1998 agreement, incorporated into Great Basin's implementation plan adopted last summer by the Environmental Protection Agency, establishes a schedule for meeting air quality standards that avoids decades of litigation, says Richard F. Harasick, a Department of Water and Power engineer in charge of the Owens Valley project.

"We're over the kicking and screaming. We want to be good stewards of the environment that's been given to us. It's a change in our way of thinking," he says.

The $100 million plan calls for flooding sections of the lake. By the end of next year, saturated surfaces and shallow pools of water will cover 13 square miles of the lake. By 2003, 16 square miles of the dry lake will be treated for dust emissions, mostly by flooding. After that, the department will treat two square miles of lakebed a year for three years until it meets federal air quality standards, Harasick says.

. . . .

Prodding the city in its self-proclaimed conversion are a litany of legal actions threatened or filed by the Lone Pine Shoshone-Paiute Tribe. Los Angeles missed deadline after federal deadline while members of the tribe continued to breathe in the dust and get sick, says Dorothy Alther, a Bishop-based attorney with California Indian Legal Services.

"It was clear that L.A. was going to do nothing unless someone complained," Alther says. "We became the gorilla in the closet, continually threatening to sue everyone."

The tribe will be monitoring the flooding project for progress and compliance with federal law. There are many more battles to be fought, says Alther.

For now, however, the federal order and the agreement it produced between Los Angeles and Owens Valley is "the best thing possible," she says. "The day the first drop comes out of the aqueduct to fix the problem, I'll be out there with champagne glasses."

———————

See Keith Rogers, *Paiutes challenge assurances about coal-fired power plant*, LAS VEGAS REVIEW JOURNAL, June 19, 2006:

Ask members of the Moapa Band of Paiutes what they think about the 40-year-old, coal-fired power plant at the edge of their reservation and their answer is: It doesn't pass the smell test.

Ask Nevada Power officials about the same plant, the 590-megawatt Reid Gardner Station that's been churning out electricity for lights and air conditioners 50 miles away in Las Vegas, and they admit there have been odor problems in the past.

But the plant, they say, has complied with the state standard for rotten-egg-smelling hydrogen sulfide gas the past two years, and they say the company is trying to be a good neighbor to the Paiutes.

....

Lalainia Benn, air quality technician for the Moapa Band, is not so convinced.

"We can truly say we don't believe anything they tell us," she said Thursday on a clear, odor-free day at the reservation, which straddles Interstate 15 northeast of the Las Vegas Valley.

"Anything they say, we have to see it to believe it because we've never seen anything yet," she said.

Her comments came a few days after she met with Nevada Division of Environmental Protection officials to repeat the tribe's concern that, though the plant recently has met the hydrogen sulfide standard, the odor emanating from the plant's ponds is still prevalent.

On some days and sometimes in the early mornings, Benn said, she has photographed "dark, yellow-brown clouds that just sit over the area, and we breathe that."

....

Even when she was a young girl living on the reservation "it's always smelled like sulfur here."

"I call this environmental injustice. Something should have been done many years ago," Benn said.

....

She said the reservation has existed since 1875, or 90 years before the Reid Gardner Station went on line. Centuries before 1875, Paiutes had lived in what is now Moapa and Hidden valleys.

The tribe is not opposed to power plants and was nearing closure of a deal for a 720-megawatt cleaner-burning, natural-gas-fired power plant two years ago.

But the deal evaporated when the company the Paiutes were dealing with to build the plant at the reservation, Calpine Corp., of San Jose, Calif., went bankrupt.

In the past, Benn said, Nevada Power has said Reid Gardner's 183 full-time workers don't get sick.

"Well, our comment to them is they don't live here 24-7, and they haven't been living here since the plant was built," she said.

....

———————

Rob Capriccioso, *Tribes urged to prepare for possible federal carbon incentives*, INDIAN COUNTRY TODAY, April 10, 2008:

Under a federally recognized cap and trade incentive plan, a coal electricity plant could offset the carbon dioxide it produces by paying for carbon credits from tribal forestry, soil or other projects that pull carbon out of the atmosphere. Tribes could then receive payments as a result of environmental stewardship.

"For tribal governments and individual Indians who have large land holdings, this could become a very real economic market," said Ted Dodge, executive director of the National Carbon Offset Coalition. The group, which focuses on the sale of carbon credits via a non-federal trade program, has worked with a handful of tribes on monetizing their carbon collection portfolios.

Many tribes already have key ingredients for making carbon capture work, namely large amounts of land, trained staff and positive commitments to the environment. Trees and crops that suck carbon out of the air are already being grown on tribal lands or could be in the future. Scientists, too, have been working on ways to safely store carbon underground and in land formations, which could one day be another way for land-rich tribes to garner carbon capture incentives.

A financial institution called the Chicago Climate Exchange is already helping some tribes achieve modest financial gains by trading carbon credits, despite the lack of a federal cap and trade system thus far. The entirely voluntary-based member institution is currently believed to be North America's only market that allows for legally binding carbon credit trading.

The Nez Perce Tribe has been a leader in trading credits on the CCX, based on tree-planting the tribe has done on its lands since 2003. The Assiniboine Sioux, Fort Peck Indian Reservation and Northern Cheyenne tribes are all believed to be currently working plans to trade carbon credits as well.

Brian Kummett, a forester for the Nez Perce tribal forestry division, has worked for the past 14 years on planting 3,500 acres of Ponderosa pines, Douglas firs and larch saplings on trust lands held by the Nez Perce. For his region of the country, these trees are some of the best at removing carbon dioxide from the air by storing it in their leaves and bark. The forests he's helped plant also serve as wildlife refuges and have become home to many traditional Native medicinal plants.

Carbon sequestration grants from the Department of Energy have helped provide seed money to grow the forestry.

Last year, the Nez Perce tribal council decided to put its trees on the market via the CCX. To make that happen, the BIA had to sign off, in effect auditing the number of trees the Nez Perce tribe has planted, and this information then had to be shared with the exchange.

Energy experts say the tribe has effectively created a model through its work with the exchange that other tribes with trust lands could follow. Under the current rules of the exchange, tribes who join the program through 2010 could be trading carbon credits for trees planted all the way back to 2003. The exchange has also recently approved selling carbon sequestration credits on rangeland and no-till agricultural fields, which both also capture carbon dioxide from the environment.

Since December, the Nez Perce Tribe has been selling its carbon sequestering abilities and has thus far traded credits amounting to almost 8,000 tons of carbon. With carbon credits currently trading at just under $5 per ton, the tribe is seeing a small return on its investment.

With talk of a federal cap and trade system in the air, Kummett is keeping a close eye on the situation. If policymakers established a cap and trade plan, the market for capturing carbon could reach $12–$15 per ton, according to some economic experts. Europe, which already has in place a market for trading carbon dioxide credits, has seen carbon trading reach more than $30 per ton.

"'The beauty of the system with the Chicago Climate Exchange right now is that because there's no federal regulation, you can count projects that you've been doing all the way back to 2003," Kummett said. "If we do have federal cap and trade down the road, it remains to be seen whether tribes could trade on their old work."

Tribal advocates have already been talking to policymakers in Washington about their carbon concerns. One of the chief areas they'd like to see addressed surrounds terrestrial sequestration, which includes initiatives like the Nez Perce tree-planting. They'd like to see terrestrial sequestration given federal incentives like those being discussed in Congress for geological sequestration, a process of carbon capture focusing on the development of new storage technologies aimed at stopping carbon dioxide from entering the atmosphere in the first place.

That might be a tough sell, according to Senate energy officials, who say there has yet to be a real clamor on Capitol Hill to create dramatic incentives for terrestrial sequestration.

"Tribes need to be out there, explaining why terrestrial sequestration is crucial in removing carbon from the environment," Dodge said. "It's a bridge to get carbon reduction now, while new geological sequestration technologies are still being developed. And there should be incentives for doing it."

He said tribes should also be looking for ways to get in on the technology of geological sequestration. As scientists look for ways to store large amounts of carbon underground and in water and above-ground rock, a tribe with those features could find itself in a position to benefit greatly from a federal cap and trade incentive program.

"The devil is strictly in the details, and that's why tribes need to be looking at this," he said. "It's all about how the system is designed and whether these types of offsets are even allowed to exist."

Notes

1. Leslie R. Dubois, *Curiosity and Carbon: Examining the Future of Carbon Sequestration and the Accompanying Jurisdictional Issues as Outlined in the Indian Energy Title of the 2005 Energy Policy Act*, 27 ENERGY L.J. 603 (2006).

2. Sophie Smyth, *Can Business Learn to Love the Environment? The Case for a U.S. Corporate Carbon Fund*, 58 RUTGERS L. REV. 451 (2005–2006).

3. Christine Zuni Cruz, *Shadow War Scholarship, Indigenous Legal Tradition, and Modern Law in Indian Country*, 47 WASH. L.J. 631, 652 (2008) ("I tell my students the Tribal Law Journal is more than a journal, it is a movement—a modest, humble movement—to encourage Indigenous Peoples to own their own law and to preserve the native intellect and philosophy").

4. David F. Coursen, *EPA's New Tribal Strategy*, 38 ENVT'L L. REP. NEWS & ANALYSIS 10643 (2008).

Discussion Draft, Indian Nations' Alliance on Climate Change: Environmental Restoration, Territorial Sovereignty and Economic Development, Office of the President, Quinault Indian Nation, Jan. 14, 2007 Draft:

Executive Summary

Goals of this Initiative:
1. Establish a platform of principles to guide tribal participation in matters pertaining to climate change.
2. Establish a formal communication network for sharing information and expertise on developments, issues, and opportunities.

Great Uncertainty and Looming Challenges from Climate Change

The science relating to climate change is in a constant state of flux and new information is continually coming to light. Climate change and global warming will have uncertain effects on tribal communities and the resources that have sustained their cultures and economies for generations. Scientifically, there is great uncertainty regarding how climate change and global warming [affects] the forests, water, soils, air, fish and wildlife that are vital to specific locales.

The news media is rife with conjecture on potential implications and sweeping generalizations, raising concern or even fear of the unknown. Nation states and corporate interests are primed to prey upon these uncertainties to the detriment of the uninformed and underprepared. For example, carbon sink projects (under the Kyoto and perhaps the Copenhagen Protocols) could well be located on lands within tribal territories without recognizing or respecting the rights and uses of those resources by tribal communities.

While one might think global warming is solely a biological or environmental question, it is also a political, diplomatic issue of utmost importance to tribal governments. Politically, regional, state, national and international forces are mounting to implement broad policies and agreements that are likely to affect tribal interests. The central political questions that must be resolved in order to protect and advance tribal rights are:

"By what process and means shall indigenous peoples have control over and benefit from the wealth in their own territories?"

"How can states' governments or corporate interests be compelled to recognize tribal rights of self-determination and prerogatives for managing and using tribal resources?"

"How can tribes gain access to the information, knowledge, skills and resources necessary to protect their interests?"

The Need for a Political Foundation for Addressing Climate Change

Tribal governments will need to assert their rights for a "place at the table" to protect and advance their interests as political developments in climate change arise. There is a need for tribal leadership to strengthen political and diplomatic capacities to directly engage and participate in policy-level negotiations and legislative or administrative initiatives pertaining to climate change. The recent adoption of the United Nations Resolution on the Rights of Indigenous Peoples serves as a prime example of how nation states can be persuaded to respect the interests of tribal communities.

It is proposed that interested tribes form an Alliance on Climate Change. The first order of business would be for participating Indian Nations to establish a firm foundation of fundamental principles, a form of political platform, for protecting and advancing tribal interests in matters pertaining to global warming and climate change. The platform should at least include planks pertaining to protection of tribal territorial sovereignty, recognition of the rights of tribes to substantively participate in the development of domestic and international policies that concern efforts to combat or mitigate global warming, principals of social equity, working in concert with other entities (*e.g.*, the Expert Mechanism on the Rights of Indigenous Peoples which was recently established by resolution of the U.N. Human Rights Council, the International Indian Treaty Council, NCIA, etc.), and commitments to share knowledge and information and to work together to effectuate the platform.

On 13 September 2007 the United Nations General Assembly adopted the Declaration on the Rights of Indigenous Peoples. The Declaration contains important new principles that can now be used by Indian nations to promote the development of new international arrangements beneficial to their political, cultural and economic interests. The recently adopted United Nations Declaration on the Rights of Indigenous Peoples will provide some help in further elevating Indian Nations' international profile.

The Alliance would establish stable and strong inter-tribal political, financial, and technical cooperation within formalized framework that would enable participating tribes to develop technical and legal capacity, undertake technical research and establish a public information capacity.

The Alliance would monitor legislative and administrative climate change policy activities of the Canadian and the U.S. governments as well as inter-state Climate Change negotiations with the goal of establishing a full and formal role for Indian governments at the final Copenhagen round by 2012.

Capacity Building:

The participating tribes would commit to increasing the capacity of Tribal Natural Resources and Legal personnel to establish a firm base of knowledge and expertise in international law, diplomacy, and the science of global warming and climate change. Much of this capacity would be shared through a formal system/network to facilitate communication among indigenous peoples in North America and world-wide on matters pertaining to global warming.

Such a mechanism would enhance the capacity of tribal communities to keep informed and muster political support to protect or advance their interests when the need arises.

A number of initiatives could be undertaken at modest cost, such as the simple step of establishing and maintaining a WWW site where interpersonal contacts and resources can be found, initiatives or policies can be proposed and debated, stories on how tribes are dealing with global warming can be shared (*e.g.,* how global warming is affecting their communities, what they think the changes they are observing mean for their ways of life, and traditional ecological knowledge regarding what needs to be done, partnerships or agreements being reached, etc.), and links to sites where information on scientific, market, or political developments of interest can be readily accessed.

Such a network would facilitate technology sharing to increase awareness of practical and effective measures that tribal communities could do to address issues relating to global warming and climate change. For example, some tribes may employ "Smart Technology" that involves infrastructure to power distribution systems which allows electricity use to be adjusted to save money and reduce the need for new power plants and transmission lines; tribes could integrate small power plants into community developments or structures to heat and generate electricity from waste wood or thinning to avoid costs of purchasing oil, gas, or electricity; market conservation easements [could] provide income while accomplishing resource management objectives.

A successful communication network would also help lay the groundwork for cooperative participation in carbon markets (if and when viable opportunities emerge). Tribal nations may be uniquely positioned to play a major role in carbon sequestration. Indigenous nations have the knowledge and territorial rights of use and access to resources that could contribute significantly to removing carbon dioxide from the atmosphere. Indian nations have a major interest in reversing global warming to protect their resources and communities, and may be able to participate in emerging carbon markets in a manner that secures their territorial sovereignty, advances resource management objectives, and earning financial returns. But carbon markets are currently fraught with uncertainty, both [with] respect to scientific merit, value, and conditions of sale. Interested tribes could benefit from sharing information on how to structure sales of carbon credits or by creating marketing consortiums to increase market presence and value.

Conclusion

Indian nations have the opportunity to assume a prominent place at regional, national, and international fora to address the consequences of global warming and climate change. To become major players, Indian nations must organize their efforts and establish the means to act.

Tribal approaches to their environments are based on balancing human want and need with the capacity of the earth to regenerate a new life. Cultural practices result in "green cultural territories"—areas of the world rich in biological diversity, sustained by a combination of traditional knowledge and modern science.

The Quinault Nation invites other tribes to forge a Climate Change Alliance that can enable tribes to play an assertive, active role in the emerging debates over global warming and climate change, and to take effective action, both within their own communities and society as a whole.

Resolution #08—08 *Supporting an Inter-Tribal Alliance on Climate Change, available at* http://earth1.epa.gov/oar/tribal/pdfs/Resolution%208-08.pdf:

Affiliated Tribes of Northwest Indians

2008 Winter Conference
Yakima, Washington
Resolution #08-08
Supporting an inter-tribal Alliance on Climate Change

PREAMBLE

We, the members of the Affiliated Tribes of Northwest Indians of the United States, invoking the divine blessing of the Creator upon our efforts and purposes, in order to preserve for ourselves and our descendants rights secured under Indian Treaties and benefits to which we are entitled under the laws and constitution of the United States and several states, to enlighten the public toward a better understanding of the Indian people, to preserve Indian cultural values, and otherwise promote the welfare of the Indian people, do hereby establish and submit the following resolution:

WHEREAS, the Affiliated Tribes of Northwest Indians (ATNI) are representatives of and advocates for national, regional, and specific tribal concerns; and

WHEREAS, the Affiliated Tribes of Northwest Indians is a regional organization comprised of American Indians in the states of Washington, Idaho, Oregon, Montana, Nevada, Northern California, and Alaska; and

WHEREAS, the health, safety, welfare, education, economic and employment opportunity, and preservation of cultural and natural resources are primary goals and objectives of Affiliated Tribes of Northwest Indians; and

WHEREAS, climate change is one of the most pressing environmental issues of our time, with strong impacts on air, water, land and the overall ecosystem. Indian tribes are facing the immediate, adverse impacts of climate change. Tribes in the Pacific Northwest are being forced to consider alternatives to the salmon on which they have subsisted for centuries; and

WHEREAS, in light of global and local initiatives to address climate change, tribal governments need to assert their rights for a "place at the table" to protect and advance their territorial sovereignty and their rights to substantively participate in the development of domestic and international policies that concern efforts to combat or mitigate for climate change; and

WHEREAS, tribal governments have the opportunity now to protect their interests and rights, to play a role in reducing their emissions as part of the global response to climate change, and to shape policy discussions and future regulatory systems; and

WHEREAS, the Quinault Indian Nation invites interested tribes to forge an Alliance on Climate Change that can enable tribes to play an active role in the emerging debates over climate change by establishing a platform of principles to guide tribal participation in matters pertaining to climate change and by establishing an inter-tribal communication network for sharing information and expertise on climate change; now

THEREFORE BE IT RESOLVED, the Affiliated Tribes of Northwest Indians supports the creation of an Alliance on Climate Change and supports the securing of funding to aid the creation of such an Alliance.

CERTIFICATION

The foregoing resolution was adopted at the 2008 Winter Conference of the Affiliated Tribes of Northwest Indians, held at the Yakima Convention Center, Yakima, Washington on January 25, 2008, with a quorum present.

Lieberman-Warner Climate Security Act of 2008 — S.2191

The Lieberman-Warner Climate Security Act of 2008 (S.2191), a bill introduced by Senators Joseph Lieberman (I-CT) and John Warner (R-V A) in October 2007, takes measurable steps to address global warming and its adverse impacts. Unlike former climate change legislation introduced in the Senate, the Lieberman-Warner bill acknowledges the nation's tribes and the need to provide them with resources to address the adverse impacts of global warming currently facing their communities. While the bill moves in the right direction by providing these resources, much more is necessary to assure that tribes are adequately equipped to protect themselves from global warming impacts.

The Lieberman-Warner bill, among other things, would cap 75 percent of the nation's greenhouse gas (GHG) emissions, with such emissions generated by the electric power, industrial and transportation sectors. The cap for these sources would be reduced below 2005 emission levels by 15 percent in 2020 and 70 percent in 2050 respectively. With these reductions and additional ones expected as a result of energy efficiency provisions in the bill, total U.S. GHG emissions would be expected to decline 53–61 percent. This is still not at the level that most scientists claim as the appropriate amount for reducing U.S. GHG emissions, namely 80 percent by no later than 2050, but it is a substantive effort on the part of the Senators nonetheless.

Global warming is perhaps the most pressing environmental issue of our time. Federally recognized tribes—sovereign nations with certain rights ensured by the U.S. Constitution, treaties and legal precedence—are facing the immediate, adverse impacts of global warming. Historically, tribal communities have borne a disproportionate weight of negative environmental consequences created by commercial and industrial operations, and in this case, those created by global warming.

To begin to address these negative environmental consequences, tribes would have access to two set-asides for Indian country as provided for under the bill. The first set-aside, namely 0.5 percent of the bill's annual emissions allowances through 2050, would be managed by the U.S. Environmental Protection Agency (EPA) and made available to tribes to undertake activities that "deliver assistance to tribal communities within the United States that face disruption or dislocation as a result of global warming" (*see* Section 3303(d)). The projected monetary value of this set-aside is between $250 million and $1.25 billion, with the value increasing over time, between 2012 and 2050. The second set-aside, namely 1 percent of the bill's Adaptation Fund financed by the proceeds from an annual emissions allowance auction, would be managed by the Department of the Interior and made available to tribes to undertake adaptation activities through the Tribal Wildlife Grants program of the U.S. Fish and Wildlife Service (*see* Section 4702(b)(4)). The projected monetary value of this set-aside is yet uncertain, but it will also likely be substantial. Along with thinking that the percentage of each set-aside should be increased, the National Tribal Environmental Council (NTEC) would argue that the scope of activities of the former set-aside be expanded to match the kind allowed for under a corresponding state set-aside, the kind of activities being renewable energy development and promotion of energy efficiency.

Along with these set-asides is a provision that could serve as a detriment to Indian tribes and more specifically to Alaskan Native Villages. Section 9004 of the bill reads: "For purposes of this Act, the Administrator may treat any federally recognized Indian tribe as a State, in accordance with section 301(d) of the Clean Air Act (42 U.S.C. §7601(d))." Under the worst case scenario, this provision could require tribes to be granted "treatment as a state" (TAS) before they could access the aforementioned 0.5 percent tribal set-aside. The EPA has been criticized by some in Indian country as to how the TAS process is managed. The Agency was also taken to task by the U.S. Government Accountability Office (GAO), which in 2005, issued a comprehensive report on EPA's performance in reviewing tribal requests to obtain TAS status. Broadly speaking, the GAO found that the Agency did not have a written strategy that establishes timeframes for reviewing tribal TAS requests nor did the TAS process have sufficient transparency. While the GAO report was issued in 2005, the EPA has failed to provide a formalized, written response of which tribes are aware and for which they may make substantive comments. In addition to the problems cited by the GAO concerning the TAS process is the inability of Alaskan Native Villages to obtain TAS status. As such, these tribes, perhaps the most in need of resources to address the immediate and adverse impacts of global warming, would be excluded from accessing the 0.5 percent tribal set-aside if having TAS status was a prerequisite.

Although the Lieberman-Warner bill moves in the right direction, much more needs to be done to improve it to the benefit of tribal needs and concerns. This will take, however, input from leaders throughout Indian country who know firsthand about the adverse impacts of global warming facing their communities. NTEC therefore stands ready to help these leaders carry their messages to Washington, D.C., where Senators are preparing for a floor debate likely to begin in May 2008, if not sooner. You are strongly encouraged to contact NTEC Executive Director, Jerry Pardilla, about how tribes can make a difference in the days ahead regarding the Lieberman-Warner bill and any other such legislation, and how NTEC might help. [Contact information redacted.]

Proposed Amendments to National Climate Protection Act Do Not Include Tribal Role in National Plans for Climate Change Adaptation

Senator Cantwell (D-WA) introduced S. 2355, known as the Climate Change Adaptation Act, on November 1, 2007. Joining as co-sponsors in December were Senators Kerry (D-MA), Klobuchar (D-MN), and Lautenberg (D-NJ). S. 2355 proposes to amend an existing law, the National Climate Protection Act (15 U.S.C. 2901), which was originally passed in 1987 and later amended in 2000. The purpose of this existing law is to assist the Nation and the world to understand and respond to natural and man-induced climate processes.

The newly proposed amendments would be a major overhaul, first by renaming the original law as the Climate Change Adaptation Act. These new amendments propose to enhance the ability of the United States to develop and implement climate change adaptation programs and policies, and for other purposes. The key provisions are summarized below:

1. The President is to provide Congress with a 5-year national strategic plan to address the impacts of climate change, and requires an update on a 5-year cycle;
2. Congress authorizes appropriations of $10 million for each of the fiscal years 2009 to 2013 to develop the strategic plan;
3. The Secretary of Commerce is required to conduct regional assessments of the vulnerability of coastal and ocean areas and resources;
4. The Secretary of Commerce is required to submit to Congress a national coastal and ocean adaptation plan;
5. The Secretary of Commerce is to provide technical planning assistance and products;
6. The Secretary shall provide grants of financial assistance to coastal states with approved coastal zone management programs; and
7. Congress authorizes $35 million for each of fiscal years 2009 to 2013 to develop the coastal and ocean adaptation plan.

In each of the key provisions outlined above, tribes are not mentioned. This is a glaring omission as state and local governments, and nongovernmental entities are specifically mentioned and accounted for in the planning processes. This bill warrants greater attention because Tribes should be part of these processes to ensure that the national strategic plan, and the coastal and ocean adaptation plan not only reflect their impacts, but also includes Tribes in the adaptation or mitigation strategies and plans.

This bill was referred to the Senate Commerce, Science and Transportation Committee, and a hearing was held on December 4, 2007. S. 2355 was favorably reported out of committee. The full text of this bill can be found at: http://thomas.loc.gov (The Library of Congress THOMAS).

Prepared by Jerry Pardilla, Executive Director, National Tribal Environmental Council (www.ntec.org).

The following principles were developed by the National Tribal Environmental Council and its Senior Policy Analyst, Robert Gruenig. They are a reference source available to tribal leaders in meetings with the Obama Transition Team and the EPA Transition Team.

Native American Principles for Climate Legislation

- Indian tribes should be specifically referenced as sovereign partners in addressing the problem of climate change; legislation should avoid the use of such terms as "tribal communities" that are vague and could open up resources to a larger number of groups beyond federally-recognized tribes; "Indian tribe" as defined under the Indian Self-Determination and Education Assistance Act, or "Indian Tribal government" as defined under the Indian Environmental General Assistance Program should be used in the "definitions" section of climate legislation to best reflect which tribes should have access to resources
- The status and rights of indigenous peoples throughout the world should be given due respect, particularly when referencing international efforts to address climate change
- Appropriate weight should be given to traditional tribal knowledge of the environment in climate legislation
- Indian tribes, states and local governments should be treated equally in climate legislation to the degree that each of these jurisdictions should have equal access to the same resources
- Indian tribes should not be required to obtain treatment-as-a-state (TAS) status or meet a similar, burdensome requirement to access resources made available under climate legislation

- Indian tribes should be provided with the resources to accurately assess and reduce their carbon footprint; these resources would go toward such activities as developing greenhouse gas emissions inventories, modeling for such emissions, and conducting subsequent monitoring
- Sufficient resources should be provided to Indian tribes for the collection of traditional knowledge and the establishment of procedures for taking such knowledge into account
- Sufficient resources should be devoted to the establishment of a federal-tribal program that researches and addresses the threats and costs to tribal cultures and lifeways as a result of climate change; additional resources should be provided for natural resource management programs that protect indigenous ecological systems, subsistence plants and animals, and promote intertribal sharing of traditional knowledge and culture
- Indian tribes should be provided with sufficient resources to address the adverse impacts facing their communities as a result of climate change through adaptive and mitigation measures that will ensure the environmental integrity of their homelands
- Tribal set-aside(s) should be established to address climate impacts; the following should be considered in establishing tribal set-aside(s) as part of climate legislation:
  - The federal trust responsibility to Indian tribes;
  - The unique situation of Indian tribes, in that their cultural survival depends on the safeguarding of their lands and resources including those resources off tribal lands preserved as a result of treaty rights; the size of the tribal set-aside(s) therefore needs to appropriately reflect this unique situation;
  - The tribal set-aside(s) should be made available in direct monies as opposed to allowances; as a general rule, most Indian tribes lack the expertise, experience and administrative capacity to manage and sell allowances and would find it much more effective to have direct monies to immediately address climate change impacts;
  - A negotiated rulemaking process should be authorized that would require the federal agency overseeing the tribal set-aside(s) to form an advisory committee with tribal leaders from across the nation to design, establish controls for, and provide overall management of the set-aside(s), assuring that effective government-to-government consultation occurs between tribes and the federal government in developing a distribution formula for the set-aside(s);
  - Indian tribes should have considerable discretion in how they use their portion of the tribal set-aside(s); examples of possible activities include promotion of energy efficiency, renewable energy and transmission development, climate change education, green job transition training, and adaptation and mitigation.
- Indian tribes should be acknowledged and provided with the necessary resources under any offsets program to best utilize their agricultural and forestry lands for sequestering carbon and providing them with substantial economic development opportunities
- Indian tribes should be provided with the necessary financial and technical assistance to enact and implement energy efficiency codes for buildings on lands within their jurisdiction; this assistance is not unlike what has been provided to state and local governments since the early 1990s
- Indian tribes should be provided with sufficient resources to improve their transportation infrastructure; tribal roads and routes need to be redesigned for better efficiency with additional resources needed to promote mass transit in locations where warranted
- Alaska Native Villages should be provided with specific funding and technical assistance to relocate their communities due to flooding and erosion, a result of climate change
- The Internal Revenue Code should be amended so as to allow Indian tribes to pass on their otherwise unused production tax credit (PTC) to joint partners in renewable energy

projects; tribes are tax exempt and have no federal liability against which they can apply the PTC, meaning that the only portion of the PTC that can be currently applied as part of a tribal renewable energy project is the ownership interest of the private investor

Secure Water Act (S. 2156) to Assess Long-Term Availability of Water Resources

The SECURE Water Act (S. 2156) was introduced by Senator Bingaman (D-NM) on October 4, 2007. This bill was co-sponsored by Senators Cantwell (D-WA), Domenici (R-NM), Johnson (D-SD), Salazar (D-CO), and Tester (D-MT). This bill proposes to authorize and facilitate the improvement of water management by the Bureau of Reclamation, to require the Secretary of the Interior and the Secretary of Energy to increase the acquisition and analysis of water resources for irrigation, hydroelectric power, municipal, and environmental uses.

S. 2156 is concerned about future adequate and safe water supplies in the United States, particularly to support increasing populations, economic growth, irrigated agriculture, energy production, and protection of aquatic ecosystems while facing the uncertainty posed by global climate change. In the findings, this bill asserts that States bear the primary responsibility and authority for managing water resources, but the federal government should support the states, regional, local and tribal governments by carrying out nationwide data collection and monitoring activities, research, and activities to increase the efficiency of water use.

S. 2156 requires specific federal agencies to: assess risks to water resources, develop strategies to ensure that long-term water resources management is sustainable, improve the understanding of variability in the water cycle, identify new supplies of water, analyze the impacts of human activity on water and ecological resources, and to assess future availability of surface and groundwater supplies.

The specific agency actions are outlined below:

The Secretary of Interior is required to carry out a number of actions to include:

1. establishing a climate change adaptation program that assesses best scientific information about presently observed and future impacts of global climate change on water resources, and assesses risks to water supply of major reclamation river basins, and develops monitoring plans and strategies to mitigate and adapt to impacts to water supplies;
2. feasibility studies for implementing each mitigation and adaptation strategy;
3. providing funding for water management improvement;
4. establishing and leading a climate change and water intergovernmental panel;
5. reviewing the national streamflow information program;
6. establishing a water use and availability assessment program; and
7. reporting to Congress about the effects and risks resulting from climate change on water resources; and a detailed assessment of availability, significant trends, usage of surface and groundwater, water use conflicts or shortages or factors that cause or will likely cause conflict or shortage.

The Secretary of Energy is required to assess the effects and risks resulting from global climate change with respect to water supplies required for hydroelectric power generation at federal water projects.

S. 2156 has some provisions for tribes, but it deserves attention and comments from tribes to ensure that tribal consultation, participation, and rights are addressed in each element of the SECURE Water Act. This bill does not explicitly recognize tribal authority with respect to water resources, and it fails to address tribal treaty and water rights. Several major river basins are specifically named in the bill, particularly the Colorado River, Columbia River, Klamath River, Missouri River, Rio Grande, Sacramento River, and San Joaquin River.

This bill was referred to the Committee on Energy and Natural Resources, and a hearing was held on December 11, 2007. The full text of S. 2156 can be found at: http://thomas.loc.gov (The Library of Congress THOMAS).

Prepared by Jerry Pardilla, Executive Director, National Tribal Environmental Council (www. ntec.org).

VI. Private Initiatives: Global Warming and the Individual

Michael Maniates, Allegheny College, WASHINGTON POST, Nov. 22, 2007, quoted in 2008 FRIEDMAN at 187:

> Never has so little been asked of so many at such a critical moment.

John C. Dernbach has picked up on the challenge of how Congress should engage individuals in the effort to address climate change *See Harnessing Individual Behavior to Address Climate Change Options for Congress*, 26 VA. ENVTL. L.J. 107, 107 (2008):

> This Article recommends a broad range of provisions, including findings and purposes, public participation, targets and timetables, numerous forms of public information, and a variety of incentives and pathways for individual action. The purpose of such provisions is to complement, not substitute for, provisions addressing major emitters. A congressional effort to engage individuals would take advantage of some of the nation's key strengths—individual initiative, engaged citizenship, and collective sense of purpose.

See id. at 160:

> Climate change legislation is likely to be much more effective if Congress engages individuals as much as possible. While there is considerable discussion over the appropriate design of a regulatory and market-based structure, it is impossible to separate those issues from issues involving the role of individuals. The problem is too daunting to focus simply on large polluters, and there is considerable reason to believe that individuals can make a significant contribution—as citizens and consumers as well as in other roles.

For a broader account, see TOM KERR, VOLUNTARY CLIMATE CHANGE EFFORTS, IN GLOBAL CLIMATE CHANGE AND U.S. LAW 591 (Michael B. Gerrard ed. 2007) (ABA Section of Environment, Energy & Resources).

Needless to say, "individuals" are engaged in countless ways as humanity confronts the issue of the ages. *See* Paul Siffo, *Human Kind is Particularly Good at Muddling, in* WHAT ARE YOU OPTIMISTIC ABOUT? TODAY'S LEADING THINKERS ON WHY THINGS ARE GOOD AND GETTING BETTER 328, 330 (Harper Collins 2007):

> the future will be what the future has always been—a mix of challenges, marvels, and endless surprise. We will do what we have always done and muddle our collective way through. Humankind is particularly good at muddling, and that is what makes me most optimistic of all.

An impressive legal literature already is appearing on this important topic. *E.g.*, Victor B. Flatt, *Act Locally, Affect Globally: How Changing Social Norms to Influence the Private Sector Shows A Path to Using Local Government to Control Environmental Harms*, 35 B.C. Envtl. Aff. L. Rev. 455 (2008); Michael P. Vandenbergh & Anne C. Steinemann, *The Carbon-Neutral Individual*, 82 N.Y.U. L. Rev. 1673 (2007).

––––––––––

For an example of what people on the other side of the globe are doing to combat climate change, *see* Siiri Aileen Wilson, *The Western Arnhem Land Fire Abatement Program* (paper prepared for seminar, "Global Warming in Indian Country" (Prof. William H. Rodgers, Jr.), Law B584, University of Washington, School of Law, Spring 2008) (footnotes renumbered):

In August of 2007, the West Arnhem Land Fire Abatement (WALFA) Team won Australia's Eureka Prize for Innovative Solutions to Climate Change.[1] The WALFA project is a landmark agreement between Aboriginal Australians, the state and federal governments and the energy industry.[2] WALFA funds the implementation of traditional methods of indigenous landscape burning and fire management in Australia's Northern Territory. The WALFA program is simple, but elegant. WALFA utilizes the reduction in greenhouse gas emissions through indigenous land management to offset emissions created by the energy industry.

....

WALFA partners the Northern Territory Government, Darwin Liquefied Natural Gas, the Northern Land Council and five Aboriginal communities from the northern coast to the headwaters of the Katherine and Mann rivers in the central Northern Territory.[3] This is the first time that a major energy company has formed a partnership with Aboriginal Traditional Owners to foster a return to traditional fire management regimes leading to a subsequent reduction in greenhouse gases.[4] The WALFA project produces an abatement in greenhouse gases by improving wildfire management in the Northern Territory's West Arnhem Land through an agreement based on traditional Indigenous ecological knowledge.[5] One of WALFA's main strengths is its potential to deliver not only positive environmental outcomes, but positive economic and socio-cultural outcomes, as well.

The WALFA program began in 1997 as a collaborative fire management project.[6] Initially, the WALFA team sought only to develop a program to reduce and manage the number of savanna wildfires in West Arnhem Land. By 2000, it had become obvious that the innovative program could also help reduce greenhouse gas emissions through both carbon offsetting and carbon sequestration.[7] This led to a 2001 funding proposal submitted to the Australian Greenhouse Office ("AGO"). Although the AGO enthusiastically supported the program, the Federal government ultimately denied the proposal.[8] As a result, the developers of the WALFA project sought private funding sources.

Because Australia is moving towards an increasingly progressive policy on combating global climate change, securing private funding for the WALFA project was an achievable goal. Aus-

––––––––––

1. Tropical Savannas CRC: *Eureka Win for West Arnhem Land Fire Project, available at* http://savanna.ntu.edu.au/news/topical_savannas109.html [hereinafter Eureka Win].

2. *Savannah Explorer: Fire Agreement to Strengthen Communities*, http://savanna.ntu.edu.au/view/250363/ppa_home/fire-agreement-to-strengthen-communities.html [hereinafter Savanna Explorer].

3. *Id.*

4. *Id.*

5. Native Title Report 2007 Chapter 12, Study: Western Arnhem Land Fire Management, http://www.hreoc.gov.au/social_justice/nt_report/ntreport07/chapter12.html [hereinafter NT Report 2007].

6. Dick Williams and Jeremy Russell-Smith, *Greenhouse Opportunities*, a presentation explaining the background (on file with author).

7. *Id.*

8. *Id.*

tralia's progressive political shift was cemented by the November 2007 election of Prime Minister Kevin Rudd. Rudd ushered in a new political era in Australia that promised to make significant changes to the national policy on climate change.[9] While the previous, conservative Howard administration had denied all scientific evidence in support of global climate change,[10] Prime Minister Rudd made signing the Kyoto Protocol ("Kyoto") the first official act of his new administration.[11] Rudd's ratification of Kyoto was quickly followed by the development of a national cap and trade program and a 627 million dollar governmental climate-change package.[12]

Recognizing Australia's growing commitment to fighting global climate change and anticipating the emergence of a national cap and trade program, many industrial polluters sought to establish carbon offsetting partnerships prior to the government's ratification of Kyoto. One such company was the Darwin Liquefied Natural Gas Company, or DNLG. As a subsidiary of petroleum giant ConocoPhillips,[13] DNLG was financially equipped to offer huge monetary incentives to anyone able to trade carbon allowances to offset the company's emissions from their Darwin Harbour plant on the shores of the Northern Territory. The 2006 WALFA agreement was the perfect solution: DNLG could offset their plant emissions by providing private funding to the innovative fire management project.

. . . .

The WALFA program mimics a cap and trade system, but is technically defined as an abatement program.[14] Under a greenhouse gas abatement program, there is a net decrease in the overall emissions of one or more greenhouse gases within a delineated area.[15] Accordingly, a cap and trade system is only one method of achieving an abatement. Greenhouse gas abatement can occur because all polluters reduce their emissions by a mandated percentage, because a single polluter reduces [its] emissions, or because pollution allowances are traded, as in the WALFA project.

. . . .

Savannah wildfires cause forty percent of all greenhouse gas emissions in the Northern Territory and account for two to four percent of Australia's total national greenhouse gas emissions.[16] Small, controlled burns implemented across the landscape can protect the Arnhem Land Plateau from these wildfires.[17] Controlled burns create firebreaks and reduce the amount of fuel available to these destructive fires. Limiting wildfires through controlled burning therefore serves a twofold purpose: it reduces the number of large-scale, uncontrolled wildfires while simultaneously reducing greenhouse gas emissions.

---

9. Patrick Barta and Rachel Pannet, *Howard Government Suffers Defeat in Australian Parliamentary Election*, THE WALL STREET JOURNAL, November 25, 2007, *available at* http://online.wsj.com/article/SB119590425426103055.html?mod=sphere_ts.

10. Joseph Romm, *Denier Bites the Dust: Australian Prime Minister Goes Down to Decisive Defeat*, GRIST: ENVIRONMENTAL NEWS AND COMMENTARY, November 24, 2007, *available at* http://gristmill.grist.org/story/2007/11/24/131846/14.

11. BBC News, *Rudd Takes Australia Inside Kyoto*, December 3, 2007, *available at* http://news.bbc.co.uk/2/hi/asia-pacific/7124236.stm.

12. Emma Young, *Australia announces "cap and trade" CO2 scheme*, NEW SCIENTIST, July 17, 2007, *available at* http://environment.newscientist.com/article/dn12279.

13. ConocoPhillips: Australia and Timor-Leste, Exploration and Production, *available at* http://conocophillips.com/about/worldwide_ops/country/australia/australia.htm.

14. *See* Paul Purdon, Gary Cooke and Peter White, *The Western Arnhem Land Fire Management Agreement — history and significance*, a presentation prepared for the Savana Fire — Ecology, Culture and Economy Forum in Darwin, Australia, May 7, 2008.

15. NT Report 2007, *supra* note 5.

16. Eureka Win, *supra* note 1.

17. Savanna Explorer, *supra* note 2.

. . . .

Fires that burn early in the dry-season are relatively "cool" and do not significantly damage the landscape; they do not burn the canopy of the trees or consume all of the fallen debris because there is still some moisture in the grasses and trees. These early dry-season fires are generally smoldering combustion fires that require less oxygen, burn at lower temperatures and produce fewer large flames.[18] Fires that burn late in the dry-season, however, burn very hot because the landscape has completely dried out or "cured." Late dry-season fires are most often flaming combustion fires that utilize large amounts of oxygen and produce large plumes and flames that can jump and travel greater distances across landscapes.[19] These late dry-season fires significantly damage the landscape, burn out the canopy of the trees and can burn out of control for months, destroying vast tracts of land.[20]

. . . .

The participating Aboriginal communities hire their own local rangers to implement WALFA's prescribed burning regime.[21] Training is provided to new rangers in order to build the skills and resources of the communities to manage the WALFA program on a long term and ongoing basis.[22] Outside consultation and coordination are available to the ranger programs, but local Aboriginal people are allowed to determine how the programs are carried out.[23] The ranger groups additionally provide a new and innovative structure for the transfer of traditional knowledge from older, more experienced members of the communities to the young.

. . . .

Aboriginal fire management is based around the concept of caring for country. Under WALFA, a return to traditional Aboriginal land management and caring for country is possible through the funding and support of the local ranger programs.[24] Community rangers are the key to successfully implementing WALFA in each of the five partner communities. These locally based rangers groups carry out the prescribed burning. These same rangers have the required local fire knowledge, experience and history, as well as the specific fire management techniques, required to create mosaic burning in a targeted fashion that maximizes biodiversity and positive land management outcomes.

. . . .

Securing sustainable and just economic outcomes for Aboriginal traditional owners and communities in the remote regions of the Northern Territory has been an elusive goal for Aboriginal people, as well as for the national and Territory governments, various public agencies and community groups.[25] The increasing value and intact environmental nature of much of the indigenous lands across northern Australia offers opportunities that create sustainable on-country development for traditional owners in the region through new and exciting economies. The West Arnhem Land Fire Abatement (WALFA) project is, hopefully, the first of many opportunities to be put into operation.[26]

---

18. *See* Gary Cook, *Fuels, Fires and Greenhouse Gasses*, a presentation made for the Savanna Fire — Ecology, Culture and Economy Forum in Darwin, Australia, May 7, 2008.

19. *Id.*

20. NT Report 2007, *supra* note 5.

21. SEAN KERINS, INDIGENOUS INVOLVEMENT IN ENVIRONMENTAL AND HERITAGE MANAGEMENT, a report prepared for the 2006 Australian State of the Environment Committee, *available at* http://www.environment.gov.au/soe/2006/publications/integrative/indigenous/northern-land-council-html.

22. *Id.*

23. *Id.*

24. NT Report 2007, *supra* note 5.

25. *Id.*

26. *Id.*

Since European settlement, Indigenous people have moved from their traditional way of life "on country" into towns and settlements.[27] The WALFA project area was once home to many Aboriginal people living traditionally and actively managing their land.[28] Forced migrations, however, have left much of the landscape unpopulated and unmanaged. It has meant that the traditional fire regimes that protected the landscape from late dry-season fires have ceased, and that the landscape has become only more prone to the very hot destructive late dry-season wildfires.

The major outcome of the WALFA agreement is its ability to provide meaningful jobs for Aboriginal people on country. One of the major challenges that people in remote indigenous communities face is the lack of culturally appropriate careers and job opportunities.[29] Working "on country," which is understood as working on one's traditional homelands, is critically important for maintaining Aboriginal identity and for achieving Aboriginal sovereignty.[30] The long term benefits to the communities involved include the transfer of indigenous knowledge between generations as elders work with young people, helping urban Aboriginal people reestablish contact with their traditional lands and families, providing Aboriginal role models and career paths for Aboriginal children and promoting successful economic partnerships between the states, the federal government and the private sector with Aboriginal communities.[31]

....

---

27. *Id.*

28. *Id.*

29. *Id.*

30. *See* WORKING ON COUNTRY: CONTEMPORARY INDIGENOUS MANAGEMENT OF AUSTRALIA'S LAND AND COASTAL REGIONS (Richard Baker, Jocelyn Davies and Elspeth Young eds., Oxford University Press 2001).

31. *See* Savanna Explorer, *supra* note 2.

Index